TWENTIETH-CENTURY
CHILDREN'S WRITERS

TWENTIETH-CENTURY
CHILDREN'S WRITERS

WITH A PREFACE BY
NAOMI LEWIS

EDITOR
D. L. KIRKPATRICK

ST. MARTIN'S PRESS
NEW YORK

CONTENTS

PREFACE

The writers listed in this book – well over 600 in all – are the main 20th-century contributors in English to one or other branch of an extraordinary literature. It probably has, in written form, no precedent in the world's past history. It is of its own kind, not a watered-down form of adult writing, but the link between the two is close. "It is not so much a question of taking up one's stand on the lower rungs of the literary ladder," wrote that notable practitioner Mrs. Molesworth in 1893, "as of standing on another ladder altogether – one which has its own steps, its higher and lower positions of excellence." These positions of excellence are almost always unpredictably filled, often by middle-aged adults who have never written in this particular field before: an Adams, a Ransome. Children do not write good children's books. One of the best novels ever written by a real pre-adolescent child is wasted on children: Daisy Ashford's *The Young Visiters*. Though the low periods of this literature (one such lasted for years in the earlier part of this century) bring the kind into disrepute, its high phases affect other writing. Thus, in the two decades or so between 1851 (*The King of the Golden River*) and 1871 (*At the Back of the North Wind* and *Through the Looking-Glass*), numbers of writers in adult fields were tempted into the genre of children's fantasy: among them Thackeray with *The Rose and the Ring*, Frances Browne with *Granny's Wonderful Chair* (1857), Kingsley with *The Water-Babies* (1863), the mathematician Dodgson (Carroll) with *Alice* (1865), Dickens with *A Holiday Romance* (1868), Jean Ingelow with *Mopsa the Fairy* (1869) – richness indeed. Several of these writers – adult novelists though they considered themselves – are remembered today by their children's books alone. Interestingly, it was a hundred years later, in the 1950's and 60's, that the next such flowering occurred.

How old is a child? It seems a modern problem, but it exercised Mrs. Trimmer, writing on "Books *for* Children and Books *for* Young Persons," in 1802: "Formerly," she complained, "all were reckoned *Children*, till they had at least attained their *fourteenth year*. Now ... we have *Young Persons* of *five* or *six years old*."

How to distinguish the child's book from the adult's? – and is the distinction important? These questions are best considered after a view of the scene. As a recognised part of publishing, English books for the pleasure (as well as the improvement) of the young go back to Newbery's mid-18th century: a piece of literary history admirably charted by Harvey Darton, M. F. Thwaite and others. What chiefly concerns us here is the strange course of children's literature in our own century: first, the casual and freakish, then the phenomenal. Suddenly, in the three decades since the war, children's books have become a major field of publishing and of international exchange; and where a prestigious medium exists, the gifted come. Would *The Mouse and His Child* have been published first for adults? Or *Smith*? Or *The Owl Service* or *A Wizard of Earthsea*?

But look back to the first half century, post-Lang, post-Barrie, post-Nesbit, and the map is puzzling, ill-defined. The reaction against Victorian taste sets in, lasts long; the war-caused paper block of the 1940's holds up change. Taste runs to the lightweight and whimsical. Books about children or fairies or both (*Dream Days*, de la Mare's *Songs of Childhood*, *Martin Pippin in the Apple Orchard*, *The Crock of Gold*, *When We Were Very Young*) are published for, and are widely read by, adults. As for books intended for children, the ordinary sort about daily or holiday doings are very thin stuff indeed when they come from the average hand: the sliced white bread of reading. They obey the time's unspoken codes: no death, disasters, poverty; no great emotions, no stern moral lessons – none of those features that gave such force to 19th-century fiction. Certainly not an echo is heard of current happenings, in Jarrow or Spain or Germany. (How unlike today, when hijacking, kidnapping, immigrants, drugs and the Irish troubles are in brisk use by the practical novelist.) The boarding school tale thrives, the glum provincial day-school reader's dream-world; enclosed in its private laws, as in its mock-Gothic walls, it generates its own emotional heat. Straight-

tale survivors from this time are few. The main one is Noel Streatfeild, who had the wit to write of children intent on work, not play, or involved in some form of expertise – tennis, say, or skating. Her *Ballet Shoes* is still in vigorous print. Ransome, of course: but he is a special case. His tales – a kind of daydream cherished through years as a foreign correspondent in revolutionary Russia – were written for no one apart from his buried youthful self.

Yet cross the frontier of reasoned fact, cross the frontier of time – in other words, move into fantasy, move into history – and the rules, taboos and the codes no longer hold: nothing is too violent or too strange. And so, in this same time, we find some of the most potent imaginative works of modern children's literature: *The Hobbit* (and later, *The Lord of the Rings*), *The Midnight Folk* and *The Box of Delights*, *The Sword in the Stone* and *Mistress Masham's Repose*, the Narnia tales of C. S. Lewis (distinct taboo-breakers with their sadism, religion and death), *The Borrowers*, *The Children of Green Knowe*, *A Traveller in Time*, *Tom's Midnight Garden*, *Henrietta's House* as well as *Poor Cecco* and *Mary Poppins*; historical tales include the splendid, early Roman stories of Mitchison, and books by Harnett, and Picard, and of course Sutcliff's *The Eagle of the Ninth*. Only a few years away are *Elidor* and *Earthfasts* and *The Dark Is Rising* and *Smith* and *The Mark of the Horse Lord*. Violence, mystery, exile, death, terror, loyalties, love and loss have been entering children's literature all the time. The very youngest have always (or should always have) met these things in nursery rhymes – the wildest, most enigmatic poetry likely to come their way for years, perhaps for always – and in the great traditional fairy tales. (*Not* to have read them early, in Dr. Bruno Bettelheim's view, is to be deprived for life.)

Fantasy (like history) is a convenient word, but really needs some defining. In verse or fiction it covers many forms. It can touch the everyday world of the supernatural (as in books by Garner or Farmer, as in most ghost stories). It can call in the past to the present (as in *Tom's Midnight Garden*). It can offer a total world, such as Earthsea, Middle-earth, Moominland. It can re-interpret myth and legend, as in *The Book of Three* or *The Owl Service* (both Mabinogion-based) or in the countless Arthurian variants, from *The Sword in the Stone* to *The Green Knight* by Vera Chapman. It includes all the tales giving life to dolls (*Miss Hickory*, *Poor Cecco*, *The Mouse and His Child*), the wish-themes (*Five Children and It*), the mirror-versions of life played out by animals (*The Wind in the Willows*, *Mrs. Frisby and the Rats of NIMH*, *Watership Down* – also a quest tale, a major form) or by *things* (Hans Andersen). It can cross into science fiction, as in many of Andre Norton's books. And it involves the great field of nonsense (not so much absence of sense as a wild variation) – the brilliant games with words. Carroll and Lear are the masters still; but *The Phantom Tollbooth* must be the best original *modern* book in the Carroll line. It must also be remarked that many of the worst as well as the greatest written works belong to the genre of fantasy. Failure waits for those who refuse to see that magic too has its laws; that every wish has its price; that the mean wisher can't wish beyond his own mean range.

What might not have been foretold by yesterday's crystal-gazer is the increasingly powerful place of fantasy in "older" children's fiction, not least in the fiction of current life. This, I believe, is a peculiarly English feature. American authors seem able to write at a high level on modern American children or adolescents in modern situations: no dreams, no dips into time, no supernatural. I find this superbly demonstrated in the work of the Cleavers and Betsy Byars. (Paula Fox keeps to the real, but *suggests* the fantasy that a child's imagination can make of fact.) For English authors though – perhaps because English life tends to become inexplicit when looked at closely; perhaps because England lacks today extremes of poverty as well as extremes of climate and landscape – the temptation to draw on dream or magic or shifts of time is hard to resist. I doubt if one of our leading writers *has* entirely resisted it (again I stress the point, in older fiction): certainly not Garner, Mayne, Farmer, Townsend, Dickinson, Garfield, Lively, Paton Walsh, Cresswell, Peyton, Aiken, Pearce – a list by no means complete. Only a strong particular theme, such as autism (Roy Brown's *The Siblings*) or animals in the human world (G. D. Griffiths' *Abandoned*) seems able to lift today's non-fantasy into (Mrs. Molesworth's phrase) "positions of excellence."

Historical fiction has its own turns of history. In the Victorian century every leading adult novelist produced at least one substantial work in the genre: *The Cloister and the Hearth*, a major work by a not-quite-major writer, has few rivals even now. But by the earlier years of the present century the genre had largely slipped into being a kind of popular costume drama (in fact, as a form of housewife's reading, it flourishes still). Its novelists, more concerned with fiction than history, tended to keep to well-trodden fields: the picturesque view of the English Civil War (Cavaliers and Roundheads), the French Revolution (and the languid English aristocrat Pimpernel), the Napoleonic Wars (good battle stuff for the boys; good home romance for the girls); Bonnie Prince Charlie, Bonnie King Charles, occasional dips into the colourful medieval, the roistering Elizabethan. Attitudes were uncomplicated: "our" side was the prettier side of the two opposing teams: the King's, the Cavaliers'. And so the appearance in 1934 of Geoffrey Trease's *Bows Against the Barons*, which neatly reversed the usual values (good peasants, bad "nobles"), remains a landmark. Trease soon grew beyond this simplistic phase, valuable though it was at the time. He is writing still (try for a recent sample his gripping *The Red Towers of Granada*), the most widely-ranging historical novelist in the calendar.

So it could be said that, in the post-war renaissance, the whole of history, much of it scarcely touched, lay open to fiction writers. Not only was a change in the old fixed attitudes now acceptable (the human and analytic rather than the easy old right and wrong), but there were many fields where, indeed, no fixed view was established. (Are we for Saxon or Norman?) Rosemary Sutcliff, throwing a brilliant personal light on the murk and mists of Ancient Britain, gave an equally fair view of Briton and Roman soldier. In a range of effective books, Treece, Trease, Harnett, Picard, Burton, Paton Walsh, Hodges, Willard, Leeson, Garfield, Carter, Ray, Crossley-Holland are among those who have notably extended a reading child's experience of the historied past. Inevitably the best are those set before the 19th century.

Near-perspective is always a difficulty. Though a number of worthy and even goodish books turn up on recent events and themes (history is at our heels, advancing every day), few are so far of memorable quality. The General Strike of 1926 (mostly noted in adult fiction or documentary as a time for carefree undergraduates to play at driving trains) *has* been approached from the miners' end – but a really convincing work still waits to be written. (The best of recent novels in this area could well be Susan Price's *Twopence a Tub*, which deals with a failed miners' strike in the 19th century.) But most younger English writers today do not understand working and workless poverty as, for instance, Mrs. Gaskell understood it in *Mary Barton*, a work that is valid still both as fiction and history.

Again, no English writer for the young has so far written with any point on the turbulent years between 1933 and 1939, when not all the young (or old) were indifferent to the unchecked spread of the Fascist disease through Europe. As for the war itself, with few exceptions the most important books for the young come from Holland (source of Anne Frank's *Diary*), Denmark, and other countries which knew the taste of Occupation. Sylvia Sherry's *Dark River, Dark Mountain*, at once perceptive and haunting, is one of the best I recall with an English setting. Currently, English junior fiction is suffering from a rash of sentimentalised novels about English children sheltering "sensitive" Luftwaffe airmen found in the bushes. Such books do nothing to lessen the sick attraction to Nazism itself – a matter about whose facts most young people today seem to know nothing at all.

More exact attention has gone to another subject: the novel which centres on the black/white or black/black story. Picture books for the very young mingle black, brown, white in their illustrations, in the most natural fashion. But pictures are more easily managed than words. (How does E.L. Konigsburg make her point in *Jennifer, Hecate, Macbeth, William McKinley, and Me, Elizabeth*, with words or pictures?) Books by English writers giving a lead place to non-white children are so far well-meant but unmemorable. Two recent winners of the breakaway Other Award should be noted, though: Jean MacGibbon's *Hal* and Bernard Ashley's *The Trouble with Donovan Croft*. Both have a black lead character, though both the authors are white. A notable Australian book of the 1960's should be listed here, H.F. Brinsmead's *Pastures of the Blue Crane*, which touches the native colour question in Queensland. So too should Elizabeth Borton de Treviño's *I, Juan de Pareja*, a striking reconstruction of Velasquez's black servant's story.

Still, it is from the United States, where black/white history runs more deep, and from black writers, that fiction of quality comes at the current time. Notable among these are Virginia Hamilton (a stunning writer and a recent Newbery winner) and Rosa Guy (*The Friends*). William H. Armstrong's *Sounder*, an earlier book, left a haunting impact, though its film version managed to miss almost every point that made the story memorable.

A more deeply rooted issue in English life is the elusive but very genuine one of "class." What shocked the readers of *Jane Eyre* (1847) was that the lead role and marital prize (battered though it might be) went to a *governess*! Even in the new century a servant remained a background figure in fiction: strict housekeeper, vulgar cook, illiterate kitchen-maid. Accepted attitudes can be as readily observed in E. Nesbit's works as anywhere. Beguiled as we are by her narrative voice, her verve and invention, we have to allow that her cooks and maids and errand boys are almost always comics, cardboard figures of fun; that her main child characters when they cannot go to expensive schools, go to no school at all; that her only poor-boy hero, the little waif Dickie Harding, turns out to owe his gentle manners to his being the lost heir to an ancient noble line. She was, to be sure (like Shakespeare), taking the easy path with plots, and these came readily to hand. But the fact that they *came* to hand makes the point. (*The Children of the House*, by Pearce and Fairfax-Lucy, a book which is based on fact, movingly shows what was also true, the close bond between "upper class" children and servants in a great house when both feared and suffered from the harsh hand of authority.) Of course, with hindsight, novelists today can effectively present the old feudal injustices that were finally broken only by the Second World War. Peyton does this notably well in her late-Edwardian *Flambards*. The truth is that arbitrary codes do make strong plots: as I may have said elsewhere, what is bad for our lives is often good for our fiction. In 20th-century children's books certain themes lived on well beyond their life in fact. Thus Pearce's fine and ingenious *Minnow on the Say* carries off its story (saving the threadbare ancestral home by finding the long-lost treasure) by the sheer skill of its telling.

Nor has class vanished yet. Publishers and librarians are known today to pause doubtfully over this or that text, murmuring the unlucky verdict "too middle-class." How would they rate the acknowledged breakthrough book, *The Family from One End Street* (1937), if it reached them now, in manuscript? Even a child might see that this well-meant, well-liked, lively book about a large cockney family is written from an outside, and, unwittingly, slightly downward view; that its characters – apart from the bookish sensitive one – are essentially "they" not "we." Yet the importance of this book in its time should not be underrated.

It should be clear by now that what runs between children's and adults' books is not a straight line but one as winding as the Thames on a map, if not quite so refractory a one as that of Norway's coast. It changes with tides and seasons; often it cannot be seen at all. It vanishes under flood. But there *is* a line. We are aware of this when a children's author seems to grow restless, begins to write of older characters, older problems, then, in the next book, steps over and is gone, for the time at least, from children's reading. This happens today to a number of leading English writers. (William Mayne, to date, is one of the few who seems able to absorb the pangs of human life into his books while staying on the side of children's literature. His most complex, probably greatest book, *The Jersey Shore*, should be studied in this light. But read it in the English edition, which does not tamper with the end.) Alan Garner has said: "Most of the people who read my books are adults, whatever their ages." You could also say that whatever a childlike child is reading is for that time a children's book. I have known a simple 9 year old to read and reread *Plain Tales from the Hills*, rejecting the *Just-So Stories*. Ah, but what did the reader find in it? The little Brontës, who knew no children's fiction as we now understand the term, read dull political newspapers – and turned the statesmen and military leaders into figures of fairy tale. The youthful mind is immensely adaptable, taking the lowest when it is there, but capable of any feat if required.

Most of the commentary here has been about middle and older fiction, for this is where change and invention chiefly lie. Younger and youngest books abound, of course, mainly in series. I mention them at this point to say that, even in a first-reader, brilliance is possible.

Arnold Lobel's *Frog and Toad, Mouse Tales, Owl at Home* are continually lit with this, a short tale in the last of these outstandingly. It is called "Tearwater Tea." Others that must be admired include Marjorie Weinman Sharmat's *Nate the Great* books, about a cool detective, not more than six years old; these say all that a story needs in their terse allotment of words. But even without such bright occasions, the standard of books for the 4 to 6, 7 to 9 year old reader is higher than it was when some of these series started. Though the approach is simple, the language clear, the subjects often belong to the larger world.

But indeed, the younger the book (or, rather, the reader, looker or listener) the greater the impact; picture books, which aim at the youngest of all, have an importance which is hard to overstate. They meet the human mind at its most susceptible. They convey at once what often cannot be comfortably said in words (the "colour" instance has already been given). They are looked at often; their words are remembered long. This is not the place to discuss their staggering range, good or bad, of manner and technique (they enter this volume primarily through the artist's invention of text and theme), but their subjects *are* to the point. When a picture book shows (and hundreds continue to do just this) a "comic" view of a man with a whip standing over a cowering circus lion or tiger, or of that no less obscene spectacle of a rodeo, it is fixing an assumption that these things are approved, amusing, accepted fun.

This holds, of course, through the whole of children's reading. Anyone who has read that remarkable (adult) short story "The Lottery" by Shirley Jackson will know what is meant by the word assumption – an obstinate and unreasoned superstition, artificially kept alive, with dire results. Somewhere along the line we have dropped the assumption that religious non-conformists should be publicly burned, that women, non-whites, and the (white, Anglo-Saxon) labouring poor are incapable of education. But assumption persists through children's books (not least in fable) that wolves are bad and must be exterminated; that whaling and fur-trapping are all right because they happen in clean adventure, and far away at that. A child who reads Roberts or Griffiths or a novel such as *Julie of the Wolves* is unlikely, in later life, to run a battery farm or work in an animal-vivisecting laboratory. Well, fairly unlikely. The trouble is that more children have seen or read *Jaws* than have ever come across the works mentioned above. Still, the books are there, and it is with the reading and listening children that creeds, taboos, and superstitions not only begin, but end.

I have called this literature paradoxical, but paradox is also another view of fact. One such fact is that the greatest children's writers rarely care much for children – give or take the selected child or two. Their works, they claim, were not aimed at the young at all. (It is only frankly commercial writers who firmly state the reverse.) The truth is that the works of Grahame and Nesbit and Andersen and Stevenson are written *from* or out of a childhood source, their own; something of their childhood selves has persisted, undissolved, into adult life. Though some particular boy or girl may have prompted the start of certain books (*Peter Rabbit, The Wind in the Willows*), the real child lay in the author. The same holds for *A Child's Garden of Verses, The Little Mermaid, The Treasure Seekers, Swallows and Amazons, The Hobbit.* Disbelievers should study biography.

What qualifies entry into this literature? Is it that there are juveniles in the cast? Yes – but a number of works (of the Crusoe and Verne kind certainly; and much science fiction) do well enough without. (What views on *Lord of the Flies* and *A High Wind in Jamaica*?) Is it that the events, however adult, should be seen throughout as from a child's view? This takes us nearer. (But then, does a laisser-passer go to *What Maisie Knew* or *The Go-Between*?) Technique, perhaps? But, at least in the teenage novel, time-sequence tricks, all-dialogue narrative, and streams-of-thought have become no novelty. On the grounds of style *Dream Days* and *The Water-Babies* have been dismissed by the pusillanimous. Perhaps it is best to say that the theme of a children's book need not be within a child's experience but within the range of a child's imagination. Well. ... One other point, and not the least significant, is that in children's literature at its best a kind of justice prevails. Justice? That ill-used word means very much to a child, the sinner no less than the sinned against. "Children who are innocent love justice; but most people are wicked, and prefer mercy." So observed Chesterton; he had been listening to youthful comments on Maeterlinck's *Blue Bird*. Man of aphorisms though he was, I doubt if he ever said anything more penetrating.

—Naomi Lewis

xi

EDITOR'S NOTE

Twentieth-Century Children's Writers includes English-language authors of fiction, poetry, and drama for children and young people. The selection of entrants is based upon the recommendations of the advisers listed on page xv.

The main part of the book covers writers most of whose work for children was published after 1900; the appendix is of some important representative writers of the later 19th century.

The entry for each writer consists of a biography, a complete list of separately published books, and a signed critical essay. Living entrants were invited to make a comment on their books for children.

Original British and United States editions of all books have been listed; other editions are listed only if they are first editions. Illustrators of first editions of children's books have been listed. Under "publications for children" we have listed books that at some time since their publication have been considered children's books. Retellings of myths and traditional tales are listed in the "other" section.

Special thanks are due to Patricia Scott who suggested the project and helped in the initial stages of research, and to R.C. Cox for his editorial assistance throughout the preparation of the manuscript. We would also like to thank the entrants and contributors for their patience and cooperation in helping us compile this book.

ADVISERS

Peggy Appiah
Gillian Avery
Dorothy Butler
Marcus Crouch
Matyelok Gibbs
Roger Lancelyn Green
Virginia Haviland
Ethel L. Heins
Naomi Lewis
Donnarae MacCann

Nellie McCaslin
Irma McDonough
Marcie Muir
Nancy J. Schmidt
Rosemary Stones
Zena Sutherland
John Rowe Townsend
Geoffrey Trease
Lee Wyndham

CONTRIBUTORS

William D. Anderson
Fran Ashdown
Gillian Avery
Janet E. Baker
Raymond W. Barber
Ann Bartholomew
Anthea Bell
Betty Boegehold
Valerie Brinkley-Willsher
Clyde Robert Bulla
Mary Mehlman Burns
Dorothy Butler
Francelia Butler
Dennis Butts
Mary Cadogan
Alasdair K. D. Campbell
Margaret Campbell
Anne Carter
Charles Causley
Charity Chang
Mary Blount Christian
Berna C. Clark
Leonard Clark
Pamela Cleaver
Mary Silva Cosgrave
Patricia Craig
Marcus Crouch
Mary Croxson
Norman Culpan
Alan Edwin Day
Brian Doyle

Peter du Sautoy
Barbara Elleman
Anne W. Ellis
A. W. England
Fred Erisman
Martha J. Fick
Tom Fitzgibbon
Rachel Fordyce
Geoff Fox
Gillian Freeman
Norma R. Fryatt
James C. Giblin
Betty Gilderdale
Cecilia Gordon
Margaret Greaves
Roger Lancelyn Green
Patrick Groff
Irene Haas
Dennis Hall
Graham Hammond
Ann G. Hay
Renée Haynes
Betsy Hearne
Peggy Heeks
Ethel L. Heins
Ravenna Helson
James E. Higgins
John Hole
Peter Hollindale
Anna Home
Karen Nelson Hoyle

Fred Inglis
Callie Israel
Clara O. Jackson
Wendy Jago
Coleman A. Jennings
Ursula M. Jones
Antony Kamm
R. Gordon Kelly
Jessica Kemball-Cook
Edward Kemp
Lee Kingman
Carolyn T. Kingston
Dolores C. Leffall
Claudia Lewis
Naomi Lewis
Mary J. Lickteig
Myra Cohn Livingston
Rebecca J. Lukens
Alan M. Lynskey
Donnarae MacCann
Anne S. MacLeod
Gertrud Mander
Gwen Marsh
Margaret R. Marshall
Bobbie Ann Mason
Margaret Maxwell
Nellie McCaslin
David McCord
Irma McDonough
Myles McDowell
Joan McGrath
Dorothy Clayton McKenzie
Walter McVitty
Margaret Meek
Leonard R. Mendelsohn
Jean F. Mercier
Susan Meyers
Joan Mills
Naomi Mitchison
Christian H. Moe
Francis J. Molson
Doris Langley Moore
Caroline Moorehead
Marcie Muir
Heather Neill
Mary Nettlefold
Janet E. Newman
Vivien Noakes
Ruth Osler

Jill Paton Walsh
Eric Quayle
Sheila G. Ray
Mary Rayner
William Ready
David Rees
James Reeves
Mae Durham Roger
James W. Roginski
James Roose-Evans
Mary Rubio
Jean Russell
Glenn Edward Sadler
Rubie Saunders
H. M. Saxby
Vivian J. Scheinmann
Nancy J. Schmidt
Mabel D. Segun
Nancy Shepherdson
Dorothy D. Siles
Barbara Smiley
John Robert Sorfleet
Kenneth J. Sterck
Madeleine B. Stern
Rosemary Stones
Jon C. Stott
Zena Sutherland
Gillian Thomas
Ann Thwaite
Eileen Totten
John Rowe Townsend
Geoffrey Trease
Alvin Tresselt
Margaret M. Tye
Peter Vansittart
Margaret Walker
Joan Ward
Aidan Warlow
Rosemary Weber
Brigitte Weeks
Joyce I. Whalley
Joy Whitby
Frank Whitehead
Winifred Whitehead
Angela Wigan
Gladys A. Williams
Barbara Ker Wilson
Jacqueline Brown Woody
Jane Yolen

TWENTIETH-CENTURY
CHILDREN'S WRITERS

Richard Adams
Joan Aiken
Ruth Ainsworth
Lloyd Alexander
Mabel Esther Allan
E. M. Almedingen
Doris Andersen
Prudence Andrew
Valenti Angelo
Joan Walsh Anglund
Peggy Appiah
Edward Ardizzone
Richard Armour
Richard Armstrong
William H. Armstrong
Ruth Arthur
Honor Arundel
Bernard Ashley
Flora B. Atkin
M. E. Atkinson
Richard Atwater
Esther Averill
Gillian Avery
Jacqueline Ayer
Natalie Babbitt
Martha Bacon
R. L. Bacon
Carolyn Sherwin Bailey
Betty Baker
Margaret J. Baker
Margaret Balderson
Martin Ballard
Angela Banner
Helen Bannerman
Kitty Barne
Anne Mainwaring Barrett
J. M. Barrie
L. Frank Baum
Nina Bawden
Nina Beachcroft
John and Patricia Beatty
Harry Behn
Hilaire Belloc
Ludwig Bemelmans
Nathaniel Benchley
Rex Benedict
Elisabeth Beresford
Leila Berg
Herbert Best
Margery Williams Bianco
Violet Bibby
Clare Bice
Val Biro
Claire Huchet Bishop
Donald Bisset

Ann Blades
Marie Halun Bloch
Judy Blume
Enid Blyton
N. M. Bodecker
Michael Bond
Frank Bonham
Crosby Bonsall
Lucy Boston
Helen Dore Boylston
Christianna Brand
Angela Brazil
Elinor Brent-Dyer
Robert Bright
Carol Ryrie Brink
H. F. Brinsmead
Joyce Lankester Brisley
L. Leslie Brooke
Walter R. Brooks
Margaret Wise Brown
Roy Brown
Dorita Fairlie Bruce
Mary Grant Bruce
Anthony Buckeridge
Mary Buff
Angela Bull
Clyde Robert Bulla
Robert Burch
Frances Hodgson Burnett
Sheila Burnford
John Burningham
Hester Burton
Virginia Lee Burton
Betsy Byars
Eleanor Cameron
Natalie Savage Carlson
Bruce Carter
Peter Carter
Arthur Catherall
Rebecca Caudill
Charles Causley
Betty Cavanna
Winifred Cawley
Nan Chauncy
Joseph E. Chipperfield
Charlotte Chorpenning
John Christopher
Richard Church
Marchette Chute
John Ciardi
Patricia Clapp
Ann Nolan Clark
Catherine Anthony Clark
Leonard Clark
Mavis Thorpe Clark

Joan Clarke
Pauline Clarke
Ewan Clarkson
Beverly Cleary
Vera and Bill Cleaver
Dorothy Clewes
Lucille Clifton
Eleanor Clymer
Elizabeth Coatsworth
Mary Cockett
Padraic Colum
Ralph Connor
Lyn Cook
Olivia Coolidge
Gordon Cooper
Lettice Cooper
Susan Cooper
Scott Corbett
Alexander Cordell
William Corlett
John Craig
Helen Cresswell
Samuel Rutherford Crockett
Richmal Crompton
Kevin Crossley-Holland
Julia W. Cunningham
Jane Curry
W. Towrie Cutt

Roald Dahl
Alice Dalgliesh
Ruth Dallas
Maureen Daly
David Scott Daniell
Marjorie Darke
James Daugherty
Edgar and Ingri Parin d'Aulaire
Peter Dawlish
C. Day Lewis
Marguerite de Angeli
Meindert De Jong
Walter de la Mare
Beatrice Schenk de Regniers
Anne de Roo
Elizabeth Borton de Treviño
Peter Dickinson
Eilís Dillon
Nance Donkin
John Donovan
Mary Alice Downie
V. H. Drummond
William Péne du Bois
Maurice Duggan
Norman Duncan
Mabel Dunham

Mary Durack
Roger Duvoisin

Edward Eager
Walter D. Edmonds
Dorothy Edwards
Monica Edwards
Cyprian Ekwensi
E. M. Ellin
Roberta Elliott
Sylvia Engdahl
Elizabeth Enright
Eleanor Estes
Marie Hall Ets
Hubert Evans
Evelyn Everett-Green

Eleanor Farjeon
Walter Farley
Penelope Farmer
Max Fatchen
Louise Fatio
Cliff Faulknor
Edward Fenton
Kathleen Fidler
Rachel Field
George Finkel
Winifred Finlay
Aileen Fisher
Dorothy Canfield Fisher
Nicholas Fisk
Louise Fitzhugh
Marjorie Flack
Sid Fleischman
James Flora
Esther Forbes
Michael Foreman
Antonia Forest
Paula Fox
Barbara C. Freeman
Don Freeman
Fiona French
Jean Fritz
Rosalie K. Fry
Roy Fuller
Rose Fyleman
J. G. Fyson

Wanda Gág
Ruth Stiles Gannett
Joyce Gard
Jane Gardam
Leon Garfield
Alan Garner
Eve Garnett
Doris Gates
Jonathan Gathorne-Hardy

Jean Craighead George
May Gibbs
Nikki Giovanni
Fred Gipson
Rumer Godden
John Gordon
Elizabeth Goudge
Eleanor Graham
Lorenz Graham
Kenneth Grahame
Hardie Gramatky
Nicholas Stuart Gray
Margaret Greaves
Roger Lancelyn Green
Bette Greene
Constance C. Greene
Graham Greene
Ted Greenwood
Grey Owl
Frederick Grice
G. D. Griffiths
Helen Griffiths
Rosa Guy

Berta and Elmer Hader
Roderick Haig-Brown
J. B. S. Haldane
Kathleen Hale
Gail E. Haley
Aylmer Hall
Virginia Hamilton
Cynthia Harnett
Aurand Harris
Christie Harris
Mary K. Harris
Rosemary Harris
Erik Haugaard
John F. Hayes
Carolyn Haywood
Robert Heinlein
Marguerite Henry
Nat Hentoff
Anita Hewett
Florence Hightower
E. W. Hildick
S. E. Hinton
Russell Hoban
C. Walter Hodges
Syd Hoff
Grace Hogarth
Isabelle Holland
Holling C. Holling
Felice Holman
Jacynth Hope-Simpson
Charlotte Hough
James A. Houston

Richard Hughes
Shirley Hughes
Ted Hughes
S. G. Hulme Beaman
Irene Hunt
Mabel Leigh Hunt
Kristin Hunter
Mollie Hunter
Norman Hunter
Laurence Hyde

Sulamith Ish-Kishor

Jesse Jackson
Will James
Randall Jarrell
Ann Jellicoe
W. E. Johns
Annabell and Edgar Johnson
Crockett Johnson
Diana Wynne Jones
June Jordan
Sesyle Joslin
Margaret Jowett
Aaron Judah
Norton Juster

Virginia Kahl
Josephine Kamm
Geraldine Kaye
Ezra Jack Keats
Charles Keeping
Harold Keith
Eric Kelly
Carol Kendall
Judith Kerr
M. E. Kerr
Barbara Kimenye
Clive King
Lee Kingman
Rudyard Kipling
Jim Kjelgaard
Norma Klein
Frank Knight
E. L. Konigsburg
Phyllis Krasilovsky
Joanna Halpert Kraus
Robert Kraus
Ruth Krauss
Joseph Krumgold
Karla Kuskin
Elisabeth Kyle

Evelyn Lampman
Jane Langton
Jean Lee Latham
Eleanor Lattimore
Ann Lawrence

5

Mildred Lawrence
Robert Lawson
Alec Lea
Munro Leaf
Benjamin Lee
Dennis Lee
Mildred Lee
Robert Leeson
Amy Le Feuvre
Ursula K. Le Guin
Adelaide Leitch
Madeleine L'Engle
Lois Lenski
C. S. Lewis
Hilda Lewis
Joan M. Lexau
Betty Jean Lifton
Norman Lindsay
Joan Lingard
Eric Linklater
Leo Lionni
William Lipkind
Joseph Wharton Lippincott
Jean Little
Penelope Lively
Myra Cohn Livingston
Anita Lobel
Arnold Lobel
Elsie Locke
Hugh Lofting
Patricia Lynch

Jean MacGibbon
Ellen MacGregor
Elisabeth MacIntyre
Constance D'Arcy Mackay
Walter Macken
Jean MacKenzie
Margaret MacPherson
Angus MacVicar
Reginald Maddock
Margaret Mahy
Rosemary Manning
Ruth Manning-Sanders
Markoosie
David Martin
Patricia Miles Martin
John Masefield
Sharon Bell Mathis
Christobel Mattingley
William Mayne
Robert McCloskey
David McCord
Phyllis McGinley
Eloise Jarvis McGraw

Iona McGregor
David McKee
Lorrie McLaughlin
Allan Campbell McLean
Janet McNeill
Stephen W. Meader
Florence Crannell Means
Cornelia Meigs
Mary Melwood
Eve Merriam
Jean Merrill
Laurence Meynell
Katherine Milhous
Madge Miller
A. A. Milne
Else Minarik
Elyne Mitchell
Naomi Mitchison
F. N. Monjo
L. M. Montgomery
Rutherford Montgomery
Diana Moorhead
Walt Morey
Alison Morgan
Farley Mowat
Dhan Gopal Mukerji

E. Nesbit
Evaline Ness
Emily Cheney Neville
Clare Turlay Newberry
Beverley Nichols
Ruth Nichols
Lilith Norman
Sterling North
Andre Norton
Mary Norton
Robert Nye

Robert C. O'Brien
Scott O'Dell
Mary O'Hara
Carola Oman
Kola Onadipe
Doris Orgel
Edward Ormondroyd
Reginald Ottley
Jenny Overton
Elsie Oxenham

C. Everard Palmer
Peggy Parish
Ruth Park
Richard Parker
Mary Elwyn Patchett
Jill Paton Walsh
Brian Patten

Philippa Pearce
Howard Pease
Richard Peck
Robert Newton Peck
Bill Peet
Lucy Fitch Perkins
Maud and Miska Petersham
Ann Petry
K. M. Peyton
Joan Phipson
Barbara Leonie Picard
Stephanie Plowman
Leo Politi
Madeleine A. Polland
Josephine Poole
Gene Stratton Porter
Sheena Porter
Beatrix Potter
Rhoda Power
Susan Price
John Pudney
Virginia Pye

Gwynedd Rae
Arthur Ransome
Ellen Raskin
Marjorie Kinnan Rawlings
Mary Ray
William Rayner
James Reaney
Leslie Rees
James Reeves
Meta Mayne Reid
H. A. and Margret Rey
Frank Richards
Laura E. Richards
Antonia Ridge
Louise Riley
Charles G. D. Roberts
Elizabeth Madox Roberts
Keith Robertson
Joan G. Robinson
Mary Rodgers
James Roose-Evans
Diana Ross
Glen Rounds
Philip Rush

Marilyn Sachs
Andrew Salkey
Malcolm Saville
Ruth Sawyer
Richard Scarry
Jack Schaefer
Ann Schlee
Miriam Schlein

Jenny Seed
George Selden
Maurice Sendak
Kate Seredy
Ian Serraillier
Ernest Thompson Seton
Dr. Seuss
David Severn
Helen Sewell
Monica Shannon
Marjorie Weinman Sharmat
Edith Sharp
Margery Sharp
Noreen Shelley
Sylvia Sherry
Louisa R. Shotwell
Isaac Bashevis Singer
Barbara Sleigh
Louis Slobodkin
Esphyr Slobodkina
C. Fox Smith
Emma Smith
William Jay Smith
Caroline Dale Snedeker
Zilpha Keatley Snyder
Donald J. Sobol
Barbara Softly
Virginia Sorensen
Ivan Southall
Elizabeth George Speare
Eleanor Spence
Armstrong Sperry
E. C. Spykman
Mary Q. Steele
William O. Steele
William Steig
John Steptoe
William Stevenson
A. C. Stewart
Mary Stolz
Phil Stong
Margaret Storey
Catherine Storr
Joyce Stranger
Noel Streatfeild
L. A. G. Strong
Elizabeth Stucley
Rodie Sudbery
Donald Suddaby
Rosemary Sutcliff
Efua Sutherland
Eve Sutton
Ronald Syme
John Symonds
Geraldine Symons

Joan Tate
Sydney Taylor
Theodore Taylor
Colin Thiele
James Thurber
Ann Thwaite
Eve Titus
Barbara Euphan Todd
H. E. Todd
J. R. R. Tolkien
Ruth Tomalin
John Rowe Townsend
P. L. Travers
Mary Treadgold
Geoffrey Trease
Henry Treece
Alvin Tresselt
Elleston Trevor
Meriol Trevor
Tasha Tudor
John R. Tunis
Brinton Turkle
Ethel Turner
Philip Turner

Yoshiko Uchida
Janice Udry
Tomi Ungerer
Nora S. Unwin
Bertha Upton
Alison Uttley

Hilda Van Stockum
John Verney
Elizabeth Gray Vining
Judith Viorst
Elfrida Vipont

Bernard Waber
Jan Wahl
David Walker

Stuart Walker
D. J. Watkins-Pitchford
Clyde Watson
Jenifer Wayne
Rosemary Weir
Ronald Welch
Barbara Wersba
Joyce West
Robert Westall
Percy Westerman
Eliza Orne White
E. B. White
T. H. White
Phyllis A. Whitney
Leonard Wibberley
Ester Wier
Kurt Wiese
Kate Douglas Wiggin
Laura Ingalls Wilder
Anne Wilkinson
Barbara Willard
Jay Williams
Ursula Moray Williams
Barbara Ker Wilson
Maia Wojciechowska
David Wood
Kerry Wood
Lorna Wood
Patricia Wrightson
Olwen Wymark
Lee Wyndham

Elizabeth Yates
Jane Yolen
Delbert A. Young
Scott Young

Paul Zindel
Gene Zion
Charlotte Zolotow

APPENDIX

Louisa May Alcott
Thomas Bailey Aldrich
R. M. Ballantyne
Lewis Carroll
Susan Coolidge
Mary Mapes Dodge
Juliana Horatia Ewing
Lucretia P. Hale
Joel Chandler Harris
G. A. Henty
Jean Ingelow
Andrew Lang

Edward Lear
George MacDonald
Mary Louisa Molesworth
Howard Pyle
Talbot Baines Reed
Anna Sewell
Robert Louis Stevenson
Frank R. Stockton
Hesba Stretton
Mark Twain
Charlotte Yonge

ADAMS, Richard. British. Born in Newbury, Berkshire, 9 May 1920. Educated at Bradfield; Worcester College, Oxford, B.A. 1948, M.A. 1953. Served in the British Army, 1940–45. Married Barbara Elizabeth Acland in 1949; has two daughters. Worked in the Ministry of Housing and Local Government, London, 1948–68; Assistant Secretary, Department of the Environment, London, 1968–74. Recipient: Library Association Carnegie Medal, 1972; *Guardian* Award, 1973. Agent: David Higham Associates Ltd., 5–8 Lower John Street, London WIR 4HA. Address: Knocksharry House, Lhergy Dhoo, Peel, Isle of Man, United Kingdom.

PUBLICATIONS

Fiction

Watership Down.   London, Rex Collings, 1972; New York, Macmillan, 1974.
Shardik.   London, Allen Lane-Rex Collings, 1974; New York, Simon and Schuster, 1975.
The Plague Dogs.   London, Allen Lane, 1977.

Verse

The Tyger Voyage, illustrated by Nicola Bayley.   London, Cape, and New York, Knopf, 1976.
The Ship's Cat, illustrated by Alan Aldridge.   London, Cape, and New York, Knopf, 1977.

Other

Nature Through the Seasons, with Max Hooper, illustrated by David Goddard and Adrian Williams.   London, Penguin, 1975.

Richard Adams comments:
I do not, myself, recognise a distinction between publications for children and for adults. It has always seemed to me that there are only books and readers, and I agree with C.S. Lewis' view that a book which is not worth reading when you are sixty is not worth reading when you are six. *Watership Down* has been marketed as a novel for readers of any age, both in Great Britain and the U.S.A., as well as in other countries. *Shardik* also is read both by children and adults. In my view, the distinction may do more harm than good by deterring children from reading books which they would enjoy if left to themselves but which they have been told are "for adults."

*   *   *

The appearance of *Watership Down* was one of the miracles of publishing history. A story told first to the author's children, in the traditional English way, it did the rounds of the major publishers, to be finally accepted by the small house set up by Rex Collings. Lengthy and expensive, it remained a "sleeper" for some time, though very well reviewed, and then suddenly everyone was reading it. Awards and paperback editions followed; it became the best-selling Puffin of all time and is now both a Penguin and a Puffin, available equally to adult and child readers.

Watership Down tells how a group of rabbits escape from their warren, destroyed by Man, and after many adventures find a new, safe warren on Watership Down (a real place on the Berkshire Downs). Though lengthy and laden with descriptive passages it became a best-seller for many reasons: its exciting plot, its nostalgic evocation of the English countryside by sight, touch and smell, and the credible description of a rabbit society superior to our own. Another feature which strengthens the book's imaginative hold is Richard Adams' invention of Rabbit Language for the regular details of rabbit life, with special words for the sun (Frith), out-door feeding (silflay), mechanical vehicles (hrududu), and many more. The rabbits' names, from wild plants and flowers, are supposedly translations from Lapine. They have their own mythology with legends of El-ahrairah, the rabbits' Robin Hood.

The thrills in the plot lie in the continual dangers the rabbits face and defeat, and here they become humanised. Although they do nothing that rabbits physically cannot do, they are given speech and reasoning powers similar (and often superior!) to human beings. Two characters particularly enlist our sympathy and keep us involved – sensitive Fiver, who can foretell danger, and Hazel, the reluctant leader. Realising that the others need him to lead them, Hazel assumes this responsibility, but without dominating them, and invents feats new to rabbits: rescuing a rabbit from a snare, raiding a farmyard hutch for does, using a boat to escape across a river.

Watership Down follows a long line of English animal fantasy. It is less like *The Wind in the Willows* (where animals live in houses, wear clothes, and eat human food) than B.B.'s *The Little Grey Men*. Adams himself says that Kipling was his model. Apart from the initial premise that rabbits think as well as humans, no magic is involved. Factual details of rabbit life come from R.M. Lockley's book *The Private Life of the Rabbit.*

Watership Down has been criticised for its "sexism" ("Old Worlds and New: Anti-Feminism in *Watership Down*" by Jane Resh Thomas, *Horn Book*, August 1974). She pointed out that rabbit society is male-dominated, does are just breeding-stock, and the female characters in the book are basically docile, and started a lively correspondence in *Horn Book* magazine. One could also criticise the fact that no alternative social structure other than a hierarchy governed by a Chief Rabbit is considered by our heroes. Richard Boston (*The Guardian*, 6 August 1976) discusses the politics of the book, relating it to Britain in the Second World War. Graham Hammond ("Trouble with Rabbits," *Children's Literature in Education*, September 1973) calls it a "somewhat outmoded view of leadership largely characterised by paternalism," and is worried about the effect on child readers, who might assimilate a wrong view of adult life.

One can partly answer these criticism with reference to Lockley, who describes a hierarchical, male-dominated structure with both sexes performing a strictly biological function, with the caveat that Lockley was not describing a completely wild community but an experimental, isolated one whose relationships, he admitted, he recorded in *human* terms and which he sometimes tampered with.

Richard Adams has also written *Shardik* and *The Tyger Voyage. Shardik* was acclaimed as the follow-up to *Watership Down*: this even longer animal saga tells of a giant bear which comes out of a forest to be received by a savage tribe as the reincarnation of its god and to be used as the figurehead for battle and conquest. It is not a children's book – politics, religion and violence have too large a place, so it is not within the scope of this essay. *The Tyger Voyage* is a collaboration with the artist Nicola Bayley to form a children's picture book, a short story in rhyming quatrains about the adventures of two tigers (whom he insists on calling "tygers"). Commissioned to inspire the artist and written in 24 hours, this verse needs no further mention.

Richard Adams is now a full-time writer. One now speculates whether his future books will have anything in common with his earlier successes. Will they all be about animals? Will they be better written or just as heavy with purple passages? Will women get a more equal share of the story? For an amateur writing in his spare time, Richard Adams has already achieved books and fame the envy of many professional writers.

—Jessica Kemball-Cook

AIKEN, Joan (Delano).   British.   Born in Rye, Sussex, 4 September 1924; daughter of the poet Conrad Aiken. Educated at Wychwood School, Oxford, 1936–40. Married Ronald George Brown in 1945 (died, 1955); has one son and one daughter. Worked for the BBC, 1942–43; Librarian, United Nations Information Centre, London, 1943–49; Sub-Editor and Features Editor. *Argosy*, London, 1955–60; Copywriter, J. Walter Thomson, London, 1960–61. Recipient: *Guardian* Award, 1969; Mystery Writers of America Edgar Allan Poe Award, 1972. Agent: A.M. Heath, 40–42 William IV Street, London WC2N 4DD; or Brandt and Brandt, 101 Park Avenue, New York, New York 10017, U.S.A. Address: White Hart House, High Street, Petworth, Sussex, England.

PUBLICATIONS FOR CHILDREN

Fiction

All You've Ever Wanted and Other Stories, illustrated by Pat Marriott.   London, Cape, 1953.

More Than You Bargained For and Other Stories, illustrated by Pat Marriott.   London, Cape, 1955; New York, Abelard Schuman, 1957.

The Kingdom and the Cave, illustrated by Dick Hart.   London and New York, Abelard Schuman, 1960.

The Wolves of Willoughby Chase, illustrated by Pat Marriott.   London, Cape, 1962; New York, Doubleday, 1963.

Black Hearts in Battersea, illustrated by Robin Jacques.   New York, Doubleday, 1964; London, Cape, 1965.

Nightbirds on Nantucket, illustrated by Robin Jacques.   London, Cape, and New York, Doubleday, 1966.

The Whispering Mountain.   London, Cape, 1968; New York, Doubleday, 1969.

A Necklace of Raindrops and Other Stories, illustrated by Jan Pienkowski.   London, Cape, and New York, Doubleday, 1968.

Armitage, Armitage, Fly Away Home, illustrated by Betty Fraser.   New York, Doubleday, 1968.

A Small Pinch of Weather and Other Stories, illustrated by Pat Marriott.   London, Cape, 1969.

Night Fall.   London, Macmillan, 1969; New York, Holt Rinehart, 1971.

Smoke from Cromwell's Time and Other Stories.   New York, Doubleday, 1970.

The Green Flash and Other Tales of Horror, Suspense, and Fantasy.   New York, Holt Rinehart, 1971.

The Cuckoo Tree, illustrated by Pat Marriott.   London, Cape, and New York, Doubleday, 1971.

The Kingdom under the Sea and Other Stories.   London, Cape, 1971.

A Harp of Fishbones and Other Stories, illustrated by Pat Marriott.   London, Cape, 1972.

Arabel's Raven.   London, BBC Publications, 1972; New York, Doubleday, 1974.

The Escaped Black Mamba, illustrated by Quentin Blake.   London, BBC Publications, 1973.

All But a Few.   London, Penguin, 1974.

The Bread Bin, illustrated by Quentin Blake.   London, BBC Publications, 1974.

Midnight Is a Place, illustrated by Pat Marriott.   London, Cape, and New York, Viking Press, 1974.

Not What You Expected: A Collection of Short Stories.   New York, Doubleday, 1974.

Mortimer's Tie, illustrated by Quentin Blake.   London, BBC Publications, 1976.

A Bundle of Nerves.   London, Gollancz, 1976.

Tale of a One-Way Street, illustrated by Jan Pienkowski.   London, Cape, 1977.

The Faithless Lollybird, illustrated by Pat Marriott.   London, Cape, 1977.

The Far Forests.   New York, Viking Press, 1977.
Go Saddle the Sea.   London, Cape, and New York, Doubleday, 1977.

Plays

Winterthing, music by John Sebastian Brown, illustrated by Arvis Stewart (produced Albany, New York, 1977). New York, Holt Rinehart, 1972; included in *Winterthing, and The Mooncusser's Daughter,* 1973.
The Mooncusser's Daughter, illustrated by Arvis Stewart.   New York, Viking Press, 1973; included in *Winterthing, and The Mooncusser's Daughter,* 1973.
Winterthing, and The Mooncusser's Daughter.   London, Cape, 1973.
Street, music by John Sebastian Brown (produced London, 1977).

Television Plays: *The Dark Streets of Kimballs Green,* 1976; *Mortimer's Tie,* 1976; *The Apple of Trouble,* 1977.

Verse

The Skin Spinners, illustrated by Ken Rinciari.   New York, Viking Press, 1976.

Other

Translator, *The Angel Inn,* by Contessa de Ségur, illustrated by Pat Marriott.   London, Cape, 1976.

PUBLICATIONS FOR ADULTS

Novels

The Silence of Herondale.   New York, Doubleday, 1964; London, Gollancz, 1965.
The Fortune Hunters.   New York, Doubleday, 1965.
Trouble with Product X.   London, Gollancz, 1966; as *Beware of the Bouquet,* New York, Doubleday, 1966.
Hate Begins at Home.   London, Gollancz, 1967; as *Dark Interval,* New York, Doubleday, 1967, London, Sphere, 1972.
The Ribs of Death.   London, Gollancz, 1967; as *The Crystal Crow.*   New York, Doubleday, 1968.
The Embroidered Sunset.   London, Gollancz, and New York, Doubleday, 1970.
Died on a Rainy Sunday.   London, Gollancz, and New York, Holt Rinehart, 1972.
The Butterfly Picnic.   London, Gollancz, 1972; as *A Cluster of Separate Sparks,* New York, Doubleday, 1972.
Voices in an Empty House.   London, Gollancz, and New York, Doubleday, 1975.
Castle Barebane.   London, Gollancz, and New York, Viking Press, 1976.
Last Movement.   London, Gollancz, 1977.
The Five-Minute Marriage.   London, Gollancz, 1977.

Short Stories

The Windscreen Weepers and Other Tales of Horror and Suspense.   London, Gollancz, 1969.

Joan Aiken comments:
My books for children fall into three categories. Collections of short stories which may be described as fairytales – i.e., magical, fantastic, supernatural, though set mainly in the present

day. Full-length books for a slightly older age-group, say 11–14. These contain no magic or supernatural elements, but are set mostly in an imaginary 19th century. Shorter stories for younger children of a semi-fantastic nature about talking or at least extra-intelligent animals – i.e., *Arabel's Raven*, "Mice and Mendelson."

*   *   *

For sheer energy and exuberance, Joan Aiken has no rival among contemporary English children's writers except perhaps Leon Garfield. Her stories heap incident on incident, invention on invention, in a spendthrift way that only a writer with endless imaginative resources could afford.

Her fiction for children, up to the time of writing, consists of six novels and several story-collections. Each of the six novels is self-contained; and there has been no attempt to shape them into a unified whole, but the same people and places frequently appear in more than one. All are set in the past, but they are not historical; indeed, they are unhistorical to a degree that demands a total suspension of disbelief. Their action takes place in a period of English history that never happened, and in most of them, it is the reign of King James III, who came to the throne in 1832 and has remained there in spite of the machinations of those who support the Hanoverian Pretender. ("Bring back, bring back, oh bring back my Georgie to me," they sing.)

Among the surprising features of this England-that-never-was is the fact, or "unfact," that the Channel Tunnel has been completed, and a great many wolves have been driven by severe winters in Europe and Russia to migrate through it into Britain. This is the background to Miss Aiken's first children's novel. *The Wolves of Willoughby Chase*. Wolves roam the bleak northern landscape in which stands the turreted stately home of Sir Willoughby Green, but even the wolves are no more fierce and predatory than the wicked governess Miss Slighcarp who usurps control after Sir Willoughby and Lady Green have gone abroad, leaving behind them their small daughter Bonnie and their niece Sylvia.

Bonnie and Sylvia, obstacles to Miss Slighcarp's nefarious schemes, are shipped off to a Squeersian orphan-school run by massive, mean Mrs. Brisket. But, escaping from it with the help of a dauntless country boy called Simon, they make their way to London, and villainy is duly exposed in a thorough, satisfying denouement.

Simon reappears in *Black Hearts in Battersea*, a book which is largely about Hanoverian conspiracies against Good King James. Among the new characters encountered in this story are the eccentric Duke of Battersea, living in pink-granite Battersea Castle; his heir, young Lord Bakerloo; and the King himself, a little, dapper, elderly Scottish gentleman who remarks, "Och, well, noo, Battersea … how's your gude lady?" There is also sharp-eyed, sharp-tongued Cockney waif Dido Twite who in turn reappears as heroine of *Nightbirds on Nantucket*. In the latter book a plan to assassinate the King by means of a long-distance cannon fired across the Atlantic from Nantucket Island is fortunately thwarted.

By the time of *The Cuckoo Tree*, James III has gone to his rest, to be succeeded by Richard IV. ("This is yer ain appointit King, Davie Jamie Charlie Neddie Geordie Harry Dick Tudor-Stuart, wishfu' tae have a crack wi' ye," the new monarch tells a crowd.) The Hanoverians are still busy, intending to dispose of his Majesty and all the great ones of the land by a dastardly deed at the Coronation, but they are foiled again when Dido Twite rides to the rescue on an elephant. In *Midnight Is a Place* the author forsakes politics and plotting, and the scene is largely a satanic Northern town at the time of the Industrial Revolution. But once again there are villainy and cliffhanging drama with virtue triumphant at the end.

As these brief summaries may suggest, Miss Aiken goes in for wild exaggeration, staggering improbability, and riotous melodrama. She does so, of course, deliberately and shamelessly. Her books are rich in humour as well as in incident, and her use of language is not only masterly but masterful. The intricate plots, energetic development, and prolific character-creation, together with a strong tendency to caricature, suggest the influence of Dickens. Nevertheless, Miss Aiken is more her own woman, more an individual and less a follower in somebody else's path, than most writers can hope to be. Obviously, there are

13

limitations. The action of her books is external, and there is not much psychological exploration or examination of moral issues – aims which would probably be incompatible with the rapid pace and high colour of her writing.

Her story-collections must receive shorter shrift here than they deserve. *All You've Ever Wanted* and *More Than You Bargained For* preceded the novels but display the same strong line in humorous fantasy and the same lavish use of ideas that could be made to stretch much farther by a thriftier writer. Several stories are about the engaging Armitage family, who take the inexplicable for granted, are unflustered by magic, and keep a pet unicorn called Candleberry. Among later collections, *A Necklace of Raindrops* is outstanding; the eight stories it tells are clearly fairy-tales, but they incorporate, in addition to the more usual fairy-tale properties, buses, trains and aeroplanes – all without any sign of strain. *Arabel's Raven* and *Mortimer's Tie* put into book form stories that were told on the B.B.C. *Jackanory* television programme. Mortimer, the irrepressible pet raven, likes diamonds and slot-machines and potato-crisps and gets into hilarious predicaments; and his vocabulary consists, with great literary appropriateness, of the one word "nevermore."

It is easy for the well-meaning writer of children's books to become excessively serious, even solemn. Joan Aiken is never likely to fall into that trap. Her work is a welcome reminder that the first aim of fiction is to give pleasure, and the better the fiction, the greater should be the pleasure. Undoubtedly there are other benefits: one might well expect Miss Aiken's books to stretch the imagination spectacularly and to stimulate a delight in words for their own sake, but any such results are incidental – a bonus.

—John Rowe Townsend

AINSWORTH, Ruth (Gallard). British. Born in Manchester, Lancashire, 16 October 1908. Educated at Ipswich High School; Froebel Training Centre, Leicester. Married Frank L. Gilbert in 1935; has three sons. Script Writer, *Listen with Mother* and *English for Schools* series, BBC, London. Address: West Cheynes, Corbridge, Northumberland NE45 5GH, England.

PUBLICATIONS FOR CHILDREN

Fiction

Tales about Tony, illustrated by Cora E.M. Paterson. London, Epworth Press, 1936.
Mr. Popcorn's Friends. London, Epworth Press, 1938.
The Gingerbread House. London, Epworth Press, 1938.
The Ragamuffins. London, Epworth Press, 1939.
Richard's First Term. London, Epworth Press, 1940.
Five and a Dog. London, Epworth Press, 1949.
"Listen with Mother" Tales, illustrated by Astrid Walford. London, Heinemann, 1951.
Rufty Tufty the Golliwog, illustrated by Dorothy Craigie. London, Heinemann, 1952.
Rufty Tufty at the Seaside, illustrated by Dorothy Craigie. London, Heinemann, 1954.
Charles Stories and Others, from "Listen with Mother," illustrated by Sheila Hawkins. London, Heinemann, 1954.
More about Charles and Other Stories, from "Listen with Mother," illustrated by Sheila Hawkins. London, Heinemann, 1954.
The Snow Bear, illustrated by Rosemary Trew. London, Heinemann, 1956.
Rufty Tufty Goes Camping, illustrated by Dorothy Craigie. London, Heinemann, 1956.
Rufty Tufty Runs Away, illustrated by Dorothy Craigie. London, Heinemann, 1957.

Five "Listen with Mother" Tales about Charles, illustrated by Matvyn Wright. London, Adprint, 1957.

Nine Drummers Drumming, illustrated by John Mackay. London, Heinemann, 1958.

Rufty Tufty Flies High, illustrated by D.G. Valentine. London, Heinemann, 1959.

Cherry Stones: A Book of Fairy Stories, illustrated by Pat Humphreys. London, Heinemann, 1960.

Rufty Tufty's Island, illustrated by D.G. Valentine. London, Heinemann, 1960.

Lucky Dip: A Selection of Stories and Verses, illustrated by Geraldine Spence. London, Penguin, 1961.

Rufty Tufty and Hattie, illustrated by D.G. Valentine. London, Heinemann, 1962.

Far-Away Children, illustrated by Felice Trentin. London, Heinemann, 1963; New York, Roy, 1968.

The Ten Tales of Shellover, illustrated by Antony Maitland. London, Deutsch, 1963; New York, Roy, 1968.

The Wolf Who Was Sorry, illustrated by Doritie Kettlewell. London, Heinemann, 1964; New York, Roy, 1968.

Rufty Tufty Makes a House, illustrated by D.G. Valentine. London, Heinemann, 1965.

Daisy the Cow, illustrated by Sarah Garland. London, Hamish Hamilton, 1966.

Horse on Wheels, illustrated by Janet Duchesne. London, Hamish Hamilton, 1966.

Jack Frost, illustrated by Jane Paton. London, Heinemann, 1966.

Roly the Railway Mouse, illustrated by Leslie Atkinson. London, Heinemann, 1967; as *Roly the Railroad Mouse*, New York, Watts, 1969.

The Aeroplane Who Wanted to See the Sea. London, Bancroft, 1968.

Boris the Teddy Bear. London, Bancroft, 1968.

Dougal the Donkey. London, Bancroft, 1968.

More Tales of Shellover, illustrated by Antony Maitland. London, Deutsch, and New York, Roy, 1968.

Mungo the Monkey. London, Bancroft, 1968.

The Old Fashioned Car. London, Bancroft, 1968.

The Rabbit and His Shadow. London, Bancroft, 1968.

The Noah's Ark, illustrated by Elsie Wrigley. London, Lutterworth Press, 1969.

The Bicycle Wheel, illustrated by Shirley Hughes. London, Hamish Hamilton, 1969.

Look, Do and Listen, illustrated by Bernadette Watts. London, Heinemann, and New York, Watts, 1969.

The Phantom Cyclist and Other Stories, illustrated by Antony Maitland. London, Deutsch, and Chicago, Follett, 1971.

Another Lucky Dip, illustrated by Shirley Hughes. London, Penguin, 1973.

The Phantom Fisherboy: Tales of Mystery and Magic, illustrated by Shirley Hughes. London, Deutsch, 1974.

Bedtime Book. Maidenhead, Berkshire, Purnell, 1974.

Three's Company, illustrated by Prudence Seward. London, Lutterworth Press, 1974.

The Bear Who Liked Hugging People and Other Stories, illustrated by Antony Maitland. London, Heinemann, 1976.

The Phantom Roundabout and Other Stories, illustrated by Shirley Hughes. London, Deutsch, 1977.

Up the Airy Mountain. London, Heinemann, 1977.

Plays

Three Little Mushrooms: Four Puppet Plays (includes *Here We Go round the Buttercups, Lob's Silver Spoon, Hide-and-Seek, Hay-Making*). London, Heinemann, 1955.

More Little Mushrooms: Four Puppet Plays (includes *Three Clever Mushrooms, Tick-Tock, Christmas Eve, The White Stranger*). London, Heinemann, 1955.

Verse

All Different, illustrated by Linda Bramley.   London, Heinemann, 1947.
The Evening Listens.   London, Heinemann, 1953.

Other

The Ruth Ainsworth Readers (*The Cottage by the Sea; Little Wife Goody; The Robber;
    The Wild Boy; A Comfort for Owl; Sugar and Spice; Fun, Fires and Friends; Black
    Bill; A Pill for Owl; Tortoise in Trouble; The Pirate Ship; Hob the Dwarf*).   London,
    Heinemann, 12 vols., 1953–55.
Look Ahead Readers, with Ronald Ridout, illustrated by John Mackay.   London,
    Heinemann, 8 vols., 1956–57.
Books for Me to Read, with Ronald Ridout:
    Red Books (*Jill and Peter; The House of Hay; Come and Play; A Name of My Own;
        The Duck That Ran Away; Tim's Hoop*), illustrated by Ingeborg Meyer-
        Rey.   London, Bancroft, 6 vols., 1964.
    Blue Books (*At the Zoo; What Are They?; Colours; Silly Billy; A Pram and a Bicycle;
        Pony, Pony*), illustrated by Gwyneth Mamlock.   London, Bancroft, 6 vols., 1965.
    Green Books (*Susan's House; What Can You Hear?; Tim's Kite; Flippy the Frog; Huff
        the Hedgehog; A House for a Mouse*), illustrated by William Robert
        Shaw.   London, Bancroft, 6 vols., 1968.
The Look about You Books (*In Woods and Fields, Down the Lane, Beside the Sea, By
    Pond and Stream, In Your Garden, In the Park*), illustrated by Jennie Corbett.
    London, Heinemann, 6 vols., 1967–69.
The Ruth Ainsworth Book, illustrated by Shirley Hughes.   London, Heinemann, and
    New York, Watts, 1970.
Dandy the Donkey (reader).   London, Bancroft, 1971.
The Wild Wood (reader).   London, Bancroft, 1971.
Fairy Gold: Favourite Fairy Tales Retold for the Very Young, illustrated by Barbara
    Hope Steinberg.   London, Heinemann, 1972.
Three Bags Full (miscellany), illustrated by Sally Long.   London, Heinemann, 1975.

Editor, *Book of Colours and Sounds*.   London, Purnell, 1968.

Ruth Ainsworth comments:
    I had a quiet childhood by the sea in Suffolk. Many of my stories have a background of
lonely beaches, sand dunes, marram grass and small prints of bare feet. Mermaids occur as
well as shrimps and anemones.
    My father died when I was a baby. I started writing as soon as I could use a pencil and
published poems in periodicals in my 'teens. I won a Gold Medal for poetry.
    I love reading, biography, letters, novels, and poetry. I specially enjoy Jane Austen and Ivy
Compton-Burnett. I like walking, architecture, looking at paintings and listening to music.
My chief joy is seeing my family and my friends informally and often. Life in this small
Northumberland town suits me pretty well, though I still feel that Suffolk is my native home.

                            *   *   *

    Ruth Ainsworth's storytelling is all for the younger reader, so the tales are short, no one is
really cruel, the endings are always happy, the lonely find friends, the bad become good. The
characters may be small children doing quite ordinary things or talking animals, fairies, and
toys who do quite surprising things.
    Each collection of ten or a dozen small stories has a variety of backgrounds. *Tales of
Shellover* and *More Tales of Shellover* begin and end with a kind old woman gathering her

pets together so that Shellover the tortoise can recount the tales, but he never interrupts between them. The only general advice is that it pays to be kind. The poor shepherd who needs to earn three gold coins in the city in order to marry his goose-girl is helped by a goose, a squirrel, and a ladybird whom he has saved on the way, while a small boy loses his magic shilling when he refuses to help a beggar girl. The behaviour of the four kittens, the wayward fairy child, and the friendly hen all have obvious appeal for small children. Disobedience always brings disaster, as with the two sisters who go into the forbidden cave, but magic rights everything.

The Bear Who Liked Hugging People and Other Stories begins with a typical Ruth Ainsworth character, a mountain bear who did no harm to anybody but would hug people because he liked them. Unfortunately, some of the people hugged were never the same again. He was saved from being shot by being given a bed quilt to hug. Most of the children have model parents. When Miranda brought a mermaid home, her mother said: "Come in, my dear, and have some tea. I will set another place." Later the mermaid returns to the sea, and Miranda stays happily on land: none of the problems Hans Andersen's mermaid suffered arise. Even the Phantom Fisherboy, in the collection with that title, is not really creepy, only returning to the place where he was happy.

There are a whole series of books about Rufty Tufty the Golliwog, all simply written in short sentences and full of domestic adventures. "If you could see Rufty Tufty the Golliwog in bed one morning, you would know why his mother called him Rufty Tufty. The bed is always smooth and tidy because Mrs. Golliwog tucks it in so well .... But what is that odd black tuft on the pillow ... is it a tangle of black wool .... No, it is a golliwog's hair."

Ruth Ainsworth has also written *Look about You* books, describing things to be seen in the country and by the sea, for the same age group, and other books with much advice on plays, games, and things to do anywhere and everywhere.

—Margaret Campbell

ALEXANDER, Lloyd (Chudley). American. Born in Philadelphia, Pennsylvania, 30 January 1924. Educated at West Chester State College, Pennsylvania, 1942; Lafayette College, Easton, Pennsylvania, 1943; the Sorbonne, Paris, 1946. Served in the United States Army Combat Intelligence and Counter-Intelligence corps; Staff Sergeant. Author-in-Residence, Temple University, Philadelphia, 1970–74. Member, Library Committee, *World Book Encyclopedia*, Chicago, 1973–74. Since 1970, Director, Carpenter Lane Chamber Music Society, Philadelphia; since 1973, Member, Editorial Advisory Board, *Cricket* magazine, La Salle, Illinois. Recipient: Jewish Book Council Isaac Siegel Memorial Award, 1959; American Library Association Newbery Medal, 1969; National Book Award, 1971. Agent: Brandt and Brandt, 101 Park Avenue, New York, New York 10017. Address: 1005 Drexel Avenue, Drexel Hill, Pennsylvania 19026, U.S.A.

PUBLICATIONS FOR CHILDREN

Fiction

Border Hawk: August Bondi, illustrated by Bernard Krigstein. New York, Farrar Straus, 1958.
The Flagship Hope: Aaron Lopez, illustrated by Bernard Krigstein. Philadelphia, Jewish Publications Society, 1960.
Time Cat: The Remarkable Journeys of Jason and Gareth, illustrated by Bill Sokol. New York, Holt Rinehart, 1963; as *Nine Lives*, London, Cassell, 1963.

The Book of Three. New York, Holt Rinehart, 1964; London, Heinemann, 1966.
The Black Cauldron. New York, Holt Rinehart, 1965; London, Heinemann, 1967.
Coll and His White Pig, illustrated by Evaline Ness. New York, Holt Rinehart, 1965.
The Castle of Llyr. New York, Holt Rinehart, 1966; London, Heinemann, 1968.
Taran Wanderer. New York, Holt Rinehart, 1967.
The High King. New York, Holt Rinehart, 1968.
The Marvelous Misadventures of Sebastian: Grand Extravaganza, Including a Performance by the Entire Cast of the Gallimaufry-Theatricus. New York, Dutton, 1970.
The King's Fountain, illustrated by Ezra Jack Keats. New York, Dutton, 1971.
The Four Donkeys, illustrated by Lester Abrams. New York, Holt Rinehart, 1972; Kingswood, Surrey, World's Work, 1974.
The Cat Who Wished to Be a Man. New York, Dutton, 1973.
The Foundling and Other Tales of Prydain, illustrated by Margot Zemach. New York, Holt Rinehart, 1973.
The Wizard in the Tree, illustrated by Laszlo Kubinyi. New York, Dutton, 1975.
The Town Cats and Other Tales, illustrated by Laszlo Kubinyi. New York, Dutton, 1977.

PUBLICATIONS FOR ADULTS

Novel

And Let the Credit Go. New York, Crowell, 1955.

Other

My Five Tigers. New York, Crowell, and London, Cassell, 1956.
Janine Is French. New York, Crowell, 1958; London, Cassell, 1960.
My Love Affair with Music. New York, Crowell, 1960; London, Cassell, 1961.
Park Avenue Vet, with Louis J. Camuti. New York, Holt Rinehart, and London, Deutsch, 1962.
Fifty Years in the Doghouse. New York, Putnam, 1964; as *Send for Ryan!,* London, W.H. Allen, 1965.

Translator, *The Wall and Other Stories,* by Jean-Paul Sartre. New York, New Directions, 1948; as *Intimacy and Other Stories,* London, Peter Nevill, 1949; New Directions, 1952.
Translator, *Nausea,* by Jean-Paul Sartre. New York, New Directions, 1949; London, Hamish Hamilton, 1962; as *The Diary of Antoine Roquentin,* London, Lehmann, 1949.
Translator, *Selected Writings,* by Paul Eluard. New York, New Directions, 1951; London, Routledge, 1952; as *Uninterrupted Poetry: Selected Writings,* New Directions, 1975.
Translator, *The Sea Rose,* by Paul Vialar. London and New York, Peter Nevill, 1952.

Critical Study: *A Tribute to Lloyd Alexander* by Myra Cohn Livingston, Philadelphia, Drexel Institute, 1976.

*   *   *

Lloyd Alexander rose to prominence in the children's book field in the United States as a result of a cycle of five books, the "Prydain" series. Before this time, Alexander had written several books for adults (*My Five Tigers, Park Avenue Vet*) and for children (*Time Cat*) which had been moderately praised. These early books, both adult and juvenile, revealed several characteristics which Alexander was to exhibit again and again in his work: a fondness for cats, a strong imaginative bent, and a witty, essentially self-deprecating, sense of humor.

The "Prydain" series, based loosely on the Welsh Mabinogion tales, takes a boy, Taran, a stray without known parentage, and sets him on a journey which ends in a sense of identity and true self-knowledge. In *The Book of Three*, Taran, then an Assistant Pig-Keeper, sets out to find his vanished charge Hen Wen, the oracular pig. By the time Taran finds Hen Wen, we've been introduced to Eilonwy, the heroine of the series and Taran's future mate; Fflewddur Fflam, a cowardly knight; Gurgi, sub-human but loyal; and Gwydion, leader of the good side against the evil, represented here by the enchantress, Achren. This first volume does an excellent job of setting the scene for the four books which follow, introducing the main characters and establishing the ebb and flow of incident which carries the books.

The Black Cauldron, perhaps the most chilling of the five, introduces the theme of sacrifice. The cauldron, in the hands of the evil Arawn, revivifies the dead thrown into it, making them immortal, and good seems certain to perish as evil flourishes. But Ellidyr, originally on Taran's side and later a defector, redeems himself by willingly jumping into the cauldron, shattering it with his own death. Taran begins to see that being a warrior means not only honor but the risk of death.

Eilonwy is kidnapped in *The Castle of Llyr*, and after many vicissitudes is rescued by Taran, aided by Fflewddur Fflam and a giant cat, Llyan. *Taran Wanderer* concentrates on Taran's journey to find his father; he's discovered that he wants to marry Eilonwy and feels that he cannot offer her the hand of an unknown. At the end of his journey, he has not found his parents, but he has discovered that it's what he himself is that is important.

In *The High King* the final battle between good and evil occurs, with much death on both sides. At its end, Gwydion and his friends sail for the Summer Country, where there is no death. Taran is invited to go with them; his sense of duty calls him to remain in Prydain, even at the cost of Eilonwy. She gives up her claims to otherworldliness to remain with Taran.

The "Prydain" cycle captures one's attention because of the convolutions of the plot, the universal appeal of the themes, and the felicity of the prose style. Interesting characters are created in great abundance, but somehow they remain cardboard figures. In spite of Taran's search and Eilonwy's trials, they change little during the course of the five books. Our first impressions of these two and the other characters in the books stand: enjoyable but static.

After the "Prydain" series, Alexander began a group of stories which perhaps display his innate talents more truly than the earlier ones. *The Marvelous Misadventures of Sebastian* is a wry, subtle comedy. Sebastian, a fiddler in the small orchestra of a nobleman in a make-believe land, is sacked when he offends an important personage. He sets out for the city, but finds the countryside in a sad state, obviously suffering from mismanagement on the sovereign's part. Sebastian meets a white cat, a princess avoiding marriage, and gains a magic violin. After many amusing adventures, the princess has claimed her throne, and Sebastian is off to prove himself worthy of her hand. The characters are stereotypes, albeit amusing ones, but the real fun is in the romp across the country and the sly twists of wit in the telling of the tale.

The Cat Who Wished to Be a Man and *The Wizard in the Tree* are essentially variations on the standard Alexander theme: proving oneself a person of worth even when one has no family background.

Alexander's later books seem penultimate to his work from 1964 through 1970. The same incidents, reworked over and over again, although with grace and enduring wit, are not enough. Characters must not simply be created; they must grow and show evidence of it. It is this task which Alexander has thus far not accomplished.

—Rosemary Weber

ALLAN, Mabel Esther. British. Born in Wallasey, Cheshire, 11 February 1915. Educated at private schools. Served in the British Women's Land Army during World War II. Recipient: Mystery Writers of America award, 1971. Agent: John Farquharson Ltd., Bell House, 8 Bell Yard, London WC2A 2JR; or, Julian Bach Literary Agency Inc., 3 East 48th Street, New York, New York 10017, U.S.A. Address: Gleng. ʳth, 11 Oldfield Way, Heswall, Wirral, Merseyside L60 6RQ, England.

PUBLICATIONS FOR CHILDREN

Fiction

The Glen Castle Mystery. London, Warne, 1948.
The Adventurous Summer, illustrated by Isobel Veevers. London, Museum Press, 1948.
The Wyndhams Went to Wales, illustrated by Beryl Thornborough. London, Sylvan Press, 1948.
Mullion, illustrated by R. Walter Hall. London, Hutchinson, 1949.
Cilia of Chiltern's Edge, illustrated by Betty Ladler. London, Museum Press, 1949.
Trouble at Melville Manor, illustrated by Isobel Veevers. London, Museum Press, 1949.
Holiday at Arnriggs. London, Warne, 1949.
Chiltern Adventure, illustrated by T.R. Freeman. London, Blackie, 1950.
Jimmy John's Journey. London, Dean, 1950.
Over the Sea to School, illustrated by W. Mackinlay. London, Blackie, 1950.
School under Snowdon. London, Hutchinson, 1950.
Everyday Island. London, Museum Press, 1950.
Seven in Switzerland, illustrated by Isobel Veevers. London, Blackie, 1950.
The Exciting River, illustrated by Helen Jacobs. London, Nelson, 1951.
Clues to Connemara, illustrated by Philip. London, Blackie, 1952.
The Maclains of Glen Gillean. London, Hutchinson, 1952.
Return to Derrykereen. London, Ward Lock, 1952.
A School in Danger, illustrated by Eric Winter. London, Blackie, 1952.
The School on Cloud Ridge. London, Hutchinson, 1952.
The School on North Barrule. London, Museum Press, 1952.
The Secret Valley, illustrated by C. Instrell. Leeds, E.J. Arnold, 1953.
Room for the Cuckoo: The Story of a Farming Year. London, Dent, 1953.
Three Go to Switzerland, illustrated by Isobel Veevers. London, Blackie, 1953.
Lucia Comes to School. London, Hutchinson, 1953.
Strangers at Brongwerne. London, Museum Press, 1953.
Meric's Secret Cottage. London, Blackie, 1954.
Adventure Royal, illustrated by C.W. Bacon. London, Blackie, 1954.
Here We Go Round: A Career Story for Girls. London, Heinemann, 1954.
Margaret Finds a Future. London, Hutchinson, 1954.
New Schools for Old. London, Hutchinson, 1954.
The Summer at Town's End, illustrated by Iris Weller. London, Harrap, 1954.
Adventures in Switzerland. London, Pickering and Inglis, 1955.
The Mystery of Derrydane, illustrated by Vera Chadwick. Huddersfield, Yorkshire, Schofield and Sims, 1955.
Changes for the Challoners. London, Ward Lock, 1955.
Glenvara. London, Hutchinson, 1955; as *Summer of Decision,* New York, Abelard Schuman, 1957.
Judith Teaches. London, Lane, 1955.
Swiss School. London, Hutchinson, 1955.
Adventure in Mayo. London, Ward Lock, 1956.

Balconies and Blue Nets: The Story of a Holiday in Brittany, illustrated by Peggy Beetles. London, Harrap, 1956.

Lost Lorrenden, illustrated by Shirley Hughes. London, Blackie, 1956.

Strangers in Skye. London, Heinemann, 1956; New York, Criterion Books, 1958.

Two in the Western Isles. London, Hutchinson, 1956.

The Vine-Clad Hill, illustrated by T.R. Freeman. London, Lane, 1956; as *Swiss Holiday*, New York, Vanguard Press, 1957.

Flora at Kilroinn. London, Blackie, 1956.

The Amber House. London, Hutchinson, 1956.

Ann's Alpine Adventure. London, Hutchinson, 1956.

At School in Skye, illustrated by Constance Marshall. London, Blackie, 1957.

Black Forest Summer. London, Bodley Head, 1957; New York, Vanguard Press, 1959.

Sara Goes to Germany. London, Hutchinson, 1957.

Ballet for Drina (as Jean Estoril), illustrated by Eve Guthrie and M.P. Steedman Davies. London, Hodder and Stoughton, 1957; New York, Vanguard Press, 1958.

Drina's Dancing Year (as Jean Estoril). London, Hodder and Stoughton, 1958.

Blue Dragon Days. London, Heinemann, 1958; as *Romance in Italy*, New York, Vanguard Press, 1962.

The Conch Shell, illustrated by T.R. Freeman. London, Blackie, 1958.

The House by the Marsh, illustrated by Sheila Rose. London, Dent, 1958.

Rachel Tandy. London, Hutchinson, 1958.

Drina Dances in Exile (as Jean Estoril). London, Hodder and Stoughton, 1959.

Drina Dances in Italy (as Jean Estoril), illustrated by Eve Guthrie and M.P. Steedman Davies. London, Hodder and Stoughton, 1959; New York, Vanguard Press, 1962.

Amanda Goes to Italy. London, Hutchinson, 1959.

Catrin in Wales. London, Bodley Head, 1959; New York, Vanguard Press, 1961.

A Play to the Festival. London, Heinemann, 1959; as *"On Stage, Flory,"* New York, Watts, 1961.

Shadow over the Alps. London, Hutchinson, 1960.

A Summer in Brittany. London, Dent, 1960; as *Hilary's Summer on Her Own*, New York, Watts, 1961.

Tansy of Tring Street, illustrated by Sally Holliday. London, Heinemann, 1960.

Drina Dances Again (as Jean Estoril). London, Hodder and Stoughton, 1960.

Drina Dances in New York (as Jean Estoril). London, Hodder and Stoughton, 1961.

Holiday of Endurance. London, Dent, 1961.

Bluegate Girl. London, Hutchinson, 1961.

The First Time I Saw Paris (as Anne Pilgrim). London and New York, Abelard Schuman, 1961.

Pendron under the Water, illustrated by T.R. Freeman. London, Harrap, 1961.

Clare Goes to Holland (as Anne Pilgrim). London, Abelard Schuman, 1962.

Drina Dances in Paris (as Jean Estoril). London, Hodder and Stoughton, 1962.

Home to the Island, illustrated by Geoffrey Whittam. London, Dent, 1962; New York, Vanguard Press, 1966.

Signpost to Switzerland. London, Heinemann, 1962; New York, Criterion Books, 1964.

Drina Dances in Madeira (as Jean Estoril). London, Hodder and Stoughton, 1963.

A Summer in Provence (as Anne Pilgrim). London and New York, Abelard Schuman, 1963.

The Ballet Family, illustrated by A.R. Whitear. London, Methuen, 1963; New York, Criterion Books, 1966.

Kate Comes to England. London, Heinemann, 1963.

New York for Nicola. New York, Vanguard Press, 1963; London, White Lion, 1977.

The Sign of the Unicorn: A Thriller for Young People, illustrated by Shirley Hughes. London, Dent, and New York, Criterion Books, 1963.

Drina Dances in Switzerland (as Jean Estoril).   London, Hodder and Stoughton, 1964.

Strangers in New York.   London and New York, Abelard Schuman, 1964.

It Happened in Arles.   London, Heinemann, 1964; as *Mystery in Arles*, New York, Vanguard Press, 1964.

The Ballet Family Again, illustrated by A.R. Whitear.   London, Methuen, 1964; as *The Dancing Garlands*, New York, Criterion Books, 1968.

Fiona on the Fourteenth Floor, illustrated by Shirley Hughes.   London, Dent, 1964; as *Mystery on the Fourteenth Floor*, New York, Criterion Books, 1965.

Drina Goes on Tour (as Jean Estoril).   Leicester, Brockhampton Press, 1965.

A Summer at Sea, illustrated by Geoffrey Whittam.   London, Dent, and New York, Vanguard Press, 1965.

Cruising to Danger (as Priscilla Hagon), illustrated by William Plummer.   Cleveland, World, 1966; London, Harrap, 1968.

Dancing to Danger (as Priscilla Hagon), illustrated by Susanne Suba.   Cleveland, World, 1966.

The Way over Windle, illustrated by Raymond Briggs.   London, Methuen, 1966.

Skiing to Danger.   London, Heinemann, 1966; as *Mystery of the Ski Slopes*, New York, Criterion Books, 1966.

In Pursuit of Clarinda, illustrated by Margaret Wetherbee.   London, Dent, 1966.

It Started in Madeira.   London, Heinemann, 1967; as *The Mystery Began in Madeira*, New York, Criterion Books, 1967.

Missing in Manhattan, illustrated by Margaret Wetherbee.   London, Dent, 1967; as *Mystery in Manhattan*, New York, Vanguard Press, 1968.

Selina's New Family (as Anne Pilgrim), illustrated by Graham Byfield.   London and New York, Abelard Schuman, 1967.

We Danced in Bloomsbury Square (as Jean Estoril).   London, Heinemann, 1967; Chicago, Follett, 1970.

Mystery at Saint-Hilaire (as Priscilla Hagon), illustrated by William Plummer.   Cleveland, World, 1968.

The Wood Street Secret, illustrated by Shirley Hughes.   London, Methuen, 1968; New York, Abelard Schuman, 1970.

The Kraymer Mystery.   New York, Criterion Books, 1969; London, Abelard Schuman, 1973.

Mystery at the Villa Bianca (as Priscilla Hagon), illustrated by William Plummer.   New York, World, 1969.

Climbing to Danger.   London, Heinemann, 1969; as *Mystery in Wales*, New York, Vanguard Press, 1971.

The Mystery of the Secret Square (as Priscilla Hagon), illustrated by Ray Abel.   New York, World, 1970.

Dangerous Inheritance.   London, Heinemann, 1970.

The Wood Street Group, illustrated by Shirley Hughes.   London, Methuen, 1970.

Christmas at Spindle Bottom, illustrated by Lynette Hemmant.   London, Dent, 1970.

The Secret Dancer, illustrated by Juliet Mozley.   London, Dent, 1971.

The May Day Mystery.   New York, Criterion Books, 1971; London, White Lion, 1977.

The Wood Street Rivals, illustrated by Shirley Hughes.   London, Methuen, 1971.

An Island in a Green Sea, illustrated by Charles Robinson.   New York, Atheneum, 1972; London, Dent, 1973.

Behind the Blue Gates.   London, Heinemann, 1972.

Time to Go Back.   London and New York, Abelard Schuman, 1972.

Mystery in Rome.   New York, Vanguard Press, 1973; as *The Bells of Rome*, London, Heinemann, 1975.

The Wood Street Helpers, illustrated by Shirley Hughes.   London, Methuen, 1973.

A Formidable Enemy.   London, Heinemann, 1973; Nashville, Nelson, 1975.

Crow's Nest.   London, Abelard Schuman, 1974.

A Chill in the Lane.   Nashville, Nelson, 1974.

The Night Wind, illustrated by Charles Robinson. New York, Atheneum, 1974.
Ship of Danger. London, Heinemann, and New York, Criterion Books, 1974.
The Secret Players, illustrated by James Russell. Leicester, Brockhampton Press, 1974.
Bridge of Friendship. London, Dent, 1975; New York, Dodd Mead, 1977.
Romansgrove, illustrated by Gail Owens. New York, Atheneum, 1975.
The Flash Children, illustrated by Gavin Rowe. London, Hodder and Stoughton, and
    New York, Dodd Mead, 1975.
Away from Wood Street, illustrated by Shirley Hughes. London, Methuen, 1976.
Trouble in the Glen, illustrated by Jutta Ash. London, Abelard Schuman, 1976.
The Rising Tide. London, Heinemann, 1976.
The Sound of Cowbells. London, Abelard Schuman, 1977.
My Family's Not Forever. London, Abelard Schuman, 1977.
The View Beyond My Father. London, Abelard Schuman, 1977.

PUBLICATIONS FOR ADULTS

Novel

Murder at the Flood. London, Stanley Paul, 1957.

Manuscript Collection: University of Southern Mississippi, Hattiesburg.

Mabel Esther Allan comments:

For some years I sold only short stories for young people, adult articles and poetry. My first book was published in 1948. Since then I have published about one hundred and thirty books. All my books are set in places I have lived in, or visited, and travelling is one of my main pleasures. I have been to New York sixteen times and have lived there for short periods. I have written many books set in my favourite city, for instance *Bridge of Friendship*, which shows both the horrors of its poverty and its beauty.

My books have changed a good deal in recent years. This change started with *An Island in a Green Sea* and *Time to Go Back*, and continued with *My Family's Not Forever* and *The View Beyond My Father*. There are fewer taboos now, and children's authors can go more deeply into emotional problems.

                              *   *   *

Mabel Esther Allan is best known as a writer of as-you-like-its for girls just entering their teens − stories, broadly speaking, with a common theme: i.e., emerging from childhood's limitations into the first joyful experience of independent, self-assured adulthood.

This, of course, is a prospect to which her young readers are themselves looking forward, and she presents them with a heroine, usually about sixteen years old, with whom they can easily identify. Dreams, rather than everyday probabilities and problems, are admittedly her stock in trade. Early troubles − loss of parents, failure to achieve some special ambition, etc. − only serve to launch her heroines (and the identifying reader) on the path to adventure and romance. Glowing prospects open up: trips to exciting places (Paris, Rome, New York) and novel experiences (a sea voyage or an unexpected legacy of three islands).

In the new, exciting world, however, mystery and danger lurk, but these only serve to call out the heroine's pluck and good sense and set the stage for the opportune arrival of a nice, handsome young man. Young love flowers with the fairy-tale ending always implied ... "and they lived happy ever after."

In short, Mabel Esther Allan is an able story-teller who is content to be just that and doesn't aspire to be a philosopher or reformer. Her dream worlds may be rather too good to be true, but, if one of the chief functions of a children's writer is to make books attractive to the less intellectual children and establish reading firmly for them as a pleasant recreation able to hold its own in competition with T.V. and broadcasting, she is a writer who certainly deserves her place in this record.

Occasionally she also writes for the seven-to-tens more prosaic tales about working-class children in the multiracial backstreets of Liverpool. Here, though uplift tends to show a little through the concealing jam (especially in the gifts and graces showered upon her non-whites), there is a sensible vein of self-help. Her children make their own adventures, find ways to earn money, and discover that healing feuds and helping neighbours can be fun.

—Gladys A. Williams

ALMEDINGEN, E.M. (Martha Edith von Almedingen). British. Born in St. Petersburg, Russia, 12 July 1898; emigrated to England in 1923; became British citizen, 1932. Educated privately; Xenia Nobility College; Petrograd University, 1916–20. Lecturer in English, medieval history and literature, Petrograd University, 1921–22; Lecturer in Russian history and literature, Oxford University, 1951. Recipient: *Atlantic Review* prize, for autobiography, 1941; *Book World* Festival award, 1968. Fellow, Royal Society of Literature, 1951. *Died 5 March 1971.*

PUBLICATIONS FOR CHILDREN

Fiction

>   *One Little Tree: A Christmas Card of a Finnish Landscape*, illustrated by Denise Brown. London, Parrish, 1963; New York, Norton, 1968.
>   *The Knights of the Golden Table*, illustrated by Charles Keeping. London, Bodley Head, 1963; Philadelphia, Lippincott, 1964.
>   *The Treasure of Siegfried*, illustrated by Charles Keeping. London, Bodley Head, 1964; Philadelphia, Lippincott, 1965.
>   *Little Katia*, illustrated by Victor Ambrus. London, Oxford University Press, 1966; as *Katia*, New York, Farrar Straus, 1967.
>   *Young Mark*, illustrated by Victor Ambrus. London, Oxford University Press, 1967; New York, Farrar Straus, 1968.
>   *A Candle at Dusk*, illustrated by Doreen Roberts. London, Oxford University Press, and New York, Farrar Straus, 1969.
>   *Fanny*, illustrated by Ian Ribbons. London, Oxford University Press, and New York, Farrar Straus, 1970.
>   *Ellen.* New York, Farrar Straus, 1970; London, Oxford University Press, 1971.
>   *Anna*, illustrated by Robert Micklewright. London, Oxford University Press, and New York, Farrar Straus, 1972.

Other

>   *Russian Fairy Tales*, illustrated by Hazel Cook. London, Muller, 1957; as *Russian Folk and Fairy Tales*, New York, Putnam, 1963.
>   *The Young Pavlova*, illustrated by Denise Brown. London, Parrish, 1960; New York, Roy, 1961.
>   *The Young Leonardo da Vinci*, illustrated by Azpelicueta. London, Parrish, 1963; New York, Roy, 1966.
>   *A Picture History of Russia*, illustrated by Clarke Hutton. London, Oxford University Press, and New York, Watts, 1964.

The Young Catherine the Great, illustrated by Denise Brown.   London, Parrish, 1965; New York, Roy, 1966.

The Retreat from Moscow, illustrated by Sheila Bewley.   London, Parrish, 1966; New York, Warne, 1968.

The Story of Gudrun, based on the Third Part of the Epic of Gudrun, illustrated by Enrico Arno.   New York, Grosset and Dunlap, 1967.

I Remember St. Petersburg, illustrated by John Sergeant.   London, Longman, 1969; as *My St. Petersburg: A Reminiscence of Childhood*, New York, Norton, 1970.

Rus into Muscovy: The History of Early Russia, illustrated by Michael Charlton. London, Longman, 1971; as *Land of Muscovy*, New York, Farrar Straus, 1972.

PUBLICATIONS FOR ADULTS

Novels

Young Catherine.   London, Constable, 1937; New York, Stokes, 1938.

The Lion of the North.   London, Constable, 1938.

She Married Pushkin.   London, Constable, 1939.

Frossia.   London, Lane, 1943; New York, Harcourt Brace, 1944; abridged edition, London, Bodley Head, 1961.

Dasha.   London, Lane, 1944; New York, Harcourt Brace, 1945.

The Inmost Heart.   London, Lane, 1949; as *The Golden Sequence*, Philadelphia, Westminster Press, 1949.

Flame on the Water.   London, Hutchinson, 1952.

The Rock.   London, Hutchinson, 1953.

Stand Fast, Beloved City.   London, Hutchinson, 1954.

Ground Corn.   London, Hutchinson, 1955.

Fair Haven.   London, Hutchinson, 1956.

Stephen's Light.   London, Hutchinson, 1956; New York, Holt Rinehart, 1969.

The Scarlet Goose.   London, Hutchinson, 1957; New York, Holt Rinehart, 1970.

The Little Stairway.   London, Hutchinson, 1960; as *The Winter in the Heart*, New York, Appleton Century Crofts, 1960.

Dark Splendour.   London, Hutchinson, 1961.

The Ladies of St. Hedwigs.   London, Hutchinson, 1965; New York, Vanguard Press, 1967.

Too Early Lilac.   London, Hutchinson, 1970; New York, Vanguard Press, 1974.

Play

Storm at Westminster.   London and New York, Oxford University Press, 1952.

Verse

Rus.   London and New York, Oxford University Press, 1939.

Poloniae Testamentum.   London, Lane, 1942.

Out of Seir.   London, Lane, 1943.

The Unnamed Stream and Other Poems.   London, Bodley Head, 1965.

Other

The Catholic Church in Russia Today.   London, Burns Oates, and New York, Kennedy, 1923.

The English Pope, Adrian IV.   London, Heath Cranton, 1925.

Women under Fire: Six Months in the Red Army.   London, Hutchinson, 1930.

St. Gregory the Great.   Dublin, Irish Messenger, 1930.

The Wanderer. Dublin, Irish Messenger, 1930.

Clear Skies at Last. Dublin, Irish Messenger, 1931.

Destiny. Dublin, Irish Messenger, 1931.

God and the Soviet. Dublin, Irish Messenger, 1931.

From Rome to Canterbury. London, Faith Press, and Milwaukee, Morehouse, 1933.

The Pilgrimage of a Soul. London, Faith Press, and Milwaukee, Morehouse, 1934.

Through Many Windows Opened by the Book of Common Prayer. London, Faith Press, and Milwaukee, Morehouse, 1935.

Tomorrow Will Come (autobiography). London, Lane, and Boston, Little Brown, 1941.

Dom Bernard Clements: A Portrait. London, Lane, 1945.

The Almond. London, Lane, 1947.

Within the Harbour. London, Lane, 1950.

Late Arrival (includes *The Almond* and *Within the Harbour*). Philadelphia, Westminster Press, 1952.

Life of Many Colours: The Story of Grandmother Ellen. London, Hutchinson, 1958; as *A Very Far Country*, New York, Appleton Century Crofts, 1958.

So Dark a Stream: A Study of the Emperor Paul I of Russia, 1754–1801. London, Hutchinson, 1959.

The Batsford Colour Book of Kittens. London, Batsford, 1961; as *Kittens in Color*, New York, Viking Press, 1961.

Catherine, Empress of Russia. New York, Dodd Mead, 1961; as *Catherine the Great: A Portrait*, London, Hutchinson, 1963.

The Empress Alexandra, 1872–1918: A Study. London, Hutchinson, 1961.

The Emperor Alexander II: A Study. London, Bodley Head, 1962.

The Emperor Alexander I. London, Bodley Head, 1964; New York, Vanguard Press, 1966.

An Unbroken Unity: A Memoir of Grand Duchess Serge of Russia, 1864–1918. London, Bodley Head, 1964.

The Romanovs: Three Centuries of an Ill-Fated Dynasty. London, Bodley Head, and New York, Holt Rinehart, 1966.

Francis of Assisi: A Portrait. London, Bodley Head, 1967; as *St. Francis of Assisi: A Great Life in Brief*, New York, Knopf, 1967.

Charlemagne: A Study. London, Bodley Head, 1968.

Leonardo da Vinci: A Portrait. London, Bodley Head, 1969.

Translator, *The Lord's Passion*, by Hrabanus Magnentius. London, Mowbray, 1938.

* * *

E.M. Almedingen's connection with writing for children has a long history. It began when her great-aunt, Catherine A. Almedingen, started to translate American and English children's classics into Russian. Then Catherine wrote her autobiography, *The Story of a Little Girl*. Published in 1874, it won the approval of Chekhov and Tolstoy and of countless Russian children until the 1917 revolution. The real Katia lived from 1829 to December 16, 1893, and, besides writing for children, she founded one of the best children's monthlies in Russia, *Rodnik*.

The book *Little Katia* is a version of *The Story of a Little Girl* by her great-niece, E.M. Almedingen. Katia was born in Russia, but was not Russian by blood-line because her father was Austro-Bavarian and her mother Danish. After living in three separate and very different homes before the age of 13, Katia then journeyed to Moscow to enter a strict upper school where she was to live for four years.

Upper-class Russian life is pictured during the reign of the Czars. Life on farms and large estates, winter and summer, provides a scintillating background of sunshine and shadow for the story of a temperamental young girl. Occasional passages show the deep chasms in the social structure of the country, such as this: " ... when I was a little girl there was a gulf between people like my father and anyone engaged in trade .... Trade meant buying and selling. Uncle Nicholas and all his neighbors certainly sold timber and cattle. .... So did my father .... But, from the social sense, the difference stood for an unsurmountable barrier. I believe that *kouptzy* (merchants) were often far more wealthy than any of us, but bags of gold as such did not matter."

In the story of *Young Mark*, a Ukrainian boy of 18th century Russia, Almedingen reconstructs his journey, mostly on foot, from his native village in the Ukraine to St. Petersburg, to see the Hetman, who, he hoped, would help him to attain his life's goal – to be a singer. It was a journey marked by formidable reverses, menace, and treachery. Almedingen has imparted the history in a way that makes a varicolored background for an unnusual story, with special attention to local custom, food, and the characters met on the road and in the marketplaces. The circumstances of the peasants are shown in clear contrast to the richness of the nobility, but not in a propagandistic way. Such, one feels, was the way it was, at that time, in that place.

Many of Almedingen's books are based on episodes in her own family history. *Anna* tells of her great-grandmother, a rare person because, for one thing, she was educated – unlike most Russian girls even in the upper classes – and excelled in languages. Again we have a picture, clear in its details, of the life in a wealthy Russian merchant's home, though unnusual because marked by devotion to study and the collecting of rare books in which even the Czarina Catherine took an interest. Religion was an integral part of this life. When Anna made a momentous discovery about herself, she paid a visit to St. Praskovia's, the church she preferred, and lighted a large wax candle in front of an icon, as a "Signature to the discovery."

A story for younger children, *One Little Tree*, tells of a more modern day, though, with its close-knit family and child-like faith, the story may seem old-fashioned to some of our children. But once having read it, one finds it hard to forget. Eight-year-old Arni in a small Finnish village finds, one year, that in order to keep his promise to his sister to get a fir tree for their Christmas he has to cross the recently closed border into Russian-held territory. What might have been a bitter ending is retrieved by a Russian soldier who is touched by Arni's bravery and faith. Arni's parents who face hunger rather than sell their children's few treasures are convincingly portrayed.

Almedingen's *Picture History of Russia* covers the story of Russia from about 500 A.D. to the date of its publication, 1964. It is necessarily a sweeping view of Russian history, but main events are highlighted, and there are movement and interesting information on every page. Like most of the author's other, more personalized narratives, it stands as an excellent introduction to that vast and still mysterious country.

—Norma R. Fryatt

ANDERSEN, Doris. Canadian. Born in Tanana, Alaska, 6 February 1909. Educated at the University of British Columbia, Vancouver, B.A. 1929; University of Washington, Seattle, B.S. in library science 1930. Married George C. Andersen in 1929; has two sons and one daughter. Library Assistant, Seattle Public Library, 1929–30; Librarian, Ottawa Public Library, 1940–43, and Canadian Legion Library, Ottawa, 1943–45; Children's Librarian, 1956–65, and Branch Head Librarian, 1965–74, Vancouver Public Library. Lecturer in Children's Literature, Capilano College, North Vancouver, 1969. Address: 1232 Esquimalt Avenue, West Vancouver, British Columbia V7T 1K3, Canada.

PUBLICATIONS FOR CHILDREN

Fiction

  Blood Brothers, illustrated by David Craig. Toronto, Macmillan, New York, St.
    Martin's Press, and London, Macmillan, 1967.
  Slave of the Haida, illustrated by Muriel Wood. Toronto, Macmillan, 1974.

PUBLICATIONS FOR ADULTS

Other

  Ways Harsh and Wild. Vancouver, Douglas, 1973.

Doris Andersen comments:
   After discovering that two living octogenarian relatives of my husband took part when
children in the trek of Norwegians from Minnesota to the wilds of Bella Coola in 1894, I was
moved to write *Blood Brothers*, the story of the boy Nels who is a fictional member of the
party. What happens when Nels accidentally arouses the anger of the Indians provides the
climax of the story. The problems arising from the enforced abolition of the potlatch are
featured here. When my interest was sparked by a brief anecdote about a Haida raid told to
me by a Salish leader, I wrote the junior novel *Slave of the Haida* about the slave-owning
societies of Canada's west coast; in this book a young Salish boy is captured by Haida
warriors. For *Ways Harsh and Wild*, which one critic recommended for the entire family, I
collected hundreds of personal anecdotes of my uncle, parents and sister and wove them into
a true adventure story of Gold Rush days in Alaska. My research for my books has included
interviews, diaries of explorers and missionaries, works of anthropologists and historians,
Indian legends, government departmental reports of the periods, old newspapers, magazines,
maps, material on flora and fauna, trips to background locations, etc. I try to show the
problems of natives and white settlers from their many conflicting viewpoints as evinced in
records of the eras covered and to avoid the stereotyped extremes in my Indian characters.
While I use action and suspense to engage interest, I hope to leave the reader with a
heightened sensitivity to his environment, its people, and their past and present problems.

*   *   *

   Both of Doris Andersen's books for children are set in the Indian culture of the Pacific
Northwest Coast of North America. The author has an extensive background knowledge of
this culture. Despite this fact, she does not seem at ease with her subject – too frequently, she
appears to be creating incidents for the express purpose of imparting information rather than
allowing the setting to become incidental to the development of her story.
   Her themes of the impact between cultures, in one case between White and Indian and in
the other between hostile Indian tribes, are treated in a simplistic manner. *Blood Brothers*, for
example, concerns an Indian boy and a young Norwegian immigrant who become blood
brothers on the occasion of their first meeting. Later, their friendship is the sole cause of the
resolution of hostilities between the Indians and the settlers, who are imposing their way of
life on the native culture. *Slave of the the Haida* relates a Salish chief's son's struggle to escape
from his Haida captors and his success due to the decision of his owner to assist him
regardless of the tribal rules. Since slaves were valuable assets it is fairly unrealistic to expect
that a Haida youth would flout tribal mores and act in such a way.
   The characterization in both books is shallow, occasionally stereotyped. The grim
European grandfather of *Blood Brothers* suffers a total unexplained change of heart for no
apparent reason at the conclusion of the book. His daughter is depicted as a warm, friendly
woman of Norwegian extraction who, nevertheless, cannot accept cultural differences and

even proclaims with regard to the Indians, "They are all savages, all of them...." Beyond physical descriptions we are given few clues as to the nature of the characters who thus fail to develop as fully rounded personalities.

Andersen tends to use repetitive sentence structure, a habit which inhibits reading ease. In many cases, emotion is conveyed by means of an exclamation point rather than by careful descriptive writing or use of dialogue.

The technical problems which have been outlined are fairly serious; however, they do not detract from the fact that Andersen is, above all, a good storyteller. Events move swiftly to satisfying conclusions, and the reader is carried along effortlessly from opening sentence to denouement. If Andersen could learn how to get inside her characters and motivate them on a less superficial level, she would overcome a major literary handicap and, in all likelihood, produce truly excellent stories for children.

—Fran Ashdown

ANDREW, Prudence (Hastings).   British.   Born in London, 23 May 1924. Educated at St. Anne's College, Oxford, B.A. (honours) in history 1946. Married G.H.L. Andrew in 1946; has two daughters. Worked in Personnel Department, Joseph Lucas Ltd., Birmingham, 1944–45; staff member, Nuffield Institute of Colonial Affairs, Oxford, 1945–47; History Teacher, St. Michael's Convent School, Monmouthshire, 1956–60. Address: 30 Lytham Close, Liverpool 10, Lancashire, England.

PUBLICATIONS FOR CHILDREN

Fiction

> *The Hooded Falcon.*   London, Hutchinson, 1960; New York, Putnam, 1961.
> *Ordeal by Silence: A Story of Medieval Times.*   London, Hutchinson, and New York, Putnam, 1961.
> *Ginger over the Wall*, illustrated by Charles Mozley.   London, Lutterworth Press, 1962.
> *A Question of Choice.*   London, Hutchinson, and New York, Putnam, 1962.
> *Ginger and Batty Bill*, illustrated by Charles Mozley.   London, Lutterworth Press, 1963.
> *The Earthworms.*   London, Hutchinson, 1963; as *The Constant Star*, New York, Putnam, 1964.
> *Ginger and Number 10*, illustrated by Charles Mozley.   London, Lutterworth Press, 1964.
> *The Christmas Card*, illustrated by Mary Russon.   London, Hamish Hamilton, 1966.
> *Ginger among the Pigeons*, illustrated by Charles Mozley.   London, Lutterworth Press, 1966.
> *Mr. Morgan's Marrow*, illustrated by Janet Duchesne.   London, Hamish Hamilton, 1967.
> *A New Creature.*   London, Hutchinson, and New York, Putnam, 1968.
> *Dog!*, illustrated by Trevor Stubley.   London, Hamish Hamilton, 1968; Nashville, Nelson, 1973.
> *A Man with Your Advantages.*   London, Hutchinson, 1970.
> *Mister O'Brien.*   London, Heinemann, 1972; Nashville, Nelson, 1973.
> *Una and Grubstreet.*   London, Heinemann, 1972; as *Una and the Heaven Baby*, Nashville, Nelson, 1975.
> *Rodge, Silvie, and Munch*, illustrated by Jael Jordan.   London, Heinemann, 1973.

Goodbye to the Rat.   London, Heinemann, 1974.
The Heroic Deeds of Jason Jones, illustrated by Jael Jordan.   London, Heinemann, 1975.
Where Are You Going To, My Pretty Maid?   London, Heinemann, 1977.

PUBLICATIONS FOR ADULTS

Novel

A Sparkle from the Coal.   London, Hutchinson, 1964.

*   *   *

Most of Prudence Andrew's books have an urban setting, identified in some cases as Liverpool. It is in such a setting that her earliest books place Ginger, the contemporary "William"-like leader of a gang of four. In the early 1960's, when the series of books about Ginger appeared, children's books were beginning to reflect the new multi-racial society of urban Britain. Prudence Andrew was one of the first writers to include black characters in her stories, although the early *Ginger and Number 10* has been criticised for the attitudes which it portrays, despite the theme of opposition to racial prejudice which runs through the book.

The Ginger series was followed by two books about lonely children who come to terms with their situations. Physically handicapped Christopher, in *Mister O'Brien*, imagines a one-legged man, vividly dressed, who appears – in the street or the school playground – or whose voice can be heard whenever Christopher has to decide between two courses of action, of which one demands a great deal of courage. It is Mr. O'Brien who is responsible for Christopher's friendship with Penny Marshall, from a slum basement flat, and this in turn leads Christopher, buoyed up by his admiration for Scott of the Antarctic, to accomplish the apparently impossible feat of walking ten miles in a sponsored charity walk.

In *Una and Grubstreet*, the latter does exist as a small toy bear, but his role in the conversation with motherless Una is that of her more responsible, sensible self. Una's wish for a baby in the family leads her to stealing one, although she herself would call it a "rescue." It is the sensible voice of Grubstreet, reminding her at the end that "If we really do want a baby brother, this girl is our best hope," which reconciles her to the idea of her father's remarriage.

These stories are eminently readable; despite the deep concern in the books with the child's inner feelings, there is plenty of action and humour to keep the plot moving. Both books have satisfactorily happy endings; the child protagonists have clearly developed as a result of their experiences.

Prudence Andrew's gifts for reproducing conversation, for accurate observation, and for creating plausible characters are apparent even when she is writing to a formula. She has produced competently written stories for both younger and older age-groups than those for which the books already discussed are intended.

Mr. Morgan's Marrow, written for the child who can read but needs practice to become fluent, has (exceptionally among her work) a strong Welsh atmosphere, helped by the names of the characters and slight turns of speech. In this and other simply written books for the younger age group, Prudence Andrew, despite the restrictions imposed by the short length, manages to create an interesting and credible story, with a fairy-tale ending.

At the other end of the scale, *Goodbye to the Rat* is a Pyramid Book, intended for the reluctant teenage reader, about three boys in Liverpool looking for jobs. The plot is well constructed, interweaving the stories of the boys – Nick, who represents the norm of the white boy without academic qualifications, Louie, the cheerful and full-of-bounce black, and Tony, who cannot rise to the heights of his mother's ambitions. Here again, the story has elements of documentary realism and plausibility of characterisation.

Most striking of Prudence Andrew's skills, apart from her ability to tell a good story, is her gift for adding authentic detail, based on accurate and kindly observation, which makes her plots convincing from an adult point of view.

—Sheila G. Ray

ANGELO, Valenti. American. Born in Massarosa, Tuscany, Italy, 23 June 1897; emigrated to the U.S.A. in 1905; naturalized citizen, 1923. Educated in California public schools. Married Maxine Grimm in 1923; has two children. Worked as field hand, in paper mills, chemical works, and steel works, and as engraver. Since 1926, free-lance illustrator. Recipient: American Institute of Graphic Arts award, 1926. Address: 1155 Jones Street, Apartment 504, San Francisco, California 94109, U.S.A.

PUBLICATIONS FOR CHILDREN (illustrated by the author)

Fiction

Nino. New York, Viking Press, 1938.
Golden Gate. New York, Viking Press, 1939.
Paradise Valley. New York, Viking Press, 1940.
A Battle in Washington Square. New York, Golden Cross Press, 1942.
Hill of Little Miracles. New York, Viking Press, 1942.
Look out Yonder. New York, Viking Press, 1943.
The Rooster Club. New York, Viking Press, 1944.
The Bells of Bleecker Street. New York, Viking Press, 1949.
The Marble Fountain. New York, Viking Press, 1951.
Big Little Island. New York, Viking Press, 1955.
The Acorn Tree. New York, Viking Press, 1958.
The Honey Boat. New York, Viking Press, 1959.
The Candy Basket. New York, Viking Press, 1960.
Angelino and the Barefoot Saint. New York, Viking Press, 1961.
The Merry Marcos. New York, Viking Press, 1963; London, Macdonald, 1965.
The Tale of a Donkey. New York, Viking Press, 1966.

PUBLICATIONS FOR ADULTS

Other

The Splendid Gift. New York, privately printed, 1940.

Bibliography: *Valenti Angelo: Author, Illustrator, Printer: A Checklist of His Work from 1926 to 1970,* Bronxville, New York, privately printed, 1970.

Illustrator: *The Letters of Amerigo Vespucci,* 1926; *Sir Francis Drake* by John Wooster Robertson, 1926; *The Book of Job,* 1926; *The Book of Ruth,* 1926; *Salome,* 1927 and 1945, and *Fairy Tales,* 1942, by Oscar Wilde; *Two Unpublished Manuscripts* by Algernon Swinburne, 1927; *The Voyage and Travaile of Sir John Maundivile,* 1928; *The Scarlet Letter,* 1928, *The House of Seven Gables,* 1936, *The Golden Touch,* 1939, and *Twice-Told Tales,* 1966, all by Nathaniel Hawthorne; *South Wind* by Norman Douglas, 1929; *The Barefoot Saint* by Stephen Vincent Benét, 1929; *American Taste* by Lewis Mumford, 1929; *A Sentimental Journey* by Laurence Sterne, 1929; *Zadig* by Voltaire, 1929; *The Fables of*

Europe, 1930; *Leaves of Grass* by Walt Whitman, 1930; *The Red Badge of Courage*, 1931, *A Battle in Greece*, 1936, and *The Blood of the Martyr*, 1939, all by Stephen Crane; *Pierrot of the Minute* by Ernest Dowson, 1932; *A Lytell Geste of Robyn Hode and His Meiny*, 1932; *California As It Is*, 1933; *Arabian Nights Tales*, 1934; *The Sermon on the Mount*, 1935; *Cherry Ripe* by A. E. Coppard, 1935; *The Rubaiyat of Omar Khayyam*, 1935; *Chinese Love Tales* translated by George Soulié, 1935; *The Song of Songs Which Is Solomon's*, 1935; *Vathek* by William Beckford, 1935; *The Book of Esther*, 1935; *Japanese Fairy Tales* by Lafcadio Hearne, 1936; *The Kasidah of Haji Abdu el Yezdi* by Richard Burton, 1936; *Not So Deep as a Well* by Dorothy Parker, 1936; *Prelude to Man* by Chard Powers Smith, 1936; *The Psalms of David*, 1936; *Roller Skates*, 1936, and *The Long Christmas*, 1941, by Ruth Sawyer; *Quattrocentisteria* by Maurice Hewlett, 1937; *A Visit from St. Nicholas* by Clement C. Moore, 1937; *The Song of Roland* translated by Charles Scott Moncrieff, 1938; *Chinese Fairy Tales*, 1938; *The Man Without a Country* by Edward Everett Hale, 1938; *Persian Fairy Tales*, 1939; *Paula* by Marguerite Vance, 1939; *King John*, 1940, *Sonnets*, 1941, *The Tragedy of Hamlet*, 1950, and *The Taming of the Shrew*, 1967, all by Shakespeare; *Dago Red* by John Fante, 1940; *The Wife of Martin Guerre* by Janet Lewis, 1941; *The Song of Hiawatha* by Henry Wadsworth Longfellow, 1942; *The Three Musketeers* by Alexandre Dumas, 1942; *The Luck of Roaring Camp* by Bret Harte, 1943; *The Animals' Christmas* edited by Anne Thaxter Eaton, 1944, and *Welcome Christmas!* by Eaton, 1955; *The Little Flowers of St. Francis of Assisi* translated by T. Okey, 1944, and *Canticle of the Sun* by St. Francis of Assisi, 1951; *A Donkey for the King* by Olive Price, 1945; *The Confessions of St. Augustine*, 1945; *The Philobiblion* by Richard De Bury, 1945; *Light of Asia* by Edwin Arnold, 1946; *Imitation of Christ* by Thomas à Kempis, 1946; *Sonnets from the Portuguese* by Elizabeth Barrett Browning, 1948; *The Fiscal Hoboes* by William Saroyan, 1949; *The Court of the Printers' Guild*, 1949; *Hey, Mr. Grasshopper!* by Floy Parkinson Gates, 1949; *Writing and Criticism: A Book for Margery Bianco* by Anne Carroll Moore and Bertha Mahony Miller, 1951; *Ode on a Grecian Urn* by John Keats, 1952; *Song of St. Francis*, 1952, *Benito*, 1961, and *St. Valentine's Day*, 1965, all by Clyde Robert Bulla; *The Birthday of Little Jesus* by Sterling North, 1952; *The Christmas Story* by Norman Vincent Peale, 1953; *The Koran*, 1953; *Joan of Arc* by Nancy W. Ross, 1953; *Journey to Bethlehem* by Delos Lovelace, 1953; *Hymn to Aphrodite* by John Edgar, 1953; *America* by Ruth Tooze, 1956; *The Second Chapter of the Gospel According to St. Luke*, 1956; *The Life of St. George*, 1957; *The Holy Bible*, 1958; *The Lives of the Saints*, 1959; *The Bible Story for Children*, 1959; *The Book of Jonah*, 1960; *The Book of Proverbs*, 1963.

*   *   *

There are two themes that run consistently through the books of Valenti Angelo, and sometimes they run side by side. One is love for Italy, the homeland where he was born, and the other is love for his adopted home, America.

As a child in Italy, he was shown a book that influenced all his later years. It was a 15th-century manuscript Book of the Hours written and illuminated by hand, and he thought of it as the most beautiful book in the world. As a young man, making his way in America, he turned toward painting, illustrating, lettering, and engraving. His studies led him to a firm that specialized in printing fine books, where he became well established as an illustrator.

When he decided to write about his childhood, "I never dreamed," he said, "that so much could be recollected of my daily life."

His first book, *Nino*, is a joyous account of a boy's life in an Italian village at the turn of the century with his text and accompanying illustrations speaking of warmth and affection for his home in the "Little Alps" of Tuscany. *Golden Gate* is the story of an Italian immigrant boy, his introduction to America, and his difficult adjustment to the customs of the strange, new land.

These two books and all the others written and illustrated by Valenti Angelo are based on recollections of the author's childhood. Most are realistic, a few are fantasy. Some are quiet tales of family life, others are rousing adventures. The settings of his stories are almost equally divided between America and Italy.

The author-illustrator is kindly and gentle, a man of religious convictions, with a lively sense of humor. It is natural that these qualities should find their way into his stories and illustrations. His books never preach, they never seek to "improve" the reader; they are meant only to give pleasure.

—Clyde Robert Bulla

———————————————

ANGLUND, Joan Walsh.   American.   Born in Hinsdale, Illinois, 3 January 1926. Studied at the Chicago Art Institute, 1944; American Academy of Art, 1945. Married Robert Lee Anglund in 1947; has two children. Apprentice to the artist Adele Roth, Chicago. Recipient: *New York Times* award, for illustration, 1958. Address: c/o Atheneum Publishers, 122 East 42nd Street, New York, New York 10017, U.S.A.

PUBLICATIONS FOR CHILDREN (illustrated by the author)

Fiction

> *A Friend Is Someone Who Likes You.*   New York, Harcourt Brace, 1958; London, Collins, 1959.
> *Look Out the Window.*   New York, Harcourt Brace, 1959; London, Collins, 1962.
> *The Brave Cowboy.*   New York, Harcourt Brace, and London, Bodley Head, 1959.
> *Love Is a Special Way of Feeling.*   New York, Harcourt Brace, and London, Collins, 1960.
> *Christmas Is a Time of Giving.*   New York, Harcourt Brace, 1961; London, Collins, 1962.
> *Cowboy and His Friend.*   New York, Harcourt Brace, and London, Collins, 1961.
> *Cowboy's Secret Life.*   New York, Harcourt Brace, 1963; London, Collins, 1964.
> *Spring Is a New Beginning.*   New York, Harcourt Brace, 1963; London, Collins, 1964.
> *Childhood Is a Time of Innocence.*   New York, Harcourt Brace, 1964; London, Collins, 1965.
> *What Color Is Love?*   New York, Harcourt Brace, 1966; London, Collins, 1967.
> *A Year Is Round.*   New York, Harcourt Brace, 1966; London, Collins, 1967.
> *Do You Love Someone?*   New York, Harcourt Brace, 1971; London, Collins, 1972.
> *The Cowboy's Christmas.*   New York, Atheneum, 1972; London, Collins, 1973.

Verse

> *A Pocketful of Proverbs.*   New York, Harcourt Brace, 1964; London, Collins, 1965.
> *Morning Is a Little Child.*   New York, Harcourt Brace, 1969; London, Collins, 1970.

Other

> *In a Pumpkin Shell: A Mother Goose ABC.*   New York, Harcourt Brace, 1960; London, Collins, 1961.
> *Nibble Nibble Mousekin: A Tale of Hansel and Gretel.*   New York, Harcourt Brace, 1962; London, Collins, 1963.
> *A Is for Always: An ABC Book.*   New York, Harcourt Brace, 1968; London, Collins, 1969.
> *A Child's Book of Old Nursery Rhymes.*   New York, Atheneum, 1973; London, Collins, 1974.

Editor, *A Book of Good Tidings from the Bible.*   New York, Harcourt Brace, 1965;
London, Collins, 1966.

P<small>UBLICATIONS FOR</small> A<small>DULTS</small>

Verse

A Cup of Sun: A Book of Poems.   New York, Harcourt Brace, 1967; London, Collins,
1968.
A Slice of Snow: A Book of Poems.   New York, Harcourt Brace, 1970; London, Collins,
1971.
Goodbye, Yesterday: A Book of Poems.   New York, Atheneum, 1974.

Illustrator: *To Church We Go* by Robbie Trent, 1948; *For You with Love: A Poem* by Louis
Untermeyer, 1961; *The Golden Treasury of Poetry*, 1959, and *The Golden Book of Poems for
the Very Young*, 1971, both edited by Louis Untermeyer.

*   *   *

Joan Walsh Anglund is a prolific author and illustrator of picture books for young
children. Her work is intended for a popular audience and she has captured the attention of
children and adults on two continents. For instance, *A Friend Is Someone Who Likes You* has
sold over a million copies in the United States and it has done well in Europe. The tone of
much of Anglund's writing is characterized by this passage from the fore-mentioned book:
love is "the happy way we feel when we save a bird that has been hurt ... or feed a lost cat ...
or calm a frightened colt." The inclusive "we" and the voice of the teacher-narrator is strong.
The theses of many of Anglund's works are simple homilies, e.g., "A friend is someone who
likes you," and "Spring is a new beginning." Much of her work revolves around simple
statements on the themes of loving, sharing, giving, and the beauty of nature. Most of the
texts of the works come full circle, reiterating the thesis in the conclusion. For example, *Do
You Love Someone?* moves from "The universe is wide and wonderful and filled with many
stars" to "For the heart is its own world, and in that world you are important!" Anglund's
works have a considerable appeal to adults who read to young children, probably because of
the honeyed moralism illustrated above, but also because of the pictures which Anglund
draws for the text. Her illustrations are still life, stop action frames of a somewhat precious
nature. Her little people have large heads, round eyes and vast looks of wonder. There is an
otherworldliness about her characters which is accentuated by old fashioned dress and
mannerisms, and the stereotyped accouterments of childhood such as balloons, teddy bears,
blocks, balls and dolls. The illustrations, however, are particularly appropriate to the texts of
the works and lend credence to the moral ideas.

—Rachel Fordyce

APPIAH, Peggy.   British.   Born in Filkins, Gloucestershire, 21 May 1921. Educated at
Norland Place and Queen's College Schools, London; Maltman's Green, Buckinghamshire;
Whitehall Secretarial College. Married Joe E. Appiah in 1953; has one son and three
daughters. Formerly, research assistant, Ministry of Information, London; secretary, Racial
Unity, London. Agent: David Higham Associates Ltd., 5–8 Lower John Street, London W1R
4HA, England. Address: P.O. Box 829, Kumasi, Ashanti, Ghana, West Africa.

PUBLICATIONS FOR CHILDREN

Fiction

The Children of Ananse, illustrated by Mora Dickson. London, Evans, 1968.
A Smell of Onions, illustrated by Percy Markwei. London, Longman, 1971.
Gift of the Mmoatia, illustrated by Nii O. Quao. Tema, Ghana Publishing Corporation, 1972.
Ring of Gold, illustrated by Laszlo Acs. London, Deutsch, 1976.
A Dirge Too Soon. Tema, Ghana Publishing Corporation, 1976.

Other

Ananse the Spider: Tales from an Ashanti Village, illustrated by Peggy Wilson. New York, Pantheon Books, 1966.
Tales of an Ashanti Father, illustrated by Mora Dickson. London, Deutsch, 1967.
The Pineapple Child and Other Tales from Ashanti. London, Deutsch, 1969.
The Lost Earring (reader), illustrated by J. Jarvis. London, Evans, 1971.
Yao and the Python (reader), illustrated by J. Jarvis. London, Evans, 1971.
Why Are There So Many Roads? (folktales), illustrated by A. A. Teye. Lagos, African Universities Press, 1972.
Why the Hyena Does Not Care for Fish and Other Tales from the Ashanti Gold Weights, illustrated by Joanna Stubbs. London, Deutsch, 1977.

Peggy Appiah comments:
All the books I have so far published have been about Ashanti, where I live. The country is full of stories, and I find the atmosphere conducive to writing. Life in Africa has much of the unexpected, and people are closely involved in each other's lives. I have tried to project its liveliness and interest in my books and to give children in other parts of the world some idea of the life of those in Ghana. I have also tried to write for Ghanaian children about themselves, as in the past they have had to depend on books with foreign backgrounds. Most of the books are about village and forest life, animals and birds. I was brought up in the country, and it is there my main interests lie. Kwaku Ananse the Spider is the Brer Rabbit of Ghana; *Aesop's Fables* are so like the Spider stories that Ghanaian children read them as such. The wind in the willows is the same one that breathes through the palm fronds. It is this universality of children's lore that I try to promote through my writing, hoping it will help to promote mutual understanding in this troubled world.

*   *   *

Peggy Appiah, first English, then, through her marriage, Ashanti, is in a singularly good position to write stories in English about Ashanti. Other parts of Ghana barely appear, but then why should they? Ashanti itself has an old and complex culture and enough stories to last a few lifetimes. People who live sociably in family and village groups without telly and newspapers are apt to be good storytellers, and when one lives among them one can't help picking up the story habit. Peggy Appiah has done just that for a double audience in two countries; her stories must be as acceptable in Ghana as they are in England. By now there are thousands of children out there speaking and reading English as their second language but probably finding most English children's books a bit boring and unintelligible – nothing they can connect with.
They must enjoy Peggy's books and so will British children who are at all interested in other countries. Her stories often have an element of folklorist fantasy, though *A Smell of Onions* is amusingly factual, a tangled tale of village life, very much as it is elsewhere and as it might be told. *The Gift of the Mmoatia* in which two little girls, one Ghanaian, the other

British, make friends and share joys and troubles, shows both Peggy's gifts and her limitations. In Ghana the wee folk of the deep forest are plausible, but the English fairies are booksy. This is surely because the author doesn't believe in them whereas she can at least suspend disbelief in the strange little Mmoatia who helped the children! Abena's reactions and puzzlements during her English visit are charmingly and beautifully observed, especially her astonishment at the long English evenings. Peggy is very happy with the children in her stories as also with the animals and insects, including Ananse, the important spider who comes into so many West Coast stories, and into her book, *Tales of an Ashanti Father*, for people live close to them and would not find it strange to speak their language — nor I think would Peggy Appiah.

—Naomi Mitchison

ARDIZZONE, Edward. British. Born with French nationality in Haiphong, Ton Kin, China, 16 October 1900; moved to England in 1905, became British citizen, 1921. Educated at Clayesmore School, Iwerne Minster, Dorset, 1913–17; Westminster School of Art, London, 1922–27. Served in the Royal Artillery, 1939–40; Official War Artist, 1940–45. Married Catherine Anderson in 1928; has one daughter and two sons. Clerk in City of London, 1920–26; Instructor in Graphic Design, Camberwell School of Art, London, 1947–52; Instructor in audio-visual aids, UNESCO, Southern India, 1952–53; Visiting Tutor in Etching and Lithography, Royal College of Art, London, 1953–60. One-man shows: Bloomsbury Gallery, 1930, Leger Gallery, 1931, Nicholson Gallery, 1939, Leicester Galleries, 1948, Mayor Gallery, 1962, Victoria and Albert Museum, 1973, New Grafton Gallery, 1975, all in London; group shows: London Group, 1935, New English Group, 1936, Royal Society of Painters in Water Colours, 1954, and Royal Academy Summer Exhibition since 1964, all in London. Recipient (for illustration): Library Association Kate Greenaway Medal, 1957, *New York Times* award, 1962, 1973. Fellow, Society of Industrial Artists; Associate, 1962, and Member, 1970, Royal Academy; Honorary Associate, Royal College of Art; Royal Designer for Industry, Royal Society of Arts, 1975. C. B. E. (Commander, Order of the British Empire), 1971. Address: 5 Vine Cottages, Rodmersham Green, Sittingbourne, Kent ME9 0PT, England.

PUBLICATIONS FOR CHILDREN (illustrated by the author)

Fiction

> *Little Tim and the Brave Sea Captain.* London and New York, Oxford University Press, 1936; revised edition, London, Oxford University Press, and New York, Walck, 1955.
> *Lucy Brown and Mr. Grimes.* London and New York, Oxford University Press, 1937; revised edition, London, Bodley Head, 1970; New York, Walck, 1971.
> *Lucy and Tim Go to Sea.* London and New York, Oxford University Press, 1938; revised edition, London, Oxford University Press, and New York, Walck, 1958.
> *Nicholas and the Fast-Moving Diesel.* London, Eyre and Spottiswoode, 1947; New York, Walck, 1959.
> *Paul, The Hero of the Fire.* London, Penguin, 1948; Boston, Houghton Mifflin, 1949; revised edition, London, Constable, 1962; New York, Walck, 1963.
> *Tim to the Rescue.* London and New York, Oxford University Press, 1949.
> *Tim and Charlotte.* London and New York, Oxford University Press, 1951.
> *Tim in Danger.* London and New York, Oxford University Press, 1953.

Tim All Alone. London and New York, Oxford University Press, 1956.
Johnny the Clockmaker. London and New York, Oxford University Press, 1960.
Tim's Friend Towser. London, Oxford University Press, and New York, Walck, 1962.
Peter the Wanderer. London, Oxford University Press, 1963; New York, Walck, 1964.
Diana and Her Rhinoceros. London, Bodley Head, and New York, Walck, 1964.
Sarah and Simon and No Red Paint. London, Constable, 1965; New York, Delacorte Press, 1966.
Tim and Ginger. London, Oxford University Press, and New York, Walck, 1965.
Tim to the Lighthouse. London, Oxford University Press, and New York, Walck, 1968.
The Wrong Side of the Bed. New York, Doubleday, 1969; as *Johnny's Bad Day,* London, Bodley Head, 1970.
Tim's Last Voyage. London, Bodley Head, 1972; New York, Walck, 1973.
Ship's Cook Ginger. London, Bodley Head, 1977.

PUBLICATIONS FOR ADULTS

Other

Baggage to the Enemy. London, Murray, 1941.
The Young Ardizzone: An Autobiographical Fragment. London, Studio Vista, and New York, Macmillan, 1970.
Diary of a War Artist. London, Bodley Head, 1974.

Bibliography: "Edward Ardizzone: A Preliminary Hand-List of His Illustrated Books, 1929–1970" by Brian Alderson, in *The Private Library* (Pinner, Middlesex), Spring 1972.

Illustrator: *In a Glass Darkly* by Sheridan Le Fanu, 1929; *The Library* by George Crabbe, 1930; *The Mediterrean* edited by Paul Bloomfield, 1935; *Tom, Dick, and Harriet* by A. Neil Lyons, 1937; *Great Expectations,* 1939, *Bleak House,* 1955, *David Copperfield,* 1955, and *Short Stories,* 1971, all by Charles Dickens; *The Local,* 1939, *Back to the Local,* 1949, *Londoners,* 1951, and *Showmen and Suckers,* 1951, all by Maurice Gorham; *Mimff,* 1939, *Mimff in Charge,* 1949, *Mimff Takes Over,* 1954, and *Mimff-Robinson,* 1958, all by H. J. Kaeser; *My Uncle Silas,* 1939, and *Sugar for the House,* 1957, by H. E. Bates; *The Battle of France* by André Maurois, 1940; *The Road to Bordeaux* by C. Denis Freeman and Douglas Cooper, 1940; *Peacock Pie,* 1946, *The Story of Joseph,* 1958, *The Story of Moses,* 1959, *The Story of Samuel,* 1960, and *Stories from the Bible,* 1961, all by Walter de la Mare; *The Poems of François Villon,* 1946; *Hey Nonny Yes* edited by Hallam Fordham, 1947; *The Pilgrim's Progress* by John Bunyan, 1947; *Three Brothers and a Lady* by Margaret Black, 1947; *The True and Pathetic History of Desbarollda the Waltzing Mouse,* 1947, and *The Land of Green Ginger,* 1966, by Noel Langley; *Camberwell School of Arts and Crafts Jubilee,* 1948; *Charles Dickens Birthday Book* edited by Enid Dickens Hawksley, 1948; *The Otterbury Incident* by C. Day Lewis, 1948; *Somebody's Rocking My Dreamboat* by Noel Langley and Hazel Pynegar, 1949; *The Tale of Ali Baba* translated by J. C. Mardrus and E. Powys, 1949; *The Comedies* by Shakespeare, 1951; *The Blackbird in the Lilac,* 1952, *Pigeons and Princesses,* 1956, *Prefabulous Animiles,* 1957, *The Wandering Moon,* 1957, *The Exploits of Don Quixote, Retold,* 1959, *Titus in Trouble,* 1959, *Hurdy-Gurdy,* 1961, *Sailor Rumbelow and Britannia,* 1962, *The Story of Jackie Thimble,* 1964, *Three Tall Tales,* 1965, *The Secret Shoemakers,* 1966, *Rhyming Will,* 1967, *The Angel and the Donkey,* 1969, *How the Moon Began,* 1971, *Complete Poems for Children,* 1973, *The Lion That Flew,* 1974, and *More Prefabulous Animiles,* 1975, all by James Reeves; *The Modern Prometheus* by Zareh Nubar, 1952; *The Warden,* 1952, and *Barchester Towers,* 1953, by Anthony Trollope; *The Fantastic Tale of the Plucky Sailor and the Postage Stamp* by Stephen Corrin, 1954; *The Newcomes,* 1954, and

Henry Esmond, 1956, by W. M. Thackeray; *The Little Bookroom*, 1955, *Jim at the Corner*, 1958, *Eleanor Farjeon's Book*, 1960, *Italian Peepshow*, 1960, *Mrs. Malone*, 1962, *Kaleidoscope*, 1963, and *The Old Nurse's Stocking-Basket*, 1965, all by Eleanor Farjeon; *The Minnow on the Say* by Philippa Pearce, 1955; *Pictures on the Pavement* by G. W. Stonier, 1955; *The Suburban Child* by James Kenward, 1955; *Sun Slower Sun Faster* by Meriol Trevor, 1955; *Marshmallow* by Clare Newberry, 1956; *Hunting with Mr. Jorrocks* by R. S. Surtees, edited by Lionel Gough, 1956; *St. Luke's Life of Christ* translated by J. B. Phillips, 1956; *A Stickful of Nonpareil* by George Scurfield, 1956; *Ding Dong Bell* by Peter Young, 1957; *Lottie*, 1957, *Elfrida and the Pig*, 1959, and *The Stuffed Dog*, 1967, all by John Symonds; *The School in Our Village* by Joan M. Goldman, 1957; *Brief to Counsel*, 1958, *Know about English Law*, 1965, and *Learn about English Law*, 1974, all by Henry Cecil; *Pinky-Pye*, 1958, *The Witch Family*, 1960, *The Alley*, 1964, *Miranda the Great*, 1967, and *The Tunnel of Hugsy Goode*, 1972, all by Eleanor Estes; *Father Brown Stories* by G. K. Chesterton, 1959; *The Godstone and the Blackymor* by T. H. White, 1959; *Holiday Trench*, 1959, and *Kidnappers at Coombe*, 1960, by Joan Ballantyne; *The Nine Lives of Island Mackenzie* by Ursula Moray Williams, 1959; *Boyhoods of Great Composers* by Catherine Gough, 2 vols., 1960, 1963; *Merry England* by Cyril Ray, 1960; *The Penny Fiddle*, 1960, and *Ann at Highwood Hall*, 1964, by Robert Graves; *The Rib of the Green Umbrella* by Naomi Mitchison, 1960; *The Adventures of Huckleberry Finn*, 1961, and *The Adventures of Tom Sawyer*, 1961, by Mark Twain; *Down in the Cellar* by Nicholas Stuart Gray, 1961; *Folk Songs of England, Ireland, Scotland, and Wales* edited by William Cole, 1961; *The Island of Fish in the Trees*, 1962, *The Land of Right Up and Down*, 1964, and *Kali and the Golden Mirror*, 1967, all by Eva-Lis Wuorio; *J. M. Barrie's Peter Pan* by Eleanor Graham, 1962; *London since 1912* by John Hayes, 1962; *Naughty Children* edited by Christianna Brand, 1962, and *Nurse Matilda*, 1964, *Nurse Matilda Goes to Town*, 1967, and *Nurse Matilda Goes to Hospital*, 1974, all by Brand; *A Ring of Bells* by John Betjeman, 1962; *The Singing Cupboard*, 1962, and *Swanhilda-of-the-Swans*, 1964, by Dana Faralla; *The Story of Let's Make an Opera!* by Eric Crozier, 1962; *Stig of the Dump* by Clive King, 1963; *Hello, Elephant*, 1964, and *The Muffletumps*, 1966, by Jan Wahl; *The Thirty-Nine Steps* by John Buchan, 1964; *The Milldale Riot* by Freda P. Nichols, 1965; *Old Perisher* by Diana Ross, 1965; *Timothy's Song* by William J. Lederer, 1965; *The Truants and Other Poems* by John Walsh, 1965; *The Year Round* by Leonard Clark, 1965; *Daddy-Long-Legs* by Jean Webster, 1966; *The Little Girl and the Tiny Doll*, 1966, and *The Night Ride*, 1973, by Aingelda Ardizzone; *The Dragon* by Archibald Marshall, 1966; *The Eleanor Farjeon Book: A Tribute*, 1966; *The Growing Summer* by Noel Streatfeild, 1966; *Long Ago When I Was Young* by E. Nesbit, 1966; *A Likely Place* by Paula Fox, 1967; *Travels with a Donkey in the Cevennes*, 1967, and *Home from Sea*, 1970, by Robert Louis Stevenson; *Robinson Crusoe* by Daniel Defoe, 1968; *Upsidedown Willie*, 1968, *Special Branch Willie*, 1969, and *Fire-Brigade Willie*, 1970, all by Dorothy Clewes; *Do You Remember What Happened* by Jean Chapman, 1969; *A Riot of Quiet* by Virginia Sicotte, 1969; *Dick Whittington, Retold* by Kathleen Lines, 1970; *The Old Ballad of the Babes in the Wood*, 1972; *Rain, Rain Don't Go Away* by Shirley Morgan, 1972; *The Second-Best Children in the World* by Mary Levin, 1972; *Ardizzone's Kilvert*, edited by William Plomer, abridged by Elizabeth Divine, 1976.

*   *   *

Edward Ardizzone's books have for over thirty years been loved by succeeding generations of children all over the world. One of the most attractive aspects of his work is its presentation of an idiosyncratic, and instantly recognizable, view of life, always affectionate and sympathetic without ever lapsing into sentimentality. This sympathetic vision springs from his readiness to enter into the texture of his characters' experience – a readiness exemplified in the precise observation of apparently casual detail which authenticates his draughtsmanship. The purity and directness of his vision and insight reveal something childlike in his own nature.

His writing is similarly perceptive and authentic. The seagoing adventures of Tim, his most famous creation, have many elements of romance – storm, shipwreck, last-minute rescue. At the same time, however, they are full of the homely detail of shipboard life. Tim may be the hero, but he is not immune from seasickness, and we see him peeling potatoes and scrubbing floors as well as detecting fires and saving the ship's cat. The narrative is always strong and economical: the illustrations, with their comic-strip captions, are never merely ornamental, and the writing always carries the story forward. This is clearly an important factor in the popularity of the tales.

But Ardizzone does not simply tell tales. His work is an unpretentious celebration of certain human qualities and moral values. Most children find it easy to identify with the heroes and heroines, who are all (especially the boys) characterised by self-reliance, courage, and fortitude in adversity. They are often lonely and far from home. Their plans and hopes are threatened, whether by natural disaster or by the scorn and bullying of hostile figures (such as the taunting schoolboys in *Johnny the Clockmaker*). But they have perseverance and self-confidence, and there are always allies as well as enemies. The hero triumphs through his own doggedness and through the loyalty and affection which bind him to his friends. After the wildest exploits he returns to the familiarity of home, and the young reader, having lived through perilous voyages, is left with a reassuring sense of warmth and companionship. It is as if we are told: Life starts at home and, after a journey of adventure, conflict and reconciliation, ends there.

—James Reeves

ARMOUR, Richard (Willard). American. Born in San Pedro, California, 15 July 1906. Educated at Pomona College, Claremont, California, B.A. 1927; Harvard University, Cambridge, Massachusetts (Dexter Scholar, 1931), M.A. 1928, Ph.D. 1933. Served as a Colonel in the United States Army, retired, 1953; with War Department General Staff during World War II: Legion of Merit (twice). Married Kathleen Stevens in 1932; has one son and one daughter. Instructor in English, University of Texas, Austin, 1928–29, and Northwestern University, Evanston, Illinois, 1930–31; Professor of English, College of the Ozarks, Clarksville, Arkansas, 1932–33; American Lecturer, University of Freiburg, Germany, 1933–34; Professor of English, Wells College, Aurora, New York, 1934–35, and Claremont Graduate School, California, 1946–63. Professor of English, 1945–63, Dean of Faculty, 1961–63, Balch Lecturer, 1963–66, and since 1966, Dean and Professor Emeritus, Scripps College, Claremont, California. Carnegie Visiting Professor, University of Hawaii, Honolulu, 1957; State Department Lecturer in Europe and Asia, 1964–67. Litt.D.: College of the Ozarks, 1944; Pomona College, 1972; Claremont Men's College, 1974; L.H.D.: Whittier College, California, 1968; Southern California College of Optometry, Los Angeles, 1972; LL.D.: College of Idaho, Caldwell, 1969. Agent: Paul R. Reynolds Inc., 12 East 42nd Street, New York, New York 10017. Address: 460 Blaisdell Drive, Claremont, California 91711, U.S.A.

PUBLICATIONS FOR CHILDREN

Verse

The Year Santa Went Modern, illustrated by Paul Galdone. New York, McGraw Hill, 1964.

The Adventures of Egbert the Easter Egg, illustrated by Paul Galdone. New York, McGraw Hill, 1965; Kingswood, Surrey, World's Work, 1966.

Animals on the Ceiling, illustrated by Paul Galdone. New York, McGraw Hill, 1966.

The Strange Dreams of Rover Jones, illustrated by Eric Gurney.   New York, McGraw Hill, 1973.

Other (in verse)

Our Presidents, illustrated by Leonard Everett Fisher.   New York, Norton, 1964.
A Dozen Dinosaurs, illustrated by Paul Galdone.   New York, McGraw Hill, 1967; Kingswood, Surrey, World's Work, 1968.
Odd Old Mammals: Animals After the Dinosaurs, illustrated by Paul Galdone.   New York, McGraw Hill, 1968; Kingswood, Surrey, World's Work, 1969.
On Your Marks: A Package of Punctuation, illustrated by Paul Galdone.   New York, McGraw Hill, 1969.
All Sizes and Shapes of Monkeys and Apes, illustrated by Paul Galdone.   New York, McGraw Hill, 1970; Kingswood, Surrey, World's Work, 1972.
Who's in Holes?, illustrated by Paul Galdone.   New York, McGraw Hill, 1971; Kingswood, Surrey, World's Work, 1973.
Sea Full of Whales, illustrated by Paul Galdone.   New York, McGraw Hill, 1974; Kingswood, Surrey, World's Work, 1977.

PUBLICATIONS FOR ADULTS

Play

To These Dark Steps, with Bown Adams (produced New York, 1943).   New York, Institute for the Education of the Blind, 1943.

Verse

Yours for the Asking: A Book of Light Verse.   Boston, Humphries, 1942.
Privates' Lives: Verses.   Boston, Humphries, 1944.
Leading with My Left.   New York, Beechhurst Press, 1946.
Golf Bawls.   New York, Beechhurst Press, 1946.
For Partly Proud Parents: Light Verse about Children.   New York, Harper, 1950.
Light Armour: Playful Poems.   New York, McGraw Hill, 1954.
Nights with Armour: Lighthearted Light Verse.   New York, McGraw Hill, 1958.
An Armoury of Light Verse.   Boston, Pocket Books, 1964.
Punctured Poems: Famous First and Infamous Second Lines.   Englewood Cliffs, New Jersey, Prentice Hall, 1966.
All in Sport.   New York, McGraw Hill, 1972.
The Spouse in the House.   New York, McGraw Hill, 1975.

Other

Barry Cornwall: A Biography of Bryan Waller Procter.   Boston, Meador, 1935.
The Literary Recollections of Barry Cornwall.   Boston, Meador, 1936.
Writing Light Verse.   Boston, The Writer, 1947; revised edition, 1958; augmented edition as *Writing Light Verse and Prose Humor*, 1971.
It All Started with Columbus.   New York, McGraw Hill, 1953; London, Hammond, 1962.
It All Started with Europa.   New York, McGraw Hill, 1955; London, Hammond, 1962.
It All Started with Eve.   New York, McGraw Hill, 1956; London, Hammond, 1957.
Twisted Tales from Shakespeare.   New York, McGraw Hill, 1957; London, Hammond, 1958.
It All Started with Marx.   New York, McGraw Hill, 1958; London, Hammond, 1959.
Drug Store Days: My Youth among the Pills and Potions.   New York, McGraw Hill,

1959; as *Pills, Potions and Granny*, London, Hammond, 1960.

The Classics Reclassified.   New York, McGraw Hill, 1960; London, Hammond, 1961.

A Safari into Satire.   Los Angeles, California Library Association, 1961.

Golf is a Four-Letter Word.   New York, McGraw Hill, and London, Hammond, 1962.

Armour's Almanac.   New York, McGraw Hill, 1962.

Through Darkest Adolescence.   New York, McGraw Hill, 1963; London, Hammond, 1964.

American Lit Relit.   New York, McGraw Hill, 1964.

Going Around in Academic Circles.   New York, McGraw Hill, 1965.

It All Started with Hippocrates.   New York, McGraw Hill, 1966.

A Satirist Looks at the World (lecture).   Ann Arbor, University of Michigan School of Business Administration, 1967.

It All Started with Stones and Clubs.   New York, McGraw Hill, 1967.

My Life with Women.   New York, McGraw Hill, 1968.

English Lit Relit.   New York, McGraw Hill, 1969.

A Diabolical Dictionary of Education.   New York, World, 1969.

A Short History of Sex.   New York, McGraw Hill, 1970.

Out of My Mind.   New York, McGraw Hill, 1972.

It All Started with Freshman English.   New York, McGraw Hill, 1973.

Going Like Sixty: A Lighthearted Look at the Later Years.   New York, McGraw Hill, 1974.

The Academic Bestiary.   New York, Morrow, 1974.

The Happy Bookers: A History of Librarians and the World.   New York, McGraw Hill, 1976.

It All Would Have Startled Columbus.   New York, McGraw Hill, 1976.

It All Started with Nudes.   New York, McGraw Hill, 1977.

Editor, with Raymond F. Howes, *Coleridge the Talker: A Series of Contemporary Descriptions and Accounts*.   Ithaca, New York, Cornell University Press, and London, Oxford University Press, 1940.

Editor, *Young Voices: A Book of Wells College Verse*.   Aurora, New York, Wells College Press, 1941.

Manuscript Collections: Scripps College Library, Claremont, California; Mugar Memorial Library, Boston University.

Richard Armour comments:

If there is anything special about my writings it is the variety of subjects and techniques. I write both light verse and light prose (after a period of writing heavy biographies), and books for children, books for adults, and books for readers of all ages. Also in most of my books, those for children as well as those for adults, I combine fact and fun, entertainment and edification. Many of my books are brought by teachers into the classroom to combat boredom. I use many large and often dull books to get the information (especially facts that are little known even by specialists in the given field) to write my playful small books. Children have livelier imaginations and a greater curiosity than adults and I try to keep this in mind when I write for them.

*   *   *

It is rather difficult to think of a learned man, author of books on literary criticism, writing humorous verse and satire on such topics as mammals, Santa, and golf. But the proof is Richard Armour, college professor, author of several serious works on literature and loads of books of verse, satire and humor for children and readers of all ages. But it should not be unusual for a man with a lively, creative mind to be a keen observer, grasp what might seem trite or commonplace and turn this into gentle satirical humor.

Younger readers, those aged 8 to 11 years, have been treated to two levels of Armour's writing. The first is his purely imaginative works: *Egbert the Easter Egg* and *The Year Santa Went Modern* are centered around two major holiday seasons. His verse enhanced, but illustrations helped the plots to unfold. But far more interesting is his use of factual information in such books as *Who's in Holes?* and *A Dozen Dinosaurs*. In these, Armour has taken well-researched, factual materials and added light verse. The result, while not great poetry, is lots of fun and entertainment while learning facts.

In all of Armour's books we get the essence of his wit, his marvelous ability to reduce the pompous to the absurd and the lofty and reserved to the simple. Literature, medicine, history, education, women, family, golf, and Shakespeare – none has been spared his satirical pen. His writing in many instances mirrors our culture. Our everyday activities, our foibles, our contradictions, our hypocrisies are reduced to a level which can only make us chuckle.

Armour is not a great writer, but he is a witty storyteller with a tremendous gift for satire in a light, breezy and humorous style. He is not aiming for depth. His brilliance lies in his ability to render the complex simple – an unusually difficult task but one which seems to come so easily to this author in all of his books.

—Dorothy D. Siles

ARMSTRONG, Richard. British. Born in Northumberland, in 1903. Educated at Walbottle Primary School, 1908–16. Worked as an errand boy, labourer, greaser, and crane driver in steelworks, Tyneside, 1916–19; sailor and radio operator, Merchant Navy, 1920–37; typist, secretary, architect's assistant, and undertaker's labourer, 1937–54. Recipient: Library Association Carnegie Medal, 1949; New York *Herald Tribune* Festival award, 1956. Agent: A.P. Watt and Son, 26–28 Bedford Row, London WC1R 4HL, England.

PUBLICATIONS FOR CHILDREN

Fiction

> *The Mystery of Obadiah*, illustrated by Marjorie Sankey. London, Dent, 1943.
> *Sabotage at the Forge*, illustrated by L.P. Lupton. London, Dent, 1946.
> *Sea Change*, illustrated by M. Leszczynski. London, Dent, 1948.
> *The Whinstone Drift*, illustrated by Michael A. Charlton. London, Dent, 1951.
> *Wanderlust: Voyage of a Little White Monkey*, illustrated by Frederick K. Crooke. London, Faber, 1952.
> *Danger Rock*, illustrated by M. Leszczynski. London, Dent, 1955; as *Cold Hazard*, Boston, Houghton Mifflin, 1956.
> *The Lost Ship: A Caribbean Adventure*, illustrated by Edward Osmond. London, Dent, 1956; New York, Day, 1958.
> *No Time for Tankers*, illustrated by Reg Gray. London, Dent, 1958; New York, Day, 1959.
> *Another Six*. Oxford, Blackwell, 1959.
> *The Lame Duck*, illustrated by D.G. Valentine. London, Dent, 1959; as *Ship Afire!*, New York, Day, 1961.
> *Before the Wind*. Oxford, Blackwell, 1959.
> *Horseshoe Reef*, illustrated by D.G. Valentine. London, Dent, 1960; New York, Duell, 1961.
> *Out of the Shallows*, illustrated by D.G. Valentine. London, Dent, 1961.

Trial Trip, illustrated by D. G. Valentine.   London, Dent, 1962; New York, Criterion Books, 1963.

The Ship Stealers (as Cam Renton), illustrated by Val Biro.   Penshurst, Kent, Friday Press, 1963.

Island Odyssey, illustrated by Andrew Dodds.   London, Dent, 1963; as *Fight for Freedom: An Adventure of World War II*, New York, McKay, 1966.

Big-Head (as Cam Renton), illustrated by Val Biro.   Penshurst, Kent, Friday Press, 1964.

The Big Sea, illustrated by Andrew Dodds.   London, Dent, 1964; New York, McKay, 1965.

The Greenhorn, illustrated by Roger Payne.   London, Nelson, 1965.

The Secret Sea, illustrated by Roger Payne.   London, Dent, and New York, McKay, 1966.

The Mutineers, illustrated by Gareth Floyd.   London, Dent, and New York, McKay, 1968.

The Albatross, illustrated by Graham Humphreys.   London, Dent, and New York, McKay, 1970.

Other

A History of Seafaring:
1. *The Early Mariners.*   London, Benn, 1967; New York, Praeger, 1968.
2. *The Discoverers.*   London, Benn, 1968; New York, Praeger, 1969.
3. *The Merchantmen.*   London, Benn, and New York, Praeger, 1969.

Themselves Alone: The Story of Men in Empty Places.   London, Benn, and Boston, Houghton Mifflin, 1972.

Powered Ships: The Beginnings.   London, Benn, 1975.

Editor, *Treasure and Treasure Hunters.*   London, Hamish Hamilton, and New York, David White, 1969.

PUBLICATIONS FOR ADULTS

Novels

The Northern Maid.   London, Dent, 1947.
Passage Home.   London, Dent, 1952.
Sailor's Luck.   London, Dent, 1959.
Storm Path.   London, Dent, 1964.

Other

Grace Darling, Maid and Myth.   London, Dent, 1965.

Richard Armstrong comments:
  My ambition was to be a school teacher, but poverty and the First World War denied me the necessary education, and when the dust settled I did the next best thing and became a writer. This accounts for the didactic element in my books. My aim has been to tell young people groping through the fantasies of adolescence (and anyone else who wants to know) what the real world looks like to me and perhaps a little something of what life is all about. But first I had to provide my family with a roof overhead and three squares a day, so the main body of my work is a compromise between what I wanted to say in it and what my publishers would accept and pay for. From time to time I chanced my arm and wrote a book regardless, but the end result was always another pile of rejection slips, an increase in my

overdraft and a frosty letter from my bank manager. Consequently what is considered by competent commentators, unconnected with the publishing trade, to be my best work to date – a novel on faith and three books for boys – remains unpublished and up for grabs.

*   *   *

The best writers of adventure stories for young people have three particular things to offer: their own experience of action, a straightforward style full of vitality, and a positive attitude to life in general. These qualities are abundantly present in the work of Richard Armstrong. You could add a talent for exciting plots, but these seem to grow naturally from his own experience of action and men.

Some of his early books were about boys in heavy industry, notably *Sabotage at the Forge* and *The Whinstone Drift*, but most of his books concern the sea and ships. Everything he writes is authentic, based on his knowledge of ships and the men who sail them – as exciting as real-life adventure. Early in his writing career it was Armstrong's avowed intention to teach young readers something of the crafts and skills of steel workers, miners and seamen, but the effect is far from didactic; he makes all the details so fascinating that one's understanding of them enhances the drama of his stories. One appreciates how much depends on a man's skill and judgment, with moral issues and conflicts of temperament contributing to the tension.

His style makes sensible use of colloquial speech; it is vigorous and descriptive. His strength lies in his complete knowledge of the scene: he is not painting for effect; he is telling it as it is and with a rare feeling for words and the rhythms of language. He credits his readers with intellect as well as feeling, but he is no mandarin writer.

Nor do his plots follow a formula. The plot line emerges from situation and character; no two are the same. Wreckers, salvage, whaling, war are only a few of his themes. Several books concern youths for whom a voyage full of natural hazards and human conflicts marks an important stage in growing up. There is often an older man, captain or mate perhaps, who wins the boy's respect. Such men are imaginative and humane; their senses and intuition are alert to the pulse of communal feeling on board ship and they never act without regard to this. They take life and death decisions without any illusions – men of ideals, but realists too.

Often the adventure is shared by two boys of contrasting temperaments, linked by friendship, as in *Horseshoe Reef* and *The Big Sea* (though these are otherwise quite different stories). Others concern the interplay of personalities in a group of young people trapped and held under pressure, as in *Danger Rock*; in *The Mutineers* where they are marooned by choice in what should have been an island paradise; in *The Albatross* where they steal a ketch and make off with treasure trove but cannot land anywhere because of the law – a tragic adventure which only one survives.

The fifteen boys of *The Mutineers* are also fleeing the law. They are all sixteen or seventeen, emigrating to Australia under a training scheme. Having taken over the ship at gunpoint for kicks, they escape the consequences by sailing away in one of the boats. Bo-bo Bolton has the know-how to sail and to find the island, but it is Chick Hinshelwood who emerges as the leader. He is a good organiser, but he imposes his authority brutally and soon shows his appetite for power. Stubby, who could have stood up to him at the beginning, refuses the responsibility of leadership. This is an awesome story of brutalized human beings in a "prison" of their own making.

This books bears striking similarities to William Golding's *Lord of the Flies*. Both books say something of deep interest about human nature and about fear and the lust for power. But their messages are quite different: Armstrong's is positive, Golding's pessimistic. The contrast highlights an essential ingredient in a book for young readers if it is to appeal to them. However sad or horrifying the story, there must be characters with inner strength to identify with. We leave Stubby, Bo-bo, and Jake wiser and stronger for their appalling experiences.

Sea stories used to be a distinct category of fiction and one of the most popular, its readers not confined to the young only. But, regrettably, this is no longer so. Richard Armstrong was undoubtedly one of the masters of the genre (writing for adults as well as young people) and served it well for twenty years. Gradually, though, times and tastes change; he sensed this and reflected these changes. There is nothing old-fashioned about the youths in his later novels. They are less naive, more of a problem to themselves than his early heroes. It is characteristic of Armstrong that he has never ceased to respond to each younger generation as it came. This sensitive rapport with his fellow men is at the heart of all his work.

—Gwen Marsh

ARMSTRONG, William H(oward). American. Born in Lexington, Virginia, 14 September 1914. Educated at Augusta Military Academy, 1929–32; Hampden-Sydney College, Virginia, 1932–36, A.B. (cum laude) 1936 (Phi Beta Kappa); University of Virginia, Charlottesville, 1937–38. Married Martha Stonestreet Williams in 1942 (died 1953); has two sons and one daughter. History teacher, Virginia Episcopal School, 1939–44, and Kent School, Connecticut, 1944–76. Recipient: National School Bell award, 1963; American Library Association Newbery Medal, 1970. Address: Kimadee Hill, Kent, Connecticut 06757, U.S.A.

PUBLICATIONS FOR CHILDREN

Fiction

> *Sounder*, illustrated by James Barkley. New York, Harper, 1969; London, Gollancz, 1971.
> *Sour Land*, illustrated by David B. Armstrong. New York, Harper, 1971.
> *The MacLeod Place*, illustrated by Eros Keith. New York, Coward McCann, 1972.
> *The Mills of God*, illustrated by David B. Armstrong. New York, Doubleday, 1973.

Other

> *Barefoot in the Grass: The Story of Grandma Moses*. New York, Doubleday, 1970.
> *Animal Tales*, illustrated by Mirko Hanák. New York, Doubleday, 1970.
> *Hadassah: Esther, the Orphan Queen*, illustrated by Barbara Byfield. New York, Doubleday, 1972.
> *My Animals*, illustrated by Mirko Hanák. New York, Doubleday, 1974.
> *The Education of Abraham Lincoln*, illustrated by William Plummer. New York, Coward McCann, 1974.

PUBLICATIONS FOR ADULTS

Other

> *Study Is Hard Work*. New York, Harper, 1956.
> *Through Troubled Waters*. New York, Harper, 1957.
> *Peoples of the Ancient World*, with Joseph Ward Swain. New York, Harper, 1959.
> *87 Ways to Help Your Child in School*. New York, Barron's, 1961.
> *Tools of Thinking*. New York, Barron's, 1961.
> *Word Power in Five Easy Lessons*. New York, Barron's, 1969.
> *Study Tapes*. New York, Barron's, 1975.

Manuscript Collection: Kerlan Collection, University of Minnesota, Minneapolis.

*   *   *

William H. Armstrong's *Sounder* portrays a black family caught in the slavery of poverty, isolation, and ignorance that prevailed as a social condition in the Old South in the years between the Civil War and 1900. The setting of the action is deliberately vague and thereby broadens the focus of the book to suggest a widespread cultural milieu. In addition, Armstrong's device of having the main action of the story reported to the author fifty years later gives the book an even wider perspective of social history.

The characters have no names other than "the boy," "the mother," "the father" – a stylistic device that tends to universalize them. What happens to these characters extends itself to represent the general conditions for blacks at that period of history. And another effect of their having no names is to portray them as they are regarded and used by the indifferent and sometimes hostile white society around them. The blacks in the story are faceless, nameless objects to be exploited as cheap labor by the whites and never to be acknowledged as equals.

Early in the plot, the father is arrested and taken away to jail for having stolen a ham and some sausage to feed his family. In the course of his arrest, the family dog, Sounder, is lamed and rendered mute. The dog's voice has been carefully described by the author as making "music as though the branches of all the trees were being pulled across silver strings." The unity of the family and its closeness to nature are equated with the music of the dog's voice. The dog is made silent when the harmony of the family is broken by the overreaction of an oppressive white society. Sounder's voice is restored only with the return of the father, an event whose importance is compared with the return of Ulysses in *The Odyssey* and the greeting given the returned warrior by the dog Argus. The comparison is ironic, however, because the father in *Sounder*, unlike Ulysses, is crippled and soon will die. The crippling of the dog at the beginning of the story is a structural foreshadowing of the injuries to the father at the climax of the book.

A subplot develops as the boy searches for his father at distant work camps. During his travels, the boy finds a book, and finally a teacher who then teaches him to read. This helps provide a solution to the boy's problems. He, like the other blacks in the story, is held in social bondage because they simply do not have the necessary knowledge and experience to make the choice to leave their menial dependence on a white landowner who had "scattered the cabins of his Negro sharecroppers far apart, like flyspecks on a whitewashed ceiling." Education opens the larger world to the boy and provides the means for his personal liberation.

Armstrong never backs away from a realistic portrayal of police brutality or of the well-motivated and justified murderous anger of the boy when he encounters sadistic jailers and deputies. The portrayal of violence is always at the service of art in *Sounder*.

—William D. Anderson

ARTHUR, Ruth (Mabel).   British.   Born in Glasgow, Lanark, 26 May 1905. Educated at St. Columbus School, Kilmacolm, Renfrewshire; Froebel Educational Institute, Roehampton, London, Froebel Certificate 1926. Married Frederick N. Huggins in 1932; has two sons and four daughters. Froebel kindergarten teacher, Laurel Bank School, Glasgow, 1927–30, and High School, Loughton, Essex, 1930–32. Agent: Curtis Brown Group Ltd., 1 Craven Hill, London W2 3EW; or, Marilyn Marlow, Curtis Brown Ltd., 575 Madison Avenue, New York, New York 10022, U.S.A. Address: 81 Bainton Road, Oxford, England.

Fiction

Friendly Stories, illustrated by C. F. Christie.   London, Harrap, 1932.

The Crooked Brownie, illustrated by R. M. Turvey.   London, Harrap, 1936.

Pumpkin Pie.   London, Collins, 1938.

The Crooked Brownie in Town, illustrated by R. M. Turvey.   London, Harrap, 1942.

The Crooked Brownie at the Seaside, illustrated by R. M. Turvey.   London, Harrap, 1942.

Cowslip Mollie.   London, Hutchinson, 1949.

Carolina's Holiday and Other Stories, illustrated by Dodie Masterman.   London, Harrap, 1957.

The Daisy Cow and Other Stories of the Channel Islands, illustrated by Lucien Lowen.   London, Harrap, 1958.

Carolina's Golden Bird and Other Stories, illustrated by Lucien Lowen.   London, Harrap, 1958.

A Cottage for Rosemary, illustrated by M. Whitaker.   London, Harrap, 1960.

Carolina and Roberto, illustrated by Lucien Lowen.   London, Harrap, 1961.

Dragon Summer, illustrated by Margery Gill.   London, Hutchinson, 1962; New York, Atheneum, 1963.

Carolina and the Sea Horse, and Other Stories, illustrated by Lucien Lowen.   London, Harrap, 1964.

My Daughter Nicola, illustrated by Fermin Rocker.   New York, Atheneum, 1965; London, Gollancz, 1966.

A Candle in Her Room, illustrated by Margery Gill.   London, Gollancz, and New York, Atheneum, 1966.

Requiem for a Princess, illustrated by Margery Gill.   London, Gollancz, and New York, Atheneum, 1967.

Portrait of Margarita, illustrated by Margery Gill.   London, Gollancz, and New York, Atheneum, 1968.

The Whistling Boy, illustrated by Margery Gill.   London, Gollancz, and New York, Atheneum, 1969.

The Saracen Lamp, illustrated by Margery Gill.   London, Gollancz, and New York, Atheneum, 1970.

The Little Dark Thorn, illustrated by Margery Gill.   London, Gollancz, and New York, Atheneum, 1971.

The Autumn People, illustrated by Margery Gill.   London, Gollancz, and New York, Atheneum, 1973; as *The Autumn Ghosts*, London, Target, 1976.

After Candlemas, illustrated by Margery Gill.   London, Gollancz, and New York, Atheneum, 1974; as *Candlemas Mystery*, London, Target, 1976.

On the Wasteland, illustrated by Margery Gill.   London, Gollancz, and New York, Atheneum, 1975.

An Old Magic, illustrated by Margery Gill.   London, Gollancz, and New York, Atheneum, 1977.

Other

Mother Goose Stories.   London, Collins, 1938.

Ruth Arthur comments:

I write about the intricacies of human relationships and the difficulties of adolescence. In my stories I try to introduce children of 11 and 12 upwards to some of the universal problems of the grown-up world such as adoption, divorce, loneliness, delinquency.

*   *   *

Since the publication of *A Candle in Her Room*, Ruth Arthur has built up a reputation as a writer of Gothic novels for girls in their teens. The novels are well-constructed and readable, and, for girls of eleven or so, they provide a useful stepping-stone to the adult fiction of Daphne du Maurier, Mary Stewart, and other writers of this kind.

Most of the novels have a similar pattern. The central character is usually a girl in her teens: in some of the books (for example *The Saracen Lamp* and *A Candle in Her Room*) there is a succession of such heroines, living at different times, whose lives are related by a common motif to link the past with the present, such as the lamp brought back from the Crusades in *The Saracen Lamp*, the French folk tune in *The Whistling Boy*, or the medallion in *Requiem for a Princess*. Many of the stories have a supernatural element, which is much to contemporary taste (*The Autumn People*, a time-travel story, was retitled *The Autumn Ghosts* for the paperback edition). Although the starting point of the story is usually the present day, there are a strong historical interest and a concern with local superstitions, traditions, and customs.

There is a general atmosphere of middle-class affluence, and the romantic approach is only to some extent offset by the introduction of contemporary problems – the feelings of the half-coloured heroine and an autistic child in *A Portrait of Margarita*, for example. In *The Whistling Boy*, in particular, the balance of the story is to some extent upset by the introduction of too many problems, none of which has any real bearing on the plot.

The stories are given a firm geographical setting, whether in Pembrokeshire (*A Candle in Her Room*), Norfolk (*The Whistling Boy*), Cornwall (*Requiem for a Princess*) or Oxfordshire (*Portrait of Margarita*) – but this is less significant than the need to provide a prevailing background of affluence and the ambience for the supernatural. The names of the supporting characters are chosen carefully to echo this atmosphere, and middle-class security is comfortably supported by a cohort of obliging servants, old nannies, and housekeepers. The heroines themselves seldom have any serious problems. They tend to be introspective, and are usually given suitably romantic names.

However, these books undoubtedly do meet the needs of a stage through which many young teenage girls pass and provide a rather richer diet than might otherwise be experienced which, caught at the right stage, may lead naturally on to adult books.

—Sheila G. Ray

ARUNDEL, Honor (Morfydd). British. Born in Llanarmon, Gwynedd, 15 August 1919. Educated at Hayes Court, Kent; Somerville College, Oxford, 1938–39. Married Alex McCrindle in 1952; three daughters and one stepdaughter. Worked as a typist; journalist; engineer; film, radio and theatre critic. *Died 8 June 1973.*

PUBLICATIONS FOR CHILDREN

Fiction

> *Green Street*, illustrated by Eileen Armitage. London, Hamish Hamilton, 1966; New York, Hawthorn Books, 1970.
> *The High House*, illustrated by Eileen Armitage. London, Hamish Hamilton, 1966; New York, Meredith Press, 1968.
> *Emma's Island.* London, Hamish Hamilton, 1968; New York, Hawthorn Books, 1970.
> *The Two Sisters.* London, Heinemann, 1968; New York, Meredith Press, 1969.

The Amazing Mr. Prothero, illustrated by Jane Paton. London, Hamish Hamilton, 1968; Nashville, Nelson, 1972.

The Longest Weekend. London, Hamish Hamilton, 1969; New York, Nelson, 1970.

The Girl in the Opposite Bed. London, Hamish Hamilton, 1970; New York, Nelson, 1971.

Emma in Love. London, Hamish Hamilton, 1970; New York, Nelson, 1972.

The Terrible Temptation. London, Hamish Hamilton, and New York, Nelson, 1971.

A Family Failing. London, Hamish Hamilton, and Nashville, Nelson, 1972.

The Blanket Word. London, Hamish Hamilton, 1973.

PUBLICATIONS FOR ADULTS

Other

The Freedom of Art. London, Lawrence and Wishart, 1965.

Editor, with Maurice Carpenter and Jack Lindsay, *New Lyrical Ballads.* London, Editions Poetry, 1945.

*   *   *

The reputation of a writer of children's books remains only as long as the books are read or revived. Before her untimely death Honor Arundel had written successfully the kind of story for which there was a known demand but no infallible formula that would win critical acclaim. Accessible fiction for girls who had more staying power than was needed for pulp novelettes and magazine short stories was in short supply. A new concern for "social realism," undefined but understood, prompted a number of writers to deal with teenage problems in narratives that seemed more contrived than spontaneous, and where the solution to unwanted pregnancy, a coloured boyfriend, or dropping out of school fell pat into the final chapter. Honor Arundel solved a number of the problems in this kind of fiction, enough at least to set her apart from more run-of-the-mill writers, and to earn the respect of both her readers and their teachers.

She had the gift of writing lightly – an underestimated style. She dealt with the emotional problems of adolescence, particularly the conflict of idealism and the awareness that parents are only human, with a plain, unstressed realism. The adults in her books are fallible, integral characters, the young people not always attractive in their self-concern. Thus most of her stories are a contrast with the staginess of much writing for this particular age-group. The class system, divorced or separated parents, feckless adults, the struggle for independence, and the inexorable demands of earning one's living are presented with detachment and humanity. Her sympathy for the plight of her heroines does not include tolerance of their self-pity, and this separates her writing from that of countless imitators. She is not too indulgent of the middle classes, whose poverty is only relative compared with that of others who are society's victims. But she does not provide fairy godmothers for those who can't afford tuition fees. Her idealism is in places – a fine old Edinburgh house, an island on the west coast of Scotland – rather than people.

In some respects Honor Arundel is "an easy read" for girls who need challenging literature, but she represents a very definite stage for some readers on the way to a more developed taste. Her sense of values confronts her readers with worthwhile issues, and she shows that "am I all right?" is a proper evaluative question to ask of a sympathetic story-teller.

—Margaret Meek

ASHLEY, Bernard. British. Born in London, 2 April 1935. Educated at the Roan School, Blackheath, London, and Sir Joseph Williamson's School, Rochester, Kent, 1947–53; Trent Park College of Education, 1955–57, Cert.Ed.; Cambridge Institute of Education, 1970–71, Cambridge Associate Diploma in Primary Education. Served in the Royal Air Force, 1953–55. Married Iris Holbrook in 1958; has three sons. Teacher, Kent Education Committee, Gravesend, 1957–65, Hertfordshire Education Committee, Hertford Heath, 1965–71, and Hartley Junior School, Newham, London, 1971–76. Since 1977, Headteacher, Charlton Manor Junior School, London. Recipient: Children's Rights Workshop Other Award, 1976. Address: 128 Heathwood Gardens, London SE7 8ER, England.

PUBLICATIONS FOR CHILDREN

Fiction

> The Trouble with Donovan Croft, illustrated by Fermin Rocker. London, Oxford University Press, 1974.
> Terry on the Fence, illustrated by Charles Keeping. London, Oxford University Press, 1975; New York, S. G. Phillips, 1977.
> All My Men. London, Oxford University Press, 1977.

Other

> Don't Run Away (reader), illustrated by Ray Whittaker. London, Allman, 1965.
> Wall of Death (reader), illustrated by Ray Whittaker. London, Allman, 1966.
> Space Shot (reader), illustrated by Laszlo Acs. London, Allman, 1967.
> The Big Escape (reader), illustrated by James Hunt. London, Allman, 1967.
> The Men and the Boats: Britain's Life-Boat Service. London, Allman, 1968.
> Weather Men. London, Allman, 1970; revised edition, 1974.

Bernard Ashley comments:
   Each of my three full-length stories tells of a boy's attempts to cope with a crisis point in his life, each crisis presenting a problem as serious at the time as any he will later have to face as an adult: Donovan Croft, a black boy seemingly rejected in an alien environment; Terry, caught up in a frightening world of juvenile crime; and Paul, in All My Men, struggling to secure his place in a new and unfriendly school. Excitement, humour and personal relationships are some of the ingredients, but conflict, both internal and external, is the meat of each story, as it is of life.

                                        *   *   *

   Bernard Ashley's experience as a North London headmaster has given him a rare insight into the stresses and strains of school and home in an urban working class environment, and his writing reveals a commitment to children affected by these pressures. But Ashley does not set out to discuss "problems," and he writes compelling fiction for children focusing on the predicament of the modern urban child.
   Ashley's dialogue and his keen eye for detail capture with brevity and authenticity the atmosphere of playground, classroom and home life, in particular the conventions and friendships, tensions and cruelties of junior-school-age children's lives. His stories move forward as he builds up a series of incidents around a child who finds himself propelled into a course of action that he regrets but cannot avoid. Ashley also draws in the adults whom he reveals to be subject to the same pressures and to be human too.
   The Trouble with Donovan Croft is about a West Indian boy who is fostered with a white family. The shock of separation from his parents has made him mute. The story deals with

the growing relationship between Donovan and Keith, his new foster brother. Ashley's treatment of a boy subjected to different kinds of racial prejudice is outstanding.

Terry on the Fence has Terry terrorised by a gang of boys from a neighbouring school into helping them with a robbery. The interaction of home and peer group pressures is tensely and inexorably drawn. In *All My Men* Paul moves from central London to a suburban estate and a new school, where he comes up against the class bully. But Paul's attempt to stand up to him is rather didactically treated, the "moral" too orchestrated.

—Rosemary Stones

ATKIN, Flora B.   American.   Born in Baltimore, Maryland, 15 May 1919. Educated at George Washington University, Washington, D.C., 1935–38; Syracuse University, New York, 1938–40, A.B. in education and English 1940; Bennington College, Vermont, 1941; Catholic University of America, Washington, D.C., 1959–61. Married Maurice Atkin in 1941; has three children. Director, Recreational Arts Department, 1940–44, and Founding Director, Creative Arts Day Camp, 1941–44, Jewish Community Center, Washington, D.C.; Instructor in Dance Education, Howard University, Washington, D.C., 1942–43; free-lance creative arts educator and children's theatre director, 1953–68; Founding Director-Playwright, In-School Players, Adventure Theatre, Montgomery County, Maryland, 1969–76. Recipient: District of Columbia One-Act Play Tournament award 1970, 1971, 1973; Eastern States Theatre Association award, 1971, 1973; Children's Theatre Association Citation, 1972. Agent: Patricia Whitton, New Plays Inc., Box 273, Rowayton, Connecticut 06853; or, Joan Turner, 60 Lambton Road, London SW20 0LP, England. Address: 5507 Uppingham Street, Chevy Chase, Maryland 20015, U.S.A.

PUBLICATIONS FOR CHILDREN

Plays

    Tarradiddle Tales (also director: produced Washington, D.C., 1969; New York, 1974).   Rowayton, Connecticut, New Plays, 1970.
    Tarradiddle Travels (also director: produced Washington, D.C., 1970; New York, 1972).   Rowayton, Connecticut, New Plays, 1971.
    Golliwhoppers! (also director: produced Washington, D.C., 1972; New York, 1975).   Rowayton, Connecticut, New Plays, 1973.
    Skupper-Duppers (also director: produced Washington, D.C., 1974; New York, 1976).   Rowayton, Connecticut, New Plays, 1975.

Flora B. Atkin comments:

I created *Tarradiddle Tales* as a pilot project for Adventure Theatre, an adult company bringing in-school performances to children in the Washington area. So successful was this project that I created a sequel, *Tarradiddle Travels*, with its own special quality (and for a broader age range), but similarly combining dance, drama, pantomime, narration, and simple musical rhythmic instruments. The Tarradiddle plays were motivated by world-wide folklore, with its universality of appeal, yet with a recognition of the varying truths and mores in different cultures. *Golliwhoppers!* and *Skupper-Duppers* evolved from American folklore in all its diversity.

In each play I try to give the audience a feeling that it is right in the middle of the unfolding story. Variety of pace, mood, and theatrical technique in each tale and in the structure of each

51

play as a whole provides a rewarding experience for performers and audience alike. It is my belief that theatre for children is relevant to the purposes of education and should be an intrinsic part of a child's learning experience. A genuine and artistically conceived dramatic production can encourage esthetic sensitivity growth, stimulate a feeling of "I can do it too," and provide enjoyment for all.

*　　*　　*

Flora B. Atkin is a playwright, director, choreographer, and educator whose work is well-known throughout the United States. She has taught rhythms, dance, creative dramatics, and music in various schools and colleges and conducted workshops for leaders in the District of Columbia Recreation Department. Her four plays – *Tarradiddle Tales*, *Tarradiddle Travels*, *Golliwhoppers!*, and *Skupper-Duppers* – have been given over 2000 performances by more than 90 producing groups, including productions at the Kennedy Center and the Smithsonian Institution in Washington, D.C.

Ms. Atkin's greatest contribution to children's theatre in the United States is her original approach to material, much of which is regional in origin. She does not use traditional folk and fairy tales, but rather dramatizes the less well-known tales of the southeastern part of the country. She adapts her work to the needs of the small touring companies and the school assembly period without losing either substance or entertainment value. She represents a complete change from the earlier, more conventional type of playwright. Her dialogue is colloquial and her ideas relevant to curricular material as well as to the interests of modern children.

Ms. Atkin's approach is innovative rather than traditional, and since 1969 she has devoted much of her time to directing plays motivated by folklore for in-school touring.

—Nellie McCaslin

ATKINSON, M(ary) E(velyn). British. Born in Highgate, London, 20 June 1899. Educated privately: Leeson House, Langton Matravers, Dorset. Served as a British Red Cross nurse during World Wars I and II. Married George Neuberg Frankau in 1951. *Died in 1974.*

Publications for Children

Fiction

    August Adventure, illustrated by Harold Jones.   London, Cape, 1936.
    Mystery Manor, illustrated by Harold Jones.   London, Lane, 1937.
    The Compass Points North, illustrated by Harold Jones.   London, Lane, 1938.
    Smugglers' Gap, illustrated by Harold Jones.   London, Lane, 1939.
    Going Gangster.   London, Lane, 1940.
    Crusoe Island, illustrated by Harold Jones.   London, Lane, 1941.
    Challenge to Adventure, illustrated by Stuart Tresilian.   London, Lane, 1942.
    The Monster of Widgeon Weir, illustrated by Stuart Tresilian.   London, Lane, 1943.
    The Nest of the Scarecrow, illustrated by Stuart Tresilian.   London, Lane, 1944.
    Problem Party, illustrated by Stuart Tresilian.   London, Lane, 1945.
    Chimney Cottage, illustrated by Dorothy Craigie.   London, Lane, 1947.
    The House on the Moor, illustrated by Charlotte Hough.   London, Lane, 1948.
    The Thirteenth Adventure, illustrated by Charlotte Hough.   London, Lane, 1949.

Steeple Folly, illustrated by Charlotte Hough.   London, Lane, 1950.
Castaway Camp, illustrated by Charlotte Hough.   London, Lane, 1951.
Hunter's Moon, illustrated by Charlotte Hough.   London, Lane, 1952.
The Barnstormers, illustrated by Charlotte Hough.   London, Lane, 1953.
Riders and Raids, illustrated by Sheila Rose.   London, Lane, 1955.
Unexpected Adventure, illustrated by Sheila Rose.   London, Lane, 1955.
Horseshoes and Handle Bars, illustrated by Sheila Rose.   London, Lane, 1958; New
    York, A. S. Barnes, 1959.
Where There's a Will, illustrated by Wendy Marchant.   London, Nelson, 1961.

Other

Editor, with G. T. Atkinson, *A Book of Giants and Dwarfs*.   London, Dent, 1929.

PUBLICATIONS FOR ADULTS

Plays

Here Lies Matilda.   London, Deane, 1931.
Beginner's Luck.   London, Deane, and Boston, Baker, 1932.
Patchwork.   London, Deane, and Boston, Baker, 1933.
The Chimney Corner.   London, Deane, and Boston, Baker, 1934.
The Day's Good Cause.   London, Deane, and Boston, Baker, 1935.
Crab-Apple Harvest.   London, Deane, and Boston, Baker, 1936.
Going Rustic.   London, Deane, and Boston, Baker, 1936.
Little White Jumbo.   London, Pinker, 1937.
Can the Leopard?   London, Deane, and Boston, Baker, 1939.
The Lights Go Up.   London, Deane, 1945.

*   *   *

M. E. Atkinson's claim to be remembered rests entirely on her long series of books about the Lockett children and their friends which appeared at regular intervals between 1936 and 1949. In her later years she wrote about another group of children (Fricka Hammond and her cousins) and also a number of not particularly good pony stories for girls. Most of the Lockett books were illustrated by two very different, but both excellent, artists – Stuart Tresilian and Harold Jones. Harold Jones' very first work was for *August Adventure*, Miss Atkinson's first novel, and his pictures give an outward distinction to many of the books, which is not entirely belied by the stories themselves.

Miss Atkinson has had little critical attention. In their histories of children's fiction, neither Frank Eyre nor John Rowe Townsend mention her, and Geoffrey Trease merely brackets her with David Severn and Malcolm Saville as one of the three outstanding exponents of the holiday adventure theme, sub-Arthur Ransome. Certainly the books carry all the familiar and much derided hallmarks of the fiction of the period. The Locketts – Jane, Bill and Oliver – are relentlessly middle-class, and their world accepts as entirely natural private schools, cooks, and even titled friends. Moreover their parents are in India, and, as their author herself puts it, "the Lockett children have a positive flair for finding themselves alone and independent." Their language is inevitably dated. Things are "perfectly beastly," "frightfully important," "frantically secret." The device of pretending that everything really happened, that the Lockett's adventures are all true (written by them with the help of a convenient Aunt Margaret) sometimes wears a little thin. There are frequent cross-references to other books in the series, and these are sometimes irritatingly self-congratulatory. It is with some reluctance that the reader realizes he feels rather similar feelings to those of Peter Richards, the referee in *Challenge to Adventure*, who "enjoyed each sentence, eager for the strange story to unravel as fast as it could yet determined to miss nothing." This book, in fact the most "in-bred" of the lot – the Locketts have been challenged to prove that things really do happen to them – is actually one of the most attractive and appealing and can still offer enormous enjoyment to young readers.

These long expansive stories (*Crusoe Island*, for instance, runs to well over three hundred pages) are still appealing because, though the plots may be rather contrived and the continual emphasis on adventure may become a little tedious, Miss Atkinson was so good at character. In a cast of dozens, hardly one is a stereotype. In many ways, she was ahead of her time. Peter Richards may think that Jane is "more like a boy than a girl." Her creator knows that there are many girls who are happy to wear their brother's old shorts and ride his old bike. Fenella, too, is not a "tomboy" but a particularly masterful individual. Her fight with Bill in *Going Gangster* lacks the self consciousness of a contemporary writer tying herself in knots in order to be non-sexist. Fenella and Nina too (whose leading part is in *Problem Party*) illustrate Miss Atkinson's excellent ability to write about "grey" characters – neither black nor white but human and convincing. She was also ahead of her time in the degree of realism she allowed herself. Writing about the provision of an earth box for the dogs in *Crusoe Island*, she says "the problem was not one about which one usually writes in the polite type of book." Reading these books again for the first time for thirty years, I was pleased to recognize that safe, lively world I enjoyed so much when I read them first as a child during the war.

—Ann Thwaite

ATWATER, Richard (Tupper).   American.   Born in Chicago, Illinois, 20 December 1892. Educated at the University of Chicago, 1907–17, Associate in Arts 1909, B.A. (honors) in Greek 1910. Married Florence H. Carroll; two daughters. Taught at the University of Chicago; Columnist, *Tribune, Evening Post* (as "Riq"), and *Daily News*, all Chicago. *Died in 1938.*

PUBLICATIONS FOR CHILDREN

Fiction

> *Doris and the Trolls*, illustrated by John Gee.   Chicago, Rand McNally, 1931.
> *Mr. Popper's Penguins*, completed by Florence Atwater, illustrated by Robert Lawson.   Boston, Little Brown, 1938; London, Harrap, 1939.

PUBLICATIONS FOR ADULTS

Verse

> *Rickety Rimes of Riq*.   Chicago, Ballou, 1925.

> Translator, *Secret History of Procopius*.   New York, Covici Friede, 1934.

*   *   *

One of the tests of good fantasy is its firm rooting in realism, and with *Mr. Popper's Penguins* Richard and Florence Atwater proved to be among the best of the early writers of this century to pass that test. Their story of a mild little housepainter whose secret wanderlust fastened on dreams of polar exploration is told in bland, sober fashion. Mr. Popper and his wife are modest people, and with their two children are a cozy family. Papa has a penchant for writing to his heroes, and is astounded when Admiral Drake thanks him via radio and then sends him a penguin. When their new pet languishes, Papa Popper writes for help – and gets another penguin. And so a new family begins, and a new career, as all the penguins are trained to perform for vaudeville. The conception of a family joyfully accepting the disruption of the Popper household is appealing to children, and the characters and dialogue have an ingenuous charm, but it is the combination of ludicrous events and the benign calm with which the authors and the Poppers alike accept them that has made the book a perennial favorite with younger children.

—Zena Sutherland

AVERILL, Esther (Holden).   American.   Born in Bridgeport, Connecticut, 24 July 1902. Educated at Vassar College, Poughkeepsie, New York, B.A. 1923; Brooklyn Museum Art School. Member of the Editorial Department, *Women's Wear Daily*, New York, 1923–25; free-lance journalist, Paris, 1925–31; Founding Publisher, Domino Press, Paris, 1931–35; worked in the children's section of the New York Public Library. Recipient: *New York Times* award, for illustration, 1954. Address: 30 Joralemon Street, Apartment 11-A, Brooklyn, New York 11201, U.S.A.

PUBLICATIONS FOR CHILDREN

Fiction (illustrated by the author)

> *Powder: The Story of a Colt, The Duchess, and a Circus*, with Lila Stanley, illustrated by Feodor Rojankovsky.   Paris, Domino Press, New York, Smith and Haas, and London, Faber, 1933.
> *Flash: The Story of a Horse, a Coach-Dog, and the Gypsies*, illustrated by Feodor Rojankovsky.   Paris, Domino Press, New York, Smith and Haas, and London, Faber, 1934.
> *Fable of a Proud Pony* (as John Domino).   Paris, Domino Press, 1934.
> *The Cat Club; or, The Life and Times of Jenny Linsky.*   New York and London, Harper, 1944.
> *The Adventures of Jack Ninepins.*   New York and London, Harper, 1944.
> *The School for Cats.*   New York and London, Harper, 1947.
> *Jenny's First Party.*   New York and London, Harper, 1948.
> *Jenny's Moonlight Adventure.*   New York, Harper, 1949.
> *When Jenny Lost Her Scarf.*   New York, Harper, 1951.
> *Jenny's Adopted Brothers.*   New York, Harper, 1952.
> *How the Brothers Joined the Cat Club.*   New York, Harper, 1953; Kingswood, Surrey, World's Work, 1959.
> *Jenny's Birthday Book.*   New York, Harper, 1954.
> *Jenny Goes to Sea.*   New York, Harper, 1957.
> *Jenny's Bedside Book.*   New York, Harper, 1959.
> *The Fire Cat.*   New York, Harper, 1960; Kingswood, Surrey, World's Work, 1961.
> *The Hotel Cat.*   New York, Harper, 1969.
> *Captains of the City Streets.*   New York, Harper, 1972.
> *Jenny and the Cat Club (The Cat Club, Jenny's First Party, When Jenny Lost Her Scarf, Jenny's Adopted Brothers, How the Brothers Joined the Cat Club).*   New York, Harper, 1973; London, Fontana, 1976.

Other

> *The Voyages of Jacques Cartier*, illustrated by Feodor Rojankovsky. New York,
> Domino Press, 1937; revised edition, as *Cartier Sails the St. Lawrence*, New York,
> Harper, 1956.
> *King Philip: The Indian Chief*, illustrated by Vera Belsky. New York, Harper, 1950.
> *Eyes of the World: The Story and Work of Jacques Collot.* New York, Funk and
> Wagnalls, 1969.

> Editor, with Lila Stanley, *Daniel Boone: Historic Adventures of an American Hunter
> among the Indians*, illustrated by Feodor Rojankovsky. Paris, Domino Press, and
> London, Faber, 1931; revised edition, New York, Harper, 1945.

> Translator, *Tales of Poindi*, by Jean Mariotti, illustrated by Feodor Rojankovsky. New
> York, Domino Press, 1938.

PUBLICATIONS FOR ADULTS

Other

> *Political Propaganda in Children's Books of the French Revolution.* New York,
> Hawthorn House, 1935.

*   *   *

Jenny Linsky is undoubtedly Esther Averill's most famous and enduring character. Over a dozen books for younger readers have been written about this shy, orphan cat with the engaging personality. Most of the stories are short enough to be read comfortably in one sitting and concern the various adventures of Jenny and her fellow members of the Cat Club.

Averill's descriptive prose is characterized by a light, delicate touch. With deft strokes of the pen she endows Jenny and her companions with distinct personalities which are in keeping with their physical appearance. Jenny's quiet courage is sympathetically and humorously portrayed in *Jenny's Moonlight Adventure*. Her agonizing decision to rescue a friend's prized possession is realistically explored as she wavers from a firm decision not to help to shame that she hasn't the courage to act and finally to the conviction that she must help her friend.

Averill's world is black and white – good deeds are rewarded, bad deeds are punished, and transgressors of the Cat Club rules are made to see the error of their ways. Moral overtones are evident throughout Averill's fiction. There is an emphasis, for example, on the praiseworthiness of facing up to one's problems, admitting guilt when one has done wrong and treating one's fellows properly. Jenny's initial encounter with the Cat Club in the book, *The Cat Club*, teaches her that shyness is a handicap which may be overcome. Likewise, fear of the unknown in *Jenny's Moonlight Adventure* is shown to be diminished by a direct stand against those fears.

The understated style of Averill's writing makes her books a delight to read. She uses words sparingly to provide a setting, describe the characters and get the story under way. Her sure sense of story is evident – even in *Jenny's Bedside Book* which lacks any action at all, the story-within-a-story technique holds the reader's attention.

The humor of Averill's work is derived from her straightforward tongue-in-cheek descriptions and the exaggerated dignity which she invests in her animal characters. Relationships between the characters are almost always positive. The books are full of tenderness and warm, loving friendships.

Definitely, her books with their gaiety and charm have made an important contribution to the genre of children's fantasy, confirmed by their continuing popularity.

—Fran Ashdown

AVERY, Gillian (Elise). British. Born in Reigate, Surrey, 30 September 1926. Educated at Dunottar School, Reigate. Married A. O. J. Cockshut in 1952; has one daughter. Junior reporter, *Surrey Mirror*, Redhill, Surrey, 1944–47; staff member, *Chambers Encyclopedia*, London, 1947–50; assistant illustrations editor, Clarendon Press, Oxford, 1950–54. Recipient: *Guardian* Award, 1972. Address: 32 Charlbury Road, Oxford OX2 6UU, England.

PUBLICATIONS FOR CHILDREN

Fiction

The Warden's Niece, illustrated by Dick Hart. London, Collins, 1957.
Trespassers at Charlcote, illustrated by Dick Hart. London, Collins, 1958.
James Without Thomas, illustrated by John Verney. London, Collins, 1959.
The Elephant War, illustrated by John Verney. London, Collins, 1960; New York, Holt Rinehart, 1971.
To Tame a Sister, illustrated by John Verney. London, Collins, 1961; Princeton, New Jersey, Van Nostrand, 1964.
The Greatest Gresham, illustrated by John Verney. London, Collins, 1962.
The Peacock House, illustrated by John Verney. London, Collins, 1963.
The Italian Spring, illustrated by John Verney. London, Collins, 1964; New York, Holt Rinehart, 1972.
Call of the Valley, illustrated by Laszlo Acs. London, Collins, 1966; New York, Holt Rinehart, 1968.
A Likely Lad, illustrated by Faith Jaques. London, Collins, and New York, Holt Rinehart, 1971.
Ellen's Birthday, illustrated by Krystyna Turska. London, Hamish Hamilton, 1971.
Ellen and the Queen, illustrated by Krystyna Turska. London, Hamish Hamilton, 1972; Nashville, Nelson, 1974.
Jemima and the Welsh Rabbit, illustrated by John Lawrence. London, Hamish Hamilton, 1972.
Freddie's Feet, illustrated by Krystyna Turska. London, Hamish Hamilton, 1976.
Huck and Her Time Machine. London, Collins, 1977.

Other

Victorian People in Life and Literature. London, Collins, and New York, Holt Rinehart, 1970.
The Echoing Green: Memories of Victorian and Regency Youth. London, Collins, and New York, Viking Press, 1974.
Book of Strange and Odd. London, Longman, 1975.

Editor, *A Flat Iron for a Farthing*, by Juliana Horatia Ewing. London, Faith Press, 1959.
Editor, *Jan of the Windmill*, by Juliana Horatia Ewing. London, Faith Press, 1960.
Editor, *The Sapphire Treasury of Stories for Boys and Girls*. London, Gollancz, 1960.
Editor, *In the Window Seat: A Selection of Victorian Stories*, illustrated by Susan Einzig. London, Oxford University Press, 1960; Princeton, New Jersey, Van Nostrand, 1965.
Editor, *Father Phim*, by Annie Keary. London, Faith Press, 1962.
Editor, *Unforgettable Journeys*, illustrated by John Verney. London, Gollancz, 1965.
Editor, *School Remembered*, illustrated by John Verney. London, Gollancz 1967; New York, Funk and Wagnalls, 1968.
Editor, *A Great Emergency, and a Very Ill-Tempered Family*, by Juliana Horatia Ewing. London, Gollancz, 1967.

Editor, *The Gold of Fairnilee and Other Stories*, by Andrew Lang.   London, Gollancz, 1967.

Editor, *Village Children*, by Charlotte Yonge.   London, Gollancz, 1967.

Editor, *Banning and Blessing*, by Margaret Roberts.   London, Gollancz, 1967.

Editor, *The Hole in the Wall and Other Stories*, illustrated by Doreen Roberts.   London, Oxford University Press, 1968.

Editor, *Victoria Bess and Others*, by Brenda, Mrs. Gatty, and Frances Hodgson Burnett.   London, Gollancz, 1968; as *Victorian Doll Stories*, New York, Schocken, 1969.

Editor, *The Wallypug of Why*, by G. E. Farrow, illustrated by Harry Furniss.   London, Gollancz, 1968.

Editor, *Froggy's Little Brother*, by Brenda.   London, Gollancz, 1968.

Editor, *My New Home*, by Mary Louisa Molesworth, illustrated by L. Leslie Brooke.   London, Gollancz, 1968.

Editor, *The Life and Adventures of Lady Anne* (anonymous), illustrated by F. D. Bedford.   London, Gollancz, 1969.

Editor, *Stephanie's Children*, by Margaret Roberts.   London, Gollancz, 1969.

Editor, *Anne's Terrible Good Nature and Other Stories for Children*, by E. V. Lucas.   London, Gollancz, 1970.

Editor, *The Rival Kings*, by Annie Keary.   London, Gollancz, 1970.

Editor, with others, *Authors' Choice 1*, illustrated by Krystyna Turska.   London, Hamish Hamilton, 1970; New York, Crowell, 1971.

Editor, *Red Letter Days*, illustrated by Krystyna Turska.   London, Hamish Hamilton, 1971.

PUBLICATIONS FOR ADULTS

Other

Mrs. Ewing.   London, Bodley Head, 1961; New York, Walck, 1964.

Nineteenth Century Children: Heroes and Heroines in English Children's Stories, 1780–1900, with Angela Bull.   London, Hodder and Stoughton, 1965.

Childhood's Pattern: A Study of the Heroes and Heroines of Children's Fiction, 1770–1950.   London, Hodder and Stoughton, 1975.

*   *   *

For two decades Gillian Avery has been producing extremely believable children's stories set in the late Victorian era. She has a sympathetic understanding of her chosen period which is evoked without sentimental inflation or a retrospective smoothness. She manages to express the past *as* the present by underlining its unevenness and normality. Stringent observation of character and manners, and a flair for humorous incident, enhance the realism of her stories.

Gillian Avery recalls that when she wrote her first book she seemed to know more about the feelings of the children of 1875 than the self-assured attitudes of young people in the 1950's. She felt that there was an affinity between her own pre-war generation with its "meek acceptance of the power of the adult world" and the Victorian child who had always been accustomed to authoritarian treatment. However, the objective of her fictional children – even the most diffident – is usually to assert themselves in some particular way. This often involves a flouting of the restraining conventions of the time, with consequent conflict or social unease. Gillian Avery makes this type of embarrassment acutely credible to readers brought up in today's more liberal environment. She also makes the most of the humorous elements which occur in these situations – especially when they arise from confrontations between children and adults. Her stories, despite their serious moments, are really domestic or social comedies.

The Warden's Niece was Gillian Avery's first book and it is still one of the most popular. She started writing it one winter as "an escape from the weeping ... skies and raw fogs" of Manchester, where she was then living; appropriately the book begins with an escape of a different kind. Maria runs away from her dispiriting boarding school to her uncle, the Warden of an Oxford college. Although she has shown no sign of academic distinction, she hopes one day to become a lecturer in Latin and Greek. Her uncle encourages this creditable ambition, arranging for Maria to have lessons with the Smith brothers – the lordly Thomas, reasonable Joshua, and outrageous James. Their eccentric temporary tutor gives the children opportunities to explore their surroundings, and Maria stumbles on a mystery concerning a 17th-century boy. She feels that he is linked with a scrawled message which she discovers on the wall of a stately home. Determination to complete this piece of original research gives Maria the courage to play truant and even to gatecrash the Bodleian. The Oxford setting and historical associations give the book a strong appeal. It has, apparently, sent people to Oxford. Gillian Avery thinks it reflects her own romantic yearnings: "As an adolescent I felt about the place as many of my contemporaries felt about Hollywood."

The Elephant War also has an Oxford background. Its heroine, Harriet Jessop, is more timid than Maria but equally convincing. The awesome Smith brothers appear once more. Harriet thinks that they typify the intellectual life of Oxford which seems excitingly attractive to her. She is recruited by a formidable aunt into a campaign to save one of the London Zoo's elephants from being sent to America – to "slavery" in Barnum's Circus. This "cause" draws Harriet into a series of farcical events, and she falls foul of the Smith family who ridicule her campaigning zeal; but unexpectedly James Smith suddenly becomes her infuriating and disruptive ally. (Gillian Avery is particularly perceptive when describing the irritation that a bumptious small boy or girl can arouse in a more sensitive older child.) The point is effectively made that enthusiasms can get out of control.

In *The Greatest Gresham* the primly brought up Julia and Henry Gresham are – like Harriet Jessop – deeply aware of their own inadequacies. These are highlighted by their relationship with the next door children. Richard and Kate Holt live in a scruffy and disordered home, but they have an independence which Julia and Henry long to emulate. The Greshams force themselves to perform difficult and embarrassing feats suggested by the Holts; this is supposed to broaden their minds. The story has an intriguingly furtive atmosphere. The children form a secret society, and the Greshams are constantly afraid that their parents will declare the Holts "undesirable" and end the association.

A desire for genteel respectability and social position plays a big part in *A Likely Lad*. It was inspired by the reminiscences of Gillian Avery's father-in-law about his Lancashire boyhood. Bookish Willy Overs is the likely lad; his self-made, shopkeeper father intends him to begin work at 13 in an insurance office. Mr. Overs sees this as the start of a successful career for his son, and also as a means of establishing the superiority of his branch of the family over that of his patronizing in-laws. Willy's apprehensive but persistent resistance to the scheme eventually persuades his father to allow him to continue his education. The atmosphere of a working-class home at the turn of the century is expressed through the effects of unvarying domestic routines on the children. For instance, on their mother's baking day Willy and his brother have to suffer banishment from the cosy kitchen/living-room to the boredom of an immaculate but icy and toyless parlour.

In the stories the sense of another time is conveyed externally: there are frequent descriptions of cold, dark rooms and the rituals of lighting fires and candles; of plush table covers, knickerbocker suits and merino dresses. The psychological tone of Gillian Avery's books, however, is modern, and lively enough to appeal to a wide range of present-day readers. Everything in the books is seen from the children's point of view. This was certainly not the case in stories which were written for real life Victorian children. The naughtiest of their heroines would never have found herself in the situation of the little girl in Gillian Avery's *Ellen and the Queen* who has an illicit peep at Queen Victoria's legs!

—Mary Cadogan

AYER, Jacqueline (Brandford). American. Born in New York City, 2 May 1932. Educated at the High School of Music and Art, New York, 1944–48; Syracuse University, New York, 1948–50; Ecole des Beaux Arts, Paris, 1950–52. Married Frederic Ayer in 1955; has two daughters. Fashion Illustrator, *Vogue* and *Jardin des Modes*, both Paris, 1952–53, and Bonwit Teller, New York, 1954; Executive Fabric and Fashion Designer, International Basic Economy Corporation, Bangkok, 1960–70; Advisor to the Indian Government on fabric and fashion export, Delhi and Bombay, 1971–74. Since 1975, free-lance fabric designer. Recipient: *Seventeen* award, for illustration, 1948; Society of Illustrators award, 1960. Address: 10 East End Avenue, New York, New York 10020, U.S.A.

PUBLICATIONS FOR CHILDREN (illustrated by the author)

Fiction

> *Nu Dang and His Kite.* New York, Harcourt Brace, 1959; London, Collins, 1960.
> *A Wish for Little Sister.* New York, Harcourt Brace, 1960; London, Collins, 1961.
> *The Paper-Flower Tree.* New York, Harcourt Brace, 1962; London, Collins, 1963.
> *Little Silk.* New York, Harcourt Brace, 1970; London, Collins, 1971.

Other

> *Oriental Costume.* London, Studio Vista, 1974; New York, Scribner, 1975.

Manuscript Collection: Children's Books Department, New York Public Library.

Illustrator: *Humpy* by Peter Yershov, 1959; *Rumpelstiltskin* by the Grimm Brothers, 1967; *Princess September* by W. Somerset Maugham, 1969.

Jacqueline Ayer comments:

My book work has always reflected an exotic view that was for me and my young children, living abroad, a daily fare we grew to love and feel comfortable within. I've tried to show, as a writer and illustrator, the emotions that make us all equivalent, and the details that enrich the differences. It has been difficult to maintain this innocent view of the world: now that my children are young adults, I feel their child's viewpoint has been lost to me. It is harder to see the simpler elements, as corruption, poverty, and ignorance have intruded our lost tropical garden.

                              *   *   *

A good picture book is a skilful blend of illustration and text. The text should be a kind of poetry, brief, suggestive and impressionistic. There should be no dichotomy of mood between text and pictures. Jacqueline Ayer's books about the Orient are superb examples of this marriage. The text matches the pictures in authenticity of mood and of place and time. The lilt of language matches the fresh lovely pictures. Her stories have substance and are interesting. They are gifts from the East for all children.

Nu Dang and His Kite is about a boy in Siam who loves to fly his kite, the boldest, bravest and most beautiful of all kites. Nu Dang's kite blows away and is lost. He journeys in his boat down the long brown river to search for it. He talks to people whose homes, shops, and restaurants are boats: vendors, buses, and butchers, all boats. He meets young priests and children lotus gathering and cloth merchants, all beautifully drawn and painted. The authenticity of her detail adds to the beauty. At the finish of this tour of river life in Siam, Nu Dang finds that the "kind wind has carried his kite gently home."

A Wish for Little Sister is a journey through the city of Bangkok through the eyes of a little girl, who, on her birthday morning, has been given a wish. She doesn't know what to wish for, so she asks ideas from all her family, people who dye, spin and weave beautiful silks. There are fine accurate drawings of silk workers at their tasks, alternating with fantasy pictures of the wishes as visualized by a Thai child. These pictures are full of wit. Little sister finds a wish, and it comes true, "just as the sun's red glow changed to the moon's white light."

Little Silk is a remarkable book. Few picture books contain such mood and emotion. There are scenes of a faded never-again China, and very real scenes of modern family life in Hong Kong, the markets and trolleys, bustle and noise. The tale she tells is a haunting story of a beautiful old doll who travels a lonely journey through many years, playing a part in the lives of three very different little girls.

The Paper-Flower Tree tells us of life in a small Thai village. The story is about a little girl whose strong belief in a fantasy is rewarded by the fantasy coming true. The color here is lovely, as are the costumes, and the characterizations are well done. Two old tales, *Humpy* and *Rumpelstiltskin* have been made into young fresh books by Jacqueline Ayer's illustrations. They are distinguished by her beautiful drawings.

—Irene Haas

BB. See WATKINS-PITCHFORD, D. J.

BABBITT, Natalie.   American.   Born in Dayton, Ohio, 28 July 1932. Educated at Laurel School for Girls, Cleveland, graduated 1950; Smith College, Northampton, Massachusetts, 1950–54, B.A. 1954. Married Samuel F. Babbitt in 1954; has two sons and one daughter. Since 1969, instructor in writing and illustrating for children, Kirkland College, Clinton, New York. Recipient: Christopher Award, 1976. Agent: Curtis Brown Ltd., 575 Madison Avenue, New York, New York 10022. Address: Harding Road, R.D. 1, Clinton, New York 13323, U.S.A.

PUBLICATIONS FOR CHILDREN (illustrated by the author)

Fiction

> *The Search for Delicious.*   New York, Farrar Straus, 1969; London, Chatto and Windus, 1975.
> *Kneeknock Rise.*   New York, Farrar Straus, 1970.
> *The Something.*   New York, Farrar Straus, 1970.
> *Goody Hall.*   New York, Farrar Straus, 1971.
> *The Devil's Storybook.*   New York, Farrar Straus, 1974; London, Chatto and Windus, 1976.
> *Tuck Everlasting.*   New York, Farrar Straus, 1975; London, Chatto and Windus, 1977.
> *The Eyes of the Amaryllis.*   New York, Farrar Straus, 1977.

Verse

> *Dick Foote and the Shark.*   New York, Farrar Straus, 1967.
> *Phoebe's Revolt.*   New York, Farrar Straus, 1968.

Illustrator: *The Forty-Ninth Magician* by Samuel F. Babbitt, 1966; *Small Poems*, 1972, and *More Small Poems*, 1976, by Valerie Worth.

Natalie Babbitt comments:

I am motivated first by a simple passion for the English language, and second by a fascination with the many faces a single reality assumes when viewed through the filter of any given individual's biases, experiences, expectations, and/or desires. Though I am categorized as a writer of fantasy, I have never written about the true fairyland as defined by Tolkien, but rather concern myself with the above-mentioned filters which lend every reality an aspect of fantasy. My stories in the main concern human beings and the effects their own fantasies/filters have upon their own realities.

*   *   *

Natalie Babbitt has made a small but special place for herself in the world of children's literature. Her stories are highly individual, notable for their humor, which is never condescending, and for their unusual themes. The messages in Babbitt's fiction are not the lessons on personal morality so commonly carried by children's books; the statements made in *Kneeknock Rise, Goody Hall*, and most memorably in *Tuck Everlasting* are philosophic and general, rather than moralistic and particular. They are comments on human ways, needs and oddities as visible to children as to adults.

One can point to problems. Some instances of Babbitt's humor are almost certainly beyond the ken of her readers, assuming those readers are children and not reviewers. The gentle parodies of Shakespeare, for example — "Rumble, rumble, foil and fumble/Choir adjourn and children mumble," or "Where the sea bucks, there buck I" — are unlikely to mean much to anyone under 12 (or maybe 22). And Babbitt's child characters are sometimes dim in comparison with the adults in the stories; quite often they are not nearly central enough to the action to satisfy a youthful reader. Talk without action is sometimes a drawback; the long prelude to the action of *Goody Hall*, amusing as it is in its scene-setting dialogue, is static and adult. It would play well on a stage, as Shakespeare's comic dialogues play well while they also inform the audience, but whether a child reader will stay with it is another question.

But even when the inaccessible is subtracted from Babbitt's stories, there is much left that is original, funny, and thoughtful. *The Devil's Storybook* is full of lighthearted malice properly ascribed to the devil and his offspring; *Kneeknock Rise* is a kindly look at the pleasures of harmless drama in everyday life; *The Search for Delicious* makes an old point about the relativity of value in a new way.

Babbitt's masterpiece to date is unquestionably *Tuck Everlasting*. She has chosen for this story a theme no less profound than the meaning and place of death in the universe of living things, yet her handling of this weighty subject is so deft and so gentle that the theme never overwhelms the characters or their poignant, believable tale.

The comparison that comes to mind is with E. B. White's *Charlotte's Web*. Both are fantasies, but barely: just enough to carry forward their themes without becoming so abstract as to lose touch with their young audiences. They are earthbound fantasies, both dealing plainly with life and death, telling stories that are sad and true and funny, all at once. The passage in which Tuck tells Winnie why she must choose mortality over life everlasting is surely one of the most moving in children's literature. He makes it simple, not just because Winnie is eleven years old and could not understand a complex discussion of immortality, but because the matter is to Tuck a simple one: "Life. Moving, growing, changing, never the same two minutes together .... Being part of the whole thing, that's the blessing."

Natalie Babbitt is an uncommon writer, whose future should be interesting to watch.

—Anne S. MacLeod

BACON, Martha (Sherman).   American.   Born in Berkeley, California, 2 April 1917. Educated at Anna Head School, Berkeley; Miss Barry's Foreign School, Florence; Barrington School, Great Barrington, Massachusetts. Married R.B. Ballinger in 1963; has three children from previous marriage, and two stepchildren. Editorial Assistant, *Atlantic Monthly*, Boston, 1954–56; Feature Editor, *Vogue*, New York, 1956–57, and *Harper's Bazaar*, New York, 1957–59; Lecturer in Creative Writing, University of Rhode Island, Kingston, 1960–63. Since 1965, Lecturer to Assistant Professor of English, Rhode Island College, Providence. Recipient: Borestone Poetry Award, 1957. Address: Department of English, Rhode Island College, Providence, Rhode Island 02908, U.S.A.

PUBLICATIONS FOR CHILDREN

Fiction

> *Sophia Scrooby Preserved*, illustrated by Donald Omar White.   Boston, Little Brown, 1968; London, Gollancz, 1971.
> *The Third Road*, illustrated by Robin Jacques.   Boston, Little Brown, 1971.
> *In the Company of Clowns: A Commedia*, illustrated by Richard Cuffari.   Boston, Little Brown, 1974.

PUBLICATIONS FOR ADULTS

Novels

> *A Star Called Wormwood*.   New York, Random House, 1948; London, Hodder and Stoughton, 1950.
> *A Masque of Exile*.   New York, Clarkson N. Potter, 1962; London, Heinemann, 1963.

Verse

> *Lament for the Chieftains and Other Poems*.   New York, Coward McCann, 1942.
> *Things Visible and Invisible*.   New York, Coward McCann, 1947.

Other

> *Puritan Promenade* (essays).   Boston, Houghton Mifflin, 1964.

> Translator, *The Child Across the River*, by Giulietta d'Alessandro.   New York, McDowell Obolensky, 1958.

Manuscript Collection: State University of New York Library, Buffalo.

Martha Bacon comments:
I began to write for children fairly recently. I found that the ideas which I wished to express were best realized in a story addressed to children. I enjoy writing these books because they allow the fancy to roam freely while the form remains disciplinary and even somewhat restricted. Clarity is essential and I enjoy pursuing it.

*   *   *

Teacher, poet, and novelist, Martha Bacon has used her knowledge of literary craftsmanship to fit diverse writing styles to the small but distinguished and varied contribution she has made to literature for children. In her first book, *Sophia Scrooby*

Preserved, set in the late 18th century, her heroine is the daughter of an African chieftain; taken as a slave, the child is brought up and educated by the Scrooby family, surpassing in elegance and virtuosity the daughter of the house. While she is captured by pirates, held in bondage by a voodoo queen, and has other high adventures, Sophia preserves the mincing decorum of the period. Even the chapter titles – "As the hart panteth on the mountain so does Pansy pant for the joys of knowledge, and so great is her desire, and so earnest her efforts that success crowns her endeavors and she decks her brows with bays" – are part of Bacon's amusing parody of the florid style of the period; while her plot is clearly concocted pen-in-cheek, it is nevertheless relentlessly vigorous.

The Third Road is a deft time-shift fantasy in which three lively children from a California household are taken by a unicorn into the formal elegance of a 17th-century Spanish court. While the merger of fantasy and realism is believable, the book lacks the ebullience of its predecessor or the cohesion of its successor, *In the Company of Clowns*. The latter is in the picaresque tradition, an adventure tale set in Italy early in the 18th century, and recreates vividly the casual and flamboyant life of the strolling players who are followed by the protagonist, a 12-year-old orphan who is bored with life as a convent scullery boy.

—Zena Sutherland

BACON, R(onald) L(eonard). New Zealander. Born in 1924. Married; has three children. Has worked as a teacher. Currently, Deputy Principal of an intermediate school. Address: Unit 3, 16 Turama Road, Royal Oak, Auckland, New Zealand.

PUBLICATIONS FOR CHILDREN

Fiction

> *The Boy and the Taniwha*, illustrated by Para Matchitt.   Auckland and London, Collins, 1966.
> *Rua and the Sea People*, illustrated by Para Matchitt.   Auckland and London, Collins, 1968.
> *Again the Bugles Blow*, illustrated by V. J. Livingston.   Auckland and London, Collins, 1973.

PUBLICATIONS FOR ADULTS

Novels

> *In the Sticks*, illustrated by David More.   Auckland, Collins, 1963.
> *Along the Road*, illustrated by David More.   Auckland and London, Collins, 1964.

Other

> *Auckland: Gateway to New Zealand*, photographs by Gregory Riethmaier.   Auckland and London, Collins, 1968.
> *Auckland: Town and Around*, photographs by Gregory Riethmaier.   Auckland and London, Collins, 1973.

*   *   *

Writing for R.L. Bacon developed as a by-product of the busy and demanding career as a rural teacher. His first novel, *In the Sticks*, written for an adult audience but of interest to older children, describes the vicissitudes, the heartbreaks, the fun, and the excitement of the teacher working in the backblocks.

His two picture books for children are both illustrated by the Maori artist, Para Matchitt. *The Boy and the Taniwha* describes the life of the little Maori boy Hemi. He lives with his grandmother according to the traditional customs before the coming of the *Pakeha*. The story tells of Hemi's growth in knowledge and in courage when he finds the taniwha and passes the test of manhood. The text is illustrated magnificently by the lively shapes and colours of Para Matchitt's drawings.

Rua and the Sea People appeared two years later and tells of another Maori boy, Rua, and his life by the sea. The climax to this tale is the arrival of Captain Cook's ship in 1769, "big, as the meeting house on the marae was big." Rua does not hold as much interest as Hemi, and Para Matchitt has used a great deal of abstraction in his illustrations. These are striking but children do not have for them the warm affection that they have for his earlier illustrations.

In *Again the Bugles Blow* there is a return to the verve of *The Boy and the Taniwha*. This short novel describes one of the great moments in those sad inter-racial conflicts of the mid-19th century, the Land Wars. The main character is another lad named Rua, a contemporary Maori boy who lives in the inner city. By some sort of time shift he finds himself in the Auckland of the early 1860's. Attached to the British Military forces during their thrust into the Waikato, Rua sees the tragic waste of war. The climax of the story describes one of the most courageous moments of the Maori warriors. Encircled at Orakau, short of food and water, under bombardment by the Armstrong guns, the defenders fought to the end. Rua had crept into the pa. He observed the call to surrender and the famous reply "We shall fight on for ever, and ever and ever."

R.L. Bacon writes a crisp, uncluttered narrative. He shows his mastery of technique in presenting a picture of a tragic dilemma through the eyes of a boy whose very innocence brings deeper understanding and a greater sense of pity to the reader. As yet, he has produced a slender output for children but has shown his very real gifts and dedication at a time when very little of quality was being written about Maori themes. It is hoped that these books are just the beginning of his contribution to writing for children.

—Tom Fitzgibbon

BAILEY, Carolyn Sherwin. American. Born in Hoosick Falls, New York, 25 October 1875. Educated at Lansingburgh Academy; Teachers College, Columbia University, New York; Montessori School, Rome; New York School of Social Work. Married Eben Clayton Hill in 1936. Principal, Jefferson Avenue Kindergarten, Springfield, Massachusetts; taught in New York City public schools; Social Worker, Warren Goddard House, New York; Editor, Children's Department, *Delineator* magazine, New York; from 1916, Editor, *American Childhood* magazine, Springfield, Massachusetts. Recipient: American Library Association Newbery Medal, 1947. *Died 23 December 1961.*

PUBLICATIONS FOR CHILDREN

Fiction

Stories for Sunday Telling. Boston, Pilgrim Press, 1916.
Stories for Any Day. Boston, Pilgrim Press, 1917.
Stories for Every Holiday. New York, Abingdon Press, 1918.

Once Upon a Time Animal Stories. Springfield, Massachusetts, Bradley, 1918.

The Outdoor Story Book. Boston, Pilgrim Press, 1918.

Everyday Stories, illustrated by Frederick Knowles. Springfield, Massachusetts, Bradley, 1919.

Hero Stories, illustrated by Frederick Knowles. Springfield, Massachusetts, Bradley, 1919.

The Enchanted Bugle and Other Stories. Dansville, New York, Owen, 1920.

The Torch of Courage and Other Stories. Springfield, Massachusetts, Bradley, 1921.

Flint: The Story of a Trail, illustrated by Charles Lassell. Springfield, Massachusetts, Bradley, 1922.

Reading Time Stories. Chicago, Whitman, 1923.

Surprise Stories. Chicago, Whitman, 1923.

When Grandfather Was a Boy: Stories. Boston, Pilgrim Press, 1923.

Friendly Tales: A Community Story Book. Springfield, Massachusetts, Bradley, 1923.

Lincoln Time Stories. Chicago, Whitman, 1924.

The Wonderful Tree and Other Golden Day Stories, illustrated by Joseph Dash. Chicago, Whitman, 1925.

Little Men and Women Stories. Chicago, Whitman, 1926.

The Wonderful Window and Other Stories, illustrated by Katherine Wireman. Nashville, Cokesbury Press, 1926.

The Wonderful Days, illustrated by C.B. Fall. Chicago, Whitman, 1929.

Read Aloud Stories, illustrated by Hildegard Lupprian. Springfield, Massachusetts, Bradley, 1929.

Li'l' Hannibal. New York, Platt and Munk, 1938.

Country-Stop, illustrated by Grace Paull. New York, Viking Press, 1942; as *Wishing-Well House*, London, Muller, 1950.

Pioneer Art in America, illustrated by Grace Paull. New York, Viking Press, 1944.

The Little Rabbit Who Wanted Red Wings, illustrated by Dorothy Grider. New York, Platt and Munk, 1945.

Miss Hickory, illustrated by Ruth Chrisman Gannett. New York, Viking Press, 1946; London, Hodder and Stoughton, 1977.

Merry Christmas Book, illustrated by Eunice Young Smith. Chicago, Whitman, 1948.

Old Man Rabbit's Dinner Party, illustrated by Robinson. New York, Platt and Munk, 1949; revised edition, 1961.

Enchanted Village, illustrated by Eileen Evans. New York, Viking Press, 1950.

Finnegan II, His Nine Lives, illustrated by Kate Seredy. New York, Viking Press, 1953.

The Little Red Schoolhouse, illustrated Dorothy Bayley Morse. New York, Viking Press, 1957.

Flickertail, illustrated by Garry MacKenzie. New York, Walck, 1962.

Plays

Plays for the Children's Hour. Springfield, Massachusetts, Bradley, 1931.

This Way to Animal Land, with Ditzy Baker. Akron, Ohio, Saalfield, 1936.

Verse

Stories and Rhymes for a Child, illustrated by Christine Wright. Springfield, Massachusetts, Bradley, 1909.

Songs of Happiness, music by Mary B. Ehrmann. Springfield, Massachusetts, Bradley, 1912.

A Christmas Party, illustrated by Cyndy Szekeres. New York, Pantheon Books, 1975.

Other

Mother Goose: Old Rhymes Reproduced in Connection with Their Veracious History, illustrated by Peter Newell. New York, Holt, 1905.

The Jingle Primer: A First Book in Reading Based on Mother Goose Rhymes and Folk Tales, with Clara L. Brown. New York, American Book Company, 1906.

Firelight Stories: Folk Tales Retold, illustrated by Diantha Horne. Springfield, Massachusetts, Bradley, 1907.

Boys' Make-at-Home Things, with Marian Elizabeth Bailey. New York, Stokes, 1912.

Girls' Make-at-Home Things. New York, Stokes, 1912.

The Children's Book of Games and Parties. Chicago, Donohue, 1913.

Every Child's Folk Songs and Games. Springfield, Massachusetts, Bradley, 1914.

Boys and Girls of Colonial Days, illustrated by Uldene Shriver. Chicago, Flanagan, 1917.

The Way of the Gate (reader), with others. New York, Macmillan, 1917.

What to Do for Uncle Sam: A First Book of Citizenship. Chicago, Flanagan, 1918.

Stories of Great Adventures, illustrated by Clara Burd. Springfield, Massachusetts, Bradley, 1919.

Folk Stories and Fables, illustrated by Frederick Nagler. Springfield, Massachusetts, Bradley, 1919.

Broad Stripes and Bright Stars: Stories of American History, illustrated by Power O'Malley. Springfield, Massachusetts, Bradley, 1919.

Wonder Stories: The Best Myths, illustrated by Clara Burd. Springfield, Massachusetts, Bradley, 1920; London, Batsford, 1924.

In- and Out-Door Play Games, illustrated by Cobb Shinn. Chicago, Whitman, 1923.

All the Year Play Games, illustrated by Cobb Shinn. Chicago, Whitman, 1924.

Boys and Girls of Pioneer Days. Chicago, Flanagan, 1924.

Stories from an Indian Cave: The Cherokee Cave Builders, illustrated by Joseph Dash. Chicago, Whitman, 1924.

Boys and Girls of Discovery Days, illustrated by Dorothy Dulin. Chicago, Flanagan, 1931.

In Nature's Fairyland. Dansville, New York, Owen, 1927.

Untold History Stories, illustrated by Lillian Titus. Dansville, New York, Owen, 1927.

Forest, Field, and Stream Stories (reader), illustrated by Dorothy Dulin. Chicago, Flanagan, 1928.

Boys and Girls of Today. Chicago, Flanagan, 1928.

Boys and Girls of Modern Days, illustrated by Dorothy Dulin. Chicago, Flanagan, 1929.

Boy Heroes in Making America, illustrated by Lea Norris and Power O'Malley. Chicago, Flanagan, 1931.

Our Friends at the Zoo (reader), with Alice Hanthorn, illustrated by Ruth Hallock. Springfield, Massachusetts, McLoughlin, 1934.

Children of the Handcrafts, illustrated by Grace Paull. New York, Viking Press, 1935.

Tell Me a Birthday Story, illustrated by Margaret Ayer. New York, Stokes, 1935.

Tops and Whistles: True Stories of Early American Toys and Children, illustrated by Grace Paull. New York, Viking Press, 1937.

From Mocassins to Wings: Stories of Our Travel Ways, illustrated by Margaret Ayer. Springfield, Massachusetts, Bradley, 1938.

Garden, Orchard, and Meadow Stories (reader), illustrated by Dorothy Dulin. Chicago, Flanagan, 1939.

Homespun Playdays, illustrated by Grace Paull. New York, Viking Press, 1941.

Editor, with Clara M. Lewis, *For the Children's Hour*, illustrated by C. William Breck. Springfield, Massachusetts, Bradley, 1906.

Editor, *Stories Children Need.* Springfield, Massachusetts, Bradley, 1916.

Editor, *Tell Me Another Story*. Springfield, Massachusetts, Bradley, 1918.

Editor, *The Three Musketeers*, by Alexandre Dumas, illustrated by Harold Brett. Springfield, Massachusetts, Bradley, 1920.

Editor, *Lorna Doone*, by R.D. Blackmore. Springfield, Massachusetts, Bradley, 1921.

Editor, *Merry Tales for Children*. Springfield, Massachusetts, Bradley, 1921.

Editor, *Evangeline*, by Henry Wadsworth Longfellow. Springfield, Massachusetts, Bradley, 1922.

Editor, *In the Animal World*. Springfield, Massachusetts, Bradley, 1924.

Editor, *Stories Children Want*, illustrated by Jack Perkins. Springfield, Massachusetts, Bradley, 1931.

Editor, *Schoolroom Plays and Projects*. Springfield, Massachusetts, Bradley, 1932.

PUBLICATIONS FOR ADULTS

Other

Daily Program of Gift and Occupation Work, with Clara M. Lewis. Springfield, Massachusetts, Bradley, 1904.

For the Story-Teller: Story Telling and Stories to Tell. Springfield, Massachusetts, Bradley, 1913.

Montessori Children. New York, Holt, 1915.

Letting in the Gang. New York, privately printed, 1916.

Everyday Play for Children. Chicago, Donohue, 1916.

Editor, *Sketches along Life's Road*, by Elizabeth Harrison. Boston, Stratford, 1930.

Editor, *The Story-Telling Hour*. New York, Dodd Mead, and London, Harrap, 1934.

*   *   *

Although the total body of Carolyn Sherwin Bailey's creative work is considerable, perhaps those works with greatest potential for lasting value are her series on pioneer arts and crafts in America and her *Miss Hickory*, which won the Newbery medal. Included in the pioneer arts and crafts series are *Children of the Handcrafts*, *Tops and Whistles*, *Homespun Playdays*, and *Pioneer Arts in America*. These works are the result of their author's genuine interest in the history and artifacts of a bygone era. *Pioneer Arts in America* is representative of the series. Details in this work as, for example, the weathervane, a wax doll, a silver teapot, a sparking lamp, the jewels of Sandwich, a fiddlin fool and others, are all touched with laudable elements of suspense and drama and a strong flavor of historical accuracy. Such stories could have been thinly skeletal and dully factual. Instead they are fully fleshed out, balanced, fluid, and historically appealing, enough so to continue to captivate and hold readers in their spell.

It remains, however, that *Miss Hickory* is the most successful and classic of Miss Bailey's works. Although Miss Bailey's story-telling talent and literary skill are clearly evident in her early works, close acquaintance with the total body of her writing indicates she experienced a gradual but steady genesis as a creative artist. With the creation of her inimitable *Miss Hickory*, Miss Bailey reached her literary apex. Like Carlo Collodi, A. A. Milne, L. Frank Baum, E. Nesbit, and other respected writers, Miss Bailey in her *Miss Hickory* has successfully used the toy device as literary motif. Her toy doll, Miss Hickory, is by no means a stillborn plaything, for into her Miss Bailey has breathed life that requires no resuscitation from readers. Although Miss Hickory is sometimes as hardheaded as the hickory nut which is, indeed, her head, she is no inert replica of any ordinary toy or real life personage.

Unlike some toys now famous in literature Carolyn Bailey's Miss Hickory does not interact, except by implication, with either her creator or with other creatures of the human world. Instead, Miss Hickory's ostensible ties are with animal friends and acquaintances imbued with human characteristics – Crow, Chipmunk, Squirrel, Hen-Pheasant, and Mr. T.

Willard-Brown, a barnyard cat. In her relationships with these friends Miss Hickory is spunky, spirited, sharp-tongued and seemingly inflexible, yet inwardly she is often vulnerable and sensitively insecure. She is, nonetheless, never a real loser. Despite numerous situations of near calamitous nature, with hickory nut for head and applewood twig for body, Miss Hickory proves herself a survivor, even after being deprived of head and brain by Squirrel, for she miraculously becomes a living, blossoming, fruit-bearing branch of an old apple tree. Thus Miss Bailey, in giving Miss Hickory a life after death, has added a new dimension to the use of the toy device as literary motif and has given to children and other readers a most satisfying instance of the creative ideal.

—Charity Chang

BAKER, Betty. American. Born in Bloomsburg, Pennsylvania, 20 June 1928. Attended school in Orange, New Jersey. Married Robert George Venturo in 1948 (divorced, 1965); has one child. Dental assistant, owner of gift shop, lecturer. Editor, *Roundup* magazine. Recipient: Western Heritage Award, 1964, 1971; Western Writers of America Spur Award, 1968. Address: 4127 East Indian School, Apartment 20, Phoenix, Arizona 85018, U.S.A.

PUBLICATIONS FOR CHILDREN

Fiction

> *The Sun's Promise*, illustrated by Juliette Palmer. New York, Abelard Schuman, 1962; London, Abelard Schuman, 1963.
> *Little Runner of the Longhouse*, illustrated by Arnold Lobel. New York, Harper, and Kingswood, Surrey, World's Work, 1962.
> *Killer-of-Death*, illustrated by John Kaufmann. New York, Harper, 1963.
> *The Shaman's Last Raid*, illustrated by Leonard Shortall. New York, Harper, 1963.
> *The Treasure of the Padres*, illustrated by Leonard Shortall. New York, Harper, 1964.
> *Walk the World's Rim*. New York, Harper, 1965.
> *The Blood of the Brave*. New York, Harper, 1966.
> *The Dunderhead War*. New York, Harper, 1967.
> *Do Not Annoy the Indians*, illustrated by Harold Goodwin. New York, Macmillan, and London, Collier Macmillan, 1968.
> *The Pig War*, illustrated by Robert Lopshire. New York, Harper, 1969; Kingswood, Surrey, World's Work, 1971.
> *And One Was a Wooden Indian*. New York, Macmillan, 1970.
> *A Stranger and Afraid*. New York, Macmillan, and London, Collier Macmillan, 1972.
> *The Big Push*, illustrated by Bonnie Johnson. New York, Coward McCann, 1972.
> *The Spirit Is Willing*. New York, Macmillan, 1974.
> *Dupper*, illustrated by Chuck Eckart. New York, Morrow, 1976.

Other

> *Arizona*. New York, Coward McCann, 1969.
> *At the Center of the World: Based on Papago and Pima Myths*, illustrated by Murray Tinkelman. New York, Macmillan, 1973.
> *Three Fools and a Horse* (Apache folktale), illustrated by Glen Rounds. New York, Macmillan, 1975.
> *Settlers and Strangers: Native Americans of the Desert Southwest and History as They Saw It*. New York, Macmillan, 1977.

Editor, *Great Ghost Stories of the Old West.* New York, Scholastic, 1968.

Manuscript Collections: University of California Library, Los Angeles; Kerlan Collection, University of Minnesota, Minneapolis.

*   *   *

Betty Baker has carved a niche for herself in the last two decades as a writer of historical fiction about the Southwestern United States and Mexico and of stories dealing with American Indians of the Southwest. Her fiction ranges from gentle, humorous tales such as that of a little Iroquois boy who loves maple sugar – this one written using a controlled vocabulary for beginning readers (*Little Runner of the Longhouse*) – to historical fiction for young adolescents. She is at her best with one of these, *Walk the World's Rim*, a tightly plotted, well characterized story of the friendship of a young Indian boy and Esteban, the negro slave who was one of the four survivors of the ill-fated expedition led by Cabeza de Vaca in the sixteenth century to the New World. A companion piece to *Walk the World's Rim* is *A Stranger and Afraid*, the story of a young plains Indian captured by the Pueblo Indians of the Southwest, who sees the expedition of Coronado as an opportunity to escape from the Pueblo Indians and to return to his people when he is given to the Spaniards as their guide.

Although Baker writes chiefly historical tales involving the American Indian, she does on occasion vary her subject. In *The Dunderhead War* she pairs an unlikely duo with seventeen-year-old Quincy Heffendorf from Missouri and his methodical German uncle Fritz. This fast-paced story of the Mexican War of 1846 tells of the dangers and adventures which befell the ill-trained, undisciplined Missouri Volunteers and Quincy and his uncle, who followed the Volunteers in a wagon train. But Baker is at her best with her sensitive and sympathetic novels dealing with the American Indian during the transition period in the Southwest when the white man first entered the area. *Killer-of-Death* is the finest of these stories. It is a moving tale of an Apache boy who comes to manhood just as the first white settlers entered Arizona – and what the coming of these strangers meant to the Apache nation.

The *Shaman's Last Raid* brings us into the twentieth century with a thoroughly modern, non-reservation living pair of Indian children. What happens when their great grandfather, an old Apache medicine man, visits them for the summer makes a funny story which children in the middle grades enjoy.

Baker's continued output of stories and novels for young people fills a real need for knowledgeable, sensitive portraits of the Southwestern American Indian and of the arid land which was his domain before the coming of the white man.

—Margaret Maxwell

BAKER, Margaret J(oyce). British. Born in Reading, Berkshire, 21 May 1918. Educated at Roland Houses School, London; King's College, London University, 1936–37. Mobile canteen driver, Church Army, during World War II. Agent: Curtis Brown Group Ltd., 1 Craven Hill, London W2 3EP; or, Curtis Brown Ltd., 575 Madison Avenue, New York, New York 10022, U.S.A. Address: Prickets, 1 Church Close, Old Cleeve, Minehead, Somerset TA24 6HW, England.

PUBLICATIONS FOR CHILDREN

Fiction

Nonsense Said the Tortoise, illustrated by Leo Bates. Leicester, Brockhampton Press,

1949; as *Homer the Tortoise*, New York, McGraw Hill, 1950; London, White Lion, 1974.

Four Farthings and a Thimble, illustrated by Decie Merwin. New York, Longman, 1950; London, Lane, 1952.

A Castle and Sixpence, illustrated by Decie Merwin. New York, Longman, 1951; London, Lane, 1953.

Treasure Trove, illustrated by T.R. Freeman. Leicester, Brockhampton Press, 1952.

Benbow and the Angels, illustrated by Dorothy Lake Gregory. New York, Longman, 1952; London, Harrap, 1956.

The Family That Grew and Grew, illustrated by Nora S. Unwin. New York, McGraw Hill, 1952; London, Nelson, 1954.

Homer Sees the Queen, illustrated by Garry MacKenzie. New York, McGraw Hill, 1953; Leicester, Brockhampton Press, 1956.

The Young Magicians, illustrated by T.R. Freeman. Leicester, Brockhampton Press, 1954.

Lions in the Potting Shed, illustrated by Marcia Lane Foster. Leicester, Brockhampton Press, 1954; as *Lions in the Woodshed*, New York, McGraw Hill, 1955.

The Wonderful Wellington Boots. Leicester, Brockhampton Press, 1955.

Acorns and Aerials, illustrated by Marcia Lane Foster. Leicester, Brockhampton Press, 1956.

The Bright High Flyer, illustrated by T.R. Freeman. Leicester, Brockhampton Press, and New York, Longman, 1957.

Tip and Run, illustrated by T.R. Freeman. Leicester, Brockhampton Press, 1958.

Homer Goes to Stratford, illustrated by T.R. Freeman. Leicester, Brockhampton Press, and Englewood Cliffs, New Jersey, Prentice Hall, 1958.

The Magic Sea Shell, illustrated by Marjorie-Anne Watts. London, Harrap, 1959; New York, Holt Rinehart, 1960.

The Birds of Thimblepins, illustrated by Elizabeth Grant. London, Harrap, 1960.

Homer in Orbit, illustrated by T.R. Freeman. Leicester, Brockhampton Press, 1961.

Into the Castle, illustrated by T.R. Freeman. Leicester, Brockhampton Press, 1962.

The Cats of Honeytown, illustrated by Keith Money. London, Harrap, 1962.

Away Went Galloper, illustrated by Norman Thelwell. London, Methuen, 1962; Chicago, Encyclopedia Britannica Press, 1964.

Castaway Christmas, illustrated by Richard Kennedy. London, Methuen, 1963; New York, Farrar Straus, 1964.

Cut Off from Crumpets, illustrated by Richard Kennedy. London, Methuen, 1964.

The Shoe Shop Bears, illustrated by C. Walter Hodges. London, Harrap, 1964; New York, Farrar Straus, 1965.

Homer Goes West, illustrated by T.R. Freeman. Leicester, Brockhampton Press, 1965.

Hannibal and the Bears, illustrated by C. Walter Hodges. London, Harrap, 1965; New York, Farrar Straus, 1966.

Porterhouse Major, illustrated by Shirley Hughes. London, Methuen, and Englewood Cliffs, New Jersey, Prentice Hall, 1967.

Bears Back in Business, illustrated by Daphne Rowles. London, Harrap, and New York, Farrar Straus, 1967.

Hi-Jinks Joins the Bears, illustrated by Leslie Wood. London, Harrap, 1968; New York, Farrar Straus, 1969.

Home from the Hill, illustrated by Richard Kennedy. London, Methuen, 1968; New York, Farrar Straus, 1969.

Teabag and the Bears, illustrated by Leslie Wood. London, Harrap, 1970.

Snails' Place, illustrated by Jan Brychta. London, Dent, 1970.

The Last Straw, illustrated by Doreen Roberts. London, Methuen, 1971.

Boots and the Ginger Bears, illustrated by Leslie Wood. London, Harrap, 1972.

The Sand Bird, illustrated by Gareth Floyd. London, Methuen, and Nashville, Nelson, 1973.

Prickets Way, illustrated by Gavin Rowe.   London, Methuen, 1973.
Lock Stock and Barrel, illustrated by Gareth Floyd.   London, Methuen, 1974.
Sand in Our Shoes, illustrated by Fermin Rocker.   London, Methuen, 1976.

Other

The Fighting Cocks (reader).   London, Pitman, 1949.
Anna Sewell and Black Beauty, illustrated by Imre Hofbauer.   London, Harrap, 1956;
   New York, Longman, 1957.

Margaret J. Baker comments:
   I like my stories to be humorous and unalarming. I want the stories meant for younger
children especially to leave them with a feeling of happiness and security. I want to help
children to understand animals and to love them. I want them to understand each other and
the older generations. I want them to value gentleness and not to confuse it with weakness.
When writing I want to show what I find lovely or funny, wonderful and strange. I think
children can comprehend anything so long as it is plainly put. Inside I believe a child's
feelings are the same as those of an adult. The only difference is that an adult can express the
feelings more easily. Maybe that's part of the job of writing children's books. The writer acts
as the children's spokesman. For this reason the writer needs to be on their side and to write
from inside the characters in the story.

*   *   *

   Margaret J. Baker writes for two age groups. *The Shoe Shop Bears* and their successive
volumes are popular, especially among small girls, because of their clearly defined characters
and also because they form a family unit of Father, Mother, and Child bear. They are
described in Mr. ShoeHorn's stocklist as "3 stuffed bears: large, medium, small, for the
comfort, amusement and edification of juvenile customers during the fitting of their
footwear." The bears become restless, wanting to see more of the world outside. Eventually
they escape and, in successive books, meet other children and other toys. In the first book
they are introduced to a very old teddy bear, Mr. Chesterfield, who articulates the archetypal
role of the teddy bear – "A bear's job is just to be there, ready to receive all the affection that
he is offered and to give it."
   Miss Baker's books for older children tend to centre on a family of children who learn to
cope with animals, people, the elements: in *Castaway Christmas* the children, unassisted by
adults, cope with floods; in *Cut Off from Crumpets* with blizzards and snow drifts. In the
latter book Miss Baker reaches out beyond her safe family circle to include others less
fortunate. In a climactic scene Letty ventures onto thin ice, alone with her problem (the adult
world in which her parents quarrel and separate) in order to rescue two dogs. When she gets
back with the dogs her brother says, "You'll be all right now," and "she knew ... that
whatever happened in the future now she would be all right and able to manage. By saving
the lives of two dogs she had saved something of her own." Miss Baker writes exciting
stories, full of practical detail and recognisable situations, but at such moments she brings a
depth of insight. For the only child who yearns for brothers and sisters, or for large families
who will recognise themselves, these books are exactly right.

—James Roose-Evans

BALDERSON, Margaret. Australian. Born in Sydney, New South Wales. Educated at high school in Sydney. Worked as a librarian in Sydney. Recipient: Australian Children's Book Council Book of the Year Award, 1969. Address: c/o Oxford University Press, Box 2784Y, Melbourne, Victoria 3001, Australia.

PUBLICATIONS FOR CHILDREN

Fiction

When Jays Fly to Barbmo, illustrated by Victor Ambrus. London, Oxford University Press, and New York, World, 1969.
A Dog Called George, illustrated by Nikki Jones. London, Oxford University Press, 1975.

* * *

When Margaret Balderson became a resident worker in Norway she experienced in a deeply personal way the innate rhythms of that land as expressed through its seasons. In particular, the Dark Time of the long Arctic winter became for her symbolic of an oppression of spirit which evaporates with the miracle of each spring, when the "whole of the radiant world" lies humble "in an attitude of silent thanksgiving," and when young people "run around in circles, laughing crazily at the patterns left ... in the deep glittering snow." *When Jays Fly to Barbmo* is Margaret Balderson's response to a land and its people. It is the slow, lyrically measured story of Ingeborg, a heroine descended in spirit from the epics of the Norsemen. Her country is under threat of invasion – a threat that fills the strongly drawn adult characters with dread and foreboding. When the invasion comes it not only destroys the quiet tenor of life, but it causes Ingeborg to question her heredity and hence her identity. Only when she is thrust into personal isolation and destroys, advisedly, her father's home – the last of all that she held dear – and completes the long and demanding trek to her Lapp grandfather can she face her own Dark Time and emerge as a person with a new life ahead. So the Germans depart, summer comes once more and Ingeborg goes "home." The land and its people return to the pattern of the seasons.

The author's second book is set in Canberra, Australia, and again reflects her gift of re-shaping emotional experience into satisfying literary expression. She owns an old, shaggy English sheep dog called George, the blue-eyed hero of *A Dog Called George* who causes his adopted master, 10-year-old Tony, to come to terms with his place in the family and in society. Above all, Tony learns that man and beast must each be himself for George was George, always "ready for him with a paw for the shaking and an ear for the scratching – happy to see him come – unconcerned to see him go .... George who would gladly share his world for as long as Tony wanted him to, and yet not drag him down, reproachfully binding him into a straight-jacket of guilt as that share became smaller and smaller."

In both books Balderson's style is demanding but so textured that her characters help bring insight to the tensions and the satisfactions of family life. Ingeborg, with her devoted dog, Benne, resolves her personal conflict in her home surrounded by the towering black hulks of Norway's mountains, and Tony with his adopted dog, George, in his home adjacent to a long, flat, narrow strip of paddock on the eastern side of Canberra.

—H. M. Saxby

BALLARD, Martin. British. Born in Bristol, 28 February 1929. Educated at St. Paul's School, London, 1941–48; Jesus College, Cambridge, 1949–52, M.A.; Balliol College, Oxford, 1952–53; Ridley Hall, Cambridge, 1956–58. Served in the British Army, 1948–49; Sergeant. Married Anne Duff in 1953 (divorced); has two sons and one daughter. Assistant District Officer, Colonial Service, Northern Nigeria, 1953–56; Clerk in Holy Orders, Church of England Sheffield Diocese, 1958–62 (resigned orders); history teacher, Bristol Education Authority, 1962–69. Director, Educational Publishers Council, 1970–72, and since 1972, Director, Book Development Council, Publishers' Association, London. Schoolmaster Fellow, Clare College, Cambridge, 1968. Agent: Michael Horniman, A.P. Watt and Son, 26–28 Bedford Row, London WC1R 4HL. Address: 103 Tottenham Road, London N.1, England.

PUBLICATIONS FOR CHILDREN

Fiction

The Emir's Son, illustrated by Gareth Floyd. London, Constable, and Cleveland, World, 1967.
The Monarch of Juan Fernandez, illustrated by A.R. Whitear. London, Constable, 1967; New York, Scribner, 1968.
Benjie's Portion, illustrated by F.D. Phillips. London, Longman, 1969; New York, World, 1970.
The Speaking Drums of Ashanti. London, Longman, 1970.
Dockie. London, Longman, 1972.

Other

Bristol: Seaport City, illustrated by Gareth Floyd. London, Constable, 1966.
The Story of Teaching. London, Longman, 1969.
Rome and Empire, A.D. 41–122, illustrated by Gareth Floyd. London, Methuen, 1970.
Faith and Violence: The Birth of Medieval Europe, A.D. 800–900, illustrated by Gareth Floyd. London, Methuen, 1970.
The Cross and the Sword: The Middle Ages, 1270–1350, illustrated by Gareth Floyd. London, Methuen, 1970.
Sails and Guns: The Era of Discovery, 1491–1534, illustrated by Gareth Floyd. London, Methuen, 1970.
Europe Reaches round the World, 1584–1632, illustrated by Gareth Floyd. London, Methuen, 1970.
Kings and Courtiers: The Era of Elegance, 1684–1716, illustrated by Gareth Floyd. London, Methuen, 1970.
Revolutions and Steam Engines, 1775–1815, illustrated by Gareth Floyd. London, Methuen, 1971.
The Age of Progress, 1848–1866, illustrated by Gareth Floyd. London, Methuen, 1971.
The World at War, 1900–1918, illustrated by Gareth Floyd. London, Methuen, 1971.
Who Am I? A Book of World Religions. London, Hutchinson, 1971.
Scholars and Ancestors: China under the Sung Dynasty. London, Methuen, 1973.
Land of the Great Moguls: Akbar's India. London, Methuen, 1973.
Uthman dan Fodio. London, Longman, 1977.

PUBLICATIONS FOR ADULTS

Other

Editor, *New Movements in the Study and Teaching of History.* London, Maurice Temple Smith, and Bloomington, Indiana University Press, 1970.

Martin Ballard comments:

With the exception of the one picture book, my work for children has all been for the 12-plus age range. It covers fiction, general non-fiction, and work for schools.

These areas are not so dissimilar as they might seem at first sight for the fiction has been centered on a researched historical background, while the school books have tried to break away from the traditional mere compilation of fact. In my best known book, *Dockie*, I have developed a social realism rather different, I hope, from the "problem books" which have been appearing recently, and my next novel will break away from the historical background to develop this theme further.

*   *   *

Martin Ballard's first novel for children was the story of Alexander Selkirk, the real Robinson Crusoe, entitled *The Monarch of Juan Fernandez*.

This version is much shorter, crisper, and easier to read than that of Defoe, and it provides an interesting character study for young people of a man who could survive alone that crucial period as a castaway and yet possess a difficult and somewhat taciturn personality when it came to the more ordinary situations in life.

Benjie's Portion, the pitiful story of a young slave in Nova Scotia, is set in the time of the great philanthropist Granville Sharp who was planning to establish a colony for free men in Sierra Leone. The hardship endured by all concerned in Nova Scotia, during the voyage, and later in Africa is related in a simple, direct style. In the sequel, *The Speaking Drums of Ashanti*, the slave-boy's son Simon accompanies the Governor of Sierra Leone on an expedition to the smaller tribes to try to win their support for the British Army against the Ashanti, who were still active slave-dealers. Young Simon is forced to recognize the cunning of both black and white men, and to set these disturbing revelations against the teaching of his own mission school background. The second story makes more compelling reading, but the style in which both are written becomes stilted at times. The author of any book on such a subject must guard against the story developing into a documentary, and this is something that Mr. Ballard has not always avoided, but the books are a real attempt to portray life in a period which is very little covered in books for children.

The author's style becomes much more alive in *Dockie*. Young Moggy Harris is waiting for the day to leave school – to do what? To follow his father as a docker, or realize his secret ambition to become a boxer? The author paints a very vivid picture of the grinding poverty of dockyard workers in the 1920s, and of the insurmountable difficulties that beset every household. After one of many rows, Moggie leaves home and finds conditions even worse. When his father becomes a blackleg in order to feed his family, the reader is treated to a first-class account of the activities of trade unionists of the day.

Martin Ballard's only picture book, *The Emir's Son*, is based on an old Hausa fable. It concerns a wealthy young man whose life was changed from one of idle pleasure to one of affection for his father's people after he had encountered a very old man planting seeds who told him: "Others have planted and I have eaten. I, too, will plant so that others may eat." Although in a format designed for younger readers, the appeal of this story is universal.

—Berna C. Clark

BANNER, Angela. Pseudonym for Angela Mary Maddison. British. Born in Bombay, India, 14 May 1923. Educated at Ancaster Gate and House, Bexhill, Sussex, 1933–37. Married Lionel Parsons in 1941; has two children. Address: The Ant and Bee Partnership, c/o Grindlays Bank, 13 St. James's Square, London SW1Y 4LF, England.

PUBLICATIONS FOR CHILDREN

Fiction

Ant and Bee: An Alphabetical Story for Tiny Tots, illustrated by Bryan Ward.   Leicester,
   Ward, 1950; New York, Watts, 1966.
More Ant and Bee, illustrated by Bryan Ward.   London, Ward, 1956; New York,
   Watts, 1960.
Mr. Fork and Curly Fork: A Time Story.   London, Ward, 1956.
One, Two, Three with Ant and Bee: A Counting Story, illustrated by Bryan
   Ward.   London, Ward, and New York, Watts, 1958.
Around the World with Ant and Bee, illustrated by Bryan Ward.   London, Ward, and
   New York, Watts, 1960.
More and More Ant and Bee: Another Alphabetical Story, illustrated by Bryan
   Ward.   London, Ward, 1961; New York, Watts, 1962.
Ant and Bee and the Rainbow: A Story about Colours, illustrated by Bryan
   Ward.   London, Ward, and New York, Watts, 1962.
Ant and Bee and Kind Dog: An Alphabetical Story, illustrated by Bryan Ward.   London,
   Ward, and New York, Watts, 1963.
Happy Birthday with Ant and Bee, illustrated by Bryan Ward.   London, Ward, and
   New York, Watts, 1964.
Ant and Bee and the ABC, illustrated by Bryan Ward.   London, Ward, and New York,
   Watts, 1966.
Ant and Bee Time, illustrated by the author.   London, Kaye and Ward, and New York,
   Watts, 1969.
Ant and Bee and the Secret, illustrated by the author.   London, Kaye and Ward, and
   New York, Watts, 1970.
Ant and Bee and the Doctor, illustrated by the author.   London, Kaye and Ward, and
   New York, Watts, 1971.
The Ant and Bee Big Buy Bag, illustrated by the author.   London, Kaye and Ward,
   1971.
Ant and Bee Go Shopping, illustrated by the author.   London, Kaye and Ward, and
   New York, Watts, 1972.
Kind Dog on Monday, illustrated by the author.   London, Ant and Bee Partnership,
   1972.
Kind Dog Up and Down the Hill, illustrated by the author.   London, Ant and Bee
   Partnership, 1972.
Which Two Will Meet?, illustrated by the author.   London, Ant and Bee Partnership,
   1972.

Angela Banner comments:
   The best reading teacher for a child is another child.
   My books are made for shared-reading between children. No child is too young to "read" a
few words from memory and so contribute to a story telling.
   Early memory "reading" leads to reading confidence: too often destroyed by educating
adults.

*   *   *

Angela Banner is the author (and sometimes also the illustrator) of the enormously popular
series about Ant and Bee. She says she chose an ant and a bee because she used to be afraid of
insects and she hoped her children would be different. But, in fact, their insectness is merely
incidental. Their smallness is nicely exploited, and Bee does a good deal of flying about, often
with Ant on his back. But they are not insects in the way that Mr. Jackson is a toad or Samuel

Whiskers a rat. And they are not trying to be. They are zany, one-dimensional characters with enormous appeal for children. They come in small, fat, colourful packets as tempting as a box of Smarties.

The text may be tedious stuff for reading-aloud parents but at least they have the consolation of some bizarre ideas and surrealistic conjunctions and the knowledge that the books are educational as well as entertaining. The books are designed to encourage reading (with key words from a limited vocabulary), counting, telling the time, knowing the colours. The least overtly educational is one of the most successful. *Happy Birthday with Ant and Bee* is supposed to make children aware of the order of the days of the week, but is in fact more of a juvenile guide to the proper conduct of a birthday party. *One, Two, Three with Ant and Bee* can be guaranteed to teach children not only how to count but how to write and read their numbers. As for the reading books, Miss Banner once said she chooses the key words first, "like cooking ingredients." Some of the key words are definitely odd. If you meet a four year old who knows a *yew*-tree and a tea-*urn* when he sees them, you can be sure he has *Ant and Bee* in his house.

The effect of the whole series is to assure a child that books are fun and small, friendly familiar objects, not glossy beautiful things that need to be treated reverently. The series could be called vulgar, brash, unsubtle, limited, marred by over-emphatic punctuation. But they combine that mixture of the rational and irrational, the strange and familiar which children delight in. They are lively, funny, inventive and instructive, and undoubtedly successful.

—Ann Thwaite

———————————

BANNERMAN, Helen (Brodie Cowan Watson).   British.   Born in Edinburgh, in 1863. Educated privately; St. Andrews University, Scotland, L.L.A. Married William Burney Bannerman in 1889 (died, 1924); two sons and two daughters. Lived in India for thirty years. *Died 13 October 1946.*

PUBLICATIONS FOR CHILDREN

Fiction (illustrated by the author)

> *The Story of Little Black Sambo.*   London, Grant Richards, 1899; New York, Stokes, 1900.
> *The Story of Little Black Mingo.*   London, Nisbet, 1901; New York, Stokes, 1902.
> *The Story of Little Black Quibba.*   London, Nisbet, 1902; New York, Stokes, 1903.
> *Little Degchie-Head: An Awful Warning to Bad Babas.*   London, Nisbet, 1903.
> *The Story of Little Kettle-Head: An Awful Warning to Bad Babas.*   New York, Stokes, 1904.
> *Pat and the Spider: The Biter Bit.*   London, Nisbet, 1904; New York, Stokes, 1905.
> *The Story of the Teasing Monkey.*   New York, Stokes, 1907.
> *The Story of Little Black Quasha.*   London, Nisbet, and New York, Stokes, 1908.
> *The Story of Little Black Bobtail.*   New York, Stokes, 1909.
> *The Little Black Sambo Story Book,* with Frank Ver Beck.   Philadelphia, Altemus, 1930.
> *Sambo and the Twins.*   New York, Stokes, 1936; London, Nisbet, 1937.
> *The Story of Little White Squibba.*   London, Chatto and Windus, 1966.

*   *   *

Helen Bannerman's *The Story of Little Black Sambo* was made up by an Englishwoman living in India in the 1890's to amuse her children. When it was published, embellished by its author's own rather crude coloured illustrations, it was an immediate success and has been continuously in print ever since. It is easy to see why so many generations of children have enjoyed having it read to them – it has even been called "one of the funniest books in existence." The language is simple; there is a picture to look at on almost every other page; and the story-line has the riveting simplicity of a folk-tale. Little Black Sambo, given a fine new Red Coat, Blue Trousers, Purple Shoes and Green Umbrella, goes out for a walk in the Jungle where he meets four Tigers who, one after another, agree not to eat him in return for one of his pieces of finery. (The Purple Shoes have to be worn as ear-muffs, while the fourth Tiger can only manage to hold the Green Umbrella by tying a knot in his tail.) The Tigers meet and quarrel over which of them is now the grandest. In the end, in a climax which small children find tremendously funny, the Tigers chase each other round a tree so fast that they simply melt away, leaving nothing but a great big pool of melted butter. Sambo's father, Black Jumbo, takes this home with him, and with it his mother, Black Mumbo, makes an enormous feast of pancakes, of which Sambo eats no fewer than "a Hundred and Sixty-nine."

In its various successors there is a similar pattern of repetition-with-variation, culminating in a ludicrous and often innocently bloodthirsty denouement: in *Little Black Mingo* the Mugger swallows the "horrid cross old woman," Black Noggy, complete with a tin of kerosene and a box of matches, with explosive results; in *Little Black Quibba* the Elephant and the Snake engage in a fight in which the Elephant falls over a cliff and ties his trunk together with the Snake into such a tight knot that the Snake (whose rear end is curled round a tree) is pulled out "longer and longer and thinner and thinner" until it breaks "with a Snap! into three pieces."

In the 1960's there was vociferous unease about the racism implicit in these stories. It is true that if one takes the naming of the characters, together with the garishly coloured clothes they are so proud of, there is evident a certain unwitting condescension towards the black human protagonists which passed unnoticed seventy-odd years ago but which properly raises qualms in the uneasy multi-racial climate of today. The fault seems to lie less in Helen Bannerman than in the diseased state of our own culture in which the name Sambo itself can be used to insult or abuse. It must be doubtful, however, whether a normal child in a normal household will take any harm from these stories, the more so since the child-reader's natural inclination, whatever his colour, is to identify whole-heartedly with the Little Black hero or heroine.

—Frank Whitehead

BARNE, Kitty (Marion Catherine Barne).   British.   Born in 1883. Educated at the Royal College of Music, London. Served in the Women's Voluntary Service during World War II. Married Eric Streatfeild. Recipient: Library Association Carnegie Medal, 1941. *Died in 1957.*

PUBLICATIONS FOR CHILDREN

Fiction

Tomorrow, illustrated by Ethel King-Martyn.   London, Hodder and Stoughton, 1912.
The Easter Holidays, illustrated by Joan Kiddell-Monroe.   London, Heinemann, 1935;
    as *Secret of the Sandhills*, New York, Dodd Mead, 1949; London, Nelson, 1955.
Young Adventurers, illustrated by Ruth Gervis.   London, Nelson, 1936.
She Shall Have Music, illustrated by Ruth Gervis.   London, Dent, 1938; New York,
    Dodd Mead, 1939.

Family Footlights, illustrated by Ruth Gervis.   London, Dent, and New York, Dodd
   Mead, 1939.
Visitors from London, illustrated by Ruth Gervis.   London, Dent, and New York, Dodd
   Mead, 1940.
May I Keep Dogs?, illustrated by Arnrid Johnston.   London, Hamish Hamilton, 1941;
   New York, Dodd Mead, 1942; as *Bracken My Dog*, London, Dent, 1949.
We'll Meet in England, illustrated by Steven Spurrier.   London, Hamish Hamilton,
   1942; New York, Dodd Mead, 1943.
Three and a Pigeon, illustrated by Steven Spurrier.   London, Hamish Hamilton, and
   New York, Dodd Mead, 1944.
In the Same Boat, illustrated by Ruth Gervis.   London, Dent, and New York, Dodd
   Mead, 1945.
Musical Honours, illustrated by Ruth Gervis.   London, Dent, and New York, Dodd
   Mead, 1947.
Dusty's Windmill, illustrated by Marcia Lane Foster.   London, Dent, 1949; as *The
   Windmill Mystery*, New York, Dodd Mead, 1950.
Roly's Dogs, illustrated by Alice Molony.   London, Dent, 1950; as *Dog Stars*, New
   York, Dodd Mead, 1951.
Barbie, illustrated by Marcia Lane Foster.   London, Dent, 1952; Boston, Little Brown,
   1969.
Admiral's Walk, illustrated by Mary Gurnat.   London, Dent, 1953.
Rosina Copper the Mystery Mare, illustrated by Alfons Purtscher.   London, Evans,
   1954; New York, Dutton, 1956.
Cousin Beattie Learns the Fiddle.   Oxford, Blackwell, 1955.
Tann's Boarders, illustrated by Jill Crockford.   London, Dent, 1955.
Rosina and Son, illustrated by Marcia Lane Foster.   London, Evans, 1956.

Plays

Tomorrow, with D.W. Wheeler.   London, Curwen, 1910.
Winds, with D.W. Wheeler, music by Kitty Barne, illustrated by Lucy Barne.   London,
   Curwen, 1912.
Timothy's Garden, verses by D.W. Wheeler, illustrated by Lucy Barne.   London,
   Curwen, 1912.
Celadine's Secret, verses by D.W. Wheeler, illustrated by J.M. Saunders.   London,
   Curwen, 1914.
Peter and the Clock.   London, Curwen, 1919.
Susie Pays a Visit.   London, Curwen, 1921.
The Amber Gate: A Pageant Play.   London, Curwen, 1925.
Philemon and Baucis.   London, Gowans and Gray, and Boston, Baker, 1926.
Madge: A Camp-Fire Play.   London, Novello, 1928.
Adventurers: A Pageant Play.   London, Deane, 1931; Boston, Baker, 1936.
The Grand Party, adaptation of the novel *Holiday House*, by Catherine Sinclair, in *The
   Theatre Window: Plays for Schools*, edited by W.T. Cunningham.   London, Arnold,
   1933.
*Two More Mimes from Folk Songs: The Wraggle, Taggle Gipsies, O!, Robin-a-
   Thrush.*   London, Curwen, 1936.
*Two Mimes from Folk Songs: The Frog and the Mouse, The Flowers in the
   Valley.*   London, Curwen, 1937.
They Made the Royal Arms.   London, Deane, and Boston, Baker, 1937.
Shilling Teas.   London, Deane, and Boston, Baker, 1938.
Days of Glory: A Pageant Play.   London, Deane, 1946.
The "Local Ass": A Documentary Pageant Play for Girl Guides.   London, Girl Guides'
   Association, 1947.
The Lost Birthday.   London, Curwen, n.d.

Other

The Amber Gate, illustrated by Ruth Gervis.   London and New York, Nelson, 1933.
Songs and Stories for Acting, illustrated by Ruth Gervis.   Glasgow, Brown and Ferguson, 1939.
Listening to the Orchestra.   London, Dent, 1941; revised edition, 1946; Indianapolis, Bobbs Merrill, 1946.
Here Come the Girl Guides.   London, Girl Guides' Association, 1947.
Elizabeth Fry: A Story Biography.   London, Penguin, 1950.
Introducing Handel, illustrated by Jill Crockford.   London, Dent, 1955; New York, Roy, 1957.
Introducing Mozart, illustrated by Jill Crockford.   London, Dent, 1955; New York, Roy, 1957.
Introducing Schubert, illustrated by Jill Crockford.   London, Dent, and New York, Roy, 1957.

PUBLICATIONS FOR ADULTS

Novels

Mother at Large.   London, Chapman and Hall, 1938.
While the Music Lasted.   London, Chapman and Hall, 1943.
Enter Two Musicians.   London, Chapman and Hall, 1944.
Duet for Sisters.   London, Chapman and Hall, 1947.
Vespa.   London, Chapman and Hall, 1950.
Music Perhaps.   London, Chapman and Hall, 1953.

*   *   *

Though she produced a good deal of earlier work, mainly plays and now forgotten, it was not until a few years before the Second World War that Kitty Barne began to explore a field of children's fiction in which she became something of a pioneer. She would probably have disclaimed a title with quite such aggressive connotations. She was, however, in her quiet way, a very serious and responsible writer. Her junior novels were intended to reflect the real world, in which young characters faced problems and struggled to solve them. She never favoured the child-insulated world in which adults appeared only as fringe characters, tolerated only when the plot demanded their entrance. At a period when most modern stories were frankly escapist, dealing with holiday adventures or improbable juvenile detection, Kitty Barne, while not making her books superficially too dissimilar, let in a much-needed draught of fresh air.

The outbreak of war in 1939 gave her inspiration and immediately enlarged opportunities. No one could any longer pretend that young readers could or should be protected from reality. In her Carnegie-winner, *Visitors from London*, she dealt with the impact of London evacuees upon a Sussex village. Later, another Cockney evacuee was a key character in *Three and a Pigeon*, another story of the home front which also involved the black market in farm produce. *In the Same Boat* tells of a Polish girl's escape to Britain and her schooldays there with her new-found English friend. Perhaps most noteworthy of all these novels is *Musical Honours*, in which the father, a returned prisoner-of-war from the Far East, faces all the problems of readjustment, not least the renewal of relationships with his elder children who remember him and with the younger who do not. This was probably one of the earliest children's books in which a parent was depicted as a flesh-and-blood person with faults, not as a love-and-authority symbol.

Both in her thought and in her language, Kitty Barne preferred to stretch her young readers, to overrate rather than underrate their capacity. She was against what she called "patronising simplicity" and "brightness." Children, she declared, did not mind long words or ideas that were a little big for them. She found an exhilaration in writing for them, and this emotion was communicated in the warmth and enthusiasm of her style.

—Geoffrey Trease

BARRETT, Anne Mainwaring. British. Born in Southsea, Hampshire, 7 May 1911. Educated at Sherborne School for Girls, Dorset. Married Hugh Myles Boxer in 1933; William Kenyon Tufnell Barrett, 1941, one daughter. Worked with Children's Film Foundation, London, 1960–65. Address: c/o Lloyds Bank, Wadhurst, Sussex, England.

PUBLICATIONS FOR CHILDREN

Fiction

Caterpillar Hill, illustrated by Catherine Cummins. London, Collins, 1950.
Stolen Summer, illustrated by John Robinson. London, Collins, 1951; New York, Dodd Mead, 1953.
The Dark Island. London, Collins, 1952.
The Journey of Johnny Rew, illustrated by Shirley Hughes. London, Collins, 1954; Indianapolis, Bobbs Merrill, 1955.
Sheila Burton: Dental Assistant. London, Bodley Head, 1956.
Songberd's Grove, illustrated by David Knight. London, Collins, and Indianapolis, Bobbs Merrill, 1957.
Midway, illustrated by Margery Gill. London, Collins, 1967; New York, Coward McCann, 1968.

Play

Screenplay: *Treasure in Malta*, 1963.

*   *   *

Anne Mainwaring Barrett is a writer of considerable power whose work, on the whole, has not been accorded the continuing praise which it merits. Her best-known books are *Songberd's Grove* and *Midway*. Her earlier books are highly imaginative but are somewhat marred by the many strands to their plots. The first four novels have very improbable themes, but are written with an almost dreamlike quality, and this style, while it makes for very enjoyable reading, also tends to date them. *Caterpillar Hall* is an adventure in time: Penelope turns the gold band of her umbrella to take her back many years, revealing the early lives of other characters. *Stolen Summer* is the summer spent by Jenny and her mother in a beautiful country house; to young readers of today the passion of James and Jenny for all things Nelsonian – to the point of making models of the ships at Trafalgar – is the most entertaining aspect. *The Dark Island* is set in Ireland, and concerns the discovery by two children of a man who has lost his memory; this turns into a kind of spy-thriller as it unfolds. *The Journey of Johnny Rew* traces the hero's search for his unknown father. This story is memorable for the many remarkable characters whom Johnny encounters – especially old Sam Brisle the hedger and the charming, trusting ladylike Miss Merrament.

Songberd's Grove is a story of the Teddyboy era. Martin, a boy of some spirit comes to live with his parents in an old tumbledown flat; in the same house dwell many diverse characters including the leader of the local spivs – Lenny. This story is more factual, and the gradual unfolding of the various situations which bring cheer to all of them – including the discovery that the street has some architectural merit – is carefully done. The architect has that "rarely met aura of true authority" which reduces Lenny to size and provides a lesson for all bullies.

In *Midway* – her finest book – Mark is the middle child of five, and as the family grew it was evident that Mark is the least clever. Gradually his father has lost interest in him, and Mark is always trying to prove his usefulness. The boy has a vivid imagination, and he invents a glorious tiger whom he calls "Midway" and in whom he confides his troubles and fears, and with whom all things are possible. Mark distrusts his father's fellow scientist, and when this rival attempts to steal his father's work, it is Mark who saves the day, so at last his father gives him the place in his affections to which Mark aspires. This is a splendid piece of writing which may well help any child who feels out of things at school or at home.

—Berna C. Clark

BARRIE, J(ames) M(atthew).   British.   Born in Kirriemuir, Forfarshire, now Angus, Scotland, 9 May 1860. Educated at Glasgow Academy, 1868–70; Forfar Academy, 1870–71; Dumfries Academy, 1873–78; Edinburgh University, 1878–82, M.A. 1882. Married the actress Mary Ansell in 1894 (divorced, 1909). Drama and book critic, *Edinburgh Courant*, 1879–82; Leader Writer, *Nottingham Journal*, 1883–84. Lived in London after 1885. President, Society of Authors, 1928–37, and Dramatists' Club, 1934–37. LL.D.: St. Andrews University, 1898; Edinburgh University, 1909. Rector, St. Andrews University, 1919–22; Chancellor, Edinburgh University, 1930–37. Order of Merit, 1922. Knighted, 1913. *Died 19 June 1937.*

PUBLICATIONS FOR CHILDREN

Fiction

> *The Boy Castaways of Black Lake Island.*   Privately printed, 1901.
> *Peter and Wendy*, illustrated by F. D. Bedford.   London, and New York, Hodder and Stoughton, 1911; as *Peter Pan and Wendy*,   London, Hodder and Stoughton, 1921.

Play

> *Peter Pan; or, The Boy Who Wouldn't Grow Up* (produced London, 1904; Washington, D.C., and New York, 1905; revised version, produced London, 1910).   London, Hodder and Stoughton, 1913; New York, Scribner, 1918.

PUBLICATIONS FOR ADULTS

Novels

> *Better Dead.*   London, Swan Sonnenschein Lowrey, 1888; Chicago, Rand McNally, 1891.
> *When a Man's Single: A Tale of Literary Life.*   London, Hodder and Stoughton, 1888; New York, Harper, 1889.
> *The Little Minister.*   London, Cassell, 3 vols., 1891; New York, Lovell, 1891.
> *Sentimental Tommy: The Story of His Boyhood.*   London, Cassell, and New York, Scribner, 1896.

Tommy and Grizel. London, Cassell, and New York, Scribner, 1900.

The Little White Bird. London, Hodder and Stoughton, 1902; as *The Little White Bird; or, Adventures in Kensington Gardens,* New York, Scribner, 1902; revised material for children, as *Peter Pan in Kensington Gardens,* 1906.

Farewell Miss Julie Logan: A Wintry Tale. London, The Times Publishing Company, 1931; New York, Scribner, 1933.

Plays

Caught Napping. Privately printed, 1883.

Ibsen's Ghost; or, Toole Up-to-Date (produced London, 1891).

Richard Savage, with H. B. Marriott Watson (produced London, 1891). Privately printed, 1891.

Walker, London (as *The Houseboat,* produced London, 1892). London and New York, French, 1907.

The Professor's Love Story (produced New York, 1892; London, 1894). Included in *Plays,* 1942.

Becky Sharp (produced London, 1893).

Jane Annie; or, The Good Conduct Prize, with Arthur Conan Doyle, music by Ernest Ford (produced London, 1893). London, Chappell, and New York, Novello Ewer, 1893.

The Little Minister, adaptation of his own novel (produced London, Washington, D.C., and New York, 1897; as *Little Mary,* produced London, 1903). Included in *Plays,* 1942.

A Platonic Friendship (produced London, 1898).

The Wedding Guest (produced London, 1900). London, Fortnightly Review, and New York, Scribner, 1900.

The Admirable Crichton (produced London, 1902; New York, 1903). London, Hodder and Stoughton, 1914; New York, Scribner, 1918.

Quality Street (produced London, 1902; New York, 1903). London, Hodder and Stoughton, 1913; New York, Scribner, 1918.

Pantaloon (produced London, 1905). Included in *Half Hours,* 1914.

Alice Sit-by-the-Fire (produced London and New York, 1905). London, Hodder and Stoughton, and New York, Scribner, 1919.

Josephine (produced London, 1906).

Punch (produced London, 1906).

What Every Woman Knows (produced London, Atlantic City, New Jersey, and New York, 1908). London, Hodder and Stoughton, and New York, Scribner, 1918.

Old Friends (produced London, 1910; New York, 1917). Included in *Plays,* 1929.

A Slice of Life (produced London, 1910; New York, 1912).

The Twelve-Pound Look (produced London, 1910; New York, 1911). Included in *Half Hours,* 1914.

Rosalind (produced London, 1912; New York, 1915). Included in *Half Hours,* 1914.

The Dramatists Get What They Want (produced London, 1912; as *The Censor and the Dramatists,* produced New York, 1913).

The Will (produced London and New York, 1913). Included in *Half Hours,* 1914.

The Adored One: A Legend of the Old Bailey (produced London, 1913; as *The Legend of Leonora,* produced New York, 1914; shortened version, as *Seven Women,* produced London, 1917). *Seven Women* included in *Plays,* 1929.

Half an Hour (produced London and New York, 1913).

Half Hours (includes *Pantaloon, The Twelve-Pound Look, Rosalind, The Will*). London, Hodder and Stoughton, and New York, Scribner, 1914.

Der Tag (produced London, 1914; as *Der Tag; or, The Tragic Man,* produced New York, 1914). London, Hodder and Stoughton, and New York, Scribner, 1914.

Rosy Rapture, The Pride of the Beauty Chorus, music by H. Darewski and Jerome Kern (produced London, 1915).

The Fatal Typist (produced London, 1915).

The New Word (produced London, 1915; New York, 1917). Included in *Echoes of the War*, 1918.

The Real Thing at Last (produced London, 1916).

Irene Vanbrugh's Pantomime (produced London, 1916).

Shakespeare's Legacy (produced London, 1916). Privately printed, 1916.

A Kiss for Cinderella (produced London and New York, 1916). London, Hodder and Stoughton, and New York, Scribner, 1920.

The Old Lady Shows Her Medals (produced London and New York, 1917). Included in *Echoes of the War*, 1918.

Reconstructing the Crime (produced London, 1917).

Dear Brutus (produced London, 1917; New York, 1918). London, Hodder and Stoughton, and New York, Scribner, 1922.

La Politesse (produced London, 1918).

A Well-Remembered Voice (produced London, 1918). Included in *Echoes of the War*, 1918.

Echoes of the War (includes *The Old Lady Shows Her Medals, The New Word, Barbara's Wedding, A Well-Remembered Voice*). London, Hodder and Stoughton, and New York, Scribner, 1918.

Barbara's Wedding (produced London, 1927; New York, 1931). Included in *Echoes of the War*, 1918.

The Truth about the Russian Dancers (produced London, 1920). New York, Dance Perspectives, 1962.

Mary Rose (produced London and New York, 1920). London, Hodder and Stoughton, and New York, Scribner, 1924.

Shall We Join the Ladies? (produced London, 1921; New York, 1925). Included in *Plays*, 1929.

Neil and Tinntinabulum. Privately printed, 1925.

Representative Plays (includes *Quality Street, The Admirable Crichton, What Every Woman Knows, Dear Brutus, The Twelve-Pound Look, The Old Lady Shows Her Medals*). New York, Scribner, 1926.

The Plays of J. M. Barrie (includes *Peter Pan, The Admirable Crichton, Alice Sit-by-the-Fire, What Every Woman Knows, A Kiss for Cinderella, Dear Brutus, Mary Rose, Pantaloon, Half an Hour, Old Friends, Rosalind, The Twelve-Pound Look, The New Word, A Well-Remembered Voice, Barbara's Wedding, The Old Lady Shows Her Medals, Shall We Join the Ladies?*). London, Hodder, and Stoughton, and New York, Scribner, 1929; augmented edition, edited by A. E. Wilson (includes *Walker, London; The Professor's Love Story; The Little Minister; The Wedding Guest; The Boy David*), Hodder and Stoughton, 1942.

The Boy David (produced Edinburgh and London, 1936; New York, 1941). London, Davies, and New York, Scribner, 1938.

Verse

Scotland's Lament: A Poem on the Death of Robert Louis Stevenson. Privately printed, 1895.

Other

The New Amphion. Edinburgh, David Douglas, 1886.

Auld Licht Idylls. London, Hodder and Stoughton, 1888; New York, Macmillan, 1891.

A Window in Thrums. London, Hodder and Stoughton, 1889; New York, Cassell, 1892.

An Edinburgh Eleven: Pencil Portraits from College Life.   London, Office of the British
   Weekly, 1889; New York, Lovell Coryell, 1892.
My Lady Nicotine.   London, Hodder and Stoughton, 1890; Chicago, Rand McNally,
   1891.
Allahakbarries C. C. (on cricket).   Privately printed, 1893.
Margaret Ogilvy, by Her Son.   New York, Scribner, and London, Hodder and
   Stoughton, 1896.
The Allahakbarrie Book of Broadway Cricket for 1899.   Privately printed, 1899.
George Meredith 1909.   London, Constable, and Portland, Maine, Thomas B. Mosher,
   1909; as *Neither Dorking nor the Abbey*, Chicago, Browne's Bookstore, 1911.
The Works (Kirriemuir Edition).   London, Hodder and Stoughton, 10 vols., 1913.
Charles Frohman: A Tribute.   Privately printed, 1915.
*Who Was Sarah Findley? by Mark Twain, with a Suggested Solution of the
   Mystery.*   Privately printed, 1917.
The Works of J. M. Barrie.   New York, Scribner, 10 vols., 1918.
*Courage: The Rectorial Address Delivered at St. Andrews University, May 3rd
   1922.*   London, Hodder and Stoughton, and New York, Scribner, 1922.
The Ladies' Shakespeare (lecture).   Privately printed, 1925.
The Works (Peter Pan edition).   New York, Scribner, 14 vols., 1929.
The Entrancing Life (address).   London, Hodder and Stoughton, and New York,
   Scribner, 1930.
The Greenwood Hat, Being a Memoir of James Anon, 1885–1887.   Privately printed,
   1930; revised edition, London, Davies, and New York, Scribner, 1937.
M'Connachie and J. M. B.: Speeches.   London, Davies, 1938.
Letters of J. M. Barrie, edited by Viola Meynell.   London, Davies, 1942.
Plays and Stories, edited by Roger Lancelyn Green.   London, Dent, 1962.

Bibliography: *Sir James M. Barrie: A Bibliography* by B. D. Cutler, New York, Greenberg,
1931.

Critical Studies: *J. M. Barrie* by F. J. Harvey Darton, London, Nisbet, 1929; *Fifty Years of
Peter Pan* by Roger Lancelyn Green, London, Davies, 1954; *J. M. Barrie* by Roger Lancelyn
Green, London, Bodley Head, 1960, New York, Walck, 1961; *J. M. Barrie: The Man Behind
the Image* by Janet Dunbar, London, Collins, 1970.

                              *   *   *

   It is not always realised that – a few private oddities apart – J. M. Barrie produced only one
work for the young. But that one, a major myth of the new century, was written in many
forms over many years, before and after the actual stage production. Indeed, it is fair to say
that no important work discussed in the present volume can have a more curious history than
Peter Pan, "that terrible masterpiece," as Peter Davies (see below) once called it. Where for a
start is its authentic form to be found? Though that first stage production was in 1904, the
play had to wait several years for a definitive printed version. The "story," the full-length
definitive narrative (the longest, best, most satisfying of all the versions) did not appear until
1911. Yet clues can be found in Barrie's quite early adult writings.
   Certain facts in Barrie's life have so fundamental a part in the making of *Peter Pan* that
they should be set out here. He was a small-town Lowlands Scot, one of a weaver's large
family. When David, the mother's favourite child, was killed in a skating accident on the eve
of his 14th birthday, James, then aged 6 and hitherto of little account, set himself to
compensate for the loss. The obsessive relationship that grew between mother and son was to
mark the whole of his life, as writer and as man. Another intense relationship began towards
the end of the century, when the once penniless young journalist had, quite rapidly, become
the rich and celebrated novelist and playwright. This was with Sylvia and Arthur Llewellyn
Davies (she was the daughter of George du Maurier) and their several – eventually five –

small sons. These boys, devoted childish listeners, were in an immediate sense the kindlers of *Peter Pan* – Jack, Peter, and Michael (as their names confirm) especially.

In print, the magic boy first appeared by name in Barrie's adult novel *The Little White Bird* (1902) a strange first-person narrative about a wealthy bachelor clubman's attachment to a little boy, David. Taking this boy for walks in Kensington Gardens, the narrator tells him of the elusive Peter Pan, who can be found in the Gardens at night, when the gates are closed. A little girl (not motherly Wendy but a sturdy likeable child called Maimie Mannering) bravely stays behind at dusk, though her brother runs away, and she becomes Peter's friend. Four years later these chapters were taken out and reprinted as a separate book called *Peter Pan in Kensington Gardens*, with pictures by Arthur Rackham: its verve and magical atmosphere make it well worth reading today. Told verbally this was the form first known to the Davies boys.

But the roots of the tale go very much further back. In *Margaret Ogilvy* (1896) Barrie recalled how his mother's childhood had ended at 8, when she had to become the family's housekeeper. "The horror of my boyhood was," he noted, "that I knew a time would come when I must also give up games, and how it was to be done, I saw not." More revealing still are his novels *Sentimental Tommy* and *Tommy and Grizel*. Tommy, a clever feckless dreamer who – disastrously – can't face adult responsibilities, plans a work of fiction:

> a reverie about a little boy who was lost. His parents find him in a wood singing joyfully to himself because he thinks he can now be a boy for ever; and he fears that if they catch him they will compel him to grow into a man, so he runs further from them into the wood and is running still, singing to himself because he is always to be a boy.

But Barrie, unlike Tommy, had a shrewd and positive streak, and the gift of turning fancy into fact. Only a writer of great assurance could have hoped for a theatrical production of *Peter Pan* with its extraordinary cast and sets and flying devices. Beerbohm Tree, who had first offer, thought it hopelessly unworkable, original to excess. But Charles Frohman was more adventurous, and the vastly successful opening productions, on both sides of the Atlantic, were his.

Like most of Barrie's work, *Peter Pan* has been adored and reviled for much the same qualities: what some perhaps call charm, others call sentimental and whimsical. Possibly neither group has taken into account Barrie's outstanding craftsmanship as a playwright, or of his easy gift for gripping a reader's interest on the printed page. The sentimental and whimsical were certainly part of his stock-in-trade, but they were not accidentally used; by the time he wrote *Peter Pan*, the hard glint in the sentimentalist's pale blue eyes becomes increasingly evident. (It is, indeed, a wonderfully *heartless* book – as Barrie was well aware: see the final line of the novel.) A touch of self-satire can possibly be observed even in the obsessional mother-theme. Wendy is given many good lines, in the novel particularly; note her watching the mermaids "combing out their hair in a lazy way that quite irritated her"; note her scornful feelings when Hook has her tied to the mast.

> No words of mine can tell you how Wendy despised those pirates. To the boys there was at least some glamour in the pirate calling, but all that she saw was that the ship had not been scrubbed for years. There was not a port-hole on the grimy glass of which you might not have written with your finger "Dirty pig"; and she had already written it several times.

Yet her role holds the seeds of its own defeat. "You need not be sorry for Wendy," writes Barrie. "She was one of the kind that likes to grow up. In the end she grew up of her own free will a day quicker than other girls." By ceasing to be a child, she rapidly loses Peter, Ariel of the child-world; she loses in every sense the power to fly. The Wendy portrait, begun with such simple charm (the name was the pet-name of Henley's short-lived little daughter) has clearly got out of hand, reflecting an unadmitted conflict in Barrie himself.

Peter Pan: landmark or signpost? The first far more than the second; it seems to have stunned imitation at any notable level. Pan-followers ran to coyness rather than wit; and this affects the work's reputation still. True, it did give an impetus to theatre for children; it can also be said that it brought into the open the growing cult of childhood and fairies in writings meant for adults. From Grahame's *The Golden Age* in the 1890's to Milne's *When We Were Very Young* in the 1920's, this cult took in work of de la Mare, Eleanor Farjeon (*Martin Pippin*), Rose Fyleman, Saki, James Stephens (*The Crock of Gold*) – and other prose and verse, now classed as children's reading, which were certainly published for adults in their day. With *Peter Pan* the process works in reverse. Both play and novel were (like *Alice*) specifically meant for the young, but are now (like *Alice*) of increasing interest to adults. *Peter Pan* mirrors its time; it mirrors, though more obliquely, its author's mind. As an instance: Barrie first made his name (and almost wrecked it in his home town) by using his local Scottish background for copy. In *Peter Pan* the Scot is hard to trace. But in fact it is the northern stranger's eye that finds such appeal in the Edwardian middle class nursery; in the social mystique of Kensington Gardens; in the *mores* of prep school and public school. Is not Hook himself, most enigmatic of pirates, abjuring "bad form" even in death, an old Etonian? James Hook ... odd that the author should give him his own name. But nothing is really simple in this work. How to explain the dog-kennel father, say, so many years pre-Thurber?

The position of *Peter Pan* today is a curious one. It is at once known and not known. Like other invented myths (Crusoe, Gulliver) its persons and ideas have currency among many who have neither read nor seen what Barrie wrote. Those who *do* read (or listen) often meet it only through feeble brief retellings (there are, alas, a number of these in print). They are missing much; the full text abounds in richnesses. *Peter Pan* is the secure child's dream of danger, of wild distances, of freedom from adult rules – but always (as in Sendak's *Where the Wild Things Are*) from a safe home base. It incorporates the traditional boy's adventure yarn which had so much delighted Barrie himself when young; indeed, much of the pirate/redskin material can be seen as a brilliant take-off of the genre. Peter himself is the absolute leader and hero-figure, the animator of action. But the children are not only onlookers; they are *in* the event, as themselves. It incorporates magic; the children actually fly. All these elements are combined on an island which accomodates redskins, pirates, mermaids, wolves with the greatest ease. For the young, the whole thing is a feast which lasts the longer by the skill – the continual sleight-of-hand – with which it is served. A "terrible masterpiece," yes, but the most complex and original of all its author's works, and a mine for Barrie-explorers.

—Naomi Lewis

BAUM, L(yman) Frank. American. Born in Chittenango, New York, 15 May 1856. Educated at schools in Syracuse, New York, and Peekskill Military Academy, New York. Married Maud Gage in 1882; four sons. Reporter, New York *World*, 1873–75; Founding Editor, *New Era*, Bradford, Pennsylvania, 1876; actor (as Louis F. Baum and George Brooks), theatre manager, and producer, New York; poultry farmer, in the 1880's; salesman, Baum's Castorine axle grease, 1886–88; Owner, Baum's Bazaar general store, Aberdeen, Dakota Territory, 1888–90; Editor, *Saturday Pioneer*, Aberdeen, 1890–91; Reporter, Chicago *Post*, Buyer, Siegel Cooper and Company, Chicago, and Salesman, Pitkin and Brooks, Chicago, 1891–97; Founder, National Association of Window Trimmers, 1897, and Founding Editor and Publisher, *The Show Window* magazine, Chicago, 1897–1902; Founding Director, Oz Film Manufacturing Company, Los Angeles, 1914. *Died 6 May 1919.*

PUBLICATIONS FOR CHILDREN

Fiction

A New Wonderland, illustrated by Frank Berbeck. New York, R. H. Russell, 1900; as
 The Surprising Adventures of the Magical Monarch of Mo, Indianapolis, Bobbs
 Merrill, 1903.
The Wonderful Wizard of Oz, illustrated by W. W. Denslow. Chicago, George M. Hill,
 1900; as *The New Wizard of Oz*, Indianapolis, Bobbs Merrill, 1903; London, Hodder
 and Stoughton, 1906.
Dot and Tot in Merryland, illustrated by W. W. Denslow. Chicago, George M. Hill,
 1901.
The Master Key: An Electrical Fairy Tale, illustrated by Fanny Cory. Indianapolis,
 Bowen Merrill, 1901; London, Stevens and Brown, 1902.
The Life and Adventures of Santa Claus, illustrated by Mary Cowles
 Clark. Indianapolis, Bowen Merrill, and London, Stevens and Brown, 1902.
The Enchanted Island of Yew, illustrated by Fanny Cory. Indianapolis, Bobbs Merrill,
 1903.
The Marvelous Land of Oz, illustrated by John R. Neill. Chicago, Reilly and Britton,
 and London, Revell, 1904.
Queen Zixi of Ix, illustrated by Frederick Richardson. New York, Century, 1905;
 London, Hodder and Stoughton, 1906.
The Woggle-Bug Book, illustrated by Ike Morgan. Chicago, Reilly and Britton, 1905.
John Dough and the Cherub, illustrated by John R. Neill. Chicago, Reilly and Britton,
 1906.
Annabel (as Suzanne Metcalf). Chicago, Reilly and Britton, 1906.
Sam Steele's Adventures on Land and Sea (as Hugh Fitzgerald). Chicago, Reilly and
 Britton, 1906; as *The Boy Fortune Hunters in Alaska* (as Floyd Akers), 1908.
Aunt Jane's Nieces (as Edith Van Dyne). Chicago, Reilly and Britton, 1906.
Aunt Jane's Nieces Abroad (as Edith Van Dyne). Chicago, Reilly and Britton, 1906.
Twinkle Tales (*Bandit Jim Crow, Mr. Woodchuck, Prairie-Dog Town, Prince Mud-
 Turtle, Sugar-Loaf Mountain, Twinkle's Enchantment*) (as Laura Bancroft), illustrated
 by Maginel Wright Enright. Chicago, Reilly and Britton, 6 vols., 1906; as *Twinkle
 and Chubbins*, 1911.
Ozma of Oz, illustrated by John R. Neill. Chicago, Reilly and Britton, 1907; as *Princess
 Ozma of Oz*, London, Hutchinson, 1942.
Sam Steele's Adventures in Panama (as Hugh Fitzgerald). Chicago, Reilly and Britton,
 1907; as *The Boy Fortune Hunters in Panama* (as Floyd Akers), 1908.
Policeman Bluejay (as Laura Bancroft), illustrated by Maginel Wright
 Enright. Chicago, Reilly and Britton, 1907; as *Babes in Birdland*, 1911.
Dorothy and the Wizard of Oz, illustrated by John R. Neill. Chicago, Reilly and
 Britton, 1908.
The Boy Fortune Hunters in Egypt (as Floyd Akers). Chicago, Reilly and Britton, 1908.
Aunt Jane's Nieces at Millville (as Edith Van Dyne). Chicago, Reilly and Britton, 1908.
The Road to Oz, illustrated by John R. Neill. Chicago, Reilly and Britton, 1909.
The Boy Fortune Hunters in China (as Floyd Akers). Chicago, Reilly and Britton, 1909.
Aunt Jane's Nieces at Work (as Edith Van Dyne). Chicago, Reilly and Britton, 1909.
The Emerald City of Oz, illustrated by John R. Neill. Chicago, Reilly and Britton,
 1910.
The Boy Fortune Hunters in Yucatan (as Floyd Akers). Chicago, Reilly and Britton,
 1910.
Aunt Jane's Nieces in Society (as Edith Van Dyne). Chicago, Reilly and Britton, 1910.
The Sea Fairies, illustrated by John R. Neill. Chicago, Reilly and Britton, 1911.
The Daring Twins, illustrated by Pauline Batchelder. Chicago, Reilly and Britton,
 1911.

The Boy Fortune Hunters in the South Seas (as Floyd Akers).   Chicago, Reilly and Britton, 1911.

Aunt Jane's Nieces and Uncle John (as Edith Van Dyne).   Chicago, Reilly and Britton, 1911.

The Flying Girl (as Edith Van Dyne).   Chicago, Reilly and Britton, 1911.

Sky Island, illustrated by John R. Neill.   Chicago, Reilly and Britton, 1912.

Phoebe Daring, illustrated by Joseph Pierre Nuyttens.   Chicago, Reilly and Britton, 1912.

Aunt Jane's Nieces on Vacation (as Edith Van Dyne).   Chicago, Reilly and Britton, 1912.

The Flying Girl and Her Chum (as Edith Van Dyne).   Chicago, Reilly and Britton, 1912.

The Patchwork Girl of Oz, illustrated by John R. Neill.   Chicago, Reilly and Britton, 1913.

The Little Wizard Series (*Jack Pumpkinhead and the Sawhorse, Little Dorothy and Toto, Ozma and the Little Wizard, The Cowardly Lion and the Hungry Tiger, The Scarecrow and the Tin Woodman, Tiktok and the Nome King*).   Chicago, Reilly and Britton, 6 vols., 1914; as *Little Wizard Stories of Oz*, Reilly and Britton, 1914; London, Simpkin, 1939.

Aunt Jane's Nieces on the Ranch (as Edith Van Dyne).   Chicago, Reilly and Britton, 1913.

Tik-Tok of Oz, illustrated by John R. Neill.   Chicago, Reilly and Britton, 1914.

Aunt Jane's Nieces Out West (as Edith Van Dyne).   Chicago, Reilly and Britton, 1914.

The Scarecrow of Oz, illustrated by John R. Neill.   Chicago, Reilly and Britton, 1915.

Aunt Jane's Nieces in the Red Cross (as Edith Van Dyne).   Chicago, Reilly and Britton, 1915.

Rinkitink in Oz, illustrated by John R. Neill.   Chicago, Reilly and Britton, 1916.

The Snuggle Tales (*Little Bun Rabbit, Once upon a Time, The Yellow Hen, The Magic Cloak, The Gingerbread Man, Jack Pumpkinhead*), illustrated by John R. Neill.   Chicago, Reilly and Britton, 6 vols., 1916–17; as *Oz-Man Tales*, 6 vols., 1920.

Mary Louise (as Edith Van Dyne).   Chicago, Reilly and Britton, 1916.

Mary Louise in the Country (as Edith Van Dyne).   Chicago, Reilly and Britton, 1916.

The Lost Princess of Oz, illustrated by John R. Neill.   Chicago, Reilly and Britton, 1917.

Mary Louise Solves a Mystery (as Edith Van Dyne).   Chicago, Reilly and Britton, 1917.

The Tin Woodman of Oz, illustrated by John R. Neill.   Chicago, Reilly and Britton, 1918.

Mary Louise and the Liberty Girls (as Edith Van Dyne).   Chicago, Reilly and Britton, 1918.

Mary Louise Adopts a Soldier (as Edith Van Dyne).   Chicago, Reilly and Lee, 1919.

The Magic of Oz, illustrated by John R. Neill.   Chicago, Reilly and Lee, 1919.

Glinda of Oz, illustrated by John R. Neill.   Chicago, Reilly and Lee, 1920.

Jaglon and the Tiger Fairies, illustrated by Dale Ulrey.   Chicago, Reilly and Lee, 1953.

A Kidnapped Santa Claus.   Indianapolis, Bobbs Merrill, 1961.

Plays

The Wizard, music by Paul Tietjens, lyrics by Baum, adaptation of the story by Baum (produced Chicago, 1902; revised version, as *There Is Something New under the Sun*, produced New York, 1903).

The Woggle-Bug (produced Chicago, 1905).

The Tik-Tok Man of Oz, music by Louis F. Gottschalk, adaptation of the story by Baum (produced Los Angeles, 1913).

Verse

By the Candelabra's Glare, illustrated by W. W. Denslow. Chicago, privately printed, 1898.

Father Goose, His Book, illustrated by W. W. Denslow. Chicago, George M. Hill, and London, Werner, 1899.

The Army Alphabet, illustrated by Harry Kennedy. Chicago, George M. Hill, 1900.

The Navy Alphabet, illustrated by Harry Kennedy. Chicago, George M. Hill, 1900.

The Songs of Father Goose, music by Alberta N. Hall, illustrated by W. W. Denslow. Chicago, George M. Hill, 1900.

Father Goose's Year Book: Quaint Quacks and Feathery Shafts for Mature Children, illustrated by Walter Enright. Chicago, Reilly and Britton, 1907.

Other

Mother Goose in Prose, illustrated by Maxfield Parrish. Chicago, Way and Williams, 1897; London, Duckworth, 1899.

American Fairy Tales, illustrated by Ike Morgan and others. Chicago, George M. Hill, 1901; augmented edition, Indianapolis, Bobbs Merrill, 1908.

L. Frank Baum's Juvenile Speaker (miscellany), illustrated by John R. Neill and others. Chicago, Reilly and Britton, 1910; as Baum's Own Book for Children, 1912.

PUBLICATIONS FOR ADULTS

Novels

The Fate of a Crown (as Schuyler Staunton). Chicago, Reilly and Britton, and London, Revell, 1905.

Daughters of Destiny (as Schuyler Staunton). Chicago, Reilly and Britton, 1906.

Tamawaca Folks (as John Estes Cooke). Macatawa, Michigan, Macatawa Press, 1907.

The Last Egyptian (published anonymously). Philadelphia, Stern, and London, Sisley, 1908.

Plays

The Maid of Arran, music and lyrics by Baum, adaptation of the novel A Princess of Thule by William Black (also director: produced Gilmore, Pennsylvania, 1881; New York, 1882).

Kilmourne (produced Syracuse, New York, 1884).

Matches (produced, 1885).

The Uplift of Lucifer, and other Uplift plays (produced Los Angeles).

Other

The Book of the Hamburgs: A Brief Treatise upon the Mating, Rearing and Management of the Different Varieties of Hamburgs. Hartford, Connecticut, Stoddard, 1886.

The Art of Decorating Dry Goods Windows and Interiors. Chicago, Show Window Publishing Company, 1900.

Our Landlady (Saturday Pioneer columns). Mitchell, South Dakota Writers' Project, 1941.

Critical Studies: The Wizard of Oz and Who He Was edited by Russel Nye and Martin Gardner, East Lansing, Michigan State University Press, 1957; Wonderful Wizard Marvelous Land by Raylyn Moore, Bowling Green, Ohio, Bowling Green State University Press, 1974.

*   *   *

I am not sure, at this late date in life, whether the average reader five or six years old considers the author of a book and the book itself as equal, or anything like equal, in importance. It seems to me now that at six I was but vaguely aware of a writer named L. Frank Baum. It was Dorothy, the Scarecrow, the Tin Woodman, the Saw-Horse, Jack Pumpkinhead, Tip, Ozma of Oz, or Toto and a few special other characters and friends who really mattered. Certainly the man who drew the wondrous pictures mattered. He was John R. Neill, brother of the registered nurse looking after my mother's elderly aunt who had mislaid her brilliant mind and spoke, whenever she did speak, in nonsense snatches of English, German, and French: a dear and Ozlike character in herself. And John R. Neill, because he signed and gave me several of the early Oz books, seemed to me quite capable of having written them himself without Mr. Baum's assistance. Mr. Neill illustrated thirteen of Baum's Oz volumes, beginning with the second. The all-important first one – *The Wizard of Oz* – carried the now-famous drawings of W. W. Denslow.

Mr. Denslow in 1899 had illustrated Baum's second venture in the book world: a commercial if not precisely a literary success called *Father Goose: His Book*. This forgotten item, the *Dictionary of American Biography* informs me – calling it Baum's first, which it was not – sold 90,000 copies in ninety days, an achievement comparable to the English sale of Sir John Betjeman's collected poems just fifty-nine years later.

Many Oz readers no longer young would surely agree that the John R. Neill drawings, which never fail to honor in skill, concept, and extension the classic Denslow originals, bear the same relation to Frank Baum's prose as the work of Tenniel does to *Alice*, Shepard to Milne, Garth Williams to *Miss Bianca* as well as to E. B. White's *Stuart Little* and *Charlotte's Web*. To some Oz readers, as surely to me, they (along with the somewhat more formal Denslows) are not only inseparable, *they are books in themselves*; they evoke the words on the page even as they translate them into action. And the Land of Oz remains, in very large part because of Denslow's and Neill's visual imagination, the most famous Never-Never Land created by an American author.

And in the present era of ever-increasing global violence, it is possibly all the more surprising and welcome (compared with TV and the comics, for example) as a place devoid of bloodshed. Baum offers Oz to all who read him as a world of perpetual wonder: no more, no less. If the Tin Woodman has to destroy a pack of wolves, he does it with his ax: "They all lay dead in a heap." But there is no picture of the heap; no gory mess; nothing but these simple words. Neither is death treated as a comic ending as in the plunges and explosions in the old animated films. Quite the opposite: in Oz dead things (like the Saw horse) come alive.

Young Dorothy of Kansas, consistently (and always by strange chance) a visitor to Oz, is the dominant character in the best books of the series. She shares with us on page after page her excitement, dangers, threats, surprises, mishaps, weird adventures, and the love (not just affection) which she bestows on her adopted companions. The reader likewise is *her* friend: he or she is *admitted* rather than invited to the Land of Oz, a sacred place; and he or she had better walk with open eyes. Apart from the earth-born Wizard himself, Dorothy remains the only living link between here and there. Her Uncle Henry's and Aunt Em's farm in Kansas has a cyclone cellar – standard equipment in Kansas – which is quite enough to suggest that Dorothy is a highly transportable character when the wind is up and the chips are down. In *The Wizard* she and her dog Toto and the house itself are blown straight into the Land of Oz. But, like the venturesome children in the Narnia Chronicles or in some of E. Nesbit's stories, she naturally (or unnaturally) has other means of travel than the wind at her disposal. Oz may be reached, for example, by some lucky storm at sea (as in *Ozma of Oz*) during which she rides a chickencoop swept from the deck of the ship. Inside the coop is Billina, a very wise old assertive talking hen – a yellow hen, since yellow and green are the Master's favorite colors. The shore upon which they are finally washed in safety and good condition is not, of course, the land one expects. But the Land of Ev is separated from the Land of Oz by nothing worse than a magically crossable desert.

As to that: by means of silver shoes, a magic belt, or other methods of teleport, young Dorothy always returns to her home and her never despairing Aunt Em and Uncle Henry at the end of each story, just as C. S. Lewis's children slip back into England through the wardrobe, attic, or whatever. And Time, unsurprisingly, tends to telescope as in some of H. G. Wells's and J. B. Priestley's writing, so that even in a lengthy visit to Oz little time on Earth is actually lost.

If Baum lacks the poetic style of Carroll, Nesbit, and Lewis, he managed a highly satisfactory style of his own; and once he has set his reader down on the enchanted surface of Oz, his creatures speak most naturally, like Rat and Mole in *The Wind in the Willows*, and not with any trace of foreign, feigned, or tricky accent in the manner of Pooh, Piglet, Donald Duck, or philosophic Snoopy. Dorothy, it is true, *does* speak at times like the little girl she is: "prob'ly," "b'lieve," "immedi'tly," " 'cause," "ign'rant." " 'spected," " 'zactly." But she doesn't do it consistently; never in order to be funny. The other characters can be funny.

"The Scarecrow sat upon the Lion's back, and the big beast walked to the edge of the gulf and crouched down. 'Why don't you run and jump?' asked the Scarecrow. 'Because that isn't the way we Lions do things,' he replied." This, in total simplicity, is the way we expect the animals of E. B. White to talk. With Baum, it is a tiny interlude of humor; and yet it does flash in our mind.

Baum has his own sly way speech, and a truly Lear-like gift with proper names. His Oz books are filled with them: Wheelers, Scoodlers, Munchkins, Glinda, Kalidahs, Buttonsbright, Skeezers, the Quadlings, Ugu, Gaylette, Ozma, Inga, Ork, Quelala. And outside the Oz continuum Baum delights in *Rinkitink, The Magical Monarch of Mo, Queen Zixie of Ix*. Also *pastoria* – possibly the corruption of the name of a popular medicine of the time. It seems to me that Lear, Swift, Carroll, and even Kipling move, however vaguely, in the background of all this; but they are English, and Baum was South Dakota, Chicago, America. As much as any of his peers or predecessors, in nonsense he proved himself an original. Some of his words – created, borrowed, or shrewdly used (like *gump*) – have stuck in the language. Oz itself is just as real today as Eden, Utopia, or Erewhon. For example, *The Illustrated London News* (December 1976) referred to "Project Ozma" of 1960, involving the powerful radiotelescope at Green Bank, West Virginia, in an attempt to identify any transmissions from the systems of two particular stars in outer space eleven light-years away.

Baum's thirty other books for children, written under two pseudonyms – one masculine, one feminine – have suffered no conflicts with oblivion. Nor is it pertinent here to discuss the continuation of the Oz book series, after Baum's death in 1919, by Ruth Plumly Thompson (nineteen of them); three by John R. Neill; two by Jack Snow; one by Rachel Cosgrove; one by Baum's son, Colonel Frank Joslyn Baum. A grand total, including the authentic ones, of forty!

But only Baum himself *is* Oz, as I have tried to show in the following verse, written in 1965 (from *All Day Long*, 1966, by permission of Little, Brown & Co., the publishers):

OZ

Is Oz?
Oz was.
I knew it well.
Is Oz?
Dear Land! It cast a spell
on me that I'm not over yet.
Can you imagine I'd forget
the Wizard? Could my mind erase
Tin Woodman, Dorothy? Misplace
Jack Pumpkinhead, the Scarecrow, Tip?
The Saw-Horse, Gump, Billina? Skip
the Cowardly Lion? I guess not!
Would Tiktok tick if one forgot
the Nome King? What would Scarecrow
do to me if I'd not tell you who
was H. M. Woggle-Bug, T. E.?
His letters still spell THEM to me.

THEM isn't all that they imply:
H.M.T.E. *is* THEM, though. Try
H (2) M(4) T(1) and E,
you'll find, just must be – oh, yes, (3).
And then there's Ozma who, of course,
was – that's a secret. Funny! Force
of habit makes me say these things.
The Wheelers? Did they fly with wings?
They rolled on wheels. The Scoodlers? Should
I blurt out *everything?* I could.
This Ozman (which I am) still keeps
his hat on even while he sleeps,
for who can say in Oz what's next?
It doesn't do to tax the text.
Just keep on going, book through book:
In Oz you see before you look.
In Oz you wake before you dream,

in Oz you're never what you seem,   Is Oz then? Yes, yes, three times yes!
in Oz you do before you dare.   *Is Oz?*
In Oz — but maybe you've been there?   You *know* it is, don't you?
A lot of people have, I guess.   I hoped you did.
                                            I thought you do.

—David McCord

BAWDEN, Nina. British. Born in London, 19 January 1925. Educated at Somerville College, Oxford, B.A. 1946, M.A. 1951; Salzburg Seminar in American Studies, 1960. Married H.W. Bawden in 1946; A.S. Kark, 1954; has three children. Since 1969, Justice of the Peace for Surrey. Member, P.E.N. Executive Committee, 1968–71. Recipient: *Guardian* Award, 1976. Fellow, Royal Society of Literature, 1970. Address: 22 Noel Road, London N1 8HA, England.

PUBLICATIONS FOR CHILDREN

Fiction

Devil by the Sea. London, Collins, and Philadelphia, Lippincott, 1957.
The Secret Passage. London, Gollancz, 1963; as *The House of Secrets*, Philadelphia, Lippincott, 1964.
On the Run. London, Gollancz, 1964; as *Three on the Run*, Philadelphia, Lippincott, 1965.
The White Horse Gang. London, Gollancz, and Philadelphia, Lippincott, 1966.
The Witch's Daughter, illustrated by Shirley Hughes. London, Gollancz, and Philadelphia, Lippincott, 1966.
A Handful of Thieves. London, Gollancz, and Philadelphia, Lippincott, 1967.
The Runaway Summer. London, Gollancz, and Philadelphia, Lippincott, 1969.
Squib, illustrated by Shirley Hughes. London, Gollancz, and Philadelphia, Lippincott, 1971.
Carrie's War. London, Gollancz, and Philadelphia, Lippincott, 1973.
The Peppermint Pig, illustrated by Alexy Pendle. London, Gollancz, and Philadelphia, Lippincott, 1975.

PUBLICATIONS FOR ADULTS

Novels

Who Calls the Tune. London, Collins, 1953; as *Eyes of Green*, New York, Morrow, 1953.
The Odd Flamingo. London, Collins, 1954.
Change Here for Babylon. London, Collins, 1955.
The Solitary Child. London, Collins, 1956.
Just Like a Lady. London, Longman, 1960; as *Glass Slippers Always Pinch*, Philadelphia, Lippincott, 1960.
In Honour Bound. London, Longman, 1961.
Tortoise by Candlelight. London, Longman, and New York, Harper, 1963.
Under the Skin. London, Longman, and New York, Harper, 1964.
A Little Love, A Little Learning. London, Longman, and New York, Harper, 1966.

A Woman of My Age.   London, Longman, and New York, Harper, 1967.
The Grain of Truth.   London, Longman, and New York, Harper, 1968.
The Birds on the Trees.   London, Longman, 1970; New York, Harper, 1971.
Anna Apparent.   London, Longman, and New York, Harper, 1972.
George Beneath a Paper Moon.   London, Allen Lane, and New York, Harper, 1974.
Afternoon of a Good Woman.   London, Macmillan, and New York, Harper, 1976.

Nina Bawden comments:
I consider my books for children as important as my adult work, and in some ways more challenging.

*   *   *

Nina Bawden is one of the very few children's authors who will admit to making a conscious adjustment to writing for children. In her early books for young readers, one can well imagine she paced a deliberate distance from the adult novels which she also writes. Perhaps because she also writes for adults she is singularly free from the temptation to write for adults on the children's list.

Miss Bawden's early children's books have been called "not always probable accounts of contemporary life." Summaries of her plots would make her seem like a writer very different from the one she is. The jewel thieves in *The Witch's Daughter*, the children-catch-villains theme of *A Handful of Thieves*, the Prime Minister's son saved from political kidnapping in *On the Run*, are typical examples. They might seem like the kinds of escapist reading that children readily like and that many lesser writers offer them. But Miss Bawden is a subtle writer, who plays her themes with a difference. In *The Witch's Daughter*, one of the children is blind; there is a spectacular account of an escape from a cave, led by the blind girl, who can find her way out through the darkness, but stumbles and is lost at the very moment when light from outside can be seen, and the others run triumphantly forwards. The Prime Minister's son comes not from Ruritania, but modern Africa; another of Miss Bawden's runaways is an illegal Pakistani immigrant.

More profound still is the difference made by the characterisation to Miss Bawden's stories. Her children may do improbable things, but they never think, feel, or say unchildlike or improbable things. Their preoccupations, ideas, hopes, and fears, their relationships with each other and with the adults around them, their weaknesses and faults as well as their basic innocent courage and goodwill are entirely realistic and believable. This is childhood seen with particular clarity.

There is also a very distinctive tone to Miss Bawden's sympathy – a particular tenderness for children having a tough time and for not very likeable children. Mary in *The Runaway Summer* is a good example. Lonely and miserable because her parents are getting divorced, she is beastly to her kind aunt, and even steals sweets, yet we never lose sympathy for her.

It is this element in Miss Bawden's outlook that comes into full prominence with *Squib*, the story of a grossly neglected child. There are brilliant insights in this book – especially the pathetic muddle of half-baked fears (of walking in the wood, of witches) which overlie the awful knowledge that Squib has been shackled in a laundry basket and simply confuse the children about what is reality and what is not, so that they hardly know if they are playing or really rescuing a real victim. However, there is also a good deal of the apparatus of adventure, that had been so strong an element in Miss Bawden's work so far – a burning tower, a disastrous raid on Squib's caravan, and so to a happy ending that involves bringing in the adults to get things right. The emotional tone of this uncomplicated complication sits rather uneasily with the real subject of Squib – the compassion and fear of a little girl, the courage of a little boy, and the suffering of Squib himself.

With the appearance of *Carrie's War*, it became plain that *Squib* had been a transitional book. *Carrie's War* is an enormous step forwards. Carrie and her brother are evacuees in a Welsh village with a narrow, bigoted shopkeeper and his kindly though brow-beaten sister.

They would have been miserable without the friendship of other villagers, especially Hebibah, who fed them love, food and stories. Once more the plot concerns the precarious hold on reality of a child's imaginings. Convinced by Hebibah's tales Carrie comes to believe that she had committed a dreadful crime, and she carries the load of guilt and grief into adult life. Only when she brings her own children back to the village can the truth emerge and all be made well again. In this book we have dispensed with the drama of external situations – there are no crooks, no villains but Carrie's own guilty fears. In a notable shift of feeling, Carrie reaches a glimpse of sympathy and understanding even for the horrible tyrant Mr. Evans. There is a portrait of a whole community of people, their oddities and their feuds, seen through the bemused and only half understanding eyes of childhood. In this profound and affectionate book one has a sense of Miss Bawden putting out her full strength as a writer as never before, and finding a way of writing with full complexity and delicacy still within the reach of children. Carrie's very partial understanding is the mainspring of the plot; yet Carrie is loving and trusting. And in important ways Miss Bawden truly shows that the happy ending is not just a deferment to children as readers but a fully justified resolution.

The Peppermint Pig is a perfect, small masterpiece about the sojourn in a country village of an Edwardian family. The true subject is the painful relationship of happiness, hope, and the inexorable passing of time. This is delicately explored in the reactions of the children to their changed circumstances, the absence of their adored father, and, above all, the death of Johnny the pet pig, whose end is inevitable. This is a charming and profound book.

Great though the development of Miss Bawden's talent has been, and large though the difference is between *The Secret Passage* and *The Peppermint Pig*, it can be said of all her work that more than any other contemporary writer for the young, she understands and respects the childhood of her readers as well as that of her characters.

—Jill Paton Walsh

BEACHCROFT, Nina. British. Born in London, 10 November 1931; daughter of the writer T.O. Beachcroft. Educated at Wimbledon High School; St. Hilda's College, Oxford, 1950–53, B.A. (honours) in English. Married Richard Gardner in 1954; has two daughters. Sub-editor, *Argosy*, London, 1953–55, and *Radio Times*, London, 1955–57. Agent: David Higham Associates Ltd., 5–8 Lower John Street, London W1R 4HA. Address: The Cottage, Datchworth Green, Knebworth, Hertfordshire, England.

PUBLICATIONS FOR CHILDREN

Fiction

Well Met by Witchlight. London, Heinemann, 1972; New York, Atheneum, 1973.
Under the Enchanter. London, Heinemann, 1974.
Cold Christmas: A Ghost Story. London, Heinemann, 1974.
A Spell of Sleep. London, Heinemann, 1976.
A Visit to Folly Castle. London, Heinemann, 1977.

Nina Beachcroft comments:

I have written, on and off, for most of my life. I wrote short stories, of which a few were published, until I worked on a short story magazine, when reading too many soon killed the urge to write them. I wrote two long unpublished (and unpublishable) adult novels, and it was not until my first daughter was about eight that I thought of trying something for children. I wrote three before I eventually got *Well Met by Witchlight* accepted by Heinemann. In trying very hard to please children, I found I was pleasing myself. I enjoy writing fantasy; fairy tales have always appealed to me, as has the best kind of science fiction. It's the imaginative idea behind the story that gets me off the ground; after that, my concern is, I suppose, to work it out in some of its implications and to tell a fast-moving, exciting story, always with its feet in everyday reality even if its head is in the clouds.

*   *   *

Nina Beachcroft's novels are concerned with kinds of enchantment and with the persistent interaction of the past and the present. Her capacity for social observation and humorous detachment was apparent from the beginning; but it was not until the publication of *Under the Enchanter* that her approach could be called truly original. The earlier *Well Met by Witchlight*, for all its skill and exuberance, is merely a conventional tale of broomstick magic.

Under the Enchanter is set in the north of England, and the bleak quality of the landscape is evoked with precision. The plot is straightforward. The Hearsts have rented a holiday farmhouse which contains, unknown to them, an Elizabethan necromancer. His appearance is the result of a night of incautious sorcery on the part of former tenants. "Mr. Strange" inhabits a loft and appears to outsiders to be an old tramp. His real nature is revealed only to the fascinated children. Laura is able to resist his attempt at enchantment, but Andrew succumbs. At this point a new emotion enters the story: the frustration of the child brought face-to-face with adult obtuseness. Laura's parents *won't* see that there is anything wrong with Andrew. It is left to his sister to hold him back from the destruction that "Mr. Strange" has planned.

This novel makes effective use of the contrast between 20th-century behaviour and attitudes and the ominous, intrusive presence of age-old forces. Unlike a great many stories of the supernatural it is neither high-flown nor sententious. Its style is impressively restrained. In *Cold Christmas*, too, the uncanny element is enhanced by the author's ironic realism. Like most good ghost stories it has a prosaic location. Josephine and her parents are invited to spend Christmas with a group of television actors and directors and their wives and obstreperous children. The predominant mood is one of tension: incompatibilities between the generations which usually are played down in children's books are made plain in this one. As the grown-ups veer between jocularity and irritation, the children themselves – particularly the heroine – are resentful, fractious and ill-at-ease – but never boring or unconvincing.

Margaret, the child-ghost, is wholly benevolent; but there are deadly undercurrents at work at the house, Cold Christmas. The moment of denouement, or disillusion, is a moment of shock that is to be savoured for the economy of its effect. A treasure-hunt leads to the discovery of part of a human skeleton: the bones that are the starting-off point for every "ghost."

A Spell of Sleep is fantasy on a more homely level: it follows the line of a fairy story where the hero is forced to use his wits to break the enchantment. Again, the present-day context gives a special richness to the use of a formal literary mode. The underlying destructive force in this story is malice, not evil: its protagonists are a couple of bad neighbours who survive for eight hundred years. As usual, Nina Beachcroft provides a satisfactory moral resolution without sacrificing credibility or imaginative vigour.

—Patricia Craig

BEATTY, John (Louis). American. Born in Portland, Oregon, 24 January 1922. Educated at Reed College, Portland, B.A. 1943; Stanford University, California, M.A. 1947;

University of Washington, Seattle, Ph.D. in history 1953. Served in the United States Army 1943–45: Silver Star, Purple Heart. Married Patricia Robbins (i.e., Patricia Beatty, *q.v.*) in 1950; one daughter. Instructor, Reed College, 1947–49, University of Washington, 1950–52, and University of Delaware, Newark, 1952–53; Assistant Professor, 1953–59, Associate Professor, 1959–75, and Professor of History, 1975, University of California, Riverside. Recipient: American Philosophical Society grant, 1959. *Died 23 March 1975.*

PUBLICATIONS FOR CHILDREN (with Patricia Beatty)

Fiction

> *At the Seven Stars*, illustrated by Douglas Gorsline.   New York, Macmillan, 1963; London, Chatto and Windus, 1966.
> *Campion Towers*.   New York, Macmillan, 1965; London, Chatto and Windus, 1967.
> *A Donkey for the King*, illustrated by Ann Siberell.   New York, Macmillan, 1966.
> *The Royal Dirk*, illustrated by Franz Altschuler.   New York, Morrow, 1966.
> *The Queen's Wizard*.   New York, Macmillan, 1967.
> *Witch Dog*, illustrated by Franz Altschuler.   New York, Morrow, 1968.
> *Pirate Royal*.   New York, Macmillan, and London, Collier Macmillan, 1969.
> *King's Knight's Pawn*.   New York, Morrow, 1971.
> *Holdfast*.   New York, Morrow, 1972.
> *Master Rosalind*.   New York, Morrow, 1974.
> *Who Comes to King's Mountain?*   New York, Morrow, 1975.

PUBLICATIONS FOR ADULTS

Other

> *Warwick and Holland, Being the Lives of Robert and Henry Rich*.   Denver, Alan Swallow, 1965.

> Editor, with Oliver A. Johnson, *Heritage of Western Civilization: Select Readings*.   Englewood Cliffs, New Jersey, Prentice Hall, 1958.

*   *   *

See the essay on Patricia Beatty and John Beatty.

BEATTY, Patricia.   American.   Born in Portland, Oregon, 26 August 1922. Educated at Reed College, Portland, B.A. in history and English 1944; University of Idaho, Moscow, 1947–50; University of Washington, Seattle, 1951. Married John Beatty, *q.v.*, in 1950 (died, 1975), one daughter; Carl G. Uhr, 1976. English and history teacher, Coeur d'Alene High School, Idaho, 1947–50; Librarian, E.I. du Pont Company, Wilmington, Delaware, 1952–53, and Riverside Public Library, California, 1953–56; Instructor in Creative Writing, University of California, Riverside, 1967–68, and Los Angeles, 1968–69. Address: 5085 Rockledge Drive, Riverside, California 92506, U.S.A.

PUBLICATIONS FOR CHILDREN

Fiction

Indian Canoe-Maker, illustrated by Barbara Beaudreau. Caldwell, Idaho, Caxton
    Press, 1960.
Bonanza Girl, illustrated by Liz Dauber. New York, Morrow, 1962.
At the Seven Stars, with John Beatty, illustrated by Douglas Gorsline. New York,
    Macmillan, 1963; London, Chatto and Windus, 1966.
The Nickel-Plated Beauty, illustrated by Liz Dauber. New York, Morrow, 1964.
Campion Towers, with John Beatty. New York, Macmillan, 1965; London, Chatto
    and Windus, 1967.
Squaw Dog, illustrated by Franz Altschuler. New York, Morrow, 1965.
A Donkey for the King, with John Beatty, illustrated by Ann Siberell. New York,
    Macmillan, 1966.
The Royal Dirk, with John Beatty, illustrated by Franz Altschuler. New York,
    Morrow, 1966.
The Queen's Own Grove, illustrated by Liz Dauber. New York, Morrow, 1966.
The Queen's Wizard, with John Beatty. New York, Macmillan, 1967.
The Lady from Black Hawk, illustrated by Robert Frankenberg. New York, McGraw
    Hill, 1967.
Witch Dog, with John Beatty, illustrated by Franz Altschuler. New York, Morrow,
    1968.
Me, California Perkins, illustrated by Liz Dauber. New York, Morrow, 1968.
Pirate Royal, with John Beatty. New York, Macmillan, and London, Collier
    Macmillan, 1969.
Blue Stars Watching. New York, Morrow, 1969.
Hail Columbia, illustrated by Liz Dauber. New York, Morrow, 1970.
The Sea Pair, illustrated by Franz Altschuler. New York, Morrow, 1970.
King's Knight's Pawn, with John Beatty. New York, Morrow, 1971.
A Long Way to Whiskey Creek. New York, Morrow, 1971.
Holdfast, with John Beatty. New York, Morrow, 1972.
O the Red Rose Tree, illustrated by Liz Dauber. New York, Morrow, 1972.
The Bad Bell of San Salvador. New York, Morrow, 1973.
Red Rock over the River. New York, Morrow, 1973.
Master Rosalind, with John Beatty. New York, Morrow, 1974.
How Many Miles to Sundown. New York, Morrow, 1974.
Who Comes to King's Mountain?, with John Beatty. New York, Morrow, 1975.
Rufus, Red Rufus, illustrated by Ted Lewin. New York, Morrow, 1975.
By Crumbs, It's Mine! New York, Morrow, 1976.
Something to Shout About. New York, Morrow, 1976.
Billy Bedamned, Long Gone By. New York, Morrow, 1977.
I Want My Sunday, Stranger. New York, Morrow, 1977.

PUBLICATIONS FOR ADULTS

Novels

Station Four. Chicago, Science Research Associates, 1969.
The Englishman's Mistress (as Jean Bartholomew). New York, Dell, 1975.

Manuscript Collection: University of California, Riverside.

Patricia Beatty comments:
    For the most part I write of the historical past for young readers – and not only because of

a personal, loving interest in history. I sense a growing disinterest among people of the English-speaking world in what has gone on before. This seems particularly true of many university students who say openly, "History began yesterday." I try to make the English and American "pasts" come to life in order to convince the 9 to 14 age group that people of the past were real people with real personalities and real problems and not text-book, dry-as-a-bone beings, mummified by time and bloodless footnotes.

*   *   *

"You have much to learn and you must be more bold or you will never be more than a pawn of other men in all your days." This advice, given in *King's Knight's Pawn*, echoes the philosophy embraced by John and Patricia Beatty in their novels of bold, resourceful girls and boys caught up in the sweep of historical events. In *Campion Towers*, an excellent adventure story, the headstrong nature of Penitence, the impoverished Puritan from Massachusetts, gets her embroiled in the English Civil War after she arrives in England to visit her dying grandmother and to collect her inheritance. In *The Royal Dirk*, another fine work filled with intrigue and suspense, Alan Macrae aids Bonnie Prince Charlie to flee the Scottish Highlands. Politics and danger are Alan's companions during his sojourn in eighteenth-century London. Young people will be captivated by *Master Rosalind*, the tale of a pastor's granddaughter who masquerades as a boy and joins the Globe Players after an unsuccessful stint as a London rogue. It is fast-moving story of a girl who rebels at the limitations placed on her being female.

The bulk of the work by the two Beattys focuses on well-researched British history, but when Patricia Beatty writes alone, she deals primarily with women's rights, the Old West, and American Indians. *Hail Columbia* is the best of her books which are concerned with the women's rights theme. Columbia, a late nineteenth-century suffragist, visits her brother's family in Oregon after a long absence. Her brother has rigid ideas of a woman's place, but his sister audaciously disputes his sexism. The town and Columbia's niece will never be the same after the fiery woman's infusion of feminist theory. In *Something to Shout About*, Hope Foster narrates an exciting and humorous chapter in the history of a new town in Montana Territory in 1875. Hope leads the women in using their wits to get the fledgling school out of a defunct, odorous chicken-coop and into a respectable building. Drawing on the expertise of a lawyer, reporter, teacher – all women – and a woman doctor disguised as a man, Hope and the town mothers achieve a sweet victory. The formula of bold girls mixed together with the Old West does not always result in success as evidenced by *Red Rock over the River* and *By Crumbs, It's Mine!* both of which move along at an undramatic pace, despite the presence of promising characters.

The Sea Pair is a departure from the others mentioned here. A woman from New York City comes to teach at a Washington reservation school and makes a profound impact on an embittered, young Indian boy. It is a revealing story of Indian life, its hardships and its deadends. Patricia Beatty's solo writing does not contain the same quality of well-laid plot construction and intricate detail as when she collaborated with her late husband. In spite of this, her subject matter usually carries the story along successfully.

—Vivian J. Scheinmann

BEHN, Harry. American. Born in Prescott, Arizona, 24 September 1898. Educated at Stanford University, California, 1918; Harvard University, Cambridge, Massachusetts, B.S. 1922. Married Alice Lawrence in 1925; one daughter and two sons. Scenario Writer, Metro-Goldwyn-Mayer, Twentieth-Century Fox, and Universal studios, Hollywood, 1925–35; Professor of Creative Writing, University of Arizona, Tucson, 1938–47. Founding Director,

Phoenix Little Theatre, 1922–23; Vice President, Tucson Regional Plan, 1940–47; Founding Editor, *Arizona Quarterly*, Tucson, 1942–47. Recipient: George G. Stone Center for Children's Books award, 1965. *Died 6 September 1973.*

PUBLICATIONS FOR CHILDREN

Fiction

    The Painted Cave, illustrated by the author.   New York, Harcourt Brace, 1957.
    Timmy's Search, illustrated by Barbara Cooney.   Greenwich, Connecticut, Seabury Press, 1958.
    The Two Uncles of Pablo, illustrated by Mel Silverman.   New York, Harcourt Brace, 1959; London, Macmillan, 1960.
    Roderick, illustrated by Mel Silverman.   New York, Harcourt Brace, 1961.
    The Faraway Lurs, illustrated by the author.   Cleveland, World, 1963; as *The Distant Lurs*, London, Gollancz, 1965.
    Omen of the Birds, illustrated by the author.   Cleveland, World, 1964; London, Gollancz, 1965.

Verse (illustrated by the author)

    The Little Hill: Poems and Pictures.   New York, Harcourt Brace, 1949.
    All Kinds of Time.   New York, Harcourt Brace, 1950.
    Windy Morning: Poems and Pictures.   New York, Harcourt Brace, 1953.
    The House Beyond the Meadow.   New York, Pantheon Books, 1955.
    The Wizard in the Well: Poems and Pictures.   New York, Harcourt Brace, 1956.
    The Golden Hive: Poems and Pictures.   New York, Harcourt Brace, 1966.
    What a Beautiful Noise, illustrated by Harold Berson.   New York, World, 1970.

Other

    Translator, *Cricket Songs: Japanese Haiku.*   New York, Harcourt Brace, 1964.
    Translator, *More Cricket Songs: Japanese Haiku.*   New York, Harcourt Brace, 1971.

PUBLICATIONS FOR ADULTS

Verse

    Siesta.   Phoenix, Golden Bough Press, 1931.
    The Grand Canyon.   Los Angeles, privately printed, 1935.
    Sombra.   Copenhagen, Christreu, 1961.

Other

    Chrysalis: Concerning Children and Poetry.   New York, Harcourt Brace, 1968.

    Translator, *The Duino Elegies*, by Rainer Maria Rilke.   Mount Vernon, New York, Peter Pauper Press, 1957.
    Translator, with Peter Beilenson, *Haiku Harvest.*   Mount Vernon, New York, Peter Pauper Press, 1962.

Manuscript Collections: Kerlan Collection, University of Minnesota, Minneapolis; University of Oregon Library, Eugene.

*   *   *

It is a fascinating and far-flung legacy which Harry Behn has left to the child-reader and to those interested in literature for children, characterized, perhaps, by his own words, "Innocence is hardly more than a willingness to wonder." How unusual it is to think of Harry as a man of innocence – born in Arizona when it was still a territory, educated at Harvard and world-traveled! And yet it is the right phrase, for his willingness to wonder and wander, his enthusiasms and curiosity moved within a changing world which he persisted in viewing, most often, through the eyes of the innocent.

His books, ranging from the child's poetic voice of *Windy Morning* through stories and novels and further poetry as well as translation of haiku, carry a thread of transcendentalism; it is the Indian Earth-Mother, the gods of the Sun People, the god Aplu, the rising of the sun, the "almost imperceptible experience of wonder, removed from knowledge." "When a child," he wrote in *Chrysalis*, "sees his first butterfly and becomes himself a flying flower, such innocence has in it more reality than any however heroic whiz around the planet." So it was that the language of a bug, a chicken, a crow, a storm, rain, or train could spell-bind him into poem or prose-making.

Like Walter de la Mare, he found elves and wizards, fairies and magical beings of whom to write; like Robert Louis Stevenson he became the child speaking in "Swing Song" or "Pirates." Yet his was an American heritage, rooted in world history. *All Kinds of Time* clearly expressed that "Seconds are bugs/minutes are children/hours are people/days are postmen/weeks are Sunday School/months are/north/south/east/west/and in between/ seasons are/wild flowers/tame flowers/golden leaves/and snow/years are/Santa Claus/ centuries are/George/Washington/and forever is God." This, and the poems within his other books of poetry for children are those of an American child and his particular wonder: "Tell me, tell me everything!/What makes it Winter/And then Spring?" he asks through the child in "Curiosity." Yet, the series of questions of the poem end with his own continuing questions, "Tell me! or don't even grown-ups know?" This search, therefore, led him on; it was not unusual that because of his love for seasons and simplicity he should turn to the translation of Japanese haiku, that he should examine the life of a crow in *Roderick* or Dawn Boy, the Indian, in *The Painted Cave*; that his mother's childhood in Denmark should inspire him to write *The Faraway Lurs* or that his questioning of the correlation between Etruscan and American civilization spun itself out in *Omen of the Birds*.

Poetry, he wrote, "must be presented with careful incompleteness of information." Incompletion thus sustains curiosity; information is not a *raison d'être* for the poet, and "willingness to wonder" is Harry Behn's unique contribution to children's literature.

—Myra Cohn Livingston

BELLOC, (Joseph) Hilaire (Pierre).   British.   Born in St. Cloud, France, 27 July 1870; naturalized British subject, 1902. Educated at Oratory School, Edgbaston; Balliol College Oxford (Brackenbury History Scholar), 1892–95, B.A. in history 1895. Served in the 10th Battery of the 8th Regiment of Artillery of the French Army, 1891. Married Elodie Agnes Hogan in 1896 (died, 1914); three sons, two daughters. Liberal Member of Parliament for South Salford, 1906–10. Head of the English Department, East London College. LL.D.: Glasgow University, 1902. Knight Commander with Star, Order of St. Gregory the Great, 1934. *Died 16 July 1953.*

PUBLICATIONS FOR CHILDREN

Verse

   The Bad Child's Book of Beasts: Verses, illustrated by Basil Blackwood.   Oxford, Alden, and New York, Dutton, 1896.

More Beasts (for Worse Children): Verses, illustrated by Basil Blackwood.   London and
New York, Arnold, 1897.

*Cautionary Tales for Children: Designed for the Admonition of Children Between the
Ages of Eight and Fourteen Years: Verses*, illustrated by Basil Blackwood.   London,
Eveleigh Nash, 1907; New York, Knopf, 1922.

New Cautionary Tales: Verses, illustrated by Nicolas Bentley.   London, Duckworth,
1930; New York, Harper, 1931.

Cautionary Verses: The Collected Humorous Poems of Hilaire Belloc.   London,
Duckworth, 1939; New York, Knopf, 1941.

Selected Cautionary Verses.   London, Duckworth, 1940.

PUBLICATIONS FOR ADULTS

Novels

Emmanuel Burden, Merchant ....   London, Methuen, 1904; New York, Scribner,
1915.

Mr. Clutterbuck's Election.   London, Eveleigh Nash, 1908.

A Change in the Cabinet.   London, Methuen, 1909.

Pongo and the Bull.   London, Constable, 1910.

The Girondin.   London, Nelson, 1911; New York, Doubleday, 1912.

The Green Overcoat.   Bristol, Arrowsmith, and New York, McBride, 1912.

The Mercy of Allah.   London, Chatto and Windus, and New York, Appleton, 1922.

Mr. Petre.   London, Arrowsmith, and New York, McBride, 1925.

The Emerald of Catherine the Great.   London, Arrowsmith, and New York, Harper,
1926.

The Haunted House.   London, Arrowsmith, 1927; New York, Harper, 1928.

But Soft — We Are Observed!   London, Arrowsmith, 1928; as *Shadowed!*, New York,
Harper, 1929.

Belinda: A Tale of Affection in Youth and Age.   London, Constable, 1928; New York,
Harper, 1929.

The Missing Masterpiece.   London, Arrowsmith, and New York, Harper, 1929.

The Man Who Made Gold.   London, Arrowsmith, 1930; New York, Harper, 1931.

The Postmaster-General.   London, Arrowsmith, and Philadelphia, Lippincott, 1932.

The Hedge and the Horse.   London, Cassell, 1936.

Verse

Verses and Sonnets.   London, Ward and Downey, 1896.

The Modern Traveller.   London, Arnold, 1898; New York, Knopf, 1923.

A Moral Alphabet.   London, Arnold, 1899.

Verses.   London, Duckworth, 1910.

Verses.   New York, L. J. Gomme, 1916.

Sonnets and Verse.   London, Duckworth, 1923; New York, McBride, 1924; revised
edition, Duckworth, 1938.

(Selected Poems).   London, Benn, 1925.

The Praise of Wine: An Heroic Poem.   London, privately printed, 1931.

Ladies and Gentlemen: For Adults Only and Mature at That: Verses.   London,
Duckworth, 1932.

Songs of the South Country.   London, Duckworth, 1951.

The Verse of Hilaire Belloc, edited by W. N. Roughead.   London, Nonesuch Press,
1954.

Collected Verse.   London, Penguin, 1958.

Complete Verse, edited by W. N. Roughead.   London, Duckworth, 1970.

Other

Danton: A Study.   London, Nisbet, and New York, Scribner, 1899.

Lambkin's Remains.   Oxford, Simpkin, and New York, M. F. Mansfield, 1900.

Paris.   London, Arnold, 1900; New York, Scribner, 1907.

Robespierre: A Study.   London, Nisbet, and New York, Scribner, 1901.

The Path to Rome.   London, George Allen, and New York, Longman, 1902.

The Aftermath; or, Gleanings from a Busy Life, Called upon the Outer Cover, for Purposes of Sale, Caliban's Guide to Letters.   London, Duckworth, and New York, Dutton, 1903.

The Great Inquiry (Only Authorised Version) Faithfully Reported.   London, Duckworth, 1903.

The Old Road.   London, Constable, 1904; Philadelphia, Lippincott, 1911.

Avril, Being Essays on the Poetry of the French Renaissance.   London, Duckworth, and New York, Dutton, 1904.

An Open Letter on the Decay of Faith.   London, Burns and Oates, 1906.

Esto Perpetua: Algerian Studies and Impressions.   London, Duckworth, 1906; New York, McBride, 1925.

Sussex, Painted by Wilfrid Ball.   London, A. and C. Black, 1906; revised edition, as *The County of Sussex*, London, Cassell, 1936.

Hills and the Sea.   London, Methuen, and New York, Scribner, 1906.

The Historic Thames.   London, Dent, and New York, Dutton, 1907.

The Eye-Witness (incidents in history).   London, Eveleigh Nash, and New York, Kings Treasuries of Literature, 1908.

The Catholic Church and Historical Truth (lecture).   Preston, Lancashire, W. Watson, 1908.

On Nothing and Kindred Subjects.   London, Methuen, 1908; New York, Dutton, 1909.

An Examination of Socialism.   London, Catholic Truth Society, 1908.

The Pyrenees.   London, Methuen, 1909; New York, Knopf, 1923.

On Everything.   London, Methuen, 1909; New York, Dutton, 1910.

Marie Antoinette.   London, Methuen, and New York, Doubleday, 1909.

The Church and Socialism.   London, Catholic Truth Society, 1910.

The Ferrer Case.   London, Catholic Truth Society, 1910.

The International.   Philadelphia, Dolphin, 1910.

On Anything.   London, Constable, and New York, Dutton, 1910.

On Something.   London, Methuen, 1910; New York, Dutton, 1911.

The Party System, with Cecil Chesterton.   London, Stephen Swift, 1911.

Socialism and the Servile State (debate with J. Ramsay Macdonald).   London, South West London Federation of the Independent Labour Party, 1911.

First and Last.   London, Methuen, 1911; New York, Dutton, 1912.

The French Revolution.   London, Williams and Norgate, and New York, Holt, 1911.

The Battle of Blenheim, Malplaquet, Waterloo, Tourcoing, and *Crecy.*   London, Stephen Swift, 5 vols., 1911–12; revised edition of *Waterloo*, London, Hugh Rees, 1915.

The Four Men: A Farrago.   London, Nelson, and Indianapolis, Bobbs Merrill, 1912.

The River of London.   London, T. N. Foulis, 1912; Boston, Phillip, n.d.

Warfare in England.   London, Williams and Norgate, 1912.

The Servile State.   London, T. N. Foulis, 1912; Boston, Phillip, 1913.

This and That and the Other.   London, Methuen, and New York, Dodd Mead, 1912.

The Battle of Poitiers.   London, Hugh Rees, 1913.

The Stane Street: A Monograph.   London, Constable, and New York, Dutton, 1913.

The Book of the Bayeux Tapestry, Presenting the Complete Work in a Series of Colour Facsimiles.   London, Chatto and Windus, and New York, Putnam, 1914.

The Hilaire Belloc Calendar: A Quotation from the Works of Hilaire Belloc for Everyday in the Year.   London, Frank Palmer, 1913.

Anti-Catholic History: How It Is Written. London, Catholic Truth Society, 1914.

Three Essays. Portland, Maine, Thomas B. Mosher, 1914.

The History of England from the First Invasion by the Romans to the Accession of King George the Fifth (volume 11 only). New York, Catholic Publications Society of America, and London, Sands, 1915.

A General Sketch of the European War: The First and *Second Phase.* London, Nelson, 2 vols., 1915–16; as *The Elements of the Great War*, New York, Hearst, 1915.

A Picked Company, Being a Selection from the Writings of Hilaire Belloc. London, Methuen, 1915.

High Lights of the French Revolution. New York, Century, 1915.

The Two Maps of Europe and Some Other Aspects of the Great War. London, C. Arthur Pearson, 1915.

Land and Water Map of the War and How to Use It. London, Land and Water, 1915.

At the Sign of the Lion and Other Essays. Portland, Maine, Thomas B. Mosher, 1916.

The Last Days of the French Monarchy. London, Chapman and Hall, 1916.

The Second Year of the War. London, Burrup Mathieson and Sprague, 1916.

The Free Press. London, Allen and Unwin, 1918.

Religion and Civil Liberty. London, Catholic Truth Society, 1918.

The House of Commons and Monarchy. London, Allen and Unwin, 1920; New York, Harcourt Brace, 1922.

Europe and the Faith. London, Constable, and New York, Paulist Press, 1920.

Pascal's Provincial Letters. London, Catholic Truth Society, 1921.

Catholic Social Reform Versus Socialism. London, Catholic Truth Society, 1922.

The Jews. London, Constable, and Boston, Houghton Mifflin, 1922.

The Contrast. London, Arrowsmith, 1923; New York, McBride, 1924.

The Road. Manchester, British Reinforced Concrete Engineering Company, and New York, Harper, 1923.

Economics for Helen. London, Arrowsmith, and New York, McBride, 1924; as *Economics for Young People ...*, London and New York, Putnam, 1925.

The Political Effort. London, True Temperance Association, 1924.

The Campaign of 1812 and the Retreat from Moscow. London and New York, Nelson, 1924.

The Cruise of the "Nona." London, Constable, and Boston, Houghton Mifflin, 1925.

England and the Faith. London, Catholic Truth Society, 1925.

A History of England. London, Methuen, and New York, Putnam, 4 vols., 1925–31.

Miniatures of French History. London, Nelson, 1925; New York, Harper, 1926.

Hilaire Belloc (essays). London, Harrap, 1926.

The Highway and Its Vehicles, edited by Geoffrey Holme. London, The Studio, 1926.

Short Talks with the Dead and Others. London, Cayme Press, and New York, Harper, 1926.

Mrs. Markham's New History of England, Being an Introduction for Young People to the Current History and Institutions of Our Times. London, Cayme Press, 1926.

A Companion to Mr. Wells's "Outline of History." London, Sheed and Ward, 1926; San Francisco, Ecclesiastical Supply Association, 1927.

Mr. Belloc Still Objects to Mr. Wells's "Outline of History." London, Sheed and Ward, 1926; San Francisco, Ecclesiastical Supply Association, 1927.

Selected Works. London, Library Press, 9 vols., 1927.

Towns of Destiny. New York, McBride, 1927; as *Many Cities*, London, Constable, 1928.

The Catholic Church and History. London, Burns Oates and Washbourne, and New York, Macmillan, 1927.

Oliver Cromwell. London, Benn, 1927.

James the Second. London, Faber, and Philadelphia, Lippincott, 1928.

How the Reformation Happened. London, Cape, and New York, Dodd Mead, 1928.

A Conversation with an Angel, and Other Essays. London, Cape, 1928; New York,

Harper, 1929.

Joan of Arc.   London, Cassell, and Boston, Little Brown, 1929.

Survival and New Arrivals.   London, Sheed and Ward, and New York, Macmillan, 1929.

Richelieu.   New York, Doubleday, 1929; London, Benn, 1930.

Wolsey.   London, Cassell, and Philadelphia, Lippincott, 1930.

A Pamphlet, July 27th, 1930.   Privately printed, 1930; as *World Conflict,* London, Catholic Truth Society, 1951.

Cranmer.   London, Cassell, 1931; as *Cranmer, Archbishop of Canterbury, 1533–1556,* Philadelphia, Lippincott, 1931.

On Translation (lecture).   Oxford, Clarendon Press, 1931.

Essays of a Catholic Layman in England.   London, Sheed and Ward, 1931; as *Essays of a Catholic,* New York, Macmillan, 1931.

How We Got the Bible.   London, Catholic Truth Society, 1932.

Napoleon.   London, Cassell, and Philadelphia, Lippincott, 1932.

The Question and the Answer.   New York, Bruce, 1932; London, Longman, 1938.

The Tactics and Strategy of the Great Duke of Marlborough.   London, Arrowsmith, 1933.

William the Conqueror.   London, Davies, 1933; New York, Appleton, 1934.

Becket.   London, Catholic Truth Society, 1933.

Charles the First, King of England.   London, Cassell, and Philadelphia, Lippincott, 1933.

Cromwell.   London, Cassell, and Philadelphia, Lippincott, 1934.

A Shorter History of England.   London, Harrap, and New York, Macmillan, 1934.

Milton.   London, Cassell, and Philadelphia, Lippincott, 1935.

Hilaire Belloc (humorous writings).   London, Methuen, 1935.

An Essay on the Restoration of Property.   London, Distribution League, 1936; as *The Restoration of Property,* New York, Sheed and Ward, 1936.

Selected Essays, edited by John Edward Dineen.   Philadelphia, Lippincott, 1936.

The Battle Ground.   London, Cassell, and Philadelphia, Lippincott, 1936.

Characters of the Reformation.   London and New York, Sheed and Ward, 1936.

The Crusade: The World's Debate.   London, Cassell, 1937; as *The Crusades: The World's Debate,* Milwaukee, Bruce, 1937.

The Crisis of Our Civilization.   London, Cassell, and New York, Fordham University Press, 1937.

An Essay on the Nature of Contemporary England.   London, Constable, and New York, Sheed and Ward, 1937.

The Issue.   New York and London, Sheed and Ward, 1937.

The Great Heresies.   London and New York, Sheed and Ward, 1938.

Monarchy: A Study of Louis XIV.   London, Cassell, and New York, Harper, 1938.

Stories, Essays, and Poems.   London, Dent, 1938.

The Case of Dr. Coulton.   London, Sheed and Ward, 1938.

Return to the Baltic.   London, Constable, 1938.

Charles II: The Last Rally.   New York, Harper, 1939; as *The Last Rally: A Story of Charles II,* London, Cassell, 1940.

The Test Is Poland.   London, Weekly Review, 1939.

The Catholic and the War.   London, Burns Oates, 1940.

On the Place of G. K. Chesterton in English Letters.   London and New York, Sheed and Ward, 1940.

On Sailing the Sea: A Collection of the Seagoing Writings of Hilaire Belloc, edited by W. N. Roughead.   London, Methuen, 1939; Fair Lawn, New Jersey, Essential Books, 1951.

The Silence of the Sea and Other Essays.   New York, Sheed and Ward, 1940; London, Cassell, 1941.

Places.   New York, Sheed and Ward, 1941; London, Cassell, 1942.

Elizabethan Commentary. London, Cassell, 1942; as *Elizabeth: Creature of Circumstance*, New York, Harper, 1942.

The Alternative. London, Distributist Books, 1947.

Selected Essays. London, Methuen, 1948.

Hilaire Belloc: An Anthology of His Prose and Verse, edited by W. N. Roughead. London, Hart Davis, and Philadelphia, Lippincott, 1951.

One Thing and Another: A Miscellany from His Uncollected Essays, edited by Patrick Cahill. London, Hollis, 1955.

Essays, edited by Anthony Forster. London, Methuen, 1955.

Selected Essays, edited by J. B. Morton. London, Penguin, 1958.

Letters from Hilaire Belloc, edited by Robert Speaight. London, Hollis and Carter, and New York, Macmillan, 1958.

Advice. London, Harvill Press, 1960.

Editor, *Extracts from the Diaries and Letters of Hubert Howard*. Oxford, H. Hart, 1899.

Editor, *The Footpath Way: An Anthology for Walkers*. London, Sidgwick and Jackson, 1911.

Editor, *Travel Notes on a Holiday Tour in France*, by James Murray Allison. London, privately printed, 1931.

Translator, *The Romance of Tristan and Iseult*, by J. Bedier. London, George Allen, 1903; New York, Boni, 1930.

Translator, *The Principles of War*, by Marshal Foch. London Chapman and Hall, 1918; New York, Holt, 1920.

Translator, *Precepts and Judgments*, by Marshal Foch. London, Chapman and Hall, 1919; New York, Holt, 1920.

Bibliography: *The English First Editions of Hilaire Belloc ...* by Patrick Cahill, privately printed, 1953.

*   *   *

There would be no place for Hilaire Belloc in a book of this kind were it not for the gift children have for annexing books designed for their elders. He was no children's writer, although it might be argued that in some important ways he remained an adolescent all his life. His passionate advocacy of improbable, and especially unpopular, theses, his gusto, his dislike of a pedantic adherence to logical processes, all hinted at a certain permanent immaturity at odds with his formidable scholarship.

Young people once liked – and may turn to them again – the "Chester-Belloc" novels, but Belloc's lasting appeal to children rests upon his group of mock cautionary tales in which he made genial fun of a literary convention which was dying, if not dead, in his own childhood. The moral tales in verse written by Elizabeth Turner and others in the early years of the nineteenth century were serious in intent, concerned with warning the young of the consequences of sin – or even mildly bad behaviour. By the end of the century these naive rhymes invited laughter. Belloc adopted the themes, and often the meters, of these archaic poems and, giving them only a slightly different emphasis, made them not merely parody but a genuinely original comic creation. Belloc's *Cautionary Tales* are not an isolated example. Among contemporaries Harry Graham in his *Ruthless Rhymes for Heartless Homes* guyed the same conventions. What gives Belloc's work its rare quality is that he, unlike others playing the same frivolous game, was a real poet. He was one of the outstanding verse technicians of the age with an absolute mastery of his craft, and he was without rival in the brevity and symmetry of his epigrams. The same perfection of craftsmanship that he devoted to "serious" verse he brought to the absurd accounts of Matilda – who cried wolf once too often – and Augustus King, the chewer of string, and Jim, who let go of nurse's hand and was eaten by a lion. Similar qualities are found, perhaps even more characteristically, in the shorter rhymes of *A Bad Child's Book of Beasts* and its sequels.

Belloc's epigrams and sonnets, and the rumbustious verses scattered through the prose works, make regular appearances in anthologies of verse for children, doubtless to the poet's posthumous amusement.

—Marcus Crouch

BEMELMANS, Ludwig. American. Born in Meran, Austria, 27 April 1898; emigrated to the United States in 1914; naturalized citizen, 1918. Educated at schools in Regensburg and Rothenburg, Bavaria. Served in the United States Army during World War I. Married Madeline Freund in 1935; one daughter. Worked as a waiter and restaurant proprietor. Recipient: New York *Herald Tribune* Festival award, 1950, 1957; *New York Times* award, for illustration, 1952, 1953, 1955; American Library Association Caldecott Medal, 1954. *Died 1 October 1962.*

PUBLICATIONS FOR CHILDREN (illustrated by the author)

Fiction

> *Hansi.* New York, Viking Press, 1934; London, Lovat Dickson, 1935.
> *The Golden Basket.* New York, Viking Press, 1936.
> *The Castle Number Nine.* New York, Viking Press, 1937.
> *Quito Express.* New York, Viking Press, 1938.
> *Rosebud.* New York, Random House, 1942.
> *A Tale of Two Glimps.* New York, CBS, 1947.
> *The Happy Place.* Boston, Little Brown, 1952.
> *The High World.* New York, Harper, 1954; London, Hamish Hamilton, 1958.
> *Parsley.* New York, Harper, 1955.

Verse

> *Madeline.* New York, Simon and Schuster, 1938; London, Verschoyle, 1952.
> *Fifi.* New York, Simon and Schuster, 1940.
> *Sunshine.* New York, Simon and Schuster, 1950.
> *Madeline's Rescue.* New York, Viking Press, and London, Verschoyle, 1953.
> *Madeline's Christmas in Texas.* Dallas, Nieman Marcus, 1955.
> *Madeline and the Bad Hat.* New York, Viking Press, 1956; London, Deutsch, 1958.
> *Madeline and the Gypsies.* New York, Viking Press, and London, Deutsch, 1959.
> *Welcome Home!* New York, Harper, 1960; London, Hamish Hamilton, 1961.
> *Madeline in London.* New York, Viking Press, 1961; London, Deutsch, 1962.
> *Marina.* New York, Harper, 1962.

PUBLICATIONS FOR ADULTS

Novels

> *Now I Lay Me Down to Sleep.* New York, Viking Press, 1943; London, Hamish Hamilton, 1944.
> *The Blue Danube.* New York, Viking Press, 1945; London, Hamish Hamilton, 1946.

Dirty Eddie.   New York, Viking Press, 1947; London, Hamish Hamilton, 1948.
The Eye of God.   New York, Viking Press, 1947; as *The Snow Mountain*, London, Hamish Hamilton, 1950.
The Woman of My Life.   New York, Viking Press, and London, Hamish Hamilton, 1957.
Are You Hungry, Are You Cold.   Cleveland, World, 1960; London, Mayflower, 1965.
The Street Where the Heart Lies.   Cleveland, World, 1963.

Short Stories

Small Beer.   New York, Viking Press, 1939; London, Lane, 1940.
I Love You, I Love You, I Love You.   New York, Viking Press, 1942; London, Hamish Hamilton, 1943.

Other

My War with the United States.   New York, Viking Press, 1937; London, Gollancz, 1938.
Life Class.   New York, Viking Press, 1938; London, Lane, 1939.
At Your Service: The Way of Life in a Hotel.   Evanston, Illinois, Row Peterson, 1941.
Hotel Splendide.   New York, Viking Press, 1941; London, Hamish Hamilton, 1942.
Hotel Bemelmans.   New York, Viking Press, 1946; London, Hamish Hamilton, 1956.
The Best of Times: An Account of Europe Revisited.   New York, Simon and Schuster, 1948; London, Cresset Press, n.d.
How to Travel Incognito.   Boston, Little Brown, 1952.
Father, Dear Father (autobiographical).   New York, Viking Press, and London, Hamish Hamilton, 1953.
To the One I Love the Best.   New York, Viking Press, 1955.
The World of Bemelmans.   New York, Viking Press, and London, Hamish Hamilton, 1955.
My Life in Art.   New York, Harper, and London, Deutsch, 1958.
How to Have Europe All to Yourself.   New York, European Travel Commission, 1960.
Italian Holiday.   Boston, Houghton Mifflin, 1961.
On Board Noah's Ark.   New York, Viking Press, 1962.
La Bonne Table (writings and drawings), edited by Donald and Eleanor Friede.   New York, Simon and Schuster, and London, Deutsch, 1964.

Editor, *Holiday in France.*   Boston, Houghton Mifflin, 1957; London, Deutsch, 1958.

Illustrator: *Noodle* by Munro Leaf, 1937; *Literary Life and the Hell with It* by Whit Burnett, 1939.

*   *   *

The reputation of Ludwig Bemelmans rests solidly on his five picture books about Madeline, that daring little girl who lived in Paris with eleven other little girls and Miss Clavel in a house "covered with vines." Most of the other Bemelmans books are out of print now – story and picture books that children never adopted as they adopted *Madeline. The High World*, however, is still in circulation, and both *Parsley* and *Hansi* are available on library reference shelves. First a word about these and two others, before we take a closer look at the *Madelines* with their casual, comical couplets, their appealing little girl, and the large bright water-color settings.

The scenes and people Bemelmans knew as a child growing up in the Austrian Tyrol are reflected in the two illustrated storybooks, *The High World* and *Hansi*. Small escapades and rich local color fill the pages of *Hansi*, while an avalanche and daring rescue based on a real incident bring *The High World* to its climax. Both books keep the reader fully involved and could in themselves have established Bemelmans as an important writer. *Parsley* is a large picture book of the *Madeline* size, filled with beautiful Bemelmans paintings of the forest where the stag named Parsley lived. It evidently failed to equal the *Madeline* books in appeal, perhaps because it verges on sentimentality and an unacceptable anthropomorphism at the end.

Quito Express, one of the very early books, is about to be reprinted – an occasion for rejoicing. This small book, illustrated in chalky cinnamon colors, is the satisfying story of little Ecuadorian Pedro, a baby who crawled onto an express train and was carried away for four days, well cared for by a kindly conductor.

It seems a pity that another of the early books, *The Golden Basket*, is no longer available. In this storybook two little girls explore Bruges with their father. And wonder of wonders, they encounter one day twelve uniformed little girls out walking two by two with their Madame Severine. The littlest girl, one Madeleine, skips and hops behind them all saying "Boo-boo-boo!" Which brings us to the famous Madeline of the well-known picture books.

The first book, *Madeline*, was an instant success. Quite apart from the appealing verses and pictures, it offered a heroine to love and hospital experience – a magnetic topic for young readers. The books that followed were true to the original characterization of the independent little Madeline and continued to blend playful, easy versification with the sweeping pictorial art of the cartoonist-painter. Readers know that foreign cities will be laid out for them to inspect in detail in the Bemelmans illustrations, glowing in color and full of movement – just as the verses move along rapidly and happily through the story. The Bemelmans touch in these books is light and warm, comical and endearing. There is nothing else quite like it. *Madeline's Rescue* brought Bemelmans the Caldecott Medal for "the most distinguished American picture book."

—Claudia Lewis

BENCHLEY, Nathaniel (Goddard).   American.   Born in Newton, Massachusetts, 13 November 1915; son of the writer Robert Benchley. Educated at Phillips Exeter Academy, Exeter, New Hampshire, 1931–34; Harvard University, Cambridge, Massachusetts, 1934–38, S.B. 1938. Served in the United States Naval Reserve, 1941–46. Married Marjorie Bradford in 1939; has two sons. City Reporter, *Herald Tribune*, New York, 1939–41; Assistant Entertainment Editor, *Newsweek*, New York, 1946–47. Recipient: Western Writers of America Spur Award, 1973. Agent: Roberta Pryor, International Creative Management, 40 West 57th Street, New York, New York 10019; or, Elaine Green Ltd., 31 Newington Green, London N16 9PU, England. Address: Box 224, Siasconset, Massachusetts. 02564, U.S.A.

PUBLICATIONS FOR CHILDREN

Fiction

    Red Fox and His Canoe, illustrated by Arnold Lobel.   New York, Harper, 1964; Kingswood, Surrey, World's Work, 1969.
    Oscar Otter, illustrated by Arnold Lobel.   New York, Harper, 1966; Kingswood, Surrey, World's Work, 1967.
    The Strange Disappearance of Arthur Cluck, illustrated by Arnold Lobel.   New York, Harper, 1967; Kingswood, Surrey, World's Work, 1968.

A Ghost Named Fred, illustrated by Ben Shecter. New York, Harper, 1968; Kingswood, Surrey, World's Work, 1969.

Sam the Minuteman, illustrated by Arnold Lobel. New York, Harper, 1969; Kingswood, Surrey, World's Work, 1977.

The Several Tricks of Edgar Dolphin, illustrated by Mamoru Funai. New York, Harper, and Kingswood, Surrey, World's Work, 1970.

The Flying Lesson of Gerald Pelican, illustrated by Mamoru Funai. New York, Harper, 1970.

Gone and Back. New York, Harper, 1970.

Feldman Fieldmouse, illustrated by Hilary Knight. New York, Harper, 1971; London, Abelard Schuman, 1975.

Small Wolf, illustrated by Joan Sandin. New York, Harper, 1972; Kingswood, Surrey, World's Work, 1973.

The Magic Sled, illustrated by Mel Furukawa. New York, Harper, 1972; as *The Magic Sledge*, London, Deutsch, 1974.

Only Earth and Sky Last Forever. New York, Harper, 1972.

The Deep Dives of Stanley Whale, illustrated by Mischa Richter. New York, Harper, 1973; Kingswood, Surrey, World's Work, 1976.

Bright Candles. New York, Harper, 1974; London, Deutsch, 1976.

Beyond the Mists. New York, Harper, 1975.

A Necessary End. New York, Harper, 1976.

Snorri and the Strangers, illustrated by Don Bolognese. New York, Harper, 1976.

George the Drummer Boy, illustrated by Don Bolognese. New York, Harper, 1977.

Kilroy and the Gull, illustrated by John Schoenherr. New York, Harper, 1977.

Other

Sinbad the Sailor, illustrated by Tom O'Sullivan. New York, Random House, 1960; London, Muller, 1964.

PUBLICATIONS FOR ADULTS

Novels

Side Street. New York, Harcourt Brace, 1950.

One to Grow On. New York, McGraw Hill, 1958.

Sail a Crooked Ship. New York, McGraw Hill, 1960; London, Hutchinson, 1961.

The Off-Islanders. New York, McGraw Hill, 1961; London, Hutchinson, 1962; as "*The Russians Are Coming, The Russians Are Coming,*" London, Penguin, 1966.

Catch a Falling Spy. New York, McGraw Hill, and London, Hutchinson, 1963.

A Winter's Tale. New York, McGraw Hill, and London, Hutchinson, 1964.

The Visitors. New York, McGraw Hill, 1964; London, Hutchinson, 1965.

A Firm Word or Two. New York, McGraw Hill, 1965.

The Monument. New York, McGraw Hill, and London, Hutchinson, 1966.

Welcome to Xanadu. New York, Atheneum, and London, Hutchinson, 1968.

The Wake of Icarus. New York, Atheneum, 1969.

Lassiter's Folly. New York, Atheneum, 1971.

The Hunter's Moon. Boston, Little Brown, 1972.

Plays

The Frogs of Spring, from his novel *Side Street* (produced New York, 1953). New York, French, 1954.

Screenplay: *The Great American Pastime*, 1956.

Other

Robert Benchley: A Biography. New York, McGraw Hill, 1955; London, Cassell, 1956.
Humphrey Bogart. Boston, Little Brown, and London, Hutchinson, 1975.

Editor, *The Benchley Roundup* (writings by Robert Benchley). New York, Harper, 1954; London, Cassell, 1956.

Manuscript Collection: Mugar Memorial Library, Boston University.

*   *   *

In 1964, the popular author of a succession of works for adults began writing equally remarkable books for the four- to eight-year-old crowd. Nathaniel Benchley's picture books are comedy-fantasies for the most part and far above the controlled-vocabulary froth offered for easy reading. Most have been counted by critics as among the best of the year when they appeared. Some are serious introductions to history: *Sam the Minuteman, Small Wolf* (which is a sad commentary on the whites' treatment of American Indians) and *Snorri and the Strangers* (about a child born in America of parents who had sailed from Greenland 1000 year ago).

In 1970 Benchley began to write a series of historical novels for older readers. The first was *Gone and Back*, the story of Obed Taylor who lived with his family in New England during the 19th century. They trek West to join the Oklahoma Land Rush, a plot which results in an absorbing story and gives the reader a memorable account of two contrasting ways of life during the infancy of the new country. Two years later, the author wrote a searing tale about an American Indian boy, Dark Elk, who joined Chief Crazy Horse and his warriors, who fought Custer at the Battle of Little Big Horn. Essentially a tragedy, *Only Earth and Sky Last Forever* is lightened by the famous Benchley wit.

Later, the author was drawn to the epic days of the Danish struggle against Nazi domination during World War II. Since he is set on making sure that his novels are built upon fact, Benchley traveled to Denmark to research the story which became *Bright Candles.* The chief actors in the drama are Jens and Ole, two youths who can't accept the takeover of their country. At first, they perform petty acts of sabotage but branch out into more daring deeds. The novel is among the few to record the heroism of the Danish underground. Slow at first to react against domination, they were impelled to reprisals after the first deportation of the Jewish citizens.

The Benchley stay in Scandanavia also gave him the background for *Beyond the Mists,* based on the 11th-century sagas. It's an authentic, interesting portrayal of the lives of the Viking raiders whose horrific ways and dreadful deaths disgust young Gunnar. Nevertheless, he sails with Leif Eriksson to the New World where encounters with "natives" point up how fear and foolishness create absurdities and conflicts.

A Necessary End tells of Ralph Bowers, Signalman Third on a P.C. subchaser during World War II. The novel reads like a *roman à clef* and is surely based on the author's own experience. He served in the U. S. Navy anti-submarine force for four years. It is an irresistible page-turner with no hint of contrivance.

Nathaniel Benchley says he began writing for young people because "It's my personal battle with television; I want to get them into reading instead of staring at the tube." So far, he's winning.

—Jean F. Mercier

BENEDICT, Rex (Arthur). American. Born in Jet, Oklahoma, 27 June 1920. Educated at Jet High School, graduated 1938; Northwestern State University, Alva, Oklahoma, B.A. 1949; University of Oklahoma, Norman, 1949–50. Served in the United States Navy Air Corps, 1942–45, 1951–53: Lieutenant. Married Giusi Maria Usai in 1966. Orchestra director, Alva, 1938–41; orchestra manager, San Diego, 1945–46; film dubber, 1953–57, and film translator, 1957–60, Rome; publisher's reader, New York 1960–65. Since 1967, Printer, Corsair Press, New York; since 1972; Reviewer, *New York Times*. Address: 23 West 88th Street, New York, New York 10024, U.S.A.

PUBLICATIONS FOR CHILDREN

Fiction

> *Good Luck Arizona Man.* New York, Pantheon Books, 1972; London, Hamish Hamilton, 1973.
> *Goodbye to the Purple Sage: The Last Great Ride of the Sheriff of Medicine Creek.* New York, Pantheon Books, 1973; London, Hamish Hamilton, 1974.
> *Last Stand at Goodbye Gulch.* New York, Pantheon Books, 1974; London, Hamish Hamilton, 1975.
> *The Ballad of Cactus Jack.* New York, Pantheon Books, 1975; London, Hamish Hamilton, 1976.

Verse

> *In the Green Grass Time.* New York, Corsair Press, 1964.

Other

> *Oh … Brother Juniper*, illustrated by Joan Berg. New York, Pantheon Books, 1963.

> Translator, *One Moonless Night* by Noële Lavaivre. New York, Braziller, 1964.
> Translator, *The Polka Dot Twins* by Augusto Lunel. New York, Braziller, 1964.

PUBLICATIONS FOR ADULTS

Verse

> *Moonwash.* New York, Corsair Press, 1969.
> *Nights in the Gardens of Glebe.* New York, Corsair Press, 1970.
> *Epitaph for a Lady.* New York, Corsair Press, 1970.
> *Haloes for Heroes.* New York, Corsair Press, 1971.

> Translator, *The Prayers of Man*, edited by Alfonso Maria di Nola. New York, McDowell Obolensky, 1961.
> Translator, *Amorous Tales from the Decameron.* New York, Fawcett, 1963.
> Translator, *Those Cursed Tuscans*, by Curzio Malaparte. Athens, Ohio University Press, 1964.

Rex Benedict comments:
   If there is one word that will catch the intent of my efforts in the novel for children, it is the word "mythical." In almost all my novels I have used the Old West as myth. Since facts of the West are so hopelessly lost in myth, I, instead of trying to disentangle them, confuse them even more in the hope of arriving at logic. There is no length to which one can not go in

writing about the West, so long as one is convincing. A professor in Canada is currently dramatizing for television one of the novels under the title *The Magic Lie*. I think, to judge by his title, he is on the right path. The treatment of the West is all a great, beautiful lie, but it is concealed by magic. In short, you don't even notice the prevarication. (I hope.)

*   *   *

In his racy comic Westerns, Rex Benedict writes of "the code of the West, not the code of civilization. The two never was the same" (*Goodbye to the Purple Sage*). Like many other writers and film-makers, he looks westward for a mythology which celebrates the simpler American virtues – the courage, heroism, and loyalty which went with the territory: "It was part of the code, the poetry, the religion, like the purple sage and the western stars and all the rest of it." The legend was undoubtedly very different from the reality, just as the legends of chivalry bear little correspondence to the actualities of the medieval world. And the tension between the legends of a bygone age and contemporary reality breeds humour, as Cervantes well knew. Certainly, there is a quixotic note in Benedict's work, only it is outlaws and marshals who tilt at windmills. Humour and nostalgia are mixed in these stories, which have chapter headings like "Fugitive Pass" and "Sunset Trail," place-names like Cuts Plenty Throats and Last Gulp Water Hole, horses like Big Mistake and Bullet Proof and a gallery of eccentric characters from Tenderleaf T., the Apache brave, to the Reverend Heavenly Cash. Quentin Blake's cover illustrations catch this flavour well.

Good Luck Arizona Man is a quest story. Good Luck Arizona Boy has been brought up among the Apaches, though he suspects and, in the course of the book, finds out that he is of white origin. His initiation test is to find the gold of the Guadaloupes. For this, white men from Coronado and the conquistadores onwards have died; to the Indians, it must remain hidden and sacred in Dead Man's Gulch. The title gives a clue as to the hero's choice; the book is not only a very funny story but also an interesting confrontation of racial values.

Goodbye to the Purple Sage shows a confrontation between lawmen and outlaws. The protagonists made a brief appearance in the earlier book. They are, on the one hand, the Pecos Gang – Cactus Jack, Cold Eyed Luke, Memphis Bill, Dalhart Ike, Three Finger Doc and Sasatone Rose – and on the other, Sagebrush Sheridan, the sheriff of Medicine Creek. This is the story of his last pursuit with a posse of Apache Comanches, Texan Rangers, and Mexican Rurales:

> A sheriff must ride
> at the rim of the sky
> A sheriff must ride
> and a sheriff must die.

Last Stand at Goodbye Gulch spells out the confrontation: to the marshal: "You're always supposed to be lookin' for wanted men and ... if there aren't any around you're supposed to go out and dig up a few because in an unlaw-abiding world like ours there is always somebody that is wanted for something"; to the outlaw: "You're supposed to be runnin' from the law all your life because you're a wanted man and even if you're innocent it doesn't matter because if you're runnin' a U.S. marshal will start chasing you and hound you to the end of your days." The only thing that makes this extraordinary is that the marshals themselves have turned outlaw and dwell in the jail in Goodbye Gulch. This book has more twists and turns of plot but is memorable chiefly for its heroine, Cherokee Waters.

The Ballad of Cactus Jack is a return to earlier form and a sequel to *Goodbye to the Purple Sage*. That showed the heroic death of the sheriff at the Last Surround. This book moves towards the death of Cactus Jack. No longer a wanted man, he droops and pines until the sheriff's grandson sets up an elaborate charade of pursuit. With his posse of Wayward Boys from Bull Bodeen's reformatory school, natural survivors all, he chases the outlaw towards the last great shoot-out at Lonely Corrals. Whatever aspect of the Wild West Rex Benedict says goodbye to in his next book, one can predict that it will be gripping, nostalgic, and uproariously funny.

—Mary Croxson

BERESFORD, Elisabeth. British. Born in Paris, France. Educated at St. Mary's Hall, Brighton; St. Catherines, Bramley; Dirchling Dame School, Sussex; Brighton and Hove High School. Served as a radio operator in the Women's Naval Service during World War II. Married Max Robertson in 1949; has one daughter and one son. Since 1948, Free-lance Journalist. Agent: A. M. Heath Ltd., 40–42 William IV Street, London WC2N 4DD, England.

PUBLICATIONS FOR CHILDREN

Fiction

    The Television Mystery. London, Parrish, 1957.
    The Flying Doctor Mystery. London, Parrish, 1958.
    Trouble at Tullington Castle. London, Parrish, 1958.
    Cocky and the Missing Castle, illustrated by Jennifer Miles. London, Constable, 1959.
    Gappy Goes West. London, Parrish, 1959.
    The Tullington Film-Makers. London, Parrish, 1960.
    Two Gold Dolphins, illustrated by Peggy Fortnum. London, Constable, 1961; Indianapolis, Bobbs Merrill, 1964.
    Danger on the Old Pull 'n Push. London, Parrish, 1962.
    Strange Hiding Place. London, Parrish, 1962.
    Diana in Television. London, Collins, 1963.
    The Missing Formula Mystery. London, Parrish, 1963.
    The Mulberry Street Team, illustrated by Juliet Pannett. Penshurst, Kent, Friday Press, 1963.
    Awkward Magic, illustrated by Judith Valpy. London, Hart Davis, 1964; as *The Magic World,* Indianapolis, Bobbs Merrill, 1965.
    The Flying Doctor to the Rescue. London, Parrish, 1964.
    Holiday for Slippy, illustrated by Pat Williams. Penshurst, Kent, Friday Press, 1964.
    Game, Set, and Match. London, Parrish, 1965.
    Knights of the Cardboard Castle, illustrated by C. R. Evans. London, Methuen, 1965.
    Travelling Magic, illustrated by Judith Valpy. London, Hart Davis, 1965; as *The Vanishing Garden,* New York, Funk and Wagnalls, 1967.
    The Hidden Mill, illustrated by Margery Gill. London, Benn, 1965; New York, Meredith Press, 1967.
    Peter Climbs a Tree, illustrated by Margery Gill. London, Benn, 1966.
    Fashion Girl. London, Collins, 1967.
    The Black Mountain Mystery. London, Parrish, 1967.
    Looking for a Friend, illustrated by Margery Gill. London, Benn, 1967.
    The Island Bus, illustrated by Robert Hodgson. London, Methuen, 1968.
    Sea-Green Magic, illustrated by Ann Tout. London, Hart Davis, 1968.
    The Wombles, illustrated by Margaret Gordon. London, Benn, 1968; New York, Meredith Press, 1969.
    David Goes Fishing, illustrated by Imre Hofbauer. London, Benn, 1969.

Gordon's Go-Kart, illustrated by Margery Gill.   London, Benn, 1970.
Stephen and the Shaggy Dog, illustrated by Robert Hales.   London, Methuen, 1970.
Vanishing Magic, illustrated by Ann Tout.   London, Hart Davis, 1970.
The Wandering Wombles, illustrated by Oliver Chadwick.   London, Benn, 1970.
Dangerous Magic, illustrated by Oliver Chadwick.   London, Hart Davis, 1972.
The Invisible Womble and Other Stories, illustrated by Ivor Wood.   London, Benn, 1973.
The Secret Railway, illustrated by James Hunt.   London, Methuen, 1973.
The Wombles in Danger.   London, Benn, 1973.
The Wombles at Work, illustrated by Margaret Gordon.   London, Benn, 1973.
Invisible Magic, illustrated by Reg Gray.   London, Hart Davis, 1974.
The Wombles Go to the Seaside.   London, World Distributors, 1974.
The Wombles Gift Book, illustrated by Margaret Gordon.   London, Benn, 1975.
The Snow Womble, illustrated by Margaret Gordon.   London, Benn, 1975.
Snuffle to the Rescue, illustrated by Gunvor Edwards.   London, Penguin, 1975.
Tomsk and the Tired Tree, illustrated by Margaret Gordon.   London, Benn, 1975.
Wellington and the Blue Balloon, illustrated by Margaret Gordon.   London, Benn, 1975.
Orinoco Runs Away, illustrated by Margaret Gordon.   London, Benn, 1975.
The Wombles Make a Clean Sweep, illustrated by Ivor Wood.   London, Penguin, 1975.
The Wombles to the Rescue, illustrated by Margaret Gordon.   London, Benn, 1975.
The MacWombles's Pipe Band, illustrated by Margaret Gordon.   London, Benn, 1976.
Madame Cholet's Picnic Party, illustrated by Margaret Gordon.   London, Benn, 1976.
Bungo Knows Best, illustrated by Margaret Gordon.   London, Benn, 1976.
Tobermory's Big Surprise, illustrated by Margaret Gordon.   London, Benn, 1976.
The Wombles Go round the World, illustrated by Margaret Gordon.   London, Benn, 1976.
The World of the Wombles, illustrated by Edgar Hodges.   London, World Distributors, 1976.

Plays

The Wombles, adaptation of her own stories (produced London, 1974).

Screenplay: *The Wombles*, 1977.

Other

The Wombles Annual 1975 to *1978*.   London, World Distributors, 4 vols., 1974–77.

Publications for Adults

Novels

Paradise Island.   London, Hale, 1963.
Escape to Happiness.   London, Hale, 1964.
Roses Round the Door.   London, Hale, 1965.
Island of Shadows.   London, Hale, 1966.
Veronica.   London, Hale, 1967.
A Tropical Affair.   London, Hale, 1967.
Saturday's Child.   London, Hale, 1968.
Love Remembered.   London, Hale, 1970.
Love and the S. S. Beatrice.   London, Hale, 1972.
Pandora.   London, Hale, 1974.

Plays

Road to Albutal, with Nick Renton (produced Edinburgh, 1976).

Television Plays: over sixty television scripts.

Elisabeth Beresford comments:
The books are roughly in three categories: 1) straight adventure, 2) magic – children with very ordinary backgrounds, to whom quite extraordinary things happen, 3) The Wombles, who, it is hoped, will make children want to fight pollution and to think up ways of "making good use of bad rubbish" (Womble family motto). And will also make readers of all ages laugh!

*   *   *

Elisabeth Beresford shares in some degree the dilemma of Conan Doyle. Doyle invented, in a lighter moment, an amateur detective, and Sherlock Holmes hung around his neck like a dead weight. Elisabeth Beresford invented the Wombles. She may not feel as bitterly about her success as Doyle did. There can be no doubt that, in writing these gently humorous tales, she is sharing with readers her own warm affection for these curious creatures. But, in achieving a runaway success with the Wombles, Elisabeth Beresford has distracted attention from her other, and not less important, writing.

She was an established writer long before she discovered her first Womble on Wimbledon Common. That she had not won high critical acclaim was due partly to the variety of her work – writers are expected to keep tidily to well-defined paths – partly to her readiness to accept the discipline of the "easy readers." A typical example of her stories with a contemporary "realistic" theme is *The Hidden Mill*. In this she takes an actual landscape, one of the decayed rivers of South London, and the derelict buildings on its banks. Three recognisable children from the back streets find that this grubby environment has a rich potential for adventure, dangerous games, and romance, all scaled down to real life. Even the happy ending is based on probability.

While writing this kind of story Elisabeth Beresford was engaged on more substantial fantasies in the E. Nesbit manner. *Dangerous Magic* is characteristic of these. A great struggle between the forces of good and evil takes place among familiar scenes in London with action mainly in a block of high-rise flats, and a great aerial battle is fought out above the Thames. Like many of the best fantasies it is a tale of high adventure told largely in comic terms. The unicorn which comes to life in a thunderstorm is firmly in the Nesbit tradition in its vanity, its colloquial speech, and its ultimate, if reluctant, heroism.

As for the Wombles, it is difficult to take a cold critical look at a legend. The original stories have been blurred by subsequent translation into other media, and the endearing characters are uncomfortably familiar as toys, puppets, and shambling pop singers. The literary Wombles belong to an ancient tradition, that of the moral tale. In their advocacy of old-fashioned virtues the Wombles are Victorian, but their insistence on conservation strikes a contemporary note. The invention in these stories lacks originality, as the writing lacks distinction, but the Wombles have acquired a life independent of the parent stories in which they first appeared. They seem destined for some kind of immortality.

—Marcus Crouch

BERG, Leila. British. Born in Salford, Lancashire, 12 November 1917. Educated at Manchester High School; London University. Married in 1940; has one son and one daughter. General Editor, Salamander Books, Thomas Nelson, publishers, London, 1965. Since 1968, free-lance editor, "Nippers" and "Little Nippers" school series, Macmillan Education Ltd., London. Recipient: Children's Book Circle Eleanor Farjeon Award, 1974. Address: 25 Streatham Common South, London S.W.16, England.

PUBLICATIONS FOR CHILDREN

Fiction

The Adventures of Chunky, illustrated by George Downs. London, Oxford University Press, 1950; as *Chunky*, 1958.
The Nightingale and Other Stories, illustrated by Garry Mackenzie. London, Oxford University Press, 1951.
The Tired Train and Other Stories, illustrated by Jean Bailey. London, Max Parrish, 1952.
Little Pete Stories, illustrated by Henrietta Garland. London, Methuen, 1952; revised edition, 1968.
Trust Chunky, illustrated by Peggy Fortnum. Leicester, Brockhampton Press, 1954.
Fire Engine by Mistake, illustrated by Val Biro. Leicester, Brockhampton Press, 1955.
The Story of the Little Car, illustrated by W. A. Sillince. London, Epworth Press, 1955; revised edition as *The Little Car Has a Day Out*, Leicester, Brockhampton Press, 1970; as *The Little Car*, London, Methuen, 1972.
Lollipops: Stories and Poems, illustrated by Kathleen Dance. Leicester, Brockhampton Press, 1957.
Andy's Pit Pony, illustrated by Val Biro. Leicester, Brockhampton Press, 1958.
The Hidden Road, illustrated by B. Chapman. London, Hamish Hamilton, 1958.
Fourteen What-Do-You-Know Stories, illustrated by Stanley Jackson. London, Epworth Press, 1958; New York, Roy, 1959.
A Box for Benny, illustrated by Jillian Willett. Leicester, Brockhampton Press, 1958; Indianapolis, Bobbs Merrill, 1961.
Three Men Went to Work, illustrated by Dorothy Clark. London, Methuen, 1960.
The Jolly Farm Book, illustrated by Lindy. London, Collins, 1960.
See How They Work, illustrated by Dorothy Clark. London, Methuen, 1962.
A Newt for Roddy, illustrated by Constance Marshall. London, Nelson, 1965.
My Dog Sunday, illustrated by Dick Hart. London, Hamish Hamilton, 1968.

Other (school texts and retellings)

Paint a Black Horse. London, Methuen, 1958.
Bamburu: Boy of Ghana. London, Methuen, 1958.
Noriko-San: Girl of Japan, illustrated by Anna Riwkin-Brick. London, Methuen, 1958.
The Singing Town, illustrated by Thorbjørn. London, Methuen, 1959.
Little Owl. London, Methuen, 1966.
How John Caught the Sea-Horse and Other Stories, illustrated by Edward Standon. London, Penguin, 1966.
Folk Tales for Reading and Telling, illustrated by George Him. Leicester, Brockhampton Press, and Cleveland, World, 1966.
The Penguin Who Couldn't Paddle and Other Stories, illustrated by Edward Standon. London, Penguin, 1967.
A Day Out, illustrated by Ferelith Eccles Williams. London, Macmillan, 1968.
Finding a Key, illustrated by Jenny Williams. London, Macmillan, 1968.

Fish and Chips for Supper, illustrated by Richard Rose.   London, Macmillan, 1968.
Jimmy's Story, illustrated by Richard Rose.   London, Macmillan, 1968.
The Jumble Sale, illustrated by George Craig.   London, Macmillan, 1968.
Lesley's Story, illustrated by George Craig.   London, Macmillan, 1968.
Julie's Story, illustrated by Richard Rose.   London, Macmillan, 1970.
Letters, illustrated by Ferelith Eccles Williams.   London, Macmillan, 1970.
Paul's Story, illustrated by Richard Rose.   London, Macmillan, 1970.
Robert's Story, illustrated by Richard Rose.   London, Macmillan, 1970.
Susan's Story, illustrated by Richard Rose.   London, Macmillan, 1970.
Doing the Pools, illustrated by Richard Rose.   London, Macmillan, 1972.
The Doctor, illustrated by Val Biro.   London, Macmillan, 1972.
Hospital Day, illustrated by Shirley Hughes.   London, Macmillan, 1972.
Knitting, illustrated by George Him.   London, Macmillan, 1972.
My Brother, illustrated by Linda Birch.   London, Macmillan, 1972.
Put the Kettle On!, illustrated by John Dyke.   London, Macmillan, 1972.
That Baby, illustrated by Margaret Belsky. London, Macmillan, 1972.
Tracy's Story, illustrated by Richard Rose.   London, Macmillan, 1972.
Well, I Never!, illustrated by George Him.   London, Macmillan, 1972.
A Band in School, illustrated by John Dyke.   London, Macmillan, 1975.
Plenty of Room, illustrated by Joan Beales.   London, Macmillan, 1975.
Grandad's Clock, illustrated by Joan Beales.   London, Macmillan, 1976.

Editor, *Four Feet and Two, and Some with None: An Anthology of Verse*, illustrated by
    Shirley Burke and Marvin Bileck.   London, Penguin, 1960.

Translator, with Ruth Baer, *Grown-Ups Don't Understand*, by Irmgard Keun, illustrated
    by Sylvia Stokeld.   London, Max Parrish, 1955; as *The Bad Example*, New York,
    Harcourt Brace, 1955.

PUBLICATIONS FOR ADULTS

Play

Raising Hell (produced Salisbury, 1972; London, 1973).

Other

Risinghill: Death of a Comprehensive School.   London, Penguin, 1968.
Children's Rights.   London, Elek, and New York, Praeger, 1971.
The Train Back: A Search for Parents, with Pat Chapman.   London, Allen Lane, 1972.
Look at Kids.   London, Penguin, 1972.
Reading and Loving.   London, Routledge, 1977.

Leila Berg comments:
    I simply explore people and situations in a way that I feel is relevant to a child's experience,
and that will hold a child through amusement, excitement or a sense of wonder. This is how
one writes for adults too – the only difference is relevance to a *child's* experience.

                                    *   *   *

    Leila Berg is a prolific writer for children and above all a story-teller whose wealth of
experience of reading to children is very apparent in her writing. Her style is pruned of
unnecessary detail, lively and colloquial, with events surely paced to reach a satisfying
conclusion. She writes for the younger age range – stories to listen to or first stories to read

for oneself. Her writing has now lost the occasional didacticism of her earlier work. It is based on her own experiences – her Salford Jewish childhood (*A Box for Benny*), her own children, the nursery she ran in her home and so forth. It has also been much shaped both by her desire to show children in literature as they really are – active, argumentative, thinking (e.g. *Little Pete Stories*) – and, more recently, by her conviction of the need for a literature where the majority of children can read about themselves ("Nippers").

In Berg's most recent work – supplementary readers for the "Nippers" series (which she also edits) – her ideas about children's literature have found their fullest expression. The series has been attacked by teachers who object to the depiction of the realities of working class life and by others who point to what they see as a stereotyped and patronising view of working people. Berg's books are not to be so lightly dismissed, however. She has an excellent ear and these latest books are clear demonstrations of her skill in conveying with verve and wit the speech patterns and vocabulary of those considered till very recently to be "uncultured." Berg also brings to her urban working-class themes the traditional story patterns and repetitions of the teller of tales – in *Fish and Chips for Supper*, for example, we have the lively use of a cumulative tale.

It is not easy to assess Berg's contribution to children's literature. Her major innovations – dialogue true to the cadences of working class speech and the presentation of positive working class characters in their own environment – have had a major impact on children's book publishing and extended the range of possibilities open to other writers.

—Rosemary Stones

BEST, (Oswald) Herbert.   British.   Born in Chester, Cheshire, 25 April 1894. Educated at King's School, Chester; Queen's College, Cambridge, LL.B. 1914. Served in the Royal Engineers, 1914–19; Lieutenant. Married the writer and illustrator Evangel Allena Champlin (pseudonym Erick Berry) in 1926. District Officer, British Colonial Civil Service, Nigeria, 1919–32. Address: Sharon, Connecticut 06069, U.S.A.

PUBLICATIONS FOR CHILDREN

Fiction

> *Garram the Hunter: A Boy of the Hill Tribes*, illustrated by Erick Berry.   New York, Doubleday, 1930; London, Lane, 1935.
> *Son of the Whiteman*, illustrated by Erick Berry.   New York, Doubleday, 1931.
> *Garram the Chief: The Story of the Hill Tribes*, illustrated by Erick Berry.   New York, Doubleday, 1932; London, Lane, 1935.
> *Flag of the Desert*, illustrated by Erick Berry.   New York, Viking Press, 1936; Oxford, Blackwell, 1937.
> *Tale of the Four Tribes*, illustrated by Erick Berry.   Oxford, Blackwell, and New York, Doubleday, 1938.
> *Gunsmith's Boy*, illustrated by Erick Berry.   Chicago, Winston, 1942; London, Newnes, 1944.
> *Young'un.*   New York, Macmillan, 1944; London, Cape, 1945.
> *Border Iron*, illustrated by Erick Berry.   New York, Viking Press, 1945; London, Newnes, 1946.
> *Watergate: A Story of the Irish on the Erie Canal*, illustrated by Erick Berry.   Philadelphia, Winston, 1951.
> *Not Without Danger: A Story of the Colony of Jamaica in Revolutionary Days*, illustrated by Erick Berry.   New York, Viking Press, 1951.

The Sea Warriors. New York, Macmillan, 1959.
Desmond's First Case, illustrated by Ezra Jack Keats. New York, Viking Press, 1961.
Bright Hunter of the Skies, illustrated by Bernarda Bryson. New York, Macmillan, 1961.
Carolina Gold. New York, Day, 1961.
Desmond the Dog Detective: The Case of the Lone Stranger, illustrated by Lilian Obligado. New York, Viking Press, 1962.
Desmond and the Peppermint Ghost: The Dog Detective's Third Case, illustrated by Lilian Obligado. New York, Viking Press, 1965.
Desmond and Dog Friday, illustrated by W.T. Mars. New York, Viking Press, 1968.
The Polynesian Triangle, with Erick Berry. New York, Funk and Wagnalls, 1968.

Other

Concertina Farm, with and illustrated by Erick Berry. London, Joseph, 1943.
The Long Portage: A Story of Ticonderoga and Lord Howe, illustrated by Erick Berry. New York, Viking Press, 1948; as *The Road to Ticonderoga; or, The Long Portage,* London, Penguin, 1954.
Ranger's Ransom: A Story of Ticonderoga, illustrated by Erick Berry. New York, Aladdin Books, 1953.
The Webfoot Warriors: The Story of UDT, the U.S. Navy's Underwater Demolition Team. New York, Day, 1962.
Parachute to Survival. New York, Day, 1964.
Men Who Changed the Map: A.D. 400 to 1914, with Erick Berry. New York, Funk and Wagnalls, 1968.

PUBLICATIONS FOR ADULTS

Novels

The Mystery of the Flaming Hut. London, Cassell, and New York, Harper, 1932.
The Skull Beneath the Eaves. London, Grayson, 1933.
Winds Whisper. London, Hurst and Blackett, 1937.
Low River. London, Hurst and Blackett, 1937.
The Twenty-Fifth Hour. London, Cape, and New York, Random House, 1940.
Whistle, Daughter, Whistle. New York, Macmillan, 1947.
The Columbus Cannon. New York, Viking Press, 1954.
Diane. New York, Morrow, 1954; London, Museum Press, 1955.
A Rumour of Drums. London, Cassell, 1962; New York, McKay, 1963.

Other

Writing for Children, with Erick Berry. New York, Viking Press, 1947; revised edition, Coral Gables, Florida, University of Miami Press, 1964.

*   *   *

Herbert Best is a prolific author; his eventful life has provided him with subject matter both variegated and fascinating. And he has proven himself able to write successfully for any audience, from the youngsters who enjoy the adventures of Desmond the dog detective to the most senior readers. By far his best-known and best-loved work, however, is *Young'un,* a favourite with all readers from adolescence upwards.

The author, though for many years a resident of the Lake Champlain district of New York State, was born in England. But any reader of *Young'un* not aware of this fact will assuredly assume that only an American born and bred could so master the rural American dialect and attitudes of long ago. He has, moreover, created a young heroine both good and likeable; a well-rounded, believable human being, feminine to her very marrow, no mean feat for any author, but requiring tremendous breadth of sensitivity and imagination from a man attempting to reveal from within the mind of a young girl just awakening to womanhood.

Young'un is the story of three almost-children, whose mother has died in a fire, and whose father, unable to face the tragedy or the losing struggle to maintain his ill-kept farm, deserts the youngsters and takes to the woods. But these youngsters are not pitiful waifs; they are proud, self-reliant and brave, and they determine to hold the remains of their family together and to make a success of their failing farm.

They face daunting difficulties, including the scepticism of their neighbours who plainly expect their valiant efforts to fail – and the account of their struggles, the good moments and the bad, make a very special story indeed. There is a ring of truth to this story of the youngsters winning through adversity to proud adulthood, a feeling that, yes, indeed, this is just how it must have been, and the people, too, just like this. The hard work, the discomfort, the independence, and the warm neighbourliness were all a part of backwoods life at the end of the 18th century, and still a part today.

For all their quaint speech and customs and their obvious lack of "book learning," Best has not made his characters bumpkins or yokels. They are highly skilled craftsmen and women, who can make or mend anything they need, and are dependent upon no repairmen, social workers, or law enforcement officers. *Young'un*'s world has about it a warm and enviable glow that no electric light can duplicate.

—Joan McGrath

BIANCO, Margery Williams.   British.   Born in London, 22 July 1881. Educated privately and at schools in Philadelphia and Sharon Hill, Pennsylvania. Married Francisco Bianco; one son and one daughter, the illustrator Pamela Bianco. *Died 4 September 1944.*

Publications for Children

Fiction

> *The Velveteen Rabbit; or, How Toys Become Real*, illustrated by William Nicolson.   London, Heinemann, and New York, Doran, 1922.
> *The Little Wooden Doll*, illustrated by Pamela Bianco.   New York, Macmillan, 1925.
> *Poor Cecco: The Wonderful Story of a Wonderful Wooden Dog Who Was the Jolliest Toy in the House until He Went Out to Explore the World*, illustrated by Arthur Rackham.   London, Chatto and Windus, and New York, Doran, 1925.
> *The Apple Tree*, illustrated by Boris Artzybasheff.   New York, Doran, 1926.
> *The Adventures of Andy*, illustrated by Leon Underwood.   New York, Doran, 1927.
> *The Skin Horse*, illustrated by Pamela Bianco.   New York, Doran, 1927.
> *The Candlestick*, illustrated by Ludovic Rodo.   New York, Doubleday, 1929.
> *Other People's Houses*.   New York, Viking Press, 1930.
> *The House That Grew Smaller*, illustrated by Rachel Field.   New York, Macmillan, 1931.
> *A Street of Little Shops*, illustrated by Grace Paull.   New York, Doubleday, 1932; Kingswood, Surrey, World's Work, 1958.
> *The Hurdy-Gurdy Man*, illustrated by Robert Lawson.   New York, Oxford University Press, 1933; London, Oxford University Press, 1937.
> *The Good Friends*, illustrated by Grace Paull.   New York, Viking Press, 1934.

Winterbound, illustrated by Kate Seredy.   New York, Viking Press, 1936.
Green Grows the Garden, illustrated by Grace Paull.   New York, Macmillan, 1936.
Franzi and Gizi, with Gisella Loeffler.   New York, Messner, 1941.
Penny and the White Horse, illustrated by Marjory Collinson.   New York, Messner, 1942.
Bright Morning, illustrated by Margaret Platt.   New York, Viking Press, 1942; London, Collins, 1945.
Forward, Commandos!, illustrated by Rafaello Busoni.   New York, Viking Press, 1944; London, Wells Gardner Darton, 1947.

Other

All about Pets, illustrated by Grace Gilkison.   New York, Macmillan, 1930.
More about Animals, illustrated by Helen Torrey.   New York, Macmillan, 1934.
Tales from a Finnish Tupa, with James Cloyd Bowman, illustrated by Laura Bannon.   Chicago, Whitman, 1936.
Rufus the Fox: Adapted from the French of Samivel.   London and New York, Harper, 1937.
The Five-and-a-Half Club (reader), with Mabel O'Donnell and Rona Munro, illustrated by Florence and Margaret Hoopes.   Evanston, Illinois, Row Peterson, 1942; London, Nisbet, 1956.
Herbert's Zoo and Other Favorite Stories, with others, illustrated by Julian.   New York, Simon and Schuster, 1949.
The New Five-and-a-Half Club (reader), with Mabel O'Donnell, illustrated by Margaret Ayer.   Evanston, Illinois, Row Peterson, 1951.
Comprehension Cards.   London, Nisbet, 24 vols., 1959.

Translator, *The African Saga*, by Blaise Cendrars.   New York, Payson and Clarke, 1927.
Translator, *Little Black Stories for Little White Children*, by Blaise Cendrars, illustrated by Pierre Pinsard.   New York, Payson and Clarke, 1929.
Translator, with Dagny Mortensen, *Sidsel Longskirt: A Girl of Norway*, by Hans Aanrud, illustrated by Ingri and Edgar Parin d'Aulaire.   Philadelphia, Winston, 1935.
Translator, with Dagny Mortensen, *Solve Suntrap: A Boy of Norway* by Hans Aanrud, illustrated by Ingri and Edgar Parin d'Aulaire.   Philadelphia, Winston, 1935.

PUBLICATIONS FOR ADULTS

Novels

The Late Returning.   London, Heinemann, and New York, Macmillan, 1902.
Spendthrift Summer.   London, Heinemann, 1903.
The Price of Youth.   London, Duckworth, and New York, Macmillan, 1904.
The Bar.   London, Methuen, 1906.
The Thing in the Woods.   London, Duckworth, 1913.

Play

Out of the Night: A Mystery Comedy, with Harold Hutchinson.   London and New York, French, 1929.

Other

Paris.   London, A. and C. Black, and New York, Macmillan, 1910.

Translator, *Four Cents an Acre: The Story of Louisiana under the French*, by Georges Oudard.   New York, Brewer and Warren, 1931.

*   *   *

Some of the greatest books – among them *Alice, The Wind in the Willows* and *The Hobbit* – have started life as private books. Conceived for the entertainment of individual children, they have only later, and then sometimes after processing, found a wider audience.

Margery Williams Bianco's *Poor Cecco* is of this company. It was made first for the author's daughter Pamela – genius out of genius; at 12 Pamela's drawings inspired Walter de la Mare to a set of charming "illustrative" verses, and she grew up to be equally distinguished as artist and writer. The "Poor Cecco" of the title was a battered wooden dog, and the other characters were out of Pamela's toy-cupboard. They live in a necessarily closely-knit community, form complicated relationships, and talk their own language. The modern reader who is privileged to look in on this private world is initially puzzled, but not for too long. *Poor Cecco* is one of the classic "toy" stories, deserving a place beside *Hitty* and *Impunity Jane* among the very best of the genre.

Mrs. Bianco knew, as all who enjoy the company of small children must, that toys are a very serious matter. There is plenty of laughter in *Poor Cecco*, but it is with, not at, the creatures whose destinies are worked out in these pages. The toys feel emotions rather like those of humans, but their actions are governed by certain physical limitations. They are animate but still made of wood, fabric, and stuffing.

They are nicely contrasted with the humans and the animals. There is a particularly convincing portrait of Murrum the cat, who comes nearest in this fundamentally kindly story to being the villain of the piece. The humans play a minor and passive role, apart from the postman who brings home Poor Cecco and his friends from their wanderings, tied together like a parcel and the postage duly paid with Poor Cecco's hard-earned pennies.

Unlike some improvised stories *Poor Cecco* is tightly constructed. The plot is very compact, even if the entry of a major character – Jensina the Dutch doll – is delayed until well into the book; this is not a flaw so much as a calculated building-up to one of the crises of the narrative. Jensina is a splendid person, strong-minded, resourceful, set against the home-bred dolls with their gossip and petty jealousies. The subtleties of characterisation are expressed always in dialogue rather than in description; each toy has his idiosyncracies of speech and his individual standpoint.

Mrs. Bianco has always been well served by her illustrators. The first edition of *Poor Cecco* had seven colour-plates in Arthur Rackham's grandest manner, and a recent edition has drawings no less decorative and perhaps more penetrating by Antony Maitland. A lesser book, *The Hurdy-Gurdy Man*, was honoured with masterly designs by Robert Lawson. The book which comes nearest to *Poor Cecco* – *The Velveteen Rabbit* – is one of the very few illustrated by one of the greatest masters of this art, Sir William Nicolson.

The Velveteen Rabbit might be regarded as a trial run for *Poor Cecco*. It too is a story of toys and of the nursery magic which can give them a reality more sharp than that of the ordinary world. But here the writer lacks confidence, and her book is tentative and uncertain, full of the sententiousness into which American writers are prone to slip when the heat of inspiration cools. The moral, instead of being implicit in the narrative, has to be stated and underlined.

Mrs. Bianco, although not prolific, ranged widely, with translations, educational readers, and a travel book about Paris. For most readers she remains, and rightly, a one-book woman. *Poor Cecco* contains the best of her: the tenderness, the sense of adventure and of fun, the sturdy commonsense. As postscript to one of her innumerable letters to Bulka, which fill one memorable chapter, Tubby writes: "I love you more than Christmas and Easter and Fairyland." These are strong words, but they are rather what the reader feels about this uniquely heart-warming book.

—Marcus Crouch

BIBBY, Violet. British. Born in Newport Pagnell, Buckinghamshire, 18 February 1908. Educated at Whitelands College; Central School of Art, London. Married Edmund Bibby in 1937; has two sons. Worked as an English and Arts and Crafts teacher. Agent: Murray Pollinger, 4 Garrick Street, London WC2E 9HB. Address: 1 Cumberland Road, Angmering, Sussex BN16 4BG, England.

PUBLICATIONS FOR CHILDREN

Fiction

    Saranne, illustrated by Hilary Abrahams.   London, Penguin, 1969.
    The Mirrored Shield, illustrated by Graham Humphreys.   London, Penguin, 1970.
    The Wildling, illustrated by Graham Humphreys.   London, Penguin, 1971.
    Many Waters.   London, Faber, 1974; as *Many Waters Cannot Quench Love*, New
        York, Morrow, 1975.
    Tinner's Quest.   London, Faber, 1977.

Violet Bibby comments:
I have a strong feeling of "place," which has set off each book so far. My writing, I am told, is very "visual." I would have been a painter if I had not turned to writing seriously. I still paint evocative landscapes.

*   *   *

A craft or a lifestyle is the true hero of every one of Violet Bibby's books. *Saranne*, her first book, uses the world of canal narrowboats as a background for an adventure and mystery story. The way of life of canal folk is beautifully described; the characters, though simple, are vivid, and the plot is elaborate in a rather old-fashioned manner. The author's affection and enthusiasm for her subject shine through the book, and make a warm and pleasing result.

The Mirrored Shield treats in a similar manner of the craft of stonemason in the fifteenth century; *The Wildling* glass workers in the Sussex Weald in the early 17th century. All these books have a particular flavour; though carefully written, their plots and characters are rather mechanical; though lively, they lack the inner life which might make them transcend their function as the author's device to allow her to write about the life of their time and setting. However, Violet Bibby is not a narrowly didactic writer, for she is able to infuse the details of her world and the minutiae of ancient crafts with the life and enthusiasm her characters never quite embody.

Many Waters might seem to be in the same mould. Once more there is an old and picturesque life-style – that of fen-dwellers in Cambridgeshire before the Dutchmen drained the marshes in the 1640's. But the character of Constancy, and her affection for a young Dutch engineer is more successful, and more subtly drawn. The mysterious world of the wetlands is still the main subject, and, though the book is a little over-plotted, it is convincing and touching.

Tinner's Quest takes her largest canvas yet. With the intricate knowledge and talent for exposition which we by now expect of her, Miss Bibby describes the life of Cornish tin miners and charts two generations of a mining family in their wanderings from Cornwall to America to Australia. Salan, the true central figure of the book, is Miss Bibby's most interesting character. Speaking the old tongue, liking the old standing stones, with an instinctive feel for the lie of the lodes in the rock, he goes native when he gets to Australia, understanding and befriending the aborigines. The mystery of his crime, and the search for him by his wife and son make up the main movement of the book; the means by which an adit is cut to drain a flooded mine into the sea is a sub-plot as powerful as the main one. No one can make such matters as comprehensible and fascinating as Miss Bibby can; this is her best book.

—Jill Paton Walsh

BICE, Clare. Canadian. Born in Durham, Ontario, 24 January 1908. Educated at Aberdeen Public School, 1913–21, and Central Collegiate, 1921–26, London, Ontario; University of Western Ontario, London, 1926–29, B.A.; Art Students' League and Grand Central School of Art, both in New York, 1930–31. Served in the Canadian Army, 1942–45: Corporal. Married Marion Agnes Reid in 1943; one son and one daughter. Curator, London Art Museum, Ontario, 1940–72. Taught at the Doon School of Art, and summer sessions at Queen's University, Kingston, Ontario; Mount Allison University, Sackville, New Brunswick; University of British Columbia, Vancouver; and University of Western Ontario. Painter: one-man shows in Montreal, and London and Hamilton, Ontario; group shows: New York World's Fair, 1939; Canadian Army Exhibition, 1944; Canadian National Exhibition; Stratford Festival, Ontario. President, Canadian Art Museums Directors' Organization, 1966–68. Recipient: Canadian Government Fellowship, 1952; Canada Arts Council Senior Fellowship, 1962, 1972; Centennial Medal, 1967. LL.D.: University of Western Ontario, 1962. Associate, 1938, Full Academician, 1964, and President, 1967–70, Royal Canadian Academy. Member, Order of Canada, 1973. *Died 18 May 1976.*

PUBLICATIONS FOR CHILDREN (illustrated by the author)

Fiction

Jory's Cove. New York, Macmillan, 1941.
Across Canada: Stories of Canadian Children. New York, Macmillan, 1949.
The Great Island. New York, Macmillan, 1954.
A Dog for Davie's Hill. Toronto, Macmillan, 1956.
The Hurricane Treasure. Toronto, Macmillan, and New York, Viking Press, 1965.

Illustrator: *Animals, Plants, and Machines* by Lucy Sprague Mitchell and Margaret Wise Brown, 1944; *T'A'int Runnin' No More*, 1946, *The Bruce Beckons*, 1952, and *Silken Lines and Silver Hooks*, 1954, all by William Sherwood Fox; *Thunder in the Mountains* by Hilda Mary Hooke, 1947; *The Golden Pine Cone*, 1950, *The Sun Horse*, 1951, *The One-Winged Dragon*, 1955, *The Silver Man*, 1958, *The Diamond Feather*, 1962, and *The Hunter and the Medicine Man*, 1966, all by Catherine Anthony Clark; *The Force Carries On* by T. Morris Longstreth, 1954; *At the Dark of the Moon* by Mabel Tinkiss Good, 1956; *The Great Canoe* by Adelaide Leitch, 1962; *Keen for Adventure* by William E. Corfield, 1967.

* * *

Clare Bice has received more attention as an artist known for fine landscapes and portraits than as a writer for children. The five juveniles which he wrote and illustrated vary in quality from the informative but uninspired *Across Canada: Stories of Canadian Children* to the exciting mystery and adventure stories which are set on the rugged Eastern Canadian seacoast. These latter books, as well as the one set in the Scottish Highlands (*A Dog for Davie's Hill*), are successful both with children and from a literary point of view.

Bice's eye as a painter is both his strength and his undoing in *Across Canada*. The realistic illustrations give an appealing pastoral vision of Canadian provincial life, but the text itself is drab. The stories are mere sketches of the landscapes he surveys – seacoasts, farms, prairies, mountains, forests, and the Canadian North; there is little dramatic action or plot. At the center of each sketch is a child, ostensibly the subject of the piece, but description consists more of the superficial visual details noticed by the painter than of character analysis by the writer.

Mystery-adventure stories like *The Great Island* and *Hurricane Treasure* are more successful. In them, Bice creates a vivid setting, and he blends landscape with character and action more skillfully. One interesting technique in *The Great Island* is seen in his manipulations of time. We meet Angus, the boy protagonist, who takes us into three levels of time: his imagination turns backwards into the historical and mythic past of pirates and buried gold; his actual present consists of poverty and loneliness because his father must work in the big city to support them; and the future is secured because Angus' search for treasure leads to the community's obtaining a new fish-freezing plant which will furnish local employment for his father. Dramatic action is sustained throughout, and the skillful juxtapositioning of the past, present, and future gives depth to the story.

The Hurricane Treasure is another mystery-adventure based on a treasure hunt. It features a haunted house which collapses in a storm, Gothic fashion, as well as Canadian Mounties on the trail of smugglers, but Bice treats this stock material realistically. One of the tensions in the story is between the local Nova Scotian villagers and the summer visitor-intruders towards whom the natives have ambivalent feelings. The conclusion, precipitated by the hurricane, furnishes a meager treasure of gold, but a greater treasure of understanding between people. When the air is cleared, blighted lives are restored, and everyone learns that appearances can deceive.

A Dog for Davie's Hill, set in the Scottish Highlands, is also successful in conveying a realistic sense of place. Basically a mystery story about sheep stealing, it is also a dog story, with a touching account of a boy and a dog's affection for each other. The book's character development gives it more depth.

Bice's strength as a writer is in conveying atmosphere and a sense of place and community. However, he also has commendable skill as a mystery-adventure story writer. His plots move quickly, and the humanitarian spirit which underlies his material rarely intrudes in the story.

—Mary Rubio

BIRO, Val (Balint Stephen Biro). British. Born in Budapest, Hungary, 6 October 1921. Educated at the Cistercian School, Budapest; Central School of Arts and Crafts, London, 1939–42. Married Vivien Woolley in 1945, one daughter; Marie-Louise Ellaway, 1970, two stepchildren. Studio Manager, Sylvan Press, London, 1944–46; Production Manager, C. and J. Temple, London, 1946–48; Art Director, John Lehmann, publishers, London, 1948–51; Urban District Councillor, 1966–70. Freelance artist and writer. Fellow, Society of Industrial Artists and Designers. Address: 95 High Street, Amersham, Buckinghamshire HP7 0DT, England.

PUBLICATIONS FOR CHILDREN

Fiction (illustrated by the author)

Bumpy's Holiday. London, Sylvan Press, 1943; New York, Transatlantic Arts, 1945.
Gumdrop: The Adventures of a Vintage Car. Leicester, Brockhampton Press, 1966; Chicago, Follett, 1967.

Gumdrop and the Farmer's Friend. Leicester, Brockhampton Press, 1967; Chicago, Follett, 1968.

Gumdrop on the Rally. Leicester, Brockhampton Press, 1968; Chicago, Follett, 1969.

Gumdrop on the Move. Leicester, Brockhampton Press, 1969; Chicago, Follett, 1970.

Gumdrop Goes to London. Leicester, Brockhampton Press, 1971.

Gumdrop Finds a Friend. Leicester, Brockhampton Press, 1973.

Gumdrop in Double Trouble. Leicester, Brockhampton Press, 1975.

Gumdrop and the Steamroller. London, Hodder and Stoughton, 1976.

Gumdrop Posts a Letter. London, Hodder and Stoughton, 1976.

Gumdrop on the Brighton Run. London, Hodder and Stoughton, 1976.

Gumdrop Has a Birthday. London, Hodder and Stoughton, 1977.

Other

The Honest Thief: A Hungarian Folktale. Leicester, Brockhampton Press, 1972.

Buster Is Lost! (reader). London, Macmillan, 1974.

A Dog and His Bone (reader). London, Macmillan, 1975.

Illustrator: *The Story of a Carrot* by Kate Barclay, 1944; *No Bombs at All*, 1944, and *Airman's Song Book*, 1945, by Cyril H.W. Jackson; *Private Gallery* by P. Tabori, 1944; *Worlds Without End* by Denys Val Baker, 1945; *Escape from the Zoo*, 1945, *A Camel from the Desert*, 1947, and *The Penguin Goes Home*, 1951, all by Richard Parker; *Crusading Holiday* by Mary F. Moore, 1946; *England, The Mysterious Island* by P. Treves, 1948; *The Story of Joseph and Pharaoh* by Frances Dale, 1950; *Pilgrim's Progress* by John Bunyan, 1951; *Serena Blandish* by Enid Bagnold, 1951; *Zoo for Zanies* by Nicholas Husk, 1952; *The South African Twins*, 1953, and *The Australian Twins*, 1954, by Daphne Rooke; *The Man Who Made Wine* by J.M. Scott, 1954; *David the Shepherd Boy* by Elizabeth Goudge, 1954; *Fit for a Bishop* by Stephen Bishop, 1955; *Fire Engine by Mistake*, 1955, *Andy's Pit Pony*, 1958, and *The Doctor*, 1972, all by Leila Berg; *The Casket and the Sword* by Norman Dale, 1956; *Tommy the Tugboat*, 1956, *Henry the Helicopter*, 1956, *Tommy Joins the Navy*, 1957, *Henry to the Rescue*, 1959, *Henry the Hero*, 1960, *Tommy's New Engine*, 1961, *Hovering with Henry*, 1961, *Henry in the News*, 1963, *Henry's Busy Winter*, 1964, *Tommy and the Lighthouse*, 1965, *Henry Joins the Police*, 1966, *Tommy and the Oil Rig*, 1967, *Henry and the Astronaut*, 1968, *Tommy and the Spanish Galleon*, 1969, *Henry and the Traction Engine*, 1970, *Tommy and the Yellow Submarine*, 1971, *Henry in the Mountains*, 1972, *Henry in Iceland*, 1973, *Ferryboat Tommy*, 1973, *Tommy in the Caribbean*, 1974, *Henry on Safari*, 1975, and *Tommy and the Island*, 1977, all by Dora Thatcher; *To Arms for the Queen* by Eric Leyland, 1956; *Kettleby's Zoo* by Margaret Holden, 1957; *Andy and [the Mascots*, 1957, *the Water Crossing*, 1958, *the Sharpshooter*, 1959, *the Display Team*, 1959, *the Secret Papers*, 1961, *the Miniature War*, 1962, *the Royal Review*, 1963, *His Last Parade*, 1968], all by Reginald Taylor; *Hideaway Johnny* by David Scott Daniell, 1959; *The Story of Scotland* by Lawrence Stenhouse, 1961; *The Prisoner of Zenda* by Anthony Hope, 1961; *What a Lark*, 1961, and *Soap-Box Derby*, 1962, by Rosemary Weir; *Man Makes Towns* by Kenneth Rudge, 1963; *The Ship Stealers*, 1963, and *Big-Head*, 1964, by Cam Renton; *The Seas of Britain* by Peter Dawlish, 1963; *The Country Year* by Thurlow Craig, 1964; *Arabian Nights*, 1965; *The Wonderful Wizard of Oz*, 1965, and *The Marvellous Land of Oz*, 1967, by L. Frank Baum; *The Sunday Telegraph Gardening Book* by Fred Whitsey, 1966; *Journal of My Service in India* by J. Corneille, 1966; *The Story of Fanny Burney* by Josephine Kamm, 1966; *The Field Bedside Book*, 1967; *The Ghost of June* by Rupert Croft-Cooke, 1968; *Kangaroo Tennis*, 1968, and *Benjie the Circus Dog*, 1969, by Donald Bisset; *One Man's Happiness* by Lord Tweedsmuir, 1968; *Sally the Seal*, 1968, *James and Sally Again*, 1970, and *Mr. Bubbus and the Railway Smugglers*, 1976, all by Joan Drake; *Home Is the North* by Walt Morey, 1968; *Discovering Chesham* by Arnold Baines, 1968; *The Untravelled World* by Eric E. Shipton, 1969; *Picture Reference Book of the Georgians* by Boswell Taylor, 1969; *Garden Glory* by Ted Humphris, 1969; *The Terrible*

Trumpet by William Wise, 1969; *Soldier Bear* by Geoffrey Morgan, 1970; *The Writ of Green Wax* by Edward Bohan, 1970; *Lovingly*, 1971, *Prayerfully*, 1972, and *Thankfully*, 1975, all by Helen Steiner Rice; *See, Hear and Speak* by Donald Sutherland, 1971; *American Wit and Wisdom* by James Dow, 1971; *The Cook Hostess' Book*, 1971, and *The Sherlock Holmes Cook Book*, 1976, by Fanny Craddock; *The Good Food Guide*, 1971; *Making Friends with Music* by James Glennon, 1971; *The Jazz Band* by Helen Solomon, 1972; *Country Talk*, 1972, *More Country Talk*, 1973, *New Country Talk*, 1975, and *New Country Talk Again*, 1977, all by J.B.H. Peel; *Mr. Purpose* by Mimi Irving, 1972; *A Reading Book* by Leslie Alexander, 1972; *Tales of the Circus* by Jane MacMichael, 1972; *Victoria in the Wings*, 1972, and *The Prince and the Quakeress*, 1976, and other novels by Jean Plaidy; *Play the Best Courses* by Peter Allen, 1973; *Cubs with a Difference*, 1973, *Cubs Away*, 1974, and *Cubs on Saturday*, 1976, all by Stephen Andrews; *The Dinghy Stories* by Dawn Bowker, 1973; *Garry the Goblin* by Gladys Williams, 1973; *The Reporter* by Michael Pollard, 1973; *The Nose Knows*, 1974, *Dolls in Danger*, 1974, *The Case of the Condemned Cat*, 1975, *The Menaced Midget*, 1975, *The Case of the Nervous Newsboy*, 1976, *The Great Rabbit Robbery*, 1976, *A Cat Called Amnesia*, 1976, and *The Case of the Invisible Dog*, 1977, all by E.W. Hildick; *Down the Kitchen Sink* by Beverley Nichols, 1974; *The Robert Carrier Cookery Course*, 1974; *The Sick Cow*, 1974, and *George the Fire Engine*, 1976, by H.E. Todd; *Brer Rabbit and the Wonderful Tar-Baby*, 1975, *Brer Rabbit is Trapped*, 1975, *Brer Rabbit and the Alligator*, 1976, and *Brer Rabbit Saves Brer Terrapin*, 1976, all by Enid Blyton; *Food and Drink from Your Garden*, 1975, and *The Rough Shoot*, 1975, by Daniel Green; *Machines on the Farm* by John Denton, 1975; *Jim's Go-Kart* by Jeffrey Bevington, 1975; *The Best Games People Play* by Richard Sharp, 1976; *British Folk Customs* by Christina Hole, 1976.

Val Biro comments:

All my "Gumdrop" books are based on my own real vintage car called Gumdrop, in reality an Austin Healey 12, 1926. I am an illustrator by training and profession, but the happy acquisition of this car in 1961 turned my thoughts to writing about it and to produce picture books as a result. Most incidents in my stories are based on fact — on things that happened to my car in real life — but imagination then takes over to create books of fiction. I now visit festivals, schools and libraries in the real Gumdrop and talk to children about it. In between my own books, I remain an illustrator of other people's books. Gumdrop has appeared on TV several times and is translated into many languages.

                    *   *   *

Val Biro has made his reputation by picture books for very young children, writing and illustrating them himself. The illustrations are as important as the text, if not more important, for this age group. His chief character is Gumdrop, a vintage car.

"He was a very old car, and his proper name was Austin Clifton Twelve-Four. But everybody called him Gumdrop. His owner, Mr. Oldcastle, was so lonely that he had to go to live with his daughter and sell his car, but he kept the old brass horn." A different incident, portrayed in large dramatic coloured pictures, follows on every page. Burglars steal Gumdrop and crash the car; various characters, including a gipsy family, secure interesting bits off the vehicle. The rest of the book is taken up with recovering everything, and ends up with a vintage car rally. The last page shows the cross-section of an Austin made in 1926.

After that Gumdrop fills many books. He drives round London tangling with crooks, is involved with tractors and cranes, animals and people. A vehicle with real personality, he appeals to the young, who take an interest in cars at a very early age.

"There was a strange sight at the Red Lion one sunny morning in June. The vintage cars had come to start their big rally of the year. Never was there such a collection of fine old cars in the yard. Each had a Rally number fixed to it. Number 1 was an Alvis Duck-Back and Number 2 a Morris Bullnose. The model T Ford was Number 3 .... And then there was a blue car with a black hood and a brass horn. It was Number 9: an Austin Clifton Heavy

Twelve-Four, vintage 1926, driven by Bill McArran. It was Gumdrop." So begins a typical story. This information occupies two pages of large well-spaced print because the vehicles themselves, their owners and some young spectators, all with expressive faces, fill the entire background.

This particular rally involves a thief, a farmyard, a horse box, a pony club rally, a carnival procession, a crowd of pigs who have to be given a lift, a blazing hayrick, a fire engine, and an angry motor cycle. Gumdrop of course had lost his way, but he was awarded a brass starting handle as a special prize for solving the crime of the stolen prizes.

The book ends on a good moral note. "Everyone cheered and all the cars sounded their horns. Gluurk-Gug and Bleep-Blip, Honk-Tonk and Tootle-Toot. Gumdrop was the happiest car in the rally because he had helped a lost little boy, a mayor in a procession, a farmer with ten little pigs ... helped put out a fire and found the silver cups."

—Margaret Campbell

BISHOP, Claire Huchet. American. Born in Brittany, France. Educated at the Sorbonne, Paris. Married to Frank Bishop. Recipient: New York *Herald Tribune* Festival award, 1947; Child Study Association of America Award, 1953. Address: 309 East 52nd Street, New York, New York 10022, U.S.A.

PUBLICATIONS FOR CHILDREN

Fiction

> *The Five Chinese Brothers*, illustrated by Kurt Wiese. New York, Coward McCann, 1938; London, Oxford University Press, 1939.
> *The Kings' Day*, illustrated by Doris Spiegel. New York, Coward McCann, 1940.
> *The Ferryman*, illustrated by Kurt Wiese. New York, Coward McCann, 1941; London, Faber, 1943.
> *The Man Who Lost His Head*, illustrated by Robert McCloskey. New York, Viking Press, 1942.
> *Augustus*, illustrated by Grace Paull. New York, Viking Press, 1945.
> *Pancakes-Paris*, illustrated by Georges Schreiber. New York, Viking Press, 1947.
> *Blue Spring Farm*. New York, Viking Press, 1948.
> *Bernard and His Dogs*, illustrated by Maurice Brevannes. Boston, Houghton Mifflin, 1952.
> *Twenty and Ten*, illustrated by William Pène du Bois. New York, Viking Press, 1952.
> *All Alone*, illustrated by Feodor Rojankovsky. New York, Viking Press, 1953.
> *The Big Loop*, illustrated by Carles Fontseré. New York, Viking Press, 1955; London, Dent, 1958.
> *Toto's Triumph*, illustrated by Claude Ponsot. New York, Viking Press, 1957; London, Dent, 1959.
> *A Present from Petros*, illustrated by Dimitris Davis. New York, Viking Press, 1961.
> *Twenty-Two Bears*, illustrated by Kurt Wiese. New York, Viking Press, 1964.
> *The Truffle Pig*, illustrated by Kurt Wiese. New York, Coward McCann, 1971.
> *Georgette*, illustrated by Ursula Landshoff. New York, Coward McCann, 1973.

Other

> *Christopher the Giant* (on St. Christopher), illustrated by Berkeley Williams, Jr. Boston, Houghton Mifflin, 1950.

Lafayette: French-American Hero. Champaign, Illinois, Garrard, 1960.
Yeshu, Called Jesus (as Claire Huchet), illustrated by Don Bolognese. New York, Farrar Straus, 1966; London, Constable, 1967.
Mozart: Music Magician, illustrated by Paul Frame. Champaign, Illinois, Garrard, 1968.
Johann Sebastian Bach: Music Giant, illustrated by Russell Hoover. Champaign, Illinois, Garrard, 1972.

Editor, *Happy Christmas: Tales for Boys and Girls,* illustrated by Ellen Raskin. New York, Stephen Daye Press, 1956.

PUBLICATIONS FOR ADULTS

Other

French Children's Books for English-Speaking Children: A ... Descriptive List .... New York, Sheridan Square Press, 1938.
France Alive. New York, McMullen, 1947.
All Things Common. New York, Harper, 1950.
Martin de Porres, Hero, illustrated by Jean Charlot. Boston, Houghton Mifflin, 1954.
French Roundabout. New York, Dodd Mead, 1960; revised edition, 1966.
Here Is France. New York, Farrar Straus, 1969.
How Catholics Look at Jews: Inquiries into Italian, French, and Spanish Teaching Methods. New York, Paulist Press, 1974.

*   *   *

Claire Huchet Bishop brings to American children a taste of Europe – of different people and different customs. In her books one can learn how truffles are found, what it was like to live in war-deprived Paris, how it feels to herd sheep on a mountain by yourself. Yet the author's interest is deeper than mere geographical or historical glimpses. She is discussing important and recurring problems in a child's life.

In *All Alone,* for example, a story designed for older children, a young sheep herder must decide whether to save a new acquaintance from death or abide by a strict village custom of having no dealings with strangers. The peasant lad is faced with a choice between two values – respect for his parents or regard for another human being. It is a serious situation, including fear of punishment, and it is one which could be the experience of any child in some form. Despite his narrow training, the hero chooses the higher law of doing good to his neighbor. Results show the wisdom of his act and encourage a child reader to think for himself.

Pancakes-Paris is still of interest, though it pictures the aftermath of World War II. Its real topic is privation. Butter, milk, orange, eggs, and cocoa are familiar words to children, but in this story these common foods are very scarce. So the custom of having delectable crêpes before Lent is unknown to the younger children and just a faint memory to the older ones. The disappearance of this tradition is symbolic of a world from which beauty and gracious occasions have been wiped away. It is a bleak scene of mud-colored dripping plaster walls, made so by long periods of no heat, of water and onion as a butter substitute, and of washing without soap. Against this dark picture stands the staunch character of Charles, the oldest child, now man of the family. It is his determination which makes it possible to celebrate the holiday with pancakes as before the war, to bring a shaft of light into the dreary monotony life has become. As in *All Alone* the reader finds a hero who meets difficulties with spirit.

Claire Bishop writes books for very young children as well as the two just discussed, designed for eight-to-twelve-year-olds. *The Truffle Pig,* like *Pancakes-Paris* takes place in France. Using words a child knows well, the author creates a story full of country sounds and smells with a lonely boy's love for a pig at its center: "It was tiny with a lovely pink color. It looked very bright. Pierre liked it at once." Pierre elegantly names his pet "Marcel" and the pig signifies his immediate attachment for the boy with loud unmistakable grunts. Pierre's loneliness dissolves.

However, pigs usually go to market and Marcel is no exception. In desperation, Pierre runs away with him. "Pierre and Marcel made for the woods. The birds had gone to bed. The smell of earth and plants filled the air. It was very quiet." What a nice description of forest-feeling tucked beside the dark problem! But while in the woods, Marcel displays a talent for finding truffles, and this delicacy delivers the pig from market, Pierre from loneliness, and Pierre's family from poverty.

Truffle Pig shows the author's versatility. She uses simple words and a cadence and format suitable for younger children to portray her vivid scenes and sensations. We do not begrudge the and-they-lived-happily-ever-after ending. Like the other books, it deals with a deep childhood problem − loneliness. Claire Bishop has no hesitation in bringing untrivial subjects to children but the writing is appropriate for the audience.

—Carolyn T. Kingston

BISSET, Donald. British. Born in London, 30 August 1910. Educated at the Warehousemen, Clerks and Drapers School, Addington, Surrey. Served in the Royal Artillery during World War II: Lieutenant. Married Nancy Bisset in 1946 (divorced); has one son. Radio, television, and stage actor. Agent: (literary) A.M. Heath, 40–42 William IV Street, London, WC2N 4DD; (theatre) Joseph and Wagg Ltd., 78 New Bond Street, London W.1. Address: 33 Andrewes House, Barbican, London EC2Y 8AB, England.

PUBLICATIONS FOR CHILDREN

Fiction

Anytime Stories, illustrated by the author.   London, Faber, 1954.
Sometime Stories, illustrated by the author.   London, Faber, 1957.
Next Time Stories, illustrated by the author.   London, Methuen, 1959.
This Time Stories, illustrated by the author.   London, Methuen, 1961.
Another Time Stories, illustrated by the author.   London, Methuen, 1963.
Little Bear's Pony, illustrated by Shirley Hughes.   London, Benn, 1966.
Hullo Lucy, illustrated by Gillian Kenny.   London, Benn, 1967.
Talks with a Tiger, illustrated by the author.   London, Methuen, 1967.
Kangaroo Tennis, illustrated by Val Biro.   London, Benn, 1968.
Nothing, illustrated by the author.   London, Benn, 1969.
Upside Down Land.   Moscow, Progress Publishers, 1969.
Benjie the Circus Dog, illustrated by Val Biro.   London, Benn, 1969.
Time and Again Stories, illustrated by the author.   London, Methuen, 1970.
Barcha the Tiger, illustrated by Derek Collard.   London, Benn, 1971.
Tiger Wants More, illustrated by the author.   London, Methuen, 1971.
Yak and the Sea Shell, illustrated by Lorraine Calaora.   London, Methuen, 1971.
Yak and the Painted Cave, illustrated by Lorraine Calaora.   London, Methuen, 1971.
Yak and the Buried Treasure, illustrated by Lorraine Calaora.   London, Methuen, 1972.
Yak and the Ice Cream, illustrated by Lorraine Calaora.   London, Methuen, 1972.
Father Tingtang's Journey, illustrated by the author.   London, Methuen, 1973.
Jenny Hopalong, illustrated by Derek Collard.   London, Benn, 1973.
Yak Goes Home, illustrated by Lorraine Calaora.   London, Methuen, 1973.

The Happy Horse, illustrated by David Sharpe. London, Benn, 1974.
The Adventures of Mandy Duck, illustrated by the author. London, Methuen, 1974.
Hazy Mountain, illustrated by Shirley Hughes. London, Penguin, 1975.
"Oh Dear," Said the Tiger, illustrated by the author. London, Methuen, 1975.
Paws with Shapes, illustrated by Tony Hutchins. Maidenhead, Berkshire, Intercontinental Books, 1976.
Paws with Numbers, with Michael Morris, illustrated by Tony Hutchins. Maidenhead, Berkshire, Intercontinental Books, 1976.
The Lost Birthday, illustrated by the author. Moscow, Progress Publishers, 1976.
The Story of Smokey Horse, illustrated by the author. London, Methuen, 1977.
This Is Ridiculous, illustrated by the author. London, Hamlyn, 1977.

Donald Bisset comments:
All my books are modern fairy stories – animistic in concept – and, on the surface, nonsensical, but nevertheless they have meanings (varied).

*   *   *

Donald Bisset writes for small children. His stories are very short; all the heroes, whether they are humans, animals or inanimate objects, talk and have most original problems comfortably solved. The author illustrates most of the books himself with small childish black and white drawings.

The tales move quickly from domestic to wild places, as in *Hullo Lucy* in which a small girl goes for a walk and meets a policeman, a king in his palace, a crocodile in a river, a Chinese boy and an African girl, a big ship, a whale, a sunflower, a milkman and various animals, but no-one says hello until she meets a kilted Scotsman. He points out that she has not said hello to them, so she writes, asking them all, except the crocodile, to tea. After that she says hello whenever she meets people.

Animals and humans mix happily. "One day Yak was in a big city among all the rush and noise of traffic and crowds of people" is how *Yak Goes Home* begins. He decides to return to the mountains and on the advice of Vulture takes peppermint creams as presents to his friends. After a restful train journey he gets a lift with an elephant in exchange for some of the peppermints.

Tiger appears in several books. He only eats words and gets very thin if not told stories, so he and the author set off together to find them. "Listen, beyond the arch, near here, on a little hill, there's a tree – the wind rustles its leaves and brings it stories from over the hills and far away." Walter the Owl, who lives in the tree, tells them about Alphonse, a friendly dragon who once a week has a fight with a knight; then Eli the elephant describes the dog that rattled and the brooms and vacuum cleaner who lived in a cupboard and had an argument. The book continues with brief adventures of kittens, a king, a pelican, a piano, a silent fish and a kite. The old beginning, "Once upon a time," is frequently used. *Talks with a Tiger* involve a Queen seeking the wisest person in her kingdom, a Beetle who met a Bulldozer, Father Neptune and the Whales, and the Tiger's tea party. All original nonsense.

Time and Again Stories begins: "Once upon a time there was a river which was made of words. It flowed down to the sea and the sea was made of story books." The tales are typical: a little penguin called Ian was sitting on an iceberg one day when the edge broke off and he fell into the sea, sitting on a small piece of ice until it floated to the Caribbean. This is followed by a quarrel between St. Pancras and King's Cross stations, which makes the clocks so furious that they go faster and faster and the trains do the same. Peace is restored when the Queen gives a medal to Euston. It is impossible to predict what will happen over the next page.

—Margaret Campbell

BLADES, Ann (Sager).   Canadian.   Born in Vancouver, British Columbia, 16 November 1947. Educated at Crofton House School, Vancouver; University of British Columbia, Vancouver, 1965–70, teaching certificate 1970; British Columbia Institute of Technology, 1972–74, registered nurse's qualification. Married Philip Michael Blades in 1966 (separated, 1971; divorced, 1975). Elementary school teacher, Peace River North School District, Mile 18, British Columbia, 1967–68, Department of Indian Affairs and Northern Development, Taché, British Columbia, 1969, and Surrey School District, British Columbia, 1969–71; clerk, London, Ontario, 1972; Registered Nurse, Vancouver General Hospital, 1974–75, and Mt. St. Joseph Hospital, Vancouver, 1975–76. Recipient: Canadian Library Association Award, 1972; Canada Council grant, 1975. Address: 3570 West 12th Avenue, Vancouver, British Columbia, Canada.

PUBLICATIONS FOR CHILDREN (illustrated by the author)

Fiction

>   *Mary of Mile 18.*   Montreal and Plattsburgh, New York, Tundra Books, 1971; London, Bodley Head, 1976.
>   *A Boy of Taché.*   Montreal and Plattsburgh, New York, Tundra Books, 1973.

Illustrator: *Jack the Woodcutter,* 1977.

Ann Blades comments:

When I was 19, I went to teach in the two-room school at Mile 18, an isolated farming community in northern British Columbia. In early spring, wanting an activity to help pass the time and impressed by the apparent lack of relevant reading material for children in rural areas, I decided to write and illustrate a book for children. I began to work on *Mary of Mile 18,* using one of my pupils, Mary, and her family as the characters in the book. I finished writing and illustrating *Mary of Mile 18* the following year, while teaching in the two-room school at Taché, an Indian reserve in central British Columbia. The next year I wrote and illustrated *A Boy of Taché,* based on a true episode that occurred while I was teaching there.

*   *   *

Requirements for a textbook rarely provoke successful literary endeavours. But the paucity of school material meaningful to children in a one-room schoolhouse tucked away in northern British Columbia became the touchstone of Ann Blades' invention. Her charges in a remote Mennonite community 18 miles off mile 73 of the Alaska Highway would comprehend little of the stoplights, sidewalks, and manicured parks which are veritable landmarks of conventional schoolbooks, but they would have intimate knowledge of the brilliant northern lights, and of isolation, solitude and an almost overwhelming sense of sameness. And it was these familiar elements which inspired *Mary of Mile 18,* in which the lifestyle of Mary Fehr, bespectacled child within a closely knit family, emerges with simple poignancy. Mary hopes that something different will happen, and she believes the northern lights to be harbingers of promised novelty. Something does happen in the appearance of a pup which is half wolf. But pets are an unaffordable luxury, and the pup cannot be Mary's until he proves capable of contributing to the sustaining pattern of existence. *Mary of Mile 18* suggests that creative pedagogy does indeed border on art.

Blades' second book, *A Boy of Taché,* presents a more elaborate text and a more involved plot. It is also more self consciously instructive with ecological concerns and observations on northern lifestyles arising from several asides. Za refuses to shoot a pregnant beaver, and it is observed that nowadays there is but an occasional eagle. The two companions pass by a nearby construction camp which is building a railway. But the learning is by no means intrusive. An intriguing theme unites change and continuity. The young Indian boy, Charlie, will now begin to hunt alone, since his beloved grandfather, whose life Charlie has saved, will be forced to retire. But the youthful hero will in fact become a hunter, and his dream of manhood differs little if at all from those of his ancestors.

A third book, as yet unpublished, *The Fowlini*, is a fairy story, the tale of a young boy who bravely encounters his fears by confronting the terrible monster who has penetrated his bedroom. The child like the author finds resources unlimited and the results are artistically compelling. Bedtime can be innocently productive, as Ann Blades discovers for her readers yet another realm of possibility plucked from a prosaic moment.

—Leonard R. Mendelsohn

BLOCH, Marie Halun. American; naturalized, 1923. Born in Komarno, Austria-Hungary, 1 December 1910. Educated at the University of Chicago, 1931–35, Ph.B. 1935. Married Donald Beaty Bloch in 1930; has one daughter. Junior Economist, Department of Labor, Washington, D.C., 1935–38, 1942–43. Recipient: Boys' Clubs of America Award, 1955. Agent: McIntosh and Otis Inc., 475 Fifth Avenue, New York, New York 10017. Address: 654 Emerson Street, Denver, Colorado 80218, U.S.A.

PUBLICATIONS FOR CHILDREN

Fiction

Danny Doffer, illustrated by Jessie Robinson.   New York and London, Harper, 1946.
Big Steve, The Double-Quick Tunnel Man, illustrated by Nicolas Mordvinoff.   New York, Coward McCann, 1952.
Herbert the Electrical Mouse, illustrated by Millard McGee.   New York, Messner, 1953; as *Leave It to Herbert*, New York, Tab, 1958.
Tony of the Ghost Towns, illustrated by Dorothy Marino.   New York, Coward McCann, 1956.
Marya of Clark Avenue, illustrated by Susanne Suba.   New York, Coward McCann, 1957.
The Dollhouse Story, illustrated by Walter Erhard.   New York, Walck, 1961.
The House on Third High, illustrated by Charles Walker.   New York, Coward McCann, 1962.
Aunt America, illustrated by Joan Berg.   New York, Atheneum, 1963.
The Two Worlds of Damyan, illustrated by Robert Quackenbush.   New York, Atheneum, 1966; London, Macdonald, 1968.
Bern, Son of Mikula, illustrated by Edward Kozak.   New York, Atheneum, 1972.

Other

Tunnels, illustrated by Nelson Sears.   New York, Coward McCann, 1954.
Dinosaurs, illustrated by George Mason.   New York, Coward McCann, 1955.
Mountains on the Move, illustrated by Robert Gartland.   New York, Coward McCann, 1960.
Look at Dinosaurs, illustrated by Jo Acheson.   London, Hamish Hamilton, 1962.
Ukrainian Folk Tales, illustrated by J. Hnizdovsky.   New York, Coward McCann, 1964; London, Hart Davis, 1965.

Ivanko and the Dragon, illustrated by Yaroslava Mills.   New York, Atheneum, 1969.

Manuscript Collection: Kerlan Collection, University of Minnesota, Minneapolis.

Marie Halun Bloch comments:
Each of my books is rooted in some enthusiasm of mine – material of such over-riding personal interest that I want to share it with others, even at the expense of weeks and months of the sometimes agonizing work of writing.

However, enthusiasm is never enough. Delving into vivid memories of my own youthful thoughts and feelings, I always search for those elements in my material that will make my story as universal as possible in order to engage the interest of the reader.

Out of my love for the mountains of Colorado, where I spend a part of each summer, have come my books *Big Steve, Tony of the Ghost Towns, Mountains on the Move, The House on Third High*, and *Dinosaurs* as well. In 1960 I made the first of several returns to my native place, in West Ukraine. The profoundly moving experience of "going home," by which I refreshed my native heritage, led me eventually to produce six books, beginning with the highly successful *Aunt America*.

Two books resulted from my nearly lifelong interest in folk tales and folklore. To me there's something thrilling in the fact that one meets similar customs and similar tales the world over. This fact says to me that folklore is the distillation of the total human experience and that a writer ought to be familiar with this fund of wisdom and the symbols of which it is composed. A writer is, in any case, a descendant of the tribal storyteller, the priest-practitioner of the magic that illuminates both the inner world of the reader and the physical world in which he lives.

                         *   *   *

Many of Marie Halun Bloch's books are based on her own experiences as a child or an adult: *Tony of the Ghost Towns* and *The House on Third High* reflect her love for the Colorado mountains where she spends summers, *The Dollhouse Story* was written at the request of a small daughter whose fascination with a dollhouse was shared by her mother, and *Aunt America* was provoked by a visit to the Ukrainian village in which the author was born, and through which her renewed interest in her background inspired *The Two Worlds of Damyan, Bern, Son of Mikula*, and two books of Ukrainian folktales.

But even before this visit, Bloch had written *Marya*, based on her own childhood. Shy, convinced that her new teacher feels that Ukrainians are inferior, Marya Polenko learns, when her parents invite the teacher to share a family holiday, that her teacher had simply not known she was shy. The story is episodic, but Bloch gives a vivid picture of the adjustment problems that a timid child has in any new situation. The folktales are useful for storytelling, but are rather stilted in writing style. *Bern, Son of Mikula* is historical fiction, based on careful research and vivid in its details of tenth-century Kiev, but it moves ponderously; of the two contemporary stories, *The Two Worlds of Damyan*, too, is a bit heavy-handed in contrasting the ideologies of Damyan's young communist friends and his old-fashioned grandmother, while in *Aunt America* Bloch makes the same kind of comparison far more effectively. It is through the eyes of visiting Aunt Lydia that young Lesya sees, with fresh perception, that her father (who had been a political prisoner) is a man of integrity, and that the uncle she had previously admired because he had been "wise" is a toady. The story gives a colorful picture of a Ukrainian village and a perceptive depiction of the ambivalence of some members of the younger generation in an Iron Curtain country. Of all Bloch's books, it best achieves the goal she has set of giving, through her stories, an intimate glimpse into the unfamiliar, an enlargement of one's world.

—Zena Sutherland

BLUME, Judy.   American.   Born in Elizabeth, New Jersey, 12 February 1938. Educated at New York University, B.A. 1960. Married John M. Blume in 1959 (divorced), one daughter and one son; Thomas A. Kitchens, 1976. Lives in northern New Mexico. Agent: Harold Ober Associates Inc., 40 East 49th Street, New York, New York 10017, U.S.A.

<small>PUBLICATIONS FOR CHILDREN</small>

Fiction

> *The One in the Middle Is the Green Kangaroo*, illustrated by Lois Axeman.   Chicago, Reilly and Lee, 1969.
> *Iggie's House.*   Englewood Cliffs, New Jersey, Bradbury Press, 1970.
> *Are You There, God? It's Me, Margaret.*   Englewood Cliffs, New Jersey, Bradbury Press, 1970.
> *Freckle Juice*, illustrated by Sonia O. Lisker.   New York, Scholastic, 1971.
> *Then Again, Maybe I Won't.*   Scarsdale, New York, Bradbury Press, 1971.
> *It's Not the End of the World.*   Scarsdale, New York, Bradbury Press, 1972.
> *Tales of a Fourth Grade Nothing*, illustrated by Roy Doty.   New York, Dutton, 1972.
> *Otherwise Known as Sheila the Great.*   New York, Dutton, 1972.
> *Deenie.*   Scarsdale, New York, Bradbury Press, 1973.
> *Blubber.*   Scarsdale, New York, Bradbury Press, 1974.
> *Forever.*   Scarsdale, New York, Bradbury Press, 1975; London, Gollancz, 1976.
> *Starring Sally J. Freedman as Herself.*   Scarsdale, New York, Bradbury Press, 1977.

Manuscript Collection: Kerlan Collection, University of Minnesota, Minneapolis.

Judy Blume comments:
Writing about young people comes naturally to me because I am blessed with almost total recall. Often young people will ask me how I know all their secrets. It's because I remember just about everything from age eight on, and many things that happened before that. I write sometimes from my own experiences, sometimes from my children's, and other times by imagining how I would feel and react if placed in a certain situation. I'm not sure where my ideas come from. And I don't like to think about that − it's too scary. I'm just grateful that when I finish one book there is usually a new idea waiting for me. I let each book evolve naturally. I find the first draft pure torture. Once that's finished I can relax, for it is the rewriting process that I really enjoy. I'm thankful for the thousands of letters I receive from my young fans each year. I owe my career to my readers!

                              *   *   *

Most of Judy Blume's fiction is written in the first person, and her stories are all bright and cheerful in the accepted American style. This is true even when the theme is ostensibly serious: in *Deenie*, for instance, the girl suffers from scoliosis but the psychological problems arising from her condition are only superficially indicated. The moral lesson is overt and it is very easily drawn: pretty Deenie is squeamish about physical deformity in others until she is forced to wear a body-brace to correct her own tendency to curvature of the spine.

Deenie is able to come to terms with the situation without too much difficulty: she faces her school friends, who are sympathetic to begin with in the wrong way, and even goes to a party wearing the brace. Tony Miglione, the central character of *Then Again, Maybe I Won't*, requires psychiatric treatment to cure his nervous stomach disorder; but the first-person narrative again ensures a light-hearted effect. The proper mode to express an adolescent viewpoint is the self-critical, unassuming, humorous one; Judy Blume has simply extended it to include acknowledgement of the sexual or slightly anti-social tendencies of her characters.

Thirteen-year-old Tony worries about wet dreams and the fact that he may have an erection in class; and in context his fear of embarrassment in this respect is presented as a suitable subject for comic treatment.

Judy Blume, in fact, has a rare ability to write about the sexual behaviour of children in a way that is neither salacious nor propagandist. Her approach is straightforward and completely natural. It is difficult to think of her as a pioneer, since she has merely transcribed the thoughts and feelings that are common to all children at certain ages; yet she *has* broken new ground. In *Are You There, God? It's Me, Margaret* (her third published book, but the first one that she felt satisfied with) she describes an eleven-year-old's preoccupation with the development of her chest and the onset of menstruation. "How can I stop worrying when I don't know if I'm going to turn out normal," Margaret wonders; the author makes her anxiety appear justifiable, and touching, without the least sign of affectation.

Margaret plays kissing games but doesn't get much out of them: "... I really like you, Margaret. How do you want me to kiss you?" "On the cheek and fast." Her sexual interests are still concentrated on mechanical appliances like bras and sanitary belts. But in *Forever* the author's attention is focused on a later stage of development. Her protagonists here are a couple of eighteen-year-olds whose sexual responses are completely mature. What they do is described in detail, but the mood of physical infatuation isn't evoked. In this sense the writing is not erotic; it has at times a clinical, instructive quality that is offset only by the narrative implication that the experience usually *is* enjoyable. But even here there is no romantic exaggeration: things can go wrong, and Judy Blume doesn't hesitate to say so.

Forever is pitched at exactly the right note to appeal to adolescent readers at the level of simple interest. There is no complexity of character or situation; the author's purpose is not symbolical or moralistic. Her honesty is startling only because it is unusual in the genre; her books make nonsense of the coyness or reticence of other children's authors who can write about the effects of sexuality without acknowledging its practical form. This is due to a failure of nerve, usually for reasons of propriety or convention. *Forever* fills a gap in children's literature that was becoming increasingly apparent. If more writing of this calibre were available, it might supplant the low-brow adult pulp-fiction that many teenagers use to provide the quality missing from their own books.

There is no puritanical morality in *Forever* but there is a certain amount of emphasis on social responsibility. Katherine and Michael don't take foolish risks; they are sensible, intelligent and well-adjusted. The affair has no unfortunate repercussions. And Judy Blume is out to repudiate the false connotations of "for ever"; as an absolute concept, it is meaningless. Katherine's ultimate attitude is entirely rational. "I'll never regret one single thing we did together," she states; and why should she? But the point needs to be stressed.

Judy Blume's books are set on the East Coast of America, in an environment of affluence and material glamour. Her central characters are all concerned to get their priorities in order, either at a communal or a personal level. Where the humour is not augmented by sexual or social outspokenness it tends to become glib or heavy-handed (*Tales of a Fourth Grade Nothing*, for example). Sometimes the author comes dangerously close to the idiom of "social problem" fiction, when reassuring doctors or teachers or birth-control specialists intervene for the children's own good. These episodes have the effect of setpieces, inserted for a non-literary purpose. Character differentiation in all cases is rudimentary. But in two novels at least – *Margaret* and *Forever* – Judy Blume is making a point that is both original and important. Her psychological observations are not deep but they are accurate – and *Forever* especially suggests that her imagination can benefit from an increased density in the fictional material that it works on.

—Patricia Craig

BLYTON, Enid (Mary). British. Born in London, 11 August 1897. Educated at St. Christopher's School for Girls, Beckenham, Surrey, 1907–15; Froebel Institute, Ipswich

High School, 1916–18. Married Hugh Pollock in 1924 (divorced, 1942), two daughters; Kenneth Darrell Waters, 1943 (died, 1967). Taught at Bickley Park School, Kent, 1919; nursery governess, Surbiton, Surrey, 1920–24. Columnist, "From My Window," 1923–27, "Letter to Children," 1927–29, and "Children's Page," 1929–45, *The Teachers' World,* London; Editor, *Sunny Stories* magazine, London, 1926–52, and *Enid Blyton Magazine,* London, 1953–59. Chairman of the Committee, Shaftesbury Society Children's Home, Beaconsfield, Buckinghamshire, 1954–67; Vice-President, Friends of the Cheyne Walk Centre, London, 1960–68. Recipient: Boys' Clubs of America award, 1948. *Died 28 November 1968.*

PUBLICATIONS FOR CHILDREN

Fiction

The Enid Blyton Book of Fairies.   London, Newnes, 1924.
The Zoo Book.   London, Newnes, 1924.
The Enid Blyton Book of Bunnies.   London, Newnes, 1925.
The Book of Brownies, illustrated by Ernest Aris.   London, Newnes, 1926.
Tales Half Told.   London, Nelson, 1926.
The Animal Book.   London, Newnes, 1927.
Let's Pretend, illustrated by I. Bennington Angrave.   London, Nelson, 1928.
Tarrydiddle Town.   London, Nelson, 1929.
Cheerio! A Book for Boys and Girls.   London, Birn, 1933.
Five Minute Tales: Sixty Short Stories for Children.   London, Methuen, 1933.
Letters from Bobs.   Privately printed, 1933.
The Old Thatch.   London, Johnston, 16 vols., 1934–35, 1938–39.
The Red Pixie Book.   London, Newnes, 1934.
Ten Minutes Tales: Twenty-Nine Varied Stories for Children.   London, Methuen, 1934.
The Children's Garden.   London, Newnes, 1935.
The Green Goblin Book.   London, Newnes, 1935; shortened version, as *Feefo, Tuppenny, and Jinks,* London, Staples Press, 1951.
Hedgerow Tales.   London, Newnes, 1935.
The Famous Jimmy, illustrated by Benjamin Rabier.   London, Muller, 1936; New York, Dutton, 1937.
Fifteen Minute Tales: Nineteen Stories for Children.   London, Methuen, 1936.
The Yellow Fairy Book.   London, Newnes, 1936.
Adventures of the Wishing Chair, illustrated by Hilda McGavin.   London, Newnes, 1937.
The Adventures of Binkle and Flip, illustrated by Kathleen Nixon.   London, Newnes, 1938.
Billy-Bob Tales, illustrated by May Smith.   London, Methuen, 1938.
Mr. Galliano's Circus.   London, Newnes, 1938.
The Secret Island.   Oxford, Blackwell, 1938.
Boys' and Girls' Circus Book, illustrated by Hilda McGavin.   London, News Chronicle, 1939.
The Enchanted Wood.   London, Newnes, 1939.
Hurrah for the Circus! Being Further Adventures of Mr. Galliano and His Famous Circus, illustrated by E.H. Davie.   London, Newnes, 1939.
Naughty Amelia Jane!   London, Newnes, 1939.
Boys' and Girls' Story Book.   London, Newnes, 1940.
The Children of Cherry Tree Farm, illustrated by Harry Rountree.   London, Country Life, 1940.
Children of Kidillin (as Mary Pollock).   London, Newnes, 1940.

The Little Tree House, Being the Adventures of Josie, Click, and Bun, illustrated by Dorothy M. Wheeler. London, Newnes, 1940; as *Josie, Click, and Bun and the Little Tree House,* 1951.

Mr. Meddle's Mischief, illustrated by Joyce Mercer and R.M. Turvey. London, Newnes, 1940.

Naughtiest Girl in the School. London, Newnes, 1940.

The Secret of Spiggy Holes. Oxford, Blackwell, 1940.

Tales of Betsy-May, illustrated by Joan Gale Thomas. London, Methuen, 1940.

Three Boys and a Circus (as Mary Pollock). London, Newnes, 1940.

The Treasure Hunters, illustrated by E. Wilson and Joyce Davies. London, Newnes, 1940.

Twenty Minute Tales. London, Methuen, 1940.

The Adventures of Mr. Pink-Whistle. London, Newnes, 1941.

The Adventurous Four. London, Newnes, 1941.

Five O'Clock Tales. London, Methuen, 1941.

The Further Adventures of Josie, Click, and Bun, illustrated by Dorothy M. Wheeler. London, Newnes, 1941.

The Secret Mountain. Oxford, Blackwell, 1941.

The Twins at St. Clare's. London, Methuen, 1941.

The Children of Willow Farm, illustrated by Harry Rountree. London, Country Life, 1942.

Circus Days Again, illustrated by E.H. Davie. London, Newnes, 1942.

Happy Story Book. London, Hodder and Stoughton, 1942.

Enid Blyton's Little Books. London, Evans, 6 vols., 1942.

Five on a Treasure Island. London, Hodder and Stoughton, 1942; New York, Crowell, 1950.

Hello, Mr. Twiddle, illustrated by Hilda McGavin. London, Newnes, 1942.

I'll Tell You a Story, illustrated by Eileen A. Soper. London, Macmillan, 1942.

I'll Tell You Another Story. London, Macmillan, 1942.

Jolly John at Christmas Time. London, Evans, 1942.

Mary Mouse and the Doll's House. Leicester, Brockhampton Press, 1942.

More Adventures on Willow Farm. London, Country Life, 1942.

The Naughtiest Girl Again. London, Newnes, 1942.

The O'Sullivan Twins. London, Methuen, 1942.

Shadow the Sheep Dog. London, Newnes, 1942.

Six O'Clock Tales: Thirty-Three Short Stories for Children, illustrated by Dorothy M. Wheeler. London, Methuen, 1942.

Mischief at St. Rollo's (as Mary Pollock). London, Newnes, 1943.

The Secret of Cliff Castle (as Mary Pollock). London, Newnes, 1943.

Bimbo and Topsy, illustrated by Lucy Gee. London, Newnes, 1943.

The Adventures of Scamp (as Mary Pollock). London, Newnes, 1943.

Dame Slap and Her School, illustrated by Dorothy M. Wheeler. London, Newnes, 1943.

Five Go Adventuring Again. London, Hodder and Stoughton, 1943; New York, Crowell, 1951.

Jolly John by the Sea. London, Evans, 1943.

Jolly John on the Farm. London, Evans, 1943.

The Magic Faraway Tree, illustrated by Dorothy M. Wheeler. London, Newnes, 1943.

Merry Story Book, illustrated by Eileen A. Soper. London, Hodder and Stoughton, 1943.

More Adventures of Mary Mouse. Leicester, Brockhampton Press, 1943.

The Mystery of the Burnt Cottage, illustrated by J. Abbey. London, Methuen, 1943; Los Angeles, W.L. McNaughton, n.d.

The Secret of Killimooin. Oxford, Blackwell, 1943.

Polly Piglet, illustrated by Eileen A. Soper.   Leicester, Brockhampton Press, 1943.

Seven O'Clock Tales: Thirty Short Stories for Children.   London, Methuen, 1943.

Smuggler Ben (as Mary Pollock).   London, Werner Laurie, 1943.

Summer Term at St. Clare's.   London, Methuen, 1943.

The Toys Come to Life, illustrated by Eileen A. Soper.   Leicester Brockhampton Press, 1943.

At Appletree Farm.   Leicester, Brockhampton Press, 1944.

Billy and Betty at the Seaside.   Dundee, Valentine and Sons, 1944.

A Book of Naughty Children.   London, Methuen, 1944.

The Boy Next Door, illustrated by A.E. Bestall.   London, Newnes, 1944.

The Dog That Went to Fairyland.   Leicester, Brockhampton Press, 1944.

Claudine at St. Clare's.   London, Methuen, 1944.

Come to the Circus, illustrated by Eileen A. Soper.   Leicester, Brockhampton Press, 1944.

Eight O'Clock Tales, illustrated by Dorothy M. Wheeler.   London, Methuen, 1944.

Five Run Away Together, illustrated by Eileen A. Soper.   London, Hodder and Stoughton, 1944.

The Island of Adventure, illustrated by Stuart Tresilian.   London. Macmillan, 1944; as *Mystery Island*, New York, Macmillan, 1945.

Jolly Little Jumbo.   Leicester, Brockhampton Press, 1944.

Jolly Story Book, illustrated by Eileen A. Soper.   London, Hodder and Stoughton, 1944.

Little Mary House Again.   Leicester, Brockhampton Press, 1944.

The Mystery of the Disappearing Cat, illustrated by J. Abbey.   London, Methuen, 1944; Los Angeles, W.L. McNaughton, 1948.

Rainy Day Stories, illustrated by Nora S. Unwin.   London, Evans, 1944.

The Second Form at St. Clare's, illustrated by W. Lindsay Cable.   London, Methuen, 1944.

Tales of Toyland, illustrated by Hilda McGavin.   London, Newnes, 1944.

The Three Golliwogs.   London, Newnes, 1944.

The Blue Story Book, illustrated by Eileen A. Soper.   London, Methuen, 1945.

The Brown Family, illustrated by E. and R. Buhler.   London, News Chronicle, 1945.

The Caravan Family, illustrated by William Fyffe.   London, Lutterworth Press, 1945.

The Conjuring Wizard and Other Stories, illustrated by Eileen A. Soper.   London, Macmillan, 1945.

The Family at Red Roofs, illustrated by W. Spence.   London, Lutterworth Press, 1945.

Fifth Formers at St. Clare's, illustrated by W. Lindsay Cable.   London, Methuen, 1945.

Five Go to Smugglers' Top.   London, Hodder and Stoughton, 1945.

Hallo, Little Mary House, illustrated by Olive F. Openshaw.   Leicester, Brockhampton Press, 1945.

Hollow Tree House, illustrated by Elizabeth Wall.   London, Lutterworth Press, 1945.

Jolly John at the Circus.   London, Evans, 1945.

The Mystery of the Secret Room.   London, Methuen, 1945; Los Angeles, Parkwood Press, 1950.

The Naughtiest Girl Is a Monitor.   London, Newnes, 1945.

Round the Clock Stories, illustrated by Nora S. Unwin.   London, National Magazine Company, 1945.

The Runaway Kitten, illustrated by Eileen A. Soper.   Leicester, Brockhampton Press, 1945.

Sunny Story Book.   London, Hodder and Stoughton, 1945.

The Teddy Bear's Party, illustrated by Eileen A. Soper.   Leicester, Brockhampton Press, 1945.

The Twins Go to Nursery-Rhyme Land, illustrated by Eileen A. Soper.   Leicester, Brockhampton Press, 1945.

Amelia Jane Again.   London, Newnes, 1946.

The Bad Little Monkey, illustrated by Eileen A. Soper.   Leicester, Brockhampton Press, 1946.

The Castle of Adventure, illustrated by Stuart Tresilian.   London, Macmillan, and New York, Macmillan, 1946.

The Children at Happy House, illustrated by Kathleen Gell.   Oxford, Blackwell, 1946.

Chimney Corner Stories, illustrated by Pat Harrison.   London, National Magazine Company, 1946.

First Term at Malory Towers.   London, Methuen, 1946.

Five Go Off in a Caravan, illustrated by Eileen A. Soper.   London, Hodder and Stoughton, 1946.

The Folk of the Faraway Tree, illustrated by Dorothy M. Wheeler.   London, Newnes, 1946.

Gay Story Book, illustrated by Eileen A. Soper.   London, Hodder and Stoughton, 1946.

Josie, Click, and Bun Again, illustrated by Dorothy M. Wheeler.   London, Newnes, 1946.

The Little White Duck and Other Stories, illustrated by Eileen A. Soper.   London, Macmillan, 1946.

Mary Mouse and Her Family, illustrated by Olive F. Openshaw.   Leicester, Brockhampton Press, 1946.

The Mystery of the Spiteful Letters, illustrated by J. Abbey.   London, Methuen, 1946.

The Put-em-Rights, illustrated by Elizabeth Wall.   London, Lutterworth Press, 1946.

The Red Story Book.   London, Methuen, 1946.

The Surprising Caravan, illustrated by Eileen A. Soper.   Leicester, Brockhampton Press, 1946.

Tales of Green Hedges, illustrated by Gwen White.   London, National Magazine Company, 1946.

The Train That Lost Its Way, illustrated by Eileen A. Soper.   Leicester, Brockhampton Press, 1946.

The Adventurous Four Again.   London, Newnes, 1947.

At Seaside Cottage, illustrated by Eileen A. Soper.   Leicester, Brockhampton Press, 1947.

Five on Kirrin Island Again.   London, Hodder and Stoughton, 1947.

The Green Story Book, illustrated by Eileen A. Soper.   London, Methuen, 1947.

The Happy House Children Again, illustrated by Kathleen Gell.   Oxford, Blackwell, 1947.

Here Comes Mary Mouse Again.   Leicester, Brockhampton Press, 1947.

The House at the Corner, illustrated by Elsie Walker.   London, Lutterworth Press, 1947.

Little Green Duck and Other Stories.   Leicester, Brockhampton Press, 1947.

Lucky Story Book, illustrated by Eileen A. Soper.   London, Hodder and Stoughton, 1947.

More about Josie, Click, and Bun, illustrated by Dorothy M. Wheeler.   London, Newnes, 1947.

The Mystery of the Missing Necklace.   London, Methuen, 1947.

Rambles with Uncle Nat, illustrated by Nora S. Unwin.   London, National Magazine Company, 1947.

The Saucy Jane Family, illustrated by Kathleen Gell.   London, Lutterworth Press, 1947.

A Second Book of Naughty Children: Twenty-Four Short Stories, illustrated by Kathleen Gell.   London, Methuen, 1947.

The Second Form at Malory Towers.   London, Methuen, 1947.

The Smith Family, Books 1–3.   Leeds, E.J. Arnold, 3 vols., 1947.

The Valley of Adventure, illustrated by Stuart Tresilian.   London, Macmillan, and New York, Macmillan, 1947.

The Very Clever Rabbit. Leicester, Brockhampton Press, 1947.

The Adventures of Pip. London, Sampson Low, 1948.

The Boy with the Loaves and Fishes, illustrated by Elsie Walker. London, Lutterworth Press, 1948; New York, Roy, 1958(?).

Come to the Circus, illustrated by Joyce M. Johnson (different book from the 1944 title). London, Newnes, 1948.

Bedtime Series. Leicester, Brockhampton Press, 2 vols., 1948.

Five Go Off to Camp. London, Hodder and Stoughton, 1948; as *Five on the Track of a Spooky Train*, New York, Atheneum, 1972.

How Do You Do, Mary Mouse. Leicester, Brockhampton Press, 1948.

Just Time for a Story, illustrated by Grace Lodge. London, Macmillan, 1948; New York, St. Martin's Press, 1952.

Jolly Tales. London, Johnston, 1948.

Let's Have a Story, illustrated by George Bowe. London, Pitkin, 1948.

The Little Girl at Capernaum, illustrated by Elsie Walker. London, Lutterworth Press, 1948.

Mister Icy-Cold. Oxford, Blackwell, 1948.

More Adventures of Pip. London, Sampson Low, 1948.

The Mystery of the Hidden House, illustrated by J. Abbey. London, Methuen, 1948.

Nature Tales. London, Johnston, 1948.

Now for a Story, illustrated by Frank Varty. Newcastle upon Tyne, Harold Hill, 1948.

The Red-Spotted Handkerchief and Other Stories, illustrated by Kathleen Gell. Leicester, Brockhampton Press, 1948.

The Sea of Adventure, illustrated by Stuart Tresilian. London, Macmillan, and New York, Macmillan, 1948.

The Secret of the Old Mill, illustrated by Eileen A. Soper. Leicester, Brockhampton Press, 1948.

Six Cousins at Mistletoe Farm, illustrated by Peter Beigel. London, Evans, 1948.

Tales after Tea. London, Werner Laurie, 1948.

Tales of the Twins, illustrated by Eileen A. Soper. Leicester, Brockhampton Press, 1948.

Three Ran Away Together, illustrated by Jeanne Farrar. Leicester, Brockhampton Press, 1948.

Third Year at Malory Towers, illustrated by Stanley Lloyd. London, Methuen, 1948.

We Want a Story, illustrated by George Bowe. London, Pitkin, 1948.

The Bluebell Story Book. London, Gifford, 1949.

Bumpy and His Bus, illustrated by Dorothy M. Wheeler. London, Newnes, 1949.

A Cat in Fairyland and Other Stories. London, Pitkin, 1949.

The Circus Book. London, Latimer House, 1949.

The Dear Old Snow Man. Leicester, Brockhampton Press, 1949.

Don't Be Silly, Mr. Twiddle. London, Newnes, 1949.

The Enchanted Sea and Other Stories. London, Pitkin, 1949.

Daffodil Story Book. London, Gifford, 1949.

Good Morning Book, illustrated by Don and Ann Goring. London, National Magazine Company, 1949.

Five Get into Trouble, illustrated by Eileen A. Soper. London, Hodder and Stoughton, 1949; as *Five Caught in a Treacherous Plot*, New York, Atheneum, 1972.

Humpty Dumpty and Belinda. London, Collins, 1949.

Jinky's Joke and Other Stories, illustrated by Kathleen Gell. Leicester, Brockhampton Press, 1949.

Little Noddy Goes to Toyland, illustrated by Harmsen Van Beek. London, Sampson Low, 1949.

Mr. Tumpy and His Caravan, illustrated by Dorothy M. Wheeler. London, Sidgwick and Jackson, 1949; Los Angeles, W.L. McNaughton, 1951.

The Mountain of Adventure, illustrated by Stuart Tresilian. London, Macmillan, and

New York, Macmillan, 1949.

The Mystery of the Pantomime Cat. London, Methuen, 1949.

Oh, What a Lovely Time. Leicester, Brockhampton Press, 1949.

The Rockingdown Mystery, illustrated by Gilbert Dunlop. London, Collins, 1949.

The Secret Seven, illustrated by George Brook. Leicester, Brockhampton Press, 1949; as *The Secret Seven and the Mystery of the Empty House,* Chicago, Children's Press, 1972.

A Story Party at Green Hedges, illustrated by Grace Lodge. London, Hodder and Stoughton, 1949.

The Strange Umbrella and Other Stories. London, Pitkin, 1949.

Tales after Supper. London, Werner Laurie, 1949.

Those Dreadful Children, illustrated by Grace Lodge. London Lutterworth Press, 1949.

Tiny Tales. Worcester, Littlebury, 1949.

The Upper Fourth at Malory Towers. London, Methuen, 1949.

Chuff the Chimney Sweep and Other Stories. London, Pitkin, 1950.

The Astonishing Ladder and Other Stories, illustrated by Eileen A. Soper. London, Macmillan, 1950.

Enid Blyton's Little Book. Leicester, Brockhampton Press, 6 vols., 1950.

Five Fall into Adventure, illustrated by Eileen A. Soper. London, Hodder and Stoughton, 1950; New York, Atheneum, 1972.

Hurrah for Little Noddy. London, Sampson Low, 1950.

In the Fifth at Malory Towers, illustrated by Stanley Lloyd. London, Methuen, 1950.

The Magic Knitting Needles and Other Stories. London, Macmillan, 1950.

Mister Meddle's Muddles, illustrated by R.M. Turvey and Joyce Mercer. London, Newnes, 1950.

Mr. Pink-Whistle Interferes. London, Newnes, 1950.

The Mystery of the Invisible Thief. London, Methuen, 1950.

The Pole Star Family, illustrated by Ruth Gervis. London, Lutterworth Press, 1950.

The Poppy Story Book. London, Gifford, 1950.

The Rilloby Fair Mystery, illustrated by Gilbert Dunlop. London, Collins, 1950.

Round the Year Stories. London, Coker, 1950.

Rubbalong Tales, illustrated by Norman Meredith. London, Macmillan, 1950.

The Seaside Family, illustrated by Ruth Gervis. London, Lutterworth Press, 1950.

Secret Seven Adventure, illustrated by George Brook. Leicester, Brockhampton Press, 1950; as *The Secret Seven and the Circus Adventure,* Chicago, Children's Press, 1972.

The Ship of Adventure, illustrated by Stuart Tresilian. London, Macmillan, and New York, Macmillan, 1950.

Six Cousins Again, illustrated by Maurice Tulloch. London, Evans, 1950.

Tales about Toys. Leicester, Brockhampton Press, 1950.

The Three Naughty Children and Other Stories, illustrated by Eileen A. Soper. London, Macmillan, 1950.

Tricky the Goblin and Other Stories, illustrated by Eileen A. Soper. London, Macmillan, 1950.

We Do Love Mary Mouse. Leicester, Brockhampton Press, 1950.

Welcome Mary Mouse, illustrated by Olive F. Openshaw. Leicester, Brockhampton Press, 1950.

What an Adventure. Leicester, Brockhampton Press, 1950.

The Wishing Chair Again. London, Newnes, 1950.

The Yellow Story Book, illustrated by Kathleen Gell. London, Methuen, 1950.

Benny and the Princess and Other Stories. London, Pitkin, 1951.

The Big Noddy Book, illustrated by Harmsen Van Beek. London, Sampson Low, 1951 (and later volumes).

The Buttercup Farm Family, illustrated by Ruth Gervis. London, Lutterworth Press, 1951.

Buttercup Story Book. London, Gifford, 1951.

Down at the Farm. London, Sampson Low, 1951.

Father Christmas and Belinda. London, Collins, 1951.

Five on a Hike Together, illustrated by Eileen A. Soper. London, Hodder and Stoughton, 1951.

The Flying Goat and Other Stories. London, Pitkin, 1951.

Gay Street Book, illustrated by Grace Lodge. London, Latimer House, 1951.

Hello Twins. Leicester, Brockhampton Press, 1951.

Here Comes Noddy Again. London, Sampson Low, 1951.

Hurrah for Mary Mouse. Leicester, Brockhampton Press, 1951.

Last Term at Malory Towers, illustrated by Stanley Lloyd. London, Methuen, 1951.

Let's Go to the Circus. London, Odhams, 1951.

The Little Spinning Mouse and Other Stories. London, Pitkin, 1951.

The Magic Snow-Bird and Other Stories. London, Pitkin, 1951.

The Mystery of the Vanished Prince, illustrated by Treyer Evans. London, Methuen, 1951.

Noddy and Big Ears Have a Picnic. London, Sampson Low, 1951.

Noddy and His Car. London, Sampson Low, 1951.

Noddy Has a Shock. London, Sampson Low, 1951.

Noddy Has More Adventures. London, Sampson Low, 1951.

Noddy Goes to the Seaside. London, Sampson Low, 1951.

Noddy Off to Rocking Horse Land. London, Sampson Low, 1951.

Noddy Painting Book. London, Sampson Low, 8 vols., 1951–57.

Noddy's House of Books. London, Sampson Low, 6 vols., 1951.

A Picnic Party with Enid Blyton, illustrated by Grace Lodge. London, Hodder and Stoughton, 1951.

Pippy and the Gnome and Other Stories. London, Pitkin, 1951.

A Prize for Mary Mouse. Leicester, Brockhampton Press, 1951.

The Proud Golliwog. Leicester, Brockhampton Press, 1951.

The Runaway Teddy Bear and Other Stories. London, Pitkin, 1951.

The Six Bad Boys, illustrated by Mary Gernat. London, Lutterworth Press, 1951.

A Tale of Little Noddy. London, Sampson Low, 1951.

"Too-Wise" the Wonderful Wizard and Other Stories. London, Pitkin, 1951.

Up the Faraway Tree, illustrated by Dorothy M. Wheeler. London, Newnes, 1951.

Well Done, Secret Seven, illustrated by George Brook. Leicester, Brockhampton Press, 1951; as *The Secret Seven and the Tree House Adventure,* Chicago, Children's Press, 1972.

Bright Story Book, illustrated by Eileen A. Soper. Leicester, Brockhampton Press, 1952.

The Circus of Adventure, illustrated by Stuart Tresilian. London, Macmillan, 1952; New York, St. Martin's Press, 1953.

Come Along Twins. Leicester, Brockhampton Press, 1952.

Five Have a Wonderful Time, illustrated by Eileen A. Soper. London, Hodder and Stoughton, 1952.

The Mad Teapot. Leicester, Brockhampton Press, 1952.

Mandy, Mops, and Cubby Find a House. London, Sampson Low, 1952.

Mandy, Mops, and Cubby Again. London, Sampson Low, 1952.

Mary Mouse and Her Bicycle, illustrated by Olive F. Openshaw. Leicester Brockhampton Press, 1952.

Mr. Tumpy Plays a Trick on Saucepan. London, Sampson Low, 1952.

The Mystery of the Strange Bundle, illustrated by Treyer Evans. London, Methuen, 1952.

Noddy and Big Ears. London, Sampson Low, 1952.

Noddy and the Witch's Wand. London, Sampson Low, 1952.

Noddy's Colour Strip Book, illustrated by Harmsen Van Beek. London, Sampson Low, 1952.

Noddy Goes to School. London, Sampson Low, 1952.
Noddy's Ark of Books. London, Sampson Low, 5 vols., 1952.
Noddy's Car Gets a Squeak. London, Sampson Low, 1952.
Noddy's Penny Wheel Car. London, Sampson Low, 1952.
The Queer Mystery, illustrated by Norman Meredith. London, Staples Press, 1952.
The Rubadub Mystery, illustrated by Gilbert Dunlop. London, Collins, 1952.
Secret Seven on the Trail, illustrated by George Brook. Leicester, Brockhampton Press, 1952; as *The Secret Seven and the Railroad Mystery,* Chicago, Children's Press, 1972.
Snowdrop Story Book. London, Gifford, 1952.
The Very Big Secret, illustrated by Ruth Gervis. London, Lutterworth Press, 1952.
Welcome Josie, Click, and Bun, illustrated by Dorothy M. Wheeler. London, Newnes, 1952.
Well Done, Noddy. London, Sampson Low, 1952.
Clicky the Clockwork Clown. Leicester, Brockhampton Press, 1953.
Five Go Down to the Sea, illustrated by Eileen A. Soper. London, Hodder and Stoughton, 1953; Chicago, Reilly and Lee, 1961.
Go Ahead Secret Seven, illustrated by Bruno Kay. Leicester, Brockhampton Press, 1953; as *The Secret Seven Get Their Man,* Chicago, Children's Press, 1972.
Gobo and Mr. Fierce. London, Sampson Low, 1953.
Here Come the Twins. Leicester, Brockhampton Press, 1953.
Mandy Makes Cubby a Hat. London, Sampson Low, 1953.
Mary Mouse and the Noah's Ark, illustrated by Olive F. Openshaw. Leicester, Brockhampton Press, 1953.
Mr. Tumpy in the Land of Wishes. London, Sampson Low, 1953.
My Enid Blyton Story Book, illustrated by Willy Schermelé. London, Juvenile Productions, 1953.
The Mystery of Holly Lane, illustrated by Treyer Evans. London, Methuen, 1953.
The New Big Noddy Book. London, Sampson Low, 1953.
New Noddy Colour Strip Book. London, Sampson Low, 1953.
Noddy and the Cuckoo's Nest. London, Sampson Low, 1953.
Noddy at the Seaside. London, Sampson Low, 1953.
Noddy's Cut-Out Model Book. London, Sampson Low, 1953.
Noddy Gets Captured. London, Sampson Low, 1953.
Noddy Is Very Silly. London, Sampson Low, 1953.
Noddy's Garage of Books, illustrated by Harmsen Van Beek. London, Sampson Low, 5 vols., 1953.
The Secret of Moon Castle. Oxford, Blackwell, 1953.
Snowball the Pony, illustrated by Iris Gillespie. London, Lutterworth Press, 1953.
Visitors in the Night. Leicester, Brockhampton Press, 1953.
Well Really Mr. Twiddle!, illustrated by Hilda McGavin. London, Newnes, 1953.
The Adventure of the Secret Necklace, illustrated by Isabel Veevers. London, Lutterworth Press, 1954.
The Castle Without a Door and Other Stories. London, Pitkin, 1954.
The Children at Green Meadows, illustrated by Grace Lodge. London, Lutterworth Press, 1954.
Friendly Story Book, illustrated by Eileen A. Soper. Leicester, Brockhampton Press, 1954.
Marigold Story Book. London, Gifford, 1954.
Noddy Pop-Up Book. London, Sampson Low, 1954.
Noddy Giant Painting Book. London, Sampson Low, 1954.
Good Work, Secret Seven!, illustrated by Bruno Kay. Leicester, Brockhampton Press, 1954; as *The Secret Seven and the Case of the Stolen Car,* Chicago, Children's Press, 1972.
Five Go to Mystery Moor. London, Hodder and Stoughton, 1954.
How Funny You Are, Noddy. London, Sampson Low, 1954.
Little Strip Picture Books. London, Sampson Low, 1954 (and other volumes).

The Little Toy Farm and Other Stories. London, Pitkin, 1954.
Mary Mouse to the Rescue. Leicester, Brockhampton Press, 1954.
Merry Mister Meddle, illustrated by R.M. Turvey and Joyce Mercer. London, Newnes, 1954.
More about Amelia Jane, illustrated by Sylvia I. Venus. London, Newnes, 1954.
The Mystery of Tally-Ho Cottage, illustrated by Treyer Evans. London, Methuen, 1954.
Noddy and the Magic Rubber. London, Sampson Low, 1954.
Noddy's Castle of Books, illustrated Harmsen Van Beek. London, Sampson Low, 5 vols., 1954.
Away Goes Sooty, illustrated by Pierre Probst. London, Collins, 1955.
Benjy and the Others, illustrated by Kathleen Gell. London, Latimer House, 1955.
Bimbo and Blackie Go Camping, illustrated by Pierre Probst. London, Collins, 1955.
Bobs, illustrated by Pierre Probst. London, Collins, 1955.
Christmas with Scamp and Bimbo. London, Collins, 1955.
Little Bedtime Books. London, Sampson Low, 8 vols., 1955.
Neddy the Little Donkey, illustrated by Romain Simon. London, Collins, 1955.
Sooty, illustrated by Pierre Probst. London, Collins, 1955.
Five Have Plenty of Fun. London, Hodder and Stoughton, 1955.
Foxglove Story Book. London, Gifford, 1955.
Gobo in the Land of Dreams. London, Sampson Low, 1955.
Golliwog Grumbled. Leicester, Brockhampton Press, 1955.
Holiday House, illustrated by Grace Lodge. London, Evans, 1955.
The Laughing Kitten, illustrated by Paul Kaye. London, Harvill Press, and New York, Roy, 1955.
Mandy, Mops, and Cubby and the Whitewash. London, Sampson Low, 1955.
Mary Mouse in Nursery Rhyme Land. Leicester, Brockhampton Press, 1955.
Mischief Again, illustrated by Paul Kaye. London, Harvill Press, and New York, Roy, 1955.
Mr. Pink-Whistle's Party. London, Newnes, 1955.
Mr. Tumpy in the Land of Boys and Girls. London, Sampson Low, 1955.
More Chimney Corner Stories, illustrated by Pat Harrison. London, Latimer House, 1955.
Noddy in Toyland. London, Sampson Low, 1955.
Noddy Meets Father Christmas. London, Sampson Low, 1955.
Ring o' Bells Mystery. London, Collins, 1955.
The River of Adventure, illustrated by Stuart Tresilian. London, Macmillan, and New York, St. Martin's Press, 1955.
Run-about Holidays, illustrated by Lilian Chivers. London, Lutterworth Press, 1955.
Secret Seven Win Through, illustrated by Bruno Kay. Leicester, Brockhampton Press, 1955; as *The Secret Seven and the Hidden Cave Adventure,* Chicago, Children's Press, 1972.
The Troublesome Three, illustrated by Leo. London, Sampson Low, 1955.
You Funny Little Noddy! London, Sampson Low, 1955.
Be Brave, Little Noddy! London, Sampson Low, 1956.
Bom the Little Toy Drummer, illustrated by R. Paul-Höye. Leicester, Brockhampton Press, 1956.
The Clever Little Donkey, illustrated by Romain Simon. London, Collins, 1956.
Colin the Cow-Boy, illustrated by R. Caillé. London, Collins, 1956.
A Day with Mary Mouse, illustrated by Frederick White. Leicester, Brockhampton Press, 1956.
Animal Tales, illustrated by Romain Simon. London, Collins, 1956.
Noddy Play Day Painting Book. London, Sampson Low, 1956.
Five on a Secret Trail, illustrated by Eileen A. Soper. London, Hodder and Stoughton, 1956.

Four in a Family, illustrated by Tom Kerr. London, Lutterworth Press, 1956.
The Mystery of the Missing Man, illustrated by Lilian Buchanan. London, Methuen, 1956.
Noddy and His Friends. London, Sampson Low, 1956.
Noddy and Tessie Bear. London, Sampson Low, 1956.
The Noddy Toy Station Books. London, Sampson Low, 5 vols., 1956.
The Rat-a-Tat Mystery. London, Collins, 1956.
Scamp at School, illustrated by Pierre Probst. London, Collins, 1956.
Three Cheers Secret Seven, illustrated by Burgess Sharrocks. Leicester, Brockhampton Press, 1956; as *The Secret Seven and the Grim Secret*, Chicago, Children's Press, 1972.
Bom and His Magic Drumstick. Leicester, Brockhampton Press, 1957.
Do Look Out, Noddy! London, Sampson Low, 1957.
Bom Painting Book. London, Dean, 1957.
Five Go to Billycock Hill, illustrated by Eileen A. Soper. London, Hodder and Stoughton, 1957.
Mary Mouse and the Garden Party, illustrated by Frederick White. Leicester, Brockhampton Press, 1957.
Mystery of the Strange Messages, illustrated by Lilian Buchanan. London, Methuen, 1957.
Noddy and Bumpy Dog. London, Sampson Low, 1957.
Noddy's New Big Book. London, Sampson Low, 1957.
Secret Seven Mystery, illustrated by Burgess Sharrocks. Leicester, Brockhampton Press, 1957; as *The Secret Seven and the Missing Girl Mystery*, Chicago, Children's Press, 1972.
The Birthday Kitten, illustrated by Grace Lodge. London, Lutterworth Press, 1958.
Bom Goes Adventuring, illustrated by R. Paul-Höye. Leicester, Brockhampton Press, 1958.
Clicky Gets into Trouble, illustrated by Molly Brett. Leicester, Brockhampton Press, 1958.
Five Get into a Fix, illustrated by Eileen A. Soper. London, Hodder and Stoughton, 1958.
Mary Mouse Goes to the Fair, illustrated by Frederick White. Leicester, Brockhampton Press, 1958.
Mr. Pink-Whistle's Big Book. London, Evans, 1958.
My Big-Ears Picture Book. London, Sampson Low, 1958.
My Noddy Picture Book. London, Sampson Low, 1958.
Noddy Has an Adventure. London, Sampson Low, 1958.
Puzzles for the Secret Seven, illustrated by Burgess Sharrocks. Leicester, Brockhampton Press, 1958; as *The Secret Seven and the Case of the Music Lover*, Chicago, Children's Press, 1972.
Rumble and Chuff, illustrated by David Walsh. London, Juvenile Productions, 2 vols., 1958.
You're a Good Friend, Noddy! London, Sampson Low, 1958.
The Noddy Shop Book. London, Sampson Low, 5 vols., 1958.
Bom and the Clown. Leicester, Brockhampton Press, 1959.
Bom and the Rainbow, illustrated by R. Paul-Höye. Leicester, Brockhampton Press, 1959.
Hullo Bom and Wuffy Dog, illustrated by R. Paul-Höye. Leicester, Brockhampton Press, 1959.
Mary Mouse Has a Wonderful Idea, illustrated by Frederick White. Leicester, Brockhampton Press, 1959.
Noddy and Bunkey. London, Sampson Low, 1959.
Noddy Goes to Sea. London, Sampson Low, 1959.
Noddy's Car Picture Book. London, Sampson Low, 1959.

Ragamuffin Mystery. London, Collins, 1959.

Secret Seven Fireworks, illustrated by Burgess Sharrocks. Leicester, Brockhampton Press, 1959; as *The Secret Seven and the Bonfire Mystery*, Chicago, Children's Press, 1972.

Adventure of the Strange Ruby, illustrated by Roger Payne. Leicester, Brockhampton Press, 1960.

Adventure Stories. London, Collins, 1960.

Bom Goes to Magic Town. Leicester, Brockhampton Press, 1960.

Cheer Up, Little Noddy! London, Sampson Low, 1960.

Clicky and Tiptoe, illustrated by Molly Brett. Leicester, Brockhampton Press, 1960.

Five on Finniston Farm, illustrated by Eileen A. Soper. London, Hodder and Stoughton, 1960.

Good Old Secret Seven, illustrated by Burgess Sharrocks. Leicester, Brockhampton Press, 1960; as *The Secret Seven and the Old Fort Adventure*, Chicago, Children's Press, 1972.

Happy Day Stories, illustrated by Marcia Lane Foster. London, Evans, 1960.

Here Comes Bom, illustrated by R. Paul-Höye. Leicester, Brockhampton Press, 1960.

Mary Mouse Goes to Sea, illustrated by Frederick White. Leicester, Brockhampton Press, 1960.

Mystery Stories. London, Collins, 1960.

Noddy Goes to the Fair. London, Sampson Low, 1960.

Noddy's Tall Blue [Green, Orange, Pink, Red, and Yellow] Book. London, Sampson Low, 6 vols., 1960.

Will the Fiddle, illustrated by Grace Lodge. London, Instructive Arts, 1960.

Tales at Bedtime, illustrated by Hilda McGavin. London, Collins, 1961.

Bom at the Seaside, illustrated by R. Paul-Höye. Leicester, Brockhampton Press, 1961.

Bom Goes to the Circus, illustrated by R. Paul-Höye. Leicester, Brockhampton Press, 1961.

Five Go to Demon's Rocks, illustrated by Eileen A. Soper. London, Hodder and Stoughton, 1961.

Happy Holiday, Clicky, illustrated by Molly Brett. Leicester, Brockhampton Press, 1961.

Mary Mouse Goes Out for the Day, illustrated by Frederick White. Leicester, Brockhampton Press, 1961.

Mr. Plod and Little Noddy. London, Sampson Low, 1961.

The Mystery of Banshee Towers, illustrated by Lilian Buchanan. London, Methuen, 1961.

The Mystery That Never Was, illustrated by Gilbert Dunlop. London, Collins, 1961.

Noddy's Toyland Train Picture Book. London, Sampson Low, 1961.

Shock for the Secret Seven, illustrated by Burgess Sharrocks. Leicester, Brockhampton Press, 1961; as *The Secret Seven and the Case of the Dog Lover*, Chicago, Children's Press, 1972.

A Day at School with Noddy. London, Sampson Low, 1962.

Five Have a Mystery to Solve, illustrated by Eileen A. Soper. London, Hodder and Stoughton, 1962.

The Four Cousins, illustrated by Joan Thompson. London, Lutterworth Press, 1962.

Fun with Mary Mouse, illustrated by R. Paul-Höye. Leicester, Brockhampton Press, 1962.

Look Out Secret Seven, illustrated by Burgess Sharrocks. Leicester, Brockhampton Press, 1962; as *The Secret Seven and the Case of the Missing Medals*, Chicago, Children's Press, 1972.

Noddy and the Tootles. London, Sampson Low, 1962.

Stories for Monday. London, Oliphants, 1962.

Stories for Tuesday. London, Oliphants, 1962.

The Boy Who Wanted a Dog, illustrated by Sally Michel. London, Lutterworth Press, 1963.

Five Are Together Again, illustrated by Eileen A. Soper. London, Hodder and Stoughton, 1963.

Fun for the Secret Seven, illustrated by Burgess Sharrocks. Leicester, Brockhampton Press, 1963; as *The Secret Seven and the Case of the Old Horse*, Chicago, Children's Press, 1972.

Sunshine Picture Story Book. Manchester, World Distributors, 1964 (and later volumes).

Happy Hours Story Book. London, Dean, 1964.

Mary Mouse and the Little Donkey, illustrated by R. Paul-Höye. Leicester, Brockhampton Press, 1964.

Noddy and the Aeroplane. London, Sampson Low, 1964.

Story Book for Fives to Sevens, illustrated by Dorothy Hall and Grace Shelton. London, Parrish, 1964.

Storytime Book. London, Dean, 1964.

Tell-a-Story Books. Manchester, World Distributors, 1964.

Trouble for the Twins. Leicester, Brockhampton Press, 1964.

The Boy Who Came Back, illustrated by Elsie Walker. London, Lutterworth Press, 1965.

Sunshine Book. London, Dean, 1965.

Treasure Box. London, Sampson Low, 1965.

The Man Who Stopped to Help, illustrated by Elsie Walker. London, Lutterworth Press, 1965.

Noddy and His Friends: A Nursery Picture Book. London, Sampson Low, 1965.

Noddy Treasure Box. London, Sampson Low, 1965.

The Fairy Folk Story Book. London, Collins, 1966.

Fireside Tales. London, Collins, 1966.

The Happy House Children. London, Collins, 1966.

John and Mary, illustrated by Fromont. Leicester, Brockhampton Press, 9 vols., 1966–68.

Pixie Tales. London, Collins, 1966.

Pixieland Story Book. London, Collins, 1966.

Stories for Bedtime. London, Dean, 1966.

Stories for You. London, Dean, 1966.

Holiday Annual Stories. London, Low Marston, 1967.

Holiday Magic Stories. London, Low Marston, 1967.

Holiday Pixie Stories. London, Low Marston, 1967.

Holiday Toy Stories. London, Low Marston, 1967.

Noddy and His Passengers. London, Sampson Low, 1967.

Noddy and the Magic Boots, Noddy's Funny Kite. London, Sampson Low, 1967.

Noddy and the Noah's Ark Adventure Picture Book. London, Sampson Low, 1967.

Noddy in Toyland Picture Book. London, Low Marston, 1967.

Noddy's Aeroplane Picture Book. London, Sampson Low, 1967.

The Playtime Story Book. Manchester, World Distributors, 4 vols., 1967.

Adventures on Willow Farm. London, Collins, 1968.

Brownie Tales. London, Collins, 1968.

The Playtime Book. Manchester, World Distributors, 8 vols., 1968.

Once upon a Time. London, Collins, 1969.

Verse

Child Whispers. London, J. Saville, 1922.

Real Fairies: Poems. London, J. Saville, 1923.

Songs of Gladness, music by Alec Rowley. London, J. Saville, 1924.

Silver and Gold, illustrated by Lewis Baumer. London, Nelson, 1925.

The Enid Blyton Poetry Book: Ninety-Six Poems for the Twelve Months of the Year. London, Methuen, 1934.

Noddy Nursery Rhymes. London, Sampson Low, 1956.
Noddy's Own Nursery Rhymes. London, Sampson Low, 1958.

Plays

A Book of Little Plays (includes *The Princess and the Swineherd, Sing a Song of Sixpence, Fairy Prisoners, Robin Hood, Peronel's Paint*). London, Nelson, 1926.
The Play's the Thing (includes *The Capture of the Robbers; Rag, Tag, and Bobtail; Rumpelstiltskin; The King's Jester; The Magic Apple; Merry Robin Hood; The King's Pocket Knife; In the Toyshop; The Cuckoo; The Rainbow Flowers; The Wishing-Glove; The Broken Statue*), music by Alec Rowley, illustrated by A.E. Bestall. London, Nelson, 1927; as *Plays for Older Children* and *Plays for Younger Children*, London, Newnes, 2 vols., 1940.
Six Enid Blyton Plays (includes *The Princess and the Enchanter, Robin Hood and the Butcher, The Enchanted Cap, A Visit to Nursery-Rhyme Land, The Squirrel's Secret, The Whistling Brownie*). London, Methuen, 1935.
How the Flowers Grow and Other Plays (includes *The Fairy in the Box, The Magic Ball, The Toys at Night-Time, Who Stole the Crown?, Santa Claus Gets Busy*), music by Cecil Shawman. Exeter, Wheaton, 1939.
Cameo Plays, Book 4 (includes *The Making of a Rainbow, Poor Mr. Twiddle, The Three Wishes, The Donkey's Tail, Santa Claus Comes down the Chimney, The Wind and the Sun, Brer Rabbit and Mr. Dog, The Little Green Imp*), edited by George H. Holroyd. London, Arnold, 1939.
The Wishing Bean and Other Plays (includes *The Hole in the Sack, Spreading the News, The Queen's Garden, Sneezing Powder, The Land of Nursery Rhymes*). Oxford, Blackwell, 1939; as *Six Plays for Schools*, 1939.
Noddy in Toyland, music by Philip Green (produced London, 1954). London, Sampson Low, 1956.
Finding the Tickets. London, Evans, 1955.
Mr. Sly-One and Cats. London, Evans, 1955.
Mother's Meeting. London, Evans, 1955.
Who Will Hold the Giant? London, Evans, 1955.

Other

Responsive Singing Games. London, J. Saville, 1923.
Reading Practice, 1–5, 8–9, 11. London, Nelson, 8 vols., 1925–26.
The Bird Book, illustrated by Ronald Green. London, Newnes, 1926.
Aesop's Fables, Retold. London, Nelson, 1928.
Let's Pretend, illustrated by I. Bennington Angrave. London, Nelson, 1928.
Old English Stories, Retold. London, Nelson, 1928.
Pinkity's Pranks and Other Nature Fairy Stories, Retold. London, Nelson, 1928.
Tales of Brer Rabbit, Retold. London, Nelson, 1928.
Nature Lessons. London, Evans, 1929.
The Knights of the Round Table. London, Newnes, 1930.
Tales from the Arabian Nights. London, Newnes, 1930.
Tales of Ancient Greece. London, Newnes, 1930.
Tales of Robin Hood. London, Newnes, 1930.
Let's Read. London, Birn, 1933.
My First Reading Book. London, Birn, 1933.
Read to Us. London, Birn, 1933.
The Adventures of Odysseus. London, Evans, 1934.
The Story of the Siege of Troy. London, Evans, 1934.
Tales of the Ancient Greeks and Persians. London, Evans, 1934.
Tales of the Romans. London, Evans, 1934.

Round the Year with Enid Blyton: Spring, Summer, Autumn, Winter. London, Evans, 4 vols., 1934.

The Children's Garden. London, Newnes, 1935.

Heyo, Brer Rabbit! Tales of Brer Rabbit and His Friends. London, Newnes, 1938.

Birds of Our Gardens, illustrated by Roland Green and Ernest Aris. London, Newnes, 1940.

The News Chronicle Boys' and Girls' Book. London, News Chronicle, 1940.

The Babar Story Book, from stories by Jean de Brunhoff. London, Methuen, 1941; shortened version, as *Tales of Babar,* 1942.

A Calendar for Children. London, Newnes, 1941.

Book of the Year, music by Alec Rowley, illustrated by Eileen A. Soper. London, Evans, 1941 (and later volumes).

Enid Blyton Readers, 1–7, 10–12. London, Macmillan, 10 vols., 1942–50.

The Further Adventures of Brer Rabbit, Being More Tales of Brer Rabbit and His Friends, illustrated by Ernest Aris. London, Newnes, 1942.

The Land of Far-Beyond, based on *Pilgrim's Progress* by John Bunyan. London, Methuen, 1942.

The Children's Life of Christ. London, Methuen, 1943.

The Christmas Book, illustrated by Treyer Evans. London, Macmillan, 1944.

Nature Lover's Book, illustrated by Donia Nachshen and Noel Hopking. London, Evans, 1944.

Nature Readers, 1–30. London, Macmillan, 30 vols., 1945–46.

The First Christmas, illustrated by Paul Henning. London, Methuen, 1945.

The Enid Blyton Holiday Book. London, Sampson Low, 1946 (and 11 later volumes).

Before I Go to Sleep: A Book of Bible Stories and Prayers for Children at Night. London, Latimer House, 1947; Boston, Little Brown, 1953.

Enid Blyton's Treasury. London, Evans, 1947.

Jinky Nature Books. Leeds, E.J. Arnold, 4 vols., 1947.

Brer Rabbit and His Friends. London, Coker, 1948.

Brer Rabbit Book, illustrated by Grace Lodge. London, Latimer House, 8 vols., 1948–58.

Let's Garden, illustrated by William McLaren. London, Latimer House, 1948.

The Enid Blyton Nature Plates, with stories and notes, and reference book. London, Macmillan, 3 vols., 1949.

The Enid Blyton Bible Stories: Old Testament, with Bible pictures and reference book. London, Macmillan, 16 vols., 1949.

My Enid Blyton Bedside Book. London, Barker, 1949 (and 11 later volumes).

A Book of Magic. London, Macmillan, 1949.

Round the Year with Enid Blyton. London, Evans, 1950.

The Queen Elizabeth Family, illustrated by Ruth Gervis. London, Lutterworth Press, 1951.

The Enid Blyton Bible Stories: New Testament, with Bible pictures and reference book. London, Macmillan, 16 vols., 1952–53.

Animal Lover's Book. London, Evans, 1952.

Enid Blyton's Omnibus, illustrated by Jessie Land. London, Newnes, 1952.

My First Nature Book, illustrated by Eileen A. Soper. London, Macmillan, 1952 (and 2 later volumes).

Enid Blyton's Christmas Story, illustrated by Fritz Wegner. London, Hamish Hamilton, 1953.

The Story of Our Queen, illustrated by F. Stocks May. London, Muller, 1953.

Little Gift Books, illustrated by Pierre Probst. London, Hackett, 1954 (and later volumes).

Enid Blyton Magazine Annual. London, Evans, 1954 (and 3 later volumes).

The Greatest Book in the World, illustrated by Mabel Peacock. London, British and Foreign Bible Society, 1954.

Bible Stories from the Old Testament, illustrated by Grace Lodge.   London, Lutterworth Press, 1955.

Bible Stories from the New Testament, illustrated by Grace Lodge.   London, Muller, 1955.

Favourite Book of Fables, from the Tales of La Fontaine.   London, Collins, 1955.

What Shall I Be?, illustrated by Pierre Probst.   London, Collins, 1955.

Playing at Home, with Sabine Schweitzer.   London, Methuen, 1955.

Let's Have a Party, illustrated by Paul Kaye.   London, Harvill Press, 1956.

A Story Book of Jesus, illustrated by Elsie Walker.   London, Macmillan, 1956.

New Testament Picture Books 1–2.   London, Macmillan, 2 vols., 1957.

The School Companion, with others.   London, New Educational Press, 1958.

A.B.C. with Noddy.   London, Sampson Low, 1959.

Old Testament Picture Books.   London, Macmillan, 1960.

Noddy's One, Two, Three Book.   London, Sampson Low, 1961.

The Big Enid Blyton Book.   London, Hamlyn, 1961.

Brer Rabbit Again, illustrated by Grace Lodge.   London, Dean, 1963.

Easy Reader.   London, Collins, 1965 (and later volumes).

Brer Rabbit's a Rascal, illustrated by Grace Lodge.   London, Dean, 1965.

Learn to Count with Noddy.   London, Sampson Low, 1965.

Learn to Go Shopping with Noddy.   London, Sampson Low, 1965.

Learn to Read about Animals with Noddy.   London, Sampson Low, 1965.

Learn to Tell the Time with Noddy.   London, Sampson Low, 1965.

Tales of Long Ago, Retold.   London, Dean, 1965.

Enid Blyton's Bedtime Annual.   Manchester, World Distributors, 1966 (and later volumes).

Enid Blyton's Playbook.   London, Collins, 1966 (and later volumes).

Noddy Toyland ABC Picture Book.   London, Sampson Low, 1967.

Editor, *Sunny Stories for Little Folks*, and *Sunny Stories 1937–52*.   London, Newnes, 27 vols., 1926–52.

Editor, *Treasure Trove Readers*, junior series.   Exeter, Wheaton, 1934.

Editor, *Nature Observation Pictures.*   London, Warne, 4 vols., 1935.

Editor, *Birds of the Wayside and Woodland*, by Thomas A. Coward.   London, Warne, 1936.

Editor, *The Children's Book of Prayers.*   London, Muller, 1953.

PUBLICATIONS FOR ADULTS

Other

The Story of My Life.   London, Pitman, 1952.

Editor, *The Teacher's Treasury.*   London, Newnes, 3 vols., 1926.

Editor, *Modern Teaching: Practical Suggestions for Junior and Senior Schools.*   London, Newnes, 6 vols., 1928.

Editor, *Modern Teaching in the Infant School.*   London, Newnes, 4 vols., 1932.

*   *   *

Although her work was first published in a magazine in 1917 and her first book, a 24-page pamphlet of verse, appeared in 1922, the stories which made Enid Blyton a household name with both adults and children did not begin to appear until the late 1930's, first in the weekly magazine *Enid Blyton's Sunny Stories*, and subsequently in book form.

Enid Blyton did not die until 1968, but most of her stories are conceived against the background of the 1930's and 1940's, and reflect the middle-class standards of suburbia of those decades, although there is little mention of the Second World War. Her books are now criticised for racism, sexism, and snobbishness; but, to her, the all-important factor was the plot. When necessary, working-class characters are very much in command of the situation, notably Jack, whose skills enable the runaways to survive in *The Secret Island*, and Andy, the fisherman's boy, in *The Adventurous Four*.

Although Enid Blyton published over 600 books, some of them (usually those in series) have made much more impact than others. Noddy is the character most frequently criticised by adults, but he probably makes most of his impression on children because of the colourful illustrations and the commercial "spin-offs" rather than because of his adventures.

Many adults recall with affection the two short fantasy series which begin respectively with *The Adventures of the Wishing Chair* and *The Enchanted Wood*. The origins of both of these may be found in the Norse legends – the wishing chair having overtones of Frey's ship, and the faraway tree of Yggdrasill – but the strange lands which the children visit are far removed from the Norse tradition. They offer plenty of opportunity for slapstick humour and memorable non-human characters, and provide vivid images on which the more imaginative child can weave his own variations.

The Secret Seven and *The Famous Five* have been shown by many reading surveys to be the most widely read series. These provide exciting and undemanding reading material at an age when plenty of reading practice is important. They motivate children to want to read, and there is little which can be offered as an alternative with the same appeal. Enid Blyton never paid any attention to the adult critic of children's literature, who in any case was not much in evidence until long after she was well-established, and she gave the children what she believed they wanted. Since 1960 other authors who have contributed titles to series designed to help the child acquire the fluency which is essential to reading for enjoyment, have also tried to win adult approval in terms of characterisation, plot and style, but have often omitted the all-important elements of adventure and excitement.

There are other series of mystery/adventure stories which are almost as well known and widely read. Enid Blyton's stories in this genre appeal to children at an age when this type of story has the most appeal for them, at a time when links with their peer group are important and membership of a gang is most children's ideal. The exclusiveness of the Blyton characters may be criticised, but it is an accurate reflection of what children are like at this age. The *Adventure* books are more complex in both plot and characterisation than any of the others, and are therefore bought and praised by librarians and teachers who are selective in their purchase of Blyton books. There are two *Mystery* series: one of them features Fatty, "the master of disguises," and his friends in their attempts to outwit Mr. Goon the policeman in solving mysteries; in the other the central character is the mysterious Barney with his unusual pet. Most memorable of the adventure stories, for those who have read them, are the five *Secret* books, in which Miss Blyton made use of traditionally British popular literary motifs – the desert island, the kidnapped Ruritanian prince and the secret Afro-Asian kingdom.

The circus life portrayed in the numerous circus stories was romanticised even for the 1940's, with the horse-drawn caravans and the lack of concern for the realities of compulsory education or regulations about children performing in public; but these stories again provide a setting for unusual characters, exciting adventures and close contact with animals – early recognised by Enid Blyton as a theme popular with children. Jimmy Brown's success with all kinds of animals in *Mr. Galliano's Circus* is a perfect wish-fulfilment story.

Most boys grow out of Blyton at the age of 10 or 11, but girls may go on reading her longer because of the existence of the school stories. Reading surveys carried out in the 1940's show that the school story was the most popular type of story among girls of 11–14. Enid Blyton's first school stories were those about *The Naughtiest Girl*, set in a progressive, self-governing, coeducational school. Presumably designed so that they would not alienate the boy readers of *Sunny Stories*, in which they appeared as serials, they proved less popular than the later stories about *St. Clare's* and *Malory Towers*. These have worn remarkably well: the girls do not run into troubles of the trivial kind found in comparable stories, which would seem absurd to a schoolgirl of the 1970's, nor did Enid Blyton rely on secret passages, lost heiresses, smugglers or spies to add interest to the stories. The action arises out of the characters, and the simple psychology, showing why people behave as they do, may well stand the girl reader in good stead in later life; there is also some good slapstick comedy. Although the school story generally has never risen to great literary heights, Enid Blyton's stories are good examples of the genre.

The nearest approach to "social realism" comes in *Six Bad Boys*, the first edition of which included a preface of praise by Sir Basil Henriques, the well-known juvenile magistrate. This book reflected ideas prevalent in the post-war period; women were being encouraged to stay at home if they had school-age children, and the six boys who eventually come before the juvenile court are shown to have unsatisfactory homes and, particularly, unsatisfactory mothers. Although this may seem over-simplified and out of date in the liberated 1970's, there is still a lot of common sense to be found within the pages of this book.

If there is one point for which Enid Blyton can be criticised it is for her over-simplification – of plot, of character and especially of language and style. The vocabulary of her books is very limited, and this leads to an overuse of words such as "horrid," "queer," "peculiar," "exciting" – simple words easily understood by children. However it is this very simplicity which constitutes the appeal for children of all abilities. Provided that the child is encouraged to move on to other books at the appropriate stage in his or her development, the reading of Blyton may well help to develop necessary reading skills.

—Sheila G. Ray

BODECKER, N(iels) M(ogens). Danish.   Born in Copenhagen, Denmark, 13 January 1922; moved to the U.S.A. in 1952. Educated at the Technical Society School of Architecture, 1939–41, School of Applied Art, 1941–44, and School of Commerce, 1942–44, all in Copenhagen. Served in the Royal Danish Artillery, 1945–47. Married Mary Ann Weld in 1952 (marriage dissolved, 1959); has three children. Free-lance writer and illustrator, Copenhagen, 1944–52, and in the U.S.A. since 1952. Recipient: Society of Illustrators award, 1965; *New York Times* award, for illustration, 1973; Christopher Award, 1974, 1976. Address: Hancock, New Hampshire 03449, U.S.A.

PUBLICATIONS FOR CHILDREN (illustrated by the author)

Fiction

    Miss Jaster's Garden.   New York, Golden Press, 1971; London, Collins, 1973.
    Good Night, Little A.B.C., with Robert Kraus.   New York, Springfellow Books, 1972; London, Cape, 1974.
    The Mushroom Center Disaster, illustrated by Erik Blegvad.   New York, Atheneum, 1974.

Verse

    Let's Marry Said the Cherry and Other Nonsense Poems.   New York, Atheneum, 1974; London, Faber, 1977.
    Hurry, Hurry, Mary Dear and Other Nonsense Poems.   New York, Atheneum, 1976.

Other

    It's Raining Said John Twaining (Danish nursery rhymes).   New York, Atheneum, and London, Macmillan, 1973.

PUBLICATIONS FOR ADULTS

Verse

> *Digtervandring* (Poets Ramble).   Copenhagen, Forum, 1943.
> *Graa Fugle* (Grey Birds).   Copenhagen, Prior, 1946.

Illustrator: *Spillebog for Hus, Hjem, og Kro* (Book of Games for House, Home, and Inn) by Sigfred Pedersen, 1948; *Oh! What a Wonderful Wedding* by Virginia Rowans, 1953; *Half Magic*, 1954, *Knight's Castle*, 1956, *Magic by the Lake*, 1957, *The Time Garden*, 1958, *Magic or Not?*, 1959, *The Well-Wishers*, 1960, and *Seven-Day Magic*, 1962, all by Edward Eager; *The Bulls and the Bees* by Roger Eddy, 1956; *Cousins*, 1956, and *Beaux*, 1958, by Evan Commager; *Songberd's Grove* by Anne Barrett, 1957; *Cadwallader: A Diversion* by Russell Lynes, 1959; *The S-Man* by Mark Caine, 1960; *Sylvester the Mouse with the Musical Ear* by Adelaide Holl, 1961; *David Copperfield* by Charles Dickens, 1962; *The Book of the Dance* by Agnes DeMille, 1963; *The Snake in the Carpool* by Miriam Schlein, 1963; *Lizzie's Twin* by Doris Adelberg, 1964; *Is There a Mouse in the House?* by Josephine Gibson, 1965; *Shoe Full of Shamrock* by Mary Francis Shura, 1965; *Good Night, Little One*, 1972, *Good Night, Richard Rabbit*, 1972, *The Night-Lite Calendar 1974* and *1975*, 1973–74, and *The Night-Lite Storybook*, 1975, all by Robert Kraus; *Mattie Fritts and the Flying Mushroom* by Michael Jennings, 1973; *A Little at a Time* by David A. Adler, 1976.

N. M. Bodecker comments:

My first collection of Danish verse, written when I was nineteen, came out in Copenhagen in 1943. Poetry was my first love, illustration came later, and writing for children later still.

I changed language and country (though not nationality) at the age of thirty, and for the next twenty years made my living as an illustrator, working on my English poetry after hours.

When my first English book came out in New York, it may have looked as if an illustrator had suddenly turned writer. Actually the illustrator had been the writer in disguise. A troublesome disguise at times, for illustrating never gave me much pleasure.

With *Let's Marry Said the Cherry* I finally picked up the thread I had dropped in Copenhagen 23 years earlier: writing and illustrating my own nonsense.

Writing for children took me by surprise, I hadn't planned it, it just happened. The child in me would out.

I'm rather a late bloomer in many ways, and the closer I get to resemble an adult, the easier I find it to give the child in me free range: to sympathize with un-rung bells and boats tugging at their moorings, longing to perform according to their nature: to know that when the longing grows strong enough, the boat sails itself and the bell rings out unaided. Certainly, at night when I'm asleep, the piano in the garden room plays "Oranges and Lemons," or a little Schubert, perhaps.

*   *   *

Gifted with rare imagination and a wonderful sense of the absurd, N. M. Bodecker has written both poetry and prose for children. His first English language work, *Miss Jaster's Garden*, is a gentle tale of a very proper English maiden lady and her good friend Hedgie, and what happens when the flower seeds that Miss Jaster inadvertently drops on Hedgie's back grow and bloom. The simple story of Miss Jaster and her hedgehog friend scarcely prepares the reader for the remarkably imaginative miniature world of *The Mushroom Center Disaster*, a story which in its cozy British warmth and tender feeling for small living things (in this case, insects) is reminiscent of Grahame's *Wind in the Willows*, but which in its exquisitely careful choice of words and in its poetic rhythm is Bodecker at his best. The story itself, a tale with ecological overtones of what happens when the remains of a picnic lunch are carelessly dropped on a tiny insect village, is slight, but the careful detail with which Bodecker describes the modus vivendi of the insects' miniature, and very humanly British, world is captivating.

Bodecker has made his greatest contribution to children's literature, however, with his nonsense verse for children, a growing corpus which has appeared beginning with *It's Raining Said John Twaining*. *It's Raining* is a translation of Danish nursery rhymes done for Bodecker's three American-born sons; integrated with Bodecker's own illustrations, the poems have a tongue-twisting rhythm and logical illogic which cry to be read aloud. Here we find Miss Jaster reincarnated as Little Miss Price who rode with her mice over the ice, the three guinea pigs who went, like "Pussycat, Pussycat" of the old English nursery rhyme, to see the King, and a host of other zanies in the best nursery-rhyme tradition. The rhythms of traditional skipping rhymes and happily inspired word play animate Bodecker's poetry, which has justly been compared with that of Edward Lear, Ogden Nash, and Lewis Carroll. His further collections (*Let's Marry Said the Cherry, Hurry, Hurry, Mary Dear*) have enlarged Bodecker's range of subject matter and cast of characters without exhausting his seemingly limitless originality and inspired nonsense.

—Margaret Maxwell

BOND, (Thomas) Michael. British. Born in Newbury, Berkshire, 13 January 1926. Educated at Presentation College, Reading, 1934–40. Served in the Royal Air Force, 1943–44; Middlesex Regiment, British Army, 1944–47. Married Brenda Mary Johnson in 1950; has one daughter. Cameraman, BBC, London, 1947–66; director, Paddington and Company (Films) Ltd. Agent: Harvey Unna and Stephen Durbridge Ltd., 14 Beaumont Mews, Marylebone High Street, London W.1. Address: 19 Beak Street, London W.1, England.

PUBLICATIONS FOR CHILDREN

Fiction

> *A Bear Called Paddington*, illustrated by Peggy Fortnum. London, Collins, 1958; Boston, Houghton Mifflin, 1960.
> *More about Paddington*, illustrated by Peggy Fortnum. London, Collins, 1959; Boston, Houghton Mifflin, 1961.
> *Paddington Helps Out*, illustrated by Peggy Fortnum. London, Collins, 1960; Boston, Houghton Mifflin, 1961.
> *Paddington Abroad*, illustrated by Peggy Fortnum. London, Collins, 1961; Boston, Houghton Mifflin, 1972.
> *Paddington at Large*, illustrated by Peggy Fortnum. London, Collins, 1962; Boston, Houghton Mifflin, 1963.
> *Paddington Marches On*, illustrated by Peggy Fortnum. London, Collins, 1964; Boston, Houghton Mifflin, 1965.
> *Here Comes Thursday*, illustrated by Daphne Rowles. London, Harrap, 1966; New York, Lothrop 1967.
> *Paddington at Work*, illustrated by Peggy Fortnum. London, Collins, 1966; Boston, Houghton Mifflin, 1967.
> *Paddington Goes to Town*, illustrated by Peggy Fortnum. London, Collins, and Boston, Houghton Mifflin, 1968.
> *Thursday Rides Again*, illustrated by Beryl Sanders. London, Harrap, 1968; New York, Lothrop, 1969.

Parsley's Good Deed, illustrated by Esor.   London, BBC Publications, 1969.
The Story of Parsley's Tail, illustrated by Esor.   London, BBC Publications, 1969.
Thursday Ahoy!, illustrated by Leslie Wood.   London, Harrap, 1969; New York, Lothrop, 1970.
Paddington Takes the Air, illustrated by Peggy Fortnum.   London, Collins, 1970; Boston, Houghton Mifflin, 1971.
Parsley's Last Stand.   London, BBC Publications, 1970.
Parsley's Problem Present.   London, BBC Publications, 1970.
Thursday in Paris, illustrated by Leslie Wood.   London, Harrap, 1971.
Book of Bears.   London, Purnell, 1971.
The Tales of Olga da Polga (*Olga Makes a Wish, Olga's New Home, Olga Counts Her Blessings, Olga Makes Her Mark, Olga Takes a Bite, Olga's Second House, Olga Makes a Friend, Olga's Special Day*), illustrated by Hans Helweg.   London, Penguin, 8 vols., 1971; New York, Macmillan, 8 vols., 1973.
Parsley the Lion, illustrated by Ivor Wood.   London, Collins, 1972.
Parsley Parade, illustrated by Ivor Wood.   London, Collins, 1972.
Paddington Bear, illustrated by Fred Banbery.   London, Collins, 1972; New York, Random House, 1973.
Paddington's Garden, illustrated by Fred Banbery.   London, Collins, 1972; New York, Random House, 1973.
Book of Mice.   London, Purnell, 1972.
The Day the Animals Went on Strike, illustrated by Jim Hodgson.   London, Studio Vista, 1972; New York, American Heritage Press, 1973.
Olga Meets Her Match, illustrated by Hans Helweg.   London, Penguin, 1973; New York, Hastings House, 1975.
Paddington at the Circus, illustrated by Fred Banbery.   London, Collins, 1973; New York, Random House, 1974.
Paddington Goes Shopping, illustrated by Fred Banbery.   London, Collins, 1973; as *Paddington's Lucky Day*, New York, Random House, 1974.
Paddington on Top, illustrated by Peggy Fortnum.   London, Collins, 1974; Boston, Houghton Mifflin, 1975.
Paddington's Blue Peter Story Book, illustrated by Ivor Wood.   London, Collins, 1974; as *Paddington Takes to T.V.*, Boston, Houghton Mifflin, 1974.
Mr. Cram's Magic Bubbles, illustrated by Gioia Fiammenghi.   London, Penguin, 1975.
Windmill, illustrated by Tony Cattaneo.   London, Studio Vista, 1975.
Paddington at the Seaside, illustrated by Fred Banbery.   London, Collins, 1975.
Paddington at the Tower, illustrated by Fred Banbery.   London, Collins, 1975.
Olga Carries On, illustrated by Hans Helweg.   London, Penguin, 1976; New York, Harvey House, 1977.
Paddington at the Station, illustrated by Barry Wilkinson.   London, Collins, 1976.
Paddington Takes a Bath, illustrated by Barry Wilkinson.   London, Collins, 1976.
Paddington Goes to the Sales, illustrated by Barry Wilkinson.   London, Collins, 1976.
Paddington's New Room, illustrated by Barry Wilkinson.   London, Collins, 1976.

Plays

The Adventures of a Bear Called Paddington, with Alfred Bradley.   London, French, 1974.
Paddington on Stage, with Alfred Bradley, illustrated by Peggy Fortnum.   London, Collins, 1974.

Television Plays: *The Herbs* series.

Other

> *Herbs Annual.*   London, BBC Publications, 2 vols., 1969, 1970.
> *The Parsley Annual.*   London, BBC Publications, 2 vols., 1971, 1972.
> *The Book of Flying Things.*   London, Studio Vista, 1975.
> *Paddington's Loose-End Book: An ABC of Things to Do*, illustrated by Ivor Wood.   London, Collins, 1976.
> *Paddington's Party Book*, illustrated by Ivor Wood.   London, Collins, 1976.
> *The Great Big Paddington Book*, illustrated by Ivor Wood.   London, Collins, 1976; New York, Collins World, 1977.

> Translator, with Eve Barwell, *The Motormalgamation*, by H. G. Fischer-Tschop and Barbara von Johnson.   London, Studio Vista, 1973.

*   *   *

It is almost impossible to think of Michael Bond without thinking of Paddington, so identified is he with his creation, one of the outstanding success stories of recent publishing. This success is due largely to the fact that Paddington is a bear. Teddies and other bears naturally appeal to children as symbolising love and security, and this one is certainly loved. His adventures, as children soon realise, are all certain to go wrong. Thus they have the pleasure of anticipation. Even very young children can become involved. In *Paddington Goes Shopping*, for instance, they can see in a few colourful pictures and brief texts what happens when Paddington is turned loose in a supermarket – he is buried under a load of groceries!

Bond's choice of a bear, although almost accidental, is very skilful. Paddington is not particularly bear-like: he behaves like a child and is generally regarded by the Browns as just another member of the family, albeit very accident-prone. By using a bear in this way, Bond has got the best of both worlds. He interests children who are fascinated by Paddington's propensity for disasters but he also attracts adults to whom the bear epitomises the well-meaning but bumbling adult whose behaviour can be so amusing. Perhaps it is too much to say that Bond uses Paddington to illustrate human frailty and failings but undoubtedly he does pin-point many situations familiar to adults. By comparison, Olga da Polga can never match the general appeal of Paddington. She is definitely a guinea pig whose adventures are restricted to her natural surroundings; her relationship with humans is strictly traditional and lacks the supreme touch of fantasy which is the hallmark of the Paddington books where the animal is accepted as "human" throughout all the stories. Nobody looks askance at his going shopping or living as part of the Brown family and it is this dual aspect of Paddington (bear-appeal to children, human personification to adults) that makes Michael Bond's creation so outstanding.

—Margaret Walker

BONHAM, Frank. American. Born in Los Angeles, California 25 February 1914. Attended Glendale College, California. Served in the United States Army, 1942–43. Married to Gloria Bailey; has three sons. Recipient: George G. Stone Center for Children's Books Award, 1967. Address: 8302 Sugarman Drive, La Jolla, California, U.S.A.

PUBLICATIONS FOR CHILDREN

Fiction

> *Burma Rifles: A Story of Merrill's Marauders.*   New York, Crowell, 1960.

War Beneath the Sea. New York, Crowell, 1962.
Deepwater Challenge. New York, Crowell, 1963.
Honor Bound. New York, Crowell, 1963.
The Loud, Resounding Sea. New York, Crowell, 1963.
Speedway Contender. New York, Crowell, 1964.
Durango Street. New York, Dutton, 1965.
Mystery in Little Tokyo, illustrated by Kazue Mizumura. New York, Dutton, 1966.
Mystery of the Red Tide, illustrated by Brinton Turkle. New York, Dutton, 1966.
The Ghost Front. New York, Dutton, 1968.
Mystery of the Fat Cat, illustrated by Alvin Smith. New York, Dutton, 1968.
The Nitty Gritty, illustrated by Alvin Smith. New York, Dutton, 1968.
The Vagabundos. New York, Dutton, 1969.
Viva Chicano. New York, Dutton, 1970.
Chief. New York, Dutton, 1971.
Cool Cat. New York, Dutton, 1971.
The Friends of the Loony Lake Monster. New York, Dutton, 1972.
Hey, Big Spender! New York, Dutton, 1972.
A Dream of Ghosts. New York, Dutton, 1973.
The Golden Bees of Tulami. New York, Dutton, 1974.
The Missing Persons League. New York, Dutton, 1976.
The Rascals at Haskell's Gym. New York, Dutton, 1977.

PUBLICATIONS FOR ADULTS

Novels

Lost Stage Valley. New York, Simon and Schuster, 1948; Kingswood, Surrey, World's Work, 1950.
Bold Passage. New York, Simon and Schuster, 1950; London, Hodder and Stoughton, 1951.
Blood on the Land. New York, Ballantine, 1952; London, Muller, 1955.
Snaketrack. New York, Simon and Schuster, 1952.
The Outcast of Crooked River. London, Hodder and Stoughton, 1953.
Night Raid. New York, Ballantine, 1954.
The Feud at Spanish Fort. New York, Ballantine, 1954.
Hardrock. New York, Ballantine, 1956; London, Muller, 1960.
Border Guns. London, Muller, 1956.
Last Stage West. New York, Dell, 1957; London, Muller, 1959.
Tough Country. New York, Dell, and London, Muller, 1958.
The Sound of Gunfire. London, World Distributors, 1960.
One for Sleep. New York, Fawcett, 1960; London, Muller, 1961.
The Skin Game. New York, Fawcett, 1961; London, Muller, 1963.
Trago .... New York, Dell, 1962.
Defiance Mountain. London, World Distributors, 1962; New York, Popular Library, 1964.
By Her Own Hand. New York, Simon and Schuster, 1963.
Cast a Long Shadow. New York, Simon and Schuster, 1964.
Rawhide Guns. New York, Popular Library, 1964.
Logan's Choice. New York, Fawcett, 1964.

Plays

Television Plays: *Wells Fargo, Restless Gun, Shotgun Slade,* and *Death Valley Days* series.

*   *   *

Frank Bonham's novels are an adroitly controlled mix of cautionary tales, encouragement and hope, spiced with earthy humor. In 1960 he published his first, *Burma Rifles*, based upon the exploits of Japanese-Americans who served with the Allies in World War II. He has been writing for young people (age 10 and up) ever since and stands as one of the most literate and effective authors of what is called realism. Most of Bonham's stories feature disadvantaged boys — Blacks and Chicanos — who are forced to tackle outsized problems. *Durango Street* dealt with the dilemma of Rufus Henry, a boy on parole trying to stay out of further trouble. This was praised by critics, and was followed by *Viva Chicano* and other singular successes in the same genre.

A skilled, inventive storyteller, Bonham has insights which could pierce a stone wall but his most noticeable asset is compassion. His stories are therefore approved by pedagogues as "useful" in that they call attention to social ills. Fortunately, that discouraging epithet is ignored by readers who have discovered that Bonham's novels are, above all, outstanding entertainments.

Recently, the author has enhanced his reputation and added to his audience with two definite departures. In these, he combines the realism he's known for with unusual and convincing darts into fantasy. *The Golden Bees of Tulami* finds Cool Hankins, a Black teenager, being leaned on by gangsters trying to force him to quit school and take up boxing for their profit. Cool meets a stranger from Africa, J. S. Kinsman, who arrives in Dogtown Ghetto with golden bees whose honey has a pacific effect on those who eat it. The miraculous substance is introduced with the hope of achieving world peace; greedy entrepreneurs, however, scotch the dream of the idealists. But Cool's relationship with Kinsman teaches the boy important lessons and he gains the courage to defy his would-be oppressors.

The Missing Persons League is suspenseful science-fiction set in a bleak future when America is run by rigid bureaucrats; the world is dying of pollution, and individuals subsist on tasteless rations based on the number of people in each family. Again a young and spunky hero, Brian Foster, faces tough odds. His mother and sister have been missing for a year — a fact he keeps secret from the authorities for obvious reasons. While trying to find his missing relations, Brian also has to contend with a deadly enemy, Lt. Atticus, who suspects the truth, and is sure that the boy is breaking the law by growing forbidden food for himself and his father. The climax is a burst of excitement as Brian and the girl he loves learn the secret of their vanished kin and join them in a new world, just as icy Atticus is about to pounce.

It's safe to say that the stories of Frank Bonham will continue to be read and enjoyed by those who appreciate the adventures of recognizable humans.

—Jean F. Mercier

BONSALL, Crosby (Newell). American. Born on Long Island, New York, 2 January 1921. Studied at American School of Design, New York; New York University School of Architecture. Married to George Bonsall. Worked in advertising agencies. Lives in Williamsport, Pennsylvania. Address: c/o Harper and Row Inc., 10 East 53rd Street, New York, New York 10022, U.S.A.

PUBLICATIONS FOR CHILDREN

Fiction

The Surprise Party, illustrated by the author.   New York, Wonder Books, 1955.

Captain Kangaroo's Book, illustrated by Evan Jeffrey.   New York, Grosset and Dunlap, 1958.

Polar Bear Brothers (as Crosby Newell), photographs by Ylla.   New York, Harper, 1960.

Kippy the Koala (as Crosby Newell), photographs by George Leavens.   New York, Harper, 1960.

Tell Me Some More, illustrated by Fritz Siebel.   New York, Harper, 1961; Kingswood, Surrey, World's Work, 1962.

Listen, Listen!, photographs by Ylla.   New York, Harper, and London, Hamish Hamilton, 1961.

Hurry Up, Slowpoke, illustrated by the author.   New York, Grosset and Dunlap, 1961.

Who's a Pest?, illustrated by the author.   New York, Harper, 1962; Kingswood, Surrey, World's Work, 1963.

Look Who's Talking, photographs by Ylla.   New York, Harper, 1962; London, Hamish Hamilton, 1963.

The Case of the Hungry Stranger, illustrated by the author.   New York, Harper, 1963; Kingswood, Surrey, World's Work, 1964.

What Spot?, illustrated by the author.   New York, Harper, and Kingswood, Surrey, World's Work, 1963.

It's Mine, illustrated by the author.   New York, Harper, 1964.

I'll Show You Cats, photographs by Ylla.   New York, Harper, 1964.

The Case of the Cat's Meow, illustrated by the author.   New York, Harper, 1965; Kingswood, Surrey, World's Work, 1966.

The Case of the Dumb Bells, illustrated by the author.   New York, Harper, 1966; Kingswood, Surrey, World's Work, 1967.

Here's Jellybean Reilly, photographs by Ylla.   New York, Harper, 1966.

Whose Eye Am I?, photographs by Ylla.   New York, Harper, 1968.

The Case of the Scaredy Cats, illustrated by the author.   New York, Harper, 1971; Kingswood, Surrey, World's Work, 1973.

The Day I Had to Play with My Sister, illustrated by the author.   New York, Harper, 1972; Kingswood, Surrey, World's Work, 1974.

Mine's the Best, illustrated by the author.   New York, Harper, 1973; Kingswood, Surrey, World's Work, 1974.

Piggle, illustrated by the author.   New York, Harper, 1973; Kingswood, Surrey, World's Work, 1974.

And I Mean It, Stanley, illustrated by the author.   New York, Harper, 1974; Kingswood, Surrey, World's Work, 1975.

Twelve Bells for Santa, illustrated by the author.   New York, Harper, 1977.

Other

Let Papa Sleep (reader), illustrated by Emily Reed.   New York, Grosset and Dunlap, 1963.

Illustrator: *August Explains* by Phil Ressner, 1963; *Go Away, Dog* by Joan L. Nodset, 1963; *Seesaw* by Joan Kahn, 1964; *Great Big Joke and Riddle Book* edited by Oscar Weigler, 1970.

*   *   *

Crosby Bonsall is one example of an author who originally wrote fairly exclusively about little boys, but who has evolved into a writer who knows that little girls can be interesting central figures as well. This is very important in the area of Bonsall's specialty, the I Can Read and Early I Can Read books. In *The Case of the Hungry Stranger*, the four clubhouse boys (who appear in *The Case of the Cat's Meow* and *The Case of the Dumb Bells*) offer to find the culprit who ate two blueberry pies. They check out the postman, the ice-cream man, the policeman, and the paperboy in their all-male world. Finally, they track down the offender, a male dog owned by Marigold, who joins them to help eat their reward (a third blueberry pie). The feast is held outside the clubhouse, for "No Girls Allowed" is emblazoned on the door. It takes Bonsall a few years for her consciouness to be raised but, subsequently, in *The Case of the Scaredy Cats*, Marigold and her friends challenge their exclusion from the clubhouse activities with their own slogan, "Girls Are As Good As Boys," and fight for recognition. Although these boys may not change, Marigold and her friends have asserted themselves, an important first step.

Within the limitations of a confining vocabulary and simple sentence structure, it is difficult to write an engaging early reader, yet Bonsall does this admirably in *And I Mean It, Stanley*. It is a charming story about a disheveled spunky girl who builds a "really, truly great thing" out of backyard litter while she directs an amusing monologue at her unseen pal. It is a sure-winner for the library story-hour. In *What Spot?* Bonsall takes small children out of their everyday world and intensifies their imagination with her illustrations and the enigma of the puzzling spot in the snow which is eyed by an old walrus, a puffin, and a bear. *Tell Me Some More* introduces children to the wonders and magic of the library, notwithstanding the book's outdated appearance. *The Day I Had to Play with My Sister* realistically portrays in the Early I Can Read format the frustrations felt by a brother when he tries valiantly, but in vain, to have fun with a younger sibling. Crosby Bonsall has many titles to her credit, making it wise to be selective in avoiding books which ignore or denigrate girls. One such book is *Who's a Pest?*, a story about poor little Homer and his identically mean-looking, nasty sisters, Lolly, Molly, Polly, and Dolly.

Bonsall can be an edifying author for the young uninitiated reader who can start picking out words and ideas from her large body of work. For this reason, titles like *And I Mean It, Stanley* and *The Case of the Scaredy Cats* are two which deserve special attention.

—Vivian J. Scheinmann

BOSTON, Lucy (Maria). British. Born in Southport, Lancashire, in 1892. Educated at Downs School, Seaford, Sussex; Somerville College, Oxford, 1914; trained in the Voluntary Aid Detachment, St. Thomas's Hospital, London. Married in 1917 (marriage dissolved, 1935). Served as a nurse in France during World War I. Recipient: Library Association Carnegie Medal, 1962. Address: The Manor, Hemingford Grey, Huntingdonshire, England.

PUBLICATIONS FOR CHILDREN

Fiction

> *The Children of Green Knowe*, illustrated by Peter Boston. London, Faber, 1954; New York, Harcourt Brace, 1955.
> *The Chimneys of Green Knowe*, illustrated by Peter Boston. London, Faber, 1958; as *Treasure of Green Knowe*, New York, Harcourt Brace, 1958.
> *The River at Green Knowe*, illustrated by Peter Boston. London, Faber, and New York, Harcourt Brace, 1959.
> *A Stranger at Green Knowe*, illustrated by Peter Boston. London, Faber, and New York, Harcourt Brace, 1961.
> *An Enemy at Green Knowe*, illustrated by Peter Boston. London, Faber, and New York, Harcourt Brace, 1964.
> *The Castle of Yew*, illustrated by Margery Gill. London, Bodley Head, and New York, Harcourt Brace, 1965.

The Sea-Egg, illustrated by Peter Boston.   London, Faber, and New York, Harcourt
Brace, 1967.
The House That Grew, illustrated by Caroline Hemming.   London, Faber, 1969.
Nothing Said, illustrated by Peter Boston.   London, Faber, and New York, Harcourt
Brace, 1971.
Memory in a House.   London, Bodley Head, 1973.
The Guardians of the House, illustrated by Peter Boston.   London, Bodley Head, 1974.
The Fossil Snake, illustrated by Peter Boston.   London, Bodley Head, 1975; New York,
Atheneum, 1976.
The Stones of Green Knowe, illustrated by Peter Boston.   London, Bodley Head, and
New York, Atheneum, 1976.

PUBLICATIONS FOR ADULTS

Novels

Yew Hall.   London, Faber, 1954.
Persephone.   London, Collins, 1969; as *Strongholds,* New York, Harcourt Brace, 1969.

Play

The Horned Man; or, Whom Will You Send to Fetch Her Away?   London, Faber, 1970.

Critical Study: *Lucy Boston* by Jasper Rose. London, Bodley Head, 1965; New York, Walck,
1966.

*   *   *

Lucy Boston is one of the children's writers who, in the 1950's, began decisively to redirect
the course of juvenile fiction. Her earliest books have an unusual delicacy and formality of
structure: at a time when predetermined adventure and pony stories were still proliferating,
she infused a new seriousness and imaginative honesty into the concept of writing for
children.

The underlying theme of the "Green Knowe" series is continuity, and this is pushed to an
extreme in *The Stones of Green Knowe,* when children from various centuries are brought
together in a climactic scene. Twelfth-century Roger is the first boy to live at the Norman
stronghold: "All [the] free reaches of the imagination were centred for Roger in the new
house that would stand to repel invaders, to receive heroes, to outlast perils, to withstand in
its living stone walls the evils of witches and demons." The stories too are centred in the
house and this economical device enables the author to deal effectively with time shifts and
episodes of magic and danger. Everything is contained within Green Knowe, which
transmits its own validity.

Mrs. Boston's "ghosts" are rendered in concrete terms, and the interaction between the
past and the present (a common aspect of recent fiction) gives an oblique fascination to the
straightforward historical events. In context the supernatural has a super-rational basis; the
convergence of different times in moments of intensity or special insight is an accepted
convention. Mrs. Boston has an unusual sensitivity, nothing to do with whimsy or free-range
airy-fairy effects: it is simply expressed in an exquisite clarity of detail (down to the small
piece of quilt, "rose-coloured ... with minute white sprays") and a judicious use of fantastical
motifs. She rarely goes too far: when she does (in several episodes in *The River at Green
Knowe,* for instance) she steps back into her stride without fuss.

The River is the weakest of the "Green Knowe" stories; the children's adventures are
balanced awkwardly between the realistic and the dreamlike, and the book lacks a
satisfactory conclusion. Of the three children, only Ping, the Chinese boy, reappears later in
the series. In *A Stranger at Green Knowe* he befriends an escaped gorilla and helps it to hide in

a bamboo thicket: this is the only one of the six books that doesn't contain an element of magic. Instead, a number of complex ideas of freedom and ethics and their violation are presented in symbolical terms. It is entirely fitting that Ping, the displaced boy, should be the hero of this story, not Tolly, great-grandson of the owner of the house.

Tolly is the boy whose special responsiveness gives literal shape to the sequence related by the old lady as she sews her patchwork quilts. The romantic 17th-century children of Green Knowe, Toby, Alexander and Linnet, with their deer, squirrel and superb horse Feste, are the most elusive and ethereal of Mrs. Boston's creations. The historical characters in the second story (*The Chimneys of Green Knowe*) have greater substance: blind Susan and her black companion Jacob are among the most entertaining and resourceful children in fiction. Susan's disability simply makes her "special"; she isn't in the least pathetic or repressed. Mrs. Boston uses the deprivation of one sense to exploit the others: "Everything that touched Susan was something she couldn't see. But far from being afraid she wanted to catch everything in the act of being real. She even put her finger in the candle-flame to see what being burnt was like .... "

This is the most perfectly realized of the stories. The narrative works on two levels on a realistic plane, and the historical evocations are highly charged in a way that complements domestic accuracy. It is an excellent blend of adventure and an exercise of the imagination. Its effect, however, is less powerful than that of *An Enemy at Green Knowe* (with its malevolent sorceress actually named Miss Melanie D. Powers). Mrs. Boston has most successfully eliminated all trace of fear from her supernatural confrontations; but in *An Enemy* she acknowledges and examines the concepts of evil and destructiveness. The other stories have a gentle aura of subtlety and precision; this bristles with apprehension and generates a real sense of malignity.

Lucy Boston has written books for younger children: of these, *The Sea-Egg* is the most original and persuasive. The basic motif, the one impossible event that is right in poetic terms, is repeated later with less conviction. The dryad of *Nothing Said*, the regenerated reptile of *The Fossil Snake*, are presented in a context too slight to sustain them. In *The Guardians of the House*, in the episode of the caves, fantasy shades into fallacy. Mrs. Boston's talent requires scope for extension of the central theme and elaboration of imagery.

Elizabeth Bowen has commented on "the insufficiency of so-called real life to the requirements of those who demand to be really alive." The "Green Knowe" books help to close the gap in one direction: that of belief in a tangible residue of the experience of past generations, the overflow of one consciousness into another, the associative and regenerative power of objects. Taken as a whole, the series is an important contribution to children's literature.

—Patricia Craig

BOYLSTON, Helen Dore. American. Born in Portsmouth, New Hampshire, 4 April 1895. Educated at Portsmouth schools; Simmons College, Boston, one year; Massachusetts General Hospital, Boston, qualified nurse 1917. Served as an anesthesiologist with Harvard Unit at British Army Hospital, France 1917–18: Captain. Head Nurse and Instructor in Anesthesia, Massachusetts General Hospital, 1918–21; Red Cross Nurse, Albania and Poland, 1921–24; Nurse, in private practice, New York, 1925–27; Head Nurse, Norwalk Hospital, Connecticut, in late 1940's. Agent: Brandt and Brandt, 101 Park Avenue, New York, New York 10017. Address: c/o Virginia P. Boyd, P.O. Box 149, Westport, Connecticut 06880, U.S.A.

Fiction

> *Sue Barton, Student Nurse*, illustrated by Forrest Orr.   Boston, Little Brown, 1936;
> London, Lane, 1939.
> *Sue Barton, Senior Nurse*, illustrated by Forrest Orr.   Boston, Little Brown, 1937;
> London, Lane, 1940.
> *Sue Barton, Visiting Nurse*, illustrated by Forrest Orr.   Boston, Little Brown, 1938;
> London, Lane, 1941.
> *Sue Barton, Rural Nurse*, illustrated by Forrest Orr.   Boston, Little Brown, 1939;
> London, Lane, 1942.
> *Sue Barton, Superintendent of Nurses*, illustrated by Forrest Orr.   Boston, Little Brown,
> 1940; London, Lane, 1942.
> *Carol Goes Backstage*, illustrated by Frederick Wallace.   Boston, Little Brown, 1941;
> as *Carol Goes on the Stage*, London, Lane, 1943.
> *Carol Plays Summer Stock*, illustrated by Major Felten.   Boston, Little Brown, 1942; as
> *Carol in Repertory*, London, Lane, 1944.
> *Carol on Broadway*, illustrated by Major Felten.   Boston, Little Brown, 1944; as *Carol
> Comes to Broadway*, London, Lane, 1945.
> *Carol on Tour*, illustrated by Major Felten.   Boston, Little Brown, 1946; London, Lane,
> 1948.
> *Sue Barton, Neighborhood Nurse*.   Boston, Little Brown, 1949; London, Lane, 1950.
> *Sue Barton, Staff Nurse*.   Boston, Little Brown, 1952; London, Lane, 1953.

Other

> *Clara Barton: Founder of the American Red Cross*, illustrated by Paula Hutchison.
> New York, Random House, 1955.

Other

> *"Sister": The War Diary of a Nurse*.   New York, Washburn, 1927.

Helen Dore Boylston comments:
Teenage girls about to decide how they propose to earn a living naturally lean toward the romantic. Nursing and acting have a romantic appeal, but young imaginations conjure up the most wildly inaccurate pictures of life in either profession. I am a nurse myself, and have loved it all my days. But nursing is quite, *quite* different from anything girls imagine. The same is true in regard to the theatre.

So, I proposed to give them as *true* a picture as I was able. The nursing books were easy, naturally. As for the acting profession – my neighbor and friend, Eva LeGallienne, is a very famous actress indeed. When I discussed my problem with her, she suggested that I spend an entire autumn and winter backstage in her theatre watching rehearsals, opening nights, and theatre life in general. I did so, and I also brought each completed manuscript to her for her criticisms and suggestions.

*   *   *

Series books created by the Stratemeyer syndicate were disavowed by educators and librarians, but in the third decade of this century Helen Dore Boylston offered to the adolescent girl two heroines who were acceptable – Sue Barton and Carol Page. These series were greeted by reviewers as either authoritative vocational stories about nursing and theatre professions respectively or falsely glamorous. Later, the author was selected by the Landmark Series editor to write a biography of the founder of the American Red Cross, Clara Barton.

In seven volumes, Sue Barton progresses from a student nurse to various professional roles in her career. Plot is the strongest element of the author's technique, combining speed and suspense. Romance, mystery and episodes of typhoid epidemic, hurricane and pneumonia propel the momentum. Early in her student days, Sue meets Dr. Bill Barry to whom she becomes married five books and seven years later. Strange noises in a rented house prompt the reader to finish the third book. A portion of each series book is devoted to reviewing earlier books and previewing the forthcoming book. The fifth book, *Sue Barton, Superintendent of Nurses*, was initially intended to conclude the series, as the couple is finally married and Sue announces a forthcoming child.

Character development is superficial, with changes in circumstances substituted for depth. Sue remains the calm and witty nurse, while Marianna merely changes from waif to sedate wife of an older man. Minor characters such as Tony, the Greek laundryman, and Veazie Ann Cooney, the New Hampshire housekeeper, offer local color through their stereotyped accents. Innumerable people have "twinkling eyes." Humor permeates the books with dialogue such as "superabundance of megalomania arising from excessive local prominence," and situations such as the dachshund sitting on Sue's wedding underwear and then becoming drunk.

Boston, New York City, and New Hampshire are settings drawn from the author's own background. Historical data is limited to the Henry Street Settlement in *Sue Barton, Visiting Nurse*. The authoritative aura created by the author is offset by cliches such as "I'm responsible for the kind of person she becomes," "Doctors should marry nurses," and "There ought always to be a baby in the house." However, there is strong support for the working woman. Sue's father advises, "Show the world what you can do before you settle down" and the nurse postpones marriage for professional experiences.

Although the Sue Barton series is a "period piece" with expressions such as "Zulu gone mad," New York described as "crawling with gangsters and Chinamen and murderers," and nursing procedures from the 1930's, the titles remain in print in the United States and in Great Britain, and have been published in other languages.

As with the nurse series, the subject of each of the four Carol Page books is introduced in the title. A girl rises from high school debut to a small part in a New York play to appenticeship with the summer theater, to Broadway and finally to a tour. Details in background are convincing and ample. As a contemporary reviewer stated, "a career story of this profession must not be rushed." Referred to as a "second string heroine" by M. L. Becker, Carol Page is currently an unknown character, and the books are out of print.

The biography of Clara Barton describes episodes in the nurse's life from age three to more than ninety, and is more substantial and readable than other juvenile biographies about the heroine. The book suffers from superlatives in describing the biographee as a faster runner, better pitcher, more politically knowledgeable and in general harder working than her contemporaries.

—Karen Nelson Hoyle

BRAND, (Mary) Christianna (Milne). British. Born in Malaya, 17 December 1909. Educated at a Franciscan convent, Taunton, Somerset. Married Roland S. Lewis in 1939; has one daughter. Agent: A.M. Heath, 40–42 William IV Street, London WC2N 4DD. Address: 88 Maida Vale, London W9 1PR, England.

PUBLICATIONS FOR CHILDREN

Fiction

Danger Unlimited. New York, Dodd Mead, 1948; as *Welcome to Danger*, London, Foley House Press, 1950.
Nurse Matilda, illustrated by Edward Ardizzone. Leicester, Brockhampton Press, and New York, Dutton, 1964.
Nurse Matilda Goes to Town, illustrated by Edward Ardizzone. Leicester, Brockhampton Press, 1967; New York, Dutton, 1968.
Nurse Matilda Goes to Hospital, illustrated by Edward Ardizzone. London, Hodder and Stoughton, and New York, Dutton, 1974.

Other

Editor, *Naughty Children: An Anthology*, illustrated by Edward Ardizzone. London, Gollancz, 1962; New York, Dutton, 1963.

PUBLICATIONS FOR ADULTS

Novels

Death in High Heels. London, Lane, 1941; New York, Scribner, 1954.
Heads You Lose. London, Lane, 1941; New York, Dodd Mead, 1942.
Green for Danger. New York, Dodd Mead, 1944; London, Lane, 1945.
The Crooked Wreath. New York, Dodd Mead, 1946; as *Suddenly at His Residence*, London, Lane, 1947.
The Single Pilgrim (as Mary Roland). London, Sampson Low, and New York, Crowell, 1946.
Death of Jezebel. New York, Dodd Mead, 1948; London, Lane, 1949.
Cat and Mouse. London, Joseph, and New York, Knopf, 1950.
London Particular. London, Joseph, 1952; as *Fog of Doubt*, New York, Scribner, 1953.
Tour de Force. London, Joseph, and New York, Scribner, 1955.
The Three-Cornered Halo. London, Joseph, and New York, Scribner, 1957.
Starrbelow (as China Thompson). London, Hutchinson, 1958.
Court of Foxes. London, Joseph, 1969; Northridge, California, Brooke House, 1977.
The Radiant Dove (as Annabel Jones). London, Joseph, 1974; New York, St. Martin's Press, 1975.
Alas, For Her That Met Me! (as Mary Ann Ashe). London, Star, 1976.
Ring of Roses. London, W.H. Allen, 1977.

Short Stories

What Dread Hand. London, Joseph, 1968.
Brand X. London, Joseph, 1974.

Other

Heaven Knows Who. London, Joseph, and New York, Scribner, 1960.

Christianna Brand comments:
I believe that children, in small families and the permissive age, have too few opportunities to be just mischievously naughty, and that they adore reading about children who *are*. The

three "Nurse Matilda" books are about a huge family of children, and each chapter starts with a list of their misdeeds: "Tora was pouring treacle into the Wellington boots. David was putting glue in the sandwiches," etc., each list ending, "And all the other children were doing simply dreadful things too." This has the children rolling about with laughter and mums write in to thank me for books they can bear to read over and over and over again. The theme is that Nurse Matilda is sent for – she is terribly ugly "with a nose like two potatoes" – and magics them all into goodness again, until they retrogress and she has to be sent for once more. It is an expansion of a story handed down through my family.

The Anthology follows the same theme, being extracts from books about naughty children through the ages, from the Bible – where they ran out upon Elijah crying, "Go to, thou baldhead!" and were deservedly eaten up by two large bears – to the present day.

*   *   *

To the vast majority of English children today, nannies are creatures as mythical as dragons, but like dragons, they have their traditional habits and characteristics enshrined in children's literature. Christianna Brand's Nurse Matilda is a late but notable addition to the small, select band which includes Nana the dog and Mary Poppins.

Nurse Matilda, "the ugliest person you ever saw in your life" with "a nose like two potatoes," descends upon the enormous family of naughty Brown children to teach them the error of their ways. Her method is simple: when they are doing something naughty she bangs her magic stick, and they find themselves unable to stop, so that soon, of course, their naughtiness is no fun at all. As their manners improve she herself grows prettier, until when at last they are reformed characters (temporarily, at least), she leaves. "When my children don't want me, but do need me: then I must stay. When they no longer need me, but they do want me: then I have to go."

This is the pattern of all three books: Nurse Matilda is set in the Browns' home, Nurse Matilda Goes to Town takes the family to terrible Great-Aunt Adelaide's London house, Nurse Matilda Goes to Hospital lands them first in hospital and then by the sea – a seaside which has almost a surrealistic touch of Lewis Carroll about it. Each story contains an ingenious set-piece of naughtiness and culminates in a dream-like chase. These are humorous moral tales set in that Edwardian nursery world which will be most familiar to modern children from the works of E. Nesbit. Part of the appeal of the Brown children's naughtiness, one suspects, lies in the implicit presence of a fairly stern discipline in that nursery world, where you knew where you were and there was no question of your being mentally disturbed rather than plain naughty if you went pouring syrup into your siblings' Wellington boots.

The author tells us that the genesis of the books lies in a story told to the children of her own family, including her cousin Edward Ardizzone, whose illustrations complement the narrative perfectly. In Christianna Brand's version these three little jeux d'esprit have great style and verve, and perhaps show their oral origin in the success with which they can be read aloud. The story races along in an extravaganza of words, stopping every now and then for a little set-piece, a recital of the various awful things the children are up to, and ending in a chorus of: "And all the other children were doing simply dreadful things too." Very short, very funny, with not a word wasted, the three "Nurse Matilda" books surely deserve to rank as minor classics of children's writing.

—Anthea Bell

BRAZIL, Angela. British. Born in Preston, Lancashire, 30 November 1869. Educated at Manchester High School; Ellerslie College, Manchester; Heatherley Studio, London. Vice-President, 1920, and President, 1928, Coventry Y.W.C.A.; Vice-President, Coventry Natural History and Scientific Society. Died 13 March 1947.

PUBLICATIONS FOR CHILDREN

Fiction

A Terrible Tomboy, illustrated by the author and Amy Brazil.   London, Gay and Bird, 1904.
The Fortunes of Philippa.   London, Blackie, 1906.
The Third Class at Miss Kaye's.   London, Blackie, 1908.
Bosom Friends: A Seaside Story.   London, Nelson, 1909.
The Nicest Girl in the School.   London, Blackie, 1909; Boston, Caldwell, 1911.
The Manor House School, illustrated by F. Moorsom.   London, Blackie, 1910; Boston, Caldwell, 1911.
A Fourth Form Friendship.   London, Blackie, 1911.
The New Girl at St. Chad's.   London, Blackie, 1911.
A Pair of Schoolgirls.   London, Blackie, 1912.
The Leader of the Lower School.   London, Blackie, 1913.
The Youngest Girl in the Fifth.   London, Blackie, 1913.
The Girls of St. Cyprian's.   London, Blackie, 1914.
The School by the Sea.   London, Blackie, 1914.
The Jolliest Term on Record, illustrated by Balliol Salmon.   London, Blackie, 1915.
For the Sake of the School.   London, Blackie, 1915.
The Luckiest Girl in the School, illustrated by Balliol Salmon.   London, Blackie, and New York, Stokes, 1916.
The Madcap of the School, illustrated by Balliol Salmon.   London, Blackie, 1917; New York, Stokes, 1922.
The Slap-Bang Boys.   London, Nelson, 1917.
A Patriotic Schoolgirl, illustrated by Balliol Salmon.   London, Blackie, 1918.
For the School Colours, illustrated by Balliol Salmon.   London, Blackie, 1918.
A Harum-Scarum Schoolgirl, illustrated by John Campbell.   London, Blackie, 1919; New York, Stokes, 1920.
The Head Girl at The Gables, illustrated by Balliol Salmon.   London, Blackie, 1919; New York, Stokes, 1920.
Two Little Scamps and a Puppy, illustrated by E. Blampied.   London, Nelson, 1919.
A Gift from the Sea.   London, Nelson, 1920.
Loyal to the School, illustrated by Treyer Evans.   London, Blackie, 1920.
A Popular Schoolgirl, illustrated by Balliol Salmon.   London, Blackie, 1920; New York, Stokes, 1921.
The Princess of the School, illustrated by Frank Wiles.   London, Blackie, 1920; New York, Stokes, 1921; as *A Princess at the School*, London, Armada, 1970.
A Fortunate Term, illustrated by Treyer Evans.   London, Blackie, 1921; as *Marjorie's Best Year*, New York, Stokes, 1923.
Monitress Merle, illustrated by Treyer Evans.   London, Blackie, 1922.
The School in the South, illustrated by W. Smithson Broadhead.   London, Blackie, 1922; as *The Jolliest School of All*, New York, Stokes, 1923.
The Khaki Boys and Other Stories.   London, Nelson, 1923.
Schoolgirl Kitty, illustrated by W.E.Wightman.   London, Blackie, 1923; New York, Stokes, 1924.
Captain Peggie, illustrated by W.E.Wightman.   London, Blackie, and New York, Stokes, 1924.
Joan's Best Chum, illustrated by W.E.Wightman.   London, Blackie, 1926; New York, Stokes, 1927.
Queen of the Dormitory and Other Stories, illustrated by P.B. Hickling.   London, Cassell, 1926.
Ruth of St. Ronan's, illustrated by F. Oldham.   London, Blackie, 1927.
At School with Rachel, illustrated by W.E.Wightman.   London, Blackie, 1928.

St. Catherine's College, illustrated by Frank Wiles. London, Blackie, 1929.
The Little Green School, illustrated by Frank Wiles. London, Blackie, 1931.
Nesta's New School, illustrated by J. Dewar Mills. London, Blackie, 1932; as
    Amanda's New School, London, Armada, 1970.
Jean's Golden Term. London, Blackie, 1934.
The School at The Turrets. London, Blackie, 1935.
An Exciting Term. London, Blackie, 1936.
Jill's Jolliest School. London, Blackie, 1937.
The School on the Cliff, illustrated by F.E.Hiley. London, Blackie, 1938.
The School on the Moor, illustrated by Henry Coller. London, Blackie, 1939.
The New School at Scawdale, illustrated by M. Mackinlay. London, Blackie, 1940.
Five Jolly Schoolgirls. London, Blackie, 1941.
The Mystery of the Moated Grange. London, Blackie, 1942.
The Secret of the Border Castle, illustrated by Charles Willis. London, Blackie, 1943.
The School in the Forest, illustrated by J. Dewar Mills. London, Blackie, 1944.
Three Terms at Uplands, illustrated by D.L.Mays. London, Blackie, 1945.
The School on the Loch, illustrated by W. Lindsay Cable. London, Blackie, 1946.

Plays

The Mischievous Brownie. Edinburgh, Patterson, 1899.
The Fairy Gifts. Edinburgh, Patterson, 1901.
Four Recitations. Edinburgh, Patterson, 1903.
The Enchanted Fiddle. Edinburgh, Patterson, 1903.
The Wishing Princess. Edinburgh, Patterson, 1904.

Other

My Own Schooldays (autobiography). London, Blackie, 1925.

Critical Study: The Schoolgirl Ethic: The Life and Work of Angela Brazil by Gillian Freeman,
London, Allen Lane, 1976.

*   *   *

Angela Brazil pioneered the girls' school story in Great Britain and created a *genre*. Her
name is synonymous with "jolly hockey sticks" fiction in spite of many excellent followers.
Her first school story, *The Fortunes of Philippa*, was based on her mother's experiences of an
English boarding school after early childhood in Rio de Janeiro, and contains a moving,
psychologically accurate account of a nervous breakdown occasioned by a persecuting
teacher. The book's success brought a commission from Blackie's, who remained her
publishers until her death in 1947, although by that time her "works," as she called them, had
deteriorated to a formula. The best are those written between 1911 (*The New Girl at St.
Chad's* and *A Fourth Form Friendship*) and 1924 (*Captain Peggie*). There was a biography in
1926 (*My Own Schooldays*) which gives a carefully scissored and romanticized account.

Angela Brazil's schooling was academically sound and emotionally disappointing. She
longed for secret societies, boarding school, hockey and amateur dramatics, and created them
for her readers. Many girls, inspired by her books, became boarders, and found that real life
in no way measured up to Brazil fiction. The books often have perfunctory plots with poor
construction. It is the girls, the teaching staffs and the intense relationships which give them
life, and there is no doubt that Angela Brazil really understood adolescent agonies. Passions,
jealousies, resentments and aims were charted with sympathy, as were the problems and
responsibilities of headmistresses who appear in a wide range of personalities. Angela Brazil
believed in education for its own sake, free from the stress of examinations; loyalty to the
family (particularly to mothers − fathers play virtually no part in her books); loyalty to

England (*A Patriotic Schoolgirl* and *For the School Colours* are the best examples) and loyalty to *friends*. Aldred and Mabel in *A Fourth Form Friendship* suffer and enjoy the emotional intensity of a heterosexual liaison, and it must be stressed that Angela Brazil was totally innocent of any underlying forces guiding her subconscious. It is interesting to note that in subsequent editions a kiss becomes a handshake, as behaviour patterns changed. In *Loyal to the School* a new principal *objected to seeing girls walking about the playground with their arms round each others waists or the display of any affections. She called such behaviour "early Victorian."*

Slang is an essential ingredient of the books and made the author unpopular with real headmistresses. Two High Mistresses of St. Paul's School for Girls (Miss Gray and Miss Strudwick) separately condemned her to two generations of pupils. Whether Angela Brazil took the slang from schoolgirls (she claimed she did and rode the commutor train from Coventry to Leamington Spa to take it down from travelling pupils) or the schoolgirls from Angela Brazil, it is difficult to decide. Some of it is incomprehensible – "it's a sneaking rag to prig their bikkies" – and some unlikely – "it's a blossomy idea, O Queen!" What is indisputable is that Angela Brazil drew continuously on her own life, so that her biography can be charted from her work. A visit to a café, a gift of chocolates, hatred of a sister-in-law and adoration of a sick nephew (*A Patriotic Schoolgirl*) are all to be found in the seemingly inflexible format. *Schoolgirl Kitty* is built on personal relationships and events, Carrington is a surname she used as an alias for Brazil, and Lesbia Carrington in *For the School Colours* is based on herself.

—Gillian Freeman

BRENT-DYER, Elinor M. British. Born in South Shields, County Durham, in 1895. Educated privately in Leeds; Leeds University. Teacher; Headmistress, Margaret Roper School, Hereford. *Died in September 1969.*

PUBLICATIONS FOR CHILDREN

Fiction

> *Gerry Goes to School*, illustrated by Gordon Broe. Edinburgh, Chambers, 1922; Philadelphia, Lippincott, 1923.
> *A Head Girl's Difficulties*, illustrated by Nina K. Brisley. Edinburgh, Chambers, 1923.
> *The Maids of La Rochelle*, illustrated by Nina K. Brisley. Edinburgh, Chambers, 1924.
> *The School at the Chalet*, illustrated by Nina K. Brisley. Edinburgh, Chambers, 1925.
> *Jo of the Chalet School*, illustrated by Nina K. Brisley. Edinburgh, Chambers, 1926.
> *A Thrilling Term at Janeways*, illustrated by F.M. Anderson. London, Nelson, 1927.
> *Seven Scamps Who Are Not at All Boys*, illustrated by Percy Tarrant. Edinburgh, Chambers, 1927.
> *The Princess of the Chalet School*, illustrated by Nina K. Brisley. Edinburgh, Chambers, 1927.
> *The Head Girl of the Chalet School*, illustrated by Nina K. Brisley. Edinburgh, Chambers, 1928.
> *Judy the Guide*, illustrated by L.A. Govey. London, Nelson, 1928.
> *The New House Mistress*. London, Nelson, 1928.
> *Heather Leaves School*, illustrated by Percy Tarrant. Edinburgh, Chambers, 1929.
> *The Rivals of the Chalet School*, illustrated by Nina K. Brisley. Edinburgh, Chambers, 1929.

Eustacia Goes to the Chalet School. Edinburgh, Chambers, 1930.
The School by the River. London, Burns and Oates, 1930.
The Chalet School and Jo, illustrated by Nina K. Brisley. Edinburgh, Chambers, 1931.
A Feud in the Fifth Remove. London, Religious Tract Society, 1931.
Janie of La Rochelle. Edinburgh, Chambers, 1932.
The Little Marie-José. London, Burns and Oates, 1932.
The Chalet Girls in Camp. Edinburgh, Chambers, 1932.
The Exploits of the Chalet Girls, illustrated by Nina K. Brisley. Edinburgh, Chambers, 1933.
The Chalet School and the Lintons, illustrated by Nina K. Brisley. Edinburgh, Chambers, 1934.
Carnation of the Upper Fourth. London, Religious Tract Society, 1934.
The New House at the Chalet School. Edinburgh, Chambers, 1935.
Jo Returns to the Chalet School, illustrated by Nina K. Brisley. Edinburgh, Chambers, 1936.
Monica Turns Up Trumps. London, Religious Tract Society, 1936.
Caroline the Second. London, Religious Tract Society, 1937.
The New Chalet School, illustrated by Nina K. Brisley. Edinburgh, Chambers, 1938.
They Both Liked Dogs. London, Religious Tract Society, 1938.
The Chalet School in Exile. Edinburgh, Chambers, 1940.
The Chalet School Goes to It, illustrated by Nina K. Brisley. Edinburgh, Chambers, 1941.
The Highland Twins at the Chalet School. Edinburgh, Chambers, 1942.
The Little Missus. Edinburgh, Chambers, 1942.
Lavender Laughs in the Chalet School. Edinburgh, Chambers, 1943.
Gay from China at the Chalet School. Edinburgh, Chambers, 1944.
Jo to the Rescue. Edinburgh, Chambers, 1945.
The Lost Staircase. Edinburgh, Chambers, 1946.
Lorna at Wynyards. London, Lutterworth Press, 1947.
Stepsisters for Lorna, illustrated by John Bruce. London, Temple, 1948.
Three Go to the Chalet School. Edinburgh, Chambers, 1949.
Peggy of the Chalet School. Edinburgh, Chambers, 1950.
The Chalet School and the Island. Edinburgh, Chambers, 1950.
Fardingdales. London, Latimer House, 1950.
The Chalet School and Rosalie. Edinburgh, Chambers, 1951.
A Quintette in Queensland. Edinburgh, Chambers, 1951.
Bess on Her Own in Canada. Edinburgh, Chambers, 1951.
Carola Storms the Chalet School. Edinburgh, Chambers, 1951.
The Chalet School in the Oberland. Edinburgh, Chambers, 1952.
The Wrong Chalet School. Edinburgh, Chambers, 1952.
Shocks for the Chalet School. Edinburgh, Chambers, 1952.
Bride Leads the Chalet School. Edinburgh, Chambers, 1953.
Changes for the Chalet School. Edinburgh, Chambers, 1953.
Janie Steps In. Edinburgh, Chambers, 1953.
The Susannah Adventure. Edinburgh, Chambers, 1953.
Nesta Steps Out. London, Oliphants, 1954.
Kennelmaid Nan. London, Lutterworth Press, 1954.
Joey Goes to the Oberland. Edinburgh, Chambers, 1954.
Chudleigh Hold. Edinburgh, Chambers, 1954.
The Condor Crags Adventure. Edinburgh, Chambers, 1954.
The Chalet School and Barbara. Edinburgh, Chambers, 1954.
Beechy of the Harbour School. London, Oliphants, 1955.
A Chalet Girl from Kenya. Edinburgh, Chambers, 1955.
The Chalet School Does It Again. Edinburgh, Chambers, 1955.
Tom Tackles the Chalet School. Edinburgh, Chambers, 1955.

Top Secret. Edinburgh, Chambers, 1955.
A Problem for the Chalet School. Edinburgh, Chambers, 1956.
Leader in Spite of Herself. London, Oliphants, 1956.
Mary-Lou of the Chalet School. Edinburgh, Chambers, 1956.
A Genius at the Chalet School. Edinburgh, Chambers, 1956; revised edition, London, Collins, 1969.
Excitements at the Chalet School. Edinburgh, Chambers, 1957.
The New Mistress at the Chalet School. Edinburgh, Chambers, 1957.
The Chalet School and Richenda. Edinburgh, Chambers, 1958.
The Coming-of-Age of the Chalet School. Edinburgh, Chambers, 1958.
Theodora and the Chalet School. Edinburgh, Chambers, 1959.
Trials for the Chalet School. Edinburgh, Chambers, 1959.
Joey & Co. in Tirol. Edinburgh, Chambers, 1960.
Ruey Richardson − Chaletian. Edinburgh Chambers, 1960.
A Leader in the Chalet School. Edinburgh, Chambers, 1961.
The Chalet School Wins the Trick. Edinburgh, Chambers, 1961.
The Feud in the Chalet School. Edinburgh, Chambers, 1962.
A Future Chalet School Girl. Edinburgh, Chambers, 1962.
The School at Skelton Hall. London, Parrish, 1962.
The Chalet School Reunion. Edinburgh, Chambers, 1963.
The Chalet School Triplets. Edinburgh, Chambers, 1963.
Trouble at Skelton Hall. London, Parrish, 1963.
Jane at the Chalet School. Edinburgh, Chambers, 1964.
Redheads at the Chalet School. Edinburgh, Chambers, 1964.
Summer Term at the Chalet School. Edinburgh, Chambers, 1965.
Adrienne and the Chalet School. Edinburgh, Chambers, 1965.
Two Sams at the Chalet School. Edinburgh, Chambers, 1967.
Althea Joins the Chalet School. Edinburgh, Chambers, 1969.
Prefects of the Chalet School. Edinburgh, Chambers, 1970.

Other

Verena Visits New Zealand. Edinburgh, Chambers, 1951.
Sharlie's Kenya Diary. Edinburgh, Chambers, 1951.
The Chalet Girls' Cook Book. Edinburgh, Chambers, 1953.

Editor, *The Chalet Book of Girls 1* to *3.* Edinburgh, Chambers, 3 vols., 1947–49.

PUBLICATIONS FOR ADULTS

Novel

Elizabeth the Gallant. London, Butterworth, 1935.

*   *   *

From the early 1920's until her death in 1969 Elinor Brent-Dyer wrote almost 100 books for girls. These included historical and adventure stories but it is for her 58 Chalet School books that this author is remembered. *The School at the Chalet* was published in 1925 and Elinor Brent-Dyer's international tri-lingual, non-denominational school in the "Austrian Tirol" soon caught the imagination of readers. It became so popular that a Chalet School Club was formed, attracting a large membership from many parts of the world.

The school, an intriguing amalgam of foreign glamour and British "grit," is founded by Madge Bettany, a young Englishwoman. Although inexperienced, Madge becomes the Chalet School's first headmistress, taking administrative, racial and language complications in her stride: she is an unconventional principal, sometimes addressing one or other of her pupils as "honey" or "darling."

The school's family atmosphere is accentuated by the presence of Madge's sister, Joey, originally a junior pupil and later Head-Girl. In adult life Joey becomes prolific as a writer of girls' stories and as a breeder (she has eleven children). Despite the variety of pupils who come and go the vitality of the series rests largely on the character of Joey. As this lively and intrepid heroine grows older it is more difficult for the author to make her integral to the stories. However, even in the last book of the series – no. 58, published posthumously in 1970 – Joey is still insisting that "if she lived to be a great-grandmother, she would be a Chalet girl to the end."

Initially the Chalet School's appeal owed a great deal to its location. Elinor Brent-Dyer ably conveys the charm of the school beside mist-swathed mountains and a lake "alive with dancing shadows." The books are sometimes over-lush. Gentians, marguerites and alpen roses have a technicolour quality: floweriness spills over into descriptions of the girls in their flame-coloured ties, brown tunics and shantung blouses. But this is counterbalanced by plenty of action. For instance *The Princess of the Chalet School* includes – as well as a flower-strewn masque, a garden party and a wedding – two kidnapping attempts and an outsize thunderstorm which breaks every window in the valley and sets the school's playing fields on fire. The school buildings are saved from total destruction only by an equally violent hailstorm which opportunely covers everything with five inches of hail in as many minutes. Girls fall into icebound rivers or are stranded on exposed mountain sides: in the first five books alone Joey manages to save the lives of six girls and one dog.

The Chalet School survives after evacuation from the Nazis. It moves first to the Channel Islands, then to Wales and later to the Oberland. Elinor Brent-Dyer exploited several of the stock ingredients of girls' fiction including animals, babies, guiding and country dance. A headmistress for many years, she understood the tastes of girls growing up between the wars although by the late 1950's her books had become anachronistic.

—Mary Cadogan

BRIGHT, Robert. American. Born in Sandwich, Massachusetts, 5 August 1902. Educated at Phillips Academy, Andover, Massachusetts; Princeton University, New Jersey. Married Katherine Bailey in 1931; has one daughter and one son. Reporter, *Baltimore Sun*, 1925–26, and *Paris Times*, 1926–27; Assistant to the President, Condé Nast Publications, New York, 1927–28; Advertising Manager, Revillon Frères, New York, 1928–36; Instructor, Massachusetts Department of Education, Boston, 1948–51; Lecturer, Emerson College, Boston, 1949; Case Worker, Department of Welfare, Taos, New Mexico, 1952; Music and Art Critic, *New Mexican*, Sante Fe, 1964–65. Agent: Marie Rodell-Frances Collin, 141 East 55th Street, New York, New York 10022. Address: 242 Laurel Street, San Francisco, California 94118, U.S.A.

PUBLICATIONS FOR CHILDREN (illustrated by the author)

Fiction

The Travels of Ching. New York, Scott, 1943; London, Collins, 1945.
Georgie. New York, Doubleday, 1944; London, Collins, 1945.
Me and the Bears. New York, Doubleday, 1951.
Hurrah for Freddie!, with Dorothy Brett. New York, Doubleday, 1953.
I Like Red. New York, Doubleday, 1955; Kingswood, Surrey, World's Work, 1964.

Georgie to the Rescue. New York, Doubleday, 1956; Kingswood, Surrey, World's Work, 1964.

Miss Pattie. New York, Doubleday, 1954.

The Friendly Bear. New York, Doubleday, 1957; Kingswood, Surrey, World's Work, 1967.

Georgie's Hallowe'en. New York, Doubleday, 1958; Kingswood, Surrey, World's Work, 1967.

My Red Umbrella. New York, Morrow, 1959.

Which Is Willy? New York, Doubleday, 1962; Kingswood, Surrey, World's Work, 1963.

Georgie and the Robbers. New York, Doubleday, 1963; Kingswood, Surrey, World's Work, 1964.

Georgie and the Magician. New York, Doubleday, 1966; Kingswood, Surrey, World's Work, 1967.

Gregory, The Noisiest and Strongest Boy in Grangers Grove. New York, Doubleday, 1969; Kingswood, Surrey, World's Work, 1970.

Georgie and the Noisy Ghost. New York, Doubleday, 1971; Kingswood, Surrey, World's Work, 1973.

Georgie Goes West. New York, Doubleday, 1973; Kingswood, Surrey, World's Work, 1975.

Georgie's Christmas Carol. New York, Doubleday, 1975.

Verse

Round, Round World (as Michael Douglas). New York, Golden Press, 1960.

My Hopping Bunny. New York, Doubleday, 1960; Kingswood, Surrey, World's Work, 1967.

Other

Richard Brown and the Dragon. New York, Doubleday, 1952; Kingswood, Surrey, World's Work, 1964.

PUBLICATIONS FOR ADULTS

Novels

The Life and Death of Little Jo. New York, Doubleday, 1944; as *Little Jo*, London, Cresset Press, 1946.

The Intruders. New York, Doubleday, 1946; London, Cresset Press, 1948.

The Olivers: The Story of an Artist and His Family. New York, Doubleday, 1947.

The Spirit of the Chase. New York, Scribner, 1956; London, Cresset Press, 1957.

Robert Bright comments:

I intended to make a career as a novelist. But by the time I had published my third novel I realized that while I was gaining critical success I was not getting sufficient return to support a family. I had to be sensible, and so, sensibly, I turned to writing and illustrating picture books for children whose imagination commanded my respect and affection. What I have tried to do in my books is to present fantasy in the way of good stories with interesting characters and lots of humor and fun but with no silliness. So much of fantasy is apt to be silly, but good fantasy is logical and true. It teaches without straining, and above all, it does not abuse the confidence of the reader. I like to think therefore that those who have been brought up and are still being brought up in part with my books may always look back with pleasure at the imaginary worlds to which these stories introduced them.

*   *   *

The picture storybooks of Robert Bright represent a curious divergence of opinion between the tastes of children and those of certain adult critics of children's literature. Bright's books continue to receive enthusiastic endorsements from young children, but he is seldom referred to in any serious discussion of children's literature, such as those written for teachers or librarians. While a note on his "Georgie" books is found in the American Library Association *Books for Elementary Schools* and in *Children's Catalog*, Bright's work is generally dismissed out of hand by most compilers of selective bibliographies, even those exclusively of picture storybooks.

Although Bright has written these kind of books with several themes, what literary recognition he has received comes almost entirely from his "Georgie" books. Their qualities help explain their attractiveness to children. These books are pleasant distortions of reality about a wise and brave but altogether gentle little ghost, named Georgie, who resides, unknown to them, with a rather docile and witless old couple. Bright recalls that the idea for Georgie stemmed from his own children badgering him to make up for them a ghost story. While they probably wanted a tale of dread and awe, it was to Bright's ultimate advantage as a publishable writer for the young that he decided against doing a genuine ghost story. Instead, he chose a tongue-in-cheek treatment of the supernatural. This is the kind of book Bright tells fulfilled his ambition to enter into the child's world so as to invest it with stories that would have delighted him as a child. But one probable reason for lack of critical acclaim lies in his decision to illustrate his Georgie books. While he does a generally good job of melding the pictures with the stories, his drawings are so utterly lacking in artistic merit that they have negatively influenced critics not perceptive to the obvious merits of his plots and dialogue.

His illustrations aside, there is little doubt that Bright has succeeded in his goal of delighting children. In each of his books about Georgie this smallish apparition heroically undertakes to set to rights some villainous action or unfortunate mishap. For example, in *Georgie and the Robbers* (to this point Georgie "never scared anybody, he was much too shy for that") Bright updates the well-known folk tale, "The Three Musicians." In this case Georgie and his animal playmates do scare away robbers hiding out in a barn and recover their loot. It is obvious here, and in other of his Georgie stories, that Bright takes advantage of some of the motifs and traditions of folk literature that children enjoy hearing about. Among these motifs are the small person journeying away from home to a confrontation with a villain, followed by a showdown between good and evil and finally a rescue of the helpless. Bright's characters, as those in folk tales, are habitual in their behavior and unchanging in their motives. They are flat fictional personages whose behavior in stress situations is easily, and therefore happily predictable by the child reader. Bright also borrows from traditional literature his manner of talking directly to the reader, his highly melodramatic climaxes, his use of repetition and refrain for the sake of emphasis, and his choice of archaic settings. Other of Bright's books are reflections of the cumulative stories of folk literature. In *My Red Umbrella* and *I Like Red*, simple, repetitive, plotless structures, in which one thing or event in a sequence is much like that which it precedes and follows, Bright demonstrates again his dependence on folk literature.

—Patrick Groff

BRINK, Carol Ryrie.   American.   Born in Moscow, Idaho, 28 December 1895. Educated at Portland Academy, 1912–14; University of Idaho, Moscow, 1914–17; University of California, Berkeley, B.A. 1918. Married Raymond Woodard Brink in 1918; has one son and one daughter. Recipient: American Library Association Newbery Medal, 1936. D.Litt.:

University of Idaho, 1965. Agent: Reese Halsey, 8783 Sunset Boulevard, Los Angeles, California 90069. Address: 2404 Loring Street, Pacific Beach, California 92109, U.S.A.

PUBLICATIONS FOR CHILDREN

Fiction

Anything Can Happen on the River!, illustrated by W.W. Berger. New York, Macmillan, 1934.
Caddie Woodlawn, illustrated by Kate Seredy. New York, Macmillan, 1935; London, Collier Macmillan, 1963.
Mademoiselle Misfortune, illustrated by Kate Seredy. New York, Macmillan, 1936.
Baby Island, illustrated by Helen Sewell. New York, Macmillan, 1937.
All over Town, illustrated by Dorothy Bayley. New York, Macmillan, 1939.
Lad with a Whistle, illustrated by Robert Ball. New York, Macmillan, 1941.
Magical Melons: More Stories about Caddie Woodlawn, illustrated by Marguerite Davis. New York, Macmillan, 1944.
Family Grandstand, illustrated by Jean McDonald Porter. New York, Viking Press, 1952.
The Highly Trained Dogs of Professor Petit, illustrated by Robert Henneberger. New York, Macmillan, 1953.
Family Sabbatical, illustrated by Susan Foster. New York, Viking Press, 1956.
The Pink Motel, illustrated by Sheila Greenwald. New York, Macmillan, 1959; London, Collier Macmillan, 1963.
Andy Buckram's Tin Men, illustrated by W.T. Mars. New York, Viking Press, 1966.
Winter Cottage, illustrated by Fermin Rocker. New York, Macmillan, 1968.
Two Are Better Than One, illustrated by Fermin Rocker. New York, Macmillan, and London, Collier Macmillan, 1968.
The Bad Times of Irma Baumlein, illustrated by Trina Schart Hyman. New York, Macmillan, and London, Collier Macmillan, 1972.
Louly, illustrated by Ingrid Fetz. New York, Macmillan, 1974.

Plays

The Cupboard Was Bare. Franklin, Ohio, Eldridge, 1928.
The Queen of the Dolls. Franklin, Ohio, Eldridge, 1928.
Caddie Woodlawn, adaptation of her own story (produced Minneapolis, 1957). New York, Macmillan, 1954.
Salute Mr. Washington, in *Plays* (Boston), March 1976.

Other

Narcissa Whitman: Pioneer to the Oregon Country, illustrated by Samuel Armstrong. Evanston, Illinois, Row Peterson, 1950.
Lafayette, illustrated by Dorothy Bayley Morse. Evanston, Illinois, Row Peterson, 1953.

Editor, *Best Short Stories for Children.* Evanston, Illinois, Row Peterson, 6 vols., 1936–41.

PUBLICATIONS FOR ADULTS (as Carol Brink)

Novels

Buffalo Coat. New York, Macmillan, 1944; London, Cassell, 1949.

Stopover.   New York, Macmillan, 1951.
The Headland.   New York, Macmillan, 1955; London, Gollancz, 1956.
Strangers in the Forest.   New York, Macmillan, 1959.
Château St. Barnabé.   New York, Macmillan, 1963.
Snow in the River.   New York, Macmillan, 1964.
The Bellini Look.   New York, Bantam, 1976.

Other

Harps in the Wind: The Story of the Singing Hutchinsons.   New York, Macmillan, 1947.
The Twin Cities (on Minneapolis – St. Paul).   New York, Macmillan, 1961.

Manuscript Collections: Kerlan Collection, University of Minnesota, Minneapolis; University of Idaho Library, Moscow.

*   *   *

Carol Ryrie Brink's books indicate that she is equally at home in the past and the present. Her strength lies in presenting realistic family relationships and vivid personal portraits, made all the more interesting by her background knowledge of history. *Caddie Woodlawn* was reprinted more than thirty times during its first thirty years. Subtitled "A Frontier Story" it tells of 11-year-old Caddie's life with her family on a farm in Wisconsin. Although set at the time of the Civil War, the war plays no part in the story, for Miss Brink has focused on the tense situation between the Indians and the white settlers. Caddie's long friendship with the Indians and their innate trust in her help to avert a threatened uprising and offer the reader an exciting and believable pioneer story. Miss Brink must have been aware that books such as *Caddie Woodlawn* play an important part in the process of growing up, for in writing about the pioneer family and their way of life she reminds the reader that frontier life required qualities from children unheard of today. They took on real responsibilities as co-workers and shared equally in the family fortunes and failures.

Caddie Woodlawn was followed in 1944 by *Magical Melons* which gives further adventures of Caddie and her brothers but was never as popular as its predecessor. She wrote many other books, one of which, *Baby Island*, put forward the absurd and delightful situation of two girls shipwrecked with a lifeboat full of babies whom they cared for with love and ingenuity on a desert island. In her foreword Miss Brink says she wrote this book for girls who love minding babies and couldn't find enough candidates. It is a delightful and amusing story lost to today's readers through the misfortunes of publishing. *Winter Cottage* tells of a city family feeling the hopelessness of the great depression. They leave the city for a winter in the country where their spirits are raised by the beauties of country living.

Whether writing of past or present, the strength of Carol Brink's books lies in the carefully observed family relationships, which provide the basis for a wider circle as the child develops.

—Ann Bartholomew

BRINSMEAD, H(esba) F(ay).   Australian.   Born in Blue Mountains, New South Wales, 15 March 1922. Married Reginald Brinsmead in 1943; has two sons. Educated through correspondence school, at high school in Wahroonga, and at Avondale College. Worked as a governess in Tasmania for two years; speech therapy teacher, western Victoria, 1945–48; kindergarten supervisor, Melbourne, 2 years; amateur actress, Box Hill City Drama Group,

Melbourne, 1950–60. Full-time writer since 1960. Recipient: Australian Children's Book Council Book of the Year Award, 1965, 1972. Agent: Dorothy Blewett Associates, View Hill Crescent, Melbourne, Victoria. Address: Weathertop, Shamara Road, Terranora, New South Wales 2485, Australia.

PUBLICATIONS FOR CHILDREN

Fiction

Pastures of the Blue Crane, illustrated by Annette Macarthur-Onslow.   London, Oxford University Press, 1964; New York, Coward McCann, 1966.

Season of the Briar, illustrated by William Papas.   London, Oxford University Press, 1965; New York, Coward McCann, 1967.

Beat of the City, illustrated by William Papas.   London, Oxford University Press, 1966; New York, Coward McCann, 1968.

A Sapphire for September, illustrated by Victor Ambrus.   London, Oxford University Press, 1967.

Isle of the Sea Horse, illustrated by Peter Farmer.   London, Oxford University Press, 1969.

Listen to the Wind, illustrated by Robert Micklewright.   London, Oxford University Press, 1970.

Longtime Passing.   Sydney and London, Angus and Robertson, 1971.

Who Calls from Afar?, illustrated by Ian Ribbons.   London, Oxford University Press, 1971.

Echo in the Wilderness, illustrated by Graham Humphreys.   London, Oxford University Press, 1972.

The Honey Forest.   Sydney, Angus and Robertson, 1977.

The Ballad of Benny Perhaps.   Melbourne, Cassell, 1977.

Other

Under the Silkwood (reader).   Sydney, Cassell, 1975.

The Wind Harp (reader).   Sydney, Cassell, 1977.

*   *   *

H.F. Brinsmead is an instinctive, uninhibited storyteller with a strong vein of irony which is usually displayed in dialogue. Her storytelling springs chiefly from development of characters and their reaction to a basic situation; characterization always dominates the plot. Another striking feature of her writing is her ability to recreate the feel of the Australian landscape, for which she has a passionate regard. There is, too, a certain aural quality in her writing which seems in some sense to give it a folkloric association. This is most notably displayed in *Longtime Passing*.

Pastures of the Blue Crane was the author's first published book; set in a coastal surfing resort in Queensland, it handles with particular skill the relationship between youth and age, and also touches on the problem of colour prejudice. The author did not again really achieve such distinction in her writing until she wrote *Longtime Passing*, which embodies much autobiographical detail of her own childhood. It is a chronicle of the Truelance family, latter-day pioneers of a tiny hamlet in the Blue Mountains of New South Wales. It is by turns funny, sad, exciting, poignant – a microcosm of life, and it also recreates most vividly the background of rain forest and bushland. In *Beat of the City*, the author tackled a background with which she felt less in accord, and consequently this novel is not so compulsive or immediate in its appeal. In some of her other novels, too, the author shows a tendency towards repetition and over-statement, a lack of discipline in her writing. In her latest work, however, she shows the sure touch and compulsive urge which distinguish *Pastures of the Blue Crane* and *Longtime Passing. The Honey Forest* is a short, beautifully constructed story for the 7–11 age-group, with a background similar to that of *Longtime Passing*. Hesba Brinsmead shows a new gentleness in writing for this younger audience. *The Ballad of Benny Perhaps* is for older teenagers, a powerful novel set in an outback opal field, which does not hesitate to draw bold scenes of drunkeness and cruelty – in fact, as in *Longtime Passing*, the author presents a full spectrum of emotions and every now and then injects the narrative with her ironic humour.

—Barbara Ker Wilson

———————————

BRISLEY, Joyce Lankester. British. Born in Bexhill, Sussex, in 1896. Educated at day school, Bexhill; Lambeth Art School, London. Free-lance illustrator. Address: Fairlight, Bluehouse Lane, Limpsfield, Oxted, Surrey RH8 0AR, England.

PUBLICATIONS FOR CHILDREN (illustrated by the author)

Fiction

> *Milly-Molly-Mandy Stories.* London, Harrap, 1928; New York, McKay, n.d.
> *More of Milly-Molly-Mandy.* London, Harrap, 1929; New York, McKay, 1977.
> *Further Doings of Milly-Molly-Mandy.* London, Harrap, and New York, McKay, 1932.
> *The Dawn Shops and Other Stories.* London, Harrap, and New York, McKay, 1933.
> *Marigold in Godmother's House.* London, Harrap, 1934.
> *Bunchy.* London, Harrap, and New York, McKay, 1937.
> *Adventures of Purl and Plain.* London, Harrap, 1941.
> *Milly-Molly-Mandy Again.* London, Harrap, 1948; New York, McKay, 1977.
> *Another Bunchy Book.* London, Harrap, 1951.
> *Milly-Molly-Mandy & Co.* London, Harrap, 1955; New York, McKay, 1977.
> *Milly-Molly-Mandy and Billy Blunt.* London, Harrap, 1967; New York, McKay, 1977.

Plays

> *Three Little Milly-Molly-Mandy Plays* (includes *Milly-Molly-Mandy Goes Errands, Keeps Shop, Meets Her Great Aunt*). London, Harrap, 1938.

Verse

> *Lambs' Tails and Suchlike: Verses and Sketches.* London, Harrap, and New York, McKay, 1930.

Other

> *My Bible-Book.* London, Harrap, 1940; New York, McKay, 1941.
> *Children of Bible Days.* London, Harrap, 1970.

> Editor, *The Wide, Wide World,* by Elizabeth Wetherell. London, University of London Press, 1950.

Illustrator: *Adventures of a Little Wooden Horse*, 1938 and *Pretenders' Island*, 1940, both by Ursula Moray Williams.

*   *   *

Most of Joyce Lankester Brisley's short stories concern the domestic events in the life of a small girl. Milly-Molly-Mandy "had a Father, and a Mother, and a Grandpa, and a Grandma, and an Uncle, and an Aunty; and they all lived together in a nice white cottage with a thatched roof."

In Milly-Molly-Mandy she has created a likeable, believable little girl who is every child's better self, a child so cheerful, affectionate and generous that she could very well seem too good to be true. It is no small achievement to have brought this off so well, and to have hit off so exactly the things which most please a child: the errands successfully run, the present for mother stitched in secret, the store-room transformed into a new bedroom all to herself, the railway carriage discovered in a field.

Her style in simple and exclamatory, designed for reading aloud; the vocabulary limited. There is little description but her own illustrations give a minimum of character to the various adults who might otherwise appear undifferentiated in their general twinkling benevolence.

Using the same basic setting of village life, in her stories about Bunchy Joyce Lankester Brisley crosses the boundary into fantasy. In a series of tales following one pattern, a lonely little girl who lives with her grandmother makes playmates for herself out of a pastry girl and cat, the figures on a scrap-work screen, the people in a pack of Happy Families cards and others. In her grandmother's absence these characters come to life and keep her company. These adventures are less convincing than the real doings of Milly-Molly-Mandy, but they have the same underlying warmth and affection for children.

Joyce Lankester Brisley's work now seems slightly dated and remote. There are an underlying condescension and sentimentality inherent, for example, in referring to a character throughout as "little-friend-Susan." She writes of a world without war or poverty or illness or anger, a world as warm and as welcoming, as comforting and as kindly as hot tea and toast beside the fire in winter, and if the country setting is romanticised, a land where every cottage is thatched and where mushrooms spring up in high summer, it is within its limitations none the worse for that, a place where everyone might like to have spent their childhood.

—Mary Rayner

BROOKE, L(eonard) Leslie.   British.   Born in Birkenhead, Cheshire, 24 September 1862. Educated at Birkenhead School; Royal Academy, London. Married Sybil Diana Brooke in 1894; two sons. Recipient: Royal Academy Armitage Medal, 1888. *Died 1 May 1940.*

PUBLICATIONS FOR CHILDREN (illustrated by the author)

Verse

Johnny Crow's Garden.   London and New York, Warne, 1903.
Johnny Crow's Party.   London and New York, Warne, 1907.
Johnny Crow's New Garden.   London and New York, Warne, 1935.

Other

Tom Thumb. London and New York, Warne, 1904.
The Golden Goose. London and New York, Warne, 1904.
The Story of the Three Bears. London and New York, Warne, 1904.
The Story of the Three Little Pigs. London and New York, Warne, 1904.
*The Golden Goose Book, Being the Stories of the Golden Goose, the Three Bears, the Three
    Little Pigs, Tom Thumb.* London and New York, Warne, 1905.
The Tailor and the Crow. London and New York, Warne, 1911.
Oranges and Lemons. London and New York, Warne, 1913.
The Man in the Moon. London and New York, Warne, 1914.
A Nursery Rhyme Picture Book. London and New York, Warne, 1914.
Nursery Rhymes, Tales and Jingles. London and New York, Warne, 1916.
Ring o' Roses. London and New York, Warne, 1922.
Little Bo-Peep. London and New York, Warne, 1922.
A Nursery Rhyme Picture Book Number Two. London and New York, Warne, 1922.
This Little Pig Went to Market. London and New York, Warne, 1922.

Illustrator: *Nurse Heatherdale's Story,* 1891, *The Girls and I,* 1892, *Mary,* 1893, *The New
Home,* 1894, *The Carved Lions,* 1895, *Sheila's Mystery,* 1895, *The Oriel Window,* 1896, and
Miss Mouse and Her Boys, 1897, all by Mary Louisa Molesworth; *The Nursery Rhyme Book*
edited by Andrew Lang, 1897; *A Spring Song* by Thomas Nashe, 1898; *Pippa Passes* by
Robert Browning, 1898; *The Jumblies and Other Nonsense Verses, Nonsense Songs,* and *The
Pelican Chorus and Other Nonsense Verses,* all by Edward Lear, 1900; *Travels 'round Our
Village* by Eleanor G. Hayden, 1901; *The House in the Wood and Other Old Fairy Stories,* by
the Grimm Brothers, 1909; *The Truth about Old King Cole* by George F. Hill, 1910; *Mad
Shepherds and Other Human Studies* by Lawrence P. Jacks, 1923; *Barchester Towers* by
Anthony Trollope, 1924; *A Roundabout Turn* by Robert H. Charles, 1930.

*   *   *

L. Leslie Brooke's stories have been described as "collector's pieces," but they are much
more than this: they are perfect examples of the kind of writing which both parent and child
can enjoy, each on his own level. The traditional tales − *The Three Little Pigs, The Three
Bears, Tom Thumb, The Golden Goose* − are told directly and simply, with the repetition
children love, and also with an ear both for the rhythms of English prose and its variety of
sentence structure which lend a tough vitality to the stories even after much re-telling. The
line drawings and colour illustrations are delightful, well integrated into the story, with a sly
sense of humour which points up significant episodes. The morning after the abortive
excursion to the turnip field, for instance, there is a picture of the wolf, waking up tardily at
four o'clock, a partly eaten turnip still on the chair by his bed, and a picture on the wall of a
wolf cooking fried back bacon, while on the next page the little pig is pictured already
precariously climbing up the apple tree, his back legs dangling as he clutches the branch
desperately with his front trotters. There is much fun for both alert adult and child in these
stories and their accompanying illustrations, as also in the cunningly illustrated nursery
rhymes of *Ring o' Roses.*
   The gem of the collection is the *Johnny Crow* series, in which a dapper Johnny Crow
creates a superb garden where he entertains a fascinating variety of farmyard and jungle
animals. The pictures are again so detailed, so full of humour and so thoroughly integrated
with the text that they enhance and expand the child's understanding, particularly in those
occasional wickedly satirical episodes which, as in Beatrix Potter's books, make no
concessions to the myth that children cannot cope with words of more than two syllables.

> Then the Stork
> Gave a Philosophic Talk
> Till the Hippopotomi
> Said: "Ask no further 'What am I?' "
> While the Elephant
> Said something quite irrelevant
> In Johnny Crow's Garden.

Here the long words roll off the adult's tongue in a manner very satisfying to the small child, for whom the accompanying illustrations make the joke explicit enough without any laboured explanations from a well-meaning parent or teacher. Most of the rhymes, of course, are much simpler than the ones just quoted; amusing, memorable verse which, together with the wealth of meaning in the drawings above them, makes the story-rite a pleasure for both parent and child, an excellent answer to the complaints of some parents that children's stories bore them stiff.

—Winifred Whitehead

BROOKS, Walter R(ollin). American. Born in Rome, New York, 9 January 1886. Educated at Rochester University, New York, 1904–06; New York Homeopathic Medical College, 1906–08. Married Anne Shepard in 1909; Dorothy Collins, 1953. Associate Editor, *Outlook*, New York, 1923–32; Member of the Editorial Staff, *New Yorker*, 1933, and *Fiction Parade*, New York, 1933–37. *Died 17 August 1958.*

PUBLICATIONS FOR CHILDREN (illustrated by Kurt Wiese)

Fiction

> *To and Again*, illustrated by Adolfo Best-Maugard. New York and London, Knopf, 1927; as *Freddy Goes to Florida*, New York, Knopf, 1949; as *Freddy's First Adventure*, London, Lane, 1949.
> *More To and Again*. New York, Knopf, and London, George Allen, 1930; as *Freddy the Explorer*, London, Lane, 1949; as *Freddy Goes to the North Pole*, Knopf, 1951.
> *Freddy the Detective*. New York, Knopf, 1932; London, Lane, 1950.
> *The Story of Freginald*. New York, Knopf, 1936; as *Freddy and Freginald*, London, Lane, 1952.
> *The Clockwork Twin*. New York, Knopf, 1937.
> *Wiggins for President*. New York, Knopf, 1939; as *Freddy the Politician*, 1948.
> *Freddy's Cousin Weedly*. New York, Knopf, 1940.
> *Freddy and the Ignormus*. New York, Knopf, 1941.
> *Freddy and the Perilous Adventure*. New York, Knopf, 1942.
> *Freddy and the Bean Home News*. New York, Knopf, 1943.
> *Freddy and Mr. Camphor*. New York, Knopf, 1944.
> *Freddy and the Popinjay*. New York, Knopf, 1945.
> *Freddy the Pied Piper*. New York, Knopf, 1946.
> *Freddy the Magician*. New York, Knopf, 1947.
> *Jenny and the King of Smithia*, illustrated by Decie Merwin. New York, Grosset and Dunlap, 1947.
> *Freddy Goes Camping*. New York, Knopf, 1948.
> *Freddy Plays Football*. New York, Knopf, 1949.

Freddy the Cowboy. New York, Knopf, 1950.
Freddy Rides Again. New York, Knopf, 1951.
Freddy the Pilot. New York, Knopf, 1952.
Freddy and the Space Ship. New York, Knopf, 1953.
Freddy and the Men from Mars. New York, Knopf, 1954.
Freddy and the Baseball Team from Mars. New York, Knopf, 1955.
Freddy and Simon the Dictator. New York, Knopf, 1956.
Freddy and the Dragon. New York, Knopf, 1958.
Henry's Dog Henry, illustrated by Aldren Watson. New York, Knopf, 1965.
Jimmy Takes Vanishing Lessons, illustrated by Don Bolognese. New York, Knopf, 1965.

Verse

The Collected Poems of Freddy the Pig. New York, Knopf, 1953.

PUBLICATIONS FOR ADULTS

Novel

Ernestine Takes Over. New York, Morrow, 1935; London, Jarrolds, 1937.

Other

New York: An Intimate Guide. New York, Knopf, 1931.

*   *   *

One of the most difficult juvenile genres to create is that of the anthropomorphic animal. Historically few of these characters have survived more than one generation, and deservedly so. One of the great American exceptions is Walter R. Brooks' Freddy the pig. This talking and thinking pig, jack of all trades and master of none, wore many hats, ranging from detective to magician to politician and beyond. For the child reader, events on Mr. Bean's farm are solely episodic, ranging from the hilarious to the darkly sinister, only slightly familiar to the present world. For the adult, the Bean farm, Freddy, and the other animals are boldly familiar archetypes of daily events and people. A little of all the human traits can be found here both through the human and animal characters. Judging the series by contemporary children's literature standards, the books are beginning to date. The illustrations denote scenes, costumes and vehicles no longer in use. Brooks' handling of stock character types, the American Indian for example, are now being regarded as overtly stereotypical and thus harmful. Valid as these criticisms may be, the series should be considered in its proper time scheme. Brooks undisputedly raised the anthropomorphic genre to a higher level with Freddy when one stops to consider the 1950's output when the series was beginning. Freddy could not help but lessen library and bookseller's shelves of romantically portrayed doe-eyed kittens and puppies by being a real (human) animal with real feelings, ideas, and faults.

—James W. Roginski

_____

BROWN, Margaret Wise. American. Born in New York City, 23 May 1910. Educated at Chateau Brilliantmont, Lausanne, Switzerland, 1923–25; Dana Hall, Wellesley,

Massachusetts; Hollins College, Virginia, B.A. 1932; Columbia University, New York; Bureau of Educational Experiments, now Bank Street College of Education, New York. Editor, William R. Scott Inc., publishers, New York, 1938–41. *Died 13 November 1952.*

PUBLICATIONS FOR CHILDREN

Fiction

When the Wind Blew, illustrated by Rosalie Slocum.   New York and London, Harper, 1937.
Bumble Bugs and Elephants, illustrated by Clement Hurd.   New York, Scott, 1938.
The Fish with the Deep Sea Smile, illustrated by Roberta Rauch.   New York, Dutton, 1938.
The Little Fireman, illustrated by Esphyr Slobodkina.   New York, Scott, 1938.
The Streamlined Pig, illustrated by Kurt Wiese.   New York and London, Harper, 1938.
Little Pig's Picnic and Other Stories, illustrated by Walt Disney Studio.   Boston, Heath, 1939; London, Collins, 1949.
Noisy Book, illustrated by Leonard Weisgard.   New York, Scott, 1939.
Country Noisy Book, illustrated by Leonard Weisgard.   New York, Scott, 1940.
Baby Animals, illustrated by Mary Cameron.   New York, Random House, 1941.
The Polite Penguin, illustrated by H.A. Rey.   New York and London, Harper, 1941.
The Poodle and the Sheep, illustrated by Leonard Weisgard.   New York, Dutton, 1941.
The Seashore Noisy Book, illustrated by Leonard Weisgard.   New York, Scott, 1941.
Don't Frighten the Lion!, illustrated by H.A. Rey.   New York and London, Harper, 1942.
Indoor Noisy Book, illustrated by Leonard Weisgard.   New York, Harper, 1942.
Night and Day, illustrated by Leonard Weisgard.   New York and London, Harper, 1942.
The Runaway Bunny, illustrated by Clement Hurd.   New York and London, Harper, 1942.
A Child's Good Night Book, illustrated by Jean Charlot.   New York, Scott, 1943.
Little Chicken, illustrated by Leonard Weisgard.   New York and London, Harper, 1943.
The Noisy Bird Book, illustrated by Leonard Weisgard and Audubon.   New York, Scott, 1943.
SHHH ... bang: A Whispering Book, illustrated by Robert de Veyrac.   New York and London, Harper, 1943.
The Big Fur Secret, illustrated by Robert de Veyrac.   New York and London, Harper, 1944.
Black and White, illustrated by Charles Shaw.   New York and London, Harper, 1944.
Horses (as Timothy Hay), illustrated by Dorothy Wagstaff.   New York and London, Harper, 1944.
Red Light, Green Light (as Golden MacDonald), illustrated by Leonard Weisgard.   New York, Doubleday, 1944.
They All Saw It, photographs by Ylla.   New York and London, Harper, 1944.
Willie's Walk to Grandmama, with Rockbridge Campbell, illustrated by Lucienne Bloch.   New York, Scott, 1944.
The House of a Hundred Windows.   New York and London, Harper, 1945.
The Little Fisherman, illustrated by Dahlov Ipcar.   New York, Scott, 1945.
Little Lost Lamb (as Golden MacDonald), illustrated by Leonard Weisgard.   New York, Doubleday, 1945.
Little Fur Family, illustrated by Garth Williams.   New York, Harper, 1946; London, Harper, 1977.

The Man in the Manhole and the Fix-It Man, with Edith Thacher Hurd (as Juniper Sage), illustrated by Bill Ballantine. New York, Scott, 1946.

The Bad Little Duckhunter, illustrated by Clement Hurd. New York, Scott, 1947.

The Golden Egg Book, illustrated by Leonard Weisgard. New York, Simon and Schuster, 1947.

The First Story, illustrated by Marc Simont. New York and London, Harper, 1947.

Goodnight, Moon, illustrated by Clement Hurd. New York, Harper, 1947; Kingswood, Surrey, World's Work, 1975.

The Sleepy Little Lion, photographs by Ylla. New York, Harper, 1947; London, Harvill Press, 1960.

The Winter Noisy Book, illustrated by Charles Shaw. New York, Harper, 1947.

Five Little Firemen, with Edith Thacher Hurd, illustrated by Tibor Gergely. New York, Simon and Schuster, 1948.

The Golden Sleepy Book, illustrated by Garth Williams. New York, Simon and Schuster, 1948.

The Little Farmer, illustrated by Esphyr Slobodkina. New York, Scott, 1948.

Wonderful Storybook, illustrated by J.P. Miller. New York, Simon and Schuster, 1948.

The Color Kittens, illustrated by Alice and Martin Provensen. New York, Simon and Schuster, 1949.

The Important Book, illustrated by Leonard Weisgard. New York, Harper, 1949.

The Little Cowboy, illustrated by Esphyr Slobodkina. New York, Scott, 1949.

My World, illustrated by Clement Hurd. New York, Harper, 1949.

A Pussycat's Christmas, illustrated by Helen Stone. New York, Crowell, 1949.

Two Little Miners, with Edith Thacher Hurd, illustrated by Richard Scarry. New York, Simon and Schuster, 1949.

Two Little Trains, illustrated by Jean Charlot. New York, Scott, 1949; Kingswood, Surrey, World's Work, 1960.

O, Said the Squirrel, photographs by Ylla. London, Harvill Press, 1950.

The Dream Book: First Comes the Dream, illustrated by Richard Floethe. New York, Random House, 1950.

The Little Fat Policeman, with Edith Thacher Hurd, illustrated by Alice and Martin Provensen. New York, Simon and Schuster, 1950.

The Peppermint Family, illustrated by Clement Hurd. New York, Harper, and London, Hamish Hamilton, 1950.

The Quiet Noisy Book, illustrated by Leonard Weisgard. New York, Harper, and London, Hamish Hamilton, 1950.

The Wonderful House, illustrated by J.P. Miller. New York, Simon and Schuster, and London, Muller, 1950; revised edition, Simon and Schuster, 1960.

Fox Eyes, illustrated by Jean Charlot. New York, Pantheon Books, 1951.

The Summer Noisy Book, illustrated by Leonard Weisgard. New York, Harper, 1951.

The Train to Timbuctoo, illustrated by Art Seiden. New York, Simon and Schuster, 1951; London, Muller, 1952.

Two Little Gardeners, with Edith Thacher Hurd, illustrated by Gertrude Elliott. New York, Simon and Schuster, 1951.

Christmas in the Barn, illustrated by Barbara Cooney. New York, Crowell, 1952.

Dr. Squash, The Doll Doctor, illustrated by J.P. Miller. New York, Simon and Schuster, 1952.

Mister Dog, The Dog Who Belonged to Himself, illustrated by Garth Williams. New York, Simon and Schuster, 1952; London, Muller, 1954.

The Moon Balloon, illustrated by Leonard Weisgard. New York, Harper, 1952.

Seven Little Postmen, with Edith Thacher Hurd, illustrated by Tibor Gergely. New York, Simon and Schuster, 1952.

The Duck, photographs by Ylla. New York, Harper, and London, Harvill Press, 1952.

The Golden Bunny and Seventeen Other Stories and Poems, illustrated by Leonard Weisgard. New York, Simon and Schuster, 1953.

The Hidden House, illustrated by Aaron Fine.   New York, Holt, 1953.

The Little Frightened Tiger (as Golden MacDonald), illustrated by Leonard Weisgard.   New York, Doubleday, 1953.

The Sailor Dog, illustrated by Garth Williams.   New York, Simon and Schuster, 1953; London, Muller, 1954.

The Friendly Book, illustrated by Garth Williams.   New York, Simon and Schuster, 1954.

The Little Fir Tree, illustrated by Barbara Cooney.   New York, Crowell, 1954.

Little Indian, illustrated by Richard Scarry.   New York, Simon and Schuster, 1954; London, Golden Pleasure Books, 1964.

Wheel on the Chimney, illustrated by Tibor Gergely.   Philadelphia, Lippincott, 1954.

Willie's Adventures, illustrated by Crockett Johnson.   New York, Scott, 1954.

The Little Brass Band, illustrated by Clement Hurd.   New York, Harper, 1955.

Seven Stories about a Cat Named Sneakers, illustrated by Jean Charlot.   New York, Scott, 1955.

Young Kangaroo, illustrated by Symeon Shimin.   New York, Scott, 1955; Kingswood, Surrey, World's Work, 1959.

Big Red Barn, illustrated by Rosella Hartman.   New York, Scott, 1956.

David's Little Indian, illustrated by Remy Charlip.   New York, Scott, 1956.

Home for a Bunny, illustrated by Garth Williams.   New York, Simon and Schuster, 1956; London, Hamlyn, 1961.

Three Little Animals, illustrated by Garth Williams.   New York, Harper, 1956.

Whistle for the Train (as Golden MacDonald), illustrated by Leonard Weisgard.   New York, Doubleday, 1956.

The Dead Bird, illustrated by Remy Charlip.   New York, Scott, 1958.

Four Fur Feet, illustrated by Remy Charlip.   New York, Scott, 1961.

On Christmas Eve, illustrated by Beni Montresor.   New York, Scott, 1961; London, Collins, 1963.

Once upon a Time in a Pigpen, illustrated by Ann Strugnell.   Reading, Massachusetts, Addison Wesley, 1977.

Verse

Big Dog, Little Dog (as Golden MacDonald), illustrated by Leonard Weisgard.   New York, Doubleday, 1943.

The Little Island (as Golden MacDonald), illustrated by Leonard Weisgard.   New York, Doubleday, 1946.

Wait till the Moon Is Full, illustrated by Garth Williams.   New York, Harper, 1948.

The Dark Wood of the Golden Birds, illustrated by Leonard Weisgard.   New York, Harper, 1950.

A Child's Good Morning, illustrated by Jean Charlot.   New York, Scott, 1952.

Where Have You Been?, illustrated by Barbara Cooney.   New York, Crowell, 1952.

Sleepy ABC, illustrated by Esphyr Slobodkina.   New York, Lothrop, 1953.

Nibble Nibble: Poems, illustrated by Leonard Weisgard.   New York, Scott, 1959.

Other

The Children's Year, illustrated by Feodor Rojankovsky.   New York and London, Harper, 1937.

The Comical Tragedy or Tragical Comedy of Punch and Judy, illustrated by Leonard Weisgard.   New York, Scott, 1940.

The Fables of La Fontaine, illustrated by André Hellé.   New York and London, Harper, 1940.

Brer Rabbit: Stories from Uncle Remus, illustrated by A.B. Frost.   New York and
London, Harper, 1941.
Animals, Plants, and Machines (reader), with Lucy Sprague Mitchell, illustrated by Clare
Bice.   Boston, Heath, 1944.
Farm and City (reader), with Lucy Sprague Mitchell.   Boston, Heath, 1944.
Pussy Willow, illustrated by Leonard Weisgard.   New York, Simon and Schuster,
1952.
The Diggers, illustrated by Clement Hurd.   New York, Harper, and London, Hamish
Hamilton, 1961.

*   *   *

In the late 1930's and early 1940's Margaret Wise Brown made a significant breakthrough
in the style and approach to writing for children. Her concept of a child and how to reach him
through words opened the door for many writers that followed. Without her pioneer work,
such people as Ruth Krauss, Maurice Sendak, Remy Charlip, not to mention myself and a
host of others, would have had a much more difficult time gaining recognition.

She was the first to really exploit the "concept" book, in which a story went beyond its
traditional bounds and incorporated important aspects of a child's world. This was
exemplified in the Noisy Books series which appeared in the early 1940's. Taking the
explorations that Lucy Sprague Mitchell had done in the world of the here-and-now,
Margaret Wise Brown turned them slightly awry, and the result was *The Fish with the Deep
Sea Smile* that included not only such zany stories as "The Steam Roller" and "Sneakers,
That Rapscallion Cat," but tender, sensitive poetry as well.

Her most profound book, philosophically speaking, is *The Little Island*, in which a fish and
a cat learn that "All lands are one land under the sea," and that there are things in this world
that must be taken just on faith. Such was her skill that she could blend profundities into a
story with a deft touch, and the result would be pure magic.

She wrote on the dust jacket of *The Fish with the Deep Sea Smile*:

> This book is an attempt to write of a child's reality, the things that seem important
> to a child of five, six, or seven – nonsense that children can recognize; getting lost
> and getting found; being good and being bad; shyness and loneliness and the sheer
> joy of living. Wonder at the colors and smells and sounds of the world so fresh to
> their brand new senses; the importance of the seasons. This book hopes to touch
> their imaginings and to suggest imaginings in the realm of a child's reality.

Her untimely death in 1952 cut off a talent that still had much to offer, and today's children
are the poorer for it.

—Alvin Tresselt

BROWN, Roy (Frederick).   British.   Born in Vancouver, British Columbia, Canada, 10
December 1921. Married to Wendy Landman; has two sons and two daughters. Primary
school teacher, 1946–69; Deputy Head, Helen Allison School for autistic children, 1969–75.
Address: 13 Clarence Place, Gravesend, Kent, England.

PUBLICATIONS FOR CHILDREN

Fiction

A Saturday in Pudney, illustrated by James Hunt.   London, Abelard Schuman, and
New York, Macmillan, 1966.

The House on the Green, illustrated by Trevor Parkin.   Edinburgh, Oliver and Boyd, 1967.

Little Brown Mouse, illustrated by Constance Marshall.   London, University of London Press, 1967.

The Wonderful Weathercock, illustrated by Ferelith Eccles Williams.   London, University of London Press, 1967.

The Viaduct, illustrated by James Hunt.   London, Abelard Schuman, 1967; New York, Macmillan, 1968.

The Day of the Pigeons, illustrated by James Hunt.   London, Abelard Schuman, and New York, Macmillan, 1968.

The Saturday Man, illustrated by Trevor Ridley.   London, BBC Publications, 1969.

The Wapping Warrior, illustrated by James Hunt.   London, Chatto and Windus, 1969.

The River, illustrated by James Hunt.   London, Abelard Schuman, 1970; as *Escape the River*, New York, Seabury Press, 1972.

The Thunder Pool, illustrated by Gareth Floyd.   London, Abelard Schuman, 1971.

The Battle of Saint Street, illustrated by James Hunt.   London, Abelard Schuman, and New York, Macmillan, 1971.

Flight of Sparrows.   London, Abelard Schuman, and New York, Macmillan, 1972.

Bolt Hole.   London, Abelard Schuman, 1973; as *No Through Road*, New York, Seabury Press, 1974.

The White Sparrow.   London, Abelard Schuman, 1974; New York, Seabury Press, 1975.

Shep the Second, illustrated by Clifford Bayly.   London, Abelard Schuman, 1975.

The Siblings.   London, Abelard Schuman, 1975; as *Find Debbie!*, New York, Seabury Press, 1976.

The Million Pound Mouse, illustrated by Joanna Stubbs.   London, Abelard Schuman, 1975.

The Cage.   London, Abelard Schuman, 1976; New York, Seabury Press, 1977.

Chubb on the Trail, illustrated by Margaret Belsky.   London, Abelard Schuman, 1976.

The Big Test, illustrated by James Hunt.   London, Hutchinson, 1976.

A Nag Called Wednesday, illustrated by Jeroo Roy.   London, Hutchinson, 1977.

Chubb to the Rescue.   London, Abelard Schuman, 1977.

Plays

Radio Plays: *News Extra!* series, 1973.

Other

A Book of Saints.   London, Cassell, 1959.

The Children's Book of Old Testament Stories, illustrated by Hugh T. Marshall.   London, Harrap, 1959.

The Children's Pinocchio, illustrated by Sheila Rose.   London, Harrap, 1960.

The Children's Heidi, illustrated by Sheila Connelly.   London, Harrap, 1963.

Port of Call, illustrated by Jack Trodd.   London and New York, Abelard Schuman, 1965.

The Legend of Ulysses, illustrated by Mario Logli and Gabriele Santini.   London, Hamlyn, 1965.

The Battle Against Fire, with William Stuart Thomson, illustrated by James Hunt.   London, Abelard Schuman, 1966.

Reynard the Fox, illustrated by John Vernon Lord.   London and New York, Abelard Schuman, 1969.

*   *   *

Among major children's writers of the 1970's Roy Brown is one particularly open to his times, in tune with their issues and concerns, and while the readability and human interest of his stories guarantee a wide readership the settings indicate a conscious desire to offer the non-academic urban child a means of identification. The years have brought development in technique but not deviation from city backgrounds and characters at risk or disadvantage in modern society.

Roy Brown first came to notice with *A Saturday in Pudney* which had an uncomplicated story line – the tracking down of a lost child and subsequent discovery of thieves – a large cast list of neighbourhood children (including two statutory girls, one West Indian), and a satisfying ending. *The Day of the Pigeons* used the twin search theme again, here the children's pursuit of the lost racing pigeons and the attempts of Mousy Lawson, on the run from an approved school, to contact his father, but this time plot structure and detailing moved forward in complexity. *The River* introduced three characters who recur with variations in later stories: the backward, disturbed child; the ex-Borstal bully; the boy who lets himself be led into crime through threats, promises or his own inadequacies. We meet them in *Bolt Hole*, where Barry drifts into criminal associations because of the failure of other relationships, and in *Flight of Sparrows*. *The Siblings* centres on the disappearance of a psychotic 14-year-old, but here we have moved up in the social scale to a block of flats, home of a local government official and his very desperate family.

One looks to Roy Brown not for stylistic qualities nor for great originality but for authenticity of setting and compassionate engagement with characters. Sympathy is shown to the petty criminal, the old and defenceless, the subnormal, who are seen as the victims of an unfeeling society: the settings with which readers grow familiar are London's river and waste grounds, its derelict houses, warehouses and building sites. At first classified with Hildick, rather dismissively, as a "cement street" writer, Roy Brown has now emerged as a key figure in the "relevant" children's fiction fashionable in the 1970's. Yet assessment of his contribution is difficult. The sentiment sometimes moves over into sentimentality: judgments like "Inside the big tough guy there's a wee laddie – maybe even a guid laddie – trying to get out" (*The Day of the Pigeons*) grate; the purple passages (see the last sequence of *The White Sparrow*) embarrass because they are out of key with the prevailing tone; characters are too often explained rather than revealed. The critical question is "If the themes weren't so topical would the literary merits be more suspect?" *The Siblings*, Roy Brown's most powerful book to date, provides a partial answer. More than compensating for the weaknesses are the mastery of pace, the accessibility and humanity of the stories, and the enlargement of the reader's sympathies.

—Peggy Heeks

BRUCE, Dorita Fairlie.   British.   Born in 1885. Lived in London for many years. *Died in September 1970.*

PUBLICATIONS FOR CHILDREN

Fiction

The Senior Prefect.   London, Oxford University Press, 1921; as *Dimsie Goes to School*, 1933.
Dimsie Moves Up, illustrated by Wal Paget.   London, Oxford University Press, 1921.
Dimsie Moves Up Again, illustrated by Gertrude D. Hammond.   London, Oxford University Press, 1922.

Dimsie among the Prefects, illustrated by Gertrude D. Hammond. London, Oxford University Press, 1923.

The Girls of St. Bride's, illustrated by Henry Coller. London, Oxford University Press, 1923.

Dimsie Grows Up, illustrated by Henry Coller. London, Oxford University Press, 1924.

Dimsie, Head-Girl, illustrated by M.S. Reeve. London, Oxford University Press, 1925.

That Boarding School Girl. London, Oxford University Press, 1925.

The New Girl and Nancy. London, Oxford University Press, 1926.

Nancy to the Rescue. London, Oxford University Press, 1927.

Dimsie Goes Back, illustrated by M.S. Reeve. London, Oxford University Press, 1927.

The New House-Captain, illustrated by M.S. Reeve. London, Oxford University Press, 1928.

The King's Curate. London, Murray, 1930.

The Best House in the School, illustrated by M.S. Reeve. London, Oxford University Press, 1930.

The Best Bat in the School. London, Oxford University Press, 1931.

The School on the Moor, illustrated by M.S. Reeve. London, Oxford University Press, 1931.

Captain of Springdale, illustrated by Henry Coller. London, Oxford University Press, 1932.

Mistress-Mariner. London, Murray, 1932.

Nancy at St. Bride's, illustrated by M.D. Johnston. London, Oxford University Press, 1933.

The New House at Springdale, illustrated by M.D. Johnston. London, Oxford University Press, 1934.

Nancy in the Sixth. London, Oxford University Press, 1935.

Dimsie Intervenes, illustrated by M.D. Johnston. London, Oxford University Press, 1937.

Nancy Returns to St. Bride's, illustrated by M.D. Johnston. London, Oxford University Press, 1938.

Prefects at Springdale, illustrated by M.D. Johnston. London, Oxford University Press, 1938.

Captain Anne, illustrated by M.D. Johnston. London, Oxford University Press, 1939.

The School in the Woods, illustrated by G.M. Anson. London, Oxford University Press, 1940.

Dimsie Carries On, illustrated by W. Bryce Hamilton. London, Oxford University Press, 1942.

Toby at Tibbs Cross, illustrated by Margaret Horder. London, Oxford University Press, 1943.

Nancy Calls the Tune, illustrated by Margaret Horder. London, Oxford University Press, 1944.

A Laverock Lilting, illustrated by Margaret Horder. London, Oxford University Press, 1945.

Wild Goose Quest. London, Lutterworth Press, 1945.

The Serendipity Shop, illustrated by Margaret Horder. London, Oxford University Press, 1947.

Triffeny, illustrated by Margaret Horder. London, Oxford University Press, 1950.

The Bees on Drumwhinnie, illustrated by Margaret Horder. London, Oxford University Press, 1952.

The Debatable Mound, illustrated by Patricia M. Lambe. London, Oxford University Press, 1953.

The Bartle Bequest, illustrated by Sylvia Green. London, Oxford University Press, 1955.

Sally Scatterbrain, illustrated by Betty Ladler. London, Blackie, 1956.

Sally Again, illustrated by Betty Ladler. London, Blackie, 1959.

Sally's Summer Term, illustrated by Joan Thompson.   London, Blackie, 1961.

*   *   *

Between the first and second world wars Dorita Fairlie Bruce was an extremely popular writer for girls. Her most memorable books – the "Dimsie," "Nancy," and "Springdale" series – have school settings and clearly defined, likeable heroines with whom several generations of schoolgirl readers have identified. Dorita Bruce has sometimes been dismissed merely as an imitator of Angela Brazil, the creator of the twentieth-century girls' school story. There *are* similarities in the intentional – and unconscious – humour of both authors, but Dorita Bruce's plots and characterizations have a subtlety and an uncontrived exuberance that are lacking in many of Angela Brazil's stories.

Dorita Bruce's main characters grow up gradually during the course of a series: they progress from being naive but endearing juniors to responsible young adults. The well-ordered life of many girls' private schools is convincingly conveyed through descriptions of regular music practices and walks in crocodile, of girls discarding gymslips for silk dresses on special occasions, or standing around for hours on the boundary, fielding at cricket matches. School is shown as the world in microcosm; there is plenty of challenge – in rivalries between individuals and groups, or in the destructive influence of one girl over another. The author is at her best in describing friendships which are "fervent" but "healthy-minded." Strong aversion to excessively sentimental relationships is the keynote of many of Dorita Bruce's books. Prefects encourage sport as a potent corrective, while Dimsie and other juniors form an effective and long lived "Anti-Soppist League" to put down "mushy" behaviour.

Dorita Bruce is less successful at manipulating the relationships in which her heroines become involved as adults. Most of them eventually marry, but schoolgirlish anti-soppism complicates the courting process: "Oh Peter … How can you say anything so horrible?" responds Dimsie when the man whom she later marries first declares his love.

The authentic backgrounds of Dorita Fairlie Bruce's stories partly derive from her own experiences as a boarding school pupil. She once wrote of her characters: "I go back to school with them …." Dorita Bruce was an officer in the Girls' Guildry and her fiction sometimes exploited this organization's character-building propensities.

She possessed a sense of scene and mood. The cosiness of a study tête-à-tête for instance, is enhanced by its contrast with a winter gale raging outside over the sodden downs. Dorita Bruce was Scottish, and several of her books contain evocative descriptions of her country's lochs, islands, and hills. As well as schoolgirls' adventures she wrote several historical short stories and novels.

Dorita Bruce's books tended to dismiss intellectuals and progressives as cranks or useless day-dreamers. Through her straightforward schoolgirls she projected her ideals of practical Christianity (which she occasionally expressed as "helping lame dogs over stiles"), patriotism, and esprit de corps. It is a measure of her skill that she did so without obtrusively moralizing. Many adults today feel that her books constructively influenced their childhood and adolescence.

—Mary Cadogan

BRUCE, Mary Grant.   Australian.   Born in Sale, Victoria. Educated at Sale local schools. Writer and broadcaster for the Australian Imperial Forces during World War I. Married George E. Bruce in 1914; one son. Member of the staff of *Age*, Melbourne; Editor, *Woman's World* and *Woman*; broadcaster. Member, Royal Society of Literature. *Died 2 July 1958*.

PUBLICATIONS FOR CHILDREN

Fiction

A Little Bush Maid, illustrated by J. Macfarlane. Melbourne and London, Ward Lock, 1910.

Mates at Billabong, illustrated by J. Macfarlane. Melbourne and London, Ward Lock, 1911.

Timothy in Bushland, illustrated by J. Macfarlane. Melbourne and London, Ward Lock, 1912.

Glen Eyre, illustrated by J. Macfarlane. Melbourne and London, Ward Lock, 1912.

Norah of Billabong, illustrated by J. Macfarlane. Melbourne and London, Ward Lock, 1913.

Gray's Hollow, illustrated by Patric Dawson. Melbourne and London, Ward Lock, 1914.

From Billabong to London, illustrated by Fred Leist. Melbourne and London, Ward Lock, 1915.

Jim and Wally, illustrated by Bruno Salmon. Melbourne and London, Ward Lock, 1916.

'Possum, illustrated by J. Macfarlane. Melbourne and London, Ward Lock, 1917.

Dick, illustrated by J. Macfarlane. Melbourne and London, Ward Lock, 1918.

Captain Jim, illustrated by J. Macfarlane. Melbourne and London, Ward Lock, 1919.

Dick Lester of Kurrajong, illustrated by J. Macfarlane. Melbourne and London, Ward Lock, 1920.

Rossiter's Farm, illustrated by Esther Paterson. Melbourne, Whitcombe and Tombs, 1920.

Back to Billabong, illustrated by J. Macfarlane. Melbourne and London, Ward Lock, 1921.

The Cousin from Town, illustrated by Esther Paterson. Melbourne, Whitcombe and Tombs, 1922.

The Twins of Emu Plains, illustrated by Dewar Mills. Melbourne and London, Ward Lock, 1923.

Billabong's Daughter, illustrated by J. Macfarlane. Melbourne and London, Ward Lock, 1924.

The Houses of the Eagle, illustrated by Harold Copping. Melbourne and London, Ward Lock, 1925.

Hugh Stanford's Luck. Sydney, Cornstalk, 1925.

The Tower Rooms, illustrated by Dewar Mills. Melbourne and London, Ward Lock, 1926.

Robin, illustrated by Edgar A. Holloway. Sydney, Cornstalk, 1926; London, Angus and Robertson, 1938.

Billabong Adventurers, illustrated by J. Macfarlane. Melbourne and London, Ward Lock, 1927.

Anderson's Jo. Sydney, Cornstalk, 1927.

Golden Fiddles, illustrated by Dewar Mills. Melbourne and London, Ward Lock, 1928.

The Happy Traveller, illustrated by Laurie Taylor. Melbourne and London, Ward Lock, 1929.

Bill of Billabong, illustrated by A.A. Kent. Melbourne and London, Ward Lock, 1931.

Road to Adventure, illustrated by Laurie Taylor. Melbourne and London, Ward Lock, 1932; New York, Minton Balch, 1933.

Billabong's Luck, illustrated by Laurie Taylor. Melbourne and London, Ward Lock, 1933.

"Seahawk," illustrated by J.F. Campbell. Melbourne and London, Ward Lock, 1934.

Wings above Billabong, illustrated by J.F. Campbell. Melbourne and London, Ward Lock, 1935.

Circus Ring, illustrated by J.F. Campbell.   Melbourne and London, Ward Lock, 1936;
New York, Putnam, 1937.

Billabong Gold, illustrated by J.F. Campbell.   Melbourne and London, Ward Lock,
1937.

Told by Peter, illustrated by J.F. Campbell.   Melbourne and London, Ward Lock, 1938.

Son of Billabong, illustrated by J.F. Campbell.   Melbourne and London, Ward Lock,
1939.

Peter and Co., illustrated by J.F. Campbell.   Melbourne and London, Ward Lock,
1940.

Karalta.   Sydney and London, Angus and Robertson, 1941.

Billabong Riders.   Melbourne and London, Ward Lock, 1942.

Other

The Stone Axe of Burkamukk: Aboriginal Legends Retold, illustrated by J.
Macfarlane.   Melbourne and London, Ward Lock, 1922.

PUBLICATIONS FOR ADULTS

Other

The Power Within: Four Broadcast Talks.   Privately printed, 1941.

*   *   *

Mary Grant Bruce not only had a devoted following in her own country but many young
English readers first learned about the hazards of the Australian bush, its strange bandicoots,
wombats, kangaroos and native bears, its exotic bell-birds and the laughing jackass, and other
indigenous creatures, including the mythical Bunyip, through well-thumbed copies of her
popular *Timothy in Bushland*. Others were introduced to aboriginal legends through *The
Stone Axe of Burkamukk*. Most of her books were first published in England, but in the
period between the first and second world wars many an Australian home gathered on its
bookshelves, for family reading, a collection of the famous *Billabong* books, a series which
began with *A Little Bush Maid* in 1910.

The Lintons of "Billabong" were a motherless family who lived on a prosperous station
property in the north of Victoria, seventeen miles from Cunjee, the nearest town.
"Billabong" is a comfortably secure world in microcosm. Threat is usually external in the
form of natural disaster – drought, flood or bushfire – or of lawless creatures such as vagrant
swagmen, cattle duffers or gold thieves. The world outside only occasionally casts its shadow
as when the Linton men are involved in World War I. But "Billabong" is always there, its
wide shady verandahs, its long lagoon in which to swim, its creek for fishing which can dry
up or run high, its scrub through which cattle roam and its open paddocks across which to
canter. Against this background Norah Linton, the little bush maid, grows from childhood to
womanhood; a fresh open country girl – stalwart yet feminine; resourceful yet lovingly
dependent on her menfolk. Her older brother Jim, too, is proudly upright and dependable,
and Norah is to marry his boisterous mate, Wally Meadows, who "laughed at life just as he
laughed at Death, when it came near to touching him." Only when trouble threatens the
Billabong folk does life become serious. This stable family group benignly ruled over by Mr.
Linton embraces the homestead servants and the station hands. Brownie, ample, motherly,
astutely aware that her cooking will hold the family together in any crisis and "regarded by
the station as a species of stout angel in petticoats" and Murty O'Toole, the dry-mouthed Irish
stockman, are closest to the family. But the arch-enemies Hogg the gardener and Lee Wing
his Chinese help, along with Black Billy the stockboy, are all treated with the same respect as
is meted to all visitors and to the many lame-dogs whom the Lintons befriend over the years.

The series reflects the social and economic climate of Australia which weathered both a world war and a depression. Gold is discovered on the property, and to meet expanding needs the Lintons turn to their own air transport in *Wings above Billabong.*

Mary Grant Bruce gives a good deal of explanatory background information, but because she is a first-class story-teller, she is able to regulate the pace of her narrative to her readers' interests. Her characters are made of stern stuff but are not unsentimental, perhaps predictable as well as being reliable. Their conflicts and alarms are always transitory and there is always a happy issue from any kind of adversity. Hence her plots are melodramatic rather than tragic. But her many books epitomised, even if they idealised, a recognisably outback Australian life-style of warm-hearted characters committed to the ideal of "mateship."

—H. M. Saxby

BUCKERIDGE, Anthony. British. Born in London, 20 June 1912. Educated at Seaford College, Sussex; University College, University of London. Served in the armed forces, 1939–45. Married Sylvia Brown; Eileen Selby; has two sons and one daughter. Worked as a teacher, actor, and broadcaster. Agent: English Theatre Guild, 1 The Pavement, London, S.W.4. Address: East Crink, Barcombe Mills, Lewes, Sussex BN8 5BL, England.

PUBLICATIONS FOR CHILDREN

Fiction

Jennings Goes to School. London, Collins, 1950.
Jennings Follows a Clue. London, Collins, 1951.
Jennings' Little Hut. London, Collins, 1951.
Jennings and Darbishire. London, Collins, 1952.
A Funny Thing Happened! London, Lutterworth Press, 1953.
Rex Milligan's Busy Term, illustrated by Mazure. London, Lutterworth Press, 1953.
Jennings' Diary. London, Collins, 1953.
According to Jennings. London, Collins, 1954.
Our Friend Jennings. London, Collins, 1955.
Rex Milligan Raises the Roof, illustrated by Mazure. London, Lutterworth Press, 1955.
Rex Milligan Holds Forth, illustrated by Mazure. London, Lutterworth Press, 1955.
Thanks to Jennings. London, Collins, 1957.
Take Jennings, For Instance, illustrated by Mays. London, Collins, 1958.
Jennings, As Usual, illustrated by Mays. London, Collins, 1959.
The Trouble with Jennings, illustrated by Mays. London, Collins, 1960.
Just Like Jennings. London, Collins, 1961.
Rex Milligan Reporting, illustrated by Mazure. London, Lutterworth Press, 1961.
Leave It to Jennings, illustrated by Mays. London, Collins, 1963.
Jennings, Of Course!, illustrated by Mays. London, Collins, 1964.
Especially Jennings!, illustrated by Mays. London, Collins, 1965.
A Bookful of Jennings. London, Collins, 1966; revised edition, as *The Best of Jennings,* 1972.
Jennings Abounding, illustrated by Mays. London, Collins, 1967.
Jennings in Particular, illustrated by Mays. London, Collins, 1968.
Trust Jennings!, illustrated by Mays. London, Collins, 1969.
The Jennings Report, illustrated by Mays. London, Collins, 1970.
Typically Jennings! London, Collins, 1971.

Speaking of Jennings.   London, Collins, 1973.
Jennings at Large.   London, Collins, 1977.

Plays

Draw the Line Somewhere (produced Ramsgate, Kent, 1948).
Happy Christmas, Jennings (produced Lewes, Sussex, 1969).

Radio Plays: *Jennings at School* series, 1948–74; *A Funny Thing Happened!*, 1963; *Liz*, 1974.

Television Plays: *Rex Milligan* series, 1954–55; *Jennings* series, 1958, 1966.

Other

Editor, *Stories for Boys 1* and *2*.   London, Faber, 1957, 1965.
Editor, *In and Out of School: Stories.*   London, Faber, 1958.

*   *   *

Anthony Buckeridge's small schoolboy hero Jennings is something of a phenomenon. The series of books about him began to appear in the early 1950's, but Jennings and his bespectacled friend Darbishire, agelessly fixed at about 10 years old, are still popular, in spite of their attending the kind of establishment preparatory school unfamiliar to most of the readers of their adventures.

It may be, however, that the sheer artificiality of the enclosed boarding-school background contributes to the continued popularity of these stories. Farce flourishes in an atmosphere where strict rules of conduct are laid down, and broken. And Mr. Buckeridge struck a rich vein of schoolboy humour with Jennings, Darbishire and their friends, tolerant Mr. Carter and choleric Mr. Wilkins, pompous headmaster Mr. Pemberton-Oakes, famous visiting Old Boy General Merridew and the rest. It is a style of humour which has much in common with Richmal Crompton's William, with P. G. Wodehouse's school stories (and some of his later novels), with the howlers of Sellar and Yeatman's *1066 and All That* and Williams and Searle's *Down with Skool* books: witness the difficulties of Jennings and Darbishire trying to converse with a friendly crew of French fishermen, Darbishire being unable to remember any French at all but "a passage which had caused him some trouble in class the previous day. So far as he had been able to judge, the translation was: *The gentleman who wears one green hat approaches himself all of a sudden.*"

The farcical situations of the books are neatly contrived, with Jennings inevitably getting caught in a web of his own mistaken but well-intentioned weaving. But what really counts is the backchat among the boys themselves. Slang such as "wizard" and "supersonic," "bate" and "bish" may date, but Mr. Buckeridge's feeling for the way small boys talk and argue and amiably insult each other does not.

Moreover, the lasting popularity of the Jennings books is not just an interesting but a cheering phenomenon in the Britain of the 1970's, where there is growing anxiety about ordinary standards of literacy among schoolchildren, because to enjoy the wilful verbal misunderstandings and intentionally dreadful puns of Jennings and his friends, the reader undoubtedly needs to be literate himself, and to quite a high degree. To get the point of Jenning's malapropism when he tries to explain to the Head that a flippant verse in his textbook was "meant meteorologically" a child has to have some knowledge of the word "metaphorically." Altogether, it is good to see this very English type of humorous school story still enjoyed; educational methods and slang may change, but small boys and their healthy sense of comedy do not.

—Anthea Bell

BUFF, Mary. American. Born in Cincinnati, Ohio, 10 April 1890. Educated at the University of Oklahoma, Norman; Bethany College, Kansas, B.A.in painting. Married the artist Conrad Buff in 1922; two sons. Taught in an elementary school, Lewistown, Montana, for three years, and in a teacher's college in Idaho for three years; Assistant Art Curator, Los Angeles Museum of History, Science and Art, 1920–22; taught art in a school in Hollywood. *Died in November 1970.*

PUBLICATIONS FOR CHILDREN (illustrated by Conrad Buff)

Fiction

Dancing Cloud the Navajo Boy. New York, Viking Press, 1937; revised edition, 1957.
Kobi, A Boy of Switzerland. New York, Viking Press, 1939.
Dash and Dart. New York, Viking Press, 1942; London, Museum Press, 1945.
Big Tree. New York, Viking Press, 1946.
Peter's Pinto. New York, Viking Press, 1949.
The Apple and the Arrow. Boston, Houghton Mifflin, 1951.
Magic Maze. Boston, Houghton Mifflin, 1953.
Hurry, Skurry, and Flurry. New York, Viking Press, 1954.
Hah-nee of the Cliff Dwellers. Boston, Houghton Mifflin, 1956.
Elf Owl. New York, Viking Press, 1958.
Trix and Vix. Boston, Houghton Mifflin, 1960.
Forest Folk. New York, Viking Press, 1962.
Kemi, An Indian Boy Before the White Man Came. Los Angeles, Ward Ritchie Press, 1966.

Other

The Colorado: River of Mystery. Los Angeles, Ward Ritchie Press, 1968.

*   *   *

A felicitous union of author and artist was the hallmark of the talented couple Mary and Conrad Buff. Mrs. Buff's rhythmic poetic prose was interpreted and enriched by Mr. Buff's superb visual dimension.

Their first book, *Dancing Cloud,* has no strong story line nor plot development but is a complete picture of the daily activities of one Navaho family. Each chapter deals with one facet of Dancing Cloud's family life. Lithograph illustrations capture the color and beauty of the desert land.

Hah-nee is a series of vignettes; the main character, Hah-nee, is used to give continuity to the description of another time. Young readers are impressed with the long-ago life of the great Pueblo cities and are left with wonder at what happened to a once-thriving culture which left the pueblos silent and decaying. Mr. Buff captured the magnificence of the pueblos in all their activity.

Set in Mr. Buff's boyhood home, *The Apple and the Arrow* is a distinguished yet simple retelling of the William Tell story. The characters are fully developed and the story is historically authentic. Full-page illustrations display the great beauty of Switzerland which Mr. Buff knew so well.

After writing of other cultures and other times, the Buffs turned to their own area and created unforgettable animal characters in *Dash and Dart* and *Forest Folk.* Simple rhythmic sentences tell of the life of two fawns. The mood and movement of the forest are shown both in story and illustration. The writing is always simple but the situations described are authentic and unsentimental, and allow Mr. Buff ample opportunity to portray wildlife in its natural setting.

197

Big Tree is considered by many to be the apex of the Buffs' writing and illustrating careers. It is the biography of Wawona, a famous giant redwood, interspersed with events taking place elsewhere in the world during Wawona's growth and development. The story begins when Wawona was a tiny seed, long before the time of man in California; he is shown when the Egyptians were building the pyramids and in the time when a national park was created to save these oldest of all living things. Mrs. Buff's cadenced imaginative writing and the scope of the story give Mr. Buff opportunity to display his artistic versatility.

—Dorothy Clayton McKenzie

BULL, Angela (Mary). British. Born in Halifax, Yorkshire, 28 September 1936. Educated at Badminton School, Bristol, 1948–54; Edinburgh University (Mackenzie Prize, 1959), 1955–59, M.A. (honours) in English; St. Hugh's College, Oxford, 1959–61. Married Martin Wells Bull in 1962; has one son and one daughter. Teacher, Casterton School, Kirkby Lonsdale, Westmorland, 1961–62; assistant, Medieval Manuscript Room, Bodleian Library, Oxford, 1962–63. Address: St. John's Vicarage, Ingrow, Keighley, West Yorkshire, England.

PUBLICATIONS FOR CHILDREN

Fiction

The Friend with a Secret, illustrated by Lynton Lamb. London, Collins, 1965; New York, Holt Rinehart, 1967.
Wayland's Keep, illustrated by Shirley Hughes. London, Collins, 1966; New York, Holt Rinehart, 1967.
Child of Ebenezer. London, Collins, 1974.
Treasure in the Fog, illustrated by Joanna Worth. London, Collins, 1976.
Griselda. London, Collins, 1977.

PUBLICATIONS FOR ADULTS

Other

Nineteenth Century Children: Heroes and Heroines in English Children's Stories, 1780–1900, with Gillian Avery. London, Hodder and Stoughton, 1965.

Angela Bull comments:
All my stories so far published have either a Victorian, or partly Victorian background. This is the result of having spent two years at Oxford doing research on Victorian children's books and having built up a collection of them since. Because of social conditions, Victorian children did not have the independence necessary for adventure of the type found in modern children's books. Their dramas tend to be inward, especially the drama of relationships, and it is this which has particularly interested me as a writer. Some action is of course necessary to the plot, but on the whole I have tried to put the emphasis on the relationships of children of dissimilar outlook and upbringing, moving towards mutual understanding and reconciliation.

*   *   *

Writers like Angela Bull who tackle the problem of writing historical novels for children set themselves a special task of demonstrating that the past was inhabited by "real" people and not just puppet figures acting out historical events and long dead stories. In *Treasure in the Fog* she demonstrates admirably that she has truly mastered the skill of handling authentic historical settings with a strong purpose of story told through lively natural child characters. Hints of Nesbit echo in the foggy streets of Victorian London where the upright Hastings children have been left in the care of the servants while their parents enjoy the warmth of Italy. Edward, at fourteen, is in command and decides that they may visit the circus, but this proves to be a more exciting expedition than they had thought; they return to find that their Butler is not quite the friend they had thought him to be. *Treasure in the Fog* provides the newly skilled reader with a lively short novel, full of action and historical detail, yet not too overwhelming.

Much more complex is the *Child of Ebenezer*, a taut anguished book in which the heroine, Little Grace Wentworth, finds herself caught between the religious bigotry of her family – members of the notorious Children of Ebenezer sect – and the humanity and tolerance of her governess and her secret friends, the fun-loving Catholic Kavanagh family. Domestic tragedy enables Grace to break the bonds of her upbringing and find her true self. One need look no further than Mrs. Bull's home town of Keighley to see the authentic Yorkshire setting for this notable novel of the 1890's.

In Angela Bull's two earlier books, *Wayland's Keep* and *The Friend with a Secret*, we feel a strong sense of loyalty and family kinship. The three cousins thrown together in the same house (in *Wayland's Keep*) begin their relationship by bickering and disliking each other, but as they unravel their family history they discover a growing respect and deepening friendship.

The strong narrative and realistic dialogue combine with authentic historical settings to make Angela Bull's novels a satisfying read, especially for girls who like their stories with substance as well as excitement and atmosphere.

—Jean Russell

BULLA, Clyde Robert. American. Born in King City, Missouri, 9 January 1914. Educated at Bray school, 1920–26; King City High School, 1926–27. Farmer until 1943; Linotype Operator and Columnist, *Tri-County News*, King City, 1943–49. Recipient: Boys' Clubs of America award, 1956; George G. Stone Center for Children's Books award, 1968; Christopher Award, 1972. Agent: Curtis Brown Ltd., 575 Madison Avenue, New York, New York 10022. Address: 1230 Las Flores Drive, Los Angeles, California 90041, U.S.A.

PUBLICATIONS FOR CHILDREN

Fiction

The Donkey Cart, illustrated by Lois Lenski. New York, Crowell, 1946.
Riding the Pony Express, illustrated by Grace Paull. New York, Crowell, 1948.
The Secret Valley, illustrated by Grace Paull. New York, Crowell, 1949.
Surprise for a Cowboy, illustrated by Grace Paull. New York, Crowell, 1950.
A Ranch for Danny, illustrated by Grace Paull. New York, Crowell, 1951.
Johnny Hong of Chinatown, illustrated by Dong Kingman. New York, Crowell, 1952.
Song of St. Francis, illustrated by Valenti Angelo. New York, Crowell, 1952.
Star of Wild Horse Canyon, illustrated by Grace Paull. New York, Crowell, 1953.
Eagle Feather, illustrated by Tom Two Arrows. New York, Crowell, 1953.

Squanto, Friend of the White Men, illustrated by Peter Burchard. New York, Crowell, 1954; as *Squanto, Friend of the Pilgrims*, New York, Crowell, 1969.
Down the Mississippi, illustrated by Peter Burchard. New York, Crowell, 1954.
White Sails to China, illustrated by Robert Henneberger. New York, Crowell, 1955.
The Poppy Seeds, illustrated by Jean Charlot. New York, Crowell, 1955.
John Billington, Friend of Squanto, illustrated by Peter Burchard. New York, Crowell, 1956.
The Sword in the Tree, illustrated by Paul Galdone. New York, Crowell, 1956.
Old Charlie, illustrated by Paul Galdone. New York, Crowell, 1957.
Ghost Town Treasure, illustrated by Don Freeman. New York, Crowell, 1957.
Pirate's Promise, illustrated by Peter Burchard. New York, Crowell, 1958.
The Valentine Cat, illustrated by Leonard Weisgard. New York, Crowell, 1959.
Three-Dollar Mule, illustrated by Paul Lantz. New York, Crowell, 1960.
The Sugar Pear Tree, illustrated by Taro Yashima. New York, Crowell, 1961.
Benito, illustrated by Valenti Angelo. New York, Crowell, 1961.
Viking Adventure, illustrated by Douglas Gorsline. New York, Crowell, 1963.
Indian Hill, illustrated by James Spanfeller. New York, Crowell, 1963.
White Bird, illustrated by Leonard Weisgard. New York, Crowell, 1966; London, Macdonald, 1969.
The Ghost of Windy Hill, illustrated by Don Bolognese. New York, Crowell, 1968.
Mika's Apple Tree: A Story of Finland, illustrated by Des Asmussen. New York, Crowell, 1968.
The Moon Singer, illustrated by Trina Schart Hyman. New York, Crowell, 1969.
New Boy in Dublin: A Story of Ireland, illustrated by Jo Polseno. New York, Crowell, 1969.
Pocahontas and the Strangers, illustrated by Peter Burchard. New York, Crowell, 1971.
Open the Door and See All the People, illustrated by Wendy Watson. New York, Crowell, 1972.
Dexter, illustrated by Glo Coalson. New York, Crowell, 1973.
The Wish at the Top, illustrated by Chris Conover. New York, Crowell, 1974.
Shoeshine Girl, illustrated by Leigh Grant. New York, Crowell, 1975.
Marco Moonlight, illustrated by Julia Noonan. New York, Crowell, 1976.
The Beast of Lor, illustrated by Ruth Sanderson. New York, Crowell, 1977.

Other

A Dog Named Penny (reader), illustrated by Kate Seredy. Boston, Ginn, 1955.
Stories of Favorite Operas, illustrated by Robert Galster. New York, Crowell, 1959.
A Tree Is a Plant, illustrated by Lois Lignell. New York, Crowell, 1960; London, A. and C. Black, 1962.
What Makes a Shadow?, illustrated by Adrienne Adams. New York, Crowell, 1962; London, A. and C. Black, 1965.
The Ring and the Fire: Stories from Wagner's Niebelung Operas, illustrated by Clare and John Ross. New York, Crowell, 1962.
St. Valentine's Day, illustrated by Valenti Angelo. New York, Crowell, 1965.
More Stories of Favorite Operas, illustrated by Joseph Low. New York, Crowell, 1965.
Lincoln's Birthday, illustrated by Ernest Crichlow. New York, Crowell, 1966.
Washington's Birthday, illustrated by Don Bolognese. New York, Crowell, 1967.
Flowerpot Gardens, illustrated by Henry Evans. New York, Crowell, 1967.
Stories of Gilbert and Sullivan Operas, illustrated by James and Ruth McCrea. New York, Crowell, 1968.
Jonah and the Great Fish, illustrated by Helga Aichinger. New York, Crowell, 1970.
Joseph the Dreamer, illustrated by Gordon Laite. New York, Crowell, 1971.

Translator, *Noah and the Rainbow*, by Max Bollinger, illustrated by Helga Aichinger. New York, Crowell, 1972.

PUBLICATIONS FOR ADULTS

Novel

These Bright Young Dreams. Philadelphia, Penn, 1941.

Manuscript Collections: Kerlan Collection, University of Minnesota, Minneapolis; University of Oregon Library, Eugene; de Grummond Collection, University of Southern Mississippi, Hattiesburg.

Music: incidental music for plays – *The Bean-Pickers*, 1952, *A Change of Heart*, 1952, *Strangers in a Strange Land*, 1952, all by Lois Lenski; songs – *We Are Thy Children*, 1952, *Songs of Mr. Small*, 1954, *Songs of the City*, 1956, *Up to Six*, 1956, *At Our House*, 1959, *When I Grow Up*, 1960. all by Lois Lenski.

Clyde Robert Bulla comments:
When I was a boy I made up my own stories. Some were high adventure, with buried treasure, perilous journeys, and hairbreadth escapes. Some were quiet, about everyday people like those I knew. Others were about the mysteries of life – things that puzzled and haunted me and left me with a sense of wonder. These are the stories I began to write a long time afterward and the stories I am writing now.

* * *

Clyde Robert Bulla attracts young people to his books by building his plots quickly and believably, using simple language without condescension. With the stage set, the characters reveal themselves through conversation and action. He skillfully interweaves the plot with a sense of good and evil, right and wrong.

His approach to writing fiction indicates a subtle change in the late 1960's. Heretofore, characters emerged from plot and conversation. The story of *White Bird* is contingent upon love as known and interpreted by the foundling boy and by the seemingly stern farmer who raises him. Plot develops from their relationship.

Bulla continued to follow the pattern of his earlier fiction in some of his books, but changes appear. In *The Moon Singer*, complex ideas are described in simple language. The peasant boy sings because he must, and sings especially well when the moon is full. His need to sing might be a microcosm of the need of any artist, the inner drive to create in spite of, rather than because of, society. There is the gentle yet persuasive suggestion that this is more than just a medieval tale of a boy who felt compelled to sing.

Shoeshine Girl is the story of stubborn and defiant ten-year-old Sarah Ida who must have money in her pocket. With no means of obtaining it, she goes to work for Al, the shoeshine man. Bulla retains his direct style, but Sarah Ida's growth towards self-acceptance and a concern for other people is believable and sound.

In *Marco Moonlight*, Marco has a recurrent dream about himself as a baby, a dream in which he is playing with his brother. He describes this again to his wealthy grandparents with whom he lives. There unfolds a series of strange events in almost Gothic style. The book may not be a critical success, but demonstrates Bulla's continuing efforts to break away from conformity in his writing.

An opera enthusiast, Bulla has retold stories of operas with knowledge, and transmits his keen interest. *Squanto, Friend of the White Men*, an early work of fictionalized biography, contains no complexity. *Pocahontas and the Strangers*, a much later fictionalized biography, retains the same uncomplicated approach but has warmth, accurate description, and the

201

added dimension of dilemma in the meeting of two cultures – American Indian and white. *Jonah and the Great Fish* and *Joseph the Dreamer* are faithful retellings of the Old Testament stories, told with dignity.

Because of the simple language, the unobservant critic might find it easy to appraise each of Bulla's books as a story told with directness of plot which, at times, might be considered thin. This is an underestimation of the author. In his more than fifty books there are consistency of integrity and respect for audience. He offers the young, and not so young, reader a range of concepts, an introduction to other times and other cultures.

—Mae Durham Roger

BURCH, Robert (Joseph). American. Born in Inman, Georgia, 26 June 1925. Educated at the University of Georgia, Athens, B.A. in agriculture 1949; Hunter College, New York, 1955. Served in the United States Army, in New Guinea and Australia, 1943–46. Civil Servant, United States Army Ordnance Depot, Atlanta, 1951–53, and in Japan, 1953–55; office worker, Muir and Company Advertising, New York, 1956–59, and Walter E. Heller and Company, New York, 1959–62. Recipient: Breadloaf Writers Conference fellowship, 1960; Women's International League for Peace and Freedom Jane Addams Award, 1967; Child Study Association of America award, 1967; George G. Stone Center for Children's Books award, 1974. Address: P.O. Box 243, Fayetteville, Georgia 30214, U.S.A.

PUBLICATIONS FOR CHILDREN

Fiction

> *The Traveling Bird*, illustrated by Susanne Suba. New York, McDowell Obolensky, 1959.
> *A Funny Place to Live*, illustrated by W.R. Lohse. New York, Viking Press, 1962.
> *Tyler, Wilkin, and Skee*, illustrated by Don Sibley. New York, Viking Press, 1963.
> *Skinny*, illustrated by Don Sibley. New York, Viking Press, 1964; London, Methuen, 1965.
> *D.J.'s Worst Enemy*, illustrated by Emily Weiss. New York, Viking Press, 1965.
> *Queenie Peavy*, illustrated by Jerry Lazare. New York, Viking Press, 1966.
> *Renfroe's Christmas*, illustrated by Rocco Negri. New York, Viking Press, 1968.
> *Joey's Cat*, illustrated by Don Freeman. New York, Viking Press, 1969.
> *Simon and the Game of Chance*, illustrated by Fermin Rocker. New York, Viking Press, 1970.
> *The Hunting Trip*, illustrated by Susanne Suba. New York, Scribner, 1971.
> *Doodle and the Go-Cart*, illustrated by Alan Tiegreen. New York, Viking Press, 1972.
> *Hut School and the Wartime Home-Front Heroes*, illustrated by Ronald Himler. New York, Viking Press, 1974.
> *The Jolly Witch*, illustrated by Leigh Grant. New York, Dutton, 1975.
> *Two That Were Tough*, illustrated by Richard Cuffari. New York, Viking Press, 1976.
> *The Whitman Kick*. New York, Dutton, 1977.

PUBLICATIONS FOR ADULTS

Other

> Translator, *A Jungle in the Wheat Field*, by Egon Mathiesen. New York, McDowell Obolensky, 1960.

Robert Burch comments:

Most of my stories are realistic. They take place in the area I know best, the rural south. Although my characters are made up, they must seem real to me before I can write about them. If I think about them until I know them quite well, they help me write the book! It becomes a matter of letting the story grow as naturally as possible out of character development and the circumstances of the time and the place in which it is set.

*   *   *

Robert Burch seems to have two distinct messages in his works. In his books for pre- and early-readers, whether he's writing anthropomorphically as in *A Funny Place to Live* and *The Traveling Bird*, realistically as in *Joey's Cat*, or tongue-in-cheek in *The Hunting Trip*, Burch writes fluently for the rights of animals to live complementary though parallel lives to humans.

But it is in his books for middle readers that he makes a personal and emotional comment on life. In a folksy, low key style he writes about the rural Georgia of his youth. The red clay land deals harshly with its inhabitants. Poverty is always an adversary, the only one in his early books (*Tyler, Wilkin and Skee* and *Skinny*), a co-adversary in his later novels. He writes of a time when transportation was limited and sacrifice was a requisite.

But there is never a poverty of spirit. The children of Burch's books perform their chores with a minimum of fuss, take disappointments in stride and are fiercely loyal to each other. Although the youngest children are denied the privileges of the older ones, like whittling and swimming "at the hole," they are appreciated for talents they possess. Skee is something of a songwriter – he makes up songs for every occasion. Renfroe is an expert imitator. Understated action and dialog demonstrate these traits without didacticism.

In *Tyler* three young brothers work hard, play kick-the-can and look forward to an occasional car ride with a neighbor although it means a two-mile walk back. Meals are sufficient but fresh fruit is unheard of (Skee didn't remember ever seeing a tangerine). Yet when a "fruit basket for the needy" was delivered to their door they protest that they aren't needy. Accepting life's blows seems to be an underlying theme. The orphan boy Skinny hates the idea of an orphanage, but he not only goes, he also gives his dog to the woman who'd cared for him in the interim.

But there's humor, too. Picture the scene in *Tyler*. It's a lazy Sunday and chores are done. A car passes on the dusty road. An hour or two later, another car. Skee turns to his brother and observes, "Somebody must've left the gate open." In *Skinny* the orphan is urged by a carnival boy to run away with him. "Where to?" Skinny wants to know. "Any place you think of. I can't do all the planning," Calvin replies. The dialogue is casual rural with expressions like "plumb peace loving" and "simmered down" and "Howdy!" scattered generously.

Burch's later books have shown more character development. In *D.J.'s Worst Enemy* he's a scrapper, a prankster ("If we don't go over there and stir up a little trouble they'll think we're scared of 'em"). Queenie Peavy in a novel by that name demonstrates fierce loyalty to her "jail bird" father and rebels against every authority and peer. Kate, the sixth-grade heroine in *Hut School and the Wartime Home-Front Heroes*, struggles with her discovery that nothing – good or bad – stays the same. In *Renfroe's Christmas*, the littlest charmer of *Worst Enemy* has aged three years and turned a bit selfish.

The land and the environment offer no compromise in Burch's books. Neither do his characters. Daddy Rabbit can't face settling down and leaves Miss Bessie to spinsterhood and Skinny to the orphanage. Queenie's father proves highly unworthy of her loyalty. But with the struggle against poverty and the devils that dwell within, there is the overpowering message of hope.

—Mary Blount Christian

BURNETT, Frances Hodgson. American. Born in Manchester, England, 24 November 1849; emigrated to the U.S.A. in 1865; became American citizen, 1905. Educated in Manchester schools. Married Swan Burnett in 1873 (divorced, 1898), two sons; Stephen Townesend, 1900 (separated, 1901; died, 1914). *Died 29 October 1924.*

PUBLICATIONS FOR CHILDREN

Fiction

Little Lord Fauntleroy. New York, Scribner, and London, Warne, 1886.
Sara Crewe; or, What Happened at Miss Minchin's. London, Unwin, 1887; New York, Scribner, 1888.
Editha's Burglar. Boston, Jordan Marsh, 1888.
Editha's Burglar, and Sarah Crewe. London, Warne, 1888.
Little Saint Elizabeth and Other Stories. New York, Scribner, and London, Warne, 1890.
Children I Have Known. London, Osgood McIlvaine, 1892; as *Giovanni and the Other: Children Who Have Made Stories,* New York, Scribner, 1892.
The Captain's Youngest and Other Stories. London, Warne, 1894; as *Piccino and Other Child Stories,* New York, Scribner, 1894.
The Two Little Pilgrims' Progress: A Story of the City Beautiful. New York, Scribner, and London, Warne, 1895.
A Little Princess, Being the Whole Story of Sara Crewe Now Told for the First Time. New York, Scribner, and London, Warne, 1905.
Racketty Packetty House. New York, Century, 1905; London, Warne, 1907.
The Troubles of Queen Silver-Bell. New York, Century, 1906; London, Warne, 1907.
The Cozy Lion, as Told by Queen Crosspatch. New York, Century, 1907; London, Stacey, 1972.
The Spring Cleaning, as Told by Queen Crosspatch. New York, Century, 1908; London, Stacey, 1973.
The Good Wolf. New York, Moffat, 1908.
Barty Crusoe and His Man Saturday. New York, Moffat, 1909.
The Land of the Blue Flower. New York, Moffat, 1909; London, Putnam, 1912.
The Secret Garden, illustrated by Charles Robinson. New York, Stokes, and London, Heinemann, 1911.
The Lost Prince. New York, Century, and London, Hodder and Stoughton, 1915.
The Way to the House of Santa Claus: A Christmas Story. New York and London, Harper, 1916.
Little Hunchback Zia. New York, Stokes, and London, Heinemann, 1916.

Plays

The Real Little Lord Fauntleroy, adaptation of her own novel (produced London, Boston, and New York, 1888).
Editha's Burglar, with Stephen Townesend, adaptation of the novel by Burnett (produced Neath, Glamorgan, 1890; as *Nixie,* produced London, 1890).
A Little Princess, adaptation of her own novel *Sara Crewe* (as *A Little Unfairy Princess,* produced London, 1902; as *A Little Princess,* produced London and New York, 1903). Published in *Treasury of Plays for Children,* edited by Montrose J. Moses, Boston, Little Brown, 1921.
Racketty Packetty House, adaptation of her own novel (produced New York, 1912).

PUBLICATIONS FOR ADULTS

Novels

That Lass o' Lowries. New York, Scribner, and London, Warne, 1877.
Dolly: A Love Story. Philadelphia, Porter and Coates, and London, Routledge, 1877; as *Vagabondia,* New York, Scribner, 1883.
Haworth's. London, Macmillan, and New York, Scribner, 1879.
Louisiana. New York, Scribner, 1880.
Louisiana, and That Lass o' Lowries. London, Macmillan, 1880.
A Fair Barbarian. Boston, Osgood, and London, Warne, 1881.
Through One Administration. Boston, Osgood, 3 vols., 1883; London, Warne, 1883.
A Woman's Will: or, Miss Defarge. London, Warne, 1877; with *Brueton's Bayou,* by John Habberton, Philadelphia, Lippincott, 1888.
The Fortunes of Philippa Fairfax. London, Warne, 1888.
The Pretty Sister of José. New York, Scribner, and London, Blackett, 1889.
A Lady of Quality ... New York, Scribner, and London, Warne, 1896.
His Grace of Osmonde .... New York, Scribner, and London, Warne, 1897.
In Connection with the De Willoughby Claim. New York, Scribner, and London, Warne, 1899.
The Making of a Marchioness. New York, Stokes, 1901; revised edition, London, Smith Elder, 1901.
The Methods of Lady Walderhurst. New York, Stokes, 1901; London, Smith Elder, 1902.
In the Closed Room. London, Hodder and Stoughton, 1904; New York, McClure, 1905.
The Dawn of a Tomorrow. New York, Scribner, 1906; London, Warne, 1907.
The Shuttle. New York, Stokes, 1908.
My Robin. New York, Stokes, 1912; London, Putnam, 1913.
T. Tembaron. New York, Stokes, and London, Hodder and Stoughton, 1913.
The White People. New York, Harper, 1917; London, Heinemann, 1920.
The Head of the House of Coombe. New York, Stokes, and London, Heinemann, 1922.
Robin. New York, Stokes, and London, Heinemann, 1922.

Short Stories

Surly Tim and Other Stories. New York, Scribner, and London, Ward Lock, 1877.
Theo: A Love Story. Philadelphia, Peterson, and London, Ward Lock, 1877.
Pretty Polly Pemberton: A Love Story. Philadelphia, Peterson, 1877; London, Routledge, 1878.
Kathleen: A Love Story. Philadelphia, Peterson, and London, Routledge, 1878.
Miss Crespigny: A Love Story. Philadelphia, Peterson, and London, Routledge, 1878.
Earlier Stories. New York, Scribner, 1878; London, Routledge, 1879.
Earlier Stories, second series. New York, Scribner, 1878; London, Chatto and Windus, 1879.
A Quiet Life, and The Tide on the Moaning Bar. Philadelphia, Peterson, 1878; London, Routledge, 1879.
Our Neighbour Opposite. London, Routledge, 1878.
Jarl's Daughter and Other Stories. Philadelphia, Peterson, 1879.
Natalie and Other Stories. London, Warne, 1879.

Plays

That Lass o' Lowries, with Julian Magnus, adaptation of the novel by Frances Hodgson Burnett (produced New York, 1878).

Esmeralda, with William Gillette (produced Newark, New Jersey, and New York, 1881; as *Young Folk's Ways*, produced London, 1883).

Phyllis, adaptation of her own novel *The Fortunes of Philippa Fairfax* (produced London, 1889).

The Showman's Daughter, with Stephen Townesend (produced Worcester, 1891; London, 1892).

The First Gentleman of Europe, with Constance Fletcher (produced New York and London, 1897).

A Lady of Quality, with Stephen Townesend, adaptation of the novel by Frances Hodgson Burnett (produced Detroit and New York, 1897; Cambridge and London, 1899).

The Pretty Sister of José, adaptation of her own novel (produced Syracuse, New York, New York City, and London, 1903).

That Man and I, adaptation of her own novel *In Connection with the De Willoughby Claim* (produced London, 1903; New York, 1904).

The Dawn of a Tomorrow, adaptation of her own novel (produced New York, 1909; Liverpool and London, 1910).

Other

The Drury Lane Boys' Club.   Washington, D.C., Moon Press, 1892.

The One I Knew the Best of All: A Memory of the Mind of a Child (autobiography).   New York, Scribner, and London, Warne, 1893.

In the Garden.   New York, Medici Society, 1925.

Critical Study: *Waiting for the Party: The Life of Frances Hodgson Burnett, 1849–1924* by Ann Thwaite, London, Secker and Warburg, and New York, Scribner, 1974.

*   *   *

The bulk of Mrs. Burnett's work for children was written in the nineteenth century but her two best books – the final version of *Sara Crewe*, called *A Little Princess*, and *The Secret Garden* – both belong to the twentieth. These are the two books which are still read and enjoyed by thousands of children every year, not as period pieces but in exactly the same way as they read contemporary writers. A third book, *Little Lord Fauntleroy*, is also enjoyed; but the critic, anyway, if not the child reader, is more affected in his judgment by the date it was written.

Mrs. Burnett was well established as a writer for adults when she published *Fauntleroy*. Her early novels were compared with those of George Eliot, and in 1883 an article in the *Century* magazine listed her as one of those with Henry James "who hold the front rank today in general estimation." Her first stories for children were short ones, which appeared in *St. Nicholas*. It was only after the phenomenal success of *Fauntleroy* that she regularly published children's books. The quality of these was variable, and her most impressive work continued to be for adults until the publication of *A Little Princess* in 1905.

The history of this book is curious and is worth going into in some detail. Indeed, a comparison of the three versions of the story gives a rewarding insight into Mrs. Burnett's working methods and her development as a children's writer. *Sara Crewe* first appeared in 1887. It was a story drawing on some of her experiences as a child at the Miss Hadfields' school in Manchester, but was set in London. Like nearly all Mrs. Burnett's stories, its theme is the reversal of fortune. In *Fauntleroy*, Cedric Erroll had left a small house in New York, wearing clothes made out of his mother's old gown, for the life of the heir to an earldom and an English castle. Sara Crewe had gone to school as an heiress and been reduced, after her bankrupt father's death, to living in an attic as a drudge and an outcast. In both cases, the moral is firmly drawn and cannot be missed by even the most unperceptive child reader: we are what we are, and our outward trappings and possessions have nothing to do with real nobility.

In 1902 Mrs Burnett turned the story of *Sara Crewe* into a play. The following year, her editor at Scribner's came up with the suggestion that she write a new, longer version of the book under the play's title, *A Little Princess*, incorporating the new material she had introduced in the play. He wanted the book quickly, the play was still running and sales would be splendid. Fortunately at that point Mrs. Burnett was committed to two other plays. The book was not rushed and was not finally finished until November 1904.

In the original version, Sara's experiences up until her father's death took no more than four and a half pages. In *A Little Princess* they take ninety. The earlier book is little more than a series of notes for the rich rewards of the full-scale novel. The basic story is an excellent one, and the final version demonstrates with what tremendous skill Mrs. Burnett was able to make the most of it. The detail is excellent too: Mrs. Burnett was always good at detail. As she once said, "It is not enough to mention they have tea; you must specify the muffins."

A Little Princess is a great deal more interesting than *Fauntleroy*, partly because Sara is seen not from the adult point of view, but from her own viewpoint. *The Secret Garden*, is even more interesting. "It is the most satisfying children's book I know," the critic Marghanita Laski once wrote, and countless people have shared that view.

Mrs. Burnett wrote much of the book in the rose garden of Great Maytham Hall in Rolvenden in Kent. All her life, she said, she had felt "a sort of curious kinship with things which grew" and *The Secret Garden* is, among many other things, an expression of this kinship.

The place is important: the atmosphere of the huge house and garden is romantic and mysterious. The small orphan from India comes to Misselthwaite across the moors. Her arrival is strongly reminiscent of that of Jane Eyre at Thornfield, and there are other points of resemblance between the two books. Mrs. Burnett did not in fact know Yorkshire well, and her setting owes more to the Brontës than to real life. She stayed with Lord Crewe at Fryston Hall in 1895, but that is her only recorded visit to the area. We don't know where she acquired her knowledge of the Yorkshire dialect Dickon and his family speak so convincingly, but she had always been interested in dialect, ever since the days as a child in Manchester and Salford when one of her greatest pleasures was to sneak out and gossip with the "back street" children.

The setting, as I say, is important, but much more important are the children. The most original thing about the book is that its heroine and one of its heroes are both thoroughly unattractive children. The first sentence makes it compulsive reading: "When Mary Lennox was sent to Misselthwaite Manor to live with her uncle, everybody said she was the most disagreeable-looking child ever seen." And Colin is a hysterical hypochondriac. It is the entirely convincing transformation of these two unhappy children that gives the story its great appeal, even to readers who do not find the natural world particularly attractive.

Other Victorian writers had made deprived children behave quite inappropriately, but Mrs. Burnett's instinct has since been confirmed by child psychologists. A child denied love does behave as Mary behaved. But *The Secret Garden* is far more than a parable or a demonstration of child behaviour. With Mrs. Burnett the story always came first, and she was far too good a writer to spoil it with propaganda. Only at the beginning of Chapter 27 does she lapse, with explicit explanations of her symbolism and a bald definition of what the rest of the book conveys so subtly: "to let a sad thought or a bad one get into your mind is as dangerous as letting a scarlet fever germ get into your body." *The Secret Garden* was a book of the new, the twentieth century. Far from encouraging the attitudes instilled in Frances as a child ("speak when you're spoken to, come when you're called ..."), it suggested children should be self-reliant and have faith in themselves, that they should listen, not to their elders and betters, but to their own hearts and consciences.

The Secret Garden did not make a great impact on its first appearance, but it has never been out of print. It is this book which establishes Mrs. Burnett as undoubtedly one of the most important writers of the century.

—Ann Thwaite

BURNFORD, Sheila (Philip Cochrane Every). Canadian.   Born in Scotland, 11 May 1918; emigrated to Canada in 1951. Educated at St. George's School, Edinburgh; Harrogate College, Yorkshire; studied in Germany. Married David Burnford in 1941; has three daughters. Served in the Royal Naval Hospitals Voluntary Aid Detachment, England, 1939–41; ambulance driver, 1941–42. Recipient: Canadian Library Association Book of the Year Medal, 1963; American Library Association Aurianne Award, 1963. Lives in Hampshire, England. Agent: David Higham Associates, 8–10 Lower John Street, London W1R 4HA, England.

PUBLICATIONS FOR CHILDREN

Fiction

> *The Incredible Journey*, illustrated by Carl Burger.   Boston, Little Brown, 1961; revised edition, London, Hodder and Stoughton, 1961.
> *Mr. Noah and the Second Flood*, illustrated by Michael Foreman.   Toronto, McClelland and Stewart, London, Gollancz, and New York, Praeger, 1973.

PUBLICATIONS FOR ADULTS

Novel

> *Bel Ria.*   London, Joseph, 1977.

Other

> *The Fields of Noon* (autobiographical essays).   Toronto, McClelland and Stewart, Boston, Little Brown, and London, Hodder and Stoughton, 1964.
> *Without Reserve* (on the Indians of Ontario).   Toronto, McClelland and Stewart, Boston, Little Brown, and London, Hodder and Stoughton, 1969.
> *One Woman's Arctic.*   London, Hodder and Stoughton, 1972; Boston, Little Brown, 1973.

*   *   *

Of Sheila Burnford's two books for children, *The Incredible Journey* is by far the most popular. In the same genre as Anna Sewell's *Black Beauty*, the story is a sentimental account of the adventures of three pets who survive incredible hardships in an attempt to return to their owners. A young Labrador Retriever, a Siamese cat and an old Bull Terrier regularly overcome tremendous problems – attack by wild animals, hunger, inclement weather, to name a few – and eventually do succeed in becoming reunited with their owners. Perhaps such an adventure is possible in reality, but it seems implausible that three house pets could so readily adapt to the rigours of wilderness survival in northern Ontario.

The author ascribes just about every human characteristic except speech to her protagonists. In fact, her animals could easily be three children since they think and act much more like people than animals. Allusions are made, for example to the terrier's "irrepressible air of sly merriment" and his "apologetic grin." The relationship between the three pets seems to be unrealistically altruistic. On one occasion, the cat attacks a bear cub in an effort to save one of the dogs and later gives up his supper in order that the dog might regain his strength. References are made to the Labrador Retriever as the group's "gentle, worried leader." All of the animals, indeed, are invested with commendable traits and human-like emotions. Burnford has created a memorable story but she has not created one that is a fair representation of the true nature of animals.

Mr. Noah and the Second Flood is an entirely different type of book. Obviously the vehicle for a strong anti-pollution crusade, this overly long contemporary fable about Noah's descendents is sometimes humorous, sometimes depressing. The theme of man's carelessness in upsetting the ecological balance is very heavily stressed to the detriment of the story. The characters tend to be stereotypes – Mrs. Noah is the epitome of the befuddled, kind-hearted grandmother and Noah is ever the serene patriarch. Most of the humor is derived from observations made by the isolated Noah family on events taking place in the world outside their mountain retreat. The story would probably be more successful in a format less reminiscent of a picture book and cut down to half of its present length.

—Fran Ashdown

BURNINGHAM, John (Mackintosh).   British.   Born in Farnham, Surrey, 27 April 1936. Educated at Summerhill School, Leiston, Suffolk; Central School of Art, London, 1956–59, diploma. Married Helen Oxenbury in 1964; has one son and one daughter. Recipient (for illustration): Library Association Kate Greenaway Medal, 1964, 1971; *New York Times* award, 1971; *Boston Globe-Horn Book* Award, 1972. Address: c/o Jonathan Cape Ltd., 30 Bedford Square, London WC1B 3EL, England.

PUBLICATIONS FOR CHILDREN (illustrated by the author)

Fiction

> *Borka: The Adventures of a Goose with No Feathers.*   London, Cape, and New York, Random House, 1963.
> *Trubloff: The Mouse Who Wanted to Play the Balalaika.*   London, Cape, 1964; New York, Random House, 1965.
> *ABC,* illustrated by the author and Leigh Taylor.   London, Cape, 1964; Indianapolis, Bobbs Merrill, 1967.
> *Humbert, Mister Firkin and the Lord Mayor of London.*   London, Cape, 1965; Indianapolis, Bobbs Merrill, 1967.
> *Cannonball Simp.*   London, Cape, 1966; Indianapolis, Bobbs Merrill, 1967.
> *Harquin: The Fox Who Went Down to the Valley.*   London, Cape, 1967; Indianapolis, Bobbs Merrill, 1968.
> *Seasons.*   London, Cape, 1969.
> *Mr. Gumpy's Outing.*   London, Cape, and New York, Holt Rinehart, 1970.
> *Mr. Gumpy's Motor Car.*   London, Cape, 1973; New York, Macmillan, 1975.
> *Come Away from the Water, Shirley.*   London, Cape, and New York, Crowell, 1977.

Other

> *Birdland: Wall Frieze.*   London, Cape, and New York, Braziller, 1966.
> *Lionland: Wall Frieze.*   London, Cape, 1966.
> *Storyland: Wall Frieze.*   London, Cape, 1966.
> *Jungleland: Wall Frieze.*   London, Cape, 1968.
> *Wonderland: Wall Frieze.*   London, Cape, 1968.
> *Around the World: Two Wall Friezes.*   London, Cape, 1972.
> *Around the World in Eighty Days.*   London, Cape, 1972.
> *The Baby* (reader).   London, Cape, 1974; New York, Crowell, 1975.
> *The Rabbit* (reader).   London, Cape, 1974; New York, Crowell, 1975.
> *The School* (reader).   London, Cape, 1974; New York, Crowell, 1975.

The Snow (reader).   London, Cape, 1974; New York, Crowell, 1975.
The Blanket (reader).   London, Cape, 1975; New York, Crowell, 1976.
The Cupboard (reader).   London, Cape, 1975; New York, Crowell, 1976.
The Dog (reader).   London, Cape, 1975; New York, Crowell, 1976.
The Friend (reader).   London, Cape, 1975; New York, Crowell, 1976.

Illustrator: *Chitty-Chitty Bang-Bang* by Ian Fleming 1964; *The Extraordinary Tug-of-War* by Letta Schatz 1968.

*   *   *

John Burningham is a born storyteller who would probably dispense with words entirely if he could. For him, the roles of author and artist are largely reversed. His books are conceived in pictures and the text is used, increasingly, simply to provide the necessary minimum of information, or else as a gloss on the visual element which carries the real strength of the narrative.

It was clear from his first book, *Borka*, which way the balance lay. *Borka*, like *Trubloff, Humbert, Cannonball Simp*, and *Harquin* which followed, falls into the pattern of the traditional picture story book, assuming a fair degree of reading skill. The writing is prosaic and slightly ungainly, matching the lumpiness of the figures, but it is the atmosphere of the pictures, their combination of the funny and familiar with something altogether wilder, more primitive, and more poetic, that gives these books their compelling power. Borka, for all her cartoon shape and mild domestic eye, is a real wild goose and no barnyard fowl, while the marshes she inhabits can be frightening as well as beautiful.

By 1970, when the first *Mr. Gumpy* book appeared, a change of manner was apparent. The proportion of text to pictures was drastically reduced and both had been fined down, lightened and developed greatly in subtlety and humour. Mr. Gumpy, with his gumboots and watering can, or punting stoutly in shirtsleeves and panama, or setting out for a peaceful drive only to be waylaid by a hopeful horde of two and four-legged friends. Mr. Gumpy, infinitely good-natured, kind and willing to be put upon, is a great comic character. In his way, he is a classic and lives on in his sunlit world of river and hill, in his neat Victorian villa, as a permanent reassurance that somewhere there will always be time for a swim before tea.

The Mr. Gumpy stories have an Aristotelian pattern of happiness, disaster and reconciliation. In the "Little Books" there is no such moral content and everything, text and pictures alike, has been pared down to essentials. There is still a recognisable thread of story; the small boy at home, in the park or in the snow, moves through a logical sequence of situations. But here the object is to capture and hold a moment's experience, simplified to the point where even the very young can approach it without help. In the process, he achieves an essential truthfulness as accessible to adults as to children.

John Burningham is an artist whose work is in continuous development. *Come Away from the Water, Shirley* combines the colour and drama of his early work with the later delicacy and economy. He is an author who must be "read" visually and in these terms commands an ever-widening range of expression.

—Anne Carter

BURTON, Hester (Wood-Hill).   British.   Born in Beccles, Suffolk, 6 December 1913. Educated at Headington School, Oxford, 1925–31; Oxford University, 1932–36, B.A. (honours) 1936. Married Reginald W.B. Burton in 1937; has three daughters. Part-time grammar school teacher; assistant editor of the Oxford Junior Encyclopedia, London, 1956–61. Recipient: Library Association Carnegie Medal, 1964; *Boston Globe-Horn Book Award*, 1971. Address: Mill House, Kidlington, Oxford, England.

PUBLICATIONS FOR CHILDREN

Fiction

The Great Gale, illustrated by Joan Kiddell-Monroe.   London, Oxford University Press,
    1960; as *The Flood at Reedsmere*, Cleveland, World, 1968.
Castors Away!, illustrated by Victor Ambrus.   London, Oxford University Press, 1962;
    Cleveland, World, 1963.
Time of Trial, illustrated by Victor Ambrus.   London, Oxford University Press, 1963;
    Cleveland, World, 1964.
No Beat of Drum, illustrated by Victor Ambrus.   London, Oxford University Press,
    1966; Cleveland, World, 1967.
In Spite of All Terror, illustrated by Victor Ambrus.   London, Oxford University Press,
    1968; New York, World, 1969.
Otmoor for Ever!, illustrated by Gareth Floyd.   London, Hamish Hamilton, 1968.
Thomas, illustrated by Victor Ambrus.   London, Oxford University Press, 1969; as
    Beyond the Weir Bridge, New York, Crowell, 1970.
Through the Fire, illustrated by Gareth Floyd.   London, Hamish Hamilton, 1969.
The Henchmans at Home, illustrated by Victor Ambrus.   London, Oxford University
    Press, 1970; New York, Crowell, 1972.
The Rebel, illustrated by Victor Ambrus.   London, Oxford University Press, 1971;
    New York, Crowell, 1972.
Riders of the Storm, illustrated by Victor Ambrus.   London, Oxford University Press,
    1972; New York, Crowell, 1973.
Kate Rider, illustrated by Victor Ambrus.   London, Oxford University Press, 1974;
    New York, Crowell, 1975.
To Ravensrigg.   London, Oxford University Press, 1976; New York, Crowell, 1977.
Tim at the Fur Fort, illustrated by Victor Ambrus.   London, Hamish Hamilton, 1977.
A Grenville Goes to Sea, illustrated by Colin McNaughton.   London, Heinemann, 1977.

Plays

Radio Play: *The Great Gale*, from her own story. 1961.

Television Play: *Castors Away!*, from her own story. 1968.

Other

Barbara Bodichon, 1827–1891.   London, Murray, 1949.
A Seaman at the Time of Trafalgar, illustrated by Victor Ambrus.   London, Oxford
    University Press, 1963.

Editor, *Coleridge and Wordsworth*.   London, Oxford University Press, 1953.
Editor, *Tennyson*.   London, Oxford University Press, 1954.
Editor, *Her First Ball: Short Stories*, illustrated by Susan Einzig.   London, Oxford
    University Press, 1959.
Editor, *A Book of Modern Stories*.   London, Oxford University Press, 1959.

Hester Burton comments:
    I have always been interested in the way ordinary people lived in times past. I love
children, and I enjoy writing; hence my historical novels for young people. My method is to
find some fairly small episode in history which catches my imagination such as a natural
disaster, a battle, or a siege or a riot − find out all I can about it − and then plunge my

imaginary young people into it and watch them struggle, usually very bravely, for honour and survival. It is the quality of the average boy and girl when put to the test which I find so surprising and inspiring.

*   *   *

Towards the end of *The Great Gale* when the flooded East Anglian village of Reedsmere has been visited both by the Queen and by the Minister of Housing, Mr. Macmillan, Mary whispers to her friend Myrtle: "I shall never forget today .... Today we were part of history." Later after hearing on the radio the full extent of the havoc wrought by the gale she has a different thought. "Perhaps, after all, it was not an exciting, but a solemn and dreadful thing to be part of history." This duality of response on the part of individuals caught up in a national crisis is very characteristic of Hester Burton's novels, whether they are set in the 17th, 18th, 19th, or 20th centuries; it is not for nothing that one of her most highly-praised books is called *Time of Trial* (though in this case the "time" is 1801, and the "trial" is in one sense that of the heroine's radical book-seller father accused of sedition). Mrs. Burton has modestly acknowledged a tendency to "find refuge" in history because the present age is becoming increasingly difficult to understand, whereas the past, in so far as historians have selected and interpreted the evidence, is easier to see in perspective. Moreover she has confessed that she is inclined to choose an historical event or theme because it echoes something she has experienced in her own life, and one can see, for instance, that *Castors Away*, with its vivid and at times harrowing account of the autumn of the Battle of Trafalgar has its parallel in some events of the Second World War, while *No Beat of Drum*, with its portrayal of the harsh poverty of the English farm-labourers in 1829 to 1831, mirrors to a certain extent the divisive class-conflicts of the 1930's. Yet in fact her most successful novel of all is the one which derives most directly from lived experience. *In Spite of All Terror* evokes for us with a wonderful visual concreteness the outbreak of war in 1939, the evacuation of an East London school to the remoteness of the Oxfordshire countryside, the trauma of Dunkirk, the excitement of the Battle of Britain, and the anguish of the bombing of London in the autumn of 1940. It is moreover the most compulsively readable of her novels, its characterisation remains convincing while covering an extremely varied range of social classes, and it has in Liz Hawtin a protagonist who is at the same time the most believable and the most engaging of all Mrs. Burton's heroines.

Even in this novel Hester Burton supplemented her own recollections with the use of books, as well as other people's memories. Her more strictly historical novels have all been thoroughly and intelligently researched, using contemporary documents and diaries as well as modern scholarship, so that they recreate for us with powerful authenticity both the atmosphere and the detailed ways of life of her chosen period. (In keeping with the spirit of her self-acknowledged selectivity she has made herself particularly at home in the period of the French Revolution and the Napoleonic Wars – *The Rebel, Rider of the Storm, Time of Trial* and *Castors Away* – and also in the period of the English Civil War – *Thomas* and *Kate Rider*.) In general her stories move at a brisk pace and are well supplied with incident; for the young adolescent reader their appeal is probably enhanced by a disposition to include, and even to work for, moments of strong feeling and uninhibited emotional release. An attractive example of her historical work at its best is *No Beat of Drum* in which the action moves from the impoverished countryside of Southern England to the penal settlements of Van Diemen's Land. One cannot fault the generosity of the author's sympathy with the exploited and starving labourers, and she shows understanding of the "Captain Swing" riots even though she does not condone them. The portrayal of life in Tasmania is as vividly detailed as that of life in Hampshire, and one's only reservation about the latter part of the book is that the plot relies rather too much on coincidence.

The "excitement" of "being part of history" has always been strongly present in Hester Burton's fiction, but in some of her later work the "solemn and dreadful" aspects have come more to the fore. Thus even in the relatively early *Castors Away* the more barbarous features of the naval warfare of the time were rendered with an unflinching realism which makes some parts of the book decidedly strong meat for juvenile stomachs. A few years later in *Thomas* Mrs. Burton seemed to have lost contact temporarily with her young readership by a too remorseless insistence on the hardships, miseries and frustrations of her three protagonists; indeed her description of the Great Plague of London makes harrowing reading for an adult.

In a slightly different way too there was evidence in her next book of a faltering in the author's sense of audience. *The Henchmans at Home* is a collection of six related stories about a country doctor's family in Victorian England, and some of these stories are among Mrs. Burton's most appealing work. However, they suffer from the disadvantage of being angled towards widely differing age-levels of reader. Elements of contrivance in her next two novels, *The Rebel* and *Riders of the Storm*, kept alive an anxiety that perhaps this author had now passed her peak. But in *Kate Rider* she returned fully to form, and produced a story about a Roundhead girl growing up in the early years of the Civil War which has all the qualities of the best of her earlier work.

—Frank Whitehead

BURTON, Virginia Lee. American. Born in Newton Center, Massachusetts, 30 August 1909. Educated at the California School of Fine Arts, San Francisco, 1926–28; Boston, Museum School, 1930. Married George Demetrios in 1931; two sons. Sketcher, *Boston Transcript*, 1928–31. Recipient: American Library Association Caldecott Medal, 1943. *Died 15 October 1968.*

PUBLICATIONS FOR CHILDREN (illustrated by the author)

Fiction

> *Choo Choo: Story of a Little Engine Who Ran Away.* Boston, Houghton Mifflin, 1937; London, Faber, 1944.
> *Mike Mulligan and His Steam Shovel.* Boston, Houghton Mifflin, 1939; London, Faber, 1941.
> *Calico the Wonder Horse; or, The Saga of Stewy Stinker.* Boston, Houghton Mifflin, 1941; London, Faber, 1942.
> *The Little House.* Boston, Houghton Mifflin, 1942; London, Faber, 1946.
> *Katy and the Big Snow.* Boston, Houghton Mifflin, 1943; London, Faber, 1947.
> *Maybelle the Cable Car.* Boston, Houghton Mifflin, 1952.

Other

> *Life Story.* Boston, Houghton Mifflin, 1962.

Illustrator: *Sad-Faced Boy* by Arna Bontemps, 1937; *Manual of American Mountaineering* edited by Kenneth A. Henderson, 1941; *Don Coyote* by Leigh Park, 1942; *Fast Sooner Hound* by Arna Bontemps and Jack Conroy, 1942; *Song of Robin Hood* edited by Ann Malcolmson, 1949; *The Emperor's New Clothes* by Hans Christian Andersen, 1949.

*   *   *

Writing her books was always the most difficult part, Virginia Lee Burton claimed – a hundred times harder than drawing pictures, of which she never tired. After her few ventures with illustrating stories written by others, she wanted to be in complete control of every aspect of her books, so she wrote them herself. But rather than let an idea develop freely into a story, she approached the text in terms of composing it to fit space on an illustrated page.

Despite this limitation, her texts are effective, especially when read aloud. Continual elimination of extra words plus trial-and-error to assure each word used was the best choice produced simple and strong texts.

Burton found a subject she wanted to draw (a machine or a house); then she worked out a story with that subject as heroine by planning a series of drawings to enliven a thin plot thread. The text length was dictated by the number of pages available and the situations for drawings to be spread over them. The actual attention to individual words came last, as she created the text to accompany the pictures. The final step came after the text was set, when she would cut or substitute words so the shape of the type pattern would be an integral part of the page design.

That *Choo Choo* is still a success after forty years says a great deal about the effectiveness of the story despite changing times. The spare but energetic text, full of read-aloud sound effects, catches the exuberant motion in the black-and-white drawings of the runaway steam engine on its dramatic adventure. A child today who has never seen nor heard a steam engine will gain a definite idea of what one was like from hearing *Choo Choo* read, and gain, too, a comforting feeling when the naughty engine is rescued and welcomed back by its crew.

Mike Mulligan and His Steam Shovel is wordier (but only because the story covers a longer span of time) and introduces more characters, and the surprise ending takes verbal as well as visual explanation. Here Burton allows her words to express more than mere accompaniment to the action of the color pictures: she introduces suspense as Mike Mulligan wonders if his long-unemployed, old-fashioned steam-shovel, Mary Anne, really can "dig as much in a day as a hundred men could dig in a week." This suspense becomes the crux of the story as Mary Anne and Mike take on a race against time, digging the cellar for the new town hall in Popperville in just one day. Then a puzzle: how can Mike get Mary Anne out of the cellar? The entire story keeps children's interest and the ingenious ending intrigues them. This is an all-time favorite among American picture books with Mary Anne and Mike Mulligan enshrined in any Hall of Fame of children's book characters.

Burton also used the theme of machine as heroine with a snowplow in *Katy and the Big Snow* and with a cable-car in *Maybelle the Cable Car*. *Katy* has the appeal inherent in fighting a bad storm, a subject all children can understand. It is told with a strong, direct text. *Maybelle* is complicated, involving technical explanations about San Francisco's cable-cars and the citizens' vote to save them; and even introducing a villain, Big Bill the bus, doesn't really make it an entertaining story.

Calico the Wonder Horse; or, The Saga of Stewy Stinker has more plot than her other books and the writing is as sharp and vivid as the drawings (some of her most exciting black-and-white work is in this book, which she drew as an antidote to the comics her sons read). It is parody of westerns and tall tales. The style, slap-bang in pace, is just right for this grand mix of funny desperados and frantic action.

A story with a lyric quality which comes partly from the repetition of words that sound well read aloud and partly from the repetition of patterns of the seasons and the years is *The Little House* who "shall never be sold for gold or silver and she will live to see our great-great-grandchildren's great-great-granchildren living in her." Bestowing feminine gender on her like a ship, Burton also gives the house human qualities – curiosity, sadness, loneliness, fear, and finally happiness when she is rescued from the engulfing city and restored to country life. Children identify with having things happen to them that they cannot prevent and, like the welcoming back of naughty *Choo Choo*, they find great satisfaction in a happy ending: the little house being lived in and loved once more. They also absorb the complex concepts of times (the sun rising and setting each day; the moon waxing and waning each month; the seasons changing each year) and of change (from country to city to country) through just such a simple and moving story as *The Little House*.

Burton conceived of *Life Story*, "The Story of Life on Our Earth from Its Beginnings Up to Now," as a drama. Her carefully detailed color paintings are framed by the proscenium arch of a stage as an astronomer, a geologist, a paleontologist, a historian, a grandmother, and the author herself stand in the spotlight to show and tell. New scientific discoveries since 1962 may alter theories of creation and evolution and the date man first existed, but *Life Story* will always be brilliant presentation of infinitely complicated material. The text is specifically written to fit each illustration and the reduction of each enormous scientific era or area of study to a few brief sentences sometimes leads to obvious oversimplification. But the brevity is an invitation to a child to discover more. The last section recapitulates *The Little House* and the author's own experience. It also projects and shares emotionally with the reader Burton's deep respect for the designs of nature and the forces of life.

—Lee Kingman

BYARS, Betsy (Cromer).   American.   Born in Charlotte, North Carolina, 7 August 1928. Educated at Furman University, Greenville, South Carolina, 1946–48; Queens College, Charlotte, 1948–50, B.A. in English 1950. Married Edward Ford Byars in 1950; has three daughters and one son. Recipient: American Library Association Newbery Medal, 1971. Address: 641 Vista Place, Morgantown, West Virginia 26505, U.S.A.

PUBLICATIONS FOR CHILDREN

Fiction

> *Clementine*, illustrated by Charles Wilton.   Boston, Houghton Mifflin, 1962.
> *The Dancing Camel*, illustrated by Harold Berson.   New York, Viking Press, 1965.
> *Rama, The Gypsy Cat*, illustrated by Peggy Bacon.   New York, Viking Press, 1966.
> *The Groober*, illustrated by the author.   New York, Harper, 1967.
> *The Midnight Fox*, illustrated by Ann Grifalconi.   New York, Viking Press, 1968; London, Faber, 1970.
> *Trouble River*, illustrated by Rocco Negri.   New York, Viking Press, 1969.
> *The Summer of the Swans*, illustrated by Ted CoConis.   New York, Viking Press, 1970.
> *Go and Hush the Baby*, illustrated by Emily McCully.   New York, Viking Press, 1971.
> *The House of Wings*, illustrated by Daniel Schwartz.   New York, Viking Press, 1972; London, Bodley Head, 1973.
> *The 18th Emergency*, illustrated by Robert Grossman.   New York, Viking Press, 1973; London, Bodley Head, 1974.
> *The Winged Colt of Casa Mia*, illustrated by Richard Cuffari.   New York, Viking Press, 1973; London, Bodley Head, 1974.
> *After the Goat Man*, illustrated by Ronald Himler.   New York, Viking Press, 1974; London, Bodley Head, 1975.
> *The Lace Snail*, illustrated by the author.   New York, Viking Press, 1975.
> *The T.V. Kid*, illustrated by Richard Cuffari.   New York, Viking Press, and London, Bodley Head, 1976.
> *The Pinballs*.   New York, Harper, and London, Bodley Head, 1977.

Betsy Byars comments:
   My books usually begin with something that really happened, a newspaper story or an event from my children's lives. But, aside from this mutual starting-point, each book has

been a different writing experience. My daughter once described one of my books by saying, "Mom just made it up as she went along." That was true, but in another book I wrote the end first and worked back.

It takes me about a year to write a book, but I spend another year thinking about it and polishing it. Living with my own teenagers has taught me that not only must I not write down to my readers, I must write up to them. Boys and girls are very sharp today, and when I visit classrooms and talk with students I am always impressed to find how many of them are writing stories and how knowledgeable they are about writing.

*   *   *

Betsy Byars won the Newbery Medal for her book *The Summer of the Swans*. It is a strong and sensitive book and epitomizes the best qualities of Miss Byars' writing. It has a consistently objective point of view, a quick and incisive style, startling realistic details of scene and characterization, and a sustained presentational quality that is almost painterly. This quality dovetails remarkably well with the tone of the book. Although Miss Byars is working with emotionally high-keyed social and moral issues, she disavows moralism. She presents characters and issues realistically and impersonally and allows the reader to make his own judgments.

The two main characters in *The Summer of the Swans* are Charlie and his sister Sara. Charlie does things, but he doesn't do them quite right. In getting out of a tent, he pulls at one side causing the other to snap loose; he stumbles a little. While eating a lollipop, he bends the stick beyond recognition and the sucker comes off repeatedly. These are the types of things every child has done once or twice in his life, and for that reason a child can sympathize with Charlie. What makes Charlie different, however, is the fact that he always does things slightly askew of what one expects of a ten-year-old – he is retarded. But the beauty of his characterization is the quiet understated way in which his little mistakes build up to portray a child, fully meriting the sympathy and affection he gets, not in spite of what he is, but because of what he is. Charlie's sister Sara is, for the majority of the book, a foil for him. Sara is defeatist; she styles herself "hung up," and has the potential of being a loser, at least in her own estimation, because she too makes little mistakes. But she is extremely aware of her mistakes and those of the people around her. She is, in fact, a sensitive child; but that word, at best, is ambivalent. Sensitivity can imply the type of person who constantly holds his fingers to his pulse asking "How do I feel? How did I feel a minute ago? How will I feel in the future?" Or it can apply to the person who is sensitive to his environment, perceptively aware, intaking, synthesizing and appreciating his surroundings. The fascinating quality of Sara's characterization is the subtle shift from the former to the latter; and again, this is done with such a lightness of touch that the shift is barely perceptible. All the reader knows is that Byars has skillfully set up a character who has the potential of being an introverted onlooker, and finally portrays a girl who grows a little when she realizes that she is in fact altruistic, loving, and unselfishly involved in the life of her retarded brother. She also learns to develop a slightly ironic point of view knowing that "A person ... can occasionally be mistaken." There are other well developed characters in *The Summer of the Swans*, and the entire novel is unified by Byars' detailed sense of place and time.

One is tempted to say of Betsy Byars' work that, like the little girl with the curl in the middle of her forehead, when she is good, she is very, very good. This does not mean that when she is bad she is horrid. Like all either-or propositions that is too simplistic and demeaning. She occasionally falters, in works such as *The 18th Emergency*, *The T.V. Kid* and *The Winged Colt of Casa Mia*, when the tone shifts and when moral implications become too patent or too fluctuating. However, the works are never didactic, and in two picture books, *The Lace Snail* and *Go and Hush the Baby*, Byars achieves the same presentational quality that makes *The Summer of the Swans* so fluid and unified. *Go and Hush the Baby* is about a somewhat over-worked mother, a young boy with a vaulting imagination, and, of course, a baby. The book is based on a series of repeated sequences in which (1) the baby fusses, (2) the mother tells the boy to go hush the baby, and (3) he does. The structure and style are simple, and the repetitiveness and predictability would be soothing to a young listening audience. What makes the work remarkable is the wide variety of very original and imaginative tricks the boy uses to hush the baby – all are fun, but none is unbelievably exaggerated. Essentially, the book is a low-keyed argument for creativity with no moral stated. *The Lace Snail* is both written and illustrated by Byars. Again, she relies heavily on the technique of repetition in structure, and variation in detail, image, and intensity. A snail is constantly asked to supply lace for a wide variety of creatures, which she does, trying to adopt her gift to the needs and personality of the receiver. For instance she makes "heavy strong lace for the hippopotamus's size and light fine lace for the hippopotamus's nature." The themes of possessiveness, selfishness, and selflessness are lightly handled, and dialogue is particularly consistent with the characters and situation. For such a short book, there is a high sense of drama, conflict, and impending doom tempered by the snail's refusal to pass judgment on her fellow creatures. Like many of Betsy Byars' characters she is intrinsically fair and honest and a bit phenomenological. The burden of her story might be a catch phrase for the majority of Byars' work. The snail says "I don't know how I move. I don't know how I breathe. And I don't know how I make lace .... It's just the way life is, I think."

—Rachel Fordyce

CAMERON, Eleanor (Butler). American. Born in Winnipeg, Manitoba, Canada, 23 March 1912. Educated at the University of California, Los Angeles, 2 years; Art Center School, Los Angeles, one year. Married Ian Stuart Cameron in 1934; has one son. Library Clerk, Los Angeles Public Library, 1930–36, and Los Angeles Schools Library, 1936–42; Special Librarian, Foote Cone and Belding Advertising, Los Angeles, 1942–43; Research Librarian, Honig Cooper and Harrington Advertising, Los Angeles, 1956–58. Recipient: *Boston Globe-Horn Book* Award, 1971; National Book Award, 1974. Lives in Pebble Beach, California. Agent: Lavinia Trevor, 1 Cleveland Square, London W2 6DH, England. Address: c/o E.P. Dutton and Co. Inc., 201 Park Avenue South, New York, New York 10003, U.S.A.

PUBLICATIONS FOR CHILDREN

Fiction

> *The Wonderful Flight to the Mushroom Planet*, illustrated by Robert Henneberger. Boston, Little Brown, 1954.
> *Stowaway to the Mushroom Planet*, illustrated by Robert Henneberger. Boston, Little Brown, 1956.
> *Mr. Bass's Planetoid*, illustrated by Louis Darling. Boston, Little Brown, 1958.
> *The Terrible Churnadryne*, illustrated by Beth and Joe Krush. Boston, Little Brown, 1959.
> *A Mystery for Mr. Bass*, illustrated by Leonard Shortall. Boston, Little Brown, 1960.
> *The Mysterious Christmas Shell*, illustrated by Beth and Joe Krush. Boston, Little Brown, 1961.
> *The Beast with the Magical Horn*, illustrated by Beth and Joe Krush. Boston, Little Brown, 1963.
> *A Spell Is Cast*, illustrated by Beth and Joe Krush. Boston, Little Brown, 1964.
> *Time and Mr. Bass*, illustrated by Fred Meise. Boston, Little Brown, 1967.
> *A Room Made of Windows*, illustrated by Trina Schart Hyman. Boston, Little Brown, 1971; London, Gollancz, 1972.

The Court of the Stone Children. New York, Dutton, 1973.
To the Green Mountains. New York, Dutton, 1975.
Julia and the Hand of God, illustrated by Gail Owens. New York, Dutton, 1977.

PUBLICATIONS FOR ADULTS

Other

The Green and Burning Tree: On the Writing and Enjoyment of Children's Books. Boston, Little Brown, 1969.

Manuscript Collection: Kerlan Collection, University of Minnesota, Minneapolis.

Eleanor Cameron comments:
Why write for children? Because, for some unexplainable reason, what the children's writer has to say, the stories he has to tell, come forth most naturally and fully and freely when related to the memories and emotions of childhood. The writer for children is most deeply released when speaking out of his own childhood (at least using autobiographical feelings), and yet his work must be as good for adults as it is for children. This cannot be stressed too much. He will, just as in writing for adults, give the best of himself and demand the best of himself. If this seems an obvious statement, it is astonishing how many otherwise intelligent people believe that it is a matter of writing down when one writes for children. This idea is, of course, insulting. Yet a young woman once told my husband very seriously that she was spending four hours a day, apart from an eight-hour job, in trying to write for children, and that she supposed the main problem was in learning how to write down properly. She should have heard Dorothy Parker's remark, concerning fiction writing in general, "It's going to be the best you can do, and it's the fact that it's the best you can do that kills you." However, in my last three novels, *A Room Made of Windows*, *The Court of the Stone Children*, and especially in *To the Green Mountains* I have found passages with which I'm not too dissatisfied.

*   *   *

Eleanor Cameron has been slow to receive the recognition she deserves. Perhaps her reputation was hurt by her breaking into print initially as a writer of juvenile science fiction, a genre only now being accepted. Perhaps, too, Cameron's role as a critic of children's books unafraid of established reputations has been held against her. In any case, a look at the quality and variety of Cameron's books and the ample signs of her continuing artistic growth should suffice to convince the disinterested observer that Cameron is a major author of children's fiction.

The Mushroom Planet books, which first brought Cameron success, continue to be popular, and for good reason: they are entertainingly written, contain lively incidents, skillfully employ some of the more immediately attractive conventions of science fiction, and feature characters, e.g., David, Chuck, and Tyco Bass, easy to identify with and like. Already evident also in these narratives is Cameron's skill in describing physical setting and suggesting the close relationship that can exist between place and character. If the Mushroom Planet books show that Cameron can tell a good story, the next several novels reveal an author deliberately seeking to broaden her scope and hone her narrative skills. For instance, *The Terrible Churnadryne*, a fantasy, breaks loose from the constraints of science fiction. Plotting becomes realistic, as *The Mysterious Christmas Shell* aptly illustrates, rejecting a dependence on magic and extrapolated technology. Theme moves into the foreground, most notably in *A Spell Is Cast*, and tends to focus on problems peculiar to growing up.

A Room Made of Windows marks the end of Cameron's apprenticeship and her emergence as an important writer. Capturing the emotional and psychological nuances of pre-adolescence, the novel describes Julia's learning to make her thoughts and feelings "windows" into her deepest self and then outward toward the world around her. The novel also depicts Julia's difficulty in accepting her mother's re-marriage as well as her fondly remembered father's inadequacies. (Incidentally, *A Room Made of Windows* is one of the few presentations – and the best by an American – of the genesis of a writer that children can comprehend.) *The Court of the Stone Children* and *To the Green Mountains* continue her exploration of feminine pre-adolescence. In the former, which combines elements of fantasy, ghost story and mystery, Nina learns that history and art can not only give immediacy to the past but heighten her perceptions and structure her life. In *To the Green Mountains*, Kath grows up, against a background of small town life at its best and worst, increasingly aware of the fact that ambitions and dreams are often thwarted because of inadequate self-knowledge, that fidelity and loyalty cannot always resolve conflicts, and that sexuality, expressed as well as repressed, does sometimes destroy. What Cameron will attempt next and its quality, obviously, cannot be known; but what she has already accomplished surely must rank her among the finest contemporary authors of children's fiction.

—Francis J. Molson

CARLSON, Natalie Savage. American. Born in Winchester, Virginia, 3 October 1906. Attended high school in California. Married Daniel Carlson in 1929; has two daughters. Reporter, *Morning Sun*, Long Beach, California, 1926–29. Recipient: New York *Herald Tribune* Festival award, 1952, 1954; Boys' Clubs of America award, 1955, 1956; Child Study Association of America award, 1966. Address: 17 Doral Mobile Home Villas, Clearwater, Florida 33515, U.S.A.

PUBLICATIONS FOR CHILDREN

Fiction

> *Alphonse, That Bearded One,* illustrated by Nicolas Mordvinoff. New York, Harcourt Brace, 1954.
> *Wings Against the Wind,* illustrated by Mircea Vasiliu. New York, Harper, 1956.
> *Hortense, The Cow for a Queen,* illustrated by Nicolas Mordvinoff. New York, Harcourt Brace, 1957.
> *The Happy Orpheline,* illustrated by Garth Williams. New York, Harcourt Brace, 1957; London, Blackie, 1960.
> *The Family under the Bridge,* illustrated by Garth Williams. New York, Harper, 1958; as *Under the Bridge,* London, Blackie, 1969.
> *A Brother for the Orphelines,* illustrated by Garth Williams. New York, Harper, 1959; London, Blackie, 1961.
> *Evangeline, Pigeon of Paris,* illustrated by Nicolas Mordvinoff. New York, Harcourt Brace, 1960; as *Pigeon of Paris,* London, Blackie, 1972.
> *The Tomahawk Family,* illustrated by Stephen Cook. New York, Harper, 1960; London, Hamish Hamilton, 1961.
> *The Song of the Lop-Eared Mule,* illustrated by Janina Domanska. New York, Harper, 1961.
> *Carnival in Paris,* illustrated by Fermin Rocker. New York, Harper, 1962; London, Blackie, 1964.
> *A Pet for the Orphelines,* illustrated by Fermin Rocker. New York, Harper, 1962; London, Blackie, 1963.

School Bell in the Valley, illustrated by Gilbert Riswold. New York, Harcourt Brace, 1963.

Jean-Claude's Island, illustrated by Nancy Eckholm Buckert. New York, Harper, 1963; London, Blackie, 1966.

The Orphelines in the Enchanted Castle, illustrated by Adrianna Saviozzi. New York, Harper, 1964; London, Blackie, 1965.

The Letter on the Tree, illustrated by John Kaufmann. New York, Harper, 1964; London, Blackie, 1967.

The Empty Schoolhouse, illustrated by John Kaufmann. New York, Harper, 1965.

Sailor's Choice, illustrated by George Loh. New York, Harper, 1966.

Chalou, illustrated by George Loh. New York, Harper, 1967; London, Blackie, 1968.

Luigi of the Streets, illustrated by Emily McCully. New York, Harper, 1967; as *The Family on the Waterfront*, London, Blackie, 1969.

Ann Aurelia and Dorothy, illustrated by Dale Payson. New York, Harper, 1968.

Befana's Gift, illustrated by Robert Quackenbush. New York, Harper, 1969; as *A Grandson for the Asking*, London, Blackie, 1969.

Marchers for the Dream, illustrated by Alvin Smith. New York, Harper, 1969; London, Blackie, 1971.

The Half Sisters, illustrated by Thomas di Grazia. New York, Harper, 1970; London, Blackie, 1972.

Luvvy and the Girls, illustrated by Thomas di Grazia. New York, Harper, 1971.

Marie Louise and Christophe, illustrated by Jose Aruego and Ariane Dewey. New York, Scribner, 1974.

Marie Louise's Heydey, illustrated by Jose Aruego and Ariane Dewey. New York, Scribner, 1975.

Runaway Marie Louise, illustrated by Jose Aruego and Ariane Dewey. New York. Scribner, 1977.

Other

The Talking Cat and Other Stories of French Canada, illustrated by Roger Duvoisin. New York, Harper, 1952.

Sashes Red and Blue, illustrated by Rita Fava. New York, Harper, 1956.

Manuscript Collections: Kerlan Collection, University of Minnesota, Minneapolis; de Grummond Collection, University of Southern Mississippi, Hattiesburg.

*   *   *

Natalie Savage Carlson acknowledges that she sought professional training to learn to write. Though this training may account for her well-structured books, her inherent ability is reflected in her graceful style and her amused and amusing observations of human behavior. Her writing has a genial overtone, derived perhaps partly from her childhood in the American South and partly from her French-Canadian roots.

One of her early books, *The Talking Cat and Other Stories of French Canada*, consists of tales told to her mother by a French relative, Michel Meloche. Her version of a well-known French-Canadian folktale about the skunk in the kitchen is a good example of her warm style and gentle humor. Another book in the same temper is *The Song of the Lop-Eared Mule* in which Janina Domanska's illustrations synchronize nicely with the story.

Perhaps her most successful work is *The Family under the Bridge*, a story which developed during an extended stay in Paris. Here, for instance, the tramp, Armand, feeds on the rich odours from a restaurant: "For two hours, Armand sat on the curb enjoying the food smells, because that is the length of time a Frenchman allows himself for lunch in the middle of the day. Then he daintily wiped his whiskered lips with his cuff and rose ...."

Another popular book which grew out of her Paris experience is *The Happy Orpheline*, with pictures by Garth Williams. The plot has a clever twist: in an orphanage outside Paris, twenty orphans don't want to be adopted, as they are happy where they are!

She attempts always to tell a story which no one else has done, or at least one which she feels she is especially able to do well. Some wry satire can be detected in *Alphonse, That Bearded One*, in which a trained bear masquerades successfully as a soldier and helps bring peace with the Indians. Less successful are her attempts to adapt her talent to social needs, as in *The Empty Schoolhouse* and *Marchers for the Dream*. *The Half Sisters* is semi-autobiographical, and an interesting account of how truth is adapted to the fictional form has been written by her daughter, Dr. Julie Carlson McAlpine (*Children's Literature*, 1976). In his work *The Nesbit Tradition: The Children's Novel, 1945–70*, Marcus Crouch praises Mrs. Carlson highly for her effortless lightness of touch and fine dialogue.

—Francelia Butler

CARTER, Bruce. Pseudonym for Richard Alexander Hough. British. Born in Brighton, Sussex, 15 May 1922. Educated at Frensham Heights School, Farnham, Surrey, 1931–40. Served as a Fighter Pilot in the Royal Air Force, 1941–45. Married Helen Charlotte Woodyatt (i.e., Charlotte Hough, *q.v.*) in 1943; has four children. General Manager and Children's Books Editor, The Bodley Head, London, 1946–55; Managing Director, Hamish Hamilton Books for Children, London, 1955–70. Chairman, Auxiliary Hospitals Committee, King Edward's Hospital Fund, 1975. Member of the Council, Navy Records Society, 1970–73 and since 1975. Recipient: *Daily Express* Best Book of the Sea Award, 1972. Agent: Curtis Brown Ltd., 1 Craven Hill, London W.2. Address: 25 St. Ann's Terrace, London NW8 6PH, England.

PUBLICATIONS FOR CHILDREN

Fiction

> *The Perilous Descent into a Strange Lost World*, illustrated by Tony Weare. London, Lane, 1952; as *Into a Strange Lost World*. New York, Crowell, 1953.
> *Speed Six!*, illustrated by Tony Weare. London, Lane, 1953; New York, Harper, 1956.
> *Peril on the Iron Road*, illustrated by Charlotte Hough. London, Hamish Hamilton, 1953.
> *Gunpowder Tunnel*, illustrated by Charlotte Hough. London, Hamish Hamilton, 1955.
> *Target Island*, illustrated by Tony Weare. London, Hamish Hamilton, 1956; New York, Harper, 1957; revised edition, Hamish Hamilton, 1967.
> *Juliet in Publishing* (as Elizabeth Churchill). London, Lane, 1956.
> *Tricycle Tim*, illustrated by Prudence Seward. London, Hamish Hamilton, 1957.
> *The Kidnapping of Kensington*, illustrated by C. Walter Hodges. London, Hamish Hamilton, and New York, Harper, 1958; as *The Children Who Stayed Behind*. London, Penguin, 1964.
> *Four-Wheel Drift*. London, Bodley Head, and New York, Harper, 1959; revised edition, London, Heinemann, 1973.
> *The Night of the Flood*, illustrated by Prudence Seward. London, Hamish Hamilton, 1959.
> *Ballooning Boy*, illustrated by Prudence Seward. London, Hamish Hamilton, 1960.
> *The Motorway Chase*, illustrated by Bernard Wragg. London, Hamish Hamilton, 1961.

The Plane Wreckers (as Pat Strong), illustrated by Bernard Wragg.   London, Hamish Hamilton, 1961.

Fast Circuit.   London, Hamish Hamilton, and New York, Harper, 1962.

The Playground, illustrated by Prudence Seward.   London, Hamish Hamilton, 1964.

The Airfield Man.   London, Hamish Hamilton, 1965; New York, Coward McCann, 1966.

The Gannet's Nest, illustrated by Constance Marshall.   London, Hamish Hamilton, 1966.

B Flight.   London, Hamish Hamilton, 1970.

Upley United, illustrated by Harry Bloom.   London, Heinemann, 1972.

The Deadly Freeze.   London, Dent, 1976.

Buzzbugs.   London, Dent, and New York, Warne, 1977.

Other

Motor Racing: A Guide for the Younger Enthusiast, with Michael Frostick.   London, Lane, 1955.

The Wright Brothers.   London, Newnes, 1955.

Neville Duke.   London, Newnes, 1955.

Tim Baker, Motor Mechanic: A Career Book.   London, Chatto and Windus, 1957.

Nuvolari and the Alfa Romeo, illustrated by Raymond Briggs.   London, Hamish Hamilton, and New York, Coward McCann, 1968.

Jimmy Murphy and the White Dusenberg, illustrated by Raymond Briggs.   London, Hamish Hamilton, and New York, Coward McCann, 1968.

The Battle of Midway (as Richard Hough).   New York, Macmillan, and London, Collier Macmillan, 1970.

The Battle of Britain (as Richard Hough).   New York, Macmillan, and London, Collier Macmillan, 1971.

The Bike Racers (reader), illustrated by John Crawley.   London, Longman, 1974.

Galapagos: The Enchanted Islands (as Richard Hough), illustrated by Charlotte Hough.   London, Dent, and Reading, Massachusetts, Addison Wesley, 1975.

Editor, *Great Motor Races.*   London, Weidenfeld and Nicolson, 1960; as *Great Auto Races*, New York, Harper, 1961.

PUBLICATIONS FOR ADULTS (as Richard Hough)

Novel

The Fighter.   London, Joseph, 1963.

Other

Six Great Railwaymen: Stephenson, Hudson, Denison, Huish, Stephen, Gresley.   London, Hamish Hamilton, 1955.

Tourist Trophy: The History of Britain's Greatest Motor Race.   London, Hutchinson, 1957.

W.O.: An Autobiography, with Walter Owen Bentley.   London, Hutchinson, 1958.

The Fleet That Had to Die.   London, Hamish Hamilton, and New York, Viking Press, 1958; abridged edition, London, Chatto and Windus, 1963.

British Grand Prix: A History.   London, Hutchinson, 1958.

Admirals in Collision.   London, Hamish Hamilton, and New York, Viking Press, 1959.

B.P. Book of the Racing Campbells.   London, Stanley Paul, 1960.

The Potemkin Mutiny.   London, Hamish Hamilton, 1960; New York, Pantheon Books, 1961.

Sky Fever, with Geoffrey de Havilland.   London, Hamish Hamilton, 1961.

A History of the World's Motorcycles, with L.J.K. Setright.   London, Allen and Unwin, 1960; New York, Harper, 1966; revised edition, Allen and Unwin, and Harper, 1973.

A History of the World's Sports Cars, with Michael Frostick.   London, Allen and Unwin, and New York, Harper, 1961.

A History of the World's Classic Cars, with Michael Frostick.   London, Allen and Unwin, and New York, Harper, 1963.

The Hunting of Force Z.   London, Collins, 1963; as *Death of the Battleship*, New York, Macmillan, 1963.

Dreadnought: A History of the Modern Battleship.   New York, Macmillan, 1964; London, Joseph, 1965; revised edition, Cambridge, Stephens, and New York, Macmillan, 1975.

The Battle of Jutland.   London, Hamish Hamilton, 1964.

A History of the World's Racing Cars, with Michael Frostick.   London, Allen and Unwin, and New York, Harper, 1965.

Rover Memories: An Illustrated Survey of the Rover Car, with Michael Frostick.   London, Allen and Unwin, 1966.

The Big Battleship; or, The Curious Career of H.M.S. Agincourt.   London, Joseph, 1966; as *The Great Dreadnought: The Strange Story of the H.M.S. Agincourt, The Mightiest Battleship of World War I*, New York, Harper, 1967.

Racing Cars.   London, Hamlyn, 1967.

A History of the World's High Performance Cars, with Michael Frostick.   London, Allen and Unwin, and New York, Harper, 1967.

Fighting Ships.   London, Joseph, and New York, Putnam, 1969.

First Sea Lord: An Authorised Biography of Admiral Lord Fisher.   London, Allen and Unwin, 1969; revised edition, London, Severn House, 1977; as *Admiral of the Fleet: The Life of John Fisher*, New York, Macmillan, 1970.

The Pursuit of Admiral von Spee.   London, Allen and Unwin, 1969; as *The Long Pursuit*, New York, Harper, 1969.

The Blind Horn's Hate.   London, Hutchinson, and New York, Norton, 1971.

Captain Bligh and Mr. Christian: The Men and the Mutiny.   London, Hutchinson, 1972; New York, Dutton, 1973.

Louis and Victoria: The First Mountbattens.   London, Hutchinson, 1974; as *The Mountbattens*, New York, Dutton, 1975.

One Boy's War: Per Astra Ad Ardua (autobiography).   London, Heinemann, 1975.

Great Admirals.   London, Weidenfeld and Nicolson, and New York, Morrow, 1977.

Editor, *First and Fastest: A Collection of the World's Great Motor Races.*   London, Allen and Unwin, 1963; as *First and Fastest: A Collection of Accounts of the World's Greatest Auto Races*, New York, Harper, 1964.

Editor, *The Enzo Ferrari Memoirs: My Terrible Joys*, by Enzo Ferrari, translated by Ivan Scott.   London, Hamish Hamilton, 1963.

Editor, *The Motor Car Lover's Companion.*   London, Allen and Unwin, and New York, Harper, 1965.

Editor, *Advice to a Grand-daughter: Letters from Queen Victoria to Princess Victoria of Hesse.*   London, Heinemann, and New York, Simon and Schuster, 1975.

Bruce Carter comments:

My writing for children stems directly from, first, the tastes of my own children, and, second, from my experience as an editor of children's books. (I started the Bodley Head children's list in 1947, the Hamish Hamilton list in 1955, and participated as a consultant editor in the redevelopment of the Heinemann list 1971–76.) Except for one or two educational books, my adventure books, historical novels, science fiction (my first *and* most recent) and motor racing stories reflect my own enthusiasms, which have been widely varied, from flying in the war to canoeing on old canals, from long-distance bicycling to ornithology. It they have had any success, I think it must be because I enormously enjoy writing them, and always turn back to writing them with relief and delight after a long, heavily researched adult work.

*   *   *

Most of Bruce Carter's stories centre on mechanical transport, and the amount of technical detail increases with the age range of the readers. His adult books are non-fiction on the same themes, suggesting sound knowledge.

His stories, even for the youngest readers, are vigorous and lively. Tim, in *Tricycle Tim*, is lost, though he hardly realises it, and Jim and Bryony in *The Gannet's Nest*, too young to appreciate the very real danger, are rescued at the vital moment. Boisterous older children fend for themselves in Robinson Crusoe situations in *Target Island* and *The Kidnapping of Kensington*. For teenage readers there are car-racing stories full of thrills and spills where the characters are all adult.

Carter's first and his most recent books – *The Perilous Descent into a Strange Lost World* and *The Deadly Freeze* – are both science fiction, two lively thrillers where the imaginative used of technology mixed with fantasy blends with politics.

Two historical novels – *Peril on the Iron Road* and *Gunpowder Tunnel* – are carefully researched accounts of tunnel building for an early railway and a pioneer canal. Local opposition is strong in both cases, but trouble in *Gunpowder Tunnel* comes from the rival contractor. Both have plenty of excitement – battles with and amongst miners and attempts to blow up the tunnels. The young people succeed in foiling the plans of the villains, but in neither book do the characters wholly convince the reader.

The car-racing stories – *Speed Six!*, *Four-Wheel Drift*, *Fast Circuit*, and the two imaginative reconstructions of real races, *Jimmy Murphy and the White Dusenberg* and *Nuvolari and the Alfa Romeo* – are good examples of the genre, by an enthusiast for enthusiasts. Team work and brilliant driving succeed against all odds, but heroism also has its place. Unfortunately, with its lower standards, big business is also involved in motor-racing; unscrupulous rivals extend the dimensions of the plot. Yet Carter shows, for instance in *Nuvolari*, that he can write a really gripping fast-moving story in quite simple language by concentrating on the race and the personality of the driver only.

Carter's best books are his air stories – *B Flight* and *The Airfield Man*. Here technicalities are submerged beneath the personalities of the characters – Will, flying fighter planes in the First World War; Simon's father, a failure as the proprietor of a hardware shop who only really lived as a wartime pilot; the deranged farmer.

Tricycle Tim and *The Kidnapping of Kensington* have a strong comic line.

War is never glorified, heroes are heroic not through bravado but through determination, and often the ending is wistful rather than happy.

—Margaret M. Tye

CARTER, Peter. British. Born in Manchester, Lancashire, in 1929. Educated at Oxford University (Mature State Scholar, 1958). Apprentice in the building trade, 1942–49; teacher in Birmingham. Address: c/o Oxford University Press, Walton Street, Oxford OX2 6DP, England.

PUBLICATIONS FOR CHILDREN

Fiction

   The Black Lamp, illustrated by David Harris.   London, Oxford University Press, 1973;
      Nashville, Nelson, 1975.
   The Gates of Paradise, illustrated by Fermin Rocker.   London, Oxford University
      Press, 1974.
   Madatan, illustrated by Victor Ambrus.   London, Oxford University Press, 1974.
   Under Goliath.   London, Oxford University Press, 1977.

Other

   Mao.   London, Oxford University Press, 1976.

*   *   *

Peter Carter has established himself with his historical novels as a writer of distinction. His themes are diverse. *The Black Lamp*, his first novel, tells of the supplanting of hand looms by machines in the Lancashire of the early 1800's and the events that culminated in the Peterloo massacre, and is thereby an important contribution to the growing number of historical novels written from the point of view of ordinary working people. *Madatan* is the tale of a Celt captured by Vikings, converted to Christianity in Northumbria, and then used as a pawn in the power struggles of the corrupt Church. In *The Gates of Paradise* Carter attempts a portrait of William Blake and thereby comes up against one of the most challenging and oft-avoided problems for the historical novelist – how to present a well-known historical figure as a person. Carter's Blake is a compassionate man who takes in a runaway apprentice and later the ruined tradesman who tried to report him for revolutionary activities. We see Blake the visionary and Blake the humanitarian, but Carter's portrait lacks the fiery genius of this most extraordinary man of art and letters. Carter's skilful weaving of invention with fact results, however, in a compelling book that will inspire young readers to seek out Blake's works for themselves.

The variety and complexity of Carter's work so far reveal him to be a writer of talent and scope. His novels are characterised by solid and credible historical backgrounds against which the reader can grasp, for example, the hardships of the Lancashire weavers' threatened way of life, the impact of Christian ideas on a Celtic convert, the mysterious inspiration of the great poet and artist William Blake. Peter Carter's particular skill lies in his ability to capture the reader's interest in and respect for the issues of the past by presenting them as burningly credible and immediate to those involved in them.

—Rosemary Stones

CATHERALL, Arthur.   British.   Born in Bolton, Lancashire, 6 February 1906. Served in the Royal Air Force, 1940–45: Staff Officer. Married Elizabeth Benson in 1936; has one daughter and one son. Agent: Leresche and Steele, 11 Jubilee Place, London SW3 3TE. Address: 31 Parkgate Drive, Bolton, Lancashire BL1 8SD, England.

PUBLICATIONS FOR CHILDREN

Fiction

   Rod o' the Rail.   London, Pearson, 1936.

The Rival Tugboats.   London, Partridge, 1937.
Adventurer's Ltd.   London, A. and C. Black, 1938.
Black Gold.   London, Pearson, 1939.
Vanished Whaler, illustrated by S. Drigin.   London, Nelson, 1939.
Phantom Patrol (as A.R. Channel).   London, Collins, 1940.
Keepers of the Khyber.   London, Nelson, 1940.
Lost with All Hands.   London, Nelson, 1940.
Raid on Heligoland.   London, Collins, 1940.
The Flying Submarine.   London, Collins, 1942.
The River of Burning Sand.   London, Collins, 1947.
The Bull Patrol.   London, Lutterworth Press, 1949.
Riders of the Black Camel.   Bath, Venturebooks, 1949.
Cock o' the Town, illustrated by Kenneth Brookes.   London, Boy Scouts Association, 1950.
Wings for a Gull.   London and New York, Warne, 1951.
Kidnapped in Kandy (as Margaret Ruthin), illustrated by C. Cane.   London, Blackie, 1951.
The Ring of the Prophet (as Margaret Ruthin).   London and New York, Warne, 1953.
Pirate Sealer.   London, Collins, 1953.
Shanghaied!   London, Collins, 1954.
Ten Fathoms Deep, illustrated by Geoffrey Whittam.   London, Dent, 1954; New York, Criterion Books, 1968.
White Horse of Hungary (as Margaret Ruthin).   London and New York, Warne, 1954.
Strange Safari (as Margaret Ruthin).   London and New York, Warne, 1955.
Jackals of the Sea, illustrated by Geoffrey Whittam.   London, Dent, 1955.
The Scuttlers, illustrated by A. Bruce Cornwell and Drake Brookshaw.   London, Nelson, 1955.
Sea Wraith.   London, Lutterworth Press, 1955.
Wild Goose Saboteur, illustrated by Kenneth Brookes.   London, Dent, 1955.
Forgotten Submarine, illustrated by Geoffrey Whittam.   London, Dent, 1956.
Land under the White Robe, illustrated by Geoffrey Whittam.   London, Dent, 1956.
Jamboree Challenge, illustrated by Kenneth Brookes.   London, Dent, and New York, Roy, 1957.
Java Sea Duel, illustrated by Geoffrey Whittam.   London, Dent, 1957.
Jungle Trap, illustrated by Paul Hogarth.   London, Dent, 1958; New York, Roy, 1968.
Coral Reef Castaway (as Peter Hallard), illustrated by Terence Greer.   London, Phoenix House, 1958; New York, Criterion Books, 1960.
Tenderfoot Trapper, illustrated by Edward Osmond.   London, Dent, 1958; New York, Criterion Books, 1959.
Sea Wolves, illustrated by Geoffrey Whittam.   London, Dent, and New York, Roy, 1959.
A Shark on the Saltings (as Dan Corby).   London, Parrish, 1959.
The Little Sealer (as Dan Corby).   London, Parrish, 1960; as *The Arctic Sealer*, New York, Criterion Books, 1961.
The Secret Pagoda (as Margaret Ruthin).   London and New York, Warne, 1960.
Jungle Nurse (as Margaret Ruthin), illustrated by Hugh Marshall.   London, Dobson, and New York, Watts, 1960.
Barrier Reef Bandits (as Peter Hallard), illustrated by Hugh Marshall.   London, Dobson, and New York, Criterion Books, 1960.
Dangerous Cargo, illustrated by Geoffrey Whittam.   London, Dent, 1960; New York, Roy, 1961.
Lapland Outlaw, illustrated by Fred Wood.   London, Dent, 1960; New York, Lothrop, 1966.
The Tunnel Busters (as A.R. Channel).   London, Collins, 1960.
The Million-Dollar Ice Floe (as A.R. Channel), illustrated by Eric Mudge-Marriott.   London, Dobson, 1961.

Operation V.2 (as A.R. Channel).   London, Collins, 1961.

Lost off the Grand Banks (as Dan Corby).   London, Parrish, 1961; New York, Criterion Books, 1962.

Reindeer Girl (as Margaret Ruthin), illustrated by Marie Whitby.   London, Dobson, 1961; as *Elli of the Northland*, New York, Farrar Straus, 1968.

Guardian of the Reef (as Peter Hallard), illustrated by Hugh Marshall.   London, Dobson, 1961.

Blue Veil and Black Gold (as Trevor Maine), illustrated by Richard Kennedy.   London, Odhams Press, 1961; New York, Roy, 1965.

China Sea Jigsaw, illustrated by Geoffrey Whittam.   London, Dent, 1961; New York, Roy, 1962.

Arctic Spy (as A.R. Channel), illustrated by Horace Gaffron.   London, Collins, 1962.

The Forgotten Patrol (as A.R. Channel).   London, Collins, 1962.

The Rogue Elephant (as A.R. Channel), illustrated by D.J. Watkins-Pitchford.   London, Dobson, 1962; Philadelphia, Macrae Smith, 1964.

Lapland Nurse (as Margaret Ruthin), illustrated by Marie Whitby.   London, Dobson, 1962.

Orphan Otter, illustrated by N. Osten-Sacken.   London, Dent, and New York, Harcourt Brace, 1962.

Vagabond Ape, illustrated by N. Osten-Sacken.   London, Dent, 1962.

Yugoslav Mystery, illustrated by Stuart Tresilian.   London, Dent, 1962; New York, Lothrop, 1964.

Man-Eater (as Dan Corby), illustrated by Richard Lewis.   London, Parrish, 1963; New York, Criterion Books, 1964.

Secret of the Shetlands (as Margaret Ruthin), illustrated by Gwen Gibson.   London, Dobson, 1963.

Prisoners under the Sea, illustrated by Geoffrey Whittam.   London, Dent, 1963.

Mission Accomplished (as A.R. Channel).   London, Collins, 1964.

Red Ivory (as A.R. Channel), illustrated by D.J. Watkins-Pitchford.   London, Dobson, and Philadelphia, Macrae Smith, 1964.

Thunder Dam (as Dan Corby), illustrated by Omar Davis.   London, Parrish, 1964; New York, Criterion Books, 1965.

Katrina of the Lonely Isles (as Margaret Ruthin), illustrated by Gwen Gibson.   London, Dobson, 1964; New York, Farrar Straus, 1965.

Lone Seal Pup, illustrated by Edward Osmond.   London, Dent, 1964; New York, Dutton, 1965.

The Strange Invader, illustrated by Stuart Tresilian.   London, Dent, 1964; as *The Strange Intruder*, New York, Lothrop, 1965.

Conqueror's Gold (as Dan Corby).   London, Parrish, 1965.

Tanker Trap, illustrated by Geoffrey Whittam.   London, Dent, 1965; New York, Roy, 1966.

Reindeer Rescue (as Linda Peters), illustrated by F.M. Johnson.   Leeds, E.J. Arnold, 1966.

Kidnapped on Stromboli (as Margaret Ruthin).   London, Dobson, 1966.

Sicilian Mystery, illustrated by Stuart Tresilian.   London, Dent, 1966; New York, Lothrop, 1967.

Jungle Rescue (as A.R. Channel), illustrated by D.J. Watkins-Pitchford.   London, Dobson, 1967; New York, Phillips, 1968.

A Zebra Came to Drink, illustrated by Edward Osmond.   London, Dent, and New York, Dutton, 1967.

Prisoners in the Snow, illustrated by Victor Ambrus.   London, Dent, and New York, Lothrop, 1967.

Death of an Oil Rig, illustrated by Geoffrey Whittam.   London, Dent, 1967; New York, Phillips, 1969.

Night of the Black Frost, illustrated by Roger Payne.   London, Dent, and New York, Lothrop, 1968.

Camel Caravan, illustrated by Joseph Papin. New York, Seabury Press, 1968; as *Desert Caravan,* London, Macdonald, 1969.

Kidnapped by Accident, illustrated by Victor Ambrus. London, Dent, 1968; New York, Lothrop, 1969.

Island of Forgotten Men, illustrated by Geoffrey Whittam. London, Dent, 1968.

Duel in the High Hills, illustrated by Stanley Smith. London, Dent, and New York, Lothrop, 1968.

Red Sea Rescue, illustrated by Victor Ambrus. London, Dent, 1969; New York, Lothrop, 1970.

Boy on a White Giraffe (as Peter Hallard), illustrated by Sheila Bewley. New York, Seabury Press, 1968; London, Macdonald, 1969.

Lost in Lapland (as Peter Hallard), illustrated by Judith Ann Lawrence. London, Macdonald, 1970; as *Puppy Lost in Lapland,* New York, Watts, 1971.

Hungarian Rebel (as Margaret Ruthin). London, Dobson, 1970.

Antlers of the King Moose, illustrated by Edward Mortelmans. London, Dent, and New York, Dutton, 1970.

The Big Tusker, illustrated by Douglas Phillips. London, Dent, and New York, Lothrop, 1970.

Keepers of the Cattle, illustrated by Bernard Brett. London, Dent, 1970.

Freedom for a Cheetah, illustrated by Shyam Varma. London, Dent, and New York, Lothrop, 1971.

Barracuda Mystery, illustrated by Gavin Rowe. London, Dent, 1971.

The Unwilling Smuggler, illustrated by Geoffrey Whittam. London, Dent, 1971.

Last Horse on the Sands, illustrated by David Farris. London, Dent, 1972; New York, Lothrop, 1973.

Kalu and the Wild Boar (as Peter Hallard), illustrated by W.T. Mars. New York, Watts, 1973.

Cave of the "Cormorant." London, Dent, 1973.

A Wolf from the Sky, illustrated by Derek Lucas. London, Dent, 1974.

Stranger on Wreck Buoy Sands. London, Dent, 1975.

Twelve Minutes to Disaster and Other Stories, illustrated by Derek Lucas. London, Dent, 1977.

The Ghost Elephant. London, Abelard Schuman, 1977.

The Last Run and Other Stories. London, Dent, 1977.

Other

Camp-Fire Stories and How to Tell Them. London, Jenkins, 1935.

The Steam and Steel Omnibus, with George W. Blow, illustrated by George W. Blow. London, Collins, 1950.

The Scout Story Omnibus. London, Collins, 1954.

The Young Baden-Powell, illustrated by William Randell. London, Parrish, 1961; New York, Roy, 1962.

Vanishing Lapland. New York, Watts, 1972.

PUBLICATIONS FOR ADULTS

Novels

Tomorrow's Hunter. London, Jenkins, 1950.

Vibrant Brass. London, Dent, 1954.

Singapore Sari (as J. Baltimore). Leicester, Fiction House, 1958.

No Bouquets for These. London, Tempest Press, 1958.

Play

Step in My Shoes, with David Reade (produced Southport, Lancashire, 1958).

Arthur Catherall comments:

As a young reader I always took for gospel whatever I got from a book. For that reason I have endeavoured throughout my life as a writer to be authentic. As far as possible I have been to the places where I set my stories. I have worked with young people for over forty years, and I have tried to get the feel of what they look for. You don't find any unnecessary clubbing or shooting in my books. Boys can be little savages without the inspiration of a story to start them off. They look for heroes in a story. I try to give them the right kind of heroes, for boys are great imitators.

*   *   *

Arthur Catherall, with his many pseudonyms, must be one of the most prolific of writers for the young, but the truly amazing thing is not so much the output as the consistently authentic standard, the fidelity to fact. The stories are all set in places which Arthur Catherall has personal knowledge of, so that although the scenes are immensely varied they are all authentic. And furthermore, he never cheats on plot in the time-honoured manner of "Spring-Heeled Jack" (for instance) who, tied to a stake amid flames and dancing savages simply bursts his bonds, leaps from the fire and speeds away amid a hail of arrows! No, Catherall takes no short cuts; he is as clever at extricating his hero from his predicament as he is at devising it.

Catherall served in World War II in various zones of action, including the Pacific; he has travelled in all parts of the British Commonwealth, Europe, North America, the Arctic – you name any place he has written about and he has been there. But his intimate knowledge of a region is no mere backcloth; it also provides the warp and weft of the plot. In other words, plot is intrinsic to place – that of *Red Sea Rescue* could never be adapted for a book about Sicily or Scotland, nor could *Jungle Trap* be adapted to the Arctic or Lancashire. Monsoons, floods, drug-smuggling, working elephants all belong to the India of *The Big Tusker*. Not only does the author know the climate and terrain but also the methods used by local smugglers, the behaviour of elephants and the way they work with timber. Every detail is thoroughly studied.

Catherall's mastery of the cliffhanger consists in exploiting to the full the hazards intrinsic to the scene and situation by bringing them into the narrative at the exact point where they will maximize the drama and create the greatest surprise.

Let us take a close look at one of his best animal stories. *Freedom for a Cheetah*. First the spellbinding atmosphere of the Indian plains. Dum-dum the cheetah had spent the two years of her life in a stable with only the occasional company of pariah dogs. The air had never been really clean. When her master hunted she was sent dashing across the dusty plains in pursuit of black buck. Now, a youth with a spite against her trainer offers the cheetah her freedom.

In the few minutes Dum-dum stood in the moonlight outside the yard gates ... she was filled with a new and a strange delight .... The light breeze she was now sniffing with such enjoyment brought scents and sounds which thrilled her. Somewhere a jackal was howling, and when he stopped a barking deer called. Both sounds were so far away that human ears could not have picked them up. Dum-dum heard them, and her eyes glowed .... Suddenly she knew what she wanted, and without a sound or a backward glance, she sprinted off in a direct line away from the big house. Her shapely paws threw up little puffs of dust which looked like smoke in the moonlight.

But freedom held many terrors for Dum-dum and the story follows her adventures with wild dogs, treacherous mud, hunger, tiger, cobra, bees, fire and finally men. Pursued by a pack of wild dogs, Dum-dum finds that the river mud which had almost fatally trapped her when first she was free now became her ally, for the dogs could not trust themselves to it. She held her position on a stepping-stone.

> As a team the wild dogs were almost unbeatable, and more than a match for any cheetah; but spread out on the stepping-stones they were not a team. The two dogs now in the path of the spitting, snarling Dum-dum refused to face her. One tried to retreat, and the other was swept into the water by a flailing blow from a powerful right paw. The other dog half turned, made a wild leap and went straight into the treacherous mud at the water's edge .... The pack began to withdraw, whining in their anxiety.

When children are the heroes, their ingenuity and intelligence are stretched to the full to deal with their predicament but always in a way that fits their young experience. In *Prisoners in the Snow* we are in the Austrian mountains. Two children are trapped with their grandfather in their farmhouse after an aeroplane crashing into the mountain causes an avalanche which buries the house in snow. Cows from the damaged cowshed have to be brought into the parlour and hay to feed them brought from the threatened hay loft; the injured pilot who bailed out has to be rescued from the roof — but the roof may collapse and it is a long fall. Grandfather assesses the risk:

> "Does that mean we can't help him?" Trudi asked, and there was a quiver in her voice.
>
> Her grandfather did not reply, but began scratching behind his right ear again.
>
> "I suppose we could bring down a lot of hay," he finally said. "That would break your fall; but I don't know that would be enough ...."
>
> "I know," and Toni's eyes were shining like stars in the lamplight at the idea which had suddenly come to him. "Do you remember when the circus came to the valley last year? There was a man who rode a bicycle across a tightrope. He carried a girl on his shoulders .... They had a net stretched underneath them —" Toni was interrupted by Trudi who gave an excited squeal and shouted:
>
> "Yes, a safety-net. I remember. I couldn't bear to look until Papa said that even if the man fell off neither he nor the girl would be hurt."

So they rig up a net, but the idea came quite naturally from the children's experience. And as will be seen from this example, the children's own excitement is yet another factor adding to the tension and excitement of the reader. It can be explicit in a way not possible in animal stories; but emotion never interferes or takes over.

Arthur Catherall in books such as the Bulldog series has written adventures with men as heroes: Jack Frodsham and Husky Hudson of the salvage tug *Bulldog* in the China seas. These resourceful fellows are always up against the same enemy, Karmey, an unscrupulous villain who is constantly balked of his plan to sink them. These are superb yarns, all the more satisfying because it is the same team of heroes being brought time and again to the brink of disaster but turning the tables on the same enemy. *Death of an Oil Rig*, *Island of Forgotten Men*, and *Ten Fathoms Deep* are a few of these marvellously thrilling novels.

It is a comment on our times that a writer of exciting adventures with real believable heroes is considered a writer for young people. To exploit the same talents in the adult market today he would have to write grisly whodunnits or novels with an anti-hero like Flashman. But this would not be Catherall at all. Throughout his long writing career he has always held up to his readers an image of a hero or heroine with courage, kindness, loyalty and spirit.

—Gwen Marsh

CAUDILL, Rebecca. American. Born in Poor Fork, Kentucky, 2 February 1899. Educated at Sumner County High School, Portland, Tennessee, graduated 1916; Wesleyan College, Macon, Georgia, 1916–20, B.A. in English 1920; Vanderbilt University, Nashville, 1921–22, M.A. 1922. Married James S. Ayars in 1931; has one daughter. English and history teacher, Sumner County High School, 1920–21; English teacher, Collegio Bennett, Rio de Janeiro, 1922–24; Editor, *Torchbearer* magazine, Nashville, 1924–30. Since 1967, Member of the Board of Trustees, Pine Mountain Settlement School, Kentucky. Address: 510 West Iowa Street, Urbana, Illinois 61801, U.S.A.

PUBLICATIONS FOR CHILDREN

Fiction

Barrie and Daughter, illustrated by Berkeley Williams. New York, Viking Press, 1943.
Happy Little Family, illustrated by Decie Merwin. Philadelphia, Winston, 1947.
Tree of Freedom, illustrated by Dorothy Bayley Morse. New York, Viking Press, 1949.
Schoolhouse in the Woods, illustrated by Decie Merwin. Philadelphia, Winston, 1949.
Up and Down the River, illustrated by Decie Merwin. Philadelphia, Winston, 1951.
Saturday Cousins, illustrated by Nancy Woltemate. Philadelphia, Winston, 1953.
The House of the Fifers, illustrated by Genia. New York, Longman, 1954.
Susan Cornish, illustrated by E. Harper Johnson. New York, Viking Press, 1955.
Schoolroom in the Parlor, illustrated by Decie Merwin. Philadelphia, Winston, 1959.
Time for Lissa, illustrated by Velma Ilsley. New York, Nelson, 1959.
Higgins and the Great Big Scare, illustrated by Beth Krush. New York, Holt Rinehart, 1960.
The Best-Loved Doll, illustrated by Elliott Gilbert. New York, Holt Rinehart, 1962.
The Far-Off Land, illustrated by Brinton Turkle. New York, Viking Press, 1964; London, Hart Davis, 1965.
A Pocketful of Cricket, illustrated by Evaline Ness. New York, Holt Rinehart, 1964; London, Harrap, 1966.
A Certain Small Shepherd, illustrated by William Pène du Bois. New York, Holt Rinehart, 1965; Edinburgh, Oliver and Boyd, 1966.
Did You Carry the Flag Today, Charley?, illustrated by Nancy Grossman. New York, Holt Rinehart, 1966.
Contrary Jenkins, with James S. Ayars, illustrated by Glen Rounds. New York, Holt Rinehart, 1969.
Somebody Go and Bang a Drum, illustrated by Jack Hearne. New York, Dutton, 1974.

Verse

Come Along!, illustrated by Ellen Raskin. New York, Holt Rinehart, 1969.
Wind, Sand, and Sky, illustrated by Donald Carrick. New York, Dutton, 1976.

Other

Florence Nightingale, illustrated by William Neebe. Evanston, Illinois, Row Peterson, 1953.
My Appalachia: A Reminiscence. New York, Holt Rinehart, 1966.

PUBLICATIONS FOR ADULTS

Other

The High Cost of Writing. Cumberland, Kentucky, Southeast Community College, 1965.

Manuscript Collections: University of Kentucky, Lexington; Kerlan Collection, University of Minnesota, Minneapolis.

Rebecca Caudill comments:

My writing for children – even the rewriting – has been an exercise in joy. Most of my books are based on experiences of my own childhood spent in Appalachian Kentucky, and so are written from the heart. The response from children has been most gratifying.

*   *   *

Significant in Rebecca Caudill's novels for older children and her stories for younger ones is the part that setting plays. Child protagonists are usually hill children from Appalachia, their lives largely determined by the setting in which they live. Pioneers and early settlers live in wild surroundings, their simple and rugged homes determining the nature of their lives. In clear descriptions that work smoothly with the action, Caudill convinces the reader of the importance of place and time – 18th or 19th century America.

Well defined conflicts in Caudill's novels for older children frequently show a girl protagonist struggling with a desire to be an individual, to maintain her principles without losing her friendships. The omniscient point of view keeps the reader fully informed about all that the heroine thinks. With action, suspense, and careful attention to historical detail, Caudill builds the story to a climax and leaves the reader satisfied. Although the romance is idealized and a bit sentimental, Caudill's teen-age girls are individuals, clearly and believably defined. Pioneer families are warm and relationships deftly sketched; parents, who might seem stern and workridden, are human and admirable.

The most notable stylistic element in Caudill's books for older children is the authentic-sounding mountain diction of the characters. Not overdone, the dialect does not call attention to itself. Although Caudill's themes are highly moralistic – behave as conscience requires, be yourself rather than a conformist – they are not didactic.

Stories for younger children show understanding of the wondering child amused by and amazed at the ordinary, simple things. Quiet, rural children gathering pinto beans and crickets, noting snakes and pretty rocks are her characters. Caudill's use of the haiku, however, as text for some of her picture books is disappointing, for the verses fail either to surprise or to intensify the vision glimpsed. Caudill's skill lies in her stories of Appalachia.

—Rebecca J. Lukens

CAUSLEY, Charles (Stanley).   British.   Born in Launceston, Cornwall, 24 August 1917. Educated at Launceston National School; Horwell Grammar School; Launceston College; Peterborough Training College. Served in the Royal Navy, 1940–46. Since 1947, has taught in Cornwall. Honorary Visiting Fellow in Poetry, University of Exeter, 1973–74. Literary Editor of BBC radio magazines, *Apollo in the West* and *Signature*, 1953–56. Member of the Arts Council Poetry (later Literature) Panel, 1962–66. Vice-President, West Country Writers' Association; Vice-President, The Poetry Society, London. Recipient: Society of Authors travelling scholarship, 1954, 1966; Queen's Gold Medal for Poetry, 1967; Cholmondeley Award, for poetry, 1971. Fellow, Royal Society of Literature, 1958. Agent: David Higham Associates Ltd., 5–8 Lower John Street, London W1R 3PE. Address: 2 Cyprus Well, Launceston, Cornwall PL15 8BT, England.

PUBLICATIONS FOR CHILDREN

Verse

Figure of 8: Narrative Poems, illustrated by Peter Whiteman.   London, Macmillan, 1969.
Figgie Hobbin: Poems for Children, illustrated by Pat Marriott.   London, Macmillan, 1970; New York, Walker, 1973.
The Tail of the Trinosaur, illustrated by Jill Gardiner.   Leicester, Brockhampton Press, 1973.
As I Went Down Zig Zag, illustrated by John Astrop.   London and New York, Warne, 1974.
Here We Go Round the Round House, illustrated by Stanley Simmonds.   Leicester, New Broom Press, 1976.
The Hill of the Fairy Calf, illustrated by Robine Clignett.   London, Hodder and Stoughton, 1976.
The Animals' Carol, illustrated by Judith Bunker.   London, Macmillan, 1977.

Other

When Dad Felt Bad (reader), illustrated by Richard Rose.   London, Macmillan, 1975.
Dick Whittington, illustrated by Antony Maitland.   London, Penguin, 1976.

Editor, *Dawn and Dusk: Poems of Our Time*, illustrated by Gerald Wilkinson.   Leicester, Brockhampton Press, 1962; New York, Watts, 1963.
Editor, *Rising Early: Story Poems and Ballads of the 20th Century*, illustrated by Anne Netherwood.   Leicester, Brockhampton Press, 1964; as *Modern Ballads and Story Poems*, New York, Watts, 1965.
Editor, *In the Music I Hear: Poems by Children*.   Gillingham, Kent, ARC Press, 1970.
Editor, *Oats and Beans and Barley: Poems by Children*.   Gillingham, Kent, ARC Press, 1971.
Editor, *The Puffin Book of Magic Verse*, illustrated by Barbara Swiderska.   London, Penguin, 1974.

PUBLICATIONS FOR ADULTS

Short Stories

Hands to Dance.   London, Carroll and Nicholson, 1951.

Plays

Runaway.   London, Curwen, 1936.
The Conquering Hero.   London, Curwen, and New York, Schirmer, 1937.
Benedict.   London, Muller, 1938.
How Pleasant to Know Mrs. Lear.   London, Muller, 1948.

Verse

Farewell, Aggie Weston.   Aldington, Kent, Hand and Flower Press, 1951.
Survivor's Leave.   Aldington, Kent, Hand and Flower Press, 1953.
Union Street: Poems.   London, Hart Davis, 1957; Boston, Houghton Mifflin, 1958.
The Ballad of Charlotte Dymond.   Dartington Hall, Devon, privately printed, 1958.
Johnny Alleluia: Poems.   London, Hart Davis, 1961.

233

Penguin Modern Poets 3, with George Barker and Martin Bell.   London, Penguin, 1962.
Ballad of the Bread Man.   London, Macmillan, 1968.
Underneath the Water: Poems.   London, Macmillan, 1968.
Pergamon Poets 10, with Laurie Lee, edited by Evan Owen.   Oxford, Pergamon Press, 1970.
Timothy Winters, music by Wallace Southam.   London, Turret Books, 1970.
Six Women.   Richmond, Surrey, Keepsake Press, 1974.
Collected Poems, 1951–1975.   London, Macmillan, and Boston, David R. Godine, 1975.

Recordings: *Here Today 1*, Jupiter; *The Poet Speaks 8*, Argo; British Council Tapes, 1960, 1966, 1968; *Causley Reads Causley*, Sentinel.

Other

Editor, *Peninsula: An Anthology of Verse from the West-Country*.   London, Macdonald, 1957.
Editor, *Modern Folk Ballads*.   London, Studio Vista, 1966.
Editor, *Selected Poems*, by Frances Bellerby.   London, Enitharmon Press, 1971.

Manuscript Collections: State University of New York, Buffalo; University of Exeter Library, Devon.

*   *   *

It would be hard to draw a firm dividing line through the work of Charles Causley: poems for adults one side, poems for children the other. He has one of the most attractively approachable gifts of all modern poets writing in English today, and young readers may well enjoy his work for adults (and vice versa). But of the volumes classified by their publishers as specifically for children, his poetry falls, very broadly speaking, into two categories.

First there is the frankly comic verse, which could attract even the child who normally steers clear of poetry altogether. This includes short pieces such as "I Saw a Jolly Hunter," from *Figgie Hobbin*, longer ones such as "My Neighbour Mr. Normanton," an ironic monologue from the same collection with a grim twist in the last verse, and narratives of considerable length such as "Stoker Rock's Baby" (*Figure of 8*), almost Gilbertian in tone with its internal rhymes and rollicking nautical atmosphere. Into the same category comes the full-length book *The Tail of the Trinosaur*, a splendidly sustained narrative about an amiable prehistoric monster which surprises and alarms the town of Dunborough by emerging from a ninety-million-year deep-frozen sleep, and frustrating all their efforts to be rid of it (including the would-be virgin sacrifice of "Miss Esmeralda Flight / The well-known toxophilite"). The verse goes along at a great pace, with numerous skilful changes of metre to vary the tone. A more lyrical verse story is *The Hill of the Fairy Calf*, the Irish tale of a young piper who wins a magic battle of wits with the Queen of the Fays, a shape-changer in the true fairy tradition.

This really brings one to the second large category of Charles Causley's verse for children, which has its roots firmly in the tradition of ballad, folk-song and singing game, and often in the atmosphere of his native Cornwall too. These poems, dramatic and tragic, like "The Song of Samuel Sweet" (*Figure of 8*), or liltingly cheerful like "My Young Man's a Cornishman" (*Figgie Hobbin*) are far from being mere pastiche. Their actual verse forms may be traditional, and so is the use of certain ballad-like elliptical narrative devices, or series of repeated questions and answers – and occasionally a phrase will call for a familiar response from the reader, as when, at the end of "The Obby Oss" (*Figure of 8*), one can practically hear the poem swing into the tune of the Padstow May Song. But the particular use of these forms is all Mr Causley's own; his sharp, bright imagery and the energy and irony of his language are products of an original and individual vision.

And among all that is racy, comic and fast-moving, bright and rhythmic, one must not forget the sprinkling of quiet little lyrics among Charles Causley's poetry for the young, where a child may come upon a sudden, apparently simple turn in the verse to catch at his imagination ("At Candlemas" – *Figgie Hobbin*):

> But still within the elder tree
> The strong sap rose, though none could see.

—Anthea Bell

CAVANNA, Betty. American. Born in Camden, New Jersey, 24 June 1909. Educated at local schools, Haddonfield, New Jersey; Douglass College, New Brunswick, New Jersey, 1925–29, Litt.B. in journalism 1929 (Phi Beta Kappa). Married Edward Talman Headley in 1940 (died, 1952), one son; George Russell Harrison, 1957. Reporter, *Bayonne Times*, New Jersey, 1929–31; worked in the publicity and advertising departments and as Art Director, Westminster Press, Philadelphia, 1931–41. Address: 170 Barnes Hill Road, Concord, Massachusetts 01742, U.S.A.

PUBLICATIONS FOR CHILDREN

Fiction

Puppy Stakes. Philadelphia, Westminster Press, 1943.

The Black Spaniel Mystery. Philadelphia, Westminster Press, 1945.

Secret Passage, illustrated by Jean MacLaughlin. Philadelphia, Winston, 1946.

Going on Sixteen. Philadelphia, Westminster Press, 1946.

A Date for Diane (as Elizabeth Headley), illustrated by Janet Smalley. Philadelphia, Macrae Smith, 1946.

Spurs for Suzanna, illustrated by Virginia Mann. Philadelphia, Westminster Press, 1947; London, Lutterworth Press, 1948.

Take a Call, Topsy! (as Elizabeth Headley), illustrated by Janet Smalley. Philadelphia, Macrae Smith, 1947.

A Girl Can Dream, illustrated by Harold Minton. Philadelphia, Westminster Press, 1948.

Puzzle in Purple (as Betsy Allen). New York, Grosset and Dunlap, 1948.

The Secret of Black Cat Gulch (as Betsy Allen). New York, Grosset and Dunlap, 1948.

The Riddle in Red (as Betsy Allen). New York, Grosset and Dunlap, 1948.

The Clue in Blue (as Betsy Allen). New York, Grosset and Dunlap, 1948.

Paintbox Summer, illustrated by Peter Hunt. Philadelphia, Westminster Press, 1949.

She's My Girl! (as Elizabeth Headley). Philadelphia, Macrae Smith, 1949; as *You Can't Take Twenty Dogs on a Date* (as Betty Cavanna). Philadelphia, Westminster Press, 1977.

The Green Island Mystery (as Betsy Allen). New York, Grosset and Dunlap, 1949.

Spring Comes Riding. Philadelphia, Westminster Press 1950; London, Lutterworth Press, 1952.

The Ghost Wore White (as Betsy Allen). New York, Grosset and Dunlap, 1950.

Two's Company, illustrated by Edward J. Smith. Philadelphia, Westminster Press, 1951.

Catchpenny Street (as Elizabeth Headley). Philadelphia, Macrae Smith, 1951; (as Betty Cavanna), Philadelphia, Westminster Press, 1976.

The Yellow Warning (as Betsy Allen). New York, Grosset and Dunlap, 1951.

Lasso Your Heart. Philadelphia, Westminster Press, 1952.

Love, Laurie. Philadelphia, Westminster Press, 1953.

The Gray Menace (as Betsy Allen). New York, Grosset and Dunlap, 1953.

Six on Easy Street. Philadelphia, Westminster Press, 1954.

The Brown Satchel Mystery (as Betsy Allen). New York, Grosset and Dunlap, 1954.

Passport to Romance. New York, Morrow, 1955.

Diane's New Love (as Elizabeth Headley). Philadelphia, Macrae Smith, 1955.

Peril in Pink (as Betsy Allen). New York, Grosset and Dunlap, 1955.

The Boy Next Door. New York, Morrow, 1956.

The Silver Secret (as Betsy Allen). New York, Grosset and Dunlap, 1956.

Angel on Skis, illustrated by Isabel Dawson. New York, Morrow, 1957.

Toujours Diane (as Elizabeth Headley). Philadelphia, Macrae Smith, 1957.

Stars in Her Eyes. New York, Morrow, 1958.

The Scarlet Sail. New York, Morrow, 1959; Leicester, Brockhampton Press, 1962.

Accent on April. New York, Morrow, 1960.

A Touch of Magic. Philadelphia, Westminster Press, 1961.

Fancy Free. New York, Morrow, 1961.

A Time for Tenderness. New York, Morrow, 1962.

Almost Like Sisters. New York, Morrow, 1963.

Jenny Kimura. New York, Morrow, 1964; Leicester, Brockhampton Press, 1966.

Mystery at Love's Creek. New York, Morrow, 1965.

A Breath of Fresh Air. New York, Morrow, 1966.

The Country Cousin. New York, Morrow, 1967.

Mystery in Marrakech. New York, Morrow, 1968.

Spice Island Mystery. New York, Morrow, 1969.

Mystery on Safari, illustrated by Joseph Cellini. New York, Morrow, 1971.

The Ghost of Ballyhooly. New York, Morrow, 1971.

Mystery in the Museum. New York, Morrow, 1972.

Petey, illustrated by Beth and Joe Krush. Philadelphia, Westminster Press, 1973.

Joyride. New York, Morrow, 1974.

Ruffles and Drums, illustrated by Richard Cuffari. New York, Morrow, 1975.

Mystery of the Emerald Buddha. New York, Morrow, 1976.

Other

The First Book of Seashells, illustrated by Marguerite Scott. New York, Watts, 1955; London, Edmund Ward, 1965.

Arne of Norway. New York, Watts, and London, Chatto and Windus, 1962.

The First Book of Wild Flowers, illustrated by Page Cary. New York, Watts, 1961.

Lucho of Peru. New York, Watts, 1961; London, Chatto and Windus, 1962.

Paulo of Brazil. New York, Watts, 1962; London, Chatto and Windus, 1963.

Pepe of Argentina. New York, Watts, 1962; London, Chatto and Windus, 1963.

Lo Chau of Hong Kong. New York, Watts, and London, Chatto and Windus, 1963.

Chico of Guatemala. New York, Watts, and London, Chatto and Windus, 1963.

Noko of Japan. New York, Watts, 1964.

Carlos of Mexico. New York, Watts, and London, Chatto and Windus, 1964.

Tavi of the South Seas. New York, Watts, 1965; London, Chatto and Windus, 1967.

Doug of Australia. New York, Watts, and London, Chatto and Windus, 1965.

Ali of Egypt. New York, Watts, and London, Chatto and Windus, 1966.

Demetrios of Greece. New York, Watts, and London, Chatto and Windus, 1966.

The First Book of Wool, with George Russell Harrison.   New York, Watts, 1966; as *Wool*, London, Watts, 1972.

The First Book of Fiji.   New York, Watts, 1968; as *Fiji*, London, Watts, 1972.

Morocco.   New York, Watts, 1970; London, Watts, 1972.

Editor, *Pick of the Litter: Favorite Dog Stories*.   Philadelphia, Westminster Press, 1952.

Manuscript Collection: de Grummond Collection, University of Southern Mississippi, Hattiesburg.

*   *   *

Betty Cavanna's books are about growing up. Primarily, she has written a string of teenage romance books which follow the conventions of the junior novel, treating emotional problems of girls as they move past adolescence. The world of Cavanna's fiction is pleasant, conventional, stereotyped, with few enormous problems.

The protagonists are wholesome, pretty American girls with cute names such as Dizzy, Carlie, Marcy, Fancy, and April. These young women are well-rounded teenagers with idealized perceptions of reality. They have an innate wisdom which might take most people a lifetime of hardship to attain. Their problems are only those minor difficulties which prevent them from having a full, mature grasp of reality.

Many of the stories are humorless books with shallow characterizations of girls worried about whether to wear lipstick, but Cavanna's books have been enormously popular and in fact have been highly recommended by critics for their attention to subjects that have reflected girls' interests. However, the heroines usually cannot succeed independently and they look up to success-seeking, industrious male figures. Cavanna has a good reputation for her sensitive treatment of those awkward transition years, and her stories have been recommended for slow readers. Although her writing style tends to be formal and functional, her vocabulary is extensive.

The plots are about the heartbreaks of growing up. In *A Date for Diane*, Diane is sensitive about her braces but discovers that the boy she likes also wears them. In *Going on Sixteen* a girl with artistic ambitions overcomes her shyness through her relationship with her dog. *The Boy Next Door* is a typical novel about first love. Jane and the boy next door have been good friends all their lives, but when he becomes romantic, Jane rejects his advances and a difficult period follows, especially when Jane's sister claims him for herself.

More recent stories challenge the older taboos of children's fiction. *Almost Like Sisters* treats a mother-daughter rivalry. Victoria's young, pretty, widowed mother dances with all the boys at the dance while Victoria stands in the shadows. Another story examines the effect of divorce. In *Jenny Kimura* the Tokyo-born daughter of a mixed marriage confronts racial and cultural prejudice in Kansas City and on Cape Cod. In *A Time for Tenderness* young people of different cultures and racial backgrounds intermingle when a Southern girl goes to Brazil with her mother.

Although junior novels of the 1970's have incorporated contemporary problems such as slum conditions and abortion, many of Cavanna's more recent books have been mystery-adventures patterned after the popular series books. *Mystery in Marrakech*, for example, uses trite tourist trappings typical of the settings of popular mysteries (medieval mosques, ominous bazaars, nomads on camels, ancient casbahs) to tell a tale about a mysterious kidnapping in the winding alleyway of a menacing foreign city, complete with an international oil intrigue. And *Spice Island Mystery*, set on the romantic Caribbean island of Grenada, bears a strong message against marijuana as the heroine battles a smuggling ring. The heroine is in some ways atypical. She is a dark-skinned West Indian girl who has gone to school in the United States. Except for a certain sensitivity to the problems of Grenada, she is a suburban American girl in disguise.

Although they are less realistic than her soap-opera style books, Cavanna's mysteries are somewhat more palatable because the energetic plots are well-sustained and the heroines more forceful.

—Bobbie Ann Mason

CAWLEY, Winifred. British. Born in Felton, Northumberland, 24 January 1915. Educated at Western Elementary School, Wallsend, Northumberland, 1921–26; Wallsend Secondary School, 1926–33; University of Durham at Newcastle (open scholar, 1933–36; Spence Watson Prize for English Literature, 1936; Ellen Phoebe Wright Prize for Education, 1937), 1933–37, B.A. (honours) in English 1936, Diploma in the Theory and Practice of Teaching 1937; University College, University of London (William Black Noble student), 1937–39. Married Arthur Clare Cawley in 1939; has one son. English teacher, English School, Cairo, 1941–44, Leeds College of Technology, 1950–54, West Park School, Leeds, 1954–58, Leeds Girls' High School, 1958–59, and 1966–73, Lourdes Hill Convent, Brisbane, Queensland, 1960–63, and Indooroopilly High School, Brisbane, 1964–65. Recipient: *Guardian* Award, 1974. Agent: Oxford University Press, Walton Street, Oxford OX2 6DP. Address: Moor Croft, Moor Road, Bramhope, Leeds LS16 9HH, England.

PUBLICATIONS FOR CHILDREN

Fiction

> *Down the Long Stairs*, illustrated by William Stobbs. London, Oxford University Press, 1964; New York, Holt Rinehart, 1965.
> *Feast of the Serpent*, illustrated by Doreen Roberts. London, Oxford University Press, 1969; New York, Holt Rinehart, 1970.
> *Gran at Coalgate*, illustrated by Fermin Rocker. London, Oxford University Press, 1974; New York, Holt Rinehart, 1975.
> *Silver Everything, and Many Mansions*, illustrated by William Stobbs. London, Oxford University Press, 1976.

Winifred Cawley comments:

Down the Long Stairs was set in motion by a building I've been aware of all my life, Tynemouth Castle; *Feast of the Serpent* by a brief, tantalising account of a 1649 Newcastle witchcraft trial in an old book, *England's Grievance*, by Ralph Gardiner (1655), which was among the many I used to try to make the 17th-century coal-trade background of my first story as accurate as possible.

Gran at Coalgate, which won the *Guardian* Award, is also set in Northeast England, but nearly 300 years later, in 1926, the year of the General Strike and the great coal strike. Yet to a young reader it probably seems as remote as the first two, for it also tells of a way of life that has vanished. I suppose it is to some extent autobiographical. Coalgate is based on Leadgate in County Durham, as I knew it. Gran is my own Gran; other characters, other people I knew there and then. Coalgate/Leadgate may seem an unlikely place to be something of an earthly paradise, yet such it was to me. I wanted present day children to catch a glimpse of its quality. *Silver Everything* and *Many Mansions* are again based on my memories, this time of life in Wallsend-on-Tyne where I grew up. Most of the events in the stories actually happened.

In the first two books I tried to imagine what it was like to be an ordinary boy or girl in long ago extraordinary times. In the next two I tried to record what it was like to be an ordinary child in very ordinary and very humble circumstances fifty years ago.

At present I am working on a novel for young adults not, this time, set in Northeast England but in Rumania in the strange years 1939 and 1940. I lived there during those years. I like my stories to be anchored in fact and spend a lot of time (which I enjoy) among old books and old newspapers.

*   *   *

Winifred Cawley's books are set in Northumberland. *Down the Long Stairs* is a first person narrative, in which Ralph Cole, now an old man, reflects on the events and personalities he met during his panic-stricken flight from the Roundheads in 1648. After a slow start, the excitement of the chase, the quieter yet vivid detail of the Border country and the warm and moving memories of the people who helped him will capture the young reader's attention. But the heart of the novel is Ralph's slowly growing awareness of the complexity of life. At fifteen his future seemed assured: this security he loses, not merely through his own wilfulness, but also through his subsequent discovery of what life down the mines was really like. He learns, too, that Royalist and Roundhead, Papist and Puritan, coalowner and coalminer are not labels which divide people straightforwardly into good and bad; and that his own attitudes and behaviour are more complex and less creditable than he had supposed, and are fraught with danger to others besides himself. These lessons on the road to maturity, in themselves a common enough theme in children's books, are here presented in a clearly realised historical setting.

In *Feast of the Serpent*, set a year later in 1649, the heroine's difficulties are compounded by a growing alienation both from her mother's Romany world and her father's Border kinsfolk; and when she also becomes involved in the Roundheads' hysterical witchhunts, the pressures of her own inner conflicts added to her terrifying prison experience bring her perilously close to accepting their accusations as justified. There is good writing here, too, and a moving analysis of the girl's predicament, but the handling of the narrative is less assured. The story is told in the third person, but from shifting viewpoints, and the unwary young reader is sometimes left bewildered by the attempt to reflect both the confusions and uncertainties of the heroine and the suspicions and hostilities of the people around her.

The third story, *Gran at Coalgate*, is set in a Northumbrian mining town of the 1920's, a time remote enough to make the young reader view this as an historical novel, too. Jinnie's father is a rigid, Puritanical man who does not hold with the Goings-on at Coalgate. When Jinnie goes there to stay with Gran she is understandably bored by her cousin's Getting-Worked-Up over the lads, but is agonisedly fascinated by the Sins-of-Dancing-and-Going-to-the-Pictures, and is also naively and unbelievably puzzled by the activities of Aunt Polly, who is No-Better-Than-She-Should-Be. The style is not entirely successful, a mixture of straightforward narrative and a reported-speech reflection of Jinnie's bewildered thoughts, which is racy and idiomatic, but too insistently sprinkled with the Capital Letters with which she views life. A melodramatic ending unfortunately prevents any really satisfactory working-out of her conflicts. After her adventurous interlude with Gran she presumably sinks quietly back into a world where Dad's blinkered values resume their hold: a disappointing conclusion considering how strikingly this theme of adolescent conflict runs through all three books.

—Winifred Whitehead

CHANCE, Stephen.   See TURNER, Philip.

CHAUNCY, Nan(cen Beryl Masterman). British. Born in Middlesex, 28 May 1900. Educated at St. Michael's Collegiate School, Hobart, Tasmania. Married Antony Chauncy in 1938; one daughter. Recipient: Australian Children's Book Award, 1958; Australian Book of the Year Award, 1959, 1961; Boys' Clubs of America award, 1961. *Died 1 May 1970.*

PUBLICATIONS FOR CHILDREN

Fiction

They Found a Cave, illustrated by Margaret Horder. Melbourne and London, Oxford University Press, 1948; New York, Watts, 1961.
World's End Was Home, illustrated by Shirley Hughes. Melbourne and London, Oxford University Press, 1952; New York, Watts, 1961.
A Fortune for the Brave, illustrated by Margaret Horder. Melbourne and London, Oxford University Press, 1954; New York, Watts, 1961.
Tiger in the Bush, illustrated by Margaret Horder. London, Oxford University Press, 1957; New York, Watts, 1961.
Devil's Hill, illustrated by Geraldine Spence. London, Oxford University Press, 1958; New York, Watts, 1960.
Tangara: "Let Us Set Off Again," illustrated by Brian Wildsmith. London, Oxford University Press, 1960; as *The Secret Friends*, New York, Watts, 1962.
Half a World Away, illustrated by Annette Macarthur-Onslow. London, Oxford University Press, 1962; New York, Watts, 1963.
The "Roaring 40," illustrated by Annette Macarthur-Onslow. London, Oxford University Press, and New York, Watts, 1963.
High and Haunted Island, illustrated by Victor Ambrus. London, Oxford University Press, 1964; New York, Norton, 1965.
The Skewbald Pony, illustrated by David Parry. London, Nelson, 1965.
Panic at the Garage, illustrated by Peter Lloyd. Edinburgh, Oliver and Boyd, 1965.
Mathinna's People, illustrated by Victor Ambrus. London, Oxford University Press, 1967; as *Hunted in Their Own Land*, New York, Seabury Press, 1973.
Lizzie Lights, illustrated by Judith White. London, Oxford University Press, 1968.
The Lighthouse Keeper's Son, illustrated by Victor Ambrus. London, Oxford University Press, 1969.

Other

Beekeeping, illustrated by Jane Walker. Melbourne, Oxford University Press, 1967.

Manuscript Collection: State Archives, Hobart, Tasmania.

*   *   *

Nan Chauncy began writing at a time when Australian children's literature was dominated by melodramatic and romantic post-war fiction. Her early stories for children were in the existing mode except that *They Found a Cave*, although retaining conventional eccentric adult characters and exploiting a strong story line, was about a group of children who emerged as dynamic interacting individuals. They exist in a strong family relationship, and the Tasmanian bush setting is recognisably real. These two characteristics were so refined and strengthened in *Tiger in the Bush* and *Devil's Hill* that both books won the Australian Children's Book of the Year Award in successive years and established the author's reputation as a realist. Indeed it can well be claimed that she established the contemporary realistic novel for children in Australia which has now been extended and developed in style and technique, as well as in content, by writers such as Patricia Wrightson and Ivan Southall.

In *Tiger in the Bush, Devil's Hill* and *The "Roaring 40"* Nan Chauncy explores the personal relationships of the Lorenny family. Badge Lorenny, "the little boy, the odd man out, the pest and the hanger-on" whom his older brother Lance and his sister Iggy call a "Bidgee burr" and a "wattle tick" because they can't do anything without his irritating presence, is the stalwart younger son of a strongly drawn family. There is Liddle-ma, a big woman in every way with strong principles and a warm heart, Dad, of few words but inspiring utter confidence in his offspring, the children, and their cousins from "outside." For "the world as Badge Lorenny knew it was just home – home tucked between the rough-wrought mountains of Tasmania like a drop of dew between cabbage leaves." To each of the children "home was home ... as soon as you opened the door you saw the great blaze of the fire in the wide black hearth ... you saw Dad slowly put down his newspaper – Liddle-ma's comforting smile." Home was a valley sanctuary hewn from the bush and accessible only by flying-fox – "The Wire." Here Badge learns that honesty and loyalty are more important than possessions or popularity, and that retaining his integrity brings a glow "greater than any sunset, uplifting him with joy and pride and a great relief." Through the incident of the lost cow in *Devil's Hill*, which had actually happened to the writer and one of her brothers, Badge's cousin, Sam, the skite, the blusterer, and the shirker learns the value of honest toil and the necessity for interdependence as well as independence to weld a family into an enduring unit.

Tangara made a different contribution to Australian children's literature. Perhaps for the first time there was a successful blending of realism with fantasy, and the plight of the aborigines who had been exterminated by white settlers in the early days of the colony of Tasmania was treated with dignity and spirituality. *Tangara* is a journey in time, a psychic rediscovery of the life of the Tasmanian aborigines through the "vision" of Lexie Pavemont whose deep affinity with her great-great-aunt Rita summons the aboriginal girl, Merrina, Rita's friend, from the past to prevent a latter-day tragedy, so that yet another debt is added to the past. The novel moves by implication and imagery to evoke insight into the unspeakable past and ends elegiacally with Merrina keening, "her thin arms reaching up imploringly," "alone and calling to her dead." A more formal lament was to be sung by Chauncy in *Mathinna's People*, a series of tableaux from the day that the young chief Wyrum gazed with awe at the white sails of the *Heemskerck* in 1642 to the death of Towterer, the chief, who went to the Old Ones broken in body and spirit by the contamination of white culture. Ironically the white man, George Robinson, who sought to do good from the highest motives is the one most responsible for a psychological affliction that was far more traumatic than bodily hurt.

Mathinna's People is Nan Chauncy's finest compostion. In *The "Roaring 40"* and *High and Haunted Island* she had written evocatively of Tasmania's lonely and threatening South-West coast, and had then created a fictitious island where a colony of Circlists act out the rituals of their religious faith. Even here, where there is a hint of the mysterious, Chauncy's writing is poetically realistic and convincing. Her last two stories, *Lizzie Lights* and *The Lighthouse Keeper's Son*, were less satisfying in that her work had come almost full circle with a return to some early weaknesses of plotting and characterisation.

In spite of a changing society and a greater sophistication in more recent writers, Nan Chauncy, through the Lorenny books and her aboriginal studies in particular, remains among the foremost Australian writers for children.

—H.M. Saxby

CHIPPERFIELD, Joseph E(ugene). British. Born in St. Austell, Cornwall, 20 April 1912. Educated privately. Married Mary Anne Tully in 1936. Editor, Author's Literary Service, London, 1930–34; editor and scriptwriter for documentary films, 1934–40. Address: c/o Hutchinson Publishing Group Ltd., 3 Fitzroy Square, London W1P 6JD, England.

PUBLICATIONS FOR CHILDREN

Fiction

Two Dartmoor Interludes. London, Boswell Press, 1935.
An Irish Mountain Tragedy. London, Boswell Press, 1936.
Three Stories (includes *Two Dartmoor Interludes, An Irish Mountain Tragedy, The Ghosts from Baylough*). London, Boswell Press, 1936.
This Earth – My Home: A Tale of Irish Troubles. Dublin, Padraic O'Follain, 1937.
Storm of Dancerwood, illustrated by C. Gifford Ambler. London, Hutchinson, 1948; New York, Longman, 1949; revised edition, Hutchinson, 1967.
Greatheart, The Salvation Hunter: The Epic of a Shepherd Dog, illustrated by C. Gifford Ambler. London, Hutchinson, 1950; New York, Roy, 1953.
Beyond the Timber Trail, illustrated by Raymond Sheppard. London, Hutchinson, 1951; New York, Longman, 1953.
Windruff of Tor Links, illustrated by Helen Torrey. New York, Longman, 1951; London, Hutchinson, 1954.
Grey Chieftain, illustrated by C. Gifford Ambler. London, Hutchinson, 1952; New York, Roy, 1954.
The Dog of Castle Crag (as John Eland Craig), illustrated by Leslie Atkinson. London, Nelson, 1952.
Silver Star, Stallion of the Echoing Mountain, illustrated by C. Gifford Ambler. London, Hutchinson, 1953; New York, Roy, 1955.
Greeka, Eagle of the Hebrides, illustrated by C. Gifford Ambler. London, Hutchinson, 1953; New York, Longman, 1954; revised edition, Hutchinson, 1962.
Rooloo, Stag of the Dark Water, illustrated by C. Gifford Ambler. London, Hutchinson, 1955; New York, Roy, 1962; revised edition, Hutchinson, 1962, Roy, 1963.
Dark Fury, Stallion of Lost River Valley, illustrated by C. Gifford Ambler. London, Hutchinson, 1956; New York, Roy, 1957.
Wolf of Badenoch: Dog of the Grampian Hills, illustrated by C. Gifford Ambler. London, Hutchinson, 1958; New York, Longman, 1959.
Ghost Horse: Stallion of the Oregon Trail, illustrated by C. Gifford Ambler. London, Hutchinson, 1959; New York, Roy, 1962.
Grasson, Golden Eagle of the North, illustrated by C. Gifford Ambler. London, Hutchinson, 1960.
Petrus, Dog of the Hill Country, illustrated by Stuart Tresilian. London, Heinemann, and New York, Longman, 1960.
Seokoo of the Black Wind, illustrated by C. Gifford Ambler. London, Hutchinson, 1961; New York, McKay, 1962.
The Grey Dog from Galtymore, illustrated by Stuart Tresilian. London, Heinemann, 1961; New York, McKay, 1962.
Sabre of Storm Valley, illustrated by C. Gifford Ambler. London, Hutchinson, 1962; New York, Roy, 1965.
A Dog Against Darkness, illustrated by F.R. Exell. London, Heinemann, 1963; as *A Dog to Trust: The Saga of a Seeing-Eye Dog,* New York, McKay, 1964.
Checoba, Stallion of the Comanche, illustrated by C. Gifford Ambler. London, Hutchinson, 1964; New York, Roy, 1966.
Boru, Dog of the O'Malley, illustrated by C. Gifford Ambler. London, Hutchinson, 1965; New York, McKay, 1966.
The Two Fugitives, illustrated by John Lathey. London, Heinemann, 1966.
Lone Stands the Glen, illustrated by Barry Driscoll. London, Hutchinson, 1966.
The Watcher on the Hills. London, Heinemann, 1968.
Rex of Larkbarrow, illustrated by Robert Hales. London, Hutchinson, 1969.
Storm Island, illustrated by Gareth Floyd. London, Hutchinson, 1970.

Banner, The Pacing White Stallion, illustrated by Robert Hales. London, Hutchinson, 1972.
Lobo, Wolf of the Wind River Range, illustrated by Robert Hales. London, Hutchinson, 1974.
Hunter of Harter Fell, illustrated by Victor Ambrus. London, Hutchinson, 1977.

Other

The Story of a Great Ship: The Birth and Death of the Steamship Titanic, illustrated by Charles King. London, Hutchinson, 1957; New York, Roy, 1959.

* * *

Joseph E. Chipperfield's *Storm of Dancerwood* has been revised and reprinted and is probably his best book. It tells of an alsatian dog and a blind vixen who have a curious, gentle relationship which ends in her death. The dog becomes gradually attached to a man who succeeds in winning his confidence. So develops that extraordinary empathy between human and animal that this author understands so well. Children understand this too because so many of them have just such close ties with their pets.

Often Chipperfield's dogs, or horses, are wild, intractable or misunderstood, which adds spice to the stories. He has been said to "revive nostalgically the dramatic quality of Jack London" and this is a fair comparison. He has the same gift for interpreting animals' reactions without becoming too anthropomorphic. Only in *A Dog Against Darkness* does one have doubts about the subtlety of the thoughts that run through Arno's brain as he is being trained to be a guide dog for the blind. But this book has its own peculiar fascination, for readers of any age, because of the descriptions of this very special training.

The horse stories are violent and vivid and greatly enriched by the background of pioneering days in America. *Banner* is a tale of men obsessively determined to capture a horse that has become a legend. Banner is the last of the wild white stallions, driven up the Colorado Rockies into a country being ravaged by men and their new railroads. He finally escapes his most persistent and crazy pursuer, leaving man and horse to the vultures. But there is no doubt left in the reader's mind that the frontiers of the west are pushing on and destroying the old ways of life.

Many of Chipperfield's books have remained in print, and *Ghost Horse* is available also in paperback. Children love animal stories. You will not find Chipperfield books learnedly analysed in manuals on children's literature, or hear them seriously discussed at conferences, but neither will you find them sitting unread on library shelves.

—Cecilia Gordon

CHORPENNING, Charlotte (Lee Barrows). American. Born 3 January 1872. Educated at Iowa Agricultural College, Ames; Cornell University, Ithaca, New York, 1892–94, B.L. 1894; Harvard University, Cambridge, Massachusetts (John Craig Prize, 1915), 1913–15. Married John C. Chorpenning. Teacher, Wolf Hall school, Denver, 1901–04; English teacher, Winona Normal School, Minnesota, 1904–13, and 1915 to early 1920's; Dramatic Director, Recreation Training School, Hull House, Chicago; Member of the Speech Department, Northwestern University, Evanston, Illinois; Head of the Children's Theatre, Goodman Theatre, Art Institute of Chicago, 1931–52; worked with the U.S.O. during World War II. Co-Founder, Children's World Theatre in the late 1940's. *Died in January 1955.*

PUBLICATIONS FOR CHILDREN

Plays

The Emperor's New Clothes, adaptation of the story by Hans Christian Andersen (produced New York, 1935). New York, French, 1932.

Rhodopis, The First Cinderella. Chicago, Coach House Press, 1934.

Jack and the Beanstalk (produced New York, 1937). Anchorage, Kentucky, Children's Theatre Press, 1935.

The Indian Captive (produced Chicago, 1936). Anchorage, Kentucky, Children's Theatre Press, 1937.

Tom Sawyer's Treasure Hunt, adaptation of the story *Tom Sawyer* by Mark Twain. New York, French, 1937.

Hans Brinker and the Silver Skates, adaptation of the story by Mary Mapes Dodge. Anchorage, Kentucky, Children's Theatre Press, 1938.

Little Black Sambo and the Tigers, adaptation of the story by Helen Bannerman (produced New Orleans, 1939). New York, Dramatists Play Service, 1938; as *Rama and the Tigers*, Chicago, Coach House Press, 1954.

The Prince and the Pauper, adaptation of the story by Mark Twain. New York, Dramatists Play Service, 1938.

Radio Rescue. New York, Dramatists Play Service, 1938.

The Return of Rip Van Winkle, adaptation of the story "Rip Van Winkle" by Washington Irving. New York, Dramatists Play Service, 1938; as *Rip Van Winkle*, Chicago, Coach House Press, 1954.

Cinderella, adaptation of the story by Charles Perrault. Anchorage, Kentucky, Children's Theatre Press, 1940.

Abe Lincoln – New Salem Days (produced Chicago, 1941). Chicago, Coach House Press, 1954.

Rumpelstiltskin (produced New York, 1947). Anchorage, Kentucky, Children's Theatre Press, 1944.

The Secret Weapon. Washington, D.C., National Education Association, 1944.

Alice in Wonderland, adaptation of the story by Lewis Carroll. Chicago, Dramatic Publishing Company, 1946.

The Adventures of Tom Sawyer, adaptation of the story by Mark Twain. Chicago, Dramatic Publishing Company, 1946.

Many Moons, adaptation of the story by James Thurber (produced New York, 1947). Chicago, Dramatic Publishing Company, 1946.

The Elves and the Shoemaker, with Nora Tully (produced Chicago, 1946). Anchorage, Kentucky, Children's Theatre Press, 1946.

Little Red Riding Hood; or, Grandmother Slyboots (produced New York, 1947). Anchorage, Kentucky, Children's Theatre Press, 1946.

The Sleeping Beauty. Anchorage, Kentucky, Children's Theatre Press, 1947.

Little Lee Bobo, Chinatown Detective, with R.H. Lee. Anchorage, Kentucky, Children's Theatre Press, 1948.

The Three Bears. Anchorage, Kentucky, Children's Theatre Press, 1949.

King Midas and the Golden Touch. Anchorage, Kentucky, Children's Theatre Press, 1950.

Flibbertygibbet (His Last Chance), with Nora Tully MacAlvay. Anchorage, Kentucky, Children's Theatre Press, 1952.

Robinson Crusoe, adaptation of the novel by Daniel Defoe. Anchorage, Kentucky, Children's Theatre Press, 1952.

The Magic Horn: A Story of Roland and Charlemagne, with Anne Nicholson. Chicago, Coach House Press, 1954.

Lincoln's Secret Messenger – Boy Detective to a President. Chicago, Coach House Press, 1955.

Hansel and Gretel, adaptation of the story by the Grimm Brothers.   Chicago, Coach House Press, 1956.

PUBLICATIONS FOR ADULTS

Other

Twenty One Years with Children's Theatre.   Anchorage, Kentucky, Children's Theatre Press, 1954.

*   *   *

Charlotte Chorpenning has been the greatest influence on playwrights writing for children in the United States. She was the first to make a serious attempt to study the reactions of children in the theatre and to use her observations in writing plays. The result was a large body of published plays which are still widely performed.

Although she wrote a few original plays, she generally preferred to adapt well-known fairy tales to the stage. Her long association with the Goodman Theatre enabled her to study the workings of the child mind within the framework of the theatre. Besides trying to interest and amuse her audience, she was convinced of the necessity of weaving long range meanings into her plays, and to give children useful experience through their identification with the characters. Though she used the conventional structure of the well-made play, large casts, and elaborate scenery, she remained faithful to the intent of the original author or folk theme. Moral values emerged from the story and characters, and happy endings were not merely imposed but grew out of the situation.

Though some of her writing seems dated today, Chorpenning is acknowledged as our first serious and successful children's playwright.

—Nellie McCaslin

CHRISTOPHER, John.   Pseudonym for C.S. Youd.   British.   Born in 1922. Recipient: Christopher Award, 1971; *Guardian* Award, 1971. Address: c/o David Higham Associates, 5–8 Lower John Street, London W1R 4HA, England.

PUBLICATIONS FOR CHILDREN

Fiction

The White Mountains.   London, Hamish Hamilton, and New York, Macmillan, 1967.
The City of Gold and Lead.   London, Hamish Hamilton, and New York, Macmillan, 1967.
The Pool of Fire.   London, Hamish Hamilton, and New York, Macmillan, 1968.
The Lotus Caves.   London, Hamish Hamilton, and New York, Macmillan, 1969.
The Guardians.   London, Hamish Hamilton, and New York, Macmillan, 1970.
The Prince in Waiting.   London, Hamish Hamilton, and New York, Macmillan, 1970.
Beyond the Burning Lands.   London, Hamish Hamilton, and New York, Macmillan, 1971.
The Sword of the Spirits.   London, Hamish Hamilton, and New York, Macmillan, 1972.
A Figure in Grey (as Hilary Ford).   Kingswood, Surrey, World's Work, 1973.

245

Dom and Va.   London, Hamish Hamilton, and New York, Macmillan, 1973.
Wild Jack.   London, Hamish Hamilton, and New York, Macmillan, 1974.
Empty World.   London, Hamish Hamilton, 1977.

Other

In the Beginning (reader), illustrated by Clyde Pearson.   London, Longman, 1972.

PUBLICATIONS FOR ADULTS

Novels

The Year of the Comet.   London, Joseph, 1955.
The Death of Grass.   London, Joseph, 1956; as *No Blade of Grass*, New York, Simon and Schuster, 1957.
The Caves of Night.   London, Eyre and Spottiswoode, and New York, Simon and Schuster, 1958.
Felix Walking (as Hilary Ford).   London, Eyre and Spottiswoode, and New York, Simon and Schuster, 1958.
Felix Running (as Hilary Ford).   London, Eyre and Spottiswoode, 1959.
A Scent of White Poppies.   London, Eyre and Spottiswoode, and New York, Simon and Schuster, 1959.
The Long Voyage.   London, Eyre and Spottiswoode, 1960; as *The White Voyage*, New York, Simon and Schuster, 1961.
The World in Winter.   London, Eyre and Spottiswoode, 1962; as *The Long Winter*, New York, Simon and Schuster, 1962.
Cloud on Silver.   London, Hodder and Stoughton, 1964; as *Sweeney's Island*, New York, Simon and Schuster, 1964.
Bella on the Roof (as Hilary Ford).   London, Longman, 1965.
The Possessors.   London, Hodder and Stoughton, and New York, Simon and Schuster, 1965.
A Wrinkle in the Skin.   London, Hodder and Stoughton, 1965; as *The Ragged Edge*, New York, Simon and Schuster, 1966.
The Little People.   London, Hodder and Stoughton, and New York, Simon and Schuster, 1967.
Pendulum.   London, Hodder and Stoughton, and New York, Simon and Schuster, 1968.
Sarnia (as Hilary Ford).   London, Hamish Hamilton, and New York, Doubleday, 1974.
Castle Malindine (as Hilary Ford).   London, Hamish Hamilton, 1975.

Short Stories

The Twenty-Second Century.   London, Grayson, 1954; New York, Lancer, 1962.

*   *   *

Publication in 1967 of *The White Mountains*, John Christopher's first book for children, was arguably the point at which science fiction began to take its proper place in English children's literature. Previously in this country, it had probably been the least-esteemed form of writing for children, associated by unsympathetic adults with pulp comics and the sillier side of television, and featuring (it was supposed) super-heroes, bug-eyed monsters, and ray-gun battles in space. *The White Mountains*, written in cool clear prose and intelligently thought out, was unmistakably a "quality" book as well as a highly readable one; and with the two titles that followed, *The City of Gold and Lead* and *The Pool of Fire*, it made up a trilogy which was successful with children and critics alike.

The books tell how three boys join the struggle of a handful of free men against the Masters, a ruling elite from a distant world who look on humans as inferior, expendable creatures – rather, in fact, as we look on animals. A second trilogy – *The Prince in Waiting, Beyond the Burning Lands* and *The Sword of the Spirits* – is set in a different kind of post-cataclysmic England, now divided into warring city-states. The hero, Luke, has a mission to unite his fragmented country, but in the end turns against his own people: a disconcerting twist which would be unimaginable in the old-fashioned boys' adventure story.

Indeed, John Christopher does not simplify any issue for the sake of young readers. *The Lotus Caves, The Guardians* and *Wild Jack*, which are three separate books and not a trilogy, present in different forms a choice for their heroes between lives of comfort but restricted liberty on one hand and of harsh, dangerous freedom on the other; and it is not pretended that this choice is an easy one. John Christopher is an experienced storyteller who knows how to make his readers want to turn the page; but when the last page is turned the book is not over-and-done-with, for there is something left in the mind for the reader to go on thinking about.

—John Rowe Townsend

CHURCH, Richard (Thomas). British. Born in London, 26 March 1893. Educated at Dulwich Hamlet School, London, 1905–08. Married Caroline Parfett in 1915; Catherina Schimmer, 1930 (died, 1965); Dorothy Beale, 1967; four children. Civil Servant, London, 1909–33; Editor, J.M. Dent, publishers, London, 1933–51. Co-Founder, *The Criterion,* London, 1921; regular contributor to *The Spectator* and *New Statesman,* London; for forty years contributor of a monthly essay to the "Home Forum Page" of the *Christian Science Monitor,* Boston. Director, English Festival of Spoken Poetry, until it merged with the Arts Council Poetry Panel. Recipient: Femina Vie Heureuse Prize, 1938; *Sunday Times* Gold Medal, 1955; Foyle Poetry Prize, 1957. President, P.E.N., 1958–59, Kent and Sussex Poetry Society, 1962, and the English Association, 1964–65. Fellow, 1950, and Vice-President, 1968, Royal Society of Literature. Fellow, Royal Society of Art, 1970. C.B.E. (Commander, Order of the British Empire), 1957. *Died 4 March 1972.*

PUBLICATIONS FOR CHILDREN

Fiction

> *A Squirrel Called Rufus,* illustrated by John Skeaping. London, Dent, 1941; Philadelphia, Winston, 1946.
> *The Cave,* illustrated by Clarke Hutton. London, Dent, 1950; as *Five Boys in a Cave,* New York, Day, 1951; revised edition, Dent, 1953.
> *Dog Toby: A Frontier Tale,* illustrated by Laurence Irving. London, Hutchinson, 1953; New York, Day, 1958.
> *Down River,* illustrated by Laurence Irving. New York, Day, 1957; London, Heinemann, 1958.
> *The Bells of Rye.* London, Heinemann, 1960; New York, Day, 1961.
> *The White Doe,* illustrated by John Ward. London, Heinemann, 1968; New York, Day, 1969.
> *The French Lieutenant: A Ghost Story for Young Readers.* London, Heinemann, 1971; New York, Day, 1972.

Publications for Adults

Novels

Oliver's Daughter: A Tale. London, Dent, 1930.
High Summer. London, Dent, 1931; New York, Smith, 1932.
The Prodigal Father. London, Dent, and New York, Day, 1933.
The Apple of Concord. London, Dent, 1935.
The Porch. London, Dent, 1937.
The Stronghold. London, Dent, 1939.
The Room Within. London, Dent, 1940.
The Sampler. London, Dent, 1942.
The Nightingale. London, Hutchinson, 1952.
The Dangerous Years. London, Heinemann, 1956; New York, Dutton, 1958.
The Crab-Apple Tree. London, Heinemann, 1959.
Prince Albert. London, Heinemann, 1963.
Little Miss Moffatt: A Confession. London, Heinemann, 1969.

Play

The Prodigal: A Play in Verse (produced Canterbury, 1953).   London, Staples Press, 1953.

Verse

The Flood of Life and Other Poems. London, Fifield, 1917.
Hurricane and Other Poems. London, Selwyn and Blount, 1919.
Philip and Other Poems. Oxford, Blackwell, 1923.
The Portrait of the Abbot: A Story in Verse. London, Benn, 1926; New York, Dial Press, 1927.
The Dream and Other Poems. London, Benn, 1927.
Mood Without Measure. London, Faber and Gwyer, 1927.
Theme with Variations. London, Benn, 1928.
The Glance Backward: New Poems. London, Dent, 1930.
News from the Mountain. London, Dent, 1932.
Twelve Noon. London, Dent, 1936.
The Solitary Man and Other Poems. London, Dent, 1941.
Twentieth Century Psalter. London, Dent, 1943.
The Lamp. London, Dent, 1946.
Collected Poems. London, Dent, 1948.
Selected Lyrical Poems. London, Staples Press, 1951.
The Inheritors: Poems, 1948–1955. London, Heinemann, 1957.
(Poems). London, Hulton, 1959.
North of Rome. London, Hutchinson, 1960.
The Burning Bush: Poems, 1958–1966. London, Heinemann, 1967.
25 Lyrical Poems. London, Heinemann, 1967.

Other

Mary Shelley. London, Howe, and New York, Viking Press, 1928.
Calling for a Spade. London, Dent, 1939.
Eight for Immortality. London, Dent, 1941; Freeport, New York, Books for Libraries Press, 1969.
Plato's Mistake. London, Routledge, 1941.

British Authors: A Twentieth Century Gallery. London, Longman, 1943; revised edition, 1948; Freeport, New York, Books for Libraries Press, 1969.

Green Tide. London, Country Life, 1945.

Richard Jefferies Centenary, 1848–1948: Memorial Lecture. Swindon, Council of the Borough of Swindon, 1948.

Kent. London, Hale, 1948.

A Window on a Hill. London, Hale, 1951.

The Growth of the English Novel. London, Methuen, 1951; New York, Barnes and Noble, 1961.

A Portrait of Canterbury. London, Hutchinson, 1953; revised edition, 1968.

Over the Bridge: An Essay in Autobiography. London, Heinemann, 1955; as *Over the Bridge: An Autobiography*, New York, Dutton, 1956.

The Royal Parks of London. London, Ministry of Works, 1956.

Small Moments. London, Hutchinson, 1957.

The Golden Sovereign: A Conclusion to "Over the Bridge." London, Heinemann, and New York, Dutton, 1957.

Country Window: A Round of Essays. London, Heinemann, 1958.

Calm October: Essays. London, Heinemann, 1961.

The Voyage Home. London, Heinemann, 1964; New York, Day, 1966.

A Stroll Before Dark: Essays. London, Heinemann, 1965.

A Look at Tradition. London, Oxford University Press, 1965.

London: Flower of Cities All. London, Heinemann, and New York, Day, 1966.

Speaking Aloud. London, Heinemann, 1968.

A Harvest of Mushrooms and Other Sporadic Essays. London, Heinemann, 1970.

The Wonder of Words. London, Hutchinson, 1970.

London in Colour. London, Batsford, and New York, Norton, 1971.

Kent's Contribution. Bath, Adams and Dart, 1972.

Editor, *Poems and Prose*, by Algernon Charles Swinburne. London, Dent, and New York, Dutton, 1940.

Editor, with M.M. Bozman, *Poems of Our Time, 1900–1942.* London, Dent, 1945.

Editor, *John Keats: An Introduction and a Selection.* London, Phoenix House, 1948.

Editor, *Poems*, by Percy Bysshe Shelley. London, Cassell, 1949.

Editor, *Poems for Speaking.* London, Dent, 1950.

Editor, *A Selection of Poems*, by Edmund Spenser. London, Grey Walls Press, 1953.

Editor, *Out of the Dark: New Poems*, by Phoebe Hesketh. London, Heinemann, 1954.

Editor, *The Spoken Work: A Selection from Twenty-Five Years of "The Listener."* London, Collins, 1955; revised edition, 1960.

Editor, *The Little Kingdom: A Kentish Collection.* London, Hutchinson, 1964.

Editor, *Essays by Divers Hands.* London, Oxford University Press, 1965.

Manuscript Collection: University of Texas, Austin.

*   *   *

Unlike many authors Richard Church is not easy to categorize; he belongs to no obvious group or movement, apparently owes nothing to older writers, and was content every so often to publish a skilful, polished, craftsmanlike story, capable of catching the attention on more than one level, that of the younger reader who might possibly remain unaware of a deeper significance, and that of the adult who is not afraid to dip into what ostensibly is a story for children and find there a satisfying and perceptive commentary on the human condition. *Dog Toby* is such a story, a moving and poignant tale which takes place on both sides of a barbed wire frontier. Three children and their two dogs, innocently oblivious of the significance of the wire, ignore the division it represents, and reach a close understanding with ordinary people on the other side. A simple allegory but none the less effective.

Similarly, *A Squirrel Called Rufus* is the story of an old-established family of red squirrels, secure in the heart of a forest, who are confronted by a deadly and ruthless enemy, a horde of grey squirrels invading their home, threatening to usurp their rights and freedoms. After a great battle, the climax of the struggle, the invaders are hurled back, to leave the red squirrels triumphant. Once again to all intents and purposes this is nothing more than an unpretentious if exciting and dramatic adventure story, but then we notice the date of publication – 1941, and so presumably written when England itself stood in the same perilous situation.

The world of nature also provides the backcloth to *The White Doe*, about Tom Winter's concern for a white doe and her fawn he befriends in the forest where his father is woodman. At the same time Tom is troubled in his mind by the effect of his parting with his close friend Billy Lander, the Squire's son away for the first time at boarding school. And then another complicating factor enters his life, the arrival of snobbish Harold Sims into the locality, with whom Tom immediately crosses swords, and whose determination to hunt the deer occasions the life-and-death climax. In this instance the angry thread of human relationships, entangled even further by Tom's friendship with Harold's sister, is thrown into sharp contrast with the orderly passing of the seasons in the forest and on the shore.

The Cave relates the exploration by a group of five boys who call themselves the Tomahawk Club of a limestone cave one of them stumbles across. Again Church focuses attention on human relationships: when danger comes the dominating Alan Hobbs fails to measure up to it and another of the group, George Reynolds, assumes authority and responsibility, and displays the qualities of leadership. Compared to this compelling series of character studies, *Down River*, the further adventures of the Tomahawk Club, is slightly pedestrian. But no author can sustain such a high level of excellence indefinitely, not even Richard Church.

—Alan Edwin Day

CHUTE, Marchette (Gaylord). American. Born in Wayzata, Minnesota, 16 August 1909. Educated at Central High School, Minneapolis, 1921–25; Minneapolis School of Art, 1925–26; University of Minnesota, Minneapolis, 1926–30, B.A. 1930 (Phi Beta Kappa). Recipient: Poetry Society of America Chap-Book Award, 1954; Women's National Book Association Constance Lindsay Skinner Award, 1959. Litt.D.: Western College, Oxford, Ohio, 1952; Carleton College, Northfield, Minnesota, 1957; Dickinson College, Carlisle, Pennsylvania, 1964. Member, American Academy of Arts and Letters; Benjamin Franklin Fellow, Royal Society of Arts. Address: Sutton Terrace North, 450 East 63rd Street, New York, New York 10021, U.S.A.

PUBLICATIONS FOR CHILDREN

Fiction

 The Innocent Wayfaring, illustrated by the author. New York, Scribner, 1943; London, Phoenix House, 1956.
 The Wonderful Winter, illustrated by Grace Golden. New York, Dutton, 1954; London, Phoenix House, 1956.

Verse (illustrated by the author)

 Rhymes about Ourselves. New York, Macmillan, 1932.

Rhymes about the Country. New York, Macmillan, 1941.
Rhymes about the City. New York, Macmillan, 1946.
Around and About. New York, Dutton, 1957.
Rhymes about Us. New York, Dutton, 1974.

Other

An Introduction to Shakespeare. New York, Dutton, 1951; as *Shakespeare and His Stage*, London, University of London Press, 1953.
Stories from Shakespeare. Cleveland, World, 1956; London, Murray, 1960.
Jesus of Israel. New York, Dutton, 1961; London, Gollancz, 1962.
The Green Tree of Democracy. New York, Dutton, 1971.

PUBLICATIONS FOR ADULTS

Plays

Sweet Genevieve, with M.G. Chute (produced New York, 1945).
The Worlds of Shakespeare, with Ernestine Perrie (produced New York, 1963). New York, Dutton, 1963.

Other

The Search for God. New York, Dutton, 1941; London, Benn, 1946.
Geoffrey Chaucer of England. New York, Dutton, 1946; London, Hale, 1951.
The End of the Search. New York, North River Press, 1947.
Shakespeare of London. New York, Dutton, 1950; London, Secker and Warburg, 1951.
Ben Jonson of Westminster. New York, Dutton, 1953; London, Hale, 1954.
Two Gentle Men: The Lives of George Herbert and Robert Herrick. New York, Dutton, 1959; London, Secker and Warburg, 1960.
The First Liberty: A History of the Right to Vote in America, 1619–1850. New York, Dutton, 1969; London, Dent, 1970.
P.E.N. American Center: A History of the First Fifty Years. New York, P.E.N. American Center, 1972.

Manuscript Collections: New York Public Library; Kerlan Collection, University of Minnesota, Minneapolis.

Marchette Chute comments:
I enjoy doing historical research and the past is very real to me, but the subject chooses me rather than my choosing the subject. I have written adult books on Shakespeare, on the Bible, and on American political history, and in each case, when long years of research have brought me the necessary perspective. I have then felt able to write non-fiction books on these subjects for young people. I have also written two novels for young people with backgrounds in English history, one in Chaucer's day and the other in Shakespeare's. The only contemporary work I have done is my verse for young children, in which I have had no research to do except to remember my own fortunate childhood.

*   *   *

Marchette Chute is a scholarly writer who specialises in the sixteenth century. She is known for her books on Shakespeare and Ben Jonson, also Geoffrey Chaucer and a children's information book on the life and times of Shakespeare and his fellow players. Her gifts for bringing factual material to life and putting her readers into the picture have been channelled into producing fictional tales of the places and people of whom she knows so much.

In *The Innocent Wayfaring* two young people run away from home and set off across country towards London. The Merrie England of Chaucer's day had its dark side too, and their eyes are opened to the realities of life. They visit the great trade fairs, one of the stately homes of England, and fall in with all kinds of travellers on the roads and in the boisterous inns. There is a wonderful sense of period and, though at no time does the author seem to be "teaching," every detail in the story can be substantiated by documentary evidence, even down to the recipe for face cream.

With *The Wonderful Winter* she moves us back into Elizabethan London. A youthful nobleman runs away with his puppy and gets taken on by Shakespeare's company of players. He becomes a boy actor and helps behind the scenes, and we learn a lot, incidentally, about the conditions of life at the Globe Theatre. At last, conscience pricking him, he confesses his true identity and returns home, a mature young man.

Informative, amusing, though not all that exciting, these stories are full of character and life and could do much to give a child a taste for historical fiction, and bring him to share the author's love for the rumbustious past of England about which she knows so much and writes so affectionately.

—Ann G. Hay

CIARDI, John (Anthony). American. Born in Boston, Massachusetts, 24 June 1916. Educated at Bates College, Lewiston, Maine, 1934–36; Tufts College, Medford, Massachusetts, B.A. (magna cum laude) 1938 (Phi Beta Kappa); University of Michigan, Ann Arbor (Hopwood Award, 1939), M.A. 1939. Served in the United States Army Air Corps, 20th Air Force, 1942–45: Air Medal, Oak Leaf Cluster. Married Myra Judith Hostetter in 1946; has one daughter and two sons. Instructor in English, Kansas City University, Missouri, 1940–42, 1946; Briggs Copeland Instructor in English, 1946–48, and Assistant Professor, 1948–53, Harvard University, Cambridge, Massachusetts; Lecturer, 1953–54, Associate Professor, 1954–56, and Professor of English, 1956–61, Rutgers University, New Brunswick, New Jersey (resigned); Lecturer, 1947–73, and Director, 1956–72, Bread Loaf Writers Conference, Vermont. Editor, Twayne Publishers, New York, 1949; Lecturer, Salzburg Seminar in American Studies, 1951; Poetry Editor, *Saturday Review*, New York, 1956–73; Host, *Accent* program, CBS-TV, 1961–62. Since 1973, Contributing Editor, *World Magazine*, New York. Recipient: Oscar Blumenthal Prize, 1943, Eunice Tietjens Memorial Prize, 1944, Levinson Prize, 1946, and Harriet Monroe Memorial Prize, 1955 (*Poetry*, Chicago); New England Poetry Club Golden Rose, 1948; American Academy in Rome Fellowship, 1956; Boys' Clubs of America Award, 1962. D.Litt.: Tufts College, 1960; Ohio Wesleyan University, Delaware, 1971; Washington University, St. Louis, 1971; Hum.D.: Wayne University, Detroit, 1963; LL.D.: Ursinus College, Collegeville, Pennsylvania, 1964; D.L.H.: Kalamazoo College, Michigan, 1964; Bates College, 1970. Member, National Institute of Arts and Letters, and American Academy of Arts and Sciences. Address: 359 Middlesex Avenue, Metuchen, New Jersey 08840, U.S.A.

PUBLICATIONS FOR CHILDREN

Fiction

The Wish-Tree, illustrated by Louis Glanzman. New York, Crowell Collier, 1962.

Verse

The Reason for the Pelican, illustrated by Madeleine Gekiere.   Philadelphia, Lippincott, 1959.

Scrappy the Puppy, illustrated by Jane Miller.   Philadelphia, Lippincott, 1960.

I Met a Man, illustrated by Robert Osborn.   Boston, Houghton Mifflin, 1961.

The Man Who Sang the Sillies, illustrated by Edward Gorey.   Philadelphia, Lippincott, 1961.

You Read to Me, I'll Read to You, illustrated by Edward Gorey.   Philadelphia, Lippincott, 1962.

John J. Plenty and the Fiddler Dan: A New Fable of the Grasshopper and the Ant, illustrated by Madeleine Gekiere.   Philadelphia, Lippincott, 1963.

You Know Who, illustrated by Edward Gorey.   Philadelphia, Lippincott, 1964.

The King Who Saved Himself from Being Saved, illustrated by Edward Gorey.   Philadelphia, Lippincott, 1965.

The Monster Den; or, Look What Happened at My House – and to It, illustrated by Edward Gorey.   Philadelphia, Lippincott, 1966.

Someone Could Win a Polar Bear, illustrated by Edward Gorey.   Philadelphia, Lippincott, 1970.

Fast and Slow, illustrated by Becky Gaver.   Boston, Houghton Mifflin, 1975.

PUBLICATIONS FOR ADULTS

Verse

Homeward to America.   New York, Holt, 1940.

Other Skies.   Boston, Little Brown, 1947.

Live Another Day: Poems.   New York, Twayne, 1949.

From Time to Time.   New York, Twayne, 1951.

As If: Poems New and Selected.   New Brunswick, New Jersey, Rutgers University Press, 1955.

I Marry You: A Sheaf of Love Poems.   New Brunswick, New Jersey, Rutgers University Press, 1958.

39 Poems.   New Brunswick, New Jersey, Rutgers University Press, 1959.

In the Stoneworks.   New Brunswick, New Jersey, Rutgers University Press, 1961.

In Fact.   New Brunswick, New Jersey, Rutgers University Press, 1962.

Person to Person.   New Brunswick, New Jersey, Rutgers University Press, 1964.

The Strangest Everything.   New Brunswick, New Jersey, Rutgers University Press, 1966.

An Alphabestiary: Twenty-Six Poems.   Philadelphia, Lippincott, 1967.

A Genesis: 15 Poems.   New York, Touchstone Publications, 1967.

The Achievement of John Ciardi: A Comprehensive Selection of His Poems with a Critical Introduction, edited by Miller Williams.   Chicago, Scott Foresman, 1969.

Lives of X.   New Brunswick, New Jersey, Rutgers University Press, 1972.

The Little That Is All.   New Brunswick, New Jersey, Rutgers University Press, 1974.

Recording: *As If*, Folkways.

Other

Dialogue with an Audience.   Philadelphia, Lippincott, 1963.

Poetry: A Closer Look, with James M. Reid and Laurence Perrine.   New York, Harcourt Brace, 1963.

Manner of Speaking (*Saturday Review* columns).   New Brunswick, New Jersey, Rutgers University Press, 1972.

Editor, *Mid-Century American Poets*.   New York, Twayne, 1950.
Editor, *How Does a Poem Mean?*   Boston, Houghton Mifflin, 1960; revised edition, with Miller Williams, 1975.

Translator, *The Inferno*, by Dante.   New Brunswick, New Jersey, Rutgers University Press, 1954.
Translator, *The Purgatorio*, by Dante.   New York, New American Library, 1961.
Translator, *The Paradiso*, by Dante.   New York, New American Library, 1970.

Bibliography: *John Ciardi: A Bibliography* by William White, Detroit, Wayne State University Press, 1959.

Manuscript Collections: Wayne State University, Detroit; Library of Congress, Washington, D.C.

John Ciardi comments:

I gather that there is a professionalism about writing for children. The professionals I have met seem to have rules, some of which make me uneasy. I began writing children's poems first as a game with my nephews, then with my own children. I do not know how to do it by rule, only by ear. I know I am happy when I reach children. I want the contact to be *fun*. A few years ago the National Council of Teachers of English surveyed American school children and had them vote for their 25 favorite poems. The poem they put at the top of the list was my "Mummy Slept Late and Daddy Fixed Breakfast." No citation has ever given me more pleasure, especially as evidence that my amateur sense of it has been right, that I am reaching children where it is fun.

*   *   *

It is one thing to write nonsense verse for children, as many do, with outrageously silly situations, concocted creatures and humorous story lines as well as attention to contemporary concerns – but quite another matter when a poet, in command of his craft, puts his mind and heart to it. John Ciardi, whose background is that of a scholar, critic and adult poet, is such a craftsman who has kept in touch with the matters which delight the young, and has, through numerous books, presented them with a wealth of observations, creatures and situations which derive their strength from pattern and rhyme which rings clear and true to the ear and often invites active participation and much laughter.

Ciardi's imagination is in tune with the young who enjoy the absurdity of ridiculous names; he has, in a sense, updated Edward Lear for the contemporary child with his "Brobinyak" who lives in the "Forest of Foffenzee/In the land of the Pshah of Psham," where one might also meet "Radio Eeels" or the "Banjo Tern" or the "Scrawny Shank," or the "Saginsack" whose "Radio Horns/And Aerials for ears" could "be listening to you." Again, in the story of "The Army Horse and the Army Jeep" there are echoes of the inanimate table and chair of Lear. Yet Ciardi is not imitating; he is his own man, unlike others writing for children who seize nonsense and preposterous names and situations and who do not, in craft or in use of symbol, measure up to Lear.

Ciardi's interest in animals, the shark, python, whale, crow, ape, boa constrictor and others permeates his books in an imaginative series of short-story poems. Nature is also given emphasis in "How to Tell the Top of a Hill" or "The River Is a Piece of Sky." Ecological concerns crop up in "And They Lived Happily Ever After for a While" all of which focus on the same wonder and imaginative speculation as in "The Reason for the Pelican" or "Fast and Slow" where the "fast young crow" does not know "... Where to go."

The occasional cuteness of "Mummy Slept Late and Daddy Fixed Breakfast" or "Prattle," although popular, seem to me to be less than Ciardi at his best. The strength and haunting quality of "There once was an Owl perched on a shed./Fifty years later the Owl was dead./

Some say mice are in the corn./Some say kittens are being born" prove his ability to soar beyond mere childishness.

In whatever form he chooses to write, his control is always admirable; his couplets, tercets,quatrains, limericks attest to his carefully constructed meter and rhyme; his technique is happily beyond what he himself calls the "spillage of raw emotion." Ciardi writes to entertain in a rhythm to which the young respond, and if occasional morals creep in now and again, they are done with a sophistication and humor that are so carefully worked into the poem that they cannot be faulted.

—Myra Cohn Livingston

CLAPP, Patricia. American. Born in Boston, Massachusetts, 9 June 1912. Attended Kimberley School, Montclair, New Jersey; Columbia University School of Journalism, New York. Married Edward della Torre Cone in 1933; has one son and two daughters. Since 1940, Member of the Board of Managers, Studio Players, Upper Montclair, New Jersey; since 1960, Librarian, New Jersey Theatre League. Address: 83 Beverley Road, Upper Montclair, New Jersey 07043, U.S.A.

PUBLICATIONS FOR CHILDREN

Fiction

> *Constance: A Story of Early Plymouth.* New York, Lothrop, 1968.
> *Jane-Emily.* New York, Lothrop, 1969.
> *King of the Dollhouse,* illustrated by Judith Gwyn Brown. New York, Lothrop, 1974.
> *I'm Deborah Sampson: A Soldier in the War of the Revolution.* New York, Lothrop, 1977.

Plays

> *Peggy's on the Phone.* Chicago, Dramatic Publishing Company, 1956.
> *Smart Enough to Be Dumb.* Chicago, Dramatic Publishing Company, 1956.
> *The Incompleted Pass.* Chicago, Dramatic Publishing Company, 1957.
> *Her Kissin' Cousin.* Cedar Rapids, Iowa, Heuer, 1957.
> *The Girl Out Front.* Chicago, Dramatic Publishing Company, 1958.
> *The Ghost of a Chance.* Cedar Rapids, Iowa, Heuer, 1958.
> *The Curley Tale.* Cedar Rapids, Iowa, Art Craft, 1958.
> *Inquire Within.* Evanston, Illinois, Row Peterson, 1959.
> *The Girl Whose Fortune Sought Her,* in *Children's Plays from Favorite Stories,* edited by Sylvia E. Kamerman. Boston, Plays Inc., 1959.
> *Edie-Across-the-Street.* Boston, Baker, 1960.
> *The Honeysuckle Hedge.* Franklin, Ohio, Eldridge, 1960.
> *Never Keep Him Waiting.* Chicago, Dramatic Publishing Company, 1961.
> *Red Heels and Roses.* New York, McKay, 1962.
> *If a Body Meets a Body.* Cedar Rapids, Iowa, Heuer, 1963.
> *Now Hear This.* Franklin, Ohio, Eldridge, 1963.
> *The Magic Bookshelf,* and *The Other Side of the Wall,* in *Fifty Plays for Junior Actors,* edited by Sylvia E. Kamerman. Boston, Plays Inc., 1966.
> *The Do-Nothing Frog,* in *100 Plays for Children,* edited by A.S. Burack. Boston, Plays Inc., 1970.

255

Other plays: *The Invisible Dragon, Yankee Doodle Came to Cranetown, A Feather in His Cap, The Wonderful Door, A Wish Is for Keeping, Susan and Aladdin's Lamp, The Signpost, The Friendship Bracelet, Christmas in Old New England, The Straight Line from Somewhere.*

Other

Dr. Elizabeth: The Story of the First Woman Doctor.   New York, Lothrop, 1974.

PUBLICATIONS FOR ADULTS

Plays

A Candle on the Table.   Boston, Baker, 1972.

Other play: *The Retirement.*

Manuscript Collection: Kerlan Collection, University of Minnesota, Minneapolis.

Patricia Clapp comments:

The Books – no current trends, tensions, problems, mores, or "hangups" – rather historical or period stories, or pure fantasy. There *are* ladies and gentlemen in the world, there are laughter, and concern for other people. Children still like to imagine things, to pretend, to be deliciously (and safely) frightened, and they like happy endings. Since such things are still possible – even in today's life – I choose to write about them.

The Plays – comedy, with enough dramatic tension to hold them together. The 30 + include historical plays, imaginary kingdom plays, everyday plays, plays with music and plays with audience participation. Plays that children can act in without having to play roles beyond their ability, and plays that children can watch just for enjoyment. Age range for young actors is from primary school through high school. The few adult plays are in a different class – rather more timely and more demanding.

*   *   *

Although most of Patricia Clapp's writing for children and young people is in the form of plays, her first novel made more impact than her earlier dramatic work in the field of children's literature, winning a place as one of the runners-up for the National Book Award in the first year there was a category for children's books. *Constance* is in journal form, and Clapp uses this literary device brilliantly in one of the most outstanding books set in the colonial period of the United States – and there are many. Constance has come over on the *Mayflower*, and she is an outspoken, lively girl of fourteen who finds America "cold, grey, hard, bleak, unfriendly," and the first winter in the Plymouth colony grim. She misses London, and she is apprehensive about her future. But, like any adolescent, she is resilient and soon becomes immersed in the affairs of the colony, in relationships with Native Americans and struggles with English backers, and, as she grows older, in the man she marries at the close of the story. The last diary entry begins "How Beautiful Plymouth is, held tight in winter!" Clapp's research is not obtrusive in historical details, but emerges in the thorough identification with the period, and her heroine is both a girl of her time and a character with universality, in a story that is smoothly written, historically accurate, and vivid in its characterization.

In *Jane-Emily* and *King of the Dollhouse* Clapp turns to fantasy. The first is told by Louisa, eighteen, who expects a quiet summer with her orphaned niece Jane and Jane's grandmother, but Jane becomes obsessed by the spirit of Emily, an aunt who had died at Jane's age and whose malice is made increasingly apparent as the story develops. The realism and fantasy are nicely blended and the story builds in suspense nicely, albeit at a slow pace. The second book is somewhat less effective, since there is no real story line and the fantasy is not as well combined with its realistic base as in *Jane-Emily*. A small girl discovers that her dollhouse is inhabited by a tiny, plump king who takes care of eleven babies of identical size while their mother the queen is off riding and hunting. The incidents are episodic rather than cohesive, and the book needs either humor or action to compensate for its static quality, although the style of the writing is competent.

As she did in *Constance*, Clapp uses first person to gain immediacy in her one biography, *Dr. Elizabeth*, the life story of Elizabeth Blackwell, the first woman to get a medical degree in the United States. Clapp avoids two of the pitfalls to which many biographers for young readers succumb: there is no note of adulation in the writing, and there is no undue attention to the biographee's childhood. Blackwell emerges as a vivid character, and her story is valuable both as a segment of medical history and as a chapter in the long struggle for women's rights.

—Zena Sutherland

CLARK, Ann Nolan. American. Born in Las Vegas, New Mexico, 5 December 1896. Educated at New Mexico Highlands University, Las Vegas. Married Thomas Patrick Clark in 1919. Assistant English teacher, Highlands University; Educational Supervisor, Bureau of Indian Affairs, 1920–62; trained teachers in Latin America, 1945–50. Education Consultant, Institute of Latin-American Affairs; United States Delegate to Unesco Conference, Brazil. Recipient: New York *Herald Tribune* Festival award, 1941, 1952; American Library Association Newbery Medal, 1953; United States Bureau of Indian Affairs Distinguished Service Award, 1962; Catholic Library Association Regina Medal, 1963. Address: P.O. Box 164, Cortaro, Arizona 95230, U.S.A.

PUBLICATIONS FOR CHILDREN

Fiction

> *Buffalo Caller: The Story of a Young Sioux Boy of the Early 1700's, Before the Coming of the Horse*, illustrated by Marian Hulsizer. Evanston, Illinois, Row Peterson, 1942.
> *Young Hunter of Picuris*, illustrated by Velino Herrara. Chilouo, Oklahoma, Bureau of Indian Affairs, 1943.
> *Little Navajo Bluebird*, illustrated by Paul Lantz. New York, Viking Press, 1943.
> *Magic Money*, illustrated by Leo Politi. New York, Viking Press, 1950.
> *Secret of the Andes*, illustrated by Jean Charlot. New York, Viking Press, 1952.
> *Looking-for-Something: The Story of a Stray Burro of Ecuador*, illustrated by Leo Politi. New York, Viking Press, 1952.
> *Blue Canyon Horse*, illustrated by Allan Houser. New York, Viking Press, 1954.
> *Santiago*, illustrated by Lynd Ward. New York, Viking Press, 1955.
> *A Santo for Pasqualita*, illustrated by Mary Villarejo. New York, Viking Press, 1959.
> *World Song*, illustrated by Kurt Wiese. New York, Viking Press, 1960.
> *Paco's Miracle*, illustrated by Agnes Tait. New York, Farrar Straus, 1962.
> *Tia Maria's Garden*, illustrated by Ezra Jack Keats. New York, Viking Press, 1963.
> *Medicine Man's Daughter*, illustrated by Don Bolognese. New York, Farrar Straus, 1963.
> *This for That*, illustrated by Don Freeman. San Carlos, California, Golden Gate Books, 1965.

257

Summer Is for Growing, illustrated by Agnes Tait. New York, Farrar Straus, 1968.
Hoofprint on the Wind, illustrated by Robert Andrew Parker. New York, Viking Press, 1972.
Year Walk. New York, Viking Press, 1975.
All This Wild Land. New York, Viking Press, 1976.

Verse

In My Mother's House, illustrated by Velino Herrara. New York, Viking Press, 1941.
Third Monkey, illustrated by Don Freeman. New York, Viking Press, 1956.
Bear Cub, illustrated by Charles Fracé. New York, Viking Press, 1965.

Other

Who Wants to Be a Prairie Dog? (reader), illustrated by Van Tishnahjinnie. Phoenix, Office of Indian Affairs, 1940.
Little Herder in Spring [Autumn, Winter, Summer] (readers), illustrated by Hoke Denetsosie. Phoenix, Office of Indian Affairs, 4 vols., 1940, 1942.
Little Boy with Three Names: Stories of Taos Pueblo (reader), illustrated by Tunita Lujan. Chilouo, Oklahoma, Office of Indian Affairs, 1940.
The Pine Ridge Porcupine (reader). Lawrence, Kansas, Office of Indian Affairs, 1941.
A Child's Story of New Mexico, with Frances Carey. Lincoln, Nebraska, University Publishing, 1941.
There Still Are Buffalo (reader), illustrated by Andrew Standing Soldier. Lawrence, Kansas, Office of Indian Affairs, 1942.
The Slim Butte Raccoon (reader), illustrated by Andrew Standing Soldier. Lawrence, Kansas, Office of Indian Affairs, 1942.
The Grass Mountain Mouse (reader), illustrated by Andrew Standing Soldier. Lawrence, Kansas, Office of Indian Affairs, 1942.
The Hen of Wahpeton (reader), illustrated by Andrew Standing Soldier. Lawrence, Kansas, Office of Indian Affairs, 1943.
Bringer of the Mystery Dog (reader), illustrated by Oscar Howe. Lawrence, Kansas, Office of Indian Affairs, 1943.
Brave Against the Enemy: A Story of Three Generations – of the Day Before Yesterday, of Yesterday, and of Tomorrow (reader), illustrated by Helen Post. Lawrence, Kansas, Office of Indian Affairs, 1944.
Sun Journey: A Story of the Zuñi Pueblo (reader), illustrated by Percy T. Sandy. Chilouo, Oklahoma, Office of Indian Affairs, 1945.
Singing Sioux Cowboy Reader, illustrated by Andrew Standing Soldier. Lawrence, Kansas, United States Indian Service, 1947.
The Little Indian Pottery Maker, illustrated by Don Perceval. Los Angeles, Melmont, 1955.
Third Monkey, illustrated by Don Freeman. New York, Viking Press, 1956.
The Little Indian Basket Maker, illustrated by Harrison Begay. Los Angeles, Melmont, 1957.
The Desert People, illustrated by Allan Houser. New York, Viking Press, 1962.
Father Kino: Priest to the Pimas, illustrated by H. Lawrence Hoffman. New York, Farrar Straus, and London, Burns and Oates, 1963.
Brother Andre of Montreal, illustrated by Harold Lang. New York, Vision Books, and London, Burns and Oates, 1967.
Along Sandy Trails, illustrated by Alfred A. Cohn. New York, Viking Press, 1969.
Circle of Seasons, illustrated by W.T. Mars. New York, Farrar Straus, 1970.

PUBLICATIONS FOR ADULTS

Other

Journey to the People.   New York, Viking Press, 1969.
These Were the Valiant: A Collection of New Mexico Profiles.   Albuquerque, Horn, 1969.

Manuscript Collections: Kerlan Collection, University of Minnesota, Minneapolis; de Grummond Collection, University of Southern Mississippi, Hattiesburg.

Ann Nolan Clark comments:
   When I entered the Bureau of Indian Affairs (B.I.A.) in the 1920's, I quickly realized that there were no textbooks which Indian children could relate to – vocabulary, background, and values in the books then available were foreign to them and could not be understood. I wrote what was then called "Third Grade Geography" which I thought would help to build concepts of people in relation to places and modes of living. Each child bound (in Indian calico) his own book and illustrated it. Someone from the B.I.A. Washington office showed a copy to May Massee at Viking Press, and the book was published as *In My Mother's House.* This lead the B.I.A. to encourage me to write Indian readers for Indian children. These were illustrated by Indian students and published at Indian schools where printing was being taught. I did a series of Pueblo, Navajo, and Papago stories, but World War II cut off our appropriation for printing. After that I continued to work for the B.I.A., and tried to write a book every year.

*   *   *

In My Mother's House is one of the most unusual books ever written for children in the United States. Ann Nolan Clark wrote it so that her small class of third graders in the tiny Tewa Indian village of Tesuque, New Mexico, would have a book that they could read and understand about the everyday life of their people.
   It is no wonder the five Indian children took the book to their hearts. It is a book filled with their ways, their world, their words; and said in a way that they would say it. Yes, the book must be *said.* If one just looks at the words it could easily be mistaken for any other primer for early readers, but when the words are given sound, the Indian child's deep feeling for nature and love of family are poetically revealed.
   Ordinarily teaching children and writing for them doesn't mix well, but then Ann Nolan Clark is no ordinary woman. Like Sylvia Ashton-Warner, the remarkable teacher-writer who worked among the Maori children of New Zealand, Mrs. Clark's writing is extraordinary because her approach to teaching was extraordinary. For instance, she found in the written work of older Indian children the quiet beauty of straight forward "Talk" that comes naturally to a person raised in the oral tradition. Here, in "Sleep," is but one of those she shares in *Journey to the People*:

The sun goes down
and night falls.
Then I close my eyes
and go to sleep
in my bed under the trees.

   These served as her models when she turned to writing books for their younger brothers and sisters, who could not as yet read or write, but whose minds and hearts she knew and understood; books like *Blue Canyon Horse* and *The Desert People* (a companion piece to *In My Mother's House*). It begins:

> I am a boy
>   of the Desert People.
>
> White men call me Indian
> White men call me Papago
>   but the wild animals
>   call me Brother
>   because they know me
>   and love me.

Simple beauty remains the most succinct and apt description of Ann Nolan Clark's books, even when one considers those that are addressed to more sophisticated readers. The plots of books like *Secret of the Andes* and *Santiago* revolve around the difficulties faced by young Indians in meeting the demands of two conflicting cultures. These works appeal most to those readers who appreciate the special delights of atmosphere and mood that are captured only by a writer who not only knows the cultures of the Indians of the Americas but who also has a reverential understanding for the people and their ways, all gained through a lifetime of living with them.

As she says: "children need children's books that have been written with honesty, accuracy, and reality. They need books that develop deeper understandings and broader acceptances, that enrich imagination. Their need is my challenge." Ann Nolan Clark has met that challenge.

—James E. Higgins

CLARK, Catherine Anthony (Smith).   British.   Born in London, 5 May 1892; emigrated to Canada in 1914. Educated at the Convent of Jesus and Mary, Ipswich, Suffolk. Married Leonard Clark in 1919; one son and one daughter. Columnist, *Prospector*, Nelson, British Columbia. Recipient: Canadian Library Association Book of the Year Medal, 1952. *Died 24 February 1977.*

PUBLICATIONS FOR CHILDREN

Fiction

> *The Golden Pine Cone*, illustrated by Clare Bice.   Toronto, Macmillan, 1950.
> *The Sun Horse*, illustrated by Clare Bice.   Toronto, Macmillan, 1951.
> *The One-Winged Dragon*, illustrated by Clare Bice.   Toronto, Macmillan, 1955.
> *The Silver Man*, illustrated by Clare Bice.   Toronto, Macmillan, 1958; London, Macmillan, 1959.
> *The Diamond Feather; or, The Door in the Mountain: A Magic Tale for Children*, illustrated by Clare Bice.   Toronto and London, Macmillan, 1962.
> *The Man with the Yellow Eyes*, illustrated by Gordon Raynor.   Toronto, Macmillan, and New York, St. Martin's Press, 1963; London, Macmillan, 1964.
> *The Hunter and the Medicine Man*, illustrated by Clare Bice.   Toronto, Macmillan, 1966.

*   *   *

As the author of six books of fantasy Catherine Anthony Clark was an important contributor to a field of writing sparsely represented in Canadian children's literature. Her books are set in British Columbia and the magic adventures they recount take place in wilderness areas and the foothills of the Rocky Mountains where the spirits of the land and the people who have inhabited it are alive. They draw strongly on the legendary figures and the beliefs of the Indians of the Pacific Northwest and indeed native peoples play an important role in all the stories. Clark has created folk spirits of the countryside, the Lake Snake, the Head Canada Goose, which add humour and imaginative vigour. On the periphery of the enchanted lands are prospectors and settlers. It is often through these characters for whom the boundaries of reality have become blurred, that the spirits are introduced.

The protagonists are children, generally a boy and girl. At odds with their lives, they are drawn to fantastic adventures in which they undertake a quest. In following it they come to a better understanding of themselves and the problems with which they must contend. While this forms the unifying theme of the plots, the author's purpose is more closely involved in portraying the land and its inheritance. Her strength as a descriptive writer is a major factor in her success. There is a marked similarity between the stories. *The Golden Pine Cone* relates the magic adventures of two children who find a golden pine cone belonging to the ruler of the lands, lakes and forests and must withstand those who seek the power it holds. In *The Sun Horse* a boy and girl search for her father who has been lured by a golden stallion into the idyllic valley of forgetfulness. The Chinese and Indian strains in British Columbia's past are brought together in *The One-Winged Dragon*, the story of an old Chinese farmer who keeps a dragon in his well and the children who, with the dragon's help, return his daughter to him. The life of native peoples of the Pacific Northwest is well reflected in their adventures. The book is more well constructed than the earlier fantasies, its characterization is fuller and more sympathetic. *The Silver Man* tells of a troubled boy who, in his dazed contemplation of a rock crystal, experiences an adventure in which he restores a lost young chieftain to his tribe. Clark's last two novels are weakened by a plethora of incident and plot. In *The Diamond Feather* an orphaned brother and sister go through the door in a mountain to the Valley at the Edge of Time in search of the children of a bitter old prospector. *The Hunter and the Medicine Man* tells of two children who explore a haunted mountain and become involved in an evil medicine man's attempt to usurp the position of a tribe's rightful chief.

The books are limited in their imaginative scope. There is often little distinction between the real world and the fantastic. Although the children are believable, their dialogue natural and colloquial, the conduct clearly expected of them is very exacting. Written with ease and inventiveness the stories are, however, entertaining reading.

Clark also produced a book of historical fiction for early readers, *The Man with the Yellow Eyes*. Set near Nelson, British Columbia, at the turn of the century it tells of a boy's race against an unscrupulous prospector to stake his father's claim to land containing rich deposits of silver. The handling of the plot is banal but the descriptions of the foothills and the practical ways of the hardworking settlers are here, as in the other books, noteworthy.

—Ruth Osler

CLARK, Leonard. British. Born in St. Peter Port, Guernsey, 1 August 1905. Educated at Monmouth School, 1917–22; Normal College, Bangor, Caernarvonshire, 1928–30, Cert.Ed. 1930. Served in the Home Guard, Devon Regiment, 1940–43. Married Jane Callow in 1954; has one son and one daughter. Taught in Gloucestershire, 1922–28, and London, 1930–36; Inspector of Schools, Devon, Yorkshire, and London, 1936–70. Since 1970, Editor, Longmans Poetry Library series (64 titles); currently, Consultant Editor, Chatto and Windus Poetry Books for the Young, London, and Thornhill Press, Gloucester. Member, Arts Council Literature Panel, 1965–69. Liveryman of Haberdashers' Company, 1965. Freeman of City of London, 1965. Honorary Associate, London Academy of Music and Dramatic Art, 1969. Fellow, Royal Society of Literature, 1953. Knight of the Order of St. Sylvester, 1970. O.B.E. (Officer, Order of the British Empire), 1966. Address: 50 Cholmeley Crescent, London N6 5HA, England.

PUBLICATIONS FOR CHILDREN

Fiction

Robert Andrew Tells a Story, illustrated by James Scargill.   Leeds, E.J. Arnold, 1965.
Robert Andrew and Tiffy, illustrated by James Scargill.   Leeds, E.J. Arnold, 1965.
Robert Andrew by the Sea, illustrated by James Scargill.   Leeds, E.J. Arnold, 1965.
Robert Andrew and the Holy Family, illustrated by James Scargill.   Leeds, E.J. Arnold, 1965.
Robert Andrew and the Red Indian Chief, illustrated by James Scargill.   Leeds, E.J. Arnold, 1966.
Robert Andrew and Skippy, illustrated by James Scargill.   Leeds, E.J. Arnold, 1966.
Robert Andrew in the Country, illustrated by James Scargill.   Leeds, E.J. Arnold, 1966.
Mr. Pettigrew's Harvest Festival, illustrated by Toffee Sanders.   Gloucester, Thornhill Press, 1974.
Mr. Pettigrew's Train, illustrated by Toffee Sanders.   Gloucester, Thornhill Press, 1975.
Mr. Pettigrew and the Bellringers, illustrated by Toffee Sanders.   Gloucester, Thornhill Press, 1976.

Verse

Daybreak: A First Book of Poems, illustrated by Selma Nakivell.   London, Hart Davis, 1963.
The Year Round: A Second Book of Poems, illustrated by Edward Ardizzone.   London, Hart Davis, 1966.
Fields and Territories.   London, Turret Books, 1967.
Good Company, illustrated by Jennie Corbett.   London, Dobson, 1968.
Near and Far, illustrated by Kozo Kakimoto and others.   London, Hamlyn, 1968.
Here and There, illustrated by Kuniro Fukazawa.   London, Hamlyn, 1969.
Secret as Toads.   London, Chatto and Windus, 1972.
Singing in the Streets: Poems for Christmas.   London, Dobson, 1972.
The Broad Atlantic.   London, Dobson, 1974.
Four Seasons, illustrated by Jennie Corbett.   London, Dobson, 1975.
Collected Poems and Verses for Children.   London, Dobson, 1975.
The Tale of Prince Igor, illustrated by Charles Keeping.   London, Dobson, 1977.

Other

When They Were Children, illustrated by William Randell.   London, Parrish, and New York, Roy, 1964.
St. Felix and the Spider.   London, Catholic Truth Society, 1974.
St. Patrick.   London, Catholic Truth Society, 1974.
St. Anthony of Egypt.   London, Catholic Truth Society, 1974.
St. Dorothea and the Flowers of Paradise.   London, Catholic Truth Society, 1974.

Editor, *The Magic Kingdom: An Anthology of Verse for Seniors*.   London, Elkin Mathews and Marrot, 1937.
Editor, *The Open Door: An Anthology of Verse for Juniors*.   London, Elkin Mathews and Marrot, 1937.

Editor, *Quiet as Moss: Thirty Six Poems*, by Andrew Young. London, Hart Davis, 1960.

Editor, *Drums and Trumpets: Poetry for the Youngest*, illustrated by Heather Copley. London, Bodley Head, 1962; Chester Springs, Pennsylvania, Dufour, 1963.

Editor, *Common Ground: An Anthology for the Young*, illustrated by M.E. Eldridge. London, Faber, 1964.

Editor, *Selected Poems by John Clare, 1793–1864*. Leeds, E.J. Arnold, 1964.

Editor, *All Things New: An Anthology*, illustrated by Ann Tout. London, Constable, 1965; Chester Springs, Pennsylvania, Dufour, 1968.

Editor, *The Poetry of Nature*. London, Hart Davis, 1965.

Editor, *Following the Sun: Poems by Children*, illustrated by Tony Dyson. London, Odhams, 1967.

Editor, *Flutes and Cymbals: Poetry for the Young*, illustrated by Shirley Hughes. London, Bodley Head, 1968; New York, Crowell, 1969.

Editor, *Sound of Battle*, illustrated by Ewart Oakeshott. Oxford, Pergamon Press, 1969.

Editor, *Poems by Children*. London, Studio Vista, 1970.

Editor, *All Along, Down Along: A Book of Stories in Verse*, illustrated by Pauline Baynes. London, Longman, 1971.

PUBLICATIONS FOR ADULTS

Verse

Poems. London, Fortune Press, 1940.
Passage to the Pole and Other Poems. London, Fortune Press, 1944.
Rhandanim. Leeds, Salamander Press, 1945.
The Mirror and Other Poems. London, Allen Wingate, 1948.
XII Poems. Birmingham, City of Birmingham School of Printing, 1948.
English Morning and Other Poems. London, Hutchinson, 1953.
Selected Poems, 1940–1957. London, Hutchinson, 1958.
Walking with Trees. London, Enitharmon Press, 1970.
Every Voice. Guildford, Surrey, Words Press, 1971.
The Hearing Heart: Poems. London, Enitharmon Press, 1974.
Winter to Winter and Other Poems. London, Dobson, 1977.

Other

Alfred Williams: His Life and Works. Oxford, Blackwell, 1945; New York, A.M. Kelly, 1969.
Ideas in Poetry. Birmingham, City of Birmingham School of Printing, 1947.
Sark Discovered: Prospect of an Island, Being a Literary and Pictorial Record of the Island of Sark. London, Dent, 1956; revised edition, London, Dobson, 1971.
Walter de la Mare: A Checklist. Cambridge, University Press, 1956.
Walter de la Mare. London, Bodley Head, 1960; New York, Walck, 1961.
Green Wood: A Gloucestershire Childhood. London, Parrish, 1962.
Andrew Young. London, Longman, 1964.
A Fool in the Forest (autobiography). London, Dobson, 1965.
Prospect of Highgate and Hampstead. London, Highgate Press, 1967.
Grateful Caliban (autobiography). London, Dobson, 1967.
A Tribute to Walter de la Mare, with Edmund Blunden. London, Enitharmon Press, 1974.
Three Poets, Two Children. Gloucester, Thornhill Press, 1975.
The Inspector Remembers (autobiography). London, Dobson, 1976.
Writing for the Public. Gloucester, Thornhill Press, 1976.

Editor, *The Kingdom of the Mind: Essays and Addresses by Albert Mansbridge, 1903–1937.* London, Dent, 1944.
Editor, *Andrew Young: Prospect of a Poet: Essays and Tributes by Fourteen Writers.* London, Hart Davis, 1957.
Editor, *The Collected Poems of Andrew Young.* London, Hart Davis, 1960.
Editor, with others, *The Complete Poems of Walter de la Mare.* London, Faber, 1969.
Editor, *The Complete Poems of Andrew Young.* London, Secker and Warburg, 1973.
Editor, *Poems of Ivor Gurney, 1890–1937.* London, Chatto and Windus, 1973.

Leonard Clark comments:

It is natural that, as the father of two children, a former teacher, and one of Her Majesty's Inspectors of Schools for many years, I should write prose and poetry for the young. In addition, as editor of many anthologies of poetry for the young, I have seen the need for providing for them, in attractive form, collections of poetry by other poets. These, I believe, together with my own books of poetry, have made a major contribution to literature for children; by children I mean an age range which extends from five to sixteen years. In essence, my poetry for the young does not differ greatly from any other poetry I write, for I have always believed that a good poem for children must be a good poem for everybody else. This poetry, which has largely concerned itself with nature, and with the thoughts and feelings of children as they grow up and inherit the world, is successful, perhaps, because I believe I am the child for whom the poems have been written. My long experience of children and my simple, straightforward style of writing have, I believe, gone a long way to establishing me as one of the significant poets of our age for the young. Although I owe a great deal to Walter de la Mare's advice and guidance, my voice is my own. It is a very English voice which tries to speak of things eternal, without any condescension, sentimentality, or undue nostalgia. It faces up to life as life is lived imaginatively, with always an eye on the visionary and mystical.

*   *   *

Despite his popular *Mr. Pettigrew* stories Leonard Clark is best known for poetry. Teaching experience enables him to speak directly to children. "You are the child for whom the poem is written," Kathleen Raine has told him. He is also the only Inspector of Schools since Matthew Arnold to publish a substantial heap of verse. After de la Mare, only he and James Reeves have produced their collected children's poems. His influence on educational literary policy has been considerable, and he originated the Arts Council's "Writers in Schools" project. He has edited many anthologies, some of poems by children themselves. All his books are very carefully designed. In *Following the Sun* the chapter headings from Traherne make a continuous and developing accompaniment to the poems themselves. In *All Things New*, seasonal changes, the Six Days and varied manifestations of Creation, the illustrations, link the verse to a subtle whole. His own poem "Earthworm" is shaped like a worm, the rhythms of "Snow" approximate that of the fall of snow itself. Clark is particularly sympathetic to the 5–12 age group but always "a poem for children must be a good poem." He never hesitates to include a difficult work, confident that even a small response is ample justification. Too much easy reading rots the imagination; a poem, wrote T.S. Eliot, can communicate before it is understood.

Clark's range is wide: the undeservedly obscure, neglected and forgotten may flank some famous name, testifying not to the insignificance but unimportance of fashion. Throughout, originality of theme is rated less than originality of perception. He is quick to notice the child who sees the ocean as an angry cat but who may yet allow people to lie on its wet back: and the teenager who sadly, memorably, wonders whether her own indifference has killed a baby. His concern with tradition places poems and individual words against total history, the changing values and perspectives. "Sleep" is shown treated by John Fletcher, Wordsworth, Tennyson, Edward Thomas, Auden. This concern informs his choices amongst contemporaries. When an Inspector, he set himself to remedy their neglect in schools. His *The Poetry of Nature*, starting with Chaucer and Lydgate, ends with Wain, Thwaite, Kirkup, Ted Hughes. A teacher, he realises that little can be taught, much implied. He seldom writes a "children's poem," but first writes, then decides the audience. His own verse includes lyrics, narratives of travel and adventure, and, above all, nature poetry in the tradition of Clare, Christina Rossetti, Frost, and Edward Thomas, with affinities to de la Mare and Andrew Young, on both of whom he is an authority. It is not the slack pastoral of nymphs and shepherds, but of observation, precise, sharp, at times ironic. Edith Sitwell once called him "a practical mystic." He sees not Man and Nature but Man with Nature. There are also echoes of Blake and Samuel Palmer. His most consistent influence is the English countryside, its centuries of order, work − he enjoys *things* in action − conflict and evolution, landscapes of peace made strong despite inescapable present pollutions and past cruelties. Quiet Somerset contains sad once-bloody Sedgemoor. With little violence but much intensity his is a poetry of special places, private dreams, secret sounds, the precious autonomy of field and wood, the gaps within silence of an abandoned house. Conflict is suggested, not between Science and Nature, but irresponsible bits of Science exploiting or ruining a Nature which, if left wholly to itself, would likewise distort and overwhelm. Throughout, Clark speaks to those for whom trees are more than timber, hedges more than barriers. Birds are simultaneously remote and personal: they are pattern and colour, carrion and myth, pet and victim.

He records the permutations of the child's day, the complex gradations of light and emotion, overlappings of morning, and afternoon, evening, of play and dream. He largely ignores current events but not history: is grieved and angered by the murder both of the Inca Atahualpa and of J.F. Kennedy. He knows that for certain minds a cave painting or Spanish ingot can be more contemporary than a transistor. Many poems, ostensibly simple, can ultimately reveal the unexpected. In his long writing life − he began publishing at 18 − he has kept an evenness of texture which may have prevented many obvious anthology pieces. This at least leaves much to be discovered. That he has always wanted to gently delight rather than bruise and crudely shock may have robbed him of some critical esteem but undeniably won him a very wide readership.

—Peter Vansittart

CLARK, Mavis Thorpe. Australian. Educated at Methodist Ladies College, Melbourne. Married to Harold Latham; has two daughters. Recipient: Australian Children's Book Council Book of the Year Award, 1967. Address: 2 Crest Avenue, Balwyn, Victoria 3103, Australia.

PUBLICATIONS FOR CHILDREN

Fiction

> *Hatherly's First Fifteen*, illustrated by F. E. Hiley. London, Oxford University Press, 1930.
> *Dark Pool Island*. Melbourne, Oxford University Press, 1949.
> *Missing Gold*. London, Hutchinson, 1949.
> *The Twins from Timber Creek*. Melbourne, Oxford University Press, 1949.
> *Home Again at Timber Creek*. Melbourne, Oxford University Press, 1950.
> *Jingaroo*. Melbourne, Oxford University Press, 1951.
> *The Brown Land Was Green*, illustrated by Harry Hudson. Melbourne and London, Heinemann, 1956.

Gully of Gold, illustrated by Anne Graham.   Melbourne and London, Heinemann, 1958.

Pony from Tarella, illustrated by Jean M. Rowe.   London and Melbourne, Heinemann, 1959.

They Came South, illustrated by Joy Murray.   London and Melbourne, Heinemann, 1963.

The Min-Min, illustrated by Genevieve Melrose.   Melbourne, Lansdowne Press, 1966; London, Angus and Robertson, 1967; New York, Macmillan, 1969.

Blue above the Trees, illustrated by Genevieve Melrose.   Melbourne, Lansdowne Press, 1967; London, Angus and Robertson, 1968; New York, Meredith Press, 1969.

Spark of Opal, illustrated by Genevieve Melrose.   Melbourne, Lansdowne Press, 1968; London, Methuen, 1971; New York, Macmillan, 1973.

Nowhere to Hide, illustrated by Genevieve Melrose.   Melbourne, Lansdowne Press, 1969.

Iron Mountain, illustrated by Ronald Brooks.   Melbourne, Lansdowne Press, and London, Methuen, 1970; New York, Macmillan, 1971.

New Golden Mountain.   Melbourne, Lansdowne Press, 1973; as *If the Earth Falls In*, New York, Seabury Press, 1973.

Wildfire.   Sydney, Hodder and Stoughton, and Leicester, Brockhampton Press, 1973; New York, Macmillan, 1974.

The Sky Is Free.   Sydney, Hodder and Stoughton, Leicester, Brockhampton Press, and New York, Macmillan, 1976.

The Hundred Islands.   Sydney and London, Hodder and Stoughton, and New York, Macmillan, 1977.

Other

John Batman (as Mavis Latham).   Melbourne, Oxford University Press, 1962.

Fishing (as Mavis Latham), illustrated by Joy Murray.   Melbourne, Oxford University Press, 1963.

A Pack Tracker, illustrated by Shirley Turner.   Melbourne and New York, Oxford University Press, 1968.

Opal Mining, illustrated by Barbara Taylor.   Melbourne, Oxford University Press, 1969.

PUBLICATIONS FOR ADULTS

Other

Pastor Doug: The Story of an Aboriginal Leader.   Melbourne, Lansdowne Press, 1965; London, Newnes, 1966; revised edition, as *Pastor Doug: The Story of Sir Douglas Nicholls, Aboriginal Leader*, Lansdowne Press, 1972.

Jane and Betty Rayner, Strolling Players.   Melbourne, Lansdowne Press, 1972.

*   *   *

Mavis Thorpe Clark is a prolific and well organized writer; her teenage novels are set in different parts of Australia, and she first investigates these backgrounds very thoroughly before she begins to write. In *Blue above the Trees* and *The Brown Land Was Green*, two early novels, she relates the experiences of two (fictional) pioneer families. In these two stories, plot and characterization can be more readily separated than in her later novels, when her skill in characterization increases to the point where events and characters interact upon each other. Her plots, however, are always strong, with events and their outcome a vital force in each story. *Nowhere to Hide*, another earlier work, is interesting as being one of the few novels for young readers which has a background of Australia during the second world war.

The Min-Min (Australian Children's Book of the Year, 1967) is undoubtedly Mavis Thorpe Clark's most outstanding work; in telling the story of an outback railway settler's family, living cut off from civilization, she displays a degree of conviction and compassion which she has not quite achieved since, perhaps because in *The Min-Min* she was content to pursue one outstanding theme. In several of her other novels, by contrast, she tends to introduce a number of parallel or sub-themes, diffusing the reader's interest between characters of almost equal importance. *The Sky Is Free* and *The Hundred Islands* are each concerned with topical and social questions, which tend now and then to dominate characterization and plot. In *The Sky Is Free*, the young hero runs away from a comfortable suburban home to the opal fields; on the way he teams up with a boy who is also on the run, from an institutional home. While this novel has many admirable qualities, including well-assimilated information about the opal fields, the plot is perhaps too neatly contrived. Conservation, especially that of the fauna of the Bass Strait islands, is the theme of *The Hundred Islands*, which contains fascinating first-hand observation of the mutton-bird, in particular; but in this novel, too, the author tends to subject characterization to the theme, and manipulate the plot a little too firmly.

—Barbara Ker Wilson

CLARKE, Joan. British. Practising pediatrician. Address: c/o Jonathan Cape Ltd., 30 Bedford Square, London WC1B 3EL, England.

PUBLICATIONS FOR CHILDREN

Fiction

The Happy Planet, illustrated by Antony Maitland. London, Cape, 1963.
Foxon's Hole, illustrated by Pat Marriott. London, Cape, 1969.
Early Rising, illustrated by Pauline Martin. London, Cape, 1974; Philadelphia, Lippincott, 1976.

*   *   *

Each of Joan Clarke's stories is different from the next and each is successful in its own way. *The Happy Planet*, her first novel, is the story of two children who return to Earth from Tuan – a planet peopled by descendants of those who had fled from a catastrophe on Earth 1000 years previously. Life on Tuan follows a design familiar in other space fantasies: a highly technological "Brave New World." There is perhaps a lack of imaginative invention in this and in the pattern of life on Earth where little that is original seems to have developed. Within this limitation, the characterisation is well-established and the tension and excitement in the plot carry the reader forward to a satisfying conclusion in which evil is overcome, danger to life on Earth averted and a happy future assured for the two children. Joan Clarke's second novel, *Foxon's Hole*, is also about someone come to Earth but from another time rather than another place. Mick, a Neanderthal boy, is brought forward from the Ice Age by an experiment with an imperfectly understood process of time travel. His position is realistically created: he is an intelligent boy, fascinated by gadgets but superficially stupid so that it seems inevitable when the well-meaning, overworked, unimaginative authorities put him in a hospital for mentally retarded children. The characterisation of the children, and of the sympathetic adults, is complete and satisfying although some minor villains tend to be stereotypes.

Early Rising is quite different. The story of Erica, second of the five children of a

267

Gloucestershire vicar at the end of the last century, is a slice of social history. It is difficult not to identify with this wild (by nineteenth-century standards), outspoken but good-hearted child in her encounters with the step-sister who brings up the family, her governesses, her teachers at school in England and France. Books based on domestic incidents such as these often appeal more to the nostalgic adult than to the child, but the strength of the characterisation and the liveliness of the telling make for an undoubted appeal to young as well as older readers. Joan Clarke is an accomplished and thoughtful writer who has a deserved reputation based on only three novels. Each has been more skilful than the last and her next is eagerly awaited.

—Valerie Brinkley-Willsher

CLARKE, Pauline. British. Born in Kirkby-in-Ashfield, Nottinghamshire, 19 May 1921. Educated at Somerville College, Oxford, B.A. (honours) in English 1943. Married Peter Hunter Blair in 1969. Recipient: Library Association Carnegie Medal, 1963. Agent: Curtis Brown Group Ltd., 1 Craven Hill, London W2 3EW. Address: 62 Highsett, Hills Road, Cambridge CB2 1NZ, England.

PUBLICATIONS FOR CHILDREN

Fiction

The Pekinese Princess, illustrated by Cecil Leslie. London, Cape, 1948.
The Great Can, illustrated by Cecil Leslie. London, Faber, 1952.
The White Elephant, illustrated by Richard Kennedy. London, Faber, 1952; New York, Abelard Schuman, 1957.
Five Dolls in a House (as Helen Clare), illustrated by Cecil Leslie. London, Lane, 1953.
Merlin's Magic (as Helen Clare), illustrated by Cecil Leslie. London, Lane, 1953.
Smith's Hoard, illustrated by Cecil Leslie. London, Faber, 1955; as *Hidden Gold*, New York, Abelard Schuman, 1957; as *The Golden Collar*, Faber, 1967.
Sandy the Sailor, illustrated by Cecil Leslie. London, Hamish Hamilton, 1956.
The Boy with the Erpingham Hood, illustrated by Cecil Leslie. London, Faber, 1956.
Bel the Giant and Other Stories (as Helen Clare), illustrated by Peggy Fortnum. London, Lane, 1956; as *The Cat and the Fiddle, and Other Stories*, Englewood Cliffs, New Jersey, Prentice Hall, 1968.
Five Dolls and the Monkey (as Helen Clare), illustrated by Cecil Leslie. London, Lane, 1956; Englewood Cliffs, New Jersey, Prentice Hall, 1967.
Five Dolls in the Snow (as Helen Clare), illustrated by Cecil Leslie. London, Bodley Head, 1957; Englewood Cliffs, New Jersey, Prentice Hall, 1965.
James the Policeman, illustrated by Cecil Leslie. London, Hamish Hamilton, 1957.
James and the Robbers, illustrated by Cecil Leslie. London, Hamish Hamilton, 1959.
Torolv the Fatherless, illustrated by Cecil Leslie. London, Faber, 1959.
Five Dolls and Their Friends (as Helen Clare), illustrated by Cecil Leslie. London, Bodley Head, 1959; Englewood Cliffs, New Jersey, Prentice Hall, 1968.
Seven White Pebbles (as Helen Clare), illustrated by Cynthia Abbott. London, Bodley Head, 1960.
The Lord of the Castle, illustrated by Cecil Leslie. London, Hamish Hamilton, 1960.
The Robin Hooders, illustrated by Cecil Leslie. London, Faber, 1960.
James and the Smugglers, illustrated by Cecil Leslie. London, Hamish Hamilton, 1961.

Keep the Pot Boiling, illustrated by Cecil Leslie.   London, Faber, 1961.
The Twelve and the Genii, illustrated by Cecil Leslie.   London, Faber, 1962; as *The Return of the Twelves*, New York, Coward McCann, 1964.
James and the Black Van, illustrated by Cecil Leslie.   London, Hamish Hamilton, 1963.
Five Dolls and the Duke (as Helen Clare), illustrated by Cecil Leslie.   London, Bodley Head, 1963; Englewood Cliffs, New Jersey, Prentice Hall, 1968.
The Bonfire Party, illustrated by Cecil Leslie.   London, Hamish Hamilton, 1966.
The Two Faces of Silenus, illustrated by Cecil Leslie.   London, Faber, and New York, Coward McCann, 1972.

Verse

Silver Bells and Cockle Shells, illustrated by Sally Ducksbury.   London and New York, Abelard Schuman, 1962.

Other

Crowds of Creatures, illustrated by Cecil Leslie.   London, Faber, 1964.

*   *   *

The greatest single achievement of Pauline Clarke is undoubtedly her original fantasy *The Twelve and the Genii*. Once the concept is accepted that the toy soldiers given to Branwell Brontë when he was eight might be rediscovered and brought to life by another young boy in the present, the rest follows with compelling and inevitable logic. The Twelve are sharply individualised characters but always retain their soldierly nature, and the saga of their final journey, helped by the children, is full of fascinating detail. Her other stories can be grouped for convenience into historical novels, contemporary adventures and first readers. Among the historical stories, *Torolv the Fatherless* is a striking example of her skill in combining a feeling of period with a strong narrative and the ability to create character. The conflict between Torolv's loyalty to his Saxon foster family and to the Viking raider to whom he owed his first allegiance is shown with compassion. Life in medieval Norwich is vividly described in *The Boy with the Erpingham Hood* and the everyday detail is combined with the excitement and heartbreak of action at Agincourt and Harfleur.

Her contemporary stories such as *Keep the Pot Boiling*, a collection of nostalgic episodes about a family trying to make money, *The White Elephant*, a fast-moving but unlikely thriller about jewel thieves in London, and *Smith's Hoard*, in which children fight to save some Iceni treasures from the scrap merchant, are mostly well-written and full of vitality with authentic backgrounds and straightforward narrative style. *The Two Faces of Silenus* is a fantasy for older readers − a difficult undertaking − in which she captures the transition between childhood and adult emotions. Pauline Clarke has a special ability in writing for the very young which sparkles from her stories *James*, *Sandy the Sailor*, and *The Bonfire Party*, for instance. She uses simple vocabulary and repetition to create interesting stories in which her knowledge of children and her ability to capture them on paper are ably demonstrated. However remote the historical setting or bizarre the fantasy, her books are enriched and given plausibility by the description of everyday events and characters: the children in *The Twelve*, the detail of London in *The White Elephant*, the skills and rivalries in *Torolv* and the factual research in *Erpingham Hood*. Above all, she has that most essential talent for writers for children: the ability to tell a story.

—Valerie Brinkley-Willsher

CLARKSON, Ewan. British. Born in Workington, Cumberland, 23 January 1929. Educated at Altrincham Grammar School, Cheshire, 1939–45. Private, Royal Army Medical Corps, 1947–49. Married Jenny Maton in 1951; has one son and one daughter. Has worked as a scientist, veterinarian, zookeeper, mink and rabbit farmer, beach photographer, truck driver, local radio broadcaster. Address: Moss Rose Cottage, Preston, Kingsteignton, Newton Abbot, Devon, England.

PUBLICATIONS FOR CHILDREN

Fiction

> *Break for Freedom: The Story of a Mink*, illustrated by David Carl Forbes. London, Newnes, 1967; as *Syla the Mink*, New York, Dutton, 1968.
> *Halic: The Story of a Grey Seal*, illustrated by Richard Cuffari. New York, Dutton, 1970; London, Hutchinson, 1971.
> *The Running of the Deer*, illustrated by David Stone. London, Hutchinson, and New York, Dutton, 1972.
> *In the Shadow of the Falcon*, illustrated by Victor Ambrus. New York, Dutton, 1973; London, Hutchinson, 1974.
> *The Badgers of Summercombe*. London, Hutchinson, and New York, Dutton, 1977.

Other

> *Wolf Country: A Wilderness Pilgrimage*, illustrated by David Stone. New York, Dutton, 1975; London, Hutchinson, 1976.

PUBLICATIONS FOR ADULTS

Play

> Television Documentary: *In the Shadow of the Falcon*, from his own book, in *The World about Us* series, 1976.

Ewan Clarkson comments:
    I look for beauty in the face of truth, and try to convey a little of what I find to the reader, in the hope that he or she will revere life the more. I try to entertain, in order to hold the reader's attention, but I also try to educate, for I believe that the only way to change mankind is by changing man's thinking, and this, as is well known, is best achieved among the young.
    Whether he likes it or not, man is a part of nature, and his fate is inextricably bound up with the fate of the wolf, the falcon, and the blue whale. If he is to save himself, he must save all other forms of life. This, over and over again, is the theme of my work. I am also deeply religious, although not tied to any dogma or creed, and my convictions must be apparent in my work.

                                        *   *   *

It is hard to know whether to describe Ewan Clarkson as a novelist who concentrates on animal subjects, or as a naturalist who portrays and explores his themes in the form of narrative. Both are probably true. Certainly, he is an extremely able writer, and his books are notably good of their kind. The point must be made, or remade, that (as with most leading authors in this genre – Roberts, G.D. Griffiths, Williamson) his books are not specifically aimed at the young – indeed, they are published in both adults' and children's lists. The chief point of difference between these writers is the placing of the humans in their work. Unlike the great purists Roberts and Griffiths, who do not even give names to their creatures and rarely to their humans, Clarkson tends to make his humans integral to the plot, sometimes (as in *The Running of the Deer*) giving them foreground roles. He is a patently unsentimental writer: he could hardly fail to be, with his sharp observing eye and his almost obsessional care for detail. But it is clear enough where his sympathies lie, and that they are backed by reason. The basic motif of every book (where he also sets out the claim of its beast or bird to life in the human economy) is that, in wantonly destroying the plant and animal kingdom, humans destroy themselves.

Break for Freedom, a notable piece of writing in the genre, has an unusual subject; a mink, which escapes from a Devon fur-farm, discovers the joys and dangers of life outside the cage. This book illustrates particularly well Clarkson's quick illuminating of detail in any scene, so that each item − rat, worm, weed, log, beetle, stone − lives suddenly in the context of its history. *Halic* follows the life of an Atlantic grey seal, born on a rocky beach off the Welsh coast. Again, it is exact and informing, not only on the seal itself (how it avoids the "bends," for instance) but on other forms of marine and coastal life; the description of a wreck taken over by sea plants and sea creatures is particularly striking. Event, in books of this genre, is often linked with disaster − met, avoided, or overcome. Killer whale, shark, and other such natural opponents provide vivid episodes, but more dire are the ills of human origin: the oil slick, the dislodged mine, the clubs of the seal cub-killers, the unattractive weapons of city "sportsmen" in submarine gear. But Halic has the hero's privilege of survival; the sea atmosphere is compulsive; whoever reads the book once will read it again.

In the Shadow of the Falcon, another effective story, centres on a pair of peregrine falcons and their young, nesting on a vertiginous ledge of remote Welsh coastal cliff. Owen Thomas, farmer, widower, philosopher of the Clarkson kind, manages to save the eggs from thieves by a ruse; next problem, how to save the young birds, the eyasses. Good drama this. But there are other hazards: fishing lines, tanker oil, factory effluents, pesticides − often as part of a cycle. A neat sentence can sum much. Thus: "The first to succumb in the gusty Pembrokeshire fields was a rook, a frugal bird who had toiled diligently, year after year, helping to rid the land of the very pests against which the farmer now dressed his seed." As for the peregrine, "Their fate is our fate," the book concludes, "for, be it good or evil, we share a common destiny .... Perhaps in saving the peregrine [men] may unwittingly save themselves."

In *The Running of the Deer* − the most ambitious and least resolved of his books − Clarkson writes of the Exmoor deer (and of heather, fern, buzzard, rabbit, acorn, oak) with his usual expertise. But humans take the foreground and act out the central problems. A young farmer, a newcomer who has married a local girl, tries to prevent the Hunt crossing his land; as a result the locals wreck his business and almost break his marriage. Yet Clarkson is less than kind to the anti-bloodsports organisation that buys the farm. Two other characters, Isaac, an aging giant, cynic and philosopher, who gives the young man sage advice, and a deerloving hunter, a perfect shot, secretly called in to deal with a "rogue" or wounded creature, add to the book's complexities.

More characteristic is *The Badgers of Summercombe*, focussing on a family of these "proud and ancient" creatures in the Devon woods. They are monogamous (we learn), are scrupulously clean, and are vast consumers of grubs, cockchafers, voles. Against them, hunger and natural foes apart, are the gun, the trap, the badger-hunter, the motorist, flood, fire, poison, and the developer's bulldozer. All these touch the story. Borun, the litter's main survivor, is also snared by gipsies for his pelt, is sold instead to a wretched little zoo, and escapes because of the shoddy work of the cage-maker (Clarkson never misses a point). He has a curious, rather touching friendship with a young lost cat. And because of a thoughtful geologist's report, the wood of his ancestral home is saved, *pro tem*, from the motor-road planner. Another compulsive yarn, with or without the final Clarkson note, "For the badgers of Summercombe and western civilisation, time was perhaps running out. The badgers at least had for the moment won a short reprieve."

—Naomi Lewis

CLEARY, Beverly (Bunn). American. Born in McMinnville, Oregon, 12 April 1916. Educated at the University of California, Berkeley, B.A. 1938; University of Washington, Seattle, B.A. in librarianship 1939. Married Clarence Cleary in 1940; has one daughter and one son. Children's Librarian, Yakima Public Library, Washington, 1939–40; Post Librarian, United States Army Hospital, Oakland, California, 1942–45. Recipient: American Library Association Laura Ingalls Wilder Award, 1975. Lives in Carmel, California. Address: c/o William Morrow and Co. Inc., 105 Madison Avenue, New York, New York 10016, U.S.A.

PUBLICATIONS FOR CHILDREN

Fiction

Henry Huggins, illustrated by Louis Darling. New York, Morrow, 1950.
Ellen Tebbits, illustrated by Louis Darling. New York, Morrow, 1951.
Henry and Beezus, illustrated by Louis Darling. New York, Morrow, 1952.
Otis Spofford, illustrated by Louis Darling. New York, Morrow, 1953.
Henry and Ribsy, illustrated by Louis Darling. New York, Morrow, 1954.
Beezus and Ramona, illustrated by Louis Darling. New York, Morrow, 1955.
Fifteen, illustrated by Beth and Joe Krush. New York, Morrow, 1956; London, Penguin, 1962.
Henry and the Paper Route, illustrated by Louis Darling. New York, Morrow, 1957.
The Luckiest Girl. New York, Morrow, 1958.
Jean and Johnny, illustrated by Beth and Joe Krush. New York, Morrow, 1959.
The Real Hole, illustrated by Mary Stevens. New York, Morrow, 1960; London, Collins, 1962.
Two Dog Biscuits, illustrated by Mary Stevens. New York, Morrow, 1961; London, Collins, 1963.
Emily's Runaway Imagination, illustrated by Beth and Joe Krush. New York, Morrow, 1961.
Henry and the Clubhouse, illustrated by Louis Darling. New York, Morrow, 1962.
Sister of the Bride, illustrated by Beth and Joe Krush. New York, Morrow, 1963.
Ribsy, illustrated by Louis Darling. New York, Morrow, 1964.
The Mouse and the Motorcycle, illustrated by Louis Darling. New York, Morrow, 1965; London, Hamish Hamilton, 1974.
Mitch and Amy, illustrated by George Porter. New York, Morrow, 1967.
Ramona the Pest, illustrated by Louis Darling. New York, Morrow, 1968; London, Hamish Hamilton, 1974.
Runaway Ralph, illustrated by Louis Darling. New York, Morrow, 1970; London, Hamish Hamilton, 1974.
Socks, illustrated by Beatrice Darwin. New York, Morrow, 1973.
Ramona the Brave, illustrated by Alan Tiegreen. New York, Morrow, and London, Hamish Hamilton, 1975.
Ramona and Her Father, illustrated by Alan Tiegreen. New York, Morrow, and London, Hamish Hamilton, 1977.

Play

The Sausage at the End of the Nose. New York, Children's Book Council, 1974.

Verse

The Hullabaloo ABC, illustrated by Earl Thollander. Berkeley, California, Parnassus Press, 1960.

Beverly Cleary comments:

As a child I had difficulty learning to read. The discovery, when I was about eight years old, that I could actually read, and read with pleasure, was one of the most exciting moments of my life. From that moment on, as I read through the shelves of the library, I searched for, but was unable to find, the books I wanted to read most of all: books about the sort of children who lived in my neighborhood, books that would make me laugh. The stories I write are the stories I wanted to read as a child, and the experience I hope to share with children is the discovery that reading is one of the pleasures of life and not just something one must do in school.

*   *   *

Beverly Cleary, who in 1975 received the Laura Ingalls Wilder Award for her "substantial and lasting contribution to literature for children," has successfully written picture books, stories for the middle graders, and novels for young teen-agers. She is equally at home with reality and fantasy. This wide range is perhaps not known to all who are acquainted with her name, because "Beverly Cleary" and "Henry Huggins" have become so closely associated.

Mrs. Cleary's first book was about 8-year-old Henry Huggins and his neighborhood friends, including Beezus and Ramona, who lived on Klickitat Street in Portland, Oregon, forty or more years ago. This humorous, true-to-life story was followed by seven others about this group of children, who naturally grew a little older as the books succeeded each other. Meanwhile, Mrs. Cleary created Henry's feminine counterpart, Ellen Tebbits, who with friends (and enemy, Otis Spofford) lived in the Tillamook Street neighborhood in Portland. These locales have been pictured very realistically by Mrs. Cleary, who spent her school years in Portland. The farming community in Oregon where she lived earlier is faithfully reflected in *Emily's Runaway Imagination*, a story about the small daily ups and downs in the life of a 4th-grade girl in the early part of the century, when airplanes and automobiles were still novelties.

It is these "small daily ups and downs" that make these books such interesting reading for children of about 7 to 10. Consider *Henry Huggins*, for instance. The 8-year-old reader has graduated from most picture books and is still too young for distant places, complex themes, and psychological depth. Yet he or she wants plot, crisis, and character. In *Henry Huggins* Beverly Cleary has elevated into plots just those crises that are real in the life of a young boy and she has made Henry the one who has to find his own way out of his troubles. He has parents who are supportive and helpful, but they don't solve his problems. It is Henry who must pay for the lost football, bring the dog home on the bus, and care for his fast-reproducing guppies. In short, here is the right transition book − full of plots, character, crises, and above all humor − for children who have left the first-readers but cannot yet tackle *Tom Sawyer*. Furthermore, Beverly Cleary writes lucidly and simply, but without condescension. She is a fine stylist for young readers, introducing them to natural dialogue and appropriate prose.

It may be objected today that Henry Huggins and Ellen Tebbits and their friends are exclusively white, middle-class children; that Henry's mother is something of a stereotype, always cooking and keeping the house neat − though she did help Henry pick up night-crawlers; that the teacher, Miss Roop, is a stereotype, too, with her Santa Claus Christmas play so far removed from the interests of boys of 8 or 9. Still it must be recognized that Beverly Cleary has created extremely real children whose lives are filled with the small and often hilarious vicissitudes common to thousands of boys and girls wherever they live.

In her novels for young teens − *Fifteen, Jean and Johnny, The Luckiest Girl*, and *Sister of the Bride* − Mrs. Cleary has likewise created very believable characters − high school girls who are just beginning to date. Her settings here are the Bay Area in California, and again we have only white, middle-class families, though with considerable variety among the parents. Also, it must be pointed out that drugs, alcohol, and sex do not touch the lives of these young people. Sex appears only as a light kiss at the end of the book, climaxing the romance. If there are any further thoughts about it − even in *Sister of the Bride*, which is solely about a coming marriage – the reader is left guessing. These stories, then, may be considered not entirely contemporary by the standards of some young readers; but they do have universality in their themes: Jane, Barbara, Jean, and Shelley are slowly discovering who they are; they gradually find new strengths in themselves and begin to formulate more mature values affecting themselves, their friends, and their parents.

Beverly Cleary's three picture books, *The Hullabaloo ABC*, *The Real Hole*, and *Two Dog Biscuits*, reflect the same kind of skill that has made her such a popular author for older ages. But she has not chosen to specialize in the picture book genre. Recently she has produced a book about twins, *Mitch and Amy*; *Socks*, a cat story; two books about Ramona of the Klickitat Street group; and *Runaway Ralph*, a sequel to her first fantasy story, *The Mouse and the Motorcycle*. With this first story of Ralph, a hotel mouse who could ride a toy motorcycle given to him by one of the guests, a young boy who could talk with him, Beverly Cleary entered that special domain of the miniature fantasy world within the real world. In Ralph she created an independent, daring and caring small fellow who may become as greatly loved as Henry Huggins. In the case of Henry, the reader believes all the way because the story is so real. In the case of Ralph, the reader willingly suspends disbelief, captivated by the fantasy and feeling that it should be real even though it isn't. In fact, Ralph may pave the way for many children straight to *Stuart Little* by E. B. White, *The Borrowers* by Mary Norton, and other ingenious stories of the everyday world as seen from the eyes of imagined miniature inhabitants.

—Claudia Lewis

CLEAVER, Vera and Bill.   American.   Vera born in Virgil, South Dakota, grew up in Florida. Bill served in the United States Air Force: Sergeant. Worked for the Air Force in Japan and France. Recipient: Western Writers of America Spur Award, 1976. Live in Winter Haven, Florida. Address: c/o J. B. Lippincott Company, East Washington Square, Philadelphia, Pennsylvania 19105, U.S.A.

PUBLICATIONS FOR CHILDREN

Fiction

Ellen Grae, illustrated by Ellen Raskin.   Philadelphia, Lippincott, 1967.
Lady Ellen Grae, illustrated by Ellen Raskin.   Philadelphia, Lippincott, 1968.
Where the Lilies Bloom, illustrated by Jim Spanfeller.   Philadelphia, Lippincott, 1969; London, Hamish Hamilton, 1970.
Grover, illustrated by Frederic Marvin.   Philadelphia, Lippincott, 1970; London, Hamish Hamilton, 1971.
The Mimosa Tree.   Philadelphia, Lippincott, 1970; London, Oxford University Press, 1977.
The Mock Revolt.   Philadelphia, Lippincott, 1971; London, Hamish Hamilton, 1972.
I Would Rather Be a Turnip.   Philadelphia, Lippincott, 1971; London, Hamish Hamilton, 1972.
Delpha Green and Company.   Philadelphia, Lippincott, 1972; London, Collins, 1975.
Ellen Grae, and Lady Ellen Grae.   London, Hamish Hamilton, 1973.
Me Too.   Philadelphia, Lippincott, 1973; London, Collins, 1975.
The Why's and Wherefore's of Littabelle Lee.   New York, Atheneum, 1973; London, Hamish Hamilton, 1974.

Dust of the Earth. Philadelphia, Lippincott, 1975; London, Oxford University Press, 1977.

Trial Valley. Philadelphia, Lippincott, and London, Oxford University Press, 1977.

PUBLICATIONS FOR ADULTS (by Vera Cleaver)

Novel

The Nurse's Dilemma. New York, Bouregy, 1966.

*   *   *

Vera and Bill Cleaver are a writing team of husband and wife who together contribute a new voice to American fiction for older children. Their narrative is spare, their dialogue authentic and their humour casual. The setting of most of their novels is the South, and they bring into children's literature the literary tradition of Southern Gothic; their work is akin to that of Carson McCullers and Flannery O'Connor. Heat and lethargy pervade their small towns, where people have personalities as eccentric as their names, and where, in the atmosphere of stagnation and distortion, only the "gutty" or courageous make something of their lives. The adults in the Cleavers' novels are far from the wise, kind, remote beings of traditional children's literature; they seem rather to have more than their fair share of fallibility, misfortune and emotional disaster. The young have to cope with a legacy of parental fecklessness, failure and abandonment. As Arbuthnot and Sutherland say in Children and Books: "These books are prime examples of the changes that have occurred in what has been considered appropriate in children's books." Excellent, too, is the portrayal of the children themselves in all the inner conflicts of the awkward age. Their "passionate struggle into conscious being," to borrow a phrase from D. H. Lawrence, is shown with a self-mocking honesty and a saving humorous sanity which distinguish them from the usual "problem novel." There is even something endearing in the characters' angers and frustrations, their rebellion against and acceptance of life's limitations, and their growth into compassion and insight. Though boys are treated as sensitively as girls, it is in the portrayal of the latter that the Cleavers' characterisation is at its best. These heroines are no tomboys or pseudo-boys but emergent women of spirit, intelligence and resilience.

Ellen Grae, in the novella of that name, lodging with the McGruders during her parents' separation and impending divorce, is a bright and sensible girl. She shows the strain of the situation only in the long fantastic stories she spins, which are obviously her way of explaining the vagaries of adult behaviour. Her troubles also enable her to treat with sympathy the finicky Rosemary, who is also staying with the McGruders because of her parents' divorce, Grover, whose mother has committed suicide, and the town freak Ira, whose real-life story is more horrific than anything in Ellen Grae's fantasies. The sequel Lady Ellen Grae has less impact. It tells of well-meaning relatives' attempts to give Ellen Grae a conventional girl's upbringing, attempts which the reader hopes are doomed to failure and which Ellen Grae makes sure are.

Grover is also dominated by Ellen Grae. It is she who helps Grover when his mother decides she cannot live with cancer and commits suicide. Grover's father is paralysed by grief, while his son is sustained by friendship and his ordinary childhood pursuits. In these three stories the sleepy, gossipy small town of Thicket, Florida, is vividly drawn.

Between the earlier stories and the later novel, the Cleavers wrote the book which to many will always be their best, Where the Lilies Bloom. The setting is the mountain country of North Carolina and the family's efforts to eke out a living by "wild-crafting" or the collecting of medicinal plants for sale give opportunity for description of the beautiful countryside and the "forgotten people" who farm it. But the book is chiefly memorable for its heroine, 14-year-old Mary Call Luther. During her father's terminal illness and after his death, it is her driving force which keeps the family together on the small-holding in Trial Valley. She mothers the two younger children, Romey and Ima Dean, though "mothering" is hardly the word for her tough and assertive ways. More feminine aspects are shown in the 18-year-old Devola, whose courtship by the wicked landlord has a hint of melodrama. The tone and pace of the book are well sustained and the scene of Luther's burial has a classic simplicity which puts it on a level with the burial scene in Steinbeck's *The Grapes of Wrath*.

I Would Rather Be a Turnip has another typical Cleaver heroine in Annie Jelks, daughter of a pharmacist in a gossipy Southern town and aunt of the illegitimate son of her older sister. She reacts violently against the boy's stay with the family and the social ostracism she suffers as a result. But, like Ellen Grae, she exorcises her demons by story-telling and by the time she has written out her troubles in long, unpublishably bad stories she has come to terms with herself. *The Mock Revolt* has an ironic title. Though the story is set in the 1930's, the hero Ussy Mock is typical of the late 1960's in his feelings of vague dissatisfaction with the older generation. Self-pity, however, gives way to social compassion when he becomes unwillingly the protector of the Wilder family, an angry, defeated father, a sickly pregnant mother, and the whining, begging Luke who claims his friendship.

Delpha Green and Company is an odd book and its reliance on astrology for its framework and character typology is rather contrived. However, what is clear is a contrast between the closed heart of Merlin Choate, the factory owner and most prominent citizen of Chinquapin Cove, and the open heart of Delpha Green and her father, ex-convict and self-styled pastor of the Church of Blessed Hope. Delpha cheers many of the townspeople with her Pollyanna act and is instrumental in the founding of a rival industry, a cosmetics factory. But she comes to realise, "Well, cheerfulness can be a friend during bad times but to meet every bitter occurrence with a smile and an excuse is not a true human quality."

Me Too is about an "exceptional" child, to use the American term. "Don't you want to be like me?" Lydia asks her autistic twin, Lornie. "Yes," whispered Lornie, "Yes, me too." During the summer when Lornie is home from her special school and in Lydia's care, her sister comes to love her with an acceptance of what she can be and to abandon her dreams of making her like herself. Other writers on this theme, like Roy Brown, Richard Parker and Eleanor Spence, have sensitively explored the effect on the immediate family of an autistic child. The Cleavers extend this to friends and neighbours. Lornie becomes a touchstone of their humanity, bringing out their fear, sentimentality, superstition and, occasionally, love and understanding.

The Why's and Wherefore's of Littabelle Lee is a book to match *Where the Lilies Bloom*. It too is a story of rural hardship in mountain country, this time the Ozarks. The heroine, Littabelle, is Mary Call two years older; she has the same fiery intelligence and indomitable spirit. An orphan, she lives with her aged grandparents and her Aunt Sorrow, who as a spinster has been left to look after them by her neglectful brothers and sisters. When Aunt Sorrow goes off to live a life of her own before it is too late she announces to Littabelle, "You are not a baby any longer. Everybody has to drop off being that when the time comes. Yours has come. Now you have got to meet your whys and wherefores face to face." Littabelle's struggles to do so involve her in teaching in Pintail Fork School, which not only gives her a thirst for education as a way out of the grinding poverty of mountain farming but also sharpens her wits; it is an unusual but effective solution to her problems to sue her rich uncles and aunts for parental neglect. Here as elsewhere the Cleavers combine a portrayal of the personal problems of adolescence with a concern for social issues.

—Mary Croxson

CLEWES, Dorothy (Mary). British. Born in Nottingham, 6 July 1907. Educated privately in Nottingham; at University of Nottingham. Married Winston David Armstrong Clewes in 1932 (died, 1957). Worked as a secretary and physician's dispenser, Nottingham,

1924–32. Agent: Curtis Brown Ltd., 575 Madison Avenue, New York, New York 10022, U.S.A. Address: Soleig, King's Ride, Alfriston, Sussex, England.

PUBLICATIONS FOR CHILDREN

Fiction

The Rivals of Maidenhurst.   London, Nelson, 1925.
The Cottage in the Wild Wood, illustrated by Irene Hawkins.   London, Faber, 1945.
The Stream in the Wild Wood, illustrated by Irene Hawkins.   London, Faber, 1946.
The Treasure in the Wild Wood, illustrated by Irene Hawkins.   London, Faber, 1947.
The Wild Wood (includes *The Cottage in the Wild Wood* and *The Stream in the Wild Wood*), illustrated by Irene Hawkins.   New York, Coward McCann, 1948.
The Fair in the Wild Wood, illustrated by Irene Hawkins.   London, Faber, 1949.
Henry Hare's Boxing Match, illustrated by Patricia W. Turner.   London, Chatto and Windus, and New York, Coward McCann, 1950.
Henry Hare's Earthquake, illustrated by Patricia W. Turner.   London, Chatto and Windus, 1950; New York, Coward McCann, 1951.
Henry Hare, Painter and Decorator, illustrated by Patricia W. Turner.   London, Chatto and Windus, 1951.
Henry Hare and the Kidnapping of Selina Squirrel, illustrated by Patricia W. Turner.   London, Chatto and Windus, 1951.
The Adventure of the Scarlet Daffodil, illustrated by R. G. Campbell.   London, Chatto and Windus, 1952; as *The Mystery of the Scarlet Daffodil*, New York, Coward McCann, 1953.
The Mystery of the Blue Admiral, illustrated by J. Marianne Moll.   New York, Coward McCann, 1954; London, Collins, 1955.
The Secret, illustrated by Peggy Beetles.   London, Hamish Hamilton, and New York, Coward McCann, 1956.
The Runaway, illustrated by Peggy Beetles.   London, Hamish Hamilton, and New York, Coward McCann, 1957.
Adventure on Rainbow Island, illustrated by Shirley Hughes.   London, Collins, 1957; as *Mystery on Rainbow Island*, New York, Coward McCann, 1957.
The Jade Green Cadillac, illustrated by Shirley Hughes.   London, Collins, 1958; as *The Mystery of the Jade-Green Cadillac*, New York, Coward McCann, 1958.
The Happiest Day, illustrated by Peggy Beetles.   London, Hamish Hamilton, 1958; New York, Coward McCann, 1959.
The Old Pony, illustrated by Peggy Beetles.   London, Hamish Hamilton, 1959; New York, Coward McCann, 1960.
Hide and Seek, illustrated by Peggy Beetles.   London, Hamish Hamilton, 1959; New York, Coward McCann, 1960.
The Lost Tower Treasure, illustrated by Shirley Hughes.   London, Collins, 1960; as *The Mystery of the Lost Tower Treasure*, New York, Coward McCann, 1960.
The Hidden Key, illustrated by Peggy Beetles.   London, Hamish Hamilton, 1960; New York, Coward McCann, 1961.
The Singing Strings, illustrated by Shirley Hughes.   London, Collins, 1961; as *The Mystery of the Singing Strings*, New York, Coward McCann, 1961.
All the Fun of the Fair, illustrated by Juliette Palmer.   London, Hamish Hamilton, 1961; New York, Coward McCann, 1962.
Wilberforce and the Slaves, illustrated by Peter Edwards.   London, Hutchinson, 1961.
Skyraker and the Iron Imp, illustrated by Peter Edwards.   London, Hutchinson, 1962.
The Purple Mountain, illustrated by Robert Broomfield.   London, Collins, 1962; as *The Golden Eagle*, New York, Coward McCann, 1962.

The Birthday, illustrated by Juliette Palmer.   London, Hamish Hamilton, 1962; New York, Coward McCann, 1963.

The Branch Line, illustrated by Juliette Palmer.   London, Hamish Hamilton, and New York, Coward McCann, 1963.

Operation Smuggle, illustrated by Shirley Hughes.   London, Collins, 1964; as *The Mystery of the Midnight Smugglers*, New York, Coward McCann, 1964.

Boys and Girls Come Out to Play, illustrated by Jane Paton.   London, Hamish Hamilton, 1964.

The Holiday, illustrated by Janet Duchesne.   London, Hamish Hamilton, and New York, Coward McCann, 1964.

Guide Dog, illustrated by Peter Burchard.   London, Hamish Hamilton, and New York, Coward McCann, 1965; as *Dog for the Dark*, London, White Lion, 1974.

Red Ranger and the Combine Harvester, illustrated by Peter Edwards.   London, Hutchinson, 1966.

Roller Skates, Skooter and Bike, illustrated by Constance Marshall.   London, Hamish Hamilton, and New York, Coward McCann, 1966.

A Boy like Walt.   London, Collins, and New York, Coward McCann, 1967.

A Bit of Magic, illustrated by Robert Hales.   London, Hamish Hamilton, 1967.

A Girl like Cathy.   London, Collins, 1968.

Adopted Daughter.   New York, Coward McCann, 1968.

Upsidedown Willie, illustrated by Edward Ardizzone.   London, Hamish Hamilton, 1968.

Peter and the Jumbie, illustrated by Robert Hales.   London, Hamish Hamilton, 1969.

Special Branch Willie, illustrated by Edward Ardizzone.   London, Hamish Hamilton, 1969.

Library Lady, illustrated by Robert Hales.   London, Chatto Boyd and Oliver, 1970; as *The Library*, New York, Coward McCann, 1971.

Fire-Brigade Willie, illustrated by Edward Ardizzone.   London, Hamish Hamilton, 1970.

Two Bad Boys, illustrated by Lynette Hemmant.   London, Hamish Hamilton, 1971.

The End of Summer.   New York, Coward McCann, 1971.

Storm over Innish.   London, Heinemann, 1972; Nashville, Nelson, 1973.

A Skein of Geese, illustrated by Janet Duchesne.   London, Chatto Boyd and Oliver, 1972.

Ginny's Boy.   London, Heinemann, 1973.

Hooray for Me, illustrated by Michael Jackson.   London, Heinemann, 1973.

Wanted − A Grand, illustrated by Robert Micklewright.   London, Chatto and Windus, 1974.

Missing from Home.   London, Heinemann, 1975.

Nothing to Declare.   London, Heinemann, 1976.

The Testing Year.   London, Heinemann, 1977.

Other

The Brown Burrows Books, illustrated by Patricia W. Turner.   London, Chatto and Windus, 4 vols., 1950−51.

Guide Dogs for the Blind.   London, Hamish Hamilton, 1966.

Editor, *The Secret of the Sea: An Anthology of Underwater Exploration and Adventure*, illustrated by Jeroo Roy.   London, Heinemann, 1973.

PUBLICATIONS FOR ADULTS

Novels

She Married a Doctor.   London, Jenkins, 1943; as *Stormy Hearts*, New York, Arcadia House, 1944.

Shepherd's Hill. London, Sampson Low, 1945.
To Man Alone. London, Jenkins, and New York, Arcadia House, 1945.
A Stranger in the Valley. London, Harrap, 1948.
The Blossom on the Bough. London, Harrap, 1949.
Summer Cloud. London, Harrap, 1951.
Merry-Go-Round. London, Hodder and Stoughton, 1954.
I Came to a Wood. London, Hale, 1956.

*   *   *

Dorothy Clewes is a prolific and versatile writer, catering for all ages of child reader. The quality of her work is as varied as her themes.

Many of her books are written in series: Willie, not quite five years old, who brightens up a dull existence in a variety of amusing and alarming ways; Penny, just starting school, and her friend Maxwell (to both Willie and Penny the Postman and the Milkman give good advice, and moreoever treat them seriously, so they think); and the slightly older Kay, Rory and Gerald, whose misdemeanours are forgiven because the adults remember they were children once. The settings are comfortable and cosy, and unfamiliar adults – gipsies, circus people – are paste-board figures. The many books about the Hadley children are for older readers, who surely would spot that despite annual summer holidays they never get any older; they delight in solving mysteries ahead of their police inspector father.

Occasionally a book has a foreign setting. *Peter and the Jumbie* is a pleasant story about a West Indian boy. *Two Bad Boys* and *The Purple Mountain* are set in Italy and *Hooray for Me* in Spain. In the two Italian stories the characters all speak irritating broken English to each other and it is hard to believe that *The Purple Mountain* and *Missing from Home* (French background) are by the same writer.

Henry Hare was a series, now forgotten, in the Alison Uttley tradition. The personalised machine appears reasonably convincingly in *Skyraker and the Iron Imp, Wilberforce and the Slaves* and *Red Danger and the Combine-Harvester.* Among other non-series stories for younger children, *A Skein of Geese* is a rather charming story about two lonely little girls whose lives are paralleled by two lonely geese.

Most of Dorothy Clewes' best works are written for teenagers. She follows the fashion for "problem stories" in *Guide Dog* (a young man recently blinded), *A Boy like Walt* (unsatisfactory home life), *A Girl like Cathy* (adoption) and *Missing from Home* (a broken marriage). *Guide Dog* was criticised as being improbable when first published, despite being founded on fact, but today a parcel bomb explosion is unfortunately too usual. Fine and convincing character-drawing shows in all these books, despite a rather self-conscious effort to tempt the boy reader through motor-cycling in *A Boy like Walt.*

—Margaret M. Tye

CLIFTON, Lucille. Afro-American. Born in Depew, New York, 27 June 1936. Educated at Howard University, Washington, D.C., 1953–55. Married Fred J. Clifton in 1958; has six children. Formerly, Visiting Writer, Columbia University School of the Arts, New York. Since 1971, Poet-in Residence, Coppin State College, Baltimore. Recipient: YM-YWHA Poetry Center Discovery Award, 1969; National Endowment for the Arts grant, 1969. Agent: M. Marlow, Curtis Brown Ltd., 575 Madison Avenue, New York, New York 10022. Address: 2605 Talbot Road, Baltimore, Maryland 21216, U.S.A.

PUBLICATIONS FOR CHILDREN

Fiction

All Us Come Cross the Water, illustrated by John Steptoe.   New York, Holt Rinehart, 1973.
Don't You Remember?, illustrated by Evaline Ness.   New York, Dutton, 1973.
The Boy Who Wouldn't Believe in Spring, illustrated by Brinton Turkle.   New York, Dutton, 1973.
The Times They Used to Be, illustrated by Susan Jeschke.   New York, Holt Rinehart, 1974.
My Brother Fine with Me, illustrated by Moneta Barrett.   New York, Holt Rinehart, 1975.
Three Wishes, illustrated by Stephanie Douglas.   New York, Viking Press, 1976.
Amifika, illustrated by Thomas di Grazia.   New York, Dutton, 1977.

Verse

Some of the Days of Everett Anderson, illustrated by Evaline Ness.   New York, Holt Rinehart, 1970.
Everett Anderson's Christmas Coming, illustrated by Evaline Ness.   New York, Holt Rinehart, 1972.
Good, Says Jerome, illustrated by Stephanie Douglas.   New York, Dutton, 1973.
Everett Anderson's Year, illustrated by Ann Grifalconi.   New York, Holt Rinehart, 1974.
Everett Anderson's Friend, illustrated by Ann Grifalconi.   New York, Holt Rinehart, 1976.
Everett Anderson's 1–2–3, illustrated by Ann Grifalconi.   New York, Holt Rinehart, 1977.

Other

The Black BC's, illustrated by Don Miller.   New York, Dutton, 1970.

PUBLICATIONS FOR ADULTS

Verse

Good Times.   New York, Random House, 1969.
Good News about the Earth.   New York, Random House, 1972.
An Ordinary Woman.   New York, Random House, 1974.

Other

Generations of Americans: A Memoir.   New York, Random House, 1976.

*   *   *

Lucille Clifton ranks! She's stolen our Black children's hearts, and hopefully their minds as well. I have not met a Black child who does not appreciate the poetic artistry of Lucille Clifton, even if he doesn't know what I mean. Children appreciate the sound of Everett Anderson's name on their small tongues, the humor of sibling rivalry/love; they appreciate Ms. Clifton's instincts as a mother, father, teacher, listener, best friend. The images she creates can make any child comfortable, as if they're actual experiences. Ms. Clifton is the ultimate in the current breed of Black writers for children. Her black femaleness is evident when she writes of love and in her positive images for Black children. She seems to know, best of all, how impressionable children are and how important it is, for Black children especially, to feel good about themselves.

Everett Anderson, for example, could have been another Black child unintentionally ignored and neglected because the adults in his world ran out of time before they got back to him. Instead Ms. Clifton created a special friend for him in *Everett Anderson's Friend*:

> someone new ....
> next door in 13A.
> A girl named Maria
> who wins at ball
> is fun to play with
> ... Why, she can say,
> "Come in with Me
> and play ... and wait
> if your Mama is working late."

This particular book of poetry, as with the other Everett Anderson poems, plus all of her poetry and stories about Black children radiate with good vibrations and the simple pleasures of childhood. Pleasures that must be first introduced (as in *Some of the Days of Everett Anderson*):

> When I am seven
> Mama can stay from work
> and play with me
> all day. I won't go to school
> ... we can talk
> and eat
> and we will laugh.

– then engaged in as Johnny and Baggy do in *My Brother Fine with Me*, when baggy decides to run away from home – "Me and him put all his stuff in a shopping bag, and he get his bat and he ready to go" – and constantly reinforced as Janice Marie helps her younger brother Jerome (*Good, Says Jerome*) to understand his Blackness:

> Black is ... a feeling inside
> about who we are and
> how strong and how free.
> Good, says Jerome
> that feels like me.

Ms. Clifton reveals the best in black writing for children: she's functional, entertaining, instructional, relevant, realistic, memorable, and fulfilling. Lucille Clifton meets all of my criteria to be the recipient of an award for "The Best Books for Black Children by a Black Writer."

—Jacqueline Brown Woody

* * *

CLYMER, Eleanor. American. Born in New York City, 7 January 1906. Educated at Barnard College, New York, 1923–35; University of Wisconsin, Madison, B.A. 1928; New York University; Bank Street College of Education, New York. Married Kinsey Clymer in

1933; has one son. Worked as a teacher in camps and nursery schools. Recipient: Child Study Association of America award, 1975. Address: 11 Nightingale Road, Katonah, New York 10536, U.S.A.

PUBLICATIONS FOR CHILDREN

Fiction

A Yard for John, illustrated by Mildred Boyle. New York, McBride, 1943.
Here Comes Pete, illustrated by Mildred Boyle. New York, McBride, 1944.
The Grocery Mouse, illustrated by Jeanne Bendick. New York, McBride, 1945.
Little Bear Island, illustrated by Ursula Koering. New York, McBride, 1945.
Teddy (as Elizabeth Kinsey), illustrated by Jeanne Bendick. New York, McBride, 1945.
Sunday in the Park (as Janet Bell), illustrated by Aline Appel. New York, McBride, 1946.
Monday-Tuesday-Wednesday Book (as Janet Bell), illustrated by Mary Stevens. New York, McBride, 1946.
Patch (as Elizabeth Kinsey), illustrated by James Davis. New York, McBride, 1946.
The Country Kittens, illustrated by Jeanne Bendick. New York, McBride, 1947.
The Trolley Car Family, illustrated by Ursula Koering. New York, McKay, 1947.
The Latch Key Club, illustrated by Corinne Dillon. New York, McKay, 1949.
Treasure at First Base, illustrated by Jean Macdonald Porter. New York, Dodd Mead, 1950.
Tommy's Wonderful Airplane, illustrated by Kurt Wiese. New York, Dodd Mead, 1951.
Thirty-Three Bunn Street, illustrated by Jane Miller. New York, Dodd Mead, 1952.
Sea View Secret (as Elizabeth Kinsey), illustrated by Mary Stevens. New York, Watts, 1952.
Donny and Company (as Elizabeth Kinsey), illustrated by Mary Stevens. New York, Watts, 1953.
Chester, illustrated by Ezra Jack Keats. New York, Dodd Mead, 1954.
This Cat Came to Stay! (as Elizabeth Kinsey), illustrated by Don Sibley. New York, Watts, 1955.
Not Too Small after All, illustrated by Tom O'Sullivan. New York, Watts, 1955.
Sociable Toby, illustrated by Ingrid Fetz. New York, Watts, 1956.
Mr. Piper's Bus, illustrated by Kurt Wiese. New York, Dodd Mead, 1961.
Benjamin in the Woods. New York, Grosset and Dunlap, 1962.
Now That You Are Seven, illustrated by Ingrid Fetz. New York, Association Press, 1963.
Harry, The Wild West Horse, illustrated by Leonard Shortall. New York, Atheneum, 1963; London, Hamish Hamilton, 1964.
The Tiny Little House, illustrated by Ingrid Fetz. New York, Atheneum, 1964.
Chipmunk in the Forest, illustrated by Ingrid Fetz. New York, Atheneum, 1965.
The Adventure of Walter, illustrated by Ingrid Fetz. New York, Atheneum, 1965.
My Brother Stevie. New York, Holt Rinehart, 1967.
The Big Pile of Dirt, illustrated by Robert Shore. New York, Holt Rinehart, 1968.
Horatio, illustrated by Robert Quackenbush. New York, Atheneum, 1968.
Belinda's New Spring Hat, illustrated by Gioia Fiammenghi. New York, Watts, 1969.
We Lived in the Almont, illustrated by David Stone. New York, Dutton, 1970.
The House on the Mountain, illustrated by Leo Carty. New York, Dutton, 1971.
The Spider, The Cave, and the Pottery Bowl, illustrated by Ingrid Fetz. New York, Atheneum, 1971.
Me and the Eggman, illustrated by David Stone. New York, Dutton, 1972.

How I Went Shopping and What I Got, illustrated by Trina Schart Hyman. New York, Holt Rinehart, 1972.
Santiago's Silvermine, illustrated by Ingrid Fetz. New York, Atheneum, 1973.
Luke Was There, illustrated by Diane de Groat. New York, Holt Rinehart, 1973.
Leave Horatio Alone, illustrated by Robert Quackenbush. New York, Atheneum, 1974.
Take Tarts as Tarts Is Passing, illustrated by Roy Doty. New York, Dutton, 1974.
Engine Number Seven, illustrated by Robert Quackenbush. New York, Holt Rinehart, 1975.
Hamburgers – And Ice Cream for Dessert, illustrated by Roy Doty. New York, Dutton, 1975.
Horatio's Birthday, illustrated by Robert Quackenbush. New York, Atheneum, 1975.

Other

Make Way for Water, illustrated by J. C. Wonsetler. New York, Messner, 1953.
Modern American Career Women, with Lillian Erlich. New York, Dodd Mead, 1959.
The Case of the Missing Link, illustrated by Robert Macguire. New York, Basic Books, 1962; revised edition, 1968.
Search for a Living Fossil: The Story of the Coelacanth, illustrated by Joan Berg. New York, Holt Rinehart, 1963; London, Lutterworth Press, 1965.
Communities at Work. Boston, Heath, 1964; revised edition, 1969.
Wheels, illustrated by Charles Goslin. New York, Holt Rinehart, 1965.
The Second Greatest Invention: Search for the First Farmers, illustrated by Lili Réthi. New York, Holt Rinehart, 1969.

PUBLICATIONS FOR ADULTS

Other

Management in the Home, with Lillian Gilbreth. New York, Dodd Mead, 1954.

Manuscript Collection: de Grummond Collection, University of Southern Mississippi, Hattiesburg.

Eleanor Clymer comments:
I began writing for children under the guidance of Lucy Sprague Mitchell, a proponent of the "Here and Now" school of children's literature. My first books were based on the everyday familiar world of the children I knew. As they grew older I wrote about their interests – baseball, airplanes, exploring, photography, pets. I also wrote about the history of science.

In the last ten years, however, I have felt I wanted to say something more important, something about the emotions and problems of children dealing with a sometimes hostile world. In My Brother Stevie I tried to tell what a child of the "inner city" might have said in talking about her own life, writing simply enough not to put off some older children who might not be facile readers but who might already have had difficult life experience. That was the first of several books in which I found myself going back to the city I knew well in the past. Some of these books are The Big Pile of Dirt, How I Went Shopping and What I Got, We Lived in the Almont, Me and the Eggman, The House on the Mountain, Luke Was There.

I have also been interested in the life of present-day native Americans. I wrote The Spider, The Cave, and the Pottery Bowl about Hopi children, and Santiago's Silvermine about Mexican children. I am now working on a book about Indians of the Northeast.

*　　*　　*

Eleanor Clymer has written fifty books for children, enough surely to earn her the title of a prolific writer. But there are other writers who turn books out regularly; the difference is that Clymer is an *excellent* as well as a prolific writer of children's books. She exhibits the same fine literary quality in a non-fiction book such as *The Search for a Living Fossil: The Story of the Coelacanth* as she does in her renowned works of fiction such as *My Brother Stevie, The House on the Mountain*, and *Luke Was There*.

Ms. Clymer writes both for the picture book crowd, young readers, and older readers from 10 up. While *My Brother Stevie* and *Luke Was There* may be catalogued for an audience of 9 to 11, adults will be as deeply moved as children by these books. Both books refute, to me, the claim that only ethnic writers can know the ethnic experience, for one of these stories is from the viewpoint of a young black girl, the other from that of a young black boy. And in both tales, the reader intensely identifies with the characters. Ms. Clymer doesn't let the environment and life style of the protagonists occupy the foreground. She is unsparing in her depiction of the problems facing the children, of the less-than-ideal treatment they receive both from their situations and from the people surrounding them. In her books, the facts of reality must be accepted; what is important to the reader is how the children cope with them. In the coping, they reveal to us some important truths about ourselves. Clymer never *tells* us; the characters and their actions *show* us. When we see Stevie's negative responses to his grandmother's punishing attitudes, and his loving response to his understanding teacher, we learn something about helping human needs. In *Luke Was There*, we live in the skin of an institutionalized child and feel in our bones his despair and anger as adults betray his trust again and again. After experiencing these books (and *The House on the Mountain*), we can never again view ghetto children as before; we have walked in their shoes. These three books alone place Eleanor Clymer in the foremost rank of children's writers.

Clymer's style is deceptively simple; but it is the simplicity that results from the painstaking paring away of superfluous or extraneous words and thoughts. Her characters' speech seems to be their natural speech; in actuality, it is Ms. Clymer's skill in subtly deleting all but the important prose yet retaining the flavor and rhythm of natural speech that allows us to understand the needs and personalities of the characters. For instance, these two lines from *The House on the Mountain*: "I tell Gloria, 'Why don't you watch the kids?' She says, 'Why don't you leave me alone?' " Here we glimpse the concern of the 10-year-old "I" who is relating the story, and his teen-age sister's indifference — in just seventeen words!

Clymer's recent books about Horace the cat, for younger children, are much more amusing and lighter in theme. Parents who are inveigled into reading them aloud will chuckle in recognition of the "characteristic cat" that is Horace. Only an appreciative watcher of cats could so unerringly portray Horace in all his set ways! Ms. Clymer must have as much fun in creating these adventures as children will in listening to them. While we enjoy these, we all await another tender and loving journey into the complex world of childhood that is Eleanor Clymer's greatest gift to all of us — children and adults alike.

—Betty Boegehold

COATSWORTH, Elizabeth (Jane). American. Born in Buffalo, New York, 31 May 1893. Educated at Park Street School, 1899–1907; Los Robles School, Pasadena, California, 1907–09; Buffalo Seminary, 1909–11; Vassar College, Poughkeepsie, New York, B.A. 1915; Columbia University, New York, M.A. 1916; Radcliffe College, Cambridge, Massachusetts. Married Henry Beston in 1929; has two daughters. Recipient: American Library Association Newbery Medal, 1931; New England Poetry Club Golden Rose, 1967. Litt.D.: University of Maine, Orono, 1955; L.H.D.: New England College, Henniker, New Hampshire, 1958. Agent: Mark Paterson, 11–12 West Stockwell Street, Colchester, CO1 18N, England. Address: Chimney Farm, Nobleboro, Maine 04555, U.S.A.

PUBLICATIONS FOR CHILDREN

Fiction

The Cat and the Captain, illustrated by Gertrude Kaye.   New York, Macmillan, 1927.
Toutou in Bondage, illustrated by Thomas Handforth.   New York, Macmillan, 1929.
The Boy with the Parrot, illustrated by Wilfred Bronson.   New York, Macmillan, 1930.
The Cat Who Went to Heaven, illustrated by Lynd Ward.   New York, Macmillan, 1930; London, Dent, 1949.
Knock at the Door, illustrated by F.D. Bedford.   New York, Macmillan, 1931.
Cricket and the Emperor's Son, illustrated by Weda Yap.   New York, Macmillan, 1932; revised edition, Kingswood, Surrey, World's Work, 1962.
Away Goes Sally, illustrated by Helen Sewell.   New York, Macmillan, 1934; London, Woodfield, 1955.
The Golden Horseshoe, illustrated by Robert Lawson.   New York, Macmillan, 1935; revised edition, as *Tamar's Wager*, London, Blackie, 1971.
Sword of the Wilderness, illustrated by Harve Stein.   New York, Macmillan, 1936; London, Blackie, 1972.
Alice-All-by-Herself, illustrated by Marguerite de Angeli.   New York, Macmillan, 1937; London, Harrap, 1938.
Dancing Tom, illustrated by Grace Paull.   New York, Macmillan, 1938; London, Combridge, 1939.
Five Bushel Farm, illustrated by Helen Sewell.   New York, Macmillan, 1939; London, Woodfield, 1958.
The Littlest House, illustrated by Marguerite Davis.   New York, Macmillan, 1940; Kingswood, Surrey, World's Work, 1958.
The Fair American, illustrated by Helen Sewell.   New York, Macmillan, 1940; London, Blackie, 1970.
A Toast to the King, illustrated by Forrest Orr.   New York, Coward McCann, 1940; London, Dent, 1941.
Tonio and the Stranger, illustrated by Wilfred Bronson.   New York, Grosset and Dunlap, 1941.
You Shall Have a Carriage, illustrated by Henry Pitz.   New York, Macmillan, 1941.
Forgotten Island, illustrated by Grace Paull.   New York, Grosset and Dunlap, 1942.
Houseboat Summer, illustrated by Marguerite Davis.   New York, Macmillan, 1942.
The White Horse, illustrated by Helen Sewell.   New York, Macmillan, 1942; as *The White Horse of Morocco*, London, Blackie, 1973.
Thief Island, illustrated by John Wonsetler.   New York, Macmillan, 1943; Kingswood, Surrey, World's Work, 1960.
Twelve Months Make a Year, illustrated by Marguerite Davis.   New York, Macmillan, 1943.
The Big Green Umbrella, illustrated by Helen Sewell.   New York, Grosset and Dunlap, 1944.
Trudy and the Tree House, illustrated by Marguerite Davis.   New York, Macmillan, 1944.
The Kitten Stand, illustrated by Kathleen Keeler.   New York, Grosset and Dunlap, 1945.
The Wonderful Day, illustrated by Helen Sewell.   New York, Macmillan, 1946; London, Blackie, 1973.
Plum Daffy Adventure, illustrated by Marguerite Davis.   New York, Macmillan, 1947; Kingswood, Surrey, World's Work, 1965.
Up Hill and Down: Stories, illustrated by James Davis.   New York, Knopf, 1947.
The House of the Swan, illustrated by Kathleen Voute.   New York, Macmillan, 1948; Kingswood, Surrey, World's Work, 1959.
The Little Haymakers, illustrated by Grace Paull.   New York, Macmillan, 1949.

The Captain's Daughter, illustrated by Ralph Ray. New York, Macmillan, 1950; London, Collier Macmillan, 1963.

First Adventure, illustrated by Ralph Ray. New York, Macmillan, 1950.

Door to the North, illustrated by Frederick Chapman. Philadelphia, Winston, 1950; Kingswood, Surrey, World's Work, 1960.

Dollar for Luck, illustrated by George and Doris Hauman. New York, Macmillan, 1951; as *The Sailing Hatrack*, London, Blackie, 1972.

The Wishing Pear, illustrated by Ralph Ray. New York, Macmillan, 1951.

The Last Fort, illustrated by Edward Shenton. Philadelphia, Winston, 1952; London, Hamish Hamilton, 1953.

Boston Belles, illustrated by Manning Lee. New York, Macmillan, 1952.

Cat Stories, illustrated by Feodor Rojankovsky. New York, Simon and Schuster, 1953; London, Publicity Products, 1955.

Dog Stories, illustrated by Feodor Rojankovsky. New York, Simon and Schuster, 1953; London, Publicity Products, 1954.

Old Whirlwind: A Story of Davy Crockett, illustrated by Manning Lee. New York, Macmillan, 1953.

Aunt Flora, illustrated by Manning Lee. New York, Macmillan, 1953.

Horse Stories, with Kate Barnes, illustrated by Feodor Rojankovsky. New York, Simon and Schuster, 1954.

The Sod House, illustrated by Manning Lee. New York, Macmillan, 1954.

Cherry Ann and the Dragon Horse, illustrated by Manning Lee. New York, Macmillan, 1955.

Hide and Seek, illustrated by Genevieve Vaughan-Jackson. New York, Pantheon Books, 1956.

The Peddler's Cart, illustrated by Zhenya Gay. New York, Macmillan, 1956.

The Dog from Nowhere, illustrated by Don Sibley. Evanston, Illinois, Row Peterson, 1958.

Down Tumbledown Mountain, illustrated by Aldren Watson. Evanston, Illinois, Row Peterson, 1958.

The Cave, illustrated by Allan Houser. New York, Viking Press, 1958; as *Cave of Ghosts*, London, Hamish Hamilton, 1971.

You Say You Saw a Camel!, illustrated by Brinton Turkle. Evanston, Illinois, Row Peterson, 1958.

Pika and the Roses, illustrated by Kurt Wiese. New York, Pantheon Books, 1959.

Desert Dan, illustrated by Harper Johnson. New York, Viking Press, 1960; London, Harrap, 1963.

Lonely Maria, illustrated by Evaline Ness. New York, Pantheon Books, 1960; London, Hamish Hamilton, 1967.

The Noble Doll, illustrated by Leo Politi. New York, Viking Press, 1961.

Ronnie and the Chief's Son, illustrated by Stefan Martin. New York and London, Macmillan, 1962.

Jock's Island, illustrated by Lilian Obligado. New York, Viking Press, 1963; London, Angus and Robertson, 1965.

Jon the Unlucky, illustrated by Esta Nesbitt. New York, Holt Rinehart, 1964; Chalfont St. Giles, Buckinghamshire, Sadler, 1968.

The Secret, illustrated by Don Bolognese. New York, Macmillan, 1965; Kingswood, Surrey, World's Work, 1967.

The Hand of Apollo, illustrated by Robin Jacques. New York, Viking Press, 1965; Kingswood, Surrey, World's Work, 1967.

The Place, illustrated by Marjorie Auerbach. New York, Holt Rinehart, 1966.

The Fox Friend, illustrated by John Hamberger. New York, Macmillan, 1966.

Chimney Farm Bedtime Stories, with Henry Beston, illustrated by Maurice Day. New York, Holt Rinehart, 1966.

Bess and the Sphinx (includes verse), illustrated by Bernice Loewenstein. New York, Macmillan, 1967; London, Blackie, 1974.

Troll Weather, illustrated by Ursula Arndt.   New York, Macmillan, 1967; Kingswood, Surrey, World's Work, 1968.
The Ox-Team, illustrated by Peter Warner.   London, Hamish Hamilton, 1967.
Bob Bodden and the Good Ship "Rover," illustrated by Ted Schroeder.   Champaign, Illinois, Garrard, 1968; London, Watts, 1972.
The Lucky Ones: Five Journeys Toward a Home, illustrated by Janet Doyle.   New York, Macmillan, 1968.
Lighthouse Island, illustrated by Symeon Shimin.   New York, Norton, 1968.
George and Red, illustrated by Paul Giovanopoulos.   New York, Macmillan, 1969.
They Walk in the Night, illustrated by Stefan Martin.   New York, Norton, 1969.
Indian Mound Farm, illustrated by Fermin Rocker.   New York, Macmillan, and London, Collier Macmillan, 1969.
Grandmother Cat and the Hermit, illustrated by Irving Boker.   New York, Macmillan, 1970.
Bob Bodden and the Seagoing Farm, illustrated by Frank Aloise.   Champaign, Illinois, Garrard, 1970; London, Watts, 1972.
The Snow Parlor and Other Bedtime Stories, illustrated by Charles Robinson.   New York, Grosset and Dunlap, 1971.
Under the Green Willow, illustrated by Janina Domanska.   New York, Macmillan, 1971.
Good Night, illustrated by Jose Aruego.   New York, Macmillan, 1972.
The Wanderers, illustrated by Trina Schart Hyman.   New York, Scholastic, 1972.
Daisy, illustrated by Judith Gwyn Brown.   New York, Macmillan, 1973.
Pure Magic, illustrated by Ingrid Fetz.   New York, Macmillan, 1973; as *The Werefox*, New York, Collier, 1975; as *The Fox Boy*, London, Blackie, 1975.
All-of-a-Sudden Susan, illustrated by Richard Cuffari.   New York, Macmillan, 1974.
Marra's World, illustrated by Krystyna Turska.   New York, Morrow, 1975.

Verse

Mouse Chorus, illustrated by Genevieve Vaughan-Jackson.   New York, Pantheon Books, 1955.
The Peaceable Kingdom and Other Poems, illustrated by Fritz Eichenberg.   New York, Pantheon Books, 1958.
The Children Come Running.   New York, Golden Press, 1960.
The Sparrow Bush: Rhymes, illustrated by Stefan Martin.   New York, Norton, 1966.
Down Half the World, illustrated by Zena Bernstein.   New York, Macmillan, 1968.

Other

Runaway Home (reader), illustrated by Gustaf Tenggren.   Evanston, Illinois, Row Peterson, 1942.
The Princess and the Lion, illustrated by Evaline Ness.   New York, Pantheon Books, 1963.
Daniel Webster's Horses, illustrated by Cary.   Champaign, Illinois, Garrard, 1971.

Editor, *Tales of the Gauchos*, by W.H. Hudson, illustrated by Henry Pitz.   New York, Knopf, 1946.
Editor, *Indian Encounters: An Anthology of Stories and Poems*, illustrated by Frederick Chapman.   New York, Macmillan, 1960.

PUBLICATIONS FOR ADULTS

Novels

Here I Stay.   New York, Coward McCann, 1938; London, Harrap, 1939.

The Trunk. New York, Macmillan, 1941.
The Enchanted: An Incredible Tale. New York, Pantheon Books, 1951; London, Dent, 1952.
Silky: An Incredible Tale. New York, Pantheon Books, and London, Gollancz, 1953.
Mountain Bride: An Incredible Tale. New York, Pantheon Books, 1954.
The White Room. New York, Pantheon Books, 1958; London, Dent, 1959.

Verse

Fox Footprints. New York, Knopf, 1923.
Atlas and Beyond. New York and London, Harper, 1924.
Compass Rose. New York, Coward McCann, 1929.
Country Poems. New York, Macmillan, 1942.
Summer Green. New York, Macmillan, 1948.
The Creaking Stair: Poems. New York, Coward McCann, 1949.
Night and the Cat. New York, Macmillan, 1950.
Poems. New York, Macmillan, 1957.

Other

The Sun's Diary: A Book of Days for Any Year. New York, Macmillan, 1929.
Country Neighborhood. New York, Macmillan, 1944.
Maine Ways. New York, Macmillan, 1947.
South Shore Town. New York, Macmillan, 1948.
Maine Memories. Brattleboro, Vermont, Stephen Greene Press, 1968.
Personal Geography (memoirs). Brattleboro, Vermont, Stephen Greene Press, 1976.

Editor, *Especially Maine: The Natural World of Henry Beston from Cape Cod to the St. Lawrence.* Brattleboro, Vermont, Stephen Greene Press, 1970.

Manuscript Collection: Kerlan Collection, University of Minnesota, Minneapolis.

*   *   *

Elizabeth Coatsworth writes about "things which touch my imagination." Her imagination is as boundless as her pen is prolific. The author of some 90 books for children, Coatsworth is expert on such diverse subjects as Viking-raided Ireland (*The Wanderers*), the ancient inhabitants of the fjords and mountains in Norway (*Troll Weather*) and a city boy's summer in *Lighthouse Island.* Her vision encompasses lonely children and their search for independence, magic dolls, refugees, forests where animals can turn into people and, above all, Nature.

Although she has travelled widely, the bulk of her work concerns America in all its phases. History books aside, she has written of the desert, the plains, the mountains, Indians, pioneers, immigrants. But it is from Maine that her finest books have come, and in Maine that she has found for decades the resources to create one lapidary tale after another.

Now in her eighties, the author still understands the perceptions of the young. One of her most successful themes is that of the lonely and different child learning to cope in an adverse world. *Lonely Maria* and *Grandmother Cat and the Hermit* both deal with this idea, as does *Marra's World* which combines the theme with Coatsworth's favorite setting – an island off the Maine Coast. With the subtle use of magic and fantasy it conveys the mood of a legend. Marra is regarded as hopeless by her teacher and schoolmates and even by her father and grandmother: "Everything about her life bewildered her." But when it comes to nature,

Marra excels. She knows everything about the island. Gradually, with the help of a friend, she accepts herself as different, and the enchantment begins. Marra's mother is Nerea, a seal who was human for a time and who returned to the sea. Here, and in *The Enchanted*, Coatsworth touches on the ancient mythic theme where one being is able to work extraordinary changes for love of another.

Coatsworth reaches her apogee in her nature writing, notably "The Incredible Tales" tetralogy about New England originally written for adults. As critic Edmund Fuller observes: "As with all Miss Coatsworth's work, *Silky* is a poet's book, mystic, delicate, lovely. With these 'Incredible Tales' she has created a rich, fresh medium that is at once original and yet the revival of a tradition neglected or distorted in this material age." *The Enchanted*, the best of the four, begins: "There is in northern Maine a township or, as they say here, a 'plantation,' called the Enchanted. It lies in the heart of the forest country and is seldom entered except by lumbermen bound for some winter logging camp from which they return with curious stories." A young man, David Ross, decides to try farming and buys a place right next to the Enchanted. His neighbors are a warm, closely-knit family named Perdry, and he falls in love with one of the daughters and marries her. For their honeymoon they camp in the forest: "The stream seemed to sing its continual braided song especially for them, and the big pine sheltered them as though it liked them. They sat for many hours between its curving roots, their backs to its wide trunk, looking out at the water flowing by, always new water, and new ripples of light, yet always essentially the same stream catching the sunlight in the same net of motion." The magic in this tale and in Coatsworth's others is not arbitrary. It is all planned, provided for. Her special gift is the weaving together of a local story and her own vivid characters. The events that conclude *The Enchanted*, the metamorphosis of the Perdrys, are at once anticipated and surprising.

It is Coatsworth's intention to instruct through her stories, but she is never pedantic. The works do not come together with quite the ease of a folk tale that has been repeated from generation to generation, but are a combination of good New England common sense and modern legend. In *All-of-a-Sudden Susan*, building a feeling of danger, Coatsworth writes: "Everything was uneasy, except people, who are always the last to notice what's happening around them." A weakened dam bursts in a storm and Susan is carried away on the flood with her magic doll, Emelida, who talks to her. Susan sees uprooted houses, bloated animals, even a dead woman. "You can't keep people from dying," Emelida comforts her. "They do it all the time and we may be doing it, too, for all we know. But meantime, enjoy yourself."

The Sod House follows immigrants from their arrival in Boston ("More than a hundred years ago a great many people left Germany, because they were no longer free to say what they thought"), to the settling of a community in Kansas. The New England Emigrant Aid Society helps the Traubels buy land on the Osage River. They are not welcome as northerners at a time when North and South are angling for control of the territory. Political reasons are carefully explained. The Indians the Traubels meet are portrayed solemnly and informatively (Coatsworth has always been interested in their way of life), and Ilse, the child in the story, is allowed to fulfill her possibilities, as are most of Coatsworth's fictive children.

The Lucky Ones, a collection of five stories about the homeless and the stateless from different parts of the world – Tibet, Algeria, Rwanda, Hungary, and Hong Kong – explains why they are refugees, and describes the adversity they meet in trying to adjust to another way of life. Each story is preceded by a poem, and while in some cases the political background is not given in enough detail, the children in the stories, and the children who read them, are treated with the respect that marks all Coatsworth's work.

Using her considerable creativeness and knowledge, her love of the natural world and her regard for children, Coatsworth is responsible for consistently fine literature for readers whose imaginations remain as young and fresh as her own.

—Angela Wigan

COCKETT, Mary. British. Born in Yorkshire, in 1915. Educated at Bedford College, University of London; London Institute of Education. Married to Reginald Cockett; has one son and one daughter. Editor, National Institute of Industrial Psychology, 1943–48, and International Congress of Mental Health, 1948–49. Address: 24 Benville Avenue, Bristol BS9 2RX, England.

PUBLICATIONS FOR CHILDREN

Fiction

Jonathan on the Farm, illustrated by Joan and Dick Robinson. London, Harrap, 1954.
Jonathan and Felicity, illustrated by Joan and Dick Robinson. London, Harrap, 1955.
Fourteen Stories about Jonathan, illustrated by Sheila Connelly. London, Harrap, 1956.
More about Jonathan, illustrated by Dick Robinson. London, Harrap, 1957.
Jan the Market Boy, illustrated by Peggy Beetles. Leicester, Brockhampton Press, 1957.
Bouncing Ball, illustrated by Peggy Beetles. London, Hamish Hamilton, 1958.
Jasper Club, illustrated by Mary Shillabeer. London, Heinemann, 1959.
When Felicity Was Small, illustrated by Dick Robinson. London, Harrap, 1959.
Rolling On, illustrated by Shirley Hughes. London, Methuen, 1960.
Seven Days with Jan, illustrated by Peggy Beetles. Leicester, Brockhampton Press, 1960.
Mary Ann Goes to Hospital. London, Methuen, 1961.
Out with Felicity and Jonathan, illustrated by Dick Robinson. London, Harrap, 1962.
Cottage by the Lock, illustrated by Shirley Hughes. London, Methuen, 1962.
Benny's Bazaar, illustrated by Jennifer Cook. Edinburgh, Oliver and Boyd, 1964.
Acrobat Hamster, illustrated by Lynette Hemmant. London, Hamish Hamilton, 1965.
The Birthday Ride, illustrated by W.F. Phillipps. Edinburgh, Oliver and Boyd, 1965.
Sunflower Giant, illustrated by Lynette Hemmant. London, Hamish Hamilton, 1966.
There for the Picking, illustrated by Maureen Eckersley. Edinburgh, Oliver and Boyd, 1966.
Ash Dry, Ash Green, illustrated by Diana Stanley. Edinburgh, Oliver and Boyd, 1966; New York, Criterion Books, 1968.
Strange Valley, illustrated by Mary Dinsdale. Edinburgh, Oliver and Boyd, 1967.
Twelve Gold Chairs, illustrated by Margery Gill. Edinburgh, Oliver and Boyd, 1967.
Something Big, illustrated by Robert Hales. Edinburgh, Oliver and Boyd, 1968.
The Wild Place, illustrated by Margery Gill. Edinburgh, Oliver and Boyd, 1968.
Rosanna the Goat, illustrated by Reginald Gray. London, Chatto Boyd and Oliver, 1969; Indianapolis, Bobbs Merrill, 1970.
Pelican Park, illustrated by Frank Francis. London, Harrap, and New York, Warne, 1969.
Another Home, Another Country, illustrated by Sandra Archibald. London, Chatto Boyd and Oliver, 1969.
Farthing Bundles, illustrated by Jane Paton. London, Chatto Boyd and Oliver, 1970.
The Joppy Stories (Joppy Crawling, and Joppy on His Feet; Joppy Steps Out, and Caught on a Tree Stump; Joppy in a Bucket, and The Moving Cat), illustrated by Mary Cossey. London, Chatto and Windus, 3 vols., 1972.
Boat Girl, illustrated by Gareth Floyd. London, Chatto and Windus, 1972.
As Big as the Ark, illustrated by Barry Wilkinson. London, Methuen, 1974.
Look at the Little One, illustrated by Margaret Palmer. London, Hodder and Stoughton, 1974; Chicago, Children's Press, 1976.
Snake in the Camp, illustrated by Joan Beales. Leicester, Brockhampton Press, 1975; Chicago, Children's Press, 1976.
Tower Raven, illustrated by Sally Launder. London, Abelard Schuman, 1975.
Backyard Hospital, illustrated by Gareth Floyd. London, Hodder and Stoughton, 1976.

Other

Roads and Travelling, illustrated by Trevor Stubley.   Oxford, Blackwell, 1964.
Bridges, illustrated by Diana Stanley.   Edinburgh, Oliver and Boyd, 1965.
Tufty (reader), illustrated by George Adamson.   London, Macmillan, 1968.
Frankie's Country Day (reader), illustrated by Mary Dinsdale.   London, Macmillan, 1968.
The Lost Money (reader), illustrated by Mary Dinsdale.   London, Macmillan, 1968.
The Wedding Tea (reader), illustrated by Mary Dinsdale.   London, Macmillan, 1970.
Magic and Gold: Tales from Northern Europe, illustrated by Peter Kesteven.   Oxford and New York, Pergamon Press, 1970.
Towns.   Oxford, Blackwell, 1971.
The Marvellous Stick (reader), illustrated by Mary Dinsdale.   London, Macmillan, 1972.
Bells in Our Lives, illustrated by Janet Duchesne.   Newton Abbot, Devon, David and Charles, 1973.
Treasure, illustrated by Desmond Knight.   London, Dent, 1973.
The Rainbow Walk (reader), illustrated by Prudence Seward.   London, Burke, 1973.
An Armful of Sparrows (reader), illustrated by George Adamson.   London, Macmillan, 1973.
Dolls and Puppets.   Newton Abbot, Devon, David and Charles, 1974.
Walls, illustrated by W.G.D. Hill.   Oxford, Blackwell, 1974.
He Cannot Really Read (reader), illustrated by Prudence Seward.   London, Oxford University Press, 1975.
The Story of Cars.   Oxford, Blackwell, 1976.
The Magician (reader), illustrated by Richard Rose.   London, Macmillan, 1976.

*   *   *

Adults and children who read Janet and John without wincing may well feel at home with Mary Cockett's prolific output for the young and very young reader. Though on the surface some of her books deal with "disadvantaged" children, in effect her books are pre-eminently a celebration of conventional proprieties. This comes partly of the author's general outlook, but mostly from her teacherly stance towards her readers and her material. One "blurb" writer, with endemic overstatement, speaks of Miss Cockett's "genius for instruction," referring no doubt to her indefatigable urge to inform, to pack every page with useful information about keeping goats, growing sunflowers or going into hospital. But to treat stories mainly as occasions for imparting factual knowledge and inculcating wholesome attitudes is to misconceive the purpose of fiction and the nature of the imagination.

Promising starting points such as a boy on his grandfather's steam roller (*Rolling On*), a den behind derelict cottages (*The Wild Place*), or a canal girl on a pleasure-boat (*Boat Girl*), are lost in the service of humdrum tasks, compulsory purchase orders and the problems of educating itinerant children. Often we have what seems to be the prelude to a story rather than the story itself. It is as though the author is reluctant to waste the fruits of her researches, so that what should be background takes over as subject, while character and incident play a subordinate role. The unrelenting explanation of inconsequential detail gives an impression of condescension and artificiality which is not helped by unlikely dialogue such as "I've come, Grum, I've come," or "Oh, mummy, you are an idiot but you're rather sweet." The author leans heavily on pets and other animals for dramatic tension and for raising the emotional temperature, as in the mawkish obsequies for Old Bess in *Boat Girl* where there is no indication that the adults, or for that matter the author herself, view the proceedings in any way different from that of the children involved. If sentimentality is an excessive show of feeling disproportionate to the object or situation, then that word applies not infrequently to these stories. They are more childish than childlike. They leave untapped the power of the imagination to inform and move in ways that transcend the merely factual and conventional.

What is reading for, one might ask, as young readers, coming off their primers, are met by this sort of fare.

—Graham Hammond

COLUM, Padraic. Irish. Born in Longford, 8 December 1881. Educated at National School, Sandycove, County Dublin. Worked as clerk in railway office, Dublin, until 1904; Founder, with James Stephens and Thomas MacDonagh, *Irish Review*, Dublin 1916. Settled in the United States, living in New York after 1939. President, James Joyce Society, New York. Recipient: Academy of American Poets Fellowship, 1952; Irish Academy of Letters Gregory Medal, 1953; Catholic Library Association Regina Medal, 1961. Member, Irish Academy of Literature and National Institute of Arts and Letters. *Died 11 January 1972.*

PUBLICATIONS FOR CHILDREN

Fiction

> *A Boy in Eirinn*, illustrated by Jack B. Yeats. London, Dent, and New York, Dutton, 1913.
> *The Boy Apprenticed to an Enchanter*, illustrated by Dugald Stuart Walker. New York, Macmillan, 1920.
> *The Peep-Show Man*, illustrated by Lois Lenski. New York, Macmillan, 1925; London, Macmillan, 1932.
> *The White Sparrow*, illustrated by Joseph Low. New York, Macmillan, 1935; as *Sparrow Alone*, London, Blackie, 1975.
> *Where the Winds Never Blew and the Cocks Never Crew*, illustrated by Richard Bennett. New York, Macmillan, 1940.

Play

> *The Destruction of the Hostel* (produced Dublin, 1910).

Other

> *The King of Ireland's Son*, illustrated by Willy Pogany. New York, Holt, 1916; London, Harrap, 1920.
> *The Boy Who Knew What the Birds Said*, illustrated by Dugald Stuart Walker. New York, Macmillan, 1918.
> *The Adventures of Odysseus and the Tale of Troy*. New York, Macmillan 1918; London, Harrap, 1920; as *The Children's Homer*, Macmillan, 1946.
> *The Girl Who Sat by the Ashes*, illustrated by Dugald Stuart Walker. New York, Macmillan, 1919; London, Collier Macmillan, 1968.
> *The Children of Odin: A Book of Northern Myths*, illustrated by Willy Pogany. New York, Macmillan, 1920; London, Harrap, 1922.
> *The Golden Fleece and the Heroes Who Lived Before Achilles*, illustrated by Willy Pogany. New York, Macmillan, 1921.
> *The Children Who Followed the Piper*, illustrated by Dugald Stuart Walker. New York, Macmillan, 1922.
> *The Six Who Were Left in a Shoe*, illustrated by Dugald Stuart Walker. Joliet, Illinois, Volland, 1923.

Tales and Legends of Hawaii: At the Gateways of the Day, and *The Bright Islands*, illustrated by Juliette May Fraser. New Haven, Connecticut, Yale University Press. 2 vols., 1924–25; as *Legends of Hawaii*, 1937.

The Island of the Mighty, Being the Hero Stories of Celtic Britain Retold from the Mabinogion, illustrated by Wilfred Jones. New York, Macmillan, 1924.

The Voyagers, Being Legends and Romances of Atlantic Discovery, illustrated by Wilfred Jones. New York, Macmillan, 1925.

The Forge in the Forest, illustrated by Boris Artzybasheff. New York, Macmillan, 1925.

The Fountain of Youth: Stories to Be Told, illustrated by Jay Van Everen. New York, Macmillan, 1927.

Orpheus: Myth of the World, illustrated by Boris Artzybasheff. New York, Macmillan, 1930; as *Myths of the Old World*, New York, Universal Library, n.d.

The Big Tree of Bunlahy: Stories of My Own Countryside, illustrated by Jack B. Yeats. New York, Macmillan, 1933.

The Frenzied Prince, Being Heroic Stories of Ancient Ireland, illustrated by Willy Pogany. Philadelphia, McKay, 1943.

The Stone of Victory and Other Tales, illustrated by Judith Gwyn Brown. New York, McGraw Hill, 1966.

Editor, *Gulliver's Travels*, by Jonathan Swift, illustrated by Willy Pogany. New York, Macmillan, 1917; London, Harrap, 1919.

Editor, *The Arabian Nights, Tales of Wonder and Magnificence*, illustrated by Lynd Ward. New York, Macmillan, 1953.

PUBLICATIONS FOR ADULTS

Novels

Castle Conquer. New York and London, Macmillan, 1923.
Three Men: A Tale. London, Elkin Mathews and Marrot, 1930.
The Flying Swans. New York, Crown, 1957.

Plays

The Children of Lir, and *Brian Boru*, in *Irish Independent* (Dublin), 1902.

The Kingdom of the Young (produced, 1902). Published in *United Irishman* (Dublin) 1903.

The Foleys, and *Eoghan's Wife*, in *United Irishman* (Dublin), 1903.

The Saxon Shillin' (produced Dublin, 1903). Published in *Lost Plays of the Irish Renaissance*, edited by Robert G. Hogan and J.F. Kilroy. Dixon, California, Proscenium Press, 1970.

The Fiddler's House (as *Broken Soil*, produced Dublin, 1903; London, 1904; revised version, as *The Fiddler's House*, produced Dublin, 1907; New York, 1941). Dublin, Maunsel, 1907; in *Three Plays*, 1916.

The Land (produced Dublin and London, 1905). Dublin, Maunsel, 1905; in *Three Plays*, 1916.

The Miracle of the Corn: A Miracle Play (produced in Dublin, 1908; London 1911). Included in *Studies*, 1907; in *Theatre Arts Magazine* (New York), October 1921.

Thomas Muskerry (produced Dublin and London, 1910). Dublin, Maunsel, 1910; in *Three Plays*, 1916.

The Desert. Dublin, Devereux Newth, 1912; as *Mogu the Wanderer; or,The Desert: A Fantastic Comedy*, Boston, Little Brown, 1917; as *Mogu of the Desert* (produced Dublin, 1931).

The Betrayal (produced Manchester, 1913; Pittsburgh, 1914).   Published in *One-Act Plays of To-Day*, vol. 4, edited by J.W. Marriott, London, Harrap, 1928; published separately, New York, French, n.d.

Three Plays: The Fiddler's House, The Land, Thomas Muskerry.   Boston, Little Brown, 1916; Dublin and London, Maunsel, 1917; revised edition, London, Macmillan, 1925.

The Grasshopper, with F.E. Washburn-Freund, adaptation of a play by Count Keyserling (produced New York, 1917).

Balloon (produced Ogunquit, Maine).   New York, Macmillan, 1929.

The Show-Booth, adaptation of a play by Alexander Blok (produced Dublin, 1948).

Moytura: A Play for Dancers.   Dublin, Dolmen Press, and London, Oxford University Press, 1963.

The Challengers: Monasterboice, Glendalough, Cloughoughter (produced Dublin, 1966).

The Road round Ireland, with Basil Burwell, adaptation of works by Colum (produced Norwalk, Connecticut, 1967; as *Carricknabauna*, produced New York, 1967).

Verse

Heather Ale: A Book of Verse.   Privately printed, 1907.

Wild Earth: A Book of Verse.   Dublin, Maunsel, 1907; revised edition, as *Wild Earth and Other Poems*, Maunsel, and New York, Holt, 1916; as *Wild Earth: Poems*, Dublin, Talbot Press, 1950.

Dramatic Legends and Other Poems.   New York and London, Macmillan, 1922.

The Way of the Cross: Devotions on the Progress of Our Lord Jesus Christ from the Judgement Hall to Calvary.   Chicago, Seymour, 1926.

Creatures.   New York, Macmillan, 1927.

Old Pastures.   New York, Macmillan, 1930; London, Macmillan, 1932.

Poems.   New York, Macmillan, 1932; revised edition, as *Collected Poems*, New York, Devin Adair, 1953.

The Story of Lowry Maen.   New York, Macmillan, 1937.

Flower Pieces: New Poems.   Dublin, Orwell Press, 1938.

The Jackdaw.   Dublin, Gayfield Press, 1939.

Ten Poems.   Dublin, Dolmen Press, 1952.

The Vegetable Kingdom.   Bloomington, Indiana University Press, 1954.

Garland Sunday.   Dublin, privately printed, 1958.

Irish Elegies.   Dublin, Dolmen Press, 1958; revised edition, 1961; London, Oxford University Press, 1963; Chester Springs, Pennsylvania, Dufour, 1965.

The Poet's Circuits: Collected Poems of Ireland.   London, Oxford University Press, 1960.

Images of Departure.   Dublin, Dolmen Press, 1969.

Other

Studies (miscellany).   Dublin, Maunsel, 1907.

My Irish Year.   London, Mills and Boon, and New York, Pott, 1912.

The Irish Rebellion of 1916 and Its Martyrs: Erin's Tragic Easter, with others, edited by Maurice Joy.   New York, Devin Adair, 1916.

The Road round Ireland.   New York, Macmillan, 1926.

Cross Roads in Ireland.   New York, Macmillan, 1930.

Ella Young: An Appreciation.   London and New York, Longman, 1931.

A Half-Day's Ride; or, Estates in Corsica.   London and New York, Macmillan, 1932.

The Legend of Saint Columba.   New York, Macmillan, 1935; London, Sheed and Ward, 1936.

Our Friend James Joyce, with Mary Colum.   New York. Doubleday. 1958: London. Gollancz, 1959.

Arthur Griffith.   Dublin, Browne and Nolan, 1959; as *Ourselves Alone! The Story of Arthur Griffith and the Origin of the Irish Free State,* New York, Crown, 1959.

Story Telling Old and New.   New York, Macmillan, 1961.

Editor, *Oliver Goldsmith.*   London, Herbert and Daniel, and Chicago, Browne. 1913.

Editor, *Broad-Sheet Ballads, Being a Collection of Irish Popular Songs.*   Dublin and London, Maunsel, 1913; Baltimore, Norman Remington, 1914.

Editor, with Joseph Harrington O'Brien, *Poems of the Irish Revolutionary Brotherhood.*   Boston, Small Maynard, 1916; revised edition, 1916.

Editor, *An Anthology of Irish Verse.*   New York, Boni and Liveright, 1922; revised edition, New York, Liveright, 1948.

Editor, *A Treasury of Irish Folklore: The Stories, Traditions, Legends, Humor, Wisdom, Ballads, and Songs of the Irish People.*   New York, Crown, 1954; revised edition. 1962, 1967.

Editor, with Margaret Freeman Cabell, *Between Friends: Letters of James Branch Cabell and Others.*   New York, Harcourt Brace, 1962.

Editor, *The Poems of Samuel Ferguson.*   Dublin, Figgis, 1963.

Editor, *Roofs of Gold: Poems to Read Aloud.*   New York, Macmillan, and London, Collier Macmillan, 1964.

Critical Study: *Padraic Colum: A Biographical-Critical Introduction* by Zack R. Bowen, Carbondale, Southern Illinois University Press, 1970.

Theatrical Activities

Actor: **Plays** – Buinne in *Dierdre* by AE, Dublin, 1902; Pupil in *The Hour-Glass* by W.B. Yeats, Dublin, 1903; A Cripple in *The King's Threshold* by W.B. Yeats. Dublin, 1903.

*   *   *

Around the glowing turf fires in the Longford workhouse where his father was Master. Padraic Colum heard the talk and tales of his people, the dispossessed, the ailing, and the old folk of the road. The story teller, from the place of honour near the fire, knew the children were listening with their elders. So it was with Colum in his many books. Some of them were written directly for children, and they, with his poems, are his best work, especially *The King of Ireland's Son* and *The Golden Fleece.*

Colum recreated many of the world's myths and legends for children. He used Greek, Scandinavian, Norse, and Irish legends, and achieved a *tour de force* in his *Tales and Legends of Hawaii.* The critic Lionel Trilling praised Colum's children's books, probably for the reason that Colum never writes down to his audience, or burdens the tales with scholarly footnotes or explanations. His story-telling is straight and direct, and accomplishes its purposes of entrancing the reader and arousing wonder.

Besides the books of legends and myths, Colum wrote several novels, of which *A Boy in Eirinn* is the first and best. He captures the vision as seen through the eyes of a child.

All his life there was the child peering out of him, even while he grew into an honoured man of letters in a literary world that has lost its zest and innocence.

—William Ready

CONNOR, Ralph. Pseudonym for Charles William Gordon. Canadian. Born in Indian Lands, Glengarry County, Ontario, 13 September 1860. Educated at St. Mary's High School, Ontario; University of Toronto, B.A., 1883; Knox College, Toronto, B.D., 1887; New College, Edinburgh, 1893–94. Served as a Major (Senior Chaplain) in the Canadian Army and British Expeditionary Force, 1915–18: mentioned in despatches, 1916. Married Helen Skinner King in 1899; one son and six daughters. High school teacher, Chatham, Ontario, 1884–86; teacher, Upper Canadian College, Toronto, 1886–87; ordained Presbyterian Minister, 1890; Missionary, Northwest Territories, 1890–93; Minister, St. Stephen's Church, Winnipeg, 1894–1937. Chairman, Joint Council of Industry, Province of Manitoba, 1920–24. D.D.: Knox College, Kingston, Ontario. Fellow, Royal Society of Canada, 1904. Companion of the Order of St. Michael and St. George, 1935. *Died 31 October 1937.*

PUBLICATIONS FOR CHILDREN

Fiction

> *Glengarry School Days: A Story of Early Days in Glengarry.* Toronto, Westminster, and Chicago, Revell, 1902; as *Glengarry Days,* London, Hodder and Stoughton, 1902.

PUBLICATIONS FOR ADULTS

Novels

> *Gwen's Canyon.* Toronto, Westminster, 1898.
> *Beyond the Marshes.* Toronto, Westminster, 1898; Chicago, Revell, 1900.
> *Black Rock: A Tale of the Selkirks.* Toronto, Westminster, New York, Crowell, and London, Hodder and Stoughton, 1898.
> *The Sky Pilot: A Tale of the Foothills.* Toronto, Westminster, Chicago, Revell, and London, Hodder and Stoughton, 1899.
> *Michael McGrath, Postmaster.* London, Sharpe, 1900.
> *The Prospector: A Tale of Crow's Nest Pass.* Toronto, Westminster, 1901; Chicago, Revell, and London, Hodder and Stoughton, 1904.
> *The Man from Glengarry.* Toronto, Westminster, and Chicago, Revell, 1901.
> *The Swan Creek Blizzard.* Chicago, Revell, 1904.
> *Gwen: An Idyll of the Canyon.* Chicago, Revell, and London, Hodder and Stoughton, 1904.
> *Breaking the Record.* New York, Revell, 1904.
> *The Doctor: A Tale of the Rockies.* Toronto, Westminster, and Chicago, Revell, 1906; as *The Doctor of Crow's Nest,* London, Hodder and Stoughton, 1906.
> *The Settler: A Tale of Saskatchewan.* New York and London, Hodder and Stoughton, 1906; as *The Foreigner: A Tale of Saskatchewan,* Toronto, Westminster, New York, Doran, and London, Hodder and Stoughton, 1909.
> *Corporal Cameron: A Tale of the North-West Mounted Police.* Toronto, Westminster, and New York, Hodder and Stoughton, 1912.
> *The Patrol of the Sun Dance Trail.* New York, Doran, and London, Hodder and Stoughton, 1914.
> *The Major.* Toronto and New York, McClelland and Stewart, and London, Hodder and Stoughton, 1917.
> *To Him That Hath.* New York, Doran, 1921; London, Hodder and Stoughton, 1922; Toronto, McClelland and Stewart, 1928.
> *The Gaspards of Pine Croft: A Romance of the Windermere.* Toronto, McClelland and Stewart, New York, Doran, and London, Hodder and Stoughton, 1923.

Treading the Winepress. Toronto, McClelland and Stewart, New York, Doran, and London, Hodder and Stoughton, 1925.

The Runner: A Romance of the Niagaras. Toronto and New York, Doubleday, 1929; London, Hodder and Stoughton, 1930.

The Rock and the River: A Romance of Quebec. Toronto, McClelland and Stewart, and New York, Dodd Mead, 1931; London, Lane, 1932.

The Arm of Gold – le Bras d'or. Toronto, McClelland and Stewart, and New York, Dodd Mead, 1932; London, Lane, 1933.

The Girl from Glengarry. Toronto, McClelland and Stewart, and New York, Dodd Mead, 1933; as *The Glengarry Girl*, London, Lane, 1934.

Torches Through the Bush: A Tale of Glengarry. Toronto, McClelland and Stewart, and New York, Dodd Mead, 1934; London, Lane, 1935.

The Rebel Loyalist. Toronto, McClelland and Stewart, and New York, Dodd Mead, 1935; London, Lane, 1936.

He Dwelt among Us. Toronto, McClelland and Stewart, New York, Revell, and London, Hodder and Stoughton, 1936.

The Gay Crusader: A Romance of Quebec. Toronto, McClelland and Stewart, and New York, Dodd Mead, 1936.

Short Stories

The Pilot at Swan Creek. London, Hodder and Stoughton, 1905.

The Friendly Four and Other Stories. New York, Doran, 1926; London, Hodder and Stoughton, 1927.

Other

The Life of James Robertson, Missionary Superintendent in the Northwest Territories (as Charles William Gordon). Toronto, Westminster, Chicago, Revell, and London, Hodder and Stoughton, 1908.

The Angel and the Star. Toronto, Westminster, Chicago, Revell, and London, Hodder and Stoughton, 1908.

The Dawn by Galilee: A Story of the Christ. Toronto, Westminster, and New York and London, Hodder and Stoughton, 1909.

The Recall of Love: A Message of Hope. Toronto, Westminster, and New York and London, Hodder and Stoughton, 1910.

Christian Hope. London, Hodder and Stoughton, 1912.

A Fight for Freedom. Toronto, McClelland and Stewart, 1917.

Postscript to Adventure: The Autobiography of Ralph Connor – Charles W. Gordon, edited by J. King Gordon. New York, Farrar and Rinehart, and London, Hodder and Stoughton, 1938.

*   *   *

Ralph Connor's beloved Glengarry world was a part of the Canadian past that has disappeared almost without a trace. The people of whom he wrote, though they might have been born and lived all their lives in Canada, nonetheless felt themselves to be somehow more Scottish than the inhabitants of Scotland; the older ones among them would doubtless have taken umbrage had anyone dared call them "Canadian."

Glengarry has faded into a dim colonial past, but should be remembered. Connor's many books enjoyed an enormous popularity not too long ago, and he helped to create an impression of Canada of which vestiges remain even today, perpetuating the image of a homespun pioneer way of life that was already but a memory in his own day.

Connor's Glengarry was a harsh place for school children, a little world sternly ruled by dour fathers who flourished the Bible and the strap to much the same purpose and with equally quelling effects. Home was a log house far from the nearest neighbours, so isolated by winter snows that younger children could only attend school during the milder months. Work was burdensome and never over: even the youngest children had to bear a hand with the ceaseless labour.

Yet if there were hardships, good things too were a part of the pioneer past: unsullied air and water, the heroic challenge of wresting a home and farm from virgin wilderness and watching it slowly become fruitful and welcoming, the simple social pleasures of the spelling bee, the sleigh-ride, and the old swimming hole.

Glengarry school days were of short duration in those hard-working times. Boys became men as soon as they were able to do a man's work, and "book learning" seldom amounted to more that the three R's. "The idea of school was to fit the children for the struggle into which their lives would thrust them, so that the boy who could spell and read the cipher was supposed to be ready for his life work." Only the minister and the doctor were likely to be learned folk, which earned them a reverential respect in their God-fearing, rather grimly pious little community. It was a hard life, but a rewarding one. Connor, no stylist, tells a simple tale of boys progressing toward sturdy manhood in the simple, straightforward language his subject demands.

In his work is to be found perhaps the fullest flowering of "muscular Christianity" in North American literature, didactic, sentimental, almost aggressively wholesome, and rather charming in its sincerity and innocence. Young readers of today will find the little log schoolhouse in the wilderness as foreign and as fascinating as Ur of the Chaldees, and for the same reasons: it is all so unimaginably different from the known and familiar. Yet if Canada has changed, people have not. Though their surroundings are quaint and even primitive, the children of Glengarry still appeal across the years to the children of the Space Age, who have much to envy them.

—Joan McGrath

COOK, Lyn. Pseudonym for Evelyn Margaret Waddell. Canadian. Born in Weston, Ontario, 4 May 1918. Educated at the University of Toronto, B.A. (honours) 1940, B.L.S. 1941. Served as a Meteorological Observer, Women's Division, Royal Canadian Air Force, 1942–46; Canada Service Medal. Married Robb John Waddell in 1949; has one son and one daughter. Librarian, Toronto Public Libraries, 1941–42; Children's Librarian, Sudbury, Ontario, Public Library, 1946–47; Script-Writer, Director and Narrator of the children's show "A Doorway to Fairyland," Canadian Broadcasting Company, Toronto, 1947–52; Children's Creative Drama Teacher, New Play Society Theatre Group, 1956–65; also story-teller and creative drama group organizer for pre-school children, Scarborough, Ontario, Public Libraries. Agent: Scargall of Markham, 1 Talisman Crescent, Markham, Ontario L3P 2C8. Address: 72 Cedarbrae Boulevard, Scarborough, Ontario M1J 2K5, Canada.

PUBLICATIONS FOR CHILDREN

Fiction

> The Bells on Finland Street, illustrated by Stanley Wyatt. Toronto and New York, Macmillan, 1950.
> The Little Magic Fiddler, illustrated by Stanley Wyatt. Toronto, Macmillan, 1951.
> Rebel on the Trail, illustrated by Ruth M. Collins. Toronto, Macmillan, and New York, St. Martin's Press, 1953.
> Jady and the General, illustrated by Murray Smith. Toronto, Macmillan, and New York, St. Martin's Press, 1955.

Pegeen and the Pilgrim, illustrated by Pat and Bill Wheeler. Toronto, Macmillan, 1957; London, Harrap, 1959.
The Road to Kip's Cove, illustrated by William Wheeler. Toronto, Macmillan, 1961; New York, St. Martin's Press, 1962.
Samantha's Secret Room, illustrated by Bill McKibbin. Toronto and London, Macmillan, 1963; New York, St. Martin's Press, 1964.
The Secret of Willow Castle, illustrated by Kelly Clark. Toronto, Macmillan, 1966.
The Magical Miss Mittens, illustrated by Mary Davies. Toronto, Macmillan, 1970.
Toys from the Sky, illustrated by Mary Davies. Toronto, Clarke Irwin, 1972.

Verse

Jolly Jean-Pierre, illustrated by Mary Davies. Toronto, Burns and MacEachern, 1973.
If I Were All These, illustrated by Peter Ivens. Toronto, Burns and MacEachern, 1974.

Other

The Brownie Handbook for Canada, illustrated by Frances Shadbolt. Toronto, Girl Guides of Canada, 1965.

PUBLICATIONS FOR ADULTS

Verse

Fragment. Islington, Ontario, privately printed, n.d.
Harvest. Islington, Ontario, privately printed, n.d.
Soliloquy. Islington, Ontario, privately printed, n.d.

Lyn Cook comments:
I have always wanted to be a story-teller, and the knowledge that many children in my own and other countries of the world have shared the characters and events of my imagination brings me great joy. My books are, for the most part, regional tales of Canada, but the letters that come to me show me that my stories have another dimension for my fans, young and old – the dimension of human relationships and the all-important landscape of the human heart.

*   *   *

The Canadian mosaic emerges as a veritable watermark on each page of Lyn Cook's fiction. Her first and perhaps most successful work, *The Bells on Finland Street*, celebrates the friendly union of young girls of differing national origins. Little Elin delights in tales of trolls and descriptions of Finnish yuletide festivities narrated by her visiting grandfather. But her wish to reside in Finland brings a gentle chastening from the old gentleman. The ways of the old country are best continued in the new. In reference to the skating competition Elin proudly proclaims "I'm Finland, I follow Chrissie, she's Czechoslovakia." Her grandfather replies, "Remember, little one, tonight you skate for Finland, and some day you skate for Canada." The new country with old traditions supplies the theme for *Jady and the General* in which a lad from an Ontario peach farm rides to glory astride a Morgan stallion whom he has renamed after his mother's ancestor – an ancestor whose ghost reputedly makes an annual ride to commemorate his role in a military encounter against the Americans.

Indelible traditions form the framework for *Samantha's Secret Room* where Samantha Wiggins, the third of that name, finally decodes the presumed ramblings of her demanding great-grandmother to discover a well-concealed secret room occupied by the original Samantha. The old order has a comfortable manner of becoming settled in Canadian environs as a Stratford, Ontario lass (*Pegeen and the Pilgrim*) discovers during the first Shakespeare festival, now an annual summer fete. The world comes to Canada and the 12-year-old would-be actress finds friends among scholars and actors from around the world. Young children with an ever intensifying sense of their past are at the centre of *Rebel on the Trail* as youthful David Cartwright becomes dangerously involved in the rebellion of 1837. *The Secret of Willow Castle* has as its setting a house that still stands, and a cousin of the heroine turns out to be the future first Prime Minister of Canada, Sir John A. MacDonald. The accretions of tradition keep building up in a Canada not all that old. *The Magical Miss Mittens* involves further intrigue with the past as a Nova Scotia boy and girl find themselves on brief excursions through time as they encounter Leif Ericsson, Socrates, Shakespeare, and Lincoln, and in true Canadian fashion making each of them their own. The ghost of the past supplies the milieu for *The Road to Kip's Cove* which also features a conscious display of the Canadian landscape. A recent picture book with bilingual text, *Jolly Jean-Pierre*, efficiently reflects French Canadian mannerisms while recalling the voyageurs in a compelling tall tale.

—Leonard R. Mendelsohn

COOLIDGE, Olivia. American. Born in London, England, 16 October 1908; naturalized American citizen. Educated at Wycombe Abbey School. Buckinghamshire, 1921–27; Somerville College, Oxford, 1927–31, B.A., 1931, M.A. 1941. Married Archibald Cary Coolidge in 1946; has four stepchildren. English teacher, Potsdam-Hermannswerder, Germany, 1931–32; classics teacher, Wimbledon High School, London, 1932–37; secretary, Education Service Bureau for Camps, New York, 1938; English teacher, Low-Heywood School, Stamford, Connecticut, 1939, and Winsor School, Boston, 1940–46. Member, Board of Trustees, Mills College of Education, New York, 1956–61. Agent: Harriet Wasserman, Russell and Volkening Inc., 551 Fifth Avenue, New York, New York 10017. Address: Box 133, R.D. 3, Cambridge, Maryland 21613, U.S.A.

PUBLICATIONS FOR CHILDREN

Fiction

> *Egyptian Adventures*, illustrated by Joseph Low.   Boston, Houghton Mifflin, 1954.
> *Cromwell's Head*, illustrated by Edward Wilson.   Boston, Houghton Mifflin, 1955.
> *Roman People*, illustrated by Lino Lipinsky.   Boston, Houghton Mifflin, 1959.
> *Men of Athens*, illustrated by Milton Johnson.   Boston, Houghton Mifflin, 1962.
> *People in Palestine*.   Boston, Houghton Mifflin, 1965.
> *The King of Men*, illustrated by Ellen Raskin.   Boston, Houghton Mifflin, 1966.
> *Marathon Looks on the Sea*, illustrated by Erwin Schrachner.   Boston, Houghton Mifflin, 1967.
> *The Maid of Artemis*, illustrated by Bea Holmes.   Boston, Houghton Mifflin, 1969.
> *Tales of the Crusades*.   Boston, Houghton Mifflin, 1970.
> *Come by Here*, illustrated by Milton Johnson.   Boston, Houghton Mifflin, 1970.

Other

> *Greek Myths*, illustrated by Edouard Sandoz.   Boston, Houghton Mifflin, 1949.
> *Legends of the North*, illustrated by Edouard Sandoz.   Boston, Houghton Mifflin, 1951.
> *The Trojan War*, illustrated by Edouard Sandoz.   Boston, Houghton Mifflin, 1952.
> *Winston Churchill and the Story of Two World Wars*.   Boston, Houghton Mifflin, 1960.

Caesar's Gallic War. Boston, Houghton Mifflin, 1961; London, Bodley Head, 1964.
Makers of the Red Revolution. Boston, Houghton Mifflin, 1963.
Edith Wharton. New York, Scribner, 1964.
Lives of the Famous Romans, illustrated by Milton Johnson. Boston, Houghton Mifflin, 1965.
Women's Rights: The Suffrage Movement in America, 1848–1920. New York, Dutton, 1966.
Eugene O'Neill. New York, Scribner, 1966.
George Bernard Shaw. Boston, Houghton Mifflin, 1968.
The Golden Days of Greece, illustrated by Enrico Arno. New York, Crowell, 1968.
Tom Paine, Revolutionary. New York, Scribner, 1969.
Gandhi. Boston, Houghton Mifflin, 1971.
The Three Lives of Joseph Conrad. Boston, Houghton Mifflin, 1972.
The Apprenticeship of Abraham Lincoln. New York, Scribner, 1974.
The Statesmanship of Abraham Lincoln. New York, Scribner, 1977.

Olivia Coolidge comments:
I write to communicate to older children some of the things that interest me. All my fictional work except for *Come by Here* is classical or early medieval. I have also found great pleasure in writing biography which is not too long for hard-pressed students to read and yet at the same time is not too simplified or too didactic for minds that are beginning to function at an adult level.

*   *   *

Most of the books written by Olivia Coolidge are about important personalities, historical events, and mythology. Mrs. Coolidge writes on subjects that interest her and on which she has conducted extensive research. As the author states (in *Something about the Author,* vol. 1, 1971): "I write about history, biography and ancient legends for teens because I am more interested in values that always have been of concern to people than I am in the form we express them in at this moment."

Coolidge's works on mythology, like *Greek Myths* and *Legends of the North,* are usually told in a style that makes them easy to read. The author's works of fiction revolve around myths and tales of gods and heroes. *Egyptian Adventures* is a collection of short stories based on Egyptian life from 1600 to 1100 B.C. The stories center around Egyptian animals, good luck charms, spirits, magicians, and the life of the Pharaoh. Each story is colorfully told and vividly recreates something that the Egyptians left to the world as a legacy. Another collection of short stories is *Men of Athens* spanning the period from 500 to 400 B.C. The stories are about great leaders and kings like King Darius and King Xerxes. The greatness of the Athenians is depicted in the great wars, as well as in the Olympic Games. The episodes are based on the deeds of such men as Pericles, the architects of the Parthenon, Socrates and Plato, and the writers Aeschylus, Sophocles, Euripides, and Aristophanes. Another Greek story is *Marathon Looks on the Sea.* This is the tale of Metiochos, a Greek boy who rises from meagre beginnings to become a political figure and ruler against the background of the Battle of Marathon and the events that led to it. Yet another work of Greek life but with a different viewpoint is *The Maid of Artemis.* The temple of Artemis at Brauron is the setting from which is derived the picturesque story of a young Greek girl's family life and growth to womanhood.

Mrs. Coolidge also uses the traditional legends about the Olympian gods and goddesses. *The King of Men* is a tale taken from the legend of Agamemnon. This legendary hero is depicted struggling to exist between two worlds – the earthly situations, and dealings with the gods and goddesses.

Mrs. Coolidge has written other works that deal with legends and myths. One of many is *Tales of the Crusades,* a well written tale about the adventures of knights and the splendor of knighthood. One work is based specifically on Negro culture, *Come by Here.* The story of Minty, a young black girl growing up in Baltimore in the early 1900's, is well-written, but it does not rank with her other works in quality of the story or the writing style.

Most of Mrs. Coolidge's works are scholarly, as well as lucid, compact, and fascinating. The author is unsurpassed in her treatment of mythology for the young reader.

—Dolores C. Leffall

COOPER, Gordon (John Llewellyn). British. Born in Melksham, Wiltshire, 27 March 1932. Educated at St. Michael's School, Melksham, 1937–43; High School for Boys, Trowbridge, Wiltshire, 1943–48. Civil Servant, 1967. Address: 6 Beanacre Road, Melksham, Wiltshire, England.

PUBLICATIONS FOR CHILDREN

Fiction

> *An Hour in the Morning,.* illustrated by Phillip Gough. London, Oxford University Press, 1971; New York, Dutton, 1974.
> *A Time in a City,* illustrated by Robin Jacques. London, Oxford University Press, 1972; New York, Dutton, 1975.
> *A Second Springtime,* illustrated by Robin Jacques. London, Oxford University Press, 1973; Nashville, Nelson, 1975.
> *Hester's Summer,* illustrated by Robin Jacques. London, Oxford University Press, 1974.
> *A Certain Courage,* illustrated by Robin Jacques. London, Oxford University Press, 1975.

Gordon Cooper comments:

An Hour in the Morning began life as a short poem "Country Girl" which I had written after seeing an old brown photograph of a group of girls with their teacher outside a village school in 1914.

I began writing *A Second Springtime* after seeing a paragraph in a local newspaper from a "March of Time" column which stated that in 1870 six girls had appeared before the magistrates in order to obtain necessary certificates authorizing their departure to Canada under a special welfare scheme.

Settings and real-life circumstances play an important part in all the books. At the end of writing each story I have always felt a deep sense of admiration for the people whose lives I have tried to portray.

*   *   *

The quiet chronicle of everyday events has a secure place in adult fiction but it is in many ways the antithesis of what children demand of a story. Adventure regularly comes top of polls of children's reading tastes, with humour, fantasy and school themes fairly close behind, and it is difficult to recall a contemporary best-selling children's author whose work does not fall into one of these categories. It cannot be claimed that Gordon Cooper's books slot in to any of these groups, or that his careful reconstructions of times just past have achieved great popularity among library borrowers. It is the adults, especially the critics, who have discerned the fascination of detail when built into a credible background, and the potential emotional richness of the everyday.

The tone of the stories is thoughtful; the chief characters live restricted domestic lives on which world events impinge but are only half understood. Duty plays a large part. Kate in *An Hour in the Morning* rises at six, lights fires, carries hot water, cleans shoes, and is never resentful of her labour-filled life. The six-year-old twins walk three miles to school and three back and never consider this a hardship.

We do, of course, meet unpleasant characters – Aunt Em in *A Time in a City*, continually complaining and critical, or brusque Mr. Pritchard and his wife – and problems, such as Ben's unfriendliness and the accusation of theft in *A Second Springtime*. There are hints of deep thoughts and moral problems, as in the whole sequence in *A Second Springtime* when Hester decides how to meet Mrs. Pollitt's attempts to make amends. Rarely, though, do we glimpse the dark side of human nature. It is fascinating to compare Nina Bawden's view of Edwardian family life in *The Peppermint Pig* and of wartime evacuation in *Carrie's War* with *An Hour in the Morning* and *A Certain Courage* respectively and assess which is nearer the truth.

The basic structure of a Cooper novel is usually simple, the chronicling of life for one central character over a year or so, filled in with a fairly large supporting cast of neighbourhood acquaintance, the charting of a course from tribulation to achievement via hard work and honesty. There is no attempt to probe deeply into motives, desires, frustrations, and the style has a flat tranquillity which makes even the small emotions described hard to transmit. " 'Happy birthday Hester' Mrs. Clarke said. 'Thank you Ma' said Hester excitedly" (*A Second Springtime*) is one of many examples of language failing to meet situation. Yet the stories have the same ring of truth which Judith St. John's reminiscences of her Canadian childhood have: they make compulsive reading just as *The Archers* make compulsive listening. The simple structure – this happened, then that – the untraumatic experiences, the optimism, the detailed guide to times within living memory, combine to make satisfying stories which leave their readers more grateful for the conditions and opportunities of the present.

—Peggy Heeks

COOPER, Lettice (Ulpha). British. Born in Eccles, Lancashire, 3 September 1897. Educated at St. Cuthbert's School, Southbourne; Lady Margaret Hall, Oxford, 1916–18, B.A. Editorial Assistant and Drama Critic, *Time and Tide*, London, 1939–40. Public Relations Officer, Ministry of Food, London, 1940–45. President, Robert Louis Stevenson Club, 1958. Since 1975, Vice-Chairman, English P.E.N. Club. Recipient: Arts Council bursary, 1968; Eric Gregory Travelling Scholarship, 1977. Agent: A.P. Watt and Son, 26–29 Bedford Row, London WC1R 4HL. Address: 95 Canfield Gardens, London NW6 3DY, England.

PUBLICATIONS FOR CHILDREN

Fiction

> *Blackberry's Kitten*, illustrated by Mary Shillabeer. Leicester, Brockhampton Press, 1961; New York, Vanguard Press, 1963.
> *The Bear Who Was Too Big*, illustrated by Nicholas Fisk. London, Parrish, 1963; Chicago, Follett, 1966.
> *Bob-a-Job*, illustrated by Mary Dinsdale. Leicester, Brockhampton Press, 1963.

Contadino, illustrated by Antony Maitland.   London, Cape, 1964.

The Twig of Cypress, illustrated by W.F. Phillipps.   London, Deutsch, 1965; New York, Washburn, 1966.

We Shall Have Snow.   Leicester, Brockhampton Press, 1966.

Robert the Spy Hunter.   London, Kaye and Ward, 1973.

Parkin, illustrated by Rosie Evans.   London, Harrap, 1977.

Other

Great Men of Yorkshire.   London, Lane, 1955.

The Young Florence Nightingale, illustrated by Denise Brown.   London, Parrish, 1960; New York, Roy, 1961.

The Young Victoria, illustrated by Denise Brown.   London, Parrish, 1961; New York, Roy, 1962.

James Watt, illustrated by W.F. Phillipps.   London, A. and C. Black, 1963.

Garibaldi, illustrated by Ronald Ferns.   London, Methuen, 1964; New York, Roy, 1966.

The Young Edgar Allan Poe, illustrated by William Randell.   London, Parrish, 1964; New York, Roy, 1965.

The Fugitive King, illustrated by Denise Brown.   London, Parrish, 1965.

A Hand upon the Time: A Life of Charles Dickens.   New York, Pantheon Books, 1968; London, Gollancz, 1971.

The Gun-Powder Treason Plot, illustrated by Elisabeth Grant.   London and New York, Abelard Schuman, 1970.

Robert Louis Stevenson.   London, Barker, 1970.

PUBLICATIONS FOR ADULTS

Novels

The Lighted Room.   London, Hodder and Stoughton, 1925.

The Old Fox.   London, Hodder and Stoughton, 1927.

Good Venture.   London, Hodder and Stoughton, 1928.

Likewise the Lion.   London, Hodder and Stoughton, 1928.

The Ship of Truth.   London, Hodder and Stoughton, and Boston, Little Brown, 1930.

Private Enterprise.   London, Hodder and Stoughton, 1931.

Hark to Rover.   London, Hodder and Stoughton, 1933.

We Have Come to a Country.   London, Gollancz, 1935.

The New House.   London, Gollancz, and New York, Macmillan, 1936.

National Provincial.   London, Gollancz, and New York, Macmillan, 1938.

Black Bethlehem.   London, Gollancz, and New York, Macmillan, 1947.

Fenny.   London, Gollancz, 1953.

Three Lives.   London, Gollancz, 1957.

A Certain Compass.   London, Gollancz, 1960.

The Double Heart.   London, Gollancz, 1962.

Late in the Afternoon.   London, Gollancz, 1971.

Tea on Sunday.   London, Gollancz, 1973.

Snow and Roses.   London, Gollancz, 1976.

Other

Robert Louis Stevenson.   London, Home and Van Thal, 1947; Denver, Alan Swallow, 1948.

Yorkshire: West Riding.   London, Hale, 1950.

George Eliot.   London, Longman, 1951; revised edition, 1960, 1964.

Manuscript Collection: The Public Library, Eccles, Lancashire.

Lettice Cooper comments:
I want to write books that children will *enjoy*, and I hope the books will stimulate their imaginations.

*   *   *

Lettice Cooper succeeds in keeping a story going amid a wealth of descriptions. The countryside of Tuscany, where she spends several weeks every year, and the way of life of the Catholic hill farmers dominate *Contadino*. Nicolo, born and brought up in America, returns to his dead mother's family farm when his father marries again. His Italian grandparents, the whole family and neighbourhood welcome him and he feels that he belongs. He loves working hard on the farm and walking in a religious procession. He goes alone to Rome to see the Count to prevent his grandparents being turned out. The author's insight into Nicolo's feelings make all his adventures vivid and interesting.

Italo, the hero of *The Twig of Cypress*, also comes from a Tuscan farming family. He and his brothers are caught up in the movement for Italian liberation and in Rome join Garibaldi's fight against the French. Italo is too young to be a soldier but, as a messenger carrying his uncle's vegetables to the General or news to his older brother, an active Red Shirt, he has an exciting and dangerous time in the besieged city. He discovers that his old enemy, a Tuscan neighbour, is signalling to the French. After a tense expedition by night he is captured and locked up but rescued in time. His brother Marco rides out with Garibaldi while Italo returns home, but a final note recounts the successful return of the Red Shirts.

Both these books are for older children and succeed in portraying the Italian people and their country. *Bob-a-Job, We Shall Have Snow* and *Blackberry's Kitten* are all for a slightly younger age group, the 7 to 10 year olds. They have a familiar English town setting, needing little description and move quickly from one incident to another. Cathy in *We Shall Have Snow* is sad at being uprooted and sent to live with a childless uncle and aunt while her family go to South America for six months. All the adults are very understanding but befriending a robin really solves her problems.

Bob-a-Job is an account of one day's efforts, most of them funny, by two scout cubs anxious to earn money honestly but easily distracted. Coal falls on them when they tidy a cellar, the children whom they try to look after cry, they lose a shopping list and buy the wrong groceries for a harassed housewife, but they succeed in learning to polish shoes and to paint a wall. An unexpected ending neatly finishes off a good story.

Lettice Cooper is particularly good at describing the feelings and behaviour of small boys at various ages. The cubs are well-meaning but clumsy and full of play, the Italian boys are older and more responsible, but things easily go wrong for all of them, only to be put right at the end.

—Margaret Campbell

COOPER, Susan (Mary). British. Born in Burnham, Buckinghamshire, 23 May 1935. Educated at Slough High School; Somerville College, Oxford, 1953–56, M.A. 1956. Married Nicholas J. Grant in 1963; has one son and one daughter. Worked as a reporter and feature writer, *Sunday Times*, London. Recipient: *Boston Globe-Horn Book* Award, 1973; American Library Association Newbery Medal, 1976. Address: 10 Leslie Road, Winchester, Massachusetts 01890, U.S.A.

PUBLICATIONS FOR CHILDREN

Fiction

The Dark is Rising:
  Over Sea, Under Stone, illustrated by Margery Gill.   London, Cape, 1965; New
    York, Harcourt Brace, 1966.
  The Dark Is Rising, illustrated by Alan Cober.   London, Chatto and Windus, and
    New York, Atheneum, 1973.
  Greenwitch.   London, Chatto and Windus, and New York, Atheneum, 1974.
  The Grey King. illustrated by Michael Heslop.   London, Chatto and Windus, and
    New York, Atheneum, 1975.
  Silver on the Tree.   London, Chatto and Windus, and New York, Atheneum, 1977.
Dawn of Fear, illustrated by Margery Gill.   New York, Harcourt Brace, 1970; London,
  Chatto and Windus, 1972.

PUBLICATIONS FOR ADULTS

Novel

Mandrake.   London, Hodder and Stoughton, 1964.

Play

Television Play: *Dark Encounter*, 1976.

Other

Behind the Golden Curtain: A View of the U.S.A.   London, Hodder and Stoughton,
  1965; New York, Scribner, 1966.
J.B. Priestley: Portrait of an Author.   London, Heinemann, 1970; New York, Harper,
  1971.

Editor, *Essays of Five Decades*, by J.B. Priestley.   London, Heinemann, 1969.

Manuscript Collection: Osborne Collection, Toronto Public Library.

Susan Cooper comments:
  Although *Dawn of Fear* is a realistic novel the remaining five books for children constitute
a sequence with the overall title of *The Dark Is Rising*. This is a fantasy dealing with the
pressures of good and evil in the world, which appears to be read by children from the age of
10 upwards, by university students, and by assorted adults.

                              *   *   *

  Whether explicitly or through the buried metaphor of fantasy, the author will be
trying always to say to the reader: Look, this is the way things are. The conflict that
is in this story is everywhere in life, even in your own nature. It is frightening but
try not to be afraid. Ever. Look, learn, remember; this is the kind of thing you will
have to deal with yourself, one day, out there.
  Perhaps a book can help with the long, hard matter of growing up, just a little.
Maybe, sometimes.

Thus spoke Susan Cooper in her speech of acceptance when presented with the Newbery Medal in 1976 for *The Grey King*, the fourth in her sequence of five novels under the general title *The Dark Is Rising*. It is an appropriate comment, for these books are as much about the process of a young person's coming to terms with maturity as about the continuous struggle between the Dark and the Light.

The first volume, *Over Sea, Under Stone*, was written initially as a single book. It was several years before she embarked on the later books in the sequence, and there is therefore a marked difference in tone between the first book and those that follow, though the magnitude of the quest is anticipated in such a passage as this: "Barney shivered with fright and sudden cold. Who are you to intrude here? the voice seemed to whisper; one small boy prying into something that is so much bigger than you can understand, that has remained undisturbed for so many years? Go away, go back, where you are safe, leave such ancient things alone."

In the second volume, *The Dark Is Rising*, the central character, Will Stanton, is, on his eleventh birthday, precipitated sharply away from all that is safe when he learns that he is the last of the Old Ones and that his quest is to join together the five remaining signs of the Light. "Come, Old One," says Merriman (the figure of Merlin who links all five books), "remember yourself. You are no longer a small boy." Like every artist, Will has to learn that he is born with a special power which he has to learn how to control. "It is a burden, make no mistake about that. Any great gift or talent is a burden ... and you will often long to be free of it. If you were born with the gift then you must serve it."

In her first book, Susan Cooper provides a gripping adventure story naturalistically told; the children are vividly depicted and are very much in control of events, whereas in the third book, *Greenwitch*, the same children and Will Stanton are little more than ciphers, while the forces of Dark and Light are left to dominate the stage. Something seems to have happened to the author in the interval between the first book and the second. It reminds one of C.S. Lewis's *That Hideous Strength*, and Jocelyn Brooke's strange tale of menace, *The Scapegoat*. Gripped by archetypal material she goes as close as is possible to freaking out, entering into the labyrinth of her unconscious, much as Martha Graham would do with her great dance creations, in order to bring back these ancient trophies. From the start she plunges the reader with force into the terror of the oncoming darkness, yet the story, with its Eliot-like sense of time present and time past being simultaneous, is firmly earthed in the detail of the large friendly family and of the surrounding countryside. This is a major book on any level, weaving together an intricate pattern of cultural threads, written with a breadth and ease of scholarship. It has much to say about the dark side of God, both in the portrayal of Herne the Hunter and in the scene set inside the village church on the morning of Christmas Day.

In *Greenwitch*, there is a sentence that sums up, I think, the weakness of this, the shortest, book (why so short? Is it a much edited version of a much longer text? or was the author unable to flesh out the theme?): "Slowly he lowered his arms and like puppets the children came back to life." Yet the confrontation in this book of Jane, the central character, with the deeper meaning of the Greenwitch (an ancient spring ritual) – the appalling loneliness of great power which can only be held in great isolation – is powerfully conveyed.

Each of her books is uniquely centred in a particular landscape – Cornwall, Buckinghamshire and, in the last two books, the mountain country of North Wales. The characterisation of the isolated Welsh farming community in *The Grey King* is amazingly accurate. It is perhaps the most haunting and gravely beautiful of her books and sings with the slow sad majesty of a Welsh lament. More than any of the previous books this has its basis in Arthurian legend, and the albino boy, Brian, is both an ally to Will Stanton and a key to the puzzle of the Grey King.

The perennial richness of the Arthurian myth as a source of inspiration to writers in this century, as of painters in the last, is worthy of a special study. To the distinguished company of Professor Tolkien, C.S.Lewis, Charles Williams, Alan Garner, T.H.White, Emma Jung, and others, we can now add Susan Cooper.

—James Roose-Evans

307

CORBETT, Scott. American. Born in Kansas City, Missouri, 27 July 1913. Educated at Kansas City Junior College, 1930–32; University of Missouri, Columbia, Bachelor of Journalism 1934. Served as a Correspondent, United States Army 42nd (Rainbow) Infantry Division, 1943–46. Married Elizabeth Grosvenor Pierce in 1940; has one daughter. Recipient: Mystery Writers of America Edgar Allan Poe Award, 1962, 1976. Agent: Curtis Brown Ltd., 575 Madison Avenue, New York, New York 10022. Address: 149 Benefit Street, Providence, Rhode Island 02903, U.S.A.

PUBLICATIONS FOR CHILDREN

Fiction

Susie Sneakers, illustrated by Leonard Shortall. New York, Crowell, 1956.
Midshipman Cruise. Boston, Little Brown, 1957.
Tree House Island, illustrated by Gordon Hansen. Boston, Little Brown, and London, Dent, 1959.
Dead Man's Light, illustrated by Leonard Shortall. Boston, Little Brown, 1960.
The Lemonade Trick, illustrated by Paul Galdone. Boston, Little Brown, 1960.
The Mailbox Trick, illustrated by Paul Galdone. Boston, Little Brown, 1961.
Cutlass Island, illustrated by Leonard Shortall. Boston, Little Brown, 1962; London, Dent, 1964.
Danger Point: The Wreck of the "Birkenhead." Boston, Little Brown, 1962.
The Disappearing Dog Trick, illustrated by Paul Galdone. Boston, Little Brown, 1963.
The Limerick Trick, illustrated by Paul Galdone. Boston, Little Brown, 1964.
The Baseball Trick, illustrated by Paul Galdone. Boston, Little Brown, 1965.
One by Sea. illustrated by Victor Mays. Boston, Little Brown, 1965.
The Cave above Delphi, illustrated by Gioia Fiammenghi. New York, Holt Rinehart, 1965.
Pippa Passes, illustrated by Judith Gwyn Brown. New York, Holt Rinehart, 1966.
The Case of the Gone Goose, illustrated by Paul Frame. Boston, Little Brown, 1966.
Diamonds Are Trouble. New York, Holt Rinehart, 1967.
The Turnabout Trick, illustrated by Paul Galdone. Boston, Little Brown, 1968.
Cop's Kid, illustrated by Jo Polseno. Boston, Little Brown, 1968.
Ever Ride a Dinosaur?, illustrated by Mircea Vasiliu. New York, Holt Rinehart, 1969.
The Hairy Horror Trick, illustrated by Paul Galdone. Boston, Little Brown, 1969.
The Case of the Fugitive Firebug, illustrated by Paul Frame. Boston, Little Brown, 1969.
Diamonds Are More Trouble. New York, Holt Rinehart, 1969.
Steady, Freddie, illustrated by Lawrence Beall Smith. New York, Dutton, 1970.
The Baseball Bargain, illustrated by Wallace Tripp. Boston, Little Brown, 1970.
The Mystery Man, illustrated by Nathan Goldstein. Boston, Little Brown, 1970.
The Case of the Ticklish Tooth, illustrated by Paul Frame. Boston, Little Brown, 1971.
The Hateful Plateful Trick, illustrated by Paul Galdone. Boston, Little Brown, 1971.
The Big Joke Game, illustrated by Mircea Vasiliu. New York, Dutton, 1972.
The Red Room Riddle, illustrated by Geff Gerlach. Boston, Little Brown, 1972.
Dead Before Docking, illustrated by Paul Frame. Boston, Little Brown, 1972.
Run for the Money, illustrated by Bert Dodson. Boston, Little Brown, 1973.
The Home Run Trick, illustrated by Paul Galdone. Boston, Little Brown, 1973.
Dr. Merlin's Magic Shop, illustrated by Joe Mathieu. Boston, Little Brown, 1973.
Take a Number. New York, Dutton, 1974.
The Hockey Trick, illustrated by Paul Galdone. Boston, Little Brown, 1974.
Here Lies the Body, illustrated by Geff Gerlach. Boston, Little Brown, 1974.
The Case of the Silver Skull, illustrated by Paul Frame. Boston, Little Brown, 1974.
The Great Custard Pie Panic, illustrated by Joe Mathieu. Boston, Little Brown, 1974.

The Boy with Will Power, illustrated by Ed Parker.   Boston, Little Brown, 1975.
The Case of the Burgled Blessing Box, illustrated by Paul Frame.   Boston, Little Brown, 1975.
The Boy Who Walked on Air, illustrated by Ed Parker.   Boston, Little Brown, 1975.
The Great McGoniggle's Gray Ghost, illustrated by Bill Ogden.   Boston, Little Brown, 1975.
The Great McGoniggle's Key Play, illustrated by Bill Ogden.   Boston, Little Brown, 1976.
The Black Mask Trick, illustrated by Paul Galdone.   Boston, Little Brown, 1976.
The Hockey Girls.   New York, Dutton, 1976.
Captain Butcher's Body, illustrated by Geff Gerlach.   Boston, Little Brown, 1976.
The Great McGoniggle Rides Shotgun, illustrated by Bill Ogden.   Boston, Little Brown, 1977.
The Hangman's Ghost Trick, illustrated by Paul Galdone.   Boston, Little Brown, 1977.

Other

What Makes a Car Go?, illustrated by Len Darwin.   Boston, Little Brown, 1963; London, Muller, 1968.
What Makes TV Work?, illustrated by Len Darwin.   Boston, Little Brown, 1965; London, Muller, 1968.
What Makes a Light Go On?, illustrated by Len Darwin.   Boston, Little Brown, 1966; London, Muller, 1968.
What Makes a Plane Fly?, illustrated by Len Darwin.   Boston, Little Brown, 1967.
What Makes a Boat Float?, illustrated by Victor Mays.   Boston, Little Brown, 1970.
What about the Wankel Engine?, illustrated by Jerome Kuhl.   New York, Scholastic, 1974.

PUBLICATIONS FOR ADULTS

Other

The Reluctant Landlord.   New York, Crowell, 1950.
Sauce for the Gander.   New York, Crowell, 1951.
We Chose Cape Cod.   New York, Crowell, 1953.
Cape Cod's Way: An Informal History.   New York, Crowell, 1955.
The Sea Fox: The Adventures of Cape Cod's Most Colorful Rumrunner, with Manuel Zora.   New York, Crowell, 1956; London, Hale, 1957.
Rhode Island.   New York, Coward McCann, 1969.

Manuscript Collections: de Grummond Collection, University of Southern Mississippi, Hattiesburg; Kerlan Collection, University of Minnesota, Minneapolis.

*

Scott Corbett comments:

I am a storyteller devoted to the proposition that suspense and humor are a worthwhile combination. My books, especially the Trick books, have been widely used in schools to trap reluctant readers and get them started on books. My most successful efforts of late have been ghost stories of a slightly more modern flavor than those Victorian chillers which today are not only period pieces but, all too often, semi-colon pieces. The What Makes It Work books were successful in explaining difficult subjects to beginning readers – mainly because I started with no knowledge of the subjects myself and thus did not make the expert's mistake of assuming too much basic understanding on the part of his readers. *What Makes a Car Go?* was published in an Arabic edition, not for children but as a workable introduction to the internal combustion engine for adult Arabs. Perhaps this was a mistake — I may have let something slip about the importance of all that oil.

*   *   *

A strange old lady gave Kerby Maxwell a magic chemistry set. Think what different comic authors might do with this beginning. What Scott Corbett did was to have Kerby and his friend Fenton concoct a lemonade which made whoever drank it *good*. There are humorous consequences for Kerby's relationships with his surprised parents, the bully next door, and for the school play. *The Lemonade Trick* turned out to be the first of the successful series of "trick books" for which Corbett is best known.

In these and most of his other stories, Corbett blends a little magic and plot with a lot of boyish humor. *Ever Ride a Dinosaur?* begins "I don't know how you feel about garbage. Personally, I agree with the fellow who said 'I can take it out, or leave it alone.' The only trouble was at my cousin Charlie's house, I seemed to do the taking out, and he did the leaving alone." As this opening suggests, Corbett establishes an amiable relationship with the reader and gets on with his story. His themes are basic ones for the pre-adolescent boy. Corbett treats these themes in such a way as to keep them fun but non-threatening. "As usual," he writes in *The Limerick Trick*, "when [Kerby] secretly worked with his chemistry set, he felt a bit guilty. What would his parents think if they knew?" In the work of Sendak, du Bois, or Dahl the explosive potential of this chemistry set would become apparent. In Corbett's stories the chemicals are used in a pro-social way. The lemonade trick makes one good, the hockey trick must be used to maintain a fair balance between the rival Panthers and Wildcats, etc. There is a fairly tight lid on the id, with the usual indirect outlets for aggression against authority figures.

Corbett's main characters are ordinary boys, not heroes, and he himself is a skillful craftsman but not a perfectionist. He can be very good, but he also includes material that is mediocre or not strictly germane in the interests of entertainment. Though his humor and invention lack the brilliance of authors who are more daring and more invested in their creativity, he is a very enjoyable author of books for juvenile boys to read themselves.

—Ravenna Helson

CORDELL, Alexander. Pseudonym for George Alexander Graber. British. Born in Colombo, Ceylon, 9 September 1914. Educated privately; at Marist Brothers' College, 1921–30. Served in the Royal Army, 1932–36; Royal Engineers, 1939–45; Major. Married Rosina Wells in 1937; has one daughter. Quantity Surveyor, 1936–68. Address: 130 Friary Park, Arbory, Isle of Man, United Kingdom.

PUBLICATIONS FOR CHILDREN

Fiction

> *The White Cockade.* Leicester, Brockhampton Press, and New York, Viking Press, 1970.
> *Witches' Sabbath.* Leicester, Brockhampton Press, and New York, Viking Press, 1970.
> *The Healing Blade.* Leicester, Brockhampton Press, and New York, Viking Press, 1971.
> *The Traitor Within*, illustrated by Victor Ambrus. Leicester, Brockhampton Press, 1971; Nashville, Nelson, 1973.

PUBLICATIONS FOR ADULTS

Novels

A Thought of Honour. London, Museum Press, 1954; as *The Enemy Within,* London, Transworld, 1975.
Rape of the Fair Country. London, Gollancz, and New York, Doubleday, 1959.
The Hosts of Rebecca. London, Gollancz, 1960; as *Robe of Honor,* New York, Doubleday, 1960.
Race of the Tiger. London, Gollancz, 1963.
The Sinews of Love. London, Gollancz, 1965; New York, Doubleday, 1966.
The Bright Cantonese. London, Gollancz, 1967; as *The Deadly Eurasian,* New York, Weybright and Talley, 1968.
Song of the Earth. London, Gollancz, 1969; New York, Simon and Schuster, 1970.
The Fire People. London, Hodder and Stoughton, 1972.
If You Believe the Soldiers. London, Hodder and Stoughton, 1973; New York, Doubleday, 1974.
The Dream and the Destiny. London, Hodder and Stoughton, and New York, Doubleday, 1975.
This Sweet and Bitter Earth. London, Hodder and Stoughton, 1977.

*   *   *

Alexander Cordell's transition from writing adult novels to writing for children was in a way a natural one, but he accepted the challenge, for challenge it was, with the same dedication and seriousness he had brought to writing for adults. He had already represented the oppressed people of Wales in the trilogy which began with *Rape of the Fair Country.* In his first essay in writing for children he chose to do the same for Ireland, taking as his focal point the 1798 rebellion. *The White Cockade, Witches' Sabbath,* and *The Healing Blade* are on one level swashbuckling spy-stories, chock-full of changes of fortune, as young John Regan takes on the mantle of his dead father as an agent for the United Irishmen, and the pace is as fast as his splendid mare Mia who carries him on his adventures. But Regan is not quite the super-human figure of romantic fantasy. He has feelings, and through his eyes too is reflected the quandary of the ordinary folk, pushed to arms against the British only because there was no alternative.

In *The White Cockade* the historical situation is set as Regan takes a message to the leader of the imminent rebellion, Lord Edward Fitzgerald. Of the three, this is the most "fictional," and the plot has twist after twist before Regan, having at one point been press-ganged into the British navy, succeeds in his mission. In *Witches' Sabbath* there is greater attention to the interpretation of historical personages and events, as Regan joins Father John Murphy, that mystical figure driven by circumstances to start the revolution before its leaders are ready. At the start of *The Healing Blade* the Wexford Rebellion has been crushed. Regan is sent to France to penetrate the English spy-ring and to protect Wolfe Tone, the man who was Ireland's last hope if she was to rise again. At the end of the book the fictional character and historical fact come together when Regan is the means whereby the knife with which the captured Tone committed suicide is put into Tone's hands. All three stories are particularly distinguished for their glorious, passionate Irish prose.

The Traitor Within reflects Cordell's great interest in the East, of which he has first-hand experience. The setting is a modern Chinese commune repeatedly threatened from Taiwan. Through the boy Ling's doubts and fears we learn of the conflict between the old Chinese culture and the new, and read the underlying message that young people, for all their different upbringings, are basically the same the world over. This utterly successful and moving story, told with humour and in language which catches admirably the Far Eastern way of speech and thought, is one of the most significant but under-rated children's novels of its time.

—Antony Kamm

CORLETT, William. British. Born in Darlington, County Durham, 8 October 1938. Educated at St. Olave's School, Ripon, Yorkshire; Fettes College, Edinburgh; Royal Academy of Dramatic Art, London, 1956–58, Diploma. Repertory and television actor in London and the provinces. Address: Cottesbrook, Great Bardfield, near Braintree, Essex, England.

PUBLICATIONS FOR CHILDREN

Fiction

> *The Gate of Eden.* London, Hamish Hamilton, 1974; Scarsdale, New York, Bradbury Press, 1975.
> *The Land Beyond.* London, Hamish Hamilton, 1975; Scarsdale, New York, Bradbury Press, 1976.
> *The I Deal Table.* London, Compton Russell, 1975.
> *The Once and Forever Christmas,* with John Moore. London, Compton Russell, 1975.
> *Return to the Gate.* London, Hamish Hamilton, 1975; Scarsdale, New York, Bradbury Press, 1977.
> *The Dark Side of the Moon.* London, Hamish Hamilton, 1976; Scarsdale, New York, Bradbury Press, 1977.

Plays

> *Orlando the Marmalade Cat Buys a Cottage,* adaptation of the story by Kathleen Hale (produced London, 1975).
> *Orlando's Camping Holiday,* adaptation of the story by Kathleen Hale (produced London, 1976).

PUBLICATIONS FOR ADULTS

Plays

> *The Gentle Avalanche* (produced Farnham, Surrey, 1962; London, 1963). London, French, 1964.
> *Another Round* (produced Farnham, Surrey, 1962). London, French, 1963.
> *Return Ticket* (produced Farnham, Surrey, 1962; London, 1965). London, English Theatre Guild, 1966.
> *The Scallop Shell* (produced Farnham, Surrey, 1963).
> *Flight of a Lone Sparrow* (produced Farnham, Surrey, 1965).
> *The Scourging of Matthew Barrow* (produced Leicester, 1966).
> *Tinker's Curse* (produced Nottingham, 1968). Published in *Plays of the Year 34,* London, Elek, 1968; New York, Ungar, 1969.
> *We Never Went to Cheddar Gorge* (televised 1968; produced Perth, 1969).
> *The Illusionist* (produced Perth, 1969).

National Trust (produced Perth, 1970).
The Deliverance of Fanny Blaydon (produced Perth, 1971).

Television Plays: *Dead Set at Dream Boy*, 1965; *We Never Went to Cheddar Gorge*, 1968; *The Story Teller*, 1969; *A Memory of Two Loves*, 1972; *Conversations in the Dark*, 1972; *Mr. Oddy*, from story by Hugh Walpole, 1975; *The Orsini Emeralds*, from story by G.B. Stern, 1975; *Emerdale Farm* series, 1975–77.

* * *

William Corlett, dramatist, writer for television, and former actor, began his career as a novelist in 1974 with *The Gate of Eden*, quickly followed by *The Land Beyond* and *Return to the Gate*. The three books, which are in the interest range of adolescents rather than of pre-teenage children, have the same narrator and form a loosely-organized trilogy.

In *The Gate of Eden* the narrator, as a boy, befriends an elderly schoolmaster. The old man – pathetic, vulnerable, increasingly dependent on him emotionally – encourages his developing literary taste, but is bound to lose him in the end, and does so to a girl who is perfectly ordinary but has the huge advantages of being young and of the other sex. *The Land Beyond* finds the narrator, as a young man, in Greece, writing his way out of depression after the breakup of a three-year relationship with another girl, and getting a renewal of spirit from a mystical identification with a charioteer of ancient Delphi. In the last book, *Return to the Gate*, the narrator is an old man surviving precariously in an authoritarian society. All three books are written with confident expertise, a fine ear for dialogue, and a good deal of technical ingenuity; yet it is possible to doubt with each one in turn whether it quite rings true emotionally, and to wonder whether the display of technique conceals some shortcoming at a deeper artistic level.

These doubts grow with Corlett's fourth book, *The Dark Side of the Moon*, in which the imprisonment of a kidnapped school-boy is described in parallel with the experience of an astronaut "out of sight of the earth and of all that is familiar." There are verbal pyrotechnics again, and cosmic questionings in which issues as huge as the meaning of life are raised and thrown around; but long before the end it seems clear that this book is on the wrong side of the sometimes-quite-narrow dividing line that can separate a good book from a bad one. It is only fair to say, however, that Corlett's work has received praise from reviewers, and that he is undeniably an inventive and technically accomplished writer.

—John Rowe Townsend

CRAIG, John (Ernest). Canadian. Born in Peterborough, Ontario, 2 July 1921. Educated at the University of Manitoba, Winnipeg (King Fellow), B.A. 1951; University of Toronto, M.A. in Canadian history. Worked for a market research firm 1953–69. Address: c/o McClelland and Stewart Ltd., 25 Hollinger Road, Toronto, Ontario M4B 3G2, Canada.

PUBLICATIONS FOR CHILDREN

Fiction

Wagons West, illustrated by Stanley Wyatt. Toronto, Dent, 1955; London, Dent, and New York, Dodd Mead, 1956.
The Long Return, illustrated by Robert Doremus. Toronto, McClelland and Stewart, and Indianapolis, Bobbs Merrill, 1959.

No Word for Good-Bye, illustrated by Harri Aalto.   Toronto, Peter Martin Associates,
1969; New York, Coward McCann, 1971.
Zach.   New York, Coward McCann, 1972; London, Gollancz, 1973.
Who Wants to Be Alone?   New York, Scholastic, 1974.
The Wormburners.   New York, Scholastic, 1976.

Other

By the Sound of Her Whistle, illustrated by Fred Craig.   Toronto, Peter Martin
Associates, 1966.

PUBLICATIONS FOR ADULTS

Novels

The Pro.   Toronto, Peter Martin Associates, 1968; as Power Play, New York, Dodd
Mead, 1973.
In Council Rooms Apart.   New York, Putman, 1971.
If You Want to See Your Wife Again ....   New York, Putnam, 1971; London, Cassell,
1973.
Superdude.   New York, Warner, 1974.
The Clearing.   London, Constable, 1975.
Close Doesn't Count.   Toronto, Macmillan, and London, Macdonald and Jane's, 1975.
All G.O.D.'s Children.   New York, Morrow, 1975.

Plays

Television Plays: Adventures in Rainbow Country and The Starlost series.

Other

How Far Back Can You Get?   Toronto and New York, Doubleday, 1974.
Canada's Olympic Chances.   New York, Simon and Schuster, 1976.

*   *   *

The most beautiful, perhaps, of John Craig's books for young readers, is No Word for
Good-Bye, the haunting story of a friendship, and of its power to bridge the gulf of prejudice
and misunderstanding. Ken is a white city boy who has "everything"; Paul an Ojibway
Indian whose family is about to be driven from the shack which is their home. Ken is
inquisitive, articulate; Paul is silent and remote. But somehow sympathy and generosity
narrow the gap between their two worlds, and the boys become friends and allies in a
hopelessly outmatched battle with big business. At summer's end life tears them apart,
perhaps never to meet again, and Paul has no word with which to say goodbye to Ken; but
their friendship has never relied upon words.

Another of Craig's young Indian heroes, Zach, of Who Wants to Be Alone? is literally alone
in the world, for he is the last surviving Agawa. He finds no trace of his vanished tribe
though he searches through much of Canada and the American midwest. All but resigned to
a life alone, he falls in with others who share his sense of dislocation – Willie, a black badly
hurt by the white college world of athletic scholarships, and D.J., a white girl fleeing a
comfortable middle-class home whose values are totally inimicable to her. Gradually they
find themselves belonging somewhere – they have become a family.

As a change of pace from wilderness settings, Craig's Wormburners is the heartening story
of an inner-city cross-country team (who run "fast enough to burn the worms in the

ground"); they are short of funds but well supplied with spirit and determination. This is a warmly satisfying story of underdogs coming from behind to win the national championship, and it has the kind of old-fashioned happy ending that leaves the reader with a warm glow of satisfaction.

Craig writes for the mature young reader, able to interpret subtle shadings and relationships without requiring exhaustive explanation. His girls and women are sketchy creations at best, but his boys and young men are painfully real: their bruises of the spirit are more poignant than the cuts and slashes of more boisterous fiction for young people.

A favorite device in Craig's work is the use of a summer place in the bush country to illustrate a deepening awareness of the realities of life with advancing years. Where the child sees only the sparkling lake and the picnic grounds, the youth begins to envision that same smiling landscape in its unwelcoming winter guise, and to speculate about the lives of those who must live the year round where others come only to holiday.

John Craig's ability to discern and to convey to others the special beauty that is so often a part of lives of rugged privation, and his generous admiration of the fortitude with which such lives are undertaken, are praiseworthy qualities.

—Joan McGrath

CRESSWELL, Helen. British. Born in Nottinghamshire, 11 July 1934. Educated at Nottingham Girls' High School; King's College. London University. B.A. (honours) in English. Married Brian Rowe in 1962; has two daughters. Worked as a literary assistant. fashion buyer, teacher. Agent: A.M. Heath and Co. Ltd., 40–42 William IV Street. London WC2N 4DD. Address: Old Church Farm. Eakring. Newark. Nottinghamshire. England.

PUBLICATIONS FOR CHILDREN

Fiction

> Sonya-by-the-Shore, illustrated by Robin Jane Wells. London. Dent. 1960.
> Jumbo Spencer, illustrated by Clixby Watson. Leicester. Brockhampton Press. 1963; Philadelphia, Lippincott. 1966.
> The White Sea Horse, illustrated by Robin Jacques. Edinburgh. Oliver and Boyd, 1964; Philadelphia. Lippincott. 1965.
> Jumbo Back to Nature, illustrated by Leslie Wood. Leicester. Brockhampton Press, 1965.
> Pietro and the Mule, illustrated by Maureen Eckersley. Edinburgh. Oliver and Boyd, and Indianapolis, Bobbs Merrill, 1965.
> Jumbo Afloat, illustrated by Leslie Wood. Leicester. Brockhampton Press. 1966.
> Where the Wind Blows, illustrated by Peggy Fortnum. London. Faber. 1966; New York, Funk and Wagnalls, 1968.
> The Piemakers, illustrated by V.H. Drummond. London. Faber. 1967; Philadelphia, Lippincott, 1968.
> A Day on Big O, illustrated by Shirley Hughes. London. Benn, 1967; Chicago, Follett, 1968.
> A Tide for the Captain, illustrated by Robin Jacques. Edinburgh. Oliver and Boyd, 1967.
> The Signposters, illustrated by Gareth Floyd. London. Faber, 1968.
> Jumbo and the Big Dig, illustrated by Leslie Wood. Leicester. Brockhampton Press, 1968.

315

The Barge Children, illustrated by Lynette Hemmant.   London, Hodder and Stoughton, 1968.

The Sea Piper, illustrated by Robin Jacques.   Edinburgh, Oliver and Boyd, 1968.

The Night-Watchmen, illustrated by Gareth Floyd.   London, Faber, and New York, Macmillan, 1969.

A Gift from Winklesea, illustrated by Janina Ede.   Leicester, Brockhampton Press, 1969.

A Game of Catch, illustrated by Gareth Floyd.   London, Chatto Boyd and Oliver, 1969; New York, Macmillan, 1977.

A House for Jones, illustrated by Margaret Gordon.   London, Benn, 1969.

The Outlanders, illustrated by Doreen Roberts.   London, Faber, 1970.

Rainbow Pavement, illustrated by Shirley Hughes.   London, Benn, 1970.

The Wilkses, illustrated by Gareth Floyd.   London, BBC Publications, 1970.

The Bird Fancier, illustrated by Renate Meyer.   London, Benn, 1971.

Up the Pier, illustrated by Gareth Floyd.   London, Faber, 1971; New York, Macmillan, 1972.

The Weather Cat, illustrated by Margery Gill.   London, Benn,1971.

The Beachcombers, illustrated by Errol Le Cain.   London, Faber, and New York, Macmillan, 1972.

Bluebirds over Pit Row, illustrated by Richard Kennedy.   London, Benn, 1972.

Jane's Policeman, illustrated by Margery Gill.   London, Benn, 1972.

The Long Day, illustrated by Margery Gill.   London, Benn, 1972.

Roof Fall!, illustrated by Richard Kennedy.   London, Benn, 1972.

Short Back and Sides, illustrated by Richard Kennedy.   London, Benn, 1972.

The Beetle Hunt, illustrated by Anne Knight.   London, Longman, 1973.

The Bongleweed, illustrated by Ann Strugnell.   London, Faber, 1973; New York, Macmillan, 1974.

The Bower Birds, illustrated by Margery Gill.   London, Benn, 1973.

Lizzie Dripping, illustrated by Jenny Thorne.   London, BBC Publications, 1973.

Lizzie Dripping by the Sea, illustrated by Faith Jaques.   London, BBC Publications,1974.

Lizzie Dripping and the Little Angel, illustrated by Faith Jaques.   London, BBC Publications, 1974.

Lizzie Dripping Again, illustrated by Faith Jaques.   London, BBC Publications, 1974.

Two Hoots, illustrated by Martine Blanc.   London, Benn, 1974.

Two Hoots Go to Sea, illustrated by Martine Blanc.   London, Benn, 1974.

More Lizzie Dripping, illustrated by Faith Jaques.   London, BBC Publications, 1974.

Butterfly Chase, illustrated by Margery Gill.   London, Penguin, 1975.

The Winter of the Birds.   London, Faber, 1975; New York, Macmillan, 1976.

Two Hoots in the Snow, illustrated by Martine Blanc.   London, Benn, 1975.

Two Hoots and the Big Bad Bird, illustrated by Martine Blanc.   London, Benn, 1975.

Two Hoots and the King, illustrated by Martine Blanc.   London, Benn, 1977.

Two Hoots Play Hide and Seek, illustrated by Martine Blanc.   London, Benn, 1977.

The Bagthorpe Saga: Ordinary Jack, illustrated by Jill Bennet.   London, Faber, and New York, Macmillan, 1977.

Donkey Days, illustrated by Shirley Hughes.   London, Benn, 1977.

Plays

Television Plays: *Lizzie Dripping* series, from her own stories, 1973, 1975; *Dick Whittington*, 1974; *Jumbo Spencer*, from her own story, 1976.

Other

Rug Is a Bear (reader), illustrated by Susanna Gretz.   London, Benn, 1968.

Rug Plays Tricks (reader), illustrated by Susanna Gretz.   London, Benn, 1968.
Rug Plays Bali (reader), illustrated by Susanna Gretz.   London, Benn, 1969.
Rug and a Picnic (reader), illustrated by Susanna Gretz.   London, Benn, 1969.
John's First Fish (reader), illustrated by Prudence Seward.   London, Macmillan, 1970.
At the Stroke of Midnight: Traditional Fairy Tales Retold, illustrated by Carolyn Dinan.   London, Collins, 1971.
The Key (reader), illustrated by Richard Kennedy.   London, Benn, 1973.
Cheap Day Return (reader), illustrated by Richard Kennedy.   London, Benn, 1974.
Shady Deal (reader), illustrated by Richard Kennedy.   London, Benn, 1974.
The Trap (reader), illustrated by Richard Kennedy.   London, Benn, 1974.

*   *   *

Although Helen Cresswell began her career as a writer of delicate poetic fantasies, her reputation was made of stronger stuff. Her major books have something fantastic, if not always of fantasy, in them. *The Piemakers*, her first outstanding success, includes no magical elements; the fantasy comes from telling a story larger than life. *The Signposters* was from a similar mould. With *The Night-Watchmen* in 1969 her work changed direction. The scene was still an enlarged version of the ordinary world, but the supernatural crept in, and it has stayed with her ever since. From *The Outlanders* to *The Winter of the Birds* her stories have occupied the frontier country between a world of commonplace niceness and nastiness and the terrors and wonders which lurk just out of sight. Part of the strength of the novels lies in their implications; she rarely brings the reader face to face with magic.

In her Lizzie Dripping stories, originally designed for television, Helen Cresswell leaves it to the reader to decide whether the supernatural exists. Lizzie is a very ordinary little girl in an ordinary family. Does she really have adventures with a witch? Television is a medium which by its nature cannot deal effectively with implications. The viewer has to see the witch as Lizzie does. In the more subtle written version options are left open. That gloriously colourful and embarrassing witch may be real, or she may exist only in Lizzie Dripping's inventive head.

Attractive as they are, the Lizzie Dripping stories are a by-product of the major novels. So too are the Jumbo Spencer stories, and the disciplined brief texts which Helen Cresswell has written for reluctant older readers, these latter perhaps the finest examples of a creative artist accepting restrictions on vocabulary, syntax and subject-matter. It is as a writer of humorous and poetic fantasies that Helen Cresswell is best known and is likely to be best remembered.

The Piemakers is the real foundation-stone of her work. This is a story of the Roller family, hereditary piemakers of Danby Dale in Yorkshire. A recurrent theme in all Helen Cresswell's books is that of craftsmanship, of work done with skill and pride. The Rollers, like the Signposters and the entertainers in *Up the Pier* and even the scavengers and beachcombers, like to do a job well. Even Gravella Roller, who hates the family trade and wants to go on the stage, recognizes her father's supreme artistry. Faced with the newly baked royal pie "faintly golden, smooth and yet promising a rough, satisfying crustiness, and decorated with the Royal Coat of Arms, a slightly deeper gold, perfect as if it had been carved from stone by the chisel of a master," Gravella breathes: "Oh, it's beautiful!" and her mother dabs her eyes with "the pinafore that wasn't there."

The Piemakers is a funny book, but it takes the fun quite seriously. It is a comedy of incongruity, achieved by blowing a commonplace situation up to gigantic proportions. Baking a pie is not funny. Baking a pie for two thousand eaters *is*, the more so because the logistics of the operation are worked out in detail. Helen Cresswell sets her very tall story neatly in a pseudo-historical context, producing archival evidence. Archaeological too; in an exquisite epilogue she takes sceptical readers back to Danby Dale to look at the duck pond on the village green. Yes, it *is* the pie-dish.

Funny as the book is, real life is sometimes funnier. Having spun *The Piemakers* out of her imagination, Helen Cresswell discovered that the piemakers of Danby Dale had really existed.

Documentary evidence was to be had, and earnest historical researchers sought her acquaintance and co-operation.

In *The Signposters* Helen Cresswell pursued a similar theme, but with a little less gusto. Again the emphasis is on craftsmanship, but the crafts are many and the effect dissipated. This is a story of the open road, and the best of it is the atmosphere and the pervasive happiness.

She is at her best in drawing eccentrics, and this is perhaps a small criticism of her work. Every fantasy needs a touchstone of reality. In *The Night-Watchmen* the story turns on a very normal little boy who lacks the sharp individuality of, for example, Alice. Consequently, instead of providing a bridge between the real and the fantastic worlds, Henry tends to be an obstacle to one's acceptance of the fantasy. The same is true, in a lesser degree, of the small lodger in *The Beachcombers*.

This apart, *The Night-Watchmen* is an absorbing novel as well as a key to Helen Cresswell's later work. The central idea is marvellous in its originality and simplicity. Josh and Caleb are tramps who have devised the perfect protection against being moved on by the police. A hole in the ground, a Danger Men at Work sign, and tramps become night-watchmen, part of the scenery and not worth a second glance. A whole comic novel could be grown from this seed, and this writer could have brought it off splendidly with such richly humorous characters as Josh and Caleb. But Helen Cresswell had already written two purely funny books, and she was pushing outwards the frontiers of her craft. So the night-watchmen are threatened by Greeneyes, a half-explained and less than half-seen terror of the night. Henry helps to frustrate the Greeneyes and Josh and Caleb catch the night train to There. The story is masterly in its rise to a climax and a swift resolution, but some readers are left with the vague feeling that they have been cheated.

Since 1969, with a major book almost every year, Helen Cresswell has strengthened and refined her art without adding substantially to her achievements. *The Winter of the Birds* is perhaps her cleverest book, but it is not necessarily for that reason more original and important than the earlier work. There are signs that with greater maturity she is becoming more serious, or more sober. There is not much sheer fun in *The Winter of the Birds*. Edward Flack, who has dedicated his life to the achievement of heroism, is a nice invention but he barely raises a smile. Patrick Finn, who *is* a hero, is one of Helen Cresswell's larger-than-life people; he is very noisy but hardly very amusing. The best touches of Cresswell humour come from the terrible MacKays, enormously anti-social small boys.

Remarkable as *The Winter of the Birds* is, and it contains some of her most powerful writing, it would be a pity if it were a sure indication that Helen Cresswell is turning away from humour. One of her most precious gifts is that of laughter. Her humour comes partly from situations but more from character, from people recognisable enough as humans but drawn, like Dickens', with sufficiently broad brush-strokes to emphasize their grotesque quality. She is the past-master among contemporary writers of the rare art of comedy. Of wonder her mastery is a little less than perfect. Here her aspiration is not yet matched with technique, so that the reader is unable to concede a total suspension of disbelief. She is, notwithstanding, among the most original and exciting writers of her generation, and one for whom the future is as promising as it is unpredictable.

—Marcus Crouch

CROCKETT, Samuel Rutherford. British. Born in Little Duchrae, Balmaghie, Kirkcudbrightshire, 24 September 1860. Educated at Laurieston Free Church School, 1865–67; Cowper's Free Church School, Castle Douglas, Kirkcudbrightshire, 1867–76;

Edinburgh University, 1876–79; Heidelberg University; New College, Edinburgh, 1882–86. Married Ruth Mary Milner in 1887; two sons and two daughters. Travelling tutor in Germany, Sicily, and Italy, 1879–82. Entered the Free Church of Scotland and ordained minister, 1886. Minister, Penicuik, Midlothian 1886–95 (resigned). Editor, *Worker's Monthly*, London, 1890–91. *Died 21 April 1914.*

PUBLICATIONS FOR CHILDREN

Fiction

Sweetheart Travellers: A Child's Book for Children, for Women, and for Men, illustrated by Gordon Browne and W.H.C. Groome. London, Wells Gardner Darton, and New York, Stokes, 1895.

The Surprising Adventures of Sir Toady Lion with Those of General Napoleon Smith: An Improving History for Old Boys, Young Boys, Good Boys, Bad Boys, Little Boys, Cowboys, and Tom-Boys, illustrated by Gordon Browne. London, Wells Gardner Darton, and New York, Stokes, 1897.

Sir Toady Crusoe, illustrated by Gordon Browne. London, Wells Gardner Darton, and New York, Stokes, 1905.

Sweethearts at Home: Assisted by Sweetheart Herself, and with Additions and Corrections by Hugh John, Sir Toady Lion, Maid Margaret, and Miss Elizabeth Fortinbras, illustrated by C.E. Brock. London and New York, Hodder and Stoughton, 1912.

Other

Editor, *Red Cap Tales Told from Ivanhoe* [*The Fortunes of Nigel, Quentin Durward, Guy Mannering, Rob Roy, The Antiquary, Waverley, The Pirate*, and *A Legend of Montrose*], by Walter Scott. London, A. and C. Black, and New York, Macmillan, 8 vols., 1904–10.

PUBLICATIONS FOR ADULTS

Novels

The Stickit Minister and Some Common Men. London, Unwin, 1893; New York, Macmillan, n.d.

The Play Actress. London, Unwin, and New York, Putnam, 1894.

The Lilac Sunbonnet. London, Unwin, and New York, Appleton, 1894.

Mad Sir Uchtred of the Hills. London, Unwin, and New York, Macmillan, 1894.

The Raiders, Being Some Passages in the Life of John Faa, Lord and Earl of Little Egypt. London, Unwin, and New York, Macmillan 1894.

The Men of the Moss Hags. London, Isbister, and New York, Macmillan, 1895.

A Galloway Herd. New York, Fenno, 1895.

The Grey Man. London, Unwin, and New York, Harper, 1896.

Cleg Kelly, Arab of the City. London, Smith Elder, and New York, Appleton, 1896.

Lochinvar. London, Methuen, 1897; New York, Harper, 1898.

The Standard Bearer. London, Methuen, and New York, Appleton, 1898.

The Red Axe. London, Smith Elder, 1898; New York, Harper, 1899.

The Silver Skull. New York, Stokes, 1898; London, Smith Elder, 1901.

The Black Douglas. London, Smith Elder, and New York, Doubleday, 1899.

Kit Kennedy: Country Boy. London, Clarke, and New York, Harper, 1899.

Ione March. London, Hodder and Stoughton, and New York, Dodd Mead, 1899.

Joan of the Sword Hand. London, Ward Lock, and New York, Dodd Mead, 1900.

Little Anna Mark. London, Smith Elder, 1900; as *The Isle of the Winds: An Adventurous Romance,* New York, Doubleday, 1900.

Cinderella. London, Clarke, and New York, Dodd Mead, 1901.

The Firebrand. London, Macmillan, and New York, McClure, 1901.

The Dark o' the Moon, Being Certain Further Histories of Folk Called "Raiders." London, Macmillan, and New York, Harper, 1902.

The Banner of Blue. New York, McClure, 1902; London, Hodder and Stoughton, 1903.

Flower o'-the-Corn. London, Clarke, 1902: New York, McClure Phillips, 1903.

The Adventurer in Spain. London, Isbister, and New York, Stokes, 1903.

The Loves of Miss Anne. London, Clarke, and New York, Dodd Mead, 1904.

Strong Mac. London, Ward Lock, and New York, Dodd Mead, 1904.

Raiderland: All about Grey Galloway. London, Hodder and Stoughton, and New York, Dodd Mead, 1904.

Maid Margaret of Galloway. London, Hodder and Stoughton, 1905; as *May Margaret: Called "The Fair Maid of Galloway,"* New York, Dodd Mead, 1905.

The Cherry Ribband. London, Hodder and Stoughton, and New York, Barnes, 1905.

Kid McGhie: A Nugget of Dim Gold. London, Clarke, 1906.

Fishers of Men. New York, Appleton, 1906.

The White Plumes of Navarre: A Romance of the Wars of Religion. London, Religious Tract Society, 1906; as *The White Plume,* New York, Dodd Mead, 1906.

Me and Myn. London, Unwin, 1907.

Vida: or, The Iron of Kirktown. London, Clarke, 1907; as *The Iron Lord,* New York, Empire Book Company, 1907.

Little Esson. London, Ward Lock, 1907.

Deep Moat Grange. London, Hodder and Stoughton, and New York, Appleton, 1908.

Princess Penniless. London, Hodder and Stoughton, 1908.

The Bloom o' the Heather. London, Nash, 1908.

The Men of the Mountain. London, Religious Tract Society, and New York, Harper, 1909.

Rose of the Wilderness. London, Hodder and Stoughton, 1909.

The Seven Wise Men. London, Religious Tract Society, 1909.

Love's Young Dream. New York, Macmillan, 1910.

The Dew of Their Youth. London, Hodder and Stoughton, 1910.

The Smugglers. London, Hodder and Stoughton, 1911.

The Lady of the Hundred Dresses. London, Nash, 1911.

Love in Pernicketty Town. London and New York, Hodder and Stoughton, 1911.

Patsy. New York, Macmillan, 1912.

Anne of the Barricades. London and New York, Hodder and Stoughton, 1912.

The Moss Troopers. London and New York, Hodder and Stoughton, 1912.

Sandy's Love Affair. London, Hutchinson, 1913; as *Sandy,* New York, Macmillan, 1914.

A Tatter of Scarlet. London, Hodder and Stoughton, 1913.

Silver Sand. London, Hodder and Stoughton, and Chicago, Revell, 1914.

Hal o' the Ironsides. London, Hodder and Stoughton, and New York, Revell, 1915.

The Azure Hand. London and New York, Hodder and Stoughton, 1917.

The White Pope, Called "The Light Out of the East." Liverpool, Books Ltd., 1920; as *The Light Out of the East,* New York, Doran, 1920.

Rogues' Island. London, Faber, 1926.

Short Stories

Bog-Myrtle and Peat: Tales, Chiefly of Galloway. London, Bliss Sands, and New York, Appleton, 1895.
Lad's Love: Tales. London, Bliss Sands, and New York, Appleton, 1897.
The Stickit Minister's Wooing and Other Galloway Stories. London, Hodder and Stoughton, and New York, Doubleday, 1900.
Love Idylls. London, Murray, and New York, Dodd Mead, 1901.
Young Nick and Old Nick: Yarns for the Year's End. London, Paul, 1910.

Verse

Dulce Cor, Being the Poems of Ford Berèton. London, Kegan Paul, 1886.

Other

My Two Edinburghs: Searchlights Through the Mists of Thirty Years. London, Cedar Press, 1909.

*   *   *

Sir Toady Lion, otherwise Arthur George Picton Smith – the *nom de guerre* derives from his early attempts to twist his tongue round the name of his favourite character in history, Richard *Coeur de Lion* – is the younger brother of Hugh John Smith who assumes the imperial title of General Napoleon Smith at the age of twelve before leading his army in a campaign against the town "Smoutchies" who are holding a pet lamb hostage in the Black Sheds, the slaughterhouse yard, and who are trespassing in the grounds of The House of Windy Standard, Sir Toady's home in the Scottish border country. The army musters in its ranks their literary sister Priscilla, Sammy and Cissy Carter from the neighbouring estate of Oaklands, and two stable boys, Mike O'Donelly and Peter Greg. And it is Sir Toady himself who stealthily rescues the lamb for all the military ardour, staffwork, and planning of the commander-in-chief after the first set encounter with the enemy had decidedly ended in the Smoutchies' favour.

Nevertheless Samuel Rutherford Crockett's *The Surprising Adventures of Sir Toady Lion with Those of General Napoleon Smith* really belongs to the elder brother as he emerges from a series of adventures with honour unblemished and his sense of duty undiminished in true romantic fashion whereas Sir Toady demands a fair measure of patience and toleration in the reader. He appears as a more sympathetic and engaging character in *Sir Toady Crusoe* when befriending an Australian boy searching for his sister, but even here his precocious cunning is in no way alleviated by the mawkish sentimentality constantly surrounding him. In many respects this is a pity because Crockett writes with a fresh and affectionate nostalgia in the earlier volume which is largely based on his own childhood upbringing. Of *Sweetheart Travellers* and *Sweethearts at Home*, described by the author as "vagrom chronicles," little need be said, their excessively sentimental approach has earned for them a truly deserved and lasting oblivion.

—Alan Edwin Day

CROMPTON, Richmal. Pseudonym for Richmal Crompton Lamburn. British. Born in Bury, Lancashire, 15 November 1890. Educated at St. Elphin's Clergy Daughters' School, Warrington, Lancashire, later Darley Dale, Derbyshire; Royal Holloway College, University of London (Driver Scholar, 1914), B.A. (honours) in classics 1914. Teacher, St. Elphin's, 1915–17; Classics Mistress, Bromley High School, Kent, 1917–24. Crippled by poliomyelitis in 1923. Served as a volunteer in the Auxiliary Fire Service, Bromley, during World War II. *Died 11 January 1969.*

PUBLICATIONS FOR CHILDREN

Fiction

Just William, illustrated by Thomas Henry. London, Newnes, 1922.
More William, illustrated by Thomas Henry. London, Newnes, 1923.
William Again, illustrated by Thomas Henry. London, Newnes, 1923.
William the Fourth, illustrated by Thomas Henry. London, Newnes, 1924.
Still William, illustrated by Thomas Henry. London, Newnes, 1925.
William the Conqueror, illustrated by Thomas Henry. London, Newnes, 1926.
William the Outlaw, illustrated by Thomas Henry. London, Newnes, 1927.
William in Trouble, illustrated by Thomas Henry. London, Newnes, 1927.
William the Good, illustrated by Thomas Henry. London, Newnes, 1928.
William, illustrated by Thomas Henry. London, Newnes, 1929.
William the Bad, illustrated by Thomas Henry. London, Newnes, 1930.
William's Happy Days, illustrated by Thomas Henry. London, Newnes, 1930.
William's Crowded Hours, illustrated by Thomas Henry. London, Newnes, 1931.
William the Pirate, illustrated by Thomas Henry. London, Newnes, 1932.
William the Rebel, illustrated by Thomas Henry. London, Newnes, 1933.
William the Gangster, illustrated by Thomas Henry. London, Newnes, 1934.
William the Detective, illustrated by Thomas Henry. London, Newnes, 1935.
Sweet William, illustrated by Thomas Henry. London, Newnes, 1936.
William the Showman, illustrated by Thomas Henry. London, Newnes, 1937.
William the Dictator, illustrated by Thomas Henry. London, Newnes, 1938.
William and A.R.P., illustrated by Thomas Henry. London, Newnes, 1939; as *William's Bad Resolution*, 1956.
William and the Evacuees, illustrated by Thomas Henry. London, Newnes, 1940; as *William the Film Star*, 1956.
William Does His Bit, illustrated by Thomas Henry. London, Newnes, 1941.
William Carries On, illustrated by Thomas Henry. London, Newnes, 1942.
William and the Brains Trust, illustrated by Thomas Henry. London, Newnes, 1945.
Just William's Luck, illustrated by Thomas Henry. London, Newnes, 1948.
Jimmy. London, Newnes, 1949.
William the Bold, illustrated by Thomas Henry. London, Newnes, 1950.
Jimmy Again, illustrated by Lunt Roberts. London, Newnes, 1951.
William and the Tramp, illustrated by Thomas Henry. London, Newnes, 1952.
William and the Moon Rocket, illustrated by Thomas Henry. London, Newnes, 1954.
William and the Space Animal, illustrated by Thomas Henry. London, Newnes, 1956.
William's Television Show, illustrated by Thomas Henry. London, Newnes, 1958.
William the Explorer, illustrated by Thomas Henry. London, Newnes, 1960.
William's Treasure Trove, illustrated by Thomas Henry. London, Newnes, 1962.
William and the Witch, illustrated by Thomas Henry and Henry Ford. London, Newnes, 1964.
William and the Pop Singers, illustrated by Henry Ford. London, Newnes, 1965.
William and the Masked Ranger, illustrated by Henry Ford. London, Newnes, 1966.
William the Superman, illustrated by Henry Ford. London, Newnes, 1968.
William the Lawless, illustrated by Henry Ford. London, Newnes, 1970.

Play

William and the Artist's Model.   London, J. Garnet Miller, 1956.

<small>PUBLICATIONS FOR ADULTS</small>

Novels

The Innermost Room.   London and New York, Andrew Melrose, 1923.
The Hidden Light.   London, Hodder and Stoughton, 1924.
Anne Morrison.   London, Jarrolds, 1925.
The Wildings.   London, Hodder and Stoughton, 1925.
David Wilding.   London, Hodder and Stoughton, 1926.
The House.   London, Hodder and Stoughton, 1926; as *Dread Dwelling.* New York,
    Boni and Liveright, 1926.
Millicent Dorrington.   London, Hodder and Stoughton, 1927.
Leadon Hill.   London, Hodder and Stoughton, 1927.
Enter − Patricia.   London, Newnes, 1927.
The Thorn Bush.   London, Hodder and Stoughton, 1928.
Roofs Off!   London, Hodder and Stoughton, 1928.
The Four Graces.   London, Hodder and Stoughton, 1929.
Abbot's End.   London, Hodder and Stoughton, 1929.
Blue Flames.   London, Hodder and Stoughton, 1930.
Naomi Godstone.   London, Hodder and Stoughton, 1930.
Portrait of a Family.   London, Macmillan, 1931.
The Odyssey of Euphemia Tracy.   London, Macmillan, 1932.
Marriage of Hermione.   London, Macmillan, 1932.
The Holiday.   London, Macmillan, 1933.
Chedsy Place.   London, Macmillan, 1934.
The Old Man's Birthday.   London, Macmillan, 1934; Boston, Little Brown, 1935.
Quartet.   London, Macmillan, 1935.
Caroline.   London, Macmillan, 1936.
There Are Four Seasons.   London, Macmillan, 1937.
Journeying Wave.   London, Macmillan, 1938.
Merlin Bay.   London, Macmillan, 1939.
Steffan Green.   London, Macmillan, 1940.
Narcissa.   London, Macmillan, 1941.
Mrs. Frensham Describes a Circle.   London, Macmillan, 1942.
Weatherley Parade.   London, Macmillan, 1944.
Westover.   London, Hutchinson, 1946.
The Ridleys.   London, Hutchinson, 1947.
Family Roundabout.   London, Hutchinson, 1948.
Frost at Morning.   London, Hutchinson, 1950.
Linden Rise.   London, Hutchinson, 1952.
The Gypsy's Baby.   London, Hutchinson, 1954.
Four in Exile.   London, Hutchinson, 1955.
Matty and Dearingroydes.   London, Hutchinson, 1956.
Blind Man's Buff.   London, Hutchinson, 1957.
Wiseman's Folly.   London, Hutchinson, 1959.
The Inheritor.   London, Hutchinson, 1960.

Short Stories

Kathleen and I, and, of Course, Veronica.   London, Hodder and Stoughton, 1926.
A Monstrous Regiment.   London, Hutchinson, 1927.

Mist and Other Stories. London, Hutchinson, 1928.
The Middle Things. London, Hutchinson, 1928.
Felicity Stands By. London, Newnes, 1928.
Sugar and Spice and Other Stories. London, Ward Lock, 1929.
Ladies First. London, Hutchinson, 1929.
The Silver Birch and Other Stories. London, Hutchinson, 1931.
The First Morning. London, Hutchinson, 1936.

                         *   *   *

Richmal Crompton's "William Books" must be among the most long-lived (almost half a century separates the first story from the last), consistent (such a personality as William's resists all change) and entirely original of all the popular boys' series.

William Brown started life in a women's magazine during the First World War, in a short story called "The Outlaws." That first story, one of Crompton's best, was later reprinted for children in *Just William* and established the characters, locale, theme and structure of over three hundred and fifty sequels. They are brilliantly contrived little melodramas of traditional village life disrupted by one well-intentional but entirely unruly little boy. His escapades are, to borrow his own description of a Western film, "blood-curdlin' an' nerve-shatterin'" for all those around him.

The setting is a very middle-class family; there are servants and occasional smart dinner parties, until the outbreak of the Second World War. Mrs. Brown is skilfully portrayed as a mild and eternally optimistic wife striving to salvage the morale, sanity and social reputation of her despairing family from the havoc created by her younger son. William, of course, has no wish to create disharmony or pain. He merely seeks a reasonable amount of freedom in which to engage in a few reckless adventures with his friends, earn enough money to buy the necessities of life such as white rats and gobstoppers, and sometimes to contribute to the welfare of the community by such laudable means as opening his own stray dogs' home, helping to attract customers to the new village shop and secretly adopting some evacuee children. Because he is enterprising, imaginative, generous and totally ingenuous, catastrophe and retribution are particularly hurtful.

The stories, at both adult and child level, are extremely funny. Even the late stories of the 1960's have a satirical bite and an inventiveness reminiscent of P.G. Wodehouse. The *nouveau riche* Bott family that settle in the village might have been created by Evelyn Waugh. Richmal Crompton never lost sight of her original adult audience and much of her humour is sophisticated and ironic; never is it crude or repetitive. Recently, her niece Richmal Ashbee has modified some of the stories for the 1970's readership; the scruffy school cap and flannel shorts are replaced by jeans and a t-shirt. But the wit and the finely observed social detail remain unspoilt.

—Aidan Warlow

CROSSLEY-HOLLAND, Kevin (John Williams). British. Born in Mursley, Buckinghamshire, 7 February 1941. Educated at Bryanston school; St. Edmund Hall, Oxford, B.A. (honours) in English language and literature. Married Ruth Marris in 1972; has two sons by first marriage. Editor, Macmillan and Company, publishers, London, 1962–71. Gregory Fellow, University of Leeds, 1969–71. Talks Producer, BBC, London, 1972. Since 1972, Editorial Director, Victor Gollancz Ltd., publishers, London; since 1975, General Editor. Mirror of Britain series, Andre Deutsch Ltd., publishers, London. Recipient: Arts Council award, for children's book, 1968. Agent: Deborah Rogers Literary Agency, 29 Goodge Street, London, W.1, England.

PUBLICATIONS FOR CHILDREN

Fiction

Havelok the Dane, illustrated by Brian Wildsmith. London, Macmillan, 1964; New York, Dutton, 1965.

King Horn, illustrated by Charles Keeping. London, Macmillan, 1965; New York, Dutton, 1966.

The Sea-Stranger, illustrated by Joanna Troughton. London, Heinemann, 1973; New York, Seabury Press, 1974.

The Fire-Brother, illustrated by Joanna Troughton. London, Heinemann, 1974; New York, Seabury Press, 1975.

The Earth-Father, illustrated by Joanna Troughton. London, Heinemann, 1975.

The Wildman, illustrated by Charles Keeping. London, Deutsch, 1976.

Other

The Green Children, illustrated by Margaret Gordon. London, Macmillan, 1966; New York, Seabury Press, 1968.

The Callow Pit Coffer, illustrated by Margaret Gordon. London, Macmillan, 1968; New York, Seabury Press, 1969.

Wordhoard: Anglo-Saxon Stories, with Jill Paton Walsh. London, Macmillan, and New York, Farrar Straus, 1969.

The Pedlar of Swaffham, illustrated by Margaret Gordon. London, Macmillan, 1971; New York, Seabury Press, 1972.

Green Blades Rising: The Anglo-Saxons. London, Deutsch, 1975; New York, Seabury Press, 1976.

Editor, *Winter's Tales for Children 3*. London, Macmillan, 1967.

Editor, *The Faber Book of Northern Legends*, illustrated by Alan Howard. London, Faber, 1977.

Translator, *Storm and Other Old English Riddles*, illustrated by Miles Thistlethwaite. London, Macmillan, and New York, Farrar Straus, 1970.

PUBLICATIONS FOR ADULTS

Verse

On Approval. London, Outposts Publications, 1961.

My Son. London, Turret Books, 1966.

Alderney: The Nunnery. London, Turret Books, 1968.

Norfolk Poems. London, Academy Editions, 1970.

A Dream of a Meeting. Frensham, Surrey, Sceptre Press, 1970.

Confessional. Frensham, Surrey, Sceptre Press, 1970.

More Than I Am. London, Steam Press, 1971.

The Wake. Richmond, Surrey, Keepsake Press, 1972.

The Rain-Giver. London, Deutsch, 1972.

Petal and Stone. Knotting, Bedfordshire, Sceptre Press, 1975.

The Dream-House. London, Deutsch, 1976.

Other

Pieces of Land: Journeys to Eight Islands. London, Gollancz, 1972.

Editor, *Running to Paradise: An Introductory Selection of the Poems of W.B. Yeats.* London, Macmillan, 1967; New York, Macmillan, 1968.
Editor, *Winter's Tales 14.* London, Macmillan, 1968.
Editor, with Patricia Beer, *New Poetry 2* (anthology). London, Arts Council, 1976.

Translator, *The Battle of Maldon and Other Old English Poems.* London, Macmillan, and New York, St. Martin's Press, 1965.
Translator, *Beowulf.* London, Macmillan, and New York, Farrar Straus, 1968.

*   *   *

Kevin Crossley-Holland's work for children seems limited only by his predilection for the re-telling of an ancient story. So far, he has avoided the challenge of the purely original, imaginative tale. But, among his contemporaries, he has few rivals as an exponent of the traditional narrative re-told.

The stories are of long ago; but character, situation, landscape – however strange and remote they may at first appear – soon declare themselves as being not merely of their own, but of all time. The narrative skill, freshness and aptness of language, quietly direct mode of address, all compel the attention, awaken the imagination, remain in the mind. It is a voice as old, and as new, as poetry.

Even the most insignificant-seeming characters are never remote, lay figures. They live, breathe and move. At the same time, they retain their mythic, mystic qualities. The underlying themes and *motifs*, the subtly-revealed eternal truths beating at the heart of all great folk-literature, are always delicately but firmly indicated.

These vital components are particularly well-represented by the quartet of medieval stories written primarily for young readers (or listeners), beginning with *The Green Children*. In each case, the basic structure is thoroughly established; and not the smallest detail is lost or distorted in the process of the story's realization. The voice of the narrator remains as anonymous an instrument as that of the minstrel or ballad-singer. The emphasis, very properly, is not on the singer but on the song. The verbal furnishing is spare, but chosen with great precision; the dramatic movement cunningly sited and sprung. Mind and imagination are continuously stimulated and fed as the tales are resolved.

In the dark legend of *The Callow Pit Coffer*, two young brothers suddenly find "strength in themselves" to resist the powers of darkness. At the mysterious close of *The Green Children*, we learn that "nobody knows – unless you do – whether the green girl lived on earth to the end of her days: or whether, one day, near the Wolfpits, she simply disappeared." The painful, but ultimately peaceful Suffolk myth *The Wildman*, telling of a merman's capture, suffering and escape, also suggests – among much else – a near-parable of each individual's entrance into this world from a bag of waters. In the more solidly grounded *The Pedlar of Swaffham*, on the other hand, the central figure takes the Gold Road to London in pursuit of his own dream, but returns with (and resolves happily) that of another: discovering, in the process, how many of us are "foreigners in our own country."

Splendidly complementary to the stories are Kevin Crossley-Holland's translations of Early English riddles collected in *Storm*: poems dazzlingly new-minted, witty, imaginatively refreshing. Again, as in so much of his work, the people and moods of a period apparently remote in time are vitalized and gently brought near. In the writer, and by attrition, in the reader, past, present and future meet. Such writing, to such effect, is a rare and notable achievement.

—Charles Causley

CUNNINGHAM, Julia W(oolfolk). American. Born in Spokane, Washington, 4 October 1916. Educated at St. Anne's School, Charlottesville, Virginia. Clerk, Guaranty Trust Company, New York, 1937–40; Co-ordinating Editor, G. Schirmer, music publishers, New York, 1940–44; Associate Editor, Dell Publishing Company, New York, 1944–47; Secretary, Air Reduction Company, New York, 1947–49; Assistant to the Advertising Manager, Sherman Clay and Company, San Francisco, 1950–51; Free-lance writer, France, 1952; Salesperson, Metropolitan Museum of Art, New York, 1953–56. Since 1957, Bookseller and children's book buyer, Tecolote Book Shop, Santa Barbara, California. Recipient: New York *Herald Tribune* Festival award, 1965. Agent: Curtis Brown Ltd., 575 Madison Avenue, New York, New York 10022. Address: 33 West Valerio Street, Santa Barbara, California 93101, U.S.A.

PUBLICATIONS FOR CHILDREN

Fiction

> *The Vision of François the Fox,* illustrated by Nicholas Angelo. Boston, Houghton Mifflin, 1960.
> *Dear Rat,* illustrated by Walter Lorraine. Boston, Houghton Mifflin, 1961.
> *Macaroon,* illustrated by Evaline Ness. New York, Pantheon Books, 1962; London, Harrap, 1963.
> *Candle Tales,* illustrated by Evaline Ness. New York, Pantheon Books, 1964.
> *Dorp Dead,* illustrated by James Spanfeller. New York, Pantheon Books, 1965; London, Heinemann, 1967.
> *Viollet,* illustrated by Alan Cober. New York, Pantheon Books, 1966.
> *Onion Journey,* illustrated by Lydia Cooley. New York, Pantheon Books, 1967.
> *Burnish Me Bright,* illustrated by Don Freeman. New York, Pantheon Books, 1970; London, Heinemann, 1971.
> *Wings of the Morning,* illustrated by Katy Peake. San Francisco, Golden Gate Books, 1971.
> *Far in the Day,* illustrated by Don Freeman. New York, Pantheon Books, 1972.
> *The Treasure Is the Rose,* illustrated by Judy Graese. New York, Pantheon Books, 1973.
> *Maybe, A Mole,* illustrated by Cyndy Szekeres. New York, Pantheon Books, 1974.
> *Come to the Edge.* New York, Pantheon Books, 1977.

Manuscript Collections: Kerlan Collection, University of Minnesota, Minneapolis; University of Oregon Library, Eugene.

*   *   *

Julia W. Cunningham's *Dorp Dead* portrays the experiences of 11-year-old Gilly Ground, first in the depersonalizing atmosphere of an orphanage, later in the near enslavement of the home of Master Kobalt, a sadistic, time-obsessed bully, and finally as Gilly escapes from Kobalt to find a new life.

Cunningham has the first person-narrator, Gilly, tell the story in the form of a record of the action after it has been completed. The limitations of language and perception inherent in the device of a child persona are avoided by the fact that Gilly, the protagonist, is "ferociously intelligent" and insightful in his observations of himself and others. As a character, Gilly deliberately avoids emotional involvement in the activities of the orphanage and the school. He calls himself a "stuffed bear from whom infrequent and inaccurate grunts of non-knowledge are extracted." His refusal to learn to spell is an effort to hide his true nature from the forces of conformity and regimentation around him. The fact that he writes "Dorp Dead" on Kobalt's door at the end of the novel indicates both his liberation and his uniqueness.

The director of the orphanage, Mrs. Heister, is characterized by her name as one who will attempt to "heist" Gilly's individuality by forcing him into the routines of the institution with its relentless loud bells. When Gilly moves to the foster home of Master Kobalt, he arrives at a house that is square and gray, suggestive of a prison, and which is linked through color with the orphanage where Gilly spent a "gray and grotty year." Master Kobalt is a man who lives obsessively in rigid routines: "I live in lanes of time; each hour is channeled," Kobalt tells Gilly. Kobalt is an ironic character: his name suggests a bright blue color but his description is of grayness; he has assumed the role of foster parent but he is actually a tyrant and a cruel master. His home appears to offer warmth and confort but in fact it is a prison. Kobalt's name also calls to mind the destructively radioactive element that will penetrate and invade matter in the same way that Kobalt the man intrudes upon the identity of Gilly.

Gilly finds refuge from the orphanage first and later from Kobalt's house in a ruined tower where he meets The Hunter, a man of strong identity and purpose as indicated by his being dressed in black instead of the gray of Master Kobalt. Gilly associates The Hunter with a book on King Arthur that he had read. The Hunter and the tower therefore appear to represent the strong, heroic character of the mythical past in opposition to the sterile institutions of society such as the orphanage and Kobalt. The Hunter as a character is akin to the seer or sage of folktales. He tells Gilly that he "hunts to see" with a gun with no bullets. The Hunter is unlike other adults Gilly knows because of his refusal to give direct advice. His enigmatic utterances are reminiscent of the psychotherapist who directs and guides the patient to find his answers from within his own personality. *Dorp Dead* is strongly existential in its theme that truth must arise from within oneself, that external codes and systems are false and inimical to the individual's quest for meaning and identity.

—William D. Anderson

CURRY, Jane (Louise). American. Born in East Liverpool, Ohio, 24 September 1932. Educated at Pennsylvania State University, State College, 1950–51; Indiana University of Pennsylvania, 1951–54, B.S. in Education 1954; University of California, Los Angeles, 1957–59; Stanford University, California (teaching assistant), 1959–61, 1964–65, 1967–68, M.A. 1966, Ph.D. 1969; Royal Holloway College, University of London (Fulbright Fellow), 1961–62; University College, University of London (Leverhulme Fellow), 1965–66. Art Instructor, Los Angeles City Schools, 1955–59; Shop Assistant, Vroman's Bookstore, Pasadena, California, 1963; Acting Instructor, Stanford University, 1967–68. Lives in Los Angeles. Address: c/o Margaret K. McElderry Books, Atheneum Publishers, 122 East 42nd Street, New York, New York 10017, U.S.A.

PUBLICATIONS FOR CHILDREN

Fiction

> *Beneath the Hill,* illustrated by Imero Gobbato. New York, Harcourt Brace, 1967; London, Dobson, 1968.
> *The Sleepers,* illustrated by Gareth Floyd. New York, Harcourt Brace, 1968; London, Dobson, 1969.
> *The Change-Child,* illustrated by Gareth Floyd. New York, Harcourt Brace, 1969; London, Dobson, 1970.
> *The Daybreakers,* illustrated by Charles Robinson. New York, Harcourt Brace, and London, Longman, 1970.

Mindy's Mysterious Miniature, illustrated by Charles Robinson.   New York, Harcourt
  Brace, 1970; as *The Housenapper*, London, Longman, 1971.
Over the Sea's Edge, illustrated by Charles Robinson.   New York, Harcourt Brace, and
  London, Longman, 1971.
The Ice Ghosts Mystery.   New York, Atheneum, 1972; London, Longman, 1973.
The Lost Farm, illustrated by Charles Robinson.   New York, Atheneum, and London,
  Longman, 1974.
Parsley Sage, Rosemary and Time, illustrated by Charles Robinson.   New York,
  Atheneum, 1975.
The Watchers.   New York, Atheneum, 1975; London, Penguin, 1976.
The Magical Cupboard, illustrated by Charles Robinson.   New York, Atheneum, 1976.
Poor Tom's Ghost, illustrated by Janet Archer.   New York, Atheneum, and London,
  Penguin, 1977.
The Birdstones.   New York, Atheneum, 1977; London, Penguin, 1978.

Other

  Down from the Lonely Mountain: California Indian Tales, illustrated by Enrico
    Arno.   New York, Harcourt Brace, 1965; illustrated by the author, London,
    Dobson, 1968.

Manuscript Collection: Kerlan Collection, University of Minnesota, Minneapolis.

Jane Curry comments:

  Most of my novels for children, whether for younger or older readers, are adventures —
usually, in part or in whole, fantasies — which in one way or another involve children of the
present in events of the past. This is not always an essentially historical past, as it is in *Poor
Tom's Ghost*. In the Abáloc stories (*Beneath the Hill, The Daybreakers, Over the Sea's Edge,
The Watchers* and *The Birdstones*), it is one that draws as much or more from both Old and
New World legend and myth as from archaeology and history.
  I find great satisfaction in involving children in other places, people and times — but from
time to time I also enjoy writing a story like *The Housenapper*, for sheer fun.

                              *   *   *

  Jane Curry is a trained historian as well as an accomplished writer. Not surprisingly,
history and legend constitute an important element in not only her first book, *Down from the
Lonely Mountain*, a children's version of California Indian tales, but virtually all her
subsequent writing. *Beneath the Hill*, an original amalgam of Welsh and American history
and legend, is her first novel and the first in a trio of loosely related fantasy narratives
concerning the mound builders of middle and southeastern America. In spite of a potentially
exciting notion that unregulated strip mining in the Pennsylvania mountains is part of some
large, vaguely described evil, the novel is uncomplicated and obvious in plot,
characterization, and theme — features that render the novel quite accessible to children.
Picking up one of the major narrative strands of its predecessor but utilizing a different set of
characters, *The Daybreakers* postulates a link among medieval Wales, the mound builders,
and the Aztecs. A time shift fantasy, the novel shuttles its protagonists back and forth
between the present and the times of the mound builders. Although requiring some
familiarity with history, *The Daybreakers* remains attractive to young readers because the
characters are many and varied, and much of the action occurs in the present. *Over the Sea's
Edge*, the third of the mound builders fantasies, is the most ambitious and demanding of
Curry's novels to date. Dependent on an extensive knowledge of history and legend to be

rewarding, the novel is stylistically dense and allusive. Complexity in characterization and an attendant ambiguity in moral values, along with the former qualities, make the work the least accessible of Curry's novels.

Several other novels are noteworthy. *The Change-Child* blends history and fantasy so expertly that the reader needs to remind himself that the elves are really creatures of faerie. *Mindy's Mysterious Miniature* and *The Lost Farm*, which describes the sometimes humorous results of Professor Kurtz's Reducer, should delight readers captivated by the idea of shrinking. *The Sleepers*, perhaps Curry's best novel, is an Arthurian fantasy which compares favourably with Mayne's *Earthfast*, Cooper's *Over Sea, Under Stone*, and Norton's Arthurian narratives. Intricate plotting, suspense, intrigue, mystery, and deft, engrossing utilization of the legend that Arthur is asleep awaiting a call to save England from its greatest peril make *The Sleepers* one of today's superior fantasies.

Curry's recent novels, *The Lost Farm* and *Parsley Sage, Rosemary and Time*, relatively slight fantasies, and *The Ice Ghosts Mystery*, suggest that she may be marking time while she ponders what direction her talent should next take. Because of her predilection for history, legend, and myth and her continuing growth as a novelist, all who have followed Curry's career trust that her already considerable achievement will be capped eventually by a major work as good as the high fantasy of Le Guin and Cooper.

—Francis J. Molson

CUTT, W(illiam) Towrie. Canadian. Born in Orkney, Scotland, 26 January 1898. Educated at Kirkwall Grammar School, Orkney; University of Alberta, Edmonton, B.A. 1942, B.Ed. 1947, M.A. 1950. Served as a private, Gordon Highlanders, France, 1916–19; instructor, Royal Canadian Air Force, 1942–44. Married Margaret Nancy Davis in 1948. Teacher, Alberta, 1928–63. Address: 624 Cornwall, Victoria, British Columbia V8V 4LI, Canada.

PUBLICATIONS FOR CHILDREN

Fiction

On the Trail of Long Tom, illustrated by Sheila Dorrell. Toronto, Collins, and London, Deutsch, 1970.
Message from Arkmae. Toronto, Collins, 1972; edited by Madean Stewart, London, Deutsch, 1972.
Seven for the Sea. London, Deutsch, 1972; Chicago, Follett, 1974.
Carry My Bones Northwest. London, Deutsch, 1973.

Other

Faraway World: An Orkney Boyhood, illustrated by Joseph Sloan. London, Deutsch, 1977.

W. Towrie Cutt comments:

Writers of children's books are advised to keep the child in view – to connect. Which children? Out of 10,000,000 Canadian and British children, 4,000 will, if I am lucky, read my book – one out of 2,000. Which one am I writing for? I have written for children who may be led to take an interest in the humble unrecorded makers of Canadian history and interested in the preservation of animal life, especially sea mammals. I deal with two half-breed boys in my Canadian historicals, one who went the way of the white man and the other who went the way of the Indian – a choice such boys had to make at one time. In my seal stories, I seek to recall Orkney folk lore. I am against books understood only by gifted youths being labelled as "children's books."

*   *   *

W. Towrie Cutt's *Message from Arkmae* and *Seven for the Sea* are really one book broken in two, though each can be read independently. Both books are an impassioned plea for the protection of wild life in the Orkneys, written with the observation and insight of a man who was born and spent his childhood in the islands and who still, in his heart, lives there.

Set on the isle of Sanday, both books concern the Ward family. Father and two sons have the distinguishing feature of a hard skin between their fingers and a red tinge on the neck which is said to denote their descent from a Ward who married a seal woman. Thus the legend. Two younger Wards, cousins, Erchie and Mansie, who spend days in their rowing boat fishing and beach combing, find themselves one day in an underground cavern where they meet a merman. It is this character who articulates the author's plea for the conservation of the island, and above all of the seals. In the sequel, the two boys, rowing to Sanday, are held up by fog and accept a lift from a strange boatman. Slowly they realise that the boatman has taken them back into the past where they witness what actually happened to their great-great grandfather, Selkie Ward, when, through his own fault, he lost his seal wife. Even though not sure afterwards whether it was perhaps only a dream, the two boys now accept as true the local legend about Selkie Ward.

The quality of life on the Orkneys a hundred years ago is beautifully captured and the freshly remembered detail firmly anchors the old Celtic fairy tale, which, in both books, is told with a strong sense of mystery and suspense.

— James Roose-Evans

DAHL, Roald. British. Born in Llandaff, South Wales, 13 September 1916. Educated at Repton School, 1929–32. Served in the Royal Air Force, 1939–45. Married the actress Patricia Neal in 1953; has one son and three daughters. Member of the Eastern Staff, Shell Company, London, 1933–37, and Shell Company of East Africa, Dar-es-Salaam, 1937–39. Recipient: Mystery Writers of America Edgar Allan Poe Award, 1952, 1954. Agent: Murray Pollinger, 4 Garrick Street, London W.C.2. Address: Gipsy House, Great Missenden, Buckinghamshire, England.

PUBLICATIONS FOR CHILDREN

Fiction

> *The Gremlins*, illustrated by Walt Disney Studio.   New York, Random House, 1943; London, Collins, 1944.
> *James and the Giant Peach*, illustrated by Nancy Burkert.   New York, Knopf, 1961; London, Allen and Unwin, 1967.
> *Charlie and the Chocolate Factory*, illustrated by Joseph Schindelman.   New York, Knopf, 1964; London, Allen and Unwin, 1967.
> *The Magic Finger*, illustrated by William Pène du Bois.   New York, Harper, 1966; London, Allen and Unwin, 1968.

Fantastic Mr. Fox, illustrated by Donald Chaffin.   New York, Knopf, and London, Allen and Unwin, 1970.

Charlie and the Great Glass Elevator: The Further Adventures of Charlie Buclat and Willie Wonka, Chocolate-Maker Extraordinary, illustrated by Joseph Schindelman.   New York, Knopf, 1972; London, Allen and Unwin, 1973.

Danny, The Champion of the World, illustrated by Jill Bennett.   London, Cape, and New York, Knopf, 1975.

The Wonderful Story of Henry Sugar and Six More.   London, Cape, and New York, Knopf, 1977.

PUBLICATIONS FOR ADULTS

Novel

Sometime Never: A Fable for Supermen.   New York, Scribner, 1948; London, Collins, 1949.

Short Stories

Over to You: 10 Stories of Flyers and Flying.   New York, Reynal and Hitchcock, 1946; London, Hamish Hamilton, 1947.

Someone Like You.   New York, Knopf, 1953; London, Secker and Warburg, 1954; revised edition, London, Joseph, 1961.

Kiss, Kiss.   New York, Knopf, and London, Joseph, 1960.

Twenty-Nine Kisses.   London, Joseph, 1969.

Selected Stories.   New York, Random House, 1970.

Penguin Modern Stories 12, with others.   London, Penguin, 1972.

Switch Bitch.   New York, Knopf, and London, Joseph, 1974.

Plays

The Honeys (produced New York, 1955).

Screenplays: *You Only Live Twice*, 1965; *Chitty-Chitty-Bang-Bang*, 1967; *The Night-Digger*, 1970; *The Lightning Bug*, 1971; *Willie Wonka and the Chocolate Factory*, 1971.

*   *   *

There are adult critics who have accused Roald Dahl of "crude vitality and vulgarity" but to condemn his books as of "questionable morality" is to misinterpret them in the child's terms — for children he truly is "the champion of the world." Since the publication of *Charlie and the Chocolate Factory*, Roald Dahl, then already well-known as a writer for adults, has established himself as a highly popular author with an inventive imagination that is totally child-centred. He presents to the 8–11-year-old-reader a "cautionary tale" in which Charlie Buckett and his Grandfather join five other children in a fantastic tour of Willy Wonka's Chocolate Factory, complete with astonishing machinery which deals out just punishment for gluttony. The factory is staffed by the mysterious Oompa-Loompas, strange pygmy creatures brought from Africa into Wonka's bondage. No less amazing is Willy Wonka's invention in *Charlie and the Great Glass Elevator*; Charlie goes off into orbital flight with three bedridden Grandparents to a wild extravaganza of publicity when their flight-path inadvertently crosses that of the staff capsule to the first United States Space Hotel. The humour is acid in parts and far removed from the folk lore and comic strip quality of the first Charlie book.

James and the Giant Peach was the first of Dahl's books to be written for children, and is his most fantastic and, in many ways, his most unsuccessful. James burrows into the sides of the giant peach before he can set off on his madcap adventures. The story lacks that easy flow for reading aloud. The use of a giant peach for the central theme is a macabre touch that echos some of Dahl's short stories for adults.

When writing for younger children the author adds magic and charm to his other skills as a writer. In *The Magic Finger* he uses very successfully the well-known vehicle of the pointed finger to bring about magic – but only when the heroine is in a temper.

Farmers Boggis, Bunce, and Bean, characters in *Fantastic Mr. Fox*, must surely be three of the most obnoxious characters in children's literature. All the reader's sympathy is with the hero, the fox who regularly raids their farms for chickens, turkeys, ducks and cider to feed his ever-growing family. The farmers' repeated assaults on his stronghold only prove just how wily a fellow Mr. Fox can be. This epic fable for 6–9-year-olds is the classic story of the underdog making good. In fact all Dahl's heros are the poor of this world whose lives are transformed by the fantastic and at times disconcerting happenings of the story. Not least of his heroes is Danny, "the champion of the world," who lives a simple life with his wonderful Father in a caravan behind their garage. Dad's only excitement is to raid the local estate for pheasants and there is nothing that he does not know about pheasant poaching. The relationship between Danny and his father is a very special one and more highly characterised than those in Dahl's earlier books.

Undoubtedly Dahl is a writer who has readability and instant appeal to children. If some sombre adults question his literary standing and morality it is because their view of children's literature is that it is for knowledge and education rather than for "wonder and delight."

—Jean Russell

DALGLIESH, Alice. American. Born in Trinidad, West Indies, 7 October 1893; emigrated to the United States, 1902; naturalized citizen. Educated at the Pratt Institute, Brooklyn, New York, diploma in kindergarten teaching; Teachers College, Columbia University, New York, A.B. in English and education, M.A. Teacher of kindergarten and elementary education for 17 years; teacher at Horace Mann School, New York; Editor, Books for Young Readers, Charles Scribner's Sons, Inc., New York, 1934–60. Contributing Editor, *Saturday Review*, New York, 1960–66. Address: P.O. Box 283, Woodbury, Connecticut 06798, U.S.A.

PUBLICATIONS FOR CHILDREN

Fiction

> *West Indian Play Days*, illustrated by Margaret Evans Price.   Chicago, Rand McNally, 1926.
> *The Little Wooden Farmer, and The Story of the Jungle Pool*, illustrated by Theodora Baumeister.   New York, Macmillan, 1930; revised edition, 1968; London, Hamish Hamilton, 1969.
> *The Blue Teapot: Sandy Cove Stories*, illustrated by Hildegard Woodward.   New York, Macmillan, 1931.
> *The Choosing Book*, illustrated by Eloise Burns Wilkin.   New York, Macmillan, 1932.
> *Relief's Rocker*, illustrated by Hildegard Woodward.   New York, Macmillan, 1932.
> *Roundabout*, illustrated by Hildegard Woodward.   New York, Macmillan, 1934.
> *Sailor Sam*, illustrated by the author.   New York, Scribner, 1935.
> *The Smiths and Rusty*, illustrated by Berta and Elmer Hader.   New York and London, Scribner, 1936.

Wings for the Smiths, illustrated by Berta and Elmer Hader.   New York and London, Scribner, 1937.

The Young Aunts, illustrated by Charlotte Becker.   New York and London, Scribner, 1939.

The Hollyberrys, illustrated by Pru Herric.   New York and London, Scribner, 1939.

Wooden Shoes in America, illustrated by Lois Maloy.   New York, Scribner, 1940.

A Book for Jennifer: A Story of London Children in the Eighteenth Century and of Mr. Newbery's Juvenile Library, illustrated by Katherine Milhous.   New York, Scribner, 1940.

Three from Greenways, illustrated by Gertrude Howe.   New York, Scribner, and London, Hodder and Stoughton, 1941.

Gulliver Joins the Army, illustrated by Ellen Segner.   New York, Scribner, 1942.

The Little Angel, illustrated by Katherine Milhous.   New York, Scribner, 1943.

The Silver Pencil, illustrated by Katherine Milhous.   New York, Scribner, 1944.

Along Janet's Road, illustrated by Katherine Milhous.   New York, Scribner, 1946.

Reuben and His Red Wheelbarrow, illustrated by Ilse Bischoff.   New York, Grosset and Dunlap, 1946.

The Davenports Are at Dinner, illustrated by Flavia Gág.   New York, Scribner, 1948.

The Davenports and Cherry Pie, illustrated by Flavia Gág.   New York, Scribner, 1949.

The Bears on Hemlock Mountain, illustrated by Helen Sewell.   New York, Scribner, 1952; London, Epworth Press, 1965.

The Courage of Sarah Noble, illustrated by Leonard Weisgard.   New York, Scribner, 1954; London, Hamish Hamilton, 1970.

Adam and the Golden Cock, illustrated by Leonard Weisgard.   New York, Scribner, 1959.

Other

A Happy School Year (reader), illustrated by Mary Spoor Brand.   Chicago, Rand McNally, 1924.

Peregrin and the Goldfish, illustrated by Tom Seidmann-Freud.   New York, Macmillan, 1929.

First Experiences with Literature (textbook).   New York, Scribner, 1932.

America Travels: The Story of a Hundred Years of Travel in America, illustrated by Hildegard Woodward.   New York, Macmillan, 1933; revised edition, 1961.

Long Live the King! A Story Book of English Kings and Queens, illustrated by Lois Maloy.   New York, Scribner, 1937.

America Begins: The Story of the Finding of the New World, illustrated by Lois Maloy.   New York and London, Scribner, 1938; revised edition, 1959.

America Builds Homes: The Story of the First Colonies, illustrated by Lois Maloy.   New York and London, Scribner, 1938.

Wings Around South America, illustrated by Katherine Milhous.   New York, Scribner, 1941.

The True Story of Fala, with Margaret Suckley.   New York, Scribner, 1942.

They Live in South America, illustrated by Katherine Milhous and Frances Lichten.   New York, Scribner, 1942.

The Thanksgiving Story, illustrated by Helen Sewell.   New York, Scribner, 1954.

The Columbus Story, illustrated by Leo Politi.   New York, Scribner, 1955.

The Fourth of July Story, illustrated by Marie Nonnast.   New York, Scribner, 1956.

Ride the Wind (on Charles Lindbergh), illustrated by Georges Schreiber.   New York, Scribner, 1956.

Editor, *Christmas: A Book of Stories New and Old,* illustrated by Hildegard Woodward.   New York, Scribner, 1934; as *A Christmas Holiday Book,* London, Dent, 1934.

Editor, *Once on a Time* (folktales), illustrated by Katherine Milhous.   New York and London, Scribner, 1938.

Editor, with Françoise, *The Gay Mother Goose*, illustrated by Françoise.   New York and London, Scribner, 1938.

Editor, *The Will James Cowboy Book*.   New York, Scribner, 1938.

Editor, *Happily Ever After: Fairy Tales*, illustrated by Katherine Milhous.   New York and London, Scribner, 1939.

Editor, *St. George and the Dragon*, by Richard Johnson, illustrated by Lois Maloy.   New York, Scribner, 1941.

Editor, *The Enchanted Book*, illustrated by Concetta Cacciola.   New York, Scribner, 1947.

PUBLICATIONS FOR ADULTS

Other

Selected Books for Young Children, with *Selected Pictures for Young Children*, by Rita Scherman.   New York, Educational Playthings, 1934.

The Horace Mann Kindergarten for Five-Year-Old Children, with Charlotte Garrison and Emma Sheehy.   New York, Columbia University Teachers College, 1937.

Editor, with Annis Duff, *Aids to Choosing Books for Your Children*.   New York, Children's Book Council, 1957.

*   *   *

Alice Dalgliesh's rich background as a British and American subject, as a kindergarten and elementary school teacher, and as a children's book editor are all reflected in her many different types of children's books, with their wide variety of locale, period, and subject matter. Perhaps Dalgliesh's information books are her most popular ones; many have gone through various editions, and, in the case of *America Travels*, the second edition is revised and enlarged. This work is characteristic of Dalgliesh's competent treatment of information and history. The style is casual, with a strong emphasis on dialogue, factual exposition, and indirect characterization. This particular work contains eight "traveling tales," as diverse as the story about a young pioneer child who travels alone by stage coach, and a story about "two boys and the first automobile that came to town." The intent of the author is to give a young reading audience a taste of a broad range of accurate subject matter related to travel.

This attention to accuracy, detail, and diversity is also characteristic of *The Thanksgiving Story, The Fourth of July Story*, and *Christmas: A Book of Stories New and Old*. The exactness of detail and perspective in the information books is reflected in Dalgliesh's juvenile historical novels, such as *Adam and the Golden Cock*, based on a true story that occurred around Newton, Connecticut, in 1781, and *The Courage of Sarah Nobel*, also a true story, about an eight-year-old child who travels through the wilderness into Indian country to cook for her father while he builds a new home. Sarah's perceptions about the Indian community and the "humanness" of its members are of real value to the child who grows up with a demeaning and stereotyped impression of American Indians superimposed on him from all sides.

Alice Dalgliesh's characters and stories are all given life and moment because of the author's attention to image, detail, and believability. For this reason, two of Dalgliesh's picture books for young children have remained perennial favorites. *The Little Wooden Farmer*, in a recent edition with fine illustrations by Anita Lobel, is a repetition book emphasizing the progressive steps one takes to produce a well-appointed farm. Because of the dialogue, repetition, and progression, the book reads well aloud. Dalgliesh apparently realized this when she first published the story in 1930 as one "to read and play." The dramatic quality of Dalgliesh's picture books is seen best is *The Bears on Hemlock Mountain*. This is a tense, suspenseful, and characteristically imaginative tale that lends itself both to reading aloud and acting out. Behind all of Dalgliesh's work is a strong sense of the child audience for which it is written, and a delight in language, detail, situation, and action.

—Rachel Fordyce

DALLAS, Ruth. New Zealander. Born in Invercargill, 29 September 1919. Educated at Southland Technical College, Invercargill. Recipient: New Zealand Literary Fund Achievement Award, 1962; University of Otago Robert Burns Fellowship, 1968. Address: 448 Leith Street, Dunedin, New Zealand.

PUBLICATIONS FOR CHILDREN

Fiction

> *The Children in the Bush*, illustrated by Peter Campbell.   London, Methuen, 1969.
> *Ragamuffin Scarecrow*, illustrated by Els Noordhof.   Dunedin, Otago University Bibliography Room, 1969.
> *A Dog Called Wig*, illustrated by Edward Mortelmans.   London, Methuen, 1970.
> *The Wild Boy in the Bush*, illustrated by Peter Campbell.   London, Methuen, 1971.
> *The Big Flood in the Bush*, illustrated by Peter Campbell.   London, Methuen, 1972.
> *The House on the Cliffs*, illustrated by Gavin Rowe.   London, Methuen, 1975.

Other

> *Sawmilling Yesterday*, illustrated by Juliet Peter.   Wellington, Department of Education, 1958.

PUBLICATIONS FOR ADULTS

Verse

> *Country Road and Other Poems 1947–52.*   Christchurch, Caxton Press, 1953.
> *The Turning Wheel.*   Christchurch, Caxton Press, 1961.
> *Experiment in Form.*   Dunedin, Otago University Bibliography Room, 1964.
> *Day Book: Poems of a Year.*   Christchurch, Caxton Press, 1966.
> *Shadow Show.*   Christchurch, Caxton Press, 1968.
> *Walking on the Snow.*   Christchurch, Caxton Press, 1976.
> *Song for a Guitar.*   Dunedin, Otago University Press, 1976.

Manuscript Collection: Hocken Library, University of Otago, Dunedin, New Zealand.

Ruth Dallas comments:
    In New Zealand when I was a child, the books I read came from England and were to a certain extent foreign, in that I had never seen the environment I was reading about: big cities, attached houses, upstairs bedrooms, nurseries, nannies, fathers who were abroad, English villages, gamekeepers, and all historical material, including very old houses – in short, the common paraphernalia of children's fiction as I first encountered it. Even the elderly people in my family had grown up in a setting that was quite different from the "old country." Between the oral New Zealand tales I heard and storybook stories from overseas,

there was a gap that disturbed me for a long time. I began to write stories about New Zealand children for the school journals in 1958. My first children's novel was published in London in 1969 and was based on tales I had heard in my own family. I had noticed that children were growing up who did not know that much of their green farmland was once covered with the forest that is now found in reserves and that not only old pioneers had lived in the bush but children, too. I plan to continue writing New Zealand stories, both historical and contemporary, as well as poetry.

*   *   *

Ruth Dallas is best known in her own country as a poet who particularly evokes the landscape of southern South Island. Both her prose and poetry for children have been made available to numerous young New Zealanders through the School Journals, enlightened publications put out by the Department of Education for reading in schools.

The connection with educational purpose may in part contribute to the slightly didactic nature of her earlier works. *The Children in the Bush, The Wild Boy in the Bush,* and *The Big Flood in the Bush* all rather self-consciously teach about the life of the Early Settlers but are made vivid by the liveliness of their characterization. All three books feature a family of four 19th-century children whose vigour, enthusiasm and propensity for getting into not unlikely scrapes in the absences of their widowed mother, the Settlement's nurse, are reminiscent of E. Nesbit's. Ruth Dallas has the rare gift of conveying a "child's eye view" and these books are recounted by the youngest – 8-year-old Jean. The angle of the narrative is convincingly hers, whether she describes laughing and talking after bedtime so that "Mrs. Bain came into the room in her petticoat" or the frequent crises with their cow, who rejoiced in the inspired name of "Hokey-Pokey."

The numerous animal stories, plays and poems published in the "Journals" have reached fruition in *A Dog Called Wig,* which must be one of the most unusual of all animal stories. Here a boy, who initially has to plead with his parents to keep the stray dog which has appeared in the garden, subsequently feels betrayed and disillusioned by the animal's attachment to his father. Only after the dog is badly injured and the boy involved in an exciting adventure with escaped Borstal inmates, is the relationship restored.

These books are all in an "easy to read" format which, while most suitable to the less confident reader, are stylistically cramping. In *The House on the Cliffs,* however, Ms. Dallas has profited by a longer book for an older reader. In this evocative story the images of shells, wind, rocks, and solitary sea-birds, which occur so frequently in her poems, become symbols of the delicate balance between loneliness and independence in the relationship between eccentric old Biddy Bristow and two present-day schoolgirls. This story has the different levels of meaning so characteristic of both good poetry and good children's literature, and in Biddy's single-minded beach searchings for "a bell to ring when the wind blows" we learn something of the nature of creative seeking. Here at last is a happy marriage between the children's writer and the poet.

—Betty Gilderdale

DALY, Maureen. American. Born in Castle Caulfield, County Tyrone, Ireland. Educated at St. Mary Springs Academy, Fond du Lac, Wisconsin; Rosary College, River Forest, Illinois, B.A. Married William P. McGivern in 1948; has two children. Police Reporter and Columnist, *Chicago Tribune,* 1946–48; Associate Editor, *Ladies' Home Journal,* Philadelphia, 1948–54; Editorial Consultant, *Saturday Evening Post,* Philadelphia, 1960–69. Agent: Lurton Blassingame, 10 East 43rd Street, New York, New York 10017. Address: 73–305 Ironwood Street, Palm Desert, California 92260, U.S.A.

PUBLICATIONS FOR CHILDREN

Fiction

> *Seventeenth Summer.* New York, Dodd Mead, 1942; London, Hollis and Carter, 1947.
> *Patrick Visits the Farm,* illustrated by Ellie Simmons. New York, Dodd Mead, 1959.
> *Patrick Takes a Trip,* illustrated by Ellie Simmons. New York, Dodd Mead, 1960.
> *Sixteen and Other Stories,* illustrated by Kendall Rossi. New York, Dodd Mead, 1961.
> *Patrick Visits the Library,* illustrated by Paul Lantz. New York, Dodd Mead, 1961.
> *Patrick Visits the Zoo,* illustrated by Sam Savitt. New York, Dodd Mead, 1963.
> *The Ginger Horse,* illustrated by Wesley Dennis. New York, Dodd Mead, 1964.
> *The Small War of Sergeant Donkey,* illustrated by Wesley Dennis. New York, Dodd Mead, 1966.
> *Rosie, The Dancing Elephant,* illustrated by Lorence Bjorklund. New York, Dodd Mead, 1967.

Other

> *What's Your P.Q. (Personality Quotient)?,* illustrated by Ellie Simmons. New York, Dodd Mead, 1952; revised edition, 1966.
> *Spain: Wonderland of Contrasts.* New York, Dodd Mead, 1965.

> Editor, *My Favorite Mystery Stories.* New York, Dodd Mead, 1966.
> Editor, *My Favorite Suspense Stories.* New York, Dodd Mead, 1968.

PUBLICATIONS FOR ADULTS

Other

> *Smarter and Smoother: A Handbook on How to Be That Way.* New York, Dodd Mead, 1944.
> *The Perfect Hostess: Complete Etiquette and Entertainment for the Home.* New York, Dodd Mead, 1948.
> *Twelve Around the World.* New York, Dodd Mead, 1957.
> *Mention My Name in Mombasa: The Unscheduled Adventures of an American Family Abroad* (as Maureen Daly McGivern), with William P. McGivern. New York, Dodd Mead, 1958.
> *Spanish Roundabout.* New York, Dodd Mead, 1960.
> *Moroccan Roundabout.* New York, Dodd Mead, 1961.

> Editor, *My Favorite Stories.* New York, Dodd Mead, 1948.
> Editor, *Profile of Youth.* Philadelphia, Lippincott, 1951.

Manuscript Collection: University of Oregon Library, Eugene.

*   *   *

"In almost everything I write," Maureen Daly has said, "I seem to travel far for the subject – or else write microscopically about things that happen right at home." She has traveled thousands of miles preparing her book on teen-agers, *Twelve Around the World,* and her other travel books. Closer to home are her books on etiquette and the social proprieties.

And right from her own home town, by the shores of Lake Winnebago in Fond du Lac, Wisconsin, came her first and most lasting stories. As a sophomore in high school, she learned, along with her classmates, to appreciate good writing under the tutelage of a gifted enthusiastic teacher. "The entire class soon wanted to become authors," she remembers. At fifteen, with a story entitled "Fifteen," she won fourth place in a national short story contest conducted by *Scholastic Magazine*. The next year, she won first place with "Sixteen," a story reprinted in the 1938 annual O. Henry Memorial Award volume. "Sixteen" is a spare first-rate story that says more in seven pages than most say in seventy. "You Can't Kiss Caroline" is memorable for its lovely surprise ending; and the true story of a nun from the nursing order of Sisters on the island of Ibiza, just off the coast of Barcelona, elicited a response from a doctor who wanted to contribute money to the good work carried on by the nuns. "Love Is a Summer Word" is an excerpt from Maureen Daly's first novel and most successful work, *Seventeenth Summer*.

Seventeenth Summer is a sensitively written sincere story of an adolescent's awakening to the raptures and anxieties of a first young love. It was an instantaneous hit. Teen-agers claimed it at once as their own. There had been teen-age books but, magically, this one was written by one of their own crowd, then a sophomore in college, who intuitively sensed the fears and doubts, the heights and depths of their emotions at that moment. The novel's personal viewpoint reflected their feelings of insecurity, of humiliation, of heavenly exhilaration; their daydreams and endless streams of speculation about themselves and their codes of behavior. For the lonely outsider, the unsophisticated girl who did not smoke or drink or pet, the heroine's innocence and natural artlessness were immensely reassuring. It was a time of blossoming, of new beginnings, of discovering values, forming relationships and growing up to one's own responsibilities.

Maureen Daly had heeded well the advice of her high school teacher who had urged her students to try to look honestly at themselves and to write what they knew about. *Seventeenth Summer* is a story written "microscopically," with distinction.

—Mary Silva Cosgrave

DANIELL, David Scott. Pseudonym for Albert Scott Daniell. British. Born in London, 1 July 1906. Educated at Bedford Modern School. Served in the Royal Engineers, Eighth Army, in Sicily and Italy, 1941–46: Captain. Married Elizabeth Mary Thirlby in 1939. Worked for the Commonwealth Trust, Gold Coast, 1929–30. *Died 29 August 1965.*

PUBLICATIONS FOR CHILDREN

Fiction

Mission for Oliver, illustrated by William Stobbs. London, Cape, 1953.
Polly and Oliver, illustrated by William Stobbs. London, Cape, 1954.
The Dragon and the Rose, illustrated by Sheila Stratton. London, Cape, 1955; New York, Abelard Schuman, 1957.
Hunt Royal, illustrated by William Stobbs. London, Cape, 1958.
Hideaway Johnny, illustrated by Val Biro. Leicester, Brockhampton Press, 1959.
The Boy They Made King, illustrated by William Stobbs. London, Cape, 1959; New York, Duell, 1960.
Polly and Oliver at Sea, illustrated by William Stobbs. London, Cape, 1960.
The Rajah's Treasure, illustrated by William Stobbs. New York, Duell, 1960.
Sandro's Battle, illustrated by Colin Spencer. London, Cape, and New York, Duell, 1962.
By Jiminy, illustrated by D. G. Valentine. Leicester, Brockhampton Press, 1962.
Saved by Jiminy, illustrated by D. G. Valentine. Leicester, Brockhampton Press, 1963.
Polly and Oliver Besieged, illustrated by William Stobbs. London, Cape, 1963.

By Jiminy Ahoy, illustrated by D. G. Valentine.   Leicester, Brockhampton Press, 1963.
By Jiminy in the Jungle, illustrated by D. G. Valentine.   Leicester, Brockhampton Press, 1964.
Polly and Oliver Pursued, illustrated by William Stobbs.   London, Cape, 1964.
Horsey and Co. and the Bank Robbers (as Richard Bowood), illustrated by A. Oxenham.   London, Golden Pleasure Books, 1965.
By Jiminy in the Highlands, illustrated by D. G. Valentine.   Leicester, Brockhampton Press, 1966.
Red Gaskell's Gold (as Richard Bowood), illustrated by Peter Kesteven.   London, Macmillan, and New York, St. Martin's Press, 1966.

Plays

Children's Theatre Plays (includes *Hide-and-Seek; The Queen and Mr. Shakespeare; The King's Messenger; Stand and Deliver; The Adventure; The Jester, The Queen, and the Hen*).   London, Harrap, 1948.
More Children's Theatre Plays (includes *Hereward the Wake, The Gascon Ring, The Stowaway, The Silver Snuff Box*), illustrated by Elizabeth Thirlby.   London, Harrap, 1951.
Costume Plays for Schools (includes *Hunt Royal, The Ring of Gold, Roses for the Queen, Tyger's Hart, Treasure Hunt*).   London, Harrap, 1955.
Faith of Our Fathers: The Story of Christianity in Britain (includes *A.D. 150–878: Go Preach in Heathen Britain, 1100–1382: The Glory of the Medieval Church, 1537–1620: The Years of Conflict, 1662–1960: Freely to Worship*), with G. W. H. Lampe.   London, University of London Press, 4 vols., 1961.
Letters for the Prince, in *Junior One-Act Plays of To-Day, Fourth Series*, edited by Harold Gardiner.   London, Harrap, 1963.

Other

Flight One to *Six: Australia, Canada, United States of America, India, Africa*, and *The Holy Land*, illustrated by Jack Matthew.   Loughborough, Leicestershire, Wills and Hepworth, 6 vols., 1958–62.
The Story of Flight (as Richard Bowood), illustrated by Robert Ayton.   Loughborough, Leicestershire, Wills and Hepworth, 1960.
The Golden Pomegranate, illustrated by George Adamson.   London, University of London Press, 1960.
Great Inventions (as Richard Bowood), illustrated by Robert Ayton.   Loughborough, Leicestershire, Wills and Hepworth, 1961.
Ladybird Book of London (as John Lewesdon).   Loughborough, Leicestershire, Wills and Hepworth, 1961.
The Story of Railways (as Richard Bowood), illustrated by Robert Ayton.   Loughborough, Leicestershire, Wills and Hepworth, 1961.
The Story of Ships (as Richard Bowood), illustrated by Robert Ayton.   Loughborough, Leicestershire, Wills and Hepworth, 1961.
Battles and Battlefields, illustrated by William Stobbs.   London, Batsford, 1961.
Discovering the Bible, with G. W. H. Lampe, illustrated by Graham Oakley.   London, University of London Press, 1961; Nashville, Abingdon Press, 1966.
The Weather (as Richard Bowood), with F. E. Newing, illustrated by J. H. Wingfield.   Loughborough, Leicestershire, Wills and Hepworth, 1962.
Explorers and Exploration, illustrated by William Stobbs.   London, Batsford, 1962.
Magnets, Bulbs and Batteries (as Richard Bowood), with F. E. Newing, illustrated by J. H. Wingfield.   Loughborough, Leicestershire, Wills and Hepworth, 1962.
Lights, Mirrors and Lenses (as Richard Bowood), with F. E. Newing, illustrated by J. H. Wingfield.   Loughborough, Leicestershire, Wills and Hepworth, 1962.

Levers, Pulleys and Engines (as Richard Bowood), with F. E. Newing, illustrated by J. H. Wingfield. Loughborough, Leicestershire, Wills and Hepworth, 1963.

Air, Wind and Flight (as Richard Bowood), with F. E. Newing, illustrated by J. H. Wingfield. Loughborough, Leicestershire, Wills and Hepworth, 1963.

The Story of Houses and Homes (as Richard Bowood), illustrated by Robert Ayton. Loughborough, Leicestershire, Wills and Hepworth, 1963.

Naples Ahead (as Richard Bowood), illustrated by David Knight. London, Macmillan, and New York, St. Martin's Press, 1964.

The Story of Clothes and Costume (as Richard Bowood), illustrated by Robert Ayton. Loughborough, Leicestershire, Wills and Hepworth, 1964.

The Story of Our Churches and Cathedrals (as Richard Bowood), illustrated by Robert Ayton. Loughborough, Leicestershire, Wills and Hepworth, 1964.

Soldiers (as Richard Bowood). London, Hamlyn, 1965.

Animals and How They Live (as Richard Bowood), with F. E. Newing, illustrated by Ronald Lampitt. Loughborough, Leicestershire, Wills and Hepworth, 1965.

Plants and How They Grow (as Richard Bowood), with F. E. Newing, illustrated by Ronald Lampitt. Loughborough, Leicestershire, Wills and Hepworth, 1965.

Discovering the Army, illustrated by Crispin Fisher. London, University of London Press, 1965.

Our Land in the Making: Earliest Times to the Norman Conquest and *Norman Conquest to Present Day* (as Richard Bowood), illustrated by Ronald Lampitt. Loughborough, Leicestershire, Wills and Hepworth, 2 vols., 1966.

Birds and How They Live (as Richard Bowood), with F. E. Newing, illustrated by Ronald Lampitt. Loughborough, Leicestershire, Wills and Hepworth, 1966.

Sea Fights. London, Batsford, 1966.

Underwater Exploration (as Richard Bowood), illustrated by B. Knight. Loughborough, Leicestershire, Wills and Hepworth, 1967.

Your Body, illustrated by Robert Ayton. Loughborough, Leicestershire, Wills and Hepworth, 1967.

PUBLICATIONS FOR ADULTS

Novels

Young English. London, Cape, 1931.
Morning's at Seven. London, Cape, 1940.
The Time of the Singing. London, Cape, 1941.
Nicholas Wilde. London, Cape, 1948.
Fifty Pounds for a Dead Parson. London, Cape, 1960.

Other

Cap of Honour: The Story of the Gloucestershire Regiment (the 28th/61st Foot), 1694–1950. London, Harrap, 1951.
Royal Hampshire Regiment, 1918–1950, vol. 3. Aldershot, Hampshire, Gale and Polden, 1955.
History of the East Surrey Regiment, 1920–1952, vol. 4. London, Benn, 1957.
4th Hussar: The Story of the 4th Queen's Own Hussars, 1685–1958. Aldershot, Hampshire, Gale and Polden, 1959.
World War 1 and *2: An Illustrated History.* London, Benn, 2 vols., 1965–66.

*   *   *

David Scott Daniell was a full-time professional writer with many interests. Whatever he wrote is distinctive for the enthusiasm he brought to his subject and for the desire to share

341

that enthusiasm with his readers. As a story-teller he tends to stand outside the action, so that the effect is as if we were watching a film or a play. Indeed his first published work for children was a collection of some of the costume plays he had written for Bertha Waddell's theatre, and from these and his work for radio come his ability to handle dialogue and his penchant for dramatic happenings and swift changes of fortune.

The five Polly and Oliver stories, two of which were originally written as radio plays, are in effect costume dramas in narrative form. Oliver is a drummer boy in the 111th Regiment of Foot at the time of the Napoleonic Wars. His long-suffering sergeant is also his uncle, whose daughter Polly accompanies the regiment everywhere and Oliver most places. The adventures of the pair of them take place on land and sea in Sicily, Spain and India, and involve soldiers and bandits, spies and subterfuges, chases and captures, misunderstandings and mistaken identities. They are fun to read and are also full of authentic military and nautical detail.

Another series of adventure stories is that woven round the lively and resourceful By Jiminy, a modern Neapolitan shoe-shine boy, and his English friends, the twins Tom and Sukie, children of an archaeologist. Though basically these are straightforward and easily assimilable variations on the theme of children versus crooks, there are sufficient characterisation, genuine humour, and accurate archaeological background to lift them above many other stories of this kind.

Of the individual historical novels *The Boy They Made King* successfully illuminates the story of Lambert Simnel. The character of Lambert himself is especially well-drawn, and his transition from shoe-maker's son to royal imposter and back again to ordinary boy is completely convincing. *Hunt Royal*, about the flight of Charles II, is along more conventional lines, but Daniell is a good enough writer to make Charles a character in his own right and to take advantage of opportunities for dramatic irony. A particularly good scene is that in which three boys staying in the house in which Charles is hiding are interrogated by Cromwell's officers.

In *Sandro's Battle*, a boy, living with his composer father and a beloved donkey in a castle in Italy during World War II, is involved with soldiers on both sides when the area becomes a no-man's land between the two armies, and the castle a strategic position. The dialogue sparkles and the fun is fast, but the underlying message is serious – war destroys innocent bystanders and causes them to lose their homes and possessions; it also makes ordinary and friendly people range themselves against each other to kill.

—Antony Kamm

DARKE, Marjorie. British. Born in Birmingham, Warwickshire, 25 January 1929. Educated at Worcester Grammar School for Girls, 1938–46; Leicester College of Art and Technology, 1946–50; Central School of Art, London, 1950. Has two sons and one daughter. Textile designer, John Lewis Partnership, London, 1951–54. Address: c/o Penguin Books, Harmondsworth, Middlesex UB7 0DA, England.

PUBLICATIONS FOR CHILDREN

Fiction

Ride the Iron Horse, illustrated by Michael Jackson. London, Longman, 1973.
The Star Trap, illustrated by Michael Jackson. London, Longman, 1974.
Mike's Bike, illustrated by Jim Russell. London, Penguin, 1974.

A Question of Courage, illustrated by Janet Archer.   London, Penguin, and New York,
    Crowell, 1975.
What Can I Do?, illustrated by Barry Wilkinson.   London, Penguin, 1975.
The Big Brass Band, illustrated by Charles Front.   London, Penguin, 1976.
Kipper's Turn, illustrated by Mary Dinsdale.   Glasgow, Blackie, 1976.
My Uncle Charlie, illustrated by Jannat Houston.   London, Penguin, 1977.
The First of Midnight, illustrated by Anthony Morris.   London, Penguin, 1977.

Marjorie Darke comments:
    Unlike many writers, I came to the craft late. Although I have always been an avid reader
the idea of writing stories did not occur until greater leisure − when my children went to
school − made me aware of an ever-growing need to do something more creative and
demanding than housework. Writing specifically for children was not a conscious choice. In
my opinion too much emphasis is placed on the dividing line between stories for children and
those for adults. I write for myself, the characters and storyline often beginning with a chance
conversation, a few words overheard in the street, something read in a book or seen on
television. Once born the people in my imagination have a curious knack of assuming a life of
their own, their actions often veering away from paths I have planned for them. I find it
difficult to pin-point the reasons why I have often chosen historical backgrounds for my
work. They may stem from a lifelong love of hearing tales told by my mother and
grandmother of "when I was a girl." Certainly it had nothing to do with school history
which I found dry and boring except for the rare times we studied the lives of ordinary
people. People, in fact, are my main concern − trying to bring back their lives and make them
as real as if they were here today.
    Stories for very young children were a later development in my writing career, requiring a
different but no less demanding technique; one must never "write down" or patronise. And
because children are clear sighted and perceptive, endeavouring to entertain them continues
to be a great challenge and an ever-growing pleasure.

              *   *   *

    Marjorie Darke writes about spirited, energetic people who attempt to take up new
challenges in times of great social change when many are hostile to that change. She has a
fine sense of period and place confidently evoked by conventions, speech, the detail of a dress
fastening or of a kitchen implement.
    Darke's first novel, Ride the Iron Horse, is a dramatic well-paced tale of conflicts of loyalty.
John, an illiterate farm labourer, dreams of becoming an engineer on the new railways. Its
sequel, The Star Trap, is the story of Squire's daughter Frances, John's friend, who runs
away from home to be an actress in defiance of conventions. While the hardships of life in a
travelling theatrical company are told with convincing lack of glamour, the book is dull and
marred by an unlikely romance across class barriers, between Frances and John. This novel
points, however, to Darke's increasing interest in the role of women in history.
    In A Question of Courage a Birmingham seamstress, Emily, is caught up in the Suffragette
movement. Despite another unlikely romance − between working-class Emily and upper-
class Peter − the book humorously reveals Emily's strong and forceful personality within the
context of her growing involvement in the cause, and it provides a rich picture of the times in
which the issues were fought out.
    In The First of Midnight Jess, an energetic and forceful Poorhouse girl, escapes the
servitude of her own existence and helps a black slave gain his freedom. Through this
attractive, dynamic heroine Darke again lays emphasis on women's role in history. Above
all, this book gives a lively picture of 18th-century Portsmouth and its economic dependence
on the slave trade by describing with wit and panache those involved − ruthless and
unscrupulous for all their respectability. This is Darke's best book so far and a promising first

volume of a trilogy that could establish her as an important historical novelist.

In her books for children just learning to read (e.g., *Mike's Bike*) Marjorie Darke demonstrates an ability to tell a simple tale in short sentences with clarity and feeling.

—Rosemary Stones

DAUGHERTY, James (Henry). American. Born in Asheville, North Carolina, 1 June 1889. Educated at Corcoran School of Art, Washington, D.C.; Pennsylvania Academy of Fine Arts, Philadelphia; London School of Art. Worked as a ship camouflager during World War I. Married Sonia Medvedeva in 1913; one son. Artist and illustrator: murals in Cleveland, and in Weston, Fairfield, and Stamford, Connecticut; retrospective exhibition, New York, 1971. Recipient: American Library Association Newbery Medal, 1940. *Died 12 February 1974.*

PUBLICATIONS FOR CHILDREN (illustrated by the author)

Fiction

    Andy and the Lion. New York, Viking Press, 1938.
    The Picnic. New York, Viking Press, 1958.

Verse

    The Wild, Wild West. Philadelphia, McKay, 1948.
    West of Boston. New York, Viking Press, 1956.

Other

    Daniel Boone. New York, Viking Press, 1939.
    Poor Richard. New York, Viking Press, 1941.
    Abraham Lincoln. New York, Viking Press, 1943.
    The Landing of the Pilgrims. New York, Random House, 1950.
    Of Courage Undaunted: Across the Continent with Lewis and Clark. New York, Viking Press, 1951.
    Trappers and Traders of the Far West. New York, Random House, 1952.
    Marcus and Narcissa Whitman, Pioneers of Oregon. New York, Viking Press, 1953.
    The Magna Charta. New York, Random House, 1956.
    William Blake. New York, Viking Press, 1960.

    Editor, *The Kingdom and the Power and the Glory: Stories of Faith and Marvel.* New York, Knopf, 1929.
    Editor, *Their Weight in Wildcats: Tales of the Frontier.* Boston, Houghton Mifflin, 1936.
    Editor, *In the Beginning, Being the First Chapter of Genesis from the King James Version.* New York and London, Oxford University Press, 1941.
    Editor, *Walt Whitman's America* (selections). Cleveland, World, 1964.
    Editor, *Henry David Thoreau, A Man of Our Time.* New York, Viking Press, 1967.
    Editor, *The Sound of Trumpets: Selections from Ralph Waldo Emerson.* New York, Viking Press, 1971.

PUBLICATIONS FOR ADULTS

Other

An Outline of Government in Connecticut, edited by Philip E. Curtiss. Hartford, Connecticut, House Committee on Public Information, 1944.

Bibliography: "James Henry Daugherty: A Bibliography" by Edward and Elaine Kemp, in Imprint: Oregon (Eugene), Fall 1975.

Manuscript Collection: University of Oregon Library, Eugene.

Illustrator: Tad Sheldon, Boy Scout by John Fleming Wilson, 1913; King Penguin by Richard Henry Horne, 1925; The Lost Gospel by Arthur Cheney Train, 1925; The Plucky Allens by Clara Pierson, 1925; The Adventures of Johnny T. Bear by Margaret McElroy, 1926; Daniel Boone: Wilderness Scout by Stewart Edward White, 1926; The Mountain of Jade by Violet Irwin and Vilhjalmur Stefansson, 1926; Drake's Quest by Cameron Rogers, 1927; Kris and Kristina by Marie Bruce, 1927; The Splendid Spur edited by Arthur Quiller-Couch, 1927; The Story of Bread, 1927, The Story of Milk, 1927, and The Story of Textiles, 1928, all by Elizabeth Watson; Abe Lincoln Grows Up 1928, and Early Moon, 1930, by Carl Sandburg; The Blacksmith and the Blackbirds by Edith Rickert, 1928; The Conquest of Montezuma's Empire by Andrew Lang, 1928; Hugh Gwyeth by Beulah Dix, 1928; Irene of Tundra Towers, 1928, and Judy of the Whale Gates, 1930, by Elizabeth Burrows; Knickerbocker's History of New York, 1928, and The Bold Dragoon, 1930, by Washington Irving; The Stream of History by Geoffrey Parsons, 1928; Tuftoo, the Clown by Howard Garis, 1928; The White Company by Arthur Conan Doyle, 1928; Wulnoth, The Wanderer by Herbert Inman, 1928; Courageous Companions by Charles Joseph Finger, 1929; Three Comedies by William Shakespeare, 1929; Uncle Tom's Cabin by Harriet Beecher Stowe, 1929; The Adventures of Johnny Appleseed by Henry Chapin, 1930; John Brown's Body by Stephen Vincent Benét, 1930; The Oregon Trail by Francis Parkman, 1931; The Adventures of Tom Sawyer by Mark Twain, 1932; Mashinka's Secret, 1932, All Things New, 1936, Vanka's Donkey, 1940, Wings of Glory, 1940, The Way of an Eagle, 1941, Ten Brave Men, 1951, Ten Brave Women, 1953, Thomas Jefferson, 1963, all by Sonia Medvedeva Daugherty; The Memoirs of Benvenuto Cellini, 1932; The Railroad to Freedom by Hildegarde Swift, 1932; The Sign of the Buffalo Skull by Peter O. Lamb, 1932; Windows on Henry Street by Lillian D. Wald, 1934; Girls of Glen Hazard, 1937, and Clue of the Faded Dress, 1938, by Maristan Chapman; Green Gravel by Dora Aydelotte, 1937; Over the Blue Wall, by Etta Lane Matthews, 1937; Call of the Mountain by Cornelia Meigs, 1940; Morgan's Fourth Son by Margaret Isabel Ross, 1940; Almanac for Americans by Willis Thornton, 1941, 1954; Barnaby Rudge by Charles Dickens, 1941; A Treasury of Best-Loved Hymns edited by Daniel Poling, 1942; Yankee Thunder, 1944, John Henry and the Double-Jointed Steam Drill, 1945, Joe Magarac and His U.S.A. Citizen Papers, 1948, and Heroes in American Folklore, 1962, all by Irwin Shapiro; Lincoln's Gettysburg Address, 1947; American Folklore and Its Old-World Backgrounds by Carl Lamsen Carmer, 1949; American Life in Literature edited by Jay Hubbell, 1949; The Authentic Revolution by Erwin Canham, 1950; Better Known as Johnny Appleseed by Mabel Leigh Hunt, 1950; Comanche by David Appel, 1951; A Long Way to Frisco by Alfred Powers, 1951; The Loudest Noise in the World, 1954, and Gillespie and the Guards 1956, by Benjamin Elkin; The Rainbow Book of American History by Earl Schenck Miers, 1955, 1968; The Last of the Mohicans by James Fenimore Cooper, 1957; Wisher, 1960, and Robert Goddard, 1964, by Charles Michael Daugherty; A Promise to Our Country by James Francis Calvert, 1961; The Three Musketeers by Alexandre Dumas, 1962.

*   *   *

Only an occasional page, such as James Daugherty's salute as illustrator to Father

345

Knickerbocker in *Knickerbocker's History of New York* foretells the remarkable command of English, the talent for melodic lines, exhibited privately in the journals young Daugherty kept while traveling as an art student of sixteen in England. That one page, along with bold, witty illustrations of typical Daugherty women and men with keen eyes, thrust jaws, and angular bodies, presaged Daugherty the writer.

Daugherty was nearly fifty when he became established as a writer, and perhaps because this talent had been dammed up for so many years, it seemed to pour forth rapidly after Daugherty completed his first book as author and illustrator, *Andy and the Lion*. The illustrations in *Andy* stand independently of the text, and, indeed, Daugherty had submitted them to his editor at Viking without words. However, with the addition of a simple, charming narration, he secured a balance between words and illustrations.

His second book, the first in which his talents as a writer are fully displayed, was *Daniel Boone*. Daugherty's appreciation, understanding, and admiration of this typically American figure are constantly evident. The prose, illustrations, and subject are a successful blend, and introduce the qualities which appear in nearly every book written by this artist, a major exponent of the Synchromist art school in the 1910's.

Daugherty's love of country, of American life and customs, the expanding frontier in American history, and of heroes, both legendary and historic, became the source for many books. Like the poet Walt Whitman, he celebrated many national events and people, but unlike Whitman, he did not sing of himself nor did he accept all American history at face value. He combined a serious regard for human values, when writing of Thoreau, Emerson, or Lincoln, with a somewhat sceptical view of the possible motivation of some American patriots. His sincere admiration for the Pilgrims (*The Landing of the Pilgrims*), the exploration of the American west (*Of Courage Undaunted: Across the Continent with Lewis and Clark*), and the hardy pioneer (*Marcus and Narcissa Whitman, Pioneers of Oregon*) is exemplified by his warm descriptions in prose and illustration. While he proclaimed in resonant prose or poetry, or both in combination, the deeds of his forebears, Daugherty was a good critic, with a turn of phrase or malicious facial expression shared with the reader; *West of Boston, The Wild, Wild, West*, and *Their Weight in Wildcats* are good examples.

Concern for fellow man, for the honest, self-reliant individual is expressed as Daugherty writes of Lincoln or introduces the transcendental philosophy of Emerson and Thoreau. Daugherty accepts the philosophy, which appears as an underlying theme in his work, while warning his reader that meditation cannot demand inward commitment: Thoreau and Emerson have obligations to their society. The matter is cause for comment in *West of Boston*.

Daugherty's place as a writer is assured in history. Although his subjects are American by birth or nature, their appeal is universal. Daugherty's mastery of language and humor, his appeal to the five senses, his celebration of life, understanding of mankind, and his love of all things fill each book. As a writer and illustrator with a good editorial sense, he knew how to combine, balance, and strengthen the art of writing and of illustration.

—Edward Kemp

---

d'AULAIRE, Edgar Parin.   American.   Born in Munich, Germany, 30 September 1898; emigrated to the United States in 1929; naturalized citizen, 1939. Educated at the Institute of Technology, 1917–19, and School of Applied Arts, 1919–22, Munich; studied art with Hans Hofmann, Munich, 1922–24, and with Andre Lhote and Pola Gauguin, Paris, 1925–29. Married Ingri Mortenson (i.e., Ingri Parin d'Aulaire, *q.v.*) in 1925; has two children. Artist: book illustrator, 1922–26; painted frescoes, Norway, 1926–27; graphic work exhibited in United States, Italy, Norway, Czechoslovakia, France. Recipient: American Library Association Caldecott Medal, 1940; Catholic Library Association Regina Medal, 1970. Address: 74 Mather Road, Georgetown, Connecticut 06829, U.S.A.

PUBLICATIONS FOR CHILDREN (with Ingri Parin d'Aulaire, illustrated by the authors)

Fiction

The Magic Rug. New York, Doubleday, 1931.
Ola. New York, Doubleday, 1932.
Ola and Blakken and Line, Sine, Trine. New York, Doubleday, 1933; revised edition, as *The Terrible Troll-Bird*, 1976.
Children of the Northlights. New York, Viking Press, 1935; London, Woodfield, 1960.
Animals Everywhere. New York, Doubleday, 1940; revised edition, 1954.
Don't Count Your Chicks. New York, Doubleday, 1943.
Wings for Per. New York, Doubleday, 1944.
Too Big. New York, Doubleday, 1945.
Nils. New York, Doubleday, 1948.
Foxie. New York, Doubleday, 1949; revised edition, as *Foxie the Singing Dog*, 1969.
The Two Cars. New York, Doubleday, 1955.
The Magic Meadow. New York, Doubleday, 1958.

Other

The Conquest of the Atlantic. New York, Viking Press, 1933.
George Washington. New York, Doubleday, 1936.
Abraham Lincoln. New York, Doubleday, 1939.
Leif the Lucky. New York, Doubleday, 1941.
Pocahontas. New York, Doubleday, 1946.
Benjamin Franklin. New York, Doubleday, 1950.
Buffalo Bill. New York, Doubleday, 1952.
Columbus. New York, Doubleday, 1955.
Book of Greek Myths. New York, Doubleday, 1962.
Norse Gods and Giants. New York, Doubleday, 1964.
Trolls (Norwegian folktales). New York, Doubleday, 1972.

Translator, *East of the Sun and West of the Moon: Twenty-One Norwegian Folktales*, by Peter Christen Asbjørnsen. New York, Viking Press, 1938; revised edition, 1966.

Manuscript Collections: Dartmouth College, Hanover, New Hampshire; University of Oregon, Eugene; Kerlan Collection, University of Minnesota, Minneapolis; de Grummond Collection, University of Southern Mississippi, Hattiesburg.

Illustrator: *Rama, The Hero of India* by Dhan Gopal Mukerji, 1930; *Blood* by Hanns J. Ewers, 1930; *Needle in a Haystack* by John Mattheson, 1930; *Coming of the Dragon Ships* by Florence McClurg Everson, 1931; *Kari* by Gabriel Scott, 1931; *Gao of the Ivory Coast* by Katherine Seabrook, 1931; with Ingri Parin d'Aulaire: *The Lord's Prayer*, 1934; *Sidsel Longskirt*, 1935, and *Solve Suntrap*, 1936, by Hans Aanrud, translated by Margery Williams Bianco and Dagay Mortenson; *The Star Spangled Banner* by Francis Scott Key, 1942; *Johnny Blossom* by Dikken Zwilgmeyer, 1948.

Edgar and Ingri Parin d'Aulaire comment:
For almost 50 years we have been working together on picture books, and still like it as much as when we first began. But when a book is finished we return to our individual paintings – which are still as different as when we first met. We have created a third personality for our books – it is not Edgar, it is not Ingri – it is a mixture of us both. We have no intention of ever becoming a monster with one head and four hands.

*   *   *

Working as a couple, the d'Aulaires have distilled over 20 picture books for children from their extensive research and travel. They become "one unity with two heads, four hands, and one handwriting when working." Producing books with Norwegian and American backgrounds predominantly, they steep themselves in the subject and locale for about a year prior to executing each one.

The most authoritative books are the seven with Norwegian settings. *Ola* incorporates Norwegian folklore motifs, customs and local color in the realistic story about a contemporary child. The sequel, *Ola and Blakken and Line, Sine, Trine* is more fanciful (and was reworked for a new edition called *The Terrible Troll-Bird*), Laplanders are followed through a year of seasonal activities in *Children of the Northlights*. Mythology is the subject matter for *Norse Gods and Giants*, while folklore is the source of *East of the Sun and West of the Moon* and *Trolls*. Three books link Norway and the United States. *Leif the Lucky* is a biography of the man who discovered Vineland on the American shores, while *The Conquest of the Atlantic* describes voyages from the Vikings to Balboa. The countries are not specifically identified in *Wings for Per*, which juxtaposes traditional law and justice with tyranny and occupation. A school boy, *Nils*, is called a sissy when he wears hand-knit stockings to school. The second generation Norwegian-American eventually achieves acceptance and respect among his classmates. While Edgar is credited for the dramatic quality, it is Ingri who inserts the humor in the text.

As immigrants to the United States, the d'Aulaires selected national heroes and patriotic subjects. *George Washington, Abraham Lincoln, Pocahontas, Benjamin Franklin, Buffalo Bill* and *Columbus* were published in a span of nineteen years. These biographies are propelled by the chronological action and consequently stiff when compared to *Ola* and the more imaginative books. The d'Aulaires came to American themes "as children," offering a fresh approach to the national anthem, *The Star Spangled Banner*. Even *The Lord's Prayer* was interpreted from the viewpoint of an American child, which annoyed Bertha E. Mahony and Marguerite M. Mitchell, who felt that children's imagination should provide the images. Even *Don't Count Your Chicks*, based on the Danish Hans Christian Andersen work, has an early American interpretation.

Research and travel have enabled the pair to produce accurate accounts. Their first book, *The Magic Rug*, was written in the style of a travelogue in response to a Norwegian child's request for information about their winter stay in Kairawan in Tunisia. To write *The Conquest of the Atlantic*, they studied in the New York Public Library and University of Norway in Oslo, and viewed ship models and costumes in the Musée de la Marine in the Louvre in Paris. They established a base in Geneva, and become acquainted with Swiss history, literature, and art before beginning *The Magic Meadow*. The authors have remarked that a thousand pages of research may be compressed into each picture book, and that they may rework a manuscript ten or twenty times before being satisfied. In an interview with Art Buchwald (*Herald Tribune*, October 30, 1956), Ingri d'Aulaire said: "We found out many wicked stories about Mr. Franklin and we were tempted to use them, but we were afraid because it would spoil the market for the children's books. The mothers and grandmothers would say 'no.' " As well as accumulating notes, the couple visit each area. While working on *Buffalo Bill*, they spent six weeks camping out on the midwest plains. They walked over George Washington's Virginia, and pitched tents along the Lincoln trail.

Unlike the biographies which have little dialogue, the imaginative books have lively conversation. *Foxie* is based in part on Anton Chekov's *Kashtanka*, about a performing theatrical dog. While Kashtanka's master is a poor carpenter and her fellow performers are a cat, a gander and a pig, Foxie returns to a boy after sharing the stage with a cat and a rooster. Ingri's humor is apparent in *The Two Cars*, for one remarks, "My paint is hardly dry behind my fenders," while the other states, "I am one hundred thousand miles old." A statement in this book, published midway in their production for children, is indicative of the manner in which the couple works – "you won the race but not the praise." Striving for perfection, they have produced both quantity and quality.

—Karen Nelson Hoyle

d'AULAIRE, Ingri (Mortenson) Parin. American. Born in Kongsberg, Norway, 27 December 1904; emigrated to the United States in 1929; naturalized citizen, 1940. Educated at Kongsberg Junior College, 1918–23; Institute of Arts and Crafts, Oslo, 1923–24; studied art with Hans Hofmann, Munich, 1924–25, and with Andre Lhote and Pola Gauguin, Paris, 1925–29. Married Edgar Parin d'Aulaire, *q.v.*, in 1925; has two children. Portrait artist. Recipient: American Library Association Caldecott Medal, 1940; Catholic Library Association Regina Medal, 1970. Address: 74 Mather Road, Georgetown, Connecticut 06829, U.S.A.

See the entry for Edgar Parin d'Aulaire.

DAWLISH, Peter. Pseudonym for James Lennox Kerr. British. Born in Paisley, Renfrewshire, 1 July 1899. Educated at North School, Paisley. Served in the Royal Naval Volunteer Reserve, 1915–19 and 1942–46: mentioned in despatches. Married Elizabeth Lamorna Birch in 1932; one son. Gold prospector; member of the British Mercantile Marine, 1919–29, 1939–42. *Died 11 March 1963.*

PUBLICATIONS FOR CHILDREN

Fiction

> *The Eye of the Earth* (as James Lennox Kerr), illustrated by F.P. Paterson. London, Nelson, 1936.
> *Peg-Leg and the Fur Pirates*, illustrated by Norman Hepple. London, Oxford University Press, 1939.
> *Captain Peg-Leg's War*, illustrated by J.D. Evans. London, Oxford University Press, 1939.
> *Peg-Leg and the Invaders*, illustrated by Jack Matthew. London, Oxford University Press, 1940.
> *Peg-Leg Sweeps the Sea*, illustrated by Leonard Boden. London, Oxford University Press, 1940.
> *Dauntless Finds Her Crew*, illustrated by P.A. Jobson. London, Oxford University Press, 1947.
> *The First Tripper*, illustrated by P.A. Jobson. London, Oxford University Press, 1947.
> *Dauntless Sails Again*, illustrated by P.A. Jobson. London, Oxford University Press, 1948.
> *Dauntless and the Mary Baines*, illustrated by P.A. Jobson. London, Oxford University Press, 1949.
> *North Sea Adventure*, illustrated by P.A. Jobson. London, Oxford University Press, 1949.
> *Dauntless Takes Recruits*, illustrated by P.A. Jobson. London, Oxford University Press, 1950.
> *MacClellan's Lake*, illustrated by Roy Sharp. London, Oxford University Press, 1951.
> *Aztec Gold*, illustrated by P.A. Jobson. London, Oxford University Press, 1951.
> *Dauntless Sails In*, illustrated by P.A. Jobson. London, Oxford University Press, 1952.
> *The Bagodia Episode*, illustrated by P.A. Jobson. London, Oxford University Press, 1953.
> *Dauntless in Danger*, illustrated by P.A. Jobson. London, Oxford University Press, 1954.
> *Way for a Soldier*. London, Oxford University Press, 1955.
> *He Went with Drake*, illustrated by P.A. Jobson. London, Harrap, 1955.
> *Sailors All*. Oxford, Blackwell, 1958.

349

The Race for Gowrie Bay, illustrated by Christopher Brooker. London, Oxford University Press, 1959.

Dauntless Goes Home, illustrated by P.A. Jobson. London, Oxford University Press, 1960.

The Boy Jacko, illustrated by William Stobbs. London, Oxford University Press, 1962; New York, Watts, 1963.

Other

Young Drake of Devon. London, Oxford University Press, 1954.

Martin Frobisher, illustrated by William Stobbs. London, Oxford University Press, 1956.

Johnno the Deep-Sea Diver: The Life Story of Diver John Johnstone as Told to Peter Dawlish. London, Harrap, and New York, Watts, 1960.

The Royal Navy, illustrated by Victor Ambrus. London, Oxford University Press, 1963.

The Seas of Britain, illustrated by Val Biro. London, Benn, 1963.

The Merchant Navy, illustrated by Victor Ambrus. London, Oxford University Press, 1966.

Editor (as James Lennox Kerr), *On – and Under – the Ocean Wave: A Book of Modern Sea Stories.* London, Nelson, 1933.

PUBLICATIONS FOR ADULTS (as James Lennox Kerr)

Novels

Old Ship. London, Constable, 1930; New York, Macmillan, 1931.

Glenshiels. London, Lane, 1932.

Ice: A Tale of Effort. London, Lane, 1933.

The Blackspit Smugglers. London, Nelson, 1935.

Woman of Glenshiels. London, Collins, 1935.

The Fool and the Tractor. London, Collins, 1936.

Other

Backdoor Guest. London, Constable, and Indianapolis, Bobbs Merrill, 1930.

The Young Steamship Officer. London, Nelson, 1933.

Cruising in Scotland; The Log of the Migrant Describing How a £35 Cruiser Gave Pleasure to a Distinguished Artist and His Family. London, Collins, 1938.

The Eager Years: An Autobiography. London, Collins, 1949.

The Great Storm, Being the Authentic Story of the Loss at Sea of the "Princess Victoria" and Other Vessels Early in 1953. London, Harrap, 1954.

The R.N.V.R.: A Record of Achievement, with Wilfred Granville. London, Harrap, 1957.

Wilfred Grenfell: His Life and Work. London, Harrap, and New York, Dodd Mead, 1959.

The Unfortunate Ship: The Story of H.M. Troopship Birkenhead. London, Harrap 1960.

Harbour Spotter. London, Newman Neame, 1962.

The Yachtsman's Log and Astronomical Position Line Formula. Privately printed, 1963.

Editor, *A Modern Sinbad: An Autobiography*, by Aylward Edward Dingle. London, Harrap, 1948.

Editor, with David James, *Wavy Navy by Some Who Served*. London, Harrap, 1950.
Editor, *Touching the Adventures of Merchantmen in the Second World War*. London, Harrap, 1953.

*   *   *

Peter Dawlish won an excellent reputation during the 1940's and 1950's as a kind of latter-day Arthur Ransome with his fine stories of the sea and ships. He was a professional sailor and wrote from his own experiences and expert know-how. After reading a handful of Dawlish stories, young readers would have a useful, practical knowledge of how to handle small (and not-so-small) boats on river and sea – and that information would have been put across in a completely painless fashion, interspersed with generous lashings of exciting adventures and incidental humour.

Dawlish's early books for boys featured a tough sea skipper named Captain Peg-Leg, but it was with his series of stories about *Dauntless* that his popularity really became established. *Dauntless* was a derelict French fishing-boat, a 45-footer, which a group of schoolboys reconditioned with the help and advice of the experienced Captain Blake and took on a series of eventful voyages. Along the way Dawlish imparts a considerable amount of navigational lore and seamanship, aided by excellent illustrations and sketches by P.A. Jobson. As with Ransome, Dawlish often makes his readers impatient to become amateur sailors themselves; his competent writing, as in this extract from *Dauntless Takes Recruits*, is full of enthusiasm, pride and technical description:

He looked upward at the gleaming mainmast and forrad to where the bowsprit had been drawn inboard for safety in narrow, crowded places and nodded his approval. The mainsail was stowed on its boom and the whole protected with a tanned canvas cover, the boom itself resting on a stout, varnished crutch. Running-rigging was coiled on its pins, spare mooring-lines on the scoured deck. Suspended on a bracket screwed to the mainmast was the ship's bell, its bracket and also the bell itself of polished brass, Tim's masterpiece of a bell lanyard dangling handsomely from the bell's tongue. Aft, the compass binnacle, the hub of the steering-wheel and the tip of the wheel's midships spoke were also of brass and gleaming like precious metal. Every detail of the *Dauntless* showed the pride her owners and crew took in her.

As well as other boys' sea and adventure stories, both modern and historical, Dawlish wrote one of the first career novels for young people. Titled *The First Tripper* it is a detailed story about a cadet's first voyage in the Merchant Navy.

—Brian Doyle

DAY LEWIS, C(ecil). Born in Ballintubber, Ireland, 27 April 1904. Educated at Sherborne School, Dorset; Wadham College, Oxford, M.A. Served as an Editor in the Ministry of Information, London, 1941–46. Married Mary King in 1928 (divorced, 1951), two sons; Jill Balcon, 1951, one son and one daughter. Assistant Master, Summerfields School, Oxford, 1927–38; Larchfield, Helensburgh, 1928–30; Cheltenham College, Gloucestershire, 1930–35; Professor of Poetry, Oxford University, 1951–56; Norton Professor of Poetry, Harvard University, Cambridge, Massachusetts, 1964–65. Clark Lecturer, 1946, and Sidgwick Lecturer, 1956, Cambridge University; Warton Lecturer, British Academy, London, 1951; Byron Lecturer, University of Nottingham, 1952; Chancellor Dunning Lecturer, Queen's University, Kingston, Ontario, 1954; Compton Lecturer, University of

Hull, Yorkshire, 1968. Director of Chatto and Windus Ltd., publishers, London, 1954–72. Member of the Arts Council of Great Britain, 1962–67. Honorary Fellow, Wadham College, Oxford, 1968. D.Litt.: University of Exeter, 1965; University of Hull, 1969; Litt.D.: Trinity College, Dublin, 1968. Fellow, 1944, Vice-President, 1958, and Companion of Literature, 1964, Royal Society of Literature; Honorary Member, American Academy of Arts and Letters, 1966; Member, Irish Academy of Letters, 1968. C.B.E. (Commander, Order of the British Empire), 1950. Poet Laureate, 1968. *Died 22 May 1972.*

PUBLICATIONS FOR CHILDREN

Fiction

> *Dick Willoughby.* Oxford, Blackwell, 1933; New York, Random House, 1938.
> *The Otterbury Incident,* illustrated by Edward Ardizzone. London, Putnam, 1948; New York, Viking Press, 1949.

Other

> *Poetry for You: A Book for Boys and Girls on the Enjoyment of Poetry.* Oxford, Blackwell, 1944; New York, Oxford University Press, 1947.

PUBLICATIONS FOR ADULTS

Novels

> *The Friendly Tree.* London, Cape, 1936; New York, Harper, 1937.
> *Starting Point.* London, Cape, 1937; New York, Harper, 1938.
> *Child of Misfortune.* London, Cape, 1939.

Novels (as Nicholas Blake)

> *A Question of Proof.* London, Collins, and New York, Harper, 1935.
> *Thou Shell of Death.* London, Collins, 1936; as *Shell of Death,* New York, Harper, 1936.
> *There's Trouble Brewing.* London, Collins, and New York, Harper, 1937.
> *The Beast Must Die.* London, Collins, and New York, Harper, 1938.
> *The Smiler with the Knife.* London, Collins, and New York, Harper, 1939.
> *Malice in Wonderland.* London, Collins, 1940; as *Summer Camp Mystery,* New York, Harper, 1940.
> *The Case of the Abominable Snowman.* London, Collins, 1941; as *Corpse in the Snowman,* New York, Harper, 1941.
> *Minute for Murder.* London, Collins, 1947; New York, Harper, 1948.
> *Head of a Traveller.* London, Collins, and New York, Harper, 1949.
> *The Dreadful Hollow.* London, Collins, and New York, Harper, 1953.
> *The Whisper in the Gloom.* London, Collins, and New York, Harper, 1954.
> *A Tangled Web.* London, Collins, and New York, Harper, 1956.
> *End of Chapter.* London, Collins, and New York, Harper, 1957.
> *A Penknife in My Heart.* London, Collins, and New York, Harper, 1958.
> *The Widow's Cruise.* London, Collins, and New York, Harper, 1959.
> *The Worm of Death.* London, Collins, and New York, Harper, 1961.
> *The Deadly Joker.* London, Collins, 1963.
> *The Sad Variety.* London, Collins, and New York, Harper, 1964.
> *The Morning after Death.* London, Collins, and New York, Harper, 1966.

The Nicholas Blake Omnibus (includes *The Beast Must Die, A Tangled Web, A Penknife in My Heart*).   London, Collins, 1966.
The Private Wound.   London, Collins, and New York, Harper, 1968.

Verse

Beechen Vigil and Other Poems.   London, Fortune Press, 1925.
Country Comets.   London, Martin Hopkinson, 1928.
Transitional Poem.   London, Hogarth Press, 1929.
From Feathers to Iron.   London, Hogarth Press, 1931.
The Magnetic Mountain.   London, Hogarth Press, 1933.
Collected Poems, 1929–1933.   London, Hogarth Press, 1935; with *A Hope for Poetry,* New York, Random House, 1935.
A Time to Dance and Other Poems.   London, Hogarth Press, 1935.
Noah and the Waters.   London, Hogarth Press, 1936.
A Time to Dance, Noah and the Waters and Other Poems, with an Essay, Revolution in Writing.   New York, Random House, 1936.
Overtures to Death and Other Poems.   London, Cape, 1938.
Poems in Wartime.   London, Cape, 1940.
Selected Poems.   London, Hogarth Press, 1940.
Word over All.   London, Cape, 1943; New York, Transatlantic, 1944.
(Poems).   London, Eyre and Spottiswoode, 1943.
Short Is the Time: Poems, 1936–1943 (includes *Overtures to Death* and *Word over All*).   New York, Oxford University Press, 1945.
Poems, 1943–1947.   London, Cape, and New York, Oxford University Press, 1948.
Collected Poems, 1929–1936.   London, Hogarth Press, 1948.
Selected Poems.   London, Penguin, 1951; revised edition, 1957, 1969.
An Italian Visit.   London, Cape, and New York, Harper, 1953.
Collected Poems.   London, Cape-Hogarth Press, 1954.
Christmas Eve.   London, Faber, 1954.
The Newborn: D.M.B., 29th April, 1957.   London, Favil Press of Kensington, 1957.
Pegasus and Other Poems.   London, Cape, 1957; New York, Harper, 1958.
The Gate and Other Poems.   London, Cape, 1962.
Requiem for the Living.   New York, Harper, 1964.
On Not Saying Anything.   Cambridge, Massachusetts, privately printed, 1964.
A Marriage Song for Albert and Barbara.   Cambridge, Massachusetts, privately printed, 1965.
The Room and Other Poems.   London, Cape, 1965.
C. Day Lewis: Selections from His Poetry, edited by Patric Dickinson.   London, Chatto and Windus, 1967.
Selected Poems.   New York, Harper, 1967.
The Abbey That Refused to Die: A Poem.   County Mayo, Ireland, Ballintubber Abbey, 1967.
The Whispering Roots.   London, Cape, 1970; as *The Whispering Roots and Other Poems,* New York, Harper, 1970.
Going My Way.   London, Poem-of-the-Month Club, 1970.
The Poems of C. Day Lewis, edited by Ian Parsons.   London, Cape, 1977.

Recording: *Poems,* Argo, 1974.

Other

A Hope for Poetry.   Oxford, Blackwell, 1934; with *Collected Poems,* New York, Random House, 1935.

Revolution in Writing. London, Hogarth Press, 1935; New York, Random House, 1936.

Imagination and Thinking, with L. Susan Stebbing. London, British Institute of Adult Education, 1936.

We're Not Going to Do Nothing: A Reply to Mr. Aldous Huxley's Pamphlet "What Are You Going to Do about It?" London, Left Review, 1936; Folcroft, Pennsylvania, Folcroft Editions, 1970.

The Poetic Image. London, Cape, and New York, Oxford University Press, 1947.

Enjoying Poetry: A Reader's Guide. London, National Book League, 1947.

The Colloquial Element in English Poetry. Newcastle upon Tyne, Literary and Philosophical Society, 1947.

The Poet's Task. Oxford, Clarendon Press, 1951; Folcroft, Pennsylvania, Folcroft Editions, 1970.

The Grand Manner. Nottingham, University of Nottingham, 1962.

The Lyrical Poetry of Thomas Hardy. London, Oxford University Press, 1953; Folcroft, Pennsylvania, Folcroft Editions, 1970.

Notable Images of Virtue: Emily Brontë, George Meredith, W. B. Yeats. Toronto, Ryerson Press, 1954; Folcroft, Pennsylvania, Folcroft Editions, 1969.

The Poet's Way of Knowledge. Cambridge, University Press, 1957.

The Buried Day (autobiography). London, Chatto and Windus, and New York, Harper, 1960.

The Lyric Impulse. Cambridge, Massachusetts, Harvard University Press, and London, Chatto and Windus, 1965.

Thomas Hardy, with R. A. Scott-James. London, Longman, 1965.

A Need for Poetry? Hull, University of Hull, 1968.

On Translating Poetry: A Lecture. Abingdon-on-Thames, Berkshire, Abbey Press, 1970.

Editor, with W. H. Auden, *Oxford Poetry 1927*. Oxford Blackwell, 1927.

Editor, with others, *A Writer in Arms*, by Ralph Fox. London, Lawrence and Wishart, 1937.

Editor, *The Mind in Chains: Socialism and the Cultural Revolution*. London, Muller, 1937; Folcroft, Pennsylvania, Folcroft Editions, 1972.

Editor, *The Echoing Green: An Anthology of Verse*. Oxford, Blackwell, 3 vols., 1937.

Editor, with Charles Fenby, *Anatomy of Oxford: An Anthology*. London, Cape, 1938.

Editor, with L. A. G. Strong, *A New Anthology of Modern Verse, 1920–1940*. London, Methuen, 1941.

Editor, with others, *Orion: Volume II* and *Volume III*. London, Nicholson and Watson, 1945, 1946.

Editor, *The Golden Treasury of the Best Songs and Lyrical Poems in the English Language*, by Francis Turner Palgrave. London, Collins, 1954.

Editor, with John Lehmann, *The Chatto Book of Modern Poetry. 1915–1955*. London, Chatto and Windus, 1956.

Editor, with Kathleen Nott and Thomas Blackburn, *New Poems 1957*. London, Joseph, 1957.

Editor, *A Book of English Lyrics*. London, Chatto and Windus, 1961; as *English Lyric Poems, 1500–1900*, New York, Appleton Century Crofts, 1961.

Editor, *The Collected Poems of Wilfred Owen*. London, Chatto and Windus, 1964; revised edition, New York, New Directions, 1964.

Editor, *The Midnight Skaters: Poems for Young Readers*, by Edmund Blunden. London, Bodley Head, 1968.

Editor, *The Poems of Robert Browning*. Cambridge, Limited Editions Club, 1969; New York, Heritage Press, 1971.

Editor, *A Choice of Keats's Verse*. London, Faber, 1971.

Editor, *Crabbe*. London, Penguin, 1973.

Translator, *The Georgics of Virgil*.   London, Cape, 1940; New York, Oxford University Press 1947.

Translator, *The Graveyard by the Sea*, by Paul Valéry.   London, Secker and Warburg, 1947.

Translator, *The Aeneid of Virgil*.   London, Hogarth Press, and New York, Oxford University Press, 1952.

Translator, *The Eclogues of Virgil*.   London, Cape, 1963; with *The Georgics*, New York, Doubleday, 1964.

Translator, with Mátyás Sárközi, *The Tomtit in the Rain: Traditional Hungarian Rhymes*, by Erzsi Gazdas.   London, Chatto and Windus, 1971.

Bibliography: *C. Day Lewis, The Poet Laureate: A Bibliography* by Geoffrey Handley-Taylor and Timothy d'Arch Smith, London and Chicago, St. James Press, 1968.

Manuscript Collections: New York Public Library; State University of New York at Buffalo; British Museum, London; University of Liverpool.

*   *   *

C. Day Lewis is best known as a children's writer for *The Otterbury Incident*. It has been "one of those books that work" to grateful teachers and librarians in the United Kingdom for more than 25 years.

His heroes attend a day school in post-war England, a departure from the timeless cloisters of boarding schools which were still a feature of boys' comics of the period. Their exploits are described by George, himself a participant in the kids-catch-crooks adventure − a device which allows confidential asides to his reader and a mock-heroic style as the boys go into action with the discipline of a commando unit. His idiom is firmly middle-class and, inevitably, of its time: chaps in the company shut up "j. quick" when their leader tells them off; a couple of spivs are "a pair of blisters" or "fearful outsiders." There are unselfconscious references to a search proving as difficult as looking for "a nigger in a dark cellar" and to a pawnbroker "jewing" the boys, and a carefree objectivity about "females."

It would be a pity if adult preoccupations of the 1970's led to the removal of the book from the English stockroom or the library shelves. A young reader in headlong pursuit of the engaging plot is unlikely to be distracted by occasional obscurity or bias. The abiding success of the book lies in the fact that it reworks, in a particularly lively way, a situation of unfailing appeal to children. A group of kids, unaided, outwit a trio of grown-ups; and since the grown-ups are criminals, the children earn the gratitude and admiration of adult society, embodied in a police inspector and their headmaster.

The basic formula was well-tried even in 1948. Day Lewis's story is distinguished by the rapid and entertaining ride he offers over a steeplechase of a plot. Each hurdle requires ingenious negotiation: inventive and comic fund-raising to pay for a broken window; bizarre detection by the local newsagent, E. Sidebotham, who suffers periodic delusions that he is Sherlock Holmes; and a satisfying denouement as the boys' practised military strategies are brought into play against a criminal with a cut-throat razor he means to use.

Characters are simply sketched, but for many children the stereotypes may provide readier access to the narrative than subtler portraits. Day Lewis had already demonstrated his control of an exciting plot peopled by boldly drawn figures in *Dick Willoughby*, where he charted the progress of a young Elizabethan. Secret tunnels, sword-play on the Spanish Main, an evil Catholic kinsman and a dash of innocent romance spice the mixture. The dialogue is entangled in what Geoffrey Trease calls "tushery": "Marry, come up, thou tun of a booby, that hairy comet of thine, that holly-bush thou grow'st to keep thy neck warm for the rope med frighten Spaniards but not a Dorset maiden," cries a serving maid to a bluff retainer "in high glee."

Even in *Dick Willoughby*, however, there are many of the qualities which mark *The Otterbury Incident*: the clarity of the issues at stake, the pace of the action, and a pervading high spiritedness.

—Geoff Fox

---

de ANGELI, Marguerite (Lofft). American. Born in Lapeer, Michigan, 14 March 1889. Educated at schools in Lapeer and Philadelphia. Married John de Angeli in 1910; has four sons and one daughter. Professional singer, 1904–21. Recipient: American Library Association Newbery Medal, 1950; Catholic Library Association Regina Medal, 1968. Address: 2601 Parkway, Philadelphia, Pennsylvania 19130, U.S.A.

PUBLICATIONS FOR CHILDREN (illustrated by the author)

Fiction

> *Ted and Nina Go to the Grocery Store.* New York, Doubleday, 1935.
> *Ted and Nina Have a Happy Rainy Day.* New York, Doubleday, 1936.
> *Henner's Lydia.* New York, Doubleday, 1936; Kingswood, Surrey, World's Work, 1965.
> *Petite, Suzanne.* New York, Doubleday, 1937.
> *Copper-Toed Boots.* New York, Doubleday, 1938; Kingswood, Surrey, World's Work, 1965.
> *Skippack School.* New York, Doubleday, 1939; Kingswood, Surrey, World's Work, 1964.
> *A Summer Day with Ted and Nina.* New York, Doubleday, 1940.
> *Thee, Hannah!* New York, Doubleday, 1940; Kingswood, Surrey, World's Work, 1962.
> *Ellin's Amerika.* New York, Doubleday, 1941; Kingswood, Surrey, World's Work, 1964.
> *Up the Hill.* New York, Doubleday, 1942.
> *Yonie Wondernose.* New York, Doubleday, 1944.
> *Turkey for Christmas.* Philadelphia, Westminster Press, 1944.
> *Bright April.* New York, Doubleday, 1946.
> *Jared's Island.* New York, Doubleday, 1947.
> *The Door in the Wall.* New York, Doubleday, 1949; Kingswood, Surrey, World's Work, 1959.
> *Just Like David.* New York, Doubleday, 1951.
> *Black Fox of Lorne.* New York, Doubleday, 1956; Kingswood, Surrey, World's Work, 1959.
> *Fiddlestrings.* New York, Doubleday, 1974.
> *The Lion in the Box.* New York, Doubleday, 1975.
> *Whistle for the Crossing.* New York, Doubleday, 1977.

Other

> *A Pocket Full of Posies: A Merry Mother Goose.* New York, Doubleday, 1961.
> *The Goose Girl.* New York, Doubleday, 1964.

Editor, *Book of Nursery and Mother Goose Rhymes.* New York, Doubleday, 1954.
Editor, *The Old Testament.* New York, Doubleday, 1960.

PUBLICATIONS FOR ADULTS

Other

Libraries and Reading: Their Importance in the Lives of Famous Americans, with others,
   edited by Donald H. Hunt.   Philadelphia, Drexel Press, 1964.
Butter at the Old Price: The Autobiography of Marguerite de Angeli.   New York,
   Doubleday, 1971.

Editor, *Book of Favorite Hymns.*   New York, Doubleday, 1963.

Illustrator: *The New Moon,* 1924, and *The Covered Bridge,* 1936, by Cornelia Meigs; *Meggy MacIntosh* by Elizabeth Janet Gray, 1930; *A Candle in the Mist* by Florence Crannell Means, 1931; *The Christmas Nightingale* by Eric Kelly, 1932; *Joan Wanted a Kitty* by Jane Brown Gemmill, 1937; *Alice-All-by-Herself* by Elizabeth Coatsworth, 1937; *Red Sky over Rome* by Anne D. Kyle, 1938; *The Princess and the Gypsy* by Jean Rosmer, 1938; *Prayers and Graces for Little Children* edited by Quail Hawkins, 1941; *They Loved to Laugh* by Kathryn Worth, 1942; *In and Out: Verses* by Tom Robinson, 1943; *The Empty Barn,* 1966, and *The Door in the Wall,* 1968, by Arthur C. de Angeli.

*   *   *

Most famous of all Marguerite de Angeli's long list of titles is *The Door in the Wall,* which won for her the coveted Newbery Medal. Set in the England of Edward III, it is a beautifully realized piece of historical fiction: the young hero's brave acceptance of his handicap and his determination to fight on against all but insuperable hardship have an inspiring message for youngsters of any era. The writer conveys with jewel-like clarity both the differences and the similarities of that distant time and this: green, wild England with its glorious, comfortless castles and noisome narrow streets, and the inhabitants in so many ways so like their counterparts of today. Robin is a boy of the 13th century, but he speaks very clearly to the 20th-century reader.

De Angeli has a gift for making the exotic, peculiar, or particular seem universal and unthreatening to young readers, who are often xenophobic in their rejection of the unfamiliar. She writes with equal sympathy and understanding of families of varied ethnic backgrounds and creeds; and just as her illustrations bring their outward appearances vividly to life, her gentle, simple stories make their daily lives and the small concerns of their children those of all loving families everywhere. If at first glance her works seem concerned with contrasting cultures, in fact her study is that of the universality of happy childhood.

She reserves the larger dramatic themes, such as war and revenge, for her few tales of the remote past; young Robin of *The Door in the Wall* is the saviour of his besieged castle in the mist; in *Black Fox of Lorne* Jan and Brus, twin Viking lads of the 10th century, avenge their father's death by treachery; but these ambitious novels for older children are atypical. De Angeli is best known and loved for her shorter stories of ordinary, day-to-day childhood concerns; of the boy who longs above all things for a pair of copper-toed boots; the working lad whose stern but loving father must be made to see that there is a place for artists as well as for miners; little Hannah who painfully discovers for herself the meaning of her drab Quaker bonnet and learns to wear it with pride; and all her other believable, loveable children.

Many of her stories and their illustrations are based upon de Angeli's own family and its folklore, and have both the strength and weakness of family tradition revealed to the outsider. There is a suggestion of the "separateness" enveloping any close-knit family, however large-hearted its members, and a natural tendency to overrate family stories and catch-phrases that have meaning only to the inner circle of intimates. But more than offsetting the effect of partiality is the depth of love, trust and understanding that informs de Angeli's writings with the glow of happiness remembered and preserved.

—Joan McGrath

DE JONG, Meindert. American. Born in Wierum, Netherlands, 4 March 1906. Educated at Calvin College, Grand Rapids, Michigan, A.B. 1928; University of Chicago. Served in the United States Army Air Corps during World War II: historian of the Chinese-American Wing, 14th Air Force. Married Hattie Overeinter in 1932; Beatrice DeClaire McElwee, 1962, five stepchildren. Lived in Mexico, 1962–67. Recipient: American Library Association Newbery Medal, 1955, and Aurianne Award, 1959; Child Study Association of America award, 1957; Hans Christian Andersen International Medal, 1962; National Book Award, 1969; Catholic Library Association Regina Medal, 1972. Agent: Sheldon Fogelman, 10 East 40th Street, New York, New York 10016. Address: 504 Lake Drive, Allegan, Michigan 49010, U.S.A.

PUBLICATIONS FOR CHILDREN

Fiction

> *The Big Goose and the Little White Duck*, illustrated by Edna Potter. New York, Harper, 1938; London, Heinemann, 1939.
> *Dirk's Dog Bello*, illustrated by Kurt Wiese. New York, Harper, 1939; London, Lutterworth Press, 1960.
> *Wheels over the Bridge*, illustrated by Aldren Watson. New York and London, Harper, 1941.
> *Bells of the Harbor*, illustrated by Kurt Wiese. New York and London, Harper, 1941.
> *The Cat That Walked a Week*, illustrated by Tessie Robinson. New York, Harper, 1943; London, Lutterworth Press, 1965.
> *The Little Stray Dog*, illustrated by Edward Shenton. New York and London, Harper, 1943.
> *Billy and the Unhappy Bull*, illustrated by Marc Simont. New York, Harper, 1946; London, Lutterworth Press, 1966.
> *Good Luck Duck*, illustrated by Marc Simont. New York, Harper, and London, Hamish Hamilton, 1950.
> *Tower by the Sea*, illustrated by Barbara Comfort. New York, Harper, and London, Hamish Hamilton, 1950.
> *Smoke above the Lane*, illustrated by Girard Goodenow. New York, Harper, 1951.
> *Shadrach*, illustrated by Maurice Sendak. New York, Harper, 1953; London, Lutterworth Press, 1957.
> *Hurry Home, Candy*, illustrated by Maurice Sendak. New York, Harper, 1953; London, Lutterworth Press, 1962.
> *The Wheel on the School*, illustrated by Maurice Sendak. New York, Harper, 1954; London, Lutterworth Press, 1956.
> *The Little Cow and the Turtle*, illustrated by Maurice Sendak. New York, Harper, 1955; London, Lutterworth Press, 1961.
> *The House of Sixty Fathers*, illustrated by Maurice Sendak. New York, Harper, 1956; London, Lutterworth Press, 1958.
> *Along Came a Dog*, illustrated by Maurice Sendak. New York, Harper, 1958; London, Lutterworth Press, 1959.

The Last Little Cat, illustrated by Jim McMullen.   New York, Harper, 1961; London, Lutterworth Press, 1962.
The Singing Hill, illustrated by Maurice Sendak.   New York, Harper, 1962; London, Lutterworth Press, 1963.
Nobody Plays with a Cabbage, illustrated by Tom Allen.   New York, Harper, 1962; London, Lutterworth Press, 1963.
Far Out the Long Canal, illustrated by Nancy Grossman.   New York, Harper, 1964; London, Lutterworth Press, 1965.
Puppy Summer, illustrated by Anita Lobel.   New York, Harper, and London, Lutterworth Press, 1966.
Journey from Peppermint Street, illustrated by Emily McCully.   New York, Harper, 1968; London, Lutterworth Press, 1969.
A Horse Came Running, illustrated by Paul Sagsoorian.   New York, Macmillan, and London, Lutterworth Press, 1970.
The Easter Cat, illustrated by Lillian Hoban.   New York, Macmillan, 1971; London, Lutterworth Press, 1972.
The Almost All-White Rabbity Cat, illustrated by H. B. Vestal.   New York, Macmillan, and London, Lutterworth Press, 1972.

Other

Bible Days, illustrated by Kreigh Collins.   Grand Rapids, Michigan, Fideler, 1949.
The Mighty Ones: Great Men and Women of Early Bible Days, illustrated by Harvey Schmidt.   New York, Harper, 1959; London, Lutterworth Press, 1960.

Manuscript Collection: Kerlan Collection, University of Minnesota, Minneapolis.

*   *   *

Great writers have a quality far more important that facility with words, more than observation and a graphic portrayal of what is observed. It is a quality which might be called compassionate perception. Certain writers of children's literature have this characteristic. Children are often loving by nature, perceptive, sensitive, and they respond to an author who is spiritually akin to them.

So we come to Meindert De Jong whose books span many years and assorted ages. That De Jong likes animals can be quickly seen from his titles: *Puppy Summer, The Last Little Cat, The Cat That Walked a Week, A Horse Came Running, Good Luck Duck.* But titles do not reveal his wonderful ability to describe sensitively but without sentimentality the shimmering love which sometimes springs up between a child and a pet.

The Easter Cat is the story of Millicent, a little girl who adored cats but was prevented from having one of her own by her Mother's allergy. Gradually the reader learns that Millicent is the only small person in a world of adults. Her desire for a kitten is really her need for a being smaller than herself who depends upon her love and care. How universal a situation from a child's eye level! In solving the problem, De Jong uses carefully selected diction. Note this description of a clock at night – "The white dial of the big clock was a murky nothing sending out its heavy tick-tocks" – or the description of an emotional reaction – "Your heart sort of gets like cheap ice cream when it melts – all watery and mushy." The vocabulary of *The Easter Cat* is familiar to little children – ice cream and tick-tocks and mush – yet De Jong's artistry is obvious. Adults may forget the pain of being always too small or too weak, but a child recognizes the feeling readily, and, in Millicent, finds a heroine who learns to cope and conquer.

In *The Wheel on the School* written for older children, De Jong begins his story in a sleepy Dutch school with a little girl's composition about storks. Storks may not be familiar to the average child, but school rooms and compositions are and so he slips easily into the barren seaside community of Shora whose children desire the return of the great birds to nest upon

359

their roofs as they did in the past. Now the roofs of Shora are all sharp, too slippery for nesting, but the children intend to entice the storks by placing a wheel on the school house roof.

This simple plot becomes complicated because the children must overcome hostility from adults, violent storms, and finally a close brush with death to rescue two bedraggled storm-weakened birds. *The Wheel on the School* is an absorbing adventure story but it has a larger meaning. It is a monumental struggle which touches a whole community. A fisherman learns that his mind and his courage can supplement the use of legs; the children find that physical strength is second to spiritual tenuousness; the whole village encounters elemental forces of wind and tide but the common project causes a deep emotional stirring which finally washes away petty feelings and unifies Shora's people. It is a lovely story and one which shows a child that he need not be unimportant just because he is not an adult.

Shadrach is a classic and as such is confined to no age group. *Shadrach* is about the finding of identity, the nucleus of being which a child must discover so that his own uniqueness may stand forth. Grandfather has promised Davie a rabbit — not just any rabbit — a black rabbit. Perceiving its specificity even before it is a reality, Davie names his rabbit carefully — a wonderful name with Biblical undertones — Shadrach. Like Millicent in *The Easter Cat*, this child needs a smaller being to care for, and his affection for his rabbit is very deep. When the rabbit is lost, the family suggests a replacement (as families do) but Davie becomes ill at the thought. He understands the animal's uniqueness. There can be no casual substitution. This child is "all-children." Will no one *see*? At last the busy adults pause and try to comprehend what a small voice is saying. At last they listen. *Shadrach* is a definition of love — perceptive, sensitive love because it rests on the ability to understand and accept each individual as special.

Meindert De Jong's books are important contributions to literature, examining problems of childhood with depth and beauty.

—Carolyn T. Kingston

---

de la MARE, Walter. British. Born in Charlton, Kent, 25 April 1873. Attended St. Paul's Cathedral Choristers' School (Founder, *The Choristers Journal*, 1889). Married Constance Elfrida Ingpen in 1899 (died, 1943); two sons and two daughters. Clerk, Anglo-American Oil Company, London, 1890–1908. Received civil list pension, 1908. Honorary Fellow, Keble College, Oxford. Recipient: James Tait Black Memorial Prize, for fiction, 1922; Library Association Carnegie Medal, 1948; Foyle Poetry Prize, 1954. D. Litt.: Oxford, Cambridge, Bristol, and London universities; LL.D.: St. Andrews University. Companion of Honour, 1948; Order of Merit, 1953. *Died 22 June 1956.*

PUBLICATIONS FOR CHILDREN

Fiction

    The Three Mulla-Mulgars, illustrated by Dorothy P. Lathrop. London, Duckworth, 1910; New York, Knopf, 1919; as *The Three Royal Monkeys; or, The Three Mulla-Mulgars*, London, Faber, 1935.
    Story and Rhyme: A Selection from the Writings of Walter de la Mare, Chosen by the Author. London, Dent, and New York, Dutton, 1921.
    Broomsticks and Other Tales, illustrated by Bold. London, Constable, and New York, Knopf, 1925.
    Miss Jemima, illustrated by Alec Buckels. Oxford, Blackwell, 1925; Poughkeepsie, New York, Artists and Writers Guild, 1935.

Lucy, illustrated by Hilda T. Miller. Oxford, Blackwell, 1927.

Old Joe, illustrated by C. T. Nightingale. Oxford, Blackwell, 1927.

The Dutch Cheese and the Lovely Myfanwy, illustrated by Dorothy P. Lathrop. New York, Knopf, 1931.

The Lord Fish and Other Tales, illustrated by Rex Whistler. London, Faber, 1933.

The Old Lion and Other Stories, illustrated by Irene Hawkins. London, Faber, 1942.

The Magic Jacket and Other Stories, illustrated by Irene Hawkins. London, Faber, 1943.

The Scarecrow and Other Stories, illustrated by Irene Hawkins. London, Faber, 1945.

The Dutch Cheese and Other Stories, illustrated by Irene Hawkins. London, Faber, 1946.

Collected Stories for Children, illustrated by Irene Hawkins. London, Faber, 1947.

A Penny a Day, illustrated by Paul Kennedy. New York, Knopf, 1960.

Play

Crossings: A Fairy Play, music by C. Armstrong Gibbs, illustrated by Randolph Schwabe (produced Hove, Sussex, 1919; London, 1925). London, Beaumont Press, 1921; New York, Knopf, 1923.

Verse

Songs of Childhood (as Walter Ramal). London, Longman, 1902; (as Walter de la Mare), 1916.

A Child's Day: A Book of Rhymes, illustrated by Carine and Will Cadby. London, Constable, 1912; New York, Holt, 1923.

Peacock Pie: A Book of Rhymes. London, Constable, 1913; New York, Holt, 1917.

Down-Adown-Derry: A Book of Fairy Poems, illustrated by Dorothy P. Lathrop. London, Constable, and New York, Holt, 1922.

Poems for Children. London, Constable, and New York, Holt, 1930.

This Year, Next Year, illustrated by Harold Jones. London, Faber, and New York, Holt, 1937.

Bells and Grass: A Book of Rhymes, illustrated by Rowland Emett. London, Faber, 1941; New York, Viking Press, 1942.

Collected Rhymes and Verses, illustrated by Berthold Wolpe. London, Faber, 1944.

Rhymes and Verses: Collected Poems for Children, illustrated by Elinore Blaisdell. New York, Holt, 1947.

Poems, edited by Eleanor Graham, illustrated by Margery Gill. London, Penguin, 1962.

Other

Told Again: Traditional Tales, illustrated by A. H. Watson. Oxford, Blackwell, 1927; as *Told Again: Old Tales Told Again*, New York, Knopf, 1927; as *Tales Told Again*, London, Faber, and Knopf, 1959.

Stories from the Bible, illustrated by Theodore Nadejen. London, Faber, and New York, Cosmopolitan, 1929.

Animal Stories, Chosen, Arranged, and in Some Part Re-Written. London, Faber, 1939; New York, Scribner, 1940.

Selected Stories and Verses, edited by Eleanor Graham. London, Penguin, 1952.

Editor, *Come Hither: A Collection of Rhymes and Poems for the Young of all Ages*, illustrated by Alec Buckels. London, Constable, and New York, Knopf, 1923; revised edition, 1928.

Editor, with Thomas Quayle, *Readings: Traditional Tales Told by the Author*, illustrated by A. H. Watson and C. T. Nightingale.   Oxford, Blackwell, 5 vols., 1926–28; New York, Knopf, 1926–28.

Editor, *Tom Tiddler's Ground: A Book of Poetry for the Junior and Middle Schools*.   London, Collins, 3 vols., 1931; New York, Knopf, 1962.

Editor, *Old Rhymes and New, Chosen for Use in Schools*.   London, Constable, 2 vols., 1932.

PUBLICATIONS FOR ADULTS

Novels

Henry Brocken: His Travels and Adventures in the Rich, Strange, Scarce-Imaginable Regions of Romance.   London, Murray, 1904; New York, Knopf, 1924.

The Return.   London, Arnold, 1910; New York, Putnam, 1911; revised edition, London, Collins, and New York, Knopf, 1922; London, Faber, 1945.

Memoirs of a Midget.   London, Collins, 1921; New York, Knopf, 1922.

Short Stories

Lispet, Lispett, and Vaine.   London, Bookman's Journal, 1923.

The Riddle and Other Stories.   London, Selwyn and Blount, 1923; as *The Riddle and Other Tales*, New York, Knopf, 1923.

Ding Dong Bell.   London, Selwyn and Blount, and New York, Knopf, 1924.

Two Tales: The Green-Room, The Connoisseur.   London, Bookman's Journal, 1925.

The Connoisseur and Other Stories.   London, Collins, and New York, Knopf, 1926.

At First Sight.   New York, Crosby Gaige, 1928.

On the Edge: Short Stories.   London, Faber, 1930; New York, Knopf, 1931.

Seven Short Stories.   London, Faber, 1931.

A Froward Child.   London, Faber, 1934.

The Nap and Other Stories.   London, Nelson, 1936.

The Wind Blows Over.   London, Faber, and New York, Macmillan, 1936.

The Picnic and Other Stories.   London, Faber, 1941.

Best Stories of Walter de la Mare.   London, Faber, 1942.

The Collected Tales of Walter de la Mare, edited by Edward Wagenknecht.   New York, Knopf, 1949.

A Beginning and Other Stories.   London, Faber, 1955.

Ghost Stories.   London, Folio Society, 1956.

Some Stories.   London, Faber, 1962.

Eight Tales.   Sauk City, Wisconsin, Arkham House, 1971.

Verse

Poems.   London, Murray, 1906.

The Listener and Other Poems.   London, Constable, 1912; New York, Holt, 1916.

The Old Men.   London, Flying Fame, 1913.

The Sunken Garden and Other Poems.   London, Beaumont Press, 1917.

Motley and Other Poems.   London, Constable, and New York, Holt, 1918.

Flora, drawings by Pamela Bianco.   London, Heinemann, and Philadelphia, Lippincott, 1919.

Poems 1901 to 1918.   London, Constable, and New York, Holt, 2 vols., 1920.

The Veil and Other Poems.   London, Constable, 1921; New York, Holt, 1922.

Thus Her Tale: A Poem.   Edinburgh, Porpoise Press, 1923.

A Ballad of Christmas.   London, Selwyn and Blount, 1924.

The Hostage. London, Selwyn and Blount, 1925.

St. Andrews, with Rudyard Kipling. London, A. and C. Black, 1926.

(Poems). London, Benn, 1926.

Alone. London, Faber, 1927.

Selected Poems. New York, Holt, 1927.

Stuff and Nonsense and So On. London, Constable, and New York, Holt, 1927; revised edition, London, Faber, 1946.

A Captive and Other Poems. New York, Bowling Green Press, 1928.

Self to Self. London, Faber, 1928.

A Snowdrop. London, Faber, 1929.

News. London, Faber, 1930.

To Lucy. London, Faber, 1931.

The Sunken Garden and Other Verses. Birmingham, Birmingham School of Printing, 1931.

Two Poems. Privately printed, 1931.

The Fleeting and Other Poems. London, Constable, and New York, Knopf, 1933.

Poems 1919 to 1934. London, Constable, 1935; New York, Holt, 1936.

Poems. London, Corvinus Press, 1937.

Memory and Other Poems. London, Constable, and New York, Holt, 1938.

Two Poems, with Arthur Rogers. Privately printed, 1938.

Haunted: A Poem. London, Linden Press, 1939.

Collected Poems. New York, Holt, 1941; London, Faber, 1942.

Time Passes and Other Poems, edited by Anne Ridler. London, Faber, 1942.

The Burning-Glass and Other Poems, Including The Traveller. New York, Viking Press, 1945.

The Burning-Glass and Other Poems. London, Faber, 1945.

The Traveller. London, Faber, 1946.

Two Poems: Pride, The Truth of Things. London, Dropmore Press, 1946.

Inward Companion: Poems. London, Faber, 1950.

Winged Chariot. London, Faber, 1951.

Winged Chariot and Other Poems. New York, Viking Press, 1951.

O Lovely England and Other Poems. London, Faber, 1953.

The Winnowing Dream. London, Faber, 1954.

Selected Poems, edited by R. N. Green-Armytage. London, Faber, 1954.

The Morrow. Privately printed, 1955.

(Poems), edited by John Hadfield. London, Vista Books, 1962.

A Choice of de la Mare's Verse, edited by W. H. Auden. London, Faber, 1963.

Envoi. Privately printed, 1965.

The Complete Poems of Walter de la Mare, edited by Leonard Clark and others. London, Faber, 1969; New York, Knopf, 1970.

Other

M. E. Coleridge: An Appreciation. London, The Guardian, 1907.

Rupert Brooke and the Intellectual Imagination (lecture). London, Sidgwick and Jackson, and New York, Harcourt Brace, 1919.

Some Thoughts on Reading (lecture). Bembridge, Isle of Wight, Yellowsands Press, 1923.

Some Women Novelists of the 'Seventies. London, Cambridge University Press, 1929.

The Printing of Poetry (lecture). London, Cambridge University Press, 1931.

The Early Novels of Wilkie Collins. London, Cambridge University Press, 1932.

Lewis Carroll. London, Faber, 1932; Folcroft, Pennsylvania, Folcroft Editions, 1970.

Poetry in Prose (lecture). London, Oxford University Press, 1935; New York, Oxford University Press, 1937.

Early One Morning in the Spring: Chapters on Children and on Childhood as It Is Revealed in Particular in Early Memories and in Early Writings. London, Faber, and New York, Macmillan, 1935.

Arthur Thompson: A Memoir. Privately printed, 1938.

An Introduction to Everyman. London, Dent, 1938.

Stories, Essays, and Poems, edited by M. M. Bozman. London, Dent, 1938.

Behold, This Dreamer! Of Reverie, Night, Sleep, Dream, Love-Dreams, Nightmare, Death, The Unconscious, The Imagination, Divination, The Artist, and Kindred Subjects. London, Faber, and New York, Knopf, 1939.

Pleasures and Speculations. London, Faber, 1940; Freeport, New York, Books for Libraries, 1969.

Private View (essays). London, Faber, 1953.

Walter de la Mare: A Selection from His Writings, edited by Kenneth Hopkins. London, Faber, 1956.

Editor, *Desert Islands and Robinson Crusoe.* London, Faber, and New York, Fountains Press, 1930; revised edition, Faber, 1932.

Editor, *Poems,* by Christina Rossetti. Newtown, Wales, Gregynog Press, 1930.

Editor, *The Eighteen-Eighties: Essays by Fellows of the Royal Society of Literature.* London, Cambridge University Press, 1930.

Editor, *Love.* London, Faber, 1943; New York, Morrow, 1946.

Bibliography: in *L'Oeuvre de Walter de la Mare: Une Aventure Spirituelle* by Luce Bonnerot, Paris, Didier, 1969.

Critical Study: *Walter de la Mare* by Leonard Clark, London, Bodley Head, 1960; New York, Walck, 1961.

*   *   *

Walter de la Mare belongs to that small company of major poets who have also written poetry for the young. It is a company which includes William Blake, Christina Rossetti, Robert Louis Stevenson, and Rudyard Kipling. In output, range, and quality he is the greatest of them all. As a poet he published, between 1902 and 1944, 9 books of poetry for, and about, children. *Collected Rhymes and Verses* contains nearly all the poems – over 300 of them – which he wrote "with the young in mind."

He was also a story writer, and a storyteller, who wrote 20 original stories for children, and 60 retellings of traditional stories. In all he published 15 books of stories for children, beginning with *The Three Mulla-Mulgars* in 1910, and ending with *Collected Stories for Children* in 1947. The retellings are contained in *Told Again, Stories from the Bible,* and *Animal Stories.*

Although, perhaps, his stories and retellings for children are not now read so widely as they once were, largely because of changing social conditions and new fashions, no editor of an anthology for children dare omit including some of his poems. At least two dozen of these have passed into the language.

In addition, Walter de la Mare was a superb anthologist. His principal anthologies are *Come Hither,* and *Tom Tiddler's Ground. Early One Morning in the Spring* is an informed book of prose and poetry, though mainly for adults, consisting of "Chapters on Children and on Childhood as it is revealed in particular in early memories and in early writings." This book established him as a brilliant and scholarly writer about children who clearly knew about children's thoughts and feelings at first hand and who had studied childhood in most of its aspects.

When his first book of poems, *Songs of Childhood,* appeared in 1902, it was apparent to everyone that a genius had arrived who possessed an individual vision and a fresh and authentic poetic voice. The secret of his craftsmanship proved to be a rare fancy, unusual vowel melody and cunning rhythms, all of which had the effect of giving to the poems haunting overtones and strangeness. De la Mare had the gift of being able to put a spell upon children, largely through the music of his poetry, so that even when children today do not know the meaning of half the words used, they are beguiled by the exquisite vowel melody. In *Songs of Childhood* he wrote about witches, ogres, dwarfs, sleep, dreamland, moonlight and fairies, all, as it were, inhabiting a world set between dawn and dusk, often sad and sometimes sinister. *Peacock Pie* is undoubtedly his masterpiece; it has gone into many editions and now exists in a fascinating one illustrated by Edward Ardizzone. The world of *Peacock Pie* is drenched in moonlight, but it also has its fantasy and fun, romance, and a deep sense of brooding. The terrain the poems explore is delightfully mad and inconsequential, very English, washed by great seas, humming with sighing winds. *Collected Rhymes and Verses* finally proves that no poet has written finer poems about fairies, witches, winter, snow, the moon, the fantastic. Blake's children were mystics enjoying heaven. Stevenson's were wistful or gay, Christina Rossetti's were very personal to her, Kipling's always had a sense of the past. But de la Mare wrote as if he were a child himself, revealing his own childhood, though with the mature gifts of the true poet. Yet although his children are true to childhood, they are not *all* children; they are de la Mare children, modest and withdrawn, in close touch with terrors, splendours and the supernatural. Fearful and fanciful at the same time, they seem to be uncorrupted by the world. Although de la Mare wrote about everyday things, his poems are never far away from "a world beyond" which he himself created. His fields and seas are English; his dreams and sleep are Nowhere.

His longest story for children, *The Three Mulla-Mulgars*, is his prose masterpiece, one of the most poetical tales ever written. An enchanting allegory, it is a mixture of realism and fantasy, telling of the adventures of the monkeys Thumb, Thimble and Nod, living "on the borders of the Forest of Munza-Mulgar." They have the most exciting adventures, and meet the most extraordinary animals and people in the course of their wanderings. "The Three Sleeping Boys of Warwickshire" is also an excellent example of de la Mare's kind of story. It is a dreamy, 18th-century tale of magic, of Jeremy Nollykins, a chimney sweep, and his apprentices, Tom, Dick and Harry, whose shadow-shapes are captivated by the music of *Boys and Girls Come out to Play*. Each night when they hear it, they rise like phantoms from their beds to join the other sleeping children of the town. The cruel Noll consults a witch who tells him how to prevent the boys getting out at night. The result is that they fall into a trance, are exhibited in Warwick Museum, and sleep on for fifty-three years until the curator's niece opens the case where they are lying. "And out pell-mell came rushing our three young friends the chimney sweeps, their dream-shapes home at last." "The Lord Fish," his most ambitious and imaginative short story, tells of the adventures of a young fisherman, John Cobbler, who fished morning, noon and night. John comes upon a mysterious house, catches a pike from a brook that runs near it, and finds a key inside the fish. Eventually he is captured by the great Lord Fish and kept by him, in a fishlike state, in his great stone house. But, helped by the maid, John gains his freedom and discovers a casket which is to make his fortune. The story is full of dazzling and gripping writing, the work of an amazing craftsman. Of the retellings, *Animal Stories* consists of 42 stories and 46 rhymes. It is a storehouse of knowledge, with hardly an animal excluded. The homely animals – hare, hedgehog, frog, pig, cat, dog, goose, ox – play the leading parts; the human beings take second place. *Stories from the Bible* contains versions of the stories of the Garden of Eden, the Flood, Joseph, Moses, Samson, Samuel, Saul, and David. They are moving and tastefully written, with a great sense of style and exquisite literary taste, and are genuine works of literature. For those who seek for the best of de la Mare's stories, they are the 17 which make up his *Collected Stories for Children*. These richly sum up a life devoted to the delight and understanding of children. Diverse in subject matter and treatment, they are the work of one who never condescended to his readers, who honoured their intelligence and powers of imagination, and who was able to share with children themselves a clear and penetrating vision.

Of the anthologies, *Come Hither*, described as "a collection of rhymes and poems for the young of all ages," is still one of the greatest anthologies in the language. Spanning 600 years, it contains 438 poems by 260 poets, and is introduced by a fascinating allegorical story of how the book came into being. As if this were not enough, there are 300 pages of scholarly comments on the poems, showing an amazing knowledge of poetry and of feeling for it. *Tom Tiddler's Ground*, with Bewick woodcut decorations, is also a fine collection. Its brief introduction gives good advice to children and adults about the reading of poetry.

To sum up, then. The real success of Walter de la Mare as a poet, storyteller and anthologist for children was that he was wonderfully consistent, a master of the English language whose work has no period limitations, who could handle fantasy without its degenerating into absurdity and sentimentality, who saw life in terms of beauty and wisdom, and who had a deep concern for all unhappiness. He saw childhood in its wholeness, recognizing it to be elemental, wayward, unfathomable and divine. It is not surprising that de la Mare was a household name in his day. His work will be read and enjoyed for years to come, not only by children but by their parents and teachers.

—Leonard Clark

---

de REGNIERS, Beatrice Schenk. American. Born in Lafayette, Indiana, 16 August 1914. Educated at the University of Illinois, Urbana, 1931–33; University of Chicago, Ph.B. 1935, and graduate student, 1936–37; University of Toulouse, 1935; the Sorbonne, Paris, 1935–36; Winnteka Graduate Teachers College, Illinois, M.Ed. 1941. Married Francis de Regniers in 1946. Member of the Eloise Moore Dance Group, Chicago, 1942–43; Copywriter, Scott Foresman, publishers, Chicago, 1943–44; Welfare Officer, UNRRA, Egypt, 1944–46; Copywriter, American Book Company, New York, 1948–49; Director of Educational Materials, American Heart Association, New York, 1949–61. Since 1961, Editor, Lucky Book Club, Scholastic Book Services, New York. Address: c/o Seabury Press Inc., 815 Second Avenue, New York, New York 10017, U.S.A.

PUBLICATIONS FOR CHILDREN

Fiction

> *The Giant Story*, illustrated by Maurice Sendak. New York, Harper, 1953.
> *A Little House of Your Own*, illustrated by Irene Haas. New York, Harcourt Brace, 1954; London, Collins, 1957.
> *What Can You Do with a Shoe?*, illustrated by Maurice Sendak. New York, Harper, 1955.
> *A Child's Book of Dreams*, illustrated by Bill Sokol. New York, Harcourt Brace, 1957.
> *Cats Cats Cats Cats Cats*, illustrated by Bill Sokol. New York, Pantheon Books, 1958.
> *The Snow Party*, illustrated by Reiner Zimnik. New York, Pantheon Books, 1959; London, Faber, 1961.
> *What Happens Next: Adventures of a Hero*, illustrated by Remo. New York, Macmillan, 1959.
> *Who Likes the Sun?*, illustrated by Leona Pierce. New York, Harcourt Brace, 1961; London, Collins, 1962.
> *The Little Book*, illustrated by the author. New York, Walck, 1961.
> *The Little Girl and Her Mother*, illustrated by Esther Gilman. New York, Vanguard Press, 1963.
> *May I Bring a Friend?*, illustrated by Beni Montresor. New York, Atheneum, 1964; London, Collins, 1966.
> *How Joe the Bear and Sam the Mouse Got Together*, illustrated by Brinton Turkle. New York, Parents' Magazine Press, 1965.

Penny, with Marvin Bileck.   New York, Viking Press, 1966.

Circus.   New York, Viking Press, 1966.

The Giant Book, illustrated by William Lahey Cummings.   New York, Atheneum, 1966.

The Day Everybody Cried, illustrated by Nonny Hogrogian.   New York, Viking Press, 1967.

The Boy, The Rat, and the Butterfly, illustrated by Haig and Regina Shekerjian.   New York, Atheneum, 1971.

Verse

Was It a Good Trade?, illustrated by Maurice Sendak.   New York, Harper, 1956; London, Collins, 1957.

Something Special, illustrated by Irene Haas.   New York, Harcourt Brace, 1958; London, Collins, 1959.

Willy O'Dwyer Jumped in the Fire: Variations on a Folk Rhyme, illustrated by Beni Montresor.   New York, Atheneum, 1968; London, Collins, 1970.

Catch a Little Fox: Variations on a Folk Rhyme, illustrated by Brinton Turkle.   New York, Seabury Press, 1970; London, Hamish Hamilton, 1971.

It Does Not Say Meow and Other Animal Riddle Rhymes, illustrated by Paul Galdone.   New York, Seabury Press, 1972; Kingswood, Surrey, World's Work, 1973.

A Bunch of Poems and Verses, illustrated by Mary Jane Dunton.   New York, Seabury Press, 1977.

Other

The Shadow Book, photographs by Isabel Gordon.   New York, Harcourt Brace, 1960.

The Abraham Lincoln Joke Book, illustrated by William Lahey Cummings.   New York, Random House, 1965.

David and Goliath, illustrated by Richard Powers.   New York, Viking Press, 1965.

Red Riding Hood, Retold in Verse ..., illustrated by Edward Gorey.   New York, Atheneum, 1972; London, Collins, 1973.

The Enchanted Forest, illustrated by Edward Gorey.   New York, Atheneum, 1974.

Little Sister and the Month Brothers (Slav folktale), illustrated by Margot Tomes.   New York, Seabury Press, 1975; London, Hamish Hamilton, 1976.

Editor, with Eva Moore and Mary M. White, *Poems Children Will Sit Still For: A Selection for Primary Grades.*   New York, Citation Press, 1969.

*   *   *

"Sometimes you just want everyone to leave you alone. No children. No grownups. Then it is a good thing to have a little house of your own. Behind a chair in a corner is a good house. A big hat is like a little house. A false face is a little house for your face."

Those lines from Beatrice Schenk de Regniers' *A Little House of Your Own* are marked by the deceptively simple style that characterizes her writing. On closer examination, one becomes aware of the pleasing rhythm, the precise choice of words, the genuinely childlike point-of-view, and the *speakability* of the lines. These are qualities that distinguish most of the more than thirty books for young children that Beatrice de Regniers has written and published since 1953.

While unified in style, her output can be separated into several distinct categories. First there are the concept books, of which *A Little House of Your Own* is a notable example. Others in this group would include the poetic *Who Likes the Sun?*, *The Shadow Book* with its lovely blend of photographs and text, and *The Little Girl and Her Mother*, which gently describes what each can, and cannot, do and ends with the little girl growing up and becoming a mother herself.

Another category to which Mrs. de Regniers has made some important contributions is that of the retold folk tale. In both *Little Sister and the Month Brothers* and *Red Riding Hood* she employs her gift for simple directness to achieve texts that young children can read by themselves, while at the same time maintaining an unobtrusive elegance – no mean accomplishment. And her original story *The Snow Party* adheres to many of the classic folk tale patterns as it recounts what happened when a bunch of snowbound people – and animals – turned what might have been a disaster into a frolic. *The Snow Party* is one of Mrs. de Regniers' most unbridled, and most zestful, books.

The largest section in her body of work is comprised of picture book variations on folk rhymes, and original texts with the same lilting, musical quality. *What Can You Do with a Shoe?* is one of the most amusing and imaginative examples, and *Was It a Good Trade?*, *Catch a Little Fox*, and *It Does Not Say Meow* have their share of sparkling moments too. *Willy O'Dwyer Jumped in the Fire* seems too frail as a text, however, perhaps because Beni Montresor's pictures for it are so dark and heavy. Earlier, Mr. Montresor won the Caldecott Medal with another of Mrs. de Regniers' texts in the folk rhyme genre, *May I Bring a Friend?* While this sustains a pleasingly gentle tone as it tells of all the animals that accompany a little boy on his visits to the King and Queen, it lacks some of the energy that infuses Mrs. de Regniers' other song-like picture books.

Occupying a special place in her *oeuvre* are the exceptions, books that fit into no particular category as they experiment with new forms and themes. *The Day Everybody Cried* explores feelings of sadness and happiness but stays on too abstract a level to make its point successfully. *Penny*, a modern reworking of the Thumbelina theme, is a fascinating attempt to create a miniature novel. And *The Boy, The Rat, and the Butterfly* attempts even more – a parable of life, death, and rebirth expressed through the relationship of the three title characters, all of whom are named Peter. "Now they are going down the road," the book ends. "The boy, the rat, and the butterflies. They don't seem to be going very far. And wherever they are going, they are not getting there very fast. And it doesn't matter, really."

There it is again – the deceptive simplicity that stamps so many of Beatrice de Regniers' books for children.

—James C. Giblin

---

de ROO, Anne (Louise). New Zealander. Born in Gore, in 1931. Educated at New Plymouth Girls' High School; University of Canterbury, Christchurch, 1949–52, B.A. 1952. Library Assistant, Dunedin Public Library, 1956; Assistant Librarian, Dunedin Teachers' College, 1957–59; governess and part-time gardener, Shropshire, England, 1962–68; part-time secretary, Hertfordshire, England, 1969–73. Since 1974, part-time medical typist, Palmerston North, New Zealand. Agent: A. P. Watt and Son, 26–28 Bedford Row, London WC1R 4HL, England. Address: Flat 3, 8 Rolleston Street, Palmerston North, New Zealand.

PUBLICATIONS FOR CHILDREN

Fiction

The Gold Dog. London, Hart Davis, 1969.
Moa Valley. London, Hart Davis, 1969.

Boy and the Sea Beast, illustrated by Judith Anson.   London, Hart Davis, 1971; New
  York, Scholastic, 1974.
Cinnamon and Nutmeg.   London, Macmillan, 1972; Nashville, Nelson, 1974.
Mick's Country Cousins.   London, Macmillan, 1974.
Scrub Fire.   London, Heinemann, 1977.

Anne de Roo comments:
  As a child in New Zealand I had only books that told of strange faraway places where
Christmas came in midwinter and children gathered bluebells in the woods in May. Books in
fact that had nothing to do with the world I saw about me. Tales of strange distant places are
fine and exciting and I like to think I provide them for English and American children – New
Zealand is a new, wild place in which exciting things can still happen. But much more
important to me are the New Zealand children who as well as strange stories of Christmas by
the fireside instead of in the summer sunshine have a right to stories that belong to the world
they see about them and to parts of their country they have not yet explored for themselves.

                              *   *   *

  Anne de Roo's first book reveals a style which is unpretentious and sparing. *The Gold Dog*
is a good, lively "yarn," skillfully constructed with vigorous scenes of outdoor adventure as
children, following their own hunches, perform feats of courage. Set in a very authentic and
distinctive part of New Zealand, the mountainous district of Central Otago, scene of the gold
discoveries of Gabriel Read in 1861, the book describes a search for lost treasure. The most
interesting part of the story concerns the reverberations of the area's romantic past when the
old digger, Seb, wins the love and respect of the little community of Marston on the Oxburn.
  Moa Valley is also set in the mountains in the southern part of the South Island of New
Zealand. The book describes courage in the face of hardship when young people become lost
in unexplored territory. An older man is again the focus of the story: Mr. Peacock dreams he
will find a living moa, a giant flightless bird, long thought extinct.
  Boy and the Sea Beast marks a stage when a new dimension enters her work. Up to this
point, it is clear that Anne de Roo is technically very effective but while the quality of
suspense is strong, the solution to the action comes too easily and character is subordinated to
the need for a happy ending. This is much less so in *Boy and the Sea Beast* which is about a
child's friendship with a dolphin. The book is inspired by the charming stories of two famous
dolphins, Pelorous Jack and Opo, who have been friends to man in New Zealand. Despite the
very indifferent illustrations which in no way convey with accuracy the Maori or his
environment, Boy-at-Last Rangi and his family who live in the far North of the North Island
of New Zealand are spontaneous and vital people. The delightful dolphin, Thunder, is saved
by Boy from exploitation but must finally leave for the free and wild life with his own kind.
  This theme is extended and deepened in *Cinnamon and Nutmeg* and *Mick's Country
Cousins*, two closely related stories of the lush rolling dairy lands of the North Island
province of Taranaki in which characters matter far more than the adventures which follow
from their predicaments. In the second novel, Mick has no father and, as a consequence,
becomes unmanageable. Sent to wholesome surroundings in the country, he feels the tension
between his old values and the newer ones on the farm. Significantly, it is the love of animals
which has a large part in the development of a feeling for those around him.
  Anne de Roo has moved a long distance from her first stories of romantic adventure to
these latter stories which possess a deeper emotional content and a feeling for living things
that cause them to linger in the mind long after they are read.

                                                        —Tom Fitzgibbon

de TREVINO, Elizabeth Borton. American. Born in Bakersfield, California, 2 September 1904. Educated at Stanford University, California, B.A. 1925 (Phi Beta Kappa); Boston Conservatory of Music. Married Luis Treviño Gomez in 1935; has two children. Reporter, *Jamaica Plain Journal*, Boston; apprentice in production and advertising, Ginn and Company, publishers, Boston; Interviewer, Boston *Herald American*, for several years. Recipient: American Library Association Newbery Medal, 1966. Lives in Cuernavaca, Mexico. Agent: McIntosh and Otis, 18 East 41st Street, New York, New York 10017. Address: c/o Doubleday and Co., 245 Park Avenue, New York, New York 10017, U.S.A.

PUBLICATIONS FOR CHILDREN

Fiction

Pollyanna in Hollywood, illustrated by H. Weston Taylor.   Boston, Page, 1931.
Our Little Aztec Cousin of Long Ago, Being the Story of Coyotl and How He Won Honor under His Kings, illustrated by Harold Cue.   Boston, Page, 1934.
Pollyanna's Castle in Mexico, illustrated by Harold Cue.   Boston, Page, 1934.
Our Little Ethiopian Cousin: Children of the Queen of Sheba.   Boston, Page, 1935.
Pollyanna's Door to Happiness, illustrated by Harold Cue.   Boston, Page, 1936.
Pollyanna's Golden Horseshoe, illustrated by Griswold Tyng.   Boston, Page, 1939.
About Bellamy, illustrated by Jessie Robinson.   New York and London, Harper, 1940.
Pollyanna and the Secret Mission, illustrated by Harold Cue.   Boston, Page, 1951.
A Carpet of Flowers, illustrated by Alan Crane.   New York, Crowell, 1955; Kingswood, Surrey, World's Work, 1956.
Nacar, The White Deer, illustrated by Enrico Arno.   New York, Farrar Straus, 1963; Kingswood, Surrey, World's Work, 1964.
I, Juan de Pareja.   New York, Farrar Straus, 1965; London, Gollancz, 1966.
Casilda of the Rising Moon: A Tale of Magic and of Faith, of Knights and a Saint in Medieval Spain.   New York, Farrar Straus, 1967; London, Gollancz, 1968.
Turi's Poppa.   New York, Farrar Straus, 1968; as *Turi's Papa*, London, Gollancz, 1969.
Beyond the Gates of Hercules: A Tale of the Lost Atlantis.   New York, Farrar Straus, and London, Gollancz, 1971.

Other

Here Is Mexico.   New York, Farrar Straus, 1970.

PUBLICATIONS FOR ADULTS

Novels

Even As You Love.   New York, Crowell, 1957.
The Greek of Toledo: A Romantic Narrative about El Greco.   New York, Crowell, 1959.
The Fourth Gift.   New York, Doubleday, 1966.
The House on Bitterness Street.   New York, Doubleday, 1970.
The Music Within.   New York, Doubleday, 1973.

Other

My Heart Lies South: The Story of My Mexican Marriage.   New York, Crowell, 1953.
Where the Heart Is (memoirs).   New York, Doubleday, 1962.
Juarez, Man of Law.   New York, Farrar Straus, 1974.
The Hearthstone of My Heart (memoirs).   New York, Doubleday, 1977.

Manuscript Collection: Boston University Library.

* * *

"All my life," writes Elizabeth Borton de Treviño, "I have been fascinated by imaginative speculation," and each of her stories is such a speculation, triggered off by some legend or historical incident.

Of her books, *I, Juan de Pareja* has had most acclaim. It is based on Velasquez' paintings, and on the known facts of his life, but the hero is Juanico, his slave, who tells the story. It is an unusual and memorable book, concerned with the problems and frustrations of slavery, and the parallel constraints imposed on artistic freedom by the requirements of court convention. Tolerance, understanding, and love of Art and Truth are its moral values, as exemplified by Velasquez himself, whose words, "Art should be Truth, and Truth, unadorned, unsentimentalised, is Beauty," lie at the centre of the book.

This attitude is explicit also in *Beyond the Gates of Hercules*, a tale of the lost Atlantis which becomes, finally, a modern moral fable. The Atlanteans are deeply religious, and committed to the civilised peaceful way of life, though one might question here their uncritical acceptance of voluntary human sacrifice to the angry Seagod. The story elaborates the idyllic life of Atlantis in a Golden Age of mutual understanding and co-operation, though its happiness is soon shot through with trouble and anxiety as events move inexorably forward. For Baka, lacking the intuitive thought-reading powers of his people, becomes a scientist, and eventually, to compensate for his increasing alienation from his family, an aggressive power-seeker. He turns his master's potentially good invention to evil use, becomes a military dictator, and Atlantis is destroyed. Its fate is clearly a warning to the Atomic Age, but the diagnosis of its ills is too superficial and simplistic. The book has charm, all the same.

Turi's Poppa, though set in post-war Europe, with echoes of its confusions and distresses, is less fraught with warnings. Turi is half gypsy. After his mother's death he and his father, a penniless violin-maker, walk to Italy where work is waiting. Turi's gypsy lore and cunning, though of great help on the journey and in encounters with border guards, are also a source of trouble and distress: the conflicting attitudes and values of father and son are recounted with engaging simplicity, though with some of the lapses into sentimentality which so mar *Casilda of the Rising Moon*. This latter book tells the legendary story of a frail, suffering, sensitive Moorish princess, whose faith transforms her into an incredibly enduring and miracle-working saint. But the writing is strained and over-insistent, and the story remains a fervidly romantic idealisation which contrasts unfavourably with the calmer achievements of the other books. *Nacar, The White Deer* is a more appealing story, with its loving and detailed account of pastoral life in seventeenth century Mexico, exciting encounters with snakes and brigands, a voyage to Spain, and a climax in which the hitherto dumb hero makes an impassioned plea for the life of his deer, now threatened with a sacrifical role in a glorious royal hunt. This story, too, is concerned to extol and defend the gentler things of life against violence and greed: a theme which runs through all these stories, and which, in spite of the sentimentality which sometimes creeps in, remains refreshing and appealing to the sensitive, thoughtful young reader.

—Winifred Whitehead

DICKINSON, Peter. British. Born in Livingstone, Zambia, 16 December 1927. Educated at Eton College, Buckinghamshire, 1941–46; King's College, Cambridge (exhibitioner), B.A. 1951. National Service, 1946–48. Married Mary Rose Barnard in 1953; has two sons and two daughters. Assistant editor, *Punch* magazine, London, 1952–69. Recipient: Crime Writers Association Golden Dagger Award, for novel, 1968, 1969;

Guardian Award, 1977; *Boston Globe-Horn Book* Award, 1977. Agent: A. P. Watt and Son, 26–28 Bedford Row, London WC1R 4HL. Address: 33 Queensdale Road, London W11 4SB, England.

PUBLICATIONS FOR CHILDREN

Fiction

The Weathermonger.   London, Gollancz, 1968; Boston, Little Brown, 1969.

Heartsease, illustrated by Robert Hales.   London, Gollancz, and Boston, Little Brown, 1969.

The Devil's Children, illustrated by Robert Hales.   London, Gollancz, and Boston, Little Brown, 1970.

Emma Tupper's Diary.   London, Gollancz, and Boston, Little Brown, 1971.

The Dancing Bear, illustrated by David Smee.   London, Gollancz, and Boston, Little Brown, 1972.

The Iron Lion, illustrated by Marc Brown.   Boston, Little Brown, 1972; London, Allen and Unwin, 1973.

The Gift, illustrated by Gareth Floyd.   London, Gollancz, 1973; Boston, Little Brown, 1974.

The Blue Hawk, illustrated by David Smee.   London, Gollancz, and Boston, Little Brown, 1976.

Annerton Pit.   London, Gollancz, and Boston, Little Brown, 1977.

Plays

Television Plays: *Mandog* series, 1972; *The Changes*, 1975.

Other

Presto! Humorous Bits and Pieces.   London, Hutchinson, 1975.

Chance, Luck and Destiny (miscellany), illustrated by David Smee and Victor Ambrus.   London, Gollancz, 1975; Boston, Little Brown, 1976.

PUBLICATIONS FOR ADULTS

Novels

Skin Deep.   London, Hodder and Stoughton, 1968; as *The Glass-Sided Ants' Nest*, New York, Harper, 1968.

A Pride of Heroes.   London, Hodder and Stoughton, 1969; as *The Old English Peep Show*, New York, Harper, 1969.

The Seals.   London, Hodder and Stoughton, 1970; as *The Sinful Stones*, New York, Harper, 1970.

Sleep and His Brother.   London, Hodder and Stoughton, and New York, Harper, 1971.

The Lizard in the Cup.   London, Hodder and Stoughton, and New York, Harper, 1972.

The Green Gene.   London, Hodder and Stoughton, and New York, Pantheon Books, 1973.

The Poison Oracle.   London, Hodder and Stoughton, and New York, Pantheon Books, 1974.

The Lively Dead.   London, Hodder and Stoughton, and New York, Pantheon Books, 1975.

King and Joker.   London, Hodder and Stoughton, and New York, Pantheon Books, 1976.

Walking Dead.   London, Hodder and Stoughton, 1977.

Peter Dickinson comments:

My purpose in writing a children's book is to tell a story, and everything else is secondary to that; but when secondary considerations arise they have to be properly dealt with. Apart from that I like my stories exciting and as different as possible from the one I wrote last time. When I write for children I'm conscious of doing a different sort of thing from what I do when I write for adults, but that doesn't mean I'm writing down. Place and feel, even of imaginary landscapes, are important to me, nuances of character less so. Most of my books have an element of fantasy in them, but where this happens I try to deal with the subject in as practical and logical a way as possible.

*   *   *

Peter Dickinson arrived on the children's book scene in 1969, and by spring of the following year could be regarded as established and successful. His first three books were published within a few months of each other and were acclaimed in terms of the highest praise. These were *The Weathermonger, Heartsease,* and *The Devil's Children*, and they are all about the Changes: a time which the author describes as "now, or soon," when people in England have turned against machinery and gone back to a dark age of ignorance and malice. The three might well be called a trilogy in reverse; for the first, *The Weathermonger,* tells how the Changes ended, while the last, *The Devil's Children,* describes what happened at the beginning. *Heartsease* comes in the middle. All three books, however, are self-contained and can be read separately.

In *The Weathermonger,* two children, Geoffrey and Sally, having escaped from benighted England to France, are sent back to find out what is going on. After a dash across country in a superb 1909 Rolls Royce, borrowed from the Beaulieu motor museum, they track down the source of the Changes. This is the famous magician Merlin of Arthurian legend, who has been revived but is lying in a drug-sick condition, in which his powerful but distorted mind is having drastic effects on the land and on the mentality of its people. The children persuade him to give up the drug, and he returns to his long rest. This extraordinary and unconvincing explanation is a major flaw in an exciting and intriguing story. Wisely, in the other two books the author says no more about Merlin, and presents the Changes without explanation, as a background both for adventure and for some extremely shrewd perceptions of human nature.

Heartsease tells how some young people find a "witch," a young man who has been stoned and left for dead. At great risk they nurse him, then smuggle him on board an old tugboat lying in Gloucester Docks, and later manage to start up the tug's engine – an act of great wickedness in these machine-abhorring times – in order to get him to sea and away. This is a considerably better book than *The Weathermonger*: more unified, and with much more credible and interesting people in it.

The Devil's Children begins with a girl called Nicola who is left on her own in London at the start of the Changes and who herself experiences the revulsion against machinery which in the other books has been seen from outside. Nicola is adopted by a group of Sikhs who are unaffected by the Changes but feel themselves to be in danger; she is to be their "canary" and will indicate by her own reactions what they can and cannot do without giving offence. The way the Sikhs establish themselves as a rural community and deal first with hostile villagers and then with a robber band provides most of the matter of the story; and the portraits of the Sikhs, both individually and collectively, are sensitive and affectionate.

The three books form rather a mixed achievement: in many ways impressive but having some weaknesses, especially in *The Weathermonger*. Peter Dickinson's subsequent books have all been very different from them and from each other; he has refused to let himself be typecast.

Emma Tupper's Diary is a high-spirited holiday adventure story, and shows what can be done with this well-worn genre. Fourteen-year-old Emma and her Scottish cousins, living on the banks of a loch, decide to surprise the television people by producing a monster, but get a glorious and much greater surprise themselves. The background to this story is somewhat aristocratic: Emma's cousins' father is the clan chief of the McAndrews, and the family are monarchs of pretty well all they survey. In contrast, *The Gift* features a fairly humble family in which Dad keeps losing jobs and Mum goes off from time to time on "holidays," from one of which she returns with two new suitcases and a black eye. The "gift" of the title belongs to their son Davy and runs in the family: it's a second sight which enables him to see the pictures formed in the minds of people who are near him. It seems fairly harmless, though a slight nuisance, until the day Davy realises he is looking at the contents of a violently disordered mind. Soon he finds that a crime is being planned and Dad is going to be involved. The plan fails; but in the end Davy, with only his gift to help him, is face to face with a potential murderer.

The Gift, like *The Weathermonger*, is not a total success: perhaps because the author, while not content to write a straightforward thriller, has failed to give his story the psychological depth that would make a serious novel out of it. However, in *The Dancing Bear* and *The Blue Hawk* Dickinson is on his best form and shows how admirably he can imagine, construct and write a book.

The Dancing Bear opens in Byzantium in the 6th century A.D. After a great household has been raided by Huns, a young slave called Silvester sets out with Holy John, the dirty old resident saint, and Bubba the bear, on a perilous mission to Hunnish lands. This is a close-textured, vigorous and often very funny story, episodic but having a firm overall shape. The contrast between the devious intricacies of Byzantium and the brutal simplicity of life among the Huns is effectively drawn. Silvester, though able and resourceful, thinks as a slave and knows his place. It takes a formal manumission to persuade him that in his adventurings he has become a free man and can have the girl he wants.

The Blue Hawk is Peter Dickinson's most impressive book so far. The setting is a country that strongly suggests ancient Egypt, though the time (unstated) seems more likely to be the remote future than the remote past. It is a society run largely by priests in the names of the Gods: a society in which there are rigid rules for everything, and nothing can ever change. A boy priest called Tron, rashly interrupting the ritual sacrifice of a blue hawk, comes into companionship with the young, active but threatened King, and helps to open up the sealed, static land. There is a deep ambiguity in Tron, a boy unsure to whom he owes his allegiance; and there are even deeper mysteries surrounding the Gods. Do they exist, and if so, what are they like? Here is material for profound speculation; but nobody of course is obliged to speculate, and the story is compelling enough if simply read at surface level. With this book and *The Dancing Bear*, Peter Dickinson has more than earned the praise which perhaps was given too easily at the start of his career as a children's writer.

—John Rowe Townsend

DILLON, Eilís. Irish. Born in Galway, 7 March 1920. Educated at Ursuline Convent, Sligo. Married Cormac O'Cuilleanain in 1940 (died 1970), one son and two daughters; Vivian Mercier, 1974. Lecturer in creative writing, Trinity College, Dublin 1971–72. Agent: David Bolt, Bolt and Watson Ltd., 8 Storey's Gate, London S.W.1, England. Address: 7 Templemore Avenue, Dublin 6, Ireland; or, 1 El Vedado Lane, Santa Barbara, California 93105, U.S.A.

PUBLICATIONS FOR CHILDREN

Fiction

An Choill Bheo (The Live Forest). Dublin, Government Publication Sale Office, 1948.
Midsummer Magic, illustrated by Stuart Tresilian. London, Macmillan, 1950.
Oscar agus an Cóiste Sé nEasóg (Oscar and the Six-Weasel Coach). Dublin, Government Publication Sale Office, 1952.

The Lost Island, illustrated by Richard Kennedy. London, Faber, 1952; New York, Funk and Wagnalls, 1954.

The San Sebastian, illustrated by Richard Kennedy. London, Faber, 1953; New York, Funk and Wagnalls, 1954.

Ceol na Coille (The Song of the Forest). Dublin, Government Publication Sale Office, 1955.

The House on the Shore, illustrated by Richard Kennedy. London, Faber, 1955; New York, Funk and Wagnalls, 1956.

The Wild Little House, illustrated by V. H. Drummond. London, Faber, 1955; New York, Criterion Books, 1957.

The Island of Horses, illustrated by Richard Kennedy. London, Faber, 1956; New York, Funk and Wagnalls, 1957.

Plover Hill, illustrated by Prudence Seward. London, Hamish Hamilton, 1957.

Aunt Bedelia's Cats, illustrated by Christopher Brooker. London, Hamish Hamilton, 1958.

The Singing Cave, illustrated by Richard Kennedy. London, Faber, 1959; New York, Funk and Wagnalls, 1960.

The Fort of Gold, illustrated by Richard Kennedy. London, Faber and New York, Funk and Wagnalls, 1961.

King Big-Ears, illustrated by Kueta Vanecek. London, Faber, 1961; New York, Norton, 1963.

A Pony and a Trap, illustrated by Monica Brasier-Creagh. London, Hamish Hamilton, 1962.

The Cats' Opera, illustrated by Kueta Vanecek. London, Faber, 1962; Indianapolis, Bobbs Merrill, 1963.

The Coriander, illustrated by Richard Kennedy. London, Faber, 1963; New York, Funk and Wagnalls, 1964.

A Family of Foxes, illustrated by Richard Kennedy. London, Faber, 1964; New York, Funk and Wagnalls, 1965.

The Sea Wall, illustrated by Richard Kennedy. London, Faber, and New York, Farrar Straus, 1965.

The Lion Cub, illustrated by Richard Kennedy. London, Hamish Hamilton, 1966; New York, Duell, 1967.

The Road to Dunmore, illustrated by Richard Kennedy. London, Faber, 1966.

The Cruise of the Santa Maria, illustrated by Richard Kennedy. London, Faber, and New York, Funk and Wagnalls, 1967.

The Key, illustrated by Richard Kennedy. London, Faber, 1967.

Two Stories: The Road to Dunmore and The Key, illustrated by Richard Kennedy. New York, Meredith Press, 1968.

The Seals, illustrated by Richard Kennedy. London, Faber, 1968; New York, Funk and Wagnalls, 1969.

Under the Orange Grove, illustrated by Richard Kennedy. London, Faber, 1968; New York, Meredith Press, 1969.

A Herd of Deer, illustrated by Richard Kennedy. London, Faber, 1969; New York, Funk and Wagnalls, 1970.

The Wise Man on the Mountain, illustrated by Gaynor Chapman. London, Hamish Hamilton, 1969; New York, Atheneum, 1970.

The Voyage of Mael Duin, illustrated by Alan Howard. London, Faber, 1969.

The King's Room, illustrated by Richard Kennedy. London, Hamish Hamilton, 1970.

The Five Hundred, illustrated by Gareth Floyd. London, Hamish Hamilton, 1972.

The Shadow of Vesuvius. Nashville, Nelson, 1977.

Other

Living in Imperial Rome, illustrated by Richard Kennedy. London, Faber, 1974; as *Rome under the Emperors*, Nashville, Nelson, 1975.

Editor, *The Hamish Hamilton Book of Wise Animals*, illustrated by Bernard Brett. London, Hamish Hamilton, 1975.

PUBLICATIONS FOR ADULTS

Novels

Death at Crane's Court.   London, Faber, 1953; New York, Walker, 1963.
Sent to His Account.   London, Faber, 1954; New York, Walker, 1969.
Death in the Quadrangle.   London, Faber, 1956; New York, Walker, 1968.
The Bitter Glass.   London, Faber, 1958; New York, Appleton Century Crofts, 1959.
The Head of the Family.   London, Faber, 1960.
Bold John Henebry.   London, Faber, 1965.
Across the Bitter Sea.   New York, Simon and Schuster, 1973; London, Hodder and Stoughton, 1974.
Blood Relations.   London, Hodder and Stoughton, and New York, Simon and Schuster, 1977.

Plays

A Page of History (produced Dublin, 1966).

Radio Play: *Manna*, 1960.

Eilis Dillon comments:
I began to write at a very early age and so unselfconsciously that it was almost inevitable that I should begin by writing children's books. I work on them exactly as I do on adult fiction, concentrating on character and background rather than on plot but usually find that a strong story soon develops. Almost all of my books for children have a strong Irish background and have their source in my knowledge of the Irish language. The exceptions are set in Italy, where I lived for six years.

*   *   *

Though some of her books for younger readers, notably *Under the Orange Grove* and *The Five Hundred*, are set in Italy, Eilis Dillon is best known as a writer of Irish adventure stories appealing especially to boys of about 9 to 13. This description alone, however, does not adequately reflect her quality, for in her authentic picture of life on the west coast of Ireland, with a sensitive portrayal of human motives and emotions, Miss Dillon has raised the conventional adventure story to a level of seriousness that is rare in children's books. Some of her subjects – boats, deserted islands, storms, wrecks, caves, assorted land and sea creatures, tinkers, horse-thieves, eccentric men and women – may not be particularly bold or original; in less skilful hands they could well receive banal and melodramatic treatment. But if her earliest books such as *The Lost Island* and *The San Sebastian* should strain credulity in places, their successors are well-constructed stories of originality and realism, with credible characters and events arising naturally out of everyday life in Connemara. What gives Miss Dillon's novels their distinctive depth is her ability to invest her material with mature significance as well as youthful excitement, and to treat important human themes in an unforced, undidactic way.

A recurrent theme is misunderstanding, discord, and ultimate reconciliation. Bad blood exists within or between families, between island and island, islanders and the mainland, or the local inhabitants and a foreign newcomer. Tension arises from superstition, suspicion, stupidity, pride, or obstinacy, and often harks back to some trivial incident or apocryphal tale in the distant past, such as the feud in *The Coriander* between the islanders of Inishgillan and those of Inishthorav over the alleged extinction of the Killaney light long ago in order to cause a lucrative wreck, or the alleged betrayal of the priest in the rebellion of 1795 that is still the occasion of bitterness between the men of Rossmore and those of Inishrone in *The Island of Horses*. Without making light of the consequences, the author plays a gentle if pointed humour upon these human foibles. It usually takes an alliance of boys and older women to bring the men to their senses, despite the men's obstructive attitudes on the place of boys, and women, in their society. As Sally MacDonagh says in *The Sea Wall*, "It happens that way in the world, that the young people have more courage than the grown-up ones." The heroes of the stories are boys of 15 or 16, approaching manhood and ready to test their growing powers in response to challenging situations, yet close enough in age and status to form a link between the boy reader and the world of adults. For in the course of their adventures with currachs and hookers which enact and match children's fantasies, these heroes encounter the harsh realities of life, including conflict of loyalties and adult unreliability. The reality of Miss Dillon's fiction is moral, social and emotional, as well as physical.

In Connemara and the islands of Galway Bay, families have dwindled and declined through emigration to America. Few return with their new skills and prosperity. Islands that once thrived are now inhabited only by animals grazing among the derelict homes. Old men remember with wild glee their deeds against the Black and Tans. The sense of community is very strong, and the power of customs and traditional beliefs is ever present. The physical scene is vividly recreated, from the populous, jostling Galway Horse Fair to the bleak tracts of moorland where the turfs are cut for the fires. Each story is separate, without formal links with any other, yet they share a distinctive atmosphere that is powerfully and sensitively evoked in language that does not strain after figurative effect or portentous symbolism but works directly. The deceptively simple drawings, contributed by Richard Kennedy throughout a remarkable 25-year partnership, subtly complement the keen sense of place and character established in the writing. Miss Dillon's books are marked for their restraint and under-statement, and for their total lack of quaintness and sentimentality.

Miss Dillon's adult characters, unlike those in so many children's books, are as convincing as the younger ones. Particularly well drawn are the irascible, alienated, or eccentric older men, such as the shipwrecked doctor in *The Coriander*, chafing at his enforced stay on Inishgillan; the grandfather and Colman Flaherty, both in *The Cruise of the Santa Maria*, who drive away those close to them by their fierce independence and insults; the remote figure of Michael Joyce in *A Herd of Deer*, mystified by his neighbours' hostility to his unwitting flouting of local custom. But Miss Dillon excels in creating strong-minded, highly individual women who have in them "the stored wisdom and charity of years," such as old Mrs. Conroy in *The Island of Horses*, making her affecting but unsentimental journey to the abandoned island where she was born; Mamó in *The Coriander*, whose patient hospitality and caring good sense win over the doctor to the islanders; Sally MacDonagh in *The Sea Wall*, striving against obstinacy and superstition to prevent another disaster; and the silent, red-haired Maggie in *The Cruise of the Santa Maria*, devotedly finishing her dead father's half-built hooker. Miss Dillon sensitively reveals as the narrative unfolds the motives and feelings of each character, major or minor, good or bad, man, woman or child, so that the moments of high drama or pathos, such as when the men of Inishgillan arrive off Inishthorav to retrieve their stolen sheep, or when Sarah is reunited with her old father, Colman Flaherty, need no elaboration but rely on an imaginative response from the reader.

Pervading the swift action and wide-ranging adventure is Miss Dillon's wise, moral, sometimes gently mocking, always compassionate reflection upon the life and lives she so perceptively observes. To have fashioned out of the child's adventure story a natural vehicle for moral significance, without obtrusive moralising, and without loss of narrative interest and excitement, is a major achievement.

—Graham Hammond

DONKIN, Nance (Clare). Australian. Born in West Maitland, New South Wales. Married Victor Donkin in 1939; has one son and one daughter. Journalist, *Daily Mercury*, Maitland, and *Morning Herald*, Newcastle. President, Children's Book Council, Victoria, 1968–76. Recipient: Australian Arts Council travel grant, 1972. Address: 297 Canterbury Road, Forest Hill, Victoria, Australia.

PUBLICATIONS FOR CHILDREN

Fiction

> *Araluen Adventures*, illustrated by Edith B. Bowden.   Melbourne, Cheshire, 1946.
> *No Medals for Meg*, illustrated by Edith B. Bowden.   Melbourne, Cheshire, 1947.
> *Julie Stands By*, illustrated by Joan Turner.   Melbourne, Cheshire, 1948.
> *Blue Ribbon Beth*.   Melbourne, Oxford University Press, 1951.
> *House by the Water*, illustrated by Astra Lacis Dick.   London, Angus and Robertson, 1969.
> *Johnny Neptune*.   Sydney, Angus and Robertson, 1971; London, Angus and Robertson, 1972.
> *The Cool Man*.   London, Angus and Robertson, 1973.
> *A Friend for Petros*, illustrated by Gavin Rowe.   London, Hamish Hamilton, 1974.
> *Patchwork Grandmother*, illustrated by Mary Dinsdale.   London, Hamish Hamilton, 1975.
> *Green Christmas*, illustrated by Gavin Rowe.   London, Hamish Hamilton, 1976.
> *Yellowgum Girl*, illustrated by Margaret Loxton.   London, Hamish Hamilton, 1976.
> *A Handful of Ghosts*.   London, Hodder and Stoughton, 1976.

Other

> *Sheep*, illustrated by Jocelyn Jones.   Melbourne, Oxford University Press, 1967.
> *Sugar*, illustrated by Jocelyn Jones.   Melbourne, Oxford University Press, 1967.
> *An Emancipist*, illustrated by Jane Robinson.   Melbourne, Oxford University Press, 1968.
> *A Currency Lass*, illustrated by Jane Walker.   Melbourne, Oxford University Press, 1969.
> *An Orphan*, illustrated by Ann Culvenor.   Melbourne, Oxford University Press, 1970.
> *Margaret Catchpole*, illustrated by Edwina Bell.   Sydney and London, Collins, 1974.

> Editor, *The Australian Children's Annual*.   Melbourne, Lothian, 1963.

Manuscript Collection: Dromkeen Trust Collection, Melbourne.

Nance Donkin comments:
   Digging into Australia's rough, tough, sad, bad past has been a satisfying and stimulating occupation. In trying to picture the past for children I hope to help them to see, even vaguely, that "history is people like you." My several books for younger children I enjoyed writing very much because I enjoy the company and the conversation of young children and have been pleased that I am apparently able to communicate with them in this other way.

*   *   *

   Perhaps the mood of Nance Donkin's writing was fashioned by the – in her own words – "web of words spun by my father, a natural story-teller of the yarn and tall story ender." Her reason for writing her books, she once said, is because "I have found writing for children gives me great satisfaction and I think there is an enormous vacuum in Australian children's writing which should be filled with lots of well-written books about ordinary lives and occasionally making extraordinary discoveries, though not of buried treasures or smugglers' caches." How far has she succeeded in attaining this goal? In her books ordinary lives abound; there is a scarcity of extraordinary discoveries.

Her early books deal with middle class suburban and country life. *Araluen Adventures, No Medals for Meg* and *Julie Stands By* have uninspired plots and much digressive conversation. "Elsie's a good stick," said Kate, "but she does get rattled, doesn't she?" Except in *Blue Ribbon Beth* where two girls assist the home help to recover his memory, there are no really dramatic moments.

Her later books are more interesting, and she shows a genuine feeling for her Australian background. In *House by the Water* there is a real family, and the dialogue is stronger and more convincing. May Reibey, having told her sons that she is an ex-convict, adds, "There's something else boys," she winked at them and put a finger up in warning, "Now you know how I was boned, don't turn conk! No whiddling to the girls." *Johnny Neptune*, set in Sydney in 1790, describes the fortunes of an orphan fighting for existence in the rough life of the new colony and, although sometimes rambling, is a pioneer story that holds one's interest.

Two later books show an appreciation and knowledge of the Australian Bush. *Yellowgum Girl* is an enjoyable story about a city boy's holiday near a nature reserve where "Desert mice that move quicker than a flash nibble silky tea tree blossom and the emu's favourite food is the bright red tops of greeny flame heath bushes." In *Green Christmas* a family spending their first camping Christmas are shown, in this so-called new country, a secret cave where the wall paintings are thousands of years old.

—Nancy Shepherdson

DONOVAN, John. American. Born in 1928. Executive Director, Children's Book Council, New York. Address: c/o Children's Book Council Inc., 67 Irving Place, New York, New York 10003, U.S.A.

PUBLICATIONS FOR CHILDREN

Fiction

> *The Little Orange Book*, illustrated by Mauro Caputo. New York, Morrow, 1961.
> *I'll Get There. It Better Be Worth the Trip.* New York, Harper, 1969; London, Macdonald, 1970.
> *Wild in the World.* New York, Harper, 1971.
> *Remove Protective Coating a Little at a Time.* New York, Harper, 1973.
> *Good Old James*, illustrated by James Stevenson. New York, Harper, 1975.
> *Family.* New York, Harper, 1976.

PUBLICATIONS FOR ADULTS

Play

> *Riverside Drive* (produced New York, 1964).

*   *   *

John Donovan's novels stand apart from each other and from most of children's literature. His characters live in a lonely world, but in each book they find a close friend to redeem them from emotional extinction. These friends are thorny and independent, giving their love with integrity, without obligation.

In *I'll Get There. It Better Be Worth the Trip*, Dave Ross is isolated by his grandmother's death. His divorced parents do not really want either him or his dog Fred, unless by occasional arrangement. The one classmate Dave is drawn to in his new school still suffers too much from the death of a best friend to let Dave near. Later, the love both boys need and begin to feel toward each other leads to a brief sexual encounter and, after Dave's beloved dog is killed, firm companionship.

Where *I'll Get There* intones the casual language of a first-person narrative, *Wild in the World* is stark, tight, and concentrated. A brief first chapter dispenses with twelve members of a mountain family, leaving only one teenage boy alive. He survives physically by his own strength and knowledge and emotionally with the help of a wild dog whom he calls Son. The two discover and care for each other with growing joy. Son endures a rattlesnake bite, but John dies of pneumonia, leaving to the dog his heritage of free affection and to readers an intensely moving memory.

Remove Protective Coating a Little at a Time returns to the desperately sophisticated New York City boy who has everything materially and very little else. Harry caused his parents' marriage by being conceived, and the marriage dictates a predictable but empty path for both his mother, an ex-prom queen whose life means nothing as her son grows older, and his father, a highschool baseball star who has succeeded in the advertising business and in staying away from home to avoid his wife's disintegration. None of Harry's peers seem to stray across his path; an old woman does – briefly and meaningfully. Amelia is a bum, but she speaks her mind and lives by it as well. By the time she disappears, Harry has finally connected with somebody for the first time in his life, deeper than surface. One knows it will happen again.

Family is beautifully written. It blends wit with tragedy, a tight plot with unforgettable characterizations, a perfectly trimmed style with an ambitiously extended theme, and an experimental mixture of genres — science fiction, fantasy, realism, and allegory. Several captive apes, more or less strangers to each other, escape from what one of them suspects will be a mutilating experiment. In finding and establishing a wild home, they revert to a natural allegiance of warmth and loyalty. A gentle Man, who symbolizes human integrity, joins them briefly, but the next visitors are late fall hunters. With the leader and baby slain, the animal narrator and his pregnant companion return to the science lab, forced to trust the mercy of man. The reader is forced to respond with compassion as a member of the universal family.

Donovan creates scenes of great impact. His ideal of the respectful common bond reaches straight and simply toward adolescents struggling with the pain both of loneliness and relationships. He has been there, and made the trip worthwhile.

—Betsy Hearne

DOWNIE, Mary Alice (Dawe). Canadian. Born in Alton, Illinois, United States, 12 February 1934. Educated at St. Clement's School, Toronto; Trinity College, University of Toronto, 1951–55, B.A. (honours) in English 1955. Married John Downie in 1959; has three daughters. Reporter, *Marketing* magazine, Toronto, 1955–56; Editorial Assistant, *Canadian Medical Association Journal*, Toronto, 1956–57; Librarian, later Publicity Director, Oxford University Press, Toronto, 1958–59. Since 1973, Book Review Editor, *Kingston Whig-Standard*. Recipient: Ontario Arts Council award, 1970, 1975; Canada Council bursary, 1971. Address: 190 Union Street, Kingston, Ontario, Canada.

PUBLICATIONS FOR CHILDREN

Fiction

> *Honor Bound*, with John Downie, illustrated by Joan Huffman.   Toronto, Oxford
> University Press, and New York, Walck, 1971.
> *Scared Sarah*, illustrated by Laszlo Gal.   Toronto, Nelson, 1974.
> *Dragon on Parade*, illustrated by Mary Lynn Baker.   Toronto, Peter Martin Associates,
> 1974.

Other

> *The Magical Adventures of Pierre* (French-Canadian fairy tale), illustrated by Yüksel
> Hassan.   Toronto, Nelson, 1974.
> *The Witch of the North: Folktales of French Canada*, illustrated by Elizabeth
> Cleaver.   Ottawa and San Francisco, Oberon Press, 1975.
> Editor, with Barbara Robertson, *The Wind Has Wings: Poems from Canada*, illustrated
> by Elizabeth Cleaver.   Toronto, Oxford University Press, and New York, Walck,
> 1968; London, Oxford University Press, 1969.

Mary Alice Downie comments:

My books are for children, and my themes are usually drawn from the Canadian past. It's a short past when you consider the country but stretches out when the heritage of the immigrant is included.

The books have resulted from a mixture of writing, translating, retelling and rediscovery of little-known materials. My aim is to entertain and occasionally inform young Canadians. My hope is that the stories and poems will appeal beyond the borders of the country and the age of childhood.

                              *   *   *

Mary Alice Downie's *Honor Bound*, written jointly with her husband, John Downie, and *Dragon on Parade* describe completely different facets of Canadian life, separated by two centuries. *Honor Bound* tells the story of a family, loyal to the British Crown, who were forced to leave their home in Philadelphia at the end of the American War of Independence. The United Empire Loyalists formed a hardy nucleus of pioneers who developed the wilderness of Upper Canada and endured many hardships. This is a lively, well-researched story of a thrilling period in Canada's history. The long and dangerous journey on horseback and by sailing ship across Lake Ontario, the rigors of a first Canadian winter and the many hair-raising adventures of the family members bring history to life in an eminently readable fashion. The insights into family relationships and the well-developed characters will appeal to 8–12-year-olds.

Dragon on Parade, a picture book, tells the story of summertime in a typical Canadian small town on the shores of Lake Huron. For children from other countries this is a charming introduction to family life in Canada, and Canadian children take it to their hearts for it tells of simple, everyday incidents which might have happened to any one of them. The story centres on the annual summer carnival in the town and the family project to construct a fearsome dragon for the opening parade. Three generations work together to produce the prize-winning entry. Detailed illustrations and a clear well-written text combine in this warm family story.

—Barbara Smiley

DRUMMOND, V(iolet) H(ilda).   British.   Born in London, 30 July 1911. Educated at The Links, Eastbourne, Sussex; St. Martin's School of Art, London. Married Anthony Swetenham in 1948; has one son by previous marriage. Since 1960, Chairman, V. H. Drummond Productions. Recipient: Library Association Kate Greenaway Medal, for illustration, 1957. Address: 24 Norfolk Road, London NW8 6HG, England.

PUBLICATIONS FOR CHILDREN (illustrated by the author)

Fiction

> *Phewtus the Squirrel.*   London and New York, Oxford University Press, 1939; revised edition, London, Constable, 1966.
> *Mrs. Easter's Parasol.*   London, Faber, 1944.
> *Miss Anna Truly.*   London, Faber, 1945; Boston, Houghton Mifflin, 1949.
> *Lady Talavera.*   London, Faber, 1946.
> *Tidgie's Innings.*   London, Faber, 1947.
> *The Charming Taxicab.*   London, Faber, 1947.
> *The Mountain That Laughed.*   London, Grey Walls Press, 1947.
> *The Flying Postman.*   London, Penguin, and Boston, Houghton Mifflin, 1948.
> *Mr. Finch's Pet Shop.*   London, Faber, 1953; New York, Oxford University Press, 1954.
> *Mrs. Easter and the Storks.*   London, Faber, 1957; New York, A.S. Barnes, 1960.
> *Little Laura's Cat.*   London, Faber, 1960.
> *Little Laura on the River.*   London, Faber, 1960.
> *Little Laura and the Thief.*   London, Nelson, 1963.
> *Little Laura and Her Best Friend.*   London, Nelson, 1963.
> *Little Laura and the Lonely Ostrich.*   London, Nelson, 1963.
> *Miss Anna Truly and the Christmas Lights.*   London, Longman, 1968.
> *Mrs. Easter and the "Golden Bounder."*   London, Faber, 1970.
> *Mrs. Easter's Christmas Flight.*   London, Faber, 1972.
> *Mrs. Easter's Parasol.*   London, Faber, 1977.

Plays

> Television Plays: *Little Laura* series, 1963.

Illustrator: *The Twelfth* by J. K. Stanford, 1944; *Here and There a Lusty Trout* by Thomas A. Powell, 1947; *Verse and Worse* by Arnold Silcock, 1947; *The Shaggy Dog Story* by Eric Partridge, 1948; *Carbonel* by Barbara Sleigh, 1955; *The Wild Little House* by Eilís Dillon, 1955; *Espirit de Corps* by Lawrence Durrell, 1957; *The Piemakers* by Helen Cresswell, 1967.

V. H. Drummond comments:
   I wrote my first children's book for my son aged four; the idea for my next book, *Mrs. Easter's Parasol,* came to me while walking with him in Kensington Gardens. In 1963 I drew the pictures and wrote the stories for the *Little Laura* series on BBC "Children's Hour," and my last three children's books were written for my three grandchildren.

*   *   *

   V. H. Drummond won the Kate Greenaway medal in 1957 but her talent as an imaginative and original writer of stories for young children is at least as great as her talent as an illustrator. Her characters, Little Laura and her beloved Nannie, Laura's best friend, Billie

Guftie, and his Aunt Mrs. Easter, even Miss Anna Truly (though she hates washing-up) inhabit a world which has so little connection with reality that surely no one could call it dated or class-ridden. Certainly, Miss Drummond has a decided preference for things that are not new-fangled and automatic, useful as the escalator is in disposing of Vilewort the Villain. And Laura may cry "What larkish fun!" This is hardly the expression of a contemporary child, but one with as much appeal for such children as her ride on the swan's back and her unselfconscious converse with the King.

Miss Drummond's characters are all tremendously spirited. The King reacts to the story of Mrs. Easter and the storks with "What courage! What a tale of romance!" We can only say the same. One of Miss Drummond's favourite words is elegant. The King's tea table is, of course, elegant. So is the main lodge in *Lady Talavera*. More surprisingly, so is the ice cream in *The Flying Postman*. And Miss Drummond's style and language are never less than elegant: "So they descended from the roof and made their way towards the harbour, followed by the grieving bird."

The Flying Postman is the best of all these delightful books. Shorter than most, with bolder yet softer artwork, the story tells of Mr. Musgrove, who delivered letters by helicopter and foolishly crashed into the church when entertaining the children with his aerobatics. The Postal Authorities dismiss him and Mr. Musgrove is forced to make a living by selling pink ice cream. Fortunately one day the Post Master General has an accident outside Mr. Musgrove's house and, in return for his kindness and the reviving elegant ice cream, reinstates him in his job – a logical, unbureaucratic procedure any child would applaud.

—Ann Thwaite

---

du BOIS, William Pène. American. Born in Nutley, New Jersey, 9 May 1916. Educated at Miss Marstow's School, New York; Lycée Hoche, Versailles, 1924–28; Lycée de Nice, 1928–29; Morristown School, New Jersey, 1930–34. Served in the United States Army, 1941–45; correspondent, *Yank* magazine. Married Jane Bouché in 1943; Willa Kim, 1955. Art editor and designer, *Paris Review*. Recipient: New York *Herald Tribune* Festival award, 1947, 1956; American Library Association Newbery Medal, 1948; *New York Times* award, for illustration, 1971. Agent: Ann Watkins Inc., 77 Park Avenue, New York, New York 10016. Address: c/o Viking Press, 625 Madison Avenue, New York, New York 10022, U.S.A.

PUBLICATIONS FOR CHILDREN (illustrated by the author)

Fiction

  Elizabeth, The Cow Ghost. New York, Nelson, 1936; London, Museum Press, 1944.
  Giant Otto. New York, Viking Press, 1936; London, Harrap, 1937.
  Otto at Sea. New York, Viking Press, 1936; London, Harrap, 1937.
  The Three Policemen; or, Young Bottsford of Farbe Island. New York, Viking Press, 1938.
  The Great Geppy. New York, Viking Press, 1940; London, Hale, 1942.
  The Flying Locomotive. New York, Viking Press, 1941; London, Museum Press, 1946.
  The Twenty-One Balloons. New York, Viking Press, 1947; London, Hale, 1950.
  Peter Graves. New York, Viking Press, 1950; Kingswood, Surrey, World's Work, 1974.
  Bear Party. New York, Viking Press, 1951; Kingswood, Surrey, World's Work, 1975.

Squirrel Hotel. New York, Viking Press, 1952.
The Giant. New York, Viking Press, 1954.
Lion. New York, Viking Press, 1956.
Otto in Texas. New York, Viking Press, 1959; Leicester, Brockhampton Press, 1961.
Otto in Africa. New York, Viking Press, 1961; Leicester, Brockhampton Press, 1962.
The Alligator Case. New York, Harper, 1965.
Lazy Tommy Pumpkinhead. New York, Harper, 1966.
The Horse in the Camel Suit. New York, Harper, 1967.
Pretty Pretty Peggy Moffitt. New York, Harper, 1968.
Porko von Popbutton. New York, Harper, 1969.
Call Me Bandicoot. New York, Harper, 1970.
Otto and the Magic Potatoes. New York, Viking Press, 1970.
Bear Circus. New York, Viking Press, 1971; Kingswood, Surrey, World's Work, 1975.

Other

The Hare and the Tortoise, and The Tortoise and the Hare, with Lee Po. New York, Doubleday, 1972.

Illustrator: *Harriet* by Charles McKinley, Jr., 1946; *Witch of Scrapfaggot Green,* 1948; *The Mousewife* by Rumer Godden, 1951; *The Young Visitors* by Daisy Ashford, 1951; *Moon Ahead* by Leslie Greener, 1951; *Twenty and Ten* by Claire Bishop, 1952; *My Brother Bird* by Evelyn Ames, 1954; *The Rabbit's Umbrella* by George Plimpton, 1955; *In France* by Marguerite Clement, 1956; *Castles and Dragons* edited by the Child Study Association, 1958; *Fierce John* by Edward Fenton, 1959; *The Owl and the Pussycat* by Edward Lear, 1962; *The Light Princess* by George MacDonald, 1962; *The Three Little Pigs,* 1962; *Dr. Ox's Experiment* by Jules Verne, 1963; *A Certain Small Shepherd* by Rebecca Caudill, 1965; *The Magic Finger* by Roald Dahl, 1966; *The Tiger in the Teapot* by Betty Yurdin, 1968; *Digging for China: A Poem* by Richard Wilbur, 1970; *The Topsy-Turvy Emperor of China* by Isaac Bashevis Singer, 1971; *Seal Pool* by Peter Matthiessen, 1972; *William's Doll,* 1972, *My Grandson Lew,* 1974, *The Unfriendly Book,* 1975, and *It's Not Fair,* 1976, all by Charlotte Zolotow; *Where's Gomer?* by Norma Farber, 1974; *Moving Day* by Tobi Tobias, 1976; *The Runaway Flying Horse* by Paul J. Bonzon, 1976.

                              *   *   *

If the prolific writings of William Pène du Bois suggest any common theme, it would have to be the celebration of eccentricity. His Newbery Medal winner, *The Twenty-One Balloons,* begins with a retired arithmetic teacher being retrieved from the Atlantic Ocean where he clung for dear life to the workings of twenty-one deflated balloons. But instead of pursuing the reason why, the author focuses instead upon outrageously idiosyncratic Professor Sherman as he rebuffs entreaties of benefactors and dignitaries – even the President of the United States – rather than relate his experiences prior to addressing the Western American Explorer's Club. His accidental landing on the island of Krakatoa had brought him into contact with people whose proclivities were if anything more peculiar than his own. The gentleman who originally discovered Sherman unconscious and naked upon the beach, waits in a stolid, butler-like stance to provide the survivor with spats, a detachable collar and a starched white dickey in order to commence a brief expedition through tropical brush and into the society of Krakatoa.

Although the virtues of loyalty and perseverence are implicitly applauded throughout du Bois' writings, overbearing commitment to excess commands the essential spotlight. In separate studies of the seven deadly sins (four of these theological fictions for children have appeared so far) he parades impish delight in excess with one central character demonstrating comic ingenuity in perpetuating an obvious psychological imbalance. There is no denunciation of vice. Porko von Popbutton's swelled belly and voracious gastronomic compulsion cast him ultimately as unlikely hero as victorious goalie against an arch rival school. Ermine Bandicoot, the youthful miser, is as well a charming teller of tales who eschews cigarettes because they are too costly. He does, however, collect the butts with the intention of reprocessing valuable tobacco. His comic lust for gain provokes the ingenious venture of using the Statue of Liberty as an advertising pedestal and he later uses a football field to roll the world's largest cigarette. *Peter Graves* features two eccentrics, Peter the fearless, who urges his school gang across the bay via sharply peaking and declining bridge cables, and Houghton F. Furlong whose horrible house and preposterous inventions scare off even the authorities. Furlong's latest concoction defies the inventor and his youthful accomplice in the search for a possible use. Five small books concern Otto, a Bunyanesque otterhound who can snuggle up to the Sphinx, fan a windmill with his tail, and casually bury 171 Arab warriors in the sand. *The Alligator Case* and its sequel *The Horse in the Camel Suit* concern a young boy's preoccupation with being a detective. His over zealous imagination is matched by equally peculiar villans, one of whom knocks bullet peas into the air with pork chop mallets, each time adroitly retrieving the vegetables in his open mouth. The comedy of humours continues throughout the du Bois opus.

—Leonard R. Mendelsohn

DUGGAN, Maurice (Noel). New Zealander. Born in Auckland, 25 November 1922. Educated at the University of Auckland. Married Barbara Platts in 1945; one child. Worked in advertising, 1961–75, with J. English Wright (Advertising) Ltd., Auckland, 1965–75. Recipient: Hubert Church Memorial Award, 1957; New Zealand Library Association Esther Glen Award, 1959; Katherine Mansfield Award, for short story, 1959; Otago University Robert Burns Fellowship, 1960; New Zealand Literary Fund Scholarship, 1966; Freda Buckland Award, 1970. *Died in January 1975.*

PUBLICATIONS FOR CHILDREN

Fiction

> *Falter Tom and the Water Boy*, illustrated by Kenneth Rowell. Auckland, Janet and Blackwood Paul, 1957; London, Faber, and New York, Criterion Books, 1958.
> *The Fabulous McFanes and Other Children's Stories*, illustrated by Richard Kennedy. Whatamorgo Bay, Cape Cattley, 1974.

PUBLICATIONS FOR ADULTS

Short Stories

> *Immanuel's Land.* Auckland, Pilgrim Press, 1956.
> *New Authors: Short Story 1*, with others. London, Hutchinson, 1961.
> *Summer in the Gravel Pit.* Auckland, Janet and Blackwood Paul, and London, Gollancz, 1965.
> *O'Leary's Orchard and Other Stories.* Chrustchurch, Caxton Press, 1970.

*   *   *

Maurice Duggan's claim to distinction as a children's author stems undoubtedly from his award-winning novel *Falter Tom and the Water Boy*. A collection of three short stories, *The Fabulous McFanes*, reveals a capacity for energetic storytelling and considerable insight into the concerns of childhood; but to *Falter Tom* must go the ultimate tribute. It remains, without doubt, the most distinguished work to have emerged so far from the pen of a New Zealand author for children.

The story is a fantasy, told in simple, almost faultless prose, the whole a mere 64 pages long. Falter Tom, an old, tale-spinning sailor whose nickname derives from a stiff leg which imparts "a peculiar style to his walk" is enticed into the underwater world by the water boy, an ageless child of the sea, a mixture of wisdom and innocence, gravity and gaiety. Duggan's sea-world is a timeless one, a setting in which the old man's age is irrelevant, his lameness unhampering. It is simultaneously a real world, inhabited by live fish, furnished with ghostly wrecks of ancient and modern ships, embellished here and there with lost treasure and spilled cargo. Duggan invents a minimum of artificial detail; even the Sea Kings, who must be consulted, ultimately, as to Falter Tom's destiny, are heard but not seen, their awesome voices intoning the conditions in unison. The boy himself is at once all-child and all-spirit, humanity and immortality.

It would be possible to theorize that Duggan, a man of robust, outdoor temperament to whom the loss of a leg was a major tragedy, and who before his early death suffered in turn a series of debilitating illnesses, saw in Falter Tom's story the enactment of his own wish fulfilment – deliverance from a world in which pain and despair must often have threatened to extinguish the wit and humour that were his by nature. Certainly, the underwater world as Falter Tom, escorted by the boy, experiences it, seems to contain all of eternity. There, the old become young, the halt and the lame are made whole.

But to the child reader, preoccupied quite properly with his own enjoyment of the story, such speculation is irrelevant. The pace and shape of the tale, the humanity of the characters, the green reality of the underwater world, and the mounting of the tension are all. Falter Tom's agony of choice (to remain forever, or to leave and resume mortal life) elevates his story to the level of high drama. His decision is an affirmation of life, his story heroic.

—Dorothy Butler

DUNCAN, Norman. Canadian. Born in Brantford, Ontario, 2 July 1871. Educated at the University of Toronto, 1891–95. Journalist, *Bulletin*, Auburn, New York, 1895–97, and *New York Evening Post*, 1897–1900; Newfoundland and Labrador Correspondent, *McClure's* magazine, 1900–04; Professor of Rhetoric, Washington and Jefferson College, Washington, Pennsylvania, 1901–06; Middle and Far East Correspondent, *Harper's* magazine, New York, 1907, 1912–13; Professor of English, University of Kansas, Lawrence, 1909–11. *Died 18 October 1916.*

PUBLICATIONS FOR CHILDREN

Fiction

> *The Adventures of Billy Topsail*. New York, Revell, and London, Hodder and Stoughton, 1906.
> *Billy Topsail and Company*. New York, Revell, 1910.
> *Billy Topsail, M.D.: A Tale of Adventure with Doctor Luke of the Labrador*. New York, Revell, 1916; London, Hodder and Stoughton, 1917.

PUBLICATIONS FOR ADULTS

Novels

> *The Way of the Sea.* New York, McClure, 1903; London, Hodder and Stoughton, 1904.
> *Doctor Luke of the Labrador.* New York, Revell, and London, Hodder and Stoughton, 1904.
> *The Mother.* New York, McClure, and London, Hodder and Stoughton, 1905.
> *The Cruise of the Shining Light.* Toronto, Oxford University Press, and New York and London, Harper, 1907.
> *Every Man for Himself.* New York, Harper, 1908.
> *The Suitable Child,* illustrated by Elizabeth S. Green. New York, Revell, 1909.
> *The Measure of a Man: A Tale of the Big Woods.* New York, Revell, 1911; London, Hodder and Stoughton, 1912.
> *The Best of a Bad Job: A Hearty Tale of the Sea.* Toronto, Oxford University Press, and New York, Revell, 1912.
> *Finding His Soul.* New York and London, Harper, 1913.
> *The Bird-Store Man: An Old-Fashioned Story.* New York, Revell, 1914.
> *Christmas Eve at Swamp's End.* New York, Revell, 1915.
> *Battles Royal Down North.* New York, Revell, 1918.
> *Harbour Tales Down North.* New York, Revell, 1918.

Short Stories

> *The Soul of the Street: Correlated Stories of the New York Syrian Quarter.* New York, McClure, 1900.

Other

> *Dr. Grenfell's Parish: The Deep Sea Fisherman.* Toronto and New York, Revell, and London, Hodder and Stoughton, 1905.
> *Higgins: A Man's Christian.* New York and London, Harper, 1909.
> *Going Down from Jerusalem: The Narrative of a Sentimental Traveller,* illustrated by Lawren S. Harris. New York and London, Harper, 1909.
> *Australian Byways: The Narrative of a Sentimental Traveller,* illustrated by George Harding. New York and London, Harper, 1915.

*   *   *

Norman Duncan wrote more than twenty books, most of which can be categorized as popular fiction for adults. However, a number of these adult books, such as *The Cruise of the Shining Light,* were read by adolescents as well as by adults. Although the characters in Duncan's books for adults are drawn from subjects as diverse as New York prostitution and the fishermen of Labrador and Newfoundland, it is generally agreed that he is at his best when writing stories of the sea. His technique is to employ a mixture of sentimentality and sharply focused realism, and his emphasis is usually on action and the documentary presentation of a particular region rather than on an in-depth exploration of character.

The popular Billy Topsail novels, which Duncan wrote specifically for young readers, are episodic adventure stories set on the Newfoundland and Labrador coast. The early years of the boy-protagonist Billy Topsail are the focus of *The Adventures of Billy Topsail;* the sequel, *Billy Topsail and Company* covers some of the same time-span, but focuses on a merchant-trading venture of Billy's adolescent years; *Billy Topsail, M. D.: A Tale of Adventure with Dr. Luke of the Labrador* again reworks some of the earlier material, but it focusses on Billy's later teen years, during which time he assists Duncan's famous Dr. Luke and decides to become a doctor himself. (The fictional Dr. Luke, based partly on the real Dr. Wilfred T. Grenfell, is the protagonist of *Doctor Luke of the Labrador*, one of Duncan's well-known works for adults.)

Despite some repetition, the novels are exciting to read, and they give the reader a sense of what it was like to grow up on the rugged, sparsely populated Canadian coast around the turn of the century. Billy Topsail is a lively, red-blooded little boy whose curiosity and sense of adventure often take him into danger on either land or sea, but his pluck, common sense, and courage always save him. One memorable portion of the first book, for instance, describes Billy and a friend's encounter with a giant squid who plays dead until the curious boys bring their boat near him; then his ubiquitous tentacles appear from all angles, behind and under their punt, and the terrified boys fight for their lives. Another scene which appears in many variations in the Topsail series is that in which Billy (or someone else, like Dr. Luke) takes a shortcut across the cove on floating ice pans in order to save a life or to do a good deed. These perilous trips, so dangerous because the boys (or men) either may slip off the ice and drown, or fall through "rotten" ice and suffocate, or float out to sea and freeze, serve to underline Duncan's admiration for the hardiness and bravery of these people of Newfoundland and Labrador. *Billy Topsail, M. D.,* for example, includes an extraordinarily effective long episode in which Billy is rushing a little lame boy across the ice in the huge bay on the fateful night that the spring ice breaks up and begins drifting out to sea. The two boys are left helplessly marooned on an ice pan with the starving, vicious, part-wolf sled dogs who try to attack and eat the weakening boys.

Duncan stresses bravery, loyalty, kindness, humour, manners, friendliness, and helpfulness to others, especially weaker people. Although he often lapses into didacticism and sentimental idealization of character, Duncan reveals remarkable narrative and descriptive powers in the Billy Topsail series.

—Mary Rubio

DUNHAM, (Bertha) Mabel. Canadian. Born in Harrison, Ontario, 29 May 1881. Educated locally, Berlin, now Kitchener, Ontario; Toronto Normal School; Victoria College, University of Toronto, B.A. 1908; McGill University Library School. Schoolteacher, 1898–1904; Chief Librarian, Berlin Public Library, 1908–44; Lecturer in Library Science, Waterloo College, Ontario, 1932–45. Recipient: Canadian Library Association Book of the Year Medal, 1949. D.Litt.: University of Western Ontario, London. *Died 21 June 1957.*

PUBLICATIONS FOR CHILDREN

Fiction

> *Kristli's Trees,* illustrated by Selwyn Dewdney. Toronto, McClelland and Stewart, 1948.

PUBLICATIONS FOR ADULTS

Novels

> *The Trail of the Conestoga.* Toronto, Macmillan, 1924.
> *Toward Sodom.* Toronto, Macmillan, 1927.
> *The Trail of the King's Men.* Toronto, Ryerson Press, 1931.

Other

Grand River   Toronto, McClelland and Stewart 1945.
Mills and Millers of Western Ontario.   London, Ontario, Lawson Memorial Library, 1946.

Editor, *So Great a Heritage: Centennial, 1841–1941, Trinity United Church, Kitchener, Ontario.*   Kitchener, Cober, 1941.

*   *   *

Mabel Dunham was descended on her mother's side from Pennsylvania German ancestors who were pro-British at the time of the American War of Independence. From this background she drew the material for her first two novels for adults, *The Trail of the Conestoga* and *Toward Sodom.* The first is based on the emigration of Mennonites in covered wagons from the United States to Canada, and the second on lives of later generations of these settlers. In her third novel, *The Trail of the King's Men,* Dunham writes of the Loyalists from whom her father was descended. *Grand River* is an historical account of the settlement of the Grand River in Ontario. All her writing for adults involves material about the Dutch Mennonites from Pennsylvania who settled in Waterloo County, Ontario for reasons of conscience, and is based on extensive detail and research, reflecting her career as a librarian.

Kristli's Trees, her only novel for children, is set in Waterloo County and recounts the life and problems of a young Mennonite boy, Kristli, growing up on a rather isolated farm. Specifically, the novel deals with the problems of being part of a minority group which is very conscious of itself as different from the society in which it lives. Like her other novels, this one is chiefly valuable for its documentary interest and its depiction of a Mennonite household, its activities and its values. The German dialect of the characters is well caught and the pervasive sense of history and the need for roots, a metaphoric extension of the book's title, are admirably conveyed. *Kristli's Trees* is a simple tale, and can at times be moving, particularly in its limpid account of the unsophisticated and quiet ways of the Mennonites' daily life. The book's characterization is, at times, sentimental. On the whole, however, *Kristli's Trees* relates an appealingly simple story in a quietly understated manner, and brings to life a relatively unknown way of life.

—Janet E. Baker

DURACK, Mary.   Australian.   Born in Adelaide, South Australia, 20 February 1913. Educated at Loreto Convent, Perth. Married Horace Clive Miller in 1938; has two sons and two daughters. Journalist, Western Australian Newspapers Ltd., Perth, 1938. President, Western Australian Branch, Fellowship of Australian Writers, Swanbourne, 1958–63. Recipient: Commonwealth Literary Grant, 1973, 1977. O.B.E. (Officer, Order of the British Empire), 1966. Agent: T. Curnow, Curtis Brown (Australia) Pty. Ltd., 24 Renny Street, Paddington, New South Wales 2021. Address: 12 Bellevue Avenue, Nedlands, Western Australia 6009, Australia.

PUBLICATIONS FOR CHILDREN

Fiction

The Way of the Whirlwind, illustrated by Elizabeth Durack.   Sydney, Consolidated Press, 1941; London, Angus and Robertson, 1956.

Plays

The Ship of Dreams (produced Fremantle, Western Australia, 1968).
The Way of the Whirlwind, adaptation of her own story (produced Broome, Western Australia, 1970).

Verse

Little Poems of Sunshine by an Australian Child.   Perth, Sampson, 1923.
Piccaninnies, illustrated by Elizabeth Durack.   Sydney, Offset Printing, 1940.
The Magic Trumpet, illustrated by Elizabeth Durack.   Melbourne, London, and New York, Cassell, 1946.
Kookanoo and Kangaroo, illustrated by Elizabeth Durack.   Adelaide, Rigby, 1963; London, Angus and Robertson, 1964; Minneapolis, Lerner, 1966.

Other

All-About: The Story of a Black Community on Argyle Station, Kimberley, illustrated by Elizabeth Durack.   Sydney, The Bulletin, 1935.
Chunuma, illustrated by Elizabeth Durack.   Sydney, The Bulletin, 1936.
Son of Djaro, illustrated by Elizabeth Durack.   Perth, Sampson, 1940.
To Ride a Fine Horse, illustrated by Elizabeth Durack.   Melbourne and London, Macmillan, and New York, St. Martin's Press, 1963.
The Courteous Savage: Yagan of Swan River, illustrated by Elizabeth Durack.   Melbourne and London, Nelson, 1964; as *Yagan of the Bibbulmun*, Melbourne, Nelson, 1976.
An Australian Settler, illustrated by David Parry.   Melbourne and London, Oxford University Press, 1964.
A Pastoral Emigrant, illustrated by David Parry.   Melbourne, London, and New York, Oxford University Press, 1965.

PUBLICATIONS FOR ADULTS

Novel

Keep Him My Country.   Sydney, Angus and Robertson, and London, Constable, 1955.

Plays

Dalgerie, music by James Penberty (produced Perth, 1966).
Swan River Saga (produced Perth, 1971).   Perth, Service Printing, 1975.

Radio Play: *The Dallying Llama*, 1959.

Other

Child Artists of the Australian Bush, with Florence Rutter.   London, Harrap, 1950.
Kings in Grass Castles.   London, Constable, 1959.
The Rock and the Sand.   London, Constable, 1969.
To Be Heirs Forever (biography of Eliza Shaw).   London, Constable, 1976.

Editor, *The Fifth Sparrow*, by M. L. Skinner.   Sydney, Sydney University Press, 1972.
Editor, *The End of Dreaming*, by Ingrid A. Drysdale.   Adelaide, Rigby, 1974; London, Hale, 1975.

*   *   *

Mary Durack and her sister Elizabeth, whose illustrations form an integral part of all her books, have a unique position in Australian children's literature. As the grandchildren of one of Australia's most picturesque pioneers who drove his flocks and herds thousands of miles through unexplored country in one of the greatest pioneering feats of the nineteenth century, their name was already known when *The Bulletin* in Sydney published their first book in 1935. This and two subsequent books depicted life on Argyle Station in remote north-western Australia, telling of the day-to-day events of the aborigines living on the station. Though the books often told of the doings of aboriginal children, they are not necessarily books *for* children. Several years later, in 1941, they produced a real fairy story, *The Way of the Whirlwind*. In the old fairy tale tradition it told of two children who set out on a quest, their adventures, and the ultimate success of their search. But in this story the children were aborigines, whose baby brother had been stolen by a whirlwind. Their search involved them with such creatures, of the spirit or animal world, that imaginary aboriginal children could possibly have encountered. The young children, for whom the book was written, could identify with the aboriginal hero and heroine, and the story was skilfully told, the suspense being maintained throughout. This was at the time the most successful attempt to create a fantasy based on aboriginal life. Though it did not purport to interpret aboriginal mythology, the device lent a new dimension to the conventional fairy story, and it enabled Australian children to relate to the aboriginal children they had probably never seen, and the country and creatures who formed their environment. This story has not the richness or conviction of imaginative power to move the reader as do the great works of the imagination, but its liveliness and originality still appeal to young children. It advanced children's stories in Australia through the authors' unselfconscious acceptance of aboriginal characters and a primitive setting, which was then an innovation.

Of Mary Durack's later books for children, the most satisfying is *The Courteous Savage*, later reprinted as *Yagan of the Bibbulmun*, a sympathetic account of the tragic relations between the early white settlers in Western Australia and the aboriginal inhabitants. Mary Durack has interpreted aboriginal life in many books for Australian children with understanding and imagination.

—Marcie Muir

DUVOISIN, Roger (Antoine). American. Born in Geneva, Switzerland, 28 August 1904; emigrated to the United States in 1927; naturalized citizen, 1938. Educated at Ecole Professionelle, Geneva, 1915–17; Ecole des Arts Decoratifs, Geneva, 1917–23, teaching diploma. Married Louise Fatio, *q.v.*, in 1925; has two sons. Stage Designer, Geneva Opera, 1922–24; manager of a ceramics firm, Ferney-Voltaire, France, 1924–25; Textile Designer, Mallinson Silk Company, New York, 1927–32; Visiting Professor, Parsons School of Art, New York, 1942–50. Free-lance Illustrator, 1932–60. Group shows: Art Alliance Gallery, Philadelphia, 1946; Museum of Modern Art, New York 1946; Durand Rue Gallery, New York, 1949; Philadelphia Museum School of Art, 1953; "Graphic Art in the U.S.A.," European tour, 1963; Bratislava Biennale; Rutgers University Museum of Art, 1973. Recipient: New York *Herald Tribune* Festival award, 1944; American Library Association Caldecott Medal, for illustration, 1948; *New York Times* award, for illustration, 1954, 1955, 1961, 1965, 1973; Society of Illustrators award, 1961; University of Southern Mississippi award, 1971; New York Academy of Science award, for non-fiction, 1975; University of Minnesota Kerlan Award, 1976. Address: Gladstone, New Jersey 07934, U.S.A.

PUBLICATIONS FOR CHILDREN (illustrated by the author)

Fiction

A Little Boy Was Drawing. New York, Scribner, 1932.
Donkey – Donkey: The Troubles of a Silly Little Donkey. Racine, Wisconsin, Whitman, 1933; London, Chatto Boyd and Oliver, 1969.
All Aboard! New York, Grosset and Dunlap, 1935.
The Christmas Cake in Search of Its Owner. New York, American Artists Group, 1941.
The Christmas Whale. New York, Knopf, 1945.
Chanticleer. New York, Grosset and Dunlap, 1947.
Petunia. New York, Knopf, 1950; London, Lane, 1958.
Petunia and the Song. New York, Knopf, 1951.
A for the Ark. New York, Lothrop, 1952; London, Bodley Head, 1961.
Petunia's Christmas. New York, Knopf, 1952; London, Bodley Head, 1960.
Petunia Takes a Trip. New York, Knopf, 1953; London, Bodley Head, 1959.
Easter Treat. New York, Knopf, 1954.
One Thousand Christmas Beards, See Smith Toy Shop, Eat at Joe's. New York, Knopf, 1955; Kingswood, Surrey, World's Work, 1975.
Two Lonely Ducks: A Counting Book. New York, Knopf, 1955; London, Bodley Head, 1966.
The House of Four Seasons. New York, Lothrop, 1956; Leicester, Brockhampton Press, 1960.
Petunia Beware! New York, Knopf, 1958; London, Bodley Head, 1962.
Day and Night. New York, Knopf, 1960.
The Happy Hunter. New York, Lothrop, 1961; Edinburgh, Oliver and Boyd, 1962.
Veronica. New York, Knopf, 1961; London, Bodley Head, 1962.
Our Veronica Goes to Petunia's Farm. New York, Knopf, 1962; as *Veronica Goes to Petunia's Farm*, London, Bodley Head, 1963.
Lonely Veronica. New York, Knopf, 1963; London, Bodley Head, 1964.
Spring Snow. New York, Knopf, 1963; Kingswood, Surrey, World's Work, 1966.
Veronica's Smile. New York, Knopf, 1964; London, Bodley Head, 1965.
Petunia, I Love You. New York, Knopf, 1965; London, Bodley Head, 1966.
The Missing Milkman. New York, Knopf, 1967; Kingswood, Surrey, World's Work, 1968.
What Is Right for Tulip. New York, Knopf, 1969.
Veronica and the Birthday Present. New York, Knopf, 1971; London, Bodley Head, 1972.
The Crocodile in the Tree. London, Bodley Head, 1972; New York, Knopf, 1973.
Jasmine. New York, Knopf, 1973; London, Bodley Head, 1974.
Petunia's Treasure. New York, Knopf, 1975; London, Bodley Head, 1977.
Periwinkle. New York, Knopf, 1976.
Crocus. New York, Knopf, and London, Bodley Head, 1977.

Other

And There Was America. New York, Knopf, 1938.
The Three Sneezes and Other Swiss Tales. New York, Knopf, 1941; London, Muller, 1943; as *Fairy Tales from Switzerland*, Muller, 1958.
They Put Out to Sea: The Story of the Map. New York, Knopf, 1943; London, University of London Press, 1947.
The Four Corners of the World. New York, Knopf, 1948.

The Miller, His Son, and Their Donkey. New York, McGraw Hill, 1962; London, Bodley Head, 1963.
See What I Am. New York, Lothrop, 1974.

Bibliography: *A Roger Duvoisin Bibliography* by Irvin Kerlan, Charlottesville, Bibliographic Society of the University of Virginia, 1958.

Manuscript Collections: Kerlan Collection, University of Minnesota, Minneapolis; Rutgers University Library, New Brunswick, New Jersey; de Grummond Collection, University of Southern Mississippi, Hattiesburg.

Illustrator: *Mother Goose* edited by William Rose Benét, 1936; *The Pied Piper of Hamelin* by Robert Browning, 1936; *Riema, Little Brown Girl of Java,* 1937, *Soomoon, Boy of Bali,* 1938, and *Jo-Yo's Idea,* 1939, all by Kathleen Morrow Elliot; *The Feast of Lamps* by Charlet Root, 1938; *Tales of the Pampas* by W. H. Hudson, 1939; *Rhamon, A Boy of Kashmir* by Helwig Washburne, 1939; *Language Arts for Modern Youth,* 1939; *The Dog Cantbark* by Marjorie Fischer, 1940; *Military French,* n.d.; *At Our House* by John G. McCullough, 1943; *A Child's Garden of Verses,* 1944, and *Travels with a Donkey,* 1956, by Robert Louis Stevenson; *Fair, Fantastic Paris* by Harold Ettlinger, 1944; *Jumpy the Kangaroo* by Janet Howard, 1944; *The Christmas Book of Legends and Stories* by Elva Smith and Alice Hazeltine, 1944; *Virgin with Butterflies* by Tom Powers, 1945; *The Happy Time* by Robert Fontaine, 1945; *Bhimsa the Dancing Bear* by Christine Weston, 1945; *"I Won't," Said the King* by Mildred Jordan, 1945; *The Life and Adventures of Robinson Crusoe* by Daniel Defoe, 1946; *The Successful Secretary* by Margaret Pratt, 1946; *At Daddy's Office* by Robert Jay Misch, 1946; *Daddies: What They Do All Day,* 1946, and *The Sitter Who Didn't Sit,* 1949, by Helen Walker Puner; *Moustachio* by Douglas Rigby, 1947; *White Snow, Bright Snow,* 1947, *Johnny Maple-Leaf,* 1948, *Sun Up,* 1949, *Follow the Wind,* 1950, *Hi, Mr. Robin!,* 1950, *Autumn Harvest,* 1951, *Follow the Road,* 1953, *I Saw the Sea Come In,* 1954, *Wake Up, Farm!,* 1955, *Wake Up, City!,* 1957, *The Frog in the Well,* 1958, *Timothy Robbins Climbs the Mountain,* 1960, *Under the Trees and Through the Grass,* 1962, *Hide and Seek Fog,* 1965, *The World in the Candy Egg,* 1967, *It's Time Now!,* 1969, and *The Beaver Pond,* 1970, all by Alvin Tresselt; *The Steam Shovel That Wouldn't Eat Dirt* by George Walters, 1948; *Christmas Pony* by William Hall, 1948; *The Little Whistler* by Frances Frost, 1949; *The Man Who Could Grow Hair* by William Attwood, 1949; *Dozens of Cousins* by Mabel Watts, 1950; *Vavache, The Cow Who Painted Pictures* by Frederic Attwood, 1950; *Love and Dishes* by Niccolo de Quattrociocchi, 1950; *The Christmas Forest,* 1950, *Anna the Horse,* 1951, *The Happy Lion,* 1954, *The Happy Lion in Africa,* 1955, *The Happy Lion Roars,* 1957, *A Doll for Marie,* 1957, *The Three Happy Lions,* 1959, *The Happy Lion's Quest,* 1961, *Red Bantam,* 1963, *The Happy Lion and the Bear,* 1964, *The Happy Lion's Vacation,* 1967, *The Happy Lion's Treasure,* 1971, *Hector Penguin,* 1973, *The Happy Lion's Rabbits,* 1974, *Marc and Pixie and the Walls in Mrs. Jones's Garden,* 1975, and *Hector and Christina,* 1976, all by Louise Fatio; *The Camel Who Took a Walk,* 1951, and *Tigers Don't Bite,* 1956, by Jack Tworkov; *Farm Wanted* by Helen Hilles, 1951; *Gian-Carlo Menotti's Amahl and the Night Visitors,* 1952; *The Talking Cat and Other Stories of French Canada* by Natalie Savage Carlson, 1952; *Busby and Co.* by Herbert Coggins, 1952; *Chef's Holiday* by Idwal Jones, 1952; *Tell Me, Little Boy* by Doris Van Liew Roster, 1953; *The Night Before Christmas* by Clement C. Moore, 1954; *Sophocles the Hyena* by James Moran, 1954; *Flash of Washington Square* by Margaret Pratt, 1954; *Little Red Nose* by Miriam Schlein, 1955; *One Step, Two ...,* 1955, *Not a Little Monkey,* 1957, *In My Garden,* 1960, and *The Poodle Who Barked at People,* 1964, all by Charlotte Zolotow; *Ride with the Sun,* edited by Harold Courlander, 1955; *Petits Contes Vrais,* by Mary Riley and Andre Humbert, 1955; *Trilium Hill* by E. L. Marsh, 1955; *Christmas on the Mayflower* by Wilma Pitchford Hays, 1956; *Bennie, The Bear Who Grew Too Fast* by Beatrice and Ferrin Fraser, 1956; *The Sweet Pattotie Doll,* 1957, *Wobble the Witch Cat,* 1958, *Houn' Dog,* 1959, *The Nine Lives of Homer C. Cat,* 1961, and *The Hungry Leprechaun,* 1962, all by Mary Calhoun; *Does Poppy Live Here?* by Arthur Gregor, 1957; *The Little Church on the Big Rock* by Hazel Allen,

1958; *Favorite Fairy Tales Told in France* edited by Virginia Haviland, 1959; *A Fish Is Not a Pet* by May Natalie Tabak, 1959; *The Pointed Brush* by Patricia Miles Martin, 1959;*The Three-Cornered Hat* by Pedro Antonio de Alarcón, 1959; *Angelique* by Janice, 1960; *Lisette*, 1962, *The Rain Puddle*, 1965, and *The Remarkable Egg*, 1968, all by Adelaide Holl; *The Lamb and the Child*, 1963, and *Days of Sunshine, Days of Rain*, 1965, by Dean Frye; *Around the Corner* by Jean B. Showalter, 1966; *Nubber Bear* by William Lipkind, 1966; *Poems from France* edited by William Jay Smith, 1967; *The Old Bullfrog*, 1968, and *The Web in the Grass*, 1972, by Berniece Freschet; *Earth and Sky* by Mona Dayton, 1969; *Which Is the Best Place?* translated by Mirra Ginsburg, 1976; *Whatever Happened to the Baxter Place?* by Pat Ross, 1976; *Heinz Hobnail and the Great Shoe Hunt* by Anne Duvoisin, 1976.

Roger Duvoisin comments:

The childhood impressions that are still alive in Louise Fatio and me help us to understand children and to communicate with them. I love the lively curiosity children show toward their surroundings; I love their questions, and the free way they have of expressing their reactions in their conversation, in their drawings and paintings, and even in their poems and letters. Adults often lose this refreshing freedom and curiosity as they form set, conventional opinions about their world. That is why it is so interesting to converse with children, to learn from them as well as to teach them.

It is good to observe that children are now more and more encouraged to express themselves, to create, and that they are taken more seriously. Because of this, making books for children is a more captivating form of art for the writer and illustrator.

*   *   *

Whether he's illustrating his own stories or those by others (including his wife, Louise Fatio), Roger Duvoisin's pictures become part of the whole. It's almost impossible to separate his visuals from the texts because Duvoisin's innate and professionally developed gifts insure that his illustrations complement the tales. And this sense of design serves him as well in the construction of a narrative; he's an artist with words as well as with his brush. Most critics would agree, however, that the reason for the author-illustrator's lasting appeal is that readers know he cares, about them and his subjects.

Specifically he is appreciated for his delicious sense of humor, the playfulness which infuses a Duvoisin production even on a serious theme. Everyone loves to laugh at "Petunia," the silly goose who convinces herself and the other farm animals that she knows everything because she owns a book. After a succession of convulsive mishaps based on Petunia's pretensions as an expert, she learns: "I can't carry wisdom under my wing ... I must learn to read." Another of Duvoisin's charming characters is the cow "Jasmine," who argues the case for individuality. Finding a fancy hat, she wears it and sticks to her principles even when the chapeau makes her the laughing-stock of the barnyard.

Jasmine, Petunia and their companions are well known to millions of children as are Duvoisin's other animal stars – cats, dogs and more exotic fauna like the hippo and the giraffe. *A for the Ark* – one of the catchiest alphabet books for beginners to cut their literary teeth on – brings a whole menagerie to joyous life. And sometimes his plots involve humans as well. In *The House of Four Seasons*, Suzy and Billy are helping their parents paint their house, a task which gives Duvoisin the chance to present a nifty lesson in how to create various colors and, not incidentally, to tell a suspenseful story. *The Missing Milkman* invigorates the maxim concerning all work and no play and vice versa. Here we follow the adventures of a dairy worker who runs away to spend a bucolic holiday until idleness palls and duty calls.

In all the original and witty books which Roger Duvoisin has been conjuring up for 45 years, he teaches implicitly while he entertains. That characteristic is no small part of his appeal.

—Jean F. Mercier

EAGER, Edward. American. Born in Toledo, Ohio. Educated at Harvard University, Cambridge, Massachusetts. Married; one son. *Died in 1964.*

PUBLICATIONS FOR CHILDREN

Fiction

Mouse Manor, illustrated by Beryl Bailey-Jones. New York, Farrar Straus, 1952.
Half Magic, illustrated by N.M. Bodecker. New York, Harcourt Brace, and London, Macmillan, 1954.
Playing Possum, illustrated by Paul Galdone. New York, Putnam, 1955.
Knight's Castle, illustrated by N.M.Bodecker. New York, Harcourt Brace, and London, Macmillan, 1956.
Magic by the Lake, illustrated by N.M.Bodecker. New York, Harcourt Brace, and London, Macmillan, 1957.
The Time Garden, illustrated by N.M. Bodecker. New York, Harcourt Brace, 1958; London, Macmillan, 1959.
Magic or Not?, illustrated by N.M.Bodecker. New York, Harcourt Brace, and London, Macmillan, 1959.
The Well-Wishers, illustrated by N.M.Bodecker. New York, Harcourt Brace, 1960; London, Macmillan, 1961.
Seven-Day Magic, illustrated by N.M.Bodecker. New York, Harcourt Brace, 1962; London, Macmillan, 1963.

Verse

Red Head, illustrated by Louis Slobodkin. Boston, Houghton Mifflin, 1951.

PUBLICATIONS FOR ADULTS

Plays

Dream with Music (lyrics only), book by Sidney Sheldon, Dorothy Kilgallen, and Ben Roberts, music by Clay Warnick (produced New York, 1944).
The Liar, with Alfred Drake, music by John Mundy, lyrics by Edward Eager, adaptation of a play by Goldoni (produced New York, 1950).
The Gambler, with Alfred Drake, adaptation of a play by Ugo Betti (produced New York, 1952).
The Adventures of Marco Polo: A Musical Fantasy (lyrics only), book by William Friedberg and Neil Simon, music by Clay Warnick and Mel Pahl (televised, 1956). New York, French, 1959.
Call It Virtue, adaptation of a play by Luigi Pirandello (produced New York, 1963).
Gentlemen, Be Seated, with Jerome Moross, music by Jerome Moross, lyrics by Edward Eager (produced New York, 1963).
Rugantino (lyrics only), book by Alfred Drake, music by Armando Trovaioli, adaptation of a play by Pietro Garinei, Sandro Giovanini, Festa Campanile, and Franciosa (produced New York, 1964).
The Happy Hypocrite, music by James Bredt, adaptation of the story by Max Beerbohm (produced New York, 1968).

Television Plays: *The Marriage of Figaro*, from the libretto by Lorenzo da Ponte, music by Mozart, 1954; *The Adventures of Marco Polo* (lyrics only), 1956.

*   *   *

Seldom has a major author been imitated so blatantly and in many ways so successfully as E. Nesbit by Edward Eager. In *Half Magic* and its sequels, Eager's indebtedness is gracefully acknowledged: Nesbit is his group of children's favorite author, and they want the sort of real magic that came into her characters' ordinary lives to enter theirs. This magic has rules that enable you to direct it, or, if they are not respected, cause the magic to thwart you.

This basic paradigm Eager takes from Nesbit, along with the family of four or five clever but believable children. The coin of *Half Magic* recalls Nesbit's amulet, *Knight's Castle* the Magic City, the Natterjack of *The Time Garden* is her Psammead, etc. The adventures are like hers and the humour is like hers, perhaps even more abundant. Sometimes there is also a scene, setting, or mood from Baum, Boston, or Carroll. Eager loved books and was a natural at entering the literary worlds of others with appreciation and zest.

Eager's experience of "magic" was almost certainly less deep than Nesbit's. Perhaps he resembled Mr. Smith in *Half Magic*, who says: "The trouble with life is that not enough impossible things happen for us to believe in, don't you agree?" In some of his best books, *Magic or Not?* and *The Well-Wishers*, Eager uses the device of tantalizing uncertainty about the reality of the magic. Nowhere in Eager's books is there the powerful force field of inner psychic happenings that Nesbit can create.

As a fantasist, Eager is looser and less compelling than his model. On the other hand, he is more interested in his characters as people in real relationships. Compare Mr. Smith in *Half Magic* with "the gentleman upstairs" in *The Story of the Amulet*. Eager is at his best when he uses his affection and perceptiveness to delineate his characters and integrate his story at the level of real life. In other books, such as *Seven-Day Magic*, he remains witty and inventive but seems to be repeating his own adaptations.

—Ravenna Helson

EDMONDS, Walter D(umaux). American. Born in Boonville, New York, 15 July 1903. Educated at Cutler School, New York, 1914–16; St. Paul's School, Concord, New Hampshire, 1916–19; Choate School, Wallingford, Connecticut, 1919–21; Harvard University, Cambridge, Massachusetts, 1921–26. A.B. 1926. Married Eleanor Livingston Stetson in 1930 (died, 1956), one son, two daughters; Katharine Howe Baker-Carr, 1956. Member of the Board of Overseers, Harvard College, 1945–50; Director, 1955–72, and President and Publisher, 1957–66, *Harvard Alumni Bulletin*. Recipient: American Library Association Newbery Medal, 1942; National Book Award, 1976; Christopher Award, 1976. Litt.D.: Union College, Schenectady, New York, 1936; Rutgers University, New Brunswick, New Jersey, 1939; Colgate University, Hamilton, New York, 1946; Harvard University, 1952. Agent: Harold Ober Associates, 40 East 49th Street, New York, New York 10017. Address: 27 River Street, Concord, Massachusetts 01742, U.S.A.

PUBLICATIONS FOR CHILDREN

Fiction

The Matchlock Gun, illustrated by Paul Lantz. New York, Dodd Mead, 1941.
Tom Whipple, illustrated by Paul Lantz. New York, Dodd Mead, 1942.
Two Logs Crossing: John Haskell's Story, illustrated by Tibor Gergely. New York, Dodd Mead, 1943.
Wilderness Clearing, illustrated by John de Martelly. New York, Dodd Mead, 1944.
Cadmus Henry, illustrated by Manning Lee. New York, Dodd Mead, 1949.
Mr. Benedict's Lion, illustrated by Doris Lee. New York, Dodd Mead, 1950.

Corporal Bess, illustrated by Manning Lee.   New York, Dodd Mead, 1952.

Hound Dog Moses and the Promised Land, illustrated by William Gropper.   New York, Dodd Mead, 1954.

Uncle Ben's Whale, illustrated by William Gropper.   New York, Dodd Mead, 1955.

They Had a Horse, illustrated by Douglas Gorsline.   New York, Dodd Mead, 1962.

Time to Go House, illustrated by Joan Berg Victor.   Boston, Little Brown, 1969.

Selected Short Stories: Seven American Stories, illustrated by William Sauts Bock.   Boston, Little Brown, 1970.

Wolf Hunt, illustrated by William Sauts Bock.   Boston, Little Brown, 1970.

Beaver Valley, illustrated by Leslie Morrill.   Boston, Little Brown, 1971.

The Story of Richard Storm, illustrated by William Sauts Bock.   Boston, Little Brown, 1974.

Bert Breen's Barn.   Boston, Little Brown, 1975.

PUBLICATIONS FOR ADULTS

Novels

Rome Haul.   Boston, Little Brown, and London, Sampson Low, 1929.

The Big Barn.   Boston, Little Brown, 1930; London, Sampson Low, 1931.

Erie Water.   Boston, Little Brown, 1933; London, Hurst and Blackett, 1934.

Drums along the Mohawk.   Boston, Little Brown, and London, Jarrolds, 1936.

Chad Hanna.   Boston, Little Brown, and London, Collins, 1940.

Young Ames.   Boston, Little Brown, and London, Collins, 1942.

In the Hands of the Senecas.   Boston, Little Brown, and London, Collins, 1947; as *The Captive Woman*, New York, Bantam, 1962.

The Wedding Journey.   Boston, Little Brown, 1947.

The Boyds of Black River.   New York, Dodd Mead, and London, Collins, 1953.

Short Stories

Mostly Canallers: Collected Stories.   Boston, Little Brown, 1934.

Other

The First Hundred Years, 1848–1948: 1848, Oneida Community; 1880, Oneida Community Limited; 1935, Oneida Ltd.   Oneida, New York, Oneida, Ltd., 1948; revised edition, 1958.

They Fought with What They Had: The Story of the Army Air Forces in the Southwest Pacific, 1941–1942.   Boston, Little Brown, 1951.

The Erie Canal: The Story of the Digging of Clinton's Ditch.   Utica, New York, Munson Williams Proctor Institute, 1960.

The Musket and the Cross: The Struggle of France and England for North America.   Boston, Little Brown, 1968.

Walter D. Edmonds comments:

I am no good at this sort of thing, but perhaps my remarks accepting the National Book Award for *Bert Breen's Barn* may be apropos.

"It's a fine thing to be given a National Book Award, and I am deeply grateful – though I'm not sure my book deserves recognition as a book for children. I'm not sure there really is such a book, anyway. The great children's classics belong equally to adults. Though I have no classics to my name, all but three of my 'children's books' appeared originally in adult magazines or were written for adult readers. The three I started out deliberately to write for children seem to me not much more so than the others – which may, I see, be a commentary on my writing. So I think categories do not mean a great deal. The story is the important thing.

"In *Bert Breen's Barn* I set out to make a story about an occurrence that happened on our place and neighborhood in upstate New York when I was a very small boy, just learning to tie my own shoes. As a matter of fact it was an old man on whom I modelled the character of Birdy Morris who showed me how to tie the laces so they never came undone, until you wanted them to. I did not write the story for children but for my own pleasure, finding myself, in the process, overwhelmed with remembrances of how things were just after the turn of the century and by the qualities of life we were brought up to think valuable.

"So to be given a National Book Award near the end of fifty years of writing means a great deal more than I can put into words. Especially as I never have been much of a hand to win a prize. Except in marriage."

*   *   *

Can you imagine a book for children written by Conrad, Maugham, or Shaw? By Hemingway, Dreiser, Edmund Wilson? No, you can't. But by H.G. Wells, yes; by George Moore, yes; by Willa Cather, J.B. Priestley, yes; even by Max Beerbohm, yes. And just to have read two or three adult volumes by Dickens, Stevenson, Kipling, Mark Twain, or E.B. White tells you *instantly* that they *must* have written something designed for the young.

So it is with Walter D. Edmonds, native and professional up-state New Yorker, whose novels (*Drums along the Mohawk*) and short stories (*Mostly Canallers*) contrive no casual fiction out of a local history which he has absorbed as by osmosis. They *are* the Mohawk and Black Rivers, German Flats; the Erie Canal — boats, locks, and towpaths; blazed trails on the first proud wilderness frontier evolving west from Albany even as the second (and the faster one) would score the plains with wagon tracks beyond St. Louis. Edmonds is no disciple of a leatherstocking Cooper on the warpath of his exegesis. He is in there with the pioneers, the Indians; the courage and the hardship; the translators of the rifle, plow, and axe.

Except for long, productive summers on his family's sprawling acres up in Boonville, New York, Edmonds has lived his adult life in either Cambridge or Concord, Massachusetts, in the shadow of Harvard or of Emerson and Thoreau. But in no way has such awkward geography or gentle environment diminished his allegiance to the New York outback up-state.

Rome Haul, his first adult novel and his first success — a book that told you he could write for the young — was in his mind before graduation from Harvard College in 1926. For the next fourteen years he gave all his writing time to adult fiction. He never actually set out to write stories for children. "All ... of my 'children's books,' " he says, "appeared originally in adult magazines or were written for adult readers. The three I started out deliberately to write for children seem to me not much more so than the others .... The story is the important thing." Apart from *Bert Breen's Barn*, let the reader guess which are the other two!

No — or yes — *The Matchlock Gun, They Had a Horse, Two Logs Crossing, Beaver Valley*, and (above all) *Bert Breen's Barn*, to name a few, are simply brief excursions in the mind of the craftsman putting words together in the long day's work. None of the adult books for which he is famous have won major prizes; but *The Matchlock Gun*, a lean, two-fisted tale of New York's Dutch pioneers and native Indian raiders, took the Newbery Medal as early as 1942. *Bert Breen's Barn* won the National Book Award in 1976. And of all his books in the juvenile field, this one (acknowledged as true in facts) seems likely to become a classic. Though it does not clamor for attention, it was written in delight, not the least embroidered, utterly strong and simple in the country idiom of the turn of the century. From the very first page on, it talks the reader down to solid earth: "a lantern carried by hand always has a kind of bob to it," "a heavy watch chain that barely made it from one pocket of his waistcoat to the other," "the best dinner he had sat down to in his life or got up from either," "by the time his mind darked up and shut off for good there was hardly more than an hour left for sleeping." Indeed, the main characters, as well-drawn as those in my favorite Edmonds adult story, "Mr. Dennett's Great Adventure," sometimes breathe straight down your neck. Which is not to say that we have lacked knowledge of this kind of boy apart from his treasure hunt, in the young hero of *Two Logs Crossing* or in the young husband (aged 17) in *They Had a Horse*. The surprise in *Bert Breen's Barn*, worked up to by a kind of literary peristalsis, seems as natural as it is often artificial in detective stories. An honest, lovable book.

For runners up on the Edmonds juvenile list, I choose *Two Logs Crossing, Tom Whipple*, and *The Matchlock Gun*. But why, I ask, has *Hound Dog Moses and the Promised Land* never made the juvenile prize-lists? There is real magic in *that* one. Would you choose Marc Connelly's play, *The Wisdom Tooth*, over *The Green Pastures*? I should hope not! Mentioning *Moses* (its original title) reminds me that I have failed to speak of Edmonds' love of animals, particularly his love of dogs, cows, and horses in that order. Surely *Moses* belongs in the any-age group with Farley Mowat's *The Dog Who Wouldn't Be*; and with valiant *Stickeen* by the great naturalist John Muir. *Stickeen* most surely remains the American masterpiece of dogdom. I'd put *Moses* second.

—David McCord

EDWARDS, Dorothy. British. Born in Teddington, Middlesex. Educated at grammar school. Married to Francis P. Edwards; has one son and one daughter. Worked as a secretary; freelance editor, BBC; lecturer and broadcaster. Recipient: Children's Rights Workshop Other Award, 1975. Address: 22 Burnham Drive, Reigate, Surrey RH2 9HD, England.

PUBLICATIONS FOR CHILDREN

Fiction

> *My Naughty Little Sister: Stories from "Listen with Mother,"* illustrated by Henrietta Garland. London, Methuen, 1952.
> *My Naughty Little Sister and Some Others*, illustrated by Caroline Guthrie. London, Methuen, 1957.
> *My Naughty Little Sister's Friends*, illustrated by Una J. Place. London, Methuen, 1962.
> *When My Naughty Little Sister Was Good*, illustrated by Shirley Hughes. London, Methuen, 1968.
> *Tales of Joe and Timothy*, illustrated by Reintje Venema. London, Methuen, 1969.
> *All about My Naughty Little Sister*, illustrated by Shirley Hughes. London, Methuen, 1969.
> *Listen, Listen!*, illustrated by Elizabeth Davies. London, BBC Publications, 1970.
> *More Naughty Little Sister Stories*, illustrated by Shirley Hughes. London, Methuen, 1970.
> *Peter Nick-Nock and the Cuckoo Clock*, illustrated by Alexy Pendle. London, Transworld, 1971.
> *Roger's Trains*, illustrated by Alexy Pendle. London, Transworld, 1971.
> *Joe and Timothy Together*, illustrated by Reintje Venema. London, Methuen, 1971.
> *Janie's Cooking Day*, illustrated by Elizabeth Davies. London, Transworld, 1973.
> *Sam's Woolly Hat*, illustrated by Elizabeth Davies. London, Transworld, 1973.
> *My Naughty Little Sister and Bad Harry*, illustrated by Shirley Hughes. London, Methuen, 1974.
> *The Magician Who Kept a Pub and Other Stories*, illustrated by Jill Bennett. London, Penguin, 1975.

A Wet Monday, illustrated by Jenny Williams.   London, Penguin, 1975; New York, Morrow, 1976.

Dad's New Car, illustrated by John Dyke.   London, Methuen, 1976.

Bad Harry's Rabbit, illustrated by Shirley Hughes.   London, Methuen, 1976.

My Naughty Little Sister Goes Fishing, illustrated by Shirley Hughes.   London, Methuen, 1977.

My Naughty Little Sister and Bad Harry's Rabbit.   London, Methuen, 1977.

Plays

Radio Plays: *The Girl Who Wanted to Eat Boys*, 1974; *The Old Woman Who Lived in a Real Glass Vinegar Bottle*, 1976; *Listen with Mother* series.

Television Scripts: *Playschool* series.

Verse

Listen and Play Rhymes One and *Two*, illustrated by Prudence Seward.   London, Methuen, 2 vols., 1973.

Other

Look, Look, A Cookery Book, illustrated by Prudence Seward.   London, Methuen, 1973.

Look, Look, My Garden Book, illustrated by Prudence Seward.   London, Methuen, 1973.

A Look, See and Touch Book, illustrated by Peter Edwards.   London, Methuen, 1976.

A Walk Your Fingers Story, illustrated by Peter Edwards.   London, Methuen, 1976.

Editor, "*Listen with Mother*" *Stories*, illustrated by Caroline Sharp.   London, BBC Publications, 1972.

Editor, *The Read-to-Me Story Book*, illustrated by Lynette Hemmant.   London, Methuen, 1974.

Editor, *The Read-Me-Another Story Book*, illustrated by Jenny Williams.   London, Methuen, 1976.

Editor, *Once, Twice, Thrice upon a Time*, illustrated by Juliette Palmer.   London, Lutterworth Press, 1976.

Editor, *Once, Twice, Thrice and Then Again*, illustrated by Juliette Palmer.   London, Lutterworth Press, 1976.

*   *   *

Writing principally for the under-sevens, Dorothy Edwards's chief character is My Naughty Little Sister. Stories about her and about Joe and Timothy were originally written to be told aloud. They are short and recounted in the first person by an adult remembering her own childhood. They usually begin: "Once when I was a little girl and my naughty little sister was a very little girl" or in similar terms. Neither child ever has a name, but the listener or reader soon ceases to be aware of the adult who is describing her past and becomes absorbed in the activities of the sister and her friends. Most young children relish descriptions of the naughtiness of their contemporaries.

In the very first story the teller is an only child when the new baby is born. She decides to love the new arrival when the baby stops crying on being nursed by her. Then the chronicles of naughtiness begin with biting Father Christmas,but the tale ends happily as all of them do. My naughty little sister apologises and gets away with the doll she wanted off the Christmas tree. The crimes usually involve disobedience, like falling into the pond when told not to go near it, or cutting up the material for a new dress which she knew she ought not to have done – but all is always forgiven. Her quick changes of mood are described simply: "She was very smiley at first." Each episode has a completely different adventure full of familiar domestic details.

Dorothy Edwards's style is conversational. In the short story about Dirty Billy, for example, there are phrases like "He was just ordinary – like you and me," or "I can't say I blame him, can you?" Billy never washed but his sister was very clean and tidy and so pretty that a smart television man came to see her. But when he discovered she could not act, he chose Billy for a soap advertisement because of "all that beautiful dirt." Billy washed it off in front of the cameras, made a good film and was so pleased to see himself clean that he was never grimy again. His sister wasn't a bit jealous; she asked him for his autograph. This illustrates the amiable tone of Dorothy Edwards's fiction.

She also writes verse for the same age group, short and cheerful, suitable for miming or singing, like "Shoes":

> I've worn a big hole
> In the sole
> Of my shoe;
> I've worn a big hole
> And my sock's poking through.
> I'll hop to the Cobbler's,
> That's what I'll do.

Dorothy Edwards has written several short stories for older children, dealing with supernatural happenings. Her style for these is quite different, quite adult. "The Roman Wood," published in *Young Winter's Tales 7*, describes the effect of a very old wood on Maudie, a strange small girl, unloved by her unmarried mother who is employed by a writer – a far cry from Naughty Little Sister.

—Margaret Campbell

EDWARDS, Monica (le Doux). British. Born in Belper, Derbyshire, 8 November 1912. Educated at Wakefield High School; Thornes House School, Wakefield; St. Brandon's School for the Daughters of the Clergy, Bristol. Married William Edwards in 1933; has one son and one daughter. Agent: Curtis Brown Group Ltd., 1 Craven Hill, London W2 3EW. Address: Cowdray Cross, Thursley, Godalming, Surrey, England.

PUBLICATIONS FOR CHILDREN

Fiction

Wish for a Pony, illustrated by Anne Bullen. London, Collins, 1947.
No Mistaking Corker, illustrated by Anne Bullen. London, Collins, 1947.
The Summer of the Great Secret, illustrated by Anne Bullen. London, Collins, 1948.
The Midnight Horse, illustrated by Anne Bullen. London, Collins, 1949; New York, Vanguard Press, 1950.
The White Riders, illustrated by Geoffrey Whittam. London, Collins, 1950.
Black Hunting Whip, illustrated by Geoffrey Whittam. London, Collins, 1950.
Punchbowl Midnight, illustrated by Charles Tunnicliffe. London, Collins, 1951.

Cargo of Horses, illustrated by Geoffrey Whittam.   London, Collins, 1951.
Spirit of Punchbowl Farm, illustrated by Joan Wanklyn.   London, Collins, 1952.
Hidden in a Dream, illustrated by Geoffrey Whittam.   London, Collins, 1952.
The Wanderer, illustrated by Joan Wanklyn.   London, Collins, 1953.
Storm Ahead, illustrated by Geoffrey Whittam.   London, Collins, 1953.
No Entry, illustrated by Geoffrey Whittam.   London, Collins, 1954.
Punchbowl Harvest, illustrated by Joan Wanklyn.   London, Collins, 1954.
The Nightbird, illustrated by Geoffrey Whittam.   London, Collins, 1955.
Frenchman's Secret, illustrated by Geoffrey Whittam.   London, Collins, 1956.
Strangers to the Marsh, illustrated by Geoffrey Whittam.   London, Collins, 1957.
Operation Seabird, illustrated by Geoffrey Whittam.   London, Collins, 1957.
The Cownappers, illustrated by Geoffrey Whittam.   London, Collins, 1958.
Killer Dog, illustrated by Sheila Rose.   London, Collins, 1959.
No Going Back, illustrated by Geoffrey Whittam.   London, Collins, 1960.
The Outsider, illustrated by Geoffrey Whittam.   London, Collins, 1961.
The Hoodwinkers, illustrated by Geoffrey Whittam.   London, Collins, 1962.
Dolphin Summer, illustrated by Geoffrey Whittam.   London, Collins, 1963; New York,
     Hawthorn Books, 1971.
Fire in the Punchbowl, illustrated by Geoffrey Whittam.   London, Collins, 1965.
The Wild One, illustrated by Geoffrey Whittam.   London, Collins, 1967.
Under the Rose, illustrated by Richard Kennedy.   London, Collins, 1968.
A Wind Is Blowing.   London, Collins, 1969.

Play

Screenplay: *The Dawn Killer*, 1958.

Other

Joan Goes Farming.   London, Lane, 1954.
Rennie Goes Riding.   London, Lane, 1956.

Publications for Adults

Other

The Unsought Farm.   London, Joseph, 1954.
The Cats of Punchbowl Farm.   London, Joseph, and New York, Doubleday, 1964.
The Badgers of Punchbowl Farm.   London, Joseph, 1966.
The Valley and the Farm.   London, Joseph, 1971.
Badger Valley.   London, Joseph, 1976.

Monica Edwards comments:
   My books for children are all based on fact. They form two series: one ("Romney Marsh")
was inspired by my own youth in a Sussex fishing village; the other ("Punchbowl Farm") by
my children's life on a Surrey farm. Both places are real, and the events can be followed on
Ordnance Survey maps for the areas.

                                        *   *   *

   From a seemingly inauspicious start in the late 1940's, with the publication of *Wish for a
Pony* and *No Mistaking Corker*, Monica Edwards developed two very real and memorable
series in the "Romney Marsh" and "Punchbowl" books. In spite of the heavy emphasis on

the pony-lovers in the first two books, there was even then a noticeable depth of character in the children, usually missing from the horse-show-and-rosette story which was published in such great numbers in the late 1940's and 1950's. Monica Edwards takes each character and builds its identity within a setting she knows and, obviously, loves.

Tamzin, Rissa, Roger and Meryon love the Romney Marsh, with its sheep and wide sky and distant sea, and their adventures in and around it often arise out of the plight of one aspect of their way of life: the fishing in *The Nightbird*, or sheep farming in *The White Riders* and *No Entry*. The author is not afraid of blood and fighting as in *Cargo of Horses*, or of the emotional problems of growing up, in *No Going Back* and *A Wind Is Blowing*.

The Thorntons of Punchbowl Farm move from Hampshire into Surrey after the caravan holiday described in the first person by Lindsey in *No Mistaking Corker*. These are much more family stories, with Andrea, Dion, Lindsey and Peter leading normal, bickering, loving family lives in the setting of the wild Devil's Punchbowl and the derelict farm they own beside it. Most of the adventures in this series arise out of normal farming crises, like the animals poisoned by yew in *Spirit of Punchbowl Farm*, or the escaping animals in *The Wanderer*. Andrea is followed through her adolescent years, Lindsey remains staunch in her defence of wild creatures and the old ways, and Dion's ever-present determination to farm the wild acres is seen to reach fruition by the last in the series – *The Wild One*. Peter alone plays no major part in any of the stories, except to preserve normality by being the imitating younger brother whose mice have always got out or who needs looking after. Touches of time travel and fantasy (in *Black Hunting Whip* and *Spirit of Punchbowl Farm*) add to the exceptional quality of these realistic tales of farm life.

As Monica Edwards herself shows from the beginning of her writing a touch of the qualities of Arthur Ransome, whose titles are often mentioned in her text, so is she now being seen to influence the writings of younger authors. Much of her style of writing is apparent in the books by Tasmanian author Anne Farrell, who quotes Monica Edwards titles as Mrs. Edwards quoted Ransome. Such developments are proof of the author's quality: that her writing ability is admirable, and that her stories are memorable.

—Mary Nettlefold

EKWENSI, Cyprian. Nigerian. Born in Minna, 26 September 1921. Educated at Government College, Ibadan; Achimota College, Ghana; School of Forestry, Ibadan; Higher College, Yaba; Chelsea School of Pharmacy, London University. Married to Eunice Anyiwo; has five children. Lecturer in Biology, Chemistry and English, Igbodi College, Lagos, 1947–49; Lecturer in Pharmacognosy and Pharmaceutics, School of Pharmacy, Lagos, 1949–56; Pharmacist, Nigerian Medical Service, and Head of Features, Nigerian Broadcasting Corporation, 1956–61. Director of Information, Federal Ministry of Information, Lagos, 1961–66, and since 1966, Director of Information Services, Enugu. Chairman, East Central State Library Board, Enugu, 1971. Member, Nigerian Arts Council. Recipient: Dag Hammarskjold International Award, 1968. Address: 50 Ogbete Street, P.O. Box 137, Enugu, Nigeria.

PUBLICATIONS FOR CHILDREN

Fiction

When Love Whispers. Onitsha, Nigeria, Tabansi Bookshop, 1947.
The Leopard's Claw. London, Longman, 1950.
Yaba Roundabout Murder. Lagos, Tortoise Series Books, 1962.

Juju Rock, illustrated by Bruce Onabrakpeya.   Lagos, African Universities Press, 1966.
Coal Camp Boy.   Lagos, Longman, 1973.
Samankwe in the Strange Forest.   Lagos, Longman, 1973.
The Rainbow-Tinted Scarf and Other Stories, illustrated by Gay Galsworthy.   London,
   Evans, 1975.
Samankwe and the Highway Robbers.   London, Evans, 1975.

Other

Ikolo the Wrestler and Other Ibo Tales.   London, Nelson, 1947.
The Drummer Boy (reader).   London, Cambridge University Press, 1960.
The Passport of Mallam Ilia (reader).   London, Cambridge University Press, 1960.
An African Night's Entertainment: A Tale of Vengeance, illustrated by Bruce
   Onabrakpeya.   Lagos, African Universities Press, and London, Deutsch, 1962.
The Great Elephant-Bird (reader), illustrated by Rosemary Tonks and John
   Cottrel.   London, Nelson, 1965.
Trouble in Form Six (reader), illustrated by Prue Theobalds.   London, Cambridge
   University Press, 1966.
The Boa Suitor (reader), illustrated by John Cottrell.   London, Nelson, 1966.

PUBLICATIONS FOR ADULTS

Novels

People of the City.   London, Dakers, 1954; Greenwich, Connecticut, Fawcett, 1969.
Jagua Nana.   London, Hutchins, 1961; Greenwich, Connecticut, Fawcett, 1969.
Burning Grass: A Story of the Fulani of Northern Nigeria.   London, Heinemann, 1962.
Beautiful Feathers.   London, Hutchinson, 1963.
Iska.   London, Hutchinson, 1966.
Survive the Peace.   London, Heinemann, 1976.

Short Stories

The Rainmaker and Other Stories.   Lagos, African Universities Press, 1965.
Lokotown and Other Stories.   London, Heinemann, 1966.
Restless City and Christmas Gold.   London, Heinemann, 1975.

Critical Study: *Cyprian Ekwensi* by Ernest Emenyonu, London, Evans, 1974.

*   *   *

Cyprian Ekwensi is one of the most prolific children's writers in Africa. He is nearly
unique among African writers in publishing stories for children as early as the 1940's, in
West African Review and T. Cullen Young's *African New Writing*, before children's literature
was emphasized, and in continuing to write for children even after becoming internationally
known as a novelist. The reissue of his stories in collections and new editions attests to his
popularity among young readers.

Ekwensi's writing for children is thoroughly grounded in the realities of contemporary life
in the three main geographical regions of Nigeria. Folk tales, including *An African Night's
Entertainment*, and adventure stories, such as *Juju Rock* and *The Passport of Mallam Ilia*, are
set in Northern Nigeria among the Hausa and Fulani people. Most of the stories in *The
Rainbow-Tinted Scarf* take place in Western Nigeria among the Yoruba people, while *Coal
Camp Boy* and the new series about Samankwe are set in Eastern Nigeria among the Igbo
people. *The Drummer Boy* and many of the stories in *The Rainmaker* have urban settings.
Ekwensi is truly a national writer, yet his work is not so localized as to prevent its being
enjoyed by children outside Nigeria.

Ekwensi's folklore, like his fiction, is told in contemporary Nigerian idiom. The folk tales reflect some of the diversity of Nigerian folklore by including tales told by several ethnic groups, tales with human as well as animal characters, and long tales like the one in *An African Night's Entertainment*. Versions of widespread themes in West African folklore, such as a woman who marries an animal, melting girl, a king who refuses to let his beautiful daughter marry, and tortoise trickster tales are found in his collections, along with local themes. Numerous stylistic features of oral narratives such as epigrammatic naming, proverbs, songs, choral responses and extensive dialogue are used, though extensively simplified for children. Ekwensi has chosen to retell folk tales with implicit or explicit morals, reflecting the strong didactic emphasis in all his writing for children.

Ekwensi's fiction includes the same elements which he enjoyed reading as a youth: truth, poetic justice, heroism, romance, folkloric mystery and adventure. His stories, most of which are about the adventures of boys and men, reflect real experiences such as going to school in the colonial and post-colonial eras, poverty in urban areas and the aftermath of the Nigerian Civil War, as well as fictional experiences prominent in the mass media, such as capturing thieves and searching for lost treasure.

Adventure is a focus of all Ekwensi's fiction, regardless of its setting. The adventure may be sheer fun, as when school boys play pranks in *Trouble in Form Six*, but more often it involves apprehending wrong-doers. The blind hero of *The Drummer Boy* unknowingly becomes involved with thieves who purport to be his friends,while the hero of *Coal Camp Boy* who resettles near Enugu after the Nigerian Civil War discovers looters who are reselling property stolen from war victims. In *Juju Rock* a search for a man lost in a boat crash leads to the discovery of a gold mine whose riches are being concealed by a group of men who use secret society rituals to frighten away potential discoverers of their wealth. In his various adventures, Samankwe encounters highway robbers, kidnappers, money doublers and illicit palm wine makers. The adventures often include fighting and violence, but those who do wrong always are punished and the heroes receive praise for their bravery and attempts to uphold justice.

—Nancy J. Schmidt

ELLIN, E(lizabeth) M(uriel). New Zealander. Born in Waiuku, 22 March 1905. Educated at secondary school in Auckland. Agent: Minerva Bookshop Ltd., C.P.O. Box 2597, 13 Commerce Street, Auckland 1. Address: 42 Beach Road, Castor Bay, Auckland 9, New Zealand.

PUBLICATIONS FOR CHILDREN

Fiction

The Children of Clearwater Bay, illustrated by Garth Tapper.   Auckland, Minerva, and London, Macmillan, 1969.
The Greenstone Axe, illustrated by Elizabeth Sutherland.   Albany, New Zealand, Stockton House, 1975.

*   *   *

E.M. Ellin's two published novels have, in high degree, what educationists currently call "readability." Both books show children coping with situations which are dangerous in a very real sense; both, by the use of a deceptively simple prose style, a swift evocation of setting and character, and sure handling of energetic narrative, ensure reader attention to the last page.

The Children of Clearwater Bay is a tale of endurance, of desperate measures taken to ensure survival in the face of catastrophe. The Cameron children, six of them ranging in age from 14 to 2-year-old twins, are real children: quarrelsome, joyful, and, in the face of danger, sensibly dismayed. This dismay emphasises their subsequent resourcefulness; in common with their counterparts in *The Greenstone Axe* (the three Archer children) they demonstrate a proper balance of anxiety evoked by consciousness of their own immaturity, and determination to do the best in the circumstances.

This capacity for bringing the characters alive and bestowing credibility on the action is the hallmark of Ellin's writing. One senses in her prose – particularly in the dialogue – a memory for the preoccupations of childhood, an effortless recapturing of childish reaction to circumstance, as well as a retention of that particular quality of zest and resilience which belongs, alone, to the healthy child.

Ellin's childhood, spent on a farm in the far north of New Zealand, obviously equipped her with a strong sense of place. This she transmits smoothly to her books, which are both set in this area. The isolation of pioneer life, the necessity for children to behave responsibly and independently, while yet retaining the ebullience of childhood, the ever-present influence of the bush and the sea, all emerge strongly.

The historical details in Ellin's stories are accurately researched and presented without comment. There are friendly Maoris and hostile Maoris; the author sees as her concern the recounting of the children's adventures against an authentic background rather than the espousal of any cause. In this – and in her predilection for banishing parents so that the action centres around the children, unencumbered and unassisted – she reflects a tradition earlier than her own in children's writing though several other modern authors (notably Southall in his earlier work) favoured this device.

If one is to believe (with Geoffrey Trease) that "whatever the other valuable elements in a story, the single indispensable one is entertainment," one must acknowledge Ellin's achievement. Her characters interact vigorously against a background which exists. The result is entertainment of a high order.

—Dorothy Butler

ELLIOTT, Roberta. New Zealander. Born in Christchurch. Educated at Auckland Training College, Teacher's Certificate. Teacher, Department of Education, New Zealand, 1949–58; organizer and presenter, children's program, New Zealand Broadcasting Corporation, 1958–61; English Teacher, Berlitz School of Languages, Helsinki, Nice, Florence, and Lisbon, and Department of Education, British Council, Rome, 1961–69; scriptwriter, education department, Australian Broadcasting Commission, Sydney, 1969–72; teacher, Carshalton, Surrey, 1972–73. Since 1973 English teacher at a boys' comprehensive school. Free-lance scriptwriter, Educational Television. Agent: Osyth Leeston, A.M. Heath and Company Ltd., 40–42 William IV Street, London WC2N 4DD.

PUBLICATIONS FOR CHILDREN

Fiction

> *Kirsti and Ruski*, illustrated by Eija Grönquist. London, Macmillan, 1965; as *Kirsti and the Bear*, New York, Harcourt Brace, 1965.
> *The Miracle*, illustrated by Hugh Marshall. London, Macmillan, 1966.
> *The Country Boy*, illustrated by Michael A.E. Beach. London, Macmillan, 1967.

The Day of the Cats, illustrated by Jeannette Giblin.   London, Macmillan, 1968.
A Lump of Gold, illustrated by Tessa Jordan.   London, Macdonald, 1970.

Roberta Elliott comments:
   The theme of most of my books has been the psychological development of the child as he encounters human problems — more often than not the problems of those older than himself. I have attempted to show that most miracles arise from caring and giving. The books have all been inspired by foreign history and tradition against which a present-day story is set. This applies particularly to the books set in Florence where I lived for four years and learnt so much more about life having experienced the 1966 Florence flood. It has taken until now for me to discover that it is, after all, not so necessary to travel abroad in search of inspiration. I am at present working on my first children's novel set in England.
   As a teacher I feel compelled to introduce vocabulary for the child to reach up to.

*   *   *

   Although Roberta Elliott is a New Zealander, all her books are set in Europe, the first, *Kirsti and Ruski*, in Finland, *The Miracle* in Portugal, and the rest in Italy. It is not surprising, therefore, to find that she tends to explore national traits rather than individual character. At the beginning of *Kirsti and Ruski*, for instance, we learn that "Finns have a special kind of courage," and even the animals in the book discuss national differences, "You're a Finn and they've got no sense of humour!" "You know quite well there are three types of Lapp, Swedish, Norwegian and Finnish ... and mighty glad I am I'm not a Russian, one minute hot and the next minute cold."
   Coming as she does from a people recently described by Gordon McLauchlan as "passionless" it is small wonder that when Roberta Elliott moves to Southern Europe she seems fascinated by the volatile temperament of its inhabitants, and she explores the pride and warmth, insults and reconciliations of uninhibited Portuguese and Italians with sympathy and delight. She shows how Italians have not only a national identity but a particularly local loyalty. Alessandro, hero of *The Country Boy*, initially sees Florentines as hostile and arrogant compared to the folk in his native Assisi until his opinions are altered by the kindness of his fellow workers. A family rift occurs in *A Lump of Gold* when the daughter marries a Neapolitan, because her hard-working Florentine parents regard all Neapolitans as lazy and dishonest.
   Miss Elliott's immigrant view is again evident in her indefatigable exploration of place, which is frequently shown through a visitor's eyes. Restaurants, trattoria, cafes, and hotels are the setting for three of the books. Often life is seen from the narrow streets where tall houses, siesta-shuttered, come quickly alive in the face of the unusual. The attractions of Florence are most convincingly described and the near-disaster of their ruin by the Arno's flood is central to both *A Lump of Gold* and *The Day of the Cats*.
   The poverty which still exists in Southern Europe is a major theme. We are shown the abject squalor of the squatter area outside Lisbon, the farm closing through lack of money in Assisi, the restaurant in difficulties in Florence, and the plight of an old signorina in *The Day of the Cats*. Ultimately, however, the message is that human relationships are more important than money. This is never more clearly stated than in *A Lump of Gold* where riches are no longer needed once the family is reconciled; in unity they have resources which overcome poverty.
   Rather predictable plots which sometimes verge perilously on the sentimental are redeemed in these books by good story-telling and lively dialogue. Miss Elliott's children, moreover, have a spontaneous warmth and unselfish sense of purpose which not only win over the adults they encounter, but tempt the reader to visit the countries which produce them.

—Betty Gilderdale

ENGDAHL, Sylvia (Louise). American. Born in Los Angeles, California, 24 November 1933. Educated at Pomona College, Claremont, California, 1950; Reed College, Portland, Oregon, 1951; University of Oregon, Eugene, 1951–52; University of California, Santa Barbara, A.B. 1955. Elementary school teacher, Portland, 1955–56; Programmer, then Computer Systems Specialist, SAGE Air Defense System, in Massachusetts, Wisconsin, Washington, and California, 1957-67. Recipient: Christopher Award, 1973. Address: Box 153, Garden Home Post Office, Portland, Oregon 97223, U.S.A.

PUBLICATIONS FOR CHILDREN

Fiction

> *Enchantress from the Stars*, illustrated by Rodney Shackell. New York, Atheneum, 1970; London, Gollancz, 1974.
> *Journey Between Worlds*, illustrated by James and Ruth McCrea. New York, Atheneum, 1970.
> *The Far Side of Evil*, illustrated by Richard Cuffari. New York, Atheneum, 1971; London, Gollancz, 1975.
> *This Star Shall Abide*, illustrated by Richard Cuffari. New York, Atheneum, 1972; as *Heritage of the Star*, London, Gollancz, 1973.
> *Beyond the Tomorrow Mountains*, illustrated by Richard Cuffari. New York, Atheneum, 1973.

Other

> *The Planet-Girded Suns: Man's View of Other Solar Systems*, illustrated by Richard Cuffari. New York, Atheneum, 1974.
> *The Subnuclear Zoo: New Discoveries in High Energy Physics*, with Rick Roberson. New York, Atheneum, 1977.

> Editor, with Rick Roberson, *Universe Ahead: Stories of the Future*, illustrated by Richard Cuffari. New York, Atheneum, 1975.
> Editor, *Anywhere, Anywhen: Stories of Tomorrow*. New York, Atheneum, 1976.

Sylvia Engdahl comments:

Though my novels are set in future or hypothetical worlds, they are directed toward a general audience rather than toward fans of genre-oriented science fiction. They are intended primarily for older teenagers, but are enjoyed by preadolescents who are advanced readers and also by many adults. Their main emphasis is on the significance of space exploration, man's place in the universe, and human values that I consider universal: all themes in which I believe today's young people are seriously interested. My chief concern is to place the future in perspective in relation to the past and present, as well as to offer an affirmative outlook toward that future, and toward a wider universe than the single planet Earth.

*   *   *

Sylvia Engdahl has written only science fiction so far in her career. Sf would appear, then, to be no passing interest but the focus of virtually all her creativity. This deep commitment may account for the shape and quality of Engdahl's fiction, for she does not go out of her way to accommodate the general reader. Engdahl's sf is not easy to read: it tends to be lengthy, eschews lively incident in favor of dialogue, and prefers analysis and commentary. Although several novels include romance, perhaps in an attempt to wed a popular young adult element to sf, Engdahl's primary intent remains presenting the latter as undiluted as possible. At the same time, her sf is neither "Buck Rogerish" nor "Star Trecky"; that is, there is no heavy emphasis on nuts and bolts procedures, futuristic technological innovations, and the conventions of "space opera." The subjects of Engdahl's sf are less glamorous but more significant: the possibility of life in outer space, the attraction of travel to the stars upon human curiosity and daring, the rigorous challenge of space colonization, and the relationship between two races and cultures, one technologically superior, the other, primitive.

Enchantress from the Stars and *The Far Side of Evil* best represent Engdahl's method and achievement. Both are detailed and overly long narratives that describe the ways a much older, more advanced and, presumably, wiser race handles a younger and technologically inferior race it encounters in space. In the first novel members of the Anthropological Service from the Foundation seek to prevent the Imperial Exploration Corps of a young, still aggressive and materialistic planet from subjugating and colonizing an even younger planet. In the second novel members of the Service become involved in a struggle between two super powers on Toris. Elana, a young woman member of the Service, figures prominently in both narratives. In *Enchantress from the Stars* Georyn, a native of the planet, believes Elana an enchantress and falls in love with her, unexpectedly complicating her mission; in *The Far Side of Evil* Elana is captured and tortured because another Federation agent unwisely falls in love and decides to interfere in Torrian affairs. Neither novel contains much overt action; what does occur is primarily psychological and emotional. But in both narratives the outcome of a seemingly inconsequential incident, taking place away from the centers of power and involving very few participants, determines the future of an entire planet. Though she explores the possible relationships which might develop between individuals from different planets, Engdahl obviously prefers to work on a relatively small and intimate scale. In this way, she trusts she can bring home quietly and persuasively, if not dramatically and excitingly, her major theme: new ideas, attitudes, and values must not be forced upon a society but allowed and encouraged to affect, first, one individual and then, gradually and naturally, others.

—Francis J. Molson

ENRIGHT, Elizabeth. American. Born in Oak Park, Illinois, 17 September 1909. Educated at Edgewood School, Greenwich, Connecticut; Art Students League, New York, 1927–28; in Paris, 1928; Parsons School of Design, New York. Married Robert Marty Gillham in 1930; three sons. Taught creative writing, Barnard College, New York, 1960–62. Recipient: American Library Association Newbery Medal, 1939; New York *Herald Tribune* Festival Award, 1957. LL.D.: Nasson College, Springvale, Maine, 1966. *Died 8 June 1968.*

PUBLICATIONS FOR CHILDREN (illustrated by the author)

Fiction

> *Kintu: A Congo Adventure.* New York, Farrar and Rinehart, 1935.
> *Thimble Summer.* New York, Farrar and Rinehart, 1938; London, Heinemann, 1939.
> *The Sea Is All Around.* New York, Farrar and Rinehart, 1940; London, Heinemann, 1959.
> *The Saturdays.* New York, Farrar and Rinehart, 1941; London, Heinemann, 1955.
> *The Four-Story Mistake.* New York, Farrar and Rinehart, 1942; London, Heinemann, 1955.
> *Then There Were Five.* New York, Farrar and Rinehart, 1944; London, Heinemann, 1956.
> *The Melendy Family* (includes *The Saturdays, The Four-Story Mistake, Then There Were Five*). New York, Farrar and Rinehart, 1947.

A Christmas Tree for Lydia. New York, Rinehart, 1951.

Spiderweb for Two: A Melendy Maze. New York, Rinehart, 1951; London, Heinemann, 1956.

Gone-Away Lake, illustrated by Beth and Joe Krush. New York, Harcourt Brace, and London, Heinemann, 1957.

Return to Gone-Away, illustrated by Beth and Joe Krush. New York, Harcourt Brace, 1961; London, Heinemann, 1962.

Tatsinda, illustrated by Irene Haas. New York, Harcourt Brace, 1963; London, Heinemann, 1964.

Zeee, illustrated by Irene Haas. New York, Harcourt Brace, 1965; London, Heinemann, 1966.

Short Stories

Borrowed Summer and Other Stories. New York, Rinehart, 1946; as *The Maple Tree and Other Stories,* London, Heinemann, 1947.

The Moment Before the Rain. New York, Harcourt Brace, 1955.

The Riddle of the Fly and Other Stories. New York, Harcourt Brace, 1959; London, Heinemann, 1960.

Doublefields: Memories and Stories. New York, Harcourt Brace, 1966; London, Heinemann, 1967.

Illustrator: *Kees,* 1930, *Annan, A Lad of Palestine,* 1931, and *Kees and Kleintje,* 1934, all by Marian King; *The Crystal Locket* by Nellie M. Rowe, 1935.

*   *   *

Elizabeth Enright's keen perception of childhood, and her remarkable gifts as a writer place her books among the select few that are timeless and enduring. In *The Sea Is All Around* one of her characters says, "I like people to look at things wholeheartedly ... learning and absorbing them so that their memories are full of accurate impressions." Her books are full of "accurate impressions"; they ring true. The children in her books, too, have this ability to look, learn and absorb whole-heartedly. They are interesting and full of life.

The heroine of *Thimble Summer* is 10-year-old Garnet Linden. Her Wisconsin summer starts out to be dull and hopeless; her family's farm is in serious trouble because of drought and it is the time of the great depression. Soon after she finds a silver thimble in a dried up river bed, the rains come and a lovely summer of adventure begins. The book is full of the feel of a mid-west farm and the dry little towns nearby, and the mood of America in the thirties. A child of the depression, an orphan named Eric whose life has been lonely wandering, accidentally finds his way to the Linden family and is cared for and eventually adopted by them. There is a tree-house adventure, a wonderful chapter about being locked in the town library after closing time, a rebellious trip to a distant city. The summer, and the book, come to an end on a note of joy when Garnet's own personal pig whom she has raised from babyhood wins the blue ribbon at the county fair.

The Sea Is All Around is full of the mood of a storm-swept wintery island thirty miles out in the Atlantic. Once a busy port and home for prosperous whaling captains, the island is rich in tradition, scenery, and characters as well. Mab Kendall is an orphan who comes from Iowa to live with an Aunt on Pokenick Island. This book is unforgettable for its description of loneliness and the awakening of contentment in a child. There are many lovely old people. Like those in another book whom Enright describes, "They carry with them memories of a long life starred with adventures." Her warm descriptions are delightful – she makes us see and feel storms and cold, snow and spring, the presence of the sea, northern lights, dune plants, swamp flowers and mosses, always called by their right names and more vivid as a result.

In the "Melendy" books the children are satisfying characters, particularly now when television gives ready-made dreams and makes watchers of us. All Enright children do things that children dream of doing. In *The Saturdays* they contrive ways of making New York City their private source of joy. *The Four-Story Mistake* takes Mona, Rush, Randy and Oliver Melendy out of the city and into an old house in the country, full of secrets and mysteries. The grounds are "thirty acres of land that hold a sample of everything delightful short of an active volcano and an ocean that one could want on his own territory: brook, woods, stable, hollow tree and summer house."

Then There Were Five continues Melendy life in the country. World War Two plays a part in this book, with Father in Washington and the children involved in at-home war efforts. The Melendy children have many talents and use them in fascinating ways. They also love to talk, and say things the way one wishes one could, and they are funny. A new Melendy comes on the scene, Mark, a young boy with no home, who adds much to the family and the book. *Spiderweb for Two* finds the older children away and Randy and Oliver home alone. For a little while their lives are empty. Then the mail brings the first of a series of clues in the form of cryptic poems, which, when deciphered, lead the children to strange hiding places and many adventures.

Gone-Away Lake and *Return to Gone-Away* are about two realistically drawn families who live in the country. Witty, original old people give a sense of history with stories of the past. Animals abound, and secrets and clubs, danger and daring, and always nature, authentic and fascinating, accessible and an accessory to what happens.

Tatsinda is a "once-upon-a-time" fairy tale, traditional in feeling. But Enright's knowing characterizations and lovely language make it special and fresh. *Zeee* is a funny down-to-earth fairy tale about a "bad" fairy, the size of a bee, who lives in the present and has personality problems. Zeee eventually finds a home and a friend and makes peace with herself and the cruel world which looms around her.

These are all beautiful books, to become deeply involved in, to absorb easily and happily and to remember always.

—Irene Haas

ESTES, Eleanor (Ruth). American. Born in West Haven, Connecticut, 9 May 1906. Attended Pratt Institute Library School, New York (Hewens Scholar), 1931–32. Married Rice Estes in 1932; has one child. Children's Librarian, New Haven Public Library, Connecticut, 1924–31, and New York Public Library, 1932–40. Recipient: New York *Herald Tribune* Festival award, 1951; American Library Association Newbery Medal, 1952. Address: 324 Willow Street, New Haven, Connecticut 06511, U.S.A.

PUBLICATIONS FOR CHILDREN

Fiction

> *The Moffats*, illustrated by Louis Slobodkin. New York, Harcourt Brace, 1941; London, Bodley Head, 1959.
> *The Middle Moffat*, illustrated by Louis Slobodkin. New York, Harcourt Brace, 1942; London, Bodley Head, 1960.
> *Rufus M.*, illustrated by Louis Slobodkin. New York, Harcourt Brace, 1943; London, Bodley Head, 1960.
> *The Sun and the Wind and Mr. Todd*, illustrated by Louis Slobodkin. New York, Harcourt Brace, 1943.
> *The Hundred Dresses*, illustrated by Louis Slobodkin. New York, Harcourt Brace, 1944.

The Sleeping Giant and Other Stories, illustrated by the author.   New York, Harcourt
   Brace, 1948.
Ginger Pye, illustrated by the author.   New York, Harcourt Brace, 1951; London,
   Bodley Head, 1961.
A Little Oven, illustrated by the author.   New York, Harcourt Brace, 1955.
Pinky Pye, illustrated by Edward Ardizzone.   New York, Harcourt Brace, 1958;
   London, Constable, 1959.
The Witch Family, illustrated by Edward Ardizzone.   New York, Harcourt Brace,
   1960; London, Constable, 1962.
The Alley, illustrated by Edward Ardizzone.   New York, Harcourt Brace, 1964.
Miranda the Great, illustrated by Edward Ardizzone.   New York, Harcourt Brace,
   1967.
The Tunnel of Hugsy Goode, illustrated by Edward Ardizzone.   New York, Harcourt
   Brace, 1971.
The Coat-Hanger Christmas Tree, illustrated by Susanne Suba.   New York,
   Atheneum, 1973; London, Oxford University Press, 1977.

Play

The Lollipop Princess: A Play for Paper Dolls, illustrated by the author.   New York,
   Harcourt Brace, 1967.

PUBLICATIONS FOR ADULTS

Novel

The Echoing Green.   New York, Macmillan, 1947.

Eleanor Estes comments:
   I like to make children laugh or cry – to feel something. And, to do that, I myself must be
amused at what I am writing, or saddened. I have no aim other than to entertain, and to do
this in the most complete and artistic way that I can.

*   *   *

To read a book by Eleanor Estes is to relive one's childhood. The sights, sounds, thoughts,
and, above all, the pace of child life are authentically reproduced. It matters not that the
setting for the majority of her characters is small town U.S.A. The children she creates are
universal figures.
   In *The Moffats* and *The Middle Moffat* we see life from the perspective of ten-year-old Jane.
Did you ever tremble at the measured pace of authority? So does Janie, and she hides from
the omniscient Chief of Police in the large bread box outside the general store. Did you ever
wish to best a braggart? So do all the Moffats, and they arrange a ghost, built upon Mama's
dress form, which frightens Peter Frost and even themselves. Do birthday celebrations
delight you? Janie has great fun enjoying the one arranged for the Oldest Inhabitant. Ever
wish for a new view of the world? Join Jane as she bends over and looks through her own
legs to see what difference that stance will make in what she sees.
   Rufus M. concentrates on Jane's five-year-old brother and his problems in handling his
world. Take the day Rufus decides that since everyone else in the family gains so much
pleasure from reading, it's time he had a library book of his own. He accomplishes the long
journey to the library on his tricycle only to find the door tightly shut. Perspiringly persistent,
Rufus looks in all the windows and tries the door, eventually discovering that the library lady
is there, quietly eating her lunch. His need is greater than hers, and he gets to fill out an
application, frowningly intent upon lettering Rufus M without ruining the nib of the pen or

splattering too much ink. Estes' use of descriptive detail makes us feel that pen between our own fingers.

While we know that the Moffats are poor, and mama is a widow, these are not the major concerns of the children. Estes does an admirable job of presenting life as the Moffat children themselves would see it. Sometimes Estes' gift is so sure that her work is painful to read. In *The Hundred Dresses* Wanda's intense hurt at the teasing of the other girls when she says she has a hundred dresses at home, although she wears the same one to school each day, is so clearly evident that guilt for one's own childhood cruelties floods the adult.

The Alley is set in New York City, on a short street inhabited by university faculty families. The 33 children who live and play on the block, rarely setting foot off it, have built a hierarchy and act within its written and unwritten rules. The tenacity of children in holding to an idea or determination with a seeming disregard for the passage of time, the child's eternal weapon against the adult, is clearly depicted here. Connie's home has been burglarized at the beginning of the book. Several months later, having taken the case on as a project and watching for the burglar whom the children are sure will reappear, Connie and her friends do indeed help to apprehend the criminal.

Pets are an important part of children's lives, and Estes based *Ginger Pye*, her Newbery Award book, on the love of Jerry Pye for his lost dog, finally recovered after six months' absence. *Pinky Pye* introduces us to a kitten that typewrites, as well as an elf owl. Jerry and Rachel are typical children of any era, interested in how mother and father met each other (on an escalator), and renowned among their friends because their Uncle Benny is younger than they.

Some may consider Estes' books dated because the settings they employ no longer exist. The mechanics of life may have changed, but the essential child has not. Her characters dream the long, long thoughts of childhood, interact believably with one another, and are interested in adult life only when it directly impinges on their own. Characters stay in the memory when details of plot are forgotten; and Estes' Jane and Rufus, Jerry and Rachel, are well worth knowing.

—Rosemary Weber

ETS, Marie Hall. American. Born near Milwaukee, Wisconsin, 16 December 1893. Educated at Lawrence College, Appleton, Wisconsin, 1915–16; New York School of Fine and Applied Art, 1916–17; University of Chicago, Ph.B. 1924, and graduate work; Art Institute, Chicago; Columbia University Law Enforcement Division, New York. Married Milton T. Rodig in 1918 (died, 1919); Harold N. Ets, 1929 (died, 1943). Artist for San Francisco and Los Angeles decorating firms, 1915–18; social worker, Department of the Navy, 1918; volunteer resident, Chicago Commons Settlement House, 1919–29; child health worker for the American Red Cross in Pilsen, Czechoslovakia, 1921–22; Agent, United States Coal Commission in West Virginia and Illinois, 1923. One-man show (drawings): Columbia University Teachers College, New York, 1963. Recipient: New York *Herald Tribune* Festival award, 1947; *New York Times* award, for illustration, 1952, 1968; American Library Association Caldecott Medal, 1960; University of Minnesota Kerlan Award, 1975. Address: c/o Viking Press, 625 Madison Avenue, New York, New York 10022, U.S.A.

PUBLICATIONS FOR CHILDREN (illustrated by the author)

Fiction

Mister Penny. New York, Viking Press, 1935; London, Woodfield, 1957.

In the Forest. New York, Viking Press, 1944; London, Faber, 1955.
My Dog Rinty, with Ellen Tarry, illustrated by Alexander and Alexandra Alland. New York, Viking Press, 1946.
Oley, The Sea Monster. New York, Viking Press, 1947.
Little Old Automobile. New York, Viking Press, 1948.
Mr. T.W. Anthony Woo: The Story of a Cat and a Dog and a Mouse. New York, Viking Press, 1951.
Another Day. New York, Viking Press, 1953; London, Faber, 1956.
Play with Me. New York, Viking Press, 1955.
Mister Penny's Race Horse. New York, Viking Press, 1956; London, Woodfield, 1958.
Cow's Party. New York, Viking Press, 1958; London, Faber, 1959.
Nine Days to Christmas, with Aurora Labastida. New York, Viking Press, 1959.
Mister Penny's Circus. New York, Viking Press, 1961.
Gilberto and the Wind. New York, Viking Press, 1963.
Automobiles for Mice. New York, Viking Press, 1964.
Just Me. New York, Viking Press, 1965; London, Angus and Robertson, 1966.
Bad Boy, Good Boy. New York, Crowell, 1967.
Talking Without Words: I Can, Can You? New York, Viking Press, 1968.
Elephant in a Well. New York, Viking Press, 1972.
Jay Bird. New York, Viking Press, 1974.

Verse

Beasts and Nonsense. New York, Viking Press, 1952.

Other

The Story of a Baby. New York, Viking Press, 1939.

PUBLICATIONS FOR ADULTS

Other

Rosa: The Life of an Italian Immigrant. Minneapolis, University of Minnesota Press, 1970.

Manuscript Collection: Kerlan Collection, University of Minnesota, Minneapolis.

Marie Hall Ets comments:
I lived in a family with several children who loved to hear stories and have me draw for them. I found it to be as enjoyable for me as for my nieces and nephew, so have tried to entertain children with my stories and pictures ever since.

*   *   *

The best work of Marie Ets is deceptively simple. Most picture books that speak directly to the young child of nursery school age stand the risk of not at first impressing the adult who selects it. Very often it is only after the adult witnesses the secret appeal that such books hold for children that he returns to examine and appreciate the subtle craftsmanship of the author-illustrator.

A book like *In the Forest* or *Play with Me* is so simple in construction and syntax that one may be tempted to say that it wouldn't be very hard to write a book like that – when in fact these are the most difficult books of all to write. The distance in years and experience between the writer and the young child is so great that only a special few, like Mrs. Ets, have been successful in creating picture books that the child intuitively recognizes as having been written expressly for him.

In these books Ets daringly selects a first person telling. In order for her to do this she not only must feel comfortable with the mental furniture of the young child's mind, but she must also be sure to select a content and a style with which the child is both familiar and comfortable. She skillfully blends fancifulness with matter-of-factness; both are integral ingredients of a child's imaginative play. Repetition, artfully employed, gives the effect of the muted chant that a child often creates when he plays alone:

> I had a new horn and a paper hat
> And I went for a walk in the forest.
>
> A big wild lion was taking a nap,
> But he woke up when he heard my horn.
>
> "Where are you going?" he said to me.
> "May I go too, if I comb my hair?"
>
> So he combed his hair and he came too
> When I went for a walk in the forest.

Her longer stories, like *Mister Penny* and *Mr. T.W. Anthony Woo* are reminiscent of the earlier stories of Hugh Lofting. Like Doctor Dolittle in fiction (and Doctor Schweitzer in life), Mr. Penny and the cobbler of Shooshko are superb adult models for children. They show a great love and reverence for all God's creatures, and they demonstrate great patience towards them, no matter how mischievous they may be. These books are alive with silly names and slapstick humor that make children laugh out loud, but beneath all the fun, and devoid of moralistic pronouncement, are such notions as: "People always hate the things they are afraid of" and "How nice it is to have peace."

The works of Marie Hall Ets are perfect for sharing; there is much to savor for both child and adult.

—James E. Higgins

EVANS, Hubert (Reginald). Canadian. Born in Vankleek Hill, Ontario, 9 May 1892. Educated at Galt Collegiate, Ontario, graduated 1909. Served in the Kootenay Battalion, Rocky Mountain Rangers in France and Flanders, 1915–19. Married Anna Winter in 1920 (died, 1960); has three children. Newspaper reporter, Toronto and British Columbia, for four years; worked for commercial fisheries and on salmon conservation as a fisheries officer; lived in Indian villages, Northern British Columbia, 1946–53. Address: Roberts Creek, Strait of Georgia, British Columbia, Canada.

PUBLICATIONS FOR CHILDREN

Fiction

Forest Friends: Stories of Animals, Fish and Birds West of the Rockies. Philadelphia, Judson Press, 1926.
Derry, Airedale of the Frontier. New York, Dodd Mead, 1928.
Derry's Partner, illustrated by Frank E. Schoonover. New York, Dodd Mead, 1929.

Derry of Totem Creek, illustrated by H.E.M. Sellen.   New York, Dodd Mead, 1930.
The Silent Call.   New York, Dodd Mead, 1930.
Mountain Dog.   Philadelphia, Westminster Press, 1956.

Verse

Whittlings, illustrated by Robert Jack.   Madera Park, British Columbia, Harbor
   Publishing, n.d.

Other

North to the Unknown: The Achievement and Adventures of David Thompson, illustrated
   by Ruth Thompson.   Toronto, McClelland and Stewart, and New York, Dodd Mead,
   1949.

PUBLICATIONS FOR ADULTS

Novels

The New Front Line.   Toronto, Macmillan, 1927.
Mist on the River.   Toronto, Copp Clark, 1954.

*   *   *

Hubert Evans' writings are concerned for the most part with the Skeena River area of
British Columbia, an area whose facets he knows very well from his life there working first
in the commercial fisheries and later as a fisheries officer. This background is evident in his
writing for adults, the two novels, *The New Front Line* and *Mist on the River*. These both
reflect his knowledge of life in the province, particularly the life of the Indians.

In his children's books Evans draws on much of his own experience of close contact with
the outdoors for his material. His two collections of animal stories, *Forest Friends: Stories of
Animals, Fish and Birds West of the Rockies* and *The Silent Call*, are told in a familiar,
anecdotal style. Their chief interest is their reflection of the natural world Evans appears to
know very well. His fictionalized biography of David Thompson (1770–1857), *North to the
Unknown*, written for teen-agers, is marred by his lack of familiarity with the historical period
about which he writes.

Perhaps his most successful writing is to be seen in his novels about Derry, an Airedale
terrier, *Derry, Airedale of the Frontier*, *Derry's Partner* and *Derry of Totem Creek*, which
appeared in Grosset's *Famous Dog Stories* series, and *Mountain Dog*. In these, Evans writes
animal biographies against a background of carefully described and obviously well-loved
settings in British Columbia. His love of nature and his desire for its conservation are evident
throughout these books. Like most attempts at rendering intelligible the thoughts and
activities of animals, these books could be accused of, at times, sentimentalizing and
anthropomorphizing dogs. While Evans can at times be accused of both practices, the stories,
with their well-observed detail and their exciting and imaginative plots, sustain interest very
well. As a writer of nature stories, and particularly of dog stories, Evans is quite successful
and much of his work bears favourable comparison with that of the two most prominent
Canadian writers of the genre, Ernest Thompson Seton and Charles G.D. Roberts.

—Janet E. Baker

EVERETT-GREEN, Evelyn.   British.   Born in London, 17 November 1856. Educated at Gower Street Preparatory School; Bedford College, University of London (Reid Scholar, 1872–73); Royal Academy, London. Worked as a nurse in a London hospital. *Died 27 April 1932.*

PUBLICATIONS FOR CHILDREN

Fiction

Tom Tempest's Victory (as H.F.E.).   Glasgow, Marr, 1880.

Carry's Christmas Gift (as H.F.E.).   London, S.P.C.K., 1881.

Fast Friends; or, David and Jonathan (as H.F.E.).   London, S.P.C.K., 1882.

Little Freddie; or, Friends in Need (as H.F.E.).   London, Shaw, 1882.

His Mother's Book (as H.F.E.).   London, Shaw, and New York, Robert Carter, 1883.

Fighting the Good Fight; or, The Successful Influence of Well Doing (as H.F.E.).   London, Nelson, 1883.

Her Husband's Home; or, The Durleys of Linely Castle.   London, Shaw, 1885; Philadelphia, American Sunday School Union, n.d.

Mr. Hatherley's Boys.   London, Religious Tract Society, 1885.

Uncle Roger; or, A Summer of Surprises.   London, Religious Tract Society, 1885.

True to Himself; or, My Boyhood's Hero.   London, Nelson, 1885; revised edition, as *True to the Last; or, My Boyhood's Hero,* London, Nisbet, and New York, Nelson, 1885.

The Head of the House: The Story of a Victory over Passion and Pride.   London, Religious Tract Society, 1886; Boston, Bradley and Woodruff, 1887.

Dulcie's Little Brother; or, Doings at Little Monksholm.   London and New York, Nelson, 1887.

Our Winnie; or, When the Swallows Go.   London, Shaw, 1887.

The Last of the Dacres.   London, Warne, 1887.

A Child Without a Name, illustrated by Charles Whymper.   London, Religious Tract Society, 1887; as *Drifted Ashore; or, A Child Without a Name,* Boston, Bradley and Woodruff, 1890.

Barbara's Brothers, illustrated by R. and E. Taylor.   Philadelphia, American Sunday School Union, 1887; London, Religious Tract Society, 1888.

All or Nothing; or, Ruthven of Ruthven.   London, Warne, 1888.

Little Lady Clare, illustrated by Robert Fowler.   London, Blackie, 1888.

Dodo: An Ugly Little Boy; or, Handsome Is That Handsome Does.   London, S.P.C.K., 1888.

The Little Midshipman and Other Stories.   London, Religious Tract Society, 1889.

My Boynie: The Story of Some Motherless Children.   London, Swan Sonnenschein, 1889.

Miriam's Ambition.   London, Blackie, 1889.

Monica.   London, Ward and Downey, 1889.

My Black Sheep.   London, Kelly, 1889.

Dulcie and Tottie: The Story of an Old-Fashioned Pair.   London and New York, Nelson, 1889.

The Percevals; or, A Houseful of Girls.   London, Religious Tract Society, and Chicago, Revell, 1890.

Little Ruth's Lady.   London, Shaw, and New York, Carter, 1890.

Bertie Clifton; or, Paul's Little Schoolfellow.   London, Shaw, 1890.

Birdie's Resolve and How It Was Accomplished.   London and New York, Nelson, 1890.

Clive's Conquest.   Edinburgh, Oliphant, 1890.

Daring Dot. Edinburgh, Oliphant, 1890.

Marcus Stratford's Charge; or, Roy's Temptation. London, Religious Tract Society, and Boston, Bradley and Woodruff, 1890.

Mischievous Moncton; or, Jest Turned to Ernest. London, Cauldwell, 1890.

Oliver Langton's Ward. Edinburgh, Oliphant, and Boston, Bradley and Woodruff, 1890.

The Stronger Will. Edinburgh, Oliphant, and Boston, Bradley and Woodruff, 1890.

A Summer Holiday: The Story of Prince. London, Religious Tract Society, 1890.

Dorothy's Vocation. Edinburgh, Oliphant, and Boston, Bradley and Woodruff, 1890.

The Secret of the Old House. London, Blackie, and New York, Scribner, 1890.

Sir Aylmer's Heir. London and New York, Nelson, 1890.

Syd's New Pony. Edinburgh, Oliphant, 1890.

The Witch of the Quarry Hut. Edinburgh, Oliphant, 1890.

Fir-Tree Farm. London, Religious Tract Society, and Chicago, Revell, 1891.

Dulcie's Love Story. London and New York, Nelson, 1891.

Loyal Hearts: A Story of the Days of "Good Queen Bess." London and New York, Nelson, 1891.

Miss Meyrick's Niece. London, Kelly, 1891.

Mrs. Romaine's Household. Edinburgh, Oliphant, and Boston, Bradley and Woodruff, 1891.

Shadow-Land; or, What Lindis Accomplished. London, Shaw, 1891.

Sydney's Secret; or, Honesty Is the Best Policy. London, S.P.C.K., 1891.

"Let's Toss for It"; or, The Gambler's Career. London, Knapp, 1891.

Fresh from the Fens: A Story of Three Lincolnshire Lasses (as Evelyn Ward). London, Seeley, 1891.

Dare Lorimer's Heritage. London, Hutchinson, 1891; Boston, Bradley and Woodruff, 1892.

Duckworth's Diamonds. London, Paul, n.d.

Dick Whistler's Tramp. London, Religious Tract Society, and Chicago, Revell, 1891.

A Pair of Originals (as Evelyn Dare). London, Seeley, 1892.

Don Carlos, Our Childhood's Hero. London, S.P.C.K., 1892.

In the Wars of the Roses. London and New York, Nelson, 1892.

The Church and the King: A Tale of England in the Days of Henry VIII. London and New York, Nelson, 1892.

The Doctor's Dozen. Edinburgh, Oliphant, and Philadelphia, American Sunday School Union, 1892.

Falconer of Falconhurst. Edinburgh, Oliphant, 1892.

A Holiday in a Manor House; or, Who Solved the Mystery. London, Biggs, 1892.

In the Days of Chivalry: A Tale of the Times of the Black Prince. London, Nelson, 1892; New York, Nelson, 1893.

The Lord of Dynevor: A Tale of the Time of Edward the First. London and New York, Nelson, 1892.

Old Miss Audrey: A Chronicle of a Quiet Village. London, Religious Tract Society, 1892; Chicago, Revell, 1893.

A Pair of Pickles. Edinburgh, Oliphant, 1892; Boston, Bradley, 1899.

Everybody's Friend; or, Hilda Danvers' Influence. London, Partridge, 1893.

St. Dunstan's Clock: A Story of 1666 (as Evelyn Dare). London, Seeley, 1893.

Evil May Day: A Story of 1517. London and New York, Nelson, 1893.

Friends or Foes? London, Shaw, 1893.

The Great Show; or, Bunny's Birthday. London, Religious Tract Society, and Chicago, Revell, 1893.

Little Miss Vixen. Edinburgh, Oliphant, and Chicago, Revell, 1893.

St. Wynfrith and Its Inmates: The Story of an Almshouse. London, Jarrolds, 1893.

Tom Heron of Sax: A Story of the Evangelical Revival of the Eighteenth Century. London, Religious Tract Society, and Chicago, Revell, 1893.

The Wilful Willoughbys: A Cathedral City Story. Edinburgh, Oliphant, and Chicago, Revell, 1893.

Golden Gwendolyn. London, Hutchinson, and Boston, Bradley, 1893.

The Lost Treasure of Trevlyn: A Story of the Days of the Gunpowder Plot. London and New York, Nelson, 1893.

Maud Melville's Marriage: A Story of the Seventeenth Century. London and New York, Nelson, 1893.

Namesakes: The Story of a Secret. London, Hutchinson, and Chicago, Revell, 1893.

Over the Sea Wall. London, S.P.C.K., and New York, Young, 1893.

Ronald Kennedy; or, A Domestic Difficulty. London, Partridge, 1893.

Afterthought House. London, S.P.C.K., 1894.

Eustace Marchmont: A Friend of the People. London, Shaw, 1894; Boston, Bradley, 1895.

The Family: Some Reminiscences of a Housekeeper. London, Religious Tract Society, 1894.

Flats. Edinburgh, Oliphant, 1894.

Keith's Trial and Victory. London, Sunday School Union, 1894.

Miss Uraca. Edinburgh, Oliphant, and Boston, Bradley, 1894.

The Secret Chamber at Chad. London, Nelson, 1894.

A Difficult Daughter. London, Sunday School Union, 1894.

Pat the Lighthouse Boy. London, Shaw, and New York, Ward and Drummond, 1894.

Two Bright Shillings. London, Religious Tract Society, 1894.

Shut In: A Tale of the Wonderful Siege of Antwerp in 1585. London and New York, Nelson, 1894.

Arnold Inglehurst the Preacher: A Story of the Fen Country. London, Shaw, 1895.

Judith, The Money-Lender's Daughter. Edinburgh, Oliphant, 1895; Boston, Bradley, 1896.

Ralph Roxburgh's Revenge. London, Sunday School Union, 1895; as *Ralph Roxburgh's Triumph,* London, Pilgrim Press, 1931.

A Soldier's Son and the Battle He Fought. London, Shaw, 1895.

A Stepmother's Strategy. London, Hutchinson, 1895.

The Sunny Side of the Street: A Story of Patient Waiting. London, Religious Tract Society, 1895.

His Choice − and Hers: The Story of an Episode, with H. Louisa Bedford. London, S.P.C.K., and New York, Young, 1895.

Duff Darlington; or, An Unsuspected Genius. London, Partridge, 1895.

Dominique's Vengeance: A Story of France and Florida. London and New York, Nelson, 1896.

Squib and His Friends. London, Nelson, 1896.

Enid's Ugly Duckling, with H. Louisa Bedford. London, Religious Tract Society, 1896.

In Taunton Town: A Story of the Rebellion of James Duke of Monmouth in 1685. London and New York, Nelson, 1896.

Olive Roscoe; or, The New Sister. London and New York, Nelson, 1896.

The Sign of the Red Cross: A Tale of Old London. London and New York, Nelson, 1897.

The Young Pioneers; or, With La Salle on the Mississippi. London and New York, Nelson, 1897.

A Clerk of Oxford and His Adventures in the Barons' War. London and New York, Nelson, 1897.

Molly Melville. London and New York, Nelson, 1897.

Battledown Boys; or, An Enemy Overcome. London, Sunday School Union, and Philadelphia, Union Press, 1898.

Esther's Charge. London, Nelson, 1898; New York, Burt, 1899.

Gladys or Gwenyth: The Story of a Mistake. London, Nelson, 1898.

Sister: A Chronicle of Fair Haven. London and New York, Nelson, 1898.

Tom Tufton's Toll.   London and New York, Nelson, 1898.

Tom Tufton's Travels.   London and New York, Nelson, 1898.

For the Queen's Sakej or, The Story of Little Sir Caspar, illustrated by John H. Bacon.   London, Nelson, 1898.

Little Lois.   London, Nelson, 1898.

Joy's Jubilee.   London, Nelson, 1898.

French and English: A Story of the Struggle in America.   London, Nelson, 1899.

Miss Marjorie of Silvermead.   London, Hutchinson, 1899; Philadelphia, G.W. Jacobs, 1901.

Sir Reginald's Ward; or, Tales of the Family.   London, Religious Tract Society, 1899.

The Probation of Mervyn Castleton.   London, James Bowden, 1899.

Cross Purposes; or, The Deanes of Dean's Croft, with Emma and Beatrice Marshall.   London, Griffith Farran, 1899.

The Heir of Hascombe Hall: A Tale of the Days of the Early Tudors.   London, Nelson, 1899; New York, Nelson, 1900.

The Mystery of Alton Grange.   London, Nelson, 1899.

Priscilla, with H. Louisa Bedford.   London, Nelson, 1899; New York, Nelson, 1900.

Bruno and Bimba: The Story of Some Little People.   London, Nister, 1900.

Eleanor's Hero, illustrated by J. Barnard Davis.   London, Sunday School Union, 1900.

The Little Match-Girl.   London, Shaw, 1900.

A Fiery Chariot.   London, Hutchinson, 1900.

In Cloister and Court; or, The White Flower of a Blameless Life: The Story of Bishop Ken.   London, Shaw, 1900.

The King's Butterfly, illustrated by Arthur A. Dixon.   London, Nister, and New York, Dutton, 1900.

The Master of Fernhurst.   London, Shaw, 1900.

Odeyne's Marriage.   London, Shaw and New York, Dutton, 1900.

The Silver Axe: The Narrative of Rupert, Earl of Herondale.   London, Hutchinson, 1900.

The Wooing of Val: The Story of Six Days.   London, Hutchinson, 1900.

Paul Harvard's Campaign.   London, Religious Tract Society, 1901.

A Gordon Highlander.   London and New York, Nelson, 1901.

Princess Fairstar: A Story of the Days of Charles I, illustrated by F.H. Michael.   London, Nister, 1901; New York, Dutton, 1902.

The Secret of Maxshelling.   London, Shaw, and New York, Dutton, 1901.

Tregg's Triumph: A Story of Stormy Days.   London, Religious Tract Society, 1901.

Holidays at the Farm, with Evelyn Fletcher and others.   London, Nister, 1901; New York, Dutton, 1913.

Bob and Bill.   London, Religious Tract Society, 1901.

After Worcester: The Story of a Royal Fugitive.   London and New York, Nelson, 1901.

True Stories of Girl Heroines, illustrated by E.F. Sherie.   London, Hutchinson, and New York, Dutton, 1901.

Alwyn Ravendale.   London, Religious Tract Society, and New York, American Tract Society, 1902.

The Boys of the Red House.   London, Melrose, 1902.

Gabriel Garth, Chartist.   London, Melrose, 1902.

In Fair Granada: A Tale of Moors and Christians.   London and New York, Nelson, 1902.

A Princess's Token, illustrated by Arthur A. Dixon.   London, Nister, 1902.

White Wyvill and Red Ruthven: A Story of the Strife of the Roses.   London, Nister, 1902.

For the Faith: A Story of the Young Pioneers of Reformation in Oxford.   London and New York, Nelson, 1902.

Short Tales from Storyland: A Volume of Thirty Stories, illustrated by Mrs. Seymour Lucas and Eveline Lance.   London, Nister, 1902.

Fallen Fortunes, Being the Adventures of a Gentleman of Quality in the Days of Queen Anne. London and New York, Nels, 1902.

My Lady Joanna, Being a Chronicle Concerning the King's Children Rendered into Modern English from the Records by Lady Edeline. London, Nisbet, 1902.

Tiny and Her Grandfather; or, A Small Beauty and an Ogre Who Was Not a Beast. London, Ward Lock, 1902.

To the Rescue: A Tale of a London Prentice Boy. London, Nister, 1902.

Audrey Marsh. London, Collins, 1903.

Cambria's Chieftain. London and New York, Nelson, 1903.

The Castle of the White Flag: A Tale of the Franco-German War. London and New York, Nelson, 1903.

The Conscience of Roger Trehern. London, Religious Tract Society, 1903; as *Roger Trehern*, Philadelphia, American Tract Society, 1903.

The Squire's Heir; or, The Secret of Rochester's Will. London, Melrose, 1903.

Under Two Queens. London, Shaw, 1903.

A Hero of the Highlands; or, The Romance of a Rebellion as Related by One Who Looked On. London and New York, Nelson, 1903.

The Children's Crusade: A Story of Adventure. London, Nelson, 1904.

The Faith of Hilary Lovel: A Story of Armada Days. London, Religious Tract Society, 1904.

The Jilting of Bruce Heriot. London, Religious Tract Society, 1904.

Ringed by Fire: A Story of the Franco-Prussian War. London, Nelson, 1904.

The Three Graces. London, Melrose, 1904.

The Sisters of Silver Sands. London, Sunday School Union, 1904.

Little Lady Val: A Tale of the Days of Good Queen Bess, illustrated by Arthur A. Dixon. London, Nister, and New York, Dutton, 1904.

Miss Greyshott's Girls, illustrated by A. Twidle. London, Melrose, 1905.

Uncle Boo. London, Nelson, 1905.

In Northern Seas. London, Nelson, 1905.

Jim Trelawny, illustrated by E.A. Pike. London, Sunday School Union, 1905.

Madam of Clyst Peveril, illustrated by C. Pearse. London, Melrose, 1905.

Smouldering Fires; or, The Kinsmen of Kinthorns. London, Nelson, 1905.

Treasure Trove: A Tale of Shark's Tooth Rocks. London, Shaw, 1905.

The Defence of the Rock. London, Nelson, 1906.

In a Land of Beasts, illustrated by Arthur A. Dixon. London, Collins, 1906.

The Master of Marshlands, illustrated by Bertha Newcombe. London, Ward Lock, 1906.

Percy Vere, illustrated by R. Lillie. London, Cassell, 1906.

Dickie and Dorrie: A Tale of Hallowdene Hall, illustrated by Gordon Browne. London, Wells Gardner Darton, 1906.

A Motherless Maid, illustrated by Dorothy Travers-Pope. London, Melrose, 1906.

Our Great Undertaking: A Grandmother's Story. London, Hodder and Stoughton, 1906.

Clanrickard Court, illustrated by N.C. Bishop-Culpeper. London, Melrose, 1907.

Miss Lorimer of Chard, illustrated by C. Pearse. London, Melrose, 1907.

Carol Carew; or, Was It Imprudent. London, Partridge, 1907; Philadelphia, McKay, 1910; as *The Imprudence of Carol Carew,* Partridge, 1933.

Knights of the Road. London, Nelson, 1907.

Ruth Ravelstan the Puritan's Daughter. London, Nelson, 1907.

Gowrie's Vengeance: The Romance of a Conspiracy. London, Nelson, 1908.

Hilary Quest, illustrated by Watson Charlton. London, Pilgrim Press, 1908.

The Cossart Cousins. London, Religious Tract Society, 1908.

Greyfriars. London, Religious Tract Society, 1908.

The Family Next Door. London, Religious Tract Society, 1908.

Stepsister Stella, illustrated by Gertrude Steel. London, Pilgrim Press, 1908.

Half-a-Dozen Sisters. London, Religious Tract Society, 1909.
A Wilful Maid. London, Partridge, 1909.
The City of the Golden Gate. London, Stanley Paul, and New York, Dodge, 1909.
A Lad of London Town: A Tale of Darkness and Light, illustrated by T. Heath Robinson. London, Pilgrim Press, 1909.
In Grandfather's Garden. London, Nelson, 1910.
Ursula Tempest, illustrated by Victor Prout. London, Religious Tract Society, 1910.
The Dean's Daughter (as Cecil Adair). London, Stanley Paul, 1910.
General John: A Story for Boy Scouts and Others, illustrated by H.R. Millar. London, Partridge, 1910.
Dickie and Dorrie at School, illustrated by Gordon Browne. London, Wells Gardner Darton, 1911.
Patricia Pendragon (as Evelyn Dare). London, White, 1911.
Cantacute Towers (as Cecil Adair). London, Stanley Paul, 1911.
A Disputed Heritage, illustrated by Saville Lumley. London, Pilgrim Press, 1911.
Aunt Patience. London, Religious Tract Society, 1912.
Miss Mallory of Mote. London, Hutchinson, 1912.
Tommy and the Owl. London, Partridge, 1912.
The Yellow Pup, illustrated by C. Fleming Williams. London, Partridge, 1912.
Francesca (as Cecil Adair). London, Stanley Paul, 1912.
Inchfallen. London, Ward Lock, 1913.
Dora's Dolls' House. London, Stanley Paul, 1914.
The House on the Cliff. London, Ward Lock, 1914.
The Heronstoke Mystery. London, Religious Tract Society, 1915.
Adventurous Anne. London, Stanley Paul, 1916.
Sweepie. London, Religious Tract Society, 1918.
Daddy's Ducklings. London, Religious Tract Society, 1921.
Crystal's Victory; or, The House of the Ghost (as Cecil Adair). London, Stanley Paul, 1921.
Queen's Manor School. London, Stanley Paul, 1921.
The Tyrant of Tylecourt. London, Stanley Paul, 1922.
Twins at Tachbury, illustrated by N. Buchanan. London, Wells Gardner Darton, 1924.
The Squire's Daughters. London, Stanley Paul, 1932.

Other

The Eversley Secrets. London, Blackie, 1886.
Paths of Peace, 1894: The Christmas Number of "The Sunday Magazine," illustrated by James Greig. London, Isbister, 1894.
Called of Her Country: The Story of Joan of Arc, illustrated by E.F. Sherie. London, Bousfield, 1903.
Guy Fulkes of the Tower. London, Hutchinson, 1906.
A Heroine of France: The Story of Joan of Arc. London, Nelson, 1906.
The Story of Joan of Arc (as Evelyn Dare). London, Oxford University Press, 1914.

Publications for Adults

Fiction

Maude Kingslake's Collect (as H.F.E.). London, S.P.C.K., 1882.
Lady Temple's Grandchildren. London, Nisbet, 1883.
Lenore Annandale's Story. London, Religious Tract Society, 1884; Boston, Bradley, 1889.
Fighting the Good Fight. New York, Nelson, 1884.

Torwood's Trust. London, Bentley, 3 vols., 1884.

Two London Homes; or, Marjorie and Muriel. London, Shaw, 1884.

Cuthbert Coningsby: A Sequel to "Maude Kinglake's Collect," London, S.P.C.K., 1884.

The Mistress of Lydgate Priory; or, The Story of a Long Life. London, Religious Tract Society, 1885; as *The Mistress of Lydgate,* Boston, Bradley, 1889.

The Cottage and the Grange. London, Religious Tract Society, 1885.

Winning the Victory; or, Di Pennington's Record. London and New York, Nelson, 1886.

Joint Guardians. London, Religious Tract Society, 1887; Boston, Bradley, 1889.

Temple's Trial; or, For Life or Death. London and New York, Nelson, 1887.

Vera's Trust. London and New York, Nelson, 1889.

Whyola. Edinburgh, Oliphant, 1892.

My Cousin from Australia. London, Hutchinson, 1894.

A Great Indiscretion. London, Isbister, 1895.

The Chatterton Mystery. London, Clarke, 1896.

Hope. New York, Ketcham, 1896.

Under the Village Elms: Stories of the Beatitudes. London, Shaw, 1900.

Olivia's Experiment. London, Hutchinson, 1901.

Where There's a Will. London, Hutchinson, 1902.

The Niece of Esther Lynne. London, Hutchinson, 1903.

Dufferin's Keep. London, Hutchinson, 1905.

The Secret of Wold Hall. London, Hutchinson, and Chicago, McClurg, 1905.

In Pursuit of a Phantom. London, Religious Tract Society, 1905.

Lady Elizabeth and the Juggernaut. London, Hodder and Stoughton, 1906.

The Magic Island, Being the Story of a Garden and Its Master. London, Hutchinson, 1906.

Married in Haste. London, Hutchinson, 1907.

Superfluous Sisters. London, Hutchinson, 1907.

The Winning of Iris Newcombe. London, Scott, 1907.

The Erincourts. London, Marshall Brothers, 1907.

In Quest of a Wife and Other Stories. London, Shaw, 1907.

The Guardianship of Gabrielle. London, Hutchinson, 1908.

Co-Heiresses. London, Stanley Paul, 1909.

The Lady of Shall Not. London, Hutchinson, 1909.

A Pair of Originals. London, Seeley, 1909.

A Queen of Hearts. London, White, 1909.

The House of Silence. London, Hutchinson, 1910.

The Wife of Arthur Lorraine. London, White, 1910.

A Will in a Well. London, Stanley Paul, 1910.

Clive Lorimer's Marriage. London, Stanley Paul, 1911.

The Lady of the Bungalow. London, Stanley Paul, 1911.

The Evolution of Sara. London, Hutchinson, 1911.

The Qualities of Mercy. London, Stanley Paul, 1911.

Galbraith of Wynyates. London, Stanley Paul, 1912.

Defiant Diana. London, Stanley Paul, 1913.

Gabriel's Garden (as Cecil Adair). London, Stanley Paul, 1913.

Marcus Quayle, M.D. London, Hutchinson, 1913.

The Price of Friendship. London, Stanley Paul, 1913.

Quadrille Court (as Cecil Adair). London, Stanley Paul, 1913; Cleveland, International Fiction Library, 1929.

Under the Incense Trees (as Cecil Adair). London, Stanley Paul, 1914.

Black Ladies. London, Hutchinson, 1914.

The Double House. London, Stanley Paul, 1914.

A Barbed Wire. London, Stanley Paul, 1914.

The Sails of Life (as Cecil Adair).   London, Stanley Paul, and New York, Brentano's, 1915.
The Mist Pool (as Cecil Adair).   London, Stanley Paul, 1915.
"Confirmed Bachelor."   London, Hutchinson, 1915.
Herndale's Heir.   London, Stanley Paul, 1915.
The Mystery of Captain York.   London, Holden and Hardingham, 1915.
The Heiress of Swallowcliffe.   London, Stanley Paul, 1915.
Dashing Dick's Daughter.   London, Stanley Paul, 1915.
The Temptation of Mary Lister.   London, Stanley Paul, 1917.
Maid of the Moonflower (as Cecil Adair).   London, Stanley Paul, 1917.
Green Dusk for Dreams (as Cecil Adair).   London, Stanley Paul, 1918.
Eyes of Eternity.   London, Stanley Paul, 1918.
The Freedom of Fenella.   London, Stanley Paul, 1918.
A Difficult Half-Dozen.   London, Jarrolds, 1919.
Firebrand.   London, Mascot Novels, 1919.
Monster's Mistress.   London, Stanley Paul, 1919.
Mrs. Desmond's Daughter.   London, Morgan and Scott, 1919.
The Cactus Hedge (as Cecil Adair).   London, Stanley Paul, 1919.
Monks-Lyonness (as Cecil Adair).   London, Stanley Paul, 1920.
Billy's Bargain.   London, Stanley Paul, 1920.
The Silver Tea-Shop.   London, Stanley Paul, 1920.
Magic Emeralds.   London, Stanley Paul, 1921.
Miss Anne Thorpe.   London, Stanley Paul, 1921.
The Azure Lake (as Cecil Adair).   London, Stanley Paul, 1921.
Happy Chance (as Cecil Adair).   London, Stanley Paul, 1922.
Where Rainbows Rest (as Cecil Adair).   London, Stanley Paul, 1922.
The Son Who Came Back.   London, Stanley Paul, 1922.
Heristal's Wife (as Cecil Adair).   London, Stanley Paul, 1923.
Angels' Tears (as Cecil Adair).   London, Stanley Paul, 1923.
The Expectation Aunt.   London, Stanley Paul, 1923.
Lynette Lynton.   London, Stanley Paul, 1923.
Lossie of the Mill.   London, Stanley Paul, 1924.
The Revolt of Waydolyn.   London, Stanley Paul, 1924; as *The Revolt of Winnie*, London, J. Leng, 1927.
Silver Star-Dust (as Cecil Adair), with Ernestine Talbot Reed.   London, Stanley Paul, 1924; New York, Greenberg, 1925.
Dawn Island (as Cecil Adair).   London, Stanley Paul, 1924; New York, Greenberg, 1925.
Iridescence (as Cecil Adair).   London, Stanley Paul, 1925.
Whispering Trees (as Cecil Adair).   London, Stanley Paul, 1925.
Ghost Hall.   London, Stanley Paul, 1925.
The Tragedy of Trifles.   London, Stanley Paul, 1925.
Dreamland and Dawn (as Cecil Adair).   London, Stanley Paul, 1926.
Grandmamma over the Sea (as Cecil Adair).   London, Stanley Paul, 1926.
The Silence of the Hills (as Cecil Adair).   London, Stanley Paul, 1926.
The Back Number.   London, Stanley Paul, 1926.
Sheila Mary.   London, Stanley Paul, 1926.
The Two Barbaras.   London, Stanley Paul, 1927.
When the Old House Dreams (as Cecil Adair).   London, Stanley Paul, 1927.
Fire Seeds (as Cecil Adair).   London, Stanley Paul, 1927.
Claude the Charmer.   London, Stanley Paul, 1927.
Uncle Quayle.   London, Stanley Paul, 1928.
Shimmering Waters (as Cecil Adair).   London, Stanley Paul, 1928; Philadelphia, Dorrance, 1929.
Blue Mist and Mystery (as Cecil Adair).   London, Stanley Paul, 1928.

A Soul Escaped (as Cecil Adair).   London, Stanley Paul, 1929.
Silver and Gold (as Cecil Adair).   London, Stanley Paul, 1929.
Miss Gosshawk and Gosshawk.   London, Stanley Paul, 1929.
Quettenden's Folly.   London, Stanley Paul, 1929.
The Genius of Gerald.   London, Stanley Paul, 1930.
Sapphire and Emerald (as Cecil Adair).   London, Stanley Paul, 1930.
Shadowland (as Cecil Adair).   London, Stanley Paul, 1930.
Golden Mists (as Cecil Adair).   London, Stanley Paul, 1931.
The Lady Asphodel: A Romance (as Cecil Adair).   London, Stanley Paul, 1931.
Tall Chimneys.   London, Stanley Paul, 1931.
The Curse of Carlyon.   London, Wright and Brown, 1931.
Monk Maltravers, V.C.   London, Stanley Paul, 1931.
The Romance of Vivian Adene.   London, Wright and Brown, 1932.
Hills of the West (as Cecil Adair).   London, Stanley Paul, 1932.
The Island of Avilion (as Cecil Adair).   London, Stanley Paul, 1932.
Shelmerdale (as Cecil Adair).   London, Stanley Paul, 1933.
The Shining Strand (as Cecil Adair).   London, Stanley Paul, 1933.
Under the Old Oaks.   London, Pickering and Inglis, 1933.
An Orchard Idyll.   London, Wright and Brown, 1933.

*   *   *

Evelyn Everett-Green provided for some 50 years popular books for the young, and the style of her writing is representative of the trends of juvenile publishing of the late 19th and early 20th centuries. Her output (an annual average of 6 or 7 volumes, rising to 11 in peak years), though large by present-day standards, was not considered unduly excessive then (her older contemporary, L.T. Meade, wrote even more). She ranged over most genres of fiction: historical novels, school stories, street arab tales, family adventures, romantic but safe tales for the girl on the brink of leaving the schoolroom ("Yet young maidens will have their dreams, and a maiden's dream requires a man to make it interesting"); she even attempted a story in 1910 for the newly emerging Boy Scout Movement.

Like most lady writers of her type, she extolled the virtues of the thoroughbred gentleman – whose children did not need to be taught the meaning of honour – and denounced the parvenu and nouveau riche – who could not learn it. Like them, too, her favourite scene was the grey-walled mansion with its tumble of roses and terraces descending to rolling parkland, and her favourite child characters the rosy-cheeked maiden with eyes of speedwell blue, the merry rogue, the scamp, the innocent pickle who leaves a trail of devastation but has a warm and loving heart. Occasionally, as in *My Boynie*, she succeeds in creating credible children. Though the plot of this is a familiar one of the period and turns on the gradual decline and ultimate death of a little boy from spinal injury – in this case through being led into mischief by a tomboy elder sister – the character of the latter is sympathetically observed, and the knowledgeable enthusiasm for gardens and for flowers is reminiscent of Mrs. Ewing's *Mary Meadow* (which indeed the author may have had in mind). She did not, however, usually allow herself time to produce books of this quality, but was content to supply giftbooks for all occasions. These were in general well-received by reviewers who praised their "excellent tone," and described them as "wholesome fiction" and "simple, attractive, healthy stories."

—Gillian Avery

FARJEON, Eleanor. British. Born in London, 13 February 1881; daughter of the novelist Benjamin Leopold Farjeon, and sister of the writer Herbert Farjeon. Educated privately. Contributed verse (as Tom Fool) to the *Daily Herald*, London, 1917–30; staff member and verse contributor (as Chimaera), *Time and Tide*, London, in the 1920's. Recipient: Hans Christian Andersen International Medal, 1956; Library Association Carnegie Medal, 1956; Catholic Library Association Regina Medal, 1959. *Died 5 June 1965.*

PUBLICATIONS FOR CHILDREN

Fiction

Martin Pippin in the Apple Orchard, illustrated by C. E. Brock. London, Collins, 1921; New York, Stokes, 1922.

Nuts and May: A Medley for Children, illustrated by Rosalind Thorneycroft. London, Collins, 1925.

Tom Cobble. Oxford, Blackwell, 1925.

Italian Peepshow and Other Tales, illustrated by Rosalind Thorneycroft. New York, Stokes, 1926; as *Italian Peepshow and Other Stories*, Oxford, Blackwell, 1934; revised edition, as *Italian Peepshow*, London, Oxford University Press, 1960.

The Wonderful Knight, illustrated by Doris Pailthorpe. Oxford, Blackwell, 1927.

Kaleidoscope. London, Collins, 1928; New York, Stokes, 1929.

The Perfect Zoo, illustrated by Kathleen Burrell. London, Harrap, and Philadelphia, McKay, 1929.

The King's Daughter Cries for the Moon, illustrated by May Smith. Oxford, Blackwell, 1929.

The Tale of Tom Tiddler, illustrated by Norman Tealby. London, Collins, 1929; New York, Stokes, 1930.

Westwoods, illustrated by May Smith. Oxford, Blackwell, 1930; Poughkeepsie, New York, Artists and Writers Guild, 1935.

The Old Nurse's Stocking-Basket, illustrated by E. H. Whydale. London, University of London, and New York, Stokes, 1931.

Perkin the Pedlar, illustrated by Clare Leighton. London, Faber, 1932.

Katy Kruse at the Seaside; or, The Deserted Islanders. London, Harrap, and Philadelphia, McKay, 1932.

Ameliaranne and the Magic Ring, illustrated by S. B. Pearce. Philadelphia, McKay, 1933.

Ameliaranne's Prize Packet, illustrated by S. B. Pearce. London, Harrap, 1933.

Pannychis, illustrated by Clare Leighton. Shaftesbury, Dorset, High House Press, 1933.

Jim at the Corner and Other Stories, illustrated by Irene Mountfort. Oxford, Blackwell, 1934; as *The Old Sailor's Yarn Box*, New York, Stokes, 1934.

Ameliaranne's Washing Day, illustrated by S. B. Pearce. London, Harrap, and Philadelphia, McKay, 1934.

The Clumber Pup, illustrated by Irene Mountfort. Oxford, Blackwell, 1934.

And I Dance My Own Child, illustrated by Irene Mountfort. Oxford, Blackwell, 1935.

Jim and the Pirates, illustrated by Roger Naish. Oxford, Blackwell, 1936.

The Wonders of Herodotus, illustrated by Edmund Nelson. London and New York, Nelson, 1937.

Martin Pippin in the Daisy-Field, illustrated by Isobel and John Morton-Sale. London, Joseph, 1937; New York, Stokes, 1938.

One Foot in Fairyland: Sixteen Tales, illustrated by Robert Lawson. London, Joseph, and New York, Stokes, 1938.

The Silver Curlew, illustrated by Ernest H. Shepard. London, Oxford University Press, 1953; New York, Viking Press, 1954.

The Little Bookroom, illustrated by Edward Ardizzone.   London, Oxford University
Press, 1955; New York, Walck, 1956.
The Glass Slipper, illustrated by Ernest H. Shepard.   London, Oxford University Press,
1955; New York, Viking Press, 1956.
Mr. Garden, illustrated by Jane Paton.   London, Hamish Hamilton, and New York,
Walck, 1966.

Plays

The Glass Slipper, with Herbert Farjeon, illustrated by Hugh Stevenson (produced
London, 1944).   London, Wingate, 1946.
The Silver Curlew: A Fairy Tale, music by Clifton Parker (produced London,
1949).   London, French, 1953.
Grannie Gray: Children's Plays and Games with Music and Without, illustrated by Joan
Jefferson Farjeon.   London, Dent, 1939.

Verse

Nursery Rhymes of London Town, illustrated by Macdonald Gill.   London, Duckworth,
1916.
More Nursery Rhymes of London Town, illustrated by Macdonald Gill.   London,
Duckworth, 1917.
All the Way to Alfriston, illustrated by Robin Guthrie.   London, Morland Press, 1918.
Singing Games for Children, illustrated by J. Littlejohns.   London, Dent, and New
York, Dutton, 1919.
A First [and *Second*] *Chap-Book of Rounds*, music by Herbert Farjeon, illustrated by
John Garside.   London, Dent, and New York, Dutton, 2 vols., 1919.
Tunes of a Penny Piper, illustrated by John Aveten.   London, Selwyn and Blount, 1922.
Songs for Music and Lyrical Poems.   London, Selwyn and Blount, 1922.
All the Year Round.   London, Collins, 1923; as *Around the Seasons: Poems*, London,
Hamish Hamilton, and New York, Walck, 1969.
The Country Child's Alphabet, illustrated by William M. Rothenstein.   London, Poetry
Bookshop, 1924.
The Town Child's Alphabet, illustrated by David Jones.   London, Poetry Bookshop,
1924.
Songs from "Punch" for Children.   London, Saville, 1925.
Young Folk and Old.   Shaftesbury, Dorset, High House Press, 1925.
Joan's Door, illustrated by Will Townsend.   London, Collins, 1926; New York, Stokes,
1927.
Singing Games from Arcady.   Oxford, Blackwell, 1926.
Come, Christmas, illustrated by Molly McArthur.   London, Collins, 1927; New York,
Stokes, 1928.
An Alphabet of Magic, illustrated by Margaret Tarrant.   London, Medici Society, 1928.
Poems for Children.   Philadelphia, Lippincott, 1931.
Kings   and   Queens,   with   Herbert   Farjeon,   illustrated   by   Rosalind
Thorneycroft.   London, Gollancz, and New York, Dutton, 1932; revised edition,
London, Dent, 1953; Philadelphia, Lippincott, 1955.
Heroes   and   Heroines,   with   Herbert   Farjeon,   illustrated   by   Rosalind
Thorneycroft.   London, Gollancz, and New York, Dutton, 1933.
Over the Garden Wall, illustrated by Gwendolen Raverat.   London, Faber, and New
York, Stokes, 1933.
Sing for Your Supper, illustrated by Isobel and John Morton-Sale.   London, Joseph,
and New York, Stokes, 1938.
A Sussex Alphabet, illustrated by M. Thompson.   Bognor Regis, Sussex, Pear Tree
Press, 1939.

Cherrystones, illustrated by Isobel and John Morton-Sale. London, Joseph, 1942;
Philadelphia, Lippincott, 1944.
A Prayer for Little Things, illustrated by Elizabeth Orton Jones. Boston, Houghton
Mifflin, 1945.
The Mulberry Bush, illustrated by Isobel and John Morton-Sale. London Joseph, 1945.
The Starry Floor, illustrated by Isobel and John Morton-Sale. London, Joseph, 1949.
Mrs. Malone, illustrated by David Knight. London, Joseph, 1950; New York, Walck,
1962.
Silver-Sand and Snow. London, Joseph, 1951.
A Puffin Quartet of Poets, with others, edited by Eleanor Graham, illustrated by Diana
Bloomfield. London, Penguin, 1953.
Children's Bells: A Selection of Poems, illustrated by Peggy Fortnum. London, Oxford
University Press, 1957; New York, Walck, 1960.
Then There Were Three: Being Cherrystones, The Mulberry Bush, The Starry Floor,
illustrated by Isobel and John Morton-Sale. London, Joseph, 1958; Philadelphia,
Lippincott, 1965.

Other

Mighty Men: Achilles to Julius Caesar, Beowulf to Harold, illustrated by Hugh
Chesterman. Oxford, Blackwell, and New York, Appleton, 2 vols., 1925.
Tales from Chaucer: The Canterbury Tales Done into Prose, illustrated by W. Russell
Flint. London, Medici Society, and Boston, Hale Cushman and Flint, 1930.
Ten Saints, illustrated by Helen Sewell. New York, Oxford University Press, 1936;
London, Oxford University Press, 1953.
Paladins in Spain ..., illustrated by Katherine Tozer. London and New York, Nelson,
1937.
The New Book of Days, illustrated by Philip Gough and M. W. Hawes. London,
Oxford University Press, 1941; New York, Walck, 1961.
Eleanor Farjeon's Book: Stories, Verses, Plays, edited by Eleanor Graham, illustrated by
Edward Ardizzone. London, Penguin, 1960.

Editor, with William Mayne, *The Hamish Hamilton Book of Kings*, illustrated by Victor
Ambrus. London, Hamish Hamilton, 1964; as *A Cavalcade of Kings*, New York,
Walck, 1965.
Editor, with William Mayne, *The Hamish Hamilton Book of Queens*, illustrated by
Victor Ambrus. London, Hamish Hamilton, 1965; as *A Cavalcade of Queens*, New
York, Walck, 1965.
Editor, *The Green Roads: Poems for Young Readers*, by Edward Thomas, illustrated by
Bernard Brett. London, Bodley Head, and New York, Holt Rinehart, 1965.

PUBLICATIONS FOR ADULTS

Novels

Gypsy and Ginger. New York, Dutton, 1920.
The Soul of Kol Nikon. London, Collins, and New York, Stokes, 1923.
Ladybrook. London, Collins, and New York, Stokes, 1931.
The Fair of St. James: A Fantasia. London, Faber, and New York, Stokes 1932.
Humming Bird. London, Joseph, 1936; New York, Stokes, 1937.
Miss Granby's Secret. London, Joseph, 1940; as *Miss Granby's Secret; or, The Bastard
of Pinsk*, New York, Simon and Schuster, 1941.
Brave Old Woman. London, Joseph, 1941.
The Fair Venetian. London, Joseph, 1943.
Golden Coney. London, Joseph, 1943.

Ariadne and the Bull.   London, Joseph, 1945.
Love Affair.   London, Joseph, 1947; New York, Macmillan, 1949.
Two Bouquets.   London, Joseph, 1948.

Short Stories

Faithful Jenny Dove and Other Tales.   London, Collins, 1925.
A Bad Day for Martha.   Oxford, Blackwell, 1928.

Plays

Floretta (opera), music by Herbert Farjeon (produced London, 1899).   London, Henderson and Spalding, 1899.
The Registry Office (opera), music by Herbert Farjeon (produced London, 1900).   London, Henderson and Spalding, 1900.
A Gentleman of the Road (operetta), music by Herbert Farjeon (produced London, 1902).   London, Boosey and Hawkes, 1903.
The Two Bouquets: A Victorian Comedy with Music, with Herbert Farjeon (produced London, 1936).   London, Gollancz, 1936.
An Elephant in Arcady, with Herbert Farjeon (produced 1938).
Aucassin and Nicolette, with Herbert Farjeon, music by Clifton Parker.   London and New York, Chappell, 1952.
A Room at the Inn: A Christmas Masque.   London, French, 1957.

Verse

Pan-Worship and Other Poems.   London, Elkin Mathews, 1908.
Dream-Songs for the Beloved.   London, Orpheus Press, 1911.
Sonnets and Poems.   Oxford, Blackwell, 1918.
Snowfall.   London, Favil Press, 1928.
A Collection of Poems.   London, Collins, 1929.
Songs of Kings and Queens, with Herbert Farjeon.   London, Arnold, 1938.
First and Second Love: Sonnets.   London, Joseph, 1947.

Other

Arthur Rackham: The Wizard at Home.   New York, Century, 1914.
Trees.   London, Batsford, 1914.
The ABC of the B.B.C.   London, Collins, 1928.
A Nursery in the Nineties (autobiography).   London, Gollancz, 1935; as *Portrait of a Family*, New York, Stokes, 1936.
Magic Casements (essays).   London, Allen and Unwin, 1941.
Dark World of Animals.   London, Sylvan Press, 1945.
Elizabeth Myers.   Aylesford, St. Albert's Press, 1957.
The Memoirs of Eleanor Farjeon: Book One: Edward Thomas, The Last Four Years.   London, Oxford University Press, 1958.

Translator, with Herbert Farjeon, *The Fan*, in *Four Comedies*, by Carlo Goldoni.   London, Cecil Palmer, 1922.

Critical Study: *Eleanor Farjeon* by Eileen Colwell,   London, Bodley Head, and New York, Walck, 1961.

*   *   *

"All ages" is written on the dust-jacket of several of Eleanor Farjeon's books but, unlike Hans Andersen who was so annoyed at his fairy stories being labelled for children, she seemed content that the eternal truths she sought to wrap up in her fiction should be for the young. She was a prolific writer of verses, plays, history and tales, many of which, like *Martin Pippin in the Apple Orchard* or *Jim at the Corner*, were recounted by a central character. Her best work lies in the selection of short stories she made herself at the age of 73, *The Little Bookroom*, which won both the Carnegie and the Hans Andersen Medals. She explained in the introduction: "When I came to write books myself they were a muddle of fiction and fact and fantasy and truth. I have never quite succeeded in distinguishing one from the other .... Seven maids with seven brooms, sweeping for half-a-hundred years, have never managed to clear my mind of its dust of vanished temples and flowers and kings, the curls of ladies, the sighing of poets, the laughter of lads and girls."

Situations are briefly created, then change swiftly, often to an unexpected end as in "The Little Dressmaker," in which the heroine marries the footman, because the hero really was a footman and not a prince in disguise, or in "The Seventh Princess," in which an unhappy queen cuts and covers with a scarf her youngest daughter's hair, so that she will not succeed her. The behaviour of adults is mocked; in *The King's Daughter Cries for the Moon* they arrest everyone on hearsay; in *Westwoods* they are afraid to go beyond a certain fence simply because they were told not to when they were children. They find happiness when they return to childhood dreams as in this story and in "The Barrel Organ," when "the traveller was dancing too, he danced as he used to when he was ten years old, till the tune of the organ was faint to hear." Some of the settings are real, as in "Pennyworth" where a small boy puts his penny in the wrong machine, so gets no chocolate but enjoys the railway station none-the-less, or absurd − a sentry guarding an empty piece of ground because years ago a beautiful flower grew there.

There is plenty of magic but no sentimentality: the very old lady has a sweet, sly, greedy smile; Susan Brown treasures her piece of coloured paper telling her future but she did not know what was in it because she could not read. There was a happy village which consulted five generations of wise Tims but did nothing "until the day came when Baby Tims died an unmarried man at 100 years of age. After that the village became as other villages and did something."

The traditional fairy story ending, with the poor little waif attaining riches, was not for Eleanor Farjeon, who did not see happiness in terms of material things. The Kind Farmer gave everything away: "for the sake of all children he had left his child with nothing. Yet in the end, you might say, he had left the whole village to little Jane Churdon, for every roof and hearth in it was hers." A compromise is reached by a lonely rich girl who sends roses floating down a river whenever she wants to enjoy herself baking bread with some poor children in their cottage.

One other tale not in this selection but worth mentioning is "Elsie Piddock Skips in Her Sleep," from *Martin Pippin in the Daisy Field*. A village child becomes such a famous skipper that the fairies get to know and teach her fresh skills in her sleep. When a hard-hearted business man tries to take the village skipping ground, she returns, a tiny old lady over a hundred, and skips in her sleep for ever to save the land for the children. *Martin Pippin in the Apple Orchard* was highly praised when it was published in 1921 for adults and was later enjoyed by teenage girls, but now makes rather slow reading. After many pages of country rhymes, Martin, a wandering troubadour, appears and sings and recites stories to a group of maidens bored stiff with guarding a love-sick girl.

Jim, an old sailor full of improbable yarns (*Jim at the Corner*), is a more interesting character. He is quite happy sitting on a box, saluting the passers-by whose cast-off clothes he is wearing, and telling a small boy of the wonderful things he did on the sea. One of the best concerns a codfish he rescued who in return gave him cod-liver oil which smelt so awful that the fierce ninth wave retreated and the ship was saved.

In *Kaleidoscope* a man returns to the countryside of his childhood and remembers his continued longing for something he could not find. Anthony as a boy, ashamed of his mother bringing a second coat to school on a cold day, dreaming of a flying horse or watching the woodworker, really comes to life again.

Fact slides into fantasy in the very readable lives of *Ten Saints*. St. Bridget, coming quickly into her cell, flung her wet mantle over a sunbeam which she mistook for a beam of wood. She then forgot and the sun went down, but the sunbeam waited patiently until the saint removed her mantle before he retired to find the sun. St. Patrick's journeys can still be traced because he "strewed his name over rocks and churches, islands and valleys, causeways and cells as a running stag scatters his scent." There are short verses about each saint.

Eleanor Farjeon was revered in her long life and regarded as a poet; her poems today are not highly considered, her play on Cinderella is dated, but her poetic feeling and humour live on in her short stories.

—Margaret Campbell

FARLEY, Walter (Lorimer). American. Born in Syracuse, New York, 26 June 1920. Educated at Erasmus High School, Brooklyn, New York; Mercersburg Academy, Pennsylvania, graduated 1936; Columbia University, New York. Served in the Fourth Armored Division, and as staff member of *Yank* magazine, United States Army, 1942–46. Married Rosemary Lutz in 1945; has four children. Lives in Pennsylvania and Florida. Address: c/o Random House Inc., 201 East 50th Street, New York, New York 10022, U.S.A.

PUBLICATIONS FOR CHILDREN

Fiction

> *The Black Stallion*, illustrated by Keith Ward. New York, Random House, 1941; London, Lunn, 1947.
> *Larry and the Undersea Raider*, illustrated by P. K. Jackson. New York, Random House, 1942; London, Muller, 1944.
> *The Black Stallion Returns*, illustrated by Harold Eldridge. New York, Random House, 1945; London, Lunn, 1947.
> *Son of the Black Stallion*, illustrated by Milton Menasco. New York, Random House, 1947; London, Collins, 1950.
> *The Island Stallion*, illustrated by Keith Ward. New York, Random House, 1948; London, Hodder and Stoughton, 1973.
> *The Black Stallion and Satan*, illustrated by Milton Menasco. New York, Random House, 1949; revised edition, London, Hodder and Stoughton, 1974.
> *The Blood Bay Colt*, illustrated by Milton Menasco. New York Random House, 1950.
> *The Island Stallion's Fury*, illustrated by Harold Eldridge. New York, Random House, 1951; London, Hodder and Stoughton, 1975.
> *The Black Stallion's Filly*, illustrated by Milton Menasco. New York, Random House, 1952.
> *The Black Stallion Revolts*, illustrated by Harold Eldridge. New York, Random House, 1953.
> *The Black Stallion's Sulky Colt*, illustrated by Harold Eldridge. New York, Random House, 1954.
> *The Island Stallion Races*, illustrated by Harold Eldridge. New York, Random House, 1955.
> *The Black Stallion's Courage*. New York, Random House, 1956.
> *The Black Stallion Mystery*, illustrated by Mal Singer. New York, Random House, 1957; London, Hodder and Stoughton, 1973.
> *The Horse-Tamer*, illustrated by James Schucker. New York, Random House, 1958.

The Black Stallion and Flame, illustrated by Harold Eldridge.   New York, Random
   House, 1960; revised edition, London, Hodder and Stoughton, 1974.
Little Black, A Pony, illustrated by James Schucker.   New York, Random House, 1961;
   London, Collins, 1963.
Little Black Goes to the Circus, illustrated by James Schucker.   New York, Random
   House, 1963; London, Collins, 1965.
The Black Stallion Challenged!, illustrated by Angie Draper.   New York, Random
   House, 1964.
The Horse That Swam Away, illustrated by Leo Summers.   New York, Random House,
   1965.
The Great Dane, Thor, illustrated by Joseph Cellini.   New York, Random House, 1966.
The Little Black Pony Races, illustrated by James Schucker.   New York, Random
   House, 1968.
The Black Stallion's Ghost, illustrated by Angie Draper.   New York, Random House,
   1969.
The Black Stallion and the Girl, illustrated by Angie Draper.   New York, Random
   House, 1971.

Other

Man o' War, illustrated by Angie Draper.   New York, Random House, 1962.

*   *   *

Beginning with a ship-wrecked stallion of Arabian origins and unknown parentage,
Walter Farley built a series of stories around the Black Stallion. The fillies and colts that the
Black Stallion sires are the subjects of books that tell of Flame, Satan, Black Minx, Bonfire
and others.

Farley's early style is choppy, rough, and occasionally awkward. In addition to frequent
exclamation points to force excitement and suspense, Farley over-uses simple, regular
sentences in subject-predicate order. The later books, however, are varied in style, using
complex sentence forms as well as vivid fragments. Always realistic in details about horse
farms, stables, and race tracks, Farley successfully pictures his setting, giving each book a
strong sense of place.

While early Black Stallion books show a minimum of distinction between human
characters, Farley's later stories develop the character of Alec Ramsay, the Black's master,
into a credible boy who is skillful with horses and a natural rider. Although many of the race-
track and stable characters seem interchangeable, occasionally some are endowed with more
life and become distinctive and memorable. Characterization of the Black Stallion and the
other race horses also changes throughout the series. Individual horses acquire personality,
but not without Farley's lapsing into an omniscient point of view that pretends to know a
horse's thoughts.

The strongest feature of Farley's stories is the successful involvement of the reader in
admiration for the horses, his true subjects; whatever the plot, the horse is the focus. Alec
Ramsay may be the protagonist, but life to Alec is the Black. Like most series books, the Black
Stallion stories tend to melt into one another, but the Black Stallion and his offspring remain
alive, more memorable than plots or people.

—Rebecca J. Lukens

FARMER, Penelope.   British.   Born in Westerham, Kent, 14 June 1939.   Educated
privately, 1945–56; St. Anne's College, Oxford, 1957–60, B.A. (honours) in history; Bedford
College, University of London, Diploma of Social Studies 1962. Married Michael John
Mockridge in 1962 (divorced); has one son and one daughter. Teacher, London County

Council, 1960–61. Agent: Deborah Owen, 78 Narrow Street, London E.14. Address: 39 Mount Ararat Road, Richmond, Surrey, England.

*   *   *

It may be that Penelope Farmer's most considerable work is already over – in the complex allegory, *A Castle of Bone* – and this not because of fading gifts but because the preoccupations informing the major books over the decade 1962–1972 have reached a stage of resolution. While some authors say "I write for myself" somewhat hypocritically, the feeling of personal involvement in Penelope Farmer's novels is particularly strong, the images, landscapes and characters seeming spun out of her own life threads.

To reduce the stories to precis is as difficult as reducing lyric poems to one sentence summaries and as irrelevant. Penelope Farmer has classified herself as a writer of introvert fantasies, concerned with "the process of consciousness or of dream," and one traces these concerns in the hallucinatory flying episodes in *The Summer Birds*, the dream sequences in *Emma in Winter*, and Hugh's dreams in *A Castle of Bone* of the forest beyond which is the castle it is his task to claim. Even the settings and landscapes have a hypnotic quality – the downs at night in full moonlight, the silver gorse flowers, the turf cold and gray, the evening star cold and white; or the somnolent heat of midsummer meadows pictured in *The Summer Birds*, the mysterious blue shadows and luminosity of a snowbound world in *Emma in Winter*, and the dark cedar tree in *Charlotte Sometimes*. Buildings match landscape in these three books, the decaying Victorian mansion, the archaic flavour of the village school with its chalk smell, noisy desk lids, round of monitorial duties and the "Silence, children, silence" fussing of Miss Hallibutt. The characters, in contrast, are sharply contemporary and clearly defined. The unpredictable nature of adults, the tensions of shifting classroom relationships ("Shall I be chosen?"; "Why did she snub me?"), the helplessness of being a child in a grown-up world, and the shadows cast by the transitory nature of childhood are presented with tact and a lightness of touch which bring fantasy and reality into equipoise.

Some fantasies grow from darkness, but the three stories of Charlotte and Emma Makepeace have a white beneficent magic. The most popular of the three, *Charlotte Sometimes*, shows a brilliant handling of the time-switch technique and a sincerity which rejects slick solutions to the dilemmas of the two heroines. The dreams of *A Castle of Bone* are of another quality, more powerful and more painful, both fantasy and reality realised with raw intensity as uncompromising as Garner's *The Owl Service*.

In addition to these major works Penelope Farmer has given her own touch of distinction to contributions to Hamish Hamilton's Antelope series, to crisp retellings of heroic tales for Collins, and to collections of short stories.

—Peggy Heeks

FATCHEN, Max. Australian. Born in Adelaide, South Australia, 3 August 1920. Educated at Angle Vale Primary School; Gawler High School. Served in the Royal Australian Air Force, 1940–45. Married Jean Wohlers in 1942; has two sons and one daughter. Journalist, *Adelaide News* and *Sunday Mail*, Adelaide, 1946–55. Since 1955, Journalist, and since 1971, Literary Editor, *The Advertiser*, Adelaide. Agent: Winant, Towers Ltd., 14 Cliffords Inn, Fetter Lane, London EC4A 1DA, England. Address: 15 Jane Street, Smithfield, South Australia 5114, Australia.

PUBLICATIONS FOR CHILDREN

Fiction

The River Kings, illustrated by Clyde Pearson. Sydney, Hicks Smith, and London, Methuen, 1966; New York, St. Martin's Press, 1968.
Conquest of the River, illustrated by Clyde Pearson. Sydney, Hicks Smith, and London, Methuen, 1970.
The Spirit Wind, illustrated by Trevor Stubley. Sydney, Hicks Smith, and London, Methuen, 1973.
Chase Through the Night, illustrated by Graham Humphreys. Sydney and London, Methuen, 1977.

Other (in verse)

Drivers and Trains, illustrated by Iris Millington. Melbourne, Longman, 1963.

Keepers and Lighthouses, illustrated by Iris Millington.   Melbourne, Longman, 1963.
The Plumber, illustrated by Iris Millington.   Melbourne, Longman, 1963.
The Electrician, illustrated by Iris Millington.   Melbourne, Longman, 1963.
The Transport Driver, illustrated by Iris Millington.   Melbourne, Longman, 1965.
The Carpenter, illustrated by Iris Millington.   Melbourne, Longman, 1965.

PUBLICATIONS FOR ADULTS

Verse

Peculia Australia : Verses.   Privately printed, 1965.

Other

Just Fancy, Mr. Fatchen! A Collection of Verse, Prose and Fate's Cruel Blows.   Adelaide, Rigby, 1967.

Manuscript Collection : South Australia State Library, Adelaide.

Max Fatchen comments:
  My work as a journalist has taken me along Australia's river systems, particularly the Murray. I have covered its floods, talked to its oldtimers, ridden on some of the last of its riverboats and thus gathered material for my two books on the Murray – *The River Kings* and *Conquest of the River.* I have also seen the Mississippi, and it was a visit there in 1963 that helped to trigger my interest in writing books myself. My assignments have also taken me to sea aboard lighthouse ships and landing servicing crews by boat and helicopter on lonely islands off the Southern Australian coast. I have also been at sea with trawlermen, naval surveyors and lobster fishermen. I know particularly the windy coastline of South Australia where the last squareriggers came to load grain for their race around the Horn. I have also roamed over Australia's outback, particularly in the area under the Gulf of Carpentaria and across the lonely rivers and coastline of Arnhem Land in the Northern Territory. Here again I have found material for my books. The sea and the land are not just background but characters in my books because I feel they are alive, have a personality of their own and react on the people I write about. So I describe weather, the moods of landscape and climate, the fact that in the loneliness of the outback, particularly at night, the land can be felt like a presence padding around in the darkness outside. I feel that children like a strong storyline, action, character, good dialogue and no humbug. I find them honest, attentive and perceptive once their interest is captured. A book is a voyage, and I don't want them just to be passengers but members of the crew.

*   *   *

  The sea, rivers, and sailing craft, combined with his deep feeling for his native South Australia, lie at the heart of Max Fatchen's writing for young readers. His first two novels (for younger teenagers) formed a slightly tentative approach into the area of children's literature. *The River Kings* and *Conquest of the River,* set in South Australia's pioneering days when riverboats used to trade and cruise along the Murray River, both follow the fortunes of teen-aged Shane, who runs away from an unhappy home and becomes a member of a riverboat crew. Both stories are well-constructed, though perhaps a little too tightly organized, and they are filled with dramatic and humorous incident and deft chracterization of typical riverboat people – a tough but kindly Cap'n, a Chinese cook, Scottish Engineer, and so forth. They are also soundly based on riverboat knowledge and research. The choice of incidents and their outcome tend to be predictable, but, given the riverboat setting, this is to some extent inevitable – fire, flood, bunyips, and races between one riverboat and another are obvious ingredients of stories set on the Murray – and Max Fatchen was one of the first to choose this setting for junior fiction. Well in the background lurks the author's almost mystic and certainly poetic feeling for the great river. Here is a sound professional journalist producing exciting and very readable fiction, with just a hint of more significant power behind him. His narrative style is exceptionally clear-cut, free of any excess verbiage.

The publication of *The Spirit Wind* marked an important new departure for Max Fatchen. This is a much deeper and more ambitious work, in which the strain of poetry and mysticism emerges strongly, linked to Aboriginal lore through the character of Nunganee, an outcast from his tribe because he once "sang" a man's death. Set, once again, in the last century, the central character is fifteen-year-old Jarl Hansen, deckhand aboard the *Hootzen*, a squarerigger out of Norway bound for Australia, and ruled by a sadistic Mate. Jarl encounters Nunganee when he jumps ship in South Australia; their destinies, as well as that of the Mate and of the *Hootzen* herself, become entwined and are eventually fulfilled during a night of fierce storm when the mysterious Spirit Wind is unleashed. In this work Max Fatchen shows new powers and has launched his writing beyond the shallower seas of predictable incident and nicely observed characterization. It will be interesting indeed to follow the future development of his work.

—Barbara Ker Wilson

FATIO, Louise. American. Born in Lausanne, Switzerland, 18 August. Educated at boarding school, Basel, Switzerland; Collège des Jeunes Filles, Geneva. Married Roger Duvoisin, *q.v.*, in 1925; has two sons. Emigrated to the U.S.A. in 1925; naturalized citizen, 1938. Address: Gladstone, New Jersey 07934, U.S.A.

PUBLICATIONS FOR CHILDREN (illustrated by Roger Duvoisin)

Fiction

The Christmas Forest. New York, Aladdin Books, 1950.
Anna the Horse. New York, Aladdin Books, 1951.
The Happy Lion. New York, McGraw Hill, 1954; London, Lane, 1955.
The Happy Lion in Africa. New York, McGraw Hill, 1955; London, Bodley Head, 1963.
The Happy Lion Roars. New York, McGraw Hill, 1957; London, Bodley Head, 1959.
A Doll for Marie. New York, McGraw Hill, 1957.
The Three Happy Lions. New York, McGraw Hill, 1959; London, Bodley Head, 1960.
The Happy Lion's Quest. New York, McGraw Hill, 1961; London, Bodley Head, 1962.
Red Bantam. New York, McGraw Hill, and London, Bodley Head, 1963.
The Happy Lion and the Bear. New York, McGraw Hill, 1964; London, Bodley Head, 1965.
The Happy Lion's Vacation. New York, McGraw Hill, 1967; as *The Happy Lion's Holiday,* London, Bodley Head, 1968.
The Happy Lion's Treasure. New York, McGraw Hill, and London, Bodley Head, 1971.
Hector Penguin. New York, McGraw Hill, and London, Bodley Head, 1973.
The Happy Lion's Rabbits. New York, McGraw Hill, 1974; London, Bodley Head, 1975.

Marc and Pixie and the Walls in Mrs. Jones's Garden. New York, McGraw Hill, 1975;
London, Hodder and Stoughton, 1977.
Hector and Christina. New York, McGraw Hill, 1977.

Manuscript Collection: Kerlan Collection, University of Minnesota, Minneapolis.

Louise Fatio comments:

As in the case of most of those who translate their thoughts and beliefs into books, my books are an extension of my life. Or, I should say, our lives, my husband's and mine, for we have similar backgrounds, share the same tastes, and collaborate on many of our books.

Our love of people, of nature, our respect for animals – all often expressed in my books – date from our childhoods. We spent many summer vacations on farms or in villages, my husband in a Savoy village or a fishing village on the Mediterranean, I in a French-Swiss village. The need for a full country life not too far from a civilized city led us to settle in New Jersey (then a farming land which deserved its name of garden state) when we came to America. It is in this country atmosphere that we composed most of our books and brought up our children.

*   *   *

Louise Fatio is best known for her Happy Lion books, a series that has general unifying qualities. Perhaps the most significant of these qualities are characterization of the happy, genial lion and the quiet themes found in each of the picture books.

The Happy Lion lives in the zoo, but thanks to his friendship with the zookeeper's son is able to wander out of the zoo whenever it suits him. Uncharacteristically gentle and thoroughly kind, the Happy Lion shows great concern for others – visitors as well as fellow zoo-dwellers. He is pensive, restless, lonely, helpful; when he is free, he occasionally frightens townspeople, but not by his fierceness.

In addition to the memorable character of the Happy Lion, the themes of the books are an important element. To love and be loved is a treasure. We need someone like ourselves, as the Happy Lion discovers when he finds a mate. Where we live is home, not where we come from, the Happy Lion discovers when he visits Africa. He challenges rules and finds that sometimes new rules are needed. In still another story he discovers that befriending others makes one happy. And finally, aggressive behavior is rewarded with aggression, kind behavior with kindness. Fatio's Hector Penguin in another kind of tale finds it important to be what you are. Don't conform is Hector's discovery.

These direct, straightforward stories with little imagery or stylistic complexity, illustrated by Roger Duvoisin, have warmth and acceptance in their tone: they are important as comfortable affirmations of love and loyalty.

—Rebecca J. Lukens

FAULKNOR, (Chauncey) Cliff(ord Vernon). Canadian. Born in Vancouver, British Columbia, 3 March 1913. Educated at the University of British Columbia, Vancouver, B.S.A. (honours) 1949. Served as a gunner, Royal Canadian Artillery, Victoria, 1937–39; Marine engineer sergeant, Canadian Army Water Transport, 1939–45. Married Elizabeth Harriette Sloan in 1943; has one son and one daughter. Ledger Keeper, Royal Bank of Canada, Vancouver, 1929–31; machine operator, Alberni Pacific Lumber, Port Alberni, and assistant ranger, British Columbia Forest Service; land inspector, British Columbia Department of Lands and Forests, Land Utilization Research and Survey Division, Victoria, 1949–54;

Associate Editor, *Country Guide* magazine, Winnipeg, 1954–55, and Calgary, 1955–75; land appraiser agrologist, Calgary, 1976. Past President, Alberta Farm Writers Association. Recipient: Canadian Farm Writers Federation award, 1961, 1968, 1969, 1973, 1974, 1975; Canadian Children's Book Award, 1965. Address: 2919 14th Avenue N.W., Calgary, Alberta T2N 1N3, Canada.

PUBLICATIONS FOR CHILDREN

Fiction

> *The White Calf: The Story of Eagle Child, The Piegan Boy, Who Found a White Buffalo Calf Said To Have Been Sent by the Above Ones*, illustrated by Gerald Tailfeathers. Toronto and Boston, Little Brown, 1965; London, Dent, 1966.
> *The White Peril*, illustrated by Gerlad Tailfeathers. Toronto and Boston, Little Brown, 1966; London, Dent, 1968.
> *The In-Betweener*, illustrated by Leonard Shortall. Toronto and Boston, Little Brown, 1967.
> *The Smoke Horse*, illustrated by W. F. Phillipps. Toronto, McClelland and Stewart, and London, Dent, 1968.
> *West to Cattle Country*, illustrated by Gordon McLean. Toronto, McClelland and Stewart, 1975.
> *Johnny Eagleclaw*. Edmonton, John LeBel, 1977.

PUBLICATIONS FOR ADULTS

Other

> *The Romance of Beef*. Winnipeg, Public Press, 1966.
> *The Pen and the Plow*. Winnipeg, Public Press, 1976.
> *Turn Him Loose*. Saskatoon, Western Prairie Books, 1977.

Manuscript Collection: University of Calgary.

Cliff Faulknor comments:

I don't consciously set out to write for children. When an idea comes to me I just sit down at my typewriter and let it work itself out. I have found that once you have created a genuine character he or she will act and react according to the natures you have given them, and the story will flow from these actions.

As for the story setting and background information, I research this very carefully. And if I am dealing with the past, my story must be true to the history of that period, and the setting must be as it was during that period.

For instance, in my Indian books, a rider cannot have his horse nibbling on a grass or shrub species not native to that area or have him swim a river in a year history records as a time of intense drought. I have read some books where the main character describes the scene from a certain mountain, and I have gone up that mountain only to find it would be impossible for him to do so. I wouldn't want that to happen in any of my books. For my Western books I went "on location," plotting the movements of my characters and locating the battle scenes. I don't attempt to be very profound in any of my writings; I like to entertain and inform.

*   *   *

Cliff Faulknor's *The White Calf, The White Peril*, and *The Smoke Horse* comprise a trilogy focussed on the life of a Piegan Blackfoot boy as he grows to manhood in the mid–19th century. *The White Calf* introduces Eagle Child at age 12, when he saves an orphaned white buffalo calf – believed to be sacred because of its colour – and raises it to near-yearling status. The novel ends with the buffalo's release and its return to the herd. In the interval, the calf fills the role of a wilful spirit, sometimes bringing good in its wake, sometimes ill. Its primary significance is as a mark of Eagle Child's own maturing process: he learns that the acclaim the calf brings him carries with it a duty, and that internalization of this sense of duty is part of what makes a man. Indeed, as the subsequent books reveal, it is through the eventual necessary retaking of the full-grown buffalo's life that Eagle Child earns his warrior name, White Bull.

The White Calf also shows Eagle Child's band on the hunt, in struggles with other tribes (wherein his older brother Tailfeathers earns his adult name, War Bonnet), and at the Sun Dance. The events are exciting, and the details of Blackfoot life are authentic, but the book suffers a little from the presence of two heroes, Eagle Child and War Bonnet. Some of the most exciting events are seen through the latter's eyes, not the former's, and this can lead to problems of reader-identification.

The White Peril opens five winters later, again beginning and ending with encounters between Eagle Child and the white buffalo, now a rogue killer. The title refers not only to the animal, however; it also implies the encroachment of white men. This danger is repeatedly mentioned, and at one point the possibility of forming an Indian confederation to war against the whites is raised. White weapons and disease make this impratical. As before, the adventures of the hunt and inter-tribal raiding parties comprise much of the novel's excitement, but the most important event is a deadly epidemic of measles. Concomitantly, the white buffalo – at one point a symbol of Indian hopes for the favour of the Above Ones – is also killed. In everything, the manifold unforeseen consequences of human acts are evident. Thus the book contains a realistic admixture of sadness and joys, with the coming of the whites viewed from an Indian perspective. This novel is carefully constructed, and the previous work's problem with dual viewpoints does not occur.

In *The Smoke Horse*, set later the same year, Eagle Child (now White Bull) learns the quality of mercy – a quality that marks his inner maturity and true manhood. The action focuses on horse raids, captures, escapes, battles – all very well depicted. It's a fine story, well-crafted and gripping, with many flashes of Faulknor's subtle humour and adept dialogue. It provides a fitting conclusion to the trilogy.

The In-Betweener also deals with the maturing process – and its difficulties – in an adolescent boy, Chad. The white protagonist and the twentieth-century West Vancouver setting mark real changes for Faulknor, and Chad's problems – compared to those of Eagle Child – reflect the less integral society to which he belongs. Like all Faulknor's work, the novel is exciting, basically realistic, and enjoyable to read.

—John Robert Sorfleet

FENTON, Edward. American. Born in New York City, 7 July 1917. Attended Amherst College, Massachusetts. Served with the American Field Service and the British 8th Army in North Africa during World War II. Married Sophia Harvati in 1963. Staff member in the print department, Metropolitan Museum of Art, New York, 1950–55. Recipient: Mystery Writers of America Edgar Allan Poe Award, 1962; Batchelder Award, for translation, 1970, 1974. Address: 24 Evrou Street, Athens 610, Greece.

PUBLICATIONS FOR CHILDREN

Fiction

Us and the Duchess, illustrated by Reisie Lonette.   New York, Doubleday, 1947.
Aleko's Island, illustrated by Dimitris Davis.   New York, Doubleday, 1948; London,
   Oxford University Press, 1953.
Hidden Trapezes, illustrated by Reisie Lonette.   New York, Doubleday, 1950.
Nine Lives; or, The Celebrated Cat of Beacon Hill, illustrated by Paul Galdone.   New
   York, Pantheon Books, 1951.
The Golden Doors, illustrated by Gioia Fiammenghi.   New York, Doubleday, 1957; as
   Mystery in Florence, London, Constable, 1959.
Once upon a Saturday, illustrated by Rita Fava.   New York, Doubleday, 1958.
Fierce John, illustrated by Williame Pène du Bois.   New York, Doubleday. 1959.
The Nine Questions, illustrated by C. Walter Hodges.   New York, Doubleday, 1959;
   Kingswood, Surrey, World's Work, 1962.
The Phantom of Walkaway Hill, illustrated by Jo Ann Stover.   New York, Doubleday,
   1961.
An Island for a Pelican, illustrated by Dimitris Davis.   New York, Doubleday, and
   Kingswood, Surrey, World's Work, 1963.
The Riddle of the Red Whale.   New York, Doubleday, 1966.
The Big Yellow Balloon, illustrated by Ib Ohlsson.   New York, Doubleday, 1967.
A Matter of Miracles.   New York, Holt Rinehart, 1967.
Penny Candy, illustrated by Edward Gorey.   New York, Holt Rinehart, 1970.
Duffy's Rocks.   New York, Dutton, and London, Hamish Hamilton, 1974.

Other

Translator, *Petros' War*, by Alki Zei.   New York, Holt Rinehart, 1968; London,
   Gollancz, 1972.

PUBLICATIONS FOR ADULTS

Novels

The Double Darkness.   New York, Doubleday, 1947; London, Cresset Press, 1948.
Anne of a Thousand Days.   New York, New American Library, 1970.

Verse

Soldiers and Strangers: Poems.   New York, Macmillan, 1945.

*   *   *

Edward Fenton has written many varied types of excellent books for children in his long
career, but despite the wide range of topics, locales, and types, there is an homogeneity about
his work: each story is characterized by wit, depth of idea and emotion, a strongly defined
atmosphere and tone, and, generally, a tantalizing irony that is linked to his extensive use of
visual and auditory detail.
   Typical of his work is a picture book entitled *Penny Candy*, illustrated by Edward Gorey.
The book is dedicated to "all those who have never tasted the delicious agony of having to
choose between one big one and five little ones for a single penny. It is also for those who
have, and remember." That sense of remembering, shared by both author and reader, is
typical of the delicate or poignant ironies that pervade much of Fenton's writing. For
instance, in this work, the put-upon youngest child finds a nickel and, despite the fact of his

earlier neglect, decides to treat his sister and her friends to candy at Widow Shinns' – even though the Widow may be a witch. In her shop, the children take on the coloration of the candy they eat in a subtle shift from reality to fantasy, presaged by the ominous Widow Shinn and her sugary, musty, and magic-smelling shop.

This attention to detail, imagery and atmosphere is mirrored in many of Fenton's longer works where he is able to expand on his impressive ability to establish a sense of place. Granted Fenton is well-traveled and speaks at least five languages, but the fact that he has lived in Italy and Greece probably only heightens his use of imagery, his attention to the rhythm of a place, and his ability to mesh plot development with atmosphere in such works as *Aleko's Island, The Golden Doors, An Island for a Pelican,* and *A Matter of Miracles.* As well as books about Italy and Greece, and a number of translations from works in Greek, Spanish, German, Dutch, Polish, French and Italian, Edward Fenton has published picture books and longer narrative fictions with a strong American background. Some of the best of these are *Fierce John,* a picture book; *Once upon a Saturday,* an outgrowth of his peripatetic youth in New York City; *The Phantom of Walkaway Hill,* winner of the Edgar Allan Poe Award in 1962, and *The Riddle of the Red Whale,* both of which borrow their setting from a farm Fenton owned in Duchess County, New York; and *Duffy's Rocks.* Of the latter, Fenton says he relied on his childhood in New York City for atmosphere and incident; however, the most remarkable thing about the book is the fact that he makes the stultifying ménage of Pittsburgh and its surrounding mill towns during the depression as alive and vibrant as if they were part and parcel of his own experience. Fenton is an eloquent and varied writer of children's books and his trademarks are fluent style, powerful imagery, sustained plot and characterization, and a pervasive and authentic sense of place.

—Rachel Fordyce

FIDLER, Kathleen (Annie). British. Born in Coalville, Leicestershire, 10 August 1899. Educated at Girls' High School, Wigan, Lancashire, 1911–18; St. Mary's College, Bangor, North Wales, 1918–20, Teacher's Certificate. Married J. H. Goldie in 1930 (died); has one son and one daughter. Headmistress, Scot Lane Evening Institute, 1924–30, and St. Paul's Girls' School, Wigan, 1925–30; script writer, Authors' Panel for Schools Broadcasting in Scotland, 1938–62. Recipient: Moscow Film Festival award, 1967. Agent: Lutterworth Press, Luke House, Farnham Road, Guildford, Surrey, England. Address: Jane Bank, Broomieknowe, Lasswade, Midlothian, Scotland.

PUBLICATIONS FOR CHILDREN

Fiction

    The Borrowed Garden. London, Lutterworth Press, 1944.
    St. Jonathan's in the Country: A Sequel to "The Borrowed Garden," illustrated by Charles Koolman. London, Lutterworth Press, 1945; revised edition, 1952.
    Fingal's Ghost. London, John Crowther, 1945.
    The Brydons at Smugglers' Creek, illustrated by H. Tilden Reeves. London, Lutterworth Press, 1946.
    The White Cockade Passes. London, Lutterworth Press, 1947.
    The Mysterious Mr. Simister. London, Lutterworth Press, 1947.
    More Adventures of the Brydons, illustrated by Victor Bertoglio. London, Lutterworth Press, 1947; revised edition, London, Hodder and Stoughton, 1971.

The Brydons Go Camping, illustrated by A. H. Watson. London, Lutterworth Press, 1948.

Mr. Simister Appears Again, illustrated by Margaret Horder. London, Lutterworth Press, 1948.

Mr. Simister Is Unlucky, illustrated by Margaret Horder. London, Lutterworth Press, 1949.

The Brydons Do Battle, illustrated by A. H. Watson. London, Lutterworth Press, 1949.

The Brydons in Summer, illustrated by A. H. Watson. London, Lutterworth Press. 1949.

Guest Castle. London, Lutterworth Press, 1949.

I Rode with the Covenanters, illustrated by E. Boye Uden. London, Lutterworth Press, 1950.

The Brydons Look for Trouble, illustrated by T. R. Freeman. London, Lutterworth Press, 1950.

The Brydons in a Pickle, illustrated by T. R. Freeman. London, Lutterworth Press, 1950.

Surprises for the Brydons, illustrated by T. R. Freeman. London, Lutterworth Press, 1950.

The White-Starred Hare and Other Stories, illustrated by A. H. Watson. London, Lutterworth Press, 1951.

The Brydons Get Things Going, illustrated by T. R. Freeman. London, Lutterworth Press, 1951; revised edition, London, Hodder and Stoughton, 1971.

The Brydons Hunt for Treasure, illustrated by T. R. Freeman. London, Lutterworth Press, 1951.

The Brydons Catch Queer Fish, illustrated by T. R. Freeman. London, Lutterworth Press, 1952.

The Brydons Stick at Nothing, illustrated by T. R. Freeman. London, Lutterworth Press, 1952.

Fedora the Donkey, illustrated by Iris Gillespie. London, Lutterworth Press, 1952.

The Stallion from the Sea, illustrated by G. S. Ronald. London, Lutterworth Press, 1953.

The Brydons Abroad, illustrated by T. R. Freeman. London, Lutterworth Press, 1953.

The Deans Move In, illustrated by Reg Forster. London, Lutterworth Press, 1953.

Pete, Pam and Jim, the Investigators, illustrated by Lunt Roberts. London, Lutterworth Press, 1954.

The Deans Solve a Mystery, illustrated by Reg Forster. London, Lutterworth Press, 1954.

The Deans Follow a Clue, illustrated by Reg Forster. London, Lutterworth Press, 1954.

The Bank House Twins, illustrated by Frank Bellamy. London, Lutterworth Press, 1955.

The Droving Lad, illustrated by Geoffrey Whittam. London, Lutterworth Press, 1955.

The Deans Defy Danger, illustrated by Reg Forster. London, Lutterworth Press, 1955.

The Brydons on the Broads, illustrated by T. R. Freeman. London, Lutterworth Press, 1955; revised edition, London, Hodder and Stoughton, 1971.

Challenge to the Brydons, illustrated by T. R. Freeman. London, Lutterworth Press, 1956.

Mr. Punch's Cap, illustrated by Shirley Hughes. London, Lutterworth Press, 1956.

The Deans Dive for Treasure, illustrated by Reg Forster. London, Lutterworth Press, 1956.

The Deans to the Rescue, illustrated by Reg Forster. London, Lutterworth Press, 1957.

The McGills at Mystery Farm, with Jack Gillespie, illustrated by Leo Davy. London, Lutterworth Press, 1958.

Lanterns over the Lune, illustrated by David Walsh. London, Lutterworth Press, 1958.

The Deans' Lighthouse Adventure, illustrated by Reg Forster.   London, Lutterworth
   Press, 1959.
More Adventures of the McGills, with Jack Gillespie, illustrated by Hodgson.   London,
   Lutterworth Press, 1959.
The Deans and Mr. Popple, illustrated by Reg Forster.   London, Lutterworth Press,
   1960.
The Brydons at Blackpool, illustrated by T. R. Freeman.   London, Lutterworth Press,
   1960.
Escape in Darkness, illustrated by Geoffrey Whittam.   London, Lutterworth Press,
   1961.
The Deans' Dutch Adventure, illustrated by Reg Forster.   London, Lutterworth Press,
   1962.
The Brydons Go Canoeing, illustrated by T. R. Freeman.   London, Lutterworth Press,
   1963.
The Little Ship Dog, illustrated by Antony Maitland.   London, Lutterworth Press,
   1963.
The Desperate Journey, illustrated by Michael Charlton.   London, Lutterworth Press,
   1964.
Flash the Sheep Dog, illustrated by Antony Maitland.   London, Lutterworth Press,
   1965.
Police Dog, illustrated by Sheila Rose.   London, Lutterworth Press, 1966.
The Boy with the Bronze Axe, illustrated by Edward Mortelmans.   Edinburgh, Oliver
   and Boyd, 1968.
Haki the Shetland Pony, illustrated by Victor Ambrus.   London, Lutterworth Press,
   1968; Chicago, Rand McNally, 1970.
Treasure of Ebba, illustrated by Trevor Ridley.   London, Lutterworth Press, 1968.
Mountain Rescue Dog, illustrated by Mary Russon.   London, Lutterworth Press, 1969.
School at Sea, illustrated by David Grice.   London, Epworth Press, 1970.
The Gold of Fast Castle, illustrated by Trevor Ridley.   London, Lutterworth Press,
   1970.
The Thames in Story.   London, Epworth Press, 1971.
Turk the Border Collie, illustrated by Mary Dinsdale.   London, Lutterworth Press,
   1975.
The Railway Runaways.   London, Blackie, 1977.

Plays

Screenplay: *Flash the Sheepdog*, 1968.

Radio Plays: *Children's Hour* series.

Television Play: *Haki the Shetland Pony*, from her own story, 1970.

Other

Stories from Scottish Heritage, with Lennox Milne.   Edinburgh, Chambers, 3 vols.,
   1951.
Tales of the North Country, illustrated by Jack Matthew.   London, Lutterworth Press,
   1952.
To the White North: The Story of Sir John Franklin, illustrated by F.
   Furnivall.   London, Lutterworth Press, 1952.
Tales of London, illustrated by Douglas Relf.   London, Lutterworth Press, 1953.
Tales of the Midlands, illustrated by Douglas Relf.   London, Lutterworth Press, 1954.

The Man Who Gave Away Millions: The Story of Andrew Carnegie, illustrated by Hodgson. London, Lutterworth Press, 1955; New York, Roy, 1956.

Tales of Scotland, illustrated by Douglas Relf. London, Lutterworth Press, 1956.

Look to the West: Tales of Liverpool, illustrated by Henry Toothill. London, Lutterworth Press, 1957.

Tales of the Islands, illustrated by Douglas Relf. London, Lutterworth Press, 1959.

Tales of Pirates and Castaways, illustrated by Charles Keeping. London, Lutterworth Press, 1960.

Tales of the West Country, illustrated by Charles Keeping. London, Lutterworth Press, 1961.

True Tales of Treasure, illustrated by W. F. Phillipps. London, Lutterworth Press, 1962.

Tales of the South Country, illustrated by W. F. Phillipps. London, Lutterworth Press, 1962.

True Tales of Escapes, illustrated by W. F. Phillipps. London, Lutterworth Press, 1965.

New Lamps for Old (reader), illustrated by John Dugan. Edinburgh, Oliver and Boyd, 1965.

Adventure Underground (reader), illustrated by Forth Studios. Edinburgh, Oliver and Boyd, 1966.

Forest Fire (reader), illustrated by Laszlo Acs. Edinburgh, Oliver and Boyd, 1966.

True Tales of Mystery, illustrated by Bonar Dunlop. London, Lutterworth Press, 1967.

True Tales of Castles, illustrated by Imre Hofbauer. London, Lutterworth Press, 1969.

Flodden Field, September 9, 1513, illustrated by F. R. Exell. London, Lutterworth Press, 1971.

Diggers of Lost Treasure. London, Epworth Press, 1972.

Stories of Old Inns. London, Epworth Press, 1973.

The '45 and Culloden, July 1745 to April 1746, illustrated by F. R. Exell. London, Lutterworth Press, 1973.

Pirate and Admiral: The Story of John Paul Jones, illustrated by Bernard Brett. London, Lutterworth Press, 1974.

Wrecks, Wreckers and Rescuers, with Ian Morrison, illustrated by Morrison. London, Lutterworth Press, 1977.

Kathleen Fidler comments:

My writing first began for my own children's interest and amusement. The "Brydon Family" books, written first as broadcasts, later as books, reflected my own happy and simple family life. As my children grew, my writing expanded into historical, biographical and archeological fields, representing my and their varied interests. I now write to interest my grandchildren. Broadcasting has been a large part of my writing, and this sharpened the focus of books and dialogue. I also give talks to children in schools and libraries, and this keeps me actively in touch with children.

*   *   *

Kathleen Fidler's books are deceptively written. They are easy and quick to read and appear to be somewhat lightweight but this very approach tends to obscure the fact that much meticulous preparation has been undertaken before a single word has been committed to paper. Her books are the result of careful research plus acute observation of human and animal behaviour.

This careful groundwork is true of all her writings but is particularly evident in books such as *Pirate and Admiral: The Story of John Paul Jones*. From his early days on the Solway up to his death, Kathleen Fidler takes the reader through all the stages of his incredible story but not once does the book become a mere catalogue of dates or events. The central figure stands out as a man of great courage and strength of character who was full of compassion and concern for his men. Yet the book is easy to read and wholly convincing.

Perhaps her skill as a writer is best shown in *The Boy with the Bronze Axe*, a story about a Stone Age settlement on Skara Brae in the Orkney Islands. The central theme concerns the lives of the children, Kali and Brockan, after the arrival of Tenko with his bronze axe. It is an exciting and vivid adventure story, as well as a brilliant reconstruction of life in that time with detailed and accurate descriptions of building techniques, domestic arrangements, and carefully contrasted characters. The descriptions of the domestic and building methods never obtrude but take their place so well in the pattern of the story that they fall into position as an essential ingredient of the tale and add to its impact on the reader.

Kathleen Fidler tells a story in a straightforward, uncomplicated manner. The action keeps moving, dialogue is brisk, and there are few, if any, distractions. The general impression given is of a simple story simply told; this is the very essence of her skill. Fortified by impeccable research, her writings are uncomplicated but compelling and vivid books with an immediate appeal.

—Margaret Walker

FIELD, Rachel (Lyman). American. Born in New York City, 19 September 1894. Educated at Springfield High School; Radcliffe College, Cambridge, Massachusetts, 1914–18. Married Arthur Siegfried Pederson in 1935; one adopted daughter. Member of the editorial department, Famous Players-Lasky film company, Hollywood, 1918–23. Recipient: Drama League of America prize, 1918; American Library Association Newbery Medal, 1930. *Died 15 March 1942.*

PUBLICATIONS FOR CHILDREN

Fiction

> *Eliza and the Elves*, illustrated by Elizabeth MacKinstry. New York, Macmillan, 1926.
> *The Magic Pawnshop: A New Year's Eve Fantasy*, illustrated by Elizabeth MacKinstry. New York, Dutton, 1927; London, Dent, 1928.
> *Little Dog Toby*, illustrated by the author. New York, Macmillan, 1928.
> *Polly Patchwork*, illustrated by the author. New York, Doubleday, 1928.
> *Hitty, Her First Hundred Years*, illustrated by Dorothy P. Lathrop. New York, Macmillan, 1929; as *Hitty: The Life and Adventures of a Wooden Doll*, London, Routledge, 1932.
> *Pocket-Handkerchief Park*, illustrated by the author. New York, Doubleday, 1929.
> *Calico Bush*, illustrated by Allen Lewis. New York, Macmillan, 1931; London, Collier Macmillan, 1966.
> *The Yellow Shop*, illustrated by the author. New York, Doubleday, 1931.
> *The Bird Began to Sing*, illustrated by Ilse Bischoff. New York, Morrow, 1932.
> *Hepatica Hawkes*, illustrated by Allen Lewis. New York, Macmillan, 1932.
> *Just Across the Street*, illustrated by the author. New York, Macmillan, 1933.
> *Susanna B. and William C.*, illustrated by the author. New York, Morrow, 1934.
> *The Rachel Field Story Book* (includes *The Yellow Shop*, *Pocket-Handkerchief Park*, *Polly Patchwork*), illustrated by Adrienne Adams. New York, Doubleday, 1958; Kingswood, Surrey, World's Work, 1960.

Plays

Everygirl, in *St. Nicholas* (New York), October 1913.
Three Pills in a Bottle (produced Cambridge, Massachusetts, 1917; New York, 1923). Included in *Six Plays*, 1924.
Rise Up, Jennie Smith (produced Cambridge, Massachusetts, 1918). New York, French, 1918.
Time Will Tell (produced Cambridge, Massachusetts, 1920).
The Fifteenth Candle. New York, French, 1921.
Six Plays (includes *Cinderella Married, Three Pills in a Bottle, Columbine in Business, The Patchwork Quilt, Wisdom Teeth, Theories and Thumbs*). New York, Scribner, 1924; *The Patchwork Quilt* published in *One-Act Plays of Today*, edited by J. W. Marriott, London, Gollancz, 1928.
The Cross-Stitch Heart and Other Plays (includes *Greasy Luck, The Nine Days' Queen, The Londonderry Air, At the Junction, Bargains in Cathay*). New York, Scribner, 1927.
Patchwork Plays (includes *Polly Patchwork; Little Square-Toes; Miss Ant, Miss Grasshopper, and Mr. Cricket; Chimney Sweeps' Holiday; The Sentimental Scarecrow*). illustrated by the author. New York, Doubleday, 1930.
First Class Matter. New York, French, 1936.
The Bad Penny. New York, French, 1938.

Verse (illustrated by the author)

The Pointed People: Verses and Silhouettes. New Haven, Connecticut, Yale University Press, and London, Oxford University Press, 1924.
An Alphabet for Boys and Girls. New York, Doubleday, and London, Heinemann, 1926.
Taxis and Toadstools: Verse and Decorations. New York, Doubleday, and London, Heinemann, 1926.
A Little Book of Days. New York, Doubleday, and London, Heinemann, 1927.
Christmas Time. New York, Macmillan, 1941.
Poems. New York, Macmillan, 1957.

Other

All Through the Night, illustrated by the author. New York, Macmillan, 1940; London, Collins, 1954.
Prayer for a Child, illustrated by Elizabeth Orton Jones. New York, Macmillan, 1944.
Fortune's Caravan, from translation by Marian Saunders of a work by Lily Jean-Javal, illustrated by Maggie Salcedo. New York, Morrow, 1933; London, Oxford University Press, 1935.

Editor, *The White Cat and Other Old French Fairy Tales*, by Marie Catherine d'Aulnoy, illustrated by Elizabeth MacKinstry. New York, Macmillan, 1928.
Editor, *American Folk and Fairy Tales*, illustrated by Margaret Freeman. New York and London, Scribner, 1929.
Editor, *People from Dickens: A Presentation of Leading Characters from the Books of Charles Dickens*, illustrated by Thomas Fogarty. New York and London, Scribner, 1935.

PUBLICATIONS FOR ADULTS

Novels

Time Out of Mind. New York, Macmillan, 1935; London, Macmillan, 1937.

To See Ourselves, with Arthur Pederson.   New York, Macmillan, 1937; London, Collins, 1939.

All This and Heaven Too.   New York, Macmillan, 1938; London, Collins, 1939.

And Now Tomorrow.   New York, Macmillan, 1942; London, Collins, 1943.

Short Story

Christmas in London.   Privately printed, 1946.

Verse

Points East: Narratives of New England.   New York, Brewer and Warren, 1930.

A Circus Garland.   Washington, D.C., Winter Wheat Press, 1930.

Branches Green.   New York, Macmillan, 1934.

Fear Is the Thorn.   New York, Macmillan, 1936.

Other

God's Pocket: The Story of Captain Samuel Hadlock, Junior, of the Cranberry Isles, Maine.   New York, Macmillan, 1934; London, Macmillan, 1937.

Ave Maria: An Interpretation from Walt Disney's "Fantasia" Inspired by the Music of Franz Schubert.   New York, Random House, 1940.

Illustrator: *Punch and Robinetta* by Ethel May Gate, 1923; *Come Christmas* by Eleanor Farjeon, 1928; *The House That Grew Smaller* by Margery Williams Bianco, 1931.

*   *   *

Rachel Field's reputation as a children's book author today rests almost solely on her book *Hitty, Her First Hundred Years* which won the Newbery Award in 1930. The book is a picaresque, first-person narrative of the memoirs of the doll Mehitable's first hundred years. The strong personality of the doll binds the narration together, although individual scenes and a wide variety of characters are given considerable dimension. The setting ranges from New England to India and eventually back again, with realistic scenes devoted to plantation life, whale sightings, the singing of Jenny Lind, and sitting for a daguerreotypist intermixed. The book is enhanced by illustrations by Dorothy P. Lathrop who frequently illustrated for Field. For a discussion of Rachel Field's work habits and how *Hitty* came into being, one should consult Louise Bechtel's *Books in Search of Children*.

Rachel Field was also an illustrator of books for children and adults, but she is best known for her literary canon which includes fantasy, historical fiction, non-fiction, poetry, and plays, as well as a selected edition of Mme. d'Aulnoy's fairy tales and a slightly saccharine *Prayer for a Child*. One aspect of her work that is largely ignored today, but merits attention, is her playwriting for children. Her best known works in this genre are five diverse plays anthologized in a volume entitled *Patchwork Plays*. These plays are good in that they are all playable, making few highly technical demands on child players but considerable demands on the child audience's imagination. Each of the plays is packed with action and believability. Perhaps a distance of forty years precludes immediacy and dramatic impact on a modern audience of a play about a sentimental scarecrow, but Miss Field would capture a modern audience with her play *Little Square-Toes*. This short work is about a young girl who is captured by Indians during King Philip's war and who is reluctant to return to "civilization" when given the chance. It is marked by highly realistic dialogue, swift action and a strong, developmental plot. Field's best known book of poetry for children is *Taxis and Toadstools*, a town-and country anthology on subjects as diverse as the conjunction of the two subjects in the title would suggest. The best poems read naturally with flowing enjambment; the weakest scan methodically and almost monotonously, though the latter are much in the minority.

—Rachel Fordyce

FINKEL, George (Irvine). Born in South Shields, County Durham, England, 13 May 1909. Educated at public primary schools; Bede Collegiate School, Sunderland, County Durham, 1919–26. Served in the Royal Auxiliary Air Force, 1930–34; Sub-Lieutenant, Royal Naval Volunteer Reserve, 1939–45; Lieutenant Commander, Royal Navy, 1945–50; Technical Training Officer, Australian Fleet Air Arm, Nowra, New South Wales, during the Korean War; Engineer Officer, Naval Air Base, Nowra, 1952–58. Married Lena Almond in 1930; three sons and one daughter. Cadet chemical engineer, 1927–34; Aviator, Imperial Airways, England, Europe, and Africa, 1934–39; professional officer and later teaching hospitals planning officer. University of New South Wales, Kensington. *Died in March 1975.*

PUBLICATIONS FOR CHILDREN

Fiction

The Mystery of Secret Beach. Sydney, Angus and Robertson, 1962; London, Angus and Robertson, 1963.
Ship in Hiding. Sydney, Angus and Robertson, 1963.
Cloudmaker. Sydney and London, Angus and Robertson, and New York, Roy, 1965.
The Singing Sands. Sydney and London, Angus and Robertson, 1966.
The Long Pilgrimage, illustrated by George Tetlow. Sydney and London, Angus and Robertson, 1967; New York, Viking Press, 1969.
Twilight Province, illustrated by George Tetlow. Sydney and London, Angus and Robertson, 1967; as *Watch Fires to the North,* New York, Viking Press, 1967.
The "Loyall Virginian." Sydney and London, Angus and Robertson, and New York, Viking Press, 1968.
Journey to Jorsala. London, Angus and Robertson, 1969.
The Peace Seekers. Sydney and London, Angus and Robertson, 1970.
The Stranded Duck, illustrated by Andrew Parnell. Sydney, Angus and Robertson, 1973.
Operation Aladdin, illustrated by Walter Stackpool. Sydney and London, Hodder and Stoughton, 1976.

Other

Navigator and Explorer: James Cook, illustrated by Amnon Sadubin. Sydney, Wentworth Press, 1969.
James Cook, Royal Navy, illustrated by Amnon Sadubin. Sydney and London, Angus and Robertson, 1970.
Community Services: Power, Transport. Melbourne, Nelson, 2 vols., 1970.
Laws: Making and Keeping Them. Melbourne, Nelson, 1970.
Migrants of Legend. Melbourne, Nelson, 1970.
Migrants Who Changed the World. Melbourne, Nelson, 1970.
Migrants Who Had No Choice. Melbourne, Nelson, 1970.
Migrants Who Made Britain. Melbourne, Nelson, 1970.
Producing Food: Cereals, Fish, Fruit, Meat. Melbourne, Nelson, 4 vols., 1970.

William Light. Sydney, Angus and Robertson, 1972.

Matthew Flinders, Explorer and Scientist, illustrated by Victor Hatcher. Sydney and London, Collins, 1973.

New South Wales, 1788–1900. Melbourne, Nelson, 1974.

Victoria, 1834–1900. Melbourne, Nelson, 1974.

The Dutchman Bold: The Story of Abel Tasman. Sydney, Angus and Robertson, 1975.

Governor Lachlan Macquarie. Melbourne, Nelson, 1975.

South Australia, 1836–1900. Melbourne, Nelson, 1975.

Antarctica: The Heroic Age. Sydney and London, Collins, 1976.

*   *   *

George Finkel began his literary career by writing a few well-structured adventure stories for boys. He then became absorbed in a much deeper vein of creative fiction, and produced a number of originally researched historical novels, as well as fictional biographies. In both novels and biographies he often presents ingenious theories and fresh viewpoints on the significance of certain events or character motivation. Thus, in *Twilight Province* he presents his view of the Arthur legend; *The "Loyall Virginian"* explores an unusual aspect of the secession of the North American colonies from Britain; *The Peace Seekers* attempts an explanation of the infiltration of a North American Indian tribe by men of Celtic stock. Attention to detail and exact explanation of, for example, mechanical parts is a recognizable facet of his writing, reflecting his own inquiring mind. The careful plotting of his novels tends to occupy first place in the scheme of work; characterization is not the dominant aspect. George Finkel's fictional biographies, especially *James Cook, Royal Navy* (he felt a particular empathy in relation to Cook for they belonged to the same part of England, and Finkel's own seagoing experience was considerable) and *William Light* – the gallant, artistic ex-Army officer who became first Surveyor General for South Australia – are clear-cut and strike a happy balance between fiction and fact. They are neither romanticized nor are they bereft of the attribute of story.

Latterly, George Finkel turned to a new form of fiction: short, compelling novels set in the present day whose main appeal is to boys in the 10–14 age-group. In *The Stranded Duck* and *Operation Aladdin*, he related two stories concerning salvage operations carried out by a family of cousins and their grandfather. But for the author's untimely death, these stories might well have developed into a continuing series. They are tightly structured, told with economy of narrative, and show a considerably deeper degree of characterization than do his longer novels.

—Barbara Ker Wilson

FINLAY, Winifred (Lindsay Crawford). British. Born in Newcastle upon Tyne, Northumberland, 17 April 1910. Educated at High School for Girls, Whitley Bay, Northumberland; King's College, University of Newcastle, 1928–33, M.A. (honours) in English. Married Evan Finlay in 1935; has one daughter. Schoolmistress and college lecturer, Newcastle upon Tyne, 1933–35, Stratford upon Avon, 1941–44, Leeds, 1944–48, and Northampton, 1948–50. Since 1965, regular contributor, *Child Education,* London. Recipient: Mystery Writers of America Edgar Allan Poe Award, 1970. Address: The Old House, Walgrave, Northamptonshire, England.

PUBLICATIONS FOR CHILDREN

Fiction

The Witch of Redesdale.   London, Harrap, 1951.
Peril in Lakeland.   London, Harrap, 1953.
Peril in the Pennines.   London, Harrap, 1953.
Cotswold Holiday, illustrated by Shirley Macgregor.   London, Harrap, 1954.
The Lost Silver of Langdon.   London, Harrap, 1955.
Storm over Cheviot.   London, Harrap, 1955.
Judith in Hanover.   London, Harrap, 1955.
Canal Holiday.   London, Harrap, 1957.
The Cruise of the "Susan."   London, Harrap, 1958.
The Castle and the Cave, illustrated by J.S. Goodall.   London, Harrap, 1960.
The Lost Emeralds of Black Howes.   London, Harrap, 1961.
Alison in Provence, illustrated by J.S. Goodall.   London, Harrap, 1963.
Mystery in the Middle Marches.   London, Harrap, 1964.
Castle for Four.   London, Harrap, 1966.
Adventure in Prague.   London, Harrap, 1967.
Danger at Black Dyke.   London, Harrap, and New York, Phillips, 1968.
The Cry of the Peacock.   London, Harrap, 1969.
Summer of the Golden Stag.   London, Harrap, 1969.
Singing Stones.   London, Harrap, 1970.
Beadbonny Ash.   London, Harrap, 1973; Nashville, Nelson, 1975.

Plays

Radio Plays: *Children's Hour* series, 1947–63, including *The Clues of the Sickle Moon,* 1961, *Mystery in the Middle Marches,* 1962, *Castle for Four,* 1963.

Other

Folk Tales from the North, illustrated by Victor Ambrus.   London, Kaye and Ward, 1968; New York, Watts, 1969.
Folk Tales from Moor and Mountain, illustrated by Victor Ambrus.   London, Kaye and Ward, 1969; New York, Roy, 1970.
Cap o' Rushes, illustrated by Victor Ambrus.   London, Kaye and Ward, and New York, Hale, 1974.
Tattercoats and Other Folk Tales, illustrated by Shirley Hughes.   London, Kaye and Ward, and New York, Hale, 1976.
Ghosts, Ghouls, and Spectres: English Ghost Stories, with Gillian Hancock, illustrated by Gavin Rowe.   London, Kaye and Ward, 1976.
Spies and Secret Agents, with Gillian Hancock, illustrated by Gavin Rowe.   London, Kaye and Ward, 1977.
The Treasure Hunters, with Gillian Hancock.   London, Kaye and Ward, 1977.

Winifred Finlay comments:
I have written stories ever since I can remember. I first wrote professionally for own daughter during the war when there was a shortage of suitable books. My stories and plays are set in real places which I know well: Britain, France, Germany, Czechoslovakia. I have tried to show that, because of the action in which they were involved, my principal characters have developed in their understanding of themselves and other people.

As a Northumbrian with Scottish parents, I have drawn chiefly on areas I knew when young: the Roman Wall, the Border Country, and the Scottish Highlands and Islands. In doing background research, I have collected fascinating folk and ghost tales, ballads and legends which I am now retelling for my grandchildren. I was taught to have a healthy respect for the English language, and I have always tried to maintain sound literary standards as I feel very strongly that only the best is good enough for children.

*   *   *

Winifred Finlay has had a prolific career as a writer of children's books and radio plays. Most of her novels have followed the same pattern: some children on holiday are involved in a mystery which they eventually solve, finding after dramatic and often dangerous events that the mystery itself was not as spectacular as they had thought. The anti-climactic conclusion keeps her stories realistic and sensible, and the hordes of international crooks and caves stuffed with treasure remain remain firmly in the children's imaginations.

She narrates not only a story, but also the emotional journey taken by one or more children who have to come to terms with a difficult relationship or one of the problems of growing up. From her observation and experience Mrs. Finlay is best qualified to describe the adolescent girl, and though her heroines are from the same mould, the different situations they face bring plenty of variety to the basic theme of a girl growing up, finding out how to relate to her mother and to boy-friends, finding a suitable career and perhaps going against her parents' wishes.

Several of her books, like *Summer of the Golden Stag* and *Adventure in Prague*, deal with a teenage girl alone, abroad. As she copes with foreigners, plus the inevitable mystery, she learns about her own personality and needs. Whether abroad or at home, the mystery element is usually associated with a genuine historical background. Mrs. Finlay is especially sympathetic to the scenery and antiquities of North Britain – the lakes, the Roman Wall, ancient stones, etc., which are described in detail, while she also ridicules childish fantasies, e.g. of Druids: "Stonehenge and mistletoe and long white beards."

In 1970 Winifred Finlay deserted the typical adventure-story for full-blooded fantasy of the Alan Garner kind, where supernatural creatures from the past come alive now. *Singing Stones* and *Beadbonny Ash* are magical adventures in Scotland's Celtic past. They resemble the earlier books in their well-drawn family relationships and historical detail, but they abandon the cynical attitude to mystery for a genuine commitment to the power of the supernatural and the war between Good and Evil.

Singing Stones is about the discovery of the ancient carved coronation stone of Scotland; *Beadbonny Ash* about a girl's rediscovery of her love for her mother, through a journey in time to the days when the Old Gods were replaced by Christ. The girl's mother is identified with the great Celtic goddess, Ugly Hag and Beautiful Lady in one, just as in real life her daughter loves and hates her.

Recently she has written several collections of folk-tales from oral and literary sources. Her retellings are not mere paraphrases, but expansions of the old tales with detail and humour. Two collections of ghost and spy stories have extended her work. But *Beadbonny Ash* is her masterpiece.

—Jessica Kemball-Cook

FISHER, Aileen (Lucia). American. Born in Iron River, Michigan, 9 September 1906. Educated at the University of Chicago, 1923–25; University of Missouri, Columbia, Bachelor of Journalism 1927. Director, Women's National Journalistic Register, Chicago, 1929–32; Research Assistant, Labor Bureau of the Middle West, Chicago, 1931–32. Recipient:

451

Western Writers of America Award, for non-fiction, 1967. Address: 505 College Avenue, Boulder, Colorado 80302, U.S.A.

PUBLICATIONS FOR CHILDREN

Fiction

Over the Hills to Nugget, illustrated by Sandra James.   New York, Aladdin Books, 1949.
Trapped by the Mountain Storm, illustrated by J. Fred Collins.   New York, Aladdin Books, 1950.
Homestead of the Free: The Kansas Story.   New York, Aladdin Books, 1953.
Timber! Logging in Michigan, illustrated by Pers Crowell.   New York, Aladdin Books, 1955.
Off to the Gold Fields, illustrated by R.M. Powers.   New York, Nelson, 1955; as *Secret in the Barrel*, New York, Scholastic, 1965.
Cherokee Strip: The Race for Land, illustrated by Walt Reed.   New York, Aladdin Books, 1956.
A Lantern in the Window, illustrated by Harper Johnson.   New York, Nelson, 1957.
Skip, illustrated by Genevieve Vaughan-Jackson.   New York, Nelson, 1958.
Fisherman of Galilee, illustrated by John De Pol.   New York, Nelson, 1959.
Summer of Little Rain, illustrated by Gloria Stevens.   New York, Nelson, 1961.
My Cousin Abe, illustrated by Leonard Vosburgh.   New York, Crowell, 1962.
Arbor Day, illustrated by Nonny Hogrogian.   New York, Crowell, 1965.
Human Rights Day, with Olive Rabe, illustrated by Lisl Weil.   New York, Crowell, 1966.

Plays

The Squanderbug's Christmas Carol.   Washington, D.C., United States Treasury Department, 1943.
The Squanderbug's Mother Goose.   Washington, D.C., United States Treasury Department, 1944.
A Tree to Trim: A Christmas Play.   Evanston, Illinois, Row Peterson, 1945.
What Happened to Toyland.   Evanston, Illinois, Row Peterson, 1945.
Nine Cheers for Christmas: A Christmas Pageant.   Evanston, Illinois, Row Peterson, 1945.
Before and After: A Play about the Community School Lunch Program.   Washington, D.C., War Food Administration, 1945.
All Set for Christmas.   Evanston, Illinois, Row Peterson, 1946.
Here Comes Christmas! A Varied Collection of Christmas-Program Materials for Elementary Schools.   Evanston, Illinois, Row Peterson, 1947.
Witches, Beware: A Hallowe'en Play.   New York, Play Club, 1948.
Set the Stage for Christmas: A Collection of Pantomimes, Skits, Recitations, Readings, Plays and Pageants.   Evanston, Illinois, Row Peterson, 1948.
Christmas in Ninety-Nine Words (lyrics only), music by Rebecca Welty Dunn.   Evanston, Illinois, Row Peterson, 1949.
Angel in the Looking -Glass, in *Plays* (Boston), ix, 1950.
The Big Book of Christmas: A Collection of Plays, Songs, Readings, Recitations, Pantomimes, Skits, and Suggestions for Things to Make and Do for Christmas.   Evanston, Illinois, Row Peterson, 1951.
Health and Safety Plays and Programs.   Boston, Plays Inc., 1953.
Holiday Programs for Boys and Girls.   Boston, Plays Inc., 1953.
United Nations Plays and Programs, with Olive Rabe.   Boston, Plays Inc., 1954.

Patriotic Plays and Programs, with Olive Rabe.   Boston, Plays Inc., 1956.
Christmas Plays and Programs.   Boston, Plays Inc., 1960.
Plays about Our Nations's Songs.   Boston, Plays Inc., 1962.
The King's Toothache, and *One-Ring Circus*, in *Thirty Plays for Classroom Reading*,
   edited by Donald D. Durrell.   Boston, Plays Inc., 1965.
Time for Mom, and *Young Abe Lincoln*, in *Fifty Plays for Holidays*, edited by Sylvia E.
   Kamerman.   Boston, Plays Inc., 1969.
Bicentennial Plays and Programs.   Boston, Plays Inc., 1975.

Verse

The Coffee-Pot Face, illustrated by the author.   New York, McBride, 1933.
Inside a Little House, illustrated by the author.   New York, McBride, 1938.
That's Why, illustrated by the author.   New York, Nelson, 1946.
Up the Windy Hill: A Book of Merry Verse with Silhouettes, illustrated by the
   author.   New York, Abelard Schuman, 1953; London, Abelard Schuman. 1958.
Runny Days, Sunny Days: Merry Verses, illustrated by the author.   New York and
   London, Abelard Schuman, 1958.
Going Barefoot, illustrated by Adrienne Adams.   New York, Crowell, 1960.
Where Does Everyone Go?, illustrated by Adrienne Adams.   New York, Crowell, 1961.
I Wonder How, I Wonder Why, illustrated by Carol Barker.   New York and London,
   Abelard Schuman, 1962.
Like Nothing at All, illustrated by Leonard Weisgard.   New York, Crowell, 1962.
I Like Weather, illustrated by Janina Domanska.   New York, Crowell, 1963.
Cricket in a Thicket, illustrated by Feodor Rojankovsky.   New York, Scribner, 1963.
Listen Rabbit, illustrated by Symeon Shimin.   New York, Crowell, 1964.
In the Middle of the Night, illustrated by Adrienne Adams.   New York, Crowell, 1965.
In the Woods, In the Meadow, In the Sky: Poems, illustrated by Margot Tomes.   New
   York, Scribner, 1965; Kingswood, Surrey, World's Work, 1967.
Best Little House, illustrated by Arnold Spilka.   New York, Crowell, 1966.
Skip Around the Year, illustrated by Gioia Fiammenghi.   New York, Crowell, 1967.
My Mother and I, illustrated by Kazue Mizumura.   New York, Crowell, 1967.
Up, Up the Mountain, illustrated by Gilbert Riswold.   New York, Crowell, 1968.
We Went Looking, illustrated by Marie Angel.   New York, Crowell, 1968.
Clean as a Whistle, illustrated by Ben Shecter.   New York, Crowell, 1969.
In One Door and Out the Other: A Book of Poems, illustrated by Lillian Hoban.   New
   York, Crowell, 1969.
Sing, Little Mouse, illustrated by Symeon Shimin.   New York, Crowell, 1969.
But Ostriches ..., illustrated by Peter Parnall.   New York, Crowell, 1970.
Feathered Ones and Furry, illustrated by Eric Carle.   New York, Crowell, 1971.
Do Bears Have Mothers Too?, illustrated by Eric Carle.   New York, Crowell, 1973.
My Cat Has Eyes of Sapphire Blue, illustrated by Marie Angel.   New York, Crowell,
   1973.
Once We Went on a Picnic, illustrated by Tony Chen.   New York, Crowell, 1975.

Other

Guess Again! (riddles).   New York, McBride, 1941.
All on a Mountain Day, illustrated by Gardell Christensen.   New York, Nelson, 1956.
*We Dickinsons: The Life of Emily Dickinson as Seen Through the Eyes of Her Brother
   Austin*, illustrated by Ellen Raskin.   New York, Atheneum, 1965.
Valley of the Smallest: The Life Story of a Shrew, illustrated by Jean Zallinger.   New
   York, Crowell, 1966.
We Alcotts: The Life of Louisa May Alcott as See Through the Eyes of "Marmee" ...,
   illustrated by Ellen Raskin.   New York, Atheneum, 1968.

Easter, illustrated by Ati Forberg. New York, Crowell, 1968.

Jeanne d'Arc, illustrated by Ati Forberg. New York, Crowell, 1970.

The Ways of Animals (in verse) (*Animal Houses*, illustrated by Jan Wills; *Animal Jackets*, illustrated by Muriel Wood; *Filling the Bill*, illustrated by Betty Fraser; *No Accounting for Taste*, illustrated by Gloria Gaulke; *Now That Days Are Colder*, illustrated by Gordon Laite; *Sleepy Heads*, illustrated by Phero Thomas; *"You Don't Look Like Your Mother," Said the Robin to the Fawn*, illustrated by Ati Forberg; *Tail Twisters*, illustrated by Albert John Pucci; *Going Places*, illustrated by Midge Quenell; *Animal Disguises*, illustrated by Tim and Greg Hildebrandt). Glendale, California, Bowmar, 10 vols., 1973–74.

The Ways of Plants (in verse) (*Plant Magic*, illustrated by Barbara Cooney; *Mysteries in the Garden*, illustrated by Ati Forberg; *Swords and Daggers*, illustrated by James Higa; *And a Sunflower Grew*, illustrated by Trina Schart Hyman; *Petals Yellow and Petals Red*, illustrated by Albert John Pucci; *Now That Spring Is Here*, illustrated by Symeon Shimin; *As the Leaves Fall Down*, illustrated by Barbara Smith; *Prize Performances*, illustrated by Margot Tomes; *A Tree with a Thousand Uses*, illustrated by James Endicott; *Seeds on the Go*, illustrated by Hans Zander). Glendale, California, Bowmar, 10 vols., 1977.

Aileen Fisher comments:

I enjoy writing for children. I especially enjoy writing verse. It gives me such a good chance for remembering how things looked and felt and *were* when I was a child.

*   *   *

Aileen Fisher draws upon observation and research to produce children's literature in the various genres. As a child, she walked four miles to school, and as an adult she scheduled a daily trek in the mountains. She has written poetry, prose in the form of nature stories and biographies, non-fiction, and plays.

Poetry has been her most significant contribution, for as one *New York Times* reviewer wrote, "She lights the commonplace moment with wonder." While in college, she published her first compilation of poems in *The Coffee-Pot Face*. Subjects which she would treat for a lifetime were here – nature, such as a ladybug and icicles, objects such as a chair, childhood conditions such as a tummy-ache, and seasons. Well-known illustrators were selected to interpret her one-poem picture books, such as *In the Middle of the Night* and *Once We Went on a Picnic*. Inspired by her verse, Adrienne Adams, Marie Angel, and Symeon Shimin earned honors for their work. While praising *Going Barefoot* for its "rare synthesis of information and imagination," a reviewer considered it too long for one sitting with a small child.

Close observation of nature and research on the Upper Peninsula in Michigan are the basis of *Timber! Logging in Michigan*. Colorado Mountains are the setting for a number of books, such as *Trapped by the Mountain Storm* and *Valley of the Smallest: The Life Story of a Shrew*. The shrew was an unusual selection of an animal for a full-length novel, but the author introduced other animals to show the natural interrelationships, and the author acknowledges a British zoologist who had published a book on the behaviour of a shrew. Virginia Haviland wrote in the *Horn Book* (December 1966): "A sharp observer, with a poet's imagination, the author records what she has seen near her mountain home. Her account is both more vivid and more suspenseful than most nature books ...."

Her biographies have fared less well under the scrutiny of reviewers. By having Simon Peter, the brother of Emily Dickinson, and the mother of the March girls tell the stories of *Fisherman of Galilee*, *We Dickinsons*, and *We Alcotts*, she ensures a fresh approach. But despite direct quotations from primary sources, the books pale when compared to the Biblical narrative and authors' autobiographical writing. *Jeanne d'Arc*, according to the reviewer Barbara Wersba in the *New York Times Review* (24 May 1970), lacks passion, and "remains less of the journey of a saint than a biography of a very nice girl." Non-fiction publications, are the result of the same elements, research, observation, and literary style. The collections of plays have the usefulness of being free of royalty fees for the performers, but for the same reason are unimpressive.

—Karen Nelson Hoyle

FISHER, Dorothy (Frances) Canfield. American. Born in Lawrence, Kansas, 17 February 1879. Educated at Ohio State University, Columbus, Ph.B. 1899; the Sorbonne, Paris; Columbia University, New York, Ph.D. 1905. Married John Redwood Fisher in 1907; two children. Secretary, Horace Mann School, New York, 1902–05. Did relief work in France, 1916–19. Member of the Vermont Board of Education, 1921–23. Recipient: Delta Kappa Gamma Society Educator's Award, 1946; Women's National Book Association Skinner Award, 1951; Sarah Josepha Hale Special Award, 1958. D.Litt.: Middlebury College, Vermont, 1921; Dartmouth College, Hanover, New Hampshire, 1922; University of Vermont, Burlington, 1922; Columbia University, 1929; Northwestern University, Evanston, Illinois, 1931; Rockford College, Illinois, 1934; Ohio State University, 1935; Williams College, Williamstown, Massachusetts, 1935; Swarthmore College, Pennsylvania, 1935; University of Nebraska, Lincoln, 1936; Mount Holyoke College, South Hadley, Massachusetts, 1936; Marlboro College, Vermont, 1951; Smith College, Northampton, Massachusetts, 1954. *Died 9 November 1958.*

PUBLICATIONS FOR CHILDREN

Fiction

> *Understood Betsy*, illustrated by Ada C. Williamson.   New York, Holt, 1917; London, Constable, 1922; as *Betsy*, London, Bodley Head, 1962; revised edition, New York, Holt Rinehart, 1971.
> *Made-to-Order Stories*, illustrated by Dorothy P. Lathrop.   New York, Harcourt Brace, 1925; London, Cape, 1926.
> *Tell Me a Story: A Book of Stories to Tell to Children*, illustrated by Tibor Gergely.   Lincoln, Nebraska, University Publishing Company, 1940; London, Mitre Press, n.d.
> *Nothing Ever Happens and How It Does*, with Sarah N. Cleghorn, illustrated by Esther Boston Bristol.   Boston, Beacon Press, 1940.
> *Something Old, Something New: Stories of People Who Are American*, illustrated by Mary D. Shipman.   Chicago, Scott Foresman, 1949.

Plays

> *A Family Talk about War.*   New York, Children's Crusade for Children, 1940.
> *Liberty and Union*, with Sarah N. Cleghorn.   New York, Book of the Month Club, 1940.

Other

> *What Shall We Do Now? Five Hundred Games and Pastimes*, with others.   New York, Stokes, 1907.
> *On a Rainy Day*, with Sarah Fisher Scott.   New York, A.S. Barnes, 1938.

In the City and on the Farm (reader), with Eunice Crabtree and Lu Verne Walker, illustrated by Terry Townsend. Lincoln, Nebraska, University Publishing Company, 1940; London, Mitre Press, n.d.

My First Book: A Reading Readiness Book, with Eunice Crabtree and Lu Verne Walker. Lincoln, Nebraska, University Publishing Company, 1940.

Runaway Toys (reader), with Eunice Crabtree and Lu Verne Walker, illustrated by Terry Townsend. Lincoln, Nebraska, University Publishing Company, 1940.

To School and Home Again (reader), with Eunice Crabtree and Lu Verne Walker, illustrated by Terry Townsend. Lincoln, Nebraska, University Publishing Company, 1940; London, Mitre Press, n.d.

More about the City and the Farm (reader), with Eunice Crabtree and Lu Verne Walker, illustrated by Terry Townsend. Lincoln, Nebraska, University Publishing Company, 1941.

Under the Roof (reader), with Eunice Crabtree and Lu Verne Walker, illustrated by Terry Townsend. Lincoln, Nebraska, University Publishing Company, 1941; London, Mitre Press, n.d.

Under the Sun (reader), with Eunice Crabtree and Lu Verne Walker, illustrated by Terry Townsend. Lincoln, Nebraska, University Publishing Company, 1941; London, Mitre Press, n.d.

Highroads and Byroads (reader), with Eunice Crabtree and Lu Verne Walker, illustrated by Mary Royt and George Buctel. Lincoln, Nebraska, University Publishing Company, 1948; London, Mitre Press, n.d.

Next Door (reader), with Eunice Crabtree and Lu Verne Walker. Lincoln, Nebraska, University Publishing Company, 1949.

Paul Revere and the Minute Men, illustrated by Norman Price. New York, Random House, 1950.

Our Independence and the Constitution, illustrated by Robert Doremus. New York, Random House, 1950.

A Fair World for All, illustrated by Jeanne Bendick. New York, McGraw Hill, 1952.

And Long Remember: Some Great Americans Who Have Helped Me, illustrated by Ezra Jack Keats. New York, McGraw Hill, 1959.

PUBLICATIONS FOR ADULTS

Novels

Gunhild: A Norwegian-American Episode. New York, Holt, 1907.

The Squirrel-Cage. New York, Holt, and London, Constable, 1912.

The Bent Twig. New York, Holt, 1915; London, Constable, 1916.

The Brimming Cup. New York, Harcourt Brace, and London, Cape, 1921.

Rough-Hewn. New York, Harcourt Brace, 1922; London, Cape, 1923.

Raw Material. New York, Harcourt Brace, 1923.

The Home-Maker. New York, Harcourt Brace, and London, Cape, 1924.

Her Son's Wife. New York, Harcourt Brace, and London, Cape, 1926.

The Deepening Stream. New York, Harcourt Brace, and London, Cape, 1930.

Bonfire. New York, Harcourt Brace, and London, Cape, 1933.

Seasoned Timber. New York, Harcourt Brace, and London, Cape, 1939.

Short Stories

Hillsboro People, verse by Sarah N. Cleghorn. New York, Holt, 1915; London, Cape, 1923.

The Real Motive. New York, Holt, and London, Constable, 1916.

Home Fires in France. New York, Holt, 1918; London, Constable, 1919.

Basque People. New York, Harcourt Brace, and London, Cape, 1931.

Fables for Parents.   New York, Harcourt Brace, 1937; London, Cape, 1938.
Four-Square.   New York, Harcourt Brace, 1949.
A Harvest of Stories, from a Half Century of Writing.   New York, Harcourt Brace, 1956.

Other

Emile Angier, Playwright-Moralist-Poet: A Study.   Columbus, Ohio State University, 1899.
Corneille and Racine in England: A Study of the English Translations of the Two Corneilles and Racine, with Especial Reference to Their Presentation on the English Stage.   New York, Columbia University Press, and London, Macmillan, 1904.
Elementary Composition, with George R. Carpenter.   New York and London, Macmillan, 1906.
A Montessori Mother.   New York, Holt, 1912; London, Constable, 1913; as *Montessori for Parents,* Cambridge, Massachusetts, Bentley, 1965.
The Montessori Manual, in Which Dr. Montessori's Teachings and Educational Occupations Are Arranged in Practical Exercises or Lessons....   Chicago, Richardson, 1913; London, Kegan Paul, 1914.
Mothers and Children.   New York, Holt, 1914; London, Constable, 1915.
A Peep into the Educational Future.   Buffalo, New York, Park School, 1915.
Self-Reliance: A...Discussion of Teaching Self-Reliance...to Modern Children.   Indianapolis, Bobbs Merrill, 1916; London, Constable, 1917.
Fellow Captains!, with Sarah N. Cleghorn.   New York, Holt, 1916.
The Day of Glory.   New York, Holt, 1919.
What Grandmother Did Not Know.   Boston, Pilgrim Press, 1922.
The French School at Middlebury.   Middlebury, Vermont, Middlebury College, 1923.
Why Stop Learning?   New York, Harcourt Brace, 1927.
Learn or Perish (lecture).   New York, Liveright, and London, Oxford University Press, 1930.
Vermont Summer Homes.   Montpelier, Vermont Bureau of Publicity, 1932.
Moral Pushing and Pulling (lecture).   Townsend, Vermont, Leland and Gray Seminary, 1933.
Tourists Accommodated: Some Scenes from Present Day Summer Life in Vermont.   New York, Harcourt Brace, 1934.
Wells College Phi Beta Kappa Address.   Aurora, New York, Wells College, 1936.
Our Young Folks.   New York, Harcourt Brace, 1943.
American Portraits.   New York, Holt, 1946.
Book Clubs (lecture).   New York, New York Public Library, 1947.
Vermont Traditions: The Biography of an Outlook on Life.   Boston, Little Brown, 1953.
Memories of My Home Town.   Privately printed, 1956.
Memories of Arlington, Vermont.   New York, Duell, 1957.

Editor, with Sidonie Matsner Brunberg, *Our Children: A Handbook for Parents.*   New York, Viking Press, 1932.

Translator, *Life of Christ,* by Giovanni Papini.   New York, Harcourt Brace, 1923.
Translator, *Work: What It Has Meant to Men Through the Ages,* by Adriano Tilgher.   New York, Harcourt Brace, and London, Harrap, 1931.

Critical Study: *Pebble in a Pool: The Widening Circles of Dorothy Canfield Fisher's Life* by Elizabeth Yates, New York, Dutton, 1958; as *The Lady from Vermont,* Brattleboro, Vermont, Stephen Greene Press, 1971.

*   *   *

Dorothy Canfield Fisher used her own background as a basis for her written work. Her unusual ability to create realistic tales was based on her own experiences as a girl and young woman. She was a professor's daughter, born in Kansas of strong New England heritage. The atmosphere of learning and the familiarity with her family history shaped her character. She had a privileged position from which to view her surroundings. Yet her Vermont values, strengthened and broadened by education and travel, helped mold an individual sensitive to the needs and aspirations of human beings.

Understood Betsy certainly reflects all of her powers of observation as well as her biases and interests. In this book a young girl, raised by two aunts in a midwestern city, must spend time with distant relatives in Vermont. Two prim, affluent, city-dwelling aunts have provided for their niece, but they have turned her into a dependent, nervous and neurotic being. It is not a pleasant view of urban life. The Vermonters who take Betsy in are deftly characterized. Uncle Harry is a taciturn yet warm-hearted man the likes of which are disappearing from New England. Cousin Ann and Aunt Abigail are the very embodiment of the stern, upright, resourceful yet loving Yankee. In this new atmosphere, Betsy learns to adjust, adapt, and grow in self-reliance and warm personal relationships. One is impressed with the characters and background in the story: they are psychologically and historically accurate. The theme of learning to overcome problems and adjust has been accomplished without becoming overbearing or maudlin.

Made-to-Order Stories is more unusual. These stories originated in tales made up for Mrs. Fisher's ten-year-old son who disliked trite and usual plots. All of the stories are based on diverse objects. For example, a ship's anchor, a library, a woodchuck, a spider, a bed, a doorknob and usually a little boy are woven into an exciting and unusual tale. Only when one reads through the innumerable stories can one fathom the incredible well of creativity from which she drew.

Mrs. Fisher's stories have entertained children for generations. Her writing, of course, reflects the rural attitudes and values of her era as well as her respect for children and their intelligence. Her characters are always real and the author never talks down to her readers. Teachers and parents who want accurate American historical and cultural material in children's literature will want to see her work on every library shelf. It is interesting to note that *Understood Betsy*, with a setting that may be unfamiliar to a late-twentieth-century urban child, is most unusual. This book about a girl growing up in the early twentieth century stresses Betsy's human rather than her feminine identity. The author's creativity, humor, insight and observation have been used to construct tales which have held and will continue to hold the attention of children from 8 to 12.

—Dorothy D. Siles

FISK, Nicholas. British. Born in London, 14 October 1923. Educated at secondary school in Sussex. Served in the Royal Air Force. Married Dorothy Fisk in 1949; has twin daughters and two sons. Head of Creative Department, Percy Lund, Humphries and Co., London. Agent: A.M. Heath, 40–42 William IV Street, London WC2N 4DD, England.

PUBLICATIONS FOR CHILDREN

Fiction

The Bouncers, illustrated by the author. London, Hamish Hamilton, 1964.
The Fast Green Car, illustrated by Bernard Wragg. London, Hamish Hamilton, 1965.
There's Something on the Roof!, illustrated by Dugald Macdougall. London, Hamish Hamilton, 1966.

Space Hostages.   London, Hamish Hamilton, 1967; New York, Macmillan, 1969.
Trillions.   London, Hamish Hamilton, 1971.
Grinny.   London, Heinemann, 1973; Nashville, Nelson, 1974.
High Way Home.   London, Hamish Hamilton, 1973.
Emma Borrows a Cup of Sugar, illustrated by Carol Barker.   London, Heinemann, 1973.
Little Green Spaceman, illustrated by Trevor Stubley.   London, Heinemann, 1974.
The Witches of Wimmering, illustrated by Trevor Stubley.   London, Pelham Books, 1976.
Time Trap.   London, Gollancz, 1976.
Wheelie in the Stars.   London, Heinemann, 1976.

Other

Look at Cars, illustrated by the author.   London, Hamish Hamilton, 1959; revised edition, London, Panther, 1969.
Look at Newspapers, illustrated by Eric Thomas.   London, Hamish Hamilton, 1962.
Cars.   London, Parrish, 1963.
The Young Man's Guide to Advertising.   London, Hamish Hamilton, 1963.
Making Music, illustrated by Donald Green.   London, Joseph, 1966; Boston, Crescendo, 1969.
Lindbergh the Lone Flier, illustrated by Raymond Briggs.   London, Hamish Hamilton, and New York, Coward McCann, 1968.
Richtofen the Red Baron, illustrated by Raymond Briggs.   London, Hamish Hamilton, and New York, Coward McCann, 1968.

Illustrator: *The Bear Who Was Too Big* by Lettice Cooper, 1963; *Tea with Mr. Timothy* by Geoffrey Morgan, 1966; *Menuhin's House of Music* by Eric Fenby, 1969; *Skiffy* by William Mayne, 1972.

*   *   *

Nicholas Fisk caters for children bred on television. His style is punchy and to the point as you might expect from a man who commutes to London on his motor bike to head the creative department of a leading printing and publishing firm. When he writes his children's books he draws extensively on his technical knowledge and first-hand experience of the commercial world. And although he subscribes to the convention that children identify best through other children, he makes few concessions to a child readership when it comes to his range of vocabulary and the sophistication of his ideas. It is his particular contribution to take something ordinary and develop it into something quite extraordinary: the old lady in *Grinny* turns out to be a sinister robot from outer space; the salvaged motor bike in *Wheelie in the Stars* becomes a symbol of freedom and individuality.

Fisk describes his approach to writing in his essay in *The Thorny Paradise* (edited by Edward Blishen, 1975): " ... How much more exciting the microscope's or telescope's viewpoint than one's own. How much more interesting the possibility than the fact ... the freedom of fantasy than the chains of present circumstance ...." This attitude has evolved over the years. He started by writing realistic novels, drawing affectionately and humorously on his own experience of family life. The children in *The Bouncers* discover a trampoline and some old circus posters in the attic of their new home and decide to put on a show. *The Fast Green Car* takes another young family on holiday to France. *There's Something on the Roof* – an old Chinaman's kite – is atmospheric but still everyday realism.

Then in 1967 came *Space Hostages*. The story follows the fortunes of a group of children hi-jacked in a spaceship by a fanatical, dying airman. Like their counterparts in *Lord of the Flies*, they are forced to sort out their pecking order *in extremis*. It was Fisk's first sci-fi offering and it made an immediate impact. But he will not be type-cast. He continues to experiment with different kinds of children's books. Within a year of each other he published *Grinny*, one of his most successful sci-fi stories; *High Way Home*, a practical account of three adolescents shipwrecked on a remote island who make their way back to civilisation by constructing an air balloon; and *Emma Borrows a Cup of Sugar*, a wry nursery tale. His most recent novels are set in the future when the worst fears of our environmentalists have been realised. The quality of life has deteriorated. Man has to be regimented in order to survive. His heroes are no longer characters but types – rebels as opposed to conformists – and there is a clear social message behind the make-believe. A most original writer, Fisk could be described as the Huxley-Wyndham-Golding of children's literature scaled but not watered down.

—Joy Whitby

FITZHUGH, Louise. American. Born in Memphis, Tennessee, 5 October 1928. Educated at Bard College, Annandale-on-Hudson, New York; Art Students' League, New York; Cooper Union, New York. Recipient: *New York Times* award, for illustration, 1969; Children's Rights Workshop Other Award, 1976. *Died 19 November 1974.*

PUBLICATIONS FOR CHILDREN (illustrated by the author)

Fiction

    Suzuki Beane, with Sandra Scoppettone.   New York, Doubleday, 1961.
    Harriet the Spy.   New York, Harper, 1964; London, Gollancz, 1974.
    The Long Secret.   New York, Harper, 1965; London, Gollancz, 1975.
    Bang, Bang, You're Dead, with Sandra Scoppettone.   New York, Harper, 1969.
    Nobody's Family Is Going to Change.   New York, Farrar Straus, 1974; London, Gollancz, 1976.

*   *   *

Louise Fitzhugh was a well known but not a prolific writer. She made her mark with her picture book *Harriet the Spy* which features an original 11-year-old heroine, Harriet, who is going to be a writer but meanwhile keeps busy as a spy. Harriet's come-uppance occurs when her schoolfriends find and read her notebook, full of candid comments about them. Innovatory when first published, and still enthusiastically included in booklists, *Harriet the Spy* now appears to have been much overrated – its long-winded and rather "psychological" account of Harriet's doings are of more interest to adult reviewers than child readers. *The Long Secret* is a sequel to *Harriet the Spy*.

Fitzhugh's last book, *Nobody's Family Is Going to Change*, is undoubtedly her best. The element that drew attention to *Harriet the Spy* – acute perception of the state of mind of young people between childhood and adolescence – is here rendered into crisp narrative full of understated punchy dialogue and caustic wit; even the minor characters glow with life.

The story deserves describing here. The Sheridans are black New Yorkers, an "ideal" American family, middle-class with maid and two children at private school. Lawyer Daddy has achieved all this for his family in his fight to escape his youth when he was spat on "every day of his life...for being black." But Emma (11) and Willie (7) do not live up to family standards. Emma (fat and with "Afro hair which for some reason did not stand up like everyone else's but grew sideways") announces her determination to be a lawyer, while Willie (slim and handsome) wants to be a dancer. Daddy thinks that men who dance are sissies and a bad example to aspiring black people, while Daddy *and* Mama disapprove of women lawyers. Mama suggests Emma might marry one instead and raise "two lovely children." Emma's struggle to help Willie and to get her own way is to convince Mama that "nobody's family is going to change." Underlying the comedy and topical issues (sexual stereotyping, children's rights, black identity), Fitzhugh reveals a sympathy for children and an understanding of their struggles that makes this book a landmark in writing for young people on contemporary themes. No easy solutions are suggested here.

Louise Fitzhugh died recently. The wisdom and warm humour of this, her last, book will remain with her readers.

—Rosemary Stones

FLACK, Marjorie. American. Born in Greenport, Long Island, New York, 23 October 1897. Attended the Art Students' League, New York, 1918–20. Married the artist Karl Larsson in 1919 (divorced, 1940), one daughter; the poet William Rose Benét, 1943 (died, 1950). Art Teacher, Bronxville, New York. *Died 29 August 1958.*

PUBLICATIONS FOR CHILDREN

Fiction (illustrated by the author)

Taktuk, An Arctic Boy, with Helen Lomen. New York, Doubleday, 1928; London, Lane, 1956.
All Around the Town. New York, Doubleday, 1929.
Angus and the Ducks. New York, Doubleday, 1930; London, Lane, 1933.
Angus and the Cat. New York, Doubleday, 1931; London, Lane, 1933.
Angus Lost. New York, Doubleday, 1932; London, Lane, 1933.
Ask Mr. Bear. New York, Macmillan, 1932.
The Story about Ping, illustrated by Kurt Wiese. New York, Viking Press, 1933; London, Lane, 1935.
Wag-Tail Bess. New York, Doubleday, 1933; as *Angus and Wag-Tail Bess,* London, Lane, 1935.
Tim Tadpole and the Great Bullfrog. New York, Doubleday, 1934.
Humphrey: One Hundred Years Along the Wayside with a Box Turtle. New York, Doubleday, 1934.
Christopher. New York and London, Scribner, 1935.
Topsy. New York, Doubleday, 1935; as *Angus and Topsy,* London, Lane 1935.
Up in the Air, illustrated by Karl Larsson. New York, Macmillan, 1935.
Wait for William. Boston, Houghton Mifflin, 1935.
What to Do about Molly, illustrated by the author and Karl Larsson. Boston, Houghton Mifflin, 1936; London, Lane, 1938.
Willy Nilly. New York, Macmillan, 1936; London, Lane, 1939.
Lucky Little Lena. New York, Macmillan, 1937.
The Restless Robin. Boston, Houghton Mifflin, 1937.
Walter, The Lazy Mouse. New York, Doubleday, 1937; Edinburgh, Chambers, 1964.
William and His Kitten. Boston, Houghton Mifflin, 1938; London, Lane, 1939.
Pedro, with Karl Larsson, illustrated by Karl Larsson. New York, Macmillan, 1940.
The New Pet. New York, Doubleday, 1943; London, Lane, 1956.
I See a Kitty, illustrated by Hilma Larsson. New York, Doubleday, 1943.
The Boats on the River, illustrated by Jay Hyde Barnum. New York, Viking Press, 1946.

Verse

> *Adolphus; or, The Adopted Dolphin and the Pirate's Daughter*, with William Rose Benét.   Boston, Houghton Mifflin, 1941.
> *Away Goes Jonathan Wheeler*, illustrated by Hilma Larsson.   New York, Doubleday, 1944.

Other

> *Neighbors on the Hill*, with Mabel O'Donnell, illustrated by Florence and Margaret Hoopes.   Evanston, Illinois, Row Peterson, 1943.

Illustrator: *Knights, Goats, and Battleships* by Terry Strickland Colt, 1930; *Scamper, The Bunny Who Went to the White House*, 1934, and *Scamper's Christmas*, 1934, both by Anne Roosevelt Dall; *Here, There, and Everywhere*, 1936, and *All Together*, 1952, both by Dorothy Aldis; *The Country Bunny and the Little Gold Shoes* by DuBose Heyward, 1939; *A Black Velvet Story* by Dee Smith, 1940; *Olaf, Lofoten Fisherman* by Fru Constance Schram, 1940.

*   *   *

Marjorie Flack's picture books are good for reading aloud to small children. Angus is a Scottie dog who chases the ducks, strongly objects to sharing his home with a cat, gets lost, and helps to overcome the excessive timidity of Bess the Airedale and to solve the problems of the spaniel Topsy. Each simple story is illustrated with clear realistic line drawings and told with a good eye for the detail of a lively young dog's life. The young child will enjoy Angus's experiences as they are also his own: the "Things Which Come Apart" though clearly they shouldn't; the fascination of things on the other side of the hedge; the terrors of being lost; and the jealousy when a rival appears in the household. There is a comforting progression in the books, too: the alarums and excursions with the ducks in the first book are followed by later episodes in which the same ducks are routed by an older and more confident Angus. These stories are for under-fives; *The Story about Ping* is a favourite with five to six-year-olds. Ping is a duckling who lives on a Chinese boat on the Yangtze River. He runs away to escape punishment, but after a frightening day alone on the river returns thankfully to the safety of his wise-eyed boat, along with his father, mother and all his other relations. This is a varied and entertaining story, with a touch of fantasy and of the exotic, illustrated with bright, quaint and intriguing pictures by Kurt Wiese.

Walter, The Lazy Mouse is a longer story for five to seven-year-olds. Walter is so lazy that he is perpetually out of phase with both home and school. Eventually, when his family forget his existence altogether and move house without him he finds refuge with a family of bullfrogs who are even more happy-go-lucky than himself. Rather perversely, he is so anxious to establish himself in their singularly unretentive memories that he becomes punctual, active and hardworking, labouring at a more-than-usually thankless task of perpetually teaching these frogs what they don't need to know and will inevitably forget. The illogicality of this teacher's nightmare, however, will not be apparent or important to the child reader, for whom the amusing detail of Walter's efforts at swimming and furniture-making and his wholly delightful first encounter with the chorus of frogs will make this a memorable tale.

Taktuk, An Arctic Boy, written in collaboration with Helen Lomen, is a very different kind of book. It gives an informative picture of the life of a ten-year-old Eskimo boy, but though the detail is good and the story simply told, the tone is a little condescending, and amid the welter of information and the rather wooden prose the Eskimo family never comes alive. It is a useful rather than an enthralling book.

—Winifred Whitehead

FLEISCHMAN, (Albert) Sid(ney). American. Born in Brooklyn, New York, 16 March 1920. Educated at San Diego State College, B.A. 1949. Served in the United States Naval Reserve, 1941–45. Married Betty Taylor in 1942; has three children. Magician in vaudeville and night clubs, 1938–41; Reporter, San Diego *Daily Journal*, 1949–50; Associate Editor, *Point* magazine, San Diego, 1950–51. Recipient: Western Writers of America Spur Award, 1964; Boys' Clubs of America Award, 1964; George G. Stone Center for Children's Books Award, 1972; Society of Children's Book Writers Golden Kite Award, 1974. Agent: Curtis Brown Ltd., 575 Madison Avenue, New York, New York 10022. Address: 305 Tenth Street, Santa Monica, California, U.S.A.

PUBLICATIONS FOR CHILDREN

Fiction

> *Mr. Mysterious and Company.* Boston, Little Brown, 1962; London, Hutchinson, 1963.
> *By the Great Horn Spoon!*, illustrated by Eric von Schmidt. Boston, Little Brown, 1963; London, Hamish Hamilton, 1965; as *Bullwhip Griffin*, New York, Avon, 1967.
> *The Ghost in the Noonday Sun*, illustrated by Warren Chappell. Boston, Little Brown, 1965; London, Hamish Hamilton, 1966.
> *McBroom Tells the Truth*, illustrated by Kurt Werth. New York, Norton, 1966.
> *Chancy and the Grand Rascal*, illustrated by Eric von Schmidt. Boston, Little Brown, 1966; London, Hamish Hamilton, 1967.
> *McBroom and the Big Wind*, illustrated by Kurt Werth. New York, Norton, 1967.
> *McBroom's Ear*, illustrated by Kurt Werth. New York, Norton, 1969.
> *Longbeard the Wizard*, illustrated by Charles Bragg. Boston, Little Brown, 1970.
> *Jingo Django.* illustrated by Eric von Schmidt. Boston, Little Brown, and London, Hamish Hamilton, 1971.
> *McBroom's Ghost*, illustrated by Robert Frankenberg. New York, Grosset and Dunlap, 1971.
> *The Wooden Cat Man*, illustrated by Jay Yang. Boston, Little Brown, 1972.
> *McBroom's Zoo*, illustrated by Kurt Werth. New York, Grosset and Dunlap, 1972.
> *McBroom's Wonderful One-Acre Farm* (includes *McBroom Tells the Truth, McBroom and the Big Wind, McBroom's Ghost*) illustrated by Quentin Blake. London, Chatto and Windus, 1972.
> *The Ghost on Saturday Night*, illustrated by Eric von Schmidt. Boston, Little Brown, 1974; London, Heinemann, 1975.
> *McBroom Tells a Lie*, illustrated by Walter Lorraine. Boston, Little Brown, 1976.
> *Here Comes McBroom* (includes *McBroom Tells a Lie, McBroom the Rainmaker, McBroom's Zoo*), illustrated by Quentin Blake. London, Chatto and Windus, 1976.
> *Me and the Man on the Moon-Eyed Horse*, illustrated by Eric von Schmidt. Boston, Little Brown, 1977.

Other

> *Mr. Mysterious's Secrets of Magic*, illustrated by Eric von Schmidt. Boston, Little Brown, 1975; as *Secrets of Magic*, London, Chatto and Windus, 1976.

PUBLICATIONS FOR ADULTS

Novels

> *The Straw Donkey Case.* New York, Phoenix Press, 1948.

Murder's No Accident.   New York, Phoenix Press, 1949.
Shanghai Flame.   New York, Fawcett, 1951; London, Fawcett, 1957.
Look Behind You, Lady.   New York, Fawcett, 1952; London, Muller, 1953; as *Chinese Crimson*, London, Jenkins, 1962.
Danger in Paradise.   New York, Fawcett, 1953; London, Muller, 1954.
Counterspy Express, with *Treachery in Trieste* by M.V. Heberden.   New York, Ace, 1954.
Malay Woman.   New York, Fawcett, 1954; London, Fawcett, 1955; as *Malayan Manhunt*, London, Jenkins, 1965.
Blood Alley,   New York, Fawcett, 1955; London, Fawcett, 1956.
Yellowleg.   New York, Fawcett, and London, Muller, 1960.
The Venetian Blonde.   New York, Fawcett, and London, Jenkins, 1968.

Plays

Screenplays: *Blood Alley*, 1955; *Good-bye My Lady*, 1956; *Lafayette Escadrille*, 1958; *The Deadly Companions*, 1961; *Scalawag*, 1972.

Sid Fleischman comments:
   While my books rarely draw upon direct personal experience, I catch ghostly glimpses of my presence on almost every page. The stories inevitably reveal my interests and enthusiasms – my taste for the comic in life, my love of adventure, the seductions (for me) of the 19th-Century American frontier, and my enchantment with the folk speech of that period. Language is a wondrous toy and I have great literary fun with it.
   Since I don't plot my stories in advance, the experience of writing a book is, for me, very much the same as reading a book. I rarely know what is going to happen next and have to sit at the typewriter to find out. My starting point is almost always a background, such as the California gold rush in *By the Great Horn Spoon!* or the age of piracy in *The Ghost in the Noonday Sun*. On other occasions I begin with an idea for a character: the magician in *Mr. Mysterious and Company*, for example, or a mid-West teller of tall tales as in the McBroom stories.

*   *   *

   The tall tale is a special branch of folklore. It has its own language, its own pacing, its own outrageous logic. But it is also tied to a specific place: rural America. Coming out of the European Munchausen tradition, the tall tale found a permanent home on the American frontier where it was frontier in spirit, style, and tone. The tall tale can still be found in its oral form in the rural southern and western United States. In its literary form it can be found, occasionally, in children's books.
   Sid Fleischman comes neither from the south or west, nor from the country at all. He is a product of the urban East. Yet he has made the particular voice of the tall tale so much his own that, if any one author can be said to be master of the genre, it is he. His oddball characters include Chancy, so skinny he has to stand twice to cast a shadow; McBroom, who owns the richest one-acre farm in the world; Jingo Hawks, the biggest liar in Mrs. Duggart's Beneficent Orphan Home – and proud of it; and hosts of others.
   Fleischman's wit and style are deceptive. His flagrant humor disguises the fact that he is a careful craftsman who chooses each scene with infinite care and sets it down straight-facedly. He may be pulling your leg, but he does it with a pokerface. His slang style, with its tall tale helpings of grandiloquence, hyperbole, and exaggeration, are the result of impeccable research. He fills looseleaf notebooks with data on names, phrases, places, all culled from period novels, newspapers, and other primary sources. For Fleischman, the tall tale is both a literary dialect and a literary folklore. He takes it seriously.

Fleischman's many novels combine adventure with history, humor with serious statement. But the stories themselves are told at such a breakneck pace that the reader is given little time to consider how finely drawn the strange characters are, how definitively rendered are the villains. Instead it seems, at first reading, that story is all. Nowhere does this craftsmanship, this use of language, this swiftness of pace show more clearly than in *Chancy and the Grand Rascal*. One part quest story, two parts braggadocio, it concerns the travels of young Chancy Dundee and his uncle (the grand rascal) by foot, by raft, by train, by steamboat and by will power through the U.S.A. as they look for the scattered remnants of their family. There are tall tales within tall tales, whoppers told offhandedly by Chancy, his Uncle Will, his sister Indiana and others. And by the time the book is through, the reader has laughed a lot, learned a great deal about frontier life, and added some marvellous new/old words to his vocabulary like yawhawin', pineries, mudshoes, jayhawkers, and beeves.

—Jane Yolen

FLORA, James (Royer). American. Born in Bellefontaine, Ohio, 25 January 1914. Educated at Urbana College, Ohio, 1931–33; Art Academy of Cincinnati, 1934–39. Married Jane Sinnickson in 1941; has five children. Co-Founding Publisher, Little Man Press, Cincinnati, 1939–42; Art Director and Sales Promotion Manager, Columbia Recording Corporation, New York and Bridgeport, Connecticut, 1942–50; lived in Mexico 1950–52; Consultant Art Director and Board Member, Benwill Publishing Corporation, Boston, 1957–62. Since 1962, Art Director and Board Member, Computer Design Publishing Company. Since 1962, free-lance magazine illustrator. Address: St. James Place, Bell Island, Rowayton, Connecticut, U.S.A.

PUBLICATIONS FOR CHILDREN (illustrated by the author)

Fiction

The Fabulous Firework Family. New York, Harcourt Brace, 1955.
The Day the Cow Sneezed. New York, Harcourt Brace, 1957.
Charlie Yup and His Snip-Snap Boys. New York, Harcourt Brace, 1959.
Leopold, The See-Through Crumbpicker. New York, Harcourt Brace, 1961.
Kangaroo for Christmas. New York, Harcourt Brace, 1962.
My Friend Charlie. New York, Harcourt Brace, 1964.
Grandpa's Farm: Four Tall Tales. New York, Harcourt Brace, 1965.
Sherwood Walks Home. New York, Harcourt Brace, 1966.
Fishing with Dad. New York, Harcourt Brace, 1967.
The Joking Man. New York, Harcourt Brace, 1968.
Little Hatchy Hen. New York, Harcourt Brace, 1969.
Pishtosh, Bullwash, and Wimple. New York, Atheneum, 1972.
Stewed Goose. New York, Atheneum, 1973.
The Great Green Turkey Creek Monster. New York, Atheneum, 1976.

Plays

Screenplays (animated films): *The Fabulous Firework Family*, 1959; *Leopold, The See-Through Crumbpicker*, 1972.

PUBLICATIONS FOR ADULTS

Other

New Orleans Wood Engravings in Portfolio. Cincinnati, Little Man Press, n.d.

Manuscript Collection: Kerlan Collection, University of Minnesota, Minneapolis.

Illustrator: *The Talking Dog and the Barking Man* by Elizabeth Seeman, 1960.

James Flora comments:

Aside from my own personal pleasure in writing and illustrating for children my only aim is entertainment. I always try to write a bang-up good story that will intrigue a child and demonstrate how much fun reading can be. The process of learning to read is so protracted, difficult, and boring in our schools that many children find it distasteful and never learn at all.

I keep my work light and rollicking and my reward is the letters I get from children telling me how much they *enjoy reading* my books. To impart the joy of reading is the single thread that runs through all my stories.

*　　*　　*

James Flora states, in *Something about the Author*, vol. 1 (1971), "Since I was trained as a visual person, I think in pictures not in words, as most writers do. When I have decided on the story I want for my next book ... I can see in my mind all the pictures that I will draw for the book. Then I sit down at the typewriter and describe what is taking place in the pictures." Flora's procedures seem evident in his books; he draws with the wild exuberance of a Dr. Seuss and his stories have a similar quality of exaggeration and nonsense humor that is most appealing to children. At times, as in *The Great Green Turkey Creek Monster*, the story seems almost captions for the pictures, as an anthropomorphic vine takes over a town and creates havoc.

Flora's zany humor occasionally becomes capricious, and in some stories it weakens the validity of the tale, as in *Stewed Goose*, in which a goose outwits a predatory bear but only because the bear, illogically, occupies himself with repetitive ploys to trap the goose although he could easily simply dispose of him. The pace of Flora's stories is often frantic and sometimes almost without plot, depending on slapstick jokes in the text and in the busy illustrations. However, the type of humor is one that young children enjoy, and they also appreciate the exciting action in all Flora's stories and, in the best of them, an opportunity to identify with characters and share their suspense.

—Zena Sutherland

FORBES, Esther. American. Born in Westborough, Massachusetts, 28 June 1891. Educated at Bradford Junior College, graduated 1912; University of Wisconsin, Madison 1916–18. Married Albert Learned Hoskins in 1926 (divorced, 1933). Staff member, Houghton Mifflin Company, publishers, Boston, 1920–26, 1942–46. Recipient: Pulitzer Prize, for history, 1943; American Library Association Newbery Medal, 1944. Litt.D.: Clark University, Worcester, Massachusetts, 1943; University of Maine, Orono, 1943; University of Wisconsin, Madison, 1949; Northeastern University, Boston, 1949; Wellesley College, Massachusetts, 1959; LL.D.: Tufts University, Medford, Massachusetts. Member, American Academy of Arts and Sciences. *Died 12 August 1967.*

PUBLICATIONS FOR CHILDREN

Fiction

> *Johnny Tremain*, illustrated by Lynd Ward.   Boston, Houghton Mifflin, 1943; London, Chatto and Windus, 1944.

Other

> *America's Paul Revere*, illustrated by Lynd Ward.   Boston, Houghton Mifflin, 1946.

PUBLICATIONS FOR ADULTS

Novels

> *O Genteel Lady!*   Boston, Houghton Mifflin, 1926; London, Heinemann, 1927.
> *Miss Marvel.*   Boston, Houghton Mifflin, 1935.
> *Paradise.*   New York, Harcourt Brace, and London, Chatto and Windus, 1937.
> *The General's Lady.*   New York, Harcourt Brace, 1938; London, Chatto and Windus, 1939.
> *The Running of the Tide.*   Boston, Houghton Mifflin, 1948; London, Chatto and Windus, 1949.
> *Rainbow on the Road.*   Boston, Houghton Mifflin, 1954; London, Chatto and Windus, 1955.

Other

> *Ann Douglas Sedgwick: An Interview.*   Boston, Houghton Mifflin, 1928.
> *A Mirror for Witches, in Which Is Reflected the Life, Machinations, and Death of Famous Doll Bilby, Who, with a More Than Feminine Perversity, Preferred a Demon to a Mortal Lover.*   Boston, Houghton Mifflin, and London, Heinemann, 1928.
> *Paul Revere and the World He Lived In.*   Boston, Houghton Mifflin, 1942.
> *The Boston Book.*   Boston, Houghton Mifflin, 1947.

*   *   *

The reputation of Esther Forbes as a writer in the children's book field has been established by one book – *Johnny Tremain*. It is her only work of fiction for children. Young people who are interested in historical fiction, however, would enjoy her other work, particularly *Rainbow on the Road*.

Esther Forbes had several unique advantages in writing *Johnny Tremain* which helped to make the book one of the most solid choices to win the Newbery Medal in the history of the award; they have also helped to make the book still worth-while – even enabling it to survive the trauma of being required reading in many a school system.

The first advantage was her detailed knowledge of Paul Revere's world – its physical conditions, its contemporary events, its political figures and their influences. Information of all kinds, gathered in her exhaustive research for her earlier *Paul Revere*, was so firm in her mind that complete scenes for *Johnny Tremain*, accurately detailed and furnished, could arise spontaneously. The creative process did not have to be interrupted and reaffirmed by research. The richness and liveliness added to the story by this ability are as rewarding as the plot and characters.

The second advantage derived also from her historical research: the curiosity and insight with which she considered people and the reasons for their behavior. She was always titillated by the quirk of thought or misunderstanding which could precipitate an historical incident. As she studied the Boston of the 1760's and 1770's, the role played by apprentices of

467

all trades intrigued her – and she promised herself the indulgence of writing a piece of fiction about them in time.

When World War II brought the issue of freedom and fighting for it once more into daily consciousness, she found the crux for her story. She could reveal the universal and timeless problems of making difficult choices, believing in a cause, being responsible for one's actions, overcoming a handicap (Johnny's burned hand), and facing grief and loss (the death of Rab) by telling the story of Johnny Tremain, apprentice to a silversmith in Boston during the American Revolution. In her Newbery Award Acceptance Speech, Esther Forbes said, "I was anxious to show young readers something of the excitement of human nature, never static, always changing, often unpredictable, and endlessly fascinating." She might well have been defining the elements needed to produce a classic – which is what she did.

The text for *America's Paul Revere* is a distillation of the man and the most important facts of his life and times, prepared for younger readers as a counterpart for Lynd Ward's illustrations.

—Lee Kingman

FOREMAN, Michael. British. Born in Pakefield, Suffolk, 21 March 1938. Educated at Notley Road Secondary Modern School; Lowestoft School of Art, Suffolk, National Diploma in Design 1958; Royal College of Art, London (Silver Medal, 1963), A.R.C.A. (honours) 1963. Married Janet Charters in 1959 (divorced); has one son. Lecturer, St. Martin's School of Art, London, 1963–65, London School of Painting, 1967, Royal College of Art, 1968–70, and Central School of Art, London, 1971–72. Art Director, *Playboy*, Chicago, 1965, and *King*, London, 1966. Since 1960, Art Director, *Ambit*, London. Recipient (for painting): Schweppes travelling scholarship, 1961–63; Festival International du Livre Silver Eagle Award, Nice, 1972; Victoria and Albert Museum Francis Williams Prize, 1972, 1977. Agent: John Locke, 15 East 76th Street, New York, New York 10021, U.S.A.; or, Gallery Elaine, 15 Rue Vernon, 75018 Paris, France. Address: St. Peters Studio, St. Peters Street, St. Ives, Cornwall, England.

PUBLICATIONS FOR CHILDREN (illustrated by the author)

Fiction

> *The Perfect Present.* London, Hamish Hamilton, and New York, Coward McCann, 1967.
> *The Two Giants.* Leicester, Brockhampton Press, and New York, Pantheon Books, 1967.
> *The Great Sleigh Robbery.* London, Hamish Hamilton, 1968; New York, Pantheon Books, 1969.
> *Horatio.* London, Hamish Hamilton, 1970; as *The Travels of Horatio*, New York, Pantheon Books, 1970.
> *Dinosaurs and All That Rubbish.* London, Hamish Hamilton, 1972; New York, Crowell, 1973.
> *Moose.* London, Hamish Hamilton, 1971; New York, Pantheon Books, 1972.
> *War and Peas.* London, Hamish Hamilton, and New York, Crowell, 1974.
> *All the King's Horses.* London, Hamish Hamilton, and Scarsdale, New York, Bradbury Press, 1976.
> *Panda's Puzzle.* London, Hamish Hamilton, and Scarsdale, New York, Bradbury Press, 1977.

Illustrator: *The General* by Janet Charters, 1961; *Making Music* by Gwen Clemens, 1966; *I'm for You and You're for Me* by Mabel Watts, 1967; *Let's Fight and Other Russian Fables* by Sergei Vladimirovich Mikhalkov, 1968; *Adam's Balm* by William Ivan Martin, 1970; *The Birthday Unicorn*, 1970, and *Alexander in the Land of Mog*, 1973, by Janet Elliott; *Fischer v. Spassky* by C.O. Alexander, 1972; *The Living Arts of Nigeria* edited by William Fagg, 1971; *The Living Treasures of Japan* by Barbara Adachi, 1973; *Mr. Noah and the Second Flood* by Sheila Burnford, 1973; *Private Zoo* by Georges McHargue, 1973; *Rainbow Rider* by Jane Yolen, 1974; *Teeny-Tiny and the Witch Woman* by Barbara K. Walker, 1974; *The Stone Book*, 1976, and *Tom Fobble's Day*, 1977, by Alan Garner; *The Pushcart War* by Jean Merrill, 1976; *Hans Christian Andersen: His Classic Fairy Tales* translated by Erik Haugaard, 1976; *Monkey and the Three Wizards* translated by Peter Harris, 1976; *Kitchen Stories* by Kurt Baumann, 1977.

* * *

Michael Foreman is a "political" writer/illustrator who expresses ideas about society and the human race allegorically through the medium of picture books. *Dinosaurs and All That Rubbish*, for example, takes pollution and the distribution of wealth as its theme, *War and Peas* the relationship between the industrialised nations and the Third World.

Foreman's books work on two different levels. Thus in *Moose* we have on one level a story about a moose who is disturbed by an eagle and a bear who throw things at each other. On another level the story can be seen to symbolise the fate of the ordinary person, or poor nation (moose), caught up unwittingly in the wars of the super-powers (eagle and bear). There is a strong element of satire in Foreman's treatment of these "serious" themes – in *All the King's Horses*, for example, the fairy tale princess-and-the-suitors convention, familiar to all children, is turned outrageously on its head as the suitors have to wrestle with the princess whose hand they are seeking and are then dispensed with as she is "heard, rushing through the nightmares of kings and the dreams of princesses."

Foreman's texts have a confident grace; their style is colloquial and witty ("it will serve my daughter right to get lumbered with a lumberjack") while introducing unselfconsciously interesting and difficult words – "unruly," "eligible," etc. Foreman's great achievement, however, lies in his ability to express complex, often topical, political ideas simply, cogently and with humour. But it would be a mistake to see Foreman as just a protest writer. As he himself says: (*Books for Your Children*, Vol. 10, No. 3) "It is not necessarily a protest. It could be a celebration of things that are going on in the world or things that are being ignored."

—Rosemary Stones

FOREST, Antonia. British. Born in London. Address: c/o Faber and Faber Ltd., 3 Queen Square, London, WC1N 2AU, England.

PUBLICATIONS FOR CHILDREN

Fiction

Autumn Term, illustrated by Marjorie Owens. London, Faber, 1948.
The Marlows and the Traitor, illustrated by Doritie Kettlewell. London, Faber, 1953.
Falconer's Lure: The Story of a Summer Holiday, illustrated by Tasha Kallin. London, Faber, 1957.

End of Term. London, Faber, 1959.
Peter's Room. London, Faber, 1961.
The Thursday Kidnapping. London, Faber, 1963; New York, Coward McCann, 1965.
The Thuggery Affair. London, Faber, 1965.
The Ready-Made Family. London, Faber, 1967.
The Player's Boy. London, Faber, 1970.
The Players and the Rebels. London, Faber, 1971.
The Cricket Term. London, Faber, 1974.
The Attic Term. London, Faber, 1976.

*   *   *

Although four of Antonia Forest's books are primarily school stories, the rest of her series about the Marlow family is set mainly outside school in holiday periods. In all these stories the upper-middle-class background is evident, but particularly in the stories set at home, which have casual references to servants, to hunting, to parties, and to private chapels, more akin to children's books of the 1930's than to the 1970's.

The most original and outstanding plot in the series is that of *Peter's Room*, a brilliant blend of reality and fantasy woven around the intense fascination of the Brontë kingdoms of Gondal and Angria for the young Marlows. The interest in these imaginary kingdoms is aroused when one of the sisters, Ginty, has to produce an essay on some aspect of the Brontës' life or work. The Marlows create their own kingdom of Angora and become utterly absorbed in it for an entire Christmas holiday. This highly successful book well deserved the commendation it received from the Library Association in 1961.

However, Antonia Forest is likely to be remembered primarily for her school stories in which she follows accepted formulae, but gives the Marlows a rare form of immortality with school years spanning a period of nearly thirty years, and also introduces ingenious variations. The twins' hopes of academic triumph are doomed to failure. Running away is an ignominious experience for Nick who is immediately sent back to school by her elder brother, and has not even been missed in her absence. Starts of term are highlighted by the incident of the pulling of the communication cord in the train or a bolt across the fields to catch an escaped merlin. Dramatics perhaps occupy an undue proportion of certain plots, but this is acceptable to even the wariest reader because of Antonia Forest's enthusiastic details.

It is not Antonia Forest's skilful handling of the school story plot, with its crippling limitations, that ensures her success, but her positive flair for characterisation: her presentation of violent clashes of personality, her understanding of the fluctuations of schoolgirl friendships, and her insight into sisterly relationships.

Antonia Forest's able handling of plot and character, combined with sound literary style, enables her to present the traditional school story in a new and lasting dimension, unlikely to have many if any successful imitators.

—Anne W. Ellis

FOX, Paula. American. Born in New York City, 22 April 1923. Married Richard Sigerson in 1948 (divorced, 1954), two children; Martin Greenberg, 1962. Recipient: Guggenheim Fellowship, 1972; National Institute of Arts and Letters Award, 1972; American Library Association Newbery Medal, 1974; National Endowment for the Arts award, 1974. Lives in Brooklyn, New York. Agent: Robert Lescher, 155 East 71st Street, New York, New York 10021, U.S.A.

PUBLICATIONS FOR CHILDREN

Fiction

Maurice's Room, illustrated by Ingrid Fetz.   New York, Macmillan, 1966.
A Likely Place, illustrated by Edward Ardizzone.   New York, Macmillan, 1967;
   London, Macmillan, 1968.
How Many Miles to Babylon?, illustrated by Paul Giovanopoulos.   New York, David
   White, and London, Macmillan, 1967.
Dear Prosper, illustrated by Steve McLachlin.   New York, David White, 1968.
The Stone-Faced Boy, illustrated by Donald Mackay.   Englewood Cliffs, New Jersey,
   Bradbury Press, 1968; London, Macmillan, 1969.
The King's Falcon, illustrated by Eros Keith.   Englewood Cliffs, New Jersey, Bradbury
   Press, 1969; London, Macmillan, 1970.
Portrait of Ivan, illustrated by Saul Lambert.   Englewood Cliffs, New Jersey, Bradbury
   Press, 1969; London, Macmillan, 1970.
Hungry Fred, illustrated by Rosemary Wells.   Englewood Cliffs, New Jersey,
   Bradbury Press, 1969.
Blowfish Live in the Sea.   Englewood Cliffs, New Jersey, Bradbury Press, 1970.
Good Ethan, illustrated by Arnold Lobel.   Scarsdale, New York, Bradbury Press, 1973.
The Slave Dancer, illustrated by Eros Keith.   Scarsdale, New York, Bradbury Press,
   1973; London, Macmillan, 1974.

PUBLICATIONS FOR ADULTS

Novels

Poor George.   New York, Harcourt Brace, and London, Bodley Head, 1967.
Desperate Characters.   New York, Harcourt Brace, and London, Macmillan, 1970.
The Western Coast.   New York, Harcourt Brace, 1972; London, Macmillan, 1973.
The Widow's Children.   New York, Dutton, 1976.

*   *   *

Devotees of good literature for children or adults have lauded the extraordinary talents of
Paula Fox. To read her children's books is an experience in delving into the emotional life of
young people. Although *The Slave Dancer* is an award-winner and rightfully so, *Blowfish
Live in the Sea* and *The Stone-Faced Boy* are equally excellent examples of Fox's superb craft.
Before we continue with the glory of Fox, mention should be made of her shortcomings
which encompass books for the beginning reader such as her first picture-book, *Hungry
Fred*, and *Good Ethan*, as well as an absurd fantasy, *Dear Prosper*. *Hungry Fred* is a dull story
about a boy who eats everything in sight, including the furniture, in a vain attempt to get
attention from his uncaring family. *Good Ethan* relates the story of a city boy whose ball
lands across the street – forbidden territory. Unfriendly people pass by and refuse assistance,
convincing Ethan to use his ingenuity in walking up buildings and down trees to effect the
rescue of his plaything. It is a spiritless tale. The five to seven age-range obviously is not Fox's
forte. *Dear Prosper*, a memoir in the form of a letter written to a boy by a dog, is a poor piece
of whimsy.

What does work well with Paula Fox is her penetrating analysis of a child's emotions,
conflicts and agonizing attempts at coping. When Fox writes in the first person, it is
particularly spare and pungent. In *Blowfish Live in the Sea*, 12-year-old Carrie is the one
person who can reach Ben, her 18-year-old half-brother. When Ben's father invites him to
Boston to meet for the first time, Ben takes Carrie along for moral support. Carrie loves Ben
and wants to help him, especially during the strained, painful encounter with his father, a
touching, hapless failure. Ben decides to leave home in an effort to bolster up the broken man

in his new venture. It is really Carrie's story, and she tells it with deep understanding and sympathy for both her rebellious brother and his bungling father.

In *Portrait of Ivan*, Fox delivers a compassionate rendering of a wealthy, motherless only child who lives with his uncommunicative father. When an empathetic artist is commissioned to draw Ivan's portrait, some of the walls of defense which surround the boy start to crumble. The artist takes Ivan to Florida on an assignment where the boy meets Geneva, a girl who is as free and unafraid as Ivan is repressed. As a result of his trip away from home and his interaction with new friends, Ivan starts to emerge from his shell. Returning home, he makes the effort to bridge the gap between his father and himself. In *Blowfish Live in the Sea* and *Portrait of Ivan* the exploration of feelings provides the reader with ample satisfaction. Other times, as in *Maurice's Room* or *A Likely Place*, we wait for something to happen and close the book admiring Fox's keen psychological insights, if a little disappointed by the lack of action.

In *The Slave Dancer*, the author has written an exciting adventure about 13-year-old Jessie Bollier of New Orleans who is impressed for service in a slave ship bound for Africa. Jessie narrates the story of his four months at sea where his task is to play the fife for the doleful blacks who are traded for gold, rum and tobacco. To Jessie's dismay, his pity for the slaves turns to contempt, "I hated their shuffling, their howling, their very suffering!" As Jessie's emotions change from one moment to the next, Fox makes his ambivalence a credible aspect of his growth. The boy's harrowing experiences aboard *The Moonlight* and his short-lived friendship with Ras, part of the human cargo, leave scars on Jessie which remain to haunt him in his later years.

Gus is the morose, middle-child of a family of five children in *The Stone-Faced Boy*. No one understands Gus, who can show neither happiness nor displeasure until Great-Aunt Hattie, a mysterious figure, appears on the scene. Shortly after her arrival, she presents Gus with a geode, a symbol of the beauty locked up inside the boy. Following his nighttime rescue of a stray dog trapped in the snow, Gus finally reacts to his hostile younger brother. When Great-Aunt Hattie departs, his sisters and brothers beg Gus to break open the geode and to let everyone look inside, but he refuses. "He knew how the stone would look inside, but he didn't choose to break it open yet." Fox has the uncanny ability to crawl inside a child's head and heart to elicit sharp, vivid characterizations.

In *How Many Miles to Babylon?* danger and terror await 10-year-old James when the sad and lonely boy runs out of school one day. Although the milieu is a poor Black ghetto, the story transcends such limitations of place. James' father is gone, his mother is ailing and absent, and his three aging aunts care for the boy in a single, shabby room. The boy seeks haven in an abandoned house where a trio of dog thieves force him to assist them in their scheme. Using his wits, the frightened boy runs from the predators at night and finds his way back home where life is much better, where people care for and about him. In *The King's Falcon*, the king runs away from home, but never returns to his nagging wife and dull kingdom after he finds contentment in being another king's falconer. Children will find it difficult to understand the moral of this story and will miss not having a young child with whom to identify.

For those readers interested in a young person's emotions, explored with sincerity and warmth, Paula Fox offers beautifully-crafted children's literature.

—Vivian J. Scheinmann

FREEMAN, Barbara C(onstance).   British.   Born in Ealing, Middlesex, 29 November 1906. Educated at Tiffin Girls' School, Kingston-upon-Thames, Surrey; Kingston School of Art. Address: Shirley, 62 Hook Road, Surbiton KT6 5BH, Surrey, England.

PUBLICATIONS FOR CHILDREN (illustrated by the author)

Fiction

> *Timi.* London, Faber, 1961.
> *Two-Thumb Thomas.* London, Faber, 1961.
> *A Book by Georgina.* London, Faber, 1962; New York, Norton, 1968.
> *Broom-Adelaide.* London, Faber, 1963; Boston, Little Brown, 1965.
> *The Name on the Glass.* London, Faber, 1964; New York, Norton, 1966.
> *Lucinda.* London, Faber, 1965; New York, Norton, 1967.
> *Tobias.* London, Faber, 1967.
> *The Forgotten Theatre.* London, Faber, 1967.
> *The Other Face.* London, Macmillan, 1975; New York, Dutton, 1976.
> *A Haunting Air.* London, Macmillan, 1976; New York, Dutton, 1977.
> *A Pocket of Silence.* London, Macmillan, 1977.

Illustrator: *Stories from Hans Andersen,* 1949; *Stories from Grimm,* 1949; *The Sleeping Beauty and Other Tales* by Charles Perrault; *The Magic Candles* by Mary Steward; *Granny's Wonderful Chair* by Frances Browne; *Jan and His Clogs,* 1951. *Jan Klaassen Cures the King,* 1952, *Puppet Plays for Children,* 1953, and *Never Run from the Lion and Another Story,* 1958, all by Antonia Ridge; pictures for *The Children's Encyclopedia.*

Barbara C. Freeman comments:

I write, I suppose, chiefly because I enjoy writing and I like living in two worlds: the one I was born into and the other (which becomes entirely real) which I write about. I'm deeply interested in the way ordinary people lived in the past and the way in which the past thrusts into the present. I believe that most writers find that their characters develop lives of their own and sometimes take charge of both conversations and plots. This, for me, is pure delight, and I allow my people all the freedom that is possible.

At art school I was trained to observe details of every kind, and it is a habit that one never grows out of. Details, especially those of the past, fascinate me.

*   *   *

Barbara C. Freeman writes easily of young girls in Victorian England; her narratives pass from one century to another, often travelling into the past, then back into modern times in one book. Sometimes, as in *The Forgotten Theatre,* where the curiosity of two Victorian cousins is aroused by an old building into discovering the life of an actress ancestor, the story is straightforward. In "Betony" magic is necessary to transport the heroine bodily into the life of her ancestors. This heroine is solitary and shy and welcomes these excursions into the past, which she makes by burying a pastille in a china ornament. The story becomes highly complicated, but Betony returns in time with added knowledge and confidence. The endings are always happy. Charlotte in *The Forgotten Theatre* no longer feels sad and unwanted when she is allowed to make the stage her career.

The Name on the Glass and *Lucinda* are both stories of Victorian family life, one set in London, one in the country, while *Tobias* moves from the seventeenth century and back again. *Broom-Adelaide* is a fantasy about a young Ruritanian Grand Duchess who outwits a witch. *A Book by Georgina* concerns two enthusiastic sisters finding out the history of an old house. In *A Haunting Air* the ghost of an unhappy Victorian child returns to a modern house and sings, but discovering her history helps two twentieth-century girls solve their own problems of loneliness and frustration.

But Barbara Freeman's best known story is about Two-Thumb Thomas, the small boy educated by Linette, a school cat, but finally readopted by humans. Linette often attends class herself, teaches Thomas his letters; then he attends school himself by hiding in the cloakroom and listening through the wall; at night he sleeps on a shelf in the stationery cupboard. When he grows too big for this, he takes over an old abandoned house, but the rats refuse to share the accommodation. Like most good fantasies, this one has an ordinary domestic setting. As Thomas tells his story, "a fat gay cuckoo swept down across the garden shouting at the top of its voice ... the lawn was dappled with long shadows and a faint breath of wood smoke came drifting from Dove Lane."

Timi is a Griffin who is too scared to use her wings and fly with the other Griffins, so makes friends with the village baker. Her affection for him lends her courage and after an adventure she is brave enough to return to her fellows. Barbara Freeman is equally at home with fantasy or ordinary humans and quite prepared to mix the two ingredients to make a good story.

—Margaret Campbell

FREEMAN, Don. American. Born in San Diego, California, 11 August 1908. Educated at Principia High School, St. Louis; Art Students' League, New York. Served in the United States Army Infantry, Rainbow Division, for two years. Married Lydia Cooley in 1931; has one son. Trumpeter in jazz band; Drama Artist, *New York Times*, 1934–52. One-man show: Margo Feiden Galleries, New York, 1975. Recipient: New York *Herald Tribune* Festival award, 1953. Address: 1932 Cleveland Avenue, Santa Barbara, California 93103, U.S.A.

PUBLICATIONS FOR CHILDREN (illustrated by the author)

Fiction

> *Chuggy and the Blue Caboose*, with Lydia Freeman. New York, Viking Press, 1951.
> *Pet of the Met*, with Lydia Freeman. New York, Viking Press, 1953.
> *Beady Bear*. New York, Viking Press, 1954.
> *Mop Top*. New York, Viking Press, 1955.
> *Fly High, Fly Low*. New York, Viking Press, 1957.
> *The Night the Lights Went Out*. New York, Viking Press, 1958.
> *Norman the Doorman*. New York, Viking Press, 1959; Leicester, Brockhampton Press, 1972.
> *Space Witch*. New York, Viking Press, 1959.
> *Cyrano the Crow*. New York, Viking Press, 1960.
> *Come Again, Pelican*. New York, Viking Press, 1961.
> *Botts, The Naughty Otter*. San Carlos, California, Golden Gate Books, 1963.
> *Ski Pup*. New York, Viking Press, 1963.
> *Dandelion*. New York, Viking Press, 1964; Kingswood, Surrey, World's Work, 1965.
> *The Turtle and the Dove*. New York, Viking Press, 1964; Kingswood, Surrey, World's Work, 1965.
> *A Rainbow of My Own*. New York, Viking Press, 1966; Kingswood, Surrey, World's Work, 1967.
> *The Guard Mouse*. New York, Viking Press, 1967; Kingswood, Surrey, World's Work, 1970.
> *Corduroy*. New York, Viking Press, 1968.
> *Quiet! There's a Canary in the Library*. San Carlos, California, Golden Gate Books, 1969.
> *Tilly Witch*. New York, Viking Press, 1969.

Forever Laughter.   San Carlos, California, Golden Gate Books, 1970.
Hattie the Backstage Bat.   New York, Viking Press, 1970.
Penguins of All People!   New York, Viking Press, 1971.
Inspector Peckit.   New York, Viking Press, 1972; Kingswood, Surrey, World's Work, 1973.
Flash and Dash.   Chicago, Children's Press, 1973.
The Seal and the Slick.   New York, Viking Press, 1974; as *The Sea Lion and the Slick*, Kingswood, Surrey, World's Work, 1976.
The Paper Party.   New York, Viking Press, 1974; Kingswood, Surrey, World's Work, 1977.
Will's Quill.   New York, Viking Press, 1975.
Bearymore.   New York, Viking Press, 1976.
The Chalk Box Story.   Philadelphia, Lippincott, 1976.

Plays

Screenplays (short films): *Lollipop Opera*, 1970; *Storymaker*, 1972.

Television Play: *The Baker (Sesame Street* series), 1971.

Other

Add-a-Line Alphabet.   San Carlos, California, Golden Gate Books, 1968.

PUBLICATIONS FOR ADULTS

Other

It Shouldn't Happen.   New York, Harcourt Brace, 1945.
Come One, Come All!   New York, Rinehart, 1949.

Illustrator: *My Name Is Aram*, 1940, and *The Human Comedy*, 1943, by William Saroyan; *Diedrich Knickerbocker's History of New York* by Washington Irving, 1940; *The White Deer* by James Thurber, 1945; *Once Around the Sun* by Brooks Atkinson, 1951; *Sauce for the Gander* by Scott Corbett, 1951; *Mike's House* by Julia Sauer, 1954; *Third Monkey*, 1956, and *This for That*, 1965, by Ann Nolan Clark; *The Uninvited Donkey* by Anne H. White, 1957; *Ghost Town Treasure* by Clyde Robert Bulla, 1957; *Best Friends*, 1967, and *Best of Luck*, 1969, by Myra Brown; *Voltaire's Micromegas* by Elizabeth Hall, 1967; *California Indian Days* by Helen Bauer, revised edition, 1968; *Seven in a Bed* by Ruth Sonneborn, 1968; *Joey's Cat* by Robert Burch, 1969; *Burnish Me Bright*, 1970, and *Far in the Day*, 1972, by Julia W. Cunningham; *Edward and the Night Horses* by Jacklyn Matthews, 1971; *The Wild Cats of Rome* by Elizabeth Cooper, 1972; *The Christmas Strangers* by Marjorie Thayer, 1976; *Monster Night at Grandma's House* by Richard Peck, 1977.

*   *   *

   Don Freeman's picture books sing out with a playfulness that strikes the child's imagination. He sees his themes and subjects with an artist's eye from which comes a flow of pictures followed by a stream of words.
   Pet of the Met, one of his first books (written in collaboration with his wife, Lydia), set a high standard for his work. He blends his intimate knowledge of the Opera House and

Mozart's *The Magic Flute* with mouse and cat antics. Mr. Petrini, the page turner at the opera house, and a *Magic Flute* enthusiast, deftly confronts a mouse's traditional enemy, Mephistopheles, the cat. There is a jauntiness of writing that gives the book a lasting spirit.

Norman the Doorman is a master at collecting mousetraps set for him in the museum where he is the doorman and guide to his relatives, including Maestro Petrini and family. He hears of a sculpture competition, enters his sculpture *Trapeese*, and wins first prize. This is a caper to be enjoyed for what it is, with an implicit commentary on the meaning of art exhibits to be detected by the more sophisticated reader. *The Guard Mouse* continues the fanciful escapades of the Petrini family. Their cousin, Clyde, a Grenadier guard at Buckingham Palace, welcomes the Petrinis. The children, Do, Re, Mi, tired after their long trip from New York, are left behind as Clyde takes the parents on a tour of London, a light-hearted romp that indicates more than a chance aquaintance with the city. In each of these books an element of surprise adds marked interest to the story. Freeman is an effective storyteller, interweaving information that can arouse the undiscovered interests of the young child.

Freeman's imagination reaches out into unlikely areas. Peary B. Penguin, in *Penguins of All People!*, is urgently requested to attend a special meeting of the United Nations, to share with the members the secret of how penguins live together so peacefully. Might the U.N. members learn from him? In *Will's Quill*, Willoughby, a country goose, is rescued by Young Will, and, to show his gratefulness for Will's kindness, tells the story with overtones of archaic language about a country goose who helped William Shakespeare in the writing of his plays.

Freeman has also created books that capture spontaneously, without ulterior motive, the imaginative world to which the young child responds. *Mop Top* is the story of a little boy who will not have his hair cut until he is mistaken for a mop. In *Dandelion*, a lion receives an invitation to a tea-and-taffy party from Jennifer Giraffe, and sets about with meticulous preparation to look his best. The results are preposterous, sustained by Freeman's clear vision and obvious zest for the development of this situation. Children can identify with the implicit, gentle wisdom. In *Corduroy*, a shopworn bear yearns for a home in which his sense of belonging can be satisfied. Lisa sees Corduroy, the bear, and empties her piggy bank to buy him. He must belong to her. Freeman develops the not-uncommon theme of a stuffed animal and a child with understanding and compassion.

Freeman's visual sense gives strength to his picture books even when his text does not reach the same height. At his best, he offers rich visual experiences with sparkle and harmony in his writing.

—Mae Durham Roger

FRENCH, Fiona. British. Born in Bath, Somerset, 27 June 1944. Educated at Croydon College of Art, Surrey, National Diploma in Design for painting and lithography, 1966. Children's art therapy teacher, Long Grove Psychiatric Hospital, Epsom, Surrey, 1967–69; design teacher, Wimbledon School of Art, 1970–71, and Leicester and Brighton polytechnics, 1973–74. Assistant to the painter Bridget Riley, 1967–72. Agent: Laura Cecil, 106 Exeter Mansions, Shaftesbury Avenue, London, W.1. Address: Flat 6, 12 Princes Avenue, Muswell Hill, London, N.10, England.

PUBLICATIONS FOR CHILDREN (illustrated by the author)

Fiction

Jack of Hearts. London, Oxford University Press, and New York, Harcourt Brace, 1970.

Huni. London, Oxford University Press, 1971.
The Blue Bird. London, Oxford University Press, and New York, Walck, 1972.
King Tree. London, Oxford University Press, and New York, Walck, 1973.
City of Gold. London, Oxford University Press, and New York, Walck, 1974.
Aio the Rainmaker. London, Oxford University Press, 1975.
Matteo. London, Oxford University Press, 1976.
Hunt-the-Thimble. London, Oxford University Press, 1977.

PUBLICATIONS FOR ADULTS

Short Stories

Un-Fairy Tales. Privately printed, 1966.

Illustrator: *Book of Magical Birds* by Margaret Mayo, 1977.

*   *   *

By steeping herself in the culture or period content of her picture books, Fiona French produces not only authentic detail but an almost tangible atmosphere, a feat perceivable in her gloriously rich illustrative style and in the entirely suitable economy and relevance of the texts.

All her books are full of the powerful elemental themes found in myth and fairy tale. Envy, greed, power appear in the first book, *Jack of Hearts,* based on the playing card Kings of Hearts, Diamonds, Clubs, and Spades, represented as happy, rich, warlike, and evil respectively, and the 18th birthday feast of Jack of Hearts. Research shows in the description of the feast, including "wild boar and peacock and paradise sauce and herring pie and hedgehog, gingerbread, sea-holly candy and rich red wine." Elemental emotions appear also in *King Tree,* in a Louis XIV Garden of Versailles setting, where Orange Tree organises nominations for king, and the oak, laurel, pomegranate, olive, and vine vie with each other in election promises; but the ladies choose Orange Tree as King. Pride and the fight between good and evil appear in *City of Gold,* a medieval, Biblical style tale of John and Thomas, brothers journeying on the roads easy and hard, thwarting the Devil in a series of encounters. *The Blue Bird* reveals the evil Enchantress when the Chinese girl Blue Jade seeks a cure for her pet bird's loss of voice, a revelation spectacularly accomplished in transition from Wedgwood blue illustration to a burst of colour when the Enchantress is demolished and her victims freed. *Matteo* too follows the practical jokers through apparent success to just retribution.

Survival and proving oneself to the gods are the themes of *Huni* and *Aio the Rainmaker.* Huni, possible successor to Pharaoh, meets some of the gods from Egyptian mythology – Ra, the cat, the serpent, Osiris – survives ordeals to prove health and strength, and is deemed fit to be the new Pharaoh. In *Aio,* African tribal art and legend are interwoven to form an African "experience" of a parched land, of Aio's powers to call on the Ancestors for rain to relieve the thirsty animals, graphically described in text and pictures.

These simple but strong emotions lend themselves to a textual treatment in which Miss French retains the essence of the concept in short yet strongly phrased sentences with the narrative flow and the underlying moral message of the oral tradition. The striking use of colour is a feature of her powerful illustrative style: playing cards based on a real design, medieval stained glass windows in *City of Gold,* Egyptian art in *Huni,* Chinese style in *The Blue Bird,* French mannered style in *King Tree,* African art in *Aio,* and Florentine style in *Matteo.*

Her picture books are not, in theme and style, for the young child, but for those over 8, for young people, and for adults who see the masterly relationship between the verbal and visual concept of each book.

—Margaret R. Marshall

FRITZ, Jean. American. Born in Hankow, China, 16 November 1915. Educated at Wheaton College, Norton, Massachusetts, B.A. 1937; Columbia University Teachers College, New York, 1938–39. Married Michael G. Fritz in 1941; has two children. Research assistant, Silver Burdett Co., New York, 1938–41; Children's Librarian, Dobbs Ferry Library, New York, 1955–57; Teacher, The Jean Fritz Writers' Workshop, Katonah, New York, 1962–70, and Board of Cooperative Educational Services, Westchester County, New York, 1971–75. Book reviewer, *New York Times*. Agent: Russell and Volkening, 551 Fifth Avenue, New York, New York 10017. Address: 50 Bellewood Avenue, Dobbs Ferry, New York 10522, U.S.A.

PUBLICATIONS FOR CHILDREN

Fiction

Bunny Hopwell's First Spring, illustrated by Rachel Dixon. New York, Wonder Books, 1954.

Help Mr. Willy Nilly, illustrated by Jean Tamburine. New York, Treasure Books, 1954.

Fish Head, illustrated by Marc Simont. New York, Coward McCann, 1954; London, Faber, 1956.

121 Pudding Street, illustrated by Sofia. New York, Coward McCann, 1955.

The Late Spring, illustrated by Erik Blegvad. New York, Coward McCann, 1957.

The Cabin Faced West, illustrated by Feodor Rojankovsky. New York, Coward McCann, 1958.

Champion Dog, Prince Tom, with Tom Clute, illustrated by Ernest Hart. New York, Coward McCann, 1958.

How to Read a Rabbit, illustrated by Leonard Shortall. New York, Coward McCann, 1959.

Brady, illustrated by Lynd Ward. New York, Coward McCann, 1960; London, Gollancz, 1966.

Tap, Tap, Lion – One, Two, Three, illustrated by Leonard Shortall. New York, Coward McCann, 1962.

I, Adam, illustrated by Peter Burchard. New York, Coward McCann, 1963; London, Gollancz, 1965.

Magic to Burn, illustrated by Beth and Joe Krush. New York, Coward McCann, 1964.

Early Thunder, illustrated by Lynd Ward. New York, Coward McCann, 1967; London, Gollancz, 1969.

George Washington's Breakfast, illustrated by Paul Galdone. New York, Coward McCann, 1969.

Other

Growing Up, illustrated by Elizabeth Webbe. Chicago, Rand McNally, 1956.

The Animals of Dr. Schweitzer, illustrated by Douglas Howland. New York, Coward McCann, 1958; Edinburgh, Oliver and Boyd, 1962.

San Francisco, illustrated by Emil Weiss. Chicago, Rand McNally, 1962.

Surprise Party (reader), illustrated by George Wiggins. New York, Initial Teaching Alphabet Publications, 1965.

The Train (reader), illustrated by Jean Simpson. New York, Grosset and Dunlap, 1965.

And Then What Happened, Paul Revere?, illustrated by Margot Tomes. New York, Coward McCann, 1973.

Why Don't You Get a Horse, Sam Adams?, illustrated by Trina Schart Hyman. New York, Coward McCann, 1974.

Where Was Patrick Henry on the 29th of May?, illustrated by Margot Tomes. New York, Coward McCann, 1975.

Who's That Stepping on Plymouth Rock?, illustrated by J.B. Handelsman. New York, Coward McCann, 1975.

Will You Sign Here, John Hancock?, illustrated by Trina Schart Hyman. New York, Coward McCann, 1976.

What's the Bid Idea, Ben Franklin?, illustrated by Margot Tomes. New York, Coward McCann, 1976.

Can't You Make Them Behave, King George?, illustrated by Tomie de Paola. New York, Coward McCann, 1977.

PUBLICATIONS FOR ADULTS

Other

Cast for a Revolution: Some American Friends and Enemies, 1728–1814. Boston, Houghton Mifflin, 1972.

Manuscript Collections: Kerlan Collection, University of Minnesota, Minneapolis; University of Oregon Library, Eugene.

Jean Fritz comments:

Although I experiment in various kinds of writing, my curiosity, I suppose, drives me most often to the past where there are more people, more stories, more truths, more secrets than I can ever hope to exhaust. I like having more than one century at my disposal. And I seem to need to put my roots down deeper and deeper into my own country.

*   *   *

Early in the 1970's Jean Fritz began to write the short, beguiling biographies which promise to make her as famous literarily as her subjects are historically. For readers aged 7 through 11 years, the books bear such jaunty titles as *George Washington's Breakfast, And Then What Happened, Paul Revere?*, and *Will You Sign Here, John Hancock?* These mini-lives include a zesty account of Plymouth Rock, a work which proves that the author can infuse even a stone with personality.

Great Bicentennial favorites, the little histories have been applauded by critics and read eagerly – not just by children but by adults who are amused by Fritz's lighthearted approach to weighty subjects. But the author is in no way guilty of debunking heroes. On the contrary, she is one of the few writers who convince us, by stressing their humanity, that the American Founding Fathers were even more remarkable than we had realized.

The current books are the logical culmination of Jean Fritz's background and interests. During the 1950's, she began to invent characters to people stories rooted in actuality. (Even her fantasies, like the adventurous *Magic to Burn*, center around British/American relations.) *The Cabin Faced West* is an affectionate *roman à clef* about her own great-great-grandmother, Ann Hamilton. When Ann was a child, her father moved his family from their staid home in Gettysburg across the Allegheny Mountains into trackless Western Pennsylvania. The little girl's initial loneliness and growing love for her new home in the wilds are the backbone of an appealing novel. Readers can't help feeling Ann's joyous excitement when George Washington stops on his travels to dine with her family in the rough cabin on Hamilton Hill in 1784.

It isn't surprising that a gifted woman author can capture and convey the days of a girl child seeking cheer in bleak, strange surroundings. But Fritz does equally well by her boy heroes. During the 1960's, she created several historical novels in which young men were featured, teenagers whose involvement in chaotic events have made the past real and interesting to modern readers. Daniel West battles split loyalties during the tense days of 1765 in Salem in *Early Thunder*, when the town in Massachusetts suffered from the conflicts between Whigs and Tories that presaged the storm which began raging in 1776. In *I, Adam* the suspenseful adventures of Adam Crane convince him that coming of age in 1850 doesn't equal attaining manhood, that part of his destiny is to work for the shaping of the young nation. Brady Minton of *Brady* is a kid who learns the hard way not to tell everything he knows. His father is helping slaves to escape, just before the outbreak of the Civil War, a secret Mr. Minton can't trust his son to keep until Brady comes through a crisis and proves he has grown reliable.

The hallmarks of all Jean Fritz's books are literary quality, authenticity, empathy with her characters, and respect for her young readers – the latter quality clearly visible in writing with no hint of condescension. And her natural, unforced sense of humor doesn't hurt a bit either.

—Jean F. Mercier

FRY, Rosalie K(ingsmill). British. Born on Vancouver Island, British Columbia, Canada, 22 April 1911. Educated at St. Margarets P.N.E.U. School, Swansea; Central School of Art, London, 1929–34. Served in the Women's Royal Naval Service, 1939–45. Address: Lark Rise, 15 East Cliff, Southgate, Swansea SA3 2AS, Wales.

PUBLICATIONS FOR CHILDREN (illustrated by the author)

Fiction

Bumblebuzz. New York, Dutton, 1938.
Ladybug! Ladybug! New York, Dutton, 1940.
Bandy Boy's Treasure Island. New York, Dutton, 1941.
Adventure Downstream. London, Hutchinson, 1946.
In a Rock Pool. London, Hutchinson, 1947.
Cherrywinkle. London, Hutchinson, 1951.
The Little Gypsy. London, Hutchinson, 1951.
Pipkin Sees the World. New York, Dutton, 1951; as *Pipkin the Woodmouse*, London, Dent, 1953.
Deep in the Forest. London, Hutchinson, 1955; New York, Dodd Mead, 1956.
The Wind Call. London, Dent, and New York, Dutton, 1955.
Lucinda and the Painted Bell. London, Dent, 1956; as *A Bell for Ringleblume*, New York, Dutton, 1957.
Child of the Western Isles. London, Dent, 1957; as *Secret of the Ron Mor Skerry*, New York, Dutton, 1959.
Secret of the Forest. London, Hutchinson, 1958.
Matelot, Little Sailor of Brittany. New York, Dutton, 1958; as *Lucinda and the Sailor Kitten*, London, Dent, 1959.
Fly Home Colombina. London, Dent, and New York, Dutton, 1960.
The Mountain Door. London, Dent, 1960; New York, Dutton, 1961.
Princess in the Forest. London, Hutchinson, 1961.
The Echo Song. London, Dent, and New York, Dutton, 1962.
The Riddle of the Figurehead. London, Dent, and New York, Dutton, 1963.
September Island, illustrated by Margery Gill. London, Dent, and New York, Dutton, 1965.

The Castle Family, illustrated by Margery Gill.   London, Dent, 1965; New York, Dutton, 1966.

Promise of the Rainbow, illustrated by Robin Jacques.   New York, Farrar Straus, 1965; London, Dent, 1967.

Whistler in the Mist, illustrated by Robin Jacques.   New York, Farrar Straus, 1968.

Gypsy Princess, illustrated by Philip Gough.   London, Dent, and New York, Dutton, 1969.

Snowed Up, illustrated by Robin Jacques.   New York, Farrar Straus, 1970; London, Dent, 1971.

Mungo, illustrated by Velma Ilsley.   New York, Farrar Straus, 1972.

Secrets.   London, Dent, 1973.

Other

Baby's Progress Book.   Cardiff, W.H. Smith, 1944.

Lost in the Dew.   Cardiff, W.H. Smith, 1944.

Many Happy Returns (birthday book).   Cardiff, W.H. Smith, 1944.

Two Little Pigs (reader).   London, Hutchinson, 3 vols., 1953.

Cinderella's Mouse and Other Fairy Tales.   New York, Dutton, 1953.

Illustrator: *The Land of Lost Handkerchiefs*, by Marjorie Knight, 1954; *The Water Babies*, by Charles Kingsley, 1957.

*   *   *

Rosalie K. Fry trained as an artist, but from the beginning she wrote her own stories to illustrate. In the 1940's and early 1950's she wrote stories for the very young with delicately coloured illustrations. She succeeded in personalizing even such unlikely creatures as hawk moths (*Cherrywinkle*) and crabs. *In a Rock Pool*, a story of the two crab friends Captain and Crusty, is a model of simple storytelling and presentation with not a word wasted.

With *Pipkin Sees the World* Rosalie Fry began storytelling at greater length for an age level of about 8 or 9. While still humanising animals, she gives more detail from nature; dramatic incidents arise from Pipkin's natural fear of the owl or from his liking for garden peas. Her line illustrations demonstrate her love of small wild animals and all the (to us) miniature splendours of their habitat. Pipkin himself is gently sentimentalized, with a hint of humour in the drawings.

Jokle, the baby bear in *Deep in the Forest*, is another cuddly animal – more so than Pipkin, for he is that dream of every child: a live toy. This little book with Rosalie Fry's lovely pictures in colour and line has everything that we think of as particularly pleasing to little girls: a spirited little heroine called Katinka plays houses, loves a pet, explores natural surroundings by herself but from the secure base of a loving home. She is moved by a lyrical feeling for the countryside and by a sense of beauty and mystery. The word "pretty" is often apt for this author's work, not used, as too often by grownups, patronizingly, but simply as a more modest and childlike word than beautiful. Rosalie Fry knows exactly what children mean by "pretty."

The Wind Call is a full-length tale of a fairy child and the last that could be produced with coloured illustrations, but at about this time she illustrated in the same charming style the Dent/Dutton edition of *The Water Babies*. She went on to write and illustrate in line slightly older books, three for instance about Lucinda who, though only 8, went abroad with her artist parents and appreciated the landscapes, lore and crafts of Brittany and Italy. Then, from *The Echo Song* onwards, her books were about children of 10 or more and were illustrated by other artists (except *Secrets*).

In these later works, which no longer draw upon fantasy, her style is still a model of clarity: thoughtful and telling details make the plots absorbing and convincing, and the characters and settings have a charm that appeals strongly to children, especially girls, entering their teens. Boating is a favourite theme but there is a variety of others, all inspired by her own experience of places: song contest and bird preservation in Wales (*The Echo Song*), exploration of a flooded estuary (*September Island*), a family mystery in Devon (*The Riddle of the Figurehead*), with, always, the interplay of character sympathetically developed.

Secrets are very well handled: secret news, secret presents, secret ambitions, or vague secrets with the charm of enchantment, such as unexplored mysterious places full of secret wild life and shadowy legends — all the secrets and private discoveries a child loves to cherish. They provide the natural suspense of the story and, in emotional terms, they provide a significant aid in a child's progress towards a strong self-image. The young reader knows the importance of lone experiences which he can keep to himself, so he responds to secrets in stories.

One secret in *Gypsy Princess* actually turns out to tell Zilda who she is. The story starts with Robert and Zilda discovering a passage running the whole length of a row of houses under the roofs. It leads to an old coach-house used by Robert's uncle as a store for antiques, and here, in a dark corner, Zilda finds a gypsy living-wagon with a bed-place, sliding panels, built-in furniture and beautiful amber glass handles and knobs. The gypsy who left it had said he would come back one day to give it to the princess to whom it rightfully belonged. When Zilda found her own name carved beneath the wagon with the words "My princess," the whole story of her own dead parents comes out. Zilda herself was, to her father at least, a princess.

Robert, at the end, says to her:

"But surely you want to know whether you truly are a princess or not?"
"Not specially."
He looked at her with a puzzled frown.
"Aren't you queer?" he murmured. "I'd simply have to know."
"Ah, but I'm a gypsy," said Zilda with a little laugh. "We are a secret people, and that's the way we like it."

The gypsy wagon, lovingly described, is irresistible. Rosalie Fry made just such a discovery of a gypsy wagon herself and owns it as an annex to her home. It is a sort of library where local children come to borrow books — where they can enjoy the "secret" experience of a good read.

—Gwen Marsh

FULLER, Roy (Broadbent).   British.   Born in Failsworth, Lancashire, 11 February 1912. Educated at private schools; qualified as a solicitor, 1933. Served in the Royal Navy, 1941–46; Lieutenant, Royal Naval Volunteer Reserve. Married Kathleen Smith in 1936; has one son, the poet John Fuller. Assistant Solicitor, 1938–58, Solicitor, 1958–69, and since 1969, Director, Woolwich Equitable Building Society, London. Chairman of the Legal Advisory Panel, 1958–69, and since 1969, Vice-President, Building Societies Association. Professor of Poetry, Oxford University, 1968–73; Member, Arts Council of Great Britain, 1976–77 (resigned). Since 1972, Governor, BBC. Chairman of the Poetry Book Society, London, 1960–68. Recipient: Arts Council Poetry Award, 1959; Duff Cooper Memorial Prize, for poetry, 1968; Queen's Gold Medal for Poetry, 1970. Fellow, Royal Society of Literature, 1958. C.B.E. (Companion, Order of the British Empire), 1969. Address: 37 Langton Way, London S.E.3., England.

PUBLICATIONS FOR CHILDREN

Fiction

>*Savage Gold*, illustrated by Robert Medley.   London, Lehmann, 1946.
>*With My Little Eye*, illustrated by Alan Lindsay.   London, Lehmann, 1948; New York,
>   Macmillan, 1957.
>*Catspaw*, illustrated by David Gollins.   London, Alan Ross, 1966.

Verse

>*Seen Grandpa Lately?*, illustrated by Joan Hickson.   London, Deutsch, 1972.
>*Poor Roy*, illustrated by Nicolas Bentley.   London, Deutsch, 1977.

PUBLICATIONS FOR ADULTS

Novels

>*The Second Curtain*.   London, Verschoyle, 1953; New York, Macmillan, 1956.
>*Fantasy and Fugue*.   London, Verschoyle, 1954; New York, Macmillan, 1956.
>*Image of a Society*.   London, Deutsch, 1956; New York, Macmillan, 1958.
>*The Ruined Boys*.   London, Deutsch, 1959; as *That Distant Afternoon*, New York,
>   Macmillan, 1959.
>*The Father's Comedy*.   London, Deutsch, 1961.
>*The Perfect Fool*.   London, Deutsch, 1963.
>*My Child, My Sister*.   London, Deutsch, 1965.
>*The Carnal Island*.   London, Deutsch, 1970.

Verse

>*Poems*.   London, Fortune Press, 1939.
>*The Middle of a War*.   London, Hogarth Press, 1942.
>*A Lost Season*.   London, Hogarth Press, 1944.
>*Epitaphs and Occasions*.   London, Lehmann, 1949.
>*Counterparts*.   London, Verschoyle, 1954.
>*Brutus's Orchard*.   London, Deutsch, 1957; New York, Macmillan, 1958.
>*Collected Poems, 1936–61*.   London, Deutsch, and Chester Springs, Pennsylvania,
>   Dufour, 1962.
>*Buff*.   London, Deutsch, and Chester Springs, Pennsylvania, Dufour, 1965.
>*New Poems*.   London, Deutsch, and Chester Springs, Pennsylvania, Dufour, 1968.
>*Pergamon Poets 1*, with R.S. Thomas, edited by Evan Owen.   Oxford, Pergamon Press,
>   1968.
>*Off Course*.   London, Turret Books, 1969.
>*Penguin Modern Poets 18*, with A. Alvarez and Anthony Thwaite.   London, Penguin,
>   1970.
>*To an Unknown Reader*.   London, Poem-of-the-Month Club, 1970.
>*Song Cycle from a Record Sleeve*.   Oxford, Sycamore Press, 1972.
>*Tiny Tears*.   London, Deutsch, 1973.
>*An Old War*.   Edinburgh, Tragara Press, 1974.
>*From the Joke Shop*.   London, Deutsch, 1975.
>*The Joke Shop Annexe*.   Edinburgh, Tragara Press, 1975.
>*An Ill-Governed Coast*.   Sunderland, Ceolfrith Press, 1976.

Other

> *Owls and Artificers: Oxford Lectures on Poetry.* London, Deutsch, and La Salle,
> Illinois, Library Press, 1971.
> *Professors and Gods: Last Oxford Lectures on Poetry.* London, Deutsch, 1973; New
> York, St. Martin's Press, 1974.

> Editor, *Byron for Today.* London, Porcupine Press, 1948.
> Editor, with Clifford Dyment and Montagu Slater, *New Poems 1952.* London, Joseph,
> 1952.
> Editor, *Supplement of New Poetry.* London, Poetry Book Society, 1964.

Manuscript Collections (verse): State University of New York, Buffalo; British Library,
London.

Roy Fuller comments:
   Though writing for children has always given me a certain sense of freedom, I have never
thought of my children's books as "written down" to an audience. Indeed, possibly I have
erred the other way; *With My Little Eye* was published in the United States as an adult crime
novel! The separation in time between the two groups of children's books is to be accounted
for by the fact that I was stimulated to write them first by my son's childhood, then my
grandchildren's. My interest continues; as I write this I am working on a book of tales for
children – "and for others" perhaps I should add! I spoke about (*inter alia*) my own writings
for children and their relation to my other work in a Sidney Robbins Memorial Fund lecture
in 1975 (printed in *Children's Literature in Education*, Spring 1976) called "The Influence of
Children on Books."

*   *   *

   Savage Gold, written for Roy Fuller's son, is the story of two lads who find themselves
caught up in a clash of interests between rival mining corporations in East Africa. It is well
told, its setting is an attractive one, the action comes at a fast and exciting pace, but in the end
Fuller's literariness leaves doubts as to whether his talents are really suitable for the writing
of junior fiction. These misgivings are reinforced by *With My Little Eye*, a boy's detective
novel which examines the effects of a court-room murder on the mind of an exceptionally
intellectual and literate adolescent, Frederick French, only son of a County Court judge, and
which follows his peripatetic efforts to hunt down the killer.
   French bears an undoubted resemblance to Michael Innes' erudite sleuth John Appleby –
he finds his first clue in Sir Walter Scott's *The Black Dwarf* – and in general *With My Little
Eye* contains the same bizarre mixture of intellectual cerebration and outlandish adventures
that characterize the early Innes detective novels. But in all seriousness we can only conclude
that Fuller sadly misdirected his inventiveness; even in 1948 the market for this type of story,
aimed at that almost indefinable range of reader between twelve and seventeen, could not
have been very large, and although the book attracted much praise from the critics, it is
difficult to believe it held much interest for that age group. Take this passage, for example,
which comes from a discussion between father and son:

> Well, on the highest level I think that the hunt for a murderer – fictional or in real
> life – satisfied a moral longing. It is all part of a revolution of our time. We – my
> generation – have no general and dogmatic views about right and wrong. And yet
> we want good to be rewarded and evil punished. Murder is a happening which
> usually is quite unarguably evil even from our disillusioned viewpoint. And so in
> that little limited sphere we have a disproportionate interest. On a lower level, of

course, the pursuit of a murderer has the interest of a puzzle. But if you go on to ask me why men are fascinated by puzzles, I am afraid I cannot answer you.

Few teenage readers, either then or now, will surely continue for very long to read even a detective novel if it stops the action to moralize in this fashion especially when the son, whose speach it is, and who also tells the story in the first person, is demonstrably in today's terms an unashamed, unrepentent elitist in his language and attitude.

Catspaw belongs to the verges of science-fiction: Victoria, a little girl, wanders into a country inhabited solely by dogs who somewhat improbably are living in constant fear of Pussia the land of the cats. A clever parable about the cold war, the whole ghastly twilight world of espionage, intelligence, and security is mirrored there in fantasy, but again the message is wasted on the wrong audience.

—Alan Edwin Day

FYLEMAN, Rose (Amy). British. Born in Basford, Nottinghamshire, 6 March 1877. Educated at University College, Nottingham; Royal College of Music, London, diploma; studied singing in Germany and Paris. Singer: first public performance, Queen's Hall, London, 1903. Teacher and lecturer; regular contributor to *Punch*, London; Founding Editor, *Merry-Go-Round* children's magazine, 1923–24. *Died 1 August 1957.*

PUBLICATIONS FOR CHILDREN

Fiction

> *The Rainbow Cat and Other Stories*, illustrated by Thelma Cudlipp Grosvenor. London, Methuen, 1922; New York, Doran, 1923.
> *Forty Good-Night Tales*, illustrated by Thelma Cudlipp Grosvenor. London, Methuen, 1923; New York, Doran, 1924.
> *The Adventure Club*, illustrated by A.H. Watson. London, Methuen, 1925; New York, Doran, 1926.
> *Letty: A Study of a Child*, illustrated by L. Hummel. London, Methuen, 1926; New York, Doran, 1927.
> *Forty Good-Morning Tales*. London, Methuen, 1926; New York, Doran, 1929.
> *Twenty Teatime Tales*. London, Methuen, 1929; as *Tea Time Tales*, New York, Doubleday, 1930.
> *The Dolls' House*, illustrated by Margaret Tempest. London, Methuen, 1930; New York, Doubleday, 1931.
> *The Katy Kruse Play Book*, illustrated by Katy Kruse. London, Harrap, and Philadelphia, McKay, 1930.
> *The Strange Adventures of Captain Marwhopple*, illustrated by Gertrude Lindsay. London, Methuen, 1931; New York, Doubleday, 1932.
> *The Easter Hare and Other Stories*, illustrated by Decie Merwin. London, Methuen, 1932.
> *Jeremy Quince, Lord Mayor of London*, illustrated by Cecil Leslie. London, Cape, 1933.
> *The Princess Dances*, illustrated by Cecil Leslie. Lond, Dent, 1933.
> *Timothy's Conjuror*. London, Methuen, 1942.
> *The Timothy Boy Trust*, illustrated by Marjorie Wratten. London, Methuen, 1944.
> *Hob and Bob: A Tale of Two Goblins*, illustrated by Charles Stewart. London, Hollis and Carter, 1944.

Adventures with Benghazi, illustrated by Peggy Fortnum. London, Eyre and Spottiswoode, 1946.
The Smith Family, Books 4–6. Leeds, E.J. Arnold, 3 vols., 1947.
Nursery Stories. London, Evans, 1949.
Lucy the Lamb. London, Eyre and Spottiswoode, 1951.
Neddy the Donkey. London, Eyre and Spottiswoode, 1951.
The Sparrow and the Goat. London, Eyre and Spottiswoode, 1951.
The Starling and the Fox. London, Eyre and Spottiswoode, 1951.
White Flower, illustrated by M.E. Stewart. Leeds, E.J. Arnold, 1953.

Plays

Eight Little Plays for Children (includes *Darby and Joan, The Fairy Riddle, Noughts and Crosses, The Weather Clerk, The Fairy and the Doll, Cabbages and Kings, In Arcady, Father Christmas*). London, Methuen, 1924; New York, Doran, 1925.
Seven Little Plays for Children (includes *The Princess and the Pirate; The Butcher, The Baker, The Candlestickmaker; The Mermaid; Peter Coffin; The Arm-Chair; Mother Goose's Party; The Coming of Father Christmas*). London, Methuen, 1928.
Happy Families: A Comic Opera, music by Thomas F. Dunhill. London, Methuen, 1933.
Nine New Plays for Children (includes *The Whisker; The Moon; Cinderella "At Home"; The Sampler; Three Naughty Imps; Surprise, The Imp; The Test; Sleeping Beauty; Father Christmas Comes to Supper*), illustrated by Eleanor L. Halsey. London and New York, Nelson, 1934.
Six Longer Plays for Children (includes *Snow-White, Porridge, Pork-Pie Night, The Bear, The Gus-Plug, The Angry Brownies*), illustrated by Eleanor L. Halsey. London, Nelson, 1936.
The Magic Pencil and Other Plays from My Tales (includes *The Carpet of Truth, Captain Marwhopple, The Rhyming Prince, The Chestnut Man, The Three Princesses, Troodle, A Legend of St. Nicholas*). London, Methuen, 1938.
The Spanish Cloak. London, Methuen, 1939.
Red-Riding-Hood, music by Will Grant. London, Oxford University Press, 1949.

Verse

The Sunny Book, illustrated by Millicent Sowerby. London, Oxford University Press, 1918.
Fairies and Chimneys. London, Methuen, 1918; New York, Doran, 1920.
The Fairy Green. London, Methuen, 1919; New York, Doran, 1923.
The Fairy Flute. London, Methuen, 1921; New York, Doran, 1923.
A Small Cruse, illustrated by Katy Kruse. London, Methuen, 1923.
The Rose Fyleman Fairy Book. London, Methuen, and New York, Doran, 1923.
Fairies and Friends. London, Methuen, 1925; New York, Doran, 1926.
The Rose Fyleman Calendar, illustrated by L. Hummel. London, Methuen, 1927.
The Katy Kruse Dolly Book, illustrated by Katy Kruse. London, Harrap, and New York, Doran, 1927.
Joy Street Poems, with others. Oxford, Blackwell, 1927.
A Princess Comes to Our Town, illustrated by Gertrude Lindsay. London, Methuen, 1927; New York, Doubleday, 1928.
Old-Fashioned Girls and Other Poems, illustrated by Ethel Everett. London, Methuen, 1928.
A Garland of Rose's: Collected Poems of Rose Fyleman, illustrated by René Bull. London, Methuen, 1928.

Gay Go Up, illustrated by Decie Merwin. London, Methuen, 1929; New York, Doubleday, 1930.

Fifty-One New Nursery Rhymes, illustrated by Dorothy Burroughes. London, Methuen, 1931; New York, Doubleday, 1932.

The Blue Rhyme Book, music by T.F. Dunhill, illustrated by M. Bantock. London, Boosey-Methuen, 1933.

Number Rhymes. Leeds, E.J. Arnold, 1946.

Rhyme Book for Adam. London, Methuen, 1949.

Other

A Little Christmas Book, illustrated by L. Hummel. London, Methuen, 1926; New York, Doran, 1927.

The Second Katy Kruse Dolly Book, illustrated by Katy Kruse. London, Harrap, 1930.

Hey! Ding-a-Ding. London, University of London, 1931.

The Rose Fyleman Birthday Book, illustrated by Muriel Dawson and Margaret Tarrant. London, Medici Society, 1932.

Bears, illustrated by Stuart Tresilian. London and New York, Nelson, 1935.

Monkeys. London and New York, Nelson, 1936.

Billy Monkey: A True Tale of a Capuchin, with E.M.D. Wilson, illustrated by Cecil Leslie. London, Nelson, 1936; New York, Nelson, 1937.

A Book of Saints: Joan of Arc to St. Nicholas, illustrated by Gertrude Mittelman. London, Methuen, 1939.

Folk-Tales from Many Lands. London, Methuen, 1939.

Daphne and Dick (An Uncle from Canada, Round and About, Adventures), illustrated by Jeannetta Vise. London, Macdonald, 3 vols., 1952.

Editor, *Round the Mulberry Bush, Being a Book of Stories and Verse for Children*. London, Partridge, and New York, Dodd Mead, 1928.

Editor, *Sugar and Spice: A Collection of Nursery Rhymes, New and Old*, illustrated by Janet Laura Scott. Racine, Wisconsin, Whitman, 1935.

Editor, *Here We Come A'Piping* (verse), illustrated by Irene Mountfort. Oxford, Blackwell, 1936; New York, Stokes, 1937.

Editor, *A'Piping Again* (verse), illustrated by Irene Mountfort. Oxford, Blackwell, 1936; New York, Stokes, 1938.

Editor, *Bells Ringing: An Anthology of Verse for Young Children*, illustrated by Irene Mountfort. Oxford, Blackwell, 1938; New York, Stokes, 1939.

Editor, *Pipe and Drum: An Anthology of Verse for Young Children*, illustrated by Irene Mountfort. Oxford, Blackwell, 1939; New York, Stokes, 1940.

Editor, *Let's Play*. London, Grout, 1943.

Editor, *Punch and Judy*, illustrated by Paul Henning. London, Methuen, 1944.

Editor, *Over the Tree Tops: Nursery Rhymes from Many Lands*. Oxford, Blackwell, 1949.

Translator, *Bibi*, by Karin Michaelis, illustrated by Hedvig Collin. London, Allen and Unwin, 1933.

Translator, *Bibi Goes Travelling*, by Karin Michaelis, illustrated by Hedvig Collin. London, Allen and Unwin, 1934.

Translator, *Widdy-Widdy-Wurkey: Nursery Rhymes from Many Lands*, illustrated by Valerie Carrick. Oxford, Blackwell, 1934; as *Picture Rhymes from Foreign Lands*, New York, Stokes, 1935; as *Nursery Rhymes from Many Lands*, New York, Dover, 1971.

Translator, *Green Island*, by Karin Michaelis, illustrated by Hedvig Collin. London, Allen and Unwin, 1936.

Translator, *Père Castor's Wild Animal Books (Bourru, The Brown Bear; Frou, The Hare; Mischief, The Squirrel; Plouf, The Wild Duck; Scaf, The Seal; Quipic, The Hedgehog; Martin, The Kingfisher; Cuckoo)*, by Lida, illustrated by Rojan. London, Allen and Unwin, 8 vols., 1937–42.

Translator, *Fireflies*, by Jan Karafiat, illustrated by Emil Weiss. London, Allen and Unwin, 1942.

Translator, *Tuck, The Story of a Snow Hare*, by Alfred Flueckiger, illustrated by Grace Huxtable. London, Lane, 1949.

Translator, *Simone and the Lilywhites*, by Marie-Louise Ventteclaye. London, Museum Press, 1949.

Translator, *The Adventures of Tommy, The Cat Who Went to Sea*, by Lillian Miozzi, illustrated by Charlotte Hough. London, Lane, 1950.

Translator, *Peter and His Friend Toby*, by Lily Martini, illustrated by Wolfgang Felten. London, Lane, 1955.

PUBLICATIONS FOR ADULTS

Play

After All. London, Methuen, 1939.

Other

Translator, *Songs.* London, Curwen, 1927.

*   *   *

Rose Fyleman is one of the people responsible for the modern tiny fairy, as distinct from the Elizabethan kind like Puck, who were full-sized, often grotesque and capable of metamorphosis. Her first poem, "There are fairies at the bottom of my garden," established for all time the tiny flower-fairies, dainty, gossamer-winged and glamorous, wearing crowns and gaily-coloured dresses. Yet they live in surroundings familiar to her young readers, as in the poem called "The Fairy House," where a little girl discovers a tiny house with

> Teeny weeny carpets
> On shiny polished floors
> Teeny weeny handles
> On little painted doors

and the rest of its furnishings to match. Fairies are at the same time wonderful yet understandable.

As a teacher she knew what appealed to little children. Some of the earlier work she produced was adapted from French and German folk tales and poems, and others, though original, have a continental flavour, as in the tale called "The Broom," where the poor crossing-sweeper gets a witch's broom by mistake and becomes rich by hiring it out for journeys, until a scientist rents it to go to the moon and meets its rightful owner.

A skilled musician, she turned many of her poems into songs and indeed composed a children's opera. Though the present taste for magic in fiction tends to be darker and more sinister, there is still a place for Rose Fyleman to give small children their first taste of the supernatural world.

—Ann G. Hay

FYSON, J(enny) G(race).   British.   Born in Bromley, Kent, 3 October 1904. Educated at St. Swithens School, Winchester, 1918–21. Married Christopher Fyson in 1940 (died). Painter, 1921–37, and weaver. Address: c/o Oxford University Press, Walton Street, Oxford OX2 6DP, England.

PUBLICATIONS FOR CHILDREN

Fiction

> *The Three Brothers of Ur*, illustrated by Victor Ambrus.   London, Oxford University Press, 1964; New York, Coward McCann, 1967.
> *The Journey of the Eldest Son*, illustrated by Victor Ambrus.   London, Oxford University Press, 1965; New York, Coward McCann, 1967.

Play

> Radio Play: *Saul and David*, 1952.

J.G. Fyson comments:
   In my two published books I have tried to fill in the background of the time of Abraham from archeological discoveries. The pitfall that one meets in trying to write religious books for children is the snare of becoming a religious propagandist: of manufacturing facts and twisting behaviour to fit a theory. I have tried all the time to let the facts speak for themselves and to make my characters complete human beings, then found they inevitably led me to conclusions unthought of.
   In *The Journey of the Eldest Son* it became clear that there was no way of freeing man from the load of guilt that his imagination has cooked up except by the intervention of the New Testament. As when a man recovers from a neurosis he sees God and is cured.

*   *   *

   Which is the more difficult historical novel to write, one of a period which is fully documented, or one where the documentation is so thin as to be virtually invisible? Jenny Fyson chose the latter and made it seem an easy matter to recreate a 4000 year-old scene. The setting of her two linked novels is Ur of the Chaldees. Here is a sophisticated society, a city-state which has achieved a highly developed form of government, fine crafts and a system of trade. Outside the city walls lies the wilderness where savages threaten the trade routes. The wealth of Teresh the Stern and the welfare of his family depend on the courage of those who will dare the dangers and trade in distant parts.
   The Three Brothers of Ur is largely a family story. Haran the youngest son is a harum-scarum, "that king of all the jackdaws of Ur," as Mushinti the Beautiful puts it neatly. His flair for mischief is the motive-force of much of the story. The malice of Maychor, the middle son, also plays a part. Shamashazir is above mischief and malice. As the elder son he is head of the house when Teresh is away; moreover he needs to have his father's agreement to travel on the next trade journey. But father will give no permission without a favourable sign from the Teraphim, the household god. Haran manages to break the Teraphim, but Shamashazir receives messages from someone greater than a clay image, a voice coming out of the White Mountains.
   In *The Journey of the Eldest Son* Shamashazir takes the trail over the mountains and is able to test both his courage and endurance and the relative power of the gods of the tribes he

meets. He also meets the Lord of All the Earth and realizes the source of the voice which he had heard from the mountains.

The advent of monotheism seems an unlikely theme on which to base two stories for children. In Jenny Fyson's hands adventure and character and philosophy become one. Many readers who delight in the fun and the excitement remain unaware that in another Book Shamashazir is called Abraham, and that they are reading the story of a great turning-point in history. It is not important. No reader can be unaware that on his adventurous journey Shamashazir discovers a great truth, even if the nature of that truth remains hidden for a time. These are not the only children's books whose true meaning is understood only in adult life.

—Marcus Crouch

GAG, Wanda (Hazel). American. Born in New Ulm, Minnesota, 11 March 1893. Educated at New Ulm High School, graduated, 1912; St. Paul Art School, 1913–14; Minneapolis Art School, 1914–17; Art Students' League, New York, 1917–18. Married Earle Marshall Humphreys in 1931. Schoolteacher, 1912–13; commercial artist, 1918–23. One-man shows: New York Public Library, 1923; Weyhe Gallery, New York 1926, 1930, 1940 (retrospective); group shows: Museum of Modern Art, New York, 1939; Metropolitan Museum, New York, 1943. Recipient: University of Minnesota Kerlan Award, 1977. *Died 27 June 1946.*

PUBLICATIONS FOR CHILDREN (illustrated by the author)

Fiction

> *Millions of Cats.*   New York, Coward McCann, 1928; London, Faber, 1929.
> *The Funny Thing.*   New York, Coward McCann, 1929; London, Faber, 1962.
> *Snippy and Snappy.*   New York, Coward McCann, 1931; London, Faber, 1932.
> *The ABC Bunny.*   New York, Coward McCann, 1933; London, Faber, 1962.
> *Nothing at All.*   New York, Coward McCann, 1941; London, Faber, 1942.

Other

> *Gone Is Gone; or, The Story of a Man Who Wanted to Do Housework.*   New York, Coward McCann, 1935; London, Faber, 1936.
> *Tales from Grimm.*   New York, Coward McCann, 1936; London, Faber, 1937.
> *Snow-White and the Seven Dwarfs.*   New York, Coward McCann, and London, Faber, 1938.
> *Three Gay Tales from Grimm.*   New York, Coward McCann, 1943; London, Heinemann, 1946.
> *More Tales from Grimm.*   New York, Coward McCann, 1947; London, Faber, 1962.

PUBLICATIONS FOR ADULTS

Other

> *Growing Pains: Diaries and Drawings for the Years 1908–1917.*   New York, Coward McCann, 1940.

Manuscript Collection: Kerlan Collection, University of Minnesota, Minneapolis.

Critical Study: *Wanda Gág: The Story of an Artist* by Alma Scott, Minneapolis, University of Minnesota Press, 1949.

Illustrator: *The Day of Doom* by Michael Wigglesworth, 1929.

*   *   *

Wanda Gág created 10 children's books in 13 years, interspersing those of her own imagination told succinctly in the style of folklore with "freely translated" editions from the Brothers Grimm *Märchen.* Her material was thoroughly steeped in a Bohemian transplant in America's Midwest, New Ulm, and yet was stamped with her individuality.

Millions of Cats was her first published book, and critics consistently state that it was her greatest literary achievement. The story had been told to youngsters in Connecticut, rescued from her "reject bin" and submitted for publication. The little old man searched for a cat to please his wife and offset their loneliness. The refrain, "Hundreds of cats, thousands of cats, millions, and billions, and trillions of cats," echoes throughout the book. The book was heralded on publication with such positive commendations as Anne Carroll Moore's statement in *The New York Herald Tribune Book Section* (9 September 1928), "It bears all the earmarks of becoming a perennial favorite among children and takes a place of its own, both for the originality and strength of its pictures and the living folktale quality of its text." Wanda Gág's editor, Ernestine Evans, wrote in *Nation* (21 November 1928),

> *Millions of Cats* is as important as the librarians say it is. Not only does it bring to book-making one of the most talented and original of American lithographers, an artist who has a following both here and abroad, but it is a marriage of picture and tale that is perfectly balanced. And the story pattern, so cunningly devised with such hearty and moral simplicity, is told in a prose as skilful as jingle.

Four imaginative books followed the book about cats, with a dragon, mice, rabbit and dogs as the central characters respectively. *The Funny Thing* is the story of Bobo's rescuing dolls from the dragon who craved them, but was satisfied with a substitution of "Jum-jills." It too had a pre-publication history of having been retold innumerable times to young friends until it was perfect. Reviewers considered the book "highly individual" and possessed of a "curious grotesque charm."

Snippy and Snappy is the story of two mice who seek cheese and adventure, and are ultimately rescued by their parents. The repetitive pattern, "We rolled it up, we rolled it down, We followed it over this and that" is less striking than in the author's first book. A review by Anne T. Eaton noted, "There is a feeling of drama in the story that pleases children, and it reads aloud well, for the author's very simple prose has distinction and style" (*New York Times*, 1 November 1931). Rachel Field wrote in *Saturday Review of Literature* (14 November 1931), "The story, too, is simply and gaily written, for fun and not for information, although it has an excellent moral about meddling."

The ABC Bunny, unlike most alphabet books, has a story line. "A for Apple, big and Red, B for Bunny snug-a-bed, C for Crash, D for Dash, E for Elsewhere in a Flash" spurs the consecutive action. The rabbit wanders, meeting animals with various alphabetical designations until its arrival in Bunnytown with a "We Welcome You" sign. Wanda's brother, Howard, lettered the text of this book as he had for her other imaginative books with the exception of *Gone Is Gone*. Alice Dalgliesh, in *Saturday Review of Literature* (18 November 1933), chose this as the best book of the year, and added, "Wanda Gág has a feeling for the rightness of words that no other maker of picture books can approach" with her "clever rhyming couplets full of pleasant words." Anne Carroll Moore (in *Books*, 12 November 1933) wrote, "No animal has suffered more from commercialized treatment in books and toys than the rabbit, and in restoring him to his place in nature, Wanda Gág has made a rich contribution to childhood in a spacious and timely picture book." *Nothing at All* was the last imaginative book from Wanda Gág's pen. The invisible dog "Whirled and twirled and swirled" at sunrise and repeated, "I'm busy Getting dizzy," and gradually acquired spots and a complete image.

Of the retellings of folktales, four of the five are directly from Grimm. The exception is the first one published, *Gone Is Gone*. In the text on the book jacket, the author explained that her childhood favorite was about a peasant who wanted to do housework, but in her searching she discovered that it was not recorded by the Brothers Grimm. "I decided to make a little book of the story, consulting no other sources except one – my own memory of how the tale was told to me when I was a little girl." She dedicated the book "To my peasant ancestors." The husband and wife exchange daily tasks, and Fritzl admits that his work is no more difficult than Liesi's.

The other folktales are "freely translated," according to the title pages. Her concern for social and political issues of the day is reflected in the selection of the tales, just as *Gone Is Gone* was an expression of her regard for women's liberation. When Walt Disney's cartoon version of *Snow White and the Seven Dwarfs* was released in 1937, Wanda Gág set out immediately to combat the erroneous image in the minds of children.

Wanda Gág considered folklore of importance, for she had been nurtured on the "Old World customs, songs and folklore" in New Ulm, Minnesota. In an essay entitled, "I Like Fairy Tales" (*Horn Book*, March–April 1939), she wrote:

> I know I should now feel bitterly cheated if, as a child, I had been deprived of all fairy lore; and it does not seem to me that we have the right to deprive any child of its rightful heritage of Fairyland. In fact, I believe it is *just* the modern children who need it, since their lives are already overbalanced on the side of steel and stone and machinery – and nowadays, one might well add, bombs, gas-masks and machine guns.

Growing Pains: Diaries and Drawings for the Years 1908–1917 reveals the candid yearnings and accomplishments of Wanda Gág from her 15th to 24th year. The book also serves as a treasure-house of information about the Midwest in the early 20th century. Her convictions about individuality and society are expressed here in a format different from, but consistent with, the picture books. The importance of music and stories in her young life is understandably expressed in the rhythm, rhyme, and repetition of her books for children. One better understands why the vain cats quarreled to death in *Millions of Cats*, why *The Funny Thing* could be cajoled, and why the invisible orphan dog in *Nothing at All* had a plan.

Wanda Gág was much respected in literary and library circles. Anne Carroll Moore, supervisor of work with children at the New York Public Library, admired and encouraged her. The May–June 1947 issue of *The Horn Book* was published "In Tribute to Wanda Gág." *Millions of Cats* was selected as a Newbery Award Honor Book, while *The ABC Bunny*, *Nothing at All* and *Snow White and the Seven Dwarfs* were runners-up to the Caldecott Award. The Kerlan Award 1977 was given to Wanda Gág posthumously, signed by the President of the University of Minnesota for "distinguished contribution to children's literature" and for inspiring "generous donation" to the Children's Literature Research Collections.

—Karen Nelson Hoyle

GANNETT, Ruth Stiles. American. Born in New York City, 12 August 1923. Educated at City and Country School; George School, Pennsylvania; Vassar College, Poughkeepsie, New York, B.A. 1944. Married Peter Kahn in 1947; has seven children. Medical technician, Boston City Hospital; radar research technician, Massachusetts Institute of Technology,

Cambridge; staff member, Children's Book Council, New York. Recipient: New York *Herald Tribune* Festival award, 1948. Address: Route 227, Trumansburg, New York 14886, U.S.A.

PUBLICATIONS FOR CHILDREN

Fiction

> *My Father's Dragon*, illustrated by Ruth Chrisman Gannett. New York, Random House, 1948; London, Macmillan, 1957.
> *The Wonderful House-Boat-Train*, illustrated by Fritz Eichenberg. New York, Random House, 1949.
> *Elmer and the Dragon*, illustrated by Ruth Chrisman Gannet. New York, Random House, 1950.
> *The Dragons of Blueland*, illustrated by Ruth Chrisman Gannett. New York, Random House, 1951.
> *Katie and the Sad Noise*, illustrated by Ellie Simmons. New York, Random House, 1961.

*   *   *

In her trilogy (*My Father's Dragon, Elmer and the Dragon, The Dragons of Blueland*), Ruth Stiles Gannett sets her pace with verve and freshness, with a childlike matter-of-factness, and an inherent logic. Her use of the fantastic reflects a sensitivity for the imagination of young children. So skillfully does she develop Elmer Elevator that the incredible becomes credible without strain. In *My Father's Dragon* her understanding of what little boys are like, especially Elmer, is apparent. The reader accepts, without question, Elmer's decision to make the journey to Wild Island to free the baby dragon. Unafraid of words, Gannett selects exactly the right ones for her tale. Clearly American in spirit, her language takes on universality.

Elmer and the Dragon continues naturally Elmer's high adventure. The humor and the nonsense are typical of the imaginative world of any child. She offers details that indicate an intuitive understanding of a child's curiosity. Whether it is food or history or even the contents of a treasure chest, everything is described with relish.

The Dragons of Blueland brings to an end Elmer's adventures as he sets out with Boris, the baby dragon, to rescue Boris' family entrapped in a cave. Although the humor and excitement are not so well sustained as in the two earlier books, this is a finale for a saga that reflects completely the child's world. One is reminded of the world of Christopher Robin. There is the same kind of naturalness, believability, and whimsey.

The author's mother, Ruth Chrisman Gannett, has illustrated the books. Her work interprets the text perfectly; they complement the text so that there is not only reading but visual pleasure.

The Wonderful House-Boat-Train, the search of Pops Pops, the retired railroad engineer, and his four grandchildren for a home, is more deliberate and lacks the quality that is associated with a natural, creative flow. *Katie and the Sad Noise* appears to be a book for the beginning reader. Katie hears strange noises and tells her parents of them. Their concern leads to a consultation with Katie's teachers. One situation follows another, building up a sense of mystery. The resolution is neatly presented, and ends with a Christmas surprise, but the complexity of plot tends to throw off course the simplicity of text.

Ruth Stiles Gannett will be remembered for her singular approach to creativity. Children, hearing or reading the Elmer Elevator books, can say, "Of course!" The cultivated adult will recognize the touch of the real storyteller who has accomplished what she has set out to do – to tell her tales with grace, childlike humor, and literary style.

—Mae Durham Roger

GARD, Joyce. Pseudonym for Joyce Reeves. British. Born in London, 13 January 1911. Educated at Wycombe Abbey School, Buckinghamshire, 1924–29; Lady Margaret Hall, Oxford, 1930–33, B.A. (honours) in English 1933. Assistant, Foreign Rights Department, Curtis Brown Ltd., London, 1934–35; teacher, Varndean School for Girls, Brighton, 1935–37; lived in Paris, 1937–39; temporary administrative assistant, Ministry of Economic Warfare, London, 1939–45; civil servant, Frankfurt and Hamburg, 1945–47; apprentice, Winchcombe Pottery, Gloucestershire, 1947–48; studio potter, London and Newhaven, Sussex, 1948–56; part-time private secretary and research assistant to Roland Penrose, Institute of Contemporary Arts, London, 1956–72. Translator and contributor, *XX Siècle* art review, Paris, 1939–70. Address: Wrens Cottage, Charing Heath, Ashford, Kent TN27 0AU, England.

PUBLICATIONS FOR CHILDREN

Fiction

Woorroo, illustrated by Ronald Benham.   London, Gollancz, 1961.
The Dragon of the Hill.   London, Gollancz, 1963.
Talargain, The Seal's Whelp.   London, Gollancz, 1964; New York, Holt Rinehart, 1965.
Smudge of the Fells.   London, Gollancz, 1965; New York, Holt Rinehart, 1966.
The Snow Firing.   London, Gollancz, 1967; New York, Holt Rinehart, 1968.
The Mermaid's Daughter.   London, Gollancz, and New York, Holt Rinehart, 1969.
Handysides Shall Not Fall, illustrated by Carolyn Dinan.   London, Kaye and Ward, 1975.
The Hagwaste Donkeys, illustrated by Gareth Floyd.   London, Pelham, 1976.

Other

Translator, *Journey to the Centre of the Earth*, by Jules Verne, illustrated by Dick Hart.   London, Hutchinson, 1961.
Translator (as Joyce Reeves), *Marc Chagall: Drawings and Water Colors for the Ballet*, by Jacques Lassaigne.   Paris, XX Siècle, and New York, Tudor, 1969.

Joyce Gard comments:
The only way I can write for children is to write for myself as a child – to become a child again, the person I was and still essentially am.

My books are not easy to introduce or categorize briefly. However, I think the basic essentials of any children's fiction, which I have tried to provide, are: 1) a good story, 2) good writing, 3) credible, interesting people, not too complex, 4) a sound setting – an individual and distinctive *place*, and 5) something *extra*.

This "extra" could be an unusual insight into a particular way of life, for instance, or a special magic or mystery. In my first children's books I attempted to recapture the ecstasy of pure physical sensation which only children, I believe, can experience unmixed: either imagined – flying like a bird in *Woorroo* – or real – ocean-swimming in *Talargain*, here enhanced by communion with the seals.

I explored other childhood dreams and obsessions, such as finding buried treasure, confronting dragons, entering into the lives of beautiful people of the past – *The Dragon of the Hill* and *Talargain*.

Then I turned to practical lives I would have liked to live – a sheep farmer in the Lake District in *Smudge of the Fells* – or had myself lived – a studio potter in *The Snow Firing*. There is as much technical know-how in these two books as I could squeeze in without, I hope, giving up the first requisite of a good story.

The Mermaid's Daughter is for an older age-group; it is the story of a girl growing up in the Scilly Isles in Roman times and her adventures as she strives to reconcile her two roles – that of the chosen mortal embodiment of the Sea Goddess of the islands and of a flesh-and-blood human being and her relationships with family and lovers, friends and enemies.

I don't believe in an explicit "message"; in my experience this causes an automatic switch-off of interest in a healthy child. I believe strongly, however, that worthwhile fiction is a power for good by feeding the imagination, as Shelley claimed for poetry.

*   *   *

Joyce Gard writes for children prepared to savour a book rather than romp through it for the sake of the story. Her novels are strongly rooted in place – the English Lakes, Gloucestershire, the Scillies – often luminously evoked. In each the author explores one of her many interests, which include pottery, sheep-farming, and archaeology, and these are the real focus of the story. Though they may begin with exciting action, such as the memorable horror and beauty of the dragon's flight, successive events move more slowly and are sometimes impeded by a straight recapitulation of events that the reader has not shared. The characters also are usually subordinate to the theme or plot, perfectly satisfactory for their purpose but not explored in any great depth and not much changed or developed by the things that happen to them. Miss Gard's best gift is that of sensory perception. *Woorroo* shares the wild joy and freedom of winged flight, *Talargain* the physical sensation, the delight and fear, of swimming with the seals, and the boy's relationship with them. In *The Snow Firing* one can feel the smooth wet clay and the warmly sensuous beauty of the finished pots.

The stories intended for younger readers will appeal only to a limited audience of rather sheltered children. But in the present spate of books for the mass there may still be a need for a few for minority groups.

It is in the novels dealing with the past that the writer shows her real quality. *The Dragon of the Hill*, *Talargain*, and *The Mermaid's Daughter* are all wholly or partly set in the period of Roman Britain. The life and manners of the time are handled convincingly and lightly; the reader can share in them without feeling burdened by conscientious social history. Gard is particularly interested in ancient cults and can identify herself imaginatively with the religious feeling of other times and countries. Woorroo's aboriginal magic, as he chants and paints in the dawn at the edge of the lake, is one of the most memorable moments in the novel. *The Mermaid's Daughter*, by far her most ambitious and successful book, attempts to recreate the cult of the Great Mother, the Sea Goddess, as it may once have existed in the Scilly Islands. The heroine, Astria, is the secret representative of the goddess among her people. The story moves between the islands and the Roman fortress at Caerleon, both vividly evoked. It develops slowly despite times of excitement, of romantic love and tragedy, but it immerses the reader completely in its own world. Individual episodes remain most vividly in the mind – the ritual marriage in the dark cave by the sea, Astria dancing on the bright spring grass beyond Caerleon, watched by the wild, shy hill people, the meeting with St. Alban in the Roman garrison. But above all one is haunted by the images of sea and sky and flowers, a sense of grace and light. This is a book of unusual quality.

—Margaret Greaves

GARDAM, Jane. British. Born in Coatham, Yorkshire, 11 July 1928. Educated at Bedford College, London University, B.A. (honours) 1949. Married David Gardam in 1952; has two sons and one daughter. Sub-editor, *Weldons Ladies Journal*, London, 1952–53; assistant literary editor, *Time and Tide*, London, 1953–55. Recipient: David Higham Prize, for fiction, 1975; Winifred Holtby Memorial Prize, for fiction, 1976. Fellow, Royal Society of Literature, 1976. Address: 53 Ridgeway Place, London SW19 4SP; or, Fell House, Hartley Kirk-by-Stephen, Westmorland, England.

PUBLICATIONS FOR CHILDREN

Fiction

> *A Few Fair Days*, illustrated by Peggy Fortnum. London, Hamish Hamilton, 1971; New York, Macmillan, 1972.
> *A Long Way from Verona*. London, Hamish Hamilton, and New York, Macmillan, 1971.
> *The Summer after the Funeral*. London, Hamish Hamilton, and New York, Macmillan, 1973.
> *Bilgewater*. London, Hamish Hamilton, 1976; New York, Morrow, 1977.

PUBLICATIONS FOR ADULTS

Novel

> *Black Faces, White Faces*. London, Hamish Hamilton, 1975; as *The Pineapple Bay Hotel*, New York, Morrow, 1976.

*   *   *

Judged by the standards that apply to more prolific writers, Jane Gardam's reputation rests on a small distinctive output to date, but there is every sign of a maturing major talent. The predominant outer landscape of her narratives is the northeast coast of England; the inner topography is the scarcely charted jungle of the feelings and self-regard of middle childhood and adolescence.

The crossing of early social, educational and sexual experience with adult expectations provides Mrs. Gardam with episodes that are sad and comic in turn. The world in which her heroines move most easily is peopled by the mildly eccentric middle-class who contain their problems by a pattern of life which, on the surface at least, is like their clothes, well-worn and familiar. The adults are innocents of the dangerous kind, well-intentioned and unperceiving. Wisdom, as in Ivy Compton-Burnett's books, is the privilege of the underlings and the extrovert children. All of the books deal with a chrysalis period in the life of the protagonists, the moment when girls face themselves, view their prospects painfully, and wish life were like literature. Each heroine has a literary counterpart, in character and prose style. Athene Price (in *The Summer after the Funeral*) is beautiful and admired, but inside all is turmoil, and she sees herself as a reincarnation of Emily Brontë. Marigold ("Bilgewater") Green is obsessed by her plump ugliness and tries to make an equation of James Joyce and Thomas Hardy. As a result there is a mild self-indulgent elitism about the writing, and the adult critic may be looking back with all too much sympathy to this kind of adolescence. But the wit of expression and the humour of situation save the books from any suggestion of post-Freudian intensity. The younger reader grows in literary awareness by virtue of a bond with an author who shows rather than tells.

A proper critical appreciation of Jane Gardam depends on an analysis of the words on the page, their pace and poise, the juxtaposition of styles – the use of the epistolary form, for example – and rhetorical variety. Sometimes the story reads like memory, sometimes it is a diary. But with Jane Gardam the story for girls moves into another phase where the inner weather of adolescence is serious and funny at once, and the adults no more help than ever.

—Margaret Meek

GARFIELD, Leon. British. Born in Brighton, Sussex 14 July 1921. Educated at grammar school, Brighton. Served in the Medical Corps, British Army, 1940–46. Married Vivien Dolores Alcock in 1948; has one daughter. Biochemical technician, Whittington Hospital, London, 1946–66. Recipient: *Guardian* Award, 1967; Library Association Carnegie Medal, 1971. Agent: Winant, Towers Ltd., 14 Cliffords Inn, London EC4A 1DA; or, Monica McCall, International Creative Management, 40 West 57th Street, New York, New York 10019, U.S.A. Address: 59 Wood Lane, London N.6, England.

PUBLICATIONS FOR CHILDREN

Fiction

Jack Holborn, illustrated by Antony Maitland.   London, Constable, 1964; New York, Pantheon Books, 1965.

Devil-in-the-Fog, illustrated by Antony Maitland.   London, Constable, and New York, Pantheon Books, 1966.

Smith, illustrated by Antony Maitland.   London, Constable, and New York, Pantheon Books, 1967.

Black Jack, illustrated by Antony Maitland.   London, Longman, 1968; New York, Pantheon Books, 1969.

Mister Corbett's Ghost, illustrated by Alan E. Cober.   New York, Pantheon Books, 1968.

Mr. Corbett's Ghost and Other Stories, illustrated by Antony Maitland.   London, Longman, 1969.

The Drummer Boy, illustrated by Antony Maitland.   New York, Pantheon Books, 1969; London, Longman, 1970.

The Restless Ghost: Three Stories, illustrated by Saul Lambert.   New York, Pantheon Books, 1969.

The Boy and the Monkey, illustrated by Trevor Ridley.   London, Heinemann, 1969; New York, Watts, 1970.

The Strange Affair of Adelaide Harris, illustrated by Fritz Wegner.   London, Longman, and New York, Pantheon Books, 1971.

The Captain's Watch, illustrated by Trevor Ridley.   London, Heinemann, 1972.

The Ghost Downstairs, illustrated by Antony Maitland.   London, Longman, and New York, Pantheon Books, 1972.

Lucifer Wilkins, illustrated by Trevor Ridley.   London, Heinemann, 1973.

The Sound of Coaches, illustrated by John Lawrence.   London, Penguin, and New York, Viking Press, 1974.

The Prisoners of September.   London, Penguin, and New York, Viking Press, 1975.

The Pleasure Garden, illustrated by Fritz Wegner.   London, Penguin, and New York, Viking Press, 1976.

Mirror, Mirror, illustrated by Antony Maitland.   London, Heinemann, 1976.

The Lamplighter's Funeral, illustrated by Antony Maitland.   London, Heinemann, 1976.

The Cloak, illustrated by Faith Jaques.   London, Heinemann, 1976.

Moss and Blister, illustrated by Faith Jaques.   London, Heinemann, 1976.

The Dumb Cake.   London, Heinemann, 1977.

Tom Titmarsh's Devil.   London, Heinemann, 1977.

The Fool.   London, Heinemann, 1977.

Rosy Starling.   London, Heinemann, 1977.

The Valentine, illustrated by Faith Jaques.   London, Heinemann, 1977.

Labour in Vain, illustrated by Faith Jaques.   London, Heinemann, 1977.

An Adelaide Ghost.   London, Ward Lock, 1977.

Other

The God Beneath the Sea, with Edward Blishen, illustrated by Charles
Keeping. London, Longman, 1970; New York, Pantheon Books, 1971.
Child o' War: The True Story of a Boy Sailor in Nelson's Navy, with David Proctor,
illustrated by Antony Maitland. London, Collins, and New York, Holt Rinehart,
1972.
The Golden Shadow, with Edward Blishen, illustrated by Charles Keeping. London,
Longman, and New York, Pantheon Books, 1973.
The House of Hanover: England in the Eighteenth Century. London, Deutsch, and
New York, Seabury Press, 1976.

Editor, Baker's Dozen: A Collection of Stories. London, Ward Lock, 1973; as Strange
Fish and Other Stories, New York, Lothrop, 1974.
Editor, The Book Lovers. London, Ward Lock, 1976.

*   *   *

Since the publication of his first novel, Jack Holborn, a vigorous tale of piracy and
adventure, Leon Garfield has produced a very considerable body of work for young people,
remarkable for its high imaginative quality and individual style. His next few books, like the
first, had 18th-century settings: Devil-in-the-Fog concerned a family of strolling actors, Smith
was the story of a sharp little London pickpocket, Black Jack took its young hero Tolly out
into the country of the same period with a group of travelling fairground folk, and The
Drummer Boy was a powerful anti-war story. With The Strange Affair of Adelaide Harris Mr.
Garfield, moving forward in time to the early 19th century, turned to high comedy. The
Sound of Coaches reflects the everyday lives of people engaged in working the stage-coaches
in their heyday, The Prisoners of September follows the fates of two young men of very
different temperaments at the time of the French Revolution, while in The Pleasure Garden a
young clergyman's love affair becomes entangled with blackmail and murder and the
mysteries of the Garden itself.

Besides these full-length novels Garfield has written short stories, some of them ghost
stories, some tales mingling adventure, romance and comedy in the manner of his novels.
Other short stories are for younger readers, including the series of "Garfield's Apprentices,"
but there is no diminution of imaginative power or the least inclination to write down. The
award-winning The God Beneath the Sea, written in collaboration with Edward Blishen, and
its successor, The Golden Shadow, are not just re-tellings of the Greek myths, but truly
creative works: the first concentrating upon myths of the gods, with Hephaestus as central
figure, and the second on legends of men, taking Heracles as focal point and making a
genuinely sympathetic human figure of one of the less immediately appealing of the Greek
heroes.

Apart from these two books, Garfield's work is usually placed under the heading of
Historical Novels, but it is far from that type of well-meaning book where the background
has been so painstakingly researched as to become all-important. History lies lightly on these
novels. Leon Garfield has certainly done his research, but the background is transmuted so
that we see it as it affects the inner lives of his characters. Now and then he may particularize:
as in The Prisoners of September, where the September Massacres are basic to the ironically
twisting plot, and young Richard Mortimer, full of the revolutionary fervour of the time, is
sadly brought to shabbier dealings and a less heroic end than he could have foreseen. But
more often he does not pinpoint actual time and place, and we feel no need to know the site
and date of the battle in France where the Drummer Boy, Charlie, beat his drum, nor what
duke commanded the army.

Certain important themes recur: notably, that all is not what it seems. In Jack Holborn the
ambiguous and amoral figure of Solomon Trumpet starts as a villain and ends up befriending
the hero. The supposedly wicked uncle in Devil-in-the-Fog turns out more pathetic than

sinister. The terrifying criminal Black Jack becomes the ally of Tolly and his Belle; Charlie not only learns the hollowness of military glory, but finds that the fat army surgeon he despised is right-thinking if unheroic. And Garfield returns to this theme again in *The Pleasure Garden*, where there are many layers of shifting illusion; the reader who, like the Rev. Martin Young, strips them away, can find beyond the ornate and fantastic details of plot and setting a compassionate study of various aspects of human love, not excluding its negation or rejection, and culminating in some beautiful use of quotation from the *Song of Songs*.

With illusion and disillusion so marked as themes, it is not surprising to find an element of the supernatural present too. Explicit if properly mysterious in the ghost stories themselves, it is half-glimpsed and half-felt elsewhere rather than spelt out. It even surfaces briefly in the bright comic world of *Adelaide Harris*, where the old nurse's spell to summon the baby's kidnapper successfully conjures up the enterprising brother who "exposed" her like Romulus and Remus and was subsequently left with the wrong baby – only the success of the spell is lost on all concerned.

In *Adelaide Harris* comedy predominates; it emerges sporadically, or is present in the form of irony, in most of Garfield's other books, and comes to the fore again in *The Prisoners of September*, though intertwined with tragedy this time. Indeed, it is this combination of comedy, high adventure, romance, mystery, and an eye for intriguing detail which is the hallmark of Garfield's rich and individual style. Of his early books, *Jack Holborn* has been described as Stevensonian, some of the others as Dickensian, but these are parallels only; there is nothing derivative. One could in fact continue to find parallels, and say there is a touch of Keats in the two books of Greek tales, with their sense of the numinous pervading nature; or that Thomas Love Peacock would surely have appreciated the posturing of Ralph Bunnion, who considers himself irresistible to women, in *Adelaide Harris*. (One might even find parallels musical as well as literary, and detect a Mozartian balance of tone here and there: it is not hard, for instance, to imagine sensible, pretty Charity of *The Drummer Boy* singing Susanna's music, or her cold counterpart Sophia as a Queen of the Night.) But Garfield's style is really unique; when he strikes notes that momentarily remind us of other notes memorably struck elsewhere, he does it in his own fashion.

For beyond the sheer narrative entertainment of these books – which is very great – there is always a search, conscious or otherwise, on the part of the young heroes for true and lasting values, and this is to be seen through the vivid surface texture of the books. To take just one example: one may trace Garfield's striking use of imagery to describe the sky, from *Jack Holborn*, with its storm cloud "like a great black tiger in the sky ... long tail and a great paw dripping down into the sea," to *The God Beneath the Sea*, where the baby god falls "like a golden needle stitching the heavens," right through to a superb moment at the end of *The Pleasure Garden* where the Cosmic Effect promised by the purveyor of fireworks finally occurs at the end of the dazzling display: "The blackness thinned and beyond, calm and distinct, shone the stars of heaven. Here was an unmasking indeed!" The synthesis of vivid language with the quiet revelation of simplicity beyond the complexities is part of the wide range of Leon Garfield's talent, and may well make classics of his books.

—Anthea Bell

GARNER, Alan. British. Born in Congleton, Cheshire, 17 October 1934. Educated at Alderley Edge Primary School, Wilmslow, Cheshire; Manchester Grammar School; Magdalen College, Oxford. Served in the Royal Artillery: Second Lieutenant. Married Anne Cook in 1956 (marriage dissolved), one son and two daughters; Griselda Greaves, 1972, one son. Recipient: Library Association Carnegie Medal, 1968; *Guardian* Award, 1968. Address: Blackden, Holmes Chapel, Crewe, Staffordshire, England.

PUBLICATIONS FOR CHILDREN

Fiction

The Weirdstone of Brisingamen: A Tale of Alderley. London, Collins, 1960; New
   York, Watts, 1961; revised edition, London, Penguin, 1963; New York, Walck,
   1970.
The Moon of Gomrath. London, Collins, 1963; New York, Walck, 1967.
Elidor, illustrated by Charles Keeping. London, Collins, 1965; New York, Walck,
   1967.
The Old Man of Mow, illustrated by Roger Hill. London, Collins, 1966; New York,
   Doubleday, 1970.
The Owl Service. London, Collins, 1967; New York, Walck, 1968.
Red Shift. London, Collins, and New York, Macmillan, 1973.
The Breadhorse, illustrated by Albin Trowski. London, Collins, 1975.
The Stone Book, illustrated by Michael Foreman. London, Collins, 1976.
Tom Fobble's Day, illustrated by Michael Foreman. London, Collins, 1977.
Granny Reardun, illustrated by Michael Foreman. London, Collins, 1977.

Plays

Holly from the Bongs, music by William Mayne (produced Goostrey, Cheshire,
   1965). London, Evans, 1966; revised version, music by Gordon Crosse (produced
   London, 1974).
Potter Thompson, music by Gordon Crosse (produced London, 1975).

Radio Play: *The Weirdstone of Brisingamen,* from his own story, 1963.

Television Play: *The Owl Service,* from his own story, 1969.

Other

The Guizer: A Book of Fools. London, Hamish Hamilton, 1975; New York, Morrow,
   1976.

Editor, *The Hamish Hamilton Book of Goblins: An Anthology of Folklore,* illustrated by
   Krystyna Turska. London, Hamish Hamilton, 1969; as *A Cavalcade of Goblins,*
   New York, Walck, 1969.

*   *   *

Alan Garner is the *enfant terrible* of contemporary English children's literature. He is an
intensely individual writer whose idiosyncrasies result in books which are few but varied, of
a recognisable tradition yet unique in themselves, seemingly without precedent. Few writers
can so confound the critics and stir up such controversy. It is a characteristic of human nature
to attack what one does not understand, and it is now impossible to guess what each new
Garner book will be like; some critics have abandoned him altogether!
   After a conventional beginning which can be seen as Tolkien-like (*The Weirdstone of
Brisingamen* and *The Moon of Gomrath*) Garner's acceptance was such that he could afford to
start expressing powerful ideas about life and relationships in his own peculiar way, making
his own rules of style as he saw fit. This has perplexed those adults who have preconceived
ideas of what books should be like. An older pre-television generation might have difficulty in
understanding the visual messages carried in a bombardment of the short, sharp shocks of

changing pictures in a film which their grandchildren can understand with ease. Alan Garner's recent books are something of a counterpart to such films, with emphasis on dialogue rather than narrative, with the abrupt tentativeness of ordinary discourse replacing the artificial conventions of literary speeches. With much of the rapid action, ideas, and words being unexplained, the reader is forced to concentrate and participate if he is to share in the experience and to extract meaning.

Alan Garner has said that his stories "have to work for *me*, to say what I want to express. In fact, I must write poetry, making words work on more than one level." For him, the discursive novelist's techniques may be inappropriate, and compact images and ideas now have to work implicitly and by association, thus demanding effort from the reader. *Red Shift* observes none of the usual criteria for excellence in children's books: if anything, it negates them. There are no explanations, not a single character is described, there is almost no narrative, there are no chapter divisions, the "he said"/"she replied" convention has been largely abandoned and the dialogue, on which comprehension depends, is both cryptic and fractured. *Red Shift* is thus more like a film than a poem, in which the realisation must take place in the reader's mind. It demands effort, but the rewards are great; the emotional impact can be considerable for those willing to experience it.

Red Shift contains three stories, which are pursued bit by bit, a small break in the type separating one time shift from another – for they take place in different centuries but in the same location. The people are interchangeable, as are their actions and words. Yet the first change is made abruptly without indication and by the last few pages the text so runs together that the reader cannot say with any certainty where he is at.

Those who find difficulty in extracting meaning from *Red Shift* probably find the peculiar scrambled medium distracting. They miss the essential point that this medium *is* the message, for Garner's over-riding theme, as in *The Owl Service*, is that we are all caught up in a dimension of time, which is only relative. It is not a continuum. *It all exists all at once.* Tom, in *Red Shift* says "We're bits of other futures" and "Nothing I say is original." Just as the relationships and events are repeated (or happen simultaneously) in *Red Shift*, so are Gwyn, Alison and Roger in *The Owl Service* caught in a conflict which has been re-enacted, with variations, century after century. The relentlessness, the irresistible inevitability of events is, thus, a determinist view of human behaviour, and it is one which Garner shares with Thucydides, not over a 2000-year gap but *now*. As Tom says in *Red Shift*, "I see everything at once."

Garner's earlier, simpler books allowed children to slip in and out of local legend, participating in it, sharing in the ancient life of their environment. Whereas the movement is "back" into a co-existing past in *The Weirdstone of Brisingamen* and *The Moon of Gomrath*, the forces of another time and place in *Elidor* also intrude on the Manchester of the present, upsetting television sets and burning out washing machines. Even in miniature works, *The Breadhorse* and *The Stone Book*, we see children experiencing the mystical power of the past; their heritage is a tremendous source of comfort and strength.

It is of interest also to note the sexual tension which gives a nervous edge to *The Owl Service*, constantly present as a powerful force. The receptive reader of *Red Shift* will experience, vicariously, a deal of sexual *activity*, there on the page, albeit implied. Better than most, Garner acknowledges the manifold energies constantly at work on all of us. Just as in life we may barely be aware of their pervasiveness, so too in Garner's novels, not just with sexuality but with class distinctions and a whole range of subtle influences.

Part of the fascination of Alan Garner's books is to enjoy the elaborate cat-and-mouse game he conducts, in which one can never know what to expect. It comes as a jolt to see Roger emerge as the positive force at the end of *The Owl Service*, when all our literary experiences would have led us to believe that only Gwyn could be the "hero." And then a major character in the same book, Alison's mother Margaret, never once *appears*, existing solely through the reporting of others. And what writer would have Roman legionaries talking like American G.I.'s, as in *Red Shift*? Yet why not?

Alan Garner's books provide absorbing experiences. In spite of all the intellectualising over them, they are basically simple stories which, in cases like *Elidor* or *The Owl Service*, build up to an overwhelming climax on the very last page or two, leaving one thrilled yet stunned. After all, Alan Garner merely wants you to keep reading to find out what happens next.

—Walter McVitty

GARNETT, Eve C.R. British. Born in Worcestershire. Educated at The Convent, Bideford, Devon; West Bank School, Devon; Alice Ottley School, Worcester; Chelsea Polytechnic School of Art, London; Royal Academy Schools, London (studentship; Creswick Prize and Silver Medal). Artist: murals for Children's House, Bow, London; exhibitions at the Tate Gallery, 1939, Le Fevre Gallery, and New English Art Club, all London. Recipient: Library Association Carnegie Medal, 1938. Address: c/o Lloyds Bank, Lewes, Sussex, England.

PUBLICATIONS FOR CHILDREN (illustrated by the author)

Fiction

> *The Family from One End Street and Some of Their Adventures.* London, Muller, 1937; New York, Vanguard Press, 1939.
> *In and Out and Roundabout: Stories of a Little Town.* London, Muller, 1948.
> *Further Adventures of the Family from One End Street.* London, Heinemann, and New York, Vanguard Press, 1956.
> *Holiday at the Dew Drop Inn: A One End Street Story.* London, Heinemann, and New York, Vanguard Press, 1962.
> *Lost and Found: Four Stories.* London, Muller, 1974.

Other

> *To Greenland's Icy Mountains: The Story of Hans Egede, Explorer, Coloniser, Missionary.* London, Heinemann, and New York, Roy, 1968.

> Editor, *A Book of Seasons: An Anthology.* London, Oxford University Press, 1952; Boston, Bentley, 1953.

PUBLICATIONS FOR ADULTS

Other

> *"Is It Well with the Child?"*, illustrated by the author. London, Muller, 1938.

Illustrator: *The London Child* by Evelyn Sharp, 1927; *The Bad Barons of Crashbania* by Norman Hunter, 1932; *A Child's Garden of Verses* by Robert Louis Stevenson, 1948; *A Golden Land* edited by James Reeves, 1958.

*   *   *

Eve Garnett wrote *The Family from One End Street* as a shot in the battle against slums, one of the first attempts to show a working-class family from within the four walls of their home rather than as stereotypes seen from outside. It was rejected by eight publishers in all as "unsuitable for children" before being accepted.

Forty years on, the Ruggles family are still refreshingly real. They face poverty with good sense and cheerfulness; it is an accepted part of their way of living. The mother, Rosie, is particularly well drawn: fiercely angry with her children over any waste of money – the loss of a new school hat by daughter Kate is the occasion of uncompromising fury – but immensely warm and loving at the same time. It is still rare in children's books to find parents so roundly drawn or the tug-of-war relationships between parents and children so realistically treated; and it is this as much as the class dimension which makes the family from One End Street memorable. If the children are less original, if one has met fat responsible Lily, the eldest child, before, or thin studious dreamy Kate (why are clever children in children's literature always *thin*?), they are wonderfully accurately observed. Eve Garnett writes from inside her characters, with a gentle sense of comedy.

Take John, walking along a river bank: "The river was a wonderful place: it breathed adventure! ... strange and patient men fished from its muddy banks and ... flowers grew beside it in beautiful squishy mud that was a delight to walk in. Above all things it was strictly forbidden by Mrs. Ruggles, and therefore doubly attractive – a sort of adventure in itself." Or this scene in the Ruggles' kitchen: " 'Will you go,' cried Rosie, 'can't you see we're worried!' The little Ruggles looked wise. 'Worried' in their experience was another name for what in a child was called 'in a shocking temper.' They scuttled off like rabbits." These are real parents up against real pressures and children who know and recognize the danger signals.

Construction is not Eve Garnett's strong point. For example, *The Family from One End Street* strings a series of events together without any overall sense of climax, and in *Further Adventures of the Family from One End Street* she devotes two-thirds of the book to Kate's visit to the country with her younger brother and sister, and then switches completely in the final third to the rest of the family back in town; it is almost two books.

However, this is of no great importance. She writes vividly and economically with a sharp feel for people and place and with a delightful sense of humour, and no amount of clever craftsmanship will ever substitute for that.

—Mary Rayner

GATES, Doris. American. Born in Mountain View, California, 26 November 1901. Educated at Fresno State College, California, 1924–26; Los Angeles Library School, 1926–27; Western Reserve University, Cleveland, 1929–30. Children's Librarian, Fresno County Library, 1930–40; Instructor, San Jose State College, California, 1940–43; Visiting Lecturer, University of California, Berkeley, 1943–45, University of Southern California, Los Angeles, 1947, and San Francisco State College, 1956. Advisory Editor and Co-author, Basic Readers series 1955–62, and 360 reading series, 1970–73, Ginn and Company, Boston. Address: 159 Spindrift Road, Carmel, California 93923, U.S.A.

PUBLICATIONS FOR CHILDREN

Fiction

> *Sarah's Idea*, illustrated by Marjorie Torrey. New York, Viking Press, 1938; London, Muller, 1947.
> *Blue Willow*, illustrated by Paul Lantz. New York, Viking Press, 1940; London, Muller, 1942.
> *Sensible Kate*, illustrated by Marjorie Torrey. New York, Viking Press, 1943; London, Muller, 1947.

Trouble for Jerry, illustrated by Marjorie Torrey.   New York, Viking Press, 1944;
London, Muller, 1954.
North Fork.   New York, Viking Press, 1945; London, Muller, 1950.
My Brother Mike.   New York, Viking Press, 1948.
River Ranch, illustrated by Jacob Landau.   New York, Viking Press, 1949.
Little Vic, illustrated by Kate Seredy.   New York, Viking Press, 1951.
The Cat and Mrs. Cary, illustrated by Peggy Bacon.   New York, Viking Press, 1962;
London, Methuen, 1964.
The Elderberry Bush, illustrated by Lilian Obligado.   New York, Viking Press, 1967.

Other

Becky and the Bandit (reader), illustrated by Paul Lantz.   Boston, Ginn, 1952.
May I Come In? (reader), with Theodore Clymer.   Boston, Ginn, 1969.
Lord of the Sky: Zeus, illustrated by Robert Handville.   New York, Viking Press, 1972.
The Warrior Goddess: Athena, illustrated by Don Bolognese.   New York, Viking Press,
1972.
The Golden God: Apollo, illustrated by Constantinos CoConis.   New York, Viking
Press, 1973.
Two Queens of Heaven: Aphrodite, Demeter, illustrated by Trina Schart Hyman.   New
York, Viking Press, 1974.
The Mightiest of Mortals: Heracles, illustrated by Richard Cuffari.   New York, Viking
Press, 1975.
A Fair Wind for Troy, illustrated by Charles Mikolaycak.   New York, Viking Press,
1976.

PUBLICATIONS FOR ADULTS

Other

Helping Children Discover Books.   Chicago, Science Research Associates, 1956.

*   *   *

The writings of Doris Gates cover a variety of subjects: classical mythology, the dust bowl
era in the San Joaquin Valley, lumbering in the High Sierras, and horse racing across the
United States to name but a few. However, in each of her books, one is aware of her strong
sense of story structure through her handling of plot, setting, and character development. In a
way, it is no accident that her most recent books have been a series of retellings of the
classical myths, for the structures of traditional stories – myths and romances – have been
implicit in all her writings. This can best be illustrated by looking in detail at two of her
novels for children, *Little Vic*, representative of her animal stories, and *Blue Willow*,
representative of her California-based stories.

Little Vic is the story of Pony Rivers and his love for Little Vic, grandson of the famous
race horse Man o' War. Basically it is a simple story, tracing the progress of the orphaned
Pony Rivers from New York City, to the winner's circle at California's Santa Anita Race
Track. He reaches this destination because of his love for Little Vic, whom he has been with
throughout the horse's young life, and in whom he had kept faith when all others had given
up. Early in the book, Pony thinks about the horse: "He isn't ever going to do anything the
way the people think he will. But he's going to be great just the same." Both boy and horse
prove themselves when, riding at night on the Arizona ranch to which the horse has been
sent for training, they rescue a group of campers from a flash flood. It is at this point that the
boy truly understands the horse's greatness, and the victory in the Santa Anita Handicap
follows quickly. One sees the age-old structure of romance, the journey of wish fulfillment to
a promised land, take the typical American form of the rags-to-riches success story.

In *Little Vic*, this romance pattern is handled very simply, with plot and character development being very straightforward. In *Blue Willow*, justly considered a minor children's classic, the pattern is more complex and more artistically presented. The plot concerns a family of migrant farm workers, the Larkins, once prosperous Texas ranchers, who escape the dust bowl to find happiness on a California ranch. The heroine, young Janey, discovers the courage necessary to help her family discover a home. Doris Gates makes careful use of setting, creating a series of symbolic scenes which reflect the family's movement to peace and security. Of the Larkin's early Texas home we are told little. Irretrievably past, it represents the security Janey now lacks and so desires. The dust-bowl area containing the shack in which the Larkins live represents the wasteland of poverty in which the Larkins now live. It is like the wilderness through which the children of Israel had to pass to reach their goal, and it is like the nightmare landscape which threatened to engulf the questing knight. The third major symbolic setting is the river which Janey and her family visit. As her mother, quoting Isaiah, says, it is as "rivers of water in a dry place." It offers the family a sense of release, a few hours of hope to offset their position as migrant workers. The Anderson farm represents the security which the Larkins once possessed and to which they ultimately return. However, the farm, like the promised land in many fairy tales and romances, is guarded by the evil ogre who must be defeated if it is to be achieved – in this case, it is Bounce Reyburn, the shady ranch foreman whom Janey courageously confronts at the climax of the novel.

Of course, the major symbol of the novel is the blue willow plate itself. Doris Gates uses Janey's changing attitudes toward the plate to indicate her growth as a person. At first, it serves as her means of fighting a feeling of inferiority and she frequently escapes into reveries about it. However, with the illness of her stepmother, she realizes that she is willing to give up the plate and her dream world to pay for a doctor. At the end of the story, she recovers the plate and places it on the mantle of the fireplace in the family's new home on the Anderson ranch. The romance journey has been completed, the land of heart's desire has been achieved – mainly through the courage of young Janey and her mother and father.

One sees in *Blue Willow* a perfect combination of realistic description of setting, careful study of character, and the structural patterns of romance, the linear journey to fulfillment. The book is Doris Gates' major literary achievement and an important contribution to American children's literature. Not only is it an excellent presentation of the migrant workers' lives of the 1930's, it is a universal story of how courage can lead one to success and happiness.

—Jon C. Stott

GATHORNE-HARDY, Jonathan. British. Born in Edinburgh, 17 May 1933. Educated at Bryanston School, 1947–51; Cambridge University, 1953–57, B.A. Military service, 1951–53. Married Sabrina Gathorne-Hardy in 1964; has one son and two daughters. Has worked as an advertising copywriter, bookseller, and book reviewer. Agent: Laura Cecil, 10 Exeter Mansions, 106 Shaftesbury Avenue, London W.1. Address: West Lodge, Compton Bassett, Calne, Wiltshire, England.

PUBLICATIONS FOR CHILDREN

Fiction

Jane's Adventures In and Out of the Book, illustrated by Nicholas Hill. London, Alan Ross, 1966.

Jane's Adventures on the Island of Peeg, illustrated by Nicholas Hill. London, Alan Ross, 1968; as *Operation Peeg*, Philadelphia, Lippincott, 1974.

Jane's Adventures in a Balloon, illustrated by Nicholas Hill. London, Gollancz, 1975; as *The Airship "Lady Ship" Adventure*, Philadelphia, Lippincott, 1977.

PUBLICATIONS FOR ADULTS

Novels

One Foot in the Clouds. London, Hamish Hamilton, 1961.
Chameleon. London, Hamish Hamilton, and New York, Walker, 1967.
The Office. London, Hodder and Stoughton, 1970; New York, Dial Press, 1971.

Other

The Rise and Fall of the British Nanny. London, Hodder and Stoughton, 1972; as *The Unnatural History of the Nanny*, New York, Dial Press, 1973.
The Public School Phenomenon. London, Hodder and Stoughton, 1977.

Jonathan Gathorne-Hardy comments:

I first started to write children's books because I liked telling stories to my young sister and later to my own children. I continued to do so partly in the hope that they would one day provide a small pension for me (children's books, I had been told, can have a longer "life" than adult novels); partly because I got pleasure from the exercise of skill necessary to produce a sufficiently enthralling narrative which I think children require; partly because I found that the sort of narrative I enjoyed they enjoyed too. I write with no Christian moral intention since I do not believe that is a function of the artist, unless it be moral to wish to stimulate, entertain, amuse and amaze young imaginations.

*   *   *

Jonathan Gathorne-Hardy is perhaps best known as a writer of adult novels and for his social histories of the British Nanny and the English public schools. However, fortunately for children, he has a younger sister with an insatiable demand for stories, the more weird and wonderful the better. Making up and telling tales for her has led to the writing of the "Jane" books.

Jane, daughter of Lord Charrington, lives in a vast Cornish castle where the servants are provided with ride-on vacuum-cleaners. In *Jane's Adventures In and Out of the Book*, she discovers an ancient volume into the pictures of which she steps and becomes involved in macabre happenings in a land of tunnels, a land where all the inhabitants are her doubles, escaping just in time to rejoin her parents on their return from the U.S.A. where her father has become converted to Socialist principles and resigned his title. Jane then goes to a boarding-school on a remote Scottish island where, in *Jane's Adventures on the Island of Peeg*, the island floats away with her and her friends. They find that the island is really a secret weapon of World War II, loaded with explosives and staffed by old soldiers who think the war is still on.

In *Jane's Adventures in a Balloon* she is alone in an airship awaiting its trial flight when it is set loose by vandals and she sails off to a series of improbable but exciting adventures in darkest Africa.

Jane is an amusing character with superb British sangfroid and a gift for succeeding in the face of impossible odds. Her adventures are excellent for reading aloud to children of about 9.

—Ann G. Hay

GEISEL, Theodor Seuss. See **SEUSS, Dr.**

GEORGE, Jean Craighead. American. Born in Washington, D.C., 2 July 1919. Educated at Pennsylvania State Universtiy, State College, B.A. 1941; Louisiana State University, Baton Rouge; University of Michigan, Ann Arbor. Married John L. George in 1944 (divorced, 1963); has three children. Reporter, International News Service, 1942–44, and *Washington Post*, 1944–46, both in Washington, D.C.; Artist, *Pageant Magazine*, New York, 1946–47. Staff Writer, 1969–74, and since 1974, Roving Editor, *Reader's Digest*, Pleasantville, New York. Recipient: Aurianne Award, 1958; George G. Stone Center for Children's Books award, 1969; *Book World* Festival Award, 1971; American Library Association Newbery Medal, 1973. Agent: Curtis Brown Ltd., 575 Madison Avenue, New York, New York 10022. Address: 20 William Street, Chappaqua, New York 10514, U.S.A.

PUBLICATIONS FOR CHILDREN

Fiction (illustrated by the author)

Vulpes the Red Fox, with John L. George. New York, Dutton, 1948.
Vison the Mink, with John L. George. New York, Dutton, 1949.
Masked Prowler: The Story of a Raccoon, with John L. George. New York, Dutton, 1950.
Meph, The Pet Skunk, with John L. George. New York, Dutton, 1952.
Bubo the Great Horned Owl, with John L. George. New York, Dutton, 1954.
Dipper of Copper Creek, with John L. George. New York, Dutton, 1956.
Snow Tracks. New York, Dutton, 1958.
My Side of the Mountain. New York, Dutton, 1959; London, Bodley Head, 1962.
The Summer of the Falcon. New York, Crowell, 1962; London, Dent, 1964.
Red Robin Fly Up! Pleasantville, New York, Reader's Digest, 1963.
Gull Number 737. New York, Crowell, 1964.
Hold Zero! New York, Crowell, 1966.
The Hole in the Tree. New York, Dutton, 1967.
Coyote in Manhattan, illustrated by John Kaufman. New York, Crowell, 1968.
All upon a Stone, illustrated by Don Bolognese. New York, Crowell, 1971.
Who Really Killed Cock Robin? An Ecological Mystery. New York, Dutton, 1971.
Julie of the Wolves, illustrated by John Schoenherr. New York, Harper, 1972; London, Hamish Hamilton, 1973.
All upon a Sidewalk, illustrated by Don Bolognese. New York, Dutton, 1974.
Hook a Fish, Catch a Mountain. New York, Dutton, 1975.
Going to the Sun. New York, Harper, 1976.
Wentletrap Trap, illustrated by Symeon Shimin. New York, Dutton, 1977.

Play

Tree House, music by Saul Aarons (produced).

Other

Spring Comes to the Ocean, illustrated by John Wilson. New York, Crowell, 1966.
The Thirteen Moons (The Moon of the Owls, Bears, Salamander, Chickadee, Monarch

Butterfly, Fox Pups, Wild Pigs, Mountain Lion, Deer, Alligator, Wolves, Winter Bird, and Mole), illustrated by John Schoenherr and others.   New York, Crowell, 13 vols., 1967–69.

Beastly Inventions: A Surprising Investigation into How Smart Animals Really Are, illustrated by the author.   New York, McKay, 1970; as Animals Can Do Anything, London, Souvenir Press, 1972.

PUBLICATIONS FOR ADULTS

Other

Everglades Wildguide.   Washington, D.C., National Park Service, 1972.
The American Walk Book.   New York, Dutton, 1977.

Manuscript Collection: Kerlan Collection, University of Minnesota, Minneapolis.

Illustrator: Hawks, Owls, and Wildlife by John Johnson Craighead, 1969.

Jean Craighead George comments:
   As a naturalist I have a profound respect for a holistic view of the Earth, and so I write about children in nature and their relationship to the complex web of life of which we are but one small part. Knowledge of the scheme of things brings security and satisfaction to the human child. I call my books "documentary novels" for the investigations into nature are scientific and carefully researched. Today a work for children must be accurate and faithful to the truth.

*   *   *

   The novels of Jean Craighead George are stories about nature. Though diverse in setting, characterization, and plot, her books have many themes in common. Her characters observe the mysteries of nature and seek answers that help them understand these mysteries. As they seek answers, they reflect on the secrets that nature holds. Typical of this reflection is that done by June, the main character in The Summer of the Falcon as she searches for answers: "There is something that all life has in common, and when I know what it is I shall know myself." This states a theme common in Jean George's books. Sam, a teen-age boy from the city, leaves his home to live in the wilderness in My Side of the Mountain. He attempts to understand nature in a search for ways he can live in harmony with it.
   Rob and Tony must find answers to a mystery in Who Really Killed Cock Robin? As in any mystery, the major events are set up in the beginning of the story. Cock Robin and Mrs. Robin arrive in the town of Saddleboro in the spring. They build their nest in the mayor's hat. The first major event of the mystery occurs when it is announced: "Cock Robin is dead." The plot thickens when Mrs. Robin also dies. "Who killed Cock Robin?" Clues are gathered, data is collected, the evidence is studied, hypotheses are made; some are supported and some are rejected. Both the elements of mystery stories and the elements of scientific research are present throughout the book. Tony and Rob gather data in a scientific way and study the behavior of robins in order to reach a conclusion about what did really kill them.
   Other mysteries of nature are presented by studying the behavior of sea gulls in Gull Number 737, the behavior of wolves in Julie of the Wolves, the ecology of a mountain stream in Hook a Fish, Catch a Mountain, the life of mountain goats in Going to the Sun and the instincts of a coyote in Coyote in Manhattan.
   As important as the realization of nature's mysteries is the method used to uncover them through careful study by using the scientific method. In each story the background of scientific data is woven into the story, often with reference to actual scientific experiments to

substantiate the facts. Throughout all her books, the collection of facts and the observation of data in the scientific method are important. In *Gull Number 737* Dr. Rivers, a professor of biology, is collecting data about the seagulls. Young Luke Rivers' impatience at the slowness of this process is contrasted with his father's thoroughness. "His father had taught him to write down all observations. Eventually many, many notes and hours and days and times would tell the story."

Spinner, a young girl from New York City, is introduced to the scientific research when she and her cousin, Alligator, attempt to solve the mystery of the large cut-throat trout she caught in *Hook a Fish, Catch a Mountain*: "The cards read: date, locale, time, water temperature, oxygen content, wind and water color. Spinner was aghast. Ecological spies were very scientific."

In some of George's books, trained scientists search for answers to questions from nature by using the scientific method learned through formal education. However, in *Julie of the Wolves*, untrained Miyax (Julie) learned about nature in an unsophisticated way. Even Sam, the young teenager living alone in the woods in *My Side of the Mountain*, takes notes. In his quest for answers, he seeks out help that books can provide by visiting the public library. This information provides a foundation for Sam, but most of his knowledge is gained through observation. These two young people have something in common with scientists: careful, patient observations and the analysis of the information after it has been gathered.

This thorough study of nature results in more than knowledge. The characters' love of the creations of nature are seen in the books. The appreciation is shown in their awe at the works of nature. In *Gull Number 737*, Luke Rivers watches the hatching of a gull and says, "I can't believe it," so impressed is he by this work of nature. Later his father adds: "You may be amazed by birth, ... but I never fail to be amazed by instinct. This little bird has never seen its mother .... It could not possibly know that pecking that spot could make its mother choke up food ... and yet [he] does it."

Another important feature of the works of Jean George is the comment on the place man has in the world of nature. In her books, man is a part of ecology. The most important lesson for Sam was his realization that he could not live in conflict with, but had to learn to use, the elements of nature, not changing them, but accepting them as they were.

The characters show an understanding of nature and a desire to protect its creatures. Many people come to the aid of the coyote who hides in Central Park in *Coyote in Manhattan*. In the words of Miss Landry who feeds the birds in Central Park, "If birds and mice and coyotes are in the Park, they're here for a reason. They have as much right as we do."

Man sometimes interferes with the way of Nature, a fact commented on in *Summer of the Falcons*: "Nature had a way, the children learned at Pritchard's, of accommodating itself to the comings-and-goings of human beings." Mice and bees were left "to tolerate the people in summer and assume their rightful ownership of the house when the people were gone."

Sometimes there is an exasperation with the way man acts, as when Rob surveys the newly-formed dump near Saddleboro in *Who Really Killed Cock Robin?* "Eight years ago ... this dump was a half-acre hole surrounded by woods .... An orchid called a pitcher plant once grew under this tree .... The orchids are gone, the tree is dead, and the dump covers over ten acres. We are a very intelligent beast." This is balanced, later in the story, when Tony reflects on his job in the Conservation Service and considers the hope for educating people: "People *will* stop polluting the earth when they see what they're doing." And the book ends on this hopeful note: "A team of people killed Cock Robin and a team of people solved the crime. And that's how it's going to be from now until the day we live in balance with all beasts and plants, and air and water."

The conflict between man and nature is shown in *Going to the Sun* as Marcus learns about mountain goats and changes his beliefs about hunting. "Marcus was a hunter." That fact is simply stated in the beginning of the book. Marcus had accepted the fact that hunting was a way to achieve balance with animals such as the mountain goats and he longed for the trophy of a mounted goat's head. But when Marcus studied the goats, he became aware that he had to reject this belief. This awareness results in a turmoil of accepting his father's ways or the ways of the mountain goats, for Marcus learned that even greatly controlled hunting of the goats was their destruction. The resolution of the story, "Marcus no longer believed in hunting," reflects his change.

The conflict between civilized man and nature is probably greatest in *Julie of the Wolves.* The two names used for the main character emphasize this conflict. She is part Miyax, the part that stands for the old ways of the Eskimos, and she is part Julie, her "white man's name" which depicts a changing attitude in Alaska. This contrast focuses on her two opposing desires, to join her pen pal in San Francisco, and to live in the wilderness. This dilemma is heightened when the wolf is killed. "Miyax buried her fingers in Kapu's fur. 'They did not even stop to get him!' she cried. 'They did not even kill him for money. I don't understand. I don't understand. *Ta vun ga vun ga*,' she cried. '*Pisupa gasu punga*.' She spoke of her sadness in Eskimo, for she could not recall any English."

Jean George has provided readers an opportunity to experience nature with a guide who understands its workings and appreciates its ways. Only occasionally do literary critics question some element of the human characterizations or the story structure. The fact that she weaves good stories while describing nature in an accurate, detailed and exciting fashion is never challenged.

—Mary J. Lickteig

GIBBS, (Cecilia) May. Australian. Born in Surrey, England, 1877; emigrated to Australia in 1881. Educated at Church of England Girls' School, Perth; Cope and Nichol School, Chelsea Polytechnic, and Henry Blackburn School of Black and White Art, London. Married B.J. Ossoli Kelly in 1913. M.B.E. (Member, Order of the British Empire). *Died 27 November 1969.*

PUBLICATIONS FOR CHILDREN (illustrated by the author)

Fiction

> *About Us.* London, Nister, and New York, Dutton, 1912.
> *Gum Blossom Babies.* Sydney, Angus and Robertson, 1916.
> *Gumnut Babies.* Sydney, Angus and Robertson, 1916.
> *Boronia Babies.* Sydney, Angus and Robertson, 1917.
> *Flannel Flowers and Other Bush Babies.* Sydney, Angus and Robertson, 1917.
> *Wattle Babies.* Sydney, Angus and Robertson, 1918.
> *Snugglepot and Cuddlepie: Their Adventures Wonderful.* Sydney, Angus and Robertson, 1918.
> *Little Ragged Blossom, and More about Snugglepot and Cuddlepie.* Sydney, Angus and Robertson, 1920.
> *Little Obelia, and Further Adventures of Ragged Blossom, Snugglepot and Cuddlepie.* Sydney, Angus and Robertson, 1921.
> *Nuttybub and Nittersing.* Melbourne, Osboldstone, 1923.
> *Chucklebud and Wunkydoo.* Melbourne, Osboldstone, 1924; as *Two Little Gumnuts,* Sydney, Cornstalk, 1929.
> *Scotty in Gumnut Land.* Sydney, Angus and Robertson, 1941; London, Angus and Robertson, 1956.
> *Mr. and Mrs. Bear and Friends.* Sydney, Angus and Robertson, 1943; London, Angus and Robertson, 1957.
> *Prince Dande Lion: A Garden Whim-Wham.* Sydney, Ure Smith, 1953; London, Angus and Robertson, 1954.

Verse

Bib and Bub: Their Adventures.   Sydney, Cornstalk, 2 vols., 1925.
The Further Adventures of Bib and Bub.   Sydney, Cornstalk, 1927.
More Funny Stories about Old Friends Bib and Bub.   Sydney, Cornstalk, 1928.
Bib and Bub in Gumnut Town.   Waterloo, New South Wales, Halstead, 1929.
Bib and Bub Painting Book: New Stories.   Sydney, Penfold, n.d.
Gumnuts.   Sydney, Angus and Robertson, 1940.

Manuscript Collection: Mitchell Library, Sydney.

Illustrator: *Barons and Kings (1215–1485)* by Estelle Ross, 1912; *Scribbling Sue and Other Stories* by Amy Eleanor Mack, 1913; *Gem of the Flat* by Constance Mackness, 1914; *A Little Bush Poppy* by Edith Graham, 1915.

*   *   *

May Gibbs gave Australian children a sense of identity with their own land. She told them amusing stories about the wild creatures of the "bush," and of appealing "buds" and "blossoms" – imaginary figures evoked from the unique Australian flora. Like Beatrix Potter, she was a talented artist before she turned to writing. Having dwelt in her childhood amidst the enchantingly beautiful West Australian bushland, she spent most of her life recreating its charm for children. She was an excellent draftsman, and meticulous in her attention to detail. After producing calendars, post-cards and the like during World War I, she wrote and illustrated some exquisite little booklets, beginning with *Gum Blossom Babies* in 1916. Their success encouraged her to create her best-known book, *Snugglepot and Cuddlepie*, which became a favourite, especially when it was later combined with two subsequent books to form *The Complete Adventures of Snugglepot and Cuddlepie*.

She also began to produce a comic strip, with the two main characters, Bib and Bub, closely resembling the gum-nuts in her stories. Each strip told a simple story in doggerel, but they were loved by children, and appeared weekly in Australian newspapers from 1925 for over forty years, so that most Australians of different generations shared one childhood experience. Her humour and invention were always entertaining, though the strips in later years were sometimes reprinted. She was not fortunate in the production of her books, though the first editions of the earlier ones were well-produced with a generous number of illustrations. Later production was of a crude quality on poor paper with blurred or faint illustrations; more recently her work has been further debased, the stories being re-told and the illustrations re-drawn in garish colours to capture the news-stall trade. As a result of this, and perhaps over-exposure to her somewhat repetitive stories, critics have under-rated her. Nevertheless, at least two of her creations, the gum-nuts themselves and the wicked "Banksia men" – grotesque characters derived from the weird-looking cones of a native tree – have become part of the Australian ethos. The charm, gentleness and fun of her stories, with their reminder to "be kind to all Bush creatures," have not diminished in the slightest, and the originality of her work is striking.

—Marcie Muir

GIOVANNI, Nikki (Yolande C. Giovanni).   American.   Born in Knoxville, Tennessee, 7 June 1943. Educated at Fisk University, Nashville, Tennessee, 1960–61, 1964–67, B.A. (honors) in history 1967; University of Pennsylvania School of Social Work, Philadelphia; Columbia University, New York. Has one son. Assistant Professor of Black Studies, Queens

College, Flushing, New York, 1968; Associate Professor of English, Livingston College, Rutgers University, New Brunswick, New Jersey, 1968–70. Editorial Consultant, *Encore* magazine, Albuquerque, New Mexico. Recipient: Ford grant, 1968; National Endowment for the Arts grant, 1969. D.H.: Wilberforce University, Ohio, 1972; D.Litt.: University of Maryland, Princess Anne, 1974; Ripon University, Wisconsin, 1974; Smith College, Northampton, Massachusetts, 1975. Address: c/o Glickman, 24 West 40th Street, New York, New York 10018, U.S.A.

PUBLICATIONS FOR CHILDREN

Verse

> *Spin a Soft Black Song*, illustrated by Charles Bible.   New York, Hill and Wang, 1971.
> *Ego Tripping and Other Poems for Young Readers*, illustrated by George Ford.   Westport, Connecticut, Lawrence Hill, 1973.

Recording: *The Reason I Like Chocolate*, Folkways, 1976.

PUBLICATIONS FOR ADULTS

Verse

> *Black Judgement.*   Detroit, Broadside Press, 1968.
> *Black Feeling, Black Talk.*   Detroit, Broadside Press, 1968.
> *Re: Creation.*   Detroit, Broadside Press, 1970.
> *Black Feeling Black Talk/Black Judgement.*   New York, Morrow, 1970.
> *Poem of Angela Yvonne Davis.*   New York, TomNik Ltd., 1970.
> *My House.*   New York, Morrow, 1972.
> *The Women and the Men.*   New York, Morrow, 1975.

Recordings: *Truth Is on Its Way*, Right On, 1971; *Like a Ripple on a Pond*, Niktom, 1973; *The Way I Feel*, Niktom, 1975; *Legacies*, Folkways, 1976.

Other

> *Gemini: An Extended Autobiographical Statement on My First Twenty-Five Years of Being a Black Poet.*   Indianapolis, Bobbs Merrill, 1971.
> *A Dialogue: James Baldwin and Nikki Giovanni.*   Philadelphia, Lippincott, 1973; London, Joseph, 1975.
> *A Poetic Equation: Conversations Between Nikki Giovanni and Margaret Walker.*   Washington, D.C., Howard University Press, 1974.

Editor, *Night Comes Softly* (anthology).   New York, Niktom, 1970.

Manuscript Collection: Mugar Memorial Library, Boston University.

*   *   *

Nikki Giovanni is a star, a superstar, probably the only "star" poet. She's an easily recognizable personality to poets, non-poets, teachers, parents and children. She has been anthologized, awarded, interviewed, televised extensively. She writes (sometimes) militantly, (sometimes) conscientiously, (sometimes) entertainingly, (sometimes) functionally, (sometimes) tenderly. She always writes artistically; her talent is not to be doubted.

Ms. Giovanni's most notable quality is her universal appeal, especially to children, all children. Generally she writes for children in the same mode as she does for adults. Her son Tommy seems to be a frequent and important inspiration. As a result, many of her poems reflect adulthood's child's eye view of life, giving them an appeal to both age levels. The poem "Fear" is an example:

> early evening fear
> comes i turn
> on the television for company
> and see
> the news.

Ms. Giovanni's own childhood seems to have been a happy one and memories of it are prevalent in her books for children, especially in *Spin a Soft Black Song*. This book, she says, came about because "we [author and illustrator Charles Bible] wanted to say things the way we said [them] when we were little ... in a book with poems and pictures for and about children cause when we were growing up there were precious few of them ... especially for us." Her idea is a good one and her purpose of re-creating childhood as she saw and felt it has been accomplished, as evident in the poems included in this book:

> "TRIPS"
> eeeveryyee time
> when i take my bath
> and put on my clean clothes
> and they all say MY
> HOW NICE YOU LOOK ...

or

> "MOMMIES"   "DADDIES"
> ... tuck you in at night   ... throw you in the air
> and kiss you   tell you GET OUT THERE AND
> and   FIGHT AND DON'T COME BACK
>   TILL YOU WIN ...

The poem "Nikki-Rosa" from the book *Ego-Tripping* is another good example of her childhood experiences; it is at its best, a semi-autobiography; it is also relevant to today's black youth, filled with images and experiences that they can understand:

> ... and though you're poor it isn't poverty that concerns you ... but only that everybody is together and you and your sister have happy birthdays ... all the while i was quite happy.

Nikki Giovanni succeeds; her poetry for children expresses hope that these *can* be happy times.

—Jacqueline Brown Woody

GIPSON, Fred(erick Benjamin).   American.   Born in Mason, Texas, 7 February 1908. Educated at Mason High School, graduated 1926; University of Texas, Austin, 1933–37. Married Tommie Eloise Wynn in 1940 (divorced, 1964); two children. Worked as farm and ranch hand, and as clerk, 1926–33. Reporter and columnist, Corpus Christi *Caller-Times*, San Angelo *Standard-Times*, and Paris *News*, all in Texas, 1938–40; Associate Editor, *True West* magazine, 1953–59; Editorial Director, *Frontier Times*, Bandera, Texas, 1958–59. President, Texas Institute of Letters, 1960. *Died 14 August 1973.*

PUBLICATIONS FOR CHILDREN

Fiction

> *The Trail-Driving Rooster.*   New York, Harper, 1955.
> *Old Yeller*, illustrated by Carl Burger.   New York, Harper, 1956; London, Hodder and
>   Stoughton, 1957.
> *Savage Sam*, illustrated by Carl Burger.   New York, Harper, and London, Hodder and
>   Stoughton, 1962.

PUBLICATIONS FOR ADULTS

Fiction

> *Hound-Dog Man.*   New York, Harper, 1949.
> *The Home Place.*   New York, Harper, 1950; London, Joseph, 1951; abridged edition,
>   as *Return of the Texas*, Edinburgh, Oliver and Boyd, 1962.
> *Recollection Creek.*   New York, Harper, 1955; revised edition, for children, 1959.

Plays

> Screenplays: *Old Yeller*, 1957; *Hound Dog Man*, 1959; *Savage Sam*, with William
> Tunberg, 1963.

> Television Play: *Brush Roper.*

Other

> *Fabulous Empire: Colonel Zack Miller's Story.*   Boston, Houghton Mifflin, 1946; as
>   *Circles round the Wagon*, London, Joseph, 1949.
> *Big Bend*, with J. Oscar Langford.   Austin, University of Texas Press, 1952.
> *Cowhand: The Story of a Working Cowboy.*   New York, Harper, 1953; London,
>   Transworld Publishers, 1957.
> *The Cow Killers: With the Aftosa Commission in Mexico.*   Austin, University of Texas
>   Press, 1956.
> *An Acceptance Speech.*   New York, Harper, 1960.

Critical Study: *Fred Gipson* by Sam H. Henderson,   Austin, Steck Vaughn, 1967.

*   *   *

American children have long been enamored of stories of the settlement of the West and Southwest during the 1800's. Fred Gipson, of Texas, created two of the most exciting and readable adventure stories of the genre for children. *Old Yeller* and *Savage Sam* are his two best stories, both using dogs as the central characters. *Yeller*, on its way to classic status, has the necessary careful balance of humor, terror, suspense, and drama to keep it timeless in appeal and readable for generations to come. Yeller is one of the most appealing dogs to appear in the twentieth century since the writing days of Eric Knight (*Lassie*) and Albert Payson Terhune (*Bob*, etc.). *Sam*, son of Old Yeller, is filled with more unresolved terror, more violence, and less humor, making it slightly less successful as a juvenile than *Yeller*. Both stories were later rewritten by Gipson for filming by the Walt Disney studios. Gipson, a strong regionalist in his writings, hoped to teach something about American history through his books, feeling that the textbook approach was seldom successful. He accomplished his aim well; few fiction books utilizing a Texas locale can match his for depth, accuracy, and historical background. His other works readable by children, *The Trail-Drivin' Rooster* and *Hound-Dog Man*, used a similarly regional atmosphere. Many people have tried to write about Texas; few have done it well; even fewer have met with Gipson's fame and success with it.

—James W. Roginski

GODDEN, (Margaret) Rumer. British. Born in Sussex, 10 December 1907. Educated privately and at Moira House, Eastbourne, Sussex. Married Laurence Sinclair Foster in 1934; James Lesley Haynes-Dixon, 1949 (died, 1973); has two daughters. Directed children's ballet school, Calcutta. Recipient: Whitbread Award, 1973. Agent: Curtis Brown Group Ltd., 1 Craven Hill, London W2 3EW. Address: 4 Mermaid Street, Rye, Sussex, England.

PUBLICATIONS FOR CHILDREN

Fiction

> *The Dolls' House*, illustrated by Dana Saintsbury. London, Joseph, 1947; New York, Viking Press, 1948.
> *The Mousewife*, illustrated by Dana Saintsbury. London, Macmillan, and New York, Viking Press, 1951.
> *Impunity Jane: The Story of a Pocket Doll*, illustrated by Adrienne Adams. New York, Viking Press, 1954; London, Macmillan, 1955.
> *The Fairy Doll*, illustrated by Adrienne Adams. London, Macmillan, and New York, Viking Press, 1956.
> *Mouse House*, illustrated by Adrienne Adams. New York, Viking Press, 1957; London, Macmillan, 1958.
> *The Story of Holly and Ivy*, illustrated by Adrienne Adams. London, Macmillan, and New York, Viking Press, 1958.
> *Candy Floss*, illustrated by Adrienne Adams. London, Macmillan, and New York, Viking Press, 1960.
> *Miss Happiness and Miss Flower*, illustrated by Jean Primrose. London, Macmillan, and New York, Viking Press, 1961.
> *Little Plum*, illustrated by Jean Primrose. London, Macmillan, and New York, Viking Press, 1963.
> *Home Is the Sailor*, illustrated by Jean Primrose. London, Macmillan, and New York, Viking Press, 1964.
> *The Kitchen Madonna*, illustrated by James Bryan. London, Macmillan, and New York, Viking Press, 1967.
> *Operation Sippacik*, illustrated by James Bryan. London, Macmillan, and New York, Viking Press, 1969.

The Old Woman Who Lived in a Vinegar Bottle, illustrated by Mairi Hedderwick. London, Macmillan, and New York, Viking Press, 1972.
The Diddakoi, illustrated by Creina Glegg. London, Macmillan, and New York, Viking Press, 1972.
Mr. McFadden's Hallowe'en, illustrated by Ann Strugnell. London, Macmillan, and New York, Viking Press, 1975.
The Rocking Horse Secret, illustrated by Juliet Stanwell Smith. London, Macmillan, 1977.

Verse

In Noah's Ark. London, Joseph, and New York, Viking Press, 1949.
St. Jerome and the Lion. London, Macmillan, and New York, Viking Press, 1961.

Other

Poetry Programmes for Schools. London, Macmillan, 1966.

Editor, *A Letter to the World: Poems for Young People*, by Emily Dickinson. London, Bodley Head, 1968.

Publications for Adults

Novels

Chinese Puzzle. London, Davies, 1936.
The Lady and the Unicorn. London, Davies, 1938.
Black Narcissus. London, Davies, and Boston, Little Brown, 1939.
Gypsy, Gypsy. London, Davies, and Boston, Little Brown, 1940.
Breakfast with the Nikolides. London, Davies, and Boston, Little Brown, 1942.
Rungli-Rungliot (Thus Far and No Further). London, Davies, 1944; as *Rungli-Rungliot Means in Paharia, Thus Far and No Further*, Boston, Little Brown, 1946.
Fugue in Time. London, Joseph, 1945; as *Take Three Tenses: A Fugue in Time*, Boston, Little Brown, 1945.
The River. London, Joseph, and Boston, Little Brown, 1946.
A Candle for St. Jude. London, Joseph, and New York, Viking Press, 1948.
A Breath of Air. London, Joseph, 1950; New York, Viking Press, 1951.
Kingfishers Catch Fire. London, Macmillan, and New York, Viking Press, 1953.
An Episode of Sparrows. New York, Viking Press, 1955; London, Macmillan, 1956.
The Greengage Summer. London, Macmillan, and New York, Viking Press, 1958.
China Court: The Hours of a Country House. London, Macmillan, and New York, Viking Press, 1961.
The Battle of the Villa Fiorita. London, Macmillan, and New York, Viking Press, 1963.
In This House of Brede. London, Macmillan, and New York, Viking Press, 1969.
The Peacock Spring. London, Macmillan, 1975; New York, Viking Press, 1976.

Short Stories

Mooltiki: Stories and Poems from India. London, Macmillan, and New York, Viking Press, 1957.
Swans and Turtles: Stories. London, Macmillan, 1968; as *Gone: A Thread of Stories*, New York, Viking Press, 1968.

Other

Bengal Journey: A Story of the Part Played by Women in the Province, 1939–1945. London, Longman, 1945.

Hans Christian Andersen: A Great Life in Brief. London, Hutchinson, and New York, Knopf, 1955.

Two under the Indian Sun, with Jon Godden (autobiography). London, Macmillan, and New York, Viking Press, 1966.

The Raphael Bible. London, Macmillan, and New York, Viking Press, 1970.

The Tale of the Tales (on the film *Tales of Beatrix Potter*). London, Warne, 1971.

Shiva's Pigeons: An Experience of India, with Jon Godden. London, Chatto and Windus, and New York, Viking Press, 1972.

The Butterfly Lions. London, Macmillan, 1977.

Editor, *Mrs. Manders' Cook Book*, by Olga Manders. London, Macmillan, and New York, Viking Press, 1968.

Translator, *Prayers from the Ark* (verse), by Carmen de Gasztold. London, Macmillan, and New York, Viking Press, 1962.

Translator, *The Creatures' Choir* (verse), by Carmen de Gasztold. London, Macmillan, 1962; New York, Viking Press, 1965.

*   *   *

"Books are meant to give a child pleasure, sheer enjoyment, and it seems to me in the writing of books nowadays, something has been lost, something that children have always wanted, obviously wanted. I believe that 'something' is the story." So Rumer Godden gave her audience a key to her own writing when she opened the 1976 Children's Book of the Year Exhibition in London. For Rumer Godden is above all else a storyteller. Her first children's story *The Dolls' House* was written because she wanted to see if she could produce a novel in miniature. Her success in writing for both adults and children has shown how well she has mastered the discipline of not producing a simplified adult novel for children, but having that clarity of thought which enables an author to stick to the story "and not philosophise."

Many of her books for children are about dolls, and the dolls house shows a tiny version of the adult world, the dolls serving to give a child's eye view of relationships, personalities and situations that come frighteningly near to reality. *Candy Floss*, about a doll stolen by a spoilt child, provides enough drama to make the reader hold his breath until he sees her safely returned. While her doll characters reflect the complexities of family life, they never lose their doll-like characteristics. In *Holly and Ivy* the much coveted doll in the toyshop which gladdens the orphan child on Christmas morning is very much a doll to be dressed and played with. Tottie Plantagenet, the farthing doll heroine of *The Dolls' House*, is a real person, and the malice which the kid-and-china doll Marchpane exerts over her is as bitter and acid as any fishwife's quarrel.

Not all Rumer Godden's stories are as emotional or poignant as that of Tottie. *Miss Happiness and Miss Flower*, two Japanese dolls, achieve great joy when Nona makes them a proper little Japanese house and a whole Japanese garden to themselves. Friendship is the theme of another story about Miss Happiness and Miss Flower when they win the heart of the round cosy little doll, Little Plum, who sits on Gem's window sill next door.

It has been said that Rumer Godden's books steer a steady course between sensitivity and sentimentality. Certainly her books reflect her early childhood in India in a beautiful house with many servants: "our life did evoke a princess quality." She has that rare gift in a writer of not overstating her case, leaving the reader to discover the people behind the characters. She is always sincere and always just. Her most outstanding children's book, *The Diddakoi*, is sentimental, emotional, middle-class and romantic; but it also and far more importantly has a

517

timeless quality enjoyed by all children regardless of status, race, or class, because essentially it is a story about people. It is people who matter to Rumer Godden, the people who, like herself when she was sent to school in England, feel out of step with the rest of the crowd. And which of us has not at some time had that experience. Kizzy, the half-gypsy girl, loses her home after her Gran dies and their wagon is burnt. She is determined not to conform, to go to school; but she will look after the horse Joe, and never "go into brick." Her story, woven with that of the crusty old Admiral with his unspoken love of Miss Brooke, the magistrate who befriends Kizzy, evokes the fullness and rightness of things that children need in their tales. They do not see that the cottage fire at the climax of the book is unrealistic; it is a logical ending, since it sets the scene for the happy-ever-after ending with which the book so beautifully ends.

Although Rumer Godden's books are essentially about people and their feelings, her three royal Pekinese ruling her home in Rye amply testify to her love and understanding of animals. From an anecdote in Dorothy Wordsworth's *Journal* about the friendship between a mouse and a caged dove, she has written the parable *The Mousewife*, a delicate tender story, just as memorable in its telling as the tragedy of many far larger heroines.

Not all Rumer Godden's writings can be classified as "tender and evocative"; as in all good stories, there is a hard core beneath, and also a large smattering of humour. *Operation Sippacik* is an adventure story with the unusual setting of Cyprus during the EOKA troubles. In *Mr. McFadden's Hallowe'en* she writes a jolly good horse story in every sense of the word, with a stubborn and determined heroine riding an even more stubborn and determined pony. Haggis loves Mr. McFadden's turnip field, but Mr. McFadden loves no one, least of all Selina and her pony. It is a humorous and witty story with great insight into human and animal behaviour in a small village.

Virginia Haviland has called Rumer Godden "a genuine writer for adults and children unaffected by pressures from without." This was shown to perfection when Rumer Godden published the much celebrated article in the *Horn Book* called "An Imaginary Correspondence." It was between Mr. V. Andal, a publisher, and the ghost of Beatrix Potter, and concerned possible publication of a modern retelling of the Peter Rabbit story. "Are children nowadays so much less intelligent than their parents?" she wrote. "I think I write carefully because I enjoy my writing and enjoy taking pains over it. I write to please myself: my usual way is to scribble and cut out and write it again and again. The shorter, the plainer – the better. And to read the Bible (unrevised version and Old Testament) if I feel my style wants chastening ... [our] real work is to enrich a child's heritage of words – not diminish it." And enrich it she certainly does.

—Jean Russell

GORDON, John. British. Born in Jarrow, County Durham, 19 November 1925. Educated at Wisbech Grammar School, Cambridgeshire. Served in the Royal Navy, 1943–47. Married Sylvia Ellen Young in 1954; has one son and one daughter. Reporter, *Isle of Ely and Wisbech Advertiser*, 1947–51; Chief Reporter and Sub-editor, *Bury Free Press*, Bury St. Edmunds, Suffolk, 1951–58; Sub-editor, *Western Evening Herald*, Plymouth, 1958–62; Sub-editor and Columnist, *Eastern Evening News*, Norwich, 1962–73. Since 1973, Sub-editor, *Eastern Daily Press*, Norwich. Address: 99 George Borrow Road, Norwich, Norfolk NR4 7HU, England.

PUBLICATIONS FOR CHILDREN

Fiction

> *The Giant under the Snow.* London, Hutchinson, 1968; New York, Harper, 1970.
> *The House on the Brink.* London, Hutchinson, 1970; New York, Harper, 1971.
> *The Ghost on the Hill.* London, Penguin, 1976; New York, Viking Press, 1977.

John Gordon comments:

I write about the supernatural because it makes a good story and disturbs the commonplace. I like to take an ordinary town or a village and make it as real as I can. This is very important because the supernatural, the imagination, are nothing if they are not anchored in reality. Once this is done it is possible to concentrate on some event which turns this world upside down, and causes the people in it to see things they had never dreamt of and experience feelings they had never known.

* * *

John Gordon is a painstaking writer whose 3 novels have been spread over 9 years. Behind the swift movement and high tension of his stories one has the sense of a man fighting to achieve a difficult mastery.

The books are about adolescents and concerned with adolescence. There are other concerns as well: the continuing influence of the past, and the supernatural or seemingly supernatural. "The boundary between imagination and reality, and the boundary between being a child and being an adult are border country, a passionate place in which to work," John Gordon wrote in his contribution to Edward Blishen's book *The Thorny Paradise.*

The Giant under the Snow is a fantasy based on the splendid idea of a Green Man – a huge legendary figure from a hillside – that once walked and now lies buried: a strange shape of mounds and ridges in the landscape. Three youngsters are caught up in the last act of a struggle between light and dark, in which an attempt is made to bring the giant to life. There is powerful material here, but too much of it; the book is overcrowded with action and not well enough organised. *The House on the Brink* was a great advance. An evil-looking log is found lying in Fenland mud. Does it move, does it leave a foul and sluglike, though invisible, trail? Could it be – or was it once – human? Is it dangerous, or is the menace in someone's mind? Or both? Dick and Helen are drawn into a quest to find out; and the answers have emotional rather than strictly factual logic.

The Ghost on the Hill is set in an isolated village; at its heart is an unquiet grave whose occupant cannot rest until repetition of an old tragedy has been averted. The style is taut, the suspense compelling, and the drawing of personal relationships precise. John Gordon emerges as a finely gifted writer who is still struggling upwards and might go much farther yet.

—John Rowe Townsend

GOUDGE, Elizabeth (de Beauchamp). British. Born in Wells, Somerset, 24 April 1900. Educated at Grassendale School, Southbourne, Hampshire; Reading University School of Art. Recipient: Library Association Carnegie Medal, 1947. Fellow, Royal Society of Literature, 1946. Agent: David Higham Associates Ltd., 5–8 Lower John Street, London WIR 4HA. Address: Rose Cottage, Peppard Common, Henley-on-Thames, Oxfordshire, England.

PUBLICATIONS FOR CHILDREN

Fiction

Sister of the Angels: A Christmas Story, illustrated by C. Walter Hodges. London, Duckworth, and New York, Coward McCann, 1939.

Smoky House, illustrated by C. Walter Hodges. London, Duckworth, and New York, Coward McCann, 1940.

The Well of the Star. New York, Coward McCann, 1941.

Henrietta's House, illustrated by Lorna R. Steele. London, University of London Press-Hodder and Stoughton, 1942; as *The Blue Hills*, New York, Coward McCann, 1942.

The Little White Horse, illustrated by C. Walter Hodges. London, University of London Press, 1946; New York, Coward McCann, 1947.

Make-Believe, illustrated by C. Walter Hodges. London, Duckworth, 1949; Boston, Bentley, 1953.

The Valley of Song, illustrated by Stephen Spurrier. London, University of London Press, 1951; New York, Coward McCann, 1952.

Linnets and Valerians, illustrated by Ian Ribbons. Leicester, Brockhampton Press, and New York, Coward McCann, 1964.

I Saw Three Ships, illustrated by Richard Kennedy. Leicester, Brockhampton Press, and New York, Coward McCann, 1969.

Other

God So Loved the World: A Life of Christ. London, Hodder and Stoughton, and New York, Coward McCann, 1951.

PUBLICATIONS FOR ADULTS

Novels

Island Magic. London, Duckworth, and New York, Coward McCann, 1934.

The Middle Window. London, Duckworth, 1935; New York, Coward McCann, 1939.

A City of Bells. London, Duckworth, and New York, Coward McCann, 1936.

Towers in the Mist. London, Duckworth, and New York, Coward McCann, 1938.

The Bird in the Tree. London, Duckworth, and New York, Coward McCann, 1940.

The Castle on the Hill. London, Duckworth, and New York, Coward McCann, 1941.

Green Dolphin Country. London, Hodder and Stoughton, 1944; as *Green Dolphin Street*, New York, Coward McCann, 1944.

The Herb of Grace. London, Hodder and Stoughton, 1948; as *Pilgrim's Inn*, New York, Coward McCann, 1948.

Gentian Hill. London, Hodder and Stoughton, and New York, Coward McCann, 1949.

The Heart of the Family. London, Hodder and Stoughton, and New York, Coward McCann, 1953.

The Rosemary Tree. London, Hodder and Stoughton, and New York, Coward McCann, 1956.

The White Witch. London, Hodder and Stoughton, and New York, Coward McCann, 1958.

The Dean's Watch. London, Hodder and Stoughton, and New York, Coward McCann, 1960.

The Scent of Water. London, Hodder and Stoughton, and New York, Coward McCann, 1963.

The Child from the Sea. London, Hodder and Stoughton, and New York, Coward McCann, 1970.

Short Stories

The Fairies' Baby and Other Stories. London, Foyle, 1919.
A Pedlar's Pack and Other Stories. London, Duckworth, and New York, Coward McCann, 1937.
The Golden Skylark and Other Stories. London, Duckworth, and New York, Coward McCann, 1941.
The Ikon on the Wall and Other Stories. London, Duckworth, 1943.
The Reward of Faith and Other Stories. London, Duckworth, 1950; New York, Coward McCann, 1951.
White Wings: Collected Short Stories. London, Duckworth, 1952.
The Lost Angel. London, Hodder and Stoughton, and New York, Coward McCann, 1971.

Plays

Three Plays: Suomi, The Brontës of Haworth, and Fanny Burney. London, Duckworth, 1939.
Fanny Burney (produced Oldham, Lancashire, 1949). Included in *Three Plays,* 1939.

Verse

Songs and Verses. London, Duckworth, 1947; New York, Coward McCann, 1948.

Other

The Elizabeth Goudge Reader, edited by Rose Dobbs. New York, Coward McCann, 1946; as *At the Sign of the Dolphin: An Elizabeth Goudge Anthology,* London, Hodder and Stoughton, 1947.
Saint Francis of Assisi. London, Duckworth, 1959; as *My God and My All: The Life of St. Francis of Assisi,* New York, Coward McCann, 1959.
The Chapel of the Blessed Virgin Mary, Buckler's Hard, Beaulieu. Privately printed, 1966.
A Christmas Book (anthology). London, Hodder and Stoughton, and New York, Coward McCann, 1967.
The Ten Gifts (anthology), edited by Mary Baldwin. London, Hodder and Stoughton, and New York, Coward McCann, 1969.
The Joy of the Snow: An Autobiography. London, Hodder and Stoughton, and New York, Coward McCann, 1974.

Editor, *A Book of Comfort: An Anthology.* London, Joseph, and New York, Coward McCann, 1964.
Editor, *A Diary of Prayer.* London, Hodder and Stoughton, and New York, Coward McCann, 1966.
Editor, *A Book of Peace: An Anthology.* London, Joseph, 1967; New York, Coward McCann, 1968.
Editor, *A Book of Faith.* London, Hodder and Stoughton, and New York, Coward McCann, 1976.

Elizabeth Goudge comments:
I have always loved writing for children; I have enjoyed writing my children's books even more than writing my novels. Of all my books the two I care for most are *The Little White Horse* and *The Valley of Song.* And I have enjoyed the children themselves, both receiving their letters and being visited by them. They have been one of the greatest joys of my life.

*   *   *

Elizabeth Goudge was in many ways a writer born out of her time, and always liable to be judged old-fashioned. Young readers, however, are themselves strongly inclined to have old-fashioned tastes, so that the best of her works, like the best of Victorian work, are unlikely to lose their appeal. The openly religious, sometimes Anglican, element which runs through all her writing may perhaps seem increasingly strange if the habit of church-going continues to decline, but her highly evocative powers of description, her gift for creating memorable characters and her ability to work through an intricately-woven plot and bring it to a satisfactory conclusion, are virtues which will surely survive. Among her other qualities one may note Miss Goudge's habit of surrounding her child characters with interesting adults, often advanced in years, and her flair for giving personality to animals, especially dogs and horses.

At their best Miss Goudge's stories are strongly rooted in everyday reality, with magic and fantasy used only to enliven; similarly, her much-criticised lapses into sentimentality and sickly-sweetness are quite rare in the two or three books on which her reputation depends. Little need be said here about *Smoky House* and *The Valley of Song*. The former is an odd mixture of smuggling adventure, fairy-story and cosy moralizing, while the latter, though palpably sincere, is too much concerned with the author's personal vision of heaven, and not enough with a child's normal interests. Two other books are interesting but uneven. *Sister of the Angels* is very sentimental, though redeemed by flashes of humour and a fine portrayal of an artist's dedication; and the collection called *Make-Believe* contains one story − "The Forester's Ride" − which one might recommend for any high-spirited ten-year-old, but otherwise it seems more suitable for nostalgic adults than for children.

Most of Miss Goudge's children's books came in the earlier part of her writing career. One exception, *Linnets and Valerians*, 1964, also happens to be in her very best vein, with a plot of nicely-judged complexity and a sparkling cast of heroes, villains and eccentrics. Ezra Oake, the one-legged sailor-servant, is certainly among her finest creations. Possibly, however, her two previous great successes, *The Little White Horse* and *Henrietta's House*, deserve higher praise by virtue of their originality. *Henrietta's House* must be almost unique in giving pride of place to a group of elderly clergymen, and the combination in this book of rollicking entertainment with a deep religious purpose is a notable achievement. *The Little White Horse* is lengthy, complicated and concerned with emotions such as sexual passion, pride, jealousy and loneliness; yet the principal characters and incidents are exceptionally captivating, and an atmosphere of joyous enchantment persists throughout. Miss Goudge's reputation could stand on this book alone.

—Alasdair K. D. Campbell

GRAHAM, Eleanor. British. Born in Walthamstow, Essex, 9 January 1896. Educated at Chingford High School, Essex, 1902–09; North London Collegiate School for Girls, 1910–14; London School of Medicine, 1914–16. Worked at Bumpus' children's book room, London, 1926–30; Children's Book Editor, William Heinemann, Ltd., publishers, London, 1930–33, and Methuen Ltd., publishers, London, 1933–36; Librarian, private children's lending library, 1936–37; Children's Book Editor and Founder of the Puffin series, Penguin Books Ltd., London, 1939–61. Children's Book Reviewer, *Sunday Times* and *The Bookman*, both London, in the 1930's. Recipient: Children's Book Circle Eleanor Farjeon Award, 1973. Address: 3 Spanish Place, London W. 1, England.

PUBLICATIONS FOR CHILDREN

Fiction

The Night Adventures of Alexis, illustrated by Winifred Langlands. London, Faber, 1925.
Six in a Family, illustrated by Alfred Sindall. London, Nelson, 1935.
The Children Who Lived in a Barn, illustrated by J. T. Evans. London, Routledge, 1938; revised edition, London, Penguin, 1955.
Head O'Mey, illustrated by Arnold Bond. London, Benn, 1947.

Other

High Days and Holidays: Stories, Legends and Customs of Red-Letter Days and Holidays, illustrated by Priscilla M. Ellingford. London, Benn, 1932; as *Happy Holidays: Stories, Legends and Customs of Red-Letter Days and Holidays*, New York, Dutton, 1933.
Change for Sixpence. London, University of London Press, 1937.
When the Fun Begins. London, University of London Press, 1937.
Adventure in Natal: A Book for Boys of Early Hunting Adventures in Natal, with George Gordon Campbell. London, Pitman, 1938.
The Making of a Queen: Victoria at Kensington Palace. London, Cape, 1940.
The Story of "The Wind in the Willows": How It Came to Be Written. London, Methuen, 1950.
True Dog Stories, with Lillian Gask. London, Harrap, 1950.
The Story of Charles Dickens, illustrated by Norman Meredith. London, Methuen, 1952; New York, Abelard Schuman, 1954.
The Story of Jesus, illustrated by Brian Wildsmith. London, Penguin, 1959.
J. M. Barrie's Peter Pan: The Story of the Play, illustrated by Edward Ardizzone. Leicester, Brockhampton Press, and New York, Scribner, 1962.

Editor, *Welcome Christmas! Legends, Carols, Stories, Riddles*, illustrated by Priscilla M. Ellingford. London, Benn, 1931; New York, Dutton, 1932.
Editor, *Tents in Mongolia: A Youth Edition*, by Henning Haslund-Christensen. London, Kegan Paul, 1935.
Editor, *More Travels and Adventures in Mongolia: A Youth Edition of "Men and Gods in Mongolia,"* by Henning Haslund-Christensen. London, Kegan Paul, 1936.
Editor, *Selected Stories and Verses*, by Walter de la Mare. London, Penguin, 1952.
Editor, *A Puffin Book of Verse*, illustrated by Claudia Freedman. London, Penguin, 1953.
Editor, *A Puffin Quartet of Poets*, illustrated by Diana Bloomfield. London, Penguin, 1958.
Editor, *Eleanor Farjeon's Book: Stories, Verses, Plays*, illustrated by Edward Ardizzone. London, Penguin, 1960.
Editor, *Poems*, by Walter de la Mare, illustrated by Margery Gill. London, Penguin, 1962.
Editor, *Secret Laughter* (anthology). London, Penguin, 1964.
Editor, *A Thread of Gold: An Anthology of Poetry*, illustrated by Margery Gill. London, Bodley Head, 1964; Freeport, New York, Books for Libraries Press, 1969.
Editor, *The Music of the Feast: Poems for Young Readers*, by Robert Herrick, illustrated by Lynton Lamb. London, Bodley Head, 1969.

PUBLICATIONS FOR ADULTS

Other

   Kenneth Grahame.   London, Bodley Head, and New York, Walck, 1963.

*   *   *

Eleanor Graham's most notable contribution to children's fiction is *The Children Who Lived in a Barn.* It merits serious consideration, as the plot offers a complete contrast to the highly successful holiday adventure plot initiated by Arthur Ransome and imitated by M. E. Atkinson, Aubrey de Selincourt, M. Pardoe and many other writers. Eleanor Graham accepts the convention of disposing of parents by means of an air crash, but this does not ensure a carefree, parentless existence. Instead, it highlights the stark realities which face a group of children left temporarily without parents. It does not prove possible to dispense with adults, and an incredibly large number of adults, pleasant and unpleasant, interfere helpfully and unhelpfully with the children's affairs. In the best tradition of Arthur Ransome, Eleanor Graham extols the virtues of self-reliance. She perhaps differs from him in her relentless emphasis on the unromanticized mechanics of everyday life. It is inevitable that some of these details are now obsolete, e.g. the wash day procedure. Perhaps the greatest weakness of the plot is the return of the parents, but these are minor criticisms of an original story.

Unlike numerous forgotten writers of the period whose characterization was so nominal as to be non-existent, Eleanor Graham succeeds with the Dunnett children in creating five individual and consistent personalities. She gives convincing details of their relationships with each other, of their quarrels, and of the problems which arise in the absence of parents. She also succeeds in giving a valid account of family solidarity in a time of crisis. The strains imposed on the eldest girl, Susan, who is only 13 years old, are particularly well handled.

By the post-World War II period a family in a similar situation would normally be caught in the safety net of the social services, although John Rowe Townsend offered an alternative in *Gumble's Yard* (1961). The young reader of today might feel that the family situation of *The Children Who Lived in a Barn* has little resemblance to any situation known to him, but he might also admire the Dunnetts' success in coming to terms with a crisis, and he might even envy them a degree of freedom unlikely today. This book was a deliberate antidote to the often far-fetched holiday adventure stories of the 1930's, and Eleanor Graham might be said to have had a definite didactic purpose in writing it. It is easy to understand that with her wide experience in the field of children's publishing, she must have felt deep concern over the proliferation of second-rate material for children, particularly in the 1920's. Her serious endeavours in the fields of publishing and editing led to an improvement in the quality of children's books in the 1930's, and ensures her a lasting place in the history of children's literature.

—Anne W. Ellis

GRAHAM, Lorenz (Bell).   American.   Born in New Orleans, Louisiana, 27 January 1902. Educated at the University of Washington, Seattle, 1921; University of California, Los Angeles, 1923–24; Virginia Union University, Richmond, 1934–36, B.A. 1936; Columbia University, New York; New York University. Married Ruth Morris in 1929; has four children. Teacher, Monrovia College, Liberia, 1924–29, and Richmond Adult Schools, Virginia, 1930–33; Educational Advisor, Civilian Conservation Corps, Virginia and Pennsylvania, 1936–42; Housing Manager, Newport News Housing Authority, Virginia, 1942–46; real estate salesman and building contractor, Long Island, New York, 1946–49;

Social Worker, Queens Federation of Churches, New York, 1948–56; Probation Officer, Los Angeles County, California, 1957–67. Since 1970, Lecturer, California State University, Pomona. Recipient: Child Study Association of America Award, 1959; *Book World* Festival award, 1969; Martin Luther King Award, 1975. Address: 1400 Niagara Avenue, Claremont, California 91711, U.S.A.

PUBLICATIONS FOR CHILDREN

Fiction

> *Tales of Momolu*, illustrated by Letterio Calapai.   New York, Reynal, 1946.
> *South Town*.   Chicago, Follett, 1958.
> *North Town*.   New York, Crowell, 1967.
> *I, Momolu*, illustrated by John Biggers.   New York, Crowell, 1966.
> *Whose Town?*   New York, Crowell, 1969.
> *Carolina Cracker*.   Boston, Houghton Mifflin, 1972.
> *Detention Center*.   Boston, Houghton Mifflin, 1972.
> *Stolen Car*.   Boston, Houghton Mifflin, 1972.
> *Runaway*.   Boston, Houghton Mifflin, 1972.
> *Return to South Town*.   New York. Crowell, 1976.

Other

> *How God Fix Jonah*, illustrated by Letterio Calapai.   New York, Reynal, 1946.
> *The Story of Jesus*, illustrated by William Walsh.   New York, Gilberton, 1955.
> *The Ten Commandments*, illustrated by Norman Nodel.   New York, Gilberton, 1956.
> *A Road Down in the Sea*, illustrated by Gregorio Prestopino.   New York, Crowell, 1971.
> *God Wash the World and Start Again*, illustrated by Clare Romano Ross.   New York, Crowell, 1971.
> *David He No Fear*, illustrated by Ann Grifalconi.   New York, Crowell, 1971.
> *John Brown's Raid: A Picture History*.   New York, Scholastic, 1972.
> *Directions*, books 3 and 4, with John Durham and Elsa Graser.   Boston, Houghton Mifflin, 1972.
> *Song of the Boat*, illustrated by Leo and Diane Dillon.   New York, Crowell, 1975.

Manuscript Collection: Kerlan Collection, University of Minnesota, Minneapolis.

Lorenz Graham comments:
I started wanting to write while I was teaching in Africa. Then and there it became startlingly clear to me that there were no honest books about Africans for young readers. Later I realized that almost no decent books about black Americans were available. I am a Black. My writings about Africans and Americans try to depict the characters as real people. While I write primarily for young readers I receive many interesting comments from adults. I believe my books have promoted understanding.

*   *   *

Lorenz Graham writes biblical stories for the young reader fluently and with conviction. The author grew up in an atmosphere of religious expression, and spent several years in Africa learning about the continent and the customs of its peoples. These experiences have allowed him to paint a vivid picture of what he believes represents Africa.

Most of his religious works are told in poetic form and in the speech pattern of modern

African youth. One of his better known works is *How God Fix Jonah*, a story of many biblical characters told in the English vernacular using African speech patterns. Graham's works have got progressively better. The stories in *David He No Fear* are told by Africans as if they were the characters in the book themselves.

Graham has also written a series which depicts the frustrations and ambitions of a young black teenager, David Williams, and his family. This series is much more popular with young readers than the author's religious works. *South Town*, the first of the series, revolves around David Williams and his family, and the bigotry and violence that they encounter. The second title in the series is *North Town* where the Williams family have come after deciding to leave the South. Here the family encounters the bigotry of the North, much more refined and subtle. *Whose Town?* continues the problems that David Williams and his family face in a northern industrial city. Graham's description of racial prejudice could readily be attributed to real situations he has encountered.

Lorenz B. Graham writes simply and with dignity and vitality.

—Dolores C. Leffall

GRAHAME, Kenneth. British. Born in Edinburgh, 8 March 1859. Educated at St. Edward's School, Oxford, 1868–75. Married Elspeth Thomson in 1899; one son. Worked for Grahame, Currie, and Spens, parliamentary agent's office, London, 1875–79. From 1879, Gentleman-Clerk, and Secretary, 1898–1908, Bank of England, London. Secretary of the New Shakespere Society, London, 1877–91. *Died 6 July 1932.*

PUBLICATIONS FOR CHILDREN

Fiction

> *The Golden Age.* London, Lane, and Chicago, Stone and Kimball, 1895.
> *Dream Days.* London and New York, Lane, 1898; revised edition, 1899.
> *The Wind in the Willows*, illustrated by Graham Robertson. London, Methuen, and New York, Scribner, 1908.
> *The First Whisper of "The Wind in the Willows,"* edited by Elspeth Grahame. London, Methuen, 1944; Philadelphia, Lippincott, 1945.

Other

> Editor, *Lullaby-Land: Songs of Childhood*, by Eugene Field, illustrated by John Lawrence. New York, Scribner, 1897; London, Lane, 1898.
> Editor, *The Cambridge Book of Poetry for Young People.* London, Cambridge University Press, 2 vols., and New York, Putnam, 1916.

PUBLICATIONS FOR ADULTS

Short Stories

> *The Headswoman.* London and New York, Lane, 1898.

Other

    Pagan Papers.   London, Elkin Mathews and Lane, 1893; Chicago, Stone and Kimball, 1894.
    The Kenneth Grahame Day Book, edited by Margery Coleman.   London, Methuen, 1937.

Critical Study: *Kenneth Grahame,* by Eleanor Graham, London, Bodley Head, and New York, Walck, 1963.

*   *   *

It was *The Golden Age,* presently followed by *Dream Days,* that "made" Kenneth Grahame's name. Indeed, so great was the success of these books, both in Britain and America, that *The Wind in the Willows* at first disappointed readers. Several publishers (including those who held the earlier books) had in fact turned down the manuscript. Publishing history is full of these wry mischances. Yet all three books have more in common than may at first appear. All have a seminal place in later fiction. And all derive so much from the accidents of their author's life that some relevant facts should first be set out here.

Grahame's childhood was one of uprooting and loss. He was born in Edinburgh in 1859, the third of four children; in his first few years the family lived in the Western Highlands, near Loch Fyne. This pleasant time was ended by the mother's death when Kenneth was five. The children were despatched to their maternal grandmother at Cookham Dene in Berkshire – a loved place that relives in Grahame's books – but three years later they were moved again. Meanwhile the advocate father, destroyed by the loss of his wife, resigned his post (as Sheriff-Substitute of Argyllshire), drifted to France and died, an alcoholic, at Le Havre. The fates of the four young Grahames (presently three, for the oldest, Willie, died at 16) lay with unimaginative southern relatives; they inflicted their worst blow on Kenneth by refusing to let him go on to Oxford, though his record at school should have made this a natural step. Such luxuries were thought unsuitable, and a place was found for him in the Bank of England. He had a conformist streak, and rose in time to one of the Bank's three top positions. But the sense of deprivation remained. His other half-life, of intense dream-fantasy, was to channel itself, by various chances, into the books we know.

Grahame's first printed writings were lightweight period essays, ephemeral stuff, though fashionable at the time. But Henley, editor of the *National Observer,* noticed one that was different: "The Olympians"; he urged Grahame to write more in this kind. Grahame did; and *The Golden Age* and *Dream Days* were the result. They are, in simplest terms, made up of events in the daily lives of five orphaned children, living in a country house with unloved relatives. Allies are mostly found among the servants, or the odd bachelor solitaries – an artist, maybe a doctor. But the adult and child worlds are distinct. The children live, with marvellous vividness, in the imagination, acting out each book they read, entering, as it were, each picture. (See "Its Walls Were As of Jasper.") One may note that when Edward the oldest goes away to school, the narrator stays behind, still in childhood. In life, Kenneth went off too. Wild Wood? Wide World? Not for Rat; not for Grahame, either.

Grahame was not by temperament an original, yet here he was an original indeed. Nobody yet had so fully pursued this sharp child's view of child and adult, seen with a child's exactness, set down with an adult's skill. The books would affect not only children's fiction (notably the Nesbit-style family story), but the whole child-cult for adults in the new century. Not widely read today, they yet will always be a brilliant find for perceptive readers.

The Wind in the Willows (whose influence can be seen in animal fantasies from Uttley to Adams), began as a series of episodes told to Grahame's 4-year-old son Alistair. Without this waiting listener the book as we know it would probably never have been written. The animal cast, which at first so much perplexed Grahame's adult readers, came naturally enough in a nursery narrative. Are they not creatures of fable and fairy tale? What else, after all? The child-theme of *The Golden Age* and *Dream Days* was, for Grahame, played out; all five children at the end of the tale were already moving towards the Olympian world. Yet animal comrades, neither old nor young, free both from childhood's rules and adult burdens (like undergraduates) exactly fitted the need. As it happens, Grahame had already given thought (expressed in his Introduction to Aesop and elsewhere) to the unjust human roles imposed on animals in didactic fables. Even so, like most major works of children's fiction, *The Wind in the Willows* is not so much a book for the young as a book for Grahame himself about himself, for the streak of childhood that stayed in him undissolved: an autobiography of the mind. Some episodes can be seen as wholly personal: "Wayfarers All," in which Rat is held by friends from the lure of bohemian wanderings, and is offered the consolation of turning the whole affair into poetry, is notably of this kind.

But the first reviews suggest the general perplexity. "For ourselves," the *Times* critic wrote, "we lay *The Wind in the Willows* reverently aside, and again, for the hundredth time, take up *The Golden Age*." "Grown-up readers," this writer adds, "will find it monstrous and elusive." For *Punch* it was "a sort of irresponsible holiday story in which the chief characters are woodland animals, who are represented as enjoying most of the advantages of civilisation." Arnold Bennett took a bolder view. "The author may call his chief characters the Rat, the Mole, the Toad – they are human beings, and are meant to be nothing but human beings .... The book is an urbane exercise in irony at the expense of the English human character and mankind. It is entirely successful."

Yet Grahame was not by intent an adult ironist. As narrative, the book is truly in key with a young child's mind, not least in the merging of outward fact with the inward fact of fantasy. Motor and train exist with mediaeval dungeon. The very size of the creatures varies easily with the scene. "The Toad was train-size; the train was Toad-size" – thus Grahame answered a query on this point. As a result, no pictures, even Shepard's, even Rackham's, are wholly satisfactory, though both are fine on the scenery. It might be worth pointing out that much that is characteristic in *The Wind in the Willows* is foreshadowed in the two earlier books – the camaraderie, the food and feasts, the secret haunts, the obsession with ships (or boats) and water, the long days of summer, the pantheism, the woods under winter snow – and the literary ambiances. But in those earlier books the Wide World is always near. In *The Wind in the Willows* the carefree days are held. It is a book which (in Peter Greene's apt comment) stops the clock. Its potent English pastoral dream – reflected too in so much Georgian poetry – remains unchanged. The earliest readers in 1908 and thereafter must have thought this permanence true of Edwardian life itself. History was soon to give the book a further asset – nostalgia, and nostalgia is one of the few commodities that do not decline with time.

And so, *The Wind in the Willows* has been for most of the century a prime best-seller and an unmistakeable landmark in child-literature. Few educated people grow up without meeting its characters, its phrases ("messing about in boats," for instance), its evocative woods and waters. Children mainly prefer the preposterous deeds of Toad (a character almost certainly evolved for the small-boy Alistair); adults more often remember Rat and Mole, in the early chapters especially. A newcomer may quite reasonably wonder what keeps the book in living currency. The style is far from simple; it abounds with absorbed quotations, parody and pastiche. Its values are not only "middle-class" but almost feudal. Not a girl or woman can be seen except when about some needed chore. But the central fusion of fact and fantasy still drives through these things.

—Naomi Lewis

GRAMATKY, Hardie. American. Born in Dallas, Texas, 12 April 1907. Educated at Stanford University, California, 1926–28; Chouinard Art School, Los Angeles, 1928–30. Served as Training Film Supervisor in the United States Air Force, 1942–45. Married

Dorothea Cooke in 1932; has one daughter. Head Animator, Walt Disney Productions, Hollywood, 1930–36. Artist and reporter, *Fortune* magazine, New York, 1937–39, and other magazines. Commissioned Air Force War Artist, Vietnam, 1966. Secretary of the American Watercolor Society, 1946–48. Address: 60 Roseville Road, Westport, Connecticut 06880, U.S.A.

PUBLICATIONS FOR CHILDREN (illustrated by the author)

Fiction

> *Little Toot.*   New York, Putnam, 1939; London, Dent, 1946.
> *Hercules: The Story of an Old-Fashioned Fire Engine.*   New York, Putnam, 1940; Kingswood, Surrey, World's Work, 1960.
> *Loopy.*   New York, Putnam, 1941; London, Dent, 1947.
> *Creeper's Jeep.*   New York, Putnam, 1948; Kingswood, Surrey, World's Work, 1960.
> *Sparky: The Story of a Little Trolley Car.*   New York, Putnam, 1952; Kingswood, Surrey, World's Work, 1959.
> *Homer and the Circus Train.*   New York, Putnam, 1957; Kingswood, Surrey, World's Work, 1960.
> *Bolivar.*   New York, Putnam, 1961; Kingswood, Surrey, World's Work, 1962.
> *Nikos and the Sea God.*   New York, Putnam, 1963; Kingswood, Surrey, World's Work, 1964.
> *Little Toot on the Thames.*   New York, Putnam, 1964; Kingswood, Surrey, World's Work, 1965.
> *Little Toot on the Grand Canal.*   New York, Putnam, 1968; Kingswood, Surrey, World's Work, 1969.
> *Happy's Christmas.*   New York, Putnam, 1970; Kingswood, Surrey, World's Work, 1971.
> *Little Toot on the Mississippi.*   New York, Putnam, 1973; Kingswood, Surrey, World's Work, 1974.
> *Little Toot Through the Golden Gate.*   New York, Putnam, 1975; Kingswood, Surrey, World's Work, 1977.

Manuscript Collections: University of Oregon Library, Eugene; Kerlan Collection, University of Minnesota, Minneapolis; de Grummond Collection, University of Southern Mississippi, Hattiesburg.

Illustrator: *Treasure Hunt* by Isabel Boyd Proudfit, 1939; *Skwee-Gee* by Darwin and Hildegarde Teilhat, 1940.

Hardie Gramatky comments:

I like to feel that my work is designed to reach out to children of the younger age group (ages 5 to 8) as a challenge to their potential imaginations. Through an exciting visual approach (paintings that I do in full color) I relate picture to story in a way that makes children love and enjoy the beauty and power of words.

Research for my books is actually done right on the spot, as it were. The background of the story is authentic, which every child seems to appreciate. Through picture and story the reader travels to far-off worlds that he may never have an opportunity to see.

This is a creative venture – working with young minds. From the amount of mail I receive I feel certain the experiment has worked.

*   *   *

Mention *Sparky: The Story of a Little Trolley Car* to anyone, child or adult, and you'll probably get a puzzled look. Say *Little Toot* and the response will be, in all likelihood, a smile and an instant nod of recognition. The trolley car is demonstrably first cousin to the famous tugboat in character and plot. But Hardie Gramatky, author-illustrator of both books and of several others, has grown rich and famous with the story of the perky tug while his other works are comparatively unknown. *Little Toot* is now over 40 years old, as much in demand as ever, as are the author's sequels to the original.

Gramatky's style is attractive; his stories are carefully constructed, simply written but never condescending. He builds on locales familiar to him, on characters children can empathize with. A prime example is *Nikos and the Sea God*, about a modern Greek boy who becomes involved with the formidable Poseidon. The text is enlivened by Gramatky's use of Greek words, readily understood in context. The author has also created *Homer and the Circus Train, Creeper's Jeep* and other satisfying entertainments.

His popularity and assurance of lasting renown, however, rest on the cornerstone of his career, *Little Toot*, and its successors. What makes some books classics and others, which seem equally appealing, also-rans, is a question which all authors (and publishers) would love to have the answer to. Most critics and readers agree that the doughty tugboat grabs and keeps its large audience, generation after generation, because of Toot's innate qualities. Always faced with overwhelming odds, sneered at because of his lack of size and strength, Little Toot is nevertheless the soul of pluck, comparable to the fellow who loses battles but wins the war. Boys and girls who are also small exult in his victories. Children respond to a well-told, suspenseful story which keeps them turning the pages to find out what happens next. But most of all, they like the assurance they get from discovering that, like their hero, they count too – little though they be. A fringe benefit of the Little Toot books (which parents and educators value) is that they give readers information about life in various parts of America, England and Italy. Still, the magnet of the stories is Gramatky's skillful adaptation of a theme at least as old as that familiar since Biblical time, the triumph of David over Goliath.

—Jean F. Mercier

———————

GRAY, Elizabeth Janet. See **VINING, Elizabeth Gray**.

———————

GRAY, Nicholas Stuart. British. Born in Scotland, 23 October 1922. Educated privately. Actor and stage director. Agent: Lawrence Fitch, 113 Wardour Street, London W.1; or, Samuel French Inc., 25 West 45th Street, New York, New York 10036, U.S.A. Address: c/o Faber and Faber Ltd., 3 Queen Square, London WC1N 3AU, England.

PUBLICATIONS FOR CHILDREN

Fiction

Over the Hills to Fabylon, illustrated by the author. London, Oxford University Press, 1954; New York, Hawthorn Books, 1970.
Down in the Cellar, illustrated by Edward Ardizzone. London, Dobson, 1961.

The Seventh Swan: An Adventure Story, illustrated by Joan Jefferson Farjeon.   London,
Dobson, 1962.

The Stone Cage, illustrated by the author.   London, Dobson, 1963.

Grimbold's Other World, illustrated by Charles Keeping.   London, Faber, 1963; New
York, Meredith Press, 1968.

The Apple-Stone, illustrated by William Stobbs.   London, Dobson, 1965; New York,
Meredith Press, 1969.

Mainly in Moonlight, illustrated by Charles Keeping.   London, Faber, 1965; New York,
Meredith Press, 1967.

The Boys, illustrated by Robin Adler.   London, Dobson, 1968.

The Further Adventures of Puss in Boots, illustrated by W.M. Hatch.   London, Faber,
1971.

The Edge of Evening, illustrated by Charles Stewart.   London, Faber, 1976.

Plays

The Haunted (produced London, 1948).

Beauty and the Beast, illustrated by Joan Jefferson Farjeon (produced London,
1950).   London, Oxford University Press, 1951.

The Tinder-Box, adaptation of a story by Hans Christian Andersen, illustrated by Joan
Jefferson Farjeon.   London, Oxford University Press, 1951.

The Princess and the Swineherd, illustrated by Joan Jefferson Farjeon (produced
London, 1952).   London, Oxford University Press, 1952.

Rapunzel (puppet play; produced London, 1953).

The Hunters and the Henwife, illustrated by Joan Jefferson Farjeon.   London, Oxford
University Press, 1954.

The Marvellous Story of Puss in Boots, illustrated by Joan Jefferson Farjeon (also
director: produced London, 1954).   London, Oxford University Press, 1955.

The Imperial Nightingale, adaptation of a story by Hans Christian Andersen, illustrated
by Joan Jefferson Farjeon (also director: produced London, 1956).   London, Oxford
University Press, 1957.

New Clothes for the Emperor, adaptation of a story by Hans Christian Andersen,
illustrated by Joan Jefferson Farjeon (produced London, 1957).   London, Oxford
University Press, 1957.

The Other Cinderella, with Due Acknowledgements to All the Earlier Versions, illustrated
by Joan Jefferson Farjeon.   London, Oxford University Press, 1958.

The Seventh Swan, illustrated by Joan Jefferson Farjeon.   London, Dobson, 1962.

The Wrong Side of the Moon, based on a story by the Grimm brothers and his own story
The Stone Cage (produced Edinburgh, 1966; London, 1968).

Lights Up (produced London, 1967).

New Lamps for Old, illustrated by Joan Jefferson Farjeon (also director: produced
Guildford, Surrey, 1968).   London, Dobson, 1968.

Gawain and the Green Knight, illustrated by Victor Ambrus.   London, Dobson, 1969.

Illustrator: *James and Macarthur* by Jenny Laird, 1951.

Theatrical Activities:

Director: **Plays** – *Beauty and the Beast*, London, 1953; *The Marvellous Story of Puss in
Boots*, London, 1954; *The Imperial Nightingale*, London, 1956; *New Clothes for the
Emperor*; *The Wrong Side of the Moon*, tour, 1967; *New Lamps for Old*, Guildford, Surrey,
1968; *The Shepherd's Play*, Gloucestershire, 1975.

Actor: **Plays** – Francis in *The Haunted*, London, 1948; understudied The Beast in *Beauty
and the Beast*, London, 1951; Prince Etienne in *The Princess and the Swineherd*, London,

1952; Puss in *The Marvellous Story of Puss in Boots*, London and tours; Second Suspicious Character, London, 1956, and later Four Winds in *The Imperial Nightingale*; Piers in *New Clothes for the Emperor*, London, 1957; Tomlyn in *The Wrong Side of the Moon*, Edinburgh, 1966, London, 1968; Slave of the Lamp in *New Lamps for Old*, Guildford, Surrey, 1968; Iago in *Othello* by Shakespeare, Malvern, Worcestershire, 1969.

*   *   *

Nicholas Stuart Gray is an actor and director, and first began writing as a dramatist. Often he develops familiar fairy tales, but with the range and subtlety to attract an adult audience as much as children. Beneath the sparkle and gaiety there are profounder themes – the beauty and kindness and terror of Death in *The Imperial Nightingale*, the inward shadows of self-distrust and the loneliness of being "different" in *Gawain and the Green Knight*. However familiar the story, the events are always unexpected. But the plays are never beyond the scope of young actors and audiences, for the very full stage directions help them to realise character and mood, and the arts of magic are contrived to be theatrically effective by very simple means. This is the kind of material, sensitive and intelligent, that children most need.

Some of the stories have been written both as plays and novels. One of the most satisfying is *The Stone Cage*, the story of Rapunzel told by Tomlyn, the witch's cat and half-unwilling, half-fascinated familiar. A daring, impudent, and devious cat, with a wry sense of humour, he believes himself to hate everyone and trust no one. His fellow-familiar, Marshall, the ancient raven, is terrified of magic. Between them they save Rapunzel, but are punished by exile to the terrible far side of the moon. Yet when Mother Gotel is caught by her own black magic, Marshall and Tomlyn elect to stay with her in her desolation until she has learned to grow a human heart again. Under Tomlyn's racy, throw-away, ironic account of things runs always the current of deeper feeling, the tragedy and triumphs of human experience. Through the witch herself, vicious, treacherous, and cruel, we become increasingly aware of pity for misery and self-inflicted loneliness as much as for the griefs of those who love.

The novels with completely original plots, such as *Down in the Cellar* and *The Apple-Stone*, give scope for the author's hilarious inventiveness but are never merely funny. Both these involve a group of redoubtable but completely credible children. In the latter book they find the fabulous Apple-Stone which will animate any inanimate object it touches. Their use of it, sometimes intentional, sometimes accidental, leads to adventures absurd, sad, or horrific, through which they slowly learn the heavy responsibility of magic. Their understanding and sympathy are enlarged in many ways before the Apple-Stone slips away again into "the untroubled quiet of the earth and the night."

The two books of short stories, *Mainly in Moonlight* and *The Edge of Evening*, exhibit the full range and versatility of Mr. Gray's writing. They have the wildly unpredictable humour, the sudden darknesses and shadows, the poise between the worlds of night and day, of magic and reality, that show their Highland origin. Their demons and hippogriffs, knights and mermaids, sad little witches and perplexed humans, are funny, touching, and fascinating. So are the animals – dogs, cats, horses, goats – beautifully drawn by a writer who loves and respects them. Some of the stories haunt the heart for a long time afterwards – the tragedy of human stupidity and misunderstanding in "The Star Beast" and its curiously inverted reflection in "The Blot on the Landscape" (both "space" stories of a very unexpected kind), the nostalgic sadness of "The Golden Beasts" or "The Stranger."

Laughter, magic, and pity are the stuff of all Mr. Gray's work. He is probably a wizard himself, with a sense of humour – a dangerous but irresistible combination.

—Margaret Greaves

GREAVES, Margaret. British. Born in Birmingham, Warwickshire, 13 June 1914. Educated at Alice Ottley School, Worcester, 1927–33; St. Hugh's College, Oxford (scholar), 1933–38, B.A. (honours) in English 1936. B. Litt. 1938, M.A. 1944. Served in the British Women's Land Army, 1941–43. English Mistress, High School, Lincoln, 1938–40, Priory School, Shrewsbury, 1940–41, and Pate's Grammar School, Cheltenham, 1943–46; Lecturer, 1946–60, and Principal Lecturer and Head of the English Department, 1960–70, St. Mary's College, Cheltenham. Address: Castle House, Winchcombe, Cheltenham, Gloucestershire GL54 5LH, England.

PUBLICATIONS FOR CHILDREN

Fiction

Gallimaufry series (includes *The Snowman of Biddle, The Rainbow Sun, King Solomon and the Hoopoes, The Great Bell of Peking*), illustrated by Jill McDonald. London, Methuen, 4 vols., 1971; Glendale, California, Bowmar, 4 vols., 1975.

The Dagger and the Bird, illustrated by Jill McDonald. London, Methuen, 1971; New York, Harper, 1975.

The Grandmother Stone. London, Methuen, 1972; as *Stone of Terror*, London, Target, and New York, Harper, 1974.

Little Jacko and the Wolf People, illustrated by Jill McDonald. London, Methuen, 1973.

The Gryphon Quest. London, Methuen, 1974.

Curfew. London, Methuen, 1975.

The Night of the Goat, illustrated by Trevor Ridley. London, Abelard Schuman, 1976.

Nothing Ever Happens on Sundays. London, BBC Publications, 1976.

Other

English for Juniors series (includes *Your Turn Next, One World and Another, Gallery, Two at Number Twenty, What Am I?*), illustrated by Jill McDonald. London, Methuen, 5 vols., 1966–72; as *Gallery Wonders*, Glendale, California, Bowmar, 1975.

Editor, *Scrap-Box: Poems for Grown-Ups to Share with Children*, illustrated by Jill McDonald. London, Methuen, 1969.

PUBLICATIONS FOR ADULTS

Other

The Blazon of Honour: A Study in Renaissance Magnanimity. London, Methuen, and New York, Barnes and Noble, 1964.

Regency Patron: Sir George Beaumont. London, Methuen, 1966.

Margaret Greaves comments:

I have never outgrown the children's books that I loved. As I have grown older I have only added to the range and depth of my imaginative reading. So, when I write for children, I write also for myself. Because I have lived nearly always in the country I think I have a particular caring for natural things, a feeling for the past, and a predisposition towards folklore and magic. But above all I care about people; and whether my stories are those of "real life" or "fantasy" (what is the distinction? – they are only different ways of presenting such glimmers of truth as one is privileged to see), the core of my interest is in human relationships.

*   *   *

In *Little Jacko and the Wolf People* Margaret Greaves presents a "western." There are dangers and courage, friendship and co-operation, ritual, magic and celebration, wolves and desperadoes. An exciting package in a story told with swift economy and but a few hundred words for the very young.

At the other end of the age-range, in *Curfew*, she explores a profound philosophical problem. Set in the early 19th century, the story is told of a boy on the run from justice whose gullibility has led him into a state where false witness can be upheld against him. His struggles to survive involve him in petty thefts and deceit, and eventually lead him to become entangled with smuggling and murder. As the boy-hero searches for honest values in a world both perfidious and generous he finds that Law and Justice are not in themselves sufficient guides to conduct. Only in probing a deeper moral understanding, he learns, will resolution be found for the dilemmas he must face. The adolescent reader who is used to having his stories neatly tied up at the end with evil overcome and triumphant virtue rewarded will find this novel's refusal to offer cut and dried answers salutary and stimulating.

If Margaret Greaves has the courage to leave her heroes (and readers!) in uncertainty and nagging doubt it is because, enriched in self-knowledge, they emerge from adventures equipped to face a more complex world. Neither the heroes and heroines of *The Dagger and the Bird* nor of *The Grandmother Stone* are assured of living happily ever after. In the former their long-lost brother has yet to adjust to the family, to fit into the warmth and harsh reality of life at the smithy after the insubstantial and wish-fulfilling faerie world. Like his brother and sister before him, he will have to learn to choose wisely between Truth and Show.

This is an excellent little book. A world of faerie magic is conjured up, as also in *The Gryphon Quest*, through a richness of language drawing concrete images. It is at once tangibly present and shiftingly insubstantial. In *The Grandmother Stone*, however, a novel likely to attract an older readership, the power of magic and its association with credulity and popular superstition are measured against courage and independence of mind. Margaret Greaves handles the themes of witchcraft, iconolatry and bigotry in a story set in Sark about the time of the civil wars. Her heroes survive in displaying a clear-sighted faith in the worth of people. They emerge, not to blaring trumpets and popular acclaim, but to a sense of personal maturity. Still isolated they are, if sadder, wiser in self-knowledge and with fewer illusions about others. A remarkable feature of this novel too is its handling of dawning sexuality. Awakening physical awareness is evoked with sensitivity and totally without prurience.

Few children's writers can have commanded the range, assurance and depth of Margaret Greaves.

—Myles McDowell

GREEN, Roger (Gilbert) Lancelyn. British. Born in Norwich, Norfolk, 2 November 1918. Educated at Dane Court, Pyrford, Surrey; Liverpool College; Merton College, Oxford, 1937–42, B.A. 1940, B. Litt. and M.A. 1944. Married June Burdett in 1948; has two sons and one daughter. Actor, Oxford and London, 1942–45; antiquarian bookseller, Oxford, 1943; Deputy Librarian, Merton College, Oxford, 1945–50; William Noble Research Fellow in English, 1950–52, and Member of Council, 1964–70, University of Liverpool. Since 1957, Editor, *Kipling Journal*, London. Andrew Lang Lecturer, St. Andrews University, Scotland,

1968. Recipient: Mythopoeic Society Award, 1975; Scout Association Chief Scout's Medal, 1976. Address: Poulton Hall, Poulton-Lancelyn, Bebington, Wirral, Cheshire L63 9LN, England.

PUBLICATIONS FOR CHILDREN

Fiction

The Wonderful Stranger: A Holiday Romance, illustrated by John Baynes. London, Methuen, 1950.

The Luck of the Lynns, illustrated by Sheila Macgregor. London, Methuen, 1952.

The Secret of Rusticoker, illustrated by Sheila Macgregor. London, Methuen, 1953.

The Theft of the Golden Cat, illustrated by Edward McGrath. London, Methuen, 1955.

Mystery at Mycenae: An Adventure Story of Ancient Greece, illustrated by Margery Gill. London, Bodley Head, 1957; New York, Barnes and Noble, 1959.

The Land Beyond the North, illustrated by Douglas Hall. London, Bodley Head, 1958; New York, Walck, 1959.

The Land of the Lord High Tiger, illustrated by J.S. Goodall. London, Bell, 1958.

The Luck of Troy, illustrated by Margery Gill. London, Bodley Head, 1961; Philadelphia, Dufour, 1965.

Other

The Sleeping Beauty and Other Tales, illustrated by Rene Cloke. Leicester, Ward, 1947.

Beauty and the Beast, and Other Tales, illustrated by Rene Cloke. Leicester, Ward, 1948.

The Story of Lewis Carroll. London, Methuen, 1949; New York, H. Schuman, 1950.

King Arthur and His Knights of the Round Table, illustrated by Lotte Reiniger. London, Penguin, 1953.

The Adventures of Robin Hood, illustrated by Arthur Hall. London, Penguin, 1956.

Old Greek Fairy Tales, illustrated by Ernest H. Shepard. London, Bell, 1958; New York, Roy, 1969.

Tales of the Greek Heroes, illustrated by Betty Middleton-Sandford. London, Penguin, 1958.

The Tale of Troy: Retold from the Ancient Authors, illustrated by Betty Middleton-Sandford. London, Penguin, 1958.

Heroes of Greece and Troy (includes *Tales of the Greek Heroes* and *The Tale of Troy*). illustrated by Heather Copley and Christopher Chamberlain. London, Bodley Head, 1960; New York, Walck, 1961; revised edition, Bodley Head, 1973.

The Saga of Asgard: Retold from the Old Norse Poems and Tales, illustrated by Brian Wildsmith. London, Penguin, 1960; as *Myths of the Norsemen*, London, Bodley Head, 1962; Philadelphia, Dufour, 1964.

The True Book about Ancient Greece, illustrated by N. G. Wilson. London, Muller, 1960.

Ancient Greece, illustrated by Carol Barker. London, Weidenfeld and Nicolson, 1962; New York, Day, 1969.

Once, Long Ago: Folk and Fairy Tales of the World, illustrated by Vojtěch Kubasta. London, Golden Pleasure Books, 1962; as *Once upon a Time: Folk and Fairy Tales of the World*, New York, Golden Press, 1962; as *My Book of Favourite Fairy Tales*, London, Hamlyn, 1969.

Authors and Places: A Literary Pilgrimage, illustrated by John Bowers. London, Batsford, 1963; New York, Putnam, 1964.

Ancient Egypt, illustrated by Elizabeth Hammond.   London, Weidenfeld and Nicolson, 1963; New York, Day, 1964.

Tales of the Greeks and Trojans, illustrated by Janet and Anne Grahame Johnstone.   London, Purnell, 1964.

Tales from Shakespeare (The Comedies and *Tragedies and Romances)*, illustrated by Richard Beer.   London, Gollancz, 2 vols., 1964–65; New York, Atheneum, 1965.

Tales the Muses Told: Ancient Greek Myths, illustrated by Shirley Hughes.   London, Bodley Head, and New York, Walck, 1965.

A Book of Myths, illustrated by Joan Kiddell-Monroe.   London, Dent, and New York, Dutton, 1965.

Myths from Many Lands, illustrated by Janet and Anne Grahame Johnstone.   London, Purnell, 1965.

Folk Tales of the World, illustrated by Janet and Anne Grahame Johnstone.   London, Purnell, and Boston, Ginn, 1966.

Sir Lancelot of the Lake, illustrated by Janet and Anne Grahame Johnstone.   London, Purnell, 1966.

Stories of Ancient Greece, illustrated by Doreen Roberts.   London, Hamlyn, 1967.

Tales of Ancient Egypt, illustrated by Heather Copley.   London, Bodley Head, 1967; New York, Walck, 1968.

Jason and the Golden Fleece, illustrated by Janet and Anne Grahame Johnstone.   London, Purnell, 1968.

The Tale of Ancient Israel, illustrated by Charles Keeping.   London, Dent, and New York, Dutton, 1969.

The Tale of Thebes, illustrated by Jael Jordan.   London and New York, Cambridge University Press, 1977.

Editor, *Modern Fairy Stories*, illustrated by Ernest H. Shepard.   London, Dent, and New York, Dutton, 1955.

Editor, *The Book of Nonsense*, illustrated by Charles Folkard.   London, Dent, and New York, Dutton, 1956.

Editor, *Fairy Stories*, by Mary Louisa Molesworth.   London, Harvill Press, 1957.

Editor, *Tales of Make-Believe*, illustrated by Harry Toothill.   London, Dent, and New York, Dutton, 1960.

Editor, *The Book of Verse for Children*, illustrated by Mary Shillabeer.   London, Dent, 1962.

Editor, *Ten Tales of Detection*.   London, Dent, and New York, Dutton, 1967.

Editor, *Stories and Poems*, by Rudyard Kipling.   London, Dent, 1970.

Editor, *Thirteen Uncanny Tales*, illustrated by Ray Ogden.   London, Dent, and New York, Dutton, 1970.

Editor, *The Hamish Hamilton Book of Dragons*, illustrated by Krystyna Turska.   London, Hamish Hamilton, 1970; as *A Calvacade of Dragons*, New York, Walck, 1970.

Editor, *Alice's Adventures in Wonderland, and Through the Looking-Glass and What Alice Found There*, by Lewis Carroll, illustrated by John Tenniel.   London and New York, Oxford University Press, 1971.

Editor, *Tales of Terror and Fantasy: Ten Stories from "Tales of Mystery and Imagination,"* by Edgar Allan Poe, illustrated by Arthur Rackham.   London, Dent, 1971.

Editor, *Ten Tales of Adventure*, illustrated by Philip Gough.   London, Dent, 1972.

Editor, *The Hamish Hamilton Book of Magicians*, illustrated by Victor Ambrus.   London, Hamish Hamilton, 1973; as *A Cavalcade of Magicians*, New York, Walck, 1973.

Editor, *Strange Adventures in Time*, illustrated by George Adamson.   London, Dent, and New York, Dutton, 1974.

Editor, *The Hamish Hamilton Book of Other Worlds*, illustrated by Victor Ambrus. London, Hamish Hamilton, 1976.

PUBLICATIONS FOR ADULTS

Novel

From the World's End: A Fantasy.   Leicester, Ward, 1948; New York, Ballantine, 1971.

Verse

The Lost July and Other Poems.   London, Fortune Press, 1945.
The Singing Rose and Other Poems.   Leicester, Ward, 1947.

Other

Tellers of Tales.   Leicester, Ward, 1946; revised edition, London, Ward, and New York, Watts, 1965.
Andrew Lang: A Critical Biography with a Short Title Bibliography of the Works of Andrew Lang.   Leicester, Ward, 1946; Folcroft, Pennsylvania, Folcroft Editions, 1973.
Poulton-Lancelyn: The Story of an Ancestral Home.   Oxford, Oxonian Press, 1948.
A.E.W. Mason: The Adventures of a Story Teller.   London, Parrish, 1952.
Fifty Years of "Peter Pan."   London, Davies, 1954.
Into Other Worlds: Space-Flight in Fiction from Lucian to Lewis.   London and New York, Abelard Schuman, 1957.
Lewis Carroll.   London, Bodley Head, 1960; New York, Walck, 1962.
J. M. Barrie.   London, Bodley Head, 1960; New York, Walck, 1961.
Mrs. Molesworth.   London, Bodley Head, 1961; New York, Walck, 1964.
Andrew Lang.   London, Bodley Head, and New York, Walck, 1962.
The Lewis Carroll Handbook, Being a New Version of a Handbook of the Literature of the Rev. C.L. Dodgson.   London, Oxford University Press, 1962; revised edition, London, Dawson, and New York, Barnes and Noble, 1970.
C.S. Lewis.   London, Bodley Head, and New York, Walck, 1963; revised edition, in *Three Bodley Head Monographs*, Bodley Head, 1969.
Kipling and the Children.   London, Elek, 1965.
C.S. Lewis: A Biography, with Walter Hooper.   London, Collins, and New York, Harcourt Brace, 1974.
"Holmes, This is Amazing": Essays in Unorthodox Research.   Privately printed, 1975.

Editor, *The Diaries of Lewis Carroll.*   London, Cassell, 2 vols., 1953; New York, Oxford University Press, 1954.
Editor, *A Century of Humorous Verse, 1850–1950.*   London, Dent, and New York, Dutton, 1959.
Editor, *The Readers' Guide to Rudyard Kipling's Work.*   Canterbury, Gibbs, 1961.
Editor, *Plays and Stories*, by J.M. Barrie.   London, Dent, and New York, Dutton, 1962.
Editor, *The Works of Lewis Carroll*, illustrated by John Tenniel.   London, Hamlyn, 1965.
Editor, *Kipling: The Critical Heritage.*   London, Routledge, and New York, Barnes and Noble, 1971.

Translator, *The Searching Satyrs*, by Sophocles.   Leicester, Ward, 1946.

Translator, *Two Satyr Plays: Euripides' Cyclops and Sophocles' Ichneutai*.   London, Penguin, 1957.

Theatrical Activities:

Actor: **Play** – Pirate Noodler in *Peter Pan* by J.M. Barrie, London and tour, 1942–43.

Roger Lancelyn Green comments:

My intention with my first four works of fiction was to write exciting adventure stories set against a background of the way of life on a country estate in the 1920's and 30's – a way of life that had almost passed away even as I wrote. But the setting was too "out of date" and not yet sufficiently "period" to satisfy the critics. None of the four reached a second edition – and two more (the set) remain unpublished.

Meanwhile, however, I had begun retelling myths, legends and fairy tales – with great success. And I set myself to give young readers as many of the great stories of the ancient world as I could – mainly of ancient Greece but also Egypt, the Middle East, Scandinavia and our own national legends. That many of these have been reprinted almost annually shows that I have at least made good a "felt want" now that Latin and Greek are so little taught.

Deep study of Greek legends and my great love for Greece and its literature led me to attempt to use Greek legends as the basis of fictional narratives – "historical romances" in which the history was that of the world of Homer: *Mystery at Mycenae*, a detective story with Odysseus as the detective; *The Land Beyond the North*, an adventure story of the Argonauts' return from Calchis with the Golden Fleece; and, the most successful, *The Luck of Troy*, a spy story told from the point of view of a Greek boy in Troy during the siege and fall.

The Land of the Lord High Tiger was a departure in the direction of the Carroll-Nesbit tradition written round my old "stuffed animals" and the stories I told them as a child. This is my own favourite (*The Luck of Troy* is my best) – but again the sequel remains unpublished.

*   *   *

Although Roger Lancelyn Green's main contribution to children's literature is his distinguished work as a compiler, editor and reteller of tales, there are in his impressively long list of titles some eight books, all, with the exception of *The Luck of Troy* (1961), published in the 1950's (and all except the last out of print), that are works of fiction in a stricter sense. It is a pity that Green should have neglected this form of writing for so long, for in the three "classical" novels for older readers, *Mystery at Mycenae*, *The Land Beyond the North*, and *The Luck of Troy*, there is evidence of a developing skill in creating intelligent and imaginative novels.

The Land of the Lord High Tiger, a whimsical tale for younger children, is a hotchpotch fantasy which Roger and Priscilla enter through a picture of a tiger on the bedroom wall. They become a prince and princess, encountering more or less predictable pieces of pantomime machinery such as three wishes, lost slippers, giants, wizards, a robber captain memorably named Habbakuk Hak, magic carpets (eaten by Tiger Moths!) and last-minute rescues. Odd oaths ("Screwtape and Slogarithma") and tortured puns ("only school-girls and tidal-waves have serge on them") have a period charm, while the villains are too funny to be frightening.

Green is much more at home in ancient Greece where his inventive flair combines well with his deep knowledge and love of classical myth, legend and literature. *Mystery at Mycenae*, the story of Helen of Troy's earlier abduction as a young girl, told in the style of a detective novel, is perhaps marred by excessive schoolmasterly explanation and lines of dialogue such as "It's all a beastly muddle," and "I hawk at higher game, ha-ha," while half way through the gaff is blown on the mystery. But the blend of classical authenticity with imaginative speculation is vindicated in the sequel, *The Luck of Troy*, which is, as it were, the inside story of the last year of the great siege as experienced by the twelve-year-old Nicostratus, Helen's son by Menelaus, who had been taken as a baby to Troy by Paris along with his mother. The complexities of the narrative are skilfully and imaginatively handled in clear, unfussy prose, while questions of loyalty, courage and civilised conduct are explored through the boy's awakening consciousness of the conflict between his Greek origin and his Trojan upbringing. With the decline of the classics in schools, this novel, together with *The Land Beyond the North*, which is an audacious but not too implausible story linking Jason's journey to the Hyperboreans with Daedalus and the building of Stonehenge, is an imaginative as well as an effective way for a young reader to become acquainted with classical antiquity.

—Graham Hammond

GREENE, Bette. American. Born in Memphis, Tennessee, 28 June 1934. Attended the University of Alabama, University, 1952; Columbia University, New York, 1955. Married Donald Sumner Greene in 1959; has two children. Recipient: Society of Children's Book Writers Golden Kite Award, 1973. Agent: Sheldon Fogelman, 10 East 40th Street, New York, New York 10016. Address: 338 Clinton Road, Brookline, Massachusetts 02146, U.S.A.

PUBLICATIONS FOR CHILDREN

Fiction

> *Summer of My German Soldier.* New York, Dial Press, 1973; London, Hamish Hamilton, 1974.
> *Philip Hall Likes Me. I Reckon Maybe*, illustrated by Charles Lilly. New York, Dial Press, 1974; London, Hamish Hamilton, 1976.
> *Morning Is a Long Time Coming.* New York, Dial Press, 1978.

Bette Greene comments:
I grew up in a small town in the Arkansas Delta (the very eye of the Bible Belt) during the war bond and pin-up picture days of World War II. My friends considered me the luckiest girl in town because, while sugar was being rationed, my parents owned a country store full of gum and candy. But on the contrary, I considered myself the unluckiest, unhappiest girl in town because my religion (Jewish) was alien to my community, my friends and especially myself. I used to sneak into the tents of itinerant Protestant preachers the way a teenager today might sneak into an X-rated movie. And as the evangelist spoke with easy familiarity of the fires of Hell, I could feel its heat. So I "caught" religion as simply as others caught colds.
And it is from these roots – of childhood sights, smells, and memories – that I write.

*   *   *

Summer of My German Soldier was an outstanding achievement as a first novel and it established Bette Greene as a first class writer from the very start. Set in the 1940's, it is a powerful story of a 12-year-old Arkansas girl who harbours an escaped German prisoner-of-war. Essentially, it tells of her alienation from immediate family and community, and her desperate need to give and receive love and recognition. The irony is that Patty Bergen, who is Jewish, and therefore an alien in a conservative, white-Anglo-Saxon town (so small that it has only one two-story house), has only an "enemy" soldier and a black housemaid to turn to for friendship. Her self-centred mother and brooding and brutal father are presented as pathetic – or even pathological – villains: it is not merely a case of a daughter at odds with her parents, unable to understand them, for they treat her as having no rights of her own, and her father's obsessive suspicion, bitterness, and self-pity cannot explain his savagely punitive attitude towards his hapless daughter.

Summer of My German Soldier is an intense and concentrated study, assured and confident. It is marred only by the unlikely portrayal of the young German soldier, whose proper conduct, eloquent language, glib philosophizing, handsome demeanor and impeccable breeding ask too much of the critical reader's willing suspension of disbelief. On the other hand, this is likely to help guarantee the book's acceptance by teen-age readers, and the idealised romanticism is one which reflects Patty's viewpoint most appropriately.

Summer of My German Soldier was such a striking and compelling first novel, with such a strong emphasis on exciting plot and serious thematic treatment that readers expecting more of the same were bound to be disappointed by *Philip Hall Likes Me. I Reckon Maybe*. It is no sequel. It is quite unlike the former book, being a series of short stories, episodes from green and pleasant childhood days in Arkansas, linked loosely through 11-year-old Beth Lambert's affection for her classmate Philip Hall. She is an intelligent, happy child, with loving parents. Nothing in the earlier book prepares the reader for the innocence, fun, optimism, and sunniness of this book. It does have the expected drive and vitality but infused in this case with tenderness and humour. The style is so direct that the unifying theme is introduced in the very first page, and the simple representation of dialogue is extraordinarily polished and convincing. Bette Greene is a writer of considerable ability, a worthy successor to the great Louise Fitzhugh (their work is similar in some respects), but with few equals anywhere, in terms of promise.

—Walter McVitty

GREENE, Constance C(larke).   American.   Born in New York City, 27 October 1924. Educated at Marymount Academy, New York, graduated, 1942; Skidmore College, Saratoga Springs, New York, 1942–44. Married Philip M. Greene in 1946; has five children. Agent: Marilyn Marlow, Curtis Brown Ltd., 575 Madison Avenue, New York, New York 10022. Address: R.F.D. 1, Poland Springs, Maine 04274. U.S.A.

PUBLICATIONS FOR CHILDREN

Fiction

A Girl Called Al, illustrated by Byron Barton.   New York, Viking Press, 1969.
Leo the Lioness.   New York, Viking Press, 1970.
The Good Luck Bogie Hat.   New York, Viking Press, 1971.
The Unmaking of Rabbit.   New York, Viking Press, 1972.
Isabelle the Itch, illustrated by Emily McCully.   New York, Viking Press, 1973.
The Ears of Louis, illustrated by Nola Langner.   New York, Viking Press, 1974.
I Know You, Al, illustrated by Byron Barton.   New York, Viking Press, 1975; London, Penguin, 1977.
Beat the Turtle Drum, illustrated by Donna Diamond.   New York, Viking Press, 1976.
Getting Nowhere.   New York, Viking Press, 1977.

Constance C. Greene comments:

If I had to categorize my books for children, I would say they were contemporary and, hopefully, funny. Maybe even a bit joyous on occasion. Children are hard-nosed, resilient, and tough little creatures. They know that life isn't a bowl of cherries but they like to laugh, perhaps even more than adults. And I hope I provide some laughter for them. My most recent book, however, is about two sisters, one of whom dies. The title, *Beat the Turtle Drum*, is taken from a musical play by Ian Serraillier. For a long time I had wanted to write about death, as I myself had a sister who died, and it was a difficult task; but I'm glad I did what I set out to do.

*   *   *

Warmth, vitality, and wit, three distinguishing marks of quality in Constance C. Greene's novels, are particularly evident in her characterizations. Her ability to draw believable characters, identifiable to the boy or girl next door, is Greene's strength and accounts for her high popularity with young readers. So strong is it, in fact, that she relies on her creations to carry the story through a usually slim, episodic plot line and successfully carries it off.

With a sharply observant eye she portrays her young protagonists, firmly roots them in reality, and rounds them out as distinct, sometimes quirky personalities who project themselves through casual, glib and often amusing dialog. The result is a range of lively characters: cool, cocky Ben who sports a black Humphrey Bogart hat in *Good-Luck Bogie Hat*, overly energetic Isabelle who arranges daily fist fights with Herbie in *Isabelle the Itch*, and non-conformist Al who continually tells her friends, "Have a weird day!" in *I Know You, Al*. Nor does Greene slight her minor characters, as evidenced by Herbie, who delights in making neck boils from wads of chewed gum in *Isabelle the Itch* or Ack-Ack Ackerman, whose greatest ambition is to make the Ten Most Wanted Criminals List in *Good-Luck Bogie Hat*.

Perhaps the most interesting of Greene's inventions, however, are the elderly, somewhat eccentric friends who bolster the protagonists' confidence, provide emotional refuge, and occasionally disperse tidbits of wisdom. There is Mrs. Stern in *Isabelle the Itch*, who continually paints her house; Mrs. Beeble in *The Ears of Louis*, who cheats at poker; and Mr. Richards in *A Girl Called Al*, who shines his kitchen floor with clothes tied to his shoes.

The underlying theme in Greene's work is self-adjustment. And, although the problem may loom large in the beholder's eye, it is often a growing-up pain such as Louie's self-consciousness about his ears, Al's fear of attending her father's wedding, or Tibb's horror at discovering her idol is pregnant and getting married in *Leo the Lioness*. The resolution is slowly brought about through the character's own realization of the problem and his or her ability to cope with it.

In *Beat the Turtle Drum* the author again permeates her story with warm, witty and vibrant characters, but her growth as a writer is clearly evident here as Greene deepens her portrayals and reaches toward creating a more complex novel. For example, Kate, the narrator, is more fully explored than the narrator in the two Al books, who doesn't even have a name. And, while still using a series of episodes to create the action, she moves each situation inevitably toward Joss' death at the climax, with the characters, though grief-stricken, able to handle the crisis. Although a death occurs in *A Girl Called Al*, it is a minor happening, whereas in *Beat the Turtle Drum*, it is the story's focus, and Greene handles it in a poignant, resourceful and sensitive way.

Time and place are unimportant in Greene's novels; rather she strikes a universal note, presenting contemporary problems laced with frankness and humor to an empathic audience of young readers.

—Barbara Elleman

GREENE, Graham. British. Born in Berkhamsted, Hertfordshire, 2 October 1904. Educated at Berkhamsted School; Balliol College, Oxford. Served in the Foreign Office, London, 1941–44. Married Vivien Dayrell-Browning in 1927; has two children. Staff Member, *The Times*, London 1926–30; Movie Critic, 1937–40, and Literary Editor, 1940–41, *Spectator*, London. Director, Eyre and Spottiswoode, publishers, London, 1944–48, and The Bodley Head, publishers, London, 1958–68. Recipient: Hawthornden Prize, 1941;James Tait Black Memorial Prize, 1949; Shakespeare Prize, Hamburg, 1968; Thomas More Medal, 1973. Litt.D.: Cambridge University, 1962; D.Litt.: Edinburgh University, 1967. Honorary Fellow, Balliol College, 1963. Companion of Honour, 1966. Chevalier of the Legion of Honour, 1969. Address: c/o The Bodley Head, 9 Bow Street, London WC2E 7AL, England.

PUBLICATIONS FOR CHILDREN (illustrated by Dorothy Craigie)

Fiction

> *The Little Train* (published anonymously). London, Eyre and Spottiswoode, 1946; New York, Lothrop, 1958.
> *The Little Fire Engine*. London, Parrish, 1950; as *The Little Red Fire Engine*, New York, Lothrop, 1952.
> *The Little Horse Bus*. London, Parrish, 1952; New York, Lothrop, 1954.
> *The Little Steam Roller: A Story of Mystery and Detection*. London, Parrish, 1953; New York, Lothrop, 1955.

PUBLICATIONS FOR ADULTS

Novels

> *The Man Within*. London, Heinemann, and New York, Doubleday, 1929.
> *The Name of Action*. London, Heinemann, 1930; New York, Doubleday, 1931.
> *Rumour at Nightfall*. London, Heinemann, 1931; New York, Doubleday, 1932.
> *Stamboul Train: An Entertainment*. London, Heinemann, 1932; as *Orient Express: An Entertainment*, New York, Doubleday, 1933.
> *It's a Battlefield*. London, Heinemann, and New York, Doubleday, 1934.
> *England Made Me*. London, Heinemann, and New York, Doubleday, 1935.
> *A Gun for Sale: An Entertainment*. London, Heinemann, 1936; as *This Gun for Hire: An Entertainment*, New York, Doubleday, 1936.
> *Brighton Rock*. London, Heinemann, 1938; as *Brighton Rock: An Entertainment*, New York, Viking Press, 1938.
> *The Confidential Agent*. London, Heinemann, and New York, Viking Press, 1939.
> *The Power and the Glory*. London, Heinemann, 1940; as *The Labyrinthine Ways*, New York, Viking Press, 1940.
> *The Ministry of Fear: An Entertainment*. London, Heinemann, and New York, Viking Press, 1943.
> *The Heart of the Matter*. London, Heinemann, and New York, Viking Press, 1948.
> *The End of the Affair*. London, Heinemann, and New York, Viking Press, 1951.
> *The Third Man: An Entertainment*. New York, Viking Press, 1950.
> *The Third Man and The Fallen Idol*. London, Heinemann, 1950.
> *Loser Takes All: An Entertainment*. London, Heinemann, 1955; New York, Viking Press, 1957.
> *The Quiet American*. London, Heinemann, 1955; New York, Viking Press, 1956.
> *Our Man in Havana: An Entertainment*. London, Heinemann, and New York, Viking Press, 1958.
> *A Burnt-Out Case*. London, Heinemann, and New York, Viking Press, 1961.

The Comedians. London, Bodley Head, and New York, Viking Press, 1966.
Travels with My Aunt. London, Bodley Head, 1969; New York, Viking Press, 1970.
The Honorary Consul. London, Bodley Head, and New York, Viking Press, 1973.
The Human Factor. London, Bodley Head, 1978.

Short Stories

The Basement Room and Other Stories. London, Cresset Press, 1935.
The Bear Fell Free. London, Grayson, 1935.
Twenty-four Stories, with James Laver and Sylvia Townsend Warner. London, Cresset Press, 1939.
Nineteen Stories. London, Heinemann, 1947; New York, Viking Press, 1949; augmented edition, as *Twenty-one Stories*, London, Heinemann, 1954.
A Visit to Morin. Privately printed, 1959.
A Sense of Reality. London, Bodley Head, and New York, Viking Press, 1963.
May We Borrow Your Husband? and Other Comedies of the Sexual Life. London, Bodley Head, and New York, Viking Press, 1967.
The Collected Stories of Graham Greene. London, Bodley Head-Heinemann, 1972; New York, Viking Press, 1973.

Plays

The Living Room (produced London, 1953; New York, 1954). London, Heinemann, 1953; New York, Viking Press, 1954.
The Potting Shed (produced New York, 1957; London, 1958). New York, Viking Press, 1957; London, Heinemann, 1958.
The Complaisant Lover (produced London, 1959; New York, 1961). London, Heinemann, 1959; New York, Viking Press, 1961.
Carving a Statue (produced London, 1964; New York, 1968). London, Bodley Head, 1964.
The Third Man: A Film, with Carol Reed. London, Lorrimer Films, 1969.
Alas, Poor Maling, adaptation of his own story (broadcast, 1975). Published in *Shades of Greene,* London, Bodley Head-Heinemann, 1975.
The Return of A. J. Raffles: An Edwardian Comedy Based Somewhat Loosely on E. W. Hornung's Characters in "The Amateur Cracksman" (produced London, 1975). London, Bodley Head, 1975; New York, Simon and Schuster, 1976.

Screenplays: *21 Days,* 1938; *The Green Cockatoo,* 1938; *The New Britain,* 1940; *Went the Day Well?,* 1942; *Brighton Rock,* with Terence Rattigan, 1946; *The Fallen Idol,* 1949; *The Third Man,* 1950; *Saint Joan,* 1957; *Our Man in Havana,* 1960; *The Comedians,* 1967.

Verse

Babbling April: Poems. Oxford, Blackwell, 1925.

Other

Journey Without Maps: A Travel Book. London, Heinemann, and New York, Doubleday, 1936.
The Lawless Roads: A Mexican Journey. London, Longman, 1939; as *Another Mexico,* New York, Viking Press, 1939.

British Dramatists. London, Collins, 1942; included in *The Romance of English Literature*, New York, Hastings House, 1944.

Why Do I Write: An Exchange of Views Between Elizabeth Bowen, Graham Greene and V. S. Pritchett. London, Marshall, 1948.

After Two Years. Privately printed, 1949.

For Christmas. Privately printed, 1950.

The Lost Childhood and Other Essays. London, Eyre and Spottiswoode, 1951; New York, Viking Press, 1952.

Essais Catholiques, translated by Marcelle Sibon. Paris, Editions de Seuil, 1953.

In Search of a Character: Two African Journals. London, Bodley Head, and New York, Viking Press, 1961.

The Revenge: An Autobiographical Fragment. Privately printed, 1963.

Victorian Detective Fiction: A Catalogue of the Collection Made by Dorothy Glover and Graham Greene, Introduced by John Carter. London, Bodley Head, 1966.

Collected Essays. London, Bodley Head, and New York, Viking Press, 1969.

A Sort of Life (autobiography). London, Bodley Head, and New York, Simon and Schuster, 1971.

The Pleasure-Dome: The Collected Film Criticism, 1935–40, of Graham Greene, edited by John Russell Taylor. London, Secker and Warburg, 1972; as *The Pleasure-Dome: Graham Greene on Film: Collected Film Criticism, 1935–40*, New York, Simon and Schuster, 1972.

The Portable Graham Greene, edited by Philip Stratford. New York, Viking Press, 1973.

Lord Rochester's Monkey: Being the Life of John Wilmot, Second Earl of Rochester. London, Bodley Head, and New York, Viking Press, 1974.

Editor, *The Old School: Essays by Divers Hands.* London, Cape, and New York, Peter Smith, 1934.

Editor, *The Best of Saki.* London, British Publishers Guild, 1950.

Editor, with Hugh Greene, *The Spy's Bedside Book: An Anthology.* London, Hart Davis, 1957.

Editor, *The Bodley Head Ford Madox Ford.* London, Bodley Head, 4 vols., 1962, 1963.

Editor, *An Impossible Woman: The Memories of Dottoressa Moor of Capri.* London, Bodley Head, 1975.

Bibliography: *Graham Greene* by J. D. Vann, Kent, Ohio, Kent State University Press, 1970.

*   *   *

On the subject of children's books nobody has written more accurately or eloquently than Graham Greene in his essay "The Lost Childhood," where he compares the child's experience of learning to read with the suddenness of "a key turned in a lock," and remembers that each book was "a crystal in which the child dreamed that he saw life moving." His own four children's stories are perhaps a little disappointing, measured against these standards, yet they have long since become classics and now make a very attractive package in their second published version, lovingly illustrated by Edward Ardizzone. Greene uses for all of them the same well-tried nostalgic formula which gives them a serial character starting with the similarity in title and main character and including the predictability of happy ending and humanistic moral.

It is the adventure tale applied to old-fashioned road and transport vehicles which have acquired slightly sentimentalised human characteristics (as do the horses which draw two of them). The little train sets out from its quiet branchline existence to see the world and discovers like Bunyan's Pilgrim that it is a confusing and frightening place where it would have got stranded but for the brotherly help of a big express train which brings it back safely to its rightful home. The little fire engine with fireman Sam Trolley and Toby, the horse, is brutally put out of work when a new motorised fire engine is brought in to serve a larger district. After brave attempts at scraping a living by peddling, Toby secretly leaves master and vehicle at Christmas only to dash back when a fire breaks out on the farm and fetch engine and fireman to put out the fire, while the new firemen are feasting, forgetful of their duty. Of course they are reinstated to serve happily ever after. The little horse bus and grocer Potter have an adventure on similar lines and get rid of their more modern, but less personal rival, the Hygienic Emporium with its elegant hansom cab, by catching two notorious thieves. And the little steam roller, on duty at London airport preparing roads and runways, outdoes the customs officers and airport police in hunting down wily goldsmuggler King.

Four stories which wittily and whimsically demonstrate the maxim "small is beautiful and still useful," displaying a slightly patronising, sentimental preference for old-fashioned personal ways as more humane than hygiene, technology and bureaucracy. But also, naturally, more colourful and thus better material for the storyteller who deals with people and the dramatic ups and downs of their lives. Greene's conservatism is thus a function of his metier. Writing for children, he pleads for the rights of the individual, for humanity rather than efficiency, for the communal spirit against greed, power and institutionalisation.

—Gertrud Mander

* * *

GREENWOOD, Ted (Edward Alister Greenwood). Australian. Born in Melbourne, Victoria, 4 December 1930. Educated at Balwyn Primary School, 1936–41; Mont Albert Central School, 1942–43; Melbourne Boys' High School, 1944; Camberwell High School, 1945–47; Melbourne Teachers' College, 1949–50; Royal Melbourne Institute of Technology, 1954–59, Diploma of Art 1959. Married Florence Lorraine Peart in 1954; has two sons and two daughters. Primary teacher, Melbourne, 1948–56; Lecturer in art education, Melbourne Teachers' College, 1956–60, and Toorak Teachers' College, Melbourne, 1960–68. Recipient: Australian Children's Book Council Picture Book of the Year Award, 1969; Churchill Fellowship, 1972; Australian Literary Fellowship, 1975; Visual Arts Board award, 1976. Address: Hilton Road, Ferny Creek, Victoria 3786, Australia.

PUBLICATIONS FOR CHILDREN (illustrated by the author)

Fiction

> *Obstreperous.* Sydney, Angus and Robertson, 1969; London, Angus and Robertson, 1970.
> *Aelfred.* Sydney, Angus and Robertson, 1970; London, Angus and Robertson, 1971.
> *V. I. P., Very Important Plant.* Sydney and London, Angus and Robertson, 1971.
> *Joseph and Lulu and the Prindiville House Pigeons.* Sydney and London, Angus and Robertson, 1972.
> *Terry's Brrrmmm GT.* Sydney, Angus and Robertson, 1974; London, Angus and Robertson, 1976.

Illustrator: *Sly Old Wardrobe,* 1968, and *The Glass Room,* 1970, by Ivan Southall; *Children Everywhere,* 1970.

Ted Greenwood comments:

I am still seeking to make a picture book which acts as a catalyst for the child's own imagination and which gives the reader/viewer enough cues to set off on his/her own line of thought. I want visual and verbal to interlock rather than for one to only echo the other. I want each to be pared down to a minimum.

*   *   *

Ted Greenwood is a free-thinking person who works from principles rather than precedent, being interested in philosophies and ideas rather than trends and formulas. Nobody in the world produces books which even *look* like his. He's not trying to be different – just being true to himself.

His background as a teacher leads him to want to challenge children, to cajole them into thinking for themselves. This approach determines the nature and shape of his books. In *V.I.P.*, for instance, where he wants to give children a feeling of the inevitable continuity of natural life, in its *cyclical* nature, he deliberately avoids capital letters, even at the start, suggesting that nothing really just *begins*. The first page contains just five words and two square inches of line drawing on the edge of the page. Thus, he forces children to participate in the experience of the book he has made. They need to ask questions in order to sort it all out, to find out what is happening, what is meant. This is the most noticeable characteristic of Ted Greenwood's work which, in both pictures and text, tends to be implicit rather than explicit. He wants children to make their own discoveries.

Ted Greenwood is an unconventional man, without pretensions. His drawings, like his language, are simple in the extreme, yet the subject is viewed from constantly changing perspectives, bombarding the mind of the reader, demanding that he participate. The text is often physically fractured in order to match the sense (e.g., in *Joseph and Lulu and the Prindiville House Pigeons* it is elongated where the buildings are tall, and in *Terry's Brrrmmm GT* it goes downhill to match the descent of the billy-cart) just as the drawings are fractured or incomplete in order to make the reader anticipate what might be on the following page.

When in *Terry's Brrrmmm GT* the child reads the line "Terry had an idea," he must work out, from the context and the accompanying drawings, what the idea is, just as, in *Obstreperous*, from the line "but the leaves were still and the trees straight," he has to discern that conditions are just not windy enough for kite-flying. Thus does this maker of unique books treat children with infinite respect, for the truth is that what is most important in Ted Greenwood's books is what is *not* said. *Terry's Brrrmmm GT* is not about a cart-race as much as the warm friendship of two children, and their interdependence.

It is possible that Ted Greenwood will develop as a writer, rather than an illustrator, and it is certain that what he produces will be characterised by the ideas it provokes and the warmth and humanity of the telling. Ted Greenwood's work stimulates a life beyond its own physical limitations.

—Walter McVitty

GREY OWL (Washaquonasin). Pseudonym for Archibald Stansfeld Belaney. Canadian. Born in Hastings, Kent, England, 18 September 1888. Educated at Hastings Grammar School. Served in the Montreal Regiment, Canadian Army, 1915–17. Married Angele Eguana in 1910, two children; Constance Holmes, 1918 (divorced, 1921); Gertrude Bernard (Anahareo), 1927, one child; Yvonne Perrier, 1937. Clerk, Cheale Brothers, timber merchants, Hastings, 1904–05; guide, trapper, mail carrier, and fire ranger, Ontario, 1907–31; Warden, Riding Mountain National Park, 1931, and Prince Albert National

Park, 1931–38. Adopted blood brother, Ojibwa tribe, 1920. Lecturer and filmmaker; regular contributor, *Forest and Outdoors* magazine, Canada, 1930–38. *Died 13 April 1938.*

PUBLICATIONS FOR CHILDREN

Fiction

    The Adventures of Sajo and Her Beaver People, illustrated by the author. London, Lovat Dickson, 1935; as *Sajo and the Beaver People,* New York, Scribner, 1936.

PUBLICATIONS FOR ADULTS

Other

    The Men of the Last Frontier. London, Country Life, 1931; New York, Scribner, 1932.
    Pilgrims of the Wild (autobiography). London, Lovat Dickson, 1934; New York, Scribner, 1935.
    Grey Owl and the Beaver, with Harper Cory. London and New York, Nelson, 1935.
    Tales of an Empty Cabin. London, Lovat Dickson, and New York, Dodd Mead, 1936.
    A Book of Grey Owl: Pages from the Writings of Wa-sha-quon-asin, edited by E. E. Reynolds. London, Davies, 1938; as *Beavers* and *On the Trail,* London, Cambridge University Press, 2 vols., 1940.
    Grey Owl's Farewell to the Children of the British Isles. London, Lovat Dickson, 1938.

Critical Studies: *Grey Owl and I: A New Autobiography* by Anahareo, London, Davies, 1972, as *Devil in Deerskins: My Life with Grey Owl,* Toronto, New Press, 1972; *Wilderness Man: The Strange Story of Grey Owl* by Lovat Dickson, London, Macmillan, 1973.

Theatrical Activities

    Director: **Films** – *The Little People,* 1930; *The Beaver Family,* 1931; *The Trail; Winter; Men Against the Snow,* 1936.

                *   *   *

Grey Owl's work indicates a great respect and affection for the wilderness and its inhabitants. In an era when these aspects of life were too quickly disappearing in the face of rapid development, and the antagonism between wilderness and civilization stood out in stark contrast, he provided a sensitive yet factual assessment of nature and its place in our culture. Four books form the nucleus of his work: *The Men of the Last Frontier, Pilgrims of the Wild, Tales of an Empty Cabin,* and *The Adventures of Sajo and Her Beaver People.* The first three books can be appreciated by readers of all ages, the last by children from 8 to 11 years.

Nature, wilderness, animal life and man's interaction with them. Grey Owl was a keen observer and through his writing one can see what is beautiful and harmonious as well as what is savage and predatory in nature.

Although Grey Owl would discount his emphasis on man, he has provided some vivid portraits of the men who inhabit these wilderness areas: courageous, honest, tale-telling, respecting each other for what they do, not for who they are, and keeping to a strict code of conduct in their work. Their hardships and joys, their pleasures and observations on life are best recorded in *The Men of the Last Frontier* and *Tales of an Empty Cabin.* He also portrayed men who abused the wilderness: men who killed wantonly, disregarding season and any thought of replenishing a species or leaving half-skinned carcasses strewn along a trail.

More important to Grey Owl was his concern with wildlife, especially the beaver. In *Tales of an Empty Cabin* and *Pilgrims of the Wild,* he vividly depicts his life of hunting and his gradual disenchantment with the instruments of death: the steel jaw trap, the use of poison, and the rifle. This disenchantment turned into positive action when he adopted two beaver kittens whose mother had been killed in an out-of-season trap. His observations on their antics, personalities, eating habits, and interaction with man and nature are delightful. The depth of this human-animal relationship provides a poignant touch.

Grey Owl combined all of his knowledge of animals and nature in his only children's story, *The Adventures of Sajo and Her Beaver People*. This combination created a realistic adventure story guaranteed to keep a child's attention to the conclusion. It is the tale of two Indian children whose father is forced to sell one of their two beaver kittens to pay a debt to a local trader. The plot develops when the children and their pet set out to find their little friend. They endure all sorts of hardships before they are finally reunited.

All of Grey Owl's works illustrate the true nature of the animal whether beaver, deer or wolf. He writes of their positive points as well as of the suffering and cruelty these creatures must endure from predatory animals, natural disaster and man. Hopefully his work has made and will continue to make people aware of wildlife and conservation. The material, written in far less sophisticated a manner than most of today's readers would demand, is still appropriate.

—Dorothy D. Siles

GRICE, Frederick. British. Born in Durham, 21 June 1910. Educated at Johnston School, Durham, 1922–28; King's College, University of London (Brewer Prize), 1928–31, B.A. (honours) in English; Hatfield College, Durham University, 1931–32, teaching diploma. Served in the Royal Air Force, 1941–46: Flight Lieutenant. Married Gwendoline Simpson in 1939; has two daughters. Assistant Master, A. J. Dawson School, County Durham, 1934–40; Head of the English Department, Worcester College of Further Education, 1946–72. Recipient: Children's Rights Workshop award, 1977. Address: 91 Hallow Road, Worcester, England.

PUBLICATIONS FOR CHILDREN

Fiction

> *Aidan and the Strollers*, illustrated by William Stobbs.   London, Cape, 1960; as *Aidan and the Strolling Players*, New York, Duell, 1960.
> *The Bonny Pit Laddie*, illustrated by Brian Wildsmith.   London, Oxford University Press, 1960; as *Out of the Mines: The Story of a Pit Boy*, New York, Watts, 1961.
> *The Moving Finger*, illustrated by Joan Kiddell-Monroe.   London, Oxford University Press, 1962; as *The Secret of the Libyan Caves*, New York, Watts, 1963.
> *A Severnside Story*, illustrated by William Papas.   London, Oxford University Press, 1964.
> *The Luckless Apple*, illustrated by Ian Ribbons.   London, Oxford University Press, 1966.
> *The Oak and the Ash*, illustrated by Trevor Ridley.   London, Oxford University Press, 1968.
> *The Courage of Andy Robson*, illustrated by Victor Ambrus.   London, Oxford University Press, 1969.
> *The Black Hand Gang*, illustrated by Doreen Roberts.   London, Oxford University Press, 1971.
> *Young Tom Sawbones*, illustrated by Ian Ribbons.   London, Oxford University Press, 1972.

Nine Days' Wonder, illustrated by Paul Ritchie.   London, Oxford University Press, 1976.

Other

Folk Tales of the North Country Drawn from Northumberland and Durham.   London, Nelson, 1944.
Folk Tales of the West Midlands, illustrated by N. J. P. Turnbull.   London, Nelson, 1952.
Folk Tales of Lancashire, illustrated by N. J. P. Turnbull.   London, Nelson, 1953.
Rebels and Fugitives, illustrated by William Stobbs.   London, Batsford, 1963; New York, Norton, 1964.
A Northumberland Missionary, illustrated by Ralph Lavers.   London, Oxford University Press, 1963.
Jimmy Lane and His Boat (reader), illustrated by Eileen Green.   London, Oxford University Press, 1963; New York, Watts, 1968.
The Rescue, and The Poisoned Dog (reader), illustrated by Gwyneth Cole.   London, Oxford University Press, 1963; New York, Watts, 1968.
Bill Thompson's Pigeon (reader), illustrated by Maureen Warren.   London, Oxford University Press, 1963; New York, Watts, 1968.
The Lifeboat Haul (reader), with *Elizabeth Woodcock* by Dora Saint, illustrated by John Lawrence.   London, Oxford University Press, 1965.
Dildrum, King of the Cats, and Other English Folk Stories, illustrated by Julia Ball.   London, Oxford University Press, 1967; New York, Watts, 1968.
Tales and Beliefs (reader), illustrated by Gunvor Edwards.   London, Nelson, 1974.

PUBLICATIONS FOR ADULTS

Verse

Night Poem and Other Pieces.   Tunbridge Wells, Kent, Peter Russell, 1955.
The Faithful City.   Privately printed, 1960.

Other

Francis Kilvert: Priest and Diarist.   Hereford, Kilvert Society, 1975.

Editor, *A Kilvert Symposium*.   Hereford, Kilvert Society, 1975.

Manuscript Collection: de Grummond Collection, University of Southern Mississippi, Hattiesburg.

Frederick Grice comments:
I was born in the North of England, within hearing distance of the bells of Durham Cathedral. My father worked in a small colliery a few miles out of Durham. I think I had the best of three worlds – the world of the pit village with its stories of strikes, evictions, lock-outs and accidents; the world of the beautiful mediaeval city of Durham where I went to school; and the world of the austerely beautiful countryside that encircled the colliery village.

The first book I wrote was a simple collection of North Country legends and folk tales. I was interested in them because they seemed to embody the spirit of the land and the people that were to be the main theme of my writing – *The Bonny Pit Laddie, The Oak and the Ash, The Courage of Andy Robson, Nine Days' Wonder*, etc. The variety of my interests, and in particular my interest in literature (for the greater part of my working life I have been a college tutor) has prompted me to investigate other themes such as the fortunes of strolling players in the late 18th and early 19th centuries, the lives of railway navvies, etc., but I write best and most authentically about the North, and these are the stories to which children most eagerly respond.

*   *   *

At a time when working-class children's stories were rare, *The Bonny Pit Laddie*, set in Frederick Grice's native Durham, came as a welcome phenomenon, its subject-matter handled with deep feeling and skilful craftsmanship. True, it did not depict the contemporary scene. Set back more than half a century, it had the nostalgia that is apt to creep into this author's fiction. Thus, *A Severnside Story* has juke-boxes and leather-jacketed motor-cyclists to denote the 1960's, but one feels that the boy-hero, and certainly the author, would have been more at home in the Worcester of Elgar's youth. That is really the atmosphere which is so sensitively and poetically evoked. Grice sticks to the locations he knows. Even in *The Moving Finger* he is utilising his North African service in World War II, but understandably this book has less intimate, affectionate feeling, and is more of a conventionally-contrived adventure story.

His strengths and weaknesses are very clearly exemplified in *Aidan and the Strollers*, a delightful tale of travelling actors of 1825. Characters and atmosphere are splendidly handled – indeed, there is a prodigality of almost Dickensian characters passing all too briefly across the ever-changing scene. Plot-construction and the maintenance of tension are less successful. Time-lapses of several weeks are cursorily bridged in a paragraph or two, leaving the reader with unanswered questions. The author has tried to pour a heady quart into a pint-pot, yet shortage of space does not deter him from introducing long Shakespearean quotations and charming but not altogether necessary descriptions of rural sights and sounds.

If Grice excels in male characterization, he seems curiously uninterested in depicting the other sex. The absence of women in the Saharan adventure is understandable, but in a theatrical story one would have expected the actresses to make their presence felt. Aidan and his friend Jeremy might appear to a modern child unbelievably blind to the girls they must have met. Possibly the author, already fifty when this book appeared, was following the tradition of his own childhood reading, when there were books for boys and books for girls, as rigidly separated as school cloakrooms.

Grice is a literary storyteller of style and integrity. For the "gentle" reader – the more bookish, imaginative child – his work offers great satisfaction.

—Geoffrey Trease

GRIFFITHS, G(ordon) D(ouglas). British. Born in Wallasey, Cheshire, 19 July 1910. Educated at Wallasey Grammar School, 1920–27; St. Luke's College, Exeter, 1957–58. Served in the Reconnaissance Corps, and acting sergeant, Intelligence Corps, British Army, 1943–46. Worked as a farmer; French, Latin, and Greek teacher, Devon preparatory schools and Exeter Cathedral School, 1959–60; publishers' reader. *Died in July 1973.*

PUBLICATIONS FOR CHILDREN

Fiction

Mattie: The Story of a Hedgehog, illustrated by Elsie Wrigley. Kingswood, Surrey, World's Work, 1967; New York, Delacorte Press, 1977.

Silver Blue: A Story of Ponies That Run Free on Dartmoor, illustrated by Elsie
   Wrigley.   Kingswood, Surrey, World's Work, 1970.
Abandoned.   Kingswood, Surrey, World's Work, 1973; Chicago, Follett, 1974.

PUBLICATIONS FOR ADULTS

Other

History of Teignmouth, with E. G. C. Griffiths.   Teignmouth, Devon, Brunswick Press,
   1965.

*   *   *

Judged by quantity only, the output of G. D. Griffiths might seem slight: no more than
three books, whose economy of writing makes each rather less in length than the average
novel. But these three books place their author in the highest rank of their special genre, the
animal narrative. (See also Roberts, Clarkson, and others.) It is a scrupulous genre, needing
both informed observation and the ability to record its findings. It does *not* include the (often
bestselling) humorous records of an author's adventures as vet or zoo-keeper. Animals are
rarely themes for comedy, especially those caught up in the human world. A central feature
of the form – and Griffiths illustrates this particularly well – is that, while neither sentimental
nor anthropomorphic, it rouses a sympathetic understanding through the explicit
presentation of its facts.

All of Griffiths' books are set in the Dartmoor region of Devon, one of the last surviving
"wild" areas in southern England. Each focusses on a particular animal, living in a natural
habitat yet affected both for good and ill by human contact. The subject of *Mattie* is a
hedgehog, one of a family born in an old neglected garden near the moor. Outside a textbook
there can be few more exact accounts of the creature's looks, behaviour, cycle of life from
birth to old age and death. Griffiths, though, is not writing a textbook but a work lit by
creative imagination; its impact stays. Characteristically, he shows how inescapably his
creature is linked with the larger world around, not only that of insects, plants, other
woodland fauna, but of the human kind. One nameless human kicks and kills; another tries
to mend the harm, puts out milk, or a grass-filled flowerpot for shelter. *Mattie* is a memorable
little book, a classic of its kind.

Silver Blue is far more ambitious in plan, but also – no doubt for this reason – the least
"popular" work of the three. As if in contrast to the minuscule scale of the hedgehog story,
this ranges widely over the moor, and over the years of the 19th century – a time when a
certain wild strain of Dartmoor pony appeared and vanished. Thus, the tale follows a line of
creatures, not one individual member. Yet it has all the essential Griffiths qualities – the
knowledge, the sense of place, the austere and moving distinction. A beautiful book, it
deserves to be better known.

Abandoned, arguably the peak work of the three, has the particularity of *Mattie* and the
wider range of *Silver Blue*. Here, the focus returns to the individual creature – in this case, a
cat. At 12 weeks old it is thrown out of a car on to a lonely Dartmoor road, and, after further
human rejections, learns to accept the life of the moor. The deep snows of winter, the
drought of summer, a heath fire (started by campers), floods when the swollen river
overflows, illegal gintraps, a fox hunt – all these the cat survives, though not without scars.
Humans betray but humans are also rescuers. A watchman at the claypits tends her after the
fire; an old "lifer" at the prison finds her half dead and frozen in the stables, and shelters her
through the winter; an elderly couple very gradually win her confidence at the end. In all the

books, but especially in *Abandoned*, the sense of the moorland seasons is Brontëan in its beauty and its vividness. At the same time, the reader is always kept aware − if only by an illuminating line or two − of the human lives that touch the creature's anxious world: now, say, a difficult husband back from sea; now a prison warder sharing his charges' isolation. This grasp of the total scene, animal, human, elemental, makes *Abandoned* more than a genre example; it is a small but distinguished novel in its own right.

—Naomi Lewis

GRIFFITHS, Helen. British and Spanish. Born in London, 8 May 1939. Educated at Balham and Tooting College of Commerce, London (Matthew Arnold Memorial Prize), 1954–57. Married Pedro Santos de la Cal in 1959 (died, 1973); has three daughters. Cow Girl, Bedfordshire, 1957; secretary, Blackstock Engineering, Cockfosters, Hertfordshire, 1958–59; office worker, Selfridges, 1959, and Oliver and Boyd, publishers, 1959–60, both London; teacher of English as a foreign language, Madrid, 1973–76. Address: 42 Newbridge Road, Bath, Avon, England.

PUBLICATIONS FOR CHILDREN

Fiction

Horse in the Clouds, illustrated by Edward Osmond. London, Hutchinson, 1957; New York, Holt Rinehart, 1958.
Wild and Free, illustrated by Edward Osmond. London, Hutchinson, 1958.
Moonlight, illustrated by Edward Osmond. London, Hutchinson, 1959.
Africano. London, Hutchinson, 1961.
The Wild Heart, illustrated by Victor Ambrus. London, Hutchinson, 1963; New York, Doubleday, 1964.
The Greyhound, illustrated by Victor Ambrus. London, Hutchinson, 1964; New York, Doubleday, 1966.
The Wild Horse of Santander, illustrated by Victor Ambrus. London, Hutchinson, 1966; New York, Doubleday, 1967.
León, illustrated by Victor Ambrus. London, Hutchinson, 1967; New York, Doubleday, 1968.
Stallion of the Sands, illustrated by Victor Ambrus. London, Hutchinson, 1968; New York, Lothrop, 1970.
Moshie Cat: The True Adventures of a Majorcan Kitten, illustrated by Shirley Hughes. London, Hutchinson, 1969; New York, Holiday House, 1970.
Patch, illustrated by Maurice Wilson. London, Hutchinson, 1970.
Federico, illustrated by Shirley Hughes. London, Hutchinson, 1971.
Russian Blue, illustrated by Victor Ambrus. London, Hutchinson, and New York, Holiday House, 1973.
Just a Dog, illustrated by Victor Ambrus. London, Hutchinson, 1974; New York, Holiday House, 1975.
Witch Fear, illustrated by Victor Ambrus. London, Hutchinson, 1975; as *Mysterious Appearance of Agnes*, New York, Holiday House, 1975.
Pablo, illustrated by Victor Ambrus. London, Hutchinson, 1977; as *Running Wild*, New York, Holiday House, 1977.

PUBLICATIONS FOR ADULTS

Novel

The Dark Swallows.   London, Hutchinson, 1966; New York, Knopf, 1967.

Helen Griffiths comments:
   I had my first book published at an early age, and my first few titles are obviously immature. Their purpose, I think, was sheer self-entertainment together with encouragement from my publishers to continue.
   The main theme behind all my work, which I have endeavoured to express from the beginning, is to show animals free from the sentimental light in which they are so often portrayed in fiction. I have not tried to write sad books, as I have been accused of doing. I have tried and continue trying to portray a section of life as I see and feel it to be.
   Many of my later books have a Spanish background, and in these I have tried to portray the country and the people as they really are, not as foreigners so often imagine them to be. I have also attempted to express how Spaniards feel towards animals, not cruel but indifferent, an attitude often misunderstood outside the country. I would like to think that these books may help people to know a little more about Spain.

*   *   *

   Helen Griffiths's first published book was written when she was a schoolgirl of 15 or 16. Though she has gained in depth and range in her many subsequent novels, her strong descriptive manner and her central kindling theme (the lot of animals – those especially linked with man – in a predatory human world) remain the same. In almost every book it is some rare child, briefly sharing the genius of the animal, who makes a link between creature and humankind. Though knowledgeable enough about her horses, dogs, and cats, she is probably more of a novelist than a naturalist writer of the Clarkson or Williamson sort. And, because of the key role given to children in her stories, she is also more aptly ranked than these as a children's novelist.
   Her first few stories were about horses in the South American plains – free wild creatures, mostly doomed to be caught and "broken" or slaughtered for their skins. The note of violence and cruelty that must attend such themes may not have lessened their popularity with the young. But she has grown towards a greater subtlety. Perhaps the two best of her horse novels are *The Wild Heart* and *The Wild Horse of Santander* (note the recurring adjective). The first of these tells of a mare born wild on the pampas; left motherless at four months and surviving only by theft, she grows up a natural loner, even among her kind. But she is coveted by traders and others for her supreme racing speed. At the end of a terrible hunt she finds strange sanctuary – in a church. A foundling boy, brought up by the village priest, has to solve the problem of how to give her both liberty and life. The second novel tells of an 8-year-old blind Spanish boy, languid and over-cosseted, who is "given" a new-born foal, born to a half-wild mare after an escapade. A deep alliance grows between the two young creatures, and presently, without either bit or bridle, the horse (which no one else is able to touch) will race along day after day with the blind boy on his back. (What most disturbs the adults is that the horse and not the human is master of the two.) This perfect trust is cracked when the boy leaves for an operation to restore his sight.
   In more recent novels she has written of dogs and cats – chiefly in the Spanish setting that she herself knows well. They are, inevitably, grim and poignant stories, though most have consoling endings. *León* is one of the most complex and important of these books – a classic of dog fiction. A clever Spanish village boy, Hilario, has the chance of going to medical school, but has to leave his beloved mongrel sheep-dog with relatives. Caught in the Civil War, and badly wounded, he does not return for several years, while León – chained,

starved, beaten, abused, abandoned – tastes the fate of most of his kind in a Latin country. It is the chance of Hilario's medical skill that at last reunites the two. In other novels, based on personal fact, a nameless human (in fact, the author herself) has an operative part in the tale, and ensures a happier end. *Just a Dog*, a vivid account of the life of mongrel strays in Madrid, is of this kind; *Moshie Cat* is another. Two characteristic tales – *The Greyhound* and *Russian Blue* – have a London setting.

Of all her books, *Witch Fear* seems most to diverge from the pattern of the rest, yet basically it is still of the Griffiths kind. This interesting tale describes the situation of what we might now call an autistic child in a superstitious European village several centuries ago – a condition in this case caused by shock: the frightful death of her mother, a herbal healer, as a witch. Unable to communicate in expected human fashion, this girl is in much the same unhappy position as an animal in the rough peasant setting – indeed, her only natural alliance is with a rescued cat. Though (since this is fiction) truth comes out and the girl is saved from death, the basic Griffiths point is sharply made.

Her novels stand up to many readings, especially as animal studies. If their note is often sombre, this is because of their truth to human behaviour, too often where the normal is the mindless, mean, and gross. Yet every group has its bright exceptions: the animals remain uncorrupt, and the reader is left with a curious sense of hope. She is neither a sentimental writer nor a propagandist one. The facts of each story, gravely observed, carry their own implicit commentary.

—Naomi Lewis

GUY, Rosa (Cuthbert). American. Born in Trinidad, West Indies, 1 September 1928. Widow of Warner Guy; has one son. Founding President, Harlem Writer's Guild. Agent: McIntosh and Otis Inc., 18 East 41st Street, New York, New York 10017. Address: c/o Holt Rinehart and Winston, 383 Madison Avenue, New York, New York 10017, U.S.A.

PUBLICATIONS FOR CHILDREN

Fiction

Bird at My Window.   Philadelphia, Lippincott, and London, Souvenir Press, 1966.
The Friends.   New York, Holt Rinehart, 1973; London, Gollancz, 1974.
Ruby.   New York, Viking Press, 1976.

PUBLICATIONS FOR ADULTS

Play

Venetian Blinds (produced New York, 1954).

Other

Editor, *Children of Longing*.   New York, Holt Rinehart, 1971.

*   *   *

Rosa Guy's writings, though small in output, are of a very high quality. She writes sensitively of Black experience, especially of those situations which in childhood and adolescence often seem of tremendous importance.

Her highly acclaimed and best book, *The Friends*, is a story set in Harlem about friendship, love and death. Friendship – developing, understanding, maintaining – is the most important theme, ever-changing, controversial. Phyllisia Cathy and Edith Jackson are two opposites who are eventually attracted into friendship, though initially with unwillingness on Phyllisia's part. Phyllisia is not really interested in being friends with Edith because she is ashamed of Edith's worn clothes and street manners. Phyllisia *needs* Edith, however, because she is strong, protective, often maternal – attributes lacking in her own life. Her father is a tyrant, her mother is dying of cancer, and her classmates constantly make fun of her. The characterization of Phyllisia, whose family has recently moved to Harlem from the West Indies, is very well-developed by Ms. Guy, surely influenced by her own West Indian heritage. The middle class aspirations of the family, the boisterous, boasting language of Mr. Cathy, the proud, proper way of life are all there, authentic, realistic. Ms. Guy has written with compassion about this transplanted, sometimes misguided but lovable family. We experience the loneliness, despair, and sensitivity of Phyllisia, her friend Edith, her mother, her father, and (in the later novel *Ruby*) her sister.

The Friends is a simple penetrating, compelling story; it is moving, and appealing to children, and shows Ms. Guy to be a very special writer.

—Jacqueline Brown Woody

HADER, Berta (Hoerner). American. Born in San Pedro, Coahuila, Mexico, in 1890. Educated at the University of Washington, Seattle, 1909–12; California School of Design, San Francisco, 1915–18. Married Elmer Hader, *q.v.*, in 1919. Staff artist, San Francisco *Bulletin*, 1916–18. Recipient: American Library Association Caldecott Medal, 1949. *Died 6 February 1976.*

PUBLICATIONS FOR CHILDREN (with Elmer Hader, illustrated by the authors)

Fiction

> *The Little Red Hen.* New York, Macmillan, 1928.
> *The Old Woman and the Crooked Sixpence.* New York, Macmillan, 1928.
> *Coming, Two Funny Clowns.* New York, Coward McCann, 1929.
> *Lions and Tigers and Elephants, Being an Account of Polly Patchin's Trip to the Zoo.* London and New York, Longman, 1930.
> *Under the Pig-Nut Tree.* New York, Knopf, and London, Allen and Unwin, 1930.
> *The Farmer in the Dell.* New York, Macmillan, 1931.
> *Tooky, The Story of a Seal Who Joined the Circus.* New York and London, Longman, 1931.
> *Chuck-a-Luck and His Reindeer.* Boston, Houghton Mifflin, 1933.
> *Spunky.* New York, Macmillan, 1933.
> *Whiffy McMann.* New York and London, Oxford University Press, 1933.
> *Midget and Bridget.* New York, Macmillan, 1934.
> *Jamaica Johnny.* New York, Macmillan, 1935.
> *Billy Butter.* New York, Macmillan, 1936.
> *Tommy Thatcher Goes to Sea.* New York, Macmillan, 1937.

Cricket, The Story of a Little Circus Pony. New York, Macmillan, 1938; Birmingham, Combridge, 1939.
Cock-a-Doodle-Do: The Story of a Little Red Rooster. New York, Macmillan, 1939.
The Cat and the Kitten. New York, Macmillan, 1940.
Little Town. New York, Macmillan, 1941.
The Story of Pancho and the Bull with the Crooked Tail. New York, Macmillan, 1942; London, Hale, 1946.
The Mighty Hunter. New York, Macmillan, 1943; London, Hale, 1947.
Rainbow's End. New York, Macmillan, 1945.
The Skyrocket. New York, Macmillan, 1946.
Big City. New York, Macmillan, 1947.
The Big Snow. New York, Macmillan, 1948.
Little Appaloosa. New York, Macmillan, 1949.
Squirrely of Willow Hill. New York, Macmillan, 1950.
Lost in the Zoo. New York, Macmillan, 1951.
Little White Foot. New York, Macmillan, 1952.
Wish on the Moon. New York, Macmillan, 1954.
Home on the Range: Jeremiah Jones and His Friend Little Bear in the Far West. New York and London, Macmillan, 1955.
The Runaways. New York, Macmillan, 1956.
Ding Dong Bell, Pussy's in the Well. New York, Macmillan, 1957.
Little Chip of Willow Hill. New York, Macmillan, 1958.
Reindeer Trail. New York, Macmillan, 1959.
Mister Billy's Gun. New York, Macmillan, and London, Macmillan, 1960.
Quack, Quack. New York, Macmillan, 1961.
Little Antelope: An Indian for a Day. New York, Macmillan, 1962.
Snow in the City. New York, Macmillan, and London, Collier Macmillan, 1963.
Two Is Company, Three's a Crowd. New York, Macmillan, and London, Collier Macmillan, 1965.

Verse

What'll You Do When You Grow Up??? New York and London, Longman, 1929.

Other

The Picture Book of Travel. New York, Macmillan, 1928.
Picture Book of Mother Goose. New York, Coward McCann, 1930.
Picture Book of the States. New York and London, Harper, 1932.
Stop, Look, and Listen. New York, Longman, 1936.
Green and Gold: The Story of the Banana. New York, Macmillan, 1936.
The Inside Story of the Hader Books. New York, Macmillan, 1937.
The Little Stone House: A Story of Building a House in the Country. New York, Macmillan, 1944.
The Friendly Phoebe. New York, Macmillan, 1953.

Manuscript Collection: University of Oregon Library, Eugene.

Illustrator, with Elmer Hader: *The Ugly Duckling, Chicken Little, Wee Willie Winkie,* and *Hansel and Gretel,* all 1927; *Donald in Numberland* by Jean Murdoch Peedie, 1927; *Goldilocks and the Three Bears,* 1928; *The Wonderful Locomotive* by Cornelia Meigs, 1928; *The Story of the Water Supply,* 1929, and *The Story of Health,* 1931, by Hope Holway; *The Story of Markets* by Ruth Orton Camp, 1929; *Garden of the Lost Key* by Forrestine Hooker, 1929; *The Story of Mr. Punch* by Octave Feuillet, 1929; *Monkey Tale,* 1929, *Little Elephant* and *Baby Bear,* 1930, *Lion Cub: A Jungle Tale,* 1931, *Humpy, Son of the Sands,* 1937, and

Stripey, A Little Zebra, 1939, all by Hamilton Williamson; *Timothy and the Blue Cart* by Elinor Whitney, 1930; *Big Fellow at Work* by Dorothy Baruch, 1930; *Sonny Elephant* by Madge Bigham, 1930; *Good Little Dog*, 1930, *Bingo Is My Name*, 1931, and *Here, Bingo!*, 1932, all by Anne Stoddard; *The Play-Book of Words* by Prescott Lecky, 1933; *Jimmy, The Groceryman* by Jane Miller, 1934; *Everyday Fun*, 1935, and *Who Knows?*, 1937, by Julia Hahn; *The Smiths and Rusty*, 1936, and *Wings for the Smiths*, 1937, both by Alice Dalgliesh; *A Visit from St. Nicholas*, by Clement C. Moore, 1937; *Marcos, A Mountain Boy of Mexico* by Melicent Lee, 1937; *The Farmer* by Henry B. Lent, 1937; *Banana Tree House* by Phillis Garrard, 1938; *Timothy Has Ideas* by Miriam E. Mason, 1943; *Mr. Peck's Pets* by Louise Hunting Seaman, 1947. Elmer Hader only: *Charm*, 1927, and *How Dear to My Heart*, 1940, by Mary Margaret McBride; *Down Ryton Water* by Eva Gaggin, 1941; *The Isle of Que* by Elsie Singmaster, 1948.

*   *   *

Berta and Elmer Hader, a husband and wife team, wrote and illustrated children's books from the 1920's through the 1960's. The upgrading of children's literature during the nearly five decades that the Haders were associated with children's books can be seen in their works. While some of their earlier works may be considered of dubious quality, their later books possess good literary style and careful coordination of pictures and text. There is variety in their books, though most of them are stories about animals. At a time when children's picture books contained anthropomorphic animals that were overly "cute," the Haders carefully created animals in all their animal dignity.

A common setting of books by the Haders is Willow Farm, which is sure to be the rural area where they lived in the little house they built themselves. The story of the building of this house is told in their picture book *The Little Stone House*. Willow Farm is the setting of *Squirrely of Willow Hill*, a story about Mr. and Mrs. McGinty who care for a squirrel, tame him and spoil him; but when spring comes, set him free in a park. Mr. and Mrs. McGinty and Willow Farm are revisited in *Little White Foot*, about the peaceful coexistence of a mouse family and a human family which results in the belling of the family cat to protect the lives of the mice.

The care and understanding of animal ways shown in both *Squirrely of Willow Farm* and *Little White Foot* are shown over and over again in the Haders' books. *Quack, Quack* is a mallard duck aided for a time by people, but allowed to return to the wilds again. The skunk and the fawn, kept for a while by the retired carpenter in *Rainbow's End*, both return to their lives in the forest. A similar event occurs in *Cock-a-Doodle Doo* when Little Red, a baby chick hatched with ducks, finds his way back to the barnyard to live with his own kind.

The best known of the Haders' works is *The Big Snow*, which received the Caldecott Award in 1949. It is a book that shows the careful detail that typifies many of their works. *The Big Snow* is an animal book. People appear in the illustrations only twice, and are important only because of their relationship with the animals. The story has three parts. The animals prepare for winter, there is a snowstorm, and animals and people cope with the results of the heavy snow. The many details of the book deserve attention. Bright blue endpapers show many designed snowflakes. On the page preceding the title page a wild goose, the late fall symbol, is shown flying into the book. The frontispiece is a full color picture of a snow scene, a promise of the major intent of the book. Central to this picture are the many animals in it: deer, raccoons, skunks, squirrels, rabbits, a cardinal and a blue jay. The title page itself is almost stark, reminiscent of a quiet heavy snowfall; it is decorated only with seven snowflakes. The back of the title page shows a man and a woman surrounded by snow, a small self portrait of the Haders, which is a trademark of a Hader book.

On the first page of the story, the geese return. These heralds of winter appear across the top of each page throughout the first half of the book guiding the reader's eye through the pages. The final appearance of the geese is a full-color page that is shared with no other animal. The geese at the top of each page have been witness to the preparation made for winter by a variety of animals. With their disappearance midway in the book, winter takes over. Snow starts to fall and the reader is witness to the simple drama of a tremendous snowfall.

The story tells of the effect of the snowfall, the shoveling out, and of an old couple who share food with animals whose survival is threatened by the heavy snow. The story ends on Ground Hog's Day when the ground hog predicts six more weeks of winter in this uncomplicated and satisfying paragraph:

> The ground hog was right. It was a long cold winter for the birds and the animals on the hill, but the little old man and the little old woman put out food for them until the warm spring came. And that was the end of the BIG SNOW.

In *Rainbow's End*, the reader sees a reflection of the main character as he examines the injured birds the children bring him to be cared for: "Toby always felt sad for these feathered creatures that made his day happier with their pretty ways and their sweet songs." So it seems this genuine appreciation for the companionship of animal life permeates Berta and Elmer Hader's books. This care is expressed through the stories – animals characterize only themselves, behave according to their instincts, and are allowed to remain happily in natural surroundings with their own kind – and is displayed even more clearly in the illustrations, beautiful representations of animals in careful proportion showing each animal as it really is. Surely this is one of the Haders' greatest contributions to children's books.

—Mary J. Lickteig

HADER, Elmer (Stanley). American. Born in Pajaro, California, in 1889. Educated at the California School of Design, San Francisco. Served in the Army Camouflage Corps during World War I. Married Berta Hoerner (i.e., Berta Hader, *q.v.*) in 1919. Worked as apprentice silversmith, surveyor's assistant and locomotive fireman, 1906–10. Recipient: American Library Association Caldecott Medal, 1949. *Died in 1973*

See the entry for Berta Hader.

HAIG-BROWN, Roderick (Langmere). Canadian. Born in Lancing, Sussex, England, 21 February 1908; emigrated to Canada in 1926. Educated at Charterhouse, Godalming, Surrey. Served in the Canadian Army, 1939–45: Major. Married Ann Elmore in 1934; one son and three daughters. Worked as a logger, trapper, fisherman, and guide, Washington, U.S.A., and British Columbia, 1926–29; Provincial Magistrate and Judge, Campbell River Children's and Family Court, British Columbia, 1941–75. Frequent broadcaster and moderator of television programs. Chancellor, University of Victoria, British Columbia, 1970–73. Recipient: Canadian Library Association Book of the Year Medal, 1947, 1964; Governor-General's Citation, 1948; Crandell Conservation Trophy, 1955; Vicky Metcalf Award, 1966. LL.D.: University of British Columbia, Vancouver, 1952. *Died 9 October 1976.*

PUBLICATIONS FOR CHILDREN

Fiction

Silver: The Life of an Atlantic Salmon, illustrated by J.P. Moreton.   London A. and C. Black, 1931.

Ki-yu: A Story of Panthers, illustrated by Kurt Wiese.   Boston, Houghton Mifflin, 1934; as *Panther*, London, Cape, 1934; Houghton Mifflin, 1973.

Starbuck Valley Winter, illustrated by Charles De Feo.   New York, Morrow, 1943; London, Collins, 1944.

Saltwater Summer.   Toronto, Collins, and New York, Morrow, 1948; London, Collins, 1949.

Mounted Police Patrol.   London, Collins, and New York, Morrow, 1954.

Fur and Gold, illustrated by Paul Duff.   Toronto, Longman, 1962.

The Whale People, illustrated by Mary Weiler.   London, Collins, 1962; New York, Morrow, 1963.

Other

Captain of the Discovery: The Story of Captain George Vancouver, illustrated by Robert Banks.   Toronto and London, Macmillan, 1956.

The Farthest Shores, illustrated by Frank Newfeld.   Toronto, Longman, 1960.

PUBLICATIONS FOR ADULTS

Novels

Pool and Rapid: The Story of a River, illustrated by C.F. Tunnicliffe.   Toronto, McClelland and Stewart, and London, A. and C. Black, 1932.

Timber: A Novel of Pacific Coast Loggers.   New York, Morrow, 1942; as *The Tall Trees Fall*, London, Collins, 1943.

On the Highest Hill.   Toronto, Collins, and New York, Morrow, 1949; London, Collins, 1950.

Other

The Western Angler: An Account of Pacific Salmon and Western Trout in British Columbia.   New York, Derrydale Press, 1939.

Return to the River: A Story of the Chinook Run.   New York, Morrow, 1941; London, Collins, 1942.

A River Never Sleeps.   Toronto, Collins, and New York, Morrow, 1946; London, Collins, 1948.

Measure of the Year.   Toronto, Collins, and New York, Morrow, 1950.

Fisherman's Spring.   Toronto, Collins, and New York, Morrow, 1951.

Spring Congregation Address, 1952: Power and People.   Vancouver, University of British Columbia, 1952.

Fisherman's Winter.   New York, Morrow, 1954.

Divine Discontent: An Address to the Annual Assembly of Victoria College.   Victoria, British Columbia, Victoria Daily Times, 1954.

The Case for the Preservation of Strathcona Park.   Victoria, British Columbia, Daily Colonist, 1955.

Fabulous Fishing in Latin America ....   New York, Pan American World Airways, 1956.

The Face of Canada, with others.   Toronto, Clarke Irwin, 1959; London, Harrap, 1960.

Fisherman's Summer.   Toronto, Collins, and New York, Morrow, 1959.

The Living Land: An Account of the Natural Resources of British Columbia.   Toronto, Macmillan, and New York, Morrow, 1961.

The Pacific Northwest, with Stewart Holbrook and Nard Jones, edited by Anthony Netboy.   New York, Doubleday, 1963.

A Primer of Fly Fishing.   Toronto, Collins, and New York, Morrow, 1964.

Fisherman's Fall.   Toronto, Collins, and New York, Morrow, 1964.

Canada's Pacific Salmon, revised edition.   Ottawa, Queen's Printer, 1967.

The Canadians 1867–1967.   Toronto, Macmillan, 1967.

The Salmon.   Ottawa, Queen's Printer, 1974.

Manuscript Collection: University of British Columbia Library, Vancouver.

Theatrical Activities:
Actor: **Films** – *Out of the North*, 1952; *Rural Magistrate.*

*   *   *

When Roderick Haig-Brown died in 1976, he left behind a body of children's books which is distinguished for its tremendous variety and uniform excellence. He achieved success in writing historical fiction and biography, modern realistic fiction, and realistic animal stories. While each book deals with a different subject matter, two qualities are common to all of his books: his knowledge and love of Canada's West Coast and his interest in analyzing the development of a character who stands alone, be he a British sea captain, a Nootka Indian chief, a modern teenager, or a mountain lion. As it is impossible to consider all of Haig-Brown's juvenile books, we shall analyze only four, each one representative of one of the literary types mentioned above.

Ki-yu (Panther) in many ways sets the tone for Haig-Brown's later works. A realistic animal story, it is set on the West Coast of Vancouver Island, and the author reveals his great knowledge of and respect for both the terrain and wild life of that area. Ki-yu, a panther, shows himself early in life to be clever and strong and instinctively senses those forces which will determine the course of his life: "Upon his determination to fight for meat, upon the degree of ferocity and persistence with which he would hunt and kill, his whole life was dependent. So the instinct to be savage and possessive when meat was within reach was all-powerful, and the first scent of meat from his mother's kill aroused that instinct until it blotted all others from him." Ki-yu's life is one of constant combat, against other panthers who would possess his mates or his food, against wolves and bears, and, most significant, against man. In fact, the main conflict is between the panther and David Milton, a professional hunter. Clearly, Haig-Brown sees this as an heroic confrontation, the most noble animal of the area and the most dedicated hunter, a man who respects and understands his adversary and who has a deep sense of the responsibility attached to his profession. Working alone with his dogs, Milton is clearly Haig-Brown's ideal hunter, a contrast to the other people in the story, the cowards, the bumblers, and the jealous rivals. However, in the end, the aging and injured Ki-yu, is not killed by Milton but, after a courageous battle, torn to pieces by a pack of wolves, a victim of the law of survival by which he had lived.

Starbuck Valley Winter is also set in the valleys of Vancouver Island. It describes the winter spent by the teenage hero Don Morgan, who struggles at trapping, hoping to make enough money to buy a boat. But more important, it is the story of the youth's growth to maturity. Because he is only 16 years old, Don has difficulty in acquiring a hunting licence. But once that problem is overcome, his real tests have just begun. Setting off with his overweight and generally ineffectual chum, Tubby Miller, he learns that trapping is not an easy business. Not only must he struggle with foul weather and bad luck along the trap line; he must also overcome his inner uncertainties and insecurities. In the end, he proves his worthiness and, more important, he comes to understand Jetson, a renegade old trapper he had viewed with suspicion and hostility.

In addition, Don acquires a virtue seen in all of Haig-Brown's heroes: a deep knowledge of and reverence for the land. Haig-Brown often stated that the only real ownership of any land is in the knowing of it. Early in the winter, Don realizes that "it was going to take time, perhaps several seasons to know it properly and learn how to use it." Don will become like David Milton of *Panther*, Atlin of *The Whale People*, and George Vancouver of *Captain of the Discovery*, each of whom Haig-Brown admires, not only for his heroism, but also for his desire to come to terms with the rugged landscape.

An historical novel dealing with the natives of Canada's West Coast, *The Whale People* again focuses on the growth to maturity of a young man. Son of the great whale chief Nit-gass, Atlin's eventual succession to chieftainship is in no doubt. The question that arises is "Will he be worthy of the title he will eventually assume?" The novel presents the tests he must undergo.

The first eleven chapters trace the early training of young Atlin. Like his father, he is ambitious and impatient – he would like to rush into the hunt without adequate preparations. However, the training, it is stressed, must be deliberate, must be taken a step at a time. It is according to ritual, but behind that ritual is the common sense understanding that lack of adequate foundations can be disastrous. Seal hunting follows salmon fishing and preceeds whale hunting – for each activity requires progressively more advanced skills. During the winter, the potlach ceremonies, which Atlin with his youthful impatience thinks unimportant, are intended to impress on both him and the tribe that he is Nit-gass' successor.

With the death of Nit-gass on a whale hunt, Atlin assumes the title of whale chief. But there are four steps he must undertake to acquire the reality as well as the title of whale chief. Following the tradition he must move the stone harpoon in his father's shrine and swim in the pool of the supernatural shark – these are the tests of strength and courage which will be necessary on the hunt. Second, he must oversee the preparation of the village for the hunt – a test of his leadership ability. Third, he must venture on the sea to kill the great whale, thus bringing food and therefore life to his people. And finally, he must soothe the strained relationships with Eskowit, a chief of the neighboring tribe, and thus prove his political ability. This he does through marrying the chief's daughter. As the book ends, he has proved his right to the title of Whale Chief.

From this brief look at the structure of Haig-Brown's *The Whale People*, we can see that there is little of the inner conflict one finds in many novels, including *Starbuck Valley Winter*, of young people growing up. Instead, there is the presentation of the logical and ritual steps of the creation of a whale chief. It is, in fact, in Haig-Brown's ability to present the dignity of this ritual movement, along with his loving and knowledgeable treatment of Canada's Pacific lands and seas, that the great beauty of the book is to be found.

In his historical writings, Haig-Brown combines factual accuracy with his interest in character and, as in his other writings, his feel for the Canadian landscape. These qualities are best seen in *Captain of the Discovery*, the biography of 18th century explorer George Vancouver.

In discussing Vancouver, Haig-Brown calls him a "quiet hero." Since the times of such early explorers as Cabot and Cartier, the science of navigation and knowledge of the world had advanced greatly. Seamen no longer feared that they might sail off the edge of the world. But there were still dangers: the sea was unpredictable, disease on ship was still difficult to control, natives could – and did – prove hostile, and much of the territory being explored was unknown and hence a threat. Haig-Brown describes Vancouver's heroism in this way: "The real story of George Vancouver is not in one great voyage or in any one spectacular deed. It is in the hundreds of lesser voyages made by the small boats ... through three long years of exploration. ... Vancouver was the driving force behind [the men], he was the strength that held them all together, the wisdom and judgment and devotion that brought them safely through, a community of men in two small ships ten thousand miles away from their nearest base of supply."

Perhaps the best way of approaching *Captain of the Discovery* is as a character study of Vancouver himself. An important influence on his life was the example of Captain James Cook, under whom he served as a ship's boy. Cook's quiet courage and his concern for the well-being of his men made a deep impression on Vancouver. In fact, one of the major motivating forces behind Vancouver's explorations was a desire to vindicate Cook's name, which had fallen into disrepute after his death.

Friendship was important to Vancouver, as is indicated in the scenes describing his relationships with the Spanish explorer Quadra and the Hawaiian king Tamaahmaah. Finally, one should notice that throughout his voyages, Vancouver had great respect for the rights of native peoples. At a time when European traders were ruthlessly exploiting Pacific islanders, Vancouver affirmed their rights to self-determination and regretted the devastating results of europeanization of the Pacific.

Although Haig-Brown is an excellent story teller, bringing his narrative details vividly to life, he will be best remembered for these two qualities we have noticed in the books we have examined: his deep feeling for the land of Canada's West Coast, and his sensitive portrayal of his quiet heroes.

—Jon C. Stott

HALDANE, J(ohn) B(urdon) S(anderson). Indian. Born in Oxford, England, 5 November 1892; brother of Naomi Mitchison, *q.v.*; became Indian citizen, 1960. Educated at Oxford Preparatory School; Eton College, Buckinghamshire; New College, Oxford, M.A. Served in the Black Watch in France and Iraq, 1914–19: Captain. Married Charlotte Franken in 1926 (marriage dissolved, 1945); Helen Spurway, 1945. Fellow of New College, 1919–22; Reader in Biochemistry, Cambridge University, 1922–23; Fullerian Professor of Physiology, Royal Institution, London, 1930–32; Professor of Genetics, 1933–37, and Professor of Biometry, 1937–57, London University. Research Professor, Indian Statistical Institute, 1961; Head of Genetics and Biometry, Government of Orissa, 1962–64. President, Genetical Society, 1932–36; Chairman of the Editorial Board, *Daily Worker*, London, 1940–49. Recipient: Royal Society Darwin Medal, 1953; Linnean Society Darwin-Wallace Medal, 1958; National Academy of Sciences Kimber Medal, 1961; Accademia dei Lincei Feltrinelli Prize, 1961. D.Sc.: University of Groningen, 1946; Oxford University, 1961; Honorary Doctorate, University of Paris, 1949; LL.D.: University of Edinburgh, 1956. Honorary Fellow, New College, 1961. Corresponding Member, Société de Biologie, 1928; Fellow, Royal Society, 1932; Chevalier, Legion of Honour, 1937; Honorary Member, Moscow Academy of Sciences, 1942; Corresponding Member, Deutsche Akademie der Wissenschaften, 1950, National Institute of Sciences of India, 1953, and Royal Danish Academy of Sciences, 1956. *Died 1 December 1964.*

PUBLICATIONS FOR CHILDREN

Fiction

> *My Friend Mr. Leakey*, illustrated by Leonard Rosoman.   London, Cresset Press, 1937; New York, Harper, 1938.

PUBLICATIONS FOR ADULTS

Novel

> *The Man with Two Memories.*   London, Merlin Press, 1976.

Other

Daedalus; or, Science and the Future: A Paper Read to the Heretics, Cambridge, on February 4th, 1923.   London, Kegan Paul Trench Trubner, and New York, Dutton, 1924.

Callinicus: A Defence of Chemical Warfare.   London, Kegan Paul Trench Trubner, and New York, Dutton, 1925.

Animal Biology, with Julian Huxley.   London, Oxford University Press, 1927.

The Last Judgment: A Scientist's Vision of the Future of Man.   New York and London, Harper, 1927.

Possible Worlds and Other Essays.   London, Chatto and Windus, 1927; as *Possible Worlds and Other Papers*, New York, Harper, 1928.

Science and Ethics (lecture).   London, C.A.Watts, 1928.

Enzymes.   London, Longman, 1930.

Materialism (miscellany).   London, Hodder and Stoughton, 1932.

The Causes of Evolution.   London, Longman, and New York, Harper, 1932.

The Inequality of Man and Other Essays.   London, Chatto and Windus, 1932; as *Science and Human Life*, New York, Harper, 1933.

Biology in Everyday Life, with John Randal Baker.   London, Allen and Unwin, 1933.

Fact and Faith.   London, C.A. Watts, 1934.

Human Biology and Politics.   London, British Science Guild, 1934.

Science and the Supernatural: A Correspondence Between Harold Lunn and J.B.S. Haldane.   London, Eyre and Spottiswoode, and New York, Sheed and Ward, 1935.

The Outlook of Science, edited by William Empson.   London, Routledge, 1935.

Science and Well-Being, edited by William Empson.   London, Routledge, 1935.

The Chemistry of the Individual (lecture).   London, Oxford University Press, 1938.

The Marxist Philosophy.   London, Birkbeck College, 1938.

A.R.P. [Air Raid Precautions].   London, Gollancz, 1938.

Heredity and Politics.   London, Allen and Unwin, and New York, Norton, 1938.

How to Be Safe from Air Raids.   London, Gollancz, 1938.

The Marxist Philosophy and the Sciences.   London, Allen and Unwin, 1938; New York, Random House, 1939.

Science and Everyday Life.   London, Lawrence and Wishart, 1939; New York, Macmillan, 1940.

Science and You.   London, Fore Publications, 1939.

Keeping Cool and Other Essays.   London, Chatto and Windus, 1940; as *Adventures of a Biologist*, New York, Harper, 1940.

Science in Peace and War.   London, Lawrence and Wishart, 1940.

New Paths in Genetics.   London, Allen and Unwin, 1941; New York, Harper, 1942.

Dialectical Materialism and Modern Science.   London, Labour Monthly, 1942.

Why Professional Workers Should Be Communists.   London, Communist Party, 1945.

A Banned Broadcast and Other Essays.   London, Chatto and Windus, 1946.

Science Advances.   London, Allen and Unwin, and New York, Macmillan, 1947.

What Is Life?   New York, Boni and Gaer, 1947; London, Lindsay Drummond, 1949.

Is Evolution a Myth? A Debate Between Douglas Dewar, L. Merson Davies and J.B.S. Haldane.   London, Paternoster Press, 1949.

Everything Has a History (essays).   London, Allen and Unwin, 1951.

The Biochemistry of Genetics.   London, Allen and Unwin, 1954; New York, Macmillan, 1956.

The Argument from Animals to Men: An Examination of Its Validity for Anthropology (lecture).   London, Royal Anthropological Institute, 1956.

Karl Pearson 1857–1957 (address).   London, Biometrika Trustees, 1958.

The Unity and Diversity of Life (lecture).   New Delhi, Ministry of Information and Broadcasting, 1965.

Science and Indian Culture.   Calcutta, New Age Publishers, 1965.

Science and Life: Essays of a Rationalist. London, Pemberton-Barrie and Rockliff, 1968.

Editor, *You and Heredity,* by Amram Scheinfeld and Morton D. Schweitzer. London, Chatto and Windus, 1939.

Critical Study: *J.B.S.: The Life and Work of J.B.S. Haldane* by Ronald W. Clark, London, Hodder and Stoughton, 1968; New York, Coward McCann, 1969.

*   *   *

It was a mathematician who wrote *Alice in Wonderland* a century ago. It was one of the greatest polymaths of our own time who wrote another of the best books for children ever published, *My Friend Mr. Leakey,* but who, unlike Lewis Carroll, left it at that. Perhaps in Carroll work and play were more sharply divided. All the zest and delight in the strangeness of the universe that illuminated Jack Haldane's scientific research, all "the power to connect things in his mind in unexpected ways" noted in Sir Peter Medawar's preface to *J.B.S.* are at their height in this volume. The paperback edition is especially valuable for a preliminary paragraph in which the author's voice speaks as directly as it does in the narrative. "Professor Haldane has been used for experiments ever since he was three .... Some of the things that have happened to him are nearly as queer as the things that happen in this book. He thinks ... science can be more exciting than magic ... the nearest things he has to a dragon in his house are two she-newts, Flosshilda and Berenice .... He is bald, weighs about 15 stone, and is fond of swimming." Children were still writing to him about the book in 1962, when he told one that "a green lizard 4 feet long" had trespassed into his Indian bathroom.

There are three minor stories in the volume: one about a man who gives rats biscuits containing powdered iron filings and then draws them by a powerful magnet into a pit, one about an anaconda fitted with status-symbolic golden teeth by his millionaire owner, and one about the naiad Miss Wandle with a magic shop in Wandsworth. All have startling freshness and ingenuity, but in the actual Mr. Leakey adventures invention tumbles over itself in glory. He is a real magician, a member of the International Congress of Sorcerers on the Brocken, and has his meals grilled by a small dragon (who wears asbestos boots when out of the fire) and served by an octopus. Strawberries are fetched from New Zealand by a jinn whose incautious colleagues get stomach ache from radio waves, find the lower air crowded with aeroplanes, and are pelted with shooting stars by angels if they fly too high. When Mr. Leakey gives a party he temporarily transforms his guests into human-sized versions of whatever they choose (a whimsy film star turned butterfly finds herself with goggly eyes and a proboscis). He travels on a magic carpet which "hovers stiffly" a foot above floors covered with books. He makes the author practise being invisible, which produces a (physiologically justified) "nasty giddy feeling." And so on. Nothing could be more characteristic of the man who wrote in his last years "the world is not only queerer than anyone has imagined but queerer than anyone *can* imagine."

—Renée Haynes

HALE, Kathleen. British. Born in Broughton, Biggar, Lanarkshire, 24 May 1898. Educated at Manchester High School for Girls; Manchester School of Art; University College, Reading (scholar), 1916–18; Central School of Art, London; East Anglian School of Painting and Drawing. Married Douglas McClean in 1926 (died, 1967); has two sons. Artist: paintings exhibited at New English Arts Club, London Group, Grosvenor Galleries, Vermont

Gallery, Warwick Public Library Gallery, Gallery Edward Harvane, New Grafton Gallery, Parkin Gallery; metal groups and pictures exhibited at Lefevre Galleries and Leicester Galleries; mural for Festival of Britain Schools Section, London, 1951; Orlando Ballet for Festival Gardens, London, 1951. Fellow, Society of Industrial Artists and Designers. O.B.E. (Officer, Order of the British Empire). Address: Tod House, near Forest Hill, Oxford, England.

PUBLICATIONS FOR CHILDREN (illustrated by the author)

Fiction

> *Orlando, The Marmalade Cat: A Camping Holiday.*   London, Country Life, and New
>   York, Scribner, 1938.
> *Orlando's Evening Out.*   London, Penguin, 1941.
> *Orlando's Home Life.*   London, Penguin, 1942.
> *Orlando, The Marmalade Cat, Buys a Farm.*   London, Country Life, 1942.
> *Henrietta, The Faithful Hen.*   London, Transatlantic Arts, 1943; New York, Coward
>   McCann, 1953.
> *Orlando, The Marmalade Cat: His Silver Wedding.*   London, Country Life, 1944.
> *Orlando, The Marmalade Cat, Becomes a Doctor.*   London, Country Life, 1944.
> *Orlando's Invisible Pyjamas.*   London, Transatlantic Arts, 1947.
> *Orlando, The Marmalade Cat: A Trip Abroad.*   London, Country Life, 1949.
> *Orlando, The Marmalade Cat, Keeps a Dog.*   London, Country Life, 1949.
> *Orlando, The Judge.*   London, Murray, 1950.
> *Orlando's Country Life: A Peep-Show Book.*   London, Chatto and Windus, 1950.
> *Puss-in-Boots: A Peep-Show Book.*   London, Chatto and Windus, 1951.
> *Orlando, The Marmalade Cat: A Seaside Holiday.*   London, Country Life, 1952.
> *Manda.*   London, Murray, 1952; New York, Coward McCann, 1953.
> *Orlando's Zoo.*   London, Murray, 1954.
> *Orlando, The Marmalade Cat: The Frisky Housewife.*   London, Country Life, 1956.
> *Orlando's Magic Carpet.*   London, Murray, 1958.
> *Orlando, The Marmalade Cat, Buys a Cottage.*   London Country Life, 1963.
> *Orlando and the Three Graces.*   London, Murray, 1965.
> *Orlando, The Marmalade Cat, Goes to the Moon.*   London, Murray, 1968.
> *Orlando, The Marmalade Cat, and the Water Cats.*   London, Cape, 1972.
> *Henrietta's Magic Egg.*   London, Allen and Unwin, 1973.

Illustrator: *I Don't Mix Much with Fairies*, 1928, and *Plain Jane*, 1929, by Mary R. Harrower; *Basil Seal Rides Again* by Evelyn Waugh, 1963.

Kathleen Hale comments:
   I began writing my books for my own children. Then I wrote for children who were deprived of family love – as I was to a certain extent – especially those evacuated during the last war, torn from their parents and sent to sometimes unsympathetic homes. I've tried to keep the parent relationship, with love and understanding, alive for children who are denied it. I also wrote the books for *my own* rather cold childhood, thereby living out a warmth that was lacking when I was a child.

*   *   *

   Kathleen Hale's numerous picture-story books about Orlando the Marmalade Cat provide an excellent example of the kind of book which is enjoyed most when it is read aloud to a child of the right age, and at the same time pored over with the fascinated alertness that brings to light new things to notice in the illustrations with every re-reading. For Orlando's adventures have come in books of varied shapes and sizes (including some very large ones); but invariably the text and the pictures have been carefully integrated so that the story-line carried by the words is echoed and often embellished by the richly inventive lithographs. As an instance of what the pictures can add to the words one might mention *Orlando's Evening Out*, where the "cots" in which the kittens are fast asleep are shown to be Master's slippers, while Master himself, with Orlando on one knee and Orlando's wife Grace on the other, is no more than a bald head hidden behind the *Daily Mews*. This story involves a visit to the circus in the course of which Orlando involuntarily becomes a star performer, and the orchestra ends up by playing "He's a Jolly Good Feline .... " It will be seen that Kathleen Hale's verbal humour relies a good deal upon puns; sometimes these are not particularly good ones, but the word-play can at times be wittily original – Tinkle's coinage "Hot Wartle" must surely have passed into the accepted lingo of not a few families.

The humour hinges also on a complex interweaving of the humanised feline world of Orlando and his family and a richly eccentric human world. One of the very best of the stories is *Orlando's Invisible Pyjamas*. This starts with Orlando slipping out one snowy evening to take a dead mouse to the nightwatchman who is guarding a hole in the road (the kitten Tinkle sees him and says: "Hello Farver, you've grown a Mousetache!"); unfortunately Mr. Pusey, the nightwatchman, does not really appreciate Orlando's gift when it is deposited in his frying-pan alongside his sausages, and in the ensuing flurry Orlando's hind quarters are drenched with paraffin. The following day Tinkle finds an embarrassed Orlando hiding in the snowy pampas grass, "quite bald from the waist to the tip of his tail." His family smuggles him home camouflaged by a "Modesty Awning," and while the kittens and Mr. Pusey do their best to entertain him as he lies in bed, Grace knits him a pair of pyjamas which look just like real fur. Trouble comes only when he meets a dog and all his fur stands on end except his pyjamas – an incident entertainingly reinforced by the illustration. The later stories have tended to become increasingly fantastical and highly elaborated, but the series as a whole offers a wealth of enjoyment – ideal, one would say, for the intelligent 6-year-old, but capable of being appreciated on some level at almost any age from four to eight.

—Frank Whitehead

HALEY, Gail E(inhart). American. Born in Charlotte, North Carolina, 4 November 1939. Educated at Richmond Professional Institute, Virginia, 1958–60; University of Virginia, Charlottesville, 1960–62. Married Joseph A. Haley in 1959; Arnold F. Arnold, 1966, one daughter. Vice-President, Manuscript Press, New York, from 1965. Recipient: American Library Association Caldecott Medal, 1971; British Library Association Kate Greenaway Medal, for illustration, 1977. Agent: Marilyn Marlowe, Curtis Brown Ltd., 575 Madison Avenue, New York, New York 10022, U.S.A.; or, A.P. Watt, 26–28 Bedford Row, London WC1R 4HL. Address: 3 Market Place, London N.2, England.

PUBLICATIONS FOR CHILDREN (illustrated by the author)

Fiction

My Kingdom for a Dragon. Crozet, Virginia, Crozet Print Shop, 1962.
The Wonderful Magical World of Marguerite. New York, McGraw Hill, 1964.
Round Stories about Things That Live on Land and *in Water.* Chicago, Follett, 2 vols., 1966.
Round Stories about Things That Grow. Chicago, Follett, 1966.

Round Stories about Our World.   Chicago, Follett, 1966.
Noah's Ark.   New York, Atheneum, 1971.
The Abominable Swamp Man.   New York, Viking Press, 1975.
The Post Office Cat.   New York, Scribner, and London, Bodley Head, 1976.
Go Away, Stay Away.   New York, Scribner, and London, Bodley Head, 1977.

Other

A Story, A Story: An African Tale, Retold.   New York, Atheneum, 1970; London,
    Methuen, 1972.
Jack Jouett's Ride.   New York, Viking Press, 1973; London, Bodley Head, 1974.
Costumes for Plays and Playing.   London, Methuen, 1977.

Illustrator: *The Skip Rope Book* edited by Francelia Butler, 1962; *One, Two, Buckle My Shoe: A Book of Counting Rhymes,* 1964; *The Three Wishes of Hu* by James Holding, 1965; *Koalas* by Bernice Kohn, 1965; *Which Is Which?* by Solveig Russell, 1966; *P.S., Happy Anniversary* by Lois Wyse 1966; *The Peek-a-Boo Book of Puppies and Kittens* by Hannah Rush, 1966; *All Together, One at a Time* by E.L. Konigsburg, 1971.

*   *   *

Gail E. Haley studied with the well-known artist Charles Smith. Her artistic gifts, however, extend beyond any professional training. She uses whatever materials are at hand – scraps of linoleum, boxwood tufts from a hedge – anything which interests her in her surroundings. Often, her pictures are transformations of people she knows or of pictures of people – from old daguerreotypes, for instance.

Though her art sometimes appears to be effortlessly done, much of it is carefully planned. Her lovely pastel over-size book, *Marguerite,* was first prepared as a small pen-and-ink pamphlet, distributed among her friends. Her first book, *My Kingdom for a Dragon,* consisted of linoleum block prints of bold design. Critics found her illustrations in *The Skip Rope Book* "fresh" and "perky." Since then, her style has become less eclectic, more inclined towards bold colors and execution.

Her artistic imagination also carries over into her writing. She has from the beginning of her literary career revealed a deep resentment of social injustice, and her highly original fantasies are usually social allegories as well. In *My Kingdom for a Dragon,* a Knight, criticized for making friends with a dragon, recognizes that if he betrays this dragon he is betraying himself: "The Sunshine in his own heart would die." In the African legend, *A Story, A Story,* for which Ms. Haley won the Caldecott Award, she captures the spirit of the original story so well in English that her version is often used by professional story-tellers for oral narration. She concludes: "This is my story which I have related. If it be sweet, or if it be not sweet, take some elsewhere, and let some come back to me." Her prose style has a poetic quality, perhaps best exemplified so far in *Jack Jouett's Ride,* written and illustrated by Ms. Haley at the suggestion of Lady Walton. It is a re-telling of the story of the innkeeper's son during the American Revolution who outwitted the British Dragoons. *The Abominable Swamp Man* is an extraordinarily imaginative achievement which goes beyond a cry for liberation as an external reality to urge freedom for fantasy as well – the right of every creature to a private fantasy life.

—Francelia Butler

HALL, Aylmer. Pseudonym for Norah E. L. Hall. British. Born in Surrey, 24 April 1914. Educated at Clifton High School, Bristol, 1927–32; St. Hugh's College, Oxford, 1932–35, B.A. (honours) in modern languages. Married Robert Aylmer Hall in 1938; has one son and one daughter. Personal Assistant to the Secretary, New Commonwealth Institute, London, 1936; Assistant Press Librarian, Royal Institute of International Affairs, London, 1937–39; Chief Press Librarian in Research Division, Ministry of Information, London, 1939–40. Agent: Winant, Towers Ltd., 14 Cliffords Inn, London E.C.4. Address: 28 Burghley Road, London S.W.19, England.

PUBLICATIONS FOR CHILDREN

Fiction

>*The Mystery of Torland Manor*, illustrated by Nat Long. London, Harrap, 1952.
>*The Admiral's Secret.* London, Harrap, 1953.
>*The K.F. Conspiracy*, illustrated by R.C.W. Meade. London, Harrap, 1955.
>*The Sword of Glendower*, illustrated by Janet Duchesne. London, Methuen, 1960; as
>   *The Search for Lancelot's Sword*, New York, Criterion Books, 1962.
>*The Devilish Plot*, illustrated by John Hodder. London, Hart Davis, 1965.
>*The Tyrant King: A London Adventure.* London, London Transport Board, 1967.
>*The Marked Man.* London, Hart Davies, 1967.
>*Colonel Bull's Inheritance.* London, Macmillan, 1968; New York, Meredith Press,
>   1969.
>*Beware of Moonlight.* London, Macmillan, 1969; New York, Nelson, 1970.
>*The Minstrel Boy.* London, Macmillan, 1970.

PUBLICATIONS FOR ADULTS

Other

>Editor (as Norah Hall). *The Chronology of the Second World War.* London, Royal
>   Institute of International Affairs, 1947.

Aylmer Hall comments:
The first five books by "Aylmer Hall" were written at the instigation of, and in collaboration with, my husband, as serial stories for our small son at his preparatory school. Later, when my husband's job became too demanding, I was a solo performer with a very good and helpful trainer. The last books, all set in Ireland, from which my family come, were inspired by our acquiring a country refuge in West Cork, but their historical setting has been very carefully prepared.

*   *   *

Aylmer Hall's earlier books have perhaps too "dated" a quality about them for the modern taste: the recent past of the immediately post-war years seems to belong to the Boys' Own era much more than to the present day. Intrepid public-schoolboys get mixed up in murky political criminality and the Great British Virtues prevail, while the settings, though strongly evoked, are redolent of much that has been popular schoolboy diet before.

For all that, Aylmer Hall is much more than just another writer in a tired tradition. In spite of the stereotyped upper-middle-class heroes with their public-school code there is a sensitively considered dimension of anxiety and self-doubt running through. Far from intrepid, in fact, her heroes are capable of almost numbing fear. If they succeed it is not without near-miss moments of failure.

Michael Mannering in *The Admiral's Secret*, tangling with sinister ex-Nazi opportunists, moves with trepidation and frequent lapses of that presence of mind so essential in your archetypal schoolboy hero. Later, in *The K.F. Conspiracy*, though older and more assured, when he finds himself in the thick of a mittel-European border war, the first elation quickly gives way to a sense of personal inadequacy, fear, and exhaustion.

The whole register of the recent past has an air of theatricality. This may be one reason why the more remote historical romances appear rather less mannered. In *Colonel Bull's Inheritance* Mrs. Hall evokes the time and place of the West of Ireland in the 18th century in a tightly constructed plot in which the boy-hero finds himself caught in the crossfire of no less than four opposing parties. This is indeed a very workmanlike novel, for the complicated elements of plot are cleverly mixed and balanced in a story that never for a moment loses its line and clarity. Where the earlier novels would tie themselves in knots but for the explanatory set speeches rather ingenuously introduced from time to time, in the later novels the dialogue springs naturally from character and incident and the plots unfold with subtle ease.

The first commitment was to a generalised ethic. The earlier heroes survived because of their fidelity to a code of conduct. Yet in working through their predicaments the code took on a deeply personal relevance. In her later books, however, codes and causes are shown to be as hollow as the strutting attitudes they beget. The only values to have any currency are those based on mutual love and respect. Sean Daly in *The Minstrel Boy* is surrounded by charismatic characters whose personal metals are found weakened under stress, while his own humbler creed stands the test of betrayal, starvation and torture. The anchor of Sean's faith is his growing love for Margaret. Mrs. Hall's concern now is with the inescapable personal dimension in moral decision.

—Myles McDowell

HAMILTON, Charles. See **RICHARDS, Frank.**

HAMILTON, Virginia (Esther). American. Born in Yellow Springs, Ohio, 12 March 1936. Educated at Antioch College, Yellow Springs, Ohio, 1952–55; Ohio State University, Columbus, 1957–58; New School for Social Research, New York. Married Arnold Adoff in 1960; has two children. Recipient: Mystery Writers of America Edgar Allan Poe Award, 1969; *Boston Globe-Horn Book* Award, 1974; National Book Award, 1975; American Library Association Newbery Medal, 1975. Agent: Dorothy Markinko, McIntosh and Otis Inc., 18 East 41st Street, New York, New York 10017. Address: Box 293, Yellow Springs, Ohio 45387, U.S.A.

PUBLICATIONS FOR CHILDREN

Fiction

Zeely, illustrated by Symeon Shimin. New York, Macmillan, 1967.
The House of Dies Drear, illustrated by Eros Keith. New York, Macmillan, 1968.
The Time-Ago Tales of Jahdu, illustrated by Nonny Hogrogian. New York, Macmillan, 1969.

The Planet of Junior Brown.   New York, Macmillan, 1971.

Time-Ago Lost: More Tales of Jahdu, illustrated by Ray Prather.   New York, Macmillan, 1973.

M.C. Higgins, The Great.   New York, Macmillan, 1974; London, Hamish Hamilton, 1975.

Arilla Sun Down.   New York, Morrow. 1976; London, Hamish Hamilton, 1977.

Other

W.E.B. Du Bois: A Biography.   New York, Crowell, 1972.

Paul Robeson: The Life and Times of a Free Black Man.   New York, Harper, 1974.

Editor, *The Writings of W.E.B. Du Bois.*   New York, Crowell, 1975.

PUBLICATIONS FOR ADULTS

Other

Illusion and Reality (lecture).   Washington, D.C., Library of Congress, 1976.

Virginia Hamilton comments:

The writing of books encompasses the whole of my life, although it isn't serious business for me in the sense that I need discuss it solemnly every moment. After all, writing has to be a part-time occupation. More than any other serious profession, it feeds and grows on living, and living is what a writer must do full-time. Living full-time takes more energy and discipline than any writing I know of. It demands that one not let herself become uninvolved with life; or forget or fear to look at it.

The making of any fiction for me is foremost a self-viewing that becomes a force for life and living. The fiction becomes greater than the sum of fact, memory and imagination that create it. At the last, it stands independent from the self and is often more mysterious than anything the writer of it may have experienced herself.

That is why I so often say that life is continuous, going in a circle. And everyone who is black who has lived and those now living have something to say to me and have something to do with the person I am. It must be that all people who have lived and those now living hold our common knowledge as humans and make us one people. That is why, although I generally write of the black experience, I place no restriction on whom or what kind of people I may write about. Writers must remain free to write as readers must have freedom of choice in order to read. Writing has to be fun for me, the writer, in the hopes that readers will respond to it with enthusiasm. Therein is an interchange of thought and feeling which has a way of bringing us together in communication.

*   *   *

Virginia Hamilton has heightened the standards for children's literature as few other authors have. She does not address children or the state of children so much as she explores with them, sometimes ahead of them, the full possibilities of boundless imagination. Even her farthest-flung thoughts, however, are carefully leashed to the craft of writing. There is clearly a hardworked development from the first two books, which were coated with some stiffness of language and incident, to three powerful novels weaving fantastic characters and situations with graceful, credible assurance.

Although comparatively awkward, the early *Zeely* and *The House of Dies Drear* leave indelible flashing impressions – one of a six-and-a-half foot swine shepherdess descended from African royalty and the other of an ancient, indomitable descendent of slaves guarding his heritage of abolitionist wealth in a secret cavern. The second book is better built but still does not fully break surface formality to the power underneath. Then, in *The Time-Ago Tales of Jahdu*, Hamilton frees her words into strong, rhythmic patterns that can fit and follow her roving imagination.

The Planet of Junior Brown unites the graceful language of Jahdu with the sustained structure of imaginative fiction. The uncanny figure of Junior Brown – hugely fat, talented and unhappy – revolves in his own troubled universe while Buddy – strong, resourceful, streetwise – swirls around him, caring. One has too much mother, the other none. Little by little their props fall. The two boys' peaceful haven, a concealed school closet in which the janitor has built a simulated solar system that lights up, is threatened and must be dissembled. Their truancy is discovered. Junior's piano teacher slips from strangeness to madness, dragging Junior with her into disturbing hallucinations. Who can Buddy trust in New York City? So many already contributed to Junior's problems, and so many could seal his psychological doom in the guise of help.

Coming to Junior's rescue, Buddy develops his own philosophy of leadership in the underground "planets" established by older homeless boys to take care of younger ones. Early on he teaches, along with techniques of survival, "The highest law is to learn to live for yourself." By the end of the book, he has found a new trust. "We are together ... because we have to learn to live for each other." Supporting such a resolution are two perfect portraits and a vivid setting.

As *The Planet* is a city book, quick in pace, *M.C. Higgins, The Great* is a country book, with slowgathering but inevitable power, natural images, and homemade music. M.C. Higgins is born of the hills and hardship. Every aspect of living requires enormous physical effort. But there are rewards: the knowledge of Sarah's Mountain, passed to the eldest son for generations; the rich, deep, abiding love of family. M.C. has passed all the land's tests of toughness but must face the outside threat of intruders upon the land – a stripminers' spoil heap that could bury his cabin any time, a music collector who takes his mother's voice on tapes for empty hints of help, a young stranger who tempts M.C.'s heart to follow her.

The pictures and the relationships and the sounds that fit together here deepen in perspective with each reading. There is a sure direction that never slips into preplanning, an opening and closure of another world that one wants to visit – a unique place where six-fingered, red-haired merino blacks have made a vegetable farming commune stretched over with a rope web where the children can climb and play. And they are as believeable as the strength M.C. finds in himself, his family, his friends, his mountain.

Arilla Sun Down is an adventurous book because it leaves the beaten paths of complete sentences and of Hamilton's previously successful award winners. That took a lot of nerve. In this first-person narrative are mixed chapters of present and past. A Midwestern girl, black with Amerind blood, gropes her way toward identity in a family that tugs strongly in different directions – her mother a black dancer, her father a nomad with an unresolved native American background, her brother a charismatic, self-defined, modern-day warrior. The chapters of Arilla's memories are written in a stream-of-consciousness flow with impressionistic child language floating among half-buried images and snatches of adult conversation remembered piecemeal. Some, such as the scene of an old man's death, have a great impact, and on the whole they work effectively to undergird the adolescent's present-tense story of finding her name and place.

There are symbols in each of Hamilton's books that could be discussed at length, but the importance of her work is more than symbolism or sounding the black experience. The importance of it lies in taking artistic integrity as far as it will go, beyond thought of popular reading, but with much thought to communicating. This is a tradition which is accepted in adult literature and which must be accepted in children's literature if it is to be considered a true art form. With plenty of books that fit easily, there must be that occasional book that grows the mind one size larger.

—Betsy Hearne

HARNETT, Cynthia (Mary). British. Born in London, 22 June 1893. Educated at private schools; Chelsea School of Arts, London; studied with the artist G. Vernon Stokes. Recipient: Library Association Carnegie Medal, 1952. Address: Little Thatch, Binfield Heath, Henley-on-Thames, Oxfordshire, England.

PUBLICATIONS FOR CHILDREN

Fiction

> *Velvet Masks,* illustrated by G. Vernon Stokes. London, Medici Society, 1937.
> *The Pennymakers,* with G. Vernon Stokes, illustrated by the authors. London, Eyre and Spottiswoode, 1937.
> *Junk, The Puppy,* with G. Vernon Stokes, illustrated by the authors. London, Blackie, 1937.
> *Banjo, The Puppy,* with G. Vernon Stokes, illustrated by the authors. London, Blackie, 1938.
> *To Be a Farmer's Boy,* with G. Vernon Stokes, illustrated by the authors. London, Blackie, 1940.
> *Mudlarks,* with G. Vernon Stokes, illustrated by the authors. London, Collins, 1940.
> *Mountaineers,* with G. Vernon Stokes, illustrated by the authors. London, Collins, 1941.
> *Ducks and Drakes,* with G. Vernon Stokes, illustrated by the authors. London, Collins, 1942.
> *Bob-Tail Pup,* with G. Vernon Stokes, illustrated by the authors. London, Collins, 1944.
> *Sand Hoppers,* with G. Vernon Stokes, illustrated by the authors. London, Collins, 1946.
> *Two and a Bit,* with G. Vernon Stokes, illustrated by the authors. London, Collins, 1948.
> *Follow My Leader,* with G. Vernon Stokes, illustrated by the authors. London, Collins, 1949.
> *The Great House,* illustrated by the author. London, Methuen, 1949; Cleveland, World, 1969.
> *Pets Limited,* with G. Vernon Stokes, illustrated by the authors. London, Collins, 1950.
> *The Wool-Pack,* illustrated by the author. London, Methuen, 1951; as *Nicholas and the Woolpack,* New York, Putnam, 1953.
> *Ring Out, Bow Bells!,* illustrated by the author. London, Methuen, 1953; as *The Drawbridge Gate,* New York, Putnam, 1954.
> *The Green Popinjay,* illustrated by the author. Oxford, Blackwell, 1955.
> *Stars of Fortune,* illustrated by the author. London, Methuen, and New York, Putnam, 1956.
> *The Load of Unicorn,* illustrated by the author. London, Methuen, 1959; as *Caxton's Challenge,* Cleveland, World, 1960.
> *A Fifteenth Century Wool Merchant,* illustrated by the author. London, Oxford University Press, 1962.
> *The Writing on the Hearth,* illustrated by Gareth Floyd. London, Methuen, 1971; New York, Viking Press, 1973.

Other

> *David's New World: The Making of a Sportsman,* with G. Vernon Stokes, illustrated by the authors. London, Country Life, 1937.
> *Getting to Know Dogs,* illustrated by G. Vernon Stokes. London, Collins, 1947.

Monasteries and Monks, illustrated by Edward Osmond.   London, Batsford, 1963.

Editor, *In Praise of Dogs: An Anthology in Prose and Verse*, illustrated by G. Vernon Stokes.   London, Country Life, 1936.

*   *   *

After the publication of *The Writing on the Hearth* Cynthia Harnett announced that it was to be her last book. Since it took her ten years to complete the research necessary before she would begin writing, and she was in her eighties then, one can see why. This is an indication of the meticulous way in which she prepared her historical novels. Every detail must be accurate. It is important that the distance between Ewelme church and the manor house be correctly stated, for example, and one can check that it is. Many children use her story *The Wool-Pack* as a basis for projects, as enough of Burford village has remained recognisable from mediaeval days for them to pace out the hero's adventures on the actual ground.

Her books are not only enjoyable historical adventures but provide a vivid reconstruction of the period, and are often used by teachers as background material for lessons without spoiling the story. *Stars of Fortune* is the story of George Washington's English forebears. *Ring Out, Bow Bells* tells of the real Dick Whittington (of pantomime fame) who was thrice Lord Mayor of London. In researching this book, the author explored bomb-blasted London at the end of World War II, using Stow's 16th-century street plans, and was able to discover the mediaeval foundations of many of the houses she describes in the story, including Whittington's own, from the ruins of which a black cat appeared to share her sandwiches!

The Load of Unicorn is an exciting tale of the rivalry between early printers and the scriveners or handwriters, and incidentally the reader absorbs a good deal about Caxton and the printing trade. Yet nowhere does it seem like a lesson. Her books are story-books first and foremost, with a wealth of corroborative detail. Illustrated by her own little line drawings interpolated into the text, her books appeal mainly to children between 9 and 13.

—Ann G. Hay

HARRIS, Aurand.   American.   Born in Jamesport, Missouri, 4 July 1915. Educated at Jamesport public schools, 1920–32; University of Kansas City, 1932–36, A.B. 1936; Northwestern University, Evanston, Illinois, 1937–39, M.A. 1939; Columbia University, New York (John Golden Prize, 1945), 1945–47. Auditorium Teacher, Gary public schools, Indiana, 1939–41; Head of the Drama Department, William Woods College, Fulton, Missouri, 1942–45. Since 1946, Drama Teacher, Grace Church School, New York. Drama Teacher, Columbia University Teachers College, New York, Summers 1958–63; Playwright-in-Residence, University of Florida, Tallahassee, 1972, and University of Texas, Austin, 1975; Drama Teacher, Western Connecticut State College, Danbury, Summer 1976. Associated with summer theatre in Cape May, New Jersey, 1946, Bennington, Vermont, 1947, Peaks Island, Maine, 1948, and Harwich, Massachusetts, 1963–75. Recipient: American Theatre Association Chorpenning Cup, 1967; National Endowment for the Arts grant, 1976. Address: 41 West 8th Street, New York, New York 10011, U.S.A.

PUBLICATIONS FOR CHILDREN

Plays

Pinocchio and the Fire-Eater (produced Gary, Indiana, 1940).   New York, McGraw Hill, 1967.

Once upon a Clothesline (produced Fulton, Missouri, 1944).   Boston, Baker, 1945.

The Doughnut Hole.   New York, French, 1947.

The Moon Makes Three.   New York, French, 1947.

Seven League Boots (produced Cleveland, 1947).   Boston, Baker, 1948.

Circus Days (produced Seattle, 1948).   New York, French, 1949; revised version, as *Circus in the Wind*, 1960.

Pinocchio and the Indians (produced Seattle, 1949).   New York, French, 1949.

Simple Simon; or, Simon Big-Ears (produced Washington, D.C., 1952; Slough, Buckinghamshire, 1964).   Anchorage, Kentucky, Children's Theatre Press, 1953.

Buffalo Bill (produced Seattle, 1953).   Anchorage, Kentucky, Children's Theatre Press, 1954.

We Were Young That Year.   New York, French, 1954.

The Plain Princess, adaptation of the book by Phyllis McGinley (produced Kalamazoo, Michigan, 1954).   Anchorage, Kentucky, Children's Theatre Press, 1955.

The Flying Prince (produced Washington, D.C., 1965).   New York, French, 1958.

Junket (No Dogs Allowed), adaptation of the story by Anne H. White (produced Louisville, Kentucky, 1959).   Anchorage, Kentucky, Children's Theatre Press, 1959.

The Brave Little Tailor (produced Charleston, West Virginia, 1960; London, 1966).   Anchorage, Kentucky, Children's Theatre Press, 1961.

Pocahontas (produced Birmingham, Alabama, 1961).   Anchorage, Kentucky, Children's Theatre Press, 1961.

Androcles and the Lion (produced New York, 1964; Sheffield, 1968).   Anchorage, Kentucky, Children's Theatre Press, 1964.

Rags to Riches, adaptation of stories by Horatio Alger, music by Eva Franklin, lyrics by Aurand Harris and Eva Franklin (produced Harwich, Massachusetts, 1965; Teddington, Middlesex, 1970).   Anchorage, Kentucky, Anchorage Press, 1966.

A Doctor in Spite of Himself, adaptation of a play by Molière (produced New York, 1966).   Anchorage, Kentucky, Anchorage Press, 1968.

The Comical Tragedy or Tragical Comedy of Punch and Judy, music by Glenn Mack (produced Atlanta, 1969).   Anchorage, Kentucky, Anchorage Press, 1970.

Just So Stories, adaptation of the stories by Rudyard Kipling (produced Tallahassee, Florida, 1971).   Anchorage, Kentucky, Anchorage Press, 1971.

Ming Lee and the Magic Tree.   New York, French, 1971.

Steal Away Home, adaptation of work by Jane Kristof (produced Louisville, Kentucky, 1972).   Anchorage, Kentucky, Anchorage Press, 1972.

Peck's Bad Boy, adaptation of the novel by George Wilbur Peck (produced Harwich, Massachusetts, 1973).   Anchorage, Kentucky, Anchorage Press, 1974.

Robin Goodfellow (produced Harwich, Massachusetts, 1974).   Anchorage, Kentucky, Anchorage Press, 1977.

Yankee Doodle (produced Austin, Texas, 1975).   Anchorage, Kentucky, Anchorage Press, 1975.

Star Spangled Salute (produced Harwich, Massachusetts, 1975).   Anchorage, Kentucky, Anchorage Press, 1975.

Six Plays for Children (includes *Androcles and the Lion, Rags to Riches, Punch and Judy, Steal Away Home, Peck's Bad Boy, Yankee Doodle*), edited by Coleman A. Jennings.   Austin, University of Texas Press, 1977.

PUBLICATIONS FOR ADULTS

Plays

Ladies of the Mop.   Evanston, Illinois, Row Peterson, 1945.

Madam Ada.   New York, French, 1948.

And Never Been Kissed, adaptation of the novel by Sylvia Dee.   New York, French 1950.

Manuscript Collection: University of Texas Library, Austin.

Critical Study: *The Dramatic Contributions of Aurand Harris to Children's Theatre in the United States* by Coleman A. Jennings, unpublished dissertation, New York University, 1974 (includes bibliography).

Aurand Harris comments:

I write for children because they and I like the same thing in theatre – a good story, interesting characters, excitement, fantasy, beauty, and fun. My plays are usually based on history, legend, myth, or children's classics, and are conceived and executed in a variety of styles ranging from commedia dell'arte to melodrama to poetic fantasy. Best of all, there is an increasing and receptive audience that lets you know when it is enjoying itself.

*   *   *

Aurand Harris, author of over twenty published plays for children, is America's most-produced children's theatre playwright. His plays, constantly produced since the late 1940's, have enormously enriched the literature of American children's theatre.

During the ten-year period from 1946 to 1955, Harris experimented with a variety of plays. He had been writing not only for audiences of children, but for teen-agers and adults as well. Writing for children, however, provided Harris with opportunities which were unfettered by the naturalistic limitations usually expected by adult audiences. Because children are imaginative and willing to accept any theatrical form if it is honestly presented, he found great satisfaction in writing for them and since 1955 has written only for children and youth.

To write successful plays for children's theatre, an author must understand the youthful audience with the same thoroughness that he knows the techniques of playwriting. An audience comprised of children of various ages, representing many stages of maturity with widely differing interests and abilities to concentrate, presents an extra dimension of challenge to the playwright. Children are sensitive, perceptive, and quick to react overtly and honestly to whatever they see and hear. Aurand Harris's sensitivity to child audiences, his desire to create plays of high quality which adults perform for youth, and his thoroughly practical knowledge of all aspects of theatre have made him the respected professional playwright he is today.

Harris's children's plays are usually derived from fairy tales and legends, history and other published writing. Harris has written three original plots, but creating new stories has obviously been of secondary interest to him. Of even greater importance is the way he has learned to shape the content. As his craftmanship has steadily increased throughout his career, so has the range of maturity in the audience for whom he writes. In his later plays he has broadened his approach to include older youth, though he continues to command the attention of the younger audience members.

In writing each of his plays, Harris has re-created a dramatic form from the adult theatre with adjustments that make it suitable for a child audience. His selection of form, such as of *commedia dell'arte*, late-nineteenth-century melodrama, comedy with sober overtones, dramatic chronicle, light-hearted farce, or musical revue is determined by the presence of intrinsic qualities which appeal to children.

Because the six elements of dramatic form, theme, plot, character, dialogue, song, and spectacle, are so closely interdependent in the plays of Aurand Harris, the works exhibit a vital theatricality to which young audiences respond. Each of his plays, unified and satisfactorily resolved, has a unique quality of its own. The most outstanding example of this unified and unique playwriting is Harris's *Androcles and the Lion.*

—Coleman A. Jennings

HARRIS, Christie (Lucy Irwin). Canadian. Born in Newark, New Jersey, United States, 21 November 1907. Educated at Provincial Normal School, Vancouver, teacher's certificate 1925. Married Thomas Arthur Harris in 1932; has three sons and two daughters. Schoolteacher, British Columbia, 1925–32; free-lance scriptwriter, Canadian Broadcasting Corporation, 1936–62; Women's Editor of a newspaper, British Columbia, 1951–57. Recipient: Canadian Library Association Book of the Year Medal, 1967; Vicky Metcalf Award, 1973. Address: Suite 302, Park Lane Apartments, 975 Chilco Street, Vancouver, British Columbia V6G 2R5, Canada.

PUBLICATIONS FOR CHILDREN

Fiction

   Cariboo Trail. Toronto and New York, Longman, 1957.
   You Have to Draw the Line Somewhere, illustrated by Moira Johnston. Toronto,
      McClelland and Stewart, and New York, Atheneum, 1964.
   West with the White Chiefs, illustrated by Walter Ferro. Toronto, McClelland and
      Stewart, and New York, Atheneum, 1965.
   Raven's Cry, illustrated by Bill Reid. Toronto, McClelland and Stewart, and New
      York, Atheneum, 1966.
   Confessions of a Toe-Hanger, illustrated by Moira Johnston. Toronto, McClelland and
      Stewart, and New York, Atheneum, 1967.
   Forbidden Frontier, illustrated by E. Carey Kenney. Toronto, McClelland and Stewart,
      and New York, Atheneum, 1968.
   Let X Be Excitement. Toronto, McClelland and Stewart, and New York, Atheneum,
      1969.
   Secret in the Stlalakum Wild, illustrated by Douglas Tait. Toronto, McClelland and
      Stewart, and New York, Atheneum, 1972.
   Sky Man on the Totem Pole?, illustrated by Douglas Tait. Toronto, McClelland and
      Stewart, and New York, Atheneum, 1975

Other

   Once upon a Totem (Indian legends), illustrated by John Frazer Mills. Toronto,
      McClelland and Stewart, and New York, Atheneum, 1963.
   Figleafing Through History: The Dynamics of Dress, with and illustrated by Moira
      Johnston. Toronto, McClelland and Stewart, and New York, Atheneum, 1971.
   Mule Lib, with Tom Harris, illustrated by Franklin Arbuckle. Toronto, McClelland
      and Stewart, 1972.
   Once More upon a Totem (Indian legends), illustrated by Douglas Tait. Toronto,
      McClelland and Stewart, and New York, Atheneum, 1973.
   Mouse Woman and the Vanished Princessess (Indian legends), illustrated by Douglas
      Tait. Toronto, McClelland and Stewart, and New York, Atheneum, 1976.
   Mouse Woman and the Mischief Makers (Indian legends), illustrated by Douglas
      Tait. Toronto, McClelland and Stewart, and New York, Atheneum, 1977.

Manuscript Collection: University of Calgary Library, Alberta.

Christie Harris comments:
   My books have grown out of my own background. Three of my five children, after they
were grown up, gave me their own case histories, which I wrote as fiction. My interest in the
early Canadian West, combined with the fact that I lived on a homestead as a child, produced

three junior historical novels. And my very great interest in the remarkable culture of our Northwest Coast Indians has led me to rewrite their legends into four collections and to use other legends in a science fiction book. Indian lore has combined with new scientific findings about the sensitivity of plants to produce a fantasy.

This same interest led me to write *Raven's Cry*, a fictionalized history of our coast told from the Indian point of view. Although it won several awards as a *children's* book, *Raven's Cry* is used in universities as a study in culture contact.

My fashion-artist daughter's enthusiasm for the psychology of dress and the recent clothing revolution sparked our collaboration on *Figleafing Through History*. And my continuing family-orientation brought my husband in with his recollections of the First World War and the incredible mule he fought with.

Three of my five children are now busy writing on their own.

*   *   *

Christie Harris is one of the more prolific Canadian authors of books for children with over a dozen books to her credit. Her output covers a number of genres – historical fiction, fictionalized biography, and retellings of Indian legends. Her most successful writing is in the area of Northwest Pacific Indian mythology. Harris is adept at taking the rich and varied material available and developing it into stories which retain the original flavor of the legends and also bear the distinctly original character of her own writing. *Once upon a Totem* is a collection of five tales based on the adventures of Indian ancestors and tales of mythical tribal heroes which were represented on the exquisitely carved and painted totem poles produced by these people. Each of Harris's retellings is prefaced by a brief description of the nature of the legend and the history behind it, a useful device which places the legends in their proper historical perspective. Her language with its dignified rhythms accurately reflects the nature of a proud intelligent and highly creative people. *Mouse Woman and the Vanished Princesses* is easily Harris's most successful book to date. The character of Mouse Woman is expertly delineated in six tales of princesses who were lured away from their tribes by spirits or "narnauks." Embodying many of the characteristics of a mouse as well as a human person, Mouse Woman's task is to give advice to the princesses and assist them to return safely to their tribes. Mouse Woman is amusingly and affectionately described; we are told that her fondness for bits of wool to be ravelled into mouse nests is the one weakness of a "very, very proper little being." The six tales reflect the universality of human nature and, at the same time, give the reader a good idea of the peculiarities of Indian coastal life.

Historical fiction is a genre in which Harris seems less comfortable. *Cariboo Trail, Raven's Cry, Forbidden Frontier* and *West with the White Chiefs* deal with such events in British Columbia history as the Cariboo gold rush, the treatment of the Haida Indians by white fur traders, and a journey across the Rockies in 1863. In *Forbidden Frontier*, for example, the friendship that finally develops between the white girl, Megan, and the half-Indian girl, Alison, seems improbable in the light of Megan's betrayal of Alison's boyfriend. Although written with reasonable competence, generally Harris's historical fiction is not memorable.

Least successful are the fictionalized biographies of Harris's own children. *Confessions of a Toe-Hanger* follows the development of an enthusiastic girl in a large family through adolescence and early married life. Feeny zips through childhood wondering what to do with her life and finally discovers that all one has to do is "be oneself." Characterization is shallow – Feeny doesn't seem to go through an observable maturing process; rather, she seems to suddenly discover a basic truth on the last page of the book.

Secret in the Stlalakum Wild, a story set in the forests of British Columbia, is partly fantasy and partly an adventure story. The theme of conservation in nature is a bit overworked but does not detract from the fact that Harris has produced a very readable story based on Indian mythology and created an extremely likable heroine. It is evident that Harris's writing skills

577

are most highly developed in dealing with Northwest Coast Indian mythology. Perhaps the restrained and dignified rhythms and cadences of the language of the original stories impose a necessary restraint on her creativity while allowing her to bring a fresh approach to the material.

—Fran Ashdown

HARRIS, Mary K(athleen).   British.   Born in Harrow, Middlesex, 22 September 1905. Educated at Harrow County School for Girls, 1915–22. *Died in 1966.*

PUBLICATIONS FOR CHILDREN

Fiction

> *Gretel at St. Bride's.*   London, Nelson, 1941.
> *The Wolf,* illustrated by Kathleen Cooper.   London, Sheed and Ward, 1946; revised edition, New York, Sheed and Ward, 1955.
> *The Niche over the Door.*   London, Sheed and Ward, 1948.
> *Henrietta of St. Hilary's.*   London and New York, Staples Press, 1953.
> *Thomas,* illustrated by Cliff Roberts.   New York, Sheed and Ward, 1956.
> *A Safe Lodging,* illustrated by Don Bolognese.   New York, Sheed and Ward, 1957.
> *Emily and the Headmistress.*   London, Faber, 1958.
> *Seraphina,* illustrated by Sheila Rose.   London, Faber, 1960.
> *Penny's Way,* illustrated by Sheila Rose.   London, Faber, 1963.
> *The Bus Girls,* illustrated by Eileen Green.   London, Faber, and New York, Norton, 1965.
> *Jessica on Her Own,* illustrated by Alison Prince.   London, Faber, 1968.

Other

> *Elizabeth,* illustrated by R.M. Sax.   New York, Sheed and Ward, 1961.
> *Helena,* illustrated by Michael Hampshire.   New York, Sheed and Ward, 1964.

PUBLICATIONS FOR ADULTS

Novels

> *Fear at My Heart.*   London and New York, Sheed and Ward, 1951.
> *My Darling from the Lion's Mouth.*   London, Chatto and Windus, 1956; as *I Am Julie,*   New York, Crowell, 1956.
> *Lucia Wilmot.*   London, Chatto and Windus, 1959.

*   *   *

Mary K. Harris had no illusions about childhood. Looking back on her own schooldays (she went to her secondary school in 1915), she recalled that "I found myself amongst a group of children who were consistently horrid to each other," but she realized later "that these hateful school children were only hateful in a mass, that, in their own secret, solitary selves they were as aghast at each other as I was." There's no doubt that, like many less intelligent people, she remained all her life obsessed by her schooldays, but she turned her obsession to splendid account and gave us some of the best school stories we have. Her writing career began slowly and her early work was mainly for Guide magazines and for Sheed and Ward, the Catholic publishers – she was a convert.

Her Faber books, to their advantage, have no special axes to grind but it is interesting to note that her early Catholic story, *The Wolf*, shows her talent much more clearly than her conventional early school stories, *Gretel at St. Bride's* and *Henrietta of St. Hilary's*. Gretel, however, is not a stock heroine. The solitary quality of childhood is seen in her in extreme form. The year is 1941 and she is a refugee from Nazi Germany whereas "all the girls at St. Bride's ever worried about was Saturday sweets and getting into the hockey eleven."

Mary Harris's progression from the boarding schools of these early books and *Emily and the Headmistress*, via the grammar-school boarding hostel of *Seraphina* to the boarder-less grammar schools of *Penny's Way* and *The Bus Girls*, and eventually to the Secondary Modern of *Jessica on Her Own*, seems almost uncannily deliberate, as if Miss Harris with each book was simply attempting to get nearer and nearer to a wider number of potential readers. In fact, her social situations are a lot more complex than this would suggest. Jessica, the first of her heroines to go to a Secondary Modern, is the daughter of a Cambridge graduate mother, a very different type from the mothers in the two previous books. After her not completely successful attempt at the Ruffles (cousins, perhaps, of Eve Garnett's Ruggles) in *Emily and the Headmistress*, Miss Harris never seemed to put a foot wrong in her social nuances. But it is imaginative conviction that counts, of course, not social awareness. Miss Harris's books are never manufactured to support a thesis, but she certainly wrote with purpose. She aimed to make ordinary life interesting and meaningful. She felt it important to help children to understand themselves and each other, to make them realize, as she herself had not realized until much later, that other children are also vulnerable.

Emily and the Headmistress rather stands alone. The typical Harris heroine is 12 or 13; Emily is only 8. But it was in this book that the author first achieved her individuality. It was followed by *Seraphina*, her only novel told in the first person, a marvellously imagined story, rich in detail, strong in plot. Miss Harris had showed there could be a school story which did not suffer from conservatism, xenophobia, snobbery, the underrating of learning (the list is Orwell's).

Nothing Miss Harris wrote was solemn; everything was entertaining. In her books she explored with amused understanding the different pressures on adolescent girls as they come to terms with life, with the conflicting demands of home and school, and the difficulties and rewards of friendship. She had an ability to create not just one or two characters in each book but a whole form, even the feeling of a whole school, of individuals. In her last book, *Jessica on Her Own*, she moved out of the pure school story. School and home were equally important.

—Ann Thwaite

HARRIS, Rosemary (Jeanne). British. Born in London, 20 February 1923. Educated at Thorneloe School, Weymouth; St. Martin's, Central, and Chelsea schools of art, London; Department of Technology, Courtauld Institute, London. Served in the Red Cross Nursing Auxiliary, Westminster Division, London, 1941–45. Picture Restorer, 1949; Reader, Metro-Goldwyn-Mayer, 1951–52; Children's Book Reviewer, *The Times*, London, 1970–73. Recipient: Library Association Carnegie Medal, 1969; Arts Council grant 1971. Agent: Michael Horniman, A.P. Watt and Son, 26/28 Bedford Row, London WC1R 4HL. Address: 33 Cheyne Court, Flood Street, London SW3 5TR, England.

PUBLICATIONS FOR CHILDREN

Fiction

The Moon in the Cloud. London, Faber, 1968; New York, Macmillan, 1969.
The Shadow on the Sun. London, Faber, and New York, Macmillan, 1970.
The Seal-Singing. London, Faber, and New York, Macmillan, 1971.
The Child in the Bamboo Grove, illustrated by Errol Le Cain. London, Faber, 1971;
    New York, S.G. Phillips, 1972.
The Bright and Morning Star. London, Faber, and New York, Macmillan, 1972.
The King's White Elephant, illustrated by Errol Le Cain. London, Faber, 1973.
The Flying Ship, illustrated by Errol Le Cain. London, Faber, 1975.
The Little Dog of Fo, illustrated by Errol Le Cain. London, Faber, 1976.
I Want to Be a Fish. London, Penguin, 1977.

Play

Television Play: *Peronik*, 1976.

Other

The Lotus and the Grail: Legends from East to West, illustrated by Errol Le
    Cain. London, Faber, 1974; abridged edition, as *Sea Magic and Other Stories of
    Enchantment*, New York, Macmillan, 1974.

PUBLICATIONS FOR ADULTS

Novels

The Summer-House. London, Hamish Hamilton, 1956.
Voyage to Cythera. London, Bodley Head, 1958.
Venus with Sparrows. London, Faber, 1961.
All My Enemies. London, Faber, 1967; New York, Simon and Schuster, 1972.
The Nice Girl's Story. London, Faber, 1968; as *Nor Evil Dreams*, New York, Simon
    and Schuster, 1974.
A Wicked Pack of Cards. London, Faber, 1969; New York, Walker, 1970.
The Double Snare. London, Faber, 1974; New York, Simon and Schuster, 1975.
Three Candles for the Dark. London, Faber, 1976.

                              *   *   *

Rosemary Harris makes nonsense of any distinction between adult and children's fiction.
She writes only for her peers of any age.
    The Egyptian trilogy begins light-heartedly, though it never shirks human evil. *The Moon
in the Cloud* tells how Reuben, the musician and animal-tamer, sets out for Kemi to obtain a
pair of lions for Noah's ark and so to earn a passage for himself and his wife Thamar. He
suffers dangers and distress, becomes chief musician to the young Pharaoh, Merenkere, and
eventually achieves his mission in surprising ways, helped by his formidable cat, Cefalu. The
two succeeding books, though witty and engaging as ever, grow increasingly sombre in
theme. *The Shadow on the Sun* is the story of Merenkere's emerging greatness and of his love
for Meri-Mekhmet. It is Reuben who rescues her when she is abducted by the evil Prince of
Punt. *The Bright and Morning Star* probes the grief of Reuben and Thamar for their sick
autistic son and that of Merenkere for his weak and treacherous heir, but is yet a celebration
of human greatness and generosity. The pace never flags, but the excitement is generated as

much by language as by action. Its vivid images and rhythms, brilliant and sometimes sinister, echo the sunlight and darkness of the characters, the contrasts of the empty desert, hollow and vast beneath the stars or the relentless day, and the sophisticated yet barbaric beauty of Kemi, or the stifling horror of the voodoo-haunted jungles of Punt. The animals are as delightfully individual as the human characters, yet always retaining their own animal nature. Their comments are often the vehicle of the story's delicate and sharp-edged irony.

In *The Seal-Singing* the author moves into the contemporary world, but her Scottish island is tainted by ancient witchcraft. She shows a sympathetic understanding of adolescents in her study of the young cousins, with their loves and jealousies and uncertainties, and a fascinating knowledge of the seals themselves. Rock and wind and sea are unforgettably present. The story is tense and exciting though lightly handled. But Rosemary Harris can write for younger children as well, and her re-telling of Oriental legends, as in *The Child in the Bamboo Grove* and *The Little Dog of Fo*, is elegant, easy, and charming.

Whatever the age of her readers, one can always be certain of the imaginative distinction of Miss Harris's style and, above all, of her compelling sense of story.

—Margaret Greaves

HAUGAARD, Erik (Christian).   Danish.   Born in Copenhagen, 13 April 1923. Attended Black Mountain College, North Carolina, 1941–42; New School for Social Research, New York, 1945–47. Served in the Royal Canadian Air Force, 1942–45; King Christian X Medal (Denmark). Married Myrna Seld in 1949; has two children. Worked as farm laborer in Denmark, 1938–40, and shepherd in Wyoming. Recipient: New York *Herald Tribune* Festival award, 1967; *Boston Globe-Horn Book* award, 1967; Women's League for Peace and Freedom Jane Addams Award, 1968; Danish Cultural Minister's Award, 1970; Chapelbrook Foundation award, 1970. Address: Toad Hall, The Quay, Ballydehob, County Cork, Ireland.

PUBLICATIONS FOR CHILDREN

Fiction

>*Hakon of Rogen's Saga*, illustrated by Leo and Diane Dillon.   Boston, Houghton Mifflin, 1963; as *Hakon's Saga*, London, Faber, 1964.
>*A Slave's Tale*, illustrated by Leo and Diane Dillon.   Boston, Houghton Mifflin, 1965; London, Gollancz, 1966.
>*Orphans of the Wind*, illustrated by Milton Johnson.   Boston, Houghton Mifflin, 1966; London, Gollancz, 1967.
>*The Little Fishes*, illustrated by Milton Johnson.   Boston, Houghton Mifflin, 1967; London, Gollancz, 1968.
>*The Rider and His Horse*, illustrated by Leo and Diane Dillon.   Boston, Houghton Mifflin, 1968; London, Gollancz, 1969.
>*The Untold Tale*, illustrated by Leo and Diane Dillon.   Boston, Houghton Mifflin, 1971.
>*A Message for Parliament*.   Boston, Houghton Mifflin, 1976.

Other

>Translator, *The Complete Fairy Tales and Stories of Hans Andersen*.   New York, Doubleday, and London, Gollancz, 1974; shortened version, as *Classical Fairy Tales*, Gollancz, 1976.

581

PUBLICATIONS FOR ADULTS

Play   (

The Heroes (produced Antioch, Ohio, 1958).

Verse

25 Poems. Tappernöje, Denmark, Squire Press, 1957.

Other

Portrait of a Poet: Hans Christian Andersen and His Fairy Tales (lecture).   Washington,
D.C., Library of Congress, 1973.

Manuscript Collections: Kerlan Collection, University of Minnesota, Minneapolis; de
Grummond Collection, University of Southern Mississippi, Hattiesburg.

Erik Haugaard comments:
I conceive of my fellow men as individuals: lonely figures trying to understand the
dilemma they are born into. To live, to survive, is to me an heroic task but not necessarily a
tragic one; victory is possible, at least on an individual level. The possibility of love and
friendship exists; it is not a matter of chance but of choice. I cannot conceive of literature
without this faith; the choiceless man going to his doom is but a silent brute, and he would
not have left behind him the literature, art, and music of which we have a right to be justly
proud.

*   *   *

Erik Haugaard is an author with a deep commitment. Gleaming through this artist's sense
of time, place, and character is his belief in the human spirit and in the dignity of mankind.
He blends a wide variety of truths that underscore this belief.
In *Hakon of Rogen's Saga*, Hakon tells his own story of love and hate, freedom and
slavery, life and death. The novel rings forth in epic language that evokes a feeling of Viking
times. *A Slave's Tale* continues the saga as Hakon sets forth from Norway to return Rark, a
former slave, to his native Brittany. Helga, the slave girl of the first novel, is a stowaway. She
recounts the starkly tragic tale with deep emotion. There is a delicate balance between the fate
of the characters (even the minor ones) and the underlying message of the meaning of war.
Again, Haugaard interprets history and gives it deeper meaning in *Orphans of the Wind*, a
tale of the sea and of the American Civil War. This is Jim's story as he sets sail as deck boy
from Bristol to the United States. Here is a master storyteller who impressively interweaves
the denigrating effect of slavery and the grimness of war.
Guido, a 12-year-old orphan in Naples during World War II, is one of *The Little Fishes*
who escapes from the degradation imposed by the Germans. With two other children, he
makes his way to Cassino where he hopes to find freedom. A harrowing odyssey, the novel
carries with it a forceful testament against war. The power of the human spirit permeates the
book and radiates a passionate urge to survive. With equal forcefulness, Haugaard traces the
search for self in *The Rider and His Horse*. The source is the writing of Josephus. The time is
72–73 A.D. when a group of Jews, the Zealots, are making a last hopeless stand against the
Romans. 15-year-old David questions the meaning of everything around him, and is caught
up in the tragic episode. He emerges with an awareness of the moment of his experiences and
a sense of identity.
The Untold Tale is a story of the war between Denmark and Sweden in the 17th century.
This is Dag's story, and it is also a story of war with its tragic overtones. *A Message for*

Parliament presents another facet of war, the 17th-century English Civil War. Young Oliver's involvement in the brutal conflict is described with pace, but, again, there are the author's keen observation and apt interpretation of history.

Throughout these novels there is the steady beat of the senselessness of war and the evils of slavery. Haugaard captures language and speech patterns that admirably suit background and characters. Situations are often grim; events, almost unbearable. With poetic prose Haugaard speaks out in a clear and unmistakable voice about the futility of war, for freedom and understanding. He accomplishes this without moralizing, without weakening the power of the story.

Recognition must be given to Erik Haugaard for his fresh and artful translation of *The Complete Fairy Tales and Stories of Hans Andersen*. His faithfulness to Andersen's language and spirit is a remarkable feat.

—Mae Durham Roger

HAYES, John F(rancis). Canadian. Born in Dryden, Ontario, 5 August 1904. Educated at the University of Toronto evening classes, 1930–45. Married Helen Eileen Casselman in 1927; has two sons and one daughter. Writer, MacLean-Hunter Publishing Company, 1925–27, Consolidated Press, 1927–29, and Saturday Night Press, 1928, all in Toronto; Sales Promotion Writer, General Motors of Canada, Oshawa, Ontario, 1929–30; Head of the Creative Department, 1930–34, and Assistant Sales Manager, 1935, Brigdens Ltd., Toronto; Sales Promotion Manager, Moffats Ltd., Weston, Ontario, 1937–40; Executive Assistant, 1940–45, Sales Manager, 1945–47, Vice-President and General Manager, 1947–50, Vice-President and General Manager of the Montreal Branch, 1950–56, and Director and Member of the Executive Committee, Southam Press Ltd., Toronto; Managing Director, Southam Printing Company, Toronto, 1956–60. Director, Toronto Graphic Arts Association. Recipient: Governor-General's Award, 1952, 1954; Quebec Government Scientific and Literary Award, 1955; Canadian Library Association Book of the Year Medal, 1959; Vicky Metcalf Award, 1964. Address: 53 Bennington Heights Drive, Toronto 17, Ontario, Canada.

PUBLICATIONS FOR CHILDREN (illustrated by Fred J. Finley)

Fiction

Buckskin Colonist. Toronto, Copp Clark, 1947; Oxford, Blackwell, 1948.

Treason at York. Toronto, Copp Clark, 1949.

A Land Divided. Toronto, Copp Clark, 1951; Philadelphia, Westminster Press, 1954.

Rebels Ride at Night. Toronto, Copp Clark, 1953.

Bugles in the Hills. Toronto, Copp Clark, 1955; Oxford, Blackwell, and New York, Messner, 1956.

The Dangerous Cove: A Story of Early Days in Newfoundland. Toronto, Copp Clark, 1957; New York, Messner, 1960.

Quest in the Cariboo. Toronto, Copp Clark, 1960.

Flaming Prairie: A Story of the Northwest Rebellion of 1885. Vancouver, Copp Clark, 1965.

The Steel Ribbon. Toronto, Copp Clark, 1967.

The Nation Builders. Toronto, Copp Clark, 1968.

On Loyalist Trails: A Story about the United Empire Loyalists, illustrated by J. Merle Smith. Vancouver, Copp Clark, 1971.

Publications for Adults

Other

The Renovation Business.   Toronto, Crane, 1962.
Switzerland.   Toronto, Air Canada, 1962.
The Challenge of Change: 50 Years, 1912–1962.   Toronto, Downtown Church
    Workers Association, 1962.
Into a Nation.   Toronto, Canadian Council of Churches, 1966.
Wilderness Mission: The Story of Sainte-Marie among the Hurons.   Toronto, Ryerson
    Press, 1969.

                                    *   *   *

The historical novels of John F. Hayes provide a near panorama, in fiction, of pre-20th-century Canadian history. The earliest setting is Newfoundland in 1676; the latest, the Prairies in 1885. Hayes deals with most regions of Canada (the Maritimes, Ontario, the Prairies, British Columbia) omitting only the far north and, significantly, Quebec. And he tackles all major conflicts – again with one important exception involving Quebec: the Battle of the Plains of Abraham which resulted in the final fall of New France to the British. Why Hayes assiduously avoids Quebec subjects seems to be due to a reluctance to confront English-French antagonisms within Canada. Accordingly, another potentially divisive topic – the removal of the Acadians *(A Land Divided)* – is treated so as to defuse the historical situation of the long-lasting hostilities felt by the actual participants. Thus the expulsion is smoothed over with pro-British justifications; thus the cruelty of the eviction is minimized; and thus the Acadian co-hero, Pierre – though his family is expelled – even joins the English Navy. The reality was starker, and passions ran deeper, than Hayes allows. Accordingly, though the novel certainly contains moments of excitement and various authentic details of the period, it nevertheless violates the spirit of the time.

Hayes' other historical novels tackle the settlement of Newfoundland *(The Dangerous Cove)*, the Loyalist emigration to Canada *(On Loyalist Trails)*, the War of 1812 *(Treason at York)*, the Selkirk settlers *(Buckskin Colonist)*, the Mackenzie Rebellion *(Rebels Ride at Night)*, the British Columbia gold rush *(Quest in the Cariboo)*, the early days of the Mounties *(Bugles in the Hills)*, the building of the Canadian Pacific Railway *(The Steel Ribbon)*, and the Riel Rebellion *(Flaming Prairie)*. In these books he is generally true to the reality of the times he treats, and the historical facts, though accurate and reasonably detailed, are usually not intrusions into the story but rather enrichments of it. The historical events are quite exciting in themselves, and this contributes to the total excitement and interest that the novels create.

Hayes' fiction typically locates a teen-age male hero plus a close friend in an exciting historical time or place. Soon the boys, for reasons often connected with their fathers, find themselves at the focal point between good and evil groups and, acting, prevent calamities from happening – or at least attenuate them. The main hero generally has a close relationship with his father, and the father's praise of his son's manly achievements is frequent. In various books *(The Dangerous Cove, A Land Divided)* the hero is even allowed the wish-fulfilment situation of rescuing his father from dangerous enemies. Further, where the hero's father is dead *(Rebels Ride at Night)*, a substitute father soon steps forth to become the beneficiary of good deeds and the source of praise that boys desire. The father's (or substitute's) occupation is often important, incidentally, for the boy frequently follows in his footsteps. Action so satisfactory of boyhood dreams and male role expectations is one of the prominent elements in the books and one of the reasons that boys like them.

The defects in Hayes' fiction are sporadic, occurring to different degrees in different books, but fatal to none. These include the improbabilities of plot, repetitious action, weak concluding paragraphs, and dialogue which is acceptable but not inspired. His strength, besides historical authenticity, is the ability to create, notwithstanding defects, tales of excitement with which a boy can easily identify because they meet his psychological needs for adventure, manly behaviour, success, and parental praise.

—John Robert Sorfleet

HAYWOOD, Carolyn. American. Born in Philadelphia, Pennsylvania, 3 January 1898. Educated at High School for Girls and Normal School, both Philadelphia; Pennsylvania Academy of Fine Arts (Cresson Traveling Scholar), 1923–25. Taught at the Friends Central School, Philadelphia; assistant in the studio of Violet Oakley; portrait painter and mural artist. Recipient: Boys' Clubs of America award, 1956. Address: c/o William Morrow and Company Inc., 105 Madison Avenue, New York, New York 10016, U.S.A.

PUBLICATIONS FOR CHILDREN (illustrated by the author)

Fiction

> *When I Grow Up.* Racine, Wisconsin, Whitman, 1931.
> *"B" Is for Betsy.* New York, Harcourt Brace, 1939.
> *Two and Two Are Four.* New York, Harcourt Brace, 1940.
> *Betsy and Billy.* New York, Harcourt Brace, 1941.
> *Primrose Day.* New York, Harcourt Brace, 1942.
> *Back to School with Betsy.* New York, Harcourt Brace, 1943.
> *Here's a Penny.* New York, Harcourt Brace, 1944.
> *Betsy and the Boys.* New York, Harcourt Brace, 1945.
> *Penny and Peter.* New York, Harcourt Brace, 1946.
> *Little Eddie.* New York, Morrow, 1947.
> *Penny Goes to Camp.* New York, Morrow, 1948.
> *Eddie and the Fire Engine.* New York, Morrow, 1949.
> *Betsy's Little Star.* New York, Morrow, 1950.
> *Eddie and Gardenia.* New York, Morrow, 1951.
> *The Mixed-Up Twins.* New York, Morrow, 1952.
> *Eddie's Pay Dirt.* New York, Morrow, 1953.
> *Betsy and the Circus.* New York, Morrow, 1954.
> *Eddie and His Big Deals.* New York, Morrow, 1955.
> *Betsy's Busy Summer.* New York, Morrow, 1956.
> *Eddie Makes Music.* New York, Morrow, 1957.
> *Betsy's Winterhouse.* New York, Morrow, 1958.
> *Eddie and Louella.* New York, Morrow, 1959.
> *Annie Pat and Eddie.* New York, Morrow, 1960.
> *Snowbound with Betsy.* New York, Morrow, 1962.
> *Here Comes the Bus!* New York, Morrow, 1963.
> *Eddie's Green Thumb.* New York, Morrow, 1964.
> *Robert Rows the River.* New York, Morrow, 1965.
> *Eddie the Dog Holder.* New York, Morrow, 1966.
> *Betsy and Mr. Kilpatrick.* New York, Morrow, 1967.
> *Ever-Ready Eddie.* New York, Morrow, 1968.
> *Taffy and Melissa Molasses.* New York, Morrow, 1969.
> *Eddie's Happenings.* New York, Morrow, 1971.
> *A Christmas Fantasy,* illustrated by Glenys and Victor Ambrus. New York, Morrow, 1972; Leicester, Brockhampton Press, 1973.

Away Went the Balloons. New York, Morrow, 1973.
"C"Is for Cupcake. New York, Morrow, 1974.
Eddie's Valuable Property. New York, Morrow, 1975.
A Valentine Fantasy, illustrated by Glenys and Victor Ambrus. New York, Morrow, 1976.
Betsy's Play School, illustrated by James Griffin. New York, Morrow, 1977.

Manuscript Collection: Free Library, Philadelphia.

*   *   *

Carolyn Haywood is a prolific writer of very popular books that appeal to children in the 7 to 10 age group. Since her first junior novel appeared over 35 years ago, her recognition as one of the premier writers of mildly-exciting adventure stories involving the typical concerns of normal, middle-class children has steadily grown.

The reasons for Haywood's immense success are numerous. One of these surely must be the attractive plots of her stories, centered on the day-by-day experiences of ordinary yet extremely vigorous, active, and dominant children. Haywood creates imaginative yet wholesome situations for these children to live through, often with problems to solve. These problem conditions, of little actual consequence except for the great deal of activity they allow her characters to perform, are typical of those found in children's lives. These are predicaments which the child reader easily recognizes as ones that could actually happen to him. They are situations spun through narrative plots much like those found in the typical social novel, that is, a telling out of ever-widening social arrangements rather than the depiction of well-developed representations of personality. As well, they use an episodic, short-story form of organization. The chapters of Haywood's books are so lightly threaded, one to the other, that each of them can be read almost by itself.

The main characters of Haywood's tales are idealized, unsophisticated, even stereotyped children. They are flat or "mythical" people who enter and leave the episodes in her stories with much of the same set of qualities. These fictional children, who seldom if ever pause to question their responses to the forces set against them, are nonetheless highly endearing to young readers. Furthermore, Haywood makes sure these readers understand fully the motives of her fictionalized subjects by describing them in direct and steadfast fashion. By this means her readers are left with little or nothing to infer about their personalities or motivations. This may seem defective writing, but it is a style that young children have repeatedly shown they prefer over an indirect or subtle development of character in books. It obviously was soon apparent to Haywood that these characters were so believable to her readers that she could successfully write a series on some of them. Thus "Betsy" and "Eddie" have emerged as main attractions in several of Haywood's different stories.

—Patrick Groff

HEINLEIN, Robert (Anson). American. Born in Butler, Missouri, 7 July 1907. Educated at the United States Naval Academy, Annapolis, Maryland, graduated and commissioned Ensign, 1929; University of California, Los Angeles, 1934. Served in the United States Navy, 1929, until retirement because of physical disability, 1934. Married Virginia Gerstenfeld in 1948. Full-time Writer since 1939. Recipient: Hugo Award, 1956, 1960, 1962, 1966; Boys' Clubs of America Award, 1959; Science Fiction Writers of America Grand Master Nebula Award, 1974. Address: c/o Lurton Blassingame, 60 East 42nd Street, New York, New York 10017, U.S.A.

PUBLICATIONS FOR CHILDREN

Fiction

Rocket Ship Galileo, illustrated by Thomas Voter.   New York, Scribner, 1947; London, New English Library, 1971.

Space Cadet, illustrated by Clifford Geary.   New York, Scribner, 1948; London, Gollancz, 1966.

Red Planet, illustrated by Clifford Geary.   New York, Scribner, 1949; London, Gollancz, 1963.

Farmer in the Sky, illustrated by Clifford Geary.   New York, Scribner, 1950; London, Gollancz, 1962.

Between Planets, illustrated by Clifford Geary.   New York, Scribner, 1952; London, Gollancz, 1968.

The Rolling Stones, illustrated by Clifford Geary.   New York, Scribner, 1952; as *Space Family Stone*, London, New English Library, 1971.

Starman Jones, illustrated by Clifford Geary.   New York, Scribner, 1953; London, Sidgwick and Jackson, 1954.

The Star Beast, illustrated by Clifford Geary.   New York, Scribner, 1954; London, New English Library, 1971.

Tunnel in the Sky.   New York, Scribner, 1955; London, Gollancz, 1965.

Time for the Stars.   New York, Scribner, 1956; London, Gollancz, 1958.

Citizen of the Galaxy.   New York, Scribner, 1957; London, Gollancz, 1969.

Have Space Suit – Will Travel.   New York, Scribner, 1958; London, Gollancz, 1970.

Starship Troopers.   New York, Putnam, and London, Four Square, 1961.

Podkayne of Mars: Her Life and Times.   New York, Putman, 1963; London, New English Library, 1969.

PUBLICATIONS FOR ADULTS

Novels

Beyond This Horizon.   Reading, Pennsylvania, Fantasy Press, 1948.

Sixth Column.   New York, Gnome, 1949; as *The Day after Tomorrow*, London, New English Library, 1971; New York, New American Library, 1974.

Waldo and Magic, Inc.   New York, Doubleday, 1950; London, Gollancz, 1966.

The Puppet Masters.   New York, Doubleday, 1951; London, Museum Press, 1953.

Revolt in 2100.   Chicago, Shasta, 1953; London, Gollancz, 1964.

Double Star.   New York, Doubleday, 1956; London, Joseph, 1958.

The Door into Summer.   New York, Doubleday, 1957; London, Gollancz, 1967.

Methuselah's Children.   New York, Gnome, 1958; London, Gollancz, 1963.

Stranger in a Strange Land.   New York, Putnam, 1961; London, New English Library, 1965.

Glory Road.   New York, Putnam, 1963; London, Four Square, 1965.

Orphans of the Sky.   London, Gollancz, 1963; New York, Putnam, 1964.

Farnham's Freehold.   New York, Putnam, 1964; London, Dobson, 1965.

The Moon Is a Harsh Mistress.   New York, Putnam, 1966; London, Dobson, 1967.

A Robert Heinlein Omnibus.   London, Sidgwick and Jackson, 1966; as *Three by Heinlein*, New York, Doubleday, 1966.

A Heinlein Triad.   London, Gollancz, 1967.

I Will Fear No Evil.   New York, Putnam, 1971; London, New English Library, 1972.

Time Enough for Love: The Lives of Lazarus Long.   New York, Putnam, 1973; London, New English Library, 1974.

Short Stories

The Man Who Sold the Moon.   Chicago, Shasta, 1950; London, Sidgwick and Jackson, 1953.
The Green Hills of Earth.   Chicago, Shasta, 1951; London, Sidgwick and Jackson, 1954.
Assignment in Eternity.   Reading, Pennsylvania, Fantasy Press, 1953; London, Museum Press, 1955.
The Menace from Earth.   New York, Gnome, 1959; London, Dobson, 1966.
The Unpleasant Profession of Jonathan Hoag.   New York, Gnome, 1959; London, Dobson, 1964; as *6 × H: Six Stories*, New York, Pyramid, 1961.
The Worlds of Robert A. Heinlein.   New York, Ace, 1966; London, New English Library, 1970.
The Past Through Tomorrow: Future History Stories.   New York, Putnam, 1967.

Plays

Screenplays: *Destination Moon*, 1950; *Project Moonbase*, 1953.

Other

Of Worlds Beyond: The Science of Science Fiction Writing, with others.   Reading, Pennsylvania, Fantasy Press, 1947; London, Dobson, 1967.
The Science Fiction Novel, with others.   Chicago, Advent, 1959.
The Best of Robert Heinlein (1939–1959), edited by Angus Walls.   London, Sidgwick and Jackson, 1973.

Editor, *Tomorrow, The Stars: A Science Fiction Anthology.*   New York, Doubleday, 1952.

Manuscript Collection: University of California Library, Santa Cruz.

*   *   *

Robert Heinlein's pioneering role in the development of juvenile science fiction has helped make him an acknowledged master of modern science fiction. Before 1947, children's science fiction was little more than Tom Swift adventures and comics featuring Buck Rogers and Flash Gordon. In 1947 Heinlein published *Rocket Ship Galileo*, clearly identifiable both as science fiction and as junior novel. Accepted favorably by readers and reviewers alike, the novel marked the first time mainstream children's literature recognized science fiction. Publication of subsequent science fiction, some by Heinlein himself and the rest by authors encouraged by his example, gained respectability for the genre as a valid subcategory of children's literature.

Rocket Ship Galileo is the story of several boys who fly to the moon in a home-made atomic-powered rocket. There they discover the ruins of an extant lunar civilization and destroy the base of some Nazis secretly planning World War III. Replete with exciting incident and gadgetry, *Rocket Ship Galileo* is also a novel in which teen-agers, like many of the novel's putative readers, worry about their vocational goals, suffer parental misunderstandings, and seek to achieve a competence that instills pride. Another positive quality of the novel is its style: terse and colloquial, fast moving, and nicely balanced between scientific terminology and everyday speech.

The best of Heinlein's other juveniles follow this pattern: a skillful blending of science fiction topics and young adult subjects. *Red Planet* narrates Jim Marlowe's adventures at school and with Willie, a ball-like animal that is actually a young Martian. Not as fast-paced as its predecessor, the novel still interests because it describes a society and Martian biology Heinlein employs in the famous *Stranger in a Strange Land. Farmer in the Sky* weaves together futuristic agricultural techniques on Ganymede and Bill Lermer's indecision whether to return to earth for additional schooling or to remain as a pioneer. Subplots concerning Bill's relationship with his parents and organizing boy scouting are also intended to appeal to youth. *Citizen of the Galaxy*, taking place in a future with conditions similar to the Roman Empire, explores various modes of structuring society and investigates several opposing economic theories. Anticipating Engdahl's characteristic emphasis, Heinlein, here, is more interested in explaining ideas than in narrating incidents.

Perhaps the most provocative of Heinlein's juveniles is *Tunnel in the Sky*. Rod Walker and his classmates participate in a test of survival techniques on an unknown planet. Unexpectedly lost and stranded, fifteen teen-agers band together. At the point where a genuine community has developed and children have even been born, the group is found and brought back to earth. Regardless of the maturity shown, most are required to revert to teen-ager roles. Especially illuminating is the novel's look at an adult society which recognizes only chronological age and sorts out and treats youth accordingly.

Although not all of Heinlein's juvenile science fiction comes up to the level of *Rocket Ship Galileo* and *Tunnel in the Sky*, his place in children's literature seems assured both on historical and literary grounds.

—Francis J. Molson

HENRY, Marguerite. American. Born in Milwaukee, Wisconsin. Married to Sidney Crocker Henry. Recipient: American Library Association Newbery Medal, 1949; Boys' Clubs of America award, 1949; Children's Reading Round Table award, 1961; Western Heritage Award, 1967; University of Minnesota Kerlan Award, 1975. Address: Rancho Santa Fe, California 92067, U.S.A.

PUBLICATIONS FOR CHILDREN

Fiction

> *Auno and Tauno: A Story of Finland*, illustrated by Gladys Blackwood. Chicago, Whitman, 1940.
> *Dilly Dally Sally*, illustrated by Gladys Blackwood. Akron, Ohio, Saalfield, 1940.
> *Geraldine Belinda*, illustrated by Gladys Blackwood. New York, Platt, 1942.
> *Their First Igloo on Baffin Island*, with Barbara True, illustrated by Gladys Blackwood. Chicago, Whitman, 1943; London, Gifford, 1945.
> *A Boy and a Dog*, illustrated by Diana Thorne and Ottilie Foy. Chicago, Wilcox and Follett, 1944.
> *The Little Fellow*, illustrated by Diana Thorne. Philadelphia, Winston, 1945; revised edition, Chicago, Rand McNally, 1975.
> *Misty of Chincoteague*, illustrated by Wesley Dennis. Chicago, Rand McNally, 1947; London, Collins, 1961.
> *Always Reddy*, illustrated by Wesley Dennis. New York and London, McGraw Hill, 1947.
> *King of the Wind*, illustrated by Wesley Dennis. Chicago, Rand McNally, 1948; London, Constable, 1957.
> *Little-or-Nothing from Nottingham*, illustrated by Wesley Dennis. New York, McGraw Hill, 1949.

Sea Star: Orphan of Chincoteague, illustrated by Wesley Dennis. Chicago, Rand McNally, 1949; London, Collins, 1968.

Born to Trot, illustrated by Wesley Dennis. Chicago, Rand McNally, 1950.

Brighty of the Grand Canyon, illustrated by Wesley Dennis. Chicago, Rand McNally, 1953; London, Collins, 1970.

Cinnabar, The One O'Clock Fox, illustrated by Wesley Dennis. Chicago, Rand McNally, 1956.

Misty, The Wonder Horse, illustrated by Clare McKinley. Chicago, Rand McNally, 1956.

Black Gold, illustrated by Wesley Dennis. Chicago, Rand McNally, 1957.

Muley-Ears, Nobody's Dog, illustrated by Wesley Dennis. Chicago, Rand McNally, 1959.

Gaudenzia, Pride of the Palio, illustrated by Lynd Ward. Chicago, Rand McNally, 1960; London, Collins, 1971.

Five O'Clock Charlie, illustrated by Wesley Dennis. Chicago, Rand McNally, 1962; London, Collins, 1963.

Stormy, Misty's Foal, illustrated by Wesley Dennis. Chicago, Rand McNally, 1963; London, Collins, 1965.

White Stallion of Lipizza, illustrated by Wesley Dennis. Chicago, Rand McNally, 1964; London, Blackie, 1976.

Mustang, Wild Spirit of the West, illustrated by Robert Lougheed. Chicago, Rand McNally, 1966; London, Collins, 1968.

San Domingo, The Medicine Hat Stallion, illustrated by Robert Lougheed. Chicago, Rand McNally, 1972; London, Collins, 1975.

Stories from Around the World. Chicago, Rand McNally, 1974.

Other

Alaska [Argentina, Brazil, Canada, Chile, Mexico, Panama, West Indies, Australia, The Bahamas, Bermuda, British Honduras, Dominican Republic, Hawaii, New Zealand, and *Virgin Islands] in Story and Pictures*, illustrated by Kurt Wiese. Chicago, Whitman, 16 vols., 1941, 1946.

Birds at Home, illustrated by Jacob Abbott. Chicago, Donohue, 1942; revised edition, Northbrook, Illinois, Hubbard Press, 1972.

Justin Morgan Had a Horse, illustrated by Wesley Dennis. Chicago, Wilcox and Follett, 1945; revised edition, Chicago, Rand McNally, 1954.

Robert Fulton, Boy Craftsman, illustrated by Lawrence Dresser. Indianapolis, Bobbs Merrill, 1945.

Benjamin West and His Cat Grimalkin, illustrated by Wesley Dennis. Indianapolis, Bobbs Merrill, 1947.

Album of Horses, illustrated by Wesley Dennis. Chicago, Rand McNally, 1951; shortened version, as *Portfolio of Horses*, 1952; as *Portfolio of Horse Paintings*, 1964.

Wagging Tails: An Album of Dogs, illustrated by Wesley Dennis. Chicago, Rand McNally, 1955; as *Album of Dogs*, 1970.

All about Horses, illustrated by Wesley Dennis. New York, Random House, 1962; London, W. H. Allen, 1963; revised edition, Chicago, Rand McNally, 1967.

Dear Readers and Riders. Chicago, Rand McNally, 1969.

Birds at Home, illustrated by Jacob Abbott. Northbrook, Illinois, Hubbard Press, 1972.

A Pictorial Life Story of Misty. Chicago, Rand McNally, 1976.

*   *   *

Mention horse stories to any young reader of the genre and the name Marguerite Henry is sure to enter the conversation. These readers are usually so passionate in their love for horses that they place little demands upon the literary quality of a book so long as it is about their favorite animal. Yet even among these readers, the works of Marguerite Henry are recognized as above and apart from the usual fare of animal adventure stories.

The quality that separates her from most writers of animal stories is her historical perspective. Her works are best appreciated if they are thought of and judged as historical romance, whether it be a fictional biography like *Benjamin West and His Cat Grimalkin*, or a fictional exploration of the events which historically trace the emergence of a particular breed of horses, as in *Justin Morgan Had a Horse* or *King of the Wind*.

It is partly because children do not come to her books thinking of them as historical works that they are so especially appealing. Teachers, and far too many writers, often ignore the needs of children, forgetting that if they are to be attracted to the study of history their interests must be aroused and their sympathies enlisted; and also forgetting that children want action, drama, adventure and heroes. All of these can be found by children in the historical animal romances of Marguerite Henry.

The use of the word "romance" here should not be interpreted as meaning trite and improbable, but rather to identify the romantic tradition for young readers sired so brilliantly by R. L. Stevenson. Although Will James' *Smoky* was based on the first hand experience of a cowboy while Mrs. Henry's stories are the result of painstaking research, both writers are in the same tradition. As writers of horse stories they demonstrate, first of all, a thorough knowledge of the breed depicted. The animals are objectively reported, and yet they are portrayed in such a way that their "character" is known and felt by humans, both within and outside the stories. The human characters, too, since most of them are actual people, are neither one-dimensional nor stereotyped.

However, it is the magical appeal of history – the merging of fact with imagination with legend – that gives the Henry books their trademark. Her stories are either implicitly or explicitly marked with prologues and epilogues, so that the web of history, the connection of things distant in time, place, person and circumstance, reaches the consciousness of the young reader. The distant past touches the more recent past of the story time, which in turn touches the present and reaches out to the future of the reader's time.

The last paragraph of the epilogue in *Brighty* is a characteristic ending of a Henry book: "Especially on moonlit nights a shaggy little form can be seen flirting along the ledges, a thin swirl of dust rising behind him. Some say it is nothing but moonbeams caught up in a cloud. But the older guides swear it is trail dust out of the past, kicked up by Brighty himself, the roving spirit of the Grand Canyon – forever wild, forever free."

—James E. Higgins

HENTOFF, Nat(han Irving). American. Born in Boston, Massachusetts, 10 June 1925. Educated at Northeastern University, Boston, B.A. 1945; Harvard University, Cambridge, Massachusetts, 1946; the Sorbonne, Paris (Fulbright Fellow), 1950. Married Miriam Sargent in 1950 (divorced, 1950); Trudi Bernstein, 1954 (divorced, 1959), two daughters; Margot Goodman, 1959, two sons. Writer, producer, announcer, WMEX Radio Station, Boston, 1944–53; Editor, *Down Beat* magazine, New York, 1953–57; Co-Founding Editor, *Jazz Review*, 1959–60. Since 1960, Staff Writer, *The New Yorker*. Columnist, *Village Voice*, New York. Faculty Member, New School for Social Research, New York. Recipient: New York *Herald Tribune* Festival award, 1965. Address: 25 Fifth Avenue, New York, New York 10003, U.S.A.

PUBLICATIONS FOR CHILDREN

Fiction

> *Jazz Country.* New York, Harper, 1965.
> *I'm Really Dragged But Nothing Gets Me Down.* New York, Simon and Schuster,
> 1968.
> *In the Country of Ourselves.* New York, Simon and Schuster, 1968.
> *This School Is Driving Me Crazy.* New York, Delacorte Press, 1976; London, Angus
> and Robertson, 1977.

Other

> *Journey into Jazz,* illustrated by David Stone Martin. New York, Coward McCann,
> 1968.

PUBLICATIONS FOR ADULTS

Novels

> *Call the Keeper.* New York, Viking Press, 1966; London, Secker and Warburg, 1967.
> *Onwards!* New York, Simon and Schuster, 1968.

Other

> *Jazz Street,* photographs by Dennis Stouk. London, Deutsch, 1960.
> *The Jazz Life.* New York, Dial Press, 1961; London, Davies, 1962.
> *Peace Agitator: The Story of A.J. Muste.* New York, Macmillan, 1963.
> *The New Equality.* New York, Viking Press, 1964.
> *Our Children Are Dying.* New York, Viking Press, 1966.
> *A Doctor among the Addicts.* Chicago, Rand McNally, 1968.
> *A Political Life: The Education of John V. Lindsay.* New York, Knopf, 1969.
> *State Secrets: Police Surveillance in America,* with others. New York, Holt Rinehart,
> 1974.
> *Jazz Is.* New York, Random House-Ridge Press, 1976.
> *Does Anybody Give a Damn?* (on education). New York, Knopf, 1977.

> Editor, with Nat Shapiro, *Hear Me Talkin' to Ya: The Story of Jazz by the Men Who
> Made It.* New York, Rinehart, and London, Davies, 1955.
> Editor, with Nat Shapiro, *The Jazz Makers.* New York, Rinehart, 1957; London,
> Davies, 1958.
> Editor, with Albert J. McCarthy, *Jazz: New Perspectives on the History of Jazz.* New
> York, Rinehart, 1959; London, Cassell, 1960.
> Editor, *The Essays of A. J. Muste.* Indianapolis, Bobbs Merrill, 1967.

*   *   *

American teen-age stories have traditionally been concerned with school functions, soda-fountain dating, keeping worn-out jalopies running, persuading parents to consent to this or that unlikely scheme, very much in the spirit of Booth Tarkington's *Seventeen* (1916). Fictional youngsters' social consciousness was bounded by the social and sport pages of the local newspaper if indeed it extended so far. But all that has changed: the young hero of *Seventeen* couldn't hack it nowadays: he'd come up against Nat Hentoff's people, and he'd be way out of his league.

Hentoff's youngsters of the 1970's are a troubled lot. They are faced with adult-sized problems not of their making; and decisions they make now, in their inexperienced adolescence, will, as they well know, affect them permanently. Tell such youngsters that they are enjoying "the happiest days of their lives," and their response will likely be a sardonic one.

Tom Curtis of *Jazz Country* cares for little in life but his trumpet. Jazz is his whole world – but his white skin shuts him out from the fellowship that means everything to him. The story of Tom's painful struggle for acceptance and excellence comes to no facile conclusion. He is still striving at the story's end, but whether he will earn his passport to Jazz Country he has yet to discover.

In *I'm Really Dragged But Nothing Gets Me Down*, Jeremy Wolf, a high-school senior, is faced with a tougher hand to play. Will he or will he not register for the draft on graduation? War still drags on in Viet Nam. Failure to comply with the law may ruin his future and destroy his parents' hopes, and he desperately fears a possible jail sentence: but Jeremy's conscience insists that to register is to recognize the government's right to order him to kill. Outside influences, the opposed arguments of friends and family, however painful in their effect, are as nothing to the conflict within. Jeremy's eventual unsatisfactory answer is no solution to his moral dilemma, and its pain remains with him. Perhaps life will anaesthetize this torment of conscience, but looking around him at the Establishment, he rather hopes it will not.

The entire school population of *In the Country of Ourselves* is faced with a threatened student revolution in an urban high school. The issues are not entirely clear even to determined revolutionaries; drug scares, two-way racism, and tough police tactics further exacerbated by a false friend to the student activists among the teaching staff, add to the complexity of the situation. One is left with the impression that to be either student or instructor in American high schools of today should be recognized as a cruel and unusual punishment.

These are the young Americans as Nat Hentoff sees them, and his hard, sharp, "insider" style is exactly suited to theirs. In spite of all that life throws at them, these bright, tough, strong-willed kids keep their cool and their mordant sense of humour. Their ways don't always jibe with those of the older generation – but why should they? They're a lot older than *Seventeen*, and they play for keeps.

—Joan McGrath

HEWETT, Anita. British. Born in Wellington, Somerset, 23 May 1918. Educated at the University of Exeter, 1936–39, Teaching Diploma, National Froebel Foundation, 1939. Served in the Women's Royal Air Force, 1940–45. Married Richard Duke in 1966. Primary school teacher, 1945–52; Principal, Shirley Hall School, Kingston Hill, Surrey, 1952–61; Producer, Schools Broadcasting Department, BBC, London, 1962–70. Address: 29 Esher Road, East Molesey, Surrey, England.

PUBLICATIONS FOR CHILDREN

Fiction

> *Elephant Big and Elephant Little, and Other Stories*, illustrated by Charlotte Hough. London, Lane, 1955; New York, A. S. Barnes, 1960.
> *The Little Yellow Jungle Frogs and Other Stories*, illustrated by Charlotte Hough. London, Lane, 1956; New York, A. S. Barnes, 1960.
> *Honey Mouse and Other Stories*, illustrated by Margery Gill. London, Lane, 1957.

Think, Mr. Platypus, illustrated by Anne Marie Jauss.   New York, Sterling, 1958.

Koala Bear's Walkabout, illustrated by Anne Marie Jauss.   New York, Sterling, 1959.

The Laughing Bird, illustrated by Anne Marie Jauss.   New York, Sterling, 1959.

A Hat for Rhinoceros and Other Stories, illustrated by Margery Gill.   London, Bodley Head, 1959; New York, A. S. Barnes, 1960.

Piccolo, illustrated by Dick Hart.   London, Bodley Head, 1960; New York, A. S. Barnes, 1961.

The Tale of the Turnip, illustrated by Margery Gill.   London, Bodley Head, and New York, McGraw Hill, 1961.

The Little White Hen, illustrated by William Stobbs.   London, Bodley Head, 1962; New York, McGraw Hill, 1963.

Piccolo and Maria, illustrated by Dick Hart.   London, Bodley Head, 1962.

The Elworthy Children, illustrated by Margery Gill.   London, Bodley Head, 1963.

Dragon from the North, illustrated by Gioia Fiammenghi.   New York, McGraw Hill, 1965.

The Pebble Nest, illustrated by Jennie Corbett.   London, University of London Press, 1965.

The Bull Beneath the Walnut Tree and Other Stories, illustrated by Geraldine Spence.   London, Bodley Head, 1966; New York, McGraw Hill, 1967.

Mrs. Mopple's Washing Line, illustrated by Robert Broomfield.   London, Bodley Head, and New York, McGraw Hill, 1966.

Fire Engine Speedy, illustrated by Edward McLachlan.   London, University of London Press, 1966.

Mr. Faksimily and the Tiger, illustrated by Robert Broomfield.   London, Bodley Head, 1967; Chicago, Follett, 1969.

Animal Story Book, illustrated by Margery Gill and Charlotte Hough.   London, Bodley Head, 1972.

Other

The Seven Proud Sisters and Other Stories (reader), illustrated by M. Jarman.   London, Ginn, 1952.

The Crocodile That Couldn't Swim (reader), illustrated by C. Instrell.   Leeds, E. J. Arnold, 1953.

Slink the Shadow (reader).   Leeds, E. J. Arnold, 1953.

*   *   *

Anita Hewett's background as a teacher is evident in her work. She writes for the children she enjoyed teaching — the little ones, the eights and under. At one stage in her career she worked as a Schools Radio producer. Most of her stories are suitably short, to be read or told at one sitting. They almost always point a moral, unobtrusively and often humorously, but the educational content is there. They make ideal standbys for the classroom bookshelf.

The majority are animal fables in the Just-So tradition but lighter and tighter in texture. In the omnibus *Animal Story Book*, the stories are grouped geographically in four sections covering Africa, Australia, South America, and South-East Asia. They are informative as well as entertaining about wild life. Most of them use the well-tried techniques of repetition and cumulative construction and, at times, these technical devices are in danger of becoming mechanical. But the style is always elegant and the pay-offs refreshingly unpredictable. In "The Leopard That Lost a Spot," for instance, Monkey teases Leopard by painting out one of his spots. When the rain washes it back, to the bewildered creature's relief, Monkey laughs and laughs till he falls out of his tree. "He did not fall on the soft leaves. Nor did he fall in the long grass. He fell where he deserved to fall — in the pot of yellow paint."

Anita Hewett's picture books benefit from the contribution of distinguished artists. But the texts deserve the pictures. *Mr. Faksimily and the Tiger* is particularly successful — a charming, original tale about an intrepid photographer who goes into the jungle to snap Terrible Tiger. All he has for protection is his umbrella – but he uses it to good effect. Again, the end comes as a surprise and gives the story an unusual, satisfying twist.

Her two novels about Piccolo, an Italian urchin, and his donkey are different in kind. These are realistic stories – the first effortless, the second somewhat contrived. But both give an English child real insight into an unfamiliar lifestyle and, again, there is educational value in the way Piccolo matures through his experiences. *The Elworthy Children*, another realistic story, also stands out from the main body of her work. With affectionate humour, Anita Hewett describes the small adventures of a typical midddle-class family. Five-year-old Polly and her older sister are the main characters and there is no doubt by the end of the book that the author understands the workings of a small child's mind.

—Joy Whitby

HIGHTOWER, Florence. American. Born in Boston, Massachusetts, 9 June 1916. Educated at Vassar College, Poughkeepsie, New York, A.B. 1937. Married James R. Hightower in 1940; has four children. Address: 321 Central Street, Auburndale, Massachusetts 02166, U.S.A.

PUBLICATIONS FOR CHILDREN

Fiction

> *Mrs. Wappinger's Secret*, illustrated by Beth and Joe Krush. Boston, Houghton Mifflin, 1956; London, Lane, 1957.
> *The Ghost of Follonsbee's Folly*, illustrated by Ati Forberg. Boston, Houghton Mifflin, 1958.
> *Dark Horse of Woodfield*, illustrated by Joshua Tolford. Boston, Houghton Mifflin, 1962; London, Macdonald, 1964.
> *Fayerweather Forecast*, illustrated by Joshua Tolford. Boston, Houghton Mifflin, 1967; London, Macdonald, 1968.
> *The Secret of the Crazy Quilt*, illustrated by Beth and Joe Krush. Boston, Houghton Mifflin, 1972.

Manuscript Collection: University of Wisconsin Library, Madison.

Florence Hightower comments:
   I write novels in which I hope intelligent, reading children will find the same sustaining pleasure which intelligent, reading adults find in novels written for them. My novels deal with children in their relations with each other, their families, and their communities. My characters, like those in adult novels, are beset by problems and conflicts. Sometimes they can and do cope. Sometimes they can't or won't. Although I rely on a mechanical plot to bring my characters together in dramatic situations, I consider the unfolding of the plot of secondary importance to the unfolding of characters in their various relationships. The effectiveness of a novel, however, depends not on the intention of the author, but on the way he uses words. A story, well told, seems to grow and blossom as naturally and beautifully as a plant. A clumsily told story, though its intentions be of the best, never comes to life. It has

been suggested to me by school teachers that I write stories using only words that are on lists which children of various ages are required in school to recognize. If I did this, my stories would be born dead. In writing each sentence, I use the best words I can think of and deploy them as skilfully as I know how. I always wish that my vocabulary were larger and my skill greater. Educators and other propagandists often expect writers for children to connive with them by sneaking doses of instruction, guidance, or uplift into their books. For a novelist, especially a children's novelist, to do this strikes me as stupid and degrading. He destroys the artistic integrity of his own work, lessens its impact, and perverts his true purpose in writing – which is to reveal insights into the human condition in such a stirring, appealing, and moving way that he fires the imagination of his reader and inspires him to sharpen his own insights, challenges him to increase his knowledge, and persuades him to enlarge his sympathies by reading more novels, that he may grow up into a cultivated, discerning, novel-reading adult.

*   *   *

Perhaps it is because much of her writing reflects the activities of her own children and of the Maine island where they spent their vacations that Florence Hightower's stories have such lively and believable characters and such convincing settings. In her first book, *Mrs. Wappinger's Secret*, the action centers on an eccentric old woman who enlists the help of a young neighbor to help her find some treasure she believes is buried on her property, but the appeal lies not only in the plot but also in the insight into the likeable if often exasperating characters, especially in the depiction of Charlie's summer-weary father.

All of the Hightower books abound in humor, and in *Dark Horse of Woodfield* the author incorporates this through her distinctive characters yet manages to give a convincing picture of the Depression Era. In this story, as in others, there is a smooth blending of elements, of main plot and minor plots. The old, once-splendid house, Woodfield, is the setting for a warm family story, a horse story, and a love story, all nicely merged, and told with credible suspense. In *The Ghost of Follonsbee's Folly*, another vigorous family story, much of the appeal lies in the compatible union of odd and everyday events. Again, in *Fayerweather Forecast*, the ebullient Fayerweather clan tolerates affectionately each member's idiosyncracies. And even uses them to advantage, as in the episode in which mother is working for a new school and employs the talents of her histrionic young daughter, who obligingly quavers a pitiful tale about how dreadfully antiquated the old school is. And yet, with all the buoyant humor, the story explores a mysterious murder. In *The Secret of the Crazy Quilt*, Hightower tells a fast-paced, intricate story of rum-runners of the Prohibition Era, but the wit and humor of her style balance the grimness of the events, which are told in retrospect by two of the characters; here she again proves adroit in weaving plot threads into a seamless whole.

—Zena Sutherland

HILDICK, E(dmund) W(allace). British. Born in Bradford, Yorkshire, 29 December 1925. Educated at Wheelwright Grammar School, Dewsbury, Yorkshire, 1937–41; City of Leeds Training College, 1948–50, Teachers Certificate. Served in the Royal Air Force, 1946–48. Married Doris Clayton in 1950. Junior Assistant, Dewsbury Public Library, 1941–42; clerk, truck repair depot, Leeds, 1942–43; Laboratory Assistant, Admiralty Signals

Establishment, Haslemere and Sowerby Bridge, 1943–46; Teacher, Dewsbury Secondary Modern School, 1950–54. Since 1954, self-employed writer. Visiting Critic and Associate Editor, *Kenyon Review*, Kenyon College, Gambier, Ohio, 1966–67. Recipient: Tom-Gallon Trust Award, 1957; Hans Christian Andersen Diploma of Honour, 1968. Agent: Mrs. J. S. Luithlen, 36 Highgate Drive, Knighton, Leicester. Address: c/o Coutts and Company Ltd., 59 The Strand, London W.C.2, England.

PUBLICATIONS FOR CHILDREN

Fiction

Jim Starling, illustrated by Roger Payne. London, Chatto and Windus, 1958.

Jim Starling and the Agency, illustrated by Roger Payne. London, Chatto and Windus, 1958.

Jim Starling and the Colonel, illustrated by Roger Payne. London, Heinemann, 1960; New York, Doubleday, 1968.

Jim Starling's Holiday, illustrated by Roger Payne. London, Heinemann, 1960.

The Boy at the Window, illustrated by Ionicus. London, Chatto and Windus, 1960.

Jim Starling Takes Over, illustrated by Roger Payne. London, Blond, 1963; revised edition, London, New English Library, 1971.

Jim Starling and the Spotted Dog, illustrated by Roger Payne. London, Blond, 1963.

Jim Starling Goes to Town, illustrated by Roger Payne. London, Blond, 1963.

Meet Lemon Kelly, illustrated by Margery Gill. London, Cape, 1963; as *Lemon Kelly*, New York, Doubleday, 1968.

Birdy Jones. London, Faber, 1963; Harrisburg, Pennsylvania, Stackpole, 1969.

Mapper Mundy's Treasure Hunt, illustrated by John Cooper. London, Blond, 1963.

Lemon Kelly Digs Deep, illustrated by Margery Gill. London, Cape, 1964.

Louie's Lot. London, Faber, 1965; New York, David White, 1968.

The Questers, illustrated by Richard Rose. Leicester, Brockhampton Press, 1966; New York, Hawthorn Books, 1970.

Calling Questers Four, illustrated by Richard Rose. Leicester, Brockhampton Press, 1967.

The Questers and the Whispering Spy, illustrated by Richard Rose. Leicester, Brockhampton Press, 1967.

Lucky Les: The Adventures of a Cat of Five Tales, illustrated by Peter Barrett. London, Blond, 1967.

Lemon Kelly and the Home-Made Boy, illustrated by Iris Schweitzer. London, Dobson, 1968.

Louie's S.O.S., illustrated by Iris Schweitzer. London, Pan, 1968; New York, Doubleday, 1970.

Birdy and the Group, illustrated by Richard Rose. London, Pan, 1968; Harrisburg, Pennsylvania, Stackpole, 1969.

Here Comes Parren, illustrated by Michael Heath. London, Macmillan, 1968; New York, World, 1972.

Back with Parren, illustrated by Michael Heath. London, Macmillan, 1968.

Birdy Swings North, illustrated by Richard Rose. London, Pan, 1969; Harrisburg, Pennsylvania, Stackpole, 1971.

Manhattan Is Missing, illustrated by Jan Palmer. New York, Doubleday, 1969; London, Tom Stacey, 1972.

Top Boy at Twisters Creek, illustrated by Oscar Liebmann. New York, David White, 1969.

Monte Carlo or Bust! London, Sphere, 1969; as *Those Daring Young Men in Their Jaunty Jalopies*, New York, Berkley, 1969.

Birdy in Amsterdam, illustrated by Richard Rose. London, Pan, 1970; Harrisburg, Pennsylvania, Stackpole, 1971.

Ten Thousand Golden Cockerels, illustrated by Richard Rose. London, Evans, 1970.

The Dragon That Lived under Manhattan, illustrated by Harold Berson. New York, Crown, 1970.

The Secret Winners, illustrated by Gustave Nebel. New York, Crown, 1970.

The Secret Spenders, illustrated by Gustave Nebel. New York, Crown, 1971.

The Prisoners of Gridling Gap: A Report, With Expert Comments from Doctor Ranulf Quitch, illustrated by Paul Sagsoorian. New York, Doubleday, 1971; London, Tom Stacey, 1973.

My Kid Sister, illustrated by Iris Schweitzer. New York, World, 1971; Leicester, Brockhampton Press, 1973.

The Doughnut Dropout, illustrated by Kiyo Komoda. New York, Doubleday, 1972.

Kids Commune, illustrated by Oscar Liebman. New York, David White, 1972.

The Active-Enzyme Lemon-Freshened Junior High School Witch, illustrated by Iris Schweitzer. New York, Doubleday, 1973.

The Nose Knows, illustrated by Unada Gliewe. New York, Grosset and Dunlap, 1973; London, Hodder and Stoughton, 1974.

Birdy Jones and the New York Heads. New York, Doubleday, 1974.

Dolls in Danger, illustrated by Val Biro. London, Hodder and Stoughton, 1974; as *Deadline for McGurk*, New York, Macmillan, 1975.

Louie's Snowstorm, illustrated by Iris Schweitzer. New York, Doubleday, 1974; London, Deutsch, 1975.

The Menaced Midget, illustrated by Val Biro. London, Hodder and Stoughton, 1975.

The Case of the Condemned Cat, illustrated by Val Biro. London, Hodder and Stoughton, and New York, Macmillan, 1975.

Time Explorers Inc., illustrated by Nancy Ohanian. New York, Doubleday, 1976.

A Cat Called Amnesia, illustrated by Val Biro. New York, David White, 1976; London, Deutsch, 1977.

The Case of the Nervous Newsboy, illustrated by Val Biro. London, Hodder and Stoughton, and New York, Macmillan, 1976.

The Great Rabbit Robbery, illustrated by Val Biro. London, Hodder and Stoughton, 1976; as *The Great Rabbit Rip-Off*, New York, Macmillan, 1977.

The Top-Flight Fully-Automated Junior High School Girl Detective, illustrated by Iris Schweitzer. New York, Doubleday, 1977.

The Case of the Invisible Dog, illustrated by Val Biro. London, Hodder and Stoughton, and New York, Macmillan, 1977.

Other

A Close Look at Newspapers [*Magazines and Comics, Television and Sound Broadcasting, Advertising*]. London, Faber, 4 vols., 1966–69.

Cokerheaton (storypack), illustrated by Roger Payne. London, Evans, 1971.

Rushbrook (storypack). London, Evans, 1971.

Storypack Teachers Book. London, Evans, 1971.

PUBLICATIONS FOR ADULTS (as Wallace Hildick)

Novels

Bed and Work. London, Faber, 1962.

A Town on the Never. London, Faber, 1963.

Lunch with Ashurbanipal. London, Faber, 1965.

Bracknell's Law. New York, Harper, 1975; London, Hamish Hamilton, 1976.

The Weirdown Experiment. New York, Harper, and London, Hamish Hamilton, 1976.

Vandals. London, Hamish Hamilton, 1977.
The Loop. London, Hamish Hamilton, 1977.

Other

Word for Word: A Study of Authors' Alterations, with Exercises. London, Faber, 1965;
abridged edition, as *Word for Word: The Rewriting of Fiction*, New York, Norton,
1966.
Writing with Care: 200 Problems in the Use of English. London, Weidenfeld and
Nicolson, and New York, David White, 1967.
Thirteen Types of Narrative. London, Macmillan, 1968; New York, Clarkson N.
Potter, 1970.
*Children and Fiction: A Critical Study in Depth of the Artistic and Psychological Factors
Involved in Writing Fiction for and about Children.* London, Evans, 1970; New
York, World, 1971; revised edition, Evans, 1974.
Only The Best: Six Qualities of Excellence. New York, Clarkson N. Potter, 1973.

E. W. Hildick comments:

In my fiction for children I have always been compelled to give an accurate reflection of
the contemporary background as I know it. That is why the first half-dozen or so books are
set in the industrial working-class North of England, where I was brought up and worked
and taught until the mid-fifties. Then comes a batch (*Meet Lemon Kelly*, the Questers books,
and others) influenced by 7 years spent in the New Town of Stevenage, near London. After
that come the stories with American settings (New York City, as in *Manhattan Is Missing*,
Ohio, and the Long Island and Connecticut suburbs where we've been living for long 5–6–7
month periods every year since the mid-sixties). Such a strong emphasis on the
contemporary always courts the danger of ephemerality – and to avoid this there must be
some kind of preservative: some acid or salt. Fortunately, my adolescent bent as the Clown of
the Class – so much the despair of my teachers at the time – seems to have stood me in good
stead as a writer, with the humour, the slapstick, the occasional wit acting so effectively as a
preservative that most of my early books are still in print. About my adult fiction in relation
to the children's books, I've been interested to note, when compiling the list, that there are
often overlapping themes and settings. Thus *Meet Lemon Kelly* was written around the same
time as *A Town on the Never* (both New Town books); *Lemon Kelly Digs Deep* (a children's
archeological quest) links with *Lunch with Ashurbanipal* (British Museum background);
while *Bracknell's Law* and *Vandals* give rather sombre accounts of the vicissitudes of British
families living in the U.S., in contrast to the lighter shades of my Anglo-U.S. children's
books.

                                        *   *   *

E. W. Hildick has firm views about children and fiction and his considerable output is
aimed at putting his theory into practice. In order to broaden the social background of
children's books he concentrates on working-class, or class-less, characters and his
pioneering has paved the way for others. His intentions sometimes dominate the story but
generally he has created lively, humorous plots, a style which is deceptively fluent, although
deliberately constructed for less able readers, and characterisation which is sound, if not
always deep. The books about Jim Starling and The Questers demonstrate a new approach to
the school story in which school is shown as an integral part of the boys' lives, not a separate
way of life as in many pre-war stories. The Cement Street Secondary Modern and its teachers
will be familiar to many readers, and the boys he writes about are recognisably those he
hopes will read the books. In *The Questers* he avoids the sentimentality inherent in the theme
by the pace and ingenuity of the plots in which the boys attempt to involve their bed-ridden
friend in their activities. Aimed similarly at nine-to-twelve-year-olds, the series about Lemon

Kelly is action-packed with a minimum of narrative and shows the imagination and humour which are typical of his work. The exuberance of Hildick's writing is especially noticeable in the stories about Louie, a highly professional milkman with a trained band of schoolboy helpers who overcome every hazard including rival milk companies, snowstorms and muggers to see that the milk gets through. The farcical situations are anchored in reality by the down-to-earth Louie, and the short, staccato sentences, particularly in *Louie's Lot*, stimulate an awareness of words, their meanings and shape. Two further groups of stories are those about Birdy Jones and McGurk, for slightly older and younger readers respectively. Keen observation of the contemporary world helps to make Birdy and his manager credible, but the concept is far-fetched and more obviously contrived to appeal to the non-reading teenager. The McGurk books are an attempt to construct a conventional detective mystery in a simple style around a trivial incident such as whether the cat was guilty of catching and eating the bird.

When an author writes with a specific purpose, it would be surprising if all his books reached the highest creative literary standards. However, E. W. Hildick has a skill with words, a gift for construction and dialogue, and a knowledge of boys which enable him to write exciting stories simply but not patronisingly. Even when he is openly didactic, as in *Mapper Mundy's Treasure Hunt*, where the successful outcome depends on the boys' skill in reading an Ordnance Survey map, he succeeds in entertaining as well as teaching. It would be churlish not to be grateful for his many books which offer action, humour, some believable characters, and lively dialogue, and which are dedicated to the idea that reading is fun.

—Valerie Brinkley-Willsher

HINTON, S.E.   American.   Born in 1950. Recipient: *Media and Methods* Award, 1975; American Library Association Newcott Caldeberry Award, 1976. Address: c/o Delacorte Press, 1 Dag Hammarskjold Plaza, New York, New York 10017, U.S.A.

PUBLICATIONS FOR CHILDREN

Fiction

The Outsiders.   New York, Viking Press, 1967.
That Was Then, This Is Now.   New York, Viking Press, and London, Gollancz, 1971.
Rumble Fish.   New York, Delacorte Press, 1975; London, Gollancz, 1976.

*   *   *

The novels of S.E. Hinton expose the poverty of many stories tailored for "reluctant readers." At their worst, such books are based on the fallacy that kids with problems want to read about Kids with Problems: Trouble down Gas Street, or Stabbings on the East Side, wherever your potential market is enduring its crises. Characterisation is often two-dimensional and even condescending. If they are to know their subjects with sympathy, adult authors need both the capacity and the opportunity to listen to urban teenagers; neither is easily acquired.

Miss Hinton was seventeen when she wrote her enormously popular *The Outsiders*, and it may well be her youthful perspective which gave an unusual immediacy to language, character and setting. Her plots are indeed concerned with violence in harsh districts of American cities, but they are distinguished from the formula stories by the mercurial, vulnerable yet often courageous qualities of the protagonists. They frequently display an adolescent capacity for self-dramatisation which is particularly evident in exaggerated imitations of older boys. Ponyboy Curtis, the central character of *The Outsiders* (who reappears in a minor role in *That Was Then, This Is Now*) is convincing to young readers because, beneath the toughness necessary for survival, his needs are as various, his generosities as warm, his irrationalities as extreme, as those of a teenager from any social background. Much of the appeal of the two novels lies in the narrators' struggles to resolve the tension, common to Miss Hinton's audience, between public image and private feeling.

Miss Hinton's plots are controlled with economy. The maelstrom of abrasive encounters may stretch credulity, but it was a platitude of the late sixties that in some American cities the events of the streets beggared fiction. In *The Outsiders*, gang rituals and class warfare, an accidental killing, a flight, lead to a poignant but just resolution. *That Was Then, This Is Now* explores the relationship between Bryon and his closest friend, his unofficially adopted brother, Mark. Events and impulses which neither can contain drive them against their wills into a hostility which culminates in Bryon turning Mark in to the police.

In *Rumble Fish*, Miss Hinton shifts her viewpoint from that of the thoughtful if confused narrators who are, she has implied, reflections of herself as a teenager. Rusty-James regrets the passing of the gang conflicts in which his idolised older brother, The Motorcycle Boy, excelled. He cannot understand the present disenchantment of his brother, for whom no relationship, no experience, offers meaning. The Motorcycle Boy's loss of innocence and hope is total, and a virtually suicidal death is inevitable. Rusty-James is left alone, without orientation. In *Rumble Fish*, some of the author's limitations begin to be confirmed: there is a suggestion of repetition in the plot, for example, and physical descriptions tend to lean upon mechanical references to hair and eyes. Yet this is also the most ambitious of Miss Hinton's novels, for her subject, Rusty-James, little understood by others or by himself, unable to make a pattern of the events and characters around him, represents an element of urban life which is at once pathetic and menacing.

—Geoff Fox

HOBAN, Russell (Conwell). American. Born in Lansdale, Pennsylvania, 4 February 1925. Attended Philadelphia Museum School of Industrial Art, 1941–43. Served in the United States Army Infantry, 1943–45; Bronze Star. Married Lillian Aberman in 1944; has four children. Magazine and advertising agency artist and illustrator; story board artist, Fletcher Smith Film Studio, New York, 1951; television art director, Batten Barton Durstine and Osborn, 1951–56, and J. Walter Thompson, 1956, both in New York; advertising copywriter, Doyle Dane Bernbach, New York. Recipient: Christopher Award, 1972; Whitbread Award, 1974. Address: c/o Jonathan Cape Ltd., 30 Bedford Square, London WC1B 3EL, England.

PUBLICATIONS FOR CHILDREN

Fiction

> *Bedtime for Frances*, illustrated by Garth Williams. New York, Harper, 1960; London, Faber, 1963.
> *Herman the Loser*, illustrated by Lillian Hoban. New York, Harper, 1961; Kingswood, Surrey, World's Work, 1972.
> *The Song in My Drum*, illustrated by Lillian Hoban. New York, Harper, 1962.
> *London Men and English Men*, illustrated by Lillian Hoban. New York, Harper, 1962.
> *Some Snow Said Hello*, illustrated by Lillian Hoban. New York, Harper, 1963.

The Sorely Trying Day, illustrated by Lillian Hoban. New York, Harper, 1964;
Kingswood, Surrey, World's Work, 1965.

A Baby Sister for Frances, illustrated by Lillian Hoban. New York, Harper, 1964;
London, Faber, 1965.

Bread and Jam for Frances, illustrated by Lillian Hoban. New York, Harper, 1964;
London, Faber, 1966.

Nothing to Do, illustrated by Lillian Hoban. New York, Harper, 1964.

Tom and the Two Handles, illustrated by Lillian Hoban. New York, Harper, 1965;
Kingswood, Surrey, World's Work, 1969.

The Story of Hester Mouse Who Became a Writer, illustrated by Lillian Hoban. New
York, Norton, 1965; Kingswood, Surrey, World's Work, 1969.

What Happened When Jack and Daisy Tried to Fool the Tooth Fairies. New York,
Scholastic, 1966.

Henry and the Monstrous Din, illustrated by Lillian Hoban. New York, Harper, 1966;
Kingswood, Surrey, World's Work, 1967.

The Little Brute Family, illustrated by Lillian Hoban. New York, Macmillan, 1966.

Save My Place, illustrated by Lillian Hoban. New York, Norton, 1967.

Charlie the Tramp, illustrated by Lillian Hoban. New York, Scholastic, 1967.

The Mouse and His Child, illustrated by Lillian Hoban. New York, Harper, 1967;
London, Faber, 1969.

A Birthday for Frances, illustrated by Lillian Hoban. New York, Harper, 1968;
London, Faber, 1970.

The Stone Doll of Sister Brute, illustrated by Lillian Hoban. New York, Macmillan,
and London, Collier Macmillan, 1968.

Harvey's Hideout, illustrated by Lillian Hoban. New York, Parents' Magazine Press,
1969; London, Cape, 1973.

Best Friends for Frances, illustrated by Lillian Hoban. New York, Harper, 1969;
London, Faber, 1971.

The Mole Family's Christmas. New York, Parents' Magazine Press, 1969; London,
Cape, 1973.

Ugly Bird, illustrated by Lillian Hoban. New York, Macmillan, 1969.

A Bargain for Frances, illustrated by Lillian Hoban. New York, Harper, 1970;
Kingswood, Surrey, World's Work, 1971.

Emmet Otter's Jug-Band Christmas, illustrated by Lillian Hoban. New York, Parents'
Magazine Press, and Kingswood, Surrey, World's Work, 1971.

The Sea-Thing Child, illustrated by Brom Hoban. New York, Harper, and London,
Gollancz, 1972.

Letitia Rabbit's String Song, illustrated by Mary Chalmers. New York, Coward
McCann, 1973.

How Tom Beat Captain Najork and His Hired Sportsman, illustrated by Quentin
Blake. New York, Atheneum, and London, Cape, 1974.

Crocodile and Pierrot, with Sylvie Selig, illustrated by Selig. London, Cape, 1975;
New York, Scribner, 1977.

A Near Thing for Captain Najork, illustrated by Quentin Blake. London, Cape, 1975;
New York, Atheneum, 1976.

Verse

Goodnight, illustrated by Lillian Hoban. New York, Norton, 1966; Kingswood,
Surrey, World's Work, 1969.

The Pedaling Man and Other Poems, illustrated by Lillian Hoban. New York, Norton,
1968; Kingswood, Surrey, World's Work, 1969.

Egg Thoughts and Other Frances Songs, illustrated by Lillian Hoban. New York,
Harper, 1972; London, Faber, 1973.

Other

> *What Does It Do and How Does It Work? Power Shovel, Dump Truck, and Other Heavy Machines.* New York, Harper, 1959.
> *The Atomic Submarine: A Practice Combat Patrol under the Sea.* New York, Harper, 1960.
> *Dinner at Alberta's,* illustrated by Lillian Hoban. New York, Crowell, 1973; London Cape, 1977.
> *Ten What? A Mystery Counting Book,* illustrated by Sylvie Selig. London, Cape, 1974; New York, Scribner, 1975.

PUBLICATIONS FOR ADULTS

Novels

> *The Lion of Boaz-Jachin and Jachin-Boaz.* New York, Stein and Day, and London, Cape, 1973.
> *Kleinzeit.* London, Cape, 1974.
> *Turtle Diary.* London, Cape, 1975; New York, Random House, 1976.

*   *   *

The virtues of Russell Hoban's Picture Books surely owe something to his early years as a television art director, copywriter and free-lance illustrator. There are an elegance and wit about them, combined with the fairly unerring selection of apt illustrations (often by Lillian Hoban) which, one suspects, are the product of a talent and industry normally summed up by the word professionalism. And though these books, because of their repetitive sentence-structures and simplified vocabularies, are sometimes included in Reading Schemes, it is important to realise that many of them are more than that implies.

The best known is probably the series about Frances the Badger, who, with her father and mother, baby sister and best friend Thelma, goes through the kinds of experiences that children between the ages of 4 and 7 enjoy reading about. The books are anthropomorphic, with the badgers wearing clothes, and talking and behaving like humans generally. But what is so captivating about them is the combination of witty observations and shrewd common sense. When Frances begins to feel that her mother is busier than usual because of the new baby, she decides to run away:

> "Well," said Frances, "things are not very good here any more. No clothes to wear. No raisins for the oatmeal. I think maybe I'll run away."
> "Finish your breakfast," said Mother. "It is about time for the school bus."
> "What time will dinner be tonight?" said Frances.
> "Half past six," said Mother.
> "Then I shall have plenty of time to run away after dinner," said Frances, and she kissed her mother goodbye and went to school.

The pattern of these stories is re-assuringly familiar and almost cosy at times, with the liberal middle-class badger parents exercising just the right degree of permissive control in dealing with Frances's problems, which are usually resolved happily. But occasionally the parents' patience wears thin, and Frances has to learn that some things have to be accepted for the way they are.

The combination of wit and elegance with something rather more formidable is also presented a shade less delicately in some of the other Picture Books, such as *The Stone Doll of Sister Brute,* for example. In the story of *How Tom Beat Captain Najork and His Hired Sportsman* (illustrated by Quentin Blake) Tom has a hilarious time outwitting his aunt Miss Fidget Wonkham-Strong and her efforts to subdue him. The very qualities of fooling around, which his aunt tries so hard to crush, prove just the thing to defeat Captain Najork at the games of Womble, Muck and Sneedball, and so a deeply serious defence of natural joy is seen to underpin this whole delightful fantasy.

Similar use of fantasy, though of an increasingly sombre kind, dominates the longer stories which have begun to appear since *The Mouse and His Child* in the mid-1960's. Increasingly recognised as a modern children's classic, or a modern classic which uses the form of children's fiction, this picaresque story describes the adventures of a clockwork-toy mouse and his son after they have been rescued from a dustbin by a passing tramp. Their wanderings through a modern urban civilisation bring them close to disaster and failure many times. They meet a variety of toys and animals, including a prophetic Frog, an aristocratic toy Elephant and a philosophical Muskrat; they constantly need rewinding, and founder for a time in a muddy lake. Above all, they are pursued by Manny Rat, a ruthless and ingenious predator, who can be viciously cruel, for example, to a broken down toy-donkey:

> "You're not well," said Manny Rat. "I can see that easily. What you need is a long rest." He picked up a heavy rock, lifted it high, and brought it down on the donkey's back, splitting him open like a walnut. "Put his works in the spare-parts can," said Manny Rat to Ralphie.

Increasingly, as this powerful, comic and disturbing narrative develops, however, we become aware that the pilgrimage of the Mouse and his Child is centred upon three very human needs, the desire for a territory or home of their own, like the one they knew in the toyshop, their desire to become self-winding and independent, and finally their desire to know what is beyond "The Last Visible Dog" they see mentioned everywhere, and which comes to represent Infinity. Again the ending is deceptively ambiguous, for though the Mouse and His Child do find the apparent security of a renovated Dolls' House and are surrounded by their friends, they also learn that there is nothing "beyond the Last Visible Dog but us," and that no one is ever completely self-winding – "That's what friends are for." Even more ominously for some readers, however, is the fact that Manny Rat himself remains at large, if apparently reformed.

The violence and witty allusiveness found in *The Mouse and His Child*, including a theatre which parodies Beckett's work, for example, is not something which all children find palatable, and one suspects that, though its reputation will continue to grow, it will appeal to children of at least 12 and upwards. *The Sea-Thing Child* may be found even more oblique by young readers, for it has none of the narrative energy of *The Mouse and His Child*, dealing, as it does, with an animal washed up on the sea-shore and his conversations mainly with a fiddler-crab and an albatross. Even so, its themes, the need for absolute honesty with oneself and being true to one's own nature, in this case trying to make a bow for a violin if you are a fiddler-crab and going back to sea if you are a sea-bird, are absolutely central to Hoban's work. There is nothing "beyond the Last Visible Dog but us."

Equally the adult novels, *The Lion of Boaz-Jachin and Jachin-Boaz*, *Kleinzeit* and *Turtle Diary* will probably prove too demanding for all but the most alert adolescent readers, though there are elements of wit and fantasy in them which many will enjoy. But even on the evidence of his achievements so far Russell Hoban stands out as one of the most original and talented of children's writers with at least one outstanding book to his credit.

—Dennis Butts

HODGES, C(yril) Walter.   British.   Born in Beckenham, Kent, 18 March 1909. Educated at Dulwich College, London, 1922–25; Goldsmiths' College School of Art, London, 1925–28. Served in the British Army, 1940–46. Married Greta Becker in 1936; has two sons. Since 1931, stage and exhibition designer, mural painter, and free-lance book, magazine and advertisement illustrator. Designer of productions, Mermaid Theatre and St. George's Theatre, London. Art Director, Encyclopaedia Britannica Films, Chicago, 1959–61. Has designed exhibitions for Lloyds and the U.K. Provident Institution, and murals for the Chartered Insurance Institute, 1934, and the U.K. Provident Institution, 1957. Recipient: Library Association Kate Greenaway Medal, for illustration, 1965. Agent: Laura Cecil, Exeter Mansions, 106 Shaftesbury Avenue, London W.1. Address: 36 Southover High Street, Lewes, Sussex, England.

PUBLICATIONS FOR CHILDREN (illustrated by the author)

Fiction

Columbus Sails.   London, Bell, and New York, Coward McCann, 1939.
The Flying House: A Story of High Adventure.   London, Benn, 1947; as *Sky High: The Story of a House That Flew*, New York, Coward McCann, 1947.
The Namesake.   London, Bell, and New York, Coward McCann, 1964.
The Marsh King.   London, Bell, and New York, Coward McCann, 1967.
The Overland Launch.   London, Bell, 1969; New York, Coward McCann, 1970.
Playhouse Tales.   London, Bell, and New York, Coward McCann, 1974.

Other

Shakespeare and the Players.   London, Bell, and New York, Coward McCann, 1948.
Shakespeare's Theatre.   London, Oxford University Press, and New York, Coward McCann, 1964.
The Norman Conquest.   London, Oxford University Press, and New York, Coward McCann, 1966.
Magna Carta.   London, Oxford University Press, and New York, Coward McCann, 1966.
The Spanish Armada.   London, Oxford University Press, 1967; New York, Coward McCann, 1968.
The English Civil War.   London, Oxford University Press, 1972; as *The Puritan Revolution*, New York, Coward McCann, 1972.
The Emperor's Elephant.   London, Oxford University Press, 1975.

PUBLICATIONS FOR ADULTS

Other

The Globe Restored: A Study of the Elizabethan Theatre.   London, Benn, 1953; revised edition, London, Oxford University Press, and New York, Coward McCann, 1968.
The Globe Playhouse 1599–1613: A Conjectural Drawing.   London, Benn, and New York, Coward McCann, 1959.
Shakespeare's Second Globe: The Missing Monument.   London, Oxford University Press, 1973.

Illustrator: *King Richard's Land*, 1933, and *Mr. Sheridan's Umbrella*, 1935, by L.A.G. Strong; *Treasures of English Verse* edited by Herbert Strang, 1934; *The Happy Mariners* by Gerald W. Bullett, 1935; *Plays in Verse and Mime* by Rosalind Vallance, 1935; *Know Ye Not Agincourt* by Leslie Barringer, 1936; *The Squirrel's Granary* by William Beach Thomas, 1936; *My Garden by the Sea* by Robert A. Foster-Melliar, 1936; *The Schoolboy King* by Mark Dallow, 1937; *Trixie (Stories of the Circus)* by Bob Barton and G. Ernest Thomas, 1937; *New Tales from Shakespeare*, 1938, *More New Tales from Shakespeare*, 1939, *New Tales from Malory*, 1939, and *New Tales of Troy*, 1940, all by G.B. Harrison; *A Book of Famous Pirates*

by A.M. Smyth, 1940; *The Watchers* by A.E.W. Mason, 1940; *Mutiny in the Caribbean* by
G.W. Keeton, 1940; *They Wanted Adventure* by Kenneth Macfarlane, 1940; *Sister of the
Angels*, 1940, *Smoky House*, 1940, *The Little White Horse*, 1946, and *Make Believe*, 1949, all
by Elizabeth Goudge; *The Ship Aground*, 1940, and *Painted Ports*, 1948, by C. Fox Smith;
They Raced for Treasure, 1946, *Flight to Adventure*, 1947, *There's No Escape*, 1950,
Mountain Rescue, 1955, and *The Silver Sword*, 1956, all by Ian Serraillier; *Adventures of
Button and Mac* by Ursula Hourihane, 1946; *The Story of the Treasure Seekers*, 1947, *The
New Treasure Seekers*, 1947, and *The Would-Be-Goods*, 1947, all by E. Nesbit; *The Swiss
Family Robinson* by Johann David and Johann Rudolf Wyss, 1949; *Cocos Gold* by Ralph
Hammond, 1950; *The Chronicles of Robin Hood*, 1950, *The Queen Elizabeth Story*, 1951, *The
Armourer's House*, 1951, *Brother Dusty-Feet*, 1952, *The Eagle of the Ninth*, 1954, and *The
Shield Ring*, 1956, all by Rosemary Sutcliff; *Redcap Runs Away* by Rhoda Power, 1952; *The
Crown of Violet*, 1952, and *Bows Against the Barons*, revised edition, 1966, by Geoffrey
Trease; *Sea-Dogs and the Pilgrim Fathers* edited by John Hampdon, 1953; *Queen Elizabeth
and the Spanish Armada* by Frances Winwar, 1954; *A Swarm in May*, 1955, *Chorister's
Cake*, 1956, and *Cathedral Wednesday*, 1960, all by William Mayne; *Will Shakespeare and
the Globe Theatre* by Anne Terry White, 1955; *The King's Snare* by Helen Lobdell, 1955;
The Adventures of Huckleberry Finn, 1955, and *The Adventures of Tom Sawyer*, 1955, by
Mark Twain; *Cold Hazard* by Richard Armstrong, 1956; *Ransom for a Knight* by Barbara
Leonie Picard, 1956; *The Three Musketeers* by Dumas, 1957; *Once-upon-a-Time Storybook*
by Rose Dobbs, 1958; *The Flight and Adventures of Charles II* by Charles Norman, 1958;
The Kidnapping of Kensington by Bruce Carter, 1958; *The Golden Stile* by Gwen Walker,
1958; *Castles and Kings* by Henry Treece, 1959; *Red Indian Folk and Fairy Tales* by Ruth
Manning-Sanders, 1960; *The Siege and Fall of Troy* by Robert Graves, 1962; *Three Against
London* by Rachel Varble, 1962; *Growing Up in the Thirteenth Century*, 1962, *The Story of
the Crusades*, 1963, and *Growing Up with the Norman Conquest*, 1965, all by Alfred Duggan;
The Shoe Shop Bears 1963, and *Hannibal and the Bears*, 1965, by Margaret J. Baker; *The
Lion in the Gateway* by Mary Renault, 1964; *The Richleighs of Tantamount* by Barbara
Willard, 1966; *The Complete Pelican Shakespeare* edited by Alfred Harbage, 1969; *The Nine
Questions* by Edward Fenton, 1969; *The Rime of the Ancient Mariner* by Samuel Taylor
Coleridge, 1971; *The Pied Piper of Hamelin* by Robert Browning, 1971; *The Sea-Beggar's
Son* by F.N. Monjo, 1974.

C. Walter Hodges comments:

It is a truth more or less universally acknowledged by those concerned with literature for
children, that children ought not to be written down to. But is the opposite also true, that they
ought not to be written up from? Surely not. Those who are nowadays called Children's
Writers (and their illustrators) are adults, engaged as adults in highly-skilled creative,
imaginative work; and children in their own imaginations are as near adult as need be for an
intelligent readership. Many of the books that most attracted me and my friends when I was
young were not specifically written as "children's books"; therefore today, though I write
mostly for children, I do not bother extremely to make my books only suitable for them at
their age. I like to make them also suitable for me at mine. Besides, I am quite sure that
children of any age ought not to be given children's books that are not suitable for adults to
read.

*   *   *

C. Walter Hodges' particular talent is for the making of novels out of historical events,
always those which have a momentum and a grandeur of their own. He is a quiet author,
using no tricks of technique, and obtruding his own personality scarcely at all. This method
gives an extraordinary verisimilitude to his stories; the author's cunning and skill become
invisible, and one is apparently reading "what really happened."

In *Columbus Sails*, Mr. Hodges' first full-length book, the story is told from three different viewpoints: that of a monk who knows about the difficulties that Columbus surmounted to get his expedition financed, that of a sailor who can relate the events of the voyage, and that of an Indian in Spain, who knows how it all ended. The diffusion of the narrative voice, and the fact that each narrator tells not really his own story – the narrators are barely characterised – but that of the voyage, establishes Mr. Hodges' predominant tone.

Alfred Daneleg, through whose eyes the early years of King Alfred are told in *The Namesake*, is a more rounded character, yet still functions largely as a clear-eyed narrator of the course of history. But the change from *Columbus Sails* is very great. In Alfred Mr. Hodges found a subject that set his imagination alight. The battles and shifts of fortune of those grim times, the iron hearts and wolf's hunger of the Danes, and the brave, thoughtful, capable and loving young man who rescued England have inspired the writer, and shine for the reader. A moral as well as a physical struggle was waged by Alfred; and that gives a depth and subtlety to the story. *The Namesake* is a fine historical novel and probably Mr. Hodges' best book.

The Marsh King, a sequel to *The Namesake*, completes the tale of Alfred's early wars. The opening page tells us that the story has been garnered from two eye-witnesses, but much more is in the book than these two could probably have known, and once again we are looking at very transparent narrators. In effect this is straight narration, lacking the central consciousness of Alfred Daneleg in *The Namesake*. This is a fast moving, adventurous story, a tale of battles and treachery, but a certain resonance is missing, and it is not quite the equal of the earlier book.

In *The Overland Launch* Mr. Hodges found a more modern subject. This is the true, though incredible story of the determination of a lifeboat coxswain to get his boat in the sea and launched on a rescue mission, even though it meant hauling it up and over a hill with the most notorious ascent and descent in the West Country, in the teeth of a terrible storm. The successful achievement of this impossible task gives Mr. Hodges an epic and thrilling subject. He catches very well the temper of West Country men, and the burr of their voices. A memorable book.

Playhouse Tales is a set of short stories all about actors and playwrights of Shakespeare's time, on which Mr. Hodges is an expert. Entirely at home in this period, not now very fashionable for historical writers, Mr. Hodges is in relaxed and humorous mood. We do not need his careful notes to tell us that many of the incidents are authentic; sunny, intricate and ornate, these tales feel right for the Elizabethan atmosphere.

Mr. Hodges is an admirable craftsman; his self-effacing manners as an author should not lead one to undervalue his skill.

—Jill Paton Walsh

HOFF, Syd(ney).   American.   Born in New York City, 4 September 1912. Educated at New York public schools; National Academy of Design. Married Dora Berman in 1937; has two children. Daily Cartoonist ("Laugh It Off"), King Features Syndicate, 1957–71. Address: c/o G.P. Putnam's Sons, 200 Madison Avenue, New York, New York 10016, U.S.A.

PUBLICATIONS FOR CHILDREN (illustrated by the author)

Fiction

Muscles and Brains.   New York, Dial Press, 1940.
Eight Little Artists.   New York, Abelard Schuman, 1954.
Patty's Pet.   New York, Abelard Schuman, 1955.

Danny and the Dinosaur. New York, Harper, 1958; Kingswood, Surrey, World's Work, 1969.

Sammy, The Seal. New York, Harper, 1959; Kingswood, Surrey, World's Work, 1960.

Julius. New York, Harper, 1959; Kingswood, Surrey, World's Work, 1960.

Ogluk, The Eskimo. New York, Holt Rinehart, 1960.

Where's Prancer? New York, Harper, 1960.

Oliver. New York, Harper, 1960; Kingswood, Surrey, World's Work, 1961.

Who Will Be My Friends? New York, Harper, 1960; Kingswood, Surrey, World's Work, 1964.

Little Chief. New York, Harper, 1961; Kingswood, Surrey, World's Work, 1962.

Albert the Albatross. New York, Harper, 1961; Kingswood, Surrey, World's Work, 1962.

Chester. New York, Harper, 1961; Kingswood, Surrey, World's Work, 1969.

Stanley. New York, Harper, 1962; Kingswood, Surrey, World's Work, 1963.

Grizzwold. New York, Harper, 1963; Kingswood, Surrey, World's Work, 1964.

Lengthy. New York, Putnam, 1964; Kingswood, Surrey, World's Work, 1965.

Mrs. Switch. New York, Putnam, 1967.

Irving and Me. New York, Harper, 1967.

Wanda's Wand. Norwalk, Connecticut, C.R. Gibson, 1968.

The Witch, The Cat, and the Baseball Bat. New York, Grosset and Dunlap, 1968.

Slithers. New York, Putnam, 1968.

Baseball Mouse. New York, Putnam, 1969.

Jeffrey at Camp. New York, Putnam, 1969.

Mahatma. New York, Putnam, 1969.

Roberto and the Bull. New York, McGraw Hill, 1969; Kingswood, Surrey, World's Work, 1971.

Herschel the Hero. New York, Putnam, 1969; Kingswood, Surrey, World's Work, 1971.

The Horse in Harry's Room. New York, Harper, 1970; Kingswood, Surrey, World's Work, 1971.

The Litter Knight. New York, McGraw Hill, 1970.

Palace Bug. New York, Putnam, 1970.

Siegfried, Dog of the Alps. New York, Grosset and Dunlap, 1970.

Wilfrid the Lion. New York, Putnam, 1970.

The Mule Who Struck It Rich. Boston, Little Brown, 1971.

Thunderhoof. New York, Harper, 1971; Kingswood, Surrey, World's Work, 1972.

When Will It Snow? illustrated by Mary Chalmers. New York, Harper, 1971.

Ida the Bareback Rider. New York, Putnam, 1972.

My Aunt Rosie. New York, Harper, 1972.

Pedro and the Bananas. New York, Putnam, 1972.

A Walk Past Ellen's House. New York, McGraw Hill, 1973.

Amy's Dinosaur. New York, Dutton, 1974.

Kip Van Wrinkle. New York, Putnam, 1974.

Katy's Kitten. New York, Dutton, 1975.

Pete's Pup. New York, Dutton, 1975.

Barkley. New York, Harper, 1975.

The Littlest Leaguer. New York, Dutton, 1976.

Walpole. New York, Harper, 1977.

Plays

Giants and Other Plays for Kids (includes *Lion in the Zoo, Children on the Moon, The Family, Wild Flowers*). New York, Putnam, 1973.

Television Plays: *Tales of Hoff* series, 1947.

Other

> *Syd Hoff's Joke Book.* New York, Putnam, 1972.
> *Jokes to Enjoy, Draw and Tell.* New York, Putnam, 1974.
> *Dinosaur Do's and Don't's.* New York, Dutton, 1975.

PUBLICATIONS FOR ADULTS

Other

> *Military Secrets.* New York, Hillair, 1943.
> *Feeling No Pain: An Album of Cartoons.* New York, Dial Press, 1944.
> *Mom, I'm Home!* (cartoons). New York, Dutton, 1945.
> *Oops! Wrong Party* (cartoons). New York, Dutton, 1951.
> *It's Fun Learning Cartooning.* New York, Stravon, 1952.
> *Oops! Wrong Stateroom!* (cartoons). New York, Washburn, 1953.
> *Out of Gas!* (cartoons). New York, Washburn, 1954.
> *Okay – You Can Look Now!* (cartoons). New York, Duell, 1955.
> *The Better Hoff* (cartoons). New York, Holt Rinehart, 1961.
> *Upstream, Downstream, and Out of My Mind.* Indianapolis, Bobbs Merrill, 1961.
> *'Twixt the Cup and the Lipton.* Indianapolis, Bobbs Merrill, 1962.
> *So This Is Matrimony* (cartoons). New York, Pocket Books, 1962.
> *Hunting, Anyone?* (cartoons). Indianapolis, Bobbs Merrill, 1963.
> *From Bed to Nurse; or, What a Way to Die* (cartoons). New York, Dell, 1963.
> *Learning to Cartoon.* New York, Stravon, 1966.
> *The Art of Cartooning.* New York, Stravon, 1973.
> *Editorial and Political Cartooning: From the Earliest Times to the Present ....* New York, Stravon, 1976.

Illustrator: *Parm Me* by Alex Kober, 1945; *Hello Muddah, Hello Fadduh!*, 1964, and *I Can't Dance!*, 1964, by Allan Sherman; *I Should Have Stayed in Bed!*, 1965, *The Homework Caper*, 1966, *The Rooftop Mystery*, 1968, all by Joan M. Lexau; *A Chanukah Fable for Christmas* by Jerome Coopersmith, 1969; *Henri Goes to the Mardi Gras* by Mildred Wright, 1971; *Donald and the Fish That Walked* by Edward R. Ricciuti, 1974; *The Snake That Couldn't Slither* by Peggy Bradbury, 1976.

                              *   *   *

Up to the creation of his *Danny and the Dinosaur* (1958) and after *Amy's Dinosaur* (1974), Syd Hoff has brought to child readers stories with recognizable settings and situations. Both child and animal subjects are usually treated with humor and are often subjected to unexpected situations – conveyed by words basically easy to grasp and follow – usually in short sentences. Hoff may use children as sole heroes: in *The Littlest Leaguer* awkward Harold comes to the rescue of his team; in the longtime favorite *Danny and the Dinosaur* the animal and the boy are the co-stars who share delight in the antics their relationship stimulates – together with the contrast of their respective sizes and the possible and impossible.

Woven through most of the stories are simple themes like cooperation; even when a chain of incidents construct the story, the eventual resolution is remarkably simple, most often with a single level interpretation; but the work invariably captures the young reader's interest – often sparked by the humor of a quick turn of phrase, sudden element of surprise, or twist of plotting detail in very readable style.

Some of Hoff's fiction, in the light of current sensitivities, tends to touch the stereotyped and the imperceptive in terms of underlying problems or common prejudices. For example, in *Little Chief* Hoff exhibits almost a lack of understanding and real appreciation of an important minority group and contributes to the maintenance of outmoded attitudes. In his longer work *Irving and Me*, Artie, the Jewish teenager whose family moves from Brooklyn to Florida (an experience the author knew from living in both areas), makes a new circle of friends. Their activities are linked with a neighborhood community center and tend to have a run-of-the-mill character. Some unfortunate ethnic undertones are present, and the texture of the story as well as the characterization tends to become rather superficial, even common in spots. While the happenings mirror some of the area lifestyles of the early 1960's in a middleclass family, the situations seem extraordinarily lean in the context of today's attitudes, problems and values.

In contrast Hoff has also tried his hand at bringing together a collection, *Giants and Other Plays for Kids*, again tapping anticipated interests of children. Perhaps his most conspicuous gift has been his reliance on subjects naturally popular with children like camping, contrasts, everyday fun, jokes, rhymes, small rivalries. Hoff matches many such children's interests with a mixture of easy familiarity and the occasional touch of the preposterous, or even the corny. The result is usually a kind of deft simplicity in content as well as style, bringing children pleasure with little threat, sometimes reinforcing a stereotype, and also staying at the surface level of understanding. The characters and stories are rarely far removed from both ordinary children and situations they might encounter on an ordinary block where children with or without animals may gather and share words for a bit of fun.

—Clara O. Jackson

HOGARTH, Grace. American. Born in Newton, Massachusetts, 5 November 1905. Educated at Newton High School, 1919–23; University of California, Berkeley, 1923–24; Vassar College, Poughkeepsie, New York, 1924–27, B.A. 1927; Massachusetts School of Art, 1927–28; Yale University School of Fine Arts, New Haven, Connecticut, 1928–29; Columbia University, New York, 1935–36. Married William David Hogarth in 1936 (died, 1965); has two children. Staff Artist, later Children's Books Editor, Oxford University Press, New York and London, 1929–38, Chatto and Windus, London, 1938–39, and Houghton Mifflin, Boston, 1940–43; English representative for Houghton Mifflin, 1943–47, and other publishers, 1947–56, London; Children's Book Editor, 1956–63, Managing Director, 1963–66, Chairman and Managing Director, 1966–72, Constable, later Longman Young Books, London. Editor, Lifetime Library, 1968–70. Governor, North London and Camden Schools for Girls, 1963–71; Member of the Executive Committee, Association of Governing Bodies of Girls' Public Day Schools Trust, 1969–71. Agent: Deborah Rogers Ltd., 29 Goodge Street, London W1P 1FD. Address: 53 Ainger Road, London N.W.3, England.

PUBLICATIONS FOR CHILDREN

Fiction

> *Lucy's League* (as Amelia Gay), illustrated by Nora S. Unwin. London, Hodder and Stoughton, 1950; as Grace Hogarth, New York, Harcourt Brace, 1951.
> *John's Journey* (as Amelia Gay), illustrated by Nora S. Unwin. London, Hodder and Stoughton, 1952; as Grace Hogarth, New York, Harcourt Brace, 1952.
> *The Funny Guy*, illustrated by Fritz Wegner. London, Hamish Hamilton, and New York, Harcourt Brace, 1955.

As a May Morning.   New York, Harcourt Brace, and London, Hamish Hamilton, 1958.
A Sister for Helen, illustrated by Pat Marriott.   London, Deutsch, 1976.

Other

Australia: The Island Continent, illustrated by Howard W. Willard.   Boston, Houghton Mifflin, 1943.

PUBLICATIONS FOR ADULTS

Novels

This to Be Love (as Grace Allen).   London, Cape, 1949.
The End of Summer.   London, Cape, 1951.
Children of This World.   London, Cape, 1953.
Murders for Sale, with Andre Norton (as Allen Weston).   London, Hammond Hammond, 1954.

Other

Editor, with Caroline Hogarth, *American Cooking for English Kitchens.*   London, Hamish Hamilton, 1957.

Manuscript Collection: Vassar College Library, Poughkeepsie, New York.

Illustrator: *A Bible ABC*, 1943.

Grace Hogarth comments:
  For nearly all of my working life I was an Editor of Children's Books rather than a writer of them. I think it is always a temptation for editors to write because they are so constantly exposed to writing, but I confess that I found publishing books for children far easier than writing them.
  My first job, after university and two years of art school, was as Staff Artist in the Oxford University Press in New York just before the depression. I survived this by illustrating and editing some of the books on the children's list and by designing jackets, laying out ads, etc. Although I am not an artist of much ability, I found this experience and training of the greatest help to me when I became a publisher of books for children.
  My most successful children's books were *The Funny Guy* and *As a May Morning*, and I wrote both of them when my own children were the appropriate ages for them. There is nothing like a young audience for honest criticism and assistance!

*   *   *

  Grace Hogarth has made a dual contribution to the field of children's books, both as an editor and an author. Her first job was as children's editor at the Oxford University Press in New York and then as children's editor for a number of publishing houses in Britain. In 1957 she started the children's list at Constable and discovered many distinguished authors and artists who are at the peak of their careers today. Although there have been talented editors in both Britain and the United States, Mrs. Hogarth is unique in her experience in the field of children's books on both sides of the Atlantic. She has been of immense value in introducing important children's writers from one country to another. There has long been a tendency to feel that children must not be subjected to books which are "too foreign" and Mrs. Hogarth has tried hard to change this attitude. In an article she wrote for the *Horn Book* in 1965 she says,

Editors on both sides of the Atlantic are apt to say "American children would never understand this" or "Whatever will English children make of these peculiar clothes?" What we tend to overlook is the obvious truth that children everywhere are keenly interested in, and ready to learn about, other children, and the odder the better.

Perhaps because she started her career as an art student her interest in book illustration has always been as keen as her insistence on quality in writing. She illustrated her own edition of *A Bible ABC* for the youngest readers.

The Funny Guy, perhaps the most popular of her children's books, takes place in America in 1900 and tells of the year when Helen Hamilton's mother goes into hospital and Helen acquires the nickname of "the funny guy" from her classmates at school. Through a subscription to *St. Nicholas* magazine Helen learns that writing is fun and can bring new friends. This book was followed by *As a May Morning*, a novel for older children which explored the pleasures and pains of leaving childhood for an alien adult world. Grace Hogarth's writing is very much concerned with human relations and the importance of coming to terms with one another. There are probably few who know that she also has a number of adult works to her credit.

—Ann Bartholomew

HOLLAND, Isabelle. American. Born in Basel, Switzerland, 16 June 1920. Educated at private schools in England; University of Liverpool, 1938–40; Tulane University, New Orleans, B.A. in English 1942. Publicity Director, Lippincott, Dell and Putnam publishing companies, New York, 1960–68. Agent: Jane Wilson, John Cushman Associates, 25 West 43rd Street, New York, New York 10036. Address: c/o J.B. Lippincott, 521 Fifth Avenue, New York, New York, 10017, U.S.A.

PUBLICATIONS FOR CHILDREN

Fiction

Cecily. Philadelphia, Lippincott, 1967.
Amanda's Choice. Philadelphia, Lippincott, 1970.
The Man Without a Face. Philadelphia, Lippincott, 1972.
The Mystery of Castle Renaldi (as Francesca Hunt). Middletown, Connecticut, American Education Publications, 1972.
Heads You Win, Tails I Lose. Philadelphia, Lippincott, 1973.
Of Love and Death and Other Journeys. Philadelphia, Lippincott, 1975.
Journey for Three, illustrated by Charles Robinson. Boston, Houghton Mifflin, 1975.
Alan and the Animal Kingdom. Philadelphia, Lippincott, 1977.
Hitchhike. Philadelphia, Lippincott, 1977.

PUBLICATIONS FOR ADULTS

Novels

Kilgaren. New York, Weybright and Talley, 1974; London, Collins, 1975.
Trelawny. New York, Weybright and Talley, 1974; as *Trelawny's Fell*, London, Collins, 1976.

Moncrieff. New York, Weybright and Talley, 1975; as *The Standish Place*, London, Collins, 1976.

Darcourt. New York, Weybright and Talley, 1976; London, Collins, 1977.

Grenelle. New York, Rawson, 1976.

The de Maury Papers. New York, Rawson, 1977.

Tower Abbey. New York, Rawson, 1977.

Manuscript Collection: Kerlan Collection, University of Minnesota, Minneapolis.

Isabelle Holland comments:

The Greek philosopher Heraclitus said "character is destiny." Some well-known contemporary writer – possibly the late Elizabeth Bowen – said "character is plot." In my books I write about what interests me most: the development of character, its growth of understanding of self, and its relationship to others. To me this is the basis of all stories, and I look upon myself primarily as a story teller.

*   *   *

Isabelle Holland is an outstanding storyteller who creates solidly established characters. Her novels have strong moral themes that are part of the fibre of the story, not grafted on to convey a message. She usually writes in the first person about both boys and girls who are flawed but sympathetic, caught in emotional or psychological dilemmas and often adrift in crumbling families. Somehow they survive the test, often with ingenuity, adventure and good humor. Their parents, on the other hand, are often found wanting, thus reinforcing the idea of the essential sanity of the young, even when entrapped in the various and sundry aberrations of the adult world.

Some of the blame for the struggles of her heroes and heroines is laid squarely at the door of progressive schools and the so-called permissive attitudes of affluent, uncaring parents. Holland herself was born and educated in Europe (the scene of her first novel, *Cecily*), which may account for her educational perspective here. She is deeply convinced that poor discipline and lack of responsibility on the part of teachers and parents are an insult to the intelligence of young people, who swiftly detect weakness and feel driven to exploit it, often to their own detriment. But Holland is not a didactic writer. She has a wonderful sense of humor. The children send up the system unmercifully. Melissa, in *Heads You Win, Tails I Lose*, is afraid to be caught reading fairy tales (which her enlightened mother regards as unhealthy) so she pretends to be reading about sex (which must not be repressed, of course). "I allowed myself to look neurotically guilty. It was better than another lecture on the dangers of escapist reading."

Alcohol abuse by adults appears in several of her novels. Her characters do not explain it away or make specious allowances. They view drinking with repugnance and anger. Justin McLeod became "The Man Without a Face" as a result of a drunken driving accident in which a pupil of his was killed; Melissa's mother drinks herself to sleep as her marriage disintegrates and thinks she is hiding the fact; Dr. Harris in *Alan and the Animal Kingdom* lets his friend Alan down in his hour of need, having drunk himself insensible. The children's judgments are old-fashioned, and hold a salutary mirror up to adulthood.

The lone adult outside the established circle figures largely in Holland's world. Justin McLeod, Dr. Harris, Manuel Santiago in *Amanda's Choice*, and Meg's father in *Of Love and Death and Other Journeys* are all people from outside the present embattled world who help the children to change direction or to find out where they are going and why. Animals also stand outside the crumbling family structure. They can be relied on to respond, although Alan, the orphan, finally realizes that they cannot replace human beings.

Among the best of Holland's novels are *The Man Without a Face* and *Of Love and Death and Other Journeys*. The former explores with gentle perception the mind of fatherless Charles at odds with his mother and sister, surrounded by women, who finds a friend and mentor in Justin McLeod. His skirting the edges of homosexual involvement is portrayed with exceptional sensitivity. *Of Love and Death and Other Journeys* is Isabelle Holland's most successful novel to date. The harsh vision of inadequate parents has softened. Meg's irresponsible, unthinking mother faces her own death, and Meg's agony, culminating in a new relationship with her previously unknown father, seems to blur the lines of battle drawn between the generations.

—Brigitte Weeks

HOLLING, Holling C(lancy). American. Born in Holling Corners, Michigan, 2 August 1900. Educated at Leslie High School, Michigan, graduated, 1917; Art Institute of Chicago, graduated, 1923. Married Lucille Webster in 1925. Member of the Zoology Department, Chicago Museum of Natural History, 1923–26; taught on the New York University World Cruise, 1926–27. After 1927, free-lance designer, advertising artist, and book illustrator. *Died 7 September 1973.*

PUBLICATIONS FOR CHILDREN

Fiction (illustrated by the author)

> *Little Big-Bye-and-Bye.* Joliet, Illinois, Volland, 1926.
> *Choo-Me-Choo*, illustrated by Lucille Holling. Minneapolis, Buzza, 1928.
> *Rum-Tum-Tummy, The Elephant Who Ate.* Akron, Ohio, Saalfield, 1928.
> *Claws of the Thunderbird: A Tale of Three Lost Indians.* Joliet, Illinois, Volland, 1928.
> *Rocky Billy: The Story of the Bounding Career of a Rocky Mountain Goat.* New York, Macmillan, 1928.
> *The Twins Who Flew round the World.* New York, Platt and Munk, 1931.
> *Little Buffalo Boy*, illustrated by Holling C. and Lucille Holling. New York, Garden City Publishing Company, 1939.
> *Paddle-to-the-Sea.* Boston, Houghton Mifflin, 1941; London, Collins, 1945.
> *Tree in the Trail.* Boston, Houghton Mifflin, 1942; London, Collins, 1948.
> *Seabird*, illustrated by Holling C. and Lucille Holling. Boston, Houghton Mifflin, 1948; London, Collins, 1960.
> *Minn of the Mississippi.* Boston, Houghton Mifflin, 1951.
> *Pagoo*, illustrated by Holling C. and Lucille Holling. Boston, Houghton Mifflin, 1957.

Other

> *New Mexico Made Easy, with Words of Modern Syllables.* Chicago, Rockwell F. Clancy, 1923.
> *The Book of Indians*, illustrated by Holling C. and Lucille Holling. New York, Platt and Munk, 1935; London, Cassell, 1938.
> *The Book of Cowboys*, illustrated by Holling C. and Lucille Holling. New York, Platt and Munk, 1936; London, Cassell, 1938.

PUBLICATIONS FOR ADULTS

Verse

> *Sun and Smoke: Verse and Woodcuts of New Mexico.* Privately printed, 1923.

Illustrator: *Blot, The Little City Cat* by Phyllis Crawford, 1930; *The Road in Storyland* edited by Watty Piper, 1932; *Children of Other Lands* by Watty Piper, 1943.

*   *   *

A writer with the consummate gift of storytelling and the ability to teach through transfer of remarkable bits and pieces of information he both longingly and desperately wanted to share with children, Holling C. Holling moved from his companion collections *The Book of Indians* and *The Book of Cowboys* of the 1930's to a group of singular books which offer blendings of rare elements. Usually in collaboration with his artist wife Lucille, he offered in these books "a unique vision of their country, each focusing first on the wild life Mr. Holling knew so well, but spreading wide into the works of men and the sweep of history ... they make a special intellectually valid contribution to modern children's books."

The first of these geo-historical-fiction volumes, *Paddle-to-the-Sea* contributed a tremendously original and arresting story recaptured first in a film utterly faithful to its text, and more recently in a film recreated by Bill Mason of the National Film Board of Canada in a freer style. This novel is a mixture of imagination and a wealth of information to which a reader may return for both the story text and the marginal drawings and related details, a technique which Holling and his wife pioneered and perfected. The story follows the fascinating adventures of Paddle, carved into a miniature canoe by an Indian boy. Paddle comes to travel from "the hills above Lake Superior" across the Great Lakes, and eventually to France, encountering suspenseful situations of many kinds. The inherent values of this story for today's readers are described fully in a penetrating current analysis, "The Teaching of Paddle-to-the-Sea" by Terry Borten in *Learning* (January 1977). He comments on the energy, simplicity, understanding, and appeal in the story. "What we teachers need is Holling's insight into the relationship between narrative action and factual information." Accented also is the allowance Holling makes for the feelings of children.

Holling's consuming interest in nature combined with history is further developed in *Tree in the Trail* which traced the beginnings (1610) of a cottonwood tree in the Great Plains to the ox yoke which "traveled with a tune" to the Santa Fe Trail. To Indians this lonely giant represented a peace-medicine tree; to other travelers a landmark until 1834 when lightning and wind struck it down. Blending anthropology and zoology with geography and history, the charming prose captures the excitement of both the historical setting and the associated adventures. Captured forever is the old Southwest – together with the realia linked with its emergence. The resultant authenticity stems from the author's personal saddle-horse contact with thousands of miles of plains, deserts, and mountains; he was able to transfer the sights, knowledge and awe to the reader in a sparkling text.

Some six years later in *Seabird* he told the intriguing story of an ivory gull carved by a young lad onto a whaling ship. Traveling on the family's vessels over four generations, this marvelous gull witnessed the enormous changes sailors and their ships experienced as they moved around the seas of the world into modern times. The saga of Ezra Brown's family and its relationships to the sea and the gull is utterly fascinating.

A mud turtle, Minn, helps spotlight another rich area of the United States in *Minn of the Mississippi*, traveling from the headwaters of the great waterway along its colorful shores to the Gulf, bringing alive the people, their work and evidences of early exploration. The stirring and adventurous saga of a hermit crab is immortalized in *Pagoo*. Its contents and making – from the idea through various production stages – is caught in the film *The Story of a Book*. Against experiences involving the author's keen observation, experimenting and plotting, the crab is drawn into a whirlwind of action described with spectacular detail. The exciting telling eventually draws him into the "endless rocking rhythms of the sea." In each of these works the reader can feel the author's participation through his throbbing text and vibrant imagery.

—Clara O. Jackson

HOLMAN, Felice. American. Born in New York City, 24 October 1919. Educated at Syracuse University, New York, B.A. 1941. Married Herbert Valen in 1941; has one child. Advertising copywriter, New York, 1944–50. Address: 158 Hillspoint Road, Westport, Connecticut 06880, U.S.A.

PUBLICATIONS FOR CHILDREN

Fiction

> *Elizabeth, The Bird Watcher*, illustrated by Erik Blegvad. New York, Macmillan, 1963.
> *Elizabeth and the Marsh Mystery*, illustrated by Erik Blegvad. New York, Macmillan, 1963; London, Collier Macmillan, 1974.
> *Elizabeth the Treasure Hunter*, illustrated by Erik Blegvad. New York, Macmillan, 1964.
> *Silently, The Cat, and Miss Theodosia*, illustrated by Harvey Dinnerstein. New York, Macmillan, and London, Collier Macmillan, 1965.
> *The Witch on the Corner*, illustrated by Arnold Lobel. New York, Norton, 1966; London, Lutterworth Press, 1967.
> *Victoria's Castle*, illustrated by Lillian Hoban. New York, Norton 1966.
> *Professor Diggins' Dragons*, illustrated by Ib Ohlsson. New York, Macmillan, and London, Collier Macmillan, 1966.
> *The Cricket Winter*, illustrated by Ralph Pinto. New York, Norton, 1967.
> *The Blackmail Machine*, illustrated by Victoria de Larrea. New York, Macmillan, 1967; London, Collier Macmillan, 1968.
> *A Year to Grow*, illustrated by Emily McCully. New York, Norton, 1968.
> *The Holiday Rat, and The Utmost Mouse*, illustrated by Wallace Tripp. New York, Norton, 1969.
> *Solomon's Search*, illustrated by Mischa Richter. New York, Grosset and Dunlap, 1970.
> *The Future of Hooper Toote*, illustrated by Gahan Wilson. New York, Scribner, 1972.
> *The Escape of the Giant Hogstalk*, illustrated by Ben Shecter. New York, Scribner, 1974.
> *Slake's Limbo*. New York, Scribner, 1974.

Verse

> *At the Top of My Voice and Other Poems*, illustrated by Edward Gorey. New York, Norton, 1970.
> *I Hear You Smiling and Other Poems*, illustrated by Laszlo Kubinyi. New York, Scribner, 1973.

Other

> *The Drac: French Tales of Dragons and Demons*, with Nanine Valen, illustrated by Stephen Walker. New York, Scribner, 1975.

Manuscript Collection: Kerlan Collection, University of Minnesota, Minneapolis.

Felice Holman comments:
I write about things that are based on life in the real world, but are separated from it by a scrim that takes the glare away.

*   *   *

In 1963, Felice Holman presented her first book for readers 5 to 8 years old but clearly aimed at an audience of girls. *Elizabeth, The Bird Watcher* was a rather predictable novel – nice but unexceptional – about a child devoted to her feathered friends. A marauding squirrel helps himself to the food Elizabeth provides for the birds, a problem resolved to the satisfaction of all, including the squirrel. The book was followed by two more on the doings of Elizabeth and by a number of other books, all of which proved the author's increasing use of the imagination.

Since Holman is essentially a poet, it's not surprising that even her minor stories are enhanced by lyrical prose, striking imagery. Then, in 1970, she published her first volume of verse for children. *At the Top of My Voice* was praised for originality, humor and point. A wonderful way of introducing young people to the power of poetry, the poems are all based solidly on situations children understand. This book was followed by *I Hear You Smiling*, and selections from both volumes continue to show up in anthologies – evidence of popular appeal.

Holman's sense of fun inspired her to write *The Escape of the Giant Hogstalk*. The story is that rare jewel, convincing absurdity, with giggles interspersed with horse laughs all the way. Anthony Wilson-Brown, a trial to his "Wealthy Aristocratic Family" – he *will* fool around instead of attending to his lessons – is sent to the Caucasus ("an out-of-the way place depending on where you happen to be, of course"). He finds a legendary plant, the Giant Hogstalk, and plants its seed back home at the Royal Botanic Gardens. Grown to immensity, the plant escapes and spreads havoc among the citizens, merriment among Holman's audience. The story has a nifty coda, suggesting further adventures of the Hogstalk.

In 1974, the author topped herself and a good many other toilers in the field of children's literature. *Slake's Limbo*, the novel of a 13-year-old boy (homeless, friendless, an experienced outcast) is a milestone. Universally praised, the story describes how Artemis Slake spends 121 days in a cave under Grand Central Station in New York, how he gets food, keeps warm and evades officialdom. The book is not only a heartening saga; it's memorable for authenticity of details on the mysterious, subterranean world of an inner city. Holman gave an absorbing account of the research which is the firm foundation of *Slake's Limbo* in *The Horn Book* (October 1976).

Her passion for authenticity is obvious in *The Drac: French Tales of Dragons and Demons*. With her collaborator, Nanine Valen, Holman investigated archives, journals, libraries and private homes tracking down the genesis of legends about supernatural things that terrorized villages in France in ancient days. A versatile and gifted author-poet, Felice Holman will certainly continue to be heard from.

—Jean F. Mercier

HOPE-SIMPSON, Jacynth. British. Born in Birmingham, Warwickshire, 10 November 1930. Educated at King Edward VI High School, Birmingham; University of Lausanne; St. Hugh's College, Oxford, M.A. 1956. Married Dermot Hope-Simpson in 1955; has one daughter. English Teacher, Bournemouth School for Girls, 1953–54; Examiner, Oxford and Cambridge General Certificate of Education, 1957–58. Address: The Red House, Hartley Road, Plymouth, Devon, England.

PUBLICATIONS FOR CHILDREN

Fiction

Anne, Young Swimmer. London, Constable, 1960.
The Stranger in the Train, illustrated by Prudence Seward. London, Hamish Hamilton, 1960.
Young Netball Player. London, Constable, 1961.
The Great Fire, illustrated by Pat Marriott. London, Hamish Hamilton, 1961; New York, Dutton, 1962.
Danger on the Line, illustrated by Janet Duchesne. London, Hamish Hamilton, 1962.
The Man Who Came Back. London, Hamish Hamilton, 1962.
The Ice Fair, illustrated by Pat Marriott. London, Hamish Hamilton, 1963.
The Ninepenny, illustrated by Janet Duchesne. London, Hamish Hamilton, 1964.
The Witches' Cave, illustrated by Janet Duchesne. London, Hamish Hamilton, 1964.
The Edge of the World, illustrated by Peter Warner. London, Hamish Hamilton, 1965; New York, Coward McCann, 1966.
The High Toby, illustrated by Lynette Hemmant. London, Hamish Hamilton, 1966.
Escape to the Castle, illustrated by Mary Russon. London, Hamish Hamilton, 1967.
The Unknown Island. London, Hamish Hamilton, 1968; New York, Coward McCann, 1969.
The Gunner's Boy. London, Heinemann, 1973.
Save Tarranmoor! London, Heinemann, 1974.
The Hijacked Hovercraft, illustrated by Jeroo Roy. London, Heinemann, 1975.
Black Madonna. London, Heinemann, 1976; Nashville, Nelson, 1977.
Vote for Victoria, illustrated by Jael Jordan. London, Heinemann, 1976.

Other

Basic Certificate English: A Revision Course in the Grammar and Structure of the English Language, with Answers. London, Hamish Hamilton, 1966.
They Sailed from Plymouth. London, Hamish Hamilton, 1970.
Elizabeth I. London, Hamish Hamilton, 1971.
Who Knows? Twelve Unsolved Mysteries. London, Heinemann, 1974; Nashville, Nelson, 1976.
Always on the Move, illustrated by Jolyne Knox. London, Heinemann, 1975.

Editor, *The Hamish Hamilton Book of Myths and Legends*, illustrated by Raymond Briggs. London, Hamish Hamilton, 1964; as *The Curse of the Dragon's Gold: European Myths and Legends*, New York, Doubleday, 1969.
Editor, *The Hamish Hamilton Book of Witches*, illustrated by Raymond Briggs. London, Hamish Hamilton, 1964; as *A Cavalcade of Witches*, New York, Walck, 1967.
Editor, *Tales in School: An Anthology of Boarding-School Life*, illustrated by John Lawrence. London, Hamish Hamilton, 1971.

PUBLICATIONS FOR ADULTS

Novels

The Bishop of Kenelminster. London, Putnam, 1961.
The Bishop's Picture. London, Putnam, 1962.
The Unravish'd Bride. London, Putnam, 1963.

Jacynth Hope-Simpson comments:

I should like to feel that I write for a wide range of children, with enough incident and pace to attract the reluctant reader with (one hopes) enough depth of content to appeal to more "bookish" readers. One of my basic beliefs is that while one may need to simplify both language and one's material in writing for children, one must never write down to them. I believe accuracy to be of the utmost importance, especially as so many ideas are formed at a surprisingly early age. On an imaginative level, I am particularly interested in places and the interaction between place and personality.

*   *   *

The earliest traditions of story telling for children were strongly moral and didactic in their intention; children were taken seriously because their instruction was a serious matter. Increasingly since the 1950's, this emphasis has changed to an attempt to evoke the nature of child-hood itself as being of prime significance.

Jacynth Hope-Simpson's position is more consistent with the older tradition. She takes her subject matter from a wide range of incident and location and its seriousness is represented more by a talent for instruction than any wish to preach. She is not unsympathetic to the more recent relish for realism, but this is of a kind that grows from mundane and continuous contact with children. In *Danger on the Line* for example the small crisis is prompted by Antony's discovery that Clare, the small daughter of the master in charge of the outdoor model steam railway, was upset because "A large piece of sharp black gravel was stuck in her left nostril." In the same way in the more ambitious *Escape to the Castle*, Vaclav's adventure begins on a hot night in his Prague attic when he becomes unendurably aware of being shut out from a larger life, an unwilling prisoner (not helped by his younger brother's preoccupation with squeezing his insect bites). He locates this larger life in the Castle where his delight in Mozart's music is challenged by a meeting with the composer weighed down by problems of his own. This theme possibly needs fuller treatment to realise its complexity; but the neat ordering of surprise – where stock stories involve improbable escapes from realistic castles, this escape is from cramping domesticity in search of an ideal in a castle – is characteristic of the author's unobtrusive originality. This originality is given fuller scope in *The Gunner's Boy*. Mark and Peter are the sons of a Dartmoor parson sent to stay with an aunt in Plymouth while their mother impatiently awaits the tardy arrival of the latest child in competition with the family cat which is similarly disadvantaged. Mark is bookish and Peter, the younger boy, is mad to go to sea. Peter runs away to join a Spanish expedition but hurts his leg on the way down to the harbour, and Mark, going to bring him back, is taken in his place and becomes the reluctant, and sensitive, narrator of the story. This, again, provides more than conventional battle scenes on *The Revenge* and hardships at sea, for Mark is taken on board the *San Pablo* after the battle and sees the humane side of the despised and hated Spaniards.

The characteristic qualities of these stories include: respect for the child reader which entails such authentic details as, in the London of *The Great Fire*, "The shop signs swung over their heads; a striped pole for the barber, a knee boot for the bootmaker"; a precise sense of place whether 17th century London, the Prague of Mozart or Drake's Plymouth and contemporary Finistère; and pre-eminently a strong sense of dramatic realism so that child adventures, of the past and of today, are consistently related to an encircling and clearly defined adult world.

—Kenneth J. Sterck

HOUGH, Charlotte.   British.   Born in Brockenhurst, Hampshire, 24 May 1924. Educated at Frensham Heights School, Farnham, Surrey. Served in the Women's Royal Naval Service.

Married Richard Hough (i.e., Bruce Carter, *q.v.*) in 1943; has four children. Address: 25 St. Ann's Terrace, London NW8 6PH, England.

PUBLICATIONS FOR CHILDREN (illustrated by the author)

Fiction

> *Jim Tiger.* London, Faber, 1956; Indianapolis, Bobbs Merrill, 1958.
> *Morton's Pony.* London, Faber, 1957.
> *The Home-Makers.* London, Hamish Hamilton, 1957.
> *The Hampshire Pig.* London, Hamish Hamilton, 1958.
> *The Story of Mr. Pinks.* London, Faber, 1958.
> *The Animal Game.* London, Faber, 1959.
> *The Trackers.* London, Hamish Hamilton, 1960.
> *Algernon.* London, Faber, 1961; New York, A. S. Barnes, 1962.
> *Anna and Minnie.* London, Faber, 1962.
> *Three Little Funny Ones.* London, Hamish Hamilton, 1962.
> *The Owl in the Barn.* London, Faber, 1964.
> *More Funny Ones.* London, Faber, 1965.
> *Red Biddy and Other Stories.* London, Faber, 1966; New York, Coward McCann, 1967.
> *Sir Frog and Other Stories.* London, Faber, 1968.
> *Educating Flora and Other Stories.* London, Faber, 1968.
> *Abdul the Awful* (includes *Sir Frog and Other Stories* and *Educating Flora and Other Stories*). New York, McCall, 1970.
> *Queer Customer.* London, Heinemann, 1972.
> *Wonky Donkey.* London, Heinemann, 1975.
> *Bad Cat.* London, Heinemann, 1975.
> *Pink Pig.* London, Heinemann, 1975.
> *Charlotte Hough's Holiday Book.* London, Heinemann, 1975.
> *The Mixture as Before.* London, Heinemann, 1976.

Verse

> *A Bad Child's Book of Moral Verse.* London, Faber, and New York, Walck, 1970.

Other

> *My Aunt's Alphabet, with Billy and Me* (reader). London, Hamish Hamilton, 1969.

Illustrator: *The House on the Moor*, 1948, *The Thirteenth Adventure*, 1949, *Steeple Folly*, 1950, *Castaway Camp*, 1951, and *The Barnstormers*, 1953, all by M. E. Atkinson; *The Adventures of Tommy* by Lillian Miozzi, 1950; *I Carried the Horn*, 1951, and *Riders from Afar*, 1954, by Christine Pullein-Thompson; *Land of Ponies* by Marjorie M. Oliver, 1951; *Barry's Exciting Year*, 1951, *Barry Gets His Wish*, 1952, and *Barry's Great Day*, 1954, all by A. Stephen Tring; *Two of Us* by Janet Branford, 1952; *Mystery at Winton's Park*, 1952, and *Hotel Doorway*, 1953, by Lorna Lewis; *The Wonderful Farm* by Marcel Aymé, 1952; *Smoky Joe*, 1952, *Smoky Joe in Trouble*, 1953, and *Smoky Joe Goes to School*, 1956, all by Laurence Meynell; *Prince among Ponies* by Josephine Pullein-Thompson, 1952; *Five Proud Riders* by Ann Stafford, 1953; *The Sheepdog Adventure* by Ethelind Fearon, 1953; *The Enchanted Horse* by April Jaffé, 1953; *Peril on the Iron Road*, 1953, and *Gunpowder Tunnel*, 1955, by Bruce Carter; *Black Beauty* by Anna Sewell, 1954; *Elephant Big and Elephant Little*, 1955, *The Little Yellow Jungle Frogs*, 1956, and *Animal Story Book*, 1972, all by Anita Hewett; *The Boy with the Green Thumb* by Barbara Euphan Todd, 1956; *The Flying Jacket* edited by Betty

Willsher, 1964; *Time for a Story* edited by Eileen Colwell, 1967; *Galapagos* by Richard Hough, 1975; *What Katy Did* by Susan Coolidge.

*   *   *

Charlotte Hough is a writer of marked individuality and versatility, qualities not easily combined. She writes in both prose and verse, and for a wide age-span, ranging from the very small children to whom *Wonky Donkey* is meant to be read aloud, to the eleven-year-olds who want junior novels such as *Queer Customer*. Further – though this is not the place to attempt an assessment of her talents as an illustrator – it must be remarked that in some of her books, notably *Wonky Donkey*, her pictures are so integrated with her text that the latter (often no more than a single sentence or a single word per page) cannot be criticised in isolation.

Within the purely verbal context, however, it can be said that all her work, for whatever age, exhibits certain consistent features. There is always a great sense of fun, an infectious enthusiasm for words, a delight in juggling with them. This dexterity is naturally most marked in her use of rhyme and assonance. *A Bad Child's Book of Moral Verse* is not unworthy to stand on the shelf beside the Belloc volumes of an earlier day. But this same verbal dexterity is also a feature of her prose, which shows much of the same neatness and economy. Exuberance without waste of words is the paradox she contrives to achieve, so that the reader is whirled along.

These high spirits and robust good humour cannot obscure the fact that Mrs. Hough is in the great moralist tradition of English children's literature. Whether writing of children or adults or of animals to whom human frailties are transferred – the conceited guinea-pig, Mr. Pinks, the maladroit Jim Tiger, or Morton's pony, the elderly and sagacious pony as reliable and protective as a grown-up – she makes her points with a light touch, so that the very weaknesses of her characters render them the more lovable.

Probably it is her shorter pieces – her animal stories and fairy-tales making fresh use of old material, giant and goblin, mermaid and princess – that represent her most original contribution. At the same time, a junior novel such as *Queer Customer*, with its central theme of a boy's natural but unnecessary dread of an operation, must not be underrated. It displays another, more realistic side to her work, and her sympathetic depiction of the characters is full of insight and humanity.

—Geoffrey Trease

HOUGH, Richard. See **CARTER, Bruce.**

HOUSTON, James A(rchibald). Canadian. Born in Toronto, Ontario, 12 June 1921. Educated at Ontario College of Art, 1938–40; Ecole Grande Chaumière, Paris, 1947–48; Un-ichi Hiratsuka, Tokyo, 1958–59. Served in the Toronto Scottish Regiment, 1940–45. Married Alma G. Houston in 1950 (divorced, 1966); Alice Watson, 1967; has two sons. Civil Administrator, Canadian Government, West Baffin, Eastern Arctic, 1953–62. Associate Director, 1962–72, and since 1972, Associate Designer, Steuben Glass, New York. Artist: one-man shows – Canadian Guild of Crafts, 1953, 1955, 1957; Robertson Galleries, Ottawa, 1953; Calgary Galleries, 1966; Canadiana Galleries, Edmonton, 1977; represented in collections of Glenbow-Alberta Museum of Art, Montreal Museum of Fine Arts, National Gallery of Art, Ottawa. Recipient: Canadian Library Association Book of the Year Medal,

1966; American Indian and Eskimo Cultural Foundation Award, 1966. D.Litt.: Carleton University, Ottawa, 1972; D. H. L.: Rhode Island College, Providence, 1975. Officer, Order of Canada. Address: Letfern, Woody Hill Road, Escoheag, Rhode Island 02821, U.S.A.

PUBLICATIONS FOR CHILDREN (illustrated by the author)

Fiction

Tikta'liktat: An Eskimo Legend.   Toronto, Longman, and New York, Harcourt Brace, 1965.
Eagle Mask: A West Coast Indian Tale.   Toronto, Longman, and New York, Harcourt Brace, 1966.
The White Archer: An Eskimo Legend.   Toronto, Longman, and New York, Harcourt Brace, 1967.
Akavak: An Eskimo Journey.   Toronto, Longman, and New York, Harcourt Brace, 1968.
Wolf Run: A Cariboo Eskimo Tale.   Toronto, Longman, and New York, Harcourt Brace, 1971.
Ghost Paddle: A Northwest Coast Indian Tale.   Toronto, Longman, and New York, Harcourt Brace, 1972.
Kiviok's Magic Journey: An Eskimo Legend.   Toronto, Longman, and New York, Atheneum, 1973.
Frozen Fire.   New York, Atheneum, 1977.

Editor, *Songs of the Dream People: Chants and Images from the Indians and Eskimos of North America.*   Toronto, Longman, and New York, Atheneum, 1972.

PUBLICATIONS FOR ADULTS (illustrated by the author)

Novels

The White Dawn: An Eskimo Saga.   Toronto, Longman, New York, Harcourt Brace, and London, Heinemann, 1971.
Ghost Fox.   Toronto, McClelland and Stewart, New York, Harcourt Brace, and London, Collins, 1977.

Plays

Screenplays: *The White Dawn*, 1973; *The Mask and the Drum*, 1975; *So Sings the Wolf*, 1976; *Kalvak*, 1976.

Other

Eskimo Prints.   Barre, Massachusetts, Barre Publishers, 1967.
Ojibwa Summer.   Barre, Massachusetts, Barre Publishers, 1972.

Illustrator: *Shoot to Live*, 1944; *Nuki*, by Alma Houston, 1955; *Ayorama*, by Raymond de Coccola and Paul King, 1956; *Tuktut/Caribou*, 1957; *The Unicorn Was There*, by Elizabeth Pool, 1966; *The Private Journal of Captain G. F. Lyon of H. M. S. Hecla, During the Recent Voyage of Discovery under Captain Parry, 1821–1823*, by George Francis Lyon, 1970.

James A. Houston comments:
In some ways children do not exist in the world of Eskimos and Northern Indians. Children to them are simply small adults in the process of growing, of reaching maturity.

There are no children's stories there, only adult myths and legends and truths about life.

My stories are not really children's stories. They are simply northern stories that are suitable for both children and adults. I consider that my adult-length books are also suitable for children.

*   *   *

James A. Houston is best known for his discovery of Inuit (Eskimo) art and his stories about Inuit life. Less known are his two tales based on the lives of the British Columbia coastal Indians. Both kinds of fiction treat native Canadian societies in a "pure" form, that is, as they were before the intrusion of European culture.

Houston's Inuit novels generally emphasize the starkness of the environment, a boy hero's successful struggle for survival, and the concomitant attainment of some special insight, often spiritual or moral in nature, which helps to mark his entrance into manhood.

Tikta'liktak, the author's first book, tells the story of an Inuit boy faced with a struggle for survival in very hostile circumstances – adrift on an ice-floe, then isolated on a barren island – who proves his spiritual strength and physical resourcefulness in overcoming his difficulties. Though the ending is a bit anti-climactic, the tale is a good one. Similar is *Wolf Run*, the story of a starving boy who ventures into the barrens to hunt food for his family; after much agony he is saved by what, in a moment of insight, he believes to be the spirits of his grandparents in the guise of two helpful wolves. This novel, though containing much good writing, also falters at the conclusion, this time due to the unconvincing *deus ex machina* denouement.

Particularly reflective of conventional morality is *The White Archer*, which tells of an Inuit boy, Kungo, whose parents are killed and whose sister is abducted by Indian raiders – who, in their turn, are reacting to the murder of an Indian by an Inuit. Kungo vows revenge and spends some years preparing for it, but by the time he has it at hand he doesn't take it. In the crucial moment he realizes that he has unconsciously learned the value of compassion from two old people who cared for him, and his act of self-restraint leads to eventual reunion with his sister and reconciliation with his former enemies. The morality is good, but unfortunately Kungo's change of heart is not entirely convincing; his passion for revenge is too easily dissipated.

More satisfying is *Akavak*. Here the Inuit boy helps his dying grandfather fulfil a last wish: to travel over formidable mountains to visit his brother. Though the grandfather dies as the trip is completed, it is not without passing on much of himself and of the secrets of the mountains to Akavak, who proves himself during the journey. The tale is stark and simple on the surface but very rich and emotionally rewarding underneath. The impact is achieved through understatement, as in Anglo-Saxon poetry. A slight criticism might be that more background could be provided. The most recent Inuit story is *Kiviok's Magic Journey*. An Arctic fairy-tale, it is both typical of its genre and enjoyable, though it lacks some of the harsh struggle characteristic of the other Inuit books.

Houston's Indian tales also mark the passage from boyhood to manhood, but they do not have the same focus on survival in a stark environment that the Inuit stories reveal. Man, not nature, provides the chief threat. The Indian books are connected through the character Hooits: in *Ghost Paddle* he is the brave youth who will marry a princess of the Eagle clan; in *Eagle Mask* he is the grandfather in the royal line of that same clan. *Eagle Mask*, written first, tells of the coming of age of Hooits' grandson, Skemshan. Skemshan's transition from youth to man is marked by his merit in confronting a bear, in going whaling, in a minor encounter with raiders, and in receiving a spiritual message from a sacred eagle. Though the details of Indian life are interesting and certain events are exciting, the book's structure is weak: difficulties with point-of-view, transitions, and a plethora of minor episodes produce an unintegrated work. *Ghost Paddle*, written more recently, is better unified. In it Hooits himself makes the jump from boyhood to manhood by virtue of his courage and compassion during an attempt to reconcile the Eagle and Raven clans. He is successful without bloodshed, and the novel ends with a statement opposing the "killing winds of war," a sentiment similar to that of *The White Archer*.

Overall, Houston's work conveys well the everyday life of the people he portrays and the environmental reality of the regions in which they live. He is at his best in presenting the plight of protagonists struggling for survival: the inner conflict against one's own flagging will as well as the external conflict against the environment. In all cases, incidentally, Houston's illustrations are indispensable to the novels.

—John Robert Sorfleet

HUGHES, Richard (Arthur Warren). British. Born in Weybridge, Surrey, 19 April 1900. Educated at Charterhouse School, Surrey; Oriel College, Oxford, B.A. 1922. Served in the British Army, 1918; in the Admiralty, London, 1940–45: O.B.E. (Officer, Order of the British Empire), 1946. Married Frances C. R. Bazley in 1932; five children. Co-Founder, and Director, Portmadoc Players, Wales, 1922–25; Vice-Chairman, Welsh National Theatre, 1924–36; Petty Constable of Langharne, 1936; Filmwriter, Ealing Studies, London, 1945–55. Recipient: Femina Vie Heureuse Prize, 1929; Arts Council Award, 1961; Welsh Arts Council Award, 1973. D.Litt.: University of Wales, Cardiff, 1956. Fellow, Royal Society of Literature, 1962. Honorary Member, American Academy of Arts and Letters (Blashfield Foundation Address, 1969). *Died 28 April 1976.*

PUBLICATIONS FOR CHILDREN

Fiction

> *The Spider's Palace and Other Stories*, illustrated by George Charlton. London, Chatto and Windus, 1931; New York, Harper, 1932.
> *Don't Blame Me! and Other Stories*, illustrated by Fritz Eichenberg. London, Chatto and Windus, and New York, Harper, 1940.
> *Gertrude's Child*, illustrated by Rick Schreiter. New York, Harlin Quist, 1966; London, W. H. Allen, 1967.
> *The Wonder-Dog: Collected Stories for Children.* London, Chatto and Windus, and New York, Morrow, 1977.

PUBLICATIONS FOR ADULTS

Novels

> *A High Wind in Jamaica.* London, Chatto and Windus, 1929; as *The Innocent Voyage*, New York, Harper, 1929.
> *In Hazard: A Sea Story.* London, Chatto and Windus, 1938; as *In Hazard*, New York, Harper, 1938.
> *The Human Predicament:*
>   1. *The Fox in the Attic.* London, Chatto and Windus, and New York, Harper, 1961.
>   2. *The Wooden Shepherdess.* London, Chatto and Windus, and New York, Harper, 1973.

Short Stories

> *A Moment of Time.* London, Chatto and Windus, 1926.
> *Burial, and The Dark Child* (verse and story). Privately printed, 1930.

Plays

>   *The Sisters' Tragedy* (produced Oxford and London, 1922).   Oxford, Blackwell, 1922.
>   *The Man Born to Be Hanged* (produced Portmadoc, 1923; London, 1924). Included in
>   *The Sisters' Tragedy and Other Plays*, 1924.
>   *A Comedy of Good and Evil* (produced London, 1924; as *Minnie and Mr. Williams*,
>   produced New York, 1948).   Included in *The Sisters' Tragedy and Other Plays*,
>   1924.
>   *Danger* (broadcast, 1924).   Included in *The Sisters' Tragedy and Other Plays*, 1924.
>   *The Sisters' Tragedy and Other Plays* (includes *The Man Born to Be Hanged, A Comedy
>   of Good and Evil, Danger*).   London, Heinemann, 1924; as *A Rabbit and a Leg:
>   Collected Plays*, New York, Knopf, 1924.

Radio Play: *Danger*, 1924.

Verse

>   *Lines Written upon First Observing an Elephant Devoured by a Roc* ....   London,
>   Golden Cockerel Press, 1922.
>   *Gipsy Night and Other Poems.*   London, Golden Cockerel Press, and Chicago, Ransom,
>   1922.
>   *Ecstatic Ode on Vision.*   Privately printed, 1923.
>   *Meditative Ode on Vision.*   Privately printed, 1923.
>   *Confessio Juvenis: Collected Poems.*   London, Chatto and Windus, 1925.

Other

>   *Richard Hughes: An Omnibus*   .New York, Harper, 1931.
>   *The Administration of War Production*, with J. D. Scott.   London, Her Majesty's
>   Stationery Office, 1956.

>   Editor, with Robert Graves and Alan Porter, *Oxford Poetry 1921*.   Oxford, Blackwell,
>   1921.
>   Editor, *Poems*, by John Skelton.   London, Heinemann, 1924.

*   *   *

Richard Hughes' understanding of the child mind is demonstrated most convincingly not in the small books which he wrote specifically for young readers, but in that remarkable novel on which his reputation was first based, *A High Wind in Jamaica.* Early in the story the children experience one of those minor earth-tremors which are commonplace in the tropics. They are told that it is an earthquake. At the end of the book, after tempest, piracy and murder, they reach safety. What they remember most is that they have been in an earthquake. The precise nature of the protective sieve through which their experiences have been filtered remains unstated, but anyone who works with children will recognize the authenticity of the author's observation.

The two volumes of short stories written for children are admittedly minor writing, trifles tossed off for particular occasions and not regarded seriously by the writer. This is not to say that he withholds part of his creative skills. Hughes was always a craftsman, with respect for his medium whatever the prospective audience. *The Spider's Palace* is a set of twenty stories written under stimulus of Hughes' friendship with Clough Williams-Ellis and his family, and the first tale − "Living in W'ales" − pays good-humoured tribute to the architect and his infectious enthusiasms. Similarly *Don't Blame Me!* is the result of the Second World War, when seven children from Merseyside arrived on the author's doorstep in North Wales. In the months before they drifted home he told them this baker's-dozen of stories.

Richard Hughes has two favourite devices. One is the literal interpretation of a colloquial expression. In "The Elephant's Picnic" in the second and better volume, the elephant fills the saucepan with water and pops the kettle in it to boil. The kettle refuses to get tender, so the elephant unpacks his trunk and sleeps comfortably in his pyjamas, while the unfortunate kangaroo, who has no trunk and consequently no night-wear, stays awake and keeps the fire going. In the morning the kettle is "as tender as tender could be." The second device is the application of fairy-tale conventions to a contemporary scene. In the title story a young man buys a motor-bike which metamorphoses into a crocodile. The humour is consistently serious, with none of the posturing which many writers for adults adopt when entertaining the young. The stories are distinguished by a plain unadorned prose. For this reason, as well as for the fertile inventiveness of the narrative and the pervading humour, they have always been popular with those who tell stories aloud. They need to be told "just-so," but the effect is one of spontaneous creation.

—Marcus Crouch

HUGHES, Shirley.   British.   Born near Liverpool, Lancashire, 16 July 1929. Educated at West Kirby High School for Girls; Liverpool Art School; Ruskin School of Art, Oxford. Married John Vulliamy in 1952; has three children. Free-lance illustrator and writer. Currently, Visiting Tutor in Illustration, Ruskin School of Art, Oxford. Recipient: Children's Rights Workshop Other Award, 1976. Agent: A.P. Watt and Son, 26–28 Bedford Row, London WC1R 4HL. Address: 63 Lansdowne Road, London W11 2LG, England.

PUBLICATIONS FOR CHILDREN (illustrated by the author)

Fiction

> *Lucy and Tom's Day.*   London, Gollancz, and New York, Scott, 1960.
> *The Trouble with Jack.*   London, Bodley Head, 1970.
> *Lucy and Tom Go to School.*   London, Gollancz, 1973.
> *Sally's Secret.*   London, Bodley Head, 1973.
> *Helpers.*   London, Bodley Head, 1975; as *George the Babysitter*, Englewood Cliffs, New Jersey, Prentice Hall, 1977.
> *Lucy and Tom at the Seaside.*   London, Gollancz, 1976.
> *Dogger.*   London, Bodley Head, 1977.

Illustrator: *World's End Was Home* by Nan Chauncy, 1952; *Follow the Footprints*, 1953, *The World Upside Down*, 1954, *The Toffee Join*, 1968, all by William Mayne; *All Through the Night* by Rachel Field, 1954; *The Bell Family*, 1954, *New Town*, 1960, *The Painted Garden*, revised edition, 1961, all by Noel Streatfeild; *The Journey of Johnny Rew* by Anne Barrett, 1954; *Mr. Punch's Cap* by Kathleen Fidler, 1956; *The Man of the House* by Allan Campbell McLean, 1956; *William and the Lorry*, 1956, and *The Merry-Go-Round*, 1963, by Diana Ross; *Guns in the Wild*, 1956, *Katy at Home*, 1957, *Katy at School*, 1959, all by Ian Serraillier; *Lost Lorrenden*, 1956, *Fiona on the Fourteenth Floor*, 1964, *The Sign of the Unicorn*, 1968, *The Wood Street Group*, 1970, *The Wood Street Secret*, 1970, *The Wood Street Rivals*, 1971, *The Wood Street Helpers*, 1973, *Away from Wood Street*, 1976, all by Mabel Esther Allan; *Adventure on Rainbow Island*, 1957, *The Jade Green Cadillac*, 1958, *The Lost Tower Treasure*, 1960, *The Singing Strings*, 1961, *Operation Smuggle*, 1964, all by Dorothy Clewes; *Rolling On*, 1960, and *Cottage by the Lock*, 1962, by Mary Cockett;

Flowering Spring, by Elfrida Vipont, 1960; *Fell Farm Campers* by Marjorie Lloyd, 1960; *Fairy Tales*, 1961, and *More Fairy Tales*, 1970, by Hans Christian Andersen; *The Bronze Chrysanthemum* by Sheena Porter, 1960; *Plain Jane*, 1961, *Place Mill*, 1962, *A Stone in a Pool*, 1964, all by Barbara Softly; *Willy Is My Brother*, by Peggy Parish, 1963; *The Shinty Boys*, 1963, and *The New Tenants*, 1968, by Margaret MacPherson; *Tim Rabbit's Dozen* by Alison Uttley, 1964; *Roller Skates*, 1964, and *Lucinda's Year of Jubilo*, 1965, by Ruth Sawyer; *The Cat and Mrs. Cary* by Doris Gates, 1964; *Stories from Grimm*, 1964; *Tales the Muses Told* by Roger Lancelyn Green, 1965; *The Twelve Dancing Princesses*, 1965; *Kate and the Family Tree*, 1965, *The Smallest Doll*, 1966, *The Smallest Bridesmaid*, 1966, all by Margaret Storey; *The Faber Book of Nursery Stories* edited by Barbara Ireson, 1966; *The Witch's Daughter*, 1966, and *Squib*, 1971, by Nina Bawden; *Little Bear's Pony*, 1966, and *Hazy Mountain*, 1975, by Donald Bisset; *Wayland's Keep* by Angela Bull, 1966; *Satchkin Patchkin*, 1966, *Mary Kate and the School Bus*, 1970, *Mary Kate*, 1972, *Mrs. Pinny and the Salty Sea Day*, 1972, *Mrs. Pinny and the Blowing Day*, 1976, all by Helen Morgan; *Porterhouse Major* by Margaret J. Baker, 1967; *Home and Away* by Ann Thwaite, 1967; *A Day on Big O*, 1968, and *Rainbow Pavement*, 1970, by Helen Cresswell; *When My Naughty Little Sister Was Good*, 1968, *All about My Naughty Little Sister*, 1969, *More Naughty Little Sister Stories*, 1970, *My Naughty Little Sister and Bad Harry*, 1974, *My Naughty Little Sister Goes Fishing*, 1976, all by Dorothy Edwards; *A Crown for a Queen*, 1968, *The Toymaker's Daughter*, 1968, *Malkin's Mountain*, revised edition, 1970, *The Three Toymakers*, revised edition, 1970, all by Ursula Moray Williams; *Flutes and Cymbals* edited by Leonard Clark, 1968; *The Bicycle Wheel*, 1969, *The Ruth Ainsworth Book*, 1970, *The Phantom Fisherboy*, 1974, all by Ruth Ainsworth; *Moshie Cat*, 1969, and *Federico*, 1971, by Helen Griffiths; *Stories for Seven-Year-Olds*, 1969, *Stories for Five-Year-Olds*, 1973, *Stories for Under-Fives*, 1974, all edited by Sara Corrin; *Cinderella* by Charles Perrault, 1970; *Eight Days to Christmas*, 1970, and *Ginger*, 1972, by Geraldine Kaye; *The Lost Angel* by Elizabeth Goudge, 1971; *The Smell of Privet* by Barbara Sleigh, 1971; *Burnish Me Bright* by Julia W. Cunningham, 1971; *The Little Broomstick* by Mary Stewart, 1971; *Dancing Day* by Robina Willson, 1971; *The Thirteen Days of Christmas* by Jenny Overton, 1972; *A House in the Square* by Joan Robinson, 1972; *The First [Second, Third] Margaret Mahy Story Book*, 1972, 1973, 1975; *Hospital Day* by Leila Berg, 1972; *Where Do We Go from Here?* by Josephine Kamm, 1972; *Mother's Help* by Susan Dickinson, 1972; *The Hollywell Family* by Margaret Kornitzer, 1973; *The Gauntlet Fair* by Alison Farthing, 1974; *Jacko and Other Stories* by Jean Sutcliffe, 1974; *Miss Hendy's House* by Joan Drake, 1974; *Peter Pan and Wendy* retold by May Byron, 1976; *The Snake Crook* by Ruth Tomalin, 1976; *Make Hay While the Sun Shines* edited by Alison Abel, 1977; *A Throne for Sesame* by Helen Young, 1977.

Shirley Hughes comments:

If all the words I've written were collected together, the result would be a very slim volume indeed. Having worked for years as an interpretive illustrator in both colour and line, I approached the business of writing through wanting to design my own picture-books. In conceiving a story, I tend to think in pictures rather than words, and the text develops out of these, like the captions to a silent film.

I feel that the words in a picture book should carry the bare bones of the narrative, constantly referring attention to the pictures where the richness and detail of the story lies. They should point up the humour and help to build up the visual climaxes, sometimes not by what they describe but what they leave for the reader to see for himself. But they must always sound well read aloud.

My own books have grown out of real situations with which very small children can identify, perhaps even at an age before they can fully appreciate fairy tales. They are mostly set in a city background – my own part of London to be exact. The domestic details are very local and English, but I hope the themes are fairly universal.

*   *   *

Adults admire artistry; children look at pictures as a representation of their world. When they are discovering books and learning to read the young need the recognition and redundancy of another point of view, to see themselves and to investigate other people, places and things. Shirley Hughes's fluent gift is for drawing solidly real children, in motion or at rest so that they come as more than design figures. They are the graphic equivalent of rounded characters, alive because they run, eat, play, sleep and explore in the way of children, scattering the detritus of childhood, boxes, scales, paint, food, not as waste, but as significant form. While children's book illustration has wound through phases of flat stylish design, Shirley Hughes has stayed in the mainstream of the English tradition. Her drawing recalls the draughtsmanship of the late 19th century wood engravers.

In the books where she is both artist and writer (*Lucy and Tom's Day, Lucy and Tom Go to School, Helpers*) there is a subtlety of social comment in the domestic detail, despite the "unproblematic" nature of the earlier books. The baby-sitter in *Helpers* is a teenage boy. The faces in the scene in the recreation park reflect multi-ethnic London. Domestic interiors offer spilling toy cupboards, a clutter of clutchable objects with fingers in corners and pots. Jeans, wellingtons, jumpers and socks are textured and folded, hair is tangibly cropped, bunched and frizzed round the individual faces. The soft and floppy pose of babies, the thickness of toddlers, and the straight seriousness of schoolgirls are all depicted against the background of teeming West London streets, playgrounds and schools. There is no casual anonymity about any of Shirley Hughes's drawings. One feels she knows these children well, in action and at rest. There is a strong suggestion that her characters all talk to each other.

For all the naturalism of her own stories Shirley Hughes is greatly in demand as an illustrator of fantasy and poetry. In addition, some well-known characters, like Dorothy Edwards' Naughty Little Sister, now seem indissolubly linked to Shirley Hughes' drawings. Whether in black and white or pen and colour they are instantly recognisable. A special success is the Bodley Head *Cinderella* where the period of the original Perrault tale is beautifully caught. A knowledge of the history of costume gives Shirley Hughes' illustrations authenticity and style.

In that there is a face that represents children in England (not necessarily white) where childhood ripens, Shirley Hughes draws it. Her work wins for her admirers who believe that her talent is underestimated because of its very distinctiveness. A retrospective exhibition of her many modes would show her to be indeed a versatile and distinctive artist in the great tradition of English illustration.

—Margaret Meek

HUGHES, Ted. British. Born in Mytholmroyd, Yorkshire, in 1930. Educated at Mexborough Grammar School, Yorkshire; Pembroke College, Cambridge, B.A. 1954, M.A. 1959. Served in the Royal Air Force for 2 years. Married the poet Sylvia Plath in 1956 (died, 1963); Carol Orchard, 1970; has one son and one daughter. Worked as a rose gardener and night watchman; Reader for the Rank Organization. Since 1965, Editor, with Daniel Weissbort, *Modern Poetry in Translation* magazine, London. Recipient: New York Poetry Center First Publication Award, 1957; Guinness Award, for verse, 1958; Guggenheim Fellowship, 1959; Maugham Award, 1960; Hawthornden Prize, for verse, 1961; City of Florence International Poetry Prize, 1969; Queen's Gold Medal for Poetry, 1974. Address: c/o Faber and Faber Ltd., 3 Queen Square, London WC1N 3AU, England.

PUBLICATIONS FOR CHILDREN

Fiction

How the Whale Became and Other Stories, illustrated by George Adamson. London, Faber, 1961; New York, Atheneum, 1964.
The Iron Man: A Story in Five Nights, illustrated by George Adamson. London, Faber, 1968; as The Iron Giant: A Story in Five Nights, New York, Harper, 1968.

Plays

Beauty and the Beast (televised, 1968; produced London, 1971). Included in The Coming of the King and Other Plays, 1970.
The Coming of the King and Others Plays (includes The Tiger's Bones; Beauty and the Beast; Sean, The Fool, The Devil and the Cats). London, Faber, 1970; augmented edition, as The Tiger's Bones and Other Plays for Children (includes Orpheus), New York, Viking Press, 1973.
Sean, The Fool, The Devil and the Cats (produced London, 1971). Included in The Coming of the King and Other Plays, 1970.
The Coming of the King (televised, 1972). Included in The Coming of the King and Other Plays, 1970.
The Iron Man, adaptation of his own story (televised, 1972). London, Penguin, 1973.

Television Plays: Beauty and the Beast, 1968; The Coming of the King, 1972; The Iron Man, 1972.

Verse

Meet My Folks, illustrated by George Adamson. London, Faber, 1961; Indianapolis, Bobbs Merrill, 1973.
The Earth-Owl and Other Moon-People, illustrated by R. A. Brandt. London, Faber, 1963; New York, Atheneum, 1964.
Nessie the Mannerless Monster, illustrated by Gerald Rose. London, Faber, and New York, Chilmark Press, 1964.
Autumn Song, illustrated by Nina Carroll. Kettering, Northamptonshire, Nina Stearne, 1970.
Season Songs, illustrated by Leonard Baskin. New York, Viking Press, 1975; London, Faber, 1976.
Moon-Whales and Other Poems, illustrated by Leonard Baskin. New York, Viking Press, 1976.

Other

Poetry Is. New York, Doubleday, 1970.

PUBLICATIONS FOR ADULTS

Plays

The Calm (produced Boston, 1961).
The Wound (broadcast, 1962). Included in Wodwo, 1967.
Seneca's Oedipus (produced London, 1968; Los Angeles, 1973). London, Faber, 1969; New York, Doubleday, 1972.
Orghast (produced Persepolis, 1971).
The Story of Vasco, music by Gordon Crosse (produced London, 1974).

Radio Plays: *The House of Aries*, 1960; *A Houseful of Women*, 1961; *The Wound*, 1962; *Difficulties of a Bridegroom*, 1963; *Dogs*, 1964.

Verse

The Hawk in the Rain.   London, Faber, and New York, Harper, 1957.
Lupercal.   London, Faber, and New York, Harper, 1960.
Selected Poems, with Thom Gunn.   London, Faber, 1962.
The Burning of the Brothel.   London, Turret Books, 1966.
Recklings.   London, Turret Books, 1966.
Scapegoats and Rabies: A Poem in Five Parts.   London, Poet and Printer, 1967.
Animal Poems.   Crediton, Devon, Gilbertson, 1967.
Five Autumn Songs for Children's Voices.   Crediton, Devon, Gilbertson, 1968.
The Martyrdom of Bishop Farrer.   Crediton, Devon, Gilbertson, 1970.
A Crow Hymn.   Frensham, Surrey, Sceptre Press, 1970.
A Few Crows.   Exeter, Rougemont Press, 1970.
Crow: From the Life and Songs of the Crow.   London, Faber, 1970; New York, Harper,
     1971; revised edition, Faber, 1972.
Corgi Modern Poets in Focus 1, with others, edited by Dannie Abse.   London, Corgi,
     1971.
Crow Wakes: Poems.   London, Poet and Printer, 1971.
Poems, with Ruth Fainlight and Alan Sillitoe.   London, Rainbow Press, 1971.
Eat Crow.   London, Rainbow Press, 1972.
Selected Poems 1957–1967.   London, Faber, 1972; New York, Harper, 1973.
In the Little Girl's Angel Gaze.   London, Steam Press, 1972.
Cave Birds.   London, Scolar Press, 1975.
Eclipse.   Knotting, Bedfordshire, Sceptre Press, 1976.
Gaudete.   London, Faber, 1977.

Other

Wodwo (miscellany).   London, Faber, and New York, Harper, 1967.

Editor, with Patricia Beer and Vernon Scannell, *New Poems 1962.*   London,
     Hutchinson, 1962.
Editor, with Thom Gunn, *Five American Poets.*   London, Faber, 1963.
Editor, *Here Today.*   London, Hutchinson, 1963.
Editor, *Selected Poems,* by Keith Douglas.   London, Faber, and New York, Chilmark
     Press, 1964.
Editor, *Poetry in the Making: An Anthology of Poems and Programmes from "Listening
     and Writing."*   London, Faber, 1967.
Editor, *A Choice of Emily Dickinson's Verse.*   London, Faber, 1971.
Editor, *A Choice of Shakespeare's Verse.*   London, Faber, 1971; as *Poems: With
     Fairest Flowers While Summer Lasts: Poems from Shakespeare,* New York,
     Doubleday, 1971.
Editor, *Selected Poems,* by Yehuda Amichai.   London, Penguin, 1971.
Editor, *Crossing the Water,* by Sylvia Plath.   London, Faber, 1971; as *Crossing the
     Water: Transitional Poems,* New York, Harper, 1971.

Translator, with Janos Csokits, *Selected Poems,* by Janos Pilinszky.   Manchester,
     Carcanet Press, 1976.

*   *   *

Bearing in mind even the precedent of T. S. Eliot and *Old Possum,* few could have expected such an *eminence noir* of contemporary poetry as Ted Hughes to have followed the fierce poetic energy, the searingly realistic view of the battle between the forces of life and death contained in *The Hawk in the Rain* and *Lupercal*, with *Meet My Folks*.

But, particularly in a writer of Hughes' formidable power and accomplishment, there are more ways than one of conveying a conception of reality; and the significance should never be forgotten of Hughes' remark in *Poetry for You*: "Poets write poems to amuse themselves, partly." Occasionally, the touch in *Meet My Folks*, a bizarre verse gallery of imaginary family portraits, is uncertain. But there is more than a hint of things to come in Hughes' work for children: the frequent, unmistakeable buzz of imaginative shock:

> That crack in the road looks harmless. My Father knows it's not.
> The world may be breaking into two and starting at that spot.

The Earth-Owl is an attempt, disturbingly and enrichingly successful, to detect and identify those secret creatures colonizing the worlds within us, inhabiting the thought-planets drifting somewhere beyond the rim of the mind, and from which perhaps our dreams arise. The often long and galumphing lines of verse sometimes drop to earth, winded; but the shorter, tauter poems are unremittingly effective and create for the reader a whole new area of imaginative experience.

Aimed at rather young children and couched mainly in lines that shamble and sprint in the manner of a pantomime horse, *Nessie the Mannerless Monster* springs to life the moment the creature rises in the loch and "smashes the water to mist." It is a joyful, life-enhancing fable: a form Hughes adopts with immensely increased authority and originality in the prose *How the Whale Became*. Equally effective as these creation-myth stories is *The Iron Man*, told in language as clear and strong as pebbles, and in which the boy Hogarth confronts the unknown with courage and a growing self-knowledge.

The story is weakened only by its somewhat predictable ending; but there can be no such reservation about *Season Songs*. These poems present an unforgettable vision: of winter's attack; of the oak as a railway station where one waits for spring ("Will it stop for you?"); of the newly-born March calf plunging "to scatter his seething joy ... to find himself himself." The hunted stag doubles back weeping as the huntsmen pull aside "the camouflage of their terrible planet"; and the famous murder of Cock Robin is re-enacted as the death of summer, a tractor ("with my gear grinding glottle") voicing its own particular lament and promise.

Nothing in the whole canon of Ted Hughes' work so clearly illuminates the qualities of mystery and revelation lying at its core: a celebration, in subtly-balanced terms, of victor and vanquished, survivor and slain. Many children enter, vicariously, the world of writers of Hughes' stature through the work of other, perhaps lesser, poets. Such an approach is unnecessary here; and the good fortune is not only the child's.

—Charles Causley

HULME BEAMAN, S(ydney) G(eorge). British. Born in Tottenham, London, in 1886. Married Maud Mary Poltock; one son and one daughter. Actor, artist, toymaker; worked for the BBC, London. *Died 4 February 1932.*

PUBLICATIONS FOR CHILDREN (illustrated by the author)

Fiction

Jerry and Joe. London, Oxford University Press, 1925.
Trouble in Toyland. London, Oxford University Press, 1925.

The Road to Toytown.   London, Oxford University Press, 1925.

The Wooden Knight.   London, Oxford University Press, 1925.

Out of the Ark Books (*Teddy's New Job, Wally the Kangaroo, Grunty the Pig, Jimmy the Baby Elephant, Ham and the Egg, Jenny the Giraffe*).   London and New York, Warne, 1927.

The Tale of the Magician.   London, Oxford University Press, 1928.

The Tales of the Inventor.   London, Oxford University Press, 1928.

The Tale of Captain Brass, The Pirate.   London, Oxford University Press, 1928.

Tales of Toytown.   London, Oxford University Press, 1928.

John Trusty.   London, Collins, 1929; New York, Collins, 1930.

Wireless in Toytown.   London, Collins, 1930.

The Toytown Book.   London and New York, Warne, 1930.

Ernest the Policeman.   New York, Oxford University Press, 1930.

The Toytown Mystery.   London, Collins, 1932.

The Mayor's Sea Voyage.   London, Collins, 1938.

Stories from Toytown.   London, Oxford University Press, 1938.

The Arkville Dragon.   London, Collins, 1938.

Dirty Work at the Dog and Whistle, illustrated by Ernest Noble. London, Lapworth, 1942.

Tea for Two, illustrated by Ernest Noble.   London, Lapworth, 1942.

The Brave Deed of Ernest the Policeman, illustrated by Ernest Noble.   London, Lapworth, 1942; as *Ernest the Brave*, London, Oldbourne, 1958.

Pistols for Two, illustrated by Ernest Noble.   London, Lapworth, 1942.

Mr. Noah's Holiday, illustrated by Ernest Noble.   London, Lapworth, 1942.

Mr. Growser Moves, illustrated by Ernest Noble.   London, Lapworth, 1943; as *Mr. Growser Moves House*, London, Oldbourne, 1962.

Dreadful Doings in Ark Street, illustrated by Ernest Noble.   London, Lapworth, 1943.

Golf (Toytown Rules), illustrated by Ernest Noble.   London, Lapworth, 1943.

Frightfulness in the Theatre Royal, illustrated by Ernest Noble.   London, Lapworth, 1943.

Larry the Lamb.   London, Collins, 1946.

The Extraordinary Affair of Ernest the Policeman, illustrated by Ernest Noble.   London, Lapworth, 1947.

A Portrait of the Mayor, illustrated by Ernest Noble.   London, Lapworth, 1947.

The Disgraceful Business at Mrs. Goose's, with Betty Hulme Beaman, illustrated by Kenneth Lovell.   London, Oldbourne, 1958.

The Enchanted Ark, with Betty Hulme Beaman, illustrated by Kenneth Lovell.   London, Oldbourne, 1958.

Toytown Goes West, with Betty Hulme Beaman, illustrated by Kenneth Lovell.   London, Oldbourne, 1958.

The Theatre Royal and Punch and Judy, with Betty Hulme Beaman, illustrated by Kenneth Lovell.   London, Oldbourne, 1958.

A Toytown Christmas Party, illustrated by Kenneth Lovell.   London, Oldbourne, 1961.

The Toytown Treasure, with Betty Hulme Beaman, illustrated by Kenneth Lovell.   London, Oldbourne, 1961.

Larry the Plumber, with Betty Hulme Beaman, illustrated by Betty Larom.   London, Oldbourne, 1961.

The Conversion of Mrs. Growser, illustrated by Betty Larom.   London, Oldbourne, 1961.

The Great Toytown War, illustrated by Betty Larom.   London, Oldbourne, 1961.

How the Radio Came to Toytown, illustrated by Kenneth Lovell.   London, Oldbourne, 1961.

The Showing Up of Larry the Lamb, illustrated by Kenneth Lovell.   London, Oldbourne, 1963.

The Toytown Pantomime, illustrated by H. Faithful.   London, Oldbourne, 1963.

Other

Aladdin, Retold.   London, Lane, 1924; New York, McBride, 1925.
The Seven Voyages of Sinbad, Retold.   London, Lane, and New York, McBride, 1926.

Illustrator: *The Strange Case of Dr. Jekyll and Mr. Hyde* by Robert Louis Stevenson, 1930.

*   *   *

S. G. Hulme Beaman was creator, writer and illustrator of the magic land of Toytown and all its enchanting characters, including Larry the Lamb, Dennis the Dachshund, Mr. Growser, Ernest the Policeman, the Mayor, the Magician, the Inventor, Mrs. Goose, et al. After his first collection, *Tales of Toytown*, was published in 1928, it caught the eye of May E. Jenkin, better-known as "Elizabeth" of the popular BBC radio programme Children's Hour, who produced it on the air with great success, in 1929. The plays were extremely successful and Beaman was commissioned to write more, turning out 36 stories over the next three years, until his untimely death in 1932 at the age of 45. The stories were broadcast in Children's Hour many times over the next thirty years and were firm favourites with children of all ages. They also appeared in book form, later winning popularity with a new generation when they appeared in a TV series in 1972, when the characters also appeared in a new children's comic-paper, *Toytown*.

Beaman's illustrations were unique inasmuch as he first carved his characters from wood, arranged them in his home-made model theatre, lit them, and then drew the resulting lay-out, so that his creations always appeared to have a wooden, but three-dimensional look about them.

The Toytown stories came over far more successfully on radio than on the printed page (probably because, after all, the vast majority were specially written to be heard) and were performed in Children's Hour flawlessly and with enormous good humour by a talented cast. Derek McCulloch ("Uncle Mac"), Head of Children's Hour, played the role of Larry the Lamb, as well as narrating the plays.

The central figures in the Toytown tales were usually the mischievous pair, Larry the Lamb and his German-accented friend Dennis the Dachshund, who were forever getting themselves into complicated scrapes and incurring the wrath of the pompous Mayor, the irritable Mr. Growser ("It's dis-grrraceful and it ought not to be allowed!") and the rural-voiced, deliberate Ernest the Policeman ("I can see some names and addresses must be taken down!"). The delightfully-eccentric Magician and Inventor (whose spells and inventions were always going wrong and ending in disaster) were also well to the fore.

In his three-dozen stories and radio plays about Toytown, S. G. Hulme Beaman created a magical and gently-amusing miniature world which will remain affectionately in the memories of at least three generations.

—Brian Doyle

———————————

HUNT, Irene. American. Born in Newton, Illinois, 18 May 1907. Educated at the University of Illinois, Urbana, B.A. 1939; University of Minnesota, Minneapolis, M.A. 1946; University of Colorado, Boulder. French teacher, Oak Park public schools, Illinois, 1930–45; Instructor in Psychology, University of South Dakota, Vermillion, 1946–50. Teacher, 1950–65, and Director of Language Arts, 1965–69, Cicero public schools, Illinois. Recipient: American Library Association Newbery Medal, 1967. Address: 2587 Roy Hanna Drive South, St. Petersburg, Florida 33712, U.S.A.

PUBLICATIONS FOR CHILDREN

Fiction

> *Across Five Aprils.*   Chicago, Follett, 1964; London, Bodley Head, 1965.
> *Up a Road Slowly.*   Chicago, Follett, 1966; London, Macdonald, 1967.
> *Trail of Apple Blossom,* illustrated by Don Bolognese.   Chicago, Follett, 1968; London,
>   Blackie, 1970.
> *No Promises in the Wind.*   Chicago, Follett, 1970.
> *The Lottery Rose.*   New York, Scribner, 1976.
> *William.*   New York, Scribner, 1977.

Manuscript Collection: Kerlan Collection, University of Minnesota, Minneapolis.

*   *   *

With her first book, *Across Five Aprils,* Irene Hunt established herself as one of America's finest historical novelists. The story begins with the outbreak of the Civil War in April 1861 and ends in April 1865, shortly after the conflict has ended. Far from the actual battle scenes, the Creightons, on their farm in Southern Illinois, feel the cruel impact of war, caught as they are between the North and South. The scope of the narrative is broad, yet details of family life are intimate. The telling is poetic, compassionate, and sometimes angry.

Up a Road Slowly, perhaps the author's best-known novel, tells of a girl's growing up. When the book was awarded the Newbery Medal in 1967, Irene Hunt said in her acceptance speech:

> Often children are troubled and in a state of guilt. One can say to them, "You are not
> unique. There is in all of us only a thin veneer of civilization that separates us from the
> primitive." It is in books that one finds there are other cowards in the world, other
> youngsters who are ashamed of their environment, other people who have strange,
> dark thoughts, who have had experiences too ugly to admit. Julie, in *Up a Road
> Slowly,* is not set apart by virtue of her high-mindedness or moral values. But for a
> watchful family she might well have stepped into the same trouble in which some of
> her young readers may find themselves ....

Irene Hunt's third book, *Trail of Apple Blossoms,* recreates the life and times of John Chapman, known as Johnny Appleseed. In the early 1800's this American folk hero traveled alone through the Ohio Valley, planting apple seeds and seedling trees as he went. *Trail of Apple Blossom* is not a biography, but a historical novel, picturing Johnny Appleseed as he may have been – a heroic man with a reverence for life whose beneficent influence touched pioneer America.

No Promises in the Wind is a story of the United States in 1932, in the depths of the Great Depression. During this troubled time, bands of children took to the roads and roamed the country, eking out an existence as best they could. The book follows the adventures of two of these children, Josh Grondowski and his brother Joey, as they run away from their home in Chicago and wander south to Louisiana where they join a carnival. While the characterizations, particularly those of the brothers, are strong, the reader is likely to remember the story most for its realistic picture of the Depression in America.

The Lottery Rose begins with the grim story of George Burgess, a battered child. Misunderstood at school, brutally abused at home, he centers all his affection and hope on the rosebush he won in a lottery. Removed from his home and placed in a school for boys, he resists the kindness he is shown. It is only gradually, through the patience of teachers and his involvement in someone else's tragedy, that he begins to reach out to others. Irene Hunt's novel is searching, poignant, and uncompromisingly honest.

—Clyde Robert Bulla

HUNT, Mabel Leigh. American. Born in Coatesville, Indiana, 1 November 1892. Educated at DePauw University, Greencastle, Indiana, 1910–12; Western Reserve University Library School, 1923–24. Children's and branch librarian, Indianapolis, 1926–38. *Died 3 September 1971.*

PUBLICATIONS FOR CHILDREN

Fiction

Lucinda, A Little Girl of 1860, illustrated by Cameron Wright. New York, Stokes, 1934.

The Boy Who Had No Birthday, illustrated by Cameron Wright. New York, Stokes, 1935.

Little Girl with Seven Names, illustrated by Grace Paull. New York, Stokes, 1936.

Susan, Beware!, illustrated by Mildred Boyle. New York, Stokes, 1937.

Benjie's Hat, illustrated by Grace Paull. New York, Stokes, 1938.

Little Grey Gown, illustrated by Ilse Bischoff. New York, Stokes, 1939.

Michel's Island, illustrated by Kate Seredy. New York, Stokes, 1940.

John of Pudding Lane, illustrated by Clotilde Funk. New York, Stokes, 1941.

Billy Button's Butter'd Biscuit, illustrated by Katherine Milhous. New York, Stokes, 1941; London, Standard Art Book Company, 1943.

Corn-Belt Billy, illustrated by Kurt Wiese. New York, Grosset and Dunlap, 1942.

Peter Piper's Pickled Peppers, illustrated by Katherine Milhous. New York, Stokes, 1942; London, Standard Art Book Company, 1943.

The Peddler's Clock, illustrated by Elizabeth Orton Jones. New York, Grosset and Dunlap, 1943.

The Young Man of the House, illustrated by Louis Slobodkin. Philadelphia, Lippincott, 1944.

Sibby Botherbox, illustrated by Marjory Collison. Philadelphia, Lippincott, 1945.

Such a Kind World, illustrated by Edna Potter. New York, Grosset and Dunlap, 1947.

The Double Birthday Present, illustrated by Elinore Blaisdell. Philadelphia, Lippincott, 1947.

Matilda's Buttons, illustrated by Elinore Blaisdell. Philadelphia, Lippincott, 1948.

The Wonderful Baker, illustrated by Grace Paull. Philadelphia, Lippincott, 1950.

The Sixty-Ninth Groundchild, illustrated by Elinore Blaisdell. Philadelphia, Lippincott, 1951.

Ladycake Farm, illustrated by Clotilde Funk. Philadelphia, Lippincott, 1952.

Singing among Strangers, illustrated by Irene Gibian. Philadelphia, Lippincott, 1954.

Miss Jellytot's Visit, illustrated by Velma Ilsley. Philadelphia, Lippincott, 1955.

Stars for Cristy, illustrated by Velma Ilsley. Philadelphia, Lippincott, 1956; London, Blackie, 1958.

Cristy at Skippinghills, illustrated by Velma Ilsley. Philadelphia, Lippincott, 1958; London, Blackie, 1960.

Cupola House, illustrated by Nora S. Unwin. Philadelphia, Lippincott, 1961.

Johnny-Up and Johnny-Down, illustrated by Harold Berson.   Philadephia, Lippincott, 1962.
Beggar's Daughter.   Philadelphia, Lippincott, 1963.

Other

"Have You See Tom Thumb?" (biography of Charles Sherwood Stratton), illustrated by Fritz Eichenberg.   New York, Stokes, 1942.
Better Known as Johnny Appleseed, illustrated by James Daugherty.   Philadelphia, Lippincott, 1950.
Tomorrow Will Be Bright (reader), illustrated by Tommy Shoemaker.   Boston, Ginn, 1958.

*   *   *

An author whose books appeal chiefly to pre-teenage girls, Mabel Leigh Hunt drew on her Quaker upbringing for several of her stories. *Lucinda*, her first book, the story of an Indiana Quaker child during the Civil War, has been praised for its well-chiseled prose and for the author's power to evoke the feeling of the Indiana countryside. A second book about a Quaker child, *Little Girl with Seven Names*, has retained its popularity, dealing as it does with a perennial childhood problem, the child who is teased in school because she is different. In Melissa-Louisa-Amanda-Miranda-Cynthia-Jane-Farlow's case, it is not her Quaker upbringing which brings her ridicule from her schoolmates, but her excessively long name. The ingenious way in which Melissa Louisa manages to rid herself of a couple of her forenames is the main thrust of the slim plot of this warm little book.

Miss Jellytot's Visit is the story of Katie O'Dea, who, after her mother has had a visitor, decides that she, too, wishes to be treated as a guest, and who, as Miss Jellytot, comes for a six-day "visit" to the O'Dea family. One of the first books to deal in a realistic, sympathetic way with a mother-child relationship, this gently humorous story still appeals to girls in the early grades.

Ladycake Farm, although it has been kept in print, has not fared as well as some of her other books at the hands of contemporary critics. One of the first books to attempt a realistic and sympathetic portrayal of blacks, it deals with a black family which buys a farm in a previously all-white area. Hard work and determination lead to the family's acceptance by their neighbors at the end of the story, but the father's advice to his children to smile in the face of insults, has been felt by many reviewers to be degrading. In comparison with most current fiction for children about blacks, *Ladycake Farm* now seems dated; few children will read it with pleasure.

Hunt's juvenile biographies are characterized by meticulous research and a feeling for the kind of interesting detail which serves to make the period come alive for a young reader. Still in print, her *Better Known as Johnny Appleseed* (1950), the life of the legendary John Chapman, was a Newbery Honor Book in 1951. Also well and accurately written is *"Have You Seen Tom Thumb?"*, a biography of the midget Charles Sherwood Stratton.

—Margaret Maxwell

HUNTER, Kristin.   American.   Born in Philadelphia, Pennsylvania, 12 September 1931. Educated at the University of Pennsylvania, Philadelphia, 1947–51, B.S. in education 1951. Married John I. Lattany in 1968. Teacher, Camden, New Jersey public schools, 1951; Copywriter, Lavenson Bureau of Advertising, Philadelphia, 1952–59; Research Assistant, School of Social Work, University of Pennsylvania, 1961–62; Copywriter, Wermen and

Schorr, Philadelphia, 1962–63; Information Officer, City of Philadelphia, 1963–64, 1965–66. Free-lance Writer since 1966. Since 1972, Lecturer in Creative Writing, University of Pennsylvania. Recipient: Fund for the Republic Prize, for television documentary, 1955; Whitney Fellowship, 1959; Sigma Delta Chi Award, for reporting, 1968; National Council on Interracial Books for Children Award, 1968; National Conference of Christians and Jews Brotherhood Award, 1969; *Book World* Festival award, 1973; Christopher Award, 1974. Agent: Harold Matson Company, 22 East 40th Street, New York, New York 10016. Address: P.O. Box 8371, Philadelphia, Pennsylvania 19101, U.S.A.

PUBLICATIONS FOR CHILDREN

Fiction

> *The Soul-Brothers and Sister Lou.*   New York, Scribner, 1968; London, Macdonald, 1971.
> *Boss Cat*, illustrated by Harold Franklin.   New York, Scribner, 1971.
> *The Pool Table War.*   Boston, Houghton Mifflin, 1972.
> *Uncle Daniel and the Raccoon.*   Boston, Houghton Mifflin, 1972.
> *Guests in the Promised Land: Stories.*   New York, Scribner, 1973.

PUBLICATIONS FOR ADULTS

Novels

> *God Bless the Child.*   New York, Scribner, 1964; London, Muller, 1965.
> *The Landlord.*   New York, Scribner, 1966; London, Pan, 1970.
> *The Survivors.*   New York, Scribner, 1975.
> *The Lakestown Rebellion.*   New York, Scribner, 1978.

Plays

> *The Double Edge* (produced Philadelphia, 1965).

> Television Play: *Minority of One*, 1956.

*   *   *

Kristin Hunter's considerable reputation is based on a small body of work. The novel *The Soul-Brothers and Sister Lou*, the short stories *Guests in the Promised Land*, and the short humorous tale *Boss Cat* are all set in the same environment, the overcrowded, poor, mainly black, urban ghettos of the United States' East Coast. In *Sister Lou*, a 14-year-old girl sees her friends on the street hassled by police, denied every opportunity – even her own family distrusts them. She sees her mother always afraid of the unknown, entrapped by her fear of need, holding back her son from any chance to make his own way. There are dirt, anger, ugliness and fear in Hunter's ghetto – the police fatally shoot Lou's unarmed friend, mistaking his epilepsy for defiance. The novel reflects the 1960's. Afro-consciousness is emerging, anger is intensifying. But there is strong love in the families that struggle together and dance together. Sister Lou ends up with a successful rock group and money for college, an ending which has been attacked as contrived. It may be statistically unlikely, but it fits the mood of the book, the essentially undaunted optimism of the author whose unequivocal message is that the spark of life burns bright among the stereotyped disadvantaged. The stories in *Guests in the Promised Land* expand and reinforce this message. Time has moved on and drugs have moved onto the streets as yet another hazard for those growing up there. A stretch in prison teaches Junior the realities of being a small-time crook; Little David talks the

King Kongs out of rumbling with the Kools; and Robert will not settle for being a guest in the promised land and reacts with violence and destruction at the white man's country club.

Children's books have generally ignored or romanticized ghetto life. Hunter's work is optimistic but not in any way idealized. Her vision is steely when it views cruelty or discrimination. Her books open a salutary window on this world for young people of other cultures and other backgrounds, but for those who know her world and live there, suddenly there is someone who not only understands, but tells it like it is.

—Brigitte Weeks

HUNTER, Mollie. Scottish. Born in Longniddry, East Lothian, 30 June 1922. Educated at Preston Lodge School, East Lothian. Married Thomas McIlwraith in 1940; has two sons. Recipient: Scottish Arts Council Literary Award, 1972; Child Study Association of America award, 1972; Library Association Carnegie Medal, 1975; May Hill Arbuthnot Lectureship, 1975. Agent: A. M. Heath and Co. Ltd., 40–42 William IV Street, London WC2N 4DF, England; or, McIntosh and Otis Inc., 475 Fifth Avenue, New York, New York 10017, U.S.A. Address: The Shieling, Milton, by Drumnadrochit, Inverness-shire, Scotland.

PUBLICATIONS FOR CHILDREN

Fiction

> *Patrick Kentigern Keenan*, illustrated by Charles Keeping. London, Blackie, 1963; as *The Smartest Man in Ireland*, New York, Funk and Wagnalls, 1965.
> *Hi Johnny*, illustrated by Drake Brookshaw. London, Evans, 1963.
> *The Kelpie's Pearls*, illustrated by Charles Keeping. London, Blackie, 1964; New York, Funk and Wagnalls, 1966.
> *The Spanish Letters*, illustrated by Elizabeth Grant. London, Evans, 1964; New York, Funk and Wagnalls, 1967.
> *A Pistol in Greenyards*, illustrated by Elizabeth Grant. London, Evans, 1965; New York, Funk and Wagnalls, 1968.
> *The Ghosts of Glencoe*. London, Evans 1966; New York, Funk and Wagnalls, 1969.
> *Thomas and the Warlock*, illustrated by Charles Keeping. London, Blackie, and New York, Funk and Wagnalls, 1967.
> *The Ferlie*, illustrated by Michael Morse. London, Blackie, and New York, Funk and Wagnalls, 1968.
> *The Bodach*, illustrated by Gareth Floyd. London, Blackie, 1970; as *The Walking Stones*, New York, Harper, 1970.
> *The Lothian Run*. New York, Funk and Wagnalls, 1970; London, Hamish Hamilton, 1971.
> *The 13th Member*. New York, Harper, and London, Hamish Hamilton, 1971.
> *The Haunted Mountain*, illustrated by Trevor Ridley. London, Hamish Hamilton, and New York, Harper, 1972.
> *A Sound of Chariots*. New York, Harper, 1972; London, Hamish Hamilton, 1973.
> *The Stronghold*. New York, Harper, and London, Hamish Hamilton, 1974.
> *A Stranger Came Ashore*. London, Hamish Hamilton, and New York, Harper, 1975.
> *The Wicked One*. London, Hamish Hamilton, and New York, Harper, 1977.
> *A Furl of Fairy Wind*, illustrated by Steven Gammel. New York, Harper, 1977.

PUBLICATIONS FOR ADULTS

Plays

> *A Love-Song for My Lady* (produced Inverness, 1961).   London, Evans, 1961.
> *Stay for an Answer* (produced Inverness, 1962).   London, French, 1962.

Other

> *Talent Is Not Enough: Writing for Children.*   New York, Harper, 1976.

Mollie Hunter comments:

I write for children because I like them *as people*; because I'm an entertainer, a teller of tales, and the way young minds work gives me an opportunity to explore in story terms the workings of my own mind. My books for young readers are drawn from a study of folklore in all its aspects, and owe their style to the tradition of the orally-transmitted tale which may sustain a high degree of poetic imagery. The language needed to attempt this permits of development on two levels – a superficial one of incident, and a deeper one of symbolism; but the same requirements of this chosen language pattern are exactly those which make the story suitable for reading aloud to children who cannot yet follow the text for themselves.

The historical novels for older readers subscribe to the traditional form of written literature. The motivation behind them is no more than a desire to dip into the past and come back with some exciting story. But this story must, in itself, be a timeless one springing from a theme which is universally human; and so, in these books, this is the point at which I always eventually aim – to write a story which will not only hold the reader's interest simply *as* a story, but in which also any reader at any time may see him or her self reflected.

*   *   *

Mollie Hunter's writings fall into two categories: history, and folklore and magic. All are written with the same vigour and feeling for atmosphere which won for her the Carnegie Medal for *The Stronghold* in 1974. No-one who heard her acceptance speech was left in any doubt of the author's involvement with her work, or, indeed, her love of it.

Her books for young children are mainly based on folklore and magic, like *The Kelpie's Pearls* and *Thomas and the Warlock*. Even those, admittedly fantasy, have magnificently credible characters and the unfailing "quality" which lifts her books out of the ordinary and makes them memorable.

Her historical novels, mainly for older children, make good use of her detailed research and come over with notable reality. She is unfailing in her technical and historical research and the success of her plots owes a great deal to design and little to accident. Her ever-present awareness of the supernatural permeates her historical novels and gives the stories that spine-chilling quality beloved of all readers.

Therein, probably, lies the weak point. "Readers" love Mollie Hunter's books, but the poorer reader may find them hard to get into, or miss a subtle point. The strength and vigour of her writing, and the brilliant use of language, while making her books outstanding in a literary sense, cut her off from a large proportion of young readers. For these children, however, they provide an excellent source for storytelling.

The author deserves acclaim for the ability she has to make all stories ring true, whether it be due to her own research (as into Orcadian history and the brochs for *The Stronghold*), or to her own personal experiences (as the adolescent girlhood described in *A Sound of Chariots*). Her imaginative writing has opened the door into fantasy and history for many young people. Long may it continue to do so.

—Mary Nettlefold

639

HUNTER, Norman (George Lorimer). British. Born in Sydenham, Kent, 23 November 1899. Educated at Beckenham County School, Kent. Served in the London Irish Rifles, and at Headquarters, 9th Division, 1918–19. Married Sylvia Mary Rangel in 1923; has three children. Chief Copywriter, S. H. Benson Ltd., London, 1938–49; P. N. Barrett Company, Johannesburg, 1949–58; Central Advertising Ltd., Johannesburg, 1958–70. Also a conjurer: has performed at Maskelyne's Theatre of Magic, St. George's Hall, London, and at the Little Theatre, London; Associate of the Inner Magic Circle. Address: 23 St. Olave's Close, Penton Road, Staines, Middlesex TW18 2LH, England.

PUBLICATIONS FOR CHILDREN

Fiction

The Bad Barons of Crashbania, illustrated by Eve Garnett. Oxford, Blackwell, 1932.
The Incredible Adventures of Professor Branestawm, illustrated by W. Heath Robinson. London, Lane, 1933.
Professor Branestawm's Treasure Hunt and Other Incredible Adventures, illustrated by James Arnold. London, Lane, 1937.
Larky Legends, illustrated by James Arnold. London, Lane, 1938; abridged edition, as *The Dribblesome Teapots and Other Incredible Stories*, London, Bodley Head, 1969.
Stories of Professor Branestawm, illustrated by W. Heath Robinson. Leeds, E. J. Arnold, 1939.
Jingle Tales. London, Warne, 1941.
The Peculiar Triumph of Professor Branestawm, illustrated by George Adamson. London, Bodley Head, 1970.
The Home-Made Dragon and Other Incredible Stories, illustrated by Fritz Wegner. London, Bodley Head, 1971.
Professor Branestawm Up the Pole, illustrated by George Adamson. London, Bodley Head, 1972.
The Frantic Phantom and Other Incredible Stories, illustrated by Geraldine Spence. London, Bodley Head, 1973.
Wizards Are a Nuisance, illustrated by Quentin Blake. London, BBC Publications, 1973.
Professor Branestawm's Great Revolution, illustrated by David Hughes. London, Bodley Head, 1974.
Dust-Up at the Royal Disco, illustrated by Fritz Wegner. London, Bodley Head, 1975.
Professor Branestawm 'round the Bend, illustrated by Derek Cousins. London, Bodley Head, 1977.

Other

Puffin Book of Magic, illustrated by Jill McDonald. London, Penguin, 1968; as *Norman Hunter's Book of Magic*, London, Bodley Head, 1974.
Professor Branestawm's Dictionary, illustrated by Derek Cousins. London, Bodley Head, 1973.
Professor Branestawm's Compendium of Puzzles, illustrated by Derek Cousins. London, Bodley Head, 1975.
Professor Branestawm's Do-It-Yourself Handbook, illustrated by Jill McDonald. London, Bodley Head, 1976.

Other

> Simplified Conjuring for All: A Collection of New Tricks Needing No Special Skill or
> Apparatus, with Suitable Patter. London, Pearson, 1923.
> Advertising Through the Press: A Guide to Press Publicity. London and New York,
> Pitman, 1925.
> New and Easy Magic: A Further Series of Novel Magical Experiments Needing No
> Special Skill or Apparatus for Their Performance, With Suitable Patter. London,
> Pearson, 1925.
> Hey Presto: A Book of Effects for Conjurers, illustrated by Sid Lorraine. London, E.
> Bagshawe, 1931.
> New Conjuring Without Skill. London, Lane, 1935.
> Successful Conjuring for Amateurs, edited by F. J. Camm. London, Pearson, 1951; as
> Successful Magic for Amateurs, New York, Arco, 1952; revised edition, as Successful
> Conjuring, Arco, 1964.

Norman Hunter comments:

I write two kinds of children's books – well, three kinds if you include my books on magic and how-to-do-it. I began by writing stories about funny kings and queens in which I took plots from traditional fairy tales and bent them out of shape a bit. These stories have now developed into a series of adventures of the King and Queen of Incrediblania. The other books deal with the adventures of Professor Branestawm, a highly-learned gentleman who spends so much time knowing about extraordinary things he has no time to think of ordinary ones. He invents machines which eventually turn on him and has the kind of adventures an absent-minded professor might well have, only a great deal more so. The magic overflows into the stories to some extent because I frequently visit libraries, schools, book exhibitions and bookshops and do a little magic show in which some of the magic is tied up with Professor Branestawm and his inventions.

I am sometimes asked what age children my books appeal to. I think the Incrediblania stories are appreciated by children from about 7 or perhaps younger, while the Professor Branestawm stories are for slightly older ones, say from 9, but a lot depends on the children. As the books are funny I also have a number of adult readers and I find Mums and Dads are quite happy to read my stories to their children and sometimes sneak the books away from the children to read themselves, which I like very much.

*   *   *

Sheer high spirits and exuberant good humour are the hallmarks of Norman Hunter's popular comic stories. *The Incredible Adventures of Professor Branestawm* and its sequel, *Professor Branestawm's Treasure Hunt* were first published in the 1930's, and have retained their comic appeal for children ever since. Taking the stock figure of the eccentric, absent-minded Professor, Mr. Hunter made an engagingly dotty and unworldly character of him, gave him two faithful companions – Colonel Dedshott of the Catapult Cavaliers, none too bright but a loyal friend, and the much-tried housekeeper Mrs. Flittersnoop, always on the point of going off to stay with sister Aggie until the latest trouble is over – and involved them in a series of crazy misadventures arising from the Professor's weird machines, which never, of course, perform in exactly the way intended.

Some of these earlier stories, though they are enjoyed by children as much as ever, show their age now, with their emphasis, for instance, on radio broadcasting and mention of the long defunct Children's Hour. But Hunter has kept his hero up with the times, and since his own retirement and return to England from South Africa has published further Professor Branestawm collections, where the Professor shows himself quite at home with television, supermarkets and so on (even if he falls foul of the Way Ahead and Right Outside Group of Advanced Artists by agreeing with Mrs. Flittersnoop that her little nephew could do better. The irate artists take their revenge on the Professor's painting machine, "loosening screws and inserting plastic spanners of very bad design into the works"). Perhaps the humour of these later collections is slightly too sophisticated, compared to that of their predecessors, to suit the taste of the modern child, but the appeal still lies in the delightfully farcical situations and the author's command of comic language, with many incidental touches such as the alarm clock which "sounded more like Robin Hood's wedding in technicolour than an alarm clock." This is a very English type of humour, including the timeless setting of the little town of Great Pagwell with its municipal bureaucracy.

Hunter's other stories have been comic fairy tales. This is a difficult genre to tackle; the dangers of coyness and whimsy lie in wait, but Hunter avoids them, again by the genial verve of his language: who could resist the King of Incrediblania's comment that he sees "a most second-hand-looking person" coming down the street, or the remark that "horses are deliberately unsuitable on battleships"? These stories are well served by the pleasingly ornate illustrations of Fritz Wegner, as was Professor Branestawm first by Heath Robinson and later by George Adamson.

—Anthea Bell

HYDE, Laurence (Evelyn).   British.   Born in London, 6 June 1914. Educated at schools in Canada. Married Elizabeth Bambridge in 1939; has one son. Since 1942, Writer, Film Director and Producer, National Film Board of Canada, Montreal. Address: 15 Crichton Street, Ottawa, Ontario K1M 2ES, Canada.

PUBLICATIONS FOR CHILDREN

Fiction

   Brave Davy Coon, illustrated by the author.   New York, Harper, 1955.
   Under the Pirate Flag, illustrated by Victor Mays.   Boston, Houghton Mifflin, 1965.
   Captain Deadlock, illustrated by Charles Geer.   Boston, Houghton Mifflin, 1968.

PUBLICATIONS FOR ADULTS

Novel

   Southern Cross: A Novel of the South Seas, Told in Wood Engravings, with a Review of Stories in Pictures from Earliest Times.   Los Angeles, Ward Ritchie Press, 1951.

*   *   *

Laurence Hyde's books for children owe more to his English background than to the character or literature of his adopted country.

Brave Davy Coon, his first book, is a picture story for young readers about a raccoon who is maligned by other animals because he sleeps during the day and roams at night. This slight, neatly produced little book is illustrated by the author with line drawings.

Hyde is better known for two lively well-paced adventure stories set in the late 18th and early 19th centuries and conceived in the style of Robert Louis Stevenson. They concern Stephen Carruthers, saved in infancy from a wreck in which his parents were lost, and raised on the south shore of Nova Scotia. In *Under the Pirate Flag* he is trapped by pirates on an off-shore island and, seeing it as his only means of escape, hides on the pirate ship. He sails in her to the West Indies, his presence known only to the ship's carpenter. There the crew attempt a mutiny against the brutal captain. In the ensuing violence Stephen finds himself pitted against the captain and the situation is finally resolved by the arrival of the British navy.

In the second book, *Captain Deadlock*, Stephen has returned to Glasgow to claim his parental inheritance. During a journey to Plymouth he becomes the innocent accomplice in a plot involving a diamond necklace, part of the French crown jewels. It leads him among pirates, highwaymen, Napoleonic blockade runners and to a dungeon in Saint Malo.

Both books are first person narratives, written in the formal English of the period in which they are set. Whereas the situations and characters are placed in plausible historical context, the emphasis is on adventure and there has been little attempt to develop settings. Major characters are drawn in some detail and sharp sketches of hard-core villains create suspense and a sense of danger which give the books credibility.

—Ruth Osler

ISH-KISHOR, Sulamith. American. Recipient: Jewish Book Council of America Charles and Bertie Schwartz Award, 1964, 1972. Lives in New York City. Address: c/o Pantheon Books, 201 East 50th Street, New York, New York 10022, U.S.A.

PUBLICATIONS FOR CHILDREN

Fiction

The Heaven on the Sea and Other Stories, illustrated by Penina Ish-Kishor. New York, Bloch, 1924.

Little Potato and Other Stories, illustrated by J. Russack. New York, Board of Education, 1937.

How the Weatherman Came, illustrated by Rebecca Andrews. New York, Board of Education, 1938.

The Palace of Eagles and Other Stories, illustrated by Alice Horodisch. New York, Schoulson Press, 1948.

The Stranger Within the Gates and Other Stories, illustrated by Alice Horodisch. New York, Schoulson Press, 1948.

A Boy of Old Prague, illustrated by Ben Shahn. New York, Pantheon Books, 1963; London, Chatto and Windus, 1966.

Our Eddie. New York, Pantheon Books, 1969.

Drusilla: A Novel of the Emperor Hadrian, illustrated by Thomas Morley. New York, Pantheon Books, 1970.

The Master of Miracle: A New Novel of the Golem, illustrated by Arnold Lobel. New York, Harper, 1971.

Other

The Bible Story. New York, United Synagogue of America, 1921.

The Children's Story of the Bible. New York, Educational Stationery House, 1930.

Children's History of Israel from the Creation to the Present Time. New York, Jordan, 3 vols., 1930–33.

643

Jews to Remember, illustrated by Kyra Markham.   New York, Hebrew Publishing
Company, 1941.
American Promise: A History of Jews in the New World, illustrated by Grace
Hick.   New York, Behrman House, 1947.
Friday Night Stories, 1, 2, and 4.   New York, Women's League of the United
Synagogue of America, 3 vols., 1949.
The Carpet of Solomon: A Hebrew Legend, illustrated by Uri Shulevitz.   New York,
Pantheon Books, 1966.
Pathways Through the Jewish Holidays, edited by Benjamin Efron.   New York, Ktav,
1967.

PUBLICATIONS FOR ADULTS

Other

Magnificent Hadrian: A Biography.   New York, Minton Balch, and London, Gollancz,
1935.
Everyman's History of the Jews.   New York, Fell, 1948.
How Theodor Herzl Created the Jewish National Fund.   New York, Jewish National
Fund, 1960.
Blessed Is the Daughter, with Meyer Wazman and Jacob Sloan.   New York, Shengold,
1960.

*   *   *

Sulamith Ish-Kishor's writing reveals substantial and sure knowledge of her subject
matter. Her contribution lies especially in two novels and a legend.

Her book *A Boy of Old Prague* represents a difficult feat. Tomás, a Christian boy, is bound
to a Jewish family. He takes with him insidious, evil tales he has heard about the Jews. As he
experiences life in the Ghetto, and a pogrom, he is drawn to Jews and develops compassion
and understanding. The plight of the Jews in the 16th century is so skillfully related that the
reader gains insight into the injustices dealt to them throughout history. Without
pyrotechnics, the author lets her story unfold, and it is her understatement that gives the
novel a quiet but gripping power. Ish-Kishor not only interprets the past but also illuminates
the present, a true mark of excellence.

Our Eddie offers another facet of Jewish life. The story of the Raphel family, first in
England and then in New York, centers on Eddie's short life. Interwoven is the effect of
Rabbi Raphel's religious fanaticism on Eddie and on the rest of the family. There is keen
perception of Eddie as a human being, and as the son of a man who cannot bring himself to a
realization of what society apart from his own vision is like. This is a tapestry of a particular
kind of Jewish life full of emotion, conflict and contrast. The author's reminiscences are
deeply moving, agonizing at times, with a masterful blending of story and style.

Ish-Kishor retells a brief but important Hebrew legend in *The Carpet of Solomon*. Her love
for the tale is evident as she describes Solomon's dream in which he goes to the end of the
Earth by means of a magic carpet. His humbling experiences draw him closer to the wisdom
for which he is known. The author creates an appropriate atmosphere and sets a dream-like
mood. The underlying message is delivered with no sermonizing.

Her knowledge of Jewish history, mores, and legends is enhanced by an intensity of style
appropriate for each book. She has the touch of the craftsman coupled with an artistic use of
language.

—Mae Durham Roger

JACKSON, Jesse. American. Born in Columbus, Ohio, 1 January 1908. Attended Ohio State University, Columbus, 1927–29; Breadloaf Writers' Conference, Vermont, 1944. Married Ann Newman in 1938; has one daughter. Worked in boys' camps and with private youth agencies, and as a juvenile probation officer; worked for the Bureau of Economic Research. Since 1974, Lecturer, Appalachian State University, Boone, North Carolina. Recipient: MacDowell Colony fellowship; National Council for the Social Studies Carter G. Woodson Award, 1975. Agent: Anita Dimant, Writers' Workshop Inc., 51 East 42nd Street, New York, New York 10017. Address: Appalachian State University, Faculty Apartment 106, Boone, North Carolina 28508, U.S.A.

PUBLICATIONS FOR CHILDREN

Fiction

Call Me Charley, illustrated by Doris Spiegel. New York, Harper, 1945.
Anchor Man, illustrated by Doris Spiegel. New York and London, Harper, 1947.
Room for Randy, illustrated by Frank Nicholas. New York, Friendship Press, 1957.
Charley Starts from Scratch. New York, Harper, 1958.
Tessie, illustrated by Harold James. New York, Harper, 1968.
The Sickest Don't Always Die the Quickest. New York, Doubleday, 1971.
The Fourteenth Cadillac. New York, Doubleday, 1972.

Other

Black in America: A Fight for Freedom, with Elaine Landau. New York, Messner, 1973.
Make a Joyful Noise unto the Lord: The Life of Mahalia Jackson, Queen of Gospel Singers. New York, Crowell, 1974.

*   *   *

Jesse Jackson's fictional works center around teenage blacks – the problems and joys of growing up in the ghetto. Jackson's works reveal his own cultural heritage, but not his his life style. His background enables him to depict with accuracy the life style of many of his characters, including Tessie or Charley. The cultural background of both characters is similar to the author's own which enables him to relate experiences about his characters in such a way that the reader can visualize and interact with Tessie and Charley.

The books in the Charley series tell about the adventures of Charles Moss growing up in the ghetto and his experiences in school. His many friendships and endeavors, problems, jobs, and athletic pursuits are vividly described.

Tessie portrays a young black girl growing up in Harlem during her teenage years. The stories tell of the joys, disappointments, and experiences encountered by Tessie and her many friends.

Jesse Jackson writes simply and believably. His characters seem vibrant and their adventures realistic. He describes each event as if he had personally lived it. In spite of the fact that his works are tinged with "ghettoism" his way with words captures his audience. His works are black-oriented, but are so written that they appeal to any ethnic group.

Jackson did stray from his works of fiction to write a biography of Mahalia Jackson. The life story of this great gospel singer is woven very gracefully into an easily readable work. The book tells of Mahalia Jackson's life from the church choir in New Orleans where she began singing at 5 years of age until she reached the peak of her career.

Jesse Jackson ranks with other writers who tell interesting and exciting tales involving the cultural heritage of which they are a part.

—Dolores C. Leffall

JAMES, Will. Pseudonym for Joseph Ernest Nephtali Dufault. Canadian. Born in St. Nazaire de Acton, Quebec, 6 June 1892. Attended Catholic primary school, Montreal; California School of Fine Arts, 1919; Yale University School of Fine Art, New Haven, Connecticut, 1921. Served in the United States Army, 1918–19. Married Alice Conradt in 1920 (separated, 1935). Worked as cowhand, rodeo rider, stunt man for Thomas Ince Studio, Hollywood. Served a prison sentence for cattle rustling, 1915. Recipient: American Library Association Newbery Medal, 1927. *Died 3 September 1942.*

PUBLICATIONS FOR CHILDREN (illustrated by the author)

Fiction

> *Smoky the Cowhorse.* New York and London, Scribner, 1926.
> *Sand.* New York and London, Scribner, 1929.
> *Sun Up: Tales of the Cow Camps.* New York and London, Scribner, 1931.
> *Big Enough.* New York and London, Scribner, 1931.
> *Uncle Bill: A Tale of Two Kinds of Cowboy.* New York and London, Scribner, 1932.
> *In the Saddle with Uncle Bill.* New York and London, Scribner, 1935.
> *Young Cowboy.* New York, Scribner, 1935.
> *Scorpion, A Good Bad Horse.* New York and London, Scribner, 1936.
> *Look-See with Uncle Bill.* New York and London, Scribner, 1938.
> *The Dark Horse.* New York and London, Scribner, 1939.
> *My First Horse.* New York, Scribner, 1940.
> *Horses I've Known.* New York, Scribner, 1940.

Other

> *Cowboys North and South.* New York and London, Scribner, 1924.
> *Drifting Cowboy.* New York and London, Scribner, 1925.
> *Lone Cowboy: My Life Story.* New York and London, Scribner, 1930.
> *Cowboy in the Making.* New York and London, Scribner, 1937.
> *The Will James Cowboy Book,* edited by Alice Dalgliesh. New York, Scribner, 1938.

PUBLICATIONS FOR ADULTS

Novels

> *The Three Mustangeers.* New York and London, Scribner, 1933.
> *Home Ranch.* New York and London, Scribner, 1935.
> *Flint Spears, Cowboy Rodeo Contestant.* New York, Scribner, 1938.
> *The American Cowboy.* New York, Scribner, 1942.

Short Stories

> *Book of Cowboy Stories.* New York, Scribner, 1951; London, Phoenix House, 1952.

Other

Cow Country.   New York and London, Scribner, 1927.
All in a Day's Riding.   New York and London, Scribner, 1933.

Illustrator: *Wild Animal Homesteads* by Enos A. Mills, 1923; *Tombstone: An Iliad of the Southwest* by Walter Noble Burns, 1933.

*   *   *

The stories written by Will James, a cowboy himself, concern cowboys and horses, all that relates to the lives of cowboys and horses. At one time controversial for its colloquial quality, James's style is the spoken language of the range-rider, or seems to be; its grammatical structures are convincingly those of idiomatic language. Despite the credible dialect of poorly educated cowhands, the stories are filled with fine stylistic elements. With visual imagery, James describes the cow country and its rugged terrain, the range and its prairie vastness. When James writes of horses, his language is equally vivid, for he recreates the squeak of saddle leather, the shaking of a corral as a pony hits the earth, the stirring of dust that looks like a "young cloud." The action of the horses, as they writhe, bucking and struggling, or plunge, gallop or buck, is convincingly vivid. The stories, despite the expected limitations of subject matter, come alive when they describe the actions of the cow ponies.

Characterization is most convincing when James writes of horses, the "crethures" he loves so well. One horse is different from another, despite the similar natures of their lives. Perhaps James assumes more knowledge of the horse's thinking than a realistic story should, but James is not overwhelmingly sentimental. He confines himself largely to telling what Smoky, his most famous horse character, sees, rather than revealing Smoky's emotions. This reserve is necessary, helpful in making the horses convincing characters. James's stories do not have clear themes beyond the unifying idea that a cowboy's life is filled with hard work that he loves.

When James's stories focus on the cowboy rather than on the horse, they lose some of their vitality. In recreating the routine, the training, the activities of cowboy life, James seems to make a typical cowboy of every character, rather than making a cowboy a believable human being.

James was his own illustrator, and he showed great skill in depicting horses in all attitudes and poses; his realistic pictures are alive with motion, and his horses seem alive with muscular vitality.

—Rebecca J. Lukens

JARRELL, Randall.   American.   Born in Nashville, Tennessee, 6 May 1914. Educated at Vanderbilt University, Nashville, B.S. (Phi Beta Kappa) in psychology 1936. M.A. in English 1939. Served as a celestial navigation tower operator in the United States Army Air Corps, 1942–46. Married Mary Eloise von Schrader in 1952. Instructor in English, Kenyon College, Gambier, Ohio, 1937–39, University of Texas, Austin, 1939–42, and Sarah Lawrence College, Bronxville, New York, 1946–47; Associate Professor, 1947–58, and Professor of English, 1958–65, Women's College of the University of North Carolina (later, University of North Carolina at Greensboro). Lecturer, Salzburg Seminar in American Civilization, 1948; Visiting Fellow in Creative Writing, Princeton University, New Jersey, 1951–52; Fellow, Indiana School of Letters, Bloomington, Summer 1952; Visiting Professor of English, University of Illinois, Urbana, 1953; Elliston Lecturer, University of Cincinnati, Ohio, 1958; Phi Beta Kappa Visiting Scholar, 1964–65. Acting Literary Editor, *The Nation*, New York,

1946–47; Poetry Critic, *Partisan Review*, New Brunswick, New Jersey, 1949–53, and *Yale Review*, New Haven, Connecticut, 1955–57; Member of the Editorial Board, *American Scholar*, Washington, D.C., 1957–65. Consultant in Poetry, Library of Congress, Washington, D.C., 1956–58. Recipient: *Southern Review* Prize, 1936; Jeanette Sewell Davis Prize, 1943, Levinson Prize, 1948, and Oscar Blumenthal Prize, 1951 (*Poetry*, Chicago); J. P. Bishop Memorial Literary Prize (*Sewanee Review*), 1946; Guggenheim Fellowship, 1946; National Institute of Arts and Letters grant, 1951; National Book Award, for verse, 1961; Oliver Max Gardner Award, University of North Carolina, 1962; American Association of University Women Award, 1964; Ingram Merrill Award, 1965. D.H.L.: Bard College, Annandale-on-Hudson, New York, 1962. Member, National Institute of Arts and Letters; Chancellor, Academy of American Poets, 1956. *Died 14 October 1965.*

PUBLICATIONS FOR CHILDREN

Fiction

The Gingerbread Rabbit, illustrated by Garth Williams.   New York, Macmillan, and London, Collier Macmillan, 1964.
The Bat-Poet, illustrated by Maurice Sendak.   New York, Macmillan, 1964; London, Collier Macmillan, 1966.
The Animal Family, illustrated by Maurice Sendak.   New York, Pantheon Books, 1965; London, Hart Davis, 1967.
Fly by Night, illustrated by Maurice Sendak.   New York, Farrar Straus, 1976; London, Bodley Head, 1977.

Verse

A Bat Is Born, illustrated by John Schoenherr.   New York, Doubleday, 1977.

Other

The Rabbit Catcher and Other Fairy Tales of Ludwig Bechstein.   New York, Macmillan, and London, Macmillan, 1962.
The Golden Bird and Other Fairy Tales by the Brothers Grimm.   New York, Macmillan, 1962.
Snow-White and the Seven Dwarfs: A Tale from the Brothers Grimm, illustrated by Nancy Ekholm Burkert.   New York, Farrar Straus, 1972; London, Penguin, 1974.
The Juniper Tree and Other Tales from Grimm, with Lore Segal, illustrated by Maurice Sendak.   New York, Farrar Straus, 1973.

PUBLICATIONS FOR ADULTS

Novel

Pictures from an Institution: A Comedy.   New York, Knopf, and London, Faber, 1954.

Play

The Three Sisters, adaptation of a play by Chekhov (produced New York, 1964).   New York, Macmillan, 1969.

Verse

Five Young American Poets, with others.   New York, New Directions, 1940.
Blood for a Stranger.   New York, Harcourt Brace, 1942.

Little Friend, Little Friend. New York, Dial Press, 1945.

Losses. New York, Harcourt Brace, 1948.

The Seven-League Crutches. New York, Harcourt Brace, 1951.

Selected Poems. New York, Knopf, 1955; London, Faber, 1956.

Uncollected Poems. Cincinnati, Ohio, privately printed, 1958.

The Woman at the Washington Zoo: Poems and Translations. New York, Atheneum, 1960.

Selected Poems. New York, Atheneum, 1964.

The Lost World: New Poems. New York, Macmillan, 1965; London, Eyre and Spottiswoode, 1966.

The Complete Poems. New York, Farrar Straus, 1969; London, Faber, 1971.

The Achievement of Randall Jarrell: A Comprehensive Selection of His Poems with a Critical Introduction, by Frederick J. Hoffman. Chicago, Scott Foresman, 1970.

Jerome: The Biography of a Poem. New York, Grossman, 1971.

Other

Poetry and the Age (essays). New York, Knopf, 1953; London, Faber, 1955.

Poets, Critics, and Readers (address). Charlottesville, University of Virginia Press, 1959.

A Sad Heart at the Supermarket: Essays and Fables. New York, Atheneum, 1962; London, Eyre and Spottiswoode, 1965.

The Third Book of Criticism (essays). New York, Farrar Straus, 1969; London, Faber, 1974.

Editor, *The Anchor Book of Stories.* New York, Doubleday, 1958.

Editor, *The Best Short Stories of Rudyard Kipling.* New York, Doubleday, 1961.

Editor, *The English in England,* by Rudyard Kipling. New York, Doubleday, 1962.

Editor, *Six Russian Short Novels.* New York, Doubleday, 1963.

Editor, *The English in India: Short Stories in the Vernacular,* by Rudyard Kipling. Gloucester, Massachusetts, Peter Smith, 1970.

Translator, with Moses Hadas, *The Ghetto and the Jews of Rome,* by Ferdinand Gregorovius. New York, Schocken Books, 1948.

Translator, *Goethe's Faust: Part One.* New York, Farrar Straus, 1974.

Bibliography: *Randall Jarrell: A Bibliography* by Charles M. Adams, Chapel Hill, University of North Carolina Press, and London, Oxford University Press, 1958; supplement in *Analects I* (Greensboro, North Carolina), Spring 1964.

*   *   *

"The trouble isn't making poems," Randall Jarrell's little bat-poet bitterly says, "the trouble's finding somebody that will listen to them." Such an assertion, made by one of America's leading contemporary poets, gives rise to a series of speculations about Jarrell and his unique contribution to children's literature. For whereas reviewers hailed *The Animal Family,* the story of a lonely hunter who finds a mermaid, a bear, a lynx and a boy who live together in understanding, it becomes apparent that joy and a happy ending are what make most readers comfortable.

In his first book, *The Gingerbread Rabbit,* Jarrell also devises a happily-ever-after. But here he was only wetting his feet. Elements of "The Gingerbread Boy" permeate this story for the very young; there is but one verse in the book, the call of the vegetable man hawking turnip-greens (published in another form as an adult poem) and yet one can find all the embryonic themes which were used in his subsequent books – innocence, loneliness, the search for a home and fulfillment, fear, love and forebodings of death.

These themes recur on a far more poetic level in *The Animal Family*, *The Bat-Poet* and *Fly by Night*, and these books, one suspects, will stir and elicit a response now and in future years by the most sensitive adults and children. For the reaction of many reviewers and critics, among these (most amazingly!) other poets, often makes it painfully clear that the entire point of what Jarrell has so beautifully done is completely misunderstood. These critics fail to recognize that they are the pompous, egotistical mockingbirds of *The Bat-Poet* who listen only to their own songs and voices, who do not hear the little bat crying out in loneliness, with a need to be heard, loved, protected and accepted for his individual contribution. The hunter and mermaid of *The Animal Family* and David of *Fly by Night* represent, among others, those with this same loneliness and search. The knowledge that they are different from others, that growth is painful and love hard-won takes a different turn in all three books; each character has his mentor, his own personality, and whether in human or animal form, the fall from innocence is dealt with on various meaningful levels.

Jarrell drew from the animal world a symbolic level that deserves careful study. Is the owl of fear and possible death in *The Bat-Poet* any relation to the owl of security and mother-love of *Fly by Night*? The symbols are many, and Jarrell explored them through beautiful prose and magnificent poetry. It is quite possible, one feels, that the lack of formal poetry in *The Animal Family* makes it a less formidable more comfortable story for some readers.

As in his adult poetry, one is ever conscious that Jarrell was laying bare his own emotions in his work for children, and never more so than in *The Bat-Poet* which is, to me, the most eloquent story ever written about the sensitivity and life of a poet, about pompous critics, or, indeed, what the making of poems is all about.

—Myra Cohn Livingston

JELLICOE, Ann. British. Born in Middlesbrough, Yorkshire, 15 July 1927. Educated at Polam Hall, Darlington; Queen Margaret's, Castle Howard, Yorkshire; Central School of Speech and Drama (Elsie Fogarty Prize, 1947), 1944–47. Married C. E. Knight-Clarke in 1950 (marriage dissolved, 1961); Roger Mayne, 1962; has two children of the second marriage. Actress, Stage Manager, Director, in London and the provinces, 1947–51; Founding Director, Cockpit Theatre Club, London, 1950–53; Lecturer and Director, Central School of Speech and Drama, 1953–55; Literary Manager, Royal Court Theatre, London, 1973–75. Committee Member, League of Dramatists. Agent: Margaret Ramsay, 14a Goodwin's Court, London WC2N 4LL, England.

PUBLICATIONS FOR CHILDREN

Plays

> *You'll Never Guess* (also director: produced London, 1973). Included in *3 Jelliplays*, 1975.
> *Two Jelliplays: Clever Elsie, Smiling John, Silent Peter, and A Good Thing or a Bad Thing* (also director: produced London, 1974). Included in *3 Jelliplays*, 1975.
> *3 Jelliplays* (includes *You'll Never Guess; Clever Elsie, Smiling John, Silent Peter; A Good Thing or a Bad Thing*). London, Faber, 1975.

Plays

> *Rosmersholm*, adaptation of the play by Ibsen (also director: produced London, 1952; revised version, produced London, 1959).   San Francisco, Chandler, 1960.
> *The Sport of My Mad Mother* (also co-director: produced London, 1958).   Published in *The Observer Plays*, London, Faber, 1958; revised version, London, Faber, 1967; in *Two Plays*, 1964.
> *The Lady from the Sea*, adaptation of the play by Ibsen (produced London, 1961).
> *The Knack* (also co-director: produced Cambridge, 1961; London, 1962; Boston, 1963; New York, 1964).   London, Encore, and New York, French, 1962.
> *The Seagull*, With Ariadne Nicolaeff, adaptation of the play by Chekhov (produced London, 1964).
> *Der Freischütz*, translation of the libretto by Friedrich Kind, music by Weber (produced London, 1964).
> *Two Plays: The Knack and The Sport of My Mad Mother.*   New York, Dell, 1964.
> *Shelley; or, The Idealist* (also director: produced London, 1965).   London, Faber, and New York, Grove Press, 1966.
> *The Rising Generation* (produced London, 1967).   Published in *Playbill 2*, edited by Alan Durband, London, Hutchinson, 1969.
> *The Giveaway* (produced Edinburgh, 1968; London, 1969).   London, Faber, 1970.

Other

> *Some Unconscious Influences in the Theatre.*   London and New York, Cambridge University Press, 1967.
> *Devon: A Shell Guide*, with Roger Mayne.   London, Faber, 1975.

Theatrical Activities:

Director: **Plays** – *The Confederacy* by Vanbrugh, London, 1952; *The Frogs* by Aristophanes, London, 1952; *Miss Julie* by Strindberg, London, 1952; *Rosmersholm* by Ibsen, London, 1952; *Saints' Day* by John Whiting, London, 1953; *The Comedy of Errors*, London, 1953; *Olympia* by Ferenc Molnar, London, 1953; *The Sport of My Mad Mother* (co-director, with George Devine), London, 1958; *For Children* by Keith Johnstone, London, 1959; *The Knack* (co-director, with Keith Johnstone), London, 1962; *Skyvers* by Barry Reckord, London, 1963; *Shelley*, London, 1965; *You'll Never Guess*, London, 1973; *Two Jelliplays*, London, 1974; *A Worthy Guest* by Paul Bailey, London, 1974; *Six of the Best*, London, 1974.

*   *   *

Ann Jellicoe's first play for children was *You'll Never Guess*, a superb version of the Rumplestiltskin story. This was followed by *Clever Elsie, Smiling John, Silent Peter* and *A Good Thing or a Bad Thing*. These two plays demonstrate many of the aspects of the style which has made her adult plays so successful. In both plays a spare, realistic dialogue is used, and there is a sense of rhythm in the text which is particularly characteristic of her writing and requires careful attention in production. There is in neither play a hint of her using a special style for children, no fear of the whimsical patronising stuff children's plays are so often made of. A mother of two lively children herself, she understands what will make them laugh or simply engage their attention.

In *Clever Elsie* she takes a traditional tale as the basis for her play. In fact several age old ideas are there, besides the tale of Elsie's overactive imagination projecting a series of future disasters, all of them based on misunderstandings. It is a play of ideas, and works well with the full age range under 11 years, but it especially appeals to infants who are quite capable of grasping the fact that the characters' simplicity and lack of logic lead them up the wrong path. The young audience is placed in a position of greater knowledge, but knowledge gained by the children using their own powers of logic, and this adds to their delight.

In *A Good Thing or A Bad Thing* the overall story or plot is of more importance – again a story using traditional elements. There are a queen, a princess in need of rescue, and a monster to threaten both her and the audience. Her rescuer, however, is not the traditional prince but a mere gardener's boy, whom we see living in very ordinary circumstances with his mother. The monster is quite imaginary – it is never seen, only heard – but in production there is not a child in the audience who fails to see it, claws and all marching across the stage and dangerously near the front row! The tale is again a simple one but the conflicts presented are extremely powerful. The play is in fact essentially about power – the power of the mother, the ruler, the unknown and feared – which is why it evokes such a strong response from children.

This play differs from *Clever Elsie* in structure, in that Ann Jellicoe leaves more room for direct contact with the audience and suggests areas where ad-libbing and consultation with the children is vital to the play. *Clever Elsie* has a much more contained, constructed feel to it, so that if played with *A Good Thing or A Bad Thing* the two nicely compliment each other in style and make up an excellent programme.

Ann Jellicoe, who has herself both acted and directed, leaves room in both plays for the actor and director to complete the production. Neither play requires elaborate settings or effects and can be played not only in theatres but on tour in schools very easily, the only vital technical requirements being a reasonable sound system.

—Joan Mills

JOHNS, W(illiam) E(arl). British. Born in Hertford, 5 February 1893. Educated at Hertford Grammar School; articled to a Hertford surveyor, 1909–13. Entered the Norfolk Yeomanry, 1913, commissioned, 1916; served in the Middle East during the First World War; transferred to the Royal Flying Corps (later Royal Air Force), 1916 and served until 1930; Captain; served in the Ministry of Information, London, 1939–45. Air Correspondent for London and Continental newspapers. Founder-Editor, *Popular Flying*, 1932, and *Flying*, 1935. *Died 21 June 1968.*

PUBLICATIONS FOR CHILDREN

Fiction

> *The Camels Are Coming.* London, John Hamilton, 1932.
> *The Cruise of the Condor: A Biggles Story.* London, John Hamilton, 1933.
> *The Spy Flyers*, illustrated by Howard Leigh. London, John Hamilton, 1933.
> *Biggles Flies Again.* London, John Hamilton, 1934.
> *"Biggles" of the Camel Squadron.* London, John Hamilton, 1934.
> *Biggles Flies East*, illustrated by Howard Leigh and Alfred Sindall. London, Oxford University Press, 1935.
> *Biggles Hits the Trail*, illustrated by Howard Leigh and Alfred Sindall. London, Oxford University Press, 1935.
> *The Black Peril: A "Biggles" Story.* London, John Hamilton, 1935.
> *The Raid.* London, John Hamilton, 1935.

Sky High. London, Newnes, 1936; revised edition, London, Latimer, 1951.

Steeley Flies Again. London, Newnes, 1936; revised edition, London, Latimer, 1951.

Biggles in Africa, illustrated by Howard Leigh and Alfred Sindall. London, Oxford University Press, 1936.

Biggles & Co., illustrated by Howard Leigh and Alfred Sindall. London, Oxford University Press, 1936.

Biggles – Air Commodore, illustrated by Howard Leigh and Alfred Sindall. London, Oxford University Press, 1937.

Biggles Flies West, illustrated by Howard Leigh and Alfred Sindall. London, Oxford University Press, 1937.

Murder by Air. London, Newnes, 1937; revised edition, London, Latimer, 1951.

Biggles Flies South. London, Oxford University Press, 1938.

Biggles Goes to War, illustrated by Howard Leigh and Martin Tyas. London, Oxford University Press, 1938.

Champion of the Main, illustrated by M. Gooderham. London, Oxford University Press, 1938.

The Murder at Castle Deeping. London, John Hamilton, 1938.

Biggles Flies North, illustrated by Howard Leigh and Will Narraway. London, Oxford University Press, 1939.

Biggles in Spain, illustrated by Howard Leigh and J. Abbey. London, Oxford University Press, 1939.

The Rescue Flight: A Biggles Story, illustrated by Howard Leigh and Alfred Sindall. London, Oxford University Press, 1939.

Wings of Romance: A "Steeley" Adventure. London, Newnes, 1939; revised edition, London, Latimer, 1951.

Biggles in the Baltic, illustrated by Howard Leigh and Alfred Sindall. London, Oxford University Press, 1940.

Biggles in the South Seas, illustrated by Norman Howard. London, Oxford University Press, 1940.

Biggles – Secret Agent, illustrated by Howard Leigh and Alfred Sindall. London, Oxford University Press, 1940.

Worrals of the W.A.A.F. London, Lutterworth Press, 1941.

Spitfire Parade: Stories of Biggles in War-Time. London, Oxford University Press, 1941.

Biggles Sees It Through, illustrated by Howard Leigh and Alfred Sindall. London, Oxford University Press, 1941.

Biggles Defies the Swastika, illustrated by Howard Leigh and Alfred Sindall. London, Oxford University Press, 1941.

Biggles in the Jungle, illustrated by Terence Cuneo. London, Oxford University Press, 1942.

Biggles Sweeps the Desert. London, Hodder and Stoughton, 1942.

Worrals Flies Again. London, Hodder and Stoughton, 1942.

Worrals Carries On. London, Lutterworth Press, 1942.

Worrals on the War-Path: A Worrals of the W.A.A.F. Story, illustrated by Leslie Stead. London, Hodder and Stoughton, 1943.

Biggles – Charter Pilot. London, Oxford University Press, 1943.

Biggles "Fails to Return", illustrated by Leslie Stead. London, Hodder and Stoughton, 1943.

Biggles in Borneo. London, Oxford University Press, 1943.

King of the Commandos, illustrated by Leslie Stead. London, University of London Press, 1943.

Biggles in the Orient, illustrated by Leslie Stead. London, Hodder and Stoughton, 1944.

Gimlet Goes Again, illustrated by Leslie Stead. London, University of London Press, 1944.

Worrals Goes East, illustrated by Leslie Stead.   London, Hodder and Stoughton, 1944.

Worrals of the Islands: A Story of the War in the Pacific.   London, Hodder and Stoughton, 1945.

Biggles Delivers the Goods, illustrated by Leslie Stead.   London, Hodder and Stoughton, 1946.

Gimlet Goes Home.   London, University of London Press, 1946.

Sergeant Bigglesworth C.I.D., illustrated by Leslie Stead.   London, Hodder and Stoughton, 1946.

Comrades in Arms.   London, Hodder and Stoughton, 1947.

Gimlet Mops Up, illustrated by Leslie Stead.   Leicester, Brockhampton Press, 1947.

Worrals in the Wilds, illustrated by Leslie Stead.   London, Hodder and Stoughton, 1947.

Biggles Hunts Big Game.   London, Hodder and Stoughton, 1948.

Biggles' Second Case, illustrated by Leslie Stead.   London, Hodder and Stoughton, 1948.

Gimlet's Oriental Quest.   Leicester, Brockhampton Press, 1948.

The Rustlers of Rattlesnake Valley.   London, Nelson, 1948.

Worrals Down Under.   London, Lutterworth Press, 1948.

Biggles Breaks the Silence, illustrated by Leslie Stead.   London, Hodder and Stoughton, 1949.

Biggles Takes a Holiday, illustrated by Leslie Stead.   London, Hodder and Stoughton, 1949.

Gimlet Lends a Hand, illustrated by Leslie Stead.   Leicester, Brockhampton Press, 1949.

Worrals Goes Afoot.   London, Lutterworth Press, 1949.

Worrals in the Wastelands.   London, Lutterworth Press, 1949.

Worrals Investigates.   London, Lutterworth Press, 1950.

Doctor Vane Answers the Call.   London, Latimer, 1950.

Biggles Gets His Men, illustrated by Leslie Stead.   London, Hodder and Stoughton, 1950.

Gimlet Bores In, illustrated by Leslie Stead.   Leicester, Brockhampton Press, 1950.

Another Job for Biggles, illustrated by Leslie Stead.   London, Hodder and Stoughton, 1951.

Biggles Goes to School.   London, Hodder and Stoughton, 1951.

Biggles Works It Out, illustrated by Leslie Stead.   London, Hodder and Stoughton, 1951.

Gimlet off the Map, illustrated by Leslie Stead.   Leicester, Brockhampton Press, 1951.

Biggles – Air Detective.   London, Latimer, 1952.

Biggles Follows On, illustrated by Leslie Stead.   London, Hodder and Stoughton, 1952.

Biggles Takes the Case, illustrated by Leslie Stead.   London, Hodder and Stoughton, 1952.

Gimlet Gets the Answer, illustrated by Leslie Stead.   Leicester, Brockhampton Press, 1952.

Biggles and the Black Peril.   London, Thames Publishing Company, 1953.

Biggles and the Black-Raider, illustrated by Leslie Stead.   London, Hodder and Stoughton, 1953.

Biggles in the Blue, illustrated by Leslie Stead.   Leicester, Brockhampton Press, 1953.

Biggles in the Gobi, illustrated by Leslie Stead.   London, Hodder and Stoughton, 1953.

Biggles of the Special Air Police.   London, Thames Publishing Company, 1953.

Biggles and the Pirate Treasure, and Other Biggles Adventures, illustrated by Leslie Stead.   Leicester, Brockhampton Press, 1954.

Biggles Cuts It Fine, illustrated by Leslie Stead.   London, Hodder and Stoughton, 1954.

Biggles, Foreign Legionnaire, illustrated by Leslie Stead.   London, Hodder and Stoughton, 1954.

Biggles, Air Fighter.   London, Thames Publishing Company, 1954.

Gimlet Takes a Job, illustrated by Leslie Stead. Leicester, Brockhampton Press, 1954.

Kings of Space, illustrated by Leslie Stead. London, Hodder and Stoughton, 1954.

Adventure Bound, illustrated by Douglas Relf. London, Nelson, 1955.

Biggles' Chinese Puzzle and Other Biggles Adventures, illustrated by Leslie Stead. Leicester, Brockhampton Press, 1955.

Biggles in Australia, illustrated by Leslie Stead. London, Hodder and Stoughton, 1955.

Biggles Learns to Fly, illustrated by Leslie Stead. Leicester, Brockhampton Press, 1955.

Return to Mars, illustrated by Leslie Stead. London, Hodder and Stoughton, 1955.

Biggles of 266. London, Thames Publishing Company, 1956.

Biggles Takes Charge, illustrated by Leslie Stead. Leicester, Brockhampton Press, 1956.

No Rest for Biggles. London, Hodder and Stoughton, 1956.

Now to the Stars. London, Hodder and Stoughton, 1956.

Adventure Unlimited, illustrated by Douglas Relf. London, Nelson, 1957.

Biggles of the Interpol, illustrated by Leslie Stead. Leicester, Brockhampton Press, 1957.

Biggles on the Home Front, illustrated by Leslie Stead. London, Hodder and Stoughton, 1957.

To Outer Space, illustrated by Leslie Stead. London, Hodder and Stoughton, 1957.

Biggles Buries a Hatchet, illustrated by Leslie Stead. Leicester, Brockhampton Press, 1958.

Biggles on Mystery Island, illustrated by Leslie Stead. London, Hodder and Stoughton, 1958.

Biggles Presses On. Leicester, Brockhampton Press, 1958.

The Edge of Beyond, illustrated by Leslie Stead. London, Hodder and Stoughton, 1958.

Biggles at World's End, illustrated by Leslie Stead. Leicester, Brockhampton Press, 1959.

The Biggles Book of Heroes. London, Parrish, 1959.

Biggles' Combined Operation, illustrated by Leslie Stead. London, Hodder and Stoughton, 1959.

Biggles in Mexico, illustrated by Leslie Stead. Leicester, Brockhampton Press, 1959.

The Death Rays of Ardilla, illustrated by Leslie Stead. London, Hodder and Stoughton, 1959.

Adventures of the Junior Detection Club. London, Parrish, 1960.

Biggles and the Leopards of Zinn, illustrated by Leslie Stead. Leicester, Brockhampton Press, 1960.

Biggles Goes Home, illustrated by Leslie Stead. London, Hodder and Stoughton, 1960.

To Worlds Unknown, illustrated by Leslie Stead. London, Hodder and Stoughton, 1960.

Where the Golden Eagle Soars, illustrated by Colin Gibson. London, Hodder and Stoughton, 1960.

The Quest for the Perfect Planet. London, Hodder and Stoughton, 1961.

Biggles and the Missing Millionaire, illustrated by Leslie Stead. Leicester, Brockhampton Press, 1961.

Biggles and the Poor Rich Boy. Leicester, Brockhampton Press, 1961.

Biggles Forms a Syndicate, illustrated by Leslie Stead. London, Hodder and Stoughton, 1961.

The Biggles Book of Treasure Hunting, illustrated by William Randell. London, Parrish, 1962.

Biggles Goes Alone, illustrated by Leslie Stead. London, Hodder and Stoughton, 1962.

Biggles Sets a Trap, illustrated by Leslie Stead. London, Hodder and Stoughton, 1962.

Orchids for Biggles, illustrated by Leslie Stead. Leicester, Brockhampton Press, 1962.

Biggles and the Plane That Disappeared, illustrated by Leslie Stead. London, Hodder and Stoughton, 1963.

Biggles Flies to Work. London, Dean, 1963.

Biggles' Special Case, illustrated by Leslie Stead.   Leicester, Brockhampton Press, 1963.

Biggles Takes a Hand, illustrated by Leslie Stead.   London, Hodder and Stoughton, 1963.

Biggles Takes It Rough.   Leicester, Brockhampton Press, 1963.

The Man Who Vanished into Space.   London, Hodder and Stoughton, 1963.

Worlds of Wonder: More Adventures in Space.   London, Hodder and Stoughton, 1962.

Biggles and the Black Mask, illustrated by Leslie Stead.   London, Hodder and Stoughton, 1964.

Biggles and the Lost Sovereigns, illustrated by Leslie Stead.   Leicester, Brockhampton Press, 1964.

Biggles Investigates and Other Stories of the Air Police.   Leicester, Brockhampton Press, 1964.

Biggles and the Blue Moon.   Leicester, Brockhampton Press, 1965.

Biggles and the Plot That Failed.   Leicester, Brockhampton Press, 1965.

Biggles Looks Back, illustrated by Leslie Stead.   London, Hodder and Stoughton, 1965.

Biggles Scores a Bull.   London, Hodder and Stoughton, 1965.

Biggles in the Terai.   Leicester, Brockhampton Press, 1966.

Biggles and the Penitent Thief.   Leicester, Brockhampton Press, 1967.

Biggles in the Underworld.   Leicester, Brockhampton Press, 1968.

The Boy Biggles.   London, Dean, 1968.

Biggles and the Deep Blue Sea.   Leicester, Brockhampton Press, 1968.

Biggles and the Little Green God.   Leicester, Brockhampton Press, 1969.

Biggles and the Noble Lord.   Leicester, Brockhampton Press, 1969.

Biggles Sees Too Much.   Leicester, Brockhampton Press, 1970.

Other

Fight Planes and Aces, illustrated by Howard Leigh.   London, John Hamilton, 1932.

Modern Boy's Book of Pirates.   London, Amalgamated Press, 1939.

Sinister Service: The Adventures of Lance Lovell, Counter-Espionage Officer. as Told by His Brother and Set Down by W. E. Johns, illustrated by Stuart Tresilian.   London, Oxford University Press, 1942.

PUBLICATIONS FOR ADULTS

Novels

Mossyface (as William Earle).   London, Mellifont Press, 1932.

Blue Blood Runs Red.   London, Newnes, 1936.

Desert Night: A Romance.   London, John Hamilton, 1938.

The Unknown Quantity.   London, John Hamilton, 1940.

No Motive for Murder.   London, Hodder and Stoughton, 1958; New York, Washburn, 1959.

The Man Who Lost His Way.   London, Macdonald, 1959.

Short Stories

Short Sorties.   London, Latimer, 1950.

Sky Fever and Other Stories.   London, Latimer, 1953.

Other

The Pictorial Flying Course, with Harry M. Schofield.   London, John Hamilton, 1932.

The Air V.C.'s.   London, John Hamilton, 1935.

The Passing Show: A Garden Diary By an Amateur Gardener. London, My Garden, 1937.

Editor, *Wings: A Book of Flying Adventures.* London, John Hamilton, 1931.
Editor, *Thrilling Flights.* London, John Hamilton, 1935.

*   *   *

English children's literature, especially the adventure-story, was in a low state after the First World War, and it was not difficult for W. E. Johns, a prolific young writer capitalising on fresh first-hand experience in the glamorous new field of air-combat, to win himself a commanding position with the boy public. The entertainment value of his fiction is beyond dispute. He made no difficult demands on his readers, whose requirements and reactions he felt that he completely understood. Plot and situation were straightforward, characterization was black and white, values were those conventionally accepted at the time, and settings, though tirelessly varied and sometimes exotic, were the scenic stereotypes that any cinema-going youth could instantly recognize.

In Biggles, eventually the hero of about sixty different books, Johns could claim to have added a character to the pantheon of juvenile fiction worthy to stand with Billy Bunter, William, and a select handful of other immensely popular favourites. Biggles was doubtless an idealized projection of the author, with the same beginnings in the Royal Flying Corps in 1916. The fictional airman, however, continued his adventurous career from the dog-fights of that year to the struggle against air smugglers and other international crime almost half a century later. In all these countless stories Biggles is the admired, resourceful leader, the fearless Britisher, attended by his faithful henchmen, Ginger and Algy. Johns was a master of the formula, and his output was formidable. He created another series round the only slightly less popular character of Gimlet, and to catch more of the feminine market he invented Worrals of the W.A.A.F. In his later years, as space exploration seized the juvenile imagination, he made a spirited effort to enter that market too. There was a wide gulf, however, between the early Biggles adventures, set in a milieu he really knew, and these inter-planetary romances for which he had not the technical background of his younger and more inspired competitors.

Johns wrote in a mediocre style. His characters communicate in long, often slangy and facetious dialogues, their remarks being "snapped," "groaned," "averred," "opined," or otherwise conveyed. John Rowe Townsend has suggested that these books leave "no residual legacy" in the young reader's mind. They have, however, been fiercely attacked by other critics on ideological grounds. Certainly, they often express chauvinistic sentiments and an aggressive conviction of British and white superiority which are unacceptable in most quarters today. It may well be that in years to come they will be read chiefly by half-incredulous research students, investigating the social values prevalent in children's fiction during the second quarter of the 20th century.

—Geoffrey Trease

JOHNSON, Annabell (Jones).   American.   Born in Kansas City, Missouri, 18 June 1921. Attended William and Mary College, Williamsburg, Virginia, 1939–40; Art Students' League, New York. Married Edgar Johnson, *q.v.*, in 1949. Recipient: Western Writers of America Spur Award, 1967. Address: 2925 South Teller, Denver, Colorado 80227, U.S.A.

PUBLICATIONS FOR CHILDREN (with Edgar Johnson)

Fiction

As a Speckled Bird (Annabell Johnson alone). New York, Crowell, 1956; London,
Hodder and Stoughton, 1958.
The Big Rock Candy. New York, Crowell, 1957.
The Black Symbol, illustrated by Brian Saunders. New York, Harper, 1959; Leicester,
Brockhampton Press, 1960.
Torrie, illustrated by Pearl Falconer. New York, Harper, 1960; Leicester,
Brockhampton Press, 1961.
The Bearcat. New York, Harper, and London, Hamish Hamilton, 1960.
The Rescued Heart. New York, Harper, 1961.
The Secret Gift (as A.E. Johnson). New York, Doubleday, and London, Hodder and
Stoughton, 1961.
Pickpocket Run. New York, Harper, 1961.
Wilderness Bride. New York, Harper, 1962.
A Golden Touch. New York, Harper, 1963.
The Grizzly, illustrated by Gilbert Riswold. New York, Harper, 1964; Bath, Chivers,
1973.
A Peculiar Magic, illustrated by Lynd Ward. Boston, Houghton Mifflin, 1965.
The Burning Glass. New York, Harper, 1966.
Count Me Gone. New York, Simon and Schuster, 1968.
A Blues I Can Whistle (as A.E. Johnson). New York, Scholastic, 1969.
The Last Knife. New York, Simon and Schuster, 1971.

Manuscript Collection (Annabell and Edgar Johnson): Kerlan Collection, University of
Minnesota, Minneapolis.

Annabell and Edgar Johnson comment:
Books by Annabell and Edgar Johnson can be counted on to concern themselves with
some aspect of life in the Western United States, either past or present. Their historical novels
have concerned such commonplace aspects of life in the mountain states as the gold rush,
unionizing the coal mines, the westward trek across the Oregon and Mormon trails, and the
early days of the fur trade, and yet reviewers have felt that these stories have immediacy and
bearing upon the lives of young people today.

*　　　*　　　*

Annabell and Edgar Johnson's stories are distinguished by a highly economical use of
detail which, without any evident labouring to do so, brings home to us just what life must
have been like on the American frontier in the 19th century. Even more impressive is the
unobtrusive but wholesomely insistent moral concern which is discreetly embodied in the
narrative texture itself; as the story unfolds we find ourselves sharing the young protagonist's
unfolding discovery of the realities of human nature in other people and in himself or herself.
In Torrie the 14-year-old heroine is unwillingly uprooted from her comfortable home in St.
Louis to undertake a 2,000 mile trek by ox-drawn wagon to California. As the hardships of
the journey unroll, only slowly does she learn to value the qualities of leadership now
revealed in her insignificant-looking schoolmaster-father, the staunchness and selflessness of
her mother, the love of her parents for each other, and for herself and her brother. Moreover
it is not till her girlish susceptibility to the attentions of a blustering roustabout, Luke Egan,
has led to a near-disastrous conflict between Luke and the family's young hired teamster Jess
that she discovers how imperceptive, selfish and frivolous-minded she has been; and it is not
till the climax of the journey, when she accidentally learns that the true prupose of her

parents in undertaking their migration has been concern for her own health, that the full extent of her misconception of herself and her parents is brought home to her. The rigours of the dangerous and exciting journey have brought a new stature as well as a new self-knowledge to each member of the family; and we leave them established in a cabin in California, with the prospect of a new pioneering farming life ahead of them, and a securely-founded love burgeoning between Torrie and Jess.

Torrie has a strong emotional appeal for girls of any age above about 12, whereas *The Black Symbol* is rather more of a boys' book, though not exclusively so. The central character is Barney, who runs away from his uncle to search for his gold-miner father, and joins a travelling medicine show run by the smooth-talking Dr. Cathcart. Dr. Cathcart and his assistant Hoke Wilson clearly owe something to "The King" and "The Duke" in *Huckleberry Finn*, and the core of the book is Barney's gradual discovery of the coldhearted sadistic ruthlessness of these two villains. The detailed trickery of the carnival is neatly worked into the plot, which involves two other reluctant members of the troupe, the frightened negro boy Billy, and the blind "Strong Man" Steve. After Barney and Steve escape, Steve is recaptured, but Barney by good luck encounters his father, and the two of them ensure that the so-called "Miracle Show" is broken up by an outraged gathering of miners, and that the enslaved Billy and Steve are freed to join in working the copper-mine now owned by Barney's father. An exciting and well-constructed story with an unusual setting, and clearly drawn yet convincing characterisation.

—Frank Whitehead

JOHNSON, Crockett. Pseudonym for David Johnson Leisk. American. Born in New York City, 20 October 1906. Educated at Cooper Union, New York, 1924; New York University, 1925. Married Ruth Krauss, *q.v.*, in 1940. Drew weekly panel "Little Man with the Eyes" for *Collier's*, 1938–41, and the syndicated comic strip "Barnaby," 1941–62, and panel "Barkis," 1955. *Died 11 July 1975.*

PUBLICATIONS FOR CHILDREN (illustrated by the author)

Fiction

>*Who's Upside Down?* New York, Scott, 1952; as *Upside Down*, Chicago, Whitman, 1969.
>*Harold and the Purple Crayon.* New York, Harper, 1955; London, Constable, 1957.
>*Harold's Fairy Tale: Further Adventures with the Purple Crayon.* New York, Harper, 1956.
>*Harold's Trip to the Sky.* New York, Harper, 1957.
>*Terrible, Terrifying Toby.* New York, Harper, 1957.
>*Time for Spring.* New York, Harper, 1957.
>*The Blue Ribbon Puppies.* New York, Harper, 1958.
>*Harold at the North Pole: A Christmas Journey with the Purple Crayon.* New York, Harper, 1958.
>*Merry Go Round.* New York, Harper, 1958.
>*Ellen's Lion: Twelve Stories.* New York, Harper, 1959; Kingswood, Surrey, World's Work, 1964.
>*The Frowning Prince.* New York, Harper, 1959.
>*Harold's Circus.* New York, Harper, 1959.
>*Will Spring Be Early or Will Spring Be Late?* New York, Crowell, 1960.

A Picture for Harold's Room: A Purple Crayon Adventure. New York, Harper, 1960;
    Kingswood, Surrey, World's Work, 1963.
Harold's ABC. New York, Harper, 1963.
The Lion's Own Story: Eight New Stories about Ellen's Lion. New York, Harper, 1963;
    Kingswood, Surrey, World's Work, 1964.
We Wonder What Will Walter Be When He Grows Up? New York, Holt Rinehart,
    1964; Kingswood, Surrey, World's Work, 1966.
Castles in the Sand, illustrated by Betty Fraser. New York, Holt Rinehart, 1965;
    Kingswood, Surrey, World's Work, 1967.
Gordy and the Pirate and the Circus Ringmaster, and the Knight, and the Major League
    Manager, and the Western Marshal, and the Astronaut, and a Remarkable
    Achievement. New York, Putnam, 1965.
The Emperor's Gifts. New York, Holt Rinehart, 1965; Kingswood, Surrey, World's
    Work, 1966.

PUBLICATIONS FOR ADULTS

Other

Barnaby. New York, Holt, 1943.
Barnaby and Mr. O'Malley. New York, Holt, 1944.
Barkis: Some Precise and Some Speculative Interpretations of the Meaning of a Dog's
    Bark at Certain Times and in Certain (Illustrated) Circumstances. New York, Simon
    and Schuster, 1956.

Illustrator: *The Carrot Seed,* 1945, *How to Make an Earthquake,* 1954, *Is This You?,* 1955,
and *The Happy Egg,* 1967, all by Ruth Krauss; *Story of Money* by Constance Foster, 1950;
Willie's Adventures by Margaret Wise Brown, 1954; *Mickey's Magnet* by Franklin and
Branley, 1956; *The Little Fish That Got Away* by Bernardine Cook, 1957.

*   *   *

Crockett Johnson was the creater of *Barnaby,* a comic strip forever cherished in the
memories of those who knew it. Mr. O'Malley, Barnaby's inefficient fairy godfather, is the
key figure. Square and squat and hatted, Mr. O'Malley has inadequate wings, a cigar for a
wand and a lifetime membership in the Little Men's Chowder and Marching Society. He is
badly miscast as a fairy godfather, and Barnaby spends most of his time extracting himself
from the messes Mr. O'Malley gets both of them into.

Crockett Johnson wrote a number of children's books as well. These are blessed with the
same clear drawings and pervasive humor as the *Barnaby* strip, though the humor is less
adult. Johnson managed the delicate feat of writing whimsically for children without falling
into sentimentality. *Harold and the Purple Crayon,* perhaps his most successful book for
children, is a virtuoso performance. The simple, convincing pictures illustrate a gently
humorous text about a little boy creating his own adventurous excursion into the world with
his purple crayon. The firm purple line grows from page to page, making a moon, a road, an
ocean, a picnic, and animals to eat the leftovers, a city full of windows (but not the right
window), until Harold, always calm and in command, draws his own window, his own bed
and his own covers to pull up, and so ends his expedition. Subsequent *Harold* books followed
the same formula, with more or less success. *A Picture for Harold's Room,* an "I Can Read
Book," is a little flatter, perhaps because of the restricted vocabulary; *Harold's ABC* may be
slightly too intricate for its audience.

Ellen's Lion and *The Lion's Own Story* demonstrate Johnson's ability to keep a nice balance
between imagination and reality. The two books are collections of very brief stories
consisting of dialogues between Ellen (perhaps 5 years old) and her stuffed lion. Ellen leads
an extremely busy and adventurous life being a knight, a mountain climber, a doctor and

planning to be a "lady fireman." She is sometimes aided, but reluctantly, by her lion, who never for a moment forgets that he is stuffed, has button eyes and no powers of locomotion. He is the realist, she the Walter Mitty; together they make two amusing books, very Crockett Johnson.

Another Walter Mitty character is Gordy, of *Gordy and the Pirate*, who encounters on the way home from school a pirate and several other romantic figures, all of whom invite him to the most tempting adventures. But Gordy remembers each time, just in time, that this is the day he promised to go straight home from school. And so, eventually, he does: "And, for Gordy, that was indeed a remarkable achievement." Unfortunately, the gentle irony of the story may well go over the heads of its intended readers.

And that, indeed, may be the principal problem with some of Johnson's stories. It is not that he was given to winking over the heads of children at the adults who might be reading the stories aloud. It is just that the perspective necessary to catch the joke may be a little beyond the child for whom the story is meant. Johnson always perceived the humor of the human ego, though kindly. Just as Mr. O'Malley's inflated self-esteem is the basis for much of the fun in *Barnaby*, so some of the humor in the two *Ellen* books and the main joke of *We Wonder What Will Walter Be When He Grows Up?* depends upon a recognition of egocentricity. But small children, who are themselves egocentric, may not see it. And some of the word play in *Walter* – the characterization of the mole as the "deepest thinker," the giraffe as the "highest thinker" and so forth – seems to rest upon an acquaintance with certain clichés which little children may not have.

—Anne S. MacLeod

JOHNSON, Edgar (Raymond).   American.   Born in Washoe, Montana, 24 October 1912. Educated at Billings Polytechnic Institute, Montana; Kansas City Art Institute; Alfred University, New York. Married Annabell Jones (i.e., Annabell Johnson, *q.v.*) in 1949. Head of the Ceramics Department, Kansas City Art Institute, 1948–49. Recipient: Western Writers of America Spur Award, 1967. Address: 2925 South Teller, Denver, Colorado 80227, U.S.A.

See the entry for Annabell Johnson.

JONES, Diana Wynne.   British.   Born in London, 16 August 1934. Educated at Friends' School, Saffron Walden, Essex, 1946–53; St. Anne's College, Oxford, 1953–56, B.A. 1956. Married J.A. Burrow in 1956; has three sons. Agent: Laura Cecil, 10 Exeter Mansions, 106 Shaftesbury Avenue, London W.1. Address: 9 The Polygon, Clifton, Bristol 8, England.

PUBLICATIONS FOR CHILDREN

Fiction

Wilkins' Tooth, illustrated by Julia Rodber.   London, Macmillan, 1973; as *Witch's Business*, New York, Dutton, 1974.
The Ogre Downstairs.   London, Macmillan, 1974; New York, Dutton, 1975.
Eight Days of Luke.   London, Macmillan, 1975.

Cart and Cwidder.   London, Macmillan, 1975; New York, Atheneum, 1977.
Dogsbody.   London, Macmillan, 1975; New York, Morrow, 1977.
Power of Three.   London, Macmillan, 1976; New York, Morrow, 1977.
Charmed Life.   London, Macmillan, 1977.
Drowned Ammet.   London, Macmillan, 1977.

Plays

The Batterpool Business (produced London, 1965).
The King's Things (produced London, 1968).
The Terrible Fisk Machine (produced London, 1969).

PUBLICATIONS FOR ADULTS

Novel

Changeover.   London, Macmillan, 1970.

Diana Wynne Jones comments:
Everything I have written so far has been fantasy, and a great deal of it comic. I want to provide exciting and amusing reading for children, and I should be bored myself if I did not. But I also try to use fantasy – just as one would use a metaphor – to say things about life. It seems to me that very complicated things can be said to children by these simple means, and appreciated by them. (In the same way, I think children can grasp difficult words if the sentence and story are lucid enough.) Each time I write a book I try to say something new, with the result that each book turns out differently from the ones before – which surprises, puzzles and pleases me in about equal proportions.

*   *   *

The novels of Diana Wynne Jones are very original, each unlike the rest, and have so far been published within a very short space of time. She has always had a talent for story-telling, which developed as her children grew up. Before the novels she wrote three plays for the Unicorn Theatre in London – pleasant knockabout stuff but ephemeral, based on stereotyped situations. But the fantasy novel, for the moment, is her métier.

In each book she has used a different fantasy theme, for example, the enchanted animal, the nasty old witch, legendary gods in modern days, tiny fairy people living in secret. Children are her main characters, usually unhappy, unsettled children to whom magic comes first as an extra problem and then – if they can master it – as a way of solving their personal crisis. The common problems of child-life – absent or hostile parents, quarrelsome siblings and powerlessness against adult capriciousness – are solved by magic operated by a child who has achieved a new self-realisation on the road to maturity. In this way she follows the tradition laid down by E. Nesbit, whose children often experienced magic adentures while their family lives were disturbed.

In *The Ogre Downstairs* two families are united when The Ogre marries a mother of three (making five children altogether). To make peace, Stepfather gives each group a chemistry set. But the chemicals are magical, and, as the children can't understand the Latin labels and experiment blindly, endless disasters are caused. The children are unable to explain without giving away the secret. When mother walks out in despair at the chaos, her children can get her back only by making friends with the other group of children and the hated stepfather.

Each book also contains realistic family situations, and the business of living, not excluding death, is seriously analysed. The heroine of *Dogsbody* is Irish, with a father in prison; he escapes and is killed. The Little People in *Power of Three*, engaged in a perpetual war to the death with another magical tribe, are threatened with extinction when humans plan to flood their moor. Moril's father in *Cart and Cwidder* is murdered, and bequeaths him a magic, lute-like "cwidder." To learn to play it (and use its magic power) Moril must undergo a ruthless examination of his personality.

In an article for the *Times Literary Supplement* (11 July 1975), Miss Jones explained how children accept tragic elements in their reading and how fantasy can help them: "tragedy is both close and frequent among children .... Possibly what they love is the core of tragedy, modified by fantasy and its sting removed by laughter." She does indeed balance the serious side with generous helpings of humour. Even family quarrels have their comic and slapstick side. *Eight Days of Luke* is a glorious send-up of Norse mythology, featuring red-haired mischief-making Luke, one-eyed Mr. Wedding and his two pet ravens, Mr. Chew, the two Frys and a certain strong man with ginger hair. *The Ogre Downstairs* is full of comic scenes as the children experiment with the magic chemicals.

In the course of her writing her technique has improved. Good basic plot and sense of climax were already there, but earlier books had too much plot. Her more recent books show that she has learned to trim away complexities, and we look forward to many more in the future.

—Jessica Kemball-Cook

JORDAN, June. American. Born in New York City, 9 July 1936. Educated at Northfield School for Girls, 1950–53; Barnard College, New York, 1953–55, 1956–57; University of Chicago, 1955–56. Married Michael Meyer in 1955 (divorced, 1966); has one son. Worked as assistant producer with the filmmaker Frederick Wiseman, 1963–64; Research Associate, Mobilization for Youth Inc., New York, 1965–66; English teacher, City College of New York, 1968–69, 1975–76, Sarah Lawrence College, Bronxville, New York, 1969–70, Yale University, New Haven, Connecticut, 1974–75, and Connecticut College, New London. Member of the Board of Directors, Teachers and Writers Collaborative Inc. Recipient: Rockefeller grant, 1969; American Academy in Rome Environmental Design prize, 1970. Lives in Brooklyn, New York. Agent: Joan Daves, 505 Madison Avenue, New York, New York 10022, U.S.A.

PUBLICATIONS FOR CHILDREN

Fiction

> *His Own Where –.*   New York, Crowell, 1971.
> *New Life, New Room*, illustrated by Ed Dron.   New York, Crowell, 1973.

Verse

> *Who Look at Me?*   New York, Crowell, 1969.

Other

> *Dry Victories.*   New York, Holt Rinehart, 1972.
> *Fannie Lou Hamer* (biography), illustrated by Albert Williams.   New York, Crowell, 1972.

> Editor, with Terri Bush, *The Voice of the Children.*   New York, Holt Rinehart, 1970.
> Editor, *Soulscript: Afro-American Poetry.*   New York, Doubleday, 1970.

PUBLICATIONS FOR ADULTS

Novel

   Okay Now.   New York, Simon and Schuster, 1977.

Verse

   Some Changes.   New York, Dutton, 1971.
   Things That I Do in the Dark: Selected Poetry.   New York, Random House, 1977.

June Jordan comments:
   Children/young people seem to me the most important, demanding readership for whom you can write. They are new lives in the world and, therefore, capable of perpetuating the society we now endure or of devising new, positive ways of being alive in humane fellowship. For this reason, I always undertake the writing of books for children as a political and moral opportunity to foster constructive social change.

*   *   *

   June Jordan's reputation as a writer for children rests largely on her highly acclaimed, award-winning novel *His Own Where* –. Let us all agree that this is perfectly fitting, desirable and acceptable – it is a masterpiece. She's a rare breed, an extremely talented writer who has captured the essence of our Black lives in so few printed pages and especially in our own language. This aptly expressed essence is love. Whether the love is selfish, romantic, benevolent, or materialistic, it is our rock against the wind. Ms. Jordan knows this and shows it in 16-year-old Buddy and 14-year-old Angel, the stars of her show. *His Own Where* – provides us with a hope, while we're young and impressionable, that the love within us can be released, fulfilled in spite of external odds. Buddy and Angela create their "own where" in a deserted cemetery, "a place for loving" where they can give and take the all of love. Considerable critical attention has been given to the author's use of "Black English" in this novel. It is my opinion, however, that this particular language style (which adds lyricism to make it exceptionally nice prose) is secondary, but necessary, to the total craftsmanship.
   His Own Where – surfaces as more than a "love story written in Black English"; it is also a commentary on much of what Ms. Jordan believes in personally. A most significant belief, and the cause to which she has dedicated so much of her time and effort, seems to be the ability of Black youths to survive in a society that is literally designed to destroy them: "Buddy leaning on the wall be thinking that the whole city of his people like a all-night emergency room. People mostly suffering, uncomfortable and waiting." But through Buddy and Angela we become aware that creativity and an instinct for survival will make it better: "Where can we go beside the cemetery .... What else is there? ... It be like a big, open box ... behind them there be a locked-up house where no one ever live .... They see how they would open it up, how they would live inside, what they would do with only the birds, the water and the skylight fallen blinding into it .... And so begins a new day of the new life in the cemetery."
   Like *His Own Where* –, all of Ms. Jordan's juvenile books reflect her concern for the future of children and being the truly spirited Black person that she is, her major thrust is toward total fulfillment for the Black child. *Who Look at Me?* said, is still saying, to the young among us – I exist, recognize me, I am/shall be a surviving force with which you must reckon, I am real/deal with me while I'm young. The use of 27 different paintings representing the Black American experience as seen by artists illustrates Ms. Jordan's vision of what it is like to "exist as Number Two .../If you deny it you should try/being Number Two." *Who Look at Me?* is extraordinary – the poetry, pictures, perception and power; it commands:

> See me brown girl ...
> I am black alive and looking back at you.

His Own Where – and *Who Look at Me?* are brilliant interpretations of and for Black youth; unfortunately, they cannot work by their mere availability. Both books must be encouraged, recommended, even pushed (sometimes) by us, the believers, the teachers who understand and recognize the strong feelings, meaningful images, positive vibrations and real truths that Ms. Jordan has so expertly revealed.

June Jordan is alert, she's vital and vibrant, she's cognizant of the needs of Black children.

—Jacqueline Brown Woody

JOSLIN, Sesyle. American. Born in Providence, Rhode Island, 30 August 1929. Educated at the School of Organic Education, Fairhope, Alabama, 1945–46; University of Miami, Coral Gables, Florida, 1946–47; Goddard College, Plainfield, Vermont, 1947–48; Antioch College, Yellow Springs, Ohio, 1948–49. Married the writer Al Hine in 1950; has three daughters. Editorial Assistant, *Holiday* magazine, 1947–49, Assistant Fiction Editor, Westminster Press, 1950–52, and Book Editor, *Country Gentleman* magazine, 1950–52, all in Philadelphia; production assistant on Peter Brook's film *Lord of the Flies*, Puerto Rico, 1963. Address: Old Mill Road, New Milford, Connecticut, U.S.A.

PUBLICATIONS FOR CHILDREN

Fiction

Brave Baby Elephant, illustrated by Leonard Weisgard. New York, Harcourt Brace, 1960; London, Collins, 1961.

Baby Elephant's Trunk, illustrated by Leonard Weisgard. New York, Harcourt Brace, 1961; London, Collins, 1963.

Señor Baby Elephant, The Pirate, illustrated by Leonard Weisgard. New York, Harcourt Brace, 1962; London, Collins, 1965.

Baby Elephant and the Secret Wishes, illustrated by Leonard Weisgard. New York, Harcourt Brace, 1962; London, Collins, 1964.

Baby Elephant Goes to China, illustrated by Leonard Weisgard. New York, Harcourt Brace, 1963; London, Collins, 1969.

Baby Elephant's Baby Book, illustrated by Leonard Weisgard. New York, Harcourt Brace, 1964.

Please Share That Peanut!, illustrated by Simms Taback. New York, Harcourt Brace, 1965.

Pinkety, Pinkety: A Practical Guide to Wishing, illustrated by Luciana Roselli. New York, Harcourt Brace, 1966.

The Night They Stole the Alphabet, illustrated by Enrico Arno. New York, Harcourt Brace, 1968; London, Collins, 1970.

Doctor George Owl, illustrated by Lisl Weil. Boston, Houghton Mifflin, 1970.

The Spy Lady and the Muffin Man, illustrated by the author. New York, Harcourt Brace, 1971.

Last Summer's Smugglers, illustrated by the author. New York, Harcourt Brace, 1973.

Verse

Is There a Mouse in the House?, with Al Hine (as Josephine Gibson), illustrated by N.M. Bodecker. New York, Macmillan, 1965.

Other

What Do You Say, Dear?, illustrated by Maurice Sendak. New York, Scott, 1958; London, Faber, 1960.
What Do You Do, Dear?, illustrated by Maurice Sendak. New York, Scott, 1961; London, Faber, 1963.
There Is a Dragon in My Bed (French primer), illustrated by Irene Haas. New York, Harcourt Brace, 1961; London, Collins, 1962.
One Day in Ancient Rome, with Al Hine (as G.B. Kirtland), illustrated by Jerome Snyder. New York, Harcourt Brace, 1961; London, Macmillan, 1963.
One Day in Elizabethan England, with Al Hine (as G.B. Kirtland), illustrated by Jerome Snyder. New York, Harcourt Brace, 1962; London, Macmillan, 1963.
Dear Dragon ... and Other Useful Letter Forms for Young Ladies and Gentlemen Engaged in Everyday Correspondence, illustrated by Irene Haas. New York, Harcourt Brace, 1962; London, Collins, 1964.
One Day in Aztec Mexico, with Al Hine (as G.B. Kirtland), illustrated by Jerome Snyder. New York, Harcourt Brace, 1963; London, Macmillan, 1964.
La Petite Famille (reader), illustrated by John Alcorn. New York, Harcourt Brace, 1964; London, Hamish Hamilton, 1965.
Spaghetti for Breakfast (Italian primer), illustrated by Katharina Barry. New York, Harcourt Brace, 1965.
There Is a Bull on My Balcony (Spanish primer), illustrated by Katharina Barry. New York, Harcourt Brace, 1966.
La Fiesta (reader), illustrated by John Alcorn. New York, Harcourt Brace, 1967.

*   *   *

"The Baby Elephant" books by Sesyle Joslin are superb books for young children. They are funny, gentle and comforting. Yet there are challenges for the young mind, big new words, words in foreign languages, situations which demand thought as well as lovely puns and jokes. Few have been able to write really funny books for children; these are funny. The dialogue is dignified and full of character. Baby Elephant's family knows what to say to give their little one importance and security. These dear, witty creatures know many tricks of the "parent" trade.

The Night They Stole the Alphabet is a book for older children. It is an exciting adventure fantasy, a middle-of-the-night chase after robbers who have stolen all the letters of the alphabet from Victoria's bedroom wallpaper as well as from the pages of her books. It is a satisfying unscrambling, cogitative and imaginative.

The first of three groups of delightful, semi-serious, pedagogical hand books is called, *What Do You Say Dear?* It is a guide to everyday social behavior. In this book, an occasion is described and illustrated. It is always a dramatic and portentous situation. "You are flying around in your aeroplane and you remember that the duchess said, 'Do drop in for tea sometime.' So you do, only it makes a rather large hole in her roof. What do you say dear?" On the next page is the correct response, illustrated. In this case it is, "I'm sorry." The understated humor of these responses is bound to make a lasting impression.

Another handbook is *What Do You Do Dear?*, a book of etiquette. The same format is used here. One is treated to zany jokes all leading to some venerable rules of behavior. One is "Swallow what you are eating before you speak." "Walk through the library quietly" is what you do when an ugly old cowboy lassoes you in the library and takes you away at gun-point to his ranch.

Dear Dragon is a "how to" book of correspondence, full of useful suggestions to handle everyday or unusual, always funny situations with the appropriate nicely worded letter. *Pinkety, Pinkety* is a practical guide to wishing. *Please Share That Peanut* celebrates the happiness and satisfaction found in sharing. Funny enough to be swallowed without a qualm.

Spaghetti for Breakfast is an Italian phrase book, *There Is a Dragon in My Bed* is French, *There Is a Bull on My Balcony*, Spanish. All offer appropriate phrases in the language and in English to accommodate a lot of sight-seeing adventures and mis-adventures met by the American child-tourist. How to say for instance "My chicken is cold" when you are dining (formal) at La Tour D'Argent in Paris and the shivering chicken sits on a platter clutching a shawl about her shoulders. All is absurd and delightful: as a result these phrases have a good chance of sticking in the mind. There is a good pronunciation guide as well.

—Irene Haas

* * * * *

JOWETT, Margaret. British. Born in Ipswich, Suffolk, 18 April 1921. Educated at Princess Mary High School, Halifax, Yorkshire; Leeds University, 1939–43, B.A. (honours) in English 1942, Dip. Ed. 1943. English Mistress, Withington Girls' School, Manchester, 1943–50; free-lance researcher and supply teacher, 1950–57; Senior Lecturer, Bretton Hall, Wakefield, 1957–67. Since 1957, Lecturer, College of Education, St. John's College, York, and currently, Principal Lecturer in Drama, College of Ripon. Address: 79 Ouse Lea, Clifton, Yorkshire YO3 6SA, England.

PUBLICATIONS FOR CHILDREN

Fiction

> *Candidate for Fame*, illustrated by Peggy Fortnum.   London, Oxford University Press, 1955.
> *A Cry of Players*, illustrated by Asgeir Scott.   London, Oxford University Press, 1961; New York, Roy, 1963.

Margaret Jowett comments:
   Both books were written for those who are neither child nor adult. They were intended for readers who will one day take their theatrical scholarship neat but are not yet of an age to do so.
   I do not think that I should have researched them more thoroughly for any thesis or dissertation. In each case major figures appear, but they are observed obliquely because I did not wish to make very emphatic statements about Shakespeare or Mrs. Siddons, for instance, to young people who would have no means of checking my views. I may have failed in this intention.

*   *   *

   Margaret Jowett's reputation rests on two carefully researched stories of theatre history, *A Cry of Players* and *Candidate for Fame*. *A Cry of Players* is set in the late 16th century at the beginning of Shakespeare's career, and *Candidate for Fame* in the 18th-century theatre of Sheridan and Mrs. Siddons. Each is the story of a child player, starting off in unpromising circumstances but with "the two-hours' traffic of the stage" irresistibly in the blood, and struggling through to ultimate triumph before a demanding London audience. Harry Lulworth, in *A Cry of Players*, sets off to find his lost father, an actor; his quest ends tragically, but in his journeyings he also finds his own theatrical vocation, and wins through from his first efforts with a group of poor Lancashire actors to fame and achievement as the first Juliet. The father of Deborah Keate, in *Candidate for Fame*, is the actor-manager of an indifferent touring company in Yorkshire. With his encouragement, but also by her own efforts and painful mistakes, Deborah learns her craft in a succession of provincial theatres and is finally acclaimed at Drury Lane.

Candidate for Fame is much the better novel of the two — more tightly constructed and richly characterised as well as having a more unfamiliar and difficult period and setting. Both, however, are far more than commonplace romances for the state-struck. They convey with great conviction the insecurity and pressures of an actor's life, the social and professional humiliations a player must endure, the unrelenting drive to learn and improve. Some excellent vignettes of actual personages (Edward Alleyn and Shakespeare, Dr. Johnson and Mrs. Siddons), combined with accurate political background, give the books historical authenticity. Above all, Miss Jowett catches the sheer magic of great acting and shows us the blend of nervous egotism and selfless imaginative sympathy from which it springs.

—Peter Hollindale

JUDAH, Aaron.   British.   Born in Bombay, India, 19 October 1923. Educated at Anglo-Indian schools, graduated, 1941. Bridge-boy on a Cunard ship, 1943–44; draughtsman in a munitions factory, London, 1945. Qualified as a physiotherapist, 1949, and currently practicing physiotherapist. Address: 10 Vicars Avenue, North Bondi, New South Wales 2026, Australia.

PUBLICATIONS FOR CHILDREN

Fiction

Tommy with the Hole in His Shoe, illustrated by Sheila Hawkins.   London, Faber, 1957.
Tales of Teddy Bear, illustrated by Sheila Hawkins.   London, Faber, 1958.
The Adventures of Henrietta Hen, illustrated by Sheila Hawkins.   London, Faber, 1958.
Miss Hare and Mr. Tortoise, illustrated by Sheila Hawkins.   London, Faber, 1959.
The Pot of Gold and Two Other Tales, illustrated by Mervyn Peake.   London, Faber, 1959; New York, A.S. Barnes, 1960.
God and Mr. Sourpuss, illustrated by Richard Kennedy.   London, Faber, 1959; New York, A.S. Barnes, 1960.
Basil Chimpy Isn't Bright, illustrated by Sheila Hawkins.   London, Faber, 1959.
Henrietta in the Snow, illustrated by Sheila Hawkins.   London, Faber, 1960.
Basil Chimpy's Comic Light, illustrated by Sheila Hawkins.   London, Faber, 1960.
Anna Anaconda: The Swallowing Wonder, illustrated by John Howson.   London, Faber, 1960.
Henrietta in Love, illustrated by Sheila Hawkins.   London, Faber, 1961.
The Proud Duck, illustrated by the author.   London, Faber, 1961.
The Elf's New House, illustrated by Sheila Hawkins.   London, Faber, 1962.
Ex-King Max Forever!, illustrated by the author.   London, Faber, 1963.
The Careless Cuckoos, illustrated by Sheila Hawkins.   London, Faber, 1963.
The Fabulous Haircut, illustrated by the author.   London, Faber, 1964.
On the Feast of Stephen, illustrated by Sheila Hawkins.   London, Faber, 1965.

PUBLICATIONS FOR ADULTS

Novels

Clown of Bombay. London, Faber, 1963; New York, Dial Press, 1968.
Clown on Fire. London, Macdonald, 1965; New York, Dial Press, 1967.
Cobweb Pennant. London, Dent, 1968.
Lillian's Dam. London, Dent, 1970.

*   *   *

Aaron Judah peoples his stories with childlike humans of all ages, and with animals. The animals inhabit both the real world of nature, where the chase and sudden death are part of the order of things, and also the anthropomorphic world in which they represent the vices and virtues. Foxes are cunning, camels haughty and selfish, monkeys irresponsible, while owls are learned, hedgehogs kindly and pandas old and wise. Nothing very unusual in all this, of course, the very stuff of the best nursery stories in the tradition of Beatrix Potter and Alison Uttley. Again, like many a good storyteller before him, Aaron Judah tells a tale to point a moral without falling into moralising attitudes.

The nursery story is an over-constrained genre: all the more remarkable that this writer should have brought a freshness to it. His language is necessarily simple, direct, used with economy (though he'll stretch the young reader where precision demands it); his images are concrete, his tone often lyrical without being coy or whimsical. There are drama, often heavily charged with emotion, rich humour and inventive characterisation. No one who has met Mr. Makeshift Monkey in *Tommy with the Hole in His Shoe* or Anna Anaconda is likely easily to forget them.

The tone is central to the success of these tales. The words leap from the page demanding to be read aloud. He *shares* the experience of the stories with the young reader or listener. His voice is that of an enthralled observer excitedly and intimately drawing attention to the wonder he sees around him. Nor is he above admitting ignorance when the wonder runs beyond his grasp. We never know what fearsome presence caused the desperate Henrietta to scurry to the hollow oak (*The Adventures of Henrietta Hen*). We cannot tell, and Mr. Judah doesn't attempt to explain, what it was that God did to change Mr. Sourpuss, but we delight in that gentleman's joy at his new-found happiness.

Miss Hare and Mr. Tortoise brings together under one title all that is best in this writer's work. There are desperate fear, tenderness, humour, lyricism, harsh reality and the celebration of wonder all artfully balanced in this exquisite love story, and what must surely be the gentlest, most reassuring low-key ending of any bedtime story ever written.

—Myles McDowell

JUSTER, Norton. American. Born in Brooklyn, New York, 2 June 1929. Educated at the University of Pennsylvania, Philadelphia, B. Arch. 1952; University of Liverpool (Fulbright Scholar), 1952–53. Served in the United States Naval Reserve Civil Engineer Corps, 1954–57. Married Jeanne Ray in 1964. Architect, Juster and Gugliotta, New York, 1960–68; Instructor, Pratt Institute, New York, 1960–70. Since 1969, Architect, Juster-Pope Associates, Shelburne Falls, Massachusetts, and since 1970, Associate Professor of Design, Hampshire College, Amherst, Massachusetts. Recipient: George G. Stone Center for Children's Books award, 1971. Agent: Sterling Lord Agency, 75 East 55th Street, New York, New York 10022. Address: R.F.D., Charlemont, Massachusetts 01339, U.S.A.

PUBLICATIONS FOR CHILDREN

Fiction

> *The Phantom Tollbooth*, illustrated by Jules Feiffer.   New York, Epstein and Carroll, 1961; London, Collins, 1962.
> *The Dot and the Line: A Romance in Lower Mathematics.*   New York, Random House, 1963; London, Nelson, 1964.
> *Alberic the Wise and Other Journeys*, illustrated by Domenico Gnoli.   New York, Pantheon Books, 1965; London, Nelson, 1966.

PUBLICATIONS FOR ADULTS

Other

> *Stark Naked: A Paranomastic Odyssey*, illustrated by Arnold Roth.   New York, Random House, 1969.

*   *   *

In Norton Juster's *The Phantom Tollbooth*, young Milo has become painfully bored with school: he regards "the process of seeking knowledge as the greatest waste of time of all." One afternoon when he dejectedly returns home from school, he discovers that a large package has mysteriously appeared in his room. The box contains a turnpike tollbooth and accompanying signs. Milo drives his pedal car past the tollbooth into the fantasy portion of the plot where enchantment, magic, and impossible events become believable.

In the fantasy realm beyond the magical tollbooth, Milo travels to the cities of Dictionopolis and Digitopolis where he encounters adventures, characters, and places that are allegories for the subjects he has studied in school. In both places, Milo encounters grotesque parodies of learning. In Dictionopolis, Milo learns from Faintly Macabre the Official Which that the problems in the Kingdom of Wisdom have resulted from the banishment of the Princesses Rhyme and Reason, who represent good sense, grace, and decorum. Their absence robs knowledge of human meaning and emotional significance. One story that Milo hears can serve as an example of this. Faintly tells Milo that, as the Official Which, she was given the task of "choosing which words were to be used for all occasions." At first she offered helpful guidelines such as "brevity is the soul of Wit." In the absence of Rhyme and Reason, however, the guide quickly became the tyrant. If brevity is good, miserliness of words is better. Soon the pronouncement "Silence is Golden" became law. Instead of enhancing communication, notions of effective language have led to silence.

Without Rhyme and Reason, the use of words and numbers can become mere games devoid of human meaning. This state of affairs directly parallels Milo's earlier disenchantment with schooling and shows how the fantasy world of *The Phantom Tollbooth* acts as a commentary on, indeed a corrective of, Milo's perceptions of his life in the actual world.

When Milo decides to set out on a quest to bring back the Princesses Rhyme and Reason from the Mountains of Ignorance, he is clearly also searching for his own identity in relationship to the subjects he studies in school. After many adventures he rescues the Princesses from the Castle in the Air. When he returns to his own room, having been away only an hour, he discovers that he has a new sense of the pleasures and beauties of the world around him. He appears to have achieved a strong identity that will not be depressed and overburdened by pressures in school. When the tollbooth disappears from his room, he regrets its loss but concludes that the real world around him provides more than ample adventure.

The Phantom Tollbooth owes much to *Alice's Adventures in Wonderland* in style and theme. As in *Alice*, the humor is developed through wordplay. Juster literalizes idioms, a device that children especially like, as seen in an episode where Milo jumps to a place called Conclusions. Puns are used throughout the book: at a banquet in Dictionopolis, for example, "rigamaroles," "ragamuffins," and "synonym buns" are served. Like Alice, Milo's growth in character is indicated by his assertion of identity against the restrictions of a foolish and sterile educational system, particularly as seen in his increasing ability to use language effectively. Unlike *Alice*, however, *The Phantom Tollbooth* is not obviously a dream fantasy but instead relies on the device of the magical tollbooth to create the structure of the fantasy world.

—William D. Anderson

KAHL, Virginia C. American. Born in Milwaukee, Wisconsin. Educated at Milwaukee-Downer College, 1936–40, B.A. 1940; University of Wisconsin, Madison, 1956–57, Master of Library Science, 1957. Library Assistant, Milwaukee Public Library, 1942–48; Librarian, Berlin, and Command Librarian, Salzburg, United States Army, 1948–55; Librarian, Madison public schools, Wisconsin, 1958–61; Library Director, Menomonee Falls Public Library, Wisconsin, 1961–68. Since 1970, Librarian, Alexandria Library, Virginia. Address: c/o Charles Scribner's Sons, 597 Fifth Avenue, New York, New York 10017, U.S.A.

PUBLICATIONS FOR CHILDREN (illustrated by the author)

Fiction

Away Went Wolfgang! New York, Scribner, 1954.
Maxie. New York, Scribner, 1956.
Droopsi. New York, Scribner, 1958.
Here is Henri!, with Edith Vacheron. New York, Scribner, 1959.
More about Henri!, with Edith Vacheron. New York, Scribner, 1961.
Giants, Indeed! New York, Scribner, 1974.

Verse

The Duchess Bakes a Cake. New York, Scribner, 1955.
Plum Pudding for Christmas. New York, Scribner, 1956.
The Habits of Rabbits. New York, Scribner, 1957.
The Perfect Pancake. New York, Scribner, 1960.
The Baron's Booty. New York, Scribner, 1963.
How Do You Hide a Monster? New York, Scribner, 1971.
Gunhilde's Christmas Booke. New York, Scribner, 1972.
Gunhilde and the Hallowe'en Spell. New York, Scribner, 1975.
How Many Dragons Are There Behind the Door? New York, Scribner, 1977.

Virginia Kahl comments:

My books will appeal, I hope, to those children who enjoy a simple fantasy and possess a sense of the ridiculous; they carry no message. I am old-fashioned enough to believe that picture books are to be enjoyed by young readers. I leave to others the job of introducing them to the seamy side of life. Early childhood, when books are introduced, should be a time of joy and gaiety. I want children to enjoy my stories, laugh at the pictures, and think back indulgently on my bumbling characters. Probably the single experience that has most influenced my writing was my sojourn in Austria. I was overwhelmed by the scenery and loved the people; and the city of Salzburg is always in the back of my mind when I write my books. As for my pictures, my first editor, Alice Dalgliesh, remarked that she had seldom seen such simple illustrations. Fortunately, they seem appropriate to the text.

*   *   *

Virginia Kahl is a humorist of the slapstick school. Her "Duchess" books are founded on exuberant exaggeration, the multiplication of some small incident until a mad chaos engulfs the dukedom. A hint of these madcap happenings comes with a mere mention of the Duchess' over-large family: "Madeleine, Gwendolyn, Jane and Clothilde,/ Willibald, Genevieve, Maud and Mathilde ... " – thirteen daughters altogether. This group is soon entangled in the Duchess' innocent-looking ventures, which somehow run riot while the Duke looks on helplessly.

Kahl's success as an entertainer is best seen in *The Duchess Bakes a Cake* – a fantasy which combines rowdy humour with serene rationality. When an over-supply of yeast sends a cake dough rising to heaven with the cook trapped on top, the crisis is resolved when the youngest Duchess child gets hungry. Then everyone simply eats enough of the dough to bring the Duchess down.

> "How lovely!" the Duchess said. "Come, let us sup."
> "I'll start eating down; you start eating up."

The winning combination in this book is apparently the clarity with which silliness and logic have been joined; the personality of the high-born, scatter-brained Duchess; the easily chanted refrain ("All I wanted to make/ was a lovely light luscious delectable cake"); the unlabored rhyme and evenly accented rhythm of the verse (which help emphasize the narrative content rather than the form); and the unfamiliar words for small children to savor: pummel, catapult, minstrel, etc.

In *The Baron's Booty* and *The Habits of Rabbits* the plot lines are more familiar: kidnappers overwhelmed by the purely childlike behavior of children they've abducted, rabbits producing an over-population of ridiculous proportions. Yet these are ideal vehicles for the Duchess character and for employing a popular motif of folktales – the central role of the youngest family member.

Another memorable creation is a milk-cart dog (in *Away Went Wolfgang!*) who is so seized by the work ethic that he dashes over the cobblestone streets and spills the milk before it can be delivered. Working out his problem entails a surprise incident which turns the milk into another saleable product: butter. But Wolfgang's characterization – the portrayal of devotion and excess energy in a young dog – outshines other features in this tale.

Such high creativity has not been maintained in works like *Gunhilde's Christmas Booke* or *Maxie*. The former presents a predictable series of episodes in which Christmas customs are explained to non-Christians. The rhymed text provides a light-hearted dimension, but the narrative lacks liveliness as well as the usual Christmas ingredients: reverence or wonder. In the latter book the dachshund, Maxie, is allowed to be an explicit moralizer, and is consequently much less attractive than Wolfgang.

Kahl is a writer whose best works for preschool and kindergarten children should not be permitted to lapse into obscurity. The inspired imagination and good craftsmanship in the early books are not often surpassed; and although runaway cake batter is a motif in folk literature, the treatment applied by Virginia Kahl is entirely unprecendented. Her work as a whole offers readers a wealth of fresh images and personalities.

—Donnarae MacCann

KAMM, Josephine (Mary). British. Born in London, 30 December 1905. Educated at Queen's College School, London, 1915–17; Parents National Educational School, Burgess Hill, Sussex, 1917–23; Triangle Secretarial College, London, 1923. Married George Emile Kamm in 1929; has one son. Shorthand Typist, British Commonwealth Union, London, 1924–26; Assistant Secretary, Empire Industries Association, London, 1926–29; Shorthand Typist, rising to Senior Information Officer, Ministry of Information, London, 1939–46; Senior Information Officer, Central Office of Information, London, 1946. Recipient: Jewish Book Council of America Isaac Siegel Memorial Award, 1963. Agent: John Johnson, 15–54 Goschen Buildings, 12–13 Henrietta Street, London WC2E 8LF. Address: 67 Elm Park Gardens, Flat 39, London SW10 9QE, England.

PUBLICATIONS FOR CHILDREN

Fiction

He Went with Captain Cook, illustrated by G.S. Ronalds. London, Harrap, 1952.
Janet Carr, Journalist. London, Lane, 1953; revised edition, Leicester, Brockhampton Press, 1972.
Student Almoner. London, Lane, 1955.
Return to Freedom, illustrated by William Stobbs. London and New York, Abelard Schuman, 1962.
Out of Step, illustrated by Jillian Willett. Leicester, Brockhampton Press, 1962.
Young Mother. Leicester, Brockhampton Press, and New York, Duell, 1965.
No Strangers Here. London, Constable, 1968.
First Job. Leicester, Brockhampton Press, 1969.
Where Do We Go from Here?, illustrated by Shirley Hughes. Leicester, Brockhampton Press, 1972.
The Starting Point. Leicester, Brockhampton Press, 1975.

Other

Abraham: A Biography, with Philip Cohen. London, Union of Liberal and Progressive Synagogues, 1948.
They Served the People (biographies). London, Lane, 1954.
Men Who Served Africa, illustrated by G.S. Ronalds. London, Harrap, 1957.
Leaders of the People. London and New York, Abelard Schuman, 1959.
The Story of Sir Moses Montefiore. London, Vallentine Mitchell, 1960.
The Story of Mrs. Pankhurst, illustrated by Faith Jaques. London, Methuen, 1961; as *The Story of Emmeline Pankhurst*, New York, Meredith Press, 1968.
Malaria Ross, illustrated by Anne Linton. London, Methuen, 1963; New York, Criterion Books, 1964.
Malaya and Singapore, illustrated by W.B. White and A.W. Gatnell. London, Longman, 1963.
A New Look at the Old Testament, illustrated by Gwyneth Cole. London, Gollancz, 1965; as *Kings, Prophets, and History*, New York, McGraw Hill, 1966.
The Story of Fanny Burney, illustrated by Val Biro. London, Methuen, 1966; New York, Meredith Press, 1967.
Joseph Paxton and the Crystal Palace, illustrated by Faith Jaques. London, Methuen, 1967.
The Hebrew People: A History of the Jews from Biblical Times to the Present Day. London, Gollancz, 1967; New York, McGraw Hill, 1968.
Explorers into Africa. London, Gollancz, and New York, Crowell Collier, 1970.

Editor, *A Tale of Two Cities*, by Charles Dickens, illustrated by Barry Wilkinson. London, Collins, 1973.

PUBLICATIONS FOR ADULTS

Novels

All Quiet at Home. London, Longman, 1936.
Disorderly Caravan. London, Harrap, 1938.
Nettles to My Head. London, Duckworth, 1939.
Peace, Perfect Peace. London, Duckworth, 1947.
Come, Draw This Curtain. London, Duckworth, 1948.

Other

Progress Toward Self-Government in the British Colonies. London, Fosh and Cross, 1945.
African Challenge: The Story of the British in Tropical Africa. London, Nelson, 1946.
Daughter of the Desert: The Story of Gertrude Bell. London, Lane, 1956; as *Gertrude Bell: Daughter of the Desert*, New York, Vanguard Press, 1956.
How Different from Us: A Biography of Miss Buss and Miss Beale. London, Bodley Head, 1958.
Hope Deferred: Girls' Education in English History. London, Methuen, 1965.
Rapiers and Battleaxes: The Women's Movement and Its Aftermath. London, Allen and Unwin, 1966.
Indicative Past: A Hundred Years of the Girls' Public Day School Trust. London, Allen and Unwin, 1971.
John Stuart Mill in Love. London, Gordon and Cremonesi, 1977.

Josephine Kamm comments:

I had hoped to write from the time I first contributed to my school magazine; but a full-time job followed by marriage delayed the plan until my only son started nursery school. I published three adult novels before the outbreak of war in 1939. Throughout the war I worked in the Ministry of Information, chiefly as a writer on Commonwealth affairs. My writing for children began in a haphazard fashion. I never thought seriously about it until I was invited to contribute *He Went with Captain Cook* to a series of novels on great explorers. I found the experience so enjoyable that I decided to continue. My wartime experience led me to concentrate from time to time on a non-fiction book about the Commonwealth for older children, but I remained equally interested in fiction. Historical and career novels were followed by novels on some of the problems which confront young people today, such as racial prejudice, illegitimacy, adoption, and early marriage. These books have been– and still – are interspersed with non-fiction books for adults.

*   *   *

"What's her problem?" – the American librarian's reply to the mother who asked for a book for her teenage daughter – might serve as a title for a series that would include Josephine Kamm's books for teenage girls. The "problems" she treats run the fashionable gamut: adolescent love, race relations, pregnant school-girls, drugs, adoption, pupil power, teachers and sex, delinquency and the non-reader, the world of work, and early marrieds living with in-laws. These cautionary tales are brisk, earnest, businesslike, and uninspired.

The author's problem is that no one seems to have told her that fiction has something to do with the imagination.

The aims, methods and even the titles of these books betray a basic misconception of how fiction works. (*Janet Carr, Journalist,* is described on the dust jacket as "A career novel [sic] incorporating the latest facts about an actual job.") Plot, character and situation are manipulated for predetermined instructional ends – a serious enough fault even if the author were sensitive to issues and capable of new insights; but she tends to give pat, conventional answers to dimly perceived moral dilemmas, to make clear what is already blindingly conspicuous. Psychological subtlety eludes the author whose simplistic outlook is expressed in stock situations, stereotyped characters, patronising attitudes and glib, unexamined assumptions. She informs without illuminating, makes statements rather than undertakes a search. A spurious realism is purveyed which, because it is not suffused and transmuted by a creative imagination, lacks the sense of reality that true fiction possesses. The characters do not come alive, nor do the situations ring true, because the author is unable to explore feelings beyond the superficial. Her books have the form, but lack the "feel" of fiction. She has convictions but no power to make them convincing. The attempt to use fiction for non-fiction purposes has failed to produce fiction in any acceptable sense.

Tell-tale signs abound. In *Young Mother* (surprisingly in its fourth impression, as much of it is out of date) before a helpful little paragraph on how social workers are trained to interview people, the social worker speculates about the attitude of the pregnant girl's mother: "She would naturally be upset: but in the light of recent changes in the law she would probably have asked about abortion if she'd known about the baby sooner." Good case-work does not make good art. In *The Starting Point,* which is about the difficulties that arise from early marriage, the poverty of creative invention is seen in the ineptly stilted motivation of the young delinquent, Cliff.

Josephine Kamm's books are widely dismissed by discerning adults, and widely read by adolescent girls, a distinction not unique to these works. They clearly answer a felt need. The sad thing is that they may confirm young readers in a false view of what life is like and what reading fiction can be, thereby creating further demand for what is stale, flat and profitable.

—Graham Hammond

* * *

KAYE, Geraldine. British. Born in Watford, Hertfordshire, 14 January 1925. Educated at Felixstowe College, Suffolk, 1934–39; Watford Grammar School, 1939–42; University of London, 1946–49, B.Sc. (honours) in economics 1949. Served in the Women's Royal Naval Service, 1943–46. Married Barrington Kaye in 1948 (divorced, 1975); has two daughters and one son. Scriptwriter, Malayan Film Unit, Malaya, 1951–52; Teacher, Methodist Girls School, Paya Lebar, Singapore, 1952–54, and Mitford Colmer School, London, 1962–64. Agent: A.M. Heath and Co. Ltd., 40–42 William IV Street, London WC2N 4DD. Address: 39 High Kingsdown, Bristol BS2 8EW, England.

Publications for Children

Fiction

> *The Boy Who Wanted to Go Fishing,* illustrated by Peggy Fortnum.   London, Methuen, 1960; as *Kassim Goes Fishing,* 1969.
> *Kwasi and the Parrot and Other Stories.*   London, Oxford University Press, 1961.
> *Kwasi Goes to Town,* illustrated by Valerie Herbst.   London and New York, Abelard Schuman, 1962.

Kofi and the Eagle, illustrated by Sheila Hawkins.   London, Methuen, 1963.

Chik and the Bottle House, illustrated by Peggy Fortnum.   London, Nelson, 1965.

The Raffle Pony, illustrated by Gareth Floyd.   Leicester, Brockhampton Press, 1966.

Oh, Essie!, illustrated by Rosemary Honeybourne.   London, Benn, 1966.

The Blue Rabbit, illustrated by Clyde Pearson.   Leicester, Brockhampton Press, 1967.

Kassim and the Sea Monkey, illustrated by Gay Galsworthy.   London, Longman, 1967.

Koto and the Lagoon, illustrated by Joanna Stubbs.   London, Deutsch, 1967; New York, Funk and Wagnalls, 1969.

The Tail of the Siamese Cat, illustrated by Ferelith Eccles Williams.   London and New York, Nelson, 1967.

The Sea Monkey, illustrated by Gay Galsworthy.   London, Longman, and Cleveland, World, 1968.

Tawno, Gypsy Boy, illustrated by Gareth Floyd.   Leicester, Brockhampton Press, 1968.

Runaway Boy, illustrated by Michal Morse.   London, Heinemann, 1971.

Nowhere to Stop, illustrated by Gareth Floyd.   Leicester, Brockhampton Press, 1972.

Marie Alone.   London, Heinemann, 1973.

The Rotten Old Car, illustrated by Leslie Wood.   Leicester, Brockhampton Press, 1973; Chicago, Children's Press, 1976.

Tim and the Red Indian Headdress, illustrated by Carolyn Dinan.   Leicester, Brockhampton Press, 1973; Chicago, Children's Press, 1976.

The Yellow Pom-Pom Hat, illustrated by Margaret Palmer.   Leicester, Brockhampton Press, 1974; Chicago, Children's Press, 1976.

Goodbye, Ruby Red, illustrated by Robin Lawrie.   Leicester, Brockhampton Press, 1974; Chicago, Children's Press, 1976.

Joanna All Alone, illustrated by Mary Dinsdale.   Newton Abbot, Devon, David and Charles, 1974; Nashville, Nelson, 1975.

A Nail, a Stick, and a Lid, illustrated by Linda Birch.   Leicester, Brockhampton Press, 1975; Chicago, Children's Press, 1976.

Billy-Boy, illustrated by Gareth Floyd.   London, Hodder and Stoughton, 1975.

Children of the Turnpike, illustrated by Gareth Floyd.   London, Hodder and Stoughton, 1976.

A Different Sort of Christmas, illustrated by Doreen Caldwell.   London, Kaye and Ward, 1976.

Where Is Fred?, illustrated by Mike Cole.   London, Hodder and Stoughton, 1976.

Penny Black.   London, Heinemann, 1976.

Other (readers)

Tales for Malayan Children.   Singapore, Donald Moore, 1956.

The Creek Near Kwarme's Village and Other Stories, illustrated by Lorna Paull.   London, Oxford University Press, 1961.

Kwaku and the Bush Baby.   London, Oxford University Press, 1961.

Kwaku Goes Shopping.   London, Oxford University Press, 1961.

Susie and Sophie and Other Stories, illustrated by Gene Adams.   London, Oxford University Press, 1961.

Nii-Ofrang and His Garden and Other Stories, illustrated by Lorna Paull.   London, Oxford University Press, 1962.

Kwabena and the Leopard, illustrated by Elizabeth Vaughan.   London, Oxford University Press, 1964.

Yaa Goes South, illustrated by Elizabeth Vaughan.   London, Oxford University Press, 1967.

Bonfire Night, illustrated by George Adamson.   London, Macmillan, 1968.

Eight Days to Christmas, illustrated by Shirley Hughes.   London, Macmillan, 1970.

In the Park, illustrated by Lynette Hemmant.   London, Macmillan, 1970.

The Rainbow Shirt, illustrated by Lynette Hemmant.   London, Macmillan, 1970.

Red Shoes. London, Oxford University Press, 1971.

Nowhere to Go. London, Oxford University Press, 1971.

The Tin Soldier. London, Oxford University Press, 1971.

Donkey Boy, illustrated by Prudence Seward. London, Oxford University Press, 1972.

Ginger, illustrated by Shirley Hughes. London, Macmillan, 1972.

The Children of the Brown Family, illustrated by Gavin Rowe. London, Oxford University Press, 1973.

A Mad Skipping Cat. London, Macmillan, 1974.

Scrap's Club. London, Macmillan, 1974.

To Catch a Thief, illustrated by Trevor Stubley. London, Oxford University Press, 1975.

Adventure in London, illustrated by Mary Dinsdale. London, Oxford University Press, 1975.

Christmas Is a Baby, illustrated by Richard Butler. Lond, Macmillan, 1975.

Pegs and Flowers, illustrated by Richard Butler. London, Macmillan, 1975.

In Portobello Road, illustrated by Mary Dinsdale. London, Oxford University Press, 1976.

In the New Forest, illustrated by Trevor Stubley. London, Oxford University Press, 1976.

Geraldine Kaye comments:

I write for the whole child age range but I have tended to write for older children and teenagers as my own children have grown up. I write quite a lot about children in different cultures and environments and I am especially interested in the child who is culturally an outsider: the Gypsy child or the child of mixed parentage. It also seems to me to be important to try to give recognition to the fact that we live in a very fluid, rapidly changing society in which there is no longer clear consensus on many issues of social behaviour.

*   *   *

It is no accident which makes Geraldine Kaye so much in demand at creative writing courses. Participants encounter no mystique, no sense of the weighty English literary tradition, no talk of inspiration and the Muse. They meet instead an unpretentious professional who makes no large claims for her work; someone ever willing to exercise her craft in a commissioned series title, yet no mere cipher but a writer with skill, individuality and conviction.

The early stories, such as *The Boy Who Wanted to Go Fishing* and *Kofi and the Eagle*, make use of Geraldine Kaye's knowledge of Malaya and Africa: their level of difficulty is indicated by their inclusion in Methuen's Read Aloud series. Within the simple form, however, is contained the typical Kaye richness. The background details are authentic and sufficient to give atmosphere without unbalancing plot; the story lines are clear and uncluttered, the observation precise, and a quiet wisdom imbues the whole. The same characteristics are seen in the longer stories, many of which are based on Geraldine Kaye's long interest in gypsies and the disadvantaged. *Runaway Boy*, for example, takes the adjustment of Danny Baker, newly escaped from an approved school, to life in the open and eventual adoption by a gypsy family, while *Billy-Boy* and *Nowhere to Stop* both explore the gap between gypsies and the communities they settle in.

Geraldine Kaye's professionalism manifests itself in her adaptation to various audiences: a year's output might range from a brief supplementary reader in Hodder's Stepping Stones series or one of Macmillan's Nippers to a Heinemann Pyramid book for "reluctant" teenagers, as well as a full length book. The results are always competent and readable, often more, but quality does vary. *The Rotten Old Car* (Stepping Stones series) is a book which manages to be short and satisfying and to include an element of ambiguity which encourages the reader to build his own interpretation; *Penny Black* (Pyramid series) is the magazine story extended, with stereotyped characters – dreamy Penny and nagging Mum – and expected outcome, the discovery of a new rapport with Mike as they queue up for evening class registration.

If one had to choose one book to typify Geraldine Kaye, *Nowhere to Stop* would have a strong claim. The pace, accessible style, warmth and fairness make this a book to both enjoy and admire. While the social conscience which is a hallmark of the 1970's is clearly informing the whole story, the dogmatic tone which also characterises much current fiction writing for children is absent. Geraldine Kaye may be unlikely to make the first rank of children's authors but she can claim to be read, understood and enjoyed by a wide audience, and for many the reading will have brought extension of sympathies as well as entertainment.

—Peggy Heeks

KEATS, Ezra Jack.   American.   Born in Brooklyn, New York, 11 March 1916. Educated in public schools. Taught in the School of Visual Arts, New York, 1947–48, and Workshop School, New York, 1955–57. Magazine and advertisement illustrator. Recipient: American Library Association Caldecott Medal, 1963; *Boston Globe-Horn Book* Award, for illustration, 1970. Address: 444 East 82nd Street, New York, New York 10028, U.S.A.

PUBLICATIONS FOR CHILDREN (illustrated by the author)

Fiction

> *My Dog Is Lost*, with Pat Cherr.   New York, Crowell, 1960.
> *The Snowy Day.*   New York, Viking Press, 1962; London, Bodley Head, 1967.
> *Whistle for Willie.*   New York, Viking Press, 1964; London, Bodley Head, 1966.
> *Jennie's Hat.*   New York, Harper, 1966.
> *Peter's Chair.*   New York, Harper, 1967; London, Bodley Head, 1968.
> *A Letter to Amy.*   New York, Harper, 1968; London, Bodley Head, 1969.
> *Goggles.*   New York, Macmillan, 1969; London, Bodley Head, 1970.
> *Hi, Cat!*   New York, Macmillan, 1970; London, Bodley Head, 1971.
> *Apt. 3.*   New York, Macmillan, 1971; London, Hamish Hamilton, 1972.
> *Pet Show!*   New York, Macmillan, and London, Hamish Hamilton, 1972.
> *Psst! Doggie–.*   New York, Watts, 1973.
> *Skates!*   New York, Watts, 1973.
> *Dreams.*   New York, Macmillan, and London, Hamish Hamilton, 1974.
> *Kitten for a Day.*   New York, Watts, 1974.
> *Louie.*   New York, Morrow, 1975; London, Hamish Hamilton, 1976.

Other

> *John Henry, An American Legend.*   New York, Pantheon Books, 1965.

> Editor, *Over in the Meadow* (verse).   New York, Scholastic, 1971; London, Hamish Hamilton, 1973.

PUBLICATIONS FOR ADULTS

Other

Editor, *God Is in the Mountain* (quotations). New York, Holt Rinehart, 1966.
Editor, *Night* (quotations), photographs by Beverly Hall. New York, Atheneum, 1969.

Manuscript Collection: Gutman Library, Harvard University, Cambridge, Massachusetts.

Illustrator: *Chester* by Eleanor Clymer, 1954; *Wonder Tales of Dogs and Cats* by Florence Carpenter, 1955; *Mystery on the Isle of Skye* by Phyllis Whitney, 1955; *A Change of Climate*, 1956, and *The Tournament of the Lions*, 1960, by Jay Williams; *Danny Dunn and the Anti-Gravity Paint*, 1956, *Danny Dunn on a Desert Island*, 1957, *Danny Dunn and the Homework Machine* 1958, and *Danny Dunn and the Weather Machine*, 1959, all by Jay Williams and Raymond Abrashkin; *Three Young Kings* by George Albee, 1956; *Sure Thing for Shep* by Elizabeth Lansing, 1956; *And Long Remember* by Dorothy Canfield Fisher, 1959; *Desmond's First Case* by Herbert Best, 1961; *In the Night* by Paul Showers, 1961; *The Rice Bowl Pet* by Patricia Miles Martin, 1962; *Tia Maria's Garden* by Ann Nolan Clark, 1963; *The Flying Cow* by Ruth Collins, 1963; *Wee Joseph* by William MacKellar, 1964; *Zoo, Where Are You?* by Ann McGovern, 1964; *In a Spring Garden* edited by Richard Lewis, 1965; *The Naughty Boy: A Poem* by John Keats, 1965; *How to Be a Nature Detective* by Millicent Selsam, 1966; *The Little Drummer Boy* by Katherine Davis, Henry Onorati, and Harry Simeone, 1968; *In the Park* by Esther Hautzig, 1968; *Two Tickets to Freedom* by Florence B. Freedman, 1971; *The King's Fountain* by Lloyd Alexander, 1971; *Penny Tunes and Princesses* by Myron Levoy, 1972.

Ezra Jack Keats comments:
My purpose in creating books for children is to share my experiences with them, ranging from the real world and feeling to fantasy. I hope children, whoever they may be, will discover that they are important, resourceful, and that they can have hope and self-esteem.

*   *   *

In his early book *Whistle for Willie* Ezra Jack Keats came forward with his own unmistakable style of illustration and text: the cut-out and gouache collage that gaily and vividly simplifies and stylises urban landscapes while the precise, almost scannable text, a separate statement for every page, concentrates the incidents of the stories – each a learning situation for under-fives – into easily memorable details. All Keats' books combine the child's excitement at discovering new abilities and attitudes – like whistling (in *Whistle for Willie*), coping with ambivalent emotions (*Peter's Chair*), outwitting tougher and older kids (*Goggles*), or helping (a blind man in *Apt.3*) with a strong sense of the grim urban reality in which their little negro heroes Peter, Archie, Sam, etc. grow up. Yet the Brooklyn street, with its litter, its grimy building fronts, and graffiti-covered walls which always serves as backdrop, has the rich and lively atmosphere of home just as much as the interior of Peter's apartment or of Sam and Ben's apartment block where every inmate is known to the boys. Keats does not gloss over the stark urban reality. He presents it as the emotionally secure child would experience it, full of solid objects like traffic lights, trees, walls and pavements to draw on and play around on. This environment is as tangible in the illustrations – which little fingers find irresistibly redrawable, particularly in *The Snowy Day* with its footprints, stickmarks and "angels" made in the snow, its piling snow mountains and sparkling snow crystals – as in the text which laconically sets out the simple facts of inner and outer landscape in description and dialogue. Small things matter: found objects like sticks, cardboard boxes, pieces of chalk, goggles (*Goggles*), cats (*Hi, Cat!, Pet Show*), landmarks like look-out pipe and traffic light, the patient attention of grownups (Peter's parents, the blind man in *Apt.3*), friendship, planned and unplanned get-togethers like birthday parties (*A Letter to Amy*) and pet-shows (*Pet Show*), or improvised street entertainment (*Hi, Cat*). The world of these little books is at once open to discovery and quite secure. It is a world peopled with children, grown-ups and animals where the child becomes socialised gently and gradually, though not without experiencing the normal ambivalent feelings of pride at achieving and envy at others being better at something, of love (for parents and friends) and jealousy (for a newly arrived baby sister), of fear when bullied and triumph when successful through using wit, persistence or reasonableness. It revolves around the simple games of small children alone or in groups, and because it uses hardly any props except animals (Willie, Peter's dachshund, and Archie's found cat) it is universal, classless and timeless. There are some development and change in the style from the first books (*Whistle for Willie, The Snowy Day*) to later work (*Apt.3*), particularly in the illustrations which have changed from witty cutout collage to highly impressionistic shadow-play. Keats tackles increasingly the emotions rather than the sense and action experience of young children.

—Gertrud Mander

KEEPING, Charles (William James).   British.   Born in London, 22 September 1924. Educated at Frank Bryant School for Boys, Kennington, London; Regent Polytechnic School of Art, London, 1946–52, National Diploma in Art and Design. Served as a telegraphist in the Royal Navy, 1942–46. Married Renate Meyer in 1952; has three sons and one daughter. Printing trade apprentice, 1938; worked as an engineer and rent collector; Visiting Lecturer in Lithography, Regent Polytechnic School of Art, 1956–63. Since 1962, Visiting Lecturer in Lithography, Croydon College of Art and Design, Surrey. Artist and book designer and illustrator. Member, Society of Industrial Artists. Recipient (for illustration): Library Association Kate Greenaway Medal, 1968; Victoria and Albert Museum Francis Williams Memorial Prize, 1972; Bratislava Biennale Golden Apple Award, 1975. Agent: B.L. Kearly, 33 Chiltern Street, London W1M 1HJ. Address: 16 Church Road, Shortlands, Bromley, Kent BR2 0HP, England.

PUBLICATIONS FOR CHILDREN (illustrated by the author)

Fiction

> *Black Dolly.*   Leicester, Brockhampton Press, 1966; as *Molly o' the Moors*, Cleveland, World, 1966.
> *Shaun and the Cart-Horse.*   London, Oxford University Press, and New York, Watts, 1966.
> *Charley, Charlotte and the Golden Canary.*   London, Oxford University Press, and New York, Watts, 1967.
> *Alfie and the Ferry Boat.*   London, Oxford University Press, 1968; as *Alfie Finds the Other Side of the World*, New York, Watts, 1968.
> *Joseph's Yard.*   London, Oxford University Press, and New York, Watts, 1969.
> *Through the Window.*   London, Oxford University Press, and New York, Watts, 1970.
> *The Garden Shed.*   London, Oxford University Press, 1971.
> *The Spider's Web.*   London, Oxford University Press, 1972.
> *The Nanny Goat and the Fierce Dog.*   London, Abelard Schuman, 1973; New York, S.G. Phillips, 1974.
> *Richard.*   London, Oxford University Press, 1973.
> *The Railway Passage.*   London, Oxford University Press, 1974.

    Wasteground Circus.   London, Oxford University Press, 1975.
    Inter-City.   London, Oxford University Press, 1976.

Plays

    Television Plays: *Joseph's Yard*, 1970, and *Through the Window*, 1970, both from his own stories.

Other

    Editor, *Tinker Tailor: Folk Songs.*   Leicester, Brockhampton Press, 1968; Cleveland, World, 1969.
    Editor, *Cockney Ding Dong.*   London, Penguin, 1975.

Illustrator: *Man Must Measure* by Ted Kavanagh, 1955; *Heute und Morgen 2* and *3* by Martha Freudenberger and Magda Kelber, 1956–57; *The Silver Branch*, 1957, *Warrior Scarlet*, 1958, *The Lantern Bearers*, 1959, *Knight's Fee*, 1960, *Dawn Wind*, 1961, *Beowulf*, 1961, *Heroes and History*, 1965, *The Mark of the Horse Lord*, 1965, *Dragon Slayer*, 1966, *The Capricorn Bracelet*, 1973, and *Blood Feud*, 1977, all by Rosemary Sutcliff; *Bridges*, 1958, *Roads*, 1959, *Canals*, 1961, *Ships*, 1962, *Railways*, 1964, *Wells*, 1965, *Dams*, 1966, and *Harbours and Docks*, 1967, all by John Stewart Murphy; *Merrily on High* by Guthrie Foote, 1959; *Riverbend Bricky*, 1960, and *Bricky and the Hobo*, 1964, by Ira Nesdale; *Tales of Pirates and Castaways*, 1960, and *Tales of the West Country*, 1961, by Kathleen Fidler; *The Queen of Trent* by Mitchell Dawson, 1961; *King Solomon's Mines* by Rider Haggard, 1961; *The Golden Age*, 1962, and *Dream Days*, 1962, by Kenneth Grahame; *Lost John* by Barbara Leonie Picard, 1962; *Tipiti the Robin* by René Guillot, 1962; *The Shadow-Line, and Within the Tides* by Joseph Conrad, 1962; *Three Trumpets* by Ruth Chandler, 1962; *Harriet and the Cherry Pie* by Clare Compton, 1963; *Knights of the Golden Table*, 1963, and *The Treasure of Siegfried*, 1964, by E.M. Almedingen; *Patrick Kentigern Keenan*, 1963, *The Kelpie's Pearls*, 1964, and *Thomas and the Warlock*, 1967, by Mollie Hunter; *The Castle and the Harp* by Philip Rush, 1963; *Grimbold's Other World*, 1963, *Mainly in Moonlight*, 1965, *The Apple-Stone*, 1969, and *Over the Hills to Fabylon*, 1970, all by Nicholas Stuart Gray; *The Horned Helmet*, 1963, *The Children's Crusade*, 1964, *The Last of the Vikings*, 1964, *Splintered Sword*, 1965, *Swords from the North*, 1967, *The Dream-Time*, 1967, and *The Invaders*, 1972, all by Henry Treece; *The Moonstone* by Wilkie Collins, 1963; *They Told Mr. Hakluyt* edited by Frank Knight, 1964; *Whitsun Warpath* by Elizabeth Grove, 1964; *The Story of Egypt* by Jacoba Sporry, 1964; *Jenny*, 1964, *The Next-Doors*, 1964, and *Mrs. Jenny*, 1966, all by Joan Tate; *Wuthering Heights* by Emily Brontë, 1964; *The King's Contest*, 1964, *The Sky-Eater*, 1966, and *Poko and the Golden Demon*, 1968, all by James Holding; *The Rain Boat* by Lace Kendall, 1965; *Elidor* by Alan Garner, 1965; *Damien the Leper's Friend* by John Reginald Milsome, 1965; *Your English* by Denys Thompson and R.J. Harris, 1965; *King Horn*, 1965, and *The Wildman*, 1976, by Kevin Crossley-Holland; *Bent Is the Bow*, 1965, and *The Red Towers of Granada*, 1966, by Geoffrey Trease; *The Life of Our Lord* by Henry Daniel-Rops, 1965; *An Owl for His Birthday*, 1966, *The Haunted Mine*, 1968, *A Boy and His Bike*, 1976, and *The Story of Tod*, all by Richard Potts; *All Quiet on the Western Front* by Erich Maria Remarque, 1966; *Island of the Great Yellow Ox*, 1966, and *The Flight of the Doves*, 1968, by Walter Macken; *Komantcia* by Harold Keith, 1966; *Celtic Folk and Fairy Tales* by Eric and N.I.S. Protter, 1967; *With Books on Her Head* by Edna Walker Chandler, 1967; *Champion of Charlemagne* by Marie Butts, 1967; *Bach* by Frederic Westcott, 1967; *The Cold Flame* by James Reeves, 1967, and *An Anthology of Free Verse* edited by Reeves, 1968; *The Christmas Story*, 1968; *The Mixture as Before*, 1968, and *Of Human Bondage*, by W. Somerset Maugham; *After Many a Summer*, 1969, and *Time Must Have a Stop*, 1969, by Aldous Huxley; *The Tale of Ancient Israel* by Roger Lancelyn Green, 1969; *The Castle of Otranto* by Horace Walpole, 1969; *Mr. Britling Sees It Through* by H.G. Wells, 1969; *Knights, Beasts and Wonders* by Margaret J. Miller, 1969; *The Heroes* by Charles Kingsley, 1970; *The God Beneath the Sea*, 1970, and *The Golden Shadow*, 1973, by Leon Garfield and Edward Blishen; *The Angry Valley* by Nigel Grimshaw, 1970; *Early Encounters* by John Watts, 1970; *Five Fables from France*, 1970, and *The Strange Feathery Beast*, 1973, by Lee Cooper; *Ruined City*, 1970, and *On the Beach*, 1970, by Nevil Shute; *The Poet's Tales* by William Cole, 1971; *The Idiot* by Feodor Dostoevsky, 1971; *Enjoy Reading!* by R.E. Rogerson, 1971; *The Valley of the Frost Giants* by Mary Francis Shura, 1971; *Wizards and Wampum* by Roger Squire, 1972; *The Twelve Labors of Hercules* by Robert Newman, 1972; *Flood Warning* by Paul Berna, 1972; *Weland, Smith of the Gods* by Ursula Synge, 1972; *I'll Tell You a Tale* by Ian Serraillier, 1973; *The Ghost Stories of M.R. James*, 1973; *Weirdies*, 1973, *Monsters, Monsters, Monsters*, 1974, and *Spooks, Spirits, and Spectres*, 1975, all by Helen Hoke; *The Birds and Other Stories* by Lewis Jones, 1973; *The Latchkey Children* by Eric Allen, 1974; *The Magic Horns* by Forbes Stuart, 1974; *The Little Book of Sylvanus* by David Kossoff, 1975; *Tower Blocks* by Marian Lines, 1975; *Terry on the Fence* by Bernard Ashley, 1975; *About Sleeping Beauty* by P.L. Travers, 1975; *Les Miserables* by Victor Hugo, 1976; *Stumpy*; *Dr. Jekyll and Mr. Hyde, The Wrecker, New Arabian Nights*, and *More New Arabian Nights* all by Robert Louis Stevenson.

Charles Keeping comments:

I suppose many of my picture books for children have grown out of something observed or overheard during my numerous long walks around London. A few relate directly to experiences from my own childhood. *The Spider's Web*, for example, came from early thoughts recalled from childhood, whereas *The Railway Passage* grew out of a conversation with a comparative stranger in a pub.

I like a picture book to be more than just entertaining or a collection of pretty pictures. It should present a variety of ideal and interesting situations to stimulate thought, but I *don't* like moral solutions.

*   *   *

Always a masterly illustrator of other people's words, Charles Keeping, like many of today's finest children's book artists, has moved over to writing and illustrating his own books. While he is not in any way a born writer, although capable of the occasional telling phrase, it is certainly true that he is at his best as an artist when working to his own inspiration. Moreover he has learned the trick of making his text a foil for the pictures and pares his words increasingly so as to convey more and more of his information visually, a technique he uses to great effect in *Richard*, the story of a day in the life of a London police horse, where no detail of stabling or grooming is omitted yet the text is reduced to hardly more than captions. In this way Keeping keeps his flat, prosaic sentences simple for young readers and relies on his pictures to provide the imaginative stimulus they need.

Keeping's style has changed much over the years but his world has remained the same, the streets and yards of London's east end and the banks of London's river which he knows deeply, almost instinctively, and portrays with a detailed and observant sympathy which makes his books a chronicle for adults as well as a pleasure for children. The bold swathes of colour he used in his cockney fairy tale *Charley, Charlotte and the Golden Canary*, which won him the Kate Greenaway Medal for 1967, and the watery brilliance of *Alfie and the Ferry Boat* – in which a small boy crosses the Thames and discovers "the other side of the world" – have given way to a subtler use of line, but his work, although more delicate, has lost nothing of its strength. It has become, if anything, more formidable.

There has always been a sombre element in Keeping's imagination – in *Joseph's Yard*, for instance, or *Through the Window* – but in recent years he can be frightening, using strange angles and weird foreshortenings to suggest the transformations that the mind can work on the physical world. The chicken seen through the fence in *The Spider's Web* becomes a crimson, glaring basilisk at one moment, a harmless fowl the next. Fortunately for the reader,

Keeping's perception of things innocent or benevolent – the horse and the spider itself in the same book – is equally acute, so that ultimately gentleness prevails. Yet there is a pessimism in him which hints that the outcome is a near thing – and for how long?

—Anne Carter

KEITH, Harold (Verne). American. Born in Lambert, Oklahoma Territory, 8 April 1903. Educated at Lambert High School, graduated, 1921; Northwestern State College, Alva, Oklahoma (Scroll Scholarship, 1922), 1921–24; University of Oklahoma, Norman, B.A. in history 1929, M.A. 1938. Married Virginia Livingston in 1931; has two children. Elementary school teacher, Amorita, Oklahoma, 1922–23; Sports Correspondent, *Daily Oklahoman*, Oklahoma City, *Tulsa World*, Oklahoma, *Kansas City Star*, Missouri, and *Omaha World-Herald*, Nebraska, 1922–29; assistant grain buyer, Red Star Milling Company, Hutchinson, Kansas, 1929–30; Sports Publicity Director, University of Oklahoma, 1930–69. President, College Sports Information Directors, 1964–65. Broke U.S. Masters national records for the two and three-mile runs, 1973, and 10,000 meters run, 1974. Recipient: American Library Association Newbery Medal, 1958; Western Heritage Award, 1975; Western Writers of America Spur Award, 1975. Agent: Oliver G. Swan, Collier's Literary Agency, 280 Madison Avenue, New York, New York 10016. Address: 2318 Ravenwood, Route 3, Norman, Oklahoma 73071, U.S.A.

PUBLICATIONS FOR CHILDREN

Fiction

> *Shotgun Shaw: A Baseball Story*, illustrated by Mabel Jones Woodbury.   New York, Crowell, 1949.
> *A Pair of Captains*, illustrated by Mabel Jones Woodbury.   New York, Crowell, 1951.
> *Rifles for Watie*.   New York, Crowell, 1957; London, Oxford University Press, 1960.
> *Komantcia*.   New York, Crowell, 1965; London, Oxford University Press, 1966.
> *Brief Garland*.   New York, Crowell, 1971.
> *The Runt of Rogers School*.   Philadelphia, Lippincott, 1971.
> *Go, Red, Go!*, illustrated by Ned Glattauer.   Nashville, Nelson, 1972.
> *The Bluejay Boarders*, illustrated by Harold Berson.   New York, Crowell, 1972.
> *Susy's Scoundrel*, illustrated by John Schoenherr.   New York, Crowell, 1974.
> *The Obstinate Land*.   New York, Crowell, 1977.

Other

> *Boys' Life of Will Rogers*, illustrated by Karl S. Woerner.   New York, Crowell, 1937.

PUBLICATIONS FOR ADULTS

Other

> *Oklahoma Kickoff* (on football).   Privately printed, 1948.
> *Sports and Games*.   New York, Crowell, 1941; revised edition, 1960.

Manuscript Collections: Northwestern State College Library, Alva, Oklahoma; University of Oklahoma Library, Norman.

Harold Keith comments:

I like to write straight at the young people themselves. I like to use a variety of fields for background – Civil War in the West, Comanche Indians, regional sports history, baseball, football, boys and girls basketball, bluejays, coyotes, the Cherokee Strip land run of 1893 – almost anything that will let me research an unfamiliar field and learn more about it. It would be very dull, I believe, to write two books about the same topic or the same sport.

Hundreds of boys and girls from all over the United States write letters to me telling me what they like or dislike about my books. This is very useful to a writer. I answer every letter I receive.

*   *   *

Harold Keith's first books for children reflected some of his own interests; *Boys' Life of Will Rogers* emanated from Keith's master's thesis on Rogers' father, and *Sports and Games*, a Junior Literary Guild selection, from his remarkable record as a competitive athlete. A prolific writer of short stories for boys' magazines, Keith also wrote several sports novels. He gives much credit for the acclaim he earned for *Rifles for Watie* to the skills he had learned at a school for writers, analyzing the elements of the book (contrast, characterization, a crucial decision) in his Newbery acceptance speech in relation to what had been taught in writing classes. The mechanics, however, are fortunately not obtrusive in the book itself, a story of the Civil War in which a young Union soldier is sent behind the Confederate lines to try to discover where Stand Watie, a Cherokee, is getting new rifles that had been intended for the Union Army. The book is a strong indictment of war, showing that there are tragedy and deprivation, as well as heroism, on both sides. The protagonist, Jeff, is captured by the Confederates and successfully pretends to be one of them, so that for a time he lives and works with his enemies – and so learns that they are young men much like himself. The change from a carefree youth who saw only one side of the issues of the war to a mature young man who could understand the viewpoint of the enemy gives the story depth of characterization. The historical details are accurate and vivid; the writing style has an easy narrative flow.

Although Keith has successfully used contemporary settings in some stories (*Susy's Scoundrel*, the story of an Amish child's pet coyote, or the story of wild pets, *The Bluejay Boarders*), he is at his best when writing about the past, for then his interest in history, especially that of the Civil War period, gives life to fiction. In *Komantcia*, based on the true story of a young Spaniard taken captive by the Comanches in 1865, Pedro adjusts to the native American culture and then embraces it; Keith makes the story completely convincing by incorporation of well-researched historical details.

—Zena Sutherland

KELLY, Eric (Philbrook). American. Born in Amesbury, Massachusetts, 16 March 1884. Educated at Dartmouth College, Hanover, New Hampshire, A.B. 1906, M.A. 1929. Married Katherine Collins Merrill in 1924. Staff member, *Westfield Times*, Massachusetts, 1906, *Springfield Union*, Massachusetts, 1906–11, *Hunterton Gazette*, High Bridge, New Jersey, 1912, *Boston Herald*, 1914–18, and *Boston Transcript*, summers 1922–24; Instructor of English, 1921–29, Professor of Journalism, 1929–54, and Emeritus Professor, 1954–60, Dartmouth College. Lecturer (Kosciuszko Foundation Scholar), University of Krakow,

Poland, 1925–26; member of mission to Mexico, Office of Foreign Relief and Rehabilitation Operations, 1943. Vice-President, Paderewski Commission; Trustee, Kosciuszko Foundation. Recipient: American Library Association Newbery Medal, 1929; Kosciuszko Foundation Gold Medal, 1956. Chevalier, 1934, and Commander, 1945, Order Polonia Restituta. *Died in January 1960.*

PUBLICATIONS FOR CHILDREN

Fiction

> *The Trumpeter of Krakow*, illustrated by Angela Pruszynska.   New York, Macmillan, 1928; London, Chatto and Windus, 1968.
> *The Blacksmith of Vilno*, illustrated by Angela Pruszynska.   New York, Macmillan, 1930.
> *The Golden Star of Halich*, illustrated by Angela Pruszynska.   New York, Macmillan, 1931.
> *The Christmas Nightingale*, illustrated by Marguerite de Angeli. New York, Macmillan, 1932.
> *Three Sides of Agiochook*, illustrated by Le Roy Appleton.   New York, Macmillan, 1935.
> *Treasure Mountain*, illustrated by Raymond Lufkin.   New York, Macmillan, 1937.
> *At the Sign of the Golden Compass*, illustrated by Raymond Lufkin.   New York, Macmillan, and Birmingham, Combridge, 1938.
> *In Clean Hay.*   Privately printed, 1940.
> *On the Staked Plain*, illustrated by Harve Stein.   New York, Macmillan, 1940.
> *From Star to Star*, illustrated by Manning Lee.   Philadelphia, Lippincott, 1944.
> *The Hand in the Picture*, illustrated by Irena Lorentowicz.   Philadelphia, Lippincott, 1947.
> *The Amazing Journey of David Ingram.*   Philadelphia, Lippincott, 1948.

Other

> *A Girl Who Would Be Queen: The Story and Diary of the Young Countess Krasinska*, with Clara Hoffmanowa, illustrated by Vera Bock.   Chicago, McClurg, 1939.
> *Polish Legends and Tales.*   New York, Polish Publication Society of America, 1971.

PUBLICATIONS FOR ADULTS

Other

> *The Hope of All the Poles in the World.*   Chicago, Polish Roman Catholic Union Archives and Museum, 1941.
> *The Land of the Polish People.*   New York, Stokes, 1943; revised edition, Philadelphia, Lippincott, 1952.

*   *   *

The larger body of Eric Kelly's creative writing results from his deep love and respect for a land and a people not his own except by adoption. Although generally regarded as literature for younger readers, Kelly's fiction has been widely enjoyed by the reading public at large. Characterized by an unerring blend of good story-telling and Poland's colorful history, his fiction has brought to readers an appreciation for the cultural and intellectual history of Poland and the aspirations and ideals of a valiant and honorable people.

Kelly's intense appreciation for medieval art and architecture, his love of natural beauty, and his eye for photographic detail have found expression in a variety of Polish tales and legends. In his "By Order of the Queen," which first appeared in 1924 in *St. Nicholas*, Kelly describes Krakow, Poland, as a city of gold — "yellow in dawn, gray in dusk, blue in the midday, but gold, gold, gold in the sweet hour of sunset." He is equally at ease with characterization. In "By Order of the Queen," for example, the buyers and sellers in the market place are seen in jocular, conversational mood; yet as though setting a stage and chiseling a special character for the engrossing and suspenseful story to follow, Kelly introduces early a woman flitting "from bargain-stall to bargain-stall, glancing within as if searching for someone." She is not an old woman, he says, "but there is that about her which tells of age in other terms than years." "By Order of the Queen" and other Eric Kelly stories which appeared in *St. Nicholas* in the mid-1920's are but earlier harbingers of his highly acclaimed trilogy of Polish cities — *The Trumpeter of Krakow, The Blacksmith of Vilno*, and *The Golden Star of Halich.*

The best known and most representative of the trilogy is *The Trumpeter of Krakow* which won for its author the Newbery Medal. The general setting of this unusual historical romance is the city of Krakow; the specific setting, the parish church of St. Mary the Virgin. This church with its Gothic architecture, the royal castle on Wawel Hill, the old and renowned Krakow University, and city streets at night time provide a proper backdrop for a dramatic, swift-moving, action-packed story. The politics of Krakow's constant threat from invading Tartars or greedy Russian tsars during the fifteenth century provide warp and woof to Mr. Kelly's exciting literary canvas, while a rich historical tradition is continued in the hourly trumpeting of the Polish *Heynal* from a tower in St. Mary's. The young trumpeter Joseph Charnetski and his family, the wise and revered Professor Jan Kanty, alchemists, hypnotists, thieves, and ruffians provide suspenseful action in a drama told in rich, poetic prose. *The Trumpeter of Krakow* is analogous in some respects to Victor Hugo's *Notre-Dame de Paris*; assuredly it places Eric Kelly among the most capable American creators of juvenile fiction of his own period or any other.

—Charity Chang

KENDALL, Carol. American. Born in Bucyrus, Ohio, 13 September 1917. Educated at Bucyrus High School, graduated, 1935; Ohio University, Athens, 1935–39, A.B. 1939 (Phi Beta Kappa). Married Paul Murray Kendall in 1939 (died, 1973); has two daughters. Address: 928 Holiday Drive, Lawrence, Kansas 66044, U.S.A.

PUBLICATIONS FOR CHILDREN

Fiction

> *The Other Side of the Tunnel*, illustrated by Lilian Buchanan. London, Lane, 1956; New York, Abelard Schuman, 1957.
> *The Gammage Cup*, illustrated by Erik Blegvad. New York, Harcourt Brace, 1959; as *The Minnipins*, London, Dent, 1960.
> *The Big Splash*, illustrated by Lilian Obligado. New York, Viking Press, 1960.
> *The Whisper of Glocken*, illustrated by Imero Gobbato. New York, Harcourt Brace, 1965; London, Bodley Head, 1967.

PUBLICATIONS FOR ADULTS

Novels

The Black Seven.   New York, Harper, 1946; London, Lane, 1950.
The Baby-Snatcher.   London, Lane, 1952.

Manuscript Collection: Ohio University Library, Athens.

Carol Kendall comments:
    Fantasy is what I most enjoy writing. I like it for its agelessness and its simplicity, probably because I like to concentrate on ageless and simple themes: truth, honor, courage, goodness. I try for morality without mawkishness; fantasy seems to me the best means of achieving it.

                                        *   *   *

    The books of Carol Kendall are distinguished for their inventiveness and mixture of comic and serious content. In *The Gammage Cup*, the author was interested in depicting stalwart, inner-directed people on the one hand, and on the other hand the pettiness and tyranny of conformists.
    Literary fantasies offer the pleasure of looking in two different directions at once: toward an imaginary place and toward the world as we know it. *The Gammage Cup* provides this diverting interplay, as well as a theme which is particularly adaptable for children. For example, the oddities of the non-conforming protagonists can be treated playfully. Kendall's heroine, Muggles, has her own system of tidiness: "All was in perfect order, ... the way she liked it – the far-corner pile, the hearthstone pile, the under-the-table pile." And since the non-conformists are outnumbered by the rest of the Minnipin villagers, their underdog position allows for exciting encounters and conflicts.
    A further necessity in fantasies is to develop a sense of solidity in imaginary realms. This entails descriptive skill and high ingenuity, notable qualities in the Kendall fantasies. The history and geography of the Minnipin valley, the system of government, the values, economy, forms of recreation – these all take shape without direct exposition. Most important, the language of the Minnipins reminds us of their world apart and at the same time its ties with the world the reader knows. Minnipins have merry-go-longs, bobble-boards, haggle-fetes, picklicks, kickety balls, wasso birds, soups with enriching huddlestone tansy. And because both *The Gammage Cup* and its sequel, *The Whisper of Glocken*, are wilderness survival tales, the books offer a double ethnology: the "civilized" Minnipin way of life and the survival tactics of the adventurers.
    One problem in the first book is based on sociological criteria. The Minnipins, after they patch up their internal political quarrel, cause the total extermination of the invading Mushroom army. Yet the Mushrooms have some human qualities. Without fully developing the Mushrooms as a symbol of total evil, the Minnipin victory seems almost like a case of genocide. In *The Whisper of Glocken* this problem doesn't arise. The new Minnipin heroes are captured by members of the threatening Hulk society, but both groups escape each other in the end. This is in keeping with the theme: cultural diversity is to be valued.
    Narratives which depend upon social commentary for meaning and cohesiveness take the risk of becoming dated. Authors often reflect a social climate which makes their work praiseworthy to one generation and objectionable to another. Kendall's fantasies are sufficiently allegorical to avoid widespread rejection on this basis. Yet in *The Gammage Cup* warfare is presumed to be inevitable (hence reasonable), and some parents are now considering this an unconscionable precept to offer to children.
    Generally speaking, Kendall's themes and craftsmanship indicate a deep respect for young readers. She is an advocate of both individuality and social commitment, yet treats this

theoretical content imaginatively. As for her style, it has that unlabored, graphic quality which heightens a tale's veracity and readability.

—Donnarae MacCann

KERR, (Anne-)Judith. British. Born in Berlin, Germany, 14 June 1923; left Germany in 1933, moved to England, 1936, naturalized citizen, 1947. Educated at schools in Germany, Switzerland, France, and England; Central School of Art, London (scholar), 1945. Married the writer Nigel Kneale in 1954; has one daughter and one son. Secretary, Red Cross, London, 1941–45; teacher and textile designer, 1946–53; Reader, Script Editor, and Script Writer, BBC-TV, London, 1953–58. Address: c/o William Collins Sons and Co. Ltd., 14 St. James's Place, London SW1A 1P5, England.

PUBLICATIONS FOR CHILDREN (illustrated by the author)

Fiction

> *The Tiger Who Came to Tea.* London, Collins, and New York, Coward McCann, 1968.
> *Mog the Forgetful Cat.* London, Collins, 1970; New York, Parents' Magazine Press, 1972.
> *When Hitler Stole Pink Rabbit.* London, Collins, 1971; New York, Coward McCann, 1972.
> *When Willy Went to the Wedding.* London, Collins, 1972; New York, Parents' Magazine Press, 1973.
> *The Other Way Round* (not illustrated). London, Collins, and New York, Coward McCann, 1975.
> *Mog's Christmas.* London, Collins, 1976; New York, Collins World, 1977.

Judith Kerr comments:
  The picture books were for my children – in fact, a lot of the ideas came from my children in the first place, and also from my husband. They were the sort of ideas which amused us all. Mog is our cat. The novels also were written for my children, but deal with my own childhood as a refugee from Hitler, first in Switzerland and France, later in England during the war. It was so different from the way they grew up that I wanted them to know about it, and I wanted also to explain that it wasn't nearly as horrific as it sounded. Perhaps most of all it was a way of remembering my own parents, now long dead.

*   *   *

  Judith Kerr's twin talents of writer and illustrator were in quantitative balance in her three popular picture books, *The Tiger Who Came to Tea, Mog the Forgetful Cat,* and *When Willy Went to the Wedding,* which were aimed, successfully, at the under-fives. With these she proved herself a thoroughly competent, professional, imaginative children's author – one among many. Real distinction, however, she achieved with her two autobiographical stories for young readers over ten which chart her exceptionally eventful childhood and adolescence as the daughter of a famous German Jewish writer and refugee from Nazi Germany. Together, *When Hitler Stole Pink Rabbit* and *The Other Way Round* tell Anna's (alias Judith's) 12-year odyssey that takes her to three countries (Switzerland, France, England) and makes her trilingual. It is a lively, detached, and objective narrative, helped by a distance of 30 years between event and writing down, a precise memory, a warm sense of humour, and profound insight into the growing self-awareness and world perception of child and teenager. Both books derive most of their interest from the interaction of outside political events with inside subjective experience of child and teenager, the first story the more poignantly so because little Anna is as yet incapable of grasping the momentous historical changes which force her universally respected father to leave his native country and end his brilliant career, thus changing their lives from wealthy middle-class to destitute stateless. Yet Judith Kerr demonstrates convincingly how all that matters for the child is family togetherness and emotional security, while lack of money or settled home is of secondary importance. Both in Switzerland and France little Anna bravely takes everything into her stride: drastically reduced living conditions, changing playmates and teachers, lack of toys and money, even adjusting to a new language and being cut by Nazi Germans on holiday in their temporary Swiss home. Only a brief separation from her parents proves traumatic, because the warm understanding in a secure family is her be-all and end-all, natural squabbling and disappointments notwithstanding. Anna thus has as happy a childhood as any child growing up in much more sheltered circumstances.

The 18-year old Anna in *The Other Way Round*, however, is learning independence the hard way because of the conditions the war and her enemy-alien status put her into, and because she feels for her aging parents in their appallingly reduced existence. They live in a cheap London hotel full of Central European refugees, her father a German-language writer without work and her mother doing menial jobs – the tragedy of exile! Yet Anna succeeds and overcomes by asserting the importance of her own life (secretary during the day, art student in the evening) in spite of her deep concern for her parents. She experiences first love and loss of love, first success and failure, the reward and monotony of work, the stirrings of creativity. Set against the richly detailed backcloth of the war, the Blitz and the Battle of Britain, rationing, air raids, buzz bombs and finally victory, Judith Kerr's story of Anna's successful transition from lost schoolgirl to self-possessed art student is a chronicle of an epoch as much as of the grim refugee life Anna and her family have to live while waiting for the war to end. Together, the two books give the young reader a bit of important contemporary history, as seen and experienced by somebody who went through it vulnerable, yet open-eyed. There is no better way for the young reader to be brought up both against recent history and the psychological implications such turbulent times had for those growing up in them.

—Gertrud Mander

KERR, M.E. Pseudonym for Marijane Meaker. American. Born in Auburn, New York, 27 May 1932. Educated at the University of Missouri, Columbia, B.A. Recipient: *Media and Methods* award, 1975. Agent: Patricia Myrer, McIntosh and Otis Inc., 475 Fifth Avenue, New York, New York 10017. Address: 12 Deep Six Drive, East Hampton, New York 11937, U.S.A.

PUBLICATIONS FOR CHILDREN

Fiction

Dinky Hocker Shoots Smack! New York, Harper, 1972; London, Gollanz, 1973.
If I Love You, Am I Trapped Forever? New York, Harper, 1973.
The Son of Someone Famous. New York, Harper, 1974; London, Gollancz, 1975.

Is That You, Miss Blue? New York, Harper, 1975.
Love Is a Missing Person. New York, Harper, 1975.
I'll Love You When You're More Like Me. New York, Harper, 1977.

M. E. Kerr comments:
I write to entertain. I hope I do.

*   *   *

All of M. E. Kerr's novels are fast-paced, witty and literate. A drawback of her fiction is the weak, passive or materialistic nature of many of her women characters. Most of her men don't fare much better when one considers their hard-drinking habits and male-chauvinist attitudes. However, in Kerr's excellent first novel, *Dinky Hocker Shoots Smack!*, there is a reasonable balance of males and females exhibiting a healthy flexibility in their relationships. Dinky Hocker's mother is the community's good Samaritan and Dinky, who is addicted to food, not to drugs, discovers the only way to get her busy mother's attention is to write the message, "Dinky Hocker Shoots Smack" on walls all over town. In this probing story, Dinky is grossly fat, sarcastic, unhappy, yet protective of her unstable cousin, Natalia. Her good-natured friend Tucker, informed that his mother wants to attend law school, readily agrees to assume the household chores with his cooperative father. Kerr exhibits a special talent for characterization with the introduction of P. John, the 15-year-old politically conservative son of an ultra-liberal father. The author is matchless in this hilarious, but serious, story of boys and girls growing up in a big city.

The loneliness of uprooted adolescents is underscored in *Is That You, Miss Blue?* Flanders Brown is estranged from her mother who has run off with a younger man but who, in reality, had run away from Flander's callous father. The 14-year-old grows up in her first three months on her own after various encounters, funny and sad, with an odd array of females at boarding school. But most of all, there is the pathetic Miss Ernestine Blue. Miss Blue is a religious fanatic who has dialogues with Jesus and, because of her fervor (despite the fact that she is an inspired science teacher), is dismissed from the faculty. A disillusioned Flanders impulsively decides to visit her mother who rejoices to receive the girl, listens with compassion, and gives Flanders a home again.

Both *Love Is a Missing Person* and *If I Love You, Am I Trapped Forever?* are narrated by the main characters. The teen-age girl and boy in these two novels reveal the hurt of growing up, of facing unpleasant truths about parents, and of having to make difficult decisions.

The Son of Someone Famous is actually two parallel stories told in alternating chapters which jump in point of view between Adam, the son of someone famous, and his sometime friend, Brenda Belle. This melange is a disappointment because we are never allowed time to mull over Adam's journal before Brenda breaks in with her "Notes for a Novel." Nevertheless, even here the author perceptively examines the very real pains, pleasures and conflicting passions which are inevitable as adolescents, especially those from fragmented families, grow up and define themselves as independent people. Unfortunately, this herculean task is inhibited when Kerr chooses not to develop positive adult models.

—Vivian J. Scheinmann

KIMENYE, Barbara. Born in East Africa. Private Secretary to the government of the Kabaka of Buganda; Journalist, *Uganda Nation*, Kampala. Since 1974, Social Worker in South London. Address: 38 Florence Street, London N.1, England.

Fiction

Moses. Nairobi, Oxford University Press, n.d.
Moses and Mildred, illustrated by Rena Fennessy. Nairobi, Oxford University Press, 1967.
Moses and the Kidnappers, illustrated by Rena Fennessy. Nairobi, Oxford University Press, 1968.
Moses in Trouble, illustrated by Rena Fennessy. Nairobi, Oxford University Press, 1968.
The Winged Adventure, illustrated by Terry Hirst. Nairobi, Oxford University Press, 1969.
Moses in a Muddle, illustrated by Rena Fennessy. Nairobi, Oxford University Press, 1970.
Moses and the Ghost, illustrated by Rena Fennessy. Nairobi, Oxford University Press, 1971.
Paulo's Strange Adventure, illustrated by Olga J. Heuser. Nairobi, Oxford University Press, 1971.
Moses on the Move, illustrated by Mara Onditi. Nairobi, Oxford University Press, 1972.
Barah and the Boy. Nairobi, Oxford University Press, 1973.
Martha the Millipede. Nairobi, Oxford University Press, 1973.
Moses and the Penpal. Nairobi, Oxford University Press, 1973.
Moses the Camper. Nairobi, Oxford University Press, 1973.

Other

The Smugglers (reader), illustrated by Roger Payne. London, Nelson, 1966.

Short Stories

Kalasanda. Nairobi and London, Oxford University Press, 1965.
Kalasanda Revisited. Nairobi and London, Oxford University Press, 1966.

*   *   *

Barbara Kimenye writes boys' adventure books, including the Moses series which are known in East, Central and West Africa. In the 10 books so far published, Barbara Kimenye has done for African children what Richmal Crompton did for English children through her famous William books. Like William, Moses is an engaging schoolboy, full of high spirits which regularly land him and his "gang" in trouble with the authorities.

But Moses is not a carbon copy of William. Whereas the setting for the William books is a middle-class home from which he emerges to harass the neighbours and his teachers, Moses' adventures are set entirely in his school. The school, which bears the pretentious name Mukibi's Educational Institute for the Sons of African Gentlemen, is really a shabby, money-making institution for throw-outs from reputable schools.

Despite the school's bad reputation, Barbara gives the reader the impression that not all the boys are really bad. She makes a distinction between high-spirited boys like Moses and bad boys such as the bully, Magara, and Wakweya, the crook masquerading as a schoolboy. Her sense of humour keeps everything in proportion as in her description of "Itchy Fingers" who when approached nicely would always return an article to the owner, though he might "absent-mindedly pick it up again later in the day."

Barbara writes about the escapades of Moses and his friends with indulgent amusement, most of them being simply unfortunate, not wicked. One such escapade is the collapse of the dormitory thatched roof over the heads of the Headmaster and his deputy while Moses is trying to retrieve his pet snake from the roof. On another occasion, the cooks go on strike and stingy Mukibi puts the boys on kitchen duty. The well-intentioned efforts of Moses and his friends to provide the school with decent meals in spite of the almost empty store lands Moses in a prickly pineapple patch and he also gets tossed by a cow during an illegal milking session at night. One cannot help feeling sorry for Moses on these occasions, especially as he gets punished by the school authorities for his pains.

The adventures of Moses and his friends are most exciting and include being kidnapped by robbers, chasing spies and ghosts, and outwitting crooked businessmen. They sound so probable that the reader tends to feel that they really happened. And this is why the books have been so successful.

Barbara Kimenye's other books are not as successful as the Moses series. *The Smugglers*, for example, reads like the script of a stereotyped cinema or television adventure. It is about three boys who tangle with gold smugglers who intend to kill them once their usefulness is over. They are saved in the nick of time.

—Mabel D. Segun

KING, (David) Clive. British. Born in Richmond, Surrey, 24 April 1924. Educated at King's School, Rochester, 1933–41; Downing College, Cambridge, 1941–43, 1946–48, B.A. in English 1948; School of Oriental and African Studies, University of London, 1966–67. Served in the Royal Navy Volunteer Reserve, 1943–46: Sub-Lieutenant. Married Jane Tuke in 1949 (divorced, 1974); Penelope Timmins, 1974; has one daughter and one son. Administrative Officer, Amsterdam, 1948–50, Student Welfare Officer, Belfast, 1950–51, Lecturer, Aleppo, Syria, 1951–54, Visiting Professor, Damascus, 1954–55, Lecturer and Director of Studies, Beirut, 1960–66, and Education Officer, Madras, 1971–73, all for the British Council; Warden, East Sussex County Council, Rye, 1955–60; Education Adviser, East Pakistan Education Centre, Dacca 1967–71. Agent: Murray Pollinger, 4 Garrick Street, London W.C.2. Address 65A St. Augustine's Road, London NW1 9RR, England.

PUBLICATIONS FOR CHILDREN

Fiction

Hamid of Aleppo, illustrated by Giovanetti. New York, Macmillan, 1958.
The Town That Went South, illustrated by Maurice Bartlett. New York, Macmillan, 1959; London, Penguin, 1961.
Stig of the Dump, illustrated by Edward Ardizzone. London, Penguin, 1963.
The Twenty Two Letters, illustrated by Richard Kennedy. London, Hamish Hamilton, 1966; New York, Coward McCann, 1967.
The Night the Water Came, illustrated by Mark Peppé. London, Longman, 1973.
Snakes and Snakes, illustrated by Richard Kennedy. London, Penguin, 1975.
Me and My Million. London, Penguin, 1976.

Plays

Poles Apart (produced London, 1975).
The World of Light (produced London, 1976).

Television Play: *Good Snakes, Bad Snakes*, 1977.

Other (readers; illustrated by Jacqueline Atkinson)

High Jacks, Low Jacks.   London, Benn, 1976.
First Day Out.   London, Benn, 1976.
Accident.   London, Benn, 1976.
The Secret.   London, Benn, 1976.

Clive King comments:
  Each of the things which I have written has been inspired by a particular place which I have visited or lived in. The settings are always as authentic as possible, and they determine the action. Some of my stories have required a great deal of research, but I try not to let it show. I am interested in putting abstract facts into the simplest and clearest language. I write best when I have a specific reader or group of readers in mind, and now that I am a full-time writer I try to keep in touch with children, preferably in informal circumstances.

                                   *   *   *

  Clive King is best known for *Stig of the Dump* (reprinted sixteen times). Its appeal to younger readers is obvious: most children have no difficulty in accepting Barney's discovery of a Stone Age cave-dweller at the bottom of a disused Kentish chalk-pit cum rubbish tip, and readily follow his adventures with Stig, first in improving the "cave" by adroit lateral thinking applied to tin cans and empty bottles, and later in their encounters with the Snargets gang, two burglars after Granny's silver, an escaped leopard at Mrs. Fawkham-Greene's fancy-dress party, and a summer solstice ceremony on the North Downs complete with Stone Age village and Standing Stones. The plot is innocent of any ingenious time-shift device: the real and fantasy worlds merely merge; and the story operates simply at the surface level, with no hint of deeper significance. Characterisation and dialogue are modest in execution, and feelings are not vividly conveyed or invoked. It is rather an engaging invention than a work or creative imagination.
  Since *Stig of the Dump*, Clive King's steady output has been marked by its versatility and a laudable refusal to repeat its commercially successful formula. *The Twenty Two Letters*, an ambitious if heavy-going 300-page project for older readers which is set in the eastern Mediterranean world of the 15th century B.C.. gives in three loosely-linked stories, each of which might with a little amplification have sufficed for a children's book on its own. the author's speculative account of the inventions of the alphabet. celestial navigation. and mounted cavalry, no less. The book is scholarly, painstaking, wide-ranging and informative, but the author's interest in myth, legend and history. stemming from his own travels in the Middle East, overrides his capacity to create character and telling incident. The illustrations by Richard Kennedy are excellent.
  Later books include such diverse themes as relief operations on Kukuri Makuri Char, a tropical island hit by a cyclone, in *The Night the Water Came*; poisonous snakes and Indian skulduggery in *Snakes and Snakes*, a tale for younger readers beautifully illustrated on almost every page, again by Richard Kennedy; and a colourful, slapstick romp through London with picture thieves in *Me and My Million*, in which the illiterate, resourceful, amoral Ringo catches the wrong bus, sleeps down a tube station, takes up with the Angels, a troupe of life-sharing carnival actors squatting in a disused fire station, rides in a Rolls, drops from a drain-pipe into a conveniently passing canal barge, and otherwise runs risks with Elvis, Angel Jim, Big Van, the Glasses gang, Eugene the chauffeur, and Sir Derrick, Director of the Lyle Gallery. If it is sometimes disappointing in execution. Clive King's work is certainly inventive and enterprising in conception.

                                                          —Graham Hammond

KINGMAN, (Mary) Lee. American. Born in Reading, Massachusetts, 6 October 1919. Educated at Colby-Sawyer College, New London, New Hampshire A.A. 1938; Smith College, Northampton, Massachusetts, B.A. 1940. Married Robert H. Natti in 1945; has two children. Assistant, 1943–44, and Juvenile Editor, 1944–46, Houghton Mifflin, publishers, Boston. Member, Folly Cove Designers, Gloucester, Massachusetts, 1946–71. Book editor, poster and calendar designer, Council Member 1964–70, and since 1970, Director, *Horn Book*, Boston. Address: Blood Ledge, Lanesville, Gloucester, Massachusetts 01930, U.S.A.

PUBLICATIONS FOR CHILDREN

Fiction

Pierre Pidgeon, illustrated by Arnold E. Bare. Boston, Houghton Mifflin, 1943.
Ilenka, illustrated by Arnold E. Bare. Boston, Houghton Mifflin, 1945.
The Rocky Summer, illustrated by Barbara Cooney. Boston, Houghton Mifflin, 1948.
The Best Christmas, illustrated by Barbara Cooney. New York, Doubleday, 1949; London, Constable, 1958.
Philippe's Hill, illustrated by Hildegard Woodward. New York, Doubleday, 1950.
The Quarry Adventure, illustrated by Barbara Cooney. New York, Doubleday, 1951; as *Lauri's Surprising Summer*, London, Constable, 1957.
Kathy and the Mysterious Statue, illustrated by Jean MacDonald Porter. New York, Doubleday, 1953.
Peter's Long Walk, illustrated by Barbara Cooney. New York, Doubleday, 1953.
Mikko's Fortune, illustrated by Arnold E. Bare. New York, Farrar Straus, 1955.
The Magic Christmas Tree, illustrated by Bettina. New York, Farrar Straus, 1956; London, Oxford University Press, 1957.
The Village Band Mystery, illustrated by Erik Blegvad. New York, Doubleday, 1956.
Flivver, The Heroic Horse, illustrated by Erik Blegvad. New York, Doubleday, 1958.
Ginny's First Secret, illustrated by Hazel Hoecker. Newton, Massachusetts, Phillips, 1958.
The House of the Blue Horse. New York, Doubleday, 1960.
The Saturday Gang, illustrated by Burt Silverman. New York, Doubleday, 1961.
Peter's Pony, illustrated by Fen Lasell. New York, Doubleday, 1963.
Sheep Ahoy!, illustrated by Lisl Weil. Boston, Houghton Mifflin, 1963.
Private Eyes: Adventures with the Saturday Gang, illustrated by Burt Silverman. New York, Doubleday, 1964.
The Year of the Raccoon. Boston, Houghton Mifflin, 1966.
The Secret Journey of the Silver Reindeer, illustrated by Lynd Ward. New York, Doubleday, 1968; Kingswood, Surrey, World's Work, 1970.
The Peter Pan Bag. Boston, Houghton Mifflin, 1970.
Georgina and the Dragon, illustrated by Leonard Shortall. Boston, Houghton Mifflin, 1972.
The Meeting Post: A Story of Lapland, illustrated by Des Asmussen. New York, Crowell, 1972.
Escape from the Evil Prophecy, illustrated by Richard Cuffari. Boston, Houghton Mifflin, 1973.
Break a Leg, Betsy Maybe! Boston, Houghton Mifflin, 1976.

PUBLICATIONS FOR ADULTS

Other

Editor, *Newbery and Caldecott Medal Books, 1956–1965*. Boston, Horn Book, 1965.

Editor, *Newbery and Caldecott Medal Award Winners and Honor Books, 1922–1968.* Boston, Horn Book, 1968.

Editor, with Joanna Foster and Ruth Giles Lontoft, *Illustrators of Children's Books, 1957–1966.* Boston, Horn Book, 1968.

Editor, *Newbery and Caldecott Medal Books, 1966–1975.* Boston, Horn Book, 1975.

Manuscript Collections: Kerlan Collection, University of Minnesota, Minneapolis; de Grummond Collection, University of Southern Mississippi, Hattiesburg.

Lee Kingman comments:

In looking back over 30 years of writing for children and over 24 published books, I find no consistent pattern, but rather a reflection of the ages and interests of my two children and their friends as they grew. The subjects range from kindergarten concerns (*Peter's Long Walk*) to young adult relationships (*The Peter Pan Bag*); the styles range from legend-like (*The Secret Journey of the Silver Reindeer*), through humorous (*Georgina and the Dragon*) to realistic (*The Year of the Raccoon*). Some are mysteries; some have Icelandic, Lapp, and Finnish-American backgrounds. I have always wanted to explore new subjects, learn new things, and tried, in writing about them, to be sensitive to the style best suited to the kind and length of the material, the potential age ranges of readers, and the subjects themselves.

*   *   *

Lee Kingman has claimed that uncharted territory, Lapland, for her own in children's literature. *The Meeting Post* replaces the northern aura of mystery with an informed and friendly familiarity. Older readers of *The Secret Journey of the Silver Reindeer* may well be intrigued to further study, for this distant land, traditional home of nomads now imprisoned by the boundaries of a nationalism foreign to them, fascinates as only forbidding and unvisited outposts can.

Her love of the far north extends to Iceland, home of the Sagas. Distant in time as well as in locale, *Escape from the Evil Prophecy* is an adventure tale of the 11th century. In an era of unrest, when Christianity struggled to overcome paganism, and democratic forms of government to replace anarchic rough justice and blood-feud, Kingman's young hero and heroine personify the generosity of youth, and the difficulties of commitment to social change in the face of established custom. Whether describing the remote past or the remote wilderness, Kingman's own affectionate sympathy renders the unfamiliar and esoteric as comprehensible as the here and now, illuminating with glowing warmth those qualities that transcend time and space to make mankind one family.

With equal facility she captures the essence of people and problems closer to home. *The Peter Pan Bag* owes its success with adolescents to her empathy with their painful *rites de passage* in a culture that makes a difficult time still more difficult by leaving its boundaries undefined.

Runaway Wendy, 17 years old, longs for a summer free from her middle-class suburban home. A hippie-haven in Boston proves intoxicatingly attractive, but offers no solutions to her identity problem. Though some of the actualities of life in a hippie pad have been glossed over, it is a tribute to Kingman's understanding of youngsters insistent upon recognition of their status as adults while living, like Peter Pan, in Never-Never Land, that her story of a lost summer is acclaimed both by Wendy's contemporaries and by those of her equally troubled parents.

Georgina and the Dragon introduces 10-year-old Georgie, who feels that even her name is evidence of disappointment at the birth of a fifth daughter to a father with no son. In this slight, cheerful, mildly feminist story, dauntless Georgie proves to herself and her family that girls are full-fledged human beings too.

The critically acclaimed *The Year of the Raccoon* is Kingman's most memorable book. Joey, an ordinary, normal 15-year-old, is sandwiched between two brilliant brothers under

695

the shadow of a successful, unconsciously domineering father, who expects great things of ALL his family.

Joey's love for Bertie, his only-partly-tame raccoon, precipitates crisis in a family that has unknowingly maintained a precarious balance on the edge of catastrophe. Anyone who has ever loved a boy, an animal, or indeed a family, will be moved by this exceptional story.

Kingman's picture books and plays for juniors do not rank with her work for more mature readers; her writings are sometimes slight and uneven, but her peaks are very, very high.

—Joan McGrath

KIPLING, (Joseph) Rudyard. British. Born in Bombay, India, 30 December 1865. Educated at United Services College, Westward Ho!, Devon, 1878–82. Married Caroline Starr Balestier in 1892; three children. Assistant Editor, *Civil and Military Gazette*, Lahore, 1882–87; Editor and Contributor, "Week's News," *Pioneer*, Allahabad, 1887–89. Free-lance writer after 1889. Lived in Brattleboro, Vermont, 1892–96, in England after 1896, and in Burwash, Sussex, after 1902. Rector, St. Andrews University, 1922–25. Honorary Fellow, Magdalene College, Cambridge, 1932–36. Recipient: Nobel Prize for Literature, 1907; Royal Society of Literature Gold Medal, 1926. LL.D.: McGill University, Montreal, 1899; D. Litt.: Durham and Oxford universities, 1907; Cambridge University, 1908; Edinburgh University, 1920; the Sorbonne, Paris, 1921; Strasbourg University, 1921; D.Phil.: Athens University, 1924. Associate Member, Académie des Science et Politiques. Refused the Poet Laureateship and the Order of Merit. *Died 18 January 1936.*

PUBLICATIONS FOR CHILDREN

Fiction

> *The Jungle Book*, illustrated by J. Lockwood Kipling and others. London, Macmillan, and New York, Century, 1894.
> *The Second Jungle Book*, illustrated by J. Lockwood Kipling. London, Macmillan, and New York, Century, 1895; revised edition, Macmillan, 1895.
> *"Captains Courageous": A Story of the Grand Banks.* London, Macmillan, and New York, Century, 1897.
> *Stalky & Co.* London, Macmillan, and New York, Doubleday, 1899; revised edition, as *The Complete Stalky & Co.*, Macmillan, 1929, Doubleday, 1930.
> *Kim*, illustrated by J. Lockwood Kipling. New York, Doubleday, and London, Macmillan, 1901.
> *Just So Stories for Little Children*, illustrated by the author. London, Macmillan, and New York, Doubleday, 1902.
> *Puck of Pook's Hill*, illustrated by H. R. Millar. London, Macmillan, and New York, Doubleday, 1906.
> *Rewards and Fairies*, illustrated by Frank Craig. London, Macmillan, and New York, Doubleday, 1910.
> *Land and Sea Tales for Scouts and Guides.* London, Macmillan, and New York, Doubleday, 1923.
> *Ham and the Porcupine.* New York, Doubleday, 1935.

Novel

> *The Light That Failed*. New York, United States Book Company, 1890; London, Macmillan, 1891.

Short Stories

> *Plain Tales from the Hills*. Calcutta, Thacker Spink, 1888; New York, Lovell, and London, Macmillan, 1890.
> *Soldiers Three: A Collection of Stories* .... Allahabad, Wheeler, 1888; London, Sampson Low, 1890.
> *The Stories of the Gadsbys: A Tale Without a Plot*. Allahabad, Wheeler, 1888; London, Sampson Low, and New York, Lovell, 1890.
> *In Black and White*. Allahabad, Wheeler, 1888; London, Sampson Low, and New York, Lovell, 1890.
> *Under the Deodars*. Allahabad, Wheeler, 1888; revised edition, London, Sampson Low, 1890.
> *The Phantom 'Rickshaw and Other Tales*. Allahabad, Wheeler, 1888; revised edition, London, Sampson Low, 1890.
> *Wee Willie Winkie and Other Child Stories*. Allahabad, Wheller, 1888; revised edition, London, Sampson Low, 1890.
> *Soldiers Three, and Under the Deodars*. New York, Lovell, 1890.
> *The Phantom 'Rickshaw, and Wee Willie Winkie*. New York, Lovell, 1890.
> *The Courting of Dinah Shadd and Other Stories*. New York, Harper, and London, Macmillan, 1890.
> *Mine Own People*. New York, United States Book Company, 1891.
> *Life's Handicaps, Being Stories from Mine Own People*. New York and London, Macmillan, 1891.
> *The Naulahka: A Story of West and East*, with Wolcott Balestier. London, Heinemann, and New York, Macmillan, 1892.
> *Many Inventions*. London, Macmillan, and New York, Appleton, 1893.
> *Soldier Tales*. London, Macmillan, 1896; as *Soldier Stories*, New York, Macmillan, 1896.
> *The Day's Work*. New York, Doubleday, and London, Macmillan, 1898.
> *The Kipling Reader*. London, Macmillan, 1900; as *Selected Stories*, 1925.
> *Traffics and Discoveries*. London, Macmillan, and New York, Doubleday, 1904.
> *Actions and Reactions*. London, Macmillan, and New York, Doubleday, 1909.
> *Abaft the Funnel*. New York, Dodge, 1909.
> *A Diversity of Creatures*. London, Macmillan, and New York, Doubleday, 1917.
> *Selected Stories*, edited by William Lyon Phelps. New York, Doubleday, 1921.
> *Debits and Credits*. London, Macmillan, and New York, Doubleday, 1926.
> *Selected Stories*. London, Macmillan, 1929.
> *Thy Servant a Dog, Told by Boots*. London, Macmillan, and New York, Doubleday, 1930; revised edition, as *Thy Servant a Dog and Other Dog Stories*, Macmillan, 1938.
> *Humorous Tales*. London, Macmillan, and New York, Doubleday, 1931.
> *Animal Stories*. London, Macmillan, 1932; New York, Doubleday, 1938.
> *Limits and Renewals*. London, Macmillan, and New York, Doubleday, 1932.
> *All the Mowgli Stories*. London, Macmillan, 1933; New York, Doubleday, 1936.
> *Collected Dog Stories*. London, Macmillan, and New York, Doubleday, 1934.
> *More Selected Stories*. London, Macmillan, 1940.
> *Twenty-One Tales*. London, Reprint Society, 1946.
> *Ten Stories*. London, Pan, 1947.
> *A Choice of Kipling's Prose*, edited by W. Somerset Maugham. London, Macmillan,

1952; as *Maugham's Choice of Kipling's Best: Sixteen Stories*, New York, Doubleday, 1953.

A Treasury of Short Stories. New York, Bantam, 1957.

(Short Stories), edited by Edward Parone. New York, Dell, 1960.

Kipling Stories: Twenty-Eight Exciting Tales. New York, Platt and Munk, 1960.

The Best Short Stories, edited by Randall Jarrell. New York, Hanover House, 1961; as *In the Vernacular: The English in India* and *The English in England*, New York, Doubleday, 2 vols., 1963.

Famous Tales of India, edited by B. W. Shir-Cliff. New York, Ballantine, 1962.

Phantoms and Fantasies: 20 Tales. New York, Doubleday, 1965.

Short Stories, edited by Andrew Rutherford. London, Penguin, 1971.

Verse

Schoolboy Lyrics. Lahore, privately printed, 1881.

Echoes (published anonymously), with Alice Kipling. Lahore, privately printed, 1884.

Departmental Ditties and Other Verses. Lahore, Civil and Military Gazette Press, 1886; London, Thacker Spink, 1890.

Departmental Ditties, Barrack-Room Ballads, and Other Verse. New York, United States Book Company, 1890.

Barrack-Room Ballads and Other Verses. London, Methuen, and New York, Macmillan, 1892.

Ballads and Barrack-Room Ballads. New York, Macmillan, 1893.

The Seven Seas. New York, Appleton, and London, Methuen, 1896.

Recessional. Privately printed, 1897.

An Almanac of Twelve Sports, illustrations by William Nicholson. London, Heinemann, and New York, Russell, 1898.

Poems, edited by Wallace Rice. Chicago, Star, 1899.

Recessional and Other Poems. Privately printed, 1899.

The Absent-Minded Beggar. Privately printed, 1899.

With Number Three, Surgical and Medical, and New Poems. Santiago, Chile, Hume, 1900.

Occasional Poems. Boston, Bartlett, 1900.

The Five Nations. London, Methuen, and New York, Doubleday, 1903.

The Muse among the Motors. New York, Doubleday, 1904.

Collected Verse. New York, Doubleday, 1907; London, Hodder and Stoughton, 1912.

A History of England (verse only), with C. R. L. Fletcher. London, Oxford University Press-Hodder and Stoughton, and New York, Doubleday, 1911; revised edition, 1930.

Songs from Books. New York, Doubleday, 1912; London, Macmillan, 1913.

Twenty Poems. London, Methuen, 1918.

The Years Between. London, Methuen, and New York, Doubleday, 1919.

Verse: Inclusive Edition, 1885–1918. London, Hodder and Stoughton, and New York, Doubleday, 3 vols., 1919; revised edition, 1921, 1927, 1933.

A Kipling Anthology: Verse. London, Methuen, and New York, Doubleday, 1922.

Songs for Youth, from Collected Verse. London, Hodder and Stoughton, 1924; New York, Doubleday, 1925.

A Choice of Songs. London, Methuen, 1925.

Sea and Sussex. London, Macmillan, and New York, Doubleday, 1926.

Songs of the Sea. London, Macmillan, and New York, Doubleday, 1927.

Poems 1886–1929. London, Macmillan, 3 vols., 1929; New York, Doubleday, 3 vols., 1930.

Selected Poems. London, Methuen, 1931.

East of Suez, Being a Selection of Eastern Verses. London, Macmillan, 1931.

Sixty Poems. London, Hodder and Stoughton, 1939.

Verse: Definitive Edition. London, Hodder and Stoughton, and New York, Doubleday, 1940.

So Shall Ye Reap: Poems for These Days. London, Hodder and Stoughton, 1941.

A Choice of Kipling's Verse, edited by T. S. Eliot. London, Faber, 1941; New York, Scribner, 1943.

Sixty Poems. London, Hodder and Stoughton, 1957.

A Kipling Anthology, edited by W. G. Bebbington. London, Methuen, 1964.

Selected Verse, edited by James Cochrane. London, Penguin, 1977.

Other

Quartette, with others. Lahore, Civil and Military Gazette Press, 1885.

The City of Dreadful Night and Other Sketches. Allahabad, Wheeler, 1890.

The City of Dreadful Night and Other Places. Allahabad, Wheeler, and London, Sampson Low, 1891.

The Smith Administration. Allahabad, Wheeler, 1891.

Letters of Marque. Allahabad, Wheeler, and London, Sampson Low, 1891.

American Notes, with *The Bottle Imp,* by Robert Louis Stevenson. New York, Ivers, 1891.

Out of India: Things I Saw, and Failed to See, in Certain Days and Nights at Jeypore and Elsewhere. New York, Dillingham, 1895.

The Kipling Birthday Book, edited by Joseph Finn. London, Macmillan, 1896; New York, Doubleday, 1899.

A Fleet in Being: Notes of Two Trips with the Channel Squadron. London, Macmillan, 1898.

From Sea to Sea: Letters of Travel. New York, Doubleday, 1899; as *From Sea to Sea and Other Sketches,* London, Macmillan, 1900.

Works (Swastika Edition). New York, Doubleday, Appleton, and Century, 15 vols., 1899.

Letters to the Family (Notes on a Recent Trip to Canada). Toronto, Macmillan, 1908.

The New Army in Training. London, Macmillan, 1915.

France at War. London, Macmillan, and New York, Doubleday, 1915.

The Fringes of the Fleet. London, Macmillan, and New York, Doubleday, 1915.

Tales of "The Trade." Privately printed, 1916.

Sea Warfare. London, Macmillan, and New York, Doubleday, 1916.

The Eyes of Asia. New York, Doubleday, 1918.

The Graves of the Fallen. London, Imperial War Graves Commission, 1919.

Letters of Travel (1892–1913). London, Macmillan, and New York, Doubleday, 1920.

A Kipling Anthology: Prose. London, Macmillan, and New York, Doubleday, 1922.

The Irish Guards in the Great War. London, Macmillan, and New York, Doubleday, 2 vols., 1923.

Works (Mandalay Edition). New York, Doubleday, 26 vols., 1925–26.

A Book of Words: Selections from Speeches and Addresses Delivered Between 1906 and 1927. London, Macmillan, and New York, Doubleday, 1928.

The One Volume Kipling. New York, Doubleday, 1928.

Souvenirs of France. London, Macmillan, 1933.

A Kipling Pageant. New York, Doubleday, 1935.

Something of Myself for My Friends Known and Unknown. London, Macmillan, and New York, Doubleday, 1937.

Complete Works (Sussex Edition). London, Macmillan, 35 vols., 1937–39; as *Collected Works* (Burwash Edition), New York, Doubleday, 28 vols., 1941 (includes revised versions of some previously published works).

A.Kipling Treasury: Stories and Poems. London, Macmillan, 1940.

Kipling: A Selection of His Stories and Poems, edited by John Beecroft. New York, Doubleday, 2 vols., 1956.

Letters from Japan, edited by Donald Richie and Yoshimori Harashima. Tokyo, Kenkyusha, 1962.

Pearls from Kipling, edited by C. Donald Plomer. New Britain, Connecticut, Elihu Burritt Library, 1963.

Rudyard Kipling to Rider Haggard: The Record of a Friendship, edited by Morton Cohen. London, Hutchinson, 1965.

The Best of Kipling. New York, Doubleday, 1968.

Stories and Poems, edited by Roger Lancelyn Green. London Dent, 1970.

Bibliography: Rudyard Kipling: A Bibliographical Catalogue by J. McG. Stewart, edited by A. W. Keats, Toronto, Dalhousie University-University of Toronto Press, 1959, London, Oxford University Press, 1960.

Critical Studies: Rudyard Kipling by Rosemary Sutcliff, London, Bodley Head, 1960, New York, Walck, 1961; Kipling and the Children by Roger Lancelyn Green, London, Elek, 1965.

*   *   *

Looking back over his work a few months before he died, Rudyard Kipling wrote: "Since the tales had to be read by children, before people realised that they were meant for grown-ups, ... I worked the material in three or four overlaid tints and textures, which might or might not reveal themselves according to the shifting light of sex, youth, and experience." He wrote this specifically of his last children's book, Rewards and Fairies, but it applies to some extent to all his children's books – and this makes it particularly difficult to write of him as a "children's author."

Kipling's approach to the writing of fiction was by way of meticulous fact, originally that of the first class journalistic reporter (a position which he held for seven years in India – before returning to London at the age of twenty-three, to find himself famous within a few months). In the experimental stage towards the end of his time in India, when his first and some of his most famous stories were written, he was learning to put himself in the place of the various types about whom he was writing, to think their thoughts and to speak their language. It was a period in literary history when writing in dialect was a growing fashion, particularly prevalent in America, and Kipling with his amazingly retentive memory was able to become an expert in many dialects – Cockney, Yorkshire and Irish for his Soldiers Three, native Indians for In Black and White, the general conversation of higher class "Anglo-Indians" at Simla in many of the Plain Tales – and it was inevitable for one who loved children as he did from an early age, that he should attempt their forms of speech and thought in the four stories of the original Wee Willie Winkie volume at the end of 1888, before he left India.

The next stories which Kipling wrote with children as their intended first readers became The Jungle Book and The Second Jungle Book – several of which made their first appearance in the American children's magazine St. Nicholas. Of these stories the eight concerning Mowgli – the Indian boy who was brought up by the wolves and became the Master of the Jungle, until he returned to his own kind in the end – became immediately among the best loved stories with young readers and a Children's Classic by the end of the century. "His stories are not animal stories in the realistic sense; they are wonderful, beautiful fairy tales," wrote Ernest Thompson Seton, the great Canadian naturalist and writer of the life-stories of real animals. Many games of "make-believe" in fact and fiction took Mowgli for their hero and his jungle for their new Fairyland, and not twenty years after the publication of The Jungle Books, Baden-Powell made such make-believe still more real for small boys all over the world by basing his Wolf-cubs – the junior Boy Scouts – on them.

As was natural for a writer of Kipling's vivid imagination, as soon as he had children of his own he began to invent stories to tell to them. Many of these were never written down, but one series became the established favourite, a series of incantatory tales that had to be told again and again, always in the same words, always "just-so." The first three appeared in *St. Nicholas* at the end of 1897. There was then a gap until mid-1900. Josephine, "the daughter that was all to him," who appears as Taffimai, died in 1899 at the age of six; but after a break Kipling was able to write down the rest of the tales he had made for her, and probably added a few more – and *Just So Stories* was published in 1902. This, the most unusual of Kipling's books, is probably the most timeless and the most enduring of his tales for children. It should be read aloud to obtain its best effect, but is enjoyed in different ways at almost any age.

Between writing the first and last of the Just So stories, Kipling published three other books which appeal strongly to boy readers as well as, and perhaps in different ways to, the adults for whom they were intended. The least well known, *"Captains Courageous"*, is a full-length sea-story set among the old fishing-fleets on the Grand Banks in the North Atlantic. The theme is one of Kipling's favourites, that of the "young cub" being "licked into shape" – as of Mowgli learning to become Master of the Jungle before returning to put his particular accomplishments at the service of his own kind. In this case Harvey Cheyne, the spoilt son of an American millionaire, falls overboard from a luxury liner and is picked up by a fishing boat and made to "work his keep" for several months before returning to his family, having by then indeed "suffered a sea-change."

The next book aims at the same goal, but in a highly debatable manner: "There came to me the idea of beginning some tracts or parables for the young," wrote Kipling. "These, for reasons honestly beyond my control, turned themselves into a series of tales called *Stalky & Co.*"

This book has probably met with more contradictory criticism than any of his other works. To the adult reader it can be enjoyed again and again as one of the greatest works of humour in the language – or it can be detested and condemned as "an unpleasant book about unpleasant boys at an unpleasant school." With boys themselves, however, it has always been a favourite, is not likely to have led them into any new forms of mischief, and is certainly now too much of a "period piece" to seem anything but a hilarious collection of yarns about a type of academy almost as obsolete as a Dame School.

Kipling's other book about a boy hero is *Kim*, which is now being classed among the great British novels – by Indian and Pakistani critics and scholars as well as British and American. It is as much as, or no more, a boy's book than *Huckleberry Finn* and is enjoyed or not at various ages as variously as Mark Twain's classic. Once again it follows the development of a small boy with exceptional chances and at first no sense of duty or obligation as he develops mentally and spiritually to fill the place in the world for which he is uniquely fitted. But in the process Kim, the little Irish orphan brought up more or less as a native Indian, passes through a series of absorbing adventures set against the most vivid and authentic literary picture we have of India as Kipling saw and knew it nearly a century ago.

None of these last three books was meant specifically for young readers; but after *Just So Stories*, written for "the vanished Josephine," Kipling realised that he had two other children fast growing up and just as desirious of tales, even if of a different kind. The family had by now settled in an early seventeenth century manor house in a secluded corner of Sussex: this, and a performance of scenes from *A Midsummer Night's Dream* which the two put on for their parents, brought forth *Puck of Pook's Hill*. These tales, and those in the sequel, *Rewards and Fairies*, cover English history, largely as it impinged on their own neighbourhood, from the end of the Roman Occupation to the days of the Napoleonic Wars, and many of them have been acclaimed as among the best historical stories ever written. The historian G. M. Trevelyan, for example, wrote in 1953: "As a piece of historical imagination I know nothing in the world better than the story in *Puck* called 'The Joyous Venture' ... I can see no fault in it, and many a merit." And next to this he set "Simple Simon" and "The Tree of Justice" in *Rewards and Fairies*.

As the stories were written for Kippling's own children, who appear in them as Dan and Una, it is only right that the second volume is more difficult than the first, to match their advance in age and understanding. And they were the last books that Kipling wrote for children. "Dan" was killed in the First World War, and, though "Una" married, she had no children – so we can but regret that Kipling wrote no "Tales of a Grandfather," while giving thanks for those stories already written: some of the greatest and most enduring of their kind in whatever compartment of literature we choose to set them.

As Patrick Chalmers wrote: he was one of those who "give their heart's best only when they give to a child."

—Roger Lancelyn Green

KJELGAARD, Jim (James Arthur Kjelgaard). American. Born in New York City, 6 December 1910. Attended Syracuse University, New York, for two years. Married Edna Dresen in 1939; one daughter. Recipient: Western Writers of America Spur Award, 1958. *Died 12 July 1959.*

PUBLICATIONS FOR CHILDREN

Fiction

> *Forest Patrol*, illustrated by Tony Palazzo. New York, Holiday House, 1941; London, Sampson Low, 1948.
> *Rebel Siege*, illustrated by Charles Wilson. New York, Holiday House, 1943.
> *Big Red*, illustrated by Bob Kuhn. New York, Holiday House, 1945.
> *Buckskin Brigade*, illustrated by Ralph Ray, Jr. New York, Holiday House, 1947.
> *Snow Dog*, illustrated by Jacob Landau. New York, Holiday House, 1948.
> *Kalak of the Ice*, illustrated by Bob Kuhn. New York, Holiday House, 1949.
> *A Nose for Trouble*, illustrated by Collett. New York, Holiday House, 1949.
> *Wild Trek*, illustrated by Faye. New York, Holiday House, 1950; London, Collins, 1964.
> *Chip, The Dam-Builder*, illustrated by Ralph Ray, Jr. New York, Holiday House, 1950.
> *Irish Red, Son of Big Red*, illustrated by Ames. New York, Holiday House, 1951; London, Collins, 1958.
> *Fire-Hunter*, illustrated by Ralph Ray, Jr. New York, Holiday House, 1951.
> *Trailing Trouble*. New York, Holiday House, 1952.
> *Outlaw Red, Son of Big Red*, illustrated by Ames. New York, Holiday House, 1953.
> *The Spell of White Sturgeon*, illustrated by Stephen Voorhies. New York, Dodd Mead, 1953.
> *Haunt Fox*, illustrated by Glen Rounds. New York, Holiday House, 1954.
> *Cracker Barrel Trouble Shooter*, illustrated by Orbann. New York, Dodd Mead, 1954.
> *Lion Hound*, illustrated by Jacob Landau. New York, Holiday House, 1955; London, Collins, 1957.
> *The Lost Wagon*, illustrated by Orbann. New York, Dodd Mead, 1955.
> *Desert Dog*, illustrated by Sam Savitt. New York, Holiday House, 1956.
> *Trading Jeff and His Dog*. New York, Dodd Mead, 1956.
> *Wold Brother*, illustrated by Charles Wilson. New York, Holiday House, 1957; London, Collins, 1963.
> *Wildlife Cameraman*, illustrated by Sam Savitt. New York, Holiday House, 1957.
> *Double Challenge*, illustrated by Chris Kenyon. New York, Dodd Mead, 1957.
> *Swamp Cat*, illustrated by Edward Shenton. New York, Dodd Mead, 1957.
> *We Were There at the Oklahoma Land Run*, illustrated by Chris Kenyon. New York, Grosset and Dunlap, 1957.

Rescue Dog of High Pass, illustrated by Edward Shenton.   New York, Dodd Mead, 1958.

The Black Fawn, illustrated by Erk.   New York, Dodd Mead, 1958.

The Land Is Bright.   New York, Dodd Mead, 1958.

Hound Dog and Other Yarns, illustrated by Paul Brown.   New York, Dodd Mead, 1958.

Stormy, illustrated by Louis Darling.   New York, Holiday House, 1959; London, Collins, 1964.

Hi Jolly, illustrated by Kendall Rossi.   New York, Dodd Mead, 1959.

Boomerang Hunter, illustrated by W.T.Mars.   New York, Holiday House, 1960.

Ulysses and His Woodland Zoo, illustrated by Kendall Rossi.   New York, Dodd Mead, 1960.

The Duck-Footed Hound, illustrated by Marc Simont.   New York, Crowell, 1960.

My Father's Collie.   New York, Dodd Mead, 1961.

Tigre, illustrated by Everett Raymond Kinstler.   New York, Dodd Mead, 1961.

Hidden Trail, illustrated by Louis Darling.   New York, Holiday House, 1962.

Fawn in the Forest and Other Wild Animal Stories, illustrated by Sam Savitt.   New York, Dodd Mead, 1962.

Two Dogs and a Horse, illustrated by Sam Savitt.   New York, Dodd Mead, 1964.

Furious Moose of the Wilderness, illustrated by Mort Künstler.   New York, Dodd Mead, 1965.

Dave and His Dog Mulligan, illustrated by Sam Savitt.   New York, Dodd Mead, 1966.

Coyote Song, illustrated by Robert MacLean.   New York, Dodd Mead, 1969.

Other

The Explorations of Père Marquette, illustrated by Stephen Voorhies.   New York, Random House, 1951.

Coming of the Mormons, illustrated by Stephen Voorhies.   New York, Random House, 1953.

The Story of Geronimo, illustrated by Charles Wilson.   New York, Grosset and Dunlap, 1958.

Editor, *The Wild Horse Roundup: A Collection of Stories by Members of the Western Writers of America*, illustrated by Paul Brown.   New York, Dodd Mead, 1957.

Editor, *Hound Dogs and Others: A Collection of Stories by Members of the Western Writers of America*, illustrated by Paul Brown.   New York, Dodd Mead, 1958.

Manuscript Collection: Kerlan Collection, University of Minnesota, Minneapolis.

*   *   *

An engaging animal, a colorful person, and a distinctive habitat are the three ingredients Jim Kjelgaard incorporated into most of his many books for young people. Using a writing mode as simple as his own life-style, he based his books on his own experiences, travels, and investigation.

His most notable books are the series about the Irish setter, his favorite dog. Different temperaments are characterized in *Big Red, Irish Red, Son of Big Red*, and *Outlaw Red, Son of Big Red*. He himself hunted with Irish setters, but he had interest in other dogs, too. His impressive list of dog books includes such breeds as the greyhound in *Desert Dog*, the husky in *Snow Dog* and *Wild Trek*, the wildfowl retriever in *Stormy*, and the collie in *Double Challenge*. Intrigued with the St. Bernard, he found it necessary to inform himself using Alfred Richard Sennett's book, *Across the Great St. Bernard*, to take notes about a place he was unable to visit. He extended his scope to other creatures of the wild such as *Kalak of the Ice*, *The Black Fawn*, *Chip*, and *Haunt Fox* about a polar bear, a deer, a beaver, and his own favorite animal respectively. In a letter to Dr. Irvin Kerlan to whom the latter book is dedicated, the author wrote, "When I was a youngster, away back in 1929, it was impossible to get any sort of job. I went into the hills with two fox hounds, and before the winter was over I had 13. Naturally I didn't make any money, but I doubt if I've since had half as much fun! ... I like red foxes, I think, better than any other animal."

In most of his books there is a human being in addition to an animal. His debut, *Forest Patrol*, describes a boy yearning to become a forest ranger. The main character in *Swamp Cat* and *Stormy* is a boy, while in *Snow Dog* it is a trapper. In the book *The Story of Geronimo* he interpreted both the Apache Indian renegade and his adversaries. *Rebel Siege* portrayed the struggle of loyalties of a group in the Carolinas in 1780, written and published in the context of World War II.

The wilderness, either contemporary or historical, is the setting for most of his books. As a child he was drawn to the woods where he observed animal life in natural habitat. During the first year after high school he and a friend spent an entire winter season in the Pennsylvania forest hunting and fishing. *Buckskin Brigade*, one of the author's favorite books, portrays pioneer life on the frontier. "Story hunts have led me from the Atlantic to the Pacific and from the Arctic Circle to Mexico City," he wrote on the jacket of *Coyote Song*. "Stories, like gold, are where you find them – 3,000 miles from home or on the doorstep." While living in Wisconsin he wrote *The Spell of the White Sturgeon* and *The Explorations of Père Marquette*, both with local settings. Historical fiction, such as *The Lost Wagon* about the Oregon Trail and *Fire-Hunter* suggesting the life of a prehistoric man, were the result of research and an educated imagination.

Kjelgaard was well-known to bibliographers seeking books for the reluctant reader and for occupational counseling. He specialized in telling a good story with simplicity, and encouraged fellow-authors to provide better reading for youth. In a letter to Dr. Kerlan he mused, "As for me, I'm 43 and a very plain sort of person. By that I mean if I had a choice between attending a party at the Stork Club or going bass fishing, I'd go fishing." Reviewers praised him for his fine plots and action. Reviewing for the *Horn Book* (August 1962), Margaret Warren Brown stated, "Much more mysterious than the mystery in *Hidden Trail* (the disappearance of an elk herd) is the author's ability to fashion an absorbing story out of such unlikely materials as a youthful photographer, a Conservation Department, an Airedale, and the migration pattern of elks."

The author's brother, John, provided the model for the forest ranger in the books. The game warden's responsibilities were outlined in *Trailing Trouble* and *A Nose for Trouble*, while the wildlife cameraman is portrayed in a book with that title, and a naturalist whose plane is forced to land in the remote Canadian wilderness is described in *Wild Trek*. An avid reader can follow his books and his life chronologically, observing that the camera is substituted for a gun in his later works. No hint is given that the author suffered for the last twenty years with arthritis.

—Karen Nelson Hoyle

KLEIN, Norma. American. Born in New York City, 13 May 1938. Educated at the Dalton School, New York, 1941–51; Elizabeth Irwin High School, 1952–56; Cornell University, Ithaca, New York, 1956–57; Barnard College, New York, 1957–60, B.A. in Russian 1960 (Phi Beta Kappa); Columbia University, New York, 1960–63, M.A. in Slavic languages 1963. Married Erwin Fleissner in 1963; has two daughters. Agent: Elaine Markson, 44 Greenwich Avenue, New York, New York 10011. Address: 27 West 96th Street, New York, New York 10025, U.S.A.

PUBLICATIONS FOR CHILDREN

Fiction

Mom, The Wolf Man, and Me.   New York, Pantheon Books, 1972.
It's Not What You Expect.   New York, Pantheon Books, 1973.
Girls Can Be Anything, illustrated by Roy Doty.   New York, Dutton, 1973.
Taking Sides.   New York, Pantheon Books, 1974.
If I Had My Way, illustrated by Ray Cruz.   New York, Pantheon Books, 1974.
Dinosaur's Housewarming Party, illustrated by James Marshall.   New York, Crown, 1974.
Naomi in the Middle, illustrated by Leigh Grant.   New York, Dial Press, 1974.
Confessions of an Only Child, illustrated by Richard Cuffari.   New York, Pantheon Books, 1974.
Sunshine.   New York, Holt Rinehart, 1975; London, Everest, 1976.
The Sunshine Years.   New York, Dell, 1975.
What It's All About.   New York, Dial Press, 1975.
Blue Trees, Red Sky, illustrated by Pat Grant Porter.   New York, Pantheon Books, 1975.
Hiding.   New York, Scholastic, 1976.

Verse

A Train for Jane, illustrated by Miriam Schottland.   New York, Feminist Press, 1974.

PUBLICATIONS FOR ADULTS

Novels

Give Me One Good Reason.   New York, Putnam, 1973.
Coming to Life.   New York, Simon and Schuster, 1974.
Girls Turn Wives.   New York, Simon and Schuster, 1976.

Short Stories

Love and Other Euphemisms.   New York, Putnam, 1972.

*   *   *

Norma Klein is a prolific writer of stories for children in all age groups. She belongs to a school of writers producing "liberated" children's literature – her work often appears in the feminist magazine *Ms.* Her central character is always a girl, and in the heroine's words she retells a wide cross-section of the dilemmas that may face today's children.

Her first novel, *Mom, The Wolf Man and Me*, remains her most appealing work. The situation of 11-year-old Brett whose mother is not, and never was, married may be irregular but her relationship with her mother is close and mutually tolerant. She relishes her unusual life. The advent of a wolf-hound owning boyfriend for her mother complicates everything, but the couple agrees "no babies" (except adopted, and Brett can pick it out) and the wolf-hound goes to the wedding. Klein handles her offbeat plot with complete confidence and draws no attention to the changing life-style motif.

In another novel, *What It's All About*, she touches again on unmarried mothers as well as trans-racial adoption, racially and religiously mixed marriage, vanishing step-fathers and working mothers. She does it here also with flair and success. Bernie has much in common with Brett. She is an appealing, toughly unsentimental 11-year-old, a city kid to her toes. Her relationship with Suzu, her little sister adopted from Vietnam, transcends the mushy "orphan" stereotype. Bernie too enjoys life.

In *Taking Sides* and the recent *Hiding*, where the subject matter is disintegrating families and sexual initiation respectively, the stories seem wrenched to include the latest familial traumas. Nell's Daddy in *Taking Sides* has a tepid affair and there are teeny hints of a lesbian relationship between estranged mommy and the college friend who gives her a home. Readers get the feeling that Nell is being forced by her creator to shoulder the woes of a whole generation. (Daddy even has a heart attack.) Krii in *Hiding* is a more extreme example of a heroine cut adrift from humanity by the weighty didactic role she bears. Her attempt to come to terms with sexual maturity and the defection of her boyfriend by hiding in the attic of her parents' home is unconvincing to the point of phoniness.

The balance between the characters, their story, and the message they carry is the key to the uneven quality of Klein's writing. Her output is large, ranging from a rhyming text for the picture book *A Train for Jane* to novels that straddle the borderline between teens and adults. Intermittently she writes a fine story that captures the essence of our times – or at least the essence of growing up in New York City. The kids in *It's Not What You Expect* who set up a summer restaurant when their parents' marital problems keep them home from summer camp are a likeable crew. Oliver, the 14-year-old gourmet, is an original young man – both his watercress soup and his handling of crises are superb. *Confessions of an Only Child* is a simple and encouraging account of how 8-year-old Antonia gradually comes to terms with the idea of a sibling.

It is when the case-book takes over the story-book that Norma Klein fails to exploit her manifest talent for communicating with young people on an informal one-to-one basis. She then risks alienating her readers from the very freedom of choice and nonsexist ideology that she is seeking to propagate.

—Brigitte Weeks

KNIGHT, Frank (Francis Edgar Knight). British. Born in London, 15 August 1905. Educated at Whitgift Middle School, Croydon, Surrey. Served as a Navigation Instructor in the Royal Air Force, 1939–45. Married Elizabeth Mildred Avice Mather in 1933; has two sons and two daughters. Apprentice, 1921–25, and successively Third, Second, and First Mate, 1926–30, Merchant Navy: certified Master Mariner, 1928, and Extra Master Mariner, 1929; worked for marine insurance and yacht broking firms, and as a free-lance journalist, 1931–39, 1940–70. Agent: A.M. Heath and Co. Ltd., 40–42 William IV Street, London WC2N 4DD, England.

PUBLICATIONS FOR CHILDREN

Fiction

> *The Albatross Comes Home*, illustrated by A.R. Morley.   London, Hollis and Carter, 1949.
> *Four in the Half-Deck*, illustrated by S. Drigin.   London, Nelson, 1950.
> *The Island of the Radiant Pearls*, illustrated by Stephen Russ.   London, Hollis and Carter, 1950.
> *The Golden Monkey*, illustrated by John S. Goodall.   London, Macmillan, and New York, St. Martin's Press, 1953.
> *Strangers in the Half-Deck*, illustrated by Robert Johnston.   London, Nelson, 1953.
> *Acting Third Mate*, illustrated by Robert Johnston.   London, Nelson, 1954.
> *Voyage to Bengal*, illustrated by P.A. Jobson.   London, Macmillan, and New York, St. Martin's Press, 1954.

Clippers to China, illustrated by P.A. Jobson. London, Macmillan, and New York, St. Martin's Press, 1955.

Mudlarks and Mysteries, illustrated by P.A. Jobson. London, Macmillan, and New York, St. Martin's Press, 1955.

Two Girls and a Boat (as Cedric Salter), illustrated by Victor Bertoglio. London, Blackie, 1956.

The Bluenose Pirate, illustrated by P.A. Jobson. London, Macmillan, and New York, St. Martin's Press, 1956.

Family on the Tide, illustrated by Geoffrey Whittam. London, Macmillan, and New York, St. Martin's Press, 1956.

Please Keep Off the Mud, illustrated by P.A. Jobson. London, Macmillan, and New York, St. Martin's Press, 1957.

The Partick Steamboat, illustrated by P.A. Jobson. London, Macmillan, 1958; New York, St. Martin's Press, 1959.

He Sailed with Blackbeard, illustrated by P.A. Jobson. London, Macmillan, and New York, St. Martin's Press, 1958.

The Sea Chest: Stories of Adventure at Sea. London, Collins, 1960; New York, Platt and Munk, 1964.

Shadows on the Mud, illustrated by P.A. Jobson. London, Macmillan, and New York, St. Martin's Press, 1960.

The Slaver's Apprentice, illustrated by P.A. Jobson. London, Macmillan, and New York, St. Martin's Press, 1961.

The Last of Lallows, illustrated by William Stobbs. London, Macmillan, and New York, St. Martin's Press, 1961.

Clemency Draper, illustrated by William Stobbs. London, Macmillan, and New York, St. Martin's Press, 1963.

The Ship That Came Home, illustrated by Derek Smouthy. London, Benn, 1963.

Up, Sea Beggars!, illustrated by John Lawrence. London, Macdonald, 1964.

Remember Vera Cruz!, illustrated by John Lawrence. London, Macdonald, 1965; New York, Dial Press, 1966.

Kit Baxter's War, illustrated by John Lawrence. London, Macdonald, 1966.

Olaf's Sword, illustrated by Andrew Sier. London, Heinemann, 1969; New York, Watts, 1970.

Other

Captain Anson and the Treasure of Spain. London, Macmillan, and New York, St. Martin's Press, 1959.

The Young Drake, illustrated by Azpelicueta. London, Parrish, 1962; New York, Roy, 1963.

John Harrison, The Man Who Made Navigation Safe. London, Macmillan, and New York, St. Martin's Press, 1962.

The Young Columbus, illustrated by Azpelicueta. London, Parrish, and New York, Roy, 1963.

Stories of Famous Ships, illustrated by Will Nickless. Edinburgh, Oliver and Boyd, 1963; Philadelphia, Westminster Press, 1966.

Stories of Famous Sea Fights, illustrated by Will Nickless. Edinburgh, Oliver and Boyd, 1963; Philadelphia, Westminster Press, 1967.

Stories of Famous Explorers by Sea, illustrated by Will Nickless. Edinburgh, Oliver and Boyd, 1964; Philadelphia, Westminster Press, 1966.

The Young Captain Cook, illustrated by Joan Howell. London, Parrish, 1964; New York, Roy, 1966.

Stories of Famous Explorers by Land, illustrated by Will Nickless. Edinburgh, Oliver and Boyd, 1965; Philadelphia, Westminster Press, 1966.

Stories of Famous Sea Adventures, illustrated by Will Nickless.   Edinburgh, Oliver and Boyd, 1966; Philadelphia, Westminster Press, 1967.

Prince of Cavaliers: The Story of the Life and Campaigns of Rupert of the Rhine, illustrated by John Lawrence.   London, Macdonald, 1967.

Rebel Admiral: The Life and Exploits of Admiral Lord Cochrane, Tenth Earl of Dundonald, illustrated by John Lawrence.   London, Macdonald, 1968.

The Hero (on Lord Nelson), illustrated by John Lawrence.   London, Macdonald, 1969.

Russia Fights Japan, illustrated by Roger Phillips.   London, Macdonald, 1969.

Ships Then and Now.   London, Benn, 1969; New York, Crowell Collier, 1970.

That Rare Captain: Sir Francis Drake, illustrated by John Lawrence.   London, Macdonald, 1970.

Christopher Columbus.   London, Burns and Oates, 1970.

The Dardanelles Campaign, illustrated by Douglas Phillips.   London, Macdonald, 1970.

General-at-Sea: The Life of Admiral Robert Blake, illustrated by Douglas Phillips.   London, Macdonald, 1971.

Ships.   London, Benn, 1973.

True Stories of the Sea, illustrated by Victor Ambrus.   London, Benn, 1973.

True Stories of Exploration, illustrated by Victor Ambrus.   London, Benn, 1973.

The Clipper Ship.   London, Collins, 1973.

True Stories of Spying, illustrated by Victor Ambrus.   London, Benn, 1975.

The Golden Age of the Galleon.   London, Collins, 1976.

Editor, *They Told Mr. Hakluyt* (from Hakluyt's *Voyages*), illustrated by Charles Keeping.   London, Macmillan, and New York St. Martin's Press, 1964.

Editor, *Captain Cook and the Voyage of the "Endeavour," 1768–1771*.   London, Nelson, 1968.

PUBLICATIONS FOR ADULTS

Novels

The Sea's Fool.   London, Ward Lock, 1960.
Captains of the Calabar.   London, Ward Lock, 1961.
Pekoe Reef.   London, Ward Lock, 1962.

Other

A Beginner's Guide to the Sea (small boat manual).   London, Macmillan, and New York, St. Martin's Press, 1955.

The Sea Story, Being a Guide to Nautical Reading from Ancient Times to the Close of the Sailing Ship Era.   London, Macmillan, and New York, St. Martin's Press, 1958.

A Guide to Ocean Navigation.   London, Macmillan, and New York, St. Martin's Press, 1959.

Frank Knight comments:

My two interests have always been the sea and history. My earliest attempts at fiction (*Four in the Half-Deck*, etc.) were derived largely from my own experiences at sea and were designed to give boys who might be bitten by the sea-bug some idea of what the life was really like. Later I decided to go further back in time, and here I drew largely upon the reminiscences of old sailors I had known in my youth – their memories of the great days of sail. The result was a series of children's novels (*The Golden Monkey*, etc.) set in various periods of nautical history, early 18th to mid-19th centuries.

Later still demand from publishers for more fact and less fiction led me into straight history, biography, etc., which I still produce occasionally.

*   *   *

Frank Knight is a prolific writer of adventure novels for older children, historical and modern, on land and sea. He deals with the confusion and brutality of war by means of fast-moving plots full of plausible coincidences. *Kit Baxter's War* plunges 12-year-old Kit into the English Civil War when he rows out to warn a neighbour's ship that the town has been captured by Royalists, and then is unable to get back to shore. His fortunes rise and fall with the fighting over the next three years; at one point he captains his father's old ship into Plymouth; at another he is press-ganged into the navy and is nearly killed at the siege of Lyme Regis. Only at the very end does he discover who murdered his father and solve the other mysteries.

Young Roger in *Remember Vera Cruz!* suffers the discomfort of sailing with John Hawkins in the slave trade, is imprisoned by the Spaniards in Mexico, almost sacrificed by the Mexicans, joins Francis Drake and returns wounded to Essex to rest before going to sea again.

In *Up, Sea Beggars!* young John has an English father and a Dutch mother, so joins the 16th-century revolt of the Dutch against Spain. He fights, at first a little bewildered, then more confidently, on land and sea as the Dutch flood the low ground. He rescues a dying priest who is being beaten up by his own side, saves a mysterious Dutch girl, Madeleine, chases a scarred villain who keeps changing his name, is imprisoned and almost hung by the Spaniards but survives and solves the riddle of Madeleine's true identity.

The Clipper series are concerned with adventure on the high seas in the days of the clipper sailing ships: *The Partick Steamboat* with the first days of steam, while *Captain Anson and the Treasure of Spain* goes back to the 18th century.

The Last of Lallow's has a young heroine, Margaret, the daughter of an English country squire overwhelmed by the English Civil War. *Clemency Draper* also has a heroine, an orphan of character who is not suppressed by the horrors of an 18th-century orphanage or overcome by the temper of her eccentric benefactor. This is a cheerful, almost rollicking story, treating the terrors of the lives of the poor in Dickensian fashion, as young Clemency minds the foundling baby left in the stage coach, helps in the village shop and with solving the mystery of the French refugee.

Please Keep Off the Mud, Family on the Tide, Mudlarks and Mysteries, and *Shadows on the Mud* are modern stories of a brother and sister and their sailing dinghy around Chichester Harbour, told in bright and breezy style. The problems are soon solved against a secure home background. There is much backchat between the children; "The young are born to be blamed," as Brenda remarks when they have turned all the Sailing Club's equipment upsidedown and some adult has thereby lost something. The same local characters appear in all four books, one of which, *Shadows on the Mud*, touches on the problems of boys in an Approved School.

—Margaret Campbell

KONIGSBURG, E(laine) L(obl). American. Born in New York City, 10 February 1930. Educated at Farrell High School, Pennsylvania; Carnegie Institute of Technology, Pittsburgh, B.S. 1952; University of Pittsburgh, 1952–54. Married David Konigsburg in 1952; has three children. Bookkeeper, Ehenago Valley Provision Company, Sharon, Pennsylvania, 1947–48; science teacher, Bartram School, Jacksonville, Florida, 1954–55, 1960–62. Recipient: American Library Association Newbery Medal, 1968. Lives in Jacksonville, Florida.

Address: c/o Atheneum Publishers, 122 East 42nd Street, New York, New York 10017, U.S.A.

PUBLICATIONS FOR CHILDREN (illustrated by the author)

Fiction

> *From the Mixed-Up Files of Mrs. Basil E. Frankweiler.* New York, Atheneum, 1967; London, Macmillan, 1969.
> *Jennifer, Hecate, Macbeth, William McKinley, and Me, Elizabeth.* New York, Atheneum, 1967; as *Jennifer, Hecate, Macbeth and Me,* London, Macmillan, 1968.
> *About the B'nai Bagels.* New York, Atheneum, 1969.
> *(George).* New York, Atheneum, 1970; as *Benjamin Dickinson Carr and His (George),* London, Penguin, 1974.
> *Altogether, One at a Time,* illustrated by Gail E. Haley and others. New York, Atheneum, 1971.
> *A Proud Taste for Scarlet and Miniver.* New York, Atheneum, 1973; London, Macmillan, 1974.
> *The Dragon in the Ghetto Caper.* New York, Atheneum, 1974.
> *The Second Mrs. Giaconda.* New York, Atheneum, 1975; London, Macmillan, 1976.
> *Father's Arcane Daughter.* New York, Atheneum, 1976; London, Macmillan, 1977.

Play

> *The Second Mrs. Giaconda,* adaptation of her own novel (produced Jacksonville, Florida, 1976).

*   *   *

E.L. Konigsburg is a patchy, unpredictable, and fascinating writer. For the most part, her contributions to children's literature can be conservatively assessed as superior; and since she is amazingly inventive and prolific, it is happily permissible to assume that there will be more very good things to come.

She is probably best and most widely known for her Newbery Award winner of 1968, *The Mixed-Up Files,* an inspired piece of wish fulfillment. What youngster with spunk and imagination hasn't dreamed of having the freedom of a great museum; liberty to roam at will, *touching everything*; to sleep in the antique fourposters, bathe in the reflecting pool, and, perhaps best of all, collect the good-luck coins from the fountain? Claudia and Jamie Kincaid do all these things and more. Their well-ordered plan for running away from home and setting up light housekeeping in New York's Metropolitan Museum of Art is neatly successful; and they return safely home in their own good time: a most satisfying adventure.

One would almost hesitate to recommend such an accurate and enticing escape manual to young readers for fear of inspiring emulation — it's enough to rouse stirrings of wanderlust even in an adult; but the story reveals the discomfort and inconvenience of camping out in the world of ancient art as well as its satisfactions. Young Claudia and Jamie make a success of their adventure, but they are a convincingly special pair of people.

So too are the heroines of *Jennifer, Hecate* .... Jennifer is a self-proclaimed grade-school witch who enlists the narrator, little Elizabeth, as her apprentice. The half-pretence private world of the two little girls is amusing and touching, and their characters are beautifully contrasted. The developing friendship of two lonely city children is drawn with strokes of feathery delicacy. Jennifer happens to be black, and Elizabeth white, but the complete irrelevance of this detail makes its point more convincingly than any amount of pious sermonizing could do.

About the B'nai Bagels is less touching and amusing, indeed altogether less effective than her earlier books. 12-year-old Mark is aghast when his mother becomes manager of his Little League baseball team, but the family members become closer and learn a lot about each other in a season of shared sportsmanship and problem solving. Unfortunately Mrs. Bagel emerges as a caricature Jewish mother, given to Yiddishisms and amateur psychiatry, and Mark is an unconvincingly precocious observer. The Bagels just don't live up to their predecessors.

But then comes *(George)*. The puzzling appearance of the title is explained by the mechanics of young Ben's split personality: it is split in a most companionable way. His invisible other self George lives within Ben's body (in parenthesis, as it were), and George and Ben help each other out. Ben sees for George, and George remembers and interprets for Ben. They need each other. George does his best to soften and humanize Ben's rather arid and unperceptive approach to life; when he feels his urgent advice being ignored, George first creates an inner static condition disruptive to examination-writing, and then withdraws into inaccessibility. Ben misses George so badly that he goes to great lengths to win back his esteem, thereby greatly improving his own character. Though most of the adults who have dealings with young Ben see him as dangerously neurotic, he gives the impression of being very well-balanced indeed, at least as long as he has George.

Altogether, One at a Time is a collection of four short stories, all having to do with compromise and the need for coming to terms with reality. From these pithy little pieces it is quite a leap to *A Proud Taste for Scarlet and Miniver*, a not too successful historic fantasy based on the life and times of Queen Eleanor of Aquitaine, seen through the eyes of her household 800 years after her death. The historic facts are accurate, but the flavor is wrong. Unmistakably the cast of characters is made up of 20th-century masqueraders in medieval garb.

From the 12th century Konigsburg returns to the present for *The Dragon in the Ghetto Caper* in which a youngster living in a closed, privileged community makes contact with the realities of life outside his small protected world. His first ventures take him into a black ghetto where he becomes involved with the local numbers runner. Andrew J. Chronister is too knowing and cynical for a sheltered child; this book seems to have been written with one eye on the adult reader, and is not entirely successful as children's literature.

The Second Mrs. Giaconda is extremely clever and intriguing. The meaning hidden in its enigmatic title remains concealed till the last page, except from canny readers who are already aware that Mrs. Giaconda is more familiarly known as Mona Lisa. This is a story of Leonardo da Vinci, but since Leonardo is so towering and remote, Konigsburg approaches the maestro through his servant, the disrespectful, impish Salai, a true historic personage. Through her brilliant historic reconstruction and imagination, Leonardo, the Duke and Duchess of Milan, and the rapscallion Salai become vividly real and alive.

Konigsburg's works to date are undeniably a mixed lot, in subject matter and in quality, but upon one point there can be no disagreement. She is the possessor of a rare talent, one that is growing and developing from book to book. Her next work will be as much of a surprise package as her first; but the name E.L. Konigsburg on the title page will ensure that it deserves close attention – it will quite probably prove to be a classic of children's literature.

—Joan McGrath

KRASILOVSKY, Phyllis. American. Born in Brooklyn, New York, 28 August 1926. Attended Brooklyn College, evenings 1944–47; Cornell University, Ithaca, New York, 1949–50. Married Bill Krasilovsky in 1948; has four children. Taught children's literature at Marymount College, Tarrytown, New York, 1969–70. Agent: Marilyn Marlow, Curtis Brown Ltd., 575 Madison Avenue, New York, New York 10022. Address: 1177 Hardscrabble Road, Chappaqua, New York 10514, U.S.A.

PUBLICATIONS FOR CHILDREN

Fiction

> *The Man Who Didn't Wash His Dishes*, illustrated by Barbara Cooney. New York,
> Doubleday, 1950; Kingswood, Surrey, World's Work, 1962.
> *The Very Little Girl*, illustrated by Ninon MacKnight. New York, Doubleday, 1953;
> Kingswood, Surrey, World's Work, 1959.
> *The Cow Who Fell in the Canal*, illustrated by Peter Spier. New York, Doubleday,
> 1957; Kingswood, Surrey, World's Work, 1958.
> *Scaredy Cat*, illustrated by Ninon MacKnight. New York, Macmillan, 1959;
> Kingswood, Surrey, World's Work, 1961.
> *Benny's Flag*, illustrated by W.T.Mars. Cleveland, World, 1960; Kingswood, Surrey,
> World's Work, 1961.
> *The Very Little Boy*, illustrated by Ninon MacKnight. New York, Doubleday, 1961;
> Kingswood, Surrey, World's Work, 1963.
> *Susan Sometimes*, illustrated by Abbi Giventer. New York, Macmillan, and London,
> Macmillan, 1962.
> *The Girl Who Was a Cowboy*, illustrated by Cyndy Szekeres. New York, Doubleday,
> and Kingswood, Surrey, World's Work, 1965.
> *The Very Tall Little Girl*, illustrated by Olivia Cole. New York, Doubleday, 1960;
> Kingswood, Surrey, World's Work, 1970.
> *The Shy Little Girl*, illustrated by Trina Schart Hyman. Boston, Houghton Mifflin,
> 1970; Kingswood, Surrey, World's Work, 1971.
> *The Popular Girls Club*, illustrated by Trina Schart Hyman. New York, Simon and
> Schuster, 1972; Kingswood, Surrey, World's Work, 1974.
> *L.C. Is the Greatest*. Nashville, Nelson, 1975.

Phyllis Krasilovsky comments:

I wrote my first book, *The Man Who Didn't Wash His Dishes*, for a 4-year-old boy who was dying of cancer. I wrote it as a letter and was told by his mother that he had to hear it "7 times a day." Considering that he was in pain most of the time, I realized I had something there. I have always enjoyed writing books for children, and telling stories to children (I do a lot of speaking and lecturing), but I was not really proud of being a children's book writer until I had to research the field for a course I was invited to give on the history of children's literature at Marymount College. At that time I became overwhelmed with the glory and the scope as well as the value of it, and ever since have been most proud and have felt most like an artist because of the children's books. It is heartwarming to realize that one can open the door to the world of reading by a good story!

*   *   *

Phyllis Krasilovsky's first picture books, appearing as they did before the flood of the 1960's (which became the deluge of the 1970's), were set firmly in the tradition already established by Margaret Wise Brown and continued by Ruth Krauss and Marie Hall Ets. First and foremost they were books for the very young child, newly ready for a real story, for the translation of a familiar theme into straightforward action, with plot and climax.

Krasilovsky's command of this deceptively simple prescription is nowhere seen as clearly as in *The Very Little Girl*. In beautifully measured prose the tale proceeds, from the opening pages in which the child is shown as "smaller than a rose bush" and "smaller than a kitchen stool" through a predictable growth spurt during which she grows daily "BIGGER!" to a delectable three-page climax in which she is discovered to be "big enough to be a big sister to her new baby brother who was very, very, very little!" Here are beauty of proportion, language which in its spareness is exquisitely satisfying, and, as theme, the universal concern of growth and normality. (Its companion volume, *The Very Little Boy*, somehow detracts from the original while failing to come alive in its own right.)

The Cow Who Fell in the Canal, *Scaredy Cat* and *The Man Who Didn't Wash His Dishes* reveal the same control of plot and language, with climax and resolution expertly handled in each case. Moreover, Krasilovsky is a master of the "list" so loved by young children. *The Man Who Didn't Wash His Dishes* uses up "all the dishes – and all the vases – and all the flowerpots" before inspiration strikes and his troubles are resolved.

The books written in the sixties are marred by a didacticism which reflected the belief (or delusion) of their decade that the child might profit from exposure, in print and picture, to his own predicament and its resolution or acceptance. *The Shy Little Girl* and *The Very Tall Little Girl*, both well-shaped, economically-recounted stories, are thinly disguised tales of planned reassurance which, one suspects, might be lost on the target readers and rejected as boring by the unafflicted. *The Girl Who Was a Cowboy*, of equally though less obviously didactic intention, risks offending on yet another score; the small female "cowboy" is brought to see the inappropriateness of her preference for her cowboy hat over her "brand new straw hat, covered with beautiful flowers"! (This is a regrettable mischance; the story was an attractive one to small girls of the sixties).

These books must be seen as casualties of their times. The earlier stories, dealing as they do with timeless concerns, have not dated, and will surely assure Krasilovsky of a deserved place in the history of the picture book in the English-speaking world.

—Dorothy Butler

KRAUS, Joanna Halpert. American. Born in Portland, Maine, 7 December 1937. Educated at Sarah Lawrence College, Bronxville, New York 1955–59, A.B. 1959; Westfield College, University of London, 1957–58; University of California, Los Angeles, 1961–63, M.A. 1963; Columbia University, New York, 1967–72, Ed.D. 1972. Married Ted M. Kraus in 1966; has one son. Associate Director, Baltimore Children's Theatre, 1960–61; Assistant Director, Clark Center for Performing Arts, New York, 1963–65; Instructor, New York City Community College, 1966–69, Columbia University Teachers College, 1970–71, and State University of New York, Purchase, 1970–72. Since 1972, Assistant Professor, New York State University College, New Paltz. Recipient: American Theatre Association Chorpenning Cup, 1971; Creative Artists Public Service grant, 1976. Agent: Ms. Patricia Hale Whitton, New Plays Inc., P.O. Box 273, Rowayton, Connecticut 06853. Address: 76 Fox Run, Poughkeepsie, New York 12603, U.S.A.

PUBLICATIONS FOR CHILDREN

Fiction

Seven Sound and Motion Stories. Rowayton, Connecticut, New Plays, 1971.

Plays

The Ice Wolf (produced New York, 1964). New York, New Plays, 1967.
Mean to Be Free (produced New York, 1968). New York, New Plays, 1968.
Vasalisa (produced Davidson, North Carolina, 1972). Rowayton, Connecticut, New Plays, 1973.
Circus Home (produced Seattle, 1977).

Two Plays from the Far East, illustrated by Marisabina.   Rowayton, Connecticut, New
Plays, 1977.

Other

*The Great American Train Ride, Using Creative Dramatics for a Multi-Disciplinary
Classroom Project.*   Rowayton, Connecticut, New Plays, 1975.

Joanna Halpert Kraus comments:
   I believe that the real purpose of theatre for young people is to illuminate in an exciting
way the concerns of children today, to bring greater understanding of both the commonplace
and the extraordinary, and to illustrate the concept of alternative choices which exist in
everyone's life.
   A play, a story, a poem are all personal statements, wrung out of conviction, wrought with
care.
   I have always worked with concepts and themes that attracted me at the start – themes of
prejudice, quests for freedom. If the vision strikes a chord of compassion in the viewer, then
the contract with the muses is fulfilled.

                                *   *   *

   In the past few years Joanna Halpert Kraus has made a considerable name for herself in the
fields of Children's Theatre and Creative Dramatics, both as an educator and as a playwright.
Her best known play, *The Ice Wolf*, is a lyric, provocative, and haunting story of an Eskimo
village controlled, mind and body, by shamans and superstitions. A fair-haired child, Anatou,
is born to parents who reject her because of village taboos, and the play is essentially a well-
honed, undogmatic plea for sanity, humanity, mercy, justice, and compassion. The flow of
language and action is at times exquisite, and the play, unlike many contemporary plays for
children, has value, in Horatian terms, to educate and entertain both children and adults. This
critical evaluation is true of all Dr. Halpert's works, especially a play entitled *Mean to Be Free*
which is a re-telling of the story of Harriet Tubman and the Underground Railway. The play
is accurate and well-researched, but the intensity of the drama goes beyond facts. Early in the
play the following speech summarizes the intensity of action, feeling and dialogue that
underlie the entire play:

> But this freedom train is goin' a long way. And the road ain't easy. You've got to
> sleep by day, walk by night. And never let folks know you're about. Watch me.
> You'll learn to hide as well as I can. You gotta walk so quiet that there's not even a
> sound of your bare feet on the earth. When you sleep, you gotta be so quiet that
> there's not a sound of breathing. Not a cough or a sneeze. Once this train starts,
> ain't no turning back.

   Another of Dr. Kraus' works is a three-act, technically involved play based on a legend of
wonder about the evil Baba Yaga, the grandmother of all witches, and Vasalisa, the
adventurous daughter of a fur merchant in 17th-century Russia. Vasalisa is a modification of
Cinderella, Pandora, and Psyche, and she manages to thwart Baba Yaga's guile by truth and
goodness, although the play is not dogmatic. *Vasalisa* is framed by an interesting use of
prologue and epilogue that involve a Skomoroki or Russian troubadour-acting company, and
the entire work is rich with balalaika music, song, dance, and many visual effects. What
should be most apparent about Joanna Kraus' plays is that they are packed with action,
visual effects, and highly believable spirited dialogue. This is perhaps nowhere more
apparent than in the anthology *Seven Sound and Motion Stories* which includes *The Winner*,
based on the Aesop fable of the sun and the wind; *Chaunteecleer*, a retelling of a Chaucerian
tale; *The First Night of Sleep*, based on the African myth about Ananse the Spider; three

contemporary stories; and a science fiction tale entitled *Veritas*. Also included is the one-act play *The Tale of Oniroku*, a re-telling of a Japanese fairy tale. Each of these tales is tight, detailed, and self-contained.

—Rachel Fordyce

KRAUS, Robert. American. Born in Milwaukee, Wisconsin, 21 June 1925. Studied at Layton Art School, Milwaukee, 1942; Art Students' League, New York, 1945. Married Pamela Wong in 1946; has two children. Cartoonist and illustrator: work published in *Saturday Evening Post, Esquire* and *New Yorker*. Since 1966, Founding President, Windmill Books, New York. Address: Windmill Books Inc., 201 Park Avenue, New York, New York 10003, U.S.A.

PUBLICATIONS FOR CHILDREN

Fiction

Junior, The Spoiled Cat, illustrated by the author. New York and London, Oxford University Press, 1955.
All the Mice Came, illustrated by the author. New York, Harper, 1955.
Ladybug, Ladybug!, illustrated by the author. New York, Harper, 1957.
I, Mouse, illustrated by the author. New York, Harper, 1958.
Mouse at Sea, illustrated by the author. New York, Harper, 1959.
The Littlest Rabbit, illustrated by the author. New York, Harper, 1961.
The Trouble with Spider, illustrated by the author. New York, Harper, 1962.
Miranda's Beautiful Dream, illustrated by the author. New York, Harper, 1964.
Penguin's Pal, illustrated by the author. New York, Harper, 1964.
The Bunny's Nutshell Library (*The Silver Dandelion, Juniper, The First Robin, Springfellow's Parade*), illustrated by the author. New York, Harper, 4 vols., 1965.
Amanda Remembers, illustrated by the author. New York, Harper, 1965.
My Son, The Mouse, illustrated by the author. New York, Harper, 1966.
The Little Giant, illustrated by the author. New York, Harper, 1967.
Unidentified Flying Elephant, illustrated by Whitney Darrow. New York, Windmill Books, 1968.
The Children Who Got Married, illustrated by Edna Eicke. New York, Windmill Books, 1969.
Hello, Hippopotamus, illustrated by the author. New York, Windmill Books, 1969.
Rumple Nose-Dimple and the Three Horrible Snaps, illustrated by Mischa Richter. New York, Windmill Books, 1969.
How Spider Saved Christmas, illustrated by the author. New York, Windmill Books, 1970.
Daddy Long Ears, illustrated by the author. New York, Windmill Books, 1970.
Whose Mouse Are You?, illustrated by Jose Aruego. New York, Macmillan, 1970; London, Hamish Hamilton, 1971.
Bunya the Witch, illustrated by Mischa Richter. New York, Windmill Books, 1971.
The Tail Who Wagged the Dog, illustrated by the author. New York, Windmill Books, 1971.
Ludwig, The Dog Who Snored Symphonies, illustrated by Virgil Partch. New York, Windmill Books, 1971.

Pip Squeak Mouse in Shining Armor, illustrated by Richard Oldden.   New York, Windmill Books, 1971.

Lillian, Morgan, and Teddy, illustrated by Edna Eicke.   New York, Windmill Books, 1971.

Leo the Late Bloomer, illustrated by Jose Aruego.   New York, Windmill Books, 1971; London, Hamish Hamilton, 1972.

The Tree That Stayed Up until Next Christmas, illustrated by Edna Eicke.   New York, Windmill Books, 1972.

Good Night, Little A.B.C., with N.M. Bodecker, illustrated by Bodecker.   New York, Springfellow Books, 1972; London, Cape, 1974.

Good Night, Little One, with N.M. Bodecker.   New York, Springfellow Books, 1972; London, Cape, 1974.

Good Night, Richard Rabbit, illustrated by N.M. Bodecker.   New York, Springfellow Books, 1972; London, Cape, 1974.

Milton the Early Riser, illustrated by Jose Aruego and Ariane Dewey.   New York, Windmill Books, 1972; London, Hamish Hamilton, 1974.

Big Brother.   New York, Parents' Magazine Press, 1973.

How Spider Saved Halloween.   New York, Parents' Magazine Press, 1973.

Pip Squeaks Through, illustrated by Richard Oldden.   New York, Springfellow Books, 1973.

Poor Mister Splinterfitzi, illustrated by Robert Byrd.   New York, Springfellow Books, 1973.

Herman the Helper, illustrated by Jose Aruego and Ariane Dewey.   New York, Dutton, 1974; London, Penguin, 1977.

The Night-Lite Story Book, illustrated by N.M. Bodecker.   New York, Dutton, 1974.

Rebecca Hatpin, illustrated by Robert Byrd.   New York, Dutton, 1974.

Owliver, illustrated by Jose Aruego and Ariane Dewey.   New York, Dutton, 1974; London, Penguin, 1976.

Pinchpenny Mouse, illustrated by Robert Byrd.   New York, Dutton, 1974; London, Hutchinson, 1976.

I'm a Monkey, illustrated by Hilary Knight.   New York, Dutton, 1975.

Three Friends, illustrated by Jose Aruego and Ariane Dewey.   New York, Dutton, 1975.

The Gondolier of Venice, illustrated by Robert Byrd.   New York, Dutton, 1976; London, Hutchinson, 1977.

Kittens for Nothing, illustrated by Diane Paterson.   New York, Dutton, 1976.

Boris Bad Enough, illustrated by Jose Aruego and Ariane Dewey.   New York, Dutton, 1976.

The Good Mousekeeper, illustrated by Hilary Knight.   New York, Dutton, 1977.

The Detective of London, with Bruce Kraus, illustrated by Robert Byrd.   New York, Dutton, 1977.

Noel the Coward, illustrated by Jose Aruego and Ariane Dewey.   New York, Dutton, 1977.

Verse

Shaggy Fur Face, illustrated by Virgil Partch.   New York, Windmill Books, 1971.

Other

Animal Etiquette, illustrated by Whitney Darrow.   New York, Windmill Books, 1969.

Don't Talk to Strange Bears, illustrated by Edward Koren.   New York, Windmill Books, 1969.

The Rabbit Brothers.   New York, Anti-Defamation League of B'nai B'rith, 1969.

Vip's Mistake Book, illustrated by Virgil Partch.   New York, Windmill Books, 1970.

Night-Lite Calendar 1976, illustrated by Hilary Knight.   New York, Dutton, 1976.
Mickey Mouse Calendar 1977, illustrated by Walt Disney Studios.   New York, Dutton,
   1976.

Editor, *Nanook of the North*, by Robert J. Flaherty.   New York, Windmill Books, 1971.

Manuscript Collection: Syracuse University, New York.

Illustrator: *Red Fox and the Hungry Tiger* by Paul Anderson, 1962; *Rabbit and Skunk and
the Big Fight*, 1964, *Rabbit and Skunk and the Spooks*, 1967, and *Rabbit and Skunk and the
Scary Rock*, 1970, all by Carla Stevens; *Animail* by Cleveland Amory, 1976.

*   *   *

Rabbits, frogs and teddy bears run rampant through Robert Kraus' books for pre- and
early readers. Although the problems and situations he depicts are altogether human, he
seems more at ease clothing them in fur – ourselves in fur coats, so to speak.

The situations about which he writes are ones which quickly appeal to youngsters. *Leo the
Late Bloomer*, for instance, is about a small tiger who hasn't quite got the knack of
achievement. He's worried over and pushed and prodded. But Leo proceeds at his own pace,
which is slow. "He's a late bloomer," his mother explains. But you can see that even she is
beginning to worry. Finally, in his own good time and without any help, Leo catches up. Leo
blooms. It's a reassuring tale for children and worried parents alike, reminding us that in
nature's own time achievement and approval come.

Some of his stories end so abruptly that you're sure he abandoned it in mid-thought. "Yes,
yes, go on," you long to say. "And then what?" Or perhaps he'll surprise you with a very
heavy subject smack in the middle of a pre-school story: in *Daddy Long Ears*, which is a
story about how the Easter bunny began, he explains, "After the birth of their thirty first
child Mrs. Long Ears ran away with a muskrat and Daddy Long Ears was left with 31
bunnies to be both father and mother to. It wasn't easy."

Kraus has written of a dog that succeeds in writing symphony music (by snoring) to
support his master, who is an unsuccessful composer. And he's written of mice, all employed
at a mouse-trap factory. In *Pinchpenny Mouse* the mice spend their money carelessly, then
run to Pinchpenny for help when the factory goes broke. With the money he's saved he buys
the factory and employs them all. The premise seems to change mid-book.

While he seems most at home with animal characters, perhaps his most successful story
features people. *Bunya the Witch* is taunted by the children of her village. When they call her
a witch she throws up her hands in despair. She's shocked when her action turns them all
into frogs. Trying to explain her actions she turns the parents into pigs. "Such a thing to
discover at my age. Magic powers. Phfui! Who needs them?" she says. When she's
sucessfully changed everyone back Bunya shrugs. "So if I'm a witch, I'm a witch. Magic
powers aren't the worst thing in the world to have." With that she treats herself to a round-
the-world trip via broomstick.

Whether fragmented or whole thoughts, Kraus' books have an exuberance about them
that makes them favorites for reading.

—Mary Blount Christian

———————

KRAUSS, Ruth.   American.   Born in Baltimore, Maryland, in 1911. Educated in public
elementary schools; Peabody Institute of Music; poetry workshops at the New School of
Social Research, New York; Maryland Institute of Art, Baltimore; Parsons School of Art,

New York, graduate. Married Crockett Johnson, *q.v.*, in 1941 (died, 1975). Address: 24 Owenoke, Westport, Connecticut 06880, U.S.A.

PUBLICATIONS FOR CHILDREN

Fiction

A Good Man and His Wife, illustrated by Ad Reinhardt. New York, Harper, 1944; revised edition, 1962.

The Carrot Seed, illustrated by Crockett Johnson. New York and London, Harper, 1945.

The Great Duffy, illustrated by Richter. New York and London, Harper, 1946.

The Growing Story, illustrated by Phyllis Rowand. New York and London, Harper, 1947.

Bears, illustrated by Phyllis Rowand. New York, Harper, 1948.

The Happy Day, illustrated by Marc Simont. New York, Harper, 1949.

The Big World and the Little House, illustrated by Marc Simont. New York, Schuman, 1949.

The Backward Day, illustrated by Marc Simont. New York, Harper, and London, Hamish Hamilton, 1950.

The Bundle Book, illustrated by Helen Stone. New York, Harper, 1951.

A Hole Is to Dig: A First Book of First Definitions, illustrated by Maurice Sendak. New York, Harper, 1952; London, Hamish Hamilton, 1963.

A Very Special House, illustrated by Maurice Sendak. New York, Harper, 1953.

I'll Be You and You Be Me, illustrated by Maurice Sendak. New York, Harper, 1954.

How to Make an Earthquake, illustrated by Crockett Johnson. New York, Harper, 1954.

Charlotte and the White Horse, illustrated by Maurice Sendak. New York, Harper, 1955; London, Bodley Head, 1977.

Is This You?, illustrated by Crockett Johnson. New York, Scott, 1955.

I Want to Paint My Bathroom Blue, illustrated by Maurice Sendak. New York, Harper, 1956.

The Birthday Party, illustrated by Maurice Sendak. New York, Harper, 1957.

Monkey Day, illustrated by Phyllis Rowand. New York, Harper, 1957.

Somebody Else's Nut Tree and Other Tales from Children, illustrated by Maurice Sendak. New York, Harper, 1958.

A Moon or a Button, illustrated by Remy Charlip. New York, Harper, 1959.

Open House for Butterflies, illustrated by Maurice Sendak. New York, Harper, and London, Hamish Hamilton, 1960.

"Mama, I Wish I Was Snow" "Child, You'd Be Very Cold," illustrated by Ellen Raskin. New York, Atheneum, 1962.

Eye Nose Fingers Toes, illustrated by Elizabeth Schneider. New York, Harper, 1964.

The Little King, The Little Queen, The Little Monster and Other Stories You Can Make Up Yourself. New York, Scholastic, 1967.

The Happy Egg, illustrated by Crockett Johnson. New York, Scholastic, 1967.

This Thumbprint: Word and Thumbprints. New York, Harper, 1967.

Little Boat Lighter Than a Cork, illustrated by Esther Gilman. New York, Walker, 1976.

Verse

I Can Fly, illustrated by Mary Blair. New York, Simon and Schuster, 1950.

A Bouquet of Littles, illustrated by Jane Flora. New York, Harper, 1963.

Everything under a Mushroom, illustrated by Margot Tomes.   New York, Farrar Straus, 1967.

What a Fine Day for ..., music by Al Carmines, illustrated by Remy Charlip.   New York, Parents' Magazine Press, 1967.

I Write It, illustrated by Mary Chalmers.   New York, Harper, 1970.

PUBLICATIONS FOR ADULTS

Poem-Plays

The Cantilever Rainbow.   New York, Pantheon Books, 1965.

There's a Little Ambiguity Over There among the Bluebells and Other Theatre Poems.   New York, Something Else Press, 1968.

If Only.   Eugene, Oregon, Toad Press, 1969.

Under Twenty.   Eugene, Oregon, Toad Press, 1970.

Love and the Invention of Punctuation.   Lenox, Massachusetts, Bookstore Press, 1973.

This Breast Gothic.   Lenox, Massachusetts, Bookstore Press, 1973.

Under Thirteen.   Lenox, Massachusetts, Bookstore Press, 1976.

Productions include *A Beautiful Day, There's a Little Ambiguity Over There among the Bluebells, Re-Examination of Freedom, Newsletter, The Cantilever Rainbow, In a Bull's Eye, Pineapple Play, Quartet, A Show, A Play – It's a Girl!, Onward, Duet* (or *Yellow Umbrella*), *Drunk Boat, If Only, This Breast,* many with music by Al Carmines, Bill Dixon, and Don Heckman, produced in New York, New Haven, Connecticut, Boston, and other places, since 1964.

Manuscript Collection: Dupont School, Wilmington, Delaware.

*   *   *

After a long silence, Ruth Krauss was heard from again in 1976 when she published a new picture book. *Little Boat Lighter Than a Cork* is almost as tiny as its title, a walnut-shell craft in which a baby sails on a fantasy voyage. The simple, unpunctuated text is a lyrical lullaby, a shoo-in candidate for bedtime-story honors and it would be greeted as a work of exceptional felicity had it come from anyone else. But since *Little Boat* is by Krauss, it must be noted that it isn't a patch on the marvels of innovation she is capable of. In only one instance of the new text does she dart into an aside reminiscent of her classics. That's when the infant passenger says to the boat, "I will rock you for the small streams and big rivers and for dolphins ... " and interrupts the litany with "... for a red apple popping out of the water or is it the sun."

Her faithful following who have found Krauss's books virtual magnets since the appearance of her first in 1944 must miss the mirthful surprises she had previously offered. Millions of readers treasure their well-worn copies of *A Hole Is to Dig: A First Book of First Definitions*. People lined up in book stores to invest in the fun that book offered during the 1950's. Kids (and the kids still alive in adults) felt the pleasant shock of recognition when they met Ruth Krauss, an author who knew what they did: of course a hole is to dig; eyebrows are to go over eyes, a face is so you can make faces, a package is to look inside, etc. Another of her welcome earlier productions was *The Carrot Seed*, still enthusiastically read and listened to in a musical adaptation on a recording. The hero is a boy who is the ultimate in passive resistance and inflexible faith. Everyone tells the lad that the carrot seed he plants won't come up. He answers not a word. He bides his time. He pulls the weeds which spring up around his plant and he waters it. For a long time, nothing happens. "And then, one day, a carrot came up. Just as the little boy knew it would."

With *I'll Be You and You Be Me, Somebody Else's Nut Tree and Other Tales* and her other satisfying stories, Krauss conveys the viewpoint of a child, the awesome imagination of a little one who knows that anything is possible. One of her most pixieish books is *The Little*

King, The Little Queen, The Little Monster and Other Stories You Can Make Up Yourself in which the same things happen to three characters who are each granted a wish by a good fairy. The repetition of plot and sameness of language here are veritable meat for the readers' fantasy feasts. The dessert is the author's wind-up, a hint to her audience that they write their own tales, and her additional suggestions: "The Little Elephant," "The Little Egg," "The Little?"

Regardless of what she may or may not contribute to literature in the future, Krauss has already earned lasting fame with the creation of timeless works, clearly understood and valued by everyone who speaks the *lingua franca* of childhood.

—Jean F. Mercier

KRUMGOLD, Joseph (Quincy). American. Born in Jersey City, New Jersey, 9 April 1908. Educated at New York University, B.A. 1928. Married Helen Litwin in 1946; has one son. Press agent, writer, and producer, MGM, Paramount, Columbia, Republic, and RKO pictures, New York, Hollywood, and Paris, 1929–40; Producer and Director, Film Associates, New York, and Office of War Information, 1940–46; President in Charge of Production, Palestine Films, New York and Jerusalem, 1946–52; Owner of Joseph Krumgold Productions, 1952–60; Writer, Director, and Producer, CBS, NBC, National Educational Television, and Westinghouse television, New York, Rome, and Istanbul, 1960–70. Recipient: American Library Association Newbery Medal, 1954, 1960; film prizes at Venice, Edinburgh, and Prague festivals. Address: Hope, New Jersey 07844, U.S.A.

PUBLICATIONS FOR CHILDREN

Fiction

> *Sweeney's Adventures*, illustrated by Tibor Gergely. New York, Random House, 1942.
> *... and Now Miguel*, illustrated by Jean Charlot. New York, Crowell, 1953.
> *Onion John*, illustrated by Symeon Shimin. New York, Crowell, 1959; London, Lutterworth Press, 1964.
> *Henry 3*, illustrated by Alvin Smith. New York, Atheneum, 1967.
> *The Most Terrible Turk*, illustrated by Michael Hampshire. New York, Crowell, 1969.

PUBLICATIONS FOR ADULTS

Novel

> *Thanks to Murder.* New York, Vanguard Press, and London, Gollancz, 1935.

Plays

> Screenplays: *Blackmailer*, with Lee Loeb and Harold Buchman, 1936; *Adventure in Manhattan*, with others, 1936; *Lady from Nowhere*, with others, 1936; *Lone Wolf Returns*, 1936; *Jim Hanvey – Detective*, with Olive Cooper, 1937; *Join the Marines*, with Olive Cooper and Karl Brown, 1937; *Speed to Burn* (contributor), 1938; *Lady Behave*, with Olive Cooper, 1938; *Main Street Lawyer*, 1939; *The Phantom Submarine*, 1940; *The Crooked Road*, with others, 1940; *Seven Miles from Alcatraz*, 1942; *Hidden Hunger*

(documentary), 1942; *Magic Town*, with Robert Riskin, 1947; *Dream No More*, 1950; *Adventure in the Bronx; The Promise*; and others.

Other

Where Do We Grow from Here: An Essay on Children's Literature. New York, Atheneum, 1968.
The Oxford Furnace 1741–1925 (local history). Belvidere, New Jersey, Warren County Historical Society, 1976.

Joseph Krumgold comments:
  The three most widely read books, *... and Now Miguel, Onion John*, and *Henry 3*, deal with a similar theme. They are a trilogy devoted to the drama of confirmation, that turn of life when a child is acknowledged to be grown-up. Whether this happens through ritual or less formally, it's a two-way process. The child is examined by the adult for his maturity and understanding. And – less obviously – the community is examined, its wisdom and values are measured with all innocence by the child. It is this fresh insight, the test we're put to by our young, that determines the shape of these stories.

*   *   *

  In his two best books for children, *... and Now Miguel* and *Onion John*, Joseph Krumgold succeeds in directing the *genre* of realistic fiction for a young audience to the same purpose of exposition and exploration that identifies the best novels for adults.
  ... and Now Miguel explores the developing awareness of a Mexican boy who lives on a sheep farm and, through Miguel's consciousness, gives us the texture and design of such a life. Krumgold is also a professional film-maker and the subject of this widely acclaimed book evolved during a film-making trip when Krumgold had the opportunity to live among families like Miguel's. Working as a film-maker has yielded not only subject matter, but also particular techniques. While Krumgold's writing is not really "cinematic," he has an intensely visual sense for the telling detail and this may well have evolved from his experience with the camera.
  In some ways *Onion John* is a more unusual book, dealing, again through the consciousness of a young boy, with the way in which Onion John, an eccentric East European, part-hobo, part-wizard, interrelates with the highly conventional expectations of small-town Middle America. Onion John has lived happily for years in his tiny self-built house using candles as his only form of lighting and storing his vegetables in numerous bathtubs in his living room. The townspeople decide to build Onion John a "proper" house. No-one realises that such a house embodies a mass of expectations about how everyday life is to be conducted and eventually Onion John, unable to accommodate himself to these narrow expectations, sadly takes to the road again. A story of this kind is unusual in a book for children and Krumgold sustains a narrative which is moving without dropping into sentimentality.
  More alert readers are likely to find Krumgold's preoccupations excessively *macho*. He is, for example, almost exclusively concerned with father-son relationships and, rather laughably, in *Henry 3* manages to discover that the flabby businessmen are really heroes under the skin when faced with a hurricane, while he turns their wives into caricatures of weakness and greed, hysterical over the loss of their furs. In this respect he can viewed as the inheritor of such early writers of the boys' adventure tale as R.M. Ballantyne and G.A. Henty who, like Krumgold, celebrate a bonding of boys and men on an exclusion of females.
  Krumgold's contribution rests less on such preoccupations than on his development of sophisticated narrative techniques. Few writers for children use the first person narrative

with comparable conviction or have a comparable sense of how that form of narrative may be employed as a lens for exploring the world surrounding the "I."

—Gillian Thomas

KUSKIN, Karla. American. Born in New York City, 17 July 1932. Educated at Elizabeth Irwin High School; Antioch College, Yellow Springs, Ohio, 1950–53; Yale University, New Haven, Connecticut, 1953–55, B.F.A. 1955. Married Charles Kuskin in 1955; has two children. Recipient: American Institute of Graphic Arts Award, 1958, 1961. Agent: Harriet Wasserman, Russell and Volkening, 551 Fifth Avenue, New York, New York 10017. Address: 96 Joralemon Street, Brooklyn, New York 11201, U.S.A.

PUBLICATIONS FOR CHILDREN (illustrated by the author)

Fiction

> *Just Like Everyone Else.* New York, Harper, 1959.
> *Which Horse Is William?* New York, Harper, 1959.
> *The Walk the Mouse Girls Took.* New York and London, Harper, 1967.
> *Watson, The Smartest Dog in the U.S.A.* New York, Harper, 1968.
> *What Did You Bring Me?* New York, Harper, 1973.

Verse

> *Roar and More.* New York, Harper, 1956.
> *James and the Rain.* New York, Harper, 1957; London, Lutterworth Press, 1960.
> *In the Middle of the Trees.* New York, Harper, 1958.
> *The Animals and the Ark.* New York, Harper, 1958; London, Lutterworth Press, 1961.
> *Square as a House.* New York, Harper, 1960.
> *The Bear Who Saw the Spring.* New York, Harper, 1961.
> *All Sizes of Noises.* New York, Harper, 1962.
> *How Do You Get from Here to There?* (as Nicholas Charles). New York, Macmillan, and London, Macmillan, 1962.
> *Alexander Soames: His Poems.* New York, Harper, 1962.
> *ABCDEFGHIJKLMNOPQRSTUVWXYZ.* New York, Harper, 1963.
> *The Rose on My Cake.* New York and London, Harper, 1964.
> *Sand and Snow.* New York, Harper, 1965.
> *Jane Anne June Spoon and Her Very Adventurous Trip to the Moon* (as Nicholas Charles). New York, Norton, 1966.
> *In the Flaky Frosty Morning.* New York, Harper, 1969.
> *Any Me I Want to Be: Poems.* New York and London, Harper, 1972.
> *Near the Window Tree: Poems and Notes.* New York, Harper, 1975.
> *A Boy Had a Mother Who Bought Him a Hat.* Boston, Houghton Mifflin, 1976.

PUBLICATIONS FOR ADULTS

Plays

Screenplays: *What Do You Mean by Design?*, 1973; *An Electric Talking Picture*, 1973.

Illustrator: *Xingu* by Violette and John Viertel, 1959; *Who Woke the Sun?* by M.S. Seidman, 1960; *Sing for Joy* by Norman and Margaret Mealy, 1961; *The Dog That Lost His Family* by Jean Latham and Bee Lewi, 1961; *Oh Ye Jigs and Juleps*, 1962, and *Credos and Quips*, 1964, by Virginia Hudson; *Harrison Loved His Umbrella*, by Rhoda Levine, 1964; *Boris the Lopsided Bear* by Gladys Schmitt, 1966; *Look at Me* by Marguerita Rudolph, 1967; *Big Enough* by Sherry Kafka, 1970; *What Shall We Do, and Allee Galloo!* by Marie Winn and Allan Miller, 1970.

Karla Kuskin comments:

The first book I wrote and illustrated for children I printed on a small motor-driven press when I was a graphic arts student at Yale University. That was *Roar and More* in which I used typography to represent animal noises. Since then my books have ranged from simple, rather humorous picture books for very young children to books of poetry for somewhat older readers. I write from imagination and memories of my own childhood – what made me laugh, what I loved reading. I am particularly fond of reading and writing poetry and think that it is something young children turn to quite naturally if they are not frightened away by over-emphasis on unfamiliar forms and subject matter. In all my books I try both to communicate my own thoughts and moods to young readers and also to elicit a response from them.

*   *   *

Since Karla Kuskin's first book, a participative poetry book entitled *Roar and More*, this talented author-illustrator has worked imaginatively and successfully with a number of literary genres, always for younger children. These have included an alphabet book (*ABCDEFGHIJKLMNOPQRSTUVWXYZ*), a fanciful animal tale (*Watson, The Smartest Dog in the U.S.A.*) a concept book (*Square as a House*), and a cumulative rhyming tale (*James and the Rain*), much in the tradition of Marjorie Flack. However, it is with her short verse that Kuskin has made her most memorable contribution to literature for children. Beginning with *In the Middle of the Trees*, we find an outpouring of short poems which are universally childlike in their concepts yet perfect in their artlessly simple language. Certain to appeal to a young child's own experience is

> I'm very good at climbing
> I nearly climbed a tree
> But just as I was almost up
> I sort of skinned my knee.

The sly humor of "Sweet Delilah," a cat so perfect that

> From miles around the people came
> To watch her winning ways
> And they had nought to say but good
> And nought to give but praise

amuses adult readers, while children laugh at the way Delilah routs a pack of hungry wolves with her "barking loud harroo – " her one flaw.

A further book of short poems, *The Rose on My Cake*, sings of winter clothing, birthday parties, and days when nothing goes right. It also includes the delightfuly nonsensical "Hughbert and the Glue" and a hauntingly lyrical poem, "Once," which tells of a mouse that was once a queen:

> The world turns.
> The sun burns.
> The moon goes down to dawn ....

Kuskin's unusually imaginative and deftly humorous gift for projecting herself into various objects, natural and mechanical, is demonstrated in this same volume with her "If I Were a ... " in which she ruminates on the feelings of a bird, a fish, a larkspur, and a sandwich. She carries this idea into a later book, *Any Me I Want to Be*, a riddle book in which each of a number of objects, from trees to parrots to mittens to a computer, describes itself. The child is encouraged to imagine what it would be like to be a tiny ant, a complacent parrot, or a rooted tree, and then to go further in expressing his "If I Were ... " ideas in verse of his own.

Kuskin's most successful poems are those which capture the essence of childish experience; her ability to think herself into a child's skin she says is due to the fact that she draws for her inspiration on memories of her own childhood. That she has been able to distill these memories into simple yet lighthearted verses which at their best are evocatively perfect for her small themes is Kuskin's lasting talent.

—Margaret Maxwell

KYLE, Elisabeth. Pseudonym for Agnes M. R. Dunlop. British. Born in Ayr, Scotland. Educated privately. Agent: A.M. Heath and Co. Ltd., 40–42 William IV Street, London WC2N 4DD, England; or, Brandt and Brandt, 101 Park Avenue, New York, New York 10017, U.S.A. Address; 10 Carrick Park, Ayr, Scotland.

PUBLICATIONS FOR CHILDREN

Fiction

> *Visitors from England.* illustrated by A. Mason Trotter. London, Davies, 1941.
> *Vanishing Island*, illustrated by A. Mason Trotter. London, Davies, 1942; as *Disappearing Island*, Boston, Houghton Mifflin, 1944.
> *Behind the Waterfall*, illustrated by A. Mason Trotter. London, Davies, 1943.
> *The Seven Sapphires*, illustrated by Nora Lavrin. London, Davies, 1944; New York, Nelson, 1957.
> *Holly Hotel*, illustrated by Nora Lavrin. London, Davies, 1945; Boston, Houghton Mifflin, 1947.
> *Lost Karin*, illustrated by Nora Lavrin. London, Davies, 1947; Boston, Houghton Mifflin, 1948.
> *The Mirrors of Castle Doone*, illustrated by Nora Lavrin. London, Davies, 1947; Boston, Houghton Mifflin, 1949.
> *West Wind*, illustrated by Francis Gower. London, Davies, 1948; Boston, Houghton Mifflin, 1950.
> *The House on the Hill*, illustrated by Francis Gower. London, Davies, 1949.

Mystery of the Good Adventure (as Jan Ralston), illustrated by A. Mason Trotter.   New York, Dodd Mead, 1950.

The Provost's Jewel, illustrated by Joy Colesworthy.   London, Davies, 1950; Boston, Houghton Mifflin, 1951.

The Lintowers, illustrated by Joy Colesworthy.   London, Davies, 1951.

The Captain's House, illustrated by Joy Colesworthy.   London, Davies, 1952; Boston, Houghton Mifflin, 1953.

The Reiver's Road illustrated by A.H. Watson.   London, Nelson, 1953; as *On Lennox Moor*, New York, Nelson, 1954.

The House of the Pelican, illustrated by Peggy Fortnum.   London and New York, Nelson, 1954.

Caroline House, illustrated by Robert Hodgson.   London, Nelson, 1955; as *Carolina House*, New York, Nelson, 1955.

Run to Earth, illustrated by Mary Shillabeer.   London, Nelson, 1957.

The Money Cat, illustrated by Cecil Leslie.   London, Hamish Hamilton, 1958.

Eagle's Nest, illustrated by Juliette Palmer.   London, and New York, Nelson, 1961.

The Stilt Walkers.   London, Heinemann, 1972.

Through the Wall, illustrated by Philip Moon.   London, Heinemann, 1973.

The Yellow Coach, illustrated by Alexy Pendle.   London, Heinemann, 1976.

The Key of the Castle, illustrated by Joanna Troughton.   London, Heinemann, 1976.

Other

Queen of Scots: The Story of Mary Stuart, illustrated by Robert Hodgson.   Edinburgh, Nelson, 1957.

Maid of Orleans: The Story of Joan of Arc, illustrated by Robert Hodgson.   Edinburgh, Nelson, 1957.

Girl with a Lantern illustrated by Douglas Relf.   London, Evans, 1961; as *The Story of Grizel*, New York, Nelson, 1961.

Girl with an Easel, illustrated by Charles Mozley.   London, Evans, 1962; as *Portrait of Lisette*, New York, Nelson, 1963.

Girl with a Pen: Charlotte Brontë, illustrated by Charles Mozley.   London, Evans, 1963; New York, Holt Rinehart, 1964.

Girl with a Song: The Story of Jenny Lind, illustrated by Charles Mozley.   London, Evans, 1964; as *The Swedish Nightingale*, New York, Holt Rinehart, 1965.

Victoria: The Story of a Great Queen, illustrated by Annette Macarthur-Onslow.   London, Nelson, 1964.

Girl with a Destiny: The Story of Mary of Orange, illustrated by Charles Mozley.   London, Evans, 1965; as *Princess of Orange*, New York, Holt Rinehart, 1966.

The Boy Who Asked for More: The Early Life of Charles Dickens.   London, Evans, 1966; as *Great Ambitions*, New York, Holt Rinehart, 1968.

Duet: The Story of Clara and Robert Schumann.   London, Evans, and New York, Holt Rinehart, 1968.

Song of the Waterfall: The Story of Edvard and Nina Grieg.   London, Evans, and New York, Holt Rinehart, 1970.

PUBLICATIONS FOR ADULTS

Novels

The Begonia Bed.   London, Constable, and Indianapolis, Bobbs Merrill, 1934.

Orangefield.   London, Constable, and Indianapolis, Bobbs Merrill, 1938.

Broken Glass.   London, Davies, 1940.

The White Lady.   London, Davies, 1941.

But We Are Exiles.   London, Davies, 1942.

The Pleasure Dome. London, Davies, 1943.
The Skaters' Waltz. London, Davies, 1944.
Carp Country. London, Davies, 1946.
Mally Lee. London, Davies, and New York, Doubleday, 1947.
A Man of Talent. London, Davies, 1950; as *A Little Fire*, New York, Appleton, 1950.
The Tontine Belle. London, Davies, 1951.
Conor Sands. London, Davies, 1952.
The Regent's Candlesticks. London, Davies, 1954.
The Other Miss Evans. London, Davies, 1958.
Return to the Alcazar. London, Davies, 1962.
Love Is for Living. London, Davies, 1966; New York, Holt Rinehart, 1967.
High Season. London, Davies, 1968.
Queen's Evidence. London, Davies, 1969.
Mirror Dance. London, Davies, 1970; New York, Holt Rinehart, 1971.
The Scent of Danger. London, Davies, 1971; New York, Holt Rinehart, 1972.
The Silver Pineapple. London, Davies, 1972.
The Heron Tree. London, Davies, 1973.
Free as Air. London, Davies, 1974.
Down the Water. London, Davies, 1975.
All the Nice Girls. London, Davies, 1976.
The Burning Hill. London, Davies, 1977.

Play

The Singing Wood, with Alec Robertson (produced Glasgow, 1957).

Other

The Mirrors of Versailles. London, Constable, 1939.
Forgotten as a Dream. London, Davies, 1953.
A Stillness in the Air. London, Davies, 1956.
Oh Say, Can You See? London, Davies, 1959.

Manuscript Collection: National Library of Scotland, Edinburgh

*   *   *

Elisabeth Kyle's many titles have made no dramatic contribution to children's literature but have provided interesting and exciting stories for young readers for the last 35 years. Her love of Scotland has been a consistent feature, giving authentic atmosphere to such titles as *Caroline House, Run to Earth*, and *The House of the Pelican*, the last a mystery conveying the contrasting moods of Edinburgh. *Caroline House* is a sentimental story and now very dated in terms of clothes, customs and attitudes, but the underlying theme concerning Caroline's ancestors, Tobacco Lords of Glasgow, is absorbing. Like *Run to Earth*, it is a tale of the miscarriage of justice, and in both books a reliance on coincidence and convenience is evident in the plot. Family relationships are well drawn in Elisabeth Kyle's stories and, despite some stereotyped characters, this is clearly demonstrated in *Eagle's Nest* where a mystery about a 10-year-old burglary is skilfully combined with a background of forestry and the breeding of a rare eagle.

Among more recent books, *The Stilt Walkers* is set in London during the Great Exhibition of 1951. Elisabeth Kyle's feeling for history enables her to recreate the atmosphere in spite of a rather melodramatic plot and some superimposed historical detail, and she creates suspense and tension in an essentially ephemeral tale. In *The Key of the Castle* she returns to Scotland for the story of a page boy who wants to rescue Mary Queen of Scots from Lochleven. She writes comfortably for 8-to-10-year-olds.

The other main group of her writing consists of fictionalised biographies. She treats her subjects with sympathy, and the story presentation may catch the interest of young readers despite the dangers of over-glamourisation. The historical subjects seem more successful than the musical ones; in particular the romantic story of Grizel Hume intertwines with that of Mary of Orange. In *Girl with a Destiny* Mary's story is told up to her accession to the English throne with William in 1688 while *Girl with a Lantern* tells of Grizel Hume's early life in Scotland, her exile with her father to Holland, and their eventual return with William and Mary. In *Girl with a Pen* the author takes some liberties with the chronology, but the details of the Brontës' family life and of Charlotte's early difficulties are accurately researched. The style is old-fashioned and not always subtle but it is an imaginative and interesting reconstruction for young readers. Elisabeth Kyle is still an accomplished writer, and her early books were valuable in their time, but many of her novels are now dated and it is to be hoped that publishers will resist the temptation to reprint them unrevised.

—Valerie Brinkley-Willsher

LAMPMAN, Evelyn (Sibley). American. Born in Dallas, Oregon, 18 April 1907. Educated at Oregon State University, Corvallis. B.S. 1929. Married Herbert S. Lampman in 1934 (died, 1943); has two daughters. Continuity writer, 1929–34, and continuity chief, 1937–45, Radio KEX, Portland, Oregon; Education Director, Radio KGW, Portland, 1945–52. Recipient: Western Writers of America Spur Award 1968, 1971. Address: 3410 West Rosemont Road, West Linn, Oregon 97068, U.S.A.

PUBLICATIONS FOR CHILDREN

Fiction

Crazy Creek, illustrated by Grace Paull. New York, Doubleday, 1948.
Treasure Mountain, illustrated by Richard Bennett. New York, Doubleday, 1949.
The Bounces of Cynthiann', illustrated by Grace Paull. New York, Doubleday, 1950; Kingswood, Surrey, World's Work, 1960.
Timberland Adventure (as Lynn Bronson). Philadelphia, Lippincott, 1950.
Elder Brother, illustrated by Richard Bennett. New York, Doubleday, 1951.
Coyote Kid (as Lynn Bronson). Philadelphia, Lippincott, 1951.
Captain Apple's Ghost, illustrated by Ninon MacKnight. New York, Doubleday, 1952; London, Hodder and Stoughton, 1953.
Rogue's Valley (as Lynn Bronson). Philadelphia, Lippincott, 1952.
Tree Wagon, illustrated by Robert Frankenburg. New York, Doubleday, 1953.
The Runaway (as Lynn Bronson). Philadelphia, Lippincott, 1953.
The Witch Doctor's Son, illustrated by Richard Bennett. New York, Doubleday, 1954.
The Shy Stegosaurus of Cricket Creek, illustrated by Hubert Buel. New York, Doubleday, 1955.
Navaho Sister, illustrated by Paul Lantz. New York, Doubleday, 1956.
Darcy's Harvest (as Lynn Bronson), illustrated by Paul Galdone. New York, Doubleday, 1956.
Rusty's Space Ship. New York, Doubleday, 1957.
Popular Girl (as Lynn Bronson). New York, Doubleday, 1957.
Rock Hounds, illustrated by Arnold Spilka. New York, Doubleday, 1958.
Special Year, illustrated by Genia. New York, Doubleday, 1959.

The City under the Back Steps, illustrated by Honoré Valintcourt. New York,
   Doubleday, 1960; London, Faber, 1962.
Princess of Fort Vancouver, illustrated by Douglas Gorsline. New York, Doubleday,
   1962.
The Shy Stegosaurus at Indian Springs, illustrated by Paul Galdone. New York,
   Doubleday, 1962.
Mrs. Updaisy, illustrated by Cyndy Szekeres. New York, Doubleday, 1963.
Temple of the Sun, illustrated by Lili Réthi. New York, Doubleday, 1964.
Wheels West, illustrated by Gil Walker. New York, Doubleday, 1965.
The Tilted Sombrero, illustrated by Ray Cruz. New York, Doubleday, 1966.
Half-Breed, illustrated by Ann Grifalconi. New York, Doubleday, 1967.
The Bandit of Mok Hill, illustrated by Marvin Friedman. New York, Doubleday, 1969.
Cayuse Courage. New York, Harcourt Brace, 1970.
Once upon Little Big Horn, illustrated by John Gretzer. New York, Crowell, 1971.
The Year of the Small Shadow. New York, Harcourt Brace, 1971.
Go Up on the Road, illustrated by Charles Robinson. New York, Atheneum, 1972.
Rattlesnake Cave, illustrated by Pamela Johnson. New York, Atheneum, 1974.
White Captives. New York, Atheneum, 1975.
The Potlatch Family. New York, Atheneum, 1976.
Bargain Bride. New York, Atheneum, 1977.

Manuscript Collection: University of Oregon Library, Eugene.

*   *   *

Evelyn Lampman, writing at times under the pen name of Lynn Bronson, has written
biographies, historical fiction, contemporary novels, and stories that are variously humorous,
fanciful, or adventure-filled. She is primarily known, however, for fiction that deals with
members of minority groups, particularly the Native American.

Among Lampman's less serious books are *The Shy Stegosaurus at Indian Springs*, the
story of two children who find a friendly dinosaur, and *Captain Apple's Ghost*, in which a
ghost returns to his former home and helps preserve it as a children's museum. Neither tale is
wholly credible, but both are lively and amusing, with affable fantasy characters. Also
cheerful, if at times contrived, is one of her earliest books, *The Bounces of Cynthiann'*; the
motherless Bounce children are taken in by the town of Cynthianna in a tale that stresses the
close ties among the children and that gives a good picture of small town life.

Special Year, one of the few serious books that does not concern an ethnic minority, is a
remarkably perceptive story about pre-adolescent girls, with credible familial and peer group
relationships, and with a realistic treatment of the conflict between adult standards and peer
group mores. In *Elder Brother* Lampman pictures the cultural conflict within a Chinese-
American family with no sons who adopt a boy from China; even at the turn of the century
the girls in the family rebel against the traditional concepts of feminine role held by their new
brother. The problems of Mexican-American migrants are examined in *Go Up on the Road*, a
book in which the plot and characterization are less effective than the exposing of the
demeaning quality of migrant life and the organized efforts to improve it.

Lampman's sympathy for Native Americans and her understanding of the persecution and
cultural conflict they have suffered have made her stories about them, whether they are
historical or invented, her best books. Of the historical fiction, three outstanding books are
The Tilted Sombrero, Cayuse Courage, and *White Captives*. The first is set at the beginning of
the Mexican War of Independence and describes the first Indian revolt against Spanish rule, a
movement led by a priest. The setting is colorful, the historical details authentic, and the plot
filled with action, but it is the picture the book gives of a stratified society and a rebellion
against oppression that has major impact. *Cayuse Courage* is the story of the Whitman
massacre told from the viewpoint of a young Indian boy, a book that enables readers to see
the reasons for an event usually seen from a viewpoint sympathetic to the white pioneers.

Lampman's objectivity in seeing both the white and the Indian point of view is particularly evident in *White Captives*, based on a report written by Olive Oatman, who was taken captive by an Apache raiding party that had killed most of the members of a Mormon wagon train. The story has pace and poignancy, but it is most notable for the strong and varied characterization of Apache and Mohave Indians.

Of her novels that are pure fiction, *Half-Breed* is set in the past, the story of a boy who is at home neither with the local Indians who spurn him because he has a white father nor the white people who reject him because his mother is a Crow. Lampman concentrates, in such stories, on Native American children who face conflicting ways of life; in books with contemporary settings, such as *Navaho Sister*, Sad Girl must adjust to the new ways she finds in a government school – but must learn to be more tolerant herself. Whether the protagonist is white, as in *Rattlesnake Cave*, and learns to respect the dignity of the Native American traditions, or – as in *The Year of the Small Shadow* – is an Indian child thrust into a white environment, Lampman emphasizes the fact that the child, resilient and courageous, can cope with change, accepting new patterns while retaining an appreciation for the old.

—Zena Sutherland

LANGTON, Jane (Gillson). American. Born in Boston, Massachusetts, 30 December 1922. Educated at Wellesley College, Massachusetts, 1940–42; University of Michigan, Ann Arbor, 1942–45, B.S., M.A.; Radcliffe College, Cambridge, Massachusetts, 1945–46, 1947–48, M.A.; Boston Museum School of Art, 1958–59. Married William Langton in 1943; has three sons. Worked for WGBH Television, Boston, 1955–56. Address: Concord Road, Lincoln, Massachusetts 01773, U.S.A.

PUBLICATIONS FOR CHILDREN

Fiction

> *The Majesty of Grace*, illustrated by the author.   New York, Harper, 1961; as *Her Majesty, Grace Jones*, 1974.
> *The Diamond in the Window*, illustrated by Erik Blegvad.   New York, Harper, 1962; London, Hamish Hamilton, 1969.
> *The Swing in the Summerhouse*, illustrated by Erik Blegvad.   New York, Harper, 1967; London, Hamish Hamilton, 1970.
> *The Astonishing Stereoscope*, illustrated by Erik Blegvad.   New York, Harper, 1971.
> *The Boyhood of Grace Jones*, illustrated by Emily McCully.   New York, Harper, 1972.
> *Paper Chains*.   New York, Harper, 1977.

PUBLICATIONS FOR ADULTS

Novels

> . *The Transcendental Murder*.   New York, Harper, 1964; as *The Minute Man Murder*, New York, Dell, 1976.
> *Dark Nantucket Noon*.   New York, Harper, 1975.

Jane Langton comments:
My own three favorites are a series that begins with *The Diamond in the Window*. These

books are set in a real house in the real town of Concord, Massachusetts, and I hope the children are like real children. But their Uncle Freddy is fantastical, and because of his devotion to Concord's local saints, Emerson and Thoreau, the children's adventures are fantastic too, and awash with transcendentalism.

*   *   *

Jane Langton has proven herself a competent writer of "Nesbitian" fantasy – but with an American flavor. Several features of E. Nesbit's distinctive blend of realism and fantasy can be distinguished also in Langton's trio of fantasies involving the Hall family, *The Diamond in the Window*, *The Swing in the Summerhouse*, and *The Astonishing Stereoscope*. One feature is the family and home background against which plot develops. Like Nesbit's fictional children, Eleanor and Edward Hall are free to enjoy their escapades because their Aunt Lily and Uncle Freddy are wrapped up in their own affairs. Unlike Nesbit's adult characters, Langton's become entangled in some of the children's own adventures, especially the humorous ones. Another feature is the use of some magical object – a diamond, a swing, or a stereoscope – whereby the Hall children can shuttle back and forth between the real world and fantasy ones. Langton is careful, as Nesbit was, to account for the objects' power. Prince Krishna, Aunt Lily's friend and master magician, gives the children the objects as gifts for their amusement, but he stipulates the conditions in which the magic works. Thus, a good part of the plotting and humor in the novels concerns the children's struggling to respect these conditions.

Langton assumes, as Nesbit did previously, the intelligence and curiosity of her intended readers and never talks down to them or reiterates the obvious. This is best demonstrated by her incorporating into her narratives many references to the history of Concord and the lives and ideas of Emerson and Thoreau. More importantly, the allusions and what the author does with them contribute to the relatively high level of thought and imaginative appeal of the novels. For in her fantasies Langton, among other things, explores the possibility of a viable link between 19th-century transcendentalism and present-day Concord. Moreover, she contrasts two different understandings of history and its uses, and the variations explain some of the humor and much of the seriousness in the novels. Uncle Freddy's earnestness and penchant for applying Emersonian principles to almost any situation may trip him up occasionally, and his financial naivete drives the family virtually bankrupt. Nevertheless, the Halls' genuine goodness and concern for others do testify that Emersonian idealism can motivate and inspire. What transpires within the Hall home and Uncle Freddy's Concord College of Transcendentalist Knowledge, even if it is sometimes silly, reflects a more appropriate and valid relationship to Concord's past and its legacy than does the chamber of commerce mentality of Mr. Preek and Miss Prawn. Uncle Freddy's rivals, who see in history only a source of tourist dollars and look upon Uncle Freddy's idealism as a lamentable lack of Yankee practicality. Perhaps the many allusions to Concord and two of its most famous citizens may intimidate some youngsters, but for those who enjoy challenges the novels are a delight.

—Francis J. Molson

LATHAM, Jean Lee. American. Born in Buckhannon, West Virginia, 19 April 1902. Educated at West Virginia Wesleyan College, Buckhannon, A.B. 1925; Ithaca College, New (York, B.O.E. 1928; Cornell University, Ithaca, New York, M.A. 1930; West Virginia Institute of Technology, Montgomery, 1942. Served as a trainer of inspectors, United States War Department Signal Corps, 1943–45: Silver Wreath. Head of the English Department, Upshur County High School, West Virginia, 1926–27; substitute teacher, West Virginia

Wesleyan College, 1927; teacher, Ithaca College, 1928–29; Editor in Chief, Dramatic Publishing Company, Chicago, 1930–36. Free-lance writer, 1936–41, and since 1945. Director, workshop in juvenile writing, Indiana University Writers' Conference, Bloomington, 1959–60, and Writers' Conference in the Rocky Mountains, 1963. Recipient: American Library Association Newbery Medal, 1956; Boys' Clubs of America award, 1957. D.Litt.: West Virginia Wesleyan College, 1956. Address: 12 Phoenetia Avenue, Coral Gables, Florida 33134, U.S.A.

PUBLICATIONS FOR CHILDREN

Fiction

Carry On, Mr. Bowditch, illustrated by John Cosgrave. Boston, Houghton Mifflin, 1955.

This Dear-Bought Land, illustrated by Jacob Landau. New York, Harper, 1957.

The Dog That Lost His Family, with Bee Lewi, illustrated by Karla Kuskin. New York, Macmillan, 1961.

When Homer Honked, with Bee Lewi, illustrated by Cyndy Szekeres. New York, Macmillan, 1961.

The Cuckoo That Couldn't Count, with Bee Lewi, illustrated by Jacqueline Chwast. New York, Macmillan, 1961.

The Man Who Never Snoozed, with Bee Lewi, illustrated by Sheila Greenwald. New York, Macmillan, 1961.

The Frightened Hero: A Story of the Siege of Latham House, illustrated by Barbara Latham. Philadelphia, Chilton, 1965.

What Tabbit the Rabbit Found, illustrated by Bill Dugan. Champaign, Illinois, Garrard, 1974.

Plays

The Alien Note. Chicago, Dramatic Publishing Company, 1930.

The Christmas Party, adaptation of the story by Zona Gale. Chicago, Dramatic Publishing Company, 1930.

Crinoline and Candlelight. Chicago, Dramatic Publishing Company, 1931.

Another Washington (as Julian Lee). Chicago, Dramatic Publishing Company, 1931.

The Christmas Carol (as Julian Lee), adaptation of the story by Charles Dickens. Chicago, Dramatic Publishing Company, 1931.

A Fiancé for Fanny (as Julian Lee). Chicago, Dramatic Publishing Company, 1931.

I Will! I Won't! (as Julian Lee). Chicago, Dramatic Publishing Company, 1931.

Keeping Kitty's Dates (as Julian Lee). Chicago, Dramatic Publishing Company, 1931.

Washington for All (as Julian Lee). Chicago, Dramatic Publishing Company, 1931.

Thanksgiving for All (as Julian Lee), with Genevieve and Elwyn Swarthout, adaptation of *The Pompion Pie* by Jane Tallman. Chicago, Dramatic Publishing Company, 1932.

Christmas for All (as Julian Lee). Chicago, Dramatic Publishing Company, 1932.

Just for Justin (as Julian Lee). Chicago, Dramatic Publishing Company, 1933.

Tiny Jim (as Julian Lee). Chicago, Dramatic Publishing Company, 1933.

The Children's Book (as Julian Lee), with Harriette Wilburr and Nellie Meader Linn. Chicago, Dramatic Publishing Company, 1933.

Lincoln Yesterday and Today (as Julian Lee). Chicago, Dramatic Publishing Company, 1933.

The Giant and the Biscuits. Chicago, Dramatic Publishing Company, 1934.

The Prince and the Patters. Chicago, Dramatic Publishing Company, 1934.

Tommy Tomorrow. Chicago, Dramatic Publishing Company, 1935.

He Landed from London (as Julian Lee). Chicago, Dramatic Publishing Company, 1935.

And Then What Happened? Chicago, Dramatic Publishing Company, 1937.

All on Account of Kelly. Chicago, Dramatic Publishing Company, 1937.

Mickey the Mighty. Chicago, Dramatic Publishing Company, 1937.

Christmas Programs for the Lower Grades (as Julian Lee), with Ann Clark. Chicago, Dramatic Publishing Company, 1937.

Thanksgiving Programs for the Lower Grades (as Julian Lee), with Ann Clark. Chicago, Dramatic Publishing Company, 1937.

The Ghost of Rhodes Manor. New York, Dramatists Play Service, 1939.

Nine Radio Plays (includes *With Eyes Turned West, Mac and the Black Cat, Stew for Six, For Mister Jim, Debt of Honor, Cupid on the Cuff, Voices, The Way of Shawn, Discipline by Dad*). Chicago, Dramatic Publishing Company, 1940.

Big Brother Barges In (as Julian Lee). Chicago, Dramatic Publishing Company, 1940.

The Ghost of Lone Cabin (as Julian Lee). Chicago, Dramatic Publishing Company, 1940.

Verse

Who Lives Here?, illustrated by Benton Mahan. Champaign, Illinois, Garrard, 1974.

Other

555 Pointers for Beginning Actors and Directors. Chicago, Dramatic Publishing Company, 1935.

The Story of Eli Whitney, illustrated by Fritz Kredel. New York, Aladdin, 1953.

Medals for Morse, Artist and Inventor, illustrated by Douglas Gorsline. New York, Aladdin, 1954.

Trail Blazer of the Seas, illustrated by Victor Mays. Boston, Houghton Mifflin, 1956.

Young Man in a Hurry: The Story of Cyrus W. Field, illustrated by Victor Mays. New York, Harper, 1958.

On Stage, Mr. Jefferson!, illustrated by Edward Shenton. New York, Harper, 1958.

Drake, The Man They Called a Pirate, illustrated by Frederick Chapman. New York, Harper, and London, Hamish Hamilton, 1960.

Samuel F. B. Morse, Artist-Inventor, illustrated by Jo Polseno. Champaign, Illinois, Garrard, 1961.

Aladdin, illustrated by Pablo Ramirez. Indianapolis, Bobbs Merrill, 1961.

Ali Baba, illustrated by Pablo Ramirez. Indianapolis, Bobbs Merrill, 1961.

Nutcracker, illustrated by José Correas. Indianapolis, Bobbs Merrill, 1961.

Puss in Boots, illustrated by Pablo Ramirez. Indianapolis, Bobbs Merrill, 1961.

The Magic Fishbone, illustrated by Pablo Ramirez. Indianapolis, Bobbs Merrill, 1961.

Jack the Giant Killer, illustrated by Pablo Ramirez. Indianapolis, Bobbs Merrill, 1961.

Hop o' My Thumb, illustrated by Arnalot. Indianapolis, Bobbs Merrill, 1961.

The Ugly Duckling, Goldilocks and the Three Bears, and The Little Red Hen, illustrated by José Correas and Pablo Ramirez. Indianapolis, Bobbs Merrill, 1962.

The Brave Little Tailor, Hansel and Gretel, and Jack and the Beanstalk, illustrated by Pablo Ramirez and José Correas. Indianapolis, Bobbs Merrill, 1962.

Man of the Monitor: The Story of John Ericsson, illustrated by Leonard Everett Fisher. New York, Harper, 1962.

Eli Whitney, Great Inventor, illustrated by Cary. Champaign, Illinois, Garrard, 1963.

The Chagres: Power of the Panama Canal. Champaign, Illinois, Garrard, 1964.

Sam Houston, Hero of Texas. Champaign, Illinois, Garrard, and London, Harper, 1965.

Retreat to Glory: The Story of Sam Houston. New York, Harper, 1965.

George W. Goethals, Panama Canal Engineer, illustrated by Hamilton Greene. Champaign, Illinois, Garrard, 1965.

The Columbia, Powerhouse of North America. Champaign, Illinois, Garrard, 1967.

David Glasgow Farragut, Our First Admiral, illustrated by Paul Frame. Champaign, Illinois, Garrard, 1967.

Anchor's Aweigh: The Story of David Glasgow Farragut, illustrated by Eros Keith. New York, Harper, 1968.

Far Voyager: The Story of James Cook. New York, Harper, 1970.

Rachel Carson, Who Loved the Sea, illustrated by Victor Mays. Champaign, Illinois, Garrard, 1973.

Elizabeth Blackwell, Pioneer Woman Doctor, illustrated by Ethel Gold. Champaign, Illinois, Garrard, 1975.

Translator, *Wa O'Ka*, by Pablo Ramirez, illustrated by Ramirez. Indianapolis, Bobbs Merrill, 1961.

PUBLICATIONS FOR ADULTS

Plays

Thanks Awfully! Chicago, Dramatic Publishing Company, 1929.

Lookin' Lovely (as Janice Gard). Chicago, Dramatic Publishing Company, 1930.

Christopher's Orphans. Chicago, Dramatic Publishing Company, 1931.

A Sign unto You. Chicago, Dramatic Publishing Company, 1931.

Lady to See You. Chicago, Dramatic Publishing Company, 1931.

Listen to Leon (as Janice Gard). Chicago, Dramatic Publishing Company, 1931.

Depend on Me (as Janice Gard). Chicago, Dramatic Publishing Company, 1932.

The Blue Teapot. Chicago, Dramatic Publishing Company, 1932.

Broadway Bound. Chicago, Dramatic Publishing Company, 1933.

Master of Solitaire (produced New York, 1936). Chicago, Dramatic Publishing Company, 1935.

The Bed of Petunias. Chicago, Dramatic Publishing Company, 1937.

Here She Comes! Chicago, Dramatic Publishing Company, 1937.

Just the Girl for Jimmy. Chicago, Dramatic Publishing Company, 1937.

Have a Heart! Chicago, Dramatic Publishing Company, 1937.

What Are You Going to Wear? Chicago, Dramatic Publishing Company, 1937.

Talk Is Cheap. Chicago, Dramatic Publishing Company, 1937.

Smile for the Lady! Chicago, Dramatic Publishing Company, 1937.

Well Met by Moonlight. Chicago, Dramatic Publishing Company, 1937.

They'll Never Look There! New York, Dramatists Play Service, 1939.

The Arms of the Law. Chicago, Dramatic Publishing Company, 1940.

Old Doc. Chicago, Dramatic Publishing Company, 1940.

Gray Bread. Evanston, Illinois, Row Peterson, 1941.

People Don't Change. Chicago, Dramatic Publishing Company, 1941.

Señor Freedom. Evanston, Illinois, Row Peterson, 1941.

Minus a Million. New York, Dramatists Play Service, 1941.

The House Without a Key, adaptation of the novel by Earl Derr Biggers. Chicago, Dramatic Publishing Company, 1942.

The Nightmare. New York, French, 1943.

Radio Plays: for *First Nighter, Grand Central Station,* and *Skippy Hollywood Theatre* programs, 1930–41.

Manuscript Collection: Kerlan Collection, University of Minnesota, Minneapolis.

*   *   *

"Never double on the trail" is the motto Jean Lee Latham adheres to in producing poetry, drama, imaginative stories, retold classics, historical fiction, and biographies for children. Her reputation is based primarily on her more than twenty biographies. She has a keen sense for selection of character and compresses technical detail into a swift narrative style. As a teacher of creative writing herself, she respects the demands of the craft.

Her list of biographies reads like a *Who Was Who in America*. Samuel Morse, Sam Houston, and David Glasgow Farragut are among those chosen. She follows a pattern occasionally of writing fictionalized biography such as *Medals for Morse* and re-working it for a younger audience as *Samuel F. B. Morse* for another publisher. In an earlier century she may have used a pseudonym, for most of her books have male heroes and appeal to the mechanically inclined. Exceptions are the biographies of a doctor, Elizabeth Blackwell, and naturalist Rachel Carson. "I chose men who had it 'rough' and yet still managed to achieve something worthwhile, despite overwhelming setbacks," she remarked in an interview for the *Nassau Guardian* (18–19 February 1956).

The author has the capacity to reduce an enormous amount of minutiae to palatable form for the young reader. During World War II she studied electronics at the West Virginia Institute of Technology and became the head civilian trainer of inspectors of the Signal Corps. It was her responsibility to train inspectors and create the curriculum. She has retained the ability to communicate data succinctly and effectively. Her most notable book, and the one for which she won the Newbery Award, *Carry On, Mr. Bowditch*, incorporates a myriad of details about astronomy and mathematics without destroying the flow of the narrative. Rather than detracting from the story line, the details add an authenticity to the story of the man who before the age of 30 had written a significant book on navigation. In *Trail Blazer of the Seas*, she used quotes from letters, sample charts, and figures to verify the text.

The construction of her stories is based on a sound understanding of the craft. When she moved to Florida, she sought solitude in which she could "take narrative writing apart and find out what made it tick." She is an exponent of the word by word, line by line building of a story. The author slashes substantial sections from her working manuscripts, apparent in her original work in the Kerlan Collection at the University of Minnesota. In a trailer lined with reference books, she wrote five books, including the Newbery Award winner. By telling a good yarn with skill, Jean Lee Latham has introduced America's native and immigrant heroes to children throughout the world.

—Karen Nelson Hoyle

LATTIMORE, Eleanor (Frances).   American.   Born in Shanghai, China, 30 June 1904. Educated at California School of Arts and Crafts, Berkeley, 1920–22; Art Students' League, New York, 1924; Grand Central Art School, New York, 1927. Married Robert Armstrong Andrews in 1934 (died, 1963); has two sons. Free-lance artist, 1925–30. Group shows: Doll and Richards Gallery, Boston, 1923; Anderson Gallery, New York, 1924; Gibbes Gallery, Charleston, South Carolina, 1939. Address: 307 Romany Road, Lexington, Kentucky 40502, U.S.A.

PUBLICATIONS FOR CHILDREN (illustrated by the author)

Fiction

  Little Pear.   New York, Harcourt Brace, 1931; London, Museum Press, 1947.
  Jerry and the Pusa.   New York, Harcourt Brace, 1932.
  The Seven Crowns.   New York, Harcourt Brace, 1933.

Little Pear and His Friends.   New York, Harcourt Brace, 1934.

The Lost Leopard.   New York, Harcourt Brace, 1935.

The Clever Cat.   New York, Harcourt Brace, 1936.

Junior, A Colored Boy of Charleston.   New York, Harcourt Brace, 1938.

Jonny.   New York, Harcourt Brace, 1939.

The Story of Lee Ling.   New York, Harcourt Brace, 1940.

Storm on the Island.   New York, Harcourt Brace, 1942.

The Questions of Li-fu.   New York, Harcourt Brace, 1942.

Peachblossom.   New York, Harcourt Brace, 1943.

First Grade.   New York, Harcourt Brace, 1944.

Bayou Boy.   New York, Morrow, 1946.

Jeremy's Isle.   New York, Morrow, 1947.

Three Little Chinese Girls.   New York, Morrow, 1948; London, Angus and Robertson, 1961.

Davy of the Everglades.   New York, Morrow, 1949.

Deborah's White Winter.   New York, Morrow, 1949.

Indigo Hill.   New York, Morrow, 1950.

Christopher and His Turtle.   New York, Morrow, 1950.

The Fig Tree.   New York, Morrow, 1951.

Bells for a Chinese Donkey.   New York, Morrow, 1951; London, Angus and Robertson, 1959.

Lively Victoria.   New York, Morrow, 1952.

Wu, The Gatekeeper's Son.   New York, Morrow, 1953; London, Angus and Robertson, 1963.

Jasper.   New York, Morrow, 1953.

Holly in the Snow.   New York, Morrow, 1954.

Diana in the China Shop.   New York, Morrow, 1955.

Willow Tree Village.   New York, Morrow, 1955; London, Angus and Robertson, 1961.

Molly in the Middle.   New York, Morrow, 1956.

Little Pear and the Rabbits.   New York, Morrow, 1956; London, Angus and Robertson, 1963.

The Monkey of Crofton.   New York, Morrow, 1957.

The Journey of Ching Lai.   New York, Morrow, 1957; London, Angus and Robertson, 1959.

Happiness for Kimi.   New York, Morrow, 1958.

Fair Bay.   New York, Morrow, 1958; London, Angus and Robertson, 1964.

The Fisherman's Son.   New York, Morrow, 1959; London, Angus and Robertson, 1962.

The Youngest Artist.   New York, Morrow, 1959.

Beachcomber Boy.   New York, Morrow, 1960.

The Chinese Daughter.   New York, Morrow, 1960; London, Angus and Robertson, 1962.

The Wonderful Glass House.   New York, Morrow, 1961.

Cousin Melinda.   New York, Morrow, 1961.

The Bittern's Nest.   New York, Morrow, 1962; London, Angus and Robertson, 1964.

Laurie and Company.   New York, Morrow, 1962.

Janetta's Magnet.   New York, Morrow, 1963.

The Little Tumbler.   New York, Morrow, 1963; London, Angus and Robertson, 1964.

Felicia.   New York, Morrow, 1964; London, Angus and Robertson, 1965.

The Mexican Bird.   New York, Morrow, 1965; London, Angus and Robertson, 1966.

The Bus Trip.   New York, Morrow, 1965.

The Search for Christina.   New York, Morrow, 1966.

The Two Helens.   New York, Morrow, 1967.

Bird Song.   New York, Morrow, 1968.

The Girl on the Deer. New York, Morrow, 1969.
The Three Firecrackers. New York, Morrow, 1970.
More about Little Pear. New York, Morrow, 1971.
A Smiling Face. New York, Morrow, 1973.
The Taming of Tiger. New York, Morrow, 1975.
Adam's Key, illustrated by Alan Tiegreen. New York, Morrow, 1976.

Manuscript Collections: Kerlan Collection, University of Minnesota, Minneapolis; de Grummond Collection, University of Southern Mississippi, Hattiesburg.

Illustrator: *Turkestan Reunion* by Eleanor Holgate Lattimore, 1934; *Picture Tales from the Chinese* by Berta Metzger, 1934; *Rainbow Bridge* by Florence Crannell Means, 1934; *All Around the City* by Esther Freivogel, 1938.

Eleanor Lattimore comments:
   I don't know quite what to say about my books except that I enjoy writing and always have been interested in children. Since I draw as well as write, I "see" my characters as I write about them. The settings are real, the characters imaginary. My stories, with one exception, are realistic. The exception is *Felicia*, about a cat who assumes the form of a girl.

                                   *   *   *

   China was introduced to young children by one author primarily – Eleanor Lattimore. Her first book, *Little Pear*, remains a classic and is a prototype for her many books for children written during a half-century. She merged an episodic plot, a strong character, and a detailed Chinese setting to produce the delightful story, and the five year old hero is memorable enough to be listed in Margery Fisher's *Who's Who in Children's Literature* (1975). Sequels were published decades apart, although in *Little Pear and His Friends* (1934) he is only one year older, and remains a youngster in *Little Pear and the Rabbits* (1956) and *More About Little Pear* (1971). The Chinese culture permeates the text so thoroughly that the story cannot be separated from the place. Clothing, food, games, and customs are integrated into the child's adventures. Published the same year as Pearl Buck's *The Good Earth*, *Little Pear* seems naive in contrast.
   The plots of her books are predictable, conforming to a pattern of a search or problem resolved. *The Fig Tree* concludes with the finding of a missing cup in a miniature tea set, while *The Fisherman's Son* solves the mystery of a stolen yellow bird. *Storm on the Island* challenges the resourcefulness of a family during a hurricane and its aftermath. A more contemporary story, *The Taming of Tiger*, follows a boy moving from the inner city to a suburb. A diversion from her usual plot is *Jonny*, describing a two year old child's entire day.
   Memorable characters linger in the mind of the reader. *Junior, A Colored Boy of Charleston* was an effective book when published in 1938, sympathetically portraying an enterprising child who earned money for the family. However, the book is long since out-of-print and is not mentioned in Augusta Baker's *The Black Experience in Children's Literature* (1971) or Charlemae Rollins' *We Build Together* (1967). There is interaction between children of two cultures in *The Story of Lee Ling*, when the Chinese girl meets an American girl with "yellow hair like corn." *The Chinese Daughter* deals with a mixed racial adoption, while *Jerry and the Pusa* sees China from the point of view of an American child. Child-like competitiveness exists in *Beachcomber Boy* when Barry's shell collecting territory on the Carolina coast is invaded by Floridians.
   In addition to China, the United States and other countries provide the background for a number of books. South Carolina is the setting for *The Youngest Artist*, New Hampshire for *The Clever Cat*. Japan, Denmark, and England serve as the backdrops for *Happiness for Kimi*, *The Seven Crowns*, and *The Lost Leopard*, respectively. *Happiness for Kimi*, S. C. Gross wrote

in the *New York Times* (2 February 1958) "opens a Japanese wing in the author's oriental gallery. It has the simplicity and truth of a proverb touched with humor."

Eleanor Lattimore's success is based on her understanding of story, children, and locale. She had *Little Pear* so clearly in mind that she wrote it in one week, according to a letter to Dr. Irvin Kerlan. Writing for the reader with one or two years of experience, she usually selects characters which appeal to that age group. Each character has at least one distinguishing feature, such as the 6-year old in *Adam's Key*. His personality is molded by being the youngest of five children and the inheritor of hand-me-downs. As M. L. Becker wrote in a review, the author "has often shown her desire to bridge the gulf of interracial misunderstanding and her power to send across it filaments of good-will from one child to another."

—Karen Nelson Hoyle

LAWRENCE, Ann (Margaret). British. Born in Tring, Hertfordshire, 18 December 1942. Educated at Hemel Hempstead Grammar School; University of Southampton, 1961–64, B.A. (honours) in English 1964. Married Alan Smith in 1971. Worked for the British Trust for Ornithology, Tring, 1964–66; Cook, Lundy Field Society, Summer 1965; Teacher, Aylesbury, Buckinghamshire, 1966–71, and Tring, 1969–71. Agent: Laura Cecil, 10 Exeter Mansions, 106 Shaftesbury Avenue, London W1V 7DH, England.

PUBLICATIONS FOR CHILDREN

Fiction

> *Tom Ass; or, The Second Gift*, illustrated by Ionicus.   London, Macmillan, 1972; New York, Walck, 1973.
> *The Travels of Oggy*, illustrated by Hans Helweg.   London, Gollancz, 1973.
> *The Half-Brothers*, illustrated by Ionicus.   London, Macmillan, and New York, Walck, 1973.
> *The Conjuror's Box*, illustrated by Brian Aldridge.   London, Penguin, 1974.
> *Mr. Robertson's Hundred Pounds*, illustrated by Elizabeth Trimby.   London, Penguin, 1976.
> *Between the Forest and the Hills*, illustrated by Chris Nolan.   London, Penguin, 1977.
> *Oggy at Home*.   London, Gollancz, 1977.

Ann Lawrence comments:

I write stories which amuse me and which I hope may amuse other people. Generally in the process of getting written they generate ideas, which are worked out and demonstrated through the characters and the development of the plot, but again these are ideas which interest me, and *may* interest someone else, rather than didactic pills hiding inside a coating of fiction. I have not the least intention of offering the young any assistance with their social adjustments, beyond that which comes as a matter of course when one makes the imaginative effort of putting oneself in someone else's shoes. I should think that books are to the older child what play is to the younger: an opportunity to try out all the roles and situations life offers in the safety of one's own imagination. I feel that this is something achieved as readily through a fairytale as through the most earnest of social documents; I cannot see that it is necessary for the reader to be able to identify with the *setting* of a story, as long as he or she can identify with the characters. Indeed my feeling is that it is easier to handle one's own emotions objectively when they are distanced by an historical or fanciful setting. I presume that this has always been the function of folktales, myths, fables and legends of all kinds, and this is the tradition of storytelling in which I should like to believe that I work. I believe that all honest art is experimental, in the sense that every piece of work poses a problem of some sort which has to be worked out in its making. One cannot impose one's own solution on it, but must follow patiently the logic of the work itself.

I am concerned beyond anything with the extraordinariness of the ordinary (and following from that, with the baffling matter-o'-factness of marvels *once they have actually happened*), and with the powerful, magical clarity of any particular present moment, as soon as one becomes conscious of its unique presentness, even though nothing much may be happening – because that is the moment when *anything* could happen. I am also fascinated by people talking and the odd, revealing things they do while they are talking. Consequently I find myself trying to cast everything I write in pictures or in scenes of dialogue, so that my people and places can as far as possible speak for themselves. I do not want to explain them, I want to *show* them to you, as I see them, and let you meet them directly. I think of each book as an object, having size and shape; but also in terms of musical form, with key, rhythm, and dynamics, when regarded as a continuum, and I am always aware of having in mind some visual style which I hope to recall. However, these, like my "diagrams" of plot, characters, and ideas, are only working drawings – I do not know whether it is of any use or interest to a reader to know about them, except perhaps for the purpose of knowing that a good deal of thought may go to make even the slightest of literature.

It is my opinion that any style of which one is aware while reading is probably bad.

*   *   *

Ann Lawrence's recent novel, *Mr. Robertson's Hundred Pounds*, is perhaps her best so far. It is a rich novel, based on fact, which tells the story of young Simon who goes to Europe with his master in 1595 in pursuit of a thief and the stolen £100. Although she ranges over questions of loyalty, love, religious tolerance, artistic ambition, and political ideology, the excitement of the chase and Simon's reluctant involvement in spying makes this a stimulating and gripping novel for the reader of 12-plus. Some of the subtleties such as Mr. Robertson's equivocal religious beliefs and his relationship with Toby, whom they meet in Spain, might escape a young reader, but the characters are brought vividly to life and the dialogue is natural.

Of her earlier works, the first – *Tom Ass; or, The Second Gift* – is a fable about a lazy, over-confident youngest son who believes that he is destined to make his fortune in London but who does not anticipate the inconvenient nature of the Elf-Woman's gifts which enable him to fulfil his ambition. The skill Ann Lawrence shows in drawing the lively background of 15th-century London foreshadowed her confident handling of the historical novel. *The Half-Brothers* and *The Conjuror's Box* are both told with the humour and insight into human nature typical of all her writing, but the former is a sophisticated tale, limited in appeal, while the latter is a rather derivative, but enjoyable, fantasy. The half-brothers are four Princes who, in their attempts to woo the young Duchess of a neighbouring province, sweep that country along with their respective enthusiasms for music, poetry, science, and politics. The author gives a broad, colourful picture of Renaissance life but encourages a slightly superior attitude in the reader which externalises him from the story. In *The Conjuror's Box*, two children help a partially enchanted cat, a fiddler and other strange characters to defeat the Green Lady – one of the old gods now resenting her lack of power and exerting an evil influence on all who come into contact with her. The narrative builds up to a dramatic climax and the book might provoke some thought about the nature of time, but neither the characters nor the plot is particularly original.

The Travels of Oggy is an appealing story for younger children about a hedgehog who travels from London to "the country" learning much, on the way, about the world and the ways of other animals. Marred only by an impossible coincidence at the end, which would not bother young readers, the story is told with a light touch in which the animal behaviour is consistently natural.

All Ann Lawrence's work has a quiet competence which fails to make the headlines but which gives pleasure to many young readers. She may yet write something outstanding.

—Valerie Brinkley-Willsher

LAWRENCE, Mildred. American. Born in Charleston, Illinois, 10 November 1907. Educated at Flint Junior College, Michigan, A.A. 1926; Lawrence College, Appleton, Wisconsin, B.A. 1928 (Phi Beta Kappa); Yale University, New Haven, Connecticut, M.A. 1931. Married Clarence A. Lawrence in 1936; has one daughter. Society Editor, 1928–29, and Feature Writer and Reviewer, 1931–37, Flint *Journal*; Vice President, Eustis Publishing Company, Eustis, Florida, 1945–47. Address: 1044 Terrace Boulevard, Orlando, Florida 32803, U.S.A.

PUBLICATIONS FOR CHILDREN

Fiction

> *Susan's Bears*, illustrated by Decie Merwin. New York, Grosset and Dunlap, 1945.
> *Peachtree Island*, illustrated by Mary Stevens. New York, Harcourt Brace, 1948.
> *Sand in Her Shoes*, illustrated by Madye Lee Chastain. New York, Harcourt Brace, 1949.
> *The Homemade Year*, illustrated by Susanne Suba. New York, Harcourt Brace, 1950.
> *Tallie*, illustrated by Paul Galdone. New York, Harcourt Brace, 1951.
> *Crissy at the Wheel*, illustrated by Marvin Bileck. New York, Harcourt Brace, 1952.
> *One Hundred White Horses*, illustrated by Oscar Liebman. New York, Harcourt Brace, 1953.
> *Dreamboats for Trudy*, illustrated by Robert Frankenberg. New York, Harcourt Brace, 1954.
> *Island Secret*, illustrated by Paul Galdone. New York, Harcourt Brace, 1955.
> *Indigo Magic*, illustrated by Oscar Liebman. New York, Harcourt Brace, 1956.
> *Good Morning, My Heart.* New York, Harcourt Brace, 1957.
> *Along Comes Spring.* New York, Harcourt Brace, 1958.
> *The Questing Heart.* New York, Harcourt Brace, 1959.
> *The Shining Moment.* New York, Harcourt Brace, 1960.
> *Forever and Always.* New York, Harcourt Brace, 1961.
> *Starry Answer.* New York, Harcourt Brace, 1962.
> *Girl on Witches' Hill.* New York, Harcourt Brace, 1963.
> *Drums in My Heart.* New York, Harcourt Brace, 1964.
> *No Slipper for Cinderella.* New York, Harcourt Brace, 1965.
> *The Treasure and the Song.* New York, Harcourt Brace, 1966.
> *Reach for the Dream.* New York, Harcourt Brace, 1967.
> *Inside the Gate.* New York, Harcourt Brace, 1968.
> *Once at the Weary Why.* New York, Harcourt Brace, 1969.
> *Gateway to the Sun.* New York, Harcourt Brace, 1970.
> *Walk a Rocky Road.* New York, Harcourt Brace, 1971.
> *Touchmark*, illustrated by Deanne Hollinger. New York, Harcourt Brace, 1975.

Manuscript Collection: de Grummond Collection, University of Southern Mississippi, Hattiesburg.

Mildred Lawrence comments:

In my books I have been interested essentially in unusual places – a Lake Erie island, a Michigan town in the early days of the "horseless carriage," a remote corner of the Blue Ridge, tumultuous Boston in the 18th century. To my mind the characters spring out of the setting, which also influences the type of problem they must deal with, and, indeed, its solution. By painting my background of other places and times, with their universal problems and pleasures, I hope to help children feel at home in an increasingly complicated world – which is perhaps the purpose of juvenile literature in addition to providing entertainment (else one's audience will be long gone).

*   *   *

Mildred Lawrence began writing stories for and about girls when her own daughter was young, and her first stories were for younger girls: *Susan's Bears, Peachtree Island, Sand in Her Shoes,* and *The Homemade Year.* As is true of many of her later books for older readers, these stories reflect both the author's belief that books should help children adjust to problems in their lives, and – in their settings – the varied experiences in her own life. Often the younger protagonists are adjusting to a new environment: Cissie adapts to a new home on Peachtree Island (the author raised peaches at one time); *Sand in Her Shoes* has a newspaper background (the author and her husband ran a weekly newspaper in Florida).

As her daughter moved into adolescence, Lawrence began writing for older girls, and all her books now have teen-age protagonists, whether they are contemporary or historical fiction. Most of her books are contemporary, with *Touchmark,* a story set during the period of the American Revolutionary War, one of the few exceptions. While the story is crowded with too much detail, it is convincing in its depiction of colonial Boston and has a lively heroine who succeeds in believable fashion in reaching her goal of becoming a pewterer, an occupation then deemed unseemly for girls. *Crissy at the Wheel* is adequate but not outstanding period fiction, a pleasant family story set in the day of the new horseless carriage. In *Indigo Magic,* Lawrence demonstrates an ability to incorporate research into an 18th-century story about growing indigo for commercial use; the period details are more convincing than the plot.

Although the characters of many Lawrence books are static or superficially drawn, they cope in logical fashion with problems that are often everyday and sometimes universal: getting along with adults, gaining status in the peer group, choosing a career, assuming responsibilities, overcoming physical handicaps. Occasionally rose-tinged, the books usually are believable and they almost always have pertinence, warmth, and vitality.

—Zena Sutherland

LAWSON, Robert. American. Born in New York City, 4 October 1892. Educated at Montclair High School, New Jersey; New York School of Fine and Applied Art, 1911–14. Served in the American Expeditionary Forces, 40th Engineers Camouflage Section, during World War I. Married Marie Abrams in 1922 (died, 1956). Free-lance magazine illustrator, New York, 1914–17; commercial artist, 1919–30; from 1930, free-lance book illustrator. One-man shows (etchings): New York, 1932, 1933. Recipient: Society of American Etchers John Taylor Arms Prize, 1931; American Library Association Caldecott Medal, 1941, and Newbery Medal, 1945. *Died 26 May 1957.*

P<small>UBLICATIONS FOR</small> C<small>HILDREN</small> (illustrated by the author)

Fiction

> *Ben and Me.*   Boston, Little Brown, 1939.
> *They Were Strong and Good.*   New York, Viking Press, 1940.
> *I Discover Columbus.*   Boston, Little Brown, 1941; London, Harrap, 1943.
> *Mr. Wilmer.*   Boston, Little Brown, 1945; London, Muller, 1946.
> *Rabbit Hill.*   New York, Viking Press, 1944; London, Harrap, 1947.
> *Mr. Twigg's Mistake.*   Boston, Little Brown, 1947.
> *McWhinney's Jaunt.*   Boston, Little Brown, 1947.
> *Robbut: A Tale of Tails.*   New York, Viking Press, 1948; London, Heinemann, 1949.
> *The Fabulous Flight.*   Boston, Little Brown, 1949.
> *Smeller Martin.*   New York, Viking Press, 1950.
> *Edward, Hoppy and Joe.*   New York, Knopf, 1952.
> *Mr. Revere and I.*   Boston, Little Brown, 1953.
> *The Tough Winter.*   New York, Viking Press, 1954.
> *Captain Kidd's Cat.*   Boston, Little Brown, and London, Muller, 1956.
> *The Great Wheel.*   New York, Viking Press, 1957; London, Angus and Robertson, 1967.

Other

> *Dick Whittington and His Cat.*   New York, Limited Editions Club, 1949.

> Editor, *Just for Fun: A Collection of Stories and Verses.*   Chicago, Rand McNally, 1940.
> Editor, *Watchwords of Liberty: A Pageant of American Quotations.*   Boston, Little Brown, 1943.

P<small>UBLICATIONS FOR</small> A<small>DULTS</small> (illustrated by the author)

Other

> *Country Colic.*   Boston, Little Brown, 1944.
> *At That Time* (autobiographical).   New York, Viking Press, 1947; London, Heinemann, 1948.
> *Robert Lawson, Illustrator: A Selection of His Characteristic Illustrations,* edited by Helen L. Jones.   Boston, Little Brown, 1972.

Illustrator: *The Wonderful Adventures of Little Prince Toofat* by George Randolph Chester, 1922; *The Wee Men of Ballywooden,* 1930, *The Roving Lobster,* 1931, and *From the Horn of the Moon,* 1931, all by Arthur Mason; *The Unicorn with Silver Shoes* by Ella Young, 1932; *Peik* by Barbara Ring, 1932; *The Hurdy Gurdy Man* by Margery Williams Bianco, 1933; *Haven's End* by J. P. Marquand, 1933; *Treasure of the Isle of Mist* by W. W. Tarn, 1934; *Slim* by William Wister Haines, 1934; *The Golden Horseshoe* by Elizabeth Coatsworth, 1935; *Drums of Monmouth,* 1935, and *Miranda Is a Princess,* 1937, by Emma Gelders Sterne; *The Story of Ferdinand,* 1936, *Wee Gillis,* 1938, *The Story of Simpson and Sampson,* 1941, and *Aesop's Fables,* 1941, all by Munro Leaf; *Seven Beads of Wampum* by Elizabeth Gale, 1936; *Betsy Ross,* 1936, and *Francis Scott Key,* 1936, by Helen Dixon Bates; *Four and Twenty Blackbirds* edited by Helen Dean Fish, 1937; *The Prince and the Pauper* by Mark Twain, 1937; *The Story of Jesus for Young People* by Walter Russell Bowie, 1937; *Under the Tent of Sky,* 1937, and *Gaily We Parade,* 1940, edited by John E. Brewton; *I Hear America Singing* by Ruth Barnes, 1937; *Wind of the Vikings* by Maribelle Cormack, 1937; *Swords and*

Statues by Clarence Stratton, 1937; *Mr. Popper's Penguins* by Richard and Florence Atwater, 1938; *One Foot in Fairyland* by Eleanor Farjeon, 1938; *A Tale of Two Cities* by Charles Dickens, 1938; *Pilgrim's Progress* by John Bunyan, 1939; *Poo-Poo and the Dragons* by C. S. Forester, 1942; *Prince Prigio* by Andrew Lang, 1942; *The Crock of Gold* by James Stephens, 1942; *Adam of the Road* by Elizabeth Janet Gray, 1942; *The Little Woman Wanted Noise* by Val Teal, 1943; *The Shoelace Robin* by William Hall, 1945; *Greylock and the Robins* by Tom Robinson, 1946; *Mathematics for Success* by Mary A. Potter, 1952.

*   *   *

The only individual to win both the Newbery and Caldecott Medals, author-illustrator Robert Lawson holds a unique position in the history of American literature for children. His works are significant not only because of the recognition they received, however, but also because they support the notion that art both reflects and informs the values of an era.

A successful commercial artist and etcher, Lawson became internationally known during the 1930's as an illustrator of children's books following his collaboration with Munro Leaf for *The Story of Ferdinand* in 1936. He assumed the dual role of author-illustrator in 1939 with the publication of *Ben and Me*, first of four comic fantasies in which loquacious pets revealed the foibles of their notable owners – Benjamin Franklin, Christopher Columbus, Captain Kidd, and Paul Revere.

Whether illustrating his own texts or the texts of others, his drawings, characterized by traditional composition and an emphasis on meticulous draftsmanship, had the narrative quality which Barbara Bader in *American Picturebooks from Noah's Ark to the Beast Within* (1976) identifies as a particularly American attribute. This narrative quality appears in the tales he wrote as a strong sense of story conveyed through the forms, personae, and techniques associated with American humor. The two elements – words and pictures – merge to create a particular vision of American ideals and the American national character.

The four historical fantasies, for example, employ the talking beast motif, a familiar folklore device, but adapted to a convention of American humor, the comic monologue delivered by an apparently insignificant character who would be expected to celebrate rather than ridicule his betters. Although this same motif is apparent in the Newbery Medal-winning *Rabbit Hill* as well as in *The Tough Winter* and *Edward, Hoppy and Joe*, these are primarily stories of animal communities in the tradition of *Wind in the Willows*. Yet the characters are basically American personalities, revealed not through lengthy description but through descriptive dialogue, complemented by explicit illustrations.

More obviously reflective of mid-20th-century American values are the Caldecott Medal-winning *They Were Strong and Good*, a picture book biography of his ancestors, and *The Great Wheel*, a period romance celebrating the ideal of America as the land of opportunity. Concurrently with these tributes to American virtues, however, Lawson satirized such American institutions as merchandising and tourism in *Mr. Wilmer*, *Mr. Twigg's Mistake*, and *The Fabulous Flight*. Similarly, *McWhinney's Jaunt*, often compared to the stories of Baron Munchausen, could also be interpreted as a humorous warning to gullible consumers; yet it is essentially a tall tale, American in style and tone, dominated by the angular figure of the Yankee peddler in 20th-century disguise.

Undoubtedly Lawson's delineation of the homely virtues thought to be particularly American and his use of literary and visual techniques considered characteristic elements in the American cultural tradition contributed much to his popularity in the 1940's and 1950's. From the perspective of the 1970's, it has been noted that his treatment of minorities failed to transcend the sociological clichés of his time. Indeed, few of his human characters have the multi-dimensional personalities of his more memorable animal creations. Essentially a fabulist, he reflected the attitudes of his own era and yet, in his historical fantasies, notably *Ben and Me*, he managed to present for children an iconoclastic version of the traditions from which many of those attitudes were derived.

—Mary Mehlman Burns

LEA, Alec (Richard). British. Born near Wolfville, Nova Scotia, Canada, in 1907. Educated at St. Edward's School, Oxford; St. John's College, Oxford, 1926–28. Married May V. Kelly in 1958; has one daughter and one son. Agent: Laura Cecil, 10 Exeter Mansions, 106 Shaftesbury Avenue, London W1V 7DH, England. Address: Malvern, Bridge of Don, Aberdeen, Scotland.

PUBLICATIONS FOR CHILDREN

Fiction

> *To Sunset and Beyond.* London, Hamish Hamilton, 1970; New York, Walck, 1971.
> *Temba Dawn.* London, Bodley Head, and New York, Scribner, 1974; as *Temba Dawn,
> My Calf,* London, Target, 1975.
> *A Whiff of Boarhound.* London, Dobson, 1974.
> *Kingcup Calling.* London, Dobson, 1976.
> *Deep Down and High Up.* London, Dobson, 1976.
> *Beth Varden at Sunset.* London, Dobson, 1977.

PUBLICATIONS FOR ADULTS

Novels

> *The Outward Urge.* London, Rich and Cowan, 1944.
> *A Bid for Freedom.* London, Rich and Cowan, 1946.
> *The Roots of a Man.* Ilfracombe, Devon, Stockwell, 1954.

Alec Lea comments:

Coming into the world of children's books late in life, I have a tendency to take them more seriously, perhaps, than is good for either them or me. The more I think about the kind of book I would most like to write for the young, the more clearly I can see that I have until now not been able to write it. In a nutshell, I want to give them a book about the future, say 50 or 60 years ahead, which is sufficiently realistic to be convincing but is at the same time hopeful and attractive and contains hints for a new philosophy of life and a new ethics – the sort of book, in other words, which would be acceptable for reading in those periods of school-time still called RE. (And I mean of course acceptable by the children.)

About the books of mine listed above, all I will say is that, as a farmer and countryman for most of my life, I have tried to depict children experiencing very intensely adventures which they can only have in the countryside, on farms or in hills or mountains.

*   *   *

Alec Lea is best known for his first novel for children, *To Sunset and Beyond.* Based on a true story, this book relates the adventures of Peter Varden, son of a Dartmoor farmer, who, one summer evening in the last century, was sent out to bring the cows home for milking and became lost in a thick fog on the moors. He was not found until 36 hours later. Although some of the excitement is lost by the author's tendency to reveal the climaxes of the story before they actually happen, the narrative is otherwise taut and compelling. The strengths of the book lie also in the accurate portrayal of farm-life, which is shown quite unsentimentally as sheer hard back-breaking work, and in the evocation of the mysterious spaces of Dartmoor: Dartmoor, in fact, is really the main "character" and the feeling left by the novel in the reader's mind is of human figures struggling impressively against this hostile, overwhelming landscape.

Temba Dawn is set in Aberdeenshire, but is also mainly concerned with life on a farm. The central character, Rob, is given a calf for his 10th birthday, and the story portrays the relationship between this rather odd, withdrawn boy (he reads passages from the Bible aloud to the calf) and his unusual pet. The farm is eventually sold, but Rob is allowed to keep Temba. Once again the background is convincing and attractive – the day-to-day routine of dairy farming, weather and landscape, the feelings of people being driven from the land they have owned for years: it all sounds very real and holds the reader's attention completely.

A Whiff of Boarhound, Kingcup Calling, and *Deep Down and High Up* are much less satisfactory. It is difficult to believe in the probability of the story in the first two, and few of the characters in all three seem very rounded or credible. There is a distinctly scoutmasterish air about them: out-of-date slang – "by jeepers," etc. – people continually imparting useful information to each other rather than talking naturally, a great emphasis on old-fashioned virtues – words like "responsible" and "sensible" abound on most pages – and a soft fuzziness in the portrayal of relationships, particularly between teenagers. These books read like Arthur Ransome gone wrong. Their intentions are too didactic (dramatised manuals on camping or what to do in the event of a mountaineering accident), and it is much to be hoped that in subsequent novels Alec Lea will return to what he can do best – the Dartmoor farmer in the Dartmoor landscape, and that he will write about children rather than teenagers.

—David Rees

LEAF, (Wilbur) Munro. American. Born in Hamilton, Maryland, 4 December 1905. Educated at the University of Maryland, College Park, A.B. 1927; Harvard University, Cambridge, Massachusetts, M.A. 1931. Served in the United States Army, 1942–46: Major. Married Margaret Butler Pope in 1926; two sons. Teacher and coach, Belmont Hill School, Massachusetts, in the 1920's; teacher, Montgomery School, Wynnewood, Pennsylvania, 1931; Editor and Director, Frederick A. Stokes Company, publishers, New York, 1932–39; Columnist, *Ladies' Home Journal*, 1938–60. *Died 21 December 1976.*

PUBLICATIONS FOR CHILDREN

Fiction

> *Lo, The Poor Indian* (as Mun), illustrated by the author. New York, Leaf Mahony Seidel and Stokes, 1934.
> *Robert Francis Weatherbee*, illustrated by the author. New York, Stokes, 1935; London, Chatto and Windus, 1936.
> *The Story of Ferdinand*, illustrated by Robert Lawson. New York, Viking Press, 1936; London, Hamish Hamilton, 1937.
> *Noodle*, illustrated by Ludwig Bemelmans. New York, Stokes, 1937; London, Hamish Hamilton, 1938.
> *Wee Gillis*, illustrated by Robert Lawson. New York, Viking Press, and London, Hamish Hamilton, 1938.
> *John Henry Davis*, illustrated by the author. New York, Stokes, 1940.
> *The Story of Simpson and Sampson*, illustrated by Robert Lawson. New York, Viking Press, 1941; London, Warne, 1944.
> *Gordon the Goat*, illustrated by the author. Philadelphia, Lippincott, 1944; London, Warne, 1947.
> *Gwendolyn the Goose* (as John Calvert), illustrated by Garrett Price. New York, Random House, 1946.

Boo, Who Used to Be Scared of the Dark, illustrated by Frances Hunter. New York, Random House, 1948; as *Boo, The Boy Who Didn't Like the Dark*, London, Publicity Products, 1954.

Sam and the Superdroop, illustrated by the author. New York, Viking Press, 1948.

The Wishing Pool, illustrated by the author. Philadelphia, Lippincott, 1960.

Turnabout. Philadelphia, Lippincott, 1967.

Other (illustrated by the author)

Grammar Can Be Fun. New York, Stokes, 1934; London, Ward Lock, 1951.

Manners Can Be Fun. New York, Stokes, 1936; London, Hamish Hamilton, 1937; revised edition, Philadelphia, Lippincott, 1958.

Safety Can Be Fun. New York, Stokes, 1938; London, Ward Lock, 1951; revised edition, Philadelphia, Lippincott, 1961.

Listen, Little Girl, Before You Come to New York, illustrated by Dick Rose. New York, Stokes, 1938.

The Watchbirds: A Picture Book of Behavior. New York, Stokes, 1939; London, Warne, 1945.

Your Library and Some People You Don't Want in It. New York, Wilson, 1939.

Fair Play. New York, Stokes, 1939; London, Warne, 1959.

More Watchbirds. New York, Stokes, 1940.

Fly Away, Watchbird! New York, Stokes, 1941.

Aesop's Fables, illustrated by Robert Lawson. New York, Heritage Press, 1941.

A War-Time Handbook for Young Americans. Philadelphia, Stokes, 1942.

Health Can Be Fun. Philadelphia, Stokes, 1943; London, Warne, 1944.

3 and 30 Watchbirds. Philadelphia, Lippincott, 1944.

Let's Do Better. Philadelphia, Lippincott, 1945; London, Warne, 1947.

How to Behave and Why. Philadelphia, Lippincott, 1946.

Arithmetic [*History, Geography, Reading, Science*] *Can Be Fun*. Philadelphia, Lippincott, 5 vols., 1949–60; London, Ward Lock, 5 vols., 1951–60; revised edition of *Geography Can Be Fun*, Lippincott, 1962.

Lucky You. Philadelphia, Lippincott, 1955.

Three Promises to You. Philadelphia, Lippincott, 1957.

Being an American Can Be Fun. Philadelphia, Lippincott, 1964.

Who Cares? I Do. Philadelphia, Lippincott, 1971.

Metric Can Be Fun. Philadelphia, Lippincott, 1976.

PUBLICATIONS FOR ADULTS

Other

You and Psychiatry, with William C. Menninger. New York and London, Scribner, 1948.

Illustrator: *The Danger of Hiding Our Heads* by the Committee on the Present Danger, 1951.

*   *   *

Familiar to three generations of children, Munro Leaf's books have become recognized American classics through his unique illustrations and his simple stories. His most familiar trademark is his starkly simple pen-and-ink child characters. They were made familiar both through his books and through a "manners" column in the *Ladies' Home Journal* which appeared monthly from 1938 to 1960. The column undoubtedly gave Leaf his widest exposure and largest adult and child readership.

Most of his writings are geared to 4–9-year-olds, and and examination of his work shows Leaf to be a latter-day moralist, a direct descendant of the Sunday School bluestockings both in England and the United States. His non-fiction manners and ... *Can Be Fun* series are filled with maxims and exhortations to the reader, whether the subject is playing with friends or cleaning up the environment. Unlike his predecessors, Leaf evokes a feeling of fun and joy in his warnings both through text and illustration without the essential message being lost and without creating a feeling of gloom and doom. Leaf's goggle-eyed children, familiar in their plainness and direct in their commonness, invariably lead the reader to apply the message at hand to himself.

Leaf's two most outstanding books are *The Story of Ferdinand* and *Wee Gillis*, both illustrated by Robert Lawson. Of the two, *Ferdinand* is the stronger. The universal message, the depth of feeling, and the wide scope of emotion of the flower-smelling bull escape no one. *Wee Gillis*, with the same message of self-fulfillment, lacks the broad appeal and universality of *Ferdinand*. The reader is able to go back to each again and again, finding something new, yet familiar, each time. Both books are far superior to Leaf's other books and to many of those by his contemporaries, and stand as superb examples of that elusive concept of "quality" in children's literature.

—James W. Roginski

LEE, Benjamin. British. Born in London, 29 April 1921. Educated at Guy's Hospital Medical School, London, qualified 1944. Served in the Royal Naval Volunteer Reserve: Surgeon Lieutenant. Married Josephine Lee in 1944; has two daughters. Since 1949, Family Doctor, London. Address: c/o The Bodley Head, 9 Bow Street, London WC2E 7AL, England.

PUBLICATIONS FOR CHILDREN

Fiction

Paganini Strikes Again, illustrated by Trevor Stubley.   London, Hutchinson, 1970.
The Man in Fifteen, illustrated by Trevor Stubley.   London, Hutchinson, 1972.
The Frog Report, illustrated by Graham Humphreys.   London, Hutchinson, 1974.
It Can't Be Helped, illustrated by Quentin Blake.   London, Bodley Head, 1976.

Plays

Screenplays: *Paganini Strikes Again*, 1972; *Newsboy*, 1975.

Benjamin Lee comments:

The first three books are intended for the 9–13 age group, and their hallmark is a mixture of realism and humour. The underlying perception of character is developed in the most recent book, for "new adults." This maintains the mixture as before, but is more concerned with the development and interplay of character, against a background of current social and sexual problems of the teenager.

Unsentimentalized but real feelings find expression primarily in familiar dialogue.

*   *   *

Benjamin Lee's first novel, *Paganini Strikes Again*, is an uneven adventure story taken at a cracking pace and scooping up rather more gems in its stride than it can comfortably hold. The crooks and real danger remain at an obscurely safe distance while two serious, cynical and cultured youngsters follow their trail all over London, improbably humping violin cases which somehow it never seems convenient for them to leave at home. The children take their affairs seriously even in the midst of chaos, while the adults are beset with doubts and confusion. Grown-up assurance exhibits itself only in potty eccentricity and plain wrong-headedness. If the comedy is hilarious, however, the "detective story" hangs on a flimsily constructed hook which few child readers will mistake for anything other than a failure of imagination.

The central character of the book lives in a comfortable middle-class home for which the author appears somewhat apologetic, nodding earnestly and with every appearance of trying to avoid condescension in the direction of the real "salt of the earth" working-class characters. This concern with class is dropped in *The Man in Fifteen*, when he tells a rather more evenly constructed though equally frenetic tale of confusion which sends his principal boy characters scurrying back and forth, this time across Italy. Again a host of self-absorbed characters each tries to impress his own eccentric interpretation on events. The improbable story gains credence from the breakneck pace and the lunatic single-mindedness of the young hero and chance acquaintances, while the parents remain confused and ineffectual in the chaotic whirl of events.

The frequent change of voice is somewhat distracting and the dialogue is less convincingly realistic than in *Paganini Strikes Again*: in the frenetic activity it sometimes appears stilted and imperfectly placed. However, in *The Frog Report*, his stylistic confidence returns. This is a beautifully balanced story using the device of a book within a book: in this case a book about a boy writing a book. What the first person narrator lacks in omniscience he makes up for in cheek, simply asking "others" to write in chapters for him. The pace is altogether gentler and the humour richer, springing naturally from well drawn characterisation; the story is more serious, dealing as it does with the illegal immigration of political refugees. The tale in fact concerns the boy's attempts to come to terms with a disturbing episode in his life and with himself and his place in his family and community, by writing out his observations of events and people. In now seeking less to entertain than to illuminate with gentle humour, Benjamin Lee appears to have found an authentic voice with which to record the world seen through a child's eyes.

—Myles McDowell

LEE, Dennis (Beynon). Canadian. Born in Toronto, Ontario, 31 August 1939. Educated at the University of Toronto, B.A. 1962, M.A. in English Literature 1964. Divorced; has two daughters. Instructor in English, University of Toronto, Rochdale College, Toronto, and York University, Toronto; Writer-in-Residence, Trent University, Peterborough, Ontario, 1975. Editor, House of Anansi Press, Toronto, 1967–73; Consulting Editor, Macmillan of Canada, Toronto, 1974–76. Recipient: Governor-General's Award, for verse, 1973; Canadian Library Association Book of the Year award, 1975. Address: c/o Macmillan, 70 Bond Street, Toronto M5B 1X3, Canada.

Publications for Children

Verse

Wiggle to the Laundromat, illustrated by Charles Pachter. Toronto, New Press. 1970.

Alligator Pie, illustrated by Frank Newfeld.   Toronto, Macmillan, 1974; Boston, Houghton Mifflin, 1975.

Nicholas Knock and Other People, illustrated by Frank Newfeld.   Toronto, Macmillan, 1974; Boston, Houghton Mifflin, 1977.

Garbage Delight, illustrated by Frank Newfeld.   Toronto, Macmillan, 1977.

PUBLICATIONS FOR ADULTS

Verse

Kingdom of Absence.   Toronto, House of Anansi, 1967.
Civil Elegies.   Toronto, House of Anansi, 1968.
Civil Elegies and Other Poems.   Toronto, House of Anansi, 1972.
The Death of Harold Ladoo.   Vancouver and San Francisco, Kanchenjunga Press, 1976.

Other

Savage Fields: An Essay in Literature and Cosmology.   Toronto, House of Anansi, 1977.

Editor, with R. A. Charlesworth, *An Anthology of Verse.*   Toronto, Oxford University Press, 1964.

Editor, with R.A. Charlesworth, *The Second Century Anthologies of Verse, Book 2.*   Toronto, Oxford University Press, 1967.

Editor, with Howard Adelman, *The University Game.*   Toronto, House of Anansi, 1968.

Editor, *T. O. Now: The Young Toronto Poets.*   Toronto, House of Anansi, 1968.

Dennis Lee comments:

I can sum up the concerns of my children's poetry in two words: "roots" and "play." Beyond that, it sinks or swims on its own merits.

*   *   *

The key to Dennis Lee's poetry, both juvenile and adult, is that he is Canadian. Lee's Canadianness has two main aspects: first, his awareness of Canada as a unique place, his home land; second, his awareness of Canada's colonial status, from which she must be liberated. In his children's poetry, these two aspects have their equivalents in the concepts of "roots" and "play." The former means literature both rooted in a particular time and place, and also articulating to the reader his own roots. The latter means literature which, in Lee's words, tries "to reanimate repressed feelings," which is emotionally released, free and joyous, full of play.

It was in response to these impulses that Lee's children's verse was written. Explaining its genesis in the epilogue to *Alligator Pie*, he writes that, when reading *Mother Goose* to his children, he began to realize the distance between the nursery rhymes and contemporary Canadian reality: "The details of *Mother Goose* – the wassails and Dobbins and pipers and pence – had become exotic: children loved them, but they were no longer home ground." At the same time, Lee recognized that Canadians "are a colonial people; leaving aside the political and economic aspects of the thing for now, we have always been a colony of the imagination, first of England and France, latterly of the United States." Lee's answer was to liberate Canadian children from the colonial mentality by creating poems rooted in the things that are part of a Canadian child's inner and outer life. And in doing so he found himself becoming liberated, regaining the ability to play.

Lee has published several volumes of children's poetry. Nursery rhymes (for pre-schoolers) appear in *Alligator Pie*, which includes poems playing with incantatory Canadian place names ("Tongue Twister," "Kahshe or Chicoutimi"), activity songs ("Bouncing Song," "Rattlesnake Skipping Song"), and short word-play poems ("Skyscraper," "Willoughby Wallaby Woo"). Such works contain much pure play: alliteration, onomatopoeia, rhyme and rhythm are so strongly stressed that the words often function as music. A few poems in the latter half of the book are more for children of school-entering age: they are longer and often more serious, sensitively exploring the child's inner world ("The Special Person," "The Friend").

For the 7–10 age group, the poems in *Nicholas Knock and Other People* are most appropriate. Most of them are longer, more complex in thought, and sometimes deal with such specialized topics as the Spadina Expressway or the Mackenzie Rebellion of 1837 (both, incidentally, anti-authoritarian people's struggles). One prominent subject is the child's imaginative world ("Mister Hoobody," "The Thing"), sometimes under threat from the adult "real" world ("Nicholas Knock"). Other poems deal with the child's reaction to close relationships ("Going Up North," "With My Foot in My Mouth"); these pieces – while rooted in a sense of self – express affection clearly though indirectly. The kind of black humour that sets children chortling is also given effective expression ("Oilcan Harry"). Play, of course, has its place in all the poems; at times, as in the Ookpik poems, it even becomes the theme, a liberating force. Lee describes Ookpik as "another of the vital figures that challenge how we are. He's a dancer, an embodiment of pure lyricism: harmless, pointless, irrepressible .... There are four Ookpik poems, and by the last one he has become a kind of totemic figure or tutelary god for the books. The theme of play and the theme of roots fuse in that poem, as they often do." Ookpik: the "tutelary god" for the books. How does the last Ookpik poem end? "Ookpik,/Ookpick/By your Grace./Help us/Live in/Our own/Space." Lee's final word, then, is directed at the need for Canadians to inhabit – both physically and imaginatively – their own space, their country.

Overall, in spite of some failures ("Street Song," "The Saint's Lament"), Dennis Lee's work represents the best in children's poetry: it dances off the page and involves the reader in its world.

—John Robert Sorfleet

LEE, Mildred. American. Born in Blocton, Alabama, 19 February 1908. Educated at Cairo High School, Georgia; Tift College, Forsyth, Georgia, 1925–26; Troy Normal College, Alabama,1927; Columbia University, New York, 1936; New York University; University of New Hampshire, Durham, 1944. Married Edward Cannon Schimpff in 1929, one daughter and one son; James Henry Scudder, 1947, one daughter. Recipient: Child Study Association of America award, 1964. Address: 1361 52nd Avenue North, St. Petersburg, Florida 33703, U.S.A.

PUBLICATIONS FOR CHILDREN

Fiction

The Rock and the Willow. New York, Lothrop, 1963; London, Oxford University Press, 1975.
Honor Sands. New York, Lothrop, 1966.
The Skating Rink. New York, Seabury Press, 1969; London, Abelard Schuman, 1972.

Fog. New York, Seabury Press, 1972.
Sycamore Year. New York, Lothrop, 1974.

PUBLICATIONS FOR ADULTS

Novel

The Invisible Sun. Philadelphia, Westminster Press, 1946.

Manuscript Collections: University of Wyoming Library, Laramie; Kerlan Collection, University of Minnesota, Minneapolis.

Mildred Lee comments:
My books are really "novels for young people" rather than Children's Books in that they all deal with the agonies and ecstasies of growing up and are suitable for readers of middle school or 'teen age.

* * *

The rain started sometime in the night. Enie woke to hear its patter on the new tin roof Papa and the boys had put on two weeks ago. As he laid his tools away Papa had predicted darkly that likely there'd be a drought now to ruin his crops if he ever got the ground broken to put them in. He said the new roof was bad luck, but Mamma's jawing him about it all winter was enough to drive a man to anything.

That opening paragraph from Mildred Lee's novel *The Rock and the Willow* introduces the landscape, tone, and feeling that characterize her best work: the poverty-stricken American rural South in the 1930's and later, peopled with characters who either struggle to better their lot in life or resign themselves to apathy. In *The Rock and the Willow*, Enie, the teenage heroine, is determined to go away and get a college education despite all the pressures on her to remain at home. *The Skating Rink* features Tuck Faraday, whose severe stutter leads his peers to call him "Dummy," but who eventually asserts his individuality and worth by developing his flair for skating. Luke, the young hero of *Fog*, must adjust to the sudden, untimely death of the father he somehow always took for granted until it was too late.

Strong on atmosphere and character detail, Miss Lee is much less confident when it comes to plotting. If her protagonists are living in fairly comfortable circumstances and are not faced with any major obstacles, as is the case in *Honor Sands* and *Sycamore Year*, then her narratives tend to be a bit slack. Suspense and dramatic tension generally spring from the plight of her central characters rather than from a tightly constructed plot.

Even in her slighter stories, though, Miss Lee's craftsmanship is always apparent. She is gifted with a keen ear for the rhythms and expressions of the Southern vernacular which she employs to lend color and veracity to her dialogue. She also has a knack for building sensual word pictures of her settings and characters in their various seasons and moods. As contemporary American writers for young teenagers go, she probably makes more demands of her readers than most in terms of concentration and reading ability, but for those who stick with her books, she probably also offers richer rewards when it comes to understanding the workings of the human heart.

In an era when many fiction writers for young people have latched onto one controversial subject after another, Mildred Lee has quietly continued to offer honest, realistic portraits of unsensational situations. Valuable in themselves, her books can also serve to point interested young readers toward such outstanding adult interpreters of the American South as Carson McCullers, Flannery O'Connor, and Eudora Welty.

—James C. Giblin

LEESON, Robert (Arthur). British. Born in Barnton, Cheshire, 31 March 1928. Educated at Sir John Deane's Grammar School (scholar), 1939–44; University of London, External B.A. (honours) 1972. Served in the British Army in the Middle East, 1946–48. Married Gunvor Hagen in 1954; has one son and one daughter. Journalist since 1944; Literary and Children's Editor, *Morning Star*, London. Since 1969, free-lance editor and writer. Address: 18 McKenzie Road, Broxbourne, Hertfordshire, England.

PUBLICATIONS FOR CHILDREN

Fiction

Beyond the Dragon Prow, illustrated by Ian Ribbons. London, Collins, 1973.
'Maroon Boy, illustrated by Michael Jackson. London, Collins, 1974.
The Third Class Genie. London, Collins, 1975.
Bess, illustrated by Christine Nolan. London, Collins, 1975.
The Demon Bike Rider, illustrated by Jim Russell. London, Collins, 1976.
The White Horse. London, Collins, 1977.

PUBLICATIONS FOR ADULTS

Other

United We Stand: An Illustrated Account of Trade Union Emblems. Bath, Adams and Dart, 1971.
Strike: A Live History, 1887–1971. London, Allen and Unwin, 1973.
Children's Books and Class Society: Past and Present. London, Children's Rights Workshop, 1977.

Robert Leeson comments:
The work falls into two parts, historical adventure which tries to blend the excitement of events with an understanding of the ideas of the time – for example the Morten trilogy takes in the Armada and the Civil War battles and the outlook and thoughts of the immense variety of people labelled "Puritans" – and modern comedy/fantasy set in a northern industrial town, where the characters are children from "ordinary" families but through whose eyes the outside world tends to take on an extraordinary aspect.
I'd like to be thought of as a story teller rather than a "writer" with an ounce of plot worth a pound of description, someone who seeks to entertain but leaves the reader something to mull over afterwards.

*   *   *

Robert Leeson is one of a new breed of writers for children – highly conscious of the changes that have taken place in our view of the past, the present and the future and attempting to reflect these changes in his writing. While the label "committed" writer can be applied to Leeson, he interprets this commitment as the multiplying of literary possibilities, and his books cover some of the new options which a changing consciousness has made us aware of. Leeson does this in his historical novels by combining the novel of ideas with the tale of historical adventure, first in *Beyond the Dragon Prow* and most convincingly in his historical trilogy – *'Maroon Boy, Bess*, and *The White Horse*.
The gadzookery of the conventional romantic historical novel is here replaced with a compelling tale that begins in Elizabethan times. A Plymouth family, the Mortens, is seen through several generations, each one caught up in the moral issues of their time and of their great seaport trading city. The English slave trade, for example, began with the Elizabethan

privateers and, like it or not, the Mortens become involved. Leeson shows us that then as now there was a spectrum of opinion and of options – albeit bounded by the custom and constraints of the time.

Leeson's style in these books is picaresque; his Mortens journey far, both in England and to the Darien shore. They are continually caught up in the intrigue and mistrust that surround their family. Leeson is a demanding writer – his characters' understated dialogue is rich with meaning that must be sought for – but the persevering young reader will be richly rewarded.

Leeson's contemporary fiction has a different style and pace – easy, colloquial, funny. At its best (*The Third Class Genie*) it is very good, but *The Demon Bike Rider* is less tightly written. *The Third Class Genie* integrates fantasy into a neighbourhood story that has a tense and humorous plot. Topical references (e.g., to the politician Enoch Powell) quickly involve the reader with the very contemporary issues that confront genie-finder Alec – racial prejudice and the threatened demolition of a local street.

—Rosemary Stones

LE FEUVRE, Amy. British. Born in Blackheath, London. Wrote serials for *Sunday at Home* and *Quiver* magazines, London. *Died 29 April 1929.*

PUBLICATIONS FOR CHILDREN

Fiction

Eric's Good News. London, Religious Tract Society, 1894; Chicago, Revell, 1896.
Probable Sons. London, Religious Tract Society, 1895; New York, Revell, 1897.
Teddy's Button! London, Religious Tract Society, and Chicago, Revell, 1896.
Dwell Deep; or, Hilda Thorne's Life Story. London, Religious Tract Society, and Chicago, Revell, 1896.
On the Edge of a Moor. London, Religious Tract Society, and Chicago, Revell, 1897.
Odd. London, Religious Tract Society, 1897; as *The Odd One*, Chicago, Revell, 1897.
A Puzzling Pair, illustrated by Eveline Lance. London, Religious Tract Society, and Chicago, Revell, 1898.
His Big Opportunity, illustrated by Sydney Cowell. London, Hodder and Stoughton, and Chicago, Revell, 1898.
Bulbs and Blossoms, illustrated by Eveline Lance. London, Religious Tract Society, and Chicago, Revell, 1898.
A Thoughtless Seven. London, Religious Tract Society, and Chicago, Revell, 1898.
The Carved Cupboard. London, Religious Tract Society, and New York, Dodd Mead, 1899.
Bunny's Friends. London, Religious Tract Society, and Chicago, Revell, 1899.
What the Wind Did. Chicago, Revell, 1899.
Roses, illustrated by Sydney Cowell. London, Hodder and Stoughton, and New York, Ketcham, 1899.
Legend-Led. London, Religious Tract Society, and New York, Dodd Mead, 1899.
Brownie, illustrated by W.H.C. Groome. London, Hodder and Stoughton, and New York, American Tract Society, 1900.
Nurv, The Shepherd Boy. London, Religious Tract Society, 1900.
Olive Tracy. London, Hodder and Stoughton, 1900; New York, Dodd Mead, 1901.

A Cherry Tree. London, Hodder and Stoughton, 1901; as *Cherry, The Cucumber That Bore Fruit*, New York, Revell, 1901.

Heather's Mistress. London, Religious Tract Society, and New York, Crowell, 1901.

A Daughter of the Sea. London, Hodder and Stoughton, and New York, Crowell, 1902.

Odd Made Even. London, Religious Tract Society, 1902.

The Making of a Woman. London, Hodder and Stoughton, 1903.

Two Tramps. London, Hodder and Stoughton, and New York, Revell, 1903.

Jill's Red Bag. London, Religious Tract Society, and New York, Revell, 1903.

His Little Daughter. London, Religious Tract Society, 1904.

A Little Maid. London, Religious Tract Society, 1904.

Bridget's Quarter Deck. London, Hodder and Stoughton, 1905.

The Buried Ring, illustrated by Gordon Browne. London, Hodder and Stoughton, 1905.

The Children's Morning Message, illustrated by Jenny Wylie. London, Hodder and Stoughton, 1905.

Christina and the Boys, illustrated by Gordon Browne. London, Hodder and Stoughton, 1906.

The Mender, illustrated by W. Rainey. London, Religious Tract Society, 1906.

Miss Lavender's Boy and Other Sketches. London, Religious Tract Society, 1906.

Robin's Heritage, illustrated by Gordon Browne. London, Hodder and Stoughton, 1907.

Number Twa! London, Religious Tract Society, 1907.

The Chateau by the Lake. London, Hodder and Stoughton, 1907.

A Bit of Rough Road, illustrated by Percy Tarrant. London, Religious Tract Society, 1908.

Me and Nobbles. London, Religious Tract Society, 1908.

Us, and Our Donkey, illustrated by W.H.C. Groome. London, Religious Tract Society, 1909.

A Country Corner. London, Cassell, 1909.

The Birthday: A Christmas Sketch, illustrated by Eveline Lance. London, Religious Tract Society, 1909.

Joyce and the Rambler. London, Hodder and Stoughton, 1910.

A Little Listener, illustrated by W.H.C. Groome. London, Religious Tract Society, 1910.

Us, and Our Empire, illustrated by W.H.C. Groome. London, Religious Tract Society, 1911.

Tested! Philadelphia, Heidelberg Press, 1911; London, Partridge, 1912.

Four Gates. London and New York, Cassell, 1912.

Laddie's Choice, illustrated by W.H.C. Groome. London, Religious Tract Society, 1912; (as Mary Thurston Dodge), New York, Dodd Mead, 1912.

Some Builders. London, Cassell, 1913.

Her Husband's Property. London, Religious Tract Society, 1913.

Herself and Her Boy. London, Cassell, 1914.

Harebell's Friends. London, Religious Tract Society, 1914.

Daddy's Sword. London and New York, Hodder and Stoughton, 1915.

Joan's Handful. London, Cassell, 1915.

Dudley Napier's Daughters. London, Morgan and Scott, 1916.

A Madcap Family; or, Sybil's Home. London, Partridge, 1916.

Us, and Our Charge. London, Religious Tract Society, 1916.

Tomina in Retreat. London, Religious Tract Society, 1917.

Joy Cometh in the Morning, illustrated by Harold Copping. London, Religious Tract Society, 1917.

Dreamikins. London, Religious Tract Society, 1918.

A Happy Woman. London, Religious Tract Society, 1918.

Terrie's Moorland Home.   London, Morgan and Scott, 1918.

Little Miss Moth.   London, Partridge, 1919.

The Chisel.   London, Religious Tract Society, 1919.

The Discovery of Damaris.   London, Religious Tract Society, 1920.

Oliver and the Twins, illustrated by Gordon Browne.   London, Religious Tract Society, 1922.

The Children of the Crescent, illustrated by Arthur Twiddle.   London, Religious Tract Society, 1923.

The Little Discoverers, illustrated by M.D. Johnston.   London and New York, Oxford University Press, 1924.

My Heart's in the Highlands.   London, Ward Lock, 1924.

A Girl and Her Ways.   London, Ward Lock, 1925.

Granny's Fairyland.   London, Sheldon Press, 1925.

Noel's Christmas Tree.   London, Ward Lock, 1926.

Three Little Girls.   London, Shaw, 1926.

Andy Man: A Story of Two Simple Souls.   London, Pickering and Inglis, 1927.

Jock's Inheritance.   London, Ward Lock, 1927.

Cousins in Devon.   London, Religious Tract Society, 1928.

Adrienne.   London, Ward Lock, 1928.

Alick's Corner.   London, Religious Tract Society, 1929.

Around a Sundial, and Dicky's Brother.   London, Pickering and Inglis, 1929.

Her Kingdom: A Story of the Westmorland Fells.   London, Ward Lock, 1929.

Under a Cloud.   London, Ward Lock, 1930.

Rosebuds: Choice and Original Short Stories.   London, Pickering and Inglis, 1931.

A Strange Courtship.   London, Ward Lock, 1931.

Mimosa's Field.   London, Lutterworth Press, 1953.

Other

The Most Wonderful Story in the World: A Life of Christ for Little Children.   London, Hodder and Stoughton, and New York, Revell, 1922; as *Little Tots' Story of Jesus*, New York, Revell, 1928.

Chats with Children; or, Pearls for Young People Strung from the Word of Truth.   London, Pickering and Inglis, 1926.

Stories of the Lord Jesus, with Lettice Bell.   London, Shaw, 1933.

*   *   *

Amy Le Feuvre was one of the Religious Tract Society's more prolific authors. Her popularity, which began in the 1890's, was maintained through the first three decades of this century, and her writing was typical of the new approach of the evangelical writers to the young reader. The stern style of the earlier 19th century was now completely outmoded. In *A Puzzling Fair* (1898) she wrote of the "hell-fire" and "day of wrath" type of preaching as something marvellously old-fashioned. The street arab story, which had been the standard type of Sunday leisure reading since the late 1860's, was over-worked. The new hero of the evangelical story was the artless child who brought a gospel message of love to the adult. There was much emphasis on "the strong and steadfast faith of childhood." As one of her characters remarked, "They live so near to the throne of the Eternal One that they draw those with whom they live to do the same."

Like many of her contemporaries she was particularly fond of the "quaint" child, "old-fashioned," with delicate health, a type modelled upon Paul Dombey. With their innocent prattle these children melted the cold, stern hearts of elders who had too long been preoccupied with material things. Her most popular story in this style was *Probable Sons*, in which the fragile, curly-haired little Milly — whose mispronunciation of "prodigal sons" is responsible for the title — brings her Uncle Edward back to Christ.

In a more robust manner, she wrote tales of family life, specializing in the outwardly naughty child, the odd one out, whose motives are consistently misunderstood by the adults. She made it clear that, unlike her evangelical predecessors, she thought that absent-minded disobedience and imaginative naughtiness were attractive childish traits and could well go hand in hand with an understanding of heavenly things. This is the theme of *Teddy's Button*, perhaps her best-known story: Teddy, whose passionate wish is to follow in his father's footsteps and be a soldier, is persuaded first to join Christ's army and fight the bad elements in his nature. The Lutterworth Press (successors to the Religious Tract Society) have kept some of Amy Le Feuvre's tales in print and these are still used as gift books in mission schools abroad.

—Gillian Avery

LE GUIN, Ursula K(roeber). American. Born in Berkeley, California, 21 October 1929. Educated at Radcliffe College, Cambridge, Massachusetts, A.B. 1951 (Phi Beta Kappa); Columbia University, New York (Faculty Fellow; Fulbright Fellow, 1953), A.M. 1952. Married Charles A. Le Guin in 1953; has two daughters and one son. Formerly, Member of the French Department, Mercer University, Macon, Georgia, and University of Idaho, Moscow; Department Secretary, Emory University, Atlanta, Georgia; has taught writing workshops at Pacific University, Forest Grove, Oregon; University of Washington, Seattle; Portland State University, Oregon; in Melbourne, Australia; and at University of Reading, England. Recipient: *Boston Globe-Horn Book* Award, 1969; Science Fiction Writers of America Nebula Award, 1969, 1975; Hugo Award, 1972, 1973, 1975; National Book Award, 1972. Agent: Virginia Kidd, Box 278, Milford, Pennsylvania. Address: 3321 N.W. Thurman Street, Portland, Oregon 97210, U.S.A.

PUBLICATIONS FOR CHILDREN

Fiction

> *The Wizard of Earthsea*, illustrated by Ruth Robbins. Berkeley, California, Parnassus Press, 1967; London, Gollancz, 1971.
> *The Tombs of Atuan*, illustrated by Gail Garraty. New York, Atheneum, 1969; London, Gollancz, 1972.
> *The Farthest Shore*, illustrated by Gail Garraty. New York, Atheneum, 1972; London, Gollancz, 1973.
> *Very Far Away from Anywhere Else.* New York, Atheneum, 1976; as *A Very Long Way from Anywhere Else*, London, Gollancz, 1976.

PUBLICATIONS FOR ADULTS

Novels

> *Rocannon's World.* New York, Ace, 1966; London, Tandem, 1972.
> *Planet of Exile.* New York, Ace, 1966; London, Tandem, 1972.
> *City of Illusion.* Berkeley, California, Parnassus Press, 1967; London, Gollancz, 1971.
> *The Left Hand of Darkness.* New York, Walker, and London, Macdonald, 1969.
> *The Lathe of Heaven.* New York, Scribner, 1971; London, Gollancz, 1972.
> *The Dispossessed: An Ambiguous Utopia.* New York, Harper, and London, Gollancz, 1974.

Short Stories

    The Wind's Twelve Quarters. New York, Harper, 1975; London, Gollancz, 1976.
    Orsinian Tales. New York, Harper, 1976.
    The Word for World Is Forest. New York, Putnam, 1976.

Verse

    Wild Angels. Santa Barbara, California, Capra Press, 1975.

Other

    Editor, *Nebula Award Stories 11*. London, Gollancz, 1976; New York, Harper, 1977.

*   *   *

    Author of both adult and juvenile science fiction and fantasy, Ursula K. Le Guin is the object of growing critical admiration. Even though her adult fiction has garnered most of the critical attention and praise, her considerable achievement in children's literature has not gone unnoticed. In 1972 *The Farthest Shore*, the last volume of the Earthsea trilogy, received the National Book Award for Children's Literature in the United States. As a matter of fact, the Earthsea trilogy has come to be accepted as one of the outstanding fantasies of recent years, being compared favorably to Lewis' Narnia series, Alexander's chronicles of Prydain, and even Tolkien's Middle Earth stories. Like the latter, Le Guin's trilogy creates an imaginary world, Earthsea, with a distinctive geography, anthropology, and even its own language, Old Speech. Like the latter, the Earthsea novels also focus on one or two usually youthful protagonists whose decisions bear unexpected consequences, ethical and otherwise, and whose eventual accepting of responsibility for all their actions signals their maturation. In short, the Earthsea trilogy is high or heroic fantasy, a subcategory of fantasy especially appropriate for youth because of its concern for showing the centrality of making ethical choices while growing up or coming of age.

    In her fictive rendering of the rite of coming of age, Le Guin concentrates on Ged, destined to be the most famous Mage of Earthsea. In *The Wizard of Earthsea*, young Ged can cross the boundary separating adolescence from adulthood only after he admits responsibility for the shadow-monster his childish arrogance and lust for power summoned from the underworld into Earthsea, thereby altering the Balance of the world. In *The Tombs of Atuan*, Ged, attempting to steal the ring of Erreth-Akbe, is captured by Arha, the first priestess of the Dark Ones which are venerated within Atuan tombs. In spite of celebrating her coming of age, Arha has not yet matured and risks permanent emotional and psychological stunting because of her unwholesome worshipping of the Dark Powers. In a way, she too is trapped. To break out of their respective traps, Arha and Ged learn to trust each other. After their escape Arha begins anew the process of coming of age, and Ged learns the necessity of mutuality. Ged, middle-aged and at the height of his power in *The Farthest Shore*, embarks on a quest to restore death to its rightful place in the universe. To accompany him Ged chooses the young, inexperienced Prince Arren, who provides invaluable help in aiding the mage's journey into the Kingdom of the Dead and successful return. The same journey turns out to be Arren's rite of passage since the traversing of the underworld signals his growth into manhood.

    Three qualities, in particular, make the Earthsea trilogy exemplary fantasy. The first is an adroit use of Jungian psychology to validate employing fantasy to recount the process of coming of age. Le Guin accepts the Jungian hypothesis that each individual must undertake a spiritual journey and inwardly experience a struggle between good and evil if that individual is to mature into adulthood. Moreover, claiming that fantasy is the "language of the inner self," she believes that it is "the natural, the appropriate language" for narrating this journey and inner struggle ("The Child and the Shadow"). Accordingly, it is no surprise that much of the plot, imagery, and symbolism of the trilogy reflects Jungian insights and archetypes. For example, there are several journeys: across the broad seas to the mythic east of origins and the legendary west of destinies; through the underworld of the dead; and into the unconscious, and feminine inner space. As another example, imagery of Dark and Shadow – representing human finitude, the human capacity for evil, and death – coexists and clashes with that of Brightness and Light – representing self-knowledge, goodness, and the fleeting beauty of mortality.

Earthsea's plausibility as a secondary world is the second quality. The detailing, inner consistency, and originality, essential to fantasy if it is going to compel belief and wonder, are present. There is specific locale – forests, islands, and, above all, seas whose smell and taste seem to permeate large sections of the narrative. There is distinctive ambiance – above ground, a constantly shifting interplay between light and dark, corresponding to the tension between equal and opposite forces that characterize the moral and ethical environment of Earthsea; and, below ground, a sterile, suffocating atmosphere suggesting the effects of an exaggerated preoccupation with self and the absence of vitality. There are special customs and beliefs – for instance, a distinction between used and true names which require disclosing the latter only to one's closest friends. There is magic as a means of achieving both limited ends such as mending sails and the more significant goal of cooperating in maintaining fundamental Equilibrium in the universe. And there are dragons, old, crafty, and able to converse in Old Speech.

The final quality is style. For the trilogy Le Guin fashioned an effective melding of subject, theme, and language. A heroic diction, eschewing archaic or pseudo-heroic vocabulary, enhances the celebration of Ged as ethical hero. An oral quality, echoing Anglo-Saxon epic and Norse saga without slavish imitation, reinforces the rendering of a culture where traditional song and story dominate. Lastly, a narrative pace, alternating between crisp summary and leisurely exposition and dialogue, subtly parallels the trilogy's presentation of the uneven, sometimes slow but always steady psychological growth peculiar to coming of age.

—Francis J. Molson

LEITCH, Adelaide. Canadian. Born in Toronto, Ontario, 10 February 1921. Educated at the University of Toronto, B.A. 1942. Married James Lennox in 1963. Reporter, *Midland Free Press*, Ontario, 1943–45; Reporter and Feature Writer, *Windsor Daily Star*, Ontario, 1945–48; Managing Editor, Guardian Press, St. John's, Newfoundland, 1952–53; Editor, *Adventures in Huronia*, Ontario, 1960–67. Free-lance photo-journalist. Recipient: Canadian Women's Press Club award, 1962. Address: 169 Hanna Road, Toronto, Ontario M4G 3N9, Canada.

PUBLICATIONS FOR CHILDREN

Fiction

> *The Great Canoe*, illustrated by Clare Bice. Toronto, Macmillan, 1962; London, Macmillan, and New York, St. Martin's Press, 1963.
> *Lukey Paul from Labrador*, illustrated by Joe Rosenthal. Toronto and London, Macmillan, and New York, St. Martin's Press, 1964.
> *Mainstream*, illustrated by J. Merle Smith. Toronto, Department of Christian Education, and New York, Friendship Press, 1966.

The Blue Roan, illustrated by Charles Robinson.   Toronto, Macmillan, and New York,
    Walck, 1971.

Other

Canada, Young Giant of the North, photographs by the author.   Toronto, New York
    and London, Nelson, 1964; revised edition, 1968.

PUBLICATIONS FOR ADULTS

Other

Flightline North.   St. John's, Newfoundland, Guardian Press, 1952.
The Visible Past: The Pictorial History of Simcoe County.   Toronto, Ryerson Press,
    1967.
Into the High Country: The Story of Dufferin, The Last 12,000 Years to 1974.   Toronto,
    Hunter Rose, 1975.

Adelaide Leitch comments:

Underlying theme in most of my work, both fiction and non-fiction, reflects an interest in
places and people and their inter-action − "humanized geography and history," if you like.
(The Blue Roan is somewhat different, concentrating on character development primarily.)
Specialization in Canadiana, also other travel − with field trips to Labrador, Yukon, Alaska, as
well as southern Canada; to Greenland, Lapland, West Indies, Central America − has
provided fiction background, as well as photo stories.

                              *   *   *

Canada has a thrilling and compelling history which is, unfortunately, too little known to
the rest of the world. The Buckskin books, published by Macmillan of Canada, are "exciting
stories for younger readers, tales of action and adventure set against the background of
rousing events in Canada's history," and The Great Canoe by Adelaide Leitch was chosen
from more than a hundred manuscripts as the first title in the series. It tells the story of Gros-
Louis, a young Huron Indian boy and his hero, Samuel de Champlain. The excellent, well-
researched background, colourful imagery and stirring adventure in this tale of Canada's
earliest days make it a fitting introduction to the series. Another title in the same series is also
by Adelaide Leitch: Lukey Paul from Labrador is an inspiring story of adventure on the wild
Labrador coast at the turn of the century. Because of his father's illness, Lukey Paul, although
only ten years old, is charged with the responsibility of trading a valuable silver fox skin for
enough supplies to feed his family for the winter. He stows away on Dr. Wilfred Grenfell's
small boat for the journey to the trading post and is a witness to the great humanity and love
of the man who meant so much to the people of Labrador. Young readers will be intrigued by
this gripping story and its surprise ending. In both these stories, the device of introducing
well-known historical figures to imaginary children is one that sparks the reader's interest.
The Blue Roan is a horse story with a difference. A lonely and self-centred boy, whose
father is too absorbed in business affairs to give him enough attention, finds a solution to his
problems and a better relationship with his father through a summer spent in training an
unpredictable and potentially dangerous horse. This is a slower-paced and much more
introspective story than the other two, but it nevertheless builds to an exciting climax.
Characters are well developed, and readers will learn a lot from this book, not only about
horses but also about human relationships.

                                                                    —Barbara Smiley

L'ENGLE, Madeleine. American. Born in New York City, 29 November 1918. Educated at Smith College, Northampton, Massachusetts, A.B. (honors) 1941; New School for Social Research, New York, 1941–42; Columbia University, New York, 1960–61. Married Hugh Franklin in 1946; has three children. Worked in the theatre, New York, 1941–47; teacher, St. Hilda's and St. Hugh's School, New York, 1960–66; Member of the Faculty, University of Indiana, Bloomington, summers 1965–66, 1971; Writer-in-Residence, Ohio State University, Columbus, 1970, and University of Rochester, New York, 1972. Since 1966, Librarian, Cathedral of St. John the Divine, New York. Recipient: American Library Association Newbery Medal, 1963. Agent: Raines and Raines, 475 Fifth Avenue, New York, New York 10017. Address: Crosswicks, Goshen, Connecticut 06756, U.S.A.

PUBLICATIONS FOR CHILDREN

Fiction

> *And Both Were Young.* New York, Lothrop, 1949.
> *Camilla Dickinson.* New York, Simon and Schuster, 1951; London, Secker and Warburg, 1952; as *Camilla,* New York, Crowell, 1965.
> *Meet the Austins.* New York, Vanguard Press, 1960; London, Collins, 1966.
> *A Wrinkle in Time.* New York, Farrar Straus, 1962; London, Constable, 1964.
> *The Moon by Night.* New York, Farrar Straus, 1963.
> *The Twenty-Four Days Before Christmas,* illustrated by Inga. New York, Farrar Straus, 1964.
> *The Arm of the Starfish.* New York, Farrar Straus, 1965.
> *The Journey with Jonah.* New York, Farrar Straus, 1968.
> *The Young Unicorns.* New York, Farrar Straus, 1968; London, Gollancz, 1970.
> *Prelude.* New York, Vanguard Press, 1969; London, Gollancz, 1972.
> *Dance in the Desert,* illustrated by Symeon Shimin. New York, Farrar Straus, and London, Longman, 1969.
> *A Wind in the Door.* New York, Farrar Straus, 1973; London, Methuen, 1975.
> *Dragons in the Waters.* New York, Farrar Straus, 1976.

Plays

> *18 Washington Square, South* (produced Northampton, Massachusetts, 1940). Boston, Baker, 1944.
> *How Now Brown Cow,* with Robert Hartung (produced New York, 1949).
> *The Journey with Jonah,* adaptation of her own story, illustrated by Leonard Everett Fisher (produced New York, 1970). New York, Farrar Straus, 1967.

Verse

> *Lines Scribbled on an Envelope and Other Poems.* New York, Farrar Straus, 1969.

Other

> *Everyday Prayers,* illustrated by Lucile Butel. New York, Morehouse Barlow, 1974.
> *Prayers for Sunday,* illustrated by Lucile Butel. New York, Morehouse Barlow, 1974.

PUBLICATIONS FOR ADULTS

Novels

> *The Small Rain.* New York, Vanguard Press, 1945; London, Secker and Warburg, 1955.

759

Ilsa. New York, Vanguard Press, 1946.
A Winter's Love. Philadelphia, Lippincott, 1957.
The Love Letters. New York, Farrar Straus, 1966.
The Other Side of the Sun. New York, Farrar Straus, 1971; London, Eyre Methuen, 1972.

Other

A Circle of Quiet (essays). New York, Farrar Straus, 1972.
The Summer of the Great Grandmother (essays). New York, Farrar Straus, 1974.
The Irrational Season (essays). New York, Seabury Press, 1977.

Editor, with William R. Green, *Spirit and Light: Essays in Historical Theology.* New York, Seabury Press, 1976.

Manuscript Collections: Wheaton College, Illinois; Kerlan Collection, University of Minnesota, Minneapolis; de Grummond Collection, University of Southern Mississippi, Hattiesburg.

Madeleine L'Engle comments:
    When I am asked why I write at least half of my books for children, especially since my first books were for adults, I answer, truthfully, that when I have something to say which I think is going to be too difficult for adults, I write it in a book for children. Children are excited by new ideas; they have not yet closed the doors and windows of their imaginations. Provided the story is a good story, and makes them want to keep turning the pages, nothing is too difficult for children. Most of my children's novels at least border on fantasy, and the response from children in hundreds of letters keeps me constantly stimulated. It is the children themselves who help me to move on from one book to the next.

*   *   *

    The Newbery Award, sometimes, is either a kiss of death or a mistake. The honored novel sits on the shelf unread except by those, either children or students of children's literature, forced to peruse or dip into it. Or a second and more detached look reveals, embarrassingly, that the novel came into the world garbed, so to speak, in the verbal equivalent of the emperor's new clothes. Fortunately, Madeleine L'Engle's *A Wrinkle in Time,* awarded the Newbery Medal in 1963, has suffered neither fate. The novel continues to be read by youngsters – voluntarily as well as involuntarily; and it readily stands up under critical scrutiny.
    A Wrinkle in Time, first of all, is a realistic family novel. The Murrys are a closely knit, affectionate, supportive, and intelligent family; and these qualities, instead of seeming incredible or, worse yet, tiresomely banal, are both plausible and attractive because they derive from the family's behavior and words. The Murry's goodness, in particular, is not innate or miraculously accounted for, but earned through hard choice and the pain of self-sacrifice. *A Wrinkle in Time* is also a serious novel that unabashedly investigates the nature of good and evil and points out how the decisions and actions of individuals contribute to or detract from, whether intended to or not, society's moral and ethical well-being. Moreover, the ethical problems explored – the proper use of knowledge, the rights of the individual versus those of society, the various demands of love, and the possibility that evil exists absolutely – are real problems. The Christian ethos of the novel, furthermore, is more implied than explicitly stated and is not preached. In short, the novel is didactic but carries its moral and ethical weight gracefully.
    Another feature of *A Wrinkle in Time* is that it is a young adult novel that honestly portrays its protagonists, Meg Murry and Calvin O'Keefe, in situations typical of many young people –

anxiety over physical appearance, unsettled parental relationships, peer and sibling rivalries, and the search for identity. The novel does all this neither by pandering to the biases of the putative young readership nor by suggesting no possible amelioration of the several situations except the morally bankrupt and psychologically irresponsible one of looking inside one's unhappy self or outside to one's peers experiencing the same problem. Both the characterization and prominence of Meg, incidentally, are a happy anticipation of the non-sexist female protagonist of today. Finally, because *A Wrinkle in Time* utilizes a futuristic mode of space travel and speculates about possible life elsewhere in the universe, it is science fiction. As such, it is a historically important book since it is the first juvenile sf novel not only admitted into the mainstream of children's literature but also honored in a significant way – thus heralding juvenile sf's coming of age.

A Wrinkle in Time, as is often the case, did not spring full grown from the author's imagination. L'Engle's early juvenile, *Camilla*, an unexceptional instance of what was then called the junior novel, features a female protagonist in somewhat atypical circumstances, who struggles not only to find herself but to work out or even work out of, as may be the case, supportive, or destructive, relationships with parents, relatives, and boys. In *Meet the Austins* L'Engle anticipated the form and achievement of her masterpiece. The Austins are also a warmly affectionate and close family whose obvious goodness is offset by enough failings to make the family believable and likeable. Pre-adolescent Vicky Austin, the main character, is an obvious predecessor of Meg Murry. The Austins, it would appear, were so liked by their creator as well as by many readers that two subsequent novels narrate their further adventures. *The Moon by Night* is a low-keyed, relatively unexciting account of a cross country vacation trek undertaken by the family. *The Young Unicorns* describes the Austins' unwilling involvement in a plot to ferment civil turmoil in New York City. More intricately plotted and more serious thematically than the other Austin novels – and in these respects similar to *A Wrinkle in Time* – the novel lacks the stylistic verve, the range of allusions, and the deft and interesting characterization that make the former superior fiction.

Two other novels deserve attention. In *The Arm of the Starfish* L'Engle altered her usual approach a bit. Instead of working outward from within the intimate family circle, she has her main character, Adam Eddington, earn his way into the O'Keefe family. Unfortunately, the rest of the plot resembles formula cloak and dagger, and the goodness of the O'Keefes is stock and unbelievable. *A Wind in the Door*, a sequel to *A Wrinkle in Time*, suffers in comparison with its predecessor. Although the human characters are virtually the same, their ethical concern sufficiently weighty, the adventures suitably fantastic, e.g., travelling into the bloodstream of Charles Wallace, and the technology plausibly extrapolated, the mixture of these elements is too contrived and predictable, and, hence, lacks freshness and interest.

Even if Madeleine L'Engle had not written *A Wrinkle in Time*, she would still be counted among the relatively few novelists who manage to entertain their young readers while honestly portraying some of the problems that vex them. When *A Wrinkle in Time* is added to her corpus, however, L'Engle must be ranked as one of the truly important writers of juvenile fiction in recent decades.

—Francis J. Molson

LENSKI, Lois (Lenore). American. Born in Springfield, Ohio, 14 October 1893. Educated at local schools in Anna, Ohio, and high school in Sidney, Ohio, graduated 1911; Ohio State University, Columbus, 1911–15, B.S. in education 1915; Art Students' League, New York, 1915–20; Westminster School of Art, London, 1920–21. Married Arthur Covey in 1921 (died, 1960); one son and two step-children. Free-lance illustrator from 1920. One-man shows: Weyhe Gallery, New York, 1927 (oils); Ferargils Gallery, New York, 1932 (watercolors); group shows: Pennsylvania Water Color Show, 1922; New York Water Color

Show; Detroit Art Institute. Recipient: American Library Association Newbery Medal, 1946; Child Study Association of America award, 1948; Catholic Library Association Regina Medal, 1969; University of Southern Mississippi award, 1969. Litt.D.: Wartburg College, Waverly, Iowa, 1959; Capital University, Columbus, 1966; Southwestern College, Winfield, Kansas, 1968; D.H.L.: University of North Carolina Women's College, Greensboro, 1962. *Died 11 September 1974.*

PUBLICATIONS FOR CHILDREN (illustrated by the author)

Fiction

> *Skipping Village.* New York, Stokes, 1927.
> *A Little Girl of 1900.* New York, Stokes, 1928.
> *Two Brothers and Their Animal Friends.* New York, Stokes, 1929.
> *Two Brothers and Their Baby Sister.* New York, Stokes, 1930.
> *Spinach Boy.* New York, Stokes, 1930.
> *Benny and His Penny.* New York, Knopf, 1931.
> *Grandmother Tippytoe.* New York, Stokes, 1931.
> *Arabella and Her Aunts.* New York, Stokes, 1932.
> *Johnny Goes to the Fair.* New York, Minton Balch, 1932.
> *The Little Family.* New York, Doubleday, 1932.
> *Gooseberry Garden.* New York and London, Harper, 1934.
> *The Little Auto.* New York and London, Oxford University Press, 1934; as *The Baby Car*, London, Oxford University Press, 1937.
> *Surprise for Mother.* New York, Stokes, 1934.
> *Sugarplum House.* New York and London, Harper, 1935.
> *Little Baby Ann.* New York and London, Oxford University Press, 1935.
> *The Easter Rabbit's Parade.* New York and London, Oxford University Press, 1936.
> *Phebe Fairchild, Her Book.* New York, Stokes, 1936.
> *The Little Sail Boat.* New York, Oxford University Press, 1937; as *The Little Sailing Boat*, London, Oxford University Press, 1937.
> *A-Going to the Westward.* New York, Stokes, 1937.
> *Bound Girl of Cobble Hill.* New York, Stokes, 1938.
> *The Little Airplane.* New York and London, Oxford University Press, 1938.
> *Ocean-Born Mary.* New York, Stokes, 1939.
> *Blueberry Corners.* New York, Stokes, 1940.
> *The Little Train.* New York and London, Oxford University Press, 1940.
> *Indian Captive.* New York, Stokes, 1941.
> *The Little Farm.* New York and London, Oxford University Press, 1942.
> *Bayou Suzette.* Philadelphia, Lippincott, 1943.
> *Davy's Day.* New York and London, Oxford University Press, 1943.
> *Let's Play House.* New York and London, Oxford University Press, 1944.
> *Puritan Adventure.* Philadelphia, Lippincott, 1944.
> *Strawberry Girl.* Philadelphia, Lippincott, 1945; London, Oxford University Press, 1951.
> *Blue Ridge Billy.* Philadelphia, Lippincott, 1946.
> *The Little Fire Engine.* New York, Oxford University Press, 1946; London, Oxford University Press, 1947.
> *Surprise for Davy.* New York, Oxford University Press, 1947.
> *Judy's Journey.* Philadelphia, Lippincott, 1947; London, Oxford University Press, 1955.
> *Mr. and Mrs. Noah.* New York, Crowell, 1948.
> *Boom Town Boy.* Philadelphia, Lippincott, 1948.
> *Cotton in My Sack.* Philadelphia, Lippincott, 1949.

Cowboy Small. New York, Oxford University Press, 1949; London, Oxford University Press, 1957.

Texas Tomboy. Philadelphia, Lippincott, 1950.

Papa Small. New York, Oxford University Press, 1951; London, Oxford University Press, 1957.

Prairie School. Philadelphia, Lippincott. 1951; London, Oxford University Press, 1959.

Peanuts for Billy Ben. Philadelphia, Lippincott, 1952.

We Live in the South. Philadelphia, Lippincott, 1952.

Mama Hattie's Girl. Philadelphia, Lippincott, 1953.

Corn-Farm Boy. Philadelphia, Lippincott, 1954.

Project Boy. Philadelphia, Lippincott, 1954.

We Live in the City. Philadelphia, Lippincott, 1954.

San Francisco Boy. Philadelphia, Lippincott, 1955.

A Dog Came to School. New York and London, Oxford University Press, 1955.

Berries in the Scoop. Philadelphia, Lippincott, 1956.

Big Little Davy. New York and London, Oxford University Press, 1956.

Flood Friday. Philadelphia, Lippincott, 1956.

We Live by the River. Philadelphia, Lippincott, 1956.

Davy and His Dog. New York and London, Oxford University Press, 1957.

Houseboat Girl. Philadelphia, Lippincott, 1957.

The Little Sioux Girl. Philadelphia, Lippincott. 1958.

Coal Camp Girl. Philadelphia, Lippincott. 1959.

We Live in the Country. Philadelphia, Lippincott, 1960; London. Oxford University Press, 1961.

Davy Goes Places. New York, Walck, 1961.

Policeman Small. New York, Walck, 1962.

We Live in the Southwest. Philadelphia, Lippincott, 1962.

Shoo-Fly Girl. Philadelphia, Lippincott, 1963.

We Live in the North. Philadelphia, Lippincott. 1965.

High-Rise Secret. Philadelphia, Lippincott, 1966.

Debbie and Her Grandma. New York, Walck, 1967; London, Oxford University Press, 1968.

To Be a Logger. Philadelphia, Lippincott, 1967.

Christmas Stories. Philadelphia, Lippincott, 1968.

Deer Valley Girl. Philadelphia, Lippincott, 1968.

Debbie and Her Family. New York, Walck, 1969.

Debbie Herself. New York, Walck, 1969.

Debbie and Her Dolls. New York, Walck, 1970.

Debbie Goes to Nursery School. New York, Walck, 1970.

Debbie and Her Pets. New York, Walck, 1971.

Plays

The Bean-Pickers: A Migrant Play, music by Clyde Robert Bulla. Washington, D.C., National Council of Churches, 1952.

A Change of Heart: A Migrant Play, music by Clyde Robert Bulla. Washington, D.C., National Council of Churches, 1952.

Strangers in a Strange Land: A Migrant Play, music by Clyde Robert Bulla. Washington, D.C., National Council of Churches, 1952.

Verse

Alphabet People. New York, Harper, 1928.

Animals for Me. New York and London, Oxford University Press, 1941.

Forgetful Tommy.   Harwinton, Connecticut, Greenacres Press, 1943.
Spring Is Here.   New York and London, Oxford University Press, 1945.
Now It's Fall.   New York, Oxford University Press, 1948.
I Like Winter.   New York and London, Oxford University Press, 1950.
We Are Thy Children (hymns), music by Clyde Robert Bulla.   New York, Crowell, 1952.
On a Summer Day.   New York and London, Oxford University Press, 1953.
Songs of Mr. Small, music by Clyde Robert Bulla.   New York, Oxford University Press, 1954.
Songs of the City, music by Clyde Robert Bulla.   New York, Marks Music, 1956.
Up to Six, Book 1, music by Clyde Robert Bulla.   New York, Hansen Music, 1956.
I Went for a Walk, music by Clyde Robert Bulla.   New York, Walck, 1958.
At Our House, music by Clyde Robert Bulla.   New York, Walck, 1959; Kingswood, Surrey, World's Work, 1964.
When I Grow Up, music by Clyde Robert Bulla.   New York, Walck, 1960.
The Life I Live: Collected Poems.   New York, Walck, 1965.
City Poems.   New York, Walck, 1971.

Other

The Wonder City: A Picture Book of New York.   New York, Coward McCann, 1929.
The Washington Picture Book.   New York, Coward McCann, 1930.
My Friend the Cow.   Chicago, National Dairy Council, 1946.
Ice Cream Is Good.   Chicago, National Dairy Council, 1948.
Living with Others.   Hartford, Connecticut Council of Churches, 1952.

Editor, *Jack Horner's Pie: A Book of Nursery Rhymes.*   New York, Harper, 1927; as *Lois Lenski's Mother Goose,* n.d.
Editor, *Susie Mariar* (folk rhyme).   New York and London, Oxford University Press, 1939.

PUBLICATIONS FOR ADULTS (illustrated by the author)

Verse

Florida, My Florida: Poems.   Tallahassee, Friends of the Florida State University Library, 1971.

Other

Adventures in Understanding: Talks to Parents, Teachers, and Librarians, 1944–1966.   Tallahassee, Friends of the Florida State University Library, 1968.
Journey into Childhood: The Autobiography of Lois Lenski.   Philadelphia, Lippincott, 1972.

Bibliography: by Esther G. Witcher, in *The Lois Lenski Collection in the University of Oklahoma Library,* Norman, University of Oklahoma Library and School of Library Science, 1963.

Manuscript Collections: University of Oklahoma Library, Norman: Florida State University Library, Tallahassee.

Illustrator: *Children's Frieze-Book,* 1918; *Dolls from the Land of Mother Goose,* 1918; *The Golden Age,* 1921, and *Dream Days,* 1922, by Kenneth Grahame; *The Green-Faced Toad* by Vera B. Birch, 1921; *Cinderella,* 1922; *My ABC Book,* 1922; *The Peep-Show Man* by Padraic

Colum, 1924; *The Monkey That Would Not Kill* by Henry Drummond, 1925; *Chimney Corner Stories*, 1925, *Chimney Corner Fairy Tales*, 1926, *Fireside Stories*, 1927, *Candle-Light Stories*, 1928, *Chimney Corner Poems*, 1930, and *Fireside Poems*, 1930, all edited by Veronica S. Hutchinson; *A Merry-Go-Round of Modern Tales*, 1927, *The Hat-Tub Tale*, 1928, and *Mr. Nip and Mr. Tuck*, 1930, all by Caroline D. Emerson; *A Book of Princess Stories*, 1927, *A Book of Enchantments*, 1928, and *There Were Giants*, 1929, all edited by Kathleen Adams and Frances Atchinson; *Prudence and Peter and Their Adventures with Pots and Pans* by Elizabeth Robins and Octavia Wilberforce, 1928; *Sing a Song of Sixpence*, 1930; *Mother Goose Rhymes*, 1930; *Little Rag Doll*, 1930, and *A Name for Obed*, 1941, by Ethel C. Phillips; *The Twilight of Magic* by Hugh Lofting, 1930; *Rustam, Lion of Persia*, 1930, and *Odysseus, Sage of Greece*, 1931, by Alan Lake Chidsey; *Jolly Rhymes of Mother Goose* edited by Watty Piper, 1932, and *The Little Engine That Could* retold by Piper, 1945; *Golden Tales of the Prairie States* [*the Far West, Canada, New England, the Southwest, the Old South*], all edited by May Becker, 1932–41; *A Scotch Circus* by Tom Powers, 1934; *Down-Town*, 1936, *Betsy-Tacy*, 1940, *Betsy-Tacy and Tib*, 1941, and *Over the Big Hill*, 1942, all by Maud Hart Lovelace; *Twenty-Two Short Stories of America* edited by E.R. Mirrielees, 1937; *Edgar, The 7:58* by Phil Stong, 1938; *Once on Christmas* by Dorothy Thompson, 1938; *Mother Makes Christmas* by Cornelia Meigs, 1940; *Indigo Treasure* by Frances Rogers, 1941; *The First Thanksgiving* by Lena Barksdale, 1942; *A Letter to Popsey* by Mabel La Rue, 1942; *They Came from France* by Clara Ingram Judson, 1943; *Five and Ten* by Roberta Whitehead, 1943; *The Surprise Place* by Mary Graham Bonner, 1945; *The Donkey Cart* by Clyde Robert Bulla, 1946; *Pinocchio* adapted by Allen Chaffee, 1946; *Read-to-Me-Storybook* by the Child Study Association, 1947.

*   *   *

Lois Lenski was a prolific author of books for children for more that 30 years. Her work, much of it still in print, is aimed at children from preschool through the middle elementary school years. Lenski's writing is best described as sober, realistic and straightforward. Her prose is easy to read, convincing but not vivid and generally quite humorless. Had she chosen to write music, it would surely have been plainsong.

Her books for very young children form one body of work by themselves. Serious, very simply written, rather flat-footed, they have had an abiding appeal for many small children who seem to find in them a satisfying exactness, a comfortable familiarity. Lenski has a sure eye for those adult occupations most visible and interesting to young children. She writes about Mr. Small as a policeman, train engineer, farmer, boat captain and cowboy, giving brief glimpses of his duties in each role. (Interesting occupations are exclusively male in Lenski's world.) The methodical activities of Mr. Small in whatever guise may strike some adults (and some children) as dull, but it is clear that many children identify closely with Lenski's characters and that, for them, the orderly, informative text is an aid to imaginative participation in the adult world at a level they can comprehend.

The second major part of Lenski's work comprises the so-called historical and regional series. Both sets of stories are fiction, both share the plain narrative style, the realism and the simplicity that characterize the books for younger children. Of the two, the regional series is probably the better known.

These books, as their name implies, explore American life in various parts of the country. Here, as in her books for young children, Lenski's interest in the working world is apparent; how a family gets its living is an important theme. Lenski's research is sound; the background facts are authentic and dialect is accurate. More unusual, particularly for the 1940's and 50's, is her focus on the poorer levels of American society. Sharecroppers are depicted in *Cotton in My Sack*, Florida "crackers" in *Strawberry Girl*, and the mountain people who scratch a bare living in the Appalachians in *Blue Ridge Billy*. In all of these, Lenski presents patterns of life often invisible in children's books. For the most part, she does so with neither condescension nor sentimentality. The haphazard financial habits of the sharecropper family in *Cotton in My Sack* are given honestly, and the makeshift household arrangements of migrant worker families described sympathetically but entirely without pathos in *Judy's Journey*. Nevertheless, Lenski's values are ultimately conventional, and her literary realism has clear limits. There are problems in her stories but no tragedies; her characters face many difficulties, but few without solution. Plots generally center around a mild (sometimes mildly improbable) success story. And success usually requires that her characters trade the hand-to-mouth ways of lower class living for something closer to middle class behavior. The values of industry, education, sobriety and thrift always triumph.

At their best, as in *Strawberry Girl*, the regional stories blend local color, simple plot and uncomplicated characterization into plausible if rather predictable wholes. When Lenski is less successful, as in *To Be a Logger*, the research seems undigested, and the book remains a conglomerate of fact and message rather than a story with a shape and life of its own.

The historical stories are generally more detailed than the regional books, appealing to a slightly older audience. Otherwise, their strengths and weaknesses parallel those of the regional stories: realism is their greatest attraction (they are based on the experiences of real people); lack of humor, pat plots and sometimes an over-abundance of incident and informative detail weaken them.

—Anne S. MacLeod

LEWIS, C(live) S(taples). British. Born in Belfast, Northern Ireland, 29 November 1898. Educated at Wynyard School, Hertfordshire, 1908–10; Campbell College, Northern Ireland, 1910; Cherbourg School, Malvern, 1911–13; privately 1914–17; University College, Oxford (Scholar; Chancellor's English Essay Prize, 1921), 1917, 1919–23, B.A. (honours) 1922. Served in the Somerset Light Infantry, 1917–19; First Lieutenent. Married Joy Davidman Gresham in 1956 (died, 1960). Philosophy Tutor, 1924, and Lecturer in English, 1924, University College, Oxford; Fellow and Tutor in English, Magdalen College, Oxford, 1924–54; Professor of Medieval and Renaissance English, Cambridge University, 1954–63. Riddell Lecturer, University of Durham, 1943; Clark Lecturer, Cambridge University, 1944. Recipient: Gollancz Prize for Literature, 1937; Library Association Carnegie Medal, 1957. D.D.: University of St. Andrews, Scotland, 1946; Docteur-ès-Lettres, Laval University, Quebec, 1952; D. Litt.: University of Manchester, 1959; Hon. Dr.: University of Dijon, 1962; University of Lyon, 1963. Honorary Fellow, Magdalen College, Oxford, 1955; University College, Oxford, 1958; Magdalene College, Cambridge, 1963. Fellow of the Royal Society of Literature, 1948; Fellow of the British Academy, 1955. *Died 22 November 1963.*

PUBLICATIONS FOR CHILDREN (illustrated by Pauline Baynes)

Fiction

> *The Lion, The Witch, and the Wardrobe.* London, Bles, and New York, Macmillan, 1950.
> *Prince Caspian: The Return to Narnia.* London, Bles, and New York, Macmillan, 1951.
> *The Voyage of the "Dawn Treader."* London, Bles, and New York, Macmillan, 1952.
> *The Silver Chair.* London, Bles, and New York, Macmillan, 1953.
> *The Horse and His Boy.* London, Bles, and New York, Macmillan, 1954.
> *The Magician's Nephew.* London, Lane, and New York, Macmillan, 1955.
> *The Last Battle.* London, Lane, and New York, Macmillan, 1956.

PUBLICATIONS FOR ADULTS

Novels

> *Out of the Silent Planet.*   London, Lane, 1938; New York, Macmillan, 1943.
> *Perelandra.*   London, Lane, 1943; New York, Macmillan, 1944; as *Voyage to Venus,* London, Pan, 1960.
> *That Hideous Strength: A Modern Fairy-Tale for Grown-Ups.*   London, Lane, 1945; New York, Macmillan, 1946.
> *Till We Have Faces: A Myth Retold.*   London, Bles, 1956; New York, Harcourt Brace, 1957.

Short Stories

> *The Dark Tower and Other Stories.*   London, Collins, 1977.

Verse

> *Spirits in Bondage: A Cycle of Lyrics* (as Clive Hamilton).   London, Heinemann, 1919.
> *Dymer* (as Clive Hamilton).   London, Dent, and New York, Macmillan, 1926.
> *Poems,* edited by Walter Hooper.   London, Bles, 1964; New York, Harcourt Brace, 1965.
> *Narrative Poems,* edited by Walter Hooper.   London, Bles, 1969; New York, Harcourt Brace, 1972.

Other

> *The Pilgrim's Regress: An Allegorical Apology for Christianity, Reason and Romanticism.*   London, Dent, 1933; New York, Sheed and Ward, 1935; revised edition, London, Bles, 1943; Sheed and Ward, 1944.
> *The Allegory of Love: A Study in Medieval Tradition.*   Oxford, Clarendon Press, and New York, Oxford University Press, 1936.
> *Rehabilitations and Other Essays.*   London and New York, Oxford University Press, 1939.
> *The Personal Heresy: A Controversy,* with E.M.W. Tillyard.   London and New York, Oxford University Press, 1939.
> *The Problem of Pain.*   London, Bles, 1940; New York, Macmillan, 1943.
> *The Weight of Glory.*   London, S.P.C.K., 1942.
> *The Screwtape Letters.*   London, Bles, 1942; New York, Macmillan, 1944; revised edition, Bles, 1961.
> *Broadcast Talks; Right and Wrong: A Clue to the Meaning of the Universe, and What Christians Believe.*   London, Bles, 1942; as *The Case for Christianity,* New York, Macmillan, 1943.
> *A Preface to "Paradise Lost"* (lecture).   London and New York, Oxford University Press, 1942.
> *Christian Behaviour: A Further Series of Broadcast Talks.*   London, Bles, and New York, Macmillan, 1943.
> *The Abolition of Man; or, Reflections on Education with Special Reference to the Teaching of English in the Upper Forms of Schools.*   London, Oxford University Press, 1943; New York, Macmillan, 1947.
> *Beyond Personality: The Christian Idea of God.*   London, Bles, 1944; New York, Macmillan, 1945.
> *The Great Divorce: A Dream.*   London, Bles, 1945; New York, Macmillan, 1946.
> *Miracles: A Preliminary Study.*   London, Bles, and New York, Macmillan, 1947.
> *Vivisection.*   London, Anti-Vivisection Society, 1948.

Transpositions and Other Addresses. London, Bles, 1949; as *The Weight of Glory and Other Addresses,* New York, Macmillan, 1949.

The Literary Impact of the Authorized Version (lecture). London, Athlone Press, 1950; Philadelphia, Fortress Press, 1963.

Mere Christianity. London, Bles, and New York, Macmillan, 1952.

Hero and Leander (lecture). London, Oxford University Press, 1952.

English Literature in the Sixteenth Century, Excluding Drama. Oxford, Clarendon Press, 1954.

De Descriptione Temporum (lecture). London, Cambridge University Press, 1955.

Surprised by Joy: The Shape of My Early Life. London, Bles, 1955; New York, Harcourt Brace, 1956.

Reflections on the Psalms. London, Bles, and New York, Harcourt Brace, 1958.

Shall We Lose God in Outer Space? London, S.P.C.K., 1959.

The Four Loves. London, Bles, and New York, Harcourt Brace, 1960.

The World's Last Night and Other Essays. New York, Harcourt Brace, 1960.

Studies in Words. London, Cambridge University Press, 1960; revised edition, 1967.

An Experiment in Criticism. London, Cambridge University Press, 1961.

A Grief Observed (as N.W. Clerk; autobiography). London, Faber, 1961; Greenwich, Connecticut, Seabury Press, 1963.

They Asked for a Paper: Papers and Addresses. London, Bles, 1962.

Beyond the Bright Blue (letters). New York, Harcourt Brace, 1963.

Letters to Malcolm, Chiefly on Prayer. London, Bles, and New York, Harcourt Brace, 1964.

The Discarded Image: An Introduction to Medieval and Renaissance Literature. London, Cambridge University Press, 1964.

Screwtape Proposes a Toast and Other Pieces. London, Collins, 1965.

Of Other Worlds: Essays and Stories, edited by Walter Hooper. London, Bles, 1966; New York, Harcourt Brace, 1967.

Letters, edited by W.H. Lewis. London, Bles, and New York, Harcourt Brace, 1966.

Studies in Medieval and Renaissance Literature, edited by Walter Hooper. London, Cambridge University Press, 1966.

Spenser's Images of Life, edited by Alastair Fowler. London, Cambridge University Press, 1967.

Christian Reflections, edited by Walter Hooper. London, Bles, and Grand Rapids, Michigan, Eerdmans, 1967.

Letters to an American Lady, edited by Clyde S. Kilby. Grand Rapids, Michigan, Eerdmans, 1967; London, Hodder and Stoughton, 1969.

Mark vs. Tristram: Correspondence Between C.S. Lewis and Owen Barfield, edited by Walter Hooper. Cambridge, Massachusetts, Lowell House Printers, 1967.

A Mind Awake: An Anthology of C.S. Lewis, edited by Clyde S. Kilby. London, Bles, 1968; New York, Harcourt Brace, 1969.

Selected Literary Essays, edited by Walter Hooper. London, Cambridge University Press, 1969.

God in the Docks: Essays on Theology and Ethics, edited by Walter Hooper. Grand Rapids, Michigan, Eerdmans, 1970; as *Undeceptions: Essays on Theology and Ethics,* London, Bles, 1971.

The Humanitarian Theory of Punishment. Abingdon, Berkshire, Marcham Books Press, 1972.

Editor, *George MacDonald: An Anthology.* London, Bles, 1946; New York, Doubleday, 1962.

Editor, *Arthurian Torso, Containing the Posthumous Fragment of "The Figure of Arthur,"* by Charles Williams. London and New York, Oxford University Press, 1948.

Critical Studies: *C.S.Lewis* by Roger Lancelyn Green, London, Bodley Head, 1963; *C.S. Lewis: A Biography* by Roger Lancelyn Green and Walter Hooper, London, Collins, and New York, Harcourt Brace, 1974; *The Secret Country of C.S. Lewis* by Anne Arnott, London, Hodder and Stoughton, 1974.

*   *   *

Ever since the first of the seven Narnia books appeared in 1950, C. S. Lewis has been perhaps the best-liked post-war "quality" writer for children in Britain. This success is all the more interesting because, at the time of publishing, these books ran directly across a number of attitudes and taboos in children's fiction – and in certain ways do so still. They contain violence, pain, and death. Their tone is often admonitory; they are morally and theologically didactic. It would be wrong, of course, to think these all disadvantages. Indeed, it could be said that C. S. Lewis won his readers not only by his stunning scenes and plot situations and by his manner – a well-gauged air of intimate authority – but by a deliberate *using* of large taboos, religion and death in particular.

In the autobiographical *Surprised by Joy*, and elsewhere, Lewis has valuably charted the reading, tastes and events of his early life that led to these children's stories. "I wrote," he declared characteristically, "the books I should have liked to read. That's always been my reason for writing ... no rot about 'self-expression.' " He was the younger of two brothers, born and brought up in Northern Ireland. Motherless at nine, with a moody Welsh solicitor father, he was accustomed to an inventive, dreaming bookish solitude. "I am a product of long corridors, empty sunlit rooms, upstair indoor silences, attics explored in solitude, distant noises of gurgling cisterns and pipes, and the noise of wind under the tiles. Also of endless books." Most in the house were adult novels and of no interest to the myth-loving young romantic. What *did* make a lasting impact were E. Nesbit's three "magic" novels, *The Amulet* in particular. "It first opened my eyes to antiquity, the dark backward and abysm of time. I can still reread it with delight." Gulliver was another favourite. Andersen's *Snow Queen* and Grahame's *Dream Days* must have been read about this time. At 12 he was caught by the spell of "Northernness" – Norse myths, Rackham's illustrations to *The Ring*, Morris's *Sigurd the Volsung*. At 16, under a private tutor, W. T. Kirkpatrick, he raced into Homer. "Day after day and month after month we drove gloriously onward, tearing the whole *Achilleid* out of the *Iliad* ... and then reading the *Odyssey* entire, till the music of the thing and the clear bitter brightness ... had become part of me." A year or so later, by way of *Phantastes*, he discovered George MacDonald – a major experience. All these, and many other early-read tales go to the making of Narnia.

Of all the books, the first, *The Lion, The Witch, and the Wardrobe*, remains the favourite (or the best-remembered, which may be the same thing). There are good enough reasons for this. It is usually the first one to be read, and the gateway to the rest; it also contains one of the great moments in children's fiction (in an empty room of an old vast rambling country house a wardrobe leads to a snowy forest, faun and dwarf and witch). But it was also the key book from Lewis's view, the one where he first set out precisely (as much to himself as to his readers) the Christ-role of Aslan, who dies to save Edmund, on the Stone Table, and then rises again; the pilgrimage role (fallible, favoured, leading to brightness) of the human children; and something more: his personal view that pagan myth and Christian gospel are not inimical. In the final Narnian story centaurs, fauns, real animals and fabulous creatures pass with humans through the golden gate.

"In a certain sense," wrote Lewis, "I have never actually 'made' a story ... I see pictures. Some of these pictures have a common flavour ... which groups them together. Keep quiet and watch and they will begin joining themselves up .... I have no idea whether this is the usual way of writing stories .... It is the only one I know; images always come first." Where there are gaps, he added, some conscious inventing must at last be done.

Images always come first – much of the impact of the Narnian tales must come from this.

In *Prince Caspian* the four Pevensie children, already met in the first book, are drawn back, by a magic horn, to the aid of Caspian, in danger of death from his evil uncle Miraz who has usurped the throne. Advised of this by his half-dwarf tutor, Dr. Cornelius, Caspian escapes and goes (with the human children) to rally supporters and to restore the land to its original honour. Among his followers are the Old People, centaurs, fauns, squirrels, ravens, "a small but genuine giant, Wimbleweather, of Deadman's Hill," even Silenus and Bacchus. ("I wouldn't have felt very safe with Bacchus and all his wild girls if we'd met them without Aslan," murmurs Susan. "I should think not," says Lucy.) In the culminating battle, Peter fights with style. He "swung to face Sopespian, slashed his legs from under him, and with the back-cut of the same stroke, walloped off his head." Lewis never fails in describing such expertise.

Though it has weaknesses (and the improbable Eustace Scrubb is the principal one) *The Voyage of the "Dawn Treader"* seems the most intoxicating (or, one might say intoxicated) of the Narnian books. The abiding influence throughout is Homeric, clearly going back to young Lewis's "glorious" race through the *Odyssey*. Edmund, Lucy, and their unloved cousin Eustace Scrubb enter a picture (like the children in Grahame's *Dream Days*). It is of an ancient dragon-prowed vessel in towering waves – and there they are on board, with young King Caspian, carrying out his vow to search for the seven loyal lords whom Miraz despatched "to the unknown Eastern Seas, beyond the Lone Islands." Eustace becomes a dragon (but recovers and mends his ways); a Sea Serpent nearly crushes the boat in its coils; and they reach the edge of the World's End, and look into Aslan's country. Only one may step into it – Reepicheep, the Knightly Mouse: "For you," says the Lamb, "the door into Aslan's country is from your own world."

But as sheer fairy tale, *The Silver Chair* should take top place of the seven. Jill and Eustace, wretched at school, call Aslan's name, and find themselves on the edge of what must be the highest cliff in all fiction. Eustace falls – but Aslan wafts him on his breath to "the west of the world." Jill follows, and the two are sent on a quest to find the lost Prince Rilian, heir to the old King of Narnia. Aslan gives four signs to Jill, which she must not forget. (She does.) A Marsh-Wiggle, Puddleglum (one of Lewis's best creations), joins the journey as guide, to the Bottom of the World, where Rilian, enslaved by a Witch Queen, sits bound in a silver chair. A superb and magical story.

The Horse and His Boy, which could seem at first glance a witty vivacious Arabian Nights pastiche, provides a new pair of human children. A fair-haired fisherman's boy in dark Calormen (in fact a foundling, cast ashore as an infant) escapes being sold into slavery and, helped by a Talking Horse called Bree (echoes of Gulliver?) and joined by a fearless runaway girl called Aravis, makes the long perilous journey to Narnia – dungeons, mountains, haunted deserts – where in fact his own identity lies. This is a first-class story and children like it well. Yet, though Aslan provides the *gravitas* (aid in crisis, admonition: three real claw-stripes for Aravis) it remains one of the lighter-weight books of the seven. The children in *The Magician's Nephew*, most Nesbit-like of the novels, live in late-Victorian London, when "Mr. Sherlock Holmes was still living in Baker Street and the Bastables were looking for treasure in the Lewisham Road"; they are Digory (Father in India, mother ill) and Polly who lives next door. Uncle Andrew, who dabbles in magic, propels the two into the Other Place, where Narnia is soon (in this book, indeed) to be created. Unfortunately through inquisitiveness (or scientific interest) Digory releases Jadis, a beautiful evil witch, from a prisoning spell; she returns with the pair to London (a riotous Nesbit episode) and (symbolically) inserts herself into the newborn Narnia. Aslan sends Digory forth to collect the magic apple whose tree may help to keep her power at bay. A cabdriver and his horse (echoes of MacDonald's *North Wind*) join the return to Narnia and are given high roles in the kingdom. More contrived ("invented") than some of the books, it is not amongst the best. Yet the facts about Narnia's making deserve attention.

The final book, *The Last Battle*, is a curious and disturbing work, fine in passages, yet over-ambitious for its scope. In the last days of Narnia an ape called Shift finds a lion-skin, wraps it about his simple donkey servant, Puzzle, and claims that Aslan has returned. Through this poor puppet he orders the cutting down of the forests; he makes commercial pacts with the evil Calormenes, and sells the Narnian creatures off to work in the mines. When young Tirian "last of the Kings of Narnia," calls for aid to "the helpers beyond the world," Jill and

Eustace appear (from a railway train) and help to gather forces for the battle on Stable Hill. This gripping and terrible confrontation provides one of Lewis's best set-pieces. Aslan appears at last; the vanquished seem the victors; the frightful stable, from which no one returns alive, seems a bright and sunlit garden for Aslan-followers. The children realise that they were killed in a railway accident; Narnia disintegrates; the sun is squeezed like an orange; as we have noted, friendly creatures from all the stories pass with the humans through the golden gates: a kind of Judgment Day. "I see," says Lucy thoughtfully, "This garden is like the Stable. It is far bigger inside than it was outside." They are in Narnia, fresh and green; they are in their English home. "The dream is ended: this is the morning," Aslan says. End of the world? or end of these children's lives? It is hard to say.

One need not be a philosopher or even an adult to note the illogic and crotchets in Lewis's work. As a boy he was deeply unhappy at conventional boarding schools. Yet, it is the "progressive" school which provokes his ire. (*Did* such schools use only surnames, favour bullying?) He had real fondness for animals (excepting the ape and the wolf) and accorded them a nobler place in his books than most writers with a strong sense of hierarchy (Kipling, for instance). To eat a Talking Animal in Narnia was not to be thought of. Yet the very word "vegetarian" lashes him into fury, and he imposes on the vegetarian Eustace (who would in life need courage to hold his views) such qualities as cowardliness, meanness, greed. A loner and a dreamer himself, he commends the military virtues.

Yet readers read only what they read, and Lewis's books are outstanding witness to this fact. Without heavy prompting, what child perceives the symbolism in, say, the Stone Table episode? Would the young Lewis himself have done so? But wardrobe and lamppost are firmly lodged in every reader's mind. For all his convert's zeal he leaves a reader not so much with a dose of theology as a sensation of noble deeds, far distances, the freedom of space and time, the sure division of right and wrong. Matter of myth: matter of fairy tale.

—Naomi Lewis

LEWIS, Hilda (Winifred). British. Born in London, in 1896. Married Michael Lewis; one son. Taught in London for a few years; lived many years in Nottingham. *Died in February 1974.*

PUBLICATIONS FOR CHILDREN

Fiction

> *The Ship That Flew.* London, Oxford University Press, 1939; New York, Criterion Books, 1958.
> *The Gentle Falcon,* illustrated by Evelyn Gibbs. London, Oxford University Press, 1952; New York, Criterion Books, 1957.
> *Here Comes Harry,* illustrated by William Stobbs. London, Oxford University Press, and New York, Criterion Books, 1960.
> *Harold Was My King.* London, Oxford University Press, 1968; New York, McKay, 1970.

PUBLICATIONS FOR ADULTS

Novels

Pegasus Yoked.   London, Hurst and Blackett, 1933.
Madam Gold.   London, Hurst and Blackett, 1933.
Full Circle.   London, Hurst and Blackett, 1935.
Pelican Inn.   London, Jarrolds, 1937.
Because I Must.   London, Jarrolds, 1938.
Said Dr. Spendlove.   London, Jarrolds, 1940.
Penny Lace.   London, Jarrolds, 1942.
Imogen under Glass.   London, Jarrolds, 1943.
Strange Story.   London, Jarrolds, 1945; New York, Random House, 1947.
Gone to the Pictures.   London and New York, Jarrolds, 1946.
The Day Is Ours.   London, Jarrolds, 1947.
More Glass Than Wall.   London, Macdonald, 1950.
No Mate, No Comrade.   London, Macdonald, 1951.
Enter a Player.   London, Macdonald, 1952.
Wife to Henry V.   London, Jarrolds, 1954; New York, Putnam, 1957.
The Witch and the Priest.   London, Jarrolds, 1956; New York, McKay, 1970.
I, Jacqueline.   London, Jarrolds, 1957.
Wife to Great Buckingham.   London, Jarrolds, 1959; New York, Putnam, 1960.
Call Lady Purbeck.   London, Hutchinson, 1961; New York, St. Martin's Press, 1962.
A Mortal Malice.   London, Hutchinson, 1963.
Wife to Charles II.   London, Hutchinson, 1965; as Catherine, New York, St. Martin's
     Press, 1966.
Wife to the Bastard.   London, Hutchinson, 1966; New York, McKay, 1967.
Harlot Queen.   London, Hutchinson, and New York, McKay, 1970.
I Am Mary Tudor.   London, Hutchinson, 1971; New York, McKay, 1972.
Mary the Queen.   London, Hutchinson, 1973.
Bloody Mary.   London, Hutchinson, 1974.
Rose of England.   London, Hutchinson, 2 vols., 1977.

                              *   *   *

Hilda Lewis won a high reputation as one of Britain's most distinguished historical novelists, noted for her painstaking research into the period and characters she was recreating. Her novels in different genres include The Day Is Ours, dealing with the problems of deaf children and later memorably filmed as Mandy. Her few books for children were all concerned with historical events and characters. They include The Gentle Falcon, a haunting story of the 7-year-old French princess who was marrried to Richard II, and Here Comes Harry, a sympathetic portrait of the boy-king Henry VI.

But it is on her outstanding children's fantasy, The Ship That Flew that her reputation as a children's writer chiefly rests. In this memorable story – with strong echoes of Nesbit's The Story of the Amulet and Kipling's Puck of Pook's Hill – young Peter finds a model Viking ship in an antique shop. The ship grows big enough to transport Peter and his brothers and sisters back through time and space – to Asgard, Ancient Egypt, and Sherwood Forest – to have many exciting adventures. The children also discover that "their" ship had been given by Odin to Frey, the Norse God, as his wedding gift and, not merely a time-travel device, it exerts its own strange influence throughout the story. Written with great imaginative flair and a superb sense of history, it is one of the great modern fantasies for children

                                                              —Brian Doyle

LEXAU, Joan M. American. Born in St. Paul, Minnesota. Educated at College of St. Thomas and College of St. Catherine, both in St. Paul; New School for Social Research, New York. Has worked as a salesperson, waitress, library clerk, and office-worker; editorial secretary, *Catholic Digest*, St. Paul, 1953–55; advertising production manager, *Glass Packer* magazine, New York, 1955–56; reporter, *Catholic News*, New York, 1956–57; correspondent, Religious News Service, New York, 1957; Children's Books Production Liaison, Harper and Row, publishers, New York, 1957–61. Recipient: Child Study Association of America award, 1963. Address: P.O. Box 270, Otisville, New York 10963, U.S.A.

PUBLICATIONS FOR CHILDREN

Fiction

Olaf Reads, illustrated by Harvey Weiss. New York, Dial Press, 1961.

Cathy Is Company, illustrated by Aliki. New York, Dial Press, 1961.

Millicent's Ghost, illustrated by Ben Shecter. New York, Dial Press, 1962.

The Trouble with Terry, illustrated by Irene Murray. New York, Dial Press, 1962.

Olaf Is Late, illustrated by Harvey Weiss. New York, Dial Press, 1963.

That's Good, That's Bad, illustrated by Aliki. New York, Dial Press, 1963.

José's Christmas Secret, illustrated by Don Bolognese. New York, Dial Press, 1963; revised edition, as *The Christmas Secret*, New York, Scholastic, 1973.

Who Took the Farmer's Hat? (as Joan L. Nodset), illustrated by Fritz Siebel. New York, Harper, 1963.

Go Away, Dog (as Joan L. Nodset), illustrated by Crosby Bonsall. New York, Harper, 1963.

Benjie, illustrated by Don Bolognese. New York, Dial Press, 1964.

Maria, illustrated by Ernest Crichlow. New York, Dial Press, 1964.

Where Do You Go When You Run Away? (as Joan L. Nodset), illustrated by Adriana Saviozzi. Indianapolis, Bobbs Merrill, 1964.

I Should Have Stayed in Bed!, illustrated by Syd Hoff. New York, Harper, 1965; Kingswood, Surrey, World's Work, 1966.

More Beautiful Than Flowers, illustrated by Don Bolognese. Philadelphia, Lippincott, 1966.

The Homework Caper, illustrated by Syd Hoff. New York, Harper, 1966.

A Kite over Tenth Avenue, illustrated by Symeon Shimin. New York, Doubleday, 1967.

Finders Keepers, Losers Weepers, illustrated by Tomie de Paola. Philadelphia, Lippincott, 1967.

Every Day a Dragon, illustrated by Ben Shecter. New York, Harper, 1967.

Three Wishes for Abner, illustrated by Gloria Kamen. Boston, Ginn, 1967.

Striped Ice Cream!, illustrated by John Wilson. Philadelphia, Lippincott, 1968.

The Rooftop Mystery, illustrated by Syd Hoff. New York, Harper, 1968; Kingswood, Surrey, World's Work, 1969.

A House So Big, illustrated by Fritz Siebel. New York, Harper, 1968.

Archimedes Takes a Bath, illustrated by Salvatore Murdocca. New York, Crowell, 1969.

Benjie on His Own, illustrated by Don Bolognese. New York, Dial Press, 1970.

Me Day, illustrated by Robert Weaver. New York, Dial Press, 1971.

Emily and the Klunky Baby and the Next-Door Dog, illustrated by Martha Alexander. New York, Dial Press, 1972.

Come Here, Cat (as Joan L. Nodset), illustrated by Steven Kellogg. New York, Harper, 1973.

I'll Tell on You, illustrated by Gail Owens. New York, Dutton, 1976.

Other (folk tales)

> *Crocodile and Hen*, illustrated by Joan Sandin.   New York, Harper, 1969.
> *It All Began with a Drip, Drip, Drip* ... , illustrated by Joan Sandin.   New York, McCall,
> 1970; Kingswood, Surrey, World's Work, 1972.
> *A T for Tommy*, illustrated by Janet Compere.   Champaign, Illinois, Garrard, 1971.
> *That's Just Fine, and Who-o-o Did It?*, illustrated by Dora Leder.   Champaign, Illinois,
> Garrard, 1971.
> *The Tail of the Mouse*, illustrated by Roberta Langman.   Boston, Ginn, 1974.

PUBLICATIONS FOR ADULTS

Other

> Editor, *Convent Life: Roman Catholic Religious Orders for Women in North
> America*.   New York, Dial Press, 1964.

Manuscript Collections: Kerlan Collection, University of Minnesota, Minneapolis; de
Grummond Collection, University of Southern Mississippi, Hattiesburg.

Joan M. Lexau comments:
I like kids, have a lot of child friends and relatives, remember being a child, how it felt. I
always wanted to write and was reintroduced to children's books while working at Harper
and Row, so I write books for children. I do a lot of easy-to-read books because I remember
vividly the explosive joy of being able to read my first real book (but nothing about the
process of learning to read). I am now getting into high interest, low vocabulary books for
older children who are having trouble reading.

*   *   *

Joan M. Lexau's first book, *Olaf Reads*, which describes the enthusiasm and trials of a
young child starting to recognize words, gave no indication of the author's direction in her
later works. In 1962, *The Trouble with Terry* was published. In it Lexau drew a sensitive
portrait of a poor, fatherless family with a tired, hard-working mother. Terry is a bright,
impulsive almost-eleven. She doesn't like to memorize and would rather fail in school than
accept answers without questioning the wisdom of her teachers. "And then she had to be
born a girl. That wasn't fair at all. Girls couldn't play football, couldn't have paper routes ....
If there had to be girls, they should be treated like anybody else." By the time Terry lives
through the summer, this irrepressible female scores a touchdown while playing with her
brother's friends, acquires a temporary paper-route, and saves a child's life. *Benjie* and *Benjie
on His Own* are two very popular and touching stories of a five-year-old Black boy living in a
ghetto with his grandmother. Lexau carefully delineates the boy's deeply felt shyness which
makes it difficult for Benjie to deal with the world. But when his grandmother desperately
needs help in *Benjie on His Own*, the child surprises himself by taking on responsibility and
facing the emergency.
Striped Ice Cream! is the bitter-sweet story of a poor family of five children who are
supported by a loving mother who works as a domestic. It is an honest treatment of what it is
like to have to scrimp and do without to get such necessities as shoes for the new school-year,
a world in which striped ice-cream is a luxury reserved for the youngest child's eighth
birthday.
The I Can Read Mysteries, *The Homework Caper* and *The Rooftop Mystery*, make a good
stab at eliciting excitement for the young reader, but here Lexau misses the mark. Her plots
aren't absorbing and the writing is unimaginative. Many of Lexau's books such as *Finders
Keepers, Losers Weepers* and *Cathy Is Company* portray girls who are vapid or mean, and

stereotypic mothers. *Come Here, Cat,* one of the books Lexau wrote under the name of Nodset, is a disarming story of a girl and a cat as they get acquainted with one another. *I'll Tell on You* has a contemporary story-line. It is an account of cooperation, of childhood friendship which crosses the boundaries of sex and race as two children try out for the local baseball team. Despite the creditable themes of friendship, honesty, and trust, *I'll Tell on You* barely skims the surface of the subject matter.

It is in the *Benjie* books, *Striped Ice Cream,* and *The Trouble with Terry* that Lexau is at her best. The author presents young people with a special reading experience only when she writes with her particular sensitivity about poverty, loneliness and family-love. This is her true métier.

—Vivian J. Scheinmann

LIFTON, Betty Jean. American. Born in New York City, 11 June 1926. Educated at Barnard College, New York, B.A. 1948. Married the writer Robert Jay Lifton in 1952; has one son and one daughter. Address: 300 Central Park West, New York, New York 10024, U.S.A.

PUBLICATIONS FOR CHILDREN

Fiction

Joji and the Dragon, illustrated by Eiichi Mitsui. New York, Morrow, 1957.
Mogo the Mynah, illustrated by Anne Scott. New York, Morrow, 1958.
Joji and the Fog, illustrated by Eiichi Mitsui. New York, Morrow, 1959.
Kap the Kappa, illustrated by Eiichi Mitsui. New York, Morrow, 1960.
The Dwarf Pine Tree, illustrated by Fuku Akino. New York, Atheneum, 1963.
Joji and the Amanojaku, illustrated by Eiichi Mitsui. New York, Norton, 1965.
The Cock and the Ghost Cat, illustrated by Fuku Akino. New York, Atheneum, 1965.
The Rice-Cake Rabbit, illustrated by Eiichi Mitsui. New York, Norton, 1966.
The Many Lives of Chio and Goro, illustrated by Yasuo Segawa. New York, Norton, 1966.
Taka-Chan and I: A Dog's Journey to Japan, by Runcible, photographs by Eikoh Hosoe. New York, Norton, 1967.
Kap and the Wicked Monkey, illustrated by Eiichi Mitsui. New York, Norton, 1968.
The Secret Seller, illustrated by Etienne Delessart. New York, Norton, 1968.
The Silver Crane, illustrated by Laszlo Kubinyi. New York, Seabury Press, 1971.
Good Night, Orange Monster, illustrated by Cyndy Szekeres. New York, Atheneum, 1972.
Jaguar, My Twin, illustrated by Ann Leggett. New York, Atheneum, 1976.

Play

Kap the Kappa, adaptation of her own story, in *Contemporary Children's Theater,* edited by Lifton. New York, Avon, 1974.

Other

The One-Legged Ghost, illustrated by Fuku Akino. New York, Atheneum, 1968.
A Dog's Guide to Tokyo, photographs by Eikoh Hosoe. New York, Norton, 1969.

The Mud Snail Son, illustrated by Fuku Akino.   New York, Atheneum, 1971.
Children of Vietnam, with Thomas C. Fox.   New York, Atheneum, 1972.

Editor, *Contemporary Children's Theater.*   New York, Avon, 1974.

PUBLICATIONS FOR ADULTS

Other

Return to Hiroshima, photographs by Eikoh Hosoe.   New York, Atheneum, 1970.
Twice Born: Memoirs of an Adopted Daughter.   New York, McGraw Hill, 1975.

*   *   *

Betty Jean Lifton's prolific work as a writer reflects the influence of sojourns in the Far East. In her children's fiction such oriental themes as non-violence and the eternal recurrence of nature are accompanied by a cavalcade of strange creatures chiefly drawn from (often moralistic) Japanese folktales.

Among the folk creatures is Joji, a peace-loving scarecrow befriended by the very crows he is supposed to frighten away from a farmer's rice field. In *Joji and the Dragon*, Joji's master discards him for a hired dragon. The crows scare off their would-be conqueror, thus enabling Joji to be restored to his rightful position. Captured by a rice-paddy-terrorizing demon in *Joji and the Amanojaku* he is again rescued by his crow friends who intimidate his ferocious captor. Joji, a lively espouser of nonviolence, is appealing to the very young.

Another protagonist is a Kappa, a legendary Japanese river elf with a monkey's face and a turtle's back. In *Kap the Kappa* the mischievous Kap leaves his river home to be adopted by a fisherman whose family disguise him as a boy. However, his incorrigible pranks disclose his identity to all, and, after realizing he cannot be a human, he returns to the river and his true parents. An inspired creation, Kap inhabits other stories as well as a similarly-titled play which evinces the author's considerable skill as a playwright for children.

A mountain demon in *The Dwarf Pine Tree* grants a tiny evergreen its wish to become a dwarf pine tree beautiful enough to cure an ailing princess. The tree patiently undergoes the necessary painful transformation, is discovered and brought to the princess whose health is restored, and then it passes away to become a tree spirit. This poignant work reflecting the gentle spirit of Buddha emerges as a minor masterpiece.

Animal characters also abound in Mrs. Lifton's books. A loyal rooster in the suspenseful and touching *The Cock and the Ghost Cat* sacrifices himself to protect his master from a ghost cat bent on stealing the household's provisions. The man-size title character of *The Rice-Cake Rabbit* makes the best rice-cakes in Japan but aspires to be a samurai, a profession reserved for men. He is banished to the moon when he succeeds. This gently ironic yarn is among the author's best. In *The Many Lives of Chio and Goro*, the trans-migrating souls of a farm couple pass through animal life back to human life with comic complications in a tale which the reader can appreciate on several levels.

Betty Jean Lifton's stories have an audience range of ages 4 to 10. They are characterized by humor, an economy of words, vivid characterizations, well-structured narratives drawn from Japanese folktales without diluting the cultural source, and handsomely imaginative and colorful brush and ink illustrations by such artists as Eiichi Mitsui and Fuku Akino. Her fiction's appeal for young children and its effectiveness in stimulating interest in oriental culture are unquestionable. These factors earn Mrs. Lifton a position of prominence in juvenile literature as an imaginative, sensitive, and skillful storyteller.

—Christian H. Moe

LINDSAY, Norman (Alfred William). Australian. Born in Creswick, Victoria, 22 February 1879. Educated at Creswick State School and Creswick Grammar School. Married Kate Parkinson in 1900 (divorced, 1920), three sons, including the writer Jack Lindsay; Rose Soady, 1920, two daughters. Artist and free-lance illustrator: for *The Hawklet* sporting paper, after 1896, and *Tocsin*, both in Melbourne; Co-Editor, *The Rambler*, Melbourne, 1899; joined the Sydney *Bulletin* in 1901, and chief cartoonist until 1923, and 1932–58; associated with *The Lone Hand*, Melbourne, 1907–21, and the Endeavour Press, Sydney, 1932–35. One-man Shows: Sydney and Melbourne, 1909; Adelaide, 1924; London, 1925; Sydney, 1968; Newcastle, New South Wales, 1969; Group Show: Exhibition of Australian Art, London, 1923. *Died 21 November 1969.*

PUBLICATIONS FOR CHILDREN (illustrated by the author)

Fiction

> *The Magic Pudding, Being the Adventures of Bunyip Bluegum and His Friends Bill Barnacle and Sam Sawnoff.* Sydney, Angus and Robertson, 1918; London, Hamish Hamilton, and New York, Farrar and Rinehart, 1936.
> *The Flyaway Highway.* Sydney, Angus and Robertson, 1936.

PUBLICATIONS FOR ADULTS

Fiction

> *A Curate in Bohemia.* Sydney, Bookstall, 1913; London, Laurie, 1937.
> *Hyperborea: Two Fantastic Travel Essays.* London, Fanfrolico Press, 1928.
> *Madam Life's Lovers: A Human Narrative Embodying a Philosophy of the Artist in Dialogue Form.* London, Fanfrolico Press, 1929.
> *Redheap.* London, Faber, 1930; as *Every Mother's Son*, New York, Cosmopolitan Book Corporation, 1930.
> *The Cautious Amorist.* London, Faber, and New York, Farrar and Rinehart, 1932.
> *Miracles by Arrangement.* London, Faber, 1932; as *Mr. Gresham and Olympus*, New York, Farrar and Rinehart, 1932.
> *Saturdee.* Sydney, Endeavour Press, 1933; London, Laurie, 1936; New York, AMS Press, 1976.
> *Pan in the Parlor.* New York, Farrar and Rinehart, 1933; London, Laurie, 1936.
> *Age of Consent.* London, Laurie, and New York, Farrar and Rinehart, 1938.
> *The Cousin from Fiji.* Sydney and London, Angus and Robertson, 1945; New York, Random House, 1946.
> *Halfway to Anywhere.* Sydney, Angus and Robertson, 1947.
> *Dust or Polish.* Sydney and London, Angus and Robertson, 1950.
> *Rooms and Houses: An Autobiographical Novel.* Sydney and London, Ure Smith, 1968.

Other

> *Norman Lindsay's Book, 1* and *2*, edited by Harold Burston. Sydney, Bookstall, 1912–15.
> *The Pen Drawings of Norman Lindsay*, edited by Sydney Ure Smith and Bertram Stevens. Sydney, Angus and Robertson, 1918.
> *Creative Effort: An Essay in Affirmation.* Sydney, Art in Australia, 1920; London, Palmer, 1924.
> *The Etchings of Norman Lindsay.* London, Constable, 1927.
> *Norman Lindsay's Pen Drawings.* Sydney, Art in Australia, 1931.

Norman Lindsay Water Colour Book: Eighteen Reproductions in Colour from Original Watercolours, with an Appreciation of the Medium. Sydney, Springwood Press, 1939; augmented edition, Sydney and London, Ure Smith, 1969.
Paintings in Oil .... Sydney, Shepherd Press, 1945.
Bohemians of the Bulletin. Sydney, Angus and Robertson, 1965.
The Scribblings of an Idle Mind. Melbourne, Lansdowne Press, 1966.
Norman Lindsay's Ship Models. Sydney, Angus and Robertson, 1966.
Selected Pen Drawings. Sydney, Angus and Robertson, 1968; New York, Bonanza, 1970.
Pencil Drawings. Sydney, Angus and Robertson, 1969.
My Mask, for What Little I know of the Man Behind It: An Autobiography. Sydney and London, Angus and Robertson, 1970.
Two Hundred Etchings, edited by Douglas Stewart. Sydney, Angus and Robertson, 1973.
Pen Drawings. Sydney, Ure Smith, 1974.
Norman Lindsay's Cats, edited by Douglas Stewart. Melbourne, Macmillan, 1974.

Editor, *The Golden Shanty: Short Stories,* by Edward Dyson. Sydney, Angus and Robertson, 1963.

Critical Studies: *Norman Lindsay* by John Aikman Hetherington, Melbourne, Oxford University Press, 1962; *Norman Lindsay: His Books, Manuscripts, and Autograph Letters in the Library of, and Annotated by, Harry F. Chaplin,* Sydney, Wentworth Press, 1969.

Illustrator: *This Is the Book of Our Selection* by Arthur H. Davis, 1903; *Petronius,* 1910; *Songs of a Campaign* by Leon Gellert, 1918; *Colombine* by H.M., 1920; *The Inns of Greece and Rome* by W.C. Firebaugh, 1923; *Lysistrata* by Aristophanes, 1926; *The Passionate Neatherd* by Jack Lindsay, 1926; *The Complete Works of Petronius,* 1927; *Propertius in Love,* 1927; *Loving Mad Tom,* 1927; *Satyrs and Sunlight* by Hugh MacCrae, 1928; *A Homage to Sappho,* 1928; *The Antichrist* by Nietzsche, 1928; *Women in Parliament* by Aristophanes, 1929; *A Defence of Women* by John Donne, 1930; *The Animals Noah Forgot* by Andrew Barton Paterson, 1933; *A Drum for Ben Boyd* by Francis Webb, 1948; *Fisher's Ghost* by Douglas Stewart, 1960; *The Letters of Rachel Henning,* 1963; *Faces and Places* by Jack Lindsay, 1974.

*   *   *

In *The Magic Pudding* an urbane young koala called Bunyip Bluegum leaves home because of nuisances created by his Uncle Wattleberry's whiskers. Nattily dressed in Edwardian leisure-wear, Bunyip soon discovers a disadvantage of genteel strolling:

> Observe my doleful plight.
>   For here am I without a crumb
>   To satisfy a raging tum —
> O what an oversight!

"As he was indulging in these melancholy reflections he came round a bend in the road, and discovered two people in the very act of having lunch. These people were none other than Bill Barnacle, the sailor, and his friend, Sam Sawnoff, the penguin bold."

These boisterous characters invite Bunyip to share their pudding, which has the advantages of being inexhaustible and as variable in kind and flavours as the eaters wish. It is also a larrikin called Albert, with sprinting ability when not being dined upon, and with unrefined speech to express contempt of all but hearty eaters:

> Eat away, chew away, munch and bolt and guzzle,
>   Never leave the table till you're full up to the muzzle!

The rest of the story is a rollick of campfire feasts and roaring songs, interrupted by desperate attempts to recover Albert from puddin' thieves. These are mostly a "snooting, snouting" Possum and his accomplice, "a bulbous, boozy-looking Wombat," but there is also "a Judge who's been poisoned/ By Puddin' and Port."

In these adventures Bill and Sam produce the necessary snout-bending pugilistics; Bunyip Bluegum supplies encouragement, inspirations, and tactics. The nonsense story is told in fluent colloquial prose, in uproarious verse, and in the vigorous drawings of Lindsay at the height of his great ability as an illustrator in black-and-white.

So much of the fun and fast movement depends on sound that children of 9 or 10, unable to read well enough to appreciate the rollicking prose and verse, often fail to enjoy the book. Read aloud, however, it's an instant success. There seems no upward limit to its "reading age."

Lindsay is said to have written the book to back one of his multitudinous opinions: that children prefer food to fairies. It may seem that, although he rejected the phoney faerie of Victorian fiction, he accepted the talking-animal mode; but perhaps his animal characters are metaphors, rather than personifications. Certainly Lindsay, a life-long experimenter in crafts, became so involved in his essay at a book for children that the story has none of the humourless stiffness of so many first attempts. In fact, *The Magic Pudding* is the only Australian children's book that is indisputably a classic.

He tried again, in 1936, but *The Flyaway Highway* lacks the glorious spontaneity of *The Puddin'*. It depends on out-dated ideas (the platitudinous themes of late-Victorian popular fiction) and on dated slang. In spite of its vigorous pen-drawings, and the presence of "the bloke with cow's hooves" (who seems to be an irreverent response to Kenneth Grahame's Pan), it fails to satisfy either children or adults.

—Dennis Hall

LINGARD, Joan (Amelia). British. Born in Edinburgh. Educated at Bloomfield Collegiate School, Belfast; Moray House Training College, General Certificate of Education. Has three children. Schoolteacher, Midlothian, 1953–61. Full-time novelist and television scriptwriter. Recipient: Scottish Arts Council Bursary, 1969. Agent: David Higham Associates, 5–8 Lower John Street, London, W1R 4HA, England. Address: 31 Scotland Street, Edinburgh EH3 6PY, Scotland.

PUBLICATIONS FOR CHILDREN

Fiction

The Twelfth Day of July.   London, Hamish Hamilton, 1970; Nashville, Nelson, 1972.
Across the Barricades.   London, Hamish Hamilton, 1972; Nashville, Nelson, 1973.
Into Exile.   London, Hamish Hamilton, and Nashville, Nelson, 1973.
Frying as Usual, illustrated by Priscilla Clive.   London, Hamish Hamilton, 1973.
The Clearance.   London, Hamish Hamilton, and Nashville, Nelson, 1974.
A Proper Place.   London, Hamish Hamilton, and Nashville, Nelson, 1975.
The Resettling.   London, Hamish Hamilton, and Nashville, Nelson, 1975.
Hostages to Fortune.   London, Hamish Hamilton, 1976; Nashville, Nelson, 1977.
The Pilgrimage.   London, Hamish Hamilton, 1976; Nashville, Nelson, 1977.
Snake among the Sunflowers.   London, Hamish Hamilton, and Nashville, Nelson, 1977.
The Reunion.   London, Hamish Hamilton, 1977.

PUBLICATIONS FOR ADULTS

Novels

    Liam's Daughter.   London, Hodder and Stoughton, 1963.
    The Prevailing Wind.   London, Hodder and Stoughton, 1964.
    The Tide Comes In.   London, Hodder and Stoughton, 1966.
    The Headmaster.   London, Hodder and Stoughton, 1967.
    A Sort of Freedom.   London, Hodder and Stoughton, 1969.
    The Lord on Our Side.   London, Hodder and Stoughton, 1970.

Joan Lingard comments:

I began to write for children after writing my sixth adult novel *The Lord on Our Side*, set in Ulster from the 1940's to the 1960's. The late Honor Arundel, fellow writer and close friend, suggested I wī 'e a book about Belfast for children. At that time – 1969 – the current troubles were just begin ing to build up. On thinking about it, I realised that I had a book more or less ready made in ṛ ⁄ head: the character Josie from my adult novel was transmuted into Sadie, her brother Billy ɔ Tommy, and I created Kevin, the Catholic boy, as a balance to Sadie and his sister Brede aː ɑ counterweight to Tommy. Thus Sadie and Kevin were born, and *The Twelfth Day of July* on its way. In this and four subsequent books I have followed them through the passage from childhood to maturity, a maturity forced upon them prematurely by the situation in Ulster, the differences in their religions, their exile, and the continuing demands of their families.

As a relief almost, in order to get a respite from thinking about Ulster and its troubles, I created Maggie, a Glasgow girl, who, unlike Sadie, does not intend to follow the traditional female role of becoming a wife and mother but wants to go to university, become a social anthropologist and push out the boundaries of her life, an ambition not understood, although tolerated, by her family. In the course of four books beginning with *The Clearance* I have explored her development through that crucial stage in which she is questioning previously held concepts and beliefs and trying to find out what she does and does not want from life.

I am particularly interested in characters caught up in social change, with all its attendant problems and stresses; also in the relationships within families, and which part of their inheritance young people retain, and which part reject, or attempt to.

*   *   *

There is an uncompromising honesty about Joan Lingard's writing. She eschews glib answers, particularly to problems of bigotry and social prejudice. Any girl identifying herself with a Joan Lingard heroine could well be daunted by life's prospect. No happy-ever-after endings, even when lovers are married. The Irish stories have been criticised as too open-ended, but this quality enhances their value to young readers. Life goes on somehow, a continuing struggle.

There are five Irish books, each a link in the chain which binds together the lives of Catholic Kevin and Protestant Sadie. In *The Twelfth Day of July*, their acquaintance as child enemies in Belfast grows into a relationship far more important to them than the senseless violence which had initially seemed only an exciting game. They manage to salvage a life of their own; but *Across the Barricades* tells how the pressure from their families intensifies to Montague-and-Capulet ferocity, until finally the murder of the one person who has tried to help them puts paid to any hope that some wise understanding adult will solve all.

So Kevin and Sadie marry, and retreat to London, only to find that life there is fraught with new problems yet still permeated with the brooding influence of the Belfast streets. Not that all is unrelieved gloom; the vigour and humour of Joan Lingard's writing provide warmth and colour throughout *Into Exile*, which ends on a note of hope and love. The reader is left agog for more, and will be grateful for the brisk arrival of the next two books, *A Proper Place* and *Hostages to Fortune*, in which Ulster's poison begins to weaken. The problems now are more domestic than political, more emotional than religious. Significantly, it is not their contemporaries but older, even elderly, people who help our star-crossed couple, and there is a recurring pattern – so familiar to many young people – of outsiders helping much more effectively than parents, in this case, mothers, loving but angry.

Other books – *The Clearance, The Resettling,* and *The Pilgrimage* – centre round Maggie McKinley. She is headstrong and rebellious, with a talent for survival as durable as Sadie's, though there is nothing in the events around her comparable with the violence and tragedy of the Ulster books. Maggie's life is complicated by the complacent middle-class values of the Frasers, who are averse to her involvement with their son James, and by the total failure of her own Scottish working-class family to understand her academic ambitions. The absorbing conflict and drama spring largely from Maggie herself, from the roughness of her own nature.

All Joan Lingard's books could be labelled "contemporary," realistically confronting such issues as sex, violence, and women's rights. Always, though, they are handled deftly and in context; and thus her stories are endowed with a quality which raises them far above the level of banal romances. She captures her readers and at the same time helps to recognise the very roots of bigotry and prejudice.

—Cecilia Gordon

LINKLATER, Eric (Robert Russell). British. Born in Penarth, South Wales, 8 March 1899. Educated at Aberdeen Grammar School; Aberdeen University (Editor, *Alma Mater,* 1921–22), M.A. 1925; studied medicine. Served as a Private in the Black Watch, 1917–19; Major in the Royal Engineers, commanding the Royal Engineers Orkney Fortress, 1939–41; Member of Staff, Directorate of Public Relations, War Office, 1941–45; Temporary Lieutenant-Colonel in Korea, 1951; Territorial Decoration. Married Marjorie MacIntyre in 1933; four children. Assistant Editor, *Times of India,* Bombay, 1925–27; Assistant to the Professor of English Literature, Aberdeen University, 1927–28; Commonwealth Fellow, Cornell University, Ithaca, New York, and the University of California, Berkeley, 1928–30. Rector of Aberdeen University, 1945–48. Deputy Lieutenant of Ross and Cromarty, Scotland, 1968. Recipient: Library Association Carnegie Medal, 1945. LL.D.: Aberdeen University, 1946. Fellow, Royal Society of Edinburgh. C.B.E. (Commander, Order of the British Empire), 1954. *Died 7 November 1974.*

PUBLICATIONS FOR CHILDREN

Fiction

> *The Wind on the Moon,* illustrated by Nicolas Bentley. London and New York, Macmillan, 1944.
> *The Pirates in the Deep Green Sea,* illustrated by William Reeves. London and New York, Macmillan, 1949.

Other

> *Karina with Love,* photographs by Karl Werner Gullers. London, Macmillan, 1958.

PUBLICATIONS FOR ADULTS

Novels

White Maa's Saga.   London, Cape, and New York, Peter Smith, 1929.
Poet's Pub.   London, Cape, 1929; New York, Farrar and Rinehart, 1930.
Juan in America.   London, Cape, and New York, Farrar and Rinehart, 1931.
The Men of Ness: The Saga of Thorlief Coalbiter's Son.   London, Cape, 1932; New
   York, Farrar and Rinehart, 1933.
Magnus Merriman.   London, Cape, and New York, Farrar and Rinehart, 1934.
The Revolution.   London, White Owl Press, 1934.
Ripeness Is All.   London, Cape, and New York, Farrar and Rinehart, 1935.
Juan in China.   London, Cape, and New York, Farrar and Rinehart, 1937.
The Sailor's Holiday.   London, Cape, 1937; New York, Farrar and Rinehart, 1938.
The Impregnable Women.   London, Cape, and New York, Farrar and Rinehart, 1938.
Judas.   London, Cape, and New York, Farrar and Rinehart, 1939.
Private Angelo.   London, Cape, and New York, Macmillan, 1946.
A Spell for Old Bones.   London, Cape, 1949; New York, Macmillan, 1950.
Mr. Byculla: A Story.   London, Hart Davis, 1950; New York, Harcourt Brace, 1951.
Laxdale Hall.   London, Cape, 1951; New York, Harcourt Brace, 1952.
The House of Gair.   London, Cape, 1953; New York, Harcourt Brace, 1954.
The Faithful Ally.   London, Cape, 1954; as *The Sultan and the Lady*, New York,
   Harcourt Brace, 1955.
The Dark of Summer.   London, Cape, 1956; New York, Harcourt Brace, 1957.
Position at Noon.   London, Cape, 1958; as *My Father and I*, New York, Harcourt
   Brace, 1959.
Roll of Honour.   London, Hart Davis, 1961.
Husband of Delilah.   London, Macmillan, 1962; New York, Harcourt Brace, 1963.
A Man over Forty.   London, Macmillan, and New York, St. Martin's Press, 1963.
A Terrible Freedom.   London, Macmillan, 1966.

Short Stories

The Crusader's Key.   London, White Owl Press, 1933; New York, Knopf, 1934.
God Likes Them Plain: Short Stories.   London, Cape, 1935.
Sealskin Trousers and Other Stories.   London, Hart Davis, 1947.
A Sociable Plover and Other Stories and Conceits.   London, Hart Davis, 1957.
The Stories of Eric Linklater.   London, Macmillan, 1968; New York, Horizon Press,
   1969.

Plays

The Devil's in the Soup.   London, Cape, 1934.
Crisis in Heaven (produced Edinburgh, 1944).   London, Macmillan, 1944; New York,
   Macmillan, 1945.
Love in Albania (produced London, 1949).   London, English Theatre Guild, 1950.
Two Comedies: Love in Albania and To Meet the MacGregors.   London and New York,
   Macmillan, 1950.
The Mortimer Touch (produced London, 1952).   London, French, 1952.
Breakspear in Gascony.   London and New York, Macmillan, 1958.

Verse

Poobie.   Edinburgh, Porpoise Press, 1925.
A Dragon Laughed and Other Poems.   London, Cape, 1930.

Other

Ben Jonson and King James: Biography and Portrait.   London, Cape, and New York,
   Farrar and Rinehart, 1931.
Mary, Queen of Scots.   London, Davies, and New York, Appleton, 1933.
Robert the Bruce.   London, Davies, and New York, Farrar and Rinehart, 1934.
The Lion and the Unicorn; or, What England Has Meant to Scotland.   London,
   Routledge, 1935.
The Cornerstones: A Conversation in Elysium.   London and New York, Macmillan,
   1941.
The Defence of Calais.   London, His Majesty's Stationery Office, 1941.
The Man on My Back (autobiography).   London and New York, Macmillan, 1941.
*The Northern Garrisons: The Defence of Iceland and the Faroe, Orkney and Shetland
   Islands.*   New York, Garden City Publishing Company, 1941.
The Raft, and Socrates Asks Why: Two Conversations.   London, Macmillan, 1942;
   New York, Macmillan, 1943.
The Highland Divisions.   London, His Majesty's Stationery Office, 1942.
The Great Ship, and Rabelais Replies: Two Conversations.   London, Macmillan, 1944;
   New York, Macmillan, 1945.
The Art of Adventure (essays).   London, Macmillan, 1947.
The Campaign in Italy.   London, Her Majesty's Stationery Office, 1952.
Our Men in Korea.   London, Her Majesty's Stationery Office, 1952.
A Year of Space: A Chapter of Autobiography.   London, Macmillan, and New York,
   Harcourt Brace, 1953.
The Ultimate Viking (essays).   London, Macmillan, 1955; New York, Harcourt Brace,
   1956.
The Merry Muse.   London, Cape, 1959; New York, Harcourt Brace, 1960.
Edinburgh.   London, Newnes, 1960.
Sweden, photographs by Karl Werner Gullers.   Stockholm, Almqvist and Wiksell,
   1964.
Orkney and Shetland: An Historical, Geographical, Social and Scenic Survey.   London,
   Hale, 1965.
The Prince in the Heather.   London, Hodder and Stoughton, 1965; New York,
   Harcourt Brace, 1966.
The Conquest of England.   London, Hodder and Stoughton, and New York,
   Doubleday, 1966.
*The Survival of Scotland: A Review of Scottish History from Roman Times to the Present
   Day.*   London, Heinemann, 1968; as *The Survival of Scotland: A New History of
   Scotland from Roman Times to the Present Day,* New York, Doubleday, 1968.
Scotland.   London, Thames and Hudson, and New York, Viking Press, 1968.
The Secret Larder.   London, Macmillan, 1969.
The Royal House of Scotland.   London, Macmillan, and New York, Doubleday, 1970.
Fanfare for a Tin Hat (autobiography).   London, Macmillan, 1970.
The Music of the North.   Aberdeen, Haddo House Choral Society, 1970.
A Corpse on Clapham Common: A Tale of Sixty Years Ago.   London, Macmillan, 1971.
Voyage of the "Challenger."   London, Murray, and New York, Doubleday, 1972.
The Black Watch, with Andro Linklater.   London, Barrie and Jenkins, 1976.

Editor, *The Thistle and the Pen: An Anthology of Modern Scottish Writers.*   London,
   Nelson, 1950.
Editor, *John Moore's England: A Selection from His Writings.*   London, Collins, 1970.

*   *   *

Eric Linklater told the story of the genesis of *The Wind on the Moon* in a letter to me which
was subsequently included in *Chosen for Children,* the Library Association's book about the

Carnegie Medal. Allowing for natural exuberance – he was always rather larger than life – this can be accepted as the true account of one man's approach to writing for children. It cannot be recommended as a method to aspiring writers, but every original creative mind is idiosyncratic.

The Wind on the Moon was an improvisation, born of the necessity to entertain a pair of demanding children. It belongs in fact to that important group of books, those devised for the private entertainment of individual children. Where it differs from *Alice* and *The Wind in the Willows* is that it was the work of a professional novelist, with whom it must be a rule of life that nothing goes to waste. Even as he spun the rich absurdities out of his mind, Linklater must have known that it must eventually become a book. Its extemporary origin is revealed in an episodic structure, but the episodes are linked and related expertly. *The Wind on the Moon* is a comic fantasy which plays with the idea of humans translated into animal form. One of these is the detective who longed to be able to see over the walls; out of this urge came, very naturally, an elongation of neck which ended only in his becoming a giraffe. This and other strange happenings are highly diverting. However, the story was devised in war-time, and although it offered plenty of scope for humour the war was no joke and neither was Nazism. Suddenly the light-hearted and frivolous tale turns serious. The children who had frolicked so joyously as kangaroos become involved in a struggle against tyranny. They suffer hardship and extreme danger and their dearest friend dies. The transition from farce to tragedy is abrupt, but Linklater is too accomplished a writer to make it less than convincing.

Linklater won a Carnegie Medal with *The Wind on the Moon*. The award amused him because he regarded his book as a trifle written for an occasion. The mastery of construction, the vividly realized adventures, the sharp portraiture and effervescent writing made it a book which transcends its origins.

When he returned later to writing for children Linklater's inspiration was lacking. *The Pirates in the Deep Green Sea* had some characteristic touches, particularly in the invention of grotesque characters, and the crazy story was told with a nautical heartiness. But it quite lacked the spontaneity and the underlying passion which made *The Wind on the Moon* outstanding among the children's books of the war years.

—Marcus Crouch

LIONNI, Leo. American. Born in Amsterdam, Netherlands, 5 May 1910; emigrated to the United States in 1939; naturalized citizen, 1945. Educated at the University of Zurich, 1928–30; University of Genoa, Ph.D. in economics 1935. Married Nora Maffi in 1931; has two sons. Free-lance designer, 1930–39; Art Director, N.W. Ayer and Son Inc., Philadelphia, 1939–47; Design Director, Olivetti Corporation, New York, 1949–59; Art Director, *Fortune* magazine, New York, 1949–62; Editor, *Panorama*, Milan, 1964–65. Head of the Graphics Design Department, Parsons School of Design, New York, 1952–54. One-man shows: Worcester Museum, Massachusetts, 1958; Philadelphia Art Alliance, 1959; Naviglio, Milan, 1963; Obelisco, Rome, 1964; Galleria dell'Ariete, Milan, 1966; Galleria del Milione, Milan, 1972; Linea 70, Verona, 1973; Il Vicolo, Geneva, 1973; Baukunst Galerie, Cologne, 1974; Klingspor Museum, Offenbach, 1974; Galleria CIAK, Rome, 1975; group shows: Museum of Modern Art, New York, 1954; Venice Biennale; Bratislava Biennale, 1967. Recipient: National Society of Art Directors award, 1955; Architectural League Gold Medal, 1956; *New York Times* award, for illustration, 1959, 1960, 1967; Bratislava Biennale Golden Apple, 1967; Teheran Film Festival award, 1970; Christopher Award, 1970. Agent: Agenzia Letteraria Internazionale, Corso Matteotti 3, Milan, Italy. Address: Porcignana, Radda in Chianti, Siena, Italy.

PUBLICATIONS FOR CHILDREN (illustrated by the author)

Fiction

Little Blue and Little Yellow. New York, McDowell Obolensky, 1959; Leicester, Brockhampton Press, 1962.
Inch by Inch. New York, Obolensky, 1961; London, Dobson, 1967.
On My Beach There Are Many Pebbles. New York, Obolensky, 1961; London, Abelard Schuman, 1977.
Swimmy. New York, Pantheon Books, 1963.
Tico and the Golden Wings. New York, Pantheon Books, 1964.
Frederick. New York, Pantheon Books, 1967; London, Abelard Schuman, 1971.
The Alphabet Tree. New York, Pantheon Books, 1968.
The Biggest House in the World. New York, Pantheon Books, 1968.
Alexander and the Wind-Up Mouse. New York, Pantheon Books, 1969; London, Abelard Schuman, 1971.
Fish Is Fish. New York, Pantheon Books, 1970; London, Abelard Schuman, 1972.
Theodore and the Talking Mushroom. New York, Pantheon Books, 1971; London, Abelard Schuman, 1972.
The Greentail Mouse. New York, Pantheon Books, 1973.
In the Rabbitgarden. New York, Pantheon Books, 1975; London, Abelard Schuman, 1976.
A Colour of His Own. London, Abelard Schuman, 1975; New York, Pantheon Books, 1976.
Pezzettino. New York, Pantheon Books, 1975; London, Hutchinson, 1977.
I Want to Stay Here! I Want to Go There! A Flea Story. New York, Pantheon Books, 1977.

PUBLICATIONS FOR ADULTS

Other

Design for the Printed Page. New York, Fortune Magazine, 1960.
Il Taccuino di Leo Lionni. Milan, Electa, 1972.
La Botanica Parallela. Milan, Adelphi, 1976; translated by Patrick Creagh, as *The Parallel Botany*, New York, Knopf, 1977.

Leo Lionni comments:

Making books for children occupies a place of prime importance in my endeavors as an artist exploring the possibilities of self expression and communication. Here, too, are hiding places for private doubts and fantasies, and for private sensual (aesthetic) pleasures. But everything, content and form, has to be simple, explicit, and logical to the utmost. This is not only an exciting challenge but an extraordinary discipline.

I try, in fact, to reduce complex, so-called adult problems (alienation, search for identity, violence, love) to the most elementary verbal and visual structures in the hope that little by little my fables will stimulate creative interpretation on all age levels, and release questions and meanings that lie hidden in the words and pictures.

*   *   *

Much about Leo Lionni's aspirations, accomplishments, and insights is revealed in his own piece, "My Books for Children" (in *Wilson Library Bulletin*, October 1964). For this creator of a wonderful variety of books, among them several Caldecott award runners-up and Caldecott honor books, each uniquely developed "for the child in us," his first book, the widely used and loved *Little Blue and Little Yellow*, "just happened." The theme of the book is family rejection; the words are few but well chosen as they relate to the colored forms and shapes which carry the action.

Gifted and versatile, Lionni went on to fashion a group of outstandingly original works, uncluttered, fresh and arresting in their simplicity and clarity. Lionni emphasizes that he poses "basic problems of choice in his books." He admits, "I deal with large themes; my books are fables and parables. They express something I think and feel .... I make them for that part of us, of myself and of my friends, which has never changed, which is still a child." The particular idea dictates the individual style associated with each title. "My characters are humans in disguise, and their little problems and situations are human problems, human situations .... Most of all I try to give children doubt ... more than anything else ... which will keep us free ...."

In *Inch by Inch*, the story of an inchworm which saves itself from death by proving it can be useful by its ability to measure, the fusion of the limited number but splendidly appropriate words in conjunction with the masterful illustrations creates a suspense that is perfectly paced. *On My Beach There Are Many Pebbles* transmits something of the "original joy and wonder" of both his childhood memories and his present home overlooking the Bay of Genoa. The look, the feel, and the symbolism of the pebbles are all unmistakable in his realization.

Swimmy heralded a new combination of elements, again with well applied words which add to its tremendous visual originality in addition to its message and heroic element. Exemplifying superb artistry in which words are combined with images, some marvelously golden, is *Tico and the Golden Wings* in which a young bird learns to use its gorgeous wings to help others and to find acceptance for itself. Some three years later the "mouse-poet" Frederick who treasures a secret saved for the long cold winter, stirred its many readers. Also reflecting some current moral values, contemporary problems and associated hopes is *Alphabet Tree*, while a small snail who figures in *The Biggest House in the World* learns something significant about the size of a suitable home. *Alexander and the Wind-Up Mouse* is seemingly a more playful concoction, yet it pits real minds against mechanical minds.

Pezzettino, set on the Island of Wham, involves a search for identity. Little Pezzettino considers himself a piece of something big, but eventually discovers that he's "uniquely himself – tiny but individual." Joyfully he shouts: "I am myself." *A Colour of His Own* relates the plight of a saddened chameleon who longs for his very own color and finally realizes his wish in conjunction with a fellow chameleon. "Why don't we stay together? We will still change color wherever we go, but you and I will always be alike." This yearning for identity and companionship is familiar in Lionni. Lionni seeks to achieve a "coherence between form and content." These books represent, each in a somewhat different way, examples of his past success, fashioned with a harmony of words and images. Knowing his creative potential, and his audience of many ages, one can only anticipate the novel aspects of future stories as he continues his "quest for quality." By his ready admission, his stories "have a beginning, a development, and an end. No matter how modest they are, they must have the ingredients of the classical drama: suspense and resolution .... More often my stories are meant to stimulate the mind, to create an awareness, to destroy a prejudice ...." It is this ability which Lionni has as an adult to transmit values through his beautifully realized books which makes him such a memorable contributor to the realm of children's literature.

— Clara O. Jackson

LIPKIND, William. American. Born in New York City, 17 December 1904. Educated at the College of the City of New York, B.A. 1927; Columbia University Law School, New York, 1928, and Graduate School, 1934–37, Ph.D. in anthropology 1937. Served in England

and Germany in the United States Office of War Information, 1944–46. Married Maria Cimino in 1937. Studied Carajá and Javahé Indians in Brazil, 1938–40; Research Associate in Anthropology, Columbia University, 1940–42; Assistant Professor of Anthropology, Ohio State University, Columbus, 1942–44; Adjunct Assistant Professor, New York University, 1948–70. *Died 2 October 1974.*

PUBLICATIONS FOR CHILDREN (as Will; illustrated by Nicolas)

Fiction

The Two Reds. New York, Harcourt Brace, 1950.
Finders Keepers. New York, Harcourt Brace, 1951; Kingswood, Surrey, World's Work, 1964.
Boy with a Harpoon (as William Lipkind), illustrated by Nicolas Mordvinoff. New York, Harcourt Brace, 1952.
Even Steven. New York, Harcourt Brace, 1952.
The Christmas Bunny. New York, Harcourt Brace, 1953.
Circus Ruckus. New York, Harcourt Brace, 1954.
Boy of the Islands (as William Lipkind), illustrated by Nicolas Mordvinoff. New York, Harcourt Brace, 1954.
Professor Bull's Umbrella (as William Lipkind), illustrated by Georges Schreiber. New York, Viking Press, 1954.
Chaga. New York, Harcourt Brace, 1955.
Perry the Imp. New York, Harcourt Brace, 1956.
Sleepyhead. New York, Harcourt Brace, 1957.
The Magic Feather Duster. New York, Harcourt Brace, 1958.
Four-Leaf Clover. New York, Harcourt Brace, 1959.
The Little Tiny Rooster. New York, Harcourt Brace, 1960.
Billy the Kid. New York, Harcourt Brace, 1961.
Russet and the Two Reds. New York, Harcourt Brace, 1962.
The Boy and the Forest. New York, Harcourt Brace, 1964.
Nubber Bear (as William Lipkind), illustrated by Roger Duvoisin. New York, Harcourt Brace, 1966; London, Faber, 1968.

Other

Days to Remember: An Almanac (as William Lipkind), illustrated by Jerome Snyder. New York, Obolensky, 1961.

PUBLICATIONS FOR ADULTS

Verse

Beginning Charm for the New Year. New York, Weekend Press, 1951.

Other

Winnebago Grammar. New York, Columbia University Press, 1945.

Manuscript Collection: Kerlan Collection, University of Minnesota, Minneapolis.

*   *   *

William Lipkind's reputation in children's literature was assured by the publication of *The Two Reds,* a runner-up for the Caldecott Medal in 1951, and *Finders Keepers,* the winner in

1952. The honor gained here by Nicolas Mordvinoff, the illustrator of these books, doubtless has reflected upon Lipkind, Mordvinoff's long-time collaborator. Although Mordvinoff's illustrations in their books over-shadowed Lipkind's literary contributions to them, one should not dismiss his effect on their success. There seems little doubt that Lipkind well understood the conventions of writing for young children. One children's author, Robert Burch, has remarked that it was a course on writing for children taught by Lipkind that gave him a healthy respect for children's books.

In general, Lipkind used two kinds of narrative plots in his picture storybooks. One is based on fables and other forms of traditional literature. The other takes a more modern approach. An example of the first kind is *Finders Keepers*. Here two dogs fight over a bone instead of sharing it (a common dilemma in fables). They find, however, that this attitude will end only in the loss of the bone. Hence, they agree not to be selfish (the moral of the tale). *Nubber Bear* also contains some of the major motifs of folk literature, e.g., the small person (bear) disobeying authority and journeying away from home on a quest (for honey) that turns out to be fraught with peril and punishment. This serious story falls below Lipkind's usually satisfactory offering, however, because his experiment in having Nubber speak in couplets dissolves into strained doggerel.

That Lipkind can be both serious and frolicsome is apparent. In *Even Steven* a runt of a horse, Steven, proves his merit by recapturing a herd of stolen horses. Thus, he gets "even" for the slight mistreatments he has suffered because of his size. *The Two Reds* is a madcap adventure, full of slapstick humor (as is *Professor Bull's Umbrella*), in which a red cat, who tried to steal a red-haired boy's fish, and the boy, find (through parallel adventures) that it is better to be friends than enemies.

The strength of Lipkind's writing is implied by these remarks. It lies for one thing in the kind of characters he chooses, the dialogue they speak, and in the understandable manner in which he describes adventure and creates humor. The weakest parts of his books (*Finders Keepers* is a notable exception) are his awkward plottings. Too often Lipkind's plots turn and twist with melodramatic, even haphazard, effects, which makes for loose-jointed and irregular structures, hard to follow – and to believe. In *Professor Bull's Umbrella* the professor's lost umbrella blows around, to no determinable effect, then miraculously (and incredibly) lands back in his hand just as it starts to rain.

If Lipkind's stories for young children generally are little more than mediocre, no such negative criticism can justifiably be lodged against his longer works for older children. *Boy of the Islands*, for example, exemplifies Lipkind's ability to depict in an easy and natural yet compelling style a historical adventure in a culture far removed from his readers' experience. Lipkind creates here an entirely convincing, well-formed, honestly motivated story of the difficulties of growing up in a primitive society. *Boy of the Islands* proves the obvious paradox that Lipkind's greatest literary success was with his lesser-selling books.

—Patrick Groff

LIPPINCOTT, Joseph Wharton. American. Born in Philadelphia, Pennsylvania, 28 February 1887. Educated at the Wharton School of Finance, University of Pennsylvania, B.S. in economics 1908. Served in the United States Naval Reserve during World War I. Married Elizabeth Schuyler Mills (died, 1943), two sons and one daughter; Virginia Jones Mathieson, 1945. Member of the staff, 1908–15, Vice-president, 1915–16, President, 1926–48, and Chairman of the Board, 1948–58, J.B. Lippincott, publishers, Philadelphia. President, Frederick A. Stokes Company, publishers, New York; President, Hibernia Mine Railroad. *Died 22 October 1976.*

PUBLICATIONS FOR CHILDREN

Fiction

Bun, a Wild Rabbit, illustrated by the author. Philadelphia, Penn, 1918; revised edition, Philadelphia, Lippincott, 1953.

Red Ben, The Fox of Oak Ridge, illustrated by the author. Philadelphia, Penn, 1919; London, Harrap, 1938; revised edition, as *Little Red, The Fox*, Philadelphia, Lippincott, 1953.

Gray Squirrel, illustrated by the author. Philadelphia, Penn, 1921; revised edition, Philadelphia, Lippincott, 1954.

Striped Coat, The Skunk, illustrated by the author. Philadelphia, Penn, 1922; revised edition, Philadelphia, Lippincott, 1954.

Persimmon Jim, The Possum, illustrated by the author. Philadelphia, Penn, 1924; revised edition, Philadelphia, Lippincott, 1955.

Long Horn, Leader of the Deer. Philadelphia, Penn, 1928; revised edition, Philadelphia, Lippincott, 1955.

The Wolf King, illustrated by Paul Bransom. Philadelphia, Penn, 1933; London, Harrap, 1934.

The Red Roan Pony, illustrated by Lynn Bogue Hunt. Philadelphia, Penn, 1934; London, Harrap, 1935; revised edition, Philadelphia, Lippincott, 1951.

Chisel-Tooth, The Beaver, illustrated by Roland V. Shutts. Philadelphia, Penn, and London, Harrap, 1936.

Wilderness Champion, illustrated by Paul Bransom. Philadelphia, Lippincott, 1944; London, Hutchinson, 1948.

Black Wings, The Unbeatable Crow, illustrated by Lynn Bogue Hunt. Philadelphia, Lippincott, 1947.

The Wahoo Bobcat, illustrated by Paul Bransom. Philadelphia, Lippincott, 1950.

The Phantom Deer, illustrated by Paul Bransom. Philadelphia, Lippincott, 1954; as *No Name the Deer*, London, Macmillan, 1956.

Old Bill, The Whooping Crane. Philadelphia, Lippincott, 1958.

Coyote, The Wonder Wolf, illustrated by Ed Dodd. Philadelphia, Lippincott, 1964.

Other

Naturecraft Creatures, with G.J. Roberts. Philadelphia and London, Lippincott, 1933.

Animal Neighbors of the Countryside, illustrated by Lynn Bogue Hunt. Philadelphia, Lippincott, 1938; London, Hutchinson, 1940.

*   *   *

Publisher by vocation and naturalist by avocation, Joseph Wharton Lippincott wrote animal stories that had exciting plots and outdoor settings, used at times by the author as vehicles to plead for conservation of wild land and wild life. Indeed, most of the creatures in Lippincott's books are wild animals, and the popularity of these books has surely been attributable in part to the sympathetic affection of the writing, an affection that never degenerates into sentimentality, and in part to the accuracy of Lippincott's observations of animal behavior. He writes without anthropomorphism, yet invests his subjects with personality; his characterization of human beings is more variable, being at times effective and at other times rather wooden.

Typical of Lippincott's earlier writing in *Persimmon Jim, The Possum*, in which a wily old possum evades the irate farmers on whose poultry he has preyed: the writing style is simplified and the plot quite patterned. With *The Red Roan Pony* and *Black Wings, The Unbeatable Crow*, he sharpened both style and pace and developed situations and characters that were colorful but realistic. In *Wilderness Champion* and its companion story, *The Wolf*

King, he uses a device perennially appealing to readers: the lost pet which becomes feral and which later is tamed again; here the red setter pup, lost and raised by a wolf, remains loyal to the wolf even when he has been happily living with his master. A more unusual story is *The Wahoo Bobcat*, which describes the friendship between a huge bobcat, struggling to survive in a changing environment, the Florida swampland, and a boy of nine who tries to help the animal to escape from hunters. The background is striking, the plea for conservation strong, and the plot developed with dramatic flair.

Several of Lippincott's stories have been revised, and a large part of his output remains in print. Although some of his people have an old-fashioned flavor, the animal characters, accurately drawn, have a lasting appeal.

—Zena Sutherland

LITTLE, (Flora) Jean. Canadian. Born in Tainan, Formosa, 2 January 1932. Educated at Victoria College, University of Toronto, B.A. in English 1955; Institute of Special Education, Salt Lake City. Visiting Instructor, Florida State University, Tallahassee; Specialist Teacher, Beechwood School for Crippled Children, Guelph, Ontario. Recipient: Canadian Children's Book Award, 1961; Vicky Metcalf Award, 1974. Address: 198 Glasgow Street North, Guelph, Ontario, Canada.

PUBLICATIONS FOR CHILDREN

Fiction

> *Mine for Keeps*, illustrated by Lewis Parker. Boston, Little Brown, 1962; London, Dent, 1964.
> *Home from Far*, illustrated by Jerry Lazare. Boston, Little Brown, 1965.
> *Spring Begins in March*, illustrated by Lewis Parker. Boston, Little Brown, 1966.
> *Take Wing*, illustrated by Jerry Lazare. Boston, Little Brown, 1968.
> *One to Grown On*, illustrated by Jerry Lazare. Boston, Little Brown, 1969.
> *Look Through My Window*, illustrated by Joan Sandin. New York, Harper, 1971.
> *Kate*. New York, Harper, 1971.
> *From Anna*, illustrated by Joan Sandin. New York, Harper, 1972.
> *Stand in the Wind*, illustrated by Emily McCully. New York, Harper, 1975.
> *Listen for the Singing*. New York, Dutton, 1977.

Verse

> *It's a Wonderful World*. Guelph, privately printed, 1947.
> *When the Pie Was Opened: Poems*. Boston, Little Brown, 1968.

*   *   *

Children who must cope with physical or psychological handicaps are central to the themes of many juvenile books in the last decade or two. Jean Little's books were in the vanguard of this type of novel. Because of her own partial sightedness, she writes with particular knowledge of these problems.

Miss Little's first book, *Mine for Keeps*, tells the story of Sal Copeland whose adjustment to a regular classroom after several years in a special school is realistically portrayed. The unique problems of the cerebral palsied child are integrated into this family story with a refreshing lack of sentimentality. The Copeland family are also featured in Miss Little's third book, *Spring Begins in March*. This time Sal's younger sister, Meg, is featured. Meg's difficulties in personal relationships are told with insight and sympathy.

Although physical handicaps appear in several of Miss Little's books, it is the child's inter-personal relationships with peers and with adults which are her central pre-occupation. *Home from Far* and *Look Through My Window* explore the complexities of sibling relationships – both natural and adopted. The difficulty of losing a beloved brother and having him replaced in the family by a foster child is the theme of *Home from Far*. *Look Through My Window* portrays the shy, withdrawn only child and her relationship with four boisterous cousins. The heroines of both these books show Miss Little's empathy and sensitivity toward the "loner" in a gregarious world.

In both *Kate* and *One to Grow On* the adult/child conflict is the central theme. Miss Little's maturity as a writer is evident in *Kate*. It is the earliest of her books to display a realistic portrayal of adults. This ability to interpret the adult characters to the child-reader is further developed in *Stand in the Wind*.

It was only in *From Anna* that Miss Little tackled the handicap most familiar to her – limited vision. Anna's family feel she is stupid and slow because they do not realize that she needs eye glasses. When this is discovered, Anna attends a special class for the partially sighted and soon blossoms into a clever, happy child.

The strength in Miss Little's writing is her ability to write convincing dialogue and to establish her characters in time and place quickly and effectively. She often tries to do too much, however. In *From Anna* the heroine not only has a vision problem to overcome but also must adjust to a move from Germany to Canada. Yet, throughout all her books, Jean Little's personal feelings of optimism are pervasive and and she continues to share her joy in living with her young readers.

—Callie Israel

LIVELY, Penelope. British. Born in Cairo, Egypt, 17 March 1933. Educated at St. Anne's College, Oxford, B.A. (honours) in modern history 1956. Married Jack Lively in 1957; has one daughter and one son. Recipient: Library Association Carnegie Medal, 1974; Whitbread Literary Award, 1976. Agent: Murray Pollinger, 4 Garrick Street, London WC2E 9BH. Address: Fieldhead, 203 Myton Road, Warwick, England.

PUBLICATIONS FOR CHILDREN

Fiction

> *Astercote*, illustrated by Antony Maitland. London, Heinemann, 1970; New York, Dutton, 1971.
> *The Whispering Knights*, illustrated by Gareth Floyd. London, Heinemann, 1971; New York, Dutton, 1976.
> *The Wild Hunt of Hagworthy*, illustrated by Juliet Mozley. London, Heinemann, 1971; as *The Wild Hunt of the Ghost Hounds*, New York, Dutton, 1972.
> *The Driftway*. London, Heinemann, 1972; New York, Dutton, 1973.
> *The Ghost of Thomas Kempe*, illustrated by Antony Maitland. London, Heinemann, and New York, Dutton, 1973.
> *The House in Norham Gardens*. London, Heinemann, and New York, Dutton, 1974.
> *Going Back*. London, Heinemann, and New York, Dutton, 1975.

Boy Without a Name, illustrated by Ann Dalton.   London, Heinemann, and Berkeley, California, Parnassus Press, 1975.

A Stitch in Time.   London, Heinemann, and New York, Dutton, 1976.

The Stained Glass Window, illustrated by Michael Pollard.   London, Abelard Schuman, 1976.

Fanny's Sister.   London, Heinemann, 1977.

Play

Television Play: *Time Out of Mind,* 1976.

Other

The Presence of the Past: An Introduction to Landscape History.   London, Collins, 1976.

PUBLICATIONS FOR ADULTS

Novel

The Road to Lichfield.   London, Heinemann, 1977.

Play

Television Plays: *Boy Dominic* series (3 episodes), 1974.

Penelope Lively comments:

All my books for children reflect, in one way or another, my own interest in the workings of memory — whether personal or collective. They all seem to come out differently — memory fantastical, memory experimental, memory pastoral or historical or comical — but somehow, so far, the theme has persisted. My only excursion into non-fiction has been a respectful tribute to the history of the English landscape which I have found such a powerful inspiration.

*   *   *

Penelope Lively's first novel was published as recently as 1970, but she has rapidly established herself as one of the most interesting and rewarding of contemporary novelists for children. The books are very different, to such an extent indeed that children (who notoriously enjoy the "mixture as before") may be disappointed when they try one after enjoying another. To an adult one of the great pleasures of her work is her ability to create entirely fresh and individual books which are yet variations on the theme "we are what we have been." Mrs. Lively's concern is with identity through historical continuity. She is particularly interested in place, in the English landscape (from which she was separated during her most formative years as a child in Egypt) and in houses: "A house is a preservative," she has written, "a record of the lives it has sheltered."

The first book, *Astercote,* reflected an obsession the writer had at the time with deserted medieval villages. Mrs. Lively was rightly criticized for her failure to create living characters and convincing dialogue but the story was intriguing — and exciting. *The Whispering Knights* and the *The Wild Hunt of Hagworthy* explore two recurrent themes in English folklore. *The Driftway* is probably her least successful novel as far as child readers are concerned, but there is a great deal in it to absorb anyone interested in Penelope Lively's view of life. In *The Driftway,* she "wanted to use landscape as a channel for historical memory." She wrote about "a road, a perfectly ordinary road, the B4525 from Banbury to Northampton, but a road that is very ancient and seemed to lend itself perfectly to a double symbolism." This sounds a little pretentious and it should be made clear at once that Mrs. Lively is never pretentious. She is not trying to convey to children an appreciation of their own past and throwing in a story to make the message more palatable. The stories are seamless garments. As one critic has put it: "The concern isn't added to the story; rather the story is written out of it .... There are real children, changing in relation to their experiences. The novels are dense with life, with flux and growth."

The stories are good ones. Most accessible of all is the Carnegie medal-winner *The Ghost of Thomas Kempe*. Mrs. Lively says that in this book she was indulging a taste for ghosts. "It is a light hearted affair on the whole, but concerned with the serious matter of a child's awaking to the concept of memory." In fact, the serious matter is absorbed wholly in the comedy. It was the first book in which the writer seemed completely relaxed and in charge of her material. A lot of the fun derives from unlikely conjuctions: the ghost of a Jacobean sorcerer loose in a world of cake mixes, phone boxes, and biros.

Clever and delightful as it is, *Thomas Kempe* is a minor book compared with its successor *The House in Norham Gardens*. This is primarily the story of a quiet winter in the life of Clare Mayfield, aged 14, who lives with her great-aunts in a house in North Oxford with relics of the past. They acquire a couple of tenants: Maureen, who works for an estate agent, and John, an anthropology student from Uganda. Clare and her friend, Liz, eat baked beans and do their Latin homework together; she goes to London with John for the day; a Norfolk cousin stays the night. She has a bit part in the school *Macbeth*, and, finally, she has a bicycle accident and breaks her arm. These are the small outward events – but in Clare's mind other things are going on. This is a book about time and continuity and the relationship between the things we possess and the people we are.

Clare's great-grandfather was an anthropologist. In the attic in the house in Norham Gardens she finds one of the tamburans or ceremonial shields which he brought back from New Guinea in 1905. She becomes obsessed by this shield and the tribe it belonged to, who had no word for love in their language, no knowledge of their past, whose dead stayed with them as spirits, represented by the shields. Clare dreams about these people and feels she must return the shield. But when she does, in the hospital sleep after her accident, she knows it is too late for them. New Guinea is transformed before her eyes: the thatched huts become concrete bungalows; it is "time for Music Roundup" on the transistor radio and too late for tamburans. Clare gives the shield to the Pitt Rivers Museum. The winter is over and she chooses for her aunt's birthday not something from the antique shop (though the woman assures her "It's fashionable having old things") but a copper beech which will flourish for two hundred years. It is time to look forward.

Everything in this subtle, rich, compelling story is part of the pattern but there is nothing forced about the pattern; it seems entirely natural. Clare (a thinking, listening girl) and her aunts (early graduates, still interested in Africa and art though not in gutters or new pence) are entirely convincing – people one is glad to get to know. Mrs. Lively has certainly written more exciting books, but it is a considerable achievement to write so honestly about the long Sunday afternoons, the creeping clocks, the boredom of being 14, without ever being boring. Her relaxed, flexible style copes equally well with visits to the butcher and the brisk, useless doctor and with "the shadows of another world and another time."

Going Back is another considerable achievement. Again it is centred on a house, this time Medleycott, a house in Somerset, built at the turn of the century, with rose garden and tennis lawn, goldfish pond, stables and kitchen gardens. There is a great deal of circumstantial detail: splendid descriptions of the natural world ("clenched by frost" or "filmy with mist, the trees waist deep in it floating") and the convincing wartime background of land-girls and spam fritters, ration books, conscientious objectors, Spitfires and Hurricanes in playground games, and the knitting of balaclava helmets. But the war is incidental. It creates the situation and reinforces the alienation between Jane and Edward and their insensitive blustering father, who ultimately sends Edward away to school and precipitates the climax of the story. The suffering is real enough to make the reader weep.

The story is for the most part quiet and slow, but not easy to read. Mrs. Lively makes few concessions to a young reader. Her style is often elliptical and the vocabulary difficult (she prefers "benign and munificent" to "kind and generous"). There is no clear time scale. "In the head all springs are one spring," and characters come into focus only at particular moments, and sometimes not at all. But the tension of the narrative is beautifully sustained and it is never dull. We care passionately about what happens to Jane and Edward, especially Edward. Less is expected of Jane, the narrator, as she is a girl; the class and sexist attitudes of the time are clear and painful. We are never sure that what we remember is what actually happened, as Mrs. Lively says, but no one reading *Going Back* could forget it.

Again in *A Stitch in Time*, which won the Whitbread Prize, a house is at the centre: a rented house in Lyme Regis. "Places," she writes, are "like clocks – full of all the time there's ever been in them, and all the people, and all the things that have happened, like the ammonites in the stones." The ammonite reference is not a casual one, because the place this time is Lyme Regis and fossils are, of course, part of the story.

Maria Foster, only child of quiet boring parents, is not, like Jane Austen's young people, "wild to see Lyme." In fact, she is decidedly lukewarm about their holiday destination. Indeed, in spite of an agreeable habit of talking to inanimate objects and hearing their replies, Maria is rather a lukewarm dull girl. The book is a little lukewarm and dull itself. It lacks the richness of *The House in Norham Gardens*, the flow of *Going Back*, and the atmosphere of both of them. Children will, however, find it a much easier and more straightforward book. There is much to enjoy: the pleasure in knowing names (quercus ilex, grass vetchling, gryphaea), the contrasting families on either side of the holiday fence, the descriptions of days which might have been entirely different ones, and the reminder of days long past when a girl called Harriet had reluctantly stitched a sampler, with a swing which still creaks in the garden where there is no swing, and a dog which still barks in a house where there are no dogs.

In a slighter story for younger children, *Boy Without a Name*, Mrs. Lively leaves her usual practice of relating the past to the present and writes a story set entirely in the reign of Charles I about a small apprentice stone mason. Successful as the story is within its limits, one hopes Mrs. Lively will not turn herself into a historical novelist but will continue to explore the territory she has made so much her own. "We are all sustained by memory," as she says, and in her novels she has provided some very sustaining fare.

—Ann Thwaite

LIVINGSTON, Myra Cohn. American. Born in Omaha, Nebraska, 17 August 1926. Educated at Sarah Lawrence College, Bronxville, New York, B.A. 1948. Married Richard R. Livingston in 1952; has two sons and one daughter. Professional French horn player, 1940–48 (studied music with Darius Milhaud, 1944); Assistant Editor, *Campus* magazine, Los Angeles, 1948–50; worked in public relations for movie and musical personalities, 1949–52; Instructor in Creative Writing for Children, Dallas Public Library, 1959–64; Instructor, Los Angeles County Museum of Art, 1966–67, Beverly Hills Public Library, 1966–74, and University of California Elementary School, Los Angeles, 1972. Instructor, 1966–71, and since 1972, Poet-in-Residence, Beverly Hills Unified School District; since 1972, Extension Instructor, University of California, Los Angeles. Has lectured on poetry and conducted writing workshops throughout the United States since 1959. Agent: McIntosh and Otis, 475 Madison Avenue, New York, New York 10017. Address: 9308 Readcrest Drive, Beverly Hills, California 90210, U.S.A.

PUBLICATIONS FOR CHILDREN

Fiction (picture books)

I'm Hiding, illustrated by Erik Blegvad.   New York, Harcourt Brace, 1961.
See What I Found, illustrated by Erik Blegvad.   New York, Harcourt Brace, 1962.
I Talk to Elephants!, photographs by Isabel Gordon.   New York, Harcourt Brace, 1962.
I'm Not Me, illustrated by Erik Blegvad.   New York, Harcourt Brace, 1963.
Happy Birthday, illustrated by Erik Blegvad.   New York, Harcourt Brace, 1964.
I'm Waiting, illustrated by Erik Blegvad.   New York, Harcourt Brace, 1966.
Come Away, illustrated by Irene Haas.   New York, Atheneum, 1974.

Verse

Whispers and Other Poems, illustrated by Jacqueline Chwast.   New York, Harcourt Brace, 1958.
Wide Awake and Other Poems, illustrated by Jacqueline Chwast.   New York, Harcourt Brace, 1959.
The Moon and a Star and Other Poems, illustrated by Judith Shahn.   New York, Harcourt Brace, 1965.
Old Mrs. Twindlytart and Other Rhymes, illustrated by Enrico Arno.   New York, Harcourt Brace, 1967.
A Crazy Flight and Other Poems, illustrated by James Spanfeller.   New York, Harcourt Brace, 1969.
The Malibu and Other Poems, illustrated by James Spanfeller.   New York, Atheneum, 1974.
The Way Things Are and Other Poems, illustrated by Jenni Oliver.   New York, Atheneum, 1974.
4-Way Stop and Other Poems, illustrated by James Spanfeller.   New York, Atheneum, 1976.

Other

Editor, *A Tune Beyond Us: A Collection of Poetry*, illustrated by James Spanfeller. New York, Harcourt Brace, 1968.
Editor, *Speak Roughly to Your Little Boy: A Collection of Parodies and Burlesques*, illustrated by Joseph Low.   New York, Harcourt Brace, 1971.
Editor, *Listen, Children, Listen: An Anthology of Poems for the Very Young*, illustrated by Trina Schart Hyman.   New York, Harcourt Brace, 1972.
Editor, *What a Wonderful Bird the Frog Are: An Assortment of Humorous Poetry and Verse*.   New York, Harcourt Brace, 1973.
Editor, *The Poems of Lewis Carroll*.   New York, Crowell, 1973.
Editor, *One Little Room, An Everywhere: Poems of Love*, illustrated by Antonio Frasconi.   New York, Atheneum, 1975.
Editor, *O Frabjous Day: Poetry for Holidays and Special Occasions*.   New York, Atheneum, 1977.

PUBLICATIONS FOR ADULTS

Other

When You Are Alone/It Keeps You Capone: An Approach to Creative Writing for Children.   New York, Atheneum, 1973.
A Tribute to Lloyd Alexander.   Philadelphia, Drexel Institute, 1976.

Myra Cohn Livingston comments:

A deep respect for the emotions, sensitivities, and thoughts of young people as they differ from those of adults has always been of importance to me. *Whispers and Other Poems*, written when I was a college freshman, is a reflection of my own childhood, and although my recent poetry encompasses a more contemporary view of childhood, I feel I have never departed from the child I was; the child I know best. I am not consciously aware of writing *for* children: my poetry seems to be born of the genre of childhood. The thousands of young people with whom I share poetry and to whom I teach something of the writing of it reinforce, for me, the feeling that the early years encompass a freshness and wonder that must be nurtured, a curiosity and celebration of the simple things which each succeeding generation discovers anew. As an anthologist I am conscious of choosing those poems which speak to the young in a diction and emotional climate to which they can relate – something of the universal experience from poets of all ages and countries which may serve as an insight toward the individual growth and humanization of the reader.

*   *   *

An unusual capacity to relate to the small child and the small child's experiences is the principal quality of Myra Cohn Livingston's poetry. As subject matter she chooses early childhood, singling out for description and for wonder such simple and yet characteristic experiences as whispers or roller skating, puddles or bus riding.

People whom the child sees regularly, like the father or the driver of the school bus, are frequently subjects of Livingston's poems. She pictures between the child and the other person relationships that are comfortable and unsentimental. Livingston writes of childhood in a way that seems to involve the child him or herself; the persona is a child as he or she sees leaves in the park, makes mudpies or wonders at the dead bird.

Much of Livingston's poetry, brief and succinct as it is, has a strong sense of place. Her subject is often the seashore with the sand, the grunions, the tides, the salt water creatures either seen or lunched on. Sea anemones and sand crabs figure with a regularity that shows familiar acquaintance with the ocean. Settings also include the mountains, as the persona climbs, gazes, or is amazed. The city child is also aware of the excitement of that environment; Livingston refers to city play, city views, city ways, city freeway, zoo, and library.

Stylistically, Livingston relies to a large extent upon imagery. Often she compares an auditory sensation to tactile or visual impressions in imaginative and detailed but brief poems. Her tone is often lively, gay with laughter or delight.

Many of Livingston's verses are casual in form or appearance; her later collections are filled with free verse. Her most successful poems, however, seem to be those in which she is insistent upon brevity and conciseness, on the intensity of experience that comes with condensation of idea into brief and explicit image. Livingston has edited a number of collections of poetry for children; these collections show wide knowledge and keen appreciation of the excellence of other poets' work.

—Rebecca J. Lukens

LOBEL, Anita. American. Born in Krakow, Poland, 3 June 1934; emigrated to the United States in 1952; naturalized, 1956. Educated at schools in Stockholm and New York City; Pratt Institute, Brooklyn, New York, graduated 1955; Brooklyn Museum Art School. Married Arnold Lobel, *q.v.*, in 1955; has one daughter and one son. Textile designer and free-lance illustrator. Recipient (for illustration): *New York Times* award, 1965; *Book World* Festival award, 1972. Address: c/o Harper and Row Inc., 10 East 53rd Street, New York, New York 10022, U.S.A.

PUBLICATIONS FOR CHILDREN (illustrated by the author)

Fiction

Sven's Bridge. New York, Harper, 1965.
The Troll Music. New York, Harper, 1966.
Potatoes, Potatoes. New York, Harper, 1967; Kingswood, Surrey, World's Work, 1969.
The Seamstress of Salzburg. New York, Harper, 1970.
Under a Mushroom. New York, Harper, 1970; Kingswood, Surrey, World's Work, 1972.
A Birthday for the Princess. New York, Harper, 1973; Kingswood, Surrey, World's Work, 1975.

Other

King Rooster, Queen Hen. New York, Morrow, and London, Macmillan, 1975.

Illustrator: *Cock-a-Doodle Doo! Cock-a-Doodle Dandy!* by Paul Kapp, 1966; *Puppy Summer* by Meindert De Jong, 1966; *The Wishing Penny and Other Stories,* 1967; *Indian Summer* by F.N. Monjo, 1968; *The Little Wooden Farmer* by Alice Dalgliesh, 1968; *The Wisest Man in the World* 1968, and *How the Tsar Drinks Tea,* 1971 by Benjamin Elkin; *The Uproar,* 1970, and *Little John,* 1972, by Doris Orgel; *Three Rolls and One Doughnut* edited by Mirra Ginsburg, 1970; *Soldier, Soldier, Won't You Marry Me?* by John Langstaff, 1972; *One for the Price of Two* by Cynthia Jameson, 1972; *Clever Kate* by Elizabeth Shub, 1973; *Christmas Crafts* by Carolyn Meyer, 1974; *Peter Penny's Dance* by Janet Quin-Harkin, 1976; *How the Rooster Saved the Day* by Arnold Lobel, 1977.

*   *   *

Anita Lobel is both a superb illustrator and a fine author. With seven books to her credit (she's illustrated an additional 18), she can be counted on to give the reader a very good time. One has the feeling that she enjoyed herself immensely when she wrote each book, and this sense of quiet fun readily comes through the printed page. Fantasy is her special domain, but even fantasy must seem real during the reading or it cannot hold the reader. Ms. Lobel is very much aware of this, and her characters, whoever – or whatever – they may be, always behave in a logical manner. Because she often illustrates the book she writes, there is a perfect union of story and pictures. It is not surprising that very young connoisseurs put Anita Lobel very high on their lists of favorite authors. Her style is clear; her language is simple without insulting the intelligence of her young readers. And she tells a whopping good story; it has the feeling of being told rather than being read. This is especially true in *A Birthday for the Princess* a delightful story with an old-fashioned fairy-tale flavor. But Ms. Lobel's books, even though aimed at the very young, often have a serious side, too. In *Potatoes, Potatoes,* she handles the subject of war and peace with skill and with an understanding of her audience. In *Under a Mushroom,* her sensitivity to children's love of detail in both pictures and words is clearly evident. Her artist's eye helps her to create word pictures that conjure up scenes in the reader's imagination – something that not many authors can achieve. Even without illustrations, many of Ms. Lobel's stories hold up; that is unfortunately not true of many picture books. While illustrations do enhance her stories, it is the tale itself that is important. Though many of her books have a long-ago-and-far-away feeling, they are modern tales with a magical, timeless quality that makes them great reading at any time, at any age.

—Rubie Saunders

LOBEL, Arnold.   American.   Born in Los Angeles, California, 22 May 1933. Educated at the Pratt Institute, Brooklyn, New York, B.F.A. 1955. Married Anita Lobel, *q.v.*, in 1955; has one daughter and one son. Recipient: *New York Times* award, for illustration, 1963, 1974 (twice), 1976; Christopher Award, 1972; Bank Street College of Education Irma Black Award, 1973. Address: c/o Harper and Row Inc., 10 East 53rd Street, New York, New York 10022, U.S.A.

PUBLICATIONS FOR CHILDREN (illustrated by the author)

Fiction

> *A Zoo for Mister Muster.*   New York, Harper, 1962.
> *A Holiday for Mister Muster.*   New York, Harper, 1963.
> *Prince Bertram the Bad.*   New York, Harper, 1963; Kingswood, Surrey, World's Work, 1970.
> *Giant John.*   New York, Harper, 1964; Kingswood, Surrey, World's Work, 1965.
> *Lucille.*   New York, Harper, and Kingswood, Surrey, World's Work, 1964.
> *The Bears of the Air.*   New York, Harper, 1965; Kingswood, Surrey, World's Work, 1966.
> *The Great Blueness and Other Predicaments.*   New York, Harper, 1968; Kingswood, Surrey, World's Work, 1970.
> *Small Pig.*   New York, Harper, 1969; Kingswood, Surrey, World's Work, 1970.
> *Frog and Toad Are Friends.*   New York, Harper, 1970; Kingswood, Surrey, World's Work, 1971.
> *Mouse Tales.*   New York, Harper, 1972; Kingswood, Surrey, World's Work, 1973.
> *Frog and Toad Together.*   New York, Harper, 1972; Kingswood, Surrey, World's Work, 1973.
> *Owl at Home.*   New York, Harper, 1975; Kingswood, Surrey, World's Work, 1976.
> *Frog and Toad All Year.*   New York, Harper, 1976.
> *How the Rooster Saved the Day*, illustrated by Anita Lobel.   New York, Morrow, and London, Hamish Hamilton, 1977.
> *Mouse Soup.*   New York, Harper, 1977.

Verse

> *Martha, The Movie Mouse.*   New York, Harper, 1966; Kingswood, Surrey, World's Work, 1967.
> *The Ice-Cream Cone Coot and Other Rare Birds.*   New York, Parents' Magazine Press, 1971.
> *On the Day Peter Stuyvesant Sailed into Town.*   New York, Harper, 1971.
> *The Man Who Took Indoors Out.*   New York, Harper, 1974; Kingswood, Surrey, World's Work, 1976.

Illustrator: *Bibletime, Hebrew Dictionary, Holiday Dictionary*, all by Sol Scharfstein, 1958; *Red Tag Comes Back* by Fred Phleger, 1961; *Little Runner of the Longhouse* by Betty Baker, 1962; *Terry and the Caterpillars*, 1962, *Greg's Microscope*, 1963, *Let's Get Turtles*, 1965, and *Benny's Animals*, 1966, all by Millicent E. Selsam; *Let's Be Indians*, 1962, *Let's Be Early Settlers with Daniel Boone*, 1967, and *Dinosaur Time*, 1974, all by Peggy Parish; *The Secret Three*, 1963, and *Ants Are Fun*, 1968, by Mildred Myrick; *The Quarreling Book*, 1963, and *Someday*, 1965, by Charlotte Zolotow; *Red Fox and His Canoe*, 1964, *Oscar Otter*, 1966, *The Strange Disappearance of Arthur Cluck*, 1967, and *Sam the Minuteman*, 1969, all by Nathaniel Benchley; *Dudley Pippin* by Phil Ressner, 1965; *The Witch on the Corner* by Felice Holman, 1966; *The Star Thief* by Andrea Di Noto, 1967; *The Four Little Children Who Went round the World*, 1968, and *The New Vestments*, 1970, by Edward Lear; *The Comic*

Adventures of Old Mother Hubbard by Sarah Catherine Martin, 1968; *Junk Day on Juniper Street* by Lilian Moore, 1969; *The Terrible Tiger*, 1969, *Circus*, 1974, and *Nightmares*, 1976, by Jack Prelutsky; *I'll Fix Anthony* by Judith Viorst, 1969; *Tot Botot and His Little Flute* by Laura E. Cathon, 1970; *Hansel and Gretel* by the Grimm Brothers, 1971; *The Master of Miracle* by Sulamith Ish-Kishor, 1971; *Hildilid's Night* by Cheli Ryan, 1971; *Seahorse* by Robert A. Morris, 1972; *Miss Suzy's Easter Surprise*, 1972, *Miss Suzy's Christmas*, 1973, and *Miss Suzy's Birthday*, 1974, all by Miriam Young; *Good Ethan* by Paula Fox, 1973; *The Clay Pot Boy* by Cynthia Jameson, 1973; *As I Was Crossing Boston Common* by Norma Farber, 1973; *As Right As Right Can Be* by Anne K. Rose, 1976; *Merry, Merry FIBruary* by Doris Orgel, 1977.

*   *   *

Arnold Lobel is not only a fine illustrator of children's books, but he is a sensitive author who can delight children (and adults, too) with his stories. The author of almost 20 books (he's illustrated over 40), Mr. Lobel combines fantasy and realism in such a smooth way that readers have no difficulty in becoming fast friends with talking mice, as in *Mouse Tales*, and other creatures. But he does not limit himself to the animal kingdom. His human characters, even in the short span of a picture book, grow and develop and behave in a logical way. Like all professional children's book authors, Mr. Lobel does not insult the intelligence of his audience, nor does he underestimate it. He knows that a good story is one that can stand many readings, both by children and their parents, without going stale. Because he is such a prolific author, it is difficult to zero in on one or two titles. While each book is different from its predecessors, each has the unmistakeable stamp of Mr. Lobel's talent. His sense of fun runs rampant in *The Comic Adventures of Old Mother Hubbard*, while *The Ice-Cream Cone Coot and Other Rare Birds* displays his sense of the ridiculous. His sensitivity is clearly shown in *Mouse Tales* – no child would have the least difficulty in identifying with these tiny creatures. There are not many authors who can convey these feelings in both words and pictures, but that double talent is what helps to make Mr. Lobel one of the leading juvenile authors of the day. While he is a reasonably prolific author, each book clearly shows great attention was paid to each detail. Each word is exactly right; each character is real (whether it's a human being or not); each plot has a logical development. The freshness of Mr. Lobel's style belies the amount of careful thought that must go into each story.

—Rubie Saunders

LOCKE, Elsie (Violet).   New Zealander.   Born in Hamilton, 17 August 1912. Educated at Waiuku school, 1917–29; Auckland University, B.A. 1933. Married John Gibson Locke in 1941; has two sons and two daughters. Secretary, Woman Today Society, and Member of the Editorial Committee, *Woman Today* magazine, Wellington, 1937–39. Member of the National Committee, New Zealand Campaign for Nuclear Disarmament, 1956–65. Recipient: Katherine Mansfield Award (*Landfall* magazine), for essay, 1958. Address: 392 Oxford Terrace, Christchurch 1, New Zealand.

PUBLICATIONS FOR CHILDREN

Fiction

   The Runaway Settlers, illustrated by Antony Maitland.   Auckland, Blackwood and
      Janet Paul, and London, Cape, 1965; New York, Dutton, 1966.

The End of the Harbour, illustrated by Katrina Mataira. Auckland, Blackwood and
    Janet Paul, and London, Cape, 1968.
Moko's Hideout, illustrated by Elisabeth Plumridge and Beatrice Foster-
    Barham. Christchurch, Whitcoulls, 1976.
The Boy with the Snowgrass Hair, with Ken Dawson, illustrated by Joan
    Oates. Christchurch, Whitcoulls, 1976.

Other

A Land Without a Master. Wellington, Department of Education, 1962.
Viet-nam. Wellington, Department of Education, 1963.
Six Colonies in One Country, illustrated by Stephen Furlonger. Wellington,
    Department of Education, 1964.
Provincial Jigsaw Puzzle, illustrated by Stephen Furlonger. Wellington, Department of
    Education, 1965.
The Long Uphill Climb: New Zealand, 1876–1891, illustrated by David A.
    Cowe. Wellington, Department of Education, 1966.
High Ground for a New Nation, illustrated by David A. Cowe. Wellington, Department
    of Education, 1967.
The Hopeful Peace and the Hopeful War, illustrated by David A. Cowe. Wellington,
    Department of Education, 1968.
Growing Points and Prickles: Life in New Zealand, 1920–1960, illustrated by Cath
    Brown and R.E. Brockie. Christchurch, Whitcombe and Tombs, 1971.
It's the Same Old Earth, illustrated by Victor Ambrus. Wellington, Department of
    Education, 1973.
Maori King and British Queen (textbook), illustrated by Murray Grimsdale.
    Amersham, Buckinghamshire, Hulton, 1974.
Look under the Leaves (ecology), edited by David Young and David Ault, illustrated by
    David Waddington. Christchurch, Pumpkin Press, 1975.
Snow to Low Levels: Interaction in a Disaster. Christchurch, Whitcoulls, 1976.
The Crayfishermen and the Sea. Christchurch, Whitcoulls, 1976.

PUBLICATIONS FOR ADULTS

Verse

The Time of the Child: A Sequence of Poems. Christchurch, privately printed, 1954.

Other

The Shepherd and the Scullery-Maid. Christchurch, New Zealand Communist Party,
    1950.
The Human Conveyor Belt. Christchurch, Caxton Press, 1968.
The Roots of the Clover: The Story of the Collett Sisters and Their Families. Privately
    printed, 1971.
Discovering the Morrisons: A Pioneer Family History. Privately printed, 1976.

Editor, *Gordon Watson, New Zealander, 1912–1945: His Life and Writings*.
    Auckland, New Zealand Communist Party, 1949.

Elsie Locke comments:
    Although as a child I walked to school with serial stories writing themselves in my head, I
did not settle down to being a writer until my own children were growing into their teens. By
that time I was thoroughly hooked on children's books, and my own ideas were budding, and

still keep budding from year to year. To me, writing a story for children is a way of sharing. Naturally I share those themes that stir my interest, imagination, sympathy, sense of fun, delight and concern. History, nature, and peace get into my books because I am keen about these matters. My grandparents and great-grandparents were pioneers in the early days of New Zealand. Around the family fireside I listened to many adventurous tales and I think today's children might like to do the same. Whether my readers live in New Zealand and enjoy the familiar settings, or somewhere else and find the settings exotic, I am giving them a small piece of a big world whose glory is the great variety of places and peoples and languages and customs – not to mention all the other living things, the sky and land and the sea. My best-known work is *The Runaway Settlers*.

*   *   *

Authenticity is the keynote of Elsie Locke's writing: authenticity of subject-matter, in the painstaking research behind her historical writing and her concern to present things "as they are"; authentic respect for the mores and rights of individuals of all ages and colours; authenticity of purpose – the explication of situations and events, and introduction of the reader to social, moral and political issues; authenticity of style – never fussy or over-written, patronising or self-indulgent but precise, lucid, economical and effective.

She is essentially a moral writer; she works with material which (then or now) involves choices and conflicts, decisions about right and wrong. Modern criticism of children's literature as elitist or escapist does not touch her, since she most often deals with the ordinary person, struggling or oppressed. The runaway Small family in *The Runaway Settlers*, the communities caught up in the spreading hostility of the New Zealand "Land Wars" in *The End of the Harbour*, the Forscutt family struggling to survive a recent major snowstorm in *Snow to Low Levels*, are all examples. Her characters are involved in moral choices – the boys David and Hona maintaining their friendship in a situation of increasing tension between Maori and pakeha; Mrs. Small defending the rights of her sons against the powerful and exploiting landowner; the inclusion of both unionisation and the New Zealand misrule of Samoa in the 20th-century history *Growing Points and Prickles*. In particular, she presents the Maoris not as inferior or quaint but as inheritors and representatives of a serious, dignified and sophisticated culture.

Though her purposes are moral, she is not moralistic; though educational, she is not a pedant; though she chooses the issues, the reader is left to judge them. Sadness and liveliness, humour and tears, the hard adventures of the early settlers, and, above all, relationships between individuals carry the story and the child reading it.

—Wendy Jago

LOFTING, Hugh (John).   British.   Born in Maidenhead, Berkshire, 14 January 1886. Educated at Mount St. Mary's College, Chesterfield, Derbyshire; Massachusetts Institute of Technology, Cambridge, 1904; London Polytechnic, 1905. Served in the Irish Guards in Flanders, 1916–17. Married Flora W. Small in 1911 (died, 1927), one son and one daughter; Katherine Harrower-Peters, 1928 (died, 1929); Josephine Fricker, 1935, one son. Prospector and surveyor in Canada, 1908–09; Civil Engineer, Lagos Railway, West Africa, 1910–11; worked for British Ministry of Information, New York, 1915. Settled in the United States, 1919. Recipient: American Library Association Newbery Medal, 1923. *Died 27 September 1947.*

PUBLICATIONS FOR CHILDREN (illustrated by the author)

Fiction

The Story of Dr. Dolittle, Being the History of His Peculiar Life and Astonishing
    Adventures in Foreign Parts. New York, Stokes, and London, Cape, 1920.
The Voyages of Dr. Dolittle. New York, Stokes, 1922; London, Cape, 1923.
Dr. Dolittle's Post Office. New York, Stokes, and London, Cape, 1923.
The Story of Mrs. Tubbs. New York, Stokes, 1923; London, Cape, 1924.
Dr. Dolittle's Circus. New York, Stokes, and London, Cape, 1924.
Dr. Dolittle's Zoo. New York, Stokes, 1925; London, Cape, 1926.
Dr. Dolittle's Caravan. New York, Stokes, 1926; London, Cape, 1927.
Dr. Dolittle's Garden. New York, Stokes, 1927; London, Cape, 1928.
Dr. Dolittle in the Moon. New York, Stokes, 1928; London, Cape, 1929.
Noisy Nora. New York, Stokes, and London, Cape, 1929.
The Twilight of Magic, illustrated by Lois Lenski. New York, Stokes, and London,
    Cape, 1930.
Gub Gub's Book: An Encyclopedia of Food. New York, Stokes, and London, Cape,
    1932.
Dr. Dolittle's Return. New York, Stokes, and London, Cape, 1933.
Tommy, Tilly and Mrs. Tubbs. New York, Stokes, 1936; London, Cape, 1937.
Dr. Dolittle and the Secret Lake. Philadelphia, Lippincott, 1948; London, Cape, 1949.
Dr. Dolittle and the Green Canary. Philadelphia, Lippincott, 1950; London, Cape,
    1951.
Dr. Dolittle's Puddleby Adventures. Philadelphia, Lippincott, 1952; London, Cape,
    1953.

Verse

Porridge Poetry: Cooked, Ornamented, and Served by Hugh Lofting. New York,
    Stokes, 1924; London, Cape, 1925.

Other

Dr. Dolittle's Birthday Book. New York, Stokes, 1935.

PUBLICATIONS FOR ADULTS

Verse

Victory for the Slain. London, Cape, 1942.

Critical Study: Hugh Lofting by Edward Blishen, in Three Bodley Head Monographs,
London, Bodley Head, 1968.

*   *   *

The stubby, square-nosed Dr. Dolittle, animal doctor extraordinary from Puddleby-on-the-Marsh, is one of the most popular and enduring of children's heroes. The man who invented him, Hugh Lofting, imagined a figure whose innocence and common sense anchored the most fantastic of adventures firmly within the limits of credibility. For it is the essentially pedestrian nature of the Doctor's style – from his unperturbed expression to his plain language and practical solutions – that makes the whole lunatic world he inhabits possible.

Hugh Lofting was a young soldier serving in Flanders during the First World War – and much concerned about the terrible conditions and fate of the Army horses – when he conceived of Dr. Dolittle, a doctor turned animal vet who, because he learns the languages of his patients, is able to enter worlds and adventures inconceivable to others.

Neither the fantasy nor the subject were wholly alien to Hugh Lofting's character. As a child he had kept a miniature zoo and wild life museum in his mother's linen cupboard and had enjoyed making up stories for his brothers and sisters. After an education in a Jesuit school, Hugh Lofting worked for a time as an architect, then became a civil engineer and visited Canada, Africa and the West Indies. These facts are important. Both the nature of his work and the places he saw provided him with a rich fund of material and settings for the Doctor's voyages – he had a keen eye for detail and an obvious love of travel.

The first Dr. Dolittle stories, written from the trenches in letters home, were intended to make his two small children laugh. Dr. Dolittle was at first a comic character, a man who got into muddles. Even his appearance, as illustrations in the margins of the letters showed, was a little ludicrous: a portly, ungainly man, wearing clothes that could have been smart and yet were somehow too big and quite inappropriate. It was only in later books, perhaps as Hugh Lofting himself became older and more disillusioned by the war, that the Doctor changes. His lightheartedness gives way to seriousness, and the compassionate side to his nature is constantly emphasised in accounts of his hatred of all aggression and bullying, his growing disapproval of hunting, ill-run zoos, and pet shops.

In the first of what were to be twelve separate books on the doctor's adventures, *The Story of Dr. Dolittle*, Dr. John Dolittle is simply an ordinary doctor, with human patients. The trouble is that he keeps so many animals as pets, appearing to prefer their company, that one by one his patients, irritated and alarmed by the other occupants of his house, forsake him. Even his sister Sarah, anxious about the dwindling income, leaves.

Finally his only remaining patient is Matthew Mugg, the Cat's-Meat-Man, who suggests that the doctor should start earning his living instead as an animal doctor. Polynesia, the doctor's wise and somewhat dictatorial parrot, offers to teach him the language of the animals, starting with the ABC of birds. Before long, Puddleby-on-the-Marsh is transformed by the presence of short-sighted cart horses in spectacles. Dr. Dolittle's success is assured. Because he can actually communicate with the animals, they can tell him what is wrong with them, rather than leaving the diagnosis up to guess-work.

Dr. Dolittle's first adventure takes him to the Land of the Monkeys in Africa to cure thousands of sick gorillas, orang outangs, chimpanzees and marmosettes. The grateful patients present him with a pushmi-pullyu, a shy animal with a head at each end who eats with one mouth and talks with another, and with a marked character of his own, like the Doctor's other friends. Chee-Chee, the monkey, is nervous, and Too-Too, the owl, wise. Dabdab is a practical duck who becomes the Doctor's housekeeper. Gub Gub the pig is very greedy, and as such the natural butt of Hugh Lofting's obvious love of puns, jokes, and comic situations. Later books introduce Dobbin the horse, Sophie the seal, and a strange and unfathomable moon cat called Iffy. There are dozens more.

The books are also something of an education. While subsequent adventures take the Doctor to ever more outlandish places – the Moon, the Secret Lake – Hugh Lofting nonetheless manages to provide a good deal of practical and detailed information about geography, vegetation, species of animal, and some history, for example, references to Wilberforce and the slave trade (approximately the period in which the stories are set).

Lofting's other books for children lack the magic of Dr. Dolittle. The first of the Doctor's adventures was published, to immediate critic success, in New York in 1920. It was illustrated, as they all were, by the author's charming, somewhat dotty pen and ink drawings, which are quite as much part of the books as the stories themselves and in some ways even more memorable.

Recently Hugh Lofting has come in for attack for his use of words like "nigger" and "coon" and for his comical portrayal of the "savages" he encounters. These are uncharacteristic and thoughtless lapses in books that are otherwise so carefully designed. But it should not be allowed to spoil their real worth: their innocence, the lack of all whimsy, and the fact that Hugh Lofting was a genuinely original writer with an unusually inventive mind and a great gift for adventure.

—Caroline Moorehead

LYNCH, Patricia (Nora). Irish. Born in Cork, 7 June 1898. Educated at convent school, and secular schools in Ireland, Scotland, England and Belgium. Married Richard Michael Fox in 1922. Feature Writer, *Christian Commonwealth*, Dublin, 1918–20. Recipient: Tailteann Festival Silver Medal, 1947. *Died 1 September 1972.*

<small>PUBLICATIONS FOR CHILDREN</small>

Fiction

The Green Dragon. London, Harrap, 1925.

The Turf-Cutter's Donkey, illustrated by Jack B. Yeats. London, Dent, 1934; New York, Dutton, 1935.

The Turf-Cutter's Donkey Goes Visiting, illustrated by George Altendorf. London, Dent, 1935; as *The Donkey Goes Visiting*, New York, Dutton, 1936.

King of the Tinkers, illustrated by Katherine C. Lloyd. London, Dent, and New York, Dutton, 1938.

The Turf-Cutter's Donkey Kicks Up His Heels, illustrated by Eileen Coghlan. New York, Dutton, 1939; London, Dent, 1952.

The Grey Goose of Kilnevin, illustrated by John Keating. London, Dent, 1939; New York, Dutton, 1940.

Fiddler's Quest, illustrated by Isobel Morton-Sale. London, Dent, 1941; New York, Dutton, 1943.

Long Ears: The Story of a Little Grey Donkey, illustrated by Joan Kiddell-Monroe. London, Dent, 1943.

Strangers at the Fair and Other Stories, illustrated by Eileen Coghlan. Dublin, Browne and Nolan, 1945; London, Penguin, 1949.

Lisheen at the Valley Farm and Other Stories, with Helen Staunton and Teresa Deevy. Dublin, Gayfield Press, 1945.

The Cobbler's Apprentice, illustrated by Alfred Kerr. London, Hollis and Carter, 1947.

Brogeen of the Stepping Stones, illustrated by Alfred Kerr. London, Kerr Cross, 1947.

The Mad O'Haras, illustrated by Elizabeth Rivers. London, Dent, 1948; as *Grania of Castle O'Hara*, Boston, Page, 1952.

The Dark Sailor of Youghal, illustrated by Jerome Sullivan. London, Dent, 1951.

The Boy at the Swinging Lantern, illustrated by Joan Kiddell-Monroe. London, Dent, 1952.

Brogeen Follows the Magic Tune, illustrated by Peggy Fortnum. London, Burke, 1952; New York, Macmillan, 1968.

Delia Daly of Galloping Green, illustrated by Joan Kiddell-Monroe. London, Dent, 1953.

Brogeen and the Green Shoes, illustrated by Peggy Fortnum. London, Burke, 1953.

Brogeen and the Bronze Lizard, illustrated by Grace Golden. London, Burke, 1954; New York, Macmillan, 1970.

Orla of Burren, illustrated by Joan Kiddell-Monroe. London, Dent, 1954.

Tinker Boy, illustrated by Harry Kernoff. London, Dent, 1955.

Brogeen and the Princess of Sheen, illustrated by Christopher Brooker. London, Burke, 1955.

The Bookshop on the Quay, illustrated by Peggy Fortnum. London, Dent, 1956.

Brogeen and the Lost Castle, illustrated by Christopher Brooker. London, Burke, 1956.

Fiona Leaps the Bonfire, illustrated by Peggy Fortnum. London, Dent, 1957; as *Shane Comes to Dublin*, New York, Criterion Books, 1958.

Cobbler's Luck, illustrated by Christopher Brooker. London, Burke, 1957.

The Old Black Sea Chest: A Story of Bantry Bay, illustrated by Peggy Fortnum. London, Dent, 1958.

Brogeen and the Black Enchanter, illustrated by Christopher Brooker.   London, Burke, 1958.
The Stone House at Kilgobbin, illustrated by Christopher Brooker.   London, Burke, 1959.
Jinny the Changeling, illustrated by Peggy Fortnum.   London, Dent, 1959.
The Runaways.   Oxford, Blackwell, 1959.
Sally from Cork, illustrated by Elizabeth Grant.   London, Dent, 1960.
The Lost Fisherman of Carrigmor, illustrated by Christopher Brooker.   London, Burke, 1960.
Ryan's Fort, illustrated by Elizabeth Grant.   London, Dent, 1961.
The Longest Way Round, illustrated by D.G. Valentine.   London, Burke, 1961.
The Golden Caddy, illustrated by Juliette Palmer.   London, Dent, 1962.
Brogeen and the Little Wind, illustrated by Beryl Sanders.   London, Burke, 1962.
The House by Lough Neagh, illustrated by Nina Ross.   London, Dent, 1963.
Brogeen and the Red Fez, illustrated by Beryl Sanders.   London, Burke, 1963.
Holiday at Rosquin, illustrated by Mary Shillabeer.   London, Dent, 1964.
Guests at the Beech Tree, illustrated by Beryl Sanders.   London, Burke, 1964.
The Twisted Key and Other Stories, illustrated by Joan Kiddell-Monroe.   London, Harrap, 1964.
Mona of the Isle, illustrated by Mary Shillabeer.   London, Dent, 1965.
Back of Beyond, illustrated by Susannah Holden.   London, Dent, 1966.
The Kerry Caravan, illustrated by James Hunt.   London, Dent, 1967.

Other

Knights of God: Stories of the Irish Saints, illustrated by Alfred Kerr.   London, Hollis and Carter, 1945; Chicago, Regnery, 1955.
The Seventh Pig and Other Irish Fairy Tales, illustrated by Jerome Sullivan.   London, Dent, 1950; revised edition, as *The Black Goat of Slievemore and Other Irish Tales*, 1959.
Tales of Irish Enchantment (legends), illustrated by Fergus O'Ryan.   Dublin, Clonmore and Reynolds, and London, Burns and Oates, 1952.

PUBLICATIONS FOR ADULTS

Other

A Story-Teller's Childhood (autobiography).   London, Dent, 1947; New York, Norton, 1962.

                                   *   *   *

Country gatherings like fairs and races and tinker encampments play a large part in Patricia Lynch's stories, and to the natural bustle and exuberance of these events and places a magic element is often added. At the fair in *The Turf-Cutter's Donkey*, Eileen and Seamus are followed around by a small man and a pig, and the children find that they can fly simply by jumping in the air. But Eileen's boots have been mended by a leprechaun, and this makes plausible the elaborate sequence of events that follows. In the Long Ears series, magic is unrestrained and owes a great deal to the type of Irish folk tale that deals in talking animals and bewildering changes in settings and objects. Usually an odd collection of characters is brought together: a couple of children, a ballad singer, an apple woman, a leprechaun, tinker, changeling, or captain of a barge. Action is continuous and always directed towards the achievement of a moral resolution. The goal of the central characters is domestic cosiness, and often they are waifs and strays to make the point more telling.

Sheila, in *The Grey Goose of Kilnevin*, is sent on an errand to Bridgie Swallow, and at once a formal pattern is established: the ritualized quest, with tests and trials at every step. Sheila gets the three pounds of butter and much else besides; like all Patricia Lynch's heroines she is clever and spirited and always ready to share her few possessions with any strangers that she may meet along the road. A number of peculiar alliances result from the latter: a fox makes friends with the little grey goose, and a scarecrow provides a coat for the Ballad singer.

The fantasy is usually down-to-earth with a strong rough-and-tumble flavour; but sometimes the characters are taken right off the ground and swept into a mythological realm. This is not always successful. The author has made good use of the standard figures of Irish legend and myth: the wise woman of the mountain; the fool who recovers his wits; the Fianna, ancient warrior band; the salmon of knowledge; the Children of Lir who were changed into swans by a malicious stepmother; and so on. But Patricia Lynch has no sense of the numinous and sometimes the magical episodes have a picture postcard element when they aren't enlivened by sheer rumbustious humour.

Two excellent stories with no supernatural overtones appeared in the 1940's: *Fiddler's Quest* and *The Mad O'Haras*. Again, in each of these we have the movement towards emotional security. In the former, Ethne Cadogan, the fiddler of the title, comes to Ireland to search for her traditional home Inniscoppal (the Island of Horses) and her itinerant grandfather. Unusually, the book has an urban setting, a courtyard in Dublin; it is also the only novel by Patricia Lynch to exploit the romantic aspect of Irish nationalism:

> "A man on *The Granuaile* told me that Dublin is the City of the Troubles," whispered Ethne. "That means fighting, doesn't it?"
> "There's always fighting somewhere," said Nono wisely. "I hate it, but I'd do anything for Nial; so would Eamon – he's a hero!"

Nial Desmond is a Republican on the run; at one point in the narrative Ethne and the Rafferty children drive a cartload of guns through an army barricade. Suspense is maintained admirably through a series of incidents that includes shooting and evacuation. The book has a kind of realism that is not found often in her work, and it is offset to good effect by the use of familiar stereotypes like the ballad singer and the storyteller.

Ethne the fiddler is a talented child; like Grania in *The Mad O'Haras* she has plans for a career. Grania won't submit to convention, unlike her cousin Sally who longs to be a jockey but works as a hairdresser, a suitable girl's occupation. Patricia Lynch's heroines face up to opposition and overcome it. Grania means to be a painter, and wins a scholarship to a Dublin art school. First, however, she helps to solve the problems of her wild relatives in whom the ramshackle, devil-may-care quality of Irish life is embodied. The romantic O'Haras have tinker blood and live in a tumbledown castle. The perennial Irish theme of "bad blood" is indicated here, but naturally in the children's book context it is muted and easily resolved.

There is no complexity of situation or motive in Patricia Lynch's stories, and little attempt at character differentiation. The central characters are effectively interchangeable. The predominant virtue is kindness, and if its rewards are sometimes disproportionate this is acceptable in terms of the rigid fairy-tale structure. Even the straightforward children's novels have a simplified moral basis. The author went on producing alternate fantasy and family tales along the lines that she had laid down in the 1930's and early 40's. In *Tinker Boy*, for instance, there is acknowledgement of the glamour of vagabond life; but the tinkers' apparent lawlessness is really an illusion. It was always easy to get the better of the dreadful King of the Tinkers with his spotted kerchief. When villainy is larger than life it ceases to be frightening, and of course many of Patricia Lynch's books are for younger children who can relish without question the white pigs and mermaids and changelings and magic boots.

Jinny the Changeling employs familiar motifs: the four swans, the quest for a missing father, the swirling mists that are conjured up to mask queer goings-on. The Clerys are a poor but generous family whose fortunes begin to change when they find a baby in a clump of bushes. ("You're a dote of a Changeling," everyone says about Jinny.) As usual when she tries to be poetic about the supernatural Patricia Lynch descends into a kind of vulgarity: it is all pretty-pretty where it should be delicate and ethereal. There is in fact a slight sense of dislocation in the stories that move from one plane to another: those that work best are completely magical or completely prosaic (though in later books like *Tinker Boy* the dreariness of small Irish towns is beginning to make itself felt).

Patricia Lynch's reputation rests on her assured evocations of fairground and bog and fairy rath, the racy outspoken quality of her dialogue, and her ability to amalgamate the traditional folk tale with the present-day children's story.

—Patricia Craig

MacGIBBON, Jean. British. Born in London, 25 January 1913. Educated at St. Leonard's School, St. Andrews, Scotland; Royal Academy of Dramatic Art, London. Married James MacGibbon in 1934; has two sons and one daughter. Editorial Director, MacGibbon and Kee, publishers, London, 1948–54. Recipient: Children's Rights Workshop Other Award, 1975. Address: The Cellars, Landscove, Newton Abbot, Devon, England.

PUBLICATIONS FOR CHILDREN

Fiction

> *Peter's Private Army*, illustrated by Janet Duchesne.   London, Hamish Hamilton, 1960.
> *Red Sail, White Sail*, illustrated by Janet Duchesne.   London, Hamish Hamilton, 1961.
> *The Red Sledge*, illustrated by Janet Duchesne.   London, Hamish Hamilton, 1962.
> *Pam Plays Doubles*.   London, Constable, 1962.
> *The View-Finder*, illustrated by Janet Duchesne.   London, Hamish Hamilton, 1963.
> *A Special Providence*, illustrated by William Stobbs.   London, Hamish Hamilton, 1964; New York, Coward McCann, 1965.
> *Liz*.   London, Hamish Hamilton, 1966; New York, Scribner, 1969.
> *Sandy in Hollow Tree House*, illustrated by Janet Duchesne.   London, Hamish Hamilton, 1967.
> *The Tall Ship*, illustrated by Janet Duchesne.   London, Hamish Hamilton, 1967.
> *The Great-Great Rescuers*, illustrated by Janet Duchesne.   London, Hamish Hamilton, 1967.
> *The Spy in Dolor Hugo*.   London, Heinemann, 1973.
> *Hal*.   London, Heinemann, 1974.
> *Jobs for the Girls*.   London, Heinemann, 1975.
> *After the Raft Race*.   London, Heinemann, 1976.

PUBLICATIONS FOR ADULTS

Novel

> *When the Weather's Changing* (as Jean Howard).   London, Putnam, 1945.

Other

> Translator, *Women of Islam*, by Assia Djébar.   London, Deutsch, 1961.
> Translator, *Girls of Paris*, by Nicole de Buron.   London, Blond, 1962.

Jean MacGibbon comments:

After writing for adults for some 20 years, I began to write for children in 1959 at the suggestion of Richard Hough. Since then I have written exclusively for children of all ages. More recently my books for older children have attracted critical attention as exemplifying a new and more realistic trend in children's fiction. *Liz* was the first of these. *Hal* went further in this genre, and was welcomed by librarians and educationists for breaking new ground in subject matter and treatment, specially of multi-racial groups in an urban setting. Since I left London for Devon the background of my books has changed. But adolescents everywhere have the same preoccupations, and, with the stimulus of a changed environment, I look forward to writing further books on similar themes, specially for "reluctant" (not "backward") readers.

*   *   *

Jean MacGibbon's varied output embraces stories for the very young, sports fiction for girls (sic), historical fiction, sailing adventures, war-time adventures, average-length "contemporary" novels for adolescent girls, and short "novels" for reluctant teenage readers. There are times, notably at the end of *Liz* and the opening of *Hal*, when the author seems on the verge of writing something out of the ordinary in children's books. However, her books operate mostly at a modest level, variously combining adventure, boats, mystery, schoolgirl and schoolboy heroics, sport, school life, and light romantic fiction. Jean MacGibbon is sympathetic towards adolescents and often writes out of social concern.

If we focus on four recent books, we should recognise their precursor in *Pam Plays Doubles*, one of a series published in the early 1960's under the ominous title *Sports Fiction for Girls*. The formula apparently was a blend of coaching and courtship, manual and melodrama, caricature grammar school mistresses and earnest, athletic, "you're-a-brick-Angela" heroines − hardly a guarantee of convincing imaginative fiction. The author seems aware of these absurdities when she writes of the paragon Pam, "Now she felt deliciously hungry, on the edge of her first real grown-up date, like a girl in a story!"

In *The Spy in Dolor Hugo*, set in war-time Cornwall, the author succeeds in conveying a sense of war time, despite the effusiveness and implausibility that make heavy weather of the juvenile heroics. An increasingly implausible plot also overtakes *Hal* after a highly original opening when the West Indian girl, Hal − short for Hallelujah, real name, Gloria − partly out of pity, partly resentment, brings Barry out from his morbid isolation into the inner urban multiracial realities of the Bute Street Site and the local comprehensive. *Liz* works the other way round: a straightforward adventure turns into a powerful drama involving death and disillusionment.

It would be all too easy (and futile) to run literary critical rings round *Jobs for the Girls* and *After the Raft Race*, both set in rural Devon; and after all, the author's and publishers' desire to widen the appeal of reading to teenagers not normally attracted to books is a worthy one. Yet there is something faintly ridiculous about mature adults running hard to keep up with the language and life-style of today's teenagers. The contrived plots, cardboard characters, unreal realism, even the daringly obligatory taboo words − writing far below the author's own adult level − seem based on the dubious assumption that "to speak to their condition" one must re-enact contemporary adolescent day-to-day actualities. Social concern, as Michael Billington wrote recently, need not be an excuse for technical sloppiness. Jean MacGibbon seems to acknowledge this when she has rugger captain Brad say of the events at the end of *After the Raft Race*, "Real corny, like a cheap B feature film." Ironically, corn may be just what is needed to do the trick of winning readers. Can it be done without?

—Graham Hammond

MacGREGOR, Ellen. American. Born in Baltimore, Maryland, 15 May 1906. Educated at schools in Garfield and Kent, Washington; University of Washington, Seattle, B.S. in library science 1926; University of California, Berkeley, 1931. Children's Librarian in Wyoming, California, Idaho, Florida, Oregon, and Hawaii; Research Librarian, International Harvester, Chicago. *Died 29 March 1954.*

PUBLICATIONS FOR CHILDREN

Fiction

    Tommy and the Telephone, illustrated by Zabeth. Chicago, Whitman, 1947.
    Miss Pickerell Goes to Mars, illustrated by Paul Galdone. New York, McGraw Hill, 1951; London, Blackie, 1957.
    Miss Pickerell and the Geiger Counter, illustrated by Paul Galdone. New York, McGraw Hill, 1953; London, Blackie, 1958.
    Miss Pickerell Goes Undersea, illustrated by Paul Galdone. New York, McGraw Hill, 1953; London, Blackie, 1959.
    Miss Pickerell Goes to the Arctic, illustrated by Paul Galdone. New York, McGraw Hill, 1954; London, Blackie, 1960.
    Theodore Turtle, illustrated by Paul Galdone. New York, McGraw Hill, 1955; London, Faber, 1956.
    Mr. Ferguson of the Fire Department, illustrated by Paul Galdone. New York, McGraw Hill, 1956.
    Mr. Pringle and Mr. Buttonhouse, illustrated by Paul Galdone. New York, McGraw Hill, 1957.
    Miss Pickerell on the Moon, with Dora Pantell, illustrated by Charles Geer. New York, McGraw Hill, 1965.
    Miss Pickerell Harvests the Sea, with Dora Pantell, illustrated by Charles Geer. New York, McGraw Hill, 1968.
    Miss Pickerell and the Weather Satellite, with Dora Pantell, illustrated by Charles Geer. New York, McGraw Hill, 1971.
    Miss Pickerell Meets Mr. H.U.M., with Dora Pantell, illustrated by Charles Geer. New York, McGraw Hill, 1974.
    Miss Pickerell Takes the Bull by the Horns, with Dora Pantell, illustrated by Charles Geer. New York, McGraw Hill, 1976.
    Miss Pickerell and the Earthquakes, with Dora Pantell, illustrated by Charles Geer. New York, McGraw Hill, 1977.

*   *   *

Good science fiction, like good nonsense or fantasy, must be firmly grounded in the world of reality, as Ellen MacGregor understood so well. A minor but genuine original in the field of science fiction for very young readers is her Miss Lavinia Pickerell, heroine of a series of slightly cockeyed scientific adventures.

Miss Pickerell is the last person you'd expect to find up in the air or down a mine shaft – until you become properly acquainted. She isn't quite the prim, spinsterly person her appearance suggests. True, she is angular and stiff, wears old-fashioned clothes and an outlandish hat: looks, indeed, like a model for New England Gothic. But she is full of fun, and always ready to try something new. She has a good memory for facts, and plenty of common sense, but is by no means an intimidating scientific genius. With her seven busy nieces and nephews, Miss Pickerell is a lot like everybody's favourite maiden aunt.

Miss Pickerell's first adventure took her to Mars – quite by mistake, as an inadvertent stowaway on a space ship. Naturally, once having arrived, Miss Pickerell made the best of her opportunity to add Martian red rocks to her famous collection. Which led indirectly to her *next* adventures, with a Geiger counter to test for radioactivity and later in an undersea search for a sunken ship containing her rock collection, lost at sea en route to an exhibition. No salvage company was going to claim HER belongings. And so on, one adventure leading into another.

To Mars, to the Arctic, above the ground or below, Miss Pickerell is dauntless, intrepid and eager. It's all good fun, but with a bonus. The scientific basis of each of the Miss Pickerell stories is scrupulously accurate. Although she was careful not to overburden her fragile plots with didactic passages explaining gravity, radiation, etc., Ellen MacGregor managed very skillfully to incorporate a good deal of information that a child reader could absorb almost without realizing it. With rare judgement, she gauged just how much to present to the 8–12's who are Miss Pickerell's audience. A clear picture in bold outline, rather than a mass of confusing and discouraging detail, is most apt to appeal to and instruct that active age group.

And such diverse information is provided! Simple but sound explanations of weightlessness in space travel, atomic energy and carbon 14 testing, nuclear-powered submarines and the continental shelf, the "bends" afflicting divers who surface too rapidly – there seems no end to it. Just as there is no end to the curiosity and enthusiasm of the young readers who love Miss Pickerell.

Ellen MacGregor herself completed only four of these well-loved books before her early death; but most fortunately for her eager young public she left boxes of notes and plans for further Miss Pickerell adventures. In the sympathetic hands of Dora Pantell, faithful to the spirit of the original works, Miss Pickerell continues to learn and to teach.

—Joan McGrath

MacINTYRE, Elisabeth. Australian. Born in Sydney, New South Wales, 1 November 1916. Educated at Sydney Church of England Girls Grammar School; Bowral High School; art student at East Sydney Technical College. Worked in the Land Army during World War II. Married John Roy Eldershaw in 1951; has one daughter. Worked in a printing factory; designer, Lever's Advertising Agency, Lintas, 1937–42; free-lance artist and feature writer, *The Age*, Melbourne, *Sunday Telegraph*, Sydney, *Australian Woman's Weekly*, and the New South Wales Education Department *School Magazine*; television cartoonist for the Australian Broadcasting Commission. Recipient: Australian Children's Book Council Picture Book of the Year Award, 1965; Australian Literature Board Writer's Fellowship, 1973–76. Agent: Winant, Towers Ltd., 14 Cliffords Inn, London EC4A 1DA, England; or, Jo Stewart, 667 Madison Avenue, New York, New York 10021, U.S.A. Address: 46 Wigram Road, Glebe, New South Wales 2037, Australia.

Publications for Children (illustrated by the author)

Fiction

    Ambrose Kangaroo: A Story That Never Ends. Sydney, Consolidated Press, 1941; New
        York, Scribner, 1942.
    The Handsome Duckling. Sydney, Dawfox, 1944.
    The Black Lamb. Sydney, Dawfox, 1944.
    The Forgetful Elephant. Sydney, Dawfox, 1944.
    The Willing Donkey. Sydney, Dawfox, 1944.
    Ambrose Kangaroo Has a Busy Day. Sydney, Consolidated Press, 1944.
    Jane Likes Pictures. New York, Scribner, and London, Collins, 1959.

Ambrose Kangaroo Goes to Town.   Sydney and London, Angus and Robertson, 1964.
Hugh's Zoo.   New York, Knopf, and London, Constable, 1964.
Ninji's Magic, illustrated by Mamoru Funai.   New York, Knopf, 1966; London, Angus and Robertson, 1967.
The Purple Mouse.   Nashville, Nelson, 1975.
It Looks Different from Here.   Sydney, Hodder and Stoughton, 1977.

Plays

Radio Serials: *The Riddle of Rum Jungle,* 1957; *The Kings of Corroboree Plains,* 1960.

Verse

Susan, Who Lives in Australia.   New York, Scribner, 1944; as *Katherine,* Sydney, Australasian Publishing Company, and London, Harrap, 1946; revised edition, Sydney and London, Angus and Robertson, 1958.
Mr. Koala Bear.   New York, Scribner, 1954; London, Angus and Robertson, 1966.
The Affable, Amiable Bulldozer Man.   New York, Knopf, 1965; London, Angus and Robertson, 1966.

Other

Willie's Woollies: The Story of Australian Wool.   Melbourne, Georgian House, 1951.

Illustrator: *Three Cheers for Piggy Grunter* by Noreen Shelley, 1959; *The Story House* by Ruth Fenner, 1960.

Elisabeth MacIntyre comments:
   Simple and lighthearted as my books may be, they are a sincere attempt to say something I really believe in. A straight book about Conservation might seem dull, but, as I see it, my *Affable, Amiable Bulldozer Man* sums up the whole subject painlessly. And a book about someone coping with a disability could be depressing; but I like to think that, in *The Purple Mouse,* it can still be a wryly amusing account of rising problems that might seem insurmountable if the girl hadn't been too worried about other things to worry about them.
   At first I wrote and illustrated picture books, using words sparingly. Now less interested in how things look, and more concerned in how they seem to *be.* I write full-length books, not so much for children, more for young adults – they seem to be coming younger every year.

                              *   *   *

   Elisabeth MacIntyre's reputation was made initially through her picture-stories, which she wrote and illustrated. Of these *Susan* (published in Australia and Britain as *Katherine*), a straighforward, amusing, uncomplicated description of a little girl "who lives in Australia/ With her toys and her pets and her paraphernalia" has proved to have the most universal and lasting appeal. Two later picture-stories, *Hugh's Zoo* (a runner-up for the Australian *Children's Book of the Year* award) and *The Affable, Amiable Bulldozer Man* were produced during the 1960's, when public awareness of nature conservation was being very actively stirred; both have this "message" to put across, and neither has quite the same sense of gaiety and fun as *Katherine.* The author's first full-length novel (for the 8–11 age-group) was *Ninji's Magic,* a well coordinated story set in contemporary New Guinea. The theme, sensitively handled, is the reaction of a primitive, superstitious village community to the introduction of a school and the white man's education, exemplified in the clash, subsequently resolved, between the boy, Ninji, and his grandfather. The considerable background research behind this work is excellently assimilated.

In *The Purple Mouse* (for the 10–13 age-group), the author tackles with empathy the problem of deafness, a subject with which she is personally familiar, and which she had wanted to write about for a long time. She shows how a teenage girl begins to overcome this handicap, and cope with the inevitable social problems it brings. The story is laced with a keen sense of humour – an ingredient so often missing from "social problem" novels.

Most recently, Elisabeth MacIntyre has turned to the older teenage audience: *It Looks Different from Here* is concerned with a heroine who decides against an abortion for her illegitimate child. Again, the narrative is striking for its gentle humour and the heroine's own sense of the ridiculous, as well as the compassion with which the author develops this situation. The new venture demonstrates the most significant development of this Australian author's skill.

—Barbara Ker Wilson

MACKAY, Constance D'Arcy. American. Born in St. Paul, Minnesota. Educated at Boston University, 1903–04. Married Roland Holt in 1923 (died, 1931). Director of Pageantry and Drama, War Camp Community Service, 1918–19. *Died 21 August 1966.*

PUBLICATIONS FOR CHILDREN

Plays

> *The Queen of Hearts* (produced Boston, 1904).
> *The House of the Heart and Other Plays* (includes *The Gooseherd and the Goblin, The Enchanted Garden, Nimble-Wit and Fingerkin, A Little Pilgrim's Progress, A Pageant of Hours, On Christmas Eve, The Elf Child, The Princess and the Pixies, The Christmas Guest*). New York, Holt, 1909.
> *The Silver Thread and Other Folk Plays* (includes *The Forest Spring, The Foam Maiden, Troll Magic, The Three Wishes, A Brewing of Brains, Siegfried, The Snow Witch*). New York, Holt, 1910.
> *The Pageant of Patriotism* (also director: produced Brooklyn, New York, 1911).
> *Patriotic Plays and Pageants for Young People* (includes *Pageant of Patriots: Princess Pocahontas; George Washington's Fortune; Daniel Boone, Patriot; Benjamin Franklin, Journeyman; The Boston Tea Party; Abraham Lincoln, Rail Splitter; The Hawthorne Pageant: Merrymount; In Witchcraft Days*). New York, Holt, 1912.
> *The Pageant of Schenectady* (also director: produced Schenectady, New York, 1912). Schenectady, New York, Gazette Press, 1912.
> *The Historical Pageant of Portland, Maine,* music by Will C. Macfarlane (also director: produced Portland, 1913). Portland, Southworth, 1913.
> *The Beau of Bath and Other One-Act Plays of Eighteenth-Century Life* (includes *The Silver Lining, Ashes of Roses, Gretna Green, Counsel Retained, The Prince of Court Painters*). New York, Holt, 1915; London, Dent, 1924.
> *Plays of the Pioneers* (includes *The Pioneers, The Fountain of Youth, May-Day, The Vanishing Race, The Passing of Hiawatha, Dame Greel o' Portland Town*). New York and London, Harper, 1915.
> *William of Stratford: Shakespeare's Tercentenary Pageant* (produced Baltimore, 1916).
> *The Forest Princess and Other Masques* (includes *The Gift of Time, A Masque of*

Conservation, The Masque of Pomona, A Masque of Christmas, The Sun Goddess). New York, Holt, 1916.

Memorial Day Pageant. New York and London, Harper, 1916.

Pageant of Sunshine and Shadow (produced New York, 1916).

Patriotic Christmas Pageant (produced San Francisco, 1918).

Victory Pageant (produced New York, 1918).

Franklin. New York, Holt, 1921.

America Triumphant: A Pageant of Patriotism. New York and London, Appleton, 1926.

Youth's Highway and Other Plays (includes *In the Days of Piers Ploughman, A Calendar of Joyful Saints, The Pageant of Sunshine and Shadow, The First Noël*). New York, Holt, 1929.

Midsummer Eve: An Outdoor Fantasy (in verse). New York and London, French, 1929.

Ladies of the White House. Boston, Baker, 1948.

A Day at Nottingham: A Festival at Which All the Playgrounds of a City Can Take Part. New York, National Recreational Association, 1952.

PUBLICATIONS FOR ADULTS

Other

Costumes and Scenery for Amateurs. New York, Holt, 1915; revised edition, 1932.

How to Produce Children's Plays. New York, Holt, 1915.

The Little Theatre in the United States. New York, Holt, 1917.

Patriotic Drama in Your Town: A Manual of Suggestions. New York, Holt, 1918.

Play Production in Churches and Sunday Schools. New York, Playground and Recreation Association of America, 1921.

Rural Drama Bibliography. New York, Playground and Recreation Association of America, n.d.

Editor, *Suggestions for the Dramatic Celebration of the 300th Anniversary of the Purchase of Manhattan, 1626–1926.* New York, Playground and Recreation Association of America, 1926.

*   *   *

Constance D'Arcy Mackay was an early patroness of community theatre in the United States, particularly theatre for children. Her work spanned several decades, commencing in the early years of the 20th century and continuing until after the second world war. Although she was particularly interested in playwriting, she was also active in various dramatic activities in the United States and in the little theatre movement that was flourishing at the time.

Miss Mackay made use of folk material and history as subject matter for her plays. She also used forms of the Guild Drama of the middle ages: the Interlude, the Morality, the Miracle play, the Pageant and the Nativity drama. All of her plays were written with little theatre groups, rather than the Broadway theatre, in mind. Her work was praised for its literary quality and its appropriateness to community and school theatre groups.

She was one of the first to distinguish between the two types of dramatic programs that she saw spreading across the country. One of these was "children's theatre" (both professional and amateur) and the other was school drama, in which children themselves took part. She contributed to both but admitted to a greater interest and stronger belief in the play that was produced for child audiences rather than in programs in which children were the participants. Throughout her lifetime she stressed the use of good literature, well produced for young spectators.

Constance D'Arcy Mackay's greatest contribution was her use of a literary style in writing for children and her insistence upon content worthy of their time and attention. Although her plays are seldom produced today, all serious students of children's theatre and playwrights for children's audiences respect the high quality of her work and her respectful attitude toward both the amateur and the young spectator. This spirit, as reflected in her various contributions to the little theatre movement in America during the twenties and thirties, unquestionably lifted the level of writing for children's theatre. She was one of the first and one of the best.

—Nellie McCaslin

MACKEN, Walter. Irish. Born in Galway, 3 May 1915. Educated at Catholic schools in Galway. Married Margaret Mary Kenny in 1937; two sons. Actor and producer, Gaelic Theatre, Galway, 1939–48; actor, Abbey Theatre, Dublin, 1948–51. *Died 22 April 1967.*

PUBLICATIONS FOR CHILDREN

Fiction

> *Island of the Great Yellow Ox*, illustrated by Charles Keeping. London, Macmillan, and New York, Macmillan, 1966.
> *The Flight of the Doves.* New York, Macmillan, 1967; London, Macmillan, 1968.

Play

> Television Play: *Island of the Great Yellow Ox*, from his own story, 1972.

PUBLICATIONS FOR ADULTS

Novels

> *Quench the Moon.* London, Macmillan, and New York, Viking Press, 1948.
> *I Am Alone.* London, Macmillan, 1949.
> *Rain on the Wind.* London, Macmillan, 1950; New York, Macmillan, 1951.
> *The Bogman.* London, Macmillan and New York, Macmillan, 1952.
> *Sunset on the Window-Pane.* London, Macmillan, 1954; New York, St. Martin's Press, 1955.
> *Sullivan.* London, Macmillan, and New York, Macmillan, 1957.
> *Seek the Fair Land.* London, Macmillan, and New York, Macmillan, 1959.
> *The Silent People.* London, Macmillan, and New York, Macmillan, 1962.
> *The Scorching Wind.* London, Macmillan, and New York, Macmillan 1964.
> *Brown Land of the Mountain.* London, Macmillan, 1967; as *Land of the Mountain: A Novel of Ireland*, New York, Macmillan, 1967.

Short Stories

> *The Green Hills and Other Stories.* London, Macmillan, and New York, St. Martin's Press, 1956.

God Made Sunday and Other Stories.   London, Macmillan, and New York, Macmillan, 1962.
The Coll Doll and Other Stories.   Dublin, Gill and Macmillan, 1969.

Plays

Mungo's Mansion: A Play of Galway Life (produced Dublin, 1946; as *Galway Handicap*, produced London, 1947).   London, Macmillan, 1946.
Vacant Possession.   London, Macmillan, 1948.
Home Is the Hero (produced Dublin, 1952; New York, 1954).   London, Macmillan, 1953.
Twilight of a Warrior (produced Dublin, 1955).   London, Macmillan, 1956.
Look in the Looking Glass (produced Dublin, 1958).
Recall the Years (produced Dublin, 1966).

*   *   *

Walter Macken wrote only two books for children, *Island of the Great Yellow Ox* and *The Flight of the Doves*. Both show resourceful, ingenious yet innocent children in danger from wicked adults.

In *Island of the Great Yellow Ox*, four boys become marooned on an island where Agnes, an archaeologist, and her husband, the Captain, are engaged in an obsessive search for a golden idol. Since the children know too much, the adults try to eliminate them. To the boys, the malice of the villains is incomprehensible, although they do share something of the excitement of the search. The problems of the youngsters are practical rather than psychological, and the account of their predicament is vivid and convincing. From our point of view, the villains are indeed explained, but their internal and mutual conflicts are not well integrated with the action of the book. Agnes is warped by her obsession and she manipulates the Captain through his guilt about drinking. We understand, but the boys, with whom we are invited to identify, do not.

If the story, to some degree, remains fantastic, the island setting, a favourite one with Macken, is firmly authentic and the natural enemies, such as storms, are more terrifying than the villains.

The Flight of the Doves is the more serious and satisfying work. Finn and Derval Dove flee across Ireland from their cruel stepfather to seek Granny. The chase allows Macken to diversify both the locations and the characters. Being themselves outside the law, the children are helped by others similarly placed. Uncle Toby, who has law on his side, is an outright villain, but most characters are capable of surprising. Mickser, a criminal, is kind to the children; Powder, a tinker, would betray them. Michael, an off-duty policeman who functions as a good fairy, is prepared to tread a legal tightrope.

The themes emerge from the interplay of character. With Finn we learn that appearances deceive, that law and justice are not necessarily identical. Most importantly, Macken explores the relationship between the rationally plausible and the intuitive. Finn inspires instinctive trust. He has a natural goodness and responsibility that certain adults lack, but he is saved from authorial idealisation to some degree by his unawareness of it. Character, in this book, is more of a piece with the action and there are splendid dramatic scenes. The final confrontation is well worthy of an author who is also a playwright.

Macken is able to observe and create the child mentality, to construct exciting narrative and to deploy a language which is direct and honest but whose terseness restrains him from over-indulging his sentimental optimism.

—A.W. England

MacKENZIE, Jean. Canadian. Born in Traynor, Saskatchewan, 22 March 1928. Educated at John Oliver High School, Vancouver. Married Edward D. MacKenzie in 1952; has two sons. Assistant cook and children's nurse, R.W.Large Memorial Hospital, Bella Bella, British Columbia, 1947–48; Display Assistant, 1948–52, and Display Manager, 1952–54, Birk's Jewellers, Vancouver; Display Manager, Firbank's, Vancouver, 1954–55. Recipient: Canadian Centennial Commission prize, 1967. Address: 3815 Merriman Drive, Victoria, British Columbia V8P 2S8, Canada.

PUBLICATIONS FOR CHILDREN

Fiction

Storm Island, illustrated by Gordon Rayner.   Toronto, Macmillan, 1968.
River of Stars, illustrated by Tom McNeely.   Toronto, McClelland and Stewart, 1971.

Jean MacKenzie comments:
The land, they say, is always a major factor in Canadian literature. It certainly is in my contributions, because I'm a British Columbia writer deeply in love with my subject. British Columbia is a part of the world that few people know of, yet its history is romantic and fascinating, its landscape infinitely varied. I first became aware of the power and charm of this part of the world when I worked for 18 months in the remote Indian village of Bella Bella, halfway up the rugged British Columbia coastline. My first two books for children sprang out of that experience. They deal with modern life in this faraway corner of the world. But its history – of palisaded Hudson's Bay Company forts, of ragged gold seekers, of storm-bound sailing ships – is equally absorbing.
I can't think of anything I'd rather do than spin stories about this lovely land and the people who live – and have lived – upon it.

                                    *   *   *

The young adult fiction of Jean MacKenzie focuses on two major aspects of life on Canada's West Coast: the struggle to survive in a harsh and often hostile environment and the tensions between the native and white cultures. In each of her novels, *Storm Island* and *River of Stars*, she places her young heroes in West Coast settings she knows very well and develops conflicts in which each is given the opportunity to grow as an individual.
Jean MacKenzie's first book, *Storm Island*, is the less successful of the two novels. It is set on a tiny lighthouse island north of Vancouver Island and tells of the two months spent there by 12-year-old Ray Lewis. Sent to live with his aunt, uncle, and two younger cousins while his mother is recovering from an automobile accident, he feels at first lost and insecure in his new and lonely surroundings. Moreover, he believes he is incurring the displeasure of Uncle George, the often moody light keeper. However, when a late November storm destroys the house and the family is driven to seek shelter in a nearby cave, Ray acts with courage and resourcefulness. The character conflict between Ray and Uncle George provides an adequate basis for the relatively thin plot, but the character of the uncle, who, it turns out, feels guilty at forcing his family to live so lonely a life, is not sufficiently developed. Jean MacKenzie is at her best when she describes the setting, as her feeling for the desolate grandeur of the island and her awe of the terrifying Pacific storms are communicated convincingly to the reader.
This love for and ability to portray British Columbia's coastal areas is also seen in *River of Stars*. However, this second novel contains a powerful and moving conflict. It is the story of the conflict between the native and white cultures and of an Indian boy's growth to maturity and to an awareness of the values of his people's traditions. Jean MacKenzie has called *River of Stars* an interim report, a story which will, she believes, be rewritten by one of the native

peoples, a person who, because he writes from within the culture, will better be able to understand the tensions and problems.

The novel has as its time structure the passage of one summer – the duration of the fishing season. There is a time conflict: by the end of the season, young Andy Hill must have saved enough money to buy the boat which will enable him and his family to live in greater dignity. At first, he's made painfully aware that he is living in a white man's world and that, as an Indian, his chances for success are slight. The hostility he faces from the whites is symbolized by Smithers, a lone wolf fisherman who takes every opportunity he can to thwart Andy's plans and to humiliate him.

After Andy's boat is gutted by an explosion and his father sent to the hospital, the hopes for the summer appear to have been dashed. However, Andy's courage emerges as he revamps the boat and searches for an adult to run the boat, as is required by law. In desperation, he turns to old Ambrose, a lonely and often drunk renegade Indian. We are told that "the old man ... belonged in a time that was gone. He was a leftover. Out of place. Out of time." The relationship between the teenage boy and the old man plays an important role in Andy's maturation process. He comes to understand Ambrose as an individual; but also, as he listens to the old man's life story, he comes to understand the past of his own people. Talking of old times, Ambrose tells Andy how these ways have been destroyed by the whites. The key scene takes place in the hospital as the dying and impoverished Ambrose holds a potlatch, giving Andy his most precious gift, the Indian name which had been intended for his dead grandson. The name Tloquemas, means strong.

But the boy must also learn to live in the present and, in this respect, the character of Williem the dutchman is important. This quiet fisherman, who had suffered under the Nazis during the Second World War, tells Andy of the dangers of hatred, urging him to respect each person, explaining that it is a world for all people – Indian and white. At the end of the summer, Andy has learned from all his experiences and is no longer a boy but a man, sure of himself and of his position within a culture.

River of Stars may well be a minor Canadian children's classic. It certainly deserves to be better known than it is. Combining as it does Jean MacKenzie's knowledge and love of Canada's West Coast, her respect for native cultures, and her ability to create convincing and moving characters, it is a book which is at once an original creation and a significant comment on an important aspect of modern Canadian life.

—Jon C. Stott

MacPHERSON, Margaret. Scottish. Born in Colinton, Midlothian, 29 June 1908. Educated privately, Edinburgh; at Edinburgh University, 1926–29, M.A. Married Duncan MacPherson in 1929 (died, 1971); has seven sons. Member, Commission of Inquiry into Crofting, Inverness, 1951–54. Since 1960, Honorary Secretary, Skye Labour Party; since 1970, Member, Consultative Council, Highlands and Islands Development Board. Address: Ardrannach, Torvaig, Portree, Isle of Skye, Scotland.

PUBLICATIONS FOR CHILDREN

Fiction

> *The Shinty Boys*, illustrated by Shirley Hughes. London, Collins, and New York, Harcourt Brace, 1963.
> *The Rough Road*, illustrated by Douglas Hall. London, Collins, 1965; New York, Harcourt Brace, 1966.

Ponies for Hire, illustrated by Sheila Rose.   London, Collins, and New York, Harcourt
    Brace, 1967.
The New Tenants, illustrated by Shirley Hughes.   London, Collins, and New York,
    Harcourt Brace, 1968.
The Battle of the Braes, illustrated by Gavin Rowe.   London, Collins, 1972.
The Boy on the Roof, illustrated by Charles Front.   London, Collins, 1974.

Margaret MacPherson comments:

I had always wanted to write a book. As a young girl I scribbled away but never had
anything published. I married a crofter and was too busy rearing a large family of boys to do
any writing. But I had not forgotten my ambition, and when the boys were well on their way
to being grown up, I started to write once again.

                                  *   *   *

Margaret MacPherson tells a galloping story, both in action and feeling. Wisely, she sticks
to her own home ground, the Gaelic speaking and politically-conscious – meaning in the
Highlands, history-conscious – Island of Skye. The boy and girl characters are well and truly
in the adult world of dealings and quarrels, deceits and jealousies, or equally passionate
loyalties, over croft land, cattle beasts, houses, as well as rights and prejudices – though I
doubt if Mrs. MacPherson has ever plumbed the darkest depths of the Free Churches! The
children are on the whole – and this is true to life – quite a lot nicer than the grown-ups,
though no little angels, and they see just as clearly the astonishing beauty of the landscape or
equally astonishing grimness.

Mrs. MacPherson knows the detail of crofting life, the heavy weight of the peat creel, the
dividing up of the small catch of fish, handling sheep at the dipping, cooking, milking, and
folk crowding into the low rooms of the black houses: "We never opened windows. Fresh
air was a thing to be kept outside." Much is done through conversation, and here the Gaelic
grammar and idiom underlying English speech in the Highlands are beautifully done.

In *The Battle of the Braes*, based on real happenings, there is a delicate shift into the
narrative of a completely Gaelic speaker of the turbulent eighties, turned into English but
giving a genuine insight into another culture with a somewhat different – dare one say
better? – set of values. Mrs. MacPherson could probably write an equally exciting, close-knit
yarn with an English background, but if so her young readers would lose the feeling of
having for a while lived somewhere else and having taken part in its vivid and active life.
There are plenty of Skye stories to be told yet, and she is the one to tell them.

                                                                —Naomi Mitchison

                          _____

MacVICAR, Angus. Scottish. Born in Argyll, 28 October 1908. Educated at
Campbeltown Grammar School, 1920–26; Glasgow University, 1926–30, M.A. 1930.
Served in the Royal Scots Fusiliers, 1940–45: Captain; mentioned in despatches. Married
Jean Smith McKerral in 1936; has one son. Reporter and Assistant Editor, *Campbeltown
Courier*, 1931–33. Honorary Sheriff Substitute of Argyll, 1967. Agent: A.M. Heath and Co.
Ltd., 40–42 William IV Street, London, WC2N 4DD, England. Address: Achnamara,
Southend, Campbeltown, Argyll PA28 6RW, Scotland.

PUBLICATIONS FOR CHILDREN

Fiction

The Crocodile Men. London, Art and Educational, 1948.
The Black Wherry. London, Foley House Press, 1948.
Faraway Island, illustrated by Denis Alford. London, Foley House Press, 1949.
King Abbie's Adventure, illustrated by James Clark. London, Burke, 1950.
Stubby Sees It Through, illustrated by Lunt Roberts. London, Burke, 1950.
The Grey Pilot. London, Burke, 1951.
Tiger Mountain, illustrated by Jack Matthew. London, Burke, 1952.
The Lost Planet. London, Burke, 1953.
Return to the Lost Planet. London, Burke, 1954.
Dinny Smith Comes Home. London, Burke, 1955.
Secret of the Lost Planet. London, Burke, 1955.
The Atom Chasers. London, Burke, 1956.
The Atom Chasers in Tibet. London, Burke, 1957.
Satellite 7. London, Burke, 1958.
Red Fire on the Lost Planet. London, Burke, 1959.
Peril on the Lost Planet. London, Burke, 1960.
Space Agent from the Lost Planet. London, Burke, 1961.
Space Agent and the Isles of Fire. London, Burke, 1962; New York, Roy, 1963.
Kilpatrick − Special Reporter. London, Burke, 1963.
The High Cliffs of Kersivay, illustrated by Douglas Relf. London, Harrap, 1964.
Space Agent and the Ancient Peril. London, Burke, 1964.
Life-Boat − Green to White, illustrated by Paul Sharp. Leicester, Brockhampton Press,
   1965.
The Kersivay Kraken, illustrated by Douglas Relf. London, Harrap, 1966.
The Cave of the Hammers, illustrated by Hilary Abrahams. London, Kaye and Ward,
   1968.
Super Nova and the Rogue Satellite. Leicester, Brockhampton Press, 1969.
Super Nova and the Frozen Man. Leicester, Brockhampton Press, 1970.

Plays

Radio Plays: has adapted 19 of his books into radio serials.

Television Plays: *The Lost Planet,* and *Return to the Lost Planet* , from his own stories.

Other

Let's Visit Scotland. London, Burke, 1966; revised edition, with John C. Caldwell,
   New York, Day, 1967.
Rescue Call: The Story of the Life-Boatmen. London, Kaye and Ward, 1967.

PUBLICATIONS FOR ADULTS

Novels

The Purple Rock. London, Paul, 1933.
Death by the Mistletoe. London, Paul, 1934.
The Screaming Gull. London, Paul, 1935.
The Temple Falls. London, Paul, 1935.
The Ten Green Brothers. London, Paul, 1936.

The Cavern.   London, Paul, 1936.
Flowering Death.   London, Paul, 1937.
The Crooked Finger.   London, Paul, 1937.
Crime's Masquerader.   London, Paul, 1938.
The Singing Spider.   London, Paul, 1938.
11 for Danger.   London, Paul, 1939.
Strangers from the Sea.   London, Paul, 1939.
The Crouching Spy.   London, Paul, 1941.
Commodore Norah.   London, Pemberton, 1942.
Death on the Machar.   London, Paul, 1947.
The Other Man.   London, Pemberton, 1947.
Greybreek.   London, Paul, 1947.
Fugitive's Road.   London, Paul, 1949.
Escort to Adventure.   London, Paul, 1952.
The Dancing Horse.   London, Long, 1961.
The Killings on Kersivay.   London, Long, 1962.
The Hammers of Fingal.   London, Long, 1963.
The Grey Shepherds.   London, Long, 1964.
Murder at the Open.   London, Long, 1965.
The Canisbay Conspiracy.   London, Long, 1966.
Night on the Killer Reef.   London, Long, 1967.
Maniac.   London, Long, 1969.
Duel in Glen Finnan.   London, Long, 1969.
The Golden Venus Affair.   London, Long, 1972.
The Painted Doll Affair.   London, Long, 1973.

Plays

Minister's Monday.   Galashiels, Selkirk, McQueen, 1957.
Final Proof.   Glasgow, Brown and Ferguson, 1958.
Mercy Flight.   Glasgow, Brown and Ferguson, 1959.
Storm Tide.   Glasgow, Brown and Ferguson, 1960.
Under Suspicion.   Glasgow, Brown and Ferguson, 1962.
Stranger at Christmas.   Glasgow, Brown and Ferguson, 1964.

Radio Plays: *The Singing Spider, Strangers from the Sea, The Dancing Horse, The Hammers of Fingal, The Canisbay Conspiracy,* and *Night on Killer Reef,* from his own novels; *The Glens of Glendale* series, 1954–59.

Television Series: *Confessions of a Minister's Son.* 1965–70.

Other

Salt in My Porridge (autobiographical).   London, Jarrolds, 1971.
Heather in My Ears (autobiographical).   London, Hutchinson, 1974.
Rocks in My Scotch (autobiographical).   London, Hutchinson, 1977.

Angus MacVicar comments:
I found myself with one talent – the ability to tell a story. For nearly half a century I have been trying hard to develop it.

*   *   *

Angus MacVicar's range is wide, including schoolboy stories, adventure tales, and science fiction. It is perhaps unfortunate that, in Britain at least, his books are out of print.

The Grey Pilot is based on a true story about Bonnie Prince Charlie's adventures after the Battle of Culloden but it is, as the author states, an adventure story, not an historical work, and the exciting part of the book is certainly the account of how Donald McLeod, the Grey Pilot, and his son Murdoch became involved in helping the Prince to escape. As in that book, so too in books like *Stubby Sees It Through* and *Kilpatrick – Special Reporter* the author is at his best when involved in fast-moving adventure with plenty of action and dialogue and with the characters only lightly sketched. The settings vary, Scotland frequently but sometimes abroad, but the approach is predictable – a group of characters, united in their love for adventure and mystery solving, lots of fast-moving action, plenty of dialogue, and a minimum of descriptive writing, all of which produce books which appeal to many children.

Oddly enough, it is in his science fiction books that Angus MacVicar produces his most descriptive writing both of scenery and human beings – "the red, pear-shaped fruit on the trees, growing upwards like fat candle-sticks, the salmon-pink rocks, sharp and unweathered like crystal, the green turf that was composed not of grass, but of fine spongy moss." It is almost as if his concentration on the scientific aspect of these books has sharpened his awareness of the countryside and its people. His characterisations are sharper, more clearly defined and much better developed. These are the kind of people who *could* be going on rocket flights.

Since it is many years since the Lost Planet books were written and present day children are now quite blasé about moon flights, it is remarkable that MacVicar's science fiction books still have the power to interest and excite. Familiarity with count-downs does not prevent the reader becoming quite tense as the moment of blast-off approaches. Obviously the author enjoyed writing these books and the challenge they presented brought forth his best writing. Although science fiction is not my favourite theme, I find MacVicar's handling of the subject quite rivetting and much more powerful than his other stories. The books pulsate with action and the atmosphere crackles with tension.

Angus MacVicar is not a sophisticated writer but he is a worthy successor to his Highland forebears, a storyteller who knows the essence of good storytelling.

—Margaret Walker

MADDOCK, Reginald (Bertram). British. Born in Warrington, Cheshire, 9 August 1912. Educated at Boteler Grammar School, Warrington, 1924–30; Chester College of Education, 1930–32, Teaching Certificate 1932. Served in the British Army in North Africa and Burma, 1940–46; mentioned in despatches. Married Louise S. Hawthorn in 1964. Headmaster, Evelyn Street School, Warrington, 1949–57, and Richard Fairclough Secondary School, Warrington, 1957–73. Agent: John Johnson, 51–54 Goschen Buildings, 12 Henrietta Street, London, WC2E 8LF. Address: 5 Pheasant Walk, High Legh, Knutsford, Cheshire WA16 6LU, England.

PUBLICATIONS FOR CHILDREN

Fiction

Corrigan and the White Cobra [Tomb of Opi, Yellow Peril, Black Riders, Golden Pagoda, Dream-Makers, Blue Crater, Green Tiger, Red Lions, Little People] (as R.B. Maddock), illustrated by Robert Hodgson. London, Nelson, 10 vols., 1956–63.
Rocky and the Lions, illustrated by Robert Hodgson. London, Nelson, 1957.

The Time Maze, illustrated by Robert Hodgson.   London, Nelson, 1960.
The Last Horizon, illustrated by Douglas Relf.   London, Nelson, 1961.
The Willow Wand. London, Nelson, 1962.
The Tall Man from the Sea, illustrated by Robert Hodgson.   London, Nelson, 1962.
Rocky and the Elephant, illustrated by Robert Hodgson.   London, Nelson, 1962.
One More River, illustrated by A.S. Douthwaite.   London, Nelson, 1963.
The Widgeon Gang, illustrated by Dick Hart.   London, Nelson, 1964.
The Great Bow. London, Collins, 1964; Chicago, Rand McNally, 1968.
The Pit. London, Collins, 1966; Boston, Little Brown, 1968.
The Dragon in the Garden. London, Macmillan, 1968; Boston, Little Brown, 1969.
Sell-Out. London, Collins, 1969; as *Danny Rowley*, Boston, Little Brown, 1969.
Northmen's Fury, illustrated by Graham Humphreys.   London, Macdonald, 1970.
Thin Ice. Boston, Little Brown, 1971.
The Big Ditch, illustrated by William Stobbs.   London, Macdonald, 1971.

Reginald Maddock comments:
Apart from *The Last Horizon* and *The Great Bow*, which are allegorical, I have always tried to write about ordinary people in ordinary situations, depending less on plot than on characters for interest.

*   *   *

Reginald Maddock's novels depend upon predictable plots, limited characterisation and a prose style remarkable chiefly for the simplicity of its vocabulary. Boys tend to be boys, and girls second-class citizens. Good never fails to triumph, and in his stories set in modern times, it comes as small surprise in the last chapter to find that our heroes thwart the villains, earning the gratitude of amazed Authority.

To dismiss Maddock as a formula writer is, however, to beg questions which preoccupy teachers if not the critical pundits. Several of his books are much enjoyed by teenagers not yet ready for more demanding fare. Mr. Maddock is a headmaster, and knows his readers. He gives them sharply focussed and rapid action. His straightforward language and clear delineation of characters offer security and pleasure of comprehension to an uncertain reader. He has been a pioneer of settings familiar to readers who do not necessarily come from the middle classes.

Mr. Maddock also means to instruct: his lessons are firmly liberal, with a certainty which is now unfashionable. *The Great Bow*, for example, is a parable for our own times. A youth discovers the bow, its power is abused, tribes with the bow menace those without, until a balance of power is achieved as every race becomes skilled in archery. The hero finally leaves to found an alternative, peaceable community. *The Big Ditch* is concerned with racial prejudice. Despite the hostility of their elders, the young people of two tribes (the fair skins have enslaved the dark) unite to fill in the artificial chasm which divides them.

The stories set in contemporary industrial towns, for which Maddock is best known, again involve the struggles of young people facing problems. Danny Rowley *(Sell-Out)* has to learn to accept the remarriage of his widowed mother. Butch Reece *(The Pit)* feels that whenever "somebody did something, I got the blame." He establishes himself in adult eyes through rescuing a teacher's son from a moorland morass. In *The Dragon in the Garden*, Blaster Stewart has been educated by his progressive parents before he is sent to Cronton Comprehensive School to learn to cope with society. Here, he defeats the bullying Fagso Brown by learning judo from his father who is not only a potter but also, happily enough, a Black Belt.

Young readers seem as untroubled by such improbabilities as they are by teachers in mortarboards and gowns in comics. The novels offer an escapist world more acceptable to adolescents of tentative imagination than the fantasies of a Tolkien or a Le Guin.

Unfortunately, Mr. Maddock's insistent liberalism is sometimes expressed in a crudely didactic, even condescending, tone. The negro boy Daylight (who admittedly appeared in an novel published as long ago as 1964, *The Widgeon Gang*), though he is treated as a comic figure with rolling eyes and fear of spirits, is declared too blatantly to be as good as anyone else. Even the malevolent Fagso is well on the way to redemption when Blaster's father shows him how to pot. What such chaps need is an Interest.

If the novels are set alongside the urban stories of Bernard Ashley and S.E. Hinton (who achieve both accessibility and subtlety) their limitations are evident. The very constraints which make the novels easily readable may promote glibness or distortion, rather than simplification of the psychological and moral dilemmas which Mr. Maddock chooses as the mainsprings of his plots.

—Geoff Fox

MAHY, Margaret. New Zealander. Born in Whakatane, 21 March 1936. Educated at the University of Auckland, B.A. 1957, Diploma of Librarianship 1958. Has two children. Librarian, School Library Service, Christchurch. Recipient: New Zealand Library Association Esther Glen Award, 1970, 1973; New Zealand Literary Fund grant, 1975. Agent: Helen Hoke Associates, 10 Alma Square, London, N.W.8, England. Address: R.D. No. 1, Lyttelton, New Zealand.

PUBLICATIONS FOR CHILDREN

Fiction

The Dragon of an Ordinary Family, illustrated by Helen Oxenbury. New York, Watts, and London, Heinemann, 1969.

A Lion in the Meadow, illustrated by Jenny Williams. New York, Watts, and London, Dent, 1969.

Mrs. Discombobulous, illustrated by Jan Brychta. New York, Watts, and London, Dent, 1969.

Pillycock's Shop, illustrated by Carol Barker. New York, Watts, and London, Dobson, 1969.

The Procession, illustrated by Charles Mozley. New York, Watts, and London, Dent, 1969.

The Little Witch, illustrated by Charles Mozley. New York, Watts, and London, Dent, 1970.

Sailor Jack and the 20 Orphans, illustrated by Robert Bartelt. New York, Watts, and London, Dent, 1970.

The Princess and the Clown, illustrated by Carol Barker. New York, Watts, and London, Dobson, 1971.

The Boy with Two Shadows, illustrated by Jenny Williams. New York, Watts, and London, Dent, 1971.

The First [Second, Third] Margaret Mahy Story Book: Stories and Poems, illustrated by Shirley Hughes. London, Dent, 3 vols., 1972–75.

The Man Whose Mother Was a Pirate, illustrated by Brian Froud. London, Dent, 1972; New York, Atheneum, 1973.

The Railway Engine and the Hairy Brigands, illustrated by Brian Froud. London, Dent, 1973.

Rooms for Rent, illustrated by Jenny Williams. New York, Watts, 1974. as *Rooms to Let*, London, Dent, 1975.

The Witch in the Cherry Tree, illustrated by Jenny Williams. London, Dent, and New York, Parents' Magazine Press, 1974.

Clancy's Cabin, illustrated by Trevor Stubley. London, Dent, 1974.

The Rare Spotted Birthday Party, illustrated by Belinda Lyon. London, Watts, 1974.

Stepmother, illustrated by Terry Burton. London, Watts, 1974.

The Bus under the Leaves, illustrated by Margery Gill. London, Dent, 1975.

The Ultra-Violet Catastrophe! or, The Unexpected Walk with Great-Uncle Magnus Pringle, illustrated by Brian Froud. London, Dent, and New York, Parents' Magazine Press, 1975.

The Great Millionaire Kidnap, illustrated by Jan Brychta. London, Dent, 1975.

Leaf Magic, illustrated by Jenny Williams. New York, Parents' Magazine Press, 1975; London, Dent, 1976.

The Boy Who Was Followed Home, illustrated by Steven Kellogg. New York, Watts, 1975; London, Dent, 1977.

The Wind Between the Stars, illustrated by Brian Froud. London, Dent, 1976.

David's Witch Doctor, illustrated by James Russell. London, Watts, 1976.

The Pirate Uncle, illustrated by Mary Dinsdale. London, Dent, 1977.

Nonstop Nonsense, illustrated by Quentin Blake. London, Dent, 1977.

Verse

Seventeen Kings and Forty Two Elephants, illustrated by Charles Mozley. London, Dent, 1972.

PUBLICATIONS FOR ADULTS

Other

New Zealand: Yesterday and Today. London, Watts, 1975.

Manuscript Collection: J.M. Dent and Sons Ltd., London.

Margaret Mahy comments:

A child's attitude to reading depends on its exposure to books and language in its home from the earliest years. I have an almost fanatical belief in the importance of reading aloud to children, so many of my stories are written with this intention. I am constantly aware of the pictorial possibilities which, for instance, animals provide so abundantly. Children particularly loves rhymes and rhythmic verse because they can join in the choruses. They can identify happily with the most extraordinary events if these are described with almost prosaic understatement and dry humour.

*   *   *

Margaret Mahy is an extremely skillful weaver of stories for children. Her picture books are perhaps the best vehicle for the expression of her vivid imagination, her originality, and her ability to create fantastic characters and situations with great appeal to children. She is sensitive to the child's own imaginative processes, recognising the way in which fantasy and reality can be blurred, and the child's need for security. Her early book, *A Lion in the Meadow*, concerns a boy's fear of a creature of his imagination and his creation of a more powerful monster to overcome it; the book's strength lies in its simplicity and its venture into the world of fantasy, while retaining an atmosphere of secure domesticity to offset the child's fear. Many of Margaret Mahy's stories are excursions into magic, into the private world of a child's imagination and its inventions. Some can be seen as pure flights of fancy *(The Procession, Seventeen Kings)*; some involve an element of magic brought into a domestic situation *(A Lion in the Meadow, The Witch in the Cherry Tree)*; and some are complete make-believe nonsense *(The Man Whose Mother Was a Pirate, The Dragon of an Ordinary Family)*. It is perhaps possible to detect a shift in her writing from the creation of external fantasies, like the marvellous *Dragon of an Ordinary Family* or *Mrs. Discombobulous*, which closely resemble folk tales in their structure though set in contemporary families, to a more internal kind of fantasy where the stories are more obviously concerned with the imagination and spirit of the characters (as in her picturebook *The Wind Between the Stars*).

Another product of Margaret Mahy's vivid imagination is her ability to create fantastic and bizarre characters: the marvellous pirate woman, wild and powerful; Mrs. Discombobulous with her scalding, scolding, nagging tongue which she uses to overcome the tyrant baron; Mr. Murgatroyd, the lean, mean and lonely landlord, with his amazing assortment of lodgers; Great Uncle Magnus Pringle; the terrifying Hairy Brigands .... She knows what appeals to children; her books are littered with dragons, pirates, and particularly witches. They are drawn several times larger than life, and a few verge on becoming caricatures though even in the most evil there is always a touch of humanity.

One notable feature is the number of strong female characters: the marvellous old pirate woman, representing perhaps the spirit of adventure and the refusal to conform; the resourceful and brave girls in *The Railway Engine and the Hairy Brigands* who save the town; Mrs. Discombobulous who stands no nonsense from anyone, and, at a more human level, Phoebe in *The Wind Between the Stars*, who regains the freedom and vitality of her youth. There is no conscious moral of "non sexism," but it is good to find material which presents strong female characters, and in which roles are less clearly defined – or even sometimes reversed, as in "The Girl Who Loved Cars" in *The Third Margaret Mahy Story Book*.

One of the marks of great children's literature is the appeal it holds at a number of levels; and in Margaret Mahy's picture books we find rich humour, excitement, vivid characterisation, and also philosophy, explorations of the world of fantasy and the human spirit. Many explore the theme of freedom. This is most directly presented in *The Man Whose Mother Was a Pirate* where mother and son leave the restrictions and conformity of everyday life and journey to the wildness and magic of the sea. A more social freedom is found in *Rooms for Rent*, where the exploited tenants of the mean and bitter Mr. Murgatroyd decide to team up with each other and find some better place to live. The spirit of freedom is often represented by the wind: in *The Wind Between the Stars* the wind which Phoebe used to hear as a child calls to her again as an old woman, alone and subdued; she follows its call and learns again how to laugh and dance, rediscovering her inner vitality. This can be seen as a kind of celebration of an inner spirit in us, often buried under the sheer weight of living.

One of the most powerful features of the picture books is the remarkable use of language; it is obvious that Margaret Mahy loves words, and she uses them often for the sheer delight of their sound and rhythm. In *The Great Millionaire Kidnap*, for example, we are told that the small but clever Likely brother "could outfox foxes and hoodwink weasles; he was a master of hanky panky and hocus pocus, jugglement and jerrymander." Her use of words is often alliterative, making the more unusual ones have meaning despite their unfamiliarity. She uses language with care so that the stories flow with rhythm; each has a pace of its own, geared to the mood of the story. And in many she uses repetition skilfully to make the stories flow along, as in the cumulation of the phrase " ... the big, roaring, yellow, whiskery lion in the meadow." These devices make the description very vivid, and this is aided by the imagery she uses. One of the best examples is found in *The Man Whose Mother Was a Pirate*; when they reach the sea, they stand and gaze: "at his feet the sea stroked the sand with soft little paws. Further out the waves pounced and bounced like puppies. And out beyond again and again the great, graceful breakers moved like kings into court, trailing the sea like a peacock patterned robe behind them." And the description of Great Uncle Magnus Pringle in *The Ultra-Violet Catastrophe* is superb: "There on the flowery couch was a very clean, scrubbed and scoured, washed-up and brushed-down little old man. Sally thought Aunt Anne must have rinsed him out, and then starched and ironed him, and then polished him with a soft cloth." However, Margaret Mahy's love of language can make her stories seem over lyrical and romantic in places, and often rather long; the use of words and complex sentence structure makes many of her picture books not within the reach of young readers.

In her books for young children to read for themselves *(The Bus under the Leaves, Clancy's Cabin)*, Margaret Mahy has had to restrain her imagination to conform to the pattern of language and form required; the books are more accessible, but in the need for simplicity they have lost much of their power and originality. She comes into her own again in her collection of short stories and poems (the three Margaret Mahy Story Books). These are a mixture of homely tales of children in domestic situations, and more fanciful tales of magic, interspersed with poems which serve as a marvellous vehicle for her imaginative use of language. Again the stories are peopled with unusual and delightful characters (with several appearances by that ever popular character the witch); and they are told with skillful construction and superb use of language.

Margaret Mahy is outstanding in the richness of her ideas and in her great storytelling ability. She has a fresh and vivid imagination which speaks directly to the imagination of the child and an ability to use language to increase the force of her imagery to great effect.

—Janet E. Newman

MANNING, Rosemary. British. Born in Weymouth, Dorset, 9 December 1911. Educated at the University of London, B.A. in classics 1933. Address: 20 Lyndhurst Gardens, London, NW3 5NR, England.

PUBLICATIONS FOR CHILDREN

Fiction

> *Green Smoke*, illustrated by Constance Marshall.   London, Constable, and New York, Doubleday, 1957.
> *Dragon in Danger*, illustrated by Constance Marshall.   London, Constable, 1959; New York, Doubleday, 1960.
> *The Dragon's Quest*, illustrated by Constance Marshall.   London, Constable, 1961; New York, Doubleday, 1962.
> *Arripay*, illustrated by Victor Ambrus.   London, Constable, 1963; New York, Farrar Straus, 1964.
> *Boney Was a Warrior*, illustrated by Lynette Hemmant.   London, Hamish Hamilton, 1966.
> *The Rocking Horse*, illustrated by Lynette Hemmant.   London, Hamish Hamilton, 1970.

Other

> *Heraldry*, illustrated by Janet Price.   London, A. and C. Black, 1966.
> *Railways and Railwaymen*.   London, Penguin, 1977.

> Editor, *The Shepherd's Play, and Noah and the Flood: Two Miracle Plays*.   Glasgow, Grant, 1955.
> Editor, *A Grain of Sand: Poems*, by William Blake, illustrated by Blake.   London, Bodley Head, 1967; New York, Watts, 1968.

Editor, *Great Expectations*, by Charles Dickens, illustrated by Gareth Floyd.   London, Collins, 1970.

PUBLICATIONS FOR ADULTS

Novels

Remaining a Stranger (as Mary Voyle).   London, Heinemann, 1953.
A Change of Direction (as Mary Voyle).   London, Heinemann, 1955.
Look, Stranger.   London, Cape, 1960; as *The Shape of Innocence*, New York, Doubleday, 1961.
The Chinese Garden.   London, Cape, 1962; New York, Farrar Straus, 1963.
Man on a Tower.   London, Cape, 1965.

Other

From Holst to Britten: A Study of Modern Choral Music.   London, Workers' Music Association, 1949.

Rosemary Manning comments:
My first three children's books (the "dragon books") were written for Sue, the small daughter of a friend. Perhaps this gives them a personal quality which comes out in the relationship between the dragon and Sue, and accounts for their popularity. *Arripay*, an historical novel, was also written for Sue, when she was somewhat older. The other children's books were all commissioned.
I must confess that my adult fiction means a great deal more to me. I doubt if I shall write more children's books, but I have returned to adult novel-writing after a long absence.

*   *   *

The puzzle for outsiders is to find the link between Rosemary Manning, the academic, business-like woman who has had considerable professional success outside writing, and the author of the bedtime stories of R. Dragon, 1,500 years old, with a weakness for almond buns.
The three Dragon stories appeared between 1957 and 1961, dedicated to Susan Elisabeth Astle who may have been their inspiration. Certainly the books appear to have roots in a familiar landscape and a close relationship with a child listener. The opening of the first book, *Green Smoke*, establishes the associations very clearly: " This is a story about a girl called Susan, or Sue for short, who went for a seaside holiday to Constantine Bay in Cornwall." The immediate, unpretentious style is maintained. Not for Rosemary Manning's readers the puzzle of sorting out detailed landscape instructions: "Just think of the rockiest rocks, the sandiest sand , the greenest sea and the bluest sky you can possibly imagine and you will have some idea of Constantine Bay."
Susan finds a dragon in a secret cove, a dragon with a fund of stories which he is willing to share – of Cornish giants and magical creatures and, especially, of King Arthur. The Arthurian theme is continued in *The Dragon's Quest*, where the dragon is missing, gone on a visit, but leaves Sue his account of his adventures at Arthur's court to keep her company. The technique is of stories within a story, a framework elaborated by Paul Biegel in *King of the Copper Mountains*, and one could complain that it provides here neither the satisfaction of an old tale retold well nor the originality of new tales. *Dragon in Danger* changes the pattern, telling what happened when R. Dragon decided to visit Sue's home near London. The Dragon stories were out of print for many years until the Puffin editions of 1967–74, and in some ways they rate as period pieces, with their cosy background of Mummy and Daddy and

827

workmen who say "Thank you kindly mum": their strength is the intimate story-telling voice which immediately commands attention.

Endearing as the stories of Sue and R. Dragon are, Rosemary Manning's most impressive children's book is *Arripay*, a story of Harry Paye, the 15th-century privateer who sailed the Dorset coast in the reign of Henry IV. In this novel, firmly founded on historical fact, Rosemary Manning tackles a theme worthy of Rosemary Sutcliff. Against a precisely realised setting of Poole harbour is a robust tale of piracy, greed and betrayal through which we follow Adam, a boy out of sorts with his family and neighbours, with no stomach for violence, nor yet the temperament for a monk's life, until he finds eventually a role which he can accept.

It is ironical that today *Arripay* is largely forgotten, lost in the anti-historical swing which followed the vogue for historical stories in the 1950's, while *Green Smoke* is in its fifth Puffin reprint. Thoughts on this paradox may well have inspired Rosemary Manning's much-quoted article, "Whatever Happened to Onion John" *(The Times Literary Supplement*, 4 December 1969) but by now the fickleness of literary fashion is likely to be of only marginal interest to an author whose writing for children ceased as Susan Elisabeth Astle grew to adulthood.

—Peggy Heeks

MANNING-SANDERS, Ruth. British. Born in Swansea, Glamorgan, in 1895. Educated at Manchester University. Married Geoffrey Manning- Sanders (died); has one son and one daughter. Travelled for two years with a circus. Address: 1 Morrab Terrace, Penzance, Cornwall, England.

PUBLICATIONS FOR CHILDREN

Fiction

> *Children by the Sea*, illustrated by Mary Shepard.   London, Collins, 1938; as *Adventure May Be Anywhere*, New York, Stokes, 1939.
> *Elephant*.   New York, Stokes, 1938; London, Collins, 1940.
> *Mystery at Penmarth*, illustrated by Anne Bullen.   London, Collins, 1940; New York, McBride, 1941.
> *Circus Book*.   London, Collins, 1947; as *The Circus*, New York, Chanticleer Press, 1948.
> *Circus Boy*, illustrated by Annette Macarthur-Onslow.   London, Oxford University Press, 1960.
> *The Smugglers*, illustrated by William Stobbs.   London, Oxford University Press, 1962.
> *The Crow's Nest*, illustrated by Lynette Hemmant.   London, Hamish Hamilton, 1965.
> *Slippery Shiney*, illustrated by Constance Marshall.   London, Hamish Hamilton, 1965.
> *The Extraordinary Margaret Catchpole*.   London, Heinemann, 1966.
> *The Magic Squid*, illustrated by Eileen Armitage.   London, Methuen, 1968.
> *The Spaniards Are Coming!*, illustrated by Jacqueline Riszi.   London, Heinemann, 1969; New York, Watts, 1970.
> *Young Gabby Goose*, illustrated by James Hodgson.   London, Methuen, 1976.

Other

> *Swan of Denmark: The Story of Hans Christian Andersen*, illustrated by Astrid Walford.   London, Heinemann, 1949; New York, McBride, 1950.

Peter and the Piskies: Cornish Folk and Fairy Tales, illustrated by Raymond Briggs. London, Oxford University Press, 1958; New York, Roy, 1966.

Red Indian Folk and Fairy Tales, illustrated by C. Walter Hodges. London, Oxford University Press, 1960; New York, Roy, 1962.

Animal Stories, illustrated by Annette Macarthur-Onslow. London, Oxford University Press, 1961; New York, Roy, 1962.

A Book of Giants [Dwarfs, Dragons, Witches, Wizards, Mermaids, Ghosts and Goblins, Princes and Princesses, Devils and Demons, Charms and Changelings, Ogres and Trolls, Sorcerers and Spells, Magic Animals, Monsters, Enchantment and Curses], illustrated by Robin Jacques. London, Methuen, 15 vols., 1962–76; New York, Dutton, 15 vols., 1964–77.

Damian and the Dragon: Modern Greek Folk-Tales, illustrated by William Papas. London, Oxford University Press, and New York, Roy, 1965.

Stories from the English and Scottish Ballads, illustrated by Trevor Ridley. London, Heinemann, and New York, Dutton, 1968.

The Glass Man and the Golden Bird: Hungarian Folk and Fairy Tales, illustrated by Victor Ambrus. London, Oxford University Press, and New York, Roy, 1968.

Jonnikin and the Flying Basket: French Folk and Fairy Tales, illustrated by Victor Ambrus. London, Oxford University Press, and New York, Dutton, 1969.

Gianni and the Ogre, illustrated by William Stobbs. London, Methuen, 1970; New York, Dutton, 1971.

A Choice of Magic, illustrated by Robin Jacques. London, Methuen, and New York, Dutton, 1971.

The Three Witch Maidens, illustrated by William Stobbs. London, Methuen, 1972.

Tortoise Tales, illustrated by Donald Chaffin. London, Methuen, 1972; Nashville, Nelson, 1974.

Sir Green Hat and the Wizard, illustrated by William Stobbs. London, Methuen, 1974.

Grandad and the Magic Barrel, illustrated by Robin Jacques. London, Methuen, 1974.

Old Dog Sirko: A Ukrainian Tale, illustrated by Leon Shtainments. London, Methuen, 1974.

Ram and Goat, illustrated by Robin Jacques. London, Methuen, 1974.

Stumpy: A Russian Tale, illustrated by Leon Shtainments. London, Methuen, 1974.

Fox Tales, illustrated by James Hodgson. London, Methuen, 1976.

Scottish Folk Tales, illustrated by William Stobbs. London, Methuen, 1976.

Old Witch Boneyleg, illustrated by Kilmeny Niland. London, Angus and Robertson, 1977.

Editor, *A Bundle of Ballads*, illustrated by William Stobbs. London, Oxford University Press, 1959; Philadelphia, Lippincott, 1961.

Editor, *Birds, Beasts and Fishes* (poetry anthology), illustrated by Rita Parsons. London, Oxford University Press, 1962.

Editor, *The Red King and the Witch: Gypsy Folk and Fairy Tales*, illustrated by Victor Ambrus. London, Oxford University Press, 1964; New York, Roy, 1965.

Editor, *The Hamish Hamilton Book of Magical Beasts*, illustrated by Raymond Briggs. London, Hamish Hamilton, 1965; as *A Book of Magical Beasts*, New York, Nelson, 1970.

Editor, *Festivals*, illustrated by Raymond Briggs. London, Heinemann, 1972; New York, Dutton, 1973.

PUBLICATIONS FOR ADULTS

Novels

The Twelve Saints. London, Christophers, 1925; New York, Clode, 1926.

Selina Pennaluna. London, Christophers, 1927.

Waste Corner. London, Christophers, 1927; New York, Clode, 1928.
Hucca's Moor. London, Faber, 1929.
The Crochet Woman. London, Faber, and New York, Coward McCann, 1930.
The Growing Trees. London, Faber, and New York, Morrow, 1931.
She Was Sophia. London, Cobden Sanderson, 1932.
Run Away. London, Cassell, 1934.
Mermaid's Mirror. London, Cassell, 1935.
The Girl Who Made an Angel. London, Cassell, 1936.
Luke's Circus. London, Collins, 1939; Boston, Little Brown, 1940.
Mr. Portal's Little Lions. London, Hale, 1952.
The Golden Ball. London, Hale, 1954.
Melissa. London, Hale, 1957.

Verse

The Pedlar and Other Poems. London, Selwyn and Blount, 1919.
Karn. Richmond, Surrey, Leonard and Virginia Woolf, 1922.
Pages from the History of Zachy Trenoy. London, Christophers, 1923.
The City. London, Benn, and New York, Dial Press, 1927.

Other

The West of England. London, Batsford, 1949.
Seaside England. London, Batsford, 1951.
The River Dart. London, Westaway Books, 1951.
The English Circus. London, Laurie, 1952.

*   *   *

To note that Ruth Manning-Sanders, undoubtedly best-known for her re-tellings of folk tales from all over the world, has also produced original work may be misleading, since the successful handling of folk material calls in itself for a high degree of creativity: a sympathy for the traditional themes and a feeling for language which enables Ms. Manning-Sanders to present her tales in a vigorous style which is neither old-fashioned nor anachronistically modernized. And it is interesting to find folk themes cropping up time and again in those stories she has written which are not re-tellings of traditional material, and which range from mystery adventure, through historical novels, to simple but attractive stories for younger readers.

Even *Mystery at Penmarth*, first published in 1940 and bearing many of the hallmarks of a dated pre-war *genre* with its ponies, children's secret societies, comic servants and Vicar, has stories of historical Cornwall and accounts of Cornish customs woven into the plot. Cornwall is again the setting for *The Smugglers*, a first-person narrative by the local Squire's son Ned of smuggling at the period when that activity seemed romantic; the revenue men are the villains of the piece, and all ends well for Ned and his much admired hero, the dashing smuggler Zach. It is the author's feeling for her Cornish background that counts here.

The ethics of smuggling are seen from a more sombre viewpoint in *The Extraordinary Margaret Catchpole*, a novel based on the real-life story of the Suffolk farm girl who took up, disastrously, with a smuggler named William Laud, was twice condemned to death – for horse-stealing and for escaping from prison – and finally transported to Australia, where she made good.

The social conditions of hardship in which the agricultural poor of the late 18th-century lived are well realized, and Margaret herself makes an attractive heroine.

However, perhaps the best of Ruth Manning-Sanders' historical novels is *Circus Boy*, another first-person narrative, presenting the world of the travelling showmen of Victorian times through the eyes of Tommy Gough. With his father's circus he travels the English and

Irish countryside, and the family suffer a fairy-tale reversal of fortune when they are engaged to perform at the Crystal Palace. There is plenty of verve in this story; the background detail is excellent, and the author enters into the spirit of circus life as lived by the artistes themselves.

For younger readers, *The Spaniards Are Coming*, written as part of the Long Ago Children series, follows the fortunes of Simon and Beth, who are peripherally involved with the Spanish Armada: a good introduction to the subject and the period. Two little stories for young children just beyond the picture book and reading primer stage are *The Magic Squid* and *The Crow's Nest*. Yet again it is interesting that even in these simple stories with their modern settings – the former in the Channel Islands, the latter in Scotland – the author makes telling use of such traditional themes as the magical sea creature, which must eventually be returned to its native element, and the thieving-magpie motif. The adult reader will be reminded of Ms. Manning-Sanders' feeling for traditional folk material and skill in handling it, and the child reader of these books will be led on to her fine collections of folk tales and ballads.

–Anthea Bell

MARKOOSIE. Canadian. Born in Port Harrison, Quebec, 19 June 1942. Educated at Port Harrison Elementary School; earned Commercial Pilot's Licence, and carpentry diploma. Married to Zipporah; has one son. Pilot, Atlas Aviation, Resolute, Canada, 1969–75; Translator, Northern Quebec Innuit Association, Montreal and Port Harrison, 1975–76. Agent: McGill-Queen's University Press, 1020 Pine Avenue West, Montreal, Quebec H3A 1A2. Address: Port Harrison, Quebec, Canada.

PUBLICATIONS FOR CHILDREN

Fiction

> *Harpoon of the Hunter*, illustrated by Germaine Arnaktauyok. Montreal and London, McGill-Queen's University Press, 1970.

Markoosie comments:

Harpoon of the Hunter is an Eskimo story handed down from one generation to the next. It tells of a boy hunter who becomes a man through one episode in his life.

*　*　*

The publication of *Harpoon of the Hunter* was significant in the history of Canadian publishing since it marked the first appearance of an Eskimo fiction story published in English. After the tale was serialized in the Eskimo newsletter *Inuttituut*, Markoosie was urged to make an English translation in order to give the story the wide audience it deserved.

Markoosie writes of the difficult struggle for survival in an inhospitable environment and the courage and indomitable fortitude displayed by the inhabitants of a bleak, forbidding land. The story begins in a dramatic fashion as a small settlement is attacked during the night by a rabid polar bear. Sixteen-year-old Kamik accompanies the small band of hunters who plan to track down and destroy this potential threat to the entire group. Their mission ends in tragedy and Kamik, the sole survivor of another attack by the now-wounded bear, is left to make his way home. He is found by searchers after suffering incredible hardships and all seems well as he and his tribe embark on a move to a larger settlement. During the move, his mother and future wife are killed and Kamik, bereft, chooses to end his life and find the peace of which his dying father had spoken.

Markoosie's spare, unembellished language gives the story the heightened impact of a Greek drama. The tragic tale has a fitting setting – the stark and silent landscape provides a contrast to the constant motion of the characters across it. The writing reminds one that the oral tradition is still very much a part of the Eskimo way of life. The story has the immediacy of the spoken word due to Markoosie's use of simple sentence structure and avoidance of descriptive passages. The writing is characterized, above all, by action. Something is continually happening or about to happen and the reader is led swiftly to the tale's conclusion. Tension is emphasized by the author's technique of shifting from one scene to another. The single-minded hatred of the wounded bear is juxtaposed effectively against the group of hunters whose hunger and inadequate weapons render them horribly vulnerable. Ooramik's dream of disaster provides an ominous hint of the death of the hunters.

Harpoon of the Hunter is a brilliantly successful portrayal of courage in the face of impossible odds. It is hoped that Markoosie will continue to write about his people for the benefit of readers of all ages.

—Fran Ashdown

MARTIN, David. British. Born in Budapest, Hungary, 22 December 1915. Educated at schools in Germany. Served in the International Brigade, Spain, 1937–38. Married Elizabeth Richenda Powell in 1941; has one son. Worked for the BBC and the *Daily Express*, and Literary Editor, *Reynolds News*, all in London, 1938–47; foreign correspondent in India, 1948–49. Settled in Australia, 1949. Since 1973, Member of the Council, Australian Society of Authors. Recipient: Australia Council Senior Fellowship, 1973–76. Agent: Curtis Brown (Australia) Pty. Ltd., 24 Renny Street, Sydney, New South Wales 2021. Address: 3 Finch Street, Beechworth, Victoria 3747, Australia.

PUBLICATIONS FOR CHILDREN

Fiction

Hughie, illustrated by Ron Brooks. Melbourne, Nelson, and New York, St. Martin's Press, 1971; London, Blackie, 1972.
Frank and Francesca. Melbourne, Nelson, 1972; London, Blackie, 1973.
Gary, illustrated by Con Aslanis. Melbourne, Cassell, 1972.
The Chinese Boy. Sydney, Hodder and Stoughton, and Leicester, Brockhampton Press, 1973.
The Cabby's Daughter. Sydney, Hodder and Stoughton, and Leicester, Brockhampton Press, 1974.
Katie, with Richenda Martin, illustrated by Noela Young. Sydney, Hodder and Stoughton, and Leicester, Brockhampton Press, 1974.
Mister P and His Remarkable Flight. London, Hodder and Stoughton, 1975.

PUBLICATIONS FOR ADULTS

Novels

Tiger Bay. London, Martin and Reid, 1946.

The Stones of Bombay. London and New York, Wingate, 1949.
The Young Wife. London, Macmillan, 1962.
The Hero of Too. London, Cassell, 1965; as *The Hero of the Town*, New York, Morrow, 1965.
The King Between. Melbourne and London, Cassell, 1966; as *The Littlest Neutral*, New York, Crown, 1966.
Where a Man Belongs. Melbourne and London, Cassell, 1969.

Short Stories

The Shoes Men Walk In. London, Pilot Press, 1946.

Plays

The Shepherd and the Hunter (produced London, 1945). London, Wingate, 1946.
The Young Wife (produced Melbourne, 1966).

Verse

Battlefields and Girls: Poems. Glasgow, Maclellan, 1942.
Trident, with Hubert Nicholson and John Manifold. London, Fore Publications, 1944.
From Life: Selected Poems. Sydney, Current, 1953.
Rob the Robber, His Life and Vindication (as Spinifex). Melbourne, Waters, 1954.
Poems, 1938–1958. Sydney, Edwards and Shaw, 1958.
Spiegel the Cat: A Story-Poem. Melbourne, Cheshire, 1961; London, Cassell, 1969; New York, Clarkson N. Potter, 1971.
The Gift: Poems 1959–1965. Brisbane, Jacaranda Press, 1966.
The Idealist. Brisbane, Jacaranda Press, 1968.

Other

On the Road to Sydney (travel). Melbourne, Nelson, 1970.

Editor, *Rhyme and Reason: 34 Poems.* London, Fore Publications, 1944.

Manuscript Collection: National Library of Australia, Canberra.

David Martin comments:
I make no sharp distinction between writing for young readers and other readers. My "young novels" are often concerned with the struggle of outsiders (Australian aborigines, Chinese on the Australian goldfields, etc.). I came to "young fiction" fairly early in life, and don't intend to concentrate on it exclusively. I like writing for teenagers because they respond honestly to an honest story: they do not require attention-whipping novelty at any price. I write about girls with as much sincerity and pleasure as I write about boys.

*   *   *

David Martin's origins – Jewish and European – are crucial to an understanding of his books for children. In raw, new Australia he is in a special position to respond to the condition of disadvantaged minorities. In his children's novels he has espoused the cause of the neglected and the persecuted, and has enriched the literature of his adopted country in terms of content and themes, if not in style.

His experience has led him to identify with the plight of Aborigines, aliens in their own land *(Hughie)* and the Chinese *(The Chinese Boy)* as well as assorted contemporary migrants

(Frank and Francesca). The Chinese Boy actually has an assortment of foreigners, all regarded as outsiders in the mountains of Kiandra in 1863. They include Americans, a black from Mauritius – and depressed and defeated Aborigines.

By dwelling on a sad history of neglect, hatred and suspicion – of the abominable human need for scapegoats – David Martin's books are unashamedly didactic and the result is a style which is somewhat heavyhanded. Yet even without the special pleading, Martin writes with an old-fashioned, melodramtic *Boys' Weekly* flavor which relies on colorful and spectacular incident rather than strong characterisation or really profound thematic treatment. Martin's books are never totally satisfying because of this dichotomy; plot and propaganda do not grow out of one another with any sense of unity. His habit of fragmenting families, sometimes by death, is an arbitrary device.

He is at his weakest in producing convincing characters – they are mainly types, and his children are quite unbelievable – or reporting everyday language with verisimilitude. His minor characters, sometimes only glimpsed, are much more successful than his heroes who are as white as snow, or his villains, those dastardly blackguards. He can handle raw humor with gusto and is at his best in exploring the thoughts – fears, hopes, and preoccupations – of children, rather than what they actually say. Martin shares Leon Garfield's love of the theatrical life and the exuberance of travelling thespians. For all his stylistic faults, he is a writer of life and zest who shares with his readers very strong emotion recollected in tranquillity. He has, indeed, a strong sense of story.

—Walter McVitty

MARTIN, Patricia Miles. Pseudonym: **Miska Miles.** American. Born in Cherokee, Kansas, 14 November 1899. Educated at East High School, Denver, graduated 1917; San Mateo College, California, 1965–66. Married Edward Richard Martin in 1942. Recipient: Christopher Award, 1972. Address: 910 Bromfield Road, San Mateo, California 94402, U.S.A.

PUBLICATIONS FOR CHILDREN

Fiction

> *Sylvester Jones and the Voice of the Forest,* illustrated by Leonard Weisgard. New York, Lothrop, 1958.
> *The Pointed Brush,* illustrated by Roger Duvoisin. New York, Lothrop, 1959; Kingswood, Surrey, World's Work, 1960.
> *Chandler Chipmunk's Flying Lesson and Other Stories,* illustrated by Margo Locke. New York, Abingdon Press, 1960.
> *Happy Piper and the Goat,* illustrated by Kurt Werth. New York, Lothrop, 1960.
> *Little Brown Hen,* illustrated by Harper Johnson. New York, Crowell, 1960.
> *Suzu and the Bride Doll,* illustrated by Kazue Mizumura. Chicago, Rand McNally, 1960; Kingswood, Surrey, World's Work, 1964.
> *The Raccoon and Mrs. McGinnis,* illustrated by Leonard Weisgard. New York, Putnam, 1961.
> *Benjie Goes into Business,* illustrated by Paul Galdone. New York, Putnam, 1961.
> *Show and Tell,* illustrated by Tom Hamil. New York, Putnam, 1962.
> *Rice Bowl Pet,* illustrated by Ezra Jack Keats. New York, Crowell, 1962.
> *The Lucky Little Porcupine,* illustrated by Lee Smith. New York, Putnam, 1963.
> *The Birthday Present,* illustrated by Margo Locke. New York, Abingdon Press, 1963.

Little Two and the Peach Tree, illustrated by Joan Berg.   New York, Atheneum, 1963.
The Greedy One, illustrated by Kazue Mizumura.   Chicago, Rand McNally, 1964;
   Kingswood, Surrey, World's Work, 1965.
No, No, Rosina, illustrated by Earl Thollander.   New York, Putnam, 1964.
Calvin and the Cub Scouts, illustrated by Tom Hamil.   New York, Putnam, 1964.
The Broomtail Bronc, illustrated by Margo Locke.   New York, Abingdon Press, 1965.
Jump Frog Jump, illustrated by Earl Thollander.   New York, Putnam, 1965.
The Bony Pony, illustrated by Glen Dines.   New York, Putnam, 1965.
Rolling the Cheese, illustrated by Alton Raible.   New York, Atheneum, 1966.
The Pumpkin Patch, illustrated by Tom Hamil.   New York, Putnam, 1966.
Mrs. Grumble and Fire Engine No. 7, illustrated by Earl Thollander.   New York,
   Putnam, 1966.
Friend of Miguel, illustrated by Genia.   Chicago, Rand McNally, 1967.
Trina's Boxcar, illustrated by Robert Jefferson.   Nashville, Abingdon Press, 1967.
Dolls from Cheyenne, illustrated by Don Almquist.   New York, Putnam, 1967.
Woody's Big Trouble, illustrated by Paul Galdone.   New York, Putnam, 1967.
A Long Ago Christmas, illustrated by Albert Orbaan.   New York, Putnam, 1968.
Grandma's Gun, illustrated by Robert Corey.   San Carlos, California, Golden Gate
   Books, 1968.
Kumi and the Pearl, illustrated by Tom Hamil.   New York, Putnam, 1968.
One Special Dog, illustrated by John and Lucy Hawkinson.   Chicago, Rand McNally,
   1968.
The Dog and the Boat Boy, illustrated by Earl Thollander.   New York, Putnam, 1969.
That Cat! 1-2-3, illustrated by Unada.   New York, Putnam, 1970.
There Goes the Tiger!, illustrated by Tom Hamil.   New York, Putnam, 1970.
Navajo Pet, illustrated by John Hamberger.   New York, Putnam, 1971.
Be Brave, Charlie, illustrated by Bonnie Johnson.   New York, Putnam, 1972.
Cat, illustrated by Jonathan Goell.   Boston, Ginn, 1974.
Hide, illustrated by Joe McIntosh.   Boston, Ginn, 1974.
How Can You Hide an Elephant?, illustrated by George Ulrich.   Boston, Ginn, 1974.

Fiction (as Miska Miles)

Kickapoo, illustrated by Wesley Dennis.   Boston, Little Brown, 1961.
Dusty and the Fiddlers, illustrated by Erik Blegvad.   Boston, Little Brown, 1962.
See a White Horse, illustrated by Wesley Dennis.   Boston, Little Brown, 1963.
Pony in the Schoolhouse, illustrated by Erik Blegvad.   Boston, Little Brown, 1964.
Mississippi Possum, illustrated by John Schoenherr.   Boston, Little Brown, 1965.
Fox and the Fire, illustrated by John Schoenherr.   Boston, Little Brown, 1966.
Teacher's Pet, illustrated by Fen Lasell.   Boston, Little Brown, 1966.
The Pieces of Home, illustrated by Victor Ambrus.   Boston, Little Brown, 1967.
Rabbit Garden, illustrated by John Schoenherr.   Boston, Little Brown, 1967.
Uncle Fonzo's Ford, illustrated by Wendy Watson.   Boston, Little Brown, 1968.
Nobody's Cat, illustrated by John Schoenherr.   Boston, Little Brown, 1969.
Apricot ABC, illustrated by Peter Parnall.   Boston, Little Brown, 1969.
Hoagie's Rifle-Gun, illustrated by John Schoenherr.   Boston, Little Brown, 1970.
Eddie's Bear, illustrated by John Schoenherr.   Boston, Little Brown, 1970.
Gertrude's Pocket, illustrated by Emily McCully.   Boston, Little Brown, 1970.
Annie and the Old One, illustrated by Peter Parnall.   Boston, Little Brown, 1971.
Wharf Rat, illustrated by John Schoenherr.   Boston, Little Brown, 1972.
Somebody's Dog, illustrated by John Schoenherr.   Boston, Little Brown, 1973.
Otter in the Cove, illustrated by John Schoenherr.   Boston, Little Brown, 1974.
Tree House Town, illustrated by Emily McCully.   Boston, Little Brown, 1974.
Swim, Little Duck, illustrated by Jim Arnosky.   Boston, Little Brown, 1976.
Chicken Forgets, illustrated by Jim Arnosky.   Boston, Little Brown, 1976.

Aaron's Door, illustrated by Alan Cober.   Boston, Little Brown, 1977.
Small Rabbit, illustrated by Jim Arnosky.   Boston, Little Brown, 1977.

Plays

Two Plays about Foolish People (includes *An Invitation to Supper* and *Little Ugo and the Foolish Ones*), illustrated by Gabriel Lisowski.   New York, Putnam, 1972.

Verse

Sing, Sailor, Sing, illustrated by Graham Booth.   San Carlos, California, Golden Gate Books, 1966; Kingswood, Surrey, World's Work, 1968.

Other

John Fitzgerald Kennedy, illustrated by Paul Frame.   New York, Putnam, 1964.
Abraham Lincoln, illustrated by Gustav Schrotter.   New York, Putnam, 1964.
Pocahontas, illustrated by Portia Takakjian.   New York, Putnam, 1964.
Daniel Boone, illustrated by Glen Dines.   New York, Putnam, 1965.
Jefferson Davis, illustrated by Salem Tamer.   New York, Putnam, 1966.
Andrew Jackson, illustrated by Salem Tamer.   New York, Putnam, 1966.
John Marshall, illustrated by Salem Tamer.   New York, Putnam, 1967.
Dolley Madison, illustrated by Unada.   New York, Putnam, 1967.
Jacqueline Kennedy Onassis, illustrated by Paul Frame.   New York, Putnam, 1969.
Zachary Taylor, illustrated by Tran Mawicke.   New York, Putnam, 1969.
The Dog Next Door and Other Stories (reader), with Theodore Clymer.   Boston, Ginn, 1972.
James Madison, illustrated by Richard Cuffari.   New York, Putnam, 1970.
Eskimos: People of Alaska, illustrated by Robert Frankenberg.   New York, Parents' Magazine Press, 1970.
Indians: The First Americans, illustrated by Robert Frankenberg.   New York, Parents' Magazine Press, 1970.
Thomas Alva Edison, illustrated by Fermin Rocker.   New York, Putnam, 1971.
Chicanos: Mexicans in the United States, illustrated by Robert Frankenberg.   New York, Parents' Magazine Press, 1971.
May I Come In? (reader), with Theodore Clymer.   Boston, Ginn, 1976.

Manuscript Collection: de Grummond Collection, University of Southern Mississippi, Hattiesburg.

Patricia Miles Martin comments:
    It is my hope that through my books children will be interested in reading – not only my work – but in further reading. It is my intention to pass on to young people my own values and standards.

*   *   *

    Patricia Miles Martin provides the young reader with an opportunity to expand his horizon to include unusual animals, cultural pluralism, and famous people. She is a craftswoman in the field, researching and writing with unusual respect for the subject.
    Flora and fauna have possessed the author, apparent since her transfer from the field of poetry to children's books two decades ago with her debut, *Sylvester Jones and the Voice of the Forest*. She selects unlikely heroes such as those of *Mississippi Possum, The Lucky Little Porcupine*, and *Wharf Rat*. Even her alphabet book, *Apricot ABC*, is an ecological story

following the web of life: "An *A*pricot tree grew knobbly and tall/Beside a rickety garden wall ... it startled a *Bee*." Mrs. Martin's feeling for the earth and for life's stages are apparent in many books, but are epitomized in *Annie and the Old One*. Natural elements are depicted in other books. "The account of the blizzard and what came of it is refreshingly down to earth, with no heroics," reviewer Mary Dunham wrote of *Pony in the Schoolhouse* for the *Christian Science Monitor* (5 November 1964). Selma G. Lanes commented in *Book Week* (3 April 1966) that in *Fox and the Fire* "Both author and illustrator are naturalists at heart, and not a single false or anthropomorphic note is struck in this simple, straight-forward tale of a fox's eye-view of a natural disaster and its aftermath." In a review of *Mississippi Possum*, Alice Dalgliesh wrote of the animal in the flood in *Saturday Review* (19 June 1965), "Simple, direct, well-written, this story succeeds in making the reader care about the little possum that lived in a hollow log and was afraid of people .... Stories like this, written in a natural way, need all the recognition that is their due."

Cultures less familiar to the general reading audience are rarely identified as ethnically or racially different. It is only by implication or verified in the illustrations that the families in *Mississippi Possum* or *Little Brown Hen* are black or that the heroine of *Teacher's Pet* is a migrant fruit picker in Colorado. The author opens the door on Japanese family life in *The Greedy One, Kumi and the Pearl*, and *Little Two and the Peach Tree*, while she documents tribal American-Indian culture in *Navajo Pet* and *Annie and the Old One*.

While many of her fiction books are written under the pseudonym Miska Miles, the non-fiction titles appear under her married name. Primarily series books, they range historically from the Supreme Court Justice John Marshall to Jacqueline Kennedy Onassis. Typical are the "See and Read Beginning to Read Biographies" directed to youngsters grade two to four. Books about the Chicana, Eskimo, and Indian cultures in what is now America are in "A Stepping Stone Book" series for youngsters.

Patricia Miles Martin chooses titles which succinctly introduce both the character and the plot, such as *Benjie Goes into Business, Calvin and the Cub Scouts, Chandler Chipmunk's Flying Lesson*, and *Chicken Forgets*. Her skill as a poet is incorporated into both verse and prose texts. *Sing, Sailor, Sing* opens, "In the year of fourteen-thirty two/There was a boy Bartholmeu/In Portugal/He lived in a time when no one knew/What was false and what was true/In Portugal."

Reviewers use words and phrases such as "heartwarming," "quiet beauty" and "gentle dignity" to describe Mrs. Martin's texts. *Annie and the Old One* has been honored as a Newbery Honor Book, in addition to receiving other awards.

—Karen Nelson Hoyle

MASEFIELD, John (Edward). British. Born in Ledbury, Herefordshire, 1 June 1878. Educated at King's School, Warwick. Served in the Red Cross in France and Gallipoli during World War I. Married Constance de la Cherois-Crommelin in 1903 (died, 1960); one son and one daughter. Indentured on the merchant training ship *Conway*, 1891–3; apprenticed on a windjammer, 1894; Sixth Officer, White Star liner *Adriatic*; worked at various odd jobs in New York City, and in carpet factory, Yonkers, New York, 1896–97; Literary Editor of *Speaker* magazine after 1900; feature writer for the *Manchester Guardian*. Member of the British Council's Book and Periodicals Committee. Recipient: Polignac Prize, for poetry, 1912; Shakespeare Prize, Hamburg University, 1938; William Foyle Prize, for poetry, 1962. D.Litt.: Oxford University, 1922; LL.D.: University of Aberdeen, 1922. Named Poet Laureate, 1930; Order of Merit, 1935; Royal Society of Literature Companion of Literature, 1961. *Died 12 May 1967.*

PUBLICATIONS FOR CHILDREN

Fiction

A Book of Discoveries, illustrated by Gordon Browne.   London, Wells Gardner, and
New York, Stokes, 1910.
Lost Endeavour.   London and New York, Nelson, 1910.
Martin Hyde, The Duke's Messenger, illustrated by T.C. Dugdale.   London, Wells
Gardner, and Boston, Little Brown, 1910.
Jim Davis; or, The Captive of the Smugglers.   London, Wells Gardner, 1911; New
York, Stokes, 1912.
The Midnight Folk.   London, Heinemann, and New York, Macmillan, 1927.
The Box of Delights; or, When the Wolves Were Running.   London, Heinemann, and
New York, Macmillan, 1935.

PUBLICATIONS FOR ADULTS

Fiction

Captain Margaret: A Romance.   London, Grant Richards, 1908; Philadelphia,
Lippincott, 1909.
Multitude and Solitude.   London, Grant Richards, 1909; New York, Kennerley, 1910.
The Street of To-Day.   London, Dent, and New York, Dutton, 1911.
Sard Harker.   London, Heinemann, and New York, Macmillan, 1924.
Odtaa.   London, Heinemann, and New York, Macmillan, 1926.
The Hawbucks.   London, Heinemann, and New York, Macmillan, 1929.
The Bird of Dawning; or, The Fortune of the Sea.   London, Heinemann, and New
York, Macmillan, 1933.
The Taking of the Gry.   London, Heinemann, and New York, Macmillan, 1934.
Victorious Troy; or, "The Hurrying Angel."   London, Heinemann, and New York,
Macmillan, 1935.
Eggs and Baker; or, The Days of Trial.   London, Heinemann, and New York,
Macmillan, 1936.
The Square Peg; or, The Gun Fella.   London, Heinemann, and New York, Macmillan,
1937.
Dead Ned: The Autobiography of a Corpse ....   London, Heinemann, and New York,
Macmillan, 1938.
Live and Kicking Ned: A Continuation of the Tale of Dead Ned.   London, Heinemann,
and New York, Macmillan, 1939.
Basilissa: A Tale of the Empress Theodora.   London, Heinemann, and New York,
Macmillan, 1940.
Conquer: A Tale of the Nika Rebellion in Byzantium.   London, Heinemann, and New
York, Macmillan, 1941.
Badon Parchments.   London, Heinemann, 1947.

Short Stories

A Mainsail Haul.   London, Elkin Mathews, 1905; revised edition, 1913; New York,
Macmillan, 1913.
A Tarpaulin Muster.   London, Grant Richards, 1907; New York, Dodge, 1908.

Plays

The Campden Wonder (produced London, 1907).   Included in *The Tragedy of Nan and
Other Plays*, 1909.

The Tragedy of Nan (produced London, 1908). Included in *The Tragedy of Nan and Other Plays*, 1909.

The Tragedy of Nan and Other Plays (includes *The Campden Wonder* and *Mrs. Harrison*). London, Grant Richards, and New York, Kennerley, 1909.

The Tragedy of Pompey the Great (produced London, 1910). London, Sidgwick and Jackson, and Boston, Little Brown, 1910; revised version (produced Manchester, 1914), Sidgwick and Jackson, and New York, Macmillan, 1914.

Anne Pedersdotter, adaptation of a play by Hans Wiers-Jenssen. Boston, Little Brown, 1917; (as *The Witch*, produced Glasgow, 1910; London, 1911), New York, Brentano's 1926.

Philip the King (produced Bristol and London, 1914). Included in *Philip the King and Other Poems*, 1914.

The Faithful (produced Birmingham, 1915; London and New York, 1919). London, Heinemann, and New York, Macmillan, 1915.

Good Friday: A Play in Verse (produced London, 1917). Letchworth, Hertfordshire, Garden City Press, 1916; in *Good Friday and Other Poems*, 1916.

The Sweeps of Ninety-Eight (produced Birmingham, 1916). Included in *The Locked Chest, and The Sweeps of Ninety-Eight*, 1916.

The Locked Chest, and The Sweeps of Ninety-Eight. Letchworth, Hertfordshire, Garden City Press, and New York, Macmillan, 1916.

The Locked Chest (produced London, 1920). Included in *The Locked Chest, and The Sweeps of Ninety-Eight*, 1916.

Melloney Holtspur (produced London, 1923). London, Heinemann, and New York, Macmillan, 1922.

Esther and Berenice, adaptations of plays by Racine. London, Heinemann, 2 vols., and New York, Macmillan, 1922.

A King's Daughter: A Tragedy in Verse (produced Oxford, 1923; London, 1928). London, Heinemann, and New York, Macmillan, 1923.

Tristan and Isolt: A Play in Verse (produced Oxford, 1923; London, 1927). London, Heinemann, and New York, Macmillan, 1927.

The Trial of Jesus (produced London, 1926). London, Heinemann, and New York, Macmillan, 1925.

Verse and *Prose Plays*. New York, Macmillan, 2 vols., 1925.

The Coming of Christ (produced Oxford, 1928). London, Heinemann, and New York, Macmillan, 1928.

Easter: A Play for Singers. London, Heinemann, and New York, Macmillan, 1929.

End and Beginning. London, Heinemann, and New York, Macmillan, 1933.

A Play for Saint George. London, Heinemann, and New York, Macmillan, 1948.

Verse

Salt-Water Ballads. London, Grant Richards, 1902; New York, Macmillan, 1913.

Ballads. London, Elkin Mathews, 1903; revised edition, as *Ballads and Poems*, 1910.

The Everlasting Mercy. London, Sidgwick and Jackson, and Portland, Maine, Smith and Sale, 1911.

The Story of a Round-House and Other Poems. New York, Macmillan, 1912; revised edition, 1913.

The Widow in the Bye Street. London, Sidgwick and Jackson, 1912; with *The Everlasting Mercy*, New York, Macmillan, 1912.

The Daffodil Fields. London, Heinemann, and New York, Macmillan, 1913.

Dauber. London, Heinemann, 1913; with *The Daffodil Fields*, New York, Macmillan, 1923.

Philip the King and Other Poems. London, Heinemann, and New York, Macmillan, 1914.

Good Friday and Other Poems. New York, Macmillan, 1916.

Sonnets. New York, Macmillan, 1916.

Poems. New York, Macmillan, 1916; revised edition, 1923, 1929; as *Collected Poems*, 1935.

Sonnets and Poems. Letchworth, Hertfordshire, Garden City Press, 1916.

Lollingdon Downs and Other Poems. New York, Macmillan, and London, Heinemann, 1917.

Rosas. New York, Macmillan, 1918.

Reynard the Fox; or, The Ghost Heath Run. New York, Macmillan, and London, Heinemann, 1919.

Animula. London, Chiswick Press, 1920.

Enslaved. New York, Macmillan, 1920.

Enslaved and Other Poems. London, Heinemann, 1920; New York, Macmillan, 1923.

Right Royal. New York, Macmillan, and London, Heinemann, 1920.

King Cole. London, Heinemann, and New York, Macmillan, 1921.

The Dream. London, Heinemann, and New York, Macmillan, 1922.

Selected Poems. London, Heinemann, 1922; revised edition, 1938.

King Cole and Other Poems. London, Heinemann, 1923.

The Dream and Other Poems. New York, Macmillan, 1923.

The Collected Poems of John Masefield. London, Heinemann, 1923; revised edition, 1935, 2 vols., 1946.

Sonnets of Good Cheer to the Lena Ashwell Players .... London, Mendip Press, 1926.

Midsummer Night and Other Tales in Verse. London, Heinemann, and New York, Macmillan, 1928.

The Wanderer of Liverpool (verse and prose). London, Heinemann, and New York, Macmillan, 1930.

Poems of the Wanderer: The Ending. Privately printed, 1930.

Minnie Maylow's Story and Other Tales and Scenes. London, Heinemann, and New York, Macmillan, 1931.

A Tale of Troy. London, Heinemann, and New York, Macmillan, 1932.

A Letter from Pontus and Other Verse. London, Heinemann, and New York, Macmillan, 1936.

The Country Scene in Poems and Pictures, illustrated by Edward Seago. London, Collins, 1937; New York, Collins, 1938.

Tribute to Ballet in Poems and Pictures, illustrated by Edward Seago. London, Collins, and New York, Macmillan, 1938.

Some Verses to Some Germans. London, Heinemann, and New York, Macmillan, 1939.

Shopping in Oxford. London, Heinemann, 1941.

Gautama the Enlightened and Other Verse. London, Heinemann, and New York, Macmillan, 1941.

Natalie Maisie and Pavilastukay: Two Tales in Verse. London, Heinemann, and New York, Macmillan, 1942.

A Generation Risen. London, Collins, 1942; New York, Macmillan, 1943.

Land Workers. London, Heinemann, 1942; New York, Macmillan, 1943.

Wonderings: Between One and Six Years. London, Heinemann, and New York, Macmillan, 1943.

On the Hill. London, Heinemann, and New York, Macmillan, 1949.

Bluebells and Other Verse. London, Heinemann, and New York, Macmillan, 1961.

Old Raiger and Other Verse. London, Heinemann, 1964; New York, Macmillan, 1965.

In Glad Thanksgiving. London, Heinemann, and New York, Macmillan, 1967.

Other

Sea Life in Nelson's Time. London, Methuen, 1905; New York, Macmillan, 1925.

On the Spanish Main; or, Some English Forays on the Isthmus of Darien .... London, Methuen, and New York, Macmillan, 1906.

Chronicles of the Pilgrim Fathers. London, Dent, and New York, Dutton, 1910.

My Faith in Woman Suffrage. London, Woman's Press, 1910.

William Shakespeare. London, Williams and Norgate, and New York, Holt, 1911; revised edition, London, Heinemann, 1954.

John M. Synge: A Few Personal Recollections .... Churchtown, Cuala Press, and New York, Macmillan, 1915.

Gallipoli. London, Heinemann, and New York, Macmillan, 1916.

The Old Front Line; or, The Beginning of the Battle of the Somme. London, Heinemann, and New York, Macmillan, 1917.

The War and the Future. New York, Macmillan, 1918; as *St. George and the Dragon*, London, Heinemann, 1919.

The Poems and Plays of John Masefield. London, Macmillan, 2 vols., 1918.

The Battle of the Somme. London, Heinemann, 1919.

John Ruskin. Privately printed, 1920.

The Taking of Helen. London, Heinemann, and New York, Macmillan, 1923.

The Taking of Helen and Other Prose Selections. New York, Macmillan, 1924.

Recent Prose. London, Heinemann, 1924; revised edition, 1932; New York, Macmillan, 1933.

Shakespeare and Spiritual Life (lecture). London and New York, Oxford University Press, 1924.

With the Living Voice (lecture). London, Heinemann, and New York, Macmillan, 1925.

Oxford Recitations. New York, Macmillan, 1928.

Chaucer (lecture). Cambridge, University Press, and New York, Macmillan, 1931.

Poetry (lecture). London, Heinemann, 1931; New York, Macmillan, 1932.

The Conway: From Her Foundation to the Present Day. London, Heinemann, and New York, Macmillan, 1933; revised edition, Heinemann, 1953.

Collected Works (Wanderer Edition). London, Heinemann, 10 vols., 1935–38.

Some Memories of W.B. Yeats. Dublin, Cuala Press, and New York, Macmillan, 1940.

In the Mill (autobiography). London, Heinemann, and New York, Macmillan, 1941.

The Nine Days' Wonder: The Operation Dynamo. London, Heinemann, and New York, Macmillan, 1941.

The Twenty Five Days. London, Heinemann, 1941.

I Want! I Want! London, National Book Council, 1944; New York, Macmillan, 1945.

New Chum (autobiography). London, Heinemann, 1944; New York, Macmillan, 1945.

A Macbeth Production. London, Heinemann, 1945; New York, Macmillan, 1946.

Thanks Before Going .... London, Heinemann, 1946; New York, Macmillan, 1947; revised edition, Heinemann, 1947.

A Book of Both Sorts: Selelctions from the Verse and Prose of John Masefield. London, Heinemann, 1947.

In Praise of Nurses. London, Heinemann, 1950.

A Book of Prose Selections. London, Heinemann, and New York, Macmillan, 1950.

St. Katherine of Ledbury and Other Ledbury Papers. London, Heinemann, 1951.

So Long to Learn: Chapters of an Autobiography. London, Heinemann, and New York, Macmillan, 1952.

An Elizabethan Theatre in London. Privately printed, 1954.

The Story of Ossian. London, Heinemann, and New York, Macmillan, 1959.

Grace Before Ploughing: Fragments of Autobiography. London, Heinemann, and New York, Macmillan, 1966.

Editor, with Constance Masefield, *Lyrists of the Restoration ....* London, Grant Richards, 1905; New York, Stokes, n.d.

Editor, *The Poems of Robert Herrick*.   London, Grant Richards, 1905.
Editor, *Dampier's Voyages* ....   London, Grant Richards, 2 vols., 1906.
Editor, *A Sailor's Garland*.   London, Methuen, and New York, Macmillan, 1906.
Editor, *The Lyrics of Ben Jonson, Beaumont, and Fletcher*.   London, Grant Richards, 1906.
Editor, with Constance Masefield, *Essays, Moral and Polite, 1660–1714*.   London, Grant Richards, 1906; Freeport, New York, Books for Libraries Press, 1971.
Editor, *An English Prose Miscellany*.   London, Methuen, 1907.
Editor, *Defoe* (selections).   London, Bell, 1909.
Editor, *The Loyal Subject*, in *The Works of Beaumont and Fletcher*, edited by A.H. Bullen.   London, Bell, 1910.
Editor, *My Favourite English Poems*.   London, Heinemann, and New York, Macmillan, 1950.

Translator, *Polyxena's Speech from the Hecuba of Euripides*.   New York, Macmillan, 1928.

Bibliography: *Bibliography of John Masefield* by C.H. Simmons, New York, Columbia University Press, 1930, London, Oxford University Press, 1931.

Critical Studies: *John Masefield* by L.A.G. Strong, London, Longman, 1952; *John Masefield* by Muriel Spark, London, Peter Nevill, 1953; *John Masefield* by Margery Fisher, London, Bodley Head, and New York, Walck, 1963.

*   *   *

Nobody tells an adventure story better than John Masefield, keeping his readers galloping on the right track – tying up all the loose ends. It is no wonder that a complete set of his books, including two, *The Midnight Folk* and *The Box of Delights*, which are officially, so to speak, "children's books," are about the same people although their adventures are picked up at different times. These books, starting with *Sard Harker* and *Odtaa*, begin among the dictatorships of South America and on the high seas: where better for adventures? And considering what strong meat is demanded by most of today's young people, it seems to me that they are all highly suitable reading.

Yet we have to ask ourselves whether Masefield's writing dates too much to be swallowed by today's reader. Yes, it certainly does date. In his time a number of words now in common use were not printable – he had enormous trouble over one "bloody" in an early poem. Yet he gets the general feel of harsh treatment and harsh language in some of his sea scenes without crossing what were the publishers' limits 40 years ago. All that grates are small pieces of harmless slang which have dropped right out of use.

But there is nothing wrong with the plots and action of the stories themselves. Take the scene where Margarita and Sard are caught, escape, get caught again and – well, it seems to me to beat most other thrillers into a frazzle! This is mostly because it is told by someone who was also no mean poet, an unsurpassed dealer in words.

The Midnight Folk is the better of the two juveniles with young Kay Harker and his animal friends, not to speak of the amiable mermaids. Naturally they frustrate the wicked governess and her coven. There are delightful interludes as when the red and white chess men play one another, each encouraged by his own side. *The Box of Delights* has Kay again, but with rather too much make-believe about it, an irritating touch of whimsy, though again there is a splendid wild imagination working through it and painting scene after scene.

Some might find the interspersed verse in all Masefield's books a trifle embarrassing. I don't, though it is of its own period, more romantic and simpler than our usual poetic diet. It goes with a basic morality, which again is somewhat out of date. The good may be physically destroyed but their names live; it is not the clever, the anti-hero, who wins. This is even clearer in Masefield's poetic dramas, a few of which, one can now say with some certainty,

842

are likely to survive so long as written English is read and appreciated. Take one of his earliest verse plays, *The Faithful*, based on the Japanese story of the 47 Ronin. I was still in my teens when I read this; other teenagers may find themselves as deeply moved by it as I was then. This is Asano about to commit harakiri:

> Sometimes in wintry springs
> Frost, on a midnight breath,
> Comes to the cherry flowers
> And blasts their prime;
> So I, with all my powers
> Unused on men or things,
> Go down the wind to death,
> And know no fruiting time.

Another survivor is surely *Reynard the Fox*, again on its own ground a thriller. Whatever views one may have on hunting, this gives both sides; the kind of society it pictures is gone; but here it is set down in a simple trotting, four-stress metre, men, women and hounds: "Their minds being memories of smells." This metre lengthens to a gallop when the fox is running. It is all done with excellent craft.

A later book that seems to me quite different and wholly successful is *Basilissa*, a novel about Byzantium in the days of Justinian and Theodora. Again there is a strong thread of right and wrong with correct intuitive choices being made, as in a fairy tale, by the right people. Now it may be that this affinity with the world of the fairy tale and the ancient moral fauna and flora of the British unconscious is no longer what we understand. This world has its own kind of security, not certainly the security of a steady job, money in the bank or even a loving family, but an inside certainty: Yea, though we walk through death's dark vale. Yet I doubt if Masefield, with his deep sympathy with the ideas of other cultures, would say that orthodox Christianity was the answer. It is, however, something that we seem to lack and which if the young could get at it might help us out of our difficulties. We need luck. We need honour. It is never too early in life to grasp these. I hope out of the reading of Masefield both these intangibles may come a little nearer to a new generation of readers.

—Naomi Mitchison

MATHIS, Sharon Bell. American. Born in Atlantic City, New Jersey, 26 February 1937. Educated at Morgan State College, Baltimore, B.A. 1958. Married Leroy F. Mathis in 1957; has two daughters and one son. Interviewer, District of Columbia Children's Hospital, 1958–59; teacher, Holy Redeemer Elementary School, 1960–65, and Charles Hart Junior High School, 1965–72, both in Washington, D.C. Since 1972, teacher, Stuart Junior High School, Washington, D.C. Writer-in-Residence, Howard University, Washington, D.C., 1972–73. Recipient: Council for Interracial Books for Children award, 1969; Breadloaf Writers Conference grant, 1970; American Library Association Coretta Scott King Award, 1974. Agent: Curtis Brown Ltd., 575 Madison Avenue, New York, New York 10022. Address: c/o Viking Press, 625 Madison Avenue, New York, New York 10022, U.S.A.

PUBLICATIONS FOR CHILDREN

Fiction

Brooklyn Story, illustrated by Charles Bible. New York, Hill and Wang, 1970.

Sidewalk Story, illustrated by Leo Carty.   New York, Viking Press, 1971.
Teacup Full of Roses.   New York, Viking Press, 1972.
Listen for the Fig Tree.   New York, Viking Press, 1974.
The Hundred Penny Box, illustrated by Leo and Diane Dillon.   New York, Viking Press, 1975.

Other

Ray Charles, illustrated by George Ford.   New York, Crowell, 1973.

*   *   *

The advent of a Black literature for children has been slow in coming in the United States. Since the resurgence of a social consciousness in the 1960's, publishers have tried to meet the demand for more books on Black subjects, written for a Black audience. Of the many writers on the subject, Sharon Bell Mathis has made one of the greatest and most articulate impacts.

She wastes little time on the trivial, choosing to place the reader into the immediate action of the story. Plot development and character analysis are direct and little is glossed over. Subplots and minor themes evolve naturally and spontaneously from the incidents and the characters. Her book and magazine stories are written expressly for Black children, but her appeal with other children is as great. Her success comes from her approach: while never losing sight of her original intent, Mathis writes in a language and a style that are comfortable to many instead of a few. Her evocative moods have wide appeal, with the underlying message of "Black is beautiful." She dominates her stories with human experience and illuminates them by race. Her subjects, always within the realm of Black experience, range from a grandmother's reverie (*The Hundred Penny Box*) to blindness (*Listen for the Fig Tree*) to forced eviction (*Sidewalk Story*).

About her writing for children, Mathis has been quoted as saying, "I write to *salute* the strength in Black children, and to say to them, 'Stay strong, stay Black, and stay alive.' " This she has unquestionably done in her books, and has done it with laudable conviction.

—James W. Roginski

MATTINGLEY, Christobel (Rosemary).   Australian.   Born in Adelaide, South Australia, 26 October 1931. Educated at Presbyterian Ladies College, Pymble, New South Wales, 1940–45; The Friends' School, Hobart, Tasmania, 1945–47; University of Tasmania, Hobart, 1948–51, B.A. (honours); Public Library of Victoria Training College, 1952, Certificate of Proficiency. Married Cecil David Mattingley in 1953; has one daughter and two sons. Librarian, Department of Immigration, Canberra, 1951, Latrobe Valley Libraries, Victoria, 1953, Prince Alfred College, Adelaide, 1956–57, and St. Peter's Girls' School, Adelaide, 1966–70; Acquisitions Librarian, 1971, and Reader Services Librarian, 1972, Wattle Park Teachers' College, Adelaide; Reader Services Librarian, Murray Park College of Adult Education, Adelaide, 1973–74. Recipient: Australia Council Fellowship, 1975; International Youth Library Scholarship, 1976. Agent: A.P. Watt and Son, 26–28 Bedford Row, London WC1R 4HL, England. Address: Allendale Grove, Stonyfell, South Australia 5066, Australia.

PUBLICATIONS FOR CHILDREN

Fiction

The Picnic Dog, illustrated by Carolyn Dinan. London, Hamish Hamilton, 1970.
Windmill at Magpie Creek, illustrated by Gavin Rowe. Leicester, Brockhampton Press, 1971.
Worm Weather, illustrated by Carolyn Dinan. London, Hamish Hamilton, 1971.
Emu Kite, illustrated by Gavin Rowe. London, Hamish Hamilton, 1972.
Queen of the Wheat Castles, illustrated by Gavin Rowe. Leicester, Brockhampton Press, 1973.
The Battle of the Galah Trees, illustrated by Gareth Floyd. Leicester, Brockhampton Press, 1973.
Show and Tell, illustrated by Helen Sallis. Sydney, Hodder and Stoughton, and Leicester, Brockhampton Press, 1974.
Tiger's Milk, illustrated by Anne Ferguson. Sydney and London, Angus and Robertson, 1974.
The Surprise Mouse, illustrated by Carolyn Dinan. London, Hamish Hamilton, 1974.
Lizard Log, illustrated by Helen Sallis. Sydney, Hodder and Stoughton, 1975.
The Great Ballagundi Damper Bake, illustrated by Will Mahony. Sydney and London, Angus and Robertson, 1975.
The Long Walk, illustrated by Helen Sallis. Melbourne, Nelson, 1976.
The Special Present, illustrated by Noela Young. Sydney and London, Collins, 1977.
New Patches for Old. London, Hodder and Stoughton, 1977.
The Big Swim. Melbourne, Nelson, 1977.
Budgerigar Blue. Sydney and London, Hodder and Stoughton, 1977.

Christobel Mattingley comments:

My memories of childhood are intense and vivid, and my development as a writer began at an early age. The power of words and the magic of books had already enthralled me before I started school, and by the age of 8 I was reading widely, writing poetry, and making up stories and plays. I was always conscious of an affinity with nature and at 9 was introduced to serious nature study by an enlightened teacher and began keeping copious diaries of careful observations. At 10 I had my first publishing acceptance, in a natural history magazine. My father's work as a civil engineer building dams and bridges in various parts of Australia made me aware of the need for harmony between man and nature and intensified my love for wilderness areas. Experiencing childhood again with my own family acted as a catalyst for writing, and my stories have evolved as a combination of everyday events, places and personalities reinforcing my own emotions of childhood.

*   *   *

Although each of Christobel Mattingley's books is distinctly individual, certain characteristics are common. Her stories usually centre on one child in a small family. Boy or girl, this child acts with resourcefulness and initiative in reaching a desired objective – a personal goal. There is an adult handy for referral, and the relationship between child and adult is free of conflict, although, realistically, the parent sometimes does impose restrictions on the child. The events are always of the ordinary, everyday kind (e.g., a kite-flying contest in *Emu Kite* or a fancy dress party in *Worm Weather*), and the problems are commonplace rather than spectacular. Cathy in *Queen of the Wheat Castles* wants to save the lives of surplus kittens by finding owners for them. Antony in *Tiger's Milk* just wants to grow bigger and stronger and the book's solution is a recipe which any child can try at home. The children *do* finally succeed in their aims and, unlike some of her contemporaries, Christobel Mattingley does not probe the deep psychological guilts and anxieties of her heroes. They are ordinary children rather than schizophrenics.

A noticeable characteristic is the didacticism which arises from the author's personal affinity with the natural world and her concern for the conservation of wild life. This extends from the close observation of the behaviour of worms in *Worm Weather* to a boy's lone campaign to stop the local council from felling mighty eucalypts in a public park in *The Battle of the Galah Trees*. The absorbing natural details of *Show and Tell* are like those in *Lizard Log*, which has its own threatening band of human despoilers. All of Christobel Mattingley's books reveal her impressive love of all things natural. Where the other children in *Show and Tell* bring inanimate, *manufactured* objects like dolls, model cars and stamps to school, Robert is different: "Robert liked things that were alive. Robert liked things that were growing, like plants and tadpoles and silkworms."

The most rewarding and pervasive quality in Christobel Mattingley's books is the warmth of the personal relationships. In the age of the problem novel, in an era which eschews sentiment, it is heartening to experience basic humanity and trust as expressed between individuals, ignoring any artificial "generation gap," in books like *Worm Weather, The Surprise Mouse*, and *Queen of the Wheat Castles*.

Christobel Mattingley's talent and integrity as a writer, and her knowledge and remembrance of what it really feels like to be a young child, are guarantees of future work of excellence. It may be that she will never produce a ponderously "great" novel, but she tells an honest story with charming warmth and humanity.

—Walter McVitty

MAYNE, William. British. Born in Hull, Yorkshire, 16 March 1928. Educated at the Choir School, Canterbury. Lecturer, Deakin University, Geelong, Victoria, 1976–77. Recipient: Library Association Carnegie Medal, 1958. Address: c/o David Higham Associates Ltd., 5–8 Lower John Street, Golden Square, London W1R 4HA, England.

PUBLICATIONS FOR CHILDREN

Fiction

Follow the Footprints, illustrated by Shirley Hughes. London, Oxford University Press, 1953.

The World Upside Down, illustrated by Shirley Hughes. London, Oxford University Press, 1954.

A Swarm in May, illustrated by C. Walter Hodges. London, Oxford University Press, and Indianapolis, Bobbs Merrill, 1955.

The Member for the Marsh, illustrated by Lynton Lamb. London, Oxford University Press, 1956.

Choristers' Cake, illustrated by C. Walter Hodges. London, Oxford University Press, 1956; Indianapolis, Bobbs Merrill, 1958.

The Blue Boat, illustrated by Geraldine Spence. London, Oxford University Press, 1957; New York, Dutton, 1960.

A Grass Rope, illustrated by Lynton Lamb. London, Oxford University Press, 1957; New York, Dutton, 1962.

The Long Night, illustrated by D.J. Watkins-Pitchford. Oxford, Blackwell, 1958.

Underground Alley, illustrated by Marcia Lane Foster. London, Oxford University Press, 1958; New York, Dutton, 1961.

The Gobbling Billy, with Dick Caesar (as Dynely James). London, Gollancz, and New York, Dutton, 1959; as William Mayne and Dick Caesar, Leicester, Brockhampton Press, 1969.

The Thumbstick, illustrated by Tessa Theobald. London, Oxford University Press, 1959.

Thirteen O'Clock, illustrated by D.J. Watkins-Pitchford. Oxford, Blackwell, 1960.

The Rolling Season, illustrated by Christopher Brooker. London, Oxford University Press, 1960.

Cathedral Wednesday, illustrated by C. Walter Hodges. London, Oxford University Press, 1960.

The Fishing Party, illustrated by Christopher Brooker. London, Hamish Hamilton, 1960.

Summer Visitors, illustrated by William Stobbs. London, Oxford University Press, 1961.

The Changeling, illustrated by Victor Ambrus. London, Oxford University Press, 1961; New York, Dutton, 1963.

The Glass Ball, illustrated by Janet Duchesne. London, Hamish Hamilton, 1961; New York, Dutton, 1962.

The Last Bus, illustrated by Margery Gill. London, Hamish Hamilton, 1962.

The Twelve Dancers, illustrated by Lynton Lamb. London, Hamish Hamilton, 1962.

The Man from the North Pole, illustrated by Prudence Seward. London, Hamish Hamilton, 1963.

On the Stepping Stones, illustrated by Prudence Seward. London, Hamish Hamilton, 1963.

Words and Music, illustrated by Lynton Lamb. London, Hamish Hamilton, 1963.

Plot Night, illustrated by Janet Duchesne. London, Hamish Hamilton, 1963; New York, Dutton, 1968.

A Parcel of Trees, illustrated by Margery Gill. London, Penguin, 1963.

Water Boatman, illustrated by Anne Linton. London, Hamish Hamilton, 1964.

Whistling Rufus, illustrated by Raymond Briggs. London, Hamish Hamilton, 1964; New York, Dutton, 1965.

Sand, illustrated by Margery Gill. London, Hamish Hamilton, 1964; New York, Dutton, 1965.

A Day Without Wind, illustrated by Margery Gill. London, Hamish Hamilton, and New York, Dutton, 1964.

The Big Wheel and the Little Wheel, illustrated by Janet Duchesne. London, Hamish Hamilton, 1965.

Pig in the Middle, illustrated by Mary Russon. London, Hamish Hamilton, 1965; New York, Dutton, 1966.

No More School, illustrated by Peter Warner. London, Hamish Hamilton, 1965.

Dormouse Tales (The Lost Thimble, The Steam Roller, The Picnic, The Football, The Tea Party) (as Charles Molin), illustrated by Leslie Wood. London, Hamish Hamilton, 5 vols., 1966.

Earthfasts. London, Hamish Hamilton, 1966; New York, Dutton, 1967.

Rooftops, illustrated by Mary Russon. London, Hamish Hamilton, 1966.

The Old Zion, illustrated by Margery Gill. London, Hamish Hamilton, 1966; New York, Dutton, 1967.

The Battlefield, illustrated by Mary Russon. London, Hamish Hamilton, and New York, Dutton, 1967.

The Big Egg, illustrated by Margery Gill. London, Hamish Hamilton, 1967.

The Toffee Join, illustrated by Shirley Hughes. London, Hamish Hamilton, 1968.

Over the Hills and Far Away. London, Hamish Hamilton, 1968; as *The Hill Road*, New York, Dutton, 1969.

The Yellow Aeroplane, illustrated by Trevor Stubley. London, Hamish Hamilton, 1968; Nashville, Nelson, 1974.

The House on Fairmount, with Fritz Wegner, illustrated by Wegner.   London, Hamish
  Hamilton, and New York, Dutton, 1968.
Ravensgill.   London, Hamish Hamilton, and New York, Dutton, 1970.
Royal Harry.   London, Hamish Hamilton, 1971; New York, Dutton, 1972.
A Game of Dark.   London, Hamish Hamilton, and New York, Dutton, 1971.
The Incline, illustrated by Trevor Stubley.   London, Hamish Hamilton, and New York,
  Dutton, 1972.
The Swallows (as Martin Cobalt).   London, Heinemann, 1972; as *Pool of Swallows*,
  Nashville, Nelson, 1974.
Robin's Real Engine, illustrated by Mary Dinsdale.   London, Hamish Hamilton, 1972.
Skiffy, illustrated by Nicholas Fisk.   London, Hamish Hamilton, 1972.
The Jersey Shore.   London, Hamish Hamilton, and New York, Dutton, 1973.
A Year and a Day, illustrated by Krystyna Turska.   London, Hamish Hamilton, and
  New York, Dutton, 1976.
Party Pants.   London, Hodder and Stoughton, 1977.
Max's Dream, illustrated by Laszlo Acs.   London, Hamish Hamilton, 1977.
It.   London, Hamish Hamilton, 1977.

Other

Editor, with Eleanor Farjeon, *The Hamish Hamilton Book of Kings*, illustrated by Victor
  Ambrus.   London, Hamish Hamilton, 1964; as *A Cavalcade of Kings*, New York,
  Walck, 1965.
Editor, with Eleanor Farjeon, *The Hamish Hamilton Book of Queens*, illustrated by
  Victor Ambrus.   London, Hamish Hamilton, 1965; as *A Cavalcade of Queens*, New
  York, Walck, 1965.
Editor (as Charles Molin), *Ghosts, Spooks, Spectres.*   London, Hamish Hamilton, 1967;
  New York, David White, 1968.
Editor, *The Hamish Hamilton Book of Heroes*, illustrated by Krystyna Turska.   London,
  Hamish Hamilton, 1967; as *William Mayne's Book of Heroes*, New York, Dutton,
  1968.
Editor, *The Hamish Hamilton Book of Giants*, illustrated by Raymond Briggs.   London,
  Hamish Hamilton, 1968; as *William Mayne's Book of Giants*, New York, Dutton,
  1969.
Editor, *Ghosts: An Anthology.*   London, Hamish Hamilton, and New York, Nelson,
  1971.

Composer: incidental music for *Holly from the Bongs* by Alan Garner, 1965.

*   *   *

William Mayne is one of the most talented and interesting authors writing for children
today. His work is much admired by critics and librarians, but whether it is as much enjoyed
by children is often questioned. He is, perhaps, a minority taste; his books are more likely to
be read by perceptive, introspective children than by a mass audience, but there is no doubt
that those who read and enjoy his books are enriched by them.

His first books were the cathedral school series, based on his own experiences at choir
school, and family stories involving treasure hunts or mysteries. The family relationships
were far better portrayed than was usual for this type of book. And in them there was always
the special Mayne child – sensitive, quirky, speaking obliquely, and viewing everything
freshly from a child's viewpoint. His dialogue is the most individual and idiosyncratic part of
his writing. It is not an exact reproduction of children's conversation but an analogue of it. It
is noticeable that there are no villains in Mayne's books and seldom deep emotions; even
when he is dealing with highly charged situations, the keynote is coolness.

With *Sand* and *Pig in the Middle*, Mayne's fiction seemed to strike a new note. The schoolboys in *Sand* are teenagers who spend much of their time thinking about girls, and there is an excellently drawn brother-and-sister, love-hate relationship in it. *Pig in the Middle* is about a gang of town boys who are trying to put an old barge in order. The emphasis is less on plot here than on sharply drawn characters. The gang leader is a big boy who cannot read and is ashamed of it; there is a boy too small to be included in the gang, a second-in-command who really runs things and protects the word-blind leader, and a hero who does not quite know what life means or what he wants it to mean.

Then came *Earthfasts*, a brilliant use of fantasy, intricately plotted, exciting and perceptive. It is based on a Yorkshire legend of an 18th-century drummer boy who disappeared underground, beating his drum. Mayne brings him out in the 20th century, drum beating, unaware of passing time. He meets David and Keith (who are more deeply realised than previous Mayne heroes) and the delicate way that David sees the drummer boy's problems when he meets the 20th century head on is masterly.

In *Over the Hills and Far Away* he uses the time slip device and makes another compelling book. Magra, a red-headed girl in post-Roman Britain, is thought to be a witch who ought to be sacrificed for the good of the tribe. While she is on a perilous journey she changes places in time with Sara, a modern red-head. The second half of the book is Sara's story. Her innocence protects her from being used as a sacrifice, and when the danger to Magra is over they change back.

Mayne's most difficult book so far is *A Game of Dark*, which makes no concessions to child readers. Donald, an adolescent boy, deals with his dislike and fear of his dying father and his guilt feelings by slipping into a dark realm of his mind where he sees himself in a mediaeval world trying to kill a loathsome worm/dragon which devours the frightened populace. He finally conquers his problem and returns to reality at the moment of his father's death; it is a sombre book, powerfully written.

I think *The Jersey Shore* is the finest thing he has done. It is set in America in the late twenties. Arthur goes to stay with his Aunt Deborah (a typical Mayne eccentric) so he can meet his grandfather, an old fenman who settled in New England when times were hard. The old man talks to Arthur, who learns a quality of listening that makes him see and become part of the East Anglian landscape and partake of its history. The descriptions are wonderfully evocative, and when Arthur is stationed in England in the war and visits the fens, he recognises everything the old man described. In the last few pages of the English edition, we realise with a sense of shock but inevitability that Arthur is coloured; his grandfather, on coming to America, married Florence who was born a slave. But in the American edition, the last four pages are quite different and this fact never comes out, doing violence to the clues laid earlier and to the spirit of the book.

A Year and a Day is for younger readers. It is about a fairy child found by two little sisters in Cornwall in the 19th century and the year and a day he spends with their family. It is lovingly told with more emotion than has hitherto appeared in his books, and, as always, his language is a delight.

William Mayne enriches his readers by the way he looks at everything whether an object like a seashell or life as a whole. He portrays everything in a way that is brand new while having an eternal verity.

—Pamela Cleaver

McCLOSKEY, (John) Robert. American. Born in Hamilton, Ohio, 15 September 1914. Educated at Vesper George Art School, Boston, 1932–34; National Academy of Design, New York (President's Award, 1936), 1934–36; American Academy in Rome (Fellow), 1939. Served as a sergeant in the United States Army Infantry, 1942–45. Married Margaret Durand in 1940; has two daughters. Artist and illustrator: painted a relief in Hamilton, 1935, and a mural in Boston. Group shows: National Academy and Tiffany Foundation, both New York; Society of Independent Artists, Boston. Recipient: American Library Association Caldecott Medal, 1942, 1958; Catholic Library Association Regina Medal, 1974. D.Litt.: Miami University, Oxford, Ohio, 1964; Mount Holyoke College, South Hadley, Massachusetts, 1967. Address: Scott Islands, Harborside, Maine 04642, U.S.A.

PUBLICATIONS FOR CHILDREN (illustrated by the author)

Fiction

> *Lentil.* New York, Viking Press, 1940.
> *Make Way for Ducklings.* New York, Viking Press, 1941; Oxford, Blackwell, 1944.
> *Homer Price.* New York, Viking Press, 1943.
> *Blueberries for Sal.* New York, Viking Press, 1948; London, Angus and Robertson, 1967.
> *Centerburg Tales.* New York, Viking Press, 1951.
> *One Morning in Maine.* New York, Viking Press, 1952; London, Penguin, 1976.
> *Time of Wonder.* New York, Viking Press, 1957.
> *Burt Dow, Deep-Water Man.* New York, Viking Press, 1963.

Manuscript Collection: May Massee Memorial Collection, William Allen White Library, Emporia State College, Kansas.

Illustrator: *Yankee Doodle's Cousins* by Anne Burnett Malcolmson, 1941; *Tree Toad* by Robert Hobart Davis, 1942; *The Man Who Lost His Head* by Claire Huchet Bishop, 1942; *Trigger John's Son* by Tom Robinson, 1949; *Journey Cake, Ho!* by Ruth Sawyer, 1953; *Junket* by Anne H. White, 1955; *Henry Reed, Inc.*, 1955, *Henry Reed's Journey*, 1963, *Henry Reed's Baby-Sitting Service*, 1966, and *Henry Reed's Big Show*, 1970, all by Keith Robertson.

*   *   *

I once read a fifth grade book report that ended with the sentence: "Robert McCloskey is a Yankee Doodle Dandy of a writer." And I thought then, and think now, that no other author for children over the past 30 years fits that description so well.

The fifth grader, of course, was writing about the book *Homer Price*, a story of a boy growing up in the small midwestern American town of McCloskey's boyhood 50 years ago. There is a lot of McCloskey in Homer, who loves to invent and tinker with all sorts of gadgets, and in Lentil, his other boy hero, who loves to play the harmonica. Like Twain's Tom Sawyer, McCloskey's boys have the knack of getting themselves into and out of fantastic adventures and misadventures. The incidents in these books are authentically shaped out of actual experience and touched with the gentle humor of a grownup's remembrance. As McCloskey says of his work: "I have one foot resting on reality and the other foot planted firmly on a banana peel."

McCloskey's stories also have the distinct quality of the grand exaggeration and broad humor that one finds in the tall tales of traditional American folklore. The episode of the doughnut machine in *Homer Price* is as well known to American children today as any of the adventures of folk characters like Paul Bunyan and Pecos Bill, and it would seem as much at home in a collection of American folklore as it would in an anthology of fiction. James Daugherty found McCloskey's "boy" books to be: "America laughing at itself with a broad and genial humanity, without bitterness or sourness or sophistication." Through these books young readers today and in the future can be in touch with the folk America of their grandparents and great-grandparents.

McCloskey's picture books for younger children usually grow out of real incidents that have occurred in actual families, either his own, as in *One Morning in Maine, Blueberries for*

Sal and *Time of Wonder*, or that of Mr. and Mrs. Mallard in *Make Way for Ducklings*. These books have won great acclaim for the illustrations, but one should not overlook the writing. McCloskey, like Daugherty and Kate Seredy, was one of those illustrators who, at the urging of that remarkable children's editor May Massee, discovered that he had a talent for writing as well as for drawing. And he brought to that writing the same painstaking integrity that marks his illustration. As he says: "It's a good feeling to be able to put down a line and know that it's right."

In the picture books McCloskey usually employs a straightforward matter-of-fact style, except for *Time of Wonder*, which is more like a prose poem, uniquely written in second-person narrative. Though he admittedly "thinks in pictures," McCloskey's stories are always skillfully tuned for the ear, so that they are particularly suited for reading aloud. They are also especially suited for the young child because they are full of gentle wisdom and reassurance, while always focussing on what's right in the world.

In more than 35 years of writing and illustrating books for children Robert McCloskey has not once produced anything that is not of the highest quality. To repeat my fifth grade friend, he is indeed "a Yankee Doodle Dandy of a writer."

—James E. Higgins

McCORD, David (Thompson Watson). American. Born in New York City, 15 November 1897. Educated at Lincoln High School, Portland, Oregon, graduated 1917; Harvard University, Cambridge, Massachusetts, A.B. 1921, A.M. 1922. Served in the Field Artillery, United States Army, 1918; Second Lieutenant. Associate Editor, 1923–25, and Editor, 1940–46, *Harvard Alumni Bulletin*; Member of the Drama Staff, Boston *Evening Transcript*, 1923–28. Executive Director, Harvard Fund Council, 1925–63; Phi Beta Kappa Poet, Harvard University, 1938; Tufts College, Medford, Massachuesetts, 1938; College of William and Mary, Williamsburg, Virginia, 1950; Massachusetts Institute of Technology, Cambridge, 1973; Lecturer, Lowell Institute, Boston, 1950; Staff Member, Bread Loaf Writers Conference, Vermont, 1958, 1960, 1962, 1964; Instructor in Creative Writing, Harvard University, summers 1963, 1965, 1966; Councilor, Harvard Society of Advanced Study and Research, 1967–72; Member, Overseers' Visiting Committee, Department of Astronomy, Harvard University. Painter: several one-man shows of water colors. Honorary Member, Phi Beta Kappa, 1938; Honorary Life Associate, Dudley House, Harvard University; Honorary Member, Senior Common Room, Lowell House, Harvard University. Recipient: New England Poetry Club Golden Rose, 1941; William Rose Benét Award, 1952; Guggenheim Fellowship, 1954; National Institute of Arts and Letters Grant, 1961; Sarah Josepha Hale Award, 1962; Miriam Kallen Award, 1976; National Council of Teachers of English award, 1977. Litt.D.: Northeastern University, Boston, 1954; University of New Brunswick, Fredericton, 1963; Williams College, Williamstown, Massachusetts, 1971; LL.D.: Washington and Jefferson College, Washington, Pennyslvania, 1955; L.H.D.: Harvard University, 1956; Colby College, Waterville, Maine, 1968; Art.D.: New England College, Henniker, New Hampshire, 1956. Fellow, American Academy of Arts and Sciences; Benjamin Franklin Fellow, Royal Society of Arts, London. Address: Harvard Club of Boston, 374 Commonwealth Avenue, Boston, Massachusetts 02215, U.S.A.

PUBLICATIONS FOR CHILDREN

Verse

Far and Few, illustrated by Henry B. Kane.   Boston, Little Brown, 1952.

Take Sky (single poem).   Darien, Georgia, privately printed, 1961.
Take Sky (collection), illustrated by Henry B. Kane.   Boston, Little Brown, 1962.
Books Fall Open (bookmark).   New York, Children's Book Council, 1964.
All Day Long, illustrated by Henry B. Kane.   Boston, Little Brown, 1966.
Every Time I Climb a Tree, illustrated by Marc Simont.   Boston, Little Brown, 1967.
For Me to Say, illustrated by Henry B. Kane.   Boston, Little Brown, 1970.
Mr. Bidery's Spidery Garden, illustrated by Henry B. Kane.   London, Harrap, 1972.
Pen, Paper, and Poem.   New York, Holt Rinehart, 1973.
Away and Ago, illustrated by Leslie Morrill.   Boston, Little Brown, 1974.
The Star in the Pail, illustrated by Marc Simont.   Boston, Little Brown, 1975.
One at a Time: Collected Poems for the Young, illustrated by Henry B. Kane.   Boston,
    Little Brown, 1977.

Recording: *The Pickety Fence and 51 Other Poems*, Pathways of Sound.

PUBLICATIONS FOR ADULTS

Short Story

The Camp at Lockjaw.   New York, Doubleday, 1952.

Verse (includes broadsheets)

Floodgate.   Cambridge, Massachusetts, Washburn and Thomas, 1927.
Oxford Nearly Visited: A Fantasy.   Cambridge, Massachusetts, Cygnet Press, 1929.
Fiftieth Anniversary Ode.   Boston, St. Botolph Club, 1930.
Chocorua.   Portland, Maine, privately printed, 1932.
The Crows: Poems.   New York and London, Scribner, 1934.
Bay Window Ballads.   New York and London, Scribner, 1935.
The Stretch.   Cambridge, Massachusetts, privately printed, 1937.
Twelve Verses from XII Night.   Boston, privately printed, 1938.
The Knowing.   Cambridge, Massachusetts, privately printed, 1938.
Reflection in Blue.   Cambridge, Massachusetts, privately printed, 1939.
And What's More.   New York, Coward McCann, 1941.
The Legend of St. Botolph.   Boston, privately printed, 1942.
Christmas, 1943.   Boston, privately printed, 1943.
On Occasion.   Cambridge, Massachusetts, Harvard University Press, 1943.
Remembrance of Things Passed.   Boston, Club of Odd Volumes, 1947.
Midway in This Middle Year of the Twentieth Century.   Cambridge, Massachusetts,
    privately printed, 1950.
A Star by Day.   New York, Doubleday, 1950.
Poet Always Next But One.   Williamsburg, Virginia, College of William and Mary,
    1951.
Blue Reflections on the Merchants Limited.   Boston, Club of Odd Volumes, 1952.
The Old Bateau and Other Poems.   Boston, Little Brown, 1953.
Ten Limericks.   Cambridge, Massachusetts, privately printed, 1953.
Odds Without Ends.   Boston, Little Brown, 1954.
By Swancote Pool.   Portland, Maine, privately printed, 1954.
Whereas to Mr. Franklin.   Boston, Old South Association, 1954.
60 Lines for Three-Score Hatch.   Boston, India Wharf Rats Club, 1957.
Sonnets to Baedecker.   Meriden, Connecticut, Meriden Gravure Company, 1965.
In Memory of Sir Winston Churchill, 25 January 1965.   Boston, privately printed, 1965.
H.R.H. H.H.R.   Cambridge, Massachusetts, privately printed, 1965.
Observation Tower.   Boston, Club of Odd Volumes, 1966.
Roland Hayes.   Portland, Maine, privately printed, 1967.

Poem for the Occasion.   Boston, Colonial Society of Massachusetts, 1970.
Spree Fever.   Boston, privately printed, 1970.
Thomas Dudley Cabot.   Boston, privately printed, 1972.
R.R.: Lines, Sharp as Serifs, on the By-Passing of His Ninetieth Birthday.   Lunenburg,
    Vermont, privately printed, 1973.
Sestina for the Queen.   Boston, Bostonian Society, 1976.

Play

Alice in Botolphland.   Boston, St. Botolph Club, 1932.

Other

Oddly Enough (essays).   Cambridge, Massachusetts, Washburn and Thomas, 1926.
Stirabout (essays).   Cambridge, Massachusetts, Washburn and Thomas, 1928.
H.T.P.: Portrait of a Critic (on Henry Taylor Parker).   New York, Coward McCann,
    1935.
Notes on the Harvard Tercentenary.   Cambridge, Massachusetts, Harvard University
    Press, 1936.
An Acre for Education, Being Notes on the History of Radcliffe College.   Cambridge,
    Massachusetts, Radcliffe College, 1938; revised edition, 1954, 1958, 1963.
About Boston: Sight, Sound, Flavor, and Inflection, illustrated by the author.   New
    York, Doubleday, 1948.
... as Built with Second Thoughts.   Boston, Centennial Commission of the Boston
    Public Library, 1953.
The Related Man.   Boston, American Academy of Arts and Sciences, 1953.
David McCord's Oregon.   Boston, Massachusetts Historical Society, 1959.
On the Frontier of Understanding (address).   Fredericton, University of New
    Brunswick, 1959.
The Language of Request: Fishing with a Barbless Hook (essays).   Washington, D.C.,
    American Alumni Council, 1961.
The Fabrick of Man: Fifty Years of the Peter Bent Brigham Hospital.   Boston, Hospital
    Celebration Committee, 1963.
In Sight of Sever: Essays from Harvard.   Cambridge, Massachusetts, Harvard
    University Press, 1963.
Art and Education (lecture), with David B. Little and Sinclair H. Hitchings.   Boston,
    Boston Public Library, 1966.
Children and Poetry (lecture).   Chicago, University of Chicago Press, 1966.
Notes from Four Cities, 1927–1953.   Worcester, Massachusetts, A.J. St. Onge, 1969.
Celebration: 1925–1975 (history of Harvard College Fund).   Lunenburg, Vermont,
    privately printed, 1975.

Editor, *Once and For All* (essays).   New York, Coward McCann, 1929.
Editor, *What Cheer: An Anthology of American and British Humorous and Witty
    Verse.*   New York, Coward McCann, 1945; as *The Pocket Book of Humorous Verse,*
    New York, Pocket Books, 1946; as *The Modern Treasury of Humorous Verse,* New
    York, Doubleday, 1951.
Editor, *Bibliotheca Medica: Physician for Tomorrow.*   Boston, Harvard Medical School,
    1966.
Editor, *New England Revisited,* by Arthur Griffin.   Boston, Houghton Mifflin, 1966.
Editor, *Stow Wengenroth's New England.*   Barre, Massachusetts, Barre Publishers,
    1969.

Manuscript Collections: Boston Public Library; Widener Library, Harvard University,
Cambridge, Massachusetts; and other collections.

David McCord comments:

Giving a rather long talk to a group of children's librarians gathered at the University of Chicago a dozen years ago, I was forced to come to grips with myself over the natural question: Why does one write for children? The most generous and general answer, I suppose, is simply: Why not? But perhaps I had a special reason.

For me the small years, as Frank Kendon calls them, were never lonely, though I had neither brother nor sister nor much of anyone to play with. Childhood, and even most of my boyhood, marred by recurring malaria but not by the resulting large amount of solitude and freedom from school, left me with time to read, work with my hands, and raise chickens. I very early built and operated, with unmalarial fever, a licensed wireless telegraph station, not unaware that the dot-dash code itself is language of pure rhythm and a kind of haunting poetry in isolation. Above all, I soon became a countryman at heart: learned to look on the sky with as much affection as on the land; to walk in silence, listen, notice things and to explore with almost equal young delight the wonders of the back yard or the wilderness. That is literally true, for I began all this in Woodmere on Long Island, New York, adjacent to a poultry farm, and finished it out west beside the wild Rogue River on my uncle's ranch in Oregon: a slice of frontier life as yet unvanished, where a boy could pan for gold for pocket money, with little chance to spend it. Thrill enough it was to have it weighed out on the big brass scales of an old bank in a town about as old as 1849.

I read and was read to aloud. And into the far west I took remembrance of my Presbyterian grandmother Reed's lovely voice and the rhythm of the King James version of the Bible. My own reading wavered on another kind of scale between the Oz books, Dickens, Ralph Henry Barbour, Mark Twain, Jules Verne; Lear, Carroll, and Gilbert; W. W. Jacobs, Jack London, and such. I also read three equally indispensable magazines: *St. Nicholas*, Gernsbach's *Modern Electrics*, and *The Reliable Poultry Journal*. By the time I was ten I had read five or six books by the New Brunswick writer, Charles G.D. Roberts, from cover to cover. I still consider *Red Fox* one of the two greatest animal stories ever written. The other one for me – of course, years later – is *Tarka the Otter* by Henry Williamson. Another thing: because I was read aloud to when very young, I came to love the sound of words as well as the look of them on paper.

I began to write verse when I was fifteen, and verse for children when just out of Graduate School at Harvard. Now, some 400 poems-for-children later, I dare to offer one or two rules for the conduct of this seemingly simple but dangerously abstruse art.

First, just be a child before you grow up and let nothing interfere with the process. Write it all *out* of yourself and *for* yourself as you remember that weasel body with the eagle eyes. Next, never take the phrase "writing verse *for* children" seriously. If you write *for* them you are lost. Ask your brain's computer what you know about a child's mind and what goes on inside it. The answer is zero. What do they think of this calamitous new world which you don't even pretend to understand? They do not compare it with the past. It is the only world they know. Don't ever even pretend you are *looking* at the young; just make sure the young are *looking* at you. Make your readers believe you are letting them into your own dark life, into your own serene confusion, not you into theirs. Never talk down; and if for weeks at a time you have absolutely nothing to say, fight the uphill fight and do not say it.

*   *   *

David McCord has often been called an acrobat with language – an apt description of this poet whose verses are filled with suprising rhythm and sound effects and inventive rhyming twists, all done with acrobatic grace and playfulness. Typical of McCord, for instance, is the characterization of a little bat as not "flight able" (to rhyme with "gable"); and a description of three flying geese as making a V "with two in the caboose and one in the/ a-po-gee"; and a combination of poem and picture in which a dangling rope and a long narrow line of print force the reader to read up the page about the grasshopper who is climbing up out of a well (all three poems in *Far and Few*).

A playful tone permeates almost all of the poems, whatever the subject matter, because exploration of the textures of language is so paramount an aim for this poet. Remembering this, one can still group the subjects loosely into five major categories: 1) Poems about small creatures – a newt, bats, frogs, crickets, ants, and many others; 2) poems written in the first person about the thoughts and feelings of a child who is flying kites, fishing, eating, drawing pictures, skating, taking castor oil, going to the dentist, making a snowman, jumping in autumn leaves – all in the course of daily living indoors and out; 3) a few poems for or about children, written from the vantage point of an adult looking back; 4) poems primarily of language exploration and word play ("You *know* the word *cathedral.*/ How about *tetartohedral?*" from "The Look and Sound of Words" in *For Me to Say*); 5) two groups of poems, in *Take Sky* and *For Me To Say*, demonstrating the writing of ten verse-forms, beginning with couplet and ending with haiku.

It is interesting to note which poems – out of this array of more than 200 – are most often reprinted by anthologists and writers of children's literature texts. My informal survey indicates that there are two top favorites, appearing over and over again: the chant about the pickety fence from "Five Chants" and "This Is My Rock" (both in *Far and Few*). The chant catches the pickety, lickety sounds and the quick, brittle rhythm of the childhood game of running along and clicking a stick on a fence. This is one of the simpler language-play poems, easy to read without stumbling on rhythm or syntax. "This Is My Rock" is also an easily read poem, but serious in tone and without word play. In fact, it is one of the least typical of McCord's poems. In it a child simply speaks about a rock where he likes to sit and watch the sun and sky and the coming of the evening. Are these two poems first choices because of their simplicity and readability, as well as their charm?

Children undoubtedly turn away from many of the more complex poems because of the language difficulties – unless, of course, an adult is helping with the interpretation. What, for instance, is an uninitiated child to make of the tricky algebra here (from "Exit *x*" in *For Me to Say*):

If *vex*
is x^2, *rex*
will equal one-no-three.

Also difficult are lines like these from the poem "O-U-G-H" in *All Day Long*: "Supposing *though's* not *tho*, but more like *thoff*,/ and *sough's sow's* not a pig that sows, but *soff?*"

McCord should be read aloud to young children who are just discovering him – read aloud by adults who enjoy the rhythms and won't trip up on the word-play. A good book to begin on is *Every Time I Climb a Tree*, a collection of 25 of the earlier poems, produced as a picture book with large bright water-color illustrations. Here are not only "This Is My Rock," the pickety fence poem, and the grasshopper poem mentioned earlier, but two short ones that show McCord at his best in the game of inventing rhymes: "Glowworm" with its rhyming "knowworm," "down belowworm," "slowworm" and "Helloworm!"; and "I Want You to Meet" in which "Lady-bug" is rhymed with "Sadiebug," "Mrs. Gradybug," "oldmaidybug," and "fraidybug." Also there are winter poems, food poems (one especially for lovers of bananas and cream), Halloween and Christmas poems, and of course the title poem about the pleasures of climbing a tree (good for ants though not for pants). Almost all are just for fun and surprise and present little reading difficulty. Not strictly for fun are "This Is My Rock" and the five-line poem "Cocoon," perhaps even more moving for adults than for children, about the little caterpillar who has three good tries before it dies.

Another collection of earlier poems for the youngest readers is *The Star in the Pail*, this one also colorfully illustrated and presented as a picture book. Here, too, are easily read poems. Most readers, however, would probably vote for *Every Time I Climb a Tree* – so full of old favorites – if a choice had to be made between the two collections.

Though a great many of McCord's poems have been in print for 40 or more years, few of them are what contemporary children might consider old-fashioned. True, there's the reference (in "The Trouble Was Simply That" in *For Me To Say*) to a boy's hat with its good crown and lining and brim. "*What?*" a boy today might wonder. And readers who are girls might wish there were more girls in the poems, and might even take offense at the attitude toward girls revealed in the lines "Little boys out for trout,/ Little girls flumped about," (from "Dr. Klimwell's Fall" in *Take Sky*). But wit with words is for both girls and boys and does not go out of date. McCord's ingenious and crisp inventions will doubtless go on pleasing readers for years to come. Might as well expect Edward Lear to move into oblivion.

—Claudia Lewis

McGINLEY, Phyllis. American. Born in Ontario, Oregon, 21 March 1905. Educated at Ogden High School, Utah; Sacred Heart Academy, Ogden; University of Utah, Salt Lake City; University of California, Berkeley. Married Charles L. Hayden in 1937; has two children. Formerly, Schoolteacher, Utah and New York; worked for an advertising agency, New York City; Staff Writer, *Town and Country*, New York. Member, Advisory Board, *The American Scholar*, Washington, D.C. Recipient (for verse): Christopher Award, 1955; Poetry Society Award, 1955; Catholic Writers Guild Award, 1955; Edna St. Vincent Millay Award, 1955; St. Catherine de Siena Medal, 1956; Catholic Institute of the Press Award, 1960; Pulitzer Prize, 1961; Catholic Poetry Society Spirit Gold Medal, 1962; Laetare Medal, Notre Dame University, 1964; Campion Award, 1967. D.Litt.: Wheaton College, Illinois, 1956; St. Mary's College, Notre Dame, Indiana, 1958; Marquette University, Milwaukee, 1960; Dartmouth College, Hanover, New Hampshire, 1961; Boston College, 1962; Wilson College, Chambersburg, Pennsylvania, 1964; Smith College, Northampton, Massachusetts, 1964; St. John's University, Jamaica, New York, 1964. Member, National Institute of Arts and Letters. Address: 60 East 66th Street, Apartment C–204, New York, New York 10021, U.S.A.

PUBLICATIONS FOR CHILDREN

Fiction

    The Horse Who Lived Upstairs, illustrated by Helen Stone. Philadelphia, Lippincott, 1944.
    The Plain Princess, illustrated by Helen Stone. Philadelphia, Lippincott, 1945.
    A Name for Kitty, illustrated by Feodor Rojankovsky. New York, Simon and Schuster, 1948; London, Muller, 1950.
    The Most Wonderful Doll in the World, illustrated by Helen Stone. Philadelphia, Lippincott, 1950.
    The Horse Who Had His Picture in the Paper, illustrated by Helen Stone. Philadelphia, Lippincott, 1951.
    Blunderbus, illustrated by William Wiesner. Philadelphia, Lippincott, 1951.
    The Make-Believe Twins, illustrated by Roberta MacDonald. Philadelphia, Lippincott, 1953.
    The B Book, illustrated by Robert Jones. New York, Crowell Collier, 1962; London, Collier Macmillan, 1968.

Verse

    All Around the Town, illustrated by Helen Stone. Philadelphia, Lippincott, 1948.
    The Year Without a Santa Claus, illustrated by Kurt Werth. Philadelphia, Lippincott, 1957; Leicester, Brockhampton Press, 1960.

Lucy McLockett, illustrated by Helen Stone.   Philadelphia, Lippincott, 1959; Leicester, Brockhampton Press, 1961.

Sugar and Spice: The ABC of Being a Girl, illustrated by Colleen Browning.   New York, Watts, 1960.

Mince Pie and Mistletoe, illustrated by Harold Berson.   Philadelphia, Lippincott, 1961.

Boys Are Awful, illustrated by Ati Forberg.   New York, Watts, 1962.

How Mrs. Santa Claus Saved Christmas, illustrated by Kurt Werth.   Philadelphia, Lippincott, 1963; Kingswood, Surrey, World's Work, 1964.

A Girl and Her Room, illustrated by Ati Forberg.   New York, Watts, 1963.

Wonderful Time, illustrated by John Alcorn.   Philadelphia, Lippincott, 1966.

A Wreath of Christmas Legends, illustrated by Leonard Weisgard.   New York, Macmillan, 1967.

PUBLICATIONS FOR ADULTS

Plays

Small Wonder (lyrics only; revue; produced New York, 1948).

Screenplay: *The Emperor's Nightingale*, 1951.

Verse

On the Contrary.   New York, Doubleday, 1934.

One More Manhattan.   New York, Harcourt Brace, 1937.

A Pocketful of Wry.   New York, Duell, 1940.

Husbands Are Difficult; or, The Book of Oliver Ames.   New York, Duell, 1941.

Stones from a Glass House: New Poems.   New York, Viking Press, 1946.

A Short Walk from the Station.   New York, Viking Press, 1951.

The Love Letters of Phyllis McGinley.   New York, Viking Press, 1954; London, Dent, 1955.

Merry Christmas, Happy New Year.   New York, Viking Press, 1958; London, Secker and Warburg, 1959.

Times Three: Selected Verse from Three Decades.   New York, Viking Press, 1960; as *Times Three: Selected Verse from Three Decades with Seventy New Poems,* London, Secker and Warburg, 1961.

Christmas con and pro.   Berkeley, California, Hart Press, 1971.

Confessions of a Reluctant Optimist, edited by Barbara Wells Price.   Kansas City, Missouri, Hallmark Editions, 1973.

Other

The Province of the Heart (essays).   New York, Viking Press, 1959; London, Catholic Book Club, 1963.

Sixpence in Her Shoe (autobiographical).   New York, Macmillan, 1964.

Editor, *Wonders and Surprises: A Collection of Poems.*   Philadelphia, Lippincott, 1968.

*   *   *

Though Phyllis McGinley is noted for her light verse for adults, she has also written several books in verse for children. One of the best known is her alphabet book, *All Around the Town*, in which the verses focus on various aspects of urban life. Helen Stone's illustrations admirably reinforce this urban emphasis. The rhythms are extremely simple tetrameter lines in jog-trot rhythm:

T's the ticking Taxicab
   That's faster than a trolley.
It answers to a whistle
   Like a terrier or a collie.
I think we'd always travel
   In a taxi to and hence
But to tell the truth about it
   It's a terrible expense.

Though she seems to favor the tetrameter rhyme, she is capable of sophisticated use of meter, particularly in variations within the line, as evidenced in "A Certain Age":

All of a sudden, bicycles are toys,
Not locomotion. Bicycles are for boys
And seventh-graders, screaming when they talk.
A girl would rather
Take vows, go hungry, put on last year's frock,
Or dance with her own father
Than pedal down the block.

Her stylistic rules for writing juvenile verse are: leanness, rhythm, and repetition, qualities seen at their best, perhaps, in her various Christmas books, including *The Year Without a Santa Claus* ; *Mince Pie and Mistletoe*, about Christmas in various places; *How Mrs. Santa Claus Saved Christmas* and *A Wreath of Christmas Legends*.

Her poetry has a wholesome, pensive quality, possibly reflecting her early life on a Colorado ranch.

—Francelia Butler

McGRAW, Eloise Jarvis. American. Born in Houston, Texas, 9 December 1915. Educated at Classen High School, Oklahoma City, graduated 1932; Principia College, Elsah, Illinois, B.A. in art 1937; Museum Art School, Portland, Oregon, 1972–76. Married William Corbin McGraw in 1940; has one son and one daughter. Instructor in Painting, Oklahoma City University, 1942–43; owned and farmed a filbert orchard, Willamette Valley, Oregon, 1952–70; teacher, Lewis and Clark College, Portland, 1960–62. Teacher, Portland State University, summers since 1971. Agent: Marilyn Marlow, Curtis Brown Ltd., 575 Madison Avenue, New York, New York 10022. Address: 1970 Indian Trail, Lake Oswego, Oregon 97034, U.S.A.

PUBLICATIONS FOR CHILDREN

Fiction

   Sawdust in His Shoes. New York, Coward McCann, 1950.
   Crown Fire. New York, Coward McCann, 1951.
   Moccasin Trail. New York, Coward McCann, 1952.
   Mara, Daughter of the Nile. New York, Coward McCann, 1953.
   The Golden Goblet. New York, Coward McCann, 1961; London, Methuen, 1964.
   Merry Go Round in Oz, with Lauren McGraw Wagner, illustrated by Dick Martin. Chicago, Reilly and Lee, 1963.

Greensleeves.   New York, Harcourt Brace, 1968.
Master Cornhill.   New York, Atheneum, 1973.
A Really Weird Summer.   New York, Atheneum, 1977.

Play

Steady, Stephanie.   Chicago, Dramatic Publishing Company, 1962.

PUBLICATIONS FOR ADULTS

Novel

Pharaoh.   New York, Coward McCann, 1958.

Other

Techniques of Fiction Writing.   Boston, The Writer, 1959.

Manuscript Collection: University of Oregon Library, Eugene.

Eloise Jarvis McGraw comments:
   Five of my books have historical settings. Three of these, *Mara, Pharoah,* and *The Golden Goblet,* are laid in ancient Egypt, the study of which was an almost obsessive hobby of mine for 25 years. One, *Moccasin Trail,* deals with the American West, specifically Oregon, in pioneer days (1845–46), and another, *Master Cornhill,* with the London of 1665–66, the years of the Great Plague and the Great Fire. I very much enjoy research, and also sharing the results of it with readers through the synthesis of fiction. My other six books are set more or less specifically in the present day, though only *A Really Weird Summer,* I think, truly could be called "contemporary." In this, and in other ways, it represents a step in a new direction for me.
   My early books are built around dramatic action plots, though at the core of the story is always emotional development and an intellectual concept or theme of some sort. But with *Greensleeves* I began plotting in a different, less rigid way, and the "tone of voice" of the later books has altered accordingly. However, their chief emphasis, as in the earlier ones, is on character. I begin with a character, invariably.
   I write about what passionately interests me at the time. I write as well and clearly as I can, and I am hard to please while writing and never really satisfied with the final result – though I make sure it is the best I am capable of producing at the moment. More than once a strong motive in my undertaking a certain book is my wish that someone had written a book about this so that I could read it. I believe I always, in the end, write for myself.

*   *   *

   Although Eloise Jarvis McGraw wrote successful short stories for children before the publication of *Sawdust in His Shoes* in 1950, it is through her full-length books that she has gained her current literary prominence. Her first four books came within a period of four years and all were acclaimed for excellence in literary craftmanship. Since then her publications have appeared only sporadically, and her total literary output has been regrettably small.
   Mrs. McGraw's first and third novels, although quite different in character and tone, both deal with adjustment, a recurring theme in children's literature. The first, *Sawdust in His Shoes,* centers around the young hero's adjustment from circus life to farm life. The story moves forward with a swift-paced action in tune with the mettle of its characters. The characters are drawn by their creator with precision and understanding and their language is

the racy, though rich, language of circus and farm. Mrs. McGraw's third book, *Moccasin Trail*, deals with the difficult adjustment of a white youth who has spent much of his young life with the tribe of Crow Indians who adopted him after he was seriously injured by a fierce grizzly. As with Mrs. McGraw's first book, this too is one with character emphasis. It is told with warmth and a perceptive understanding of the two-way adjustments necessary for the hero's acceptance of and acceptance by his own family.

Crown Fire, like her first and her third books, has a strong character emphasis and plenty of suspenseful, rapidly-moving, dramatic action. The book's title is a logging term used to describe fire raging uncontrollably across tree tops. Although the story has colorful and authentic details about logging, the book's title is a symbol for the hero's temper, an explosive, uncontrollable "fire." Setting, action, pace, and literary style combine to make *Crown Fire* another artistic achievement for its author.

As a departure from works influenced by her own childhood, Mrs. McGraw successfully casts *Mara, Daughter of the Nile* in the Egypt of the Pharoahs. As its title suggests, this is a story with a heroine, not a hero. It is also less a book of character than of action, sometimes brutal action. Yet, like her earlier books, this one too has a lucid, literary style with the ring of authenticity so characteristic of all the novels Mrs. McGraw has produced to date.

The Golden Goblet is also set in ancient Egypt. This is basically the story of Ranofer, a young Egyptian lad who longs to be a goldsmith like his father. For a long while it appears that Ranofer's ambition is forever to be thwarted by his wicked half-brother, Gebu, with whom Ranofer lives after their father's death. The climax of the drama is reached when Ranofer, with the help of two friends, unravels the mystery of a golden goblet by trapping his evil brother and the brother's equally evil accomplice in the tomb they are attempting to rob.

The Golden Goblet fully reiterates Eloise Jarvis McGraw's literary competence for here again her flair for vivid characterization, suspenseful action, and intricate plot are highly evident.

—Charity Chang

McGREGOR, Iona. British. Born in Aldershot, Hampshire, 7 February 1929. Educated at Monmouth School for Girls; University of Bristol, B.A. (honours) 1950. Sub-Editor, *Dictionary of the Older Scottish Tongue*, Edinburgh University Press, 1951–57; Classics Teacher, Simon Langton Girls' School, Canterbury, 1958–62, and Beaverwood School, Chislehurst, Kent, 1962–69. Currently, Latin Teacher, St. George's School for Girls, Edinburgh. Address: c/o Faber and Faber Ltd., 3 Queen Square, London WC1N 2AU, England.

PUBLICATIONS FOR CHILDREN

Fiction

> *An Edinburgh Reel.* London, Faber, 1968.
> *The Popinjay.* London, Faber, 1969.
> *The Burning Hill.* London, Faber, 1970.
> *The Tree of Liberty.* London, Faber, 1972.
> *The Snake and the Olive.* London, Faber, 1974.

PUBLICATIONS FOR ADULTS

Play

Radio Play: *A Kind of Glory*, 1971.

Iona McGregor comments:

As a writer I have always needed the stimulus of "history" to set an edge on my imagination, although by this I mean the minutiae of daily living and the impatience of new ideas rather than great events or the people who initiated them. Eastern Scotland, the background I most enjoy writing about, is visually still close to its past. I could say that in a very small way I am searching for lost time, since it is the effort to strip these scenes and places of modern accretions which brings my characters alive for me.

*   *   *

When reading Iona McGregor's books one is reminded of the drawings by Hogarth and Rowlandson – the scene is a mass of people. Her aim is to interpret these characters as flesh and blood realities, and she succeeds very well. She is at her best when dealing with her native Scotland, and her interest in history is the peg on which many of her stories are hung. However, she has to thank her training in the Classics for her exactness in speech.

In *The Popinjay* we are immediately introduced to the central character, 16-year-old David Lindsay, the popinjay of the title. Summoned from Bordeaux in 1546 by the Cardinal Archbishop Beaton to St. Andrews, his future looks rosy and his insolence is matched only by his dreams. However, soon all is changed, the Archbishop murdered, David a wounded fugitive – and it is at this point that Iona McGregor really gets to grips with her characters. David begins to learn what life is like in the terror-stricken and plague-infested town, and his development to maturity through his involvement with the fishergirl, Elspeth, and Father Anthony from the Priory, shows evidence of the author's acute understanding of human nature. The whole story rings true and the reader is completely involved throughout.

No doubt it is because the author is so interested in the 18th century that she writes about it so confidently and convincingly, especially in her re-creation of Edinburgh at this time. Her touch is so sensitive and the writing so vivid that the reader can almost smell the stench and hear the noises of the crowds and carriages in the Lawnmarket and Canongate. This is the setting which inspires Iona McGregor to some of her finest writing, and *An Edinburgh Reel* is as lively as the dance itself. Christine's father, embittered by his experience as a prisoner after Culloden, returns to Edinburgh vowing vengeance on his unknown betrayer after the battle, whereas his daughter wants him to forgive and forget. The pages are scattered with fascinating characters – Lord Balmuir, the elderly judge, Lucky Robertson who owns the pie shop, Ewan McDonnell who tries to tempt Christine's father back into Jacobite plotting, and many more. Iona McGregor blends them all into a colourful picture of Edinburgh life, pulsating with vigour and vitality. Everything in the book echoes the authenticity of her writing, the marvellous dialogue, the jostling crowds, the personal hatreds and hopes, and the contrasting natures of the main protagonists. It is a glorious piece of writing, compulsive and exhilarating and a fine example of Iona McGregor at her best.

—Margaret Walker

McKEE, David (John).   British.   Free-lance painter, illustrator, and cartoonist. Address: c/o Abelard-Schuman Ltd., 450 Edgware Road, London W2 1EG, England.

PUBLICATIONS FOR CHILDREN (illustrated by the author)

Fiction

Bronto's Wings.   London, Dobson, 1964.
Two Can Toucan.   London and New York, Abelard Schuman, 1964.
Mr. Benn, Red Knight.   London, Dobson, 1967; New York, McGraw Hill, 1968.
Mark and the Monocycle.   London and New York, Abelard Schuman, 1968.
Elmer: The Story of a Patchwork Elephant.   London, Dobson, and New York, McGraw Hill, 1968.
123456789 Benn.   London, Dobson, and New York, McGraw Hill, 1970.
The Magician Who Lost His Magic.   London and New York, Abelard Schuman, 1970.
Six Men.   Montchaldorf, Switzerland, Nord-Sud Verlag, 1971; London, A. and C. Black, 1972.
Lord Rex: The Lion Who Wished.   London and New York, Abelard Schuman, 1973.
The Magician and the Sorcerer.   London, Abelard Schuman, and New York, Parents' Magazine Press, 1974.
The Day the Tide Went Out, and Out, and Out ....   London, Abelard Schuman, 1975; New York, Abelard Schuman, 1976.
Elmer Again and Again.   London, Dobson, 1975.
The Magician and the Petnapping.   London, Abelard Schuman, 1976; Boston, Houghton Mifflin, 1977.
Two Admirals.   London, Hutchinson, and Boston, Houghton Mifflin, 1977.
The Magician and the Balloon.   London, Abelard Schuman, 1977.

Plays

Screenplay: *Greenback Hell,* 1974.

Television Plays: *Mr. Benn* series.

Verse

Okki-Tokki-Unga: Action Songs.   London, A. and C. Black, 1976.

Other

Hans in Luck.   London and New York, Abelard Schuman, 1967.
Mathematics Everywhere.   London, Longman, 1969.
The Man Who Was Going to Mind the House: A Norwegian Folk-Tale.   London, Abelard Schuman, 1972; New York, Abelard Schuman, 1973.
Mr. Benn Annual.   London, Argus Press, 1972.
A Twister of Twists, A Tangler of Tongues: Tongue Twisters.   London, Pan, 1976.

Illustrator: *The Poor Farmer and the Robber Knights* by Walter Kreye, 1969; *Hector's House Annual,* 1969–73; *Bertha the Tanker* by Liane Smith, 1969; *Vamos Amigos* by Heloise Lewis, 1971; *Mr. Drackle and His Dragons* by Elizabeth Hull Froman, 1971; *Joseph the Border Guard,* 1972, *Joachim the Dustman,* 1974, and *Joachim the Policeman,* 1975, all by Kurt Baumann; *Kids' London* by Elizabeth Holt, 1972; *Fire,* 1973, and *The Day We Went to the Seaside,* 1973, by David Mackay; *Piccolo Book of Parties and Party Games* by Deborah Manley, 1973; *Follyfoot Pony Quiz Book* by Christine Pullein-Thompson, 1974; *Yan and the Gold Mountain Robbers,* 1974, and *Yan and the Firemonsters,* 1976, by Sydney Paulden; *Cook for Your Kids!* by Merry Archard, 1975; *Fiery Frederica* by Christine Nostlinger, 1975; *Helping* by Caroline Moorehead, 1975; *Tomfoolery,* 1975, and *Witcracks,* 1975, by Alvin Schwartz; *A Book of Elephants* edited by Katie Wales, 1977.

*　　　*　　　*

Robust humour is the hallmark of the work of David McKee. His picture books meet the needs of the 5 to 8-year-old readers who are just ready for a look at the outside world, to see a little of its intricacies and complexities. David McKee understands how children think, and his books are about people and their foibles, rather than about objects.

David McKee uses folk tale themes and transforms them into modern dress. His books read aloud well and he uses words sparingly, relying rather on his brilliant pictures to tell the tale. His *Elmer* must surely rival Dumbo as the most appealing elephant in history. Elmer is different. All the other elephants in the herd are grey, Elmer is patchwork; by painting himself grey he makes more problems than he solves. This finely-balanced story uses pattern and colour both in words and pictures to maximum effect.

Children readily identify with his characters, for they combine the absurd with the practical, the fantastic with the everyday. *Mr. Benn, Red Knight* is the epitome of the bold, swashbuckling hero lurking beneath the sombre city-suited gentleman. It needs only a casual remark from Mr. Benn such as "It's time I took a long walk" (in *123456789 Benn*) and off he goes to the fancy dress shop and another rollicking adventure. Everyone wishes that he had an uncle like Mr. Benn.

The Man Who Was Going to Mind the House retells the well-known Norwegian folk tale and treats it to a full colour, hilarious rendering. The farmer decides that he needs a rest and will take his wife's place in the house, but he soon finds that work in the fields is easier than household chores.

Books ought to be the means for young children to explore themselves and their relationships with other people. David McKee achieves a nice balance between the pure entertainment quality of words and pictures and deeper probing questions – what would YOU do if, like Lord Rex, you were discontented with being a lion and wished that you had wings like a butterfly, a trunk like an elephant, a parrot's tail, a kangaroo's hind leg, and a giraffe's neck, and suddenly found that you had them all.

In *The Magician and the Petnapping*, he has broadened his scope and design to use comic strip and busy, busy pictures to complement a witty story of the devotion of a King and his subjects to their pets. *Okki-Tokki-Unga*, a collection of action songs with brilliantly funny illustrations, is the best book of its kind I have ever seen.

A questing, questioning artist, David McKee has much to give to young children.

—Jean Russell

McLAUGHLIN, Lorrie (Bell). Canadian. Born in Hamilton, Ontario, 5 May 1924. Educated at schools in Hamilton. Married George Beatty McLaughlin in 1944; one daughter. Secretary, Royal Finance Company, Hamilton, 1940–44; taught creative writing, McMaster University, Hamilton, 1961–65. Recipient: Canadian Women's Press Club award, 1957; W. J. Gage Writing for Young Canada Award, 1963; Vicky Metcalf Award, 1968. *Died 13 September 1971.*

PUBLICATIONS FOR CHILDREN

Fiction

West to the Cariboo, illustrated by Joe Rosenthal. Toronto, Macmillan, 1962; New York, St. Martin's Press, and London, Macmillan, 1963.

The Trouble with Jamie, illustrated by Lewis Parker.   Toronto, Macmillan, and New York, St. Martin's Press, 1966; London, Macmillan, 1967.

The Cinnamon Hill Mystery, illustrated by Leonard Shortall.   New York, Crowell, 1967.

Days and Days of Darling Sam, illustrated by Jane Snyder.   Nashville, Abingdon Press, 1968.

Shogomoc Sam, illustrated by Randy Jones.   Toronto, Macmillan, and New York, St. Martin's Press, 1970.

PUBLICATIONS FOR ADULTS

Other

Is Your Child on Drugs?, with Ralph E. Wendeborn and Michael E. Palko.   Toronto, Mil-Mac Publications, 1970.

Editor, *A Canadian Market List for Writers*, revised edition.   Dundas, Ontario, Carrswood Press, 1964.

*   *   *

Lorrie McLaughlin's writing for children was often characterized by recurring themes of the power of mind over matter and the necessity of resourcefulness and flexibility by which her main characters triumph over great odds by means of their innovative thinking.

Her two earliest books, *West to the Cariboo* and *The Trouble with Jamie*, are perhaps her weakest. Their characterization is rather superficial and their historical settings are not powerfully depicted. *West to the Cariboo* tells of a journey made by two young boys from Queenston, Ontario, to Georgetown on the Red River in the 1870's in search of their father, a prospector looking for gold. *The Trouble with Jamie* is a story of a boy in Liverpool, Nova Scotia, at the turn of the 19th century when the town was a busy port. He inadvertently becomes a stowaway aboard the brig *Rover*, and subsequent events involve him in privateering on the Spanish Main.

Problems of identity and the coming of maturity through responsibility and self-reliance are central to both these books, as well as to what is perhaps McLaughlin's most successful novel for adolescents, *The Cinnamon Hill Mystery*. It is an absorbing suspense story told with vigor, interest, and humour in the first person by a very likable 12-year old girl, Trina. The author's insight into this character's mind, as well as into that of the book's young hero, William, is appealing for its credibility and sensitivity. *The Cinnamon Hill Mystery* is satisfying both as a member of the genre of adolescent mystery stories and for the depth of its characterization. William, who, like the brothers in *West to the Cariboo*, is anxious to be reunited with his absent father and strives to make himself worthy in his father's eyes, is perhaps, with Shogomoc Sam, McLaughlin's most remarkable creation.

Shogomoc Sam returns, after two books ostensibly set in the United States, to a Canadian scene – New Brunswick, and the logging camps of the 1850's. It, like *West to the Cariboo* and *The Cinnamon Hill Mystery*, is based on the search of a young adopted boy for his biological parents. In her creation of a Paul Bunyan-like figure of mythical proportions, McLaughlin achieves some effective and whimsical writing, and the book successfully combines elements of psychological realism with the tall tale familiar to loggers' yarns.

McLaughlin's work showed evidence of development in both thematic interest and in characterization as well as an increasing technical control of her material.

—Janet E. Baker

McLEAN, Allan Campbell. British. Born in Walney Island, Lancashire, 18 November 1922. Educated at Walney Island Elementary School and Barrow-in-Furness Junior Technical School, Lancashire. Served in the Royal Air Force in North Africa, Sicily, and Italy, 1941–46. Married Margaret Elizabeth White in 1946; has two sons and one daughter. Clerk, J. F. Dobson Co. Accountants, Barrow-in-Furness, 1938–41. Recipient: Frederick Niven Award, for fiction, 1962; Scottish Arts Council Award, 1972. Agent: A. M. Heath and Co. Ltd., 40–42 William IV Street, London WC2N 4DD, England. Address: Anerley Cottage, 16 Kingsmills Road, Inverness, Scotland.

PUBLICATIONS FOR CHILDREN

Fiction

> *The Hill of the Red Fox.* London, Collins, 1955; New York, Dutton, 1956.
> *The Man of the House*, illustrated by Shirley Hughes. London, Collins, 1956; as *Storm over Skye*, New York, Harcourt Brace, 1957; Collins, 1968.
> *Master of Morgana.* New York, Harcourt Brace, 1959; London, Collins, 1960.
> *Ribbon of Fire.* London, Collins, and New York, Harcourt Brace, 1962.
> *A Sound of Trumpets.* New York, Harcourt Brace, 1966; London, Collins, 1967.
> *The Year of the Stranger.* London, Collins, 1971; New York, Walck, 1972.

PUBLICATIONS FOR ADULTS

Novels

> *The Carpet-Slipper Murder.* London, Ward Lock, 1956; New York, Washburn, 1957.
> *Death on All Hallows.* London, Ward Lock, and New York, Washburn, 1958.
> *Deadly Honeymoon.* London, Ward Lock, 1958.
> *Murder by Invitation.* London, Ward Lock, 1959.
> *Stand-In for Murder.* London, Ward Lock, 1960.
> *The Islander.* London, Collins, 1962; as *The Gates of Eden*, New York, Harcourt Brace, 1962.
> *The Glasshouse.* New York, Harcourt Brace, 1968; London, Calder and Boyars, 1969.

Other

> *Explore the Highlands and Islands.* Inverness, Highlands and Islands Development Board, 1972.
> *The Highlands and Islands of Scotland.* London, Collins, 1976; New York, Crown, 1977.

Allan Campbell McLean comments:

All my historical novels for young people – *Ribbon of Fire, A Sound of Trumpets, The Year of the Stranger* – are based upon actual historical happenings in the Isle of Skye. My aim has been to present the young reader with a picture of 19th-century life in the Scottish Highlands that he or she would be unlikely to acquire from school textbooks.

*   *   *

To read Allan Campbell McLean's novels is to be transported straightway into the Highlands and islands of Scotland which provide the authentic background to his full-blooded adventure stories. He uses the main character as narrator, and this personal involvement adds realism and excitement to the tales. An Englishman who has lived many years in Scotland, McLean has a poet's ear for language, and his attention to the cadences and rhythms of the speech of the people results in truly authentic dialogue. His writing is frequently centred on social injustice and hardship, but this is historically true of the period and setting of his books and reinforces the impact of his writing.

Master of Morgana is probably the book least inspired by his social conscience, but it is a vehicle for powerfully dramatic descriptions of the lives of fishermen in Skye. Niall is seeking the man responsible for his brother's near fatal accident, and his adventures are gripping and exciting. Yet it is frequently the drama of the boy and his fellow fishermen struggling with the stormy sea which makes the greatest impression. Salmon fishing technique is minutely described, and the power of the sea in all its fury is fully equalled by the author's descriptive prose and skill in creating atmosphere. However, it is in *The Year of the Stranger* that McLean's writing reaches its heights. A tale of injustice and harshness, it grips the reader from the very first sentence: "Something wet and cold hit me across the belly, jerking me awake .... " Tension and excitement build up though interspersed with passages of poetic beauty, and soon the story becomes an allegory with visionary splendour breathtaking in its effect. Here is an ideal mixture of harshness and gentleness, excitement and peace, history and hope, all skilfully interwoven to produce a thought-provoking story.

Allan Campbell McLean is a writer so attuned to his background and environment that his writing always rings true. Description and action are finely balanced to produce first rate adventure stories which linger in the memory for a long time.

—Margaret Walker

McNEILL, Janet. British. Born in Dublin, Ireland, 14 September 1907. Educated at Birkenhead School, Cheshire, 1914–24; St. Andrews University, Scotland, M.A. in classics 1929. Married Robert P. Alexander in 1933 (died, 1973); has two living sons and one daughter. Secretary, Belfast *Telegraph*, 1930–33. Agent: A. P. Watt and Son, 26–28 Bedford Row, London WC1R 4HL. Address: 3 Grove Park, Redland, Bristol BS6 6PP, England.

PUBLICATIONS FOR CHILDREN

Fiction

My Friend Specs McCann, illustrated by Rowel Friers.   London, Faber, 1955.
A Pinch of Salt, illustrated by Rowel Friers.   London, Faber, 1956.
A Light Dozen: Eleven More Stories, illustrated by Rowel Friers.   London, Faber, 1957.
Specs Fortissimo, illustrated by Rowel Friers.   London, Faber, 1958.
This Happy Morning, illustrated by Rowel Friers.   London, Faber, 1959.
Special Occasions: Eleven More Stories, illustrated by Rowel Friers.   London, Faber, 1960.
Various Specs, illustrated by Rowel Friers.   London, Faber, 1961; New York, Nelson, 1971.
Try These for Size, illustrated by Rowel Friers.   London, Faber, 1963.
The Giant's Birthday, illustrated by Walter Erhard.   New York, Walck, 1964.
Tom's Tower, illustrated by Mary Russon.   London, Faber, 1965; Boston, Little Brown, 1967.
The Mouse and the Mirage, illustrated by Walter Erhard.   New York, Walck, 1966.
The Battle of St. George Without, illustrated by Mary Russon.   London, Faber, and Boston, Little Brown, 1966.

I Didn't Invite You to My Party, illustrated by Jane Paton.   London, Hamish Hamilton, 1967.

The Run-Around Robins, illustrated by Monica Brasier-Creagh.   London, Hamish Hamilton, 1967.

Goodbye, Dove Square, illustrated by Mary Russon.   London, Faber, and Boston, Little Brown, 1969.

Dragons, Come Home! and Other Stories, illustrated by John Lawrence.   London, Hamish Hamilton, 1969.

Umbrella Thursday, illustrated by Carolyn Dinan.   London, Hamish Hamilton, 1969.

Best Specs: His Most Remarkable Adventures, illustrated by Rowel Friers.   London, Faber, 1970.

The Other People.   Boston, Little Brown, 1970; London, Chatto and Windus, 1973.

The Youngest Kite, illustrated by Elizabeth Haines.   London, Hamish Hamilton, 1970.

The Prisoner in the Park.   London, Faber, and Boston, Little Brown, 1971.

Much Too Much Magic, illustrated by Carolyn Harrison.   London, Hamish Hamilton, 1971.

A Helping Hand, illustrated by Jane Paton.   London, Hamish Hamilton, 1971.

Wait for It and Other Stories.   London, Faber, 1972.

A Monster Too Many, illustrated by Ingrid Fetz.   Boston, Little Brown, 1972.

A Snow-Clean Pinny, illustrated by Krystyna Turska.   London, Hamish Hamilton, 1973.

A Fairy Called Andy Perks, illustrated by John Lawrence.   London, Hamish Hamilton, 1973.

We, Three Kings.   London, Faber, and Boston, Little Brown, 1974.

Ever After.   London, Chatto and Windus, and Boston, Little Brown, 1975.

The Magic Lollipop, illustrated by Linda Birch.   Leicester, Brockhampton Press, 1975; Chicago, Children's Press, 1976.

The Three Crowns of King Hullabaloo, illustrated by Mike Cole.   Leicester, Brockhampton Press, 1975; Chicago, Children's Press, 1976.

Just Turn the Key, illustrated by Douglas Hall.   London, Hamish Hamilton, 1976.

Plays

Finn and the Black Hag, music by Raymond Warren.   London, Novello, 1962.

Switch On — Switch Off and Other Plays (includes *Can I Help You?, There's a Man in That Tree, Clothes-Line, Three from Four Leaves One, Burning Topic*).   London, Faber, 1968.

Graduation Ode, music by Raymond Warren (produced Belfast, 1968).

Other (readers)

It's Snowing Outside, illustrated by Carol Barker.   London, Macmillan, 1968.

The Day They Lost Grandad, illustrated by Julius.   London, Macmillan, 1968.

The Nest Spotters, illustrated by Geraldine Spence.   London, Macmillan, 1972.

The Family Upstairs, illustrated by Trevor Stubley.   London, Macmillan, 1973.

My Auntie, illustrated by George Him.   London, Macmillan, 1975.

Go On, Then, illustrated by Terry Reid.   London, Macmillan, 1975.

Growlings, illustrated by Richard Rose.   London, Macmillan, 12 vols., 1975.

PUBLICATIONS FOR ADULTS

Novels

A Child in the House.   London, Hodder and Stoughton, 1955.

Tea at Four O'Clock.   London, Hodder and Stoughton, 1956.

The Other Side of the Wall.   London, Hodder and Stoughton, 1956.
A Furnished Room.   London, Hodder and Stoughton, 1958.
Search Party.   London, Hodder and Stoughton, 1959.
As Strangers Here.   London, Hodder and Stoughton, 1960.
The Early Harvest.   London, Bles, 1962.
The Maiden Dinosaur.   London, Bles, 1964; as *The Belfast Friends*, Boston, Houghton
    Mifflin, 1966.
Talk to Me.   London, Bles, 1965.
The Small Widow.   London, Bles, 1967; New York, Atheneum, 1968.

Plays

Gospel Truth.   Belfast, Carter, 1951.

More than 20 radio plays.

Janet McNeill comments:
I began writing fantasy for children because an active and agile imagination is a great help
to a child confronted by the facts of a largely materialistic world. I then found it possible, and
interesting, to write of the children in this world and their reaction to it. I am always glad if I
can make a child laugh and remember laughing.

                                        *   *   *

Janet McNeill is a godsend equally to adults who advocate reading for enjoyment and to
children who want to enjoy what they read. She has a special brand of quirky humour and
lightness of touch, even when writing about intrinsically serious subjects. Few authors have
such empathy with children, from the very young to confused adolescents.

In the books for younger readers – even in those tailored to the demands and format of a
particular series – all the children show a perceptiveness typified by little Madge in *A Helping
Hand.* Though led by naive logic to some odd conclusions about the characteristics of old age,
she creates a satisfying relationship with the crotchety couple next door.

For pre-adolescents, there is the ludicrous world of Specs McCann and his friend Curly,
the close-knit society of schoolboys, with their in-jokes and their extraordinary speech
patterns. The hazards and misfortunes of being a growing boy in a world controlled by (to
him) unpredictable and prejudiced adults have never been better portrayed. Likewise, Matt
and his friends, in *The Battle of St. George Without*, are involved with eccentric yet believable
adults. Janet McNeill sees oddities of character with the child's eye, that perception which is
so devastating in the classroom; yet the comic element sharpens perspective, especially when
the largely make-believe gang-life of adolescents impinges on the adult world of real crime
and danger.

The same characters, grown older, reappear in *Goodbye, Dove Square*, coping with
typically urban stress and change. Rehoused in a high-rise flat, Matt looks back nostalgically
to the warm untidy life when walls were thicker and people "took things the way they were."
The environment is constricting and nasty, the gang is splitting up, Matt alone is still at
school. Internal adjustments are difficult; his mates now enjoy enviable wealth and freedom;
for them, displacement is alleviated by compensations which he cannot share. Everything
exacerbates his feeling that there are many things he cannot understand, even about himself,
much less about other people and their bewildering relationships.

Kate, in *The Other People*, also has problems of coming to terms with a new life. Her
difficulty is more a matter of adjusting to a reality which proves entirely different from her
rosy expectations. Like Matt, she finds a way of piecing together the complicated jigsaws of
adult life. Each of them reaches some understanding of the separateness and of the individual
importance of other people.

Janet McNeill not only has her own distinctive way of writing "realistic" stories. She has a gift, too, for letting elements of fantasy creep into tales firmly set in the everyday world. The vivid evocation of school life in *Tom's Tower*, for example, slides convincingly into the realms of fancy. Many of her short stories, too, contain some twist of circumstance, some unexpected slant. Even the commonplace is never banal, and what *seems* quite ordinary turns out to be rather odd – not far-fetched, not forced, but perceived as more-than-ordinary by an author who makes a truth of the truism that some people can see more than meets the eye.

—Cecilia Gordon

MEADER, Stephen W(arren). American. Born in Providence, Rhode Island, 2 May 1892. Educated at Rochester High School; Moses Brown School, Providence; Haverford College, Pennsylvania, A. B. 1913. Married Elizabeth White Hoyt in 1916 (died, 1962), two sons and two daughters; Patience R. Ludlam, 1963. Case worker, Children's Aid Society, Newark, New Jersey, 1913–14; Secretary, Essex County Big Brother Movement, Newark, 1915; Member of the Publicity Department, Reilly and Britton, publishers, Chicago, 1916; Assistant Editor, *Country Gentleman* magazine, Philadelphia, 1916–21; advertising writer, Holmes Press, Philadelphia, 1921–27; copy writer, 1927–57, and Associate Copy Director, 1941–57, N. W. Ayer and Son, Philadelphia. Address: c/o Harcourt Brace Jovanovich Inc., 757 Third Avenue, New York, New York 10017, U.S.A.

PUBLICATIONS FOR CHILDREN

Fiction

> *The Black Buccaneer*, illustrated by the author.   New York, Harcourt Brace, 1920.
> *Down the Big River*, illustrated by the author.   New York, Harcourt Brace, 1924.
> *Longshanks*, illustrated by Edward Caswell.   New York, Harcourt Brace, 1928.
> *Red Horse Hill*, illustrated by Lee Townsend.   New York, Harcourt Brace, 1930.
> *Away to Sea*, illustrated by Clinton Balmer.   New York, Harcourt Brace, 1931.
> *King of the Hills*, illustrated by Lee Townsend.   New York, Harcourt Brace, 1933.
> *Lumberjack*, illustrated by Henry Pitz.   New York, Harcourt Brace, 1934; London, Bell, 1955.
> *The Will to Win and Other Stories*, illustrated by John Gincano.   New York, Harcourt Brace, 1936.
> *Who Rides in the Dark?*, illustrated by James MacDonald.   New York, Harcourt Brace, 1937; Oxford, Blackwell, 1938.
> *T-Model Tommy*, illustrated by Edward Shenton.   New York, Harcourt Brace, 1938.
> *Boy with a Pack*, illustrated by Edward Shenton.   New York, Harcourt Brace, 1939.
> *Bat, The Story of a Bull Terrier*, illustrated by Edward Shenton.   New York, Harcourt Brace, 1939.
> *Clear for Action!*, illustrated by Frank Beaudouin.   New York, Harcourt Brace, 1940.
> *Blueberry Mountain*, illustrated by Edward Shenton.   New York, Harcourt Brace, 1941; London, Bell, 1960.
> *Shadow in the Pines*, illustrated by Edward Shenton.   New York, Harcourt Brace, 1942.
> *The Sea Snake*, illustrated by Edward Shenton.   New York, Harcourt Brace, 1943.
> *The Long Trains Roll*, illustrated by Edward Shenton.   New York, Harcourt Brace, 1944.

Skippy's Family, illustrated by Elizabeth Korn.   New York, Harcourt Brace, 1945.
Jonathan Goes West, illustrated by Edward Shenton.   New York, Harcourt Brace, 1946.
Behind the Ranges, illustrated by Edward Shenton.   New York, Harcourt Brace, 1947.
River of the Wolves, illustrated by Edward Shenton.   New York, Harcourt Brace, 1948.
Cedar's Boy, illustrated by Lee Townsend.   New York, Harcourt Brace, 1949.
Whaler 'round the Horn, illustrated by Edward Shenton.   New York, Harcourt Brace, 1950; London, Museum Press, 1953.
Bulldozer, illustrated by Edwin Schmidt.   New York, Harcourt Brace, 1951.
The Fish Hawk's Nest, illustrated by Edward Shenton.   New York, Harcourt Brace, 1952.
Sparkplug of the Hornets, illustrated by Don Sibley.   New York, Harcourt Brace, 1953.
The Buckboard Stranger, illustrated by Paul Calle.   New York, Harcourt Brace, 1954.
Guns for the Saratoga, illustrated by John Cosgrave.   New York, Harcourt Brace, 1955.
Sabre Pilot, illustrated by John Polgreen.   New York, Harcourt Brace, 1956.
Everglades Adventure, illustrated by Charles Beck.   New York, Harcourt Brace, 1957.
The Commodore's Cup, illustrated by Don Sibley.   New York, Harcourt Brace, 1958.
The Voyage of the Javelin, illustrated by John Cosgrave.   New York, Harcourt Brace, 1959.
Wild Pony Island, illustrated by Charles Beck.   New York, Harcourt Brace, 1959.
Buffalo and Beaver, illustrated by Charles Beck.   New York, Harcourt Brace, 1960.
Snow on Blueberry Mountain, illustrated by Don Sibley.   New York, Harcourt Brace, 1961.
Phantom of the Blockade, illustrated by Victor Mays.   New York, Harcourt Brace, 1962.
The Muddy Road to Glory, illustrated by George Hughes.   New York, Harcourt Brace, 1963.
Stranger on Big Hickory, illustrated by Don Lambo.   New York, Harcourt Brace, 1964.
A Blow for Liberty, illustrated by Victor Mays.   New York, Harcourt Brace, 1965.
Topsail Island Treasure, illustrated by Marbury Brown.   New York, Harcourt Brace, 1966.
Keep 'em Rolling, illustrated by Al Savitt.   New York, Harcourt Brace, 1967.
Lonesome End, illustrated by Ned Butterfield.   New York, Harcourt Brace, 1968.
The Cape May Packet, illustrated by Robert Frankenberg.   New York, Harcourt Brace, 1969.

Other

Trap Lines North.   New York, Dodd Mead, and London, Harrap, 1936.

*   *   *

Stephen W. Meader is one of America's most prolific writers: he has written more than 40 books. Most of them are about boyhood adventures in various regions of the United States; he has also written books about ships and the sea, a few sports stories, and some wartime tales.

Many of the adventures in which Mr. Meader's characters engage were actually experienced by the author. Because of his own experiences and knowledge of the regions and time periods about which he writes, the author is able to write convincingly about the exploits of Buck Evans in *Blueberry Mountain* as Buck struggles to create a prosperous business by selling blueberries in the Pocono mountain region. *Jonathan Goes West* is another adventure story; it takes place in 1845. The hero of the story, Jonathan, travels from the Northeast to the Midwest in search of his father and the book revolves around the experiences that Jonathan encounters on his voyage on a schooner, by rail, on a steamboat, on foot, as well as while being a driver for a blind bookseller.

Toby Mortan in *Everglades Adventure* explores the swamp country in the state of Florida. His exploits in the everglades are enhanced by his sharing his experiences with a naturalist and his daughter. One of the author's other regional stories is *Buffalo and Beaver*, the story of the exploits of a teenager in the Rocky Mountain wilderness.

Trap Lines North is an adventure story of the true-life experiences of a fur-trapper. Based on the life of Jim Vanderbeck, and his diary, the work contains excellent photographs.

Away to Sea is one of several of Mr. Meader's fine sea stories. A young teacher sails to Africa aboard a slave ship. His adventures with pirates are imaginative, yet believable, and a thrilling episode in the book. Other sea stories deal with a fictional account of Abraham Lincoln and the Mississippi River, *Longshanks*, and *Whaler 'round the Horn*, the story of a whaling adventure.

Tales about wars include *A Blow for Liberty*, a story set during the Revolutionary War; it involves a seafaring venture too. *Guns for the Saratoga* is also set during the period of the Revolutionary War. *Phantom of the Blockade* is a story of the Civil War.

Mr. Meader's sports stories include a collection of short stories about football, baseball, track, and races, *The Will to Win*. *Lonesome End* is an exceptionally exciting football story, and *Sparkplug of the Hornets* is a basketball story that is just as thrilling.

The characterization in all of Mr. Meader's stories is excellent, and most of the author's stories are filled with exciting adventures. The plots are believable. Mr. Meader fluently, convincingly, and lucidly captures the beauty as well as the ruggedness of any region about which he writes. Even though the author's works span a wide range of subjects and various historical periods − stories of the Revolutionary War to modern sports stories − all of his books are appealing to young readers.

—Dolores C. Leffall

MEANS, Florence Crannell. American. Born in Baldwinsville, New York, 15 May 1891. Educated at Henry Read School of Art, Denver, 1910–12; Kansas City Baptist Theological Seminary, 1912; McPherson College, Kansas, summers 1922–29; University of Denver, 1923–24. Married Carleton Bell Means in 1912 (died, 1973); has one daughter. Since 1912, free-lance writer and lecturer. Recipient: Child Study Association of America award, 1946. Address: 595 Baseline Road, Boulder, Colorado 80302, U.S.A.

PUBLICATIONS FOR CHILDREN

Fiction

Rafael and Consuelo, with Harriet Louise Fullen.   New York, Friendship Press, 1929.
A Candle in the Mist, illustrated by Marguerite de Angeli.   Boston, Houghton Mifflin, 1931.
Ranch and Ring, illustrated by Henry Peck.   Boston, Houghton Mifflin, 1932.
Dusky Day, illustrated by Manning Lee.   Boston, Houghton Mifflin, 1933.
A Bowlful of Stars, illustrated by Henry Pitz.   Boston, Houghton Mifflin, 1934.
Rainbow Bridge, illustrated by Eleanor Lattimore.   New York, Friendship Press, 1934.
Penny for Luck, illustrated by Paul Quinn.   Boston, Houghton Mifflin, 1935.
Tangled Waters, illustrated by Herbert Morton Stoops.   Boston, Houghton Mifflin, 1936.
The Singing Wood, illustrated by Manning Lee.   Boston, Houghton Mifflin, 1937.
Shuttered Windows, illustrated by Armstrong Sperry.   Boston, Houghton Mifflin, 1938.

Adella Mary in Old New Mexico, illustrated by Herbert Morton Stoops. Boston, Houghton Mifflin, 1939.

Across the Fruited Plain, illustrated by Janet Smalley. New York, Friendship Press, 1940.

At the End of Nowhere, illustrated by David Hendrickson. Boston, Houghton Mifflin, 1940.

Children of the Promise, illustrated by Janet Smalley. New York, Friendship Press, 1941.

Whispering Girl, illustrated by Oscar Howard. Boston, Houghton Mifflin, 1941.

Shadow over Wide Ruin, illustrated by Lorence Bjorklund. Boston, Houghton Mifflin, 1942.

Teresita of the Valley, illustrated by Nicholas Panesis. Boston, Houghton Mifflin, 1943.

Peter of the Mesa, illustrated by Janet Smalley. New York, Friendship Press, 1944.

The Moved-Outers, illustrated by Helen Blair. Boston, Houghton Mifflin, 1945.

Great Day in the Morning, illustrated by Helen Blair. Boston, Houghton Mifflin, 1946.

Assorted Sisters, illustrated by Helen Blair. Boston, Houghton Mifflin, 1947.

The House under the Hill, illustrated by Helen Blair. Boston, Houghton Mifflin, 1949.

The Silver Fleece, with Carl Means, illustrated by Edwin Schmidt. Philadelphia, Winston, 1950.

Hetty of the Grande Deluxe, illustrated by Helen Blair. Boston, Houghton Mifflin, 1951.

Alicia, illustrated by William Barss. Boston, Houghton Mifflin, 1953.

The Rains Will Come, illustrated by Fred Kabotie. Boston, Houghton Mifflin, 1954.

Knock at the Door, Emmy, illustrated by Paul Lantz. Boston, Houghton Mifflin, 1956.

Reach for a Star. Boston, Houghton Mifflin, 1957.

Borrowed Brother, illustrated by Dorothy Bayley Morse. Boston, Houghton Mifflin, 1958.

Emmy and the Blue Door, illustrated by Frank Nicholas. Boston, Houghton Mifflin, 1959.

But I Am Sara. Boston, Houghton Mifflin, 1961.

That Girl Andy. Boston, Houghton Mifflin, 1962.

Tolliver. Boston, Houghton Mifflin, 1963.

It Takes All Kinds. Boston, Houghton Mifflin, 1964.

Us Maltbys. Boston, Houghton Mifflin, 1966.

Our Cup Is Broken. Boston, Houghton Mifflin, 1969.

Smith Valley. Boston, Houghton Mifflin, 1970.

Other stories: *Frankie and Willie May Go a Far Piece, All "Round Me Shinin'," Some California Poppies and How They Grew*, and others, published by the Baptist Board of Education, New York, in the 1940's.

Plays

Pepita's Adventure in Friendship. New York, Friendship Press, 1929.

Other plays: *The Black Tents: A Junior Play of Life among the Bedouins of Syria, Tara Finds the Door to Happiness*, and several missionary plays.

Other

Children of the Great Spirit: A Course on the American Indian, with Frances Somers Riggs. New York, Friendship Press, 1932.

Carvers' George: A Biography of George Washington Carver, illustrated by Harve Stein. Boston, Houghton Mifflin, 1952.

PUBLICATIONS FOR ADULTS

Other

> *Sagebrush Surgeon* (biography of Clarence G. Salsbury).   New York, Friendship Press,
> 1955.
> *Sunlight on the Hopi Mesas: The Story of Abigail E. Johnson.*   Philadelphia, Judson
> Press, 1960.
> Pamphlets on American Indian tribes for the Baptist Missionary Society.

Manuscript Collection: University of Colorado Library, Boulder.

Florence Crannell Means comments:

Flossy Crannell, six years old, charted her future in staggering capitals: she would be a *great* writer, a *great* painter, a kindergartener, a missionary. My father was a Baptist clergyman in up-state New York and we lived in a sea of books. Our house was often enlivened by visitors of every kind and color, unusual at the end of the 19th century when the United States was both isolationist and isolated, before the airplane, the radio, the T.V. So it was not strange that I began to write – and sell – little stories about children of other kinds and colors, some of them illustrated by the author, since I had had some art school training. I got material from visiting and retired missionaries, from government reports on Indian work, and from the blessed public library. Finally, a Hopi Indian love story brought me a check that allowed me to visit the Hopi reservation.

I had been asked, two years earlier, to write *Rafael and Consuelo*, about Mexicans in the U.S. My first full-length book, *A Candle in the Mist*, was based on the pioneering of my maternal grandparents in 1872, but my emphasis became increasingly on the beauty and needs of our ethnic minorities. I went alone, except during my husband's vacations, to visit the Hopi and several other tribes – Navajo, Mono, Otomi, Crow. I visited the blacks of our tidal islands and Carolina low country, the beautiful old villages of the Spanish Americans in Colorado and New Mexico, California's oriental groups, even the unbelievable Chinese village ruled by rival tongs.

What I found was much beauty, much poverty, and grace and love – and far too often a great painful loneliness. So, with my husband's help, I did my best to bring what I saw to our children and young adults.

                    *   *   *

As more children's book departments were established in American publishing companies during the 1930s, a new need also grew: books for "young adults." One of the first writers to fill this need was Florence Crannell Means. Moreover, she went far beyond the "career" type of story which soon became popular to tackle difficult real-life situations with characters presented in depth. She was one of the first to write sympathetically about minority groups, articulating their struggle for dignity, security, and education – or just plain survival.

Her first stories were in the pioneer genre. But though her plots may have been built out of typical frontier activities, her characters are not stereotyped. They have individuality and strength. *A Candle in the Mist*, first published in 1931, is still in print today, as are a dozen more of her many books.

It was probably natural to follow pioneer stories with Indian stories; but Mrs. Means did not write typical Indian stories. A Baptist minister's daughter, she grew up in a household where people of many nationalities and races were welcomed wholeheartedly; thus she developed sympathy and insight into the problems of minorities, with a special interest in Indians of the Southwest. Among others, she portrayed Navajos (*Tangled Waters*) and Hopis (*Whispering Girl*). She took time to observe people on their home territory before writing about them. She always put her characters first, bringing out their habits and problems as an integral part of their personalities and their stories.

This concern for human values accounts for the survivability of her stories. Although *Shuttered Windows* and *Great Day in the Morning* are now "period pieces" (blacks are called negroes, and their worlds are basically separate from whites), the books are still valid as to story and character and valuable as social history. The same can be said of *The Moved-Outers* which dealt with *nisei* (American-born children of Japanese parents) in internment camps on the West Coast during World War II. Reading this now, one wonders if the young people could really have been so mild and cooperative with officials; but they were patriotic, as well as heart-broken; it is still a moving story − and it stands as an obvious yardstick for the change to the cynical outspokenness of today's young people.

In more recent books, Mrs. Means presented with great honesty the discouragement and bitterness of a 20-year old Hopi Indian girl (*Our Cup Is Broken*) and the unflattering selfishness in desperate times of some members of a young girl's family in Colorado in the early 1900's (*Smith Valley*). In other words, her multi-layered stories of all kinds of people are not goody-goody, missionary-inspirational; they are honest, realistic, and, always, interesting and well-written.

—Lee Kingman

MEIGS, Cornelia (Lynde). American. Born in Rock Island, Illinois, 6 December 1884. Educated at Bryn Mawr College, Pennsylvania, A. B. 1907. English teacher, St. Katherine's School, Davenport, Iowa, 1912–13; Instructor, Professor of English, and Professor Emeritus, Bryn Mawr College, 1932–50. Worked for United States War Department, Washington, D.C., 1942–45. Recipient: Drama League Prize, 1915; American Library Association Newbery Medal, 1934; Women's International League for Peace and Freedom Jane Addams Award, 1971. L.H.D.: Plano University, Texas, 1967. *Died 8 October 1973.*

PUBLICATIONS FOR CHILDREN

Fiction

> *The Kingdom of the Winding Road,* illustrated by Frances White. New York and London, Macmillan, 1915.
> *Master Simon's Garden.* New York and London, Macmillan, 1916.
> *The Island of Appledore* (as Adair Aldon), illustrated by W. B. King. New York, Macmillan, 1917.
> *The Pirate of Jasper Peak* (as Adair Aldon). New York, Macmillan, 1918.
> *The Pool of Stars.* New York, Macmillan, 1919.
> *At the Sign of the Two Heroes* (as Adair Aldon), illustrated by S. Gordon Smyth. New York, Century, 1920.
> *The Windy Hill.* New York, Macmillan, 1921.
> *The Hill of Adventure* (as Adair Aldon), illustrated by J. Clinton Shepherd. New York, Century, 1922.
> *The New Moon,* illustrated by Marguerite de Angeli. New York, Macmillan, 1924.
> *Rain on the Roof,* illustrated by Edith Ballinger Price. New York, Macmillan, 1925.
> *The Trade Wind,* illustrated by Henry Pitz. Boston, Little Brown, 1927; London, Hodder and Stoughton, 1928.
> *As the Crow Flies.* New York, Macmillan, 1927.
> *Clearing Weather,* illustrated by Frank Dobias. Boston, Little Brown, 1928.
> *The Wonderful Locomotive,* illustrated by Berta and Elmer Hader. New York, Macmillan, 1928.

The Crooked Apple Tree, illustrated by Helen Mason Grose. Boston, Little Brown, 1929.

The Willow Whistle, illustrated by E. Boyd Smith. New York, Macmillan, 1931.

Swift Rivers, illustrated by Forrest Orr. Boston, Little Brown, 1932.

Wind in the Chimney, illustrated by Louise Mansfield. New York, Macmillan, 1934.

The Covered Bridge, illustrated by Marguerite de Angeli. New York, Macmillan, 1936.

Young Americans: How History Looked to Them While It Was in the Making. Boston, Ginn, 1936.

The Scarlet Oak, illustrated by Elizabeth Orton Jones. New York, Macmillan, 1938; Birmingham, Combridge, 1939.

Call of the Mountain, illustrated by James Daugherty. Boston, Little Brown, 1940.

Mother Makes Christmas, illustrated by Lois Lenski. New York, Grosset and Dunlap, 1940.

Vanished Island, illustrated by Dorothy Bayley. New York, Macmillan, 1941.

Mounted Messenger, illustrated by John Wonsetler. New York, Macmillan, 1943.

The Two Arrows. New York, Macmillan, 1949.

The Dutch Colt, illustrated by George and Doris Hauman. New York, Macmillan, 1952.

Fair Wind to Virginia, illustrated by John Wonsetler. New York, Macmillan, 1955.

Wild Geese Flying, illustrated by Charles Geer. New York, Macmillan, 1957.

Mystery at the Red House, illustrated by Robert Maclean. New York, Macmillan, 1961.

Plays

The Steadfast Princess. New York, Macmillan, 1916.

Helga and the White Peacock. New York, Macmillan, 1922.

Other

Invincible Louisa: The Story of the Author of "Little Women." Boston, Little Brown, 1933; as *The Story of Louisa Alcott*, London, Harrap, 1935.

Jane Addams: Pioneer for Social Justice: A Biography. Boston, Little Brown, 1970.

Editor, *Glimpses of Louisa: A Centennial Sampling of the Best Short Stories*, by Louisa May Alcott. Boston, Little Brown, 1968.

PUBLICATIONS FOR ADULTS

Novel

Railroad West. Boston, Little Brown, 1937.

Other

The Violent Men: A Study of Human Relations in the First American Congress. New York, Macmillan, 1949.

What Makes a College? A History of Bryn Mawr. New York, Macmillan, 1956.

Saint John's Church, Havre de Grace, Maryland, 1809–1959. Havre de Grace, Democratic Ledger, 1959.

The Great Design: Men and Events in the United Nations from 1945 to 1963. Boston, Little Brown, 1963.

Louisa May Alcott and the American Family Story. London, Bodley Head, 1970; New York, Walck, 1971.

Editor and part author, *A Critical History of Children's Literature.* New York, Macmillan, 1953; revised edition, 1969; London, Collier Macmillan, 1969.

*   *   *

Although Cornelia Meigs, who has also written under the pseudonym of Adair Aldon, is best remembered for her Newbery Award biography of Louisa May Alcott, *Invincible Louisa,* and for her comprehensive, astute *A Critical History of Children's Literature* (revised in 1969), she also made a significant contribution in several genres to children's literature with historical fiction, mysteries, and drama. Her particular interest in the development of the United States was reflected in many books; her experiences of storytelling within the family circle were a source of her sense of narrative flow; her empathy for children was echoed repeatedly in stories in which they are faced with obstacles and rise to conquer their problems.

Meigs' first book for children, *The Kingdom of the Winding Road,* was published in 1915 but is now out of print, as are many of her other titles. Her second book, *Master Simon's Garden,* received wider critical acclaim; it is a strikingly effective message about intolerance: in a rigidly Puritan Massachusetts town, Master Simon is reviled for wasting time and space on a beautiful garden, an expression of his love and tolerance, but his legacy is appreciated by future generations. Her interest in the past is also evident in *The Willow Whistle,* a tale of pioneer life in the Middle West; in *Wind in the Chimney,* in which two English children are instrumental in helping their widowed mother keep her new home in America just after the American Revolution; and in *The Covered Bridge,* set in Vermont in 1788, which has a strong sense of local history and the New England countryside.

Meigs' play *The Steadfast Princess* won the Drama League Award in 1915, and her dramatic flair is repeatedly clear in such mystery stories as *Mystery at the Red House,* which has a plot that is exciting despite the book's slow pace. In this book, as well as in *The Dutch Colt* and *Wild Geese Flying,* young protagonists rise to the occasion and solve problems in an exciting but believable manner.

While Meigs seldom created memorable characters or drew her characters in depth, her plots are absorbing, her historical backgrounds authoritative but unobtrusive, and her themes – especially in historical fiction – strong. She wrote with perspective and polish. If all her writing is not great, many of her books have elements of greatness. Reviewing another author's book, she wrote, "No book can be said to have even the elements of greatness unless it can stand the task of recollection," and many of Cornelia Meigs' stories can indeed stand that task.

—Zena Sutherland

MELWOOD, (Eileen) Mary. British. Born in Carlton-on-Lindwick, Nottinghamshire. Educated at Retford County High School for Girls, Nottinghamshire. Married Morris Lewis in 1939; has two sons. Recipient: Arts Council Award, 1964, 1966. Agent: Patricia Whitton, New Plays Inc., Box 273, Rowayton, Connecticut 06853, U.S.A. or, C. J. Productions, Arts Theatre Club, Great Newport Street, London W. 1. Address: 5 Hove Lodge Mansions, Hove Street, Hove, Sussex BN3 2TS, England.

PUBLICATIONS FOR CHILDREN

Fiction

Nettlewood. London, Deutsch, 1974; New York, Seabury Press, 1975.

Plays

The Tingalary Bird (produced London, 1964).   New York, New Plays, 1964.
Five Minutes to Morning (produced London, 1965).   New York, New Plays, 1966.
Masquerade (produced Nottingham, 1970).
The Small Blue Hoping Stone, music by Nancy Kelel (produced Detroit, 1976).

Radio Play: *It Isn't Enough*, 1957.

*   *   *

Mary Melwood's first play, *The Tingalary Bird*, arrived in an unpromising world. For a form of entertainment that is so much appreciated there is remarkably little demand for Children's Theatre. Certainly there is none from its audience. A high percentage of children in England don't know what theatre is, and those that do would surely not be capable of registering a protest were all children's theatre to disappear overnight. Such demand as exists is manufactured by a few adults working in the field or by the occasional parent looking for something to take the kids to as a change from the zoo. If children's theatre is at the mercy of this handful of adults, naturally its playwrights are too. *The Tingalary Bird* had a lot of surviving to do.

Since 1945 children's theatre had been dominated by small heroic touring companies taking their work into schools with desperately limited facilities. Inevitably they looked for small-cast plays with no technical requirements whatever. Writers had to provide this kind of play or not be performed at all. Circumstances created a very restricted art form which those that cared came to regard as the only thing children wanted. In the 1960's, when Theatre in Education got under way, custom-built plays were wanted and were frequently assembled by the companies themselves, thus cutting out the playwright entirely. Any playwright with ambitions to write a work for children with a quarter of the staging difficulties of *Peter Pan* was doomed. Children's theatre began to petrify. John Osborne had happened in adult theatre, but children's plays had scarcely put a toe out of the fairy ring.

By some miracle, Melwood, a teacher in Nottingham, knew none of this and blithely sent her play, with a small cast but with massive technical needs, to Caryl Jenner, who had the good sense to hire a theatre and put it on. The play was successful, the Arts Council of Great Britain granted it an award (the first ever for a kids play), and Children's Theatre had taken a great leap forward.

As the curtain went up on a pleasant sailor singing an equally pleasant song, the audience in 1964 could not have the slightest idea that Melwood was going to ask seven-year-olds to examine with her the breakdown of a marriage.

An ancient couple living in a failed inn are terrified to discover a huge caged bird has arrived in their living room during a thunder storm. Through this electrifying visitor, Melwood looks at the causes of their shattered relationship. At first they seem very simple; plainly the old woman is nasty, plainly the old man is nice. A subtler conflict emerges as one realises that each character holds a different version of the truth; the old man sees the bird's eyes are golden, the old woman says they are green. Both are correct. The audience begins to see that each has driven the other into these extremes of their personalities and, since nobody leaves, a suspicion that each finds their bitter tussle necessary is confirmed by the old woman's line, of her husband, "I should have missed him if he'd got away."

All stormy night the battle goes on. By dawn the beautiful bird has gone, the old man is heart broken and the old woman utterly routed. Her horde of gold has been revealed, her dusty doll's cradle, kept for a child she never had, is broken, the key to her bare food cupboard is in her husband's possession and, believe it or not, it has been funny lots of the time. The old woman throws down her broomstick, symbol of her authority, opts out of trying to keep the forest tidy and goes to bed. But as she sneaks back to recover the doll occupant of the cradle one feels she is not so much defeated as diminished, and that this is all to the good. She is no longer frantically being clean enough and thrifty enough or selfish enough for two. The Tingalary Bird has set her husband free from her, but it has also set her free from having to compensate for the old man's delightful deficiencies. The relationship will never be reasonable but it has been reasoned. The audience leaves her wiser and well entertained.

Thereafter Melwood began to write specifically for Caryl Jenner's Unicorn company and particularly for Matyelok Gibbs, its present Artistic Director, who created all Melwood's dashing unsentimentalised old ladies and for whom *The Small Blue Hoping Stone* was written.

Five Minutes to Morning is resolved by another "all nighter." Set in a ruined schoolroom, the play involves a boy who has recently inherited the property, and who resists his clear duty to allow Mrs. Venny, the old school teacher, to continue to occupy the premises. The second act reworks, in a dream sequence, the struggle within himself between enlightenment and chaos as represented by Mrs. Venny and Tom Skinch, the would-be buyer of the property. With this play Melwood is suggesting to her audience that the true excitement in our lives lies not in that furtively thrilling, brutal side of us but in the more dangerous area of our flights of fancy (at one point the schoolroom apparently takes off and flies) and, more sombrely, in learning. Not a fashionable theme.

To convey this theme, Melwood deliberately confuses vision with perception. Significantly, Jolyon, the boy, loses his spectacles at old Mrs. Venny's front door and doesn't get them back till the end of the play. From there on it is the schoolmarm's surprisingly racy and tart version of the world that he must adopt. During his nightmare he sometimes magnifies things to clarify the truth for himself. A vast squirrel cavorts with a football-size hazel nut, the cat is a sleek, affectionate giantess, but the wild white pony, a sort of fierce, living grail, is a reversal of itself and comes tamely to Mrs. Venny's door to be fed. Skinch, in the first act a belligerent landowner, turns total killer and becomes the Unruly Creature. Everything has a changed perspective so that Jolyon can understand and decide. He does – at five minutes to morning. He chooses Mrs. Venny while yet acknowledging that the tension and balance between the Venny and Skinch in him is his fundamental vitality.

In my experience, the danger of this play is that Skinch's naughty boy act and his very amusing flouting of authority in the early stages of the nightmare sequence so endears him to the children that they are inclined to see him as a sort of William grown up, not as the malignant destroyer of us all that Melwood intends. The play loses direction.

Still, Melwood remains a writer for children of the first order. My one regret is that though England spawned her it has been left to America to perform *The Small Blue Hoping Stone*. It is always an adventure to be involved in a Melwood production. I envy my colleagues across the water.

—Ursula M. Jones

MERRIAM, Eve. American. Born in Philadelphia, Pennsylvania, 19 July 1916. Educated at Cornell University, Ithaca, New York; University of Pennsylvania, Philadelphia, A. B. 1937; University of Wisconsin, Madison; Columbia University, New York. Married to Leonard Case Lewin; has two sons. Copywriter, 1939–42; radio writer, 1942–46; moderator of weekly program on poetry, WQXR Radio, New York, 1942–46; feature editor, *Deb* magazine, New York, 1946; fashion copy editor, *Glamour* magazine, New York, 1947–48; member of the staff, Bank Street College of Education, New York 1958–60; teacher, College of the City of New York, 1966–69. Recipient: Yale Series of Younger Poets Award, 1945; CBS-TV fellowship, 1959. Agent: Betty Anne Clarke, International Creative Management, 40 West 57th Street, New York, New York 10019. Address: 548 Riverside Drive, New York, New York 10027, U.S.A.

PUBLICATIONS FOR CHILDREN

Fiction

A Gaggle of Geese, illustrated by Paul Galdone.   New York, Knopf, 1960.
What Can You Do with a Pocket?, illustrated by Harriet Sherman.   New York, Knopf, 1964.
Do You Want to See Something?, illustrated by Abner Graboff.   New York, Scholastic, 1965.
Small Fry, illustrated by Garry MacKenzie.   New York, Knopf, 1965.
Miss Tibbett's Typewriter, illustrated by Rick Schreiter.   New York, Knopf, 1966.
Andy All Year Round, illustrated by Margo Hoff.   New York, Funk and Wagnalls, 1967.
Epaminondas, illustrated by Trina Schart Hyman.   Chicago, Follett, 1968; London, Collins, 1969.
Project 1–2–3, illustrated by Harriet Sherman.   New York, McGraw Hill, 1971.
Boys and Girls, Girls and Boys, illustrated by Harriet Sherman.   New York, Holt Rinehart, 1972.

Verse

There Is No Rhyme for Silver, illustrated by Joseph Schindelman.   New York, Atheneum, 1962.
Funny Town, illustrated by Evaline Ness.   New York, Crowell Collier, 1963.
It Doesn't Always Have to Rhyme, illustrated by Malcolm Spooner.   New York, Atheneum, 1964.
Don't Think about a White Bear, illustrated by Murray Tinkelman.   New York, Putnam, 1965.
Catch a Little Rhyme, illustrated by Imero Gobbato.   New York, Atheneum, 1966.
Independent Voices, illustrated by Arvis Stewart.   New York, Atheneum, 1968.
Finding a Poem, illustrated by Seymour Chwast.   New York, Atheneum, 1970.
I Am a Man: Ode to Martin Luther King, Jr., illustrated by Suzanne Verrier.   New York, Doubleday, 1971.
Out Loud, illustrated by Harriet Sherman.   New York, Atheneum, 1973.
Rainbow Writing.   New York, Atheneum, 1976.

Other

The Real Book about Franklin D. Roosevelt, illustrated by Bette J. Davis.   New York, Doubleday, 1952; London, Dobson, 1961.
The Real Book of Amazing Birds, illustrated by Paul Wenck.   New York, Doubleday, 1952; London, Dobson, 1960.
The Voice of Liberty: The Story of Emma Lazarus.   New York, Farrar Straus, 1959.
Mommies at Work, illustrated by Beni Montresor.   New York, Knopf, 1961.
What's in the Middle of a Riddle?, illustrated by Murray Tinkelman.   New York, Collier, 1963.
The Story of Ben Franklin, illustrated by Brinton Turkle.   New York, Scholastic, 1965.
Bam, Zam, Boom: A Building Book, illustrated by William Lightfoot.   New York, Walker, 1972.
AB to Zogg: A Lexicon for Science Fiction and Fantasy Readers, illustrated by Al Lorenz.   New York, Atheneum, 1977.

Editor, with Nancy Larrick, *Male and Female under 18: Frank Comments by Young People about Their Sex Roles Today*.   New York, Discus Books, 1973.

PUBLICATIONS FOR ADULTS

Novel

A Husband's Notes about Her: Fictions.   New York, Macmillan, 1976.

Plays

Inner City, music by Merriam (produced New York, 1971).
Out of Our Fathers' House (produced New York, 1975).
The Club, music by Merriam (produced New York, 1976).

Television Play: We the Women, 1975.

Verse

Family Circle.   New Haven, Connecticut, Yale University Press, 1946.
Tomorrow Morning: Poems.   New York, Twayne, 1953.
The Double Bed from the Feminine Side.   New York, Cameron, 1958.
The Trouble with Love: Poems.   New York, Macmillan, 1960.
Basics: An I-Can-Read Book for Grownups.   New York, Macmillan, 1962.
The Inner City Mother Goose.   New York, Simon and Schuster, 1969.
The Nixon Poems.   New York, Atheneum, 1970.

Other

Montgomery, Alabama, Money, Mississippi, and Other Places.   New York, Cameron,
   1956.
Emma Lazarus: Woman with a Torch.   New York, Citadel Press, 1956.
Figleaf: The Business of Being in Fashion.   Philadelphia, Lippincott, 1960.
After Nora Slammed the Door: American Women in the 1960's: The Unfinished
   Revolution.   Cleveland, World, 1964.
Man and Woman: The Human Condition.   Denver, Research Center on Women, 1968.
Equality, Identity, and Complementarity: Changing Perspectives of Man and Woman,
   with others, edited by Robert H. Amundson.   Denver, Research Center on Woman,
   1968.

Editor, Growing Up Female in America: Ten Lives.   New York, Doubleday, 1971.

Manuscript Collections: Kerlan Collection, University of Minnesota, Minneapolis; de
Grummond Collection, University of Southern Mississippi, Hattiesburg.

*   *   *

Eve Merriam has a way with the word and a wry humor, especially evident in her poetry.
With her work and that of poets like John Ciardi, children are given an opportunity to
appreciate the beauty and uses of a poetic scheme they can comprehend. Merriam does
wonderful things with her ideas in collections such as Out Loud, Catch a Little Rhyme, It
Doesn't Always Have to Rhyme, and There Is No Rhyme for Silver in which "Two from the
Zoo" appears:

> There is an animal known as skink,
> And no matter what you might happen to think

Or ever have thunk,
A skink —
Unlike a skunk —
Does not stink.
A skink is a skink.

Learning is fun and filled with excitement when Merriam uses her talent to explore the every-day world with children. But her words have a moral tone as well, especially when she looks to the future and the possibilities there: "Eternal sunrise, immortal sleep, or cars piled up in a rusty heap?" In the collection *Finding a Poem*, Merriam's verse is rife with the examples of what we are losing amid the plenty of our plastic society. Young readers will increase their vocabulary, their general knowledge and learn to exercise their imagination.

In 1961, prior to the re-emergence of a vocal and visible women's movement, when women were still torn between a career or family (but never thinking they could have both), *Mommies at Work* appeared. In this picture-book Merriam showed mothers at jobs ranging from elevator operators to bridge-builders to office workers. *Independent Voices* contains portraits in verse of important men and women such as Ida B. Wells, Black newspaper editor; Elizabeth Blackwell, first woman physician in the U.S.; and Henry Thoreau, man of solitude. In *Boys and Girls, Girls and Boys*, the author depicts children engaged in all kinds of interesting gender-free activities. *Project 1–2–3* is a different kind of counting book using a city housing project as the background for a numerical trip through a busy place. *What Can You Do with a Pocket?* is a terrible disappointment. The exercise in imagination is lead astray when pocket-treasures conjure up a cowboy, Indian, fisherman, policeman, orchestra conductor with ensemble, and railroad engineer – all males. What is left for the female is the anachronistic, fairy-tale role of princess. It is regrettable that a farsighted author took this giant step backward after her earlier, original contribution, *Mommies at Work*. In *I Am a Man: Ode to Martin Luther King, Jr.*, Merriam wrote: "Slowly, slowly dawning new days/ beginning to change the land and its ways." Moving slowly is difficult enough to endure; moving backwards is unthinkable.

—Vivian J. Scheinmann

MERRILL, Jean (Fairbanks). American. Born in Rochester, New York, 27 January 1923. Educated at Allegheny College, Meadville, Pennsylvania, B.A. in English 1944; Wellesley College, Massachusetts, M.A. 1945; University of Madras (Fulbright Fellow), 1952–53. Assistant Feature Editor, 1945–46, and Feature Editor, 1946–49, *Scholastic* magazine, New York; Associate Editor, 1950–51, and Editor, 1956–57, *Literary Cavalcade*, New York; Associate Editor, 1965–66, and Consultant, 1969–71, Bank Street College of Education Publications Division, New York. Recipient: Boys' Clubs of America award, 1965. Agent: Curtis Brown Ltd., 575 Madison Avenue, New York, New York 10022. Address: Angel's Ark, 29 South Main Street, Randolph, Vermont 05060, U.S.A.

PUBLICATIONS FOR CHILDREN

Fiction

Henry, The Hand-Painted Mouse, illustrated by Ronni Solbert. New York, Coward McCann, 1951.
The Woover, illustrated by Ronni Solbert. New York, Coward McCann, 1952.
Boxes, illustrated by Ronni Solbert. New York, Coward McCann, 1953.

The Tree House of Jimmy Domino, illustrated by Ronni Solbert.   New York and London, Oxford University Press, 1955.

The Travels of Marco, illustrated by Ronni Solbert.   New York, Knopf, 1956.

A Song for Gar, illustrated by Ronni Solbert.   New York, McGraw Hill, 1957.

The Very Nice Things, illustrated by Ronni Solbert.   New York, Harper, 1959.

Blue's Broken Heart, illustrated by Ronni Solbert.   New York, McGraw Hill, 1960.

Tell Us about the Cowbarn, Daddy, illustrated by Lili Wronker.   New York, Scott, 1963.

The Pushcart War, illustrated by Ronni Solbert.   New York, Scott, 1964; London, Hamish Hamilton, 1973.

The Elephant Who Liked to Smash Small Cars, illustrated by Ronni Solbert.   New York, Pantheon Books, 1967.

Red Riding, illustrated by Ronni Solbert.   New York, Pantheon Books, 1968.

The Black Sheep, illustrated by Ronni Solbert.   New York, Pantheon Books, 1969.

Mary, Come Running, illustrated by Ronni Solbert.   New York, McCall, 1970.

Here I Come — Ready or Not!, illustrated by Frances Scott.   Chicago, Whitman, 1970.

How Many Kids Are Hiding on My Block?, illustrated by Frances Scott.   Chicago, Whitman, 1970.

Please, Don't Eat My Cabin, illustrated by Frances Scott.   Chicago, Whitman, 1971.

The Second Greatest Clown in the World.   Boston, Houghton Mifflin, 1971.

The Jackpot.   Boston, Houghton Mifflin, 1971.

The Toothpaste Millionaire, illustrated by Jan Palmer.   Boston, Houghton Mifflin, 1972.

Maria's House, illustrated by Frances Scott.   New York, Atheneum, 1974.

Plays

Tightrope Act, in *Isn't That What Friends Are For?*, edited by Bank Street College of Education.   Boston, Houghton Mifflin, 1972.

Television Play: *The Claws in the Cat's Paw*, 1956.

Verse

Emily Emerson's Moon, illustrated by Ronni Solbert.   Boston, Little Brown, 1960.

Other

Shan's Lucky Knife: A Burmese Folktale, illustrated by Ronni Solbert.   New York, Scott, 1960; Kingswood, Surrey, World's Work, 1961.

The Superlative Horse: A Tale of Ancient China, illustrated by Ronni Solbert.   New York, Scott, 1961.

High, Wide and Handsome and Their Three Tall Tales, illustrated by Ronni Solbert.   New York, Scott, 1964.

The Bumper Sticker Book, illustrated by Frances Scott.   Chicago, Whitman, 1973.

Editor, with Ronni Solbert, *A Few Flies and I* (haiku), by Issa Kobayashi, translated by R. H. Blyth and Nobuyuki Yuasa.   New York, Pantheon Books, 1969.

Manuscript Collections: Rare Book Division, University of Wyoming Library, Laramie; de Grummond Collection, University of Southern Mississippi, Hattiesburg; Kerlan Collection, University of Minnesota, Minneapolis.

Jean Merrill comments:

As to my general motivation as a writer, I would say that it is to celebrate those aspects of the human experience that affirm the creative and life-reverencing instinct in man. To the extent that a writer for children occasionally glimpses himself, as does any adult directing his concern to children, I am conscious of more specific motivations, among them:

– *to educate* – in the sense of socializing the child in the direction of a constructive use of his potential;

– *to entertain* – to encourage the capacity for joy by enticing the free play of a child's curiosity, humor and inventiveness;

– *to liberate* – by opening up the child to emotional as well as to intellectual experience.

Though I am referring to "the child" as if he were a receptacle, the child for whom one essentially writes is oneself, and at base writing is motivated by one's own need to resolve the enigma of life. I am always the imagined reader, as well as writer, of my books.

Writers for children are often asked whether they feel limitations on subject matter or theme in writing for children. I have never felt constrained in writing for children about anything that concerned me as an adult; what I perceive as touchstones of the human experience are as appropriate, indeed essential, to books for very young readers as to books for the literate 14-year-old.

One must obviously be selective of the language and metaphor that will most readily translate one's perceptions to children of various ages, but this necessity is no more a limitation than trying to converse with adults of background or experience different from one's own. And finding the word or symbol that will translate my feeling into a form accessible to a child is to me the essential challenge of writing.

My interest in writing children's books may have derived from the impact certain books had on me as a child, and a wish to recreate the quality of that experience. Certainly, one of the satisfactions of writing for children is the intensity of caring young readers lavish on the books they like.

It is often the books we read as children that stay with us the longest, whose titles, characters, plots and emotional tone we never forget. Their significance with repeated readings is imprinted on memory until they are as much a part of the landscape that forever colors our perception and expectation of the world as the faces of our parents and the look and smell of the houses we grew up in.

Given this extra durability that may attach to what children read, whatever a writer feels may be worth communicating seems to me to be additionally worth communicating to children. And seems also to require of those of us who write for children that we be uncompromising enemies of the shoddy, meretricious, or sentimental in our work.

*   *   *

Jean Merrill has earned her solid reputation as a children's writer by the consistently fine quality of her books. Her themes and formats are varied. Her interest in the Far East has produced some fine books such as *High, Wide and Handsome, Shan's Lucky Knife*, and *The Superlative Horse*. Her picture books are clever, original and appealing to young listeners. One good example of this genre is *The Elephant Who Liked to Smash Small Cars*. *Elephant* presents the conflict between "doing your own thing" and harming others; it is also a story of growing up, of becoming aware of others' needs. While some adults worry about the violence – i.e., the elephant's delight in smashing small cars and the "tit-for-tat" treatment he receives – young children seem to be deeply satisfied both by the portrayal of Elephant's antisocial drives and the resolution of them.

Ms. Merrill writes equally effectively for older children. Though one of her earlier and most famous books, *The Pushcart War*, is identified as for children 9 to 12, it really is for ages 9 to 90. The humorous wisdom and courageous actions of the pushcart owners in resisting the onslaughts of the powerful trucking concerns appeal to adults as well as children.

The Pushcart War exemplifies a favorite theme of Ms. Merrill – the struggle of the small and weak against the strong and mighty. In a delightful book for older readers, *The Toothpaste Millionaire* (also shown on film as a television special), the young black boy, Rufus, invents an effective toothpaste from simple materials. As his product oversells the established brands by nearly 100%, the enraged manufacturers try to put him out of business. As in *The Pushcart War*, the big corporations meet their comeuppance, even though Rufus is already dreaming up new enterprises.

Ms. Merrill's humanistic concerns are evident in all her books. In *The Superlative Horse*, merit doesn't depend on outward trappings but on inward ability. In *The Black Sheep*, a book for younger children, there is gentle insight into the worth of the "different" individual.

Ms. Merrill not only catches the flow and flavor of real children's language but structures it in such naturalistic speech that even poor readers become absorbed in her stories. She blends long and short sentences, sentence fragments, phrases and dialogue so skillfully that it reads as "real talk written down"; and the young reader immediately identifies with the characters. She has mastered the subtle art of "immediacy" – the reader is there and the adventure is happening to him or her.

One last observation: Jean Merrill is also intrigued by mathematics. Her pleasure in this science often makes it more meaningful to the reader than most textbooks on the subject. Rufus can become a toothpaste millionaire because he can understand cost and profit; in *The Pushcart War*, a professor carries percentage to its ultimate absurdity; in "The Seventeen Horses of Ali" (a story in *Discoveries: An Individualized Approach to Reading*), she presents a playful puzzle in fractions that might well awaken delight in mathematics.

A craftswoman with words, a prolific and creative writer, a humorous mathematician and a fine story-teller – Jean Merrill is all these things; but above all, she is a tender but strong affirmer of human rights.

—Betty Boegehold

MEYNELL, Laurence (Walter). Pseudonym: **A. Stephen Tring.** British. Born in Wolverhampton, Staffordshire, 9 August 1899. Educated at St. Edmund's College, Ware, Hertfordshire. Served in the Honourable Artillery Company during World War I; Royal Air Force, 1939–45: mentioned in despatches. Married Shirley Ruth Darbyshire in 1932 (died, 1955), one daughter; Joan Belfrage, 1956. Articled pupil in a land agency in the 1920's; worked as a schoolteacher and an estate agent. General Editor, Men of the Counties series, Bodley Head, publishers, London, 1955–57; Literary Editor, *Time and Tide*, London, 1958–60. Address: 9 Clifton Terrace, Brighton, Sussex BN1 3HA, England.

PUBLICATIONS FOR CHILDREN

Fiction

Smoky Joe, illustrated by Charlotte Hough. London, Lane, 1952.
Smoky Joe in Trouble, illustrated by Charlotte Hough. London, Lane, 1953.
Policeman in the Family, illustrated by Neville Dear. London, Oxford University Press, 1953.
Under the Hollies, illustrated by Ian Ribbons. London, Oxford University Press, 1954.
Bridge under the Water, illustrated by John S. Goodall. London, Phoenix House, 1954; New York, Roy, 1957.
Jane: Young Author (as Valerie Baxter). London, Lane, 1954.
Elizabeth: Young Policewoman (as Valerie Baxter). London, Lane, 1955.
Shirley: Young Bookseller (as Valerie Baxter). London, Lane, 1956.
Animal Doctor, illustrated by Raymond Sheppard. London, Oxford University Press, 1956.
Smoky Joe Goes to School, illustrated by Charlotte Hough. London, Lane, 1956.

Hester: Ship's Officer (as Valerie Baxter). London, Lane, 1957.
Sonia Back Stage. London, Chatto and Windus, 1957.
The Young Architect, illustrated by David Knight. London, Oxford University Press,
    1958.
District Nurse Carter. London, Chatto and Windus, 1958.
Nurse Ross Takes Over. London, Hamish Hamilton, 1958.
The Hunted King. London, Bodley Head, 1959.
Nurse Ross Shows the Way. London, Hamish Hamilton, 1959.
Monica Anson, Travel Agent. London, Chatto and Windus, 1959.
Nurse Ross Saves the Day. London, Hamish Hamilton, 1960.
Bandaberry. London, Bodley Head, 1960.
Nurse Ross and the Doctor. London, Hamish Hamilton, 1962.
The Dancers in the Reeds. London, Hamish Hamilton, 1963.
Good Luck, Nurse Ross. London, Hamish Hamilton, 1963.
Scoop. London, Hamish Hamilton, 1964.
The Empty Saddle. London, Hamish Hamilton, 1965.
Break for Summer. London, Hamish Hamilton, 1965.
Shadow in the Sun. London, Hamish Hamilton, 1966.
The Suspect Scientist. London, Hamish Hamilton, 1966.
The Man in the Hut, illustrated by Tony Hart. London, Kaye and Ward, 1967.
Peter and the Picture Thief, illustrated by Tony Hart. London, Kaye and Ward, 1969.
Jimmy and the Election, illustrated by Tony Hart. London, Kaye and Ward, 1970.
Tony Trotter and the Kitten, illustrated by Peter Edwards. London, Kaye and Ward,
    1971.
The Great Cup Tie, illustrated by Gareth Floyd. London, Kaye and Ward, 1974.

Fiction (as A. Stephen Tring)

The Old Gang, illustrated by John Camp. London, Oxford University Press, 1947.
Penny Dreadful, illustrated by T. R. Freeman. London, Oxford University Press, 1949.
The Cave by the Sea, illustrated by T. R. Freeman. London, Oxford University Press,
    1950.
Barry's Exciting Year, illustrated by Charlotte Hough. London, Oxford University
    Press, 1951.
Barry Gets His Wish, illustrated by Charlotte Hough. London, Oxford University
    Press, 1952.
Young Master Carver: A Boy in the Reign of Edward III, illustrated by Alan
    Jessett. London, Phoenix House, 1952; New York, Roy, 1957.
Penny Triumphant, illustrated by T. R. Freeman. London, Oxford University Press,
    1953.
Penny Penitent, illustrated by T. R. Freeman. London, Oxford University Press, 1953.
Barry's Great Day, illustrated by Charlotte Hough. London, Oxford University Press,
    1954.
Penny Puzzled, illustrated by T. R. Freeman. London, Oxford University Press, 1955.
The Kite Man. Oxford, Blackwell, 1955.
Penny Dramatic, illustrated by T. R. Freeman. London, Oxford University Press,
    1956.
Penny in Italy, illustrated by T. R. Freeman. London, Oxford University Press, 1957.
Frankie and the Green Umbrella, illustrated by Richard Kennedy. London, Hamish
    Hamilton, 1957.
Pictures for Sale, illustrated by Christopher Brooker. London, Hamish Hamilton,
    1958.
Penny and the Pageant, illustrated by Kathleen Gell. London, Oxford University Press,
    1959.
Peter's Busy Day, illustrated by Raymond Briggs. London, Hamish Hamilton, 1959.

The Man with the Sack, illustrated by Peter Booth.   London, Hamish Hamilton, 1963.
Ted's Lucky Ball, illustrated by James Russell.   London, Hamish Hamilton, 1961.
Penny Says Good-bye, illustrated by Kathleen Gell.   London, Oxford University Press, 1961.
Chad, illustrated by Joseph Acheson.   London, Hamish Hamilton, 1966.

Other

Builder and Dreamer: A Life of Isambard Kingdom Brunel, illustrated by Lee Kenyon.   London, Lane, 1952; revised version, as *Isambard Kingdom Brunel*, London, Newnes, 1955.
Rolls, Man of Speed: A Life of Charles Stewart Rolls.   London, Lane, 1953; revised version, as *The Hon. C. S. Rolls*, London, Newnes, 1955.
Great Men of Staffordshire.   London, Lane, 1955.
The First Men to Fly: A Short History of Wilbur and Orville Wright.   London, Laurie, 1955.
James Brindley: The Pioneer of Canals.   London, Laurie, 1956.
Our Patron Saints, illustrated by John Turner.   London, Acorn Press, 1957.
Thomas Telford: The Life Story of a Great Engineer, illustrated by Donald Forster.   London, Lane, 1957.
Farm Animals, illustrated by Jennifer Miles.   London, Ward, 1958.
Airmen on the Run: True Stories of Evasion and Escape by British Airmen of World War II, illustrated by Richard Kennedy.   London, Odhams Press, 1963.
The Beginning of Words: How English Grew, with Colin Pickles.   London, Blond, 1970; New York, Putnam, 1971.

PUBLICATIONS FOR ADULTS

Novels

Mockbeggar.   London, Harrap, 1924; New York, Appleton, 1925.
Lois.   London, Harrap, and New York, Appleton, 1927.
Bluefeather.   London, Harrap, and New York, Appleton, 1928.
Death's Eye.   London, Harrap, 1929; as *The Shadow and the Stone*, New York, Appleton, 1929.
Camouflage.   London, Harrap, 1930.
Mystery at Newtown Ferry.   Philadelphia and London, Lippincott, 1930.
Asking for Trouble.   London, Ward Lock, 1931.
Consummate Rose.   London, Hutchinson, 1931.
Storm Against the Wall.   London, Hutchinson, and Philadelphia, Lippincott, 1931.
The House on the Cliff.   London, Hutchinson, and Philadelphia, Lippincott, 1932.
Paid in Full.   London, Harrap, 1933; as *So Many Doors*, Philadelphia, Lippincott, 1933.
Watch the Wall.   London, Harrap, 1933; as *Gentlemen Go By*, Philadelphia, Lippincott, 1934.
Odds on Bluefeather.   London, Harrap, 1934; Philadelphia, Lippincott, 1935.
The Pattern (as Robert Eton).   London, Harrap, 1934.
Inside Out! or, Mad as a Hatter (as Geoffrey Ludlow).   London, Harrap, 1934.
Third Time Unlucky.   London, Harrap, 1935.
The Dividing Air (as Robert Eton).   London, Harrap, 1935.
The Bus Leaves for the Village (as Robert Eton).   London, Nicholson and Watson, 1936.
Women Had to Do It! (as Geoffrey Ludlow).   London, Nicholson and Watson, 1936.
On the Night of the 18th ....   London, Nicholson and Watson, and New York, Harper, 1936.
The Door in the Wall.   London, Nicholson and Watson, and New York, Harper, 1937.

The House in the Hills. London, Nicholson and Watson, 1937; New York, Harper, 1938.

Not in Our Stars (as Robert Eton). London, Nicholson and Watson, 1937.

The Dandy. London, Nicholson and Watson, 1938.

The Hut. London, Nicholson and Watson, 1938.

The Journey (as Robert Eton). London, Nicholson and Watson, 1938.

Palace Pier (as Robert Eton). London, Nicholson and Watson, 1938.

His Aunt Came Late. London, Nicholson and Watson, 1939.

And Be a Villain. London, Nicholson and Watson, 1939.

The Legacy (as Robert Eton). London, Nicholson and Watson, 1939.

The Faithful Years (as Robert Eton). London, Nicholson and Watson, 1939.

The Corner of Paradise Place (as Robert Eton). London, Nicholson and Watson, 1940.

The Creaking Chair. London, Collins, 1941.

The Dark Square. London, Collins, 1941.

Strange Landing. London, Collins, 1946.

The Evil Hour. London, Collins, 1947.

St. Lynn's Advertiser (as Robert Eton). London, Nicholson and Watson, 1947.

The Bright Face of Danger. London, Collins, 1948.

The Echo in the Cave. London, Collins, 1949.

The Dragon at the Gate (as Robert Eton). London, Nicholson and Watson, 1949.

The Lady on Platform One. London, Collins, 1950.

Party of Eight. London, Collins, 1950.

The Man No One Knew. London, Collins, 1951.

The Frightened Man. London, Collins, 1952.

Danger round the Corner. London, Collins, 1952.

Too Clever by Half. London, Collins, 1953.

Give Me the Knife. London, Collins, 1954.

Where Is She Now? London, Collins, 1955.

Saturday Out. London, Collins, 1956; New York, Walker, 1962.

The Sun Will Shine. London, Transworld, 1956.

The Breaking Point. London, Collins, 1957.

One Step from Murder. London, Collins, 1958.

The Abandoned Doll. London, Collins, 1960.

The House in Marsh Road. London, Collins, 1960.

The Pit in the Garden. London, Collins, 1961.

Moon over Ebury Square. London, Hale, 1962.

Virgin Luck. London, Collins, 1963; New York, Simon and Schuster, 1964.

Sleep of the Unjust. London, Collins, 1963.

More Deadly Than the Male. London, Collins, 1964.

Double Fault. London, Collins, 1965.

The Imperfect Aunt. London, Hale, 1966.

Die by the Book. London, Collins, 1966.

Week-end in the Scampi Belt. London, Hale, 1967.

The Mauve Front Door. London, Collins, 1967.

Death of a Philanderer. London, Collins, 1968; New York, Doubleday, 1969.

Of Malicious Intent. London, Collins, 1969.

The Shelter. London, Hale, 1970.

The Curious Crime of Miss Julia Blossom. London, Macmillan, 1970.

The End of the Long Hot Summer. London, Hale, 1972.

Death by Arrangement. London, Macmillan, and New York, McKay, 1972.

A Little Matter of Arson. London, Macmillan, 1972.

A View from the Terrace. London, Hale, 1972.

The Fatal Flaw. London, Macmillan, 1973.

The Thirteen Trumpeters. London, Macmillan, 1973.

The Fortunate Miss East. London, Hale, 1973.

The Woman in Number Five.   London, Hale, 1974; as *Burlington Square*, New York, Coward McCann, 1975.
The Fairly Innocent Little Man.   London, Macmillan, 1974.
The Footpath.   London, Hale, 1975.
Don't Stop for Hooky Hefferman.   London, Macmillan, 1975.
Hooky and the Crock of Gold.   London, Macmillan, 1975.
The Lost Half Hour.   London, Macmillan, 1976.
The Vision Splendid.   London, Hale, 1976.
The Folly of Henrietta Dyke.   London, Hale, 1976.
The Little Kingdom.   London, Hale, 1977.
Folly to Be Wise.   London, Hale, 1977.
Hooky Gets the Wooden Spoon.   London, Macmillan, 1977.

Verse

The Ballad of Pen Fields, with a Plan of the Battlefield.   Privately printed, 1927.

Other

Bedfordshire.   London, Hale, 1950.
Famous Cricket Grounds.   London, Phoenix House, 1951.
"Plum" Warner.   London, Phoenix House, 1951.
Exmoor.   London, Hale, 1953.

*   *   *

A. Stephen Tring, better known as Laurence Meynell, deserves to be ranked with Geoffrey Trease and E. W. Hildick for his endeavours to introduce realism and vitality into stories for boys.

His first boys' school story, *The Old Gang*, follows traditional formulae although he abandons the prestigious boarding-school setting to deal with grammar school and secondary modern school rivalries. This racy novel is told in the first person by a member of "the old gang," Frank Dilmot. It is highly readable, packed with incident, with a strong emphasis on various sports and feuds, rivalries and pranks. Authenticity is reduced by the introduction of an incredible mystery, and unacceptable attitudes tend to prevail, but regardless of such faults *The Old Gang* remains in print with its lively, convincing dialogue, its quick humour and its notable schoolboy trio, Frank, Joe and Mickey.

In the three books about Barry Briggs, A. Stephen Tring breaks free from the accepted patterns of an earlier period to create a strong central character, whose hopes, fears and fantasies are vividly presented to the reader in a highly realistic framework, particularly of family life on a council housing estate. This series shows more originality and realism than *The Old Gang* and was unusual in the 1950's for its rounded portrayal of parents. In this series the mystery elements are more feasible than in some of A. Stephen Tring's other books, but the introduction of upper-class characters detracts from the otherwise excellent realism of this series.

The Penny series for girls is less memorable than either *The Old Gang* or the Barry series. *Penny Dreadful* shows a degree of originality and zest not maintained in later titles of the series. The young heroine and her family are reasonably well drawn and plots are packed with action, but the fairly affluent background of the series has little relevance to the readership of a later period. As in *The Old Gang*, rather incredible mystery situations are introduced and unacceptable attitudes persist.

As an experienced writer of stories for both adults and for children A. Stephen Tring has proved willing to use his expertise to cater for particular contemporary needs: no easy task. His success is partly due to his readable, sometimes deceptively easy style of writing, and also to his combination of action with realism. His most successful work in this area is without doubt the series of books about Barry Briggs.

—Anne W. Ellis

MILES, Miska. See **MARTIN, Patricia Miles.**

MILHOUS, Katherine. American. Born in Philadelphia, Pennsylvania, 27 November 1894. Educated at Philadelphia College of Art; Pennsylvania Academy of Fine Arts (Cresson Travelling Scholar), Philadelphia. Staff Artist, Philadelphia *Record*, 1925–29; Supervisor, and muralist and poster artist, for the Pennsylvania Federal Arts Project. Group show: New York World's Fair, 1939. Recipient: American Library Association Caldecott Medal, 1951; Drexel Institute Citation, 1967. Address: 1534 Pine Street, Philadelphia, Pennsylvania 19102, U.S.A.

PUBLICATIONS FOR CHILDREN (illustrated by the author)

Fiction

> *Lovina.* New York and London, Scribner, 1940.
> *Herodia, The Lovely Puppet.* New York, Scribner, 1942.
> *Corporal Keeperupper.* New York, Scribner, 1943.
> *The First Christmas Crib.* New York, Scribner, 1944.
> *Snow over Bethlehem.* New York, Scribner, 1945.
> *The Egg Tree.* New York, Scribner, 1950.
> *Patrick and the Golden Slippers.* New York, Scribner, 1951.
> *Appolonia's Valentine.* New York, Scribner, 1954.
> *With Bells On.* New York, Scribner, 1955.

Other

> *Through These Arches: The Story of Independence Hall.* Philadelphia, Lippincott, 1964.

> Editor, with Alice Dalgliesh, *Once on a Time.* New York, Scribner, 1938.

Manuscript Collection: Kerlan Collection, University of Minnesota, Minneapolis.

Illustrator: *Happily Ever After* edited by Alice Dalgliesh, 1939, and *A Book for Jennifer*, 1940, *Wings Around South America*, 1941, *They Live in South America*, 1942, *The Little Angel*, 1943, *The Silver Pencil*, 1944, and *Along Janet's Road*, 1946, all by Dalgliesh; *Billy Button's Buttered Biscuit*, 1941, and *Peter Piper's Pickled Peppers*, 1942, by Mabel Leigh Hunt; *Old Abe* by Lorraine Sherwood, 1946; *The Brownies* by Juliana Horatia Ewing, 1946.

*   *   *

Pennsylvania is the setting of 9 of the 10 books Katherine Milhous has written herself. The state's rich historical and ethnic heritage is the substance of the texts. The Irish-Quaker author-illustrator steeped herself in the Pennsylvania Dutch traditions while creating murals and posters and collecting art designs as supervisor of the Federal Arts Project in the state.

History is interpreted for children in all books, but particularly in *Herodia, The Lovely Puppet*, the patriotic *Corporal Keeperupper*, and *Through These Arches: The Story of Independence Hall*. The state archivist provided her with an outline of the story about the lifesize marionette show traveling in the 1870's. In an autobiographical essay, the author relates her rigorous attempt to gain first-hand knowledge of the area: "I know the old barns and the woodlands and pasturelands of Pennsylvania. Once two friends and I hitched a plough-horse to a Dearborn wagon and caravanned along old dirt roads. We painted by day and slept in a tent by night. This was later to become the background for my regional books" (unpublished manuscript in the Kerlan Collection, University of Minnesota).

Corporal Keeperupper was published in the midst of the American involvement in World War II, and traces a boy's wooden soldier to the founding father of the republic, George Washington. M. L. Becker wrote in *Weekly Book Review* (23 May 1943), "In wartime a story must have more than looks to live; this ... [is] a morale-builder for an American nursery ...." Independence Hall in Philadelphia, "the cradle of liberty," is highlighted in the third book. M. S. Libby stated in a review, "The text is somewhat like an overlong script for one of those dramatic readings accompanied by light and sound affects known as 'son et lumière' ... at historical sites here and abroad" (*Book Week*, 28 June 1964).

Customs and art objects are devices used to help children appreciate the varied backgrounds in Pennsylvania. *Lovina* was the first book written by Katherine Milhous, and describes an Amish girl whose seven household plates date to the time of George Washington. The book is so filled with motives of art and culture that it serves as a source book on antiques. *The Egg Tree* is a narrative about a grandmother who shares the joy and ability of recreating a custom. Inspired by seeing an egg tree with 1,400 eggs exhibited by the Historical Society of Reading, the author fused childhood memories of her own grandmother who planted onions for practical beauty and also studied their design. The book won for the author-illustrator the coveted Caldecott medal for distinguished illustration, and was heralded by the American Graphics Art Institute. However, the weak text could not stand alone. *Appolonia's Valentine* re-introduces the same girl character in a one-room Pennsylvania school, this time making traditional hearts. The single exception to books about Pennsylvania is *The First Christmas Crib*, which tells of St. Francis of Assisi, who, according to legend, established the tradition.

The third category of books is the celebration of events. *Snow over Bethlehem* tells of the contemporary reenactment of the Moravians, in the town named for the Biblical Nazareth, warning the inhabitants of the nearby town of an Indian attack. *Patrick and the Golden Slippers* describes the Mummer's Parade held in the state capitol in Philadelphia every New Year's Day. An old Pennsylvania custom of making a miniature "putz" manger scene is described in *With Bells On: A Christmas Story*.

Katherine Milhous' books for children have strength in the illustrations rather than in the text. The text merely provides a web upon which the substantial and accurately described folk art is hung. Her attempt to share the past with contemporary children has more local than universal appeal, and is more appropriate for children living in Pennsylvania than elsewhere.

—Karen Nelson Hoyle

MILLER, Madge. American. Born in Pittsburgh, Pennsylvania, 31 May 1918. Educated at Chatham College, Pittsburgh, B.A. 1939; Case Western Reserve University, Cleveland, A.M. 1940. Married Howard R. Eulenstein in 1955; has one son and one daughter. Teacher of English, French, and Spanish, Pittsburgh public schools, 1941–45; Speech and Drama Teacher, Fillion Studios, Pittsburgh, 1946–49; Playwright, Pittsburgh Children's Theatre,

1947–50; Playwright-Director, Knickerty-Knockerty Players, Pittsburgh, 1950–71. Recipient: American Theatre Association Chorpenning Cup, 1970. Agent: Anchorage Press, P.O. Box 8067, New Orleans, Louisiana 70182. Address: 365 McCully Street, Pittsburgh, Pennsylvania 15216, U.S.A.

PUBLICATIONS FOR CHILDREN

Plays

The Land of the Dragon (produced Pittsburgh, 1945). Anchorage, Kentucky, Children's Theatre Press, 1946.

The Princess and the Swineherd (produced Pittsburgh, 1953). Chicago, Dramatic Publishing Company, 1946.

The Pied Piper of Hamelin (produced Pittsburgh, 1948). London, Dobson, 1948; Anchorage, Kentucky, Children's Theatre Press, 1951.

Hansel and Gretel (produced Pittsburgh, 1949). London, Dobson, 1949; Anchorage, Kentucky, Children's Theatre Press, 1951.

Pinocchio (produced Pittsburgh, 1950). Anchorage, Kentucky, Children's Theatre Press, 1954.

Puss in Boots (produced Pittsburgh, 1950). Anchorage, Kentucky, Children's Theatre Press, 1954.

Snow White and Rose Red (produced Pittsburgh, 1951). Anchorage, Kentucky, Children's Theatre Press, 1954.

Robinson Crusoe, adaptation of the novel by Daniel Defoe (produced Pittsburgh, 1951). Anchorage, Kentucky, Children's Theatre Press, 1954.

Alice in Wonderland, adaptation of the story by Lewis Carroll (produced Pittsburgh, 1951). Anchorage, Kentucky, Children's Theatre Press, 1953.

The Emperor's Nightingale (produced Richmond, Virginia, 1962). Anchorage, Kentucky, Children's Theatre Press, 1961.

The Unwicked Witch: An Unlikely Tale (produced Pittsburgh, 1964). Anchorage, Kentucky, Children's Theatre Press, 1964.

Other plays: *Ali Baba, Beauty and the Beast, The Emperor's New Clothes, The Little Mermaid, Merlin the Magician, The Red Shoes, OPQRS*; and *The Elves and the Shoemaker, Hok Lee and the Dwarfs, Princess Pocahontas, Rapunzel, The Sleeping Beauty*, and *St. George and the Dragon*, all with Larry Villani.

Madge Miller comments:

I am an advocate of fantasy. The fairy tales which make up the bulk of my playwriting material are to me the best possible literary form with which first to delight the child, then as he is emotionally ready to help him experience a greater awareness of the inner problems of human beings. He learns that he is not alone in his fears and his confusions. He identifies with those on stage who fight against great odds to win independence and "live happily." As a subtle dividend he receives a valuable moral education which suggests to him the advantage of right behavior. The universality and timelessness of these age-old themes furnish his mind with valuable inner resources to last a lifetime. I write to create a real world of make-believe from which the child can gain a better understanding of the sometimes unbelievable world of reality.

*   *   *

Madge Miller has written and produced over 40 plays for young people, eleven of which have been published in the United States. She has been a teacher of English, Spanish and

French in the Pittsburgh public schools and a teacher of drama and speech in private studios and colleges. She is a frequent lecturer on playwriting for children.

The majority of her plays are adaptations of folk and fairy tales, though *The Land of the Dragon* is an original play. Madge Miller uses traditional material in general but her plays have a modernity and are regularly produced in America today. She is a writer who is able to make the familiar stories live through faithful adherence to the story and the theme, but she has a word choice and tempo that are comprehensible to children of the seventies. I doubt that she influences other writers, but she is one of the most respected of children's playwrights, who can be depended upon for work of quality in a period of great social and artistic change.

—Nellie McCaslin

MILNE, A(lan) A(lexander). British. Born in London, 18 January 1882. Educated at Westminster School, London (Queen's Scholar), 1893–1900; Trinity College, Cambridge (Editor, *Granta*, 1902), 1900–03, B.A. in mathematics 1903. Served in the Royal Warwickshire Regiment, 1914–18. Married Dorothy de Sélincourt in 1913; one son, Christopher Robin Milne. Free-lance journalist, 1903–06; Assistant Editor, *Punch*, London, 1906–14. *Died 31 January 1956.*

PUBLICATIONS FOR CHILDREN

Fiction

> *Once on a Time*, illustrated by H. M. Brock.   London, Hodder and Stoughton, 1917; New York, Putnam, 1922.
> *A Gallery of Children*, illustrated by Saida.   London, Stanley Paul, and Philadelphia, McKay, 1925.
> *Winnie-the-Pooh*, illustrated by Ernest Shepard.   London, Methuen, and New York, Dutton, 1926.
> *The House at Pooh Corner*, illustrated by Ernest Shepard.   London, Methuen, and New York, Dutton, 1928.
> *Prince Rabbit, and The Princess Who Could Not Laugh*, illustrated by Mary Shepard.   London, Ward, and New York, Dutton, 1966.

Plays

> *Make-Believe*, music by George Dorlay, lyrics by C. E. Burton (produced London, 1918).   Included in *Second Plays*, 1921.
> *The Man in the Bowler Hat: A Terribly Exciting Affair* (produced New York, 1924; London, 1925).   London and New York, French, 1923.
> *The Princess and the Woodcutter*, in *Eight Modern Plays for Juniors*, edited by John Hampden.   London, Nelson, 1927.
> *Toad of Toad Hall*, music by H. Fraser-Simson, adaptation of the story *The Wind in the Willows* by Kenneth Grahame (produced Liverpool, 1929; London, 1930).   London, Methuen, and New York, Scribner, 1929.
> *The Ugly Duckling.*   London, French, 1941.

Verse (illustrated by Ernest Shepard)

When We Were Very Young. London, Methuen, and New York, Dutton, 1924.
Now We Are Six. London, Methuen, and New York, Dutton, 1927.
Sneezles and Other Selections. New York, Dutton, 1947.

Other

The Very Young Calendar 1930, illustrated by Ernest Shepard. New York, Dutton, 1930.

PUBLICATIONS FOR ADULTS

Novels

Mr. Pim. London, Hodder and Stoughton, 1921; New York, Doran, 1922.
The Red House Mystery. London, Methuen, and New York, Dutton, 1922.
Two People. London, Methuen, and New York, Dutton, 1931.
Four Days' Wonder. London, Methuen, and New York, Dutton, 1933.
One Year's Time. London, Methuen, 1942.
Chloe Marr. London, Methuen, and New York, Dutton, 1946.

Short Stories

The Secret and Other Stories. London, Methuen, and New York, Fountain Press, 1929.
Birthday Party and Other Stories. New York, Dutton, 1948; London, Methuen, 1949.
A Table Near the Band and Other Stories. London, Methuen, and New York, Dutton, 1950.

Plays

Wurzel-Flummery (produced London, 1917). London and New York, French, 1921; revised version, in *First Plays,* 1919.
Belinda: An April Folly (produced London and New York, 1918). Included in *First Plays,* 1919.
The Boy Comes Home (produced London, 1918). Included in *First Plays,* 1919.
First Plays (includes *Wurzel-Flummery, The Lucky One, The Boy Comes Home, Belinda, The Red Feathers*). London, Chatto and Windus, and New York, Knopf, 1919.
The Red Feathers (produced Leeds, 1920; London, 1921). Included in *First Plays,* 1919.
The Lucky One (produced New York, 1922; Cambridge, 1923; London, 1924). Included in *First Plays,* 1919.
The Camberley Triangle (produced London, 1919). Included in *Second Plays,* 1921.
Mr. Pim Passes By (produced Manchester, 1919; London, 1920; New York, 1921). Included in *Second Plays,* 1921.
The Romantic Age (produced London, 1920; New York, 1922). Included in *Second Plays,* 1921.
The Stepmother (produced London, 1920). Included in *Second Plays,* 1921.
Second Plays (includes *Make-Believe, Mr. Pim Passes By, The Camberley Triangle, The Romantic Age, The Stepmother*). London, Chatto and Windus, 1921; New York, Knopf, 1922.
The Great Broxopp: Four Chapters in Her Life (produced New York, 1921; London, 1923). Included in *Three Plays,* 1922.
The Truth about Blayds (produced London, 1921; New York, 1922). Included in *Three Plays,* 1922.

The Dover Road (produced New York, 1921; London, 1922).   Included in *Three Plays*, 1922.

Three Plays (includes *The Dover Road, The Truth about Blayds, The Great Broxopp*).   New York, Putnam, 1922; London, Chatto and Windus, 1923.

Berlud, Unlimited (produced London and New York, 1922).

Success (produced London, 1923; as *Give Me Yesterday*, produced New York, 1931).   London, Chatto and Windus, 1923; New York, French, 1924.

The Artist: A Duologue.   London and New York, French, 1923.

To Have the Honour (produced London, 1924; as *To Meet the Prince*, produced New York, 1929).   London and New York, French, 1925.

Ariadne; or, Business First (produced New York, 1924; London, 1925).   London and New York, French, 1925.

Portrait of a Gentleman in Slippers: A Fairy Tale (produced Liverpool, 1926; London, 1927).   London and New York, French, 1926.

Four Plays (includes *To Have the Honour, Ariadne, Portrait of a Gentleman in Slippers, Success*).   London, Chatto and Windus, 1926.

Miss Marlow at Play (produced London, 1927; New York, 1940).   London and New York, French, 1936.

The Ivory Door: A Legend (produced New York, 1927; London, 1929).   New York, Putnam, 1928; London, Chatto and Windus, 1929.

Let's All Talk about Gerald (produced London, 1928).

Gentleman Unknown (produced London, 1928).

The Fourth Wall: A Detective Story (produced London, 1928; as *The Perfect Alibi*, produced New York, 1928).   New York, French, 1929; London, French, 1930.

Michael and Mary (produced New York, 1929; London, 1930).   London, Chatto and Windus, 1930; New York, French, 1932.

They Don't Mean Any Harm (produced New York, 1932).

Four Plays (includes *Michael and Mary, To Meet the Prince, The Perfect Alibi, Portrait of a Gentleman in Slippers*).   New York, Putnam, 1932.

Other People's Lives (produced London, 1933).   London and New York, French, 1935.

More Plays (includes *The Ivory Door, The Fourth Wall, Other People's Lives*).   London, Chatto and Windus, 1935.

Miss Elizabeth Bennet, adaptation of the novel *Pride and Prejudice* by Jane Austen (produced London, 1938).   London, Chatto and Windus, 1936.

Sarah Simple (produced London, 1937; New York, 1940).   London, French, 1939.

Before the Flood.   London and New York, French, 1951.

Verse

For the Luncheon Interval: Cricket and Other Verses.   London, Methuen, and New York, Dutton, 1925.

Behind the Lines.   London, Methuen, and New York, Dutton, 1940.

The Norman Church.   London, Methuen, 1948.

Other

Lovers in London.   London, Alston Rivers, 1905.

The Day's Play (*Punch* sketches).   London, Methuen, 1910; New York, Dutton, 1925.

The Holiday Round (*Punch* sketches).   London, Methuen, 1912; New York, Dutton, 1925.

Once a Week (*Punch* sketches).   London, Methuen, 1914; New York, Dutton, 1925.

Happy Days (*Punch* sketches).   New York, Doran, 1915.

Not That It Matters.   London, Methuen, 1919; New York, Dutton, 1920.

If I May.   London, Methuen, 1920; New York, Dutton, 1921.

The Sunny Side.   London, Methuen, 1921; New York, Dutton, 1922.

(Selected Works).   London, Library Press, 7 vols., 1926.

The Ascent of Man.   London, Benn, 1928.

By Way of Introduction.   London, Methuen, and New York, Dutton, 1929.

Those Were the Days: The Day's Play, The Holiday Round, Once a Week, The Sunny Side.   London, Methuen, and New York, Dutton, 1929.

When I Was Very Young (autobiography).   London, Methuen, and New York, Fountain Press, 1930.

A. A. Milne (selections).   London, Methuen, 1933.

Peace with Honour: An Enquiry into the War Convention.   London, Methuen, and New York, Dutton, 1934; revised edition, 1935.

It's Too Late Now: The Autobiography of a Writer.   London, Methuen, 1939; as *Autobiography*, New York, Dutton, 1939.

War with Honour.   London, Macmillan, 1940.

War Aims Unlimited.   London, Methuen, 1941.

Going Abroad?   London, Council for Education in World Citizenship, 1947.

Books for Children: A Reader's Guide.   London, Cambridge University Press, 1948.

Year In, Year Out.   London, Methuen, and New York, Dutton, 1952.

On Lewis Carroll.   Lexington, Helm Press, 1964.

Critical Study: *A. A. Milne* by Thomas Burnett Swann, New York, Twayne, 1971.

*   *   *

A. A. Milne was a successful writer and dramatist for many years before and after the publication of the children's books for which he is famous. Even in children's literature, the Christopher Robin stories and verses were not his only achievement. *Once on a Time*, a comic fantasy about the war between Euralia and Barodia, was still in print in the mid-1970's, and *Toad of Toad Hall*, a play based on Kenneth Grahame's *The Wind in the Willows*, is still performed frequently. But Milne's reputation rests immovably on the four Christopher books: two of stories, *Winnie-the-Pooh* and *The House at Pooh Corner*, and two of verses, *When We Were Very Young* and *Now We Are Six*.

All four were published in the space of five years, while Milne's son Christopher was a small boy. Clearly Christopher was the inspiration; and Pooh and Piglet, Tigger and Eeyore, Kanga and Roo were originally his toys. Mrs. Milne had already brought them to life and given them individual voices, said Milne in his autobiography, and the artist E. H. Shepard "drew them as one might say from the living model." It should be said, incidentally, that this is one of the few, exceptional cases – the Alice books are another – where the illustrator could claim to rank as co-creator. Christopher Robin, Pooh, Piglet and the rest are Shepard's characters as well as Milne's.

The setting of the stories that make up *Winnie-the-Pooh* and *The House at Pooh Corner* is the Hundred-Acre Wood: a happy, self-contained Arcadian world in which all animals are equal and none more equal than others, a reassuring world in which nobody will ever come to any harm. For the child reader or hearer, there is pleasant scope for condescension towards Pooh, the Bear of Very Little Brain, or towards Owl, whose wisdom and spelling fall so far short of his pretensions; whereas the child can identify contentedly with Christopher Robin, who always knows what to do, and to whom the animals go for help as if to an adult.

The characters themselves are drawn with two or three simple strokes: Piglet is small, squeaky and timid, Eeyore the donkey is gloomy, Tigger bouncy, Kanga maternal; and Pooh – admitted by the author to be the favourite among them all – is slow-witted, vain, greedy, and yet, in the way of teddy-bears, extremely lovable. The incidents are not only funny but curiously memorable. Few adults who grew up on *Winnie-the-Pooh* can have forgotten Pooh dangling from a sky-blue balloon and pretending to be a cloud, or Pooh and Piglet trying to trap a Heffalump or tracking a Woozle round the spinney in the snow. The Expotition to the North Pole, the problem of What Tiggers Like to Eat, and the game of Pooh-sticks are lodged by now in what could almost be called the folk-memories of the 20th century.

One of the pleasures of these books is the way they move effortlessly into verse from time to time; Pooh is constantly singing a song or humming a hum. Milne was an extremely accomplished versifier. The two books of poems, *When We Were Very Young* and *Now We Are Six*, are notable for their ingenuity. Stanza forms and rhyme schemes are handled with such mastery that one hardly notices how intricate they often are. Milne was well aware of this; whatever else his verses lacked, he said, they were technically good.

Many of the verses are extremely funny: for example "The King's Breakfast" ("I do like a little bit of butter to my bread") or "The Little Black Hen" or "The Knight Whose Armour Didn't Squeak." Others are pitched precisely at the small child's eye level ("John had/ Great big/ Waterproof/ Boots on" or "Halfway down the stairs/ Is a stair/ Where I sit./ There isn't any/ Other stair/ Quite like/ It.") Charges of sentimentality have been levelled at Milne, especially over "Vespers" ("Little Boy kneels at the foot of the bed") but, interestingly, he himself said in a "preface to parents" that in his poems he had tried to indicate "the uncharming part of a child's nature: the egotism and the heartlessness"; and he pointed out that in "Vespers" it was not "God bless Mummy, because I love her so," but "God bless Mummy, I know that's right"; not "God bless Daddy because he buys me food and clothes," but "God bless Daddy, I quite forgot." Admittedly, when Milne goes on to say that "the truth about a child is also that, fresh from its bath, newly powdered and curled, it is a lovely thing, God wot," one is reminded that from a good deal of internal evidence it seems unlikely that he ever bathed the baby himself; and the world of Pooh and Christopher Robin is undoubtedly a comfortable, bourgeois, nanny-protected world. But then, that was the world in which, half a century ago, Christopher Milne was a small boy.

The four books have one essential quality that makes children's books last: they appeal both to the child and to the adult who has pleasure in reading them aloud; indeed, they are never really outgrown. They have bubbling humour, easy and skilful craftsmanship, quick, light characterisation, and the much-maligned but genuine quality of charm.

—John Rowe Townsend

MINARIK, Else (Holmelund). American. Born in Denmark; emigrated to the United States when four years old. Educated at Queens College, New York. Married the journalist Homer Bigart in 1970; has one daughter by previous marriage. Reporter, *Daily Sentinel*, Rome, New York; teacher, Commack, Long Island, in the 1940's. Address: c/o Harper and Row Inc., 10 East 53rd Street, New York, New York 10022, U.S.A.

PUBLICATIONS FOR CHILDREN

Fiction

  Little Bear, illustrated by Maurice Sendak. New York, Harper, 1957; Kingswood, Surrey, World's Work, 1965.
  No Fighting, No Biting!, illustrated by Maurice Sendak. New York, Harper, 1958; Kingswood, Surrey, World's Work, 1969.
  Father Bear Comes Home, illustrated by Maurice Sendak. New York, Harper, 1959; Kingswood, Surrey, World's Work, 1960.
  Cat and Dog, illustrated by Fritz Siebel. New York, Harper, 1960; Kingswood, Surrey, World's Work, 1969.
  Little Bear's Friend, illustrated by Maurice Sendak. New York, Harper, 1960; Kingswood, Surrey, World's Work, 1961.

Little Bear's Visit, illustrated by Maurice Sendak. New York, Harper, 1961; Kingswood, Surrey, World's Work, 1962.
Little Giant Girl and the Elf Boy, illustrated by Garth Williams. New York and London, Harper, 1963.
A Kiss for Little Bear, illustrated by Maurice Sendak. New York, Harper, 1968; Kingswood, Surrey, World's Work, 1969.

Verse

The Winds That Come from Far Away and Other Poems, illustrated by Joan Berg. New York, Harper, 1964.

Other

Translator, *My Grandpa Is a Pirate*, by Jan Lööf. New York, Harper, 1968.

*   *   *

Else Minarik's reputation was established with her first book – *Little Bear*. Four series titles followed, interspersed with three other books and a collection of poetry. The texts are within the realistic and imaginative realms of the child and are noteworthy for their story, craft, and purpose.

The fairy world, as real to a child as hiccups, is reflected in *Little Giant Girl and the Elf Boy* and a chapter in *Father Bear Comes Home*. The animals such as Owl and Duck, a child, and a doll interrelate with no difficulty. Little Bear is the best man at the skunks' wedding in *A Kiss for Little Bear* and only the doll remains inanimate. Family relationships are especially warm, with the parents providing a strong sense of security. In *Little Bear*, Mother Bear assures her child, "I did not forget your birthday and never will," and the grandfather offers his paw in *Little Bear's Visit*. With a child-like imagination, Little Bear prepares to go to the moon, and yet accepts elderly behavior such as grandfather falling asleep in *Little Bear's Visit*. Humor permeates the stories, both in episode and dialogue. In *Cat and Dog* the characters are equally mischievous. Mother Bear gently urges the youngster to remove his clothes so he will be warm in the snow. As the bear sits in the tree, he remarks that "I can always fly down. I can't fly up or sideways." The cat is reluctant to pass a kiss to the skunk, but the two skunks pass it to each other continually.

Craft is apparent in these easy-to-read books. Having been a first grade teacher, the author uses a limited vocabulary without sacrificing meaning. Unlike many series books, there is no reference made to other titles. Yet the characters reappear in the books, and the device of the cumulative tale is used.

Else Minarik's goal is to provide recreational reading material for the beginning reader, but skills in reading and writing are also emphasized in the books. Joan, in *No Fighting, No Biting*, wants to be left in peace to read, but agrees to tell stories for an interlude. Both grandparents in *Little Bear's Visit* promise to relate a story, and in *Father Bear Comes Home* the elder asks the youngster how he can read with all the racket. In *Little Bear's Friend* the bear uses a pen to write a letter.

In her single book of poetry, *The Winds That Come from Far Away*, seasonal and holiday verses are interspersed with subjects of people, flora and fauna. The concluding poem, "With Dewy Eyes," is reminiscent of Walter de la Mare. Ruth Ersted, State Supervisor of School Libraries in Minnesota, wrote of the first title: "This is what we have all been waiting for! Teachers and elementary school librarians have long been seeking a creative story that would reveal the magic and the fun of reading. *Little Bear* is magic – useful, delightfully funny, and very welcome magic."

—Karen Nelson Hoyle

MITCHELL, (Sibyl) Elyne (Keith).   British/Australian.   Born in Melbourne, Victoria, 30 December 1913. Educated at St. Catherines, Melbourne. Married Thomas Walter Mitchell in 1935; has three children. Agent: Curtis Brown Ltd., 1 Craven Hill, London W2 3EW, England, or, P.O. Box 19, Paddington, Sydney, New South Wales 2021. Address: Towong Hill, Corryong, Victoria 3707, Australia.

PUBLICATIONS FOR CHILDREN

Fiction

> *The Silver Brumby*, illustrated by Ralph Thompson.   London, Hutchinson, 1958; New York, Dutton, 1959.
> *Silver Brumby's Daughter*, illustrated by Grace Huxtable.   London, Hutchinson, 1960; as *The Snow Filly*, New York, Dutton, 1961.
> *Kingfisher Feather*, illustrated by Grace Huxtable.   London, Hutchinson, 1962.
> *Winged Skis*, illustrated by Annette Macarthur-Onslow.   London, Hutchinson, 1964.
> *Silver Brumbies of the South*, illustrated by Annette Macarthur-Onslow.   London, Hutchinson, 1965.
> *Silver Brumby Kingdom*, illustrated by Annette Macarthur-Onslow.   London, Hutchinson, 1966.
> *Moon Filly*, illustrated by Robert Hales.   London, Hutchinson, 1968.
> *Jinki, Dingo of the Snows*, illustrated by Michael Cole.   London, Hutchinson, 1970.
> *Light Horse to Damascus*, illustrated by Victor Ambrus.   London, Hutchinson, 1971.
> *Silver Brumby Whirlwind*, illustrated by Victor Ambrus.   London, Hutchinson, 1973.
> *The Colt at Taparoo*, illustrated by Victor Ambrus.   Richmond, Victoria, and London, Hutchinson, 1976.
> *Son of the Whirlwind*, illustrated by Victor Ambrus.   Richmond, Victoria, and London, Hutchinson, 1977.

PUBLICATIONS FOR ADULTS

Novels

> *Flow River, Blow Wind.*   Sydney, Australasian Publishing Company, and London, Harrap, 1953.
> *Black Cockatoos Mean Snow.*   London, Hodder and Stoughton, 1956.

Other

> *Australia's Alps.*   Sydney and London, Angus and Robertson, 1942.
> *Speak to the Earth.*   Sydney and London, Angus and Robertson, 1945.
> *Soil and Civilization.*   Sydney and London, Angus and Robertson, 1946.
> *Images in Water.*   Sydney, Angus and Robertson, 1947.
> *Australian Treescape: A Photographic Study.*   Sydney, Ure Smith, 1950.

Elyne Mitchell comments:
The children's books simply grew out of the life we led. I had had six adult books published, and a growing family. The children were on Correspondence School work, which I had to teach. So *The Silver Brumby* was written for the eldest − something exciting about wild horses to introduce her to the mountain world which I loved so much. Very soon after it was written, the first road was built through the mountains, the Silver Brumby country. Some of the wilderness was no longer wilderness, but it was possible to take very young children skiing and walking, and the whole family grew to love the snow country. More

Brumby stories were written, and a boy ski story for Harry, then a dingo story, and the story of World War I, in which the hero is a horse in my father's Light Horse, and more brumby stories.

*   *   *

In the Australian Alps where the Granite Tors of the Ramshead Range stretch between Mt. Kosciusko and the icy waters of the Crackenback River, the wind roars as it flattens the springy snowgrass, dark storms sweep across the skyline, and snow falls in silent flakes or comes in wild tremendous blizzards. In summer the gums and tussocks bow to the breezes and sunset turns every ridge and hill-top into gold and the valleys into "long fingers of blue shadow." This is the home country of Elyne Mitchell which she loves as passionately as she does her own horses and the wild horses who roam free. She writes lovingly of brumbies who move across the landscape together or alone, the colts who run together and fight for a herd of their own as each young stallion establishes a claim to his own mares.

This is the country in which Bel Bel, the cream brumby mare, "gave birth to a colt foal, pale like herself or paler in a wild, black storm." So Thowra, the silver brumby, whose name means wind, born in the wind and as fleet as the wind, begins a long fight for supremacy over man and fellow beast. The initial story, *The Silver Brumby*, is written with a deeply lyrical feeling for the wild horses and the territory over which they roam, and was highly commended by the judges of the Australian Children's Book of the Year Award in 1959, and the sequel, *Silver Brumby's Daughter*, was commended in 1961. *Winged Skis*, a mystery adventure set in the ski resorts of the Australian Alps, was highly commended in 1965.

Elyne Mitchell has been criticised in her own country for the anthropomorphism of her horses who, in the earlier stories, talk together in human terms. However, her brumby stories are widely read not only by children in Australia but have been translated into Spanish, German and Finnish, and are published both in Britain and the United States. They are strongly felt regional novels, connected as a series by the struggle for survival of each generation in freedom and dignity. There are savage and bloody battles between stallions, tender and loyal familial relationships between sire and progeny, the sexual pursuits of his mate by the male, and, in the last of the saga, *Silver Brumby Whirlwind*, a mystical farewell and a sense of destiny fulfilled as Thowra bids farewell to his true friend Benni, the kangaroo. Then the whirlwind of the south encircles him, and he returns to his own country forever.

Elyne Mitchell's tendency to a mannered style – overmuch repetition and too many broken statements – which becomes intrusive in the later *Brumby* books, is an irritation in *Jinki* where there is no circling dance of the brumbies to justify her elliptical use of language. *Light Horse to Damascus* is the story of a Queenslander, Dick Osborne, and his horse Karloo who with the Australian Light Horse beat their way across the desert to war and to Damascus. Literary techniques which succeeded when the author was writing from personal involvement are no longer valid. It is for her Silver Brumby that Elyne Mitchell will be remembered as a writer.

—H. M. Saxby

MITCHISON, Naomi (Margaret). British. Born in Edinburgh, 1 November 1897. Educated at Dragon School, Oxford; St. Anne's College, Oxford. Served as a volunteer nurse, 1915. Married G. R. Mitchison (who became Lord Mitchison, 1964) in 1916 (died, 1970); has five children. Labour Candidate for Parliament, for the Scottish Universities Constituency, 1935; Member of the Argyll County Council, 1945–66; Member of the Highland Panel, Scotland, 1947–64. Since 1966, Member of the Highland and Island Advisory Council, Scotland. Since 1963, Tribal Adviser, and Mmarona (Mother), to the Bakgatla of Botswana.

Recipient: Palmes de L'Académie Française, 1921. D. Univ.: University of Stirling, Scotland, 1976. Address: Carradale, Campbeltown, Argyll, Scotland.

PUBLICATIONS FOR CHILDREN

Fiction

The Hostages and Other Stories for Boys and Girls. London, Cape, 1930; New York, Harcourt Brace, 1931.
Boys and Girls and Gods. London, Watts, 1931.
The Big House. London, Faber, 1950.
Graeme and the Dragon, illustrated by Pauline Baynes. London, Faber, 1954.
The Land the Ravens Found, illustrated by Brian Allderidge. London, Collins, 1955.
Little Boxes, illustrated by Louise Annand. London, Faber, 1956.
The Far Harbour, illustrated by Martin Thomas. London, Collins, 1957.
Judy and Lakshmi, illustrated by Avinash Chandra. London, Collins, 1959.
The Rib of the Green Umbrella, illustrated by Edward Ardizzone. London, Collins, 1960.
Karensgaard: The Story of a Danish Farm. London, Collins, 1961.
The Fairy Who Couldn't Tell a Lie, illustrated by Jane Paton. London, Collins, 1963.
Henny and Crispies. Wellington, New Zealand School Publications, 1964.
Ketse and the Chief, illustrated by Christine Bloomer. London, Nelson, 1965.
Friends and Enemies, illustrated by Caroline Sassoon. London, Collins, 1966; New York, Day, 1968.
The Big Surprise. London, Kaye and Ward, 1967.
Don't Look Back, illustrated by Laszlo Acs. London, Kaye and Ward, 1969.
The Family at Ditlabeng, illustrated by Joanna Stubbs. London, Collins, 1969; New York, Farrar Straus, 1970.
Sun and Moon, illustrated by Barry Wilkinson. London, Bodley Head, 1970; Nashville, Nelson, 1973.
Sunrise Tomorrow. London, Collins, and New York, Farrar Straus, 1973.
A Danish Teapot, illustrated by Patricia Frost. London, Kaye and Ward, 1973.
Snake!, illustrated by Polly Loxton. London, Collins, 1976.
The Two Magicians, with Dick Mitchison. London, Dobson, 1977.

Plays

Nix-Nought-Nothing: Four Plays for Children (includes *My Ain Sel', Hobyah! Hobyah!, Elfen Hill*). London, Cape, and New York, Harcourt Brace, 1929.
An End and a Beginning and Other Plays (includes *The City and the Citizens, For This Man Is a Roman, In the Time of Constantine, Wild Men Invade the Roman Empire, Charlemagne and His Court, The Thing That Is Plain, Cortez in Mexico, Akbar, But Still It Moves, The New Calendar, American Britons*). London, Cape, 1937.

Other

The Young Alexander the Great, illustrated by Betty Middleton-Sanford. London, Parrish, 1960; New York, Roy, 1961.
The Young Alfred the Great, illustrated by Shirley Farrow. London, Parrish, 1962; New York, Roy, 1963.
Alexander the Great, illustrated by Rosemary Grimble. London, Longman, 1964.
Highland Holiday. Wellington, New Zealand School Publications, 1967.
African Heroes, illustrated by William Stobbs. London, Bodley Head, 1968; New York, Farrar Straus, 1969.

The Brave Nurse and Other Stories (reader), illustrated by Polly Loxton.   Cape Town, Oxford University Press, 1977.

Editor, *An Outline for Boys and Girls and Their Parents*.   London, Gollancz, 1932.

PUBLICATIONS FOR ADULTS

Novels

The Conquered.   London, Cape, and New York, Harcourt Brace, 1923.
Cloud Cuckoo Land.   London, Cape, 1925; New York, Harcourt Brace, 1926.
The Corn King and the Spring Queen.   London, Cape, and New York, Harcourt Brace, 1931; as *The Barbarian*, New York, Cameron, 1961.
The Powers of Light.   London, Cape, and New York, Smith, 1932.
Beyond This Limit, with Wyndham Lewis.   London, Cape, 1935.
We Have Been Warned.   London, Constable, 1935; New York, Vanguard Press, 1936.
The Blood of the Martyrs.   London, Constable, 1939; New York, McGraw Hill, 1948.
The Bull Calves.   London, Cape, 1947.
Lobsters on the Agenda.   London, Gollancz, 1952.
Travel Light.   London, Faber, 1952.
To the Chapel Perilous.   London, Allen and Unwin, 1955.
Behold Your King.   London, Muller, 1957.
Memoirs of a Spacewoman.   London, Gollancz, 1962.
When We Become Men.   London, Collins, 1965.
Cleopatra's People.   London, Heinemann, 1972.
Solution 3.   London, Dobson, 1975.

Short Stories

When the Bough Breaks and Other Stories.   London, Cape, and New York, Harcourt Brace, 1924.
Black Sparta: Greek Stories.   London, Cape, and New York, Harcourt Brace, 1928.
Barbarian Stories.   London, Cape, and New York, Harcourt Brace, 1929.
The Delicate Fire: Short Stories and Poems.   London, Cape, and New York, Harcourt Brace, 1933.
The Fourth Pig.   London, Constable, 1936.
Five Men and a Swan: Short Stories and Poems.   London, Allen and Unwin, 1958.

Plays

The Price of Freedom, with L. E. Gielgud (produced Cheltenham, 1949).   London, Cape, 1931.
As It Was in the Beginning, with L. E. Gielgud.   London, Cape, 1939.
The Corn King, music by Brian Easdale, adaptation of her own story (produced London, 1950).
Spindrift, with Denis Macintosh (produced Glasgow, 1951).   London, French, 1951.

Verse

The Laburnum Branch.   London, Cape, 1926.
The Alban Goes Out.   N.p., Raven Press, 1939.

Other

Anna Comnena.   London, Howe, 1928.

Comments on Birth Control.   London, Faber, 1930.

The Home and a Changing Civilisation.   London, Lane, 1934.

Vienna Diary.   London, Gollancz, and New York, Smith and Haas, 1935.

Socrates, with R. H. S. Crossman.   London, Hogarth Press, 1937; Harrisburg, Pennsylvania, Stackpole, 1938.

The Moral Basis of Politics.   London, Constable, 1938.

Kingdom of Heaven.   London, Heinemann, 1939.

Men and Herring, with Denis Macintosh.   Edinburgh, Serif Books, 1949.

The Swan's Road (history).   London, Naldrett Press, 1954.

Other People's Worlds (travel).   London, Secker and Warburg, 1958.

Presenting Other People's Children.   London, Hamlyn, 1961.

A Fishing Village on the Clyde, with G. W. L. Paterson.   London, Oxford University Press, 1961.

Return to the Fairy Hill (autobiography and sociology).   London, Heinemann, and New York, Day, 1966.

The Africans: A History.   London, Blond, 1970.

Small Talk: Memories of an Edwardian Childhood.   London, Bodley Head, 1973.

A Life for Africa; The Story of Bram Fischer.   London, Merlin Press, 1973.

Oil for the Highlands?   London, Fabian Society, 1974.

All Change Here: Girlhood and Marriage (autobiography).   London, Bodley Head, 1975.

Editor, *Re-Educating Scotland.*   Glasgow, Scoop Books, 1944.

Editor, *What the Human Race Is Up To.*   London, Gollancz, 1962.

Manuscript Collections: National Library of Scotland, Edinburgh; University of Texas, Austin.

Naomi Mitchison comments:

I like writing for children because it means writing straight: not putting in clever bits or the kind of passage which is only there to impress and perhaps confuse the reader. Children are very critical and they want a good story. I think I am essentially a story teller, not an observer of manners or morals. I hope young people will get from my stories what I got from E. Nesbit's. I have been lucky to have a critical audience – children of my own and later grandchildren – who have kept me on my toes. I like reading my books aloud and they have been willing to listen and tell me, for instance, what I have left out and ought to have told the reader.

One big pleasure of writing children's books is that I need not be ashamed of having a happy ending, something I like increasingly as real life gets further away from it.

*   *   *

Naomi Mitchison's lifelong devotion to travel and the study of history and social problems is reflected in the wide variety of backgrounds she chooses when writing for the young. She has lived for years among the West Highlanders and the people of Botswana, learning how the very poor survive.

Her knowledge of the language and folklore of the Scottish Highlands may make *The Big House,* written in Gaelic idioms, a little difficult for some readers, but she does create a convincing atmosphere in which everything seems reasonable. The local people all dress up for Hallowe'en, and no one is surprised when the fairy prince comes and goes at will. The friendship between the girl from the big house and the fisherman's son flourishes even when they commute to and from the dangerous past.

Friendship between children of different social classes recurs in other books. *Judy and Lakshmi,* about modern India, disguises plenty of political theory under the touching story of two girls from very different homes. In *The Rib of the Green Umbrella* a middle-class boy happily risks death, running messages with two children of very poor communist partisans. This is a most exciting adventure set in a small Italian town during the German occupation; tension is kept up from the first page to the last.

Fact and fiction mingle well in *Karensgaard*, in which a Danish boy explores the history of his own farmstead and then of his country. The Viking civilisation is the background for *The Land the Ravens Found*. *The Far Harbour* is a realistic picture of Scottish fishermen.

The struggle to stay alive dominates *The Family at Ditlabeng*, a Botswana story in which everyone goes hungry and no school fees can be paid when the crops fail. The resentments as well as the games of the children who have to fetch water and herd cattle, often at the expense of their education, are well brought out. In this story the bright girl of the family gets her chance to go to Denmark, so it ends on a hopeful note. *Sunrise Tomorrow* is also about Botswana and the careers of a group of teenagers. The heroine Seloi becomes a nurse in spite of her mother's opposition and enjoys wearing European clothes. But she realises that problems remain, that being African is as important as being modern. Plenty of drama is used to convey the theme.

The Fairy Who Couldn't Tell a Lie, unlike the other works, is for a younger age group. Two human children wander into the fairy hill in the Highlands and meet Brec, a fairy who must tell the truth, which puts her at odds with everyone else in the hill. Clare is involved in the battle between the swan fairies and the seals, but her cousin Sam is turned into a puppy and spends the story happily playing with other dogs. There is a lot of interaction between the characters, who mix dislike with affection in a variety of doses.

—Margaret Campbell

MONJO, F(erdinand) N(icolas, III). American. Born in Stamford, Connecticut, 28 August 1924. Educated at Stamford High School; Columbia University, New York, B.A. 1946. Married Louise Elaine Lyczak in 1950; has three sons and one daughter. Editor, Golden Books, Simon and Schuster, New York, 1953–58; Editor, American Heritage Junior Library, New York, 1958–61; Assistant Director, Books for Boys and Girls, Harper and Row, New York, 1961–69. Since 1969, Vice President and Editorial Director, Books for Boys and Girls, Coward McCann and Geoghegan, New York. Agent: Marilyn Marlow, Curtis Brown Ltd., 575 Madison Avenue, New York, New York 10022. Address: c/o Coward McCann and Geoghegan, 200 Madison Avenue, New York, New York 10016, U.S.A.

PUBLICATIONS FOR CHILDREN

Fiction

Indian Summer, illustrated by Anita Lobel. New York, Harper, 1968; Kingswood, Surrey, World's Work, 1969.
The Drinking Gourd, illustrated by Fred Brenner. New York, Harper, 1970; Kingswood, Surrey, World's Work, 1971.
The One Bad Thing about Father, illustrated by Rocco Negri. New York and London, Harper, 1970.
Pirates in Panama, illustrated by Wallace Tripp. New York, Simon and Schuster, 1970.
The Jezebel Wolf, illustrated by John Schoenherr. New York, Simon and Schuster, 1971; London, Dent, 1973.

The Vicksburg Veteran, illustrated by Douglas Gorsline. New York, Simon and
Schuster, 1971.

Slater's Mill, illustrated by Laszlo Kubinyi.   New York, Simon and Schuster, 1972.

Rudi and the Distelfink, illustrated by George Kraus.   New York, Dutton, 1972.

The Secret of the Sachem's Tree, illustrated by Margot Tomes.   New York, Coward
McCann, 1972.

Poor Richard in France, illustrated by Brinton Turkle.   New York, Holt Rinehart,
1973.

Me and Willie and Pa, illustrated by Douglas Gorsline.   New York, Simon and
Schuster, 1973.

Grand Papa and Ellen Aroon, illustrated by Richard Cuffari.   New York, Holt Rinehart,
1974.

The Sea-Beggar's Son, illustrated by C. Walter Hodges.   New York, Coward McCann,
and London, Chatto and Windus, 1974.

King George's Head Was Made of Lead, illustrated by Margot Tomes.   New York,
Coward McCann, 1974.

Letters to Horseface, Being the Story of W.A. Mozart's Journey to Italy, 1769–1770 ...,
illustrated by Don Bolognese and Elaine Raphael.   New York, Viking Press, 1975.

Gettysburg: Tad Lincoln's Story, illustrated by Douglas Gorsline.   New York, Dutton,
1976.

*Willie Jasper's Golden Eagle, Being an Eyewitness Account of the Great Steamboat Race
Between the "Natchez" and the "Robert E. Lee,"* illustrated by Douglas
Gorsline.   New York, Doubleday, 1976.

Zenas and the Shaving Mill, illustrated by Richard Cuffari.   New York, Coward
McCann, 1976.

A Namesake for Nathan, illustrated by Eros Keith.   New York, Coward McCann, 1977.

The House on Stink Alley: A Story about the Pilgrims in Holland, illustrated by Robert
Quackenbush.   New York, Holt Rinehart, 1977.

Other

Clarence and the Burglar, illustrated by Paul Galdone.   New York, Coward McCann,
1973; Kingswood, Surrey, World's Work, 1975.

Translator, with Nina Ignatowicz, *The Crane*, by Reiner Zimnik, illustrated by
Zimnik.   New York, Harper, 1970; London, Penguin, 1974.

*   *   *

F.N. Monjo's sense of history is people-centered. His historical books, novels, novelettes,
easy-reading history books and young biographies revolve around both the great and the
near-great of the past. His own sense of family history is equally people-centered. He grew up
surrounded by Americana in the stories his family told of his father's fur-merchant ancestors
and his mother's plantation-bred forebears. Monjo determined his own writing course,
having noted as an editor that "most of the fun of history lay in the details most children's
books seemed to omit."

Monjo's ability to capture those detailed glimpses and transmit them to eager readers can
be measured by the success of three of his many books: *The Drinking Gourd, Indian Summer*
and his extremely popular *Poor Richard in France*.

The Drinking Gourd is both fact and fiction in an easy-to-read format. Written in a straightforward, unadorned style, it is Monjo's second book, and it established both his reputation
and the direction of his work. The story of an Underground Railway stop and the young
minister's son who helps a family of black fugitives, the book appeals to both head and heart
of the young reader. Monjo is not patronizing to either.

His first book, *Indian Summer*, was also well received. But recent events in American publishing and the awareness of librarians has made the book a problem for Monjo. It is the story of a pioneer family and of the mother and children who fight off an attack by cowardly marauding Indians. Monjo's talent for frill-less, direct storytelling was already very apparent in this story. But organizations like the Council on Interracial Books have been critical of the tale. And in her introduction to a selected bibliography, *American Indian Authors for Young Readers*, Mary Gloyne Byler escalated the attack. Monjo countered in a persuasive article in *School Library Journal* saying that an author has an obligation to inform himself on a topic but has the right to choose that topic and its point of view. Still, the controversy has not died.

In his National Book Award nominee, *Poor Richard in France*, Monjo is at his unassailable best. Here his sense of humor – slightly impish and impious – can be plainly seen. In the five years between this book and his first, Monjo perfected his simple style. There is not a loose word or unnecessary phrase in the book, a charming anecdotal view of Franklin through his grandson's eyes. It is a technique Monjo has used again and again in later books to great advantage. The use of the child narrator is a common juvenile book technique, but Monjo has made the child's voice authentically his own. And his gimlet eye, slightly softened by the child's lens through which he peers, gives us a fresh and appealing look at any number of otherwise overworked periods of history.

Except for his friend and colleague Jean Fritz, F.N. Monjo has no peer in the writing of easy-reading history books.

—Jane Yolen

MONTGOMERY, L(ucy) M(aud). Canadian. Born in Clifton, Prince Edward Island, 30 November 1874. Educated at school in Cavendish, Prince Edward Island; Prince of Wales College, Charlottetown, Prince Edward Island, teacher's certificate 1894, teacher's license 1895; Dalhousie College, Halifax, Nova Scotia, 1895–96. Married Ewan Macdonald in 1911; two sons. Schoolteacher, Bideford, 1894–95, 1896–97, and Lower Bedeque, 1897–98, both in Prince Edward Island; Assistant Postmistress, Cavendish, 1898–1911; Staff Member, Halifax *Echo*, 1901–02. Fellow, Royal Society of Arts, 1923. O.B.E. (Officer, Order of the British Empire), 1935. *Died 24 April 1942.*

Publications for Children

Fiction

> *Anne of Green Gables*, illustrated by M.A. and W.A. Claus. Boston, Page, and London, Pitman, 1908.
> *Anne of Avonlea*. Boston, Page, and London, Pitman, 1909.
> *Kilmeny of the Orchard*, illustrated by George Gibbs. Boston, Page, and London, Pitman, 1910.
> *The Story Girl*. Boston, Page, and London, Pitman, 1911.
> *Chronicles of Avonlea*. Boston, Page, and London, Sampson Low, 1912.
> *The Golden Road*. Boston, Page, 1913; London, Cassell, 1914.
> *Anne of the Island*. Boston, Page, and London, Pitman, 1915.
> *Anne's House of Dreams*. New York, Stokes, and London, Constable, 1917.
> *Rainbow Valley*. Toronto, McClelland and Stewart, and New York, Stokes, 1919; London, Constable, 1920.
> *Further Adventures of Avonlea ...*, illustrated by John Goss. Boston, Page, 1920; London, Harrap, 1953.

Rilla of Ingleside. Toronto, McClelland and Stewart, New York, Stokes, and London, Hodder and Stoughton, 1921.

Emily of New Moon. New York, Stokes, and London, Hodder and Stoughton, 1923.

Emily Climbs. New York, Stokes, and London, Hodder and Stoughton, 1925.

The Blue Castle. Toronto, McClelland and Stewart, New York, Stokes, and London, Hodder and Stoughton, 1926.

Emily's Quest. New York, Stokes, and London, Hodder and Stoughton, 1927.

Magic for Marigold. Toronto, McClelland and Stewart, New York, Stokes, and London, Hodder and Stoughton, 1929.

A Tangled Web. New York, Stokes, 1931; as *Aunt Becky Began It*, London, Hodder and Stoughton, 1931.

Pat of Silver Bush. New York, Stokes, and London, Hodder and Stoughton, 1933.

Mistress Pat: A Novel of Silver Bush. New York, Stokes, and London, Harrap, 1935.

Anne of Windy Poplars. New York, Stokes, 1936; as *Anne of Windy Willows*, London, Harrap, 1936.

Jane of Lantern Hill. Toronto, McClelland and Stewart, New York, Stokes, and London, Harrap, 1937.

Anne of Ingleside. New York, Stokes, and London, Harrap, 1939.

The Road to Yesterday. New York, McGraw Hill, 1974; London, Angus and Robertson, 1975.

PUBLICATIONS FOR ADULTS

Verse

The Watchman and Other Poems. Toronto, McClelland and Stewart, 1916; New York, Stokes, 1917; London, Constable, 1920.

Other

Courageous Women, with Marian Keith and Mabel Burns McKinley. Toronto, McClelland and Stewart, 1934.

The Green Gables Letters to Ephraim Weber, 1905–1909, edited by Wilfrid Eggleston. Toronto, Ryerson Press, 1960.

Critical Studies: *The Wheel of Things: A Biography of L.M. Montgomery ...* by Mollie Gillen, London, Harrap, 1976; *L.M. Montgomery: An Assessment* by John Robert Sorfleet, Guelph, Canadian Children's Press, 1976.

*   *   *

At times, L.M. Montgomery's work challenges conventional opinion about what makes a children's book. Is it a child or adolescent protagonist? Then what does one do with such books as *Anne's House of Dreams* and *Anne of Ingleside*, wherein Anne is a married mother with, eventually, five children? Is it comparatively innocuous subject matter? Then what does one do with the bitterness and jealousies evident in extended family relationships in many of the novels, or the marital hatred of Olivia and Peter Kirk in *Anne of Ingleside*, or the actual separation of the protagonist's parents in *Jane of Lantern Hill* – not to mention the frequent deaths of children and adults in the books? In fact, virtually all of Montgomery's fiction – including *The Blue Castle* and *A Tangled Web*, sometimes termed "adult" novels – is read and enjoyed by children and adolescents. This is because Montgomery deals with the psychological realities and conflicts of childhood and adolescence: need for an independent identity and for respect in an unjust and repressive world run by adults; flare-ups of hatred as well as of love for family, relatives, and others; cross-sex hostility as well as affection; stirrings of passion versus fear of the changes it implies and inner perspectives it reveals; and so on. Indeed, a Freudian analysis of Montgomery's work, related to what we know of her inner life, could be at least as interesting – and revealing – as existing analyses of Lewis Carroll's *Alice in Wonderland*.

Her best known book is *Anne of Green Gables*, first of a long series. This tale of an orphaned girl, sent by mistake to an elderly couple who expect a boy, was enormously successful, and its heroine was termed by Mark Twain "the dearest, and most lovable child in fiction since the immortal Alice." The novel counterpoises child and adult perspectives, and this provides the basis for much of the novel's humour as well as some pathos. Anne is childhood spontaneity and imagination confronting adult conventionalism and dogmatism – both social and religious. Her words and actions effectively undermine the hypocrisy of the adult world and deflate its pretensions, while at the same time asserting the value of imaginative reality in a society which tends to deny it. And, while portraying Anne and the other characters – not to mention the land and the psychological relationships – realistically, Montgomery adds force to her depiction by drawing on the powers of fairytale archetype: the orphaned heroine coming to an unknown land, where she is involved in a case of mistaken identity, gains protectors, demonstrates her worth, defeats her enemies, and is finally reconciled with her Prince Charming, Gilbert Blythe.

Anne of Green Gables was followed by five other Anne books plus associated works such as *Rainbow Valley* and *Rilla of Ingleside* in which she appears. These later books show a considerable falling-away from the qualities of the first, as the original inspiration, a red-haired hoyden, inevitably, growing up, encounters the more stringent social pressures and realities facing a young woman. Only *Anne of the Island*, which focuses on the exciting period of Anne's college years and her various courtships, comes anywhere near the readability of the first Anne book.

With *Emily of New Moon*, Montgomery initiated her second series. The Emily trilogy presents what might be called a "Portrait of the Artist" in the successive stages of girl, teenager, and young woman. As might be expected, these novels draw upon Montgomery's own childhood experiences even more extensively than her other books. The first novel reveals that, like Anne, Emily is an orphan, though her father's death is not antecedent to the book's beginning but occurs in the third chapter. Besides being a writer by nature and circumstance, Emily is notable for her "flashes" of mystical insight and moments of second sight. As for literary considerations, *Emily of New Moon* – like its sequels, *Emily Climbs* and *Emily's Quest* – competently relates symbolism, characterization, irony, and other stylistic concerns to a coherent and consistent exposition of theme and plot. In fact, except for a slightly over-rich effect in some of the passages representing Emily's thoughts, as a group this trilogy is better integrated and more satisfying than the Anne series.

Among Montgomery's later novels are *The Blue Castle* and *A Tangled Web*, appealing especially to adolescent girls. The former is clearly the better: except for some momentary falterings, it's a good, enjoyable book of its type – the identity crisis *cum* love story – which has a solid technical underpinning (e.g. the symbolism) as well. Reading it leads one to wonder – with reason – about the state of Montgomery's own mind and marriage at the time. *A Tangled Web*, by contrast, has the defects its title implies: there are too many threads of plot and unbelievable situations, resulting in a not really satisfactory book.

In the fiction of Montgomery's final decade, two new protagonists are introduced. The first is Pat Gardiner – unusual in Montgomery's work because she has both parents living – who appears in *Pat of Silver Bush* and its sequel, *Mistress Pat*. The earlier of the two is slightly the better. Its theme is the child's fear of change in the face of its inevitability. There are a few tear-jerking passages, and children might laugh at Judy Plum's Irish dialect when read aloud, but overall it is not a memorable book, perhaps because Pat is an Anne without spirit, an Emily without ability.

Montgomery's final heroine is Jane Stuart in *Jane of Lantern Hill*. Though with no outstanding talents, Jane has a hard core of selfhood which enables her to survive the bitter hostility of a tyrannical grandmother whose interference has maintained a ten-year marital separation between Jane's parents. Further, eventually Jane's self-direct actions enable her to become the instrument for her parents' reconciliation. This tale of tyranny, self-identity, and reunion is one that rewards psychological analysis. Also suggestive are the settings, rural Prince Edward Island and urban Toronto – the latter a notable innovation in Montgomery's novels. It's a book well worth a child's reading.

Overall, L. M. Montgomery's work is marked by a succession of unforgettable heroines backdropped by a beautiful Prince Edward Island landscape. Within them their isolated selves struggle to flourish against a set of outside pressures that urge conformity and denial of selfhood as the price of social acceptance. Yet they do not submit, and eventually their struggles are rewarded by their acceptance as them*selves*, not as mere specious semblances. And further, the outer Island landscape tends to operate in parallel to the heroines' inner lives, bringing comfort when needed, as it did for Montgomery herself. Indeed, in showing the importance of heroic inner struggle at the same time as stressing the outer physical landscape, Montgomery reveals herself to be operating within the mainstream of the Canadian literary tradition.

—John Robert Sorfleet

MONTGOMERY, Rutherford (George).   American.   Born in Straubville, North Dakota, 12 April 1894. Educated at schools in Velva, North Dakota; Colorado Agricultural College, Fort Collins; Western State College, Gunnison, Colorado; University of Nebraska, Lincoln. Served as a sergeant in the United States Army Air Corps, 1917–18. Married Eunice Opal Kirks in 1930; has one son and two daughters. Teacher, Hot Springs Elementary School, Wyoming, 1915–17; Teacher and Principal, Delta County High Schools, Cedaredge, Colorado, 1921–24; Principal, Montrose County Junior High School, Colorado, 1924–28; Manager, Chamber of Commerce, 1928–32, and Judge, Court of Records, 1932–37, Gunnison County, Colorado; State Budget and Efficiency Commissioner, Denver, 1937–39; creative writing teacher, adult education classes, Los Gatos, California, 1955–57; writer, Walt Disney Studios, Burbank, California, 1958–62. Free-lance Writer, 1939–74; ghost writer for Dick Tracy series, 1941–46. Recipient: New York *Herald Tribune* Festival award, 1956; Boys' Clubs of America award, 1956; Western Writers of America Spur Award, 1966. Address: 33 Walnut Avenue, Los Gatos, California 95030, U.S.A.

PUBLICATIONS FOR CHILDREN

Fiction

   Troopers Three, illustrated by Zhenya Gay.   New York, Doubleday, 1932.
   Broken Fang, illustrated by Lynn Bogue Hunt.   Chicago, Donohue, 1935.
   Carcajou, illustrated by L. D. Cram.   Caldwell, Idaho, Caxton, 1936; London, Arrowsmith, 1937.
   Yellow Eyes, illustrated by L. D. Cram.   Caldwell, Idaho, Caxton, 1937; London, Blackie, 1939.
   Gray Wolf, illustrated by Jacob Bates Abbott.   Boston, Houghton Mifflin, 1938; London, Hutchinson, 1939.
   Timberline Tales, illustrated by Jacob Bates Abbott.   Philadelphia, McKay, 1939; London, Hutchinson, 1951.
   The Trail of the Buffalo, illustrated by Kurt Wiese.   Boston, Houghton Mifflin, 1939.
   Orphans of the Wild, illustrated by Janet Dean.   London, Arrowsmith, 1939.
   Midnight, illustrated by Jacob Bates Abbott.   New York, Holt, 1940; London, Hutchinson, 1944.

Stan Ball of the Rangers, illustrated by Jacob Bates Abbott. Philadelphia, McKay, 1941.

Ice Blink, illustrated by Rudolph Freund. New York, Holt, 1941; London, Hutchinson, 1949.

A Yankee Flier with the R.A.F. [*in the Far East, in North Africa, in the South Pacific, in Italy, over Berlin, in Normandy, on a Rescue Mission, under Secret Orders*] (as Al Avery), illustrated by Paul Laune and Clayton Knight. New York, Grosset and Dunlap, 9 vols., 1941–46.

Thumbs Up!, illustrated by E. Franklin Wittmack. Philadelphia, McKay, 1942; London, Hutchinson, 1943.

Hurricane Yank, illustrated by James Shimer. Philadelphia, McKay, 1942; London, Hutchinson, 1943.

Ghost Town Adventure, illustrated by Russell Sherman. New York, Holt, 1942.

Husky, Co-Pilot of the Pilgrim, illustrated by Jacob Landau. New York, Holt, 1942; London, Ward Lock, 1949.

Spike Kelly of the Commandos, illustrated by J. R. White. Racine, Wisconsin, Whitman, 1942.

Out of the Sun, illustrated by Clayton Knight. Philadelphia, McKay, 1943; London, Wells Gardner Darton, 1947.

War Wings, illustrated by Clayton Knight. Philadelphia, McKay, 1943; London, Wells Gardner Darton, 1948.

Trappers' Trail, illustrated by Harold Cressingham. New York, Holt, 1943; London, Hutchinson, 1948.

Warhawk Patrol, illustrated by Clayton Knight. Philadelphia, McKay, 1944; London, Wells Gardner Darton, 1948.

The Last Cruise of the "Jeanette" (as Everitt Proctor). Philadelphia, Westminster Press, 1944.

Big Brownie, illustrated by Jacob Landau. New York, Holt, 1944; London, Hutchinson, 1947.

Sea Raiders Ho!, illustrated by E. Franklin Wittmack. Philadelphia, McKay, 1945; London, Wells Gardner Darton, 1947.

Thunderboats Ho!, illustrated by E. Franklin Wittmack. Philadelphia, McKay, 1945; London, Wells Gardner Darton, 1948.

Thar She Blows (as Everitt Proctor). Philadelphia, Westminster Press, 1945; London, Pictorial Art, 1947.

Rough Riders Ho!, illustrated by E. Franklin Wittmack. Philadelphia, McKay, 1946.

Blue Streak and Doctor Medusa, illustrated by Francis Kirn. Racine, Wisconsin, Whitman, 1946.

Men Against the Ice (as Everitt Proctor), illustrated by Isa Barnett. Philadelphia, Westminster Press, 1946.

The Mystery of the Turquoise Frog, illustrated by Millard McGee. New York, Messner, 1946; London, Hutchinson, 1951.

Kildee House, illustrated by Barbara Cooney. New York, Doubleday, 1949; London, Faber, 1953.

The Mystery of Crystal Canyon, illustrated by Taylor Oughton. Philadelphia, Winston, 1951.

Hill Ranch, illustrated by Barbara Cooney. New York, Doubleday, 1951.

The Capture of the Golden Stallion, illustrated by George Giguere. Boston, Little Brown, 1951.

Wapiti, The Elk, illustrated by Gardell Christiansen. Boston, Little Brown, 1952.

Mister Jim, illustrated by Paul Galdone. London, Faber, 1952; Cleveland, World, 1957.

McGonnigle's Lake, illustrated by Garry Mackenzie. New York, Doubleday, 1953; London, Faber, 1957.

White Mountaineer, illustrated by Gardell Christiansen. Boston, Little Brown, 1953.

The Golden Stallion's Revenge, illustrated by George Giguere. Boston, Little Brown, 1953; London, Hodder and Stoughton, 1955.

The Golden Stallion to the Rescue, illustrated by George Giguere. Boston, Little Brown, 1954; London, Hodder and Stoughton, 1956.

Amikuk, illustrated by Marie Nonnast. Cleveland, World, 1955.

The Golden Stallion's Victory, illustrated by George Giguere. Boston, Little Brown, 1956; London, Hodder and Stoughton, 1957.

Claim Jumpers of Marble Canyon, illustrated by William Moyers. New York, Knopf, 1956.

Beaver Water, illustrated by Robert Doremus. Cleveland, World, 1956.

Mountain Man. Cleveland, World, 1957.

Jets Away! New York, Dodd Mead, 1957.

Tom Pittman, U.S.A.F., illustrated by Sam Kueskin. New York, Duell Sloan Pearce, 1957.

White Tail, illustrated by Marie Nonnast. Cleveland, World, 1958.

In Happy Hollow, illustrated by Harold Berson. New York, Doubleday, 1958.

The Silver Hills, illustrated by Robert Frankenberg. Cleveland, World, 1958.

Kent Barstow, Special Agent, illustrated by Sam Kueskin. New York, Duell Sloan Pearce, 1958.

The Golden Stallion and the Wolf Dog, illustrated by Percy Leason. Boston, Little Brown, and London, Hodder and Stoughton, 1958.

A Horse for Claudia and Dennis, with Natlee Kenoyer. New York, Duell Sloan Pearce, 1958.

Jet Navigator, Strategic Air Command, with Grover Heiman. New York, Duell Sloan Pearce, 1959.

The Golden Stallion's Adventure at Redstone, illustrated by Percy Leason. Boston, Little Brown, 1959; London, Hodder and Stoughton, 1960.

Tim's Mountain, illustrated by Julian de Miskey. Cleveland, World, 1959.

Missile Away. New York, Duell Sloan Pearce, 1959.

Mission Intruder, illustrated by Larry Lurin. New York, Duell Sloan Pearce, 1960.

The Odyssey of an Otter, illustrated by Hamilton Greene. New York, Golden Press, 1960; London, Purnell, 1962.

Weecha, The Raccoon, illustrated by Lawrence Tyler Dresser. New York, Golden Press, 1960; London, Purnell, 1962.

King of the Castle, illustrated by Russell Peterson. Cleveland, World, 1961.

Kent Barstow, Space Man, illustrated by Albert Orban. New York, Duell Sloan Pearce, 1961.

Klepty, illustrated by Polly Montgomery Hecathorn. New York, Duell Sloan Pearce, 1961.

Cougar, illustrated by Robert Magnusen. New York, Golden Press, 1961; London, Purnell, 1962.

El Blanco, illustrated by Gloria Stevens. New York, Golden Press, 1961.

The Capture of West Wind, illustrated by Albert Micale. New York, Duell Sloan Pearce, 1962.

Monte, The Bear Who Became a Celebrity, illustrated by Charles Geer. New York, Duell Sloan Pearce, 1962.

Kent Barstow and the Commando Flight, illustrated by George Wilson. New York, Duell Sloan Pearce, 1963.

The Defiant Heart, illustrated by Paul Laune. New York, Duell Sloan Pearce, 1963.

McNulty's Holiday, illustrated by Charles Geer. New York, Duell Sloan Pearce, 1963.

Kent Barstow on a B-70 Mission. New York, Duell Sloan Pearce, 1964.

Kent Barstow Aboard the Dyna Soar, illustrated by George Wilson. New York, Duell Sloan Pearce, 1964.

Crazy Kill Range, illustrated by Lorence Bjorklund. Cleveland, World, 1965.

Ghost Town Gold, illustrated by Lorence Bjorklund. Cleveland, World, 1965.

The Stubborn One, illustrated by Don Miller.   New York, Duell Sloan Pearce, 1965.
Into the Groove.   New York, Dodd Mead, 1966.
Thornbush Jungle, illustrated by Lorence Bjorklund.   Cleveland, World, 1966.
A Kinkajou on the Town, illustrated by Lorence Bjorklund.   Cleveland, World, 1967.
The Golden Stallion and the Mysterious Feud, illustrated by Albert Michini.   Boston,
    Little Brown, 1967; Leicester, Brockhampton Press, 1970.
Corey's Sea Monster, illustrated by Harvey Kidder.   New York, World, 1969.
Pekan, The Shadow, illustrated by J. D. Nenninger.   Caldwell, Idaho, Caxton, 1970.
Big Red, A Wild Stallion, illustrated by Pers Crowell.   Caldwell, Idaho, Caxton, 1971.
Rufus, illustrated by J. D. Nenninger.   Caldwell, Idaho, Caxton, 1973.

Plays

Screenplays: *Killers of the High Country*, 1959; *The Hound That Thought He Was a
Raccoon*, with Albert Aley, 1960; *Flash, The Teenage Otter*, with Albert Aley, 1961;
Sancho, The Homing Steer, 1961; *Ida, The Off-Beat Eagle*, 1962; *El Blanco, The Legend
of a White Stallion*, 1962.

Other

See Catch (reader), illustrated by Ralph Crosby Smith.   Boston, Ginn, 1955.
The Golden Stallion Picture Book, illustrated by Al Brulé.   New York, Grosset and
    Dunlap, 1962.
Snowman.   New York, Duell Sloan Pearce, 1962.
The Living Wilderness, illustrated by Campbell Grant.   New York, Torquil, 1964.
Dolphins as They Are.   New York, Duell Sloan Pearce, 1966.

Editor, *A Saddlebag of Tales: A Collection of Stories by Members of the Western Writers
of America*, illustrated by Sam Savitt.   New York, Dodd Mead, 1959.

PUBLICATIONS FOR ADULTS

Novels

Call of the West.   New York, Grosset and Dunlap, 1933.
Anything for a Quiet Life (as A. A. Avery).   New York, Farrar and Rinehart, 1942.
Black Powder Empire.   Boston, Little Brown, 1955; London, Ward Lock, 1957.
Posted Water.   London, Ward Lock, 1959.
Sex Isn't Everything.   New York, Torquil, 1961.
Smoky Trail.   London, Ward Lock, 1967.

Other

High Country.   New York, Derrydale Press, 1938.

Manuscript Collection: University of Oregon Library, Eugene.

*   *   *

Rutherford Montgomery has written many works of fiction – adventure stories depicting
the outdoors. His love and knowledge of animals, and his early years on a ranch, have
enabled him to write with authenticity many books dealing with animals and the West.
   One such book is *Kildee House*, which was a Newbery Medal runner-up. This is a tale
about a mountaineer, Jerome Kildee, the house that he built under a giant redwood tree and

the many friends he made there. The comparison made by the author between people and animals is remarkable. Jerome Kildee finds that his animal friends are no different from people. These newfound friends take advantage of him. Many are selfish. Many are thieves – the raccoons, skunks, deer, foxes, possums, and birds. Jerome Kildee has so many friends who eventually encamp within his walls and under his floor that he has to find larger and more suitable homes for them. Most of them are sent to the zoo, but the old faithful animals remain under the redwood tree in Kildee House.

Another work *Carcajou* (1936) is a tale of Indians and white trappers as well as animals. A wolverine, Carcajou, is the villain of the story – a regular killer feared and hated by animals and men. The author spins a web of intrigue as he describes the constant struggle for livelihood that goes on among the creatures in the Northern wilderness.

Many of the author's other works deal specifically with animals and their interactions with people. *McGonnigle's Lake* is the story of Mike McGonnigle, an old pioneer of the West, and his adventures with his many animal friends. The story revolves around Frog Lake and Mike's efforts to maintain the lake. *Hill Ranch* is the story of two teenagers who attempt to make a success of a ranch. Their difficulties and successes are underscored by the animals who are underfoot. There is Stumpy the cat and a fighting rooster named B–29. Like *McGonnigle's Like*, *Hill Ranch* also deals with efforts to maintain and develop something of worth – in this instance a farm.

Among Montgomery's animal stories about horses are *The Capture of the Golden Stallion*, and *Golden Stallion and the Wolf Dog*. The first tells of the capture of a wild horse (Golden Boy) by a 16-year-old boy. The second is one of a continuation of the Golden Stallion Series and tells more of the horse's numerous adventures. The seven titles in the series are exciting and adventure-filled.

Montgomery's stories are written in such a fashion that the reader is able to fathom much about the life and habits of animal life. The story about a wild black stallion of the Western plateau, *Midnight*, pictures the struggle for existence by the wild stallion and other animals.

Rutherford Montgomery also wrote *Ice Blink* and *Beaver Water* – this last book won two coveted awards for him. *Ice Blink* tells the story of an Eskimo boy in Alaska around 1750, and *Beaver Water* describes two brothers excitedly furtrapping in the Old Northwest in 1836. The author's other interest is aviation. Because of his involvement in the Air Corps of the U.S. Army during World War I, Mr. Montgomery has a great deal of experience to draw on in writing his stories.

He has also written works on aviation and mysteries with a tinge of science fiction.

The easy flow of words in the majority of Montgomery's works increases one's interest and holds one's attention. Many of his works begin with enthusiastic expectations and continuously build to a great crescendo. The reader is rarely disappointed.

—Dolores C. Leffall

MOORHEAD, Diana. New Zealander. Born in Horsell, Surrey, England, 28 May 1940. Educated at St. Mary's, Horsell, 1946–51; St. Catherine's, Bramley, Surrey, 1951–52; Waihi College, New Zealand, 1953–57; Auckland University (Lissie Rathbone Scholar, 1958), 1958–60, B.A. in English 1961. Married Raymond John Moorhead in 1962; has one son and one daughter. Sales Assistant, Whitcombe and Tombs, booksellers, Auckland, 1961–62; Play Centre Supervisor, Swanson and Te Atatu, 1967–69. Since 1969, Librarian, Massey High School, Auckland. Recipient: International Youth Library bursary, 1976. Address: 58 Yeovil Road, Te Atatu, Auckland 8, New Zealand.

PUBLICATIONS FOR CHILDREN

Fiction

> *In Search of Magic*, illustrated by Keith Clark.   Auckland and Leicester, Brockhampton
> Press, 1971.
> *The Green and the White*, illustrated by Victor Ambrus.   Leicester, Brockhampton
> Press, 1974.
> *Gull Man's Glory*, illustrated by Sam Thompson.   London, Hodder and Stoughton,
> 1976.

Diana Moorhead comments:
Apart from *In Search of Magic* (an early work for younger readers), my books are fantasies for the 10–12 age group. I try to create an exact and inherently logical setting for each one, as background for the themes I am exploring; and in fact the setting is often in my mind long before the plot develops. I write partly for myself, but mostly to share with others the delight that fantasy has always given me.

*   *   *

Diana Moorhead's first book, *In Search of Magic*, while it gave some hint of her ability to produce a simple, well-rounded story for younger children, was unremarkable; her reputation as a children's novelist began with the appearance of the second book, *The Green and the White*.

Here, her capacity for telling a well-paced story with dexterity and economy is demonstrated beyond doubt. Jochim, the young king of Verdontis, is charged by his wizard to enter the northern mountains, home of the feared Shrinn, in search of the Luck Charm which alone can arrest the blight which is upon his kingdom. Ostensibly an adventure story, the tale has depths which explore human prejudice and superstitions. Before all else, it has an exploration of the power of good over evil, of intelligent persistence in the face of ignorance.

The characters are created precisely. A hint of sentimentality in the handling of the relationship between Jochim and his betrothed, Elise, does not mar the whole. The novel is clearly intended for the 9-to-11 age-group for which subtlety of sexual relationship is irrelevant. In fact, Moorhead handled a sophisticated theme deftly, ensuring access at all stages of the book to children of this age-group.

Gull Man's Glory predicts a world which, presumably recoving from nuclear devastation, has assumed a form dictated by the aridness of the land. A race of winged humans, accidentally produced before the catastrophe by irresponsible genetic experiment, now forms colonies of sea-birds on the cliffs. Flet, a young gull man who has been taught to read secretly by the Meddick, or wise man, becomes involved with Lorraine, ward of the Lord of Southmark (one of the small feudal kingdoms into which the land has been divided). Flet is a youth of spirit and intelligence, whose dawning realisation that it is possible to question, added to his dangerous, if chivalrous decision to protect Lorainne from her uncle's plotting, leads him, by route of fast-moving adventures, to both an acceptance of his own difference and the vision of richer possibilities in life.

Again, direct, simple language is used skilfully, to create a place the reader can believe in and characters who live. The difficult parable form is used with apparent ease; the tale is credible, the issues real.

This ease – the natural ability to tell a story which flows – is Moorhead's chief strength. The fact that it brings her books within reach of the less intellectual child, while still providing depths of underlying significance, is fortuitously good, a characteristic regrettably rare in work of quality.

—Dorothy Butler

MOREY, Walt(er Nelson).   American.   Born in Hoquiam, Washington, 3 February 1907. Educated at Benkhe Walker Business College, 1927. Married Rosalind Alice Ogden in 1934 (died, 1976). Construction worker, millworker, and theatre manager in Oregon and Washington in the 1930's; burner foreman and superintendent, Kaiser Shipyards, Vancouver, Washington, 1940–45; deep-sea diver and fish trap inspector, Alaska, 1951; Director, Oregon Nut Cooperative, Newberg, 1960–61. Since 1937, filbert farmer. Address: c/o E. P. Dutton and Company Inc., 201 Park Avenue South, New York, New York 10023, U.S.A.

PUBLICATIONS FOR CHILDREN

Fiction

> *Gentle Ben*, illustrated by John Schoenherr.   New York, Dutton, 1965; London, Dent, 1966.
> *Home Is the North*, illustrated by Robert Shore.   New York, Dutton, 1967; London, Dent, 1968.
> *Kävik, The Wolf Dog*, illustrated by Peter Parnall.   New York, Dutton, 1968; London, Dent, 1969.
> *Angry Waters*, illustrated by Richard Cuffari.   New York, Dutton, 1969; London, Dent, 1970.
> *Gloomy Gus*.   New York, Dutton, 1970; as *The Bear at Friday Creek*, London, Dent, 1971.
> *Deep Trouble*.   New York, Dutton, 1971; London, Dent, 1972.
> *Scrub Dog of Alaska*.   New York, Dutton, 1971; London, Sidgwick and Jackson, 1975.
> *Canyon Winter*.   New York, Dutton, 1972; London, Dent, 1974.
> *Runaway Stallion*.   New York, Dutton, 1973.
> *Run Far, Run Fast*.   New York, Dutton, 1974.
> *Year of the Black Pony*.   New York, Dutton, 1976.

Other

> *Operation Blue Bear*.   New York, Dutton, 1975.

PUBLICATIONS FOR ADULTS

Other

> *North to Danger*, with Virgil Burford.   New York, Day, 1954; revised edition, Caldwell, Idaho, Caxton, 1969.

Manuscript Collection: University of Oregon Library, Eugene.

*   *   *

Walt Morey is a writer in the Jack London tradition; most of his books are animal stories set in Alaska. Morey's Alaska is that of the 1950's, the years just before the territory achieved statehood, and he writes from his experience of living and working there, primarily in the occupations concerning salmon-fishing on which the economy of the area depended. Life in small settlements like Orca City is rough and tough; many of the people are as migrant as the salmon on their annual run, and while qualities such as courage and endurance are valued, ruthless exploitation is equally a condition of survival. The message of many of Morey's novels is a questioning of this situation; their formula is often that of an adolescent boy who is for some reason a "loner"; he befriends an animal whom he has to defend from adults who would use or kill it. These stories do not stay long on library shelves; their vivid descriptions of icy wastes combined with the warmth of their emotional tone make them popular reading.

Gentle Ben is still one of the best-loved. Ben, contrary to generally held opinions of the nature of bears, especially those soured by ill-treatment in captivity, becomes the pet of young Mark Andersen and is saved by him not only from the villagers of Orca City but also from big-game hunters from the outside world.

Home Is the North and *Kävik, The Wolf Dog* both have Malamute dogs as their animal heroes, and both contrast the land of the wild and free with civilisation as represented by Seattle, the port of embarkation for Alaska. In the first, the orphan Brad fights to stay and work on the fishing boats rather than join his aunt in Seattle, especially as this means giving up his dog, Mickie. In the second, Kävik survives ill treatment and privation in his attempts to make the long journey home to the north. The latter, perhaps because it centres on the animal's reactions rather than humans', is the better book; it is both moving and powerful.

Angry Waters has less drive. Set on the Columbia River, it tells how a young man on parole repays the kindness of the couple who employ him by saving them from his convict friends and a flood in an exciting climax to the story. In *Gloomy Gus*, Eric Strong's pet bear is sold by his elders to a circus and filial loyalty leads him to accept this, much as he dislikes it. *Deep Trouble* reflects Morey's experience as an inspector of salmon fish-traps. The descriptions of diving are not only authentic but also thrilling, as are those of life at sea and wild life of the deep. *Scrub Dog of Alaska* is another story of making good. Dave Martin, son of an Indian mother and a white father, has to stand up to the racist sneers of his father's relatives in the States. His dog Scrub develops from being the weakest of the litter to being the leader of the pack.

Canyon Winter is an exciting survival story of a boy who is marooned by a plane crash in the Cascade Mountains over the winter. This experience and the influence of the old recluse who saves him make him, on his return to civilisation, a fierce conservationist. Respect and concern for wild life and the wild places of the earth are more overt here than in the earlier books, but they are Morey's message throughout.

—Mary Croxson

MORGAN, Alison (Mary). British. Born in Bexley, Kent, 23 April 1930. Educated at St. Helen's School, Northwood, Middlesex, 1943–47; Somerville College, Oxford, 1949–52, B.A. (honours) 1952; University of London, 1952–53. Married John Morgan in 1960; has two sons. Taught in secondary modern school, Malvern, Worcestershire, 1953–54, and in girls' grammar school, Newtown, Montgomery, 1954–59. Since 1964, Justice of the Peace. Recipient: Welsh Arts Council award, 1973. Agent: A. P. Watt and Son, 26–28 Bedford Row, London WC1R 4HL. Address: Talcoed, Llanafan, near Builth Wells, Powys, Wales.

PUBLICATIONS FOR CHILDREN

Fiction

> *Fish*, illustrated by John Sergeant. London, Chatto and Windus, 1971; as *A Boy Called Fish*, New York, Harper, 1973.
> *Pete*. London, Chatto and Windus, 1972.
> *Ruth Crane*. London, Chatto and Windus, 1973.
> *The Raft*, illustrated by Trevor Parkin. London, Abelard Schuman, 1974.
> *At Willie Tucker's Place*, illustrated by Trevor Stubley. London, Chatto and Windus, 1975; Nashville, Nelson, 1976.

River Song, illustrated by John Schoenherr.   New York, Harper, 1975; London, Chatto
and Windus, 1976.

Alison Morgan comments:
Fish, *Pete*, *Ruth Crane*, and *At Willie Tucker's Place* form a quartet of stories set in a
hypothetical mid-Wales with different children from the village community as major
characters in each case. *The Raft* is a short story concerned with two boys, one disabled and
the other afraid of water, who in the course of a dangerous adventure learn to understand
something of each other's problems. *River Song* traces a year in the life of a group of riverside
birds.

*   *   *

Alison Morgan's first novel, *Fish*, was widely praised, and established her as a major
writer for children; her next 3 books follow on from her initial success and are strongly
linked both in style and place. All are set in a small Welsh village community and one of the
most powerful features is the refreshing realism of the setting, characters and dialogue; the
interlocking and complex relationships of the village are skilfully drawn and are portrayed
through the eyes and understanding of the child characters. The atmosphere of this slower
and more intricate way of life, and the countryside in which it is set, are captured by the
skilful use of detail; the author draws a convincing picture of a village with its straggle of
farms and houses, the quiet respectability of its inhabitants. In each case this is disrupted by
the events of the story; each involves children facing difficulties in one form or another, and
in the resolution of the plots each involves a strong adventure element and a good deal of
tension and excitement is built up. However, unusual in adventure stories, the adults are not
relegated to minor roles nor dismissed altogether; the relationship between child and adult is
drawn in a realistic and sympathetic way, and it is the adults who explain, criticise, rescue
and support.
   Fish is the story of a relative newcomer to Llanwern, a boy who is something of an
outsider in the community. He tentatively makes friends with Jimmy, through whose eyes
the story is told; but his confidence is boosted and he begins to grow in his own eyes, and so
in the eyes of others, through his adoption of a stray dog, Floss, and their adventure together.
Pete concerns an older boy in the same community. Like *Fish*, this book works at different
levels: as an exciting adventure story, and as an imaginative and sensitive study of a teenage
boy. *Pete* was awarded the 1973 Welsh Arts Council Literature Prize. In *Ruth Crane*
Llanwern is seen through the eyes of an American outsider, a clever, sensitive teenage girl
who has just undergone a car accident in which her father was killed and her mother and
sister badly injured. The story centres around Ruth's "rescue" of her younger brother when
he decides to visit their sister in hospital some distance away and sets off with a tramp-like
figure, another of Alison Morgan's "misfits," as guide. And with *At Willie Tucker's Place*, we
return to the younger age group to which *Fish* appealed, and which perhaps best suits her
style.
   All four books involve adventure in the form of children testing themselves against the
elements, and all pay strict attention to details of time, place and event so that the reader can
follow the minutiae of the plot and become truly absorbed by it. The balance between
adventure and the development of characters and relationships is well maintained, except
perhaps in *Ruth Crane*; here the crisis situation facing Ruth is not developed; we are not told
how she feels or how she learns to cope with the drastic changes in her life, and the older
reader may become impatient with the adventure element which takes over the latter half of
the book.
   River Song is a new departure. It is the story of the summer life of birds living along a
river, living their everyday lives, making friends, and coping with dangers from further
afield. As usual the details of the countryside and its life are depicted with close observation

and great skill; yet this book is for me less successful since the style of anthropomorphism used perhaps only really works for a younger age group.

—Janet E. Newman

MOWAT, Farley (McGill). Canadian. Born in Belleville, Ontario, 12 May, 1921. Educated at public schools in Trenton, Belleville, Windsor, Richmond Hill, and Toronto, Ontario, and Saskatoon, Saskatchewan; University of Toronto, B.A. 1949. Served in the Canadian Army Infantry and Intelligence Corps, 1940–46: Captain. Married Frances Thornhill, two sons; Claire Angel Wheeler. Self-employed writer. Recipient: University of Western Ontario President's Medal, for short story, 1952; Anisfield-Wolf Award, for non-fiction, 1952; Governor-General's Award, 1957; Canadian Library Association Book of the Year Medal, 1958; Leacock Medal, 1970. Honorary degrees: University of Toronto; University of Lethbridge, Alberta; Laurentian University, Sudbury, Ontario, 1970. Address: c/o McClelland and Stewart Ltd., 25 Hollinger Road, Toronto, Ontario M4B 3G2, Canada.

PUBLICATIONS FOR CHILDREN

Fiction

> *Lost in the Barrens*, illustrated by Charles Geer.   Boston, Little Brown, 1956; London, Macmillan, 1957.
> *The Black Joke*, illustrated by D. Johnson.   Toronto, McClelland and Stewart, 1962; Boston, Little Brown, 1963; London, Macmillan, 1964.
> *The Curse of the Viking Grave*, illustrated by Charles Geer.   Boston, Little Brown, 1966.

Other

> *Owls in the Family*, illustrated by Robert Frankenberg.   Boston, Little Brown, 1961; London, Macmillan, 1963.

PUBLICATIONS FOR ADULTS

Short Stories

> *The Snow Walker.*   Boston, Little Brown, 1975; London, Heinemann, 1977.

Plays

> Television Scripts: *Sea Fare* (*Telescope* series), 1964; *Diary of a Boy on Vacation*, 1964; and others.

Other

> *People of the Deer* (on the Ihalmiut Eskimos).   Boston, Little Brown, and London, Joseph, 1952.
> *The Regiment* (on the Hastings and Prince Edward Regiment).   Toronto, McClelland and Stewart, 1955.
> *The Dog Who Wouldn't Be.*   Boston, Little Brown, 1957; London, Joseph, 1958.

The Grey Seas Under.   Boston, Little Brown, 1958; London, Joseph, 1959.

The Desperate People (on the Ihalmiut Eskimos).   Boston, Little Brown, 1959; London, Joseph, 1960.

The Serpent's Coil (on salvaging ships).   Toronto, McClelland and Stewart, 1961; Boston, Little Brown, and London, Joseph, 1962.

Never Cry Wolf.   Toronto, McClelland and Stewart, and Boston, Little Brown, 1963; London, Secker and Warburg, 1964.

Westviking: The Ancient Norse in Greenland and North America.   Boston, Little Brown, 1965; London, Secker and Warburg, 1966.

Canada North.   Boston, Little Brown, 1967.

This Rock Within the Sea: A Heritage Lost (on Newfoundland), photographs by John de Visser.   Boston, Little Brown, 1969.

The Boat Who Wouldn't Float.   Toronto, McClelland and Stewart, 1969; Boston, Little Brown, and London, Heinemann, 1970.

Sibir: My Discovery of Siberia.   Toronto, McClelland and Stewart, 1970; as *The Siberians*, Boston, Little Brown, 1970; London, Heinemann, 1972.

A Whale for the Killing.   Toronto, McClelland and Stewart, and Boston, Little Brown, 1972; London, Heinemann, 1973.

Wake of the Great Sealers.   Boston, Little Brown, 1973.

Editor, *Coppermine Journey: An Account of a Great Adventure*, by Samuel Hearne.   Toronto, McClelland and Stewart, and Boston, Little Brown, 1958.

Editor, *The Top of the World:*

1. *Ordeal by Ice.*   Toronto, McClelland and Stewart, 1960; Boston, Little Brown, and London, Joseph, 1961.
2. *The Polar Passion: The Quest for the North Pole, with Selections From Arctic Journals.*   Toronto, McClelland and Stewart, 1967; Boston, Little Brown, 1968.
3. *Tundra: Selections from the Great Accounts of Arctic Land Voyages.*   Toronto, McClelland and Stewart, 1973.

Manuscript Collection: McMaster University, Hamilton, Ontario.

Farley Mowat comments:

I am a simple fellow and I like simple things. Particularly do I like natural things, and this includes people who live natural lives (Eskimos, fishermen, northern Indians, seamen under sail, etc.). These are the kind of people I have always chosen to write about – people who are attuned to the natural world and who feel competent and at home with natural existence. Cities give me the pip. High civilizations scare the hell out of me since they inevitably lead their populations into holocausts.

*   *   *

Farley Mowat is an important and abundant writer, the author of some 20 books and innumerable essays, letters, and reviews. His father early introduced him to the outdoors, to sailboats and canoes; he went birdwatching in the Arctic when he was a boy; he was an ecologist long before it became the vogue. He embraces nature. Native peoples, seas and tundra, all the wild life that is part of the earth and lives in harmony with it, must be protected from Admass society. Essentially Mowat is an ethnologist, a nature writer and a historian, often embroiled in protest with the befouling Establishment of his beloved Canadian North.

Mowat has written three books designed for the young. About writing for children he has said, "The hardest books in the world to write are books for young people. They are also by far the most rewarding. Books written by adults, for adults, rarely have any prolonged effect upon their readers, no matter how good they may be. A good book for youngsters can influence the whole future life of the young reader."

    Lost in the Barrens is the first and best of his books for children; *The Curse of the Viking Grave* is its unsuccessful sequel. *The Black Joke* is a sea story that, like the curate's egg, is good in parts.

    Mowat, like many other good Canadian writers, eschews fiction in favour of creative fact. The success of *Lost in the Barrens*, a tale of two lads bereft in the frozen North, comes from the reality with which the writer endows the North, whose cruel and austere beauty he has learned to love. The two lost boys in the true North, and their wooing of their lives from the environment, makes this book worthy of greater success than it has yet enjoyed outside of Canada. *The Curse of the Viking Grave* is a follow-up, and one can almost hear the author's groans as he tries to breathe literary life into it.

    The Black Joke nearly suceeds, for Mowat is a sailor of sorts, and the theme is a good one that is pressed too hard. The smuggler skipper and his two sons remain shrouded. The sea, as depicted by the author in labour, lacks the reality and the beauty with which he endows the frozen North. Moreover the dialogue between the two sons and the French of Miquelon remain stilted and absurd.

    Nevertheless these three books are redolent of Canada and of the author. Well accepted by children, their teachers and librarians, they serve as good introduction to the land and to its people. They impart a feeling for the vast waste of snow that permits living only on its own terms. The thrill of discovery, and the ever widening trail of the Norsemen makes for good mulch to nourish a child's imagination and dream, while the smack of the sea against the canvas and planks, the brine, the spume and the smell bring to *The Black Joke* an atmosphere that young readers will relish.

—William Ready

MUKERJI, Dhan Gopal. Born near Calcutta, 6 July 1890; emigrated to the United States, 1910. Educated at Indian schools; Hindu priest-initiate, 1904–06; University of Calcutta, 1908; Tokyo University, 1909; University of California, Berkeley, 1910–13; Stanford University, California, Ph. B. 1914. Married Ethel Ray Dugan in 1918; one son. Lecturer. Lived in New Milford, Connecticut. Recipient: American Library Association Newbery Medal, 1928. *Died 14 July 1936.*

PUBLICATIONS FOR CHILDREN

Fiction

    Kari the Elephant, illustrated by J.E. Allen. New York, Dutton, 1922; London, Dent, 1923.
    Jungle Beasts and Men, illustrated by J.E. Allen. New York, Dutton, 1923; London, Dent, 1924.
    Hari the Jungle Lad, illustrated by Morgan Stinemetz. New York, Dutton, 1924.
    Gay-Neck: The Story of a Pigeon, illustrated by Boris Artzybasheff. New York, Dutton, 1927; London, Dent, 1928.
    Ghond the Hunter, illustrated by Boris Artzybasheff. New York, Dutton, 1928; London, Dent, 1929.
    The Chief of the Herd, illustrated by Mahlon Blaine. New York, Dutton, and London, Dent, 1929.
    Bunny, Hound and Clown, illustrated by Kurt Wiese. New York, Dutton, 1931.
    The Master Monkey, illustrated by Florence Weber. New York, Dutton, 1932.
    Fierce-Face: The Story of a Tiger, illustrated by Dorothy P. Lathrop. New York, Dutton, 1936.

Other

Hindu Fables for Little Children, illustrated by Kurt Wiese.   New York, Dutton, 1929.
Rama, The Hero of India: Valmiki's "Ramayana" Done into a Short English Version,
    illustrated by Edgar Parin d'Aulaire.   New York, Dutton, 1930; London, Dent,
    1931.

PUBLICATIONS FOR ADULTS

Novel

The Secret Listeners of the East.   New York, Dutton, 1926.

Plays

Chintamini: A Symbolic Drama, with Mary Carolyn Davies, adaptation of a play by
    Girish C. Ghose.   Boston, Badger, 1914.
Layla-Majnu.   San Francisco, Paul Elder, 1916.
The Judgment of Indra, in Drama, edited by A.D. Dickinson.   New York, Doubleday,
    1922; in Fifty One-Act Plays, edited by Constance M. Martin, London, Gollancz,
    1934.

Verse

Rajani: Songs of the Night.   San Francisco, Paul Elder, 1916.
Sandhya: Songs of Twilight.   San Francisco, Paul Elder, 1917.

Other

Caste and Outcast (autobiography).   New York, Dutton, and London, Dent, 1923.
My Brother's Face.   New York, Dutton, 1924; London, Butterworth, 1925.
The Face of Silence (on Ramakrishna).   New York, Dutton, 1926; London, Wassenaar,
    1973.
A Son of Mother India Answers.   New York, Dutton, 1928.
Visit India with Me.   New York, Dutton, 1929.
Devotional Passages from the Hindu Bible.   New York, Dutton, 1929.
Disillusioned India.   New York, Dutton, 1930.
Daily Meditation; or, The Practice of Repose.   New York, Dutton, 1933.
The Path of Prayer.   New York, Dutton, 1934.

Editor and Translator, The Song of God: Translation of the Bhagavad-Gita.   New York,
    Dutton, 1931; London, Dent, 1932.

*   *   *

Dhan Gopal Mukerji wrote the kind of books for children first made popular by Ernest
Thompson Seton, stories of wild life in which the landscape plays almost as important a part
as the animals and birds whose lives are described. "Grey Owl" is another writer in the same
genre, and was Mukerji's contemporary.
    For the most part his books are anecdotal, a stringing together of incidents from his
boyhood in Northern India. For example in Ghond the Hunter Ghond describes village life
and ceremonies, recalls journeys to Agra, Delhi and Kashmir, and tells stories of various
animals he has befriended – a mongoose, a pet panther. Kari the Elephant and Jungle Beasts
and Men consist of similar assorted incidents.
    The Chief of the Herd is in the classic animal-story mould. It tells the life of Sirdar the

elephant, leader of the herd: election as leader, a mate, a son, a forest fire, a flood. The book is packed with interesting observations on animal lore. He writes in a clear prose which occasionally topples over into lushness − "heavy kine throbbing with fat draw their silken flanks through the grain fields" − but which is in the main vivid and lively in its evocation of the Indian scene.

His prize-winning book *Gay-Neck* lacks the narrative power of a Kipling or a Henry Williamson, but must have had for its readers the charm of an exotic setting and the excitement of patriotic sentiment. Gay-Neck the pigeon is trained by his young master in Calcutta, travels to the Himalayas and is then loaned during the 1914−18 War to the Indian army. He carries vital messages across the trenches from behind enemy lines, survives his ordeal and is returned, wounded and frightened, to his beloved master in India where the healing powers of the Lama in a Himalayan monastery set him once more at peace and give him the courage to fly again.

Mukerji's creatures are not credited with as much human sentiment as Kipling's in the *Jungle Books*. It is illuminating to contrast the two: the outsider Englishman's exotic Jungle with its animals each addressing each other in a curious stylised biblical language, each animal strongly characterised as an individual but nevertheless obeying the Law of the Jungle, an invention of Kipling's, older of course than man-made laws but still an evolved code with, one cannot help but suspect, affinities with English Law; and the native-born Mukerji's more accurately observed jungle where the animals when they speak utter a plainer prose but where the natural world fits into a divine scheme of things, where "you cannot destroy one species of animal without upsetting the balance of life. Life is a whole. There is no escape from this." These words were written in 1929. Mukerji, with a view of life arising out of the same oriental philosophy that, however, diluted, has produced the hippy trail to Katmandu, foresaw dangers which the west is only now choosing to recognise.

—Mary Rayner

NESBIT, E(dith). British. Born in London, 15 August 1858. Educated at an Ursuline convent in Dinan, France, 1869, and in schools in Germany and Brighton. Married the writer Hubert Bland in 1880 (died, 1914), two sons, one daughter, one adopted daughter, and one adopted son; Thomas Terry Tucker, 1917. Journalist, elocutionist, greeting cards decorator; Poetry Critic, *Athenaeum* magazine, London, in the 1890's; Co-Editor, *Neolith* magazine, London, 1907−08; General Editor, The Children's Bookcase series, Oxford University Press and Hodder and Stoughton, 1908−11. Founding Member, 1884, and member of the Pamphlet Committee, Fabian Society. Granted a Civil List pension, 1915. *Died 4 May 1924.*

PUBLICATIONS FOR CHILDREN

Fiction

> *Listen Long and Listen Well*, with others.   London, Raphael Tuck, 1893.
> *Sunny Tales for Snowy Days*, with others.   London, Raphael Tuck, 1893.
> *Told by Sunbeams and Me*, with others.   London, Raphael Tuck, 1893.
> *Hours in Many Lands*, with others.   London, Raphael Tuck, 1894.
> *Fur and Feathers: Tales for All Weathers*, with others.   London, Raphael Tuck, 1894.

Lads and Lassies, with others.   London, Raphael Tuck, 1894.

Tales That Are True, for Brown Eyes and Blue, with others, edited by Edric Vredenburg, illustrated by M. Goodman.   London, Raphael Tuck, 1894.

Tales to Delight from Morning till Night, with others, edited by Edric Vredenburg, illustrated by M. Goodman.   London, Raphael Tuck, 1894.

Hours in Many Lands: Stories and Poems, with others, edited by Edric Vredenburg, illustrated by Frances Brundage.   London, Raphael Tuck, 1894.

Doggy Tales, illustrated by Lucy Kemp-Welch.   London, Ward, 1895.

Pussy Tales, illustrated by Lucy Kemp-Welch.   London, Ward, 1895.

Tales of the Clock, illustrated by Helen Jackson.   London, Raphael Tuck, 1895.

Dulcie's Lantern and Other Stories, with Theo Gift and Mrs. Worthington Bliss.   London, Griffith Farran, 1895.

Treasures from Storyland, with others.   London, Raphael Tuck, 1895.

Tales Told in Twilight: A Volume of Very Short Stories.   London, Nister, 1897.

Dog Tales, and Other Tales, with A. Guest and Emily R. Watson, edited by Edric Vredenburg, illustrated by R.K. Mounsey.   London, Raphael Tuck, 1898.

Pussy and Doggy Tales, illustrated by Lucy Kemp-Welch.   London, Dent, 1899; New York, Dutton, 1900.

The Story of the Treasure Seekers, Being the Adventures of the Bastable Children in Search of a Fortune, illustrated by Gordon Browne and Lewis Baumer.   London, Unwin, and New York, Stokes, 1899.

The Book of Dragons, illustrated by H.R. Millar.   London and New York, Harper 1900.

Nine Unlikely Tales for Children, illustrated by H.R. Millar and Claude Shepperson.   London, Unwin, and New York, Dutton, 1901.

The Wouldbegoods, Being the Further Adventures of the Treasure Seekers, illustrated by Arthur H. Buckland and John Hassell.   London, Unwin, 1901; New York, Harper, 1902.

Five Children and It, illustrated by H.R. Millar.   London, Unwin, 1902; New York, Dodd Mead, 1905.

The Revolt of the Toys, and What Comes of Quarrelling, illustrated by Ambrose Dudley.   London, Nister, and New York, Dutton, 1902.

Playtime Stories.   London, Raphael Tuck, 1903.

The Rainbow Queen and Other Stories.   London, Raphael Tuck, 1903.

The Phoenix and the Carpet, illustrated by H.R. Millar.   London, Newnes, and New York, Macmillan, 1904.

The Story of the Five Rebellious Dolls.   London, Nister, 1904.

The New Treasure Seekers, illustrated by Gordon Browne and Lewis Baumer.   London, Unwin, and New York, Stokes, 1904.

Cat Tales, with Rosamund Bland, illustrated by Isabel Watkin.   London, Nister, and New York, Dutton, 1904.

Pug Peter: King of Mouseland, Marquis of Barkshire, D.O.G., P.C. 1906, Knight of the Order of the Gold Dog Collar, Author of Doggerel Lays and Days ... , illustrated by Harry Rountree.   Leeds, Alf Cooke, 1905.

Oswald Bastable and Others, illustrated by C.E. Brock and H.R. Millar.   London, Wells Gardner, 1905; New York, Coward McCann, 1960.

The Story of the Amulet, illustrated by H.R. Millar.   London, Unwin, 1906; New York, Dutton, 1907.

The Railway Children, illustrated by C.E. Brock.   London, Wells Gardner, and New York, Macmillan, 1906.

The Enchanted Castle, illustrated by H.R. Millar.   London, Unwin, 1907; New York, Harper, 1908.

The House of Arden, illustrated by H.R. Millar.   London, Unwin, 1908; New York, Dutton, 1909.

Harding's Luck, illustrated by H.R. Millar.   London, Hodder and Stoughton, 1909; New York, Stokes, 1910.

The Magic City, illustrated by H.R. Millar. London, Macmillan, 1910; New York, Coward McCann, 1958.

The Wonderful Garden; or, The Three C's, illustrated by H.R. Millar. London, Macmillan, 1911; New York, Coward McCann, 1935.

The Magic World, illustrated by H.R. Millar and Spencer Pryse. London and New York, Macmillan, 1912.

Wet Magic, illustrated by H.R. Millar. London, Laurie, 1913; New York, Coward McCann, 1937.

Our New Story Book, with others, illustrated by Elsie Wood and Louis Wain. London, Nister, and New York, Dutton, 1913.

The New World Literary Series, Book Two, edited by Henry Cecil Wyld. London, Collins, 1921.

Five of Us — And Madeline, edited by Mrs. Clifford Sharp, illustrated by Nora S. Unwin. London, Unwin, 1925; New York, Adelphi, 1926.

Fairy Stories, edited by Naomi Lewis, illustrated by Brian Robb. London, Benn, 1977.

Play

Cinderella (produced London, 1892). London, Sidgwick and Jackson, 1909.

Verse

Songs of Two Seasons, illustrated by J. MacIntyre. London, Raphael Tuck, 1890.

The Voyage of Columbus, 1492: The Discovery of America, illustrated by Will and Frances Brundage. London, Raphael Tuck, 1892.

Our Friends and All about Them. London, Raphael Tuck, 1893.

As Happy as a King, illustrated by S. Rosamund Praeger. London, Ward, 1896.

Dinna Forget, with G.C. Bingham. London, Nister, 1897; New York, Dutton, 1898.

To Wish You Every Joy. London, Raphael Tuck, 1901.

Other

The Children's Shakespeare, edited by Edric Vredenburg, illustrated by Frances Brundage. London, Raphael Tuck, 1897; Philadelphia, Altemus, 1900.

Royal Children of English History, illustrated by Frances Brundage. London, Raphael Tuck, 1897.

Twenty Beautiful Stories from Shakespeare: A Home Study Course, edited by E.T. Roe, illustrated by Max Bihn. Chicago, Hertel and Jenkins, 1907.

The Old Nursery Stories, illustrated by W.H. Margetson. London, Oxford University Press-Hodder and Stoughton, 1908.

My Sea-Side Book, with George Manville Fenn. London, Nister, and New York, Dutton, 1911.

Children's Stories from Shakespeare, with *When Shakespeare Was a Boy*, by F.J. Furnivall. Philadelphia, McKay, 1912.

Children's Stories from English History, with Doris Ashley, edited by Edric Vredenburg, illustrated by John H. Bacon and Howard Davie. London, Raphael Tuck, 1914.

Long Ago When I Was Young, illustrated by Edward Ardizzone. London, Whiting and Wheaton, and New York, Watts, 1966.

Editor, with Robert Ellice Mack, *Spring [Summer, Autumn, Winter] Songs and Sketches*. London, Griffith Farran, and New York, Dutton, 4 vols., 1886.

Editor, with Robert Ellice Mack, *Eventide Songs and Sketches*. London, Griffith Farran, 1887; as *Night Songs and Sketches*, New York, Dutton, 1887.

Editor, with Robert Ellice Mack, *Morning Songs and Sketches*. London, Griffith Farran, 1887; as *Noon Songs and Sketches*, New York, Dutton, 1887.

Editor, with Robert Ellice Mack, *Lilies and Heartsease: Songs and Sketches.*   New
   York, Dutton, 1888(?).
Editor, *The Girl's Own Birthday Book.*   London, Drane, 1894.
Editor, *Poet's Whispers: A Birthday Book.*   London, Drane, 1895.
Editor, *A Book of Dogs, Being a Discourse on Them, with Many Tales and Wonders ...* ,
   illustrated by Winifred Austin.   London, Dent, and New York, Dutton, 1898.
Editor, *Winter Snow*, illustrated by H. Bellingham Smith.   New York, Dutton, 1898(?).

PUBLICATIONS FOR ADULTS

Novels

The Prophet's Mantle, with Hubert Bland (as Fabian Bland).   London, Drane, 1885;
   Chicago, Belford Clarke, 1889.
The Secret of the Kyriels.   London, Hurst and Blackett, and Philadelphia, Lippincott,
   1899.
The Red House.   London, Methuen, and New York, Harper, 1902.
The Incomplete Amorist.   London, Constable, and New York, Doubleday 1906.
Daphne in Fitzroy Street.   London, George Allen, and New York, Doubleday, 1909.
Salome and the Head: A Modern Melodrama.   London, Alston Rivers, 1909; as *The
   House with No Address*, New York, Doubleday, 1909; London, Newnes, 1914.
Dormant.   London, Methuen, 1911; as *Rose Royal*, New York, Dodd Mead, 1912.
The Incredible Honeymoon.   New York, Harper, 1916; London, Hutchinson, 1921.
The Lark.   London, Hutchinson, 1922.

Short Stories

Something Wrong.   London, Innes, 1893.
Grim Tales.   London, Innes, 1893.
The Butler in Bohemia, with Oswald Barron.   London, Drane, 1894.
In Homespun.   London, Lane, and Boston, Roberts, 1896.
Thirteen Ways Home.   London, Anthony Treherne, 1901.
The Literary Sense.   London, Methuen, and New York, Macmillan, 1903.
Man and Maid.   London, Unwin, 1906.
These Little Ones.   London, George Allen, 1909.
Fear.   London, Stanley Paul, 1910.
To the Adventurous.   London, Hutchinson, 1923.

Verse

Lays and Legends.   London and New York, Longman, 2 vols., 1886, 1892.
The Lily and the Cross.   London, Griffith Farran, and New York, Dutton, 1887.
The Star of Bethlehem.   London, Nister, 1897.
Leaves of Life.   London and New York, Longman, 1888.
The Better Part and Other Poems.   London, Drane, 1888.
Easter-Tide: Poems, with Caris Brooke.   London, Drane, and New York, Dutton,
   1888.
The Time of Roses, with Caris Brooke and others.   London, Drane, 1888.
By Land and Sea.   London, Drane, 1888.
Landscape and Song.   London, Drane, and New York, Dutton, 1888.
The Message of the Dove: An Easter Poem.   London, Drane, and New York, Dutton,
   1888.
The Lilies Round the Cross: An Easter Memorial, with Helen J. Wood.   London,
   Nister, and New York, Dutton, 1889.
Corals and Sea Songs.   London, Nister, 1889.

Life's Sunny Side, with others.   London, Nister, 1890.

Sweet Lavender.   London, Nister, 1892.

Flowers I Bring and Songs I Sing (as E. Bland), with H.M. Burnside and A. Scanes.   London, Raphael Tuck, 1893.

Holly and Mistletoe: A Book of Christmas Verse, with Norman Gale and Richard Le Gallienne.   London, Ward, 1895.

A Pomander of Verse.   London, Lane, and Chicago, McClurg, 1895.

Rose Leaves.   London, Nister, 1895.

Songs of Love and Empire.   London, Constable, 1898.

The Rainbow and the Rose.   London and New York, Longman, 1905.

Ballads and Lyrics of Socialism, 1883–1908.   London, Fabian Society, 1908.

Jesus in London: A Poem.   London, Fifield, 1908.

Ballads and Verses of the Spiritual Life.   London, Elkin Mathews, 1911.

Garden Poems.   London, Collins, 1912.

Many Voices: Poems.   London, Hutchinson, 1922.

Plays

A Family Novelette, with Oswald Barron (produced London, 1894).

The King's Highway (produced London, 1905).

The Philandrist; or, The Lady Fortune-Teller, with Dorothea Deakin (produced London, 1905).

The Magicians's Heart (produced London, 1907).

Unexceptionable References (produced London, 1912).

Other

Wings and the Child; or, The Building of Magic Cities.   London, Hodder and Stoughton, and New York, Doran, 1913.

Editor, *Battle Songs.*   London, Max Goschen, 1914.

Editor, *Essays*, by Hubert Bland.   London, Max Goschen, 1914.

Critical Studies: *E. Nesbit: A Biography* by Doris Langley Moore, London, Benn, 1933, revised edition, Philadelphia, Chilton, 1966, Benn, 1967; *Magic and the Magician: E. Nesbit and Her Children's Books* by Noel Streatfeild, London, Benn, and New York, Abelard Schuman, 1958; *E. Nesbit* by Anthea Bell, London, Bodley Head, 1960, New York, Walck, 1964.

*   *   *

E. Nesbit was one of those writers who do not perceive when they have found their level, and repine for the career they think they should have had in some other field of literature. She believed in herself primarily as a poet, but her quite numerous books of verse are now wholly neglected while the tales she wrote for children "to keep the house going" are recognized as little masterpieces of ingenuity and humour.

They fall into two categories, those based on magic and fantasy as in fairy tales from time immemorial, and those which are realistic and credible comedies of juvenile behaviour. To the first group belongs the trilogy which comprises *Five Children and It, The Phoenix and the Carpet*, and *The Story of the Amulet*. The major works in the second group also form a trilogy, *The Story of the Treasure Seekers, The Wouldbegoods*, and *The New Treasure Seekers*. Each volume can be read independently of the others. It is hard to choose between the two *genres*, in both of which, though imitated, E. Nesbit remains inimitable.

The protagonists, whether the plot hinges on magic or the adventures and misadventures of the human child, are usually families of what was then average size – four or five – with parents who are often got out of the way by absence abroad or some other simple expedient for leaving the children to their own world. Since they are differentiated by age as well as character, young readers can identify either with the eldest, aged about 11 to 14, or the little ones from 6 upwards. The smallest may be an infant. With no trace of priggishness, the elder ones, whether girls or boys, feel protective responsibility towards the others. E. Nesbit had little interest in school life and her *dramatis personae* seldom appear in situations where conformity and discipline are admired. Their virtues are courage, kindliness, a high sense of honour, and good manners, on which she lays particular stress.

Unlike most of her Victorian predecessors, she never intrudes religion, there are no pious death-bed scenes, no conversions or serious repentances. Wrongdoers are assigned only minor parts. "She was not a nice woman, and I am glad to say that she goes out of this story almost at once" – such is her typical way of dismissing a necessary but dislikable instrument of the story in *Harding's Luck*. Except when they can be given amusing roles, of which fortunately she creates many, her grown-ups tend to be somewhat sentimentalized.

The children's background is in general a rather hard-up section of the middle class. There is little pocket money, and treats that have to be paid for are scarce. E. Nesbit was an active pioneering socialist and a founder member of the Fabian Society, but she was able to combine its tenets, not very consistently, with unashamed imperialism and conventional, though unobtrusive, patriotism. In this respect her children are as truly Edwardian as the clothes they wear in the delightful illustrations, chiefly by H.R. Millar.

Although she occasionally touches with sympathy on the overworked and unprivileged, she does not allow political creeds to shape her narratives, and indeed she is more inclined to idealize the pre-industrial past than to look forward to a progressive future. The hero of *Harding's Luck*, a sequel to *The House of Arden*, is a crippled boy from the slums of Deptford. She describes both him and his squalid home with down-to-earth conviction, for she knew the living conditions of the poor through the charities she organized, but she provides him with aristocratic ancestors and noble aspirations, nor, when she has her youthful audience in view, does she recommend any subversion of the existing social order. She took a pride in not preaching at children and never writing down to them. Her prose, lucid and unpretentious but not over-simplified, lends itself perfectly to being read aloud.

The authors who influenced her most were probably Dickens, to whom she was devoted, though, in her youth, he had been decidedly out of fashion, Rudyard Kipling, and F. Anstey. The last-named certainly inspired the turn her imagination took when she depicted normal, everyday people caught up in amazing supernatural situations. Like him, she dealt with such manifestations humorously and avoided – at least in stories for juveniles – anything that might be frightening. Her magical creatures, the Psammead, the Phoenix, and the Mouldiwarp, are all endearing personalities in their own right. When she introduced historic scenes or distant lands, she took considerable trouble over the correctness of local colour, but always with a light touch and a knack for singling out features entertaining to a child.

After her comic sense, perhaps her greatest strength is her keen memory for the details which catch the eyes and ears of childhood, and which somehow she contrives to bring copiously into every tale without in the least slowing up her answers to the eager question: "What happens next?"

—Doris Langley Moore

NESS, Evaline. American. Born in Union City, Ohio, 24 April 1911. Educated at Ball State Teachers College, Muncie, Indiana, 1931–32; Chicago Art Institute, 1933–35; Corcoran School of Art, Washington, D.C., 1943–45; Art Students' League, New York, 1947; Accademia Della Belles Artes, Rome, 1951–52. Married the law enforcement officer Eliot Ness in 1938 (died, 1957). Teacher of children's art classes, Corcoran School of Art,

1945–46, and Parsons School of Design, New York, 1959–60; fashion illustrator, Saks Fifth Avenue, New York, and magazine illustrator, 1946–49. Since 1959, free-lance illustrator. Recipient: *New York Times* award, for illustration, 1961, 1964, 1965; American Library Association Caldecott Medal, 1967. Address: c/o Charles Scribner's Sons Inc., 597 Fifth Avenue, New York, New York 10017, U.S.A.

PUBLICATIONS FOR CHILDREN (illustrated by the author)

Fiction

> *A Gift for Sula Sula.* New York, Scribner, 1963.
> *Josefina February.* New York, Scribner, 1963; London, Chatto Boyd and Oliver, 1970.
> *Exactly Alike.* New York, Scribner, 1964; Edinburgh, Oliver and Boyd, 1968.
> *Pavo and the Princess.* New York, Scribner, 1964.
> *A Double Discovery.* New York, Scribner, 1965.
> *Sam, Bangs, and Moonshine.* New York, Holt Rinehart, 1966; London, Bodley Head, 1967.
> *The Girl and the Goatherd; or, This and That and Thus and So.* New York, Dutton, 1970.
> *Do You Have the Time, Lydia?* New York, Dutton, 1971; London, Bodley Head, 1972.
> *Yeck Eck.* New York, Dutton, 1974.

Other

> *Long, Broad, and Quickeye.* New York, Scribner, 1969; London, Chatto Boyd and Oliver, 1971.
> *American Colonial Paper House: To Cut Out and Color.* New York, Scribner, 1975.
> *A Paper Palace: To Cut Out and Color.* New York, Scribner, 1976.
> *Four Rooms from the Metropolitan Museum of Art: To Cut Out and Color.* New York, Scribner, 1977.

> Editor, *Amelia Mixed the Mustard and Other Poems* (anthology). New York, Scribner, 1975.

Illustrator: *The Story of Ophelia* by Mary J. Gibbons, 1954; *The Bridge* by Charles Ogburn, Jr., 1957; *The Sherwood Ring* by Elizabeth Pope, 1958; *Lonely Maria*, 1960, and *The Princess and the Lion*, 1963, by Elizabeth Coatsworth; *Ondine* by Maurice Osborne, 1960; *Across from Indian Shore* by Barbara Robinson, 1962; *Where Did Josie Go?*, 1962, *Josie and the Snow*, 1964, and *Josie's Buttercup*, 1967, all by Helen Buckley; *Thistle and Thyme* edited by Sorche Nic Leodhas, 1962, and *All in a Morning Early*, 1963, and *Kellyburn Braes*, 1968, by Nic Leodhas; *Macaroon*, 1962, and *Candle Tales*, 1964, by Julia W. Cunningham; *Funny Town* by Eve Merriam, 1963; *A Pocketful of Cricket* by Rebecca Caudill, 1964; *Coll and His White Pig*, 1965, and *The Truthful Harp*, 1967, by Lloyd Alexander; *Favorite Fairy Tales Told in Italy* edited by Virginia Haviland, 1965; *Tom Tit Tot: An English Folk Tale*, 1965; *Pierino and the Bell* by Sylvia Cassedy, 1966; *Mr. Miacca: An English Folk Tale*, 1967; *Some of the Days of Everett Anderson*, 1970, *Everett Anderson's Christmas Coming*, 1972, and *Don't You Remember?*, 1973, all by Lucille Clifton; *Joey and the Birthday Present*, 1971, and *The Wizard's Tears*, 1975, by Maxine Kumin; *Old Mother Hubbard and Her Dog* by Sarah Catherine Martin, 1972; *The Woman of the Wood* by Algernon Black, 1973; *The Steamroller* by Margaret Wise Brown, 1975; *The Lives of My Cat Alfred* by Nathan Zimelman, 1976; *The Warmint* by Walter de la Mare, 1976.

*   *   *

Evaline Ness is, in my opinion, the most brilliant and original illustrator of children's books in America today. But she has also written as well as illustrated several books, has created two books on doll houses, and has assembled a collection of children's poetry called *Amelia Mixed the Mustard and Other Poems*.

Each of her own books is for younger children, and each I consider an excellent example of that category. Like another writer-illustrator, Maurice Sendak, who is usually billed above her (but not by me), her texts are as carefully conceived as is her artwork; and both are blended into so satisfactory a whole that it's difficult to consider them separately.

Take *Yeck Eck*, for example. It begins, "This small person, Tana Jones, had everything she wanted except the thing she wanted most. A BABY." As the humorous fantasy unfolds, a friend with numerous younger siblings donates a baby to Tana (which she promptly names Agift). Agift cries, "Yeck, Eck!" – words interpreted by Tana to mean, "Take me!" As more and more babies are donated to her, the text spills over onto the bibs and dresses and walls – the words become part of the art. But even dream wishes end, when the babies prefer an adult caregiver to Tana. Now hearing their burbling cries, Tana sadly asks herself, "What does Yeck-Eck mean?" And herself answers, "Only a baby knows."

If the art and text interweave here to create a charming whole, what of the message? In the age of Women's Lib, how does Ms. Ness dare to create a heroine who wants to play with babies rather than paints, skates or trucks? (Shh! Many children still agree with Tana!)

The answer is, Evaline Ness never cuts her cloth – or her stories – to fit the fad of the moment; but, on the other hand, she is often in advance of the current trend. In a book called *The Girl and the Goatherd*, written before the Women's Movement gained national notice, a girl seeks the traditional gift of beauty. But before she receives that desired beauty, she wins the love of the Goatherd who likes her as she is; and beauty, once attained, proves worthless. A crotchety, stubborn heroine who comes to comprehend the superficial value of physical perfection? An unlikely theme for those days!

Or consider *Do You Have the Time, Lydia?* A hectic activist, Lydia races from one non-traditional interest to another. Yet, unlike that of the present crop of feminist writers, the activism here is only the background of the story, which focuses rather on Lydia's inability to finish a job and her insensitivity to her younger brother. Though the story's theme is a universal one of changing values, the background images may well linger longer in young readers' memories than the more strident messages received from some feminist presses.

All Ms. Ness' protagonists are girls except one – the boy in her illustrations to the scary English folktale, *Mr. Miacca*. And each girl is a unique creation both in character and in the problems she faces; perhaps, considering the interchangeability of more prolific authors' characters, in Ms. Ness' case, less is more. And not only do the girls assume a three-dimensional reality, the adults too, when present, are unique individuals. The only three families shown are single-parent families. The girl in *Exactly Alike* lives with younger twin brothers and a mother constantly busy with sewing to sustain the family. The girl must take care of the naughty, teasing twins, a job that would tax an adult's patience. But she learns to cope with the situation by persistence and initiative.

In *Yeck Eck*, Tana lives with a father who drives a taxicab; Josefina, in *Josefina February*, lives with a poor farmer uncle; and in Ms. Ness' most famous book, *Sam, Bangs, and Moonshine* (a Caldecott Award winner), the young Samantha, called Sam, lives with a fisherman father.

Sam has "the reckless habit of lying." Or, as her father implores her, "Talk real, not moonshine .... Moonshine is flummadiddle. Real is the opposite." Sam's mother is dead – but not to Sam. In the "moonshine" she spins to her cat Bangs, to her friend Thomas, and to herself, she sees her mother as a mermaid. Then she sends Thomas on a quest for an imaginary kangaroo which has gone to live with her mermaid mother in a seacave; and she ignores her conscience, which speaks through Bangs, of the dangers of the incoming tide. Bangs goes after Thomas, and both seem lost when a sudden storm hits the coast.

At this point, a dedicated feminist might have Sam involved in the active rescue work; but Ms. Ness gives Sam the harder job – that of waiting alone with her suffering. And in that suffering (which all of us sometimes endure), Sam finally recognizes that "real" is Thomas, is

Bangs, is no mother. But her perceptive father reassures her that "there is good moonshine and bad moonshine – it's just important to know the difference." And Sam, like Josefina February, is able to make a hard choice to help a friend.

Evaline Ness' words speak for themselves; their poetry, their clarity, their honesty well match her subtle but straightforward portraits of children. Unlike the present trend of presenting "ugly" children under the guise of reality, Evaline Ness gives us, in both words and pictures, children as they really are – beautiful, straight and honest, involved in the pleasures and problems of life.

—Betty Boegehold

NEVILLE, Emily Cheney. American. Born in Manchester, Connecticut, 28 December 1919. Educated at Oxford School, 1931–36; Bryn Mawr College, Pennsylvania, A.B. 1940; Albany Law School, New York, J.D. 1976; admitted to the New York bar, 1977. Married Glenn T. Neville in 1948 (died, 1965); has three daughters and two sons. Office worker, 1940–41, and Feature Writer, 1941–44, New York *Daily Mirror.* Recipient: American Library Association Newbery Medal, 1964; Women's International League for Peace and Freedom Jane Addams Award, 1966. Address: Keene Valley, New York 12943, U.S.A.

PUBLICATIONS FOR CHILDREN

Fiction

It's Like This, Cat, illustrated by Emil Weiss. New York, Harper, 1963; London, Angus and Robertson, 1969.
Berries Goodman. New York, Harper, 1965; London, Angus and Robertson, 1970.
The Seventeenth Street Gang, illustrated by Emily McCully. New York, Harper, 1966.
Traveler from a Small Kingdom, illustrated by George Mocniak. New York, Harper, 1968.
Fogarty. New York, Harper, 1969.
Garden of Broken Glass. New York, Delacorte Press, 1975.

Manuscript Collection: Kerlan Collection, University of Minnesota, Minneapolis.

Emily Cheney Neville comments:
I enjoy writing conversation and dialogue, and having characters show themselves by what they say. Therefore the characters are somewhat fragmentary and do not have clearly narrated roles or purposes. No heavy messages. You can show a reader how you think people talk or act, but the child reader can draw his or her own conclusions. I like my books to be a bit funny.

*   *   *

Emily Cheney Neville is the author of several books for children. *Berries Goodman, Fogarty, Garden of Broken Glass,* and *Traveler from a Small Kingdom* among others. One of her books, however, *It's Like This, Cat* has been awarded the Newbery medal. It is notable for its honest rendering of the scenes and sounds of New York City, the natural language of its teenage hero, Dave Mitchell, and the telling of some events not for the squeamish.

It's Like This, Cat is a far cry from the saccharine stories which flooded the children's book market for years about blonde white children who always lived in the suburbs, in pleasant houses, with idyllically married parents — stories which left those children whose circumstances were less rosy feeling deprived. Writers like Emily Neville realize that children face many problems and well designed books can help them clarify and meet their troubles. *It's Like This, Cat* does all this and more.

For one thing, Dave Mitchell's language "feels right." He says, "My pop is full of hot air," or "It must be lousy to be in the city without any family or friends," or "Why do I have a nut for a friend?"

Is this literature for children? Yes, when juxtaposed against the realistic slang-filled speech, we can find the hero describing his day at Coney Island like this: "I kick off my shoes and stand with my feet in the ice water and the sun hot on my chest. Looking out at the horizon with its few ships and some sea gulls and planes overhead, I think: It's mine, all mine. I could go anywhere in the world, I could. Maybe I will." What freedom, what daydreams are conveyed and how natural for a city boy to feel such sensations away from buildings and cement! The words are simple, yet given brightness by contrast. And there is depth, too — the probing of a child's innermost thoughts. These short quotes are only a glimpse of the art with which Emily Neville has crafted this story. New York's skyscrapers, back alleys, parks and zoos are a backdrop for the hero's adventures and difficulties. We suffer with him in his father's lack of understanding, sympathize with him when a kitten is thoughtlessly killed, and enjoy his conversations with the Tom cat that fills a void in his life.

Today's teenager may find some of the expressions dated but the events discussed are recurrent, always new. Dave Mitchell's world, like that of F. Scott Fitzgerald, is a moment of historical time. Parts of it such as Fulton Fish Market have vanished forever, but it is fun to step back and walk through places which cannot be seen again or to find their reality in books even though you have never known the originals.

It's Like This, Cat is satisfying on several levels — it is a good story, well told, and it has something important to say about life. Such qualifications make any book literature and this one has a special niche in children's stories.

— Carolyn T. Kingston

NEWBERRY, Clare Turlay. American. Born in Enterprise, Oregon, 10 April 1903. Educated at the University of Oregon, Eugene, 1921–22; Portland Art Museum School, Oregon, 1922–23; California School of Fine Arts, San Francisco, 1923–24; La Grand Chaumière, Paris, 1930–31. Married Henry Trujillo; one son by first marriage. Painter and illustrator. *Died 12 February 1970.*

PUBLICATIONS FOR CHILDREN (illustrated by the author)

Fiction

Herbert the Lion. New York, Brewer Warren and Putnam, 1931.
Mittens. New York, Harper, 1936; London, Hamish Hamilton, 1937.
Babette. New York, Harper, 1937; London, Hamish Hamilton, 1938.
Barkis. New York, Harper, 1938; London, Hamish Hamilton, 1939.
Cousin Toby. New York and London, Harper, 1939.
April's Kittens. New York, Harper, 1940; London, Hamish Hamilton, 1944.
Lambert's Bargain. New York and London, Harper, 1941.
Marshmallow. New York, Harper, 1942; London, Hamish Hamilton, 1945.
Pandora. New York, Harper, 1944; London, Hamish Hamilton, 1946.

Smudge. New York, Harper, 1948; London, Hamish Hamilton, 1950.
T-Bone, The Baby-Sitter. New York, Harper, 1950.
Percy, Polly, and Pete. New York, Harper, 1952.
Ice Cream for Two. New York, Harper, 1953.
Widget. New York, Harper, 1958.
Frosty. New York, Harper, 1961.

Verse

The Kittens' ABC. New York, Harper, 1946; London, Hamish Hamilton, 1947; revised edition, Harper, 1965.

Other

Cats: A Portfolio. New York and London, Harper, 1943.
Cats and Kittens: A Portfolio of Drawings. New York, Harper, 1956.

PUBLICATIONS FOR ADULTS

Other

Drawing a Cat. New York and London, The Studio, 1940; as *Drawing Cats,* 1943.

*   *   *

Clare Turlay Newberry enjoyed the best of all worlds any writer for young children could hope for. For one thing, many of her simple picture books have been bestsellers. Her works doubtless have a great appeal for many librarians and teachers – and children, of course. Indeed, few writers of picture storybooks could boast of the Newberry accomplishment, that of having one's first book still in print, after almost fifty years. As well, Newberry has received the highest of honors from the critics of her books. Four of her books of fiction have been chosen as runners-up for the prestigious Caldecott Medal. It is obvious that many critics of children's literature find her picture books "charming" (the accolade given her first book by the *Horn Book*).

Newberry gained these distinctions by writing almost exclusively about the lives of domesticated cats. The names Newberry and cats, in fact, have become almost synonymous in children's literature. Newberry obviously depended heavily on her drawings of cats for her stories, sometimes basing her texts on artistic studies of cats she had previously done. With notable exceptions, for example, *Herbert the Lion, Cousin Toby,* and *Lambert's Bargain,* all her books have cats as their central figures. It is said that Newberry, at one point weary of writing exclusively about cats, suggested in half-jest that she do one on a hyena. Curiously enough this came to pass, as *Lambert's Bargain.*

Widget and *April's Kittens* are prime examples of the differing viewpoints Newberry takes in her stories. In *Widget,* as in *Smudge,* for example, she attributes near-human personal characteristics to her animals. They are thus made to think, talk to each other, and react emotionally in human terms. In these instances Newberry knows and tells all that happens in each cat's mentality, discussing the meaning of their behavior. Humans in such books, when they do appear, are shadowy figures of little importance.

In *April's Kittens* and in *Mittens,* however, the cats in her tales are objectively reported with fidelity to the characteristics of their species. Here they become the adjuncts of people, who dominate the action.

Common to Newberry's stories, aimed at the 4 to 7 age-group, is the straightforwardness of her narratives. Each of her books has a simple, easily understandable plot, full of concise, detailed and highly-realistic details. There is almost never any hint of social commentary or irony and few if any surprises. Most often her books revert to little more than the most obvious of cat behavior. While Newberry sometimes allows a human type of communication among her cats, the humans with whom they are associated are always shown to be their lovable masters (yet kept out of the range of feline discourse). With this warm human-cat relationship in mind, Newberry keeps the tone of her books compassionate and highly sentimental. (*Lambert's Bargain* is the exception here. Its slapstick antics and somewhat broad humor contrast sharply with Newberry's other books.) Her obvious intent is to evoke in the young child friendly and responsible attitudes toward animals and, indirectly, healthy feelings toward parents. For example, the mother cat's solicitude in *Widget* is something a child is sure to apprehend.

As for the quality of Newberry's literary output, it is Arbuthnot's judgment that her "little books have no importance as literature." This critic opines that it is only the kindly and tender appeal of her illustrations that make her books worthwhile. This is an unfair critique, however, especially when applied to all of Newberry's works. It is more accurate to say that her texts are bewilderingly uneven in quality. The pointlessness of texts such as *Smudge*, a book almost totally lacking in inventiveness or in any movement to a literary end, is Newberry at her worst. On the other hand, several of them do have some literary merit. In *April's Kittens*, for example, Newberry's power in handling dialogue and dramatic action are evident. Here she develops, in a highly empathetic manner, honest emotional scenes depicting the young child's versus the adult's view of life. While this story closes on a melodramatic note, it nonetheless does maintain an aura of suspense and anticipation. Here we probably have the best in Newberry's contribution to children's literature.

—Patrick Groff

NICHOLS, (John) Beverley. British. Born in Bristol, 9 September 1898. Educated at Marlborough College; Balliol College, Oxford (Editor, *Isis*; Founding Editor, *The Oxford Outlook*; President, Oxford Union), B.A. Drama Critic, *The Weekly Dispatch*, 1926; Editor, *The American Sketch*, New York, 1928–29. Address: Sudbrook Cottage, Ham Common, Surrey, England.

PUBLICATIONS FOR CHILDREN

Fiction

The Tree That Sat Down, illustrated by Isobel and John Morton Sale. London, Cape, 1945.
The Stream That Stood Still, illustrated by Richard Kennedy. London, Cape, 1948.
The Mountain of Magic, illustrated by Peggy Fortnum. London, Cape, 1950.
The Wickedest Witch in the World, illustrated by Robin Jacques. London, W.H. Allen, 1971.

PUBLICATIONS FOR ADULTS

Novels

Prelude. London, Chatto and Windus, 1920.
Patchwork. London, Chatto and Windus, 1921; New York, Holt, 1922.
Self. London, Chatto and Windus, 1922.
Crazy Pavements. London, Cape, and New York, Doran, 1927.
Evensong. London, Cape, and New York, Doubleday, 1932.

Revue. London, Cape, and New York, Doubleday, 1939.

Men Do Not Weep. London, Cape, 1941; New York, Harcourt Brace, 1942.

Laughter on the Stairs. London, Cape, 1953; New York, Dutton, 1954.

No Man's Secret. London, Hutchinson, and New York, Dutton, 1954.

The Moonflower. London, Hutchinson, 1955; as *The Moonflower Murder*, New York, Dutton, 1955.

Death to Slow Music. London, Hutchinson, and New York, Dutton, 1956.

Sunlight on the Lawn. London, Cape, and New York, Dutton, 1956.

The Rich Die Hard. London, Hutchinson, 1957; New York, Dutton, 1958.

Murder by Request. London, Hutchinson, and New York, Dutton, 1960.

Plays

Picnic (revue; composer only) (produced London, 1927).

Many Happy Returns (revue; composer only), by Herbert Farjeon (produced London, 1928).

The Stag (produced London, 1929). Included in *Failures*, 1933.

Cochran's 1930 Revue, music by Nichols and Vivian Ellis (produced London, 1930).

Avalanche (produced Edinburgh, 1931; London, 1932). Included in *Failures*, 1933.

Evensong, with Edward Knoblock, adaptation of the novel by Nichols (produced London, 1932; New York, 1933). London and New York, French, 1933.

When the Crash Comes (produced Birmingham, 1933). Included in *Failures*, 1933.

Failures: Three Plays (includes *The Stag, Avalanche, When the Crash Comes*). London, Cape, and New York, Peter Smith, 1933.

Mesmer (produced London, 1938). London, Cape, 1937.

Floodlight, music by Nichols (produced London, 1937).

Shadow of the Vine (produced London, 1954). London, Cape, 1949.

Other Plays: *Song on the Wind*, 1948; *Lady's Guide*, 1950; *La Plume de ma tante*, 1953.

Other

25, Being a Young Man's Candid Recollections of His Elders and Betters. London, Cape, and New York, Doran, 1926.

Are They the Same at Home? Being a Series of Bouquets Diffidently Distributed. London, Cape, and New York, Doran, 1927.

The Star-Spangled Manner. London, Cape, and New York, Doubleday, 1928.

Women and Children Last. London, Cape, and New York, Doubleday, 1931.

Down the Garden Path. London, Cape, and New York, Doubleday, 1932.

For Adults Only. London, Cape, 1932; New York, Doubleday, 1933.

In the Next War I Shall Be a Conscientious Objector. London, Friends' Peace Committee, 1932.

Cry Havoc! London, Cape, and New York, Doubleday, 1933.

Puck at Brighton: The Official Handbook of the Corporation of Brighton. Brighton, Corporation of Brighton, 1933.

A Thatched Roof. London, Cape, and New York, Doubleday, 1933.

The Valet as Historian. London, Forsyth, 1934.

A Village in a Valley. London, Cape, and New York, Doubleday, 1934.

How Does Your Garden Grow? (broadcast talks), with others. London, Allen and Unwin, and New York, Doubleday, 1935.

The Fool Hath Said. London, Cape, and New York, Doubleday, 1936.

No Place Like Home (travel). London, Cape, and New York, Doubleday, 1936.

News of England; or, A Country Without a Hero. London, Cape, and New York, Doubleday, 1938.

Green Grows the City: The Story of a London Garden. London, Cape, and New York, Harcourt Brace, 1939.

Verdict on India. London, Cape, and New York, Harcourt Brace, 1944.

All I Could Never Be: Some Recollections. London, Cape, 1949; New York, Dutton, 1952.

Yours Sincerely (*Woman's Own* articles), with Monica Dickens. London, Newnes, 1949.

Uncle Samson (on America). London, Evans, 1950.

Merry Hall. London, Cape, 1951; New York, Dutton, 1953.

A Pilgrim's Progress. London, Cape, 1952.

The Queen's Coronation Day: The Pictorial Record of the Great Occasion. London, Pitkin, 1953.

Cat Book. London, Nelson, 1955.

The Sweet and Twenties. London, Weidenfeld and Nicolson, 1958.

Cats' ABC. London, Cape, and New York, Dutton, 1960.

Cats' XYZ. London, Cape, and New York, Dutton, 1961.

Garden Open Today. London, Cape, and New York, Dutton, 1963.

Forty Favourite Flowers. London, Studio Vista, 1964; New York, St. Martin's Press, 1965.

Flowers That Be. London, Cape, and New York, St. Martin's Press, 1966.

A Case of Human Bondage (on Somerset Maugham). London, Secker and Warburg, 1966.

The Art of Flower Arrangement. London, Collins, and New York, Viking Press, 1967.

Garden Open Tomorrow. London, Heinemann, 1968; New York, Dodd Mead, 1969.

The Sun in My Eyes; or, How Not to Go Around the World. London, Heinemann, 1969.

Father Figure (on alcoholism). London, Heinemann, and New York, Simon and Schuster, 1972.

Down the Kitchen Sink (autobiography). London, W.H. Allen, 1974.

Cats' A-Z. London, W.H. Allen, 1977.

Editor, *A Book of Old Ballads.* London, Hutchinson, and New York, Loring and Mussey, 1934.

*   *   *

To adults, Beverley Nichols is a journalist and literary personality, but to children of the 1950's he was something else – the author of three marvellous stories about the animals of the Magic Wood, where Good battles Evil on behalf of the innocent animals who live there.

The Tree That Sat Down tells of Judy and her grandmother who run the Shop under the Willow Tree, selling items such as food, herbs, toys for young animals, quills for porcupines, gargle for nightingales, menus for moths …. Competition arrives when Old and Young Sam, an unpleasant couple, open their own shop to make a profit and cheat the animals, and when they can't beat the good humans, employ a witch. Miss Smith, the Witch, is a great comic creation, 383 years old, a not-very-successful witch whose pets are three darling toads. She is utterly evil, poisons the whole stock of the Shop under the Tree, and nearly poisons Judy too, but in the end Good triumphs, Miss Smith and the Sams flee the wood and Judy marries a fairytale Prince.

In *The Stream That Stood Still* Young Sam and Miss Smith plan revenge on Judy through her children Jack and Jill. They turn Jack into a fish, and Jill has to find the magic to live underwater so that she can search for him, with the fishes' help. He has been trapped by the witch's ally, the evil pike who was once a wicked businessman in the City (satirical touch). To save him the loyal Beavers build a dam which halts the stream, trapping the pike in the dry bed.

The last of the trilogy, *The Mountain of Magic*, takes Jack and Jill to explore the Mountain with its animals, together with the mysterious Imp. Miss Smith and Sam also return to finish off the children, and are finally defeated. This book has the most dramatic climax and pathetic ending, first with Mr. Butterfly's desperate flight up the Mountain to fetch help, and then with Mr. Crow's heroic self-sacrifice and death to save the other animals.

These fairy-tales combine old-fashioned elements like talking animals and witches with modern satire in dialogue and character. Witches have brought their magic up to date: they read newspapers like *The Weekly Cauldron* and *The Witch's Evening Wail*, keep magical ingredients in the fridge and disguise their broomsticks as vacuum cleaners. Animal society has much in common with human society in its hierarchical structure, with snobs, social climbers and the pompous head of the local community, Mr. Justice Owl of the Wood, Lord Salmon of the Stream (to whom one must *not* mention cans), and Mr. Eagle of the Mountain. Most touching are the Beavers, compulsive dam-builders. Even so, we can agree with Mr. Justice Owl's opinion of humans: "I have very little hope for the human race ... very little. It will take them at least a million years to reach the level of animals ...."

Twenty years later Beverley Nichols tried to repeat his success with *The Wickedest Witch in the World*. Miss Smith reappears, starts a Wicked Laundry, and is foiled by Judy and her grandmother. Although it is not up to the standard of the trilogy, as the ideas are repetitious and the way he addresses his child readers has become sentimental, fans of Miss Smith will enjoy seeing her defeated once again.

—Jessica Kemball-Cook

———————————

NICHOLS, Ruth. Canadian. Born in Toronto, Ontario, 4 March 1948. Educated at the University of British Columbia, Vancouver, B.A. (honours) 1969; McMaster University, Hamilton, Ontario, M.A. 1972, Ph.D. 1977. Married W.N. Houston in 1974. Recipient: Canada Council Fellowship, 1972, 1973, 1974. Address: c/o Macmillan Company of Canada Ltd., 70 Bond Street, Toronto, Ontario M5B 1X3, Canada.

PUBLICATIONS FOR CHILDREN

Fiction

> *A Walk Out of the World*, illustrated by Trina Schart Hyman.   Toronto, Longman, and New York, Harcourt Brace, 1969.
> *The Marrow of the World*, illustrated by Trina Schart Hyman.   Toronto, Macmillan, and New York, Atheneum, 1972.

PUBLICATIONS FOR ADULTS

Novels

> *Ceremony of Innocence.*   London, Faber, 1969.
> *Song of the Pearl.*   Toronto, Macmillan, and New York, Atheneum, 1976.

Manuscript Collection: Mills Memorial Library, McMaster University, Hamilton, Ontario.

Ruth Nichols comments:
    The process of my development can be followed in print since my earliest published book, *A Walk Out of the World*, was published when I was 21, and other books have followed at

regular intervals. Most of these are fantasy. I believe fantasy provides a valid and important means of examining the human passions and the nature of our relationship to reality.

*   *   *

For its readers fantasy embodies the will's ability to transcend the known. But the rationale for that metaphysical act must be expressed in a time-tested formula that leads the way through the labyrinths of fantasy to a satisfying conclusion. If the body cannot follow the mind in its passage through eons of time past, time to come, and worlds in space, the compensation for this lack lies in the reality of words to say that it can be done.

In her autobiographical novel, *Ceremony of Innocence* Ruth Nichols traces her precocious contact with her memory of eternity: she professes a metaphysical contact that gives her stories the roots of reality and the limbs of fantasy. Her almost total recall of childhood encounters and conversations allows her to develop her plot on several planes, one of which is the intuitive. This novel seems to state the apologia for her familiarity with the psychic world.

Ruth Nichols writes about what she knows, the first principle of convincing composition. She begins her two fantasies for children in places known to her: in Ontario's Georgian Bay cottage country in *The Marrow of the World; A Walk Out of the World* is into a Vancouver park out of a crowded apartment house. But she intuits so much more than the given physical settings that place her books in Canada. She is first of this world, then of another, a remembered one in which her second self finds a friendly ambience to range metaphysically.

She understands the majesty of ritual, and she initiates her heroes in ritual. She tells the reader too that there is a way that things are done, and that way has an almost fateful logic. Her disciplined pen hews to the moral line as good vanquishes evil; she is quite sure what good is. The other-worldly characters are all her own wishes come true – they do as she bids, even in the delicious pursuit of evil. For it is never in question, the ending. The way however must be strewn with pitfalls so that the good can be fully and finally appreciated. But even it has a bitter sweetness. This world must be borne yet a space, while the untranscended life measures out its days on earth. Then the promised second walk out of the world for Tobit and Judith will be the last one. In *The Marrow of the World* Philip and Linda carry tangible marks of their time travel; their promised gift they will carry even during their terrestrial life.

These chosen earthlings feel emotion and sensations like pain, but they intuit more than they understand of their roles through the uncharted forests of fantasy. They only know they must be good people. Judith and Tobit are more sympathetic characters than Philip and Linda in *The Marrow*; they are not so remote from their readers' longing for the impossible. In *The Marrow* the author has perfected the stylization of her quest fantasy and the characters are altogether more decisive, colder. And their readers fear the shadows more, and do not trust the author as totally.

Ruth Nichols wrote *A Walk Out of the World* when she was 18, and won the Canadian Association of Children's Librarians' Bronze Medal for the best book of the year in 1972 for *The Marrow of the World*. These first works are exemplars of style; she learned the rudiments early. Now only the elements will be expanded as she matures, and she may yet develop into Canada's very best fantasist.

—Irma McDonough

NORMAN, Lilith.   Australian.   Born in Sydney, New South Wales, 27 November 1927. Educated at Sydney Girls' High School, 1940–44. Library Assistant, Newtown Library, Sydney, 1947–49; Telephonist, Bonnington Hotel, London, 1950–51; Sales Assistant, Angus and Robertson Books, Sydney, 1952–53; Nurse, Balmain District Hospital, Sydney,

1953–56; Library Assistant, 1956–58, Research Officer, 1958–66, and Children's Librarian, 1966–70, Sydney Public Library. Assistant Editor, 1970–76, and since 1976, Editor, New South Wales Department of Education *School Magazine*. Agent: Curtis Brown (Australia) Pty. Ltd., P.O. Box 19, Paddington, New South Wales 2021, Australia.

Publications for Children

Fiction

Climb a Lonely Hill.   London, Collins, 1970; New York, Walck, 1972.
The Shape of Three.   London, Collins, 1971; New York, Walck, 1972.
The Flame Takers.   Sydney and London, Collins, 1973.
A Dream of Seas.   Sydney, Collins, 1978.

Plays

Television Play: in *Catch Kandy* series, 1973.

Short plays published in *School Magazine*, Sydney.

Other

Mockingbird-Man (reader).   Sydney, Hodder and Stoughton, 1977.

Publications for Adults

Other

The City of Sydney: Official Guide.   Sydney, City Council, 1959.
Facts about Sydney.   Sydney, City Council, 1959.
Asia: A Select Reading List.   Sydney, City Council, 1959.
Some Notes on the Early Land Grants at Potts Point.   Sydney, City Council, 1959.
A History of the City of Sydney Public Library.   Sydney, City Council, 1960.
Notes on the Glebe.   Sydney, City Council, 1960.
Historical Notes on Paddington.   Sydney, City Council, 1961.
Historical Notes on Newtown.   Sydney, City Council, 1962.

Manuscript Collection: School of Librarianship, University of New South Wales, Kensington.

Lilith Norman comments:

I managed to avoid becoming a writer for quite a long time, mainly, I think, because it seemed like very hard work for a very speculative result. It wasn't until I started working as a children's librarian that I realised *these* were the books I wanted to write. I was lucky, for as well as being perhaps the most rewarding and personal form of writing, it was also one of the most disciplined. And I believe discipline is the forgotten word of our times. Discipline in writing, to me, means honing your style, your rhythm, and, most of all, your own thinking, till everything has a true sharp edge, as precise and delicate as a craftsman's tool. I like to write about ordinary children trying to cope, for I believe that most of us can cope with whatever is thrown at us, *if we really have to* -- otherwise we'd all be living in caves still. I've written about realistic situations in *Climb a Lonely Hill* and *The Shape of Three*, but I've written fantasy in *The Flame Takers*. And there's the rub! Having put a tentative toe in the great ocean of fantasy, everything else seems flat and commonplace. I want to swim and dive in that ocean, I want it to become my home. I don't know if I can, but I shall have to try, with, perhaps, occasional forays back to land for relaxation.

*   *   *

If there is any theme common to Lilith Norman's very diverse books, it is the effect of environment on character. Her children are products of their backgrounds, which are quite different in every novel.

In *Climb a Lonely Hill* there is an almost totally deprived home where the mother's early death caused the father to squander what little money he had on drink. Jack, his teenage son, reacts to this by being conformist and reluctant to make decisions, whereas Susan, his daughter, is sharp and resourceful beyond her years. Yet when the children have to survive in the harsh outback after a car crash which kills their uncle, it is Jack who has to take command because Susan's foot is injured, and in the fight against heat, dust, thirst and flies he finally learns initiative and with it self-respect.

The exploration of heredity and environment is central to *The Shape of Three*. Here fraternal twins Shane and Greg Herbert accidentally meet Bruce Cunningham, who is the exact replica of Greg. Subsequent investigation reveals that they were all born in Sydney on the same night but a hospital emergency had caused the babies to be muddled. Greg and Bruce are the true identical twins and Shane is the Cunningham. The climax of the story comes when the children are restored to their rightful families and bewildered Bruce finds himself in the hurly-burly of a large warm Roman Catholic lower-middle class home, whereas the bereft Shane has to adjust to being the only child of a wealthy Protestant estate-agent father and neurotic perfectionist mother. The convincing contrast drawn between the Herbert and Cunningham households highlights the poignancy of Bruce and Shane's dilemmas as they struggle not only with uprooting but with vague feelings of hereditary kinship for their new-found relatives.

The background of *The Flame Takers* is different again, and there is another original theme – that of the sudden and inexplicable dying of talent. Here not only professional actor parents but also their musical son suddenly lose their inspirational flame and become bourgeois and materialistic. These changes are somehow connected with a sadistic schoolmaster and a fat chess-playing German, but no real explanation is given and the book's strengths lie less in plot than in the exploration of yet another type of family and of central Sydney rather than the suburbs of the previous novel.

Lilith Norman has shown courage and originality in tackling unusual subjects. She has a keen ear for Australian speech patterns and dialogue. She is an astute observer and whether depicting people or places she accurately portrays the diversity of an emerging nation in a time-worn continent.

—Betty Gilderdale

NORTH, Sterling. American. Born near Edgerton, Wisconsin, 4 November 1906. Educated at the University of Chicago, A.B. 1929. Married Gladys Buchanan in 1927; one son and one daughter. Reporter, 1929–31, and Literary Editor, 1932–43, Chicago *Daily News*; Literary Editor, New York *Post*, 1943–49, and New York *World Telegram and Sun*, 1949–56; Founding Editor, North Star Books, Houghton Mifflin, publishers, Boston, 1957–64. *Died 21 December 1974.*

PUBLICATIONS FOR CHILDREN

Fiction

The Five Little Bears, illustrated by Clarence Biers and Hazel Frazee.   Chicago, Rand
   McNally, 1935; London, Shaw, 1940.
The Zipper ABC Book, illustrated by Keith Ward.   Chicago, Rand McNally, 1937.
Greased Lightning, illustrated by Kurt Wiese.   Philadelphia, Winston, 1940.
Midnight and Jeremiah, illustrated by Kurt Wiese.   Philadelphia, Winston, 1943.
The Birthday of Little Jesus, illustrated by Valenti Angelo.   New York, Grosset and
   Dunlap, 1952; Manchester, World Distributors, 1953.
Son of the Lamp-Maker: The Story of a Boy Who Knew Jesus, illustrated by Manning
   Lee.   Chicago, Rand McNally, 1956.
The Wolfling, illustrated by John Schoenherr.   New York, Dutton, 1969; London,
   Heinemann, 1970.

Other

Abe Lincoln: Log Cabin to White House, illustrated by Lee Ames.   New York, Random
   House, 1956.
George Washington, Frontier Colonel, illustrated by Lee Ames.   New York, Random
   House, 1957.
Young Thomas Edison, illustrated by William Barss.   Boston, Houghton Mifflin, 1958.
Thoreau of Walden Pond, illustrated by Harve Stein.   Boston, Houghton Mifflin, 1959.
Captured by the Mohawks and Other Adventures of Radisson, illustrated by Victor
   Mays.   Boston, Houghton Mifflin, 1960.
Mark Twain and the River, illustrated by Victor Mays.   Boston, Houghton Mifflin,
   1961.
The First Steamboat on the Mississippi, illustrated by Victor Mays.   Boston, Houghton
   Mifflin, 1962.
Rascal: A Memoir of a Better Era, illustrated by John Schoenherr.   New York, Dutton,
   1963; as *Rascal: The True Story of a Pet Raccoon*, London, Hodder and Stoughton,
   1963; abridged edition, as *Little Rascal*, New York, Dutton, 1965; Leicester,
   Brockhampton Press, 1966.

PUBLICATIONS FOR ADULTS

Novels

Midsummer Madness.   New York, Grosset and Dunlap, 1933.
Tiger.   Chicago, Reilly and Lee, 1933.
Plowing on Sunday.   New York, Macmillan, 1934.
Night Outlasts the Whippoorwill.   New York, Macmillan, 1936; London, Cobden
   Sanderson, 1937.
Seven Against the Years.   New York, Macmillan, 1939.
So Dear to My Heart.   New York, Doubleday, 1947; London, Odhams Press, 1949.
Reunion on the Wabash.   New York, Doubleday, 1952.

Verse

(Poems).   Chicago, University of Chicago Press, 1925.

Other

The Pedro Gorino: The Adventures of a Negro Sea-Captain in Africa, with Harry
   Dean.   Boston, Houghton Mifflin, 1929; as *Umbala*, London, Harrap, 1929.

The Writings of Mazo De La Roche.   Boston, Little Brown, n.d.

Being a Literary Map of These United States Depicting a Renaissance No Less Astonishing Than That of Periclean Athens or Elizabethan London, with Gladys North, map by Frederic J. Donseif.   New York, Putnam, 1942.

Hurry Spring!   New York, Dutton, 1966.

Raccoons Are the Brightest People.   New York, Dutton, 1966; as *The Raccoons of My Life,* London, Hodder and Stoughton, 1967.

Editor, with Carl Kroch, *So Red the Nose; or, Breath in the Afternoon: Literary Cocktails* (recipes).   New York, Farrar and Rinehart, 1935.

Editor, with C.B. Boutell, *Speak of the Devil: An Anthology of the Appearances of the Devil in the Literature of the Western World.*   New York, Doubleday, 1945.

*   *   *

Sterling North began his literary career at the age of 8 by having a poem published in the *St. Nicholas* magazine, and demonstrated, in a varied and prolific literary career, his continuing interest in a young audience. One of his earliest books, *So Dear to My Heart,* the story of a boy and a lamb in rural Indiana at the turn of the century, was produced in a film version. Among other awards, North received a publisher's award for *The Wolfling,* a story based on the boyhood of his father, and four awards for *Rascal,* which was also a Newbery Honor Book (then called a "runner-up").

Although he wrote biographies of George Washington, Abraham Lincoln, and Thomas Alva Edison for young readers, North is best known to children as the author of *Rascal* or its adaptation *Little Rascal.* The writing is direct and simple, the story tinged with nostalgia and with an affection for Rascal, the pet raccoon that North had adopted when he was eleven and that he eventually set free. He is always objective in observing animal behavior, and he writes of the Wisconsin countryside half a century ago with grace and humor; the story can entertain any reader but has particularly delighted adults and children who enjoy animals or outdoor life. For younger children, the adaptation is simplified just enough and the print enlarged just enough to make the engaging story easier to read without eliminating either the major episodes of the story or its warmth.

North did not, unfortunately, retain a high standard in writing specifically for children; in *The Five Little Bears,* he tells a pointless story of five little black bears who paint themselves white to pretend they are polar bears. Rejected by the zoo polar bear, they come home and are scrubbed by their mother. Some have found the names of the black bears objectionable: Eenie, Meenie, Meinie, Mo, and Nig. The book has a mawkish touch that is absent in North's tender story of an imagined (and imaginative) account of the 7th birthday of Jesus, *The Birthday of Little Jesus.* Mary tells Jesus the story of His birth at the end of a day when He has sought and found a lost lamb.

—Zena Sutherland

NORTON, Andre.   Pseudonym for Alice Mary Norton.   American.   Born in Cleveland, Ohio. Educated at Western Reserve University, Cleveland. Children's Librarian, Cleveland Public Library, 1932–50; Special Librarian, Library of Congress, Washington, D.C., during World War II; Editor, Gnome Press, New York, 1950–58. Recipient: Boys' Clubs of America award, 1965. Agent: Larry Sternig, 742 Robertson Street, Milwaukee, Wisconsin 53213. Address: 2588 Lake Howell Lane, Maitland, Florida 32751, U.S.A.

Fiction

The Prince Commands, illustrated by Kate Seredy.   New York and London, Appleton Century, 1934.

Ralestone Luck, illustrated by James Reid.   New York and London, Appleton Century, 1938.

Follow the Drum.   New York, Penn, 1942.

The Sword Is Drawn, illustrated by Duncan Coburn.   Boston, Houghton Mifflin, 1944; London, Oxford University Press, 1946.

Scarface, illustrated by Lorence Bjorklund.   New York, Harcourt Brace, 1948; London, Methuen, 1950.

Sword in Sheath, illustrated by Lorence Bjorklund.   New York, Harcourt Brace, 1949; as *Island of the Lost*, London, Staples Press, 1953.

Star Man's Son, 2250 A.D., illustrated by Nicolas Mordvinoff.   New York, Harcourt Brace, 1952; London, Staples Press, 1953; as *Daybreak, 2250 A.D.*, New York, Ace, 1954.

Star Rangers.   New York, Harcourt Brace, 1953; London, Gollancz, 1968; as *The Last Planet*, New York, Ace, 1953.

At Swords' Points.   New York, Harcourt Brace, 1954.

The Stars Are Ours! Cleveland, World, 1954.

Sargasso of Space (as Andrew North).   New York, Gnome Press, 1955; as Andre Norton, London, Gollancz, 1970.

Yankee Privateer, illustrated by Leonard Vosburgh.   Cleveland, World, 1955.

Star Guard.   New York, Harcourt Brace, 1955; London, Gollancz, 1969.

The Crossroads of Time, with *Mankind on the Run*, by G.R. Dickinson.   New York, Ace, 1956; published separately, London, Gollancz, 1976.

Plague Ship (as Andrew North).   New York, Gnome Press, 1956; as Andre Norton, London, Gollancz, 1971.

Stand to Horse.   New York, Harcourt Brace, 1956.

Sea Siege.   New York, Harcourt Brace, 1957.

Star Born.   Cleveland, World, 1957; London, Gollancz, 1973.

Star Gate.   New York, Harcourt Brace, 1958; London, Gollancz, 1970.

The Time Traders.   New York, Harcourt Brace, 1958.

The Beast Master.   New York, Harcourt Brace, 1959; London, Gollancz, 1966.

Galactic Derelict.   Cleveland, World, 1959.

Storm over Warlock.   Cleveland, World, 1960.

Sioux Spaceman.   New York, Ace, 1960; London, Hale, 1976.

Shadow Hawk.   New York, Harcourt Brace, 1960; London, Gollancz, 1971.

Ride Proud, Rebel! Cleveland, World, 1961.

Catseye.   New York, Harcourt Brace, 1961; London, Gollancz, 1962.

The Defiant Agents.   Cleveland, World, 1962.

Lord of Thunder.   New York, Harcourt Brace, 1962; London, Gollancz, 1966.

Rebel Spurs.   Cleveland, World, 1962.

Key out of Time.   Cleveland, World, 1963.

Judgment on Janus.   New York, Harcourt Brace, 1963; London, Gollancz, 1964.

Ordeal in Otherwhere.   Cleveland, World, 1964.

Night of Masks.   New York, Harcourt Brace, 1964; London, Gollancz, 1965.

The X Factor.   New York, Harcourt Brace, 1965; London, Gollancz, 1967.

Quest Crosstime.   New York, Viking Press, 1965; as *Crosstime Agent*, London, Gollancz, 1975.

Steel Magic, illustrated by Robin Jacques.   Cleveland, World, 1965; London, Tandem, 1970.

Moon of Three Rings.   New York, Viking Press, 1966; London, Longman, 1969.

Victory on Janus. New York, Harcourt Brace, 1966; London, Gollancz, 1967.
Octagon Magic, illustrated by Mac Conner. Cleveland, World, 1967; London, Hamish Hamilton, 1968.
Operation Time Search. New York, Harcourt Brace, 1967.
Dark Piper. New York, Harcourt Brace, 1968; London, Gollancz, 1969.
Fur Magic, illustrated by John Kauffmann. Cleveland, World, 1968; London, Hamish Hamilton, 1969.
The Zero Stone. New York, Viking Press, 1968; London, Gollancz, 1974.
Postmarked the Stars. New York, Harcourt Brace, 1969; London, Gollancz, 1971.
Uncharted Stars. New York, Viking Press, 1969; London, Gollancz, 1974.
Dread Companion. New York, Harcourt Brace, 1970; London, Gollancz, 1972.
Ice Crown. New York, Viking Press, 1970; London, Longman, 1971.
Android at Arms. New York, Harcourt Brace, 1971; London, Gollancz, 1972.
Exiles of the Stars. New York, Viking Press, 1971; London, Longman, 1972.
The Crystal Gryphon. New York, Atheneum, 1972; London, Gollancz, 1973.
Dragon Magic, illustrated by Robin Jacques. New York, Crowell, 1972.
Breed to Come. New York, Viking Press, 1972; London, Longman, 1973.
Forerunner Foray. New York, Viking Press, 1973; London, Longman, 1974.
Here Abide Monsters. New York, Atheneum, 1973.
The Jargoon Pard. New York, Atheneum, 1974; London, Gollancz, 1975.
Lavender-Green Magic, illustrated by Judith Gwyn Brown. New York, Crowell, 1974.
Iron Cage. New York, Viking Press, 1974; London, Penguin, 1975.
Outside, illustrated by Bernard Colonna. New York, Walker, 1974; London, Blackie, 1976.
The Day of the Ness, with Michael Gilbert, illustrated by Gilbert. New York, Walker, 1975.
Knave of Dreams. New York, Viking Press, 1975; London, Penguin, 1976.
No Night Without Stars. New York, Atheneum, 1975; London, Gollancz, 1976.
Red Hart Magic, illustrated by Donna Diamond. New York, Crowell, 1976; London, Hamish Hamilton, 1977.
Wraiths of Time. New York, Atheneum, 1976; London, Gollancz, 1977.
Star Ka'at, with Dorothy Madlee, illustrated by Bernard Colonna. New York, Walker, 1976; London, Blackie, 1977.
The Opal-Eyed Fan. New York, Dutton, 1977.
Star Ka'at World, with Dorothy Madlee, illustrated by Jean Jenkins. New York, Walker, 1977.

Other

Rogue Reynard, illustrated by Laura Bannon. Boston, Houghton Mifflin, 1947.
Huon of the Horn, illustrated by Joe Krush. New York, Harcourt Brace, 1951.
Bertie and May, with Bertha Stemm Norton, illustrated by Fermin Rocker. New York, World, 1969; London, Hamish Hamilton, 1971.

Editor, with Ernestine Donaldy, *Gates to Tomorrow: An Introduction to Science Fiction.* New York, Atheneum, 1973.
Editor, *Small Shadows Creep: Ghost Children.* New York, Dutton, 1974; London, Chatto and Windus, 1976.

PUBLICATIONS FOR ADULTS

Novels

Murder for Sale, with Grace Hogarth (as Allen Weston). London, Hammond Hammond, 1954.

Secret of the Lost Race.   New York, Ace, 1959.
Voodoo Planet (as Andrew North).   New York, Ace, 1959.
Star Hunter.   New York, Ace, 1961.
Eye of Monster.   New York, Ace, 1962.
Witch World.   New York, Ace, 1963; London, Tandem, 1970.
Web of the Witch World.   New York, Ace, 1964; London, Tandem, 1970.
Three Against Witch World.   New York, Ace, 1965; London, Tandem, 1970.
Year of the Unicorn.   New York, Ace, 1965; London, Tandem, 1970.
Warlock of the Witch World.   New York, Ace, 1967; London, Tandem, 1970.
Sorceress of the Witch World.   New York, Ace, 1968; London, Tandem, 1970.
Garan the Eternal.   Alhambra, California, Fantasy Publishing, 1972.
Merlin's Mirror.   New York, Daw, 1975; London, Sidgwick and Jackson, 1976.
The White Jade Fox.   New York, Dutton, 1975; London, W.H. Allen, 1976.
Wolfshead.   London, Hale, 1977.
Velvet Shadows.   New York, Fawcett, 1977.

Short Stories

High Sorcery.   New York, Ace, 1970.
Spell of the Witch World.   New York, Daw, 1972.
Perilous Dreams.   New York, Daw, 1976.

Other

The Many Worlds of Andre Norton, edited by Roger Elwood.   Radnor, Pennsylvania,
   Chilton, 1974.

Editor, *Bullard of the Space Patrol*, by Malcolm Jameson.   Cleveland, World, 1951.
Editor, *Space Service.*   Cleveland, World, 1953.
Editor, *Space Pioneers.*   Cleveland, World, 1954.
Editor, *Space Police.*   Cleveland, World, 1956.

Manuscript Collection: George Arents Research Library, Syracuse University, New York.

Andre Norton comments:
   I enjoy writing imaginative fiction and always have. I began writing historical, adventure,
and spy stories, since at that time book-length science fiction or fantasy was not acceptable. I
do a great deal of research for each book and over the years I've collected a large reference
library. It is pleasing when a book of mine interests a reader and causes him or her to want to
know more about some particular point I have mentioned. I consider sci-fi and fantasy
excellent stretchers of anyone's imagination and keys to speculation which may lead to
unusual discoveries.

*   *   *

   The science fiction novels of Andre Norton are remarkable for their fast action and
evocation of strange places, and can make an important contribution to the development of
wonder and imagination in young adolescent boys, whose reading of fiction can too easily be
confined to brutal violence in a seedy modern underworld. Not that girls do not read them:
girls are often included among the protagonists, and in some stories play the main part,
notably in *Ice Crown* and *Dread Companion.* Basically Miss Norton writes straight-forward
adventure stories in which the conflict is between Good and Evil, and the qualities of
courage, endurance, friendship, unselfishness, loyalty, and resourcefulness are assumed in
the heroes and heroines, as are complete freedom from callousness and vindictiveness. Some

of the novels are conventional science fiction, as *Sargasso of Space, Plague Ship* and *Postmarked the Stars*, in all of which Dave Thorsen pursues his occupation of Galactic trader; many, such as *Catseye* and *The Beast Master*, relate adventures on distant planets between men and strange aborigines at some time in the future; while a few, such as *Steel Magic, Fur Magic* and *Dread Companion*, deal in outright magic.

The most common initial situations are migration to new planets caused by world destruction, or exploratory missions to undeveloped worlds by members of communities which are highly developed technologically. In either case there is a mingling of medieval and future technologies: stunners and blasters with bows and arrows, flitters with animal-drawn vehicles; and more likely than not powerful machines, left behind by now vanished Forerunners, will be discovered and become the focus of the plot. Almost always atmosphere, climate, and topographical features will be similar to what can be found on earth, and it is this, perhaps more than any other factor, which marks the work as science fantasy rather than science fiction, so far as distinction can be made.

Miss Norton is greatly interested in animals, and radiation-mutated animals, capable of telepathic communication with man, and helping him, are very common, as in *Catseye* and *The Beast Master*. In *Breed to Come*, cat mutants are the main characters, and rival man, whereas in *Iron Cage* bear mutants, though not technologically advanced, are the moral superiors of man. In *Steel Magic, Fur Magic* and *The Jargoon Pard* human beings are for a while turned into animals, and the resulting physical sensations well imagined. Labyrinthine underground passages are commonly encountered, and it is here in particular that brilliance is displayed in the evocation of lurking menace. As when dealing with imagined technology she displays considerable art in promoting suspension of disbelief by what she leaves unsaid.

Doubt of identity and parallel worlds in time are two familiar SF themes she uses. In *Android at Arms*, Andras, fighting to regain his kingdom, is uncertain until the end of the story whether he is, indeed, Andras, or a humanoid counterfeit. In *The Crossroads of Time* and *Crosstime Agent* a kind of cross-time Interpol provides extremely fast action. In *Knave of Dreams*, one of her best novels, the two themes are combined, for Ramsay Kimble awakens in a world of which he has dreamed, inhabiting the body of a young prince, who, the focal point of warring factions, has just died.

Entirely in the world of magic are *Fur Magic*, which takes Cory into mythological worlds of the North American Indian, *Steel Magic*, a bizarre but successful incursion into the Arthurian world of Merlin, and *Dread Companion*, probably her most remarkable achievement, in which Kilda penetrates a kind of Gaelic mythology world of illusion, perpetually shifting and changing.

There are two books of a quite different kind, though both successful: *Bertie and May*, which describes the lives of two young girls in the Ohio countryside of the 1880's, and *Shadow Hawk*, a historical novel of Ancient Egypt.

For the most part Miss Norton's style is unobtrusively effective, but pseudo-archaisms do intrude occasionally, as in the *Janus* books, while experiments in construction are not wholly successful in *Iron Cage* and *The Crystal Gryphon*.

—Norman Culpan

NORTON, Mary. British. Born in London, in 1903. Educated at a convent school. Married Robert C. Norton in 1927; has two daughters and two sons. Actress, Old Vic Theatre Company, London, 1925–26; lived in Portugal, 1927–39; worked for the British Purchasing Company, New York, 1940–43; actress, 1943–45. Recipient: Library Association Carnegie Medal, 1953. Address: c/o J.M. Dent and Sons Ltd., 26 Albemarle Street, London, W1X 4QY, England.

Fiction

The Magic Bed-Knob; or, How to Become a Witch in Ten Easy Lessons, illustrated by Waldo Peirce.   New York, Hyperion Press, 1943.

The Magic Bed-Knob, illustrated by Joan Kiddell-Monroe.   London, Dent, 1945.

Bonfires and Broomsticks, illustrated by Mary Adshead.   London, Dent, 1947.

The Borrowers, illustrated by Diana Stanley.   London, Dent, 1952; New York, Harcourt Brace, 1953.

The Borrowers Afield, illustrated by Diana Stanley.   London, Dent, and New York, Harcourt Brace, 1955.

Bedknob and Broomstick (revised version of *The Magic Bed-Knob* and *Bonfires and Broomsticks*), illustrated by Erik Blegvad.   London, Dent, and New York, Harcourt Brace, 1957.

The Borrowers Afloat, illustrated by Diana Stanley.   London, Dent, and New York, Harcourt Brace, 1959.

The Borrowers Aloft, illustrated by Diana Stanley.   London, Dent, and New York, Harcourt Brace, 1961.

Poor Stainless, illustrated by Diana Stanley.   London, Dent, and New York, Harcourt Brace, 1971.

Are All the Giants Dead?, illustrated by Brian Froud.   London, Dent, and New York, Harcourt Brace, 1975.

*   *   *

Mary Norton is already acknowledged as a writer of classic children's novels. She creates a particular kind of fantasy, the charm of which lies in its absolute logic. Her first novel, *The Magic Bed-Knob*, appeared in Britain in 1945 when fantasy was less fashionable than it is now. Miss Price, the respectable village spinster who turns out to be a practising witch, is one of the memorable characters of children's literature. She is completely real, although sadly there are few ladies like her in today's villages: "She wore grey coats and skirts and had a long thin neck with a scarf round it (made of Liberty silk with a Paisley pattern). Her nose was sharply pointed and she had very clean pink hands. She rode on a high bicycle with a basket in front, and she visited the sick and taught the piano." But Miss Price has other gifts. Her magic provides the children, Paul, Carry and Charles, with a flying bed, but after a memorable visit to a South Sea Island and a magic contest with a witch doctor Miss Price decides to give up magic "for the duration." Happily she is persuaded to come out of retirement for the sequel *Bonfires and Broomsticks* (both books were later re-published together as *Bedknob and Broomstick*), when Miss Price and the children rescue a 17th-century necromancer from the stake.

In 1952 the first of "The Borrowers" books appeared. (The others are *The Borrowers Afield*, *The Borrowers Afloat*, *The Borrowers Aloft*, and *Poor Stainless*.) Again the Borrowers books are satisfying because they are so logical. Mary Norton set out with the basic premise that something must happen to all those apparently unconnected everyday things which disappear without trace; as Kate says, there must be someone borrowing them. "Because of all the things that disappear – safety pins, for instance. Factories go on making safety pins, and every day people go on buying safety pins and yet, somehow, there never is a safety pin just when you want one. Where are they all? Where do they all go to?" The answer of course is that they are borrowed by people just like Pod, Homily, and Arriety.

Mary Norton describes the world of The Borrowers in loving detail – the gates barred with hair slides and safety pins, the walls papered with old letters, the blotting paper carpet and the bath which had once held paté de foie gras. There are wonderful descriptions of Pod's borrowing technique and his method of curtain climbing. The security of this small world, a security which Arriety feels is more of an imprisonment, is threatened and ultimately disrupted by the appearance of "a boy"!

Miss Norton is very good at boys. Paul in *The Magic Bed-Knob* is a strong and stubborn character, with a vein of practical common sense. James in the later *Are All The Giants Dead?* is another. He finds it hard to be taken visiting to the world of Fairy Tales when his chosen reading is Science Fiction. The boy in *The Borrowers* is large and clumsy and curious, but he is brave too and he does all he can to save the Borrowers after he has caused their discovery. I feel that the original Borrowers is the best of the series; once they are out in the big wide world they seem a little diminished, although there are marvellous moments in all the books and Homily, Arriety's houseproud, fussing mother, is always splendid.

Are All The Giants Dead? creates another fantasy world and is again based on a very simple thought: "What happens to all the characters in the fairy tales when they 'live happily ever after'?" The answer seems to be that they age gradually – Jack and the Beanstalk, Jack the Giant Killer, Beauty and the Beast etc. But their world is not quite as calm and content as it should be, for all the giants are *not* dead and that is where the problem lies. James, although faintly disapproving throughout of all these romantic people, helps the Princess Dulcabel to win her Prince. James' guide to this alien world is another of Mary Norton's splendid ladies, Mildred, social correspondent and deliverer of royal journals. Again the detail is very good:

"I think Boofy's chef is wonderful with onions," said the lady at the card table. "I can always recognise it," said the dark lady, turning over a page. Then she looked up at Mildred. "Why do you put this bit about going to the hairdresser?" "Because people are always asking me," said Mildred. "I have such a busy life, you see, they wonder how I fit it in."

Mary Norton is a traditional writer in the best sense. She writes with style, wit and humour and she never condescends to her readers. Her books will surely last.

—Anna Home

NYE, Robert. British. Born in London, 15 March 1939. Educated at Dormans Land, Sussex; Hamlet Court, Westcliff, Essex; Southend High School. Married Judith Pratt in 1959 (divorced); Aileen Campbell, 1966; has four sons and two daughters. Free-lance writer. Since 1967, Poetry Editor, *The Scotsman*; since 1971, Poetry Critic, *The Times*, London. Writer-in-Residence, University of Edinburgh, 1976–77. Recipient: Eric Gregory Award, for verse, 1963; Scottish Arts Council bursary, 1970, 1973, publication award, 1970, and award, 1977; James Kennaway Memorial Award, 1970; *Guardian* Prize, for novel, 1976. Address: 18 Lonsdale Terrace, Edinburgh 3, Scotland.

PUBLICATIONS FOR CHILDREN

Fiction

Taliesin, illustrated by Sheila Hawkins. London, Faber, 1966; New York, Hill and Wang, 1967.
March Has Horse's Ears, illustrated by Sheila Hawkins. London, Faber, 1966; New York, Hill and Wang, 1967.
Wishing Gold, illustrated by Helen Craig. London, Macmillan, and New York, Hill and Wang, 1970.
Poor Pumpkin, illustrated by Derek Collard. London, Macmillan, and New York, Hill and Wang, 1971.
The Mathematical Princess and Other Stories. New York, Hill and Wang, 1972.

Cricket: Three Tales, illustrated by Shelley Freshman.   Indianapolis, Bobbs Merrill,
  1975.
Out of the World and Back Again.   London, Collins, 1977.

Other

Bee Hunter: The Adventures of Beowulf, illustrated by Aileen Campbell. London,
  Faber, and New York, Hill and Wang, 1968; as *Beowulf, The Bee Hunter*, Faber,
  1972.

PUBLICATIONS FOR ADULTS

Novels

Doubtfire.   London, Calder and Boyars, 1967; New York, Hill and Wang, 1968.
Falstaff.   London, Hamish Hamilton, and Boston, Little Brown, 1976.

Short Stories

Tales I Told My Mother.   London, Calder and Boyars, and New York, Hill and Wang,
  1969.
Penguin Modern Stories 6, with others.   London, Penguin, 1970.

Plays

Sawney Bean, with William Watson (produced Edinburgh, 1969; London,
  1972).   London, Calder and Boyars, 1970.
Sisters (broadcast, 1969; produced Edinburgh, 1973).   Included in *Three Plays*, 1976.
The Seven Deadly Sins: A Mask, music by James Douglas (produced Stirling,
  1973).   Rushden, Northamptonshire, Omphalos Press, 1974.
Mr. Poe (produced Edinburgh and London, 1974).
Three Plays (includes *Fugue*, *Sisters*, and *Penthesilea*, adaptation of the play by Heinrich
  von Kleist).   London, Calder and Boyars, 1976.

Radio Plays: *Sisters*, 1969; *Devil's Jig* (libretto), 1977.

Verse

Juvenilia 1.   Lowestoft, Suffolk, Scorpion Press, 1961.
Juvenilia 2.   Lowestoft, Suffolk, Scorpion Press, 1963.
Darker Ends.   London, Calder and Boyars, and New York, Hill and Wang, 1969.
Agnus Dei.   Rushden, Northamptonshire, Sceptre Press, 1973.
Two Prayers.   Richmond, Surrey, Keepsake Press, 1974.
Five Dreams.   Rushden, Northamptonshire, Sceptre Press, 1974.
Divisions on a Ground.   Manchester, Carcanet Press, 1976.

Other

Editor, *A Choice of Sir Walter Ralegh's Verse.*   London, Faber, 1972.
Editor, *William Barnes of Dorset: A Selection of His Poems.*   Cheadle, Cheshire,
  Carcanet Press, 1973.
Editor, *A Choice of Swinburne's Verse.*   London, Faber, 1973.
Editor, *The English Sermon 1750–1850.*   Manchester, Carcanet Press, 1976.
Editor, *The Faber Book of Sonnets.*   London, Faber, 1976; as *A Book of Sonnets*, New
  York, Oxford University Press, 1976.

Manuscript Collections: University of Texas, Austin; Colgate University, Hamilton, New York; National Library of Scotland, Edinburgh.

*   *   *

Robert Nye is a Rabelaisian story-teller of reckless heroes, feckless kings, vampire-ridden fens, and headless horses. Widows play chess with blackbirds, a king grows horse's ears, failed suitors get beheaded. Enormous respect for the possibilities of words pervades his work. Imagery is simple but vivid, conveying the joys of climbing, sailing, dreaming, loving, becoming a hare, used with sufficient demands to make the reader think imaginatively, yet drawn from quotidian life. "Even the light had a brief look about it, as though it were a trespasser." A boy sees a buzzard, high, "like a full-stop scratched on the sun." Details, funny, preposterous, homely, are incessantly invented but the plot, so essential to the young, is carefully preserved. Jack will get Jill, the riddles be answered, the youngest son win treasure, true poets outmatch bad poets. Nevertheless, by a small twist of narrative, unexpected line of dialogue, old heroes are given more humanity, more realism. Magic has its place, but is generally kept in its place by elementary human needs. Splendour is shot through with earthiness. The villainous Unferth "began gnawing at his finger nails. They tasted of dirt and where he had been poking at his boil. Unferth hated the taste of himself, but he had to have it." Such figures relate to recognisable loneliness, unpopularity, the humour and tensions of family and communal life, the casual feelings that may accompany the most grandiose exploits. Panting from slaying the dragon, Beowulf develops toothache, the great poet Taliesin shows sly, schoolboy mischief. A dragon may have legitimate grievance, a villain or monster have pathos, a golden warrior reveal flaws. The rhythms, adroit repetitions, the unusual words carefully planted, make these stories excellent for reading aloud.

—Peter Vansittart

———————

O'BRIEN, Robert C.   Pseudonym for Robert Leslie Conly. American.   Born in Brooklyn, New York, 11 January 1918. Educated at schools in Amityville, Long Island, New York; Williams College, Williamstown, Massachusetts, 1935–37; Juilliard School of Music, New York; Columbia University, New York; University of Rochester, New York, B.A. in English 1940. Married Sally McCaslin in 1943; one son and three daughters. Worked in an advertising agency, 1940; researcher and writer, *Newsweek* magazine, New York, 1941–44; Reporter, *Times-Herald*, 1944–46, and *Pathfinder* magazine, 1946–51, both Washington, D.C.; member of the staff, rising to Senior Assistant Editor, *National Geographic* magazine, Washington, D.C., 1951–73. Recipient: American Library Association Newbery Medal, 1972; Mystery Writers of America Edgar Allan Poe Award, 1976. *Died 5 March 1973.*

PUBLICATIONS FOR CHILDREN

Fiction

> *The Silver Crown*, illustrated by Dale Payson.   New York, Atheneum, 1968; London, Gollancz, 1973.
> *Mrs. Frisby and the Rats of NIMH*, illustrated by Zena Bernstein.   New York, Atheneum, 1971; London, Gollancz, 1972.
> *Z for Zachariah*.   New York, Atheneum, 1974; London, Gollancz, 1975.

PUBLICATIONS FOR ADULTS

Novel

A Report from Group 17.   New York, Atheneum, 1972; London, Gollancz, 1973.

*   *   *

Robert C. O'Brien was a serious writer; that is to say, he dealt with important moral themes in some depth. He was, like C.S.Lewis, a notable example of a sophisticated writer who found the flexible conventions of children's fiction a convenient medium for exploring his own ideas.

Only his second novel, *Mrs. Frisby and the Rats of NIMH*, has achieved wide popularity as well as critical acclaim. At the level of children's animal story, it describes the heroic efforts of a mother fieldmouse to save her invalid child from imminent death from the farmer's plough. In the course of her struggle, she gets involved with a colony of hyper-intelligent rats who have escaped from a research laboratory. These rats are confronting the questions that face industrial man and clearly obsess O'Brien: whether to use technological expertise to create a competitive mechanised society that exploits and eventually destroys its environment, or whether to opt for a civilisation that respects the individual and natural resources. These are hackneyed topics among dissident American youth, but O'Brien's use of talking rats who are testing out the options for themselves provides a fresh new focus; the problems somehow appear clearer and more real in the context of an animal story than they ever could in a conventional "human" novel. O'Brien's inoffensive didacticism is carried easily by a most moving and original narrative.

His earlier novel, *The Silver Crown*, is again about a civilisation, this time our own, threatened by exploitation and destruction. An evil power, oddly derived from the 5th century St. Jerome, is about to infiltrate society first with muggings, race riots, and arson and eventually through the control of everybody's minds. O'Brien seems to have a firm belief in the notion of Evil as the source of man's troubles. His third children's book, *Z for Zachariah*, takes us to the stage when our civilisation *has* destroyed itself through a nuclear holocaust; a 16-year-old girl survivor records her macabre experiences in the form of a daily diary that reminds one of a French New Wave novel.

O'Brien's output was slender and uneven, but characterised by remarkable inventiveness, dramatic power, and a clear narrative style that enabled complex ideas to be felt as well as understood.

—Aidan Warlow

O'DELL, Scott.   American.   Born in Los Angeles, California, 23 May 1903. Educated at Occidental College, Los Angeles, 1919; University of Wisconsin, Madison, 1920; Stanford University, California, 1920–21; University of Rome, 1925. Served in the United States Air Force during World War II. Married Jane Rattenbury in 1948. Film cameraman in the 1920's; Book Editor of a Los Angeles newspaper in the 1940's. Recipient: American Library Association Newbery Medal, 1961; Hans Christian Andersen International Medal, 1972; University of Southern Mississippi award, 1976. Address: c/o Houghton Mifflin Co., 1 Beacon Street, Boston, Massachusetts 02107, U.S.A.

PUBLICATIONS FOR CHILDREN

Fiction

    Island of the Blue Dolphins. Boston, Houghton Mifflin, 1960; London, Constable, 1961.
    The King's Fifth, illustrated by Samuel Bryant. Boston, Houghton Mifflin, 1966; London, Constable, 1967.
    The Black Pearl, illustrated by Milton Johnson. Boston, Houghton Mifflin, 1967; London, Longman, 1968.
    The Dark Canoe, illustrated by Milton Johnston. Boston, Houghton Mifflin, 1968; London, Longman, 1969.
    Journey to Jericho, illustrated by Leonard Weisgard. Boston, Houghton Mifflin, 1969.
    Sing Down the Moon. Boston, Houghton Mifflin, 1970; London, Hamish Hamilton, 1972.
    The Treasure of Topo-el-Bampo, illustrated by Lynd Ward. Boston, Houghton Mifflin, 1972.
    Child of Fire. Boston, Houghton Mifflin, 1974.
    The Hawk That Dare Not Hunt by Day. Boston, Houghton Mifflin, 1975.
    The 290. Boston, Houghton Mifflin, 1976; London, Oxford University Press, 1977.
    Zia, illustrated by Ted Lewin. Boston, Houghton Mifflin, 1976; London, Oxford University Press, 1977.
    Carlota. Boston, Houghton Mifflin, 1977.

Other

    The Cruise of the Arctic Star. Boston, Houghton Mifflin, 1973.

PUBLICATIONS FOR ADULTS

Novels

    Woman of Spain. Boston, Houghton Mifflin, 1934.
    Hill of the Hawk. Indianapolis, Bobbs Merrill, 1953; London, Transworld, 1955.
    The Sea Is Red. New York, Holt Rinehart, 1958.

Other

    Representative Photoplays Analyzed. Hollywood, Palmer Institute of Authorship, 1924.
    Man Alone, with William Doyle. Indianapolis, Bobbs Merrill, 1953; as *Lifer,* London, Longman, 1954.
    Country of the Sun: Southern California: An Informal History and Guide. New York, Crowell, 1957.
    The Psychology of Children's Art, with Rhoda Kellogg. Del Mar, California, CRM Associates, 1967.

Manuscript Collection: University of Oregon Library, Eugene.

           *   *   *

It's a pity if any adult reader who loves historical adventure stories of the first rank misses the works of Scott O'Dell merely because they are labeled as "juveniles." It has only been in recent years, with the explicit depiction of sex and violence, that much of the adult fare in this genre, which has its roots in the works of Scott and Dumas, has become unsuitable for younger readers. If O'Dell were writing 30 or 40 years ago he would undoubtedly have been in the company of such writers as C. S. Forester, Nordhoff and Hall, and Kenneth Roberts; and a generation or two before that with Stevenson, Henty, Marryat, Dana, and Jack London. These writers had broad appeal, but perhaps their most enthusiastic audience consisted of readers between the ages of 12 and 16. Scott O'Dell, after a long and successful career as a journalist, historian and writer for adults, found that audience with the publication of *Island of the Blue Dolphins*.

When O'Dell speaks of himself as a practitioner in the field of children's literature he uses the term "writer of books that children read," rather than "writer of children's books." Indeed, O'Dell's strength as a writer for children is best explained by the fact that he does not write directly for them. As he says: "Books of mine which are classified officially as books written for children, were not written for children. Instead, and in a very real sense, they were written for myself. There is about them, however, one distinction which I feel is important to this form of literature: they were written consistently in the emotional area that children share with adults." O'Dell also recognizes that the young reader "has the ability, which in adults is either eroded or entirely lost, to identify himself with the characters of a story." So rather than write with a child audience in mind, O'Dell aesthetically disciplines himself by selecting a young person to narrate his tales. Indeed, he is a master of first-person narrative, which in itself is not only the unifying and coherent influence which heightens the truth and significance of his stories, but also the element which assimilates into the tales all of the author's research, personal knowledge and experience, without a single trace of pedantic or didactic intrusion.

O'Dell is, in a very real way, a different person each time he tells a story. This gives each of his books an individual quality that is uniquely suited for its natural and cultural setting. The cadence of the narrative voice, the metaphorical symbols, and the limiting perimeters of the narrator's scope, all unite to produce a story that is plausible and consistent, and poetically satisfying as well.

Karana, the Indian girl of *Island of the Blue Dolphins*, begins her story: "I remember the day the Aleut ship came to our island. At first it seemed like a small shell afloat in the sea. Then it grew longer and was a gull with folded wings." In contrast, Bright Morning, in *Sing Down the Moon*, tells a Navajo story in the natural rhythms and allusions of Navajo speech: "The day the waters came was a wonderful day. I heard the first sounds of their coming while I lay awake in the night. At first it was a whisper, like a wind among the dry stalks of our cornfield. After a while it was a sound like the feet of warriors' dancing. Then it was a roar that shook the earth."

Not only are O'Dell's stories peopled by characters whom he knows intimately, but they are also vivid in locale. He is both a native and an historian of the regions in which the stories take place. His books have in them either the sound of the sea or the feeling of the frontier. The coastal region of Southern California in the early days is the setting for *The Black Pearl* and *The Dark Canoe*, while *The King's Fifth* is set farther inland around the canyon country of the southwestern United States.

No two of O'Dell's stories are alike in structure, content, or style. *The King's Fifth* and *The Dark Canoe*, perhaps, demand a slightly more sophisticated reader. However, the others are not "easier" because of any condescension toward the young reader, but rather because they are true to the voice of the particular narrator. Young readers deserve more writers of O'Dell's stature: writers who, like him, willingly and confidently share the responsibility for the success of the story with them.

—James E. Higgins

O'HARA, Mary. Pseudonym for Mary O'Hara Alsop. American. Born in Cape May Point, New Jersey, 10 July 1885. Educated at Packer Institute, Brooklyn, New York. Married

Kent K. Parrot in 1905 (divorced), one daughter and one son; Helge Sture-Vasa, 1922 (divorced, 1947). Address: 5507 Grove Street, Chevy Chase, Maryland 20015, U.S.A.

PUBLICATIONS FOR CHILDREN

Fiction

My Friend Flicka. Philadelphia, Lippincott, 1941; London, Eyre and Spottiswoode, 1943.
Thunderhead. Philadelphia, Lippincott, 1943; London, Eyre and Spottiswoode, 1945.
Green Grass of Wyoming. Philadelphia, Lippincott, 1946; London, Eyre and Spottiswoode, 1947.

PUBLICATIONS FOR ADULTS

Novels

The Son of Adam Wingate. New York, McKay, and London, Eyre and Spottiswoode, 1952.
Wyoming Summer. New York, Doubleday, 1963.

Play

The Catch Colt, music by O'Hara (produced Washington, D.C.). New York, Dramatists Play Service, 1964.

Other

Let Us Say Grace (as Mary Sture-Vasa). Boston, Christopher, 1930.
Novel-in-the-Making. New York, McKay, 1954.
A Musical in the Making. Chevy Chase, Maryland, Markane Publishing, 1966.

Music: Esperan, 1943, May God Keep You, 1946, Windharp, and other works for piano.

*   *   *

Mary O'Hara's reputation as a children's author rests upon her trilogy of American ranch life, My Friend Flicka, Thunderhead, and Green Grass of Wyoming. Based on the author's experiences as a Wyoming rancher, the novels record 7 years in the life of Ken McLaughlin, the younger son of Rob McLaughlin, a West Point graduate who has left the Army to raise thoroughbred horses, and his wife, Nell, an artistic Bryn Mawr graduate. The three books are unified by their account of Ken's recurring clashes with his strong-willed father, the boy's gradual maturing and reconciliation with Rob, and the adult McLaughlins' long-standing financial troubles at their Goose Bar Ranch.

The works are closely linked. My Friend Flicka introduces the McLaughlin family, establishes their financial straits, and relates 10-year-old Ken's efforts to tame his colt, Flicka, a descendant of a wild white range stallion, the Albino. Thunderhead resumes the narrative two years later, telling of the birth and training of Flicka's first foal, a white colt resembling the Albino. The story of Ken's two-year-long opposition to his father's determination to geld the fractious Thunderhead is intensified by a growing estrangement between Rob and Nell; the tensions, however, are eased by the family's achieving a degree of financial security and by Nell's pregnancy. Green Grass of Wyoming, the most traditionally constructed of the books, tells two stories: that of Rob McLaughlin's grudging but eventual acceptance of Thunderhead as the Goose Bar stud and that of the developing romance between 17-year-old Ken and the grandniece of a wealthy horse-breeder.

Although working within the conventions of the realistic animal story, Mary O'Hara avoids the usual pitfalls of the genre. She does not blink at the biological facts of life, but sets reproduction and the transmission of genetic types at the heart of the novels. Nor does she gloss over the occasional conflicts of family life. She makes the subtle antagonisms between Rob and Nell and the quarrels between the day-dreaming Ken and the determined Rob as much a part of the books as the genuine love that all three share. She deals, in fact, with all of the facets of life, from the impact of climate and space to that of politics and economics, making the works accounts of believably fallible persons who are trying, at considerable cost to themselves, to live the life of their dreams.

—Fred Erisman

OMAN, Carola (Mary Anima). British. Born in Oxford, 11 May 1897; daughter of the historian Charles Oman. Educated at Wychwood School, Oxford, 1906. Worked for the British Red Cross Service, 1916–19, 1938–58 (President, Hertfordshire Branch, 1947–58). Recipient (for biography): *Sunday Times* prize, 1947; James Tait Black Memorial Prize, 1954. Fellow, Royal Historical Society; Fellow, Society of Antiquaries; Fellow, Royal Society of Literature. Address: Bride Hall, Welwyn, Hertfordshire AL6 9DB, England.

PUBLICATIONS FOR CHILDREN

Fiction

Ferry the Fearless. London, Pitman, 1936.
Johel, illustrated by Janne Beever. London, Pitman, 1937.
Alfred, King of the English, illustrated by E. Boye Uden. London, Dent, and New York, Dutton, 1939.
Baltic Spy. London, Pitman, 1940.

Other

Robin Hood, The Prince of Outlaws: A Tale of the Fourteenth Century from the "Lytell Geste," illustrated by Jack Matthews. London, Dent, and New York, Dutton, 1937.

PUBLICATIONS FOR ADULTS

Novels

The Road Royal. London, Unwin, 1924.
Princess Amelia. London, Unwin, and New York, Duffield, 1924.
King Heart. London, Unwin, 1926.
Mrs. Newdigate's Window. London, Unwin, and New York, Appleton, 1927.
The Holiday. London, Unwin, and New York, Appleton, 1928.
Crouchback. London, Hodder and Stoughton, and New York, Holt, 1929.
Miss Barrett's Elopement. London, Hodder and Stoughton, 1929; New York, Holt, 1930.
Fair Stood the Wind .... London, Hodder and Stoughton, 1930.
Major Grant. London, Hodder and Stoughton, 1931.
The Empress. London, Hodder and Stoughton, and New York, Holt, 1932.
The Best of His Family. London, Hodder and Stoughton, 1933.

Over the Water.   London, Hodder and Stoughton, 1935.
Nothing to Report.   London, Hodder and Stoughton, 1940.
Somewhere in England.   London, Hodder and Stoughton, 1943.

Verse

The Menin Road and Other Poems.   London, Hodder and Stoughton, 1919.

Other

Prince Charles Edward.   London, Duckworth, 1935.
Henrietta Maria.   London, Hodder and Stoughton, and New York, Macmillan, 1936.
Elizabeth of Bohemia.   London, Hodder and Stoughton, 1938; revised edition, 1964.
Britain Against Napoleon.   London, Faber, 1942; as *Napoleon at the Channel,* New
    York, Doubleday, 1942.
Nelson.   New York, Doubleday, 1946; London, Hodder and Stoughton, 1947.
Sir John Moore.   London, Hodder and Stoughton, 1953.
Lord Nelson.   London, Collins, 1954; Hamden, Connecticut, Archon, 1968.
David Garrick.   London, Hodder and Stoughton, 1958.
Mary of Modena.   London, Hodder and Stoughton, 1962.
Ayot Rectory.   London, Hodder and Stoughton, 1965.
Napoleon's Viceroy: Eugène de Beauharnais.   London, Hodder and Stoughton, 1966;
    New York, Funk and Wagnalls, 1968.
*The Gascoyne Heiress: The Life and Diaries of Frances Mary Gascoyne-Cecil,
    1802–1839.*   London, Hodder and Stoughton, 1968.
The Wizard of the North: The Life of Sir Walter Scott.   London, Hodder and
    Stoughton, 1973.
An Oxford Childhood (autobiography).   London, Hodder and Stoughton, 1976.

*   *   *

Carola Oman's children's books represent a brief period in her long and distinguished
career as a historian. Writing for children was probably not her metier, though her
approaches are varied, and the reader sees quite painlessly what life was like at the time of
which she is writing.

Ferry the Fearless and *Johel* are linked, as the title characters are brothers. A five-year gap
separates the two stories, so that while Ferry is a little boy the slightly older Johel appears as a
young man. For various reasons both are left alone and must make their way in the world;
neither seems to suffer from this social deprivation. *Ferry* is lacking in plot and the *leitmotif* of
the view from Ferry's bedroom window is over-sophisticated; the events of *Johel* take place
in 19 days and the story is far more dramatic, without recourse to the flashbacks of the earlier
book. The mingling of Norman and Saxon is just beginning; aristocratic and humble ways of
life are contrasted. Particularly Johel's speech in *Ferry* is archaic and not to today's taste – it is
not clear whether this is supposed to differentiate the characters or to give "flavour." Without
it the later book is generally easier to read.

Alfred, King of the English and *Robin Hood* re-create well-known mediaeval tales. Alfred's
life is seen through the eyes of Denewulf, a serf who just happens to be there when the
recorded incidents take place, including the burning of the cakes. The device is effective –
Denewulf is a pleasant character with a life of his own against which Alfred's can be set.
Both have their troubles and perhaps their compensations. *Robin Hood* is a straight narrative,
using or hinting at traditions and sources throughout the book. The legendary and faery
associations are suggested, and discussion of the hero by Caxton's apprentices when printing
the tale allows an explanation of the blurring of the details through the passage of time, while
Robin Hood dies, as it were, off-stage for the young reader.

Baltic Spy differs from the other books in style and in period and could hold its own with many an adult spy story. The few characters are adult – the only young ones appear briefly at the beginning. The two episodes of Father Robinson's spying career in the Napoleonic Wars provide plenty of excitement, with secret codes and narrow escapes. The charm of the story lies in its delightful insouciance and masterly use of understatement and the balance of suspense and humour.

—Margaret M. Tye

ONADIPE, (Nathaniel) Kola(wole).   Nigerian.   Educated at the Baptist College, Iwo, Oyo State; University of London, B.S. in economics; read law; called to the bar, 1961. Teacher for several years; Principal, Olu-Iwa College, Ijaba-Ode, 1950–59; practiced law, 1961–62; District Manager, British Petroleum, Nigeria, 1962–66; General Manager, African Universities Press and Pilgrim Books, Lagos, 1966–71. Currently, Managing Director, Amonat (Nigeria) Ltd., Lagos. Address: 3 Osinbajo Close, Obanikoro, P.O. Box 985, Lagos, Nigeria.

PUBLICATIONS FOR CHILDREN

Fiction

> The Adentures of Souza, The Village Lad, illustrated by Adebayo Ajayi.   Lagos, African Universities Press, 1963; revised edition, 1965.
> Sugar Girl, illustrated by Bruce Onabrakpeya.   Lagos, African Universities Press, 1964.
> Koku Baboni, illustrated by Frances Effiong.   Lagos, African Universities Press, 1965.
> The Slave Boy, illustrated by J. K. Oyewole.   Lagos, African Universities Press, 1966.
> The Magic Land of Shadows.   Lagos, African Universities Press, 1971.
> The Forest Is Our Playground, with M. Murphy.   Lagos, African Universities Press, 1971.

*   *   *

Kola Onadipe has not written many books for children but the few he has written have made tremendous impact on African children who use them as school supplementary readers.

His *Sugar Girl* tells the story of Ralia, a sweet-natured, helpful girl, who gets lost in the forest. She falls into the hands of a witch-like woman, escapes, has other adventures, and is finally rescued by a prince who reunites her with her family.

Koku Baboni is the story of an abandoned child adopted by a rich, childless woman, Adia. While helping an old woman to rescue her daughter from bondage, Koku discovers his origin and this discovery leads to the stoppage of twin-killing in the village.

In The Adventures of Souza, a boy and his "gang" have adventures with various creatures of the wild – wild bees, leopards, snakes – and with wild humans such as irate fathers and outraged local women.

Onadipe's stories have traditional folklore elements which come out most clearly in his book *The Magic Land of Shadows* – a story in which a motherless girl, Ajua, who is ill-treated by her father's second wife, falls inside a pool and is sucked downwards, finding herself in a magic land inhabited by "Shadows." Because she obeys the instructions of one of the "Shadows," she acquires strange powers which make her rich. Her envious stepmother descends into the magic land with disastrous consequences. The supernatural also comes out, less strongly, in *Koku Baboni* in which a woman in white gives her instructions to Adia in her dreams.

Onadipe's insistence on goodness and the triumph of good over bad is reminiscent of traditional Nigerian morality plays and the moral tag at the end of African folk tales. Sugar Girl, Ralia, is a very good, lovable girl, Koku is rich and physically powerful, but humble, while Ajua is an obedient girl. Souza, however, is different. He is much closer to primeval nature. A healthy, active outdoor type, he grows up with little supervision except when he is reported to his stern father who misguidedly thinks the whip is the answer to his son's misdemeanour. Even then, Souza shows some remorse at the end when babies are stung by wasps he has vengefully unleashed on a crowd of young spectators at a "show."

Onadipe employs a very simple style suitable for the age-group (6–12) he is writing for and their cultural background. He captivates children's interest, not only through exciting action and sustained plot interest, but also by providing familiar local colour through incidents revealing local beliefs in medicine men, love potions and charms. He gives the reader a glimpse into local customs such as secret cults and initiation rites, masquerades, hunting procedures and burial rites.

— Mabel D. Segun

ORGEL, Doris.   American.   Born 15 August 1929 in Vienna, Austria; emigrated to the United States in 1940. Educated at Radcliffe College, Cambridge, Massachusetts, 1946–48; Barnard College, New York, B.A. (cum laude) 1950 (Phi Beta Kappa). Married Shelley Orgel in 1949; has two sons and one daughter. Agent: Curtis Brown Ltd., 575 Madison Avenue, New York, New York 10022, U.S.A.

PUBLICATIONS FOR CHILDREN

Fiction

> *Sarah's Room*, illustrated by Maurice Sendak.   New York, Harper, 1963; London, Bodley Head, 1972.
> *Cindy's Snowdrops*, illustrated by Ati Forberg.   New York, Knopf, 1966; London, Hamish Hamilton, 1967.
> *Cindy's Sad and Happy Tree*, illustrated by Ati Forberg.   New York, Knopf, 1967.
> *In a Forgotten Place*, illustrated by James McMullan.   New York, Knopf, 1967.
> *Whose Turtle?*, illustrated by Martha Alexander.   Cleveland, World, 1968.
> *On the Sand Dune*, illustrated by Leonard Weisgard.   New York, Harper, 1968.
> *Phoebe and the Prince*, illustrated by Erik Blegvad.   New York, Putnam, 1969.
> *Merry, Rose, and Christmas-Tree June*, illustrated by Edward Gorey.   New York, Knopf, 1969.
> *Next Door to Xanadu*, illustrated by Dale Payson.   New York, Harper, 1969.
> *The Uproar*, illustrated by Anita Lobel.   New York, McGraw Hill, 1970.
> *The Mulberry Music*, illustrated by Dale Payson.   New York, Harper, 1971.
> *Bartholomew, We Love You!*, illustrated by Pat Grant Porter.   New York, Knopf, 1973.
> *A Certain Magic*.   New York, Dial Press, 1976.

Verse

> *Grandma's Holidays* (as Doris Adelberg), illustrated by Paul Kennedy.   New York, Dial
> Press, 1963.
> *Lizzie's Twins* (as Doris Adelberg), illustrated by N.M. Bodecker.   New York, Dial
> Press, 1964.
> *The Good-byes of Magnus Marmalade*, illustrated by Erik Blegvad.   New York,
> Putnam, 1966.
> *Merry, Merry FIBruary*, illustrated by Arnold Lobel.   New York, Parents' Magazine
> Press, 1977.

Other

> *The Tale of Gockel, Hinkel, and Gackeliah*, illustrated by Maurice Sendak.   New York,
> Random House, 1961.
> *Schoolmaster Whackwell's Wonderful Sons: A Fairy Tale*, illustrated by Maurice
> Sendak.   New York, Random House, 1962.
> *The Heart of Stone: A Fairy Tale*, illustrated by David Levine.   New York, Macmillan,
> and London, Collier Macmillan, 1964.
> *The Story of Lohengrin, The Knight of the Swan*, illustrated by Herbert Danska.   New
> York, Putnam, 1966.
> *A Monkey's Uncle*, illustrated by Mitchell Miller.   New York, Farrar Straus, 1969.
> *Baron Munchausen: Fifteen Truly Tall Tales*, illustrated by Willi Baum.   Reading,
> Massachusetts, Addison Wesley, 1971.
> *The Child from Far Away*, illustrated by Michael Eagle.   Reading, Massachusetts,
> Addison Wesley, 1971.
> *Little John*, illustrated by Anita Lobel.   New York, Farrar Straus, 1972.

> Translator, *Dwarf Long-Nose*, by Wilhelm Hauff, illustrated by Maurice Sendak.   New
> York, Random House, 1960.
> Translator, *The Enchanted Drum*, by Walter Grieder, illustrated by Grieder.   New
> York, Parents' Magazine Press, 1969.
> Translator. *The Grandma in the Apple Tree*, by Mira Lobe, illustrated by Judith Gwyn
> Brown.   New York, McGraw Hill, 1970.

*   *   *

Acclaimed in 1960 for her translation of Wilhelm Hauff's *Dwarf Long-Nose* and again in
the following year for her retelling of *The Tale of Gockel, Hinkel, and Gackeliah* (by Clemens
Brentano), Doris Orgel has continued her talents for translation and for retelling the tales of
others. Meanwhile, with the publication of her own highly successful *Sarah's Room* in 1963,
Ms. Orgel demonstrated yet another facet of her strong literary capability. In the years since
then, Doris Orgel has produced an impressive number of very ably written books for
children. In addition to *Sarah's Room* the best known of these include *Cindy's Sad and
Happy Tree*, *Phoebe and the Prince*, *The Mulberry Music*, and *A Certain Magic*.

More often than not Ms. Orgel employs deceptively simple subject matter and theme, often
basing her stories upon personal experience. Although sibling jealousy is a somewhat over-
worked theme in contemporary books for children, in *Sarah's Room* this theme in no way
borders on the trite or monotonous. On the contrary *Sarah's Room*, a simple little prose
poem, deals with sibling jealousy in a purely delightful manner. The poem-story begins and
moves forward in a pleasing rhythmic pace which lends itself well to oral reading. Little
Jenny, the poem's protagonist, longs to play in the room of her older sister, Sarah. In Sarah's
room trees grow and flowers bloom on the walls, but in Jenny's room no pretty wallpaper
has yet been placed since, when small, Jenny marked her walls "with smudges and smears."
In Sarah's very tidy room there are toys which Jenny longs to touch, but Sarah forbids her to

do so. But Doris Orgel gives Jenny another chance, through dream-fantasy, to enter Sarah's room. This time the toys beg Jenny to stay, but she finally bids them good-night promising to come again. Happily Jenny awakens from her dream-fantasy to discover that she has grown tall enough to reach the latch on Sarah's door. This time, happily for both girls, Jenny has also grown by outgrowing her earlier inclination to mess up and destroy things. Sarah decides that Jenny has grown up enough to be allowed the use of Sarah's room whenever she chooses. Jenny will now enjoy her own room, too, for Doris Orgel has seen to it that Jenny's room is also a place "where trees grow tall ... and morning glories bloom upon the wall."

Lengthier and far more serious in tone and content, are *The Mulberry Music* and *A Certain Magic*. Both are successful books which illustrate the very special attachment a child may have for an older adult relative. In *The Mulberry Music* 11-year-old Libby feels a special attachment to her Grandma Liza; in *A Certain Magic* 11-year-old Jenny loves her Aunt Trudl as much as or more than she loves her own parents. In the first of these books, the author maneuvers her child heroine through the mental anguish of coping with the serious illness and death of the grandmother; in the second, the child heroine must cope with the anxiety and guilt she feels from having discovered and read the secret childhood diary of her Aunt Trudl. The ultimate victory in *The Mulberry Music* is Libby's discovery of how love can survive beyond death; in *A Certain Magic* Jenny's victory is a dual one: conquering of loneliness and coming to terms with the fascination of evil, either real or imagined. In each of these works, the first a novel of camaraderie and courage and the second a novel of camaraderie and suspense, Doris Orgel has presented her material with honesty and integrity and with a total absence of the maudlin flavor which could have crept into such stories.

Cindy's Sad and Happy Tree depicts the anguish a little girl feels when a tree surgeon condemns her favorite elm tree to be cut down. This particular story is an excellent example of the skill of Doris Orgel in avoiding the maudlin in her sensitive portrayal of the delicate, though deep, emotions of a child experiencing loss.

Bearing a certain kinship to *Sarah's Room* in lightness and tone, *Phoebe and the Prince* also lends itself well to oral reading. The light-hearted story of a high-falutin' flea discovered by a little girl on the ear of her pet dog, *Phoebe and the Prince* is swift-moving, crisp in dialog, and interlaced with funning and punning. After the flea has told Phoebe his story and convinced her of the royal blood in his veins, he hops out of her life as suddenly and unceremoniously as he has hopped into it.

Consistently well-written and varied in style and content, the books of Doris Orgel reveal their author's unique sensitivity to the everyday problems which most children experience during emotional, social, moral, physical, and psychical development. Encompassing, as they do, the serious, the sad, the happy, the comic, the tragic experiences of children, Doris Orgel's books are never mundane.

—Charity Chang

ORMONDROYD, Edward. American. Born in Wilkinsburg, Pennsylvania, 8 October 1925. Educated at the University of California, Berkeley, A.B. 1951 (Phi Beta Kappa), M.L.S. 1958. Served in the United States Naval Reserve, 1943–45. Married to Joan Ormondroyd; has three children from previous marriage. Has worked as merchant seaman, bookstore clerk, paper factory machine operator. Currently, Technical Services Librarian, Finger Lakes Library System, Ithaca, New York. Address: R.D. 2, Newfield, New York 14867, U.S.A.

PUBLICATIONS FOR CHILDREN

Fiction

> *David and the Phoenix*, illustrated by Joan Raysor.   Chicago, Follett, 1957.
> *The Tale of Alain*, illustrated by Robert Frankenberg.   Chicago, Follett, 1960.
> *Time at the Top*, illustrated by Peggie Bach.   Berkeley, California, Parnassus Press, 1963; London, Heinemann, 1976.
> *Theodore*, illustrated by John Larrecq.   Berkeley, California, Parnassus Press, 1966.
> *Michael, The Upstairs Dog*, illustrated by Cyndy Szekeres.   New York, Dial Press, 1967.
> *Broderick*, illustrated by John Larrecq.   Berkeley, California, Parnassus Press, 1969.
> *Theodore's Rival*, illustrated by John Larrecq.   Berkeley, California, Parnassus Press, 1971.
> *Castaways on Long Ago*, illustrated by Ruth Robbins.   Berkeley, California, Parnassus Press, 1973.
> *Imagination Greene*, illustrated by John Lewis.   Berkeley, California, Parnassus Press, 1973.
> *All in Good Time*, illustrated by Ruth Robbins.   Berkeley, California, Parnassus Press, 1975.

Verse

> *Jonathan Frederick Aloysius Brown*, illustrated by Suzi Spector.   San Carlos, California, Golden Gate Books, 1964.

Edward Ormondroyd comments:
   The child I once was, and still am, somewhere, loved certain kinds of books. I try to write those kinds of books to please him. I am delighted when I succeed in beguiling not only him, and myself, but other children as well.

*   *   *

Edward Ormondroyd's particular contribution to children's literature has been his novel and convincing approach to the time-travel *genre*. *Time at the Top* employs a much more sophisticated narrative technique than one generally expects to find in a book intended for children. Ormondroyd tells the story as if in his own person, piecing together fragments of information about the mysterious disappearance of Susan Shaw and, later on, of her father. The narrator's only link with the Shaws is that they are neighbours in an apartment building and share the same cleaning lady. Ormondroyd's technique of allowing his characters to travel through time is an extremely innovative one, using as he does the elevator of the apartment building as a kind of time machine: "It was the strangest sensation − as if the elevator were forcing its way up through something sticky in the shaft, like molasses or chewing gum."

   His main character, Susan Shaw, takes the elevator one day out of a sense of ennui and discontentment with the claustrophobia of life in the apartment. She intends to look out of the 7th floor window, but discovers that the elevator mysteriously continues upwards beyond what should be the top floor. When the doors open she gets out of the elevator into a house which had stood on the same site a hundred years earlier.

   The adventures in which Susan becomes involved once she has passed through this time warp often seem slightly contrived but not so seriously as to mar the whole texture of the tale, for Ormondroyd soon introduces another unusual innovation. In general in books for children which deal with time travel, the characters return to their own time at the end of the tale. By contrast, Ormondroyd's Susan Shaw decides that middle-class life in the 1860's is preferable to her present day apartment dwelling, and she resolves not only to abandon the 20th century but also to engineer a marriage between her widowed father and the young widow who is the mother of her 19th-century friend.

The tale ends with the narrator holding the proof of this successful abduction in his hand in the form of a faded family photograph posed against the house, a "perfect example of the Hudson River Bracketed style," and identifying Susan's father:

> This man does have a mustache, a very imposing one; and behind it is the happy but faintly bewildered expression of one who has been led against his better judgement to the foot of the rainbow, and has found, contrary to all commonsense and education, a pot of gold there.

—Gillian Thomas

OTTLEY, Reginald (Leslie). British. Born in London. Educated at St. Mary Magdalene's Church of England School, London. Served in the Australian Remount Corps, 1939–45. Prior to World War II, seaman; farm worker, cattle drover, horse breaker in Australia; cattle ranch manager, Fiji; after World War II, race horse trainer, Sydney; property manager, New South Wales; worked for British Colonial Administration in Guadalcanal, Solomon Islands; cattle ranch manager, New Caledonia, French Pacific Islands. Recipient: New York *Herald Tribune* Festival award, 1966. Address: 37 Henry Street, Chapel Hill, Brisbane, Queensland 4069, Australia.

PUBLICATIONS FOR CHILDREN

Fiction

> *By the Sandhills of Yamboorah*, illustrated by Clyde Pearson. London, Deutsch, 1965; as *Boy Alone*, New York, Harcourt Brace, 1966.
> *The Roan Colt of Yamboorah*, illustrated by David Perry. London, Deutsch, 1966; as *The Roan Colt*, New York, Harcourt Brace, 1967.
> *Rain Comes to Yamboorah*, illustrated by Robert Hales. London, Deutsch, 1967; New York, Harcourt Brace, 1968.
> *Giselle.* London, Collins, and New York, Harcourt Brace, 1968.
> *Brumbie Dust: A Selection of Stories*, illustrated by Douglas Phillips. London, Collins, and New York, Harcourt Brace, 1969.
> *The Bates Family.* London, Collins, and New York, Harcourt Brace, 1969.
> *Jim Grey of Moonbah.* London, Collins, and New York, Harcourt Brace, 1970.
> *No More Tomorrow.* New York, Harcourt Brace, 1971; London, Collins, 1972.
> *The War on William Street.* London, Collins, 1971; Nashville, Nelson, 1973.
> *A Word about Horses.* London, Collins, 1973.
> *Mum's Place.* London, Collins, 1974.

Play

> Radio Play: *The Feather Shoes*, 1964.

PUBLICATIONS FOR ADULTS

Novel

Stampede. London, Laurie, 1961.

*　　*　　*

An Australian through having once lived and wandered the Outback, Reginald Ottley is claimed by Australians because of his starkly perceptive pictures of the isolated "inland" and its inhabitants. In his novels he describes the wide and lonely spaces and the rugged characters who will not allow the conditions of their lives to diminish them in any way. His most memorable portrait is the nameless boy in the *Yamboorah* trilogy, which also contains his best writing. *By the Sandhills of Yamboorah, The Roan Colt of Yamboorah,* and *Rain Comes to Yamboorah* are studies in the effect of isolation on a sensitive, introspective, and inarticulate wood-and-water-joey on a large station property near the edges of the South Australian desert. The boy's need for companionship, which he satisfies through the dog Rags and the roan colt, is given poignancy by old Kanga's tough, unsentimental and unspoken mateship. In the third book the boy eventually repays his debt to Kanga and is shown maturing to the harsh conditions of a relentless land.

Ottley extends his theme of refinement through endurance in *The Bates Family,* the epic of an itinerant droving family. Drought, flood, and fire are added to inner loneliness and stoical physical suffering, particularly in the case of Albie whose hip is crippled by a fall from a horse. The lives of the family gain stature as they look ahead to hardship seemingly as endless as the country they traverse. *No More Tomorrow* is a reminiscent tale of isolation and mateship told by a swagman of an era which is now past. The old man trudges the sandy stretches with no companion but his dog Blue, whose loyalty, devotion, and single-mindedness underscore the battler's condition. Mateship, eccentricity, the bond between man and his horse or his dog, a sparse and demanding country are further explored in the wry, sometimes near-tragic anecdotes and tales of *Brumbie Dust* and *A Word about Horses.*

Giselle was a departure for Ottley and came from his roamings in New Caledonia. It explores a few weeks in the life of a French girl and her friendship with a native boy whose ambition is to be a priest. It is more delicate in tone than his studies of the Outback and more successful than *Jim Grey of Moonbah,* a predictable and sentimental story of a compliant lad who helps his mother run a sheep station in the Snowy Mountains. *The War on William Street* is an exploration of toughness in a teen-age gang who roam Sydney in the 1930's, while *Mum's Place* is another study of the comradeship between a boy and an older man, both of whom are ashamed to admit mutual dependence. Ottley works hard at appearing unsentimental, but as a writer has become increasingly nostalgic, so that sentiment, at times, is just below the surface.

—H. M. Saxby

OVERTON, Jenny (Margaret Mary). British. Born in Cranleigh, Surrey, 22 January 1942. Educated at Guildford County Grammar School, Surrey, 1953–60; Girton College, Cambridge, 1961–64, B.A. (honours) 1964, M.A. 1966. Appeals Secretary, 1965–66, and Principal's Private Secretary, 1966–67, Newnham College, Cambridge; Assistant Editor, Aluminium Federation, London, 1967–69; Editor, Macmillan, publishers, Basingstoke, Hampshire, 1969–71. Since 1971, Editor, Lutterworth Press, Guildford. Address: c/o J.F. Overton, Crest Hill, Peaslake, Guildford, Surrey, England.

PUBLICATIONS FOR CHILDREN

Fiction

Creed Country.   London, Faber, 1969; New York, Macmillan, 1970.
The Thirteen Days of Christmas, illustrated by Shirley Hughes.   London, Faber, 1972;
   Nashville, Nelson, 1974.
The Nightwatch Winter.   London, Faber, 1973.

*   *   *

With a small output of work to date, Jenny Overton has established herself as an original and gifted novelist. Her skill lies in capturing the many-sided experience of life in a large family, spanning an age-range from mid-childhood to early adult life. The forced co-existence of touchy, competitive and vulnerable young people, each at his or her own uniquely stressful stage of growth, each with individual doubts, problems and ambitions, forms the background to all of her first three books, though in other respects *The Thirteen Days of Christmas* seems an unlikely product of the same imagination as *Creed Country* and its sequel *The Nightwatch Winter*.

The Thirteen Days of Christmas is a comic fantasy, enjoyed by children across a wide age-range. Its subject is a crazily improbable version of the carol "The Twelve Days of Christmas." The carol is interpreted literally, with truly awesome implications for the sheer number of presents cast upon the besieged heroine. At the centre of the fantasy is a highly practical domestic situation – the desire of two young boys to marry off their elder sister, whose household accomplishments unfortunately exclude the gift of cookery, to an ardent lover who is so rich that the defect will not matter. The story is imaginatively conceived and wittily told.

Jenny Overton's eye and ear for family comedy, as shown in this light tale, are also at work in the more complex and realistic situations of *Creed Country* and *The Nightwatch Winter*, novels of some complexity which require an older, more sophisticated reader. In these books the humour works in counterpoint against the explosive emotional tensions of adolescence. In *Creed Country*, for example, evidence of Sarah's first emotional entanglement is the subject of banter and mockery in her crowded family circle, and we are made aware how funny it is to adolescents who are callously uninvolved; but the story also brings out fully her embarrassment, uncertainty and pain.

Other elements are common to all three novels: a remarkable (and very rare) ability to communicate the difficulty and the wonder of music; an often playful and sardonic but nonetheless serious concern with religious belief and observance; and a sense of cycle, change, and festival, both in the seasonal landscape and in human society, with all its periodic rituals of school and home. *Creed Country* and *The Nightwatch Winter* are, in part, stories of tension and crisis, but their distinction lies especially in their humour and psychological insight, in their rich sense of place and history, and in the highly professional control of demanding and intricate plots.

—Peter Hollindale

OXENHAM, Elsie.   Pseudonym for Elsie Jeanette Dunkerley.   British.   Daughter of the writer John Oxenham. *Died 9 January 1960.*

PUBLICATIONS FOR CHILDREN

Fiction

Goblin Island, illustrated by T. Heath Robinson.   London, Collins, 1907.
A Princess in Tatters.   London, Collins, 1908.
The Conquest of Christina, illustrated by G.B. Foyster.   London, Collins, 1909.
The Girl Who Wouldn't Make Friends.   London, Nelson, 1909.
Mistress Nanciebel, illustrated by James Durden.   London, Hodder and Stoughton, 1910.
A Holiday Queen, illustrated by E.A. Overnell.   London, Collins, 1910.
Rosaly's New School, illustrated by T.J. Overnell.   Edinburgh, Chambers, 1913.
Girls of the Hamlet Club.   Edinburgh, Chambers, 1914.
Schoolgirls and Scouts, illustrated by Arthur Dixon.   London, Collins, 1914.
At School with the Roundheads, illustrated by H.C. Earnshaw.   Edinburgh, Chambers, 1915.
Finding Her Family.   London, S.P.C.K., 1915.
The Tuck-Shop Girl.   Edinburgh, Chambers. 1916.
A School Camp Fire.   Edinburgh, Chambers, 1917.
The School of Ups and Downs, illustrated by H.C. Earnshaw.   Edinburgh, Chambers, 1918.
A Go-Ahead Schoolgirl, illustrated by H.C. Earnshaw.   Edinburgh, Chambers, 1919.
Expelled from School, illustrated by Victor Prout.   London, Collins, 1919.
The Abbey Girls, illustrated by Arthur Dixon.   London, Collins, 1920.
The School Torment, illustrated by H.C. Earnshaw.   Edinburgh, Chambers, 1920.
The Twins of Castle Charming.   London, Swarthmore Press, 1920.
The Girls of Abbey School, illustrated by Elsie Wood.   London, Collins, 1921.
The Two Form-Captains, illustrated by Percy Tarrant.   Edinburgh, Chambers, 1921.
The Abbey Girls Go Back to School, illustrated by Elsie Wood.   London, Collins, 1922.
The Captain of the Fifth, illustrated by Percy Tarrant.   Edinburgh, Chambers, 1922.
Patience Joan, Outsider.   London, Cassell, 1922; New York, Funk and Wagnalls, 1923.
The Junior Captain.   Edinburgh, Chambers, 1923.
The New Abbey Girls, illustrated by Elsie Wood.   London, Collins, 1923.
The Abbey Girls Again.   London, Collins, 1924.
The Girls of Gwynfa.   London and New York, Warne, 1924.
The School Without a Name, illustrated by Nina K. Brisley.   Edinburgh, Chambers, 1924.
"Tickles"; or, The School That Was Different.   London, Partridge, 1924.
The Abbey Girls in Town, illustrated by Rosa Petherick.   London, Collins, 1925.
The Testing of the Torment, illustrated by P.B. Hickling.   London, Cassell, 1925.
Ven at Gregory's, illustrated by Nina K. Brisley.   Edinburgh, Chambers, 1925.
The Camp Fire Torment, illustrated by Nina Browne.   Edinburgh, Chambers, 1926.
Queen of the Abbey Girls, illustrated by E.J. Kealey.   London, Collins, 1926.
The Troubles of Tazy, illustrated by Percy Tarrant.   Edinburgh, Chambers, 1926.
Jen of the Abbey School, illustrated by F. Meyerheim.   London, Collins, 1927.
Patience and Her Problems, illustrated by M. Benator.   Edinburgh, Chambers, 1927.
Peggy Makes Good!, illustrated by H.L. Bacon.   London, Religious Tract Society, 1927.
The Abbey Girls Win Through.   London, Collins, 1928.
The Abbey School.   London, Collins, 1928.
The Crisis in Camp Keema, illustrated by Percy Tarrant.   Edinburgh, Chambers, 1928.
The Abbey Girls at Home, illustrated by I. Burns.   London, Collins, 1929.
Deb at School, illustrated by Nina K. Brisley.   Edinburgh, Chambers, 1929.
The Girls of Rocklands School.   London, Collins, 1929.
The Abbey Girls Play Up.   London, Collins, 1930.

Dorothy's Dilemma, illustrated by Nina K. Brisley.   Edinburgh, Chambers, 1930.
The Second Term at Rocklands.   London, Collins, 1930.
The Abbey Girls on Trial.   London, Collins, 1931.
Deb of Sea House, illustrated by Nina K. Brisley.   Edinburgh, Chambers, 1931.
The Third Term at Rocklands.   London, Collins, 1931.
Biddy's Secret.   Edinburgh, Chambers, 1932.
The Camp Mystery.   London, Collins, 1932.
The Girls of Squirrel House.   London, Collins, 1932.
The Reformation of Jinty.   Edinburgh, Chambers, 1933.
Rosamund's Victory.   London, Harrap, 1933.
Jinty's Patrol.   London, Newnes, 1934.
Maidlin to the Rescue, illustrated by R. Cloke.   Edinburgh, Chambers, 1934.
Joy's New Adventure.   Edinburgh, Chambers, 1935.
Peggy and the Brotherhood.   London, Religious Tract Society, 1936.
Rosamund's Tuck-Shop.   London, Religious Tract Society, 1937.
Sylvia of Sarn.   London and New York, Warne, 1937.
Damaris at Dorothy's.   London, S.P.C.K., 1937.
Maidlin Bears the Torch.   London, Religious Tract Society, 1937.
Schooldays at the Abbey.   London, Collins, 1938.
Rosamund's Castle.   London, Girl's Own Paper, 1938.
Secrets of the Abbey, illustrated by Heade.   London, Collins, 1939.
Stowaways in the Abbey.   London, Collins, 1940.
Damaris Dances.   London, Oxford University Press, 1940.
Patch and a Pawn.   London and New York, Warne, 1940.
Adventure for Two, illustrated by Margaret Horder.   London, Oxford University Press, 1941.
Jandy Mac Comes Back.   London, Collins, 1941.
Pernel Wins, illustrated by Margaret Horder.   London, Muller, 1942.
Maid of the Abbey, illustrated by Heade.   London, Collins, 1943.
Elsa Puts Things Right, illustrated by Margaret Horder.   London, Muller, 1944.
Two Joans at the Abbey, illustrated by Margaret Horder.   London, Collins, 1945.
Daring Doranne.   London, Muller, 1945.
The Abbey Champion, illustrated by Margaret Horder.   London, Muller, 1946.
Robins in the Abbey.   London, Collins, 1947.
The Secrets of Vairy, illustrated by Margaret Horder.   London, Muller, 1947.
Margery Meets the Roses.   London, Lutterworth Press, 1947.
A Fiddler for the Abbey, illustrated by Margaret Horder.   London, Muller, 1948.
Guardians of the Abbey, illustrated by Margaret Horder.   London, Muller, 1950.
Schoolgirl Jen at the Abbey.   London, Collins, 1950.
Selma at the Abbey.   London, Collins, 1952.
Rachel in the Abbey, illustrated by M.D. Neilson.   London, Muller, 1952.
A Dancer from the Abbey.   London, Collins, 1953.
The Song of the Abbey.   London, Collins, 1954.
The Girls at Wood End.   London, Blackie, 1957.
Tomboys at the Abbey.   London, Collins, 1957.
Two Queens at the Abbey.   London, Collins, 1959.
Strangers at the Abbey.   London, Collins, 1963.

*   *   *

Elsie Oxenham wrote over eighty books for girls between 1909 and 1959. She has sometimes been described as a writer of school stories, but few of her books strictly come within this category. They cover a wide range of themes and embody a seriousness and a depth of characterization that are unusual in the genre.

Like Angela Brazil, Dorita Fairlie Bruce, and Elinor Brent-Dyer, Elsie Oxenham wrote numerous short stories for girls' magazines as well as full-length books, providing an accurate picture of the life of many British middle-class girls in the 1920's and 30's. By the 1940's her stories had an old-fashioned flavour: some readers, however, found this – and the books' religious overtones – intriguing.

The author was a Guardian in the Camp Fire Association, an organization which never achieved the same popularity in England as in America. It is featured in several of her books. Elsie Oxenham also wrote about the Girl Guide Movement, for which she judged several folk dance contests. The theme of her *Peggy and the Brotherhood* is the conflicting appeal of these two organizations. Elsie Oxenham presents both groups sympathetically, the Camp Fire standing "for beauty and poetry" and Guiding representing "bigness" and, of course, practicality.

Many of Elsie Oxenham's books are grouped into series. The Abbey series is the largest (approximately 40 books) and the most addictive. It combines several attractive elements. There is a romanticized sense of history, expressed through an ancient Abbey. This forms a picturesque background for the folk dancing and other activities of the Hamlet Club, which is the linking factor of the series. The Club is founded initially to bring together the girls of Miss Macey's school who live in isolated hamlets; also to counterbalance the snobbish influence of the school's sophisticated "Townies." The Hamlet Club stresses the "other meaning" of Hamlet – "To be or not to be" – which Elsie Oxenham interprets as an exhortation to sacrifice one's own interests for others.

For young readers the Hamlet Club's main appeal was probably its adoption of the May Queen rituals, which involved a lot of dressing up and colourful symbolism. Elsie Oxenham apparently derived these from the May Day ceremony instituted by John Ruskin in 1881 at Whitelands Training College in London. Frequent descriptions of country dancing reflect the author's interest in the work of the English Folk Dance and Song Society, some of whose leading lights (including Cecil Sharp) are portrayed in the Abbey books.

The series is permeated by Elsie Oxenham's feeling for the countryside; this creates a mellow mood but is not overdone. (There are suggestions of mud as well as glowing sunshine in the beechwoods, of perspiration as well as prettification in the folk dance sequences.) Elsie Oxenham's ability to combine realism with romance has indelibly impressed her characters – and the values which they represent – on the minds of readers. Many adults still enthusiastically collect her books.

—Mary Cadogan

PALMER, C(yril) Everard. Canadian. Born in Kendal, Jamaica, 15 October 1930. Educated at Mico Training College, Jamaica, Teaching diploma 1955; Lakehead University, Thunder Bay, Ontario, B.A. 1973. Since 1971, teacher, Red Rock, Ontario. Address: Box 31, Nipigon, Ontario POT 2J0, Canada.

PUBLICATIONS FOR CHILDREN (illustrated by Laszlo Acs)

Fiction

The Cloud with the Silver Lining. London, Deutsch, 1966; New York, Pantheon Books, 1967.
Big Doc Bitteroot. London, Deutsch, 1968; Indianapolis, Bobbs Merrill, 1971.
The Sun Salutes You. London, Deutsch, 1970.
The Hummingbird People. London, Deutsch, 1971.

A Cow Called Boy, illustrated by Charles Gaines. Indianapolis, Bobbs Merrill, 1972;
    London, Deutsch, 1973.
The Wooing of Beppo Tate. London, Deutsch, 1972.
Baba and Mr. Big. Indianapolis, Bobbs Merrill, 1972; London, Deutsch, 1974.
My Father Sun-Sun Johnson. London, Deutsch, 1974.

PUBLICATIONS FOR ADULTS

Novel

A Broken Vessel. Kingston, Jamaica, Pioneer Press, 1960.

*   *   *

The Jamaican village of Kendal is the setting for C. Everard Palmer's rich studies of West
Indian life. Of his early work he has written, "These books are intended to revive for adults
fast-disappearing or totally extinct aspects of Jamaican life and for children creating them
because they have missed them." Kendal, Palmer's own birthplace, is remote in place as well
as time: it is 130 miles from Kingston and 4 miles up the hill road from the coastal hamlet of
Green Island. It is rural and largely self-sufficient; it is easy to see from these books why a
West Indian calls his village "my community." The rise and fall of reputations, the feuds and
the power struggles provide the plot dynamics, and each story culminates in a set-piece – a
hurricane, a fire, a trial or some village festivity which re-affirms the bonds of the
community. The stories have strong characterisation, racing narratives, and abundant and
colourful detail. Palmer has a vivid and exuberant humour and a highly individual style; he
makes full use of dialect. Except to West Indian readers, who will appreciate these novels as
literature of their heritage, the setting may appear strange and exotic. But their ambience, the
world of the village, is universal.

The Cloud with the Silver Lining is a warm and gentle story of two boys who keep the
family smallholding going when the breadwinner, their grandfather, is immobilized by an
accident. Big Doc Bitteroot contains Palmer's most memorable character, Kelso Crane. He is a
larger-than-life itinerant quack doctor who dazzles the unsophisticated villagers until one of
his cures goes wrong and he is brought to trial. The Sun Salutes You again treats of village
politics when Mike Johnson challenges Matt Southern's control not only of the trucking
business but also of the villagers' lives. While Matt corrupts the police to stay in power, Mike
enlists the aid of superstition in the person of a Pocomanian prophetess, Shepherdess Annie.
The Hummingbird People tells of rival villages' plans to celebrate the return from war of three
airmen. The "jollifying" of their plans and counter-plans has the book humming with
exuberance.

The Wooing of Beppo Tate is a comedy of courtship between Mr. Tate and Mrs. Belmont
and between the latter's daughter, Daphne, and the former's adopted son, Beppo. Beppo has
enough trouble in his new role without falling in love. But all ends happily in this successful
story for older children. A Cow Called Boy is a simple anecdotal tale of Josh whose pet calf
follows him to school and causes chaos in the classroom. The enforced sale of Boy which
results involves the whole village. Baba and Mr. Big tells of the kinship between an old man
and a hawk. It is Jim Anderson, a newcomer, who brings them together, for capturing the
hawk is the price of his initiation into the village gang; but in the process he learns new
values.

My Father Sun-Sun Johnson is Palmer's best book so far and is again for older readers.
Rami Johnson takes his father's side when his parents part and his mother marries Jake, a
man with a driving need for success. But Sun-Sun Johnson and his son too have their success
in rebuilding their lives and conquering adversity.

—Mary Croxson

PARISH, Peggy (Margaret Cecile Parish). American. Born in Manning, South Carolina. Educated at the University of South Carolina, Columbia, B.A. in English 1948; Peabody College, Nashville. Teacher in Kentucky and Oklahoma, and at the Dalton School, New York. Lives in South Carolina. Address: c/o Macmillan Publishing Co. Inc., 866 Third Avenue, New York, New York 10022, U.S.A.

PUBLICATIONS FOR CHILDREN

Fiction

Good Hunting, Little Indian, illustrated by Leonard Weisgard.   New York, Scott, 1962.
Willy Is My Brother, illustrated by Shirley Hughes.   New York, Scott, and London, Gollancz, 1963.
Amelia Bedelia, illustrated by Fritz Siebel.   New York, Harper, 1963; Kingswood, Surrey, World's Work, 1964.
Thank You, Amelia Bedelia, illustrated by Fritz Siebel.   New York, Harper, 1964; Kingswood, Surrey, World's Work, 1965.
Amelia Bedelia and the Surprise Shower, illustrated by Fritz Siebel.   New York, Harper, 1966; Kingswood, Surrey, World's Work, 1967.
Key to the Treasure, illustrated by Paul Frame.   New York, Macmillan, 1966.
Clues in the Woods, illustrated by Paul Frame.   New York, Macmillan, and London, Collier Macmillan, 1968.
Little Indian, illustrated by John E. Johnson.   New York, Simon and Schuster, 1968.
A Beastly Circus, illustrated by Peter Parnall.   New York, Simon and Schuster, 1969.
Granny and the Indians, illustrated by Brinton Turkle.   New York, Macmillan, 1969.
Jumper Goes to School, illustrated by Cyndy Szekeres.   New York, Simon and Schuster, 1969.
Granny and the Desperadoes, illustrated by Steven Kellogg.   New York, Macmillan, 1970.
Ootah's Lucky Day, illustrated by Mamoru Funai.   New York, Harper, 1970; Kingswood, Surrey, World's Work, 1971.
Snapping Turtle's All-Wrong Day, illustrated by John E. Johnson.   New York, Simon and Schuster, 1970.
Come Back, Amelia Bedelia, illustrated by Wallace Tripp.   New York, Harper, 1971; Kingswood, Surrey, World's Work, 1973.
Haunted House, illustrated by Paul Frame.   New York, Macmillan, and London, Collier Macmillan, 1971.
Granny, The Baby, and the Big Gray Thing, illustrated by Lynn Sweat.   New York, Macmillan, 1972; Kingswood, Surrey, World's Work, 1973.
Play Ball, Amelia Bedelia, illustrated by Wallace Tripp.   New York, Harper, 1972; Kingswood, Surrey, World's Work, 1973.
Too Many Rabbits, illustrated by Leonard Kessler.   New York, Macmillan, 1974; Kingswood, Surrey, World's Work, 1975.
Pirate Island Adventure, illustrated by Paul Frame.   New York, Macmillan, 1975.
Good Work, Amelia Bedelia, illustrated by Lynn Sweat.   New York, Morrow, 1976; Kingswood, Surrey, World's Work, 1977.
Teach Us, Amelia Bedelia, illustrated by Fritz Siebel.   New York, Morrow, 1977.
Hermit Dan, illustrated by Paul Frame.   New York, Macmillan, 1977.

Other

My Book of Manners, illustrated by Richard Scarry.   New York, Golden Press, 1962; London, Golden Pleasure Books, 1963.
Let's Be Indians, illustrated by Arnold Lobel.   New York, Harper, 1962.

The Story of Grains: Wheat, Corn, and Rice, with W.W. Crowder, illustrated by William Moyers.   New York, Grosset and Dunlap, 1965.

Let's Be Early Settlers with Daniel Boone, illustrated by Arnold Lobel.   New York, Harper, 1967.

Costumes to Make, illustrated by Lynn Sweat.   New York, Macmillan, 1970; London, Collier Macmillan, 1971.

Sheet Magic: Games, Toys, and Gifts from Old Sheets, illustrated by Lynn Sweat.   New York, Macmillan, and London, Collier Macmillan, 1971.

Dinosaur Time, illustrated by Arnold Lobel.   New York, Harper, 1974; Kingswood, Surrey, World's Work, 1975.

December Decorations: A Holiday How-To Book, illustrated by Barbara Wolff.   New York, Macmillan, 1975.

Let's Celebrate: Holiday Decorations You Can Make, illustrated by Lynn Sweat.   New York, Morrow, 1976.

*   *   *

Peggy Parish has a knack for combining those special elements that spark a child's interest and whet his appetite for more. She has written several successful series of which Amelia Bedelia is the most well known. First introduced in *Amelia Bedelia*, the character continues to grow in appeal with each ridiculous episode. Amelia Bedelia is remarkably adept at taking directions quite literally. On her first day as a maid at the Rogers' house, she blithely dusts the furniture with dusting powder, draws the drapes by sketching them, and dresses the chicken in pants and socks. Only her delicious lemon meringue pie prevents her dismissal. In *Amelia Bedelia and the Surprise Shower*, she and Cousin Alcolu help Mrs. Rogers throw a surprise bridal shower, complete with gifts and a shower from the garden hose. Finally in *Come Back, Amelia Bedelia*, she's discharged to pound the pavements for a new job. After wreaking havoc everywhere, she returns happily reinstated. Most comical is her literal interpretation of the game of baseball in *Play Ball, Amelia Bedelia*. From stealing bases, to tagging and running home, she never fails to misunderstand. Her predicaments are just obvious enough to allow the sophistication of a play on words.

In *Granny and the Indians*, Parish has created another unique and likable character. Alone, with a gun that doesn't shoot, Granny Guntry proves herself competent in dealing with Indians, desperadoes, and wolves. She's a nice, sweet, tough, and independent old lady who wants things done her way. Her brushes with danger are just enough to be exciting and the action never ceases until she manages to get things settled to her liking.

Parish's mystery series with Jed, Liza, and Bill Roberts are longer but just as involving. The children always manage to keep their secrets from the adults while unraveling the mysteries. Grandpa Roberts provides the initial clues for two of the mysteries that involve word scrambles, secret codes, and picture clues. Though easy to read, the mysteries provide enough action to maintain the suspense. Deciphering the clues becomes absorbing and involves the reader in the intrigue. The characters are defined through their actions and drawn well enough to seem realistic.

In contrast to her more successful series, her books about Indians are not as amusing nor as well thought out. The lack of names for the Indians in *Good Hunting, Little Indian* is offensive. Referring to the characters as Mama Indian, Papa Indian and Little Indian lacks originality and seems to imply that they might be objects rather than people. In *Little Indian*, the Indian boy must earn a name. It seems to imply all Indians are called "Little Indian" until they earn a name. The notion is preposterous, and the books do not do justice to the Indians nor the enlightened concept of presenting an accurate portrait of all peoples.

—Martha J. Fick

PARK, (Rosina) Ruth (Lucia).   Australian.   Born in Auckland, New Zealand. Educated at
St. Benedict's College; University of Auckland. Married the writer D'Arcy Niland in 1942
(died, 1967). Teacher and journalist. Recipient: Sydney *Morning Herald* prize, for novel,
1948. Lives on Norfolk Island. Address: c/o Angus and Robertson Publishers, 102 Glover
Street, Cremorne Junction, New South Wales 2090, Australia.

PUBLICATIONS FOR CHILDREN

Fiction

> *The Hole in the Hill*, illustrated by Jennifer Murray.   Sydney, Ure Smith, 1961;
>   London, Macmillan, 1962; as *The Secret of the Maori Cave*, New York, Doubleday,
>   1964.
> *The Ship's Cat*, illustrated by Richard Kennedy.   London, Macmillan, and New York,
>   St. Martin's Press, 1961.
> *Uncle Matt's Mountain*, illustrated by Laurence Broderick.   London, Macmillan, and
>   New York, St. Martin's Press, 1962.
> *The Road to Christmas*, illustrated by Noela Young.   London, Macmillan, and New
>   York, St. Martin's Press, 1962.
> *The Road under the Sea*, illustrated by Jennifer Murray.   Sydney, Ure Smith, 1962;
>   London, Macmillan, 1963; New York, Doubleday, 1966.
> *The Muddle-Headed Wombat*, illustrated by Noela Young.   Sydney, Educational Press,
>   1962; London, Angus and Robertson, 1963.
> *Shaky Island*, illustrated by Iris Millington.   London, Constable, and New York,
>   McKay, 1962.
> *The Muddle-Headed Wombat on Holiday*, illustrated by Noela Young.   Sydney,
>   Educational Press, and London, Angus and Robertson, 1964.
> *Airlift for Grandee*, illustrated by Sheila Hawkins.   London, Macmillan, and New
>   York, St. Martin's Press, 1964.
> *The Muddle-Headed Wombat in the Treetops*, illustrated by Noela Young.   Sydney,
>   Educational Press, and London, Angus and Robertson, 1965.
> *The Muddle-Headed Wombat at School*, illustrated by Noela Young.   Sydney,
>   Educational Press, and London, Angus and Robertson, 1966.
> *The Muddle-Headed Wombat in the Snow*, illustrated by Noela Young.   Sydney,
>   Educational Press, and London, Angus and Robertson, 1966.
> *Ring for the Sorcerer*, illustrated by William Stobbs.   Sydney, Hurwitz Martin, 1967.
> *The Sixpenny Island*, illustrated by David Cox.   Sydney, Ure Smith, and London,
>   Macmillan, 1968; as *Ten-Cent Island*, New York, Doubleday, 1968.
> *The Muddle-Headed Wombat on a Rainy Day*, illustrated by Noela Young.   Sydney,
>   Educational Press, 1969; London, Angus and Robertson, 1970.
> *Nuki and the Sea Serpent*, illustrated by Zelma Blakely.   London, Longman, 1969.
> *The Muddle-Headed Wombat in the Springtime*, illustrated by Noela Young.   Sydney,
>   Educational Press, and London, Angus and Robertson, 1970.
> *The Muddle-Headed Wombat on the River*, illustrated by Noela Young.   Sydney,
>   Educational Press, 1970; London, Angus and Robertson, 1971.
> *The Muddle-Headed Wombat and the Bush Band*, illustrated by Noela Young.   Sydney,
>   Angus and Robertson, 1973.
> *Callie's Castle*, illustrated by Kilmeny Niland.   Sydney and London, Angus and
>   Robertson, 1974.
> *The Gigantic Balloon*, illustrated by Kilmeny and Deborah Niland.   Sydney, Collins,
>   1975; London, Collins, and New York, Parents' Magazine Press, 1976.
> *The Muddle-Headed Wombat on Clean-Up Day*, illustrated by Noela Young.   London,
>   Angus and Robertson, 1976.
> *The Muddle-Headed Wombat and the Invention*, illustrated by Noela Young.   London,
>   Angus and Robertson, 1976.

Plays

The Uninvited Guest.   Sydney and London, Angus and Robertson, 1948.

Radio Plays: The Muddle-Headed Wombat series.

PUBLICATIONS FOR ADULTS

Novels

The Harp in the South.   Sydney, Angus and Robertson, London, Joseph, and Boston,
    Houghton Mifflin, 1948.
Poor Man's Orange.   Sydney, Angus and Robertson, 1949; London, Joseph, 1950; as
    12¹/₂ Plymouth Street, Boston, Houghton Mifflin, 1951.
The Witch's Thorn.   Sydney, Angus and Robertson, 1951; London, Joseph, and
    Boston, Houghton Mifflin, 1952.
A Power of Roses.   Sydney, Angus and Robertson, and London, Joseph, 1953.
Pink Flannel.   Sydney, Angus and Robertson, 1955.
One-a-Pecker, Two-a-Pecker.   Sydney, Angus and Robertson, 1957; London, Joseph,
    1958; as Frost and the Fire, Boston, Houghton Mifflin, 1958; London, Pan, 1962.
The Good-Looking Women.   Sydney, Angus and Robertson, 1961; London, Joseph,
    1962.
Serpent's Delight.   New York, Doubleday, 1962.

Other

The Drums Go Bang (autobiographical), with D'Arcy Niland.   Sydney, Angus and
    Robertson, 1956.
The Companion Guide to Sydney.   Sydney and London, Collins, 1973.

*   *   *

When Ruth Park created The Muddle-Headed Wombat for a radio programme, she introduced Australian children to a delightful and endearing character whose adventures are related in a popular and timeless series of books for younger children, with satisfyingly complementary illustrations. A lively sense of logical nonsense and a gift for zany dialogue are perhaps the outstanding ingredients of these stories. Ruth Park, in fact, belongs to that select body of writers who have successfully conceived a "cult" figure within children's literature. And, for Australian children, there is a special delight in the Muddle-Headed Wombat because he is a "dinkum Aussie," a home-bred creature to place alongside the imported bears, elephants and woodland creatures in books that originate overseas.

A gifted adult novelist and a distinguished journalist, Ruth Park is perhaps the most unassuming and least pretentious of Australia's writers for the young. In Callie's Castle (runner-up for the Australian Book of the Year award, 1975) she turned to a new form of fiction, for young teenagers. Set in Sydney, this is a gentle, understated story about a girl, growing up, who longs for solitude within her family circle. The author brings to Callie's story the same perception and eye for detail as she shows in her occasional short stories for young readers (for example, "The Freedom of the City," in the anthology The Cool Man) and in her regular adult articles for newspapers and journals.

She has made an interesting observation on her attitude towards creating a character. She writes: "I don't portray real children in stories; I create a fictional child very much as a gipsy makes a blanket ... a rag here, a tuft of wool there. I pick up a habit of speech, a mannerism, colour of eye ... and try to make somebody real out of the bits. I don't always succeed but I do find it a joyful business trying." She is now engaged on a historical novel for teenagers, set on Norfolk Island, where she has lived for some time.

—Barbara Ker Wilson

PARKER, Richard. British. Born in Stanmore, Middlesex, 15 February 1915. Educated at Kingsbury County Training College, London. Served in the British Army during World War II. Married Kathleen Hook in 1939; has five children. Library Assistant, Maidstone Public Library, Kent, 1934–36; Secretary to Rupert Croft-Cooke, 1937–38; reporter, *Kent Messenger*; primary school teacher for many years. Lives in Herne Bay, Kent. Address: c/o Hodder and Stoughton Children's Books, Arlen House, Salisbury Road, Leicester LE1 7QS, England.

PUBLICATIONS FOR CHILDREN

Fiction

Escape from the Zoo, illustrated by Val Biro. London, Sylvan Press, 1945.

A Camel from the Desert, illustrated by Val Biro. London, Sylvan Press, 1947.

The Penguin Goes Home, illustrated by Val Biro. London, Chatto and Windus, 1951.

A Moor of Spain: The Story of a Rogue, illustrated by John Harwood. London, Penguin, 1953.

The Three Pebbles, illustrated by Prudence Seward. London, Collins, 1954; New York, McKay, 1956.

The Sword of Ganelon. London, Collins, 1957; New York, McKay, 1958.

Lion at Large, illustrated by Paul Hogarth. Leicester, Brockhampton Press, 1959; New York, Nelson, 1961.

More Snakes than Ladders, illustrated by Jillian Willett. Leicester, Brockhampton Press, 1960; as *Almost Lost*, New York, Nelson, 1962.

New Home South, illustrated by Prudence Seward. Leicester, Brockhampton Press, 1961; as *Voyage to Tasmania*, Indianapolis, Bobbs Merrill, 1961.

A Valley Full of Pipers, illustrated by Richard Kennedy. London, Gollancz, and Indianapolis, Bobbs Merrill, 1962.

The House That Guilda Drew, illustrated by Prudence Seward. Leicester, Brockhampton Press, 1963; Princeton, New Jersey, Van Nostrand, 1964.

The Boy Who Wasn't Lonely, illustrated by Prudence Seward. Leicester, Brockhampton Press, 1964; Indianapolis, Bobbs Merrill, 1965.

Perversity of Pipers, illustrated by Richard Kennedy. London, Gollancz, and Princeton, New Jersey, Van Nostrand, 1964.

Private Beach, illustrated by Victor Ambrus. London, Harrap, 1964; New York, Duell, 1966.

Second-Hand Family, illustrated by Gareth Floyd. Leicester, Brockhampton Press, 1965; Indianapolis, Bobbs Merrill, 1966.

M for Mischief, illustrated by Juan Ballesta. London, Constable, 1965; New York, Duell, 1966.

The Punch Back Gang, illustrated by John Plant. London, Harrap, 1966; as *New in the Neighborhood*, New York, Duell, 1966.

One White Mouse, illustrated by Rene Hummerstone. Leicester, Brockhampton Press, 1966; as *No House for a Mouse*, Chicago, Follett, 1968.

The Hendon Fungus. London, Gollancz, 1967; New York, Meredith Press, 1968.

A Sheltering Tree.   New York, Meredith Press, 1969; London, Gollancz, 1970.

Spell Seven, illustrated by Trevor Ridley.   London, Longman, and New York, Nelson, 1971.

Old Powder Line.   London, Gollancz, and New York, Nelson, 1971.

Paul and Etta, illustrated by Gavin Rowe.   Leicester, Brockhampton Press, 1972; Nashville, Nelson, 1973.

Frank's Fire.   London, Macmillan, 1972.

John Morris's Mermaid.   London, Macmillan, 1972.

Not at Home.   London, Macmillan, 1972.

One Green Bottle, illustrated by Michael Jackson.   London, Heinemann, 1973.

A Time to Choose.   London, Hutchinson, 1973; New York, Harper, 1974.

He Is Your Brother, illustrated by Gareth Floyd.   Leicester, Brockhampton Press, 1974; Nashville, Nelson, 1976.

Snatched, illustrated by Peter Kesteven.   Newton Abbot, Devon, David and Charles, 1974; as *Three by Mistake,* Nashville, Nelson, 1974.

Beyond the Back Gate, illustrated by Peter Dennis.   London, Abelard Schuman, 1975.

Boy into Action, illustrated by Trevor Parkin.   London, Abelard Schuman, 1975.

The Fire Curse, illustrated by Trevor Stubley.   London, Heinemann, 1975.

Hugo Takes Off, illustrated by Trevor Stubley.   London, Hodder and Stoughton, 1976; as *The Runaway,* Nashville, Nelson, 1977.

Quarter Boy.   London, Heinemann, and Nashville, Nelson, 1976.

In and Out the Window.   London, Hutchinson, 1976.

Digging for Treasure, illustrated by Trevor Stubley.   London, Benn, 1976.

Flood, illustrated by Trevor Stubley.   London, Benn, 1976.

Sausages on the Shore, illustrated by Trevor Stubley.   London, Benn, 1976.

The Sunday Papers, illustrated by Trevor Stubley.   London, Benn, 1976.

Plays

Six Plays for Boys (includes *The New Football Boots, The Rabbit Hutch, The Wish, The Medicine Man, The Raft, No Excitement*).   London, Methuen, 1951.

Seven Plays for Boys (includes *The Rehearsal, The Hut, The Waxworks, Lazy Jack, The Dilemma, A Message to the Kite, The Coconut Shy*).   London, Methuen, 1953.

Other (readers)

Brother Turgar and the Vikings, illustrated by Joan Milroy.   London, Ginn, 1959.

The Kidnapped Crusaders, illustrated by Richard Kennedy.   London, Ginn, 1959.

The Green Highwayman, illustrated by Richard Kennedy.   London, Ginn, 1960.

Goodbye to the Bush, illustrated by Kenneth Brown.   London, Ginn, 1963.

Lost in a Shop, illustrated by Carol Barker.   London, Macmillan, 1968.

Me and My Boots, illustrated by George Adamson.   London, Macmillan, 1968.

Keeping Time, illustrated by Jane Hickson.   London, Heinemann, 1973.

PUBLICATIONS FOR ADULTS

Novels

Only Some Had Guns.   London, Collins, 1952.

The Gingerbread Man.   London, Collins, 1953; New York, Scribner, 1954.

A Kind of Misfortune.   London, Collins, 1954; New York, Scribner, 1955.

Draughts in the Sun.   London, Collins, 1955.

Harm Intended.   New York, Scribner, 1956; London, Secker and Warburg, 1957.

Fiddler's Place.   London, Davies, 1961.

Boy on a Chain.   London, Davies, 1964; as *Killer,* New York, Doubleday, 1964.

Richard Parker comments:

I began writing for children when I became a teacher, and to begin with the stories were largely a by-product. They were written to give enjoyment to or to help some particular group of children, sometimes technically and sometimes emotionally. Some stories were written for individuals, some for the class I happened to be teaching at the time. After two years (1959–61) in the Australian education system, however, I became less interested in education and more concerned with writing as a profession. Nowadays I find myself writing a story because it seems a good one and presents interesting problems, and worry far less about who will read it.

*   *   *

In the course of a life full of varied experience – as writer and librarian, soldier, teacher (in England and Australia), and as father and grandfather – Richard Parker has deeply observed many places, many people, many situations, and a storehouse of vivid recollection seems to underlie his fresh, original, camera-conscious stories. With an almost televisual technique he presents, in quick, clear, unmistakable word pictures, a succession of scenes first grasped visually, then mentally – "he plodded the stale path to a familiar door"; "the morning sun slapped him across the face like a challenge"; "stranded on the yellow beach of the new day."

Originality of phrase and style, however, is firmly anchored to a practical, no-nonsense realism. He has, above all things, the ability to see life from the point of view of the young. He knows how children talk, act, and think. He doesn't see them or life through rose-coloured spectacles, and understands that they don't either. He knows they are often torn apart by the conflict between their fresh vision of life's possibilities and its stark reality. He knows all about the stresses of family life, the blindness of many adults to the viewpoint of their children, and all the pain of being young.

Many of his best stories are for adolescents and young adults, and deal with such subjects as parental quarrels and threatened divorce, adoption and the strain of adjustment, a handicapped member in the family, pressure to follow an uncongenial occupation. But he never makes the mistake of letting some didactic aim absolve him from a writer's primary duty – to tell a story so compelling that the reader reads for the joy of it and only discovers in retrospect that somehow the tale has made him more aware, more tolerant in his viewpoint, and a bit better able himself to take life's stresses, to harness and direct his own burning impatience and frustration.

—Gladys A. Williams

PATCHETT, Mary Elwyn (Osborne). Australian. Born in Sydney, New South Wales, 2 December 1897. Educated at New England Girls' School, Armidale; Church of England Girls' Grammar School, Sydney. Journalist in Sydney for five years. Agent: Bolt and Watson Ltd., 8–12 Old Queen Street, London S.W.1. Address: 235 Latymer Court, London W6 7JZ, England.

PUBLICATIONS FOR CHILDREN

Fiction

Ajax, The Warrior, illustrated by Eric Tansley. London, Lutterworth Press, 1953; as *Ajax, Golden Dog of the Australian Bush*, Indianapolis, Bobbs Merrill, 1953.

973

Kidnappers of Space.   London, Lutterworth Press, 1953; as *Space Captives of the Golden Men*, Indianapolis, Bobbs Merrill, 1953.

The Lee Twins: Beauty Students.   London, Lane, 1953.

Tam the Untamed, illustrated by Joan Kiddell-Monroe.   London, Lutterworth Press, 1954; Indianapolis, Bobbs Merrill, 1955.

Lost on Venus.   London, Lutterworth Press, 1954; as *Flight to the Misty Planet*, Indianapolis, Bobbs Merrill, 1954.

Evening Star, illustrated by Olga Lehmann.   London, Lutterworth Press, 1954.

Adam Troy, Astroman.   London, Lutterworth Press, 1954.

"Your Call, Miss Gaynor," illustrated by Bill Martin.   London, Lutterworth Press, 1955.

Treasure of the Reef, illustrated by Joan Kiddell-Monroe.   London, Lutterworth Press, 1955; as *The Great Barrier Reef*, Indianapolis, Bobbs Merrill, 1958.

Undersea Treasure Hunters, illustrated by Joan Kiddell-Monroe.   London, Lutterworth Press, 1955; as *The Chance of Treasure*, Indianapolis, Bobbs Merrill, 1957.

Send for Johnny Danger.   London, Lutterworth Press, 1956; New York, McGraw Hill, 1958.

Return to the Reef, illustrated by Joan Kiddell-Monroe.   London, Lutterworth Press, 1956.

Sally's Zoo, illustrated by Pat Marriott.   London, Hamish Hamilton, 1957.

Outback Adventure, illustrated by Joan Kiddell-Monroe.   London, Lutterworth Press, 1957.

Caribbean Adventurers, illustrated by William Stobbs.   London, Lutterworth Press, 1957.

The Mysterious Pool, illustrated by Pat Marriott.   London, Hamish Hamilton, 1958.

The Brumby, illustrated by Juliet McLeod.   London, Lutterworth Press, 1958; as *Brumby, The Wild White Stallion*, Indianapolis, Bobbs Merrill, 1959.

The Call of the Bush, illustrated by Brian Wildsmith.   London, Lutterworth Press, 1959.

The Quest of Ati Manu, illustrated by Stuart Tresilian.   London, Lutterworth Press, 1960; Indianapolis, Bobbs Merrill, 1962.

Warrimoo, illustrated by Roger Payne.   Leicester, Brockhampton Press, 1961; Indianapolis, Bobbs Merrill, 1963.

Come Home, Brumby, illustrated by Stuart Tresilian.   London, Lutterworth Press, 1961; as *Brumby, Come Home*, Indianapolis, Bobbs Merrill, 1961.

The End of the Outlaws, illustrated by Roger Payne.   London, Lutterworth Press, and Indianapolis, Bobbs Merrill, 1961.

Dangerous Assignment, illustrated by Roger Payne.   Leicester, Brockhampton Press, 1962; Indianapolis, Bobbs Merrill, 1964.

The Golden Wolf, illustrated by Roger Payne.   London, Lutterworth Press, 1962; Indianapolis, Bobbs Merrill, 1965.

Circus Brumby, illustrated by Stuart Tresilian.   London, Lutterworth Press, 1963.

The Venus Project, illustrated by Roger Payne.   Leicester, Brockhampton Press, 1963.

Ajax and the Haunted Mountain, illustrated by Roger Payne.   London, Lutterworth Press, 1963; Indianapolis, Bobbs Merrill, 1966.

Tiger in the Dark, illustrated by Roger Payne.   Leicester, Brockhampton Press, 1964; New York, Duell Sloan Pearce, 1966.

Ajax and the Drovers, illustrated by Roger Payne.   London, Lutterworth Press, 1964.

Stranger in the Herd, illustrated by Stuart Tresilian.   London, Lutterworth Press, 1964; New York, Duell Sloan Pearce, 1966.

The White Dingo, illustrated by Peter Kesteven.   London, Lutterworth Press, 1965.

Brumby Foal, illustrated by Victor Ambrus.   London, Lutterworth Press, 1965.

Summer on Wild Horse Island, illustrated by Roger Payne.   Leicester, Brockhampton Press, 1965; New York, Meredith Press, 1967.

The Terror of Manooka, illustrated by Roger Payne.   London, Lutterworth Press, 1966.

Summer on Boomerang Beach, illustrated by Roger Payne.   Leicester, Brockhampton Press, 1967.
Festival of Jewels, illustrated by Roger Payne.   Leicester, Brockhampton Press, 1968.
Farm Beneath the Sea, illustrated by H. Johns.   London, Harrap, 1969.
Quarter Horse Boy, illustrated by Roger Payne.   London, Harrap, 1970.
The Long Ride, illustrated by Michael Charlton.   London, Lutterworth Press, 1970.
Rebel Brumby, illustrated by Roger Payne.   London, Lutterworth Press, 1972.
Roar of the Lion, illustrated by Douglas Phillips.   London, Lutterworth Press, 1973.

PUBLICATIONS FOR ADULTS

Novels

Wild Brother.   London, Collins, 1954.
Cry of the Heart.   London, Collins, 1956; New York, Abelard Schuman, 1957.
The Saffron Woman.   London, Heinemann, 1958.
Brit.   London, Hodder and Stoughton, 1961.
In a Wilderness.   London, Hodder and Stoughton, 1962; as *Dingo*, New York, Doubleday, 1963.
The Last Warrior.   London, Hodder and Stoughton, 1965; New York, Doubleday, 1966.
Hunting Cat.   London, Abelard Schuman, 1976.

Other

The Proud Eagles.   London, Heinemann, 1960; Cleveland, World, 1961.
A Budgie Called Fred.   London, Barker, 1964.
Bird of Jove (as David Bruce).   New York, Putnam, 1971.

Mary Elwyn Patchett comments:
All my books, for adults and for children, concern my main interests – animals, falconry, undersea exploration, interplanetary flight, history – and almost all are factual adventure. The animals concerned range from a great Berkut eagle from Central Asia to a small hunting cat from Trinidad. I often use Australian background and animals, and I work on accuracy.
If I had another life to live it would be spent with animals; not to tame them, or to sentimentalize over them, nor to make them replicas of myself or improve their love-lives, but simply to understand them and, if I could, to compensate a little for the hideous things which man has done, and is doing, to them.
I don't think I write especially for children, with the exception of a few books for small children. I just think of an idea and write the book in the best way I can.

*   *   *

Though some of her early books are on other subjects, Mary Elwyn Patchett's main theme, and her best, is animal life. She makes an attempt to understand the natures of animals as themselves and not merely as adjuncts to human life. This sympathy, together with her concern for their often threatened lives and her intimate knowledge of their surroundings, gives her books vision and vigour. The movement and freedom of her writing, the independence of her characters, and their ability to deal with the unexpected and dangerous, could well be the inheritance from an Australian birth and an upbringing in the bush.
Her best book by most counts is *Tiger in the Dark*, a quest in the Australian interior for the supposedly extinct Australian marsupial tiger-wolf. A blind Aboriginal child serves as guide. *Roar of the Lion*, an African story, is about a boy's struggle to come to terms with the inevitable separation from his pet lioness cub when, at maturity, she must return to her life in

the wild. In the Brumbies books, a series about wild horses in Australia, Joey Muhan tries, against great odds, to protect the brumbies from hunters and to build up a herd in a place where they can live in safety. The Ajax books describe the life of a girl on a cattle station in the Australian outback. *Quarter Horse Boy*, also a story of the outback, is about an Aboriginal boy's skill with horses and his affectionate adoption by the human family for whom he works.

Other books include *Farm Beneath the Sea*, which combines science fiction with facts about marine life and some evocative descriptions. The Dexter family, having undergone a lung operation to make them breathe like fish, descend a hundred feet below the surface of the Pacific among the "incredible blaze of multi-coloured corals. They looked almost lush in the way flowers do. The small fishey-life swarmed about them like bees around spring flowers." Here they live and set up an experimental attempt to farm the sea bed. A friendly dolphin helps. *Summer on Wild Horse Island* is, again, set beside the Great Barrier Reef amongst the sharks and barracudas.

—Nancy Shepherdson

PATON WALSH, Jill (Gillian Paton Walsh).   British.   Born in London, 29 April 1937. Educated at St. Michael's Convent, North Finchley, London, 1943–55; St. Anne's College, Oxford, 1955–59, Dip. Ed. 1959, M.A. (honours) in English. Married Antony Edmund Paton Walsh in 1961; has one son and two daughters. English Teacher, Enfield Girls Grammar School, Middlesex, 1959–62. Recipient: *Book World* Festival award, 1970; Whitbread Literary Award, 1974; *Boston Globe-Horn Book* Award, 1976; Arts Council Creative Writing Fellowship, 1976. Address: 60 Mount Ararat Road, Richmond, Surrey, England.

Publications for Children

Fiction

> *Hengest's Tale*, illustrated by Janet Margrie.   London, Macmillan, and New York, St. Martin's Press, 1966.
> *The Dolphin Crossing.*   London, Macmillan, and New York, St. Martin's Press, 1967.
> *Fireweed.*   London, Macmillan, 1969; New York, Farrar Straus, 1970.
> *Goldengrove.*   London, Macmillan, and New York, Farrar Straus, 1972.
> *Toolmaker*, illustrated by Jeroo Roy.   London, Heinemann, 1973; New York, Seabury Press, 1974.
> *The Dawnstone*, illustrated by Mary Dinsdale.   London, Hamish Hamilton, 1973.
> *The Emperor's Winding Sheet.*   London, Macmillan, and New York, Farrar Straus, 1974.
> *The Butty Boy*, illustrated by Juliette Palmer.   London, Macmillan, 1975; as *The Huffler*, New York, Farrar Straus, 1975.
> *Unleaving.*   London, Macmillan, and New York, Farrar Straus, 1976.
> *The Walls of Athens.*   London, Heinemann, 1977.

Other

> *Wordhoard: Anglo-Saxon Stories*, with Kevin Crossley-Holland.   London, Macmillan, and New York, Farrar Straus, 1969.
> *The Island Sunrise: Prehistoric Culture in the British Isles.*   London, Deutsch, 1975; New York, Seabury Press, 1976.

PUBLICATIONS FOR ADULTS

Novel

Farewell, Great King.   London, Macmillan, and New York, Coward McCann, 1972.

Jill Paton Walsh comments:
  My books do not really make up a coherent body of work to which I could write an introduction: I write about whatever I am fascinated by at the time, which makes each book different. My governing principle is to make whatever I am doing as simple and accessible as possible. I do that not merely to appeal to children, but as a point of honour − I think it pretentious to do anything else. But also my preferred subjects have lain in that large area of human experience that adults and children have in common. And the making of an adult statement about that common area that is transparent enough for children is endlessly challenging and interesting technically. The rewards and the discipline of writing for the young are very enriching.

                              *   *   *

  Jill Paton Walsh is one of the most exciting children's writers around today, and her work is still developing, moving more and more into the complex world of adolescent emotions. This is not to say that she writes books only for adolescents; her novels can be enjoyed by younger children too and by adults. They combine a strong story line with emotional intensity and clarity of vision. The stories may be about the fall of Constantinople, the death of a Saxon king, or the relief of Dunkirk, but they are also movingly about people and how they search for love, honour and the truth.
  A vital element of Jill Paton Walsh's work is that it is exceptionally well-researched. In *Hengest's Tale* she weaves a story "the broken pieces of which are in the very oldest English poetry, written long before the Norman conquest." Her tale is of Hengest, mid-fifth-century ruler of Kent, who looks back on his youth and how his attempts to combine honour and loyalty result in his killing his best friend. It is a rough tale but a moving one. As Jill Paton Walsh says in her prologue, "Nobody knows how it should really be told; but it might perhaps be like this."
  In *The Dolphin Crossing* and *Fireweed* she explores a more modern setting, that of the Second World War. In both novels she writes poignantly about children caught up in the war and their need for action to relieve their feeling of impotence. In *The Dolphin Crossing* John and Pat, two boys from totally different backgrounds, take a small boat across to Dunkirk to help the soldiers from the beach. The story ends with John, from the wealthy family, returning safe to his home. It is Pat, the evacuee, who disappears back into the hell from which they have come, in his obsession to reach the soldiers − one of whom might have been his Dad. *Fireweed* is set in the Blitz and follows the fate of Bill and Julie, again from different backgrounds, who start by having an exciting runaway time in London on their own and end by almost being killed. The mood of the book changes from exhilaration in the early scenes to tenderness as the two teenagers try to cope with an abandoned toddler and make a home for themselves in a bomb-damaged house. The relationship between Bill and Julie in *Fireweed* foreshadows Jill Paton Walsh's most recent theme, that of young people learning to grow up. The final pages of *Fireweed* are restrained, yet as moving as any she has written.
  Her next major novel, *Goldengrove*, describes a summer in the life of Madge and Paul, seemingly cousins who turn out to be even more closely related. They spend a few well-synchronised weeks with their grandmother in Cornwall, a summer in which for the first time they draw apart. Madge becomes involved in reading to a blind professor, seeing in him her own Mr. Rochester, while Paul still wants only to sail boats and play in the sand. It is the last summer of Madge's childhood − her growing up is to be seen completed in Jill Paton Walsh's sequel, *Unleaving.*

But in between *Goldengrove* and *Unleaving* comes one of her greatest achievements. *The Emperor's Winding Sheet* is a fascinating and complex story of the fall of Constantinople and of how young Piers Barber, a boy from Bristol, becomes talisman to the last Emperor of the Romans and sees the magnificent city destroyed. Piers is caught up in the Emperor's fortunes by mischance, and begins by being afraid to die when the inevitable assault on the city comes, yet at the end he performs the tenderest last rites for his master and wishes he could have died for him. This novel is so absorbing, so stretches the imagination and the emotions, that I felt on reading it that Jill Paton Walsh had perhaps achieved the ultimate in her work.

But her recent novel, *Unleaving*, marks a new passage for her. *Unleaving* is about young people, but it is so adult in concept that it could as easily fall into the category of adult novel. In *Unleaving* there are conscious or unconscious echoes of Virginia Woolf as thoughts and events pass in a dream-like sequence. The story of Madge and Paul is taken up again and is told entirely in the present tense, but the passage of the summer holidays is also the passage of time, the Gran of the book is both Madge's own Gran and herself as a grandmother. The thoughts of Madge cover sixty years and play a counter-point between emotion and logic. It is an immensely satisfying book, a book with a completeness which yet leaves the reader wondering, and wanting more from this exceptionally gifted writer.

Jill Paton Walsh's books are not essentially about death, or divorce, or war, or battle – though she writes of all these things. Using different levels of time, real events that happened, she poses the reader with the questions that these events create, and recommends to us always that life is never easy but always worthwhile. As Madge says at the end of *Unleaving*: "What shall we sing? O, the beauty of the world!"

—Eileen Totten

PATTEN, Brian. British. Born in Liverpool, Lancashire, 7 February 1946. Educated at Sefton Park Secondary School, Liverpool. Formerly, Editor, *Underdog*, Liverpool. Recipient: Eric Gregory Award, for verse, 1967; Arts Council grant, 1969. Address: c/o Allen and Unwin Ltd., 40 Museum Street, London WC1A ILU, England.

PUBLICATIONS FOR CHILDREN

Fiction

The Elephant and the Flower: Almost-Fables, illustrated by Meg Rutherford.   London, Allen and Unwin, 1970.
Manchild.   London, Covent Garden Press, 1973.
Two Stories.   London, Covent Garden Press, 1973.
Mr. Moon's Last Case, illustrated by Mary Moore.   London, Allen and Unwin, 1975; New York, Scribner, 1976.
Emma's Doll, illustrated by Mary Moore.   London, Allen and Unwin, 1976.

Plays

The Pig and the Junkle (produced Nottingham, 1975; London, 1977).

Radio Play: *The Hypnotic Island*, 1977.

Verse

> *The Sly Cormorant and the Three Fishes*, illustrated by Errol Le Cain.   London,
> Penguin, 1977.

Other

> *Jumping Mouse* (American Indian Tale), illustrated by Mary Moore.   London, Allen
> and Unwin, 1972.

PUBLICATIONS FOR ADULTS

Verse

> *Portraits.*   Liverpool, privately printed, 1962.
> *The Mersey Sound: Penguin Modern Poets 10,* with Adrian Henri and Roger
> McGough.   London, Penguin, 1967.
> *Little Johnny's Confession.*   London, Allen and Unwin, 1967; New York, Hill and
> Wang, 1968.
> *Atomic Adam.*   London, Fulham Gallery, 1967.
> *Notes to the Hurrying Man: Poems, Winter '66—Summer '68.*   London, Allen and
> Unwin, and New York, Hill and Wang, 1969.
> *The Home Coming.*   London, Turret Books, 1969.
> *The Irrelevant Song.*   Frensham, Surrey, Sceptre Press, 1970.
> *Little Johnny's Foolish Invention: A Poem* (bilingual edition), translated by Robert
> Sanesi.   Milan, Tipographia Bertieri, 1970.
> *At Four O'Clock in the Morning.*   Frensham, Surrey, Sceptre Press, 1971.
> *The Irrelevant Song and Other Poems.*   London, Allen and Unwin, 1971.
> *When You Wake Tomorrow.*   London, Turret Books, 1972.
> *The Eminent Professors and the Nature of Poetry as Enacted Out by Members of the
> Poetry Seminar One Rainy Evening.*   London, Poem-of-the-Month Club, 1972.
> *The Unreliable Nightingale.*   London, Rota, 1973.
> *Vanishing Trick.*   London, Allen and Unwin, 1976.

> Recordings: *Selections from Little Johnny's Confession and Notes to the Hurrying Man
> and New Poems,* Caedmon, 1969; *Vanishing Trick,* Tangent, 1972; *The Sly Cormorant,*
> Argo, 1977.

Other

> Editor, with Pat Krett, *The House That Jack Built: Poems for Shelter.*   London, Allen
> and Unwin, 1973.

*   *   *

Much of Brian Patten's verse is as accessible to children as to adults. The gentle tone, the air of approachability, the delicacy of his imagination, are all contributory factors. So is the hard underlying muscle of thought and organisation contained in his best work: something his art conceals by a deceptive and casual-seeming simplicity of manner.

Often, he presents a child-like, but never childish, view of town and city life. As with a child, the eye is not always entirely innocent. He gazes, with unwavering curiosity, at the minutiae of existence, and at its complexities and clichés. He reveals a sensibility profoundly aware of the ever-present possibility of the magical and the miraculous, as well as of the granite-hard realities. He is a poet very much of his age, and writes in unintimidating present-day terms: one important means, certainly, by which a child might first begin to recognise the poetry of the everyday and the apparently commonplace.

Each of his published books of "adult" verse yields something for the child. *Notes to the Hurrying Man* for example, includes the now celebrated fable "You'd Better Believe Him:"

> Discovered an old rocking-horse in Woolworth's,
> He tried to feed it but without much luck
> So he stroked it, had a long conversation about
> The trees it came from, the attics it had visited.

There is the allegorical love-song that is at the same time the surface-story of a small dragon found nesting among the coal in a wood-shed:

> If you believed in it I would come
> hurrying to your house to let you share my wonder,
> but I want instead to see
> if you yourself will pass this way.

There are also such less-anthologised but equally effective pieces as "Bombscare," "Mr. Jones Takes Over," "The Necessary Slaughter." These are all undiluted poems, beautifully calculated, informed – even in their darkest moments – with courage and hope. Patten, uncompromisingly, goes all out for the poem, not the audience: and the rest follows. The publication of a selection, primarily for children, of his "adult" poems seems overdue.

The Elephant and the Flower, prose "near-fables" for younger children, demonstrates his inventiveness and remarkable ear for the undecorated but wholly persuasive tunes and tones of a simple narrative form. The novel *Mr. Moon's Last Case*, for older children, is more ambitious in scope: a mixture of sober realism and wild fancy on the alluring subject of the possible existence of parallel worlds. But as a prose-writer, Patten is at his best with the shorter piece. His re-telling of a Plains Indian creation-myth under the title *Jumping Mouse* is a small masterpiece: an authoritative realization of the complicated theme of the inter-relationship of all earthly creatures. It has a compassionate simplicity, an inevitability of movement, and – particularly towards the close – a nobility of voice, and marks a creative writer unusually well-attuned to the imaginative needs of the child. Once received and absorbed, Brian Patten's best work is something incapable of ever being entirely lost or discarded.

—Charles Causley

PEARCE, (Ann) Philippa.   British.   Born in Great Shelford, Cambridgeshire. Educated at Perse Girls' School, 1929–39; Girton College, Cambridge, B.A. (honours) in English and history 1942, M.A. Married Martin Christie in 1963 (died); has one daughter. Civil Servant, 1942–45; Scriptwriter and Producer, 1945–58, and Free-lance Producer, 1960–62, BBC Radio, London; Assistant Editor, Educational Department, Oxford University Press, Oxford, 1958–60; Children's Editor, André Deutsch Ltd., publishers, London, 1960–67. Free-lance reviewer and lecturer. Recipient: Library Association Carnegie Medal, 1959; New York *Herald Tribune* Festival award, 1963. Address: c/o Kestrel Books, 17 Grosvenor Gardens, London SW1W 0BD, England.

PUBLICATIONS FOR CHILDREN

Fiction

Minnow on the Say, illustrated by Edward Ardizzone. London, Oxford University
   Press, 1955; as *The Minnow Leads to Treasure*, Cleveland, World, 1958.
Tom's Midnight Garden, illustrated by Susan Einzig. London, Oxford University
   Press, and Philadelphia, Lippincott, 1958.
Still Jim and Silent Jim. Oxford, Blackwell, 1960.
Mrs. Cockle's Cat, illustrated by Antony Maitland. London, Constable, and
   Philadelphia, Lippincott, 1961.
A Dog So Small, illustrated by Antony Maitland. London, Constable, 1962;
   Philadelphia, Lippincott, 1963.
The Strange Sunflower, illustrated by Kathleen Williams. London, Nelson, 1966.
The Children of the House, with Brian Fairfax-Lucy, illustrated by John
   Sergeant. London, Longman, and Philadelphia, Lippincott, 1968.
The Elm Street Lot, illustrated by Mina Martinez. London, BBC Publications, 1969.
The Squirrel Wife, illustrated by Derek Collard. London, Longman, 1971; New York,
   Crowell, 1972.
What the Neighbours Did and Other Stories, illustrated by Faith Jaques. London,
   Longman, 1972; New York, Crowell, 1973.
The Shadow-Cage and Other Tales of the Supernatural, illustrated by Janet
   Archer. London, Penguin, and New York, Crowell, 1977.

Other

From Inside Scotland Yard, with Sir Harold Scott, illustrated by Anne
   Linton. London, Deutsch, 1963; New York, Macmillan, 1965.
Beauty and the Beast, illustrated by Alan Barrett. London, Longman, 1972.

Editor, *Stories from Hans Christian Andersen*, illustrated by Pauline Baynes. London,
   Collins, 1972.

*   *   *

Philippa Pearce's books probe the experiences of childhood at many levels. They compel
belief with precise descriptions of the external environment and an imaginative unfolding –
as if from the inside – of the characters' thoughts and feelings. Stimulating shifts of time and
mood accentuate the enquiring nature of the stories; this is expressed at one level simply as a
seeing of familiar situations with a new eye, at another as the opportunity to explore a
magical garden.
   The author's first book, *Minnow on the Say*, is about a treasure hunt by two boys. It is one
of Philippa Pearce's more extroverted stories, but intermingled with the thrills of the search is
a feeling for history as clues from old documents are painstakingly studied and unravelled.
The river setting is particularly appropriate for the book's twists and changing moods. There
is the exhilaration of solving mysteries, the frustration of false trails, the boys' satisfaction in
technical achievement when they first test on the water the canoe that they have repaired.
Philippa Pearce's keen sense of place finds expression in river scenes based on the
Cambridgeshire countryside which she has known since childhood. *Minnow on the Say*
conveys some of the river's fascinations for children – boating and fishing, twisted old
willows to climb and "reed beds that might hide the nests of moorhens."
   In *Tom's Midnight Garden* a feeling for the outdoors is very differently presented. Instead
of the brilliant, sunlit river atmosphere the mood is dreamlike and secret. Quarantined
because of his brother's measles, Tom has to stay with an aunt and uncle in their flat, part of a
converted old house that has no garden. Tom feels cooped up and lonely until he discovers

that at midnight (when the grandfather clock mysteriously strikes thirteen) he can go out into a large garden which used to exist in late-Victorian days. Here he becomes friendly with Hatty, a small girl as lonely as himself.

Tom realizes that in the garden time can "dodge about in [an] unreliable, confusing way." To him, Hatty seems to be a ghost from the past; to her, he is a ghost from the future − but each is part of the other's tangible, waking experience. Here is magic without whimsy. Clear-cut images of the haunted garden and the shifting time sequences suggest the impact of past and future upon the present. In this context the reader is invited to explore questions of visibility and invisibility, of substance and weightlessness, and the effectiveness of mind or imagination in overcoming material limitations. Few children can resist the supernatural overtones. They are, however, firmly linked to reality. The core of the story is an extremely human need for companionship − a desire that is strong enough in Tom and Hatty to break through the barriers of time.

The theme of loneliness recurs in *A Dog So Small*. Ben is excluded from the companionship existing between his two older sisters and that of his younger brothers. From the sense of separateness grows an intense longing for a dog. In his imagination Ben creates Chiquitito, a remarkably intelligent and courageous dog, "so small that ... you could only see it with your eyes shut." Ben's fantasy life with his idealized dog begins to blot out reality, and he is run over crossing a London street in a withdrawn, semi-trance state. The accident kills off the make-believe pet, but eventually Ben becomes the owner of a real and initially less fulfilling dog; he has then "to learn to live with ... his heart's desire." This book shows how well the author can get beneath the skin of a character. It also closely observes the difficulties of a sensitive child in a rather crowded home that denies physical privacy while it produces psychological isolation.

Philippa Pearce has also written several stories for very young children. *Mrs. Cockle's Cat* describes how an elderly London balloon-seller who has lost her cat is one day caught up with her enormous bunch of balloons by a sudden gust of wind and made airborne. Her exuberant, half-bouncing, half-floating progress all the way to the sea − where the cat has gone in search of fish − is reminiscent of the flying dreams of childhood.

Her books for 8 to 12 year-olds often appeal to younger children if read aloud. Philippa Pearce's feeling for the sound of words was developed by her work as a radio scriptwriter and producer; the writing of school broadcasts of 20 minutes' duration increased her interest in the short story medium. *What the Neighbours Did* is a collection of short stories which have depth as well as liveliness. These feature boys more frequently than girls − possibly because this gives the author scope to produce a wider range of adventures.

In *The Shadow-Cage* inner and outer experiences coalesce. Like *Tom's Midnight Garden* these stories suggest that a heightened experience or a strong need can provide the stimulus for a supernatural event. Long forgotten objects in neglected attics and the mysteriously chilling atmosphere of certain rooms are beautifully evoked, and every effect is harnessed to produce a build-up of suspense. Each episode is a fantasy, but because of its inner logic and consistency it does not seem far-fetched. These stories are likely to give unusual exercise to the imaginations of young readers.

—Mary Cadogan

PEASE, Howard. American. Born in Stockton, California, 6 September 1894. Educated at Stanford University, California, A.B. 1923. Served in the American Expeditionary Forces at Base Hospital 3, France, 1918–19. Married Pauline Nott in 1927 (died), one son; Rossie Ferrier, 1956. Merchant seaman in the early 1920's; teacher in public and private schools, California, 1924–25, 1928–34; Instructor in English, Vassar College, Poughkeepsie, New

York, 1926–27. Recipient: Child Study Association of America award, 1947; Boys' Clubs of America award, 1949. *Died 14 April 1974.*

PUBLICATIONS FOR CHILDREN

Fiction

The Tattooed Man, illustrated by Mahlon Blaine. New York, Doubleday, and London, Heinemann, 1926.

The Jinx Ship, illustrated by Mahlon Blaine. New York, Doubleday, and London, Heinemann, 1927.

Shanghai Passage, illustrated by Paul Forster. New York, Doubleday, 1929.

The Gypsy Caravan, illustrated by Harrie Wood. New York, Doubleday, 1930.

Secret Cargo, illustrated by Paul Forster. New York, Doubleday, 1931.

The Ship Without a Crew. New York, Doubleday, 1934.

Wind in the Rigging. New York, Doubleday, 1935.

Hurricane Weather. New York, Doubleday, 1936.

Foghorns, illustrated by Anton Otto Fischer. New York, Doubleday, 1937.

Captain Binnacle, illustrated by Charles E. Pont. New York, Dodd Mead, 1938; London, Harrap, 1939.

Jungle River, illustrated by Armstrong Sperry. New York, Doubleday, 1938.

Highroad to Adventure, illustrated by Frank Dobias. New York, Doubleday, 1939.

Long Wharf. New York, Doubleday, 1939.

The Black Tanker. New York, Doubleday, 1941.

Night Boat and Other Tod Moran Mysteries. New York, Doubleday, 1942.

Thunderbolt House, illustrated by Armstrong Sperry. New York, Doubleday, 1944.

Heart of Danger. New York, Doubleday, 1946.

Bound for Singapore. New York, Doubleday, 1948.

The Dark Adventure. New York, Doubleday, 1950.

Captain of the "Araby." New York, Doubleday, 1953.

Shipwreck. New York, Doubleday, 1957.

Mystery on Telegraph Hill. New York, Doubleday, 1961.

*   *   *

In the Tod Moran mysteries Howard Pease created a popular series, readily read and enjoyed by many young readers. This series of books contains more than 13 titles from *The Tattooed Man* (1926) to *Mystery on Telegraph Hill* (1961), ranging from adventure and mystery (*Hurricane Weather* and *The Black Tanker*) to dynamite-packed war-time stories (*Heart of Danger*). *Hurricane Weather*, an absorbing tale, is about adventures in the South Sea Island waters: descriptions of the beauty of deep sea life and the roughness of the undercurrent are breathtaking. In *The Black Tanker*, Rance, the hero, and Tod sail to China and encounter intrigue and shady dealings; the clues and climax produce an enthralling adventure. *Heart of Danger* is a story about Tod and the hero, Rudy Behrens, and their role in aiding the United States against a German traitor during World War II. The most popular work of the series is *The Jinx Ship*, which pits Tod against many devilish and daring odds.

Other adventures of the sea include *Secret Cargo*, a lively and vigorous account of one youth's experiences on a freighter bound for Tahiti. *Shipwreck* is the story of Renny Mitchum, a 16-year-old mess boy on a schooner headed for the Copra Islands. The author draws heavily on his own experiences of sea life, which enhances the authenticity of the books.

Although all of Mr. Pease's stories are action-filled, suspenseful, and convincing, the characters are vibrant and alive, and the reality of his stories contributes to the excitement of each book.

—Dolores C. Leffall

PECK, Richard. American. Born in Decatur, Illinois, 5 April 1934. Educated at De Pauw University, Greencastle, Indiana, 1952–56, B.A. 1956; University of Exeter, Devon, 1954–55; Southern Illinois University, Carbondale, M.A. 1959. Served in the United States Army in Germany, 1956–58. Formerly, schoolteacher; member of the faculty, Hunter College, New York; Assistant Director, Council for Basic Education, Washington, D.C. Recipient: Mystery Writers of America Edgar Allan Poe Award, 1977. Address: 139 Maple Street, Englewood, New Jersey 07631, U.S.A.

PUBLICATIONS FOR CHILDREN

Fiction

>   *Don't Look and It Won't Hurt.* New York, Holt Rinehart, 1972.
>   *Dreamland Lake.* New York, Holt Rinehart, 1973.
>   *Through a Brief Darkness.* New York, Viking Press, 1973; London, Collins, 1976.
>   *Representing Super Doll.* New York, Viking Press, 1974.
>   *The Ghost Belonged to Me.* New York, Viking Press, 1975; London, Collins, 1977.
>   *Are You in the House Alone?* New York, Viking Press, 1976.
>   *Monster Night at Grandma's House,* illustrated by Don Freeman. New York, Viking Press, 1977.
>   *Ghosts I Have Been.* New York, Viking Press, 1977.

Other

>   *The Creative Word 2,* with Stephen N. Judy. New York, Random House, 1973.

>   Editor, *Urban Studies: A Research Paper Casebook.* New York, Random House, 1973.
>   Editor, *Transitions: A Literary Paper Casebook.* New York, Random House, 1974.
>   Editor, *Pictures That Storm Inside My Head* (poetry anthology). New York, Avon, 1976.

PUBLICATIONS FOR ADULTS

Other

>   *Old Town: A Compleat Guide,* with Norman Strasma. Chicago, 1965.
>   *A Consumer's Guide to Educational Innovations,* with Mortimer Smith and George Weber. Washington, D.C., Council for Basic Education, 1972.

>   Editor, with Ned E. Hoopes, *Edge of Awareness: Twenty-Five Contemporary Essays.* New York, Dell, 1966.
>   Editor, *Sounds and Silences.* New York, Delacorte Press, 1970.
>   Editor, *Mindscapes: Poems for the Real World.* New York, Delacorte Press, 1971.

Richard Peck comments:

The focus of my books is to introduce younger adolescents to the reading of fiction and contemporary poetry. Though the themes of my novels are meant to be serious reflections of adolescents' concerns, I try to write in forms popular with them: comedy, melodrama, wish-fulfillment, the supernatural, and mystery.

*   *   *

One of the most consistently entertaining of contemporary writers for adolescents, Richard Peck is noted for vivid characterization and lively dialogue. His themes generally deal with problems faced by young people trying to come to terms with society and their own lives. Most of his novels reflect his own mid-western American background, as his first, *Don't Look and It Won't Hurt*. The story's title reflects the hard-won philosophy of the young heroine, Carol, who has learned to back away from problems which otherwise might overwhelm her — advice which Carol gives her older sister, Ellen, unmarried and pregnant, awaiting the birth of her baby in a foster home in Chicago, when Ellen is tormented with the prospect of giving her baby up for adoption.

Dreamland Lake is a somber tale steeped in an atmosphere of impending doom as two boys, Brian and Flip, discover the body of a tramp in an abandoned amusement park. Flip's vivid imagination turns the episode into a full-blown disaster culminating in the bizarre death of Elvan, a pitifully bumbling fat boy with a yearning for importance and friendship.

Through a Brief Darkness is a tightly plotted thriller involving motherless Karen, daughter of a big-time criminal leader, who is kidnapped by his rivals. Karen's escape, aided by a somewhat too circumstantial young Etonian, makes up the action of the book; her gradual awareness of and willingness to face up to her father's criminal activities is the emotional climax.

Probably the most satisfying of Peck's books, in terms of theme, realistic character development, and plotting, is *Representing Super Doll*. Told by Verna, a delightfully wholesome girl from a midwest farm family, the book deals with Darlene, not too bright and much too beautiful, who is pushed by an ambitious mother to win a national contest, Miss Teen Super Doll. Verna's attempts to protect Darlene from contemptuous schoolmates and to cover for her on a disastrous promotional trip to New York City bring her to a realization that real beauty involves much more than regular features and a dazzling smile.

The Ghost Belonged to Me is alternately funny and frightful, but some of the characters, particularly the young hero Alexander's mother and his older sister, are overdrawn to the point of caricature. And only a writer as skilful as Peck would dare include as one of the main characters a soggy girl ghost whose principal ambition is to have her bones exhumed and laid to rest in the family burial plot, a problem which triggers the rest of the somewhat preposterous story, as Alexander, his 85 year old great-uncle, and a shrewdly intelligent young neighbor with the improbable name of Blossom Culp take the bones back to New Orleans, pursued in classic cloak-and-dagger fashion by the villain, a reporter from the New Orleans *Delta Daily*.

Before writing *Are You In the House Alone?*, Peck did considerable research, talking with doctors, lawyers, and hospital emergency room personnel. The story is told through the eyes of the victim, Gail Osburne, a suburban teenager who is raped by one of the most "respectable" boys in town. The anguish of Gail's family and friends, the refusal of the police to believe her story, and Gail's own horror as she relives the numbing terror of the rape episode and waits for the rapist to strike again make a disturbingly powerful story. But as Peck said of the book, "*Are You In the House Alone?* is not a book to reassure, nor even to please. If it's to be honest, the story's victim continues to be victimized by public opinion in many small ways. And the story cannot have a happy ending; in fact it can't really have an ending at all."

—Margaret Maxwell

PECK, Robert Newton. American. Born in Vermont. Educated at Rollins College, Winter Park, Florida, B.A. 1953. Served in the 88th Infantry Division, United States Army, 1945–47. Married Dorothy Houston in 1958; has one son and one daughter. Lumberjack, paper mill worker, hog killer; advertising executive. Writer of songs and television commercials and jingles. Recipient: *Media and Methods* award, 1975. Address: 500 Sweetwater Club Circle, Longwood, Florida 32750, U.S.A.

PUBLICATIONS FOR CHILDREN

Fiction

A Day No Pigs Would Die. New York, Knopf, 1972; London, Hutchinson, 1973.
Millie's Boy. New York, Knopf, 1973.
Soup, illustrated by Charles Gehm. New York, Knopf, 1974.
Soup and Me, illustrated by Charles Lilly. New York, Knopf, 1975.
Wild Cat, illustrated by Hal Frenck. New York, Holiday House, 1975.
I Am the King of Kazoo, illustrated by William Bryan Park. New York, Knopf, 1976.
Rabbits and Redcoats, illustrated by Laura Lydecker. New York, Walker, 1976.
Hamilton, illustrated by Laura Lydecker. Boston, Little Brown, 1976.
Hang for Treason. New York, Doubleday, 1976.
Last Sunday, illustrated by Ben Stahl. New York, Doubleday, 1977.
Trig, illustrated by Pamela Johnson. Boston, Little Brown, 1977.
Patooie, illustrated by Ted Lewin. New York, Knopf, 1977.

Play

King of Kazoo, music and lyrics by Peck, illustrated by William Bryan Park. New York, Knopf, 1976.

Verse

Bee Tree and Other Stuff, illustrated by Laura Lydecker. New York, Walker, 1975.

Other

Path of Hunters: Animal Struggle in a Meadow, illustrated by Betty Fraser. New York, Knopf, 1973; London, Macdonald and Jane's, 1974.

PUBLICATIONS FOR ADULTS

Novels

The Happy Sadist. New York, Doubleday, 1962.
Fawn. Boston, Little Brown, 1975.
The King's Iron. Boston, Little Brown, 1977.

Robert Newton Peck comments:
I want kids to know that pork chops are not made by DuPont out of soybeans. Pigs are killed because man is a predator; all of Nature is predatory ... even a carrot.
In my books, authority figures (parents, teachers, etc.) are strong and kind and respected by the kids in the story ... as Soup and I revered Miss Kelly.

*   *   *

Robert Newton Peck is a prolific author whose stories hold the reader's attention from the first word to the last. Most of his books, such as *A Day No Pigs Would Die,* are set in rural Vermont during the 1920's and are loosely based on his own childhood. These stories have a charm and a realistic quality that are reminiscent – but certainly not imitations – of Mark Twain's *Tom Sawyer*. Like Tom, Mr. Peck's hero is a young boy full of mischief and action – a thoroughly likeable protagonist. One cannot but feel slightly envious of his life on that Vermont farm of 50 years ago, even though it was, for the boy, rife with problems.

All of Mr. Peck's books do not deal with his personal experiences, however. He is fascinated with the history of Colonial and Revolutionary America, and has studied that period thoroughly. *Hang for Treason* is but one of his books set in those turbulent years, but it is much more than a story of wartime action. Basically, it is the story of a boy growing into manhood. In the hands of a skilled author such as Mr. Peck, that idea gives the book a feeling of today.

Perhaps that is Mr. Peck's greatest talent – regardless of the period of which he writes, regardless of the scene he selects for his books, the characters are real and their development is logical. That is what gives his fiction the believability so essential to a good story. He is also very much aware that while times have changed, people haven't, so youngsters reading his work today can easily identify with one or more of his characters. It would not surprise this reviewer if Mr. Peck's novels become classics that are read for many years.

—Rubie Saunders

PEET, Bill (William Bartlett Peet). American. Born in Grandview, Indiana, 29 January 1915. Educated at John Herron Art Institute, Indianapolis, 1933–37. Married Margaret Brunst in 1937; has two sons. Writer-illustrator, Walt Disney Studio, Hollywood, 1937–64. Address: 11478 Laurel Crest Road, Studio City, California 91604, U.S.A.

PUBLICATIONS FOR CHILDREN (illustrated by the author)

Fiction

> *Farewell to Shady Glade.* Boston, Houghton Mifflin, 1966; London, Deutsch, 1967.
> *Capyboppy.* Boston, Houghton Mifflin, 1966; London, Deutsch, 1969.
> *Buford the Little Bighorn.* Boston, Houghton Mifflin, 1967; London, Deutsch, 1968.
> *Jennifer and Josephine.* Boston, Houghton Mifflin, 1967; London, Deutsch, 1970.
> *Fly Homer Fly.* Boston, Houghton Mifflin, 1969; London, Deutsch, 1974.
> *The Whingdingdilly.* Boston, Houghton Mifflin, and London, Deutsch, 1970.
> *The Wump World.* Boston, Houghton Mifflin, 1970; London, Deutsch, 1976.
> *How Droofus the Dragon Lost His Head.* Boston, Houghton Mifflin, 1971; London, Deutsch, 1972.
> *The Ant and the Elephant.* Boston, Houghton Mifflin, 1972; London, Deutsch, 1975.
> *The Spooky Tail of Prewitt Peacock.* Boston, Houghton Mifflin, 1972.
> *Merle the High Flying Squirrel.* Boston, Houghton Mifflin, 1974.
> *Cyrus the Unsinkable Sea Serpent.* Boston, Houghton Mifflin, 1975; London, Deutsch, 1977.
> *The Gnats of Knotty Pine.* Boston, Houghton Mifflin, 1975; London, Deutsch, 1977.
> *Big Bad Bruce.* Boston, Houghton Mifflin, 1977.

Plays

> Screenplays (with others): *Pinnochio*, 1940; *Dumbo*, 1941; *Fantasia*, 1941; *Song of the South*, 1946; *Cinderella*, 1950; *Alice in Wonderland*, 1951; *Peter Pan*, 1953; *Sleeping*

Beauty, 1959; *One Hundred and One Dalmatians,* 1961; *The Sword in the Stone,* 1963; and short subjects.

Verse

> *Hubert's Hair-Raising Adventure.*   Boston, Houghton Mifflin, 1959; London, Deutsch, 1960.
> *Huge Harold.*   Boston, Houghton Mifflin, 1961; London, Deutsch, 1964.
> *Smokey.*   Boston, Houghton Mifflin, 1962; London, Deutsch, 1966.
> *The Pinkish Purplish Bluish Egg.*   Boston, Houghton Mifflin, 1963; London, Deutsch, 1967.
> *Ella.*   Boston, Houghton Mifflin, 1964; London, Deutsch, 1966.
> *Randy's Dandy Lions.*   Boston, Houghton Mifflin, 1964.
> *Kermit the Hermit.*   Boston, Houghton Mifflin, 1965; London, Deutsch, 1967.
> *The Caboose Who Got Loose.*   Boston, Houghton Mifflin, 1971; London, Deutsch, 1974.
> *Countdown to Christmas.*   San Carlos, California, Golden Gate Books, 1972.

Bill Peet comments:

Many years ago I illustrated the works of others, but found it to be frustrating. In writing my own stories I am able to choose the subject matter, the things I enjoy drawing, which is far more satisfactory, and far more creative. I am not an author who illustrates, but an illustrator who writes. Such freedom is a luxury after working for over 27 years at the Disney Studio where so many cooks can spoil the broth.

*   *   *

Bill Peet's widely-read picture books for young children have an exotic patina of fantasy and realistic detail with simple but imaginatively sympathetic illustrations by the author. Although the majority of Peet's texts are in prose, he uses a number of poetic devices to enhance his text, namely alliteration, assonance, consonance, and internal rhyme. Also, the texts have a balance and poise that are characteristic of the work of an author who gives attention to rhythm and the crystallizing properties of good versification, even though he is writing in prose. While his play of words and sounds may be a bit saccharine for an adult audience, children love it; and while many children forget titles of stories that have been read to them, because of Peet's repetition of sound, few forget *Kermit the Hermit, The Wingdingdilly, Huge Harold* or *The Caboose Who Got Loose.* Peet's characters are equally memorable because they all have a peculiarity or singularity that takes them off the level of stereotypes. Droofus, in *How Droofus the Dragon Lost His Head,* is a *grass-eating* dragon, not just a kind and good one. Scamp, the dog in *The Wingdingdilly,* wants to be a horse, but "Not just any horse. Scamp wanted to be a great horse like Palomar the giant Percheron who lived on the farm just across the road." The structural pattern of most of Peet's works is consistent. The main character is introduced, there is enough exposition to set the scene before conflict is introduced, and then follows a straightforward, lively, and suspense-filled narration. The climax comes swiftly and the resolution is satisfying. Typical emotions are fear and anticipation coupled with gratification at the end of the story.

Peet's illustrations fit very well with his texts. There is a slight sense of exaggeration and elongation, even awkwardness or gawkiness in the characters that is charming rather than demeaning. Perhaps the most appealing quality in the pictures of main characters, however, is their eyes and mouths, both of which are highly expressive and not without a sense of irony, perspective, and introspection. Bill Peet's stories for children are eminently readable, and the pictures are strong enough to stand on their own.

—Rachel Fordyce

PERKINS, Lucy Fitch.   American.   Born in Maples, Indiana, 12 July 1865. Educated at Old Union School, Kalamazoo, Michigan; Kalamazoo High School, 1879–83; Museum of Fine Arts School, Boston, 1883–86. Married Dwight Heald Perkins in 1891; one daughter, one son. Illustrator, Prang Educational Company, Boston, 1886, and Chicago, 1893–1903; teacher at the Pratt Institute School of Fine Arts, Brooklyn, 1887–91. *Died 18 March 1937.*

PUBLICATIONS FOR CHILDREN (illustrated by the author)

Fiction

> *The Dutch Twins.*   Boston, Houghton Mifflin, and London, Constable, 1911.
> *The Japanese Twins.*   Boston, Houghton Mifflin, 1915; London, Cape, 1955.
> *The Irish Twins.*   Boston, Houghton Mifflin, 1913; London, Cape, 1922.
> *The Eskimo Twins.*   Boston, Houghton Mifflin, 1914; London, Cape, 1922.
> *The Mexican Twins.*   Boston, Houghton Mifflin, 1915; London, Cape, 1955.
> *The Cave Twins.*   Boston, Houghton Mifflin, 1916; London, Cape, 1922.
> *The Belgian Twins.*   Boston, Houghton Mifflin, 1917; London, Cape, 1940.
> *The French Twins.*   Boston, Houghton Mifflin, 1918; London, Cape, 1939.
> *The Spartan Twins.*   Boston, Houghton Mifflin, 1918; London, Cape, 1936.
> *Cornelia: The Story of a Benevolent Despot.*   Boston, Houghton Mifflin, 1919.
> *The Scotch Twins.*   Boston, Houghton Mifflin, 1919; London, Cape, 1922.
> *The Italian Twins.*   Boston, Houghton Mifflin, 1920; London, Cape, 1952.
> *The Puritan Twins.*   Boston, Houghton Mifflin, 1921; London, Cape, 1955.
> *The Swiss Twins.*   Boston, Houghton Mifflin, 1922; London, Cape, 1936.
> *The Filipino Twins.*   Boston, Houghton Mifflin, 1923; London, Cape, 1949.
> *The Colonial Twins of Virginia.*   Boston, Houghton Mifflin, 1924; London, Cape, 1949.
> *The American Twins of 1812.*   Boston, Houghton Mifflin, 1925; London, Cape, 1951.
> *The American Twins of the Revolution.*   Boston, Houghton Mifflin, 1926; London, Cape, 1943.
> *Mr. Chick, His Travels and Adventures.*   Boston, Houghton Mifflin, 1926.
> *The Pioneer Twins.*   Boston, Houghton Mifflin, 1927; London, Cape, 1943.
> *The Farm Twins.*   Boston, Houghton Mifflin, 1928.
> *Kit and Kat: More Adventures of the Dutch Twins.*   Boston, Houghton Mifflin, 1929.
> *The Indian Twins.*   Boston, Houghton Mifflin, 1930; London, Cape, 1938.
> *The Pickaninny Twins.*   Boston, Houghton Mifflin, 1931.
> *The Norwegian Twins.*   Boston, Houghton Mifflin, 1933; London, Cape, 1936.
> *The Spanish Twins.*   Boston, Houghton Mifflin, 1934; London, Cape, 1952.
> *The Chinese Twins.*   Boston, Houghton Mifflin, 1935; London, Cape, 1936.
> *The Dutch Twins and Little Brother*, completed by Eleanor Ellis Perkins.   Boston, Houghton Mifflin, 1938.

Verse

> *The Goose Girl: A Mother's Lap-Book of Rhymes and Pictures.*   Chicago, McClurg, 1906.

Other

> *Aesop's Fables.*   New York, Stokes, 1908.
> *The Dutch Twins Primer.*   Boston, Houghton Mifflin, 1917.

> Editor, *Robin Hood: His Deeds and Adventures as Recounted in the Old English Ballads.*   New York, Stokes, and London, Jack, 1906.

Editor, *The Twenty Best Fairy Tales by Hans Andersen, Grimm, and Miss Mulock.* New York, Stokes, and London, Harrap, 1907.

Editor, *A Midsummer-Night's Dream for Young People*, based on the play by Shakespeare. New York, Stokes, and London, Harrap, 1907.

PUBLICATIONS FOR ADULTS

Other

A Book of Joys: The Story of a New England Summer. Chicago, McClurg, 1907.

Illustrator: *A Wonder Book* by Nathaniel Hawthorne, 1908; *Stories of the Pilgrims* by Margaret Blanche Pumphrey, 1912; *Little Pioneers* by Maude Warren, 1916; *News from No-Town* by Eleanor Ellis Perkins, 1919; *The Children's Year Book* edited by Maud Summers, 1923; *The Fairyland Reader* by Edgar Dubs Shimer, 1935; *Mother Goose Book*; *The Enchanted Peacock and Other Stories* by Julia Brown.

*   *   *

Lucy Fitch Perkins drew inspiration from two experiences: a visit to Ellis Island in New York where she saw the polyglot oppressed people who were immigrating to the United States in the 1920's – and a visit to a Chicago school where she marveled at what the teachers were accomplishing with children of 27 different nationalities.

Her fame as a writer for children rests upon her "Twins" series for ages 8 to 10. The series began with *The Dutch Twins* in 1911 and soon included many more. An early comment on these titles by Bertha E. Mahony and Elinor Whitney in their book *Realms of Gold* (1929) read: "Each book tells of the doings of children in various countries with truth, simplicity, and genuine skill in holding the interest of young readers .... The fact that Mrs. Perkins has been able to maintain freshness and life in so long a series is worthy of appreciation."

Mrs. Perkins later added several stories with American historical backgrounds (for example, *The American Twins of 1812* and *The Colonial Twins of Virginia*) and had published twenty-four Twins books by the time of her death at age 72. Their enduring vitality and usefulness are proven by the fact that ten or more of them have just been reissued for today's youngsters. Although a few critics have felt that the Twins books tended to stereotype nationalities and to "emphasize differences," is that bad? They serve to crystallize children's ideas of how other peoples live and to show what values immigrant children have contributed to American life. The author's goal was to foster just such cross-cultural understanding.

—Norma R. Fryatt

PETERSHAM, Maud (Sylvia Fuller). American. Born in Kingston, New York, 5 August 1889. Educated at Vassar College, Poughkeepsie, New York, graduated 1912. Married Miska Petersham, *q.v.* (died, 1960); one son. Worked for International Art Service, New York. Recipient: American Library Association Caldecott Medal, 1946. *Died 29 November 1971.*

PUBLICATIONS FOR CHILDREN (with Miska Petersham, illustrated by the authors)

Fiction

Miki.   New York, Doubleday, 1929.
The Ark of Father Noah and Mother Noah.   New York, Doubleday, 1930.
Auntie and Celia Jane and Miki.   New York, Doubleday, 1932.
Get-a-Way and Háry János.   London, Viking Press, 1933; London, Lovat Dickson, 1935.
Miki and Mary: Their Search for Treasure.   New York, Viking Press, 1934; London, Lovat Dickson, 1935.
The Box with Red Wheels.   New York, Macmillan, 1949; London, Macmillan, 1958.
The Circus Baby.   New York, Macmillan, 1950; London, Macmillan, 1958.
Off to Bed: Seven Stories for Wide-Awakes.   New York, Macmillan, 1954.
The Boy Who Had No Heart.   New York, Macmillan, 1955.
The Peppernuts.   New York, Macmillan, and London, Macmillan, 1958.

Other

The Story Book of Clothes [*Food, Houses, Things We Use, Transportation, Earth's Treasures, Gold, Iron and Steel, Oil, Ships, Trains, Wheels, Coal, Aircraft, Foods from the Field, Rice, Sugar, Wheat, Corn, Cotton, Rayon, Silk, Things We Wear, Wool*].   Philadelphia, Winston, 24 vols., 1933–39; *Coal, Iron and Steel, Oil, Houses, Food, Clothes, Gold, Transportation, Wheels, Aircraft, Ships, Trains,* London, Dent, 12 vols., 1936–38; *Cotton, Rayon, Rice, Wheat, Wool, Corn,* London, Wells Gardner Darton, 6 vols., 1947–48.
David.   Philadelphia, Winston, and London, Dent, 1938.
Joseph and His Brothers.   Philadelphia, Winston, and London, Dent, 1938.
Moses.   Philadelphia, Winston, and London, Dent, 1938.
Ruth.   Philadelphia, Winston, and London, Dent, 1938.
An American ABC.   New York, Macmillan, 1941.
America's Stamps: The Story of One Hundred Years of United States Postage Stamps.   New York, Macmillan, 1947.
The Story of the Presidents of the United States of America.   New York, Macmillan, 1953; revised edition, 1966.
The Silver Mace: A Story of Williamsburg.   New York, Macmillan, 1956.

Illustrator: *The Shepherd Psalm,* 1962; with Miska Petersham: *Children of Ancient Britain* by Louise Lamprey, 1921; *Rootabaga Stories,* 1922, and *Rootabaga Pigeons,* 1923, by Carl Sandburg; *Tales from Shakespeare* by Charles Lamb, 1923; *Poppy Seed Cakes* by Margery Clark, 1924; *The F-U-N Book,* 1924, *In Animal Land,* 1924, *Billy Bang Book,* 1927, *Little Indians,* 1930, and *Zip the Toy Mule and Other Stories,* 1932, all by Mabel La Rue; *Nursery Friends from France,* 1925, and *Tales Told in Holland,* 1926, by Olive B. Miller; *Pathway to Reading* by Bessie Coleman and others, 1925; *Little Ugly Face* by Florence Coolidge, 1925; *Marquette Readers,* 1925; *History Stories* by John Wayland, 1925; *Philippine National Literature* by Harriet Fansler and Isidoro Panlasgui, 1925; *Number Friends* by Inez Howard and others, 1927; *Children of the Mountain Eagle,* 1927, *Pran of Albania,* 1929, and *Young Trajan,* 1931, all by Elizabeth Cleveland Miller; *Where Was Bobby?* by Marguerite Clément, 1928; *Everyday Canadian Primer,* 1928; *Pleasant Pathways,* 1928, *Winding Roads,* 1928, *Faraway Hills,* 1929, and *Heights and Highways,* 1929, all edited by Wilhelmina Harper and A.J. Hamilton; *The Magic Doll of Roumania* by Marie, Queen of Romania, 1929; *The Christ Child,* 1931; *Beckoning Road, Rich Cargoes, Treasure Trove,* and *Wings of Adventure,* edited by S.V. Rowland, W.D. Lewis, and E.J. Marshall, 4 vols., 1931; *Martin the Goose Boy,* 1932, and *The Four and Lena,* 1938, by Marie Barringer; *Heidi* by Johanna Spyri, 1932; *Pinocchio* by C. Collodi, 1932; *The Picnic Book* by Jean Y. Ayer, 1934; *Albanian Wonder Tales* by Post

Wheeler, 1936; *Susannah the Pioneer Cow* by Miriam Evangeline Mason, 1941; *A Little Book of Prayers* by Emilie Johnson, 1941; *Jesus' Story*, 1942; *Literature* edited by E.A. Cross, 7 vols., 1943–48; *The Rooster Crows: A Book of American Rhymes and Jingles*, 1945; *Told under the Christmas Tree*, 1948; *A Bird in the Hand: Sayings from Poor Richard's Almanac* by Benjamin Franklin, 1951; *Rip van Winkle, and The Legend of Sleepy Hollow* by Washington Irving, 1951; *In Clean Hay* by Eric Kelly, 1953.

*   *   *

"I don't think any American can appreciate this country as I do," Miska Petersham stated during his acceptance speech for the Caldecott Medal in 1946. This remark was properly directed towards adults, for what did it matter to a child poring over the books of the Petershams in the 1920's, 1930's and even today that Miska came from Hungary and Maud was born in the United States?

Yet, the adventures of *Miki* and his trip to Hungary – climbing into a feather pillow bed, dancing to gypsy music, warming himself against a white clay stove, listening to shepherds' tales of warriors who raced across the Milky Way, watching Sari, the goose, dressed in strudel dough – this was the magic, the touchstone to another world that the Petershams' own backgrounds made possible. So it was with *Miki and Mary* – children boarding a ship to visit distant lands – as well as a seemingly-forgotten book, *Auntie*. There were children like Celia Jane, Flossie, and Trailing Arbutus in America's multi-racial world, with stern Puritan figures like Grandfather and Auntie, the schoolteacher: the Petershams mixed a sense of haunting mystery about adults with touches of levity – the magic table and a schoolroom scene bordering on hilarity.

The child, it seems to me, is not concerned with who writes the text or illustrates any given book, but rather that both words and pictures enrich as a whole. It was the Petershams' talent that their backgrounds and interests spurred them to bridge many worlds, places and themes, whether illustrating the story of *The Christ Child*, which reflected the deeply religious aspect of their being, or using Benjamin Franklin's wisdom as the text for *A Bird in the Hand*, or satisfying a young reader's curiosity for facts in their Story Books of Things We Use.

Their love for animals is omnipresent in all of their books, yet dominant in such as *Off to Bed* or *The Circus Baby*. The animals in *Miki* and *Auntie*, however, seem more credible than in the later books where they often become almost cartoon-like and a bit too precious. *The Rooster Crows: A Book of American Rhymes and Jingles* (a questionable subtitle, for many of the verses originated in England) brings together many elements of the Petersham's art, yet seems less successful to me than their earlier books, where their own sense of story, of broadening worlds with an appropriate dash of dignity, discovery and humor, prevails.

Certainly in dozens of books Miska Petersham showed his appreciation for America and Maud her religious background in a blending which showed respect for other cultures and races, with a regard for the child who wished his facts to be presented with visual accompaniment. Although the Petersham texts may appear to be somewhat simplistic today, it is well to remember that their concern for multi-ethnic and racial consciousness made its first appearance in book form in 1929, many years before other authors and illustrators took into account this important aspect of books for the young reader.

—Myra Cohn Livingston

PETERSHAM, Miska (Mihaly Petrezselyen).   American.   Born in Törökszentmiklos, Hungary, 20 September 1888; emigrated to England in 1911 and the United States in 1912. Educated at the Royal Academy of Art, Budapest. Married Maud Fuller (i.e., Maud

Petersham, *q.v.*); one son. Commercial artist. Recipient: American Library Association Caldecott Medal, 1946. *Died 15 May 1960.*

See the entry for Maud Petersham.

PETRY, Ann (Lane).   American.   Born in Old Saybrook, Connecticut, 12 October 1908. Educated at Connecticut College of Pharmacy, now University of Connecticut School of Pharmacy, 1928–31, Ph.G. 1931; Columbia University, New York, 1943–44. Married George D. Petry in 1938; has one daughter. Pharmacist, James Pharmacy, Old Saybrook and Old Lyme, Connecticut, 1931–38; Writer and Reporter, *Amsterdam News,* New York, 1938–41; Women's Editor, *People's Voice,* New York, 1941–44. Visiting Professor of English, University of Hawaii, Honolulu, 1974–75. Secretary, Authors League of America, 1960. Agent: Russell and Volkening Inc., 551 Fifth Avenue, New York, New York 10017. Address: 113 Old Boston Post Road, Old Saybrook, Connecticut 06475, U.S.A.

PUBLICATIONS FOR CHILDREN

Fiction

> *The Drugstore Cat,* illustrated by Susanne Suba.   New York, Crowell, 1949.
> *Tituba of Salem Village.*   New York, Crowell, 1964.

Other

> *Harriet Tubman: Conductor on the Underground Railroad.*   New York, Crowell, 1955;
>   as *A Girl Called Moses: The Story of Harriet Tubman.* London, Methuen, 1960.
> *Legends of the Saints,* illustrated by Anne Rockwell.   New York, Crowell, 1970.

PUBLICATIONS FOR ADULTS

Novels

> *The Street.*   Boston, Houghton Mifflin, 1946; London, Joseph, 1947.
> *Country Place.*   Boston, Houghton Mifflin, 1947; London, Joseph, 1948.
> *The Narrows.*   Boston, Houghton Mifflin, 1953; London, Gollancz, 1954.

Short Stories

> *Miss Muriel and Other Stories.*   Boston, Houghton Mifflin, 1971.

Manuscript Collection: Mugar Memorial Library, Boston University.

Ann Petry comments:
   Because I was born black and female, I write about survivors (especially when I write for children): a bad-tempered little cat (*The Drugstore Cat*); a slave indicted for witchcraft (*Tituba of Salem Village*); a runaway slave who risks her life in order to guide other slaves to the North and freedom (*Harriet Tubman*); men and women persecuted for their religious beliefs (*Legends of the Saints*).

*   *   *

Besides novels and stories for adults, acknowledged for their "finely controlled narrative skill," Ann Petry has written works of fiction and history in a different vein for children and young people. *The Drugstore Cat* is an everyday story with a pleasing charm. Of greater impact and reflective of the author's deep-seated interest in adding to both the accuracy and adequacy of the history of slavery in the United States is her magnificently drawn *Harriet Tubman: Conductor on the Underground Railroad*. In reconstructing her subject's life she "in delicate and evocative words which carry an underlying sturdiness and dignity ... makes Harriet Tubman into a living figure and recreates in vivid scenes an era of struggle, hardship, and unshakable faith."

We follow this legendary Moses (born in Tidewater, Maryland and influenced by the rebel Denmark Vesey) as she "walked, ran, hid, coaxed, cajoled, and prayed until some 300 of her people had been delivered into freedom." The structure of the fictionalized biography is fascinating for maintaining and heightening interest: to each chapter the author appends related events of the time, revealing the larger picture, the historical backdrop which lends further associations, perspective, and weight to the story. The description of the plantation where Harriet spent most of her formative years, the drastically different life patterns of the whites and Blacks, the conversational exchanges, the family involvements: all spring to life. In the outdoor world which she finally reaches Harriet is overcome by the "hard-bought thing" freedom represents. "There was such glory over everything, the sun came like gold through the trees, and over the field, and I felt like I was in heaven."

Tituba of Salem Village focuses on a Black woman slave, originally from Bridgewater, Barbados, who is one of the accused during the height of the witchcraft hysteria. The reconstruction of the several settings, the characterization of Tituba's harsh master, a "wrathful" and "impatient" man, and other members of his family, her husband John Indian, together with the pictures of the uneasy times and the surrounding atmosphere as it enveloped both children and adults, draw a reader to share intimately the mounting tension and irrationality. "They're catchin' witches in Salem Village just like they was chickens on a roost." Tituba emerges full-bodied and magnificent.

In great contrast, both in theme and telling, is the author's *Legends of the Saints*, which reveals her storytelling powers in still different ways. This "wise and gentle book" presents glimpses of ten holy people from many lands and follows their experiences with simple dignity. Covered are: Christopher, Genesius, George, Blaise, Catherine of Alexandria, Nicholas, Francis of Assisi, Joan of Arc, Thomas More, and Martin de Porres, the Black barber-surgeon of Peru. The author captures the flavor of their times and touches their heroism. The style is direct and strong; simple sentences predominate, bulk description is emphasized, and conversational exchanges are introduced. This little volume can be for its readers a first step to wishing for more information about the individuals and the countries from which they came.

—Clara O. Jackson

PEYTON, K.M. Pseudonym for Kathleen W. Peyton. British. Born in Birmingham, Warwickshire, 2 August 1929. Educated at Wimbledon High School; Manchester Art School, Art Teacher's Diploma 1951. Married Michael Peyton in 1950; has two daughters. Art Teacher, Northampton High School, 1953–55. Recipient: Library Association Carnegie Medal, 1970; *Guardian* Award, 1970. Address: Rookery Cottage, North Fambridge, Essex, England.

PUBLICATIONS FOR CHILDREN

Fiction

Sabre, The Horse from the Sea (as Kathleen Herald), illustrated by Lionel
    Edwards. London, A. and C. Black, 1948; New York, Macmillan, 1963.
The Mandrake (as Kathleen Herald), illustrated by Lionel Edwards. London, A. and C.
    Black, 1949.
Crab the Road (as Kathleen Herald), illustrated by Peter Biegel. London, A. and C.
    Black, 1953.
North to Adventure. London, Collins, 1958; New York, Platt and Munk, 1965.
Stormcock Meets Trouble. London, Collins, 1961.
The Hard Way Home, illustrated by R.A. Branton. London, Collins, 1962; as Sing a
    Song of Ambush, New York, Platt and Munk, 1964.
Windfall, illustrated by Victor Ambrus. London, Oxford University Press, 1962; as
    Sea Fever, Cleveland, World, 1963.
Brownsea Silver. London, Collins, 1964.
The Maplin Bird, illustrated by Victor Ambrus. London, Oxford University Press,
    1964; Cleveland, World, 1965.
The Plan for Birdsmarsh, illustrated by Victor Ambrus. London, Oxford University
    Press, 1965; Cleveland, World, 1966.
Thunder in the Sky, illustrated by Victor Ambrus. London, Oxford University Press,
    1966; Cleveland, World, 1967.
Flambards, illustrated by Victor Ambrus. London, Oxford University Press, 1967;
    Cleveland, World, 1968.
Fly-by-Night, illustrated by the author. London, Oxford University Press, 1968;
    Cleveland, World, 1969.
The Edge of the Cloud, illustrated by Victor Ambrus. London, Oxford University
    Press, 1969; New York, World, 1970.
Flambards in Summer, illustrated by Victor Ambrus. London, Oxford University
    Press, 1969; New York, World, 1970.
Pennington's Seventeenth Summer, illustrated by the author. London, Oxford
    University Press, 1970; as Pennington's Last Term, New York, Crowell, 1971.
The Beethoven Medal, illustrated by the author. London, Oxford University Press,
    1971; New York, Crowell, 1972.
A Pattern of Roses, illustrated by the author. London, Oxford University Press, 1972;
    New York, Crowell, 1973.
Pennington's Heir, illustrated by the author. London, Oxford University Press, 1973;
    New York, Crowell, 1974.
The Team, illustrated by the author. London, Oxford University Press, 1975; New
    York, Crowell, 1976.
The Right-Hand Man. London, Oxford University Press, 1977.
Prove Yourself a Hero. London, Oxford University Press, 1977.

*   *   *

As a small, suburban schoolgirl, K.M. Peyton longed to own a pony. It was a hopeless
obsession. So at the age of 9, to cure her frustration, she began to write about horses. Her first
story was published when she was 15, and ever since writing has been as necessary a
condition of life as eating and sleeping.

Instead of going to Oxbridge as her parents and teachers expected, she chose Art School.
Later she eloped with a fellow student and this sense of purpose – following gut instincts and
braving opposition to achieve what really mattered to her at the time – is a characteristic trait
in almost all her heroes and heroines. They express Mrs. Peyton's own nature. Ruth Hollis in
Fly-by-Night is the dogged little girl, mad about horses, as she once was. Tim, in A Pattern of

Roses, rebelling against his parents' educational plans, is herself facing the transition from school to college.

With her husband, she contributed articles and stories to newspapers. In 1958, one of their weekly pot-boilers for the *Scout Magazine* was published as a complete novel, *North to Adventure*. The heroes are two boys, and it is worth noting that in all her books Mrs. Peyton continues to write as easily about males as females. Many of her best characters *are* male, like Gil in *Thunder in the Sky*, Uncle Russell, Will, Mark and Dick in *Flambards* and Penn, the hero of her Pennington trilogy. Whether the hero is male or female, you *care* what happens to him or her and identify with their fortunes. Other adventure serials with the same antecedents followed. *Stormcock Meets Trouble* is about a pair of boys caught up in a yachting melodrama. *The Hard Way Home* was based on the Peytons' own experience as a young couple travelling rough across Canada.

If Mrs. Peyton's obsession was horses, her husband's was boats. She continues to explore both themes throughout her writing. *Windfall*, a story about fishing under sail, and in her own words "my first pure book" (pure in the sense that she wrote it because she wanted to and not primarily for bread-and-butter), established her as a serious novelist. Her husband remains a powerful background influence both as inspiration and critic. But from the 1960's onwards Mrs. Peyton has developed steadily on her own to become one of our leading children's writers. In 1970 she won the Carnegie Award for *The Edge of the Cloud* and the Guardian Award for the *Flambards* trilogy.

The way people begin their careers is usually crucial to their later development. Mrs. Peyton's artistic background gave her, she says, "the best of all trainings in observation." (She still, incidentally, likes to illustrate her own stories where possible and regards the paintbrush as far superior to the pen as a creative outlet.) Her descriptive writing is so vivid that your mind is filled with pictures as you read. She has a remarkable gift for evoking atmosphere. You are inside the skin of her characters, smelling the hay with Dick and Christina in the stables of Flambards and choked by their conflicting emotions of love, hate, and nostalgia. It makes ideal film material – *Flambards* is currently being turned into a long-running television series.

Many of her settings must be unfamiliar to her readers – the exclusive Pony Club world of *The Team* (a sequel to *Fly-by-Night*) and the bleak Essex coast along which the Maplin Bird sailed so dangerously. Her own knowledge gives the reader the illusion of direct experience. And where she herself is breaking new ground, her research is so thorough that she achieves the same effect. If you want to learn about the competitive, fruity life of a Georgian coachman, read *The Right-Hand Man*. *The Edge of the Cloud* offers an oily insight into the harsh realities behind the glamour of early flying. The Pennington books explore the contemporary music scene from the viewpoint of an unlikely but talented young pianist.

Mrs. Peyton says she writes books like these quite deliberately to get away from boats and horses. And once away, as she says, "I do get carried away!" She is, unashamedly, a romantic, a spell-binder in the old tradition.

Mrs. Peyton learnt her craft through journalistic disciplines, paid by the week to feed lesser mortals' imaginations and keep them hungry with cliff-hangers. Her pot-boilers, as well as the prestigious groups of associated novels for which she has become famous, demonstrate her professionalism. To say that she is a "children's writer" is misleading. She writes with particular sympathy about adolescent passions. But her stories are enjoyed as much by adults as children. *A Pattern of Roses* is one of her most moving books. It contrasts two boys' struggle for identity at different periods of time. Tom is the product of that underprivileged rural society that preceded the Great War. Tim is suffering from the material affluence but spiritual poverty of our own day. This delicate, subtle ghost-story is readable as a pot-boiler but it also lingers in the imagination as a true work of literature.

—Joy Whitby

PHIPSON, Joan (Margaret). Australian. Born in Warrawee, New South Wales, 16 November 1912. Educated at Frensham School, Mittagong, New South Wales. Married Colin Hardinge Fitzhardinge in 1944; has one daughter and one son. Secretary, London, 1935–37; Librarian, Frensham School, 1937–39; Copy-writer, Radio Station 2-GB, Sydney, 1939–41; telegraphist in the WAAFF, 1941–44. Recipient: Australian Children's Book Award, 1953; Australian Book Council Book of the Year Award, 1963; New York *Herald Tribune* Festival Award, 1964; Australian Authors' Award, 1975. Agent: A.P. Watt and Son, 26–28 Bedford Row, London WC1R 4HL, England.

PUBLICATIONS FOR CHILDREN

Fiction

> *Good Luck to the Rider*, illustrated by Margaret Horder. Sydney and London, Angus and Robertson, 1953; New York, Harcourt Brace, 1968.
> *Six and Silver*, illustrated by Margaret Horder. Sydney and London, Angus and Robertson, 1954; New York, Harcourt Brace, 1971.
> *It Happened One Summer*, illustrated by Margaret Horder. Sydney, Angus and Robertson, 1957; London, Hamish Hamilton, 1964.
> *The Boundary Riders*, illustrated by Margaret Horder. Sydney, Angus and Robertson, and London, Constable, 1962; New York, Harcourt Brace, 1963.
> *The Family Conspiracy*, illustrated by Margaret Horder. Sydney, Angus and Robertson, and London, Constable, 1962; New York, Harcourt Brace, 1964.
> *Threat to the Barkers*, illustrated by Margaret Horder. Sydney, Angus and Robertson, and London, Constable, 1963; New York, Harcourt Brace, 1965.
> *Birkin*, illustrated by Margaret Horder. Melbourne, Lothian, and London, Constable, 1965; New York, Harcourt Brace, 1966.
> *A Lamb in the Family*, illustrated by Lynette Hemmant. London, Hamish Hamilton, 1966.
> *The Crew of the "Merlin,"* illustrated by Janet Duchesne. Sydney, Angus and Robertson, and London, Constable, 1966; as *Cross Currents*, New York, Harcourt Brace, 1967.
> *Peter and Butch.* London, Longman, and New York, Harcourt Brace, 1969.
> *The Haunted Night.* Melbourne, Macmillan, and New York, Harcourt Brace, 1970.
> *Bass and Billy Martin*, illustrated by Ron Brooks. Melbourne and London, Macmillan, 1972.
> *The Way Home.* London, Macmillan, and New York, Atheneum, 1973.
> *Polly's Tiger*, illustrated by Gavin Rowe. London, Hamish Hamilton, 1973; New York, Dutton, 1974.
> *Helping Horse.* London, Macmillan, 1974; as *Horse with Eight Hands*, New York, Atheneum, 1974.
> *The Cats.* London, Macmillan, and New York, Atheneum, 1976.
> *Hide till Daytime*, illustrated by Mary Dinsdale. London, Hamish Hamilton, 1977.
> *Fly into Danger.* New York, Atheneum, 1977.

Other

> *Christmas in the Sun*, illustrated by Margaret Horder. Sydney and London, Angus and Robertson, 1951.
> *Bennelong*, illustrated by Walter Stackpool. Sydney and London, Collins, 1975.

Joan Phipson comments:
I began to write for children almost by accident. The fact that I had reasonable success and

enjoyed this branch of writing persuaded me to continue. I have become more and more interested, finding more and more scope for imaginative writing in this field, and would not now wish for any other. I find I enjoy the discipline of simple statements – the clarity of thought and expression necessary – and the obligation to be humble. The enthusiasm of children is genuine and heart-warming, if transitory, and the fact that each child grows up and away forces the writer to meet the demands of on-coming generations.

*   *   *

Joan Phipson's novels are of two types. The first, in a tradition established a hundred years ago, tells of the adventures of new comers to a rugged and romantic Australian outback bush setting, with its superficially glamorous rural life and natural hazards such as bush-fire and flood. A later development, a contemporary one, introduces strong thematic contrasts between urban and rural life, and even the corruption to be found in country towns and "civilised" values.

In most of her books, Joan Phipson dwells on the need of the individual for acceptance. In books like *Peter and Butch* or *The Boundary Riders*, a young child with unwelcomed physical characteristics gives undue admiration to others – people who are older, wealthier or urbane and handsome. Joan Phipson then places the contrasting characters in a situation of crisis, allowing the lowly gradually to assume leadership through their inherent, natural affinity with the earth, which proves to be more productive, constructive and dependable than the superficial veneer of acquired learning embodied in their slick city cousins.

In books such as *A Lamb in the Family*, *Polly's Tiger* or *It Happened One Summer*, acceptance by others comes simply as a result of the protagonist taking some sort of admirable initiative to resolve a situation of conflict or distress. Yet the psychological depth is always seriously plumbed, whether simply in *Polly's Tiger*, where a girl copes with her feelings of alienation through an imagined affinity with an object associated with threat, or more complexly as in *Peter and Butch*, in which a boy struggles with conflicting self-images.

A recent development retains the innocence/experience thematic paradox yet sets it in a nightmare landscape of a timeless Australia in which three children explore their inter-relationship and the whole ethos of this ancient and unknowable land in the company of a sort of pantheistic being. *The Way Home* is a remarkable novel, capable of infinite interpretation. Where *The Boundary Riders* took a literary cliché and, with directness and flair, infused it with contemporary thematic seriousness, *The Way Home* is unique in its concept and its depth of meaning. The movement has been from innocence to experience, from adventure to profundity.

Joan Phipson is a prolific writer whose eloquence has sometimes resulted in tedious novels written in inflated or convoluted style, yet her range is wide and, at her best, when dealing with subject matter close to her heart, her books are immediately appealing and, in the case of *The Way Home*, profoundly moving.

—Walter McVitty

PICARD, Barbara Leonie. British. Born in Richmond, Surrey, 4 December 1917. Educated at St. Katharine's School, Wantage, Berkshire, 1930–34. Address: c/o Oxford University Press, Walton Street, Oxford OX2 6DP, England.

PUBLICATIONS FOR CHILDREN

Fiction

The Mermaid and the Simpleton, illustrated by Philip Gough. London, Oxford
   University Press, 1949; New York, Criterion Books, 1970.
The Faun and the Woodcutter's Daughter, illustrated by Charles Stewart. London,
   Oxford University Press, 1951; New York, Criterion Books, 1964.
The Lady of the Linden Tree, illustrated by Charles Stewart. London, Oxford
   University Press, 1954; New York, Criterion Books, 1962.
Ransom for a Knight, illustrated by C. Walter Hodges. London, Oxford University
   Press, 1956; New York, Walck, 1967.
Lost John, illustrated by Charles Keeping. London, Oxford University Press, 1962;
   New York, Criterion Books, 1963.
The Goldfinch Garden: Seven Tales, illustrated by Anne Linton. London, Harrap,
   1963; New York, Criterion Books, 1965.
One Is One, illustrated by Victor Ambrus. London, Oxford University Press, 1965;
   New York, Holt Rinehart, 1966.
The Young Pretenders, illustrated by Victor Ambrus. London, Edmund Ward, and
   New York, Criterion Books, 1966.
Twice Seven Tales, illustrated by Victor Ambrus. London, Kaye and Ward, 1968.

Other

The Odyssey of Homer, illustrated by Joan Kiddell-Monroe. London, Oxford
   University Press, and New York, Walck, 1952.
Tales of the Norse Gods and Heroes, illustrated by Joan Kiddell-Monroe. London,
   Oxford University Press, 1953.
French Legends, Tales, and Fairy Stories, illustrated by Joan Kiddell-
   Monroe. London, Oxford University Press, and New York, Walck, 1955.
Stories of King Arthur and His Knights, illustrated by Roy Morgan. London, Oxford
   University Press, and New York, Walck, 1955.
German Hero-Sagas and Folk-Tales, illustrated by Joan Kiddell-Monroe. London,
   Oxford University Press, and New York, Walck, 1958.
The Iliad of Homer, illustrated by Joan Kiddell-Monroe. London, Oxford University
   Press, and New York, Walck, 1960.
The Story of Rāma and Sītā, illustrated by Charles Stewart. London, Harrap, 1960.
Tales of the British People, illustrated by Eric Fraser. London, Edmund Ward, and
   New York, Criterion Books, 1961.
The Tower and the Traitors (history), illustrated by William Stobbs. London, Batsford,
   and New York, Putnam, 1961.
Hero-Tales from the British Isles, illustrated by Gay Galsworthy. London, Edmund
   Ward, and New York, Criterion Books, 1963.
Celtic Tales: Legends of Tall Warriors and Old Enchantments, illustrated by Gay
   Galsworthy. London, Edmund Ward, and New York, Criterion Books, 1964.
The Story of the Pāndavas, Retold from the Mahābhārata, illustrated by Charles
   Stewart. London, Dobson, 1968.
William Tell and His Son, from a translation by Bettina Hürlimann, illustrated by Paul
   Nussbaumer. London, Sadler, 1969.
Three Ancient Kings: Gilgamesh, Hrolf Kraki, Conary, illustrated by Philip
   Gough. London, Kaye and Ward, and New York, Warne, 1972.
Tales of Ancient Persia, Retold from the Shah-Nāma of Firdausi, illustrated by Victor
   Ambrus. London, Oxford University Press, 1972; New York, Walck, 1973.

Editor, *Encyclopedia of Myths and Legends of All Nations*, revised edition.   London, Edmund Ward, 1962.

Barbara Leonie Picard comments:

From very early years I had intended to be a writer – but I came to be a children's writer by accident. My first books were original fairy stories told in the traditional vein, and were written entirely for my own amusement. When they were published, their success encouraged my publishers to persuade me to continue writing for young people on the subjects which held most interest for me: mythology, legends, and folk-lore. I have also written several historical novels for older children and teen-agers on themes which attracted me. I never write any book unless it is to please myself.

*   *   *

Not surprisingly, because of her experience as a reteller of old tales, Barbara Leonie Picard's original writing lies in the two fields of the invented fairy story and the historical novel.

The collections of fairy tales – *The Mermaid and the Simpleton*, *The Faun and the Woodcutter's Daughter*, and *Twice Seven Tales* (which includes *The Lady of the Linden Tree*) – derive from the main traditions of Europe and the East, but courtly romance preponderates. The motifs of the true folk tale are often used but generally the themes are more orderly. The setting of court or castle is less idealized, with considerable descriptive detail, the product of research rather than the peasant's imagination. Maidens, except when enchanted, are always good and beautiful, and heroes, whether peasant or king, are deserving of whatever good fortune they gain. Moral virtues are always stressed, though trickery is permitted when it is the only way of overcoming evil. Some stories, in the Andersen tradition, lack a happy ending.

The historical novels are fine pieces of writing, considerably longer than the average children's book.

Ransom for a Knight has a single-strand plot, but the determined little Alys and the not-very-bright Hugh, the serf's child, come through as satisfactory characters. All shades of mediaeval society are included: the baronial hall, the rich merchant's house, the peasant's hovel with its fleas. Alys's childish eagerness wins over most of the people she meets, and kind and unkind hearts are found amongst the wealthy and the poor, the honest and the dishonest, the Scots and the English.

Lost John is an absorbing story of conflicting loyalties. Fighting is for killing, not for the exercise of knightly arts: the outlaws with whom John throws in his lot are not romantic Robin Hood figures. Too often, as in real life, motives are misunderstood and the wrong reactions follow. The ending may sound contrived, but does not seem so.

In *One Is One* Stephen fulfills all his ambitions, but is the cost worth it? The sensitive, artistic boy, rejected by his family, learns three times to love, in each case to lose its object through death. In its stress on knightly combat the book owes much to Picard's own retelling of Malory. Sir Pagan is too idealised to be real, yet this is how Stephen sees him. Through the three tragedies Stephen learns where his own future lies and that his prayers were after all answered.

The "great house" setting of *The Young Pretenders* is attractive. The depiction of the main characters is remarkably acute. The theme is unusual – a rogue masquerading as a fleeing Jacobite to save his life. The children are never found out, but the story ends rather sadly because life goes on just as it did before Seumas came into it. Historical details are worked in effortlessly and understandably and never obtrude as they did just occasionally in *Ransom for a Knight*.

—Margaret M. Tye

PLOWMAN, Stephanie. British. Educated at the University of London, B.A. (honours) in history. Married A.R. Hamilton-Dee (died). Gulbenkian Research Fellow, Cambridge University, 1969–72. Address: 2 The Knell, Harcourt Road, Mathon, Malvern, Worcestershire, England.

PUBLICATIONS FOR CHILDREN

Fiction

Sixteen Sail in Aboukir Bay, illustrated by Richard Kennedy. London, Methuen, 1956.
To Spare the Conquered. London, Methuen, 1960.
The Road to Sardis. London, Bodley Head, 1965; Boston, Houghton Mifflin, 1966.
Three Lives for the Czar. London, Bodley Head, 1969; Boston, Houghton Mifflin, 1970.
My Kingdom for a Grave. London, Bodley Head, 1970; Boston, Houghton Mifflin, 1971.
A Time to Be Born and a Time to Die. London, Bodley Head, 1975.
The Leaping Song. London, Bodley Head, 1976.

Other

Nelson, illustrated by Richard Kennedy. London, Methuen, 1955.

PUBLICATIONS FOR ADULTS

Play

Radio Play: *The Royal Exiles,* 1953.

Stephanie Plowman comments:
   The gestation period of my becoming a writer of historical fiction began when, as a 16 year old, I was required to write an essay criticising the policy of Napoleon after 1807. The sheer lunacy of this made me start working out privately why I wanted to go on learning history – certainly not to be able to pontificate on the "mistakes" made by the greatest military intelligence of modern times when I myself possibly couldn't run a village post-office. To learn about people, then? What it was like to live during certain happenings? To make the past present?
   Nowadays there are two stages. An age or incident takes possession, and the obsessive reading begins. And in the course of this, a sentence, or even a few words, call a character into being, i.e., a young officer who rode with his squadron from Novgorod in a futile attempt to save the Tsar, a single title among the list of books left by the Imperial children at Ekaterinburg. After this the manuscript writes itself.

                              *   *   *

   The distinction between adult and children's literature is fine enough to encourage many people, including some of the most notable of writers of children's books, to believe that the distinction does not exist. Certainly it is difficult to think of Stephanie Plowman except as a novelist whose appeal is to a certain kind of reader, not to readers of a certain age. Her blend of passion and scholarship is so rare and precious that adults and children who are able to meet its demands are richer for the experience.
   Stephanie Plowman's major books fall into two groups, those of classical Greece and those

dealing with the last days of Imperial Russia. The latter are perhaps the more successful, but both groups show the same qualities of historical irony and personal involvement.

It is the essence of these stories that they deal with historical figures, even though the central characters are invented. Seeing the real people through fictional eyes somehow gives them a sharper reality. There is a good example of this in *The Road to Sardis* where, at the lowest point of Athens' degradation, the hero sees a stranger examining the dismantled Long Walls with a professional eye. This is Thucydides, balancing despair at the destruction of his city against a historian's concern to prove the theory that Themistocles had built the walls in haste. There are equally telling portraits of Euripides and Socrates and a brilliant hostile thumb-nail sketch of Xenophon.

The Road to Sardis is mainly the story of the war between Athens and Sparta and the decline of democracy. Stephanie Plowman showed Athens in her glory in *The Leaping Song*, which begins with Marathon and ends with Salamis when the Persian fleet was destroyed in the narrow seas. This is a more mature work, particularly in the control of narrative (which is occasionally difficult to follow in the earlier book), but the blend of fiction and history is similar and as effective.

Between the two Greek stories Stephanie Plowman studied the Russian Revolution and wrote the two novels *Three Lives for the Czar* and *My Kingdom for a Grave*. In these a young Russo-Scotsman witnesses the decline and fall of the Romanov dynasty and the outbreak of revolution. Alexei Hamilton is committed by traditional loyalty and personal affection to the Russian royal family, but neither blinds him to the fatal weakness which has doomed them. These are deeply moving novels, in which major research has been completely digested so that, although the writer's authority is never in question, the story is nearer to Greek tragedy than to modern history. The reader, with the narrator, is the helpless witness of world-shaking events. One hesitates, so near the time of publication, to prophesy classic status, but here, if anywhere in modern children's literature, one is in the presence of greatness.

— Marcus Crouch

POLITI, Leo. American. Born in Fresno, California, in 1908. Educated at the National Art Institute, Monza, Italy, six years. Artist and illustrator. Recipient: American Library Association Caldecott Medal, 1950; Catholic Library Association Regina Medal, 1966. Address: c/o Charles Scribner's Sons Inc., 597 Fifth Avenue, New York, New York 10017, U.S.A.

PUBLICATIONS FOR CHILDREN (illustrated by the author)

Fiction

Little Pancho. New York, Viking Press, 1938.
Pedro, The Angel of Olvera Street. New York, Scribner, 1946.
Juanita. New York, Scribner, 1948.
Song of the Swallows. New York, Scribner, 1949.
A Boat for Peppe. New York, Scribner, 1950.
Little Leo. New York, Scribner, 1951.
The Mission Bell. New York, Scribner, 1953.
The Butterflies Come. New York, Scribner, 1957.
Moy Moy. New York, Scribner, 1961.
Rosa. New York, Scribner, 1963.
Lito and the Clown. New York, Scribner, 1964.

Piccolo's Prank.   New York, Scribner, 1965.
Mieko.   San Carlos, California, Golden Gate Books, 1969.
Emmet.   New York, Scribner, 1971.
The Nicest Gift.   New York, Scribner, 1973.
Three Stalks of Corn.   New York, Scribner, 1976.

Other

Young Giotto.   Albuquerque, Horn, 1947.
Saint Francis and the Animals.   New York, Scribner, 1959.

PUBLICATIONS FOR ADULTS

Other

Bunker Hill, Los Angeles: Reminiscences of Bygone Days.   Palm Desert, California,
    Desert Southwest, 1964.
Tales of the Los Angeles Parks.   Palm Desert, California, Best West Publications, 1966.
The Poinsietta.   Palm Desert, California, Best West Publications, 1968.

Illustrator: *The Least One* by Ruth Sawyer, 1941; *Aqui se Habla Espanol* by Margarita
Lopez, 1942; *Angelo, The Naughty One* by Helen Garrett, 1944; *Stories from the Americas*
edited by Frank Henius, 1944; *The Three Miracles* by Catherine Blanton, 1946; *El Coyote,
The Rebel* by Louis Perez, 1947; *Vamos a Habla Espanol* by Margarita Lopez and Esther
Brown, 1949; *At the Palace Gates* by Helen Parish, 1949; *Magic Money*, 1950, and *Looking-
for-Something*, 1952, by Ann Nolan Clark; *The Columbus Story* by Alice Dalgliesh, 1955;
The Noble Doll by Elizabeth Coatsworth, 1961; *All Things Bright and Beautiful* by Cecil
Frances Alexander, 1962.

*   *   *

Leo Politi is an artist and author who has given authentic and sympathetic interpretations
about children of different cultural and ethnic backgrounds.

His best known stories are set in or near the Los Angeles area and include *Pedro, The Angel
of Olvera Street.* Told in simple narrative form, it is the story of one small Mexican boy and
his participation in the annual Christmas Posado procession. Because Pedro sang "like an
angel" he was chosen to lead the Posado. The story, as well as the colorful illustrations, are
authentic, and through Pedro children all over have learned of this colorful festivity.

Song of the Swallows tells of the friendship between Juan, a small Mexican boy, and Julian,
the old bell-ringer at the Mission of San Juan Capistrano. Julian tells Juan about the old days
at the mission, and together they ring the bells to welcome the swallows as they come flying
in from the sea on St. Joseph's day. Soft, warm pictures beautifully capture the charm of the
old mission and give a feel for old California. Mr. Politi was awarded the Caldecott Medal for
Song of the Swallows, and in his acceptance speech he said that he tries to emphasize a "love
for people, animals, birds and flowers and a love for the simple, warm and earthy things."

Juanita is again set on Olvera Street and describes the annual pre-Easter ceremony, The
Blessing of the Animals. Other picture stories which treat Mexican-American children with
great empathy are *Lito and the Clown* and *Piccolo's Prank.*

Three Stalks of Corn tells some of the legends of the Tarahumares Indians of Quetzalcoatl,
through the device of a girl asking for stories of her grandmother's childhood in Mexico. The
illustrations are gay, colorful and typical.

Mr. Politi has written about the Chinese children who live in the area in *Moy Moy*, a small
girl who is fascinated with preparations for the New Year festival in Chinatown. Warm
family relationships characterize *Moy Moy*, as well as *Mieko* which is a simple narrative of
Japanese life in Los Angeles.

While Mr. Politi's children are always representative of their cultural background and stylized, they are never stereotyped. He follows a simple story line and imbues the daily activities of the children he depicts with great warmth and empathy. Leo Politi has contributed an unsurpassed body of work for all children from which they can understand other cultural backgrounds.

—Dorothy Clayton McKenzie

POLLAND, Madeleine A(ngela).   British.   Born in County Cork, Ireland, 31 May 1918. Educated at Hitchin Girls' Grammar School, Hertfordshire, 1929–37. Served in the Women's Auxiliary Air Force, 1942–45. Married Arthur Joseph Polland in 1946; has one daughter and one son. Assistant Librarian, Letchworth Public Library, Hertfordshire, 1939–42, and 1945–46. Agent: Hilary Rubinstein, A.P. Watt and Son, 26–28 Bedford Row, London WC1R 4HL, England. Address: Sierra Mijas, Torre 2, 10/D, Los Boliches, Malaga, Spain.

PUBLICATIONS FOR CHILDREN

Fiction

> *Children of the Red King*, illustrated by Annette Macarthur-Onslow. London, Constable, 1960; New York, Holt Rinehart, 1961.
> *The Town Across the Water*, illustrated by Brian Wildsmith.   London, Constable, 1961; New York, Holt Rinehart, 1963.
> *Beorn the Proud*, illustrated by William Stobbs.   London, Constable, 1961; New York, Holt Rinehart, 1962.
> *Fingal's Quest*, illustrated by W.T. Mars.   New York, Doubleday, and London, Burns and Oates, 1961.
> *The White Twilight*, illustrated by William Stobbs.   London, Constable, 1962; New York, Holt Rinehart, 1965.
> *Chuiraquimba and the Black Robes*, illustrated by Juan Carlos Barberis.   New York, Doubleday, and London, Burns and Oates, 1962.
> *City of the Golden House*, illustrated by Leo Summers.   New York, Doubleday, 1963; Kingswood, Surrey, World's Work, 1964.
> *The Queen's Blessing*, illustrated by William Stobbs.   London, Constable, 1963; New York, Holt Rinehart, 1964.
> *Flame over Tara*, illustrated by Omar Davis. New York, Doubleday, 1964; Kingswood, Surrey, World's Work, 1965.
> *Mission to Cathay*, illustrated by Peter Landa. New York, Doubleday, 1965; Kingswood, Surrey, World's Work, 1966.
> *Queen Without Crown*, illustrated by William Stobbs.   London, Constable, 1965; New York, Holt Rinehart, 1966.
> *Deirdre*, illustrated by Sean Morrison. New York, Doubleday, and Kingswood, Surrey, World's Work, 1967.
> *To Tell My People*, illustrated by John Holder.   London, Hutchinson, and New York, Holt Rinehart, 1968.
> *Stranger in the Hills*, illustrated by Victor Ambrus.   New York, Doubleday, 1968; London, Hutchinson, 1969.
> *To Kill a King*, illustrated by John Holder.   London, Hutchinson, 1970; New York, Holt Rinehart, 1971.

Alhambra, illustrated by Mary Frances Gaaze. New York, Doubleday, 1970; London, Hutchinson, 1971.

A Family Affair, illustrated by Trevor Stubley. London, Hutchinson, 1971.

Daughter to Poseidon, illustrated by John Holder. London, Hutchinson, 1972; as *Daughter of the Sea*, New York, Doubleday, 1972.

Prince of the Double Axe, illustrated by Gareth Floyd. London, Abelard Schuman, 1976.

PUBLICATIONS FOR ADULTS

Novels

Thicker Than Water. New York, Holt Rinehart, 1964; London, Hutchinson, 1967.

The Little Spot of Bother. London, Hutchinson, 1967; as *Minutes of a Murder*, New York, Holt Rinehart, 1967.

Random Army. London, Hutchinson, 1969; as *Shattered Summer*, New York, Doubleday, 1970.

Package to Spain. London, Hutchinson, and New York, Walker, 1971.

Double Shadow (as Frances Adrian). New York, Fawcett, and London, Macdonald and Jane's 1977.

Manuscript Collection: Mugar Memorial Library, Boston University.

Madeleine A. Polland comments:

Almost without exception my books for children may be said to be the product of my own intense consciousness of the reality of history, and the reality of historical figures as people. It has always been my idea to try to portray events in which children become involved in the dramatic past. And it is, of course, infinitely more plausible to create dramatic adventures for children in past centuries, when it was perfectly possible for them to be abandoned with the need to look after themselves. Except in times of war, which television presents in all its heartbreaking contemporary detail (leaving no imagination necessary), children's lives at the present tend to run on more scheduled lines, leaving adventure to the days of history.

*   *   *

Madeleine A. Polland is noted for her impressive list of historical novels with backgrounds as various as her own native Ireland, China, Viking Denmark, Norman England, mediaeval Scotland, Moorish Spain, and ancient Crete. However, two of her last five books are contemporary, and one is a mixture of ancient and modern. If we take her books published in the 1970's as representative of her skill in writing for young people, we may conclude that she offers, whether historical or contemporary, a cultivated and thickly textured species of adolescent romantic fiction. These books illustrate what Frank Eyre may have had in mind when he included Madeleine Polland in a small group of modern children's writers who "have produced books that in a less demanding age would have been outstanding."

Although the narrative of *To Kill a King* hinges on a Saxon plot to assassinate William the Conqueror, the main interest lies in the love of Merca and Edward which blossoms during the dangers of their flight to Scotland. Edward's love "saves" Merca from the contemplative life towards which her misery following her parents' slaughter by the Normans has led her. In *Alhambra*, the dramatic conflict is supplied by the young Juanito's longing for Princess Nahid despite his fiercely patriotic rejection of the Moors with whom he has lived since early childhood. In *A Family Affair*, it is true, the incipient teenage romantic attachment of Alex, the English girl, to Christian, the Danish boy, during the family annual holiday in Copenhagen, is muted to allow more prominence to the improbable mystery thriller involving eccentric aunts and inept thefts from picture galleries. But young love is the principal theme in *Daughter to Poseidon*, both in the contemporary framework story of Saran's dependence upon the love of Miklos, the Greek student, in assuaging her grief and feelings of guilt over her parents' death in a car crash, and also in the parallel though much bulkier historical narrative in which Saran is rescued from the sea by Mikolai, the Cretan youth who with Saran's resolute support saves Knossos from infiltration by the Hellenes. The interweaving of these two levels is imaginatively done, as is the exciting build up to the earthquake and the overthrow of Paradocles.

Madeleine Polland's historical researches may seldom provide more than a vivid romanticised background to the drama she unfolds, and her plots on occasion may slip into the implausible. In her concern to convey emotion and describe mental states she may at times prolong the agony at the expense of narrative pace and indulge in slightly inflated prose, often marked by a trick of repeating names or other words as in "she would be safer, safer against the threat of war" and "Saran felt the soft, soft touch of fine linen on her legs." But she portrays her characters in bitter conflict, cruel dilemmas; they suffer pain and permanent injury on the road to self-knowledge. To the older reader who has not yet fully entered the world of adult fiction she may well provide a not inconsiderable bridge.

—Graham Hammond

POOLE, (Jane Penelope) Josephine. British. Born in London, 12 February 1933. Educated at Fyling Hall School, Cumberland, 1941–45; Queensgate School, London, 1945–50. Married Timothy Ruscombe Poole in 1956, four daughters; Vincent John Hawker Helyar, 1975, one daughter and one son. Solicitors' secretary, London, 1951–54; secretary, BBC Features Department, London, 1954–56. Agent: A.P. Watt and Son, 26–28 Bedford Row, London WC1R 4HL. Address: Poundisford Lodge, Poundisford, Taunton, Somerset, England.

PUBLICATIONS FOR CHILDREN

Fiction

A Dream in the House, illustrated by Peggy Fortnum.   London, Hutchinson, 1961.
Moon Eyes.   London, Hutchinson, 1965; Boston, Little Brown, 1967.
Catch as Catch Can.   London, Hutchinson, 1969; New York, Harper, 1970.
Billy Buck.   London, Hutchinson, 1972; as *The Visitor*, New York, Harper, 1972.
Touch and Go.   London, Hutchinson, and New York, Harper, 1976.

Play

Television Play: *The Inheritance*, in *Shadows* series, 1976.

Other

When Fishes Flew (English legends).   London, Benn, 1978.

PUBLICATIONS FOR ADULTS

Novels

The Lilywhite Boys.   London, Hart Davis, 1968.
Yokeham.   London, Murray, 1970.

Play

Television Play: *The Harbourer*, in *Country Tales* series, 1975.

Josephine Poole comments:
I enjoy writing for children. I hope this makes the books enjoyable.

*   *   *

Josephine Poole is a specialist in mystery: the mystery of the supernatural as in *Moon Eyes*, of a stranger falling off a train in *Catch as Catch Can*, the mysterious disappearance of an old woman from a hospital bed in *Touch and Go*. She is expert at building up tension from small details and creating menace out of a smiling, apparently normal scene. In her handling of *la chasse humaine* she rivals the mastery of Geoffrey Household, whom as a writer she in many ways resembles. The scene in *Touch and Go*, perhaps her most accomplished work to date, in which the heroine, Emily, is hunted round unfamiliar farm buildings in the dark and the fog by unknown attackers, and for reasons obscure to her, is a masterpiece of its kind.
     The plot of *Touch and Go*, a complex mixture of the racy, the outrageous, and the all too horribly plausible, is characteristic Poole country. Emily and her with-it, intellectual mother – Mrs. Poole also has a knack of brief, astringent pen portraits as merciless as they are funny – have booked for a "farmhouse" holiday in Devon. On the way they crash the car and Emily, recovering overnight in hospital, stumbles on the first clue in a sequence which leads her, with her friend Charles, ultimately to a gang of terrorists planning an explosion in the local naval college. The narrative ranges from the creepily sinister to the downright hilarious: the dialogue is crisp and realistic. In addition, there is something else which lifts all Mrs. Poole's writing a long way out of the common. This is her treatment of the heroine, and it is a constant thread that runs through all her books. She is not portraying exceptional children. Emily is plump and unsophisticated for her age, the heroine of *Moon Eyes* imaginative but intellectually idle; but both are intensely real and so, witches and smugglers notwithstanding, is the world in which they live. These are children in the process of coming to terms with life, learning to read its mystifying signals and accept its peculiarities. This sensitivity to the characters' own uncertainties enhances the mysteries – where all is uncertain, how to tell the abnormal from the normal? But it is also what gives the books an atmosphere which is remembered long after the plot is forgotten.

—Anne Carter

PORTER, Gene Stratton (Geneva Grace Stratton Porter).   American.   Born in Wabash County, Indiana, 17 August 1863. Attended public schools. Married Charles Darwin Porter in 1886; one daughter. Regular contributor, *McCall's Magazine*; Photographic Editor,

Recreation magazine; member of the natural history department, *Outing* magazine; natural history photography specialist, *Photographic Times Annual Almanac*, four years. Founded Gene Stratton Porter Productions film company, 1922. *Died 6 December 1924.*

PUBLICATIONS FOR CHILDREN

Fiction

Freckles, illustrated by E. Stetson Crawford. New York, Doubleday, 1904; London, Murray, 1905.
A Girl of the Limberlost, illustrated by Wladyslaw T. Benda. New York, Doubleday, 1909; London, Hodder and Stoughton, 1911.
The Magic Garden, illustrated by Lee Thayer. New York, Doubleday, and London, Hutchinson, 1927.

Play

Screenplay: *A Girl of the Limberlost*, 1924.

Verse

Morning Face, illustrated by the author. New York, Doubleday, and London, Murray, 1916.

PUBLICATIONS FOR ADULTS

Novels

The Song of the Cardinal: A Love Story. Indianapolis, Bobbs Merrill, 1903; London, Hodder and Stoughton, 1913.
At the Foot of the Rainbow. New York, Outing Publishing Company, 1907; London, Hodder and Stoughton, 1913.
The Harvester. New York, Doubleday, and London, Hodder and Stoughton, 1911.
Laddie: A True-Blue Story. New York, Doubleday, and London, Murray, 1913.
Michael O'Halloran. New York, Doubleday, and London, Murray, 1915.
A Daughter of the Land. New York, Doubleday, and London, Murray, 1918.
Her Father's Daughter. New York, Doubleday, and London, Murray, 1921.
The White Flag. New York, Doubleday, and London, Murray, 1923.
The Keeper of the Bees. New York, Doubleday, and London, Hutchinson, 1925.

Verse

The Fire Bird. New York, Doubleday, and London, Murray, 1922.
Jesus of the Emerald. New York, Doubleday, and London, Murray, 1923.

Other

What I Have Done with Birds: Character Studies of Native American Birds. Indianapolis, Bobbs Merrill, 1907; revised edition, New York, Doubleday, 1917; as *Friends in Feathers*, London, Curtis Brown, 1917.
Birds of the Bible. Cincinnati, Jennings and Graham, 1909; London, Hodder and Stoughton, 1910.

Music of the Wild, illustrated by the author. Cincinnati, Jennings and Graham, and London, Hodder and Stoughton, 1910.

Moths of the Limberlost, illustrated by the author. New York, Doubleday, 1912; London, Hodder and Stoughton, 1913.

After the Flood. Indianapolis, Bobbs Merrill, 1912.

Birds of the Limberlost. New York, Doubleday, 1914.

Homing with the Birds. New York, Doubleday, and London, Murray, 1919.

Wings. New York, Doubleday, 1923.

Tales You Won't Believe (natural history). New York, Doubleday, and London, Heinemann, 1925.

Let Us Highly Resolve (essays). New York, Doubleday, and London, Heinemann, 1927.

Critical Study: *The Lady of the Limberlost: The Life and Letters of Gene Stratton Porter* by Jeanette Porter Meehan, New York, Doubleday, 1928; as *Life and Letters of Gene Stratton Porter*, London, Hutchinson, 1928.

*   *   *

Although Gene Stratton Porter's novels might now be called old-fashioned, they have several timeless qualities. Herself a naturalist and a resident of the Limberlost area of northern Indiana, Porter's motive was first of all to interest readers in the world of nature. Her books are filled with descriptions of birds and moths particularly. The focal significance of the lives of some of her characters is the wilderness in which Elnora Comstock, the Bird Woman, and Freckles observe and collect, make notes and entice converts to nature study.

Characters depicted by Porter seem perhaps to contemporary readers incredibly dedicated to the Golden Rule; they behave in an idealized manner, their anger shortlived and responding to reason, their selfishness recognized and yielding to love. Surprisingly, however, many of these characters are memorable, most significantly those who live close to their natural environments. The city dwellers are more flat and therefore less believable, but Porter makes even them transcend their sinful natures for late conversions to goodness.

Two themes seem apparent in Porter's writing: first, a thematic reverence for nature and a Christian mystic's appreciation for a world that God has made perfect; and second, her optimism about human behavior and its perfectability.

Porter's nonfiction about birds and moths is accompanied by her own photographic illustrations, painstakingly filmed and meticulously accurate in color effects. In her fiction Porter's word pictures are equally carefully painted; her words clothe in natural detail the romantic stories of love that wins despite hardship and of vicious hatred that turns to incredible generosity. Sentimental as they seem to readers of today, Porter's novels had great readership during the early years of the century.

—Rebecca J. Lukens

PORTER, Sheena. British. Born in Melton Mowbray, Leicestershire, 19 September 1935. Educated at King Edward VII Grammar School, Melton Mowbray, 1947–54; Loughborough College School of Librarianship, Leicestershire, 1955–56. Married Patrick Lane in 1966; has two daughters. Library Assistant, Leicester City Library, 1954–57; Regional Children's Librarian, Nottinghamshire County Library, 1957–60; Editorial Assistant, Oxford University Press, London, 1960–61; Regional Children's Librarian, Shropshire County Library, 1961–62. Recipient: Library Association Carnegie Medal, 1965. Address: 23 Gravel Hill, Ludlow, Shropshire, England.

PUBLICATIONS FOR CHILDREN

Fiction

The Bronze Chrysanthemum, illustrated by Shirley Hughes. London, Oxford University Press, 1961; Princeton, New Jersey, Van Nostrand, 1965.
Hills and Hollows, illustrated by Victor Ambrus. London, Oxford University Press, 1962.
Jacob's Ladder, illustrated by Victor Ambrus. London, Oxford University Press, 1963.
Nordy Bank, illustrated by Annette Macarthur-Onslow. London, Oxford University Press, 1964; New York, Roy, 1967.
The Knockers, illustrated by Gareth Floyd. London, Oxford University Press, 1965.
Deerfold, illustrated by Victor Ambrus. London, Oxford University Press, 1966.
The Scapegoat, illustrated by Doreen Roberts. London, Oxford University Press, 1968.
The Valley of Carreg-Wen, illustrated by Doreen Roberts. London, Oxford University Press, 1971.
The Hospital, illustrated by Robin Jacques. London, Oxford University Press, 1973.

*   *   *

Sheena Porter's stories are those of an author with varied highly successful skills and a deep sense of history. She received the Carnegie Medal of the Library Association for *Nordy Bank*, a haunting holiday adventure story set in Shropshire with an impelling dog interest. In this book, Bron, the main character, is not gifted with heroine-like qualities, but is shy, quiet, and introverted. In the course of the story she becomes difficult, aggressive, and withdrawn under the influence of the historic atmosphere pervading Nordy Bank. This strong awareness of place and past is subtly blended with down-to-earth factual detail of the minutiae of camping: a combination which enables different types of reader to enjoy this book at various levels. Sheena Porter adds to a sound setting peopled with convincing characters the intense drama of an escaped Alsatian dog. Bron successfully captures the dog, and in winning his confidence regains her own. The reader shares Bron's anguish over the fate of Griff, a deaf army dog in need of retraining, but the climax of the book is reached with the choice which Bron has to make: a decision which involves conflicting loyalties and which is finally made for her by her parents.

Nordy Bank has qualities of other books by Sheena Porter: the authentic, identifiable background; the evolution of the leading character; relationships with parents and friends; convincing detail of family life and its various ramifications. *The Bronze Chrysanthemum* showed considerable potential, and this was fulfilled with *Jacob's Ladder* and *Nordy Bank*. Unlike many writers Sheena Porter has not been content to find a successful formula and slavishly repeat it. Her plots are remarkable for their wide range of location and of theme. By the late 1960's an increasing number of writers tended to deal with contemporary problems: a trend now in danger of being carried to extremes. Sheena Porter is perhaps marginally less successful in her novels on such themes, but she handles the serious problem of mental illness with acute sensitivity in *The Hospital*, environmental problems with awareness in *The Valley of Carreg-Wen*, and the timeless stepmother problem with understanding in *The Scapegoat*.

Sheena Porter, more than many contemporary writers for children, covers widely different themes. She wrote initially with the deliberate intention of providing a bridge between the easy adventure story and the more demanding material of writers like Lucy Boston and William Mayne, but she has developed as a distinguished writer for children in her own right. Children's literature is the richer by her contribution.

—Anne W. Ellis

POTTER, (Helen) Beatrix.   British.   Born in London, 6 July 1866. Educated privately. Married William Heelis in 1913. Settled in Sawrey, Lancashire as a farmer and sheep-breeder. Chairman, Herdwick Breeders' Association. Artist: Drawings Exhibition, Victoria and Albert Museum, London, 1972; National Book League, London, 1976. *Died 22 December 1943.*

PUBLICATIONS FOR CHILDREN (illustrated by the author)

Fiction

> *The Tale of Peter Rabbit.*   Privately printed, 1900; revised edition, London and New York, Warne, 1902.
> *The Tailor of Gloucester.*   Privately printed, 1902; revised edition, London and New York, Warne, 1903; as *The Tailor of Gloucester from the Original Manuscript,* 1969.
> *The Tale of Squirrel Nutkin.*   London and New York, Warne, 1903.
> *The Tale of Benjamin Bunny.*   London and New York, Warne, 1904.
> *The Tale of Two Bad Mice.*   London and New York, Warne, 1904.
> *The Tale of Mrs. Tiggy-Winkle.*   London and New York, Warne, 1905.
> *The Pie and the Patty-Pan.*   London and New York, Warne, 1905.
> *The Tale of Mr. Jeremy Fisher.*   London and New York, Warne, 1906.
> *The Story of a Fierce Bad Rabbit.*   London and New York, Warne, 1906.
> *The Story of Miss Moppet.*   London and New York, Warne, 1906.
> *The Tale of Tom Kitten.*   London and New York, Warne, 1907.
> *The Tale of Jemima Puddle-Duck.*   London and New York, Warne, 1908.
> *The Roly-Poly Pudding.*   London and New York, Warne, 1908; as *The Tale of Samuel Whiskers; or, The Roly-Poly Pudding,* London, Warne, 1926.
> *The Tale of the Flopsy Bunnies.*   London and New York, Warne, 1909.
> *Ginger and Pickles.*   London and New York, Warne, 1909.
> *The Tale of Mrs. Tittlemouse.*   London and New York, Warne, 1910.
> *The Tale of Timmy Tiptoes.*   London and New York, Warne, 1911.
> *The Tale of Mr. Tod.*   London and New York, Warne, 1912.
> *The Tale of Pigling Bland.*   London and New York, Warne, 1913.
> *The Tale of Johnny Town-Mouse.*   London and New York, Warne, 1918.
> *The Fairy Caravan.*   Philadelphia, McKay, and London, privately printed, 1929.
> *The Tale of Little Pig Robinson.*   Philadelphia, McKay, and London, Warne, 1930.
> *Sister Anne,* illustrated by Katharine Sturges.   Philadelphia, McKay, 1932.
> *Wag-by-Wall.*   Boston, Horn Book, and London, Warne, 1944.
> *The Tale of the Faithful Dove,* illustrated by Marie Angel.   London, Warne, 1955; New York, Warne, 1956.
> *The Sly Old Cat.*   London and New York, Warne, 1971.
> *The Tale of Tuppenny,* illustrated by Marie Angel.   London and New York, Warne, 1973.

Verse

> *Appley Dapply's Nursery Rhymes.*   London and New York, Warne, 1917.
> *Cecil Parsley's Nursery Rhymes.*   London and New York, Warne, 1922.

Other

> *Peter Rabbit's Painting Book.*   London and New York, Warne, 1911.
> *Tom Kitten's Painting Book.*   London and New York, Warne, 1917.
> *Jemima Puddle-Duck's Painting Book.*   London and New York, Warne, 1925.
> *Peter Rabbit's Almanac for 1929.*   London and New York, Warne, 1928.

PUBLICATIONS FOR ADULTS

Other

>   *The Art of Beatrix Potter: Direct Reproductions of Beatrix Potter's Preliminary Studies*
>   *and Finished Drawings, Also Examples of Her Original Manuscript*, edited by Leslie
>   Linder and W.A. Herring.   London and New York, Warne, 1955; revised edition,
>   1972.
>   *The Journal of Beatrix Potter from 1881 to 1897, Transcribed from Her Code Writing by*
>   *Leslie Linder.*   London and New York, Warne, 1966.
>   *Letters to Children.*   Cambridge, Massachusetts, Harvard College Library Department
>   of Printing and Graphic Arts, 1967.
>   *Beatrix Potter's Birthday Book*, edited by Enid Linder.   London and New York,
>   Warne, 1974.
>   *A History of the Writings of Beatrix Potter, Including Unpublished Work*, by Leslie
>   Linder.   London and New York, Warne, 1971.

Manuscript Collection (includes watercolours and sketches): Leslie Linder Bequest, Victoria
and Albert Museum, London.

Critical Studies: *The Tale of Beatrix Potter: A Biography* by Margaret Lane, London and New
York, Warne, 1946, revised edition, 1968; *Beatrix Potter* by Marcus Crouch, London, Bodley
Head, 1960, New York, Walck, 1961; *The History of the Tale of Peter Rabbit*, London and
New York, Warne, 1976.

Illustrator: *A Happy Pair* by F.E. Weatherley, 1893(?); *Comical Customers*, 1894(?).

*   *   *

Beatrix Potter's tales for children are remarkable in that few of them include any children —
or indeed any humans at all. Other writers for children had of course used animals as the
main protagonists of their stories, and indeed by the time that Beatrix Potter started writing at
the beginning of the 20th century, the tradition of the animal story was well-established. But
most stories were quite obviously about humans in animal form, with human attitudes and
behaviour — a genre that goes back to Aesop. What particularly distinguished Beatrix Potter's
work was that her animals were primarily animals, in a world where the human was
intrusive and unnecessary. Her natural history drawings are the key to her later work, for
from a child she had shown great interest in the natural world, and had recorded it as she saw
it, from the hesitant flower sketches of her childhood to the competent microscopic drawings
of her late teens. She studied her own pet rabbit meticulously, and likewise the other
creatures that aroused her interest: spiders, flies, ducks, mice, etc. She made many
scientifically accurate drawings, including a remarkable series of fungi, which astonish those
who only know her from her Peter Rabbit books. She also had a great feeling for place, and
her interest in landscape was heightened by a further interest in photography, a pursuit
which she shared with her father on many a countryside photographic expedition. All this
made her a careful and precise recorder of the natural scene and the little creatures that
inhabit it.

With such a background she could have developed into a good artist and illustrator, but
would not necessarily have become a good writer. However, it is quite obvious that for
Beatrix Potter the word and the picture were complementary. We can see this from the fact
that some of the famous stories originated in pictorial letters, sent earlier in her life to children
of her acquaintance. For she saw even as she wrote, and the picture and the tale made a
coherent whole. Only later in life, when the imaginative faculty was weakening did she
attempt to write round her pictures, while the fragmentary scraps of original writing not
allied to illustrations show how bereft of inspiration she became when the cohesion of the

word and its visual counterpart were lacking. Her drawings were made originally for her own pleasure, but she wasted nothing. She borrowed back the picture letters she had originally sent to the Moore children and re-worked them to make her books; she remembered the story she had been told about an old tailor in Gloucester; even the mice that sat down to spin did so on chairs she had seen in her grandmother's house. She could see, both in her mind's eye and with her pencil, so accurately that readers who know the stories well can go about the countryside she knew and loved and say "That is in *Peter Rabbit*," or "That is the path in *Tom Kitten*." In the same way, the staff of the Textile Department in the Victoria and Albert Museum, London, were able to recognise the 18th-century costumes which she drew there many years before for use in *The Tailor of Gloucester*.

Nevertheless, out of these remembered incidents and re-used sketches, Beatrix Potter created a whole new world of characters who are as alive today as they were 75 years ago, when Peter Rabbit first appeared. For many of us, Jemima Puddleduck, Mrs. Tiggy-Winkle, and Jeremy Fisher have personalities that transcend time and place, and how much, we may wonder, have the Potter tales affected the attitude to mice and rabbits of several generations of children! For the adult, faced with repeated requests for re-reading a favourite tale, it is also important that the language in which Beatrix Potter chose to write her children's books was both simple and direct, with no attempt to write down to the young listener — indeed her use of the word "soporific" in *The Flopsy Bunnies* is notorious. As a result, her stories are as easy to read aloud as to listen to.

Beatrix Potter was always very concerned about the actual appearance of her books, the text as much as the illustrations. She herself occasionally altered the amount of text appearing on the printed page, moving a word or two overleaf if she felt it would produce the page appearance that she desired. The format of the Peter Rabbit books was quite distinctive at the time when they made their first appearance, and in spite of changes in the style of children's books during the century, they remain much the same as when they were first published (except that the colour printing has deteriorated). An attempt to issue *The Pie and the Patty Pan* and *The Roly-Poly Pudding* in a larger format was not a success and they too eventually conformed to the established pattern of a size which fits so comfortably into small hands. The length of the stories too is right for the young child, being fairly short, with simple uncrowded events which can be understood by the very youngest listener.

It is difficult to sum up the reason for the popularity which Beatrix Potter has enjoyed for the last three-quarters of a century — a popularity which shows no sign of diminishing in any of the many countries where her works have been published. Moreover, as a recent exhibition of her works showed, she appeals equally to all ages, if for varying reasons, and has become something of a cult on both sides of the Atlantic. Undoubtedly part of the attraction must lie in the aptness of her illustrations to the text, and the perfection of the art work itself. But in the end the stories must stand or fall by the writing, and there is no doubt that as a story-teller she was able to create a complete world in which the characters go about their normal daily life, and into which we are allowed merely a brief peep. They inhabit a twilight world between reality and imagination, in which the very young child can also share. But for those long past their childhood she offers a gallery of characters whose personalities are so fixed in our minds that Benjamin Bunny, Squirrel Nutkin and the rest exist forever in the timeless countryside of her own beloved Lakeland.

—Joyce I. Whalley

POWER, Rhoda (Dolores). British. Born in Altrincham, Cheshire, in 1890. Educated at Oxford High School for Girls, 1903–09; Girton College, Cambridge, 1909–12. Director of Children's Broadcasting, BBC Radio, London, in the 1920's and 1930's. *Died 9 March 1957.*

PUBLICATIONS FOR CHILDREN

Fiction

> *Boys and Girls of History*, with Eileen Power.   London, Cambridge University Press,
> 1926; New York, Macmillan, 1927; revised edition, London, Dobson, 1968; New
> York, Roy, 1970.
> *More Boys and Girls of History*, with Eileen Power.   London, Cambridge University
> Press, and New York, Macmillan, 1928.
> *Ten Minute Tales and Dialogue Stories*, illustrated by Gwen White.   London, Evans,
> 1943.
> *Here and There Stories*, illustrated by Phyllis Bray.   London, Evans, 1945.
> *Redcap Runs Away*, illustrated by C. Walter Hodges.   London, Cape, 1952; Boston,
> Houghton Mifflin, 1953.
> *We Were There*, illllustrated by Charl.   London, Allen and Unwin, 1955.
> *We Too Were There: More Stories from History*, illustrated by Charl.   London, Allen
> and Unwin, 1956.
> *From the Fury of the Norsemen and Other Stories*, illustrated by Pauline
> Baynes.   Boston, Houghton Mifflin, 1957.

Other

> *Union Jack Saints: Legends*, with others.   London, Constable, 1920.
> *Twenty Centuries of Travel: A Simple Survey of British History*, with Eileen
> Power.   London, Pitman, 1926.
> *Cities and Their Stories: An Introduction to the Study of European History*, with Eileen
> Power.   London, A. and C. Black, and Boston, Houghton Mifflin, 1927.
> *The Age of Discovery from Marco Polo to Henry Hudson.*   London and New York,
> Putnam, 1927.
> *How It Happened: Myths and Folktales*, illustrated by Agnes Miller
> Parker.   Cambridge, University Press, 1930; Boston, Houghton Mifflin, 1936.
> *Richard the Lionheart and the Third Crusade*, edited by Eileen Power.   London and
> New York, Putnam, 1931.
> *Stories from Everywhere*, illustrated by Nina K. Brisley.   London, Evans, and New
> York, Macmillan, 1931; as *The Big Book of Stories from Many Lands*, New York,
> Watts, 1970.
> *Great People of the Past.*   Cambridge, University Press, and New York, Macmillan,
> 1932.
> *The Kingsway Histories for Juniors* (*From Early Days to Norman Times, Norman Times
> and the Middle Ages, The Peasants' Revolt to James I, From James I to Modern Times*),
> illustrated by E. Hamilton Thompson.   London, Evans, 4 vols., 1937–38.

PUBLICATIONS FOR ADULTS

Other

> *Under Cossack and Bolshevik.*   London, Methuen, 1919; as *Under the Bolshevik Reign
> of Terror*, New York, McBride and Nast, 1919.

*   *   *

In the 1930's intelligent school librarians and parents were always on the look-out for a
new book by Rhoda Power. She could give young readers an interest in history which would
last and take them on to serious study. Her *Boys and Girls of History*, written in collaboration
with her sister, Eileen, the historian, were outstanding of their kind. They were halfway

between fiction and solid history. She told her stories of these boys and girls through minor characters mostly, unless there happened to be a very well documented child, like, for example, the young Mary Queen of Scots. On the whole they are the stories of apprentices, of children on the outskirts of some great event: the Bristol lad or the Burmese child attaching himself first to the extraordinary stranger Ralph Fitch, first Englishman to visit Burma, but deserting him for the greater honour of tending a white elephant.

By today's standards these are long stories with no talking down or easy vocabulary, but they are compulsive reading for anyone interested in the past and must have helped many a history teacher as well as her pupils. They range the world with endpaper maps showing the voyages; and they are packed with authentic details described so vividly that they are never boring. In the voyage to the Bermudas in 1609 everyone is bailing the ships after a storm: "The richer ones looking strangely bedraggled for the colours in their silk doublets were running and the stuffing in their bombasted britches was so clogged with water that it smelt of wet hay." This I think gives a taste of her writing. When I collaborated with her in a BBC series she always knew exactly where I could get the right reference; she would never let me guess! Her *How It Happened* ranged the world of folklore (and has outstanding illustrations by Agnes Miller Parker), and here equally there is no talking down. She never sets herself above her child audience but expects them to be her equals. This was her strength.

—Naomi Mitchison

PRICE, Susan.   British.   Born in Round's Green, Staffordshire, 8 July 1955. Educated at Tividale Comprehensive School. Shop Assistant, Co-operative Society Grocery, Dudley, Worcestershire, 1972–74. Recipient: Children's Rights Workshop Other Award, 1975. Agent: Osyth Leeston, A.M. Heath and Co., 40–42 William IV Street, London WC2N 4DD. Address: 77 Barncroft Road, Tividale, Warley, Worcestershire, England.

PUBLICATIONS FOR CHILDREN

Fiction

> *The Devil's Piper.*   London, Faber, 1973; New York, Morrow, 1976.
> *Twopence a Tub.*   London, Faber, 1975.
> *Sticks and Stones.*   London, Faber, 1976.
> *Home from Home.*   London, Faber, 1977.

Susan Price comments:

I write about the people, problems, and places I know best and am most interested in. The people I write about are usually of the age I still feel myself to be, so perhaps my stories are more "about us" than "about them." But that must be true of every writer for young people.

*   *   *

Although she has published only four books so far, Susan Price has already shown herself to be an instinctive writer with an ability to get inside her characters and make their stories seem real and immediate, whether they are in fantasy, historical or contemporary settings.

The Devil's Piper was written when she was only 16 and showed the confidence and originality which have developed in subsequent titles. It is an exciting story with lively dialogue and convincing characters which give solidity to the enchanted world into which an evil-natured Leprechaun leads the four children.

In *Twopence a Tub* she turned from fantasy to the very real problems facing the miners who were involved in the disastrous pit strike in Dudley in 1851. Her considerable achievement in recreating this situation was recognised by the Children's Rights Workshop which named *Twopence a Tub* winner of The Other Award, a new annual award designed to honour books which reflect the real situations in which children find themselves rather than to recognise solely aesthetic and literary merit. Susan Price draws on family records and memories to help her recreate the squalid poverty of the miners' lives, their spirit and their brutality, and she contrasts this with the affluence of the pit owners. Young Jek Davies is confused by the different arguments: he "knows" that the strike is right but deplores some of the results, such as the hatred between strikers and blacklegs, the deaths and disease. Lesser writers might have been trapped into manufacturing a happy ending, but Susan Price does not shirk the bitterness and frustration when the miners are forced to return to work accepting a reduction in their wages instead of the hoped for increase.

16-year-old Graeme, in *Sticks and Stones*, faces similar problems to Jek, but this time the story has a contemporary setting. He too has a physically dominant father who pushes his son through life without considering what the boy wants for himself. Graeme's struggle is not against starvation and violence, as Jek's is, but rather against the well-meaning but unimaginative care of his parents. His older brother has already left home to escape his father, but Graeme takes what is, perhaps, the harder path: to stay in the family flat but persuade his parents to let him give up his job in a supermarket, with managerial prospects, and fulfil his newly realised ambition to become a park gardener. The young author shows great skill in getting inside the mind of her hero, and the story is told with the humour which is evident in all her writing.

Her first children's book was an accomplished beginning. Her later works have given Susan Price as assured place among writers for children over eleven who will find much to identify with in her stories.

—Valerie Brinkley-Willsher

PUDNEY, John (Sleigh).   British.   Born in Langley, Buckinghamshire, 19 January 1909. Educated at Gresham's School, Holt, Norfolk. Served in the Royal Air Force, 1940–45. Married Crystal Herbert in 1934 (divorced, 1955); Monica Forbes Curtis, 1955; has three children. Producer and Writer for the BBC, London, 1934–37; Correspondent for the *News Chronicle*, London, 1937–41; Book Critic, *Daily Express*, London, 1947–48; Literary Editor, *News Review*, London, 1948–50. Director of Putnam and Company, publishers, London, 1953–63. Recipient: C. P. Robertson Memorial Trophy, 1965. Address: 4 Macartney House, Chesterfield Walk, London SE10 8HJ, England. *Died 10 November 1977.*

PUBLICATIONS FOR CHILDREN

Fiction

> *Saturday* [*Sunday, Monday, Tuesday, Wednesday, Thursday, Friday*] *Adventure*, illustrated by Ley Kenyon and Douglas Relf.   London, Lane, 2 vols., 1950–51, and Evans, 5 vols., 1952–56.
> *The Grandfather Clock*, illustrated by Peggy Beetles.   London, Hamish Hamilton, 1957.
> *Crossing the Road*, illustrated by Janet Grahame and Anne Johnstone.   London, Hamish Hamilton, 1958.

Spring [*Summer, Autumn, Winter*] *Adventure*, illustrated by Douglas Relf.   London,
  Evans, 4 vols., 1961–65.
The Hartwarp Light Railway [*Dump, Balloon, Circus, Bakehouse, Explosion, Jets*],
  illustrated by Ferelith Eccles Williams.   London, Hamish Hamilton, 7 vols.,
  1962–67.
Tunnel to the Sky, illustrated by Christine Marsh.   London, Hamish Hamilton, 1965.

Other

Six Great Aviators.   London, Hamish Hamilton, 1955.

PUBLICATIONS FOR ADULTS

Novels

Jacobson's Ladder.   London, Longman, 1938.
Estuary: A Romance.   London, Lane, 1948.
Shuffley Wanderers: An Entertainment.   London, Lane, 1948.
The Accomplice.   London, Lane, 1950.
Hero of a Summer's Day.   London, Lane, 1951.
The Net.   London, Joseph, 1952.
A Ring for Luck.   London, Joseph, 1953.
Trespass in the Sun.   London, Joseph, 1957.
Thin Air.   London, Joseph, 1961.
The Long Time Growing Up.   London, Dent, 1971.

Short Stories

And Lastly the Fireworks: Stories.   London, Boriswood, 1935.
Uncle Arthur and Other Stories.   London, Longman, 1939.
It Breathed Down My Neck: A Selection of Stories.   London, Lane, 1946; as *Edna's
  Fruit Hat and Other Stories*, New York, Harper, 1946.
The Europeans: Fourteen Tales of the Continent.   London, Lane, 1948.

Plays

The Little Giant (produced London, 1972).
Ted (televised, 1972; produced Leatherhead, Surrey, 1974).

Screenplay: *Fuss over Feathers*, 1955.

Television Play: *Ted*, 1972.

Verse

Spring Encounter.   London, Methuen, 1933.
Open the Sky: Poems.   London, Boriswood, 1934; New York, Doubleday, 1935.
Dispersal Point and Other Air Poems.   London, Lane, 1942.
Beyond This Disregard: Poems.   London, Lane, 1943.
South of Forty: Poems.   London, Lane, 1943.
Almanack of Hope: Poems.   London, Lane, 1944.
Ten Summers: Poems [1933–1943].   London, Lane, 1944.
Flight above Cloud.   New York, Harper, 1944.
Selected Poems.   London, Lane, 1946.
Selected Poems.   London, British Publishers Guild, 1947.

Low Life: Verses. London, Lane, 1947.
Commemorations: Poems. London, Lane, 1948.
Sixpenny Songs. London, Lane, 1953.
Collected Poems. London, Putnam, 1957.
The Trampoline. London, Joseph, 1959.
Spill Out: Poems and Ballads. London, Dent, 1967.
Spandrels: Poems and Ballads. London, Dent, 1969.
Take This Orange. London, Dent, 1971.
Selected Poems 1967–1973. London, Dent, 1973.
For Johnny: Poems of World War Two. London, Shepheard Walwyn, 1976.

Other

The Green Grass Grew All Round. London, Lane, 1942.
Who Only England Knows: Log of a Wartime Journey of Unintentional Discovery of Fellow-Countrymen. London, Lane, 1943.
World Still There: Impressions of Various Parts of the World in Wartime. London, Hollis and Carter, 1945.
Music on the South Bank: An Appreciation of the Royal Festival Hall. London, Max Parrish, 1951.
His Majesty George VI: A Study. London, Hutchinson, 1952.
The Queen's People. London, Harvill Press, 1953.
The Thomas Cook Story. London, Joseph, 1953.
The Smallest Room: A History of Lavatories. London, Joseph, 1954; New York, Hastings House, 1955; revised edition, as *The Smallest Room: With an Annexe*, Joseph, 1959.
The Seven Skies: A Study of the British Overseas Airways Corporation and Its Forerunners. London, Putnam, 1959.
Home and Away: An Autobiographical Gambit. London, Joseph, 1960.
A Pride of Unicorns: Richard and David Atcherley of the R.A.F. London, Oldbourne, 1960.
Bristol Fashion: Some Accounts of the Earlier Days of British Aviation. London, Putnam, 1960.
The Camel Fighter. London, Hamish Hamilton, 1964.
The Golden Age of Steam. London, Hamish Hamilton, 1967.
Suez: De Lesseps' Canal. London, Dent, 1968.
A Draught of Contentment. London, New English Library, 1971.
Crossing London's River. London, Dent, 1972.
Brunel and His World. London, Thames and Hudson, 1973.
London's Docks. London, Thames and Hudson, 1975.
Lewis Carroll and His World. London, Thames and Hudson, and New York, Scribner, 1976.

Editor, with Henry Treece, *Air Force Poetry.* London, Lane, 1944.
Editor, *Laboratory of the Air: An Account of the Royal Aircraft Establishment of the Ministry of Supply, Farnborough.* London, Central Office of Information, 1948.
Editor, *Pick of Today's Short Stories.* London, Odhams, Putnam and Eyre and Spottiswoode, 13 vols., 1949–1963.
Editor, *Popular Poetry.* London, News of the World, 1953.
Editor, *The Book of Leisure.* London, Odhams, 1957.
Editor, *The Harp Book of Toasts.* London, Harp Lager, 1963.
Editor, *The Batsford Colour Book of London.* London, Batsford, 1965; New Rochelle, New York, Soccer Associates, 1966.
Editor, *Flight and Flying.* London, Hamish Hamilton, and New York, David White, 1968.

Manuscript Collection: University of Texas, Austin.

*   *   *

"All that a boy's book should be." "A crowded and exciting yarn." The reviewers greeted John Pudney's Fred and I stories enthusiastically 20 odd years ago when they first appeared. Writing in the first person, Pudney presents the two boys, presumably in their early teens, at boarding school and on their holidays with Uncle George. He lives his life either at Fort X, doing mysterious research, or else receiving urgent calls and dashing off on top secret jobs. These are very hush-hush, but the boys always get involved. Uncle explodes with wrath over their mistakes, but invariably needs them to rescue him.

They are a resourceful outdoor couple, good at swimming, climbing, and boating; one has an interest in languages, one in history. Their attitude to girls is summed up by the comment on Lulu in *Summer Adventure*: "We found her quite a good sort, as girls go."

The books are called after the days of the week and seasons of the year. Each adventure begins quickly and dangerously; the pace keeps up to the safe ending. The backgrounds vary. The *Tuesday Adventure* opens with the writer "I" taking a photograph of Fred on a mountain train in Norway, but Fred fiddles with a lever just before the camera clicks. The truck instantly plunges off down the track into the dark heart of a mountain where it sinks. There they find the stranger who behaved so suspiciously on the boat coming over from Newcastle and the story is away.

In *Friday Adventure*, while fiddling with a television set, they get an unexplained extra channel. After an embarrassing time in the toy department of a large London store – the boys blush easily – they get locked in a cupboard which precipitates them down into the bowels of the shop where strange drugged figures are at work and the man they saw on TV appears. This is considered the most dangerous episode of them all, during which Uncle George is kidnapped.

There are always a few laughs. The comic relief in *Summer Adventure* is provided by a goat that eats some of Uncle's papers and has to be taken by boat to France where a gang of smugglers threaten to kill it. Other stories are located on the Thames and in Malta: anywhere can, in no time at all, be converted into a setting in which international crooks can operate.

The Hartwarp series are equally full of action of a different kind, designed for a younger age group. The stories are shorter, the perils are milder. Hartwarp is a very accident-prone village with characters like Charley, Olly Took, and the Gaffer. By mistake the signal box may be blown up, but it lands safely in the village pond, as everything always ends happily. Even making cakes and delivering them becomes hazardous when Olly Took takes over the bakehouse. His self-raising flour causes the inhabitants to float in the air, but that makes the village so famous it appears on television and everybody is delighted.

—Margaret Campbell

PYE, Virginia (Frances Kennedy).   British.   Born in London, 27 October 1901; sister of the writer Margaret Kennedy. Educated privately. Married Sir David Pye in 1926; has one daughter and two sons. Address: Cuttmill Cottage, Shackleford, Godalming, Surrey, England.

PUBLICATIONS FOR CHILDREN (illustrated by Richard Kennedy)

Fiction

Red-Letter Holiday, illustrated by Gwen Raverat.   London, Faber, 1940.
Snow Bird.   London, Faber, 1941.

Primrose Polly.   London, Faber, 1942.
Half-Term Holiday.   London, Faber, 1943.
The Prices Return.   London, Faber, 1946.
The Stolen Jewels.   London, Faber, 1948.
Johanna and the Prices.   London, Faber, 1951.
Holiday Exchange.   London, Faber, 1953.

PUBLICATIONS FOR ADULTS

Short Stories

St. Martin's Summer.   London, Heinemann, 1930.

Virginia Pye comments:
   I wrote my children's books during and after the Second World War. They have, therefore, the background of war and post-war England and in this sense they are dated. I re-read them recently and thought them even funnier than when I wrote them. The application for translation into German was made because "they give such a true picture of English family life." I believe this aspect is entirely undated and the relationship and interplay between the four children and their adult contacts is as true now as it was then and was in the books of E. Nesbit.
   I am enchanted by most of the drawings by my cousin Richard Kennedy, particularly the small expressive ones which recapture perfectly the humour of a situation (for example, each child's rosy vision of the prospective return to London after the war in *The Prices Return*).
   The Prices Return is my favourite. *Half-Term Holiday* is hilarious, but dated. *The Stolen Jewels* was written at the request of a children's librarian and was intended to be a carrot for slow readers; it didn't really come off. *Red-Letter Holiday* has a splendid ending and would make an excellent television episode. *Johanna and the Prices* (short stories) would make a nice paperback for a long journey or measles: very popular. *Primrose Polly* has a goodish, rather romantic, plot. *Snow Bird* and *Holiday Exchange* are, I think, averagely entertaining reading.

*   *   *

   Virginia Pye's books were published between 1940 and 1953, and it is hard to believe that the modern holiday adventure story, inspired by Ransome's *Swallows and Amazons*, was only ten years old when the first of them, *Red-Letter Holiday*, was published. By 1940 the holiday adventure formula was in danger of being abused and stereotyped, but Virginia Pye, while using the conventions of the formula, provided a refreshing element of humour. Published during what was, for children's books, a rather bleak period because of wartime shortages and restrictions, it is not surprising that the Pye books were warmly welcomed by children's librarians and are uniformly praised in articles and conference papers of the period. What is surprising is that the books have been allowed to go out of print, particularly as they are hardly dated by internal references.
   Virginia Pye's most striking gifts are for portrayal of character and humour. Most of the books are concerned with the holiday adventures of the Price family – Susan, Tom, and Alan with the occasional involvement of their friend Johanna Allard. These four children come over as very real personalities. Alan, the youngest, is inclined to act without thinking, which sometimes involves the family in unexpected situations, as when he decides to improve on the idea of running a tea garden by displaying a notice "licensed to sell wines, spirits and tobacco" (*Red-Letter Holiday*), or, on a grander scale, to arrange with his Swiss pen-friend that their families should exchange houses (*Holiday Exchange*). However, when he is rendered *hors de combat* in *Primrose Polly*, Tom and Susan become involved in adventures without his help. Tom, though competent, is far from being the know-all elder brother, while Susan is well ahead of her time (except that she wears a skirt instead of jeans) in that she does

not automatically assume the female role of feeding, and generally ministering to the wants of, her brothers. Johanna is even more unconventional, providing an outside catalyst for those adventures in which she features. Introduced to the Price family (*Red-Letter Holiday*) through a photograph which shows her wearing a white dress and playing a violin, she seems determined to give the lie to this image. Having acquired a black eye and a cut lip before setting out for Cornwall to join the Prices, she manages to lose the train en route and consequently arrives later then expected. She is also ready with the original suggestion which turns the action in a new direction.

The plot of *Red-Letter Holiday* was also well ahead of its time in that the central incident is concerned with the finding of the skeleton of a prehistoric monster – the kind of theme which was to become popular twenty years later. This book, like the other Pye stories, is packed with incident and moves quickly from one unlikely situation to another; but the succession of events is made credible by the observed detail of life around and the attention paid to the minor figures.

The characters, their conversations, and the humour stay in the mind long after the details of the adventures are forgotten.

—Sheila G. Ray

RAE, Gwynedd. British. Born in London, 23 July 1892. Educated at Manor House School, Brondesbury, London, 1907–09; Villa St. George's School, Paris, 1909–10. Served in the Voluntary Aid Detachment during World War I. Formerly, social worker. Agent: Laurence Pollinger Ltd., 18 Maddox Street, London W1R 0EU. Address: Tott Close, Burwash, Sussex, England.

PUBLICATIONS FOR CHILDREN (illustrated by Irene Williamson)

Fiction

> *Mostly Mary*, illustrated by Harry Rountree. London, Mathews and Marrot, 1930; New York, Morrow, 1931.
> *All Mary*, illustrated by Harry Rountree. London, Mathews and Marrot, 1931.
> *Mary Plain in Town.* London, Cobden Sanderson, 1935.
> *Mary Plain on Holiday.* London, Cobden Sanderson, 1937.
> *Mary Plain in Trouble.* London, Routledge, 1940.
> *Mary Plain in War-Time.* London, Routledge, 1942; as *Mary Plain Lends a Paw*, 1949.
> *Mary Plain's Big Adventure.* London, Routledge, 1944.
> *Mary Plain Home Again.* London, Routledge, 1949.
> *Mary Plain to the Rescue.* London, Routledge, 1950.
> *Mary Plain and the Twins.* London, Routledge, 1952.
> *Mary Plain Goes Bob-a-Jobbing.* London, Routledge, 1954.
> *Mary Plain Goes to America.* London, Routledge, 1957.
> *Mary Plain, V.I.P.* London, Routledge, 1961.
> *Mary Plain's Whodunit.* London, Routledge, 1965.

PUBLICATIONS FOR ADULTS

Novels

 And Timothy Too. London, Blackie, 1934.
 Leap Year Born. London, Blackie, 1935.

* * *

The continuing popularity of Gwynedd Rae's Mary Plain, "an unusual first-class bear from the bear-pits at Berne," is shown by the publication in 1976 of an omnibus edition of four of the early stories. Although she has never achieved the fame of other bears such as Paddington or Winnie-the-Pooh, Mary has always had her admirers among several generations of readers.

The books were given early publicity by broadcast readings in the BBC Radio programme *Children's Hour*, but there are also qualities inherent in the books which have ensured their lasting popularity: the warm, appealing character of the bear cub, the fun for children in decoding Mary's pictographic writing, and the humour which, without ever being unkind, often arises because the reader is cleverer than Mary. The animals, of course, are anthropomorphic, but children recognise the cub's behaviour as that of a naughty small girl who can enjoy mischief denied to the young reader. The other bears also have their own natures: fussy, ineffectual Friska, greedy Bunch, and revered Big/Wool.

Many of the stories were topical and some, such as those set in wartime, may now seem dated to adults but perhaps historical to the child. The domestic incidents are usually more successful than the wilder fantasies, such as Mary's starring role in a Hollywood film, but the universal nature of the young bear's behaviour gives her something to say to each generation. Although superficially the stories are suitable for very young children, the skills needed to read the quite long texts and to appreciate the jokes make the books most suitable for 8 to 10-year-olds.

—Valerie Brinkley-Willsher

RANSOME, Arthur (Michell). British. Born in Leeds, Yorkshire, 18 January 1884. Educated at Old College, Windermere, 1893–97; Rugby College, Warwickshire, 1897–1901; Yorkshire College, now Leeds University, 1901. Married Ivy Walker in 1909 (divorced, 1924), one daughter; Evgenia Shelepin, 1924. Office boy, Grant Richards, publishers, London, 1901–02; Assistant, Unicorn Press, London, 1902–03; free-lance writer, ghost writer, and publishers reader, after 1903; Assistant Editor, *Temple Bar* magazine, London, 1905–06; Russian Correspondent, *Daily News*, 1915–19, and *The Observer*, 1917–19; Correspondent in Russia, 1919–24, Egypt, 1924–25, 1929–30, and China, 1926–27, and columnist, *Manchester Guardian*. Recipient: Library Association Carnegie Medal, 1937. Litt.D.: Leeds University, 1952; M.A.: University of Durham. C.B.E. (Commander, Order of the British Empire), 1953. *Died 3 June 1967.*

PUBLICATIONS FOR CHILDREN

Fiction

 Swallows and Amazons, illustrated by Helene Carter. London, Cape, 1930; Philadelphia, Lippincott, 1931.

Swallowdale, illustrated by Clifford Webb. London, Cape, 1931; Philadelphia, Lippincott, 1932.

Peter Duck, illustrated by the author. London, Cape, 1932; Philadelphia, Lippincott, 1933.

Winter Holiday, illustrated by the author. London, Cape, 1933; Philadelphia, Lippincott, 1934.

Coot Club, illustrated by the author and Helene Carter. London, Cape, 1934; Philadelphia, Lippincott, 1935.

Pigeon Post, illustrated by the author. London, Cape, 1936; Philadelphia, Lippincott, 1937.

We Didn't Mean to Go to Sea, illustrated by the author. London, Cape, 1937; New York, Macmillan, 1938.

Secret Water, illustrated by the author. London, Cape, 1939; New York, Macmillan, 1940.

The Big Six, illustrated by the author. London, Cape, 1940; New York, Macmillan, 1941.

Missee Lee, illustrated by the author. London, Cape, 1941; New York, Macmillan, 1942.

The Picts and the Martyrs; or, Not Welcome at All, illustrated by the author. London, Cape, and New York, Macmillan, 1943.

Great Northern? London, Cape, 1947; New York, Macmillan, 1948.

Verse

Aladdin and His Wonderful Lamp, illustrated by Mackenzie. London, Nisbet, 1919.

Other

The Child's Book of the Seasons. London, Treherne, 1906.

The Things in Our Garden. London, Treherne, 1906.

Pond and Stream. London, Treherne, 1906.

Highways and Byways in Fairyland. London, Alston Rivers, 1906; New York, McBride, 1909.

The Imp and the Elf and the Ogre (includes *The Child's Book of the Seasons, The Things in Our Garden, Pond and Stream*). London, Nisbet, 1910.

Old Peter's Russian Tales, illustrated by Dmitri Mitrokhin. London, Jack, 1916; New York, Stokes, 1917.

The Soldier and Death: A Russian Folk Tale Told in English. London, Wilson, 1920; New York, Huebsch, 1922.

PUBLICATIONS FOR ADULTS

Novel

The Elixir of Life. London, Methuen, 1915.

Other

The Souls of the Streets and Other Little Papers. London, Langham, 1904.

The Stone Lady, Ten Little Papers, and Two Mad Stories. London, Langham, 1905.

Bohemia in London. London, Chapman and Hall, and New York, Dodd Mead, 1907.

A History of Story-Telling: Studies in the Development of Narrative. London, Jack, 1909; New York, Stokes, 1910.

Edgar Allan Poe: A Critical Study. London, Secker, and New York, Kennerley, 1910.

The Hoofmarks of the Faun. London, Secker, 1911.

Oscar Wilde: A Critical Study.   London, Secker, 1912; New York, Haskell House, 1971.

Portraits and Speculations.   London, Macmillan, 1913.

Radek and Ransome on Russia, Being Arthur Ransome's "Open Letter to America" with a New Preface by Karl Radek.   New York, Socialist Publication Society, 1918.

Six Weeks in Russia in 1919.   London, Allen and Unwin, 1919; as *Russia in 1919*, New York, Huebsch, 1919.

The Crisis in Russia.   London, Allen and Unwin, and New York, Huebsch, 1921.

Racundra's First Cruise.   London, Allen and Unwin, and New York, Huebsch, 1923.

The Chinese Puzzle.   London, Allen and Unwin, 1927.

Rod and Line: Essays, Together with Aksakov on Fishing.   London, Cape, 1929.

Fishing.   Cambridge, University Press, 1955.

Mainly about Fishing.   London, A. and C. Black, 1959.

The Autobiography of Arthur Ransome, edited by Rupert Hart-Davis.   London, Cape, 1976.

Editor, *The World's Story Tellers.*   London, Jack, and New York, Dutton, 12 vols., 1908–09.

Editor, *The Book of Friendship* [and *Love*]: *Essays, Poems, Maxims, and Prose Passages.*   London, Jack, 2 vols., 1909–10; New York, Stokes, 2 vols., 1910–11.

Translator, *A Night in the Luxembourg,* by Rémy de Gourmont.   London, Stephen Swift, 1912.

Translator, *A Week,* by Y.N. Libedinsky.   London, Allen and Unwin, 1923.

Critical Study: *Arthur Ransome* by Hugh Shelley, London, Bodley Head, 1960; New York, Walck, 1964.

Illustrator: his own books *Swallowdale,* 1938, and *Swallows and Amazons,* 1938.

*   *   *

"It always rained on that day, both indoors and out of doors," wrote Arthur Ransome in his autobiography, recalling the mournful ending of the summer holidays, the return to Leeds from the farm in the Lakes where, until his father died when Arthur was 13, the Ransome family settled themselves for the Long Vacation. "The rain would stream down the window outside, and we with our noses pressed to the glass were blinded by our tears."

Beside this holiday everything else in his childhood was shadowy, it seemed, and when he came, late in life, to write his children's books it was only the holidays that he chose to record, recalling the intensity of delight of the sight of the lakeside farm at last, the ritual dipping of the hand in the water to prove that one had indeed "come home," the greeting of the familiar faces, all to find a place in the books: the kind farmer's daughter (a Swainson there, as she was in real life) who darned threadbare knickerbockers "in situ," the charcoal burners in the woods, the woodcutters, the friendly postman.

Of his 12 books for children only 5 concern the Lakes, but for most readers this is the background with which they identify Arthur Ransome. In *Coot Club, Secret Water, The Big Six,* and *Great Northern?,* the Norfolk Broads scenery is real enough, but one senses that for the author it has not the magic that sent him, during his bohemian years in London, hurrying to Euston whenever he could scrape together the fare to the north.

When the Swallows and Amazons sail Lake Windermere we are in landscape with all the elements that a child most wants, a lake like an inland sea, with islands in it where nobody goes, hills, streams, woods, places to light your own fires without interference. One can wander on the fells all day and meet nothing more than a crag-fast sheep. The natives churn up and down the lakes in their steamers in the distance, but they have no real existence in the children's minds. The characters exist in their holidays only; we are told nothing else of them and nothing else matters. It would be a betrayal to try to imagine them at school; they move for us in their own world where they are Authority. In so far as adult authority – their parents – exists, they co-operate, but the parents tacitly admit their children's holiday supremacy, and make no demands that the children cannot recognize as valid. When unjust authority descends in the shape of great-aunt, then children and mother and uncle are united in silent resistance. It is a dream-world thought up by a writer who still remembered with resentment how inadequate he had been throughout his school career, slow, stupid, pitifully short-sighted, the butt of both masters and boys.

Perfectly Arthur Ransome recaptures the child's deep absorption in himself and his doings, and succeeds in conveying the intense importance and excitement of day-to-day details when one is fending for oneself. He can recall it minutely, so that he can describe the ascent of a tree foothold by foothold, naming the branches that call for particular care. Success is blended with occasional failure. Certainly the children manipulate their camps and their boats with serene efficiency; when they set out to divine water they find it; they can build a hut that does not fall down; their signalling systems work, their homing pigeons really do carry messages to reassure the grownups. But now and then even these children are fallible; the *Swallow* is wrecked and all the ecstatic holiday happiness temporarily with it: "it was as if the summer itself had been the cargo of the little ship and had gone with her to the bottom of the lake."

The children themselves are a blend of fantasy and reality. Captain Nancy, bold and swashbuckling and defiant, could have no existence outside a storybook, but the Walker family are all aspects of the author himself. Roger, "ship's boy," is the child Arthur, enthusiastic, unthinking, confident that his elders will sort everything out; Titty, a rather older Arthur, fanciful, a worrier, but often the unexpected victor; John, the calm and business-like captain whom Arthur would have liked to have been, the boy whose commands are unquestioningly obeyed (as no elder brother's ever are). Susan, the brisk school matron, stands alone, Arthur Ransome's concession to the mothers of the 1930's anxious for the dry feet, clean teeth and proper bedtime of their young. No one quarrels with Susan's dictatorial fussiness; to quarrel would be undignified. Arthur Ransome has given to his child characters a dignity and a stature that real children would dearly like to possess; it is one of the elements of his eternal appeal.

—Gillian Avery

RASKIN, Ellen. American. Born in Milwaukee, Wisconsin, 13 March 1928. Educated at the University of Wisconsin, Madison, 1945–49. Married Dennis Flanagan in 1960; has one daughter by a previous marriage. Since 1954, freelance artist and designer, New York; group shows – 50 Years of Graphic Arts in America, 1966; Biennale of Illustrations, Bratislava, 1969; Biennale of Applied Graphic Art, Brno, 1972; Contemporary American Illustrators of Children's Books, toured U.S.A. Recipient: *New York Times* award, for illustration, 1966, 1968; New York *Herald Tribune* Festival award, 1966; *Boston Globe-Horn Book* award, 1973; Mystery Writers of America Edgar Allan Poe Award, 1975. Address: 12 Gay Street, New York, New York 10014, U.S.A.

PUBLICATIONS FOR CHILDREN (illustrated by the author)

Fiction

Nothing Ever Happens on My Block. New York, Atheneum, 1966.
Spectacles. New York, Atheneum, 1968.
Ghost in a Four-Room Apartment. New York, Atheneum, 1969.

And It Rained.   New York, Atheneum, 1969.
A & The; or, William T.C. Baumgarten Comes to Town.   New York, Atheneum, 1970.
The Mysterious Disappearance of Leon (I Mean Noel).   New York, Dutton, 1971.
The World's Greatest Freak Show.   New York, Atheneum, 1971.
Franklin Stein.   New York, Atheneum, 1972.
Moe Q. McGlutch, He Smoked Too Much.   New York, Parents' Magazine Press, 1973.
Moose, Goose, and Little Nobody.   New York, Parents' Magazine Press, 1974.
Figgs and Phantoms.   New York, Dutton, 1974.
The Tattooed Potato and Other Clues.   New York, Dutton, 1975; London, Macmillan, 1976.
Twenty-Two, Twenty-Three.   New York, Atheneum, 1976.

Verse

Silly Songs and Sad.   New York, Crowell, 1967.
Who, Said Sue, Said Whoo?   New York, Atheneum, 1973.

Manuscript Collections: Milwaukee Public Library, Wisconsin; Kerlan Collection, University of Minnesota, Minneapolis.

Illustrator: *Happy Christmas* edited by Claire Bishop, 1956; *A Child's Christmas in Wales* by Dylan Thomas, 1959; "*Mama, I Wish I Was Snow*" "*Child, You'd Be Very Cold*" by Ruth Krauss, 1962; *We Dickinsons,* 1965, and *We Alcotts,* 1968, by Aileen Fisher and Olive Rabe; *Poems of Edgar Allan Poe,* 1965; *The King of Men* by Olivia Coolidge, 1966; *Songs of Innocence* by William Blake, 1966; *The Jewish Sabbath* by Molly Cone, 1966; *D.H. Lawrence* by William Cole, 1967; *Ellen Grae,* 1967, and *Lady Ellen Grae,* 1968, by Vera and Bill Cleaver; *Poems* by Robert Herrick, edited by Winfield Townley Scott, 1967; *Probability, The Science of Chance,* 1967, *This Is 4,* 1967, *Symmetry,* 1968, and *Three and the Shape of Three,* 1969, all by Arthur Razzell; *Books* by Susan Bartlett, 1968; *Inatuk's Friend* by Suzanne Stark Morrow, 1968; *A Paper Zoo!* by Renée Weiss, 1968; *Piping down in the Valleys Wild* by Nancy Larrick, 1968; *Come Along!* by Rebecca Caudill, 1969; *Shrieks at Midnight* edited by Sara Brewton, 1969; *Goblin Market* by Christina Rossetti, 1970.

Ellen Raskin comments:

The only difference between words and pictures is that words describe verbal ideas, pictures delineate graphic ideas. In books they serve the same function: to tell a story. No matter what story I tell, my message is the same: books can be fun. Through words and pictures and the design of the book itself I try to create a world of surprises, waiting to be discovered by the child who opens the cover and turns the pages of my book.

*   *   *

Ellen Raskin's unusual combination of talents has found expression in a large number of idiosyncratic children's books. Raskin is an exuberant artist, skilled in the effective use of line and blocks of color. She illustrates and designs her own books as well as those of other writers. Raskin is an author – both of picture books and of three novels for older children. And she is very funny – often zany. Over and above these talents she is a fantasist, a neo-surrealist whose vision is lightened by both humor and compassion. So individual is her sense of story that her picture books provoke extreme reactions from young children. They either love them, delighting in their reiterative fantasy, caricature-style pictures and sense of fun, or they fail to grasp their intricacies and turn away frustrated. *Moose, Goose, and Little Nobody* is often successful with children. A simple lost-and-found plot leads readers into word plays with "moose," "goose," and "mouse," as the central characters try to reunite their castaway friend with his mother.

Raskin is a New Yorker and her books reflect the city environment in such quirky visual tales as *Nothing Ever Happens on My Block* and the cumulative rhyming story of *Ghost in a Four-Room Apartment*. Her rhyming counting book *Twenty-Two, Twenty-Three*, however, is too long, too involved with rhymes and word games and has no discernible plot to carry along young readers. Few children do more than idly turn the pages, wondering at the accomplished and minutely detailed illustrations.

Her largest output has been in picture books for 4 to 8-year-olds and both her plots and illustrations show the author's endless powers of invention; but in making the transition to longer books Raskin moves her fantasy from the drawing table to the typewriter with impressive results. Her imagination is not for the faint-hearted. No dreamlike, soft visions of success, happiness or riches. Death, natural and violent, plays its part, as do deformity, poverty and social ostracism. Raskin loves mysteries and her first novel, *The Mysterious Disappearance of Leon (I Mean Noel)*, is fast-moving and outrageous, although once again the games and puzzles get in the way of the story.

Figgs and Phantoms, an unlikely tale of a clan of eccentrics named Figg, suffers from the same problem of overloading. The author can't seem to discipline her inventiveness within manageable bounds. One of the Figgs is married (of course) to a Newton, and they live in Pineapple and subscribe (some of them) to an esoteric family religion named Capri. Mona Lisa Newton, the heroine of the tale, manages to pass over into Capri to meet her beloved Uncle Florence in a rather strained flight of fancy. It is characteristic of Raskin that, in the midst of outrageous fantasy, Uncle Florence's death is genuinely sad and in no way glossed over.

Most successful of the mysteries is the recent *The Tattooed Potato and Other Clues*. Its daring improbability is hilarious, yet at the same time the portrait of Dickory Dock as a 17-year-old art student is grittily realistic. She is poor, alone – her parents murdered in a robbery attempt on their pawn shop – streetwise and gutsy. Two stories intertwine: the parody detective cases Dickory and her boss, the portrait painter Garson, solve for the police department; and Garson's own tragic secret involving his brain-damaged companion, Isaac Bickerstaffe. The humor and the sadness weave smoothly together with a discipline lacking in the earlier novels.

Raskin is a prolific author and illustrator who seems to be slowly increasing the range of her humor and fantasy, as if feeling her way with each new book. It is this development, this search for the limits of credulity, that makes her work so satisfying despite its uneven quality. Her sense of design flows easily from words to pictures and she draws readers along on her journey, making the going smooth with laughter and exciting with wild leaps of the imagination.

—Brigitte Weeks

RAWLINGS, Marjorie Kinnan. American. Born in Washington, D.C., 8 August 1896. Educated at Western High School, Washington, D.C.; University of Wisconsin, Madison, B.A. 1918 (Phi Beta Kappa). Married Charles Rawlings in 1919 (divorced, 1933); Norton Sanford Baskin, 1941. Editor, YWCA National Board, New York, 1918–19; Assistant Service Editor, *Home Sector* magazine, 1919; staff member, *Louisville Courier Journal* and *Rochester Journal*, New York, 1920–28; syndicated verse writer ("Songs of a Housewife"), United Features, 1926–28. Lived in Florida after 1928. Recipient: O. Henry Award, for short story, 1933; Pulitzer Prize, 1939. LL.D.: Rollins College, Winter Park, Florida, 1939; L.H.D.: University of Florida, Gainesville, 1941; honorary degree, University of Tampa, Florida. Member, National Institute of Arts and Letters, 1939. *Died 14 December 1953.*

PUBLICATIONS FOR CHILDREN

Fiction

> *The Yearling*, illustrated by Edward Shenton. New York, Scribner, and London, Heinemann, 1938.
> *The Secret River*, illustrated by Leonard Weisgard. New York, Scribner, 1955.

PUBLICATIONS FOR ADULTS

Novels

> *South Moon Under.* New York, Scribner, and London, Faber, 1933.
> *Golden Apples.* New York, Scribner, 1935; London, Heinemann, 1939.
> *Jacob's Ladder.* Coral Gables, Florida, University of Miami Press, 1950.
> *The Sojourner.* New York, Scribner, and London, Heinemann, 1953.

Short Stories

> *When the Whippoorwill* —. New York, Scribner, and London, Heinemann, 1940.

Other

> *Cross Creek.* New York, Scribner, and London, Heinemann, 1942.
> *Cross Creek Cookery.* New York, Scribner, 1942; as *The Marjorie Kinnan Rawlings Cookbook*, London, Hammond Hammond, 1960.
> *The Marjorie Kinnan Rawlings Reader*, edited by Julia Scribner Bigham. New York, Scribner, 1956.

Critical Studies: *Frontier Eden: The Literary Career of Marjorie Kinnan Rawlings* by Gordon E. Bigelow, Gainesville, University of Florida Press, 1972; *Marjorie Kinnan Rawlings* by Samuel I. Bellman, New York, Twayne, 1974.

*   *   *

Marjorie Kinnan Rawlings is a regional writer. Her work is inhabited by the simple people and natural settings of the Florida backwoods which she adopted as her home. Often paramount in her novels is the struggle against the vicissitudes of an uncertain existence by the poor white — the Florida cracker — commonly epitomized in an archetypical young protagonist with frontier virtues. Her first three major novels and much of her short fiction hold marked appeal for adolescent as well as adult readers.

South Moon Under depicts the difficulties of a hunter scratching out a living as a moonshiner in the Florida scrub country. The novel combines vividly descriptive scenes of rural existence with strong characterizations and an eventful plot. *Golden Apples* recounts the efforts of an orphaned and impoverished brother and sister to survive in late 19th-century northern Florida. They "squat" on the estate of an exiled and embittered young Englishman whom they patiently regenerate. The resourceful protagonist is a more convincing figure than the vaguely sketched Englishman in this flawed but dramatically forceful novel. In the novella *Jacob's Ladder* a rootless and destitute young cracker couple encounter adversities in luckless attempts to wrest a living from a bounteous but treacherous environment. The pair's deep mutual reliance and indomitable spirit are a poignant and emotionally powerful testament.

The author's internationally acclaimed novel *The Yearling* represents her finest achievement. The hero is 12-year-old Jody Baxter, who lives with his parents in the Florida hammock country of the 1870's. As his marginally-existing family undergoes severe setbacks,

Jody tames a fawn which becomes his forest-roaming companion. When, however, his pet cannot be restrained from eating the precious crops, it must be killed. The anguished boy feels betrayed by his father and severs their close relationship. Eventually they are reconciled. Tragedy has made a man of him. Throughout the story weave such themes as man's need to belong to the land which, in turn, belongs to those who lovingly cultivate it, and the inevitability of unfair and unexpected betrayal by man and nature. Mrs. Rawlings' compellingly truthful portrait of a boy and his tender relationships is universally appealing. Her striking description of nature's elemental forces and the simple but significant events in the lives of people close to the land enrich an absorbingly ingenuous story. This distinguished novel stands as a classic of adult and children's literature.

Intended primarily for young children is the posthumously published story *The Secret River*. Its heroine is a little girl who on her own helps her empty-handed father by finding in the forest a fish-filled secret river. After sharing her catch with forest animals, she returns home with enough fish to restore her father's modest prosperity which, consequently, restores that of his neighbors. When she looks for the river again it has vanished, since the need for it has gone. Charmingly illustrated, this woodland idyll with simple story and message offers enchantment for the small child.

Mrs. Rawlings is a pastoral writer of percipience and power whose stories – besides her memorable *The Yearling* – can be enjoyed by young people.

—Christian H. Moe

RAY, Mary (Eva Pedder). British. Born in Rugby, Warwickshire, 14 March 1932. Educated at Rugby High School, 1937–50; College of Arts and Crafts, Birmingham, 1950–52; College of the Ascension, Birmingham, 1952–57. London Diploma of Social Studies and Cambridge Certificate of Religious Knowledge. Parish Worker, Sheffield Diocese, 1958–61; Assistant Matron, Warwickshire County Council Old People's Homes, Solihull, 1961–62. Civil Servant, Export Credits Guarantee Department, Birmingham, 1962–64, and, since 1965, London. Address: Pandora, 24 Richmond Drive, Herne Bay, Kent, England.

PUBLICATIONS FOR CHILDREN

Fiction

> *The Voice of Apollo*, illustrated by John Cooper. London, Cape, 1964; New York, Farrar Straus, 1965.
> *The Eastern Beacon*, illustrated by Janet Duchesne. London, Cape, 1965; New York, Farrar Straus, 1966.
> *Standing Lions*, illustrated by Janet Duchesne. London, Faber, 1968; New York, Meredith Press, 1969.
> *Spring Tide*, illustrated by Janet Duchesne. London, Faber, 1969.
> *Shout Against the Wind*, illustrated by Peter Branfield. London, Faber, 1970.
> *A Tent for the Sun*. London, Faber, 1971.
> *The Ides of April*. London, Faber, 1974; New York, Farrar Straus, 1975.
> *Sword Sleep*. London, Faber, 1975.
> *Beyond the Desert Gate*. London, Faber, 1977.

Other

> *Living in Earliest Greece*, illustrated by Peter Branfield. London, Faber, 1969.

Mary Ray comments:

After a gap since my early teens (when I had produced very horrific historical fiction and poetry), I began to write again quite suddenly in my late twenties when a friend told me that she had started a book and I could think of no good reason why I shouldn't too. It seemed obvious to me that I should write for children, as I was still very much under the influence of books that I had read as a child, and also that the books should have a classical setting. Since about the age of 6 I had never felt any strangeness or distance about what I had learned of the people of Greece and Rome and of earlier civilisations; I was at home in the period in the way that some people are at home in a place or a country. I started with Roman Britain, because I knew what the places looked like, and for me it is important that the three strands of the actual geographical first-hand knowledge, historical research, and imagination should all be as strong as I can make them. After I was able to go to Greece regularly I particularly enjoyed writing about people who lived there. I became fascinated by what was the same for me – smells and weather and mountains and ants – and what was quite different because the way that earlier people thought and the things they expected and accepted were different – slavery, pain, and the worship of different gods.

Looking back I can see that certain themes are usually important in my books. Creative people have a habit of turning up as characters, as making things, from jam to fine art, is very important to me, and my creative people often have to fight to be able to practice their skills as one does in real life. I also enjoy writing about the very old and the very young, which is a hang-over from working in residential homes for mothers and babies and the old when I was a social science student. I am also obsessed by a theme very common in children's books – how and when you become able to come to terms with what life brings. I suppose this is because to children's writers their own childhood is still very alive. We remember what it hurt to learn, what we had to fight for and what we had to accept; the characters in our books follow where we went, or go the way we wish we had gone.

*   *   *

The historical novels of Mary Ray bear witness to a passionate interest in early Western civilisation, as manifested in Ancient Greece, Rome, and Britain, especially at times of turbulence and cultural change such as the birth of Christianity. Concepts which might be thought too complex for children's reading are bravely tackled by this committed writer who often hints at far more than she can express within the confines of a children's book.

Her attitude to the classical world is ambivalent. Although she is attracted to – even obsessed with – ancient culture, as shown in her detailed, loving descriptions of the landscape and the daily life, there are terrible drawbacks. Life is rigidly stratified and many of her characters are poor, enslaved, condemned to drudgery or forced marriage. Women are especially powerless. Although Roman civilisation is a highly-organised creation, it needs the Christian philosophy to perfect it.

Mary Ray has written of the Mycenean period in *Standing Lions* and *Shout Against the Wind*. In the former she uses the theories of Robert Graves and others about the Mother Goddess and the annual sacrifice of the King in a tale of invasion and court intrigue. *Shout Against the Wind* is about refugees from the Dorian invasions, a group of people of different rank who sink these differences to make a new life.

Religion is an important element in her work, and all her main characters feel the need to communicate with some Power, to find the right god and make the right offering. In her later books she moves on to the story of the new religion, Christianity, when it was still a secret underground cult. *A Tent for the Sun*, set in Corinth when Paul was writing his Epistles to the Corinthians, makes one feel the excitement and complete surrender of the soul demanded by the new faith.

Two stories about Camillus and the slave Hylas continue the Christian theme. In *The Ides of April*, set in Rome, Hylas is suspected of murder and Camillus helps him to freedom. Hylas is sheltered by a secret Christian, and it is suggested that Christ's power has brought the truth to light. In *Sword Sleep*, set in Athens, their friendship has become closer and more romantic:

Hylas is now a Christian, and an unhappy young boy, befriended by them both, makes a third in this emotional bond. It is clear that the themes which inspired Mary Renault are also dear to Mary Ray: Mycenean Greece and the cult of the Mother Goddess; the Athenian setting with its flashbacks to the wars of Alexander; and intense male friendships which could be described as quasi-love-affairs. Her new book, *Beyond the Desert Gate*, brings together characters from the last three books in a story about the growth of Christianity in the 1st century A.D.

Mary Ray's style also recalls Renault (and Rosemary Sutcliff), as she has also chosen to evoke the ancient world in a formal, metaphoric style. Her books' titles also have symbolic force, e.g., *Spring Tide* which refers to the gradual approach of the new faith. Having specialised in a particular theme and period and chosen an appropriate formal, metaphoric style of phrasing has inevitably endeared her to critics rather than the majority of children; but each book is rightly acclaimed as an advance on the last.

—Jessica Kemball-Cook

RAYNER, William. British. Born in Barnsley, Yorkshire, 1 January 1929. Educated at Holgate Grammar School, Barnsley; Wadham College, Oxford, B.A. (honours) in English 1952. Married Pamela Rayner in 1953; has three sons. Formerly, teacher and lecturer. Agent: William Collins Sons Ltd., 14 St. James's Place, London SW1A 1PS. Address: Spurriers Close, West Porlock, near Minehead, Somerset, England.

PUBLICATIONS FOR CHILDREN

Fiction

> *Stag Boy.* London, Collins, 1972; New York, Harcourt Brace, 1973.
> *Big Mister.* London, Collins, 1974.

Other

> *Chief Joesph.* London, Collins, 1978.

PUBLICATIONS FOR ADULTS

Novels

> *The Reapers.* London, Faber, 1961.
> *The Barebones.* London, Faber, 1962.
> *The Last Days.* London, Joseph, 1968; New York, Morrow, 1969.
> *The Knife-man: The Last Journal of Judas Iscariot.* London, Joseph, and New York, Morrow, 1969.
> *The World Turned Upside Down.* London, Joseph, and New York, Morrow, 1970; as *Redcoat,* London, Sphere, 1971.
> *The Bloody Affray at Riverside Drive.* London, Collins, 1972; as *Seth and Belle and Mr. Quarles and Me: The Bloody Affray at Lakeside Drive,* New York, Simon and Schuster, 1973.
> *The Trail to Bear Paw Mountain.* London, Collins, 1974; New York, Ballantine, 1976.
> *A Weekend with Captain Jack.* London, Collins, 1975; New York, Ballantine, 1976.
> *The Day of Chaminuka.* London, Collins, 1976; New York, Atheneum, 1977.

Eating the Big Fish. London, Collins, 1977; as *Interface Transfer,* New York, Atheneum, 1978.

Other

The Tribe and Its Successors: An Account of African Traditional Life and European Settlement in Southern Rhodesia. London, Faber, and New York, Praeger, 1962.

William Rayner comments:

I began writing for older children only a few years ago and so far my serious work has taken the form of two novels, *Stag Boy* and *Big Mister.* Both these novels call on fantasy to help explore themes important to all of us, but particularly to young people as they enter adolescence – themes such as the awakening of sexuality, the recognition of evil, and the need to oppose selfish exploitation of others by understanding and love.

Stag Boy is set in the country and calls on magical beliefs of an ancient rural kind. *Big Mister* is concerned with magic of a different order – that of the infernal conjuror or illusionist. By his means, the two children who are the main characters in the book find themselves carried back into the harsh world of the early Industrial Revolution, which they experience not only on a realistic level but also in terms of magical or visionary events. The book is influenced by Blakeian ideas.

*   *   *

A comparative newcomer, William Rayner has already made an important contribution to fiction for adolescents. He combines the mystical with the matter of fact and blends a care for greater understanding between human beings with a passion for socialist reform. There is, thus, a strong crusading element, a pervading didacticism, which would ruin Rayner's work were it not for an accompanying broad sense of humor to keep it all in perspective.

Stag Boy is a truly remarkable novel, a powerful work which stimulates and excites and haunts the memory. Its theme is the corrupting force of materialist, capitalist, industrial society as a despoiler of older, earthier, rural values of a life close to the soil and the natural rhythms of things. Jim has to return to his roots in Exmoor to regain his health, lost in the hideousness of Wolverhampton. Through an ancient antlered helmet, he achieves affinity with a noble stag which is being hunted for blood sport, so that human and animal, made one, possess and guide each other. As stag, Jim is able to win the affections of susceptible Mary away from a trendy and affluent young rival who is the embodiment of city values and superficial attractions. The sensitive and sensuous relationship between stag and Mary is explored in passages of erotic beauty reminiscent of the work of D.H. Lawrence, all moonlight and fecundity.

Rayner reinforces his basic theme throughout in small ways. He shows farms turned into caravan parks, and, worse still, into rural factories, producing vast quantities of broiler chickens raised unnaturally on artificial light and food. Rayner sees this "battery farming" image as a metaphor for the possible destiny of contemporary, soul-less, inhuman industrialist society.

Big Mister is of wider scope but is less controlled and the didacticism is heavy-handed. It is set in the industrial horror of England in 1823, with children working in coal mines and as chimney sweeps, at a time when people were regarded as a dispensible commodity, infinitely replaceable. It is an exposé of the exploitation and degradation of humanity by the wealthy pious moneyed classes. It also contains some bawdy characterisation and a good deal of raw humor, and it is a rough, nightmarish book after the quiet control of *Stag Boy.*

—Walter McVitty

REANEY, James (Crerar). Canadian. Born near Stratford, Ontario, 1 September 1926. Educated at Elmhurst Public School, Easthope Township, Perth County; Stratford High School; University College, Toronto (Epstein Award, 1948), M.A. in English 1949, Ph.D. 1956. Married Colleen Thibaudeau in 1951; has two living children. Member of the English Department, University of Manitoba, Winnipeg, 1949–56. Since 1960, Member of the English Department, Middlesex College, University of Western Ontario, London. Founding Editor, *Alphabet* magazine, London, 1960–71. Active in little theatre groups in Winnipeg and London. Recipient: Governor General's Award, for verse, 1950, 1959, for drama, 1963; University of Western Ontario President's Medal, for verse, 1955, 1958; Chalmers Award, for drama, 1974, 1975. Agent: Sybil Hutchinson, Apartment 409, Ramsden Place, 50 Hillsboro Avenue, Toronto, Ontario M5R 1S8. Address: Department of English, University of Western Ontario, London, Ontario, Canada.

PUBLICATIONS FOR CHILDREN

Fiction

> *The Boy with an "R" in His Hand*, illustrated by Leo Rampen. Toronto, Macmillan, 1965.

Plays

> *Names and Nicknames* (produced Winnipeg, Manitoba, 1963). Included in *Apple Butter*, 1973; published separately, New York, New Plays for Children.
> *Apple Butter* (puppet play; also director; produced London, Ontario, 1965). Included in *Apple Butter*, 1973.
> *Let's Make a Carol*, music by John Beckwith. Waterloo, Ontario, Waterloo Music Company, 1965.
> *Listen to the Wind* (produced London, Ontario, 1965; Woodstock, New York, 1967). Vancouver, Talonbooks, 1972.
> *Colours in the Dark* (produced Stratford, Ontario, 1967). Vancouver and Toronto, Talonbooks-Macmillan, 1970.
> *Geography Match* (broadcast, 1967). Included in *Apple Butter*, 1973.
> *Apple Butter and Other Plays for Children* (includes *Names and Nicknames, Ignoramus, Geography Match*). Vancouver, Talonbooks, 1973.
> *All the Bees and All the Keys*, music by John Beckwith (produced Toronto, 1972). Erin, Ontario, Press Porcépic, 1976.

> Radio Play: *Geography Match*, 1967.

PUBLICATIONS FOR ADULTS

Plays

> *Night-Blooming Cereus* (broadcast, 1959; produced Toronto, 1960). Included in *The Killdeer and Other Plays*, 1962.
> *The Killdeer* (produced Toronto, 1960; Glasgow, 1965). Included in *The Killdeer and Other Plays*, 1962; revised version (produced Vancouver, 1970), in *Masks of Childhood*, 1972.
> *One-Man Masque* (produced Toronto, 1960). Included in *The Killdeer and Other Plays*, 1962.
> *The Easter Egg* (produced Hamilton, Ontario, 1962). Included in *Masks of Childhood*, 1972.
> *The Killdeer and Other Plays* (includes *Sun and Moon, One-Man Masque, Night-Blooming Cereus*). Toronto, Macmillan, 1962.

Sun and Moon (produced Winnipeg, Manitoba, 1971).   Included in The Killdeer and
Other Plays, 1962.
Three Desks (produced Calgary, 1967).   Included in Masks of Childhood, 1972.
Masks of Childhood (includes The Killdeer, Three Desks, Easter Egg).   Toronto, New
Press, 1972.
The Donnellys: A Trilogy:
    1. Sticks and Stones (produced Toronto, 1973).   Erin, Ontario, Press Porcépic, 1976.
    2. The Saint Nicholas Hotel (produced Toronto, 1974).   Erin, Ontario, Press
    Porcépic, 1976.
    3. Handcuffs (produced Toronto, 1975).   Erin, Ontario, Press Porcépic, 1976.

Radio Play: Night-Blooming Cereus, 1959.

Verse

The Red Heart.   Toronto, McClelland and Stewart, 1949.
A Suit of Nettles.   Toronto, Macmillan, 1958.
Twelve Letters to a Small Town.   Toronto, Ryerson Press, 1962.
The Dance of Death at London, Ontario.   London, Alphabet, 1963.
Poems.   Toronto, New Press, 1972.

Bibliography: in James Reaney: A Biography by James Stewart Reaney, Toronto, Gage,
1976.

Theatrical Activities:

Director: **Plays** – One-Man Masque and Night-Blooming Cereus, Toronto, 1960; Apple
Butter, London, Ontario, 1965.

Actor: **Plays** – in One-Man Masque and Night-Blooming Cereus, Toronto, 1960.

                                        *   *   *

James Reaney's work reflects an unashamed Canadian identity that he communicates with
conviction. He has said that a Canadian literary statement is as important as those of other
and older nations. His own contribution is far from narrowly provincial, however. What's
more, his uncommonly informed intellect allows his creative imagination to range
intimately, allusively in the larger world.
    In The Boy with an "R" in His Hand, his approach provokes readers to take sides in the
1826 type-riot in William Lyon Mackenzie's printing office. He compels them to ask why the
Tories hated Mackenzie, why there was a riot, why young Alex helped to exonerate Rebecca
who had been unjustly branded as a robber. Reaney's clear understanding leads readers to a
discovery of the operative historical and psychological processes – and history comes alive
for them through each character's role. The initial worldly innocence of two young orphan
brothers soon departs when events influence their allegiances, one to Mackenzie's, the other
to their Tory uncle's side. Children can grasp the larger events through what happens to these
boys. The novel's design is dramatic and anticipates Reaney's ultimate choice of drama as his
favourite mode. Each chapter is a complete scene, and the whole divides easily into three acts.
    In Apple Butter he presents the format for four plays, one of them for marionettes. He
encourages the players and the audience to try on the formats and alter them to their own
dimensions. The audiences are every bit as important as the players, as the playwright, as the
plays. It is quite clear that people (on and off stage) are at Reaney's centre stage, and it is how
people interact, react and trans-act that concerns him always. Reaney actually provides the
format for play in the sense of children's amusement through play – play on words and
feelings, play on sounds and actions – that is, play within a play that also moves within a
loose dramatic framework to a climax of fun.

Reaney says that *Geography Match* is "a shamelessly patriotic play and should be played recklessly and with all the stops pulled out." This kind of stage direction surely leads to the extravagances that communicate pure enjoyment to and from players and audience cumulatively. Each performance could be a new and different experience.

John Beckwith has composed musical accompaniments for Reaney's "Great Lakes Suite," six poems, and *All the Bees and All the Keys*, a fable. Reaney's inventions are natural springboards for Beckwith's ingenious embellishments. Their creative impulses harmonize playfully. Children can enjoy Reaney through the added musical dimension, although unaccompanied readings of both works are pure pleasure too.

Reaney displays his competence in works for children with the same creative involvement that he accords his work for older audiences.

—Irma McDonough

REES, (George) Leslie (Clarke). Australian. Born in Perth, Western Australia, 28 December 1905. Educated at Perth Modern School; University of Western Australia, Nedlands, 1924–29, B.A.; University College, London University, 1930. Married Coralie Clarke in 1931 (died, 1972); has two daughters. Drama Critic, *Era*, London, 1931–35; Co-Founder, 1937, and Honorary Chairman, Playwrights Advisory Board, Sydney; Federal Drama Editor, and Deputy Director of Drama until 1966, Australian Broadcasting Commission. Writer-in-Residence, Mt. Lawley College of Advanced Education, Perth, 1975. President, Sydney Centre of International P.E.N., 1967–75. Recipient: Australian Children's Book Award, 1946. Address: 4/5 The Esplanade, Balmoral Beach, New South Wales 2088, Australia.

PUBLICATIONS FOR CHILDREN

Fiction

> *Digit Dick on the Great Barrier Reef* [*and the Tasmanian Devil, in Black Swan Land, and the Lost Opals*], illustrated by Walter Cunningham. Sydney, John Sands, 4 vols., 1942–57.
> *The Story of Shy the Platypus* [*Karrawingi the Emu, Sarli the Barrier Reef Turtle, Shadow the Rock Wallaby, Aroora the Red Kangaroo, Wy-Lah the Cockatoo, Russ the Australian Tree Kangaroo*], illustrated by Walter Cunningham. Sydney, John Sands, 7 vols., 1944–64.
> *Gecko, The Lizard Who Lost His Tail*, illustrated by Walter Cunningham. Sydney, John Sands, 1944.
> *Mates of the Kurlalong*, illustrated by Alfred Wood. Sydney, John Sands, 1948.
> *Bluecap and Bimbi, The Blue Wrens*, illustrated by Walter Cunningham. Sydney, Trinity House, 1948.
> *The Story of Kurri Kurri the Kookaburra* [*Koonaworra the Black Swan*], illustrated by Margaret Senior. Sydney, John Sands, 2 vols., 1950, 1957.
> *Quokka Island*, illustrated by Arthur Horowicz. London, Collins, 1951.
> *Two Thumbs: The Story of a Koala*, illustrated by Margaret Senior. Sydney, John Sands, 1953.
> *Danger Patrol: A Young Patrol Officer's Adventures in New Guinea*. Sydney and London, Collins, 1954.

Boy Lost on Tropic Coast: Adventure with Dexter Hardy.   Sydney, Ure Smith, 1968.
Mokee the White Possum, illustrated by Tony Oliver.   Sydney, Hamlyn, 1973.
Panic in the Cattle Country.   Adelaide, Rigby, 1974.

Other

A Treasury of Australian Nature Stories.   Sydney, Ure Smith, 1974.

PUBLICATIONS FOR ADULTS

Other

Towards an Australian Drama.   Sydney and London, Angus and Robertson, 1953.
Spinifex Walkabout: Hitch-Hiking in Remote North Australia, with Coralie Rees.   Sydney, Australasian Publishing Company, and London, Harrap, 1953.
Westward from Cocos: Indian Ocean Travels, with Coralie Rees.   Sydney, Australasian Publishing Company, and London, Harrap, 1956.
The Coasts of Cape York: Travels Around Australia's Pearl-Tipped Peninsula, with Coralie Rees.   Sydney, Angus and Robertson, 1960.
People of the Big Sky Country, with Coralie Rees.   Sydney, Ure Smith, 1970.
The Making of Australian Drama: A Historical and Critical Survey from the 1830's to the 1970's.   Sydney, Angus and Robertson, 1973.
Australian Drama in the 1970's.   Sydney, Angus and Robertson, 1978.

Editor, *Australian Radio Plays.*   Sydney, Angus and Robertson, 1946.
Editor, *Modern Short Plays.*   Sydney and London, Angus and Robertson, 1951.
Editor, *Mask and Microphone: Plays.*   Sydney, Angus and Robertson, 1963.

Leslie Rees comments:
   I think children like exploring, recognising, discovering; they like adventure, meeting strange and interesting people, animals and birds, they like laughing, play-acting, narrow escapes; but in the long run feeling secure with someone and something to put their faith in. I like these things too, because there's still a child and still a boy in me. I also like sharing with children the fun and excitement I've had in travelling and getting to know Australian creatures of the wild, and reaching unusual Australian places. And with this emphasis and this incentive I go to work finding a method and an idiom that will catch the interest of the young. I am gratified to find that some of my books have reached child audiences in most English-speaking countries, and in some non-English-speaking countries, with especially large audiences in Russia.

*   *   *

   The contribution of Leslie Rees to Australian children's literature has been threefold: the development of fantasy for young readers; a loving concern for the wild-life of his country; and the keeping alive of the fast-moving adventure story for boys.
   Digit Dick, an Australian Tom Thumb, has the universal appeal of diminutive creatures as well as an engaging personality of his own. In that Digit Dick's adventures take him to the Great Barrier Reef and other remote areas of the continent, Leslie Rees introduces his readers to an exotic landscape which he peoples with strangely exciting but authentic sea and bush creatures. Inseparable from the Digit Dick stories are the somewhat cartoon-like illustrations of Walter Cunningham which elaborate the author's word play and verbal exaggeration. But it was with *Mates of the Kurlalong* that Rees made his most significant contribution to the development of nonsense fantasy in Australia. Here he is less didactic than in his other stories for young children, and he exploits an hilarious central situation in which the hero "not

exactly a wombat although he looked like one" and "not exactly a boy although he always behaved like one" commandeers a Sydney Harbour ferry. With an animal crew from Taronga Park Zoo a gloriously fantastic day of freedom begins, to end in a glorification of the endlessly possible adventures of uninhibited childhood.

It is in his series of Nature Tales, also faithfully and beautifully illustrated by Walter Cunningham, from *The Story of Shy the Platapus* through *The Story of Karrawingi the Emu*, the first recipient of the Australian Children's Book of the Year Award, to *Mokee the White Possum*, that Rees has made his most serious contribution to writing for children. Each story is a carefully detailed and authentic study of wild life in which the title character moves inevitably and dramatically through his cycle of life. The writing is clearer, cleaner and less wordy than in the Digit Dick stories. Developing readers easily identify with the struggle to survive and to maintain an ordained life-style of Shy the platypus, who "with the consciousness of motherhood upon her" turns from her cherished pool to the dark entrances of her tunnel under the surface of the earth. There is ready sympathy too, for Karrawingi, the emu, who races through the bush at midnight, proclaiming his fatherhood – of eighteen oval eggs.

Rees has also written full-blooded, tense adventure stories for older boys such as *Danger Patrol*, based on a young Patrol Officer's adventures in a still primitive New Guinea, and *Panic in the Cattle Country*, which explores the mystery of cattle in the Outback slaughtered and left with huge tearing wounds, by persons or creatures unknown. Rees's fascination with a geologically ancient continent, its aboriginal inhabitants and the white men who live in its remote vastness, its wild life and the sweep of its rugged scenery, gives a peculiarly Australian flavour to a yarn belonging firmly in the tradition of the robust boys' adventure story.

—H. M. Saxby

REEVES, James. British. Born in London, 1 July 1909. Educated at Stowe School, Buckinghamshire; Cambridge University, M.A. (honours) in English 1931. Married Mary Phillips in 1936 (died, 1966); has one son and two daughters. Taught in schools and colleges of education, 1933–52. Since 1951, General Editor, The Poetry Bookshelf series, William Heinemann Ltd., London; since 1960, General Editor, Unicorn Books, London. Fellow, Royal Society of Literature. Agent: Laura Cecil, 10 Exeter Mansions, 106 Shaftesbury Avenue, London W1V 7DH. Address: Flints, Rotten Row, Lewes, Sussex, England.

PUBLICATIONS FOR CHILDREN

Fiction

> *Pigeons and Princesses*, illustrated by Edward Ardizzone.   London, Heinemann, 1956.
> *Mulbridge Manor*, illustrated by Geraldine Spence.   London, Heinemann, 1958.
> *Titus in Trouble*, illustrated by Edward Ardizzone.   London, Bodley Head, 1959.
> *Sailor Rumbelow and Britannia*, illustrated by Edward Ardizzone.   London, Heinemann, 1962.
> *The Strange Light*, illustrated by Lynton Lamb.   London, Heinemann, 1964.
> *The Pillar-Box Thieves*, illustrated by Dick Hart.   London, Nelson, 1965.
> *Rhyming Will*, illustrated by Edward Ardizzone.   London, Hamish Hamilton, 1967; New York, McGraw Hill, 1968.
> *Mr. Horrox and the Gratch*, illustrated by Quentin Blake.   London, Abelard Schuman, 1969.

The Path of Gold, illustrated by Krystyna Turska.   London, Hamish Hamilton, 1972.
The Lion That Flew, illustrated by Edward Ardizzone.   London, Chatto and Windus, 1974.
Clever Mouse, illustrated by Barbara Swiderska.   London, Chatto and Windus, 1976.

Plays

Mulcaster Market: Three Plays for Young People (includes *Mulcaster Market, The Pedlar's Dream, The Stolen Boy*), illustrated by Dudley Cutler.   London, Heinemann, 1951; as *The Peddler's Dream and Other Plays*, New York, Dutton, 1963.
The King Who Took Sunshine.   London, Heinemann, 1954.

Verse

The Wandering Moon, illustrated by Evadne Rowan.   London, Heinemann, 1950; New York, Dutton, 1960.
The Blackbird in the Lilac: Verses, illustrated by Edward Ardizzone.   London, Oxford University Press, and New York, Dutton, 1952.
A Puffin Quartet of Poets, with others, edited by Eleanor Graham, illustrated by Diana Bloomfield.   London, Penguin, 1958.
Prefabulous Animiles, illustrated by Edward Ardizzone.   London, Heinemann, 1957; New York, Dutton, 1961.
Ragged Robin, illustrated by Jane Paton.   London, Heinemann, and New York, Dutton, 1961.
Hurdy-Gurdy: Selected Poems for Children, illustrated by Edward Ardizzone.   London, Heinemann, 1961.
The Story of Jackie Thimble, illustrated by Edward Ardizzone.   London, Chatto and Windus, 1964.
Complete Poems for Children, illustrated by Edward Ardizzone.   London, Heinemann, 1973.
More Prefabulous Animiles, illustrated by Edward Ardizzone.   London, Heinemann, 1975.

Other

English Fables and Fairy Stories, Retold, illustrated by Joan Kiddell-Monroe.   London, Oxford University Press, 1954; New York, Walck, 1960.
The Exploits of Don Quixote, Retold, illustrated by Edward Ardizzone.   London, Blackie, 1959; New York, Walck, 1960.
Fables from Aesop, Retold, illustrated by Maurice Wilson.   London, Blackie, 1961.
Three Tall Tales, Chosen from Traditional Sources, illustrated by Edward Ardizzone.   London and New York, Abelard Schuman, 1965.
The Road to a Kingdom: Stories from the Old and New Testaments, illustrated by Richard Kennedy.   London, Heinemann, 1965.
The Secret Shoemakers and Other Stories, illustrated by Edward Ardizzone.   London and New York, Abelard Schuman, 1966.
The Cold Flame, Based on a Tale from the Collection of the Brothers Grimm, illustrated by Charles Keeping.   London, Hamish Hamilton, 1967; New York Meredith Press, 1969.
The Trojan Horse, illustrated by Krystyna Turska.   London, Hamish Hamilton, 1968; New York, Watts, 1969.
Heroes and Monsters: Legends of Ancient Greece Retold, illustrated by Sarah Nechamkin.   London, Blackie, 2 vols., 1969, 1971.

The Angel and the Donkey, illustrated by Edward Ardizzone. London, Hamish Hamilton, 1969; New York, McGraw Hill, 1970.

Maildun the Voyager, illustrated by John Lawrence. London, Hamish Hamilton, 1971.

How the Moon Began, illustrated by Edward Ardizzone. London, Abelard Schuman, 1971.

The Forbidden Forest and Other Stories, illustrated by Raymond Briggs. London, Heinemann, 1973.

The Voyage of Odysseus: Homer's Odyssey Retold. London, Blackie, 1973.

Two Greedy Bears, illustrated by Gareth Floyd. London, Hamish Hamilton, 1974.

Quest and Conquest: Pilgrim's Progress Retold, illustrated by Joanna Troughton. Glasgow, Blackie, 1976.

Editor, *Orpheus: A Junior Anthology of English Poetry*. London, Heinemann, 2 vols., 1949, 1950.

Editor, *Heinemann Junior Poetry Books*. London, Heinemann, 4 vols., 1954.

Editor, *The Merry-Go-Round: A Collection of Rhymes and Poems for Children*, illustrated by John Mackay. London, Heinemann, 1955.

Editor, *A Golden Land: Stories, Poems, Songs New and Old*, illustrated by Gillian Conway and others. London, Constable, and New York, Hastings House, 1958.

Editor, *A First Bible: An Abridgement for Young Readers*, illustrated by Geoffrey Fraser. London, Heinemann, 1962.

Editor, *The Christmas Book*, illustrated by Raymond Briggs. London, Heinemann, and New York, Dutton, 1968.

Editor, *One's None: Old Rhymes for New Tongues*, illustrated by Bernadette Watts. London, Heinemann, 1968; New York, Watts, 1969.

Editor, *The Springtime Book: A Collection of Prose and Poetry*, illustrated by Colin McNaughton. London, Heinemann, 1976.

Editor, *The Autumn Book: A Collection of Prose and Poetry*, illustrated by Colin McNaughton. London, Heinemann, 1977.

Translator, *Primrose and the Winter Witch*, by Frantisek Hrubin, illustrated by Jiri Trnka. London, Hamlyn, 1964.

Translator, *The Golden Cockerel*, by Alexander Pushkin, illustrated by Ján Lebis. London, Dent, and New York, Watts, 1969.

Translator, *The Shadow of the Hawk*, by Marie de France, illustrated by Anne Dalton. London, Collins, 1975; New York, Seabury Press, 1977.

PUBLICATIONS FOR ADULTS

Play

A Health to John Patch: A Ballad Operetta. London, Boosey and Hawkes, 1957.

Verse

The Natural Need. Deyá, Mallorca, Seizin Press, and London, Constable, 1936.

The Imprisoned Sea. London, Editions Poetry, 1949.

XII Poems. Privately printed, 1950.

The Password and Other Poems. London, Heinemann, 1952.

The Talking Skull. London, Heinemann, 1958.

Collected Poems 1929–1959. London, Heinemann, 1960.

The Questioning Tiger. London, Heinemann, 1964.

Selected Poems. London, Allison and Busby, 1967; revised edition, 1977.

Subsong. London, Heinemann, 1969.

Poems and Paraphrases. London, Heinemann, 1972.

Collected Poems 1929–1974.   London, Heinemann, 1974.
Arcadian Ballads.   London, Whittington Press, 1977.

Other

The Critical Sense: Practical Criticism of Prose and Poetry.   London, Heinemann, 1956.
Teaching Poetry: Poetry in Class Five to Fifteen.   London, Heinemann, 1958.
A Short History of English Poetry 1340–1940.   London, Heinemann, 1961; New York, Dutton, 1962.
Understanding Poetry.   London, Heinemann, 1965; New York, Barnes and Noble, 1968.
Essays: Commitment to Poetry.   London, Heinemann, 1969; as *Commitment to Poetry*, New York, Barnes and Noble, 1969.
Inside Poetry, with Martin Seymour-Smith.   London, Heinemann, and New York, Barnes and Noble, 1970.
How to Write Poems for Children.   London, Heinemann, 1971.
The Reputation and Writings of Alexander Pope.   London, Heinemann, and New York, Barnes and Noble, 1976.
The Ballad.   London, Harrap, 1976.

Editor, *The Modern Poet's World.*   London, Heinemann, 1935; revised edition, as *Poet's World*, 1948, 1957.
Editor, with Denys Thomson. *The Quality of Education: Methods and Purposes in the Secondary Curriculum.*   London, Muller, 1947.
Editor, *The Writer's Way: An Anthology of English Prose.*   London, Christophers, 1948.
Editor, with Norman Culpan, *Dialogue and Drama.*   London, Heinemann, 1950.
Editor, *Selected Poems*, by D. H. Lawrence.   London, Heinemann, 1951.
Editor, *The Speaking Oak: English Poetry and Prose: A Selection.*   London, Heinemann, 1951.
Editor, *Selected Poems*, by John Donne.   London, Heinemann, 1952; New York, Macmillan, 1958.
Editor, *The Bible in Brief: Selection from the Text of the Authorized Version of 1611.*   London, Wingate, 1954.
Editor, *Selected Poems*, by John Clare.   London, Heinemann, 1954; New York, Macmillan, 1957.
Editor, *Gulliver's Travels: The First Three Parts.*   London, Heinemann, 1955.
Editor, *Selected Poems*, by Gerard Manley Hopkins.   London, Heinemann, 1956; New York, Macmillan, 1957.
Editor, *Selected Poems*, by Robert Browning.   London, Heinemann, 1956; New York, Macmillan, 1957.
Editor, *The Idiom of the People: English Traditional Verse from the Manuscripts of Cecil Sharp.*   London, Heinemann, and New York, Macmillan, 1958.
Editor, *Selected Poems*, by Emily Dickinson.   London, Heinemann, 1959; New York, Barnes and Noble, 1966.
Editor, *Selected Poems*, by Samuel Taylor Coleridge.   London, Heinemann, 1959.
Editor, *The Personal Vision ....*   London, Poetry Book Supplement, 1959.
Editor, *The Rhyming River: An Anthology of Verse.*   London, Heinemann, 4 vols., 1959.
Editor, with William Vincent Aughterson, *Over the Ranges.*   Melbourne, Heinemann, 1959.
Editor, *The Everlasting Circle: English Traditional Verse.*   London, Heinemann, and New York, Macmillan, 1960.
Editor, with Desmond Flower, *The War 1939–45.*   London, Cassell, 1960.

Editor, *Great English Essays*. London, Cassell, 1961.

Editor, *Selected Poems and Prose*, by Robert Graves. London, Hutchinson, 1961.

Editor, *Georgian Poetry*. London, Penguin, 1962.

Editor, *Gulliver's Travels: Parts I-IV*. London, Heinemann, 1964.

Editor, *The Cassell Book of English Poetry*. London, Cassell, and New York, Harper, 1965.

Editor, *Selected Poems*, by Jonathan Swift. London, Heinemann, and New York, Barnes and Noble, 1967.

Editor, with Martin Seymour-Smith, *A New Canon of English Poetry*. London, Heinemann, and New York, Barnes and Noble, 1967.

Editor, *An Anthology of Free Verse*. Oxford, Blackwell, 1968.

Editor, *The Reader's Bible*. London, Tandem, 1968.

Editor, *The Sayings of Dr. Johnson*. London, Baker, 1968.

Editor, *Poets and Their Critics*, vol. 3. London, Hutchinson, 1969.

Editor, *Homage to Trumbull Stickney*. London, Heinemann, 1968.

Editor, with Martin Seymour-Smith, *The Poems of Andrew Marvell*. London, Heinemann, and New York, Barnes and Noble, 1969.

Editor, *A Vein of Mockery* (anthology). London, Heinemann, 1973.

Editor, *Selected Poems*, by Thomas Gray. London, Heinemann, 1973; as *The Complete English Poems of Thomas Gray*, New York, Barnes and Noble, 1973.

Editor, *Five Late Romantic Poets*. London, Heinemann, 1974.

Editor, with Martin Seymour-Smith, *Selected Poems*, by Walt Whitman. London, Heinemann, 1976.

*   *   *

"We must always provide poetry in such a way that it creates and nourishes a continuing craving for poetry and does not kill it by making poetry seem something childish," said James Reeves once at a conference, condemning cosy and sloppy verse and praising nursery rhymes and Walter de la Mare. He has succeeded in keeping this advice in mind in his own poems, of which the humorous ones are most often quoted, like "Cows" from *The Blackbird in the Lilac*:

> Half the time they munched the grass, and all the time they lay
> Down in the water-meadows, the lazy month of May
> A-chewing
> A-chewing
> To pass the hours away
> "Nice weather," said the brown cow
>   "Ah," said the white.
> "Grass is very tasty
>   Grass is all right."

All of the poems are short with a dancing rhythm and plenty of nonsense. They catch a mood quickly and lightly, like these examples from *The Wandering Moon*:

> So grim and gloomy
> Are the caves beneath the sea
> Oh, rare but roomy
> And bare and boomy
> Those soft sea caverns be.

or:

> Waiting, waiting, waiting
> For the party to begin

> Waiting, waiting, waiting
> For the laughter and the din.
> Waiting, waiting, waiting
> With hair just so
> And clothes trim and tidy
> From topknot to toe.

or:

> Slowly the hands move round the clock,
> Slowly the dew dies on the dock.
> Slow is the snail — but slowest of all
> The green moss spreads on the old brick wall.

When the poet turns to stories for younger children, he creates unusual characters and backgrounds, like sailor Rumbelow, the little figure on the ship in a bottle, who loved Britannia in the glass ball, or Foo the clumsy Chinese potter, as well as the more usual royal families with Queens who bake cakes and Kings who hunt. Human failings, particularly pomposity or bad temper, are suitably mocked; kindness always wins in the end. Magic appears now and again, as in "The Old Woman and the Four Noises," in which friendly elves reassure the old countrywoman that they cause the noises in her cottage: "Don't be afraid ... you cannot see me but I live in your front door and I bring you luck. Every time the door is opened or closed, I squeak just to remind you I am here." "What an odd thing," said the old woman, "I never knew before that there was such a thing as a door elf that squeaked, but now I come to think about it, I see no reason why there shouldn't be."

The Strange Light is a longer fantasy about a small girl who discovers, on the other side of a hedge in a field of sunshine, all the characters who are waiting for writers to use them in their books, an ingenious idea. Their faces take on a strange purple glow when an author is thinking of them. This fades when he changes his mind or becomes brighter when they are summoned to go off into a story. One unattractive boy, who is never chosen, leads a revolt, but the heroine rushes back through the hedge to her uncle, who then writes a story about him and his gang, so all is well.

Mulbridge Manor is also set in the English country in summer but has a longer plot for older readers. A group of village children, led by the doctor's son, befriend an eccentric old lady at the Manor, help find a will, and defeat a criminal. Events move swiftly and unexpectedly and, as in the short stories, virtue is rewarded with a happy ending, but fate plays some funny tricks on the way. The background and the characters are all briefly introduced; no words are wasted: "Mulcaster ... was a sleepy place at the best of times ... the bells in the cathedral tower dropped four notes on the silent air, almost apologetically, as if sorry to disturb the city in its sleep." The children enter at once on their bicycles, each with a characteristic gesture.

James Reeves, besides writing his own very original verse and fiction, retells old fairy stories, Aesop's Fables and the Bible. In *Sailor Rumbelow* he includes the folk tales Rapunzel and Simple Jack, adding some spirited touches; in *The Forbidden Forest and Other Stories* he rescues ten of the lesser known of the Grimm brothers' collection. His short crisp sentences get swiftly to the point; none of the characters bandies words or minces matters.

When James Reeves tackled *The Exploits of Don Quixote*, he kept closer to the original Spanish text than many of his fellow countrymen and obviously enjoyed the humour. In his introduction he wrote: "Knight and squire represent two sides of human nature — the desire to lead and the desire to serve, the need for a spiritual aim and the need for material well-being; the balance between madness and commonsense, illusion and reality, courage and prudence."

Perhaps James Reeves welcomes Cervantes's creations as fitting companions to some of his own. But the last words on his talent must come from one of his poems:

The sea is a hungry dog
Giant and grey
He rolls on the beach all day.
With his clashing teeth and shaggy jaws
Hour upon hour he gnaws
The rumbling, tumbling stones,
And "Bones, bones, bones, bones,"
The giant sea-dog moans,
Licking his greasy paws.

But on quiet days in May or June
When even the grasses on the dune
Play no more their reedy tune,
With his head between his paws
He lies on the sandy shores
So quiet, so quiet, he scarcely snores.

—Margaret Campbell

REID, Meta Mayne. British. Born in Woodlesford, Yorkshire, 23 January 1905. Educated at Leeds Girls' High School; Manchester University, 1924–27. B.A. (honours) in English. Married E. Mayne Reid in 1935; has two sons. Chairman, Belfast P.E.N., 1960–61; President, Irish P.E.N., Dublin, 1970–72. Recipient: Listowel Festival Trophy, for verse, 1974. Agent: A.P. Watt and Son, 26–28 Bedford Row, London WC1R 4HL, England. Address: Crawfordsburn, Bangor BT19 1JG, Northern Ireland.

PUBLICATIONS FOR CHILDREN

Fiction

Phelim and the Creatures, illustrated by Sydney Passmore. London, Chatto and Windus, 1952.
Carrigmore Castle, illustrated by Richard Kennedy. London, Faber, 1954.
All Because of Dawks, illustrated by Geoffrey Whittam. London, Macmillan, and New York, St. Martin's Press, 1955.
Dawks Does It Again, illustrated by Geoffrey Whittam. London, Macmillan, and New York, St. Martin's Press, 1956.
Tiffany and the Swallow Rhyme, illustrated by Richard Kennedy. London, Faber, 1956.
The Cuckoo at Coolnean, illustrated by Richard Kennedy. London, Faber, 1956.
Dawks on Robbers' Mountain, illustrated by Geoffrey Whittam. London, Macmillan, and New York, St. Martin's Press, 1957.
Strangers in Carrigmore, illustrated by Richard Kennedy. London, Faber, 1958.
Dawks and the Duchess. London, Macmillan, 1958.
The McNeills at Rathcapple, illustrated by Brian Wildsmith. London, Faber, 1959.
Storm on Kildoney, illustrated by Geoffrey Whittam. London, Macmillan, and New York, St. Martin's Press, 1961.
Sandy and the Hollow Book, illustrated by Richard Kennedy. London, Faber, 1961.
The Tombermillin Oracle, illustrated by Richard Kennedy. London, Faber, 1962.
With Angus in the Forest, illustrated by Zelma Blakely. London, Faber, 1963.

The Tinkers' Summer, illustrated by Peggy Fortnum.   London, Faber, 1965.
The Silver Fighting Cocks.   London, Faber, 1966.
The House at Spaniard's Bay.   London, Faber, 1967.
The Glen Beyond the Door.   London, Faber, 1968.
The Two Rebels.   London, Faber, 1969.
Beyond the Wide World's End, illustrated by Antony Maitland.   London, Lutterworth Press, 1972.
The Plotters of Pollnashee, illustrated by Gareth Floyd.   London, Lutterworth Press, 1973.
Snowbound by the Whitewater, illustrated by Peter Dennis.   London, Abelard Schuman, 1975.
The Noguls and the Horse, illustrated by Tony Morris.   London, Abelard Schuman, 1976.

PUBLICATIONS FOR ADULTS

Novels

The Land Is Dear.   London, Melrose, 1936.
Far-Off Fields Are Green.   London, Melrose, 1937.

Verse

No Ivory Tower.   Walton-on-Thames, Surrey, Outposts Publications, 1974.

Manuscript Collection: de Grummond Collection, University of Southern Mississippi, Hattiesburg.

Meta Mayne Reid comments:
Although all the literary tradition is on my husband's side of the family I have written since I was very young. I am fortunate in being able to write any time and any place – at the station, on the bus, with my back to the TV set, among family talk. Poetry, perhaps, gives the greatest pleasure, but writing for children aged 8 to 12 is a kind of poetry. It must transfix the moment, heighten the sense of wonder, and all the time allow the narrative to leap ahead on the backs of firmly-drawn characters. I have written straightforward adventure stories, but I prefer fantasy or history as they present the challenge of making a new world credible.

My tales move on an Irish country background, and, since my family has lived in Northern Ireland for centuries, much of my detail springs from family stories. To be happy I must write something every day, which accounts for the 400–500 letters I send every year, most of them based on daily minutiae – a rich source of material since both fantasy and history demand practical foundations. My own favourites are *With Angus in the Forest* (Viking period) and *The Silver Fighting Cocks* (Napoleonic period).

*   *   *

Meta Mayne Reid's fiction is set in Ulster, usually in Down or Derry, and the books fall roughly into two categories: the straightforward historical novel and the present-day story with a basis of fantasy. Of the two, the former is the more successful. The time-travelling, magical, or symbolical formula usually produces an element of contrivance: the parallel episodes aren't always successfully integrated. Sometimes the author simply goes too far: the children turned into animals, for instance, in the Carrigmore series, are not convincing.

The House at Spaniard's Bay is one modern story that doesn't rely too heavily on the supernatural. A lively tale of illicit distilling, adolescent ambition, and infatuation, it has one exotic character – the tinker Judith – to embody the fey Irish quality that distinguishes the books. But the author can't resist introducing a figure from the past – the mythical Gráinne – who makes a rather theatrical appearance in a mountain cave. In *The Glen Beyond the Door*, past and present are intertwined in an episodic, unsatisfactory way.

A recent story for 10–12-year-olds, *The Noguls and the Horse*, uses the topical theme of terrorist bombing to show how a child can come to terms with her shaken sense of personal security. But Meta Mayne Reid is at her best when she writes about the Planter community of the years between 1798 and 1810. The industry of the Scottish Presbyterian settlers in Ulster is posited as an alternative to the traditional fecklessness of the native Irish hill farmer. But the author is well aware of the potent romantic aspects of dispossession and insurrection. *The Two Rebels* gives an excellent account of the aftermath of the '98 Rebellion, when the countryside was swarming with soldiers and men on the run. The rebels of the title are typical insurgents: a young Presbyterian farmer and a liberal Protestant aristocrat.

Red-coats and revenue officers are the blustering authoritarian figures outwitted incessantly by resourceful children. The historical context gives point and vigour to the unoriginal themes, and domestic detail adds credibility. Complex social and racial distinctions are simplified effectively. The heroine is usually a well-adjusted but naturally exuberant girl who has been allowed to run wild: Priscilla McCurdy, for instance (in *The Silver Fighting Cocks*) thinks sadly that "she must stop pretending that she was a boy, and Jamie her dear brother, and be a demure young miss, learning how to be a good wife in five years' time or so." Her friend Jamie is Catholic, and therefore in a lower social class: in *The Plotters of Pollnashee* the 11-year-old farmer's daughter is befriended by a gentleman's son – the point being made about natural affinities is still valid.

In *Beyond the Wide World's End* a couple of ragamuffins set off on a quest for emotional security – and find it, though there is a twist in the end. The year is 1810 and the author's research as usual has been meticulous.

Ulster has an intricate and sometimes romantic history that seems to offer enormous scope for the children's novelist – but so far Meta Mayne Reid has been the only author to exploit it.

—Patricia Craig

REY, H(ans) A(ugusto). American. Born in Hamburg, Germany, 16 September 1898; emigrated to the United States in 1940; naturalized citizen, 1946. Educated at University of Munich, 1919–20; University of Hamburg, 1920–23. Served in the German Infantry and Medical Corps, France and Russia, 1916–19. Married Margret Rey, *q.v.*, in 1935. Salesman for import firm, Rio de Janeiro, 1924–36. Free-lance writer and illustrator in Paris, 1936–40, New York, 1940–63, and from 1963, in Cambridge, Massachusetts. Recipient: *New York Times* award, for illustration, 1957. *Died 26 August 1977.*

PUBLICATIONS FOR CHILDREN (illustrated by the author)

Fiction (with Margret Rey)

How the Flying Fishes Came into Being. London, Chatto and Windus, 1938.
Raffy and the Nine Monkeys. London, Chatto and Windus, 1939; as *Cecily G. and the Nine Monkeys*, Boston, Houghton Mifflin, 1942.
How Do You Get There? Boston, Houghton Mifflin, 1941; London, Folding Books, 1951.
Curious George. Boston, Houghton Mifflin, 1941; as *Zozo*, London, Chatto and Windus, 1942.

Elizabite: The Adventures of a Carnivorous Plant.   New York, Harper, 1942; London, Chatto and Windus, 1964.
Curious George Takes a Job [*Rides a Bike, Gets a Medal, Flies a Kite, Learns the Alphabet, Goes to the Hospital*].   Boston, Houghton Mifflin, 6 vols., 1947–66; as *Zozo Takes a Job* [*Rides a Bike, Gets a Medal, Flies a Kite, Learns the Alphabet, Goes to the Hospital*], London, Chatto and Windus, 6 vols., 1954–67.

Verse (with Margret Rey)

Anybody at Home?   London, Chatto and Windus, 1939.
Tit for Tat.   New York and London, Harper, 1942.
Where's My Baby?   Boston, Houghton Mifflin, 1943; London, Folding Books, 1950.
Feed the Animals.   Boston, Houghton Mifflin, 1944; London, Folding Books, 1950.
See the Circus.   Boston, Houghton Mifflin, and London, Chatto and Windus, 1956.

Other

Zebrology (drawings).   London, Chatto and Windus, 1937.
Aerodrome for Scissors and Paint.   London, Chatto and Windus, 1939.
Au Clair de la Lune and Other French Nursery Songs.   New York, Greystone Press, 1941.
Farm (as Uncle Gus).   Boston, Houghton Mifflin, 1942.
Circus (as Uncle Gus).   Boston, Houghton Mifflin, 1942.
Christmas Manger (as Uncle Gus).   Boston, Houghton Mifflin, 1942.
Look for the Letters: A Hide-and-Seek Alphabet.   New York, Harper, 1945.
Mary Had a Little Lamb, with Margret Rey.   London, Penguin, 1951.
Find the Constellations.   Boston, Houghton Mifflin, 1954.

PUBLICATIONS FOR ADULTS

Other

The Stars: A New Way to See Them.   Boston, Houghton Mifflin, 1952; as *A New Way to See the Stars*, London, Hamlyn, 1966; revised edition, Houghton Mifflin, 1967.

Illustrator: *The Polite Penguin*, 1941, and *Don't Frighten the Lion!*, 1942, by Margaret Wise Brown; *Humpty Dumpty and Other Mother Goose Songs*, 1943; *Katy No-Pocket* by Emmy Payne, 1944; *The Park Book* by Charlotte Zolotow, 1944; *We Three Kings and Other Christmas Carols*, 1944; *Pretzel*, 1944, *Spotty*, 1945, *Pretzel and the Puppies*, 1946, and *Billy's Picture*, 1948, all by Margret Rey; *The Daynight Lamp and Other Poems* by Christian Morgenstern, 1973.

*   *   *

It matters little that the names Margret and H.A. Rey are practically unknown among the kindergarten set; what does matter is that their fictional offspring, Curious George, or Zozo in Great Britain, is instantaneously recognized and applauded by millions of children throughout the world. George, the curious little monkey, first saw light of day in the early 1940's when the world was wracked by war, and he immediately gained superstar status in the picture book world, maintaining it to this day.

It is easy, perhaps, for a critic to pass glibly over books like *Curious George* and its sequels when he is considering classic works in the field of children's literature. Such a critic might feel that there is an abyss between the comic strip and "the book," and that his job is to point out those elements which basically separate the two. For there is no denying that the Reys' work has strong links with the traditional comic strip, but therein one finds not only its energy and unique attraction to young children, but also the very subtle craftmanship of its creators. (Yes *subtle* – for the best practitioners in broad physical humor achieve their effects in a seemingly effortless fashion.)

Since *Curious George* consistently heads the popularity list of what children themselves call "funny books," it is worth our attention to see if we can identify those components in *George* which help it maintain that high rank. As already mentioned, much of the humor in the *George* books is found in physical situations. This is the slapstick humor to be found not only in the comic strips and cartoon films, but in the traditional tall tales as well, and in the films of such comic greats as Chaplin. The humor is the same: a comic character steps into an everyday, ordinary situation and the world immediately turns topsy-turvy. The difference is that George is a child character who gets involved in the everyday incidents in which children often find themselves.

George is always simply introduced on the opening page (as in *Curious George Goes to the Hospital*):

> This is George
> He lived with his friend, the man with the yellow hat. He was a good little mon-
> key, but he was always curious.
> Today George was curious about the big box on the man's desk.

The child audience half knows and half waits to be surprised by the mischief and hilarity that will follow. It is indeed a simple story formula, but one that demands a writer (in this case a team) with a gifted sense of childlike humor and an endless inventiveness.

One last point about these books that adults should not miss. From children's responses to the *George* books it is evident that the man with the yellow hat is the kind of grownup that they most admire and respect. They constantly look for his yellow hat in the crowd, especially when George is center stage and up to his ears in trouble. They know that though he never intrudes, George's grownup friend is always there when he's needed.

—James E. Higgins

REY, Margret. American. Born in Hamburg, Germany, in May 1906; emigrated to the United States in 1940; naturalized citizen, 1946. Educated at Bauhaus, Dessau, 1927; Dusseldorf Academy of Art, 1928–29; art school, Berlin. Married H.A. Rey, *q.v.*, in 1935 (died, 1977). Reporter and advertising copywriter, Berlin, in the late 1920's; photographer in London, Hamburg, and Brazil, 1930–35. One-man shows (watercolors): Berlin, 1929–34. Free-lance writer in Paris, 1936–40, New York, 1940–63, and since 1963, in Cambridge, Massachusetts. Agent: A.P. Watt and Son, 26–28 Bedford Row, London WC1R 4HL, England. Address: 14 Hilliard Street, Cambridge, Massachusetts 02138, U.S.A.

PUBLICATIONS FOR CHILDREN (illustrated by H.A. Rey)

Fiction

> *How the Flying Fishes Came into Being*, with H.A. Rey. London, Chatto and Windus, 1938.
> *Raffy and the Nine Monkeys*, with H.A. Rey. London, Chatto and Windus, 1939; as *Cecily G. and the Nine Monkeys*, Boston, Houghton Mifflin, 1942.
> *How Do You Get There?*, with H.A. Rey. Boston, Houghton Mifflin, 1941; London, Folding Books, 1951.

Curious George, with H.A. Rey.   Boston, Houghton Mifflin, 1941; as *Zozo*, London, Chatto and Windus, 1942.
Elizabite: The Adventures of a Carnivorous Plant, with H.A. Rey.   New York, Harper, 1942; London, Chatto and Windus, 1964.
Pretzel.   New York, Harper, 1944; London, Folding Books, 1950.
Spotty.   New York, Harper, 1945; London, Folding Books, 1950.
Pretzel and the Puppies.   New York, Harper, 1946.
Curious George Takes a Job [*Rides a Bike, Gets a Medal, Flies a Kite, Learns the Alphabet, Goes to the Hospital*], with H.A. Rey.   Boston, Houghton Mifflin, 6 vols., 1947–66; as *Zozo Takes a Job* [*Rides a Bike, Gets a Medal, Flies a Kite, Learns the Alphabet, Goes to the Hospital*], London, Chatto and Windus, 6 vols., 1954–67.
Billy's Picture.   New York, Harper, 1948; London, Chatto and Windus, 1964.

Verse (with H.A. Rey)

Anybody at Home?   London, Chatto and Windus, 1939.
Tit for Tat.   New York and London, Harper, 1942.
Where's My Baby?   Boston, Houghton Mifflin, 1943; London, Folding Books, 1950.
Feed the Animals.   Boston, Houghton Mifflin, 1944; London, Folding Books, 1950.
See the Circus.   Boston, Houghton Mifflin, and London, Chatto and Windus, 1956.

Other

Mary Had a Little Lamb, with H.A. Rey.   London, Penguin, 1951.

*   *   *

See the essay on H.A. Rey and Margret Rey.

RICHARDS, Frank. Pseudonym for Charles Harold St. John Hamilton.   British.   Born in Ealing, Middlesex, 8 August 1876. Educated at Thorn House School, Ealing. Song writer, with Percy Harrison. Free-lance journalist, and staff member, as Martin Clifford, for *Pluck*, 1906, and *The Gem*, 1907–39; as Frank Richards, for *The Magnet*, 1908–40; as Owen Conquest and Ralph Redway, for *Boys Friend*, from 1915; as Hilda Richards, for *School Friend*, and *The Magnet*, 1919–40; as Charles Hamilton, for *Modern Boy*, from 1928. *Died 24 December 1961*.

PUBLICATIONS FOR CHILDREN

Fiction

Schoolboy series (*The Secret of the School, The Black Sheep of Sparshott, First Man In, Looking after Lamb*).   London, Merrett, 4 vols., 1946.
Headland House series (as Hilda Richards) (*Winifred on the Warpath, The Girls of Headland House, Under Becky's Thumb*).   London, Merrett, 3 vols., 1946.
Billy Bunter at Greyfriars School, illustrated by R.J. Macdonald.   London, Skilton, 1947.
Mascot Schoolboy series (*Top Study at Topham, Bunny Binks on the War-Path, The Dandy of Topham, Sent to Coventry*).   London, John Matthew, 4 vols., 1947.
Mascot Schoolgirl series (as Hilda Richards).   London, John Matthew, 1947.

Billy Bunter's Balling-Out, illustrated by R.J. Macdonald.   London, Skilton, 1948.
Billy Bunter's Banknote.   London, Skilton, 1948.
Billy Bunter in Brazil.   London, Skilton, 1949.
Billy Bunter's Christmas Party, illustrated by R.J. Macdonald.   London, Skilton, 1949.
Bessie Bunter of Cliff House School (as Hilda Richards), illustrated by R.J. Macdonald.   London, Skilton, 1949.
The Secret of the Study (as Martin Clifford).   London, Mandeville, 1949.
Tom Merry and Co. of St. Jim's (as Martin Clifford).   London, Mandeville, 1949.
Billy Bunter among the Cannibals, illustrated by R.J. Macdonald.   London, Skilton, 1950.
Billy Bunter's Benefit, illustrated by R.J. Macdonald.   London, Skilton, 1950.
Jack of All Trades.   London, Mandeville, 1950.
Rallying Round Gussy (as Martin Clifford).   London, Mandeville, 1950.
Billy Bunter Butts In, illustrated by R.J. Macdonald.   London, Skilton, 1951.
Billy Bunter's Postal Order, illustrated by R.J. Macdonald.   London, Skilton, 1951.
The Rivals of Rookwood School (as Owen Conquest).   London, Mandeville, 1951.
The Scapegrace of St. Jim's (as Martin Clifford).   London, Mandeville, 1951.
Talbot's Secret (as Martin Clifford).   London, Mandeville, 1951.
Billy Bunter and the Blue Mauritius, illustrated by R.J. Macdonald.   London, Skilton, 1952.
Billy Bunter's Beanfeast, illustrated by R.J. Macdonald.   London, Cassell, 1952.
Gold Hawk series (as Martin Clifford).   London, Mandeville, 1952.
Billy Bunter's Brain-Wave, illustrated by R.J. Macdonald.   London, Cassell, 1953.
Billy Bunter's First Case, illustrated by R.J. Macdonald.   London, Cassell, 1953.
Billy Bunter the Bold, illustrated by R.J. Macdonald.   London, Cassell, 1954.
Bunter Does His Best, illustrated by R.J. Macdonald.   London, Cassell, 1954.
Backing Up Billy Bunter, illustrated by C.H. Chapman.   London, Cassell, 1955.
Billy Bunter's Double, illustrated by R.J. Macdonald.   London, Cassell, 1955.
The Banishing of Billy Bunter, illustrated by C.H. Chapman.   London, Cassell, 1956.
Lord Billy Bunter.   London, Cassell, 1956.
Billy Bunter Afloat, illustrated by C.H. Chapman.   London, Cassell, 1957.
Billy Bunter's Bolt, illustrated by C.H. Chapman.   London, Cassell, 1957.
Billy Bunter the Hiker, illustrated by C.H. Chapman.   London, Cassell, 1958.
Billy Bunter's Bargain, illustrated by C.H. Chapman.   London, Cassell, 1958.
Bunter Comes for Christmas, illustrated by C.H. Chapman.   London, Cassell, 1959.
Bunter Out of Bounds, illustrated by C.H. Chapman.   London, Cassell, 1959.
Bunter Keeps It Dark, illustrated by C.H. Chapman.   London, Cassell, 1960.
Bunter the Bad Lad.   London, Cassell, 1960.
Billy Bunter at Butlin's, illustrated by C.H. Chapman.   London, Cassell, 1961.
Billy Bunter's Treasure-Hunt, illustrated by C.H. Chapman.   London, Cassell, 1961.
Bunter the Ventriloquist, illustrated by C.H. Chapman.   London, Cassell, 1961.
Billy Bunter's Bodyguard, illustrated by C.H. Chapman.   London, Cassell, 1962.
Bunter the Caravanner, illustrated by C.H. Chapman.   London, Cassell, 1962.
Just Like Bunter, illustrated by C.H. Chapman.   London, Cassell, 1963.
Big Chief Bunter, illustrated by C.H. Chapman.   London, Cassell, 1963.
Bunter the Stowaway, illustrated by C.H. Chapman.   London, Cassell, 1964.
Thanks to Bunter, illustrated by C.H. Chapman.   London, Cassell, 1964.
Bunter and the Phantom of the Towers.   London, May Fair Books, 1965.
Bunter the Racketeer.   London, May Fair Books, 1965.
Bunter the Sportsman, illustrated by C.H. Chapman.   London, Cassell, 1965.
Bunter the Tough Guy of Greyfriars.   London, May Fair Books, 1965.
Bunter's Holiday Cruise.   London, May Fair Books, 1965.
Bunter's Last Fling, illustrated by C.H. Chapman.   London, Cassell, 1965.
Billy Bunter and the Man from South America.   London, Hamlyn, 1967.
Billy Bunter and the School Rebellion.   London, Hamlyn, 1967.

Billy Bunter's Big Top. London, Hamlyn, 1967.
Bessie Bunter and the Gold Robbers (as Hilda Richards). London, Hamlyn, 1967.
Bessie Bunter Joins the Circus (as Hilda Richards). London, Hamlyn, 1967.
Billy Bunter and the Bank Robber. London, Hamlyn, 1968.
Billy Bunter, Sportsman. London, Hamlyn, 1968.
Billy Bunter and the Crooked Captain. London, Hamlyn, 1968.
Billy Bunter's Convict. London, Hamlyn, 1968.
Bessie Bunter and the Missing Fortune. London, Hamlyn, 1968.
Bessie Bunter and the School Informer. London, Hamlyn, 1968.
A Strange Secret (as Martin Clifford). Maidstone, Kent, Old Boys Book Club, 1968.
The Greyfriars Cowboys. London, Howard Baker, 1975.
Yarooh! A Feast of Frank Richards, edited by Gyles Brandreth. London, Eyre Methuen, 1976.

Other

Tom Merry's Own (annual; as Martin Clifford and Frank Richards). London, Mandeville, 4 vols., 1952–55.
Billy Bunter's Own (annual). London, Mandeville, 7 vols., 1953–59; London, Oxonhoath, 1 vol., 1960.

PUBLICATIONS FOR ADULTS

Play

Radio Play: *Plus ça Change; or, The 8:45 from Surbiton,* 1945.

Other

The Autobiography of Frank Richards. London, Skilton, 1952.

Critical Study: *The World of Frank Richards* by W.O.G. Lofts and D.J. Adley, London, Howard Baker, 1975.

*   *   *

Charles Hamilton was a phenomenon. Under his many pen-names he arguably created more memorable and well-loved characters than any writer since Charles Dickens. He wrote his first story at the age of 17 and went on to turn out literally thousands of boys' tales for a wide variety of juvenile papers and comics (and, later, hard-cover books) using over twenty pseudonyms. In the boys' paper *The Gem* (1906–39) he created Tom Merry, his friend Manners and Lowther, and the aristocratic Arthur Augustus D'Arcy, of St. Jim's. In another, even more famous paper, *The Magnet* (1908–40) he created the world's most popular fat boy, Billy Bunter of Greyfriars School, together with such other characters as Harry Wharton, Bob Cherry, Frank Nugent, Hurree Jamset Ram Singh and Johnny Bull (known collectively as The Famous Five), Herbert Vernon-Smith (the Bounder of the Remove Form), Lord Mauleverer, Horace Coker (the Duffer of the Fifth), Loder (the Bully of the Sixth), not forgetting such Masters as Quelch, Prout and Hacker, and Headmaster, Dr. Locke. For *The Gem,* he wrote as Martin Clifford, for *The Magnet* as Frank Richards. As Owen Conquest he wrote of Jimmy Silver and Co. of Rookwood School, whose adventures ran in *The Boys' Friend,* starting in 1915. As Hilda Richards he began the exploits of Bessie Bunter of Cliff House School, in the pages of *The Schoolfriend* (though these stories were later taken over by other writers). It would take up pages to detail his other work. For year after year he wrote the entire cover-to-cover stories in *The Magnet* and *The Gem* (though substitute writers filled in from time to time), in addition to countless other stories, averaging around 80,000 words a week. During his lifetime his total output was at least 72 million words – equivalent to about 2,000 full-length novels. This makes Hamilton almost certainly the most prolific writer of all time.

In Billy Bunter, Charles Hamilton created one of the minor immortals of English literature. Bunter, with all his faults, his love of food (especially jam-tarts) and the lengths he would go to obtain it, his never-arriving postal-order, his perpetual cadging, his cries of "I say, you chaps!," "Beast!" and "Yarooooh!," his eavesdropping, tittle-tattling, stupidity, his tight-checked trousers, bow-tie and round glasses, have surely put The Fat Owl of the Remove Form at Greyfriars up there with such household characters as Sherlock Holmes, Pickwick, Hamlet and Tarzan. Hamilton's prose has a cosy, button-holing readability, humour, and vividness which make excellent escapist reading to this day. He could portray a character in a few graphic sentences – though, at the other end of the scale, he could be guilty of padding, which, however, could also be defended as an integral part of his unique style. Many Hamilton stories were dramatic and exciting; others were hilariously funny and often out-Wodehoused Wodehouse in descriptive form and humour content. After World War II, Hamilton wrote a series of 38 hard-cover Greyfriars books as well as many paper-backs. And currently a British publisher is reprinting, in bound facsimile-form, many of Hamilton's original boys' paper stories.

—Brian Doyle

RICHARDS, Laura E(lizabeth).   American.   Born in Boston, Massachusetts, 27 February 1850; daughter of the poet Julia Ward Howe. Attended Miss Caroline Wilby's School, Boston. Married Henry Richards in 1871; four daughters, two sons. Associated with District Nurse Association and the National Child Labor Committee; Founder, 1895, and President for 26 years, Woman's Philanthropic Union; Founded Camp Merryweather, 1900; President, Maine Consumers League, 1905–11. Recipient: Pulitzer Prize, for biography, 1915. D.H.L.: University of Maine, Orono, 1936. *Died 14 January 1943.*

PUBLICATIONS FOR CHILDREN

Fiction

> *Five Mice in a Mouse-Trap, by the Man in the Moon, Done in Vernacular, from the Lunacular,* illustrated by Kate Greenaway and others.   Boston, Estes, 1880.
> *Little Tyrant.*   Boston, Estes, 1880.
> *Our Baby's Favorite.*   Boston, Estes, 1881.
> *The Joyous Story of Toto,* illustrated by E.H. Garrett.   Boston, Roberts, 1885; London, Blackie, 1886.
> *Tell-Tale from Hill and Dale,* illustrated by A. Hochstein.   Troy, New York, Nims, 1886.
> *Kasper Kroak's Kaleidoscope,* with H. Baldwin, illustrated by A. Hochstein.   Troy, New York, Nims, 1886.
> *Toto's Merry Winter.*   Boston, Roberts, 1887.
> *Queen Hildegarde.*   Boston, Estes, and London, Gay and Bird, 1889.
> *Hildegarde's Holiday.*   Boston, Estes, and London, Gay and Bird, 1891.
> *Captain January.*   Boston, Estes, and London, Gay and Bird, 1891.
> *Hildegarde's Home.*   Boston, Estes, 1892.
> *Melody.*   Boston, Estes, 1893; London, Gay and Bird, 1895.

Marie.   Boston, Estes, 1894.

Narcissa; or, The Road to Rome, and In Verona: Two Tales.   Boston, Estes, 1894.

Nautilus.   Boston, Estes, 1895.

Five Minute Stories, illustrated by A.R. Whelan and E.B. Barry.   Boston, Estes, 1895; London, Allenson, 1906.

Hildegarde's Neighbors.   Boston, Estes, 1895.

Jim of Hellas; or, In Durance Vile, and Bethesda Pool.   Boston, Estes, 1895.

Isla Heron, illustrated by Frank Merrill.   Boston, Estes, 1896.

"Some Say," and Neighbors in Cyrus.   Boston, Estes, 1896.

Three Margarets, illustrated by Etheldred Barry.   Boston, Estes, 1897.

Hildegarde's Harvest.   Boston, Estes, 1897.

Rosin the Beau.   Boston, Estes, 1898.

Margaret Montfort, illustrated by Etheldred Barry.   Boston, Estes, 1898.

Peggy, illustrated by Etheldred Barry.   Boston, Estes, 1899.

Quicksilver Sue, illustrated by W.D. Stevens.   New York, Century, 1899.

Chop-Chin and the Golden Dragon.   Boston, Little Brown, 1899.

The Golden-Breasted Koo-Too.   Boston, Little Brown, 1899.

Rita, illustrated by Etheldred Barry.   Boston, Estes, 1900.

Fernley House, illustrated by Etheldred Barry.   Boston, Estes, 1901.

The Green Satin Gown, illustrated by Etheldred Barry.   Boston, Estes, 1903.

More Five-Minute Stories, illustrated by Wallace Goldsmith.   Boston, Estes, 1903.

The Merryweathers, illustrated by Julia Ward Richards.   Boston, Estes, 1904.

The Golden Windows: A Book of Fables for Young and Old.   Boston, Little Brown, and London, Allenson, 1904.

The Armstrongs, illustrated by Julia Ward Richards.   Boston, Estes, 1905.

The Silver Crown.   Boston, Little Brown, and London, Allenson, 1906.

The Pig Brother and Other Fables and Stories.   Boston, Little Brown, 1908.

A Happy Little Time.   Boston, Estes, 1910.

The Naughty Comet and Other Fables and Stories.   London, Allenson, 1910; revised edition, 1925.

The Little Master.   Boston, Estes, 1913; as *Our Little Feudal Cousin of Long Ago,* Boston, Page, 1922.

Three Minute Stories, illustrated by Josephine Bruce.   Boston, Page, 1914.

Honor Bright, illustrated by Frank Merrill.   Boston, Page, 1920.

Honor Bright's New Adventure, illustrated by Elizabeth Withington.   Boston, Page, 1925.

Star Bright, illustrated by Frank Merrill.   Boston, Page, 1927.

Harry in England, illustrated by Reginald Birch.   New York and London, Appleton Century, 1937.

Plays

The Pig Brother Play-Book (includes *The Pig Brother; The Shadow; For You and Me; The Useful Coal; The Sailor Man; The Cooky; Oh, Dear!; "Go" and "Come"; Child's Play; The Naughty Comet; The Tangled Skein; The Cake; Hokey Pokey; About Angels; The Great Feast; The Wheat-Field*).   Boston, Little Brown, 1915.

Fairy Operettas (includes *Cinderella, The Babes in the Wood, Beauty and the Beast, Bluebeard, The Three Bears, Good King Arthur, Puss in Boots, The Sleeping Beauty*), illustrated by Mary Robertson Bassett.   Boston, Little Brown, 1916.

Verse

Sketches and Scraps, illustrated by Henry Richards.   Boston, Estes, 1881.

In My Nursery.   Boston, Roberts, 1890.

Sun Down Songs.   Boston, Little Brown, 1899.

The Hurdy-Gurdy.   Boston, Estes, 1902.
The Piccolo.   Boston, Estes, 1906.
Jolly Jingles.   Boston, Estes, 1912.
Tirra Lirra: Rhymes Old and New, illustrated by Marguerite Davis.   Boston, Little
  Brown, 1921; London, Harrap, 1933.
Merry-Go-Round: New Rhymes and Old, illustrated by Winifred Lefferts.   New York
  and London, Appleton, 1935.
I Have a Song to Sing You, illustrated by Reginald Birch.   New York and London,
  Appleton Century, 1938.

Other

The Old Fairy Tales (Beauty and the Beast and *Hop o' My Thumb),* illustrated by Gordon
  Browne.   Boston, Roberts, and London, Blackie, 2 vols., 1886.
When I Was Your Age (autobiography).   Boston, Estes, 1894.
Snow-White; or, The House in the Wood.   Boston, Estes, 1900.
Florence Nightingale, The Angel of Crimea.   New York and London, Appleton, 1909.
Two Noble Lives: Samuel Grindley Howe, Julia Ward Howe.   Boston, Estes, 1911.
Elizabeth Fry, The Angel of the Prisons.   New York and London, Appleton, 1916.
Abigail Adams and Her Times.   New York and London, Appleton, 1917.
Joan of Arc.   New York and London, Appleton, 1919.
Laura Bridgman: The Story of an Opened Door.   New York and London, Appleton,
  1928.

Editor, *Four Feet, Two Feet, and No Feet; or, Furry and Feathery Pets and How They
  Live.*   Boston, Estes, 1885.

Novels

Love and Rocks.   Boston, Estes, 1898.
Geoffrey Strong.   Boston, Estes, 1901; London, Simpkin, 1912.
Mrs. Tree.   Boston, Estes, 1902; London, Simpkin, 1912.
Mrs. Tree's Will.   Boston, Estes, 1905.
Grandmother: The Story of a Life That Never Was Lived.   Boston, Estes, 1907.
The Wooing of Calvin Parks.   Boston, Estes, 1908.
"Up to Calvin's."   Boston, Estes, 1910.
On Board the Merry Sands.   Boston, Estes, 1911.
Miss Jiminy.   Boston, Estes, 1913.
Pippin, A Wandering Flame.   New York and London, Appleton, 1917.
A Daughter of Jehu.   New York and London, Appleton, 1918.
In Blessed Cyrus.   New York and London, Appleton, 1921.
The Squire.   New York and London, Appleton, 1923.

Short Stories

For Tommy and Other Stories.   Boston, Estes, 1900.

Plays

Seven Oriental Operettas.   Boston, Baker, 1924.
Acting Charades.   Boston, Baker, 1924.

Verse

> *To Arms! Songs of the Great War.*   Boston, Page, 1918.
> *The Hottentot and Other Ditties*, music by Twining Lynes.   New York, Schirmer, 1939.

Other

> *Glimpses of the French Court: Sketches from French History.*   Boston, Estes, 1893.
> *Julia Ward Howe, 1819–1910*, with Maud Howe Elliott.   Boston, Houghton Mifflin, 2 vols., 1915.
> *Stepping Westward* (autobiography).   New York and London, Appleton, 1931.
> *Samuel Grindley Howe.*   New York and London, Appleton Century, 1935.
> *E.A.R.* (on Edwin Arlington Robinson).   Cambridge, Massachusetts, Harvard University Press, 1936.
> *"Please."*   Privately printed, 1936.
> *What Shall the Children Read?*   New York and London, Appleton Century, 1939.
> *Laura E. Richards and Gardiner* (collection).   Augusta, Maine, Gannett, 1940.

> Editor, *Letters and Journals of Samuel Grindley Howe.*   Boston, Estes, 2 vols., 1906, 1909; London, Lane, 2 vols., 1907, 1909.
> Editor, *The Walk with God: Extracts from Julia Ward Howe's Private Journals.*   New York, Dutton, 1919.

*   *   *

Laura E. Richards was a successful writer of both prose and poetry for children during the "golden age" of children's literature in the late 19th and early 20th centuries. Her work was widely published, but she is probably best remembered for her association with the famous *St. Nicholas* magazine, in which many of her verses appeared.

Except for a very few reprint editions, Mrs. Richards' prose works for children are unavailable today. She wrote a number of biographies, mostly of women (Abigail Adams, Florence Nightingale, Elizabeth I and others) using the semi-fictional approach common to most biographies for children of the time. Though she strengthened her accounts with excerpts from diaries, letters, and journals, Mrs. Richards also greatly oversimplified both the characters of her subjects and the historical context of their lives. This, together with an old-fashioned style, has dated the biographies, and they are unlikely to be revived. The same must be said for such fiction as the "Queen Hildegarde" and "Three Margarets" series, both very popular in their time but now of interest mainly as period pieces.

It is in fact only her verse that has kept Laura Richards' name alive in the field of children's literature. *Tirra Lirra* is in print and is included in most library poetry collections for children. The dominant mood of the verses in *Tirra Lirra* is cheerful and humorous. Lightheartedness was generally characteristic of the author, though some of Mrs. Richards' verse published in *St. Nicholas* before the turn of the century reflected the sentimental attitudes of that period.

On the whole, however, Laura Richards was a good deal less sentimental in her approach to children and poetry than were many of her contemporaries. Indeed, a slight acidity, surely welcome in the customarily earnest atmosphere of the late 19th century, often flavors her work. The wicked mockingbird whose practical joke caused the frog of Okefenokee to break his lovely green neck does not get off scot-free: "I'm happy to say/He was drowned the next day/In the waters of Okefenokee." Similarly, the aged cook dispatches without a quaver of remorse one of the seven little tigers who propose to eat him. No high-minded conclusions are ever drawn; Mrs. Richards was not inclined to moralize.

Technically, Laura Richards was a competent and facile versifier. She used a variety of rhythms and rhyme schemes, mostly strong, unsubtle tetrameters, ballad forms, and limericks, though she never handled them with the intricacy of interest that, say, A.A. Milne could produce at his best. (On the other hand, she was never as far away from a child's point of view as Milne at his nostalgic worst.) She was fond – perhaps overfond – of nonsense words and repetition, certainly reflecting the influence of Edward Lear and Lewis Carroll. And while her made-up words were neither as witty as Carroll's nor as unselfconscious as Lear's, such inventions as the wigglewasticus and the ichthyosnortoryx gave her poems a nice sense of freedom. "Eletelephony," undoubtedly her best-known nonsense poem, is a truly funny play on tangled words, and "An elderly lady named Mackintosh/[who] set out to ride in a hackintosh" anticipates Ogden Nash.

Laura E. Richards deserves her niche in children's literature. If she was never highly original, still she was humorous, irreverent and pleasant to the ear. Unlike her prose, her verse is surprisingly undated.

—Anne S. MacLeod

RIDGE, Antonia.   British.   Born in Amsterdam, Netherlands, 7 October 1895. Educated at schools in Holland and England. Married James Henry Ridge in 1926; has one daughter and one son. Writer and free-lance broadcaster. Recipient: Writers' Guild award, for radio play, 1969. Address: 5 Cranbrook Drive, Esher, Surrey KT10 8DL, England.

PUBLICATIONS FOR CHILDREN

Fiction

> *The Handy Elephant and Other Stories*, illustrated by A.E. Kennedy.   London, Faber, 1946.
> *Rom-Bom-Bom and Other Stories*, illustrated by A.E. Kennedy.   London, Faber, 1946.
> *Hurrah for Muggins and Other Stories*, illustrated by Francis Gower.   London, Faber, 1947.
> *Endless and Co.*, illustrated by A.E. Kennedy.   London, Faber, 1948.
> *Galloping Fred*, illustrated by A.E. Kennedy.   London, Faber, 1950.
> *Leave It to Brooks!*, illustrated by Nora S. Unwin.   London, National Magazine Company, 1950.
> *Jan and His Clogs*, illustrated by Barbara C. Freeman.   London, Faber, 1951; New York, Roy, 1952.
> *Stories from France (The Market, The Station, The Village, The Farm, The Mountain, The Seaside)*.   Leicester, Brockhampton Press, 6 vols., 1956–57.
> *The Little Red Pony*, with Mies Bouhuys, illustrated by Dick De Wilde.   London, Harrap, 1960; Indianapolis, Bobbs Merrill, 1962.
> *Hurrah for a Dutch Birthday*, with Mies Bouhuys, illustrated by Jillian Willett.   London, Faber, 1964.
> *Melodia: A Story from Holland*, with Mies Bouhuys, illustrated by Leslie Wood.   London, Faber, 1969.

Plays

> *Puppet Plays for Children* (includes *Spring Magic, Melodious Mixture, The Tropical Island, Blue Beans, A Cure for Lions, All Aboard the "Bookworm Belle"*), illustrated by Barbara C. Freeman.   London, Faber, 1953.
> *Six Radio Plays* (includes *Under the Monkey-Bread Tree, Hare and the Field of Millet, Three Mice for the Abbot, Emhammed of the Red Slippers, The Legend of Saint Basil,*

Saint Martha and the Tarasque of Tarascon). Leeds, E.J. Arnold, 1954.
The Poppenkast; or, How Jan Klaassen Cured the Sick King. London, Faber, 1958; as How Jan Klaassen Cured the King, 1969.

Other

Jan Klaassen Cures the King: An Old Dutch Story, illustrated by Barbara C. Freeman. London, Faber, 1952.
Never Run from the Lion and Another Story (Algerian folktales), illustrated by Barbara C. Freeman. London, Faber, 1958; New York, Walck, 1959.

Translator, Père Castor Books (Singing Bird House, Three Little Goats, The Moon Game, My Son Scamp, The Sun Box, Three Little Pigs, Me and My Master, The Good Friends, The Story of a Mouse, Little Goat Goes to Market, The Three Little Cats, The Breadcrumbs, The Animals Who Went Looking for Summer, A Rabbit Story, A Dog's Life, The Story of a Baby Lion Who Wasn't Hungry, Some Strange Animals, Come On, Neddy!, Snowball, Kathy's New Dress, The Old Grey Mare and the Little White Hen), illustrated by Albertine Deletaille, Gerda Muller, and Lucile Butel. London, Harrap, 21 vols., 1960–70.
Translator, Mission Underground, by Norbert Casteret, illustrated by H. Johns. London, Harrap, 1968.

PUBLICATIONS FOR ADULTS

Novels

Family Album. London, Faber, and New York, Harper, 1952.
Cousin Jan. London, Faber, 1954.
Grandma Went to Russia. London, Faber, 1959.
The Thirteenth Child. London, Faber, 1962; as The Royal Pawn, New York, Appleton Century Crofts, 1963.
The Man Who Painted Roses: The Story of Pierre Joseph Redouté. London, Faber, 1974.

Short Stories

By Special Request. London, Faber, 1958.

Plays

Radio Plays: Maria Lafarge, with Edith Saunders, 1968; The Little French Clock, 1969; Au Clair de la Lune, 1970; Gentleman's Agreement, 1972; and others.

Other

For Love of a Rose. London, Faber, 1965.

Editor, A String of Beads, by Dorothy McCall. London, Faber, 1960.

*   *   *

Antonia Ridge is one of the best short story writers for children that we have. To quote one reviewer – "she knows how to turn a tale well – as juicy as pippins in autumn." Her output is prolific, and in the children's field alone she is the author of many broadcast scripts as well as amusing and entertaining volumes of short stories such as Rom-Bom-Bom, Hurrah for

Muggins, Endless and Co., and *Galloping Fred.* These stories feature the animal characters with which she is associated – Fred the donkey, Muggins the dog, and Endless who is of course a Manx cat. A different kind of tale appears in *Never Run from the Lion,* which consists of two traditional folk-tales based on the theme of courage, admirable choices for reading aloud.

Much of Antonia Ridge's work reveals her Dutch inheritance. This is particularly so in the case of her best-known play *The Poppenkast; or, How Jan Klassen Cured the Sick King,* adapted from an old Dutch puppet play.

During the last ten years Antonia Ridge has collaborated with the Dutch author Mies Bouhuys in producing a picture-book illustrating the stress laid in Dutch family life on a child's birthday, called appropriately enough *Hurrah for a Dutch Birthday.* Mies Bouhuys has also been her co-author in the writing of *Melodia,* the story of a Dutch street organ. The scene is well set, the Dutch landscape with its dykes and windmills. Grandpa Brack, who owns Melodia, is a great favourite with the local children, but he and his wife are always hoping to visit their own six grandchildren in faraway America. The fairytale theme of the rich American visitor who makes it possible for this to happen is a well-worn one but very satisfying in the context of this story. The text is slightly marred, however, by a conversational style, wholly suitable for reading aloud, which becomes condescending in print.

Although Antonia Ridge is particularly good when writing for very young children – the English text to the Père Castor series of young picture-books proves this – it is also true to say that her stories for adults, such as *The Thirteenth Child* and *Family Album* are much enjoyed by older children. Their values are very sound, and they can be heartily recommended.

—Berna C. Clark

RILEY, Louise. Canadian. Born in Calgary, Alberta, in 1904. Educated at St. Hilda's School for Girls, Calgary; McGill University, Montreal; University of Wisconsin, Madison; Columbia University, New York (American Library Association Fellow), 1942. Children's Librarian, Calgary Public Library. Recipient: Canadian Library Association Book of the Year Medal, 1956. *Died in 1957.*

PUBLICATIONS FOR CHILDREN

Fiction

> *The Mystery Horse,* illustrated by John Merle Smith.   Toronto, Copp Clark, and New York, Messner, 1950; Oxford, Blackwell, 1957.
> *Train for Tiger Lily,* illustrated by Christine Price.   Toronto, Macmillan, and New York, Viking Press, 1954.
> *A Spell at Scoggin's Crossing,* illustrated by David Knight.   New York and London, Abelard Schuman, 1960.

PUBLICATIONS FOR ADULTS

Novel

> *One Happy Moment.*   Toronto, Copp Clark, 1951.

*   *   *

Louise Riley was a writer whose work was firmly grounded in the Canadian west. Her first book, *The Mystery Horse*, is set on a ranch near Calgary, Alberta. The story is a familiar one to readers of animal stories. 16-year-old Bob raises a stray horse, only to have mysterious strangers threaten to take it from him. In the end, the horse's mysterious origin is uncovered, and Bob is allowed to keep the animal. In spite of its hackneyed plot and dated dialogue, the book has some genuine moments of interest. Details of the sort of small-time ranch life now fast disappearing from the Western plains are well-integrated into the story. Bob's family is a close-knit one, with the character of the mother emerging as a strong force in this one-parent family. *The Mystery Horse* has long been out of print, but should the contemporary young reader find a copy, it would still fill demands for yet "another horse story."

Fantasy has not been a strong tradition in Canadian juvenile publishing. Miss Riley's book *Train for Tiger Lily* and its sequel *A Spell at Scoggin's Crossing* were two of the earliest. Both have trains as the setting for the adventures. Both Tiger Lily and Scoggin's Crossing are imaginary stops on the transcontinental railroad line that spans the Canadian shores. The stops can only be reached by the Second-Class magic of Gus, the Negro porter on the train. When a family of five children find themselves the only passengers on the train upon its arrival at these stops, they become involved with a series of strange characters and magical situations. It is significant that Miss Riley chose the train as the means of transportation into her fantasy world. Prairie children are very familiar with long lines of railroad cars snaking across their wide landscapes. How many dreams of unfamiliar places and strange characters must pervade their dreams and fantasies!

The weakness of Miss Riley's work is not in the quality of imagination she employs but in her failure to weld together the elements of magic and reality into that believable whole that is the mark of good fantasy. Her ability to develop characterization that is both appropriate to the story and believable to the reader is evident in all her books. The descriptive and narrative passages in her books tend to display her uneven style.

—Callie Israel

ROBERTS, Charles G(eorge) D(ouglas). Canadian. Born in Douglas, New Brunswick, 10 January 1860. Educated at Collegiate School, Fredericton, New Brunswick, 1874–76; University of New Brunswick, Fredericton (Douglas Medal in Latin and Greek, Alumni Gold Medal for Latin Essay), B.A. (honours) in mental and moral science and political economy 1879, M.A. 1881. Served in the British Army, 1914–15; Captain; transferred to the Canadian Army, 1916; Major; subsequently worked with Lord Beaverbrook on the Canadian War Records. Married Mary Isabel Fenety in 1880 (died, 1930), three sons, one daughter; Joan Montgomery, 1943. Headmaster, Chatham Grammar School, New Brunswick, 1879–81, and York Street School, Fredericton, 1881–83; Editor, *This Week*, Toronto, 1883–84; Professor of English and French, 1885–88, and Professor of English and Economics, 1888–95, King's College, Windsor, Nova Scotia; Associate Editor, *The Illustrated American*, New York, 1897–98; Co-Editor, The Nineteenth Century series, 1900–05. Lived in England, 1911–25. Recipient: Lorne Pierce Medal, 1926. LL.D.: University of New Brunswick, 1906. Fellow, 1890, and President of Section II, 1933, Royal Society of Canada; Fellow, Royal Society of Literature, 1892; Member, National Institute of Arts and Letters, 1898. Knighted, 1935. *Died 26 November 1943.*

<small>PUBLICATIONS FOR CHILDREN</small>

Fiction

Around the Campfire, illustrated by Charles Copeland.   New York, Crowell, 1896; London, Harrap, 1906.

Earth's Enigmas: A Book of Animal and Nature Life, illustrated by C.L. Bull.   Boston, Lamson Wolffe, 1896; revised edition, Boston, Page, 1903; London, Duckworth, 1904.

The Raid from Beauséjour, and How the Carter Boys Lifted the Mortgage: Two Stories of Acadie.   New York, Hunt and Eaton, 1894; *The Raid from Beauséjour* published as *The Young Acadian*, Boston, Page, 1907.

Reube Dare's Shad Boat: A Tale of the Tide Country.   New York, Hunt and Eaton, 1895; as *The Cruise of the Yacht "Dido": A Tale of the Tide Country*, Boston, Page, 1906.

The Kindred of the Wild: A Book of Animal Life, illustrated by C.L. Bull.   Boston, Page, 1902; London, Duckworth, 1903.

The Watchers of the Trails: A Book of Animal Life, illustrated by C.L. Bull.   Boston, Page, and London, Duckworth, 1904.

Red Fox: The Story of His Adventurous Career in the Ringwaak Wilds, and of His Final Triumph over His Enemies, illustrated by C.L. Bull.   Boston, Page, and London, Duckworth, 1905.

The Haunters of the Silences: A Book of Animal Life, illustrated by C.L. Bull.   Boston, Page, and London, Duckworth, 1907.

In the Deep of the Snow, illustrated by Deaman Fink.   New York, Crowell, 1907.

The House in the Water: A Book of Animal Life, illustrated by C.L. Bull and F.U. Smith.   Boston, Page, 1908; London, Ward Lock, 1909.

The Backwoodsmen.   New York, Macmillan, and London, Ward Lock, 1909.

Kings in Exile, illustrated by Paul Bransom and C.L. Bull.   London, Ward Lock, 1909; New York, Macmillan, 1910.

Neighbours Unknown, illustrated by Paul Bransom.   London, Ward Lock, 1910; New York, Macmillan, 1911.

More Kindred of the Wild, illustrated by Paul Bransom.   London, Ward Lock, and New York, Macmillan, 1911.

Babes of the Wild, illustrated by Paul Bransom.   London and New York, Cassell, 1912; as *Children of the Wild*, New York, Macmillan, 1913.

The Feet of the Furtive, illustrated by Paul Bransom.   London, Ward Lock, 1912; New York, Macmillan, 1913.

Hoof and Claw, illustrated by Paul Bransom.   London, Ward Lock, 1913; New York, Macmillan, 1914.

The Secret Trails, illustrated by Paul Bransom and Warwick Reynolds.   New York, Macmillan, and London, Ward Lock, 1916.

The Ledge on Bald Face, illustrated by Paul Bransom.   London, Ward Lock, 1918; as *Jim: The Story of a Backwoods Police Dog*, New York, Macmillan, 1919.

Wisdom of the Wilderness.   London, Dent, and New York, Dutton, 1922.

They Who Walk in the Wild, illustrated by C.L. Bull.   New York, Macmillan, 1924; as *They That Walk in the Wild*, London, Dent, 1924.

Eyes of the Wilderness, illustrated by Dorothy Burroughes.   New York, Macmillan, and London, Dent, 1933.

Further Animal Stories.   London, Dent, 1935.

Thirteen Bears, edited by Ethel Hume Bennett, illustrated by John A. Hall.   Toronto, Ryerson Press, 1947.

Forest Folk, edited by Ethel Hume Bennett, illustrated by John A. Hall.   Toronto, Ryerson Press, 1949.

King of Beasts and Other Stories, edited by Joseph Gold.   Toronto, Ryerson Press, 1967.

Other

> *A History of Canada for High Schools and Academies.*   Boston, Lamson Wolffe, 1897;
> London, Kegan Paul, 1898.

Fiction

> *The Forge in the Forest, Being the Narrative of the Acadian Ranger, Jean de
> Mer.*   Boston and London, Lamson Wolffe, 1896.
> *A Sister to Evangeline, Being the Story of Yvonne de Lamourie.*   Boston, Lamson
> Wolffe, 1898; London, Lane, 1900; as *Lovers in Acadie*, London, Dent, 1924.
> *The Heart of the Ancient Wood.*   New York, Silver Burdett, 1900; London, Methuen,
> 1902.
> *Barbara Ladd.*   Boston, Page, and London, Constable, 1902.
> *The Prisoner of Mademoiselle: A Love Story.*   Boston, Page, and London, Constable,
> 1904.
> *The Heart That Knows.*   Boston, Page, and London, Duckworth, 1906.
> *A Balkan Prince.*   London, Everett, 1913.

Short Stories

> *By the Marshes of Minas.*   New York, Silver Burdett, 1900.
> *The Red Oxen of Bonval.*   New York, Dodd Mead, 1908.
> *Cock Crow.*   New York, Federal Printers, 1913.
> *In the Morning of Time.*   London, Hutchinson, and New York, Stokes, 1919.
> *The Last Barrier and Other Stories.*   Toronto, McClelland and Stewart, 1958.

Verse

> *Orion and Other Poems.*   Philadelphia, Lippincott, 1880.
> *Later Poems.*   Fredericton, privately printed, 1881.
> *Later Poems.*   Fredericton, Crockett, 1882.
> *In Divers Tones.*   Boston, Lothrop, 1886.
> *Autotochthon.*   Windsor, Nova Scotia, privately printed, 1889.
> *Ave: An Ode for the Centenary of the Birth of P.B. Shelley, 4th August, 1792.*   Toronto,
> Williamson, 1892.
> *Songs of the Common Day, and Ave: An Ode for the Shelley Centenary.*   London,
> Longman, 1893.
> *The Book of the Native.*   Toronto, Copp Clark, and London, Lamson Wolffe, 1896.
> *New York Nocturnes and Other Poems.*   Boston and London, Lamson Wolffe, 1898.
> *Poems.*   New York, Silver Burdett, 1901; London, Constable, 1903.
> *The Book of the Rose.*   Boston, Page, 1903; London, R. Brimley Johnson, 1904.
> *Poems.*   Boston, Page, 1907.
> *New Poems.*   London, Constable, 1919.
> *The Sweet o' the Year and Other Poems.*   Toronto, Ryerson Press, 1925.
> *The Vagrant of Time.*   Toronto, Ryerson Press, 1927; revised edition, 1927.
> *Be Quiet Wind; Unsaid.*   Toronto, privately printed, 1929.
> *The Iceberg and Other Poems.*   Toronto, Ryerson Press, 1934.
> *Selected Poems.*   Toronto, Ryerson Press, 1936.
> *Twilight over Shaugamauk and Three Other Poems.*   Tornoto, Ryerson Press, 1937.
> *Canada Speaks of Britain and Other Poems of the War.*   Toronto, Ryerson Press, 1941.
> *Selected Poems*, edited by Desmond Pacey.   Toronto, Ryerson Press, 1956.
> *Poets of the Confederation*, with others, edited by Malcolm Mackenzie Ross.   Toronto,
> McClelland and Stewart, 1960.

Other

> The Canadian Guide-Book: The Tourist's and Sportsman's Guide to Eastern Canada and
>   Newfoundland.   New York, Appleton, 1891; London, Heinemann, 1892.
> The Land of Evangeline and the Gateways Thither ... for Sportsman and
>   Tourist.   Kentville, Nova Scotia, Dominion Atlantic Railway Company, 1894.
> , Discoveries and Explorations in the Century (nineteenth century series).   Philadelphia,
>   Linscott, 1904.
> Canada in Flanders, vol. 3.   London, Hodder and Stoughton, 1918.

> Editor, Poems of Wild Life.   London, Scott, 1888.
> Editor, Northland Lyrics, by William Carmon Roberts, Theodore Roberts, and Elizabeth
>   Roberts McDonald.   Boston, Small Maynard, 1899.
> Editor, Alastor and Adonais, by P.B. Shelley.   Boston, Silver Burdett, 1902.
> Editor, with Arthur L. Tunnell, A Standard Dictionary of Canadian Biography: The
>   Canadian Who Was Who.   Toronto, Trans-Canada Press, 2 vols., 1934, 1938.
> Editor, with Arthur L. Tunnell, The Canadian Who's Who, vols. II and III.   Toronto,
>   Trans-Canada Press, 1936, 1939.
> Editor, Flying Colours: An Anthology.   Toronto, Ryerson Press, 1942.

> Translator, The Canadians of Old, by Philippe Aubert de Gaspé.   New York, Appleton,
>   1890; as Cameron of Lochiel, Boston, Page, 1905.

Critical Study: Charles G.D. Roberts by William J. Keith, Toronto, Copp Clark, 1969.

*   *   *

Charles G.D. Roberts, one of the first three Canadians to be knighted (1935), probably received that honor because he was well known as a poet, possibly even deserving the title "father of Canadian poetry." In Ten Canadian Poets Desmond Pacey analyzes the achievement of Sir Charles solely as a poet, critically and with skill. But he makes no more than a passing note of what to me and to thousands of Sir Charles's readers at the end of the old century and the first of this was inescapable: Roberts stood head and shoulders above his few North American contemporaries, such as Ernest Thompson Seton, as a nature writer who made the wild animals, birds, fish, and even dragonflies of back-woods New Brunswick come alive on the printed page. He despised any anthropomorphic approach: fox was fox, lynx lynx, porcupine porcupine, bear bear, eagle eagle, grouse grouse, owl owl, a wise old trout a wise old trout. No nicknames; no concealing of nature's cruelty, the disaster of sub-zero weather or forest fire. He wrote the prose of a poet: color in his words, economy in style, drama in his action, rhythm in the wilderness life of hunter and hunted. Beyond all this, what set Sir Charles's stories apart was his unwavering respect for the dignity of life – the dignity of death – among these creatures of the wild.

Of his dozen books which gathered these stories together five or six stand out: Red Fox (a novel), The Kindred of the Wild, The Watchers of the Trails, The Haunters of the Silences, The Feet of the Furtive, Kings in Exile. The masterpiece is Red Fox, surely the one wild animal story in English to stand beside Henry Williamson's Tarka the Otter (the gem of them all) and Jack London's The Call of the Wild. But there is a purity about Red Fox, a spareness, a kind of breathlessness, isolation from human creatures, which it alone possesses. Are these books for children? They are for all ages, just as much as The Wind in the Willows, The Jungle Books, Hudson's Far Away and Long Ago, Sally Carrighar's One Day on Beetle Rock, H.M. Tomlinson's The Brown Owl.

Roberts was fortunate in his two illustrators: Charles Livingston Bull and Paul Bransom, and fortunate in his typographers too. The original books were (and remain) works of art to look at, a delight to handle. Could any child who has never paddled a canoe, camped in the wilderness, worn snowshoes, seen a raccoon fishing in a stream, or watched a dragonfly emerge from her private cellophane on a rock in the sun by a river fail to be enchanted by one of these books alone? I doubt it.

Let me close this tribute to Sir Charles by saying that three years on my uncle's ranch in the old frontier by the wild Rogue River in Oregon when I was 12 to 15 gave me a chance to verify some of the things I had read about earlier in *Red Fox* and the other books. Two short stories in *The Watchers of the Trails* – "The Little Wolf of the Pool" (about the larva of the dragonfly) and "The Little Wolf of the Air" (about the dragonfly itself) – have a timeless pure magic in their fascination for young readers; they bring the wilderness to one's back door. They have the very look of everlastingness.

Years later, when I began to write poems for children I, too, was fortunate in my illustrator. For the naturalist – artist Henry B. Kane had read Roberts when *he* was a boy. *Red Fox* had made me wish to try to become a writer. The illustrations by Charles Livingston Bull had made Mr. Kane wish to become an artist.

—David McCord

ROBERTS, Elizabeth Madox. American. Born in Perryville, Kentucky, 30 October 1886. Educated at Covington Institute, Springfield, Kentucky; Covington High School, Kentucky, 1886–1900; University of Chicago (Fisk Prize, 1921), 1917–21, Ph.B. in English 1921 (Phi Beta Kappa). Private tutor and teacher in public schools, 1900–10. Recipient: John Reed Memorial Prize (*Poetry*, Chicago) 1928. Member, National Institute of Arts and Letters, 1940. *Died 13 March 1941.*

PUBLICATIONS FOR CHILDREN

Verse

   Under the Tree. New York, Huebsch, 1922; London, Cape, 1928; revised edition, New York, Viking Press, 1930.

PUBLICATIONS FOR ADULTS

Novels

   The Time of Man. New York, Viking Press, 1926; London, Cape, 1927.
   My Heart and My Flesh. New York, Viking Press, 1927; London, Cape, 1928.
   Jingling in the Wind. New York, Viking Press, 1928; London, Cape, 1929.
   The Great Meadow. New York, Viking Press, and London, Cape, 1930.
   A Buried Treasure. New York, Viking Press, 1931; London, Cape, 1932.
   He Sent Forth a Raven. New York, Viking Press, and London, Cape, 1935.
   Black Is My Truelove's Hair. New York, Viking Press, 1938; London, Hale, 1939.

Short Stories

   The Haunted Mirror: Stories. New York, Viking Press, 1932; London, Cape, 1933.
   Not by Strange Gods: Stories. New York, Viking Press, 1941.

Verse

In the Great Steep's Garden: Poems.   Colorado Springs, Gowdy Simmons, 1915.
Song in the Meadow: Poems.   New York, Viking Press, 1940.

Critical Study: *Elizabeth Madox Roberts* by Frederick P.W. McDowell, New York, Twayne,
1963 (includes bibliography).

*   *   *

Elizabeth Madox Roberts, Kentucky-born novelist and poet who died in 1941, is best
remembered for two of her several distinguished novels: *The Time of Man* (1926) and *The
Great Meadow* (1930). In 1940 she published an uneven book of poems called *Song in the
Meadow*. But way back in 1922 she had already produced her one undoubted masterpiece: a
gentle, quiet book of verse for children, called very gently and quietly *Under the Tree*. It was
revised and reissued in 1930 with enchanting illustrations by F. D. Bedford. Any discussion
of her merit as a writer for children centers entirely on this collection, even though three or
four of the poems included in the early part of *Song in the Meadow* sound like worthy echoes
from the 1922 volume. And very clear as well as worthy echoes too.

So what does one say of this undiminished book, still in print in hard cover? It should, of
course, be available also in soft cover. For Elizabeth Madox Roberts, without question,
remains absolutely unique in the field of verse for children. To me she is the only poet, man
or woman, writing in the English language who possessed and consistently used the
undisguised, uninterrupted voice of childhood. Excepting Emily Dickinson, not Blake, nor
Lear, Carroll, Stevenson, Eugene Field, Christina Rossetti, Laura E. Richards, Eleanor
Farjeon, Milne, Eve Merriam, Norma Farber, Marchette Chute, Aileen Fisher, Myra Cohn
Livingston, Reeves, or Serraillier — no one who wrote or writes poems for children
commanded or commands, as she did, not only the vocabulary but the attitude and voice-
inflection of a small girl lost in wonder:

> A little light is going by.
> Is going up to see the sky.
> A little light with wings.
>
> I never could have thought of it.
> To have a little bug all lit
> And made to go on wings.

She was born to notice things and actions. The world implied, and she was ready to infer.
When her small brother Clarence begins his country school days, what does she do?

> We climb up on the fence and gate
> And watch until he's small and dim,
> Far up the street, and he looks back
> To see if we keep on watching him.

The average post-Georgian poet, I think, would have said, "To see if we keep watching him,"
omitting the "on." But not a child; not Miss Roberts; not a poet of her special genius. Could
the Greek and Latin poets with their gift for onomatopoeia manage to describe the unexisting
sound of a silent vanishing dirt Kentucky road as she does here?

> The road was going on and on
> Beyond to reach some other place ....

Or look back into all the brook poetry you can think of, including Tennyson and Robert
Frost, and try to match the flawless order of these first three lines of the fourth and last stanza

of "The Branch," so settled in their utter calm that in the fourth line not one syllable and certainly not the magic of the perfect adjective "rough" will escape you:

> And where it is smooth there is moss on a stone.
> And where it is shallow and almost dry
> The rocks are broken and hot in the sun,
> And a rough little water goes hurrying by.

Two other things. In the total assembly of poems about Christmas, save for Thomas Hardy's "The Oxen," I can think of none to equal Miss Roberts' "Christmas Morning" – her wondrous imaginary visit to Bethlehem. Length forbids quoting all ten stanzas. Here is the last one:

> While Mary put the blankets back
> The gentle talk would soon begin.
> And when I'd tiptoe softly out
> I'd meet the wise men going in.

Twice in the course of the fifty-nine poems in *Under the Tree* there appears a certain small boy named with a certain not-quite-hidden tone of secret admiration. He's not called Tiny Tim or Huckleberry Finn or Christopher Robin. He has the far more romantic handle of Joe B. Kirk. Through many rereadings of this book I have often wondered about him: did he live to grow up? and what has he done with his life? His one big moment in the poems is in (or at) "The Picnic" when Miss Kate-Marie, the Sunday school teacher, kisses all the children. How marvellous, how real, how visible is Joe B. Kirk's reaction:

> She kissed us all and Joe B. Kirk;
> But Joe B. didn't mind a bit.
> He walked around and swung his arms
> And seemed to be very glad of it.

Among my personal desert island books – *Far Away and Long Ago, Come Hither, The Sea and the Jungle, The Country of the Pointed Firs, The Oregon Trail, The Tempest, My Antonia, Moby Dick*, all of Max Beerbohm, *Walden*, Emerson's *Essays*, *The Crock of Gold, Delight, The Mirror of the Sea*, and *Peer Gynt* – I include a copy of *Under the Tree* to go with *The Wind in the Willows*.

—David McCord

ROBERTSON, Keith (Carlton). American. Born in Dows, Iowa, 9 May 1914. Educated at the United States Naval Academy, Annapolis, Maryland, B.S. 1937. Served in the United States Navy: radioman on a battleship, 1930–33; officer, on destroyers, 1941–45; Captain, United States Naval Reserve. Married Elisabeth Hexter in 1946; has two daughters and one son. Refrigeration engineer, 1937–41; worked for a publisher, 1945–47; free-lance writer, 1947–58; President, Bay Ridge Speciality Co. Inc., ceramics manufacturer, Trenton, New Jersey. Address: c/o Viking Press, 625 Madison Avenue, New York, New York 10022, U.S.A.

PUBLICATIONS FOR CHILDREN

Fiction

Ticktock and Jim, illustrated by Wesley Dennis. Philadelphia, Winston, 1948; as *Watch for a Pony*, London, Heinemann, 1949.

Ticktock and Jim, Deputy Sheriffs, illustrated by Everett Stahl.   Philadelphia, Winston, 1949.

The Dog Next Door, illustrated by Morgan Dennis.   New York, Viking Press, 1950.

The Missing Brother, illustrated by Rafaello Busoni.   New York, Viking Press, 1950; London, Faber, 1952.

The Lonesome Sorrel, illustrated by Taylor Oughton.   Philadelphia, Winston, 1952.

The Mystery of Burnt Hill, illustrated by Rafaello Busoni.   New York, Viking Press, 1952.

Mascot of the Melroy, illustrated by Jack Weaver.   New York, Viking Press, 1953.

Outlaws of the Sourland, illustrated by Isami Kashiwagi.   New York, Viking Press, 1953.

Three Stuffed Owls, illustrated by Jack Weaver.   New York, Viking Press, 1954.

The Wreck of the Saginaw, illustrated by Jack Weaver.   New York, Viking Press, 1954.

Ice to India, illustrated by Jack Weaver.   New York, Viking Press, 1955.

The Phantom Rider, illustrated by Jack Weaver.   New York, Viking Press, 1955.

The Pilgrim Goose, illustrated by Erick Berry.   New York, Viking Press, 1956.

The Pinto Deer, illustrated by Isami Kashiwagi.   New York, Viking Press, 1956.

The Crow and the Castle, illustrated by Robert Grenier.   New York, Viking Press, 1957.

Henry Reed, Inc., illustrated by Robert McCloskey.   New York, Viking Press, 1958.

If Wishes Were Horses, illustrated by Paul Kennedy.   New York, Harper, 1958.

Henry Reed's Journey [Baby-Sitting Service, Big Show], illustrated by Robert McCloskey.   New York, Viking Press, 3 vols., 1963–70.

The Year of the Jeep, illustrated by W.T. Mars.   New York, Viking Press, 1968.

The Money Machine, illustrated by George Porter.   New York, Viking Press, 1969.

In Search of a Sandhill Crane, illustrated by Richard Cuffari.   New York, Viking Press, 1973.

Tales of Myrtle the Turtle.   New York, Viking Press, 1974.

Other

The Navy: From Civilian to Sailor, illustrated by Charles Geer.   New York, Viking Press, 1958.

New Jersey.   New York, Coward McCann, 1969.

PUBLICATIONS FOR ADULTS (as Carlton Keith)

Novels

The Diamond-Studded Typewriter.   New York, Macmillan, 1958; London, Heinemann, 1960; as *Gem of a Murder*, New York, Dell, 1959.

Missing, Presumed Dead.   New York, Doubleday, 1961.

Rich Uncle.   New York, Doubleday, 1963; London, Hale, 1965.

The Hiding-Place.   New York, Doubleday, 1965; London, Hale, 1966.

The Crayfish Dinner.   New York, Doubleday, 1966; as *The Elusive Epicure*. London, Hale, 1968.

A Taste of Sangria.   New York, Doubleday, 1968; as *The Missing Book-keeper*. London, Hale, 1969.

*   *   *

Keith Robertson's boys are the natural descendants of Tom Sawyer and Penrod: bright, ambitious, inquisitive and inventive; never still for a moment; often in hot water but safely out again before there is serious cause for alarm. They are boys who never grow up, just as Tom Sawyer remains a boy forever. Not in the magical sense of Peter Pan's Never Never Land agelessness: simply because boyishness is their very essence.

Henry Reed always has some enterprise on hand; his world is divided between those who understand the necessity of rabbit-keeping and running small businesses having to do with earthworm culture, babysitting, or rodeo organization, and those of the older generation or even unsympathetic young people who object to such undertakings on trumped-up adult grounds such as trespass and game laws. All the Henry Reed books hang on some plot peg such as a babysitting agency (whose clients can only be described as fiendish), or a cross-country motor trip; but they are usually episodic and rambling: one harmless complication follows another, with never a dull moment spent on the boring business of life as most of us live it. No one could wish that Henry's sunny existence should change in any particular; he's such a contented young man it does one's heart good to meet him even in print.

Robertson's alternate heroes, the young Carson Street Detectives Neil and Swede, are, like Henry Reed, model American boys of about 1950 vintage, clean-cut, wholesome, bright young fellows with short haircuts who would do credit to any senior Boy Scout Troop. It is a restful pleasure to encounter these uncomplicated kids, after struggling through various tomes dealing with the tortured life and psyche of the typical mixed-up young hero of today's often harrowing fiction for children.

Henry, Neil and Swede are not milksops; they encounter more adventures in a chapter than most of us do in a lifetime: but they are untroubled by problems beyond their power to solve. Their temporary difficulties may be complex in the extreme, but they *always* come out all right in the end: Mom is usually busy whipping up a batch of pies, and Dad has never yet failed to come through in a pinch. This is the mythical middle-America upon which nostalgia for a golden past is built. Home was never like this – but how nice if it had been! No wonder young readers enjoy the adventures of Henry Reed and the Carson Street Detectives. They leave you feeling that it isn't such a bad old world after all. An uncommonly pleasant sensation.

—Joan McGrath

ROBINSON, Joan (Mary) G(ale).   British. Born in Gerrard's Cross, Buckinghamshire. Educated privately and at Chelsea Illustrators' Studio, London. Married Richard Gavin Robinson in 1941; has two daughters. Address: The Unicorn House, Burnham Market, King's Lynn, Norfolk, England.

PUBLICATIONS FOR CHILDREN (illustrated by the author)

Fiction

My Book about Christmas (as Joan Gale Thomas).   London, Mowbray, 1946; New York, Morehouse, 1947.
My Garden Book (as Joan Gale Thomas).   London, Mowbray, 1947.
Debbie Robbie's Day Nursery.   London, University of London Press, 1950.
Susie at Home.   London, Harrap, 1953.
Teddy Robinson.   London, Harrap, 1953.
More about Teddy Robinson.   London, Harrap, 1954.
Teddy Robinson's Book.   London, Harrap, 1955.
Dear Teddy Robinson.   London, Harrap, 1956.
Mary-Mary.   London, Harrap, 1957.
Teddy Robinson Himself.   London, Harrap, 1957.

More Mary-Mary. London, Harrap, 1958.
Another Teddy Robinson. London, Harrap, 1960.
Madam Mary-Mary. London, Harrap, 1960.
Keeping Up with Teddy Robinson. London, Harrap, 1964.
Mary-Mary Stories (from *Mary-Mary, More Mary-Mary, Madam Mary-Mary*). London, Harrap, 1965; New York, Coward McCann, 1968.
When Marnie Was There, illustrated by Peggy Fortnum. London, Collins, 1967; New York, Coward McCann, 1968.
Charley, illustrated by Prudence Seward. London, Collins, 1969; New York, Coward McCann, 1970.
The House in the Square, illustrated by Shirley Hughes. London, Collins, 1972.
The Summer Surprise, illustrated by Glenys Ambrus. London, Collins, 1977.

Verse (as Joan Gale Thomas)

A Stands for Angel. London, Mowbray, 1939; as *A Is for Angel,* New York, Lothrop, 1953.
Our Father. London, Mowbray, 1940; New York, Lothrop, 1952.
If Jesus Came to My House. London, Mowbray, 1941; New York, Lothrop, 1951.
God of All Things. London, Mowbray, 1948.
One Little Baby. London, Mowbray, 1950; New York, Lothrop, 1956.
Little Angels. London, Mowbray, 1951.
The Happy Year. London, Mowbray, 1953.
If I'd Been Born in Bethlehem. London, Mowbray, 1953; New York, Lothrop, 1954.
I Ask a Blessing. London, Mowbray, 1955.
Where Is God? London, Mowbray, 1957; New York, Lothrop, 1959.
The Christmas Angel. London, Mowbray, 1961.
Seven Days. London, Mowbray, 1964.

Other

Monsieur Charbon, défense de fumer (reader), with Gale Young, illustrated by Dick Robinson. London, Harrap, 1962.

Illustrator: *Tales of Betsy-May* by Enid Blyton, 1940; *The Dip Bucket,* 1941, *Lift Up the Latch,* 1942, *When the Fire Burns Blue,* 1944, and *Shadows on the Stairs,* 1946, all by Dorothy Ann Lovell; *Beryl's Wonderful Week* by Madeleine Collier, 1944; *Janey,* 1953, and *Janey and Her Friends,* 1953, by Irene Pearl; *Jonathan on the Farm,* 1954, and *Jonathan and Felicity,* 1955, by Mary Cockett; *The House under the Tree,* 1954, and *The House in Hyde Park,* 1956, by Jennifer Ford; *The Carol Book,* 1959.

Joan G. Robinson comments:
I write slowly and laboriously, always hoping to achieve that final "spontaneity and simplicity" that I remember once being credited with in some review. I try to write from a child's-eye-view without going down on all fours; to entertain not only the child but, in stories for younger children, the patient adult reading aloud – but never at the child's expense.
The Joan Gale Thomas books stemmed from originally designing Christmas cards for Mowbrays, and then as material to illustrate.
The longer books for older children came as a welcome escape from the strict discipline of vocabulary and subject matter which governs the earlier books. These longer books were also an opportunity to write about the loner, the odd one out, the not-so-jolly – though not entirely without humour, I hope. This writing, too, proved to have its own discipline.

*   *   *

Joan G. Robinson has written many well-crafted tales for the very young, including the Teddy Robinson and the slightly more sophisticated Mary-Mary series. Teddy Robinson the Bear, humorous, with make-believe but no magic, must have entered much family folklore. Nevertheless, her three novels for older children, *When Marnie Was There*, *Charley*, and *The House in the Square*, have really established her serious reputation.

All these books are realised through a lonely, sensitive girl in a strange place, the loner, non-joiner, reticent and perforce ungiving, who "spoils everything," wanting both too little and too much, painfully enduring the dreamy poetry of growing up. One gets a direct feel of the child's day, the moments of wanting to be injured and misunderstood, the vindictive retorts stored up for defence, the puzzled resentment when only others get invited to the party, the expectation of disappointment. There is a sense of firelit rooms with a single mute figure in the dark outside, or a solitary mysterious human shadow at a high window. But also the joys of sudden acceptance in a big, cheerful family or of unexpected intimacies with a stranger, glamorous, strangely sympathetic, who may become the legendary, elusive "best friend." Happiness exists, even if too often beyond reach. Life and people are exciting but unreliable. Mrs. Robinson's careful observation often contains a drop of fantasy, a hint of fairy-tale glimmering amongst solid adventure, practical problems, the quarrels and thoughtlessness. Sudden betrayals can crack the world. An adopted child is shocked to discover that foster-parents are paid to love, that generous friendly adults can cheat and lie. The novels have strong awareness of place: wide Norfolk landscapes where creeks and marshes lie silent but alive, and a windmill is uncannily stark against the sky: and a London of tall soundless houses, empty gardens, statues that sometimes seem to breathe.

—Peter Vansittart

RODGERS, Mary. American. Born in New York City, 11 January 1931; daughter of the composer Richard Rodgers. Educated at Brearley School, New York, graduated 1948; Mannes College of Music, New York, 1943–48; Wellesley College, Massachusetts, 1948–51. Married Julian B. Beaty, Jr., in 1951 (divorced, 1958), one son and two daughters; Henry Guettel, 1961, two sons. Script editor and assistant to the producer, New York Philharmonic Young People's Concerts, CBS-TV, 1957–71; script writer, Hunter College Little Orchestra Society, New York, 1958–59. Columnist ("Of Two Minds"), with Dorothy Rodgers, *McCalls* magazine, New York. Composer and lyricist. Recipient: *Book World* Festival award, 1972; Christopher Award, 1973, 1975. Agent: Shirley Bernstein, Paramuse Artists Inc., 1414 Avenue of the Americas, New York, New York 10019. Address: 115 Central Park West, New York, New York 10023, U.S.A.

PUBLICATIONS FOR CHILDREN

Fiction

The Rotten Book, illustrated by Steven Kellogg. New York, Harper, 1969.
Freaky Friday. New York, Harper, 1972; London, Hamish Hamilton, 1973.
A Billion for Boris. New York, Harper, 1974; London, Hamish Hamilton, 1975.

Plays

Davy Jones' Locker (for marionettes; music and lyrics only), book by Arthur Birnkrant and Waldo Salt (produced New York, 1959).

Three to Make Music, music by Linda Rodgers Melnick, lyrics by Rodgers (produced New York, 1959).
Pinocchio (for marionettes) (produced, New York, 1973).

Screenplay: Freaky Friday, 1977.

PUBLICATIONS FOR ADULTS

Other

A Word to the Wives, with Dorothy Rodgers.   New York, Knopf, 1970.

Music: **Plays** − Once upon a Mattress by Jay Thompson, Marshall Barer, and Dean Fuller, 1958; Hot Spot by Jack Weinstock and Willie Gilbert, 1963; Young Mark Twain, 1964; The Mad Show by Larry Siegel and Stan Hart, 1966; **Television** − Mary Martin Spectacular, 1959; Feathertop, 1961.

*   *   *

Humor is a scarce but precious commodity in the technological society of the 1970's. Mary Rodgers breathes laughter into the situations, the characters, and the language of her books.

A child's imagination runs rampant in The Rotten Book, as Simon thinks of ways of being naughty. Fantasy is superimposed on a realistic background in Freaky Friday and its sequel, A Billion for Boris. Annabel Andrews awakens to find she has the body of her mother, while the ordinary events of life transpire. She witnesses the washing machine overflowing, and she mistakenly identifies her boyfriend Boris' mother as a cleaning lady, but she also participates in the parent-teacher conference in which she herself is discussed. Near tragedy is averted in A Billion for Boris when the television set projects tomorrow's news: the soup suspected of botulism can be destroyed, and people are persuaded to divert their plans.

The characters themselves are hilarious. Boris' eccentric artist mother has no organizational or financial skills, and he has balanced her checkbook since his ninth year. The participants in the school conference are caricatures of every child's teacher. Teen-age Virginia has "theatrical aspirations, and correct grammar." Language and dialogue are wrought for their entertaining qualities. Even the dedication of the third book gives insight into the author's humor − "to my small sons, Adam and Alec, without whom I was finally able to finish it." According to the critic Betsy Wade, the author "appears to have a sharp ear for the particular tone adults use on children." Yet when the parents disagree about camp and a raincoat for Annabel, they use contemporary sophisticated adult expressions. The latter two books are narrated in the first person by 13 and then 14-year-old Annabel Andrews, and parentheses are used generously for asides directed to the reader.

Jane Langton notes in her review of Freaky Friday that "the pages rush by, right now in 1972, and it might all be happening in the apartment next door." The very incidents and phrases which make the books so specific will unfortunately also date them. Teen-age pranks go in and out of fashion, and burning kleenex in the toilet is now passe. The telephone ad "let your fingers do the walking" and reference to the noted criminal lawyer, F. Lee Bailey, will fall dead on the ears of the next reading generation. Even now "hi-fi" has been replaced by "tapes" and the "hoover" is rarely used to refer to the vacuum cleaner. Slang such as "zing one of those carts" and aluding to the "monthly excuse" will contribute to the eventual demise of the books except as representative of an era.

Nevertheless, the books are very popular. Alix Nelson, in the New York Times Book Review (24 November 1974), notes that A Billion for Boris "assumes an urban and sophisticated frame of reference on the part of the reader, and it evokes so much New York City local color (from the Village to 125th Street by way of Central Park West, Lord & Taylor and a walk-up on West 53rd) that it really is the perfect New York City book."

Mary Rodgers is the daughter of Richard Rodgers, and has composed children's musicals such as *Davy Jones' Locker, Young Mark Twain,* and *Pinocchio.*

—Karen Nelson Hoyle

ROOSE-EVANS, James. British. Born in London, 11 November 1927. Educated at St. Benet's Hall, Oxford, B.A. 1952, M.A. 1957. Served in the Royal Army Educational Corps, 1947–49. Artistic Director, Maddermarket Theatre, Norwich, 1954–55; Member of the Faculty, Juilliard School of Music, New York, 1955–56; Staff Member, Royal Academy of Dramatic Art, London, 1957–62. Founding Director, Hampstead Theatre Club, London, 1959–69. Since 1969, Founding Director, Stage Two Theatre Workshop, London. Children's book reviewer for *Financial Times* and *Hampstead and Highgate Express.* Agent: David Higham Associates, 5–8 Lower John Street, London W1R 4HA, England.

PUBLICATIONS FOR CHILDREN (illustrated by Brian Robb)

Fiction

The Adventures of Odd and Elsewhere. London, Deutsch, 1971.
The Secret of the Seven Bright Shiners. London, Deutsch, 1972.
Odd and the Great Bear. London, Deutsch, 1973.
Elsewhere and the Gathering of the Clowns. London, Deutsch, 1974.
The Return of the Great Bear. London, Deutsch, 1975.
The Secret of Tippity-Witchit. London, Deutsch, 1975.
The Lost Treasure of Wales. London, Deutsch, 1977.

PUBLICATIONS FOR ADULTS

Plays

The Little Clay Cart, adaptation of a work by Henry Wells (produced London, 1964). London, Elek, 1965.

Radio Documentaries: *The Female Messiah,* 1975; *Acrobats of God,* 1976; *The Third Adam,* 1977; *Your Isadora,* 1977; *Topsy and Ted* (play), 1977.

Other

Directing a Play: James Roose-Evans on the Art of Directing and Acting. London, Studio Vista, and New York, Theatre Arts, 1968.
Experimental Theatre from Stanislavsky to Today. London, Studio Vista, and New York, Universe Books, 1970; revised edition, Studio Vista, 1973.
London Theatre: From the Globe to the National. London, Phaidon Press, and New York, Dutton, 1977.

Theatrical Activities:
Director: **Plays** – at the Maddermarket Theatre, Norwich, 1954–55, and the Belgrade Theatre, Coventry, 1957–59; *Nothing to Declare,* on tour, 1959; Pitlochry Festival (6 plays), 1960; *The Dumb Waiter* by Harold Pinter, London, 1960; *Under Milk Wood* by Dylan Thomas, London, 1961; at the Hampstead Theatre Club, London: *The Seagull* by

Chekhov, 1962, *In at the Kill* by Frederick Bradnum, *Private Lives* by Noël Coward, *The Square* by Marguerite Duras, *Cider with Rosie* by Laurie Lee, and *The Singing Dolphin* by Beverley Cross, 1963, *The Cloud* and *The Tower* by Barry Bermange, *The Little Clay Cart, The Corn Is Green* by Emlyn Williams, and *He Who Gets Slapped* by Leonid Andreyev. 1964, *Hippolytus* by Andrew Sinclair from a book by Dylan Thomas, *Flashing into the Dark*, and *Letters from an Eastern Front*, 1966, *Country Dance* by James Kennaway, *The Happy Apple* by Jack Pulman, *Nathan and Tabileth, and Oldenberg* by Barry Bermange, and *The Two Character Play* by Tennessee Williams, 1967, *Spitting Image* by Colin Spencer, 1968; *An Ideal Husband* by Wilde, London, 1965; *The Happy Apple* by Jack Pulman, London, 1967; *Chester Mystery Plays*, Chester, 1973; *The Taming of the Shrew*, London, 1974; *A Streetcar Named Desire* by Tennessee Williams, South Africa tour, *The Vortex* and *Fallen Angels*, both by Noel Coward, 1975; *Romeo and Juliet*, London, 1976; and others.

* * *

The seven Odd and Elsewhere stories are conceived by James Roose-Evans as a single saga, though they can all be read separately. During their adventures Odd, the teddy-bear, and Elsewhere, the toy clown, achieve a sense of their own identity, an understanding of responsibility and a purpose in life; in short, they begin to grow up. But as this process involves some muscular adventure, a good deal of humour, and a constant awareness of the joy of discovery — the reader may learn about, among other things, the National Trust, butterflies, Grimaldi, bee-keeping and even a few words of Welsh — there is little danger of solemnity overwhelming the narrative. This is not to say that there are no serious moments; the Great Bear and the King of the Clowns, the respective mentors of Odd and Elsewhere, have much to teach, but the author manages to avoid a patronizing tone, even when the occasional "moral" creeps in.

James Roose-Evans has spent much of his working life in the theatre, and he is especially good at describing the excitement and anguish of public performance, a constant theme. Circuses and Arthurian myth, liberally modified, have provided inspiration for his stories — all of which are set in Fenton House, Hampstead, and Wales — but the main thread is the traditional one of the defeat of Evil by Good. The methods, though, are often unusual. Butterflies, birds and bees, at different times, all play a crucial part in rescuing the heroes and their friends, and this reflects the general delight in Nature that informs the books.

The small bear and his friend begin as toys (Odd even loses an arm which is repaired in the first book), but they progress to being a real bear and a real clown and are sometimes indistinguishable from small boys who bleed when cut and experience shock, humiliation and triumph. To an adult this may seem a fault, but Roose-Evans claims the device is a deliberate reflection of the way children identify with their toys.

Despite a few other infelicities — the out-of-place grotesquerie of Mr. Goodman and Arbuthnot on their first appearance, the killing off of enemies without regret, and the almost invariable consigning of females to kitchens — these books have a pace and inventiveness, a feeling for language and an appreciation of lovable eccentricity that will make them delightful companions to generations of children.

Incidentally, Roose-Evans is well served by his illustrator, Brian Robb, who captures the tone exactly.

—Heather Neill

ROSS, Diana. British. Born in Valetta, Malta, 8 July 1910. Educated at Kensington High School, London; Girton College, Cambridge, B.A. (honours) in history 1931; Central School of Art, London, 1932–34. Married Antony Denney in 1939 (divorced, 1948); has twin daughters and one son. Art teacher, 1930–34. Address: Minster House, Shaw, Milksham, Wiltshire, England.

PUBLICATIONS FOR CHILDREN

Fiction

> *The Story of the Beetle Who Lived Alone*, illustrated by Margaret Kaye.   London, Faber, 1941.
> *Uncle Anty's Album*, with Antony Denney.   London, Faber, 1942.
> *The Golden Hen and Other Stories*, illustrated by Gri.   London, Faber, 1942.
> *The Little Red Engine Gets a Name*, illustrated by Lewitt and Him.   London, Faber, 1942.
> *The Wild Cherry*, illustrated by Gri.   London, Faber, 1943.
> *Nursery Tales*, illustrated by Nancy Innes.   London, Faber, 1944.
> *The Story of the Little Red Engine*, illustrated by Leslie Wood.   London, Faber, 1945.
> *The Story of Louisa*, illustrated by Margaret Kaye.   London, Penguin, 1945.
> *The Little Red Engine Goes to Market [Goes to Town, Goes Travelling, and the Rocket, Goes Home, Goes to Be Mended, and the Taddlecombe Outing, Goes Carolling]*, illustrated by Leslie Wood.   London, Faber, 8 vols., 1946–71.
> *Whoo, Whoo, the Wind Blew*, illustrated by Leslie Wood.   London, Faber, 1946.
> *The Tooter and Other Nursery Tales*, illustrated by Irene Hawkins.   London, Faber, 1951.
> *The Enormous Apple Pie and Other Miss Pussy Tales*, illustrated by Peggy Fortnum.   London, Lutterworth Press, 1951.
> *Ebenezer the Big Balloon*, illustrated by Leslie Wood.   London, Faber, 1952.
> *The Bridal Gown and Other Stories*, illustrated by Gri.   London, Faber, 1952.
> *The Bran Tub*, illustrated by Gri.   London, Lutterworth Press, 1954.
> *William and the Lorry*, illustrated by Shirley Hughes.   London, Faber, 1956.
> *Child of Air*, illustrated by Gri.   London, Lutterworth Press, 1957.
> *The Dreadful Boy*, illustrated by Prudence Seward.   London, Hamish Hamilton, 1959.
> *The Merry-Go-Round*, illustrated by Shirley Hughes.   London, Lutterworth Press, 1963.
> *Old Perisher*, illustrated by Edward Ardizzone.   London, Faber, 1965.
> *Nothing to Do*, illustrated by Constance Marshall.   London, Hamish Hamilton, 1966.
> *I Love My Love with an A: Where Is He?*, illustrated by Leslie Wood.   London, Faber, 1972.

Other

> *The World at Work (Getting You Things, Making You Things)*.   London, Country Life, 2 vols., 1939.

Diana Ross comments:

I always told stories from early childhood to my brother and sister. I began to write down my stories when I was teaching – to start the class off, I read my stories then they read theirs. The Red Engine series began as a goodnight story for my nephew John Scott who lived in a house above a railway cutting on a very branch line. Most of the nursery tale and "true" type of story were based on incidents from family life. The ones I have most enjoyed writing have been the fairy stories written for myself – and most of all the Miss Pussy and old Jackanapes stories. Gri – who illustrated some of my books when I could persuade publishers of his merits – was in fact my cat who would sit on top of my drawings as I worked on them.

*   *   *

Diana Ross writes two kinds of stories: nursery tales for very young children and magical tales for anyone who enjoys the fiction of fairyland. She has produced both kinds concurrently over a period spanning more than 30 years. Her writing draws inspiration from knowledge and love of country matters. It also owes much to her artistic training – as Gri she illustrated many of her own books. Pleasure in her family circle is a third, formative influence.

When she was a child, Diana Ross told stories to her brother and sister. Later, as teacher, mother, aunt and grandmother, she went on telling them. And this first-hand awareness of small children *listening* to stories like *Whoo, Whoo, the Wind Blew*, shaped her style. Her nursery tales make constant use of repetition, alliteration, and the cumulative tricks that delight small children. She does not waste words. At the same time, there is a great deal of accurately observed detail – the kind that educates as well as entertains. *Ebeneezer the Big Balloon* is a good example. It was no accident that BBC producers seized on her work. The 1950's was a time of expansion in children's radio and television, and Diana Ross was a pioneer contributor.

She helped to develop a new kind of nursery realism – what she herself calls coat-and-gumboot stories about ordinary children doing ordinary things, like 4-year-old Johnny in "The Tooter." She was also one of the first to explore a new kind of hero. As anthropomorphic as Pooh and Piglet, the Little Red Engine was no longer a privileged middle-class, cuddly toy. He was a worker serving the whole community, in tune with the classless, mechanised society of post-war England. It is worth noting here that the first Little Red Engine story was published four years before the Reverend Awdry's first railway book came into print.

The Miss Pussy stories are her most interesting fairytales, written as much for her own pleasure as to entertain her readers. The language and unusual use of the present tense is often very sophisticated. Miss Pussy is a feline Miss Matty in another *Cranford*. Old Tom Cat is her Captain Brown. But in their village there is an adversary – Jackanapes. And magic is an everyday occurrence. There is much quiet wisdom buried in these romantic tales. Diana Ross writes mockingly but you sense her underlying compassion. She understands human frailty and even makes it appear endearing. In a moment of stress, Miss Pussy considers her ambivalent feelings for Jackanapes, lying sick and sorry for himself in his sleazy lodgings. "Perhaps," she thinks, "in the pattern of our lives we need the bad as much as the good. There is no sun without shadow, and I am as much in debt to Jackanapes for the tricks he has played upon me as perhaps I am to another for the good they have done me." Not to everybody's taste, but rare meat for a connoisseur.

—Joy Whitby

ROUNDS, Glen (Harold). American. Born near Wall, South Dakota, 4 April 1906. Educated at Kansas City Art Institute, 1926–27; Art Students' League, New York, 1930–31. Served in the United States Army Coast Artillery and Infantry, 1942–45; Staff Sergeant. Married Margaret Olmsted in 1938 (died, 1968); has one son. Worked as a cowboy, baker, sign painter, textile designer; full-time writer since 1936. Recipient: American Association of University Women award, 1961, 1967. Address: Box 763, Southern Pines, North Carolina, U.S.A.

PUBLICATIONS FOR CHILDREN (illustrated by the author)

Fiction

    Lumber Camp.   New York, Holiday House, 1937; as *The Whistle Punk of Camp 15*, 1959.
    Pay Dirt.   New York, Holiday House, 1938.
    The Blind Colt.   New York, Holiday House, 1941.
    Whitey's First Round-Up.   New York, Grosset and Dunlap, 1942.
    Whitey's Sunday Horse.   New York, Grosset and Dunlap, 1943.
    Whitey Looks for a Job.   New York, Holiday House, 1944.
    Whitey and Jinglebob.   New York, Grosset and Dunlap, 1946.
    Stolen Pony.   New York, Holiday House, 1948; revised edition, 1969.
    Whitey and the Rustlers.   New York, Holiday House, 1951.
    Hunted Horses.   New York, Holiday House, 1951.
    Whitey and the Blizzard.   New York, Holiday House, 1952.
    Buffalo Harvest.   New York, Holiday House, 1952.
    Lone Muskrat.   New York, Holiday House, 1953.
    Whitey Takes a Trip.   New York, Holiday House, 1954.
    Whitey Ropes and Rides.   New York, Holiday House, 1956.
    Whitey and the Wild Horse.   New York, Holiday House, 1958.
    Wild Orphan.   New York, Holiday House, 1961.
    Whitey and the Colt-Killer.   New York, Holiday House, 1962.
    Whitey's New Saddle.   New York, Holiday House, 1963.
    Once We Had a Horse.   New York, Holiday House, 1971.
    The Day the Circus Came to Lonetree.   New York, Holiday House, 1973.
    Mr. Yowder and the Lion Roar Capsules.   New York, Holiday House, 1976.
    Mr. Yowder and the Steamboat.   New York, Holiday House, 1977.

Plays

    Radio Scripts: *School of the Air*, 1938–39.

Other

    Ol' Paul, The Mighty Logger.   New York, Holiday House, 1936; revised edition, 1949, 1976.
    Rodeo: Bulls, Broncos, and Buckaroos.   New York, Holiday House, 1949.
    Swamp Life: An Almanac.   Englewood Cliffs, New Jersey, Prentice Hall, 1957.
    Wildlife at Your Doorstep: An Illustrated Almanac.   Englewood Cliffs, New Jersey, Prentice Hall, 1958.
    Beaver Business: An Almanac.   Englewood Cliffs, New Jersey, Prentice Hall, 1960.
    Rain in the Woods and Other Small Matters.   Cleveland, World, 1964.
    The Snake Tree.   Cleveland, World, 1966.
    The Treeless Plains.   New York, Holiday House, 1967.
    The Prairie Schooners.   New York, Holiday House, 1968.
    Wild Horses of the Red Desert.   New York, Holiday House, 1969.
    The Cowboy Trade.   New York, Holiday House, 1972.
    The Beaver: How He Works.   New York, Holiday House, 1976.

    Editor, *Trail Drive*, from *Log of a Cowboy*, by Andy Adams.   New York, Holiday House, 1965; London, Whiting and Wheaton, 1966.
    Editor, *Mountain Men*, by George F. Ruxton.   New York, Holiday House, 1966.
    Editor, *The Boll Weevil.*   San Carlos, California, Golden Gate Books, 1967.
    Editor, *Casey Jones.*   San Carlos, California, Golden Gate Books, 1968.

Editor, *The Strawberry Roan*.   San Carlos, California, Golden Gate Books, 1970.
Editor, *Sweet Betsy from Pike*.   Chicago, Children's Press, 1973.

Illustrator: *Flipper, A Sea Lion* by Irma S. Black, 1940; *Tall Tale America* by Walter Blair, 1944; *"E" Company* by Frank O'Rourke, 1945; *Tatoosh* by Martha Hardy, 1947; *Uncle Swithin's Inventions* by Wheaton P. Webb, 1947; *Aesop's Fables*, 1949; *We Always Lie to Strangers*, 1951, *Who Blowed Up the Church House?*, 1952, *The Devil's Pretty Daughter*, 1955, *The Talking Turtle*, 1957, and *Sticks in the Knapsack*, 1958, all by Vance Randolph; *Grass, Our Greatest Crop* by Sarah J. Riedman, 1952; *Haunt Fox* by Jim Kjelgaard, 1954; *Those Glorious Mornings* by Paul Hyde Bonner, 1954; *Fire-Fly* by Paul M. Sears, 1956; *In the Arms of the Mountain* by Elizabeth Seeman, 1961; *A Wild Goose Tale*, 1961, *Dan and the Miranda*, 1962, *Big Blue Island*, 1964, *Mike's Toads*, 1970, *Squash Pie*, 1976, and *Down in the Boondocks*, 1977, all by Wilson Gage; *The Crocodile's Mouth*, 1966, and *American Tall Tale Animals*, 1968, by Adrien Stoutenberg; *Billy Boy* edited by Richard Chase, 1966; *How the People Sang the Mountains Up* by Maria Leach, 1967; *Lucky Ladybugs*, 1968, and *Tarantula, The Giant Spider*, 1972, by Gladys Conklin; *Contrary Jenkins* by Rebecca Caudill and James Ayars, 1969; *Folklore of the Great West* by John Greenway, 1969; *Ballads of the Great West* by Austin and Alta Fife, 1970; *Go Find Hanka!* by Alexander L. Crosby, 1970; *Farmer Hoo and the Baboons* by Ida Chittum, 1971; *A Twister of Twists: A Tangler of Tongues*, 1972, *Witcracks*, 1973, *Cross Your Fingers, Spit in Your Hat*, 1974, and *Kickle Snifters*, 1976, all edited by Alvin Schwartz; *I'm Going on a Bear Hunt* by Sandra S. Sivulich, 1973; *Tomfoolery*, 1973, and *Whoppers, Tall Tales, and Other Lies*, 1975, by Alvin Schwartz; *Jennie Jenkins* by Mark Taylor, 1975; *3 Fools and a Horse* by Betty Baker, 1975; *Lizard in the Sun*, 1975, *The Happy Dromedary*, 1976, and *Little Bear Goes for a Walk*, 1977, all by Berniece Freschet; *Tony, Granny and George* by Robbie Branscum, 1976.

*   *   *

Glen Rounds specializes in subject matter with which he is completely acquainted, and expresses himself distinctively. The occupations, regions, and tall tales which he describes are written authoritatively. For a number of years, the author "drifted" around the country, and was hired for a myriad of jobs. His book *Pay Dirt* tells of mining, while *Lumber Camp* focuses on lumbering, and several books depict aspects of the life of a cowboy. *The Cowboy Trade*, in contrast to glamorous versions of life in the west, is authentic, based in part on his childhood.

Rounds' realistic books are invariably set in two regions – the plains, particularly a ranch near Ekalaka, Montana, and near Southern Pines, North Carolina. His eleven Whitey books are reminiscent of his relationship with the cowboys on his father's ranch. *The Treeless Plains* is based on homesteaders' memories and his return to the territory as an adult. Even his single book about the American Indian, *Buffalo Harvest*, limits itself to the tribe in his area.

Wildlife is treated with keen observation and sensitivity, and an authenticity based on hours spent on an abandoned farm and a swamp in North Carolina. While *Wild Orphan* is a documentary of the first year of a beaver kit whose parents fell prey to traps, *Lone Muskrat* follows an aging animal. *Rain in the Woods and Other Small Matters* is more ecological, describing inter-relationships of flora and fauna.

While most of his books are realistic, the tall tales of his first book, *Ol' Paul*, come from Rounds' imagination, for the Paul Bunyan character was a device created for a lumber company's advertising campaign. The author is a good listener, and weaves anecdotes in his humorous books such as *The Day the Circus Came to Lonetree* and *Mr. Yowder and the Lion Roar Capsules*.

Rounds writes succinctly, but effectively. Like a cowboy who must minimize his motions to save energy, the author is a master at economy of words. *Wild Horses of the Red Desert* opens with the sentence, "The Red Desert is a barren land of high rocky ridges and dusty sagebrush flats, where men seldom go." He uses the vernacular in the dialogue of his characters. Whitey wanted the "purtiest" colt on the ranch for his "Sunday" horse. In *Lumber Camp*, a paragraph in the chapter, "Whiffler" reads, "Right away a gangling swamper by the name of Shikepoke spoke up. 'Reckon thet's a Sidehill Whiffler, Bub,' he said. 'They's quite a lot of 'em round right now. Yuh wanta be on the lookout for 'em.' " His robust folk humor is evident in the tall tales, but also in the dialogue of the characters. Because his books have a simple and direct approach, they are read by 7 to 10-year-old children, while adolescents needing "high interest low vocabulary" books also read them. Reviewers inevitably remind the adult that Rounds' ecology books such as *The Snake Tree* and books about the west should not be relegated only to the child's shelf.

—Karen Nelson Hoyle

RUSH, Philip. British. Born in Palmers Green, London, 24 February 1908. Educated at Southgate Grammar School; London School of Economics. Married Geraldine Rush in 1931; has one son and two daughters. Local Government Officer, East Ham, London, 1930–63; Chief Inspector of Weights and Measures, East Ham, 1963–65, and Borough of Bexley, London, 1965–68. Address: 45 Castle Street, Canterbury, Kent CT1 2PY, England.

PUBLICATIONS FOR CHILDREN

Fiction

> *He Sailed with Dampier*, illustrated by Richard Ogle. London and New York, Boardman, 1947.
> *A Cage of Falcons*, illustrated by Serena Chance. London, Collins, 1954.
> *Queen's Treason*, illustrated by F. Partridge. London, Collins, 1955.
> *The Minstrel Knight*, illustrated by Martin Thomas. London, Collins, 1955; Indianapolis, Bobbs Merrill, 1956.
> *King of the Castle*, illustrated by Martin Thomas. London, Collins, 1956.
> *Red Man's Country*, illustrated by Brian Keogh. London, Collins, 1957.
> *My Brother Lambert*, illustrated by David Walsh. London, Phoenix House, and New York, Roy, 1957.
> *He Went with Dampier*, illustrated by P.A. Jobson. London, Harrap, 1957; New York, Roy, 1958.
> *He Went with Franklin*, illustrated by Anthony Douthwaite. London, Harrap, 1960.
> *Apprentice at Arms*, illustrated by Christopher Brooker. London, Collins, 1960.
> *The Castle and the Harp*, illustrated by Charles Keeping. London, Collins, 1963; New York, McGraw Hill, 1964.
> *Frost Fair*, illustrated by Philip Gough. London, Collins, 1965; New York, Roy, 1967.
> *That Fool of a Priest and Other Tales of Early Canterbury*, illustrated by David Knight. Oxford, Pergamon Press, 1970.
> *A Face of Stone*, illustrated by David Harris. Leicester, Brockhampton Press, 1973.
> *Guns for the Armada*, illustrated by Sheila Bewley. London, Hodder and Stoughton, 1975.
> *Death to the Strangers!* London, Hodder and Stoughton, 1977.

Other

> *Great Men of Sussex*, illustrated by Peter Rush. London, Lane, 1956.
> *Strange People: The Later Hanoverians, 1760–1837*, illustrated by Peter Rush. London, Hutchinson, 1958.

More Strange People: The Early Hanoverians, 1714–1760, illustrated by Peter Rush.
   London, Hutchinson, 1958.
London's Wonderful Bridge, illustrated by Nancy Sayer.   London, Harrap, 1959.
Strange Stuarts, 1603–1714, illustrated by Peter Rush.   London, Hutchinson, 1959.
How Roads Have Grown, illustrated by Caroline Norton.   London, Routledge, 1960.
The Young Shelley, illustrated by Anne Linton.   London, Parrish, 1961; New York,
   Roy, 1962.
Weights and Measures, with John A. O'Keefe.   London, Methuen, 1962; New York,
   Roy, 1964.
The Book of Duels, illustrated by Peter Rush.   London, Harrap, 1964.

PUBLICATIONS FOR ADULTS

Novels

Rogue's Lute.   London, Dakars, 1944.
Mary Read, Buccaneer.   London and New York, Boardman, 1945.
Freedom Is the Man.   London, Dakars, 1946.
Crispin's Apprentice.   London, Dakars, 1948.

Philip Rush comments:
The past has always fascinated me and my published work has always been historical.

*   *   *

   Most of Philip Rush's stories are set in the middle ages, often in the area round Canterbury,
and all centre on a particular historical event or character, generally seen through the eyes of
a young person. An author's note identifies sources and separates fiction from fact, though
Rush's attitude, particularly where social class is involved in conflict, is often ambivalent.
Historical details are given plentifully and generally palatably.
   Red Man's Country (which could have been called "He went with Captain John Smith"),
He Went with Dampier, and *He Went with Franklin* are successful pieces of formula writing.
He Went with Franklin, which has no invented young hero, reads like a particularly gripping
travel book rather than a novel. Always the characters are clearly differentiated and racial
prejudice (towards Indians and Eskimos) is shown to be misguided. *The Young Shelley* and
My Brother Lambert present equally convincing and psychologically accurate portraits.
   Other stories are more variable. In *Apprentice at Arms* and *The Castle and the Harp* fact
reads like fiction, and *Frost Fair* is totally unconvincing. *King of the Castle* and *A Face of
Stone* are both accounts of the Wat Tyler rebellion, the later book showing a real
improvement of quality; Adam, the apprentice stonemason, is a likelier character than the
callous and unattractive Sylvester.
   The worst violence – the murder of the garrison of Bedford Castle in *The Castle and the
Harp* – is shown off-stage, but in general battle and killing are plentiful. Hardship,
particularly in the *He Went with ...* stories, is related unflinchingly, and young readers are
given an unglamourised picture. The same is also true of mediaeval life in the one book of
short stories, *That Fool of a Priest.*
   Philosophical and religious topics are dealt with openly – in the Tudor stories *Apprentice at
Arms* and *Guns for the Armada* and in *The Minstrel Knight,* a retelling of an Anglo-Norman
family history poem. Often, as in *Queen's Treason* and *A Face of Stone,* discussion of
religious topics is a prominent feature.
   Happy endings prevail because these are books for children, but where fortunate chance
does not intervene there is always a slight melancholy.

—Margaret M. Tye

SACHS, Marilyn. American. Born in New York City, 18 December 1927. Educated at Hunter College, New York, B.A. 1949; Columbia University, New York, M.S. in library science 1952. Married Morris Sachs in 1947; has one daughter and one son. Librarian, Brooklyn Public Library, 1949–60, and San Francisco Public Library, 1960–65. Address: 733 31st Avenue, San Francisco, California 94121, U.S.A.

PUBLICATIONS FOR CHILDREN

Fiction

> *Amy Moves In*, illustrated by Judith Gwyn Brown. New York, Doubleday, 1964.
> *Laura's Luck*, illustrated by Ib Ohlsson. New York, Doubleday, 1965.
> *Amy and Laura*, illustrated by Tracy Sugarman. New York, Doubleday, 1966.
> *Veronica Ganz*, illustrated by Louis Glanzman. New York, Doubleday, 1968; London, Macdonald, 1969.
> *Peter and Veronica*, illustrated by Louis Glanzman. New York, Doubleday, 1969; London, Macdonald, 1970.
> *Marv*, illustrated by Louis Glanzman. New York, Doubleday, 1970.
> *The Bears' House*, illustrated by Louis Glanzman. New York, Doubleday, 1971.
> *The Truth about Mary Rose*, illustrated by Louis Glanzman. New York, Doubleday, and London, Macdonald, 1973.
> *A Pocket Full of Seeds*, illustrated by Ben Stahl. New York, Doubleday, 1973.
> *Matt's Mitt*, illustrated by Hilary Knight. New York, Doubleday, 1975.
> *Dorrie's Book*, illustrated by Anne Sachs. New York, Doubleday, 1975; London, Macdonald and Jane's, 1976.
> *A December Tale*. New York, Doubleday, 1976.

Play

> *Reading Between the Lines* (produced New York, 1971). New York, Children's Book Council, 1971.

Manuscript Collection: Kerlan Collection, University of Minnesota, Minneapolis.

Marilyn Sachs comments:

All my life, as a child and now as an adult, books have remained one of the more dependable pleasures. Friends come and go, days are not always sunny, and chocolate often gives me rashes. Whenever something hurts I have always been able to pick up a book and forget my troubles. I like to feel my books may be doing just this for children looking for comfort and pleasure.

*   *   *

Seldom does any author's work demonstrate such a strong and steady pattern of growth as does that of Marilyn Sachs. Her earliest books appeared as amiable, run-of-the-mill stories for girls. The Stern sisters, Amy and Laura, cope or fail to cope with the trials and tribulations of the pre-adolescent, as pleasant and unremarkable young heroines have done through generations of children's books.

But from the background of *Amy and Laura* a really formidable character begins to emerge: the school bully, and the bane of Laura's career as monitor, Veronica Ganz, is a breakthrough, a genuine literary creation. Veronica is big, mean, and friendless; everyone is afraid of her until smart-aleck shrimp Peter Wedemeyer challenges her reign of terror by first goading her to frenzy with his taunts, then with the help of two friends beating her severely.

Veronica can hardly believe what has happened. Nor can Peter. He becomes so ashamed he offers to let Veronica, who is half again his size, hit him while he holds his hands behind his back. This bizzare notion is too much for Veronica. Once her hysterical laughter subsides, the two thrash things out: she can't help hitting people smaller than she is; EVERYBODY is smaller than she is. He, the runt, has always seen bigness as of all things the most desirable, and must now look at things from a new angle.

Peter and Veronica sees the two now best of friends. More of Veronica's unhappy homelife is revealed, and their two families' prejudices become a problem in the matter of Peter's bar mitzvah. The youngsters learn that friendship is sometimes painful, but worth the pain.

A generation later, *The Truth about Mary Rose* introduces Veronica's troubled daughter whose life is shadowed by the legend of her child-aunt Mary Rose who died in an apartment fire. The second Mary Rose must learn to let the past bury its dead. This book tends to trouble child readers, both by its tragic subject matter, and by the shock of finding the beloved Veronica suddenly a grown woman ("But she's MY age ...").

Still more pathetic, indeed perhaps too powerful for junior readers, is *The Bears' House*. The most unfortunate of child heroines, little Fran Ellen, lives in horrible squalor. Abandoned by her husband, Fran Ellen's mother suffers a nervous breakdown and lies weeping in her filthy bedroom. The five children, the eldest 12 and the youngest an infant, try to conceal the truth in fear of an institution and separation. Fran Ellen has one refuge: there is a beautiful dolls' house with a family of bears, and in a fantasy life she escapes into this tiny perfect world where she is loved and petted, has pretty clothes and good food. Her real and fantasy lives are on a collision course. This is strong meat to offer young readers. So is *A Pocket Full of Seeds*, but in a broader, more philosophical sense. Fran Ellen's story is a purely personal tragedy; Nicole Nieman's is the tragedy of a people. Swept up in the holocaust of World War II, she develops from a jaunty, unthinking child into a courageous teenager who may have to face life without her beloved family but will carry them forever in her heart.

And what next? Peter, Veronica and Marv may have other friends yet to be introduced; Fran Ellen's and Nicole's stories left the reader still wondering. Is it permissible to hope that they are "to be continued"?

—Joan McGrath

SALKEY, (Felix) Andrew (Alexander).   Jamaican.   Born in Colon, Panama, 30 January 1928. Educated at St. George's College, Kingston, Jamaica; Munro College, St. Elizabeth, Jamaica; University of London (Thomas Helmore Poetry Prize, 1955), B.A. in English 1955. Married Patricia Verden in 1957; has two sons. English teacher in a London comprehensive school, 1957–59. Since 1952, regular outside contributor, as interviewer and scriptwriter, BBC External Services (Radio), London. Recipient: Guggenheim Fellowship, 1960. Address: Flat 8, Windsor Court, Moscow Road, Queensway, London W.2, England.

P∪BLICATIONS FOR CHILDREN

Fiction

> *Hurricane*, illustrated by William Papas.   London, Oxford University Press, 1964.
> *Earthquake*, illustrated by William Papas.   London, Oxford University Press, 1965.
> *Drought*, illustrated by William Papas.   London, Oxford University Press, 1966.
> *Riot*, illustrated by William Papas.   London, Oxford University Press, 1967.
> *Jonah Simpson*, illustrated by Gerry Craig.   London, Oxford University Press, 1969.

Joey Tyson. London, Bogle L'Ouverture, 1974.
The River That Disappeared. London, Bogle L'Ouverture, 1977.

Other

The Shark Hunters (reader), illustrated by Peter Kesteven. London, Nelson, 1966.

PUBLICATIONS FOR ADULTS

Novels

A Quality of Violence. London, Hutchinson, 1959.
Escape to an Autumn Pavement. London, Hutchinson, 1960.
The Late Emancipation of Jerry Stover. London, Hutchinson, 1968.
The Adventures of Catullus Kelly. London, Hutchinson, 1969.
Come Home, Malcolm Heartland. London, Hutchinson, 1975.

Short Stories

Anancy's Score. London, Bogle L'Ouverture, 1973.

Verse

Jamaica. London, Hutchinson, 1973.
Land. London, Readers and Writers Publishing Cooperative, 1976.

Other

Havana Journal. London, Penguin, 1971.
Georgetown Journal: A Caribbean Writer's Journey from London via Port of Spain to Georgetown, Guyana, 1970. London, New Beacon Books, 1972.

Editor, *West Indian Stories.* London, Faber, 1960.
Editor, *Stories from the Caribbean.* London, Elek, 1965; as *Island Voices: Stories from the West Indies*, New York, Liveright, 1970.
Editor, Caribbean Section, *Young Commonwealth Poets '65.* London, Heinemann, 1965.
Editor, *Caribbean Prose.* London, Evans, 1967.
Editor, *Breaklight: An Anthology of Caribbean Poetry.* London, Hamish Hamilton, 1971; as *Breaklight: The Poetry of the Caribbean*, New York, Doubleday, 1972.
Editor, with others, *Savacou 3 and 4.* Kingston, Jamaica, and London, Caribbean Artists Movement, 1972.
Editor, *Caribbean Essays.* London, Evans, 1973.
Editor, *Writing in Cuba since the Revolution.* London, Bogle L'Ouverture, 1976.

*   *   *

A particular interest in Andrew Salkey's writing lies in the way he presents West Indian tradition and culture to English readers. In no way does he compromise this to make it "easy" for reading but seems to assume, quite rightly, that what his readers miss through particular language they will gain through context. The value of this writing in an increasingly multi-racial society will be obvious.

The main body of his work – *Drought, Earthquake, Hurricane,* and, to some extent, *Riot* and *The Shark Hunters* – is concerned with natural disaster and its effect on the group of people concerned. These stories are told very much through the eyes and viewpoints of the children involved. These children are far more realistic, believable characters than the adults whose behaviour is unfairly stereotyped, at least to adult ears. It is easy to understand why children identify with the children of the stories as they attempt to understand, participate in and overcome the difficulties with which they are surrounded. They have thoughts and fears which sometimes have to be kept from adults but which can be shared with children. It is because of this, and because of the predictability of the plots, that I would classify the author as a writer for juveniles – with nothing derogatory intended in that. As can be expected from the titles the plots have an intrinsic excitement which he sustains well – helped by subdividing the chapters into short sections. However, in this group of work it is the events themselves, and not their effects on characters, which seem to dominate.

Jonah Simpson is different. It is a far more complex story involving the hero in the history and legend of Port Royal and weaving his fantasies into what turns out to be a modern adventure situation. This story has compelling threads of intrigue and mystery which transform ordinary events in the boy's life and force him to go deeper and deeper into the puzzle which increasingly seems to surround him. In Uncle Leonard, Samuel Palmer, and the castaway the author has built his strongest adult characters while Jonah himself grows throughout the story. This is the best of Andrew Salkey's work.

—Alan M. Lynskey

SAVILLE, (Leonard) Malcolm. British. Born in Hastings, Sussex, 21 February 1901. Educated at Richmond Hill School, Surrey, and other private schools. Married Dorothy May McCoy in 1926; has two sons and two daughters. Member of the Publicity Department, Cassell and Company, publishers, London, 1920–22; Member of the Publicity Department, and Sales Promotion Manager, Amalgamated Press, London, 1922–36; Sales Promotion Manager, 1936–40, and Editor of "Sunny Stories" series and Editor of General Books, 1955–66, George Newnes, London; Associate Editor, *My Garden* magazine, London and Guildford, Surrey 1947–52; Publicity and Feature Writer, Kemsley Newspapers, London, 1952–55. Address: Chelsea Cottage, Winchelsea, East Sussex, England.

PUBLICATIONS FOR CHILDREN

Fiction

Mystery at Witchend, illustrated by G.E. Breary. London, Newnes, 1943; as *Spy in the Hills*, New York, Farrar and Rinehart, 1945.
Seven White Gates, illustrated by Bertram Prance. London, Newnes, 1944.
The Gay Dolphin Adventure. London, Newnes, 1945.
Trouble at Townsend. London, Transatlantic Arts, 1945.
The Secret of Grey Walls. London, Newnes, 1947.
The Riddle of the Painted Box, illustrated by Lunt Roberts. London, Transatlantic Arts, 1947.
Redshank's Warning, illustrated by Lunt Roberts. London, Lutterworth Press, 1948.
Two Fair Plaits, illustrated by Lunt Roberts. London, Lutterworth Press, 1948.
Lone Pine Five, illustrated by Bertram Prance. London, Newnes, 1949.
Strangers at Snowfell, illustrated by Wynne. London, Lutterworth Press, 1949.
The Master of Maryknoll, illustrated by Alice Bush. London, Evans, 1950.
The Sign of the Alpine Rose, illustrated by Wynne. London, Lutterworth Press, 1950.
The Flying Fish Adventure, illustrated by Lunt Roberts. London, Murray, 1950.

All Summer Through, illustrated by Joan Kiddell-Monroe. London, Hodder and Stoughton, 1951.

The Elusive Grasshopper, illustrated by Bertram Prance. London, Newnes, 1951.

The Buckinghams at Ravenswyke, illustrated by Alice Bush. London, Evans, 1952.

The Luck of Sallowby, illustrated by Tilden Reeves. London, Lutterworth Press, 1952.

The Ambermere Treasure, illustrated by Marcia Lane Foster. London, Lutterworth Press, 1953; as *The Secret of the Ambermere Treasure*, New York, Criterion Books, 1967.

Christmas at Nettleford, illustrated by Joan Kiddell-Monroe. London, Hodder and Stoughton, 1953.

The Secret of the Hidden Pool, illustrated by Lunt Roberts. London, Murray, 1953.

The Neglected Mountain, illustrated by Bertram Prance. London, Newnes, 1953.

Spring Comes to Nettleford, illustrated by Joan Kiddell-Monroe. London, Hodder and Stoughton, 1954.

The Long Passage, illustrated by Alice Bush. London, Evans, 1954.

Susan, Bill and the Ivy-Clad Oak [*Wolf-Dog, Golden Clock, Vanishing Boy, Dark Stranger, "Saucy Kate," Bright Star Circus, Pirates Bold*], illustrated by Ernest Shepard and T.R. Freeman. London, Nelson, 8 vols., 1954–61.

Saucers over the Moor, illustrated by Bertram Prance. London, Newnes, 1955.

Where the Bus Stopped. Oxford, Blackwell, 1955.

The Secret of Buzzard Scar, illustrated by Joan Kiddell-Monroe. London, Hodder and Stoughton, 1955.

Young Johnnie Bimbo, illustrated by Lunt Roberts. London, Murray, 1956.

Wings over Witchend. London, Newnes, 1956.

Lone Pine London. London, Newnes, 1957.

Treasure at the Mill, illustrated by Harry Pettit. London, Newnes, 1957.

The Fourth Key, illustrated by Lunt Roberts. London, Murray, 1957.

The Secret of the Gorge. London, Newnes, 1958.

Mystery Mine. London, Newnes, 1959.

Four-and-Twenty Blackbirds, illustrated by Lilian Buchanan. London, Newnes, 1959; as *The Secret of Galleybird Pit*, London, Armada, 1968.

Sea Witch Comes Home. London, Newnes, 1960.

Not Scarlet But Gold, illustrated by A.R. Whitear. London, Newnes, 1962.

A Palace for the Buckinghams, illustrated by Alice Bush. London, Evans, 1963.

Three Towers in Tuscany. London, Heinemann, 1963.

The Purple Valley. London, Heinemann, 1964.

Treasure at Amorys, illustrated by T.R. Freeman. London, Newnes, 1964.

Dark Danger. London, Heinemann, 1965.

White Fire. London, Heinemann, 1966.

The Thin Grey Man, illustrated by Desmond Knight. London, Macmillan, and New York, St. Martin's Press, 1966.

Man with Three Fingers, illustrated by Michael Whittlesea. London, Newnes, 1966.

Strange Story. London, Mowbray, 1967.

Power of Three. London, Heinemann, 1968.

Rye Royal. London, Collins, 1969.

Strangers at Witchend. London, Collins, 1970.

The Dagger and the Flame. London, Heinemann, 1970.

The Secret of Villa Rosa. London, Collins, 1971.

Where's My Girl? London, Collins, 1972.

Diamond in the Sky. London, Collins, 1974.

Other

Country Scrap Book. London, National Magazine Company, 1944; revised edition, London, Gramol, 1945.

Open-Air Scrap Book. London, Gramol, 1945.
Seaside Scrap Book. London, Gramol, 1946.
Jane's Country Year, illustrated by Bernard Bowerman. London, Newnes, 1946.
Adventure of the Life-Boat Service. London, Macdonald, 1950.
Coronation Gift Book. London, Daily Graphic-Pitkins, 1952.
King of Kings (life of Christ). London, Nelson, 1958; revised edition, Berkhamsted,
    Hertfordshire, Lion Publishing, 1975; Huntingdon, Indiana, Our Sunday Visitor,
    1977.
Small Creatures, illustrated by John Kenney. London, Ward, 1959.
Country Book. London, Cassell, 1961.
Seaside Book. London, Cassell, 1962.
Come to London [*Cornwall, Devon, Somerset*]. London, Heinemann, 1 vol., Benn, 3
    vols., 1967–70.
Eat What You Grow, illustrated by Robert Micklewright. London, Carousel, 1975.
Portrait of Rye, illustrated by Michael Renton. East Grinstead, Sussex, Goulden, 1977.
Discovering the Woodland, illustrated by Elsie Wrigley. London, Carousel, 1978.
Countryside Quiz, illustrated by Robert Micklewright. London, Carousel, 1978.

*   *   *

When Malcolm Saville decided to write his first children's book in 1942, he wrote the sort
of story he knew *he* would have enjoyed as a boy – a mystery story with plenty of action,
likeable and credible characters, and set in a real geographical locale, minutely and
colourfully described. The result was *Mystery at Witchend*, set in the highlands of Shropshire,
which introduced a group of young people subsequently known as "The Lone Piners," later
to be featured in a further 18 titles, and probably Saville's most popular and enduring
creations. That first book was an enormous success (concurrently broadcast as a serial in the
BBC Children's Hour programme) and, since then, Saville has produced nearly 80 books of
many kinds, featuring other popular characters such as The Jillies, The Buckinghams,
Michael and Mary, and Susan and Bill. His series of loosely-linked secret-service thrillers
about Marston Baines, a bachelor agent in his early twenties, his friends and occasional girl-
friends, usually set in European countries, has been written to "bridge the gap" for young
readers between children's stories and adult novels, and Saville has found the public's
response highly encouraging.

Apart from his fiction, Saville has written children's books on the countryside (*Jane's
Country Year* remains his own personal favourite), the seaside, gardening, and religious
subjects (*King of Kings*, the story of Christ told in simple and moving prose, is outstanding).
Most of his stories are written against the background of actual places (Shropshire, Sussex,
Romney Marsh, Yorkshire, Dartmoor, the West Country) which his readers can, and often
do, visit for themselves.

In the main, his stories are entertaining, well-written and extremely popular with his
young readers, who write Saville about 3,000 letters a year. He not only answers every one
personally but also sends out a regular news-sheet about his current books and activities.

Malcolm Saville has probably been seriously underrated by "establishment" reviewers of
children's books over the years. All too often, his latest books are not even granted the favour
of a critical notice. This is a fate that has frequently overtaken popular and successful writers
for adults as well as for children. Saville gives his readers what he knows they want and what
he knows they enjoy – stories about nice, civilized, realistic youngsters having exciting (but
believable) adventures, laced with atmosphere, humour and good dialogue, in superlatively
described settings. And his readers are well-satisfied.

—Brian Doyle

SAWYER, Ruth. American. Born in Boston, Massachusetts, 5 August 1880. Educated at Mrs. Brackett's School, 1887; Garland Kindergarten Normal School, Boston, graduated 1900; Columbia University, New York, B.S. 1904. Married Albert C. Durand in 1911; one son and one daughter. Helped organize kindergartens in Cuba, 1900; correspondent in Ireland for New York *Sun*, 1905, 1907; professional story-teller and lecturer, from 1908. Lived in Spain, 1931–32. Recipient: American Library Association Newbery Medal, 1937, and Laura Ingalls Wilder Medal, 1965; Catholic Library Association Regina Medal, 1965. *Died 3 June 1970.*

PUBLICATIONS FOR CHILDREN

Fiction

Tale of the Enchanted Bunnies. New York and London, Harper, 1923.
Toño Antonio, illustrated by F. Luis Mora. New York, Viking Press, 1934.
Roller Skates, illustrated by Valenti Angelo. New York, Viking Press, 1936; London, Bodley Head, 1964.
The Year of Jubilo, illustrated by Edward Shenton. New York, Viking Press, 1940; as *Lucinda's Year of Jubilo,* London, Bodley Head, 1965.
The Least One, illustrated by Leo Politi. New York, Viking Press, 1941.
The Christmas Anna Angel, illustrated by Kate Seredy. New York, Viking Press, 1944; London, Cassell, 1948.
Old Con and Patrick, illustrated by Cathal O'Toole. New York, Viking Press, 1946.
The Little Red Horse, illustrated by Jay Hyde Barnum. New York, Viking Press, 1950.
Maggie Rose, Her Birthday Christmas, illustrated by Maurice Sendak. New York, Harper, 1952.
A Cottage for Betsy, illustrated by Vera Bock. New York, Harper, 1954.
The Enchanted Schoolhouse, illustrated by Hugh Troy. New York, Viking Press, 1956; Leicester, Brockhampton Press, 1958.
The Year of the Christmas Dragon, illustrated by Hugh Troy. New York, Viking Press, 1960.
Daddles: The Story of a Plain Hound-Dog, illustrated by Robert Frankenberg. Boston, Little Brown, 1964.

Verse

A Child's Year Book, illustrated by the author. New York and London, Harper, 1917.

Other

This Way to Christmas. New York and London, Harper, 1916; revised edition, New York, Harper, 1967.
Picture Tales from Spain, illustrated by Carlos Sanchez. New York, Stokes, 1936.
The Long Christmas, illustrated by Valenti Angelo. New York, Viking Press, 1941; London, Bodley Head, 1964.
This Is the Christmas: A Serbian Folk Tale. Boston, Horn Book, 1945.
Journey Cake, Ho!, illustrated by Robert McCloskey. New York, Viking Press, 1953.
Dietrich of Berne and the Dwarf-King Laurin: Hero Tales of the Austrian Tirol, with Emmy Mollès, illustrated by Frederick Chapman. New York, Viking Press, 1963.
Joy to the World: Christmas Legends, illustrated by Trina Schart Hyman. Boston, Little Brown, 1966.
My Spain: A Story-Teller's Year of Collecting. New York, Viking Press, 1967.

Recording: *Ruth Sawyer, Storyteller,* 1965.

PUBLICATIONS FOR ADULTS

Novels

The Primrose Ring. New York and London, Harper, 1915.
Seven Miles to Arden. New York and London, Harper, 1916.
Herself, Himself, and Myself: A Romance. New York and London, Harper, 1917.
Doctor Danny. New York and London, Harper, 1918.
Leerie. New York and London, Harper, 1920.
The Silver Sixpence. New York and London, Harper, 1921.
Four Ducks on a Pond. New York and London, Harper, 1928.
Gladiola Murphy. New York and London, Harper, 1930.
Folkhouse. New York and London, Appleton, 1932.
The Luck of the Road. New York and London, Appleton, 1934.
Gallant: The Story of Storm Veblen. New York and London, Appleton, 1936.

Plays

The Sidhe of Ben-Mor: An Irish Folk Play. Boston, Badger, 1910.
The Awakening (produced New York, 1918).

Other

The Way of the Storyteller. New York, Viking Press, 1942; London, Harrap, 1944;
    revised edition, Viking Press, 1962.

Critical Study: *Ruth Sawyer* by Virginia Haviland, London, Bodley Head, and New York,
Walck, 1965.

*   *   *

For most of her adult life a storyteller with consummate gifts — whose tales both oral and written could be characterized as living folk-art — Ruth Sawyer received both the Laura Ingalls Wilder and the Regina medals for her numerous distinguished contributions to children's literature. Something of her strong positive personality and her unlimited creative power are conveyed by Virginia Haviland in her delightfully intimate and revealing monograph, *Ruth Sawyer.* In one characterization, Miss Haviland says of her: "Sentences flowed full and colorful, projected in the still rich and vibrant voice — one more revelation of the teller's oral gifts. She was ever the story-teller, 'the way' shining through everything she had to say."

The procession of Ruth Sawyer's work had several emphases: stories she drew from her remembered childhood, legends and tales she collected from several countries, including some she visited over an extended time period, e.g. Cuba, Ireland, Spain (the setting for *Toño Antonio* and *Picture Tales from Spain*), and finally the works related to the festival of Christmas which she used as both a strong spiritual symbol and the focus for warm human ingathering.

Drawn from the recollections of her growing years is *Roller Skates,* Newbery award winner, featuring a 10-year-old tomboy, Lucinda Wyman, in an 1890 New York City setting. She mirrors her "higgledy-piggledy" life during a tremendous year of growth and learning. Its sequel, *The Year of Jubilo,* follows Lucinda after her father's death when she and her family resettle in their summer cottage in Maine. In this volume are more "impetuosities, brutal honesties, crudities" and examples of "cock-sure independence." Especially noteworthy are the letters written by Lucinda to those left behind in New York.

The author's rich and loving humor and her warmth — together with her appreciation of the richness of commonality as well as the festival quality in Christmas — is reflected in *This*

Way to Christmas, real stories told to a lonesome boy stranded in northern New York. *The Long Christmas* contains Christmas legends and carols from around the world, together with a song of Saint Stephen with music. *The Christmas Anna Angel* follows the preparations of a Hungarian family during the Second World War for a bare Christmas, but the young heroine is resolute in her belief that her angel will provide cake for their tree. *This Is the Christmas*, a Serbian folk tale, is told by a Serbian grandmother and features a blind boy shepherd who pipes to a carol. *Maggie Rose, Her Birthday Christmas* follows the daughter of an impoverished family in Maine who tries to raise some money so that her family can enjoy a birthday Christmas party. *The Year of the Christmas Dragon*, also set in Maine, presents a charming story, contrasting the long ago ancient times with "the time called now" and embedded with a wonderful spring promise. Referred to as "woven magic," *Joy to the World: Christmas Legends* contains a group of legends from ancient Arabia, Serbia, and Spain, with carols interlarded.

Other stories include: *Journey Cake, Ho!*, a lovely version of the old folk tale, and *The Enchanted Schoolhouse*, the story of a young immigrant from Ireland. Eager to carry a bit of his beloved country with him, he captures "a wee fairyman" and conceals him in a teapot all the way to "Maine, USA where the two of them turned Lobster Cove topsy-turvy." Something of the relationship emerges in the fairyman's plea: "Laddy, laddy, let me loose. This is no country to be coming to. All the wizards in the world must have made it." The hero tales *Dietrich of Berne and the Dwarf-King Laurin* are drawn from the mountain people of the Austrian Tyrol. In life the hero Dietrich becomes Theodoric the Great, on whose shield the Red Lion rested. *My Spain: A Story-Teller's Year of Collecting* can be enjoyed by young people as well as adults for its picture of Spain and the charming adventures and people encountered in gathering these materials.

Ruth Sawyer's composite work is "gloriously alive; all the warmth and delightful chuckliness of her personality flood through the stories she tells .... She writes as a jongleur might speak, in a fashion much more intense and exalted and heightened than is usual." Her long and productive life and the treasured writing she left behind provide multiple and richly varied examples of "the way of the storyteller." As Ruth Sawyer remembered her Irish nurse Johanna's influence on her, she herself succeeded in handling words so that they "join hands and dance, making a fairy ring that completely encircled" her readers.

—Clara O. Jackson

SCARRY, Richard (McClure). American. Born in Boston, Massachusetts, 5 June 1919. Educated at the Boston Museum School of Fine Arts, 1938–41, 1969–71. Served in the United States Army in North Africa and the Mediterranean, 1941–46: Captain. Married Patricia Murphy in 1948; has one son. Recipient: Mystery Writers of America Edgar Allan Poe Special Award, 1976. Address: Chemin de Beau-Rivage 10, 1006 Lausanne, Switzerland.

PUBLICATIONS FOR CHILDREN (illustrated by the author)

Fiction

    The Great Big Car and Truck Book. New York, Simon and Schuster, 1951.
    Rabbit and His Friends. New York, Simon and Schuster, 1953; London, Muller, 1954.
    Naughty Bunny. New York, Golden Press, and London, Muller, 1959.
    Tinker and Tanker. New York, Doubleday, 1960; London, Hamlyn, 1969.

Tinker and Tanker Out West.   New York, Doubleday, 1961; London, Hamlyn, 1969.
Tinker and Tanker and Their Space Ship.   New York, Doubleday, 1961.
Tinker and Tanker and the Pirates.   New York, Doubleday, 1961.
Tinker and Tanker, Knights of the Round Table.   New York, Doubleday, 1963; London, Hamlyn, 1969.
Tinker and Tanker in Africa.   New York, Doubleday, 1963; London, Hamlyn, 1969.
Best Wordbook Ever.   New York, Golden Press, 1963; London, Hamlyn, 1964.
Polite Elephant.   New York, Golden Press, 1964.
Teeny Tiny Tales.   New York, Golden Press, 1965; London, Hamlyn, 1970.
The Santa Claus Book.   New York, Golden Press, 1965.
The Bunny Book.   New York, Golden Press, 1965; London, Golden Pleasure Books, 1966.
Busy Busy World.   New York, Golden Press, 1965; London, Hamlyn, 1966.
Is This the House of Mistress Mouse?   New York, Golden Press, 1966.
The Egg in the Hole Book.   New York, Golden Press, 1967.
Best Storybook Ever.   New York, Golden Press, 1968; London, Hamlyn, 1969.
The Early Bird.   New York, Random House, 1968; London, Collins, 1970.
The Great Pie Robbery.   New York, Random House, and London, Collins, 1969.
The Supermarket Mystery.   New York, Random House, and London, Collins, 1969.
Great Big Schoolhouse.   New York, Random House, and London, Collins, 1969.
Great Big Air Book.   New York, Random House, and London, Collins, 1971.
Funniest Storybook Ever.   New York, Random House, and London, Collins, 1972.
Nicky Goes to the Doctor.   New York, Golden Press, and London, Hamlyn, 1972.
Hop Aboard, Here We Go!   New York, Random House, and London, Hamlyn, 1972.
Silly Stories.   New York, Golden Press, 1973; London, Hamlyn, 1974.
Babykins and His Family.   New York, Golden Press, 1973; London, Hamlyn, 1974.
Great Steamboat Mystery.   New York, Random House, 1975; London, Collins, 1976.
Look-Look Books.   New York, Golden Press, 1976.
Busiest People Ever.   New York, Random House, 1976; London, Collins, 1977.
Favorite Storybook.   New York, Random House, and London, Collins, 1976.
Busy Town, Busy People.   New York, Random House, and London, Collins, 1976.

Verse

Hickory Dickory Clock Book.   New York, Doubleday, 1961.

Other

Nursery Tales.   New York, Simon and Schuster, 1958.
Manners.   New York, Golden Press, 1962.
What Animals Do.   New York, Golden Press, 1963.
A Tinker and Tanker Coloring Book.   New York, Doubleday, 1963.
The Rooster Struts.   New York, Golden Press, 1963; as *The Golden Happy Book of Animals*, 1964; as *Animals*, London, Hamlyn, 1964.
Animal Mother Goose.   New York, Golden Press, 1964; London, Hamlyn, 1965.
Best Nursery Rhymes Ever.   New York, Golden Press, 1964; London, Hamlyn, 1971.
Storybook Dictionary.   New York, Golden Press, 1966.
Planes.   New York, Golden Press, 1967.
Trains.   New York, Golden Press, 1967; with *Cars*, London, Golden Pleasure Books, 1969.
Boats.   New York, Golden Press, 1967; with *Planes*, London, Hamlyn, 1969.
Cars.   New York, Golden Press, 1967.
What Do People Do All Day?   New York, Random House, and London, Collins, 1969.
ABC Word Book.   New York, Random House, 1971; London, Collins, 1972.
Look and Learn Library (*Best Stories Ever, Fun with Words, Going Places, Things to Know*).   New York, Golden Press, 4 vols., 1971.

Find Your ABC's. New York, Random House, 1973.
Please and Thank You Book. New York, Random House, 1973.
Best Rainy Day Book Ever. New York, Random House, 1974; London, Hamlyn, 1975.
European Word Book. London, Hamlyn, 1974.
Cars and Trucks and Things That Go. New York, Golden Press, and London, Collins, 1974.
Animal Nursery Tales. New York, Golden Press, and London, Collins, 1975.
Best Counting Book Ever. New York, Random House, 1975; London, Collins, 1976.
Early Words. New York, Random House, 1976; London, Collins, 1977.
Color Book. New York, Random House, 1976; London, Collins, 1977.
Laugh and Learn Library. London, Collins, 1976.
Picture Dictionary. London, Collins, 1976.
Teeny Tiny ABC. New York, Golden Press, and London, Hamlyn, 1976.
Little ABC. New York, Random House, and London, Collins, 1976.
Things to Know. New York, Random House, and London, Collins, 1976.
Best Make-It Book Ever. New York, Random House, 1977.

Editor, *Fables*, by Jean de La Fontaine. New York, Doubleday, 1963.

Illustrator: *Boss of the Barnyard*, 1946; *Two Little Miners* by Margaret Wise Brown and Edith Thatcher Hurd, 1949, and *Little Indian* by Brown, 1954; *Let's Go Fishing*, 1949, *Mouse's House*, 1949, *Duck and His Friends*, 1949, *Brave Cowboy Bill*, 1950, *The Animals' Merry Christmas*, 1950, and *The Golden Bedtime Book*, 1955, all by Kathryn Jackson; *Little Benny Wanted a Pony* by Oliver Barrett, 1950; *The Animals of Farmer Jones* by Leah Gale, 1953; *Danny Beaver's Secret*, 1953, *Pierre Bear*, 1954, and *Just for Fun*, 1960, all by Patricia Scarry; *Smokey the Bear* by Jane Werner, 1955; *Mon petit dictionnaire géant* by Mary Maud Reed, 1958; *My Nursery Tale Book*, 1961; *My Book of Manners* by Peggy Parish, 1962; *I Am a Bunny* by Ole Risom, 1963; *Animal Mother Goose*, 1964; *Rudolph the Red-Nosed Reindeer* by Barbara Shook Hazen, 1964; *The Golden Book of 365 Stories*, 1966; *Best Mother Goose Ever*, 1970; *Mother Goose*, 1972; *All Day Long, At Work, My House, On Holiday, On the Farm*, and *With the Animals*, all edited by Jeffrey Bevington, 1975.

*   *   *

Richard Scarry's literary output enjoys a huge following among today's children. Part of his success may be attributed to the fact that his works are closely related in style to the medium of film or television in their emphasis on action. *What Do People Do All Day?*, a typical Scarry title, contains pages crammed with drawings depicting everyday activities in minute detail. The accompanying text is usually limited to a description of the particular action taking place. Occasionally, flip comments give the straightforward explanations an added dimension. Scarry's characters are both human and animal. In many cases animal figures intended to represent people and human figures are used in the same drawing, a technique which provides humor (e.g., a schoolbus loaded with owl pupils) and interest. The illustrations tend to have an air of cosyness and cuteness due to Scarry's use of rounded angles and a perspective which makes the characters appear to be operating in a miniature setting. All the characters smile, even in such unlikely situations as the fire brigade rescue in *Hop Aboard, Here We Go!*

Scarry's books are usually lacking in plot – rather they are a cumulation of bits of information in various spheres of knowledge. A typical Scarry title, *Great Big Schoolhouse* contains a series of approximately twenty 2–3 page vignettes centred on the theme of school activities. The author details in chronological order the events and activities in which school children are apt to be involved. The text is very like the dialogue one would expect to find in an educational television program – questions are asked, admonitions are made (with regard to dangerous objects, for example), and comments are made on the behaviour of the illustrated characters. Humor is often derived from a straightforward comment juxtaposed against a ridiculous drawing.

Like Seuss, Scarry has hit on a formula for success which he uses repeatedly. His books with their endearing characters have a certain charm. However, in exchange for commercial success he has probably forfeited any real creative development as an artist and as a writer.

—Fran Ashdown

SCHAEFER, Jack (Warner). American. Born in Cleveland, Ohio, 19 November 1907. Educated at Oberlin College, Ohio, A.B. in English 1929; Columbia University, New York, 1929–30. Married Eugenia Hammond Ives in 1931 (divorced, 1948), three sons and one daughter; Louise Wilhide Deans, 1949, three stepchildren. Reporter, United Press, New Haven, Connecticut, 1930–31; Assistant Director of Education, Connecticut State Reformatory, Cheshire, 1931–38; Associate Editor, 1932–39, and Editor, 1939–42, New Haven *Journal-Courier*; Editorial Writer, Baltimore *Sun*, 1942–44; Associate Editor, Norfolk *Virginian-Pilot*, 1944–48; Associate, Lindsay Advertising Company, 1949. Editor and Publisher, *Theatre News*, 1935–40, *The Movies*, 1939–41, and *Shoreliner*, 1949, all New Haven. Agent: Harold Matson Co. Inc., 22 East 40th Street, New York, New York 10016. Address: 2434 Anacapa Street, Santa Barbara, California 93105, U.S.A.

PUBLICATIONS FOR CHILDREN

Fiction

> *Shane.* Boston, Houghton Mifflin, 1949; London, Deutsch, 1954.
> *First Blood.* Boston, Houghton Mifflin, 1953; London, Deutsch, 1954.
> *The Canyon.* Boston, Houghton Mifflin, 1953; augmented edition, as *The Canyon and Other Stories*, London, Deutsch, 1955.
> *Old Ramon*, illustrated by Harold West. Boston, Houghton Mifflin, 1960; London, Deutsch, 1962.
> *The Plainsmen*, illustrated by Lorence Bjorklund. Boston, Houghton Mifflin, 1963.
> *Stubby Pringle's Christmas*, illustrated by Lorence Bjorklund. Boston, Houghton Mifflin, 1964.
> *Mavericks*, illustrated by Lorence Bjorklund. Boston, Houghton Mifflin, 1967, London, Deutsch, 1968.

Other

> *New Mexico.* New York, Coward McCann, 1967.

PUBLICATIONS FOR ADULTS

Novels

> *The Pioneers.* Boston, Houghton Mifflin, 1954; London, Deutsch, 1957.
> *Company of Cowards.* Boston, Houghton Mifflin, 1957; London, Deutsch, 1958.
> *Monte Walsh.* Boston, Houghton Mifflin, 1963; London, Deutsch, 1965.

Short Stories

> *The Big Range.* Boston, Houghton Mifflin, 1953; London, Deutsch, 1955.

The Kean Land and Other Stories.   Boston. Houghton Mifflin. 1959; London, Deutsch,
    1960.
Collected Stories.   Boston, Houghton Mifflin, 1966.

Other

The Great Endurance Horse Race.   Sante Fe, New Mexico, Stagecoach Press, 1963.
Heroes Without Glory: Some Goodmen of the Old West.   Boston, Houghton Mifflin,
    1965; London, Deutsch, 1966.
Adolphe Francis Alphonse Bandelier.   Sante Fe, New Mexico, Press of the Territorian,
    1966.
An American Bestiary.   Boston, Houghton Mifflin, 1975.

Editor, *Out West: An Anthology of Stories.*   Boston, Houghton Mifflin, 1955; London,
    Deutsch, 1959.

Manuscript Collection: Western History Research Center, University of Wyoming, Laramie.

Jack Schaefer comments:
  I have never deliberately and consciously written stories for children. I do not believe
anyone should do so — except a writer aiming at youngsters just learning to read. I have
always written my stories for people, for readers, regardless of age, doing the best job I could
in each instance according to the tune and the tone and the possibilities of the material I was
using. None of my books is solely for children — or solely for adults. My mail through the
years has shown that the books have done what I hoped they would do: attracted readers of
all ages.

                                    *   *   *

  Jack Schaefer's fiction-writing career began in 1949 with *Shane*, an understated tale of a
gunman's involvement with a homesteading family in Wyoming, told from the point of view
of their son. It ended in 1967 with *Mavericks*, the movingly evocative reminiscences of Old
Jake Hanlon, a dying cowboy lost in his memories of the long-extinct American West. These
two books typify Schaefer's writings for young readers; they are the terminal points of a
group of works uniformly concerned with the theme of growing up and stressing the
responsibility that comes with experience and maturity.
  Shane, although not originally written for a youthful audience, has grown increasingly
popular with young readers. Its story is simple, its point clear. The book's first-person
narration gives immediacy to the emotional tensions between Shane and the Starrett family.
Young Bob Starrett, the narrator, is torn between his admiration for Shane and his love for
his parents, and gradually learns of the complex responsibilities of adulthood. And Shane
himself, a reformed gunfighter who reluctantly resumes his violent craft to preserve the
stable lives of Joe and Marion Starrett, is a poignant, dignified personification of the
responsible individual.
  Old Ramon continues the theme of growing up. As Ramon, an aged Mexican sheepherder,
leads his patron's son through a summer's work in the pastures, the boy comes to see that
independence and responsibility go hand-in-hand, and the truly mature person is the one
who accepts them both. Less substantial is *Stubby Pringle's Christmas*, a tall tale about a
cowpoke who substitutes for Santa Claus. Even this slight work, however, reveals Schaefer's
view of responsibility, for Pringle gives up a night's festivities to make gifts for a penniless
family.
  Mavericks is the ultimate extension of Schaefer's recurring theme. Jake Hanlon, recalling
his 70-odd years as ranch-hand and cowboy, discovers that he has contributed to the
destruction of the West that he loves. He sees at last the cost of progress, and is sickened by

his vision. The responsible person, Schaefer implies, must see what Jake sees: that actions have consequences, and that modern comforts come at the expense of a cruder but more vital world. Maturity, therefore, means accepting one's responsibilities to the world, the environment, and one's self. Schaefer heeds his own advice; since 1967 he has devoted himself to writing of mankind's effect upon the Western environment and its inhabitants.

—Fred Erisman

SCHLEE, Ann. British. Born in Greenwich, Connecticut, United States, 26 May 1934. Educated at Downe House, Oxford, 1953–56, B.A. 1956. Married D.N.R. Schlee in 1956; has three daughters and one son. Address: c/o Macmillan Press Ltd., 4 Little Essex Street, London, WC2R 3LF, England.

PUBLICATIONS FOR CHILDREN

Fiction

> *The Strangers*, illustrated by Pat Marriott. London, Macmillan, 1971; New York, Atheneum, 1972.
> *The Consul's Daughter*. London, Macmillan, and New York, Atheneum, 1972.
> *The Guns of Darkness*. London, Macmillan, 1973; New York, Atheneum, 1974.
> *Ask Me No Questions*. London, Macmillan, 1976.
> *Lost*. London, Heinemann, 1977.

*   *   *

Four historical novels for older children, each taking as its point of departure a little-known incident in English history, might easily be dismissed as a minor contribution to children's literature. But Ann Schlee has a rare gift. She writes with such clarity that nothing stands between the reader and the scenes she is inventing. It is like looking through clear glass. This is true style; there is no straining after original imagery which can so often work like a bead curtain, fragmenting the vision with carefully-turned lumps of "beautiful writing."

Her first novel, *The Strangers*, is an adventure story culminating in the capture of the island of Tresco in the Scillies by the Parliamentary fleet in 1651, but it is also the story of a child face to face with strangers from a world completely new to her.

The Consul's Daughter relies less on the trappings of a conventional children's adventure story (secret cave, coded inscription) and explores more obliquely the emotional maturing of a young girl involved in the siege of Algiers in 1816. The girl's jealousy of her father's young wife and new baby, her tentative relationship with one of the young officers on board the naval frigate in which they escape, her friendship with the ship's surgeon are all delicately and accurately drawn. Above all the stifling shuttered heat of Algiers and then the life on board ship are brilliantly conveyed, and there is a fine battle scene. Suddenly you know what it must have felt like to be a young officer trained for fighting and at last on board a ship within sight of the enemy; Trafalgar is over, Nelson dead, and you are desperately anxious not to have missed a last chance of action.

The Guns of Darkness is a more ambitious novel with a much wider sweep of narrative, taking as its theme the fall of Emperor Theodore of Abyssinia. The story is told through the eyes of Louisa, whose older sister has married one of the Swiss missionaries who are forced by the Emperor to make him the cannons with which he hopes to save his kingdom. There is something of a failure with the central character; Louisa is too impassive. With an Abyssinian mother and an English father she could be expected to suffer some conflict of loyalties and confusion of identities when her people are at war with the English, but this is not fully explored.

Ann Schlee's fourth novel, *Ask Me No Questions*, is superbly imagined. Here the conflicting demands made on a child having for the first time to make her own moral decisions in a terrifying situation are fully developed. Laura, sent to stay with unsympathetic relatives to escape the cholera, becames aware that the building next door houses hundreds of children being kept in a state of squalor, starvation, and disease. The book is haunting in the true sense of the word, a book that disturbs and distresses but which I would not hesitate to press into the hands of every well-fed child over the age of 12 whom I could find.

—Mary Rayner

SCHLEIN, Miriam. American. Born in New York City. Educated at Brooklyn College, New York. Has one daughter and one son. Address: c/o Four Winds Press, 50 West 44th Street, New York, New York 10036, U.S.A.

PUBLICATIONS FOR CHILDREN

Fiction

A Day at the Playground, illustrated by Eloise Wilkin. New York, Simon and Schuster, 1951.
Tony's Pony, illustrated by Van Kaufman. New York, Simon and Schuster, 1952.
Shapes, illustrated by Sam Berman. New York, Scott, 1952.
Go with the Sun, illustrated by Symeon Shimin. New York, Scott, 1952.
The Four Little Foxes, illustrated by Luis Quintanilla. New York, Scott, 1953.
When Will the World Be Mine?, illustrated by Jean Charlot. New York, Scott, 1953.
The Sun Looks Down, illustrated by Abner Graboff. Nashville, Abelard Schuman, 1954; London, Abelard Schuman, 1958.
How Do You Travel?, illustrated by Paul Galdone. Nashville, Abingdon Press, 1954.
Elephant Herd, illustrated by Symeon Shimin. New York, Scott, 1954; Kingswood, Surrey, World's Work, 1967.
Oomi, The New Hunter, illustrated by George Mason. New York, Abelard Schuman, 1955; London, Abelard Schuman, 1958.
Little Red Nose, illustrated by Roger Duvoisin. New York and London, Abelard Schuman, 1955.
Puppy's House, illustrated by Katherine Evans. Chicago, Whitman, 1955; Edinburgh, Chambers, 1969.
Big Talk, illustrated by Harvey Weiss. New York, Scott, 1955.
Lazy Day, illustrated by Harvey Weiss. New York, Scott, 1955.
Henry's Ride, illustrated by Vane Earle. Nashville, Abingdon Press, 1956.
Deer in the Snow, illustrated by Leonard Kessler. New York and London, Abelard Schuman, 1956.
Something for Now, Something for Later, illustrated by Leonard Kessler. New York, Harper, 1956.
Little Rabbit, The High Jumper, illustrated by Theresa Sherman. New York, Scott, 1957.

Amazing Mr. Pelgrew, illustrated by Harvey Weiss.   New York and London, Abelard Schuman, 1957.

A Bunny, A Bird, A Funny Cat, illustrated by Harvey Weiss.   London and New York, Abelard Schuman, 1957.

Here Comes Night, illustrated by Harvey Weiss. Chicago, Whitman, 1957; Edinburgh, Chambers, 1967.

The Big Cheese, illustrated by Joseph Low.   New York, Scott, 1958; London, Hamish Hamilton, 1965.

The Bumblebee's Secret, illustrated by Harvey Weiss.   New York and London, Abelard Schuman, 1958.

Home, The Tale of a Mouse, illustrated by E. Harper Johnson.   New York, Abelard Schuman, 1958.

Herman McGregor's World, illustrated by Harvey Weiss.   Chicago, Whitman, 1958; Kingswood, Surrey, World's Work, 1972.

The Raggle Taggle Fellow, illustrated by Harvey Weiss.   New York and London, Abelard Schuman, 1959.

Little Dog Little, illustrated by Hertha Depper.   New York, Abelard Schuman, 1959.

The Fisherman's Day, illustrated by Harvey Weiss.   Chicago, Whitman, 1959.

The Sun, The Wind, The Sea, and the Rain, illustrated by Joe Lasker.   New York and London, Abelard Schuman, 1960.

Laurie's New Brother, illustrated by Elizabeth Donald.   New York and London, Abelard Schuman, 1961.

Amuny, Boy of Old Egypt, illustrated by Thea Dupays.   New York and London, Abelard Schuman, 1961.

The Pile of Junk, illustrated by Harvey Weiss.   New York and London, Abelard Schuman, 1962.

Snow Time, illustrated by Joe Lasker. Chicago, Whitman, 1962; Edinburgh, Chambers, 1966.

The Snake in the Carpool, illustrated by N.M. Bodecker.   New York and London, Abelard Schuman, 1963.

The Way Mothers Are, illustrated by Joe Lasker.   Chicago, Whitman, 1963.

Who?, illustrated by Harvey Weiss.   New York, Walck, 1963.

The Big Green Thing, illustrated by Elizabeth Dauber.   New York, Grosset and Dunlap, 1963; London, Muller, 1968.

Big Lion, Little Lion, illustrated by Joe Lasker.   Chicago, Whitman, 1964; Edinburgh, Chambers, 1966.

Billy, The Littlest One, illustrated by Lucy Hawkinson.   Chicago, Whitman, 1966; Edinburgh, Chambers, 1969.

The Best Place, illustrated by Erica Merkling.   Chicago, Whitman, 1968.

My House, illustrated by Joe Lasker.   Chicago, Whitman, 1971.

The Rabbit's World, illustrated by Peter Parnall.   New York, Scholastic, 1973.

The Girl Who Would Rather Climb Trees, illustrated by Judith Gwyn Brown.   New York, Harcourt Brace, 1975.

Bobo the Troublemaker, illustrated by Ray Cruz.   New York, Scholastic, 1976.

Other

Fast Is Not a Ladybug: A Book about Fast and Slow Things.   New York, Scott, 1953; as *Fast Is Not a Ladybird*, Kingswood, Surrey, World's Work, 1961.

Heavy Is a Hippopotamus, illustrated by Leonard Kessler.   New York, Scott, 1954.

It's about Time, illustrated by Leonard Kessler.   New York, Scott, 1955.

City Boy, Country Boy, illustrated by Katherine Evans.   Chicago, Children's Press, 1955.

Kittens, Cubs, and Babies, illustrated by Jean Charlot.   New York, Scott, 1959.

My Family, illustrated by Harvey Weiss. New York, Abelard Schuman, 1960;
   London, Abelard Schuman, 1964.
Moon-Months and Sun-Days, illustrated by Shelly Sacks. New York, Scott, 1972.
*Juju-Sheep and the Python's Moonstone, and Other Moon Stories from Different Times
   and Different Places*, illustrated by Joe Lasker. Chicago, Whitman, 1973.
What's Wrong with Being a Skunk?, illustrated by Ray Cruz. New York, Scholastic,
   1974.
Metric: The Modern Way to Measure, illustrated by Jan Pyk. New York, Harcourt
   Brace, 1975.
Careers in a Department Store (as Lavinia Stanhope). Milwaukee, Raintree Editions,
   1976.
Giraffe, The Silent Giant, illustrated by Betty Fraser. New York, Scholastic, 1976.

                          *   *   *

In the past 25 years, Miriam Schlein has produced more than 40 books for children, many
of them non-fiction. The titles clearly indicate what to expect and what her subjects are: *Deer
in the Snow, It's about Time, How Do You Travel?, Laurie's New Brother, The Big Cheese*. In
many of her books Schlein appears to be a better teacher than she is an inspired writer. We
look for excitement, passion, humor, realism and a combination of some or all of these. In
early books like *Oomi, The New Hunter* and *Amuny, Boy of Old Egypt* the author presents
interesting facts in an exotic setting, but the lifeless prose is a definite liability.

Now, under the impetus of current feminist rhetoric, Schlein has written *The Girl Who
Would Rather Climb Trees* — the kind of book which children will enjoy reading and
rereading. Librarians will find it to be a good selection for their story-telling hour. Although
in our culture it is difficult to believe that a girl of about 5 or 6 has never had a doll, that is the
premise of this role-free book. Melissa is an active, good-natured child who is interested in
everything — roller-skating, reading, cooking, ball playing— everything except dolls. When
she receives one as a present, she uses her imagination to think up ways to play with this
inanimate mass. She would much prefer playing with her baby cousin. Melissa's predicament
and the way she solves it without hurting the gift-givers' feelings will hold the attention of
young readers, male as well as female.

In Schlein's more recent attempt at writing a humorous story, *Bobo the Troublemaker*, the
tale gets bogged down in its spiritless style. It is to be hoped that Schlein, once having entered
the fertile, fairly untilled, field of the non-sexist book, will return to it and give us more of the
ilk of *The Girl Who Would Rather Climb Trees*.

                                                          —Vivian J. Scheinmann

                          _____

SEED, Jenny (Cecile Eugenie Seed).   South African.   Born in Cape Town, 18 May 1930.
Educated at Ellerslie High School, Cape Town. Married Robert Edward Seed in 1954; has
one daughter and three sons. Address: 10 Pioneer Crescent, Northdene, Natal 4093, South
Africa.

PUBLICATIONS FOR CHILDREN

Fiction

The Dancing Mule, illustrated by Joan Sirr. London, Nelson, 1964.
The Always-late Train, illustrated by Pieter de Weerdt. Parow, South Africa,
   Nasionale Boekhandel, 1965.

Small House, Big Garden, illustrated by Lynette Hemmant. London, Hamish
   Hamilton, 1965.
Peter the Gardener illustrated by Mary Russon. London, Hamish Hamilton, 1966.
Tombi's Song, illustrated by Dugald MacDougall. London, Hamish Hamilton, 1966;
   Chicago, Rand McNally, 1968.
To the Rescue, illustrated by Constance Marshall. London, Hamish Hamilton, 1966.
Stop Those Children!, illustrated by Mary Russon. London, Hamish Hamilton, 1966.
Timothy and Tinker, illustrated by Lynette Hemmant. London, Hamish Hamilton,
   1967.
The River Man, illustrated by Dugald MacDougall. London, Hamish Hamilton, 1968.
The Voice of the Great Elephant, illustrated by Trevor Stubley. London, Hamish
   Hamilton, 1968; New York, Pantheon Books, 1969.
Canvas City, illustrated by Lynette Hemmant. London, Hamish Hamilton, 1968.
The Prince of the Bay, illustrated by Trevor Stubley. London, Hamish Hamilton, 1970;
   as *Vengeance of the Zulu King,* New York, Pantheon Books, 1970.
The Great Thirst, illustrated by Trevor Stubley. London, Hamish Hamilton, 1971;
   Scarsdale, New York, Bradbury Press, 1973.
The Red Dust Soldiers, illustrated by Andrew Sier. London, Heinemann, 1972.
The Broken Spear, illustrated by Trevor Stubley. London, Hamish Hamilton, 1972.
The Sly Green Lizard, illustrated by Graham Humphreys. London, Hamish Hamilton,
   1973.
Warriors on the Hills, illustrated by Pat Ludlow. London, Abelard Schuman, 1975.
The Unknown Land, illustrated by Jael Jordan. London, Heinemann, 1976.
Strangers in the Land, illustrated by Trevor Stubley. London, Hamish Hamilton, 1977.

Other

Kulumi the Brave: A Zulu Tale, illustrated by Trevor Stubley. London, Hamish
   Hamilton, and New York, World, 1970.
The Bushman's Dream: African Tales of the Creation, illustrated by Bernard
   Brett. London, Hamish Hamilton, 1974; Scarsdale, New York, Bradbury Press,
   1975.

Jenny Seed comments:
   My mother was a wonderful teller of tales, especially bedtime stories, and my father was a
writer whose hand-written manuscripts filled the cupboards of his bedroom. Bearing these
two facts in mind, it is not surprising that from an early age I too had a great desire to work
with words, and that later, after my marriage when I began to try to write in earnest, my
inclination was towards stories for children.
   In some ways any writing career must be like a snowball rolling down a hill, gathering
momentum and increasing in size the further it goes. Soon short snippets for the children's
pages in newspapers and magazines lengthened out into small novels for younger readers,
and as the books grew I found myself wanting not only an exciting plot but a deeper and
more meaningful theme as well. Aware of the tremendous influence an author of children's
books may have on a young and impressionable mind, this involved much thought and soul
searching in an attempt to find answers that were at once simple enough for the reader and
yet as honest as I could make them. Later when I turned to historical novels for the early
teens this seeking became more accentuated. Though I did not realize it at the time my novels
were probably an expression of my own need to find the reality of God.
   It has been said that history is His Story. For me this was true. The more I delved into and
became absorbed in the shattering and dramatic events of African history, the more I came to
see that all was not just meaningless chaos. Behind the human triumphs and tragedies there
was a great hand holding all together with unswerving purpose and uncompromising truth.
   For me personally the searching came to an end in 1974 when I became a Christian. For

my books, the quest continues, but with a difference. I seem now to be able to write from a firmer standpoint, not so much blindly seeking after what is unknown, but rather reaching forward into a new country which is somehow already known.

*   *   *

Jenny Seed retells South African folk tales and writes historical novels and young children's fantasies for white South African children. This gives her work a distinctive Eurocentric bias, reinforced by the 19th- and early 20th-century sources upon which she bases both her folk tales and fiction. Whereas this bias has made her writing popular with white nationalists in South Africa, it has not gained an equally favorable response from the non-white majority in South Africa and others who value a more African and balanced perspective in South African life.

Jenny Seed's best work is her historical fiction, of which very little has been written by African authors. She writes primarily of the settlement of South Africa by the Boers and the conflicts among African political units, which she calls "tribes" rather than states, during and after the period of settlement. To incorporate historical background in her fiction she has consulted diaries, letters, and documents written by explorers, traders, missionaries and government officials, all of whom were Europeans.

Persons who really lived are included among the characters in Seed's novels, but the heroes and most of the action are fictitious. Regardless of whether the characters are European or African, they speak in the same type of formal English. All actions are presented in a Eurocentric framework: Europeans are depicted as kind and genteel, while Africans are savage and cruel. The Africans who were defending their land against European encroachment are always presented as the adversaries of the Europeans who were trying to settle and alter the Africans' customs.

Jenny Seed's attitude toward South African history is clearly stated in an introductory note to *The Broken Spear*. She views the fall of the Zulu kings at the hands of the Boer Trekkers as part of a larger conflict between "savages" and "civilization," and the wars that occurred as part of a worldwide conflict in which "primitive weapons" were pitted against firearms. She contrasts the "despotism" of Dingane the Zulu leader with the "enormous courage and determination" of the Boers. There is no mention of the Zulu perspective of defending their land, cattle, and people against encroachment by uncompromising foreigners.

Throughout *The Broken Spear* and her other historical fiction, Jenny Seed reflects her Eurocentric perspective by repeated use of vocabulary with negative connotations when referring to Africans. African leaders are referred to as "wicked" and "arrogant," African songs have "deep hissing notes," headdresses are "grotesque," dance music has "frenzied rhythm," is "wild and exciting," dancers have "hideous scars" on their faces, a "witch doctor" has a "hideous smile," people "jabber with excitement" and emit "blood curdling yells" and "terrible screams." This type of depiction of Africans is contrasted to the "sure foundation of Christianity" in accordance with which the Boers live. The Africans are always presented as incapable of "proper" behavior without European assistance. In *The Broken Spear* it is the missionaries who serve as intermediaries and attempt to contain the vigorous Zulu defense of their homeland. While this type of historical fiction reflects white nationalist views and was the core of popular 19th-century adventure stories by G.A. Henty, so one-sided a view of South African history is out-of-tune with contemporary historical scholarship and the sensitive and volatile nature of race relations in Southern Africa today.

—Nancy J. Schmidt

SELDEN, George. Pseudonym for George Selden Thompson. American. Born in Hartford, Connecticut, 14 May 1929. Educated at Loomis School, 1943–47; Yale University

New Haven, Connecticut (Fulbright Fellow, 1951), B.A. 1951. Recipient: Christopher Award, 1970. Address: c/o Farrar Straus and Giroux Inc., 19 Union Square West, New York, New York 10003, U.S.A.

PUBLICATIONS FOR CHILDREN

Fiction

> The Dog That Could Swim under Water, illustrated by Morgan Dennis. New York, Viking Press, 1956.
> The Garden under the Sea, illustrated by Garry MacKenzie. New York, Viking Press, 1957; as Oscar Lobster's Fair Exchange, New York and London, Harper, 1966.
> The Cricket in Times Square, illustrated by Garth Williams. New York, Farrar Straus, 1960; London, Dent, 1961.
> I See What I See!, illustrated by Robert Galster. New York, Farrar Straus, 1962.
> The Mice, The Monks, and the Christmas Tree, illustrated by Jan Balet. New York, Macmillan, and London, Collier Macmillan, 1963.
> Sparrow Socks, illustrated by Peter Lippman. New York, Harper, 1965.
> The Dunkard, illustrated by Peter Lippman. New York, Harper, 1968.
> Tucker's Countryside, illustrated by Garth Williams. New York, Farrar Straus, 1969; London, Dent, 1971.
> The Genie of Sutton Place. New York, Farrar Straus, 1973.
> Harry Cat's Pet Puppy, illustrated by Garth Williams. New York, Farrar Straus, 1974; London, Dent, 1978.

Plays

> The Children's Story, adaptation of the work by James Clavell. New York, Dramatists Play Service, 1966.

Television Play: The Genie of Sutton Place.

Other

> Heinrich Schliemann: Discoverer of Buried Treasure, illustrated by Lorence Bjorklund. New York, Macmillan, and London, Collier Macmillan, 1964.
> Sir Arthur Evans: Discoverer of Knossos, illustrated by Lee Ames. New York, Macmillan, and London, Collier Macmillan, 1964.

*   *   *

After two early works, The Dog That Could Swim under Water and The Garden under the Sea, George Selden achieved an enduring place in children's literature with The Cricket in Times Square. He has also written a sequel, Tucker's Countryside, Sparrow Socks, a fantasy for younger children, and several other books. Like E.B. White, with whose work his is often compared, Selden has a gentle humour, a style notable for its clarity and simplicity, and a warm appreciation of human friendship portrayed through anthropomorphic fantasy. His chief character, Tucker Mouse, is a memorable creation.

The Cricket in Times Square and Tucker's Countryside are sophisticated versions of the fable of the town mouse and the country mouse. The "country mouse" is the childlike and musical Chester the cricket, whose chirping provides a different kind of music from the rattling of trains in the underground railway station which is the setting of the story. Perhaps his coming to New York from the Connecticut countryside represents Selden's growing up in Hartford and settling in New York. And an outsider's view of its citizens is seen in the cultured and soft-moving Harry the cat and the quick-witted, loquacious and money-loving Tucker. The image of the city as a subterranean place, swarming with dirt and vitality, is also interesting. The few humans who stand out from the hurrying crowds are exotic, like the two old Chinese men who provide Chester with a cricket cage and the desperately poor, music-loving Bellinis whose news-stand becomes his home. It is for the Bellinis that Chester sings snatches of opera, and his last concert for them, which brings not only the subway station but also the whole of Times Square to a stand-still, is a most effective scene.

Tucker's Countryside takes the New Yorkers Harry and Tucker to visit Chester in his meadow home, threatened by property developers. *In More Books by More People*, by Lee Bennett Hopkins (1974), Selden writes, "Although I had hundreds of requests for a sequel, I put it off until I thought I had an equally good idea, for the conservation theme is dear to me. I used my own childhood home and the meadow across the street as the book's setting." Thus the subject is a contemporary one, but the book is more traditional than its predecessor. It is good to meet the characters again, and the tone is pleasant and relaxed as the various inhabitants of the meadow are described. But it lacks the pace and originality of the earlier book which, by giving animal fantasy an urban setting, is a truly unusual book.

—Mary Croxson

SENDAK, Maurice (Bernard). American. Born in Brooklyn, New York, 10 June 1928. Educated at Art Students' League, New York, 1949–51. Worked for All American Comics in the 1940's; window display artist, Timely Service, New York, 1946, and F.A.O. Schwartz, New York, 1948–51. One-man shows: Gallery of Visual Arts, New York, 1964; Rosenbach Foundation, Philadelphia, 1970, 1975; Trinity College, Hartford, Connecticut, 1972; Galerie Daniel Keel, Zurich, 1974; Ashmolean Museum, Oxford, 1975. Recipient (for illustration): 18 *New York Times* awards, 1952–76; American Library Association Caldecott Medal, 1964; Hans Christian Andersen International Medal, 1970. L.H.D.: Boston University, 1977. Address: 200 Chestnut Hill Road, Ridgefield, Connecticut 06877, U.S.A.

PUBLICATIONS FOR CHILDREN (illustrated by the author)

Fiction

> *Kenny's Window.* New York, Harper, 1956.
> *Very Far Away.* New York, Harper, 1957; Kingswood, Surrey, World's Work, 1959.
> *The Sign on Rosie's Door.* New York, Harper, 1960; London, Bodley Head, 1969.
> *Where the Wild Things Are.* New York, Harper, 1963; London, Bodley Head, 1967.
> *Higglety Pigglety Pop! or, There Must Be More to Life.* New York, Harper, 1967; London, Bodley Head, 1969.
> *In the Night Kitchen.* New York, Harper, 1970; London, Bodley Head, 1971.

Plays

> *Really Rosie*, adaptation of his own stories *The Sign on Rosie's Door* and *Nutshell Library* (televised, 1975); revised version, music by Carole King. New York, Harper, 1975.

Television Play: *Really Rosie*, 1975.

Verse

> The Nutshell Library (Alligators All Around, Chicken Soup with Rice, One Was Johnny, Pierre: A Cautionary Tale). New York, Harper, 4 vols., 1962; London, Collins, 4 vols., 1964.
> Seven Little Monsters. New York, Harper, and London, Bodley Head, 1977.

Other

> Ten Little Rabbits. Philadelphia, Rosenbach Foundation, 1970.
> Pictures. New York, Harper, 1971; London, Bodley Head, 1972.
> Some Swell Pup; or, Are You Sure You Want a Dog?, with Matthew Margolis. New York, Farrar Straus, 1976.

PUBLICATIONS FOR ADULTS

Other

> Fantasy Sketches. Philadelphia, Rosenbach Foundation, 1970.
> Questions to an Artist Who Is Also an Author: A Conversation Between Virginia Haviland and Maurice Sendak. Washington, D.C., Library of Congress, 1972.
> A Conversation with Maurice Sendak, by Jeffrey Jon Smith. Elmhurst, Illinois, Smith, 1975.

Manuscript Collection: Rosenbach Foundation, Philadelphia.

Theatrical Activities:

Director: **Television** – Really Rosie, 1975.

Illustrator: Atomics for the Millions by M.C. Eidinoff and others, 1947; Wonderful Farm, 1951, and Magic Pictures, 1954, by Marcel Aymé; Good Shabbos, Everybody! by Robert Garvey, 1951; A Hole Is to Dig, 1952, A Very Special House, 1953, I'll Be You and You Be Me, 1954, Charlotte and the White Horse, 1955, I Want to Paint My Bathroom Blue, 1956, The Birthday Party, 1957, Somebody Else's Nut Tree, 1959, and Open House for Butterflies, 1960, all by Ruth Krauss; Maggie Rose by Ruth Sawyer, 1952; The Giant Story, 1953, and What Can You Do with a Shoe?, 1955, by Beatrice Schenk de Regniers; Shadrach, 1953, Hurry Home, Candy, 1953, The Wheel on the School, 1954, The Little Cow and the Turtle, 1955, The House of Sixty Fathers, 1956, Along Came a Dog, 1958, and The Singing Hill, 1962, all by Meindert De Jong; The Tin Fiddle by Edward Tripp, 1954; Mrs. Piggle-Wiggle's Farm by Betty MacDonald, 1954; The Happy Rain, 1956, and Circus Girl, 1957, by Jack Sendak; Little Bear, 1957, No Fighting, No Biting!, 1958, Father Bear Comes Home, 1959, Little Bear's Friend, 1960, Little Bear's Visit, 1961, and A Kiss for Little Bear, 1968, all by Else Minarik; What Do You Say, Dear?, 1958, and What Do You Do Dear?, 1961, by Sesyle Joslin; Seven Tales by Hans Christian Andersen, 1959; The Moon Jumpers, 1959, and Let's Be Enemies, 1961, by Janice Udry; Dwarf Long-Nose by Wilhelm Hauff, 1960; The Tale of Gockel, Hinkel, and Gackeliah, 1961, Schoolmaster Whackwell's Wonderful Sons, 1962, and Sarah's Room, 1963, all by Doris Orgel; The Big Green Book by Robert Graves, 1962; Mr. Rabbit and the Lovely Present by Charlotte Zolotow, 1962; She Loves Me, She Love Me Not! by Robert Keeshan, 1963; Nikolenka's Childhood by Leo Tolstoy, 1963; How Little Lori Visited Times Square by Amos Vogel, 1963; Pleasant Fieldmouse by Jan Wahl, 1964; The Bee-Man of Orn, 1964, and The Griffin and the Minor Canon, 1964, by Frank Stockton; The Bat-Poet, 1964, The Animal Family, 1965, and Fly by Night, 1976, by Randall Jarrell; Hector Protector, and As I Went over the Water: Two Nursery Rhymes, 1965; Lullabies and Night Songs edited by William Engvick, 1965; Zlateh the Goat by Isaac Bashevis Singer, 1966;

Randall Jarrell, 1914–1965 edited by Robert Lowell, Peter Taylor, and Robert Penn Warren, 1967; *Poems from William Blake's Songs of Innocence,* 1967; *The Golden Key,* 1967, and *The Light Princess,* 1969, by George MacDonald; *King Grisly-Beard,* 1973, and *The Juniper Tree and Other Tales,* 1973, by the Grimm Brothers; *Fortunia* by Marie Catherine Aulnoy, 1974.

*   *   *

Maurice Sendak can be viewed as a writer with typically modern characteristics. He deals readily with content related to the subconscious – the childhood fear of rejection, need for self-control, etc. He balances the positive and negative aspects of life on a relatively equal basis, carefully avoids whatever is literal or prosaic, and values play for its own sake.

Sendak's reputation rests largely upon one book: *Where the Wild Things Are.* This tale shows his skill in dealing with something which has more than casual interest to young children: the compulsion to be contrary. When the hero, Max, dreams of untameable monsters and becomes their king, he submerges himself in wildness. But suddenly he says "Stop" to the other "Wild Things" and they obey. When four and five-year-olds hear this read aloud, there is quick comprehension, as well as relief and delight. Max is forgiven and welcomed home, but the most meaningful moment appears to be when he finds that amazing capacity – to stop.

The brief text is swift and repetitious, suiting the literary preferences of very young children. There is also a good phrase to chant: "they roared their terrible roars and gnashed their terrible teeth and rolled their terrible eyes and showed their terrible claws"; and the child is immersed in action with the opening words: "The night Max wore his wolf suit and made mischief ...." A spontaneous blend of form and content, plus a sharp focus on one psychological need in childhood, are the qualities which may account for the book's success.

Four tiny books for the preschool audience are written in traditional form: the cautionary tale *Pierre,* the alphabet book *Alligators All Around,* the counting book *One Was Johnny,* and the book of months *Chicken Soup with Rice.* Sendak calls their rhymed texts doggerel, but this is a self-effacing judgment which hardly fits the pleasantly giddy verses: "In May/ I truly think it best/ to be a robin/ lightly dressed/ concocting soup/ inside my nest./ Mix it once/ mix it twice/ mix that chicken soup/ with rice."

Pierre is especially appealing because it blends nonsense with a recognizable childhood urge. The hero is perfectly believable in wanting to cast off the constraints of his home life. This is achieved with a nonchalant retort: "His father said,/ 'Get off your head/ or I will march you/ up to bed!'/ Pierre said,/ 'I don't care!'/ 'I would think/ that you could see –'/ 'I don't care!'/ 'Your head is where/ your feet should be!'/ 'I don't care!' " Finally he is swallowed and coughed up whole by a lion.

While these four volumes (boxed together as *The Nutshell Library)* represent a less original Sendak, they reveal his fine sense of the ridiculous and his love of sheer entertainment.

Very Far Away is an early book which deserves more attention. It is a fable about running away, and displays Sendak's talent for understatement and allusion. The talking animals are so exactly like humans in their dissatisfactions and quarrels that the brief text has a keenly authentic, as well as whimsical ring.

Higglety Pigglety Pop!, despite its cheerful title, is a book about death and needs a mature child audience. The narrative appears to offer a mere random series of encounters if children are too young to understand the "Castle Yonder" – the after-life destination of the dog Jennie. The many slapstick scenes simply mislead children if they don't perceive that Jennie is about to die, and that heaven will be symbolically treated as a performance in a play called Higglety Pigglety Pop! Sendak's insistence upon revealing everything in both a negative and positive light is demonstrated in the characterization of Jennie. She is selfish, cruel, ungrateful, but finally makes a sacrifice for someone else as the climax approaches. Her questions about life's emptiness are partially answered when she hears a tree complain about its own cycle: fulfillment, discontent and ultimately "winter ... and the empty frozen night." To portray dog heaven as the place where your pet is Leading Lady, can show off everyday, and eat nothing but her favorite dinner is a bizarre but moving solution to the loss of a pet. But the story sustains its coherence, spontaneity and emotional strength only when the life/death implications – not made explicit until the epilogue – are understood.

Sendak's lesser creations include *In the Night Kitchen*, which hardly seems intended for children except in its adventures in a toy-like city. The book's oblique references to old-fashioned cookie advertisements, Laurel and Hardy movies, and various styles of graphic design have little impact upon young readers. A dream experience has insufficient force or form if it offers no meaningful allusions or convincing climaxes. And a climax usually depends upon some kind of life-like tension. Sendak credits the idea of the "night kitchen" dream to his own childhood – his belief that bakers must have all the fun while he must waste the night in sleep. But even this observation seems vapid when its narrative statement has so little shape.

Versatility is something we expect from Sendak. He has been the creator of conventional books such as *Alligators All Around*, unconventional books such as *Where the Wild Things Are*, and books which are so private their durability is hard to predict (as for example, *Higglety Pigglety Pop!*). His reputation as an author is to some degree an offshoot of his early success as an illustrator, especially when in partnership with Ruth Krauss. Nonetheless he has demonstrated his own capacity to be imaginative, lucid, economical, humorous, and immensely appealing to young audiences. His work often expresses a typically 20th-century insight: that childhood is a blend of frustration and bliss. This point has been seldom made in preschool books.

Sendak may not warrant such accolades as "magician" or "Pied Piper" of children's books, but his fame as an innovator and an innately deft fantasist seems entirely justified.

—Donnarae MacCann

SEREDY, Kate. American. Born in Budapest, Hungary, 10 November 1899; emigrated to the United States in 1922. Educated at Academy of Arts, Budapest, art teacher's diploma. Commercial artist and free-lance illustrator. Recipient: American Library Association Newbery Medal, 1938. *Died 7 March 1975.*

PUBLICATIONS FOR CHILDREN (illustrated by the author)

Fiction

    The Good Master. New York, Viking Press, 1935; London, Harrap, 1937.
    Listening. New York, Viking Press, 1936.
    The Singing Tree. New York, Viking Press, 1939; London, Harrap, 1940.
    A Tree for Peter. New York, Viking Press, 1941.
    The Open Gate. New York, Viking Press, 1943; London, Harrap, 1947.
    The Chestry Oak. New York, Viking Press, 1948; London, Harrap, 1957.
    Gypsy. New York, Viking Press, 1951; London, Harrap, 1952.
    Philomena. New York, Viking Press, 1955; London, Harrap, 1957.
    The Tenement Tree. New York, Viking Press, 1959; London, Harrap, 1960.
    A Brand-New Uncle. New York, Viking Press, 1961.
    Lazy Tinka. New York, Viking Press, 1962; London, Harrap, 1964.

Other

    The White Stag. New York, Viking Press, 1937; London, Harrap, 1938.

Illustrator: *The Prince Commands* by Andre Norton, 1934; *Broken Son* by Sonia Daugherty, 1934; *The Selfish Giant*, 1935, and *Gunniwolf*, 1936, edited by Wilhelmina Harper; *Caddie Woodlawn*, 1935, and *Mademoiselle Misfortune*, 1936, by Carol Ryrie Brink; *With Harp and Lute*, 1935, *The Oldest Story*, 1943, and *A Candle Burns for Frances*, 1946, all by Blanche Thompson, and *Bible Children*, 1937, edited by Thompson; *Winterbound* by Margery Williams Bianco, 1936; *Smiling Hill Farm*, 1937, and *A House for Ten*, 1949, by Miriam Mason; *An Ear for Uncle Emil* by Eva Roe Gaggin, 1939; *Michel's Island* by Mabel Leigh Hunt, 1940; *The Christmas Anna Angel* by Ruth Sawyer, 1944; *Hoot-Owl* by Mabel La Rue, 1946; *Adopted Jane*, 1947, *Mary Montgomery, Rebel*, 1948, and *Pilgrim Kate*, 1949, all by Helen Daringer; *Little Vic* by Doris Gates, 1951; *Finnegan II* by Carolyn Sherwin Bailey, 1953; *A Dog Named Penny* by Clyde Robert Bulla, 1955.

*   *   *

Kate Seredy first made her mark as a writer in 1935 when May Massee, the children's editor at Doubleday, suggested that she write a book about her childhood in Hungary. Miss Seredy did just that, and *The Good Master* was the result. Not only did May Massee become one of the outstanding children's book editors of her time, but Kate Seredy went on to win the Newbery Medal in 1938 for *The White Stag* and to make many distinguished contributions to the field of children's literature.

The Good Master is set on a farm on the great Hungarian plains, the home of the "good master," his son Jancsi, and Jancsi's turbulent cousin Kate. Since Miss Seredy spent most of her summers on the plains, she is able to describe vividly the people and customs of Hungary. Harvest festivals, household crafts, and even the local cooking add colour to the warm family story. Since Miss Seredy's first training was as an artist she contributed sensitive and detailed illustrations to all her own and to other people's books. Her stories depict the human situation, the hopes and beliefs of mankind. *The Good Master* was followed by *The Singing Tree* which tells about the effects of war on the "good master's" household. The Magyar legends she heard as a child inspired *The White Stag* and, though it was a prize-winning book, many people regard *The Good Master* as her best book.

Kate Seredy is one of the first children's writers to have dealt with the problems of the alien. *The Singing Tree* tells of the life of Russian prisoners in Hungary during the war, as well as German refugee children who arrive to be restored to health. In *The Chestry Oak* a homeless little boy from Hungary is sent to America where he struggles to become part of that country. Although the hero is young the ideas are adult and explore the ways in which children are affected by the tragedy of war.

Although Kate Seredy was Hungarian by birth and upbringing, she wrote English prose with no trace of foreign idiom. Her books explore values and characteristics familiar to us all, but freshly interesting against an unfamiliar background. In being both author and artist she gave her books an authenticity which is rare.

—Ann Batholomew

SERRAILLIER, Ian (Lucien). British. Born in London, 24 September 1912. Educated at Brighton College, 1926–30; St. Edmund Hall, Oxford, 1931–35, M.A. Married Anne Margaret Rogers in 1944; has three daughters and one son. Schoolmaster, Wycliffe College, Stonehouse, Gloucestershire, 1936–39, Dudley Grammar School, Worcestershire, 1940–46, and Midhurst Grammar School, Sussex, 1946–61. Since 1950, Founder and General Editor, with Anne Serraillier, "New Windmill" series (225 titles), Heinemann Educational Books, London. Recipient: Boys' Clubs of America award, 1960. Address: c/o Heinemann Educational Books Ltd., 48 Charles Street, London W1X 8AH, England.

PUBLICATIONS FOR CHILDREN

Fiction

They Raced for Treasure, illustrated by C. Walter Hodges.   London, Cape, 1946;
abridged edition, as *Treasure Ahead*, London, Heinemann, 1954.

Flight to Adventure, illustrated by C. Walter Hodges.   London, Cape, 1947; abridged
edition, as *Mountain Rescue*, London, Heinemann, 1955.

Captain Bounsaboard and the Pirates, illustrated by Michael Bartlett and Arline
Braybrooke.   London, Cape, 1949.

There's No Escape, illustrated by C. Walter Hodges.   London, Cape, 1950; New York,
Scholastic, 1973.

Making Good, illustrated by Vera Jarman.   London, Heinemann, 1955.

The Silver Sword, illustrated by C. Walter Hodges.   London, Cape, 1956; New York,
Criterion Books, 1959; as *Escape from Warsaw*, New York, Scholastic, 1963.

The Cave of Death, illustrated by Stuart Tresilian.   London, Heinemann, 1965.

Fight for Freedom, illustrated by John S. Goodall.   London, Heinemann, 1965.

Play

A Pride of Lions, music by Phyllis Tate (produced Nottingham, 1970).   London, Oxford
University Press, 1971.

Verse

The Weaver Birds, illustrated by the author.   London, Macmillan, 1944; New York,
Macmillan, 1945.

Thomas and the Sparrow, illustrated by Mark Severin.   London, Oxford University
Press, 1946.

The Ballad of Kon-Tiki and Other Verses, illustrated by Mark Severin.   London, Oxford
University Press, 1952.

Belinda and the Swans, illustrated by Pat Marriott.   London, Cape, 1952.

Everest Climbed, illustrated by Leonard Rosoman.   London, Oxford University Press,
1955.

A Puffin Quartet of Poets, with others, edited by Eleanor Graham, illustrated by Diana
Bloomfield.   London, Penguin, 1958.

Poems and Pictures.   London, Heinemann, 1958.

The Windmill Book of Ballads, illustrated by Mark Severin and Leonard
Rosoman.   London, Heinemann, 1962.

Happily Ever After, illustrated by Brian Wildsmith.   London, Oxford University Press,
1963.

The Midnight Thief, music by Richard Rodney Bennett, illustrated by Tellosa.   London,
BBC Publications, 1963.

Ahmet the Woodseller, music by Gordon Crosse, illustrated by John Griffiths.   London,
BBC Publications, 1965.

The Challenge of the Green Knight, illustrated by Victor Ambrus.   London, Oxford
University Press, 1966; New York, Walck, 1967.

The Turtle Drum, music by Malcolm Arnold, illustrated by Charles Pickard.   London,
BBC Publications, 1967.

Robin in the Greenwood, illustrated by Victor Ambrus.   London, Oxford University
Press, 1967; New York, Walck, 1968.

Robin and His Merry Men, illustrated by Victor Ambrus.   London, Oxford University
Press, 1969; New York, Walck, 1970.

The Ballad of St. Simeon, illustrated by Simon Stern.   London, Kaye and Ward, and
New York, Watts, 1970.

The Tale of Three Landlubbers, illustrated by Raymond Briggs. London, Hamish
   Hamilton, 1970; New York, Coward McCann, 1971.
The Bishop and the Devil, illustrated by Simon Stern. London, Kaye and Ward, and
   New York, Warne, 1971.
Marko's Wedding, illustrated by Victor Ambrus. London, Deutsch, 1972.
Suppose You Met a Witch, illustrated by Ed Emberley. Boston, Little Brown, 1973.
I'll Tell You a Tale: A Collection of Poems and Ballads, illustrated by Charles Keeping
   and Renate Meyer. London, Longman, 1973; revised edition, London, Penguin,
   1976.
The Robin and the Wren, illustrated by Fritz Wegner. London, Penguin, 1974.
How Happily She Laughs and Other Poems. London, Longman, 1976.

Other

Jungle Adventure (based on story by R. M. Ballantyne), illustrated by Vera
   Jarman. London, Heinemann, 1953.
The Adventures of Dick Varley (based on story by R. M. Ballantyne), illustrated by Vera
   Jarman. London, Heinemann, 1954.
Beowulf the Warrior (in verse), illustrated by Mark Severin. London, Oxford
   University Press, 1954; New York, Walck, 1961.
Guns in the Wild (based on story by R. M. Ballantyne), illustrated by Shirley
   Hughes. London, Heinemann, 1956.
Katy at Home (based on story by Susan Coolidge), illustrated by Shirley
   Hughes. London, Heinemann, 1957.
Katy at School (based on story by Susan Coolidge), illustrated by Shirley
   Hughes. London, Heinemann, 1959.
The Ivory Horn: Retold from the Song of Roland, illustrated by William
   Stobbs. London, Oxford University Press, 1960.
The Gorgon's Head: The Story of Perseus, illustrated by William Stobbs. London,
   Oxford University Press, 1961; New York, Walck, 1962.
The Way of Danger: The Story of Theseus, illustrated by William Stobbs. London,
   Oxford University Press, 1962; New York, Walck, 1963.
The Clashing Rocks: The Story of Jason, illustrated by William Stobbs. London,
   Oxford University Press, 1963; New York, Walck, 1964.
The Enchanted Island: Stories from Shakespeare, illustrated by Peter Farmer. London,
   Oxford University Press, and New York, Walck, 1964; abridged edition, as *Murder at
   Dunsinane*, New York, Scholastic, 1967.
A Fall from the Sky: The Story of Daedalus, illustrated by William Stobbs. London,
   Nelson, and New York, Walck, 1966.
Chaucer and His World. London, Lutterworth Press, 1967; New York, Walck, 1968.
Havelok the Dane, illustrated by Elaine Raphael. New York, Walck, 1967; as *Havelok
   the Warrior*, London, Hamish Hamilton, 1968.
Heracles the Strong, illustrated by Rocco Negri. New York, Walck, 1970; London,
   Hamish Hamilton, 1971.
Have You Got Your Ticket? (reader), illustrated by Douglas Hall. London, Longman,
   1972.
The Franklin's Tale, Retold, illustrated by Philip Gough. London, Kaye and Ward,
   and New York, Warne, 1972.
Pop Festival (reader), illustrated by Douglas Hall. London, Longman, 1973.

Editor, with Ronald Ridout, *Wide Horizon Reading Scheme*. London, Heinemann, 4
   vols., 1953–55.

Translator, with Anne Serraillier, *Florina and the Wild Bird*, by Selina Chönz, illustrated
   by Alois Carigiet. London, Oxford University Press, 1952.

PUBLICATIONS FOR ADULTS

Verse

Three New Poets, with Roy McFadden and Alex Comfort.   Billericay, Essex, Grey
   Walls Press, 1942.

*   *   *

Ian Serraillier's great strength is above all as a teller of tales. In his retellings, in his verse,
and in his fiction, it is his skill as a story-teller that is most in evidence. He knows exactly how
to sustain the tension of a story and hold his readers, what to leave out and what to dwell on,
and it is this which makes his versions of the ancient legends – of Heracles, Jason, or Theseus,
of Beowulf or Sir Gawain – so effective. There are a simple strength and vigour in his
writing, an enjoyment of physical skills and courage, and a fine narrative sense which makes
the old stories work marvellously well for the average child who might not otherwise
approach them.
   His stories, prose and verse, read well aloud. He obviously composes with the spoken word
in mind. All his writing appeals strongly to boys, if it is permissible these days to say so, and
is enjoyable from, say, the age of 8.
   He has put together several anthologies which include rewritten ballads and the like as well
as his own verse. Though the force of the originals is sometimes weakened, he makes the old
poems once more accessible to those who would be put off by archaic or dialect words. His
own best verse is quirky and original, as in this "Tickle Rhyme":

> "Who's that tickling my back?" said the wall.
> "Me," said a small
> Caterpillar. "I'm learning
> To crawl."

As far as his original fiction goes, he has written one very fine story based on fact (*The Silver
Sword*) and several rather unremarkable adventure stories. For example, *There's No Escape* is
a war story set in a fictitious country in the Alps. The hero is dropped by parachute to rescue
a missing scientist. England is at war with a fictitious enemy who bears a close resemblance
to the German villains of cliché. It is perhaps unfair to quote at 20 years' remove, but to
present-day readers the cliché verges at times on the comic. Even his middle-aged central
European scientist talks like a British public schoolboy: "Well, Peter, we cannot remain here
for ever. We must – how do you say – face the music alone now." There are a skilful build-
up of excitement and a fine chase over the mountains, but such books cannot really compete
with the good adult thrillers which are also available to this age-group.
   The Silver Sword is another matter. It is a fine achievement. The story is based on true
events and is beautifully fitted to Ian Serraillier's talent. It is the tale of the wanderings of a
family of Polish children across war-torn Europe in search of their father and mother; it has
a happy ending, for the three children are finally reunited with their parents in Switzerland,
and Jan, the child who never finds anyone belonging to him, stays with them. The locale and
the enemy do not have to be invented, and the simple matter-of-fact style in which the story is
told makes it the more convincing and moving. Furthermore this is not a simple goodies-
versus-baddies tale. Not every German is portrayed as unsympathetic, and there is food for
thought in the effect of wartime morality upon Jan, the boy who has joined the Balicki
children in their quest and who has turned himself in order to survive into a brilliant and
convincing liar.

—Mary Rayner

SETON, Ernest (Evan) Thompson.   American.   Born in South Shields, County Durham, England, 14 August 1860; emigrated to Canada, 1866; became United States citizen, 1931. Educated at Elizabeth Street and Victoria Street schools and Collegiate High School, Toronto; Toronto School of Art, 1877–79; Royal Academy School of Painting and Sculpture, London, 1881; Art Students' League, New York, 1884; Académie Julian, Paris, 1891. Married Grace Gallatin in 1896 (divorced, 1935), one daughter; Julia Moss Buttree, 1935, one adopted daughter. Artist for Wilhelms and Betzig, lithographic publishers, New York, 1883–84; illustrator for *The Century Dictionary*, New York, 1885–86; resort manager, Lake Ontario, 1887–90; Manitoba government naturalist after 1892. Free-lance illustrator, naturalist, and lecturer. Founder of the Woodcraft Indians, later the Woodcraft League, 1902; Chairman of the Founding Committee, 1910, and Chief Scout, 1910–15, Boy Scouts of America; Founding President, Seton Institute, Santa Fe, New Mexico, 1930–46. Recipient (for naturalist illustrations): Camp-Fire Gold Medal, 1909; Société d'Acclimatation de France medal, 1918; National Institute of Science Elliott Gold Medal, 1927; John Burroughs Medal, 1928; David Girou Medal, 1930. Associate, Royal Canadian Academy of Art; Member, National Institute of Arts and Letters. *Died 23 October 1946.*

PUBLICATIONS FOR CHILDREN (illustrated by the author)

Fiction

> *Wild Animals I Have Known, Being the Personal Histories of Lobo, Silverspot, Raggylug, Bingo, The Springfield Fox, The Pacing Mustang, Wully, and Redruff.*   New York, Scribner, 1899; London, Nutt, 1900.
> *The Trail of the Sandhill Stag.*   New York, Scribner, and London, Nutt, 1899.
> *Raggylug the Cottontail Rabbit and Other Animal Stories.*   London, Nutt, 1900.
> *The Biography of a Grizzly.*   New York, Century, and London, Hodder and Stoughton, 1900.
> *Lives of the Hunted.*   New York, Scribner, 1901; London, Nutt, 1902.
> *Two Little Savages.*   Montreal, Montreal News Company, and New York, Doubleday, 1903; London, Grant Richards, 1904.
> *Monarch, The Big Bear of Tallac.*   New York, Scribner, 1904; London, Constable, 1905.
> *Animal Heroes, Being the Histories of a Cat, a Dog, a Pigeon, a Lynx, Two Wolves, and a Reindeer.*   New York, Scribner, 1905; London, Constable, 1906.
> *Woodmyth and Fable.*   Toronto, Briggs, and New York, Century, 1905.
> *The Natural History of the Ten Commandments.*   New York, Scribner, 1907; as *The Ten Commandments of the Animal World*, New York, Doubleday, 1923.
> *The Biography of a Silver-Fox; or, Domino Reynard of Goldur Town.*   New York, Century, and London, Constable, 1909.
> *Rolf in the Woods.*   New York, Doubleday, and London, Constable, 1911.
> *Wild Animals at Home.*   Toronto, Briggs, New York, Doubleday, and London, Hodder and Stoughton, 1913.
> *The White Reindeer, Arnaux, and The Boy and the Lynx.*   London, Constable, 1915.
> *The Slum Cat, Snap, and The Winnipeg Wolf.*   London, Constable, 1915.
> *Wild Animal Ways.*   New York, Doubleday, and London, Hodder and Stoughton, 1916.
> *The Preacher of Cedar Mountain: A Tale of the Open Country.*   New York, Doubleday, and London, Hodder and Stoughton, 1917.
> *Woodland Tales.*   New York, Doubleday, and London, Hodder and Stoughton, 1921.
> *Bannertail: The Story of a Gray Squirrel.*   New York, Scribner, 1922; London, Hodder and Stoughton, 1923.
> *Katug the Snow Child.*   Oxford, Blackwell, 1929.
> *Krag, The Kootenay Ram and Other Animal Stories.*   London, University of London Press, 1929.

Johnny Bear, Lobo, and Other Stories.   New York, Scribner, 1935.
Great Historic Animals: Mainly about Wolves.   New York, Scribner, 1937; as *Mainly about Wolves,* London, Methuen, 1937.
The Biography of an Arctic Fox.   New York, Appleton Century, 1937.
Trail and Camp-Fire Stories, edited by Julia M. Seton.   New York and London, Appleton Century, 1940.
Santana, The Hero Dog of France.   Los Angeles, Phoenix Press, 1945.

Play

The Wild Animal Play for Children.   New York, Doubleday, and London, Nutt, 1900.

Other

How to Play Indian.   Philadelphia, Curtis, 1903; as *The Red Book; or, How to Play Indian,* New York, privately printed, 1904.
The Birch-Bark Roll of the Woodcraft Indians.   New York, Doubleday, 1906.
Boy Scouts of America: A Handbook of Woodcraft, Scouting, and Life-Craft.   New York, Doubleday, 1910.
The Book of Woodcraft and Indian Lore.   New York, Doubleday, and London, Constable, 1912.
The Forester's Manual; or, The Forest Trees of Eastern North America.   New York, Doubleday, 1912.
Woodcraft Boys, Woodcraft Girls.   New York, Edgar, 1915.
Sign Talk: A Universal Signal Code.   New York, Doubleday, and London, Curtis Brown, 1918.

Editor, *Famous Animal Stories: Animal Myths, Fables, Fairy Tales, and Stories of Real Animals.*   New York, Brentano's, 1932; London, Lane, 1933.

PUBLICATIONS FOR ADULTS (illustrated by the author)

Other

A List of Animals in Manitoba.   Toronto, Oxford University Press, 1886.
The Birds of Manitoba.   Washington, D.C., United States National Museum, 1891.
Studies in the Art and Anatomy of Animals.   London and New York, Macmillan, 1896.
The National Zoo at Washington, Washington, D.C., Smithsonian Institution, 1901.
Pictures of Wild Animals.   New York, Scribner, 1901.
Bird Portraits, text by Ralph Hoffman.   Boston, Ginn, 1901.
Life-Histories of Northern Animals: An Account of the Mammals of Manitoba.   New York, Scribner, 2 vols., 1909; London, Constable, 2 vols., 1910.
The War Dance and the Fire-Fly Dance.   New York, Doubleday, 1910.
The Arctic Prairies: A Canoe Journey of 2000 Miles in Search of the Caribou. Being an Account of a Voyage to the Region North of Aylmer Lake ....   New York, Scribner, 1911; London, Constable, 1912.
Lives of Game Animals: An Account of Those Land Animals in America North of the Mexican Border Which Are Considered "Game" ....   New York, Doubleday, and London, Hodder and Stoughton, 4 vols., 1925–28.
Animals Worth Knowing.   New York, Doubleday, 1934.
The Trail of an Artist-Naturalist: The Autobiography of Ernest Thompson Seton.   New York, Scribner, 1940; London, Hodder and Stoughton, 1951.
Ernest Thompson Seton's America: Selections from the Writings of the Artist-Naturalist, edited by Farida A. Wiley.   New York, Devin Adair, 1954.
Animal Tracks and Hunter Signs, with Julia M. Seton.   New York, Doubleday, 1958; London, Edmund Ward, 1959.

By a Thousand Fires: Nature Notes and Extracts from the Life and Unpublished Journals,
   edited by Julia M. Seton.   New York, Doubleday, 1967.
The Worlds of Ernest Thompson Seton, edited by John G. Samson.   New York, Knopf,
   1976.

Editor, with Julia M. Seton, *The Gospel of the Redman: An Indian Bible.*   New York,
   Doubleday, 1936; London, Methuen, 1937.

Critical Study: *Ernest Thompson Seton, Naturalist* by Shannon and Warren Garst, New
York, Messner, 1959.

Illustrator: *Bird-Life* by F. M. Chapman, 1887; *Four-Footed Americans* by Mabel Wright,
1898; *First Across the Continent* by Noah Brooks, 1901; *The Rhythm of the Redman* by Julia
Buttree, 1930.

*   *   *

The writings of Ernest Thompson Seton display the savvy of first-hand experience and the
fascination of first time enterprise. His autobiography, *The Trail of an Artist-Naturalist*,
published when he was 80, reflects the same excited agony of discovery found in his first
book, *Wild Animals I Have Known*. Even though his works abound in precise detail and acute
observation derived from unrelenting study (a number of his books, including *Life-Histories
of Northern Animals*, are essentially well-decorated catalogues of the fauna of a particular
region), his controlled ebullience and knowing naivete demonstrate that Seton is legitimately
within the ranks of writers for children.

His characters, arising from naturalists' notations, become distinct and appealing
individuals. Lobo, now subject of a Walt Disney feature, appears in *Wild Animals I Have
Known* as a stylized portrait of a predator. Rejecting the usual inclination of the leader to
assemble an expansive pack, this singular wolf heads a select marauding band of but five
lupines, each pre-eminent in some respect of size, agility, instinct, or aesthetics. The
adventure-laden tale alternates between a wolf's and artist's eye view, and succeeds in
ennobling predation decades prior to any ecologist's outcry. Lobo's uncanny capacity for
rejecting poisoned segments of an animal carcass, his apparent appetite for practical jests, and
his strongly suggested love of beauty fail to romanticize him out of belief. Ultimately the
noble pack is violently exterminated, an end which Seton observed was the way of nature
and thus inseparable from her beauties.

While Seton's description never strays from the facts of nature, the subjects of his
narratives are invariably distinct and individual. To know nature is never to generalize but
"to know one creature from his fellow." Accordingly the life story of a crow from *Wild
Animals* includes on the same page the precise musical notation for specified signals in crow
communication and a description of the hero Silverspot's predilection for toying with a
carefully concealed collection of clam shells, white pebbles, bits of tin, and an old china cup.
Wahb, solitary subject of *The Biography of a Grizzly*, likewise is at once typical and unique.
The biggest grizzly in the park, he reputedly "knows more about plants and roots than a
whole college of botanists." Such almost endearing respect for this savage hunter parallels
Seton's approach to cruelty and violence. An incident in which a callous hunter cuts down a
mother and three cubs leaving Wahb an orphan and a loner throughout life, is presented
without moralizing, though Seton with supple understatement concludes the narration with
"That is why the post office is called Four-Bears. The Colonel seemed pleased with what he
had done; indeed he told of it himself." *Lives of the Hunted*, comprising 8 indelible
biographies of preyed-upon creatures, also conveys compassion for wildlife without intrusive
sentimentality. Death, sudden and cruel, is inevitable, but then so is the will to thrive.

While a significant number of Seton's books have been expropriated for children, not
infrequently he writes explicitly for them. In 1900 he adapted *Wild Animals* into *The Wild
Animal Play for Children*, a drama which contains "an alternate reading for very young

children," with staging, music, costumes, and other dramatic effects carefully detailed by the author. The style, even of the simplified version, appears more suited for Jacobean masque than childhood recitation, but the conception provides ample scope for impersonation of woodland inhabitants, wildmen, and even of angels. His attention to children is by no means casual. He founded the Woodcraft League, served as its chief and was author, editor and illustrator of its guidebook. *The Birch-Bark Roll* is a compendium of outdoor life and lore. *Woodland Tales*, among others, is specifically addressed to a younger audience, while *Rolf in the Woods*, an elaborate series of adventures of a boy scout, a dog, and an Indian, is dedicated to the Boy Scouts of America.

His classic composition, *Two Little Savages*, is a thinly-veiled autobiography of his youthful years which were stamped by an ingenuously impassioned determination to live as an Indian. With a companion, Yan, the youthful naturalist embarks upon an often awkward return to aborigine ways. The book is replete with moments touching and comic, and ideals deflated and irrepressible, but the young hero learns from a sequence of false starts and ends up assembling a hard-earned but substantial accumulation of primitive lifestyles.

Seton's principal concern, however, continued to be the animals themselves. A second grizzly became the study for biography in *Monarch, The Big Bear of Tallac*. Unlike the earlier tale of Wahb, *Monarch* shows the interaction of human and animal becoming more conspicious and less opposed. Seton's animal characters, posed against a natural landscape and confronting circumstances conforming to the environs, retain a lively caricature quite surpassing the dull personifications which dominate and denude animal denizens of many a children's book. His hallmark, individualized realistic fantasy, is applied to domestic creatures as well. *Animal Heroes* contains a low-keyed odyssey of a slum cat who prevails in a world designed and denigrated by man. Another chapter chronicles a game though smallish homing pigeon whose legendary perseverence is finally cut short by an eyrie of peregrines. The human figures become progressively more prominent, intereacting with lynxes, bull terriers and jack rabbits. Mankind even in its youth is cruel, but it can learn compassion. Seton's involvements seem to stress that repeated experience heartens rather than hardens the soul.

—Leonard R. Mendelsohn

SEUSS, Dr. Pseudonym for Theodor Seuss Geisel. American. Born in Springfield, Massachusetts, 2 March 1904. Educated at Dartmouth College, Hanover, New Hampshire, A.B. 1925; Lincoln College, Oxford, 1925–26. Served in the United States Army Signal Corps and Information and Education Division, 1943–46; Lieutenant-Colonel; Legion of Merit. Married Helen Marion Palmer in 1927 (died, 1967); Audrey Stone Diamond, 1968. Free-lance magazine humorist and cartoonist from 1927; advertising illustrator, Standard Oil Company of New Jersey, 1928–41, and for Ford Motor Company; editorial cartoonist, *PM* magazine, New York, 1940–42; publicist, War Production Board, 1940–42; correspondent, *Life* magazine, Japan, 1954. Since 1957, Founding President and Editor-in-Chief, Beginner Books, Random House Inc., New York. One-man shows: San Diego Fine Arts Museum, 1950; Dartmouth College, 1975; Toledo Museum of Art, Ohio, 1975; La Jolla Museum of Contemporary Arts, 1976. Recipient: Academy Award, for documentary, 1946, 1947, for animated cartoon, 1951; Peabody Award, for television cartoon, 1971 (twice); Zagreb International Cartoon Festival award, 1972. L.H.D.: Dartmouth College, 1956; American International College, Springfield, Massachusetts, 1968; Lake Forest College, Illinois, 1977. Address: 7301 Encelia Drive, La Jolla, California 92037, U.S.A.

PUBLICATIONS FOR CHILDREN (illustrated by the author)

Plays

Screenplay: *Gerald McBoing-Boing* (cartoon), 1951.

Television Plays: *How the Grinch Stole Christmas*; *Horton Hears a Who*; *The Cat in the Hat*; *The Lorax*; *Dr. Seuss on the Loose*; *Hoober Bloob Highway*.

Verse

And to Think That I Saw It on Mulberry Street. New York, Vanguard Press, 1937; London, Country Life, 1939.

The 500 Hats of Bartholomew Cubbins. New York, Vanguard Press, 1938; London, Oxford University Press, 1940.

The King's Stilts. New York, Random House, 1939; London, Hamish Hamilton, 1942.

Horton Hatches the Egg. New York, Random House, 1940; London, Hamish Hamilton, 1942.

McElligot's Pool. New York, Random House, 1947; London, Collins, 1975.

Thidwick, The Big-Hearted Moose. New York, Random House, 1948; London, Collins, 1968.

Bartholomew and the Oobleck. New York, Random House, 1949.

If I Ran the Zoo. New York, Random House, 1950.

Scrambled Eggs Super! New York, Random House, 1953.

Horton Hears a Who! New York, Random House, 1954.

On Beyond Zebra. New York, Random House, 1955.

If I Ran the Circus. New York, Random House, 1956; London, Collins, 1969.

The Cat in the Hat. New York, Random House, 1957; London, Hutchinson, 1958.

How the Grinch Stole Christmas. New York, Random House, 1957.

The Cat in the Hat Comes Back! New York, Random House, 1958; London, Collins, 1961.

Yertle the Turtle and Other Stories. New York, Random House, 1958; London, Collins, 1963.

Happy Birthday to You! New York, Random House, 1959.

One Fish, Two Fish, Red Fish, Blue Fish. New York, Random House, 1960; London, Collins, 1962.

Green Eggs and Ham. New York, Random House, 1960; London, Collins, 1962.

Ten Apples Up on Top! (as Theo Le Sieg), illustrated by Roy McKie. New York, Random House, 1961; London, Collins, 1963.

The Sneetches and Other Stories. New York, Random House, 1961; London, Collins, 1965.

Sleep Book. New York, Random House, 1962; London, Collins, 1964.

Hop on Pop. New York, Random House, 1963; London, Collins, 1964.

ABC. New York, Random House, 1963; London, Collins, 1964.

I Wish That I Had Duck Feet (as Theo Le Sieg), illustrated by B. Tobey. New York, Random House, 1965; London, Collins, 1967.

The Fox in Socks. New York, Random House, 1965; London, Collins, 1966.

I Had Trouble in Getting to Solla Sollew. New York, Random House, 1965; London, Collins, 1967.

Come Over to My House (as Theo Le Sieg), illustrated by Richard Erdoes. New York, Random House, 1966; London, Collins, 1967.

The Foot Book. New York, Random House, 1968; London, Collins, 1969.

The Eye Book (as Theo Le Sieg), illustrated by Roy McKie. New York, Random House, 1968; London, Collins, 1969.

I Can Lick 30 Tigers Today and Other Stories. New York, Random House, 1969; London, Collins, 1970.

Mr. Brown Can Moo! Can You? New York, Random House, 1970; London, Collins, 1971.

The Lorax. New York, Random House, 1971; London, Collins, 1972.

In a People House (as Theo Le Sieg), illustrated by Roy McKie. New York, Random House, 1972; London, Collins, 1973.

Marvin K. Mooney, Will You Please Go Now? New York, Random House, 1972; London, Collins, 1973.

The Many Mice of Mr. Brice (as Theo Le Sieg), illustrated by Roy McKie. New York, Random House, 1973; London, Collins, 1977.

Did I Ever Tell You How Lucky You Are? New York, Random House, 1973; London, Collins, 1974.

The Shape of Me and Other Stuff. New York, Random House, 1973; London, Collins, 1974.

Wacky Wednesday (as Theo Le Sieg), illustrated by George Booth. New York, Random House, 1974; London, Collins, 1975.

There's a Wocket in My Pocket! New York, Random House, 1974; London, Collins, 1975.

Great Day for Up!, illustrated by Quentin Blake. New York, Random House, 1974; London, Collins, 1975.

Would You Rather Be a Bullfrog? (as Theo Le Sieg), illustrated by Roy McKie. New York, Random House, 1975.

Oh, The Thinks You Can Think. New York, Random House, 1975; London, Collins, 1976.

Hooper Humperdink ... ? Not Him!, illustrated by Charles Martin. New York, Random House, 1976; London, Collins, 1977.

Please Try to Remember the First of Octember (as Theo Le Sieg), illustrated by Arthur Cumings. New York, Random House, 1977.

Other

The Cat in the Hat Dictionary, by the Cat Himself, with Philip D. Eastman. New York, Random House, 1964.

The Cat in the Hat Songbook. New York, Random House, 1967.

My Book about Me – By Me, Myself. I Wrote It! I Drew It!, illustrated by Roy McKie. New York, Random House, 1969.

I Can Draw It Myself. New York, Random House, 1970.

I Can Write – By Me, Myself (as Theo Le Sieg). New York, Random House, 1971.

The Cat's Quizzer. New York, Random House, 1976; London, Collins, 1977.

PUBLICATIONS FOR ADULTS

Short Story

The Seven Lady Godivas. New York, Random House, 1939.

Plays

Screenplays: *Your Job in Germany (Hitler Lives),* 1946; *Design for Death,* with Helen Palmer Geisel, 1947; *The 5000 Fingers of Dr. T.,* with Allan Scott, 1953.

Other

Signs of Civilization! (as Seuss).   La Jolla, California, La Jolla Town Council, 1956.
Lost World Revisited: A Forward Looking Backward Glance.   New York, Award
   Books, 1967.

Manuscript Collection: Special Collections, University of California Library, Los Angeles.

Illustrator: Boners, and More Boners, both 1931.

*   *   *

A whole library of entertaining books has been created by Theodor Geisel, commonly
known as Dr. Seuss. The stories are all famous for their fanciful invention, yet they offer
considerable variety. How the Grinch Stole Christmas is a seasonal book, his Sleep Book is a
bedtime story, and The Fox in Socks is a collection of such tongue-twisters as "Through three
cheese trees three free fleas flew." The Sneetches, Horton Hears a Who, and the "Grinch"
story are moral tales, and The 500 Hats of Bartholomew Cubbins resembles a folktale. Seuss
also varies his style with the use of verse, prose, limited and unlimited vocabularies.

The limited vocabulary books such as The Cat in the Hat (with 223 different words) and
Green Eggs and Ham (with 50) constitute the beginning of a new genre in children's books:
publications which are not comparable to textbooks intended to increase skill, but a literature
designed for early, pleasurable reading. In 1957 Dr. Seuss demonstrated for the first time a
high standard of readability in books the first grader could be expected to read independently.
Only someone with untold patience and a keen love of language could have continued the
beguiling "cat in the hat" within a verbal formula. This creature performs hair-raising tricks
to enliven a rainy day for housebound children. Of course the mayhem is unseen by the
unsuspecting parents.

In his earliest children's book, And to Think That I Saw It on Mulberry Street, Dr. Seuss
established the pattern for books which consist of loosely joined imaginative scenes. Being
daydreams, they lack a dynamic progression; but each scene is an appealing improvisation
whenever it contains ingenuity, humor, and intriguing word play. These are consistently
present in McElligot's Pool, Scrambled Eggs Super!, Dr. Seuss' Sleep Book, If I Ran the
Circus, If I Ran the Zoo, and On Beyond Zebra.

Seuss' passion for words is extreme but not reckless. In If I Ran the Circus he announces
the trapeze artist with this grammatical absurdity: "My Zoom-a-Zoop Troupe from West
Upper Ben-Deezing/ Who never quite know, while they zoop and they zoom,/ Whether
which will catch what one, or who will catch whom/ Or if who will catch which by the
what and just where,/ Or just when and just how in which part of the air!"

Inventing eccentrics is one of Seuss' most singular achievements, and the pages of the
daydream books are overrun with odd creatures. There is one who eats hot pebbles in order
to blow smoke from his ears. Another bites his over-long tail before bedtime, and the
sensation wakes him up exactly eight hours later. Such character sketches are brief, vivid,
and concrete.

In the Sleep Book, everyday experiences are intermixed with the fantastic, producing a
pleasing variation and that reminder of home which young children find particularly
satisfying. "Sleep thoughts/ Are spreading/ Throughout the whole land./ The time for night-
brushing of teeth is at hand./ Up at Herk-Heimer Falls, where the great river rushes/ And
crashes down crags in great gargling gushes,/ The Herk-Heimer Sisters are using their
brushes./ Those falls are just grand for tooth-brushing beneath/ If you happen to be up that
way with your teeth."

The moral tales and those stories in the folk tradition display a skillful treatment of
characters, incidents, and themes. The 500 Hats of Bartholomew Cubbins includes a peasant
hero, a king, a magically performing hat, and an unscrupulous duke. The style makes use of
the parallel phrases of fairy tales, as well as parallel happenings. A key feature is the logic

underlying the dramatic encounter of the hero with the king and the Royal Executioner. With spooked hats reproducing themselves, the protagonist cannot obey the protocol – "hats off to the king" – nor remove his hat to be beheaded (a rule in the executioner's book). These bureaucratic realities anchor the story to human experience, while at the same time the magic is exuberant. The sequel, *Bartholomew and the Oobleck*, suffers from a trite ending and from repetitious slapstick images of the gooey "oobleck" falling like rain and sticking everything together. But in other respects this book repeats the attractions of its predecessor.

Among the themes in the moral tales we find such problems as uninvited guests, greed, racial prejudice, and disdain for the small. This latter abuse is overcome by an unflaggingly heroic elephant in *Horton Hears a Who*, yet the motto is stated in low key and in a natural context. Horton finds a speck of dust which turns out to be a very small person – a "Who" – living on top of a clover. "Who" voices are inaudible to any but elephant ears, and thus the whole jungle is full of non-believers. They decide to tie up Horton and do away with the speck. Saving the microscopic "Who" community makes an intensely dramatic climax.

Dr. Seuss is a well-disciplined nonsense poet. In America his name is a household word, and this reputation stems from his exceptional wit, inimitable characters, ingenious images, substantial themes, and meticulous rhymes and rhythm. Sometimes he draws upon the forms, motifs and gross exaggerations of tall tales. But the full secret of his childlike humor is hard to determine. Ultimately it must derive from a deeply intuitive grasp of the child's perspective and free spirit.

—Donnarae MacCann

SEVERN, David. Pseudonym for David Storr Unwin. British. Born in London, 3 December 1918; son of the publisher Sir Stanley Unwin. Educated at Abbotsholme School, Derbyshire, 1933–36. Married Bridget Mary Herbert in 1945; has twin daughter and son. Editorial Assistant, League of Nations Secretariat, Geneva, 1938; worked for Unwin Brothers, printers, Woking, Surrey, 1939, and Basil Blackwell, booksellers, Oxford, 1940; Member of the Production Department, George Allen and Unwin, publishers, London, 1941–43. Address: St. Michaels, Helions Bumstead, Haverhill, Suffolk, England.

PUBLICATIONS FOR CHILDREN

Fiction

Rick Afire!, illustrated by Joan Kiddell-Monroe. London, Lane, 1942.
A Cabin for Crusoe, illustrated by Joan Kiddell-Monroe. London, Lane, 1943; Boston, Houghton Mifflin, 1946.
Waggon for Five, illustrated by Joan Kiddell-Monroe. London, Lane, 1944; Boston, Houghton Mifflin, 1947.
A Hermit in the Hills, illustrated by Joan Kiddell-Monroe. London, Lane, 1945.
Forest Holiday, illustrated by Joan Kiddell-Monroe. London, Lane, 1946.
Ponies and Poachers, illustrated by Joan Kiddell-Monroe. London, Lane, 1947.
Bill Badger and the Pine Martens [*Bathing Pool, Buried Treasure*], illustrated by Geoffrey Higham. London, Lane, 3 vols., 1947–50.
Wily Fox and the Baby Show [*Christmas Party, Missing Fireworks*], illustrated by Geoffrey Higham. London, Lane, 3 vols., 1947–50.
The Cruise of the "Maiden Castle," illustrated by Joan Kiddell-Monroe. London, Lane, 1948; New York, Macmillan, 1949.

Treasure for Three, illustrated by Joan Kiddell-Monroe. London, Lane, 1949; New York, Macmillan, 1950.

Dream Gold, illustrated by A. K. Lee. London, Lane, 1949; New York, Viking Press, 1952.

Crazy Castle, illustrated by Joan Kiddell-Monroe. London, Lane, 1951; New York, Macmillan, 1952.

Burglars and Bandicoots, illustrated by Joan Kiddell-Monroe. London, Lane, 1952.

Drumbeats!, illustrated by Richard Kennedy. London, Lane, 1953.

Blaze of Broadfurrow Farm, illustrated by Kiff and Wilmore. London, Lane, 1955.

Walnut Tree Meadow, illustrated by Kiff and Wilmore. London, Lane, 1955.

The Future Took Us, illustrated by Jillian Richards. London, Lane, 1958.

The Green-Eyed Gryphon, illustrated by Prudence Seward. London, Hamish Hamilton, 1958.

Foxy-Boy, illustrated by Lynton Lamb. London, Bodley Head, 1959; as *The Wild Valley*, New York, Dutton, 1963.

Three at the Sea, illustrated by Margery Gill. London, Bodley Head, 1959.

Jeff Dickson, Cowhand, illustrated by Patrick Williams. London, Cape, 1963.

Clouds over the Alberhorn. London, Hamish Hamilton, 1963.

A Dog for a Day, illustrated by Joseph Acheson. London, Hamish Hamilton, 1965.

The Girl in the Grove. London, Allen and Unwin, 1974.

The Wishing Bone. London, Allen and Unwin, 1977.

Other

My Foreign Correspondent Through Africa, illustrated by Peter White. London, Meiklejohn, 1951.

PUBLICATIONS FOR ADULTS (as David Unwin)

Novels

The Governor's Wife. London, Joseph, 1954; New York, Dutton, 1955.

A View of the Heath. London, Joseph, 1956.

David Severn comments:
The series of straightforward adventure stories, with which I made my name in the 1940's, provided entertainment in their time, but I would choose to be remembered not for them but for a handful of off-beat works: *Dream Gold*, *Drumbeats!*, *Foxy-Boy*, and *The Girl in the Grove*. I feel that my fantasies are the most interesting – and certainly the most original – of all my books.

*   *   *

David Severn's work falls into two basic groups: his "holiday-adventure" family stories and his three semi-fantasies, two of which are outstanding. His first children's book, *Rick Afire!*, was written as an "escape" when he was working in wartime London and this, together with its four successors, are entertaining but fairly typical "sub-Ransome" countryside family adventures. The same can basically be said of his subsequent family adventures about the Warners (Alan, Joan, and Christopher). His Bill Badger books for younger children were nicely-done and won wide popularity.

But it was with *Dream Gold* and *Drumbeats!* that Severn's reputation really soared. In the first, two schoolboys in Cornwall share an identical dream, which transports them to a Pacific island to re-create an ancient adventure involving treasure and pirates. In the second, a group of children at a co-educational school discover an old African native – and bewitched –

drum which, when beaten upon, causes them to re-live the experiences of a doomed jungle expedition. In both stories the children are well-characterized and the atmosphere hauntingly created. In *The Future Took Us*, a well-written but slightly dated story, two schoolboys are taken forward in time to the year 3000, with only one of them returning to the present. Another of Severn's memorable books is *Foxy-Boy*, about a boy who runs on all-fours and who was brought up by the foxes.

Severn's stories are told in good, workmanlike prose, with occasional passages of brilliance and power — and it is on *Dream Gold* and *Drumbeats!* that his reputation will surely rest.

—Brian Doyle

SEWELL, Helen (Moore). American. Born in Mare Island, California, 27 June 1896. Educated at Packer Institute; Pratt Institute Art School, New York; Archipenko's Art School, New York. Free-lance illustrator. Recipient: *New York Times* award, for illustration, 1955. *Died 24 February 1957.*

PUBLICATIONS FOR CHILDREN (illustrated by the author)

Fiction

> *A Head for Happy.* New York, Macmillan, 1931.
> *Blue Barns.* New York, Macmillan, 1933; London, Woodfield, 1955.
> *Ming and Mehitable.* New York, Macmillan, 1936.
> *Peggy and the Pony.* New York and London, Oxford University Press, 1937.
> *Jimmy and Jemima.* New York, Macmillan, 1940.
> *Peggy and the Pup.* New York and London, Oxford University Press, 1941.
> *Birthdays for Robin.* New York, Macmillan, 1943; London, Hale, 1947.
> *Belinda the Mouse.* New York and London, Oxford University Press, 1944.
> *Three Tall Tales,* with Elena Eleska. New York, Macmillan, 1947.

Other

> Editor, *Words to the Wise: A Book of Proverbs.* New York, Dodd Mead, 1932.

Illustrator: *Mr. Hermit Crab* by Mimsey Rhys, 1929; *A Round of Carols* by Thomas Noble, 1929; *ABC for Everyday,* 1930; *The Christmas Tree in the Woods* by Susan Smith, 1932; *Little House in the Big Woods,* 1932, *Farmer Boy,* 1933, *Little House on the Prairie,* 1935, *On the Banks of Plum Creek,* 1937, *By the Shores of Silver Lake,* 1939, *The Long Winter,* 1940, and *Little Town on the Prairie,* all by Laura Ingalls Wilder; *Broomstick and Snowflake* by Johan Falkberget, 1933; *Where Is Adelaide?,* 1933, and *Ann Frances,* 1935, by Eliza Orne White; *A First Bible,* 1934; *Cinderella,* 1934; *Away Goes Sally,* 1934, *Five Bushel Farm,* 1939, *The Fair American,* 1940, *The White Horse,* 1942, and *The Wonderful Day,* 1946, all by Elizabeth Coatsworth; *Bluebonnets for Lucinda,* 1934, and *Tag-along Tooloo,* 1941, by Frances Clarke Sayers; *Peter and Gretchen of Old Nuremberg* by Viola May Jones, 1935; *Pinocchio* by C. Collodi, 1935; *Ten Saints* by Eleanor Farjeon, 1936; *The Magic Hill and Other Stories,* 1937, and *The Princess and the Apple Tree and Other Stories,* 1937, by A. A. Milne; *Baby Island* by Carol Ryrie Brink, 1937; *Jane Eyre* by Charlotte Brontë, 1938; *The Young Brontës* by Mary Louise Jarden, 1938; *Pride and Prejudice* by Jane Austen, 1940; *The Blue-Eyed Lady* by Ferenc Molnár, 1942; *Book of Myths* by Thomas Bulfinch, 1942; *Christmas Magic* by James S. Tippett, 1944; *Once There Was a Little Boy* by Dorothy

Kunhardt, 1946; *Brave Bantam* by Louise Seaman, 1946; *Azor,* 1948, *Azor and the Haddock,* 1949, and *Azor and the Blue-Eyed Cow,* 1951, all by Maude Cowley; *Secrets and Surprises* by Irmengarde Eberle, 1951; *Mrs. McThing* by Mary Chase, 1952; *The Bears on Hemlock Mountain,* 1952, and *The Thanksgiving Story,* 1954, by Alice Dalgliesh; *Poems* by Emily Dickinson, 1952; *Colonel's Squad,* 1952, *In the Beginning,* 1954, and *The Three Kings of Saba,* 1955, all by Alf Evers; *Grimm's Tales,* 1954.

*   *   *

Helen's Sewell's contributions to children's literature have invariably been favorably commented on by her critics. It is virtually impossible, therefore, to discover a serious discussion of children's books that does not deal with her offerings on positive terms. This well-deserved high regard, which places Sewell in the upper echelon of the field of children's books, has come about, however, because of her illustrations for these books rather than for her efforts as a writer. In the latter half of her career, from roughly the mid-1940's onward, Sewell gave up almost entirely the writing of picture storybooks. She concentrated on illustrations, to become one of the most honored of her profession, and very famous writers for children vied for her services as the illustrator of their texts. She remains, as well, one of the most adaptable. She revealed in one instance how she used the attractions children find in comic books to her advantage (in *Three Tall Tales* she imitated as nearly as possible the layout for the words as they are used in comics).

Far less familiar, even to the critics of children's literature, are the writings she did for children in the first half of her career. These books have never received the honors nor the attention of her illustrations. And rightly so, one must admit, since while the language of the studiously abbreviated picture storybooks which Sewell both wrote and illustrated is by and large thoughtfully pleasant, clear in the way it relates concepts, and even at times amusing, it is not distinguished in either the themes or in their dramatic effects.

All of her early books are now obscure and out of print (with the exception of *Blue Barns*). *A Head for Happy* is told with few words, indeed. In fact, some of its pictures are given no explanation at all. The words Sewell uses are there to punctuate a story line of three little sisters who make a doll and then go around the world searching for a proper head to fit its body. *Blue Barns* is an amusing, gentle, and true story of a farm, a funny gander, and some wild geese. It is a small picture book, for beginning readers, whose brief text prohibits any remarkable literary effect by its author. The slight plot of *Ming and Mehitable* (a "closet drama," as one critic called it) illustrated another theme which would concern only a very young child. Here the heroine's dog runs away after being pestered by being dressed up in baby clothes. Since after a search its master can find no animal so friendly, she promises the dog freedom from such minor mistreatment if he will return. *Peggy and the Pony* likewise is a story of a preoccupation only a young child would appreciate, the unrequited wish for a pony. After a number of frustrations the girl in this tale does get her request. These quiet stories, very feminine in tone, have few psychological involvements.

But Sewell's attempts at rather more complicated plots of an obviously greater psychological nature, as in *Jimmy and Jemima* and in *Belinda the Mouse*, do little to advance her reputation as a distinctive writer. The ordinary language found here fails for that purpose. As noted, it was at about this point in her life that Sewell probably wisely decided to limit her work almost entirely to the illustration of works of writers more talented than she. It is important to note, as well, that the girlish stories of this outstanding illustrator, but rather ordinary writer, happily have lost little of their original attractiveness by the passage of time. They can still be enjoyed by today's children.

—Patrick Groff

SHANNON, Monica. American. Born in Canada; moved to the United States as an infant. Educated at schools in Seattle and Idaho; Bachelor of Library Science from school in California. Married. Worked in the Los Angeles Public Library. Recipient: American Library Association Newbery Medal, 1935. *Died 13 August 1965.*

P∪BLICATIONS FOR CHILDREN

Fiction

California Fairy Tales, illustrated by C. E. Millard. New York, Doubleday, and London, Heinemann, 1926.
Eyes for the Dark, illustrated by C. E. Millard. New York, Doubleday, 1928; as *More Tales from California,* 1935.
Tawnymore, illustrated by Jean Charlot. New York, Doubleday, 1931.
Dobry, illustrated by Atanas Katchamakoff. New York, Viking Press, 1935; London, Harrap, 1936.

Verse

Goose Grass Rhymes, illustrated by Neva Kanaga Brown. New York, Doubleday, 1930.

*   *   *

Monica Shannon has to her credit five children's books – *California Fairy Tales, Eyes for the Dark, Goose Grass Rhymes, Tawnymore,* and *Dobry.* The first two are books of artistic fairy tales; the third, a book of light-hearted verse; the fourth, a pirate story of a half-breed boy; and the fifth, the story of a Bulgarian peasant boy with aspirations to become a great artist.

Collectively Miss Shannon's books attest to her intense appreciation of nature and environment; her respect and appreciation of human, plant, and animal life; and her regard and appreciation of the cultural traditions in her own family background and that of others. Traces of Monica Shannon's pleasant childhood spent in the mountains of Montana and California are evident in *Tawnymore,* in *Dobry,* and in her two books of California fairy tales. From the Bulgarian immigrants who worked on her father's ranch young Monica learned about Bulgarian customs and folkways, and from the extensive mountain ranch lands over which she roamed freely during her childhood, she learned about animals, plants and other natural life. Her keen eye for observing nature and the environment around her and her penchant for descriptive, colorful, and figurative language are clearly at work in all her writings. In "It's Going to Rain" from *Goose Grass Rhymes,* for example, Miss Shannon describes in pictorial words and with poetic ease sun and shade playing tag, winds running races, and linen dancing on the clothes-lines. In "The Tree Toad," with equal ease, the poet shows readers a neat creature "with tidy rubbers on his feet," a creature who knows nothing but embarrassment. She knows the toad is embarrassed because "his color comes, his color goes." And as to the lowly caterpillar, Miss Shannon is of the opinion that "he giggles, as he wiggles, across a hairy leaf."

The delightful tales published in *California Fairy Tales* and in *Eyes for the Dark* are numerous and varied – an amalgamation of Spain, America, Ireland, and Fairyland itself. The tales begin with such interest-capturing openers as "Now it is true that three old witch women did live under a Judas tree, right where two parts of Kaweah River run together like jabbering gossips" or "Now, once upon a time, when the Elder Berries were very young Berries and the Sierra Nevada Mountains were still down under the Pacific Ocean, a certain Pigwidgeon lived alongside the sea." Obviously tales beginning in such a fashion lend themselves well to oral telling and/or reading. It is therefore not surprising that a number of the tales have recently appeared in phonodisc format.

Dobry, by far the most widely known of Miss Shannon's.works, is the inspiring story of a young Bulgarian peasant boy who determines to be a great sculptor; many of the incidents are based on the experiences of Atanas Katchamakoff, the Bulgarian-born sculptor who provided the illustrations for the book. Dobry lives with his mother, Roda, and his grandfather in a peaceful Bulgarian village. Dobry's father has been killed in war, and the mother's only ambition for her son is that "he be learning to take his father's place in the fields one day." Being too hard-working and practical-minded herself to understand her son's artistic bent, Roda is prone to remind Dobry that the big peasant he will grow up to be will have no time for picture making. But Dobry's grandfather, whose personal philosophy is that people should wish to be different rather than alike, gently coaxes Roda to an understanding that her son must be allowed to develop in directions other than those she has dreamed. It is this development that constitutes the narrative of the book, through which readers learn not only about Dobry but also about Bulgarian village life and the stability and strength of people who live close to the soil. The major characters in *Dobry* are strong and well-delineated Grandfather being one of the chief among them. He is something of a homespun philosopher and storyteller, admired not only by his grandson but by everyone. Several of Grandfather's tales, such as the "Poplar Tree Story" and "The Story of Hadutzi-Dare" are cleverly interwoven into the fabric of *Dobry*. The pages which reveal the artistic, as well as the physical, development of Dobry are filled with colorful descriptions and imagery.

Although Monica Shannon's literary works for children were all published between 1926 and 1934, the fact that three of them, *Dobry, California Fairy Tales*, and *More Tales from California* (originally *Eyes for the Dark*), still remain in print attests to their literary quality and universality of appeal.

—Charity Chang

SHARMAT, Marjorie Weinman. American. Born in Portland, Maine, 12 November 1928. Educated at Lasell Junior College, Auburndale, Massachusetts, 1946–47; Westbrook Junior College, Portland, 1947–48, graduated 1948. Married Mitchell B. Sharmat in 1957; has two sons. Member, Circulation Staff, Yale University Library, 1951–54, and Yale Law Library, 1954–55, New Haven, Connecticut. Address: 8801 East Calle Playa, Tucson, Arizona 85715, U.S.A.

PUBLICATIONS FOR CHILDREN

Fiction

Rex, illustrated by Emily McCully. New York, Harper, 1967.
Goodnight Andrew Goodnight Craig, illustrated by Mary Chalmers. New York, Harper, 1969.
Gladys Told Me to Meet Her Here, illustrated by Edward Frascino. New York, Harper, 1970.
A Hot Thirsty Day, illustrated by Rosemary Wells. New York, Macmillan, and London, Collier Macmillan, 1971.
51 Sycamore Lane, illustrated by Lisl Weil. New York, Macmillan, and London, Collier Macmillan, 1971; as *The Spy in the Neighborhood*, New York, Collier, and London, Collier Macmillan, 1974.
Getting Something on Maggie Marmelstein, illustrated by Ben Shecter. New York, Harper, 1971; London, Abelard Schuman, 1975.
A Visit with Rosalind, illustrated by Lisl Weil. New York, Macmillan, 1972.

Nate the Great, illustrated by Marc Simont.   New York, Coward McCann, 1972;
   Kingswood, Surrey, World's Work, 1974.
Sophie and Gussie, illustrated by Lillian Hoban.   New York, Macmillan, 1973;
   Kingswood, Surrey, World's Work, 1974.
Morris Brookside, A Dog, illustrated by Ronald Himler.   New York, Holiday House,
   1973.
Morris Brookside Is Missing, illustrated by Ronald Himler.   New York, Holiday House,
   1974.
Nate the Great Goes Undercover, illustrated by Marc Simont.   New York, Coward
   McCann, 1974.
I Want Mama, illustrated by Emily McCully.   New York, Harper, 1974.
Walter the Wolf, illustrated by Kelly Oechsli.   New York, Holiday House, 1975.
I'm Not Oscar's Friend Anymore, illustrated by Tony DeLuna.   New York, Dutton,
   1975.
Nate the Great and the Lost List, illustrated by Marc Simont.   New York, Coward
   McCann, 1975; Kingswood, Surrey, World's Work, 1977.
Burton and Dudley, illustrated by Barbara Cooney.   New York, Holiday House, 1975.
Maggie Marmelstein for President, illustrated by Ben Shecter.   New York, Harper,
   1975.
The Lancelot Closes at Five, illustrated by Lisl Weil.   New York, Macmillan, 1976.
The Trip and Other Sophie and Gussie Stories, illustrated by Lillian Hoban.   New York,
   Macmillan, 1976.
Edgemont, illustrated by Cyndy Szekeres.   New York, Coward McCann, 1976.
Mooch the Messy, illustrated by Ben Shecter.   New York, Harper, 1976.
I Don't Care, illustrated by Lillian Hoban.   New York, Macmillan, 1977.
I'm Terrific, illustrated by Kay Chorao.   New York, Holiday House, 1977.
Nate the Great and the Phony Clue, illustrated by Marc Simont.   New York, Coward
   McCann, 1977.

Marjorie Weinman Sharmat comments:
   I write picture books, easy readers, and novels for children. I have a resident pest in my
head and that's why I'm a writer. This pest is never satisfied and constantly furnishes me
with new ideas and nags me to get them on paper. I like to write funny books because I think
that life is basically a serious business and needs a humorous counterbalance.

                              *   *   *

   A versatile author of books for younger children, Marjorie Weinman Sharmat writes
successfully for three age groups. Her first book, *Rex*, is a drolly imaginative tale of a small
boy who has decided to be a dog and who is willing to bring the man next door his
newspaper and slippers in his teeth to prove it. The gentle humor of her first story for
preschoolers foreshadowed some of Sharmat's strongest features: a real originality in story
concept and the ability to work within the constraints of a simplified vocabulary list in a fresh
and original manner. *Nate the Great*, a tale with echoes of James Bond's Secret Agent 007,
tells of a dead-pan 9-year-old detective, Nate, who can solve any case, provided he is properly
primed with pancakes, from finding a lost cat to unearthing a purloined picture, but who is
glad as he walks off into the rain at the end of the book that he has taken his mother's advice
and has worn his rubbers.
   In contrast to the fresh originality and real ingenuity of *Nate the Great*, a second controlled
vocabulary series, the *Sophie and Gussie* stories, is written in a dull, rather pedestrian manner
which displays none of Sharmat's understated wit and her unusual ability to create a small
literary tour-de-force within the constraints of a controlled vocabulary as in the *Nate* books.
   Children who like the humor of *Nate the Great* also enjoy *Walter the Wolf*, a slyly
humorous tale of a perfect young wolf who after years of practicing his violin, writing

poetry, and never biting anybody, decides to go into the biting business professionally. After his first "victim" bites him back, he decides that, although he is through trying to be perfect, biting is probably not the best way to make a living.

Representative of another literary genre exploited successfully in several of Sharmat's books for young children is her *I'm Not Oscar's Friend Anymore*. In this juvenile "stream of consciousness" concept book, Oscar's "former friend" thinks of all his reasons for being mad at Oscar and thinks how sad Oscar must be feeling now that he has just lost his best friend. He finally decides he will do Oscar a big favor and make up. Sharmat's attempt to recreate the thought process of a young child is handled with charm and wit and has the ring of truth about it.

For children in the middle grades, two books about Maggie Marmelstein, an urban sixth grader and her sometime friend Thad Smith (*Getting Something on Maggie Marmelstein* and *Maggie Marmelstein for President*) tell in a light-hearted and realistic manner the trials of being a sub-teenager. Thad relates the first story and Maggie the second.

The Lancelot Closes at Five moves out of the city and into the suburbs where we are introduced to Abby and Hutch, two girls in their early teens, who carry through an ingenious scheme to run away – to a model home in a new housing development a few doors from their own homes. How their plan, which seems a little pointless, backfires into a free bit of publicity for the villain of the piece, the unscrupulous promoter of the development, provides the rather thin thread of plot.

Although Sharmat has proved herself a successful writer for children of all ages, she is at her best when she is writing for the youngest children. The droll humor and the subtle charm of the best of her little books set them off as minor classics for preschoolers.

—Margaret Maxwell

SHARP, Edith (Lambert). Canadian. Born near Carroll, Manitoba, 7 March 1917. Educated at Penticton High School, British Columbia; Vancouver School of Art; Smithsonian Institution, Washington, D.C. Has taught creative writing in evening classes and summer schools. Recipient: Canadian Children's Book Award, 1958; Governor-General's Award, 1959. Address: c/o Little Brown and Company, 34 Beacon Street, Boston, Massachusetts 02106, U.S.A.

PUBLICATIONS FOR CHILDREN

Fiction

   Nkwala, illustrated by William Winter.   Boston, Little Brown, 1958; London, Dent, 1959.

PUBLICATIONS FOR ADULTS

Plays

   The Little People of Crazy Mountain.   New York, Nelson, 1963.

   Radio Plays: *Kaminkin; Let the Grey Smoke Rise; Now in Fire; Enemy Firewood*.

*   *   *

Far too many tales perpetuate the image of the North American Indian as a painted savage, fierce, quarrelsome and cruel. There will never be enough stories of the quality of Edith Sharp's *Nkwala* to counteract the stereotyped false and misleading image; pearls of great price are few and far between. This is a book of rare and satisfying beauty. It happens to concern the Spokan Indians of British Columbia, but it is about living, breathing people, who, though they lived many years ago, might as easily live today, for their humanity transcends arbitrary man-made boundaries.

Nkwala is a Salish boy of the Spokan tribe, whose laws demand that he find a guardian spirit through lonely nights of prayer, fasting and ordeal; but try as he may, no spirit comes to Nkwala through many vigils.

His tribe have lived in industrious peace for many years in the same village, but prolonged drought drives them out of their parched homeland. Reluctantly, carrying such goods as they can, they leave to seek some new hospitable home. As the trek goes on for many days, scouts begin to find signs of trouble. Others are on the march, and some travel not in peace but as raiders. The Spokan must follow the trail of evil men who have left a thirst for revenge in their wake. There are graves, too, of those the raiders have murdered, left often without the proper rites of passage along the white sky trail that will lead their spirits to rest. In pity, the Spokan pause for their shaman to help these spirits find their way to the Good Happy Place; but many lost ones were tiny children, afraid of strangers, used to the ways of women. Bright-eyes, mother of Nkwala, bravely stays through the awesome night to mother the lost children, her soft lullaby assuring them that here they will find only love.

At last the new home is found, but enemies are already in possession. Believing the Spokan to be the raiders, Okanagon warriors attack. Nkwala manages to delay them until his people reach safety; in the time he has gained, a parlay takes place. A treaty is reached, but the Okanagon claim Nkwala as a son of their tribe and a pledge of peace. Indian law dictates that he must go without a backward glance, though his heart breaks inwardly.

Then the Spokan shaman tells of his night among the spirits of the lost little ones, and of the woman who braved all terror to bring them peace. The Okanagon, moved by heroism, reward it by returning Nkwala to his mother's arms. Each tribe recognizes generosity in the other. Together they will put down the raiders, and live as brothers in peace; and among them Nkwala will grow to be a great and wise leader of men.

The story is simply told in language that sings. The great love and respect of the Indian for his environment and for his fellow man has the ring of truth, and should be exemplary to all readers. This is a rare piece of work, not only for children, though young readers love *Nkwala*, but for anyone who has the good fortune to encounter it.

—Joan McGrath

SHARP, Margery. British. Born in 1905. Educated at Streatham Hill High School, London; Bedford College, University of London, B.A. (honours) in French. Married Major Geoffrey Castle in 1938. Army Education Lecturer in World War II. Lives in London. Address: c/o William Heinemann Ltd., 15–16 Queen Street, London W1X 8BE, England.

PUBLICATIONS FOR CHILDREN

Fiction

The Rescuers, illustrated by Judith Brook.   London, Collins, and Boston, Little Brown, 1959.

Miss Bianca, illustrated by Garth Williams. London, Collins, and Boston, Little
  Brown, 1962.
The Turret, illustrated by Garth Williams. Boston, Little Brown, 1963; London,
  Collins, 1964.
Lost at the Fair, illustrated by Rosalind Fry. Boston, Little Brown, 1965; London,
  Heinemann, 1967.
Miss Bianca in the Salt Mines, illustrated by Garth Williams. London, Heinemann,
  and Boston, Little Brown, 1966.
Miss Bianca in the Orient, illustrated by Erik Blegvad. London, Heinemann, and
  Boston, Little Brown, 1970.
Miss Bianca in the Antarctic, illustrated by Erik Blegvad. London, Heinemann, 1970;
  Boston, Little Brown, 1971.
Miss Bianca and the Bridesmaid, illustrated by Erik Blegvad. London, Heinemann,
  and Boston, Little Brown, 1972.
The Magical Cockatoo, illustrated by Faith Jaques. London, Heinemann, 1974.
The Children Next Door, illustrated by Hilary Abrahams. London, Heinemann, 1974.
Bernard the Brave, illustrated by Faith Jaques. London, Heinemann, 1976; Boston,
  Little Brown, 1977.

Other

Mélisande, illustrated by Roy McKie. London, Collins, and Boston, Little Brown,
  1960.

PUBLICATIONS FOR ADULTS

Novels

Rhododendron Pie. London, Chatto and Windus, and New York, Appleton, 1930.
Fanfare for Tin Trumpets. London, Barker, 1932; New York, Putnam, 1933.
The Nymph and the Nobleman. London, Barker, 1932.
The Flowering Thorn. London, Barker, 1933; New York, Putnam, 1934.
Sophy Cassmajor. London, Barker, and New York, Putnam, 1934.
Four Gardens. London, Barker, and New York, Putnam, 1935.
The Nutmeg Tree. London, Barker, and Boston, Little Brown, 1937.
Harlequin House. London, Collins, and Boston, Little Brown, 1939.
The Stone of Chastity. London, Collins, and Boston, Little Brown, 1940.
*Three Companion Pieces: Sophy Cassmajor, The Tigress on the Hearth, and The Nymph
  and the Nobleman.* Boston, Little Brown, 1941; London, Collins, 1955.
Cluny Brown. London, Collins, and Boston, Little Brown, 1944.
Britannia Mews. London, Collins, and Boston, Little Brown, 1946.
The Foolish Gentlewoman. London, Collins, and Boston, Little Brown, 1948.
Lise Lillywhite. London, Collins, and Boston, Little Brown, 1951.
The Gypsy in the Parlour. London, Collins, and Boston, Little Brown, 1954.
The Eye of Love. London, Collins, and Boston, Little Brown, 1957.
Something Light. London, Collins, 1960; Boston, Little Brown, 1961.
Martha in Paris. London, Collins, 1962; Boston, Little Brown, 1963.
Martha, Eric and George. London, Collins, and Boston, Little Brown, 1964.
The Sun in Scorpio. London, Heinemann, and Boston, Little Brown, 1965.
In Pious Memory. Boston, Little Brown, 1967; London, Heinemann, 1968.
Rosa. London, Heinemann, 1969; Boston, Little Brown, 1970.
The Innocents. London, Heinemann, 1971; Boston, Little Brown, 1972.
The Faithful Servants. London, Heinemann, and Boston, Little Brown, 1975.
Summer Visits. London, Heinemann, 1977.

Short Stories

>   *The Lost Chapel Picnic and Other Stories.*   London, Heinemann, and Boston, Little
>   Brown, 1973.

Plays

>   *Meeting at Night* (produced London, 1934).
>   *Lady in Waiting,* adaptation of her novel *The Nutmeg Tree* (produced New York,
>   1940). New York, French, 1941.
>   *The Foolish Gentlewoman,* adaptation of her own novel (produced London,
>   1949). London, French, 1950.

Television Play: *The Birdcage Room,* 1954.

Manuscript Collection: Houghton Library, Harvard University, Cambridge, Massachusetts.

*   *   *

Margery Sharp, as a children's writer, is primarily the creator of Miss Bianca. When, in
The Magical Cockatoo, she abandons this enchanting mouse for the adventures of a little
Victorian girl, her work seems thinner. Although the book has Miss Sharp's usual wit and
some entertaining social satire, Lally's adventures are mostly too trivial to arouse much
suspense or sympathy. But the Miss Bianca series is caviare for any age – a sophisticated taste,
addictive to those who acquire it.

The first of them, *The Rescuers,* is still for many readers the most delightful of all. It is here
we first see the Mouse Prisoners' Aid Society in action, when Miss Bianca, the white mouse
from the Embassy (later the Society's President), sets out with the plebeian Bernard and the
nautical Norwegian mouse Nils, to rescue a poet from the Black Castle. Their horrific
encounters with the warder's cat arouse real suspense and excitement.

In the later stories we are often reminded of the minute size of the mice, but in other
respects they are more anthropomorphic than rodent. The characters remain unchanged,
except that the low-born Bernard's devotion to Miss Bianca, originally rather touching,
becomes imperceptibly a satirical absurdity. But Miss Sharp's inventiveness is inexhaustible.
Miss Bianca finds herself in the most dramatic and exciting situations, whether freezing in
Antarctic wastes, lost in a salt-mine, exploring the main drain of the Embassy, or playing the
harp to a cruel Ranee whose attendants are all too frequently condemned to be trampled to
death by elephants. Her hairbreadth escapes from these dangers are as wittily contrived as
they are unexpected. Bernard's mackintosh is inflated as a raft and wafted by cheerful gangs
of juvenile delinquent bats; Miss Bianca captivates an elephant; they encounter a group of
marble angels in a crypt, dispossessed from an old churchyard but consoling themselves with
a rendering of "All Things Bright and Beautiful" – naturally in the manner of "a perfectly
trained ladies-voice choir" with harp accompaniment.

Much of the humour derives from ironic contrast – the elegant sophistication of Miss
Bianca's life and surroundings, mouse though she is, or her aristocratic culture set against
Bernard's worthy but innocently vulgar tastes.

Only a child who reads well can fully enjoy these books, for their subtlest appeal is that of
language itself, a delight in words and the rhythm of words for their own sake, a pleasure in a
consciously mannered and elaborate diction akin to the pleasures of social ceremony, and the
satirist's pleasure in impish and unexpected bathos:

>   "What traces could there be but of blood upon these bricks, from the child's tender,
>   bare feet? If only she had her bedroom slippers!" sighed Miss Bianca. "To be
>   unshod makes for one danger more."

"You mean she might pick up athlete's foot?" suggested Bernard sympathetically.

These are books for the connoisseur, and blessedly have no design at all upon the reader except that of entertainment.

—Margaret Greaves

———————

SHELLEY, Noreen. Australian. Born in Lithgow, New South Wales. Educated at the Methodist Ladies' College, Burwood, New South Wales; Julian Ashton School. Has one son and one daughter. Taught in elementary schools for four years; Lecturer in Art, Sydney Teachers' Training College, and Abbotsleigh College, Wahroonga, New South Wales; Writer, Australian Broadcasting Commission, Sydney, 1943–45; Assistant Editor, 1949–60, and Editor, 1960–69, *School Magazine*, Sydney. Recipient: Australian Book Council Book of the Year Award, 1973. Address: 20 Bromborough Road, Roseville, New South Wales 2069, Australia.

PUBLICATIONS FOR CHILDREN

Fiction

> *Piggy Grunter's Red Umbrella* [*Nursery Rhymes, at the Fire, at the Circus*], illustrated by Ralph Shelley. Sydney, Johnson, 4 vols., 1944.
> *Animals of the World*, illustrated by Adye Adams. Melbourne, Robertson and Mullens, 1952.
> *The Runaway Scooter*, illustrated by Adye Adams. Melbourne, Robertson and Mullens, 1953.
> *Piggy Grunter Stories*, illustrated by Ralph Shelley. Sydney and London, Angus and Robertson, 1954.
> *Snowboy*, illustrated by Margaret Senior. Sydney, John Sands, 1958.
> *Three Cheers for Piggy Grunter*, illustrated by Elisabeth MacIntyre. Sydney, Angus and Robertson, 1959; London, Angus and Robertson, 1960.
> *Family at the Lookout*, illustrated by Robert Micklewright. London, Oxford University Press, 1972.
> *Faces in a Looking-Glass*, illustrated by Astra Lacis Dick. London, Oxford University Press, 1974.
> *Cat on Hot Bricks*, illustrated by Robert Gibson. London, Oxford University Press, 1975.

Plays

> *King of Spain and Other Plays* (includes *Silly Billy, The Toys That Came Alive, The Five Little Rabbits, A Different Santa Claus*). Melbourne, Robertson and Mullens, 1953.

> Other Plays: *Puss in Boots; Little Red Riding Hood*.

Other

> *The Baker* [*Dentist, Life Savers, Postman*], illustrated by Iris Millington. Melbourne, Longman, 4 vols., 1963.

Roundabout 1 (reader), illustrated by Astra Lacis Dick.   Sydney, Horwitz Martin, 1967.
Legends of the Gods: Strange and Fascinating Tales from Around the World, illustrated
by Astra Lacis Dick.   London, Angus and Robertson, 1976.

*   *   *

Noreen Shelley writes with an immediacy that grasps the reader's interest and holds it until her story is told. Her years as editor of the New South Wales Education Department's *School Magazine* gave her an extremely sound professional training, and although she had been writing stories since her Teachers' Training days, her writing has developed and reached maturity only within the past few years. Her serious work consists of three novels written for older children, beginning with the prize-winning *Family at the Lookout*, published in 1972, and a collection of myths and legends. Her novels could be described as family adventure stories, and do indeed involve families, including parents, and not just boy and girl protagonists with a scattering of adult characters for the sake of credibility. They are realistic, topical stories which show the author's understanding of children's interests and attitudes to the events around which the books are built. The interplay between characters – children and adults – is interesting and convincing, for the characters develop and change as a result of the events of the story. Noreen Shelley has an excellent ear for dialogue, and her style is attractive to young readers as she has the knack of writing from their level without straining after effect. There is nothing ostentatiously Australian about her books, but her characters are unmistakeably Australian.

The books flow with a deceptive ease, and add up to a more accomplished whole than the bare outline of the strong, and in some ways commonplace, plots would suggest. Incidents such as the inheritance of a very large house, romantically situated in the mountains, the kidnapping of a baby, an attempted hijack of a plane could provide plots for sensational and hackneyed stories, but a strong plot can be an advantage, and these books certainly do involve their readers. While such events are somewhat more romantic than everyday life, they are presented realistically in a recognisable society, and readers would not find it difficult to identify themselves with her characters. Her books are made more attractive to some children because of the security of the warm family atmosphere, evoked with its natural mixture of humour, minor rivalry, and irritation, as well as affection and understanding. The backgrounds to her stories are always presented vividly and authentically, varying from suburban Sydney, to the Blue Mountains, and to a family's experiences on a trip to Europe: such varied and interesting settings add to the impact of the stories themselves.

—Marcie Muir

SHERRY, Sylvia. British.   Born in Newcastle upon Tyne, Northumberland. Educated at Heaton High School, and Kenton Lodge College of Education, both Newcastle; King's College, University of Durham (Spence Watson Prize), B.A. in English. Married to Norman Sherry. Assistant Mistress, Primary School and Girls' High School, and Lecturer, College of Education, 1955–60, all Newcastle; lived in Singapore, 1960–64. Agent: Jonathan Clowes Ltd., 20 New Cavendish Street, London W.1. Address: 6 Gillison Close, Melling, near Carnforth, Lancashire LA6 2AD, England.

Fiction

>*Street of the Small Night Market.* London, Cape, 1966; as *Secret of the Jade Pavilion*, Philadelphia, Lippincott, 1967.
>*Frog in the Coconut Shell.* London, Cape, and Philadelphia, Lippincott, 1968.
>*A Pair of Jesus-Boots.* London, Cape, 1969; as *The Liverpool Cats*, Philadelphia, Lippincott, 1969.
>*The Loss of the "Night Wind."* London, Cape, 1970; as *The Haven Screamers*, Philadelphia, Lippincott, 1970.
>*A Snake in the Old Hut.* London, Cape, 1972; Nashville, Nelson, 1973.
>*Dark River, Dark Mountain.* London, Cape, 1975.
>*Mat, The Little Monkey*, illustrated by Janusz Grabianski. London, Dent, and New York, Scribner, 1977.

Plays

>Television Plays: *Little Pig*, 1976; *It's Our Turn* series, 1977.

Sylvia Sherry comments:

A novel for me begins with a place – a village, town, or particular area – and I do a lot of work finding out about the place and the people who live there. I hope to find the people I will write about in that setting. For example, Ah Wong, hero of my first novel, derived from a boy I saw working at a food stall in a street in Singapore at midnight. He was about 12 and was walking along the street tapping two pieces of bamboo together to tell people the noodle dish his stall made was ready. I hope also that the story will come out of the setting and will be an adventure that could happen only there. *The Loss of the "Night Wind"* was based on the loss of an actual fishing boat off the Northumberland coast. I like to travel and so my novels have a variety of settings. My aim is to create authentic characters in an authentic setting with an adventure plot.

* * *

Sylvia Sherry's books have a number of common characteristics but show that shift of emphasis and priority that stamp her as a developing writer.

The settings of *Street of the Small Night Market*, *A Snake in the Old Hut*, and *Frog in a Coconut Shell*, though exotic, anchor the stories in everyday reality. Yusuf, in the third of these, exemplifies her preference for boy heroes. He longs for excitement and gets it in a tangle with Indonesian raiders. Plot interest predominates, and with ghosts, miraculous pets, and recognisable baddies we are near to the world of the comic paper. A more serious book is *A Pair of Jesus-Boots*. The dangers and the limited horizons are easier to appreciate. Rocky O'Rourke gets his kicks from crime in an attempt to ape his brother, Joey. The idol falls as Joey shows his yellow streak, but the withdrawal of adulation is helped by caretaker Mr. Oliver. The real villain, the professional, Jim Simpson, has no redeeming features. The action crowds into the final pages and the theme, in this case hero-worship, has moved into centre-stage.

Back in a fishing village, *The Loss of the "Night Wind"* keeps us guessing as to who swamped a "coble." The twists of the plot require alertness in the reader, and there is tension between the story as mystery and the story as vehicle for psychological study and philosophical comment. The investigator is a boy, John Watt, who has the cocky cleverness of many boy heroes, but here it is carefully distanced, a fact which does stop him irritating us too much. The same cannot be said of eccentric Holy Island Joe, John's foil, who functions by instinct and speaks in sententious and self-conscious riddles. Villain Will Martin is "a man you couldn't say was good or bad." This marks a definite advance, but Mrs. Sherry's desire to baffle us prevents the character's satisfactory development.

Dark River, Dark Mountain has a similarly inscrutable villain in John Dale, and the setting is also England, this time during the war. Excitement is in the air, with spies and threats of invasion, and death is no joke. Colin is like John Watt, a precocious outsider, and significantly the heroes are now the narrators. In this book, sex rears a pretty French head, although the owner's attractions have largely to be taken on trust. The tale is absorbing, but the writer's increasing interest in states of mind, lyrically explored, vies for attention with the mystery. Mrs. Sherry's later books have more to offer an older reader than her earlier ones did. They tempt one to speculate that she finds the earlier formulae too constricting for her talent and ambitions.

—A.W. England

SHOTWELL, Louisa R(ossiter). American. Born in Chicago, Illinois, 1 May 1902. Educated at Wellesley College, Massachusetts, B.A. 1924; Stanford University, California, M.A. 1928. Formerly, high school English teacher and college dean of women. Address: 184 Columbia Heights, Brooklyn, New York 11201, U.S.A.

PUBLICATIONS FOR CHILDREN

Fiction

> *Roosevelt Grady*, illustrated by Peter Burchard. Cleveland, World, 1963; London, Bodley Head, 1966.
> *Adam Bookout*, illustrated by W.T. Mars. New York, Viking Press, 1967.
> *Magdalena*, illustrated by Lilian Obligado. New York, Viking Press, 1971.

Other

> *Beyond the Sugar Cane Field: UNICEF in Asia.* Cleveland, World, 1964.

PUBLICATIONS FOR ADULTS

Play

> *The Dark Valley.* New York, Friendship Press, 1964.

Other

> *This Is the Indian American* [*Your Neighbor, the Migrant*]. New York, Friendship Press, 3 vols., 1955–58.
> *The Harvesters: Story of the Migrant People.* New York, Doubleday, 1961.

> Editor, with Elsie C. Pickhard, *Every Tribe and Tongue*. New York, Friendship Press, 1960.

Manuscript Collection: University of Wyoming, Laramie.

*   *   *

Louisa R. Shotwell is a good, dependable writer of readable books for children: her stories concern boys and girls of today, kids with problems to face and solve. Adam Bookout, for example, must realize and accept the fact that his parents have been killed in a plane crash. He has been unable to face the disaster, has fantasized that his parents are really still alive and will one day unexpectedly return, till at last, unable to remain in the neighbourhood so haunted by his memories, he runs away from the Aunties who are his guardians, to confront reality in the mixed milieu of the big city. It's a smoothly written book, with all ends neatly tied at its close.

Similarly with *Magdalena*. A Puerto Rican girl living in Brooklyn, Magdalena has problems in assimilation. Her long, lustrous black braids are a source of pride to her old-country grandmother and a misery to Magdalena. She doesn't want to look prim and old-fashioned beside the other girls in her school; she longs for a short smart, smooth haircut. But when she is tempted into a hairdresser's shop, and confronts her Nani with neatly clipped hair, the old woman is sure she has been bewitched and sets about exorcising her. A rather slight plot, smoothly handled, with a colourful and eccentric cast of characters and a neatly satisfactory happy ending.

But Shotwell's *Roosevelt Grady* falls into another category altogether. Roosevelt too is a boy with a problem, but his story is a special event in children's literature. This is a great book, and not only for child readers. Roosevelt's family are itinerant fruit pickers in the south-western U.S.A., which means that they never stay more than a few weeks in any one place, for they must follow the crops to make a scanty living. Schooling becomes a very patchy business under these conditions – a few weeks here, a few weeks there. Roosevelt has been taught all about "taking away from" three or four times, but he never seems to get past that boring lesson to the one he longs for, the one that will teach him "putting into."

Roosevelt and his mother share a secret dream, of settling down to stay in one place, of Roosevelt and Sister going to a regular school, of little brother Matthew having the treatment that will perhaps cure his lameness, of baby Princess Anne growing up in a proper house with real curtains. In a bravely good-spirited story that is never consciously pathetic but often deeply moving, Roosevelt and his best friend Manowar, a nameless waif, do all that two small boys can do to alter the Grady family's way of life.

This story too has at least a temporary happy ending: the longed-for home is a derelict bus, but to Roosevelt it is a dream come true. This is a story of dauntless courage, the ordinary, everyday kind that all too often passes unnoticed. Louisa Shotwell noticed.

—Joan McGrath

SINGER, Isaac Bashevis. American. Born in Radzymin, Poland, 14 July 1904; emigrated to the United States in 1935; naturalized citizen, 1943. Educated at Tachkemoni Rabbinical Seminary, Warsaw, 1920–22. Married Alma Haimann in 1940; has one son. Proof Reader and Translator, *Literarishe Bleter*, Warsaw, 1922–33. Since 1935, Journalist, *Jewish Daily Forward*, New York. Recipient: Louis Lamed Prize, 1950, 1956; National Institute of Arts and Letters grant, 1959; Daroff Memorial Award, 1963; National Endowment for the Arts grant, 1966 (twice); Brandeis University Creative Arts Award, 1969; National Book Award, for children's literature, 1970, for fiction, 1974; Agnon Gold Medal, 1975. Ph.D.: Hebrew University, Jerusalem; D.H.L.: Hebrew Union College, Los Angeles, 1963; D. Litt.: Texas Christian University, Fort Worth; Colgate University, Hamilton, New York, 1972; Litt.D.: Bard College, Annandale on Hudson, New York, 1974. Member, National Institute of Arts and Letters, 1965; American Academy of Arts and Sciences, 1969; Jewish Academy of Arts and Sciences; Polish Institute of Arts and Sciences. Agent: Robert Lescher, 155 East 71st Street, New York, New York 10021. Address: 209 West 86th Street, New York, New York 10024, U.S.A.

PUBLICATIONS FOR CHILDREN (translated by the author and Elizabeth Shub)

Fiction

Zlateh the Goat and Other Stories, illustrated by Maurice Sendak. New York, Harper, 1966; London, Secker and Warburg, 1967.
Mazel and Shlimazel; or, The Milk of a Lioness, illustrated by Margot Zemach. New York, Farrar Straus, 1967.
The Fearsome Inn, illustrated by Nonny Hogrogian. New York, Scribner, 1967; London, Collins, 1970.
When Schlemiel Went to Warsaw and Other Stories, illustrated by Margot Zemach. New York, Farrar Straus, 1968.
Joseph and Koza; or, The Sacrifice to the Vistula, illustrated by Symeon Shimin. New York, Farrar Straus, 1970.
Alone in the Wild Forest, illustrated by Margot Zemach. New York, Farrar Straus, 1971.
The Topsy-Turvy Emperor of China, illustrated by William Pène du Bois. New York, Harper, 1971.
The Fools of Chelm and Their History, illustrated by Uri Shulevitz. New York, Farrar Straus, 1973.
A Tale of Three Wishes, illustrated by Irene Lieblich. New York, Farrar Straus, 1976.
Naftali the Storyteller and His Horse, Sus, and Other Stories, illustrated by Margot Zemach. New York, Farrar Straus, 1976; London, Oxford University Press, 1977.

Other

A Day of Pleasure: Stories of a Boy Growing Up in Warsaw (autobiographical), photographs by Roman Vishniac. New York, Farrar Straus, 1969.
Elijah the Slave: A Hebrew Legend Retold, illustrated by Antonio Frasconi. New York, Farrar Straus, 1970.
The Wicked City, illustrated by Leonard Everett Fisher. New York, Farrar Straus, 1972.
Why Noah Chose the Dove, illustrated by Eric Carle. New York, Farrar Straus, 1974.

PUBLICATIONS FOR ADULTS

Novels

The Family Moskat, translated by A.H. Gross. New York, Knopf, 1950; London, Secker and Warburg, 1966.
Satan in Goray, translated by Jacob Sloan. New York, Farrar Straus, 1955; London, Peter Owen, 1958.
The Magician of Lublin, translated by Elaine Gottlieb and Joseph Singer. New York, Farrar Straus, 1960; London, Secker and Warburg, 1961.
The Slave, translated by the author and Cecil Hemley. New York, Farrar Straus, 1962; London, Secker and Warburg, 1963.
The Manor, translated by Elaine Gottlieb and Joseph Singer. New York, Farrar Straus, 1967; London, Secker and Warburg, 1968.
The Estate, translated by Joseph Singer, Elaine Gottlieb, and Elizabeth Shub. New York, Farrar Straus, and London, Cape, 1970.
Enemies: A Love Story, translated by Alizah Shevrin and Elizabeth Shub. New York, Farrar Straus, 1972.

Short Stories

Gimpel the Fool and Other Stories, translated by Saul Bellow and others.   New York,
    Farrar Straus, 1957; London, Peter Owen, 1958.
The Spinoza of Market Street and Other Stories, translated by Elaine Gottlieb and
    others.   New York, Farrar Straus, 1961; London, Secker and Warburg, 1962.
Short Friday and Other Stories, translated by Ruth Whitman and others.   New York,
    Farrar Straus, 1964; London, Secker and Warburg, 1967.
Selected Short Stories.   New York, Modern Library, 1966.
The Séance and Other Stories, translated by Ruth Whitman and others.   New York,
    Farrar Straus, 1968; London, Cape, 1970.
A Friend of Kafka and Other Stories.   New York, Farrar Straus, 1970; London, Cape,
    1972.
A Crown of Feathers and Other Stories.   New York, Farrar Straus, 1973; London,
    Cape, 1974.
Passions and Other Stories.   New York, Farrar Straus, 1975; London, Cape, 1976.

Plays

The Mirror (produced New Haven, Connecticut, 1973).
Schlemiel the First (produced New Haven, Connecticut, 1974).
Yentl, The Yeshiva Boy, with Leah Napolin, adaptation of a story by Singer (produced
    New York, 1974).

Other

In My Father's Court (autobiography), translated by Channah Kleinerman-Goldstein
    and others.   New York, Farrar Straus, 1966; London, Secker and Warburg, 1967.
The Hasidin: Paintings, Drawings, and Etchings, with Ira Moskowitz.   New York,
    Crown, 1973.
A Little Boy in Search of God: Mysticism in a Personal Light, with Ira Moskowitz.   New
    York, Doubleday, 1976.

Editor, with Elaine Gottlieb, *Prism 2*.   New York, Twayne, 1965.

Translator, *Pan*, by Knut Hamsen.   Warsaw, Wilno, 1928.
Translator, *All Quiet on the Western Front*, by Erich Maria Remarque.   Warsaw,
    Wilno, 1930.
Translator, *The Magic Mountain*, by Thomas Mann.   Warsaw, Wilno, 4 vols., 1930.
Translator, *The Road Back*, by Erich Maria Remarque.   Warsaw, Wilno, 1930.
Translator, *From Moscow to Jerusalem*, by Leon S. Glaser.   New York, privately
    printed, 1938.

Bibliography: in *Bulletin of Bibliography* (Boston), January-March 1969.

*   *   *

Isaac Bashevis Singer is one of the few writers for children who successfully and
unselfconsciously employs magic in his storytelling. The stories are not fairy tales but folk
tales, based firmly in the traditions from which Singer came: he is a Polish Jew from Warsaw
whose father was a rabbi. The use of the supernatural in his fables illuminates and makes
more universal a world that is enclosed in time and space. For Singer does not write of
contemporary Europe or America. The place is usually a *shtetl* (a small Jewish village in
Poland), and the time is the early part of the century. The tales reflect the superstitions,
customs, folklore and the innate humor of a ghetto culture that has almost vanished.

Singer not only writes of a disappearing way of life, but he also writes in a language that is dying. When he left Europe in 1935, Yiddish was spoken by 10 million people. Now, because of the Holocaust – and because of assimilation – less than half that number speak it. But Yiddish is Singer's first language, and has remained his mode of expression because it "contains vitamins that other languages don't have." Though his narration is straightforward, he manages to leap from the old world that provides the setting for his stories to the new, through the wryness of his characters – a wryness not lost by his many translators. Thus Zelig, a character in the title story of *Naftali the Storyteller and His Horse, Sus,* discovers an imp in a sack of what he thought was sugar, and simply remarks: "There is something here that is not as it should be."

It is no coincidence that some of Singer's tales bring Hans Christian Andersen to mind, in spite of their different religious backgrounds. In Singer's culture there were no books written specifically for children, who were expected to get their stories from the Bible. But Singer read Andersen in Yiddish and acknowledges the influence of this writer on his work. The magic in the tales of his predecessor was derived from tradition and not just pulled out of an allegorical hat. Their perceptions of the world were also similar – neither storyteller ever quite lost his childhood.

Singer did not start writing for children until he was past 60. He confesses a certain disenchantment with the literature of this epoch, and feels that children are the best readers – partly because they read what they really like. "No writer," he has said, "can bribe his way to the child's attention with false originality, literary puns and puzzles, arbitrary distortions of the order of things, or muddy streams of consciousness which often reveal nothing but a writer's boring and selfish personality. I came to the child because I see in him a last refuge from a literature gone berserk and ready for suicide."

In Singer's universe mystery resides everywhere. In a tale called "The Lantuch" (house demon or sprite) from the *Naftali* collection, Aunt Yentl, obviously speaking for the author, says: "Yes, there is such a spirit as a lantuch. These days people don't believe in such things, but in my time they knew that everything can't be explained away with reason. The world is full of secrets." The *lantuchs* in the story are not malicious. One even provides for a sick mother and her blind daughter so that they need not go to the poorhouse. Singer does deal with evil, though – good does not rule everything. He believes in God but also in the lower powers (imps, devils, demons) who rule the dominion of torment, illness and despair.

One of Singer's gifts is the ability to express things in a way that confirms the child's own experience of the often confusing world in which he lives. He has spoken out against didactic writing for children – writing that teaches without enlightening. As critic Richard M. Elman has said of Singer's craft: "To have one's sense of awe, to allow experience its mystery, to recall a delight in nature tinged with a wonder about its origins ... is to gain admittance to any child's mind with integrity." "What's life, after all?" asks an ancient character and lover of tales in *Naftali the Storyteller.* "The future isn't here yet and you cannot foresee what it will bring. The present is only a moment and the past is one long story. Those who don't tell stories and don't hear stories live only for the moment, and that isn't enough."

The Fools of Chelm is an acute parable of government – or what government can be if it falls into the wrong hands. The council of Chelm wants to solve a crisis in the town ("The moment the word 'crisis' appeared in the language, the people realized there was a crisis in Chelm") and decide to do it by declaring war. The conflict is disastrous and is followed by revolution, followed by counterrevolution. The events and characters are farcical, but behind the humor lies the certainty that *The Fools of Chelm* is uncomfortably about the whole world.

A Tale of Three Wishes encompasses religion, superstition and miracles. Three children wish for wisdom, knowledge and beauty and learn that they can only be achieved by experience and hard work. One of the children who, at the end of the story is an old man, and a rabbi, says: "For those who are willing to make an effort, great miracles and wonderful treasures are in store. For them the gates of heaven are always open." It is an atypically gentle story, low-key and rather preachy.

In the beautifully illustrated *Why Noah Chose the Dove* (paintings by Eric Carle) Noah tells the animals: "I love all of you, but because the dove remained modest and silent while the rest of you bragged and argued, I choose it to be my messenger." The narrator concludes: "The truth is that there are in the world more doves than there are tigers, leopards, wolves, vultures and other ferocious beasts. The dove lives happily without fighting. It is the bird of peace."

A true storyteller, Singer writes in such a way that he transports his readers far beyond their own environments into an alien world.

—Angela Wigan

SLEIGH, Barbara. British. Born in Acock's Green, Worcestershire, 9 January 1906. Educated at St. Catherine's School, Bramley, Surrey; West Bromwich School of Art, Birmingham, 1922–25; Clapham High School Art Teacher's Training College, London, 1925–28, Art Teacher's Diploma. Married David Davis in 1935; has one son and two daughters. Art Teacher, Smethwick High School, Staffordshire, 1927–29; Lecturer, Goldsmith's Teacher Training College, London, 1929–32; Assistant, "Children's Hour" program, BBC Radio, London, 1932–35. Since 1935, Free-lance Broadcaster and Radio Writer. Agent: Harvey Unna and Stephen Durbridge Ltd., 14 Beaumont Mews, Marylebone High Street, London WIN 4HE. Address: 18 Mount Avenue, London W5 2LR, England.

PUBLICATIONS FOR CHILDREN

Fiction

> *Carbonel*, illustrated by V.H. Drummond.   London, Parrish, 1955; Indianapolis, Bobbs Merrill, 1957.
> *Patchwork Quilt*, illustrated by Mary Shillabeer.   London, Parrish, 1956.
> *The Singing Wreath and Other Stories*, illustrated by Julia Comper.   London, Parrish, 1957.
> *The Seven Days*, illustrated by Susan Einzig.   London, Parrish, 1958; New York, Meredith Press, 1968.
> *The Kingdom of Carbonel*, illustrated by D.M. Leonard.   London, Parrish, 1959; Indianapolis, Bobbs Merrill, 1960.
> *No One Must Know*, illustrated by Jillian Willett.   London, Collins, 1962; Indianapolis, Bobbs Merrill, 1963.
> *Jessamy*, illustrated by Philip Gough.   London, Collins, and Indianapolis, Bobbs Merrill, 1967.
> *Pen, Penny, Tuppence*, illustrated by Meg Stevens.   London, Hamish Hamilton, 1968.
> *The Snowball*, illustrated by Patricia Drew.   Leicester, Brockhampton Press, 1969.
> *West of Widdershins: A Gallimaufry of Stories Brewed in Her Own Cauldron*, illustrated by Victor Ambrus.   London, Collins, 1971; as *Stirabout Stories*, Indianapolis, Bobbs Merrill, 1971.
> *Ninety-Nine Dragons*, illustrated by Gunvor Edwards.   Leicester, Brockhampton Press, 1974.
> *Charlie Chumbles*.   London, Hodder and Stoughton, 1977.
> *Grimblegraw and the Wuthering Witch*.   London, Hodder and Stoughton, 1978.

Other

> *North of Nowhere: Stories and Legends from Many Lands*, illustrated by Victor Ambrus.   London, Collins, 1964; New York, Coward McCann, 1966.

Funny Peculiar: An Anthology, illustrated by Jennie Garratt.   Newton Abbot, Devon, David and Charles, 1975.

Numerous radio plays.

PUBLICATIONS FOR ADULTS

Other

The Smell of Privet (autobiography).   London, Hutchinson, 1971.

Barbara Sleigh comments:
I largely write fantasy, but, I hope, of a down-to-earth kind, avoiding mere whimsy. I feel strongly this leads young readers to wider horizons, and later to imaginative adult reading.

*   *   *

Like many talented and versatile writers, Barbara Sleigh suffers the irritating injustice of being associated too exclusively with one outstandingly popular creation. In her case it is *Carbonel*, an admittedly splendid and brilliantly observed feline character. But with all due respect to Carbonel (and he is emphatically a cat who demands respect), Barbara Sleigh as a writer stands for a good deal more.

She did not produce her first book until she had served a long and fruitful apprenticeship in the craft of storytelling. She worked for the BBC during the best years of sound radio, a medium in which the word was all-important, before television arrived to destroy the famous daily programme *Children's Hour*, and offer young people an easy alternative that made little or no mental demands. Barbara Sleigh learnt what demands *could* safely be made on a child, in subject-matter and vocabulary, provided that the storyteller knew his job. That she knows hers is demonstrated not only in the Carbonel tales but in numerous other volumes.

These vary from collections of short stories, such as *West of Widdershins*, in which a deft economy of words is combined with a prodigality of ingenious ideas, to full-length books like *Jessamy*, in which a favourite old theme − the child who slips back in time, 1914 in this case − is developed with originality. The author's personal attitude to magic and fantasy is stated in a brief intoductory note to *West of Widdershins*, and her preference for rooting them firmly in everyday life is nowhere better illustrated than in one of the stories, "Miss Peabody," set in a prosaic school classroom. Humour runs strongly through all her work. *Ninety-Nine Dragons* is especially full of it, and, though the good-natured, rather than fearsome, dragon has become almost a stereotype in recent children's fiction, Barbara Sleigh demonstrates once more her flair for giving a new brightness to whatever material she handles.

In what has proved to be, with Mary Norton, Alan Garner and many others, something of a golden age of fantasy, she has earned a high place.

—Geoffrey Trease

SLOBODKIN, Louis. American.   Born in Albany, New York, 19 February 1903. Educated at Beaux Arts Institute of Design, New York, 1918−23. Married Florence Gersh in 1927; two sons. Sculptor in studios in U.S.A. and France, 1931−35; Head of the Sculpture Department, Master Institute of United Arts, Roerich Museum, New York, 1934−37; Instructor in Sculpture, Art League, New York, 1935−36; Head of Sculpture Division, New York City Art Project, 1941−42. Awarded commissions and executed sculptures, reliefs, and statues for buildings in New York, Washington, D.C., Johnstown, Pennsylvania, and North Adams, Massachusetts, 1935–39. Numerous museum exhibitions. Member, Board of Directors, Sculptors Guild, 1939–41; President, National Sculpture Society American Group, 1940–42; Chairman, American Institute of Graphic Arts Artists Committee, 1946. Recipient: American Library Association Caldecott Medal, for illustration, 1944. *Died 8 May 1975.*

PUBLICATIONS FOR CHILDREN (illustrated by the author)

Fiction

> *The Friendly Animals.*   New York, Vanguard Press, 1944.
> *Clear the Track for Michael's Magic Train.*   New York, Macmillan, 1945.
> *The Adventures of Arab.*   New York, Macmillan, 1946.
> *Hustle and Bustle.*   New York, Macmillan, 1948.
> *Bixxy and the Secret Message.*   New York, Macmillan, 1949.
> *Mr. Mushroom.*   New York, Macmillan, 1950.
> *Dinny and Danny.*   New York, Macmillan, 1951.
> *The Spaceship under the Apple Tree.*   New York, Macmillan, 1952.
> *Circus, April 1st.*   New York, Macmillan, 1953.
> *The Horse with High-Heeled Shoes.*   New York, Vanguard Press, 1954.
> *Mr. Petersand's Cats and Kittens.*   New York, Macmillan, 1954.
> *The Amiable Giant.*   New York, Macmillan, 1955; London, Macmillan, 1958.
> *The Little Mermaid Who Could Not Sing.*   New York, Macmillan, 1956.
> *Melvin the Moose Child.*   New York, Macmillan, 1957; London, Macmillan, 1958.
> *The Space Ship Returns to the Apple Tree.*   New York and London, Macmillan, 1958.
> *The Wide-Awake Owl.*   New York, Macmillan, 1958.
> *Trick or Treat.*   New York and London, Macmillan, 1959.
> *Gogo, The French Sea Gull.*   New York, Macmillan, 1960.
> *A Good Place to Hide.*   New York, Macmillan, 1961.
> *Picco, The Sad Italian Pony.*   New York, Vanguard Press, 1961.
> *The Three-Seated Space Ship.*   New York, Macmillan, 1962.
> *The Late Cuckoo.*   New York, Vanguard Press, 1962.
> *Luigi and the Long-Nosed Soldier.*   New York, Macmillan, and London, Collier Macmillan, 1963.
> *Moon Blossom and the Golden Penny.*   New York, Vanguard Press, 1963.
> *The Polka-Dot Goat.*   New York, Macmillan, and London, Collier Macmillan, 1964.
> *Colette and the Princess.*   New York, Dutton, 1965.
> *Yasu and the Strangers.*   New York, Macmillan, and London, Collier Macmillan, 1965.
> *Round Trip Space Ship.*   New York, Macmillan, and London, Collier Macmillan, 1968.
> *The Space Ship in the Park.*   New York, Macmillan, and London, Collier Macmillan, 1972.
> *Wilbur the Warrior.*   New York, Vanguard Press, 1972.

Verse

> *Magic Michael.*   New York, Macmillan, 1944.
> *The Seaweed Hat.*   New York, Macmillan, 1947.
> *Our Friendly Friends.*   New York, Vanguard Press, 1951.
> *Millions and Millions and Millions!*   New York, Vanguard Press, 1955.
> *One Is Good But Two Are Better.*   New York, Vanguard Press, 1956.
> *Nomi and the Lovely Animals.*   New York, Vanguard Press, 1960.
> *Up High and Down Low.*   New York, Macmillan, 1960.

Other

Thank You — You're Welcome.   New York, Vanguard Press, 1957.
The First Book of Drawing.   New York, Watts, 1958.
Excuse Me! Certainly!   New York, Vanguard Press, 1959.
Read about the Policeman [*Postman, Busman, Fireman*].   New York, Watts, 4 vols.,
    1966–67.

PUBLICATIONS FOR ADULTS

Other

Fo'castle Waltz.   New York, Vanguard Press, 1945.
Sculpture: Principles and Practice.   Cleveland, World, 1949.

Manuscript Collection: University of Oregon Library, Eugene.

Illustrator: *The Moffats,* 1941, *The Middle Moffat,* 1942, *Rufus M,* 1943, *The Sun and the Wind and Mr. Todd,* 1943, *The Hundred Dresses,* 1944, and *Ginger Pye,* 1951, all by Eleanor Estes; *Many Moons* by James Thurber, 1943; *Peter the Great,* 1943, *Garibaldi,* 1944, and *Lenin,* 1945, all by Nina Baker; *The Young Man of the House* by Mabel Leigh Hunt, 1944; *Robin Hood* by J. Walter McSpadden, 1946; *The Adventures of Tom Sawyer* by Mark Twain, 1946; *Jonathan and the Rainbow,* 1948, and *The King and the Noble Blacksmith,* 1950, by Jacob Blanck; *Gertie and the Horse Who Thought and Thought* by Margarite Glendinning, 1951; *Red Head* by Edward Eager, 1951; *The Magic Fishbone* by Charles Dickens, 1953; *The Alhambra* by Washington Irving, 1953; *Evie and the Wonderful Kangeroo,* 1955, and *Evie and Cooky,* 1957, by Irmengarde Eberle; *Pysen,* 1955, *The Saucepan Journey,* 1955, and *Little O,* 1957, all by Edith Unnerstad; *Shoes Fit for a King* by Helen E. Bill, 1957; *Love and Knishes,* 1956, and *Mazel Tov Y'all,* 1968, by Sara Kasdan; *The Warm-Hearted Polar Bear* by Robert Murphy, 1957; *Upside Down Town* by F. Amerson Andrews, 1958; *Too Many Mittens,* 1958, *The Cowboy Twins,* 1960, *Io Sono,* 1962, *Mr. Papadilly and Willy,* 1964, and *Sarah Somebody,* 1969, all by Florence Slobodkin; *Martin's Dinosaur* by Reda Davis, 1959; *Clean Clarence,* 1959, and *Marshmallow Ghost,* 1960, by Priscilla and Otto Friedrich; *Mr. Spindles and the Spiders* by Andrew Packard, 1961; *The Lovely Culpeppers* by Martha Uppington, 1963.

*   *   *

Louis Slobodkin was a prolific children's book author and illustrator who began to publish in the 1940's. He is best known for books which he has both written and illustrated, though his illustrations for James Thurber's *Many Moons* and the recent work he did with his wife Florence should be noted.

Slobodkin's picture books are representative of a broad range of types within a category. The early picture books are faintly didactic, the emphasis being on an instructive lesson (*Dinny and Danny*) or an implied moral (*Magic Michael*). The use of picture books as *exemplum,* however, is played down, and the illustrations do not accentuate the moral aspect of his works. Slobodkin also wrote obviously and intentionally didactic works, such as the courtesy books *Thank You — You're Welcome* and *Excuse Me! Certainly!,* as well as a "Read About" series on busmen, postmen, firemen, and policemen. This series contains narrative histories of the various professions accompanied by episodic vignettes related to a child's perception of the profession. Slobodkin's primary text for children who are interested in learning to illustrate is held in high repute by teachers of art, and the illustrations for Florence Slobodkin's dual language text *Io Sono/I Am* enhance the instructive level of the work.

Slobodkin is also noted for a series of juvenile fiction books on the themes of space travel, space inhabitants, and a child's imaginative relationship with his world and other-worldliness. Representative titles are *The Space Ship under the Apple Tree*, *The Space Ship in the Park*, and *The Three-Seated Space Ship*. Most of these works are centered on a peripatetic hero called Eddie and his friend from the planet Martinea.

Slobodkin's illustrations are very simple and functional – rarely more than suggestive of the actions discussed in the text. Yet the fact that Slobodkin was a sculptor obviously influenced his illustrating; movement, tension, and the dynamics of living figures read clearly through his illustration. Slobodkin's role as illustrator reached an apex in Eleanor Estes' stories about the Moffats and James Thurber's *Many Moons*, for which he received the Caldecott Medal.

—Rachel Fordyce

SLOBODKINA, Esphyr. American. Born in Siberia, Russia, 22 September 1908; emigrated to the United States in 1928; naturalized citizen, 1935. Educated at a Russian high school, Harbin, Manchuria; National Academy of Design, New York. Married Ilya Bolotowsky in 1933 (divorced, 1936); William L. Urquhart, 1960 (died, 1963). President, Art Development Co., New York, 1945–68; Assistant Export Manager, CBS/Hytron, Denver and New York, 1948–57; President, Urquhart-Slobodkina Inc., Great Neck, New York, 1968–76. Recipient: two Yaddo Fellowships; three MacDowell Fellowships. Address: 20 West Terrace Road, Great Neck, New York 11021, U.S.A.

PUBLICATIONS FOR CHILDREN (illustrated by the author)

Fiction

Caps for Sale. New York, Scott, 1940; Kingswood, Surrey, World's Work, 1959.
The Wonderful Feast. New York, Lothrop, 1955.
Little Dog Lost, Little Dog Found. New York, Abelard Schuman, 1956.
The Clock. New York and London, Abelard Schuman, 1956.
The Little Dinghy. New York and London, Abelard Schuman, 1958.
Behind the Dark Window Shade. New York, Lothrop, 1958.
Billie, illustrated by Meg Wohlberg. New York, Lothrop, 1959.
Pinky and the Petunias. New York, Abelard Schuman, 1959; London, Abelard Schuman, 1962.
Moving Day for the Middlemans. New York and London, Abelard Schuman, 1960.
Jack and Jim. New York and London, Abelard Schuman, 1961.
The Long Island Ducklings. New York, Lantern Press, 1961.
Boris and His Balalaika, illustrated by Vladimir Bobri. New York and London, Abelard Schuman, 1964.
Pezzo the Peddler and the Circus Elephant [*and the Thirteen Silly Thieves*]. New York and London, Abelard Schuman, 2 vols., 1967, 1970.
The Flame, The Breeze, and the Shadow. Chicago, Rand McNally, 1969.

PUBLICATIONS FOR ADULTS

Other

Notes for a Biographer.   Great Neck, New York, Urquhart Slobodkina, 1977.

Illustrator: *The Little Fireman*, 1938, *The Little Farmer*, 1948, *The Little Cowboy*, 1949, and *Sleepy ABC*, 1953, all by Margaret Wise Brown; *Hiding Places* by Louise Woodcock, 1943.

*   *   *

In her picture storybooks Esphyr Slobodkina often uses for her purposes the "functions," as they are called, that appear in traditional folk literature. Slobodkina, born in old Russia, practices her dependency on this aged genre by relying on these old tales for the general structures of many of her stories. She borrows the essentials found in their accumulative plot schemes, their repetitive actions, and their mounting sense of suspense. Then she combines all these factors with a reduced form of language that very young children can comprehend. The resultant product proves to have a merit that exceeds the praise that she has received for this work. Her picture storybooks do have a distinctive integrity that is hers alone, although her work is sometimes confused (in name only) with that of the more highly successful Louis Slobodkin.

Slobodkina's most distinguished effort, without any doubt, has been *Caps for Sale*. The sales of this book testify that it is among the most popular of any of its kind written so far. Reported to have sold over a million copies, it easily has found its place on the all-time best seller list. Young children are smitten by this uncomplicated yet intriguing tale of a simple cap seller, who after a disappointing day takes a rest under a tree. As soon as he dozes off, however, a band of monkeys descends and steals his caps. No amount of scolding on his part can get them back, he later finds. When he shakes his fist the monkeys merely return the gesture. Finally, in total exasperation he throws his own cap to the ground, and lo, so do all the monkeys — which nicely ends the story.

None of Slobodkina's later picture storybooks have reached this exceptional level of success. This does not mean they are lacking in merit, however. On the contrary, some of her books for the very young are near-perfect examples of the cumulative tale, a format fancied by many picture book writers, many of whom do not carry it off as well as she does. *The Wonderful Feast* is a prime example of Slobodkina's success with this "house-that-Jack-built" type of story. Here a farmer gives his horse some feed. Then, in order, a goat ate what the horse left; a hen what the goat left; a mouse what the hen left; and an ant ate the very last grain. All thought it a "wonderful feast." Highly simplistic stories of this nature need illustrations of notable excellence. Since Slobodkina is an artist of undoubted ability (her abstract art has been given much praise) she is able to infuse the simple words of her cumulative tales with a vigor far beyond that which they inherently contain. Instead of the art work in her books overshadowing their literary content, it magnifies and focuses it.

This arrangement seems to work the best (see *The Clock*), however, when Slobodkina stays with the very short text required for the cumulative story. In some of her longer displays of verbal text her limited ability to sustain a satisfactory fictional drama is apparent. In her *Pezzo the Peddler* books, for example, she tries to concoct spin-offs of *Caps for Sale*. Here a cap peddler loses and retrieves his caps in various ways. Even Slobodkina's use of many short sentences, a great deal of dialogue, and explicit descriptions cannot overcome the repetitive plots, which are simply too weak to sustain these books. On the other hand, Slobodkina has demonstrated, as in *Boris and His Balalaika*, that when she depends on her imagination rather than her past success she is fully able to write admirable longer plots.

—Patrick Groff

SMITH, C(icely) Fox.   British.   Born in Manchester, Lancashire, in 1882. *Died 8 April 1954.*

PUBLICATIONS FOR CHILDREN

Fiction

Three Girls in a Boat, with Madge Smith.   London, Oxford University Press, 1938.
The Ship Aground, illustrated by C. Walter Hodges.   London and New York, Oxford University Press, 1940.
Painted Ports, illustrated by C. Walter Hodges.   London and New York, Oxford University Press, 1948.
Knave-Go-By, illustrated by Ian Ribbons.   London, Oxford University Press, 1951.
Seldom Seen, with Madge Smith, illustrated by Peggy Fortnum.   London, Oxford University Press, 1954.
The Valiant Sailor, illustrated by Neville Dear.   London, Oxford University Press, 1955; New York, Criterion Books, 1957.

Other

True Tales of the Sea, illustrated by Rowland Hilder.   London, Oxford University Press, 1932.
All the Other Children: A Book of Young Creatures.   London, Methuen, 1933.

PUBLICATIONS FOR ADULTS

Novels

The City of Hope.   London, Sidgwick and Jackson, 1914.
Singing Sands.   London, Hodder and Stoughton, 1918.
Peregrine in Love.   London, Hodder and Stoughton, 1920.
Peacock Pride, with Madge Smith.   London, Muller, 1934.

Short Stories

Tales of the Clipper Ships.   London, Methuen, 1926.

Verse

Songs of Greater Britain and Other Poems.   London, Simpkin, 1899.
The Foremost Trail.   London, Sampson Low, 1899.
Sailor Town: Sea Songs and Ballads.   London, Mathews, 1900; New York, Doran, 1919.
Wings of the Morning.   London, Mathews, 1904.
Lancashire Hunting Songs and Other Moorland Lays.   Manchester, Cornish, 1909.
Songs in Sail and Other Chantys.   London, Mathews, 1914.
The Naval Crown: Ballads and Songs of the War.   London, Mathews, 1915.
Small Craft.   London, Mathews, 1917.
Small Craft: Sailor Ballads and Chantys.   New York, Doran, 1919.
Songs and Chanties, 1914–1916.   London, Mathews, 1919.
Rhymes of the Red Ensign.   London, Hodder and Stoughton, 1919.
Ships and Folks.   London, Mathews, 1920.
Rovings: Sea Songs and Ballads.   London, Mathews, 1921.
Sea Songs and Ballads, 1917–1922.   London, Methuen, 1923; Boston, Houghton Mifflin, 1924.

Full Sail: More Sea Songs and Ballads. London, Methuen, and Boston, Houghton Mifflin, 1926.
Sailor's Delight. London, Methuen, 1931.

Other

Fighting Men. London, Mathews, 1900.
Sailor Town Days. London, Methuen, and Boston, Houghton Mifflin, 1923.
A Book of Famous Ships. London, Methuen, and Boston, Houghton Mifflin, 1924.
The Return of the "Cutty Sark." London, Methuen, 1924; Boston, Lauriat, 1925.
Ship Alley: More Sailor Town Days. London, Methuen, and Boston, Houghton Mifflin, 1925.
Ancient Mariners: Some Salt Water Yesterdays. London, Methuen, 1928.
There Was a Ship: Chapters from the History of Sail. London, Methuen, 1929; Hartford, Connecticut, Mitchell, 1930.
The Thames. London, Methuen, 1931.
Ocean Racers. London, Philip Allan, 1931; New York, McBride, 1932.
Anchor Lane. London, Methuen, 1933.
All the Way Round: Sea Roads to Africa. London, Joseph, 1938.
The Story of Grace Darling. London, Oxford University Press, 1940.
The Voyage of the Trevessa's Boats. London, Oxford University Press, 1940.
Thames Side Yesterdays. Leigh-on-Sea, Essex, Lewis, 1945.
Here and There in England with the Painter Brangwyn. Leigh-on-Sea, Essex, Lewis, 1945.
Country Days and Country Ways: Trudging Afoot in England. Leigh-on-Sea, Essex, Lewis, 1947.
Ship Models. London, Country Life, 1951.

Editor, *A Book of Shanties.* London, Methuen, and Boston, Houghton Mifflin, 1927.
Editor, *A Sea Chest: An Anthology of Ships and Sailormen.* London, Methuen, and Boston, Houghton Mifflin, 1927.
Editor, *The Man Before the Mast, Being the Story of Twenty Years Afloat,* by George Sorrell. London, Methuen, 1928.
Editor, *Adventures and Peril, Being Extracts from the "Mariners Chronicle" and Other Sources ....* London, Joseph, 1936; New York, Dodge, 1937.

*   *   *

The literary career of C. Fox Smith must be almost unique, since she turned to children's books only after some 40 years of varied authorship, most of which was concerned with either the English countryside or maritime history. Convincing background detail of land or sea is indeed an outstanding feature of all Miss Smith's children's books, which also have the virtue of being continuously exciting and adventurous in the old-fashioned manner of Stevenson or Rider Haggard. As regards character and plot, these books are somewhat variable in quality. Usually the story is told by a teenage boy who has nothing particular about him except courage and endurance; the villains and eccentrics, however, are often quite lively, and just occasionally there are insights into the complexity of human behaviour and relationships. The style of plotting ranges from a barely perceptible framework to an intriguing tightly-woven mystery, but always tending to rely too much on gigantic coincidences.

Miss Smith is now chiefly known for three fairly similar historical sea-adventures. *The Ship Aground* is a straightforward tale of piracy and hidden treasure, quite exciting but rarely memorable. Its sequel, *Painted Ports,* is more of a chronicle than a standard adventure story, some of its episodes being quite light-hearted and some exeedingly grim. The author is at her very best in describing the Castle of Comfort island, where the young hero finds a gang of escaped convicts practising a reign of terror. *The Valiant Sailor*, published posthumously, is distinctly more ambitious than the other two. Here one of the principal characters, the narrator's father, is sensitively portrayed as the victim of his own conscience, and there are opportunities for the discerning reader to become aware of some universal moral issues and dilemmas.

Miss Smith's remaining children's novels are land-based and set mainly in Devonshire. *Seldom Seen* was written with Madge Smith, and is concerned with farming in the immediate post-war era. Although infused with plenty of authentic detail and a good measure of tension in the later stages, it lacks the spark of inspiration needed to make a lasting impression. *Knave-Go-By*, on the other hand, is an historical novel with qualities which put it very near the highest class. As well as presenting an entirely convincing picture of various levels of society in the early 19th century, it includes a skilfully unravelled mystery and a host of colourful characters, including a fine comic creation in Professor Abracadabra. This is a book of the fairly rare sort that can be offered to either the studious or the impatient reader, with good hopes of satisfying both equally.

—Alasdair K.D. Campbell

SMITH, Emma. British. Born in Newquay, Cornwall, 21 August 1923. Married R.L. Stewart-Jones in 1951 (died, 1957); has two children. Recipient (for fiction): Atlantic Award, 1947; Rhys Memorial Prize, 1949; James Tait Black Memorial Prize, 1950. Agent: Peter Janson-Smith Ltd., 31 Newington Green, London N16 9PU, England.

PUBLICATIONS FOR CHILDREN

Fiction

> *Emily: The Story of a Traveller*, illustrated by Katherine Wigglesworth. London, Nelson, 1959; as *Emily: The Travelling Guinea Pig*, New York, McDowell Obolensky, 1959.
> *Emily's Voyage*, illustrated by Margaret Gordon. London, Macmillan, and New York, Harcourt Brace, 1962.
> *Out of Hand*, illustrated by Antony Maitland. London, Macmillan, 1963; New York, Harcourt Brace, 1964.
> *No Way of Telling*. London, Bodley Head, and New York, Atheneum, 1972.

PUBLICATIONS FOR ADULTS

Novels

> *Maidens' Trip*. London, Putnam, 1948.
> *The Far Cry*. London, MacGibbon and Kee, 1949; New York, Random House, 1950.

*   *   *

Emma Smith is an all too occasional writer for children. There is a shortage of family adventure stories in which the emphasis is firmly on good plotting, well-organised narrative structure, compulsive pace, tension, and excitement, but in which the author also respects the intelligence of young readers and does not try to over-simplify the disconcerting muddle of emotions that children have to cope with or the inevitable rifts of understanding between child and adult. Emma Smith has written two novels of exceptional quality in which this balance of attention is sustained with great professional skill.

Out of Hand is a "post-Ransome" story of holiday adventure. A family of lively children are sent to spend their summer at the primitive but delightful country farmhouse where their elderly Cousin Polly lives alone. The first part of the book is an idyllic celebration of the perfect open-air holiday. When Cousin Polly breaks her ankle, however, the idyll is spoilt by the intrusion of two strait-laced spinster cousins, who set out to impose a cheerless and deadening order. The rest of the novel traces a mounting feud between the children and the interlopers. As the narrative heart of the story this is always exciting and often funny, and it culminates in satisfying "victory." Yet it is also a maturing experience for the children, who come to feel a surprised compassion for their enemy and recognise that problems and motives are less simple than they seem. Children's feelings and attitudes are fairly balanced against those of the adults, and awkward conflicts of loyalty are not evaded. The book is a fine, zestful adventure story with an ending which, though reassuring, is not simplistic.

A midwinter blizzard in the Welsh hills is the focus of Emma Smith's thriller, *No Way of Telling*. Basically the plot is both hackneyed and improbable, a melodrama of pursuers and pursued, romantic heroism and lethal villainy. What sets the book apart is the situation summarised in its title. The girl Amy lives with her elderly grandmother in an isolated, snowbound cottage. The two of them are swept up into this violent winter of murderous conflict, knowing that good and evil are at war around them, but with no way of knowing which is which. The claustrophobic nightmare of their predicament is excellently rendered, and so is Amy's brave, resourceful answer to the dangerous truth. The vivid realism of the setting, and the sensitive observation of the central relationship between child and grandmother, give depth, conviction and originality to this exciting story.

For small children, Emma Smith's story *Emily's Voyage* is deservedly popular. Emily is a guinea pig with a practical nature, respectable habits, and a fondness for tea. Her addiction to travel is the pretext for an incongruous comic adventure, expertly told with the directness and economy, warmth and sensitivity that also characterise Emma Smith's distinguished and under-estimated work for older readers.

—Peter Hollindale

SMITH, William Jay. American. Born in Winnfield, Louisiana, 22 April 1918. Educated at Blow School, St. Louis, 1924–31; Cleveland High School, 1931–35; Washington University, St. Louis, 1935–41, B.A. 1939, M.A. in French, 1941; Institut de Touraine, Tours, France, 1938; Columbia University, New York, 1946–47; Wadham College, Oxford (Rhodes Scholar), 1947–48; University of Florence, 1948–50. Served as a Lieutenant in the United States Naval Reserve, 1941–45. Married the poet Barbara Howes in 1947 (divorced, 1965), two sons; Sonja Haussmann in 1966, one step-son. Assistant in French, Washington University, 1939–41; Instructor in English and French, 1946–47, and Visiting Professor of Writing and Acting Chairman, Writing Division, 1973, 1974–75, Columbia University; Instructor in English, 1951, and Poet-in-Residence and Lecturer in English, 1959–64, 1966–67, Williams College, Williamstown, Massachusetts. Writer-in-Residence, 1965–66, and Professor of English, 1967–68, and since 1970, Hollins College, Virginia. Consultant in Poetry, 1968–70, and Honorary Consultant, 1970–74, Library of Congress, Washington, D.C. Poetry Reviewer, *Harper's*, New York, 1961–64; Editorial Consultant, Grove Press, New York, 1968–70. Democratic Member, Vermont House of Representatives, 1960–62. Recipient: Young Poets Prize, 1945, and Union League Civic and Arts Foundation Prize, 1964 (*Poetry*, Chicago); Alumni Citation, Washington University, 1963; Ford Fellowship, for drama, 1964; Henry Bellamann Major Award, 1970; Loines Award, 1972; National Endowment for the Arts grant, 1972. D. Litt.: New England College, Henniker, New

Hampshire, 1973. Agent: Martha Winston, Curtis Brown Ltd., 575 Madison Avenue, New York, New York 10022. Address: Upper Bryant Road, West Cummington, Massachusetts 01265, U.S.A.

PUBLICATIONS FOR CHILDREN

Verse

> *Laughing Time*, illustrated by Juliet Kepes. Boston, Little Brown, 1955; London, Faber, 1956.
> *Boy Blue's Book of Beasts*, illustrated by Juliet Kepes. Boston, Little Brown, 1957.
> *Puptents and Pebbles: A Nonsense ABC*, illustrated by Juliet Kepes. Boston, Little Brown, 1959; London, Faber, 1960.
> *What Did I See?*, illustrated by Don Almquist. New York, Crowell Collier, 1962.
> *My Little Book of Big and Little* (*Little Dimity, Big Gumbo, Big and Little*), illustrated by Don Bolognese. New York, Macmillan, 3 vols., 1963.
> *Ho for a Hat!*, illustrated by Ivan Chermayeff. Boston, Little Brown, 1964.
> *If I Had a Boat*, illustrated by Don Bolognese. New York, Macmillan, 1966; Kingswood, Surrey, World's Work, 1967.
> *Mr. Smith and Other Nonsense*, illustrated by Don Bolognese. New York, Delacorte Press, 1968.
> *Around My Room and Other Poems*, illustrated by Don Madden. New York, Lancelot Press, 1969.
> *Grandmother Ostrich and Other Poems*, illustrated by Don Madden. New York, Lancelot Press, 1969.

Other

> Editor, with Louise Bogan, *The Golden Journey: Poems for Young People*, illustrated by Fritz Kredel. Chicago, Reilly and Lee, 1965; London, Evans, 1967.
> Editor, *Poems from France*, illustrated by Roger Duvoisin. New York, Crowell, 1967.
> Editor, *Poems from Italy*, illustrated by Elaine Raphael. New York, Crowell, 1972.

> Translator, *Children of the Forest*, by Elsa Beskow, illustrated by Beskow. New York, Delacorte Press, 1970.
> Translator, *The Pirate Book*, by Lennart Hellsing, illustrated by Poul Ströyer. New York, Delacorte Press, and London, Benn, 1972.
> Translator, *The Telephone*, by Kornei Chukovsky, illustrated by Blair Lent. New York, Delacorte Press, 1976.

PUBLICATIONS FOR ADULTS

Play

> *The Straw Market*, music by the author (produced Washington, D.C., 1965; New York, 1969).

Verse

> *Poems*. Pawlet, Vermont, Banyan Press, 1947.
> *Celebration at Dark: Poems*. London, Hamish Hamilton, and New York, Farrar Straus, 1950.
> *Typewriter Birds*. New York, Caliban Press, 1954.
> *The Bead Curtain: Calligrams*. Florence, privately printed, 1957.

Poems 1947–1957.   Boston, Little Brown, 1957.
Prince Souvanna Phouma: An Exchange Between Richard Wilbur and William Jay Smith.   Williamstown, Massachusetts, Chapel Press, 1963.
The Tin Can and Other Poems.   New York, Delacorte Press, 1966.
New and Selected Poems.   New York, Delacorte Press, 1970.
A Rose for Katherine Anne Porter.   New York, Albondocani Press, 1970.
At Delphi: For Allen Tate on His Seventy-Fifth Birthday, 19 November 1974.   Williamstown, Massachusetts, Chapel Press, 1974.

Other

The Spectra Hoax (criticism).   Middletown, Connecticut, Wesleyan University Press, 1961.
Children and Poetry: A Selective Annotated Bibliography, with Virginia Haviland.   Washington, D.C., Library of Congress, 1969.
Louise Bogan: A Woman's Words.   Washington, D.C., Library of Congress, 1971.
The Streaks of the Tulip: Selected Criticism.   New York, Delacorte Press, 1972.

Editor and Translator, *Selected Writings of Jules Laforgue.*   New York, Grove Press, 1956.
Editor, *Herrick.*   New York, Dell, 1962.

Translator, *Scirroco,* by Romualdo Romano.   New York, Farrar Straus, 1951.
Translator, *Poems of a Multimillionaire,* by Valéry Larbaud.   New York, Bonaccio and Saul, 1955.
Translator, *Two Plays by Charles Bertin: Christopher Columbus and Don Juan.*   Minneapolis, University of Minnesota Press, 1970.

Manuscript Collection: Washington University, St. Louis.

*   *   *

William Jay Smith represents an unusual phenomenon, that of a serious poet for adults trying to be funny – for children. It is understandable, then, that when this prize-winning poet showed a colleague his first attempts he was greeted with hoots of surprise bordering on reproach. This does not mean that Smith went into this new venture half-cocked, however. Smith was also a critic of poetry, and had given much thought as to what poetry should be and do. Smith's contributions to children's literature, therefore, present a rare opportunity to find out if a writter's work lives up to his expectations. There is a further interest, since Smith tells us that writing children's poems has given him the chance to explore themes he developed in his works for adults.

In Smith's books of poetry for children it can be seen, first, that his writing does fulfill to a large extent one of his major goals, to "risk everything and play for the highest stakes." It is clear that Smith's books of poetry for children offer many cleverly written bits of infectious nonsense on a wide range of topics. From page to page there is no telling what Smith will do next.

Second, most of Smith's poems for children reflect the technical soundness of good adult poetry, a standard which Smith has set for poems for the young. In general, his rhymes are usually bright and strong, his topics are the kind with appeal for children, and his figures of speech are far from clichés, yet well within the intellectual grasp of his readers (e.g., "Toaster": "a silver-scaled Dragon with Jaws of flaming red"). In Smith's collections of adult poetry he has been praised for "much leaving out, and stern self-correction." While there are bewildering exceptions to this seen in his poems for children, by and large they do reflect his studious effort. While some of his lines diminish into simple chatter, often of a playground variety (e.g., "Over and under/Over and under/Crack the whip/And hear it thunder"), and while Smith reverts at times to practical matters (e.g., in his poem "Dictionary"), his offerings to children usually aim to explore and try out new things and to maintain a sense of poesy.

Another goal Smith has set for poetry is that variety is everything. His poems for children certainly do explore a wide range of unexpected topics. The exasperation one often feels in reading conventional anthologies of poetry for children, with their seemingly endless items on nature and goodness ("sentimental drivel," Smith calls them), never applies to Smith. His heterogeneous offerings are a buffer against this. This exemption is also partly achieved from a fulfillment of another of his precepts for poetry, that it should be humorous. The chuckles abound in his books, almost on every page.

Finally, it is also true that in general Smith gets to his poem-making for children with "directness and élan — and without fuss," as he has said it should be done. His poems are playfully graphic, full of imagery, and song-like. This aspect of his writing is enhanced by his intensive use of verbs and nouns to carry the impact of what he says. Smith's direct approach to his task is also shown by his lack of pretension and condescension: he is obviously excited about experimenting with language for children, and the excitement shows.

—Patrick Groff

———————

SNEDEKER, Caroline Dale. American. Born in New Harmony, Indiana, 23 March 1871. Educated at College of Music, Cincinnati. Married Charles Henry Snedeker in 1903. Concert pianist and composer in early 1900's. *Died 22 January 1956.*

PUBLICATIONS FOR CHILDREN

Fiction

> *The Coward of Thermopylae.* New York, Doubleday, 1911; as *The Spartan,* Doubleday, 1912; London, Hodder and Stoughton, 1913.
> *The Perilous Seat.* New York, Doubleday, and London, Methuen, 1923.
> *Theras and His Town,* illustrated by Mary Haring. New York, Doubleday, and London, Heinemann, 1924.
> *Downright Dencey,* illustrated by Maginel Wright Barney. New York, Doubleday, and London, Heinemann, 1927.
> *The Beckoning Road,* illustrated by Manning Lee. New York, Doubleday, 1929.
> *The Forgotten Daughter,* illustrated by Dorothy P. Lathrop. New York, Doubleday, 1933.
> *Uncharted Ways,* illustrated by Manning Lee. New York, Doubleday, 1935.
> *The White Isle,* illustrated by Fritz Kredel. New York, Doubleday, 1940.
> *Luke's Quest,* illustrated by Nora S. Unwin. New York, Doubleday, 1947.
> *A Triumph for Flavius,* illustrated by Cedric Rogers. New York, Lothrop, 1955.
> *Lysis Goes to the Play,* illustrated by Reisie Lonette. New York, Lothrop, 1962.

Other

> *The Black Arrowhead: Legends of Long Island.* New York, Doubleday, 1929.

PUBLICATIONS FOR ADULTS

Novel

    Seth Way (as Caroline Dale Owen).   Boston, Houghton Mifflin, 1917.

Other

    The Town of the Fearless (on New Harmony, Indiana).   New York, Doubleday, 1931.

*   *   *

Many of the details of Caroline Dale Snedeker's life are important in a discussion of her writing, for her work was much influenced by certain people and places. Her birthplace, New Harmony, Indiana, had been founded as an ideal Utopian community by her great-grandfather, Robert Owen. From her grandmother she heard stories about the town's early days, and she used this narrative material in three of her books. Her family was a cultivated one, much interested in art, literature, and music. In her autobiographical essays she spoke of nine Italian paintings of Greek gods and goddesses which hung in her house when she was a child, and she pointed out their influence on her later work: "These same gods and goddesses ... peopled my childish world and have never gone away. I have truly felt that to write about ancient Greece is a privilege."

It was Caroline's husband, the dean of St. Paul's Cathedral in Cincinnati and an excellent critic and teacher, who encouraged her to write. With his help she embarked upon a study of the classics, which provided her with the background of her first novel and of several of her subsequent ones. *The Coward of Thermopylae* did not achieve the recognition it deserved until it was reissued in a format more appealing to young readers under a new title, *The Spartan*. Not for several years did she write another novel; but *The Perilous Seat* enjoyed the same wide popularity as its predecessor. Mrs. Snedeker traveled abroad – to Greece and Italy and to England, where her experiences in Cornwall and Devon brought her the keen interest in early Christianity in Britain, which is evident in *The White Isle*; her account of a first-century church service "has been noted and cited as a reliable description."

A visit to Nantucket gave the author the inspiration for *Downright Dencey*, written while she was grief-stricken over the death of her husband. One of the few of her books still in print, the story re-creates the unique atmosphere of the island in the early nineteenth century; its chief character is an impulsive, warmhearted Quaker girl. Beautifully written with an intensity of feeling, the book has been an enduring source of reading pleasure.

For many years Caroline Dale Snedeker's books were avidly read by young people – and older ones as well. Her careful, scholarly research gave her work vividness and authenticity; and her integration of historical fact with highly imaginative plots as well as her sympathetic handling of characters added great vitality.

—Ethel L. Heins

SNYDER, Zilpha Keatley. American. Born in Lemoore, California, 11 May 1928. Educated at Whittier College, California, 1944–48, B.A. 1948; University of California, Berkeley, summers 1958–60. Married Larry A. Snyder in 1950; has one daughter and two sons. Elementary school teacher, California, New York, Washington, D.C., and Alaska, 1948–62. Recipient: New York *Herald Tribune* Festival award, 1967; Christopher Award, 1969, 1972; George G. Stone Center for Children's Books award, 1975. Address: 4257 Petaluma Hill Road, Santa Rosa, California 95404, U.S.A.

PUBLICATIONS FOR CHILDREN

Fiction (illustrated by Alton Raible)

> *Season of Ponies.*   New York, Atheneum, 1964.
> *The Velvet Room.*   New York, Atheneum, 1965.
> *Black and Blue Magic*, illustrated by Gene Holtan.   New York, Atheneum, 1966.
> *The Egypt Game.*   New York, Atheneum, 1967.
> *Eyes in the Fishbowl.*   New York, Atheneum, 1968.
> *The Changeling.*   New York, Atheneum, 1970; London, Lutterworth Press, 1976.
> *The Headless Cupid.*   New York, Atheneum, 1971; London, Lutterworth Press, 1973.
> *The Witches of Worm.*   New York, Atheneum, 1972.
> *The Princess and the Giants*, illustrated by Beatrice Darwin.   New York, Atheneum, 1973.
> *The Truth about Stone Hollow.*   New York, Atheneum, 1974.
> *Below the Root.*   New York, Atheneum, 1975.
> *And All Between.*   New York, Atheneum, 1976.
> *Until the Celebration.*   New York, Atheneum, 1977.

Verse

> *Today Is Saturday*, photographs by John Arms.   New York, Atheneum, 1969.

Manuscript Collection: Kerlan Collection, University of Minnesota, Minneapolis.

Zilpha Keatley Snyder comments:
I am a fiction writer with a decided list towards the fantastical. Like most writers I write for the joy of it, to exorcise old ghosts, and because I can't seem to stop, but I am also aware of a very personal motivation. I write as a legitimate means of indulging in an apparently inborn vice – the tendency to make things up. I write for middle-aged children (9–14) because they are magical people.

*   *   *

Fantasy is the most difficult genre in the field of children's literature, and few American authors have written it as successfully as Zilpha Keatley Snyder. Since the mid-1960's she has published a book every year, almost all of them novel-length. Some are pure fantasy, while others verge on the edge of magic. Her books are embued with strong plot, haunting characters, and intricate style.

In her debut, *Season of Ponies*, a magic amulet makes it possible for Pamela to visit the gypsy boy and herd similar to the blown glass figurines on her bookcase. A recent trilogy, consisting of *Below the Root*, *And All Between*, and *Until the Celebration*, is carefully wrought with an intricate, balanced system. A girl dreams of castle, kingdom, and a prince in *The Princess and the Giants*, contradicted by the illustrator's depiction of the reality of her workaday world. Elements of magic are introduced in other books. In *The Egypt Game*, the youngsters wearing special garb meet in their temple to perform rituals. *Eyes in the Fishbowl* involves seemingly supernatural happenings in the Alcott-Simpson department store. Jessica observes the unusual behavior of a cat in *The Witches of Worm*, and suspects the worst. In all the books, there is clear a delineation between true fantasy and suspected supernatural elements by the conclusion of the story.

While characters include both adults and children, the sad, lonely girl is usually the focal point. Robin Williams, in *The Velvet Room*, is a member of a tough migrant worker family, but has unusual sensitivity and love of reading. Fairy-like Ivy leads shy Martha through many an adventure in *The Changeling*, but admits finally that she is not what she claimed to be. Martha, like Pamela in *Season of Ponies*, is strengthened by another individual. Raamo observes that his sister Pomma is brought back to health while in the company of the girl Teera in *And All Between*. Despite an attempt to provide a more rambunctious boy in *Black and Blue Magic*, the author can't resist penetrating deeply into the personality.

An entire system is supported with a myriad of details in the trilogy. The physical description of Greensky, with the contrast between the airy seven cities above ground among the branches and the world beneath the forest floor is gripping. Greensky is actually introduced in *The Changeling*, published in 1970, but is developed differently in *Below the Root*, which appeared five years later. Characters glide from place to place, and some can't resist devouring quantities of Wissenberries, which cause a sensation of drowsiness. While internal consistency is necessary in fantasy, there must be enough of the familiar to convince the reader of its plausibility. In Zilpha Snyder's most recent books there are occupations such as harvesting and embroidering, and schools for youngsters, although the fruit is "pan" and the instruction is given in the "Garden of Song and Story."

Fantasy is a good vehicle for conveying wisdom, and in *The Truth about Stone Hollow*, Amy is confronted with a new definition of the virtue. In *Below the Root*, Raamo must disobey in order to follow a higher directive, his integrity. Good is victorious, although threatened. When Neric asks, "What steps can be taken?" Hiro responds, "Small ones at first. Only evil comes from great changes made too swiftly." In her collection of poetry, *Today Is Saturday*, Zilpha Snyder recreates children's perception of reality and emotions. She captures the yearning of a girl in "Horse Fever" and the expectation of a third grader in "The One Who Holds the Flag." Her sense of humor emerges in "The Housing Specialist" in a manner unreleased in longer texts.

Zilpha Snyder is an author "in process," producing fine books, but with the potential to surpass what she has already accomplished. Her forte is fantasy, and she is one of the few American authors to provide children with this means of learning the philosophy of an adult.

—Karem Nelson Hoyle

SOBOL, Donald J. American. Born in New York City, 4 October 1924. Educated at Fieldston School, New York, 1942; Oberlin College, Ohio, B.A. 1948; New School for Social Research, New York, 1949–51. Served in the United States Army Corps of Engineers, 1943–46. Married Rose Tiplitz in 1955; has one daughter and three sons. Reporter, New York *Sun*, 1946–47, and *Long Island Daily Press*, New York, 1947–52; Buyer, R.H. Macy's, New York, 1953–55. Wrote "Two-Minute Mystery" syndicated newspaper series, 1959–68. Recipient: Mystery Writers of America Edgar Allan Poe Award, 1976. Lives in Miami. Agent: McIntosh and Otis Inc., 475 Fifth Avenue, New York, New York 10017, U.S.A.

PUBLICATIONS FOR CHILDREN

Fiction

> *The Double Quest*, illustrated by Lili Réthi. New York, Watts, 1957.
> *The Lost Dispatch*, illustrated by Anthony Palumbo. New York, Watts, 1958.
> *Encyclopedia Brown, Boy Detective, [and the Case of the Secret Pitch, Finds His Clues, Gets His Man, Solves Them All, Keeps the Peace, Saves the Day, Tracks Them Down, Shows the Way, Takes the Case, Lends a Hand, and the Case of the Dead Eagles, and the Midnight Visitor]*, illustrated by Leonard Shortall. New York and Nashville, Nelson, 13 vols., 1963–77.
> *Secret Agents Four*, illustrated by Leonard Shortall. New York, Scholastic, 1967.

Greta the Strong, illustrated by Trina Schart Hyman.   Chicago, Follett, 1970.
Milton, The Model A, illustrated by Joan Drescher.   New York, Harvey House, 1971.

Other

The First Book of Medieval Man, illustrated by Lili Réthi.   New York, Watts, 1959;
  revised edition, as *The First Book of Medieval Britain*, London, Mayflower, 1960.
Two Flags Flying (biographies of Civil War leaders), illustrated by Jerry
  Robinson.   New York, Platt and Munk, 1960.
The Wright Brothers at Kitty Hawk, illustrated by Stuart Mackenzie.   New York,
  Nelson, 1961.
The First Book of the Barbarian Invaders, A.D. 375–511, illustrated by W. Kirtman
  Plummer.   New York, Watts, 1962; London, Edmund Ward, 1963.
The First Book of Stocks and Bonds, with Rose Sobol.   New York, Watts, 1963.
Lock, Stock, and Barrel (biographies of American Revolutionary War leaders),
  illustrated by Edward J. Smith.   Philadelphia, Westminster Press, 1965.
The Amazons of Greek Mythology.   South Brunswick, New Jersey, A.S. Barnes, and
  London, Yoseloff, 1972.
True Sea Adventures.   Nashville, Nelson, 1975.

Editor, *A Civil War Sampler*, illustrated by Henry S. Gillette.   New York, Watts, 1961.
Editor, *An American Revolutionary War Reader*.   New York, Watts, 1964.
Editor, *The Strongest Man in the World*, illustrated by Cliff Schule.   Philadelphia,
  Westminster Press, 1967.

Donald J. Sobol comments:
  I have tried to write the kinds of books I wanted to read when I was a boy but could not
find.

*   *   *

  Donald J. Sobol is best known by young readers for his detective and mystery series of a
dozen books about Encyclopedia "Leroy" Brown. The first book in the series, *Encyclopedia
Brown, Boy Detective*, tells of events with which Leroy Brown becomes involved as he helps
his Chief of Police father, as a silent partner, solve crimes. Leroy is called Encyclopedia
because he carries so many facts in his head, and he is full of ideas and clues that are helpful
in solving criminal cases. Most of the books in the Encyclopedia Brown Series are composed
of one story in a single chapter and/or a collection of short stories where crimes are solved
and criminals apprehended. Mr. Sobol creates cases for Encyclopedia Brown that are
refreshing as well as suspenseful and thrilling. There are no catches or tricks to solving the
criminal cases. Mr. Sobol makes sure that each case has a solution and can be solved by
straight, matter-of-fact, intelligent thinking. Encyclopedia Brown is an excellent, rewarding,
and worthwhile series.
  Mr. Sobol has other works to his credit that deal with teenagers and their many exploits,
such as *Secret Agents Four*. The author has also written historical books, for example *The
Double Quest* which is a story of medieval England during the reign of Henry II and more of
a mystery than an historical novel. Other books about the Middle Ages are *The First Book of
Medieval Man* and *The First Book of the Barbarian Invaders*. He has also written some
biographical works, including *The Wright Brothers at Kitty Hawk*, and a book on stocks and
bonds, and edited two history collections, *A Civil War Sampler* and *An American
Revolutionary War Reader*.

—Dolores C. Leffall

SOFTLY, Barbara. British. Born in Ewell, Surrey, 12 March 1924. Educated at Nonsuch County Grammar School, Cheam, Surrey, 1938–42; Froebel Teachers Training College, London, 1942–44. Married Alan Softly in 1951. English and History Teacher, Manor House School, Little Bookham, Surrey, 1944–55. Address: 13 Windmill Lane, Ewell, Surrey, England.

PUBLICATIONS FOR CHILDREN

Fiction

>   *Plain Jane*, illustrated by Shirley Hughes. London, Macmillan, 1961; New York, St. Martin's Press, 1962.
>   *Place Mill*, illustrated by Shirley Hughes. London, Macmillan, and New York, St. Martin's Press, 1962.
>   *A Stone in a Pool*, illustrated by Shirley Hughes. London, Macmillan, and New York, St. Martin's Press, 1964.
>   *Ponder and William* [*on Holiday, at Home, at the Weekend*], illustrated by Diana John. London, Penguin, 4 vols., 1966–74.
>   *Hippo, Potta and Muss*, illustrated by Tony Veale. London, Chatto Boyd and Oliver, 1969; New York, Harvey House, 1970.
>   *A Lemon-Yellow Elephant Called Trunk*, illustrated by Tony Veale. London, Chatto Boyd and Oliver, and New York, Harvey House, 1971.
>   *Geranium*, illustrated by Margaret Wetherbee. London, Hutchinson, 1972.

Other

>   *Magic People*, illustrated by Gunvor Edwards. Edinburgh, Oliver and Boyd, 1966; New York, Holt Rinehart, 1967.
>   *More Magic People*, illustrated by Gunvor Edwards. London, Chatto Boyd and Oliver, 1969; as *Magic People Around the World*, New York, Holt Rinehart, 1970.

PUBLICATIONS FOR ADULTS

Other

>   *The Queens of England.* Newton Abbot, Devon, David and Charles, and New York, Stein and Day, 1976.

Barbara Softly comments:

History was my main interest in school, and this resulted in three historical novels for older children. When the publishers indicated that "history" was no longer marketable, my thoughts turned to other projects – stories and non-fiction for children of varying ages. Having taught children from 4–14 during my teaching days, I did not find this as difficult as it might seem, and in the range of my children's books so far there is pretty well something for everyone. It was a child's question about the wives of kings that made me plan *The Queens of England*, a non-fiction work for adults.

*   *   *

Barbara Softly is best known for her books for very young children. Her *Ponder and William* tales are about the curious friendship of a pyjama case in the form of a Panda and a small boy called William. Together they get in and out of mischief and have cosy adventures. Ponder's talent is for little songs about the rain and buttercups and other things (with which the stories are interspersed); William is best at being helpful. Their friends are three cats and Woggly-Wobbly-Wolley-Dod-Dog whom Cousin Winifred made from a stuffed sock and orange velvet to lie along the bottom of the door to keep out the draughts.

For older children she writes historical novels. *A Stone in a Pool* (on the picturesque old Royalist side) is about Charles I's imprisonment in Carisbrooke Castle, and a schoolboy who helps to plan an escape. *Plain Jane*, another Civil War adventure in the same traditional mood, is set in Cornwall in 1643.

—Nancy Shepherdson

SORENSEN, Virginia. American. Born in Provo, Utah, 17 February 1912. Educated at Brigham Young University, Provo, A.B. 1934. Married Fred C. Sorensen in 1933 (divorced), one daughter and one son; the writer Alec Waugh, 1969. Writer-in-Residence, State University of Oklahoma, Edmond, 1966–67. Recipient: Guggenheim Fellowship, 1946, 1954; Child Study Association of America Award, 1956; American Library Association Newbery Medal, 1957. Agent: Curtis Brown Ltd., 575 Madison Avenue, New York, New York 10022, U.S.A. Address: Avenue Sidi Mohammed Ben Abdallah 97, Tangier, Morocco.

PUBLICATIONS FOR CHILDREN

Fiction

> *Curious Missie*, illustrated by Marilyn Miller.   New York, Harcourt Brace, 1953.
> *The House Next Door: Utah, 1896*, illustrated by Lili Cassel.   New York, Scribner, 1954.
> *Plain Girl*, illustrated by Charles Geer.   New York, Harcourt Brace, 1955.
> *Miracles on Maple Hill*, illustrated by Beth and Joe Krush.   New York, Harcourt Brace, 1956; Leicester, Brockhampton Press, 1967.
> *Lotte's Locket*, illustrated by Fermin Rocker.   New York, Harcourt Brace, 1964.
> *Around the Corner*, illustrated by Robert Weaver.   New York, Harcourt Brace, 1971.
> *Companions of the Road*.   New York, Atheneum, 1978.

PUBLICATIONS FOR ADULTS

Novels

> *A Little Lower Than the Angels*.   New York, Knopf, 1942.
> *On This Star*.   New York, Reynal and Hitchcock, 1946.
> *The Neighbors*.   New York, Reynal and Hitchcock, 1947.
> *The Evening and the Morning*.   New York, Harcourt Brace, 1949.
> *The Proper Gods*.   New York, Harcourt Brace, 1951.
> *Many Heavens*.   New York, Harcourt Brace, 1954.
> *Kingdom Come*.   New York, Harcourt Brace, 1960.
> *The Man with the Key*.   New York, Harcourt Brace, 1974.

Short Stories

> *Where Nothing Is Long Ago: Memories of a Mormon Childhood.*   New York, Harcourt Brace, 1963.

Manuscript Collection: Special Collections, Boston University Library.

*   *   *

In Virginia Sorensen's world, people are very important and precious, and especially so as members of a family. It is the strong sense of family that animates her works and which evokes such a warm response from her readers. Perhaps her best-loved work, the 1957 Newbery Medal-winning *Miracles on Maple Hill*, most successfully brings to life a family and a community.

Father has returned at last from the war to a family that never gave up hope. But the savagery he has seen, and the months in prison camp, have changed him. The family, Father, Mother, Joe and Marly, have become tense and uneasy with Father's tension. Little things, voices, noises, small frustrations, cause trouble. Mother becomes convinced that the cure can be found in the countryside, at Grandmother's old place in Maple Hill. Daddy is not convinced – the whole idea of retreat to the country strikes him as far-fetched and simplistic – but, unwillingly, he agrees: and the miracles begin. They are the simple miracles of nature, of healing and growth; but they seem miraculous indeed to a city child. Father becomes interested in the maple sugar business run by the elderly neighbours Mr. and Mrs. Chris: he begins to think that, indeed, life in the country, outdoor work, fresh air and elbow room, will help him to become again the man he was before the war. It's a gentle story. The climax comes when Mr. Chris has a heart attack just as the sugaring time begins, on which his whole small income depends. Can the city family, so new to country ways and work, save the precious sugar crop? Predictably enough they can and do, but the story is surprisingly suspenseful. Throughout the book, there is the warm strength of caring – for family, for neighbours, for the lonely old hermit living nearby among his goats. The message that people matter is one that bears repeating and remembering.

Plain Girl shares the same warmth, with even more respect for old country ways and traditions. It tells of Esther, only daughter in a family of Plain People – the Amish. Esther feels sadly like an only child, for her brother Daniel has flouted the strict ways of the People and gone off to see the world. He has cut his hair, wears buttons on his clothes, – even drives a car! Esther is shocked but at the same time curious. When the time comes for Esther to go to school as the law dictates, she becomes friends with a little girl who is the very opposite of Plain, who wears pink frilly dresses and ribbons in her hair. Esther feels the forbidden longing to try these pretty, different unPlain garments, to trade clothes with her friend Mary. But on Daniel's return, saddened by his contact with the world and eager to be Plain once more, Esther learns to value her Amish ways.

As in her other stories for children, Mrs. Sorensen's pages are filled with a wholesome philosophy of love and caring. Her works are dated and quaint when contrasted with the hard-hitting, no-holds-barred children's literature of today, but it will be a sad world when there is no place left in it for gentle kindliness.

—Joan McGrath

SOUTHALL, Ivan (Francis). Australian. Born in Canterbury, Victoria, 8 June 1921. Educated at Chatham State School; Mount Albert Central School; Box Hill Grammar School. Served in the Australian Army, 1941, and the Royal Australian Air Force, 1942–46; Distinguished Flying Cross. Married Joyce Blackburn in 1946 (marriage dissolved), one son and three daughters; Susan Stanton, 1976. Engraver, *Herald and Weekly Times*, Melbourne, 1936–41, 1947. Gertrude Clarke Whittall Lecturer, Library of Congress, Washington, D.C., 1973; May Hill Arbuthnot Lecturer, University of Washington, Seattle, 1974. Foundation

President, Knoxbrooke Training Centre for the Handicapped, Victoria. Recipient: Australian Children's Book Council Book of the Year Award, 1966, 1968, 1969 (for picture book), 1971, 1976; British Library Association Carnegie Medal, 1972; Australian Writers Award, 1974. Address: P.O. Box 184, Forestville, New South Wales 2087, Australia.

PUBLICATIONS FOR CHILDREN

Fiction

Meet Simon Black, illustrated by Frank Norton. Sydney and London, Angus and Robertson, 1950.

Simon Black in Peril [*in Space, in Coastal Command, in China, and the Spaceman, in the Antarctic, Takes Over, at Sea*], illustrated by I. Maher and Wal Stackpool. Sydney and London, Angus and Robertson, 8 vols., 1951–62.

Hills End. Sydney and London, Angus and Robertson, 1962; New York, St. Martin's Press, 1963.

Ash Road, illustrated by Clem Seale. Sydney, Angus and Robertson, 1965; London, Angus and Robertson, and New York, St. Martin's Press, 1966.

The Fox Hole, illustrated by Ian Ribbons. Sydney, Hicks Smith, London, Methuen, and New York, St. Martin's Press, 1967.

To the Wild Sky, illustrated by Jennifer Tuckwell. Sydney and London, Angus and Robertson, and New York, St. Martin's Press, 1967.

Sly Old Wardrobe, illustrated by Ted Greenwood. Melbourne, Cheshire, and London, Angus and Robertson, 1968; New York, St. Martin's Press, 1969.

Let the Balloon Go, illustrated by Ian Ribbons. Sydney, Hicks Smith, London, Methuen, and New York, St. Martin's Press, 1968.

Finn's Folly. London, Angus and Robertson, and New York, St. Martin's Press, 1969.

Chinaman's Reef Is Ours. Sydney and London, Angus and Robertson, and New York, St. Martin's Press, 1970.

Bread and Honey. Sydney and London, Angus and Robertson, 1970; as *Walk a Mile and Get Nowhere*, Englewood Cliffs, New Jersey, Bradbury Press, 1970.

Josh. Sydney and London, Angus and Robertson, 1971; New York, Macmillan, 1972.

Over the Top, illustrated by Ian Ribbons. Sydney, Hicks Smith, and London, Methuen, 1972; as *Benson Boy*, New York, Macmillan, 1973.

Head in the Clouds, illustrated by Richard Kennedy. Sydney and London, Angus and Robertson, 1972; New York, Macmillan, 1973.

Matt and Jo. Sydney, Angus and Robertson, and New York, Macmillan, 1973; London, Angus and Robertson, 1974.

What about Tomorrow? Sydney, Angus and Robertson, 1976; London, Angus and Robertson, and New York, Macmillan, 1977.

Other

Journey into Mystery: A Story of the Explorers Burke and Wills, illustrated by Robin Goodall. Melbourne, Lansdowne Press, 1961.

Rockets in the Desert: The Story of Woomera. Sydney, Angus and Robertson, 1964; London, Angus and Robertson, 1965.

Lawrence Hargrave. Melbourne, Oxford University Press, 1964.

Indonesian Journey. Melbourne, Lansdowne Press, 1965; London, Newnes, and Boston, Ginn, 1966.

The Sword of Esau: Bible Stories Retold, illustrated by Joan Kiddell-Monroe. Sydney, Angus and Robertson, 1967; New York, St. Martin's Press, 1968.

The Curse of Cain: Bible Stories Retold, illustrated by Joan Kiddell-Monroe. Sydney, Angus and Robertson, and New York, St. Martin's Press, 1968.

Bushfire!, illustrated by Julie Mattox.   Sydney, Angus and Robertson, 1968.
Seventeen Seconds.   Sydney and London, Hodder and Stoughton, 1973; New York, Macmillan, 1974.
Fly West.   London, Angus and Robertson, 1974; New York, Macmillan, 1975.

Play

Screenplay: *Let the Balloon Go*, from his own story, 1975.

PUBLICATIONS FOR ADULTS

Novels

Third Pilot.   Sydney, Horwitz, 1958.
Flight to Gibraltar.   Sydney, Horwitz, 1958; as *Terror Flight*, 1962.
Mediterranean Black.   Sydney, Horwitz, 1959.
Sortie in Cyrenaica.   Sydney, Horwitz, 1959.
Mission to Greece.   Sydney, Horwitz, 1959.
Atlantic Pursuit.   Sydney, Horwitz, 1960.

Short Stories

Out of the Dawn: Three Short Stories.   Privately printed, 1942.

Other

The Weaver from Meltham (biography of Godfrey Hirst).   Melbourne, Whitcombe and Tombs, 1950.
They Shall Not Pass Unseen.   Sydney, Angus and Robertson, 1956.
The Story of the Hermitage: The First Fifty Years of the Geelong Church of England Girls' Grammar School.   Melbourne, Cheshire, 1956.
A Tale of Box Hill: Day of the Forest.   Box Hill, Victoria, Box Hill City Council, 1957.
Bluey Truscott: Squadron Leader Keith William Truscott, R.A.A.F., D.F.C. and Bar.   Sydney, Angus and Robertson, 1958.
Softly Tread the Brave: A Triumph over Terror, Devilry, and Death by Mine Disposal Officers John Stuart Mould and Hugh Randal Syme.   Sydney, Angus and Robertson, 1960.
Woomera.   Sydney, Angus and Robertson, 1962.
Parson on the Track: Bush Brothers in the Australian Outback.   Melbourne, Lansdowne Press, 1962.
Indonesia Face to Face.   Melbourne, Lansdowne Press, 1964; London, Angus and Robertson, 1965.
A Journey of Discovery: On Writing for Children.   London, Penguin, 1975; New York, Macmillan, 1976.

Editor, *The Challenge — Is the Church Obsolete? An Australian Response to the Challenge of Modern Society* (essays).   Melbourne, Lansdowne Press, 1966.

Manuscript Collection: National Library of Australia, Canberra.

Ivan Southall comments:
   In my books for children I see my own growth as a writer. It is my basic philosophy to regard the person who reads my work, whether the person be child or adult, as my emotional and intellectual equal. This means I make few, if any, concessions to the age of the reader.

The reader must come to me. I cannot go to the reader. Yet, in my books for children, I have striven to identify (in the full sense of the term) with the emotional and physical state of being a young person, or experiencing life (or those areas of life about which I have written), with the emotional intensity of a young person. I believe I have had more to say in this particular way than in any other. It has been a writing experience, over a number of years, of some excitement, and some adventure, and some fulfilment.

*   *   *

Ivan Southall is the best known and most discussed Australian children's writer of the 1960's and 1970's. His present reputation is as an author of unusual power and fierce, sometimes harsh integrity: one who makes no concessions for the sake of easy popularity. Yet all through the 1950's, before producing any of the work on which this reputation is founded, Southall had been turning out approximately a book a year of a very different kind about the adventures of Squadron Leader Simon Black of the Royal Australian Air Force.

Simon — wrote his creator in an article in the *Horn Book* in June 1968 — "possessed in incredible measure virtue, honour, righteous anger, courage and inventiveness. Every incredible difficulty he cheerfully overcame with dignity, grandeur, and a very stiff upper lip." Southall grew tired of him, and found his limitations frustrating. In 1960, he decided he was not going to write for children any more. Then, looking at his own children and their friends, he began to suspect that in their lives, "interacting one upon the other at an unknown depth ... lay an unlimited source of raw material." And he wrote a further book, *Hills End* which, with its successor *Ash Road*, was to be the start of a different professional and personal life.

Both books confront groups of children and young people with catastrophes — flood in *Hills End*, fire in *Ash Road* — which they are ill-equipped to cope with. They muddle through precariously, with intermittent courage and resourcefulness, but also at times with silliness, squabbling and confusion. Stiff upper lips are notably absent. These are real children, behaving as children might be expected to behave in such emergencies.

Southall's next three full-length novels dealt with somewhat similar, and in two cases even more harrowing, situations. In *To the Wild Sky* half a dozen youngsters from a crashed aircraft are stranded on a remote coast with little food and no water. The story describes their struggle to survive, but does not carry it through to its logical conclusion (death or rescue). The reader is never told what happens to them. In *Finn's Folly* three adults are killed in a road crash, a hillside is littered with drums of deadly cyanide, a mentally-retarded boy is perilously at large, and a teenage couple talk love in the wreckage beside the body of the girl's father. The disaster in *Chinaman's Reef Is Ours* is man-made rather than natural: the assault of a mining company on a not-quite-abandoned ghost town which it intends to demolish in order to start mining again.

In all these books, characters are shown at the end of their tethers; the viewpoint moves around among several people; the technique is somewhat like that of a chess game in which the pieces are moved independently and yet combined in an overall strategy. By 1970 it had begun to seem that this was Southall's established formula. However, his full-length novels after *Chinaman's Reef* showed a clear change of direction exploring in growing depth the inner experience of a central main character.

With hindsight it can be seen that the way ahead had been indicated in a short book called *Let the Balloon Go*, published in 1968. This tells how a spastic boy, determined to be "a boy like any other boy," climbs to the top of an 80-foot tree, then faces the problem of getting down. It is a dizzyingly tense story, yet its true action takes place inside one boy's mind; and this is essentially true of three succeeding major novels.

In *Bread and Honey* the day is Anzac Day, when Australians commemorate their part in two world wars. Michael, aged 13, misses seeing the great parade in his town, encounters a strange girl of 9 who lives in an imaginative world of her own, and in her company meets the local bully and thrashes the bully's henchman. Summarized in such terms it seems a slight story; but a great deal is happening inside Michael. He is worrying away at various problems of conduct and values: among them the ethics of meeting violence with violence (and on a bigger scale the glory and horror of war); the struggle between literal-minded and imaginative, conventional and spontaneous. Above all — an increasingly recurrent Southall theme — he is coming through an ordeal which is in some sense an initiation into manhood.

Josh, with which Southall won the Carnegie Medal, is an absorbing and disturbing story. Josh, a highly-strung, poetry-writing 14-year-old from the city, goes to remote Ryan's Creek, where members of his family were once leading citizens, and becomes highly unpopular with the local youngsters, from whom he suffers psychological and physical violence. Josh wins through to some kind of respect, and perhaps brings Ryan's Creek a useful catharsis. But at the end he will not be reconciled with the locals; he sets off to walk back to the city, on his own. It is the only way he can remain himself. The point of view is from right inside the tortured Josh, whose stream of consciousness is effectively, painfully presented.

In *What about Tomorrow?* there is again a profound sense of identification of the author with his central character. Sam, a 14-year-old boy in 1931, has crashed his bike and lost eight shillings' worth of newspapers he is delivering: an economic disaster that drives him into running away from home. Most of the book describes his journeyings over the next few days, during which he has encounters with several adults (mostly helpful) and falls in love with three girls in rapid succession. As with *Bread and Honey* and *Josh*, the experience is essentially that of growing up; but *What about Tomorrow?* also looks ahead to Sam's maturity, for there are forward-flashes interspersed at intervals with the narrative, showing Sam as captain of a seaplane in World War II, flying to meet his fate.

The question is not only of growing up, but also of what one is growing up towards. Sam is no Simon Black. There is a preoccupation with fear, courage, the achievement of manhood through ordeal, and the nature of glory that is characteristic of the later Southall, as is the fierce and searching light he directs on human nature. His books have seldom been, in any easy or obvious sense of the word, enjoyable; and often he has seemed to be challenging his readers, as if to see how much agony they can take. Yet the books are widely read — a fact that seems to indicate that there *are* youngsters who can take what Southall offers and who find the experience rewarding.

—John Rowe Townsend

SPEARE, Elizabeth George. American. Born in Melrose, Massachusetts, 21 November 1908. Educated at Smith College, Northampton, Massachusetts, 1926–27; Boston University, A.B. 1930, M.A. 1932. Married Alden Speare in 1936; has one son and one daughter. English teacher, high schools in Rockland, Massachusetts, 1932–35, and Auburn, Massachusetts, 1935–36. Recipient: American Library Association Newbery Medal, 1959, 1962. Address: Bibbins Road, R.F.D. 1, Fairfield, Connecticut 06430, U.S.A.

PUBLICATIONS FOR CHILDREN

Fiction

The Witch of Blackbird Pond. Boston, Houghton Mifflin, 1958; London, Gollancz, 1960.
Calico Captive, illustrated by W.T. Mars. Boston, Houghton Mifflin, 1959; London, Gollancz, 1963.
The Bronze Bow. Boston, Houghton Mifflin, 1961; London, Gollancz, 1962.

Other

   Life in Colonial America.   New York, Random House, 1963.

Novel

   The Prospering.   Boston, Houghton Mifflin, and London, Gollancz, 1967.

Other

   Child Life in New England, 1790–1840.   Sturbridge, Massachusetts, Old Sturbridge
   Village, 1961.

Manuscript Collection: Mugar Memorial Library, Boston University.

*   *   *

   Calico Captive is Elizabeth George Speare's learning experience, a natural antecedent to
her second book (the first to be published), *The Witch of Blackbird Pond*. Speare's first effort is
slow and plodding, despite the presence of elements of good fiction, and a strong female
character. The story, based on fact, focuses on Miriam Willard's capture in New Hampshire,
prior to the French and Indian War, by a small band of hostile Indians; the long trek to
Montreal; and her life as a prisoner awaiting ransoming. While in Montreal, the fiery-
tempered Miriam becomes a gifted seamstress and is able to support herself until she gains
her freedom. In attempting to lay the groundwork for her book, Speare over-extended
herself, employing a leaden narrative and an over-done interior monologue. The racist
language used in describing the Indians is deplorable, especially in a children's book.
   In *The Witch of Blackbird Pond*, Speare created a far superior literary offering in which she
avoided the errors of *Calico Captive*. The central figure is 16-year-old Kit who comes from
sunny Barbados to a cold, stiff Connecticut town to seek refuge with her aunt's family. Speare
succeeds in admirably defining her characters, especially Kit, the ebullient, acute, but
penniless orphan who flees the West Indian island following her grandfather's death. In
Barbados, Kit was happiest "running free as the wind in a world filled with sunshine." Now
she must stir vats of soap, weed the onion patch, and lead an austere life in a spare household.
It is a difficult adjustment for the granddaughter of a Loyalist who had been knighted by the
king of England, a girl who had learned to read and write in the comfort of her kin's vast,
rich library. Speare handles Kit's anger, dismay, resentment, and maturing with a deft hand.
It is with Hannah Tupper, a gentle, outcast Quaker that Kit is able to regain the feeling of
independence and self-assurance with which she grew up. It is at Hannah's that she becomes
reacquainted with Nathaniel Eaton, the sea-captain's son whose ship brought Kit to the
Puritan colony. When a fever sweeps across the town, angry townspeople go on a witch-
hunt and burn down Hannah's poor cottage. Kit rescues the old woman, but the young girl
herself is held for trial as a witch. Speare maintains the reader's interest throughout this
special book.
   After *Blackbird Pond*, Speare wrote *The Bronze Bow*, a tedious piece of work. The story is
about an ancient Israelite, an "angry, young man," who bears vengeance in his heart against
the conquering Romans until Jesus convinces him, "The only thing stronger than hate is
love." Although the message is laudable, children will find the density of this book an
overwhelming obstacle. It is unfortunate that Speare did not continue writing in the style of
The Witch of Blackbird Pond.

—Vivian J. Scheinmann

SPENCE, Eleanor. Australian. Born in Sydney, New South Wales, 21 October 1928. Educated at Erina Primary School, 1935–40; Gosford High School, 1941–45; Sydney University, 1946–48, B.A. Married John A. Spence in 1952; has two sons and one daughter. Teacher, Methodist Ladies' College, Burwood, New South Wales, 1949; Librarian, Commonwealth Public Service Board, 1950–52; Children's Librarian, Coventry City Libraries, Coventry, England, 1953–54. Teacher's Aide, 1974–75, and since 1976, Teacher, Autistic Children's School, Sydney. Recipient: Australian Children's Book Council Book of the Year Award, 1964. Address: 11 Handley Avenue, Turramurra, New South Wales 2074, Australia.

PUBLICATIONS FOR CHILDREN

Fiction

> *Patterson's Track*, illustrated by Alison Forbes. Melbourne, Oxford University Press, 1958; London, Angus and Robertson, 1959.
> *The Summer in Between*, illustrated by Marcia Lane Foster. London, Oxford University Press, 1959.
> *Lillipilly Hill*, illustrated by Susan Einzig. London, Oxford University Press, 1960; New York, Roy, 1963.
> *The Green Laurel*, illustrated by Geraldine Spence. London, Oxford University Press, 1963; New York, Roy, 1965.
> *The Year of the Currawong*, illustrated by Gareth Floyd. London, Oxford University Press, and New York, Roy, 1965.
> *The Switherby Pilgrims*, illustrated by Corinna Gray. London, Oxford University Press, and New York, Roy, 1967.
> *Jamberoo Road*, illustrated by Doreen Roberts. London, Oxford University Press, and New York, Roy, 1969.
> *The Nothing Place*, illustrated by Geraldine Spence. London, Oxford University Press, 1972; New York, Harper, 1973.
> *Time to Go Home*, illustrated by Fermin Rocker. London, Oxford University Press, 1973.
> *The Travels of Hermann*, illustrated by Noela Young. Sydney, Collins, 1973.
> *The October Child*, illustrated by Malcolm Green. London, Oxford University Press, 1976; as *The Devil Hole*, New York, Lothrop, 1977.
> *A Candle for St. Antony*. London, Oxford University Press, 1977.

Other

> *A Schoolmaster*, illustrated by Jane Walker. Melbourne, Oxford University Press, 1969.
> *A Cedar-Cutter*, illustrated by Barbara Taylor. Melbourne, Oxford University Press, 1971.

Eleanor Spence comments:
  With the exception of *The Travels of Hermann* my novels have generally been for readers from age 11 to young teens. All have Australian backgrounds and many of the experiences described were similar to episodes in my own (rural) childhood. In my later stories I have turned more to modern city life as background, and have twice used handicapped children as central characters – a deaf boy in *The Nothing Place* and an autistic boy in *The October Child*.

                         *   *   *

  Eleanor Spence is a pioneer among those writers who in the last twenty years have established a children's literature which is distinctively Australian in style and ethos. Her novels are distinguished by well-realised settings, sensitive characterisation and quiet humour. Two themes are recurrent. One is the universal theme of self-examination during the early years of adolescence: "She was dimly aware of mysteries ahead, of problems not to be neatly solved like the sums in her arithmetic book, of a whole world of experience – in brief she had her first glimpse of growing up" (*The Green Laurel*). The other is a particular interest in Australian heritage from colonial settlement to post-war immigration: "He was beginning now to find fascination in the history of his own country, and of this history men like the Swagman were an essential element" (*The Year of the Currawong*).

Both themes are to be found in *Patterson's Track*. 13-year-old Karen is interested in Convict Cove and its association with a 19th-century runaway. In retracing with a group of friends and her brothers the path of the convict she learns as much about herself as about the mystery. *The Summer in Between* has the same setting (all Eleanor Spence's novels are about Sydney and its environs). Faith Melville writes a play about Victorian settlers at her home at Booralee for her friends to act, and again self discovery results. *Lillipilly Hill* is a historical novel; Victorian restraints upon the behaviour of young ladies are defied by Harriet Wilmot in her adjustment to the rural community in New South Wales to which the family have emigrated. *The Green Laurel*, Eleanor Spence's most highly regarded novel, is about the need for roots. This is shown in the character of the heroine, Lesley Somerville, from a fairground family, in her choice of architecture as a career and in her attempts to make a community of their new home in the immigrants' suburb of Blackbutt Hill. *The Year of the Currawong* takes as its centre of interest a disused silver mine on which the interests of the Kendall family converge when they move from the city to the isolated village of Currawong.

The Switherby Pilgrims and its sequel *Jamberoo Road* are popular Australian historical novels. In the 1840's, Miss Arabella Braithwaite, a figure reminiscent of the redoubtable Mrs. Caroline Chisholm, emigrates from Switherby in Yorkshire to Illawarra in New South Wales. She takes with her an assortment of destitute children to which she adds an aboriginal orphan, Cammy. With the help of their convict servant Ebenezer, they wrest a living out of virgin soil. The sequel gives the further histories of the children, especially Cassie Brown, who rejects the prosperous Edward Marlow of Falls Farm, Jamberoo for Ebenezer.

There are new directions in the novels that follow. Boys rather than girls are the chief characters and social concern replaces the historical theme. *Time to Go Home* is a relaxed and humorous teenage novel about the competing claims of sport and work and home and school. But Rowan Price also takes time to coach a team of younger children in a poor neighbourhood. The other two novels are about handicapped boys. Glen Calder, in *The Nothing Place*, is struggling with deafness as a result of illness, as well as with the boredom of living in the vast anonymous suburb to which the family has moved. Keith Mariner, in *The October Child*, has an autistic younger brother and the effects of this on the whole family are depicted with frankness and sensitivity.

—Mary Croxson

SPERRY, Armstrong. American. Born in New Haven, Connecticut, 7 November 1897. Educated at Yale School of Fine Arts, New Haven, 1918; Art Students' League, New York, 1919–21; Académie Colarossis, Paris, 1922. Served in the United States Navy, 1917. Married Margaret Mitchell in 1930; one son and one daughter. Assistant Ethnologist, *Kaimiloa* expedition to the South Pacific, 1925–26; commercial artist and illustrator. Recipient: American Library Association Newbery Medal, 1941; New York *Herald Tribune* Festival award, 1944. *Died in April 1976.*

PUBLICATIONS FOR CHILDREN (illustrated by the author)

Fiction

One Day with Manu.   Philadelphia, Winston, 1933.
One Day with Jambi in Sumatra.   Philadelphia, Winston, 1934.
One Day with Tuktu, An Eskimo Boy.   Philadelphia, Winston, 1935.
All Sail Set.   Philadelphia, Winston, 1936; London, Lane, 1946.
Wagons Westward: The Old Trail to Sante Fe.   Philadelphia, Winston, 1936; London,
    Lane, 1948.
Call It Courage.   Philadelphia, Winston, 1936; as *The Boy Who Was Afraid*, London,
    Lane, 1942.
Little Eagle, A Navajo Boy.   Philadelphia, Winston, 1938.
Lost Lagoon.   New York, Doubleday, 1939; London, Lane 1943.
Coconut, The Wonder Tree.   New York, Macmillan, 1942; London, Lane, 1946.
Bamboo, The Grass Tree.   New York, Macmillan, 1942; London, Lane, 1946.
No Brighter Glory.   New York, Macmillan, 1942; London, Hutchinson, 1944.
Storm Canvas.   Philadelphia, Winston, 1944.
Hull-Down for Action.   New York, Doubleday, 1945; London, Lane, 1948.
The Rain Forest.   New York, Macmillan, 1947; London, Lane, 1950.
Danger to Windward.   Philadelphia, Winston, 1947; London, Lane, 1952.
Black Falcon.   Philadelphia, Winston, 1949.
River of the West, illustrated by Henry Pitz.   Philadelphia, Winston, 1952; London,
    Lane, 1954.
Thunder Country.   New York, Macmillan, 1952; London, Lane, 1953.
Frozen Fire.   New York, Doubleday, 1956; London, Lane, 1957.
South of Cape Horn.   Philadelphia, Winston, 1958.

Other

The Voyages of Christopher Columbus.   New York, Random House, 1950.
John Paul Jones, Fighting Sailor.   New York, Random House, 1955.
Pacific Islands Speaking.   New York, Macmillan, 1955.
Captain Cook Explores the South Seas.   New York, Random House, 1955; revised
    edition, as *All about Captain Cook*, London, W.H. Allen, 1960.
All about the Arctic and Antarctic.   New York, Random House, 1957.
All about the Jungle.   New York, Random House, 1959; London, W.H. Allen, 1960.
The Amazon, River Sea of Brazil.   Champaign, Illinois, Garrard, 1961; London,
    Muller, 1962.
Great River, Wide Land: The Rio Grande Through History.   New York, Macmillan,
    and London, Collier Macmillan, 1967.

Editor, *Story Parade: A Collection of Modern Stories for Boys and Girls*.   Philadelphia,
    Winston, 5 vols., 1938–42.

Illustrator: *Stars to Steer By*, 1934, and *House Afire!*, 1941, by Helen T. Follett; *Shuttered
Windows* by Florence Crannell Means, 1938; *Jungle River*, 1938, and *Thunderbolt House*,
1944, by Howard Pease; *Boat Builder* by Clara I. Judson, 1940; *Nicholas Arnold, Toolmaker*
by Marion Lansing, 1941; *Winabojo, Master of Life* by James Cloyd Bowman, 1941; *Dogie
Boy* by Edith Heal Berrien, 1943; *Sky Highways* by Trevor Lloyd, 1945; *Story of Hiawatha*
edited by Allen Chaffee, 1951.

*   *   *

Though no more than nouvelle-length, *Call It Courage* (published in Britain as *The Boy
Who Was Afraid*) has an epic mythopoeic quality which fully justifies its presentation as a

story which the Polynesians "even today ... sing in their chants and tell over the evening fire." Ever since his terrible experience as a child of three in the hurricane in which his mother lost her life, Mafatu has been afraid of the sea – the element which his people live by contending against. Shamed by their contemptuous indifference, the boy sets out in a canoe, accompanied by his only two friends, a nondescript yellow dog named Uri and Kivi, a lamed albatross, to "face the thing he feared the most." He survives a violent storm which carries away his mast, paddle, and all his other gear, and thereafter drifts helplessly on a mysterious ocean current to a mountainous island, presumably one of the Solomon Islands. Here he discovers a Sacred Place with a hideous idol to whom cannibals from a neighbouring island periodically make human sacrifices, and daringly he removes from it the spear which he needs as a weapon. On this island he proves his courage and skill by making tools to fish with and a raft to fish from, by killing a shark, a wild boar, and a giant octopus, and by building a canoe from a tamanu tree. On the very day when his preparations are complete, the cannibals return, and he narrowly escapes in his sailing-canoe, pursued by the savages who paddle vengefully after him for a day and a night. The arduous days and nights he endures on the journey back to his own island, against the current and against a fitful wind, are vividly described, as is his triumphant arrival – he wears a necklace of boar's teeth and brandishes a splendid spear – which vindicates him in the eyes of the Chief, his father. Armstrong Sperry achieves a fascinating evocation of setting both at sea and on the two contrasting islands, and also gives a superbly detailed account of the skills by which the Polynesians survive in it. The archetypal character of the story (a boy's testing of himself which takes on the nature of an initiation into manhood) ensures a strong appeal for a book which seems certain to survive as a "children's classic."

Two other books by the same author, *Lost Lagoon* and *Hull-Down for Action*, have a similar geographical setting, no less vividly portrayed; however, in each case the plot and characterisation (belonging to the period before and just after Pearl Harbor) are more standard boys'-adventure-story fare, and though the books are exciting enough, some of the personae, the villains in particular (inscrutable Jap, arrogant Nazi agent), are no more than conventional stereotypes.

—Frank Whitehead

SPYKMAN, E(lizabeth) C(hoate).   American.   Born in Southboro, Massachusetts, 17 July 1896. Educated at Westover School, Middlebury, Connecticut, graduated 1914. Married Nicholas John Spykman in 1931 (died, 1943); two daughters. *Died 7 August 1965.*

PUBLICATIONS FOR CHILDREN

Fiction

A Lemon and a Star.   New York, Harcourt Brace, 1955; London, Macmillan, 1956.
The Wild Angel.   New York, Harcourt Brace, 1957; London, Macmillan, 1958.
Terrible, Horrible Edie.   New York, Harcourt Brace, 1960; London, Macmillan, 1961.
Edie on the Warpath.   New York, Harcourt Brace, 1966; London, Macmillan, 1967.

PUBLICATIONS FOR ADULTS

Other

Westover.   Middlebury, Connecticut, Westover School, 1959.

*   *   *

E.C. Spykman's four novels – the turn-of-the-century saga of the Cares family of Summerton, Massachusetts – are one of the treasures of children's literature. The four younger Cares, Ted, Jane, Hubert, and Edie, are independent, argumentative, and intelligent. They live in a comfortably well-off world of servants, sailboats, summers by the sea, and exciting new motor cars. Reminiscent of E. Nesbit's Bastable children, they spend most of their time plotting adventures and figuring out ways to circumvent the unreasonable rules and regulations of the adult world.

Though all four children are vivid and highly individualistic characters, Edie, the youngest, emerges as Mrs. Spykman's most finely drawn portrait. In the first book – *A Lemon and a Star* – 10-year-old Jane is the central figure while 5-year-old Edie is merely an annoying younger sibling. But in the course of the next three books, Edie moves to center stage. Impetuous, self reliant, always on the lookout for adventure, Edie Cares is one of the most spirited heroines ever to live between the covers of a children's book. She lops off her long hair and rides with the boys in a sheep round-up. She plots to capture an imagined kidnapper. She marches with the suffragettes. Yet throughout she maintains an inner tenderness and sensitivity which marks her as a fully developed – though not fully grown – human being, rather than a stereotypical "tomboy" character.

The great achievement of E.C. Spykman was this ability to create full and utterly believable characters, while at the same time presenting a richly evocative picture of the time and place in which they lived. With no sense of nostalgia, she presents in equal portions the joys and the sorrows of being young. The books live, for both children and adults, because they remain consistently true to the child's perception of the world. A concern for fairness and justice is ever present, but adult moralizing is absent. Humor, lightheartedness, and moments of tenderness make reading the books a delight. An underlying recognition of the fact that, in spite of the fun, growing up is a serious business, makes the memory of them linger long after the covers are closed.

—Susan Meyers

STEELE, Mary Q(uintard). Pseudonym: **Wilson Gage.**   Born in Chattanooga, Tennessee, 8 May 1922. Educated at the University of Chattanooga, B.S. 1943. Married William O. Steele, *q.v.*, in 1943; has two daughters and one son. Recipient: Aurianne Award, 1966. Address: P.O. Box 193, Signal Mountain, Tennessee 37377, U.S.A.

PUBLICATIONS FOR CHILDREN

Fiction

Journey Outside, illustrated by Rocco Negri.   New York, Viking Press, 1969; London, Macmillan, 1970.
The First of the Penguins, illustrated by Susan Jeffers.   New York, Macmillan, 1973; London, Macmillan, 1974.

Because of the Sand Witches There, illustrated by Paul Galdone. New York, Morrow, 1975; London, Macmillan 1976.
The Eye in the Forest, with William O. Steele. New York, Dutton, 1975.
The True Men. New York, Morrow, 1976.

Fiction (as Wilson Gage)

The Secret of the Indian Mound [*Crossbone Hill*, *Fiery Gorge*], illustrated by Mary Stevens. Cleveland, World, 3 vols., 1958–60.
A Wild Goose Tale, illustrated by Glen Rounds. Cleveland, World, 1961.
Dan and the Miranda, illustrated by Glen Rounds. Cleveland, World, 1962.
Miss Osbone-the-Mop, illustrated by Paul Galdone. Cleveland, World, 1963.
Big Blue Island, illustrated by Glen Rounds. Cleveland, World, 1964.
The Ghost of Five Owl Farm, illustrated by Paul Galdone. Cleveland, World, 1966; London, Faber, 1967.
Mike's Toads, illustrated by Glen Rounds. New York, World, 1970.
Squash Pie, illustrated by Glen Rounds. New York, Morrow, 1976.
Down in the Boondocks, illustrated by Glen Rounds. New York, Morrow, 1977.

PUBLICATIONS FOR ADULTS

Other

The Living Year: An Almanac for My Survivors (essays). New York, Viking Press, 1972.

Manuscript Collection: Kerlan Collection, University of Minnesota, Minneapolis.

Mary Q. Steele comments:

My primary interest is in natural history, and especially birds. And the puzzle of humanity's place in the scheme of things follows as the night the day, and I suppose this is what I am talking about in my books, however light-hearted they may be. Which sounds a little pompous and I pray forgiveness.

I would hope my books would be enjoyed; I like to think the books make readers laugh. But I would hope too for the occasional reader who closes one of my books and ever after looks at the world of living things with some small measure of my own sense of astonishment and gratitude.

*   *   *

Although Mary Q. Steele has long been a competent writer of children's books under the pseudonym of Wilson Gage, her most innovative writing so far is represented in her first book under her own name, *Journey Outside*.

Journey Outside tells the story of Dilar, one of the Raft People whose tribe travels on an underground river in search of the "Better Place" recorded in their traditional lore. With a growing conviction that the rafts are only travelling in a circle and will never reach a "Better Place," Dilar leaps from the flotilla and accidentally finds a way to the upper world. There he is rescued by the People Against the Tigers, a hedonistic tribe of gatherers, who fix their thoughts on the present moment just as exclusively as Dilar's own people thought only of the future. Leaving them because they cannot fulfill his need to know whether the Raft People's journey is indeed a circular one, he crosses the mountains and is temporarily cared for by Wingo, a giant gourmet whose very kindness, both to Dilar and to the small creatures he feeds, turns out to be a heedless cruelty. Finally Dilar crosses the desert and reaches the sea. On the shore he meets the first character who seems to know the answer to his questions.

Vigan, the ancient and ugly goatherd is an unlikely *guru*, but through trickery he teaches Dilar that the only wisdom worth finding is already within himself: "Wisdom is like water: there comes a point where it runs into the ground and if you want it you must dig it out yourself." The book ends with Dilar setting off to retrace his steps in the dangerous and possibly pointless quest to bring his people out to the "Better Place."

Journey Outside is one of the most remarkable children's books to be published in recent years, not only because Steele solidly realizes an imaginary world, but also because she succeeds in offering her readers wisdom as well as an exciting story. In this respect *Journey Outside* may be compared with Ursula Le Guin's outstanding Earthsea trilogy. Very few writers of children's books attempt to deal with philosophical concepts, and this is curious in view of the way in which children frequently have an intense interest in philosophical inquiry. It may well be that Mary Q. Steele will emerge as one of the pathfinders in exploring subject matter of this kind.

—Gillian Thomas

STEELE, William O(wen).   American.   Born in Franklin, Tennessee, 22 December 1917. Educated at Cumberland University, Lebanon, Tennessee, 1936–40, B.A. 1940; University of Chattanooga, Tennessee, 1951. Served in the United States Air Force during World War II. Married Mary Quintard Govan (i.e., Mary Q. Steele, *q.v.*) in 1943; has two daughters and one son. Recipient: New York *Herald Tribune* Festival award, 1954; Women's International League for Peace and Freedom Jane Addams Award, 1958. Address: P.O. Box 193, Signal Mountain, Tennessee 37377, U.S.A.

PUBLICATIONS FOR CHILDREN

Fiction

The Golden Root, illustrated by Fritz Kredel.   New York, Aladdin, 1951.
The Buffalo Knife, illustrated by Paul Galdone.   New York, Harcourt Brace, 1952.
Over-Mountain Boy, illustrated by Fritz Kredel.   New York, Aladdin, 1952.
Wilderness Journey, illustrated by Paul Galdone.   New York, Harcourt Brace, 1953.
John Sevier, Pioneer Boy, illustrated by Sandra James.   Indianapolis, Bobbs Merrill, 1953.
Winter Danger, illustrated by Paul Galdone.   New York, Harcourt Brace, 1954; London, Macmillan, 1963.
Tomahawks and Trouble, illustrated by Paul Galdone.   New York, Harcourt Brace, 1955.
We Were There on the Oregon Trail, illustrated by Jo Polseno.   New York, Grosset and Dunlap, 1955.
David Crockett's Earthquake, illustrated by Nicolas.   New York, Harcourt Brace, 1956.
We Were There with the Pony Express, illustrated by Frank Vaughn.   New York, Grosset and Dunlap, 1956; Folkestone, Kent, Bailey Brothers and Swinfen, 1973.
The Lone Hunt, illustrated by Paul Galdone.   New York, Harcourt Brace, 1956; London, Macmillan, 1957.
Flaming Arrows, illustrated by Paul Galdone.   New York, Harcourt Brace, 1957; London, Macmillan, 1958.
Daniel Boone's Echo, illustrated by Nicolas.   New York, Harcourt Brace, 1957.

The Perilous Road, illustrated by Paul Galdone.   New York, Harcourt Brace, 1958; London, Macmillan, 1960.

Andy Jackson's Water Well, illustrated by Michael Ramus.   New York, Harcourt Brace, 1959.

The Far Frontier, illustrated by Paul Galdone.   New York, Harcourt Brace, 1959; London, Macmillan, 1960.

The Spooky Thing, illustrated by Paul Coker.   New York, Harcourt Brace, 1960.

The Year of the Bloody Sevens, illustrated by Charles Beck.   New York, Harcourt Brace, 1963.

Wayah of the Real People, illustrated by Isa Barnett.   Williamsburg, Virginia, Colonial Williamsburg Inc., 1964.

The No-Name Man of the Mountain, illustrated by Jack Davis.   New York, Harcourt Brace, 1964.

Trail Through Danger, illustrated by Charles Beck.   New York, Harcourt Brace, 1965.

Tomahawk Border, illustrated by Vernon Wooten.   Williamsburg, Virginia, Colonial Williamsburg Inc., 1966.

Hound Dog Zip to the Rescue, illustrated by Mimi Korach.   Champaign, Illinois, Garrard, 1970.

Triple Trouble for Hound Dog Zip, illustrated by Mimi Korach.   Champaign, Illinois, Garrard, 1972.

John's Secret Treasure, illustrated by R. Dennis.   New York, Macmillan, 1975.

The Eye in the Forest, with Mary Q. Steele.   New York, Dutton, 1975.

The Man with the Silver Eyes.   New York, Harcourt Brace, 1976.

Other

The Story of Daniel Boone, illustrated by Warren Baumgartner.   New York, Grosset and Dunlap, 1953; London, Muller, 1957.

Francis Marion: Young Swamp Fox, illustrated by Dick Gringhuis.   Indianapolis, Bobbs Merrill, 1954.

De Soto: Child of the Sun, illustrated by Lorence Bjorklund.   New York, Aladdin, 1956.

The Story of Leif Ericson, illustrated by Pranas Lapé.   New York, Grosset and Dunlap, 1954; London, Sampson Low, 1960.

Westward Adventure: The True Stories of Six Pioneers.   New York, Harcourt Brace, 1962.

The Old Wilderness Road: An American Journey.   New York, Harcourt Brace, 1968.

The Wilderness Tattoo: A Narrative of Juan Ortiz.   New York, Harcourt Brace, 1972.

Henry Woodward of Carolina: Surgeon, Trader, Indian Chief, illustrated by Hoyt Simmons.   Columbia, South Carolina, Sandlapper Press, 1972.

Manuscript Collections: Kerlan Collection, University of Minnesota, Minneapolis; Special Collections, John Brister Library, Memphis State University, Tennessee.

William O. Steele comments:

My fiction for the 8 to 12-year-old reader has mostly been concerned with pioneer and Indian struggles in the southeastern U.S. during the 18th century when the red and white cultures clashed at the cutting edge of the frontier. I try always to see the past as it was, to put into my books, not 20th-century characters with a fake pioneer dress of split cow hide, but 18th-century boys and men with buckskin shirts rubbing against their shoulder blades, and the smell of sweat and woodsmoke around them, and their bellies only half-full of dried deer meat and gritty ashcake. What I am trying to get over to my readers is not events but people who make the events. History textbooks can give a reader the high spots — but it takes more than textbooks to give you the heart-squeezed hopelessness and fear that the sound of Indian warwhoops can cause.

In my books I try to give a true picture of what the unspoiled frontier country was like when it began to be settled, of the dangers and hardships and rewards of settling it. Above all I try to convey something of the real essence of the times, something of the restless, tough-bodied, forward-looking pioneer who pushed further and further into the wilderness. And I try to accomplish this in as entertaining a fashion as I can.

In the 1950's and 60's I could write historical fiction from the white pioneer's viewpoint and not be criticised as slighting the Indian's side. Now in the 1970's I would not want to write that kind of book and probably would find no publisher if I did on account of today's ethnic sensitivity. In the future, so as to not waste a quarter of a century of research on the frontier period, I may switch to the Indian viewpoint in his struggles against the whites on the frontier. I would prefer however to go back in time to the fascinating prehistoric Indian groups of Eastern America. It will be a challenge, but it seems to be a wide open field.

*   *   *

William O. Steele writes what used to be confidently called "boys' books." Vigorous novels of pioneering, wilderness travel, and Indian fighting, written for readers of the middle years but strong enough for "reluctant readers" of 12 to 14, are his main stock in trade. Steele provides for maximum reader involvement: the major protagonist is always a young boy of 10 to 12 who is portrayed as staunch and resourceful, but never unrealistically brave or infallible. Most stories are set in the Tennessee wilderness during the pioneering period of American history, a background all but guaranteeing adventure.

The overarching theme of the novels usually involves a step by the young protagonist toward maturity; in the course of his adventures, he learns something important about himself and about life. In *Flaming Arrows*, young Chad Rabun learns tolerance of others; in *The Buffalo Knife*, Andy gains confidence in his own courage. At the very least, the outlook of the young hero is expanded: the Indian boy in *Wayah of the Real People* discards some of his superstitious fear of whites, as does Talatu in *The Man with the Silver Eyes*. But Steele never allows such themes to interfere with his central purpose, which is to tell a fast-moving, exciting story. In some books, indeed, the growing-and-learning motif is nearly smothered under an avalanche of physical adventure. In more thoughtful novels, like *Winter Danger* and *The Man with the Silver Eyes*, the elements are better balanced.

Characterization in Steele's stories centers on the young protagonist and is fairly simple. The boys are meant to be typical; one can be distinguished from the other mainly by the particular fear with which he comes to terms in the story. Adults, especially parents, are usually stock figures, brave, kind, supportive, but generalized. There are occasional exceptions: Caje's father, in *Winter Danger*, is a footloose "woodsy" whose character is briefly but sharply sketched; Camp Green, the Daniel Boone-like "Long Hunter" and Mr. Rhea, the dolorous trader, both of *Wilderness Journey*, are memorable.

Since the mid-sixties, Steele has from time to time shifted the viewpoint in his stories, giving Indian-white encounters from the Indian's side. *Wayah of the Real People* shows white society in the Williamsburg of 1752 through the eyes of a young Cherokee boy sent to Brafferton Hall for a year of schooling. Adventure is minor, but the point of view is fresh. *The Man with the Silver Eyes*, a far more somber story of an Indian boy who discovers that he is half-white, acknowledges the inherent tragedy in the clash of cultures. Though its climax is overly theatrical, this book is a welcome departure from the simplistic view of Indian-as-enemy that prevails in most of Steele's early books.

Steele's novels are credible in period detail, lively in incident, and colorful with vernacular speech. They are sometimes glib and unconvincing at any deeper level; character change is often accomplished with unrealistic ease, and incidents of physical peril and violence frequently seem contrived or gratuitous.

Steele is also author of several tall tales drawn from Tennessee mountain lore. *Andy Jackson's Water Well, The No-Name Man of the Mountain*, and several other short books tell exaggerated tales with proper deadpan style and expressive local language. The language and humor of these tales are richer and livelier than those of the adventure fiction, but for young readers, they lack the strong narrative power and the sense of identification provided by the adventure novels.

—Anne S. MacLeod

STEIG, William. American. Born in New York City, 14 November 1907. Educated at the College of the City of New York, 1923–25; National Academy of Design, 1925–29. Married Elizabeth Mead in 1936 (divorced), one daughter and one son; Kari Homestead, 1950 (divorced, 1963), one daughter; Stephanie Healey, 1964 (divorced, 1966); Jeanne Doron, 1969. Since 1930, free-lance humorous artist. One-man shows: Downtown Gallery, New York, 1939; Smith College, Northampton, Massachusetts, 1940. Recipient: American Library Association Caldecott Medal, 1970; *New York Times* award, for illustration, 1971; Christopher Award, 1973. Address: R.F.D. 1, Box KH 2, Kent, Connecticut 06757, U.S.A.

PUBLICATIONS FOR CHILDREN (illustrated by the author)

Fiction

> *Roland, The Minstrel Pig.* New York, Windmill Books, 1968; London, Hamish Hamilton, 1974.
> *Sylvester and the Magic Pebble.* New York, Windmill Books, 1969; London, Abelard Schuman, 1972.
> *The Bad Island.* New York, Windmill Books, 1969.
> *Amos and Boris.* New York, Farrar Straus, 1971; London, Hamish Hamilton, 1972.
> *Dominic.* New York, Farrar Straus, 1972; London, Hamish Hamilton, 1973.
> *The Real Thief.* New York, Farrar Straus, 1973; London, Hamish Hamilton, 1974.
> *Farmer Palmer's Wagon Ride.* New York, Farrar Straus, 1974; London, Hamish Hamilton, 1975.
> *Abel's Island.* New York, Farrar Straus, 1976; London, Hamish Hamilton, 1977.
> *The Amazing Bone.* New York, Farrar Straus, 1976.
> *Caleb and Kate.* New York, Farrar Straus, 1977.

Verse

> *An Eye for Elephants.* New York, Windmill Books, 1970.

Other

> *C D B!* New York, Windmill Books, 1968.
> *The Bad Speller* (reader). New York, Windmill Books, 1970.

PUBLICATIONS FOR ADULTS

Other (drawings)

> *Man about Town.* New York, Long and Smith, 1932.
> *About People: A Book of Symbolical Drawings.* New York, Random House, 1939.
> *The Lonely Ones.* New York, Duell Sloan Pearce, 1942.

All Embarrassed. New York, Duell Sloan Pearce, 1944.

Small Fry (*New Yorker* cartoons). New York, Duell Sloan Pearce, 1944; London, Phoenix House, 1947.

Persistent Faces. New York, Duell Sloan Pearce, 1945.

Till Death Do Us Part: Some Ballet Notes on Marriage. New York, Duell Sloan Pearce, 1947.

The Agony in the Kindergarten. New York, Duell Sloan Pearce, 1950.

The Rejected Lovers. New York, Knopf, 1951.

Dreams of Glory and Other Drawings. New York, Knopf, 1953.

The Steig Album. New York, Duell Sloan Pearce, 1953.

Continuous Performance (cartoons). New York, Duell Sloan Pearce, 1963.

Male/Female. New York, Farrar Straus, 1971.

Illustrator: *How to Become Extinct* by Will Cuppy, 1941; *Mr. Blandings Builds His Dream House* by Eric Hodgins, 1947; *Listen Little Man: A Document from the Archives of the Orgone Institute* by William Reich, 1948.

*   *   *

William Steig's books for children are blessed with amiability. Indeed, amiable is too mild a term: joy is the staple ingredient of Steig's work. Every story, whether picture book or diminutive novel, is filled with the pleasure of living. The illustrations are sensuous and tenderly humorous; the characters share a passionate delight in the green earth, the blue sky, pebbles, grass, trees and sunshine. To an animal, Steig's protagonists (all non-human) welcome the opportunity to adventure, to live. Eager and optimistic, they are all, to use Steig's own phrase from *Amos and Boris*, "full of wonder, full of enterprise, and full of love for life."

Another characteristic of Steig heroes and heroines is their healthy affection for themselves. They are neither arrogant nor egotistic, yet they enjoy firm self-regard; they know they are important to themselves and to others, and their strengths spring naturally from this confidence. Dominic's generosity, Abel's staunch resistance to despair on his isolated island, Amos's hopefulness, all have their base in cheerful self-respect – surely a psychologically sound notion. The self-doubt, anxiety and occasional despair that afflicts, say, Hoban's Mouse and his Child, never invade a Steig story.

The forms of Steig's novels parallel some classic standards. *Dominic* is a picaresque novel made up of loosely gathered episodes and climaxed by an ending quite unrelated to the rest of the story. It is held together by the winning personality of its dog hero, Dominic, and by its fairy-tale features of kindness rewarded and evil routed. *Abel's Island* is Robinsonade, a survival story with an underlying theme of self-discovery through diversity. The picture books, too, are sometimes faintly reminiscent of old, familiar tales. Roland, in *Roland, The Minstrel Pig*, in his ambitious naivete, falls prey to the treacherous fox, even as Henny Penny and dim, trusting Jemima Puddleduck. In *Amos and Boris*, Amos the mouse, rescued and befriended by Boris the whale, finds a way to return the favor to his enormous friend, just as did the rat in the old story of the Lion and the Rat.

The best of Steig's work combines persuasive characterization and a strong narrative line. *Sylvester and the Magic Pebble* is a simple tale of lost and found, told and illustrated with emotional intensity. It is very domestic, very germane to a young child's interests and feelings, a satisfying drama for children that is also endearingly funny to an adult. *The Amazing Bone* shares many of *Sylvester*'s virtues: lyrical delight in the natural world is entry and background for a dramatic story of danger and rescue which is rounded with the surprises of magic and the satisfactions of warmhearted friendship.

Steig's prose style is literate, even somewhat formal, lending his tales an air of traditional dignity as well as a humor which is perhaps more apparent to an adult than to a child. The balance is delicate but successful; the absence of most colloquialisms and the formality of conversation among characters gives an effect at once amusing and timeless, like a fairy tale, though less serious. At his very best, Steig has a knack akin to E.B. White's for the exact, unexpected phrase: Amos, when he has finished building his sailboat, uses "his most savage strength" to push it into the water. In a time of much flat-footed, didactic writing for children, Steig's work is welcome for its eloquence, warmth, and humor. Most of all, it gives pleasure by its pleasure; Steig extends to his readers a share of his own apparently boundless enthusiasm for the living world.

—Anne S. MacLeod

STEPTOE, John (Lewis).   American.   Born in Brooklyn, New York, 14 September 1950. Educated at the New York School of Art and Design, 1964–67. Married Stephanie Douglas in 1969; has one daughter and one son. Free-lance illustrator; teacher, Brooklyn Museum School, summer 1970. Recipient: Society of Illustrators Gold Medal, 1970; Bank Street College of Education Irma Black Award, 1975; American Library Association Newcott Award, 1976. Address: 840 Monroe Street, Brooklyn, New York 11221, U.S.A.

PUBLICATIONS FOR CHILDREN (illustrated by the author)

Fiction

Stevie.   New York, Harper, 1969; London, Longman, 1970.
Uptown.   New York, Harper, 1970.
Train Ride.   New York, Harper, 1971.
Birthday.   New York, Holt Rinehart, 1972.
My Special Best Words.   New York, Viking Press, 1974.
Marcia.   New York, Viking Press, 1976.

Illustrator: *All Us Come Across the Water* by Lucille Clifton, 1973; *She Come Bringing Me That Little Baby Girl* by Eloise Greenfield, 1974.

*   *   *

John Steptoe, a young black writer who wrote and illustrated *Stevie* when he was only 17, fills his books with the children and neighborhoods of his own life. Except for the idealized community in *Birthday*, these neighborhoods are ghettoes, but Steptoe's pictures of them are glowing, and his children are coping well with their lives.
     The stories are mainly sketches from life, with little plot. The uniquely Steptoe illustrations, suggesting Rouault in their outlines and large shapes of color, vary from book to book as the artist experiments. The grammar and vocabulary are always that of urban black children, more recognizably so in some of the books than in others.
     Stevie has remained the most popular. Its situation is universal – the jealousy and annoyance of a boy of 7 or 8 – Robert – whose mother helps out a neighbor by taking in her little son for a few weeks. This could happen to black or white family; and the language is colloquial in a way that is hard to identify as strictly "black." What happens to Robert in the end has universality, too. After all the irritation has been expressed, positive feelings find their way in. Stevie is missed when he has gone.
     In *Uptown*, two black boys simply talk about what they're going to be when they grow up. Harlem comes vividly to life here as the boys speak of what's "boss" and of junkies and Brothers, karate, hippies, and cops. The words they use as they talk of the clothing they like –

playboys, beavers, bad silks – could baffle the uninitiated. Teachers argue about the advisability of placing this book in their classrooms.

In *Train Ride* a group of small boys dare to sneak a subway ride into Times Square. The story emphasizes their ingenuity and ability to cope, but doesn't leave out the beatings they get from their concerned parents when they arrive home late at night.

In *Birthday, My Special Best Words*, and *Marcia*, Steptoe changes the scene. *Birthday* details a celebration of a black boy's 8th birthday in an imagined rural community where the warm spirit of cooperation and intimacy becomes the main point of the story. In *My Special Best Words* Steptoe writes a book for the very young about 3-year-old Bweela and her year-old brother, Javaka, who live alone with their father. Bweela tells in black baby talk – not always easily read aloud – about the events of daily life, including attempts to toilet-train Javaka. The scenes are intimate, honest, and loving. In *Marcia* Steptoe moves up into teen-age territory, writing a gentle love story with a sex problem at the center. Here, too, the language is the natural speech of the black characters, the tone is hopeful – so hopeful, in fact, that the story rises in the end toward an almost declamatory pitch.

Steptoe's next direction cannot be predicted. He has demonstrated marked ability to move, change, and experiment.

—Claudia Lewis

STEVENSON, William (Henri).   Canadian.   Born in 1925. Address: c/o Harcourt Brace Jovanovich Inc., 757 Third Avenue, New York, New York 10017, U.S.A.

PUBLICATIONS FOR CHILDREN

Fiction

> *The Bushbabies*, illustrated by Victor Ambrus.   Boston, Houghton Mifflin, 1965; London, Hutchinson, 1966.

PUBLICATIONS FOR ADULTS

Other

> *The Yellow Wind: An Excursion in and Around Red China.*   Boston, Houghton Mifflin, and London, Cassell, 1959.
> *After Nehru, What?*   Toronto, Globe and Mail, 1961.
> *Canada and the World.*   Toronto, Globe and Mail, 1962.
> *Birds' Nests in Their Beards* (travel in Malaysia).   Boston, Houghton Mifflin, 1964; London, Hutchinson, 1965.
> *Strike Zion!*   New York, Bantam, 1967; as *Israeli Victory*, London, Transworld, 1967.
> *Zanek! A Chronicle of the Israeli Air Force.*   New York, Viking Press, 1971.
> *The Borman Brotherhood.*   New York, Harcourt Brace, and London, Barker, 1973.
> *A Man Called Intrepid: The Secret War.*   New York, Harcourt Brace, and London, Macmillan, 1976.

*   *   *

William Stevenson has written a number of books on current affairs for adult readers, as well as *A Man Called Intrepid*, a highly successful biography of Sir William Stephenson. His only book for children, *The Bushbabies*, is based on a family incident which took place in 1964 when he was stationed in Kenya.

On an impulse Jackie Rhodes, a 13-year-old English girl, leaves the ship carrying her family away from Africa, at Mombasa. She means to return her pet bushbaby to its natural home. Tembo, her father's headman, joins her and becomes her guide and support in a dangerous journey across Kenya. Their trek up a river, over plains and through jungle is made perilous by animals, by forest fire and flood and also by man, for word has gone out that Tembo has kidnapped the white girl and is to be shot on sight. The central characters are real and memorable. Tembo is resourceful, dignified in the knowledge of his past and his place. He speaks often in tales and parables and understands his country with knowledge learned through a way of life centuries old. Contrasted to him is the impulsive, frank girl, bright and quick, self-confident in her western way. Each has something to learn from the other and from the experience. Descriptions of the animal life and terrain of Africa are closely observed and vivid. Stevenson writes with simplicity, punctuating his prose with striking figures of speech. His characters reveal themselves in action and natural dialogue.

While the book is to be enjoyed primarily as a story it contains a picture of modern Africa in transition and a statement of the continent's unique character and culture. The West may contribute to African development, but Africa is its own master. This theme, implicit in the relationship of the central figures, is stated directly in the book's closing chapters and in the summation all the main characters make of their African experience.

—Ruth Osler

STEWART, A(gnes) C(harlotte). British. Born in Liverpool, Lancashire, 9 March. Educated privately. Married to Robert Frederick Stewart; has one daughter. Recipient: Mystery Writers of America Edgar Allan Poe Award, 1972; Scottish Arts Council Award, 1977. Address: Knowetop, Corsock, Castle Douglas, Kirkcudbrightshire DG7 3EB, Scotland.

PUBLICATIONS FOR CHILDREN

Fiction

> *The Boat in the Reeds*, illustrated by Christopher Brooker.   London, Blackie, 1960; Englewood Cliffs, New Jersey, Bradbury Press, 1970.
> *Falcon's Crag.*   London, Blackie, 1969.
> *The Quarry Line Mystery.*   London, Faber, 1971; Nashville, Nelson, 1973.
> *Elizabeth's Tower.*   London, Faber, and New York, Phillips, 1972.
> *Dark Dove.*   New York, Phillips, 1974; London, Macmillan, 1975.
> *Ossian House.*   Glasgow, Blackie, 1974; New York, Phillips, 1976.
> *Beyond the Boundary.*   Glasgow, Blackie, 1976.
> *Silas and Con.*   Glasgow, Blackie, and New York, Atheneum, 1977.

A.C. Stewart comments:

I find it very difficult to write about my books: for any author so much of what goes into his books is unconscious and so when one comes to analyse them they are full of surprises for oneself. My chief concern is to tell a good story that will entertain; this is, I believe, what writing novels is about. Into my stories is bound to go much of what I believe in and care about, but if at the same time any form of advice to children gets in it is because it is part of the story and belongs in it – not as a lecture to the reader. I never meant to write for children but it has come about that way and now I find a greater interest and satisfaction in doing so than when writing for adults. Perhaps this is one reason why my children's books are accepted and not my adult ones; though conversely – and rather strangely – adults read and appear to enjoy my children's novels.

* * *

In A.C. Stewart's novels the narrative is much less significant than the setting. Place and character are fully and sensitively evoked as the narrative unfolds, at times almost somnolently. These are books about enduring human values rooted in the spirits of time and place, and to absorb these values her young heroes and heroines must learn to own with the heart. There are adventures to be sure, and gripping ones at that, told with arresting skill, but they rest less on the meeting of adversaries than on a human struggle against the vicissitudes of nature in lonely and remote places.

Ian eventually sails the Shearwater of *The Boat in the Reeds*, and indeed sails it close to disaster over the bar. But this is no ordinary tale of courage at sea. He has earned his right to sail the boat in rebuilding it with loving care. The sailing is almost incidental to the owning, and the reader will remember the child pouring his heart and imagination into the derelict dinghy long after he forgets the near-fatal first sailing. Similarly, few adventures befall John in *Ossian House* as he roams his grandfather's lands, but as the slow tale unfolds the boy becomes a part of the continuity of the world of fells and glens, linking past, present and foreseeable future in his growing love for his heritage. In *Dark Dove* Margaret draws strength from her roots in the Highlands, turning always to home exactly as her pigeons return to the loft.

If setting and the slow unfolding of character are central concerns of A.C. Stewart's novels, a distinguishing and recurring theme is the child-adult relationship. Each of her books brings a child and an adult together in mutual respect. And it is a remarkable quality of her writing that, though the child's perceptions are consistently at the centre, the principal grown-up characters are sensitively and fully adult. Child and adult complement each other while each remains true to his own station. There is nothing either patronizing or whimsical here. Adults are totally uncondescending; children are never precociously wise. Elizabeth leans on the crippled Lawrence in *Elizabeth's Tower* even as he draws strength from her mixture of practical good sense and child-like dependence. In each novel a similar relationship is developed; John and Duncan the shepherd in *Ossian House*; Margaret and Callum, the local laird, in *Dark Dove*; Ian and Tim the idler in *The Boat in the Reeds*.

It is in *Falcon's Crag* that A.C. Stewart's recurring concern with place and character and relationships is expressed at its most profound. Biddy grows to understand her Uncle Neil and Great Uncle Dermot as through her growing love for Craigengill she becomes attuned to the spirit of the place and its morose history. In this most absorbing of A.C. Stewart's novels she expresses perhaps most deeply what her other excellent novels have sought to clarify, that human values, like life, are found in the living, and are assayed as much in the heart as in the head.

—Myles McDowell

———

STOLZ, Mary (Slattery). American. Born in Boston, Massachusetts, 24 March 1920. Educated at Birch Wathen School, New York; Columbia University, New York, 1936–38; Katherine Gibbs School, New York. Married Stanley Stolz (divorced), one son; Thomas C. Jaleski, 1965. Worked at R.H. Macy's, New York, and as secretary at Columbia University Teachers College. Recipient: Child Study Association of America award, 1954; New York

Herald Tribune Festival award, 1957; Boys' Clubs of America award. Agent: Roslyn Targ Literary Agency, 250 West 57th Street, Suite 1932, New York, New York 10019. Address: P.O. Box 82, Longboat Key, Florida 33548, U.S.A.

PUBLICATIONS FOR CHILDREN

Fiction

To Tell Your Love. New York, Harper, 1950.
The Organdy Cupcakes. New York, Harper, 1951.
The Sea Gulls Woke Me. New York, Harper, 1951.
The Leftover Elf, illustrated by Peggy Bacon. New York, Harper, 1952.
In a Mirror. New York, Harper, 1953.
Ready or Not. New York, Harper, 1953; London, Heinemann, 1966.
Pray Love, Remember. New York, Harper, 1954.
Two by Two. Boston, Houghton Mifflin, 1954; London, Hodder and Stoughton, 1955; revised version, as *A Love, or a Season,* New York, Harper, 1964.
Rosemary. New York, Harper, 1955.
Hospital Zone. New York, Harper, 1956.
The Day and the Way We Met. New York, Harper, 1956.
Good-by My Shadow. New York, Harper, 1957; London, Penguin, 1964.
Because of Madeline. New York, Harper, 1957.
And Love Replied. New York, Harper, 1958.
Second Nature. New York, Harper, 1958.
Emmett's Pig, illustrated by Garth Williams. New York, Harper, 1959; Kingswood, Surrey, World's Work, 1963.
Some Merry-Go-Round Music. New York, Harper, 1959.
The Beautiful Friend and Other Stories. New York, Harper, 1960.
A Dog on Barkham Street, illustrated by Leonard Shortall. New York, Harper, 1960.
Belling the Tiger, illustrated by Beni Montresor. New York, Harper, 1961.
Wait for Me, Michael. New York, Harper, 1961.
The Great Rebellion, illustrated by Beni Montresor. New York, Harper, 1961.
Frédou, illustrated by Tomi Ungerer. New York, Harper, 1962.
Pigeon Flight, illustrated by Murray Tinkleman. New York, Harper, 1962.
Siri, The Conquistador, illustrated by Beni Montresor. New York, Harper, 1963.
The Bully of Barkham Street, illustrated by Leonard Shortall. New York, Harper, 1963.
Who Wants Music on Monday? New York, Harper, 1963.
The Mystery of the Woods, illustrated by Uri Shulevitz. New York, Harper, 1964.
The Noonday Friends, illustrated by Louis Glanzman. New York, Harper, 1965.
Maximilian's World, illustrated by Uri Shulevitz. New York, Harper, 1966.
A Wonderful, Terrible Time, illustrated by Louis Glanzman. New York, Harper, 1967.
Say Something, illustrated by Edward Frascino. New York, Harper, 1968.
The Dragons of the Queen, illustrated by Edward Frascino. New York, Harper, 1969.
The Story of a Singular Hen and Her Peculiar Children, illustrated by Edward Frascino. New York, Harper, 1969.
Juan, illustrated by Louis Glanzman. New York, Harper, 1970.
By the Highway Home. New York, Harper, 1971.
Leap Before You Look. New York, Harper, 1972.
Lands End, illustrated by Dennis Hermanson. New York, Harper, 1973.
The Edge of Next Year. New York, Harper, 1974.
Cat in the Mirror. New York, Harper, 1975.
Ferris Wheel. New York, Harper, 1977.

PUBLICATIONS FOR ADULTS

Novel

Truth and Consequence.   New York, Harper, 1953.

Manuscript Collection: Kerlan Collection, University of Minnesota, Minneapolis.

Mary Stolz comments:
All children's book writers are asked why they don't write for adults. I have never
formulated an answer satisfactory to a questioner. I don't attempt to formulate one for myself
beyond the fact that I want to write for children, and the older I get the more I tend to do
what I want to do. Long ago I wrote an adult book that was pleasantly received. From time to
time I write short stories or articles for adults. But what I do best and most happily is write for
children. I don't think it's easier than writing for adults. I don't think it's more difficult. It's
different. The difference pleases me, so this is the part of the forest I remain in.

*   *   *

Mary Stolz has been a successful writer of children's fiction for over 25 years. The range of
her work is broad, extending from books written for very young readers (*Emmett's Pig,
Belling the Tiger*) to her many novels for teenagers. In between are such stories as *The Bully
of Barkham Street, The Noonday Friends* and *A Wonderful, Terrible Time,* aimed at children
of middle elementary school age. With some exceptions, Stolz's books are "girls' stories,"
with girls as the major protagonists.
    Whatever the intended audience, all Stolz stories have a good many features in common.
They are primarily concerned with character rather than with plot, which serves largely to
precipitate and demonstrate character change. Settings are domestic rather than exotic,
realistic rather than imaginative, contemporary rather than historical. (*Cat in the Mirror,* a
recent work, is a rare exception with its slight time fantasy.) Characters are nearly always
middle-class people whose lives and concerns Stolz knows well. Their financial worries, their
expectations and disappointments, their efforts to communicate across generations are
standard elements in most Stolz plots.
    Stolz is interested in problems of human relationships, of self-knowledge, communication,
and the development of maturity. The central point in most stories is an increased
understanding by the protagonist of self and others, which in turn increases his or her feeling
of control over the events and difficulties of life. Thus, Martin, the "bully of Barkham Street,"
modifies his behavior as he begins to perceive the reasons behind it, and Janine, of *Leap
Before You Look,* is able to cope with her parents' divorce when she learns to accept their
human needs and limitations. Communication, which Stolz idealizes, is a major theme.
    Stolz's strongest qualification as a writer for young readers is her always evident respect for
the young. Her characters are articulate and literate, often interested in music, art, or poetry.
Though most of her young adult stories are romances, they rarely imply, as so many others
have, that boy-girl relationships encompass the entire meaning of life. And while her
romances of the 1950's and 1960's surely fall under the indictment of sexism, few are as
claustrophobic as most teen novels of that time.
    Stolz's most consistent weakness is a tendency to overburden a story with themes, issues,
and characters. In *By the Highway Home,* for example, death, guilt, and the Vietnam war are
added to the usual concerns about family relationships, friendship, maturing, and first love.
Moreover, over the years, themes and characterizations have often been repeated very
closely; the sisters with contrasting temperaments in *Who Wants Music on Monday?* are very
like those in *By the Highway Home,* and parental dialogues sound much alike in many books.
    Nevertheless, the glimpses of character are frequently sharp. Certainly, the passive, critical
mother of *Leap* is a more complex characterization than most of the overdrawn parents so

popular in current teenage fiction. She is surely a failure, not only as a mother but as a human being, but she is an interesting fictional creation, and Stolz manages to convey sympathy for her as well as for those whose happiness she blights, as she also does for the limited, snobbish mother in *Who Wants Music*.

Mary Stolz is too hasty, too superficial to be a great writer, but she is often perceptive and compassionate. More than many authors writing for teenaged readers over the past 25 years, she has touched, not profoundly but with genuine concern, some of the perennial questions of human relationships.

—Anne S. MacLeod

STONG, Phil(ip Duffield). American. Born in Keosauqua, Iowa, 27 January 1899. Educated at Drake University, Des Moines, Iowa, A.B. 1919, 1924–25; Columbia University, New York, 1920–21; University of Kansas, Lawrence, 1923–24. Married Virginia Maude Swain in 1925. High school athletic director and journalism teacher, Iowa, 1919–23; Editorial Writer, Des Moines *Register*, 1923–25; Wire Editor, Associated Press, New York, 1925–26; Copy Editor, North American Newspaper Alliance, 1926–27; Correspondent, *Liberty* magazine, New York, 1928, *Editor and Publisher*, New York, 1929, and New York *World*, 1929–31. Fellow, American Geological Society. Recipient: New York *Herald Tribune* Festival award, 1939. Litt. D.: Parsons College, Fairfield, Iowa, 1939; LL.D.: Drake University, 1947. *Died 26 April 1957.*

PUBLICATIONS FOR CHILDREN (illustrated by Kurt Wiese)

Fiction

Farm Boy. New York, Doubleday, 1934.
Honk: The Story of a Moose. New York, Dodd Mead, 1935; London, Harrap, 1936.
No-Sitch, The Hound. New York, Dodd Mead, 1936; London, Harrap, 1937.
High Water. New York, Dodd Mead, 1937.
Edgar, The 7:58, illustrated by Lois Lenski. New York, Farrar and Rinehart, 1938.
Young Settler. New York, Dodd Mead, 1938.
Cowhand Goes to Town. New York, Dodd Mead, 1939.
The Hired Man's Elephant, illustrated by Doris Lee. New York, Dodd Mead, 1939.
Captain Kidd's Cow. New York, Dodd Mead, 1941.
Way Down Cellar. New York, Dodd Mead, 1942.
Missouri Canary. New York, Dodd Mead, 1943.
Censored, The Goat. New York, Dodd Mead, 1945.
Positive Pete! New York, Dodd Mead, 1947.
The Prince and the Porker. New York, Dodd Mead, 1950.
Hirum the Hillbilly. New York, Dodd Mead, 1951.
Mississippi Pilot. New York, Doubleday, 1954.
A Beast Called an Elephant. New York, Dodd Mead, 1955.
Mike: The Story of a Young Circus Acrobat. New York, Dodd Mead, 1957.

PUBLICATIONS FOR ADULTS

Novels

State Fair.   New York, Century, and London, Barker, 1932.
The Stranger's Return.   New York, Harcourt Brace, and London, Barker, 1933.
Village Tale.   New York, Harcourt Brace, and London, Barker, 1934.
Week-end.   New York, Harcourt Brace, 1935.
The Farmer in the Dell.   New York, Harcourt Brace, 1935.
Career.   New York, Harcourt Brace, and London, Barker, 1936.
The Rebellion of Lennie Barlow.   New York, Farrar and Rinehart, 1937.
Ivanhoe Keeler.   New York, Farrar and Rinehart, 1939; London, Cassell, 1941.
The Long Lane.   New York, Farrar and Rinehart, 1939.
The Princess.   New York, Farrar and Rinehart, 1941.
The Iron Mountain.   New York, Farrar and Rinehart, 1942.
One Destiny.   New York, Reynal and Hitchcock, 1942.
Jessamy John.   New York, Doubleday, 1947.
Forty Pounds of Gold.   New York, Doubleday, 1951.
Return in August.   New York, Doubleday, 1953; London, Barker, 1954.
Blizzard.   New York, Doubleday, 1955; London, Hodder and Stoughton, 1956.
The Adventures of "Horse" Barsby.   New York, Doubleday, 1956.

Verse

Buckskin Breeches.   New York, Farrar and Rinehart, and London, Barker, 1937.

Other

County Fair.   New York, Stackpole, 1938.
Horses and Americans.   New York, Stokes, 1939.
If School Keeps.   New York, Stokes, 1940.
Hawkeyes: A Biography of the State of Iowa.   New York, Dodd Mead, 1940.
Marta of Muscovy: The Fabulous Life of Russia's First Empress.   New York, Doubleday, 1945.
Gold in Them Hills, Being an Irreverent History of the Great 1849 Gold Rush.   New York, Doubleday, 1947.

Editor, *The Other Worlds.*   New York, Wilfred Funk, 1941; as *25 Modern Stories of Mystery and Imagination,* New York, Doubleday, 1942.

*   *   *

Phil Stong's emergence into children's literature was the rare example of a highly successful writer for adults who decided that writing for children was necessary to remind himself that directness, simplicity, and suspense are the critical ingredients of all good narrative writing. Stong was also convinced that the writer's roots must be the sources for his literary production. Born and raised in rural Iowa, Stong based all his better books on animals and the incidents of his youth.

The most famous of his books for children, *Honk: The Story of a Moose,* (a runner-up for the 1936 Newbery Medal) is still in print. For a children's book to have this kind of staying power means it contains the ageless qualities that are associated with children's classics. *Honk* is a strongly masculine story in which boys joyfully indulge (traditionally, girls have read what boys like). Its slow-paced story allows Stong the space to flesh out his characters and to give marvelous descriptions of the northern midwest setting. It concerns some boys who one snowy winter find a hungry but decidedly friendly moose ensconced in their livery stable.

Their failed attempts to dislodge Honk – and the attempts of the father, the police, the mayor and even the city council – provides Stong's reader with many humorously incongruent scenes. While this plot of a moose happy in his refuge is slight, Stong makes up for this with natural yet energetic dialogue, some of the best in children's literature. Included here are interesting and revealing comments on Finnish ethnolinguistics and culture which give the book a tone of studied authenticity.

Stong continued his powerful writing, on the level of *Honk*, for several years. His *The Hired Man's Elephant*, for instance, won the New York *Herald Tribune* award for children's literature in 1939. Then, for some inexplicable reason, in the later years of his writing for children Stong seemed progressively to forget the formula that made such heralded accomplishments of his earlier books.

An example of his decline is *The Prince and the Porker*. This book evolves around the fantasy of a pig and a show horse, the best of friends, who carry on private conversations. The idea of a horse who cannot win prizes unless accompanied by a pig is too small a one to sustain even this slim volume, however, and its highly repetitive plot and its indecisive dialogue would thoroughly bore the modern child. It is punishing to observe here how the very standards Stong set for writers of children's books are so badly violated. The decline of Stong's capacity to concoct stories children appreciate is further evident in *Hirum the Hillbilly* and in *A Beast Called an Elephant*. Both of these books lack adventure. Instead, they involve slow-moving, drably explanatory plots. Their stilted dialogue is matched by their failed attempts at humor and their lack of suspense. Worst of all, they do not center around children. As a whole, then, they contain nothing with which today's children can identify. (The copy of *A Beast Called an Elephant* I read for this review had not been checked out of a large library for twenty years!)

Stong did recover somewhat, from what was obviously the low point in his career, with *Mike: The Story of a Young Circus Acrobat*, which does have elements of adventure and suspense. But by and large it is true that the longer Stong wrote the lesser became his accomplishments. It is significant that an anthology of Stong's stories, *Phil Stong's Big Book*, issued in 1961, contains three of the first four stories he wrote for children.

—Patrick Groff

STOREY, Margaret. British. Born in London, 27 June 1926. Educated at Sutton High School, Surrey; Samuel King's School, Alston, Cumbria; St. Paul's Girls' School, London; Girton College, Cambridge, B.A. (honours) in English 1948, M.A. 1953. Private tutor, 1956–59; English Teacher, Miss Ironside's School, London, 1959–69; Senior Teacher, Vale School, London, 1969–72; Senior English Teacher, The Study, Wimbledon, 1972–77, and Putney Park School, London, 1977. Address: c/o Faber and Faber Ltd., 3 Queen Square, London WC1N 3AU, England.

PUBLICATIONS FOR CHILDREN

Fiction

> *Kate and the Family Tree*, illustrated by Shirley Hughes.   London, Bodley Head, 1965; as *The Family Tree*, Nashville, Nelson, 1973.
> *Pauline.*   London, Faber, 1965; New York, Doubleday, 1967.
> *The Smallest Doll*, illustrated by Shirley Hughes.   London, Faber, 1966.
> *The Smallest Bridesmaid*, illustrated by Shirley Hughes.   London, Faber, 1966.

Timothy and Two Witches, illustrated by Charles Stewart. London, Faber, 1966; New York, Dell, 1974.

The Stone Sorcerer, illustrated by Charles Stewart. London, Faber, 1967.

The Dragon's Sister, and Timothy Travels, illustrated by Charles Stewart. London, Faber, 1967; New York, Dell, 1974.

A Quarrel of Witches, illustrated by Doreen Roberts. London, Faber, 1970.

The Mollyday Holiday, illustrated by Janina Ede. London, Faber, 1971.

The Sleeping Witch, illustrated by Janina Ede. London, Faber, 1971.

Wrong Gear. London, Faber, 1973.

Keep Running. London, Faber, 1974; as *Ask Me No Questions*, New York, Dutton, 1975.

A War of Wizards, illustrated by Janina Ede. London, Faber, 1976.

Margaret Storey comments:

I write because I like writing; it's communicating ideas that interests me. I write for children because I work with them. No one in my books is a portrait of anyone I know, but places are often real ones. I have an acute recall of much of my childhood, a memory of frustrations, triumphs, failure to be understood, pleasures, and friends.

*   *   *

Margaret Storey began by writing for younger children. Her collections of tales about witches and magic, such as *The Dragon's Sister* and *A Quarrel of Witches* balance excitement and humour. *The Smallest Bridesmaid* and *The Mollyday Holiday* are true-to-life stories of a little girl's joy when at last she is chosen to be a bridesmaid and, in the second story, when she goes on her long-awaited holiday. The drawings by Shirley Hughes are delightful. Most children will find something with which to identify in these stories of events which, at their age, are redletter days.

Her later books are for older girls, and invite them to identify with real-life situations which may be troubling them. *Pauline* is the story of a recently-orphaned girl growing up with unsympathetic foster-parents who disapprove of her new friends. Margaret Storey does not talk down to her readers, nor does she resort to glib solutions to the problems she poses. The adolescent girl reading her books has to put something of herself into the situation.

In *Wrong Gear* a child of divorced parents is torn between loves and loyalties. She runs away from her father and his new wife to her mother, who is unable to take her in. Unexpected help comes from school, and she learns to grow up more happily. *Keep Running* is also a case of divided loyalty. A kidnapped girl builds up a complex relationship with her captor. While wanting to escape, she feels that having given her parole she owes him something and does not want to cause him trouble.

Since most teenagers at times feel torn between "want" and "ought," these books by an author who views their problems with sympathetic insight may well have a cathartic effect and prove helpful.

—Ann G. Hay

STORR, Catherine. British. Born in London, 21 July 1913. Educated at St. Paul's Girls' School, London; Newnham College, Cambridge, 1932–36, 1939–41, B.A. (honours) in English 1935; West London Hospital, 1941–44, qualified medical practitioner 1944; Licensee, Royal College of Physicians; Member, Royal College of Surgeons. Married Anthony Storr in 1942, three daughters; Thomas Balogh, 1970. Assistant Psychiatrist, West

London Hospital, 1948–50; Senior Hospital Medical Officer, Department of Psychological Medicine, Middlesex Hospital, London, 1950–62; Assistant Editor, Penguin Books Ltd., London, 1966–70. Agent: A.D. Peters Ltd., 10 Buckingham Street, London WC2N 6BU. Address: 14 Hampstead High Street, London N.W.3, England.

PUBLICATIONS FOR CHILDREN

Fiction

> *Ingeborg and Ruthy.* London, Harrap, 1940.
> *Clever Polly and Other Stories,* illustrated by Dorothy Craigie. London, Faber, 1952.
> *Stories for Jane,* illustrated by Peggy Jeremy. London, Faber, 1952.
> *Clever Polly and the Stupid Wolf,* illustrated by Marjorie-Ann Watts. London, Faber, 1955.
> *Polly, The Giant's Bride,* illustrated by Marjorie-Ann Watts. London, Faber, 1956.
> *The Adventures of Polly and the Wolf,* illustrated by Marjorie-Ann Watts. London, Faber, 1957; Philadelphia, M. Smith, 1970.
> *Marianne Dreams,* illustrated by Marjorie-Ann Watts. London, Faber, 1958; as *The Magic Drawing Pencil,* New York, A.S. Barnes, 1960; revised edition, as *Marianne Dreams,* London, Penguin, 1964.
> *Marianne and Mark,* illustrated by Marjorie-Ann Watts. London, Faber, 1960.
> *Lucy,* illustrated by Dick Hart. London, Bodley Head, 1961; Englewood Cliffs, New Jersey, Prentice Hall, 1969.
> *Lucy Runs Away,* illustrated by Dick Hart. London, Bodley Head, 1962; Englewood Cliffs, New Jersey, Prentice Hall, 1969.
> *Robin,* illustrated by Peggy Fortnum. London, Faber, 1962; as *The Freedom of the Seas,* New York, Duell, 1965.
> *The Catchpole Story.* London, Faber, 1965.
> *Rufus,* illustrated by Peggy Fortnum. London, Faber, and Boston, Gambit, 1969.
> *Puss and Cat,* illustrated by Carolyn Dinan. London, Faber, 1969.
> *Thursday.* London, Faber, 1971; New York, Harper, 1972.
> *Kate and the Island,* illustrated by Gareth Floyd. London, Faber, 1972.
> *The Painter and the Fish,* illustrated by Alan Howard. London, Faber, 1975.
> *The Chinese Egg.* London, Faber, and New York, McGraw Hill, 1975.
> *The Story of the Terrible Scar,* illustrated by Gerald Rose. London, Faber, 1976.
> *Who's Bill?* London, Macmillan, 1976.
> *Hugo and His Grandma,* illustrated by Nina Sowter. London, Dent, 1977.

Plays

> *Flax into Gold: The Story of Rumpelstiltskin* (libretto), music by Hugo Cole. London, Chappell, 1964.

Television Plays: *Starting Out* series, 1973–78.

PUBLICATIONS FOR ADULTS

Novels

> *A Question of Abortion* (as Helen Lourie). London, Bodley Head, 1962.
> *Freud for the Jung; or, Three Hundred and Sixty Six Hours on the Couch* (as Irene Adler). London, Cresset Press, 1963.
> *The Merciful Jew.* London, Barrie and Rockliff, 1968.
> *Black God, White God.* London, Barrie and Jenkins, 1972.
> *Unnatural Fathers.* London, Quartet, 1976.

Short Stories

Tales from the Psychiatrist's Couch.   London, Quartet, 1977.

Other

Cook's Quick Reference: Essential Information on Cards.   London, Penguin, 1971.
Growing Up: A Practical Guide to Adolescence for Parents and Children.   London,
   Arrow Books, 1975.

Editor, *On Children's Literature*, by Isabelle Jan.   London, Allen Lane, 1973.

Catherine Storr comments:
   I am a compulsive writer and a natural story teller, which is why I'm better and more
successful at writing for children, who want a story above everything else, than I am at
writing fiction for adults. I'm mainly interested in the area of the different faces of reality:
hence the preoccupation with the possibilities of explaining events in more than one way –
the "scientific" and "magical" explanations. I'm often classed as a writer of fantasy, but I
prefer to think that I write in a sort of symbolic language which is no more obscure or
pompous than that of folk or fairy stories.
   I write for myself, only secondarily for a particular child, and then only if the child
happens to want something I want to write. I consider writing to be for me a kind of auto-
psycho-therapy, for which I'm fortunate enough to get paid by other people's attention and
money as well as by what it does for me.

                                        *   *   *

   With any novelists, the fact of their profession is incidental: relevant, certainly, but not the
main thing. Catherine Storr is widely known by the adults who buy her books approvingly to
be a psychologist, and indeed there are details in her books which come from psychological
interests, together with larger structures – the systematic duality of her stories, for instance,
such that appearance and reality for the heroines run in clear and separate parallel throughout
the narrative – which are surely the product of the analytic psychologist's frame of mind. Far
more to the point, however, are the richly human characteristics of an unusually modest
writer – modest in that one has constantly the sense that these books are lightly and easily
written. The modesty belies great gifts: with greater ambitions, Catherine Storr could surely
write as brilliantly and beautifully as the very best of children's novelists – do something as
good as *Tom's Midnight Garden*, say, or *The Whispering Mountain*. As it is, these bold, direct,
continent tales are most stylishly directed to a few particular points of attention which are
filled in with greater detail while the surrounding narrative moves briskly and briefly to the
conclusion.
   The duality I mentioned comes out most straightforwardly in the excellent *Polly* books. She
takes the deeply traditional – if you like, Freudian-traditional – big bad wolf of fairy tale and
makes him, in a rich, comic implausibility, into the inept, relentlessly stupid marauder of
clever Polly's amiable suburban life. Persistent, gullible, dim, unfailingly goofy, the wolf pads
round Chislehurst or Altrincham or Sutton Coldfield or wherever Polly lives, and – always
promising to do his wolfish duty and gobble her up – is always outwitted by Polly's serene
and patronizingly imperturbable good sense. One's only objection might be that Catherine
Storr anaesthetizes the terrors which fairy tales embody so conveniently in any old big, bad,
black omnivore rather too comfortably. Terrors still do walk abroad, after all, and if you
don't call them "wolf," what name can they have? But little girls, it may be replied, have
plenty to be frightened of, and it can only be exhilarating and strengthening to follow an
example of such calm and affectionate (the heroine is often sorry for her wolf) resolution and
adequacy as Polly.

The *Polly* books perfectly fit a congruence of tone, vocabulary, structure of sentiment and suspense to that of a normally impressionable little girl of, say, 7 years old. The *Lucy* books move at the same gentle but variously paced walk. To adapt a phrase, these stories walk like a child; they show a child's variety of attention, now closely focussed, now darting on to tell you what happens next, now coming comfortably to a close. The *Lucy* books would be an excellent first experience of reading a whole novel, but while making that rather limp developmental point of praise, I would also emphasize their warm sympathy, their recognisability, their loving faithfulness to the facts of a 7 or 8 year old's way of making up fictions in her head. The first *Lucy* book is perhaps a touch weaker than *Lucy Runs Away*. The duality here is between the real, tomboy, Lucy, who very believably wants nothing better than to *be* a boy, and her own lived fiction, Lew the detective. The brief little tale in which Lucy stows away in a robber's furniture van and effects the thieves' capture may even be found by a child to be less touching and to my mind certainly less real than the sequel in which the heroine carries out her threat to run away from her fantasy life into the real world, sounds the alarm to save a swimmer in trouble, and sometimes frightened, sometimes tired, always indomitable, comes safely home. The best of this endearing, graceful, tale, as it is of *Rufus*, is the delicate registration of railway journey and seaside, the sense Catherine Storr has of child's eye clarity of vision and child's pace which never fails her. I think it is best put by saying that hers are stories *told* to *listeners*, rather than novels written for readers.

This is true of the books written in a more major key, *Thursday* and the *Marianne* books, which mark the point at which the adult reader finds her enjoying larger and more demanding themes. A thriller like *The Catchpole Story* is thoroughly well done – a reworking of *Lucy* perhaps – where the moral interest is largely focussed on the interplay of 13-year-old girl and 7-year-old brother, and the way in which his perfectly spontaneous cheerfulness and tearfulness require her to maintain a grown-up courage and steadiness which she can, in a scarey adventure, only just manage. But the significance of neither novel lies in characterization, but rather in the truths to be learned about and from a reality which appears to be merely fantastic. In *Marianne Dreams*, Marianne's long convalescence is the opportunity for entering the intense and vivid world of the dream house in which she constructs a model of the process of convalescence itself, and constructs it moreover on behalf of the invalid boy Mark, and in the face of the threats of death and destruction themselves. So the story is a metaphor for nursing, itself the noblest symbol in our pictures of femininity: of altruism, patience, gentleness – and gentleness, as the novel makes clear, is in no way incompatible with a tough insistence on self-determination. I think it is her best book, although the sequel moves into an altogether larger and more populated world and is the longest of Catherine Storr's novels. It is good of course, but shrewd rather than fine, gingerly rather than delicate about adolescent love and softness. *Marianne Dreams* has gravity and power (for all that it overworks suspense), and it correctly interweaves the psyche and morality.

None of these books is thin; each, like their heroines and heroes, is small and solid, and if Catherine Storr is an occasional rather than a dedicated writer, a good storyteller rather than an artist, and wholesome rather than really creative, her gifts and qualities are strong, humorous, motherly, and indispensable.

—Fred Inglis

STRANGER, Joyce. Pseudonym for Joyce Muriel Wilson. British. Born in Forest Gate, London, 26 May. Educated at County School for Girls, Dartford, Kent; University College, London, B.Sc. 1942. Married Kenneth B. Wilson in 1944; has two sons and one daughter. Research Chemist, Imperial Chemical Industries, Manchester, 1942–46. Lecturer and writer on dog training. Lives in Anglesey, Wales. Agent: Hughes Massie Ltd., 69 Great Russell Street, London WC1B 3DH, England.

PUBLICATIONS FOR CHILDREN

Fiction

Wild Cat Island, illustrated by Joe Acheson. London, Methuen, 1961.
Circus All Alone, illustrated by Sheila Rose. London, Harrap, 1965.
Jason – Nobody's Dog, illustrated by Douglas Phillips. London, Dent, 1970.
The Honeywell Badger, illustrated by Douglas Phillips. London, Dent, 1972.
Paddy Joe. London, Collins, 1973.
The Hare at Dark Hollow, illustrated by Charles Pickard. London, Dent, 1973.
Trouble for Paddy Joe. London, Collins, 1973.
The Secret Herds: Animal Stories, illustrated by Douglas Reay. London, Dent, 1974.
Paddy Joe at Deep Hollow Farm. London, Collins, 1975.
The Fox at Drummer's Darkness, illustrated by William Geldart. London, Dent, 1976; New York, Farrar Straus, 1977.
The Wild Ponies, illustrated by Robert Rothero. London, Kaye and Ward, 1976.

Verse

Joyce Stranger's Book of Hanák Animals, illustrated by Mirko Hanák. London Dent, 1976.

PUBLICATIONS FOR ADULTS

Novels

The Running Foxes. London, Hammond Hammond, 1965; New York, Viking Press, 1966.
Breed of Giants. London, Hammond Hammond, 1966; New York, Viking Press, 1967.
Rex. London, Harvill Press, 1967; New York, Viking Press, 1968.
Casey. London, Harvill Press, 1968; as *Born to Trouble*. New York, Viking Press, 1968.
Rusty. London, Harvill Press, 1969; as *The Wind on the Dragon*. New York, Viking Press, 1969.
One for Sorrow. London, Corgi, 1969.
Zara. London, Harvill Press, and New York, Viking Press, 1970.
Chia, The Wildcat. London, Harvill Press, 1971.
Lakeland Vet. London, Harvill Press, and New York, Viking Press, 1972.
Walk a Lonely Road. London, Harvill Press, 1973.
Never Count Apples. London, Harvill Press, 1974.
Never Tell a Secret. London, Harvill Press, 1975.
Flash. London, Harvill Press, 1976.
Kym: The True Story of a Siamese Cat. London, Joseph, 1976; New York, Coward McCann, 1977.
Khazan. London, Harvill Press, 1977.

Short Stories

A Dog Called Gelert and Other Stories. London, Corgi, 1973.

Other

Two's Company (on dog training).   London, Joseph, 1977.

Joyce Stranger comments:
I trained as a biologist. I have always spent my spare time watching animals, as I specialised in animal behaviour. Many books, especially those for children, are inaccurate, or sentimentalise or humanise the animal. Animals exist in their own right, live in worlds which impinge on ours but in no way are similar to ours. I try to show how (as far as a human can) animals live in a world that is real to *them*. In my adult books I am portraying country life in a state of change — the old ways and the little farms, the country sports that over-civilised urban people may end for ever — to our great loss, as human and animal need to co-exist for balance, sanity, and to improve the quality of life. Man in an urban surrounding is doomed to increasing lack of mental stability. Those who retain the link with nature remain balanced — even the presence of a dog in the house restores proportion, if the dog is studied. No one is a hero or a great man to his dog — it speedily removes delusions of grandeur. The human-animal partnership is vital to all of us — but too many of us have lost the knowledge of this.
Too many believe the human is above the animals. We are animals. We experience pain, fear, panic; the expression in the eyes of a mouse with her young is that of a mother with her child. The reaction to danger is the same. We need to marvel at the intricacies of creation, the immense variety in the animal world, and we need to fight for the right to inherit wildlife in variety and not to reduce the marvels of creation to human tidiness and concrete prisons away from sun and trees and flowers. Suburban gardens and the cult of the family pet show men's needs — yet how many children's writers are aware of the tremendous bond between a boy who cares about animals and his dog, or the girl and her horse (and not on pony club levels)?

*   *   *

Joyce Stranger's work has a wide appeal. Many of her adult novels, especially those which are about animals, are enjoyed by children too. She has a knack with storylines which is hard to define. Indeed, how define the qualities which make a bestseller? *The Running Foxes*, which first established her reputation, was a bestseller, and many of her other novels share the same simplicity of outline and the same sympathetic insight into animal nature. A favourite theme is friendship between man (or boy) and animal — no new theme, granted, but nevertheless given lively renewal in many of her books: *Jason — Nobody's Dog*, the *Paddy Joe* books and *Walk a Lonely Road*.
Where human beings play a major role, the tone and style are quite different from the tone and even the style when she is writing about animals. There is a deep pessimism in her people. They lack the resilience and spirit of her animals. *The Honeywell Badger*, for instance, is about a boy and girl who are so keen to have a badger for a pet they pay a poacher for one and learn too late what problems they have brought upon themselves and the poor animal. The author faces these problems with characteristic thoroughness but, compared with the spontaneity of her animal stories, there is a sense of strain and heaviness. She moralizes about the harm men do.
The Hare at Dark Hollow, on the other hand, is a book of real distinction. It tells a year in the life of a young hare entirely from the animal's point of view and is the sort of *tour de force* that proclaims a unique talent. The prose is so fresh and flowing it seems as if Joyce Stranger has drunk from the well of the Poets' Muse. The reader, through the hare's eyes, learns that Dark Hollow is to be developed as building land. We see the emigration or destruction of wild life, the chain reaction in a habitat once busy with small creatures, the new fears and dangers for survivors. The ending, a happy one, is also true: hares find refuge from human hunters and other predators on the grassy expanses of airfields.
In *The Hare at Dark Hollow* the tension, always present in Joyce Stranger's books,

between animals' right to live and mankind's careless destructiveness provides a current of controlled passion throughout the book. In her novels with human heroes this tension slackens because the negative tug of despondence and fatalism wins. Mankind knows its own guilt; conscience makes us more cowardly than animals. The effect can be very depressing, as in *Trouble for Paddy Joe.* The boy has neglected the training of his young Alsatian, Storm. Consequently the dog, ignoring Paddy Joe's call, wanders off and gets lost in a Scottish wilderness. Everything that happens during the boy's long search for the dog makes a convincing and interesting narrative − the finding of an old diary confirming a legend, the exploring of the island, the storm and the solitary boat trip − but the reader is all this time in the company of Paddy Joe who is no coward but desperately sad, lonely and guilty; his thoughtless launching of the boat in which he nearly dies from exposure is like a beckoning to death.

In *The Fox at Drummer's Darkness* she has found artistic form and expression which resolve the conflicting elements in her talent. It is an extraordinary achievement, transcending all the problems that dogged her earlier efforts to relate man and beast in one literary frame. Conceived, it seems, in one daemonic impulse of creation, it has something of the epic, something of the ballad. Its few human characters are simple, unchanging figures like statues; the constantly recurring themes of burning drought, ghostly army, threat of industrial poison, give the book a structural rhythm that works inexorably towards its climax. The farmer projects all his primitive fears upon the fox, the senile huntsman lives a fantasy of hunts that never will be, and Johnny Toosmall, nightwatchman at the factory, befriends the starving, scavenging animal. But it is the animal, the fox itself, who is at the centre, alive in every detail, its intelligence and endurance stretched to the utmost and described with loving insight and understanding.

> Men were asleep. The glowing street lamps showed nothing but the fox's shadow, growing eerily long, shrinking uncannily, fading, and re-appearing on the opposite side of him, worrying him. He was used to sun shadow and moon shadow, predictable as dusk and starset, but he had never seen ranked lamps before, nor watched the change as he ran between them.
>
> At first, as the shadow flashed along the ground, he froze, watching the unnerving shape freeze with him. Then, as he ran, it began to play again, first large, then small, a fleeting silent darkness glued to his paws by a magic that he never understood.
>
> A cat sped in front of him, turned, horrified, and swiftly slashed his face in quick daring. It knew the free ways better than he, so that it leaped, lightning fast, over a wall and vanished under a garden shed ....

We find the same poetic style in the short pieces she has written for Hanák's animals. She has been refining this vivid, flowing language all her professional life. It seems so sure and strong now, one feels that it is irrespressible and may well dictate the form of future work.

—Gwen Marsh

STREATFEILD, Noel.   British.   Born in Amberley, Sussex, 24 December 1895. Educated at schools in St. Leonard's on Sea, Sussex; Laleham School, Eastbourne, Sussex; Academy of Dramatic Art, London. Actress in the 1920's; joined Women's Voluntary Services in 1939. Recipient: Library Association Carnegie Medal, 1939. Address: 51 Elizabeth Street, Eaton Square, London SW1W 9PP, England.

PUBLICATIONS FOR CHILDREN

Fiction

   Ballet Shoes, illustrated by Ruth Gervis.   London, Dent, 1936; New York, Random
      House, 1937.
   Tennis Shoes, illustrated by D.L. Mays.   London, Dent, 1937; New York, Random
      House, 1938.
   The Circus Is Coming, illustrated by Steven Spurrier.   London, Dent, 1938; revised
      edition, 1948, 1960; as *Circus Shoes*, New York, Random House, 1939.
   The House in Cornwall, illustrated by D.L. Mays.   London, Dent, 1940; as *The Secret
      of the Lodge*, New York, Random House, 1940.
   The Children in Primrose Lane, illustrated by Marcia Lane Foster.   London, Dent,
      1941; as *The Stranger in Primrose Lane*, New York, Random House, 1941.
   Harlequinade, illustrated by Clarke Hutton.   London, Chatto and Windus, 1943.
   Curtain Up, illustrated by D.L. Mays.   London, Dent, 1944; as *Theater Shoes; or,
      Other People's Shoes*, New York, Random House, 1945.
   Party Frock, illustrated by Anna Zinkeisen.   London, Collins, 1945; as *Party Shoes*,
      New York, Random House, 1947.
   The Painted Garden, illustrated by Len Kenyon.   London, Collins, 1949; revised
      edition, London, Penguin, 1961; as *Movie Shoes*, New York, Random House, 1949.
   Osbert, illustrated by Susanne Suba.   Chicago, Rand McNally, 1950.
   The Theater Cat, illustrated by Susanne Suba.   Chicago, Rand McNally, 1951.
   White Boots, illustrated by Milein Cosman.   London, Collins, 1951; as *Skating Shoes*,
      New York, Random House, 1951.
   The Fearless Treasure, illustrated by Dorothy Braby.   London, Joseph, 1952.
   The Bell Family, illustrated by Shirley Hughes.   London, Collins, 1954; as *Family
      Shoes*, New York, Random House, 1954.
   The Grey Family, illustrated by Pat Marriott.   London, Hamish Hamilton, 1956.
   Wintle's Wonders, illustrated by Richard Kennedy.   London, Collins, 1957; as *Dancing
      Shoes*, New York, Random House, 1958.
   Bertram, illustrated by Margery Gill.   London, Hamish Hamilton, 1959.
   New Town, illustrated by Shirley Hughes.   London, Collins, 1960; as *New Shoes*, New
      York, Random House, 1960.
   Apple Bough, illustrated by Margery Gill.   London, Collins, 1962; as *Traveling Shoes*,
      New York, Random House, 1962.
   Lisa Goes to Russia, illustrated by Geraldine Spence.   London, Collins, 1963.
   The Children on the Top Floor, illustrated by Jillian Willett.   London, Collins, 1964;
      New York, Random House, 1965.
   Let's Go Coaching, illustrated by Peter Warner.   London, Hamish Hamilton, 1965.
   The Growing Summer, illustrated by Edward Ardizzone.   London, Collins, 1966; as
      The Magic Summer, New York, Random House, 1967.
   Old Chairs to Mend, illustrated by Barry Wilkinson.   London, Hamish Hamilton, 1966.
   Caldicott Place, illustrated by Betty Maxey.   London, Collins, 1967; as *The Family at
      Caldicott Place*, New York, Random House, 1968.
   Gemma, illustrated by Betty Maxey.   London, May Fair Books, 1968.
   Gemma and Sisters, illustrated by Betty Maxey.   London, May Fair Books, 1968.
   The Barrow Lane Gang.   London, BBC Publications, 1968.
   Gemma Alone.   London, May Fair Books, 1970.
   Goodbye Gemma.   London, May Fair Books, 1970.
   Thursday's Child, illustrated by Peggy Fortnum.   London, Collins, and New York,
      Random House, 1970.
   Ballet Shoes for Anna, illustrated by Mary Dinsdale.   London, Collins, 1972.
   When the Siren Wailed, illustrated by Margery Gill.   London, Collins, 1974; as *When
      the Sirens Wailed*, New York, Random House, 1977.

Far to Go, illustrated by Charles Mozley.   London, Collins, 1976.

Plays

The Children's Matinée, illustrated by Ruth Gervis (includes *The Fourum, Me-ow, Olympus, The Princess and the Pea, The Cat, The Lily, Gentlemen of the Road, The Thirteenth Fairy*).   London, Heinemann, 1934.

Radio Plays: *The Bell Family* series, 1949–51; *New Town* series; *Kick Off*, 1973, and others.

Verse

Dennis the Dragon, illustrated by Ruth Gervis.   London, Dent, 1939.

Other

The Picture Story of Britain, illustrated by Ursula Koering.   New York, Watts, 1951.
The First Book of Ballet.   New York, Watts, 1953; London, Bailey Brothers and Swinfen, 1956; revised edition, London, Ward, 1963.
The First Book of England, illustrated by Gioia Fiammenghi.   New York, Watts, and London, Bailey Brothers and Swinfen, 1958; revised edition, London, Ward, 1963.
Queen Victoria, illustrated by Robert Frankenberg.   New York, Random House, 1958; London, W.H. Allen, 1961.
The Royal Ballet School.   London, Collins, 1959.
Ballet Annual.   London, Collins, 1959.
The January [February, March, April, May, June, July, August, September, October, November, December] Baby.   London, Barker, 12 vols., 1959.
Look at the Circus, illustrated by Constance Marshall.   London, Hamish Hamilton, 1960.
The Thames: London's River.   Champaign, Illinois, Garrard, 1964; London, Muller, 1966.
Enjoying Opera, illustrated by Hilary Abrahams.   London, Dobson, 1966; as *The First Book of the Opera*, New York, Watts, 1966.
Before Confirmation.   London, Heinemann, 1967.
The First Book of Shoes, illustrated by Jacqueline Tomes.   New York, Watts, 1967; London, Watts, 1971.
Red Riding Hood, illustrated by Svend Otto.   London, Benn, 1970.
The Boy Pharaoh, Tutankhamen.   London, Joseph, 1972.
A Young Person's Guide to Ballet, illustrated by Georgette Borbier.   London and New York, Warne, 1975.

Editor, *The Years of Grace* (essays).   London, Evans, 1950; revised edition, 1956.
Editor, *By Special Request: New Stories for Girls.*   London, Collins, 1953.
Editor, *Growing Up Gracefully*, illustrated by John Dugan.   London, Barker, 1955.
Editor, *Confirmation and After.*   London, Heinemann, 1963.
Editor, *Priska*, by Merja Otava, translated by Elizabeth Portch.   London, Benn, 1964.
Editor, *Nicholas*, by Marlie Brande, translated by Elisabeth Boas.   London, Benn, and Chicago, Follett, 1968.
Editor, *Sleepy Nicholas*, by Marlie Brande, translated by Elisabeth Boas.   London, Benn, and Chicago, Follett, 1970.
Editor, *The Christmas Holiday [Summer Holiday, Easter Holiday, Birthday Story, Weekend Story] Book*, illustrated by Sara Silcock.   London, Dent, 5 vols., 1973–77.

PUBLICATIONS FOR ADULTS

Novels

The Whicharts. London, Heinemann, 1931; New York, Coward McCann, 1932.
Parson's Nine. London, Heinemann, 1932; New York, Doubleday, 1933.
Tops and Bottoms. London, Heinemann, and New York, Doubleday, 1933.
Shepherdess of Sheep. London, Heinemann, 1934; New York, Reynal and Hitchcock, 1935.
It Pays to Be Good. London, Heinemann, 1936.
Caroline England. London, Heinemann, 1937; New York, Reynal and Hitchcock, 1938.
Luke. London, Heinemann, 1939.
The Winter Is Past. London, Collins, 1940.
I Ordered a Table for Six. London, Collins, 1942.
Myra Carrol. London, Collins, 1944.
Saplings. London, Collins, 1945.
Grass in Piccadilly. London, Collins, 1947.
Mothering Sunday. London, Collins, and New York, Coward McCann, 1950.
Aunt Clara. London, Collins, 1952.
Judith. London, Collins, 1956.
The Silent Speaker. London, Collins, 1961.

Plays

Wisdom Teeth (produced London, 1936). London, French, 1936.
Many Happy Returns, with Roland Pertwee (produced Windsor, 1950). London, English Theatre Guild, 1953.

Other

Magic and the Magician: E. Nesbit and Her Children's Books. London, Benn, and New York, Abelard Schuman, 1958.
A Vicarage Family (autobiographical). London, Collins, and New York, Watts, 1963.
Away from the Vicarage (autobiographical). London, Collins, 1965; as On Tour, New York, Watts, 1965.
Beyond the Vicarage (autobiographical). London, Collins, 1971; New York, Watts, 1972.
Gran-Nannie. London, Joseph, 1976.

Editor, The Day Before Yesterday: Firsthand Stories of Fifty Years Ago. London, Collins, 1956.

Critical Study: Noel Streatfeild by Barbara Ker Wilson, London, Bodley Head, 1961; New York, Walck, 1964.

*   *   *

Noel Streatfeild has an assured place as one of the pioneers of the modern novel for young readers. In retrospect, the reason for the immediate success of her first children's novel, Ballet Shoes, seems very plain: she simply brought to writing for children the same degree of integrity, the same concern for style and expression, the same perception for character, that she had employed in her first adult novel (The Whicharts). It did not occur to her to do anything else. (But it scarcely occurred to any other writer at that time — 1936 — that writing for children was something to be undertaken seriously.) From the start, too, her writing for young readers held another quality, a certain reassuring warmth, or "heart" as she herself has described it, which is most satisfactory allied to a strong vein of commonsense.

Like Edith Nesbit, Noel Streatfeild celebrates in her stories the concept of the family. The Fossils of *Ballet Shoes*, the Heaths of *Tennis Shoes*, the Forbes of *Curtain Up*, the Winters of *The Painted Garden*, the Bell Family and all the other parents and siblings (and devoted family factotums): all emphasize the author's belief in this concept – especially, perhaps, the Fossils, who are in fact a family made up through adoption. Noel Streatfeild once wrote (in *Magic and the Magician*, her biography of Edith Nesbit): "One way of gauging the aliveness of a family in a children's book is to ask yourself: 'Would I know them, if they sat opposite to me in a bus?' The answer in the best family books is invariably 'yes.' Who could fail to know the March girls, not individually but as a group? Or to take a modern example, who could miss the Ruggles of One End Street? The Bastables would not have time to sit down before everyone who knew them would be whispering 'Look who's here.' " One feels that Noel Streatfeild's own fictional families would pass the bus test quite easily, and that her readers would recognize with delight the three Fossils, the red-haired Heaths, the Bells and all the others.

In her conception and planning of certain of the stories which followed *Ballet Shoes* – *Tennis Shoes*, *The Circus Is Coming*, *White Boots* and *Curtain Up* in particular – Noel Streatfeild might be said to have hit on a "formula," in that each one describes, accurately and from first-hand observation, the training required for a particular activity and the lifestyle surrounding it. This is certainly a common factor – but the author's other qualities of style, characterization and "heart" lift each story well beyond the field of mere formula writing.

In *Magic and the Magician* Noel Streatfeild wrote: "The background and personality of a writer of adult fiction is not necessarily revealed in their books, but something of the background and personality of a good children's author is almost always discernible; for it is their ability to remember with all their senses their own childhood, and what it felt like to be a child, that makes their work outstanding." This statement is also most relevant to Noel Streatfeild's own writing. Each of her novels reflects something of her own vividly recalled childhood, crowded with family memories. And her general attitude, which forms a basis for her storytelling, reflects her consciousness of the way of life in which she was brought up. Her families are middle-class English families, not very well off – in fact often hard put to find money for school fees or new curtains, tennis coaching or a party frock. She faithfully reflects the mores and moral attitudes of her own experience of life. A child of the Vicarage, she developed as she grew up a somewhat equivocal attitude towards religious observance. Religion (the Church of England) has a background place in her family stories, but it is never over-stressed. A certain conscious nostalgia for the recent past pervades her charming anthology, *The Day Before Yesterday*; and her autobiographical works, *A Vicarage Family*, *Away from the Vicarage* and *Beyond the Vicarage*, which appeal to young and adult readers alike, reveal a child and a young woman who has much in common with many of her fictional characters.

Although Noel Streatfeild is far too skilful a writer to keep too tight a rein on her narrative, the reader is nevertheless constantly aware of her personality as the storyteller. This awareness arises from her unmistakable style, her turns of phrase, and idiosyncratic dialogue which occasionally, in repartee, verges on the sarcastic. She emerges from behind her narrative as a benevolent personality whose aim is primarily to entertain her audience. She does touch, occasionally and briefly, in her children's novels, on tragic happenings, and four books were written during and about the war years. But the darker side of life does not impinge very noticeably upon the more important, everyday events of family life which form the essential stuff of her stories. The young reader who picks up one of Noel Streatfeild's stories and becomes immersed in such events is a recruit, for a while, to a reassuring, amiable world where standards are clearly defined and all's well that ends well.

—Barbara Ker Wilson

STRONG, L(eonard) A(lfred) G(eorge). British. Born in Plymouth, Devon, 8 March 1896. Educated at Brighton College, Sussex; Wadham College, Oxford (Open Classical Scholar), 1915–16, 1919–20, M.A. Married Sylvia Brinton in 1926. Assistant Master, Summer Fields School, Oxford, for ten years; Visiting Tutor, Central School of Speech and Drama, London; Series Editor for Gollancz, Nelson and Blackwell, in the 1930's; Director, Methuen Ltd., publishers, London, 1938–58. Recipient: James Tait Black Memorial Prize, for biography, 1946. Member, Irish Academy of Letters; Fellow, Royal Society of Literature. *Died 17 August 1958.*

PUBLICATIONS FOR CHILDREN

Fiction

Patricia Comes Home, illustrated by Ruth Cobb. Oxford, Blackwell, 1929.
The Old Argo, illustrated by Ruth Cobb. Oxford, Blackwell, 1931.
King Richard's Land, illustrated by C. Walter Hodges. London, Dent, 1933; New York, Knopf, 1934.
Fortnight South of Skye. Oxford, Blackwell, 1934; New York, Loring and Mussey, 1935.
The Westward March, illustrated by L.R. Brightwell. Oxford, Blackwell, 1934.
Mr. Sheridan's Umbrella, illustrated by C. Walter Hodges. London and New York, Nelson, 1935.
The Fifth of November, illustrated by Jack Matthew. London, Dent, 1937.
Odd Man In, illustrated by P. Lefroy. London, Pitman, 1938.
They Went to the Island, illustrated by Rowland Hilder. London, Dent, 1940.
Wrong Foot Foremost. London, Pitman, 1940.
House in Disorder. London, Lutterworth Press, 1941.
Sink or Swim. London, Lutterworth Press, 1945.

Verse

Amalia, Ye Aged Sowe, illustrated by Moubray Leigh. Oxford, Blackwell, 1932.

Other

Henry of Agincourt, illustrated by Jack Matthew. London and New York, Nelson, 1937.
The Man Who Asked Questions: The Story of Socrates, illustrated by Katharine Tozer. London and New York, Nelson, 1937.
English for Pleasure (broadcasts). London, Methuen, 1941.

PUBLICATIONS FOR ADULTS

Novels

Dewer Rides. London, Gollancz, and New York, Boni, 1929.
The Jealous Ghost. London, Gollancz, and New York, Knopf, 1930.
The Garden. London, Gollancz, and New York, Knopf, 1931.
The Big Man. London, Jackson, 1931.
The Brothers. London, Gollancz, and New York, Knopf, 1932.
Sea Wall. London, Gollancz, and New York, Knopf, 1933.
Corporal Tune. London, Gollancz, and New York, Knopf, 1934.
The Seven Arms. London, Gollancz, and New York, Knopf, 1935.
The Last Enemy. London, Gollancz, and New York, Knopf, 1936.

The Swift Shadow. London, Gollancz, 1937; as *Laughter in the West*, New York,
   Knopf, 1937.
The Open Sky. London, Gollancz, and New York, Macmillan, 1939.
The Bay. London, Gollancz, 1941; Philadelphia, Lippincott, 1942.
Slocombe Dies. London, Collins, 1942.
The Unpractised Heart. London, Gollancz, 1942.
All Fall Down. London, Collins, and New York, Doubleday, 1944.
The Director. London, Methuen, 1944.
Othello's Occupation. London, Collins, 1945; as *Murder Plays an Ugly Scene*, New
   York, Doubleday, 1945.
Trevannion. London, Methuen, 1948.
Which I Never: A Police Diversion. London, Collins, 1950; New York, Macmillan,
   1952.
The Hill of Howth. London, Methuen, 1953.
Deliverance. London, Methuen, 1955.
Light above the Lake. London, Methuen, 1958.
Treason in the Egg: A Further Police Diversion. London, Collins, 1958.

Short Stories

Doyle's Rock and Other Stories. Oxford, Blackwell, 1925.
The English Captain and Other Stories. London, Gollancz, 1929; New York, Knopf,
   1931.
Don Juan and the Wheelbarrow, and Other Stories. London, Gollancz, 1932; New
   York, Knopf, 1933.
Tuesday Afternoon and Other Stories. London, Gollancz, 1935.
Two Stories. London, Corvinus Press, 1936.
The Nice Cup o' Tea. London, Favil, 1938.
Evening Piece. Privately printed, 1939.
Sun on the Water and Other Stories. London, Gollancz, 1940.
Travellers: Thirty-One Selected Short Stories. London, Methuen, 1945.
The Doll. Leeds, Salamander Press, 1946.
Darling Tom and Other Stories. London, Methuen, 1952.

Plays

The Absentee. London, Methuen, 1939.
Trial and Error. London, Methuen, 1939.
The Director, adaptation of his own novel (produced Dublin, 1951).
Sea Winds, with Norah Lloyd (produced Farnham, Surrey, 1954).
It's Not Very Nice. London, Deane, 1954.

Verse

Dallington Rhymes. Oxford, Holywell Press, 1919.
Twice Four. Oxford, Holywell Press, 1921.
Dublin Days. Oxford, Blackwell, 1921; New York, Boni and Liveright, 1923.
Says the Muse to Me, Says She. Oxford, Holywell Press, 1922.
Eight Poems. Oxford, Holywell Press, 1923.
The Lowery Road. Oxford, Blackwell, 1923; New York, Boni and Liveright, 1924.
Seven Verses: Christmas, 1924. Oxford, Holywell Press, 1924.
Seven Verses: Christmas, 1925. Oxford, Holywell Press, 1925.
Difficult Love. Oxford, Blackwell, 1927.
At Glenan Cross: A Sequence. Oxford, Blackwell, 1928.
Northern Light. London, Gollancz, 1930.

Christmas 1930. Oxford, Holywell, 1930.
Selected Poems. London, Hamish Hamilton, 1931; New York, Knopf, 1932.
March Evening and Other Verses. London, Favil, 1932.
Call to the Swan. London, Hamish Hamilton, 1936.
Low's Company: Fifty Portraits, with Helen Spalding. London, Methuen, 1952.
The Body's Imperfection: The Collected Poems. London, Methuen, 1957.

Other

Common Sense about Poetry. London, Gollancz, 1931; New York, Knopf, 1932.
A Defence of Ignorance (essay). New York, House of Books, 1932.
A Letter to W.B. Yeats. London, Hogarth Press, 1932; Folcroft, Pennsylvania, Folcroft Editions, 1971.
Life in English Literature: An Introduction for Beginners, with Monica Redlich. London, Gollancz, 3 vols., 1932; Boston, Little Brown, 3 vols., 1934.
The Hansom Cab and the Pigeons, Being Random Reflections upon the Silver Jubilee of King George V. London, Golden Cockerel Press, 1935.
Common Sense about Drama. London, Nelson, and New York, Knopf, 1937.
The Minstrel Boy: A Portrait of Tom Moore. London, Hodder and Stoughton, and New York, Knopf, 1937.
Shake Hands and Come Out Fighting (on boxing). London, Chapman and Hall, 1938.
John McCormack: The Story of a Singer. London, Methuen, and New York, Macmillan, 1941.
John Millington Synge. London, Allen and Unwin, 1941.
An Informal English Grammar. London, Methuen, 1943.
Authorship. London, Ross, 1944.
A Tongue in Your Head. London, Pitman, 1945.
Light Through the Cloud. London, Friends Book Centre, 1946.
The Art of the Short Story (lecture). London, Royal Society of Literature, 1947.
Maud Cherrill. London, Parrish, 1949.
The Sacred River: An Approach to James Joyce. London, Methuen, 1949; New York, Pellegrini and Cudahy, 1951.
John Masefield. London and New York, Longman, 1952.
Personal Remarks (essays). London, Nevill, 1953; New York, Liveright, 1954.
The Writer's Trade. London, Methuen, 1953.
The Story of Sugar. London, Weidenfeld and Nicolson, 1954.
Dr. Quicksilver, 1660–1742: The Life and Times of Thomas Dover M.D. London, Melrose, 1955.
Flying Angel: The Story of Missions to Seamen. London, Methuen, 1956.
The Rolling Road: The Story of Travel on the Roads of Britain. London, Hutchinson, 1956.
A Brewer's Progress, 1757–1957: A Survey of Charrington's Brewery. London, privately printed, 1957.
Courtauld Thompson: A Memoir. Privately printed, 1958.
Instructions to Young Writers. London, Museum Press, and New Rochelle, New York, Sportshelf, 1958.
Green Memory (autobiography). London, Methuen, 1961.

Editor, *Eighty Poems: An Anthology.* Oxford, Blackwell, 1924; as *By Haunted Stream: An Anthology of Modern English Poets,* New York, Appleton, 1924.
Editor, *The Best Poems of 1923* to *1927.* London, Bird, 5 vols., 1924–28; Boston, Small and Maynard, 2 vols., 1924, and New York, Dodd Mead, 3 vols., 1925–28.
Editor, *Beginnings* (anthology of autobiographical essays). London, Nelson, 1935.
Editor, with C. Day Lewis, *A New Anthology of Modern Verse, 1920–1940.* London, Methuen, 1941.

Editor, *English Domestic Life During the Last 200 Years: An Anthology Selected from the Novelists.* London, Allen and Unwin, 1942.
Editor, *Sixteen Portraits of People Whose Houses Have Been Preserved by the National Trust.* London, Naldrett Press, 1951.
Editor, *Fred Bason's Second Diary.* London, Wingate, 1952.
Editor, *Lorna Doone,* by R.D. Blackmore. London, Collins, 1958.

*   *   *

L.A.G. Strong's contribution to juvenile literature has been undeservedly, if understandably, obscured by his wider reputation as novelist and short story writer, poet, critic, and publisher. That he took children's fiction seriously is indicated not only by his own writing in that field but also by his pioneering efforts as editor of Basil Blackwell's series "Tales of Action" in the late 1930's, to enlist first-class authors for the then-despised adventure-story and to demonstrate that excitement and literary quality were not incompatible.

Besides story-biographies of Socrates and Henry V, he himself produced a handful of junior novels, and such was his versatility that even in this genre there were hardly two that could be exactly classified together. Three were historical, but whereas *King Richard's Land* treated a great event, the Peasants' Revolt of 1381, *Mr. Sheridan's Umbrella* was pure invention, a light period piece set in Regency Brighton. *The Fifth of November,* though again dominated by an actual historical episode, was varied by the device (less hackneyed in 1937 than since) of allowing a modern child to travel back in time. All three books had one thing in common, a conscientiously researched background brought to life by a sensitive and dynamic imagination.

The modern books were even more different. *Wrong Foot Foremost* was a school story, fairly described by John Rowe Townsend as "the last flowering of the Talbot Baines Reed tradition." Nostalgic it may have been — Strong's well-filled life included ten years as a schoolmaster — but it had a theme, the problem of merging two schools, which has since acquired a new relevance. *Odd Man In* dealt with the adventures of a young police detective. *Fortnight South of Skye,* an exciting tale of yachting in Scottish waters, was an early example of the "holiday adventure" written before Arthur Ransome had fully established that popular mode.

Strong occupies an intermediate position, part traditionalist, part innovator. He took a fresh and deeper look at history. He treated death and violence with an honesty which, though less unusual now, at the time brought the accusation of producing "unsuitable material." On the other hand, he belongs to an age when there were still mainly "books for boys" and "books for girls," clearly distinguished. He wrote the former kind, and though many girls must have read them, their lack of feminine interest seems a regrettable deficiency today.

—Geoffrey Trease

STUCLEY, Elizabeth (Florence). British. Born in Devon, 9 February 1906. Educated at St. James's School, West Malvern, Worcestershire, 1914–21; London School of Economics, 1933–35. Volunteer driver for French Army during World War II; mentioned in despatches, 1939. Married J.G.L. Northmore in 1955. Headmistress, St. Cuthbert's School; social worker. *Died 26 July 1974.*

PUBLICATIONS FOR CHILDREN

Fiction

Star in the Hand.   London, Collins, 1946.
The Pennyfeather Family: A Family Chronicle with Suitable Morals.   London, Nicholson and Watson, 1947.
The Secret Pony, illustrated by Richard Kennedy.   London, Faber, 1950.
Magnolia Buildings, illustrated by Dick Hart.   London, Bodley Head, 1960; as *Family Walk-Up,* New York, Watts, 1961.
Springfield Home, illustrated by Charles Mozley.   London, Bodley Head, 1961; as *The Contrary Orphans,* New York, Watts, 1962.
Miss Georgie's Gang.   London and New York, Abelard Schuman, 1970.

Other

Pollycon: A Book for the Young Economist, illustrated by Hugh Chesterman.   Oxford, Blackwell, 1933.

PUBLICATIONS FOR ADULTS

Novels

The House Will Come Down.   London, Duckworth, 1938.
Louisa.   London, Duckworth, 1939.
Trip No Further.   London, Low, 1946.
To End the Storm.   London, Hutchinson, 1957.

Play

The Promised Land (produced Bideford, Devon, 1951).

Other

The Village Organizer (autobiography).   London, Methuen, 1935.
Hebridean Journey with Johnson and Boswell.   London, Christopher Johnson, 1956.
Teddy Boys' Picnic (miscellany).   London, Blond, 1958.
Life Is for the Living: The Erratic Life of Elizabeth Stucley.   London, Blond, 1959.

*   *   *

In Elizabeth Stucley's *Teddy Boys' Picnic,* she says of herself:

All I can say is that I am six feet tall, impetuous, excitable, and optimistic.
I had been warned of the wild creatures that lurked in the Block.
No one had taught them manners!

These words had emerged from the beginnings of Elizabeth Stucley's real thinking about the "underprivileged" – what a different way of life from her own widely-travelled, "knowing," and "informed" existence! Then through the eyes of *Magnolia Buildings* she had re-looked and re-thought her first introductions to the "block dwellers." She had begun to find them. Problems? There were plenty, but her self-described "optimism" came to the fore. These "block dwellers" seemed to become People.

In *Magnolia Buildings,* we see a family: Mum, Dad, 12-year-old Val who finds trouble by trying hard to avoid it, Ally, 14 and glamour-crazy, the studious Doreen, and Len who is just beginning to take a peek at the outside world, which is looking a little cold from here! Problems amount to Wishes which curl their way out of a cosy well-protected world inside a cramped family existence.

What will the children remember when they grow up? – the bath under the kitchen table, longing for a bike, Ally's yearning "to attain glamour, even if it killed her," running from gangs in alleyways ...? Elizabeth Stucley paints an atmospheric picture of what will lurk in the memories of the Magnolia Building kids. As Ally says, "but Mum makes it OK!" Mum's laughter rings throughout the book, even when the reader weeps with and for her at times, even when today's reader might shake a knowing head and see where it might all be leading to. We join the kids to look at Dad ... with bitterness? His trips to the local for "half-pints," his honoured "savings," his offer to help to clean the house only as a very last-resort afterthought. So, our sophisticated Today looks at Elizabeth Stucley's Yesterday within *Magnolia Buildings*, a good story from which oozes warmth, and security that, maybe, epitomises an opposite to Ally's dreamworld outside.

Take some of the author's lovely descriptions: Aunt Glad's wedding when "even Aggie sniffed into a lace-edged hanky right through the service"; the beginning of the holiday – "Cor, isn't it grand!" and the bonfire, when "as the rockets went up and broke into a myriad of coloured stars, red, green, and orange, their hearts seemed to soar too and explode in sparks of pleasure" – all showing the corresponding use of wealthy language to fit the scene and the time.

Through this warm and amusing story, the young reader will look to today. Where are the premium bonds from Aunt Glad? Is there a job around the corner, offering just the right compromise for Ally to approach her dreams, and the right ship for Val to board just in time? "I believe you kids are going to turn out all right after all. What with Doreen being a school teacher, and Val going for a sailor, and you getting to the West End. Why, Ally, you may meet a Duke or someone grand, and get married and be a posh lady!" Do we "half believe" her, as Ally does? Perhaps we can merely say that *Magnolia Buildings* is a "good story," talk about it today, even look into tomorrow, and then leave it there.

—Joan Ward

SUDBERY, Rodie. British. Born in Chelmsford, Essex, 22 April 1943. Educated at Girton College, Cambridge, B.A. in mathematics 1964. Married Anthony Sudbery in 1964; has two daughters. Address: 5 Heslington Croft, Fulford, York YO1 4NB, England.

PUBLICATIONS FOR CHILDREN

Fiction

The House in the Wood. London, Deutsch, 1968; as *A Sound of Crying*, New York, McCall, 1970.
Cowls. London, Deutsch, 1969.
Rich and Famous and Bad. London, Deutsch, 1970.
The Pigsleg. London, Deutsch, 1971.
Warts and All. London, Deutsch, 1972.
A Curious Place. London, Deutsch, 1973.
Inside the Walls, illustrated by Sally Long. London, Deutsch, 1973.
Ducks and Drakes. London, Deutsch, 1975.

Lightning Cliff, illustrated by Sally Long. London, Deutsch, 1975.
The Silk and the Skin. London, Deutsch, 1976.
Long Way Round, illustrated by Sally Long. London, Deutsch, 1977.

*   *   *

All Rodie Sudbery's fiction has a comfortable middle-class setting, with pleasant though not necessarily indulgent parents and families where there are usually a large number of children. This is not to say that she is a "cosy" writer: her favourite kind of plot consists of children getting themselves into some kind of danger – physical, or in their relationships with each other and with adults – which is often the result of a seemingly innocuous joke or game that gets out of hand. She is in some ways the Ivy Compton-Burnett of children's writers: her novels contain an enormous amount of dialogue, complex family relationships, a sharp and witty sense of humour, and a touch of acid.

Five of her books are about Polly Devenish, her family and friends, and they take Polly from the age of 12 in the first, *The House in the Wood,* to being an undergraduate of 18 at York University in the last, *Ducks and Drakes.* The most interesting is probably the second, *Cowls,* which uses a very hackneyed theme – the haunted house in which the ghost is finally unmasked as a boy who wants to terrify the other children – but which treats the idea in an entirely new and refreshing manner. *The House in the Wood* is also notable for being a successful excursion into fantasy (only one other of Rodie Sudbery's books – *The Silk and the Skin* – is a fantasy); in this case she places the present and what happened long ago side by side to show the relevance of place, lives, and incidents of the past to people living now: a theme Penelope Lively was later to take up and explore so memorably. The last two, *Warts and All* and *Ducks and Drakes,* show some falling-off: the story-lines are weaker, and the author shows an inability to handle the complexities of relationships between teenagers of the opposite sex: the adolescent boys in particular seem cardboard thin – vague, feminine creations.

Easily her best book is *The Pigsleg,* a masterpiece of neat construction in which she explores the relationships between four families (7 adults and 9 children) without ever once leaving the reader in any confusion about who is who or feeling that any of the characters is unnecessary or ignored – no mean technical feat in itself. Its theme is the cutting down to size of Cressida, the delightful but intolerably bossy leader of a gang of children whose parents are all university dons. The gang exists, apparently, to indulge in ever more dangerous "dares," but in fact for the self-gratification of Cressida. When the dares begin to involve stealing and the punishment of one of the gang members by the others (she is dared not to speak for a year, and proceeds to try and keep totally silent), a great deal of trouble ensues with the adults, and Cressida is eventually brought under control. The book is extremely funny and also very satisfying: it certainly deserves to be considered among the finest novels for children by an English writer in recent years.

—David Rees

SUDDABY, Donald.   British.   Born in Leeds, Yorkshire, in 1900. Educated at Manchester Cathedral School. Married twice; had children. Journalist, broadcaster, and free-lance writer. *Died 17 March 1964.*

PUBLICATIONS FOR CHILDREN

Fiction

Lost Men in the Grass (as Alan Griff), illustrated by Eric Newton. London, Oxford University Press, 1940.
Masterless Swords: Variations on a Theme. London, Laurie, 1947.
New Tales of Robin Hood, illustrated by T. Heath Robinson. London, Blackie, 1950.
The Star Raiders, illustrated by Carl Haworth. London, Oxford University Press, 1950.
The Death of Metal, illustrated by William Stobbs. London, Oxford University Press, 1952.
Merry Jack Jugg, Highwayman, illustrated by Jack Matthew. London, Blackie, 1954.
Village Fanfare; or, The Man from the Future, illustrated by F.R. Exell. London, Oxford University Press, 1954.
The Moon of Snowshoes, illustrated by Leonard Rosoman. London, Oxford University Press, 1956.
Prisoners of Saturn, illustrated by Harold Jones. London, Lane, 1957.
Fresh News from Sherwood, illustrated by William Stobbs. London, Bodley Head, 1959; New York, A.S. Barnes, 1961.
Crowned with Wild Olive, illustrated by William Stobbs. London, Collins, 1961.
Tower of Babel. London, Collins, 1962.
A Bell in the Forest. London, University of London Press, 1964.
Robin Hood's Master Stroke. London, Blackie, 1965.

PUBLICATIONS FOR ADULTS

Short Story

Scarlet-Dragon: A Little Chinese Phantasy. Blackburn, Lancashire, privately printed, 1923.

*   *   *

Donald Suddaby was that rare being, a distinguished writer of science fiction and fantasy for children. His literary roots lay in Verne and Wells, and his contemporaries included John Wyndham and John Christopher. But they all wrote adult fantasy (though much of it was read also by young readers), whereas Suddaby wrote his tales specifically for children, though they could be (and were) enjoyed too by appreciative adults.

Suddaby wrote only 14 books in 25 years and every one is well worth reading. His first book *Lost Men in the Grass,* is an exciting imaginative fantasy about three men reduced to the size of ants, and their battles against insects, animals and birds. It was a remarkable tour-de-force but, unfortunately, tended to be overlooked by reviewers due to the timing of its publication. After a 10-year gap came a regular series of remarkable books of many kinds, involving space-journeys to Venus and Saturn, mysterious and sinister visitors to Earth from other worlds, Robin Hood tales, historical adventures, and stories set in Biblical and mythological times. Outstanding, perhaps, were *The Death of Metal,* a sobering story about the effect of the disintegration of all metals upon people's everyday lives, and *Village Fanfare,* which dealt with the arrival of a strange visitor (or an army of identical visitors) to a sleepy Edwardian Shropshire village and the remarkable results which followed.

One of the most unusual talents in the field of children's literature, Donald Suddaby brought a poet's sweep and descriptive power to his writing, allied to originality and humour.

—Brian Doyle

SUTCLIFF, Rosemary. British. Born in West Clanden, Surrey, 14 December 1920. Educated at Bideford School of Art, Devon. Member, Royal Society of Miniature Painters. Recipient: Library Association Carnegie Medal, 1960; New York *Herald Tribune* Festival award, 1962; *Boston Globe-Horn Book* Award, 1972. O.B.E. (Officer, Order of the British Empire), 1975. Address: Swallowshaw, Walberton, Arundel, Sussex, England.

PUBLICATIONS FOR CHILDREN

Fiction

The Armourer's House, illustrated by C. Walter Hodges. London and New York, Oxford University Press, 1951.
Brother Dusty-Feet, illustrated by C. Walter Hodges. London, Oxford University Press, 1952.
Simon, illustrated by Richard Kennedy. London, Oxford University Press, 1953.
The Eagle of the Ninth, illustrated by C. Walter Hodges. London, Oxford University Press, 1954; New York, Walck, 1961.
Outcast, illustrated by Richard Kennedy. London, Oxford University Press, 1955.
The Shield Ring, illustrated by C. Walter Hodges. London, Oxford University Press, 1956; New York, Walck, 1962.
The Silver Branch, illustrated by Charles Keeping. London, Oxford University Press, 1957; New York, Walck, 1959.
Warrior Scarlet, illustrated by Charles Keeping. London, Oxford University Press, and New York, Walck, 1958.
The Lantern Bearers, illustrated by Charles Keeping. London, Oxford University Press, and New York, Walck, 1959.
The Bridge-Builders. Oxford, Blackwell, 1959.
Knight's Fee, illustrated by Charles Keeping. London, Oxford University Press, and New York, Walck, 1960.
Dawn Wind, illustrated by Charles Keeping. London, Oxford University Press, 1961; New York, Walck, 1962.
The Mark of the Horse Lord, illustrated by Charles Keeping. London, Oxford University Press, 1965.
The Chief's Daughter, illustrated by Victor Ambrus. London, Hamish Hamilton, 1967.
A Circlet of Oak Leaves, illustrated by Victor Ambrus. London, Hamish Hamilton, 1968.
The Witch's Brat, illustrated by Robert Micklewright. London, Oxford University Press, and New York, Walck, 1970.
The Truce of the Games, illustrated by Victor Ambrus. London, Hamish Hamilton, 1971.
Heather, Oak, and Olive: Three Stories (includes *The Chief's Daughter, A Circlet of Oak Leaves, A Crown of Wild Olive*), illustrated by Victor Ambrus. New York, Dutton, 1972.
The Capricorn Bracelet, illustrated by Charles Keeping. London, Oxford University Press, and New York, Walck, 1973.
The Changeling, illustrated by Victor Ambrus. London, Hamish Hamilton, 1974.
We Lived in Drumfyvie, with Margaret Lyford-Pike. Glasgow, Blackie, 1975.
Blood Feud, illustrated by Charles Keeping. London, Oxford University Press, and New York, Dutton, 1977.
Shifting Sands, illustrated by Laszlo Acs. London, Hamish Hamilton, 1977.
Sun Horse, Moon Horse, illustrated by Shirley Felts. London, Bodley Head, 1977.

Other

The Chronicles of Robin Hood, illustrated by C. Walter Hodges. London, Oxford
University Press, 1950.

The Queen Elizabeth Story, illustrated by C. Walter Hodges. London, Oxford
University Press, 1950.

Houses and History, illustrated by William Stobbs. London, Batsford, 1960.

Beowulf, illustrated by Charles Keeping. London, Bodley Head, 1961; New York,
Dutton, 1962; as Dragon Slayer, London, Penguin, 1966.

The Hound of Ulster (Cuchulain Saga), illustrated by Victor Ambrus. London, Bodley
Head, and New York, Dutton, 1963.

A Saxon Settler, illustrated by John Lawrence. London, Oxford University Press,
1965.

Heroes and History, illustrated by Charles Keeping. London, Batsford, and New York,
Putnam, 1965.

The High Deeds of Finn Mac Cool, illustrated by Michael Charlton. London, Bodley
Head, and New York, Dutton, 1967.

Tristan and Iseult, illustrated by Victor Ambrus. London, Bodley Head, and New
York, Dutton, 1971.

Publications for Adults

Novels

Lady in Waiting. London, Hodder and Stoughton, 1956; New York, Coward
McCann, 1957.

The Rider of the White Horse. London, Hodder and Stoughton, 1959; as Rider on a
White Horse, New York, Coward McCann, 1959.

Sword at Sunset. London, Hodder and Stoughton, 1963; New York, Coward
McCann, 1964.

The Flowers of Adonis. London, Hodder and Stoughton, 1969; New York, Coward
McCann, 1970.

Other

Rudyard Kipling. London, Bodley Head, 1960; New York, Walck, 1961.

Critical Study: Rosemary Sutcliff by Margaret Meek. London, Bodley Head, and New York,
Walck, 1962.

*   *   *

In Rosemary Sutcliff's hands the children's historical novel has gained passion, insight and
depth. She makes demands of her readers, but that is right, for the best of her books are as
satisfying also to the most discerning adult. Her main themes could be termed the continuity
of history and the contiguity of peoples – the Light and the Dark, Pict and Scot, Roman and
Briton, Briton and Saxon, Saxon and Norman. She is concerned with recreating history itself
more than events and with interpreting the movements and relationships of peoples. She
seems to have an instinctive communion with the past, and while she has suffered since
childhood from a severely restricting arthritic condition, it is as though her very lack of
mobility has given her an intensity of concentration which enables her to see and describe
details that hardly occur to other writers. Her sense of place, and her feelings for the land and
those who work it, add extra dimensions; and her command and understanding of military
tactics and the very feeling of battle are not far short of astonishing.

Even with hindsight it is hard to find in her four earliest books the writer she has become.

The dialogue tends to be archaic – she solved this problem magnificently later; and the stories have an idyllic cosiness about them, at times almost mawkishness. These are period pieces, but they contain hints of ancient rituals lost in folklore, such as she has since recreated particularly in her Roman-British novels. *Brother Dusty-Feet* has another recurrent *leitmotiv*, the rejected orphan. In fact, however, better introductions for children to her work are the four short books published much later, *A Circlet of Oak Leaves, The Chief's Daughter, The Truce of the Games*, and *The Changeling*.

Simon is unusual in presenting the Civil War from both sides. There is much historical background which has to be explained, but pointers to future works are the problems presented by divided loyalties, the determination that life shall continue despite political or military upheavals, and the motivation of characters loyal to their convictions.

The Eagle of the Ninth has a situation and setting more to Rosemary Sutcliff's liking. This is the first novel of a sequence, the others being *The Silver Branch* and *The Lantern Bearers*. An actual and a symbolic link between them emphasises the view that history is continuous: a main character in all three belongs to the same Roman family, and in each appears a signet ring passed on from father to son; it also features in *Dawn Wind* and *The Shield Ring*. In *The Eagle of the Ninth* Marcus Aquila, invalided out of the army, searches for clues to the fate of his father's legion which had marched out into the mists of northern Britain, and disappeared. Primarily an adventure story, culminating in a heart-stopping chase of Aquila who has found the legion's eagle, the book's distinction lies also in its presentation of the meeting of two worlds, Roman and British, and in its atmosphere – ancient rituals; Hadrian's Wall as a living, vital, sprawling community – and the terrain – bracken, heather, mist, furze, and rain.

Beric, in *Outcast*, is an archetypal Sutcliff hero. A Roman orphan, rescued from shipwreck, he is rejected by the British tribe that fostered him, becomes a slave in Rome, and, later, returns to Britain, and to freedom. This is an episodic novel, depending to some extent on coincidence, but with powerful sequences, notably when Beric serves as a galley-slave. For *The Shield Ring* she created a community of Vikings in the Lake District withstanding for years Norman attempts to eliminate them, until their fateful last stand. The sense of place is nowhere bettered, but the action shifts awkwardly from person to person, possibly because the main character is female, an experiment Rosemary Sutcliff has not repeated since.

The pattern of history of the time and the reach of the tentacles of Rome, even in the throes of destruction, are clearly revealed in *The Silver Branch*. Two cousins desert from the Roman Army to support the cause of Carausius, murdered Emperor of Britain, against the usurper Allectus. In fact they fight for their beliefs rather than for Rome, and for the retention of some element of peaceful coexistence among peoples; and the eagle of the lost Ninth Legion reappears as a symbol now of unity. This is basically an adventure story, but *The Lantern Bearers* is more a slice of history, studded also with human conflicts and emotions. "We have been here four hundred years," says his commandant to the decurion Aquila, "and in three days we shall be gone." But Aquila, whose roots and family are in Britain, chooses to turn his back on Rome, and stays. Saxons kill his father and abduct his sister Flavia. Left to die, he is taken by a Jutish band to their homeland as a thrall. The community, Aquila among them, emigrate to Britain, and he finds his sister, now married to a Saxon. But she will not leave her husband, a choice Aquila understands only later when his own wife of political convenience sticks by him. He joins the cause of Ambrosius against Vortigern and Hengest, only to meet his own nephew in the height of battle. This is a book with excellent characterisation, whose main theme is the restoration of order out of chaos.

In *Warrior Scarlet*, the copper and scarlet of the Golden People, worshippers of the sun, contrast strongly with the mysteries of the earth itself and the Little Dark People, who still live on, but as outcasts. This is not just a superb reconstruction of a people, a period and an actual part of the South Downs, founded on meticulous research and prodigious powers of imagination, but also a sensitive and convincing account of a boy finding himself and ultimately his adult place in life. *Knight's Fee* and *Dawn Wind* are primarily about bringing peoples together. In the former the bickering of William II's barons highlights the need to unite Norman and Saxon; in the latter it is once again light and dark, Saxon and native

Briton. In each book a boy has to make his own way in life to survive. Owain, in *Dawn Wind*, is perhaps Rosemary Sutcliff's most interesting hero in that not only does his progress from being a boy who has lost his whole world depend largely on his own determination and effort, but also he is faced on the way with several agonising choices.

The Mark of the Horse Lord is arguably her finest novel, for adults or children. Certainly it is a book of supreme assurance and maturity of style, construction and content. The action is almost continuous, covering just two years, and from the tremendous opening sequence in the gladiatorial ring, climax follows climax. Phaedrus, a freed gladiator, agrees to impersonate the Lord of the Horse People. His insecure hold on his leadership, his strange but utterly plausible relationship with his ritual wife, and the struggle and differences of outlook between the Horse People and their neighbours, the Caledones, are staged against rites and dark mysteries, marvellously evoked and described. And in the last stark paragraph, which provides a totally unexpected ending, Phaedrus becomes what he really is, a tragic hero in the epic mould.

In 1965–77 Rosemary Sutcliff published no major work for older children, though she produced many radio scripts for BBC Scotland. Some of these she rewrote as *The Capricorn Bracelet*, a panoramic view of Roman Britain. *The Witch's Brat*, originally written as a magazine serial, tells of the founding of St. Bartholomew's Hospital and follows the fortunes of an orphan boy cast out by the community that has reared him.

With *Blood Feud* she entered the lists again, taking as her background the Viking excursions to the Black Sea and their support of the Emperor Basil II of Byzantium. The story is told in the first person by Jestyn, an English lad forced to leave his home and sold into slavery to a Viking master, Thormod. Slavery turns to blood-brotherhood as Jestyn becomes involved in Thormod's feud over his father's murder. This feud links the historical incidents and motivates the characters. This is a finely-wrought story with a very moving and satisfying conclusion. If at times it is rough and even violent, then so were the Vikings themselves, and their humour and loyalties, as well as their way of life, are splendidly recaptured, particularly in the dialogue. Indeed, after her earliest books, it has been one of Rosemary Sutcliff's most distinctive attributes that she makes her characters talk in ways that are completely in period and in tune with a situation by the introduction of subtle changes to the order and rhythm of modern speech.

—Antony Kamm

SUTHERLAND, Efua (Theodora). Ghanaian. Born in Cape Coast, 27 June 1924. Educated at St. Monica's School and Training College, Cape Coast; Homerton College, Cambridge; School of Oriental and African Studies, London. Married William Sutherland in 1954. Schoolteacher in Ghana, 1951–54. Founding Director, Experimental Theatre Players, now Ghana Drama Studio, Accra, since 1958. Founder, Kusum Agoromba, a children's theatre group at the University of Ghana School of Drama, Legon; Founder of Ghana Society of Writers, now the University of Ghana Writers Workshop. Co-Founder, *Okyeame* magazine, Accra. Lives in Ghana. Address: c/o Longman Group, 74 Grosvenor Street, London W1X 0AS, England.

PUBLICATIONS FOR CHILDREN

Plays

   Vulture! Vulture! Two Rhythm Plays (includes *Tahinta*). Accra, Ghana Publishing House, 1968; New York, Panther House, 1970.

Other plays: *Ananse and the Dwarf Brigade*; version of *Alice in Wonderland*.

Verse

> *Playtime in Africa*, photographs by Willis E. Bell. London, Brown Knight and
> Truscott, 1960; New York, Atheneum, 1962.

Other

> *The Roadmakers*, photographs by Willis E. Bell. Accra, Ghana Information Services,
> and London, Neame, 1961.

PUBLICATIONS FOR ADULTS

Plays

> *Edufa*, based on *Alcestis* by Euripides (produced Accra, 1964). London, Longman,
> 1967; in *Plays from Black Africa*, edited by Frederic M. Litto, New York, Hill and
> Wang, 1968.
> *Anansegoro: You Swore an Oath*, in *Présence Africaine 22* (Paris), Summer 1964.
> *Foriwa*. Accra, Ghana Publishing House, 1967; New York, Panther House, 1970.
> *The Marriage of Anansewa: A Storytelling Drama*. London, Longman, 1974.

> Other plays: *Odasani*, version of *Everyman*; adaptation of Chekhov's *The Proposal*; *The
> Pineapple Child*; *Nyamekye*.

*   *   *

Efua Sutherland is best known in Ghana as the creator of popular dramas in English and
Twi which are performed on the radio as well as on the stage. She is also a story writer and
poet who has collaborated with photographer Willis E. Bell in producing picture books for
Ghanaian children.

Many of Efua Sutherland's plays are based on Akan folklore, especially about Ananse the
spider, and employ the dramatic techniques of Akan oral literature. Prose, poetry, songs and
music are part of Akan story telling sessions and are integral to Sutherland's plays, as is
audience response. As Sutherland's plays are performed repeatedly they are altered in relation
to audience response, just as tellers of Akan folk tales up-date and renew their stories with
repeated tellings to different audiences.

In Sutherland's plays, as in Akan folklore, Ananse represents everyman and is artistically
exaggerated to serve as a medium for social reflection. In *Ananse and the Dwarf Brigade*, for
example, greedy Ananse plants a farm near a sacred grove which he keeps secret from his
wife and children. Since Ananse also is lazy, he encourages dwarves to work his farm,
although Ananse's misbehavior ultimately results in his workers ruining his farm. The play
begins like a story telling session. Ananse has a song which he sings at appropriate junctures
in the plot, and leader-chorus responses are incorporated into the dialogue.

Some of Sutherland's plays, poems and stories are about Ghanaian children. *Tahinta* is a
one act verse play about a Ghanaian boy, which utilizes the leader-chorus pattern
throughout. The chorus provides rhythmic background for the action through chanting and
hand-clapping, while the three main characters, the boy, his father, and a ghost, speak their
lines and act their parts. Through alternation of the characters' lines and the chorus
responses, the story is told of a boy who sets his fish trap and casts his net, at first without
success. After he finally catches a mud fish and happily begins his journey home, a ghost robs
him of his fish. Even his brave father is unable to retrieve the fish from the ghost.

The immediacy of Sutherland's verse plays also is found in her verse picture books. In
Playtime in Africa short poems about children being themselves as they dance, play marbles,

tell stories, fish, swim, cook, play drums, weave and fly kites are illustrated with photographs which depict Ghanaian children's delight in their activities.

Efua Sutherland's work for children is permeated both with Ghanaian tradition and the realities of contemporary children's lives. Through simple but dramatic presentation, it engages children in selected facets of their own world, whether they live in Ghana or other parts of the world.

—Nancy J. Schmidt

SUTTON, Eve(lyn Mary). New Zealander. Born in Preston, Lancashire, England, 14 September 1906; emigrated to New Zealand in 1949; became citizen, 1955. Educated at the Park School, Preston, 1917–24; Goldsmiths' College, University of London, 1925–27, teachers' training diploma. Married Alfred Sutton in 1931; has two sons. Recipient: New Zealand Library Association Esther Glen Award, 1975. Address: 84 Kohimarama Road, Flat 1, Auckland 5, New Zealand.

PUBLICATIONS FOR CHILDREN

Fiction

> *My Cat Likes to Hide in Boxes*, illustrated by Lynley Dodd. London, Hamish Hamilton, 1973; New York, Parents' Magazine Press, 1974.
> *Green Gold*, illustrated by Paul Wright. London, Hamish Hamilton, 1976.
> *Tuppenny Brown*, illustrated by Paul Wright. London, Hamish Hamilton, 1977.
> *Johnny Sweep*, illustrated by Paul Wright. London, Hamish Hamilton, 1977.

Eve Sutton comments:

My first venture into the field of children's literature, the picture book *My Cat Likes to Hide in Boxes*, came as the result of an amiable conversation with my cousin Lynley Dodd – "Wouldn't it be fun to do a book together?" But I like the actual writing and plotting, so it seemed natural to turn to books for older children. The early New Zealand scene has interested me ever since we came here and makes a natural background for my stories.

*   *   *

Eve Sutton's preferred field is a problematical one: that which caters, simultaneously, for able readers of 7 and over, and slower readers of 11 and 12. Its requirements are exacting. The principal character must fall within the upper age group and yet be accessible to the sympathies of the younger, a limiting consideration by which few writers would care to be bound. Emotional exploration of character is virtually prohibited, the resultant hero usually emerging as a somewhat vacuous personality, independent and resourceful on the one hand, but inclined to excessive virtue on the other. But there are advantages; intelligent 7-year-olds are likely to be bored by stories about their peers, who are all too likely to be bound by the very constraints of over-protected family life which they themselves find so irksome. And less able 12-year-olds, if they can be reached, provide a ready ear for stories which are exciting, uncomplicated and simply told.

Sutton contrives to avoid the pitfalls, while capitalising on the advantages. Certainly not one of her three youthful heroes, each obliged to make his own way alone in the wild young colony that was New Zealand in the mid-19th century, lacks individuality. Her use of the first person contributes to this success. Adam, Tuppenny, and Johnny emerge, in their different ways, as real boys, credible products of the backgrounds from which they have been plucked in England, and exposed to a bombardment of new impressions on the other side of the world. The story, in each case, is engrossing.

The apparent simplicity of the text of these short novels conceals, to some extent, Eve Sutton's capacity for establishing place and character, and for managing a pace which is both swift enough to ensure interest and deliberate enough to avoid confusion. A surprising amount of detail is included: the horrors of the outward voyage, the brash jauntiness of the early colony, the rigours of breaking in virgin land for farming, the thrilling yet sickening experience of whaling, the backbreaking toil of gum-digging – and through it all, the pervasive sense of hope, of beginning, of man's willingness to risk death and face hardship in search of freedom.

Sutton's only book for very young children, *My Cat Likes to Hide in Boxes*, reveals a facility with language, rhythm, and rhyme, and a sure feeling for the nonsense-humour of early childhood. Its competence is undoubted; but the author's real aptitude – and preference – seems to be in books for older children.

—Dorothy Butler

SYME, (Neville) Ronald. Irish. Born in Lancashire, 13 March 1910. Educated at Durham School, 1924–26; Collegiate School, Wanganui, New Zealand, 1926–29. Served in the British Army Intelligence Corps, 1940–45: Major. Married Marama Amoa in 1960; has one daughter. Cadet and Officer, 1930–34, and Gunner, 1939–40, British Merchant Service; reporter and foreign correspondent, 1934–39; Assistant Editor, John Westhouse and Peter Lunn Ltd., publishers, London, 1946–48; Public Relations Officer, British Road Federation, London, 1948–50. Recipient: Boys' Clubs of America award, 1951. Address: c/o William Morrow Inc., 105 Madison Avenue, New York, New York 10016, U.S.A.

PUBLICATIONS FOR CHILDREN

Fiction

> *That Must Be Julian*, illustrated by William Stobbs.   London, Lunn, 1947.
> *Julian's River War*, illustrated by John Harris.   London, Heinemann, 1949.
> *Ben of the Barrier*, illustrated by J. Nicholson.   London, Evans, 1949.
> *The Settlers of Carriacou*.   London, Hodder and Stoughton, 1953.
> *Gipsy Michael*, illustrated by William Stobbs.   London, Hodder and Stoughton, 1954.
> *They Came to an Island*, illustrated by William Stobbs.   London, Hodder and Stoughton, 1955.
> *Isle of Revolt*, illustrated by William Stobbs.   London, Hodder and Stoughton, 1956.
> *Ice Fighter*, illustrated by William Stobbs.   London, Hodder and Stoughton, 1956.
> *The Amateur Company*.   London, Hodder and Stoughton, 1957.
> *The Great Canoe*.   London, Hodder and Stoughton, 1957.
> *The Forest Fighters*, illustrated by William Stobbs.   London, Hodder and Stoughton, 1958.
> *River of No Return*, illustrated by William Stobbs.   London, Hodder and Stoughton, 1958.
> *The Spaniards Came at Dawn*, illustrated by William Stobbs.   London, Hodder and Stoughton, 1959.
> *Thunder Knoll*, illustrated by William Stobbs.   London, Hodder and Stoughton, 1960.

The Buccaneer Explorer, illustrated by William Stobbs. London, Hodder and Stoughton, 1960.

The Mountainy Men, illustrated by Richard Payne. London, Hodder and Stoughton, 1961.

Coast of Danger, illustrated by Richard Payne. London, Hodder and Stoughton, 1961.

Nose-Cap Astray, illustrated by Roger Payne. London, Hodder and Stoughton, 1962.

Two Passengers for Spanish Fork, illustrated by Brian Keogh. London, Hodder and Stoughton, 1963.

Switch Points at Kamlin, illustrated by Brian Keogh. London, Hodder and Stoughton, 1964.

The Dunes and the Diamonds, illustrated by Brian Keogh. London, Hodder and Stoughton, 1964.

The Missing Witness. London, Hodder and Stoughton, 1965.

The Saving of the Fair East Wind, illustrated by A.R. Whitear. London, Dent, 1967.

Other (illustrated by William Stobbs)

Full Fathom Five (not illustrated). London, Lunn, 1946.

Hakluyt's Sea Stories. London, Heinemann, 1948.

Bay of the North: The Story of Pierre Radisson, illustrated by Ralph Ray. New York, Morrow, 1950; London, Hodder and Stoughton, 1951.

The Story of British Roads. London, British Road Federation, 1951.

Cortes of Mexico. New York, Morrow, 1951; as *Cortez, Conqueror of Mexico*, London, Hodder and Stoughton, 1952.

I, Mungo Park [*Captain Anson, Gordon of Khartoum*]. London, Burke, 3 vols., 1951–53.

Champlain of the St. Lawrence. New York, Morrow, 1952; London, Hodder and Stoughton, 1953.

Columbus, Finder of the New World. New York, Morrow, 1952.

The Story of Britain's Highways (not illustrated). London, Pitman, 1952.

La Salle of the Mississippi. New York, Morrow, and London, Hodder and Stoughton, 1953.

Magellan, First Around the World. New York, Morrow, 1953.

John Smith of Virginia. New York, Morrow, and London, Hodder and Stoughton, 1954.

Henry Hudson. New York, Morrow, 1955; as *Hudson of the Bay*, London, Hodder and Stoughton, 1955.

Balboa, Finder of the Pacific. New York, Morrow, 1956.

De Soto, Finder of the Mississippi. New York, Morrow, 1957.

The Man Who Discovered the Amazon. New York, Morrow, 1958.

Cartier, Finder of the St. Lawrence. New York, Morrow, 1958.

On Foot to the Arctic: The Story of Samuel Hearne. New York, Morrow, 1959; as *Trail to the North*, London, Hodder and Stoughton, 1959.

Vasco Da Gama, Sailor Towards the Sunrise. New York, Morrow, 1959.

Captain Cook, Pacific Explorer. New York, Morrow, 1960.

Francis Drake, Sailor of the Unknown Seas. New York, Morrow, 1961.

First Man to Cross America: The Story of Cabeza de Vaca. New York, Morrow, 1961.

Walter Raleigh. New York, Morrow, 1962.

The Young Nelson, illustrated by Susan Groom and Trevor Parkin. London, Parrish, 1962; New York, Roy, 1963.

African Traveler: The Story of Mary Kingsley, illustrated by Jacqueline Tomes. New York, Morrow, 1962.

Francisco Pizarro, Finder of Peru. New York, Morrow, 1963.

Invaders and Invasions. London, Batsford, 1964; New York, Norton, 1965.

Nigerian Pioneer: The Story of Mary Slessor, illustrated by Jacqueline Tomes. New York, Morrow, 1964.

Alexander Mackenzie, Canadian Explorer. New York, Morrow, 1964.

Sir Henry Morgan, Buccaneer. New York, Morrow, 1965.

Francisco Coronado and the Seven Cities of Gold. New York, Morrow, 1965.

Quesada of Colombia. New York, Morrow, 1966.

William Penn, Founder of Pennsylvania. New York, Morrow, 1966.

Garibaldi, The Man Who Made a Nation. New York, Morrow, 1967.

Bolivar, The Liberator. New York, Morrow, 1968.

Captain John Paul Jones, America's Fighting Seaman. New York, Morrow, 1968.

Amerigo Vespucci, Scientist and Sailor. New York, Morrow, 1969.

Frontenac of New France. New York, Morrow, 1969.

Benedict Arnold, Traitor of the Revolution. New York, Morrow, 1970.

Vancouver, Explorer of the Pacific Coast. New York, Morrow, 1970.

Toussaint, The Black Liberator. New York, Morrow, 1971.

Zapata, Mexican Rebel. New York, Morrow, 1971.

John Cabot and His Son Sebastian. New York, Morrow, 1972.

Juarez, The Founder of Modern Mexico, illustrated by Richard Cuffari. New York, Morrow, 1972.

Verrazano, Explorer of the Atlantic Coast. New York, Morrow, 1973.

Fur Trader of the North: The Story of Pierre de la Verendrye, illustrated by Richard Cuffari. New York, Morrow, 1973.

John Charles Fremont, The Last American Explorer, illustrated by Richard Cuffari. New York, Morrow, 1974.

Marquette and Joliet, Voyagers on the Mississippi. New York, Morrow, 1974.

Geronimo, The Fighting Apache, illustrated by Ben Stahl. New York, Morrow, 1975.

Osceola, Seminole Leader, illustrated by Ben Stahl. New York, Morrow, 1976.

PUBLICATIONS FOR ADULTS

Other

The Windward Islands (Frontiers of the Caribbean, Islands of the Sun, A Schooner Voyage in the West Indies), photographs by the author. London, Pitman, 3 vols., 1953.

The Story of New Zealand (We Dip into the Past, Life in New Zealand Today, A Tour of New Zealand). London, Pitman, 3 vols., 1954.

The Cook Islands. London, Pitman, 1955.

The Travels of Captain Cook, photographs by Werner Forman. New York, McGraw Hill, 1971; London, Joseph, 1972.

Isles of the Frigate Bird (on the Cook Islands). London, Joseph, 1975.

*   *   *

Ronald Syme is best known for his exciting adventure ●tories for boys, moving at a fast pace and set in exotic settings in remote parts of the globe – although when the mood takes him, he is clearly capable of investing his plots with serious themes. *The Amateur Company*, for example, tells how Joe and Uncle Ben develop the natural resources of the island of Arorangi in the South Seas. When they depart, leaving behind them the destruction of a simple but tranquil and contented Arcadian community, both of them are troubled by some nagging doubts as to the lasting benefits of the changes arriving in the wake of their alien energy and technical know-how. And in *They Came to an Island* the same theme of the impact of an alien culture upon a primitive people is again discernible in the incident-packed story of mutiny and shipwreck, exploration and treasure hunting, but it is never obtrusive; the reader is not distracted.

If Syme has a fault it is the continuous piling up of climax upon climax. No sooner is one stirring episode out of the way than another is looming up; there is no time for reflection, and the story jerks along, breathless and impatient. But who would deny the inventiveness that allows the author this luxury? Nobody, certainly, has ever heard his readers complain.

The South Seas is often the locale of Syme's fiction: *Nose-Cap Astray*, the recovery of a space rocket by two boys, white and native, and *The Saving of the Fair East Wind*, the salvaging of an overloaded and abandoned cargo vessel, both feature the entertaining Prince Oro of Manapoa. But he is equally at home in the Caribbean of the 18th century. *Isle of Revolt* concerns a negro revolt against the English planters, and is seen through the eyes of Bill Holdsworth the 15-year-old son of a planter and his cousin Harry fresh out from England, while *The Settlers at Carriacou* relates the struggles of a small band of English colonists against powerful French attacks on the tiny island of Dominica. Another English cousin pops up in *Julian's River War*, in which Julian is a young Australian inventor who, with his assistant Snoddy, his sister Jannine, Percival Pomeroy the English cousin, and Uncle Eric, becomes involved in all sorts of mechanical contrivances, notably a car that sprouts wings and flies. At its own level this is a delightful book although the cast is really no more than a collection of stock characters.

But Syme no doubt realised that young readers welcome easily recognizable characters and situations. At this stage reading should essentially be full of fun and excitement, and these Ronald Syme provides in plenty.

—Alan Edwin Day

SYMONDS, John. British. Address: c/o Gerald Duckworth Ltd., The Old Piano Factory, 43 Gloucester Crescent, London NW1 7DY, England.

PUBLICATIONS FOR CHILDREN

Fiction

William Waste, illustrated by André François. London, Low and Marston, 1947.
The Magic Currant Bun, illustrated by André François. Philadelphia, Lippincott, 1952; London, Faber, 1953.
Travellers Three, illustrated by André François. Philadelphia, Lippincott, 1953.
The Isle of Cats, with Gerard Hoffnung. London, Laurie, 1955.
Away to the Moon, illustrated by Pamela Bianco. Philadelphia, Lippincott, 1956.
Lottie, illustrated by Edward Ardizzone. London, Lane, 1957.
Elfrida and the Pig, illustrated by Edward Ardizzone. London, Harrap, 1959; New York, Watts, 1960.
Dapple Grey: The Story of a Rocking-Horse, illustrated by James Boswell. London, Harrap, 1962.
The Story George Told Me, illustrated by André François. London, Harrap, 1963; New York, Pantheon Books, 1964.
Tom and Tabby, illustrated by André François. New York, Universe Books, 1964.
Grodge-Cat and the Window Cleaner, illustrated by André François. New York, Pantheon Books, 1965.
The Stuffed Dog, illustrated by Edward Ardizzone. London, Dent, 1967.
Harold: The Story of a Friendship, illustrated by Pauline Baynes. London, Dent, 1973.

PUBLICATIONS FOR ADULTS

Novels

The Lady in the Tower.   London, Chapman and Hall, 1951.
The Bright Blue Sky.   London, Chapman and Hall, 1956.
A Girl among Poets.   London, Chapman and Hall, 1957.
The Only Thing That Matters.   London, Unicorn Press, 1960; New York, Horizon Press, 1961.
Bezill.   London, Unicorn Press, 1962.
Light over Water.   London, Unicorn Press, 1963.
With a View on the Palace.   London, Baker, 1966.
The Hurt Runner.   London, Baker, 1968; New York, Day, 1969.
Prophecy and Parasites.   London, Duckworth, 1973; New York, Braziller, 1975.
The Shaven Head.   London, Duckworth, 1974.
Letters from England.   London, Duckworth, 1975.
The Child: Prologue to an Earthquake.   London, Duckworth, 1976.

Plays

Sheila (produced London, 1953).
The Bicycle Play, and The Winter Forest.   London, Duckworth, 1976.

Radio Play: *The Other House,* 1963.

Television Play: *I, Having Dreamt, Awake,* 1961.

Other

The Great Beast: The Life of Aleister Crowley.   London, Rider, 1951; New York, Roy, 1952; revised edition, London, Macdonald, 1971.
The Magic of Aleister Crowley.   London, Muller, 1958.
Madame Blavatsky: Medium and Magician.   London, Odhams Press, 1959; as *The Lady with the Magic Eyes,* New York, Yoseloff, 1960; as *In Astral Light,* London, Panther, 1965.
Thomas Brown and the Angels: A Study in Enthusiasm.   London, Hutchinson, 1961.
Conversations with Gerald.   London, Duckworth, 1974.

Editor, with Kenneth Grant, *The Confessions of Aleister Crowley: An Autohagiography,* abridged edition.   London, Cape, 1969; New York, Bantam, 1971.
Editor, with Kenneth Grant, *The Magical Record of Beast 666: The Diaries of Aleister Crowley, 1914–1920.*   London, Duckworth, 1972.
Editor, with Kenneth Grant, *Magick,* by Aleister Crowley.   London, Routledge, 1973.
Editor, with Kenneth Grant, *White Stains,* by Aleister Crowley.   London, Duckworth, 1973.
Editor, with Kenneth Grant, *The Complete Astrological Writings of Aleister Crowley.*   London, Duckworth, 1974.
Editor, with Kenneth Grant, *Moonchild,* by Aleister Crowley.   London, Sphere, 1974.

*   *   *

John Symonds's fantasies are shorter than most novels for older children, and his stories move quickly: they can be enjoyed by anyone over the age of about 7. Toys speak and have problems; children or playthings from the past meet children from this century and create a mutual understanding. *Lottie* is about the adventures of a doll and a dog in the 18th century;

Dapple Grey is about a rocking horse trying to find his way home. The tone is always cheerful, often witty, and the endings satisfactory.

In *The Stuffed Dog* two modern schoolgirls, exploring an attic full of a miscellaneous collection of things bought at auction sales, discover a ventriloquist's doll a hundred years old. She tells the girls how the ventriloquist bullied her – so she stole his voice and ran away to hide in a box and fell asleep, but she is now repentant and wants to return his voice. The girls give her tea and take her to see the ventriloquist's house, where the doll is horrified to see that his dog has been stuffed. In the churchyard they find the grave with a carved headstone reading: "Poor Gerald is no more. Died dumb October 25, 1867." So they know it is all true. The doll asks to be returned to the box, where she lies looking so beautiful and peaceful.

This slightly eerie tale is told in a matter-of-fact way. The doll over tea remarks: "They're all dead, dead, dead," then fetches a deep sigh and says : "Please may I have another slice of cake?" The description of the tea table is original: "a gorgeous green cake raising its head proudly and a plate of bread and butter which crouched low with envy." The modern children have quite an adventure in the attic: the trunk that houses the doll's box is so large that one of them falls inside; she discovers a telescope through which she can see "pancakes and what looked like the prow of a ship painted pink. Gosh! It was Daisy's nose and the pancakes were her freckles and what appeared to be great white rocks were her teeth."

Harold is the story of a friendship between 20th-century Octavius, an only child, and an 18th-century ghost. Octavius's parents are always busy; he is left on his own. During their holiday in a house by the sea he meets a very old lady, Agnes Golightly, who has always lived in the attic and only comes down at night. She introduces him to Harold, who was killed falling off the church tower while looking at the gargoyles. Harold's punishment is that he must wander around until he can spend a week playing with another boy, so he and Octavius enjoy exploring a shipwreck together, and Octavius is tremendously happy at having helped him. Agnes Golightly's observations on all the inhabitants of the house provide the humour. The descriptions are all short but effective: "And the sea. It was as blue as the nose of a frozen child."

—Margaret Campbell

SYMONS, (Dorothy) Geraldine. British. Born in Newera Eliya, Ceylon, 13 August 1909. Educated at Godolphin School, Salisbury, Wiltshire, 1920–27. Served with the Voluntary Aid Detachment during World War II. Has worked as a secretary, waitress, chambermaid, and guide. Agent: Curtis Brown Ltd., 1 Craven Hill, London W2 3EW. Address: 4 de Vaux Place, Salisbury, Wiltshire, England.

PUBLICATIONS FOR CHILDREN

Fiction

> *Minnie the Minnow*, illustrated by the author.   Ewell, Surrey, Tally Ho Books, n.d.
> *The Rose Window*, illustrated by F.R. Exell.   London, Heinemann, 1964; New York, Duell Sloan Pearce, 1966.
> *Morning Glory* (as Georgina Groves), illustrated by Carol Barker.   London, Whiting and Wheaton, 1966.
> *The Quarantine Child*, illustrated by F.R. Exell.   London, Heinemann, 1966.
> *The Workhouse Child*, illustrated by Alexy Pendle.   London, Macmillan, 1969; New York, Macmillan, 1971.

Miss Rivers and Miss Bridges, illustrated by Alexy Pendle.   London, Macmillan, 1971;
   New York, Macmillan, 1972.
Mademoiselle, illustrated by Alexy Pendle.   London, Macmillan, 1973.
Now and Then.   London, Faber, 1977.

PUBLICATIONS FOR ADULTS

Novels

All Souls.   London and New York, Longman, 1950.
French Windows.   London and New York, Longman, 1952.
The Suckling.   London, Macmillan, 1969.

Other

Children in the Close (autobiography).   London, Batsford, 1959.

*   *   *

Geraldine Symons has written several books for children, five in a sequence that covers the years 1909–14. In these the central characters are Pansy and Atalanta, a complementary pair whose exploits are chronicled with rationality and gusto. Pansy on her own is less impressive, as *The Rose Window* shows; she is a conventional heroine without the formidable presence of Atalanta to set her off.

Atalanta is a triumph of characterization. She is stolid, logical, and down-to-earth without being in the least bit priggish. She is well-informed, rather blasé in manner and slapdash in appearance, and speaks with the gruff precision of a bored don. Pansy is more impressionable and frivolous: the combination of the two girls is enough to spark off the alarming or amusing events that the novels relate. In *The Workhouse Child*, Pansy flees from the terrible matron of an orphanage and is forced to take refuge on the bloody floor of a butcher's shop. After a rather exciting afternoon, she finds Atalanta sitting calmly "on a molehill by a gorse bush reading *The Wide Wide World*." She goes on reading.

Miss Rivers and Miss Bridges, in the book of that title, are Atalanta and Pansy disguised as a couple of middle-aged suffragettes. This is the most remarkable and effective novel of the series: its surface humour doesn't detract in the least from the seriousness of the theme. It was published in 1971; it took roughly 60 years for the suffragette movement to get sympathetic treatment in children's literature. "If the Government persists in its pigheaded policy, I have no intention of stopping at a brick," Atalanta states. In fact she jumps off Westminster Bridge, and the two schoolgirls are later detained briefly in a prison cell. "Gross inefficiency" Atalanta concludes, after looking around. She becomes interested in prison reform.

In *Mademoiselle* the friends are staying in Paris just before the outbreak of war. *Mademoiselle* is really *fräulein*, a German spy who has walked into a diplomatic trap. In fact the whole spy genre in subtly parodied in this book. A faint mocking detachment is evident in the dedication ("To all patriotic sleuths"), but *Mademoiselle* is also an excellent adventure story. The precision of its detail raises the farcical moments to high comedy. And it has Atalanta to keep it firmly based on the ground. "Don't be so melodramatic and silly," she tells Pansy repressively.

The heroine of *Now and Then* is called Jassy, and she is one of those uncanny fictional children who can step into another era. She has only to walk down the garden to find herself back in 1940, digging a grave for two dogs that have been killed by enemy action or helping to apprehend a German pilot in a wood. The book is in a lower key than the Pansy and Atalanta stories; but it is none the less a distinguished addition to "time-travelling" fiction.

—Patricia Craig

TATE, Joan. British. Born in Tonbridge, Kent, 23 September 1922. Married; has two daughters and one son. Free-lance writer, translator, and publishers reader. Address: 32 Kennedy Road, Shrewsbury, Shropshire SY3 7AB, England.

PUBLICATIONS FOR CHILDREN

Fiction

Jenny, illustrated by Charles Keeping. London, Heinemann, 1964.
The Crane, illustrated by Richard Willson. London, Heinemann, 1964.
The Rabbit Boy, illustrated by Hugh Marshall. London, Heinemann, 1964.
Coal Hoppy, illustrated by J. Yunge-Bateman. London, Heinemann, 1964.
The Next-Doors, illustrated by Charles Keeping. London, Heinemann, 1964; New York, Scholastic, 1976.
The Silver Grill, illustrated by Hugh Marshall. London, Heinemann, 1964; New York, Scholastic, 1976.
Picture Charlie, illustrated by Laszlo Acs. London, Heinemann, 1964.
Lucy, illustrated by Richard Willson. London, Heinemann, 1964.
The Tree, illustrated by George Tuckwell. London, Heinemann, 1966; as *Tina and David*, Nashville, Nelson, 1973.
The Holiday, illustrated by Leo Walmsley. London, Heinemann, 1966.
Tad, illustrated by Leo Walmsley. London, Heinemann, 1966.
Bill, illustrated by George Tuckwell. London, Heinemann, 1966.
Mrs. Jenny, illustrated by Charles Keeping. London, Heinemann, 1966.
Bits and Pieces, illustrated by Quentin Blake. London, Heinemann, 1967.
The New House. Stockholm, Almqvist and Wiksell, 1967.
The Soap Box Car. Stockholm, Almqvist and Wiksell, 1967.
The Old Car. Stockholm, Almqvist and Wiksell, 1967.
The Great Birds. Stockholm, Almqvist and Wiksell, 1967; Glasgow, Blackie, 1976.
The Train. Stockholm, Almqvist and Wiksell, 1967.
Polly. Stockholm, Almqvist and Wiksell, 1967; London, Cassell, 1976.
The Circus and Other Stories, illustrated by Timothy Jaques. London, Heinemann, 1967.
Letters to Chris, illustrated by Mary Russon. London, Heinemann, 1967.
Wild Martin, and The Crow, illustrated by Richard Kennedy. London, Heinemann, 1967.
Luke's Garden, illustrated by Quentin Blake. London, Heinemann, 1967; augmented edition, London, Hodder and Stoughton, 1976.
Sam and Me. London, Macmillan, 1968; New York, Coward McCann, 1969.
Out of the Sun. London, Heinemann, 1969.
Whizz Kid. London, Macmillan, 1969; as *Not the Usual Kind of Girl*. New York, Scholastic, 1974.
The Letter. Stockholm, Almqvist and Wiksell, 1969.
Puddle's Tiger. Stockholm, Almqvist and Wiksell, 1969.
The Caravan. Stockholm, Almqvist and Wiksell, 1969.
Edward and the Uncles. Stockholm, Almqvist and Wiksell, 1969.
The Secret. Stockholm, Almqvist and Wiksell, 1969.
Varieties:
  1. *The Ball, The Lollipop Man, The Nest*, illustrated by Mary Dinsdale, John Dyke, and Prudence Seward. London, Macmillan, 1969.
  2. *The Cheapjack Man, The Gobblydock, The Treehouse*, illustrated by Richard Rose, Jenny Williams, and Mary Dinsdale. London, Macmillan, 1969.
Clipper. London, Macmillan, 1969; as *Ring on My Finger*, 1971; New York, Scholastic, 1976.

The Long Road Home. London, Heinemann, 1971.

Gramp, illustrated by Robert Geary. London, Chatto Boyd and Oliver, 1971.

Wild Boy, illustrated by Trevor Stubley. London, Chatto Boyd and Oliver, 1972; New York, Harper, 1973.

Wump Day, illustrated by John Storey. London, Heinemann, 1972.

Ben and Annie, illustrated by Mary Dinsdale. Leicester, Brockhampton Press, 1973; New York, Doubleday, 1974.

Dad's Camel, illustrated by Margaret Power. London, Heinemann, 1973.

Jock and the Rock Cakes, illustrated by Carolyn Dinan. Leicester, Brockhampton Press, 1973; Chicago, Children's Press, 1976.

Grandpa and My Little Sister Bee, illustrated by Leslie Wood. Leicester, Brockhampton Press, 1973; Chicago, Children's Press, 1976.

Taxi! Paderborn, Schöningh, 1973.

Night Out. Stockholm, Almqvist and Wiksell, 1973.

The Match. Stockholm, Almqvist and Wiksell, 1973.

Dinah. Stockholm, Almqvist and Wiksell, 1973.

Journal for One. Stockholm, Almqvist and Wiksell, 1973.

The Man Who Rang the Bell. Stockholm, Almqvist and Wiksell, 1973.

Ginger Mick. London, Heinemann, 1974.

The Runners, illustrated by Douglas Phillips. Newton Abbot, Devon, David and Charles, 1974.

Dirty Dan. Stockholm, Almqvist and Wiksell, 1974.

Sandy's Trumpet. Stockholm, Almqvist and Wiksell, 1974.

Zena. Stockholm, Almqvist and Wiksell, 1974.

The Thinking Box. Stockholm, Almqvist and Wiksell, 1974.

The New House, illustrated by Douglas Chalk. London, Pelham, 1976.

The House That Jack Built. London, Pelham, 1976.

Crow and the Brown Boy, illustrated by Gay Galsworthy. London, Cassell, 1976.

Polly and the Barrow Boy, illustrated by Gay Galsworthy. London, Cassell, 1976.

Billoggs, illustrated by Trevor Stubley. London, Pelham, 1976.

You Can't Explain Everything. London, Longman, 1976.

See You and Other Stories. London, Longman, 1977.

Other

Going Up. Stockholm, Almqvist and Wiksell, 3 vols., 1969–74.

Your Town, illustrated by Virginia Smith. Newton Abbot, Devon, David and Charles, 1972.

How Do You Do? Paderborn, Schöningh, 1973.

The Living River, illustrated by David Harris. London, Dent, 1974.

Your Dog, illustrated by Babette Cole. London, Pelham, 1975.

Disco Books (Big Fish, Tom's Trip, The Day I Got the Sack, Girl in the Window, Supermarket, Gren, Day Off, Moped), illustrated by Gay Galsworthy, Jill Cox, and George Craig. London, Cassell, 8 vols., 1975.

On Your Own 1. Exeter, Devon, Wheaton, 1977.

Translator, *River Boy,* by Ralph Herrmanns. London, Collins, and New York, Harcourt Brace, 1965.

Translator, *Katrin,* by Nan Inger. London, Hamish Hamilton, 1967.

Translator, *Admission to the Feast,* by Gunnel Beckman. London, Macmillan, 1971; as *19 Is Too Young to Die,* 1971.

Translator, *A Room of His Own,* by Gunnel Beckman. New York, Viking Press, 1972; London, Bodley Head, 1973.

Translator, *The Sit-in Game,* by Doris Dahlin. London, Bodley Head, and New York, Viking Press, 1972.

Translator, *That Emil*, by Astrid Lindgren.   Leicester, Brockhampton Press, 1973.

Translator, *Mia*, by Gunnel Beckman.   London, Bodley Head, 1974.

Translator, *Alban*, by Barbro Lindgren.   London, A. and C. Black, 1974.

Translator, *The Brothers Lionheart*, by Astrid Lindgren, illustrated by Ilon Wikland.   Leicester, Brockhampton Press, and New York, Viking Press, 1975.

Translator, *The Loneliness of Mia*, by Gunnel Beckman.   London, Bodley Head, 1975; as *Mia Alone*, New York, Viking Press, 1975.

Translator, *Otto Is a Rhino*, by Ole Lund Kirkegaard.   London, Pelham, 1975.

Translator, *Scatty Ricky*, by Jerete Kruuse.   London, Pelham, 1975.

Translator, *The Threat*, by Lennart Frick.   London, Hodder and Stoughton, 1975.

Translator, *Emil and the Bad Tooth*, by Astrid Lindgren.   London, Hodder and Stoughton, 1976.

Translator, *Operation Cobra*, by Anders Bodelsen.   London, Pelham, 1976.

Translator, *Witch Fever*, by Lief Esper Anderson.   London, Pelham, 1976.

Translator, *Summer Girl*, by Max Lundgren.   London, Macmillan, 1976.

Translator, *That Early Spring*, by Gunnel Beckman.   New York, Viking Press, 1977.

Translator, *For the Love of Lisa*, by Max Lundgren.   London, Macmillan, 1977.

Translator, *Tim and Trisha*, by Svend Otto S.   London, Pelham, 1977.

Translator, *Denmark Is Like This*, by Stig Weimar.   London, Kaye and Ward, 1977.

Translator, *Jasper the Taxi Dog*, by Svend Otto S.   London, Pelham, 1977.

Translator, *The Goldmaker's House*, by Irmelin Sandman Lilius, illustrated by Ionicus.   London, Oxford University Press, 1977.

PUBLICATIONS FOR ADULTS

Other

Translator, *Do You Believe in Angels?*, by John E. Aberg.   London, Hutchinson, 1963.

Translator, *Black Sister*, by Dagmar Edqvist.   London, Joseph, and New York, Doubleday, 1963.

Translator, *A Need to Love*, by Märtha Burén.   London, Joseph, and New York, Dodd Mead, 1964.

Translator, *Noah*, by Berndt Ohlsson.   London, Hutchinson, 1964.

Translator, *Camilla*, by Märtha Burén.   London, Joseph, and New York, Dodd Mead, 1965.

Translator, *The Assignment*, by Per Wahlöö.   London, Joseph, and New York, Knopf, 1965.

Translator, *The History of Diseases*, by Folke Henschen.   London, Longman, 1966; as *The History and Geography of Diseases*. New York, Dial Press, 1967.

Translator, *A Wreath for the Bride*, by Maria Lang.   London, Hodder and Stoughton, 1966.

Translator, *Murder on the 31st Floor*, by Per Wahlöö.   London, Joseph, 1966.

Translator, *The Roman*, by Mika Waltari.   New York, Putnam, 1966.

Translator, *No More Murders*, by Maria Lang.   London, Hodder and Stoughton, 1967.

Translator, *Death Awaits Thee*, by Maria Lang.   London, Hodder and Stoughton, 1967.

Translator, *The Lorry*, by Per Wahlöö.   London, Joseph, 1968; as *A Necessary Action*. New York, Pantheon Books, 1969.

Translator, *From Island to Island*, by Sven Gillsäter.   London, Allen and Unwin, 1968.

Translator, *Queen Louise of Sweden*, by Margit Fjellman.   London, Allen and Unwin, 1968.

Translator, *Ibsen: A Portrait of the Artist*, by Hans Heiberg.   London, Allen and Unwin, 1969.

Translator, *The Deep Well*, by Carl Nylander.   London, Allen and Unwin, 1969.

Translator, *The Man Who Went Up in Smoke*, by Maj Sjöwall and Per Wahlöö.   New York, Pantheon Books, 1969; London, Gollancz, 1970.

Translator, *The Fire Engine That Disappeared*, by Maj Sjöwall and Per Wahlöö. New York, Pantheon Books, 1970; London, Gollancz, 1972.

Translator, *Why Does Your Dog Do That?*, by Göran Bergman. London, Popular Dogs, 1970.

Translator, *The Steel Spring*, by Per Wahlöö. London, Joseph, and New York, Delacorte Press, 1970.

Translator, *Freezing Point*, by Anders Bodelsen. New York, Knopf, 1970; London, Joseph, 1971.

Translator, *The Generals*, by Per Wahlöö. New York, Pantheon Books, 1973; London, Joseph, 1974.

Translator, *My Sister, Isak Dinesen*, by Thomas Dinesen. London, Joseph, 1974.

Translator, *The Debt*, by Olle Edvard Hogstrand. New York, Pantheon Books, 1974; London, Hale, 1976.

Translator, *The Bjorn Borg Story*. London, Pelham, 1975.

Translator, *The Race*, by Kare Holt. New York, Delacorte Press, and London, Joseph, 1976.

Translator, *The Terrorists*, by Maj Sjöwall and Per Wahlöö. New York, Pantheon Books, 1976.

Joan Tate comments:

I have always thought that a very high proportion of books published for children are totally irrelevant to children, and that it would make no difference to the world in general if they all fell into the sea tomorrow. The only books worth their salt are those that are of interest to anyone, child, adolescent or adult − however briefly to the adult − if they do not interest, excite, amuse, entertain, dismay, distress an adult, then they are useless to any child, too.

                                        *   *   *

There are many children who for various reasons cannot or do not wish to read, and it is for this group that Joan Tate writes the majority of her books. Not all these children have actual reading problems, but many are bored by the majority of books they see. Joan Tate writes books like *Whizz Kid*, short, topical, full of snappy dialogue, and with a plot that is relevant and interesting to teenagers. These are the books which many reluctant readers will pick up; they are designed to be read by the 12–16 age group, but have an actual reading age of 9–10 years. The vivid stories have a simple vocabulary, an easy style and are set in a working-class area with teenage motor mechanics, shop assistants (*The Rabbit Boy*), nurses (*Letters to Chris*) as their main characters.

The everyday problems of urban living are tackled in a straightforward way which can capture the imagination of both boys and girls: the young marrieds in *Sam and Me*; the problem neighbours in *The Next-Doors*; the young West Indian couple in *Mrs. Jenny* coping with housing difficulties and the strange winter cold. The majority of these books have attractive, often dramatic covers designed to catch the eye. The type is big and bold, well-spaced but still looking like the good long read to be found in other paperbacks for teenagers. It is this physical attractiveness and boldness which help to popularise the books among teenage readers.

Wild Boy, first published as a short story in *Wild Martin, and The Crow*, has a strong story line. After Will finds a wild boy living on the Yorkshire Moors above his home, the reader is intrigued enough to read on to find out what happens. There are never too many characters in her books to confuse the plot and the reader always feels drawn to identify with the hero and heroine. The expanded version has a deeper plot and more finely drawn characters than the short story.

Joan Tate has also written a number of books for younger children; *Grandpa and My Little Sister Bee* and *Jock and the Rock Cakes* are examples of her simple picture stories with domestic settings and realistic dialogue for the 5–7-year-olds. In books such as *The New House* and *Billoggs* the author uses everyday settings but allows her characters more flights of fancy, more imagination than in some stories. In *Billoggs* the old tramp decides that the scrap car will make an ideal home without realising that Susan, George, and Ester have used it as a base for their adventure.

Joan Tate is a prolific writer who has specialised in that very difficult area, of writing for a specific audience rather than children at large. She has reached out to those young people who are not by instinct readers. Recently she has been using the environment much more in her themes, and *The Living River* is a leisurely and attractive look at the River Severn with a strong conservation message.

—Jean Russell

TAYLOR, Sydney (Brenner). American. Born in New York City, 31 October 1904. Educated at New York University. Married Ralph Taylor in 1925; has one daughter. Actress, Lenox Hill Players, New York, 1925–29; Dancer, Martha Graham Dance Company, New York, 1930–35. Since 1942, Instructor in Dance and Dramatics, Cejwin Camps, Port Jervis, New York. Recipient: Jewish Book Council of America Isaac Siegel Memorial Award, 1952; Boys' Clubs of America award, 1962. Address: 250 West 24th Street, New York, New York 10011, U.S.A.

PUBLICATIONS FOR CHILDREN

Fiction

> *All-of-a-Kind Family*, illustrated by Helen John.   Chicago, Willcox and Follett, 1951; London, Blackie, 1961.
> *More All-of-a-Kind Family*, illustrated by Mary Stevens.   Chicago, Follett, 1954; London, Blackie, 1967.
> *All-of-a-Kind Family Uptown*, illustrated by Mary Stevens.   Chicago, Follett, 1958.
> *Mr. Barney's Beard*, illustrated by Charles Geer.   Chicago, Follett, 1961.
> *Now That You Are Eight*, illustrated by Ingrid Fetz.   New York, Association Press, 1963.
> *A Papa Like Every One Else*, illustrated by George Porter.   Chicago, Follett, 1966.
> *The Dog Who Came to Dinner*, illustrated by John E. Johnson.   Chicago, Follett, 1966.
> *All-of-a-Kind Family Downtown*, illustrated by Beth and Joe Krush.   Chicago, Follett, 1972.

Author, director, and choreographer of many plays for children's camps.

Manuscript Collection: Kerlan Collection, University of Minnesota, Minneapolis.

*   *   *

An amateur writer, Sydney Taylor initially told the story of her own childhood in an orthodox Jewish family to her daughter at bedtime. Her books are purposeful, and despite soaring moments of brilliance, lack the careful development of plot, character, setting, and style.

The intent of the series books is to describe a family in New York City at the turn of the century, and to instill an attitude of pride in the reader. *All-of-a-Kind Family* introduces the reader to six siblings and to Jewish customs and holidays. The author writes knowingly, as she herself is the Sarah in the stories. Stimulated by letters from readers, she wrote chronologically about the blossoming family; the series covers five years, but were published over a period of 21 years. Two beginning-to-read books, *Mr. Barney's Beard* and *The Dog Who Came to Dinner* were intended to help children master vocabulary.

Sydney Taylor's method of creating plot is episodic: Mama places twelve buttons around the room for the child to find while dusting, or Henny charges her friends a penny each to see the baby bathed. Interweaving of the plot is limited, as the author did not originally plan to write four books. There is some foreshadowing, such as in *All-of-a-Kind Family* in which Charlie finds his long lost love, the library lady whom the children already know. Bachelor Uncle Hiram marries the woman who rescued the little brother in *More All-of-a-Kind Family*.

Characters mature chronologically rather than by inner growth. The five sisters and brother, born at the close of the first book, father, mother, uncle and aunt have stable characteristics, and change little. Henrietta is consistently mischievous, and is reprimanded at school as well as at home. In *All-of-a-Kind Family Uptown*, Ella does state, "guess this is what growing up really means, Grace. Standing on your own two feet and being your own mountain." Aunt Lena becomes morose after being victimized by polio, but returns to her cheerful self following a single lecture from Mama.

The specific setting of the series books is well handled. New York's east side, uptown, downtown, and the beach are the areas in which the children move, and the junk shop, library, market and school are sketched in detail. References to the Fourth of July, settlement houses, and knitting for the Red Cross support the uniqueness of place and time, and there are constant examples of Jewish foods in the home: "Teiglech are fried balls of dough soaked in honey" and gefilte fish on Friday are important on the menu.

Anecdotes are expanded into entire chapters, and are spiced with humor and evidence of the Jewish ethnic group. When Henny wore her sister's dress without permission and spilled tea on it, she dyed the entire garment in tea. In another chapter in *All-of-a-Kind Family Uptown* the children ate dinner set on the table, as they thought they were in an aunt's apartment. Yiddish words and the word order of immigrants are interspersed throughout the text, such as "Schlumper (untidy one)" and "get away from the sink already" in *More All-of-a-Kind Family*. Mama states adages, such as "do your work with good will and it'll get done twice as fast" or "there's nothing like keeping busy to help a person over a bad time." The point-of-view is inconsistent, as the narrator may relate the thoughts of one person, such as the library lady, but not another, such as Charlie. Sydney Taylor keeps the story moving swiftly in the series books, but uses the cumulative tale pattern in *Mr. Barney's Beard*. While the family stories introduce children to Jewish holidays and customs, the easy readers are limited to one hundred-fifty common words.

Sydney Taylor's "All-of-a-Kind Family" books have remained in print in the United States since their initial publication. They have been compared to Margaret Sidney's *The Five Little Peppers* and Herman Wouk's *City Boy*. The author has endeared herself to librarians by providing stories in which the library is a focal point, while at the same time introducing children to an ethnic group in a pluralistic society.

—Karen Nelson Hoyle

TAYLOR, Theodore. American. Born in Statesville, North Carolina, 23 June 1921. Educated at Cradock High School, Virginia; Fork Union Military Academy, Virginia, 1939–40; United States Merchant Marine Academy, Kings Point, New York, 1942–44. Served in the United States Merchant Marine, 1945–46, and Navy, 1950–55; Lieutenant. Married Gweneth Ann Goodwin in 1946 (divorced, 1977); has two sons and one daughter.

Sports Editor, Portsmouth *Star*, Virginia, 1941, and Bluefield *News*, West Virginia, 1946–47; Assistant Public Relations Director, New York University, 1947–49; Reporter, Orlando *Sentinel*, Florida, 1949–50; Story Editor, 1955–56, and Associate Producer, 1956–61, Perlberg-Seaton Productions, Hollywood; Free-lance Press Agent for Hollywood studios, 1961–68. Producer and Director of documentary films. Recipient: Women's International League for Peace and Freedom Jane Addams Award, 1970. Agent: A. Watkins Inc., 77 Park Avenue, New York, New York 10016. Address: 340 Moss Street, Laguna Beach, California 92651, U.S.A.

PUBLICATIONS FOR CHILDREN

Fiction

> *The Cay.*   New York, Doubleday, 1969; London, Bodley Head, 1970.
> *The Children's War.*   New York, Doubleday, 1971.
> *The Maldonado Miracle.*   New York, Doubleday, 1973.
> *Teetoncey*, illustrated by Richard Cuffari.   New York, Doubleday, 1974.
> *Teetoncey and Ben O'Neal*, illustrated by Richard Cuffari.   New York, Doubleday, 1975.
> *The Odyssey of Ben O'Neal*, illustrated by Richard Cuffari.   New York, Doubleday, 1977.

Play

> Television Play: *Sunshine, The Whale*, 1974.

Other

> *People Who Make Movies.*   New York, Doubleday, 1967.
> *Air Raid – Pearl Harbor!*, illustrated by W. T. Mars.   New York, Crowell, 1971.
> *Rebellion Town: Williamsburg, 1776*, illustrated by Richard Cuffari.   New York, Crowell, 1973.
> *Battle in the Arctic Seas: The Story of PQ 17*, illustrated by Robert Andrew Parker.   New York, Crowell, 1976.

PUBLICATIONS FOR ADULTS

Plays

> Screenplay: *Showdown*, 1974.

> Television Play: *Tom Threepersons*, 1964.

Other

> *The Magnificent Mitscher.*   New York, Norton, 1954.
> *Fire on the Beaches.*   New York, Norton, 1958.
> *The Body Trade.*   New York, Fawcett, 1968.
> *Special Unit Senator: An Investigation of the Assassination of Senator Robert F. Kennedy*, with Robert A. Houghton.   New York, Random House, 1970.
> *A Shepherd Watches, A Shepherd Sings*, with Louis Irigaray.   New York, Doubleday, 1977.

Manuscript Collection: Kerlan Collection, University of Minnesota, Minneapolis.

Theodore Taylor comments:

I don't approach a book for children any differently than I do a work for adults. I write the story as I see it and feel it. Above all, I try very hard not to "write down" to the young reader. I'm more at home dealing with adventure. I prefer action simply because it is fun to write and hopefully offers the reading enjoyment which, to me, writing is all about.

*　　　*　　　*

The Cay was Theodore Taylor's first novel for children; yet on its publication in 1969 it gained wide recognition in the United States. Its success is due in part to the relevance of its theme – the racial harmony achieved by a black adult and a white child marooned on a desert island and therefore becoming mutually interdependent. It is also due to the quality of the writing; much of Taylor's own experiences and abilities have gone into the making of the book.

Taylor is now a film-maker living in California; his primary focus is therefore visual, and this is evident in the style of the book. It has indeed been made into a successful film. The blindness of the white boy, Phillip, is symbolic as well as actual, for he has to learn that friendship is colour-blind. It also means that he has to see the island through the eyes of Timothy very much in the way that any reader of any book has to see the created world of the writer through borrowed eyes. The book, then, is stylistically interesting.

Most of Taylor's creative work has been documentary rather than fictional. This is true not only of his films but also of his books. His only work for children before *The Cay* was *People Who Make Movies*, and he has written several non-fiction works for them since. This approach helps to give that verisimilitude so necessary in a desert island tale. Finding food, building a shelter, lighting a fire, and signalling for help are all meticulously described. Taylor has lived in the Caribbean and so achieves geographical authenticity; the island is real and so is the hurricane. Similarly his wartime naval service is used to good effect in the first part of the book, when the boat on which the two are sailing, Timothy as one of the crew and Phillip as an evacuee from Aruba, is wrecked by a German U-boat. The factual background and setting cannot be faulted.

Taylor began his career as a journalist and this is reflected in his competent handling of the sensitive topic of race relationship. Even so, the book has attracted adverse criticism, notably from Albert V. Schwartz, whose 1971 article is reprinted in *Racist and Sexist Images in Children's Books*, 1975. Schwartz calls it "an adventure story for white colonialists – however enlightened – to add to their racist mythology." He feels that Phillip's attitudes undergo only a minor change from the extreme views expounded by his mother. And when Phillip asks "Timothy, are you still black?" he deplores Timothy's deprecatory laugh which helps to show that in the book Timothy "is denied history, parents, family, children. He is denied all social ties except one and that single tie is with a white boy for whom in the end he is denied his life." Many would find this view extreme, especially given the historical setting, and would praise the book for its warm and generous spirit. Each age re-interprets the myth of *Robinson Crusoe* as an image of the human condition and *The Cay* is certainly a more hopeful one than *Lord of the Flies*.

—Mary Croxson

THIELE, Colin (Milton). Australian. Born in Eudunda, South Australia, 16 November 1920. Educated at Adelaide Teachers College, South Australia, 1937–38; University of Adelaide, B.A. 1941, Dip.Ed. 1947, Dip.T. Served in the Royal Australian Air Force, 1942–45. Married Rhonda Gill in 1945; has two daughters. Taught at Port Lincoln High School, South Australia 1946–55, and Brighton High School, 1956. Lecturer, 1957–62,

Senior Lecturer in English, 1962–63, Vice-Principal, 1964, and Principal, 1965–72, Wattle Park Teachers College, Adelaide; Director, Murray Park College of Advanced Education, 1973. Since 1973, Principal, Wattle Park Teachers Centre. Formerly, National Book Reviewer, Australian Broadcasting Commission; Commonwealth Literary Fund Lecturer in Australian Literature. Member, 1964–68, and since 1969, Fellow, Australian College of Education; since 1967, Council Member, Australian Society of Authors. Recipient: W. J. Miles Memorial Prize for verse, 1944; Commonwealth Jubilee Radio Play Prize, 1951; Fulbright Scholarship, 1959; Grace Leven Prize, for verse, 1961; Commonwealth Literary Fund Fellowship, 1967. Address: 24 Woodhouse Crescent, Wattle Park, South Australia 5066, Australia.

PUBLICATIONS FOR CHILDREN

Fiction

The Sun on the Stubble.   Adelaide, Rigby, 1961; London, White Lion, 1974.
Storm Boy, illustrated by John Baily.   Adelaide, Rigby, 1963; London, Angus and Robertson, 1964; Chicago, Rand McNally, 1966.
February Dragon.   Adelaide, Rigby, 1965; London, White Lion, 1975; New York, Harper, 1976.
Mrs. Munch and Puffing Billy, illustrated by Nyorie Bungey.   Adelaide, Rigby, 1967.
Yellow-Jacket Jock, illustrated by Clifton Pugh.   Melbourne, Cheshire, 1969.
Blue Fin, illustrated by Roger Haldane.   Adelaide, Rigby, 1969; New York, Harper, 1974; London, Collins, 1976.
Flash Flood, illustrated by Jean Elder.   Adelaide, Rigby, 1970.
Flip Flop the Tiger Snake, illustrated by Jean Elder.   Adelaide, Rigby, 1970.
The Fire in the Stone.   Adelaide, Rigby, 1973; New York, Harper, 1974.
Albatross Two.   Adelaide, Rigby, 1974; London, Collins, 1975; as *Fight Against Albatross Two,* New York, Harper, 1976.
Magpie Island, illustrated by Roger Haldane.   Adelaide, Rigby, 1974; London, Collins, 1975.
Uncle Gustav's Ghosts.   Adelaide, Rigby, 1974.
The Hammerhead Light.   Adelaide, Rigby, 1976; New York, Harper, 1977.

Verse

Gloop the Gloomy Bunyip, illustrated by John Baily.   Brisbane, Jacaranda Press, 1962; as *Gloop the Bunyip,* Adelaide, Rigby, 1970.

Other

The State of Our State.   Adelaide, Rigby, 1952.
Looking at Poetry.   London, Longman, 1960.

Editor, with Greg Branson, *One-Act Plays for Secondary Schools.*   Adelaide, Rigby, 3 vols., 1962, 1964; revised version, as *Setting the Stage* and *The Living Stage,* 1969, 1970.
Editor, with Greg Branson, *Beginners, Please.*   Adelaide, Rigby, 1964.
Editor, with Greg Branson, *Plays for Young Players.*   Adelaide, Rigby, 1970.

PUBLICATIONS FOR ADULTS

Novel

Labourers in the Vineyard.   Adelaide, Rigby, and London, Hale, 1970.

Short Stories

   The Rim of the Morning.   Adelaide, Rigby, 1966.

Plays

   Burke and Wills (broadcast, 1949).   Included in *Selected Verse (1940–1970)*, 1970.

   Radio Plays: *Burke and Wills*, 1949; *Edge of Ice*, 1951; *The Shark Fishers*, 1953; *Edward John Eyre*, 1962.

Verse

   Progress to Denial.   Adelaide, Jindyworobak Publications, 1945.
   Splinters and Shards.   Adelaide, Jindyworobak Publications, 1945.
   The Golden Lightning: Poems.   Adelaide, Jindyworobak Publications, 1951.
   Man in a Landscape.   Adelaide, Rigby, 1960.
   In Charcoal and Conté.   Adelaide, Rigby, 1966.
   Selected Verse (1940–1970).   Adelaide, Rigby, 1970.

Other

   Barossa Valley Sketchbook.   Adelaide, Rigby, and San Francisco, Tri-Ocean, 1968.
   Heysen of Hahndorf (biography).   Adelaide, Rigby, and San Francisco, Tri-Ocean, 1968.
   Coorong.   Adelaide, Rigby, 1972.
   Range Without Man.   Adelaide, Rigby, 1974.
   The Little Desert.   Adelaide, Rigby, 1975.
   Grains of Mustard Seed (on state education).   Adelaide, South Australia Education Department, 1975.
   Heysen's Early Hahndorf.   Adelaide, Rigby, 1976.
   The Bight.   Adelaide, Rigby, 1976.

   Editor, *Jindyworobak Anthology.*   Adelaide, Jindyworobak Publications, 1953.
   Editor, with Ian Mudie, *Australian Poets Speak.*   Adelaide, Rigby, 1961.
   Editor, *Favourite Australian Stories.*   Adelaide, Rigby, 1963.
   Editor, *Handbook to Favourite Australian Stories.*   Adelaide, Rigby, 1964.

Colin Thiele comments:
   I have always believed that writers for children are educators whether they intend to be or not. I also believe that writers are greatly influenced by their own lives – by the sights, sounds, smells, and tastes of their childhood, by the cities, hills, valleys, and rivers they knew, by the customs, character, and speech of the people they grew up with. These convictions have certainly influenced my own writing for children. They have led me to concentrate on the regions and people I really know, and so almost all of my books have been set in South Australia.
   One of the functions of literature for a reader of any age is the revelation of mankind to man – to comment on the variousness of the human condition, to heighten his awareness of the miraculous diversity of life. But the writer for young people has a different, perhaps a far greater, responsibility: he must lead his young followers with what humanity and compassion he can compass to travel a worthwhile road to adulthood, avoiding brutality on the one hand and sentimentality on the other.
   Whether he sets his story within the horizons of a family of potato growers or fishermen or gold miners or city businessmen does not matter in the least. For the edges of life may be as

blunt or as sharp there as anywhere else. Love and bitterness, stupidity, excitement, envy and gratitude – the enjoyment and understanding of one's fellow man and of the earth and all its creatures – these may be dealt with as tellingly in Sleepy Hollow as in the most cosmopolitan crossroads of the world. Illumination is in the individual rather than the mass; the universal lies in the heart of man, not in any facade of streets, or hills, or houses.

*   *   *

Colin Thiele is among Australia's most versatile and best-known writers. His children's fiction, chiefly directed to the adolescent reader, commonly favors isolated South Australian locales from the Coorong to the Outback where man makes his living from sea or land, where youth gains stature when confronting elemental forces. Themes persistently stress tenacity and courage and man's need to conserve nature's balance.

An award-winner, *Blue Fin* is Thiele's finest novel. A tuna fisherman considers his son a bungler. But the boy redeems himself when, on a fishing expedition, he heroically saves his father and the boat from a tornado-swept sea. This exciting adventure story is also rich with colourful details about tuna fishing.

Other fine sea stories are *Storm Boy, Albatross Two*, and *Magpie Island*. The title character of *Storm Boy* lives on the Coorong with his beachcomber father and makes a pet of a pelican. When the bird is callously killed by hunters, its grieving young master leaves to pursue an education in the city. The boy's affection for his seabird is touchingly narrated. In *Albatross Two*, an off-shore oil rig explodes, polluting the sea and endangering its creatures. A boy and his sister are caught in the conflict between the fishing community and the oil-drillers in this informative, timely, and swiftly-paced story protesting man's rapacity in exploiting the natural environment. For pre-adolescent readers, *Magpie Island* poignantly depicts the lonely exile of a magpie blown to an off-coast island.

Other stories encompass a range of inland settings. *February Dragon* (a metaphor for late-summer fire) introduces a scrub country family afflicted by the devastation of a huge, carelessly-caused bushfire. The terrible aftermath is a graphic warning against human negligence in a novel both instructive and absorbing. In *The Fire in the Stone*, a boy in the Outback strikes precious opals when digging in an old mine, and then is joined by an Aborigine and European friend in defying dangers to hunt down an opal thief. A compelling and less melodramatic adventure story is "The Water-Trolly," in the adult short-story collection *The Rim of the Morning*. Here, a resourceful youth from an Outback sheep station journeys across the desert, buffeted by the elements, to fetch desperately needed water for his family, and proves his own measure as a man. Other stories in the collection range from the hilariously comic ("Lock-Out," "Dan Ran a Fowl Run," and "Fish Scales") to the tragically ironic ("The Shell"). South Australia's farming district is the milieu of *The Sun on the Stubble*. A youth's exploits in home and countryside are viewed with humor and nostalgia, and are unpretentiously evocative of the special character and customs of the Australian-German farm family.

Appealing to children under ten are *Gloop the Bunyip*, a verse tale of an Australian folklore beastie whose frightening reputation is threatened when white settlers invade his Outback haunts, and *Mrs. Munch and Puffing Billy*, in which a responsible little girl braves a flood to bring goat's milk to her ailing sister on a mountaintop farm.

Colin Thiele is a masterful story-teller of commitment. International in appeal, his work is enriched by dimensional characterization, humor, regional color, and illuminating descriptions of endeavours from fishing and farming to opal mining and oil-drilling. Committed to man's better understanding of nature, Thiele is persuasive without being pontifical, informative without being pedantic; he never forgets to spin a good yarn.

—Christian H. Moe

THURBER, James (Grover).   American.   Born in Columbus, Ohio, 8 December 1894. Educated at Ohio State University, Columbus. Married Althea Adams in 1922 (divorced, 1935), one daughter; Helen Wismer, 1935. Code Clerk, American Embassy, Paris, 1918–20; reporter, *Columbus Dispatch*, 1920–24, Paris edition of Chicago *Tribune*, 1924–26, and New York *Evening Post*, 1926–27; editor, then writer, 1927–37, then free lance-contributor, *New Yorker* magazine. Litt.D.: Kenyon College, Gambier, Ohio, 1950; Yale University, New Haven, Connecticut, 1953; L.H.D.: Williams College, Williamstown, Massachusetts, 1951. *Died 2 November 1961.*

Publications for Children

Fiction

> *Many Moons*, illustrated by Louis Slobodkin.   New York, Harcourt Brace, 1943; London, Hamish Hamilton, 1945.
> *The Great Quillow*, illustrated by Doris Lee.   New York, Harcourt Brace, 1944.
> *The White Deer*, illustrated by the author and Don Freeman.   New York, Harcourt Brace, 1945; London, Hamish Hamilton, 1946.
> *The 13 Clocks*, illustrated by Marc Simont.   New York, Simon and Schuster, 1950; London, Hamish Hamilton, 1951.
> *The Wonderful O*, illustrated by Marc Simont.   New York, Simon and Schuster, and London, Hamish Hamilton, 1955.

Publications for Adults

Short Stories and Sketches (illustrated by the author)

> *The Owl in the Attic and Other Perplexities.*   New York and London, Harper, 1931.
> *The Seal in the Bedroom and Other Predicaments.*   New York and London, Harper, 1932.
> *My Life and Hard Times.*   New York and London, Harper, 1933.
> *The Middle-Aged Man on the Flying Trapeze: A Collection of Short Pieces.*   New York, Harper, and London, Hamish Hamilton, 1935.
> *Let Your Mind Alone! and Other More or Less Inspirational Pieces.*   New York, Harper, and London, Hamish Hamilton, 1937.
> *Cream of Thurber* ....   London, Hamish Hamilton, 1939.
> *The Last Flower: A Parable in Pictures.*   New York, Harper, and London, Hamish Hamilton, 1939.
> *Fables for Our Time and Famous Poems Illustrated.*   New York, Harper, and London, Hamish Hamilton, 1940.
> *My World – and Welcome to It.*   New York, Harcourt Brace, and London, Hamish Hamilton, 1942.
> *Men, Women, and Dogs: A Book of Drawings.*   New York, Harcourt Brace, 1943; London, Hamish Hamilton, 1945.
> *The Thurber Carnival.*   New York, Harper, and London, Hamish Hamilton, 1945.
> *The Beast in Me, and Other Animals: A New Collection of Pieces and Drawings about Human Beings and Less Alarming Creatures.*   New York, Harcourt Brace, 1948; London, Hamish Hamilton, 1949.
> *The Thurber Album: A New Collection of Pieces about People.*   New York, Simon and Schuster, and London, Hamish Hamilton, 1952.
> *Thurber Country: A New Collection of Pieces about Males and Females, Mainly of Our Own Species.*   New York, Simon and Schuster, and London, Hamish Hamilton, 1953.

Thurber's Dogs: A Collection of the Master's Dogs, Written and Drawn, Real and Imaginary, Living and Long Ago. New York, Simon and Schuster, and London, Hamish Hamilton, 1955.

A Thurber Garland. London, Hamish Hamilton, 1955.

Further Fables for Our Time. New York, Simon and Schuster, and London, Hamish Hamilton, 1956.

Alarms and Diversions. New York, Harper, and London, Hamish Hamilton, 1957.

Lanterns and Lances. New York, Harper, and London, Hamish Hamilton, 1961.

Credos and Curios. New York, Harper, and London, Hamish Hamilton, 1962.

Vintage Thunder: A Collection ... of the Best Writings and Drawings of James Thurber. London, Hamish Hamilton, 2 vols., 1963.

Thurber and Company. New York, Harper, 1966; London, Hamish Hamilton, 1967.

Plays

The Male Animal, with Elliott Nugent (produced New York, 1940; London, 1949). New York, Random House, 1940; London, Hamish Hamilton, 1950.

A Thurber Carnival, adaptation of his own stories (produced Columbus and New York, 1960). New York, French, 1962.

Wrote the books for the following college musical comedies: *Oh My, Omar*, with Hayward M. Anderson, 1921; *Psychomania*, 1922; *Many Moons*, 1922; *A Twin Fix*, with Hayward M. Anderson, 1923; *The Cat and the Riddle*, 1924; *Nightingale*, 1924; *Tell Me Not*, 1924.

Other

Is Sex Necessary? or, Why You Feel the Way You Do, with E.B. White. New York, Harper, 1929; London, Heinemann, 1930.

Thurber on Humor. Columbus, Martha Kinney Cooper Ohioana Library Association, 1953(?).

The Years with Ross. Boston, Little Brown, and London, Hamish Hamilton, 1959.

Bibliography: *James Thurber: A Bibliography* by Edwin T. Bowden. Columbus, Ohio State University Press, 1968.

Critical Study: *Thurber: A Biography* by Burton Bernstein. New York, Dodd Mead, 1975.

Illustrator: *No Nice Girl Swears* by Alice Leone Moates, 1933; *Her Foot Is on the Brass Rail* by Don Marquis, 1935; *Men Can Take It* by Elizabeth Hawes, 1939; *In a Word* by Margaret Samuels, 1939; *How to Raise a Dog ...* by James R. Kinney and Ann Honeycutt, 1953.

*   *   *

James Thurber, an American original in humor, satire, nonsense, drawing, and patently a wild tyrannothesaurus type when on the hunt for words, slipped into the field of children's literature by the back front gate, like a cat "walking on velvet" – an expression of his own. By 1943 he was well established through *The New Yorker*: (a) in prose; (b) in his childlike drawings of dominant women, dominated men, and semisomnolent dogs; and (c), apart from *The New Yorker*, for such wry pieces of psychological foolery as "The Secret Life of Walter Mitty" and "The Night the Bed Fell." In that year, without any warning, *Many Moons* appeared: a very slight but delicately enchanting fairy tale involving royalty and an itemized royal retinue in the royal peck order of a Lord High Chamberlain, Royal Wizard, Royal Mathematician, Court Jester, and Royal Goldsmith. The King's daughter had fallen ill and wanted the moon. It takes but half an hour to tell you how she got it.

Many Moons was followed by *The Great Quillow*, designed perhaps for a somewhat older group, if one stops to consider its plot and the generous play of its language. And then, though surely *not* aimed just at children, came a trinity: *The White Deer*, *The 13 Clocks*, and *The Wonderful O*. Call them fairy tales, or parodies of fairy tales or pseudo fables; they are, it seems to me, entirely suitable for all readers between 9 and 99 who have imagination and a true sense of the ridiculous. The anatomy of these five books is interchangeable: impossible tasks, indomitable courage, improbable solutions, appropriate wizardry, and nothing so serious or warped as not to be funny.

The Great Quillow, a first-rate tale in concept and execution, offers an outsized giant, instead of a king, who plumps himself down on the edge of a village and not in it. To get rid of him and his crippling daily demands for food and entertainment is the problem facing the village council — tailor, butcher, candymaker, blacksmith, baker, candlemaker, lamplighter, cobbler, carpenter, and locksmith; plus the toymaker, not of the council, but the David of the story, with a mind more useful than a slingshot, and a blueprint of action which only a Thurber could have given him.

The White Deer follows the old fairy tale prescription of tasks set by a princess, and three princes (rated A, D minus, and E) to accomplish them. *The 13 Clocks*, by all odds the one masterpiece of the quintet, was written in Bermuda instead of whatever it was that Thurber went there to write: delightfully complex, dexterously sinister, mathematically proportional. *The Wonderful O* is all about disappointed pirates on the Island of Ooreo who set about removing the o's from all words that contain them. An attenuated tale, as if the life work of an oölogist (lgist) were reduced t chas befre yur eyes r rbs.

Auden once said he would test a prospective poet by asking if he (or she) likes to make lists of things. No need to ask this of Thurber who comes across with endless lists so curious they would have delighted Lear, Carroll, Rabelais, and Herman Melville. He loves to ring vowel changes — Rango, Rengo, Ringo, Rongo, Rungo, for example — in dozens of concatenations livelier than the catalogues of ships and whales. And at times he outdoes even L. Frank Baum in nonsense names, words, and phrases: Mok-Mok, Tocko, Duff of the Dolorous Doom, Thag, Wag, Gag; Prince Jorn, Hunder, St. Nillin's Day; Lobo, Bolo, Olob, Obol; Woddly; Golux, Zorn of Zorna, Xingu, the Todal who gleeped; puppybabble, whupple, thrug; "I'll slit you from your guggle to your zatch"; a blob of glup.

Another conspicuous hallmark of Thurber the fairy tale teller is an increasing use, in the last three of these books, of rhyme *written as prose*, swimming like the scum on cocoa: " 'I like the taste of wine,' he said, 'the feel of leather. I'll ride or drink your father down in any weather.' " You will find this going on more lyrically in E. B. White's *Stuart Little*, published in the same year as Thurber's *The White Deer*. Mr. White writes (as in straight prose): "She comes from fields once tall with wheat, from pastures deep in fern and thistle; she comes from vales of meadowsweet, and she loves to whistle." Not a new trick, but Thurber makes much of it. Perhaps too much of it: " 'A bell of triumph, or a knell?' 'Time,' the old man said, 'will tell.' "

But his own best trick is a solitary one in that marvelous book *The 13 Clocks*: a couple of limericks done in an inverted style original, I think, with him:

> There was an old coddle so molly,
> He talked in a glot that was poly,
> His gaws were so gew
> That his laps became dew,
> And he ate only pops that were lolly.

Two of these books — *The 13 Clocks* and *The Wonderful O* — are illustrated in color by Marc Simont, winner of the 1957 Caldecott Medal. This reader considers Mr. Simont's work in *The 13 Clocks* his absolute masterpiece, inseparable from the text as Tenniel's from *Alice*.

—David McCord

THWAITE, Ann. British. Born in London, 4 October 1932. Educated at Marsden Collegiate School, Wellington, New Zealand, 1942–45; Queen Elizabeth's Girls' Grammar School, Barnet, Hertfordshire, 1945–51; St. Hilda's College, Oxford, B.A. 1955, M.A. 1959. Married the writer Anthony Thwaite in 1955; has four daughters. Lecturer, Tokyo Women's University, 1956–57; publishers reader, 1958–65. Since 1963, regular reviewer for *Times Literary Supplement*, London, and other publications; since 1974, Contributing Editor, *Cricket* magazine, La Salle, Illinois. Address: The Mill House, Low Tharston, Norfolk NR15 2YN, England.

PUBLICATIONS FOR CHILDREN

Fiction

> *The House in Turner Square*, illustrated by Robin Jacques. London, Constable, 1960; New York, Harcourt Brace, 1961.
> *A Seaside Holiday for Jane and Toby*, illustrated by Janet Martin. London, Constable, 1962.
> *Toby Stays with Jane*, illustrated by Janet Martin. London, Constable, 1962.
> *Jane and Toby Start School*, illustrated by Janet Martin. London, Constable, 1965.
> *Toby Moves House*, illustrated by Janet Martin. London, Constable, 1965.
> *Home and Away*, illustrated by Shirley Hughes. Leicester, Brockhampton Press, 1967; as *The Holiday Map*, Chicago, Follett, 1969.
> *The Travelling Tooth*, illustrated by George Thompson. Leicester, Brockhampton Press, 1968.
> *The Day with the Duke*, illustrated by George Him. Leicester, Brockhampton Press, and New York, World, 1969.
> *The Camelthorn Papers*. London, Macmillan, 1969.
> *The Only Treasure*, illustrated by Glenys Ambrus. Leicester, Brockhampton Press, 1970.
> *The Poor Pigeon*, illustrated by Glenys Ambrus. Leicester, Brockhampton Press, 1974; Chicago, Children's Press, 1976.
> *Rose in the River*, illustrated by John Dyke. Leicester, Brockhampton Press, 1974; Chicago, Children's Press, 1976.
> *Horrible Boy*, illustrated by Glenys Ambrus. Leicester, Brockhampton Press, 1975; Chicago, Children's Press, 1976.

Other

> *The Young Traveller in Japan.* London, Phoenix House, 1958.

> Editor, *Allsorts 1* to *7*. London, Macmillan, 5 vols., 1969–72, and Methuen, 2 vols., 1974–75.

PUBLICATIONS FOR ADULTS

Other

> *Waiting for the Party: The Life of Frances Hodgson Burnett, 1849–1924*. London, Secker and Warburg, and New York, Scribner, 1974.

> Editor, *My Oxford*. London, Robson, 1977.

Ann Thwaite comments:
My work over twenty years has been almost entirely devoted to children's books –

reviewing, editing, talking about them, writing them. My main interests have been in bringing good reading and children together, and in preserving in fictional form my own experiences of children and places. My interest in children's writers of the past led me to spend four years writing a definitive biography of Frances Hodgson Burnett, and this book has taken me at last outside the field of children's books. I am now working on a full-scale biography of Edmund Gosse, but I am still involved in many different ways with children's reading.

*   *   *

Ann Thwaite has produced about 20 books, but is best known for her splendid annual miscellany called *Allsorts*. *Allsorts* is a "rag bag of entertainment," a collection of poems, puzzles, stories, word games, riddles and pictures, jokes and things-to-do. Many well-known authors and artists such as Joan Aiken, Trevor Storey, and Vernon Scannell have contributed works imaginatively woven by Ann Thwaite into this bumper Christmas package. *Allsorts* is for 7–10-year-olds, "for allsorts of children with allsorts of interests." It is sophisticated and of high quality, and THE Christmas annual for reading children.

Much of Ann Thwaite's work is for 5 to 8-year-olds who are just learning to read a whole book for themselves. *Jane and Toby Start School* shows the children in their fine new uniforms finding that the dinner, the painting, and the games at school are all very acceptable. Simple drawings give reassurance and meaning to this and the other Jane and Toby books. *The Day with the Duke* adds the spice of that special British humour which only a stately home with a noble duke in tattered old clothes being mistaken for the gardener can bring. For slightly older junior school children she has written a number of very readable day-to-day adventure stories (*The Only Treasure* and *Home and Away*).

Ann Thwaite has also written a number of exciting adventure stories for children in those difficult middle years when they have just learnt to read a long book and need a fast-moving interesting plot to keep their enthusiasm for the story. Notable among these is *The House in Turner Square*, a story of London grammar school girls who, through their interest in Georgian architecture, overcome their very different backgrounds and personalities. *The Camelthorn Papers* uses Libya to provide an exciting background to a story of treasure, kidnapping, and a poem written during World War II.

Ann Thwaite is also known to adult readers as a reviewer for the *Times Literary Supplement* and other periodicals, and as the author of the outstanding scholarly biography of Frances Hodgson Burnett, *Waiting for the Party*.

—Jean Russell

TITUS, Eve. American. Born in New York City, 16 July 1922. Educated at New York University. Divorced; has one son. Professional pianist. Address: c/o McGraw-Hill Book Co. Inc., 1221 Avenue of the Americas, New York, New York 10020, U.S.A.

PUBLICATIONS FOR CHILDREN

Fiction (illustrated by Paul Galdone)

Anatole. New York, McGraw Hill, 1956; London, Lane, 1957.
Anatole and the Cat. New York, McGraw Hill, 1957; London, Lane, 1958.
Basil of Baker Street. New York, McGraw Hill, 1958.
My Dog and I (as Nancy Lord). New York, McGraw Hill, 1958.

Anatole and the Robot.   New York, McGraw Hill, 1960; London, Bodley Head, 1961.

Anatole over Paris.   New York, McGraw Hill, 1961; London, Bodley Head, 1962.

The Mouse and the Lion, illustrated by Leonard Weisgard.   New York, Parents' Magazine Press, 1962.

Basil and the Lost Colony.   New York, McGraw Hill, 1964; London, Hodder and Stoughton, 1975.

Anatole and the Poodle.   New York, McGraw Hill, 1964; London, Bodley Head, 1966.

Anatole and the Piano.   New York, McGraw Hill, 1966; London, Bodley Head, 1967.

Anatole and the Thirty Thieves.   New York, McGraw Hill, and London, Bodley Head, 1969.

Mr. Shaw's Shipshape Shoeshop, illustrated by Larry Ross.   New York, Parents' Magazine Press, 1970.

Anatole and the Toyshop.   New York, McGraw Hill, 1970.

Basil and the Pygmy Cats.   New York, McGraw Hill, 1971; London, Hodder and Stoughton, 1977.

Why the Wind God Wept, illustrated by James Barkley.   New York, Doubleday, 1972.

Anatole in Italy.   New York, McGraw Hill, 1973; London, Bodley Head, 1974.

Basil in Mexico.   New York, McGraw Hill, 1976.

Other

The Two Stonecutters, illustrated by Yoko Mitsuhashi.   New York, Doubleday, 1967.

Manuscript Collection: Case Collection, Wayne State University, Detroit.

*   *   *

Eve Titus is known primarily for her Anatole and Basil books, but she has written several individual stories for magazines and in book form. The series stories maintain a high standard in plot and style, and have the precision and rhythm expected of a musician.

Anatole was her first published book, and has remained the most prominent. Anatole is a French mouse whose occupation is cheese tasting for M'sieu Duval. Either the cheese factory or Anatole's family is threatened in a different manner in each book, and the mouse *magnifique* comes to the rescue. The specific character or situation is obvious from the title. The belling of the cat is the classical theme used for the second story, while the robot Cheezak provides the challenge in the third book. The next six books deal with his family stranded on the Eiffel tower, the kidnapping of the model poodle Juliette, the salvaging of pearls from a grand piano, the foiling of thieves, the rescuing of his family from the clutches of a toyshop owner, and his visit to a cheese factory in Italy. *Anatole and the Toyshop* is the most dramatic, for the proprietor forces his six youngsters to ride their bicycles around the window display continually to attract an audience of shoppers.

The swiftly moving stories are sprinkled with French phrases and words. Repetition is used in introducing Anatole's wife Doucette, and their children, Paul, Paulette, Claude, Claudette, Georges and Georgette. The three suspects in the Great Cheese Robbery are Baptiste, the Baker, Blanchard, the Barber, and Bernard, the Bookseller. Rhythmical phrasing is incorporated, such as "Concerning cheese, the world agrees a mouse's nose is better than a policeman's." Eve Titus' sense of humor is revealed both in the situations and in the language, such as "And be quiet as mice!"

While Anatole is French, Basil is British and the books about him are written in the style of Arthur Conan Doyle's *Sherlock Holmes*. Basil lives at Baker Street, Number 221-B and solves mysteries with his doctor companion, David Q. Dawson. Plots, characters, and language have parallels with the Sherlockian canon. The introductory paragraphs tantalize, digress, and then proceed to the basic story. Conclusions invariably point to another adventure, as in *Basil and the Pygmy Cats* where there is reference to a Mexican adventure, and in *Basil and the Lost Colony* a mysterious note arrives. In the latter book, the detective and companion visit Tellmice, in which the inhabitants are unaware that Switzerland has regained her freedom in1291. "Relda,", the mouse opera star is introduced in the book, while Professor Ratigan, leader of the mouse underworld captures the adventurers in *Basil and the Pygmy Cats.*

The language used alludes to both mice and to Holmes. "Pawhand" and "shortpaw" refer to writing, while "Mouseland Yard" and "Mousemoor Prison" are locations, and after a heroic episode Basil is elected to lifetime membership in the Royal Academy of Mousology. In Holmesian tradition, Basil uses his deductive powers, wears a Persian robe, plays the violin, and enjoys Mrs. Judson's cheese soufflé. There is even the identification, " 'Basil of Baker Street, I presume?' " Inconsistencies are rare, but Basil's pipe is described as being both "berrywood" and "meerwood" in *Basil of Baker Street.*

Eve Titus has written other stories, but they don't have the inventiveness of those about Anatole and Basil. *My Dog and I,* written under the pseudonym Nancy Lord, is a slight picture book. *The Two Stonecutters* is a free adaptation from the Japanese, and too elaborate for a folktale. There is only a reference to the historic meeting in *The Mouse and the Lion,* a "Reading Readiness book" in which the lion visited the world of people and the mouse has almost no role. *Mr. Shaw's Shipshape Shoeshop* has rhythm and a strong plot, but is too long. The Anatole and Basil books far outweigh the others in impact and popularity. The two characters are important enough to be represented by entries in Margery Fisher's *Who's Who in Children's Literature.* Since the audience reading Basil books is considerably younger than those reading the Sherlock Holmes books, they may serve as preparation for the Victorian detective rather than a pastiche.

—Karen Nelson Hoyle

TODD, Barbara Euphan. British. Born near Doncaster, Yorkshire. Educated at St. Catherine's School, Bramley, Surrey. Served in the Voluntary Aid Detachment, 1914–18. Married John Graham Bower in 1932 (died, 1940). Regular contributor to *Punch,* London. *Died 2 February 1976.*

PUBLICATIONS FOR CHILDREN

Fiction

> *The 'normous Saturday Fairy Book,* with Marjory Royce and Moira Meighn.   London,
>   Paul, 1924.
> *The 'normous Sunday Story Book,* with Marjory Royce and Moira Meighn.   London,
>   Paul, 1925.
> *The Very Good Walkers,* with Marjory Royce, illustrated by H.R. Millar.   London,
>   Methuen, 1925.
> *Mr. Blossom's Shop.*   London, Nelson, 1929.
> *Happy Cottage,* with Marjory Royce.   London, Collins, 1930.
> *South Country Secrets* (as Euphan), with Klaxon.   London, Burns and Oates, 1935.
> *The Touchstone,* with Klaxon.   London, Burns and Oates, 1935.

Worzel Gummidge; or, The Scarecrow of Scatterbrook, illustrated by Elizabeth Alldridge. London, Burns and Oates, 1936.

Worzel Gummidge Again, illustrated by Elizabeth Alldridge. London, Burns and Oates, 1937.

The Mystery Train. London, University of London Press, 1937.

The Splendid Picnic. London, University of London Press, 1937.

More about Worzel Gummidge. London, Burns and Oates, 1938.

Mr. Dock's Garden, illustrated by Ruth Westcott. Leeds, E.J. Arnold, 1939.

Gertrude the Greedy Goose, illustrated by Benjamin Rabier. London, Muller, 1939.

The House That Ran Behind, with Esther Boumphrey. London, Muller, 1943.

Worzel Gummidge, The Scarecrow of Scatterbrook Farm (from *Worzel Gummidge; or, The Scarecrow of Scatterbrook* and *Worzel Gummidge Again*), illustrated by Ursula Koering. New York, Putnam, 1947.

Worzel Gummidge and Saucy Nancy, illustrated by Will Nickless. London, Hollis and Carter, 1947.

Worzel Gummidge Takes a Holiday, illustrated by Will Nickless. London, Hollis and Carter, 1949.

Aloysius Let Loose, with Klaxon, illustrated by A.E. Batchelor. London, Collins, 1950.

Earthy Mangold and Worzel Gummidge, illustrated by Jill Crockford. London, Hollis and Carter, 1954.

Worzel Gummidge and the Railway Scarecrows, illustrated by Jill Crockford. London, Evans, 1955.

Worzel Gummidge at the Circus, illustrated by Jill Crockford. London, Evans, 1956.

The Boy with the Green Thumb, illustrated by Charlotte Hough. London, Hamish Hamilton, 1956.

The Wizard and the Unicorn, illustrated by Prudence Seward. London, Hamish Hamilton, 1957.

Worzel Gummidge and the Treasure Ship, illustrated by Jill Crockford. London, Evans, 1958.

The Shop Around the Corner, illustrated by Olive Coughlan. London, Hamish Hamilton, 1959.

Detective Worzel Gummidge, illustrated by Jill Crockford. London, Evans, 1963.

The Shop by the Sea, illustrated by Sarah Garland. London, Hamish Hamilton, 1966.

The Clock Shop, illustrated by Jill Crockford. Kingswood, Surrey, World's Work, 1967.

The Shop on Wheels, illustrated by Jill Crockford. Kingswood, Surrey, World's Work, 1968.

The Box in the Attic, illustrated by Lynette Hemmant. Kingswood, Surrey, World's Work, 1970.

The Wand from France, illustrated by Lynette Hemmant. Kingswood, Surrey, World's Work, 1972.

Plays

The Frog Prince, with Mabel Constanduros. London, French, 1956.

The Sleeping Beauty, with Mabel Constanduros. London, French, 1956.

Verse

Hither and Thither. London, Harrap, 1927.

The Seventh Daughter (as Euphan). London, Burns and Oates, 1935.

Other

Stories of the Coronations (as Euphan), with Klaxon. London, Burns and Oates, 1937.

PUBLICATIONS FOR ADULTS

Novel

Miss Ranskill Comes Home (as Barbara Bower).   London, Chapman and Hall, and New York, Putnam, 1946.

*　　*　　*

The fame of Barbara Euphan Todd will rest on the stories which feature Worzel Gummidge and his fellow scarecrows. Typically, in *Worzel Gummidge; or, The Scarecrow of Scatterbrook*, John and Susan, aged 10 and 12, spend holidays at Scatterbrook Farm where they have hilarious and singularly credible adventures protecting the nature and escapades of these walking, talking scarecrows from discovery by adults. These stories are for sharing, and are excellent for reading aloud to children of 8 or 9 in chapters sufficiently self-contained to make satisfactory reading units. The dialogue of the scarecrows, such as " 'Tain't disgustin' " will present problems to some children who try to read the stories for themselves, but there is a strong incentive to succeed.

The older people, especially the patronising though well-meaning Mrs. Bloomsbury-Barton, tend to be caricatures of "not-understanding" adults. But they are merely foils: the scarecrows themselves are strongly individualised and have real life breathed into them. Chief among these is Worzel Gummidge himself, with his turnip head, broomstick arms, and bottle-straw boots; he is full of professional pride, unpredictable, and almost always irritatingly right. Earthy Mangold is not very bright, and is professionally most inept, but she "allus tries to be comfortin' "; it is typical of her that she shoos away the hens so that the sparrows may get the grain, and that she cannot think of her hedgerow origin without aching once more to shelter the nests of the small birds and feel their wings flutter among her boughs. Little Upsidaisy, made from a milking stool, isn't very bright either, but she is always cheerful, while valetudinarian Hannah Harrow suffers from a variety of extraordinary complaints, from the "damping off" to "the mice" – for which complaint she is advised by her friends to swallow a mousetrap.

In all these stories, the excitement lies in the adventures, and the fun in the dialogue, especially in the scarecrows' irrefutable logic from quaint premises. Here is Gummidge's justification for his threat to wish that all human beings were turned into earwigs: "Nobody wouldn't think as grass could turn into milk, but it does," argued Gummidge. "And humans is more the shape o' earwigs than grass is the shape o' milk. Stands to reason."

The stories without Gummidge in the title have no scarecrows in them, and so lack their author's most magic tough, though they are mostly about magic: for instance, Fred has a Green Thumb, which brings to life a donkey cut in a hedge and causes a red hot poker plant to set fire to a sweet shop, while candytuft becomes real candy to replace lost sweets. These books, also, are good for reading aloud in convenient chapter units, and are easier than the Gummidge books for young children to read for themselves.

—Norman Culpan

TODD, H(erbert) E(atton).   British.   Born in London, 22 February 1908. Educated at Christ's Hospital, Horsham, Sussex, 1919–25. Served in the Royal Air Force, 1940–45: Squadron Leader. Married Bertha Joyce Hughes in 1932 (died, 1968); has two living sons. Clerk, Houlder Brothers Ltd., London, 1925–27, and British Foreign and Colonial Corporation, London, 1927–29; hosiery buyer, Bourne and Hollingsworth Ltd., London, 1929–31; salesman, 1931–47, and Director and Sales Manager, 1947–69, F.G. Wigley and

Company Ltd., London. Since 1946, broadcaster and lecturer. Agent: Winant, Towers Ltd., 14 Cliffords Inn, London EC4A 1DA. Address: 2 Brownlow Road, Berkhamsted, Hertfordshire HP4 1HB, England.

PUBLICATIONS FOR CHILDREN (illustrated by Lilian Buchanan)

Fiction

> *Bobby Brewster and the Winkers' Club*, illustrated by Bryan Ward. Leicester, Ward, 1949.
> *Bobby Brewster.* Leicester, Brockhampton Press, 1954.
> *Bobby Brewster – Bus Conductor.* Leicester, Brockhampton Press, 1954.
> *Bobby Brewster's Shadow.* Leicester, Brockhampton Press, 1956.
> *Bobby Brewster's Bicycle.* Leicester, Brockhampton Press, 1957.
> *Bobby Brewster's Camera.* Leicester, Brockhampton Press, 1959.
> *Bobby Brewster's Wallpaper.* Leicester, Brockhampton Press, 1961.
> *Bobby Brewster's Conker.* Leicester, Brockhampton Press, 1963.
> *Bobby Brewster – Detective.* Leicester, Brockhampton Press, 1964.
> *Bobby Brewster's Potato.* Leicester, Brockhampton Press, 1964.
> *Bobby Brewster and the Ghost.* Leicester, Brockhampton Press, 1966.
> *Bobby Brewster's Kite.* Leicester, Brockhampton Press, 1967.
> *Bobby Brewster's Scarecrow.* Leicester, Brockhampton Press, 1968.
> *Bobby Brewster's Torch.* Leicester, Brockhampton Press, 1969.
> *Bobby Brewster's Balloon Race.* Leicester, Brockhampton Press, 1970.
> *Bobby Brewster's First Magic.* Leicester, Brockhampton Press, 1970.
> *Bobby Brewster's Typewriter.* Leicester, Brockhampton Press, 1971.
> *Bobby Brewster's Bee.* Leicester, Brockhampton Press, 1972.
> *Bobby Brewster's Wishbone.* Leicester, Brockhampton Press, 1974.
> *The Sick Cow*, illustrated by Val Biro. Leicester, Brockhampton Press, 1974; Chicago, Children's Press, 1976.
> *Bobby Brewster's First Fun.* Leicester, Brockhampton Press, 1974.
> *Bobby Brewster's Bookmark.* London, Hodder and Stoughton, 1975.
> *George the Fire Engine*, illustrated by Val Biro. London, Hodder and Stoughton, 1976.
> *The Changing of the Guard.* London, Hodder and Stoughton, 1978.

Manuscript Collection: de Grummond Collection, University of Southern Mississippi, Hattiesburg.

Incidental Music: *Blackbird Pie* (play), by Capel Annand, 1956.

H.E. Todd comments:

All my stories are about Bobby Brewster, a small boy with a round face, blue eyes, and a nose like a button. He is part of me, part of my sons, and part of all the girls as well as boys to whom I tell stories. He is nearly 9 years old now – 35 years ago he was three-and-a-half. That is when I started telling stories about him to my one son at the time, and since then I have told stories about him to thousands of children of all ages, races, creeds, colours all over the world, live, and also on radio and television.

I do not claim to write stories of great literary merit, or to teach a lesson or point a moral. I write and tell stories simply for fun. And my stories are written in exactly the same language as I tell them, for *telling* stories was my first joy and I was only persuaded to write them because people seemed to enjoy hearing them.

*   *   *

While H.E. Todd's stories are not necessarily in the mainstream of modern children's literature, his influence on children's reading has been profound. Even before his retirement from business he had become an assiduous and regular public story-teller of magnetic appeal, with a vast repertoire of tales of magic and other oddities in the life of his boy character Bobby Brewster. Bobby himself, and his parents, friends, teachers and relations, are primarily vehicles round and by means of whom the magic takes effect. What is so good about the stories is that they are founded on everyday situations and everyday things – a wristwatch, pyjamas, parties, school, trying to get to sleep, domestic animals, a piece of chalk, musical instruments. Many of the situations are really funny. The stories have witty touches of detail, and they are told in public with the professional expertise, timing, and verve of many years' practice. A typical piece of Todd nonsense which yet has the ring of logic about it concerns Bobby's clothes hanging on the line which are objecting to not being worn to a party. So he finds out what occasions each prefers, and makes a list, including, "Pants don't mind what parties they go to because they can't see anyway. They prefer to hang on the line."

However, to speak well and to write well require different techniques. Some of the stories in the books have suffered in transition because they have not fully been translated into the medium of the printed word: asides which are acceptable in public become self-conscious in print. And though many of the situations have actually been suggested by children, the vein of profitable imagination and skilful working out of a plot is sometimes thin. Certainly the books of what one might call the middle period (i.e., late 1960's) are the best, notably *Bobby Brewster and the Ghost* and *Bobby Brewster's Typewriter*.

—Antony Kamm

TOLKIEN, J(ohn) R(onald) R(euel). British. Born in Bloemfontein, South Africa, 3 January 1892; emigrated to England in 1896. Educated at King Edward VI School, Birmingham; Exeter College, Oxford, B.A. 1915, M.A. 1919. Served with the Lancashire Fusiliers, 1915–18. Married Edith Mary Bratt in 1916; four children. Worked as an Assistant on the Oxford English Dictionary, 1918–20. Reader in English, 1920–23, and Professor of the English Language, 1924–25, University of Leeds, Yorkshire. At Oxford University: Rawlinson and Bosworth Professor of Anglo-Saxon, 1925–45; Fellow, Pembroke College, 1926–45; Leverhulme Research Fellow, 1934–36; Merton Professor of English Language and Literature, 1945–59; Emeritus Fellow, Merton College, and Honorary Fellow, Exeter College. Andrew Lang Lecturer, St. Andrews University, 1939; W.P. Ker Lecturer, University of Glasgow, 1953. Artist: one-man show, Oxford, 1977. Recipient: New York *Herald Tribune* Festival award, 1938; International Fantasy Award, 1957. D.Litt.: University College, Dublin, 1954; University of Nottingham, 1970; Dr. en Phil. et Lettres: Liège, 1954. Fellow, Royal Society of Literature, 1957: awarded Benson Medal, 1966. C.B.E (Commander, Order of the British Empire), 1972. *Died 2 September 1973.*

PUBLICATIONS FOR CHILDREN

Fiction

> *The Hobbit; or, There and Back Again.* London, Allen and Unwin, 1937; Boston, Houghton Mifflin, 1938.
> *Farmer Giles of Ham.* London, Allen and Unwin, 1949; Boston, Houghton Mifflin, 1950.
> *Smith of Wootton Major.* London, Allen and Unwin, and Boston, Houghton Mifflin, 1967.

The Father Christmas Letters, edited by Baillie Tolkien, illustrated by the
author.   London, Allen and Unwin, and Boston, Houghton Mifflin, 1976.

Verse

The Adventures of Tom Bombadil and Other Verses from the Red Book, illustrated by
Pauline Baynes.   London, Allen and Unwin, 1962; Boston, Houghton Mifflin, 1963.
Bilbo's Last Song, illustrated by Pauline Baynes.   London, Allen and Unwin, and
Boston, Houghton Mifflin, 1974.

PUBLICATIONS FOR ADULTS

Novels

The Lord of the Rings:
  The Fellowship of the Ring.   London, Allen and Unwin, and Boston, Houghton
    Mifflin, 1954; revised edition, Allen and Unwin, 1966, Houghton Mifflin, 1967.
  The Two Towers.   London, Allen and Unwin, and Boston, Houghton Mifflin, 1955;
    revised edition, Allen and Unwin, 1966, Houghton Mifflin, 1967.
  The Return of the King.   London, Allen and Unwin, and Boston, Houghton Mifflin,
    1956; revised edition, Allen and Unwin, 1966, Houghton Mifflin, 1967.
The Silmarillion.   London, Allen and Unwin, and Boston, Houghton Mifflin, 1977.

Verse

Songs for the Philologists, with others.   London, privately printed, 1936.
The Road Goes Ever On, music by Donald Swann.   Boston, Houghton Mifflin, 1967;
London, Allen and Unwin, 1968.

Other

A Middle English Vocabulary.   London and New York, Oxford University Press, 1922.
Beowulf: The Monsters and the Critics.   London, Oxford University Press, 1937;
Folcroft, Pennsylvania, Folcroft Editions, 1972.
Tree and Leaf (includes short story and essay).   London, Allen and Unwin, 1964;
Boston, Houghton Mifflin, 1965.
The Tolkien Reader.   New York, Ballantine, 1966.
*Tree and Leaf, Smith of Wootton Major, The Homecoming of Beorhtnoth Beorhthelm's
Son.*   London, Allen and Unwin, 1975.

Editor, with E.V. Gordon, *Sir Gawain and the Green Knight*.   London and New York,
Oxford University Press, 1925.
Editor, *Ancrene Wisse*.   London, Oxford University Press, 1962; New York, Oxford
University Press, 1963.

Translator, *Sir Gawain and the Green Knight, Pearl, and Sir Orfeo*, edited by Christopher
Tolkien.   London, Allen and Unwin, and Boston, Houghton Mifflin, 1975.

Manuscript Collection: Wade Collection, Wheaton College, Illinois.

Critical Studies: *Tolkien and the Critics* edited by N.D. Isaacs and R.A. Zimbardo, Notre
Dame, Indiana, University of Notre Dame Press, 1968; *Master of Middle-Earth: The Fiction
of J.R.R. Tolkien* by Paul Kocher, Boston, Houghton Mifflin, 1972; *Tolkien's World* by
Randel Helms, London, Thames and Hudson, and Boston, Houghton Mifflin, 1974; *The
Tolkien Companion* by J.E.A. Tyler, London, Macmillan, 1975, New York, St. Martin's

Press, 1976; *J.R.R. Tolkien: A Biography* (includes bibliography) by Humphrey Carpenter, London, Allen and Unwin, 1977.

*   *   *

The fantasy world of J.R.R. Tolkien, scholar and professor of mediaeval literature, had its base in stories he told to himself during his adolescence, which he elaborated during the First World War into the saga of *The Silmarillion*, the love-story of a beautiful Elf-woman and a mortal man. The story gave substance to a language he had invented − Elvish − and was probably inspired by his own love-affair with his future wife. *The Silmarillion* remained unpublished until 1977, but other stories about his imaginary world of Middle-earth became world-famous. Although Tolkien's Middle-earth is based on our world, a new geography of mountain-ranges and coast-lines has been superimposed. In this essay I will deal with the Middle-earth fantasies *The Hobbit* and *The Lord of the Rings* (a work, probably, for adults, but one which is certainly enjoyed by many children) and the minor children's stories *Farmer Giles of Ham, Smith of Wootton Major*, "Leaf by Niggle," and *The Father Christmas Letters*.

In the traditional English way his first published story came about as a family tale told to his children in the 1930's. The word "hobbit" swam into his head, and soon he had invented the genus of hole-dwelling manikins, 3−4 feet high, domesticated yet tough, idealised versions of the Olde English countryman. Published in 1937, *The Hobbit* was an extraordinary book for its time. The mood of children's books was realistic and anti-magical; critics and teachers demanded books about working-class urban life and thought magic was babyish. The fact that attitudes have changed so much in 30 years is due in no small measure to Tolkien. His readers, enjoying his books so much, had to justify themselves, and inspired by his own essay "On Fairy-Stories" found good reasons for reading fairy-tales in anthropological theories of human development. The human psyche, according to Jung, needed the emotional nourishment of tales of Quest, Victory of the Youngest Son, Defeat of the Dragon, if it was ever to mature. Primitive tribes knew this instinctively − modern man needed to relearn it.

The Hobbit is a comic and tragic tale, rich in magical adventure. Characters like the cantankerous old wizard Gandalf, the dragon Smaug, evil Gollum, and the 13 dwarves are all famous now. Bilbo, the Hobbit, undergoes great trials to discover courage and maturity. Although the climax is a terrible battle the moral crux of the book comes earlier. Thorin, the chief dwarf, owes his treasure to the hero who slew the dragon, but refuses to give him any reward, although he and his fellow Lake-men are made homeless when the dragon dies. Thorin fails the test, but Bilbo redeems him by giving the men an ancestral treasure of the dwarves to help their bargaining. One can only marvel at the imagination which created the sequence of exciting adventures in which elements from Norse and Teutonic myth have been blended − trolls, elves, giant spiders, a were-bear, dragon, wild wolves and goblins all appear.

A sequel to *The Hobbit* was demanded, and for years Tolkien laboured to fit this story into the framework of Middle-earth history he had begun with *The Silmarillion*. To continue the story of the magic ring of invisibility which Bilbo "stole" from Gollum, Tolkien would have to start thousands of years after *The Silmarillion* takes place. The main characters would still be elves and men, and they would fight Sauron, servant of Morgoth who stole the silmarils of the earlier book. But he now had his hobbits as well, as comic commentary on the epic situation, and so his theme could be, as with *The Hobbit*, the triumph of weak over strong.

The Lord of the Rings tells how Frodo, Bilbo's nephew, inherits Bilbo's magic invisible ring, and with it a great burden. The ring can make its owner Ruler of the World (as in Wagner's Ring Cycle) and so it must be destroyed before Sauron, Lord of the Rings, who made it, can find it again. Frodo has to make the long and desperately dangerous journey to Sauron's country, Mordor, to throw the Ring into the Cracks of Doom.

Once more we marvel at the author's imagination, as the narrative is sustained through three long volumes. New adventures, heroes, and horrors meet us in every chapter. After volume 1 the fellowship of the Ring divides and we follow the fortunes of three separate groups. We encounter terrors like the Mines of Moria, Shelob the Spider, and the invisible Black Riders; beauty in Goldberry the River's daughter, Lórien the hidden forest; and fight the battles of Helm's Deep and the Pelennor Fields.

With a book so strong in plot, other elements must be weaker. There is no subtle characterisation: just good and evil, white and black. Moral choices are easily perceived, though not so easily made for all that: Boromir, for instance, makes the wrong choice, though basically a good man, and both Gollum and Saruman have a chance to repent. One cannot criticise Tolkien, however, for keeping to the laws of his genre and failing to give us the complex character-analysis of the 20th-century novel. In a prose epic modelled on fairy-tale many characters are unrounded because they are essentially archetypal. And so we have Aragorn and Hero, Arwen the Princess, Éowyn the Amazon, Galadriel the Enchantress, and Gandalf the Wizard.

In an epic where good must eventually triumph, fate and luck often work on the side of Good, and Tolkien occasionally hints that a Power is influencing events, though the characters still have the free will to take or reject these opportunities. So coincidence is frequently used: rescues happen in the nick of time, people meet by chance – yet those in tune with higher powers, such as Gandalf and Tom Bombadil, question whether chance is really the right word, if a Higher Power is at work.

Tolkien's epic style is often a stumbling-block to his critics. *The Lord of the Rings* is far from completely epic in diction, and the hobbits' conversation and jokes are informal enough, but when Heroes talk with Elves and Wizards, an antique style is used in which the language derives from Old English. "Verily," said Gandalf, " ... that way lies our hope, where sits our greatest fear. Doom hangs still on a thread." The society of the horse-riders of Rohan is deliberately modelled on Anglo-Saxon culture, and their poetry, which Tolkien quotes, paraphrases Old English verse. However, while some critics complain of hackneyed clichés, others welcome the historical insight the style affords, especially teachers who have found Tolkien a great inspiration to students to return to the original sagas and epics. Certainly where children are concerned, *The Lord of the Rings* is a book which opens the door to adult literature. (It can be read by good readers from the age of 8 upwards.)

Tolkien's minor works also became best-sellers. There was *Farmer Giles of Ham*, about a dragon less successful than Smaug, which also gave the supposed origins of the Oxfordshire villages of Thame and Worminghall. Two shorter stories, *Smith of Wootton Major* and "Leaf by Niggle," are really parables about Tolkien at the end of his career, the former about giving up trips to fairyland and the latter about facing death with his work unfinished. For *The Silmarillion*, the first child of his imagination, was still unpublished, pestering from fans continually interrupted him, and since *The Lord of the Rings* was published there had been many inconsistencies to correct.

The first fictional work to be published since his death was *The Father Christmas Letters* written yearly to his children in the guise of Father Christmas. Illustrated by the author, they are destined to become a children's classic. Father Christmas is helped, and hindered, by accident-prone Polar Bear, a new kind of comic character for Tolkien.

Critics have argued since Edmund Wilson's criticism in 1956 about whether *The Lord of the Rings* is a great book. W.H. Auden sprang to the defence in 1968, and Nicholas Tucker in 1976. Most critics now are favourable, though Manlove is an exception who believes that Tolkien's world is not credible. To many, however, the real world is less credible than Middle-earth, such is the power of Tolkien's imagination. Perhaps that is what his detractors hate: his book has the power to induce obsessional re-reading and a compulsion to acquire every book and article that he wrote. Such is not a bad achievement for one who never set out to be a professional children's book writer. Sir Stanley Unwin says in *The Truth about a Publisher*, 1960, that *The Lord of the Rings* is "a book for all time, which will be selling long after my departure from this world ... a great work." The Tolkien cult has passed its phase of intense growth and publicity to be revived among small groups of readers whenever they discover a common interest in Tolkien's world. As a classic of world literature it will bear out Stanley Unwin's prophecy and be read for years to come.

—Jessica Kemball-Cook

TOMALIN, Ruth. British. Born in Piltown, County Kilkenny, Ireland. Educated at Chichester High School, Sussex; King's College, University of London, Diploma of Journalism 1939. Served in the Women's Land Army, 1941–42. Married Vernon Leaver in 1942 (divorced), one son; William N. Ross, 1971. Reporter for newspapers in Hampshire, Sussex, Dorset, and Hertfordshire, 1942–61. Since 1961, part-time Press Reporter, London Magistrates' Courts and Crown Courts. Address: c/o Barclays Bank, 15 Langham Place, London W.1, England.

PUBLICATIONS FOR CHILDREN

Fiction

> *Green Ink* (as Ruth Leaver). London, Harrap, 1951.
> *The Sound of Pens* (as Ruth Leaver), illustrated by Betty Ladler. London, Blackie, 1955.
> *The Daffodil Bird*, illustrated by Brian Wildsmith. London, Faber, 1959; New York, A.S. Barnes, 1960.
> *The Sea Mice*, illustrated by Sheila Rose. London, Faber, 1962.
> *A Green Wishbone*, illustrated by Gavin Rowe. London, Faber, 1975.
> *A Stranger Thing*, illustrated by Robin Jacques. London, Faber, 1975.
> *The Snake Crook*, illustrated by Shirley Hughes. London, Faber, 1976.

PUBLICATIONS FOR ADULTS

Novels

> *All Souls.* London, Faber, 1952.
> *The Garden House.* London, Faber, 1964.
> *The Spring House.* London, Faber, 1968.
> *Away to the West.* London, Faber, 1972.

Verse

> *Threnody for Dormice.* London, Fortune Press, 1947.
> *Deer's Cry.* London, Fortune Press, 1952.

Other

> *The Day of the Rose: Essays and Portraits.* London, Fortune Press, 1947.
> *W.H. Hudson* (biography). London, Witherby, and New York, Philosophical Library, 1954.

> Editor, *Best Country Stories.* London, Faber, 1969.

Ruth Tomalin comments:

Most of my stories are about people and things of the English countryside. All are set in places well known to me at different times, ranging from a copse full of wild life (*The Daffodil Bird*) to Broadcasting House, London (*The Sea Mice*); and from a glass "watch-house" in a nature preserve (*A Stranger Thing*) to a reporters' room on a provincial evening paper (*Green Ink*).

*   *   *

Ruth Tomalin's work falls into two distinct categories. There are several short novels for children of 9 to 10, the best of which is *A Stranger Thing*. There is also a group of novels concerned with the childhood and youth of Ralph Oliver and latterly his young cousin Rowan – *The Garden House, The Spring House*, and *Away to the West*: these are longer and far more exacting works, so difficult to classify that in the judgement of some critics they are adult novels and cannot be regarded as children's books at all.

Certainly the Ralph Oliver novels are far beyond the comprehension of the small children who will enjoy *The Sea Mice, The Daffodil Bird*, or *A Stranger Thing. The Garden House*, with its subtle vision of early childhood, is thematically recondite for adolescent readers and best regarded as an adult novel. But *The Spring House* and *Away to the West* are admirable stories for the right teenage reader, though their appeal is highly specialised. Unless readers share Ruth Tomalin's intimate knowledge and love of wild life, her care for the English countryside, and her concern for the impact of humanity on landscape and fauna alike, the novels cannot be understood at their deepest imaginative level. But for those who do share these affections and concerns, they have much to offer. They are also, after all, about young people growing up – the problems of choosing a career, of coping with uncomprehending parents, of living through the anguish of first love. These are important themes in the novels, treated with sympathy, tact, and humour, and with acute, uncondescending insight.

The stories for young readers are also concerned with wild life, but they are much wider in their potential appeal. Plots are usually simple. At their centre is the relationship between children and animals, and the hidden world of childhood where such relationships are strangely private and reclusive. The bond between small boy and small mouse has never been better observed than in *The Sea Mice* and *A Stranger Thing*.

Young children respond keenly to Ruth Tomalin's exceptional understanding of their lonely and secretive adventures. Her shorter tales have their own distinctive tension and enchantment, rooted for instance in the onset and healing of childhood perplexity and fear. They are touched with the magic of secret places and fugitive children, but it is a magic emanating from a real and intimately rendered world. Like the Ralph Oliver novels, they are the product of a richly sensitive imagination and an infectious zest for the sheer diversity of life.

—Peter Hollindale

TOWNSEND, John Rowe. British. Born in Leeds, Yorkshire, 10 May 1922. Educated at Leeds Grammar School, 1933–40; Emmanuel College, Cambridge, 1947–49, B.A. 1949, M.A. 1954. Served in the Royal Air Force, 1942–46: Flight Sergeant. Married Vera Lancaster in 1948 (died, 1973); has two daughters and one son. Reporter, *Yorkshire Post*, Leeds, 1946, and *Evening Standard*, London, 1949; Sub-Editor, 1949–53, and Art Editor, 1953–55, Manchester *Guardian*, and Editor, *Guardian Weekly*, 1955–69. Since 1969, part-time Children's Books Editor, *Guardian*, Manchester and London. Visiting Lecturer, University of Pennsylvania, Philadelphia, 1965, and University of Washington, Seattle, 1969, 1971; May Hill Arbuthnot Lecturer, Atlanta, 1971; Anne Carroll Moore Lecturer, New York Public Library, 1971; Gertrude Clarke Whittall Lecturer, Library of Congress, Washington, D.C., 1976. Recipient: *Boston Globe-Horn Book* Award, 1970; English P.E.N. Award, 1970; Mystery Writers of America Edgar Allan Poe Award, 1971. Address: 19 Eltisley Avenue, Newnham, Cambridge CB3 9JG, England.

PUBLICATIONS FOR CHILDREN

Fiction

Gumble's Yard, illustrated by Dick Hart. London, Hutchinson, 1961; as *Trouble in the Jungle*, Philadelphia, Lippincott, 1969.

Hell's Edge. London, Hutchinson, 1963; New York, Lothrop, 1969.

Widdershins Crescent. London, Hutchinson, 1965; as *Good-bye to the Jungle,* Philadelphia, Lippincott, 1967.

The Hallersage Sound. London, Hutchinson, 1966.

Pirate's Island, illustrated by Douglas Hall. London, Oxford University Press, and Philadelphia, Lippincott, 1968.

The Intruder, illustrated by Graham Humphreys. London, Oxford University Press, 1969; Philadelphia, Lippincott, 1970.

Goodnight, Prof, Love, illustrated by Peter Farmer. London, Oxford University Press, 1970; as *Goodnight, Prof, Dear,* Philadelphia, Lippincott, 1971.

The Summer People, illustrated by Robert Micklewright. London, Oxford University Press, and Philadelphia, Lippincott, 1972.

A Wish for Wings, illustrated by Philip Gough. London, Heinemann, 1972.

Forest of the Night. London, Oxford University Press, 1974; Philadelphia, Lippincott, 1975.

Noah's Castle. London, Oxford University Press, 1975; Philadelphia, Lippincott, 1976.

Top of the World, illustrated by Nikki Jones. London, Oxford University Press, 1976; Philadelphia, Lippincott, 1977.

The Xanadu Manuscript. London, Oxford University Press, 1977; as *The Visitors,* Philadelphia, Lippincott, 1977.

Other

Editor, *Modern Poetry: A Selection.* London, Oxford University Press, 1971; Philadelphia, Lippincott, 1974.

PUBLICATIONS FOR ADULTS

Other

Written for Children: An Outline of English Children's Literature. London, J. Garnet Miller, 1965; New York, Lothrop, 1967; revised edition, London, Penguin, and Philadelphia, Lippincott, 1974.

A Sense of Story: Essays on Contemporary Writers for Children. London, Penguin, and Philadelphia, Lippincott, 1971.

John Rowe Townsend comments:

I wear two hats in connection with children's books: as a writer of them and as a writer about them.

In the former capacity I began my career in the early 1960's with a sense that books dealing with the rougher side of real life, and with the problems and joys of growing up in contemporary society, were far too scarce in Britain. Hence *Gumble's Yard, Hell's Edge,* and *Widdershins Crescent.* Later, the feeling that these gaps were now being adequately filled, together with the continual urge to do something different, led me to broaden my fictional scope. I might try anything now.

Under my other hat I have for some years reviewed and review-edited children's books for the *Guardian.* I have also produced an historical survey of children's literature (*Written for Children*) and a set of essays on contemporary children's writers (*A Sense of Story*). I tend to discuss children's books as literature rather than as influences in social, educational, or psychological development – but I hasten to add that literary criticism does not have to be narrowly aesthetic; it can and should take account of many aspects of a book. One thing I am certain of is that a good book for children must be a good book, period.

*   *   *

John Rowe Townsend's first children's book was written out of a horrified realisation of the gap between the lives of real children – he had been covering, as a journalist, the activities of the N.S.P.C.C. in Manchester, – and the subject-matter and style of the children's books that came to him for review. *Gumble's Yard* deals with what happens to Kevin and Sandra when their inadequate parents both desert the family home at the same time. The children go into hiding in a derelict warehouse by the canal, and cross the paths of others, dangerous characters who are also using the place to hide. There followed *Widdershins Crescent*, an exploration of the fortunes of the same family rehoused, but not much changed, and *Pirate's Island*, with a landscape and some characters in common with the earlier two books. In *Hell's Edge*, the author moves on to explore differences of viewpoint brought about by differences of class – his heroine is a university teacher's daughter, his hero wants to be a motor mechanic – and of region – the impact of northern on southern people.

Townsend's early work deserves credit for originality of subject; with the sole exception of Eve Garnett's *Family from One End Street*, published in 1937, he was the first considerable writer on the children's list to deal with working-class life. Unlike Eve Garnett he sees it from the inside, with profound sympathy, and sees it as normal, rather than a form of local exotic. These early books are shaped by the author's evident belief that children need drama-packed, thrilling "plots" and these he lavishly provides, not always with great subtlety or credibility. His admirable talent for characterisation and powerful evocation of the northern landscape pull him the other way, so that his people seem to exist in a world more concrete and vivid than anything that happens to them.

With *The Intruder*, Mr. Townsend achieved a synthesis. The plot, still full of tension and swiftly paced, concerns the arrival in a remote coastal village of a sinister stranger with a bullying manner, who insists that he is the rightful bearer of the hero's name. The outward events of the story are in full harmony with the inner life of the character, and the work has immense symbolic force. Elements of the earlier books – intense awareness of landscapes, consciousness of social class dividing people from one another – are here used with mastery to illuminate the central concern of the book – who is Arnold?

Now fully confident as a writer, Mr. Townsend moved next to the difficult, and at that time unexplored territory of adolescent love, the subject of both *Goodnight, Prof, Love* and *The Summer People*. *Goodnight, Prof, Love* charts the doomed relationship of Graham, brainy, overprotected middle class boy, and Lynn, vulgar, warm, and no better than she should be. Technically Mr. Townsend was experimenting; the book is focussed sharply on the two protagonists, and stripped bare of inessentials to the point of austerity, managing for long passages with nothing but dialogue. By contrast *The Summer People* surrounds the two young people in love with busy scenes – friends, family, and setting in place and time – a seaside holiday overshadowed by the approach of war. In both books the apparatus of plot has largely been discarded, and the characters *are* the story. In both books a view of young love emerges that is both realistic (it is unlikely to last) and deeply understanding (it is of profound value, all the same).

With *Forest of the Night* Mr. Townsend abandoned the matrix of realism that he had worked in so long, and embarked upon fantasy. We are still in distinctively Townsend country, roaming a terrifying urban landscape by night, and still on a quest for identity, though this time it is also a flight from knowledge, and from an image of Blake's tyger. The long movements of pure dialogue used realistically in *Goodnight, Prof, Love* appear again, though here the exchanges are between inner voices. Perhaps because of the disturbing power of the theme – a symbolic exploration of sexuality – to trouble adult equanimity, this strange, compelling, and brilliant book had a baffled reception, and for the moment Mr. Townsend has not followed it up.

With *Noah's Castle*, he returned to the realistic mode. *Noah's Castle* is a moral drama. In some not very distant future England's currency has collapsed and people are starving. Barry's father has stocked the house with food and barricaded it against the world. His children are torn between loyalty to family and to society. Fascinating in its exploration of the situation, this is nevertheless a bleak book. By contrast, *The Xanadu Manuscript*, which followed next, is sparkling and summery. These recent books show Mr. Townsend at the height of his powers. They are technically accomplished, and highly accessible. The elaborate plots of his earlier work have developed into a subtle narrative gift, an enviable power to grip and intrigue the reader. He continues to create vivid and totally believable people; he has a rare talent for describing strongly individual characters who are ordinary people, not distorted, patronised, or exaggerated for the sake of effect, but simply life-sized. With quiet insistence Mr. Townsend's work offers a deeply humane view of life in which the ordinary lives of everyday people are of the profoundest interest and concern.

—Jill Paton Walsh

———————————

TRAVERS, P(amela) L(yndon). British. Born in Queensland, Australia, in 1906. Educated privately. Journalist, actress, and dancer, in the 1920's; regular contributor to the *Irish Statesman*, Dublin, in 1920's and 1930's; worked for the British Ministry of Information in the United States during World War II. Writer-in-Residence, Radcliffe College, Cambridge, Massachusetts, 1965–66; Smith College, Northampton, Massachusetts, 1966–67; Scripps College, Claremont, California, 1970. O.B.E. (Officer, Order of the British Empire), 1977. Agent: David Higham Associates Ltd., 5–8 Lower John Street, London W1R 4HA. Address: c/o William Collins Sons Ltd., 14 St. James's Place, London SW1A 1P5, England.

PUBLICATIONS FOR CHILDREN

Fiction

Mary Poppins, illustrated by Mary Shepard.   London, Howe, and New York, Reynal and Hitchcock, 1934.

Mary Poppins Comes Back, illustrated by Mary Shepard.   London, Dickson and Thompson, and New York, Reynal and Hitchcock, 1935.

Happy Ever After, illustrated by Mary Shepard.   New York, Reynal and Hitchcock, 1940.

I Go by Sea, I Go by Land, illustrated by Gertrude Hermes.   London, Davies, and New York, Harper, 1941.

Mary Poppins Opens the Door, illustrated by Mary Shepard and Agnes Sims.   New York, Reynal and Hitchcock, 1943; London, Davies, 1944.

Mary Poppins in the Park, illustrated by Mary Shepard.   London, Davies, and New York, Harcourt Brace, 1952.

The Fox at the Manger, illustrated by Thomas Bewick.   New York, Norton, 1962; London, Collins, 1963.

Mary Poppins from A to Z, illustrated by Mary Shepard.   New York, Harcourt Brace, 1962; London, Collins, 1963.

Friend Monkey.   New York, Harcourt Brace, 1971; London, Collins, 1972.

Other

About Sleeping Beauty, illustrated by Charles Keeping.   New York, McGraw Hill, 1975; London, Collins, 1977.

Mary Poppins in the Kitchen: A Cookery Book with a Story, with Maurice Moore-Betty, illustrated by Mary Shepard.   New York, Harcourt Brace, 1975; London, Collins, 1976.

PUBLICATIONS FOR ADULTS

Other

> *Moscow Excursion.* London, Dickson and Thompson, and New York, Reynal and Hitchcock, 1935.
> *Aunt Sass.* New York, privately printed, 1941.
> *Ah Wong.* New York, privately printed, 1943.
> *In Search of the Hero: The Continuing Relevance of Myth and Fairy Tale* (lecture). Claremont, California, Scripps College, 1970.

*   *   *

Before Mary Poppins – that most intriguing of English nannies – blew into children's fiction on an east wind in 1934 her author's reputation as a poet and dramatic critic had already been established. P.L. Travers' ability to combine poetic insight with a feeling for dramatic situation brought a balance and an inner intensity to her stories.

Mary Poppins is a many-faceted character. Superficially she seems the prim, archetypal nannie, reading "Everything a Lady Should Know" and exuding a competent aura of boot polish and Sunlight Soap. She crackles, however, not only with starch but with an elemental and challenging magic: the startlingly blue eyes of her Dutch Doll face can see "over the rim of the world" as well as into the minds of her charges. The children of the Banks family find that in Mary's company their fantasy exploits often find exciting expression. Magical adventures might arise at any moment from commonplace circumstances. For instance, Mary Poppins can casually pick up a plum painted on the pavement by a street artist and take a bite from it. P.L. Travers firmly believes that in children's stories an ordinary environment is an essential background for magic. "To climb or to fly you need a solid basis from which to take off; otherwise everything becomes too fey."

Certainly there is nothing sentimental or amorphous about Mary Poppins. She can be imaginative or sternly practical as occasion demands. Her actions often have a catalytic effect. The magic which she brings into the lives of the Banks children sharpens their understanding of themselves and reality: it is exuberant but not escapist. Unlike many other fictional immortals Mary never makes "happily ever after" promises. She implies that the only security is an ability to accept constant change; the temporary nature of her own presence in the Banks household is stressed by the fact of her sleeping on a camp bed. Her ever present parrot-headed umbrella and capacious carpet bag too are reminders that she is always ready to travel at a moment's notice.

The original *Mary Poppins* in 1934 was quickly followed by *Mary Poppins Comes Back. Mary Poppins Opens the Door* was intended as the last of the series. In its final pages Mary leaves the Banks family for ever, although "the gifts she had brought would remain .... " However in response to readers' demands a further volume *Mary Poppins in the Park* was produced in 1952, but its action takes place during the visits of Mary Poppins that were chronicled in the 3 previous books. This is true too of *Mary Poppins in the Kitchen*, published as recently as 1975. Mary becomes temporary cook for the Banks family and teaches the children to prepare attractive meals. The book consists of a story and some recipes for each day of the week.

The series was written over several years – but always firmly set against a background of nursery cosiness common to many English homes in the 1930's. (In the Walt Disney film there was a transposition to the Edwardian period but a similar atmosphere was conveyed.) Yet there is about the Mary Poppins stories something of the timeless appeal of the classic fairy tales.

There are no magical overtones in *I Go by Sea, I Go by Land*. This account of two English children's wartime evacuation to the U.S.A. catches the atmosphere of the period – a grim acceptance of the "backs to the wall" situation coupled with a dogged optimism. For Sabrina and James there are also the excitement and apprehension of the U-boat-menaced sea trip to

America, and a new life far away from home and parents. Their responses to change and challenge make lively reading. The wonders of the World's Fair and the Statue of Liberty possibly impress them less than the sophistication of American children – like their hostess's daughter who has permanently waved hair; or the satisfaction of having constant supplies of Coca-Cola, sweet corn and out-of-season strawberries: "You can't wonder that the Americans are proud of their country." But underlying all the new discoveries and fulfilments is the fear about what might be happening to their parents left behind in England, exposed to the Blitz and the threat of invasion. P.L. Travers does not gloss over the severely disrupting effect on many young people of this wartime break-up of family life; but, as in the Mary Poppins books, her fictional children are nudged by circumstances into an acceptance of their responsibilities and an ability to cope with difficulties.

In *The Fox at the Manger* and *Friend Monkey* P.L. Travers brings together her interest in mythology and religion and her appreciation of nature. In her stories animals are more likely to be wild than domestic, as she considers that the latter have often been debased and made sycophantic by man. It is characteristic of her unsentimental attitude towards animals that the fox who joins the domesticated animals at the manger should give the Christ-child the rather surprising gift of his cunning – and that the child appreciates this above all the other gifts which are showered upon him.

In *Friend Monkey* the animal hero is equally robust. He is based upon Hanuman, the monkey lord of Hindu mythology, and his engaging efforts to help the human family who have adopted him usually result in chaos. Like most of P.L. Travers' stories this book implies that life cannot be tied up into neat packages. Monkey gives his friends no resting place, no panaceas. He opens their eyes frequently to deeper and more challenging aspects of life.

About Sleeping Beauty is a re-telling of a traditional story. This suggests that fairyland "intersects our mortal world at every point and at every second. The two of them together make one web woven fine." The literal and symbolic immortality of Mary Poppins – P.L. Travers' most famous character – underlines the truth of this.

—Mary Cadogan

TREADGOLD, Mary. British. Born in London, 16 April 1910. Educated at Ginner-Mawer School of Dance and Drama, 1916–22; Challoner School, London, 1921–23; St. Paul's Girls' School, London, 1923–28; Bedford College, University of London, 1930–36, M.A. (honours) in English. Children's Editor, William Heinemann Ltd., London, 1938–40; Producer and Literary Editor, BBC, London, 1940–60. Recipient: Library Association Carnegie Medal, 1942. Address: 61 Swan Court, London S.W.3, England.

PUBLICATIONS FOR CHILDREN

Fiction

> *We Couldn't Leave Dinah*, illustrated by Stuart Tresilian.   London, Cape, 1941; as *Left till Called For*, New York, Doubleday, 1941.
> *No Ponies*, illustrated by Ruth Gervis.   London, Cape, 1946.
> *The "Polly Harris."*   London, Cape, 1949; as *The Mystery of the "Polly Harris,"* New York, Doubleday, 1951; revised edition, London, Hamish Hamilton, 1968; New York, Nelson, 1970.
> *The Heron Ride*, illustrated by Victor Ambrus.   London, Cape, 1962.
> *The Winter Princess*, illustrated by Pearl Falconer.   Leicester, Brockhampton Press, 1962; Princeton, New Jersey, Van Nostrand, 1964.

Return to the Heron, illustrated by Victor Ambrus. London, Cape, 1963.

The Weather Boy, illustrated by Robert Geary. Leicester, Brockhampton Press, 1964; Princeton, New Jersey, Van Nostrand, 1965.

Maids' Ribbons, illustrated by Susannah Holden. London, Nelson, 1965; New York, Nelson, 1967.

Elegant Patty, illustrated by Lynette Hemmant. London, Hamish Hamilton, 1967.

Poor Patty, illustrated by Lynette Hemmant. London, Hamish Hamilton, 1968.

This Summer, Last Summer, illustrated by Mary Russon. London, Hamish Hamilton, 1968.

The Humbugs, illustrated by Faith Jaques. London, Hamish Hamilton, 1968.

The Rum Day of the Vanishing Pony. Leicester, Brockhampton Press, 1970.

PUBLICATIONS FOR ADULTS

Novel

The Running Child. London, Cape, 1951.

Mary Treadgold comments:

I regard myself as a good example of the "hobby-writer" – writing is something I've enjoyed doing, never taken over-seriously. I am delighted when people take me seriously and when anyone tells me he or she has enjoyed what I've written!

*   *   *

Mary Treadgold's first novel, *We Couldn't Leave Dinah*, won the Carnegie Medal for 1941, which lifts her well above the run of pony-adventure story writers. In fact, she is a novelist of very considerable power and while both ponies and adventure have continued to feature prominently in her books they have never come near to monopolising it or blurring a shrewd eye for character and relationships.

Both *We Couldn't Leave Dinah* and its successor, *No Ponies*, are essentially war stories. In the first, which deals with the Nazi invasion of a mythical Channel island, Clerinel, Mick and Caroline Templeton are confronted with adult problems of collaboration and divided loyalties, as well as the more ordinary excitements of a spy story. The second opens just after the war when the London-bred Atherleys travel to their aunt's lovely pre-war home in the south of France, their happiness at being Abroad only marred by the thought of the ponies and the riding that awaits them when their athletic cousins arrive. But when they reach Beaubassin, the ponies are not there and the subsequent adventure proves to the children that wars are not always over with the fighting, but that the damage to people's minds may be harder to cure.

Compared with more recent books about the war, they still stand up extremely well. Some things have dated – child-adult relationships seem oddly formal, the triplets are said to be 14 but could be 12 – yet in other ways there is a greater maturity than we have grown used to, a kind of objectivity, perfectly convincing, which makes these children seem older.

The same lack of self-centredness is felt in *The "Polly Harris"* which finds the reluctant Templetons enrolled at a London crammer's. The sensitive Caroline is both aware and highly critical of her own childishness. The plot here is in some ways much ahead of its time, with terrorists as well as smugglers (but no ponies), while running through the book at a deeper level is the idea of loneliness, one of Mary Treadgold's haunting themes. It recurs in a more overt form in the later, and less successful, *The Heron Ride* and *Return to the Heron*, but it is in *The "Polly Harris"* that it finds its clearest expression:

For the first time [Caroline] was appalled to her soul at the way people could fail other people – could misunderstand their very nature, wound the delicate structure of their human spirit, and then send them back about their ways, uncomforted and quite alone .... To her now came the knowledge that people could also misunderstand her as she had misunderstood David — could fail her, wound her and even destroy her. Not yet — there was no one yet to do it, but she knew that she had a long life before her. As she reached the lower landing, the burden of her long life lay on her, heavy as frost.

—Anne Carter

TREASE, (Robert) Geoffrey. British. Born in Nottingham, 11 August 1909. Educated at Nottingham High School, 1920–28; Queen's College, Oxford (Scholar), 1928–29. Served in the British Army, 1942–46. Married Marian Boyer in 1933; has one daughter. Social worker and journalist, London, 1929–32; teacher, Clacton-on-Sea, Essex, 1933. Since 1933, Freelance Writer. Chairman, British Children's Writers Group, 1962–63. Chairman, 1972–73, and since 1974, Member of the Council, Society of Authors. Recipient: New York *Herald Tribune* Festival award, for non-fiction, 1966. Address: The Croft, Colwall, Malvern, Worcestershire WR13 6EZ, England.

PUBLICATIONS FOR CHILDREN

Fiction

> *Bows Against the Barons*, illustrated by Michael Boland. London, Lawrence, 1934; revised edition, Leicester, Brockhampton Press, and New York, Meredith Press, 1966.
> *Comrades for the Charter*, illustrated by Michael Boland. London, Lawrence, 1934.
> *Call to Arms*. London, Lawrence, 1935.
> *Red Comet*, illustrated by Fred Ellis. Moscow, Co-operative Publishing Society of Foreign Workers, 1936; London, Lawrence and Wishart, 1937.
> *Missing from Home*, illustrated by Scott. London, Lawrence and Wishart, 1937.
> *The Christmas Holiday Mystery*, illustrated by Alfred Sindall. London, A. and C. Black, 1937; as *The Lakeland Mystery*, 1942.
> *Mystery on the Moors*, illustrated by Alfred Sindall. London, A. and C. Black, 1937.
> *Detectives of the Dales*, illustrated by A.C.H. Gorham. London, A. and C. Black, 1938.
> *In the Land of the Mogul*, illustrated by J.C.B. Knight. Oxford, Blackwell, 1938.
> *North Sea Spy*. London, Fore Publications, 1939.
> *Cue for Treason*, illustrated by Beatrice Goldsmith. Oxford, Blackwell, 1940; New York, Vanguard Press, 1941.
> *Running Deer*, illustrated by W. Lindsay Cable. London, Harrap, 1941.
> *The Grey Adventurer*, illustrated by Beatrice Goldsmith. Oxford, Blackwell, 1942.
> *Black Night, Red Morning*, illustrated by Donia Nachsen. Oxford, Blackwell, 1944.
> *Army Without Banners*. London, Fore Publications, 1945.
> *Trumpets in the West*, illustrated by Alan Blyth. Oxford, Blackwell, and New York, Harcourt Brace, 1947.
> *Silver Guard*, illustrated by Alan Blyth. Oxford, Blackwell, 1948.
> *The Hills of Varna*, illustrated by Treyer Evans. London, Macmillan, 1948; as *Shadow of the Hawk*, New York, Harcourt Brace, 1949.
> *The Mystery of Moorside Farm*, illustrated by Alan Blyth. Oxford, Blackwell, 1949.
> *No Boats on Bannermere*, illustrated by Richard Kennedy. London, Heinemann, 1949; New York, Norton, 1965.

The Secret Fiord, illustrated by H.M. Brock.   London, Macmillan, 1949; New York, Harcourt Brace, 1950.

Under Black Banner, illustrated by Richard Kennedy.   London, Heinemann, 1950.

The Crown of Violet, illustrated by C. Walter Hodges.   London, Macmillan, 1952; as *Web of Traitors*, New York, Vanguard Press, 1952.

The Baron's Hostage, illustrated by Alan Jessett.   London, Phoenix House, 1952; revised edition, Leicester, Brockhampton Press, 1973; Nashville, Nelson, 1975.

Black Banner Players, illustrated by Richard Kennedy.   London, Heinemann, 1952.

The New House at Hardale.   London, Lutterworth Press, 1953.

The Silken Secret, illustrated by Alan Jessett.   Oxford, Blackwell, 1953; New York, Vanguard Press, 1954.

Black Banner Abroad.   London, Heinemann, 1954; New York, Warne, 1955.

The Fair Flower of Danger.   Oxford, Blackwell, 1955.

Word to Caesar, illustrated by Geoffrey Whittam.   London, Macmillan, 1956; as *Message to Hadrian*, New York, Vanguard Press, 1956.

The Gates of Bannerdale.   London, Heinemann, 1956; New York, Warne, 1957.

Mist over Athelney, illustrated by R.S. Sherriffs and J.L. Stockle.   London, Macmillan, 1958; as *Escape to King Alfred*, New York, Vanguard Press, 1958.

The Maythorn Story, illustrated by Robert Hodgson.   London, Heinemann, 1960.

Thunder of Valmy, illustrated by John S. Goodall.   London, Macmillan, 1960; as *Victory at Valmy*, New York, Vanguard Press, 1961.

Change at Maythorn, illustrated by Robert Hodgson.   London, Heinemann, 1962.

Follow My Black Plume, illustrated by Brian Wildsmith.   London, Macmillan, and New York, Vanguard Press, 1963.

A Thousand for Sicily, illustrated by Brian Wildsmith.   London, Macmillan, and New York, Vanguard Press, 1964.

The Dutch Are Coming, illustrated by Lynette Hemmant.   London, Hamish Hamilton, 1965.

Bent Is the Bow, illustrated by Charles Keeping.   London, Nelson, 1965; New York, Nelson, 1967.

The Red Towers of Granada, illustrated by Charles Keeping.   London, Macmillan, 1966; New York, Vanguard Press, 1967.

The White Nights of St. Petersburg, illustrated by William Stobbs.   London, Macmillan, and New York, Vanguard Press, 1967.

The Runaway Serf, illustrated by Mary Russon.   London, Hamish Hamilton, 1968.

A Masque for the Queen, illustrated by Krystyna Turska.   London, Hamish Hamilton, 1970.

Horsemen on the Hills.   London, Macmillan, 1971.

A Ship to Rome, illustrated by Leslie Atkinson.   London, Heinemann, 1972.

A Voice in the Night, illustrated by Sara Silcock.   London, Heinemann, 1973.

Popinjay Stairs.   London, Macmillan, 1973.

The Chocolate Boy, illustrated by David Walker.   London, Heinemann, 1975.

The Iron Tsar.   London, Macmillan, 1975.

When the Drums Beat, illustrated by Janet Marsh.   London, Macmillan, 1976.

Violet for Bonaparte.   London, Macmillan, 1976.

The Seas of Morning, illustrated by David Smee.   London, Penguin, 1976.

The Spy Catchers, illustrated by Geoffrey Bargery.   London, Hamish Hamilton, 1976.

The Field of the Forty Footsteps.   London, Macmillan, 1977.

The Claws of the Eagle, illustrated by Ionicus.   London, Heinemann, 1977.

Plays

The Dragon Who Was Different and Other Plays (includes *The Mighty Mandarin, Fairyland Limited, The New Bird*).   London, Muller, 1938.

The Shadow of Spain and Other Plays (includes *The Unquiet Cloister* and *Letters of Gold*).   Oxford, Blackwell, 1953.

Radio Play: *Popinjay Stairs*, from his own story, 1973.

Other

Fortune, My Foe: The Story of Sir Walter Raleigh, illustrated by Norman Meredith. London, Methuen, 1949; as *Sir Walter Raleigh, Captain and Adventurer*, New York, Vanguard Press, 1950.
The Young Traveller in India and Pakistan [England and Wales, Greece]. London, Phoenix House, 3 vols., 1949–56; New York, Dutton, 3 vols., 1953–56.
Enjoying Books. London, Phoenix House, 1951; revised edition, 1963.
The Seven Queens of England. London, Heinemann, and New York, Vanguard Press, 1953; revised edition, Heinemann, 1968.
Seven Kings of England, illustrated by Leslie Atkinson. London, Heinemann, and New York, Vanguard Press, 1955.
Edward Elgar, Maker of Music. London, Macmillan, 1959.
Wolfgang Mozart: The Young Composer. London, Macmillan, 1961; New York, St. Martin's Press, 1962.
The Young Writer: A Practical Handbook, illustrated by Carl Hollander. London, Nelson, 1961.
Seven Stages. London, Heinemann, 1964; New York, Vanguard Press, 1965.
This Is Your Century. London, Heinemann, and New York, Harcourt Brace, 1965.
Seven Sovereign Queens. London, Heinemann, 1968; New York, Vanguard Press, 1971.
Byron: A Poet Dangerous to Know. London, Macmillan, and New York, Holt Rinehart, 1969.
D.H. Lawrence: The Phoenix and the Flame. London, Macmillan, 1973; as *The Phoenix and the Flame: D.H. Lawrence, A Biography*, New York, Viking Press, 1973.
Days to Remember: A Garland of Historic Anniversaries, illustrated by Joanna Troughton. London, Heinemann, 1973.
Britain Yesterday, illustrated by Robert Hodgson. Oxford, Blackwell, 1975.

Editor, *Six of the Best: Stories.* Oxford, Blackwell, 1955.

Translator, *Companions of Fortune*, by René Guillot, illustrated by Pierre Collot. London, Oxford University Press, 1952.
Translator, *The King's Corsair*, by René Guillot, illustrated by Pierre Rousseau. London, Oxford University Press, 1954.

PUBLICATIONS FOR ADULTS

Novels

Such Divinity. London, Chapman and Hall, 1939.
Only Natural. London, Chapman and Hall, 1940.
Snared Nightingale. London, Macmillan, 1957; New York, Vanguard Press, 1958.
So Wild the Heart. London, Macmillan, and New York, Vanguard Press, 1959.

Short Stories

The Unsleeping Sword. London, Lawrence, 1934.

Plays

After the Tempest (produced Welwyn, Hertfordshire, 1938; London, 1939). Published in *Best One-Act Plays of 1938*, edited by J.W. Marriott, London, Harrap, 1939; published separately, Boston, Baker, n.d.

Colony (produced London, 1939).
Time Out of Mind (televised, 1956; produced London, 1967).

Radio Plays: *Mr. Engels of Manchester 'Change*, 1947; *Henry Irving*, 1947; *Lady Anne*, 1949; *The Real Mr. Ryecroft*, 1949; *Elgar of England*, 1957.

Television Plays: *Time Out of Mind*, 1956; *Into Thin Air*, 1973.

Verse

The Supreme Prize and Other Poems.   London, Stockwell, 1926.

Other

Walking in England.   Wisbech, Cambridgeshire, Fenland Press, 1935.
Clem Voroshilov, The Red Marshal.   London, Pilot Press, 1940.
Tales Out of School: A Survey of Children's Fiction.   London, Heinemann, 1949; revised edition, 1964.
The Italian Story: From the Earliest Times to 1946.   London, Macmillan, 1963; New York, Vanguard Press, 1964.
The Grand Tour.   London, Heinemann, and New York, Holt Rinehart, 1967.
Nottingham: A Biography.   London, Macmillan, 1970.
The Condottieri: Soldiers of Fortune.   London, Thames and Hudson, 1970; New York, Holt Rinehart, 1971.
A Whiff of Burnt Boats: An Early Autobiography.   London, Macmillan, and New York, St. Martin's Press, 1971.
Samuel Pepys and His World.   London, Thames and Hudson, and New York, Putnam, 1972.
Laughter at the Door: A Continued Autobiography.   London, Macmillan, and New York, St. Martin's Press, 1974.
London: A Concise History.   London, Thames and Hudson, and New York, Scribner, 1975.

Editor, *Matthew Todd's Journal: A Gentleman's Gentleman in Europe, 1814–1820.*   London, Heinemann, 1968.

Manuscript Collections: Nottingham Central Library; Kerlan Collection, University of Minnesota, Minneapolis.

Critical Study: *Geoffrey Trease* by Margaret Meek, London, Bodley Head, 1960; New York, Walck, 1964.

Geoffrey Trease comments:
   Realism, I suppose, is what I have always aimed at, since I began writing for children in revulsion against the sentimental romanticism then pervading historical fiction. With the years I hope I have widened and deepened my vision, still cultivating factual accuracy but recognising that there are even more valuable qualities. I am not a "children's writer" in the sense that I concern myself with any insulated "magic world of childhood" – it is the adult world which absorbs me and which I want to present and interpret to the young reader inexorably growing up into it. To him I want to communicate my own interests, enthusiasms, emotions, and (unfashionable though this may sound) values. Even when I write about ancient Athenian democracy, anti-Semitism in Edward I's England, or corruption in Pepys's London, I always seek a modern relevance which I hope will not be lost on the more discerning child.

*   *   *

To survey the work of Geoffrey Trease is to write the history of children's books in England for the past 45 years. His career began before the Second World War, when, apart from the innovative work of Arthur Ransome, writing for children commanded neither respect nor reward. The story-telling vein of 19th-century writers for boys, Ballantyne, Marryat, Stevenson, and Cooper was worked, and there was a dearth of new reading matter to stand between the comics and the classics.

Trease saw that few children's books reflected the everyday concerns of their readers or offered them any perspective on contemporary events. His first novel, *Bows Against the Barons* depicts Robin Hood as a primitive revolutionary with the sentiments of Trease's own Spanish Civil War generation, and *Comrades for the Charter* is more propaganda than history. Yet despite the fact that these books now seem naive alongside the rich later crop of Trease's historical novels and those of other distinguished practitioners in this kind, the seeds of a whole generation of English writing for children were sown in these early days. *Cue for Treason* showed the pattern of the books to come: a fast-moving plot, clearly defined villainy, an exciting climax, and satisfactory ending. This is the tradition of the *yarn* which Trease kept alive and developed in that his readers were never disappointed in a "what happens next" approach to reading.

Trease also made a clear distinction in these early books between the historical novel and the costumed period piece. Authenticity and historical accuracy are now taken so much for granted as part of the craft of historical novelists that the debt to Trease is often forgotten. When one remembers how Baroness Orczy shaped the stereotyped picture of the French Revolution for more than a generation of English readers, it is the more interesting to note how Trease often takes the popular side, as in *The Thunder of Valmy*, which has been translated for French children. He writes in his best imaginative form about countries (Italy in *Follow My Black Plume*) and causes that draw their inspiration from threats to the rights of the individual.

At all times Geoffrey Trease has a strong awareness of his readers. This has made him an innovator in ways that are often overlooked when more style-conscious successors follow his lead. The school story, a kind which more than most betrays the social sympathies of the writer, moved into the day school with *No Boats on Bannermere* and its sequels. In this series the parents are neither dead nor banished and the characters grow older with the books. Some of the themes that writers for "new adults" now tackle in the present permissive atmosphere made their first appearance in a tentative form in these books. Although readers in the 1970's would find them dated – Trease's experiences as a schoolmaster lie behind them – in their time they brought the family story out of the doldrums of both formula fiction and the sentimental tale. They are also mercifully free from the self-indulgence that later writers have mistaken for social realism.

His excursions outside the narrower field of children's fiction have kept Geoffrey Trease alive to current views about writing for the young. His continuing love-affair with the theatre, his historical writing and biographical studies have resulted in a development of his craft which is spiral rather than linear. For example, as autobiographical and biographical writing have come to claim larger adult audiences than the novel, Trease has written books on Byron and D. H. Lawrence which bring these authors into the area of the readers' concerns. He combines in these studies the historical narrative that he does so well with insightful criticism of the revolutionary poet and the novelist, personalities that speak to the condition of the adolescent reader.

Criticism of books for children is now a voluminous business, but when *Tales Out of School* appeared in 1949 it was a new departure, an attempt by a practitioner to define his role and his craft and to set standards for his fellow writers. It is still a good corrective to the attempt to make children's literature an exclusive testing ground for critics. Trease pleads for the accessibility of books for children and insists that children's authors are artists in their own right, a claim that his own work substantiates.

—Margaret Meek

TREECE, Henry. British. Born in Wednesbury, Staffordshire, 22 December 1911. Educated at Wednesbury High School for Boys; Birmingham University, B.A. 1933, Dip.Ed. 1934. Served in the Royal Air Force, 1941–46: Flight Lieutenant. Married Mary Woodman in 1939; has two sons and one daughter. Teacher, Leicestershire Home Office School, Shustoke, 1934; English Master, The College, Cleobury Mortimer, Shropshire, 1934–35, and Tynemouth School for Boys, Northumberland, 1935–38; English Master, 1938–41, and Senior English Master, 1946–59, Barton on Humber Grammar School, Lincolnshire. Recipient: Arts Council prize, for play, 1955. *Died 10 June 1966.*

PUBLICATIONS FOR CHILDREN

Fiction

Legions of the Eagle, illustrated by Christine Price.   London, Lane, 1954.
The Eagles Have Flown, illustrated by Christine Price.   London, Lane, 1954.
Desperate Journey, illustrated by Richard Kennedy.   London, Faber, 1954.
Ask for King Billy, illustrated by Richard Kennedy.   London, Faber, 1955.
Viking's Dawn, illustrated by Christine Price.   London, Lane, 1955; New York, Criterion Books, 1956.
Hounds of the King, illustrated by Christine Price.   London, Lane, 1955.
Men of the Hills, illustrated by Christine Price.   London, Lane, 1957; New York, Criterion Books, 1958.
The Road to Miklagard, illustrated by Christine Price.   London, Lane, and New York, Criterion Books, 1957.
Hunter Hunted, illustrated by Richard Kennedy.   London, Faber, 1957.
Don't Expect Any Mercy!   London, Faber, 1958.
The Children's Crusade, illustrated by Christine Price.   London, Bodley Head, 1958; as *Perilous Pilgrimage,* New York, Criterion Books, 1959.
The Return of Robinson Crusoe, illustrated by Will Nickless.   London, Hulton Press, 1958; as *The Further Adventures of Robinson Crusoe,* New York, Criterion Books, 1958.
The Bombard, illustrated by Christine Price.   London, Bodley Head, 1959; as *Ride to Danger,* New York, Criterion Books, 1959.
Wickham and the Armada, illustrated by Hookway Cowles.   London, Hulton Press, 1959.
Viking's Sunset, illustrated by Christine Price.   London, Bodley Head, and New York, Criterion Books, 1960.
Red Settlement.   London, Bodley Head, 1960.
The Jet Beads, illustrated by W. A. Sillince.   Leicester, Brockhampton Press, 1961.
The Golden One, illustrated by William Stobbs.   London, Bodley Head, 1961; New York, Criterion Books, 1962.
Man with a Sword, illustrated by William Stobbs.   London, Bodley Head, 1962; New York, Pantheon Books, 1964.
War Dog, illustrated by Roger Payne.   Leicester, Brockhampton Press, 1962; New York, Criterion Books, 1963.
Horned Helmet, illustrated by Charles Keeping.   Leicester, Brockhampton Press, and New York, Criterion Books, 1963.
The Last of the Vikings, illustrated by Charles Keeping.   Leicester, Brockhampton Press, 1964; as *The Last Viking,* New York, Pantheon Books, 1966.
The Bronze Sword, illustrated by Mary Russon.   London, Hamish Hamilton, 1965; augmented edition, as *The Centurion,* New York, Meredith Press, 1967.
Splintered Sword, illustrated by Charles Keeping.   Leicester, Brockhampton Press, 1965; New York, Duell, 1966.
Killer in Dark Glasses.   London, Faber, 1965.

Bang, You're Dead! London, Faber, 1966.

The Queen's Brooch. London, Hamish Hamilton, 1966; New York, Putnam, 1967.

Swords from the North, illustrated by Charles Keeping. London, Faber, and New York, Pantheon Books, 1967.

The Windswept City, illustrated by Faith Jaques. London, Hamish Hamilton, 1967; New York, Meredith Press, 1968.

Vinland the Good, illustrated by William Stobbs. London, Bodley Head, 1967; as *Westward to Vinland*, New York, S. G. Phillips, 1967.

The Dream-Time, illustrated by Charles Keeping. Leicester, Brockhampton Press, 1967; New York, Meredith Press, 1968.

The Invaders: Three Stories, illustrated by Charles Keeping. Leicester, Brockhampton Press, and New York, Crowell, 1972.

Plays

Hounds of the King, with Two Radio Plays (includes *Harold Godwinson* and *William, Duke of Normandy*), illustrated by Stuart Tresilian. London, Longman, 1965.

Radio Plays: *Harold Godwinson*, 1954; *William, Duke of Normandy*, 1954.

Other

Castles and Kings, illustrated by C. Walter Hodges. London, Batsford, 1959; New York, Criterion Books, 1960.

The True Book about Castles, illustrated by G. H. Channing. London, Muller, 1960.

Know about the Crusades. London, Blackie, 1963; as *About the Crusades*, Chester Springs, Pennsylvania, Dufour, 1966.

Fighting Men: How Men Have Fought Through the Ages, with Ewart Oakeshott. Leicester, Brockhampton Press, 1963; New York, Putnam, 1965.

The Burning of Njal (saga retold), illustrated by Bernard Blatch. London, Bodley Head, and New York, Criterion Books, 1964.

PUBLICATIONS FOR ADULTS

Novels

The Dark Island. London, Gollancz, and New York, Random House, 1952; as *The Savage Warriors*, New York, Avon, 1959.

The Rebels. London, Gollancz, 1953.

The Golden Strangers. London, Lane, 1956; New York, Random House, 1957; as *The Invaders*, New York, Avon, 1960.

The Great Captains. London, Lane, and New York, Random House, 1956.

Red Queen, White Queen. London, Bodley Head, and New York, Random House, 1958; as *The Pagan Queen*, New York, Avon, 1959.

The Master of Badger's Hall. New York, Random House, 1959; as *A Fighting Man*, London, Bodley Head, 1960.

Jason. London, Bodley Head, and New York, Random House, 1961.

The Amber Princess. New York, Random House, 1962; as *Electra*, London, Bodley Head, 1963.

Oedipus. London, Bodley Head, 1964; as *The Eagle King*, New York, Random House, 1965.

The Green Man. London, Bodley Head, and New York, Putnam, 1966.

Short Stories

I Cannot Go Hunting Tomorrow: Short Stories. London, Grey Walls Press, 1946.

Plays

Carnival King (produced Nottingham, 1954).   London, Faber, 1955.
Footsteps in the Sea (produced Nottingham, 1955).

Verse

38 Poems.   London, Fortune Press, 1940.
Towards a Personal Armageddon.   Prairie City, Illinois, Press of James A. Decker, 1941.
Invitation and Warning.   London, Faber, 1942.
The Black Seasons.   London, Faber, 1945.
Collected Poems.   New York, Knopf, 1946.
The Haunted Garden.   London, Faber, 1947.
The Exiles.   London, Faber, 1952.

Other

How I See Apocalypse.   London, Drummond, 1946.
Dylan Thomas: "Dog among the Fairies."   London, Drummond, 1949; New York, de Graff, 1954; revised edition, London, Benn, and New York, de Graff, 1956.
The Crusades.   London, Bodley Head, and New York, Random House, 1962.

Editor, with J. F. Hendry, *The New Apocalypse.*   London, Fortune Press, 1939.
Editor, with J. F. Hendry, *The White Horseman: Prose and Verse of the New Apocalypse.*   London, Routledge, 1941.
Editor, with Stefan Schimanski, *Wartime Harvest.*   London, Bale and Staples, 1943.
Editor, with Stefan Schimanski, *Transformation.*   London, Gollancz, 1943.
Editor, with Stefan Schimanski, *Transformation Two, Three,* and *Four.*   London, Drummond, 3 vols., 1944, 1945, 1947.
Editor, *Herbert Read: An Introduction.*   London, Faber, 1944; Port Washington, New York, Kennikat Press, 1969.
Editor, with John Pudney, *Air Force Poetry.*   London, Lane, 1944.
Editor, with Stefan Schimanski, *A Map of Hearts: A Collection of Short Stories.*   London, Drummond, 1944.
Editor, with J. F. Hendry, *The Crown and the Sickle: An Anthology.*   London, King and Staples, 1945.
Editor, with Stefan Schimanski, *Leaves in the Storm: A Book of Diaries.*   London, Drummond, 1947.
Editor, *Selected Poems,* by Algernon Charles Swinburne.   London, Grey Walls Press, 1948.
Editor, with Stefan Schimanski, *New Romantic Anthology.*   London, Grey Walls Press, 1949.

Critical Study: *Henry Treece* by Margery Fisher (includes bibliography by Antony Kamm), in *Three Bodley Head Monographs,* London, Bodley Head, 1969.

*   *   *

Henry Treece died at 52 when even better work may have been before him. All his children's books were written within not much more than 12 years, and certainly universal recognition of his contribution to children's literature came only after his death. He had the poet's aptitude for precision of language and the enthusiasm of the gifted teacher. And the teacher in him regarded a children's book not just as an art-form *per se* but as an art-form *for children.* He was a master-technician who planned each book meticulously, storing up ideas for future novels and sequences as he went, and often writing more than was necessary so that he could select the material that would make up the most effective end-product. His ear for sound (he was pianist and composer as well as poet) led him to develop a form of historical speech which is both natural to modern ears and appropriate to period and character. With practice and conscious experiment with form and language he came to write historical novels for children of different ages from about 8 upwards, sometimes treating the same theme at two or more levels. He abhorred violence, distrusted victory, and felt that war was inglorious and horrid; yet he admired and respected the skill of the fighter (he was himself a university boxing captain), especially the brave fighter. He was primarily a story-teller who created a background and characters to fit the story he wanted to tell. The six adolescent thrillers he wrote for Faber, though technically modern stories, are in effect 20th-century fantasies of spies and crooks, action and mystery, hunter and hunted, guns, knives, and fists, laced with real humour and genuine topographical backgrounds. Otherwise, with the exception of *The Jet Beads*, a short novel of situation centred on a boy's eleven-plus problems, all his fiction is historical.

Treece's preoccupation with what he called "the cross-roads of history" led him to write stories set at times of change, like *Legions of the Eagle*, *Hounds of the King*, *The Bombard*, *The Queen's Brooch*, and the two Viking trilogies. Another recurrent theme is the rationalisation of historical legend, for example *The Eagles Have Flown* (Artos the Bear), *Man with a Sword* (Hereward), *The Last of the Vikings* (Harald Hardrada), *The Windswept City* (Troy). The many books which are built round a "home-cycle" in which characters return home, or those in which a son searches for a father, reflect Treece's own sorrow at the early death of his elder son. In some books, notably the earlier ones, he followed convention by having young heroes participate in the historical action rather than motivate it, serving as devices through which people, events and periods can be seen and interpreted with a child's eyes. In *War Dog*, his work for younger children, a dog serves the same purpose. This device failed him artistically just once in *The Children's Crusade*. The first half of the book covers this fateful journey as far as Marseilles through the eyes of two children caught by the magnetism of Stephen of Cloyes and of the sinister Pied Piper figure introduced into the story with supreme effect. The second half describes the pair's adventures in returning home from North Africa. The two halves do not knit.

Harald Sigurdson, hero of *Viking's Dawn*, *The Road to Miklagard*, and *Viking's Sunset*, starts as a youth but grows to manhood during the course of the trilogy. These are basically rich tales of travel, peopled with typical Vikings as Treece saw them — larger than life, brave, loyal but sometimes misguided, and capable of both sympathy and humour. *Man with a Sword* has a hero who *is* the action, and the book is significant also for other ways in which Treece consciously broke new ground. Though the story itself is long and complex (covering 46 years up to Hereward's death) the book is constructed in short chapters, paragraphs, and sentences, and has the unity and effect of a carefully forged narrative poem. In this book in particular, the poet and the novelist come together for the first time.

The books of the second Viking trilogy, written ostensibly for younger readers than the first, are shorter but have more depth than the Sigurdson stories. In each the main character is the centre of the action. Beorn, in *Horned Helmet*, has lost his father, but finds a substitute in the baresark Starkad, to whom he ultimately returns. This is a gem of controlled language and understatement, in the tradition of the sagas themselves. In *The Last of the Vikings* the title character is Harald Hardrada, recreated from just the first two chapters of Snorri Sturluson's *Heimskringla*, and framed with a prologue and epilogue which cover his death at Stamfordbridge. In fact Harald as a character is almost up-staged by the mystical Arsleif Summerbird who finally sacrifices himself so that Harald and his companions shall live. The boy Runolf, in *Splintered Sword*, is a psychological throwback, a Viking misfit in a world in which baresarks no longer have any value.

The last book of all that Treece completed was *The Dream-Time*. In period it goes back roughly to the prehistoric times of *Men of the Hills* and his adult novel *The Golden Strangers*; in control to *Horned Helmet* and *Man with a Sword*; but in construction and simplicity of thought and language it was entirely new. Above all it is the statement of an artist caught up in a society warring within itself for survival. To achieve his aim Treece telescoped history to bring different cultures in contrast with each other and developed an utterly simple language to represent primitive thought, all so skilfully done that one is not conscious of the fact that sentences are pared to the bone, words are mainly monosyllabic, and punctuation is kept to a minimum. Treece was concerned with cross-roads. *The Dream-Time* is a signpost. In terms of even greater contribution to children's literature, we shall never know in what direction it was pointing.

—Antony Kamm

TRESSELT, Alvin. American. Born in Passaic, New Jersey, 30 September 1916. Educated at Passaic High School, graduated 1934. Married Blossom Budney in 1949; has two daughters. Worked in a defense plant, 1943–46; display designer and advertising copywriter, B. Altman Co., New York, 1946–52; Editor, *Humpty Dumpty's Magazine*, New York, 1952–65; Editor, 1965–67, and Executive Editor and Vice President, 1967–74, Parents' Magazine Press, New York. Since 1974, Instructor and Dean of Faculty, Institute of Children's Literature, Redding Ridge, Connecticut. Recipient: New York *Herald Tribune* Festival award, 1949. Address: 53 Dorethy Road, West Redding, Connecticut 06896, U.S.A.

PUBLICATIONS FOR CHILDREN

Fiction

> *Rain Drop Splash*, illustrated by Leonard Weisgard.   New York, Lothrop, 1946.
> *White Snow Bright Snow*, illustrated by Roger Duvoisin.   New York, Lothrop, 1947.
> *Johnny Maple-Leaf*, illustrated by Roger Duvoisin.   New York, Lothrop, 1948.
> *The Wind and Peter*, illustrated by Gary MacKenzie.   New York, Oxford University Press, 1948.
> *Bonnie Bess, The Weathervane Horse*, illustrated by Marylin Hafner.   New York, Lothrop, 1949.
> *Sun Up*, illustrated by Roger Duvoisin.   New York, Lothrop, 1949; Kingswood, Surrey, World's Work, 1966.
> *Little Lost Squirrel*, illustrated by Leonard Weisgard.   New York, Grosset and Dunlap, 1950.
> *Follow the Wind*, illustrated by Roger Duvoisin.   New York, Lothrop, 1950.
> *Hi, Mr. Robin!*, illustrated by Roger Duvoisin.   New York, Lothrop, 1950.
> *Autumn Harvest*, illustrated by Roger Duvoisin.   New York, Lothrop, 1951.
> *A Day with Daddy*, photographs by Helen Heller.   New York, Lothrop, 1953.
> *Follow the Road*, illustrated by Roger Duvoisin.   New York, Lothrop, 1953.
> *I Saw the Sea Come In*, illustrated by Roger Duvoisin.   New York, Lothrop, 1954; Kingswood, Surrey, World's Work, 1967.
> *Wake Up Farm!*, illustrated by Roger Duvoisin.   New York, Lothrop, 1955; Kingswood, Surrey, World's Work, 1966.
> *Wake Up City!*, illustrated by Roger Duvoisin.   New York, Lothrop, 1957.
> *The Rabbit Story*, illustrated by Leonard Weisgard.   New York, Lothrop, 1957.
> *The Frog in the Well*, illustrated by Roger Duvoisin.   New York, Lothrop, 1958; Edinburgh, Oliver and Boyd, 1966.
> *The Smallest Elephant in the World*, illustrated by Milton Glaser.   New York, Knopf, 1959.

Timothy Robbins Climbs the Mountain, illustrated by Roger Duvoisin. New York, Lothrop, 1960; Kingswood, Surrey, World's Work, 1967.

An Elephant Is Not a Cat, illustrated by Tom Vroman. New York, Parents' Magazine Press, 1962.

Hide and Seek Fog, illustrated by Roger Duvoisin. New York, Lothrop, 1965; Kingswood, Surrey, World's Work, 1966.

The Old Man and the Tiger, illustrated by Albert Aquino. New York, Grosset and Dunlap, 1965; London, Muller, 1970.

A Thousand Lights and Fireflies, illustrated by John Moodie. New York, Parents' Magazine Press, 1965.

The World in the Candy Egg, illustrated by Roger Duvoisin. New York, Lothrop, 1967.

The Fox Who Travelled, illustrated by Nancy Sears. New York, Grosset and Dunlap, 1968.

It's Time Now!, illustrated by Roger Duvoisin. New York, Lothrop, 1969; Kingswood, Surrey, World's Work, 1971.

Other (folktales)

Under the Trees and Through the Grass (ecology), illustrated by Roger Duvoisin. New York, Lothrop, 1962.

The Mitten: An Old Ukrainian Folktale, illustrated by Yaroslava. New York, Lothrop, 1964; Kingswood, Surrey, World's Work, 1965.

How Far Is Far? (science), illustrated by Ward Brackett. New York, Parents' Magazine Press, 1964.

The Tears of the Dragon, illustrated by Chihiro Iwasaki. New York, Parents' Magazine Press, 1967.

Legend of the Willow Plate, with Nancy Cleaver, illustrated by Joseph Low. New York, Parents' Magazine Press, 1968; London, Hamish Hamilton, 1969.

The Crane Maiden, illustrated by Chihiro Iwasaki. New York, Parents' Magazine Press, 1968.

Helpful Mr. Bear, illustrated by Kozo Kakimoto. New York, Parents' Magazine Press, 1968.

Ma Lien and the Magic Brush, illustrated by Kei Wakana. New York, Parents' Magazine Press, 1968.

How Rabbit Tricked His Friends, illustrated by Yasuo Segawa. New York, Parents' Magazine Press, 1969.

The Rolling Rice Ball, illustrated by Saburo Watanabe. New York, Parents' Magazine Press, 1969.

The Fisherman under the Sea, illustrated by Chihiro Iwasaki. New York, Parents' Magazine Press, 1969.

The Land of Lost Buttons, illustrated by Kayako Nishimaki. New York, Parents' Magazine Press, 1970.

Eleven Hungry Cats, illustrated by Noboru Baba. New York, Parents' Magazine Press, 1970.

Gengoroh and the Thunder God, illustrated by Yasuo Segawa. New York, Parents' Magazine Press, 1970.

The Beaver Pond (ecology), illustrated by Roger Duvoisin. New York, Lothrop, 1970; Kingswood, Surrey, World's Work, 1971.

A Sparrow's Magic, illustrated by Fuyuji Yamanaka. New York, Parents' Magazine Press, 1970.

The Hare and the Bear and Other Stories, illustrated by Yoshiharu Suzuki. New York, Parents' Magazine Press, 1971.

Stories from the Bible, illustrated by Lynd Ward. New York, Coward McCann, 1971.

Ogre and His Bride, illustrated by Shosuke Fukuda. New York, Parents' Magazine Press, 1971.

Lum Fu and the Golden Mountain, illustrated by Daihacki Ohta.   New York, Parents'
      Magazine Press, 1971.
The Little Mouse Who Tarried, illustrated by Kozo Kakimoto.   New York, Parents'
      Magazine Press, 1971.
Wonder Fish from the Sea, illustrated by Irmgard Lucht.   New York, Parents'
      Magazine Press, 1971.
The Dead Tree (ecology), illustrated by Charles Robinson.   New York, Parents'
      Magazine Press, 1972.
The Little Green Man, illustrated by Maurice Kenelski.   New York, Parents' Magazine
      Press, 1972.
The Nutcracker, illustrated by Seiichi Horiuchi.   New York, Parents' Magazine Press,
      1974.

Manuscript Collection: Kerlan Collection, University of Minnesota, Minneapolis.

Alvin Tresselt comments:
   My books are mostly about nature, the weather and seasons, although I have also written
fantasy, humor, and here-and-now stories as well as a number of free adaptations of Japanese
folktales. In my nature stories I have avoided a didactic approach and striven for a poetic
prose style that would nurture in children a feeling for words and language, even while they
were reading about the journey of rain to the sea, the mysteries of fog, or the importance of a
dead tree. I generally use a cyclical plot when writing these stories, letting the progression of
a natural phenomenon dictate the form rather than casting the event within the confines of a
conventional story.
   All of my books have been in the 4 to 8 picture book range.

                              *   *   *

                  White snow, bright snow, smooth and deep.
                  Light snow, night snow, quiet as sleep.
                  Down, down, without a sound;
                  Down, down, to the frozen ground.

                  Covering roads and hiding fences,
                  Sifting in cracks and filling up trenches.
                  Millions of snowflakes, tiny and light.
                  Softly, gently, in the secret night.

Those two stanzas from the prologue to his *White Snow Bright Snow* suggest why Alvin
Tresselt was one of the pathbreaking American picture book authors of the late 1940's and
early 1950's. Along with Margaret Wise Brown and others, he helped to establish the
patterns of the "mood" picture book which sought to catch and hold the attention of young
listeners and readers by projecting the essence of a familiar experience in vivid yet simple
language.
   White Snow Bright Snow, for which illustrator Roger Duvoisin won the Caldecott Medal,
is a prime example of the Tresselt technique. Although there is no central character, and no
plot in the classic sense, Tresselt does introduce representative characters – the postman, the
farmer, the policeman – who recur throughout the narrative. And he structures the text in a
dramatic way, starting with the low gray sky that presages the snow-storm and ending with
the first spring robin that signals the season of snow is over.
   Tresselt pioneered this approach to nature subjects in an earlier picture book. *Rain Drop
Splash*, in which he traced the path of a raindrop from a puddle to the ocean. He continued it

in such books as *Hi, Mr. Robin!*, *Wake Up Farm!*, and *Hide and Seek Fog*, which details the impact of a thick fog that blankets a Cape Cod fishing village for three days.

Not surprisingly the Tresselt mood nature books spawned a horde of imitators. They seemed so simple to write – after all, who hadn't observed some process of nature, whether a butterfly emerging from a chrysalis or a pair of wrens building a nest, hatching eggs, and raising a new family. Why not write a picture book text about it? Hundreds if not thousands of writers tried their hand at such manuscripts. The great majority were never published, but many others did get into print. They inevitably tended to lessen the impact of some of Alvin Tresselt's own later books, especially when he seemed to repeat himself in titles like *Under the Trees and Through the Grass*.

At this juncture, Tresselt happily widened his range by turning to folk tales and fantasy. *The Mitten* was his delightful rendition of the Ukrainian tale about all the shivering forest animals that tried to crowd for warmth into the little boy's lost mitten. And even though it suffered from an uncertain point-of-view, *The World in the Candy Egg* contained some of Mr. Tresselt's loveliest writing, like this climactic extract:

> Magic world, little world, made for a child's delight,
> Where time doesn't pass and it never gets cold,
> And the shepherd and shepherdess never grow old ...
> The sheep nibble grass and crows fly away, fly away, fly away,
> In the make-believe world of the egg.

Then, in the late 1960's and early 1970's, Alvin Tresselt returned to nature themes. *It's Time Now!*, *The Dead Tree*, and *The Beaver Pond* proved that his touch was as sure as ever. Like the beavers who built first one dam and then another, he could still take the most ordinary material from nature and shape it into something fresh and special for children.

—James C. Giblin

TREVOR, Elleston. British. Born in Bromley, Kent, 17 February 1920. Educated at Yardley Court Preparatory School, 1928–32; Sevenoaks School, Kent, 1932–38. Served in the Royal Air Force, 1939–45. Married Jonquil Burgess in 1947; has one son. Lived in France, 1958–73. Recipient: Mystery Writers of America Edgar Allan Poe award, for novel, 1965. Agent: Ziegler Associates Inc., 9255 Sunset Boulevard, Los Angeles, California 90069. Address: Ocotillo Grove, Fountain Hills, Arizona 85268, U.S.A.

PUBLICATIONS FOR CHILDREN

Fiction

Into the Happy Glade (as T. Dudley-Smith). London, Swan, 1943.
By a Silver Stream (as T. Dudley-Smith), illustrated by W. A. Ward. London, Swan, 1944.
Wumpus, illustrated by John McCail. London, Swan, 1945.
Deep Wood, illustrated by David Williams. London, Swan, 1945; New York, Longman, 1947.
Heather Hill, illustrated by David Williams. London, Swan, 1946; New York, Longman, 1948.
More about Wumpus, illustrated by John McCail. London, Swan, 1947.

The Island of the Pines, illustrated by David Williams. London, Swan, 1948.
The Secret Travellers, illustrated by David Williams. London, Swan, 1948.
Where's Wumpus?, illustrated by John McCail. London, Swan, 1948.
Badger's Beech, illustrated by Leslie Atkinson. London, Falcon Press, 1948;
  Nashville, Aurora, 1970.
The Wizard of the Wood, illustrated by Leslie Atkinson. London, Falcon Press, 1948.
Badger's Moon, illustrated by Leslie Atkinson. London, Falcon Press, 1949.
Ants' Castle, illustrated by David Williams. London, Falcon Press, 1949.
Mole's Castle, illustrated by Leslie Atkinson. London, Falcon Press, 1951.
Sweethallow Valley, illustrated by Leslie Atkinson. London, Falcon Press, 1951.
Challenge of the Firebrand. London, Jenkins, 1951.
Secret Arena. London, Jenkins, 1951.
The Racing Wraith (as Trevor Burgess). London, Hutchinson, 1953.
A Spy at Monk's Court (as Trevor Burgess). London, Hutchinson, 1954.
Forbidden Kingdom. London, Lutterworth Press, 1955.
Badger's Wood, illustrated by Leslie Atkinson. London, Heinemann, 1958; New
  York, Criterion Books, 1959.
The Crystal City, illustrated by David Williams. London, Swan, 1959.
Green Glades, illustrated by David Williams. London, Swan, 1959.
Squirrel's Island, illustrated by David Williams. London, Swan, 1963.

Other

Animal Life Stories (*Rippleswim the Otter, Scamper-foot the Pine Marten, Shadow the
  Fox*). London, Swan, 3 vols., 1943–45.

PUBLICATIONS FOR ADULTS

Novels

Over the Wall (as T. Dudley-Smith). London, Swan, 1943.
Double Who Double Crossed (as T. Dudley-Smith). London, Swan, 1944.
The Immortal Error. London, Swan, 1946.
Escape to Fear (as T. Dudley-Smith). London, Swan, 1948.
Now Try the Morgue (as T. Dudley-Smith). London, Swan, 1948.
The Mystery of the Missing Book (as Trevor Burgess). London, Hutchinson, 1950.
Chorus of Echoes. London and New York, Boardman, 1950.
Image in the Dust (as Warwick Scott). London, Davies, 1951; as *Cockpit* (as Adam
  Hall), Chicago, Remploy, 1972.
Knight Sinister (as Simon Rattray). London and New York, Boardman, 1951.
Dead on Course (as Mansell Black). London, Hodder and Stoughton, 1951.
Redfern's Miracle. London and New York, Boardman, 1951.
Tiger Street. London and New York, Boardman, 1951.
Sinister Cargo (as Mansell Black). London, Hodder and Stoughton, 1951.
The Domesday Story (as Warwick Scott). London, Davies, 1952; as *Doomsday* (as
  Adam Hall), Chicago, Remploy, 1972.
A Blaze of Roses. London, Heinemann, and New York, Harper, 1952; as *The Fire-
  Raiser*, London, New English Library, 1970.
Queen in Danger (as Simon Rattray). London and New York, Boardman, 1952.
The Passion and the Pity. London, Heinemann, 1953.
Bishop in Check (as Simon Rattray). London and New York, Boardman, 1953.
Dead Silence (as Simon Rattray). London, Boardman, 1954; as *Pawn in Jeopardy* (as
  Adam Hall), Chicago, Remploy, 1972.
Naked Canvas (as Warwick Scott). London, Davies, 1954.
The Big Pick-Up. London, Heinemann, and New York, Macmillan, 1955.

Squadron Airborne.   London, Heinemann, 1955; New York, Macmillan, 1956.
Dead Circuit (as Simon Rattray).   London, Boardman, 1955; as *Rook's Gambit* (as Adam Hall), Chicago, Remploy, 1972.
The Killing-Ground.   London, Heinemann, 1956; New York, Macmillan, 1957.
Gale Force.   London, Heinemann, 1956; New York, Macmillan, 1957.
The Pillars of Midnight.   London, Heinemann, 1957; New York, Morrow, 1958.
Heat Wave (as Caesar Smith).   London, Wingate, 1957; New York, Ballantine, 1958.
Dream of Death.   London, Brown and Watson, 1958.
Silhouette.   London, Swan, 1959.
The V.I.P.   London, Heinemann, 1959; New York, Morrow, 1960.
The Billboard Madonna.   London, Heinemann, 1960; New York, Morrow, 1961.
The Mind of Max Duvine.   London, Swan, 1960.
The Burning Shore.   London, Heinemann, 1961; as *The Pasang Run*, New York, Harper, 1962.
The Volcanoes of San Domingo (as Adam Hall).   London, Collins, 1963; New York, Simon and Schuster, 1964.
The Flight of the Phoenix.   London, Heinemann, and New York, Harper, 1964.
The Berlin Memorandum (as Adam Hall).   London, Collins, 1965; as *The Quiller Memorandum*, New York, Simon and Schuster, 1965; Collins, 1967.
The Second Chance.   London, World Distributors, 1965.
Weave a Rope of Sand.   London, World Distributors, 1965.
The Shoot.   London, Heinemann, and New York, Doubleday, 1966.
The 9th Directive (as Adam Hall).   London, Heinemann, 1966; New York, Simon and Schuster, 1967.
The Freebooters.   London, Heinemann, and New York, Doubleday, 1967.
A Blaze of Arms (as Roger Fitzalan).   London, Davies, 1967.
A Place for the Wicked.   London, Heinemann, 1968.
The Striker Portfolio (as Adam Hall).   New York, Simon and Schuster, 1968; London, Heinemann, 1969.
Bury Him among Kings.   London, Heinemann, and New York, Doubleday, 1970.
The Warsaw Document (as Adam Hall).   London, Heinemann, and New York, Doubleday, 1971.
The Tango Briefing (as Adam Hall).   London, Collins, and New York, Doubleday, 1973.
Expressway (as Howard North).   London, Collins, and New York, Simon and Schuster, 1973.
The Mandarin Cypher (as Adam Hall).   London, Collins, and New York, Doubleday, 1975.
The Paragon.   London, New English Library, 1975; as *Night Stop*, New York, Doubleday, 1975.
The Kobra Manifesto.   London, Collins, and New York, Doubleday, 1976.
The Theta Syndrome.   New York, Doubleday, and London, New English Library, 1977.
Blue Jay Summer.   London, New English Library, and New York, Dell, 1977.
Seven Witnesses.   London, Remploy, 1977.

Short Stories

Elleston Trevor Miscellany.   London, Swan, 1944.

Plays

The Last of the Daylight (produced Bromley, Kent, 1959).
Murder by All Means (produced Madrid, 1960; Farnham, Surrey, and London, 1961).
A Pinch of Purple (produced Bradford, 1971).

A Touch of Purple (produced Leatherhead, Surrey, and London, 1972). London, French, 1973.

Manuscript Collection: Boston University Library.

Elleston Trevor comments:
Pure escapism.

*   *   *

Now internationally-known as the best-selling novelist Elleston Trevor, Trevor Dudley-Smith began his writing career in the early 1940's with a series of children's books published under his own name by the now-defunct publishing company of Gerald G. Swan. Evidently heavily influenced by *The Wind in the Willows* (and no worse for that) the stories featured humanized animals and birds in their natural habitat (usually a wooded forest) undergoing everyday amusing or exciting experiences. The first two books, *Into the Happy Glade* and *By a Silver Stream*, included such characters as Sapiens Owl, Hector Woodpecker, Little Push and Little Pull, the Field-Mice, Cyril Squirrel, and Boggy-the-Frog. Subsequent titles (*Deep Wood, Heather Hill, The Secret Travellers, Sweethallow Valley*) featured Old Stripe the Badger, Potter the Otter, Skip Squirrel, Woo the Owl, Scruff the Fox, and Mole-the-Miller. There were several other books, some of which were broadcast as radio plays on the BBC *Children's Hour* in the late 1940's and early 1950's.

Once the reader gets over the "twee-ness" of the animal-characters' names, the stories make for amusing and entertaining reading. There is also an endearing glow of cosiness about the writing, illustrated here by the final paragraph of *Into the Happy Glade*: "Out in the cold Glade, where the snow shimmered deep and white under a starlit heaven, you could see the countless little windows, gleaming redly through the trees and under the hedges, for they had all banked up fires to keep their houses warm for going to bed .... But brightest of all were the windows of Owl's house in the big oak, from which the faint noise of toasting and laughter drifted out on to the quiet snow, under the stars." An enterprising publisher could do worse than reissue some of these early books, complete with the original illustrations by W. A. Ward and David Williams.

—Brian Doyle

TREVOR, (Lucy) Meriol. British. Born in London, 15 April 1919. Educated at Perse Girls' School, Cambridge; St. Hugh's College, Oxford, 1938–42, B.A. 1942. Recipient: James Tait Black Memorial Award, for biography, 1963. Fellow, Royal Society of Literature. Agent: David Bolt, Bolt and Watson Ltd., 8–12 Old Queen Street, London S.W.1. Address: 70 Pulteney Street, Bath, Avon BA2 4DL, England.

PUBLICATIONS FOR CHILDREN

Fiction

The Forest and the Kingdom, illustrated by Philip Hepworth. London, Faber, 1949.
Hunt the King, Hide the Fox, illustrated by Philip Hepworth. London, Faber, 1950.
The Fires and the Stars, illustrated by Philip Hepworth. London, Faber, 1951.

Sun Slower, Sun Faster, illustrated by Edward Ardizzone. London, Collins, 1955; New York, Sheed and Ward, 1957.

The Other Side of the Moon, illustrated by Martin Thomas. London, Collins, 1956; New York, Sheed and Ward, 1957.

Merlin's Ring, illustrated by Martin Thomas. London, Collins, 1957.

The Treasure Hunt, illustrated by Constance Marshall. London, Hamish Hamilton, 1957.

The Caravan War, illustrated by Janet Pullan. London, Hamish Hamilton, 1958.

Four Odd Ones, illustrated by Martin Thomas. London, Collins, 1958.

The Sparrow Child, illustrated by Martin Thomas. London, Collins, 1958.

The Rose Round. London, Hamish Hamilton, 1963; New York, Dutton, 1964.

William's Wild Day Out, illustrated by Raymond Briggs. London, Hamish Hamilton, 1963.

The Midsummer Maze, illustrated by Hugh Marshall. London, Macmillan, and New York, St. Martin's Press, 1964.

Lights in a Dark Town, illustrated by Hilda Offen. London, Macmillan, 1964.

The King of the Castle, illustrated by Hugh Marshall. London, Macmillan, 1966.

PUBLICATIONS FOR ADULTS

Novels

The Last of Britain. London, Macmillan, and New York, St. Martin's Press, 1956.

The New People. London, Macmillan, and New York, St. Martin's Press, 1957.

A Narrow Place. London, Macmillan, 1958.

Shadows and Images. London, Macmillan, 1960; New York, McKay, 1962.

The City and the World. London, Dent, 1970.

The Holy Images. London, Dent, 1971.

The Two Kingdoms. London, Constable, 1973.

The Fugitives. London, Hodder and Stoughton, 1973; New York, Pocket Books, 1974.

The Marked Man. London, Hodder and Stoughton, and New York, Pocket Books, 1974.

The Enemy at Home. London, Hodder and Stoughton, and New York, Pocket Books, 1974.

The Forgotten Country. London, Hodder and Stoughton, 1975.

The Fortunate Marriage. London, Hodder and Stoughton, and New York, Dutton, 1976.

The Treacherous Paths. London, Hodder and Stoughton, 1976.

The Civil Prisoners. London, Hodder and Stoughton, and New York, Dutton, 1977.

Verse

Midsummer, Midwinter. Aldington, Kent, Hand and Flower Press, 1957.

Other

Newman: Pillar of the Cloud (biography). London, Macmillan, and New York, Doubleday, 1962.

Newman: Light in Winter (biography). London, Macmillan, 1962; New York, Doubleday, 1963.

Newman Today. London, Catholic Truth Society, 1963.

Newman, A Portrait Restored: An Ecumenical Revaluation, with John Coulson and A. M. Allchin. London, Sheed and Ward, 1965.

Apostle of Rome: A Life of Philip Neri, 1515–1595. London, Macmillan, 1966.

Pope John. London, Macmillan, and New York, Doubleday, 1967.

Prophets and Guardians: Renewal and Tradition in the Church. London, Hollis and Carter, and New York, Doubleday, 1969.
The Arnolds: Thomas Arnold and His Family. London, Bodley Head, and New York, Scribner, 1973.

Meriol Trevor comments:

I wrote some children's books because I wanted to, and I dedicated them to the children of friends, who all seemed to enjoy reading them. I still sometimes hear from children who have read and enjoyed my books. I have had no books for children published since 1966, though I have written some more stories for them. In all my stories I have tried to involve the children in the lives and problems of sympathetic young adults often by putting the loves and hates among and between the generations at one remove, because I think this makes it easier for children to understand, or to recognise, their own emotions.

*   *   *

Meriol Trevor has written books for children in several different genres. Her favourite medium is a kind of fantasy that is peculiarly her own, mixing myth, magic, traditional folk-lore, and Christian allegory. A number of these books, such as *The Forest and the Kingdom* and *Hunt the King, Hide the Fox,* derive from a fictitious world, The World Dionysus, which the author and a friend, Margaret Priestley, invented when they were children. Together and separately the two women have written several World Dionysus stories rather as the Brontë sisters invented and wrote about Gondal. Meriol Trevor has also produced realistic novels – *The Sparrow Child* and *The Rose Round* are examples – and stories for younger children in the Antelope and Reindeer series.

Nearly all Meriol Trevor's writing is suffused by her deeply-held Roman Catholic beliefs. This means that her books often have a specialist interest, being perhaps more easily appreciated by people of that religious persuasion than by Protestant or agnostic readers. At times, the didactic intention shows through too much, as in *The Sparrow Child,* where the story becomes somewhat implausible when the Christian myth of the grail is given too much prominence in the closing chapters.

The structure of her novels is always competent – *The Rose Round* is an interesting example of a complex story that is handled skilfully enough for the plot to seem quite simple – and there is a heavy reliance on dialogue, which is not always so convincing, sometimes failing to portray the differences of thought and feeling between the characters adequately. Perhaps her most successful books are the short novels for young readers, *William's Wild Day Out, The Treasure Hunt* and *The Caravan War,* which, slight though they may be, are distinguished by a lively sense of humour and an assurance of tone in the writing that do not always appear in the longer, more serious novels.

—David Rees

TUDOR, Tasha. American. Born in Boston, Massachusetts. Educated privately and at Spring Hill School, Litchfield, Connecticut. Has four children. Recipient: Catholic Library Association Regina Medal, 1971. Address: c/o Thomas Y. Crowell Co., 666 Fifth Avenue, New York, New York 10019, U.S.A.

PUBLICATIONS FOR CHILDREN (illustrated by the author)

Fiction

Pumpkin Moonshine. New York and London, Oxford University Press, 1938.
Alexander the Gander. New York and London, Oxford University Press, 1939; augmented edition, New York, Walck, 1961.
The County Fair. New York and London, Oxford University Press, 1940.
A Tale for Easter. New York and London, Oxford University Press, 1941.
Snow Before Christmas. New York and London, Oxford University Press, 1941.
Dorcas Porcus. New York and London, Oxford University Press, 1942.
The White Goose. New York and London, Oxford University Press, 1943.
Linsey Woolsey. New York, Oxford University Press, 1946.
Thistly B. New York, Oxford University Press, 1949.
The Dolls' Christmas. New York and London, Oxford University Press, 1950.
Amanda and the Bear. New York and London, Oxford University Press, 1951.
Edgar Allan Crow. New York, Oxford University Press, 1953.
Becky's Birthday. New York, Viking Press, 1960.
Becky's Christmas. New York, Walck, 1961.
First Delights. New York, Platt and Munk, 1966.
Corgiville Fair. New York, Crowell, 1971; London, Collins, 1973.

Verse

A Is for Annabelle. New York, Oxford University Press, 1954.
1 Is One. New York and London, Oxford University Press, 1956.
Around the Year. New York, Walck, 1957.

Other

A Time to Keep: The Tasha Tudor Book of Holidays. Chicago, Rand McNally, 1977.

Editor, *Book of Fairy Tales.* New York, Platt and Munk, 1961; London, Collins, 1963.
Editor, *Wings from the Winds.* Philadelphia, Lippincott, 1964.
Editor, *Favorite Stories.* Philadelphia, Lippincott, 1965.
Editor, *Take Joy!* Cleveland, World, 1966; London, Lutterworth Press, 1967.

Illustrator: *Mother Goose*, 1944; *Fairy Tales from Hans Christian Andersen*, 1945; *A Child's Garden of Verses* by Robert Louis Stevenson, 1947; *The Doll's House* by Rumer Godden, 1948; *Jackanapes* by Juliana Horatia Ewing, 1948; *First Prayers*, 1952; *Biggity Bantam*, 1954, and *Pekin White*, 1955, by Thomas Leighton McReady; *First Graces*, 1955; *And It Was So: Bible Stories*, 1958; *My Brimful Book*, edited by Dana Bruce, 1960; *The Secret Garden*, 1962, and *The Little Princess*, 1963, by Frances Hodgson Burnett; *A Round Dozen*, 1963, and *Little Women*, 1969, by Louisa May Alcott; *The Twenty-Third Psalm*, 1965; *The Wind in the Willows* by Kenneth Grahame, 1966; *First Poems of Childhood*, 1967; *The Real Diary of a Real Boy*, 1967, and *Brite and Fair*, 1968, by Henry Augustus Shute; *More Prayers*, 1968; *The Christmas Cat*, 1976, and *Amy's Goose*, 1977, by Efner Tudor Holmes; *The Night Before Christmas* by Clement Moore, 1976; *Bedtime Book*, 1977.

* * *

Since she is human, Tasha Tudor had undoubtedly known unhappiness, frustrations, and disappointments. But in none of the many books she has written for children, during a long and honored career, has she ever expressed concern for serious problems. While other authors address themselves to divorce, death, despair, and drugs, Tudor continues as she began in the 1930's, celebrating the joys of life, particularly its bucolic pleasures. This is not to say that her stories are soppy or bland. She is unmistakably sharing honest experiences, and she has attracted an enviable host of fans who revel in her quaint, sensitive, and graceful telling. Mention *Pumpkin Moonshine* and females from 5 through 40 are likely to say, in the words of a brisk librarian: "I 'dore it. I wouldn't lend my copy to my best friend." This book made its bow in 1938 and is still going strong. *Pumpkin* and another book of the same period epitomize the worst thing that can happen to a Tudor character. Sylvie Ann is "a very sweet wee person," pushing a big pumpkin home when it gets away from her. It careers down a slope, creates havoc among the farm animals, and knocks down Mr. Hemmelskamp who's toting a pail full of whitewash. Polite Sylvie helps the man up and apologizes to the ruffled animals. "Grandpawp" carves the pumpkin into a fierce Moonshine, to terrify passers-by gratifyingly and Sylvie Ann saves the seeds to plant and provide fun for the next year. Sylvie Ann is also the heroine of *Alexander the Gander*; in this book, the gander tries her patience sorely as he pesters his mistress and Sylvie's hostess, Mrs. Fillow. Despite their vigilance, the fowl (sorry!) desperado keeps getting into the garden and devouring his notion of a delicacy, Mrs. Fillow's prized heliotrope pansies.

First Delights: A Book about Five Senses invites young readers to follow a girl, Sally, as she experiences the initial signs of changing seasons on the farm where she lives. She sees spring's first flowers, new leaves; she hears robins sing, brooks run; she smells spring in daffodils and warm earth; she touches spring, holding new kittens; she tastes spring in syrup from maple trees. Throughout the book, she goes on using all her senses to take in the welcome offerings of summer, fall and winter. A simple story, simply told is simply lovely. It is one of the Tudor books most effectively summed up by the critic who noted that "children love them to pieces."

—Jean F. Mercier

TUNIS, John R(oberts). American. Born in Boston, Massachusetts, 7 December 1889. Educated at Harvard University, Cambridge, Massachusetts, A.B. 1911. Served in the United States Army in France during World War I. Married Lucy Rogers. Sportswriter, New York *Evening Post*, 1925–32, and Universal Service, New York, 1932–35; Tennis Commentator, NBC, New York. Recipient: New York *Herald Tribune* Festival award, 1938; Child Study Association of America award, 1944; Boys' Clubs of America award, 1949. *Died 4 February 1975.*

PUBLICATIONS FOR CHILDREN

Fiction

The Iron Duke, illustrated by Johan Bull. New York, Harcourt Brace, 1938.
The Duke Decides, illustrated by James MacDonald. New York, Harcourt Brace, 1939.
Champion's Choice, illustrated by Jay Hyde Barnum. New York, Harcourt Brace, 1940.
The Kid from Tomkinsville, illustrated by Jay Hyde Barnum. New York, Harcourt Brace, 1940.
World Series, illustrated by Jay Hyde Barnum. New York, Harcourt Brace, 1941.
All-American, illustrated by Hans Walleen. New York, Harcourt Brace, 1942.
Keystone Kids. New York, Harcourt Brace, 1943.
Rookie of the Year. New York, Harcourt Brace, 1944.
Yea! Wildcats! New York, Harcourt Brace, 1944.

A City for Lincoln. New York, Harcourt Brace, 1945.
The Kid Comes Back. New York, Morrow, 1946.
Highpockets. New York, Morrow, 1948.
Son of the Valley. New York, Morrow, 1949.
Young Razzle. New York, Morrow, 1949.
The Other Side of the Fence. New York, Morrow, 1953.
Go, Team, Go! New York, Morrow, 1954.
Buddy and the Old Pro, illustrated by Jay Hyde Barnum. New York, Morrow, 1955.
Schoolboy Johnson. New York, Morrow, 1958.
Silence over Dunkerque. New York, Morrow, 1962.
His Enemy, His Friend. New York, Morrow, 1967.
Grand National. New York, Morrow, 1973.

Other

Million-Miler: The Story of an Air Pilot. New York, Messner, 1942.

PUBLICATIONS FOR ADULTS

Novel

American Girl. New York, Brewer and Warren, 1930.

Other

$port$, Heroics, and Hysterics. New York, Day, 1928.
Was College Worth While? New York, Harcourt Brace, 1936.
Choosing a College. New York, Harcourt Brace, 1940.
Sport for the Fun of It. New York, A. S. Barnes, 1940; revised edition, 1950.
Democracy and Sport. New York, A. S. Barnes, 1941.
This Writing Game: Selections from Twenty Years of Free-Lancing. New York, A. S. Barnes, 1941.
Lawn Games. New York, A. S. Barnes, 1943.
The American Way of Sport. New York, Duell, 1958.
A Measure of Independence (autobiography). New York, Atheneum, 1964.

*   *   *

John R. Tunis attended Harvard University where he played on the tennis team and ran distance events in track. After overseas service in World War I he began to write for newspapers and magazines, while at the same time announcing major sports events. He was 49 when he wrote his first book for children, *The Iron Duke.* This was followed by other now well-known works: *All-American, Young Razzle,* and *His Enemy, His Friend.*

· His work, characterized by authentic background, attention to detail, and fast sports action, owes much to his experience as champion athlete and sports announcer. His novels are marked by their realism and sense of social values. In the 1940's he was one of the few juvenile authors to discuss the problem of race relations in sports (*All-American* and *Yea! Wildcats!*). His plots are often repetitious and didactic, but the convincing humanity of his characters gives unusual strength and appeal to his novels. *Yea! Wildcats!* and *A City for Lincoln* are frankly political and are the least popular of his works. He is at his best when describing baseball, tennis, or basketball, as in *Schoolboy Johnson, Keystone Kids,* or *All-American,* though *Grand National* seems somewhat contrived. In *Silence over Dunkerque* Tunis departs from the sports theme to portray a British sergeant faced with disaster.

Tunis always felt that his books were written for adults which perhaps accounts for the fact that he never talks down to children.

—Raymond W. Barber

TURKLE, Brinton. American. Born in Alliance, Ohio, 15 August 1915. Educated at Carnegie Institute of Technology, Pittsburgh, 1933–36; Museum of Fine Arts School, Boston, 1938–40. Married Yvonne Foulston in 1948; has one daughter and two sons. Freelance illustrator. Recipient: *Book World* Festival award, 1969; Christopher Award, 1973. Address: c/o Viking Press, 625 Madison Avenue, New York, New York 10022, U.S.A.

PUBLICATIONS FOR CHILDREN (illustrated by the author)

Fiction

> *Obadiah the Bold.* New York, Viking Press, 1965.
> *The Magic of Millicent Musgrave.* New York, Viking Press, 1967.
> *The Fiddler of High Lonesome.* New York, Viking Press, 1968.
> *Thy Friend, Obadiah.* New York, Viking Press, 1969.
> *The Sky Dog.* New York, Viking Press, 1969.
> *Mooncoin Castle; or, Skulduggery Rewarded.* New York, Viking Press, 1970.
> *The Adventures of Obadiah.* New York, Viking Press, 1972.
> *It's Only Arnold.* New York, Viking Press, 1973.
> *Deep in the Forest.* New York, Dutton, 1976.

Illustrator: *You Say You Saw a Camel!* by Elizabeth Coatsworth, 1959; *Danny Dunn on the Ocean Floor,* 1960, and *Danny Dunn and the Fossil Cave,* 1961, by Jay Williams and Raymond Abrashkin; *War Cry of the West* by Nathaniel Burt, 1964; *Indian Children of America* by Margaret Farquhar, 1964; *If You Lived in Colonial Times* by Ann McGovern, 1964; *The Far-Off Land* by Rebecca Caudill, 1964; *Four Paws into Adventure* by Claude Cenac, 1965; *The Doll in the Bakeshop* by Carol Beach York, 1965; *How Joe the Bear and Sam the Mouse Got Together,* 1965, and *Catch a Little Fox,* 1970, by Beatrice Schenck de Regniers; *The Story of Ben Franklin* by Eve Merriam, 1965; *Mystery of the Red Tide* by Frank Bonham, 1966; *Belinda and Me* by Bettye Hill Braucher, 1966; *High-Noon Rocket* by Charles May, 1966; *A Special Birthday Party for Someone Very Special,* 1966, *Sam and the Impossible Thing,* 1967, and *Jake,* 1969, all by Tamara Kitt; *The Lollipop Party* by Ruth A. Sonneborn, 1967; *The Troublesome Tuba* by Barbara Rinkoff, 1967; *That's What Friends Are For* by Florence Parry Heide and S. W. Van Clief, 1968; *Granny and the Indians* by Peggy Parish, 1969; *Yvette* by Leon Harris, 1970; *Anna and the Baby Buzzard* by Helga Sandburg, 1970; *C Is for Circus* by Bernice Chardiet, 1971; *Who Likes It Hot?* by Mary Garelick, 1972; *The Ballad of William Sycamore* by Stephen Vincent Benét, 1972; *The Boy Who Wouldn't Believe in Spring,* by Lucille Clifton, 1973; *Poor Richard in France* by F. N. Monjo, 1973; *Over the River and Through the Wood* by Lydia Child, 1974; *The Elves and the Shoemaker* by Freya Littledale, 1975; *Island Time* by Bette Lamont, 1976.

*   *   *

The most appealing of Brinton Turkle's books for younger readers are those telling the adventures of Obadiah, a Quaker boy of Nantucket Island. Filled with quaint humor and true-to-life incident, these picture books with their humorous drawings bring smiles to the faces of both adults and children. So far three have been published: *The Adventures of Obadiah, Thy Friend, Obadiah,* and *Obadiah the Bold.*

These and two books for older readers amply demonstrate the writer's skill in distilling the essence of a locale, a period in history, and a dialect or special vocabulary to create a separate world. In the Obadiah books, Mr. Turkle portrays Nantucket of the 1800's, the Quaker characters' simplicity of speech salted by sea-farers' talk. In *The Fiddler of High Lonesome,* the vernacular is colorful and ungrammatical. The story is redolent of the piney woods of the southern mountains of the United States and of the tall tales of a frontier America. "Old Man Fogle allowed as how he once shot a deer and a bobcat and a gopher snake with just one bullet." The plot centers on whether a young boy fiddler who turns up is really "kin" to the Fogles, the fight'nest family in the valley. This fiddler left a legend, too, when he departed.

Mooncoin Castle is more sophisticated, and appropriately so for older readers. It is basically a plea for historic places (in this case an old Irish castle) as opposed to glass and concrete shopping malls. And it includes a hilarious satirization of 1970's pop music. An aristocratic ghost of Cromwell's time is mistaken for one of The Unmentionables, a pop singing group that performs at the castle one night.

Action and humor of various shades are inherent in both of these stories.

Brinton Turkle has repeatedly shown that he can write for almost any age. He also designs all the books he illustrates except those for older boys and girls.

—Norma R. Fryatt

TURNER, Ethel (Sybil). Australian. Born in Doncaster, Yorkshire, England, 24 January 1872; moved to Australia in 1881. Educated at Girls' High School, Sydney. Married H. R. Curlewis in 1896; one son and one daughter. Founding Editor, with Lilian Turner, *The Parthenon* magazine, Sydney, 1889–92; Children's Editor, *Illustrated Sydney News*, later *Australian Town and Country Journal*, 1892–1919, and Sydney *Sun*, 1921–31. *Died 8 April 1958.*

PUBLICATIONS FOR CHILDREN

Fiction

    Seven Little Australians, illustrated by A. J. Johnson. London, Ward Lock, 1894; Philadelphia, McKay, 1904.
    The Family at Misrule, illustrated by A. J. Johnson. London, Ward Lock, 1895.
    The Little Larrikin, illustrated by A. J. Johnson. London, Ward Lock, 1896.
    Miss Bobbie, illustrated by Harold Copping. London, Ward Lock, 1897.
    The Camp at Wandinong, illustrated by Frances Ewan and others. London, Ward Lock, 1898.
    Three Little Maids, illustrated by A. J. Johnson. London, Ward Lock, 1900.
    The Wonder-Child, illustrated by Gordon Browne. London, Religious Tract Society, 1901.
    Little Mother Meg, illustrated by A. J. Johnson. London, Ward Lock, 1902.
    Betty & Co. London, Ward Lock, 1903.
    Mother's Little Girl, illustrated by A. J. Johnson. London, Ward Lock, 1904.
    A White Roof-Tree. London, Ward Lock, 1905.
    In the Mist of the Mountains, illustrated by J. Macfarlane. London, Ward Lock, 1906.
    The Stolen Voyage, illustrated by J. Macfarlane. London, Ward Lock, 1907.
    That Girl, illustrated by Frances Ewan. London, Unwin, 1908.
    Fugitives from Fortune, illustrated by J. Macfarlane. London, Ward Lock, 1909.
    The Apple of Happiness, illustrated by A. N. Gough. London, Hodder and Stoughton, 1911.
    An Ogre Up-to-Date, illustrated by H. C. Sandy and D. H. Souter. London, Ward Lock, 1911.
    The Secret of the Sea. London, Hodder and Stoughton, 1913.
    Flower o' the Pine, illustrated by J. H. Hartley. London, Hodder and Stoughton, 1914.
    The Cub: Six Months in His Life, illustrated by Harold Copping. London, Ward Lock, 1915.

John of Daunt, illustrated by Harold Copping.   London, Ward Lock, 1916.
St. Tom and the Dragon, illustrated by Harold Copping.   London, Ward Lock, 1918.
Brigid and the Cub, illustrated by Harold Copping.   London, Ward Lock, 1919.
Laughing Water, illustrated by Harold Copping.   London, Ward Lock, 1920.
King Anne, illustrated by Harold Copping.   London, Ward Lock, 1921.
Jennifer, J., illustrated by Harold Copping.   London, Ward Lock, 1922.
The Sunshine Family: A Book of Nonsense, with Jean Curlewis, illustrated by D. H.
    Souter and H. Bancks.   London, Ward Lock, 1923.
Nicola Silver, illustrated by Harold Copping.   London, Ward Lock, 1924.
Funny, illustrated by W. E. Wightman.   London, Ward Lock, 1926.
Judy and Punch, illustrated by Harold Copping.   London, Ward Lock, 1928.
The Child of the Children, illustrated by Frances Ewan.   London, Ward Lock, 1959.

Verse

Happy Hearts ..., with others, illustrated by D. H. Souter.   London, Ward Lock, 1908.
The Tiny House and Other Verses.   London, Ward Lock, 1911.
Captain Cub, illustrated by Harold Copping.   London, Ward Lock, 1917.

Other

Gum Leaves, with Oddments by Others (miscellany), illustrated by D. H.
    Souter.   Sydney, Brooks, 1900.
Ethel Turner Birthday Book.   London, Ward Lock, 1909.

PUBLICATIONS FOR ADULTS

Novels

Fair Ines.   London, Hodder and Stoughton, 1910.
The Ungardeners.   London, Ward Lock, 1925.

Short Stories

The Story of a Baby.   London, Ward Lock, 1895.
The Little Duchess.   London, Ward Lock, 1896.

Verse

Fifteen and Fair.   London, Hodder and Stoughton, 1911.
Oh, Boys in Brown.   Sydney, Australian Wounded Soldiers Fund, 1914.

Other

Ports and Happy Havens (travel).   London, Hodder and Stoughton, 1912.

Editor, with Bertram Stevens, *Australian Soldiers' Gift Book*.   Sydney, Voluntary
    Workers Association, 1918.

*   *   *

In the second half of the 19th century, Australian children's literature was usually
produced by English writers – most of whom had never visited the country – for English
readers. With its vast size, its remoteness, its natural hazards of bush fire and flood, its
resident "colorful savages," and its acquired highwaymen (bushrangers) and its gold rushes,

it provided a suitably romantic setting for stereotyped but appealing adventure yarns usually about a recently-arrived English family settling into a rugged and exciting rural life free of real tension or conflict.

Ethel Turner's *Seven Little Australians* was a milestone in Australian children's literature when it appeared in 1894 because it was without precedent. It ignored the established stereotype adventure yarns, and it set a new standard of realistic family stories of the type written decades later by Eleanor Spence, Joan Phipson, and Nan Chauncy. Though born in England, Ethel Turner had lived in Australia for most of her young life. Although she wrote with an English audience in mind, the family was, without apology, Australian, and the setting was both rural and urban. The family was not the usual cosy picture of jollity and comradeship, for Captain Woolcot, without explanation, was presented as being at odds with his children, whose own mother was now dead.

The plot was concerned not with sensational action of an external kind (e.g., bushfires) but with the inner conflicts of characters, their own idiosyncrasies and their relationships within the family. The conflict between paranoid father and high-spirited, assertive teenage daughter – leading to her ultimate death – gives *Seven Little Australians* a peculiarly modern quality. It has much of the flavor of the contemporary realistic problem novel and is as interesting and relevant as ever. For all its melodramatic aspects, and its dated style, it has a basic universality which seems bound to assure its longevity. Feminist readers of today have even more reason to identify with Judy than did their grandparents – and greatgrandparents.

A characteristic of Ethel Turner's books is her obvious affinity with and knowledge of children – how they think, act and feel – and her ability to create thoroughly believable child characters. Each is felt by the reader to be real, to be knowable, yet each is quite distinct and individual. They are lovable, happy, irritating, noisy, mischievous. There is usually someone with whom any young reader can identify, and the action in each story is usually vigorous enough to sustain interest throughout. The solutions to major problems – usually of misbehaviour – are melodramatic and sentimental in the spirit of the times. Death is both a constant threat and a reality in her books, and her naughty children are severely punished by wrathful adults.

Implied didacticism is very strong in Ethel Turner's books, at least as far as respectable middle-class values are concerned, with attendant rewards and punishments. Good taste and modesty are championed, the outward show of the vulgar rich being as reprehensible as the improprieties of the gutter. It therefore is natural that most of her stories deal with decent but poor families nobly struggling to attain or maintain standards of genteel decency. And because of her focus on children, and her positive belief in their basic goodness, successful family relationships are usually attained through their initiatives. They tend to rally round, to rise to the occasion, to hold the family unit together, through their innate sense of decency, fair play, unfettered humor, and a strong bond of love. Later in her career, Ethel Turner developed a strong sense of anger about social injustice and, in books such as *The Cub* and *Captain Cub*, she tried to stir the consciences of her readers, many of whom were adults, along socialist lines. Yet as early as *The Little Larrikin* she had characters rejecting the notion of rich-and-poor: "All the world ought to be respectably comfortable."

Ethel Turner's books are notable for their strong atmosphere of the benign story teller who cares for her readers. *Seven Little Australians*, *The Family at Misrule*, *Miss Bobbie*, and *The Little Larrikin* deal with the sorts of issues encountered in today's problem novels but with an exuberance and a loving concern which makes much modern writing seem clinical and heartless.

—Walter McVitty

TURNER, Philip (William).   Pseudonym: **Stephen Chance.**   British.   Born in Rossland, British Columbia, Canada, 3 December 1925. Educated at Worcester College, Oxford,

1946–49, B.A. 1950, M.A. 1962; Chichester Theological College, Sussex, 1949–51, ordained priest, Church of England, 1951. Served in the Royal Naval Volunteer Reserve, 1943–46; Sub-Lieutenant. Married Margaret Diana Samson in 1951; has two sons and one daughter. Anglican Parish Priest, St. Bartholomew's, Armley, Leeds, 1951–55; St. Peter's, Crawley, Sussex, 1955–60; St. Matthew's, Northampton, 1960–65; Head of Religious Broadcasting, BBC Midland Region, 1965–70; Teacher, Droitwich High School, Worcestershire, 1970–73; Chaplain, Eton College, Buckinghamshire, 1973–75. Since 1975, part-time teacher, Malvern College, Worcestershire. Recipient: Library Association Carnegie Medal, 1966. Agent: Bolt and Watson Ltd., 8–12 Old Queen Street, London S.W.1. Address: St. Francis, 181 West Malvern Road, Malvern, Worcestershire, England.

PUBLICATIONS FOR CHILDREN

Fiction

> *Colonel Sheperton's Clock*, illustrated by Philip Gough.   London, Oxford University Press, 1964; Cleveland, World, 1966.
>
> *The Grange at High Force*, illustrated by William Papas.   London, Oxford University Press, 1965; Cleveland, World, 1967.
>
> *Sea Peril*, illustrated by Ian Ribbons.   London, Oxford University Press, 1966; Cleveland, World, 1968.
>
> *Steam on the Line*, illustrated by Trevor Ridley.   London, Oxford University Press, and Cleveland, World, 1968.
>
> *War on the Darnel*, illustrated by Doreen Roberts.   London, Oxford University Press, and New York, World, 1969.
>
> *Wig-wig and Homer*, illustrated by Graham Humphreys.   London, Oxford University Press, 1969; New York, World, 1970.
>
> *Devil's Nob.*   London, Hamish Hamilton, 1970; Nashville, Nelson, 1973.
>
> *Powder Quay.*   London, Hamish Hamilton, 1971.
>
> *Dunkirk Summer.*   London, Hamish Hamilton, 1973.
>
> *Skull Island.*   London, Dent, 1977.

Fiction (as Stephen Chance)

> *Septimus and the Danedyke Mystery.*   London, Bodley Head, 1971; Nashville, Nelson, 1973.
>
> *Septimus and the Minster Ghost.*   London, Bodley Head, 1972.
>
> *Septimus and the Stone of Offering.*   London, Bodley Head, 1976; Nashville, Nelson, 1977.

Other

> *The Christmas Story: A Carol Service for Children.*   London, Church Information Office, 1964.
>
> *The Bible Story*, illustrated by Brian Wildsmith.   London, Oxford University Press, 1968; as *Illustrated Bible Stories*, New York, Watts, 1969.

PUBLICATIONS FOR ADULTS

Plays

> *Christ in the Concrete City* (produced Hinckley, Yorkshire, 1953).   London, S.P.C.K., 1956; revised edition, 1960; Boston, Baker, 1965.
>
> *Mann's End* (produced Armley, Yorkshire, 1953).   Included in *Tell It With Trumpets*, 1959.

Passion in Paradise Street (produced Armley, Yorkshire, 1954). Included in *Tell It with Trumpets*, 1959.

Cry Dawn in Dark Babylon: A Dramatic Mediation (as *Benny Death and His Old Bones*, produced Durham, 1957). London, S.P.C.K., 1959.

Tell It with Trumpets: Three Experiments in Drama and Evangelism (includes *Mann's End, Passion in Paradise Street, Six-Fifteen to Eternity*, with Jack Windross). London, S.P.C.K., 1959.

Casey: A Dramatic Meditation on the Passion (produced Crawley, Sussex, 1961). London, S.P.C.K., 1962.

This Is the Word, and Word Made Flesh. London, S.P.C.K., 1962.

So Long at the Fair. Melbourne, Board of Christian Education of Australia and New Zealand, 1966.

Men in Stone. Boston, Baker, 1966.

Cantata for Derelicts. London, S.P.C.K., 1967.

Madonna in Concrete. London, S.P.C.K., and Boston, Baker, 1971.

The Pantomime of Septimus Totter. Privately printed, n.d.

Other

Peter Was His Nickname. London, Waltham Forest Books, 1965.

Philip Turner comments:

It has never seemed to me that writing for children is different from writing for anyone else – except that there are some (not many) parts of adult experience that are of no interest to children because they are not yet old enough to have come across them. I write about what interests me and about what I enjoy. If other people – whether 7 or 70 – enjoy it as well, that is splendid. In prose most of what I write comes out as children's stories because of the common interest in "the wonderful oddity of things." In drama I tend to get a bit long-faced and theological for the young.

*   *   *

Philip Turner is an able but uneven writer, whose gifts have never, perhaps, been fused with complete success in a single book. Occasional failures of tone, weakening of imaginative stamina, and lapses of characterisation, occur as minor blemishes in otherwise spirited and enjoyable stories. On the other hand, he has major qualities which are infrequently found in more technically consistent novelists, and lift his work far above the ordinary. Turner's lapses seem due to some uncertainty about his own role and purposes, and especially to sporadic retreat from the seriousness that his themes demand. Inopportune humour explains certain failures of psychological conviction: he has a strange technique of transferred detachment, attributing to his young characters – often at incongruous moments of intense responsibility and crisis – a wry and amused perspective on their perils which is properly the author's own. Turner is an accomplished humorist, and hilarious episodes abound in his stories of present-day adventure, but the humour sometimes jars against a more sombre prevailing mood.

Despite the blemishes, Turner's holiday adventures are a considerable achievement. He has created his own distinctive landscape. It reaches from the little seaport of Darnley Mills, inland and up-river across a country estate, to the hill quarries and bleak open moors. Much of its length is traversed and linked by a narrow-gauge railway, which figures largely both as a focus of adventure and as an index of social history in several novels set in previous generations, and is revived in the modern adventure *War on the Darnel*. This is the setting for Turner's present-day adventures, in which three schoolboys, very different in character but close friends, play and work and grow up. *The Grange at High Force* and *War on the Darnel* are good examples of these books, which follow a similar pattern. There are comedy and high jinks, and there is also a serious crisis in which play is forgotten and the boys' responsibility tested. In *The Grange at High Force* there is much fun with the firing of an 18th-century cannon and a reconstructed Roman ballista, but there is also an appalling blizzard which sends the boys out to rescue the sheep from the high fells and a middle-aged recluse from her snowbound cottage. In *War on the Darnel* there is mock warfare between rival groups of Christian aid collectors, but there is also a dangerous flood in which lives are threatened. The natural rhythm of boyhood is here, in which games and horseplay and ingenious technical experiment prepare for the demands of adult life, recreation and duty can overlap at any time, and childlike pleasure be swamped by emergency. These are good stories, full of vigorous action, but they also successfully depict Christian worship as a natural part of life, and pause at times in reverent stillness before the natural world.

More serious, and more uniformly successful, are the books which explore the adventures of former generations in this same landscape, *Steam on the Line*, *Devil's Nob*, and *Powder Quay*. In these three books the changing fortunes of the little railway are the focus of wider movements of social change and historical experience. Turner admirably catches the lift and decline of lives and ways of life, of families and generations. These books have an emotional and political dimension which is missing in the present-day stories. *Devil's Nob* and *Powder Quay* both describe adolescent love, each with a moving realism, honesty, and tenderness. The books are concerned with class differences, the realities of poverty and social injustice, the harshness of economic catastrophe or war. Turner approaches these with evident discomfort and indignation: he is a traditionalist writer, affirming established values which his individual sympathies at times compel him to dispute. The result is some loss of ideological cohesion but a great gain in emotional force and complexity. The books have a manifest urgency and relevance which historical novels do not commonly achieve.

Turner has written for younger children, notably a charming story of two runaway piglets, *Wig-wig and Homer*. And under the name Stephen Chance he has published several stories of crime and mayhem for older readers. In *Septimus and the Danedyke Mystery* the chief character is a retired London detective who, having somewhat improbably turned country parson, finds even more improbably that his former concerns refuse to desert him. The books are an amusing and modestly successful attempt to fill an an evident gap in adolescent fiction, but they do not seriously rival the achievement of the Darnley Mills stories.

—Peter Hollindale

UCHIDA, Yoshiko. American. Born in Alameda, California, 24 November 1921. Educated at the University of California, Berkeley, A.B. (cum laude) 1942; Smith College, Northampton, Massachusetts (Graduate Fellow), M.Ed. 1944. Teacher, Frankford Friends School, Philadelphia, 1944–45; Secretary, Institute of Pacific Relations, New York, 1946–47, United Student Christian Council, New York, 1947–52, and Lawrence Radiation Laboratory, University of California, Berkeley, 1957–62. Wrote series of articles on folk arts and crafts for *Nippon Times*, Tokyo, 1953–54, and *Craft Horizons*, New York, 1955–64. Lives in Berkeley. Recipient: Ford Foundation Fellowship, 1952. Agent: Ellen Levine, Curtis Brown Ltd., 575 Madison Avenue, New York, New York 10022, U.S.A.

PUBLICATIONS FOR CHILDREN

Fiction

New Friends for Susan, illustrated by Henry Sugimoto. New York, Scribner, 1951.
The Full Circle, illustrated by the author. New York, Friendship Press, 1957.

Takao and the Grandfather's Sword, illustrated by William Hutchinson. New York, Harcourt Brace, 1958; Edinburgh, Oliver and Boyd, 1966.

The Promised Year, illustrated by William Hutchinson. New York, Harcourt Brace, 1959.

Mik and the Prowler, illustrated by William Hutchinson. New York, Harcourt Brace, 1960.

Rokubei and the Thousand Rice Bowls, illustrated by Kazue Mizumura. New York, Scribner, 1962.

The Forever Christmas Tree, illustrated by Kazue Mizumura. New York, Scribner, 1963.

Sumi's Prize, illustrated by Kazue Mizumura. New York, Scribner, 1964.

Sumi's Special Happening, illustrated by Kazue Mizumura. New York, Harcourt Brace, 1966.

In-Between Miya, illustrated by Susan Bennett. New York, Scribner, 1967; London, Angus and Robertson, 1968.

Sumi and the Goat and the Tokyo Express, illustrated by Kazue Mizumura. New York, Scribner, 1969.

Hisako's Mysteries, illustrated by Susan Bennett. New York, Scribner, 1969.

Makoto, The Smallest Boy, illustrated by Akihito Shirakawa. New York, Crowell, 1970.

Journey to Topaz, illustrated by Donald Carrick. New York, Scribner, 1971.

Samurai of Gold Hill, illustrated by Ati Forberg. New York, Scribner, 1972.

The Birthday Visitor, illustrated by Charles Robinson. New York, Scribner, 1975.

The Rooster Who Understood Japanese, illustrated by Charles Robinson. New York, Scribner, 1976.

Other

The Dancing Kettle and Other Japanese Folk Tales, illustrated by Richard Jones. New York, Harcourt Brace, 1949.

The Magic Listening Cap: More Folk Tales from Japan, illustrated by the author. New York, Harcourt Brace, 1955.

The Sea of Gold and Other Tales from Japan, illustrated by Marianne Yamaguchi. New York, Scribner, 1965.

PUBLICATIONS FOR ADULTS

Other

We Do Not Work Alone: Kanjiro Kawai. Kyoto, Folk Art Society, 1953.

The History of Sycamore Church. El Cerrito, California, privately printed, 1974.

Margaret da Patta (exhibition catalogue). Oakland, California, Oakland Museum, 1976.

Manuscript Collection: University of Oregon Library, Eugene.

Yoshiko Uchida comments:

Because I felt I could make the best contribution by writing from my own cultural heritage, all my books have been about the Japanese people. In my earlier books I wrote about Japan in the hope that American children would not only learn to understand and respect its culture, but would identify with the Japanese people as fellow human beings. Because of the growing awareness of the various ethnic groups in the United States, however, I am now writing books based on the relatively unexplored history of the Japanese people living in America. I hope these books will help dispel long-existing stereotypic images and also increase among Japanese-American young people an understanding of their own history and pride in their identity. Ultimately, however, I try to write of meaningful relationships between human beings, to celebrate our common humanity.

*   *   *

Yoshiko Uchida has limited her writing to three categories related to her ethnic background, using skill in creating plot, characterization, and setting. Her familiarity with Japanese folk tales, Japanese culture, and Japanese American society is apparent in her more than twenty books.

Her first book, *The Dancing Kettle*, adaptations of folklore she heard as a child, was very well received. *The Magic Listening Cap* was less successful, but made its way onto lists of recommended books. The author specifically states that she adapted the tales so they would be more meaningful to American children. She notes the source for each, and includes both a glossary and pronunciation guide in the books, including *The Sea of Gold*. Stories such as "New Year's Hats for the Statues" and "The Terrible Black Snake's Revenge" in *The Sea of Gold* are less familiar than tales more like those in the western tradition.

Periodic trips to Japan have made it possible for the author to write authentically about another milieu. While Old Japan is the setting for *Rokubei and the Thousand Rice Bowls*, most of the books have a contemporary theme. *Takao and Grandfather's Sword* has an intricate plot about a boy who causes a fire in his potter father's workshop and tries to make amends. Seven-year old Sumi's adventures are told in a three-book series. The heroine of *In-Between Miya* is disgruntled as the daughter of a humble Buddhist priest and teacher, but is unsuccessful in assisting her wealthy aunt in Tokyo.

Japanese Americans are depicted in the balance of her books. In *Journey to Topaz*, the author deals with the subject of the relocation of the Japanese to Utah during World War II. The young man in *Mik and the Prowler* is more Americanized than most of her characters. Miss Uchida's books frequently include a visitor from Japan to the United States, as in *The Promised Year*, in which Keiki visits an aunt and uncle in California, and *The Birthday Visitor* involving Rev. Okura's arrival in time for Emi's seventh birthday.

The plots are intricate, and yet sturdy. In *New Friends for Susan*, the author describes a third grader's adaptation to a new school in Berkeley after an earthquake. In this first realistic story, she avoids any racial reference. Having experienced relocation herself, Miss Uchida uses restraint in her novels. Only in *Journey to Topaz* does she relate the agony of eleven-year-old Yuri, his brother and mother, and she avoids bitterness in the telling. Even the picture book, *The Rooster Who Understood Japanese*, has a substantial text about the threatened pet which had to be taken away from the city.

Rich characters abound in most of her books, emerging through both description and dialogue. Emi, in *The Birthday Visitor*, fears that the minister will spoil her celebration, but her mood changes when she discovers that he has taken off his shoes under the table. Keiko, in *The Promised Year*, adjusts to a new culture and matures when visiting her California relatives. In *Makoto, The Smallest Boy*, a youngster practices and excels in painting. Assuming responsibility is a motif in *Mik and the Prowler*, as it is in *Takao and Grandfather's Sword*. The girl fails to cope with a challenge in *In-Between Miya*, but is warmly welcomed back to her community. Interrelationships among people of ethnic backgrounds are sketched in *The Rooster Who Understood Japanese*. In *Hisako's Mysteries* the youngster learns that her artist father is not dead, but living in Paris.

Setting is apparent in the background description and in the cultural differences of the people. *Samurai of Gold Hill* is specific about the first Japanese immigrants to California in 1859. Raising carnations provides the backdrop and occasionally the impetus in *The Promised Year*. In *The Forever Christmas Tree*, Japanese Takahashi yearns to celebrate a holiday he has only heard about. Respect for old age is the cultural characteristic in *Sumi's Special Happening*, in which a ninety-year-old man is honored.

Miss Uchida's books are highly successful, and have been widely recommended. The author has worked diligently in describing an ethnic group and interpreting the cultural patterns for the "creating of one world."

—Karen Nelson Hoyle

UDRY, Janice (May). American. Born in Jacksonville, Illinois, 14 June 1928. Educated at Northwestern University, Evanston, Illinois, B.S. 1950. Married Richard Udry in 1950; has two daughters. Address: 412 Elliott Road, Chapel Hill, North Carolina, U.S.A.

PUBLICATIONS FOR CHILDREN

Fiction

> *Little Bear and the Beautiful Kite*, illustrated by Hertha Depper. Racine, Wisconsin, Whitman, 1955.
> *A Tree Is Nice*, illustrated by Marc Simont. New York, Harper, 1956; Kingswood, Surrey, World's Work, 1971.
> *Theodore's Parents*, illustrated by Adrienne Adams. New York, Lothrop, 1958.
> *The Moon Jumpers*, illustrated by Maurice Sendak. New York, Harper, 1959.
> *Danny's Pig*, illustrated by Mariana. New York, Lothrop, 1960.
> *Alfred*, illustrated by Judith Roth. Chicago, Whitman, 1960.
> *Let's Be Enemies*, illustrated by Maurice Sendak. New York, Harper, 1961.
> *Is Susan Here?*, illustrated by Peter Edwards. New York and London, Abelard Schuman, 1962.
> *The Mean Mouse and Other Mean Stories*, illustrated by Ed Young. New York, Harper, 1962.
> *End of the Line*, illustrated by Hope Taylor. Chicago, Whitman, 1962.
> *Betsy-Back-in-Bed*, illustrated by Hope Taylor. Chicago, Whitman, 1963.
> *Next Door to Laura Linda*, illustrated by Meg Wohlberg. Chicago, Whitman, 1965; London, Muller, 1968.
> *What Mary Jo Shared*, illustrated by Eleanor Mill. Chicago, Whitman, 1966.
> *If You're a Bear*, illustrated by Erica Merkling. Chicago, Whitman, 1967.
> *Mary Ann's Mud Day*, illustrated by Martha Alexander. New York, Harper, 1967.
> *What Mary Jo Wanted*, illustrated by Eleanor Mill. Chicago, Whitman, 1968.
> *Glenda*, illustrated by Marc Simont. New York, Harper, 1969.
> *Emily's Autumn*, illustrated by Erik Blegvad. Chicago, Whitman, 1969; Kingswood, Surrey, World's Work, 1976.
> *The Sunflower Garden*, illustrated by Beatrice Darwin. Irvington-on-Hudson, New York, Harvey House, 1969.
> *Mary Jo's Grandmother*, illustrated by Eleanor Mill. Chicago, Whitman, 1970.
> *Angie*, illustrated by Hilary Knight. New York, Harper, 1971.
> *How I Faded Away; or, The Invisible Boy*, illustrated by Monica De Bruyn. Chicago, Whitman, 1976.
> *Oh No, Cat!*, illustrated by Mary Chalmers. New York, Coward McCann, 1976.

*   *   *

Janice Udry's second book, *A Tree Is Nice*, harks back to Joyce Kilmer's immortal poem. In this simple, almost poetic work, Udry presents the delights, charms and uses of trees. In addition to its entertainment and instructional value, the book is ecologically sound in its intent. Children will not only look at trees with a fresh eye, but they will want to "go home and plant a tree too," as a result of their contact with this book.

Udry is primarily known for her Mary Jo series, stories about a little Black girl. They are the kind of "happy ever after" tales which children like to listen to, and they are reminiscent of the stories which parents, teachers, and librarians have always told to children. Young people are comfortable with the familiar which makes *What Mary Jo Shared* (her father), *What Mary Jo Wanted* (a puppy), and *Mary Jo's Grandmother* (thematically identical to Lexau's *Benjie on His Own*) popular books. However, the less well-known *The Sunflower Garden* is a tale with far greater substance, evoking stronger emotional reactions from the reader. It is the story of Pipsa, an Indian girl of the Algonkian tribe, who feels rejected by her father. He never speaks proudly of her accomplishments – berry-picking, gathering wood, basket-weaving, making clothes – but is quick to praise his sons. The time comes when Pipsa proves her capabilities by cultivating the village's first sunflower garden and by saving the life of her baby brother. Thereafter, not only her father, but the entire village voice their pride in Pipsa, her useful new plant, and her clever ideas.

Udry creates original females in *Angie* and *Glenda*, but the episodes are uneven and no character development is displayed. The prose is flat. The author is at her best in *The Sunflower Garden* and *A Tree Is Nice*.

—Vivian J. Scheinmann

UNGERER, Tomi (Jean Thomas Ungerer). American and French. Born in Strasbourg, France, 28 November 1931; moved to the United States in 1957. Educated at Academie d'Alsace, Strasbourg, 1951–52. Served in the Camel Caravan, French Desert Police, Algeria, 1953. Married Miriam Lancaster in 1959 (marriage dissolved); Yvonne Deborah Wright, 1971; has two daughters. Free-lance Illustrator and commercial artist; Founder, Wild Oats Film Company. One-man shows: Haus am Lutzowplatz, Berlin, 1962; D'Arcy Galleries, New York, 1963; Galerie Daniel Keel, Zurich, 1969, 1972–75; Waddel Gallery, New York, 1970; Kestner Gesellschaft, Hannover, Germany, 1972; Galerie Wolfgang Gurlitt, Munich, 1972; Taxis Palais, Innsbruck, 1973; Museum des 20, Vienna, 1973; Galerie Bloch, Innsbruck, 1975; and many others. Recipient: New York *Herald-Tribune* Festival award, 1958, 1967; Society of Illustrators Gold Medal, 1960; *New York Times* award, for illustration, 1962, 1971, 1974; American Institute of Graphic Arts award, 1969. Address: c/o Diogenes Verlag, Sprecherstrasse 8, CH-8032 Zurich, Switzerland.

PUBLICATIONS FOR CHILDREN (illustrated by the author)

Fiction

The Mellops Go Flying. New York, Harper, 1957; London, Methuen, 1962.
The Mellops Go Diving for Treasure. New York, Harper, 1957.
The Mellops Strike Oil. New York, Harper, 1958.
Crictor. New York, Harper, 1958; London, Methuen, 1959.
Adelaide. New York, Harper, 1959.
Emile. New York, Harper, 1960.
Christmas Eve at the Mellops'. New York, Harper, and London, Hamish Hamilton, 1960.
Rufus. New York, Harper, 1961.
Snail, Where Are You? New York, Harper, 1962.

The Three Robbers.   New York, Atheneum, and London, Methuen, 1962.
The Mellops Go Spelunking.   New York and London, Harper, 1963.
Orlando the Brave Vulture.   New York, Harper, 1966; London, Methuen, 1967.
Moon Man.   London, Whiting and Wheaton, 1966; New York, Harper, 1967.
Zeralda's Ogre.   New York, Harper, 1967; London, Bodley Head, 1970.
Basil Ratski.   Zurich, Diogenes, 1967.
Ask Me a Question.   New York, Harper, 1968.
The Hat.   New York, Parents' Magazine Press, 1970; London, Bodley Head, 1971.
The Beast of Monsieur Racine.   New York, Farrar Straus, 1971; London, Bodley Head, 1972.
I Am Papa Snap and These Are My Favorite No-Such Stories.   New York, Harper, 1971; London, Methuen, 1973.
No Kiss for Mother.   New York, Harper, 1973; London, Methuen, 1974.
Allumette: A Fable, with Due Respect to Hans Christian Andersen, the Grimm Brothers, and the Honorable Ambrose Bierce.   New York, Parents' Magazine Press, 1974; London, Methuen, 1975.

Verse

One, Two, Where's My Shoe?   New York and London, Harper, 1964.

Other

Editor, *A Storybook from Tomi Ungerer.*   New York, Watts, and London, Collins, 1974.

PUBLICATIONS FOR ADULTS (drawings)

Other

Inside Marriage: Wedding Pictures.   New York, Grove Press, 1960.
Horrible: An Account of the Sad Achievements of Progress.   New York, Atheneum, and London, Hamish Hamilton, 1960.
Der Herzinfarkt.   Zurich, Diogenes, 1962.
A Television Notebook.   New York, CBS, 1963.
The Underground Sketch Book of Tomi Ungerer.   New York, Viking Press, and London, Bodley Head, 1964.
The Party.   New York, Paragraphic Books, 1966.
Fornicon.   New York, Rhinoceros Press, 1969.
Portfolio.   Zurich, Diogenes, 1970.
Compromises.   New York, Farrar Straus, and London, Bodley Head, 1970.
The Poster Art of Tomi Ungerer, edited by Jack Rennart.   New York, Darien House, 1970; London, Constable, 1973.
Der Sexmaniak.   Zurich, Diogenes, 1971.
Der Spiegelmensch.   Zurich, Diogenes, 1973.
Adam and Eve: A Collection of Cartoons.   Zurich, Diogenes, 1974; London, Cape, 1976.
America.   Zurich, Diogenes, 1975.
Freut Euch des Lebens.   Zurich, Diogenes, 1975.
Das grosse Liederbuch.   Zurich, Diogenes, 1975.
Das kleine Liederbuch.   Zurich, Diogenes, 1975.
Totempole.   Zurich, Diogenes, 1976.

Illustrator: *The Brave Coward* by Art Buchwald, 1957; *Agee on Film* by James Agee, 1958; *Seeds and More Seeds* by Millicent E. Selsam, 1959; *Amerika fuer Angaenger* by Paul

Rothenhäusler, 1960; *The Backside of Washington* by Dick West, 1961; *Comfortable Words* by Bergen Evans, 1962; *The Book of Gambling* edited by David Newman, 1962; *Riddle Dee Dee* by Bennett Cerf, 1962; *Frédou* by Mary Stolz, 1962; *Frances Face-Maker*, 1963, and *That Pest, Jonathan*, 1970, by William Cole, and *A Cat-Hater's Handbook*, 1963, *Beastly Boys and Ghastly Girls*, 1964, *Oh, What Nonsense!*, 1966, *A Case of the Giggles*, 1966, *What's Good for a Four-Year-Old*, 1967, *This Is Ridiculous*, 1967, *Oh, How Silly!*, 1970, *The Book of Giggles*, 1970, and *Oh, That's Ridiculous!*, 1972, all edited by Cole; *Owls and More Owls* by John Hollander, 1963; *Come into My Parlor*, 1963, and *The Too Hot to Cook Book*, 1966, by Miriam Ungerer; *The Girls We Leave Behind*, 1963, and *The Clambake Mutiny*, 1964, by Jerome Beatty; *Der Spottsdrossel* by Ambrose Bierce, 1963; *All about Women* edited by Saul Maloff, 1963; *Erlesene Verbrechen und Makellose Morde*, 1964, and *Ein Buendel Geschichten fuer Luesterne Leser*, 1967, by Henry Slesar; *Games, Anyone?* by Robert Thomson, 1964; *Dear N.A.S.A., Please Send Me a Rocket* by Tait Trussel and Paul Hencke, 1964; *Flat Stanley* by Jeff Brown, 1964; *A Collection of French Poetry*, 1966; *Warwick's Three Bottles*, 1966, and *Cleopatra Goes Sledding*, 1968, by André Hodeir; *Mr. Tall and Mr. Small* by Barbara Brenner, 1966; *The Donkey Ride* by Jean B. Showalter, 1967; *Nonsense Verses* by Edward Lear, 1967; *The Sorcerer's Apprentice* by Barbara Shook Hazen, 1969; *New York fuer Anfaenger* by Herbert Feuerstein, 1969; *Der Gestohlene Bazillus* by H.G. Wells, 1969; *The Consumer in American Society* by A.W. Troelstrup, 1970; *School Life in Paris*, 1970; *Kneipenlieder* by Rainer Brambach and Frank Geerk, 1974.

*   *   *

One of Tomi Ungerer's many talents is that of lending charm and appeal to various denizens of the human or animal population not generally loved or admired by the public. Among his host of unlikely animal heroes are to be found Emile the octopus, Rufus the bat, Crictor the heroic boa constrictor, the Mellops family of handsome and amiable pigs, and Orlando the brave vulture. In more or less human guise come the child-devouring ogre who is eventually humanized into marriageability by sweet Zeralda, the three grim robbers of the black capes and ominous eyes, and M. Racine's friend the peculiar looking and unidentifiable Beast, to name but a few. Each represents some form of life or fantastic order of being usually regarded as repulsive, threatening, or disgusting, yet in Ungerer's light-hearted picture stories all are transformed into the World's Valentines.

That this is so must be attributed at least in part to the winning way in which Ungerer has drawn them: it is quite impossible to think of Tomi Ungerer's text without reference to his pictures, for the two are inseparable. (When Crictor's acrobatic body forms letters of the alphabet, should the result be described as art or literature?) Pictures give point to his spare and economical prose, while his wickedly sly text underscores his pictorial wit. His work is dotted with "visual puns," a little piggy-boy has (of course) a human-shaped penny bank; Emile at the grand piano plays "La Mer" in concert style.

If Ungerer's animal and reptile heroes are almost-human creatures of fantasy, his human creations, however fantastic their adventures, are solidly down-to-earth. Young Zeralda, the ogre-tamer, has the self-possession of an Alice in Wonderland: no matter how bizarre the situation in which she finds herself, she holds firmly to the one essential principle that a hungry man (or ogre) must be fed. Her businesslike, matter-of-fact behaviour makes her a memorably charming young heroine. Little orphan Tiffany is made of the same sturdy stuff. Kidnapped by three fierce robbers, she remains poised and in control of the situation. Her reasonable inquiries as to the purpose of their activities lead the robbers to reconsider their antisocial behaviour and become philanthropists. Allumette, the ragged match girl suddenly deluged by inexplicable treasure from the sky, is not stunned by the situation as we should be: she immediately opens a welfare office in order to distribute largess in an orderly fashion. Their unruffled, reasonable behaviour is the secret of Ungerer's little peoples' charm.

He can take a tired old theme, give it a twist no-one else could have dreamt of – and the end result is both unpredictable and somehow inevitable and satisfying. His is an unprejudiced eye, able to discover admirable qualities in unlikely places, and, better still, he is able to make his readers do the same.

—Joan McGrath

UNWIN, Nora S(picer).   British.   Born in Surbiton, Surrey, 22 February 1907. Educated at Surbiton High School; Leon Underwood's Studio, London, 1924–26; Kingston School of Art, Surrey, 1926–28; Royal College of Art, London, 1928–32, Diploma in Design 1932. Painter, illustrator, and engraver: one-man shows in Boston, 1948, and other cities in the United States, 1950–69; group shows throughout the United States, South America, Europe, and Near East; collections in Contemporary Art Society, London; Boston Public Library; Fitchburg Art Museum, Massachusetts; Library of Congress, Washington, D.C.; New York Public Library. Part-time art teacher and director. Associate, 1935, and Fellow, 1946, Royal Society of Painter-Etchers and Engravers; Associate, Royal College of Art. Address: Pine-Apple Cottage, Old Street Road, Peterborough, New Hampshire 03458, U.S.A.

PUBLICATIONS FOR CHILDREN (illustrated by the author)

Fiction

> *Lucy and the Little Red Horse*, with *Mrs. Mouse and Family* and *Lucy and the Fairy Feasts*, by Gwendy Caroe.   London, Moring, 1943.
> *Doughnuts for Lin.*   New York, Aladdin, 1950.
> *Proud Pumpkin.*   New York, Aladdin, 1953.
> *Poquito, The Little Mexican Duck.*   New York, McKay, 1959; London, Hutchinson, 1961.
> *Two Too Many.*   New York, McKay, 1962; London, Hutchinson, 1965.
> *Joyful the Morning.*   New York, McKay, 1963.
> *The Midsummer Witch.*   New York, McKay, 1966; London, Hutchinson, 1969.
> *Sinbad the Cygnet.*   New York, Day, 1970.

Verse

> *Round the Year: Verses and Pictures.*   London, Chatto and Windus, 1939; New York, Holiday House, 1940.

Other

> *The Way of the Shepherd: The Story of the Twenty-Third Psalm.*   New York, McGraw Hill, 1963; Kingswood, Surrey, World's Work, 1964.

Manuscript Collection: University of Oregon Library, Eugene.

Illustrator: *Five of Us – And Madeline* by E. Nesbit, 1925; *How Does Your Garden Grow?* by Beverley Nichols and others, 1935; *Hans and Frieda*, 1939, *Under the Little Fir*, 1942, *Mountain Born*, 1943, *Joseph*, 1947, *Once in the Year*, 1947, *Summer Green*, 1948, *The Christmas Story*, 1949, *Amos Fortune, Free Man*, 1950, *Children of the Bible*, 1950, *A Place for Peter*, 1952, *Prudence Crandall*, 1955, *Gifts of True Love*, 1958, *Carolina's Courage*,

1964, *An Easter Story*, 1967, *With Pipe, Paddle, and Song*, 1968, *Sarah Whitcher's Story*, 1971, and *Up the Road Through Sandwich Notch*, 1973, all by Elizabeth Yates, and *Gathered Grace*, 1938, *The White Ring*, 1949, and *Your Prayers and Mine*, 1954, all edited by Yates; *The Doll Who Came Alive* by Enys Tregarthen, 1942; *Rainy Day Stories*, 1944, *Round the Clock Stories*, 1945, and *Rambles with Uncle Nat*. 1947, all by Enid Blyton; *Rosemary Isle and Other Rhymes* by Dorothy U. Ratcliffe. 1944; *My Own Picture Prayer Book* edited by Nan Dearmer, 1946; *First Alphabet and Jingle Book* by Hetty S. Burnett, 1946; *Bobby Bunnyfly* by Kay Roberts, 1947; *The House That Ran Behind* by Barbara Euphan Todd and Esther Boumphrey, 1947; *Footnotes on Nature* by John Kiernan, 1947; *Holly Hotel*, 1947. *Lost Karin*, 1948, *The Mirrors of Castle Doone*, 1949, and *The Provost's Jewel*. 1951, all by Elisabeth Kyle; *Luke's Quest* by Caroline D. Snedeker. 1947; *Andy, The Musical Ant* by William McGreal, 1947; *The Secret Garden* by Frances Hodgson Burnett. 1949; *Peter Pan* by J.M. Barrie, 1950; *Leave It to the Brooks* by Antonia Ridge, 1950; *Lucy's League* by Amelia Gay, 1950; *The Good Rain* by Alice E. Goudey. 1950; *The Princess and the Goblin* by George MacDonald, 1951; *The Reward of Faith and Other Stories* by Elizabeth Goudge. 1951; *The Family That Grew and Grew* by Margaret J. Baker. 1952; *Jack and Jill Books*, 8 vols., 1955–56; *Two for the Fair*. 1958, and *A Dog Like No Other*. 1965. by William MacKellar; *Tabby Magic*, 1959, and *More Tabby Magic*. 1961, by Cecile De Banke; *How the Manx Lost Its Tail* by Blanche Young. 1959; *Cupola House* by Mabel Leigh Hunt. 1961.

*   *   *

Primarily an artist. Nora S. Unwin wrote *Round the Year*. which was published in both Great Britain and the United States some nineteen years after her debut as an illustrator. During a span of thirty-one years. she wrote ten stories which were suitable for her own illustrations. Her books have an individuality in subject matter. characterization. and style.

The subjects come from her background and imagination. and are primarily about animals or holidays. *The Way of the Shepherd* is an elaboration on the twenty-third psalm. in which aged Reuben demonstrates to Azor how meaningful the Biblical passage is to people who work with sheep. The animals drink from water which is still. and the staff is used to assist a struggling sheep. Miss Unwin champions the smallest animals in two other books. In *Sinbad the Cygnet*. the smaller of the hatched birds must use his own ingenuity in ascending the waterfall.

The kittens in *Two Too Many* are abandoned by their owner. but become indispensible to a witch. The latter story is appropriate for Halloween. as is *Proud Pumpkin*. *The Midsummer Witch* could be enjoyed especially during two seasons. *Joyful the Morning* is a Christmas story. the title taken from a song.

Enterprising people and animals provide the substance for her books. *Doughnuts for Lin* is the story of the author's own dog. who finally persuades Mrs. Twinkle that it is worth her while to provide him with the food she had prepared for the birds. In *Poquito. The Little Mexican Duck* the fowl can't keep up with the adult ducks. but a child rescues him. At the conclusion of the story. she shows her value and prevents herself being made into soup by laying an egg. The pumpkin is made into a jack-o-lantern instead of a pie. and eventually a chipmunk uses it for a home in *Proud Pumpkin*. The kittens in *Two Too Many* provide the witch with taillights as they hang on to her broom when she makes the Grand Race over the moon.

Nora Unwin has a special touch in incorporating traditional themes and elements into her stories. and giving attention to detail. The scarecrow. who is followed by children in a Pied Piper manner in *The Midsummer Witch*. brings them to a bonfire. Poquito is a duck raised among turkeys in a Mexican town. rather than the swan among ducks in Hans Christian Andersen's fairy tale. "Pride goeth before the fall" is an adage developed in the *Proud Pumpkin*. Indeed. he is not eaten. but he is humbled ultimately. *Joyful the Morning*. which is autobiographical. describes a traditional English Christmas of about 60 years ago.

Her training as an artist is apparent in her stories. The Mexican town and village. based on her stay in San Miguel de Allende and environs is appropriate. She had obviously seen a duckling raised among turkeys, and peasants interacting with one another. In *The Way of the Shepherd*, she acknowledged the Zion Research Library of Brookline where she had used books and materials pertaining to the Holy Land. When the pumpkin is made into a lantern by Billy, he perceives "a dreadful draught blowing into my insides." *Joyful the Morning* is filled with reminiscences, including the mood of the twins, as she herself was a twin.

Three of Nora Unwin's books were in print in 1976. They will undoubtedly be outlasted by the scores of books she illustrated for others, which will be her major legacy.

—Karen Nelson Hoyle

UPTON, Bertha (Hudson).   American.   Born in 1849. *Died in 1912.*

PUBLICATIONS FOR CHILDREN (illustrated by Florence K. Upton)

Verse

The Adventures of Two Dutch Dolls – and a Golliwogg.   London and New York, Longman, 1895.
The Golliwogg's Bicycle Club.   London and New York, Longman, 1896.
The Vege-Men's Revenge.   London and New York, Longman, 1897.
Little Hearts.   London, and New York, Routledge, 1897.
The Golliwogg at the Sea-side.   London and New York, Longman, 1898.
The Golliwogg in War!   London and New York, Longman, 1899.
The Golliwogg's Polar Adventures.   London and New York, Longman, 1900.
The Golliwogg's Auto-Go-Cart.   London and New York, Longman, 1901.
The Golliwogg's Air-Ship.   London and New York, Longman, 1902.
The Golliwogg's Circus.   London and New York, Longman, 1903.
The Golliwogg in Holland.   London and New York, Longman, 1904.
The Golliwogg's Fox-Hunt.   London and New York, Longman, 1905.
The Golliwogg's Desert Island.   London and New York, Longman, 1906.
The Golliwogg's Christmas.   London and New York, Longman, 1907.
The Golliwogg in the African Jungle.   London and New York, Longman, 1909.

*   *   *

With the publication in 1895 of *The Adventures of Two Dutch Dolls*, two young American women launched a career in children's book writing and illustrating that was to have a lasting effect on the content and format of children's literature for many years. The young women were the sisters Bertha and Florence Upton; their works, because the family resided predominately in England after 1893, were published in Great Britain; and the main character of most of their works, the Golliwogg, has gone down in the annals of children's literature as a vastly sympathetic, active and interesting example of a fantasy character who achieved a considerable degree of reality in the minds of its child audience. Bertha Upton wrote the text for the Golliwogg books and her sister Florence illustrated them using mid- and late-Victorian dolls as models for the characters. The texts of the books in the Golliwogg series are consistently lively, well thought out episodes concerning the activities of the Golliwogg and (eventually) 5 Dutch dolls, Peg, Weg, Meg, Sarah Jane, and the diminutive

Midget. Typical of the movement of the patterned verse in this series is the following inductive stanza from *The Adventures of Two Dutch Dolls — and a Golliwogg*:

> Get up! get up, dear Sarah Jane!
> Now strikes the midnight hour,
> When dolls and toys
> Taste human joys,
> And revel in their power.

The narrative verse is rarely characterized by enjambment, yet the flow of the lines, the spontaneity of the ideas and characters, and the short syllabic value of words allows for rapid reading of the verse and equally rapid assimilation of the ideas and images.

It would be difficult to calculate the overall influence of the Golliwogg books on future works such as Rachel Field's *Hitty, Her First Hundred Years*, and there are numerous earlier analogues for the Golliwogg. The Golliwogg series, as a whole, exhibits a picaresque pattern without the satire. The adventures are widely diversified, showing the Golliwogg's experiences at the sea side, in Holland, on a desert island, in war, in the African Jungle, and so forth, and in all the episodes Upton maintains the strong sense of realism so necessary to good fantasy.

—Rachel Fordyce

UTTLEY, Alison (Alice Jane Uttley). British. Born in Cromford, Derbyshire, 17 December 1884. Educated at Lady Manners School, Bakewell, Yorkshire; Manchester University, B.Sc. (honours) in physics. Married James A. Uttley in 1911 (died, 1930); one son. Science teacher, Fulham Secondary School for Girls, London, 1908–11. Litt.D.: Manchester University, 1970. *Died 7 May 1976.*

PUBLICATIONS FOR CHILDREN

Fiction

> *The Squirrel, The Hare, and the Little Grey Rabbit*, illustrated by Margaret Tempest. London, Heinemann, 1929.
> *How Little Grey Rabbit Got Back Her Tail*, illustrated by Margaret Tempest. London, Heinemann, 1930.
> *The Great Adventure of Hare*, illustrated by Margaret Tempest. London, Heinemann, 1931.
> *Moonshine and Magic*, illustrated by Will Townsend. London, Faber, 1932.
> *The Story of Fuzzypeg the Hedgehog*, illustrated by Margaret Tempest. London, Heinemann, 1932.
> *Squirrel Goes Skating*, illustrated by Margaret Tempest. London, Collins, 1934.
> *Wise Owl's Story*, illustrated by Margaret Tempest. London, Collins, 1935.
> *The Adventures of Peter and Judy in Bunnyland*, illustrated by L. Young. London, Collins, 1935.
> *Candlelight Tales*, illustrated by Elinor Bellingham-Smith. London, Faber, 1936.
> *Little Grey Rabbit's Party*, illustrated by Margaret Tempest. London, Collins, 1936.

The Knot Squirrel Tied, illustrated by Margaret Tempest. London, Collins, 1937.

The Adventures of No Ordinary Rabbit, illustrated by Alec Buckels. London, Faber, 1937.

Mustard, Pepper, and Salt, illustrated by Gwen Raverat. London, Faber, 1938.

Fuzzypeg Goes to School, illustrated by Margaret Tempest. London, Collins, 1938.

A Traveller in Time. London, Faber, 1939; New York, Putnam, 1940.

Tales of the Four Pigs and Brock the Badger, illustrated by Alec Buckels. London, Faber, 1939.

Little Grey Rabbit's Christmas, illustrated by Margaret Tempest. London, Collins, 1939.

Moldy Warp, The Mole, illustrated by Margaret Tempest. London, Collins, 1940.

The Adventures of Sam Pig, illustrated by Francis Gower. London, Faber, 1940.

Sam Pig Goes to Market, illustrated by A.E. Kennedy. London, Faber, 1941.

Six Tales of Brock the Badger, illustrated by Alec Buckels and Francis Gower. London, Faber, 1941.

Six Tales of Sam Pig, illustrated by Alec Buckels and Francis Gower. London, Faber, 1941.

Six Tales of the Four Pigs, illustrated by Alec Buckels. London, Faber, 1941.

Ten Tales of Tim Rabbit, illustrated by Alec Buckels and Francis Gower. London, Faber, 1941.

Hare Joins the Home Guard, illustrated by Margaret Tempest. London, Collins, 1942.

Little Grey Rabbit's Washing-Day, illustrated by Margaret Tempest. London, Collins, 1942.

Nine Starlight Tales, illustrated by Irene Hawkins. London, Faber, 1942.

Sam Pig and Sally, illustrated by A.E. Kennedy. London, Faber, 1942.

Cuckoo Cherry-Tree, illustrated by Irene Hawkins. London, Faber, 1943.

Sam Pig at the Circus, illustrated by A.E. Kennedy. London, Faber, 1943.

Water-Rat's Picnic, illustrated by Margaret Tempest. London, Collins, 1943.

Little Grey Rabbit's Birthday, illustrated by Margaret Tempest. London, Collins, 1944.

Mrs. Nimble and Mr. Bumble, illustrated by Horace Knowles, with *This Duck and That Duck*, by Herbert McKay. London, Barmerlea, 1944.

The Spice Woman's Basket and Other Tales, illustrated by Irene Hawkins. London, Faber, 1944.

The Adventures of Tim Rabbit, illustrated by A.E. Kennedy. London, Faber, 1945.

The Speckledy Hen, illustrated by Margaret Tempest. London, Faber, 1945.

The Weather Cock and Other Stories, illustrated by Nancy Innes. London, Faber, 1945.

Little Grey Rabbit and the Weasels, illustrated by Margaret Tempest. London, Collins, 1947.

Grey Rabbit and the Wandering Hedgehog, illustrated by Margaret Tempest. London, Collins, 1948.

John Barleycorn: Twelve Tales of Fairy and Magic, illustrated by Philip Hepworth. London, Faber, 1948.

Sam Pig in Trouble, illustrated by A.E. Kennedy. London, Faber, 1948.

The Cobbler's Shop and Other Tales, illustrated by Irene Hawkins. London, Faber, 1950.

Macduff, illustrated by A.E. Kennedy. London, Faber, 1950.

Little Grey Rabbit Makes Lace, illustrated by Margaret Tempest. London, Collins, 1950.

The Little Brown Mouse Books (*Snug and Serena Meet a Queen, Snug and Serena Pick Cowslips, Going to the Fair, Toad's Castle, Mrs. Mouse Spring-Cleans, Christmas at the Rose and Crown, The Gypsy Hedgehogs, Snug and the Chimney-Sweeper, The Mouse Telegrams, The Flower Show, Snug and the Silver Spoon, Mr. Stoat Walks In*), illustrated by Katherine Wigglesworth. London, Heinemann, 12 vols., 1950–57.

Yours Ever, Sam Pig, illustrated by A.E. Kennedy. London, Faber, 1951.

Hare and the Easter Eggs, illustrated by Margaret Tempest.   London, Collins, 1952.

Little Grey Rabbit Goes to Sea, illustrated by Margaret Tempest.   London, Collins, 1954.

Little Red Fox and the Wicked Uncle, illustrated by Katherine Wigglesworth.   London, Heinemann, 1954; Indianapolis, Bobbs Merrill, 1962.

Sam Pig and the Singing Gate, illustrated by A.E. Kennedy.   London, Faber, 1955.

Hare and Guy Fawkes, illustrated by Margaret Tempest.   London, Collins, 1956.

Little Red Fox and Cinderella, illustrated by Katherine Wigglesworth.   London, Heinemann, 1956.

Magic in My Pocket: A Selection of Tales, illustrated by Judith Brook.   London, Penguin, 1957.

Little Grey Rabbit's Paint-Box, illustrated by Margaret Tempest.   London, Collins, 1958.

Little Grey Rabbit and the Magic Moon, illustrated by Katherine Wigglesworth.   London, Heinemann, 1958.

Snug and Serena Count Twelve, illustrated by Katherine Wigglesworth.   London, Heinemann, 1959; Indianapolis, Bobbs Merrill, 1962.

Tim Rabbit and Company, illustrated by A.E. Kennedy.   London, Faber, 1959.

Sam Pig Goes to the Seaside: Sixteen Stories, illustrated by A.E. Kennedy.   London, Faber, 1960.

Grey Rabbit Finds a Shoe, illustrated by Margaret Tempest.   London, Collins, 1960.

John at the Old Farm, illustrated by Jennifer Miles.   London, Heinemann, 1960.

Grey Rabbit and the Circus, illustrated by Margaret Tempest.   London, Collins, 1961.

Snug and Serena Go to Town, illustrated by Katherine Wigglesworth.   London, Heinemann, 1961; Indianapolis, Bobbs Merrill, 1963.

Little Red Fox and the Unicorn, illustrated by Katherine Wigglesworth.   London, Heinemann, 1962.

The Little Knife Who Did All the Work: Twelve Tales of Magic, illustrated by Pauline Baynes.   London, Faber, 1962.

Grey Rabbit's May Day, illustrated by Margaret Tempest.   London, Collins, 1963.

Tim Rabbit's Dozen, illustrated by Shirley Hughes.   London, Faber, 1964.

Hare Goes Shopping, illustrated by Margaret Tempest.   London, Collins, 1965.

The Sam Pig Storybook, illustrated by Cecil Leslie.   London, Faber, 1965.

The Mouse, The Rabbit, and the Little White Hen, illustrated by Jennie Corbett.   London, Heinemann, 1966.

Enchantment, illustrated by Jennie Corbett.   London, Heinemann, 1966.

Little Grey Rabbit's Pancake Day, illustrated by Margaret Tempest.   London, Collins, 1967.

The Little Red Fox and the Big Big Tree, illustrated by Jennie Corbett.   London, Heinemann, 1968.

Little Grey Rabbit Goes to the North Pole, illustrated by Katherine Wigglesworth.   London, Collins, 1970.

Lavender Shoes: Eight Tales of Enchantment, illustrated by Janina Ede.   London, Faber, 1970.

The Brown Mouse Book: Magical Tales of Two Little Mice, illustrated by Katherine Wigglesworth.   London, Heinemann, 1971.

Fuzzypeg's Brother, illustrated by Katherine Wigglesworth.   London, Heinemann, 1971.

Little Grey Rabbit's Spring Cleaning Party, illustrated by Katherine Wigglesworth.   London, Collins, 1972.

Little Grey Rabbit and the Snow-Baby, illustrated by Katherine Wigglesworth.   London, Collins, 1973.

Fairy Tales, edited by Kathleen Lines, illustrated by Ann Strugnell.   London, Faber, 1975.

Hare and the Rainbow, illustrated by Katherine Wigglesworth.   London, Collins, 1975.

Plays

Little Grey Rabbit to the Rescue, illustrated by Margaret Tempest. London, Collins, 1945.
The Washerwoman's Child: A Play on the Life and Stories of Hans Christian Andersen, illustrated by Irene Hawkins. London, Faber, 1946.
Three Little Grey Rabbit Plays (includes *Grey Rabbit's Hospital, The Robber, A Christmas Story*). London, Heinemann, 1961.

PUBLICATIONS FOR ADULTS

Novels

High Meadows. London, Faber, 1938.
When All Is Done. London, Faber, 1945.

Other

The Country Child. London, Faber, and New York, Macmillan, 1931.
Ambush of Young Days. London, Faber, 1937.
The Farm on the Hill. London, Faber, 1941.
Country Hoard. London, Faber, 1943.
Country Things. London, Faber, 1946.
Carts and Candlesticks. London, Faber, 1948.
Buckinghamshire. London, Hale, 1950.
Plowmen's Clocks. London, Faber, 1952.
The Stuff of Dreams. London, Faber, 1953.
Here's a New Day. London, Faber, 1956.
A Year in the Country. London, Faber, 1957.
The Swans Fly Over. London, Faber, 1959.
Something for Nothing. London, Faber, 1960.
Wild Honey. London, Faber, 1962.
Cuckoo in June. London, Faber, 1964.
A Peck of Gold. London, Faber, 1966.
Recipes from an Old Farmhouse. London, Faber, 1966.
The Button Box and Other Essays. London, Faber, 1968.
The Ten O'Clock Scholar and Other Essays. London, Faber, 1970.
Secret Places and Other Essays. London, Faber, 1972.

Editor, *In Praise of Country Life: An Anthology*. London, Muller, 1949.

*   *   *

Like most if not all creative writers Alison Uttley drew extensively on memories of her childhood; she found in them an inexhaustible source of inspiration and of the facts of country life that she needed to provide the right setting for her stories.

She is probably best known as the author of the *Little Grey Rabbit* books and there is a lot of Mrs. Uttley herself in the character of Grey Rabbit: the resourceful countrywoman, the lover of traditional customs and festivals, the sensitive observer who enjoyed all the signs and sounds and smells of the countryside. In fact in one special foreword she made the clear statement: "The country ways of Grey Rabbit were the country ways known to the author." But Grey Rabbit has her own character and so do her companions, boastful but basically kind Hare, timid and sometimes rather foolish Squirrel, and all the friends who visit them, Wise Owl, Fuzzypeg and the rest. Mrs. Uttley was fortunate in her main illustrator, Margaret Tempest, whose pictures gave visible form to the group of animal characters.

But one set of stories was by no means enough for Alison Uttley who kept three publishers busy. More or less simultaneously with Grey Rabbit, Sam Pig came to life, with a quite separate collection of farmyard characters: Sally the Mare, several other little pigs, and their knowledgeable friend Brock and Badger. Sam Pig became very popular, reflecting perhaps Alison Uttley's experience of small boys she knew. And at about the same time Tim Rabbit appeared, "No Ordinary Rabbit," who had some rather extraordinary experiences. But this was not all. Two further groups of characters appeared later: Snug and Serena (in the *Little Brown Mouse* books) and Little Red Fox, who had quite a substantial series of his own.

In addition there are the charming books of Fairy Tales. But it should not be thought that there is a clear cut division between these and the animal stories. It is characteristic of Alison Uttley that magic and fantasy play a part in all her writing. This element was a fundamental part of her mind and her imagination, with the result that throughout the animal stories, though they are soundly based on direct knowledge of country life, there is always the possibility that the characters will be faced with some fantastic experience which is accepted without any questioning. There is continuity between the stories about animals and the stories that can be regarded as fairy tales proper, and the connection works both ways. As Kathleen Lines says in her introduction to a selection of fairy tales: "The stories ... reveal to the willing eye and ear, the usually unsuspected magic in the countryside and in the lives of humble village people." And Alison Uttley herself is quoted as saying: "So each and every tale holds everyday magic, and each is connected with awareness of everyday life, where reality is made visible, and one sees what goes on with new eyes." Here is the essence of much of Alison Uttley's writing for children.

The Washerwoman's Child is a play written round the life of Hans Andersen, introducing versions of seven of his fairy tales. Hans Andersen's stories clearly had a special appeal for Alison Uttley, as on the one hand they were often concerned with everyday things and simple people – a pair of scissors or an iron, a chimney sweep or a shepherdess – and on the other told of those traditional characters almost equally familiar to Alison Uttley as a storyteller, such as the Snow Queen, or imaginary Princes and Princesses and Emperors. But for her these characters were often seen in a more homely setting. To quote Kathleen Lines again: "The traditional 'princess' is a beautiful country maiden, the 'prince' a fine, upstanding shepherd or farm labourer, whose rival in love is either a member of the fairy folk or a manifestation of some natural force."

But once, and in her most original and important work of fiction, she wrote about a real queen. The stories described above are for younger children; *A Traveller in Time* is for those who are older, perhaps particularly girls (though the book is gripping for anyone) as the protagonist is a young schoolgirl, surely Alison Uttley herself, in spite of the fact that the heroine is called Penelope and the name Alison is given to Penelope's elder sister. Here all Mrs. Uttley's skills and special qualities are seen at their best. The scene is the Derbyshire farm where she was born and brought up, but woven into this simple background is the dream world which always meant a very great deal to her; and the core of the story is the girl's journeys in time to the period when Mary Queen of Scots spent part of her imprisonment in a nearby Derbyshire manor house. The girl, Penelope, moves in fantasy, or in dream, between the farm she knows in her real contemporary life and the 16th-century drama enacted by the Babington family in their attempts to rescue the imprisoned Queen. Anthony Babington, later to go to his death on account of the Babington plot, is the leading character in this side of the story, but it is his younger brother Francis whom Penelope specially loves with a romantic affection which seems to have caught hold of the writer herself. By the skill of her writing Alison Uttley manages to make the story of the Babingtons and Mary Queen of Scots more "real" than the simple story of Penelope's visits to the farm. This is Mrs. Uttley's finest achievement and an outstandingly imaginative work that is uniquely her own.

—Peter du Sautoy

Van STOCKUM, Hilda. American. Born in Rotterdam, Netherlands, 9 February 1908; emigrated to the United States in 1934; naturalized citizen, 1936. Educated at Amsterdam Academy of Art; Dublin School of Art; Corcoran School of Art, Washington, D.C., 1936–37; Andre Lhote Studio, Paris, and Ernest Fuchs Studio, Jerusalem. Married Ervin R. Marlin in 1932; has four daughters and two sons. Art teacher in Ireland and illustrator for Browne and Nolan, publishers, Dublin, in late 1920's; Montessori Instructor, Child Education Foundation, New York, 1934; Instructor in Art and Creative Writing, Institute of Lifetime Learning, Washington, D.C., 1965–74. One-man shows: Painters Gallery, Dublin, 1953; Difas Gallery, Geneva, 1964; De Kuyl Gallery, Bilthoven, Netherlands, 1964; Venables Gallery, Washington, D.C., 1974; Den Arts Gallery, Ottawa, 1974; group shows: Montreal Museum of Fine Arts, 1957; Royal Academy, London, 1961, 1977; van der Straeten Gallery, New York, 1973, and many others. President, Children's Book Guild, Washington, D.C., 1972–74. Member, Women Geographers. Address: 32 Castle Hill Avenue, Berkhamsted, Hertfordshire, England.

PUBLICATIONS FOR CHILDREN

Fiction (illustrated by the author)

> *A Day on Skates.* New York and London, Harper, 1934.
> *The Cottage at Bantry Bay.* New York, Viking Press, 1938; London, Muller, 1946.
> *Francie on the Run.* New York, Viking Press, 1939; London, Muller, 1941.
> *Kersti and Saint Nicholas.* New York, Viking Press, 1940; London, Muller, 1944.
> *Pegeen.* New York, Viking Press, 1941; London, Muller, 1944.
> *Andries.* New York, Viking Press, 1942; London, Muller, 1946.
> *Gerrit and the Organ.* New York, Viking Press, 1943; London, Muller, 1948.
> *The Mitchells.* New York, Viking Press, 1945.
> *Canadian Summer.* New York, Viking Press, 1948.
> *Angels' Alphabet.* New York, Viking Press, 1948.
> *Patsy and the Pup.* New York, Viking Press, 1950.
> *King Oberon's Forest,* illustrated by Brigid Marlin. New York, Viking Press, 1957; London, Constable, 1958.
> *Friendly Gables.* New York, Viking Press, 1960.
> *Little Old Bear.* New York, Viking Press, 1962; London, Constable, 1963.
> *The Winged Watchman.* New York, Farrar Straus, 1962; London, Constable, 1964.
> *Jeremy Bear.* London, Constable, 1963.
> *Bennie and the New Baby.* London, Constable, 1964.
> *New Baby Is Lost.* London, Constable, 1964.
> *Mogo's Flute,* illustrated by Robin Jacques. New York, Viking Press, 1966; London, Constable, 1967.
> *Penengro.* New York, Farrar Straus, 1972.
> *Rufus Round and Round,* illustrated by Joanna Worth. London, Longman, 1973.
> *The Borrowed House.* New York, Farrar Straus, 1975; London, Collins, 1977.

Other

> Translator, *Tilio, A Boy of Papua,* by Rudolf Voorhoeve, illustrated by Van Stockum. Philadelphia, Lippincott, 1937; London, Hutchinson, 1939.
> Translator, *Marian and Marion,* by J.M. Selleger-Elout, illustrated by B. Midderigh-Bokhurst. New York, Viking Press, 1949.
> Translator, *Corso, The Donkey,* by Christina Pothast-Gimberg, illustrated by Elly van Beek. London, Constable, 1962.
> Translator, *The Curse of Laguna Grande,* by Siny R. van Iterson. New York, Morrow, 1973.
> Translator, *The Smugglers of Buenaventura,* by Siny R. van Iterson. New York, Morrow, 1974.

Translator, *In the Spell of the Past*, by Siny R. van Iterson.   New York, Morrow, 1975.
Translator, *Bruno*, by Achim Bröger, illustrated by Ronald Himler.   New York, Morrow, 1975.
Translator, *Kasimir*, by Achim Bröger.   New York, Morrow, 1976.

Manuscript Collections: de Grummond Collection, University of Southern Mississippi, Hattiesburg; May Massee Collection, Kansas State Teachers College, Emporia; Kerlan Collection, University of Minnesota, Minneapolis.

Illustrator: *Afke's Ten* by Sjoukje Troelstra, 1936; *Beggar's Penny*, 1943, and *The Bells of Leyden Sing*, 1944, by Catherine Coblentz; *The Burro of Barnegat Road* by Delia Goetz, 1945; *Hans Brinker* by Mary Mapes Dodge, 1946; *Little Women*, 1946, and *Little Men*, 1950, by Louisa May Alcott; *Willow Brook Farm* by Katherine D. Christ, 1948; *The Rainbow Book of Bible Stories* edited by May Becker, 1948; *Stryd voor een molen* by Jan den Tex, 1952.

*   *   *

Hilda Van Stockum has written some books available in translation and some for very young children, but in *The Winged Watchman* she has made an outstanding contribution to literature for older children. The story is set in Holland during the Nazi occupation and deals with the effects of war on the lives of the members of one Dutch family and their milieu. It is a stressful situation well chosen to test the fiber of one's character.

On a down-to-earth level, and familiar to children who usually have an aversion to "tattle-tales," is the Nazi way of rewarding those who inform on family and friends. In *The Winged Watchman* Leendert Schenderhans advances himself by watching and reporting to the enemy anything that could be damaging to his friends. He is an example of what not to be. By contrast, the courageous leader of the underground stands out, showing what greatness the human spirit may achieve during difficult times. This leader is the uncle of Joris, the story's protagonist. The events happening around him "try his soul." Joris has not yet become as brave as his uncle, and he detests Leendert, but he is deeply religious and asks questions which all of us have probably asked or wanted to ask. After a particularly unhappy experience with the Nazi conquerors, the boy seeks a priest to wonder, "Why does [God] let them go on and on, doing awful things to people when He is almighty and could stop them?" Father Kobus explains that God is concerned with all souls and even the enemy must have a chance to repent.

Joris confronts an even more troubled wrestling with his faith when S.S. troops take away the family next door, but Joris' mother rescues the baby who has been hidden in the garden. Later, when questioned, she stoutly maintains that the baby is her own. Joris accuses her of lying after the questioner is gone. "When you know that the other person is going to use the truth to rob and maim and kill, do you think he still has a right to it?" asks mother. And so the boy learns a new dimension to the words "right" and "wrong."

Hilda Van Stockum has all the courage of the underground leader in presenting these deep questions, yet she does this in terms and situations understandable to children. It is no mean accomplishment. *The Winged Watchman* is a good story, but it has extension that goes far beyond. Vietnam showed how deep war reaches into the spirits of men. Perhaps it is healthy to confront some of its problems in books before reality makes them personal experience.

—Carolyn T. Kingston

_____

VERNEY, John, Second Baronet. British. Born in London, 30 September 1913. Educated at Eton College, Buckinghamshire; Christ Church, Oxford, B.A. (honours) in history 1935. Served in the North Somerset Yeomanry, Special Air Service: mentioned in despatches; Military Cross, 1944; Légion d'Honneur, 1945. Married Lucinda Musgrave in 1939; has one son and five daughters. Painter and illustrator: group shows at Royal Society of British Artists, London; London Group; Leicester, Redfern, and Zwemmer galleries, London. Member, Farnham Urban District Council, 1968–74. Address: The White House, Clare, Suffolk, England.

PUBLICATIONS FOR CHILDREN

Fiction

Friday's Tunnel, illustrated by the author.   London, Collins, 1959; revised edition, London, Penguin, 1962; New York, Holt Rinehart, 1966.
February's Road, illustrated by the author.   London, Collins, 1961; New York, Holt Rinehart, 1966.
The Mad King of Chichiboo, illustrated by the author.   London, Collins, and New York, Watts, 1963.
ismo, illustrated by the author.   London, Collins, 1964; New York, Holt Rinehart, 1967.
Seven Sunflower Seeds.   London, Collins, 1968; New York, Holt Rinehart, 1969.
Samson's Hoard.   London, Collins, 1973.

Other

Look at Houses, illustrated by the author.   London, Hamish Hamilton, 1959; revised edition, London, Mayflower, 1970.

Editor, with Patricia Campbell, *Under the Sun: Stories, Poems, Articles from Elizabethan Sources*.   London, Constable, 1964.

PUBLICATIONS FOR ADULTS

Novels

Every Advantage.   London, Collins, 1961.
Fine Day for a Picnic.   London, Hodder and Stoughton, 1968.

Other

Verney Abroad, illustrated by the author.   London, Collins, 1954.
Going to the Wars: A Journey in Various Directions.   London, Collins, and New York, Dodd Mead, 1955.
A Dinner of Herbs (autobiographical).   London, Collins, 1966.

Illustrator: *The Odyssey* translated by George P. Kerr, 1958; *James Without Thomas*, 1959, *The Elephant War*, 1960, *To Tame a Sister*, 1961, *The Greatest Gresham*, 1962, *The Peacock House*, 1963, and *The Italian Spring*, 1964, all by Gillian Avery, and *Unforgettable Journeys*, 1965, and *School Remembered*, 1967, edited by Avery; *Diary of an Old Man* by Chaim Bermant, 1966; *Our Friend Jennings* by Anthony Buckeridge, 1967; *The Puffin Book of Horses* edited by Susan Chitty and Anne Parry, 1975; *The Dodo-Pad* (annual telephone table journal).

John Verney comments:
Having six children, much of my life has been occupied with trying to amuse, and thereby

educate, the young, one way or another. My novels for the young are really aimed at all who are young in heart, of whatever age. They are essentially about family life as it is affected by events in the adult world (e.g., a world crisis in *Friday's Tunnel*, a plot to assassinate President de Gaulle in *ismo*).

*   *   *

John Verney's chronicles of the huge Callendar family have never really achieved the runaway popular success they merit. At the back of the mind lurks the suspicion that it only needs one slight, unforseen chance and Gus Callendar, his wife, and his children, Friday, February, Gail, Barry, Des and Chrys, and Hildbrand, would become as familiar figures in the world of children's books as the Famous Five or the Secret Seven. There are drawbacks, of course; the stories are witty, literate, original, ingenious, and deserve and repay careful reading, but no other author writing for children approaches Verney's mastery in capturing the precise manner in which children become enmeshed in their parents' affairs and activities. Above all he writes naturally and can in no way be charged with that awful air of condescension that afflicts so many children's writers.

Gus Callendar, the *paterfamilias*, is a famous newspaper correspondent, a convenient career from the author's point of view in that he will be attracted in the normal course of events to odd incidents and will become closely involved in successive local, national, and even international issues. This implies in turn that his lively and likeable family are accustomed to being drawn in.

There is too an air of plausibility about each episode no matter how inherently implausible a situation really is. In *Friday's Tunnel*, for example, the action is centred round a sudden political crisis in the Mediterranean and the discovery of a very-much-in-demand mineral. The whole family find themselves inextricably bound up in this; they meet the personalities directly involved, and yet, at the end of the day, the problem is resolved in the tunnel Friday is digging in the paddock of their home on the Sussex downs. To maintain the narrative on these two levels, homely familiar Sussex and exotic Mediterranean, demands a high level of technical competence in novel writing, to say nothing of an imperturbable aplomb.

February's Road, arguably the best in the series, concerns a new London-Portsmouth trunk road which threatens to run straight through the bottom of their garden, and in this case it is February Callendar who pits her wits against the whole complex machinery of local politics and ministerial policy. In *Seven Sunflower Seeds* it is Barry who suspects that these are somehow mixed up in simultaneous plots to "fix" the Grand National steeplechase and to edge Britain into the Common Market. And in *Samson's Hoard* they all become heavily embroiled in local elections, a treasure hunt, business deals, and conservation, when Mr. Callendar stands as Independent candidate for the council. These are recognizeable situations confronting the members of one family who perhaps because of their own individual qualities appear as old friends as their continuing saga unfolds.

—Alan Edwin Day

VINING, Elizabeth Gray. American. Born in Philadelphia, Pennsylvania, 6 October 1902. Educated at Bryn Mawr College, Pennsylvania, A.B. 1923; Drexel Institute of Technology, Philadelphia, M.S. in library science 1926. Married Morgan Fisher Vining in 1929 (died, 1933). Tutor to Crown Prince of Japan, 1946–50; Vice President, Board of Trustees, 1952–71, and Vice Chairman, Board of Directors, 1952–71, Bryn Mawr College. Recipient: American Library Association Newbery Medal, 1943; New York *Herald Tribune* Festival award, 1945; Women's National Book Association Skinner Award, 1954. Litt.D.: Drexel Institute, 1951; Tufts College, Medford, Massachusetts, 1952; Douglass College,

Rutgers University, New Brunswick, New Jersey, 1953; Women's Medical College, Philadelphia, 1953; Lafayette College, Easton, Pennsylvania, 1956; L.H.D.: Russell Sage College, Troy, New York, 1952; Haverford College, Pennsylvania, 1958; Western College, Oxford, Ohio, 1959; Cedar Crest College, Allentown, Pennsylvania, 1959; Moravian College, Bethlehem, Pennsylvania, 1961; Wilmington College, New Castle, Delaware, 1962; International Christian University, Tokyo, 1966; D.Ed.: Rhode Island College of Education, Providence, 1956. Third Order of the Sacred Crown, Japan, 1950. Address: Kendal at Longwood, Box 194, Kennett Square, Pennsylvania 19348, U.S.A.

PUBLICATIONS FOR CHILDREN (as Elizabeth Janet Gray)

Fiction

    Merediths' Ann, illustrated by G.B. Cutts.   New York, Doubleday, and London, Heinemann, 1927.
    Tangle Garden, illustrated by G.B. Cutts.   New York, Doubleday, 1928.
    Tilly-Tod, illustrated by Mary Hamilton Frye.   New York, Doubleday, 1929.
    Meggy MacIntosh, illustrated by Marguerite de Angeli.   New York, Doubleday, 1930.
    Jane Hope.   New York, Viking Press, 1933; London, Dickson, 1935.
    Beppy Marlowe of Charles Town, illustrated by Loren Barton.   New York, Viking Press, 1936.
    The Fair Adventure, illustrated by Alice K. Reischer.   New York, Viking Press, 1940.
    Adam of the Road, illustrated by Robert Lawson.   New York, Viking Press, 1942; London, A. and C. Black, 1943.
    Sandy.   New York, Viking Press, 1945.
    The Cheerful Heart, illustrated by Kazue Mizumura.   New York, Viking Press, 1959; London, Macmillan, 1961.
    I Will Adventure, illustrated by Corydon Bell.   New York, Viking Press, 1962; Edinburgh, Oliver and Boyd, 1964.
    The Taken Girl (as Elizabeth Gray Vining).   New York, Viking Press, 1972.

Other

    Young Walter Scott.   New York, Viking Press, 1935; London, Nelson, 1937.
    Penn, illustrated by George Whitney.   New York, Viking Press, 1938.
    Mr. Whittier (as Elizabeth Gray Vining).   New York, Viking Press, 1974.

PUBLICATIONS FOR ADULTS

Novels

    The Virginia Exiles.   Philadelphia, Lippincott, 1955.
    Take Heed of Loving Me.   Philadelphia, Lippincott, 1964; London, Davies, 1965.
    I, Roberta.   Philadelphia, Lippincott, 1967.

Other

    The Contributions of the Quakers.   Philadelphia, F.A. Davis, 1939.
    Windows for the Crown Prince (autobiographical).   Philadelphia, Lippincott, and London, Joseph, 1952.
    The World in Tune.   Wallingford, Pennsylvania, Pendle Hill, 1952.
    Friend of Life: The Biography of Rufus M. Jones.   Philadelphia, Lippincott, 1958; London, Joseph, 1959.
    Return to Japan.   Philadelphia, Lippincott, 1960; London, Joseph, 1961.

Japanese Young People Today (address). Philadelphia, Atheneum of Philadelphia, 1961.

Quiet Pilgrimage (autobiography). Philadelphia, Lippincott, 1970.

Flora: A Biography. Philadelphia, Lippincott, 1966; as *Flora MacDonald, Her Life in the Highlands of America*, London, Bles, 1967.

William Penn: Mystic. Wallingford, Pennsylvania, Pendle Hill, 1969.

The May Massee Collection: Creative Publishing for Children, with Annis Duff. Emporia, Kansas, William Allen White Library, 1972.

*   *   *

Elizabeth Gray Vining takes to her historical romances and novels, her biographies and family stories, a commitment to time, place, and subject. Her writing reflects a deep interest in and concern for accuracy and credible interpretation.

Penn reaches beyond the man as an historic figure. His conversion to the Quaker religion caused significant conflict with his father and impaired his career in England. Vining develops Penn's character and personality with intuitive understanding which paves the way to an understanding of his significance in early American history. Her insight into Penn as a human being, as a deep believer, gives the reader not only a picture of the man himself but also of the man as a product of his time.

There is the same spirit in *Young Walter Scott* – yet with a romantic touch. If the child is the father of the man, those indications are in the book: Scott's early years are developed with care and interest, a natural bridge to his later accomplishments. Vining's impeccable sense of history and personality permeates the book even though the romanticism effects a lesser historical document than *Penn*.

Meggy MacIntosh and *Jane Hope* have been popular historical romances. Based on the true chronicles of Flora MacDonald and the Scottish Highland clansmen in North Carolina, this facet of British and American history comes alive through Meggy MacIntosh's experiences first in England, then in America. *Jane Hope* is a story of the Civil War period in which the Southern viewpoints and sentiments are patent. Meggy and Jane are spirited heroines, real people. These period pieces are reminiscent of the style of writing acclaimed in the 1930's. *Meggy MacIntosh* remains on firm ground as an historical romance. The attitudes depicted in *Jane Hope* might be questioned today, even though they are true to the period they reflect.

Vining received the John Newbery Award for the *Adam of the Road* in 1943. Her panoramic study of Chaucer's England involves the use of the five senses. Adam is important not so much as a young boy of the period but rather as a means for interpreting the historical period. What holds the book together is her style, and her use of language, which gives texture to the novel.

I Will Adventure follows a pattern similar to *Adam of the Road*. Andrew, on his way to London, meets Shakespeare, and moves into his world. The reader sees Shakespeare through Andrew's young eyes, a picture somewhat different from the commonly recognized one. The author's enthusiasm for her subject gives the book its power.

Tutor to Crown Prince Akihito from 1946 to 1950, she tells of her experiences in *Windows for the Crown Prince*. Written for adults, the book offers the young reader insight into another culture. From her subsequent visits to Japan came *The Cheerful Heart*. The story of Tomi, who returns with her family after three years as evacuees in the country, is full of gentle spirit. The poignant description of her hopes and dreams adds a universal quality.

No matter what her subject is, Vining is able to identify with her characters and select the most appropriate incidents. Although her books do not always emerge as a living reality, her interpretation of her subjects and her integrity are the striking qualities in a writing career that spans more than half a century.

—Mae Durham Roger

VIORST, Judith (Stahl). American. Born in Newark, New Jersey. Educated at Rutgers University, New Brunswick, New Jersey, B.A. in history (Phi Beta Kappa). Married Milton Viorst in 1960; has three sons. Columnist, Washington Star Syndicate, 1970–72. Since 1972, Columnist, *Redbook* magazine, New York. Recipient: Emmy Award, for television script, 1970. Address: c/o Atheneum Publishers, 122 East 42nd Street, New York, New York 10017, U.S.A.

PUBLICATIONS FOR CHILDREN

Fiction

> *Sunday Morning*, illustrated by Hilary Knight. New York, Harper, 1968.
> *I'll Fix Anthony*, illustrated by Arnold Lobel. New York, Harper, 1969.
> *Try It Again, Sam*, illustrated by Paul Galdone. New York, Lothrop, 1970.
> *The Tenth Good Thing about Barney*, illustrated by Erik Blegvad. New York, Atheneum, 1971; London, Collins, 1972.
> *Alexander and the Terrible, Horrible, No Good, Very Bad Day*, illustrated by Ray Cruz. New York, Atheneum, 1972; London, Angus and Robertson, 1973.
> *My Mama Says There Aren't Any Zombies, Ghosts, Vampires, Creatures, Demons, Monsters, Fiends, Goblins, or Things*, illustrated by Kay Chorao. New York, Atheneum, 1973.
> *Rosie and Michael*, illustrated by Lorna Tomei. New York, Atheneum, 1974.

Other

> *Projects: Space*. New York, Washington Square Press, 1962.
> *150 Science Experiments Step-by-Step*, illustrated by Dennis Telesford. New York, Bantam, 1963.
> *The Natural World: A Guide to North American Wildlife*. New York, Bantam, 1965.
> *The Changing Earth*, illustrated by Feodor Rimsky. New York, Bantam, 1967.

> Editor, with Shirley Moore, *Wonderful World of Science*, illustrated by Don Trawin. New York, Bantam, 1961.

PUBLICATIONS FOR ADULTS

Verse

> *The Village Square*. New York, Coward McCann, 1965.
> *It's Hard to Be Hip over Thirty and Other Tragedies of Married Life*. Cleveland, World, 1968; London, Angus and Robertson, 1973.
> *People and Other Aggravations*. New York, World, 1971; London, Angus and Robertson, 1973.
> *How Did I Get to Be Forty and Other Atrocities*. New York, Simon and Schuster, 1976.
> *A Visit from St. Nicholas (To a Liberated Household)*. New York, Simon and Schuster, 1977.

Other

> *The Washington, D.C., Underground Gourmet*, with Milton Viorst. New York, Simon and Schuster, 1970.
> *Yes, Married: A Saga of Love and Complaint* (collected prose). New York, Saturday Review Press, 1972.

                              *   *   *

Witty, urbane, and sensitive, Judith Viorst has continuously tackled the once thought "difficult" subjects of children's emotional stress in her books for children. Her non-sexist stories, appearing in both popular periodical and in book form, contain the right balance of humor and pathos, without losing the real message or issue. This is especially true of her picture book stories, whether it be of a pet's death (*The Tenth Good Thing about Barney*), bad days (*Alexander and the Terrible, Horrible, No Good, Very Bad Day*), boy-girl friendship (*Rosie and Michael*), or night fears (*My Mama Says*).

Most of her juveniles are based on actual experiences inside her family. Her boy characters, contrary to traditional masculine roles, do not suffer the less for demonstrating affection, fears, or tears. They become all the more human because of this portrayal, instead of demonstrating bravado where none exists. Her girl characters, like the boys, also run counter to societal stereotypes. They are often seen as aggressive, open, physically strong, and, at times, revengeful. Instead of losing in femininity as many fear, they actually gain in growth. Viorst has challenged traditional role models for boys and girls in her books and has challenged them unusually well.

She handles her subjects with depth and perception, never once assuming a position of guilt or opinion for any one side; instead, she brings out all points – adult and juvenile – on an issue, leading the reader to the logical and human position or action. Viorst can be viewed as a sophisticated and impartial recorder of human drama for children. In her books – adult and juvenile – no one loses; rather, everyone wins, especially the reader.

—James W. Roginski

VIPONT, Elfrida. British. Born in Manchester, Lancashire, 3 July 1902. Educated at Manchester High School for Girls; The Mount School, York. Married Robinson Percy Foulds in 1926 (died, 1954); has four daughters. Headmistress, Quaker Evacuation School, Yealand Manor, Lancashire, 1939–45. Recipient: Library Association Carnegie Medal, 1951. Address: Green Garth, Yealand Conyers, near Carnforth, Lancashire LA5 9SG, England.

PUBLICATIONS FOR CHILDREN

Fiction

> *Blow the Man Down* (as Charles Vipont), illustrated by Norman Hepple. London, Oxford University Press, 1939; Philadelphia, Lippincott, 1952.
> *The Lark in the Morn*, illustrated by T.R. Freeman. London, Oxford University Press, 1948; Indianapolis, Bobbs Merrill, 1951.
> *The Lark on the Wing*, illustrated by T.R. Freeman. London, Oxford University Press, 1950; Indianapolis, Bobbs Merrill, 1951.
> *The Family at Dowbiggins*, illustrated by T.R. Freeman. London, Lutterworth Press, and Indianapolis, Bobbs Merrill, 1955.
> *The Heir of Craigs* (as Charles Vipont), illustrated by Tessa Theobald. London, Oxford University Press, 1955.
> *The Spring of the Year*, illustrated by T.R. Freeman. London, Oxford University Press, 1957.
> *The Secret of Orra*, illustrated by D.J. Watkins-Pitchford. Oxford, Blackwell, 1957.
> *More about Dowbiggins*, illustrated by T.R. Freeman. London, Lutterworth Press, 1958; as *A Win for Henry Conyers*, London, Hamish Hamilton, 1968.
> *Changes at Dowbiggins*, illustrated by T.R. Freeman. London, Lutterworth Press, 1960; as *Boggarts and Dreams*, London, Hamish Hamilton, 1969.

Flowering Spring, illustrated by Shirley Hughes.   London, Oxford University Press, 1960.

Search for a Song, illustrated by Peter Edwards.   London, Oxford University Press, 1962.

Stevie, illustrated by Raymond Briggs.   London, Hamish Hamilton, 1965.

Larry Lopkins, illustrated by Pat Marriott.   London, Hamish Hamilton, 1965.

Rescue for Mittens, illustrated by Jane Paton.   London, Hamish Hamilton, 1965.

The Offcomers, illustrated by Janet Duchesne.   London, Hamish Hamilton, 1965; New York, McGraw Hill, 1967.

Terror by Night: A Book of Strange Stories.   London, Hamish Hamilton, 1966; as *Ghosts' High Noon*, New York, Walck, 1967.

The China Dog, illustrated by Constance Marshall.   London, Hamish Hamilton, 1967.

The Secret Passage, illustrated by Ian Ribbons.   London, Hamish Hamilton, 1967.

A Child of the Chapel Royal, illustrated by John Lawrence.   London, Oxford University Press, 1967.

The Pavilion, illustrated by Prudence Seward.   London, Oxford University Press, 1969; New York, Holt Rinehart, 1970.

Michael and the Dogs, illustrated by Pat Marriott.   London, Hamish Hamilton, 1969.

The Elephant and the Bad Baby, illustrated by Raymond Briggs.   London, Hamish Hamilton, and New York, Coward McCann, 1969.

Children of the Mayflower, illustrated by Evadne Rowan.   London, Heinemann, 1969; New York, Watts, 1970.

Plays

Radio Plays: *A True Tale*, 1952; *John Crook, Quaker*, 1954; *Kitty Wilkinson*, 1956; *Dr. Dinsdale in Russia*, 1956.

Other

Good Adventure: The Quest of Music in England, illustrated by Estella Canziani.   Manchester, Heywood, 1931.

Colin Writes to Friends House, illustrated by Elisabeth Brockbank.   London, Friends' Book Centre, 1934; revised edition, London, Bannisdale Press, 1946.

A Lily among Thorns: Some Passages in the Life of Margaret Fell of Swarthmoor Hall.   London, Friends Home Service Committee, 1950.

Sparks among the Stubble, illustrated by Patricia Lambe.   London, Oxford University Press, 1950.

Henry Purcell and His Times, illustrated by L.J. Broderick.   London, Lutterworth Press, 1959.

The Story of Christianity in Britain, illustrated by Gaynor Chapman.   London, Joseph, 1961.

What about Religion?, illustrated by Peter Roberson.   London, Museum Press, 1961.

Some Christian Festivals.   London, Joseph, 1963; New York, Roy, 1964.

Weaver of Dreams: The Girlhood of Charlotte Brontë.   London, Hamish Hamilton, and New York, Walck, 1966.

Towards a High Attic: The Early Life of George Eliot.   London, Hamish Hamilton, 1970; New York, Holt Rinehart, 1971.

A Little Bit of Ivory: A Life of Jane Austen.   London, Hamish Hamilton, 1977.

Editor, *The High Way: An Anthology*.   London, Oxford University Press, 1957.

Editor, *Bless This Day: A Book of Prayer*, illustrated by Harold Jones.   London, Collins, and New York, Harcourt Brace, 1958.

Editor, *The Bridge: An Anthology*, illustrated by Trevor Brierley Lofthouse.   London, Oxford University Press, 1962.

PUBLICATIONS FOR ADULTS

Novel

Bed in Hell. London, Hamish Hamilton, 1974; New York, St. Martin's Press, 1975.

Other

Quakerism: An International Way of Life (as E.V. Foulds). Manchester, 1930 Committee, 1930.

Lift Up Your Lamps: The Pageant of a Friends' Meeting (as E.V. Foulds). Manchester, 1930 Committee, 1939.

The Birthplace of Quakerism: A Handbook for the 1652 Country (as E.V. Foulds). London, Friends Home Service Committee, 1952; revised edition, 1968, 1973.

Let Your Lives Speak: A Key to the Quaker Experience (as E.V. Foulds). Wallingford, Pennsylvania, Pendle Hill, 1953; London, Friends Home Service Committee, 1954.

The Story of Quakerism, 1652–1952. London, Bannisdale Press, 1954; as *The Story of Quakerism Through Three Centuries*, 1960.

Living in the Kingdom (as E.V. Foulds). Philadelphia, Young Friends Movement, 1955.

The Quaker Witness: Yesterday and Today (as E.V. Foulds). Richmond, Indiana, Friends United Press, 1955.

Arnold Rowntree: A Life. London, Bannisdale Press, 1955.

Ackworth School, From Its Foundation in 1779 to the Introduction of Co-Education in 1946. London, Lutterworth Press, 1959.

A Faith to Live By. Philadelphia, Friends General Conference, 1962; as *Quakerism: A Faith to Live By*, London, Bannisdale Press, 1966.

George Fox and the Valiant Sixty. London, Hamish Hamilton, 1975.

Elfrida Vipont comments:
When people learn that I am a writer, they often ask, "What do you write?" When I reply, "Mainly books for children and young people," they say "Oh" rather sadly, as if to imply, "Poor thing, obviously she can't write for adults." Personally, I think writing for children is one of the most rewarding jobs imaginable. Lascelles Abercrombie used to speak of the "significant world" – "the world we never quite get except in art." If we do no more than offer a key to that significant world, our work will be well worth while. It is, of course, perfectly possible to offer a key to an ephemeral world instead, a world peopled by puppets in contrived situations, but most children's writers would rather fail in an attempt to create a living world, peopled by living characters, than succeed in presenting an artificial "readymix."

*   *   *

Though she has written many books, historical as well as modern, Elfrida Vipont is best known for *The Lark in the Morn*, its Carnegie-winning sequel *The Lark on the Wing*, and the two other loosely-connected stories, *The Spring of the Year* and *Flowering Spring*, continuing the Haverard family saga. Even of these, it is the first two that enjoy a particular popularity. Perhaps they reveal the deepest feeling. For, along with their Quakerism (which pervades all Elfrida Vipont's writing), they are about music, the other interest closest to her heart. She trained and performed as a professional singer, and readers are quick to recognise the authenticity of these books. Also, they broke new ground, appearing at a time when the girls' school story still mainly followed the pattern cut by Angela Brazil, and children's fiction in general was only starting that subtler exploration of emotions and relationships which is now expected of any good junior novel. Finally, *The Lark in the Morn* had the special freshness of an early work, drawing on an author's untapped reservoir of experience, rich in this case since, when the book was published, its creator was already in her mid-forties and had four daughters. The book is no flawless masterpiece, but it bids fair to survive as a classic, loved for the "naturalness and sincerity" which caused as perceptive a critic as Kathleen Lines to bracket it with *Little Women*.

If a writer should be judged by her best books, so should those books be assessed more on their excellences than on their minor blemishes. For all their originality, the *Lark* stories carry traces of the Brazilian model from which they were breaking free. There is an admired senior girl whose "mop of fair curls" and "elfin face" are mentioned more than once, and critics have justifiably deprecated the way in which characters "rap out," "explode," and otherwise deliver dialogue which is itself well written and full of character. Others have found the books a little sentimental – occasionally true, but far outweighed by the genuinely intense feeling of most passages – while others again, unsympathetic to the Quakerism, have accused them of "cultural snobbery" and "exclusiveness." These objections seem overstated but not entirely incomprehensible.

Yet when the stylistic blemishes are admitted, and it is conceded that the uncompromising moral values are unfashionable in some quarters today, there remains a memorable and moving story, full of vivid characters – especially the elder ones, with a dedicated young heroine who involves our sympathy. If the education of the emotions is a function of the junior novel, Elfrida Vipont's achievement must be rated high.

—Geoffrey Trease

WABER, Bernard. American. Born in Philadelphia, Pennsylvania, 27 September 1924. Educated at the University of Pennsylvania, Philadelphia; Museum School of Fine Art, Philadelphia, 1946–50; Pennsylvania Academy of Fine Arts, Philadelphia, 1950–51. Served in the United States Army, Panama Canal Zone, 1942–45: Staff Sergeant. Married Ethel Bernstein in 1952; has three children. Commercial Artist, Conde Nast Publications, New York, and *Seventeen* magazine, New York, 1952–54; Graphic Designer, *Life* magazine, New York, 1955–72. Since 1974, Graphic Designer, *People* magazine, New York. Lives in Baldwin Harbor, New York. Address: c/o Houghton Mifflin Co., 1 Beacon Street, Boston, Massachusetts 02107, U.S.A.

Publications for Children (illustrated by the author)

Fiction

> *Lorenzo.* Boston, Houghton Mifflin, 1961.
> *The House on East 88th Street.* Boston, Houghton Mifflin, 1962; as *Welcome, Lyle,* London, Chatto Boyd and Oliver, 1969.
> *Rich Cat, Poor Cat.* Boston, Houghton Mifflin, 1963.
> *How to Go About Laying an Egg.* Boston, Houghton Mifflin, 1963.
> *Lyle, Lyle, Crocodile.* Boston, Houghton Mifflin, 1965; Edinburgh, Oliver and Boyd, 1966.
> *Lyle and the Birthday Party.* Boston, Houghton Mifflin, 1966; Edinburgh, Oliver and Boyd, 1967.
> *"You Look Ridiculous," Said the Rhinoceros to the Hippopotamus.* Boston, Houghton Mifflin, 1966; London, Hamish Hamilton, 1967.

An Anteater Named Arthur. Boston, Houghton Mifflin, 1967; London, Chatto Boyd and Oliver, 1969.
Cheese. Boston, Houghton Mifflin, 1967.
A Rose for Mr. Bloom. Boston, Houghton Mifflin, 1968.
Lovable Lyle. Boston, Houghton Mifflin, 1969; London, Chatto Boyd and Oliver, 1970.
A Firefly Named Torchy. Boston, Houghton Mifflin, 1970.
Ira Sleeps Over. Boston, Houghton Mifflin, 1972.
Lyle Finds His Mother. Boston, Houghton Mifflin, 1974; London, Chatto and Windus, 1976.
I Was All Thumbs. Boston, Houghton Mifflin, 1975.
But Names Will Never Hurt Me. Boston, Houghton Mifflin, 1976.
Goodbye, Funny Dumpy-Lumpy. Boston, Houghton Mifflin, 1977.
Mice on My Mind. Boston, Houghton Mifflin, 1977.

Other

Just Like Abraham Lincoln. Boston, Houghton Mifflin, 1964.
Nobody Is Perfick (cartoons). Boston, Houghton Mifflin, 1971; London, Angus and Robertson, 1973.

*   *   *

Bernard Waber infuses his books with warmth, a freshness of style, and a ready wit. He has proven himself equally capable in the spheres of fantasy and reality. Most memorable are his adventures involving a whimsical crocodile named Lyle, who first appears in a bathtub in *The House on East 88th Street.* With remarkable aplomb and a bit of razzle-dazzle, Lyle wins the affection of the Primms: he becomes established in the family. His next adventure, *Lyle, Lyle, Crocodile,* finds him up against the irascible Mr. Grumps and his cat who arrange for his removal to the local zoo. The series is culminated by *Lyle Finds His Mother,* in which his early mentor, Hector P. Valenti, reappears with a money-making scheme to lure Lyle away on a trip in search of his mother. Laughter and humor abound, evoked by the fast pace, the ridiculous antics and the preposterous manner in which Lyle's existence is casually accepted. Waber's text merges dynamically with his illustrations to produce a creative balance of fantasy and reality in which feelings can be explored without threat.

In the same vein, yet with a different slant, is *An Anteater Named Arthur,* a warm and delightful look at a mother and son relationship. Waber uses a conversational format to recreate five short tableaux which gently poke fun at the problems inherent in such a relationship. It can only be fully appreciated when read aloud. In contrast to his fantasy, *Just Like Abraham Lincoln* is an attempt to enliven biography through a modern day Lincoln look-alike, who relates anecdotes and stories about Lincoln. The story labors in parts where the similarities between Mr. Potts and Lincoln seem overdrawn.

Waber's ability to portray feelings realistically is most successfully explored in *Ira Sleeps Over,* an insightful probe of a small boy's attachment to his teddy bear. He faithfully captures children's dialect while portraying sibling rivalry and peer relationships. Ira's indecision about taking his teddy bear on his overnight stay at Reggie's house creates a tension that is intensified by the taunting and harassment of his sister. Magically, Waber commands the reader's participation and involvement in Ira's decision. A gentle touch of irony and charm is evoked by the disclosure that Reggie lives next door.

Waber's recent realistic journey, *But Names Will Never Hurt Me,* is amusing but lacks the personal impact of *Ira Sleeps Over.* It probes the resentment of a child named Alison Wonderland brought about by her name. Some of its force is lost on an audience too young to appreciate the significance of the name. His word play is more successful in *Nobody Is Perfick* and *A Rose for Mr. Bloom.*

—Martha J. Fick

WAHL, Jan. American. Born in Columbus, Ohio, 1 April 1933. Educated at Cornell University, Ithaca, New York, 1950–53, B.A. 1953; University of Copenhagen (Fulbright Fellow), 1953–54; University of Michigan, Ann Arbor (Avery Hopwood Prize), 1955–58, M.A. Secretary to Isak Dinesen, Denmark, 1957–58. Address: 2116 Potomac Drive, Toledo, Ohio 43607, U.S.A.; or, Apartado Postal 33, San Miguel de Allende, Guanajuato, Mexico.

PUBLICATIONS FOR CHILDREN

Fiction

> *Pleasant Fieldmouse*, illustrated by Maurice Sendak. New York, Harper, 1964; Kingswood, Surrey, World's Work, 1969.
> *The Howards Go Sledding*, illustrated by John E. Johnson. New York, Holt Rinehart, 1964.
> *Hello, Elephant*, illustrated by Edward Ardizzone. New York, Holt Rinehart, 1964.
> *Cabbage Moon*, illustrated by Adrienne Adams. New York, Holt Rinehart, 1965.
> *The Muffletumps: The Story of Four Dolls*, illustrated by Edward Ardizzone. New York, Holt Rinehart, 1966.
> *Christmas in the Forest*, illustrated by Eleanor Schick. New York, Macmillan, 1967.
> *Pocahontas in London*, illustrated by John Alcorn. New York, Delacorte Press, 1967.
> *The Furious Flycycle*, illustrated by Fernando Krahn. New York, Delacorte Press, 1968; London, Longman, 1970.
> *Push Kitty*, illustrated by Garth Williams. New York, Harper, 1968.
> *Cobweb Castle*, illustrated by Edward Gorey. New York, Holt Rinehart, 1968.
> *Rickety Rackety Rooster*, illustrated by John E. Johnson. New York, Simon and Schuster, 1968.
> *A Wolf of My Own*, illustrated by Lillian Hoban. New York, Macmillan, 1969.
> *How the Children Stopped the Wars*, illustrated by Mitchell Miller. New York, Farrar Straus, 1969; London, Abelard Schuman, 1975.
> *The Fishermen*, illustrated by Emily McCully. New York, Norton, 1969.
> *May Horses*, illustrated by Blair Lent. New York, Delacorte Press, 1969.
> *The Norman Rockwell Storybook*, illustrated by Rockwell. New York, Windmill Books, 1969.
> *The Prince Who Was a Fish*, illustrated by Robin Jacques. New York, Simon and Schuster, 1970.
> *The Mulberry Tree*, illustrated by Feodor Rojankovsky. New York, Grosset and Dunlap, 1970.
> *The Wonderful Kite*, illustrated by Uri Shulevitz. New York, Delacorte Press, 1970.
> *Doctor Rabbit*, illustrated by Peter Parnall. New York, Delacorte Press, 1970; London, Longman, 1972.
> *The Animals' Peace Day*, illustrated by Victoria Chess. New York, Crown, 1970.
> *Abe Lincoln's Beard*, illustrated by Fernando Krahn. New York, Delacorte Press, 1971.
> *Anna Help Ginger*, illustrated by Lawrence Di Fiori. New York, Putnam, 1971.
> *Crabapple Night*, illustrated by Steven Kellogg. New York, Holt Rinehart, 1971.
> *Margaret's Birthday*, illustrated by Mercer Mayer. New York, Scholastic, 1971.
> *The Six Voyages of Pleasant Fieldmouse*, illustrated by Peter Parnall. New York, Delacorte Press, 1971.
> *Lorenzo Bear & Company*, illustrated by Fernando Krahn. New York, Putnam, 1971.
> *The Very Peculiar Tunnel*, illustrated by Steven Kellogg. New York, Putnam, 1972.
> *Magic Heart*, illustrated by Trina Schart Hyman. New York, Seabury Press, 1972; Kingswood, Surrey, World's Work, 1973.
> *Grandmother Told Me*, illustrated by Mercer Mayer. Boston, Little Brown, 1972.
> *Cristóbal and the Witch*, illustrated by Janet McCaffery. New York, Putnam, 1972.

Juan Diego and the Lady, illustrated by Leonard Everett Fisher.   New York, Putnam, 1972.

S.O.S. Bobomobile! or, The Further Adventures of Melvin Spitznagle and Professor Mickimecki, illustrated by Fernando Krahn.   New York, Delacorte Press, 1973; London, Longman, 1975.

The Five in the Forest, illustrated by Erik Blegvad.   Chicago, Follett, 1974.

Pleasant Fieldmouse's Halloween Party, illustrated by Wallace Tripp.   New York, Putnam, 1974; Kingswood, Surrey, World's Work, 1976.

Mooga Mega Mekki, illustrated by Fernando Krahn.   Chicago, O'Hara, 1974.

Jeremiah Knucklebones, illustrated by Jane Zalben.   New York, Holt Rinehart, 1974.

The Muffletump Storybook, illustrated by Cyndy Szekeres.   Chicago, Follett, 1975.

The Clumpets Go Sailing, illustrated by Cyndy Szekeres.   New York, Parents' Magazine Press, 1975; Kingswood, Surrey, World's Work, 1977.

The Bear, The Wolf, and the Mouse, illustrated by Kinoku Kraft.   Chicago, Follett, 1975.

The Screeching Door; or, What Happened at the Elephant Hotel, illustrated by J. Winslow Higginbottom.   New York, Scholastic, 1975.

The Muffletumps' Christmas Party, illustrated by Cyndy Szekeres.   Chicago, Follett, 1975; Kingswood, Surrey, World's Work, 1977.

Follow Me, Cried Bee, illustrated by John Wallner.   New York, Crown, 1976.

Great-Grandmother Cat Tales, illustrated by Cyndy Szekeres.   New York, Pantheon Books, 1976.

Grandpa's Indian Summer, illustrated by Joanne Scribner.   Englewood Cliffs, New Jersey, Prentice Hall, 1976.

The Pleasant Fieldmouse Storybook, illustrated by Erik Blegvad.   Englewood Cliffs, New Jersey, Prentice Hall, 1977; Kingswood, Surrey, World's Work, 1978.

Doctor Rabbit's Foundling, illustrated by Cyndy Szekeres.   New York, Pantheon Books, 1977.

Carrot Nose, illustrated by James Marshall.   New York, Farrar Straus, 1977.

Frankenstein's Dog, illustrated by Kay Chorao.   Englewood Cliffs, New Jersey, Prentice Hall, 1977.

The Muffletumps' Halloween Scare, illustrated by Cyndy Szekeres.   Chicago, Follett, 1977.

Dracula's Cat, illustrated by Kay Chorao.   Englewood Cliffs, New Jersey, Prentice Hall, 1977.

Pleasant Fieldmouse's Valentine Trick, illustrated by Erik Blegvad.   New York, Dutton, 1977.

Verse

The Beast Book, illustrated by E. W. Eichel.   New York, Harper, 1964.

Other

Runaway Jonah and Other Tales, illustrated by Uri Shulevitz.   New York, Macmillan, 1968.

Crazy Brobobalou, illustrated by Paula Winter.   New York, Putnam, 1973.

The Woman with the Eggs, illustrated by Ray Cruz.   New York, Crown, 1975.

PUBLICATIONS FOR ADULTS

Play

Paradiso! Paradiso! (produced Ithaca, New York, 1954).

Manuscript Collections: Jan Wahl Collection, University of Wyoming, Laramie; Kerlan Collection, University of Minnesota, Minneapolis.

Jan Wahl comments:

Even in my so-called "adult" fiction – stories printed in various magazines – I realized I was writing about the qualities of childhood and therefore it occured to me to write directly for children, that is, for the child in *me*, by means of fables and picture book stories. I see picture books themselves as small films and several of my artists (Maurice Sendak and Uri Shulevitz, for example) have agreed with me. I try to follow no trends but to write what I would wish to read if I, today, were a child. I find it, always, a satisfying, exciting occupation.

*   *   *

The bright sun, the pride of spring, popped into the sky like a flying orange. The forest stirred, then morning began, shaking its new green shades. Red cardinals and yellow finches darted among the trees like bold-painted arrows.

Somebody was hammering a sign beside the thick black oak. This somebody was Pleasant Fieldmouse, who lived inside the oak, at the bottom. *I Am a Fireman* it said on the sign. Pleasant Fieldmouse was wearing a fine red hat which was really a cap from a bottle. *Tipsy Cola*, the cap was labeled, but you were not supposed to look at him from the top.

Those opening paragraphs from Jan Wahl's first book for children, *Pleasant Fieldmouse*, inadvertently reveal some of the main strengths and weaknesses that run through much of Mr. Wahl's writing output. On the positive side stand imagination, a gentle whimsicality, humor, and fresh imagery. But balancing and sometimes outweighing these good qualities are the author's tendency to strain too hard for the unusual word or phrase, and his frequent descents into archness.

Jan Wahl has published a wide range of books in the last dozen or so years, from brief picture book texts like *A Wolf of My Own* and *Follow Me, Cried Bee*, to original fairy tales (*Cobweb Castle*, *Magic Heart*), to unusual short biographies (*Abe Lincoln's Beard*, *Pocahontas in London*), to humorous novels for the 8-to-12-year-old audience (*The Furious Flycycle*, *The Screeching Door*). However, the majority of his published work falls into the picture book category.

Wahl's picture books are filled with surprises – an unusual word that juts out from the text, a fantastic character who suddenly enters the scene, a startling new situation that develops unexpectedly. Accompanying the surprises, though, is what often seems like a lack of control over the material and the narrative as a whole. Story lines wander off on colorful but inconclusive tangents; interesting characters appear, take center stage for a while and then vanish, never to reappear again. Sometimes the texts actually read like dreams that Jan Wahl wrote down as soon as he awoke in the morning and then never touched again.

In a sense Wahl could probably be described as a victim of the boom in children's book publishing that flared up in the United States during the years of President Lyndon B. Johnson's so-called "Great Society" (1964–1969). That was the period when generous appropriations of federal funds were being spent on the creation and expansion of school libraries all across the country. A prolific author like Jan Wahl could – and did – sell just about everything he wrote to one publisher or another, even fragmentary pieces like *Pocahontas in London* and *May Horses*. Inevitably these slight books diminished Mr. Wahl's reputation, and there came a time in the 1970's when critics seemed to be on the verge of dismissing some of his richer and more unified books along with his weaker ones.

If that had happened, it would have been a shame – not only for Mr. Wahl but for the field of children's literature. Uneven, unsatisfying, and exasperating as Jan Wahl's stories sometimes are, he can still come through with marvelous new approaches and insights as in

Runaway Jonah, his retelling of five Old Testament stories. And he also has to his credit a true modern classic in *Push Kitty*, which dramatizes the ultimate in smothering love as the little girl narrator describes how she dresses up her kitten and tries to make him into her baby. "Baby, you are pretty lucky to have a mama like me. DON'T YOU AGREE?"

If only for *Push Kitty* and *Pleasant Fieldmouse*, Jan Wahl would have a secure niche in any chronicle of American children's books of the 1960's and 1970's.

—James C. Giblin

WALKER, David (Harry). Canadian. Born in Dundee, Scotland, 9 February 1911; became Canadian citizen, 1957. Educated at Shrewsbury School, Shropshire, 1924–29; Royal Military College, Sandhurst, Surrey, 1929–30. Married Willa Magee in 1939; has four children. Served in the British Army, in the Black Watch, 1931–47; served in India, 1932–36, and in the Sudan, 1936–38; Aide-de-Camp to the Governor-General of Canada, 1938–39; Prisoner-of-War in France, 1940–45; Instructor at the Staff College, Camberley, Surrey, 1945–46; Comptroller to the Viceroy of India, 1946–47; retired as Major, 1947; M.B.E (Member, Order of the British Empire), 1946. Full-time Writer since 1947. Member of the Canada Council, 1957–61. Canadian Commissioner, since 1965, and Chairman, 1970–72, Roosevelt Campobello International Park Commission. Recipient: Governor-General's Award, for novel, 1953, 1954. D.Litt.: University of New Brunswick, Fredericton, 1955. Fellow, Royal Society of Literature, 1950. Address: Strathcroix, St. Andrews, New Brunswick, Canada.

PUBLICATIONS FOR CHILDREN

Fiction

> *Sandy Was a Soldier's Boy*, illustrated by Dobson Broadhead. London, Collins, and Boston, Houghton Mifflin, 1957; as *Sandy*, Collins, 1961.
> *Dragon Hill*, illustrated by Ray Keane. Boston, Houghton Mifflin, 1962; London, Collins, 1963.
> *Pirate Rock*, illustrated by Victor Mays. London, Collins, and Boston, Houghton Mifflin, 1969.
> *Big Ben*, illustrated by Victor Ambrus. Boston, Houghton Mifflin, 1969; London, Collins, 1970.

PUBLICATIONS FOR ADULTS

Novels

> *The Storm and the Silence*. Boston, Houghton Mifflin, 1949; London, Cape, 1950.
> *Geordie*. Boston, Houghton Mifflin, and London, Collins, 1950.
> *The Pillar*. Boston, Houghton Mifflin, and London, Collins, 1952.
> *Digby*. London, Collins, and Boston, Houghton Mifflin, 1953.
> *Harry Black*. London, Collins, and Boston, Houghton Mifflin, 1954.
> *Where the High Winds Blow*. London, Collins, and Boston, Houghton Mifflin, 1960.
> *Winter of Madness*. London, Collins, and Boston, Houghton Mifflin, 1964.
> *Mallabec*. London, Collins, and Boston, Houghton Mifflin, 1965.
> *Come Back, Geordie*. London, Collins, and Boston, Houghton Mifflin, 1966.

Devil's Plunge. London, Collins, 1968; as *CAB–Intersec*, Boston, Houghton Mifflin, 1968.

The Lord's Pink Ocean. London, Collins, and Boston, Houghton Mifflin, 1972.

Black Dougal. London, Collins, 1973; Boston, Houghton Mifflin, 1974.

Ash. London, Collins, and Boston, Houghton Mifflin, 1976.

Pot of Gold. London, Collins, 1977.

Short Stories

Storms of Our Journey and Other Stories. Boston, Houghton Mifflin, 1962; London, Collins, 1963.

*   *   *

David Walker is far removed in background, birth and breeding from the average Canadian. Born in Dundee, Scotland, and educated at a British public school and at Sandhurst, he became the military aide to the Governor-General of Canada in 1938, and it was during that appointment that his love for Canada flowered.

Often military men like Walker make very good writers for children. They are aware of, and answerable to, the unwritten and unspoken demands of children for law, love, and order. There is something in art as in nature that requires order and law in order to survive, and children in their literature most certainly demand that writing be ordered, however fanciful and fantastic it may seem to be. Walker's books – *Big Ben*, *Dragon Hill*, *Pirate Rock*, and *Sandy Was a Soldier's Boy* – satisfy that desire for order; they are books of outdoor adventure, artful in their apparent simplicity.

All these books were written especially for the young, and they form a package that can be opened up for children anywhere, especially in the old Commonwealth nations. They form a universal prototype – like the Western cowboy. Walker provides fresh air in children's literature and an illuminating light that children desire and need.

—William Ready

WALKER, Stuart (Armstrong). American. Born in Augusta, Kentucky, 4 March 1880. Educated at Woodward High School, Cincinnati; University of Cincinnati, B.S. in engineering 1903; American Academy of Dramatic Arts, New York, 1908. One adopted son. Shipping Clerk, Southern Creosoting Company, Slidell, Louisiana, 1904; play reader, actor, and stage manager for David Belasco, 1909–14; director of repertory theatres in Buffalo and Detroit for Jessie Bonstelle, 1914; Founding director, Portmanteau Theatre, 1915–17; Director, Indianapolis Repertory Company, 1917–23, 1926–28, and Cincinnati Repertory Company, later the Stuart Walker Repertory Company, 1922–31; Film Director, Paramount, 1931–34, and Universal, 1934–35, and Producer, Paramount, 1936–41. *Died 13 March 1941.*

PUBLICATIONS FOR CHILDREN

Plays

Portmanteau Plays (includes *The Trimplet*, *Nevertheless*, *The Medicine Show*, *Six Who Pass While the Lentils Boil*), edited by Edward Hale Bierstadt (produced New York, 1916). Cincinnati, Stewart Kidd, 1917.

More Portmanteau Plays (includes *A Lady of the Weeping Willow Tree, The Very Naked Boy, Jonathan Makes a Wish*), edited by Edward Hale Bierstadt (*A Lady of the Weeping Willow Tree* and *The Very Naked Boy* produced New York, 1916; *Jonathan Makes a Wish* produced New York, 1918). Cincinnati, Stewart Kidd, 1917.
Portmanteau Adaptations (includes *Gammer Gurton's Needle, The Birthday of the Infanta*, adaptation of the story by Oscar Wilde, *Sir David Wears a Crown, Nellijumbo*), edited by Edward Hale Bierstadt (*Gammer Gurton's Needle* and *The Birthday of the Infanta* produced New York, 1916). Cincinnati, Stewart Kidd, 1921.
Five Flights Up (produced 1922).
The King's Great Aunt Sits on the Floor (produced 1923). New York, Appleton, 1925.
Seventeen, with Hubert S. Stange and Stannard Mears, adaptation of the novel by Booth Tarkington (produced on tour). New York, French, 1924.
The Book of Job (produced on tour).
The Demi-Reps, with Gladys Unger (produced 1936).

Screenplay: *Seventeen*, 1940.

Theatrical Activities:

Director: **Films** — *Secret Call*, 1931; *False Madonna*, 1931; *Misleading Lady*, 1932; *Evenings for Sale*, 1932; *Tonight Is Ours*, 1933; *The Eagle and the Hawk*, 1933; *White Woman*, 1933; *Romance in the Rain*, 1934; *Great Expectations*, 1934; *The Mystery of Edwin Drood*, 1935; *Werewolf of London*, 1935; *Manhattan Moon*, 1935; *Her Excellency the Governor*, 1935.

*   *   *

One of the early contributors to the development of children's theatre in the United States was the producer and playwright, Stuart Walker. After graduating from the University of Cincinnati he went to New York to study at the American Academy of Dramatic Art. In 1914 he organized one of the first off-Broadway groups, the Portmanteau Theatre, which toured plays of literary quality to different parts of New York City. Although the Portmanteau Theatre was not organized primarily as a children's theatre, it included in its repertory plays suitable for children and it emphasized fantasy rather than realistic adult drama.

Prior to this, Stuart Walker had been teaching dramatic art at Christadora Settlement House in New York City. Despite the interest of the settlement in his work, lack of funds made impossible the building of a playhouse in which it could be carried on. Walker's previous six years in the professional theatre gave him a background in modern stagecraft, which was to be invaluable to him in the solution of the problem. He was aware of the new trends in scenic design which emphasized simplicity and discarded the traditional heavy scenery and backdrops. With this principle of simplicity in mind, he devised a portable stage that could be packed up in ten lightweight boxes. His plays, written for this stage, were simple and easily adapted to his touring schedule.

His best known plays are: *Six Who Pass While the Lentils Boil, The Trimplet, The Birthday of the Infanta, The Medicine Show*, and *Sir David Wears a Crown*. Stuart Walker wrote for the Broadway theatre as well; best known of these works is the comedy *Seventeen*, based on the novel by Booth Tarkington.

Stuart Walker brought knowledge of the theatre to his writing, a background possessed by few writers and producers of children's theatre in the first decades of the twentieth century. His ability to use words in an interesting and original way, his gentle humor, his handling of fantasy and his wisdom set a high standard for other dramatists of the mid-1910's. Walker was most successful in such one-act plays as *Six Who Pass While the Lentils Boil*. The charm and the reality of the characters in this fantasy make it a timeless favorite of young theatre groups in America. It is this quality that keeps the play from being dated, whereas others written at the same time hold little interest for today's young people.

—Nellie McCaslin

WATKINS-PITCHFORD, D(enys) J(ames). Pseudonym: **BB.** Born in Lamport, Northamptonshire, 25 July 1905. Educated privately and at Royal College of Art, London, Associate, Royal College of Art Painting School. Served in the Territorial Royal Horse Artillery, 1927–29 (King's Cup Medal); Captain, Home Guard, during World War II. Married Cecily Mary Adnitt in 1939; one daughter and one son (deceased). Assistant Art Master, Rugby School, Warwickshire, 1930–47. Since 1947, free-lance author and illustrator. Recipient: Library Association Carnegie Medal, 1943. Fellow, Royal Society of Arts. Agent: David Higham Associates Ltd., 5–8 Lower John Street, London W1R 4HA. Address: The Round House, Sudborough, Kettering, Northamptonshire, England.

PUBLICATIONS FOR CHILDREN (as BB; illustrated by the author)

Fiction

> *Wild Lone.* London, Eyre and Spottiswoode, and New York, Scribner, 1938.
> *Sky Gipsy: The Story of a Wild Goose.* London, Eyre and Spottiswoode, 1939; as *Manka, The Sky Gipsy,* New York, Scribner, 1939.
> *The Little Grey Men.* London, Eyre and Spottiswoode, 1942; New York, Scribner, 1949.
> *Brendon Chase.* London, Hollis and Carter, 1944; New York, Scribner, 1945.
> *Down the Bright Stream.* London, Eyre and Spottiswoode, 1948.
> *The Forest of Boland Light Railway.* London, Eyre and Spottiswoode, 1955; as *The Forest of the Railway,* New York, Dodd Mead, 1957.
> *Monty Woodpig's Caravan.* London, Ward, 1957.
> *Ben the Bullfinch.* London, Hamish Hamilton, 1957.
> *Wandering Wind.* London, Hamish Hamilton, 1957.
> *Alexander.* Oxford, Blackwell, 1957.
> *Monty Woodpig and His Bumblebuzz Car.* London, Ward, 1958.
> *Mr. Bumstead.* London, Eyre and Spottiswoode, 1958.
> *The Wizard of Boland.* London, Ward, 1959.
> *Bill Badger's Winter Cruise.* London, Hamish Hamilton, 1959.
> *Bill Badger and the Pirates.* London, Hamish Hamilton, 1960.
> *Bill Badger's Finest Hour.* London, Hamish Hamilton, 1961.
> *Bill Badger's Whispering Reeds Adventure.* London, Hamish Hamilton, 1962.
> *Lepus, The Brown Hare.* London, Benn, 1962.
> *Bill Badger's Big Mistake.* London, Hamish Hamilton, 1963.
> *Bill Badger and the Big Store Robbery.* London, Hamish Hamilton, 1967.
> *The Whopper.* London, Benn, 1967.
> *At the Back o' Ben Dee.* London, Benn, 1968.
> *Bill Badger's Voyage to the World's End.* London, Kaye and Ward, 1969.
> *The Tyger Tray.* London, Methuen, 1971.
> *The Pool of the Black Witch.* London, Methuen, 1974.
> *Lord of the Forest.* London, Methuen, 1975.
> *Stories of the Wild,* with A. L. E. Fenton and A. Windsor-Richards. London, Benn, 1975.

Recollections of a Longshore Gunner. Ipswich, Boydell Press, 1976.
More Stories of the Wild, with A. Windsor-Richards. London, Benn, 1977.

Other

Meeting Hill: BB's Fairy Book. London, Hollis and Carter, 1948.
The Wind in the Wood. London, Hollis and Carter, 1952.
The Badgers of Bearshanks. London, Benn, 1961.
The Pegasus Book of the Countryside. London, Dobson, 1964.

PUBLICATIONS FOR ADULTS (as BB; illustrated by the author)

Short Stories

5 More Stories, with others. Oxford, Blackwell, 1957.

Other

The Idle Countryman. London, Eyre and Spottiswoode, 1943.
The Wayfaring Tree. London, Hollis and Carter, 1945.
A Stream in Your Garden. London, Eyre and Spottiswoode, 1948.
Be Quiet and Go A-Angling (as Michael Traherne). London, Lutterworth Press, 1949.
Confessions of a Carp Fisher. London, Eyre and Spottiswoode, 1950; revised edition, London, Witherby, 1970.
Tide's Ending. London, Hollis and Carter, and New York, Scribner, 1950.
Letters from Compton Deverell. London, Eyre and Spottiswoode, 1950.
Dark Estuary. London, Hollis and Carter, 1953.
A Carp Water: Wood Pool and How to Fish It. London, Putnam, 1958.
The Autumn Road to the Isles. London, Kaye, 1959.
The White Road Westwards. London, Kaye, 1961.
September Road to Caithness and the Western Sea. London, Kaye, 1962.
The Summer Road to Wales. London, Kaye, 1964.
A Summer on the Nene. London, Kaye and Ward, 1967.

Editor, *The Sportsman's Bedside Book.* London, Eyre and Spottiswoode, 1937.
Editor, *The Countryman's Bedside Book.* London, Eyre and Spottiswoode, 1941.
Editor, *The Fisherman's Bedside Book.* London, Eyre and Spottiswoode, 1945; New York, Scribner, 1946.
Editor, *The Shooting Man's Bedside Book.* London, Eyre and Spottiswoode, and New York, Scribner, 1948.

Illustrator: *Sport in Wildest Britain* by H. V. Prichard, 1936; *Winged Company* by R. G. Walmsley, 1940; *England Is a Village* by Clarence H. Warren, 1940; *Southern English* by Eric Benfield, 1942; *Narrow Boat* by L. T. C. Rolt, 1944; *Red Vagabond* by Gerald D. Adams, 1946; *It's My Delight* by Brian V. Fitzgerald, 1947; *Philandering Angler* by Arthur Applin, 1948; *A Sportsman Looks at Eire* by J. B. Drought, 1949; *Landmarks* by Arthur G. Street, 1949; *Fairy Tales of Long Ago* edited by Mabel C. Carey, 1952; *The White Foxes of Gorfenletch*, 1954, *Beasts of the North Country*, 1961, and *To Do With Birds*, 1965, all by Henry S. Tegner; *The Secret of Orra* by Elfrida Vipont, 1957; *The Long Night*, 1958, and *Thirteen O'Clock*, 1960, by William Mayne; *Vix*, 1960, *Birds of the Lonely Lake*, 1961, *The Cabin in the Woods*, 1963, and *The Wild White Swan*, 1965, all by Arthur Richards; *Prince Prigio and Prince Ricardo* by Andrew Lang, 1961; *The Rogue Elephant*, 1962, *Red Ivory*, 1964, and *Jungle Rescue*, 1967, all by Arthur Catherall; *Granny's Wonderful Chair* by Frances Browne, 1963; *King Todd* by Norah Burke, 1963; *The Lost Princess* by George MacDonald, 1965; *Where Vultures Fly* by Gerald Summers, 1974.

D. J. Watkins-Pitchford comments:

Though some of my best-selling books were written for young people, most – if not all – are appreciated equally by adults and I take this as a great compliment! A keen observation is essential to a successful author. I write because I find it an intensely rewarding thing, and it is fun to illustrate my own books.

*   *   *

More familiar to us as BB, D. J. Watkins-Pitchford is known above all for his wildlife books. An enthusiastic natural historian, he is able to convey vividly his wide knowledge and deep love of the countryside. *Sky Gipsy* is the story of a wild goose, telling with sympathetic insight of the beautiful but harsh life of these birds. *Wild Lone* is a moving but unsentimental account of the life of a fox in the Pytchley Hunt country. *Brendon Chase* is also about survival in the wild, but here it is two boys playing truant to live in the woods and finding that open-air living has its disadvantages.

For younger children he has created the enchanted forest of Boland, a place where anything can happen. Absurd humour which tickles the palates of the under-tens predominates in *The Wizard of Boland*, where incompetence in high places produces hilarious results. *The Forest of Boland Light Railway* is similarly delightful. His animal heroes Bill Badger and the hedgehog Monty Woodpig have adventures in the woodland and by the canal which appeal greatly to sixes and sevens and are splendid for reading aloud.

One of his books won the Carnegie Medal in 1943, and is still a prime favourite, *The Little Grey Men*; and its sequel *Down the Bright Stream* was illustrated by the author in scraperboard, though in later editions he painted in oils. These are truly delightful tales and make ideal bedtime stories. They deal with three dwarves, Dodder, Balemoney, and Sneezewort (all old country wildflower names) and their quest for their long-lost brother, using a clockwork toy boat which they find.

In all his books, the English countryside is not merely supportive but a leading character, making them pleasurable reading for all ages.

—Ann G. Hay

WATSON, Clyde. American. Born in New York City, 25 July 1947. Educated at Smith College, Northampton, Massachusetts, A.B. in music 1968. Teacher, The Common School, Amherst, Massachusetts, 1968–70, and Indian Township School, Maine, 1971–73. Agent: Marilyn Marlow, Curtis Brown Ltd., 575 Madison Avenue, New York, New York 10022. Address: Lyme, New Hampshire 03768, U.S.A.

PUBLICATIONS FOR CHILDREN (illustrated by Wendy Watson)

Fiction

Tom Fox and the Apple Pie. New York, Crowell, 1972; London, Macmillan, 1973.

Verse

Father Fox's Pennyrhymes. New York, Crowell, 1971; London, Macmillan, 1972.
Hickory Stick Rag. New York, Crowell, 1976.

Other

> *Quips and Quirks* (collection of epithets).   New York, Crowell, 1975.
> *Binary Numbers.*   New York, Crowell, 1977.

Music: *Fisherman Lullabies*, 1968; *Carol to a Child*, lyrics by Nancy Dingman Watson, 1969.

*   *   *

The key to Clyde Watson's writing is the fact that she is a musician. Her poems are often song lyrics, her prose has a musical ring. She writes quasi-Mother Goose rhyme that is influenced by three things: the old poems, her New England background, and her musical ability.

Her first works were the straightforward musical arrangements for her sister's *Fisherman Lullabies* and her mother's *Carol to a Child*. She seemed to be riding into the publishing world on her family's coattails.

However, with *Father Fox's Pennyrhymes* Clyde Watson came into her own. It is the best of all the Watson family's many books. The book is a collection of short, simple, spirited and highly original nonsense rhymes, many of which are actually lyrics to songs Clyde composed. The impeccable rhythms, the melodic flow of the full and slant rhymes all bespeak the author's musical background:

> The sky is dark, there blows a storm,
> Our cider is hot, the fire is warm,
> The snow is deep and the night is long:
> Old Father Fox, will you sing us a song?

The poems obviously come from a folkloric tradition — Mother Goose, English ballads, lullabies, and jump-rope rhymes. But instead of the 17th-century English countryside or the streets of London, they celebrate New England and especially rural Vermont where Clyde Watson was brought up. The verses range from the decidedly impish to the boisterously aggressive to some that are as soft as a cradle song. They are instantly memorized by young listeners. The pictures in the book, again by her sister, are colorful and inventive, in a comic strip format. The details in both the rhymes and the illustrations are both personal (family jokes are enshrined, the Putney farm is pictured) and universal. The book, in fact, was recognized as a modern classic on publication, winning, among other prizes, a National Book Award nomination. Quite simply, it is a beautiful, individual volume, certainly one of the few in the 1970's that is destined to outlast its decade — and even its century.

Clyde Watson's next books *Tom Fox and the Apple Pie* (a simple prose sequel), *Quips and Quirks* (a witty assemblage of name-calling epithets), and *Hickory Stick Rag* (rhyming verse immortalizing the turn-of-the-century rural school house and its denizens) — are all clever and childlike and full of appealing mischief. But none of them reaches the depth of *Father Fox's Pennyrhymes* nor do any of them have its range of color, tone, and musical appeal.

—Jane Yolen

———————

WAYNE, (Anne) Jenifer.   British.   Born in London, in 1917. Educated at Blackheath High School, London; Somerville College, Oxford, 1936–39. Married C. R. Hewitt in 1948; has two daughters and one son. Worked for the London Ambulance Service, 1939; Junior

English Mistress, Newark High School, Nottinghamshire, 1940–41; Writer and Producer, BBC Radio Features Department, London, 1941–48. Address: Rushett Edge, Bramley, Guildford, Surrey GU5 0LH, England.

PUBLICATIONS FOR CHILDREN

Fiction (illustrated by Marg ret Palmer)

Clemence and Ginger, illustrated by Patricia Humphreys.   London, Heinemann, 1960.
The Day the Ceiling Fell Down, illustrated by Dodie Masterman.   London, Heinemann, 1961.
The Night the Rain Came In, illustrated by Dodie Masterman.   London, Heinemann, 1963.
Kitchen People.   London, Heinemann, 1963; Indianapolis, Bobbs Merrill, 1965.
Merry by Name.   London, Heinemann, 1964.
The Ghost Next Door.   London, Heinemann, 1965.
Saturday and the Irish Aunt.   London, Heinemann, 1966.
Someone in the Attic.   London, Heinemann, 1967.
Ollie.   London, Heinemann, 1969.
Sprout.   London, Heinemann, 1970; New York, McGraw Hill, 1976.
Something in the Barn.   London, Heinemann, 1971.
Sprout's Window-Cleaner.   London, Heinemann, 1971; New York, McGraw Hill, 1976.
Sprout and the Dog-Sitter.   London, Heinemann, 1972; New York, McGraw Hill, 1977.
The Smoke in Albert's Garden.   London, Heinemann, 1974.
Sprout and the Helicopter.   London, Heinemann, 1975; New York, McGraw Hill, 1977.
Sprout and the Conjuror.   London, Heinemann, 1976; as *Sprout and the Magician*, New York, McGraw Hill, 1977.

PUBLICATIONS FOR ADULTS

Play

Radio Play: *The Queen of the Castle*, 1969.

Verse

The Shadows and Other Poems.   London, Secker and Warburg, 1959.

Other

This Is the Law: Stories of Wrongdoers by Fault or Folly.   London, Sylvan Press, 1948.
Brown Bread and Butter in the Basement: A Twenties Childhood.   London, Gollancz, 1973.

*   *   *

A warm love of children, a delight in family life, and an almost Puckish glee in the ridiculous – these are the attributes that make Jenifer Wayne one of the most endearing of writers for the young. Blending innocence and maturity in a particularly satisfying way, she presents her children with a candid realism and no apologies – their optimism and simple, devastating logic; their passionate, all-committed devotion to awkward animals, unprepossessing people and impossible causes; their irrefutable sense of justice and fair-dealing; their unhesitating willingness to turn the whole world upside-down without flicking an eyelash – and invites the whole world to share the glorious, hair-raising fun of being a parent. Her stories are gay, quick-moving, family affairs with happy endings. Her children certainly have problems – falling ceilings, deluges of rain, friends in trouble, odd things happening in neighbours' gardens, thick-headed adults – but these are matters the young can deal with perfectly well given time and no adult interference.

Particularly successful are her stories about her lovable young scamp, Sprout, keyed effortlessly to the understanding of the 7-to-9's, but so ruefully true to family-life at its most wit-shattering that adults of all ages, from big sisters and baby-sitters to Grandmas and Grandads, join the chorus of hilarious laughter. But hers is no gross, custard-pie humour, the ponderous adult condescending to "entertain": rather, with just a few deft, quick flicks of the artist's brush, she makes characters we all recognize spring to life and warm our hearts – "the large, obliging Mrs. Chad"; Albina, Mrs. Chad's "pin-like only child" (whose name rhymes with China); Eileen, the Irish seaside maid "whose accent never changed, though the colour of her hair did"; young sister Tilly, with her "great gift for falling over"; and Sprout's bedside-rug of a dog, "woolly and joyful." And never, never anywhere is there an unkind stroke!

—Gladys A. Williams

WEIR, Rosemary. British. Born in Kimberley, South Africa, 22 July 1905. Educated at schools in South Africa and England. Married Napier Weir in 1931 (died, 1973); has one daughter. Has worked as an actress, farmer, and teacher. Agent: Charles Lavell Ltd., 176 Wardour Street, London, W1V 3AA. Address: Little Arden, Ashill, Cullompton, Devon, England.

PUBLICATIONS FOR CHILDREN

Fiction

The Secret Journey. London, Parrish, 1957.
The Secret of Cobbetts Farm. London, Parrish, 1957.
No. 10 Green Street. London, Parrish, 1958.
Island of Birds. London, Parrish, 1959.
The Honeysuckle Line. London, Parrish, 1959; as *Robert's Rescued Railway,* New York, Watts, 1960.
The Hunt for Harry. London, Parrish, 1959.
Great Days in Green Street. London, Parrish, 1960.
Pineapple Farm, illustrated by Hugh Marshall. London, Parrish, 1960.
Little Lion's Real Island, illustrated by. W.F. Phillipps. London, Harrap, 1960.
The House in the Middle of the Road. London, Parrish, 1961.
Albert the Dragon, illustrated by Quentin Blake. London and New York, Abelard Schuman, 1961.
What a Lark, illustrated by Val Biro. Leicester, Brockhampton Press, 1961.
Tania Takes the Stage. London, Hutchinson, 1961.
Top Secret. London, Parrish, 1962.
The Star and the Flame, illustrated by William Stobbs. London, Faber, 1962; New York, Farrar Straus, 1964.

Soap Box Derby, illustrated by Val Biro. Leicester, Brockhampton Press, 1962; Princeton, New Jersey, Van Nostrand, 1965.

Black Sheep. London, Parrish, 1963; as *Mystery of the Black Sheep*, New York, Criterion Books, 1964.

The Smallest Dog on Earth, illustrated by Charles Pickard. London and New York, Abelard Schuman, 1963.

Further Adventures of Albert the Dragon, illustrated by Quentin Blake. London and New York, Abelard Schuman, 1964.

Mike's Gang, illustrated by Charles Pickard. London and New York, Abelard Schuman, 1965.

A Patch of Green. London, Parrish, 1965.

Devon Venture (as Catherine Bell). London, Collins, 1965.

The Real Game, illustrated by Aedwin Darroll. Leicester, Brockhampton Press, 1965; as *The Heirs of Ashton Manor*, New York, Dial Press, 1966.

The Boy from Nowhere, illustrated by Dennis Turner. London and New York, Abelard Schuman, 1966.

High Courage, illustrated by Ian Ribbons. London, Faber, and New York, Farrar Straus, 1967.

Pyewacket, illustrated by Charles Pickard. London and New York, Abelard Schuman, 1967.

Boy on a Brown Horse. London, Hamish Hamilton, 1967; New York, Hawthorn Books, 1971.

The Foxwood Flyer, illustrated by Robert Hales. London, Hamish Hamilton, 1968.

Albert the Dragon and the Centaur, illustrated by Quentin Blake. London and New York, Abelard Schuman, 1968.

No Sleep for Angus, illustrated by Elisabeth Grant. London and New York, Abelard Schuman, 1969.

Summer of the Silent Hands, illustrated by Lynette Hemmant. Leicester, Brockhampton Press, 1969.

The Lion and the Rose, illustrated by Richard Cuffari. New York, Farrar Straus, 1970; London, Abelard Schuman, 1972.

The Three Red Herrings. Nashville, Nelson, 1972.

Uncle Barney and the Sleep-Destroyer, illustrated by Carolyn Dinan. London, Abelard Schuman, 1974.

Uncle Barney and the Shrink-Drink, illustrated by Carolyn Dinan. London, Abelard Schuman, 1977.

Albert and the Dragonettes, illustrated by Gerald Rose. London, Abelard Schuman, 1977.

Other

A Dog of Your Own: or, Dogs Without Tears: Do's and Don't's for Young Dog Owners, illustrated by K.F. Barker. London, Harrap, 1960.

The Young David Garrick, illustrated by Anne Linton. London, Parrish, 1963; New York, Roy, 1964.

The Man Who Built a City: A Life of Sir Christopher Wren. New York, Farrar Straus, 1971.

Blood Royal, illustrated by Richard Cuffari. New York, Farrar Straus, 1973.

PUBLICATIONS FOR ADULTS

Play

Radio Play: *The Off-White Elephant*, 1958.

Rosemary Weir comments:

I began to write for children when my own daughter was grown up and I myself was over 50. I remembered my own childhood very clearly and perhaps my books for children were a way of returning to a happy time of my life. On the whole I have most enjoyed writing for younger children, *The Smallest Dog on Earth* being my own favourite.

*   *   *

Rosemary Weir's books are for a wide range of readers, from very simple stories to straight historical adventure and novels for much older children.

Albert, the peaceful dragon, and Pyewacket, the ferocious old alley-cat, have adventures original and entertaining enough to lure the inexperienced reader to books. The humour and interest depend almost wholly upon external situation, but they are excellent for their purpose. Longer books, still for young children, such as *What a Lark* and *Soap Box Derby*, are cheerful, convincing, and undemanding. One feels they may have been written to meet the demand by some librarians and teachers for "neighbourhood stories," and many children will enjoy them.

The historical adventures offer far more. They are well researched but not too heavily cumbered with details of contemporary events or manners. They remain stories, not history lessons. *High Courage*, set in the time of Simon de Montfort, brings alive the violence and tragedy of civil wars, the constricting life of a mediaeval castle, the contrasts of wealth and poverty. *The Lion and the Rose* tells of a lad ambitious to be a master stone-carver, who works on the rebuilding of St. Paul's. The feeling for the quality of stone itself, and the impressions of St. Paul's and the Portland quarries, are lively and memorable. These novels tell a good straightforward story with pace and interest. They are more concerned with events than character; the persons are satisfactorily rounded but not studied in any depth.

Rosemary Weir's best work is in the novels for older readers. *The Real Game* tells of two children from the Australian outback who discover that their father is the heir to an earldom. Their only knowledge of the English aristocracy is derived from a battered copy of *Little Lord Fauntleroy*, found by mere chance; but when they are sent home to Ashton Court the slow adjustment from dream to reality is both funny and touching. Sebastian, shy, nervous, always too dependent on his loving but bossy sister, is deeply troubled until at last he discovers his true gift and becomes a person in his own right. This is a book full of warmth and humour and kindness, with a very sensitive understanding of the anxieties and uncertainties and embarrassments of childhood. The same ability to probe and interpret experience is seen in *Summer of the Silent Hands*, which concerns a brilliant boy pianist suddenly deprived by an accident of his gift and of the only life he knows. Through loneliness and anxiety, friendship and laughter, he has slowly to find his way in the uncharted world of family life and ordinary childhood.

It is these books for older readers that show Rosemary Weir as an original and perceptive writer. The characterization is strong and clear, including satisfactory and fruitful relationships with adults as well as children. She stimulates interest by developing an unusual situation, but through it she explores the emotional experiences common to most children. She is concerned with the problems of growing up, but she makes them the material of art and not of social therapy.

—Margaret Greaves

WELCH, Ronald. Pseudonym for Ronald Oliver Felton. British. Born in Aberavon, Glamorganshire, 14 December 1909. Educated at Berkhamsted School, Hertfordshire, 1922–28; Clare College, Cambridge, M.A. (honours) in history 1931. Served in the

Territorial Army, 1933–39; Welch Regiment during World War II: Company Commander and Staff Major. Married Betty Llewellyn Evans in 1934; has one daughter. Assistant History Master, Berkhamsted School, 1931–33; Senior Teacher, Bedford Modern School, 1933; Headmaster, Okehampton Grammar School, Devon, 1947–63. Recipient: Library Association Carnegie Medal, 1955. Address: c/o Oxford University Press, Walton Street, Oxford OX2 6DP, England.

PUBLICATIONS FOR CHILDREN

Fiction

> *The Black Car Mystery.*   London, Pitman, 1950.
> *The Clock Stood Still.*   London, Pitman, 1951.
> *The Gauntlet*, illustrated by T.R. Freeman.   London and New York, Oxford University
>   Press, 1951.
> *Knight Crusader*, illustrated by William Stobbs.   London, Oxford University Press,
>   1954.
> *Sker House* (as Ronald Felton).   London, Hutchinson, 1954.
> *Captain of Dragoons*, illustrated by William Stobbs.   London and New York, Oxford
>   University Press, 1956.
> *The Long Bow.*   Oxford, Blackwell, 1957.
> *Mohawk Valley*, illustrated by William Stobbs.   London, Oxford University Press, and
>   New York, Criterion Books, 1958.
> *Captain of Foot*, illustrated by William Stobbs.   London, Oxford University Press,
>   1959.
> *Escape from France*, illustrated by William Stobbs.   London, Oxford University Press,
>   1960; New York, Criterion Books, 1961.
> *For the King*, illustrated by William Stobbs.   London, Oxford University Press, 1961;
>   New York, Criterion Books, 1962.
> *Nicholas Carey*, illustrated by William Stobbs.   London, Oxford University Press, and
>   New York, Criterion Books, 1963.
> *Bowman of Crécy*, illustrated by Ian Ribbons.   London, Oxford University Press, 1966;
>   New York, Criterion Books, 1967.
> *The Hawk*, illustrated by Gareth Floyd.   London, Oxford University Press, 1967; New
>   York, Criterion Books, 1969.
> *Sun of York,* illustrated by Doreen Roberts.   London, Oxford University Press, 1970.
> *The Galleon*, illustrated by Victor Ambrus.   London, Oxford University Press, 1971.
> *Tank Commander*, illustrated by Victor Ambrus.   London, Oxford University Press,
>   1972.
> *Zulu Warrior*, illustrated by David Harris.   Newton Abbot, Devon, David and Charles,
>   1974.
> *Ensign Carey*, illustrated by Victor Ambrus.   London, Oxford University Press, 1976.

Other

> *Ferdinand Magellan*, illustrated by William Stobbs.   London, Oxford University Press,
>   1955; New York, Criterion Books, 1956.

*   *   *

In his historical novels, Ronald Welch takes one aspect of the past, military history, and makes it his own. No other historical novelist for children is as good on battles as he is. His books are extremely well-researched, full of authentic detail, and always excitingly plotted.
The Gauntlet is a time slip story in which Welch was feeling his way – a modern boy

experiences his ancestors' adventures in a Welsh castle in the 14th century – but with *Knight Crusader* (a well-deserved Carnegie medal winner) Welch had found his metier and his style. It tells the adventures of a young crusading knight, Philip d'Aubigny, in the Holy Land in the 12th century who, at the end of the book, goes home to Wales to take up his inheritance and to found the Carey family, whose fortunes Welch followed in many of his books.

Charles Carey fights with Marlborough's army in *Captain of Dragoons*, Alan Carey is with Wolfe at Quebec in *Mohawk Valley*, Richard Carey helps to rescue French kinsmen from the revolution in *Escape from France*, Neil Carey is a Royalist soldier in the Civil War in *For the King*, Nicholas Carey fights in the Crimea in *Nicholas Carey*, and Harry Carey takes to the sea in Elizabethan England in *The Hawk*. Best of the Carey books are his superb evocation of the 1914–18 war in *Tank Commander* and *Captain of Foot*, in which Christopher Carey serves under Wellington in the Peninsular. In this book the famous diarists of the period, George Simmons and John Kincaid, are drawn upon, giving this book characters more rounded than usual.

Not Carey stories, but with jumping off points in the Welsh border country were an Elizabethan story, *The Galleon*, and *Bowman of Crécy*, an enthralling story, full of authentic detail about the Hundred Years War. Less successful, perhaps, is another Carey book, *Zulu Warrior*, which is not only pedestrian but expresses the Jingoistic sentiments of the characters which are right for the times portrayed but out of mesh with today's attitudes both to Africa and to war.

Ronald Welch's great achievement has been to produce exciting stories full of accurate information about the weapons and warfare of the times he has writing about; he has never glorified war, but has made it quite clear that mud and discomfort, wounds and death were part of soldiering as well as comradeship and adventure. Welch has been a soldier as well as a history teacher, and he has drawn on both experiences in making his historical novels for boys.

—Pamela Cleaver

WERSBA, Barbara. American. Born in Chicago, Illinois, 19 August 1932. Educated at Bard College, Annandale-on-Hudson, New York, B.A. 1954; studied acting at Neighborhood Playhouse and Paul Mann Actors Workshop, both New York. Professional stage and television actress, 1944–59. D.H.L.: Bard College, 1977. Address: Oak Tree Road, Palisades, New York 10964, U.S.A.

PUBLICATIONS FOR CHILDREN

Fiction

The Boy Who Loved the Sea, illustrated by Margot Tomes. New York, Coward McCann, 1961.
The Brave Balloon of Benjamin Buckley, illustrated by Margot Tomes. New York, Atheneum, 1963.
The Land of Forgotten Beasts, illustrated by Margot Tomes. New York, Atheneum, 1964; London, Gollancz, 1965.
A Song for Clowns, illustrated by Mario Rivoli. New York, Atheneum, 1965; London, Gollancz, 1966.
The Dream Watcher. New York, Atheneum, 1968.
Run Softly, Go Fast. New York, Atheneum, 1970.
Let Me Fall Before I Fly. New York, Atheneum, 1971.

Amanda Dreaming, illustrated by Mercer Mayer.   New York, Atheneum, 1973.
The Country of the Heart.   New York, Atheneum, 1975.
Tunes for a Small Harmonica.   New York, Harper, 1976.

Play

The Dream Watcher, adaptation of her own story (produced Westport, Connecticut, 1975).

Verse

Do Tigers Ever Bite Kings?, illustrated by Mario Rivoli.   New York, Atheneum, 1966.

*   *   *

For more than 15 years Barbara Wersba has toiled in the field of children's literature – as a novelist, poet, and as critic for the *New York Times.* The tipoff to a Wersba story is compassion for young people, especially teenagers.

Two of her novels are especially notable as examples of her reaching out to those facing hurtful problems. *The Dream Watcher* zeroes in on Albert Scully, an adolescent misfit. "I'm not square and I'm not hip," says Albert; he hates rock and roll, likes gardening and collecting recipes. A fortunate friendship with Orpha Woodfin, grande dame, results in Albert's coming to terms with himself. *The Dream Watcher* has been produced by the great actress, Eva La Gallienne, who played the part of Mrs. Woodfin in Wersba's dramatization. *The Country of the Heart* is a later novel which also describes a relationship between an older woman and a youth. Hadley is fortyish, a famous poet, angry and dying. Steven is a boy who falls in love with her but gets only snubs and mockery until she softens. The result is a brief, poignant affair and the "necessary end." Here is a story that could have been insufferably maudlin but which, in Wersba's deft hands, rises to art.

The only time Wersba could be viewed as a failure in part is in another novel about the generation gap (seemingly an irresistible theme to authors during the tumultuous 1960's), *Run Softly, Go Fast.* David is the son of a prosperous father who rebels outright against the Establishment. He sinks into the East Village (New York) subculture, gets into drugs and has an affair with a girl runaway. The book is presented as David's diary in which he spews out his loathing of his father. But in a pathetic and unconvincing finale, the boy suddenly pours out sympathy for his dominating parent.

In no other instance does the author disappoint expectations. And, even with its weaknesses, *Run Softly, Go Fast,* is a cut above most novels of the genre.

Among Wersba's stories are several fantasies, thoroughly believable and invested with a core of intelligent philosophy. Outstanding and popular in this category is *A Song for Clowns,* a nimble fable set in a mythical England of the middle ages. A youth named Humphrey Tapwell becomes a wandering minstrel and attracts other uprooted men to his company. The little band travels about, performing acts to amuse citizens who need diversion badly. Their country is saddled with a crazy king. He's a ruler who abolishes things and people out of hand because nothing and nobody can be judged perfect by his standards. When he abolishes minstrels, Humphrey and friends dare death by confronting the king and showing him the error of his ways. A popular modern fable, the book is spiced by Wersba's rhymes, protest songs which speak to the questing children of today.

With good reason, critics rank Barbara Wersba as one of the most significant authors of children's books of our time. She has style, imagination, and the courage to tackle difficult subjects.

—Jean F. Mercier

WEST, Joyce (Tarlton).   British.   Born in Auckland, New Zealand. Educated in Maori schools and by correspondence courses. Address: 88 Eighteenth Avenue, Tauranga, New Zealand.

PUBLICATIONS FOR CHILDREN (illustrated by the author)

Fiction

> *Drovers Road.*   London, Dent, 1953.
> *The Year of the Shining Cuckoo.*   Hamilton, Paul's Book Arcade, 1961; London, Dent, 1963; New York, Roy, 1964.
> *Cape Lost.*   Auckland, Paul's Book Arcade, and London, Dent, 1963.
> *The Golden Country.*   Hamilton, Blackwood and Janet Paul, and London, Dent, 1965.
> *The Sea Islanders.*   London, Dent, and New York, Roy, 1970.

PUBLICATIONS FOR ADULTS

Novels

> *Sheep Kings.*   Wellington, Tombs, 1936.
> *Fatal Lady,* with Mary Scott.   Hamilton, Paul's Book Arcade, 1960.
> *Such Nice People,* with Mary Scott.   Hamilton, Paul's Book Arcade, 1962.
> *The Mangrove Murder,* with Mary Scott.   Auckland, Paul's Book Arcade, and London, Angus and Robertson, 1963.
> *No Red Herrings,* with Mary Scott.   London, Angus and Robertson, 1964.
> *Who Put It There?,* with Mary Scott.   Hamilton, Blackwood and Janet Paul, and London, Angus and Robertson, 1965.
> *Lineman's Ticket* (as Manu Gilbert).   Hamilton, Blackwood and Janet Paul, 1967.

Joyce West comments:

My own childhood was spent in the remote country districts of New Zealand where my parents were teachers in the Maori schools. We lived far from towns, in a world of bush roads and river crossings; we rode horseback everywhere, and kept a large menagerie of dogs, cats, kittens, ducks, turkeys, pet lambs, and goats. It always seemed to be summertime. When I began to write, it was with the wish that I might save a little of the charm and flavour of those times and places for the children of today.

*   *   *

In New Zealand, Joyce West is best known for an early work, *Drovers Road,* which describes in episodic form the humorous adventures of Gay, who, though deserted by both her parents, enjoys a happy and secure life with her Aunt Belle, her uncle Dunsany, and several cousins on a rather isolated sheep station on the East Coast of the North Island of New Zealand. In many ways the book demonstrates the best qualities of this author. There are the warmth and love of a united family, a deep feeling and a sensitivity to nature and to animals. Despite some sentimentality, Joyce West, with her shrewd characterisation, her gift for comedy, and her racy style, very satisfyingly demonstrates one type of New Zealand child who lives still very much in the English tradition.

We meet the characters of *Drovers Road* in further novels. In *The Golden Country,* for example, the former schoolgirl who had appeared in an intervening novel entitled *Cape Lost,* is now the owner of an old homestead and coastal station at Cape Lost. While the book is still blemished by the element of fairy tale, the writing is confident and compelling, the characterisation realistic and memorable with, unfortunately, some instances of mawkishness. Gay's tenacious search for independence and her agonising over the choice of Mr. Right take place in the context of the hardships and the isolation of hill country sheep farming.

The Year of the Shining Cuckoo is set in another inaccessible spot: this time in dairying country bordering a tidal harbour. In this story of a boy's efforts to buy a filly, the chief interest lies in the adult characters, Grandfather and Aunt Garance, both larger than life, lovable and memorable. The themes of loneliness and the compensating warmth of family and community life are accompanied by scenes such as that at the horse fair which reveal Miss West's comic gifts and acute observation. The same delight in all living things, and in the bush, the sea, and the hills, gives her writing a flavour of the appeal of the backblocks. *The Sea Islanders*, in presenting a group of children in a Robinson Crusoe setting, allows Miss West plenty of freedom to explore flora and fauna of a tiny island.

Miss West illustrates all her books, and these illustrations, along with her sensitive descriptions, make her contribution to children's literature something very special. Along with these qualities are her ability to create a comic scene and her strength in the observation of the delightful quirks of all the country characters whom she describes. These qualities more than make up for any weaknesses in plot and sentimentality of character.

—Tom Fitzgibbon

WESTALL, Robert. British. Born in Tynemouth, Northumberland, 7 October 1929. Educated at Tynemouth High School, 1941–48; Durham University, 1948–53, B.A. (honours) in fine art; Slade School, University of London, 1955–57, diploma 1957. Served in the Royal Signals, 1953–55; Lance-Corporal. Married Jean Underhill in 1958; has one son. Art Master, Erdington Hall Secondary Modern School, Birmingham, 1957–58, and Keighley Boys' Grammar School, Yorkshire, 1958–60. Since 1960, Head of Art, and since 1970, Head of Careers, Sir John Deane's Grammar School, Chester. Writer, Whitehorn Press, Manchester, 1968–71; Northern Art Critic, *Guardian*, London, 1970. Since 1962, Art Critic, Chester *Chronicle*. Director, Telephone Samaritans of Mid-Cheshire, 1966–75. Recipient: Library Association Carnegie Medal, 1976. Address: 2 Dyar Terrace, Winnington, Northwich, Cheshire CW8 4DN, England.

PUBLICATIONS FOR CHILDREN

Fiction

> *The Machine-Gunners.* London, Macmillan, 1975; New York, Morrow, 1976.
> *The Wind Eye.* London, Macmillan, 1976; New York, Morrow, 1977.
> *The Watch House.* London, Macmillan, 1977.

Robert Westall comments:

The only common factor I can see in the books I have written so far (both published and unpublished) is that the children in them must have power of some sort to affect events drastically. Thus the children in my books are faced with moral dilemmas. I also have a marked dislike for descriptions of the appearance of people and landscape, unless absolutely essential. I find them boring in other people's work and dread them holding up the action in mine.

*   *   *

Robert Westall's first book, *The Machine-Gunners*, was greeted with widespread acclaim, winning one of the two major prizes for children's books, and being runner-up for the other. The setting of the story is Newcastle in the Second World War. Gangs of children compete with collections of souvenirs — shrapnel and shells, and such like. When a German aircraft crashes in a wood the turret machine gun is stolen by the hero, a rough small boy, and the authorities search for it in vain. This is a violent book about violent times. The children's need to hide the gun is the source of a deeply ambivalent situation; to keep it they need really only hide it, but they do in fact set it up for use. The hideout they make is a lifesaving support for one of their number whose father is dead, and whose mother is demoralised; it makes a protective fantasy round all of them, and can even briefly protect an enemy airman. But the means that must be taken to keep the secret become nastier, and when adult reality intrudes on the children's world people really get hurt.

Marvellously vivid and forceful as *The Machine-Gunners* is, it is a very undisciplined book, taking on more and more as it goes, like a snowball on a slope. Though nothing strictly implausible happens, fictional credibility is sometimes lost in this rapidly expanding and luxuriating plot. It is also a deeply class-conscious book; the behaviour of the few middle-class characters — Captain's widow gone bad, cowardly father fleeing in car full of black market petrol — seems conceived in contempt, in marked contrast to the human understanding the author can bring to bear on the sadism and cruelty shown by members of the children's gang. The merits of this book are, however, formidable. The uncompromising toughness of Mr. Westall's vision, blended with a cool tenderness that consists mainly in understanding for his characters, will make his book accessible to many children too hard-bitten for most of the children's list; his fascinated revulsion against violence means that his book raises and considers questions of conduct in bleak areas outside the scope of most other children's writers, and treats them with seriousness and a unique and distinctive tone of voice. Above all *The Machine-Gunners* has an intensity and energy on the page which is the mark of a true writer.

Mr. Westall's second book, *The Wind Eye*, is as unlike his first in subject and conception as it well could be. It is a fantasy account of the impact on a divided and quarrelsome modern family of St. Cuthbert, a ferocious old saint, still feared and revered by the locals, and encountered by means of a battered and very ancient boat with a tendency to voyage in time as well as in space. Far removed as it is from the hard-headed realism of *The Machine-Gunners*, the fantasy element in *The Wind Eye* is handled with confidence and conviction. Still the reader's main interest is likely to be in the vivid and realistic portrayal of the family, with step-brothers and sisters struggling to come to terms with each other and their bickering parents. The father is rationalist man, not always convincingly drawn. He is to be destroyed, root and branch, his vision of the world shattered, and replaced by a role as a mystic recluse. The violence in this book is psychological, and participated in by the author, whose view of his characters is highly personal and partisan. But it is a powerful and fascinating piece of work.

—Jill Paton Walsh

WESTERMAN, Percy (Francis). British. Born in Portsmouth, Hampshire, in 1876. Educated at Portsmouth Grammar School. Served in the Royal Navy and Royal Flying Corps during World War I, and in Dorset Home Guard during World War II. Married Florence Wager in 1900. Admiralty Clerk, Portsmouth Dockyard, 1896–1911. Lived many years in Wareham, Dorset. *Died 22 February 1959.*

PUBLICATIONS FOR CHILDREN

Fiction

A Lad of Grit, illustrated by E.S. Hodgson. London, Blackie, 1908.
The Winning of Goldenspurs. London, Nisbet, 1911.
The Young Cavalier, illustrated by Gordon Browne. London, Pearson, 1911.
The Flying Submarine. London, Nisbet, 1912.
Captured at Tripoli, illustrated by Charles Sheldon. London, Blackie, 1912.
The Quest of the "Golden Hope," illustrated by Frank Wiles. London, Blackie, 1912.
The Sea Monarch, illustrated by E.S. Hodgson. London, A. and C. Black, 1912.
The Scouts of Seal Island, illustrated by Ernest Prater. London, A. and C. Black, 1913;
     New York, Macmillan, 1922.
The Rival Submarines, illustrated by C. Fleming Williams. London, Partridge, 1913.
The Stolen Cruiser. London, Jarrolds, 1913.
When East Meets West, illustrated by C.M. Padday. London, Blackie, 1913.
Under King Henry's Banners, illustrated by John Campbell. London, Pilgrim Press,
     1914.
The Sea-Girt Fortress, illustrated by W.E. Wigfull. London, Blackie, 1914.
The Sea Scouts of the "Petrel." London, A. and C. Black, 1914; New York,
     Macmillan, 1924.
The Log of a Snob, illustrated by W.E. Wigfull. London, Chapman and Hall, 1914.
'Gainst the Might of Spain. London, Pilgrim Press, 1914.
Building the Empire. London, Jarrolds, 1914.
The Dreadnought of the Air. London, Partridge, 1914
The Dispatch-Riders. London, Blackie, 1915.
The Fight for Constantinople. London, Blackie, 1915.
The Nameless Island. London, Pearson, 1915.
A Sub. of the R.N.R. London, Partridge, 1915.
Rounding Up the Raider, illustrated by E.S. Hodgson. London, Blackie, 1916.
The Secret Battleplane. London, Blackie, 1916.
The Treasures of the "San Philipo." London, Religious Tract Society, 1916.
A Watch-Dog of the North Sea. London, Partridge, 1917.
Deeds of Pluck and Daring in the Great War. London, Blackie, 1917.
The Fritz Strafers. London, Partridge, 1918; as *The Keepers of the Narrow Seas*, 1931.
Under the White Ensign. London, Blackie, 1918.
Billy Barcroft, R.N.A.S. London, Partridge, 1918.
A Lively Bit of the Front, illustrated by Wal Paget. London, Blackie, 1918.
The Secret Channel and Other Stories. London, A. and C. Black, 1918; New York,
     Macmillan, 1919.
The Submarine Hunters. London, Blackie, 1918.
To the Fore with the Tanks!, illustrated by Dudley Tennant. London, Partridge, 1918.
Wilmshurst of the Frontier Force. London, Partridge, 1918.
With Beatty off Jutland. London, Blackie, 1918.
Winning His Wings, illustrated by E.S. Hodgson. London, Blackie, 1919.
The Thick of the Fray at Zeebruge, April 1918, illustrated by W.E. Wigfull. London,
     Blackie, 1919.
A Sub and a Submarine. London, Blackie, 1919.
'Midst Arctic Perils. London, Pearson, 1919.
The Airship "Golden Hind." London, Partridge, 1920.
The Mystery Ship. London, Partridge, 1920.
The Salving of the "Fusi Yama," illustrated by E.S. Hodgson. London, Blackie, 1920.
Sea Scouts All, illustrated by Charles Pears. London, Blackie, 1920.
Sea Scouts Abroad. London, Blackie, 1921.
The Third Officer, illustrated by E.S. Hodgson. London, Blackie, 1921.

Sea Scouts Up-Channel, illustrated by C.M. Padday. London, Blackie, 1922.

The Wireless Officer, illustrated by W.E. Wigfull. London, Blackie, 1922.

The War of the Wireless Waves, illustrated by W.E. Wightman. London, Oxford University Press, 1923.

The Pirate Submarine. London, Nisbet, 1923.

A Cadet of the Mercantile Marine, illustrated by W.E. Wigfull. London, Blackie, 1923.

Clipped Wings, illustrated by E.S. Hodgson. London, Blackie, 1923.

Captain Cain. London, Nisbet, 1924.

The Good Ship "Golden Effort," illustrated by W.E. Wigfull. London, Blackie, 1924.

The Mystery of Stockmere School. London, Partridge, 1924.

Sinclair's Luck. London, Partridge, 1924.

The Treasure of the Sacred Lake. London, Pearson, 1924.

Unconquered Wings, illustrated by E.S. Hodgson. London, Blackie, 1924.

Clinton's Quest, illustrated by R.B. Ogle. London, Pearson, 1925.

East in the "Golden Gain," illustrated by Rowland Hilder. London, Blackie, 1925.

The Boys of the "Puffin," illustrated by G.W. Goss. London, Partridge, 1925.

The Buccaneers of Boya, illustrated by William Rainey. London, Blackie, 1925.

Annesley's Double. London, A. and C. Black, and New York, Macmillan, 1926.

King of Kilba. London, Ward Lock, 1926.

The Luck of the "Golden Dawn," illustrated by Rowland Hilder. London, Blackie, 1926.

The Riddle of the Air, illustrated by Rowland Hilder. London, Blackie, 1926.

The Sea Scouts of the "Kestrel." London, Seeley, 1926.

Tireless Wings. London, Blackie, 1926.

The Terror of the Seas. London, Ward Lock, 1927.

Mystery Island. London, Oxford University Press, 1927.

Captain Blundell's Treasure, illustrated by J. Cameron. London, Blackie, 1927.

Chums of the "Golden Vanity," illustrated by Rowland Hilder. London, Blackie, 1927.

In the Clutches of the Dyaks, illustrated by F. Marston. London, Partridge, 1927.

The Junior Cadet, illustrated by Rowland Hilder. London, Blackie, 1928.

On the Wings of the Wind, illustrated by W.E. Wigfull. London, Blackie, 1928.

A Shanghai Adventure, illustrated by Leo Bates. London, Blackie, 1928.

Pat Stobart in the "Golden Dawn," illustrated by Rowland Hilder. London, Blackie, 1928.

Rivals of the Reef, illustrated by Kenneth Inns. London, Blackie, 1929.

Captain Starlight, illustrated by W.E. Wigfull. London, Blackie, 1929.

Captain Sang. London, Blackie, 1930.

Leslie Dexter, Cadet. London, Blackie, 1930.

A Mystery of the Broads, illustrated by E.A. Cox. London, Blackie, 1930.

The Secret of the Plateau, illustrated by W.E. Wigfull. London, Blackie, 1931.

The Senior Cadet, illustrated by Rowland Hilder. London, Blackie, 1931.

In Defiance of the Ban, illustrated by E.S. Hodgson. London, Blackie, 1931.

All Hands to the Boats!, illustrated by Rowland Hilder. London, Blackie, 1932.

The Amir's Ruby, illustrated by W.E. Wigfull. London, Blackie, 1932.

Fosdyke's Gold, illustrated by E.S. Hodgson. London, Blackie, 1932.

King for a Month, illustrated by Comerford Watson. London, Blackie, 1933.

Rocks Ahead! London, Blackie, 1933.

The White Arab, illustrated by Henry Coller. London, Blackie, 1933.

The Disappearing Dhow, illustrated by D.L. Mays. London, Blackie, 1933.

Chasing the "Pleiad." London, Blackie, 1933.

The Westow Talisman, illustrated by W.E. Wigfull. London, Blackie, 1934.

Tales of the Sea, with others, illustrated by Terence Cuneo. London, Tuck, 1934.

Andy-All-Alone, illustrated by D.L. Mays. London, Blackie, 1934.

The Black Hawk, illustrated by Rowland Hilder. London, Blackie, 1934.

Standish of the Air Police. London, Blackie, 1935.

The Red Pirate, illustrated by Rowland Hilder.   London, Blackie, 1935.
Sleuths of the Air, illustrated by Comerford Watson.   London, Blackie, 1935.
On Board the "Golden Effort."   London, Blackie, 1935.
The Call of the Sea, illustrated by D.L. Mays.   London, Blackie, 1935.
Captain Flick, illustrated by E.S. Hodgson.   London, Blackie, 1936.
His First Ship.   London, Blackie, 1936.
Midshipman Raxworthy.   London, Blackie, 1936.
Ringed by Fire.   London, Blackie, 1936.
Winged Might.   London, Blackie, 1937.
Under Fire in Spain, illustrated by Ernest Prater.   London, Blackie, 1937.
The Last of the Buccaneers.   London, Blackie, 1937.
Midshipman Webb's Treasure, illustrated by D.L. Mays.   London, Blackie, 1937.
Haunted Harbour, illustrated by John de Walton.   London, Blackie, 1937.
His Unfinished Voyage, illustrated by D.L. Mays.   London, Blackie, 1937.
Cadet Alan Carr, illustrated by D.L. Mays.   London, Blackie, 1938.
Standish Gets His Man, illustrated by W.E. Wigfull.   London, Blackie, 1938.
Sea Scouts Alert!   London, Blackie, 1938.
Standish Loses His Man, illustrated by W.E. Wigfull.   London, Blackie, 1939.
In Eastern Seas.   London, Blackie, 1939.
The Bulldog Breed, illustrated by E. Boye Uden.   London, Blackie, 1939.
At Grips with the Swastika, illustrated by Leo Bates.   London, Blackie, 1940.
Eagles' Talons.   London, Blackie, 1940.
In Dangerous Waters.   London, Blackie, 1940.
When the Allies Swept the Seas, illustrated by J.C.B. Knight.   London, Blackie, 1940.
Standish Pulls It Off.   London, Blackie, 1940.
The War – And Alan Carr, illustrated by E. Boye Uden.   London, Blackie, 1940.
War Cargo.   London, Blackie, 1941.
Sea Scouts at Dunkirk.   London, Blackie, 1941.
Standish Holds On.   London, Blackie, 1941.
Fighting for Freedom.   London, Blackie, 1941.
Alan Carr in the Near East.   London, Blackie, 1942.
Destroyer's Luck.   London, Blackie, 1942.
On Guard for England, illustrated by J.C.B. Knight.   London, Blackie, 1942.
Secret Flight.   London, Blackie, 1942.
With the Commandoes, illustrated by S. Van Abbe.   London, Blackie, 1943.
Sub-Lieutenant John Cloche, illustrated by H. Pym.   London, Blackie, 1943.
Alan Carr in Command, illustrated by Terence Cuneo.   London, Blackie, 1943.
Alan Carr in the Arctic, illustrated by E. Boye Uden.   London, Blackie, 1943.
Combined Operations, illustrated by S. Van Abbe.   London, Blackie, 1944.
Engage the Enemy Closely, illustrated by Terence Cuneo.   London, Blackie, 1944.
Secret Convoy, illustrated by Terence Cuneo.   London, Blackie, 1944.
One of the Many, illustrated by Ellis Silas.   London, Blackie, 1945.
Operations Successfully Executed, illustrated by S. Drigin.   London, Blackie, 1945.
By Luck and Pluck, illustrated by Terence Cuneo.   London, Blackie, 1946.
Return to Base, illustrated by Leslie Wilcox.   London, Blackie, 1946.
Squadron Leader, illustrated by Terence Cuneo.   London, Blackie, 1946.
Unfettered Night, illustrated by S. Jezzard.   London, Blackie, 1947.
Trapped in the Jungle, illustrated by A.S. Forrest.   London, Blackie, 1947.
The Phantom Submarine, illustrated by J.C.B. Knight.   London, Blackie, 1947.
The "Golden Gleaner," illustrated by M. Mackinlay.   London, Blackie, 1948.
First Over, illustrated by Ellis Silas.   London, Blackie, 1948.
Mystery of the Key, illustrated by Ellis Silas.   London, Blackie, 1948.
Missing, Believed Lost, illustrated by Will Nickless.   London, Blackie, 1949.
Contraband, illustrated by A. Barclay.   London, Blackie, 1949.
Beyond the Burma Road, illustrated by Victor Bertoglio.   London, Blackie, 1949.

Sabarinda Island, illustrated by A. Barclay. London, Blackie, 1950.
Mystery of Nix Hall, illustrated by D.C. Eyles. London, Blackie, 1950.
By Sea and Air. London, Blackie, 1950.
Desolation Island, illustrated by W. Gale. London, Blackie, 1950.
Held to Ransom, illustrated by Ellis Silas. London, Blackie, 1951.
The Isle of Mystery, illustrated by Philip. London, Blackie, 1951.
Working Their Passage, illustrated by Ellis Silas. London, Blackie, 1951.
Sabotage!, illustrated by Ellis Silas. London, Blackie, 1952.
Round the World in the "Golden Gleaner," illustrated by Jack Matthew. London, Blackie, 1952.
Dangerous Cargo, illustrated by W. Gale. London, Blackie, 1952.
Bob Strickland's Log, illustrated by Jack Matthew. London, Blackie, 1953.
The Missing Diplomat, illustrated by R.G. Campbell. London, Blackie, 1953.
Rolling Down to Rio, illustrated by R.G. Campbell. London, Blackie, 1953.
Wrested from the Deep, illustrated by Robert Johnston. London, Blackie, 1954.
A Midshipman of the Fleet, illustrated by P.A. Jobson. London, Blackie, 1954.
The Ju-Ju Hand. London, Blackie, 1954.
The Dark Scout, illustrated by Victor Bertoglio. London, Blackie, 1954.
Daventry's Quest, illustrated by P.A. Jobson. London, Blackie, 1955.
The Lure of the Lagoon, illustrated by E. Kearon. London, Blackie, 1955.
Held in the Frozen North, illustrated by Edward Osmond. London, Blackie, 1956.
The Mystery of the "Sempione," illustrated by P.B. Batchelor. London, Blackie, 1957.
Jack Craddock's Commission, illustrated by Edward Osmond. London, Blackie, 1958.
Mistaken Identity, illustrated by Robert Johnston. London, Blackie, 1959.

*   *   *

Between the wars Percy Westerman was a popular writer of boys' adventure stories: inside the cover of *Standish of the Air Police*, for example, sixty titles are listed. Yet today he is out of print in both England and America. He owed his popularity to skill as "a spinner of yarns," usually with a nautical or flying background, with strong suspense elements involving clashes with unspecified foreign enemies of law and order. This mixture today spells total neglect. Writing of an attempt to land an airship on a tropical island, Westerman wrote, "It was a sort of gamble – everything depended on foresight and chance, and a fortunate combination of the two alone could bring success." In his own case foresight was lacking and chance has been unkind. In story-telling, foresight does not depend on an ability to supply market calculations, but on the quality of an author's imaginative sympathy for his fictions.

Westerman's writing falls too easily into cliché and his characters into stereotypes. Thus swindles are invariably "bare-faced," meals are usually "square" and civilian life is "full of pitfalls" for unsuspecting servicemen. And the heroic character depends as much on the force of muscle as of mind. McAlastair in *The Bulldog Breed* is typical, "Although long-limbed he possessed enormous muscular development...." Intelligence is properly limited to resourceful action in dealing with such everyday situations as piloting ships through typhoons and airships through mid-air collisions. Likewise the villains fall naturally into stock situations: "The occupant of the tent turned. He held a hair brush in each hand. His glossy black hair reeked of perfumed oil." In these matters Westerman falls short of the proper demands of his trade. But change of fashion has also deprived him of his readership. His accounts of machinery and "inventions," like the Crophelium gas which powers the airship Black Comet II, have been left behind by the commonplaces of post-war technology. In the same way the actions which asserted the self-assurance of imperialism, the unquestioning obedience to authority, the stress on courage and clean-living were inappropriate to England's declining economic power during the years of depression. It is not that the heroes and their deeds are unworthy within their own limits, but in showing themselves unaware of large areas of the life of their time, they have come to stand for the values which an anti-heroic age finds least bearable.

—Kenneth J. Sterck

WHITE, Eliza Orne. American. Born in Keene, New Hampshire, 2 August 1856. Educated at schools in Keene, and at Miss Hall's School for Girls, Roxbury, Massachusetts. Lived in Brookline, Massachusetts, 1881–1947. *Died 23 January 1947.*

PUBLICATIONS FOR CHILDREN

Fiction

When Molly Was Six, illustrated by Katharine Pyle.   Boston, Houghton Mifflin, 1894.
A Little Girl of Long Ago.   Boston, Houghton Mifflin, 1896.
Ednah and Her Brothers, illustrated by Margaret Bush-Brown.   Boston, Houghton Mifflin, 1900.
An Only Child, illustrated by Katharine Pyle.   Boston, Houghton Mifflin, 1905.
A Borrowed Sister, illustrated by Katharine Pyle.   Boston, Houghton Mifflin, 1906.
Brothers in Fur.   Boston, Houghton Mifflin, 1910.
The Enchanted Mountain, illustrated by E. Pollak-Ottendorff.   Boston, Houghton Mifflin, 1911.
The Blue Aunt, illustrated by Katharine Pyle.   Boston, Houghton Mifflin, 1918.
The Strange Year, illustrated by Alice Preston.   Boston, Houghton Mifflin, 1920.
Peggy in Her Blue Frock, illustrated by Alice Preston.   Boston, Houghton Mifflin, 1921.
Tony, illustrated by Alice Preston.   Boston, Houghton Mifflin, 1924.
Joan Morse, illustrated by M.A. Benjamin.   Boston, Houghton Mifflin, 1926.
Diana's Rosebush, illustrated by Constance Whittemore.   Boston, Houghton Mifflin, 1927.
The Adventures of Andrew.   Boston, Houghton Mifflin, 1928.
Sally in Her Fur Coat, illustrated by Lisl Hummel.   Boston, Houghton Mifflin, 1929.
The Green Door, illustrated by Lisl Hummel.   Boston, Houghton Mifflin, 1930.
When Abigail Was Seven, illustrated by Lisl Hummel.   Boston, Houghton Miffiin, 1931.
The Four Young Kendalls, illustrated by Lisl Hummel.   Boston, Houghton Mifflin, 1932.
Where Is Adelaide?, illustrated by Helen Sewell.   Boston, Houghton Mifflin, 1933.
Lending Mary, illustrated by Grace Paull.   Boston, Houghton Mifflin, 1934.
Ann Frances, illustrated by Helen Sewell.   Boston, Houghton Mifflin, 1935.
Nancy Alden, illustrated by Mildred Boyle.   Boston, Houghton Mifflin, 1936.
The Farm Beyond the Town, illustrated by Mildred Boyle.   Boston, Houghton Mifflin, 1937.
Helen's Gift House, illustrated by Helen Blair.   Boston, Houghton Mifflin, 1938.
Patty Makes a Visit, illustrated by Helen Blair.   Boston, Houghton Mifflin, 1939.
The House Across the Valley, illustrated by Lois Maloy.   Boston, Houghton Mifflin, 1940.
I: The Autobiography of a Cat, illustrated by Clarke Hutton.   Boston, Houghton Mifflin, 1941.
Training Sylvia, illustrated by Dorothy Bayley.   Boston, Houghton Mifflin, 1942.

When Esther Was a Little Girl, illustrated by Connie Moran. Boston, Houghton Mifflin, 1944.

PUBLICATIONS FOR ADULTS

Novels

Miss Brooks. Boston, Roberts, 1890.
Winterborough. Boston, Houghton Mifflin, 1892.
The Coming of Theodora. Boston, Houghton Mifflin, and London, Smith and Elder, 1895.
A Lover of the Truth. Boston, Houghton Mifflin, and London, Smith and Elder, 1898.
John Forsyth's Aunts. New York and London, McClure Phillips, 1901.
Lesley Chilton. Boston, Houghton Mifflin, 1903.
The Wares of Edgefield. Boston, Houghton Mifflin, 1909.
The First Step. Boston, Houghton Mifflin, 1914.

Short Stories

The Browning Courtship and Other Stories. Boston, Houghton Mifflin, and London, Smith and Elder, 1897.

Other

Editor, *William Orne White: A Record of Ninety Years* (letters). Boston, Houghton Mifflin, 1917.

*   *   *

Most writers of successful books for children have found – though never conceivably in anything like perfect balance – an ongoing audience of boys and girls, girls and boys. Boys of my own dim day could stomach those *Five Little Peppers*, including Phronsie, through all their serial growing pains. We read the Pepper books, but we didn't boast about it. So what of the currently enchanting Miss Bianca and her four-foot Women's Lib? I for one read every Margery Sharp book just as fast as it comes off the press. Why not? After all, isn't Louisa May Alcott really but a younger edition of Jane Austen, working in the same old vineyard? For do not *Emma* and *Little Women* share in common the unfailing readership of full-grown men? Common? Surely Virginia Woolf's "common reader" is not divided, cell-like, sex by sex. Neither is the youthful "common reader" of *Alice*, the *Oz* books, *The Wind in the Willows, Martin Pippin in the Apple Orchard, Charlotte's Web, Millions of Cats, Tom, Dick, and Harriet, Peacock Pie,* Howard Pyle's *The Wonder Clock,* Henry Beston's *The Starlight Wonder Book.* Beyond that, it is more than (worse than) idle, in listing such books to set up these silly horizontal milestones for the age groups: fourth grade, sixth grade, pre- and post-teenagers. Aren't we always in our separate lives alike in easy reach of the cookie jar as well as of Bernard Shaw, Henry James, Wallace Stevens, Thoreau, Hudson, Proust, *The Road to Xanadu*?

And so we come to Eliza Orne White, a now faded figure in children's literature: an American Victorian writer whose father had a parish, and whose maternal grandfather was Chester Harding, the well-known painter. She appears to have been popular enough in her day (1856–1947) to have published in all some twenty-five novels and stories for the very young. And most specifically, in her case, stories for very young girls, *not* boys. All her life she dearly loved little girls and cats. Her cats were characters in themselves.

Her two most popular books were for the very young, *When Molly Was Six* and *A Little Girl of Long Ago.* All her books, I think, are now out of print. The young of 1977 could not and would not enter the world of unbelievable innocence that she describes.

She was born in Keene, New Hampshire, a pleasant town through which I have often driven: a pretty, partially industrial town whose Main Street is surely the widest in all New England. It was a town which obviously should have produced at least one literary figure. It produced Eliza Orne White, who lived there until she was twenty-two. Let her describe it:

> It was just the right sort of a place for a little girl to live in who was to write stories for other little girls when she grew up, for there were all the things to be found there that children most like. The town was very beautiful, with the hills around it, and Monadnock to be seen from the lower end of Main Street, and the Ashuelot River and Beaver Brook, with the woods near them, made splendid places for picnics or drives.
> In the winter, like Molly, "when she was six," my father would take me and some small friend coasting on a big black sled, down a snowy hill and across an icy pond, and we had sleigh-rides to the accompaniment of jingling sleigh-bells, and less speedy rides when we fastened our sleds to slowly moving ox teams.

She was from first to last a period piece. Her style, a sweet stillwater as old-fashioned as the flowers in her garden, as respectful as my own Presbyterian grandmother who always spoke of my Pennsylvania grandfather as "Mr. Reed." You may learn (in *When Molly Was Six*) of the difference between cows and bossies; of "pink-and-white dyaletras"; of hanging "over the *balusters*," not "banisters"; of playing jackstraws – a game of my own youth; of words like rowboats and ponycarts spelled with a hyphen; of Mammá, not Mámma or Mom; of a time when one ran *into* and not *in* the house. That is, we are told, through little twists and tags of speech, of an almost insufferable formality of deportment and confected give-and-take. Most of these books' adventures seem tame enough – as though the lives of little girls of eighty years ago were lived in greater part in a doll's house. Hence "a pew-door seemed made on purpose for little children." In *A Little Girl of Long Ago*, when a somewhat older and more gregarious heroine than Molly, along with her younger sister and brother, struggles to help another young brother free his head which he had squeezed through the back of a chair, we find the victim wailing, "Oh, dear, how you hurt!" Take a look at the prose of E. Nesbit in *The Railway Children*: it is not at all like that. But at least there is scarcely any moralizing; and when Miss White, in one of her rare didactic moments, says a word about cheating, or abandons reality to show the child reader the dreadful danger of (a) deep water or (b) setting one's clothes and hair accidently on fire, she does not labor the message; nor does she repeat it. Miss White's obvious lack is a sense of humor to leaven all her gentleness, kindness, and Sehnsucht. And, as Ethel Heins more importantly points out, her *real* failure (unlike E. Nesbit, for example) is not dealing in any way with fantasy pure and simple. Fantasy is what lasts.

—David McCord

WHITE, E(lwyn) B(rooks). American. Born in Mt. Vernon, New York, 11 July 1899. Educated at Mt. Vernon High School; Cornell Univeristy, Ithaca, New York, A.B. 1921. Served as a private in the United States Army, 1918. Married Katharine Sergeant Angell in 1929 (died, 1977); has one son. Reporter, Seattle *Times*, 1922–23; advertising copywriter, 1924–25; Columnist ("One Man's Meat"), *Harper's* magazine, New York, 1938–43. Since 1926, Contributing Editor, *The New Yorker* magazine. Recipient: National Association of Independent Schools award, 1955; American Academy of Arts and Letters Gold Medal, for essays, 1960; Presidential Medal of Freedom, 1963; American Library Association Laura Ingalls Wilder Award, 1970; George G. Stone Center for Children's Books Award, 1970; National Medal for Literature, 1971. Litt.D.: Dartmouth College, Hanover, New Hampshire,

1948; University of Maine, Orono, 1948; Yale University, New Haven, Connecticut, 1948; Bowdoin College, Brunswick, Maine, 1950; Hamilton College, Clinton, New York, 1952; Harvard University, Cambridge, Massachusetts, 1954; L.H.D.: Colby College, Waterville, Maine, 1954. Fellow, American Academy of Arts and Sciences; Member, National Institute of Arts and Letters; Member, American Academy of Arts and Letters. Address: North Brooklin, Maine 04661, U.S.A.

PUBLICATIONS FOR CHILDREN

Fiction

>*Stuart Little*, illustrated by Garth Williams. New York, Harper, 1945; London, Hamish Hamilton, 1946.
>*Charlotte's Web*, illustrated by Garth Williams. New York, Harper, and London, Hamish Hamilton, 1952.
>*The Trumpet of the Swan*, illustrated by Edward Frascino. New York, Harper, and London, Hamish Hamilton, 1970.

PUBLICATIONS FOR ADULTS

Verse

>*The Lady Is Cold: Poems.* New York and London, Harper, 1929.
>*The Fox of Peapack and Other Poems.* New York and London, Harper, 1938.

Other

>*Is Sex Necessary? or, Why You Feel the Way You Do*, with James Thurber. New York, Harper, 1929; London, Heinemann, 1930.
>*Ho Hum.* New York, Farrar and Rinehart, 1931.
>*Another Ho Hum.* New York, Farrar and Rinehart, 1932.
>*Alice Through the Cellophane.* New York, Day, 1933.
>*Every Day Is Saturday.* New York and London, Harper, 1934.
>*Farewell to Model T.* New York, Putnam, 1936.
>*Quo Vadimus? or, The Case for the Bicycle.* New York and London, Harper, 1939.
>*One Man's Meat.* New York, Harper, 1942; London, Gollancz, 1943; augmented edition, Harper, 1944.
>*The Wild Flag: Editorials from the New Yorker on Federal World Government and Other Matters.* Boston, Houghton Mifflin, 1946.
>*Here Is New York.* New York, Harper, 1949.
>*The Second Tree from the Corner.* New York, Harper, and London, Hamish Hamilton, 1954.
>*The Points of My Compass: Letters from the East, The West, The North, The South.* New York, Harper, 1962; London, Hamish Hamilton, 1963.
>*An E.B. White Reader*, edited by William W. Watt and Robert W. Bradford. New York, Harper, 1966.
>*Letters of E.B. White*, edited by Dorothy Lobrano Guth. New York, Harper, 1976.

>Editor, with Katharine S. White, *A Subtreasury of American Humor.* New York, Coward McCann, 1941.

Manuscript Collection: Cornell University Library, Ithaca, New York.

*   *   *

It takes a book like this collection to remind us that more than one famous writer — but not many more than one — has turned aside at some time from his major literary task, not only to write a book for or about children, but to produce an undisputed masterpiece, the very name of which has come to revolve, like a binary star, about his own: Mark Twain and *Huckleberry Finn*, for example. Among these very different writers are Dickens, Stevenson, Kingsley, George MacDonald, Kipling, Barrie, Belloc, Milne, C.S. Lewis, James Thurber, and E.B. White. Parallel to them, of course, are Edward Lear (a landscape painter) and Lewis Carroll (a mathematician). And who will not agree that *Treasure Island, The Jungle Books, Huckleberry Finn, Alice,* and *Charlotte's Web* by themselves are quite enough to assure their authors immortality? I mean in this case an immortality based on affectionate regard. Youth has enjoyed something and taken something to heart, and will not forget the degree to which it is still a part of him or her. And that is not at all the world's impersonal or blind acceptance of Newton and gravity, Einstein and relativity.

What about women? The George Eliots, Edith Whartons, Willa Cathers, Katherine Mansfields, and Virginia Woolfs appear to have left their monuments in other fields. Those who have indeed produced the genuine masterpieces for or about children are not women equally known, or so I think, by other kinds of writing: Louisa May Alcott, Beatrix Potter, E. Nesbit, Wanda Gág, P.L. Travers, let us say. Of course, Eleanor Farjeon, Margery Sharp, Rumer Godden are three possible exceptions.

Well, if this seems a long way round to *Charlotte's Web*, it is because I want to assure myself that I am seeing it in good light and in fair perspective. *Huckleberry Finn* stands a bit higher than *Tom Sawyer*, doesn't it? But among the seven volumes of the *Narnia Chronicles* by Lewis, which one deserves the crown? White has written three books for children — all successful, all making money; but, more important, making friends and even addicts in the good sense of that bad word, and holding hard the line for millions of young readers who can read but speak, like, only Uno, right? — one totaled Esperanto of no hope. My choice is *Charlotte's Web*, hands down, to bless this trinity, a sort of triskele speeding happily on all three legs.

But *Stuart Little*, which has sold over half a million copies in hard cover alone by 1975, has strong support including mine. *The Trumpet of the Swan*, good as it is, and splendidly written as all of White's books are, seems in its contriving to be intimate but not endearing. Unlike the lucky pig in *Charlotte's Web*, or tiny Stuart Little, human in the shape of a mouse, a swan knows how to keep its distance, trumpeting or not, stimulated or not (in White's words to an old friend in a letter) "by the tossed salad of springtime passion." Ducks are my dish, and perhaps I am prejudiced. So for some it must be like the old con game: under which of three shells is the pea? This amounts to saying again that White has produced, over reflective intervals between 1945 and 1970, three remarkable, memorable, and quite different books for the young in heart.

In the United States today, E.B. White stands alone as our one genuine, widely read, persistently influential essayist. He was born with a built-in deceptively easy style: engaging, witty, salty as the man himself. Only at some rare moment does a sudden verbal handspring tell you he has cabbaged or latched onto something relevant that Thoreau at an earlier date would not have missed. Take any scrap of essay, story, nonsense, parody, reporting, satire, verse, or burst of rightly righteous indignation; it will read, sound, look in print as spare and tidy as the work of some old master scythesman sweeping through a summer field of hay.

So then, being all of one such piece, there was no need for change of voice or vision or for pace itself in the style which White would use to write three books for children. Indeed, the genesis of *Stuart Little* (1945) can be found in the opening story called "Orville" in *Quo Vadimus?* (1939). Orville is a perky male English sparrow who attempts to tow a wren (with a piece of string) from Madison Square, New York City, up to 110th Street (above Central Park) just at the time when gliders were coming into popularity. Stuart Little, the mouse born of human parents, is not only small like Orville, he has the voice and determination of Orville. White, incidentally, calls Stuart a mouse but once — page 36 — and that, he is quick to admit, by oversight. The small bird which Stuart's human mother rescues one day from the window sill is either a wall-eyed vireo (in quotes) or a wren (also in quotes): a comely female, name of Margalo. The later vanishing of Margalo from the Little household, and Stuart impulsively setting out in search of her, control the crazy but exciting sequence of adventures through half the book. Compare, now, Orville's sparrow talk of 1939 with Stuart's mouse speech as of 1945. Only a stepping stone between them:

> Orville came to his wife with a question. "Are you through with that string?" he asked, nodding toward the trailing strand.
> "Are you crazy?" she replied, sadly.
> "I need it for something."
> His wife gazed up at him. "You're going to wreck the nest if you go pulling important strings out."
> "I can get it out without hurting anything," said Orville. "I want it for a towline."
> "A what?"
> "Listen," said Orville, "I'm going to fly to 110th Street tomorrow, towing a wren."
> The hen sparrow looked at him in disgust. "Where are you going to get a wren?"
> "I can get a wren," he said, wisely.

Now here is Stuart in a sailor suit at the sailboat pond in Central Park where the model boats are being sailed and turned back into the wind with sticks. Stuart is accosting a man — for grown men make and sail these vessels — who is turning a big black model schooner flying the American flag. White, again incidentally, sails his own boat, and his son Joel now runs a boatyard down in Maine.

> She had a clipper bow, and on her foredeck was mounted a three-inch cannon. She's the ship for me, thought Stuart. And the next time she sailed in, he ran over to where she was being turned around.
> "Excuse me, sir," said Stuart to the man who was turning her, "but are you the owner of the schooner Wasp?"
> "I am," replied the man, surprised to be addressed by a mouse in a sailor suit.
> "I'm looking for a berth in a good ship," continued Stuart, "and I thought perhaps you might sign me on. I'm strong and I'm quick."
> "Are you sober?" asked the owner of the Wasp.
> "I do my work," said Stuart, crisply.

I shall never understand how the late Anne Carroll Moore, "doyenne of the children's book world" and sometime (long time) children's librarian at the New York Public Library, not only failed to appreciate *Stuart Little* but urged both author and publisher not to publish it. She didn't like *Charlotte's Web*, either; and in *Horn Book* for December 1952 said that "Fern, the real center of the book, is never developed. The animals never talk. They speculate." My respect for Miss Moore was so great that it pains me to say, Nonsense! Nonsense on every count.

Unlike *Stuart Little*, when we come to *Charlotte's Web* we have a concentrated barnyard story about a pig: a runt named Wilbur, an unforgettable girl of eight named Fern who successfully entreats her father to spare Wilbur's life and let her bring him up; a spider named Charlotte who is to perform the miracle of writing English words on her web in praise of the fast-growing Wilbur; a clever rat named Templeton; Fern's brother Avery (ten); the children's parents, named Arable — good choice for farmers; sheep, geese, assorted human characters; and the barn itself.

My generation, which is Andy White's, grew up on endless talking birds and animals in the Oz books, including man-made talking characters like the Scarecrow and Tiktok who wound up with a key. Stuart Little himself took off in his unfinished search for Margalo in a toy automobile that runs on a few drops of gas. But in *Charlotte's Web*, though the animals and spider talk and Charlotte sings, the only other miracle is Charlotte's writing in the web. Total persuasion is at work, as I don't think it is in *The Trumpet of the Swan*. And there is no allegory, either: bibliotherapists might note. As White himself says: "*Charlotte's Web* is a tale of the animals in my barn, not of the people in my life. When you read it just relax."

Long ago I pleased myself by solving all the anagrams in Walter de la Mare's introduction to his great anthology, *Come Hither*. It seems to me now that White chose the name of Fern – she was introduced so fortunately into the book when he rewrote the manuscript – from the lovely snatch of verse written as prose (one of the several snatches; a trick of Thurber's also) in *Stuart Little*:

> She comes from fields once tall with wheat, from pastures deep in fern and thistle;
> she comes from vales of meadowsweet, and she loves to whistle.

And I would bet that he got the tremendous name of Templeton for the rat from the telephone exchange of that name in the Manhattan directory.

Of one thing I am sure: no scholar-critic will ever tear apart the fabric of *Charlotte's Web* as were it something that never should have been put together in the first place. *Esto perpetua.*

—David McCord

WHITE, T(erence) H(anbury).   British.   Born in Bombay, India, 29 May 1906. Educated at Cheltenham College, 1920–24; Queens' College, Cambridge (Exhibitioner), 1925–27, 1928–29, B.A. 1929. Taught at a preparatory school, 1930–32, and Stowe School, Buckinghamshire, 1932–36. Lived in Ireland, 1939–46, and in Jersey, 1946–47, and Alderney, 1947–64, Channel Islands. *Died 17 January 1964.*

PUBLICATIONS FOR CHILDREN

Fiction

> *The Sword in the Stone*, illustrated by the author.   London, Collins, 1938; New York, Putnam, 1939; revised edition, in *The Once and Future King*, 1958.
> *The Witch in the Wood*, illustrated by the author.   New York, Putnam, 1939; London, Collins, 1940; revised edition, as *The Queen of Air and Darkness*, in *The Once and Future King*, 1958.
> *The Ill-Made Knight*, illustrated by the author.   New York, Putnam, 1940; London, Collins, 1941; revised edition, in *The Once and Future King*, 1958.
> *Mistress Masham's Repose*, illustrated by Fritz Eichenberg.   New York, Putnam, 1946; London, Cape, 1947.
> *The Master: An Adventure Story*.   London, Cape, and New York, Putnam, 1957.
> *The Once and Future King*.   London, Collins, and New York, Putnam, 1958.
> *The Book of Merlyn*.   Austin and London, University of Texas Press, 1977.

PUBLICATIONS FOR ADULTS

Novels

> *Dead Mr. Nixon*, with R. McNair Scott.   London, Cassell, 1931.
> *Darkness at Pemberley*.   London, Gollancz, 1932; New York, Century, 1933.

They Winter Abroad (as James Aston).   London, Chatto and Windus, and New York, Viking Press, 1932.

First Lesson (as James Aston).   London, Chatto and Windus, 1932; New York, Knopf, 1933.

Farewell Victoria.   London, Collins, 1933; New York, Smith and Haas, 1934.

Earth Stopped; or, Mr. Marx's Sporting Tour.   London, Collins, 1934; New York, Putnam, 1935.

Gone to Ground.   London, Collins, and New York, Putnam, 1935.

The Elephant and the Kangaroo.   New York, Putnam, 1947; London, Cape, 1948.

Verse

Loved Helen and Other Poems.   London, Chatto and Windus, and New York, Viking Press, 1929.

The Green Bay Tree; or, The Wicked Man Touches Wood.   Cambridge, Heffer, 1929.

Verses.   Privately printed, 1962.

Other

England Have My Bones.   London, Collins, and New York, Macmillan, 1936.

Burke's Steerage; or, The Amateur Gentleman's Introduction to Noble Sports and Pastimes.   London, Collins, 1938; New York, Putnam, 1939.

The Age of Scandal: An Excursion Through a Minor Period.   London, Cape, and New York, Putnam, 1950.

The Goshawk (on falconry).   London, Cape, 1951; New York, Putnam, 1952.

The Scandalmonger (on English scandals).   London, Cape, and New York, Putnam, 1952.

The Godstone and the Blackymor (on Ireland).   London, Cape, and New York, Putnam, 1959.

America at Last: The American Journal of T.H. White.   New York, Putnam, 1965.

The White/Garnett Letters, edited by David Garnett.   London, Cape, and New York, Viking Press, 1968.

Editor and Translator, *The Book of Beasts, Being a Translation from a Latin Bestiary of the Twelfth Century.*   London, Cape, 1954; New York, Putnam, 1955.

Critical Study: *T.H. White: A Biography* by Sylvia Townsend Warner, London, Cape-Chatto and Windus, 1967.

*   *   *

Each of T.H. White's fantasies usually assigned to children is a highly personal statement of a brilliant original, the paradoxes of whose life were endless. *Mistress Masham's Repose,* the most childlike of the works, tells of a lonely little girl on a huge estate who finds by a lake in the grounds a group of little beings – descendants of Gulliver's Lilliputians. Her ally and mentor is an old professor who sees that she does not behave like a Yahoo to the doll-size creatures. Her awful guardians, a governess and a vicar, seek to capture them and are foiled. *The Master,* an eerie piece of science fiction about an aged seer on Rockall island, was dedicated to Stevenson. But White's island has none of the extrovert daylight dangers of Treasure Island.

His major work, one which he wrote and rewrote over half his life, is his retelling of the Arthurian legend. Every age produces a characteristic Arthur, and White's could well be called the version of the 1940's. *The Sword in the Stone* is the best of his stories, the genesis of his great work *The Once and Future King.* The whole epic ranges from knockabout fun to the deepest darkness and dread. There is a pupil-teacher relation as Merlyn makes a great king out of the neglected and rejected Wart. "The best thing for being sad," says Merlyn, "is to learn something." White had learnt much in his life, scholarly, odd, and practical, and most of it finds a place in this tale.

—William Ready

WHITNEY, Phyllis A(yame). American. Born in Yokohama, Japan, 9 September 1903. Educated at McKinley High School, Chicago, graduated 1924. Married George A. Garner in 1925, one daughter; Lovell F. Jahnke, 1950 (died). Dance instructor, San Antonio, Texas, one year; Children's Books Editor, Chicago *Sun*, 1942–46, and Philadelphia *Inquirer*, 1947–48; Instructor in Juvenile Fiction Writing, Northwestern University, Evanston, Illinois, 1945, and New York University, 1947–58. Member, Board of Directors, 1959–62, and President, 1975, Mystery Writers of America. Recipient: Mystery Writers of America Edgar Allan Poe Award, 1961, 1964. Lives on Long Island, New York. Address: c/o McIntosh and Otis Inc., 475 Fifth Avenue, New York, New York 10017, U.S.A.

PUBLICATIONS FOR CHILDREN

Fiction

A Place for Ann, illustrated by Helen Blair. Boston, Houghton Mifflin, 1941.
A Star for Ginny, illustrated by Hilda Frommholz. Boston, Houghton Mifflin, 1942.
A Window for Julie, illustrated by Jean Anderson. Boston, Houghton Mifflin, 1943.
The Silver Inkwell, illustrated by Hilda Frommholz. Boston, Houghton Mifflin, 1945.
Willow Hill. New York, Reynal and Hitchcock, 1947.
Ever After. Boston, Houghton Mifflin, 1948.
Mystery of the Gulls, illustrated by Janet Smalley. Philadelphia, Westminster Press, 1949.
Linda's Homecoming. Philadelphia, McKay, 1950.
The Island of Dark Woods, illustrated by Philip Wishnefsky. Philadelphia, Westminster Press, 1951; as *Mystery of the Strange Traveler*, 1967.
Love Me, Love Me Not. Boston, Houghton Mifflin, 1952.
Mystery of the Black Diamonds, illustrated by John Gretzer. Philadelphia, Westminster Press, 1954; as *Black Diamonds*, Leicester, Brockhampton Press, 1957.
Step to the Music. New York, Crowell, 1953.
A Long Time Coming. Philadelphia, McKay, 1954.
Mystery on the Isle of Skye, illustrated by Ezra Jack Keats. Philadelphia, Westminster Press, 1955.
The Fire and the Gold. New York, Crowell, 1956.
The Highest Dream. Philadelphia, McKay, 1956.
Mystery of the Green Cat, illustrated by Richard Horwitz. Philadelphia, Westminster Press, 1957.
Secret of the Samurai Sword. Philadelphia, Westminster Press, 1958.
Creole Holiday. Philadelphia, Westminster Press, 1959.
Mystery of the Haunted Pool, illustrated by H. Tom Hall. Philadelphia, Westminster Press, 1960.
Secret of the Tiger's Eye, illustrated by Richard Horwitz. Philadelphia, Westminster Press, 1961.
Mystery of the Golden Horn, illustrated by Georgeann Helms. Philadelphia, Westminster Press, 1962.
Mystery of the Hidden Hand, illustrated by H. Tom Hall. Philadelphia, Westminster Press, 1963.

Secret of the Emerald Star, illustrated by Alex Stein.   Philadelphia, Westminster Press, 1964.

Mystery of the Angry Idol, illustrated by Al Fiorentino.   Philadelphia, Westminster Press, 1965.

Secret of the Spotted Shell, illustrated by John Mecray.   Philadelphia, Westminster Press, 1967.

Secret of Goblin Glen, illustrated by Al Fiorentino.   Philadelphia, Westminster Press, 1968.

The Mystery of the Crimson Ghost.   Philadelphia, Westminster Press, 1969.

Secret of the Missing Footprint, illustrated by Alex Stein.   Philadelphia, Westminster Press, 1969.

The Vanishing Scarecrow.   Philadelphia, Westminster Press, 1971.

Nobody Likes Trina.   Philadelphia, Westminster Press, 1972.

Mystery of the Scowling Boy, illustrated by John Gretzer.   Philadelphia, Westminster Press, 1973.

Secret of Haunted Mesa.   Philadelphia, Westminster Press, 1975.

Secret of the Stone Face.   Philadelphia, Westminster Press, 1977.

PUBLICATIONS FOR ADULTS

Novels

Red Is for Murder.   New York, Ziff Davis, 1943; as *The Red Carnelian*, New York, Warner, 1965; London, Coronet, 1976.

The Quicksilver Pool.   New York, Appleton Century Crofts, 1955.

The Trembling Hills.   New York, Appleton Century Crofts, 1956; London, Coronet, 1974.

Skye Cameron.   New York, Appleton Century Crofts, 1957; London, Hurst and Blackett, 1959.

The Moonflower.   New York, Appleton Century Crofts, 1958; as *The Mask and the Moonflower*, London, Hurst and Blackett, 1960.

Thunder Heights.   New York, Appleton Century Crofts, 1960; London, Coronet, 1973.

Blue Fire.   New York, Appleton Century Crofts, 1961; London, Hodder and Stoughton, 1962.

Window on the Square.   New York, Appleton Century Crofts, 1962.

Seven Tears for Apollo.   New York, Appleton Century Crofts, 1963; London, Coronet, 1969.

Black Amber.   New York, Appleton Century Crofts, 1964; London, Hale, 1965.

Sea Jade.   New York, Appleton Century Crofts, 1965; London, Hale, 1966.

Columbella.   New York, Doubleday, 1966; London, Hale, 1967.

Silverhill.   New York, Doubleday, 1967; London, Heinemann, 1968.

Hunter's Green.   New York, Doubleday, 1968; London, Heinemann, 1969.

The Winter People.   New York, Doubleday, 1969; London, Heinemann, 1970.

Lost Island.   New York, Doubleday, 1970; London, London, Heinemann, 1971.

Listen for the Whisperer.   New York, Doubleday, and London, Heinemann, 1972.

Snowfire.   New York, Doubleday and London, Heinemann, 1973.

The Turquoise Mask.   New York, Doubleday, 1974; London, Heinemann, 1975.

Spindrift.   New York, Doubleday, and London, Heinemann, 1975.

The Golden Unicorn.   New York, Doubleday, 1976.

The Stone Bull.   New York, Doubleday, and London, Heinemann, 1977.

Other

Writing Juvenile Fiction.   Boston, The Writer, 1947; revised edition, 1960.

Writing Juvenile Stories and Novels.   Boston, The Writer, 1976.

*   *   *

Phyllis A. Whitney's juvenile fiction is primarily of two types – junior novels with sentimental maturation themes and mystery-adventure stories. Her novels about growing up are similar to those of Betty Cavanna, but she does venture into unusual territory for the junior novel with its long-standing but recently eased taboos on serious, controversial matters.

Willow Hill straightforwardly confronts the problems of an integrated community. The heroine, Val Coleman, covets the editorship of the school newspaper, but the teacher gives the job to an attractive black girl who lives in the new housing project. Val, who instinctively accepts quality but is hurt because of the teacher's choice, is forced to come to terms with her own potential racism and that of the community. Her mother, who gets her cue from a Mrs. Manning, a community stalwart, opposes the housing project, but her father, a wise gym teacher, welcomes integration. The book seems daringly ahead of its time in its sympathy and in its honest portrayal of race relations.

Although Whitney has written a number of these serious novels about the drama of growing up (such as *Linda's Homecoming*, which deals with a girl's gradual acceptance of her new stepfather), most of her stories are lively, light mysteries similar to the Nancy Drew stories. The protagonists are often 12-year-old girls, young detectives who tend to be normal kids with shortcomings and frustrations, rather than sophisticated, independent, idealized heroines. Thus Whitney has been praised for her honesty, realism, and intellectually stimulating themes. However, the appeal of her books is much the same as that of the slicker commercial series books with repeated plot formulas. The basic appeal is reader identification with a vicarious adventure, one which girls would not encounter in their ordinary lives, but an adventure which leads them safely home in the end to the comfortable security of a familiar world. The reader wants to be excited and reassured simultaneously, and most popular entertainment accomplishes this dual goal.

Whitney frequently writes of dislocation – a child longing for stability, a house with a neat yard and picket fence and dog, and a room with a ruffled bedspread. There are several characters with nomadic parents. In *Mystery of the Black Diamonds*, the father, who has to travel to do research for his writing, is a stimulus to investigation of the mystery, while mom wants desperately to settle down in a house with a washing machine. The heroine wants both domesticity and adventure, and this desire is doubly satisfying for the reader. Thus the settings of Whitney novels are important, for the danger and excitement of the adventure must be contrasted with the security and coziness of quaint, old-fashioned places. In *Mystery of the Gulls* the setting is fog-shrouded Mackinac Island during a summer at a quaint resort hotel, where the heroine encounters the mysterious folkways of the local Indians. *Mystery of the Black Diamonds* is about a Colorado ghost town. Other settings include Staten Island, New Orleans, Scotland, and Japan – all provided with extensive information on the history and culture.

—Bobbie Ann Mason

WIBBERLEY, Leonard (Patrick O'Connor). Irish. Born in Dublin, 9 April 1915. Educated at Ring College, Waterford, Ireland; Abbey House, Romsey, Hampshire; Cardinal Vaughan's School, London, 1925–30; El Camino College, Torrance, California. Served as a lance bombardier in the Trinidad Artillery Volunteers, 1938–40. Married Katherine Hazel Holton in 1948; has four sons and two daughters. Reporter, *Sunday Dispatch*, 1931–32, *Sunday Express*, 1932–34, and *Daily Mirror*, 1935–36, all London; Editor, Trinidad *Evening News*, 1936; oilfield worker, Trinidad, 1936–43; Cable Editor, Associated Press, New York, 1943–44; New York Correspondent and Bureau Chief, London *Evening News*, 1944–46;

Editor, *Independent Journal*, San Rafael, California, 1947–49; Reporter and Copy Editor, Los Angeles *Times*, 1950–54. Agent: McIntosh and Otis Inc., 475 Fifth Avenue, New York, New York 10017. Address: Box 522, Hermosa Beach, California 90254, U.S.A.

PUBLICATIONS FOR CHILDREN

Fiction

    The Lost Harpooner (as Patrick O'Connor).   New York, Washburn, 1947; London, Harrap, 1959.

    The King's Beard, illustrated by Christine Price.   New York, Farrar Straus, 1952; London, Faber, 1954.

    The Secret of the Hawk, illustrated by Christine Price.   New York, Farrar Straus, 1953; London, Faber, 1956.

    Deadmen's Cave, illustrated by Tom Leamon.   New York, Farrar Straus, and London, Faber, 1954.

    The Flight of the Peacock (as Patrick O'Connor), illustrated by Rus Anderson.   New York, Washburn, 1954.

    The Society of Foxes (as Patrick O'Connor), illustrated by Clifford Geary.   New York, Washburn, 1954.

    The Wound of Peter Wayne.   New York, Farrar Straus, 1955; London, Faber, 1957

    The Watermelon Mystery (as Patrick O'Connor).   New York, Washburn, 1955.

    Gunpowder for Washington (as Patrick O'Connor).   New York, Washburn, 1956.

    The Black Tiger (as Patrick O'Connor).   New York, Washburn, 1956.

    Mexican Road Race (as Patrick O'Connor).   New York, Washburn, 1957.

    Kevin O'Connor and the Light Brigade.   New York, Farrar Straus, 1957; London, Harrap, 1959.

    Matt Tyler's Chronicle (as Christopher Webb).   New York Funk and Wagnalls, 1958; London, Macdonald, 1966.

    Black Tiger at Le Mans (as Patrick O'Connor).   New York, Washburn, 1958.

    The Five-Dollar Watch Mystery (as Patrick O'Connor).   New York, Washburn, 1959.

    John Treegate's Musket.   New York, Farrar Straus, 1959.

    Mark Toyman's Inheritance (as Christopher Webb).   New York, Funk and Wagnalls, 1960.

    Pete Treegate's War.   New York, Farrar Straus, 1960.

    Black Tiger at Bonneville (as Patrick O'Connor).   New York, Washburn, 1960.

    Treasure at Twenty Fathoms (as Patrick O'Connor).   New York, Washburn, 1961.

    Sea Captain from Salem.   New York, Farrar Straus, 1961.

    The Time of the Lamb, illustrated by Fritz Kredel.   New York, Washburn, 1961.

    Treegate's Raiders.   New York, Farrar Straus, 1962.

    The River of Pee Dee Jack (as Christopher Webb).   New York, Funk and Wagnalls, 1962.

    Black Tiger at Indianapolis (as Patrick O'Connor).   New York, Washburn, 1962.

    The Quest of the Otter (as Christopher Webb).   New York, Funk and Wagnalls, 1963; London, Macdonald, 1965.

    The Raising of the Dubhe (as Patrick O'Connor).   New York, Washburn, 1964.

    Seawind from Hawaii (as Patrick O'Connor).   New York, Washburn, 1965.

    The "Ann and Hope" Mutiny (as Christopher Webb).   New York, Funk and Wagnalls, 1966; London, Macdonald, 1967.

    South Swell (as Patrick O'Connor).   New York, Washburn, 1967; London, Macdonald, 1968.

    Encounter near Venus, illustrated by Alice Wadowski-Bak.   New York, Farrar Straus, 1967; London, Macdonald, 1968.

    Attar of the Ice Valley.   New York, Farrar Straus, 1968; London, Macdonald, 1969.

Beyond Hawaii (as Patrick O'Connor).   New York, Washburn, 1969; London
    Macdonald, 1970.
Eusebius, The Phoenician (as Christopher Webb).   New York, Funk and Wagnalls,
    1969; London, Macdonald, 1970.
A Car Called Camellia (as Patrick O'Connor).   New York, Washburn, 1970.
Journey to Untor.   New York, Farrar Straus, 1970; London, Macdonald, 1971.
Leopard's Prey.   New York, Farrar Straus, 1971.
Flint's Island.   New York, Farrar Straus, 1972; London, Macdonald, 1973.
Red Pawns.   New York, Farrar Straus, 1973.
The Last Battle.   New York, Farrar Straus, 1976.

Verse

The Ballad of the Pilgrim Cat.   New York, Washburn, 1962.
The Shepherd's Reward, illustrated by Thomas Fisher.   New York, Washburn, 1963.

Other

The Coronation Book: The Dramatic Story in History and Legend.   New York, Farrar
    Straus, 1953.
The Epics of Everest, illustrated by Genevieve Vaughan-Jackson.   New York, Farrar
    Straus, 1954; London, Faber, 1955.
The Life of Winston Churchill.   New York, Farrar Straus, 1956; revised edition, 1965.
John Barry, Father of the Navy.   New York, Farrar Straus, 1957.
Wes Powell, Conqueror of the Grand Canyon.   New York, Farrar Straus, 1958.
Zebulon Pike, Soldier and Explorer.   New York, Funk and Wagnalls, 1961.
Man of Liberty: A Life of Thomas Jefferson.   New York, Farrar Straus, 1968.
    1. *Young Man from the Piedmont: The Youth of Thomas Jefferson.*   New York, Farrar
       Straus, 1963.
    2. *A Dawn in the Trees: Thomas Jefferson, The Years 1776 to 1789.*   New York,
       Farrar Straus, 1964.
    3. *The Gales of Spring: Thomas Jefferson, The Years 1789 to 1801.*   New York,
       Farrar Straus, 1965.
    4. *Time of the Harvest: Thomas Jefferson, The Years 1801 to 1826.*   New York,
       Farrar Straus, 1966.
Guarneri: Violin Maker of Genius.   New York, Farrar Straus, 1974; London,
    Macdonald and Jane's, 1976.

PULBICATIONS FOR ADULTS

Novels

Mrs. Searwood's Secret Weapon.   Boston, Little Brown, 1954; London, Hale, 1955.
The Mouse That Roared.   Boston, Little Brown, 1955; as *The Wrath of Grapes,*
    London, Hale, 1955.
McGillicuddy McGotham.   Boston, Little Brown, 1956; London, Hale, 1957.
Take Me to Your President.   New York, Putnam, 1957.
Beware of the Mouse.   New York, Putnam, 1958.
The Quest of Excalibur.   New York, Putnam, 1959.
The Saint Maker (as Leonard Holton).   New York, Dodd Mead, 1959.
A Pact with Satan (as Leonard Holton).   New York, Dodd Mead, 1960.
The Hands of Cormac Joyce.   New York, Putnam, 1960; London, Muller, 1962.
Secret of the Doubting Saint (as Leonard Holton).   New York, Dodd Mead, 1961.
Stranger at Killknock.   New York, Putnam, 1961; London, Muller, 1963.
The Mouse on the Moon.   New York, Morrow, 1962; London, Muller, 1963.

Deliver Us from Wolves (as Leonard Holton). New York, Dodd Mead, 1963.
Flowers by Request (as Leonard Holton). New York, Dodd Mead, 1964.
A Feast of Freedom. New York, Morrow, 1964.
The Island of the Angels. New York, Morrow, 1965.
The Centurion. New York, Morrow, 1966.
Out of the Depths (as Leonard Holton). New York, Dodd Mead, 1966.
The Road from Toomi. New York, Morrow, 1967.
Adventures of an Elephant Boy. New York, Morrow, 1968.
A Touch of Jonah (as Leonard Holton). New York, Dodd Mead, 1968.
The Mouse on Wall Street. New York, Morrow, 1969.
A Problem in Angels (as Leonard Holton). New York, Dodd Mead, 1970.
Meeting with a Great Beast. New York, Morrow, 1971; London, Chatto and Windus, 1972.
The Mirror of Hell (as Leonard Holton). New York, Dodd Mead, 1972.
The Testament of Theophilus. New York, Morrow, 1973; as *Merchant of Rome*, London, Cassell, 1974.
The Last Stand of Father Felix. New York, Morrow, 1974.
The Devil to Play (as Leonard Holton). New York, Dodd Mead, 1974.
One in Four. New York, Morrow, 1977.

Plays

Black Jack Rides Again. Chicago, Dramatic Publishing Company, 1971.
1776 – And All That. New York, Morrow, 1975.
Once, In a Garden. Chicago, Dramatic Publishing Company, 1975.

Other

The Trouble with the Irish (or the English, Depending on Your Point of View). New York, Holt, 1956; London, Muller, 1958.
The Coming of the Green. New York, Holt, 1958.
No Garlic in the Soup (on Portugal). New York, Washburn, 1959; London, Faber, 1960.
The Land That Isn't There: An Irish Adventure. New York, Washburn, 1960.
Yesterday's Land: A Baja California Adventure. New York, Washburn, 1961.
Ventures into the Deep: The Thrill of Scuba Diving. New York, Washburn, 1962.
Ah Julian! A Memoir of Julian Brodetsky. New York, Washburn, 1963.
Fiji: Islands of the Dawn. New York, Washburn, 1964.
Toward a Distant Island: A Sailor's Odyssey. New York, Washburn, 1966.
Something to Read. New York, Washburn, 1967.
Hound of the Sea. New York, Washburn, 1969.
Voyage by Bus. New York, Morrow, 1971.
The Shannon Sailors: A Voyage to the Heart of Ireland. New York, Morrow, 1972.

Manuscript Collection: University of Southern California, Los Angeles.

*   *   *

The very first book that Leonard Wibberley remembers was Robert Louis Stevenson's *Treasure Island*, which was read to him by a teacher when he was about 8 years old. It remains to this day his favorite. Even without this biographical knowledge, however, the reader of Wibberley's prolific and versatile work cannot help but notice the influence that Stevenson had upon him as a writer. Wibberley possesses the same romantic charm as Stevenson, in that he writes out of the perpetual boy that is in him. He continues to delight in putting forth the opening request of the traditional story-teller: "Make believe!" He captures the spirit of romantic youth by seeking out where joy resides, so that he may give it voice. (The very joy that so many writers for today's children would take away from them.) Whether it is in his historical novels, like those in his *Treegate Chronicles*, or in his "nonfiction fiction," as exemplified by his four-volume biography of Thomas Jefferson, Wibberley's books, like those of Stevenson, present the world as an expansive stage, bustling with romantic incident. Action is the mirror in which the characters are reflected, and the vision of the characters remains clear, vivid and uncomplicated.

Wibberley's works most often have an historical setting, not only because he strongly believes that today's young must know the past in order to understand the society and culture which they have inherited, but also because the times he selects, the American Revolution, for example, provide him with a cast of characters whose human passions are not yet hidden by the conventionalities of civilization. His books are masculine, and those he chooses to write about, real as well as fictional, are men who possess some part of his vigorous ideal of manhood: courage, intelligence, loyalty, delight in living – in short, men worth knowing and respecting. Some readers may not take to the blood and violence, but this too is not only historically accurate, but it also is in the tradition of the adventure romance. The young find in his books justification for their own hopes, dreams, and ideas.

Wibberley's writing, again like Stevenson's, is distinctively marked by his Gaelic temperament. One sometimes finds a touch of the moral philosopher, but it is always balanced by an engaging sense of humor, and never is it didactic. Above all Wibberley is a craftsman with a love for lovely words. And yet there is nothing bookish about him. He loves to travel; he loves the sea and ships and the men who sail them. His books reflect his uncanny skill in uncovering the spirit of place and the fascination of time: past, present and future.

When a youngster reads a Wibberley book he is sharing a few hours of storytelling with a man who is, according to Susan Cooper, "one of the best writers for children in the United States." It matters little whether the book be one of those already mentioned, or one of his auto-racing stories written under the pseudonym of Patrick O'Connor, or *Flint's Island*, his marvellous sequel to *Treasure Island*, or one of his adult novellas, like *The Hands of Cormac Joyce*, for each of them bears the signature of a quality writer.

—James E. Higgins

WIER, Ester (Alberti). American. Born in Seattle, Washington, 17 October 1910. Educated at Southeastern Teachers College, Durant, Oklahoma, 1929–30; University of California, Los Angeles, 1931–32. Married Henry Robert Wier in 1934; has one son and one daughter. Address: 2534 S.W. 14th Drive, Gainesville, Florida 32608, U.S.A.

PUBLICATIONS FOR CHILDREN

Fiction

> *The Loner*, illustrated by Christine Price. Philadelphia, McKay, 1963; London, Constable, 1966.
> *Gift of the Mountains*, illustrated by Richard Lewis. Philadelphia, McKay, 1963.
> *The Rumptydoolers*, illustrated by W.T. Mars. New York, Vanguard Press, 1964.
> *Easy Does It*, illustrated by W.T. Mars. New York, Vanguard Press, 1965.
> *The Barrel*, illustrated by Carl Kidwell. Philadelphia, McKay, 1966.
> *The Wind Chasers*, illustrated by Kurt Werth. Philadelphia, McKay, 1967; London, Constable, 1968.
> *The Winners*, illustrated by Ursula Koering. Philadelphia, McKay, 1967.

The Space Hut, illustrated by Leon Summers.   Harrisburg, Pennsylvania, Stackpole,
   1967.
Action at Paradise Marsh, illustrated by Earl Blust.   Harrisburg, Pennsylvania,
   Stackpole, 1968.
The Long Year, illustrated by Ursula Koering.   Philadelphia, McKay, 1969.
The Straggler, illustrated by Leonard Vosburgh.   Philadelphia, McKay, 1970.
The White Oak, illustrated by Anne Jauss.   Philadelphia, McKay, 1971.
The Partners, illustrated by Anna Maria Ahl.   Philadelphia, McKay, 1972.
The Hunting Trail, illustrated by Richard Cuffari.   New York, Walck, 1974.
The King of the Mountain.   New York, Walck, 1975.

PUBLICATIONS FOR ADULTS

Other

The Answer Book on Naval Social Customs [and *Air Force Social Customs*], with Dorothy
   Hickey.   Harrisburg, Pennsylvania, Military Service Publishing, 2 vols., 1956–57.
Army Social Customs.   Harrisburg, Pennsylvania, Military Service Publishing, 1958.
What Every Air Force Wife Should Know.   Harrisburg, Pennsylvania, Military Service
   Publishing, 1958.

Manuscript Collections: Kerlan Collection, University of Minnesota, Minneapolis; de
Grummond Collection, University of Southern Mississippi, Hattiesburg.

Ester Wier comments:
   I have tried to make my books understandable and acceptable to young readers. Each event
in each story could have happened to some child somewhere in the course of his everyday
existence. The backgrounds have been of great importance to me since here was my chance
to acquaint children with other places while allowing them to see that life goes on pretty
much the same no matter where you are. If I have aroused curiosity in them about peers
living in other locations and led them to search out more about different places, then I have
succeeded in what I have intended. And if I have been able to instill in them a love and feeling
of responsibility for animals, then I am content.

*   *   *

   Writer of dozens of stories, Ester Wier developed her writing skills considerably beyond
the point of *The Loner*. The body of her work contains many stories of children, primarily
boys, who are seeking acceptance by themselves or others. Wier shows strong understanding
of youth's efforts to stand on its own, and yet she accepts its real needs to belong to
someone else somewhere. The need to achieve and to be accepted motivates her characters,
whether they live in the Southwest of the United States and are surrounded by plains and
plateaus, or live in the Everglades of Florida and are surrounded by alligators and razorbacks.
   Perhaps the best of Wier's stories are those with nature settings, in sheep country or
shellfish shorelands. Her depictions of the natural environment are detailed without
becoming boring, integrated with the story, and yet vivid enough to convince the reader of
their reality. Research must surely be part of Wier's preparation, for many of the stories
capture the flavor of spoken dialogue.
   Although early Wier books are filled with telling rather than showing, telling the reader
the thoughts and feelings of the protagonist rather than showing the action that results from
feelings and thoughts, later stories contain well-drawn and believable characters. When the
subject of Wier's story is a wild creature, as it occasionally is, the scientific facts are evident
without being intrusive.
   Wier's skill lies in her ability to interweave imagery with action and dialogue.

Regionalism, much of it tropical or subtropical Florida, shows the way of life, the influence of environment upon people, the motivations that make the characters local and yet universal.

—Rebecca J. Lukens

WIESE, Kurt. American. Born in Minden, Germany, 22 April 1887. Educated at schools in Germany. Married Gertrude Hansen in 1930. Export trade apprentice in Hamburg; merchandise salesman in China for six years; captured in Sino-Japanese war and spent five years in Hong Kong and Australia as prisoner; free-lance illustrator in Germany and Brazil, 1920–28, and from 1928 in the United States. *Died 27 May 1974.*

PUBLICATIONS FOR CHILDREN (illustrated by the author)

Fiction

> *Karoo the Kangaroo.* New York, Coward McCann, 1929.
> *The Chinese Ink Stick.* New York, Doubleday, 1929.
> *Lian and Lo.* New York, Doubleday, 1930.
> *Wallie the Walrus.* New York, Coward McCann, 1930.
> *Ella the Elephant.* New York, Coward McCann, 1931.
> *Joe Buys Nails.* New York, Doubleday, 1931.
> *The Parrot Dealer.* New York, Coward McCann, 1932.
> *Buddy the Bear.* New York, Coward McCann, 1936.
> *The Rabbits' Revenge.* New York, Coward McCann, 1940.
> *Little Boy Lost in Brazil.* New York, Dodd Mead, 1942.
> *Fish in the Air.* New York, Viking Press, 1948.
> *Happy Easter.* New York, Viking Press, 1952.
> *The Dog, The Fox, and the Fleas.* New York, McKay, 1953.
> *The Cunning Turtle.* New York, Viking Press, 1956.
> *The Groundhog and His Shadow.* New York, Viking Press, 1959.
> *Rabbit Bros. Circus: One Night Only.* New York, Viking Press, 1963.
> *The Thief in the Attic.* New York, Viking Press, 1965.

Other

> *You Can Write Chinese.* New York, Viking Press, 1945.

Manuscript Collections: Kerlan Collection, University of Minnesota, Minneapolis; University of Oregon Library, Eugene.

Illustrator of more than 300 books.

*   *   *

Kurt Wiese wrote nearly 20 books from 1929 to 1964, the first published when he was 42. By the time he arrived in the United States, he had already lived for six years in China, three years in Australia, had returned to his birthplace in Germany, and then spent four years in Brazil. His writings are based on first hand knowledge of places he lived and animals he observed, coupled with his imagination; unfortunately, his books are weak in craftsmanship.

Authenticity is derived from experience, and Wiese's books can be divided into subjects according to where he lived. Because the immigration quota system in the 1930's limited Asians, China was considered exotic to Americans, so *The Chinese Ink Stick, Lian and Lo, You Can Write Chinese*, and *Fish in the Air*, all dealing with China, found ready audiences. His debut was with a book set in Australia, *Karoo the Kangaroo*, and a decade later he produced *Buddy the Bear* with similar background and format.

Brazil was the background for *The Parrot Dealer*, a novel intended for teenagers. The story is based on Senhor Carlos de Alvarez gathering monkeys, parrots, and other fauna in the jungles and then selling them. In a picture book, *Little Boy Lost in Brazil*, Wiese tells of customs such as sending paper balloons with a wish to St. John, and foods, such as the alligator pear. The church's role in the lives of the people, as well as the fantastic "sarcies," are apparent. *Rabbit Bros. Circus* is based in part on his study of animals while working on backgrounds for a film company founded by members of a circus family in Germany.

Animals on his wooded acreage on the Delaware River in New Jersey provided the initial inspiration for the balance of his books. They range from the imaginative *The Groundhog and His Shadow* to the "why" and "how" stories, such as *The Cunning Turtle*. Having observed that a fox and four young can live under the roots of a dead maple tree, and that a raccoon, oppossum, screech owl and woodpecker might live in the hollow, Wiese placed them in an "apartment house tree" in *The Thief in the Attic*. Humor pervades the stories. In *Fish in the Air*, a Chinese boy is carried with his kite by the wind. The mother reaches the store before her son she sent on an errand in *Joe Buys Nails*. In *The Groundhog and His Shadow*, the rodent rolls up his companion and attempts to sell it to a weatherman and then to a fox, but is ultimately joined by his shadow.

Unfortunately, the author lacked complete mastery of narrative techniques. In correspondence with Dr. Irvin Kerlan, Kurt Wiese complained about the slight texts he was solicited to illustrate. However, when he wrote the text himself, he introduced too many characters. The koala, in *Buddy the Bear*, encounters every one of his possible enemies, from dingo to lizard to wombat, and each is introduced on a double-page spread in the published book. A parade of animals is listed in *Joe Buys Nails*, more for the purpose of illustration than for story line. They include a robin, crow, frog, turtle, raccoon, catbird, horse, dog, chickenhawk, rooster, chicken, rabbit, and pheasant. There is also an explanation of why the robin's breast is red and even a story within a story interpreting why a turtle's shell is cracked. Strangely, *The Cunning Turtle* provides a different explanation for the same phenomenon. In the latter, the reptile hid in the buzzard's guitar when he flew to a cloud for a musical gathering, but fell to the ground on the return trip.

While his initial concepts for a story had possibilities, Wiese tended to allow the plot to be undeveloped and poorly balanced. *The Dog, The Fox, and the Fleas* has too much description, while *Happy Easter* has too little. In the former, the fox makes a fool of the dogs and gets to the chicken coop, while in the latter the rabbits paint the eggs just before they hatch. In *The Rabbits' Revenge*, the punishment for the man who wanted a rabbit fur suit is inappropriate, for the rabbits would have given their fur for a child's cap gladly.

While the introductions of most of the books are acceptable, the conclusions are weak. An American boy learns the characters in *You Can Write Chinese*, but the story concludes with the teacher dismissing the class without any reference to Peter. *Lian and Lo* went off in search of a dragon, but fell asleep on the back of the buffalo. It is the buffalo whose words conclude the book, "These boys are making a laughing-stock of me but nevertheless I like them." In *Wallie the Walrus*, the friend Tusky is introduced on the last page of text, and yet the story ends, "they promised each other always to be friends.... And they did."

In conclusion, Kurt Wiese's contribution as an author was less impressive than as an illustrator. His books about China provided a role appropriate for the first half of the century, but other books have now taken their place. His literary folktales lacked the succinctness and style to make them memorable. The stories he wrote for children are far less important than the more than three hundred books written by others which he illustrated.

—Karen Nelson Hoyle

WIGGIN, Kate Douglas. American. Born in Philadelphia, Pennsylvania, 28 September 1856. Educated at Gorham Female Seminary, Maine; Morison Academy, Baltimore; Abbot Academy, Andover, Massachusetts; Mrs. Severance's Kindergarten Training School, Los Angeles, 1877. Married Samuel Wiggin in 1881 (died, 1889); George Christopher Riggs, 1895. Head of a private kindergarten, Santa Barbara, California, 1877; Founder, with Felix Adler, Silver Street Free Kindergarten, San Francisco, 1878; Founder, with Nora A. Smith, California Kindergarten Training School, San Francisco, 1880. Litt. D.: Bowdoin College, Brunswick, Maine, 1904. *Died 24 August 1923.*

PUBLICATIONS FOR CHILDREN

Fiction

> *The Story of Patsy: A Reminiscence.* San Francisco, Murdock, 1883; London, Gay and Bird, 1889.
> *The Birds' Christmas Carol.* San Francisco, Murdock, 1887; London, Gay and Bird, 1891.
> *A Summer in a Cañon.* Boston, Houghton Mifflin, 1889; London, Gay and Bird, 1896.
> *Timothy's Quest.* Boston, Houghton Mifflin, 1890; London, Gay and Bird, 1893.
> *The Story Hour*, with Nora A. Smith. Boston, Houghton Mifflin, 1890.
> *Polly Oliver's Problem.* Boston, Houghton Mifflin, and London, Gay and Bird, 1893.
> *A Cathedral Courtship, and Penelope's English Experiences*, illustrated by C. Carleton. Boston, Houghton Mifflin, and London, Gay and Bird, 1893.
> *Penelope's Progress.* Boston, Houghton Mifflin, and London, Watt, 1898.
> *Penelope's Irish Experiences.* Boston, Houghton Mifflin, and London, Gay and Bird, 1901.
> *The Diary of a Goosegirl*, illustrated by Claude Shepperson. Boston, Houghton Mifflin, and London, Gay and Bird, 1902.
> *Rebecca of Sunnybrook Farm.* Boston, Houghton Mifflin, and London, Gay and Bird, 1903.
> *Half-a-Dozen Housekeepers*, illustrated by Mills Thompson. Philadelphia, Altemus, and London, Gay and Bird, 1903.
> *Rose o' the River*, illustrated by George Wright. Boston, Houghton Mifflin, and London, Constable, 1905.
> *New Chronicles of Rebecca.* Boston, Houghton Mifflin, and London, Constable, 1907; as *More about Rebecca of Sunnybrook Farm*, London, A. and C. Black, 1930.
> *Mother Carey's Chickens.* Boston, Houghton Mifflin, 1911; as *Mother Carey*, London, Hodder and Stoughton, 1911.
> *A Child's Journey with Dickens.* Boston, Houghton Mifflin, and London, Hodder and Stoughton, 1912.
> *Penelope's Postscripts: Switzerland, Venice, Wales, Devon, Home.* Boston, Houghton Mifflin, and London, Hodder and Stoughton, 1915.
> *The Romance of a Christmas Card*, illustrated by Alice Hunt. Boston, Houghton Mifflin, and London, Hodder and Stoughton, 1916.
> *Twilight Stories*, with Nora A. Smith, illustrated by Kathryn Draper. Boston, Houghton Mifflin, 1925.

Plays

> *Rebecca of Sunnybrook Farm*, with Charlotte Thompson, adaptation of the story by Wiggin (produced Springfield, Massachusetts, 1909; New York, 1910; London, 1912). New York and London, French, 1932.
> *The Birds' Christmas Carol*, with Helen Ingersoll, adaptation of the story by Wiggin. Boston, Houghton Mifflin, 1914.

Bluebeard: A Musical Fantasy.   New York and London, Harper, 1914.

Mother Carey's Chickens, with Rachel Crothers, adaptation of the story by Wiggin (produced Poughkeepsie, New York, and New York City, 1917).   New York and London, French, 1925.

Other

Kindergarten Chimes: Manual and Song Book for Kindergartners.   Boston, Ditson, 1888.

The Arabian Nights, Retold, with Nora A. Smith, illustrated by Maxfield Parrish.   New York, Scribner, and London, Laurie, 1909.

Editor, with Nora A. Smith, Hymns for Kindergartners.   San Francisco, Froebel Society, 1881.

Editor, with Nora A. Smith, Golden Numbers: A Book of Verse.   New York, McClure, 1902.

Editor, with Nora A. Smith, The Posy Ring: A Book of Verse.   New York, McClure, 1903; as Poems Every Child Should Know, New York, Doubleday, 1942.

Editor, with Nora A. Smith, The Library of Fairy Literature (The Fairy Ring, Magic Casements, Tales of Laughter, Tales of Wonder, The Talking Beasts).   New York, McClure, 5 vols., 1906–11.

Editor, with Nora A. Smith, Pinafore Palace: A Book of Rhymes.   New York, McClure, 1907.

Editor, with Nora A. Smith, An Hour with the Fairies.   New York, Doubleday, 1911.

Editor, with Nora A. Smith, Christmas Stories.   New York, Grosset and Dunlap, 1916.

Editor, with Nora A. Smith, Stories and Poems, by Rudyard Kipling.   New York, Grosset and Dunlap, 1916.

Editor, with Nora A. Smith, The Scottish Chiefs, by Jane Porter, illustrated by N.C. Wyeth.   New York, Scribner, and London, Hodder and Stoughton, 1921.

Editor, with Nora A. Smith, Pinafore Palace Series (Baby's Friend and Nursery Heroes and Heroines, Baby's Plays and Journeys, Nursery Nonsense, Palace Bedtime, Palace Playtime), illustrated by Ruth Hambridge.   New York, Doubleday, 5 vols., 1923.

PUBLICATIONS FOR ADULTS

Novels

The Village Watch-Tower.   Boston, Houghton Mifflin, and London, Gay and Bird, 1895.

Marm Lisa.   Boston, Houghton Mifflin, and London, Gay and Bird, 1896.

The Affair at the Inn, with others.   Boston, Houghton Mifflin, and London, Gay and Bird, 1904.

The Old Peabody Pew: A Christmas Romance of a Country Church.   Boston, Houghton Mifflin, and London, Constable, 1907.

Susanna and Sue.   Boston, Houghton Mifflin, and London, Hodder and Stoughton, 1909.

Robinetta, with others.   Boston, Houghton Mifflin, and London, Gay and Hancock, 1911.

The Story of Waitstill Baxter.   Boston, Houghton Mifflin, and London, Hodder and Stoughton, 1913.

Ladies in Waiting.   Boston, Houghton Mifflin, and London, Hodder and Stoughton, 1919.

Quilt of Happiness.   Boston, Houghton Mifflin, 1923.

Love by Express.   Buxton, Maine, privately printed, 1923.

Short Stories

>   *Creeping Jenny and Other New England Stories.*   Boston, Houghton Mifflin, 1924.

Plays

>   *The Old Peabody Pew*, adaptation of her own novel.   New York, French, 1917.
>   *A Thorn in the Flesh*, adaptation of a play by Ernest Legouvé.   New York and London, French, 1926.
>   *Fragments of a Play*, in *Poet Lore 40* (Boston), 1929.

Verse

>   *Nine Love Songs and a Carol.*   Boston, Houghton Mifflin, and London, Gay and Bird, 1896.

Other

>   *The Relation of Kindergarten to the Public School.*   San Francisco, Murdock, 1891.
>   *Children's Rights: A Book of Nursery Logic*, with Nora A. Smith.   Boston, Houghton Mifflin, and London, Gay and Bird, 1892.
>   *The Republic of Childhood (Froebel's Gifts, Froebel's Practices, Kindergarten Principles and Practice)*, with Nora A. Smith.   Boston, Houghton Mifflin, 3 vols., 1895–96; London, Gay and Bird, 3 vols., 1896.
>   *The Girl and the Kingdom: Learning to Teach.*   Los Angeles, City Teachers' Club, 1915.
>   *My Garden of Memory: An Autobiography.*   Boston, Houghton Mifflin, 1923; London, Hodder and Stoughton, 1924.
>   *A Thanksgiving Retrospect; or, Simplicity of Life in Old New England.*   Boston, Houghton Mifflin, 1928.

>   Editor, *The Kindergarten.*   New York, Harper, 1893.
>   Editor, *A Book of Dorcas Dishes: Family Recipes Contributed by the Dorcas Society of Hollis and Buxton.*   Cambridge, Massachusetts, privately printed, 1911.

Critical Studies: *Kate Douglas Wiggin as Her Sister Knew Her* by Nora A. Smith, Boston, Houghton Mifflin, and London, Gay and Hancock, 1925; *Kate Douglas Wiggin's Country of Childhood* by Helen F. Benner, Orono, University of Maine Press, 1956.

*   *   *

Kate Douglas Wiggin was an intellectual who wrote one of the most popular children's books ever published in the United States. This book, *Rebecca of Sunnybrook Farm*, was so vivid a picture of the experience of many little girls at the turn of the century in America that, as their "fan" mail to the author indicated, they often thought the work was a picture of their own lives. Though the identification no longer holds on a realistic level, the story still carries considerable emotional impact. It is a good story, with vibrancy and feeling, and likely to be read for a long time.

Some critics, however, have taken a negative view of the work. A critic in the *Dictionary of American Biography* wrote that the book "never exhibited imaginative flights nor aimed at any constructive picture of life, nor essayed the human comedy, as such, from any broad angle of theory or observation." Mark Twain, nevertheless, pronounced it "beautiful and warm and satisfying," and Clifton Fadiman praised the characterization of the heroine. As a child, Kate Douglas Wiggin had an interview on a train with Charles Dickens, and her work as an adult seems to have been marked by this early contact: it has a Dickensian flavor, albeit a limited one.

Though not so popular as *Rebecca, Mother Carey's Chickens* has the same folksy style and dry humor. For instance, when the four children of Mrs.Carey are growing up, a disagreeable relative, young Julia, is forced on the household:

> "Julia never did a naughty thing in her life, nor spoke a wrong word," said her father once, proudly.
> "Never mind, she's only ten, and there's hope for her yet," Captain Carey had replied cheerfully.

Less well-known is *The Birds' Christmas Carol*, a briefer work in her characteristic style, but with more pathos.

—Francelia Butler

WILDER, Laura Ingalls. American. Born in Pepin, Wisconsin, 7 February 1867. Educated at schools in Minnesota, and in De Smet, Dakota Territory. Married Almanzo James Wilder in 1885 (died, 1949); one daughter. Schoolteacher, De Smet, 1882–85; farmer in De Smet, 1885–94, and from 1894 in Mansfield, Missouri. Recipient: New York *Herald Tribune* Festival award, 1943; American Library Association Laura Ingalls Wilder Award, 1954. *Died 10 January 1957.*

PUBLICATIONS FOR CHILDREN

Fiction

> *Little House in the Big Woods*, illustrated by Helen Sewell.   New York, Harper, 1932; London, Methuen, 1956.
> *Farmer Boy*, illustrated by Helen Sewell.   New York, Harper, 1933; London, Lutterworth Press, 1965.
> *Little House on the Prairie*, illustrated by Helen Sewell.   New York, Harper, 1935; London, Methuen, 1957.
> *On the Banks of Plum Creek*, illustrated by Helen Sewell and Mildred Boyle.   New York, Harper, 1937; London, Methuen, 1958.
> *By the Shores of Silver Lake*, illustrated by Helen Sewell and Mildred Boyle.   New York, Harper, 1939; London, Lutterworth Press, 1961.
> *The Long Winter*, illustrated by Helen Sewell and Mildred Boyle.   New York, Harper, 1940; London, Lutterworth Press, 1962.
> *Little Town on the Prairie*, illustrated by Helen Sewell and Mildred Boyle.   New York, Harper, 1941; London, Lutterworth Press, 1963.
> *These Happy Golden Years*, illustrated by Helen Sewell and Mildred Boyle.   New York, Harper, 1943; London, Lutterworth Press, 1964.
> *The First Four Years*, illustrated by Garth Williams.   New York, Harper, 1971; London, Lutterworth Press, 1973.

PUBLICATIONS FOR ADULTS

Other

> On the Way Home: The Diary of a Trip from South Dakota to Mansfield, Missouri, in
> 1894, with Rose Wilder Lane.   New York, Harper, 1962.
> West from Home: Letters from Laura Ingalls Wilder, San Francisco 1915, edited by
> Roger Lea MacBride.   New York, Harper, 1974; London, Lutterworth Press, 1976.

Manuscript Collection: Laura Ingalls Wilder Home and Museum, Mansfield, Missouri.

*   *   *

Laura Ingalls Wilder was in her 60's when, at her daughter's urging, she began to set down in written form her extraordinarily vivid memories of childhood during the 1870's and 1880's in the pioneer Middle West. The result was not a simple autobiography but a cycle of shorter books whose third-person device gave them the agreeable perspective of fiction. Published in America in the 1930's and '40's they soon achieved classic status both as history and as narrative – a superb set of stories, most of them as apt for the very young as for other readers. Though, oddly, they did not appear in England until well after the War (which blocked so much publication), the Wilder books are as much admired today on this side of the Atlantic as on the other.

The first of the books, *Little House in the Big Woods*, establishes the characters if not the essential intimate solitude of the best of the later tales. The family – parents and three little girls, Mary, Laura, and baby Carrie – live in a log cabin in the Wisconsin woods. The children have never seen a town or store, but they know how cheese and butter are made, how skins are turned into leather, how an old-fashioned rifle is cleaned and reloaded – a long slow business, so the first shot has to kill. Mary is golden-haired, obedient and good. Laura, even at 5 years old is restless, fearless, inquisitive, quick to turn thought into action: she is often in trouble, and discipline is stern. But behind the rules is father (Pa) who, with only an axe and some trees can make houses, tables, beds; who can please Laura by refraining from shooting a wolf or even an animal needed for food when its behaviour interests him; who will take down his fiddle each night and teach them songs and dances. We are made aware too of the uncomplaining resourceful mother, ready to take up her roots again and again, and create an orderly home wherever they next alight.

For even now too many people are settling near the woods for Pa's liking. And so, in *Little House on the Prairie* (one of the best of all the books) the westward journeying starts. They leave in the chill and early spring, for their covered wagon, drawn by two horses, must cross the Mississippi before the ice can thaw. And indeed, once they are over the ominous cracks are heard. Another river is crossed on a raft; at a flooded fording place father has to swim with the terrified horses, the wagon sagging, half-submerged, behind. A site for a home is found; log by log (carefully watched by Laura) Pa builds house and furniture. A reader could do the same (on model scale, at least) from the description. Cowboys drive their huge herds past the door; Pa helps, and earns a cow and calf. The family are all struck down by "fever and ague" (malaria); the dog, which normally hates strangers, goes out to look for help. And Mr. Edwards, their bachelor neighbour, turns up on Christmas Eve. Like one of those Bret Harte characters at Roaring Camp he has gone to the town, forty miles away, to find presents for the children, and has swum with them through the creek. (This, with Edwards's account of his meeting with Santa Claus, is a splendid episode.)

But never far from the doorstep, or from the family's thoughts, are the Indians, whose land it really is. Of course, as Pa says, "when white settlers move into a country the Indians have to move on." Or is this too simple? A threatened attack on the house is quelled only by the intervention of an Indian chief, one of the Osage people, a noble and enigmatic warrior known as Soldat du Chene. And yet, the Ingalls must move on, for the new line drawn by the government sets them in Indian territory.

On the Banks of Plum Creek takes the family to Minnesota, after the usual long slow journey; now they are near enough to a town for Laura and Mary to walk each day to school. They timidly go to a party given by the storekeeper's vulgar and spoilt little daughter. (What clothes should one wear? how behave?) All their new security now lies with the wheat, a magnificent crop which is soon to be harvested. Pa will be able to have new boots at last, Laura reflects. But why is the light so queer? A cloud seems to be blotting out the sun:

> It was not like any cloud they had ever seen before. It was a cloud of something like snowflakes, but they were larger than snowflakes, and thin and glittering. Light shone through each flickering particle. There was no wind. The grasses were still and the hot air did not stir but the edge of the cloud came on across the sky faster than wind. The hair stood up on dog Jack's neck.

Something hits Laura's head and falls to the ground; it is a grasshopper, in the van of a vast invasion. The creatures ravage all growing things for scores of miles; then they lay their eggs in the fields for the following season. There can be no more school that year for the girls; no boots for Pa. *By the Shores of Silver Lake* tells, at the start, of a new baby, Grace. But Mary is now blind, after scarlet fever, and the land has been so weakened by locusts that they move on again. Pa takes a timekeeper's job at a railway camp in Dakota Territory, and when the camp is closed for the winter the family stays alone on the shores of the lake, 60 miles away from human dwellings. Spring will be time enough to trek to the town to file the claim for the perfect piece of land that Pa has found. Or *will* he be in time?

The Long Winter, which follows, is surely the most memorable of all the Wilder books. An October Indian summer changes overnight to ice and blizzard – and the ice and blizzard continue for an incredible seven months. The train with supplies is blocked in a mountain of hard-packed snow, and must stay there until spring. The inhabitants of the little town survive as well as they can on what they have. When fuel gives out in the Ingalls home, Pa and the girls endlessly plait hard twists of hay for burning. Wheat grains are continually ground in the coffee mill to make a kind of bread, almost their only food. In the "dark twilight" of the day, Laura feels that she can never escape from

> the hateful ceaseless pounding of the storm. The coffee mill's handle ground round and round, it must not stop. It seemed to make her part of the whirling winds driving the snow round and round over the earth and in the air, whirling and beating at Pa on the way to the stable, whirling and shrieking at the lonely houses, whirling the snow between them and up to the sky and far away, whirling forever over the endless prairie.

Then, when the last of the wheat gives out, two young men, Almanzo Wilder and his equally reckless friend Cap Garland, set out over 20 miles of trackless wastes to find a rumoured settler who *might* have a hoard of grain. Their journey and the return, horses and sacks constantly falling into holes and airpockets, are described in characteristic unstressed detail. It is a miniature epic, none the less.

Little Town on the Prairie covers the years when Laura is 14 and 15, a schoolgirl hoping to qualify for being a teacher at 16 and so help to pay towards Mary's fees at a college for the blind. The dashing Almanzo Wilder, whom all the girls admire, sees her home. Though still under age, she is offered her first schoolteaching post, at a settlement some 12 miles of prairie away. And so, at the start of *These Happy Golden Years* she leaves home for the first time. Some of the pupils at the tiny school, boys as well as girls, are older than she is herself (she is not yet 16). Her lodgings are with a half-deranged slatternly housewife who desperately longs to be back in town; the weather is bitterly cold. Yet on Friday afternoon she hears the sound of sleigh bells; Almanzo has come to take her home (and brings her back on the Sunday); so he continues to do, in the worst of weathers, until the term's contract ends. And the book closes with a fresh beginning, as Laura, at 18, now Mrs. Wilder, steps into her new home on "the tree claim." To avoid an expensive family wedding they have married without fuss in the local minister's parlour, she in her new homemade black cashmere and old blue-lined poke bonnet. Characteristically, she has asked for the word "obey" not to be used. "I cannot make a promise that I will not keep." (Almanzo's early story can be found in *Farmer Boy*, actually the second book written in the series.) Finally, *The First Four Years*, a curiously moving book, tells how the marriage took shape. Those years were hard – sickness, accidents, poverty, farming disasters. Two children were born; one died. But, the four years over, Laura knows that after all, for good or ill, she and Almanzo will live their lives on the land.

What are the qualities that keep these books alive? As tales in the "family" genre they have, of course, immense appeal – yet readers drawn to themes of solitude find them of no less interest. For one thing, they present a small close group of people alone in ranges of uninhabited country, a geographical isolation that gives peculiar intensity to the compact sheltering home, where both necessities and luxuries (including birthday and Christmas gifts) – pastimes too – must so often be made, found, grown or improvised. (This is the atmosphere that television versions have signally failed to understand or present.) In our overcrowded scene today, the Ingalls' life seems less like fact than fantasy. What must be said is that Laura Ingalls Wilder was a more gifted writer than she knew. Her power of exact recall is matched by her ability, long years after, to fix in words what was seen, heard, felt by the observing child. At the end of the first book Laura voices something of the immediacy that is her most shining trait.

> She was glad that the cosy house, and Pa and Ma, and the firelight and the music, were now. They could not be forgotten she thought, because now is now. It can never be a long time ago.

—Naomi Lewis

WILKINSON, Anne (Cochran Boyd). Canadian. Born in Toronto, Ontario, 21 September 1910. Educated privately. Married Frederik R. Wilkinson in 1932 (marriage dissolved, 1953); two sons and one daughter. Co-Founding Editor, *Tamarack Review*, Toronto, 1956. *Died 10 May 1961.*

PUBLICATIONS FOR CHILDREN

Fiction

Swann and Daphne.   Toronto, Oxford University Press, 1960.

PUBLICATIONS FOR ADULTS

Verse

Counterpoint to Sleep.   Montreal, First Statement Press, 1951.
The Hangman Ties the Holly.   Toronto, Macmillan, 1955.
The Collected Poems of Anne Wilkinson, and a Prose Memoir, edited by A.J.M. Smith.   Toronto, Macmillan, and New York, St. Martin's Press, 1968.

Other

Lions in the Way: A Discursive History of the Oslers. Toronto, Macmillan, 1956; London, Macmillan, 1957.

*   *   *

Swann and Daphne, Anne Wilkinson's only children's book, is a modern Canadian fairy-tale. The plot is readily summarized. The Whites and the Greens are next-door neighbours in whose large combined back garden appear, one summer evening, a swan and a birch tree. Mrs. White, a bird-watcher, lovingly strokes the swan, while Mrs. Green, a gardener, caresses the birch. Their affection is rewarded; the next morning the childless couples find, in place of the bird and tree, two babies: a boy with hair of feathers, a girl with hair of leaves. The former becomes Swann White; the latter, Daphne Green. They grow up in relative isolation from other children until they turn 7 and are confronted with the school inspector and the law of compulsory education. Their misadventures in society – with teacher, principal, classmates, parents, and television people – eventually prompt the children to leave home and to search for a half-remembered pastoral paradise in the north. There they are happy until some passing swans half-persuade Swann to leave with them. Loving Daphne, at first he demurs, but Daphne, loving Swann, reverts to birch shape so that he too will feel free to realize his destiny. He resumes bird form and departs – but during every spring and fall migration the pair are joyously reunited.

Among the prominent fairy-tale features of the story are the elements of magical transformation, mysterious origins, foster parents, a quest, achievement of destiny, and of course some links with the stories of the Goose Girl, Baucis and Philemon, and the legendary Daphne. Prominent too is the humour: not only such instances as the watering of Daphne's hair/leaves, but also the whole concept of two such children. Especially enjoyable is the gentle absurdity of Swann and Daphne in a "real-life" situation – one all children must confront and come to terms with – the undeniable, unavoidable fact of school. As one might expect from an author who was privately educated, public school law is shown to be "a ass."

Also real – as a substitution of race for feathers and religion for leaves would show – is the harassment directed at the two "different" children by other people. Ironically, the only alternative to societal bigotry is adulation, celebrity status. With adulation comes the economic exploitation upon which Western society is built, represented by the television man's payment of money to the parents for a show which sensationalizes the children's peculiarities. The effect of such harassment, adulation, and exploitation is to indict Western society. Accordingly, a difference of values forces the children into the northland of Canada, where they can practice self-sacrificing – and self-fulfilling – love. Though the story becomes a bit flat after the children leave human society, which provides the focus for much of the story's humour, the book offers its readers both things to enjoy and things to ponder – all in the appealing context of a contemporary fairy-tale.

—John Robert Sorfleet

———————————

WILLARD, Barbara. British. Born in Brighton, Sussex, 12 March 1909. Educated at Convent of La Sainte Union, Southampton. Recipient: *Guardian* Award, 1974. Agent: David Higham Associates Ltd., 5–8 Lower John Street, London W1R 4HA. Address: Forest Edge, Nutley, Uckfield, Sussex, England.

Fiction

Snail and the Pennithornes, illustrated by Geoffrey Fletcher.   London, Epworth Press,
   1957.
Snail and the Pennithornes Next Time, illustrated by Geoffrey Fletcher.   London,
   Epworth Press, 1958.
Son of Charlemagne, illustrated by Emil Weiss.   New York, Doubleday, 1959;
   London, Heinemann, 1960.
The House with Roots, illustrated by Robert Hodgson.   London, Constable, 1959; New
   York, Watts, 1960.
Snail and the Pennithornes and the Princess, illustrated by Geoffrey Fletcher.   London,
   Epworth Press, 1960.
The Dippers and Jo, illustrated by Jean Harper.   London, Hamish Hamilton, 1960.
Eight for a Secret, illustrated by Lewis Hart.   London, Constable, 1960; New York,
   Watts, 1961.
The Penny Pony, illustrated by Juliette Palmer.   London, Hamish Hamilton, 1961.
If All the Swords in England, illustrated by Robert M. Sax.   New York, Doubleday, and
   London, Burns and Oates, 1961.
The Pram Race, illustrated by Constance Marshall.   London, Hamish Hamilton, 1961.
Stop the Train!, illustrated by Jean Harper.   London, Hamish Hamilton, 1961.
The Summer with Spike, illustrated by Anne Linton.   London, Constable, 1961; New
   York, Watts, 1962.
Duck on a Pond, illustrated by Mary Rose Hardy.   London, Constable, 1962; New
   York, Harcourt Brace, 1963.
Hetty, illustrated by Pamela Mara.   London, Constable, 1962; New York, Harcourt
   Brace, 1963.
Augustine Came to Kent, illustrated by Hans Guggenheim.   New York, Doubleday,
   1963; Kingswood, Surrey, World's Work, 1964.
The Battle of Wednesday Week, illustrated by Douglas Hall.   London, Constable, 1963;
   as *Storm from the West*, New York, Harcourt Brace, 1964.
The Dippers and the High-Flying Kite, illustrated by Maureen Eckersley.   London,
   Hamish Hamilton, 1963.
The Suddenly Gang, illustrated by Lynette Hemmant.   London, Hamish Hamilton,
   1963.
A Dog and a Half, illustrated by Jane Paton.   London, Hamish Hamilton, 1964; New
   York, Nelson, 1971.
Three and One to Carry, illustrated by Douglas Hall.   London, Constable, 1964; New
   York, Harcourt Brace, 1965.
The Wild Idea, illustrated by Douglas Bissett.   London, Hamish Hamilton, 1965.
Charity at Home, illustrated by Douglas Hall.   London, Constable, 1965; New York,
   Harcourt Brace, 1966.
Surprise Island, illustrated by Jane Paton.   London, Hamish Hamilton, 1966; New
   York, Meredith Press, 1969.
The Richleighs of Tantamount, illustrated by C. Walter Hodges.   London, Constable,
   1966; New York, Harcourt Brace, 1967.
The Grove of Green Holly, illustrated by Gareth Floyd.   London, Constable, 1967; as
   Flight to the Forest, New York, Doubleday, 1967.
The Pet Club, illustrated by Lynette Hemmant.   London, Hamish Hamilton, 1967.
To London! To London!, illustrated by Antony Maitland.   London, Longman, and New
   York, Weybright and Talley, 1968.
Hurrah for Rosie!, illustrated by Gareth Floyd.   London, Hutchinson, 1968.
Royal Rosie, illustrated by Gareth Floyd.   London, Hutchinson, 1968.
The Family Tower.   London, Constable, and New York, Harcourt Brace, 1968.

The Toppling Towers.   London, Longman, and New York, Harcourt Brace, 1969.
The Pocket Mouse, illustrated by Mary Russon.   London, Hamish Hamilton, and New York, Knopf, 1969.
Mantlemass:
  The Lark and the Laurel, illustrated by Gareth Floyd.   London, Longman, and New York, Harcourt Brace, 1970.
  The Sprig of Broom, illustrated by Paul Shardlow.   London, Longman, 1971; New York, Dutton, 1972.
  A Cold Wind Blowing.   London, Longman, 1972; New York, Dutton, 1973.
  The Iron Lily.   London, Longman, 1973; New York, Dutton, 1974.
  Harrow and Harvest.   London, Penguin, 1974; New York, Dutton, 1975.
  The Miller's Boy, illustrated by Gareth Floyd.   London, Penguin, and New York, Dutton, 1976.
  The Eldest Son.   London, Penguin, 1977.
Priscilla Pentecost, illustrated by Doreen Roberts.   London, Hamish Hamilton, 1970.
The Reindeer Slippers, illustrated by Tessa Jordan.   London, Hamish Hamilton, 1970.
The Dragon Box, illustrated by Tessa Jordan.   London, Hamish Hamilton, 1972.
Jubilee!, illustrated by Hilary Abrahams.   London, Heinemann, 1973.
Bridesmaid, illustrated by Jane Paton.   London, Hamish Hamilton, 1976.
The Convent Cat, illustrated by Bunshu Iguchi.   New York, McGraw Hill, 1976.

Other

Junior Motorist: The Driver's Apprentice, with Frances Howell, illustrated by Ionicus.   London, Collins, 1969.
Chichester and Lewes, illustrated by Graham Humphreys.   London, Longman, 1970.

Editor, *Hullabaloo! About Naughty Boys and Girls*, illustrated by Fritz Wegner.   London, Hamish Hamilton, and New York, Meredith Press, 1969.
Editor, *Happy Families* (anthology), illustrated by Krystyna Turska.   London, Hamish Hamilton, and New York, Macmillan, 1974.
Editor, *Field and Forest*, illustrated by Faith Jaques.   London, Penguin, 1975.

Translator, *The Giants' Feast*, by Max Bolliger, illustrated by Monika Laimgruber.   London, Hamish Hamilton, 1975.

PUBLICATIONS FOR ADULTS

Novels

Love in Ambush, with Elizabeth Helen Devas.   London, Howe, 1930.
Ballerina.   London, Howe, 1931.
Candle Flame.   London, Howe, 1932.
Name of Gentleman.   London, Howe, 1933.
Joy Befall Thee.   London, Howe, 1934.
As Far as in Me Lies.   London, Nelson, 1936.
The Dogs Do Bark.   London, Macmillan, 1938.
Set Piece.   London, Nelson, 1938.
Personal Effects.   London, Macmillan, 1939.
Portrait of Philip.   London, Macmillan, 1950.
Proposed and Seconded.   London, Macmillan, 1951.
Celia Scarfe.   New York, Appleton Century Crofts, 1951.
Echo Answers.   London, Macmillan, 1952.
He Fought for His Queen.   London, Heinemann, and New York, Warne, 1954.
Winter in Disguise.   London, Joseph, 1958.

Plays

> *Brother Ass and Brother Lion*, adaptation of the story "St. Jerome, The Lion, and the
> Donkey" by Helen Waddell. London, J. Garnet Miller, 1951.
> *One of the Twelve*. London, French, 1954.
> *Fit for a King*. London, J. Garnet Miller, 1955.

Radio Play: *Duck on a Pond*, from her own book, 1962.

Television Play: *Merry Go Round*, 1965.

Other

> *Sussex.* London, Batsford, 1965; New York, Hastings House, 1966.

> Editor, *"I ...": An Anthology of Diarists*. London, Chatto and Windus, 1972.

Barbara Willard comments:

As I have been writing for such years and years it may seem strange when I say that only in the past ten years or so have I found myself writing what I must always have wanted to write. It took me a long while to find my way into children's fiction, and then some more time to make my way to *Mantlemass*, which is the historical sequence, not yet concluded, based on the Wealden area of Sussex where I live. These stories begin at the conclusion of the Wars of the Roses in 1485 and cover 250 years or so. They tell the tale of two intermingled families living within the forest pale. They are horsebreeders, foresters, iron workers – modest ordinary people, though in fact there does run in their blood a nobler strain. I have tried to imagine how they would have lived, and how they would have been affected by the events in the outside world – the change of dynasty from Plantagenet to Tudor, the Reformation, the Civil War.

Because these people have come to seem so real to me, living as I do on their ground, I think perhaps they have some reality for readers – who, in fact, are not all young readers.

*   *   *

Barbara Willard has written many books for children, set both in the present and the past; there are historical novels like *Augustine Came to Kent*, modern family sagas like the Towers series and books for younger children such as *The Penny Pony*, *The Dragon Box*, and *A Dog and a Half*, all of which are good reading, but her best books by far are her Mantlemass series of historical novels. What she does in this sequence is to explore the human consequences of social change, breathing life into history-book facts like the Reformation and the Dissolution of the Monasteries or the iron-workings in the Wealden Forest.

The Mantlemass books are set in the Ashdown Forest and span 250 years, following the fortunes of two families, the Mallorys and the Medleys, from the time Cecily Jolland comes to Mantlemass in the 15th century (*The Lark and the Laurel*) until Mantlemass is burned down in the 17th century in *Harrow and Harvest*.

Her books are full of a sense of place; she writes of the forest and life there lovingly and with knowledge gained from living in it as well as research. Her descriptions of the landscape are perceptive and evocative. She is a historical novelist who is drawn to the similarities of the past and the present rather than to their strange differences. But her great forte is her character drawing. One feels that every person in her books has a full, rounded existence inside and outside the novel. She is a very honest writer who does not hesitate to show us defects in her characters, or the ugly consequences of certain actions. She does not gloss over the harsh barbarities of the Reformation in *A Cold Wind Blowing* or the betrayals of which men and women are capable in time of civil war in *Harrow and Harvest*.

She has created some very strong women characters, tough ladies like Dame Elizabeth in *The Lark and the Laurel* and Lilias in *The Iron Lily* who are more than equal to the men they live among and trade with. She writes well about romantic love without being sentimental and deals as well with sorrow as with joy. Her touch with dialogue, often a pitfall for historical novelists, is very sure. She makes her characters use forest dialect which has a local and period flavour.

The Lark and the Laurel, which explored the consequences of child marriage for political ends, was followed by *The Sprig of Broom*, which brought a bastard son of Richard III to live in hiding in the forest after his father's death. *A Cold Wind Blowing*, a sombre book, was about the aftermath of the Dissolution of the Monasteries, and *The Iron Lily* (a *Guardian* Award winner) continued the history of the families and went into detail about the iron workings in the forest. *Harrow and Harvest* jumps several generations, being set at the time of the English Civil War and appears to be the end of the sequence with the destruction of Mantlemass and the heroine about to embark for the Americas. But the ring bearing the lark and laurel crest which appears in every episode of the saga is still in existence at the end of the book, so the sequence may go on. Certainly Ms. Willard is filling in the gaps in the series. *The Miller's Boy* goes back to the 15th century and introduces Lewis Mallory before he appears in *The Lark and the Laurel*, several short stories round out various episodes, and *The Eldest Son* fits in before *The Iron Lily*.

As the series has developed, the books have grown away from being only children's books as the first ones were. I would call *A Cold Wind Blowing*, *The Iron Lily*, and *Harrow and Harvest* books for *people* which are accessible to children rather than children's books. How many books, even nowadays, have one of the principal child characters with whom the reader will have identified, killed in what could have been his moment of triumph? I am not saying that in *Harrow and Harvest* Edmund should not have died – indeed to make an artistic whole, he had to; I am merely saying that it is unusual. Also, Mantlemass, the house we have come to love through the series almost as much as the characters themselves, is violently destroyed. And worst of all, at the very end Cecilia decides that she will bury the evidence that proves her descent from Richard III – what a blow to romantics and devotees of the cosy ending!

What a reader takes away from reading this sequence is a sense of the continuity of history, of a real family in all its complex relationships (in each novel we usually see three generations at a time) and above all, the knowledge that great events affect ordinary lives, but seldom in the ways one would expect.

—Pamela Cleaver

WILLIAMS, Jay. American. Born in Buffalo, New York, 31 May 1914. Educated at the University of Pennsylvania, Philadelphia, 1931–32; Columbia University, New York, 1933–34. Served in the United States Army, 1941–45; Purple Heart. Married Barbara Girdansky in 1941; has one son and one daughter. Recipient: Guggenheim Fellowship, 1949; Boys' Clubs of America Award, 1949; Bank Street College of Education Irma Black Award, 1977. Lives in Newport, Rhode Island. Agent: Harriet Wasserman, Russell and Volkening Inc., 551 Fifth Avenue, New York, New York 10017, U.S.A.; or, Laurence Pollinger Ltd., 18 Maddox Street, London W1R 0EU, England.

PUBLICATIONS FOR CHILDREN

Fiction

The Stolen Oracle, illustrated by Frederick Chapman.   New York, Oxford University Press, 1943.

The Counterfeit African.   New York and London, Oxford University Press, 1944.

The Sword and the Scythe, illustrated by Edouard Sandoz.   New York, Oxford University Press, 1946.

The Roman Moon Mystery.   New York, Oxford University Press, 1948.

The Magic Gate, illustrated by John Brimer.   New York, Oxford University Press, 1949.

Eagle Jake and Indian Pete, illustrated by John Brimer.   New York, Rinehart, 1947.

Danny Dunn and the Antigravity Paint [*on a Desert Island, and the Homework Machine, and the Weather Machine, on the Ocean Floor, and the Fossil Cave, and the Heat Ray, Time Traveler, and the Automatic House, and the Voice from Space, and the Smallifying Machine, and the Swamp Monster, Invisible Boy, Scientific Detective, and the Universal Glue*], with Raymond Abrashkin, illustrated by Ezra Jack Keats, Brinton Turkle, Owen Kampen, Leo Summers, and Paul Sagsoorian.   New York, McGraw Hill, 15 vols., 1956–77; Leicester, Brockhampton Press, 2 vols., 1956, 1960; London, Macdonald, 13 vols., 1965–77.

The Question Box, illustrated by Margot Zemach.   New York, Norton, 1965.

Philbert the Fearful, illustrated by Ib Ohlsson.   New York, Norton, 1966.

What Can You Do with a Word?, illustrated by Leslie Goldstein.   New York, Macmillan, 1966.

Puppy Pie, illustrated by Wayne Blickenstaff.   New York, Crowell Collier, 1962.

The Cookie Tree, illustrated by Blake Hampton.   New York, Parents' Magazine Press, 1967.

To Catch a Bird, illustrated by Jo Polseno.   New York, Crowell Collier, 1968.

The King with Six Friends, illustrated by Imero Gobbato.   New York, Parents' Magazine Press, 1968.

The Good-for-Nothing Prince, illustrated by Imero Gobbato.   New York, Norton, 1969.

The Practical Princess, illustrated by Friso Henstra.   New York, Parents' Magazine Press, 1969.

School for Sillies, illustrated by Friso Henstra.   New York, Parents' Magazine Press, 1969.

A Box Full of Infinity, illustrated by Robin Lawrie.   New York, Norton, 1970.

Stupid Marco, illustrated by Friso Henstra.   New York, Parents' Magazine Press, 1970.

The Silver Whistle, illustrated by Friso Henstra.   New York, Parents' Magazine Press, 1971.

A Present from a Bird, illustrated by Jacqueline Chwast.   New York, Parents' Magazine Press, 1971.

The Hawkstone.   New York, Walck, 1971; London, Gollancz, 1972.

The Youngest Captain, illustrated by Friso Henstra.   New York, Parents' Magazine Press, 1972.

Magical Storybook, illustrated by Edward Sorel.   New York, American Heritage Press, 1972.

The Hero from Otherwhere.   New York, Walck, 1972.

Petronella, illustrated by Friso Henstra.   New York, Parents' Magazine Press, 1973.

Forgetful Fred, illustrated by Friso Henstra.   New York, Parents' Magazine Press, 1974.

The People of the Ax.   New York, Walck, 1974; London, Macdonald and Jane's, 1975.

A Bag Full of Nothing, illustrated by Tom O'Sullivan.   New York, Parents' Magazine Press, 1974.

Everyone Knows What a Dragon Looks Like, illustrated by Mercer Mayer.   New York, Scholastic, 1976.

The Burglar Next Door, illustrated by DeAnne Hollinger.   New York, Scholastic, 1976; as *Daylight Robbery*, London, Penguin, 1977.

The Reward Worth Having, illustrated by Mercer Mayer.   New York, Scholastic, 1977.

The Time of the Kraken.   New York, Scholastic, and London, Gollancz, 1977.

Pettifur, illustrated by Hilary Knight.   New York, Scholastic, 1977.

Verse

I Wish I Had Another Name, illustrated by Winifred Lubell.   New York, Atheneum, 1962.

Other

Augustus Caesar.   Evanston, Illinois, Row Peterson, 1951.

The Battle for the Atlantic.   New York, Random House, 1959.

The Tournament of the Lions, illustrated by Ezra Jack Keats.   New York, Walck, 1960.

Medusa's Head, illustrated by Steele Savage.   New York, Random House, 1960; London, Muller, 1963.

Knights of the Crusades.   New York, American Heritage Press, 1962; London, Cassell, 1963.

Joan of Arc.   New York, American Heritage Press, 1963; London, Cassell, 1964.

Leonardo da Vinci.   New York, American Heritage Press, 1965; London, Cassell, 1966.

The Spanish Armada.   New York, American Heritage Press, and London, Cassell, 1966.

Life in the Middle Ages.   New York, Random House, 1966; London, Nelson, 1967.

The Sword of King Arthur, illustrated by Louis Glanzman.   New York, Crowell, 1968.

The Horn of Roland, illustrated by Sean Morrison.   New York, Crowell, 1968.

Seven at One Blow, illustrated by Friso Henstra.   New York, Parents' Magazine Press, 1972.

Moon Journey (based on works by Jules Verne), illustrated by Daniel le Noury.   London, Macdonald and Jane's, 1976; New York, Crown, 1977.

PUBLICATIONS FOR ADULTS

Novels

The Good Yeoman.   New York, Appleton Century Crofts, 1948; London, Macdonald, 1956.

The Rogue from Padua.   Boston, Little Brown, 1952; London, Macdonald, 1954.

The Siege.   Boston, Little Brown, and London, Macdonald, 1955.

The Witches.   New York, Random House, 1957; London, Macdonald, 1958.

Solomon and Sheba.   New York, Random House, and London, Macdonald, 1959.

The Forger.   New York, Atheneum, and London, Macdonald, 1961.

Tomorrow's Fire.   New York, Atheneum, 1964; London, Macdonald, 1965.

Smiling, The Boy Fell Dead (as Michael Delving).   New York, Scribner, 1966; London, Macdonald, 1967.

Uniad.   New York, Scribner, 1968; London, Murray, 1969.

The Devil Finds Work (as Michael Delving).   New York, Scribner, 1969; London, Collins, 1970.

Die Like a Man (as Michael Delving).   London, Collins, 1970; New York, Scribner, 1971.

A Shadow of Himself (as Michael Delving).   New York, Scribner, and London, Collins, 1972.

Bored to Death (as Michael Delving).   New York, Scribner, 1975; as Wave of Fatalities, London, Collins, 1975.

The China Expert (as Michael Delving).   London, Collins, 1976; New York, Scribner, 1977.

Other

Fall of the Sparrow.   New York, Oxford University Press, 1951.

A Change of Climate (on Majorca).   New York, Random House, and London, Macdonald, 1956.

The World of Titian.   New York and London, Time-Life Books, 1968.

Stage Left.   New York, Scribner, 1974.

Manuscript Collection: Mugar Memorial Library, Boston University.

Jay Williams comments:

At the age of 12 I won a prize (it was a book) for the best original ghost story told round the campfire in a boys' camp. The experience went to my head and I have been telling stories to children ever since. I don't think of myself as anything but a spinner of tales; I have no pretensions to being educator, moralist, or propagandist, although inevitably, unless a writer has perfect insulation between himself and his writing, into every work one's beliefs, enjoyments, and sense of morality will find their way like mice into a country kitchen. Even my non-fiction has grown out of subjects which attracted me because they were good stories. And what is a good story? I have no universal definition, but for me it is one which binds teller as much as reader in a web of surprise, tension, and wonderment. To all intents and purposes, I'm still back at that campfire.

*   *   *

One of the widest ranging writers for children today is Jay Williams. The gamut runs from ancient Rome to contemporary science fiction, and includes Medieval history and delightful tongue-in-cheek fairy tales. Along the way he has also managed to write a number of adult novels, a treatise on the American stage in the 1930's, and a half dozen highly acclaimed mystery stories. He is a willing and able writer, bristling with ideas and highly receptive to proposals from others. Given a suggestion for a writing project, his response will be, "Let me think about it," and within days he will have prepared a first draft. When I was his editor at Humpty Dumpty's Magazine and later at Parents' Magazine Press, this happened several times.

His early Danny Dunn books, written in collaboration with the late Raymond Abrashkin, made a significant contribution to the development of science fiction for children. Being Jay, he did it with his own special twist. While the books have all the appeal of sci-fi fantasy, they involve real children, and are based on carefully researched, very here-and-now scientific principles.

Well before the Women's Liberation movement had started raising the consciousness of both men and women, before many people were aware of the insidiousness of sexist role-playing in children's books, Jay was doing his turn-about fairy tales (for example, The Practical Princess, Stupid Marco, and Petronella), in which the princess not infrequently rescued the prince. He did this with grace and style, so that there was no hint of polemic in the stories which resulted.

To see Jay at his best is to watch him with a group of youngsters. Having had a theatrical background, he knows just how to handle an audience, and within minutes he has the children in the palm of his hand, joining in his enthusiasm for the story he is telling.

Although he takes his writing very seriously, he readily laughs at himself and the foibles of his fellow humans, and this is so often evident in his stories for children. With subtle wit and good humor woven into unhackneyed plots, he has created an enviable list of books for the delight of countless young people.

—Alvin Tresselt

WILLIAMS, Ursula Moray. British. Born in Petersfield, Hampshire, 19 April 1911. Educated privately and at schools in Annecy, France, and Winchester. Married Peter John in 1935 (died, 1974); has four sons. Agent: Curtis Brown Ltd., 1 Craven Hill, London W2 3EW. Address: c/o Chatto and Windus Ltd., 40–42 William IV Street, London WC2N 4DF, England.

PUBLICATIONS FOR CHILDREN

Fiction

    Jean-Pierre, illustrated by the author. London, A. and C. Black, 1931.
    The Pettabomination, illustrated by the author. London, Archer, 1933; revised edition, London, Lane, 1948.
    Kelpie, The Gipsies' Pony, illustrated by the author and Barbara Moray Williams. London, Harrap, 1934; Philadelphia, Lippincott, 1935.
    Anders and Marta, illustrated by the author. London, Harrap, 1935.
    Adventures of Anne, illustrated by the author. London, Harrap, 1935.
    The Twins and Their Ponies, illustrated by the author. London, Harrap, 1936.
    Sandy-on-the-Shore, illustrated by the author. London, Harrap, 1936.
    Tales for the Sixes and Sevens, illustrated by the author. London, Harrap, 1936.
    Dumpling, illustrated by the author. London, Harrap, 1937.
    Elaine of LaSigne, illustrated by the author and Barbara Moray Williams. London, Harrap, 1937; as *Elaine of the Mountains*, Philadelphia, Lippincott, 1939.
    Adventures of Boss and Dingbat, photographs by Peter John. London, Harrap, 1937.
    Adventures of the Little Wooden Horse, illustrated by Joyce Lankester Brisley. London, Harrap, 1938; Philadelphia, Lippincott, 1939.
    Adventures of Puffin, illustrated by Mary Shillabeer. London, Harrap, 1939.
    Peter and the Wanderlust, illustrated by Jack Matthew. London, Harrap, 1939; Philadelphia, Lippincott, 1940; revised edition, as *Peter on the Road*, London, Hamish Hamilton, 1963.
    Pretenders' Island, illustrated by Joyce Lankester Brisley. London, Harrap, 1940; New York, Knopf, 1942.
    A Castle for John-Peter, illustrated by Eileen Soper. London, Harrap, 1941.
    Gobbolino the Witch's Cat. London, Harrap, 1942.
    The Three Toymakers, illustrated by the author. London, Harrap, 1945; revised edition, London, Hamish Hamilton, 1970; New York, Nelson, 1971.
    Malkin's Mountain, illustrated by the author. London, Harrap, 1948; revised edition, London, Hamish Hamilton, 1970; New York, Nelson, 1972.
    The Story of Laughing Dandino, illustrated by the author. London, Harrap, 1948.
    Jockin the Jester, illustrated by Barbara Moray Williams. London, Chatto and Windus, 1951; Nashville, Nelson, 1973.
    The Binklebys at Home, illustrated by the author. London, Harrap, 1951.
    The Binklebys on the Farm, illustrated by the author. London, Harrap, 1953.

The Secrets of the Wood, illustrated by the author.   London, Harrap, 1955.

Grumpa, illustrated by the author.   Leicester, Brockhampton Press, 1955.

Goodbody's Puppet Show, illustrated by the author.   London, Hamish Hamilton, 1956.

Golden Horse with a Silver Tail, illustrated by the author.   London, Hamish Hamilton, 1957.

Hobbie, illustrated by the author.   Leicester, Brockhampton Press, 1958.

The Moonball, illustrated by the author.   London, Hamish Hamilton, 1958; New York, Meredith Press, 1967.

The Noble Hawks.   London, Hamish Hamilton, 1959; as *The Earl's Falconer*, New York, Morrow, 1961.

The Nine Lives of Island Mackenzie, illustrated by Edward Ardizzone.   London, Chatto and Windus, 1959; as *Island Mackenzie*, New York, Morrow, 1960.

Beware of This Animal, illustrated by Jane Paton.   London, Hamish Hamilton, 1964; New York, Dial Press, 1965.

Johnnie Tigerskin, illustrated by Diana Johns.   London, Harrap, 1964; New York, Duell Sloan Pearce, 1966.

O for a Mouseless House!, illustrated by the author.   London, Chatto and Windus, 1964.

High Adventure, illustrated by Prudence Seward.   London, Nelson, 1965.

Cruise of the "Happy-Go-Gay," illustrated by Gunvor Edwards.   London, Hamish Hamilton, 1967; New York, Meredith Press, 1968.

A Crown for a Queen, illustrated by Shirley Hughes.   London, Hamish Hamilton, and New York, Meredith Press, 1968.

The Toymaker's Daughter, illustrated by Shirley Hughes.   London, Hamish Hamilton, 1968; New York, Meredith Press, 1969.

Mog, illustrated by Faith Jaques.   London, Allen and Unwin, 1969.

Boy in a Barn, illustrated by Terence Dudley.   London, Allen and Unwin, and New York, Nelson, 1970.

Johnnie Golightly and His Crocodile, illustrated by Faith Jaques.   London, Chatto Boyd and Oliver, 1970; New York, Harvey House, 1971.

Traffic Jam, illustrated by Robert Hales.   London, Chatto and Windus, 1971.

Man on a Steeple, illustrated by Mary Dinsdale.   London, Chatto and Windus, 1971.

Mrs. Townsend's Robber, illustrated by Gavin Rowe.   London, Chatto and Windus, 1971.

Out of the Shadows, illustrated by Gavin Rowe.   London, Chatto and Windus, 1971.

Castle Merlin.   London, Allen and Unwin, and Nashville, Nelson, 1972.

A Picnic with the Aunts, illustrated by Faith Jaques.   London, Chatto and Windus, 1972.

The Kidnapping of My Grandmother, illustrated by Mike Jackson.   London, Heinemann, 1972.

Tiger-Nanny, illustrated by Gunvor Edwards.   Leicester, Brockhampton Press, 1973; Nashville, Nelson, 1974.

Grandpapa's Folly and the Woodworm-Bookworm, illustrated by Faith Jaques.   London, Chatto and Windus, 1974.

The Line, illustrated by Barry Wilkinson.   London, Penguin, 1974.

No Ponies for Miss Pobjoy, illustrated by Pat Marriott.   London, Chatto and Windus, 1975; Nashville, Nelson, 1976.

Plays

Autumn Sweepers and Other Plays (includes *Mother Josephine Bakes Bread, Forfeits, Tavi of Gold, The Organ Grinder: A Mime, A Sea Ballet*), illustrated by the author.   London, A. and C. Black, 1933.

The Good Little Christmas Tree, illustrated by the author.   London, Harrap, 1942.

The House of Happiness, illustrated by the author.   London, Harrap, 1946.
The Pettabomination, from her own story.   London, French, 1951.

Verse

Grandfather, illustrated by the author.   London, Allen and Unwin, 1933.

Other

For Brownies: Stories and Games for the Pack and Everybody Else, illustrated by the
   author.   London, Harrap, 1932.
More for Brownies, illustrated by the author.   London, Harrap, 1934.
Children's Parties, and Games for a Rainy Day.   London, Corgi, 1972.

*   *   *

Ursula Moray Williams has written over fifty children's stories and plays, notable for the
variety of their appeal to a range of ages from 3 to 13. They have in common a good story
line, a simple and often compelling lucidity of language, and a firm though not overpowering
moral attitude. Kindness, compassion, and concern for others are set against selfish greed,
heartlessness, trickery, and violence, a confrontation which is most explicit in three stories
about a beautiful but heartless and often maliciously spiteful doll, Marta. *The Three
Toymakers*, *Malkin's Mountain*, and *The Toymaker's Daughter* are set in a fantasy kingdom
of peasants, mountain scenery, and magic, with a strong folk-lore element in the telling,
though they are less astringent than the traditional folk-tale, and verge at times on the
sentimental. Akin to these tales are *Adventures of the Little Wooden Horse* and *Gobbolino, The
Witch's Cat*. They share the fantasy folk-tale element, but the observation of the complexities
of good and evil is sharper and less sentimental, and would be thought-provoking for
children older than the 6 or 7-year-olds to whom these stories are most often read. As the
stories are episodic they are well-suited to reading aloud in instalments and the two main
characters, the "quiet little horse" and the unhappy witch's cat, have charm and sure appeal
for children.

In a different, lighthearted and amusing vein of fantasy are two recent picture-books with
an Edwardian flavour, the ingenious *Grandpapa's Folly and the Woodworm-Bookworm* and
A Picnic with the Aunts; the absurdly lunatic *Johnnie Golightly and His Crocodile*; *Tiger-
Nanny*, the story of a tiger-cub who loves children – to look after, not to eat; *The Kidnapping
of My Grandmother*, a Parisian adventure with a Paul Berna flavour; and *Mog*, a zany story of
two eccentric old ladies.

In most of these stories the characters are presented with a straightforward simplicity
suited to younger children, but there are also a number of books for older readers, attempting
a greater complexity of plot and character. Among these are *Boy in a Barn*, an adventure with
a mountain peasant background similar to that of the earlier fantasies, but set in postwar
Europe; *The Noble Hawks*, an historical story of a 14th-century yeoman's son who longed to
be a falconer; *Castle Merlin*, a story set in the present day, but exploiting the current
popularity of Time fantasies; and *The Line*, an imaginative story of a magical modern
invention. In these stories there is still some stereotyping in the minor characters, and there
are some uncertainties in handling the more complex plots; but the main characters are seen
to develop in self-awareness and maturity, and there are witty and satirical undertones to the
writing which, while bearing affinity to the slyly wicked humour of some of the earlier
books, add a new dimension to this author's storytelling. For she is an inventive as well as
prolific writer, and in their different ways her books are well written, pleasantly intriguing,
and occasionally achieve a haunting power and a delightfully sharp and witty observation of
the foibles of mankind.

—Winifred Whitehead

WILSON, Barbara Ker. British. Born in Sunderland, County Durham, 24 September 1929. Educated at North London Collegiate School, 1938–48. Married Peter Richard Tahourdin in 1956; has two daughters. Assistant Editor, Oxford University Press, London, 1949–54; Children's Books Editor, John Lane, London, 1954–57; William Collins, London, 1957–62; Angus and Robertson, Sydney, 1965–73; Hodder and Stoughton, Sydney, 1973–76. Since 1976, Free-lance Consultant Editor. Agent: Curtis Brown Ltd., 575 Madison Avenue, New York, New York 10022, U.S.A. Address: 109 Darling Point Road, Darling Point, New South Wales 2027, Australia.

PUBLICATIONS FOR CHILDREN

Fiction

> *Path-Through-the-Woods*, illustrated by Charles Stewart. London, Constable, and New York, Criterion Books, 1958.
> *The Wonderful Cornet*, illustrated by Raymond Briggs. London, Hamish Hamilton, 1958.
> *The Lovely Summer*, illustrated by Marina Hoffer. London, Constable, and New York, Dodd Mead, 1960.
> *Last Year's Broken Toys*. London, Constable, 1962; as *In Love and War*, Cleveland, World, 1966.
> *Ann and Peter in Paris* [and *in London*], illustrated by Harry and Ilse Toothill. London, Muller, 2 vols., 1963–65.
> *A Story to Tell: Thirty Tales for Little Children*, illustrated by Sheila Sancha. London, J. Garnet Miller, 1964.
> *Beloved of the Gods*. London, Constable, 1965; as *In the Shadow of Vesuvius*, Cleveland, World, 1965.
> *A Family Likeness*, illustrated by Astra Lacis Dick. London, Constable, 1967; as *The Biscuit-Tin Family*, Cleveland, World, 1968.
> *Hiccups and Other Stories: Thirty Tales for Little Children*, illustrated by Richard Kennedy. London, J. Garnet Miller, 1971.

Other

> *Scottish Folk Tales and Legends*, illustrated by Joan Kiddell-Monroe. London, Oxford University Press, and New York, Walck, 1954.
> *Fairy Tales of Germany*, illustrated by Gertrude Mittelmann, [*Ireland, Mexico*, and *Persia*, all illustrated by G.W. Miller, *India*, illustrated by Rene Mackensie, *Russia*, illustrated by Jacqueline Athram, *France*, illustrated by William McLaren, *England*, illustrated by John S. Goodall]. London, Cassell, and New York, Dutton, 8 vols., 1959–61.
> *Look at Books*, illustrated by John Woodcock. London, Hamish Hamilton, 1960.
> *Legends of the Round Table*, illustrated by Marra Calati. London, Hamlyn, 1966.
> *Greek Fairy Tales*, illustrated by Harry Toothill. London, Muller, 1966; Chicago, Follett, 1968.
> *Animal Folk Tales*, illustrated by Mirko Hanák. London, Hamlyn, 1968; New York, Grosset and Dunlap, 1971.
> *Australia, Wonderland Down Under*. New York, Dodd Mead, 1969.
> *Tales Told to Kabbarli: Aboriginal Legends*, illustrated by Harold Thomas. Sydney and London, Angus and Robertson, and New York, Crown, 1972.
> *The Magic Fishbones*, illustrated by Suzanne Dolesch. London, Angus and Robertson, 1972.
> *The Magic Bird*, illustrated by Suzanne Dolesch. London, Angus and Robertson, 1973.

Editor, *The Second Young Eve*. London, Blackie, 1962.

Editor, *What A Girl* [and *Boy*] *Should Know about Sex*, by Bernhardt Gottlieb. London, Constable, 2 vols., 1962.

Editor, *Australian Kaleidoscope*, illustrated by Margery Gill. Sydney and London, Collins, 1968; New York, Meredith Press, 1969.

Editor, *A Handful of Ghosts* (anthology). London, Hodder and Stoughton, 1976.

Editor, *Alice's Adventures in Wonderland*, by Lewis Carroll, translated into Pitjantjatjara by Nancy Sheppard, illustrated by Byron Sewell. Adelaide, Adelaide University Press, 1976.

PUBLICATIONS FOR ADULTS

Other

Writing for Children. London, Boardman, 1960; New York, Watts, 1961.
Noel Streatfeild. London, Bodley Head, 1961; New York, Walck, 1964.

Barbara Ker Wilson comments:

Social history, with a special background interest in the historical position of women, seems, in retrospect, to have formed the springboard for my teenage-reader novels: *Path-Through-the-Woods*, *The Lovely Summer*, *Last Year's Broken Toys*, and *A Family Likeness*. My main aim, however, was and will for future work remain to tell a *story*. This enjoyment in story-telling extends, too, to collections of stories for very young children, and most of the tales in my two collections *A Story to Tell* and *Hiccups* are often broadcast and televised. My other very strong interest is in folklore where I feel the often artificial borderline between literature for the young and for the adult most satisfyingly disappears.

                                    *   *   *

Barbara Ker Wilson's background is part English, part Australian, and though most of the stories in *A Story to Tell* and *Hiccups* would be acceptable to the under-fives from either country, some depend on Australian setting. Some are short invented fairy tales, but most are designed to stimulate imaginative parents who make up stories for and about their own small children.

Ann and Peter in Paris and *Ann and Peter in London* are formula writing, but with enough plot to make the information palatable. Ann and Peter, like most natives, know less about London than the average visitor, an ingenious device which gives Peter the opportunity to read up the guide book before their journeys.

Path-Through-the-Woods is the story behind a patchwork quilt. In a series of pictures of the life of a Victorian family – unusual because the eldest sister breaks from convention and becomes a pioneer woman doctor – the middle-class atmosphere is well conveyed. Jemima's death coincides with the launching of the Great Eastern and generally facts are conveyed incidentally.

The Lovely Summer is really several summers, just before and during the First World War. The campaign for women's suffrage and implicitly the feminist movement is shown in the lives of three girls of different social classes. This is a convincing and readable book, with a fairly broad-minded approach to its theme – violence versus non-violence.

Probably the best book she will ever write, *Last Year's Broken Toys*, reflects the author's own childhood before and during the last war. In a sense the war is the "hero." There are dozens of characters but however brief the glimpses they are all real people. There is no straight plot, boy and girl friendships change, odd coincidences happen though the participants are not always aware of them. Some die, most survive. All the ends are tied up for the reader but not for the people involved – this is real life.

Beloved of the Gods is a competent and thoroughly researched novel about ancient Rome and the destruction of Pompeii, but there is perhaps too much concern with historical detail so that the characters only come alive occasionally.

A Family Likeness is an Australian story paralleling and contrasting the lives of the present-day girl and her mid-19th-century forbears. The switches are cleverly done, but one feels that the Victorian episodes were thought of first and that therefore the modern Debbie is less alive and less interesting. The history seems to intrude more than it did in *Last Year's Broken Toys* although there was so much more of it in the earlier book. Perhaps there is more need to "explain" things of a century ago, especially in Australia.

—Margaret M. Tye

WOJCIECHOWSKA, Maia (Teresa). American. Born in Warsaw, Poland, 7 August 1927; emigrated to the United States in 1942; naturalized citizen, 1950. Educated at Sacred Heart Academy, Los Angeles; Immaculate Heart College, Hollywood, 1945–46. Married Selden Rodman in 1950 (divorced, 1957); Richard Larkin, 1972; has two daughters. Translator, Radio Free Europe, New York, 1949–51; worked for William Burns Detective Agency, 1951–69; Assistant Editor, Retail Wholesale and Department Store Union *Record*, New York, 1953–55; copy girl, *Newsweek* magazine, New York, 1953–55; Assistant Editor, *American Hairdresser* magazine, New York, 1955–57; agent and editor, Kurt Hellmer Literary Agency, New York, 1958–61; Publicity Manager, Hawthorn Books, New York, 1961–65. Since 1949, professional tennis instructor. Recipient: American Library Association Newbery Medal, 1965. Agent: Scott Meredith Literary Agency Inc., 845 Third Avenue, New York, New York 10022. Address: 1776 Fort Union Drive, Santa Fe, New Mexico 87501, U.S.A.

PUBLICATIONS FOR CHILDREN

Fiction

> *Market Day for Ti André*, illustrated by Wilson Bigaud. New York, Viking Press, 1952.
> *Shadow of a Bull*, illustrated by Alvin Smith. New York, Atheneum, and London, Hamish Hamilton, 1964.
> *A Kingdom in a Horse*. New York, Harper, 1965.
> *The Hollywood Kid*. New York and London, Harper, 1966.
> *A Single Light*. New York, Harper, 1968.
> *Tuned Out*. New York, Harper, 1968.
> *Hey, What's Wrong with This One?*, illustrated by Joan Sandin. New York, Harper, 1969.
> *Don't Play Dead Before You Have To*. New York, Harper, 1970.
> *The Rotten Years*. New York, Doubleday, 1971.
> *The Life and Death of a Brave Bull*, illustrated by John Groth. New York, Harcourt Brace, 1972.
> *Through the Broken Mirror with Alice*. New York, Harcourt Brace, 1972.

Other

> *Odyssey of Courage: The Story of Alvar Núñez Cabeza de Vaca*, illustrated by Alvin Smith. New York, Atheneum, 1965; London, Burns and Oates, 1967.

Till the Break of Day.   New York, Harcourt Brace, 1972.
Winter Tales from Poland, illustrated by Laszlo Kubinyi.   New York, Doubleday, 1973.

PUBLICATIONS FOR ADULTS

Play

All at Sea, adaptation of a work by Slawomir Mrozek (produced New York, 1968).

Other

The International Loved Look.   New York, American Hairdresser, 1964.

Translator, *The Bridge to the Other Side*, by Monika Kotowska.   New York, Doubleday, 1970.

Manuscript Collection: Kerlan Collection, University of Minnesota, Minneapolis.

Maia Wojciechowska comments:
In my Newbery acceptance speech I wrote, "When you know what life has to sell, for how much, and what it can give away free, you will not live in darkness. I hope that in my books you'll find your light, and that by this light you may cross from one shore of love to another, from your childhood into your adulthood. I hope that some of the light will come from my books and that, because of this light, life will lose its power to frighten you." I am most concerned about children and how little they know of their inner resources. I believe that in writing for the young an author has an obligation to "enlighten" as well as entertain. I deplore the insipid books about rodents and other four-legged creatures that are the fare for the very young – they grow up thinking human beings less interesting than animals. I deplore the shoddiness of the books for older kids and the waste of time and energy that goes into producing them.

I keep hoping that Man (collectively, all of us) is coming into a Messianic age where "this is the earthly goal of man, to evolve his intellectual powers to their fullest, to arrive at the maximum of consciousness, to open the eyes of his understanding upon all things so that upon the tablet of his soul the order of the whole universe may be enrolled," as Aquinas said, will become our imperative. I seem incurably, romantically in love with the human potential, with that part of us that links us to our maker, that part that can be found in the best of literature and in the best moments of our own lives, that mysterious drive within us that reaches ever upwards. What drives me bananas is when this drive is curtailed or stopped by petty concerns, shortening of sights, wrong priorities, materialistic pursuits. I am a lay preacher in whatever writing I do, preaching the possibility of rising above our mere survival into that other plane, spiritual, if you wish, where the mind directs, unfailingly, the heart.

*   *   *

Courage. That is what the people who inhabit the world of Maia Wojciechowska must possess if they are to be victorious over the adversity which threatens to overwhelm them. And love, that is what everyone needs from someone else – or at least the memory of that love as in the surrealistic adventure *Through the Broken Mirror with Alice*. To read most of the novels of Wojciechowska is to feel the *Weltschmerz* which the author reveals when she writes of the hurt, anxiety, and even danger felt by those who inhabit her novels. Her characters are middle-class, poor, rich, but they all suffer at the hands of fate, their parents, society. There is one trait they all exhibit – a certain degree of courage with which to conquer fear and face their hardships. Whether it is the 12-year-old foster-child, Alice, existing in one home after another and preyed upon by the local junkie; 16-year-old Jim of *Tuned Out*, trying desperately to help his older brother escape from dependence on LSD; or lonely, frustrated Bryan in *The Hollywood Kid* – Wojciechowska wants them all "on speaking terms with life ...."

The best way to understand Wojciechowska's philosophy is to read *The Rotten Years* (that impossible time between 12 and 15). In the guise of Elsie Jones, a renegade junior high school teacher, the author elaborates on her distrust of the educational system, and the total lack of respect which adults often display toward adolescents. It is a powerful piece of writing which is a combination of fiction and textbook. Young people reading it during their own "rotten years" will find an empathetic ally.

The misanthropy of ignorant villagers and the goodness of a young mute girl are starkly contrasted in *A Single Light*. This work has a special, haunting quality about it, a well-developed religious theme centering on the harsh life of an unwanted, unloved child.

The big disappointment in Wojciechowska's writing is *A Kingdom in a Horse*, which is very difficult to accept as a serious piece of literature. Old people playing games on horseback, secret midnight rides, a teen-age runaway, and a mystical experience – they are all there, unjelled. Contrarily, *Don't Play Dead Before You Have To* contains an odd mixture which fits together cohesively. Charlie is only 5 when Byron first babysits for him. Although the young child doesn't speak directly to the reader throughout the entire novel, his tragedy is deeply felt. Charlie and the peripheral characters are all understood through their impact on Byron. It is an unusual story of an acutely perceptive teen-age boy who reaches out to others, and of his relationship to a younger boy whom he grows to love.

In *Shadow of a Bull*, a beautiful story, the author describes the difficulties which the son of a great bullfighter faces. It takes great courage for Manolo to turn his back on what society expects of him as he searches for his place in the world – outside the bullring. Love and courage. Wojciechowska tells us all about them.

—Vivian J. Scheinmann

WOOD, David. British. Born in Sutton, Surrey, 21 February 1944. Educated at Chichester High School for Boys, 1957–63; Worcester College, Oxford, 1963–66, B.A. (honours) in English. Married Sheila Ruskin in 1966 (marriage dissolved); Jacqueline Stanbury, 1975, one daughter. Agent: Margaret Ramsay Ltd., 14a Goodwin's Court, London WC2N 4LL, England.

Publications for Children

Plays

    The Tinder Box, adaptation of a story by Hans Christian Andersen (produced Worcester, 1967).
    The Owl and the Pussycat Went to See ..., with Sheila Ruskin, music and lyrics by Wood, adaptation of works by Edward Lear (produced Worcester, 1968; London, 1969). London, French, 1970.
    Larry the Lamb in Toytown, with Sheila Ruskin, music and lyrics by Wood, adaptation of stories by S.G. Hulme Beaman (produced Worcester, 1969; London, 1973). London, French, 1977.
    The Plotters of Cabbage Patch Corner, music and lyrics by Wood (produced Worcester, 1970; London, 1971). London, French, 1972.
    Flibberty and the Penguin, music and lyrics by Wood (produced Worcester, 1971). London, French, 1974.

The Papertown Paperchase, music and lyrics by Wood (produced Worcester, 1972;
   London, 1973). London, French, 1976.
Hijack over Hygenia, music and lyrics by Wood (produced Worcester, 1973). London,
   French, 1974.
Old Mother Hubbard, music and lyrics by Wood (produced Hornchurch, Essex,
   1975). London, French, 1976.
Old Father Time, music and lyrics by Wood (produced Hornchurch, Essex,
   1976). London, French, 1977.
The Gingerbread Man, music and lyrics by Wood (produced Basildon, Essex,
   1976). London, French, 1977.

Screenplay: *Swallows and Amazons*, 1974.

Television Plays: *Playaway* series, 1973–77.

<h2>Publications for Adults</h2>

Plays

Hang Down Your Head and Die, with David Wright (produced Oxford, London, and
   New York, 1964).
Sketches, with John Gould, in *Four Degrees Over* (produced Edinburgh and London,
   1966).
A Present from the Corporation (lyrics only; produced Worcester, 1966).
A Life in Bedrooms, with David Wright (produced Edinburgh, 1967; as *The Stiffkey
   Scandals of 1932*, produced London, 1968).
And Was Jerusalem, with Mike Sadler and John Gould (produced Oxford, 1967;
   London, 1968).
Three to One On, with John Gould (produced Edinburgh, 1968).
Postscripts, with John Gould (produced London, 1969).
Down Upper Street, with John Gould (produced London, 1971).
Just the Ticket, with John Gould (produced Leatherhead, Surrey, 1973).
Rock Nativity, music by Tony Hatch and Jackie Trent, lyrics by Wood (produced
   Newcastle upon Tyne, 1974; as *A New Tomorrow*, produced Wimbledon,
   1976). London, Weinberger, 1977.
Maudie, with Iwan Williams (produced Leatherhead, Surrey, 1974).
Think of a Number, with John Gould (produced Peterborough, 1975).
Chi-Chestnuts, with Bernard Price and Julian Sluggett (produced Chichester, 1975).
More Chi-Chestnuts, with Bernard Price and Julian Sluggett (produced Chichester,
   1976).
Tickle (produced Norwich and London, 1977).

Theatrical Activities:

Actor: **Plays** – in *Hang Down Your Head and Die*, Oxford and London, 1964; Geoff Manham
in *A Spring Song* by Ray Mathew, Edinburgh and London, 1964; Wagner in *Dr. Faustus* by
Christopher Marlowe, Oxford, 1966; in Worcester, Watford, Edinburgh, Windsor, and
Salisbury repertory companies, 1966–69; Roger in *After Haggerty* by David Mercer, London,
1970, 1971; The Son in *A Voyage round My Father* by John Mortimer, London, 1970,
Toronto, 1972; James in *Me Times Me*, toured 1971; Frank in *Mrs. Warren's Profession* by
G.B. Shaw, Leatherhead, Surrey, 1972; *Just the Ticket* (revue), Leatherhead, Surrey, 1972;
Constant in *The Provok'd Wife* by Vanbrugh, London, 1973; Bingo Little in *Jeeves* by Alan
Ayckbourn, London, 1975; *Three to One On* (revue), Peterborough, 1975. **Films** – *If ...*,
1968; *Aces High*, 1975. **Television** – *Mad Jack*, *Fathers and Sons*, *The Vamp*, and other plays,
since 1964.

David Wood comments:

Children's Theatre in Great Britain has for too long been regarded within and without the profession as second or even third division theatre. I hope I may be making a small contribution towards its elevation to a higher division! After all, if live theatre is to survive it is up to those of us who work in it to interest our *potential* audiences as early as possible. I try to combine a strong story-line with hummable songs and imaginative characters. I try never to patronize the children and never to "play to the adults." Although fantasy often plays a strong part, I hope the plays have enough substance to evoke discussion and a continuation of the experience after the curtain has fallen. And I hope they make people laugh too.

                                        *   *   *

In 1968, David Wood came to work at the Swan Theatre, Worcester as a member of the permanent company and during his first year with the company a musical of his was performed with some success. Subsequent to this, the Theatre Director, John Hole, invited David to write the Christmas show and since that time, David Wood has written 10 major shows for children which have, in many respects, altered the mode of popular entertainment for children in the theatre. In the last few years, in fact, David has become a spokesman for children's theatre in this country and a one-man lobby for a national touring children's theatre to perform large scale works especially for children.

His musical plays originally written for Christmas time have rigidly turned aside from those elements in pantomime which exist to attract adults only, but he has used the elements of pantomime extensively where they work well for children. The prime motive of all his writing has been the provision of a strong story line to which children and his audience can become committed and the story has been fleshed out with genuine character writing, and the humour that stems from such characters, and with numbers which, rather than hold up the action, make the story progress.

His plays have been performed all over the world and by repertory theatres and amateur societies throughout the length of the United Kingdom.

—John Hole

————————————

WOOD, Kerry.   Pseudonym for Edgar Allardyce Wood.   Canadian.   Born in New York, New York, United States, 2 June 1907; moved to Canada in 1909. Educated at Calgary Elementary School, 1914–1918, and elementary and high schools, Red Deer, Alberta, 1918–24. Married Marjorie Marshall in 1936; has two daughters and one son. Full time Freelance Writer and Broadcaster. Correspondent and Columnist for newspapers including Edmonton *Bulletin*, Edmonton *Journal*, Calgary *Herald*, and Calgary *Albertan*, 1926–73. Made archery tackle, 1937–44. Member of the Board, Alberta Natural History Society, 1936–64. Since 1924, Federal Migratory Bird Officer. Recipient: Ewart Foundation grant, 1954, 1957; Governor-General's Award, 1956, 1958; Canada Council grant, 1960; Vicky Metcalf Award, 1963; Alberta Historical Society award, 1964. LL.D.: University of Alberta, Edmonton, 1969. Address: Site 3, Rural Route 2, Red Deer, Alberta T4N 5E2, Canada.

PUBLICATIONS FOR CHILDREN

Fiction

   Cowboy Yarns for Young Folk.   Toronto, Copp Clark, 1951.
   Wild Winter, illustrated by Victor Mays.   Boston, Houghton Mifflin, 1954.

Great Horned MacOwl.   Red Deer, Alberta, Kerry Wood, 1962.
The Boy and the Buffalo, illustrated by Audrey Teather.   Toronto and London,
   Macmillan, and New York, St. Martin's Press, 1963.
Mickey the Beaver and Other Stories.   Toronto, Macmillan, 1964.
Samson's Long Ride, illustrated by Audrey Teather.   Toronto, Collins, 1968.

Other

The Map-Maker: The Story of David Thompson, illustrated by William
   Wheeler.   Toronto, Macmillan, 1955.
The Great Chief: Maskepetoon, Warrior of the Crees, illustrated by John Hall.   Toronto,
   Macmillan, 1957; New York, St. Martin's Press, and London, Macmillan, 1958.
The Queen's Cowboy: Colonel Macleod of the Mounties, illustrated by Joseph
   Rosenthal.   Toronto and London, Macmillan, 1960.
Bessie, The Coo, illustrated by Marjorie Wood.   Red Deer, Alberta, Kerry Wood, 1975.

PUBLICATIONS FOR ADULTS

Other

The Magpie Menace.   Red Deer, Alberta, Kerry Wood, 1936.
*Robbing the Roost: The Marquis of Roostburg Rules Governing the Ancient and
   Dishonourable Sport.*   Red Deer, Alberta, Kerry Wood, 1938.
I'm a Gaggle Man, Myself.   Red Deer, Alberta, Kerry Wood, 1940.
Three Mile Bend.   Toronto, Ryerson Press, 1945.
Birds and Animals in the Rockies.   Saskatoon, Larson, 1947.
A Nature Guide for Farmers.   Saskatoon, Larson, 1947.
The Sanctuary.   Red Deer, Alberta, Kerry Wood, 1952.
A Letter from Alberta.   Red Deer, Alberta, Kerry Wood, 1954.
A Letter from Calgary.   Red Deer, Alberta, Kerry Wood, 1954.
Willowdale.   Toronto, McClelland and Stewart, and London, Barker, 1956.
A Lifetime of Service: George Moon.   Red Deer, Alberta, Kerry Wood, 1966.
A Corner of Canada: A Personalized History of the Red Deer River Country.   Red Deer,
   Alberta, Kerry Wood, 1966.
A Time for Fun.   Red Deer, Alberta, Kerry Wood, 1967.
The Medicine Man.   Red Deer, Alberta, Kerry Wood, 1968.
The Creek.   Red Deer, Alberta, Kerry Wood, 1970.
The Icelandic-Canadian Poet Stephan G. Stephansson: A Tribute.   Red Deer, Alberta,
   Kerry Wood, 1974.
Red Deer, A Love Story.   Red Deer, Alberta, Kerry Wood, 1975.

Kerry Wood comments:
   My love of nature developed in early childhood, and from its study came an interest in the
Indians and their history. My scholarly father encouraged me to read widely and made sure
that I understood what I read. From him, and the helpfulness of librarians, came my
determination to write. I have always felt that writing for children is an important part of my
work.
   A children's book should be sincere and accurate; it should be a story of achievement,
though sadness is also appropriate. It should have natural characters, some humour, be of
interest to both children and adults, and reveal enduring values. Nonsense and fantasy share
about one-third portion of importance in children's literature, but sarcasm and satire should
never be used. Children's books should instruct, entertain, and inspire in varying degrees,
according to the story.

                              *   *   *

Kerry Wood is the prototype of the Canadian regional writer. He has lived all of his life in Red Deer, Alberta, and writes of that province with insight and love. His children's books elaborate the lives of its people – Indians, explorers, early and modern settlers. The flora and fauna are particular interests of this ardent conservationist.

Two of Wood's fictional biographies have won the Governor-General's Medal: *The Map-Maker: The Story of David Thompson* and *The Great Chief: Maskepetoon, Warrior of the Crees*. These and *The Queen's Cowboy: Colonel Macleod of the Mounties* add three colourful chapters to the Great Stories of Canada, a series of readable histories for 8-12-year-old children. Wood's appreciation of these heroes is a measure of his own human dimensions. They emerge as men of integrity, industry, and compassion. He writes straightforward chronological narratives that span the lifetime of each hero. They were people whose fate included the assumption of leadership, and Wood highlights their accomplishments dramatically. Maskepetoon's story is recorded in a lyrical style that recalls the best aspects of native life and lore, and serves children well.

Stories for very young readers ought to be works of creative literature as well as easy to read. Wood follows this principle in *The Boy and the Buffalo* and *Samson's Long Ride*, both written with immature sensibilities in mind. Both are based on real events that reveal young heroes in the making. O-Shees lived a year with a buffalo herd, adopted by two lactating mares left calfless, and survived to join his Cree family again. Ten-year-old Samson leaves mission school and travels 400 miles to find his beloved family in the Alberta mountains. Although simple in plot and style, the stories explore the human dilemma with understanding and respect for children's developing humanity. Many of Wood's 6000 short stories were written for children. Some of them were collected in *Mickey the Beaver* and *Cowboy Yarns for Young Folk*, short dramatic incidents written sympathetically and plainly.

The highlight of Wood's work for children is *Wild Winter*, a novel based on his own experiences. From the age of 16 he spent two winters alone in the Alberta wilds to prove his independence. He writes spare, moving prose about a young man's search for maturity. His stark experiences with the elements and the privations he suffered afford an example for young people finding their way.

—Irma McDonough

WOOD, Lorna. British. Born in Pex Hill, Lancashire 16 June 1913. Educated privately, and at Convent of Notre Dame, Mount Pleasant, Liverpool. Married J. Swire (divorced); has one daughter and one son. Worked for BBC Monitoring Service, London, 1942–75: Head, Central African Unit, 1974. Address: c/o Williams and Glyn's Bank Ltd., Market Square, Reading, Berkshire, England.

PUBLICATIONS FOR CHILDREN

Fiction

> *The Smiling Rabbit and Other Stories*, illustrated by Ernest Aris.   London, Harrap, 1939.
> *The Travelling Tree and Other Stories*, illustrated by Ernest Aris.   London, Harrap, 1943.
> *Ameliaranne Goes Digging*, illustrated by Susan Pearse.   London, Harrap, 1948.
> *The Finicky Mouse and Other Stories*, illustrated by R.S. Sherwood.   London, Arnold, 1949.
> *The Handkerchief Man*, illustrated by C. Instrell.   London, Arnold, 1951.

The People in the Garden, illustrated by Joan Kiddell-Monroe.   London, Dent, 1954.
Rescue by Broomstick, illustrated by Joan Kiddell-Monroe.   London, Dent, 1954.
The Hag Calls for Help, illustrated by Joan Kiddell-Monroe.   London, Dent, 1957.
Holiday on Hot Bricks, illustrated by Sheila Rose.   London, Dent, 1958.
Seven-League Ballet Shoes, illustrated by Joan Kiddell-Monroe.   London, Dent, 1959.
Climb by Candlelight, illustrated by Sheila Rose.   London, Dent, 1959.
Hags on Holiday, illustrated by Joan Kiddell-Monroe.   London, Dent, 1960.
The Golden-Haired Family, illustrated by Wendy Marchant.   London, Dent, 1961.
Hag in the Castle, illustrated by Joan Kiddell-Monroe.   London, Dent, 1962.
Hags by Starlight, illustrated by Joan Kiddell-Monroe.   London, Dent, 1970.
The Dogs of Pangers, illustrated by A.R. Whitear.   London, Dent, 1970.
Pangers Pup, illustrated by A.R. Whitear.   London, Dent, 1972.

Other

The Brave Adventures of a Shoemaker's Boy, from translation by Theresa Mravintz and
   Branko Brusar of work by Ivana Brlic-Mazuranic, illustrated by Robert
   Bartelt.   London, Dent, 1971.

Editor, *Here I Was a Child* (anthology), illustrated by Rosemary Hird.   London,
   Arnold, 4 vols., 1952.

PUBLICATIONS FOR ADULTS

Novels

The Crumb-Snatchers.   London, Cape, 1933.
Gilded Sprays.   London, Long, 1935.
The Hopeful Travellers.   London, Long, 1936.

*   *   *

Lorna Wood's writing career began very early; she was still in her teens when her first
book appeared, the adult novel called *The Crumb-Snatchers*, about a mother and daughter
who live on their wits. This novel and the two that followed were romantic comedies, very
amusing and well observed. Her heroines show a spirited attitude towards life's ups and
downs.

Lorna Wood's first children's stories appeared just as the Second World War began. By
this time she had two children herself. She loves writing and has never let domesticity or
anything else stop her, but it was easier, of course, to write short tales than to concentrate on
full-length novels. *The Smiling Rabbit and Other Stories* is a delightful collection, varied and
rich in fantastical invention. The stories are well constructed, with a twist at the end. There
were better outlets then for short stories (for whatever age); writers who grew up in the
1920's and 1930's had a highly professional respect for the genre.

The Hag Dowsabel, Lorna Wood's best-known creation, made her first appearance in this
collection, giving a wish at a prince's christening. She also turned up in two of the stories in
the next collection, *The Travelling Tree*, and it was here too that the Hag's long-suffering cat,
Sootylegs, made his debut. Later, she wrote a series of 6 full-length children's books about the
Hag, who now resided at the bottom of the Lindleys' garden. Cleverly the author creates
what Tolkien has called a Secondary World, a fantasy utterly consistent within itself. The
Lindley parents never see the Hag or give their full attention, let alone credence, to the
strange goings-on the four children get happily involved in with their eccentric friend. The
Hag appeals to one's love of exaggeration and the grotesque. She is uninhibitedly self-centred
but she will champion anyone who is put upon for grownup or other inadequate reasons. She
has no use for money and doesn't approve of the children wanting the thousand pound

reward offered by the *Daily Speed* (in *Hags by Starlight*) for finding the Alsotanian ambassador, but when the newspaper lord goes back on his offer she turns him into a bat. She does everything with panache.

The secondary characters are original and zestful too, the Hag's witch friends, for instance, and, in *Seven-League Ballet Shoes*, the boy giant Flounderbore. *The Hag Calls for Help* is particularly rich in colourful characters. There are the Boggarts, father and daughter, Rascallito the Rook, a sorry failure of an outlaw, Verdigris the Vulture who's a crook, and Uncle Harold the bird-watcher, shrunk by magic to the size of a small rook but untroubled as only an Englishman brought up on *Alice* could be.

During the same period as the Hag books Lorna Wood wrote four adventure stories. Then in 1970 came *The Dogs of Pangers*, followed by *Pangers Pup*. I think these two may prove to wear the best of all her stories. In creating these canine characters of the Pangers Dogs' Club she has indulged her fondness for dogs and her marvellous sense of fun; A.R. Whitear, the illustrator, has responded in the same spirit. The hero of *The Dogs of Pangers* is Bertram the Boxer, who "had definitely been behind the door when brains were given out." Mum and Pop Denholm-Stringfellow who are his family love him dearly; when they hear that the new occupant of the River House is a dog psychologist they decide to send Bertram to him to improve his IQ, though of course, as Mum says, "It will cost a bomb ...." Recounting these words at the Club, Bertram causes a sensation. Pedro, the elderly spaniel president growled for order. " 'Dogs of Pangers! The important thing is to find out why Mr. – Pegleg, did you say? – *wants* a bomb. To me it sounds as though he is up to no good. British dogs never shall be slaves and since you, Bertram, are going to stay with him, you will be in the best position to find out.' " And they're off.

Compton Mackenzie said of Lorna Wood's first novel: "If she can keep her zest for writing fresh, and temper it with life's experience, Miss Lorna Wood is secure of a wide popularity." Despite having had a sometimes embarrassing share of "life's experience," her zest for writing is indeed as fresh as ever. She is busy writing magazine stories and poems for the adult market and has certainly earned her popularity among bright young readers who revel in her rare brand of humour and invention.

—Gwen Marsh

WRIGHTSON, (Alice) Patricia. Australian. Born in Lismore, New South Wales, 21 June 1921. Educated at State Correspondence School; St. Catherine's College, Stanthorpe, Queensland. Married in 1943 (divorced, 1953); has one daughter and one son. Secretary and Administrator, Bonalbo District Hospital, 1946–60, and Sydney District Nursing Association, 1960–64; Assistant Editor, 1964–70, and Editor, 1970–75, *School Magazine*, Sydney. Recipient: Australian Children's Book Award, 1956; *Book World* Festival award, 1968; Australian Children's Book Council Book of the Year Award, 1974. Address: 1 Monteith Street, Turramurra, New South Wales 2074, Australia.

PUBLICATIONS FOR CHILDREN

Fiction

The Crooked Snake, illustrated by Margaret Horder. Sydney and London, Angus and Robertson, 1955.
The Bunyip Hole, illustrated by Margaret Horder. Sydney and London, Angus and Robertson, 1958.

The Rocks of Honey, illustrated by Margaret Horder.   Sydney, Angus and Robertson,
   1960; London, Angus and Robertson, 1961.
The Feather Star, illustrated by Noela Young.   London, Hutchinson, 1962; New York,
   Harcourt Brace, 1963.
Down to Earth, illustrated by Margaret Horder.   New York, Harcourt Brace, and
   London, Hutchinson, 1965.
I Own the Racecourse!, illustrated by Margaret Horder.   London, Hutchinson, 1968; as
   A Racecourse for Andy, New York, Harcourt Brace, 1968.
An Older Kind of Magic, illustrated by Noela Young.   London, Hutchinson, and New
   York, Harcourt Brace, 1972.
The Nargun and the Stars.   London, Hutchinson, 1973; New York, Atheneum, 1974.
The Ice Is Coming.   New York, Atheneum, and London, Hutchinson, 1977.

Editor, *Beneath the Sun: An Australian Collection for Children*.   Sydney, Collins, 1972;
   London, Collins, 1973.
Editor, *Emu Stew* (anthology).   London, Penguin, 1977.

Patricia Wrightson comments:
My books represent a continuous process of learning to write, but I think critical essays
have been right in discerning that the books have developed towards exploring the "other"
point of view; and that this has inevitably led, as my son affirms, to fantasy as the prime
medium for the exploration. I have at present two preoccupations: this richness of fantasy as
a means; and the use of Aboriginal folk-spirits (fairies and monsters) to enrich Australia's
contemporary fantasy.

                                        *   *   *

Dorothy Sayers once classified poets as those who make a statement and those who invite
their readers to participate with them in a search. Patricia Wrightson is one of the latter, and
her books, like poetry, can be read at different levels. Like a poet she uses symbols – an axe, a
feather-star, a racecourse, or a comet – as keys to the inner question. While on one level she is
telling a lively story with humour about a group of children in some interesting situation, she
is at a deeper level exploring the relationship of our world in the cosmos: "He felt the earth
rolling on its way through the sky, and rocks and trees clinging to it, and seas and the strands
of rivers pressed to it, and flying birds caught in its net of air." She looks at the different time
levels of Australia, the old land now violated by machinery, whose rhythms are not its own,
at the old legendary creatures, the aboriginal tribes, and the final imposition of a new alien
culture whose "false city magic" hides the light of the stars. She has a strong feeling for the
land, particularly for rock, "the living rock" where petrification is only an abeyance of life.
This may be partly aboriginal animism or simply recognition that rock is the common
element between earth and stars. Certainly it must be treated cautiously, "for stone is stone
and men whose drills break into living stone should take care, they may find what they do not
expect."
   Concern for the land naturally leads to a strong feeling for conservation from her first book
onwards and it is particularly appropriate for an Australian to explore the concept of
"ownership" because traditionally aborigines thought that land could not be owned. City-
bred Simon in *The Nargun and the Stars* is outraged by Charlie Water's message to the
Potkoorok (a water creature):

      "Say Charlie Waters sent me. He used to be a boy in this place but now he's
   the man in charge. He wants to talk to you."
      "But you're not the man in charge! You OWN it!"
      "Do I? For sixty years or so maybe, but how long do you think the Potkoorok's
   owned it?"

Ownership is discussed in *The Rocks of Honey*, but it is central to *I Own the Racecourse*, one of the most delightfully original stories ever written. Andy, a simple-minded boy, never understands the "pretend" game of "monopoly" played by his friends who "buy" and "sell" Sydney landmarks, so when an old tramp offers to "sell" him Beecham Park Racecourse he "buys" it for $3. His friends are divided between those who feel that Andy must be made to see that he does not "own" the racecourse and those who prefer to leave him with his illusions – after all, "you can own the horses but you can't own the race." Andy, who cares as much for weeds and mongrels as for flowers and thoroughbreds, causes everyone to re-think their values not only about ownership but about reality: "Real?" said Mike, "What's real? The trainers speak to him in the street and let him lead their dogs and call him 'The Owner.' That's real isn't it?"

The question of what is "real" is also explored in her previous book *Down to Earth*, in which Martin, a spaceman visiting Sydney, explains that there can be no certainty about what we see: "When I'm awake you see me in your usual way, as I've explained, because your mind responds to the stimulus of another intelligence and makes the only sort of picture it can." Similarly we cannot be sure what we hear: "There is the problem of communication. How can you and I speak to each other about anything that lies outside our own minds? We borrow from each other the words that we use, but what do the words mean?"

The great value of *Down to Earth* is that it gives us a fresh humorous look at ourselves, but both here and in *I Own the Racecourse* Patricia Wrightson brings Sydney vividly to life. Her children love the changing moods of the city, the lure of evening lights, the jostling crowds that can contain both the ordinary and eccentric, and the quiet early-morning streets. This joyous celebration of the city palls somewhat in *An Older Kind of Magic*. Here it is the "lovely but terrible city" in which commerce gets out of hand when business tycoon Sir Mortimer Wyvern tries to build a car-park in the Botanical Gardens. Yet even as its values are questioned, Selina – the heroine – is still fascinated by its magic. It is, however, a false magic of self-interested advertising agents contrasted with the old magic of a comet which appears only once every thousand years.

In *An Older Kind of Magic* and *The Nargun and the Stars* Patricia Wrightson explores the possibilities of indigenous fantasy and rejects European folklore in favour of legendary aboriginal creatures of water, rock, and tree. They are very different from Northern "little people" in their neutrality; they do not side with good or evil – "Good," asked the Potkoorok, "What is good?" – nor do they manipulate natural laws; they can only work within them. The Nargun, for instance, is both villain and hero. The slow progress of this strange stone creature to Wongadilla is set against the sudden displacement of Simon, who went there to live with cousins when his parents were killed. Simon, however, is accepted by the old creatures of Wongadilla, but the Nargun remains a hostile stranger. Yet, although Simon is instrumental in incarcerating it under the mountain, he feels pity for the Nargun. In the end, on a cosmic scale, the Nargun will win. A stone can wait "for a mountain to crumble or a river to break through," while Simon, for all his youth and vitality, will be like his name carved in fading lichen, "only a whisper in the dark."

—Betty Gilderdale

WYMARK, Olwen. American. Widow of the actor Patrick Wymark. Writer-in-Residence, Unicorn Theatre for Young People, London, 1974–75. Currently, Writer-in-Residence, Kingston Polytechnic, Surrey. Recipient: Zagreb Drama Festival Prize, 1967. Agent: Felix De Wolfe and Associates, 1 Robert Street, Adelphi, London WC2N 6BH, England.

PUBLICATIONS FOR CHILDREN

Plays

> *No Talking* (produced London, 1970).
> *Daniel's Epic*, with Daniel Henry (produced London, 1972).
> *Chinigchinich* (produced London, 1973).
> *The Bolting Sisters* (produced London, 1974).
> *Southwark Originals* (collaborative work; produced London, 1975).
> *Starters* (collaborative work; includes *The Giant and the Dancing Fairies, The Time Loop, The Spellbound Jellybaby, The Robbing of Elvis Parsley, I Spy*) (produced London, 1975; Wausau, Wisconsin, 1976).
> *Three For All* (collaborative work; includes *Box Play, Family Business, Extended Play*) (produced London, 1976).

PUBLICATIONS FOR ADULTS

Plays

> *Lunchtime Concert* (produced Glasgow, 1966)   Published in *The Best Short Plays 1975*, edited by Stanley Richards, Radnor, Pennsylvania, Chilton, 1975.
> *Triple Image* (includes *Coda, Lunchtime Concert, The Inhabitants*) (produced Glasgow, and New York, 1967; *The Inhabitants* produced London, 1974).   Published as *Three Plays*, London, Calder and Boyars, 1967.
> *The Gymnasium* (produced Edinburgh, 1967; London, 1971).   Included in *The Gymnasium and Other Plays*, 1972.
> *The Technicians* (produced Leicester, 1969; London, 1971).   Included in *The Gymnasium and Other Plays*, 1972.
> *Stay Where You Are* (produced Edinburgh, 1969, London, 1973).   Included in *The Gymnasium and Other Plays*, 1972; in *The Best Short Plays 1972*, edited by Stanley Richards, Philadelphia, Chilton, 1972.
> *Neither Here Nor There* (produced London, 1971).   Included in *The Gymnasium and Other Plays*, 1972.
> *Speak Now* (produced Edinburgh, 1971; revised version, produced Leicester, 1975).
> *The Committee* (produced London, 1971).
> *Jack the Giant Killer* (produced Sheffield, 1972).   Included in *The Gymnasium and Other Plays*, 1972.
> *The Gymnasium and Other Plays* (includes *The Technicians, Stay Where You Are, Jack the Giant Killer, Neither Here Nor There*).   London, Calder and Boyars, 1972.
> *Watch the Woman*, with Brian Phelan (produced London, 1973).
> *The Twenty-Second Day* (broadcast, 1975; revised version produced London, 1975).
> *We Three*, and *After Nature, Art* (produced London, 1977).   Published in *Play Ten*, edited by Robin Rook, London, Arnold, 1977.
> *Find Me* (produced Kingston, Surrey, 1977).

> Radio Plays: *The Ransom*, 1957; *That Unexpected Country*, 1957; *California Here We Come*, 1958; *Stay Where You Are*, 1969; *The Twenty-Second Day*, 1975; *You Come Too*, 1977.

> Television Plays: *Mrs. Moresby's Scrapbook*, 1973; *Vermin*, 1974; *Marathon*, 1975; *Mother Love*, 1975; *Dead Drunk*, 1975.

Olwen Wymark comments:
    In 1966 I was commissioned by the late Caryl Jenner, founder of The Unicorn Theatre, to

write my first children's play *No Talking*. I'd had no experience of plays specially written for children and had no idea if you did it differently; I think you don't. Under the tireless protective encouragement from Script Editor and Playwright/Actor Christopher Guinnee I managed to finish this play in about eleven months. *Chinigchinich* I wrote in a day to enter in a contest with *No Talking* (both one-acters) which I didn't win. In 1974 Chattie Salaman and Frank Whitton of The Common Stock Company asked me to work with them and a horde of kids (aged two to fifteen) in Whitechapel on a kid's play which was to be evolved in collaboration. It was absolute agony and the most exciting time I'd had in the theatre for years. The result was *Daniel's Epic*, an hour long piece. My collaborator was a 9-year-old genius called Daniel Henry.

In 1974 and 1975 at The Unicorn Theatre I had another go at collaborating with children in playwriting. The first time was with 104 kids from four Southwark schools. Each class wrote a play with me which they performed themselves with me doing what might have been called directing but was more like sustained frenzy. We called the show *Southwark Originals* and we all had a very good time. Though tiring. The 1975 project was *Starters* in which I collaborated with eight kids between six and nine on five plays which were then performed at the Unicorn by professional actors and in 1976 in Wisconsin by children. In 1976 I worked with actress-director Janet Henfrey, Lucy Parker and director Greville Hallam with a kids workshop that was run by the Sidney Webb Teacher Training College in London and with this group of forty kids we wrote together *Three For All* (which was performed by children).

Writing is, as has been said by all writers I think, a very isolated and rather lonely profession. Doom and self-hatred and extreme paranoia seem to be crucial elements in this solitary trade. Working with other people of any age on group-evolved plays is stimulating, nerve-wracking and reassuring. Out of nothing something eventually happens and everybody gets very excited. It's very hard work because your material is hundreds of improvisations and random notions all of which have to be shaped and structured and the gaps filled in by the playwright − generally under considerable pressure because there is never enough time. I would like to write lots more plays for those people we designate as children. It always seems to turn into a celebration and confirms one that the work one has chosen to do does some people some good some of the time − including oneself.

*   *   *

In the recent and rapid development of theatre for children, Olwen Wymark's *No Talking* is an important landmark. Written in 1967 when plays for under-12's inclined to be, at best, well-dramatised fairy tales, at worst, a kind of kiddy-kit, Petrushka with words, Wymark's script made a tremendous impact. The play gave children a taut exploration of the appalling consequences to its hero of his somewhat flippant resolve to stop talking in protest against the triteness of other people's conversation. It did so in a frame of reference within the child's often conservative expectation of its own culture. There are witch-like ladies, clowns, changelings, spies and so on, but, contrary to expectation, these characters happened to run electrical supply shops, land up in concentration camps, get shot, go blind, and fall in love, not prettily either but with a great deal of effort, pain, and joy. At the time, this theme, and its treatment, were revolutionary, and perhaps Wymark was applauded too much for daring and innovation and not enough for her craftmanship and the kind of grip this gaudy, poetic, and shamelessly theatrical play has on young audiences. Similarly, its partner play, *Chinigchinich* uses a familiar context − this time a Red Indian tribe − to examine the nature of authority but likewise makes a few illuminating departures from the audience preconception on "injun" behaviour which light heartedly invites them to apply a little scepticism in their own dealings with power and those who administer it.

Her first two plays were written at the request of Unicorn Theatre for Young People; her next, a collaboration with a small West Indian called Daniel, came about through her work with Common Stock. They produced *Daniel's Epic* after Wymark had done what she modestly calls an editing job, on the astonishing, cast-of-thousands fantasy he recorded at the company's workshop. This led to another collaboration with one hundred 9-year-old Southwark school children who performed their *Southwark Originals* at the Unicorn, under Wymark's direction. The plays proved an extraordinary mixture of adventure and surrealism and gave the bemused audience of parents and educationalists the heartening bonus of a totally unselfconscious culture cross. This occurred in a play that combined a London dockside family with Anansi, the West Indian folk Hero. Further collaboration with children resulted in *Starters*, a five-play programme intended for performance by adult actors although they are equally suitable for children to act.

Written after much of her work with child authors, *The Bolting Sisters* shows a tendency in Wymark to dismiss her own maturity as playwright for kids, and to write for young audiences with the belief that a child is only capable of responding to that which it could express or articulate itself. If this were true, art would long since have festered to death at toddler level. However, it is a common error and Wymark makes it rarely. Certainly she remains one of the richest talents working for Children's Theatre.

—Ursula M. Jones

WYNDHAM, Lee. Pseudonym for Jane Lee Hyndman. American. Born in Melitople, Russia, 16 December 1912; emigrated to the United States in 1923; naturalized citizen, 1942. Educated at schools in Turkey and the United States; New York University. Married Robert Hyndman in 1933 (died, 1973); has one son and one daughter. Secretary and model in New York in 1930's; Children's Book Editor, *Daily Record*, Morristown, New Jersey, 1949–58, and Philadelphia *Inquirer*, 1950–63; Instructor and Lecturer, New York University Writing Center, 1958–72. Consultant, and Director of the Masters Program, Institute of Children's Literature, Redding Ridge, Connecticut. Address: 16 Blackwell Avenue, Morristown, New Jersey 07960, U.S.A.

PUBLICATIONS FOR CHILDREN

Fiction

> *Sizzling Pan Ranch*, illustrated by Robert Logan. New York, Crowell, 1951.
> *Slipper under Glass*, illustrated by Vera Bock. New York, Longman, 1952.
> *Golden Slippers*, illustrated by Vera Bock. New York, Longman, 1953.
> *Buttons and Beaux*, with Louise Barnes Gallagher. New York, Dodd Mead, 1953.
> *Silver Yankee*, illustrated by Janet Smalley. Philadelphia, Winston, 1953.
> *A Dance for Susie*, illustrated by Jane Miller. New York, Dodd Mead, 1953.
> *Showboat Holiday*, illustrated by Jean MacDonald Porter. Philadelphia, Winston, 1954.
> *Binkie's Billions*, illustrated by Raymond Abel. New York, Knopf, 1954.
> *Susie and the Dancing Cat*, illustrated by Jane Miller. New York, Dodd Mead, 1954.
> *Camel Bird Ranch*, illustrated by Bob Riger. New York, Dodd Mead, 1955.
> *Susie and the Ballet Family*, illustrated by Jane Miller. New York, Dodd Mead, 1955.
> *Ballet Teacher*. New York, Messner, 1956.
> *The Lost Birthday Present*, illustrated by Paul Brown. New York, Dodd Mead, 1957.
> *Lady Architect*. New York, Messner, 1957.
> *On Your Toes, Susie*, illustrated by Jane Miller. New York, Dodd Mead, 1958; London, Hutchinson, 1960.

Dance to My Measure. New York, Messner, 1958.

Candy Stripers. New York, Messner, 1958.

The Timid Dragon, illustrated by Kurt Werth. New York, Lothrop, 1960.

The Little Wise Man, with Robert Wyndham, illustrated by Anthony D'Adamo. Indianapolis, Bobbs Merrill, 1960.

Chip Nelson and the Contrary Indians, illustrated by David Stone. New York, Watts, 1960.

Susie and the Ballet Horse, illustrated by Jean MacDonald Porter. New York, Dodd Mead, 1961.

Bonnie, illustrated by Nina Albright. New York, Doubleday, 1961.

Beth Hilton, Model. New York, Messner, 1961.

The Family at Seven Chimneys House, illustrated by Jo Polseno. New York, Watts, 1963.

Other

First Steps in Ballet, with Thalia Mara, illustrated by George Bobrizsky. New York, Doubleday, 1955; as *Ballet: Home Practice for Beginners,* London, Constable, 1955.

Games and Stunts for All Occasions, revised edition. Philadelphia, Lippincott, 1957.

Year 'round Party Book, revised edition. Philadelphia, Lippincott, 1957.

Ballet for You, illustrated by Catherine Scholz. New York, Grosset and Dunlap, 1959.

The How and Why Wonderbook of Ballet, illustrated by Rafaello Busoni. New York, Grosset and Dunlap, 1961.

Folk Tales of India. Indianapolis, Bobbs Merrill, 1962.

Thanksgiving, illustrated by Hazel Hoecker. Champaign, Illinois, Garrard, 1963.

Folk Tales of China. Indianapolis, Bobbs Merrill, 1963.

Tales from the Arabian Nights, illustrated by Robert J. Lee. Racine, Wisconsin, Whitman, 1965.

Mourka, The Mighty Cat (folktale), illustrated by Charles Mikolaycak. New York, Parents' Magazine Press, 1969.

Russian Tales of Fabulous Beasts and Marvels, illustrated by Charles Mikolaycak. New York, Parents' Magazine Press, 1969.

Florence Nightingale, Nurse to the World, illustrated by Richard Cuffari. New York, World, 1969.

The Winter Child: An Old Russian Folk Tale, illustrated by Yaroslava. New York, Parents' Magazine Press, 1970.

Tales the People Tell in Russia, illustrated by Andrew Antal. New York, Messner, 1970.

Tales the People Tell in China, with Robert Wyndham. New York, Messner, 1971.

Holidays in Scandinavia, illustrated by Gordon Laite. Champaign, Illinois, Garrard, 1975.

Editor, *The King's General,* by Daphne du Maurier. New York, Doubleday, 1954.

Editor, *National Velvet,* by Enid Bagnold, illustrated by Al Brulé. New York, Grosset and Dunlap, 1961.

Editor, *Dancers, Dancers, Dancers!* (anthology). New York, Watts, 1961.

Editor, with Helen J. Estes, *A Tale of Two Cities,* by Charles Dickens. Englewood Cliffs, New Jersey, Prentice Hall, 1962.

Editor, *The Prince and the Pauper,* by Mark Twain. Chicago, Whitman, 1962.

Editor, *Acting, Acting, Acting!* (anthology). New York, Watts, 1962; London, Chatto and Windus, 1964.

Editor, with Robert Wyndham, *Chinese Mother Goose Rhymes,* illustrated by Ed Young. Cleveland, World, 1968.

PUBLICATIONS FOR ADULTS

Other

> *Writing for Children and Teenagers.* Cincinnati, Writer's Digest, 1968; revised
> edition, 1972.

Manuscript Collection: University of Oregon Library, Eugene.

*   *   *

Lee Wyndham is one of the few authors who can write successfully both for the very young child and for older children. This is a very special talent, and Ms. Wyndham makes the most of it.

Her picture books frequently involve animals – cats especially. *Mourka, The Mighty Cat* is really for feline fanciers of all ages. Based on an old tale, Mourka comes alive for English-speaking readers, thanks to Ms. Wyndham's skilled treatment. Old tales, especially those from eastern Europe, fascinate Ms. Wyndham, and she seems to have made it her personal crusade to bring these stories to the present generation of young American readers. While keeping the original flavor of these tales, she gives them her special touch that endears them to modern youngsters.

When writing for older children, Ms. Wyndham chooses subjects that are dear to their hearts. What pre-teen-age girl hasn't, at least once, wished she were old enough to be a Candy Striper – those teen-agers who do volunteer work in hospitals? In *Candy Stripers* Ms. Wyndham shows that, on the inside, it's not all glamor and fun; it's real work. She manages to do this without destroying a youngster's natural desire to do something worthwhile.

Perhaps it is because Ms. Wyndham is a well-known and well-respected teacher of juvenile writing courses that she is able to keep her finger on the pulse of what young readers want. Whatever the reason, her name on a novel or a short story inevitably tells the reader that here is something worth reading. The characters in her "older" books are very much a part of the contemporary scene; they give one the feeling that one has met them already. But, at the same time, one is always eager to find out what's going to happen to them. Her stories move along briskly; her language is vivid and her plots often keep one on the edge of the seat. She knows how to use suspense to hold a young reader's attention, but she never cheats by using obvious solutions.

—Rubie Saunders

YATES, Elizabeth.   American.   Born in Buffalo, New York, 6 December 1905. Educated at the Franklin School, Buffalo; Oaksmere, Mamaroneck, New York. Married William McGreal in 1929 (died, 1963). Trustee, Town Library, Peterborough, New Hampshire; Commissioner, State Library Commission, Concord, New Hampshire; President, New Hampshire Association for the Blind, Concord. Recipient: New York *Herald Tribune* Festival award, 1943, 1950; American Library Association Newbery Medal, 1951; Boys' Clubs of America award, 1953; Women's International League for Peace and Freedom Jane Addams Award, 1955; Sarah Josepha Hale Award, 1970. Litt.D.: Aurora College, Illinois, 1965; Ripon College, Wisconsin, 1970; L.H.D.: Eastern Baptist College, St. Davids, Pennsylvania, 1966; University of New Hampshire, Durham, 1967; New England College, Henniker, New Hampshire, 1972. Address: 381 Old Street Road, Peterborough, New Hampshire 03458, U.S.A.

PUBLICATIONS FOR CHILDREN

Fiction

High Holiday. London, A. and C. Black, 1938.

Hans and Frieda in the Swiss Mountains, illustrated by Nora S. Unwin. New York and London, Nelson, 1939.

Climbing Higher. London, A. and C. Black, 1939; as *Quest in the North-land,* New York, Knopf, 1940.

Haven for the Brave. New York, Knopf, 1941.

Under the Little Fir and Other Stories, illustrated by Nora S. Unwin. New York, Coward McCann, 1942.

Around the Year in Iceland, illustrated by Jon Nielsen. Boston, Heath, 1942.

Patterns on the Wall. New York, Knopf, 1943.

Mountain Born, illustrated by Nora S. Unwin. New York, Coward McCann, 1943.

Once in the Year, illustrated by Nora S. Unwin. New York, Coward McCann, 1947.

A Place for Peter, illustrated by Nora S. Unwin. New York, Coward McCann, 1952.

Sam's Secret Journal, illustrated by Allan Eitzen. New York, Friendship Press, 1964.

Carolina's Courage, illustrated by Nora S. Unwin. New York, Dutton, 1964; as *Carolina and the Indian Doll,* London, Methuen, 1965.

An Easter Story, illustrated by Nora S. Unwin. New York, Dutton, 1967.

With Pipe, Paddle, and Song, illustrated by Nora S. Unwin. New York, Dutton, 1968.

Sarah Whitcher's Story, illustrated by Nora S. Unwin. New York, Dutton, 1971.

Other

Joseph (Bible story), illustrated by Nora S. Unwin. New York, Knopf, 1947.

The Young Traveller in the U.S.A. London, Phoenix House, 1948.

The Christmas Story, illustrated by Nora S. Unwin. New York, Aladdin, 1950.

Children of the Bible, illustrated by Nora S. Unwin. New York, Aladdin, 1950; London, Meiklejohn, 1951.

Amos Fortune, Free Man. New York, Aladdin, 1950.

David Livingstone. Evanston, Illinois, Row Peterson, 1952.

Rainbow 'round the World: A Story of UNICEF, illustrated by Betty Alden. Indianapolis, Bobbs Merrill, 1954.

Prudence Crandall, Woman of Courage, illustrated by Nora S. Unwin. New York, Aladdin, 1955.

Gifts of True Love: Based on the Old Carol "The Twelve Days of Christmas," illustrated by Nora S. Unwin. Wallingford, Pennsylvania, Pendle Hill, 1958.

Someday You'll Write. New York, Dutton, 1962.

New Hampshire. New York, Coward McCann, 1969.

Skeezer, Dog with a Mission, illustrated by Joan Drescher. New York, Harvey House, 1973.

Editor, *Piskey Folk: A Book of Cornish Legends,* by Enys Tregarthen. New York, Day, 1940.

Editor, *The Doll Who Came Alive,* by Enys Tregarthen, illustrated by Nora S. Unwin. New York, Day, 1942; London, Faber, 1944.

Editor, *The White Ring,* by Enys Tregarthen, illustrated by Nora S. Unwin. New York, Harcourt Brace, 1949.

Editor, *Sir Gibbie,* by George MacDonald. New York, Dutton, 1963; London, Blackie, 1967.

Novels

Wind of Spring.   New York, Coward McCann, 1945; London, Cassell, 1948.
Nearby.   New York, Coward McCann, 1947; London, Cassell, 1950.
Beloved Bondage.   New York, Coward McCann, 1948.
Guardian Heart.   New York, Coward McCann, 1950; London, Museum Press, 1952.
Brave Interval.   New York, Coward McCann, 1952; London, Dakars, 1953.
Hue and Cry.   New York, Coward McCann, 1953.
The Carey Girl.   New York, Coward McCann, 1956.
The Next Fine Day.   New York, Day, 1962; London, Dent, 1964.
On That Night.   New York, Dutton, 1969.

Other

Pebble in a Pool: The Widening Circles of Dorothy Canfield Fisher's Life.   New York,
   Dutton, 1958; as *The Lady from Vermont,* Brattleboro, Vermont, Stephen Greene
   Press, 1971.
The Lighted Heart (autobiographical).   New York, Dutton, 1960.
Howard Thurman: Portrait of a Practical Dreamer.   New York, Day, 1964.
Up the Golden Stair.   New York, Dutton, 1966.
Is There a Doctor in the Barn? A Day in the Life of Forrest F. Tenney, D.V.M.   New
   York, Dutton, 1966.
The Road Through Sandwich Notch.   Brattleboro, Vermont, Stephen Greene Press,
   1973.
A Book of Hours.   New York, Seabury Press, 1976.
Call It Zest.   Brattleboro, Vermont, Stephen Greene Press, 1977.

Editor, *Gathered Grace: A Short Selection of George MacDonald's Poems.*   Cambridge,
   Heffer, 1938.
Editor, *Your Prayers and Mine.*   Boston, Houghton Mifflin, 1954.

Manuscript Collection: Special Collections, Mugar Memorial Library, Boston University.

Elizabeth Yates comments:
   I have a strong feeling that the purpose of life is good, and this − in some way or another −
might be held to be the motivation in my work.

                              *   *   *

   In a small volume called *Someday You'll Write,* composed in response to the questions of
an 11-year-old girl who wishes to become a writer, Elizabeth Yates shares with readers the
essence of her own development as creative artist. She compares the creative growth process
to that of natural growth − a long, slow, evolving process of moving from birth to maturity.
She believes that writers must be able to look deeply within, reaching outward and upward, if
they are to grow. In her own case Miss Yates did not hurry the creative process. Instead, she
took sufficient time to allow ideas and imagination to incubate.
   Miss Yates is perhaps best known in the field of children's literature for two powerful
biographies for older children − *Amos Fortune, Free Man* and *Prudence Crandall, Woman of
Courage.* Based on extensive research and characterized by a fine narrative style, both books
are compassionate yet void of didacticism. Each deals with an unusual New England citizen
whose life, despite almost insurmountable hardships, was dedicated to the betterment of the
lives of others. The biographee in the first case is a black man; in the second, a white woman.

Amos Fortune's story can still be read, in brief, on the weathered headstone marking his grave in a little churchyard in Jaffrey, New Hampshire: "Born free in Africa, a slave in America, he purchased liberty, professed Christianity, lived reputably, and died hopefully, November 17, 1801." The story of Prudence Crandall can be read in state records where for more than fifty years she was listed as a criminal, her "crime" an attempt to provide equal education to white and black girls in the private school which she established in Canterbury, Connecticut in 1833. The success and appeal of both books come to a large extent from the at-easeness and compatibility which Miss Yates feels for her subjects and from her combining of fact and vision in presenting the compelling hopes and dreams that motivate the actions of Amos Fortune and Prudence Crandall. Throughout each book there is a pervasive sense that right will ultimately prevail if the protagonist can, despite all injustice, hold firm to honorable principles and remain free from the blight of prejudice, bitterness, and resentment. Amos Fortune and Prudence Crandall do remain free of blight, and each epitomizes in behavior the philosophy of usefulness which permeates the writings of Elizabeth Yates.

Carolina's Courage and *Patterns on the Wall* are works of fiction in which Miss Yates gives the protagonist of each a particular kind of usefulness. On the long overland journey she makes with her family from old New Hampshire to the Nebraska territory where they will homestead, little Carolina Putnam of *Carolina's Courage* demonstrates usefulness and courage admirable for one so young. When the coveted goal is almost in sight, Carolina's family meet up with owners of other wagons heading west. They stop to camp together near a creek they are afraid to cross – fearful of going further because of news of hostile Indians ahead. Straying from camp, taking her beloved doll Lydia-Lou, Carolina meets a little Indian girl who also has a doll. When Carolina is called back to camp for supper, the Indian child insists on exchanging dolls. When the campers break camp and move forward next day, Carolina is heart-broken to leave Lydia-Lou behind but she realizes that her father is right in feeling that the Indian doll she now has will gain safety for her own and other families of the wagon train when they meet Indians later. Readers are not told that Carolina and Lydia-Lou will sometime meet again. Miss Yates cleverly avoids an ending which leaves nothing for the reader to do.

Patterns on the Wall is about another kind of usefulness. This book is the touching and inspirational story of a sensitive New Hampshire lad in the early 1800's who grew up to be a famous wall stenciller. Like *Amos Fortune* and *Prudence Crandall*, *Patterns on the Wall* is the result of thorough and painstaking research, and its characters are believable and real. Miss Yates interprets her literary characters with a skill and intensity no less effective than that of a great actor interpreting a role. Hence, Jared Austin of *Patterns on the Wall* comes alive for readers. One can almost believe him to be the stenciller who left patterns on the wall in the old farmhouse in Peterborough, New Hampshire which has been the home of Miss Yates for many years.

To leave unnoticed two other very special books for children – *Mountain Born* and its sequel, *A Place for Peter* – would be unfair to Miss Yates. Together these books constitute a pastoral tale of a small New Hampshire lad who grows into useful manhood rooted to the soil both by rearing and by personal inclination. These stories are a testament to their author's faith in the nobility of all nature, to her love of land, of animals, and of people. One of her finest characterizations in these two books, aside from that of Peter, is that of old Benj, the trusted farmhand. Few who read *A Place for Peter* can forget the scene in which old Benj destroys eight rattlesnakes "first asking their forgiveness." Because of his sincere reverence for life, old Benj did not like the thought of what had to be done but, faced with the decision of destroying the snakes or the possibility of their destroying man or beast, the greater good determined his actions. Miss Yates' remarkable talent for descriptive writing is here at its best. The scene in which Peter is about to be bitten by a rattler because Shep, his faithful dog, has refused, in her excitement, to obey, is a case in point. Seeing three rattlers hurrying back to their den among the rock ledges Shep flings herself in their path. Threatened, the snakes coiled and "with their scaly yellow and black sides gleaming like velvet in the shade cast by an overhanging rock, gave warning with raised and singing tails that intrusion would not be tolerated."

It is fair to say that in all her books for children Miss Yates has held to the standard given to her by a former teacher that "the written word should be clean as a bone, clear as light, firm as stone." And in adhering to this standard she has provided a large body of work clearly characterized by gentleness and serenity, by a love of nature and all life, and by genuine concern for the oppressed and down-trodden. There has been about all great writers, Miss Yates feels, an ability to see the "equality of mankind and the inter-relation of life." Surely she must be one among them. Miss Yates acknowledges indebtedness to the Bible, to William Blake, and to George Eliot. These influences are unmistakably present in many of her writings.

—Charity Chang

YOLEN, Jane. American. Born in New York City, 11 February 1939. Educated at Staples High School, Westport, Connecticut, graduated 1956; Smith College, Northampton, Massachusetts, B.A. 1960; New School for Social Research, New York; University of Massachusetts, Amherst. Married David W. Stemple in 1962; has one daughter and two sons. Assistant Editor, Gold Medal Books, New York, 1960–61; Associate Editor, Rutledge Books, New York, 1961–62; Assistant Editor, Alfred A. Knopf Juvenile Books, New York, 1962–65. Member, Board of Directors, Society of Children's Book Writers, and Children's Literature Association. Massachusetts Delegate, Democratic National Convention, Miami, 1972. Recipient: Boys' Clubs of America award, 1968; Society of Children's Book Writers Golden Kite Award, 1974. Agent: Marilyn Marlow, Curtis Brown Ltd., 575 Madison Avenue, New York, New York 10022. Address: Phoenix Farm, 31 School Street, Box 27, Hatfield, Massachusetts 01038, U.S.A.

PUBLICATIONS FOR CHILDREN

Fiction

> The Witch Who Wasn't, illustrated by Arnold Roth. New York, Macmillan, and London, Collier Macmillan, 1964.
> Gwinellen, The Princess Who Could Not Sleep, illustrated by Ed Renfro. New York, Macmillan, 1965.
> Trust a City Kid, with Anne Huston, illustrated by J.C. Kocsis. New York, Lothrop, 1966; London, Dent, 1967.
> Isabel's Noel, illustrated by Arnold Roth. New York, Funk and Wagnalls, 1967.
> The Emperor and the Kite, illustrated by Ed Young. Cleveland, World, 1967; London, Macdonald, 1969.
> The Minstrel and the Mountain, illustrated by Anne Rockwell. Cleveland, World, and Edinburgh, Oliver and Boyd, 1968.
> Greyling, illustrated by William Stobbs. Cleveland, World, 1968; London, Bodley Head, 1969.
> The Longest Name on the Block, illustrated by Peter Madden. New York, Funk and Wagnalls, 1968.
> The Wizard of Washington Square, illustrated by Ray Cruz. New York, World, 1969.
> The Inway Investigators; or, The Mystery at McCracken's Place, illustrated by Allan Eitzen. New York, Seabury Press, 1969.
> The Seventh Mandarin, illustrated by Ed Young. New York, Seabury Press, and London, Macmillan, 1970.

Hobo Toad and the Motorcycle Gang, illustrated by Emily McCully. New York, World, 1970.

The Bird of Time, illustrated by Mercer Mayer. New York, Crowell, 1971.

The Girl Who Loved the Wind, illustrated by Ed Young. New York, Crowell, 1972; London, Collins, 1973.

The Girl Who Cried Flowers and Other Tales, illustrated by David Palladini. New York, Crowell, 1974.

The Rainbow Rider, illustrated by Michael Foreman. New York, Crowell, 1974; London, Collins, 1975.

The Adventures of Eeka Mouse, illustrated by Myra Gibson McKee. Stamford, Connecticut, Xerox, 1974.

The Boy Who Had Wings, illustrated by Helga Aichinger. New York, Crowell, 1974.

The Magic Three of Solatia, illustrated by Julia Noonan. New York, Crowell, 1974.

The Little Spotted Fish, illustrated by Friso Henstra. New York, Seabury Press, 1975.

The Transfigured Hart, illustrated by Donna Diamond. New York, Crowell, 1975.

Moon Ribbon and Other Tales, illustrated by David Palladini. New York, Crowell, 1976; London, Dent, 1977.

Milkweed Days, photographs by Gabriel Amadeus Cooney. New York, Crowell, 1976.

The Sultan's Perfect Tree, illustrated by Barbara Garrison. New York, Parents' Magazine Press, 1977.

The Seeing Stick, illustrated by Remy Charlip and Demetra Maraslis. New York, Crowell, 1977.

The Hundredth Dove and Other Tales, illustrated by David Palladini. New York, Crowell, 1977

The Giant's Farm, illustrated by Tomie de Paola. New York, Seabury Press, 1977.

Hannah Dreaming, photographs by Alan Epstein. Springfield, Massachusetts, Springfield Museum of Art, 1977.

Play

Robin Hood, music by Barbara Green (produced Boston, 1967).

Verse

See This Little Line?, illustrated by Kathleen Elgin. New York, McKay, 1963.

It All Depends, illustrated by Don Bolognese. New York, Funk and Wagnalls, 1969.

An Invitation to the Butterfly Ball, illustrated by Jane Breskin Zalben. New York, Parents' Magazine Press, and Kingswood, Surrey, World's Work, 1977.

Other

Pirates in Petticoats, illustrated by Leonard Vosburgh. New York, McKay, 1963.

World on a String: The Story of Kites. Cleveland, World, 1968.

Friend: The Story of George Fox and the Quakers. New York, Seabury Press, 1972.

The Wizard Islands, illustrated by Robert Quackenbush. New York, Crowell, 1973.

Ring Out! A Book of Bells, illustrated by Richard Cuffari. New York, Seabury Press, 1975; London, Evans, 1977.

Simple Gifts: The Story of the Shakers, illustrated by Betty Fraser. New York, Viking Press, 1976.

Editor, *The Fireside Song Book of Birds and Beasts*, music by Barbara Green, illustrated by Peter Parnall. New York, Simon and Schuster, 1972.

Editor, *Zoo 2000: Twelve Stories of Science Fiction and Fantasy Beasts*. New York, Seabury Press, 1973; London, Gollancz, 1975.

Editor, *Rounds about Rounds*, music by Barbara Green, illustrated by Gail Gibbons. New York, Watts, 1977; London, Watts, 1978.

PUBLICATIONS FOR ADULTS

Other

Writing Books for Children.   Boston, The Writer, 1973.

Manuscript Collection: Kerlan Collection, University of Minnesota, Minneapolis.

Jane Yolen comments:

"Prolific" is a word often used to describe me, but I would rather say that I have a very low threshold of boredom. And so I have tried many different kinds of writing: picture books, fantasy, fairy tale, straight fiction, verse, and non-fiction. Perhaps I am best known as a writer of Literary or Art Fairy Tales, stories that use the elements of old stories − the cadences, the characters, the magical settings of objects − but concern themselves with modern themes. Because of this, my stories are better known to more sophisticated and romantically-inclined young people, and college students. I am a folk singer as well as a story teller, and I hope my tales sound as if they could be sung.

*   *   *

In an article published in the October 1975 issue of *The Horn Book*, Jane Yolen wrote: "I see books for children in terms of mythology because of the way I write for children. I create literary folk or fairy tales .... The story itself is an extended image, a dream crafted by the wide-awake dreamer. They are folk tales in the sense that they use and re-use traditional material: oral cadences, stock characters, status-conferring imagery, formulaic settings or plot. They are not, in the scholarly sense, folk − that is, out of oral tradition."

Actually, Ms. Yolen's prolific output as a writer for children and young people has by no means been limited to the literary folk or fairy tale, although such books do account for the bulk of her published work. She has written picture books, collections of original tales featuring folk and fairy tale motifs, novels, and non-fiction works, several of the latter containing some of her strongest writing. Pride of place should go, however, to her folk and fairy tales.

The Emperor and the Kite (a Caldecott Medal Honor Book for Ed Young's illustrations) is one of the most successful of the picture books. A reworking of the old theme of the smallest proving to be the bravest and truest, this is the story of a tiny Chinese princess who demonstrates her great love for her father, the Emperor, after he is deposed from the throne by his courtiers and forgotten by his other children. All of Ms. Yolen's strengths are on display in this tale: her feeling for the rhythm of language and the striking image; her skillful repetition of words and phrases − so important in a picture book aimed at young children; and her firm sense of pace and the dramatic moment. *The Emperor and the Kite* is blessed with an additional element that some of her other tales lack: the strong feelings of the little princess which evoke equally strong feelings in the reader or listener.

Polished as Ms. Yolen's writing always is, the characters and situations in her stories occasionally seem too cool and remote to engage the emotions of the reader. That was the case with some of the tales in her collection *The Girl Who Cried Flowers* and in her "quest" novel *The Magic Three of Solatia*. When such remoteness invades her writing, it may end up appearing to be facile or shallow − adjectives that critics of her work have sometimes employed, while at the same time never denying her flair for words. Warmth of character and situation is perhaps more frequent in some of Jane Yolen's less ambitious books, like the humorous, easy-reading mystery story, *The Inway Investigators*, which centers on the unmasking of a petnapping ring by a group of children. Even in such stories, though, her sense of style and structure sometimes seems to inhibit the natural impulses of the characters.

Interestingly, it is in her non-fiction titles like *World on a String: The Story of Kites*, *Ring Out! A Book of Bells*, and especially *Friend: The Story of George Fox and the Quakers* that

Jane Yolen has achieved some of her most balanced and satisfying writing. Perhaps it is because non-fiction benefits even more than fiction from her qualities of discipline, control, and organization. At any rate, the folklore and folk tales that she injects into *World on a String* and *Ring Out!* lend color and depth to these books, and relate them to her fiction works in this genre. And in *George Fox*, the raw material of Fox's life appears to release her and encourages her to create a more rounded portrait of this dedicated, obsessive religious leader than she has attained with some of her fictional heroes and heroines.

—James C. Giblin

YOUNG, Delbert A(lton).   Canadian.   Born in Chalk River, Ontario, 26 November 1907. Educated at normal school: Teaching Certificate. Served in the Canadian Militia during World War II. Married Phyllis Collier in 1946. Schoolteacher for one year; farmer, 17 years; railroad worker, miner, and construction worker, 8 years; carpenter and builder, 1949–56. *Died in January 1975.*

PUBLICATIONS FOR CHILDREN

Fiction

> *Mutiny on Hudson Bay*, illustrated by Doug Sneyd.   Toronto, Gage, 1964.
> *Last Voyage of the Unicorn*, illustrated by Mary Cserepy.   Toronto, Clarke Irwin, 1969.
> *The Ghost Ship*, illustrated by William Taylor.   Toronto, Clarke Irwin, 1972.

PUBLICATIONS FOR ADULTS

Other

> *The Mounties.*   Toronto and London, Hodder and Stoughton, 1968.
> *According to Hakluyt.*   Toronto, Clarke Irwin, 1973.

*   *   *

Delbert A. Young's work for young readers presupposes a rather sophisticated audience. It is carefully detailed in its reconstruction of the period with which Young is most involved – the seafaring world of the 16th century.

In his two books for adults, Young's careful research, documentation, and skillful telling of stories are to be seen. *The Mounties* is a well-written account of the history of the Royal Canadian Mounted Police, and *According to Hakluyt* is an adaptation for modern readers of Richard Hakluyt's stirring chronicle of Elizabethan seafaring which has been called "the prose epic of the English nation."

This dramatic period of history was obviously fascinating to Young, who set all three of his novels for young readers in the 16th century. The first, *Mutiny on Hudson Bay*, relates the story of the last voyage of Henry Hudson as seen through the eyes of a young boy who was on board. In *Last Voyage of the Unicorn*, Young again tells the story – this time of the Danish ship *Unicorn* commanded by Captain Jens Munck in search of the Northwest Passage – by means of the first person narrative of a young boy, Niels Olsen, who actually went on the expedition and was one of three to survive. The tale is told in realistic and accurate detail and conveys an extremely vivid impression of the events Young describes. In *The Ghost Ship* Young again chooses as narrator a boy who sailed with Sir Francis Drake on the *Golden Hind* in search of Spanish treasure. This novel is remarkable in that it includes an unusual and skillful transition from the present century to the time of Drake, the narrator having been conveyed to the 16th century by a type of astral travel made credible and gripping by the author's obvious familiarity and ease in dealing with his topic. The characterization in this book, as well as in the others, is realistic and convincing; the presentation of Elizabethan speech is notable as well. The comparison between the two centuries, the 20th and the 16th, is often implicit in Young's books: in *The Ghost Ship* the comparison is made explicit and the author's knowledge of the earlier century gives depth to the book.

In these novels Young very skillfully carried his readers imaginatively into a world he knew intimately, and his writing was subtle, lively, and, at times, powerful. Young's writing of historical fiction for young readers was a welcome addition to an area of Canadian prose that had previously been undistinguished.

—Janet E. Baker

YOUNG, Scott (Alexander).   Canadian.   Born in Glenboro, Manitoba, 14 April 1918. Educated in Glenboro and Winnipeg schools. Served in the Canadian Navy during World War II. Married twice; has two sons and two daughters. Sports Columnist, Winnipeg *Free Press*, 1937–40; writer, *Maclean's* magazine, Toronto, 1945–48; Sports Editor, Toronto *Telegram*, 1970–71. Columnist, 1957–69, and since 1971, Toronto *Globe and Mail*. Recipient: National Newspaper award, for sportswriting, 1958; Wilderness Medal, for television documentary, 1963. Address: R.R. 2, Cavan, Ontario L0A 1C0, Canada.

PUBLICATIONS FOR CHILDREN

Fiction

> *Scrubs on Skates*, illustrated by James Ponter.   Toronto, McClelland and Stewart, and Boston, Little Brown, 1952.
> *Boy on Defense*, illustrated by James Ponter.   Toronto, McClelland and Stewart, and Boston, Little Brown, 1953.
> *The Clue of the Dead Duck*, illustrated by Douglas Johnson.   Boston, Little Brown, 1962.
> *A Boy at the Leafs' Camp*, illustrated by Doug Sneyd.   Boston, Little Brown, 1963.
> *Big City Office Junior*, with Astrid Young.   Toronto, Ryerson Press, 1964.
> *Face-Off Series (Face-Off in Moscow, Learning to Be Captain, The Moscow Challenger, The Silent One Speaks Up)*, illustrated by Kenneth Shields.   St. Paul, EMC Corporation, 4 vols., 1973.

Other

> *Hockey Heroes Series (Bobby Hull, Superstar; Frank Mahovlich, The Big M; Gil Perrault Makes It Happen; Stan Mikita, Tough Kid Who Grew Up)*.   St. Paul, EMC Corporation, 4 vols., 1974.

PUBLICATIONS FOR ADULTS

Novels

> *The Flood*.   Toronto, McClelland and Stewart, and London, Joseph, 1956.
> *Face-Off*, with George Robertson.   Toronto, Macmillan, 1971.

Short Stories

> *We Won't Be Needing You, Al: Stories of Men and Sport.* Toronto, Ryerson Press, 1968.

Other

> *Red Shield in Action: A Record of Canadian Salvation Army War Services in the Second Great War.* Toronto, Clarke, 1949.
> *Sports Stories.* Toronto, Ryerson Press, 1965.
> *The Leafs I Knew* (sports columns). Toronto, Ryerson Press, 1966.
> *O'Brien* (biography of Michael John O'Brien), with Astrid Young. Toronto, Ryerson Press, 1967.
> *Hockey Is a Battle: Punch Imlach's Own Story*, with Punch Imlach. New York, Crown, 1969.
> *Goodbye Argos*, with Leo Cahill. Toronto, McClelland and Stewart, 1973.
> *Silent Frank Cochrane: The North's First Great Politician*, with Astrid Young. Toronto, Macmillan, 1973.
> *War on Ice* (Canada-Russia hockey series). Toronto, McClelland and Stewart, 1976.
> *Canada Cup 1976.* Toronto, Worldsport, 1976.

*   *   *

A great sports writer can bring a hockey game on paper to such vivid life that it becomes more real and charged with suspense than one seen on television. Scott Young is such a writer, but his talent is not circumscribed by the boundaries of the sports arena. In his stories, as often in life, the team games so important to youngsters are milestones of their progress towards maturity. From the self-centered egotism of the child who at first plays only for himself must develop the adult who can become a true team member, can learn to rub along with inimical personalities, can put his own interest aside for the good of all.

Typical of his best work, *Scrubs on Skates* is a readable and satisfying story of growth and maturation. Pete Gordon, forced to attend the newly-built local high school rather than his father's alma mater, upon which all his hopes have centered, is bitter and resentful. The hockey team at his new school has high hopes that such a promising new player will help them to build a team to be proud of, but at first their hopes are dashed: his heart is not in it. Pete feels himself wasted among these "scrubs" of the raw new school, and fails to pull his weight. Before long, through disappointment and indignation at his attitude, his new teammates develop an understandable dislike for him. At this low point, Pete takes a good long look at what he is letting himself become, and resolves to do better. His self-improvement campaign is a tough uphill climb, and it makes a rattling good read all the way. Pete and his teammates become a force to be reckoned with as they grow out of petty enmities and into a fighting team that will put their new school on the hockey map. No longer pining after the hallowed halls and crowded trophy cabinets of his father's old school, Pete longs to help provide his own new school with its first championship photograph; to help lay the cornerstone of a proud new tradition, rather than merely adding to an old one.

For more mature young readers, *We Won't Be Needing You, Al* is a perceptive behind-the-scenes look at the men who make sports headlines. Young's impressive collection of short pieces deals chiefly with bad moments, whether peculiar to sports pros or common to mankind — events such as a death in the family, loss of work through superannuation or injury, or being let go from training camp, knowing that it's forever. The heroes in team uniform are brought into focus as sensitive, vulnerable human beings.

Scott Young's fiction is an education in depth perception, and readers need not be sports fans to find his work engrossing and enjoyable.

—Joan McGrath

ZINDEL, Paul. American. Born in Staten Island, New York, 15 May 1936. Educated at Wagner College, New York, B.S., M.A. Married Bonnie Hildebrand in 1973. Chemistry Teacher, Tottenville, New York, 1960–69. Recipient (for drama): Obie Award, 1970; Vernon Rice Drama Desk Award, 1970; New York Drama Critics Circle Award 1970; Pulitzer Prize, 1971. D.H.L.: Wagner College, 1971. Agent: Gilbert Parker, Curtis Brown Ltd.,575 Madison Avenue, New York, New York 10022. Address: c/o Harper and Row Inc., 10 East 53rd Street, New York, New York 10022, U.S.A.

PUBLICATIONS FOR CHILDREN

Fiction

> *The Pigman.* New York, Harper, 1968; London, Bodley Head, 1969.
> *My Darling, My Hamburger.* New York, Harper, 1969; London, Bodley Head, 1970.
> *I Never Loved Your Mind.* New York, Harper, 1970; London Bodley Head, 1971.
> *I Love My Mother,* illustrated by John Melo. New York, Harper, 1975.
> *Pardon Me, You're Stepping on My Eyeball!* New York, Harper, and London, Bodley Head, 1976.
> *Confessions of a Teenage Baboon.* New York, Harper, 1977.

PUBLICATIONS FOR ADULTS

Plays

> *Dimensions of Peacocks* (produced New York, 1959).
> *Euthanasia and the Endless Hearts* (produced New York, 1960).
> *A Dream of Swallows* (produced New York, 1962).
> *The Effect of Gamma Rays on Man-in-the-Moon Marigolds* (produced Houston, 1965; New York, 1970; Guildford, Surrey, 1972; London, 1973). New York, Harper, 1971; in *Plays and Players* (London), December 1972.
> *And Miss Reardon Drinks a Little* (produced Los Angeles, 1967; New York, 1971; London, 1976). New York, Random House, 1972.
> *The Secret Affairs of Mildred Wild* (produced New York, 1972).
> *Ladies at the Alamo* (produced Philadelphia and New York, 1977).

> Screenplays: *Up the Sandbox,* 1973; *Mame,* 1974.

*   *   *

Paul Zindel's books published for "young adults" are set against the idealism and despair of American middle-class teenagers in the late 1960's and 1970's. They are novels of disorientation. Zindel's adults have betrayed their young, abandoning them without resources to resolve the dilemmas of late adolescence. Parents and teachers – and the homes and schools they make – are without living roots, brittle in language and principle, afraid of sex, of nonconformity, of loss of their precarious dignity. One mother's fear that her daughter will be impregnated by males-wanting-only-one-thing is surpassed only by another's anxiety that her child will be too unattractive to capture the right-sort-of-boy. "In the forest of romance, she's a desert," confides Mrs. Shinglebox to the school psychologist in front of her daughter in *Pardon Me, You're Stepping On My Eyeball!*

Zindel's capacity for epigrammatic dialogue is one of the most remarkable features of the novels – witty, sometimes cruel, slickly East Coast American. The embarrassed tension between young and middle-aged is so sharply sustained as to make uncomfortable reading. He is also brilliantly graphic in the set-pieces – commonly parties – which provide explosive climaxes to the rebellions of his young protagonists. The sadness is that these rebellions are invariably impotent, often destructive. John and Lorraine *(The Pigman)* are involved in the death of the one wholly sympathetic adult in the novels, the elderly, childlike Mr. Pignati. When Liz becomes pregnant *(My Darling, My Hamburger)*, Sean leaves her, adopting the attitude of a father whose insensitivity he loathes: "A man's got to protect himself." The repercussions of their separation destroy the gentler friendship of Maggie and Dennis. Dewey Daniels *(I Never Loved Your Mind)* tests and then rejects the commune life-style of Yvette: he scorns "that Love Land crap. And I'm not going to give civilization a kick in the behind, because I might need an appendectomy sometime." For Marsh, unable to accept the death of his father, in *Pardon Me, You're Stepping On My Eyeball,* there is at least the consolation of Edna's understanding.

The desperation and pessimism are relieved by the implied, rather than the manifest, potential of Zindel's youthful characters. He believes, "We've stifled their sexuality, we've refused to look at the blossoming strength and beauty and energy and change that they can contribute ...." Yet when Liz and Sean make love, they do so strictly "off the page," and our exclusion from their pleasure in one another unfortunately reinforces the secretive parental attitude to sex. His teenagers never succeed in combining spontaneity with perseverance, and rarely have enough personal security to exercise cheerful common-sense. His stories are almost without adults who retain the capacity for growth and change, though the period was notable amongst all age groups for a vigorous liberal response to conservatism.

By these omissions, then, his account of the sector of American life with which he deals seems limited. His young characters have grown: but Zindel allows them only a clearer recognition of the inanities, the inequalities, and the necessity for compromise which make up their inheritance.

—Geoff Fox

ZION, Gene (Eugene Zion). American. Born in New York City, 5 October 1913. Educated at schools in Ridgefield and Fort Lee, New Jersey, 1919–27; Textile High School, New York, 1928–31; Pratt Institute, New York, 1932–36, diploma in pictorial illustration; New School for Social Research, New York, 1940–42. Served in the Anti-Aircraft Artillery Visual Training Aids Section, United States Army, 1942–44. Married Margaret Bloy Graham in 1948. Designer, Esquire Publications, New York, 1940–42; Designer and Assistant Art Director, CBS, New York, 1944–46; Graphic Designer, Conde Nast Publications, New York, 1947–51. *Died 5 December 1975.*

PUBLICATIONS FOR CHILDREN (illustrated by Margaret Bloy Graham)

Fiction

> *All Falling Down.* New York, Harper, 1951; Kingswood, Surrey, World's Work, 1969.
> *Hide and Seek Day.* New York, Harper, 1954.
> *The Summer Snowman.* New York, Harper, 1955.
> *Harry, The Dirty Dog.* New York, Harper, 1956; London, Bodley Head, 1960.
> *Really Spring.* New York, Harper, 1956.
> *Jeffie's Party.* New York, Harper, 1957.
> *Dear Garbage Man.* New York, Harper, 1957; as *Dear Dustman,* London, Bodley Head, 1962.
> *No Roses for Harry!* New York, Harper, 1958; London, Bodley Head, 1961.
> *The Plant Sitter.* New York, Harper, 1959; London, Bodley Head, 1966.

Harry and the Lady Next Door. New York, Harper, 1960; Kingswood, Surrey, World's Work, 1962.
The Meanest Squirrel I Ever Met. New York, Scribner, 1962.
The Sugar Mouse Cake. New York, Scribner, 1964.
Harry by the Sea. New York, Harper, 1965; London, Bodley Head, 1966.

*   *   *

Gene Zion had an exceptional talent for maintaining a child's perspective in everything he wrote. His characters are essentially children but appear in the guise of a dog, a trash collector, and a squirrel. Their logic is a child's logic, and their actions are subjected to adult interpretation and judgment within the story. Zion enables the child to see how his actions could be understood by others, yet in a nonthreatening way devoid of seriousness and full of humor.

His initial attempts to explore a child's logic reflect an understanding of thought concepts. *All Falling Down* investigates a child's beginning awareness of the concept of falling, while *Hide and Seek Day* explores a child's perception of the world in terms of his understanding of the game hide and seek. Both books have a passive tone which unfortunately produces a flat, unimaginative quality, lacking plot and character development.

His growth is apparent in *The Summer Snowman,* which takes a child's fantasy of saving a snowman until summer and explores the fun and enjoyment it produces. He develops a believable character in the little boy who wishes to play a joke on his older brother, and couples it with a delightful fantasy that crystallizes as an amusing plot and a successful story. *Really Spring,* similar in its development, concerns a boy who ignites the town's interest with the idea of painting everything to look like spring. The climax comes when rain washes all the paint away, and overnight it becomes "really spring." Its effect, while humorous, is not as believable nor as personally involving as *The Summer Snowman.*

Dear Garbage Man appeals to a child's fascination with trash and cleverly dramatizes the idea of rescuing everything and redistributing it. Zion's climax, with all the trash reappearing on the street, its realistic and his probing of behavior is insightful. It's an original treatment of an amusing story.

Zion's most successful creation was Harry, a dog who embodies the spirit of excitement, curiosity, and mischief of a child. Harry first captivates his admirers in *Harry, The Dirty Dog,* which explores the fantasy of escaping from a bathtub to play in the dirtiest parts of town. The humorous twist comes when his family doesn't acknowledge him and he's forced to beg for a bath to be recognized. Harry's success stems from the child's ability to empathize with his problems. In *No Roses for Harry,* he gets a sweater with roses all over it. He feels so ridiculous in it that he's forced to lose it. This familiar problem immediately involves the reader in the solution. An understanding grandma enables a happy satisfying climax. In *Harry by the Sea,* his bothersome behavior makes him a nuisance at the beach. He inadvertently gets lost, reappearing covered with sea weed. The sea monster effect injects comic relief that helps to create an imaginative story, exploring rejection and the trauma of being lost in a sea of umbrellas at the beach. With Harry, Zion generates a personality that invites warmth, involvement, and understanding.

—Martha J. Fick

ZOLOTOW, Charlotte. American. Born in Norfolk, Virginia, 26 June 1915. Educated at the University of Wisconsin, Madison. Married Maurice Zolotow in 1938 (divorced, 1969); has one son and one daughter. Member of the Children's Book Department, 1938–44, 1962–65, Senior Editor, 1965–76, and since 1976, Editorial Director, Harper Junior Books, and Associate Publisher and Vice President, Harper and Row Inc., New York. Recipient: Harper Gold Medal for Editorial Excellence, 1974; Christopher Award, 1975. Address: 29 Elm Place, Hastings-on-Hudson, New York 10706, U.S.A.

PUBLICATIONS FOR CHILDREN

Fiction

> *The Park Book*, illustrated by H.A. Rey.   New York, Harper, 1944.
> *But Not Billy*, illustrated by Lys Cassal.   New York and London, Harper, 1944.
> *The Storm Book*, illustrated by Margaret Bloy Graham.   New York, Harper, 1952.
> *The Magic Word*, illustrated by Eleanor Dart.   New York, Wonder Books, 1952.
> *The City Boy and the Country Horse* (as Charlotte Bookman), illustrated by William Moyers.   New York, Treasure Books, 1952.
> *Indian, Indian*, illustrated by Leonard Weisgard.   New York, Simon and Schuster, 1952.
> *The Quiet Mother and the Noisy Little Boy*, illustrated by Kurt Werth.   New York, Lothrop, 1953.
> *One Step, Two ...* , illustrated by Roger Duvoisin.   New York, Lothrop, 1955; London, Bodley Head, 1968.
> *Not a Little Monkey*, illustrated by Roger Duvoisin.   New York, Lothrop, 1957.
> *Over and Over*, illustrated by Garth Williams.   New York, Harper, 1957.
> *Do You Know What I'll Do?* illustrated by Garth Williams.   New York, Harper, 1958.
> *Sleepy Book*, illustrated by Vladimir Bobri.   New York, Lothrop, 1958; Kingswood, Surrey, World's Work, 1960.
> *The Bunny Who Found Easter*, illustrated by Betty Peterson.   Berkeley, California, Parnassus Press, 1959.
> *Aren't You Glad.*   New York, Golden Press, 1960.
> *The Little Black Puppy*, illustrated by Lilian Obligado.   New York, Golden Press, 1960.
> *Big Brother*, illustrated by Mary Chalmers.   New York, Harper, 1960.
> *The Three Funny Friends*, illustrated by Mary Chalmers.   New York, Harper, 1961.
> *The Night When Mother Went Away.*   New York, Lothrop, 1961; as *The Summer Night*, New York, Harper, 1974; Kingswood, Surrey, World's Work, 1976.
> *The Man with the Purple Eyes*, illustrated by Joe Lasker.   New York, Abelard Schuman, 1961; London, Abelard Schuman, 1963.
> *Mr. Rabbit and the Lovely Present*, illustrated by Maurice Sendak.   New York, Harper, 1962; London, Bodley Head, 1968.
> *The Sky Was Blue*, illustrated by Garth Williams.   New York, Harper, 1963; Kingswood, Surrey, World's Work, 1976.
> *The Quarreling Book*, illustrated by Arnold Lobel.   New York, Harper, 1963.
> *The White Marble*, illustrated by Lilian Obligado.   New York and London, Abelard Schuman, 1963.
> *A Tiger Called Thomas*, illustrated by Kurt Werth.   New York, Lothrop, 1963.
> *I Have a Horse of My Own*, illustrated by Yoko Mitsuhashi.   New York and London, Abelard Schuman, 1964.
> *The Poodle Who Barked at the Wind*, illustrated by Roger Duvoisin.   New York, Lothrop, 1964; Kingswood, Surrey, World's Work, 1965.
> *A Rose, A Bridge, and a Wild Black Horse*, illustrated by Uri Shulevitz.   New York and London, Harper, 1964.
> *When I Have a Little Girl [a Son]*, illustrated by Hilary Knight.   New York, Harper, 2 vols., 1965–67.
> *Someday*, illustrated by Arnold Lobel.   New York, Harper, 1965; Kingswood, Surrey, World's Work, 1966.
> *If It Weren't for You*, illustrated by Ben Shecter.   New York, Harper, 1966.

Big Sister and Little Sister, illustrated by Martha Alexander.   New York, Harper, 1966;
   Kingswood, Surrey, World's Work, 1968.
Flocks of Birds, illustrated by Joan Berg.   New York and London, Abelard Schuman,
   1966.
I Want to Be Little, illustrated by Tony de Luna.   New York and London, Abelard
   Schuman, 1967.
Summer Is ... , illustrated by Janet Archer.   New York and London, Abelard
   Schuman, 1967.
The New Friend, illustrated by Arvis Stewart.   New York and London, Abelard
   Schuman, 1968.
My Friend John, illustrated by Ben Shecter.   New York, Harper, 1968.
The Hating Book, illustrated by Ben Shecter.   New York, Harper, 1969; Kingswood,
   Surrey, World's Work, 1971.
The Old Dog (as Sara Abbot).   New York, Coward McCann, 1969.
Where I Begin (as Sara Abbot).   New York, Coward McCann, 1970.
You and Me, illustrated by Robert Quackenbush.   New York, Macmillan, 1971.
Wake Up and Goodnight, illustrated by Leonard Weisgard.   New York, Harper, 1971;
   Kingswood, Surrey, World's Work, 1972.
A Father Like That, illustrated by Ben Shecter.   New York, Harper, 1971.
William's Doll, illustrated by William Pène du Bois.   New York, Harper, 1972.
Hold My Hand, illustrated by Thomas di Grazia.   New York, Harper, 1972.
The Beautiful Christmas Tree, illustrated by Ruth Robbins.   Berkeley, California,
   Parnassus Press, 1972.
Janey, illustrated by Ronald Himler.   New York, Harper, 1973; Kingswood, Surrey,
   World's Work, 1974.
My Grandson Lew, illustrated by William Pène du Bois.   New York, Harper, 1974;
   Kingswood, Surrey, World's Work, 1976.
The Unfriendly Book, illustrated by William Pène du Bois.   New York, Harper, 1975.
It's Not Fair, illustrated by William Pène du Bois.   New York, Harper, 1976.
May I Visit?, illustrated by Erik Blegvad.   New York, Harper, 1976; Kingswood,
   Surrey, World's Work, 1977.

Verse

All That Sunlight, illustrated by Walter Stein.   New York, Harper, 1967.
Some Things Go Together, illustrated by Sylvie Selig.   New York, Abelard Schuman,
   1969.
River Winding, illustrated by Regina Shekerjian.   New York and London, Abelard
   Schuman, 1970.

Other

In My Garden, illustrated by Roger Duvoisin.   New York, Lothrop, 1960; Kingswood,
   Surrey, World's Work, 1963.
When the Wind Stops, illustrated by Joe Lasker.   New York, Abelard Schuman, 1962;
   London, Abelard Schuman, 1964.
A Week in Yani's World: Greece, photographs by Donald Getsug.   New York, Crowell
   Collier, and London, Collier Macmillan, 1969.
A Week in Lateef's World: India, photographs by Ray Shaw.   New York, Crowell
   Collier, 1970.

Editor, *An Overpraised Season: Ten Stories of Youth*.   New York, Harper, 1973;
   London, Bodley Head, 1974.

*   *   *

In the more than 50 books which Charlotte Zolotow has written since her first, *The Park Book*, she has never raised her voice. This is true even when she constructs stories about quarreling or other extremes of emotion. Her hallmark is artful understatement; the bedrock of her success is her almost eerie sense of what matters to the young. For example, *Janey* describes the desolation of a little girl whose best friend moves far away. The touching tale is a comfort to readers in the same situation, particularly since Zolotow avoids the bathos of a phoney happy ending.

All the Zolotow titles are popular; several are award-winning classics. *William's Doll* argues the case of a perfectly virile boy who yearns for a doll to the disgust of his he-man pals and the dismay of his father. William's wise grandmother buys him a doll and tells his father the boy needs it "so that when he's a father like you, he'll know how to take care of his baby." Blessed by the woman's movement, the book is included automatically in all non-sexist anthologies and on all lists of such literature, and has been seen on television. Zolotow was also among the first to tackle the long-taboo subject of death in a picture book. *My Grandson Lew* tells of a boy whose mother avoids all mention of the death of his grandfather until she recognizes that children, like adults, need to mourn when they lose loved ones.

In other works, the author displays a talent for displaying credible fantasies and quiet comedies. Widely enjoyed is *Mr. Rabbit and the Lovely Present*, in which a little girl matter-of-factly accepts the friendship of a tall bunny. As they wander companionably through the woods near her house, Mr. Rabbit helps the girl gather the makings of a birthday present for her mother. Equally appealing though decidedly different is *A Rose, a Bridge, and a Wild Black Horse*. Here we meet a feisty small boy, promising that he'll deliver unimaginable wonders to his sister, when he's grown up. In the finale, Zolotow scores a direct hit at male chauvinism and endears herself to underestimated females. Brother's oration concludes when he says he will not forget to bring his sister a friend to keep her company "while I explore the world."

On occasion, critics have complained that Charlotte Zolotow's books are slight and/or plotless. That opinion is not shared by readers who always hear her, quiet though she is, because they know she is as close as children themselves to what is happening in their world.

—Jean F. Mercier

APPENDIX

ALCOTT, Louisa May. American. Born in Germantown, Pennsylvania, 29 November 1832; daughter of the philosopher Amos Bronson Alcott. Educated at home, with instruction from Thoreau, Emerson, and Theodore Parker. Teacher; army nurse during the Civil War; seamstress; domestic servant. Edited the children's magazine *Merry's Museum* in the 1860's. *Died 6 March 1888.*

PUBLICATIONS FOR CHILDREN

Fiction

Flower Fables. Boston, Briggs, 1855.
The Rose Family: A Fairy Tale. Boston, Redpath, 1864.
Morning-Glories and Other Stories, illustrated by Elizabeth Greene. New York, Carleton, 1867.
Three Proverb Stories. Boston, Loring, 1868.
Kitty's Class Day. Boston, Loring, 1868.
Aunt Kipp. Boston, Loring, 1868.
Psyche's Art. Boston, Loring, 1868.
Little Women; or, Meg, Jo, Beth, and Amy, illustrated by Mary Alcott. Boston, Roberts, 2 vols., 1868–69; as *Little Women* and *Good Wives,* London, Sampson Low, 2 vols., 1871.
An Old-Fashioned Girl. Boston, Roberts, and London, Sampson Low, 1870.
Will's Wonder Book. Boston, Fuller, 1870.
Little Men: Life at Plumfield with Jo's Boys. Boston, Roberts, and London, Sampson Low, 1871.
Aunt Jo's Scrap-Bag: My Boys, Shawl-Straps, Cupid and Chow-Chow, My Girls, Jimmy's Cruise in the Pinafore, An Old-Fashioned Thanksgiving. Boston, Roberts, and London, Sampson Low, 6 vols., 1872–82.
Eight Cousins; or, The Aunt-Hill. Boston, Roberts, and London, Sampson Low, 1875.
Rose in Bloom: A Sequel to "Eight Cousins." Boston, Roberts, 1876.
Under the Lilacs. London, Sampson Low, 1877; Boston, Roberts, 1878.
Meadow Blossoms. New York, Crowell, 1879.
Water Cresses. New York, Crowell, 1879.
Jack and Jill: A Village Story. Boston, Roberts, and London, Sampson Low, 1880.
Proverb Stories. Boston, Roberts, and London, Sampson Low, 1882.
Spinning-Wheel Stories. Boston, Roberts, and London, Sampson Low, 1884.
Jo's Boys and How They Turned Out: A Sequel to "Little Men." Boston, Roberts, and London, Sampson Low, 1886.
Lulu's Library: A Christmas Dream, The Frost King, Recollections. Boston, Roberts, and London, Sampson Low, 3 vols., 1886–89.
A Garland for Girls. Boston, Roberts, and London, Blackie, 1888.
A Round Dozen: Stories, edited by Anne Thaxter Eaton. New York, Viking Press, 1963.
Glimpses of Louisa: A Centennial Sampling of the Best Short Stories, edited by Cornelia Meigs. Boston, Little Brown, 1968.
Louisa's Wonder Book: An Unknown Alcott Juvenile, edited by Madeleine B. Stern. Mount Pleasant, Michigan, Clarke Historical Library, 1975.

PUBLICATIONS FOR ADULTS

Novels

Moods. Boston, Loring, 1865; London, Routledge, 1866; revised edition, Boston, Roberts, 1882.

The Mysterious Key and What It Opened. Boston, Elliott Thomes and Talbot, 1867.
V.V.; or, Plots and Counterplots (as A.M. Barnard). Boston, Elliott Thomes and Talbot, 1871.
Work: A Story of Experience. Boston, Roberts, 1873; London, Sampson Low, 2 vols., 1873.
Beginning Again, Being a Continuation of "Work." London, Sampson Low, 1875.
A Modern Mephistopheles (published anonymously). Boston, Roberts, 1877.
A Modern Mephistopheles, and A Whisper in the Dark. Boston, Roberts, 1889.
Behind a Mask: The Unknown Thrillers, edited by Madeleine B. Stern. New York, Morrow, 1975.
Plots and Counterplots: More Unknown Thrillers, edited by Madeleine B. Stern. New York, Morrow, 1976; London, W.H. Allen, 1977.

Short Stories

On Picket Duty and Other Tales. Boston, Redpath, 1864.
Silver Pitchers, and Independence: A Centennial Love Story. Boston, Roberts, 1876; as *Silver Pitchers and Other Stories,* London, Sampson Low, 1876.

Plays

Comic Tragedies Written by "Jo" and "Meg" and Acted by the "Little Women." edited by A.B. Pratt. Boston, Roberts, and London, Sampson Low, 1893.

Other

Hospital Sketches. Boston, Redpath, 1863; revised edition, as *Hospital Sketches and Camp and Fireside Stories,* Boston, Roberts, 1869.
Nelly's Hospital. Washington, D.C., United States Sanitary Commission, 1868.
Something to Do. London, Ward Lock, 1873.
A Glorious Fourth. Boston, The Press, 1887.
What It Cost. Boston, The Press, 1887.
Jimmy's Lecture. Boston, The Press, 1887.
Louisa May Alcott: Her Life, Letters, and Journals, edited by Ednah D. Cheney. Boston, Roberts, and London, Sampson Low, 1889.
Recollections of My Childhood's Days. London, Sampson Low, 1890.
A Sprig of Andromeda: A Letter on the Death of Henry David Thoreau. New York, Pierpont Morgan Library, 1962.

Bibliography: in *Louisa's Wonder Book,* edited by Madeleine B. Stern, Mount Pleasant, Michigan, Clarke Historical Library, 1975.

Critical Studies: *Louisa May Alcott* by Madeleine B. Stern, Norman, University of Oklahoma Press, 1950, London, Peter Nevill, 1952; *Miss Alcott of Concord* by Marjorie Worthington, New York, Doubleday, 1958; *Louisa May Alcott and the American Family Story* by Cornelia Meigs, London, Bodley Head, 1970, New York, Walck, 1971.

*   *   *

In 1868 when, at the request of Thomas Niles of Roberts Brothers, Louisa May Alcott sat down to write a household story for girls, the domestic novel as evolved by Susan Warner, Maria Cummins, Ann Stephens and Mrs. E.D.E.N. Southworth consisted of commonplace episodes worked into a trite plot involving pious and insipid characters. Bronson Alcott's opinion of juvenile literature, recorded in his diary for 1839, had, in the generation that followed, been given no cause for alteration. In 1868 it was still true that the "literature of childhood" had not been written. If such extraordinarily moral tales as *The Wide, Wide World*, the Rollo books, the Lucy books, and the first of the Elsie books became unbearable, there was compensation for a youthful reader only in grave-and-horror stories, Hawthorne's legendary tales or "Peter Parley's" edifying descriptions of natural wonders.

The times were ripe for Louisa Alcott and she was well equipped to fill the gap in domestic literature. With the publication of *Little Women* (1868–1869) she created a domestic novel for children destined to influence writers in that genre for generations to come. Responding to her publisher's request, she drew her characters from those of her own sisters, her scenes from the New England where she had grown up, and many of her episodes from those she and her family had experienced. In all this she was something of a pioneer, adapting her autobiography to the creation of a juvenile novel and achieving a realistic but wholesome picture of family life with which young readers could readily identify.

The literary influence of Bunyan and Dickens, Carlyle and Hawthorne, Emerson, Theodore Parker and Thoreau can be traced in her work, but primarily she drew upon autobiographical sources for her plot and her characters, finding in her family and neighbors the groundwork for her three-dimensional characters. Her perceptively drawn adolescents, the Marches, modeled upon her sisters and herself, were not merely lifelike but alive. Her episodes, from the opening selection of a Christmas gift to the plays in the barn, from Jo March's literary career to Beth's death, were thoroughly believable for they had been lived. The Alcott humor which induced a chuckle at a homely phrase was appreciated by children. The Alcott poverty was sentimentalized; the eccentric Alcott father was an adumbrated shadow; yet, for all the glossing over, the core of the domestic drama was apparent. Reported simply and directly in a style that obeyed her injunction "Never use a long word, when a short one will do as well," the narrative embodied the simple facts and persons of a family and so filled a gap in the literature of childhood. Louisa Alcott had unlatched the door to one house, and "all find it is their own house which they enter." 20th-century writers for children who aim at credibility and verisimilitude in their reconstructions of contemporary family life are all, in one way or another, indebted to Louisa May Alcott.

By the time she created *Little Women* she had served a long apprenticeship and was already a professional writer. She had edited a juvenile monthly, *Merry's Museum*, and produced several books aimed at a juvenile readership: her first published book, *Flower Fables*, "legends of faery land"; *The Rose Family: A Fairy Tale*; and *Morning-Glories and Other Stories*, readable short stories in which autobiographical details were combined with nature lore and moral tidbits.

Alcott had also written in a variety of genres for a wide range of adult readers, weaving stories of sweetness and light, dramatic narratives of strong-minded women and poor lost creatures, realistic episodes of the Civil War, and blood-and-thunder thrillers of revenge and passion whose leading character was usually a vindictive and manipulating heroine. From the exigencies of serialization for magazines she had developed the skills of the cliff-hanger and the page-turner. Her first full-length novel, *Moods*, was a narrative of stormy passion and violence, death and intellectual love in which she attempted to apply Emerson's remark: "life is a train of moods like a string of beads." Off and on, she had worked at her autobiographical and feminist novel *Success*, subsequently renamed *Work: A Story of Experience*. By 1868, Alcott had run a gamut of literary experimentation from stories of virtue rewarded to stories of vice unpunished. She had attempted tales of escape and realism and stirred her literary ingredients in a witch's cauldron before she kindled the fire in a family hearth.

With few exceptions – notably *A Modern Mephistopheles* in which she reverted to the sensational themes of her earlier blood-and-thunders – Louisa Alcott clung to that family hearth during the remainder of her career. Between 1868 when Part One of *Little Women* appeared and 1888 when she died, she produced in her so-called *Little Women Series* a string of wholesome domestic narratives more or less autobiographical in origin, simple and direct in style, perceptive in the characterization of adolescents. *An Old-Fashioned Girl, Little Men, Eight Cousins, Rose in Bloom, Under the Lilacs, Jack and Jill*, and *Jo's Boys* are all in a sense sequels to *Little Women* though none of them quite rises to its level. *An Old-Fashioned Girl* is a domestic drama in reverse, exposing the fashionable absurdities of the Shaw home by contrast with Polly, the wholesome representative of domesticity. The Campbell clan of *Eight Cousins* exalts the family hearth again. In *Jack and Jill* the author enlarges upon the theme of domesticity, describing the home life of a New England village rather than of a single family.

Despite her experimentation with a diversity of literary techniques, despite the fact that she was a complex writer drawn to a variety of themes, Louisa Alcott has inevitably achieved fame as the "Children's Friend" and the author of a single masterpiece. Thanks to its psychological perceptions, its realistic characterizations and its honest domesticity, *Little Women* has become an embodiment of the American home at its best. Consciously or unconsciously all subsequent writers who have attempted the domestic novel for children have felt its influence for in *Little Women* the local has been transmuted into the universal and the incidents of family life have been translated to the domain of literature.

—Madeleine B. Stern

ALDRICH, Thomas Bailey. American. Born in Portsmouth, New Hampshire, 11 November 1836. Attended school in Portsmouth. Married Lilian Woodman in 1865; twin sons. Clerk in New York, 1852–55. Staff member, *Evening Mirror*, 1855–56, Editor of *Home Journal*, 1856–59, Associate Editor, *Saturday Press*, 1858–60, and Editor, *Illustrated News*, 1863, all in New York; Editor, *Every Saturday*, Boston, 1866–74, and *Atlantic Monthly*, Boston, 1881–90. M.A.: Yale University, New Haven, Connecticut, 1881; Harvard University, Cambridge, Massachusetts, 1896; LL.D.: University of Pennsylvania, Philadelphia, 1906. *Died 19 March 1907.*

PUBLICATIONS FOR CHILDREN

Fiction

> *The Story of a Bad Boy.* Boston, Fields Osgood, 1869; London, Sampson Low, 1870.

Other

> Translator, *The Story of a Cat*, by Emile de la Bédollière. Boston, Houghton Osgood, 1879.

PUBLICATIONS FOR ADULTS

Novels

> *Daisy's Necklace and What Came of It: A Literary Episode.* New York, Derby and Jackson, 1856.
> *Out of His Head: A Romance.* New York, Carleton, 1862.
> *Pansy's Wish: A Christmas Fantasy with a Moral.* Boston, Marion, 1870.
> *Prudence Palfrey.* Boston, Osgood, and London, Routledge, 1874.
> *The Queen of Sheba.* Boston, Osgood, and London, Routledge, 1877.
> *The Stillwater Tragedy.* Boston, Houghton Mifflin, 1880; Edinburgh, Douglas, 1886.
> *The Second Son*, with Margaret and Wilson Oliphant. Boston, Houghton Mifflin, 1888.
> *An Old Town by the Sea.* Boston, Houghton Mifflin, 1893.

Short Stories

Père Antoine's Date-Palm.   Privately printed, 1866.
Marjorie Daw and Other People.   Boston, Osgood, and London, Routledge, 1873.
A Midnight Fantasy, and The Little Violinist.   Boston, Osgood, 1877.
Miss Mehetabel's Son.   Boston, Osgood, 1877.
A Rivermouth Romance.   Boston, Osgood, 1877.
Two Bites at a Cherry with Other Tales.   Edinburgh, Douglas, and Boston, Houghton Mifflin, 1894.
A Sea Turn and Other Matters.   Boston, Houghton Mifflin, and London, Watt, 1902.
For Bravery on the Field of Battle.   London, Covent Garden Press, 1970.

Play

Judith of Bethulia, adaptation of his own poem *Judith and Holofernes* (produced New York, 1904).   Boston, Houghton Mifflin, 1904.

Verse

The Bells: A Collection of Chimes.   New York, Derby, 1855.
The Course of True Love Never Did Run Smooth.   New York, Rudd and Carleton, 1858.
The Ballad of Babie Bell and Other Poems.   New York, Rudd and Carleton, 1859.
Pampinea and Other Poems.   New York, Rudd and Carleton, 1861.
Poems.   New York, Carleton, 1863.
The Poems of Thomas Bailey Aldrich.   Boston, Ticknor and Fields, 1865; revised edition, 1882; Boston, Houghton Mifflin, 1885, 1897.
Cloth of Gold and Other Poems.   Boston, Osgood, and London, Routledge, 1874.
Flower and Thorn: Later Poems.   London, Routledge, 1876; Boston, Osgood, 1877.
Baby Bell.   London, Routledge, 1878.
Friar Jerome's Beautiful Book and Other Poems.   Boston, Houghton Mifflin, and London, Sampson Low, 1881.
XXXVI Lyrics and XII Sonnets.   Boston, Houghton Mifflin, 1881.
Baby Bell and Other Poems.   Glasgow, Bryce, 1883.
Mercedes and Later Lyrics.   Boston, Houghton Mifflin, 1884.
Wyndham Towers.   Edinburgh, Douglas, 1889; Boston, Houghton Mifflin, 1890.
The Sisters' Tragedy and Other Poems, Lyrical and Dramatic.   Boston, Houghton Mifflin, and London, Macmillan, 1891.
Unguarded Gates and Other Poems.   Boston, Houghton Mifflin, 1895.
Later Lyrics.   Boston, Houghton Mifflin, and London, Lane, 1896.
Judith and Holofernes.   Boston, Houghton Mifflin, 1896.
A Book of Songs and Sonnets.   Boston, Houghton Mifflin, 1906.

Other

Jubilee Days: An Illustrated Daily Record of the Humorous Features of the World's Peace Jubilee, with William Dean Howells.   Boston, Osgood, 1872.
From Ponkapog to Pesth.   Boston, Houghton Mifflin, 1883.
The Works of Thomas Bailey Aldrich.   Boston, Houghton Mifflin, 8 vols., 1896; vol. 9, 1907.
Ponkapog Papers.   Boston, Houghton Mifflin, 1904.

Editor, with E.C. Stedman, *Cameos Selected from the Works of Walter Savage Landor.*   Boston, Osgood, 1874.

Critical Studies: *The Life of Thomas Bailey Aldrich* by Ferris Greenslet, London, Constable, and Boston, Houghton Mifflin, 1908; *Thomas Bailey Aldrich* by Charles E. Samuels, New York, Twayne, 1966.

*   *   *

Although Thomas Bailey Aldrich first achieved literary renown as a poet in the mid-19th century, it is as a novelist and short story writer that he is chiefly remembered today.

His short stories, like his poems, many of which still retain their distinction, are impeccably crafted, disciplined, restrained, sparse, precise, and refined. Throughout Aldrich's works, there is artistic integrity, a subtle blending of sentiment and wit, and, ever present, a blithe young spirit that led Mark Twain to remark that he was tired of waiting for Aldrich to grow old. What does remain eternally, innocently childlike is his autobiographical novel, *The Story of a Bad Boy*. Aldrich wished to distinguish his young Tom, "an amiable, impulsive lad ... and no hypocrite ... from the faultless young gentlemen who generally figure in narratives of this kind."

His somewhat idealized story parallels the actual events of his own boyhood: early years in New Orleans, schooling in New Hampshire in preparation for Harvard until the death of his father precluded college, completing his education in Portsmouth (Rivermouth in the book). Aldrich recalls these years affectionately, amusingly, nostalgically. On his arrival in Boston from the South, he was surprised to see no Indians on Long Wharf – either they "were early risers" or "they were away just then on the warpath." And, "speaking of the Pilgrim Fathers," why was there never any "mention of the Pilgrim Mothers." Gently, he satirized the "old Puritan austerity" that cropped out on Sundays in the Nutter household where in the oppressive atmosphere of that one day a week, they ate "a dead cold dinner" that was "laid out yesterday." He vowed ever after to make Sundays cheerful days. The most haunting, poignant memory – a wholly fictitious happening – was the tragedy of poor little Binny Wallace who drifted out to sea in a gale and now sleeps in the Old South Burying Ground. One of the early regional novels, the story glows with local color, characteristic eccentricities, and traditions. In that old declining privateer port of Rivermouth, boys cruised down the river, island-hopping on excursions and learning about the sea and ships; they presented amateur theatricals in the barn, celebrated holidays properly, and not so properly burned an old stage coach, jumped jail, and waged frigid snow fights on Slater's Hill.

To Ferris Greenslet, Aldrich's official biographer and an editorial alumnus of *The Atlantic Monthly*, the book "marked an epoch in the history of juvenile literature." One of the first critics to discern that Aldrich had "done a new thing ... in American literature" was William Dean Howells, then editor of the *Atlantic*. Howells' review appeared in the January 1870 issue: "No one else seems to have thought of telling the story of a boy's life with so great desire to show what a boy's life is, and with so little purpose of teaching what it should be; certainly no one has thought of doing this for the American boy!" Howells noted that the story of Aldrich's boyhood had suggested similar books, including his own *A Boy's Town*, Charles Dudley Warner's *Being a Boy*, Mark Twain's *Tom Sawyer* and *Huckleberry Finn*. Not so, declared Bernard DeVoto, one of Twain's fellow Westerners and an historian ever alert to catch any misconceptions concerning Twain. DeVoto deemed it idle to speculate over the origins of *Tom Sawyer*, and whether Aldrich had had any influence on it, for when Mark Twain had come around to writing *Tom Sawyer*, he had "at last arrived at the theme that was most harmonious with his interest, his experience, and his talents ... Mark Twain was predestined to this work." Well, perhaps: but Howells was there! He was Twain's friend and editor. He read *Tom Sawyer* in manuscript, at Twain's request. By deleting some of the profanity and toning down the section where Becky tears a page of the teacher's book of anatomy, Howells may have slanted the story toward the juvenile market – Twain had intended it for adults. "It is not a boy's book at all," he had written to Howells. Also, by 1871, Twain and Aldrich had become friends. Twain must have been aware that what Aldrich had done for the waning years of New England Puritanism, he would do for the early years of Western frontier life. While one is genteel and polite, the other is rugged and lusty, but both cover much the same kind of boyish pranks and activities: climbing out of windows in the dead of night, running away, camping out, falling miserably in love. Aunt Polly is to one, what Grandfather Nutter is to the other: Injun Joe was starved "entirely to death in the cave" (incidentally, he ate candle wax in his struggle to survive just as, in Aldrich's story "A Struggle for Life," Philip Wentworth had in the tomb) for the same kind of heightened literary effect that Aldrich had used in letting Binny Wallace float helplessly out to sea. In his autobiography, Twain praised Aldrich's brilliance and wit, but referred blisteringly to Aldrich's prose as "diffuse, self-conscious, barren of distinction ...," grudgingly conceding that "his fame as a writer ... is based on half a dozen small poems which are not surpassed in our language for exquisite grace and beauty and finish."

The poem that Aldrich had written in honor of Longfellow's centennial – a poem that was read one month later at Aldrich's funeral – is also a fitting tribute to his boyhood story: "They do not die who leave their thoughts/ Imprinted on some deathless page./ Themselves may pass; the spell they wrought/ Endures on earth from age to age." *The Story of a Bad Boy* wrought a spell that has wound its way down the years from Lucretia Peabody Hale to Sarah Orne Jewett, from Laura Ingalls Wilder to Maureen Daly, from Esther Forbes to Jack Schaefer, from J.D. Salinger to John Donovan.

—Mary Silva Cosgrave

BALLANTYNE, R(obert) M(ichael). British. Born in Edinburgh, 24 April 1825. Educated at Edinburgh Academy, 1835–37, and privately. Married Jane Dickson Grant in 1866; four sons and two daughters. Apprentice clerk, Hudson's Bay Company, in Canada, 1841–47; clerk, North British Railway Company, Edinburgh, 1847–49; staff member, Alexander Cowan and Company, paper-makers, Edinburgh, 1849; junior partner, Thomas Constable and Company, printers, Edinburgh, 1849–55. Lecturer and free-lance writer after 1855. Member, 1858, Ensign, 1859, and Captain, 1860, Edinburgh Volunteers. Lived in Harrow, Middlesex, after 1883. *Died 8 February 1894.*

PUBLICATIONS FOR CHILDREN

Fiction

> *Snowflakes and Sunbeams; or, The Young Fur Trader: A Tale of the Far North,* illustrated by the author. London and New York, Nelson, 1856.
> *Three Little Kittens* (as Comus), illustrated by the author. London and New York, Nelson, 1856.
> *Ungava: A Tale of Esquimeaux-Land,* illustrated by the author. London and New York, Nelson, 1857.
> *The Coral Island: A Tale of the Pacific Ocean,* illustrated by the author. London and New York, Nelson, 1857.
> *Mister Fox* (as Comus), illustrated by the author. London and New York, Nelson, 1857.
> *My Mother* (as Comus), illustrated by the author. London and New York, Nelson, 1857; as *Chit-Chat by a Penitent Cat,* 1874.
> *The Butterfly's Ball and the Grasshopper's Feast* (as Comus), illustrated by the author. London and New York, Nelson, 1857.
> *The Life of a Ship from the Launch to the Wreck.* London and New York, Nelson, 1857.
> *The Robber Kitten* (as Comus). London and New York, Nelson, 1858.

Martin Rattler; or, A Boy's Adventures in the Forests of Brazil, illustrated by the author. London and New York, Nelson, 1858.

The World of Ice; or, Adventures in the Polar Regions. London and New York, Nelson, 1859.

Mee-a-ow! or, Good Advice to Cats and Kittens, illustrated by the author. London and New York, Nelson, 1859.

The Dog Crusoe: A Tale of the Western Prairies. London and New York, Nelson, 1861; as *The Dog Crusoe and His Master*, 1869.

The Gorilla Hunters: A Tale of the Wilds of Africa. London and New York, Nelson, 1861.

The Golden Dream; or, Adventures in the Far West. London, Shaw, 1861; New York, Nelson, 1878.

The Red Eric; or, The Whaler's Last Cruise: A Tale, illustrated by Coleman. London, Routledge Warne, 1861; New York, Burt, n.d.

The Wild Man of the West: A Tale of the Rocky Mountains, illustrated by J. B. Zwecker. London, Routledge Warne, 1862; Boston, Crosby and Nichols, 1864.

Gascoyne, The Sandal-Wood Trader: A Tale of the Pacific. London, Nisbet, 1863; New York, Lovell, n.d.

Fighting the Whales; or, Doings and Dangers on a Fishing Cruise. London, Nisbet, 1863; Philadelphia, Porter and Coates, n.d.

Away in the Wilderness; or, Life among the Red Indians and the Fur-Traders. London, Nisbet, 1863; Philadelphia, Davis Porter, 1865.

Fast in the Ice; or, Adventures in the Polar Region. London, Nisbet, 1863; Philadelphia, Davis Porter, 1865.

The Lifeboat: A Tale of Our Coast Heroes, illustrated by the author. London, Nisbet, 1864; Boston, Lee and Shepard, 1866.

Chasing the Sun; or, Rambles in Norway. London, Nisbet, 1864.

Freaks on the Fells; or, Three Months' Rustication, and Why I Did Not Become a Sailor. London, Routledge Warne, 1864; Philadelphia, Porter and Coates, 1865.

The Lighthouse, Being the Story of a Great Fight Between Man and the Sea, illustrated by the author. London, Nisbet, 1865.

Shifting Winds: A Tough Yarn. London, Nisbet, and Philadelphia, Porter and Coates, 1866.

Fighting the Flames: A Tale of the London Fire Brigade. London, Nisbet, 1867; Philadelphia, Lippincott, 1868.

Silver Lake; or, Lost in the Snow. London, Jackson Walford and Hodder, 1867; Philadelphia, Lippincott, 1868.

Deep Down: A Tale of the Cornish Mines. London, Nisbet, and New York, Burt, 1868.

Erling the Bold: A Tale of the Norse Sea-Kings, illustrated by the author. London, Nisbet, 1869; New York, Burt, n.d.

Sunk at Sea: or, The Adventures of Wandering Will in the Pacific. London, Nisbet, 1869.

Lost in the Forest; or, Wandering Will's Adventures in South America. London, Nisbet, 1869.

Over the Rocky Mountains; or, Wandering Will in the Land of the Red Skin. London, Nisbet, 1869.

Saved by the Lifeboat: A Tale of Wreck and Rescue on the Coast. London, Nisbet, 1869.

The Cannibal Islands; or, Captain Cook's Adventures in the South Seas. London, Nisbet, 1869.

Hunting the Lions; or, The Land of the Negro. London, Nisbet, 1869.

Digging for Gold; or, Adventures in California. London, Nisbet, 1869.

Up in the Clouds; or, Balloon Voyages. London, Nisbet, 1869.

The Battle and the Breeze; or, The Fights and Fancies of a British Tar. London, Nisbet, 1869.

The Floating Light of the Goodwin Sands: A Tale, illustrated by the author. London, Nisbet, and Philadelphia, Porter and Coates, 1870.

The Iron Horse; or, Life on the Line: A Tale of the Grand National Trunk Railway. London, Nisbet, 1871.

The Pioneers: A Tale of the Western Wilderness, Illustrative of the Adventures and Discoveries of Sir Alexander Mackenzie. London, Nisbet, 1872.

The Norsemen in the West; or, America Before Columbus: A Tale. London, Nisbet, and New York, Nelson, 1872.

Life in the Red Brigade. London and New York, Routledge, 1873.

Black Ivory: A Tale of Adventure among the Slavers of East Africa. London, Nisbet, and New York, Nelson, 1873.

The Pirate City: An Algerine Tale. London, Nisbet, and New York, Nelson, 1874.

Rivers of Ice: A Tale Illustrative of Alpine Adventure and Glacier Action. London, Nisbet, 1875.

The Story of the Rock; or, Building on the Eddystone. London, Nisbet, 1875.

Under the Waves; or, Diving in Deep Waters: A Tale. London, Nisbet, 1876.

The Settler and the Savage: A Tale of Peace and War in South Africa. London, Nisbet, 1876; New York, Nelson, 1877.

In the Track of the Troops: A Tale of Modern War. London, Nisbet, 1878.

Jarwin and Cuffy: A Tale. London, Warne, and New York, Scribner, 1878.

Philosopher Jack: A Tale of the Southern Seas. London, Nisbet, 1879.

The Lonely Island; or, The Refuge of the Mutineers. London, Nisbet, and New York, Nelson, 1880.

Post Haste: A Tale of Her Majesty's Mails. London, Nisbet, and New York, Nelson, 1880.

The Red Man's Revenge: A Tale of the Red River Flood. London, Nisbet, 1880.

My Doggie and I. London, Nisbet, 1881.

The Giant of the North; or, Poking Around the Pole. London, Nisbet, and New York, Nelson, 1881.

The Battery and the Boiler; or, Adventures in the Laying of Submarine Electric Cables, illustrated by the author. London, Nisbet, and New York, Nelson, 1882.

The Kitten Pilgrims; or, Great Battles and Grand Victories, illustrated by the author. London, Nisbet, 1882.

Dusty Diamonds Cut and Polished: A Tale of City-Arab Life and Adventure. London, Nisbet, and New York, Nelson, 1883.

Battles with the Sea; or, Heroes of the Lifeboat and Rocket. London, Nisbet, 1883.

The Thorogood Family. London, Nisbet, 1883.

The Madman and the Pirate. London, Nisbet, 1883.

The Young Trawler: A Story of Life and Death and Rescue on the North Sea. London, Nisbet, 1884.

Twice Bought: A Tale of the Oregon Gold Fields. London, Nisbet, 1884.

The Rover of the Andes: A Tale of Adventure in South America. London, Nisbet, and New York, Nelson, 1885.

The Island Queen; or, Dethroned by Fire and Water: A Tale of the Southern Hemisphere. London, Nisbet, 1885.

Red Rooney; or, The Last of the Crew. London, Nisbet, and New York, Nelson, 1886.

The Prairie Chief: A Tale. London, Nisbet, 1886.

The Lively Poll: A Tale of the North Sea. London, Nisbet, 1886.

The Big Otter: A Tale of the Great Nor'west. New York and London, Routledge, 1887.

The Fugitives; or, The Tyrant Queen of Madagascar. London, Nisbet, and New York, Nelson, 1887.

Blue Lights; or, Hot Work in the Soudan: A Tale of Soldier Life in Several of Its Phases. London, Nisbet, and New York, Nelson, 1888.

The Middy and the Moors: An Algerine Story. London, Nisbet, 1888; as *Slave of the Moors*, London, Latimer House, 1950.

The Crew of the Water Wagtail: A Story of Newfoundland. London, Nisbet, 1889.

The Eagle Cliff: A Tale of the Western Isles. London, Partridge, 1889.

Blown to Bits; or, The Lonely Man of Rakata: A Tale of the Malay Peninsula, illustrated by the author. London, Nisbet, 1889.

The Garret and the Garden; or, Low Life High Up, and Jeff Benson; or, The Young Coastguardsman. London, Nisbet, 1890; New York, Dodd Mead, n.d.

Charlie to the Rescue: A Tale of the Sea and the Rockies, illustrated by the author. London, Nisbet, 1890.

The Buffalo Runners: A Tale of the Red River Plain, illustrated by the author. London, Nisbet, and New York, Nelson, 1891.

The Coxwain's Bride; or, The Rising Tide: A Tale of the Sea, and Other Tales, illustrated by the author. London, Nisbet, 1891; New York, Dodd Mead, n.d.

The Hot Swamp: A Romance of Old Albion. London, Nisbet, and New York, Nelson, 1892.

Hunted and Harried: A Tale of the Scottish Covenanters. London, Nisbet, 1892; Boston, Bradley, 1893.

The Walrus Hunters: A Romance of the Realms of Ice. London, Nisbet, 1893.

Reuben's Luck: A Tale of the Wild North. London, S.P.C.K., 1896.

Other

The Northern Coasts of America, and the Hudson's Bay Territories: A Narrative of Discovery and Adventure, by Patrick Fraser Tytler, with continuation by R.M. Ballantyne, illustrated by Birket Foster after sketches by R.M. Ballantyne. London, Nelson, 1853.

Discovery and Adventure in the Polar Seas and Regions, by Sir John Leslie and Hugh Murray, with continuation by R.M. Ballantyne. London and New York, Nelson, 1860.

Man on the Ocean. London and New York, Nelson, 1862; revised edition, 1874.

The Ocean and Its Wonders. London and New York, Nelson, 1874.

Editor, *Naughty Boys; or, The Sufferings of Mr. Delteil,* by Champfleury, translated by Jane Ballantyne, illustrated by R.M. Ballantyne. Edinburgh, Constable, 1855.

PUBLICATIONS FOR ADULTS

Other

Hudson's Bay; or, Every-Day Life in the Wilds of North America ..... Edinburgh, Blackwood, 1848.

Handbook to the New Gold Fields: A Full Account of the Richness and Extent of the Fraser and Thompson River Gold Mines ..... Edinburgh, Strahan, 1858.

Environs and Vicinity of Edinburgh. London, Nelson, 1859.

Ships: The Great Eastern and Lesser Crafts. London, Nelson, 1859.

The Lakes of Killarney. London, Nelson, 1859.

How Not to Do It: A Manual for the Awkward Squad; or, A Handbook of Directions Written for the Instruction of Raw Recruits in Our Rifle Volunteer Regiments (published anonymously). Edinburgh, Constable, 1859.

The Volunteer Levee; or, The Remarkable Experiences of Ensign Sopht (published anonymously), illustrated by the author. Edinburgh, Constable, 1860.

Ensign Sopht's Volunteer Almanack for 1861 (published anonymously). Edinburgh, Nimmo, 1861.

Photographs of Edinburgh, with Archibald Burns. Glasgow, Duthie, 1868.

Our Seamen: An Appeal. Privately printed, 1873.

Six Months at the Cape; or, Letters to Periwinkle from South Africa. London, Nisbet,
   1878; New York, Dodd Mead, n.d.
The Collected Works of Ensign Sopht, Late of the Volunteers. London, Nisbet, 1881.
Personal Reminiscences in Book-Making. London, Nisbet, 1893.

Bibliography: *R.M.Ballantyne: A Bibliography of First Editions* by Eric Quayle. London,
Dawsons, 1968.

Critical Study: *Ballantyne the Brave: A Victorian Writer and His Family* by Eric
Quayle, London, Hart Davis, 1967.

*   *   *

In his own lifetime R.M. Ballantyne gained the distinction of being identified in the minds
of his young readers with the bravest of the deeds performed by the manly characters in the
fictional tales he wrote. His photographs, which showed him as a handsome, bearded figure
with the shoulder-length hair of a typical North American trapper, complete with long-
barrelled gun and powder-horn across his knees, went far to confirm this impression. His
autobiographical experiences as a youth employed by the Hudson's Bay Company were
related in his first book, *Hudson's Bay; or, Every-Day Life in the Wilds of North America*, and
his early life in Rupert's Land formed the background to many of his tales.

His first fictional work for the young appeared in 1856 as *Snowflakes and Sunbeams; or,
The Young Fur Trader*; but it was *The Coral Island* (1857) that made his name as a juvenile
novelist. This was the book which Robert Louis Stevenson acknowledged as the formative
influence of his own love of the South Seas, a work which later led to his writing the
immortal classic *Treasure Island*, with its dedicatory allusion to "Ballantyne the Brave."

Ballantyne was one of the first writers of fictional adventure tales for the young to apply
himself seriously to the background research so necessary to render the stories realistic.
Unlike G.A. Henty, who wrote fictional tales set against historical backgrounds in the
manner of Sir Walter Scott, Ballantyne almost without exception set himself the task of living
and often working for weeks or months in the geographical location where he meant to set
his story. Thus for *The Lifeboat* he lived at Deal with the lifeboat crew; for *The Lighthouse* he
spent several weeks on the Bell Rock Lighthouse; for *Fighting the Flames* he was with the
London Fire Brigade waiting for days on end for the bells to signal a fire; for *Deep Down: A
Tale of the Cornish Mines* he lived with the tin-miners of St. Just for over three months. The
same could be said for *The Floating Light of the Goodwin Sands*, for which he endured weeks
of sea-sickness on the Gull Lightship, and for *The Iron Horse; or, Life on the Line*, for which
he acted as fireman on board the tender of the London-to-Edinburgh express. The result of all
these and countless other expeditions both at home and abroad was a series of well over 80
full-length juvenile novels embodying a realism never before seen in works for teenage boys.

He was the hero of Victorian youth; but his weakness lay in his being straitjacketed by his
puritanism. Unlike Stevenson, he was unable to write a romantic and exciting story of
adventure that was unmoralised and unashamed. Too often the action in Ballantyne's tales
was braked by the gum of piety and the evangelistic soliloquising of the often bloodthirsty
young characters he made his heroes. They lightheartedly slaughtered the fauna and the
natives of the islands and jungles where they found themselves marooned with an impartial
vigour, before falling on their knees to thank God for His infinite mercy and a successful
day's sport. *The Gorilla Hunters* is a typical example of unrelenting cruelty by young
teenagers that passed without comment in the mid-19th-century. He wrote, as we all do, for
the age in which he lived.

Nevertheless, Ballantyne opened for the sons of the rapidly expanding *literati* of middle-
and working-class families an exciting new vista of a world spiced with romance and danger
which lay waiting for the young men of Britain to grow up and explore. He projected into
lives which were often drab and humdrum a realistically coloured image, mirroring his
readers in the figures of his heroes, and leaving them tantalised with the knowledge that they,

too, could equally well have overcome the fearful odds against which Ralph, Jack, and Peterkin grappled so bravely. He employed what was soon a well-tried formula, by giving full rein to youthful emotions within the strict bounds for what then passed as Christian morality, while leading his readers through dramatically bloody chapters of shipwreck, slaughter, capture and escape, to the inevitable happy ending of a wealthy and pious old age.

He portrayed a world where the good were terribly good, and the bad were terribly bad, and the British were terribly British – and worth ten of any foreigners alive, by Jingo! For any writer of his time to dare to suggest otherwise would have been considered the blackest heresy by the young men of Victoria's England. For these were the boys who, in their turn, were to become the soldiers and sailors, the explorers and trail-blazers, the missionaries and merchant adventurers, the exploiters, the Word-spreaders, the successes and failures of the great British Empire on which the sun would never set.

—Eric Quayle

———————

CARROLL, Lewis. Pseudonym for Charles Lutwidge Dodgson. British. Born in Daresbury, Cheshire, 27 January 1832. Educated at school in Richmond, Surrey, 1844–46; Rugby School, Warwickshire, 1846–49; Christ Church, Oxford (Boultor Scholar, 1851), B.A. 1854, M.A. 1857. Fellow, and Master of the House, 1855, Sub-Librarian, 1855, Bostock Scholar, 1855, teaching staff member, 1856–81, and Curator of the Common Room, 1882–92, Christ Church, Oxford. Ordained, 1861. *Died 14 January 1898.*

PUBLICATIONS FOR CHILDREN

Fiction

> *Alice's Adventures in Wonderland*, illustrated by John Tenniel.   London, Macmillan, 1865; New York, Appleton, 1866; revised edition, 1886, 1897.
> *Through the Looking-Glass, and What Alice Found There*, illustrated by John Tenniel.   London and New York, Macmillan, 1871; revised edition, 1897.
> *Alice's Adventures Underground*, illustrated by the author.   London, and New York, Macmillan, 1886.
> *The Nursery Alice.*   London and New York, Macmillan, 1889.
> *The "Wonderland" Postage-Stamp-Case.*   Oxford, Emberlin, 1890.

Verse

> *Phantasmagoria and Other Poems.*   London and New York, Macmillan, 1869.
> *The Hunting of the Snark: An Agony in Eight Fits*, illustrated by Henry Holiday. London, Macmillan, and Boston, Osgood, 1876.
> *Rhyme? and Reason?*, illustrated by Arthur B. Frost and Henry Holiday.   London, Macmillan, 1883; New York, Macmillan, 1884.
> *Sylvie and Bruno*, illustrated by Harry Furniss.   London and New York, Macmillan, 1889.
> *Sylvie and Bruno Concluded*, illustrated by Harry Furniss.   London and New York, Macmillan, 1893.
> *Three Sunsets and Other Poems*, illustrated by E. Gertrude Thomson.   London and New York, Macmillan, 1898.
> *The Collected Verse of Lewis Carroll*, edited by J.F. McDermott.   New York, Dutton, 1929; London, Macmillan, 1932.

For the Train: Five Poems and a Tale, edited by Hugh J. Schonfield.   London, Archer,
   1932.
The Humorous Verses of Lewis Carroll, edited by J.E. Morpurgo.   London, Grey Walls
   Press, 1950.
Useful and Instructive Poetry, edited by Derek Hudson.   London, Bles, 1954.
The Poems of Lewis Carroll, edited by Myra Cohn Livingston.   New York, Crowell,
   1973.

Other

A Tangled Tale: A Series of Mathematical Questions, illustrated by Arthur B.
   Frost.   London and New York, Macmillan, 1885.
Symbolic Logic, part 1.   London and New York, Macmillan, 1895.
*The Lewis Carroll Picture Book: A Selection from the Unpublished Writings and
   Drawings*, edited by Stuart Dodgson Collingwood.   London, Unwin, 1899; as
   Diversions and Digressions, New York, Dover, 1961.
Further Nonsense Verse and Prose, edited by Langford Reed, illustrated by H.M.
   Bateman.   London, Unwin, and New York, Appleton, 1926.
The Lewis Carroll Book, edited by Richard Herrick.   New York, Dial Press, 1931.
The Book of Nonsense, edited by Roger Lancelyn Green.   London, Dent, 1956.
Symbolic Logic, parts 1–2, edited by W.W. Bartley, III.   New York, Clarkson N.
   Potter, 1977.

Editor, *The Rectory Magazine*.   Austin, University of Texas Press, 1976.

PUBLICATIONS FOR ADULTS (as C.L. Dodgson)

Other

The Fifth Book of Euclid Treated Algebraically ....   Oxford, Parker, 1858; revised
   edition, 1868.
A Syllabus of Plane Algebraical Geometry ...., part 1.   Oxford, Parker, 1860.
Notes on the First Two Books of Euclid.   Oxford, Parker, 1860.
Notes on the First Part of Algebra.   Oxford, Parker, 1861.
The Formulae of Plane Trigonometry ....   Oxford, Parker, 1861.
An Index to "In Memoriam" (published anonymously).   Oxford, Edward Moxon,
   1862.
*The Enunciation of the Propositions and Corollaries with Questions in Euclid, Books 1 and
   2*.   London, Oxford University Press, 1863; revised edition, 1873.
A Guide to the Mathematical Student ...., part 1.   Oxford, Parker, 1864.
Notes by an Oxford Chiel (published anonymously) (includes *The Dynamics of a Particle,
   with an Excursus on the New Method of Evaluation as Applied to Pi; Facts, Figures,
   and Fancies Relating to the Elections to the Hebdomadal Council ....; The New Belfrey
   of Christ Church, Oxford; The Vision of the Three T's: A Threnody; The Blank
   Cheque: A Fable*).   Oxford, Parker, 5 vols., 1865–74.
An Elementary Treatise on Determinants ....   London, Macmillan, 1867.
Algebraic Formulae for Responsions.   London, Oxford University Press, 1868.
Algebraic Formulae and Rules.   London, Oxford University Press, 1870.
Enunciations, Euclid, 1–4.   London, Oxford University Press, 1873.
Preliminary Algebra, and Euclid, Book 5.   London, Oxford University Press, 1874.
Suggestions as to the Best Methods of Taking Votes ....   Oxford, Hall and Stacy, 1874.
Some Popular Fallacies about Vivisection (as Lewis Carroll).   Privately printed, 1875.
Doublets: A Word Puzzle.   London, Macmillan, 1879.
Euclid and His Modern Rivals.   London, Macmillan, 1879; revised edition, 1885.

Lawn Tennis Tournaments: The True Method of Assigning Prizes .... London, Macmillan, 1883.

Twelve Months in a Curatorship, by One Who Has Tried. Privately printed, 1884; revised edition, 1884.

The Principles of Parliamentary Representation. London, Harrison, 1884.

Three Years in a Curateship. Privately printed, 1886.

The Game of Logic (as Lewis Carroll). London and New York, Macmillan, 1886.

Curiosa Mathematica. London, Macmillan, 2 vols., 1888–93.

Feeding the Mind (as Lewis Carroll). London, Chatto and Windus, 1907.

Some Rare Carrolliana. Privately printed, 1924.

Six Letters by Lewis Carroll. Privately printed, 1924.

Novelty and Romancement. Boston, B.J. Brimmer, 1925.

Tour in 1867. Privately printed, 1928.

Two Letters to Marion. Bristol, D. Cleverdon, 1932.

The Rectory Umbrella, and Misch-Masch. London, Cassell, 1932.

A Selection from the Letters of Lewis Carroll ... to His Child-Friends, edited by Evelyn M. Hatch. London, Macmillan, 1933.

Logical Nonsense, edited by Philip C. Blackburn and Lionel White. New York, Putnam, 1934.

The Russian Journal and Other Selections from the Work of Lewis Carroll, edited by J.F. McDermott. New York, Dutton, 1935.

The Complete Works. New York, Random House, and London, Nonesuch Press, 1937; revised edition, 1949.

How the Boots Got Left Behind. Privately printed, 1943.

The Diaries of Lewis Carroll, edited by Roger Lancelyn Green. London, Cassell, 2 vols., 1954; New York, Oxford University Press, 1954.

The Works of Lewis Carroll, edited by Roger Lancelyn Green. London, Hamlyn, 1965.

Lewis Carroll Observed: A Collection of Unpublished Photographs, Drawings, Poetry, and New Essays, edited by Edward Guiliano. New York, Clarkson N. Potter, 1976.

Editor, *Euclid, Books 1–2.* Oxford, Parker, 1875; revised edition, London, Macmillan, 1882.

Critical Studies: *Life of Lewis Carroll* by Langford Reed, London, Foyle, 1932; *Lewis Carroll* by Derek Hudson, London, Constable, 1954; *Lewis Carroll* by Roger Lancelyn Green, London, Bodley Head, 1960, New York, Walck, 1962; *The Annotated Alice*, edited by Martin Gardner, New York, Clarkson N. Potter, 1960, London, Blond, 1964; *The Annotated Snark*, edited by Martin Gardner, New York, Clarkson N. Potter, 1962; *The Lewis Carroll Handbook* by Roger Lancelyn Green, 1962; *Lewis Carroll and His World* by John Pudney, London, Thames and Hudson, and New York, Scribner, 1976; *Lewis Carroll: Fragments of a Looking-Glass* by Jean Gattégno, New York, Crowell, 1976, London, Allen and Unwin, 1977.

*   *   *

Little that is not general knowledge can be said about the Rev. Charles Lutwidge Dodgson whose books for children were published over the pseudonym of Lewis Carroll. After the Bible and Shakespeare, he is probably the most quoted author in the English language, and nearly every character from *Alice's Adventures in Wonderland* and *Through the Looking-Glass and What Alice Found There* is known and recognised almost universally. At the time of his death Andrew Lang wrote that Carroll was, "With the possible exception of Thackeray and Hans Andersen, the most successful writer of stories for children that the world has ever seen. *Alice's Adventures* and *Through the Looking-Glass* are books of which a child with an active mind never tires. They are equally full of imagination and humour. They suggest so much more than they say, that those who have grown up with them have found more in them every year."

The appearance and popularity of *Alice* (we may consider it as a single unity in two volumes, like *Sylvie and Bruno* towards the end of his life) brought about the greatest revolution so far in the literature of childhood. Apart from a few volumes of fairy tales – Perrault, Grimm, Andersen, in various forms – and *The Rose and the Ring*, which appeared ten years before *Wonderland* – the books a child might read (other than adult works like the Waverley Novels) were still of an improving or moralistic kind, however well writers like Charlotte Yonge, or Mrs. Craik might manage to transcend their limitations. But, in spite of Thackeray and Ruskin, whose inspiration overcame the moral and indeed turned it to their own use, *Alice* was something completely new. It was, as Harvey Darton wrote in 1932, "the coming to the surface, powerfully and permanently, the first unapologetic, undocumented appearance in print, for readers who sorely needed it, of liberty of thought in children's books. Henceforth fear had gone, and with it shy disquiet. There was to be in hours of pleasure no more dread about the moral value, the ponderable, measured quality and extent, of pleasure itself. It was to be enjoyed and even promoted with neither forethought nor remorse."

It is possible to a certain extent to understand how the circumstances of his life and character made Dodgson the author of *Alice*. He grew up as an elder brother in a large family with girls predominating, and living in parsonages remote and self-contained. From an early age he was accustomed to the society of children younger than himself, and to entertaining them in various ways, the writing (and probably telling) of stories and verses being one of the chief ways in which he did this. While still an undergraduate at Christ Church, Oxford he was telling stories to children whom he met during "reading holidays" and writing nonsense letters to his youngest sister and brother, who were still children. The fact that instead of growing out of these pastimes with children he pursued them more and more eagerly was due in a considerable extent to the fact that he suffered all his life from a stammer – which left him in the company of children, and of little girls in particular. Consequently he spent more and more time with his child-friends and achieved an understanding of them and their outlook which has probably never been equalled by any other author.

Chance – and a particularly good story out of many – caused him to write out *Alice's Adventures Underground* for Alice Liddell and another chance caused the novelist Henry Kingsley to pick up and read Alice's manuscript copy, and urge Mrs. Liddell to persuade the author to publish it. Chance again made Dodgson, doubtful of the story's appeal to children other than those for whom it was written, lend his own copy to George MacDonald, himself an outstanding writer for the young, to be read to his children – whose response was so enthusiastic that Dodgson at once began revising the story and adding other incidents from his retentive memory – from which rich source came also most of the incidents in *Through the Looking-Glass* a few years later.

All this might have produced only some glorified variant in *The Rose and the Ring* genre, had not Dodgson been a professional mathematician and logician – and already an accomplished manipulator of the English language. The exact logician making use lightheartedly of the illogicalities of daily speech – and occasionally making "portmanteau" words by weaving together two other words in an exactly balanced synthesis – was able to follow where fancy led, but always in strict obedience to the discipline which he seems to have evolved spontaneously. In fact Lewis Carroll, the adult writer who was able to look at life through a child's eyes, and C.L. Dodgson, the academic lecturer on mathematics and logic, formed the perfect union from which *Alice* could be born. They were still in harmony when *The Hunting of the Snark* – the only real nonsense-epic in existence – came into being; but the marriage of two minds was falling apart when *Sylvie and Bruno* was being forced into existence: the don was imposing his will consciously upon the dreamer – and the result was what Derek Hudson has so aptly called "the most interesting failure in English literature."

Though not itself numinous, *Alice* once and for all flung wide the "magic casement opening on the foam of perilous seas in faery lands forlorn": she was the ancestor of all the great children's books that were to follow her, however different in kind they may seem – of *The Midnight Folk* and *The Lion, The Witch and the Wardrobe* as well as more obvious descendants such as *The Just So Stories* and *Winnie the Pooh*. But unlike most progenitors,

Alice is in no danger of growing old or being forgotten: she is as fresh and vivid today as she was a hundred years ago, and an everlasting delight to readers of all ages.

—Roger Lancelyn Green

COOLIDGE, Susan. Pseudonym for Sarah Chauncy Woolsey. American. Born in Cleveland, Ohio, 29 January 1835. Educated at private schools, Cleveland; Mrs. Hubbard's Select Family School for Young Ladies, Hanover, New Hampshire. Did hospital work and helped organize nursing service during the Civil War. Consulting Reader for Roberts Brothers, publishers, Boston. *Died 9 April 1905.*

PUBLICATIONS FOR CHILDREN

Fiction

> *The New Year's Bargain,* illustrated by Addie Ledyard. Boston, Roberts, and London, Warne, 1872.
> *What Katy Did,* illustrated by Addie Ledyard. Boston, Little Brown, 1872; London, Ward, 1873.
> *What Katy Did at School.* Boston, Roberts, and London, Ward, 1874.
> *Little Miss Mischief and Other Stories,* illustrated by Addie Ledyard. London, Ward, 1874.
> *Mischief's Thanksgiving and Other Stories,* illustrated by Addie Ledyard. Boston, Roberts, 1874; London, Routledge, 1875.
> *Nine Little Goslings.* Boston, Roberts, 1875.
> *For Summer Afternoons.* Boston, Roberts, 1876.
> *Eyebright.* Boston, Roberts, and London, Routledge, 1879.
> *A Guernsey Lily; or, How the Feud Was Healed.* Boston, Roberts, 1881.
> *A Round Dozen.* Boston, Roberts, 1883.
> *A Little Country Girl.* Boston, Roberts, 1885.
> *What Katy Did Next,* illustrated by Jessie McDermot. Boston, Roberts, 1886; London, Ward, 1887.
> *Clover,* illustrated by Jessie McDermot. Boston, Roberts, 1888.
> *Just Sixteen.* Boston, Roberts, 1889.
> *In the High Valley.* Boston, Roberts, 1891; London, Blackie, 1959.
> *The Barberry Bush and Eight Other Stories about Girls for Girls.* Boston, Roberts, 1892.
> *Not Quite Eighteen.* Boston, Roberts, 1894.
> *An Old Convent School in Paris and Other Papers.* Boston, Roberts, 1895.
> *Curly Locks.* Boston, Little Brown, 1899.
> *A Little Knight of Labor.* Boston, Little Brown, 1899.
> *Little Tommy Tucker.* Boston, Little Brown, 1900.
> *Two Girls.* Boston, Little Brown, 1900.
> *Uncle and Aunt.* Boston, Little Brown, 1900.
> *The Rule of Three,* illustrated by Joseph Johnson Ray. Philadelphia, Altemus, 1904.
> *A Sheaf of Stories,* illustrated by J.W.F.Kennedy. Boston, Little Brown, 1906.

Verse

> *Rhymes and Ballads for Boys and Girls,* illustrated by Harriet Roosevelt Richards and others. Boston, Roberts, 1892.

Other

Cross-Patch and Other Stories, illustrated by Ellen Oakford.   Boston, Roberts, and
London, Bogue, 1881.
Little Bo-Peep.   Boston, Little Brown, 1901.

Editor, The Day's Message.   Boston, Roberts, 1890; London, Methuen, 1911.

PUBLICATIONS FOR ADULTS

Verse

Verses.   Boston, Roberts, 1880.
A Few More Verses.   Boston, Roberts, 1889.
Last Verses.   Boston, Little Brown, 1906.

Other

A Short History of the City of Philadelphia from Its Foundation to the Present
Time.   Boston, Roberts, 1887.

Editor, The Autobiography and Correspondence of Mrs. Delany.   Boston, Roberts, 2
vols., 1879.
Editor, The Diary and Letters of Frances Burney, Mrs. D'Arblay.   Boston, Roberts, 2
vols., 1880.
Editor, Letters of Jane Austen.   Boston, Roberts, 1892.

*   *   *

Susan Coolidge gained her reputation from the Katy books, although she had some
contemporary success as a critic. At first reading What Katy Did appears to be in the mainstream of Victorian children's fiction – the motherless family "mothered" by the heroine, the
general religious ambiance and the moral retribution for wrong-doing – but a closer
inspection reveals that Susan Coolidge was in fact the forerunner of the 20th-century genre of
British girls' school stories, her literary influence being greater in the United Kingdom than in
her native United States. Figuratively speaking, she may be placed midway between the piety
of L.T. Meade's A World of Girls with its sanctimonious principal dispensing sweetness and
light to the pupils of Lavender House, and the feuds and frolics in the works of Angela Brazil.
Very probably Susan Coolidge took her inspiration from Louisa May Alcott. Certainly
Katy embodies some of the foibles of the outspoken Jo March. Like Jo, Katy endeared herself
to her readers by her very human faults and spontaneous behaviour; like Jo, she was
immediately popular, with her followers demanding a sequel; like Jo's, her popularity was
not confined to her compatriots, and English girls readily identified with her. Susan Coolidge
received (in The Independent) the curious and confusing accolade that she was on her way to
becoming a second "Aunt Jo." That Jo was a recognizable self-portrait of Louisa Alcott has to
account for the mixed reference to the real and the fictional ladies.
Susan Coolidge seems to have "written out" her Victorianism in What Katy Did. Her own
upbringing and the expectations of teachers, ministers and parents demanded a stereotyped
"good angel" figure and it is significant that the author did not select her heroine for the role
but a somewhat peripheral character, crippled Cousin Helen. Katy had disobeyed authority
and used the garden swing. In the Victorian tradition she had to be "punished" and became
bedridden from the consequent fall. Instead of saintly suffering, Katy demonstrated
untidiness, irritable temper and general misery. It was left to the visiting cousin to fulfil the
moral function.
"God is going to let you go to his school," Cousin Helen explained to Katy when she
complained.

"But what is the school?" asked Katy. "It is called The School of Pain," replied Cousin Helen, with her sweetest smile. "There's the lesson of Patience. That's one of the hardest studies ... and there's the lesson of Cheerfulness. And the lesson of Making the Best of Things ...."

Cousin Helen helped Katy to see her condition in a new light, and thus motivated the plot, but her formal utterances give a note of unreality to an otherwise natural and lively account. This must have occurred to Susan Coolidge, for Cousin Helen made no other real contribution, and by the end of the sequel volume, *What Katy Did at School*, she does not even appear, merely sending two illuminated religious texts for Katy and her sister Clover on their homecoming: "The girls thought they had never seen anything so pretty." So much for Cousin Helen, the symbol of perfect behaviour, the model for the aspiring Victorian child.

What Katy Did at School is the most significant book in the series (*What Katy Did Next*, *Clover* and *In the High Valley* followed) since it predates the entire output of girls' school stories which virtually dominated the reading of British middle-class girls until the 1940's. Adult books (such as *Jane Eyre*) might cast aspersions on the teaching profession, but for the youthful reader authority was irreproachable. There is a chasm between the approach of L.T.Meade to the pious principal Mrs. Willis and Susan Coolidge's ironic appraisal of Mrs. Florence, who lost interest in her pupils once she had decided to leave the school, and made no real effort to mete out justice. Susan Coolidge's own experiences at Mrs. Hubbard's Boarding School in Hanover, New Hampshire, had given her insight into both staff-room and dormitory and the economic strategy behind the school meals. Rebellion among the pupils at "The Nunnery," the nickname given to Hillsover by Katy's companions, was seen from the point of view of the girls, and the character of Rose Red (real name Rosamund Redding) reappeared in various guises in almost every 20th-century school story from Angela Brazil's American Gipsy Latimer in *The Leader of the Lower School* to Enid Blyton's heroine of *The Naughtiest Girl in the School*. Always defiant, ultimately likable, struggling against the system which may or may not be just, these girls form a continuous thread throughout girls' fiction, together with a casual use of slang which gives a sparkling spontaneity to the dialogue. Susan Coolidge's schoolgirls were as iconoclastic over "correct" speech as they were over behaviour. With Katy as president of the *Society for the Suppression of Unladylike Conduct*, a title bestowed with conscious mockery, established precepts were overthrown. One of the main aims was to have a good time combined with the pursuit of virtue. Victorian writers for children would have considered that a contradiction in terms.

—Gillian Freeman

DODGE, Mary Mapes. American. Born in New York City, 26 January 1831. Educated privately. Married William Dodge in 1851 (died, 1858); two sons. Helped her father edit *The Working Farmer* magazine, 1847; Home-Making Editor, *Hearth and Home* magazine, 1870–73; Founding Editor, *St. Nicholas* magazine, 1873–1905. Recipient: French Academy Montyon Prize. *Died 21 August 1905.*

PUBLICATIONS FOR CHILDREN

Fiction

The Irvington Stories, illustrated by F.O.C.Darley. New York, James O'Kane, 1865; revised edition, Chicago, Donohue, 1898.

Hans Brinker; or, The Silver Skates: A Story of Life in Holland, illustrated by F.O.C.Darley and Thomas Nast. New York, James O'Kane, 1865; as *The Silver Skates*, London, Sampson Low, 1867.
Donald and Dorothy. Boston, Roberts, and London, Warne, 1883.
The Land of Pluck. New York, Century, 1894.
The Golden Gate. Chicago, Donohue, 1903.
Po-no-kah: An Indian Tale of Long Ago. Chicago, Donohue, 1903.

Verse

When Life Is Young. New York, Century, 1894.

Other

Editor, *Baby Days.* New York, Scribner, 1877.
Editor, *Baby World: Stories, Rhymes, and Pictures for Little Folks.* New York, Century, 1884.
Editor, *A New Baby World: Stories, Rhymes, and Pictures for Little Folk.* New York, Century, 1897.
Editor, *The Children's Book of Recitation.* New York, De Witt, 1898.

PUBLICATIONS FOR ADULTS

Verse

Rhymes and Jingles. New York, Scribner Armstrong, 1874; London, Gay and Bird, 1904.
Along the Way. New York, Scribner, 1879; as *Poems and Verses*, New York, Century, 1904.

Other

A Few Friends and How They Amused Themselves. Philadelphia, Lippincott, 1869.
Theophilus and Others. New York, Scribner Armstrong, and London, Sampson Low, 1876.

*   *   *

With the publication of her *Irvington Stories*, Mary Mapes Dodge was widely recognized in the United States as a promising new writer of literature for children. Reviewers and readers praised the eight tales, which derived from American colonial history and from stories told in the author's family, for their blend of realistic detail, engaging humor, and appropriate moral tone. Encouraged by the book's success, Mrs. Dodge's publisher, James O'Kane, urged her to begin a second work and, with the Civil War approaching an end, suggested a timely theme — a boy leaving his family to enlist in the Union Army. Unenthusiastic about the idea, Mrs. Dodge turned instead to notes she had retained from her reading of Motley's *Story of the Dutch Republic* years before as well as to stories she had heard from Dutch immigrant neighbors and began work on a story set in Holland.

Reluctantly, O'Kane agreed to publish the completed manuscript, *Han Brinker and the Silver Skates*. An outstanding commercial success from the start, *Hans Brinker* quickly established itself as a classic children's book. As in the *Irvington Stories* there is an abundance of closely observed detail, abstracted from her sources (Mrs. Dodge did not visit Holland until years after the book was written) and combined with a clear moral purpose. Not notably inventive or original, Mrs. Dodge drew heavily on familiar popular conventions for the structure of the story. Hans Brinker and his sister Gretel are the impoverished but virtuous children of a dike engineer, a mute, uncomprehending invalid since he was injured ten years before the events of the story take place. This premise, the incapacitation of a family's father and breadwinner and the subsequent suffering, however salutary, of his dependents, was one of the stock conventions of late 19th-century children's literature. For good measure, the plot involves a missing sum of money, a mysterious watch, and a father estranged from his son, as well as the ice skating race that gives the book its title – all familiar devices to create suspense in what is essentially a static book – a series of set pieces, detailing the characteristic and distinctive scenes, social types, customs, dress, and culture of Holland: the festival of St. Nicholas, the windmills and canals, the cities of Haarlem, Leyden, and the Hague.

The central chapters of *Hans Brinker* – and much the longest narrative sequence – detail a skating expedition undertaken by five of Hans' friends, boys from wealthier families who can afford the diversion. As a consequence, Hans and sister disappear from the story entirely. In order to get the necessary Anglo-American perspective on Dutch culture, Mrs. Dodge makes one of the five boys an English visitor, and it is through his eyes that the reader sees the charming peculiarities of the Dutch. Enlivened somewhat by differences in temperament among the boys and by an occasional adventure – they capture a robber at one point – the expedition provides Mrs. Dodge with the means and justification for a close, sympathetic, sometimes condescending description of Dutch life.

In the final third of the book, the focus returns to the Brinker family. The father is restored to health by the leading surgeon in Holland, whom Hans has chanced to meet early in the story. With his reason restored, Hans' father recalls hiding the family savings as well as the circumstances surrounding his possession of the mysterious watch. The young man from whom he had received it turns out to be the estranged son of the eminent surgeon. The Brinker family, tested by ten years of poverty, is restored to comfortable affluence, and the surgeon is reconciled with his son – and to his son's legitimate desire to have a vocation different from his father's. A conventional final chapter describes the fate of the several children introduced in the story, apportioning happiness and success to the virtuous, especially Hans and Gretel whose fortitude, perseverance, faith, and selfless devotion through years of poverty and care exemplify character at its best.

In its affectionate and detailed description of foreign peoples and places, *Hans Brinker* was a distinct improvement over the earlier travelogues of "Peter Parley" and a harbinger of greater attention to realistic detail in American fiction for children in the late 19th century. Its moral values, however, are quite representative of much children's literature written from the 1830's to the end of the century and beyond. Although Mrs. Dodge was the pre-eminent children's periodical editor of her generation, she cannot be said to have made a very notable contribution to children's literature, *Hans Brinker* excepted. *The Irvington Stories* are deservedly forgotten, except by a few specialists, and *The Land of Pluck*, while testifying to her affection for Holland, represents no improvement on the similar sketches in *Hans Brinker*; many of her stories are simply cautionary tales of a kind indistinguishable in style or sentiment from the mass of homiletic narrative to be found in many a late 19th-century children's periodical – even the justly praised *St. Nicholas*.

—R. Gordon Kelly

EWING, Juliana Horatia. British. Born in Ecclesfield, Yorkshire, 3 August 1841; daughter of the children's writer Margaret Gatty. Married Alexander Ewing in 1867. Associated with her mother and sister in editing *Aunt Judy's Magazine*, 1866–85. *Died 13 May 1885.*

PUBLICATIONS FOR CHILDREN

Fiction

Melchior's Dream and Other Tales, edited by Mrs. Gatty, illustrated by
M.S.G. London, Bell and Daldy, 1862; Boston, Roberts, 1886.

Mrs. Overtheway's Remembrances, illustrated by J.A. Pasquier and J. Wolf. London,
Bell and Daldy, 1869; Boston, Roberts, 1881.

The Brownies and Other Tales, illustrated by George Cruikshank. London, Bell and
Daldy, 1870; New York, Hurst, 1901.

A Flat Iron for a Farthing; or, Some Passages in the Life of an Only Son. London, Bell
and Daldy, 1872; Boston, Roberts, 1884.

Lob Lie-by-the-Fire; or, The Luck of Lingborough and Other Tales, illustrated by
George Cruikshank. London, Bell. 1874; New York, Young, 1875.

Six to Sixteen. London, Bell, and Boston, Roberts, 1875.

Jan of the Windmill: A Story of the Plains, illustrated by Helen Allingham. London,
Bell, 1876; Boston, Roberts, 1877.

A Great Emergency and Other Tales. London, Bell, and Boston, Roberts, 1877.

We and the World. London, S.P.C.K., and New York, Young, 1880.

Old Fashioned Fairy Tales, illustrated by A.W. Bayes and Gordon Browne. London,
S.P.C.K., 1882; Boston, Little Brown, n.d.

Brothers of Pity and Other Tales of Beasts and Men. London, S.P.C.K., and New York,
Young, 1882.

The Story of a Short Life, illustrated by Gordon Browne. London, S.P.C.K., and New
York, Young, 1882.

Jackanapes, illustrated by Randolph Caldecott. London, S.P.C.K., and New York,
Young, 1884.

Daddy Darwin's Dovecot: A Country Tale, illustrated by Randolph Caldecott. London,
S.P.C.K., and New York, Young, 1884.

Grandmother's Spring, illustrated by R. André. London, S.P.C.K., and New York,
Young, 1885.

Mary's Meadow, and Letters from a Little Garden, illustrated by Gordon
Browne. London, S.P.C.K., and New York, Young, 1886.

Dandelion Clocks and Other Tales, illustrated by Gordon Browne and others. London,
S.P.C.K., and New York, Young, 1887.

The Peace Egg, and A Christmas Mumming Play, illustrated by Gordon
Browne. London, S.P.C.K., and New York, Young, 1887.

*Snapdragon: A Tale of Christmas Eve, and Old Father Christmas: An Old-Fashioned
Tale of the Young Days of a Grumpy Old Godfather*, illustrated by Gordon
Browne. London, S.P.C.K., and New York, Young, 1888.

Last Words: A Final Collection of Stories. Boston, Roberts, 1891.

The Ewing Book: Scenes from the Tales, edited by E.M. Allsopp. London, Bell, 1930.

Verse (illustrated by R. André)

Blue and Red; or, The Discontented Lobster. London, S.P.C.K., and New York,
Young, 1883.

A Soldier's Children and Five Other Tales in Verse. London, S.P.C.K., and New York,
Young, 1883.

The Blue Bells on the Lea and Ten Other Tales in Verse. London, S.P.C.K., and New
York, Young, 1884.

Mother's Birthday Reviews and Seven Other Tales in Verse. London, S.P.C.K., and
New York, Young, 1888.

Other

Collected Works. London, S.P.C.K., 18 vols., 1894–96.
Works. Boston, Little Brown, 11 vols., 1909(?).

Critical Studies: *Mrs. Gatty and Mrs. Ewing* by Christabel Maxwell, London, Constable, 1949; *Mrs. Ewing, Mrs. Molesworth, and Mrs. Hodgson Burnett* by Marghanita Laski, London, Barker, 1950; *Mrs. Ewing* by Gillian Avery, London, Bodley Head, 1961, New York, Walck, 1964.

*   *   *

Mrs. Ewing succeeded, better than any other Victorian writer for the young, in conveying the high spirits of childhood, and remembering its laughter and sheer enjoyment of life. She did not fall into the trap of presenting children's happiness as undiluted. She herself pointed out that "it is probably from an imperfect remembrance of their nursery lives that some people believe that the griefs of one's childhood are light, its joys uncomplicated, and its tastes simple." But she recorded light and shadow, rough and smooth, without moral reflections on their implication to the child that experienced them. It was a style very different from her mother, Mrs. Gatty, who, in the manner of her generation, had felt obliged to improve the occasion whenever she could. The early Victorian writers for the young could never forget their role as governess. Mrs. Ewing, though no conscious innovator, did forget. She used much the same material as her mother – large, happy families; she was fundamentally just as serious-minded, but she was fortunate in being born into a generation that saw no harm in *enjoying* writing for children.

No one could ever doubt the seriousness of her religious faith, but, perhaps because it was so strong, it was rarely directly stated, though one senses its influence in all she wrote. She could allow herself the occasional frivolous comment, poking gentle fun at the child who had morbid notions about sickbed piety; she could even be flippant about that sacred cow of the Victorians, Sabbath observance. She criticized the way that parents and teachers treated children; once she even so far forgot herself as to introduce an elopement into the beginning of a story. (Charlotte Yonge advised those reading *Jackanapes* aloud to omit this incident.) She sympathized with the boisterous rough ways of boys, even defended them, and, in *We and the World*, could take their side against their father – a unique occasion in Victorian children's literature. She was equally convincing when she presented a very different type of boy in *A Flat Iron for a Farthing*, a motherless only child, quaint but never muffish, who takes himself rather too seriously (though the author never does).

Perhaps she was at her best when writing of the Yorkshire scenes from which it was such anguish for her to be parted (none of the Gatty children ever wanted to live anywhere else in the world but the vicarage at Ecclesfield where they had been brought up) and of the exuberant life that young Victorians lived when families were large enough to mount private theatricals, to run their own journals and societies; when houses had space to accommodate a mass of different hobbies, and everybody could have his separate plot in the garden and a pet of his own.

Her forgetfulness of her readers sometimes transformed books for a specific class – such as Victorian publishers then produced – into books beyond their reach. *Lob Lie-by-the-Fire* and *Daddy Darwin's Dovecot*, which set out to be the sort of book about the poor boy who became a steady, decent artisan (a type produced by the ton by Anglican wives and daughters for the consumption of children in church schools), finished as exquisitely worked miniatures of Victorian social life.

Some of her longer works tend to sprawl and suffer from a plethora of sub-plot and too many ideas (the result of their being originally written in serial form for her mother's magazine, *Aunt Judy's*) but all of them are beautifully and fastidiously written. She was possibly the most literary of all the Victorian writers of the juvenile domestic tale, and the only one whose works were gathered into a complete edition. Many writers have testified to their affection for her, Kipling and Arthur Ransome among them; authors as various as Frances Hodgson Burnett and Angela Brazil have lifted (perhaps unconsciously) whole episodes from her books; *A Great Emergency* is the precursor of E. Nesbit's Bastable stories.

If one had to remember her by a single work then one might choose the short story "Our Field," so much admired by Ruskin. The plot turns on the efforts of a family of children to save enough for a dog licence, but though their anxiety about this is the shadow, during the day the children forget it because they have found a field where nobody goes, where they can play undisturbed. The field has everything, a stream with freshwater shrimps, a hollow oak, bluebells, cowslips, blackberries. The fact that there are holly berries on the bushes and daisies in the grass at the same season does not matter; Mrs. Ewing is describing an earthly paradise that only a child could know.

—Gillian Avery

HALE, Lucretia P(eabody). American. Born in Boston, Massachusetts, 2 September 1820; sister of the writer Edward Everett Hale. Educated at Susan Whitney's, Miss Peabody's, and George B. Emerson's schools. Taught for a correspondence school, and private history tutor. Member of the Boston School Committee, 1874. *Died 12 June 1900.*

PUBLICATIONS FOR CHILDREN

Fiction

> *The Peterkin Papers*, illustrated by the author.   Boston, Osgood, 1880; Kingswood, Surrey, World's Work, 1964.
> *Alone in Rome.*   Rome, Gould Memorial Home, 1883.
> *The Last of the Peterkins, with Others of Their Kin.*   Boston, Roberts, 1886.
> *Sunday School Stories for Little Children on the Golden Texts of the International Lessons of 1889*, with Mrs. Bernard Whitman.   Boston, Roberts, 1889.
> *Stories for Children, Containing Simple Lessons in Morals.*   Boston, Leach Shewell and Sanborn, 1892.
> *The Queen of the Red Chessmen.*   New York, Happy Hour Library, n.d.

PUBLICATIONS FOR ADULTS

Novels

> *The Struggle for Life.*   Boston, Walker Wise, 1861.
> *An Uncloseted Skeleton*, with Edwin Lassetter Bynner.   Boston, Ticknor, 1888.
> *The New Harry and Lucy: A Story of Boston in the Summer of 1891*, with Edward Everett Hale.   Boston, Roberts, 1892.

Other

> *The Lord's Supper and Its Observance.*   Boston, Walker Fuller, 1866.
> *The Art of Knitting.*   Boston, Tilton, 1881.
> *Three Hundred Decorative and Fancy Articles for Presents, Fairs, etc. etc.*, with Margaret E. White.   Boston, Tilton, 1885.
> *Fagots for the Fireside* ... (games).   Boston, Ticknor, 1888; revised edition, Boston, Houghton Mifflin, 1894.

Editor, *Seven Stormy Sundays*.   Boston, American Unitarian Association, 1858.
Editor, *The Service of Sorrow*.   Boston, American Unitarian Association, 1867.
Editor, *Art Needlework*, by Eliza Savage.   Boston, Tilton, 5 vols., 1879.

*   *   *

As a children's writer, Lucretia P. Hale is known principally for *The Peterkin Papers*, a collection of humorous sketches that had previously appeared in the children's periodicals *Our Young Folks* and its distinguished successor *St. Nicholas*. A sequel, *The Last of the Peterkins*, was far less popular than the *Papers*, which made the Peterkins a household word.

The Peterkin Papers consists of 22 sketches of the ludicrous and improbable misadventures of the Peterkins, an astonishingly inept family consisting of *père* and *mère*, together with their six children: Agamemnon ("who had been to college"), Elizabeth Eliza, Solomon John, and three unnamed little boys, chiefly notable for the India rubber boots which they seem incessantly to be putting on and taking off. The sketches, which tend to be repetitive in form, begin with a problem that grows more formidable the more the family's collective wisdom is invoked to solve it: what to do with a cup of coffee into which Mrs. Peterkin has stirred salt instead of sugar; how to make the family wise; what to do about a piano placed with its keyboard against a window so that it can only be played by standing on the porch and reaching through the window; what to do with a Christmas tree that is too tall for the back parlor.

Once the premise is established, the rest of the sketch recounts the efforts of the family, attempting to work in concert and sometimes with the advice of neighbors, to remedy the situation. In the case of the salted coffee, the local chemist is consulted and tries to counter the presence of the salt with an array of chemicals. Miss Hale is at her comic best cataloguing his inspired – but, alas, futile – efforts: "Then he tried, each in turn, some oxalic, cyanic, acetic, phosphoric, chloric, hyperchloric, sulphuric, boracic, silicic, nitric, formic, nitrous nitric, and carbonic acids. Mrs. Peterkin tasted each and said the flavor was pleasant, but not precisely that of coffee." In this instance, as in most of the sketches, the Peterkin's comic fixation with a futile strategem is broken finally by the cool common sense of their friend Mrs. Leslie, "the lady from Philadelphia," who sensibly suggests throwing out the offending coffee and making a new cup – or moving the piano so that its keyboard faces into the room. Although she is not present to suggest sawing a foot or two from the overly large Christmas tree, and Mr. Peterkin will not accept the carpenter's advice to do so but has him raise a portion of the ceiling instead, the thoughtful lady does provide the Peterkins with a box of Christmas ornaments, for which, with characteristic improvidence, they had neglected to plan.

The sequel, *The Last of the Peterkins*, seems, in retrospect, to be distinctly inferior to the earlier sketches. Convinced, perhaps, that she had explored most of the domestic difficulties likely to beset even a family as impractical as the Peterkins, Miss Hale shifts her focus from the family as a whole to its several members and from the narrowly local setting to one that, in the end, is international. In the first episode of *The Last of the Peterkins*, Elizabeth Eliza prepares and delivers a paper on "The Sun" to the local women's cultural society, the Circumambient Club. Such a setting provides ample scope for Miss Hale's gentle satire. In successive episodes, the family undertakes travel – first to grandfather's for maple syrup but eventually to Europe and the Middle East. Increasingly, the sketches describe the fragmentation of the family as, not surprisingly, travel connections are missed, baggage goes astray, and messages are misunderstood. In the final chapter, the family are briefly reunited, but, with the exception of the three little boys, each has seen enough of the world to have a different dream. Elizabeth Eliza marries a Russian; Agamemnon is last heard of bound for Madagascar; and Mr. and Mrs. Peterkin are headed for Yakoutsk. Their misadventures as a family are over, and even the lady from Philadelphia could not retrieve them from the far ends of the earth, to which Miss Hale consigns them.

The Peterkin Papers and its sequel enjoyed a considerable popularity with children and a measure of critical approval as well. Most of the sketches proceed from such obvious premises that children doubtless relished the absurd antics of the Peterkins, secure in knowing precisely what the lady from Philadelphia would prescribe when she should eventually appear on the scene. Despite the labored quality of the humor, on occasion, and the repetitious form of the episodes, Miss Hale is often a clever and acute observer of human foibles. In contrast to much of the earnest moralizing characteristic of late 19th-century American children's literature, *The Peterkin Papers* is delightful nonsense – virtually the first example that we have. Moreover, it is humor, however gentle and affectionate, at the expense of the family, the institution then widely regarded as the fundamental social unit. Miss Hale's mildly satirical view of the claustrophobic togetherness that was one aspect of Victorian family life marked a refreshing and popular alternative to the solemnity with which her contemporaries treated the family in books for children.

—R. Gordon Kelly

HARRIS, Joel Chandler. American. Born near Eatonton, Georgia, 9 December 1848. Educated at local schools. Married Esther LaRose in 1873; three daughters and two sons. Printers' devil and typesetter, *The Countryman* weekly, published at the Turnwoid Plantation, 1862–66; staff member, Macon *Telegraph*, Georgia, 1866, New Orleans *Crescent Monthly*, 1866–67, *Monroe Advertiser*, Forsyth, Georgia, 1867–70, Savannah *Morning News*, Georgia, 1870–76, and Atlanta *Constitution*, 1876–1900. Founder, with his son Julian, *Uncle Remus's Magazine*, later *Uncle Remus – The Home Magazine*, 1907–08. Member, American Academy of Arts and Letters, 1905. *Died 2 July 1908.*

PUBLICATIONS FOR CHILDREN

Fiction

> *Uncle Remus: His Songs and His Sayings: The Folklore of the Old Plantation*, illustrated by Frederick Church and J.H. Moser. New York, Appleton, 1881; as *Uncle Remus and His Legends of the Old Plantation*, London, Bogue, 1881; as *Uncle Remus; or, Mr. Fox, Mr. Rabbit, and Mr. Terrapin*, London, Routledge, 1881; revised edition, Appleton, and London, Osgood, 1895.
> *Nights with Uncle Remus: Myths and Legends of the Old Plantation*, illustrated by Frederick Church. Boston, Osgood, 1883; London, Routledge, 1884.
> *Daddy Jack the Runaway and Short Stories Told after Dark*, illustrated by E.W. Kemble. New York, Century, and London, Unwin, 1889.
> *Uncle Remus and His Friends: Old Plantation Stories, Songs, and Ballads, with Sketches of Negro Character*, illustrated by A.B. Frost. Boston, Houghton Mifflin, 1892; London, Osgood, 1893.
> *Little Mr. Thimblefinger and His Queer Country: What the Children Saw and Heard There*, illustrated by Oliver Herford. Boston, Houghton Mifflin, and London, Osgood, 1895.
> *Mr. Rabbit at Home*, illustrated by Oliver Herford. Boston, Houghton Mifflin, and London, Osgood, 1895.
> *The Story of Aaron (So Named), The Son of Ben Ali, Told by His Friends and Acquaintances*, illustrated by Oliver Herford. Boston, Houghton Mifflin, and London, Osgood, 1896.
> *Aaron in the Wildwoods*, illustrated by Oliver Herford. Boston, Houghton Mifflin, and London, Harper, 1897.
> *The Chronicles of Aunt Minervy Ann*, illustrated by A.B. Frost. New York, Scribner, and London, Dent, 1899.

Wally Walderon and His Story-Telling Machine, illustrated by Karl Moseley. New York, McClure, 1903; London, Richards, 1904.

Told by Uncle Remus: New Stories of the Old Plantation, illustrated by A.B. Frost and others. New York and London, McClure, 1905.

Uncle Remus and Brer Rabbit. New York, Stokes, 1907.

The Bishop and the Boogerman ..., illustrated by Charlotte Harding. New York, Doubleday, and London, Murray, 1909.

The Shadow Between His Shoulder-Blades .... Boston, Small Maynard, 1909.

Uncle Remus and the Little Boy. Boston, Small Maynard, 1910; London, Richards, 1912.

Uncle Remus Returns. Boston, Houghton Mifflin, 1918.

The Witch Wolf: An Uncle Remus Story. Cambridge, Massachusetts, Bacon and Brown, 1921.

Stories from Uncle Remus, edited by Mrs. Joel Chandler Harris. Akron, Ohio, Saalfield, 1934.

Seven Tales of Uncle Remus, edited by Thomas H. English. Atlanta, Emory University Library, 1948.

The Favorite Uncle Remus, edited by George Van Santvoord and Archibald C. Coolidge. Boston, Houghton Mifflin, 1948.

The Complete Tales of Uncle Remus, edited by Richard Chase. Boston, Houghton Mifflin, 1955.

Verse

The Tar-Baby and Other Rhymes of Uncle Remus, illustrated by A.B. Frost and E.W. Kemble. New York, Appleton, 1904.

PUBLICATIONS FOR ADULTS

Novels

A Plantation Printer: The Adventures of a Georgia Boy During the War. London, Osgood, 1892; as *On the Plantation: A Story of a Georgia Boy's Adventures During the War*, New York, Appleton, 1892.

Sister Jane, Her Friends and Acquaintances .... Boston, Houghton Mifflin, 1896; London, Constable, 1897.

Gabriel Tolliver: A Story of Reconstruction. New York, McClure, 1902.

A Little Union Scout: A Tale of Tennessee During the Civil War. New York, McClure, 1904; London, Duckworth, 1905.

Qua: A Romance of the Revolution, edited by Thomas H. English. Atlanta, Emory University Library, 1946.

Short Stories

Mingo and Other Sketches in Black and White. Boston, Osgood, and Edinburgh, Douglas, 1884.

Free Joe and Other Georgian Sketches. New York, Scribner, 1887; London, Routledge, 1888.

Balaam and His Master and Other Sketches and Stories. Boston, Houghton Mifflin, and London, Osgood, 1891.

Stories of Georgia. New York, American Book Company, 1896; revised edition, 1896.

Tales of the Home Folks in Peace and War. Boston, Houghton Mifflin, and London, Unwin, 1898.

Plantation Pageants. Boston, Houghton Mifflin, and London, Unwin, 1899.

On the Wings of Occasions .... New York, Doubleday, and London, Murray, 1900.

The Making of a Statesman and Other Stories. New York, McClure, 1902.

Other

Editor and Essayist: Miscellaneous Literary, Political, and Social Writings, edited by
   Julia C. Harris.   Chapel Hill, University of North Carolina Press, 1931.

Editor, *Life of Henry W. Grady, Including His Writings and Speeches: A Memorial
   Volume*.   New York, Cassell, 1890.
Editor, *The Book of Fun and Frolic*.   Boston, Hall Locke, 1901; as *Merrymaker*, 1902.
Editor, *World's Wit and Humor*.   New York, Doubleday, 1904.

Translator, *Evening Tales*, by Frederic Ortoli.   New York, Scribner, 1893.

Manuscript Collection: Emory University Library, Atlanta.

Critical Study: *Joel Chandler Harris: A Biography* by Paul M. Cousins, Baton Rouge,
Louisiana State University Press, 1968.

*   *   *

Joel Chandler Harris was twelve years old when the Civil War – the War Between the
States – broke out in 1860. He was sixty when he died in 1908. Born somewhere near
Eatonton, Georgia, his southern plantation background is better understood today by people
north of the Mason-Dixon line than it was in 1880, when *Uncle Remus: His Songs and His
Sayings*, in cotton-pickers' dialect, was published. Better still, most northerners in 1977
suddenly knew a great deal about one typical small Georgian town than their forebears had
known in 1880, or they themselves as late as 1976, thanks to President Jimmy Carter.
Eatonton, it seems, lies but a hundred miles or so from Plains, Georgia, as the crow (but not
the circling buzzard) flies over my open atlas. The circling buzzard? "Tooby sho! W'y dat's
Brer Tukkey Buzzard hisse'f."
   And with these words we are into the first and, with *Nights with Uncle Remus*, by far the
best of the nine volumes of Uncle Remus stories which stretched, in publication, across sixty-
eight years (1880–1948) to the varying benefit of eight different American publishers. In 1955
The Complete Tales of Uncle Remus appeared, with the original black and white illustrations
of five different artists. After sixty-five years, I clearly see now, as I thought then, that the best
of these artists – best by all odds – was A.B. Frost. The spirit of the language and the animals
was on him as it was not with any generous magic on the others. He was and is as Tenniel to
Carroll, as Shepard to Milne. It was Frederick Church who illustrated the first *Uncle Remus*
in 1880; but Frost took over the new and revised edition of 1896; did the fourth and parts of
the fifth and eighth books as well. How those marvellous pictures stick in the mind: rabbit,
fox, coon, possum, wolf, bear, Sis Cow, the mice (Miss Meadows en de gals); roughly
dressed in well-worn pants, shirt, and suspenders; sometimes a vest, sometimes a tail coat
flying in the wind. Long dresses for the females. Shoes never. Frog, terrapin, birds generally
as is. "All de creeturs, horn, claw, and wing."
   And always old black Uncle Remus in his cabin – no *Uncle Tom's Cabin*, mind you! –
half-soling a pair of shoes, perhaps; blowing the ashes from a smoking yam, weaving long
strips of "wahoo" bark into horse-collars, or scratching his head with the point of his awl,
telling the little white boy – Miss Sally's little boy – from the big house those wondrous
animal fables long after and mostly unconnected with Grimm, Andersen, or LaFontaine, as
well as long before them, but almost certainly in essence somewhere out of Africa.
Mysterious to me as a young boy; and still mysteriously unchanged today as are the deepest
of the Negro Spirituals which, apart from original New Orleans jazz, survive unwearied as
the New World's one unequalled contribution to music. "Among the unforgettable books of
American literature," says the *Dictionary of American Biography*.
   So then, what makes *Uncle Remus*, the work of a sometime casual and untroubled country
journalist, undistinguished in his other quite orthodox books, so hauntingly alive, so

enchantingly memorable? Humor, of course; but also ingenuity of plot and situation; perfect rhythmic pacing – though one nervous nerveless rabbit paradoxically is he who seems to set it. "What brevity is to wit," said Desmond MacCarthy, speaking of Maupassant, "concision is to the art of story-telling." No stories in any collected series I can think of approach the concision of these; not even those in Maugham's *Cosmopolitans*; and they, of course, aren't woven with a common thread. Then, too, Brer Rabbit's infinite resourcefulness, his crafty smalltalk, the dependable gullibility of his friends and enemies; the quiet anthropomorphic satire sometimes present but often overlooked in the almost total absence of human characters and human tension. And above all – what I could not appreciate when young – the enormous dignity as a human being of Uncle Remus, the story-teller, himself. Uncle Remus who has, as Harris tells us in 1880, "all the prejudices of caste and pride of family that were the natural results of the system."

Over the centuries, who among the myriad devotees of Horace has rejected in *Carminum Liber*, I, 38, "Percosis odi, puer, apparatus ...." simply because puer (the boy) was a slave? To be sure, Uncle Remus was most certainly a slave before 1865; but this is 1880, still a long way from civil rights. Yet here he is, an old unbittered man in the evening of life; and in the actual evening of day after Georgian day, patiently mending those shoes, smoking his pipe, reflecting on the past, since "ole times is about all we got lef'." But on what sort of past? On whose "ole times"? Not his. Not really any man's, black or white, with two or three quite casual exceptions, but on his other talkative active world of Brer Rabbit, Brer Fox, Brer Tukkey Buzzard, Brer Tarrypin, Sis Cow, Miss Meadows en de gals (the mice), viewed in animal isolation. And always the comic side of it; of predator and prey outsmarting and outsmarted, outdoing and outdone; but every bit of it in word and deed of mythical concept beyond man's crazier conflict world of violence, cruelty, and bloodshed. Mean, unbloody deaths sometimes occur; but the dead are usually resurrected later on. Off to one side, the role of Uncle Remus is that of the Stage Manager in Wilder's *Our Town*, a one-man Greek Chorus. And if his is not the voice of Anselm, the Christ-like lion figure in Lewis's *Narnia*, it remains no less a voice as philosophical, patient, persuasive, and neutral in reaction as any story-teller's should be. Here is a sample of that voice recorded in the famous "Wonderful Tar-Baby Story":

> "Brer Rabbit come prancin' 'long twel he spy de Tar-Baby, en den he fotch up on his behime legs like he wuz 'stonished. De Tar-Baby, she sot dar, she did, en Brer Fox, he lay low.
>
> " 'Mawnin'!' sez Brer Rabbit, sezee – 'nice wedder dis mawnin',' sezee.
>
> "Tar-Baby ain't sayin' nothin', en Brer Fox, he lay low.
>
> " 'How duz yo' sym'tums seem ter segashuate?' sez Brer Rabbit, sezee.
>
> "Brer Fox, he wink his eye slow, en lay low, en de Tar-Baby, she ain't sayin' nothin'.
>
> " 'How you come on, den? Is you deaf?' sez Brer Rabbit, sezee. 'Kaze if you is, I kin holler louder,' sezee.
>
> "Tar-Baby stay still, en Brer Fox, he lay low.
>
> " 'You er stuck up, dat's w'at you is,' says Brer Rabbit, sezee, 'en I'm gwine ter kyore you, dat's w'at I'm gwine ter do,' sezee.
>
> "Brer Fox, he sorter chuckle in his stummick, he did, but Tar-Baby ain't sayin' nothin'.
>
> " 'I'm gwine ter larn you how ter talk ter 'spectubble folks ef hit's de las' ack,' sez Brer Rabbit, sezee. 'Ef you don't take off dat hat en tell me howdy, I'm gwine ter bus' you wide open,' sezee.
>
> "Tar-Baby stay still, en Brer Fox, he lay low.
>
> "Brer Rabbit keep on axin' 'im, en de Tar-Baby, she keep on sayin' nothin', twel present'y Brer Rabbit draw back wid his fis', he did, en blip he tuck 'er side er de head. Right dar's whar he broke his merlasses jug. His fis' stuck, en he can't pull loose. De tar hilt 'im. But Tar-Baby, she stay still, en Brer Fox, he lay low.
>
> " 'Ef you don't lemme loose, I'll knock you agin,' sez Brer Rabbit, sezee, en wid

dat he fotch 'er a wipe wid de udder han', en dat stuck. Tar-Baby, she ain't sayin' nothin', en Brer Fox, he lay low.

" 'Tu'n me loose, fo' I kick de natchul stuffin' out'n you,' sez Brer Rabbit, sezee, but de Tar-Baby, she ain't sayin' nothin'. She des hilt on, en den Brer Rabbit lose de use er his feet in de same way. Brer Fox, he lay low."

What, I would ask, does the average citizen of the United Kingdom make of this language of *Uncle Remus*? There is nothing even approximate in tone or inflection in *Punch*'s weekly version of southern accent in "Miz Lillian Writes" (summer of 1977). In *Uncle Remus* we are listening to black plantation talk transferred to animals and birds. And young Harris, sometime and long-time staff member of the famous Atlanta *Constitution*, possessed the true alembic to distill the last least syllable accurately heard and poetically remembered. To the average American London cockney even when written can be difficult in spots; so can the lovely west country dialect poems of William Barnes; so can the local Aberdonian speech of my ancestors as I myself have heard it. Well, James Stephens once said to me in London, after reciting "The County Mayo" in Gaelic: "You don't learn French. You take it in through the pores."

Likewise with the language of *Uncle Remus*: tricky, but not too difficult since the spelling is phonetic, full of sibilants, and reliably consistent. A few words out of *Uncle Remus* were coin of the realm of my youth: *talk biggity, smole a smile, turkentime* (for turpentine); *Eavedrapper*; *bobby-cue*; low-register English-Greek frog talk such as "*knee deep, knee deep; wade in, wade in*"; *start naked* for stark naked; *swivel up and die*; the now fading but still beautiful verb *segashuate*: "How duz yo' sym'tums seem ter segashuate?"; "Is I'm a tale, or is de tale me?"; "so he ain't kin run"; *I'shmuns* (for Irishmen); etc. *So he ain't kin run!* Can anyone *possibly* miss the liquefaction of such? A couple of glossaries in the collected *Uncle Remus* are sadly incomplete.

To speak of another Harris book for children, *Little Mr. Thimblefinger and His Queer Country*, in the wake (1895) of *Uncle Remus* (1880) is somewhat like looking into Melville's *The Confidence Man* after emerging from *Moby Dick*. But *Mr. Thimblefinger* had some success in its day. Carefully illustrated with a certain grotesque charm by the gifted Oliver Herford, it is just another children's venture into a Never-Never Land: this time down through a spring and under water to a lower middle earth. These adventures were written, said Harris apologetically, "in the midst of daily work on a morning newspaper" – the Atlanta *Constitution*. "Some," he explains, "are Middle Georgia folklore, and no doubt belong to England." I cannot begin to assess this statement. But occasional references to *Uncle Remus* – the tar baby, for example – and the fact that Miss Meadows is now Mrs. Meadows somehow fail to enchant. The book is composed largely in straight English, with characters named Sweetest Susan, Chickamy Crany Crow, Tickle-My-Toes, and so on. Drusela the Negro nurse is something of a tonic, yet she talks rather like a Brer Rabbit reject.

But *Uncle Remus* today deserves true immortality. The great Spirituals have it; but music under and over them carries the lovely poetic language. Can the unforced, undying humor of *Uncle Remus* carry it in this diminishing world now, *a cappela*?

—David McCord

HENTY, G(eorge) A(lfred).   British.   Born in Trumpington, Cambridgeshire, 8 December 1832. Educated at Westminster School, London, 1847–52; Caius College, Cambridge, 1852. Served in the Hospital Commisariat and the Purveyor's Department during the Crimean War; helped organize Italian hospitals, 1859; served in Belfast and Portsmouth; Turkish Order of the Medjidie. Married Elizabeth Finucane in 1858, two sons and two daughters; Bessie Keylock. Crimean War Correspondent, *Morning Advertiser*, London; Staff

Correspondent, in Europe, Africa, Asia, and North America, *The Standard*, London, 1865–76. Editor, *Union Jack* magazine, London, 1880–83, and *Beeton's Boy's Own Magazine*, London, 1888–90, and later annuals, 1890–93. *Died 16 November 1902.*

PUBLICATIONS FOR CHILDREN

Fiction

Out on the Pampas; or, The Young Settlers, illustrated by J.B. Zwecker. London, Griffith and Farran, 1871; New York, Dutton, 1872(?).

The Young Franc-Tireurs and Their Adventures in the Franco-Prussian War, illustrated by R.T. Landells. London, Griffith and Farran, 1872; New York, Burt, n.d.

The Young Buglers: A Tale of the Peninsular War, illustrated by John Proctor. London, Griffith and Farran, and New York, Dutton, 1879.

Seaside Maidens, illustrated by Harry Furniss. London, Tinsley, 1880.

In Times of Peril: A Tale of India, illustrated by Frank Feller. London, Griffith and Farran, and New York, Dutton, 1881.

The Cornet of Horse: A Tale of Marlborough's Wars, illustrated by H. Petherick. London, Sampson Low, 1881; New York, Burt, n.d.

Winning His Spurs: A Tale of the Crusades. London, Sampson Low, 1882; as *The Boy Knight*, New York, Burt, 1883; as *Fighting the Saracens*, Boston, Brown, 1892.

Facing Death; or, The Hero of the Vaughan Pit: A Tale of the Coal Mines, illustrated by Gordon Browne. London, Blackie, and New York, Scribner, 1882.

Under Drake's Flag: A Tale of the Spanish Main, illustrated by Gordon Browne. London, Blackie, and New York, Scribner, 1882.

With Clive in India; or, The Beginnings of an Empire, illustrated by Gordon Browne. London, Blackie, 1883; New York, Burt, n.d.

By Sheer Pluck: A Tale of the Ashanti Wars, illustrated by Gordon Browne. London, Blackie, and New York, Scribner, 1883.

Jack Archer: A Tale of the Crimea. London, Blackie, 1883; Boston, Roberts, 1884; as *The Fall of Sebastopol*, Boston, Brown, 1892.

Friends, Though Divided: A Tale of the Civil War. London, Griffith and Farran, 1883; New York, Dutton, 1885.

True to the Old Flag: A Tale of the American War of Independence, illustrated by Gordon Browne. London, Blackie, and New York, Scribner, 1884.

In Freedom's Cause: A Story of Wallace and Bruce, illustrated by Gordon Browne. London, Blackie, and New York, Scribner, 1884.

St. George for England: A Tale of Cressy and Poitiers, illustrated by Gordon Browne. London, Blackie, and New York, Scribner, 1884.

The Lion of the North: A Tale of the Times of Gustavus Adolphus and the Wars of Religion, illustrated by John Schönberg. London, Blackie, 1885; New York, Burt, n.d.

The Young Colonists. London and New York, Routledge, 1885.

The Dragon and the Raven; or, The Days of King Alfred, illustrated by C.J. Staniland. London, Blackie, and New York, Scribner, 1885.

For Name and Fame; or, Through the Afghan Passes, illustrated by Gordon Browne. London, Blackie, and New York, Scribner, 1885.

Through the Fray: A Tale of the Luddite Riots, illustrated by H.M. Paget. London, Blackie, and New York, Scribner, 1885.

Yarns on the Beach: A Bundle of Tales, illustrated by J.J. Proctor. London, Blackie, and New York, Scribner, 1885.

With Wolfe in Canada; or, The Winning of a Continent, illustrated by Gordon Browne. London, Blackie, and New York, Scribner, 1886.

The Bravest of the Brave; or, With Peterborough in Spain, illustrated by H.M. Paget. London, Blackie, and New York, Scribner, 1886.

A Final Reckoning: A Tale of Bush Life in Australia, illustrated by W.B. Wollen. London, Blackie, and New York, Scribner, 1886.

The Young Carthaginian; or, A Struggle for Empire, illustrated by C.J. Staniland. London, Blackie, and New York, Scribner, 1886.

Bonnie Prince Charlie: A Tale of Fontenoy and Culloden, illustrated by Gordon Browne. London, Blackie, 1887; New York, Scribner, 1890(?).

For the Temple: A Tale of the Fall of Jerusalem, illustrated by Solomon J. Solomon. London, Blackie, and New York, Scribner, 1887.

In the Reign of Terror: The Adventures of a Westminster Lad, illustrated by John Schönberg. London, Blackie, and New York, Scribner, 1887.

Sturdy and Strong; or, How George Andrews Made His Way, illustrated by Robert Fowler. London, Blackie, 1887; New York, Burt, n.d.

The Cat of Bubastes: A Tale of Ancient Egypt, illustrated by J.R. Weguelin. London, Blackie, and New York, Scribner, 1888.

The Lion of St. Mark: A Tale of Venice, illustrated by Gordon Browne. London, Blackie, and New York, Scribner, 1888.

Captain Bayley's Heir: A Tale of the Gold Fields of California, illustrated by H.M. Paget. London, Blackie, and New York, Scribner, 1888.

Orange and Green: A Tale of the Boyne and Limerick, illustrated by Gordon Browne. London, Blackie, and New York, Scribner, 1888.

One of the 28th: A Tale of Waterloo, illustrated by W.H. Overend. London, Blackie, and New York, Scribner, 1889.

By Pike and Dyke: A Tale of the Rise of the Dutch Republic, illustrated by Maynard Brown. London, Blackie, and New York, Scribner, 1889.

Camps and Quarters, with Archibald Forbes and Charles Williams. London and New York, Ward Lock, 1889.

Tales of Daring and Danger. London, Blackie, and New York, Scribner, 1889.

The Plague Ship. London, S.P.C.K., and New York, Young, 1889.

With Lee in Virginia: A Story of the American Civil War, illustrated by Gordon Browne. London, Blackie, and New York, Scribner, 1889.

By Right of Conquest; or, With Cortez in Mexico, illustrated by W.S. Stacey. London, Blackie, and New York, Scribner, 1890.

By England's Aid; or, The Freeing of the Netherlands (1585–1604), illustrated by Alfred Pearse. London, Blackie, and New York, Scribner, 1890.

A Chapter of Adventures; or, Through the Bombardment of Alexandria, illustrated by W.H. Overend. London, Blackie, and New York, Scribner, 1890; as *The Young Midshipman: A Story of the Bombardment of Alexandria,* New York, Street and Smith, 1902.

Maori and Settler: A Story of the New Zealand Wars, illustrated by Alfred Pearse. London, Blackie, and New York, Scribner, 1890.

Redskin and Cowboy: A Tale of the Western Plains, illustrated by Alfred Pearse. London, Blackie, and New York, Scribner, 1891.

The Dash for Khartoum: A Tale of the Nile Expedition, illustrated by Joseph Nash and John Schönberg. London, Blackie, and New York, Scribner, 1891.

Held Fast for England: A Tale of the Siege of Gibraltar (1779–1883), illustrated by Gordon Browne. London, Blackie, and New York, Scribner, 1891.

In Greek Waters: A Story of the Grecian War of Independence (1821–1827), illustrated by W.S. Stacey. London, Blackie, and New York, Scribner, 1892.

Beric the Briton: A Story of the Roman Invasion, illustrated by W. Parkinson. London, Blackie, and New York, Scribner, 1892.

Condemned as a Nihilist: A Story of Escape from Siberia, illustrated by Walter Paget. London, Blackie, and New York, Scribner, 1892.

The Ranche in the Valley. London, S.P.C.K., and New York, Young, 1892.

A Jacobite Exile, Being the Adventures of a Young Englishman in the Service of Charles XII of Sweden, illustrated by Paul Hardy.   London, Blackie, and New York, Scribner, 1893.

Tales from the Works of G.A. Henty.   London, Blackie, 1893; as *Tales from Henty,* 1925.

St. Bartholomew's Eve: A Tale of the Huguenot Wars, illustrated by H.J. Draper.   London, Blackie, and New York, Scribner, 1893.

Through the Sikh War: A Tale of the Conquest of the Punjaub, illustrated by Hal Hurst.   London, Blackie, and New York, Scribner, 1893.

In the Heart of the Rockies: A Story of Adventure in Colorado, illustrated by G.C. Hindley.   London, Blackie, and New York, Scribner, 1894.

When London Burned: A Story of Restoration Times and the Great Fire, illustrated by T. Finnemore.   London, Blackie, and New York, Scribner, 1894.

Wulf the Saxon: A Story of the Norman Conquest, illustrated by Ralph Peacock.   London, Blackie, and New York, Scribner, 1894.

The Tiger of Mysore: A Story of the War with Tippoo Saib, illustrated by W.H. Margetson.   London, Blackie, and New York, Scribner, 1895.

A Woman of the Commune: A Tale of the Two Sieges of Paris, illustrated by Hal Hurst.   London, White, 1895; as *Cuthbert Hartington: A Tale of the Siege of Paris,* London, Partridge, 1899; as *A Girl of the Commune,* New York, Fenno, n.d.; as *Two Sieges of Paris; or, A Girl of the Commune,* Fenno, n.d.

A Knight of the White Cross: A Tale of the Siege of Rhodes, illustrated by Ralph Peacock.   London, Blackie, and New York, Scribner, 1895.

Through Russian Snows: A Story of Napoleon's Retreat from Moscow, illustrated by W.H. Overend.   London, Blackie, and New York, Scribner, 1895.

On the Irrawaddy: A Story of the First Burmese War, illustrated by W.H. Overend.   London, Blackie, and New York, Scribner, 1896.

At Agincourt: A Tale of the White Hoods of Paris, illustrated by Walter Paget.   London, Blackie, and New York, Scribner, 1896.

Bears and Decoits and Other Stories.   London, Blackie, 1896.

With Cochrane the Dauntless: A Tale of the Exploits of Lord Cochrane in South American Waters, illustrated by W.H. Margetson.   London, Blackie, and New York, Scribner, 1896.

In Battle and Breeze: Sea Stories, with George Manville Fenn and W. Clark Russell.   London, Partridge, 1896.

With Moore at Corunna: A Tale of the South African War, illustrated by William Rainey.   London, Blackie, and New York, Scribner, 1897.

A March on London, Being the Story of Wat Tyler's Insurrection, illustrated by W.H. Margetson.   London, Blackie, and New York, Scribner, 1897.

With Frederick the Great: A Story of the Seven Years' War, illustrated by Walter Paget.   London, Blackie, and New York, Scribner, 1897.

Among Malay Pirates.   New York, Hurst, 1897; as *Among the Malays,* Chicago, Donohue, 1900(?).

At Aboukir and Acre: A Story of Napoleon's Invasion of Egypt, illustrated by William Rainey.   London, Blackie, and New York, Scribner, 1898.

Both Sides the Border: A Tale of Hotspur and Glendower, illustrated by Ralph Peacock.   London, Blackie, and New York, Scribner, 1898.

Under Wellington's Command: A Tale of the Peninsular War, illustrated by Walter Paget.   London, Blackie, and New York, Scribner, 1898.

The Golden Cañon.   New York, Mershon, 1899.

No Surrender! A Tale of the Rising in La Vendée, illustrated by Stanley L. Wood.   London, Blackie, and New York, Scribner, 1899.

On the Spanish Main.   London, Chambers, 1899.

Won by the Sword: A Tale of the Thirty Years' War, illustrated by Charles M. Sheldon.   London, Blackie, and New York, Scribner, 1899.

In the Irish Brigade: A Tale of War in Flanders and Spain, illustrated by Charles M. Sheldon. London, Blackie, and New York, Scribner, 1900.

In the Hands of the Cave-Dwellers. New York and London, Harper, 1900.

With Buller in Natal: or, A Born Leader, illustrated by William Rainey. London, Blackie, and New York Scribner, 1900.

Out with Garibaldi: A Story of the Liberation of Italy, illustrated by William Rainey. London, Blackie, and New York, Scribner, 1900.

A Roving Commission; or, Through the Black Insurrection of Hayti, illustrated by William Rainey. London, Blackie, and New York, Scribner, 1900.

The Sole Survivors. London, Chambers, 1901.

With Roberts to Pretoria: A Tale of the South African War, illustrated by William Rainey. London, Blackie, and New York, Scribner, 1901.

At the Point of the Bayonet: A Tale of the Mahratta War, illustrated by Walter Paget. London, Blackie, and New York, Scribner, 1901.

John Hawke's Fortune: A Story of Monmouth's Rebellion. London, Chapman and Hall, 1901.

To Herat and Cabul: A Story of the First Afghan War, illustrated by Charles M. Sheldon. London, Blackie, and New York, Scribner, 1901.

With Kitchener in the Soudan: A Story of Atbara and Omdurman, illustrated by William Rainey. London, Blackie, and New York, Scribner, 1902.

With the British Legion: A Story of the Carlist Wars, illustrated by Walter Paget. London, Blackie, and New York, Scribner, 1902.

The Treasure of the Incas: A Tale of Adventure in Peru, illustrated by Walter Paget. London, Blackie, and New York, Scribner, 1902.

With the Allies to Pekin: A Tale of the Relief of the Legations, illustrated by Walter Paget. London, Blackie, and New York, Scribner, 1903.

Through Three Campaigns: A Story of Chitral, Tirah, and Ashantee, illustrated by Walter Paget. London, Blackie, and New York, Scribner, 1903.

By Conduct and Courage: A Story of Nelson's Days, edited by C.G. Henty, illustrated by William Rainey. London, Blackie, and New York, Scribner, 1904.

Gallant Deeds, illustrated by Arthur Rackham and W. Boucher. London, Chambers, 1905.

In the Hands of the Malays and Other Stories, illustrated by J. Jellico. London, Blackie, 1905.

Redskins and Colonists; or, A Boy's Adventures in the Early Days of Virginia; Burton and Son; The Ranche in the Valley; Sole Survivors. New York, Stitt, 1905.

A Soldier's Daughter and Other Stories, illustrated by Frances Ewan. London, Blackie, 1906.

Other

Editor, *Yule Logs*. London and New York, Longman, 1898.
Editor, *Yule-Tide Yarns*. London and New York, Longman, 1899.

PUBLICATIONS FOR ADULTS

Novels

A Search for a Secret. London, Tinsley, 3 vols., 1867.
All But Lost. London, Tinsley, 3 vols., 1869.
Gabriel Allen, M.P. London, Spenser Blackett, 1888.
The Curse of Carne's Hold: A Tale of Adventure. London, Spenser Blackett and Hallam, 2 vols., 1889; New York, Lovell, 1889.
A Hidden Foe. New York, United States Book Company, 1890; London, Sampson Low, 2 vols., 1891.

Rujub, The Juggler. London, Chatto and Windus, 3 vols., 1893; as *In the Days of the Mutiny: A Military Novel*, New York, Taylor, 1893.
Dorothy's Double. London, Chatto and Windus, 3 vols., 1894; as *Dorothy's Double: The Story of a Great Deception*, Chicago, Rand McNally, 1895.
The Queen's Cup. London, Chatto and Windus, 3 vols., 1897; New York, Appleton, 1898.
Colonel Thorndyke's Secret. London, Chatto and Windus, 1898; as *The Brahmin's Treasure; or, Colonel Thorndyke's Secret*, Philadelphia, Lippincott, 1899.
The Lost Heir. London, James Bowden, 1899; New York, Hurst, n.d.

Other

The March to Magdala. London, Tinsley, 1868.
The March to Coomassie. London, Tinsley, 1874.
Those Other Animals. London, Henry, 1891.
The Sovereign Reader: Scenes from the Life and Reign of Queen Victoria. London, Blackie, 1887; revised edition, as *Queen Victoria: Scenes from Her Life and Reign*, 1901.

Editor, *Our Sailors ...*, by William H.G. Kingston, continued by G.A. Henty. London, Griffith Farran, 1882.
Editor, *Our Soldiers ...*, by William H.G. Kingston, continued by G.A.Henty. London, Griffith Farran, 1886.
Editor, *Famous Travels.* Boston, Hall and Locke, 1902.

Bibliographies: *Bibliography of G.A. Henty and Hentyana* by R.S. Kennedy and B.J. Farmer, London, B.J. Farmer, 1956; *G.A. Henty: A Bibliography* by Robert L. Dartt, Cedar Grove, New Jersey, Dar-Web, and Altrincham, Cheshire, John Sherratt and Son, 1971.

Critical Study: *George Alfred Henty: The Story of an Active Life* by G. Manville Fenn, London, Blackie, 1907.

*   *   *

G.A. Henty belongs to that class of authors whose influence has far outstripped their literary achievement. His biographer and contemporary, Manville Fenn, claimed that he "taught more lasting history to boys than all the schoolmasters of his generation." It was a limited conception of history, but Henty's enthusiasm certainly infected his young readers and brought the past to life for them. His influence was in fact three-fold: besides making history palatable to boys, he inspired numerous imitators and set the adventure-story in a mould that was not broken until long after his death, while the ideology he propounded – the cult of "manliness" and the British Empire – had a far-reaching effect which rates consideration in a more than purely literary context. It has been argued that Henty and his followers helped to produce the type of adventurous young man who (wrote Edgar Osborne) "went overseas and did much towards building up our present Commonwealth of Nations." Less friendly critics have expressed this differently. Nearly 40 years after Henty's death, George Orwell complained: "Boys' fiction is sodden in the worst illusions of 1910."

Henty was of course the epitome of Victorianism, being born just five years before the queen's accession and outliving her by little more than a year. A delicate child, bullied at public school, he took lessons in "the noble art of self-defence" and had good reason thereafter to believe in the efficacy of Christian manliness, expressed in a straight left to the jaw. As a war correspondent on innumerable campaigns, he found it easy to identify himself with the conquering Empire-builders. In later life, as a popular London clubman, he had little cause to question the current assumptions of his class.

His success sprang from his ability to take a colourful theme, whether from recent or from remote history, and then, helping out the facts with invented incident and character, spin what approving parents and pedagogues called "a rattling good yarn." He worked to a formula, as his titles show – *With Clive in India, With Wolfe in Canada, With Kitchener in the Soudan,* or, for variation, *Facing Death, True to the Old Flag,* and *Held Fast for England.* His young heroes ran similarly to type, manly, middle-class, and intellectually unremarkable. The great adventurers of real history, Ralegh and Burton and T.E. Lawrence, would have fitted less comfortably into his stock-size frame.

Many of his books were based on first-hand observation. He walked the field of Inkerman among the unburied Russian dead, and the Crimean story he eventually wrote, *Jack Archer,* is one of his most vivid. He reported the Franco-Prussian War: within a year he had written *The Young Franc-Tireurs.* He accompanied Garibaldi in Italy, the Turks in their savage Balkan wars, and British expeditions into West Africa and Abyssinia. None of the slaughter he witnessed dimmed his vision of military glory. Even in his posthumously published story of the Boxer rising, *With the Allies to Pekin,* there is undiminished gusto in his account of two intrepid lads who, caught in a confined space with a dozen murderous Chinese, use their magazine-loading rifles to wipe out their adversaries in a few moments.

Henty was a methodical worker. He would lie on a sofa in his weapon-festooned study, dictating to a male secretary – and then never look at the story again until he corrected the proofs. In a six-hour day he could produce over 6000 words. In the last 33 years of his life he packed something like fourteen million words into about 90 fat volumes. It would be optimistic to seek, in such a mass, either striking originality of ideas or fastidious use of language. He at least achieved English which, if not quite as "good" as admiring schoolmasters declared it, never fell below a certain level. It was the prose of the period, rather too wordy for our own taste, and betraying his habit of unrevised dictation. Characters, after being "for a minute or two speechless with indignation," would then immediately plunge into paragraph-long speeches of advice or explanation.

Even when handling themes outside his own experience, Henty could invest his narrative with a good deal of verisimilitude, thanks to the analogous events in which he had participated. Occasionally he was lazy. His Cortez story, *By Right of Conquest,* reads like paraphrased Prescott. He makes only a feeble attempt to create his own characters and plot inside the historical framework. His conventional English boy hero, Roger – so implausibly present at the conquest of Mexico – is often forgotten for several pages at a time.

Henty set a pattern which many lesser writers adapted to the 1914 war and other themes, but by the mid-20th century his values were unfashionable, and, as the general quality of historical fiction improved, it became less heretical to criticise his literary weaknesses. Today his books are rather "collected" as Victoriana than read by boys. They have not won a place upon the shelf with the children's classics that are loved from generation to generation.

—Geoffrey Trease

INGELOW, Jean. British. Born in Boston, Lincolnshire, 17 March 1820. Educated at home. Lived in London after 1850. Editor, *Youth Magazine,* 1855. *Died 20 July 1897.*

PUBLICATIONS FOR CHILDREN

Fiction

Tales of Orris (published anonymously). Bath, Binns and Goodwin, 1860; as *Stories Told to a Child,* London, Strahan, 1865; Boston, Roberts, 1866.

Studies for Stories (published anonymously).   London, Strahan, 2 vols., 1864; Boston,
     Roberts, 1865.
A Sister's Bye-Hours.   London, Strahan, and Boston, Roberts, 1868.
Mopsa the Fairy.   London, Longman, and Boston, Roberts, 1869.
The Little Wonder-Horn.   London, King, 1872.
The Little Wonder Box.   London, Griffith Farran, 6 vols., 1887.
Very Young, and Quite Another Story.   London, Longman, 1890.
Quite Another Story.   New York, Lovell, 1890.
The Black Polyanthus and Widow Maclean.   London, Wells Gardner, 1903.

PUBLICATIONS FOR ADULTS

Novels

Allerton and Drieux; or, The War of Opinion (published anonymously).   London,
     Wertheim, 2 vols., 1857.
Off the Skelligs.   London, King, 4 vols., 1872; Boston, Roberts, 1872.
Fated to Be Free.   London, Tinsley, 3 vols., 1875; Boston, Roberts, 1875.
Sarah de Berenger.   London, King, and Boston, Roberts, 1879.
Don John.   London, Sampson Low, 3 vols., 1881; Boston, Roberts, 1881.
John Jerome, His Thoughts and Ways: A Book Without Beginning.   London, Sampson
     Low, and Boston, Roberts, 1886.
A Motto Changed.   New York, Harper, 1894.

Verse

A Rhyming Chronicle of Incidents and Feelings, edited by Edward Harston (published
     anonymously).   London, Longman, 1850.
Poems.   London, Longman, and Boston, Roberts, 1863.
Songs of Seven.   Boston, Roberts, 1866.
The Complete Poems.   Boston, Roberts, 1869.
A Story of Doom and Other Poems.   London, Longman, and Boston, Roberts, 1867; as
     Poems, Second Series, Longman, 1874.
The Monitions of the Unseen, and Poems of Love and Childhood.   Boston, Roberts, 1871.
One Hundred Holy Songs, Carols, and Sacred Ballads.   London, Longman, 1878.
High Tide on the Coast of Lincolnshire 1571.   Boston, Roberts, 1883.
Poems, Third Series.   London, Longman, 1885.
Poems of the Old Days and the New.   Boston, Roberts, 1885.
Lyrical and Other Poems.   London, Longman, 1886.
Poetical Works.   London, Longman, 1898.
Poems.   London, Muses Library, 1906.
Poems, edited by Andrew Lang.   London and New York, Longman, 1908.
Poems, 1850–1869.   London, Oxford University Press, 1913.

Critical Study: *Jean Ingelow: An Appreciation* by Eustace A. Stedman,   London, Chiswick
Press, 1935.

*   *   *

One novel and a handful of anthology poems keep Jean Ingelow's name alive today; but
these works are not negligible. They can suggest why, in her time, she was something of a
celebrity,both as adult novelist and poet; why her work was admired by such fellow writers
as Tennyson, Edward Fitzgerald, the Rossettis. She was even thought a possible Laureate
when the post fell vacant in 1892, but admittedly this was a very thin time. More pointed is
the fact that, 16 years after her death, she rated an Oxford edition of her poems. They tend to
be ballad-like and reverberating, with sharp and haunting cadences and a mysterious thread

of narrative; their appeal is not hard to understand. *High Tide on the Coast of Lincolnshire*, where the energy of the theme absorbs the sentiment, is one of the best examples.

Still, most of her poetry is for the private discoverer or devotee; so too are her shorter mildly didactic tales for the young, written in a good brisk readable style but lacking the power of flight to travel far. Very few, indeed, are accessible now, though one charming tale, "My Grandmother's Shoe," has been revived in one of Gillian Avery's collections.

Jean Ingelow's one long work for the young, her remarkable novel *Mopsa the Fairy*, is a different matter. Written within that short and dazzling period when so many leading Victorian authors experimented in children's fantasy, it remains, in its genre, a major achievement, one of those single, odd yet memorable works that make up so much of English literature. Influences? Certainly. Take the most Carrollian passage in *Mopsa*, when a ballad sung by Jack includes the lines:

> And the lark said, give us glory!
> And the dove said, give us peace!

"A very good song indeed," said the dame at the other end of the table, "only you made a mistake in the first verse. What the dove really said was, no doubt, 'Give us peas.' "

"It isn't peas, though," said Jack. However, the court historian was sent for to write down the song ... as the dame said it ought to be.

Flamingoes stand on military guard; there is an oddly macabre episode in which a gypsy's baby turns out to be a bundle of clothes with a turnip head. A further Carrollian echo surely sounds in Jack's disputation with the ravens:

> "Why," said Jack, "I see a full moon lying down there among the water-flags, and just going to set, and there is a half-moon overhead plunging among those great grey clouds, and just this moment I saw a thin crescent moon peeping out between the branches of that tree."
>
> "Well," said all the ravens at once, "did the young master never see a crescent moon in the men and women's world?"
>
> "Yes, of course," said Jack, "but they are all the same moon. I could never see all three of them at the same time."
>
> The ravens were very much surprised at this.

But the voice and the detail are essentially Ingelow's. Even the book's opening, which has been likened to the opening of *Alice*, sheers off at once in its own direction. A boy, Jack, is going through a meadow of buttercups. He leans against a hollow tree while eating a slice of plum cake, hears a twittering and climbs inside. Up above is a nest of white wool and moss. It is a nest of very young fairies; one is "creeping about rather like an old baby, and had on a little frock and pinafore." An albatross arrives, and off they fly to Fairyland, the fairies in Jack's pocket. "We are going the back way," says the albatross. "You could go in two minutes by the usual route; but these young fairies want to go before they are summoned, and therefore you and I are taking them." Does this flight echo George MacDonald? *At the Back of the North Wind* was being serialized when *Mopsa* was published, though it would not appear as a book until the following year.

Another episode, where they come to a great bay of becalmed ships, where the wind never blows, recalls another contemporary. How did the ships come to be there? asks Jack.

> Some of them had captains who abused their cabin-boys, some were pirate ships and others were going out on evil errands. ... Many ships which are supposed by men to have foundered lie becalmed in this quiet sea. Look at these five grand ones with the high poops ... they were part of the Spanish Armada; and the open boats with blue sails belonged to the Romans, they sailed with Caesar when he invaded Britain.

Kingsley, certainly. *Westward Ho!* had been published in 1855, *The Water Babies* in 1863. Yet even this probable debt has its own sea-change in *Mopsa*. A visit made to a very different writer, Anna Sewell, at Shanklin in March 1868 illuminates a further episode. Jack and Mopsa land at a border country where horses, cruelly used in the human world, cab horses, race horses, are allowed to grow back to their youth, carefully tended by clockwork people. Why *clockwork*? It is not the only occasion in the book where one feels that the author's unconscious symbolism is rather more interesting than she could have known. But the voice that speaks on the ill-used horses is so remarkably like the voice of *Black Beauty*'s author that the episode could have been written almost immediately after the meeting. *Black Beauty* itself was not published until 9 years later. And nowhere in Jean Ingelow's writing does the subject recur.

But the real originality of the tale is increasingly evident. Whatever you *can* do in this fairyland, you *may* do, Jack is told. But *can* has also its rules. It is a place that even holds the occasional human, like the apple-woman, who stays, still keeping a little stall with cherries on sticks and a few dry nuts. She could wish herself back into the world but has not the courage. "It would come into my head that I should be poor or that my boys would have forgotten me, or that my neighbours would look down on me, and so I always put off wishing for another day." Invention does not flag. Jack and Mopsa, in flight from certain primitive beasts, reach their boat and are offered the protection of a Craken's coils, arch after arch, endlessly reaching away. The water drips about them; the boat trembles "either because of its great age, or because it felt the grasp of the coil underneath." Then, as they sail on, they perceive the arches closing in; soon they have to crouch down in the boat. C.S. Lewis must have recalled this scene in *The Voyage of the "Dawn Treader."* The next arch almost touched the water. "No! that I cannot bear," cries Jack. "Somebody else may do the rest of the dream!" "Why don't you wake?" says Mopsa, as if amused.

But Mopsa is no ordinary fairy. She and Jack escape by night, crossing over the purple mountain, so that she need not rule over the unknown deer-people; so that she need not rule at all, only stay with Jack. And yet, their journey takes them to where they were fleeing from; it is her kingdom after all; there is even a shadow Jack to keep her company. But the real Jack, a human boy, must go home.

And here the book presents the basic difference between the real folk fairy tale and the invented kind, the Victorian sort especially. Jack remains a boy, delightfully so, throughout. But Mopsa, through human contact, gradually changes from child and girl, first pet, then playmate, ally in danger, to a mystical Pre-Raphaelite adult queen. From a child's view, this should not be. Morals work well enough, of the straight pragmatic kind, but emotions, no. Goosegirl and prince may turn, in time, into ageing Queen and King but essentially they are children still, playing at kingdoms. Perhaps a really good illustrator (which *Mopsa* has so far lacked) could solve the problem of Mopsa's transformation. Indeed, older readers may find the end a necessary part of the whole experience. For experience it is. Victorian fantasy, rich as it is, offers few more remarkable journeys to any fairy tale reader.

—Naomi Lewis

LANG, Andrew. British. Born in Selkirk, Scotland, 31 March 1844. Educated at Selkirk High School; Edinburgh Academy, 1854–61; St. Andrews University (Editor, *St. Leonard's Magazine*), 1861–63; Glasgow University, 1863–64; Loretto School, Musselburgh, 1864; Balliol College, Oxford (Snell Exhibitioner), 1864–68, B.A. 1866. Married Leonora Blanche Alleyne in 1875. Fellow, Merton College, Oxford, 1868–75; free-lance writer after 1875. Gifford Lecturer, St. Andrews University, 1888; Ford Lecturer, Oxford University, 1904. General Editor, English Worthies series, Longmans, 1885–87, and Bibliothèque de Corabas series, Nutt, 1887–96. LL.D.: St. Andrews University, 1885; Oxford University, 1904. *Died 20 July 1912.*

Fiction

The Princess Nobody: A Tale of Fairyland, illustrated by Richard Doyle. London, Longman, 1884.

The Gold of Fairnilee, illustrated by E.A. Lemann and T. Scott. Bristol, Arrowsmith, and New York, Longman, 1888.

Prince Prigio, illustrated by Gordon Browne. Bristol, Arrowsmith, 1889; in *My Own Fairy Book*, 1895.

Prince Ricardo of Pantouflia, Being the Adventures of Prince Prigio's Son, illustrated by Gordon Browne. Bristol, Arrowsmith, and New York, Longman, 1893.

My Own Fairy Book (includes *The Gold of Fairnilee, Prince Prigio, Prince Ricardo of Pantouflia*), illustrated by Gordon Browne and others. Bristol, Arrowsmith, and New York, Longman, 1895.

Tales of a Fairy Court, illustrated by A.A. Dixon. London, Collins, 1907.

The Gold of Fairnilee and Other Stories, edited by Gillian Avery. London, Gollancz, 1967.

Other

The Story of the Golden Fleece. London, Kelly, and Philadelphia, Altemus, 1903.

The Story of Joan of Arc. London, Jack, and New York, Dutton, 1906.

Tales of Troy and Greece, illustrated by H.J. Ford. London and New York, Longman, 1907.

Old Friends among the Fairies. London, Longman, 1926.

The Rose Fairy Book, illustrated by Vera Bock. New York, Longman, 1948; London, Longman, 1951.

Fifty Favourite Fairy Tales, edited by Kathleen Lines, illustrated by Margery Gill. London, Nonesuch Press, 1963; New York, Watts, 1964.

More Favourite Fairy Tales, edited by Kathleen Lines, illustrated by Margery Gill. London, Nonesuch Press, and New York, Watts, 1967.

Editor, *Perrault's Popular Tales*. Oxford, Clarendon Press, 1888.

Editor, *The Blue [Red, Green, Yellow, Pink, Grey, Violet, Crimson, Brown, Orange, Olive, Lilac] Fairy Book*, illustrated by H.J. Ford and others. London and New York, Longman, 12 vols., 1889–1910.

Editor, *The Blue Poetry Book*, illustrated by H.J. Ford and Lancelot Speed. London and New York, Longman, 1891.

Editor, *The True Story Book*, illustrated by H.J. Ford and others. London and New York, Longman, 1893.

Editor, *The Red True Story Book*, illustrated by H.J. Ford. London and New York, Longman, 1895.

Editor, *The Animal Story Book*, illustrated by H.J. Ford.. London and New York, Longman, 1896.

Editor, *The Nursery Rhyme Book*, illustrated by L. Leslie Brooke. London and New York, Warne, 1897.

Editor, *The Arabian Nights Entertainments*. London, Longman, 1898.

Editor, *The Red Book of Animal Stories*, illustrated by H.J. Ford. London and New York, Longman, 1899.

Editor, *The Book of Romance*, illustrated by H.J. Ford. London and New York, Longman, 1902.

Editor, *The Red Romance Book*, illustrated by H.J. Ford. London and New York, Longman, 1905.

Editor, *The Book of Princes and Princesses*, by Leonora Lang, illustrated by H.J. Ford. London and New York, Longman, 1908.

Editor, *The Red Book of Heroes*, by Leonora Lang, illustrated by A. Wallis Mills. London and New York, Longman, 1909.

Editor, *The All Sorts of Stories Book*, by Leonora Lang, illustrated by H.J. Ford. London and New York, Longman, 1911.

Editor, *The Book of Saints and Heroes*, by Leonora Lang, illustrated by H.J. Ford. London and New York, Longman, 1912.

Editor, *The Strange Story Book*, by Leonora Lang, illustrated by H.J. Ford. London and New York, Longman, 1913.

Translator, *Johnny Nut and the Golden Goose*, by Charles Deulin, illustrated by A. Lynen. London, Longman, 1887.

PUBLICATIONS FOR ADULTS

Novels

Much Darker Days (as A Huge Longway). London, Longman, 1884; revised edition, 1885.

That Very Mab (published anonymously), with May Kendall. London, Longman, 1885.

The Mark of Cain. Bristol, Arrowsmith, and New York, Scribner, 1886.

He, by the Author of It ..., with W.H. Pollock. London, Longman, 1887; as *He, A Companion to She ...*, New York, Munro, 1887.

The World's Desire, with H. Rider Haggard. London, Longman, and New York, Harper, 1890.

A Monk of Fife: A Romance of the Days of Jeanne d'Arc .... London and New York, Longman, 1895.

Parson Kelly, with A.E.W. Mason. London and New York, Longman, 1899.

The Disentanglers. London and New York, Longman, 1901.

Short Stories

In the Wrong Paradise and Other Stories. London, Kegan Paul, and New York, Harper, 1886.

Plays

The Black Thief. Privately printed, 1882.

The New Pygmalion. Privately printed, 1962.

Verse

Ballads and Lyrics of Old France, with Other Poems. London, Longman, 1872.

XXII Ballades in Blue China. London, Kegan Paul, 1880.

XXII and X: XXXII Ballades in Blue China. London, Kegan Paul, 1881; revised edition, 1888.

Helen of Troy. London, Bell, and New York, Scribner, 1882.

Rhymes à la Mode. London, Kegan Paul, 1884; New York, Longman, 1907.

Ballades and Verses Vain, edited by Austin Dobson. New York, Scribner, 1884.

Lines on the Inaugural Meeting of the Shelley Society, edited by Thomas J. Wise. Privately printed, 1886.

Grass of Parnassus: Rhymes Old and New. London and New York, Longman, 1888; revised edition, as *Grass of Parnassus: First and Last Rhymes*, 1892.

Ban and Arrière Ban: A Rally of Fugitive Rhymes.   London and New York, Longman, 1894.

The Young Ruthven.   Privately printed, 1902.

New Collected Rhymes.   London and New York, Longman, 1905.

Ode on a Distant Memory of "Jane Eyre," edited by Clement K. Shorter.   Privately printed, 1912.

The Poetical Works of Andrew Lang, edited by Leonora Lang.   London and New York, Longman, 4 vols., 1923.

(*Poems*).   London, Benn, 1926.

Other

Oxford: Brief Historical and Descriptive Notes ....   London, Seeley, 1880; New York, Macmillan, 1890.

The Library.   London and New York, Macmillan, 1881.

Notes on a Collection of Pictures by Mr. J.E. Millais ....   London, J.S. Virtue, 1881.

Custom and Myth.   London, Longman, 1884; New York, Harper, 1885; revised edition, Longman, 1885.

The Politics of Aristotle: Introductory Essays.   London, Longman, 1886.

Letters to Dead Authors.   London, Longman, and New York, Scribner, 1886; revised edition, as *New and Old Letters to Dead Authors,* London and New York, Longman, 1907.

Books and Bookmen.   New York, G.J. Coombes, and London, Longman, 1886.

Myth, Ritual, and Religion.   London, Longman, 2 vols., 1887.

Pictures at Play; or, Dialogues of the Galleries by Two Art-Critics (published anonymously), with W.E. Henley.   London, Longman, 1888.

Letters on Literature.   London and New York, Longman, 1889.

Lost Leaders, edited by Pett Ridge.   London, Kegan Paul, and New York, Longman, 1889.

Old Friends: Essays in Epistolary Parody.   London and New York, Longman, 1890.

How to Fail in Literature (lecture).   London, Field and Tuer, 1890.

Life, Letters, and Diaries of Sir Stafford Northcote, First Earl of Iddesleigh.   Edinburgh, Blackwood, 2 vols., 1890.

Angling Sketches.   London and New York, Longman, 1891.

Essays in Little.   London, Henry, and New York, Scribner, 1891.

The Tercentenary of Izaak Walton.   Privately printed, 1893.

Homer and the Epic.   London and New York, Longman, 1893.

St. Andrews.   London and New York, Longman, 1893.

Cock Lane and Common-Sense.   London, Longman, 1894.

The Voices of Jeanne d'Arc.   Privately printed, 1895.

The Life and Letters of John Gibson Lockhart ....   London, J.C. Nimmo, and New York, Scribner, 2 vols., 1896.

Modern Mythology.   London and New York, Longman, 1897.

The Book of Dreams and Ghosts.   London and New York, Longman, 1897.

Pickle the Spy; or, The Incognito of Prince Charles.   London and New York, Longman, 1897.

The Making of Religion.   London and New York, Longman, 1898.

The Companions of Pickle.   London, Longman, 1898.

Prince Charles Edward Stuart.   London and New York, Goupil, 1900; revised edition, London and New York, Longman, 1903.

A History of Scotland from the Roman Occupation.   Edinburgh, Blackwood, and New York, Dodd Mead, 4 vols., 1900–07.

Notes and Names in Books.   Privately printed, 1900.

The Mystery of Mary Stuart.   London and New York, Longman, 1901; revised edition, 1904.

Alfred Tennyson. Edinburgh, Blackwood, and New York, Dodd Mead, 1901.
Magic and Religion. London and New York, Longman, 1901.
Adventures among Books. Privately printed, 1901.
Bibliomania. Privately printed, 1902.
James VI and the Gowrie Mystery. London and New York, Longman, 1902.
Social Origins, with *Primal Law,* by J.J. Atkinson. London and New York, Longman, 1903.
The Valet's Tragedy and Other Studies in Secret History. London and New York, Longman, 1903.
Historical Mysteries. London, Smith Elder, 1904; New York, Longman, 1905.
The Puzzle of Dickens's Last Plot. London, Chapman and Hall, 1905; Folcroft, Pennsylvania, Folcroft Editions, 1976.
The Secret of the Totem. London and New York, Longman, 1905.
Adventures among Books (collection). London and New York, Longman, 1905.
The Clyde Mystery: A Study in Forgeries and Folklore. Glasgow, MacLehose, 1905.
John Knox and the Reformation. London and New York, Longman, 1905.
Homer and His Age. London and New York, Longman, 1906.
Life of Sir Walter Scott. London, Hodder and Stoughton, and New York, Scribner, 1906.
Portrait and Jewels of Mary Stuart. Glasgow, MacLehose, 1906.
The King over the Water, with Alice Shield. London and New York, Longman, 1907.
The Origins of Religion and Other Essays. London, Watts, 1908.
The Maid of France, Being the Story of the Life and Death of Jeanne d'Arc. London and New York, Longman, 1908.
The Origin of Terms of Human Relationship. London, Oxford University Press, 1909.
Sir George MacKenzie, King's Advocate of Rosehaugh: His Life and Times, 1636(?)–1691. London and New York, Longman, 1909.
La "Jeanne d'Arc" de M. Anatole France. Paris, Perrin, 1909.
The World of Homer. London and New York, Longman, 1910.
Sir Walter Scott and the Border Minstrelsy. London and New York, Longman, 1910.
Method in the Study of Totemism. St. Andrews, St. Andrews University, 1911.
A Short History of Scotland. Edinburgh, Blackwood, and New York, Dodd Mead, 1911.
Shakespeare, Bacon, and the Great Unknown. London and New York, Longman, 1912.
A History of English Literature from "Beowulf" to Swinburne. London and New York, Longman, 1912.
Highways and Byways in the Border, with John Lang. London, Macmillan, 1913.
(Essays). London, Harrap, 1926.
Andrew Lang and St. Andrews: A Centenary Anthology, edited by J.B. Salmond. St. Andrews, St. Andrews University, 1944.

Editor, *The Poems of Edgar Allan Poe.* London, Kegan Paul, 1881.
Editor, *Ballads of Books.* London and New York, Longman, 1888.
Editor, *Euterpe, Being the Second Book of the Famous History of Herodotus,* translated by Barnaby Rich. London, Nutt, 1888.
Editor, *The Strife of Love in a Dream,* by Francesco Colonna. London, Nutt, 1890.
Editor, *Selected Poems,* by Robert Burns. London, Kegan Paul, 1891.
Editor, *The Lyrics and Ballads of Sir Walter Scott.* London, Dent, 1894.
Editor, *Border Ballads.* London and New York, Laurence and Bullen-Longman, 1895.
Editor, *Poetical Works,* by Sir Walter Scott. London, Black, 2 vols., 1895.
Editor, *The Compleat Angler,* by Izaak Walton. London, Dent, 1896.
Editor, *The Poems and Songs of Robert Burns.* London, Methuen, 1896.
Editor, *A Collection of Ballads.* London, Chapman and Hall, 1897.

Editor, *Selections from the Poets: Wordsworth, Coleridge.*   London, Longman, 2 vols., 1897–98.

Editor, *The Gowrie Conspiracy: Confessions of George Sprot.*   London, Roxburghe Club, 1902.

Editor, *The Apology for William Maitland of Lethington, 1610.*   Edinburgh, Scottish History Society, 1904.

Editor, *Poets' Country.*   London, Jack, 1907.

Editor, *Poems,* by Jean Ingelow.   London and New York, Longman, 1908.

Editor, *Poems and Plays,* by Sir Walter Scott.   London, Dent, 2 vols., 1911.

Editor, *The Annesley Case.*   Edinburgh, Hodge, 1912.

Editor, *Molière's Les Precieuses Ridicules.*   Oxford, Clarendon Press, 1926.

Translator, *The Odyssey of Homer, Book 6* (published anonymously).   Privately printed, 1877.

Translator, *Specimens of a Translation of Theocritus.*   Privately printed, 1879.

Translator, with S.H. Butcher, *The Odyssey of Homer.*   London and New York, Macmillan, 1879.

Translator, with Walter Leaf and Ernest Myers, *The Iliad of Homer.*   London and New York, Macmillan, 1883.

Translator, *Theocritus, Bion and Moschus.*   London, Macmillan, 1880; New York, Macmillan, 1889.

Translator, *Aucassin and Nicolette.*   London, Nutt, 1887; as *The Song-Story of Aucassin and Nicolette,* New Rochelle, New York, Elston Press, 1902.

Translator, *The Dead Leman and Other Tales from the French.*   London, Swan Sonnenschein, and New York, Scribner, 1889.

Translator, *The Miracles of Madame Saint Katherine of Fierbois,* by J.J. Bourassé.   Chicago, Way and Williams, 1897.

Translator, *The Homeric Hymns: A New Prose Translation and Essays.*   London, Allen, and New York, Longman, 1899.

Translator, *In Praise of Frugality,* by Pope Leo XII.   Privately printed, 1912.

Translator, *Ode to the Opening Century,* by Pope Leo XII.   Privately printed, 1912.

Critical Studies: *Andrew Lang: A Critical Biography,* Leicester, Ward, 1946, and *Andrew Lang,* London, Bodley Head, and New York, Walck, 1962, both by Roger Lancelyn Green.

*   *   *

Writing in 1889 in *The Child and His Book,* Mrs. E.M. Field stated that "At the present moment the fairy-tale seems to have given way entirely in popularity to the child's story of real life, the novel of childhood, in which no effort is spared to make children appear as they are." But just before the publication of the book early in 1891, she added a note: "Since the above was written eighteen months ago, the tide of popularity seems to have set strongly in the direction of the old fairy stories."

These two quotations epitomise Andrew Lang's most important contribution in the development of the literature of childhood: and this came about largely because of the scholarly interest in folklore which made him one of the most important of the folklorists and anthropologists of his age. From the point of view of the folklorists, Andrew Lang first became notable for his essay "Mythology and Fairy Tales" in 1873, his introduction to Mrs. Hunt's complete translation of the Grimm's *Märchen* in 1884, and his two books, *Custom and Myth* (1884) and *Myth, Ritual, and Religion* (1887), the second of which contained a long section on folk-tales and fairy lore generally.

His writings for children began rather tentatively in 1884 with the short fairy story *The Princess Nobody* which he constructed most ingeniously to fit a large number of illustrations by Richard ("Dicky") Doyle which had appeared in 1869 to accompany (but not illustrate) poems by William Allingham. This charming tale was constructed on the lines of a traditional fairy tale: issued in an edition of 10,000 copies it did not, however, reach a second edition, and was buried in oblivion until 1955 when it was included in *Modern Fairy Stories* in Dent's Illustrated Children's Classics, edited by Roger Lancelyn Green, since when it has been reprinted in various forms.

He followed this with *The Gold of Fairnilee*, a tale based on the Scottish Ballads and the fairy lore of the Border Country which was his home from his birth in 1844 until 1868. As a boy he and his brother and several others from his home-town of Selkirk were accustomed to meet every Saturday evening in a barn to hear local folk tales and legends told by an old shepherd. Lang wrote that people in the Border Country believed in fairies "even when my father was a boy," and it is to the Fairyland, "which paid a fiend to Hell," that Randal of Fairnilee is carried by the Fairy Queen, even as Thomas the Rhymer had been, and from which Jean rescues him as Janet had rescued Tamlin in the ballad – in time to find the legendary Gold of Fairnilee for which Lang and his brother John had so often searched in vain.

The Fairyland of traditional belief did not prove popular, though of the few literary expeditions thither Lang's is outstandingly the best. Perhaps for this reason his next venture was into the realm explored by the ladies of the *Cabinet des Fées* and so brilliantly exploited by Thackeray in *The Rose and the Ring*.

Prince Prigio and its slightly less successful sequel, *Prince Ricardo*, make an outstanding contribution to the literary fairy story as opposed to the traditional type, and seems to be accepted now as a classic in its own particular genre. In both these books Lang's knowledge of the Märchen of the world is given brilliant play, accepting the "rules" of the typical literary Fairyland with absolute gravity and following them to their logical conclusions. The humour and a tang of underlying irony make them two books which can be enjoyed by adults as well as children. *Prince Prigio* certainly illustrates C.S. Lewis's dictum that "a children's book which is enjoyed by children only is a bad children's book: the good ones last."

Lang turned back once more to Prigio's Kingdom of Pantouflia in *Tales of a Fairy Court*, but with little of his earlier success, though in one or two of the stories the magic touch is still visible.

But good though the best of his original stories are, their excellencies have, from the start, tended to be eclipsed by the series of traditional tales which he chose, edited and occasionally retold, of which the first volume, *The Blue Fairy Book*, appeared in time for the same Christmas of 1889 as *Prince Prigio*; and it was on account of the unexpected popularity of this and its first sequel, *The Red Fairy Book*, the following year that Mrs. Field felt herself obliged to add the foot-note quoted above.

The Blue Fairy Book was a complete gamble which Lang must have persuaded his friend and publisher, Charles Longman, to undertake – and which Longman probably risked on the strength of Lang's name, which was still very high in the literary world of the day. It appeared in an edition of 5,000 copies, and its success was instantaneous. By the time *The Yellow Fairy Book* (the fourth) appeared in 1894, the first edition was of 15,000.

The series finally consisted of twenty-five annual volumes, twelve of which were Fairy Books. But several others such as *The Arabian Nights*, two *Romance* books and the final *Strange Story Book* come almost within the category of Fairy Stories. And a volume outside the series, *Tales of Troy and Greece*, presents the greatest of the ancient Greek stories entirely in Lang's own retelling, and is still rivalled only by Kingsley's *The Heroes* (1856). This also has been reprinted recently, besides the major portion of it as *The Adventures of Odysseus* in Dent (and Dutton)'s series of Children's Illustrated Classics.

In the preface to the last of the actual Fairy Books (the *Lilac*) Lang wrote: "My part has been that of Adam, according to Mark Twain, in the Garden of Eden. Eve worked, Adam superintended; I find out where the stories are, and advise, and, in short, superintend. *I do not write the stories out of my own head*. The reputation of having written all the fairy books (a European reputation in nurseries and the United States of America) is 'the burden of an honour unto which I was not born' ...."

But Lang's vast knowledge of the wide world's folk-lore and his magic touch in preparing the work of others for publication (and helped by the superbly complementary accompaniment of H.J. Ford's illustrations), make classics of these unrivalled collections, and, even more than his outstanding contribution to the history of Fairyland, ensure him a high place in the history of children's literature.

—Roger Lancelyn Green

LEAR, Edward. British. Born in London, 12 May 1812. Studied at Sass's School of Art, London, 1835, 1849; Royal Academy, London, 1850–52; studied painting with Holman Hunt. Free-lance artist after 1827, and teacher after 1830; assistant to the artists Prideaux Selby and John Gould; illustrated the animals at the home of the Earl of Derby, 1832–37; lived in Rome, 1837–45; gave drawing lessons to Queen Victoria, 1846; lived in Italy and the Mediterranean, 1846–49, and in San Remo, Italy, 1868–88. *Died 29 January 1888.*

PUBLICATIONS FOR CHILDREN (illustrated by the author)

Verse

A Book of Nonsense (published anonymously). London, Thomas Maclean, 1846; revised edition, as Edward Lear, London, Routledge, 1861; Philadelphia, Hazard, 1863.
Nonsense Songs, Stories, Botany, and Alphabets. London, Bush, 1870.
More Nonsense, Pictures, Rhymes, Botany, etc. London, Bush, 1871.
Laughable Lyrics: A Fourth Book of Nonsense, Poems, Songs, Botany, Music, etc. London, Bush, 1876.
Nonsense Songs and Stories. London, Warne, 1894.
Queery Leary Nonsense, edited by Lady Strachey. London, Mills and Boon, 1911.
The Complete Nonsense Book, edited by Lady Strachey. New York, Duffield, 1912.
The Lear Omnibus, edited by M.L. Mégroz. London and New York, Nelson, 1938; as *A Book of Lear,* London, Penguin, 1939.
The Complete Nonsense, edited by Holbrook Jackson. London, Faber, 1947; New York, Dover, 1951.
Teapots and Quails and Other New Nonsense, edited by Angus Davidson and Philip Hofer. London, Murray, and Cambridge, Massachusetts, Harvard University Press, 1953.
A Book of Bosh: Lyrics and Prose, edited by Brian Alderson. London, Penguin, 1975.
Lear in the Original, edited by Herman W. Liebert. New York, Kraus, 1975.

Other

The Lear Coloured Bird Book for Children. London, Mills and Boon, 1912.

PUBLICATIONS FOR ADULTS

Other

Illustrations of the Family of Psittacidae, or Parrots .... Privately printed, 1832.
Views in Rome and Its Environs. London, Thomas Maclean, 1841.
Gleanings from the Menagerie and Aviary at Knowsley Hall, Knowsley. Privately printed, 1846.
Illustrated Excursions in Italy. London, Thomas Maclean, 2 vols., 1846.

Journal of a Landscape Painter in Albania, etc.   London, Richard Bentley, 1851.
Journal of a Landscape Painter in S. Calabria, etc.   London, Richard Bentley, 1852.
Views in the Seven Ionian Islands.   Privately printed, 1863.
Journal of a Landscape Painter in Corsica.   London, Bush, 1870.
Tortoises, Terrapins, and Turtles, with James de Carle Sowerby.   London, Southeran
  Baer, 1872.
Letters, and *Later Letters,* edited by Lady Strachey.   London, Unwin, 2 vols., 1907–11.
Lear in Sicily ..., May-July 1847, edited by Granville Proby.   London, Duckworth,
  1938.
Journals: A Selection, edited by Herbert Van Thal.   London, Barker, and New York,
  Coward McCann, 1952.
Indian Journal: Watercolours and Extracts from the Diary (1873–1875), edited by Ray
  Murphy.   London and New York, Jarrolds, 1953.
Lear's Corfu, edited by Lawrence Durrell.   Corfu, Corfu Travel, 1965.

Critical Studies: *Edward Lear: Landscape Painter and Nonsense Poet* by Angus Davidson,
London, John Murray, 1938; *Edward Lear: The Life of a Wanderer* by Vivien Noakes,
London, Collins, 1968, Boston, Houghton Mifflin, 1969.

Illustrator: *A Century of Birds from the Himalayan Mountains,* 1831, *A Monograph of the
Ramphastidae, or Family of Toucans,* 1834, and *Birds of Europe,* 1837, all by John Gould;
The Gardens and Menageries of the Zoological Society Delineated, edited by E.T. Bennett,
1831; *Illustrations of British Ornithology,* 1834; *Transactions of the Zoological Society,* vol. 1,
1835; *The Zoology of Captain Beechey's Voyage,* 1839; *The Zoology of the Voyage of H.M.S.
Beagle,* 1841; *Pigeons* and *Parrots,* in *The Naturalist's Library* by William Jardine, 1843; *The
Genera of Birds* by G.R. Gray, 1849; *Poems of Alfred, Lord Tennyson,* 1889.

*   *   *

When Edward Lear was a young man, he went to live at Knowsley Hall, the home of the
Earls of Derby. At this time he was a natural history illustrator, and he had been
commissioned to paint the birds and animals in Lord Derby's menagerie. At Knowsley he
met "half the fine people of the day," but did not altogether like them. He wrote to a friend:
"The uniform apathetic tone assumed by lofty society irks me *dreadfully,* nothing I long for
half so much as to giggle heartily and to hop on one leg down the great gallery – but I dare
not." Instead, he began to write his limericks:

> There was an old person of Shoreham,
> Whose habits were marked by decorum;
> He bought an Umbrella, and sate in the cellar,
> Which pleased all the people of Shoreham.

As apathy denied life, so also did the improving tale, for it disclaimed children as they were
in favour of children as they ought to be:

> There was an old man of Hong Kong,
> Who never did anything wrong;
> He lay on his back, with his head in a sack,
> That innocuous old man of Hong Kong.

With the decorous and perfectly innocuous safely hidden away, Lear's real people could
indulge in amiable excess:

> There was a Young Girl of Majorca,
> Whose aunt was a very fast walker;
> She walked seventy miles, and leaped fifteen stiles,
> Which astonished that Girl of Majorca.

Their standards were so essentially worthwhile:

> There was an old person of Bray,
> Who sang through the whole of the day
> To his ducks and his pigs, whom he fed upon figs,
> That valuable person of Bray.

Beyond the restraints of propriety were those imposed by life itself. "There's something in the world amiss will be unravelled by and by," Lear would quote in his diary. In his own case, epilepsy imposed an isolating barrier which he never broke down.

In his writing such anomalies might cause embarrassment: they could also be the source of real suffering. In the Pelican Chorus, the apparent affliction suffered by the King of the Cranes is politely ignored. With the Daddy Long-Legs and the Fly, however, it is all far more serious and distressing. Each to the other seems fine and composed, and yet ... "Why," asks Mr. Daddy Long-Legs, "do you never come to court?"

> "O Mr. Daddy Long-legs,"
> Said Mr. Floppy Fly,
> "It's true I never go to court,
> And I will tell you why.
> If I had six long legs like yours,
> At once I'd go to court!
> But oh! I can't, because *my* legs
> Are so extremely short.
> And I'm afraid the King and Queen
> (One in red, and one in green)
> Would say aloud, 'You are not fit,
> You Fly, to come to court a bit!' "

Mr. Daddy Long-legs also has his secret sadness. He, who once sang so beautifully, can no longer do so:

> For years I cannot hum a bit,
> Or sing the smallest song;
> And this the dreadful reason is,
> My legs are grown too long!
> My six long legs, all here and there,
> Oppress my bosom with despair;
> And if I stand, or lie, or sit,
> I cannot sing one single bit!

But there is a remedy: they can escape to a land where none of this will matter any more:

> Then Mr. Daddy Long-legs
> And Mr. Floppy Fly
> Rushed downward to the foamy sea
> With one sponge-taneous cry;
> And there they found a little boat,
> Whose sails were pink and gray;
> And off they sailed among the waves,
> Far, and far away.
> They sailed across the silent main
> And reached the great Gromboolian plain;
> And there they play for evermore
> At battlecock and shuttledoor.

This is where Lear takes his children. Together they set out on their long and difficult journey. You must have courage to go to sea in a sieve, or indeed to sail away for a year and a day, but this courage is rewarded. There is no chance of the fainthearted following you. Critical, unimaginative adults are left behind. When the Jumblies returned home,

> ... every one said, "If we only live,
> We too will go to sea in a Sieve, –
> To the hills of the Chankly Bore!"

but we know perfectly well that they will not.

Of course, you may discover, when you reach the sunset isles of Boshen, that you have moved from loneliness into loneliness: neither the Yonghy Bonghy Bò nor the Dong could redeem their isolation. There is sadness even here. But, in the end, it is all a game, perhaps of battlecock and shuttledoor, certainly of words and of the imagination. This is what gives it its safety. "There only remains a general, but very strong, pervading sense of well-being and innate rectitude from the standpoint of eight years," a child friend said of Lear. "I knew he was 'safe' and that I was safe and that we were all safe together, and that suspicions might at once be put aside." In a potentially alien world, Lear made children feel secure:

> How pleasant to know Mr. Lear!
> Who has written such volumes of stuff!
> Some think him ill-tempered and queer,
> But a few think him pleasant enough.
>
> His mind is concrete and fastidious,
> His nose is remarkably big;
> His visage is more or less hideous,
> His beard it resembles a wig.

As a child you may feel yourself to be strange and different, you know you can never be perfect; but there is no need to worry, for in an imaginary world where people have unlikely noses and legs and weird modes of expression, where they seek out oddities with whom they can identify themselves, and where they find kindness and spontaneity, you are never likely to feel alone. It is in this that we find Lear's influence on the children's writers who came after him.

—Vivien Noakes

MacDONALD, George. British. Born near Huntly, Aberdeenshire, 10 December 1824. Educated at King's College, University of Aberdeen, 1840–45, M.A. 1845; Highbury Theological College, London, 1848–50. Married Louisa Powell in 1850 (died, 1902); eleven children. Private tutor, 1845–48, London; Minister of Trinity Congregational Church, Arundel, Sussex, 1850–53; lecturer and preacher in Manchester, 1853–56, Hastings, 1857–59, and London after 1859. Received Civil List pension, 1877. Lived in Bordighera, Italy for over 20 years. Editor, with Norman MacLeod, *Good Words for the Young* magazine, 1870–72. LL.D.: University of Aberdeen, 1868. *Died 18 September 1905.*

PUBLICATIONS FOR CHILDREN

Fiction

Dealings with the Fairies, illustrated by Arthur Hughes.　London, Strahan, 1867; New York, Routledge, 1891.

At the Back of the North Wind, illustrated by Arthur Hughes.　London, Strahan, 1870; New York, Routledge, 1871.

Ranald Bannerman's Boyhood, illustrated by Arthur Hughes.　London, Strahan, and New York, Routledge, 1871.

The Princess and the Goblin, illustrated by Arthur Hughes.　New York, Routledge, 1871; London, Strahan, 1872.

Gutta-Percha Willie, The Working Genius, illustrated by Arthur Hughes.　London, King, and Boston, Hoyt, 1873.

The Wise Woman: A Parable.　London, Strahan, 1875; as *A Double Story*, New York, Dodd Mead, 1876; as *The Lost Princess*, London, Wells Gardner Darton, 1895.

Sir Gibbie.　London, Hurst and Blackett, 3 vols., 1879; Philadelphia, Lippincott, 1879.

The Princess and Curdie, illustrated by James Allen.　Philadelphia, Lippincott, 1882; London, Chatto and Windus, 1883.

A Rough Shaking, illustrated by W. Parkinson.　New York, Routledge, 1890; London, Blackie, 1891.

The Fairy Tales of George MacDonald, edited by Greville MacDonald.　London, Fifield, 5 vols., 1904.

The Light Princess and Other Tales of Fantasy, edited by Roger Lancelyn Green.　London, Gollancz, 1961.

The Gifts of the Child Christ: Fairy Tales and Stories for the Childlike, edited by Glenn Edward Sadler.　Grand Rapids, Michigan, Eerdmans, 2 vols., 1973.

PUBLICATIONS FOR ADULTS

Novels

Phantastes: A Faerie Romance for Men and Women.　London, Smith Elder, 1858; Boston, Loring, 1870.

David Elginbrod.　London, Hurst and Blackett, 3 vols., 1863; New York, Munro, 1879.

Adela Cathcart.　London, Hurst and Blackett, 3 vols., 1864; New York, Munro, 1882.

The Portent: A Story of the Inner Vision of the Highlanders, Commonly Called the Second Sight.　London, Smith Elder, 1864; New York, Munro, 1885.

Alec Forbes of Howglen.　London, Hurst and Blackett, 3 vols., 1865; New York, Harper, 1872.

Annals of a Quiet Neighbourhood.　London, Hurst and Blackett, 3 vols., 1867; New York, Harper, 1867.

Guild Court.　London, Hurst and Blackett, 3 vols., 1867; New York, Harper, 1868.

Robert Falconer.　London, Hurst and Blackett, 3 vols., 1868; Boston, Loring, n.d.

The Seaboard Parish.　London, Tinsley, 3 vols., 1868; New York, Routledge, 1868.

The Vicar's Daughter: An Autobiographical Story.　Boston, Roberts, 1871; London, Tinsley, 3 vols., 1872.

Wilfrid Cumbermede.　London, Hurst and Blackett, 3 vols., 1872; New York, Scribner, 1872.

Malcolm.　London, King, 3 vols., 1875; Philadelphia, Lippincott, 1875.

St. George and St. Michael.　London, King, 3 vols., 1876; New York, Ford, 1876(?).

Thomas Wingfold, Curate.　London, Hurst and Blackett, 3 vols., 1876; New York, Munro, 1879.

The Marquis of Lossie.　London, Hurst and Blackett, 3 vols., 1877; Philadelphia, Lippincott, 1877.

Paul Faber, Surgeon. London, Hurst and Blackett, 3 vols., 1879; Philadelphia, Lippincott, 1879.

Mary Marston. London, Sampson Low, 3 vols., 1881; Philadelphia, Lippincott, 1881.

Warlock o' Glen Warlock. New York, Harper, 1881; as *Castle Warlock: A Homely Romance,* London, Sampson Low, 3 vols., 1882.

Weighed and Wanting. London, Sampson Low, 3 vols., 1882; New York, Harper, 1882.

Donal Grant. London, Kegan Paul, 3 vols., 1883; New York, Harper, 1883.

What's Mine's Mine. London, Kegan Paul, 3 vols., 1886; New York, Harper, 1886.

Home Again. London, Kegan Paul, and New York, Appleton, 1887.

The Elect Lady. London, Kegan Paul, and New York, Munro, 1888.

There and Back. London, Kegan Paul, 3 vols., 1891; Boston, Lothrop, n.d.

The Flight of the Shadow. London, Kegan Paul, and New York, Appleton, 1891.

Heather and Snow. London, Chatto and Windus, 2 vols., 1893; New York, Harper, 1893.

Lilith: A Romance. London, Chatto and Windus, and New York, Dodd Mead, 1895.

Salted with Fire. London, Hurst and Blackett, and New York, Dodd Mead, 1897.

Short Stories

The Gifts of the Child Christ and Other Tales. London, Sampson Low, 2 vols., 1882; New York, Munro, 1882; as *Stephen Archer and Other Tales,* Sampson Low, 1883; Philadelphia, McKay, n.d.

Far above Rubies. New York, Dodd Mead, 1899.

Verse

Within and Without: A Dramatic Poem. London, Longman, 1855; New York, Scribner, 1872.

Poems. London, Longman, 1857.

A Hidden Life and Other Poems. London, Longman, 1864; New York, Scribner, 1872.

The Disciple and Other Poems. London, Strahan, 1867.

Dramatic and Miscellaneous Poems. New York, Scribner, 2 vols., 1876.

A Book of Strife, in the Form of the Diary of an Old Soul. Privately printed, 1880.

A Threefold Cord: Poems by Three Friends, with John Hill MacDonald and Greville Matheson, edited by George MacDonald. Privately printed, 1883.

The Poetical Works of George MacDonald. London, Chatto and Windus, 2 vols., 1893.

Rampolli: Growths from a Long-Planted Root, Being Translations Chiefly from the German, Along with a "Year's Diary of an Old Soul." London, Longman, 1897.

Other

Unspoken Sermons. London, Strahan and Longman, 3 vols., 1867, 1886, 1889; New York, Routledge, n.d.

England's Antiphon. London, Macmillan, 1868; Philadelphia, Lippincott, n.d.

The Miracles of Our Lord. London, Strahan, and New York, Randolph, 1870.

Works of Fancy and Imagination. London, Strahan, 10 vols., 1871.

Orts. London, Sampson Low, 1882; as *The Imagination and Other Essays,* Boston, Lothrop, 1883; revised edition, as *A Dish of Orts,* Sampson Low, 1893.

The Tragedie of Hamlet, Prince of Denmark: A Study of the Text of the Folio of 1623. London, Longman, 1885.

The Hope of the Gospel (sermons). London, Ward Lock, and New York, Appleton, 1892.

The Hope of the Universe. London, Victoria Street Society for the Protection of Animals from Vivisection, 1896.

George MacDonald: An Anthology, edited by C.S. Lewis. London, Bles, 1946; New York, Macmillan, 1947.

Editor, *A Cabinet of Gems, Cut and Polished by Sir Philip Sidney, Now for the More Radiance Presented Without Their Setting.* London, Elliot Stock, 1892.

Translator, *Twelve of the Spiritual Songs of Novalis.* Privately printed, 1851.

Translator, *Exotics: A Translation of the Spiritual Songs of Novalis, The Hymn Book of Luther, and Other Poems from the German and Italian.* London, Strahan, 1876.

Bibliography: *A Centennial Bibliography of George MacDonald* by John Malcolm Bullock, Aberdeen, University Press, 1925.

Critical Studies: *George MacDonald and His Wife* by Greville MacDonald, London, Allen and Unwin, 1924; *The Golden Key: A Study of the Fiction of George MacDonald* by R.L. Wolfe, New Haven, Connecticut, Yale University Press, 1961.

*   *   *

George MacDonald was a singular 19th-century writer whose outstanding talent for crossing literary types and age barriers makes critical discussion of his writings difficult. More than any of his time, he understood the symbolic richness of the traditional fairytale and worked to expand its dimensions. As a teller of fanciful tales, he is unequalled. It is his unusual mastery of the parable form, converting it, as he did, into a sort of allegorical fantasy, called a *fairytale,* which continues to attract modern writers of children's books to his stories. He possessed a fully integrated genius, whereby the creations of faerie lore and the realities of his own childhood were one; and it is this feature that characterizes him best.

Typical of his lifelong experimentation with the parable-fairy-tale form, or as he later designated it, "the double story," is his first and quite successful prose narrative. *Phantastes.* Into it, he put a multifarious assortment of lyrics, chivalric Spenserian ballads, frame-stories and imaginative beings related to his reading of Hoffmann's *Golden Pot,* Novalis, and Fouqué's *Undine,* his favorite fairytale. In type, *Phantastes* defies strict classification; it is in subject-matter most like the *volksmärchen*: an episodic string of nature-parables focusing around the youthful hero Anodos and his lessons of self-renunciation. What the plot lacks in consistency of design, it compensates for by its symbolic depth. Contained in this story and its later companion, *Lilith,* are passages of double parable-writing – for example the tale of Cosmo – which place MacDonald, unrivalled in this form, with Bunyan and Spenser.

During the 1870's MacDonald did most of his best writing for children. He edited *Good Words for the Young* and serialized *At the Back of the North Wind* in it, following with a story of his boyhood reminiscences, *Ranald Bannerman's Boyhood.* And in 1872 he published his second classic, *The Princess and the Goblin,* and *The Wise Woman: A Parable,* three years later. In these books – not originally limited to any certain age – MacDonald fully demonstrated his craft as a writer of children's books.

All of his stories have in them the moral fabric of parables. Educational in thrust, each tale contains a basic plot – Diamond, the coachman's son, takes up with Mistress North Wind who becomes his flying tutoress (*At the Back of the North Wind*); Princess Irene and Curdie, the miner's son, rid the royal city of Gwyntystorm of its corruptors (The Princess and Curdie books); and in *The Wise Woman,* his most lucid and long parable, Princess Rosamond and a shepherd's daughter are taught by a beatific old woman in a cottage in the woods. Simple contrasts are readily made between rich and poor, greed and charity, beauty and ugliness, youth and age, selfishness and true obedience – popular lessons of fairyland. Cannily the reader learns that appearances are not everything ("Little Daylight"), that true knowledge comes by acceptance of self-sacrifice and dependency on another ("The History of Photogen and Nycteris"), and, finally, in the best symbolic tale, "The Golden Key," that the source of all desire (imagination?) itself is found in a cosmic search up into the rainbow. But in spite of the teasing enchantment and obvious didacticism at work in the stories, there is always – most critics contend – something more than allegorical meaning in them.

As a writer MacDonald claimed that his "aim" was to bring about "logical conviction" in his readers by creating a "mood-engendering" sensation: "The best thing you can do for your fellow, next to rousing his conscience, is – not to give him things to think about, but to wake things up that are in him; or say, to make him think things for himself." Transparency of thought and feeling is what one reacts to most in his stories. Like the Princess and Curdie, as they stand before the youthful but wise grandmother, the reader continually asks:

> "What does it all mean, Grandmother?" she sobbed and burst into fresh tears.
> "It means, my love, that I did not mean to show myself. Curdie is not yet able to believe some things. Seeing is not believing – it is only seeing."

Meaning in all stories is linked up, at one point, with an attitude of childlikeness, his lifelong theme and concern.

There is throughout his writings a philosophical preoccupation with the conversion of evil into goodness and death into life. Graphically he sketches – in his best work – *Phantastes, At the Back of the North Wind,* The Princess books, "The Golden Key," *The Wise Woman, Sir Gibbie,* and *Lilith* – his own reformed picture of Scottish Calvinism transposed into fairytale language and scenes. This he does by placing the child in the center; predestination, for instance, becomes the prodding voice of North Wind, who explains to Diamond that he is limited only by what he *really* wants to do, which is the best way home. Good and Evil are no longer absolutes in his parables, as they are in most fairytales, but take part in the living process of getting better, of recovering from the illness of self. One mounts repeatedly in his fantasies the narrow stairs of curious submission that leads to the grandmother's garret room of rebirth and instruction.

All of this is to say that MacDonald's strong beliefs and cosmic vision of the role of the child in the universe quite naturally led him to select the fairytale-parable as the ideal form: in it he found poetic liberty of expression, symbolic regularity, and a disregard for age levels which allowed him to retell many of his childhood dreams and discoveries in Huntly, where he had known the art of castle-building as well as harsh discipline. As he grew older, he used the ordinary fairytale to convey, through his own sacramental symbolism in *Lilith,* his visionary romance of growing old, what C.S. Lewis defined as "good Death": the happy ending.

The word "homesickness" can be applied to all of MacDonald's books. His children's classics have in them crystal, descriptive and cosy passages of interlacing filial relationships which are in their beauty and provocative strength unsurpassed by any other author of the period. And with the recent return to the family unit in many modern children's books and revival of interest in the fairytale, it can safely be predicted that MacDonald will go on being rediscovered as the patriarch of the child and of the Victorian household.

—Glenn Edward Sadler

MOLESWORTH, Mary Louisa. British. Born in Rotterdam, Netherlands, 29 May 1839; grew up in Manchester, England. Attended school in Lausanne, Switzerland; attended classes given by William Gaskell. Married Richard Molesworth in 1861 (separated, 1879); seven children. Lived in France and Germany, and in London after 1884. *Died 20 July 1921.*

PUBLICATIONS FOR CHILDREN

Fiction

Tell Me a Story (as Ennis Graham), illustrated by Walter Crane. London and New York, Macmillan, 1875.

Carrots: Just a Little Boy (as Ennis Graham), illustrated by Walter Crane.   London, and New York, Macmillan, 1876.

The Cuckoo Clock (as Ennis Graham), illustrated by Walter Crane.   London, Macmillan, and New York, Caldwell, 1877.

Grandmother Dear, illustrated by Walter Crane.   London and New York, Macmillan, 1878.

The Tapestry Room: A Child's Romance, illustrated by Walter Crane.   London and New York, Macmillan, 1879.

A Christmas Child: A Sketch of a Boy-Life, illustrated by Walter Crane.   London, Macmillan, 1880; New York, Macmillan, 1896.

Hermy: The Story of a Little Girl, illustrated by Mary Ellen Edwards.   London and New York, Routledge, 1880.

The Adventures of Herr Baby, illustrated by Walter Crane.   London, Macmillan, 1881; New York, Macmillan, 1886.

Hoodie, illustrated by Mary Ellen Edwards.   London, Routledge, 1881.

Rosy, illustrated by Walter Crane.   London and New York, Macmillan, 1882.

The Boys and I, illustrated by Mary Ellen Edwards.   London and New York, Routledge, 1882.

Summer Stories for Boys and Girls.   London and New York, Macmillan, 1882.

Two Little Waifs, illustrated by Walter Crane.   London and New York, Macmillan, 1883.

Christmas-Tree Land, illustrated by Walter Crane.   London and New York, Macmillan, 1884.

The Little Old Portrait, illustrated by W. Gunston.   London, S.P.C.K., and New York, Young, 1884; as *Edmee: A Tale of the French Revolution*, London, Macmillan, 1916.

Lettice, illustrated by Frank Dadd.   London, S.P.C.K., and New York, Young, 1884.

Us: An Old-Fashioned Story, illustrated by Walter Crane.   London and New York, Macmillan, 1885.

A Charge Fulfilled, illustrated by R. Caton Woodville.   London, S.P.C.K., and New York, Young, 1886.

Silverthorns, illustrated by J. Noel Paton.   London, Hatchards, 1886; New York, Dutton, n.d.

Four Winds Farm, illustrated by Walter Crane.   London and New York, Macmillan, 1886.

The Palace in the Garden, illustrated by Harriet M. Bennett.   London, Hatchards, and New York, Whittaker, 1887.

Little Miss Peggy: Only a Nursery Story, illustrated by Walter Crane.   London and New York, Macmillan, 1887.

The Abbey by the Sea, illustrated by Frank Dadd.   London, S.P.C.K., 1887.

A Christmas Posy, illustrated by Walter Crane.   London and New York, Macmillan, 1888.

Five Minutes' Stories, illustrated by Gordon Browne and others.   London, S.P.C.K., and New York, Young, 1888.

The Third Miss St. Quentin.   London, Hatchards, and New York, Whittaker, 1888.

Neighbours, illustrated by Mary Ellen Edwards.   London, Hatchards, 1889; New York, Whittaker, 1890.

A House to Let, illustrated by W.J. Morgan.   London, S.P.C.K., 1889.

The Old Pincushion; or, Aunt Clotilda's Guests, illustrated by Mrs. Adrian Hope.   London, Griffith and Farran, 1889; New York, Dutton, 1890.

The Rectory Children, illustrated by Walter Crane.   London and New York, Macmillan, 1889.

Nesta; or, Fragments of a Little Life.   London, Chambers, 1889.

Great Uncle Hoot-Toot, illustrated by Gordon Browne and others.   London, S.P.C.K., 1889.

Twelve Tiny Tales, illustrated by W.J. Morgan. London, S.P.C.K., and New York, Young, 1890.

Family Troubles, illustrated by W.J. Morgan. London, S.P.C.K., and New York, Young, 1890.

The Children of the Castle, illustrated by Walter Crane. London and New York, Macmillan, 1890.

Little Mother Bunch, illustrated by Mary Ellen Edwards. London, Cassell, 1890; New York, Burt, 1903.

The Green Casket and Other Stories, illustrated by Robert Barnes and W.J. Morgan. London, Chambers, 1890.

The Story of a Spring Morning and Other Tales, illustrated by Mary Ellen Edwards. London and New York, Longman, 1890.

The Red Grange, illustrated by Gordon Browne. London, Methuen, and New York, Whittaker, 1891.

The Bewitched Lamp, illustrated by Robert Barnes. London, Chambers, 1891.

The Lucky Ducks and Other Stories, illustrated by W.J. Morgan. London, S.P.C.K., 1891.

Nurse Heatherdale's Story, illustrated by L. Leslie Brooke. London and New York, Macmillan, 1891.

Sweet Content, illustrated by William Rainey. London, Griffith and Farran, and New York, Dutton, 1891.

Imogen; or, Only Eighteen, illustrated by Herbert A. Bone. London, Chambers, and New York, Whittaker, 1892.

An Enchanted Garden: Fairy Stories, illustrated by W.J. Hennessy. London, Unwin, and New York, Cassell, 1892.

The Girls and I, illustrated by L. Leslie Brooke. London and New York, Macmillan, 1892.

Farthings: The Story of a Stray and a Waif, illustrated by G.M. Broadley. London, Gardner Darton, and New York, Young, 1892.

The Man with the Pan-Pipes and Other Stories, illustrated by W.J. Morgan. London, S.P.C.K., and New York, Young, 1892.

Robin Redbreast, illustrated by Robert Barnes. London, Chambers, and New York, Whittaker, 1892.

The Next-Door House, illustrated by W. Hatherell. New York, Cassell, 1892; London, Chambers, 1893.

Studies and Stories, illustrated by Walter Crane. London, A.D. Innes, 1893.

The Thirteen Little Black Pigs and Other Stories, illustrated by W.J. Morgan. London, S.P.C.K., 1893; New York, Burt, 1901.

Mary: A Nursery Story for Very Little Children, illustrated by L. Leslie Brooke. London and New York, Macmillan, 1893.

Blanche, illustrated by Robert Barnes. London, Chambers, 1893; New York, Whittaker, 1894.

Olivia, illustrated by Robert Barnes. London, Chambers, 1894; Philadelphia, Lippincott, 1895.

My New Home, illustrated by L. Leslie Brooke. London, Macmillan, 1894; New York, Macmillan, 1898.

The Carved Lions, illustrated by L. Leslie Brooke. London and New York, Macmillan, 1895.

Opposite Neighbours and Other Stories, illustrated by W.J. Morgan. London, S.P.C.K., and New York, Young, 1895.

Sheila's Mystery, illustrated by L. Leslie Brooke. London and New York, Macmillan, 1895.

White Turrets, illustrated by William Rainey. London, Chambers, and New York, Whittaker, 1895.

Friendly Joey and Other Stories, illustrated by W.J. Morgan. London, S.P.C.K., 1896.

The Oriel Window, illustrated by L. Leslie Brooke.   London and New York, Macmillan, 1896.

Philippa, illustrated by J. Finnemore.   Philadelphia, Lippincott, 1896; London, Chambers, 1897.

Stories for Children in Illustration of the Lord's Prayer, illustrated by Gordon Browne and others.   London, Gardner Darton, 1897.

Meg Langholme; or, The Day after Tomorrow, illustrated by William Rainey.   London, Chambers, and Philadelphia, Lippincott, 1897.

Miss Mouse and Her Boys, illustrated by L. Leslie Brooke.   London and New York, Macmillan, 1897.

Greyling Towers, illustrated by Percy Tarrant.   London, Chambers, 1898.

The Magic Nuts, illustrated by Rosie M.M. Pitman.   London and New York, Macmillan, 1898.

The Grim House, illustrated by Warwick Goble.   London, Nisbet, 1899; New York, Whittaker, 1900.

This and That: A Tale of Two Tinies, illustrated by Hugh Thomson.   London and New York, Macmillan, 1899.

The Children's Hour.   London, Nelson, 1899; New York, Nelson, 1901.

The Three Witches, illustrated by Lewis Baumer.   London, Chambers, and Philadelphia, Lippincott, 1900.

The House That Grew, illustrated by Alice B. Woodward.   London and New York, Macmillan, 1900.

The Wood-Pigeons and Mary, illustrated by H.R. Millar.   London and New York, Macmillan, 1901.

"My Pretty" and Her Little Brother "Too," and Other Stories, illustrated by Lewis Baumer.   London, Chambers, and New York, Whittaker, 1901.

The Blue Baby and Other Stories, illustrated by Maud C. Foster.   London, Unwin, 1901; New York, Dutton, 1904.

Peterkin, illustrated by H.R. Millar.   London and New York, Macmillan, 1902.

The Mystery of the Pinewood, and Hollow Tree House, illustrated by A.A. Dixon.   London, Nister, 1903.

The Ruby Ring, illustrated by Rosie M.M. Pitman.   London and New York, Macmillan, 1904.

The Bolted Door and Other Stories, illustrated by Lewis Baumer.   London, Chambers, 1906.

Jasper, illustrated by Gertrude Demain Hammond.   London and New York, Macmillan, 1906.

The Little Guest, illustrated by Gertrude Demain Hammond.   London and New York, Macmillan, 1907.

Fairies — of Sorts, illustrated by Gertrude Demain Hammond.   London, Macmillan, 1908.

The February Boys, illustrated by Mabel Lucie Atwell.   London, Chambers, and New York, Dutton, 1909.

The Story of a Year, illustrated by Gertrude Demain Hammond.   London, Macmillan, 1910.

Fairies Afield, illustrated by Gertrude Demain Hammond.   London, Macmillan, 1911.

Stories, edited by Sidney Baldwin.   New York, Duffield, 1922.

Fairy Stories, edited by Roger Lancelyn Green.   London, Harvill Press, 1957; New York, Roy, 1958.

Other

Stories of the Saints for Children.   London and New York, Longman, 1892.

PUBLICATIONS FOR ADULTS (as Ennis Graham)

Novels

> *Lover and Husband.*   London, Skeet, 3 vols., 1869.
> *She Was Young and He Was Old* (published anonymously).   London, Tinsley, 3 vols., 1872.
> *Not Without Thorns.*   London, Tinsley, 3 vols., 1873; Boston, Osgood, 1873.
> *Cicely: A Story of Three Years.*   London, Tinsley, 3 vols., 1874.
> *Hathercourt Rectory.*   London, Hurst and Blackett, 3 vols., 1878; as *Hathercourt*, New York, Holt, 1878.
> *Miss Bouverie.*   London, Hurst and Blackett, 3 vols., 1880; New York, Harper, 1880.
> *Marrying and Giving in Marriage.*   London, Longman, and New York, Harper, 1887.
> *Leona.*   London and New York, Cassell, 1892.
> *The Laurel Walk.*   London, Isbister, and Philadelphia, Biddle, 1898.

Short Stories

> *Four Ghost Stories.*   London and New York, Macmillan, 1888.
> *That Girl in Black, and Bronzie.*   London, Chatto and Windus, 1889; New York, Lovell, 1899.
> *Uncanny Tales.*   London, Hutchinson, and New York, Longman, 1896.
> *The Wrong Envelope and Other Stories.*   London and New York, Macmillan, 1906.

Other

> *French Life in Letters.*   London and New York, Macmillan, 1889.

Critical Studies: *Mrs. Ewing, Mrs. Molesworth, and Mrs. Hodgson Burnett* by Marghanita Laski, London, Barker, 1950; *Mrs. Molesworth* by Roger Lancelyn Green, London, Bodley Head, 1961, New York, Walck, 1964.

*   *   *

On re-reading Mrs. Molesworth's stories after a long interval — or perhaps reading some of them for the first time — one is immediately struck by the fact that they are indeed very readable. She was above all else a good teller of tales. Yet when we come to analyse the content of the stories themselves, there is little in the way of dramatic events to account for this. The drama, and thereby the interest of the story, comes from the life of the characters in what is largely an everyday setting. Her stories — the best ones at any rate, for she was uneven in the quality of her writing — pick up the characters at a particular period in their lives, usually between about 5 and 12 years old. But we feel that each one had a life of his own before the story started and will continue to develop after the book has closed, whereas the events in so many children's books appear to exist in their own world, without a past or a future.

Perhaps one of the most noticeable characteristics of Mrs. Molesworth's books is their ordinariness. Her children are all very "genteel," and even if they are poor they tend to have a middle-class background. For the most part the stories are set in the comfortably solid world of nurseries and nannies, of brothers and sisters in plenty, and loving mothers (who may alas often have to go to India, or, as in *Carrots*, to Algeria). The daily routing is firmly sketched and indeed provides a useful social study of the upper-middle-class child-world of the latter 19th century. Even the names given to the children are redolent of class and period: Hermione, Rosalys, Mavis. In the case of *Four Winds Farm*, where she is dealing with a boy from a *farm*, she gives him the improbable name of Gratian, to show his "difference."

Magic does of course come into a number of her stories, especially the more successful ones like *The Cuckoo Clock* and *The Tapestry Room*, but for the most part even here it is everyday life which provides the frame of the story, though some at least of the magic comes from the twilight world between reality and fantasy. It is the insight into the child's mind, with its inability to distinguish between actuality and imagination, which sets Mrs. Molesworth apart from so many of her contemporaries. Behind many of her characters are careful observations of real children, their speech, their behaviour, and, even more important, their minds. There is poor Carrots, who genuinely believes he has found a "yellow sixpenny piece," and in no way connects it with the missing half-sovereign – "sovereigns" is a game about kings and queens! And Hermy, in the book of the same name, has great problems as to what is meant by truth, as far as the adults in her life are concerned. Mrs. Molesworth is aware that such little things assume enormous proportions in the life of the very young. But there is one big difference at that age, in that time for the young is so relative. If you are only 5, last week can be as far away as yesterday, and next year, when you will be 6, is a lifetime away.

In her descriptions of school life, Mrs. Molesworth is fair and understanding. Her school teachers, who cause so much trouble to the young (in *The Carved Lions* and *Hermy*, for example), are given their due, as if *we* should not find them so bad. For here, too, much of the trouble lies once more with the child's limited understanding of the grown-up world, and his own ability to explain a situation in everyday terms. We have all known the child for whom a toy, or even an invisible companion, were as real, if not more so, than the people around him, and the "untruths" arising from this state of affairs cannot be dealt with as with older children. It is to Mrs. Molesworth's credit that in the days before there was so much talk of child psychology, she saw and understood this aspect of child behaviour, and wrote about it as a normal part of growing up, with all its fears and confidences, and in a way that small children would understand and accept. Her world of magic, too, is gentle and charming, of the sort to banish fear, coming in the wind or with dreams. But she can also give her fairy characters a personality of their own: the North and East Winds in *Four Winds Farm*, the Raven in *The Tapestry Room*, and the Cuckoo in *The Cuckoo Clock*, are not always sweet and obliging, but can be cross and need humouring every bit as much as the kindliest adult in the real world.

Perhaps Mrs. Molesworth's real fault lies in the amount she wrote, for some of her later books (and she lived until 1921) were repetitive, thin, and with a tendency to the sentimental, which the best of her books avoid. But her best is very good indeed. The merit of *The Cuckoo Clock*, *The Carved Lions*, *The Tapestry Room*, *Us* and many others is manifest in the fact that they can still be read and enjoyed by young children of today, because they are good straightforward stories still, even if the world of nannies has passed away with the Indian Empire to which parents were so conveniently banished.

—Joyce I. Whalley

PYLE, Howard. American. Born in Wilmington, Delaware, 5 March 1853. Educated at Friends' School and Clark and Taylor's School, Wilmington; Mr. Van der Weilen's school, Philadelphia, 1868–72. Married Anne Poole in 1881. Free-lance illustrator, for *St. Nicholas Magazine*, *Harper's*, and *Harper's Young People*. Taught at Drexel Institute, Philadelphia, 1894–1900, and at his own art school in Wilmington, 1900–10. Muralist. *Died 9 November 1911.*

PUBLICATIONS FOR CHILDREN (illustrated by the author)

Fiction

Pepper and Salt; or, Seasoning for Young Folks. New York, Harper, 1886.

The Wonder Clock; or, Four and Twenty Marvellous Tales, Being One for Each Hour of the Day, Embellished with Verses by Katharine Pyle. New York, Harper, and London, Osgood, 1888.

Otto of the Silver Hand. New York, Scribner, and London, Sampson Low, 1888.

Men of Iron. New York, Harper, and London, Osgood, 1892.

The Story of Jack Ballister's Fortunes .... New York, Century, 1895; London, Osgood 1897.

The Garden Behind the Moon: A Real Story of the Moon Angel. New York, Scribner, and London, Laurence Bullen, 1895.

Twilight Land. New York, Harper, and London, Osgood, 1895.

Stolen Treasure. New York, Harper, 1907.

Other

The Merry Adventures of Robin Hood of Great Renown in Nottinghamshire. New York, Scribner, and London, Sampson Low, 1883; shortened version, as *Some Merry Adventures of Robin Hood of Great Renown in Nottinghamshire,* Scribner, 1902.

The Story of King Arthur and His Knights. New York, Scribner, and London, Newnes, 1903.

The Story of the Champions of the Round Table. New York, Scribner, and London, Newnes, 1905.

The Story of Sir Launcelot and His Companions. New York, Scribner, and London, Chapman and Hall, 1907.

The Story of the Grail and the Passing of Arthur. New York, Scribner, and London, Bickers, 1910.

Book of Pirates: Fiction, Fact and Fancy Concerning the Buccaneers and Marooners of the Spanish Main, edited by Merle Johnson. New York and London, Harper, 1921.

Book of the American Spirit: The Romance of American History, Pictured by Howard Pyle, edited by Merle Johnson and Francis J. Dowd. New York and London, Harper, 1923.

PUBLICATIONS FOR ADULTS

Novels

Within the Capes. New York, Scribner, 1885.

The Rose of Paradise .... New York, Harper, 1888.

A Modern Aladdin; or, The Wonderful Adventures of Oliver Munier: An Extravaganza in Four Acts. New York, Harper, 1892.

The Price of Blood: An Extravaganza of New York Life in 1807. Boston, Richard G. Badger, 1899.

Rejected of Men: A Story of To-Day. New York, Harper, 1903.

The Ruby of Kishmoor. New York, Harper, 1908.

Other

A Catalogue of Drawings Illustrating the Life of General Washington and of Colonial Life .... Philadelphia, Drexel Institute of Art, 1897.

(Paintings). New York, Peacock Press-Bantam, 1976.

Bibliography: *Howard Pyle: A Record of His Illustrations and Writings* by Willard S. Morse and Gertrude Brinckle, Wilmington, Delaware, Wilmington Society of Fine Arts, 1921.

Manuscript and Archive Collections: Delaware Art Center, Wilmington; Free Library of Philadelphia.

Critical Studies: *Howard Pyle: A Chronicle* by Charles D. Abbott, New York and London,
Harper, 1925; *Howard Pyle* by Elizabeth Nesbitt, London, Bodley Head, and New York,
Walck, 1966; *Howard Pyle: Writer, Illustrator, Founder of the Brandywine School* by Henry
C. Pitz, New York, Clarkson N. Potter, 1975.

Illustrator: *Yankee Doodle*, 1881; *The Lady of Shalott* by Alfred Lord Tennyson, 1882; *The
Story of Siegfried*, 1882, and *A Story of the Golden Age*, 1887, by James Baldwin; *Farm
Ballads* by Will Carleton, 1882; *The History of New York* by Washington Irving, 1886; *The
One Hoss Shay and Its Companion Poems*, 1892, *Dorothy Q.....*, 1893, and *The Autocrat of the
Breakfast Table*, 1894, all by Oliver Wendell Holmes; *Stops of Various Quills* by William
Dean Howells, 1895; *In Ole Virginia* by Thomas Nelson Page, 1896; *George Washington* by
Woodrow Wilson, 1896; *The First Christmas Tree* by Henry Van Dyke, 1897; *Evangeline*
by Henry Wadsworth Longfellow, 1897; *Hugh Wynne, Free Quaker* by S. Weir Mitchell,
1897; *The Story of the Revolution* by Henry Cabot Lodge, 1898; *Old Chester Tales* by
Margaret Deland, 1899; *The Man with the Hoe and Other Poems* by Edwin Markham, 1900;
The Bibliomania, or Book-Madness by Thomas Frognall Dibdin, 1903; *The Line of Love*,
1905, *Chivalry*, 1909, and *The Soul of Melicent*, 1913, all by James Branch Cabell; *Saint Joan
of Arc* by Mark Twain, 1919.

*   *   *

Howard Pyle must be considered a giant in American literature for children. An
innovative, vastly productive artist-writer-teacher, he was a modest man totally concerned
with inspiring good artists and creating good books. But the term giant just might have
appealed to him as a description, for his imagination was tuned in to the days of good knights
and evil villains, heroes and dragons, magic stools and clever magicians, beautiful maidens
and wicked queens, good boys, foolish men, and, surely among them, giants. And of course,
King Arthur and Robin Hood.

In his fifty-eight years he accomplished an amazing amount of enduring work. His
importance as an artist as well as writer must be mentioned here for several reasons. First, his
work spanned a period of vital change in children's books. It began in an era when moralistic
stories had themes of illness, suffering, and death, and were usually illustrated by inept
saccharine pictures; standards for writing and illustrating were low. It ended with his work,
both words and pictures, having produced the highest standards for others to follow. The
author-artist Robert Lawson, writing in *Illustrators of Children's Books 1744–1945*, stated,
"It is small wonder that the clean-cut, healthy, joyous work of Howard Pyle came to ...
children ... like a fresh breeze flooding a fetid sickroom." Second, his illustration and stories
intertwined and enhanced each other, growing equally from his concept of the subject
undertaken, even though, to an extent rarely equalled by any other author-artist, each
element is strong enough to stand alone. Third, any piece of artwork takes a great deal of time
to produce. Thus to research, absorb, recreate and retell the Robin Hood ballads and the vast
lore of King Arthur was a gigantic, time-consuming task. He was a truly prodigious worker.

Although he could easily "see things in image-terms or in the continuity of words," as
Henry C. Pitz describes his dual abilities, he was a deliberate craftsman. He actually
experimented with various writing styles to achieve the effect of the archaic speech of Robin
Hood's days and yet have it understandable to children. Reading it aloud today, now that we
are even used to *you* taking the place of *thee-and-thou* in versions of the Bible, it sounds more
unreal than ever to hear, "Now will I go too, for fain would I draw a string for the bright
eyes of my lass, for so goodly a prize as that," or hear Pauline ask poor little Otto about his
mother, "And didst thou never see her?" Such is thoroughness in setting scene, delineating
character, and sweeping all action forward in a dynamic plot – particularly in his own stories
such as *Otto of the Silver Hand*, *Men of Iron* and his pirate tales – that one quickly accepts the
language as another rich element of his writing skill.

Although *Merry Adventures of Robin Hood* was his first book to be published, *Pepper and
Salt* and *The Wonder Clock* contained stories and fables Pyle had written and illustrated for

children's magazines. *Twilight Land* was more influenced by Eastern folk tales. While at first he borrowed and retold old tales in different guises ("The Salt of Life" is the well-known Catskin motif of universal folk-lore), so steeped was he in folk and fairy lore that eventually he could turn his own rich imagination out into these forms to perfection, just as Andersen did. *The Garden Behind the Moon*, a long allegorical fantasy, is less derivative than his short stories and it contains such strong beautiful prose that it makes him a classic writer of fantasy.

With the grim sad story of medieval revenge, *Otto of the Silver Hand*, and that of 15th-century adventure, *Men of Iron*, and in his tales of Robin Hood and King Arthur, Pyle achieved new heights in literature for children: he gave them an immediate sense of their past, complete with authentic convincing details, replete with drama and pageantry, and taut with adventure.

Elizabeth Nesbitt, commenting on Pyle in *A Critical History of Children's Literature*, mentioned that the era in which Pyle developed his work has been called the Golden Age of children's literature and that "It is difficult to do justice to his contribution to the shining quality of that era. The magnitude and diversity of his work elude definition."

—Lee Kingman

REED, Talbot Baines. British. Born in Hackney, London, 3 April 1852. Educated at Priory House School, London; City of London School, 1864–68. Married Elizabeth Greer in 1876; two daughters and one son. Joined his father's London type-founding firm, 1868; managing director after 1881. Regular contributor to *Boy's Own Paper*, London, and *Leeds Mercury*. Co-Founder, and Secretary, 1892–93, Bibliographical Society. Fellow of the Society of Antiquaries, 1893. *Died 28 November 1893.*

PUBLICATIONS FOR CHILDREN

Fiction

> *The Adventures of a Three-Guinea Watch.* London, Religious Tract Society, 1883.
> *"Follow My Leader"; or, The Boys at Templeton,* illustrated by W.S. Stacey. London, Cassell, 1885.
> *The Fifth Form at St. Dominic's.* London, Religious Tract Society, 1887; Chicago, Revell, 1891.
> *The Willoughby Captains,* illustrated by Alfred Pearse. London, Hodder and Stoughton, 1887.
> *Parkhurst Sketches and Other Stories,* edited by G. Andrew Hutchison. London, Religious Tract Society, 1889.
> *My Friend Smith,* illustrated by Gordon Browne. London, Religious Tract Society, 1889.
> *Sir Ludar: A Story of the Days of the Great Queen Bess,* illustrated by Alfred Pearse. London, Sampson Low, 1889.
> *Roger Ingleton, Minor,* illustrated by J. Finnemore. London, Religious Tract Society, 1891.
> *The Cockhouse at Fellsgarth.* London, Religious Tract Society, 1893; as *The House at Fellsgarth,* Chicago, Revell, 1893.
> *Reginald Cruden: A Tale of City Life.* London, Religious Tract Society, 1894.
> *A Dog with a Bad Name.* London, Religious Tract Society, 1894.
> *The Master of the Shell.* London, Religious Tract Society, 1894.
> *Tom, Dick, and Harry.* London, Religious Tract Society, 1894.

Kilgorman: A Story of Ireland in 1798.   London and New York, Nelson, 1894.
A Book of Short Stories.   London, Religious Tract Society, 1897.

PUBLICATIONS FOR ADULTS

Other

A History of the Old English Letter Foundries ....   London, Stock, and New York,
     Armstrong, 1887.
John Baskerville, Printer (lecture).   Privately printed, 1892.

Critical Study: Talbot Baines Reed: Author, Bibliographer, Typefounder by Stanley Morrison,
privately printed, 1960.

*   *   *

It was perhaps appropriate that Talbot Baines Reed's first fictional published words were:
"It was a proud moment in my existence when Wright, captain of our football club, came up
to me in school one Friday and said, 'Adams, your name is down to play in the match against
Craven tomorrow.' " This comprised the opening of the first of his series of sketches of
sporting life at Parkhurst School, titled "My First Football Match" and appeared on the first
page of the first issue of the famous Boy's Own Paper on 18 January 1879. It set the style, tone
and content for his many tales of public school life to come, most of which first ran as
extremely popular serials in the Boy's Own Paper. His earliest and shorter contributions to the
magazine appeared anonymously. Then, in 1880, came his first full-scale serial, The
Adventures of a Three-Guinea Watch, followed by a further ten serials, mainly about public
schools, though some described life in the offices of the City of London. The included some of
the most famous school stories ever written: The Fifth Form at St. Dominic's, The Willoughby
Captains, The Master of the Shell and The Cockhouse at Fellsgarth. Although, ironically,
Reed himself attended a day-school, his fine descriptions of public boarding-school life are
generally agreed to be extremely accurate for their period.
     Although Thomas Hughes' Tom Brown's Schooldays (1857) and Frederic Farrar's Eric; or,
Little by Little (1858) had virtually established the English public school story as a genre, it
was undoubtedly Reed who shaped and developed this popular type of tale as readers later
came to know and love it. Hughes and (especially) Farrar had dominated their stories with the
dark side of Victorian boarding-school life (death, disgrace, bullying, sin and tears), allied
with perhaps over-generous lashings of religion and prayer. Reed's boys tended to be much
more extrovert, healthy, mischievous, and authentic — more "boy-like," in fact. He created
superbly the essentially self-contained world of school, its rules and its traditions. But, if he
was apt to concentrate upon the brighter side of the scholastic life, he by no means ignored
the darker. There were, for instance, the bullies, cheats, and scoundrels. There was a certain
amount of religion — and conversions of would-be or actual sinners. George Hutchinson,
editor of the Boy's Own Paper during Reed's time, once referred to his personal background
of "simple, cheerful Puritanism," and this is the quality that often comes to the foreground in
Reed's writings. And it's none the worse for that. The Boy's Own Paper was, after all,
published by the highly-respectable Religious Tract Society, and everything published in it
was supposed to instil, in as entertaining and painless a way as possible, the right thoughts
into its healthy, manly young Christian readers.
     It was Reed who really created and established many of the situations and character-types
later to be copied by numerous succeeding boys' school story writers. There were the fine,
upstanding heroes, the weak, easily-led boys, the "bounders" who broke out after lights-out
to frequent gambling-dens or (dare it be said?) music-halls, the "swots," the sportsmen, the
bullies, and the jokers. There were the inter-house rivalries, the school magazines, the
sporting contests, the "town-versus-gown" feuds, the different types of masters (both
sympathetic and un-sympathetic) the "fagging" and the dormitory midnight feasts. It was

generally a cosy world, later to become something of a formula and to be written about, in a variety of ways, by such successful school story writers as Harold Avery, R.S. Warren-Bell, Richard Bird, Hylton Cleaver, Gunby Hadath, Edwy Searles Brooks, and (most prolific of them all) Charles Hamilton. In his writing, Reed was an excellent story-teller, wrote good, realistic dialogue, had a fine descriptive flair and, most of all, made his characters come vividly to life.

—Brian Doyle

SEWELL, Anna.   British.   Born in Great Yarmouth, Norfolk, 30 March 1820; daughter of the poet Mary Sewell. Educated privately, and a school in Stoke Newington, London. Semi-invalid from youth. Lived in Brighton, 1836–45, and later in Sussex, Gloucestershire, Bath, and Norwich. Taught at the Working Man's Evening Institute, Wick, Gloucestershire, in the early 1860's. *Died 25 April 1878.*

PUBLICATIONS FOR CHILDREN

Fiction

> *Black Beauty, His Grooms and Companions: The Autobiography of a Horse, Translated from the Original Equine.*   London, Jarrolds, 1877; New York, Angell, 1878.

Critical Study: *The Woman Who Wrote "Black Beauty": A Life of Anna Sewell* by Susan Chitty, London, Hodder and Stoughton, 1971.

*   *   *

Black Beauty is the imaginary autobiography of a horse. We follow his career from its gentle beginning in the care of a farmer, up through society via the squirearchy to the nobility, and thence sadly downwards, finally pulling a cab for a sordid villain called Skinner.

It is an unashamedly didactic book. Anna Sewell wrote that "its special aim" was "to induce kindness, sympathy, and an understanding treatment of horses." This, she believed, would "bring the thoughts of men more in harmony with the purposes of God on this subject." The model owner, Squire Gordon, upbraids a neighbour who is beating a pony with the words "By giving way to such passions you injure your own character as much, nay more, than you injure your horse, and remember, we shall all be judged according to our works, whether they be towards man or towards beast."

The book's moral influence was enormous. It was adopted and distributed by The Royal Society for the Prevention of Cruelty to Animals, and by its American counterpart. Within a short time, the fashionable but cruel habit of pulling the horse's head up high with bearing-reins was abandoned and the treatment of cab horses came under far closer scrutiny. Ignorance about the care and needs of horses is condemned as bitterly as plain brutality.

The didacticism at some points goes further than the care of animals. Like many 18th and 19th century fictitious autobiographies, it surveys critically a variety of social strata and finds as much to abhor in the life of the aristocracy as in the baser world of the East End. One of the best chapters consists of a well-argued debate about the rights of cab drivers to have a day off on Sunday rather than drive the gentry off to church. And the supreme villainy of Skinner is that he not only abuses his own cab horses but that he rents his cabs out to other drivers at appallingly high rates. One of the drivers, known as Seedy Sam, has to pay Skinner eighteen shillings a week for the use of the vehicle and also maintains and feeds the two horses, before he can earn a penny for himself and his hungry family. Small wonder that his horses are broken with exhaustion and he himself suddenly dies of the strain. The phrase "economic exploitation" had not entered Anna Sewell's vocabulary, but that is what she meant.

What makes *Black Beauty* unique among Victorian children's books is the breadth of its appeal after a century. A major national survey of British children's reading preferences published in 1977 records it as the clear number one favourite book for 10 year-olds. The explanation may be two-fold: it is superbly written, and horses are extremely appealing characters.

Anna Sewell's simple narrative style matches the straightforwardness of her moral intentions – as monosyllabic and as undecorated as the English language will allow. Plain but not naive. The technique of allowing the horse to tell its own tale in the first person, though absurd if one pauses to reflect on it, seems the most natural – in fact the only possible – way in which to convey the range of experiences that Black Beauty goes through. The horse describes what happens and how he feels with the articulate understanding of a human being – because it is a human view of his suffering that Anna Sewell is trying to promote. She is not concerned with the inner realities of a horse's mind – its natural instincts and stages of development. She merely explains evident emotional behaviour in response to various forms of human treatment. And a great strength of the book is the precise and detailed technical account of the processes of breaking in, harnessing, maintaining and riding horses, the means by which the horse's nature is changed by human beings for better and for worse.

It is hard to imagine a horsey book of such emotional interest being written in a contemporary setting of Pony Club or racing stable. In Black Beauty's day, horses worked alongside humans to earn their keep and their careers had close affinities with those of working men in terms of exploitation and reward. This close resemblance between the life of man and beast in society may partly account for the intense concern that the reader has for Black Beauty. And we react with deep emotion to the revelation of human callousness and ingratitude. The end of the story is pleasing but improbable: the hero rediscovered by chance and restored to his former country background – a just reward for long suffering service to man.

—Aidan Warlow

STEVENSON, Robert Louis (Robert Lewis Balfour Stevenson). British. Born in Edinburgh, 13 November 1850. Educated at Edinburgh Academy; Edinburgh University, 1866–71; studied law in the office of Skene, Edwards and Gordon, Edinburgh; called to the Scottish Bar, 1875. Married Fanny Vandegrift Osbourne in 1880; two stepchildren, including the writer Lloyd Osbourne. Tubercular: lived in Davos, Switzerland, Hyères, France, Bournemouth, England, and the South Seas, settling in Samoa. *Died 3 December 1894.*

PUBLICATIONS FOR CHILDREN

Fiction

> *Treasure Island.* London, Cassell, 1883; Boston, Roberts, 1884.
> *Kidnapped, Being Memoirs of the Adventures of David Balfour in the Year 1715* .... London, Cassell, and New York, Scribner, 1886.
> *The Black Arrow: A Tale of the Two Roses.* New York, Scribner, and London, Cassell, 1888.
> *Catriona: A Sequel to "Kidnapped"* .... London, Cassell, 1893; as *David Balfour,* New York, Scribner, 1893.

Verse

Penny Whistles. Privately printed, 1883.
A Child's Garden of Verses. London, Longman, and New York, Scribner, 1885.

Other

A Child's Robert Louis Stevenson, edited by Patrick Braybrooke. London, Cecil Palmer, 1929.

PUBLICATIONS FOR ADULTS

Novels

Prince Otto: A Romance. London, Chatto and Windus, 1885; Boston, Roberts, 1886.
Strange Case of Dr. Jekyll and Mr. Hyde. New York, Scribner, and London, Longman, 1886.
The Master of Ballantrae: A Winter's Tale. London, Cassell, and New York, Scribner, 1889.
The Wrong Box, with Lloyd Osbourne. London, Longman, and New York, Scribner, 1889.
The Wrecker, with Lloyd Osbourne. London, Cassell, and New York, Scribner, 1892.
Weir of Hermiston. Chicago, Stone and Kimball, 1896; as *Weir of Hermiston: An Unfinished Romance*, London, Chatto and Windus, 1896.
St. Ives, Being the Adventures of a French Prisoner in England, completed by A.T. Quiller-Couch. New York, Scribner, and London, Heinemann, 1897.

Short Stories

New Arabian Nights. London, Chatto and Windus, 2 vols., 1882; New York, Munro, 1882.
More New Arabian Nights: The Dynamiter, with Fanny Stevenson. London, Longman, and New York, Holt, 1885.
The Merry Men and Other Tales and Fables. London, Chatto and Windus, and New York, Scribner, 1887.
The Misadventures of John Nicholson: A Christmas Story. New York, Munro, 1887.
The Bottle Imp. New York, Munro, 1893 (?)
Island Nights' Entertainments. New York, Scribner, 1893; as *Island Nights' Entertainments, Consisting of The Beach of Falesá, The Bottle Imp, The Isle of Voices*, London, Cassell, 1893.
The Ebb-Tide: A Trio and Quartette, with Lloyd Osbourne. Chicago, Stone and Kimball, and London, Heinemann, 1894.
The Body-Snatcher. New York, Merriam, 1895.
The Amateur Emigrant from the Clyde to Sandy Hook. Chicago, Stone and Kimball, and London, Chatto and Windus, 1895.
The Strange Case of Dr. Jekyll and Mr. Hyde, with other Fables. London, Longman, 1896.
Fables. New York, Scribner, 1896.
The Waif Woman. London, Chatto and Windus, 1916.
When the Devil Was Well. Boston, Bibliophile Society, 1921.

Plays

Deacon Brodie; or, The Double Life: A Melodrama, with W.E. Henley (produced Bradford, 1882; London, 1884; New York, 1887). Privately printed, 1880; in *Three Plays*, 1892.

Admiral Guinea: A Melodrama, with W.E. Henley (produced London, 1897). Privately printed, 1884; in *Three Plays*, 1892.

Beau Austin, with W.E. Henley (produced London, 1890). Privately printed, 1884; in *Three Plays*, 1892.

Macaire: A Melodramatic Farce, with W.E. Henley (produced London, 1900). Privately printed, 1885.

The Hanging Judge, with Fanny Stevenson. Privately printed, 1887.

Three Plays: Deacon Brodie, Beau Austin, Admiral Guinea, with W.E. Henley. London, Nutt, and New York, Scribner, 1892.

The Plays of W.E. Henley and Robert Louis Stevenson (includes *Deacon Brodie, Beau Austin, Admiral Guinea, Macaire*). London, Heinemann, 1896.

Monmouth, edited by Charles Vale. New York, Rudge, 1928.

Verse

Underwoods. London, Chatto and Windus, and New York, Scribner, 1887.

Ticonderoga. Privately printed, 1887.

Ballads. New York, Scribner, and London, Chatto and Windus, 1890.

Songs of Travel and Other Verses. London, Chatto and Windus, 1895.

Poems and Ballads. New York, Scribner, 1896; revised edition, 1913.

Three Short Poems. Privately printed, 1898.

Teuila. Privately printed, 1899.

Poems. London, Longman, 1913.

Poetical Fragments. Privately printed, 1915.

An Ode of Horace, Book 2, Ode 3. Privately printed, 1916.

Poems Hitherto Unpublished, edited by George S. Hellman. Boston, Bibliophile Society, 2 vols., 1916; as *New Poems and Variant Readings*, London, Chatto and Windus, 1918; additional volume, edited by George S. Hellman and William P. Trent, Bibliophile Society, 1921.

Moral Emblems and Other Poems. London, Chatto and Windus, and New York, Scribner, 1921.

Collected Poems, edited by Janet Adam Smith. London, Hart Davis, 1950.

Other

The Pentland Rising: A Page of History, 1666. Privately printed, 1866.

The Charity Bazaar: An Allegorical Dialogue. Privately printed, 1871.

An Appeal to the Clergy .... Edinburgh, Blackwood, 1875.

An Inland Voyage. London, Kegan Paul, 1878; Boston, Roberts, 1883.

Edinburgh: Picturesque Notes. London, Seeley, 1879; New York, Macmillan, 1889.

Travels with a Donkey in the Cevennes. London, Kegan Paul, and Boston, Roberts, 1879.

Virginibus Puerisque and Other Papers. London, Kegan Paul, 1881; New York, Scribner, 1887.

Familiar Studies of Men and Books. London, Chatto and Windus, and New York, Scribner, 1882.

The Silverado Squatters: Sketches from a Californian Mountain. London, Chatto and Windus, 1883; Boston, Roberts, 1884.

Memories and Portraits. London, Chatto and Windus, and New York, Scribner, 1887.

Thomas Stevenson, Civil Engineer. Privately printed, 1887.

Memoir of Fleeming Jenkin. New York, Scribner, 1888; London, Longman, 1912.

Father Damien: An Open Letter to the Reverend Dr. Hyde of Honolulu. Privately printed, 1890.

The South Seas: A Record of Three Cruises. Privately printed, 1890.
Across the Plains, with Other Memories and Essays. London, Chatto and Windus, and New York, Scribner, 1892.
A Footnote to History: Eight Years of Trouble in Samoa. London, Cassell, and New York, Scribner, 1892.
The Works (Edinburgh Edition), edited by Sidney Colvin. London, Chatto and Windus, 28 vols., 1894–98.
The Novels and Tales (Thistle Edition). New York, Scribner, 27 vols., 1895–1912.
Vailima Letters, Being Correspondence Addressed to Sidney Colvin, November 1890-October 1894. Chicago, Stone and Kimball, 2 vols., 1895; London, Methuen, 1895.
In the South Seas .... New York, Scribner, 1896; London, Chatto and Windus, 1900.
Familiar Epistle in Verse and Prose. Privately printed, 1896.
A Mountain Town in France: A Fragment. New York, Lane, 1896.
The Stevenson Reader, edited by Lloyd Osbourne. London, Chatto and Windus, 1898.
The Morality of the Profession of Letters. New York, Brothers of the Book, 1899.
The Letters of Robert Louis Stevenson to His Family and Friends, edited by Sidney Colvin. London, Methuen, and New York, Scribner, 2 vols., 1899; revised edition, 4 vols., 1911.
A Stevenson Medley, edited by Sidney Colvin. London, Chatto and Windus, 1899.
The Best of Stevenson, edited by Alexander Jessup. Boston, Page, 1902.
Some Letters. New York, Ingalls Kimball, 1902.
Essays and Criticism. Boston, Roberts, 1903.
Prayers Written at Vailima. New York, Scribner, and London, Chatto and Windus, 1903.
Essays of Travel. London, Chatto and Windus, 1905.
Essays in the Art of Writing. London, Chatto and Windus, 1905.
Essays, edited by William Lyon Phelps. New York, Scribner, 1906.
The Works (Household Edition). New York, Lamb, 10 vols., 1906.
The Works (Pentland Edition), edited by Edmund Gosse. London, Cassell, 20 vols., 1906–07.
The Works (Autobiographical Edition). New York, Scribner, 31 vols., 1908–12.
Lay Morals and Other Papers. London, Chatto and Windus, 1911.
Selections, edited by Henry Seidel Canby and Frederick Erastus Pierce. New York, Scribner, 1911.
The Works (Swanston Edition). London, Chatto and Windus, 25 vols., 1911–12.
Records of a Family of Engineers. London, Chatto and Windus, 1912.
Memoirs of Himself. Privately printed, 1912.
Some Letters of Robert Louis Stevenson, edited by Lloyd Osbourne. London, Methuen, 1914.
On the Choice of a Profession. London, Chatto and Windus, 1916.
Diogenes in London. San Francisco, John Howell, 1920.
Hitherto Unpublished Writings, edited by Henry H. Harper. Boston, Bibliophile Society, 1921.
Stevenson's Workshop, with Twenty-Nine MS. Facsimiles, edited by William P. Trent. Boston, Bibliophile Society, 1921.
Confessions of a Unionist: An Unpublished "Talk on Things Current," Written in the Year 1888 ...., edited by F.V. Livingston. Privately printed, 1921.
[Works] (Vailima Edition), edited by Lloyd Osbourne and Fanny Stevenson. London, Heinemann, 26 vols., 1922–23.
The Best Thing in Edinburgh (address), edited by Katharine D. Osbourne. San Francisco, John Howell, 1923.
[Works] (Skerryvore Edition). London, Heinemann, 30 vols., 1924–26.
[Works] (Tusitala Edition). London, Heinemann, 35 vols., 1924.
[Works] (South Seas Edition). New York, Scribner, 32 vols., 1925.
The Castaways of Soledad, edited by George S. Hellman. Privately printed, 1928.

The Manuscripts of "Records of a Family of Engineers": The Unfinished Chapters, edited
   by J. Christian Bat. Chicago, Walter M. Hill, 1930.
Novels and Stories. London, Pilot Press, 1945.
Selected Writings, edited by Saxe Commins. New York, Random House, 1947.
The Stevenson Companion, edited by John Hampden. London, Phoenix House, 1950.
Essays, edited by Malcolm Elwin. New York, Coward McCann, 1950.
Tales and Essays, edited by G.B. Stern. London, Falcon Press, 1950.
Silverado Journal, edited by J.E. Jordan. San Francisco, Book Club of California,
   1954.
RLS: Stevenson's Letters to Charles Baxter, edited by De Lancey Ferguson and M.
   Waingrow. New Haven, Connecticut, Yale University Press, 1956.
From Scotland to Silverado, edited by J.D. Hart. Cambridge, Massachusetts, Harvard
   University Press, 1966.

Manuscript Collections: Beinecke Collection, Yale University, New Haven, Connecticut;
Huntington Library, San Marino, California.

Critical Studies: *Voyage to Windward: The Life of Robert Louis Stevenson* by J.C. Furnas,
New York, Sloane, 1951, London, Faber, 1952; *He Wrote Treasure Island: The Story of
Robert Louis Stevenson* by G.B. Stern, London, Heinemann, 1954; *Portrait of a Rebel: The
Life and Work of Robert Louis Stevenson* by Richard Aldington, London, Evans, 1957;
Robert Louis Stevenson by Dennis Butts, London, Bodley Head, and New York, Walck, 1966.

*   *   *

Nearly all Robert Louis Stevenson's mature fiction, with the exception of *Dr. Jekyll*, takes
the form of the historical romance. *Treasure Island, Kidnapped, Catriona, The Master of
Ballantrae, St. Ives*, and *Weir of Hermiston* all fall into this category, with the action mainly
taking place in 18th-century Scotland. The two exceptions are *The Black Arrow*, which is set
in the Middle Ages, and *Treasure Island*, which has an English and exotic background.

The plots are nearly always concerned with long journeys, the search for treasure, or flight
from capture, and they are usually fraught with great hazards — piracy, murder, intrigue —
against which the hero, normally a young person of some resourcefulness, struggles to
survive. But Stevenson does not merely use the ingredients of the historical romance for
dramatic effects; he also tries to integrate them into a design by which they throw light on
various aspects of the human situation as he saw it.

Many of the stories have not a single hero at the centre, but a pair. David and Alan in
Kidnapped, Jim and Long John in *Treasure Island*, Dr. Jekyll and Mr. Hyde, are the best
known examples, and they seem to achieve a kind of complementarity as if each partner
compensates for the defects of the other. Many of the books also deal with conflicts between
clearly defined sides, such as pirates versus honest sailors, English versus Scots, or York
versus Lancaster. But there is usually a good deal of changing sides between these
antagonists. Long John Silver, for example, begins as an apparently honest sea-cook, reveals
himself as leader of the mutiny, then deserts the pirates, and finishes up by even jumping
Captain Smollett's ship. Dick Shelton in *The Black Arrow* switches his allegiance from
Lancaster to York, while Alan Breck actually deserts King George at the Battle of
Prestonpans. James in *The Master of Ballantrae* seems to have the best of both worlds,
fighting for Bonnie Prince Charlie but spying for the other side. Finally, there is a good deal
of intrigue and duplicity in the way Stevenson's characters behave, and physical disguises are
frequently adopted. In *Catriona* the heroine pretends to be David's sister; in *The Black Arrow*
Joanna passes herself off as a boy; and Dr. Jekyll's disguise is even more fundamental.

Stevenson's use of the dual-hero, the changing of sides, and the adoption of disguises is not
only appropriate to the kinds of stories he wrote, and adds to their dramatic effectiveness, but
reveals his passionate concern with the problems of identity and morality. From Stevenson's
biographers we know of the ambiguities of his own life, his troubled relations with his

parents, whom he adored, and with Scotland, which he worshipped from afar. It may be that his literary interests developed there, but, from the evidence of the fiction, it is clear that Stevenson saw man's nature as constantly shifting, and therefore all the more difficult to define and come to terms with. Dr. Jekyll, who can transform himself physically into a murderous villain, and Deacon Brodie, the clergyman who becomes a house-breaker at night-time, are simply extreme examples of such shifts. Long John Silver and Alan Breck are much more equivocal as their personalities and virtues fluctuate.

Long John, for example, is a pirate, thief and murderer in *Treasure Island*, and, as such, quite ruthless in pursuit of the gold. But he is also cheerful, brave, witty, and above all kind to Jim, who has no father. In this way Stevenson is constantly challenging out responses. Who is good or bad? he seems to be saying. In your final judgement, do you find Long John sympathetic or not? Are these sorts of questions even relevant? David Balfour operates as a kind of moral censor of Alan Breck's behaviour in *Kidnapped*, but in the end, though he may be "right" in his quarrel with Alan in "The Flight in the Heather," he comes to see that their love complicates the whole matter of knowing who is right or wrong.

Stevenson's influence on later writers is less specific, more pervasive. The historical romance, first established by Scott at the beginning of the 19th century, and then adapted for children by such authors as Marryat and Henty, went from strength to strength, until it reached its Victorian peak with Stevenson himself. Though the quality of many early 20th-century historical novels deteriorated, honourable exceptions can be found in the work of John Masefield and Geoffrey Trease, and from the 1950's the emergence of such writers as Leon Garfield, Cynthia Harnett and Rosemary Sutcliff has sparked a renaissance of the form.

Though the influence of Stevenson on the specific narrative techniques of the adventure story is doubtful, the influence of his moral values issuing into literary attitudes is everywhere absolutely pervasive, even amongst those authors who would say they had never read him, and this for two reasons. First, he showed how it was possible to write books for children that were both thrilling in the most fundamental sense, and yet at the same time deeply serious. The loss of innocence – for example, by Jim Hawkins – is as prevalent in Stevenson's work as in that of Henry James, and the friendship of the two writers was, of course, very significant. And second, in his treatment of the complexities of human behaviour, in his refusal to compartmentalise characters as either "good" or "bad," his writing revealed a maturity which the best children's writers of today can only hope to emulate but not excel. It is significant that a novelist like Leon Garfield, whose stories of the 18th century differ so much from Stevenson's, should return time and again to the equivocal nature of human relationships, and the difficulties of distinguishing appearance from reality in exciting books such as *Smith* and *Jack Holborn*. Without the achievement of Stevenson so much of today's best writing would never have appeared.

—Dennis Butts

STOCKTON, Frank R. (Francis Richard Stockton). American. Born in Philadelphia, Pennsylvania, 5 April 1834. Educated at Zane Street School, 1840–48, and Central High School, 1848–52, both in Philadelphia. Married Mary Ann Tuttle in 1860. Apprenticed as a wood-engraver, 1852, and worked as an engraver until 1870. Assistant Editor, *Hearth and Home*, 1868–73, and *St. Nicholas* magazine, 1873–78. Regular contributor to *Scribner's Magazine*. Died 20 April 1902.

PUBLICATIONS FOR CHILDREN

Fiction

Ting-a-Ling.   Boston, Hurd and Stoughton, 1870; London, Ward and Downey, 1889.

What Might Have Been Expected. New York, Dodd Mead, 1874; London, Routledge, 1875.

A Jolly Friendship. New York, Scribner, and London, Kegan Paul, 1880.

The Floating Prince and Other Fairy Tales. New York, Scribner, and London, Ward and Downey, 1881.

Ting-a-Ling Tales. New York, Scribner, 1882.

The Story of Viteau. New York, Scribner, and London, Sampson Low, 1884.

The Bee-Man of Orn and Other Fanciful Tales. New York, Scribner, 1887; London, Sampson Low, 1888.

The Queen's Museum. New York, Scribner, 1887.

The Clocks of Rondaine and Other Stories. New York, Scribner, and London, Sampson Low, 1892.

Fanciful Tales, edited by Julia E. Langworthy. New York, Scribner, 1894.

Captain Chap; or, The Rolling Stones. Philadelphia, Lippincott, and London, Nimmo, 1896; as *The Young Master of Hyson Hall,* Lippincott, and London, Chatto and Windus, 1899.

Kate Bonnet. New York, Appleton, and London, Cassell, 1902.

Stories of the Spanish Main. New York, Macmillan, 1913.

The Poor Count's Christmas. New York, Stokes, 1927.

Other

Roundabout Rambles in Lands of Fact and Fancy. New York, Scribner, 1872.

Tales Out of School. New York, Scribner, 1875.

Personally Conducted. New York, Scribner, and London, Sampson Low, 1889.

New Jersey, from the Discovery of the Scheyichbi to Recent Times. New York, Appleton, 1896; as *Stories of New Jersey,* New York, American Book Company, 1896.

The Buccaneers and Pirates of Our Coasts. New York, Macmillan, 1898.

PUBLICATIONS FOR ADULTS

Novels

The Late Mrs. Null. New York, Scribner, and London, Sampson Low, 1886.

The Hundredth Man. New York, Century, and London, Sampson Low, 1887.

The Great War Syndicate. New York, Collier, and London, Longman, 1889.

The Stories of the Three Burglars. New York, Dodd Mead, and London, Sampson Low, 1890.

The Merry Chanter. New York, Century, and London, Sampson Low, 1890.

Ardis Claverden. New York, Dodd Mead, and London, Sampson Low, 1890.

The House of Martha. Boston, Houghton Mifflin, and London, Osgood, 1891.

The Squirrel Inn. New York, Century, and London, Sampson Low, 1891.

Pomona's Travels. New York, Scribner, and London, Cassell, 1894.

The Adventures of Captain Horn. New York, Scribner, and London, Cassell, 1895.

Mrs. Cliff's Yacht. New York, Scribner, and London, Cassell, 1896.

The Girl at Cobhurst. New York, Scribner, and London, Cassell, 1898.

The Novels and Stories. New York, Scribner, 23 vols., 1899–1904.

A Bicycle in Cathay. New York, Harper, 1900.

The Captain's Toll Gate, edited by Marian E. Stockton. New York, Appleton, and London, Cassell, 1903.

Short Stories

Rudder Grange. New York, Scribner, 1879; Edinburgh, Douglas, 1883.

The Lady or the Tiger? and Other Stories. New York, Scribner, and Edinburgh, Douglas, 1884.

The Transferred Ghost. New York, Scribner, 1884.

The Casting Away of Mrs. Lecks and Mrs. Aleshine. New York, Century, and London, Sampson Low, 1886.

A Christmas Wreck and Other Stories. New York, Scribner, 1886; as *A Borrowed Month and Other Stories*, Edinburgh, Douglas, 1887.

The Dusantes. New York, Century, and London, Sampson Low, 1888.

Amos Kilbright, His Adscititious Experiences, with Other Stories. New York, Scribner, and London, Unwin, 1888.

The Rudder Grangers Abroad. New York, Scribner, and London, Sampson Low, 1891.

The Watchmaker's Wife and Other Stories. New York, Scribner, 1893; as *The Shadrach and Other Stories*, London, W.H. Allen, 1893.

A Chosen Few. New York, Scribner, 1895.

A Story-Teller's Pack. New York, Scribner, and London, Cassell, 1897.

The Great Stone of Sardis. New York and London, Harper, 1898.

The Associate Hermits. New York and London, Harper, 1898.

The Vizier of the Two-Horned Alexander. New York, Century, and London, Cassell, 1899.

Afield and Afloat. New York, Scribner, 1900; London, Cassell, 1901.

John Gayther's Garden. New York, Scribner, 1902; London, Cassell, 1903.

The Magic Egg and Other Stories. New York, Scribner, 1907.

Other

The Science Fiction of Frank R. Stockton, edited by Richard Gid Powers. Boston, Gregg Press, 1976.

Critical Study: *Frank R. Stockton* by Martin I.J. Griffin, Philadelphia, University of Pennsylvania Press, 1939 (includes bibliography).

*   *   *

One of the most prolific contributors to children's literature in the last third of the 19th century, Frank R. Stockton is perhaps best remembered for such modern fairy tales as "Ting-a-Ling," "The Griffin and the Minor Canon," "Old Pipes and the Dryad," and "The Queen's Museum." But taken as a whole, his work is richly varied. During his long association with the quality children's periodical *St. Nicholas*, first as assistant editor and later as a regular contributor, he wrote such realistic tales of adventure as *What Might Have Been Expected*, in which a brother and sister manage to provide economic security for their aged and feeble aunt. *Personally Conducted* is a collection of travel sketches originally written for *St. Nicholas*. Stockton also produced two juvenile histories: *New Jersey, from the Discovery of the Scheyichbi to Recent Times*, an anecdotal account of some dramatic occasions in the state's history, and *Buccaneers and Pirates of Our Coasts*. *Tales Out of School*, like its predecessor *Roundabout Rambles*, consists of informative stories, mostly dealing with natural history. In *The Story of Viteau*, Stockton attempted a tale of medieval life that reveals his general inability to realize in his fiction a vivid sense of place. The same difficulty can be seen in *What Might Have Been Expected*, set in the American South. Unlike many Northerners, Stockton was familiar with life in the South (his wife was from South Carolina) and his Negro characters have a substantiality not often found in children's literature of the period; but he was less successful in rendering the South as a locale. His principal interest throughout his career as a writer was in delineating character and situation. As assistant editor of *St. Nicholas*, Stockton adopted two pseudonyms, Paul Fort and John Lewees, under which he wrote numerous informative articles and such slight moralistic sketches as "Tommy Hooper's Choice," which describes the mildly humorous difficulties encountered by the youngTommy when he tries to decide how to spend 25 cents – a magnificent sum to a child in the 1870's.

Stockton's best work for children, and the most interesting, consists of his fairy tales, or "fanciful tales" as he liked to call them, beginning with the adventures of Ting-a-Ling, a diminutive elf, who first appeared in *The Riverside Magazine* in 1867. Even as a student, Stockton had wanted to write fairy tales of a particular sort. Of his approach, he later commented: "I wanted the fanciful creatures who inhabited the world of fairy-land to act, as far as possible for them to do so, as if they were inhabitants of the real world. I did not dispense with monsters and enchanters, or talking beasts and birds, but I obliged these creatures to infuse into their extraordinary actions a certain leaven of common sense." Stockton's efforts to infuse "realism" into the traditional elements of the fairy tale had both a formal and a psychological dimension. He made no attempt to render the world of faery through archaic language, for example, but told his tales simply, directly, and matter-of-factly, without archness. He was neither patronizing nor condescending to his audience, and his tales are remarkably free of the overt moralizing that often crept into the period's literature for children. Throughout the tales runs a strongly individualistic psychology – a contempt for dependence, authoritarianism, and timid conformity; a celebration of independence, sturdy self-reliance, and personal courage – that fits well with the ethic of individualism prominent in 19th-century American thought and evident in much post-Civil War literature for children. In his "fanciful tales," Stockton expressed a deft, sure touch, a gentle humor, a sweetness of temper that he rarely achieved in his other children's fiction.

The publication in the 1880's of "The Bee-Man of Orn," "The Griffin and the Minor Canon," and similar tales, as well as a series of yearly Christmas stories for *St. Nicholas*, marked the high point of Stockton's juvenile writing. By 1885, he was writing increasingly for an adult audience, who had acclaimed his short story "The Lady or the Tiger?" and in that year he undertook the writing of his first novel. Stockton produced little of note for children after the appearance in 1887 of "The Crooks of Rondaine" in *St. Nicholas*.

—R. Gordon Kelly

STRETTON, Hesba. Pseudonym for Sarah Smith. British. Born in Wellington, Shropshire, 27 July 1832. Educated at Old Hall Girls Day School, Wellington. Lived in Manchester, 1863–70, and in London after 1870. Co-founder of London Society for the Prevention of Cruelty to Children. *Died 8 October 1911.*

PUBLICATIONS FOR CHILDREN

Fiction

> *Fern's Hollow.* London, Religious Tract Society, 1864; Philadelphia, Presbyterian Board of Publication, n.d.
> *The Children of Cloverley.* London, Religious Tract Society, 1865; Boston, Hoyt, 1872.
> *Enoch Roden's Training.* London, Religious Tract Society, 1866.
> *The Fishers of Derby Haven.* London, Religious Tract Society, 1866; as *Peter Killip's King; or, The Fishers of Derby Haven,* Boston, Hoyt, 1873(?).
> *Pilgrim Street: A Story of Manchester Life.* London, Religious Tract Society, 1867; Boston, Hoyt, 1875.
> *Jessica's First Prayer.* London, Religious Tract Society, 1867; New York, American Tract Society, 1868.
> *Little Meg's Children.* London, Religious Tract Society, 1868; Boston, Hoyt, 1869.

Alone in London.   London, Religious Tract Society, and New York, American Tract Society, 1869.

Max Krömer: A Story of the Siege of Strasbourg.   London, Religious Tract Society, 1871; New York, Dodd Mead, 1873.

Bede's Charity.   London, Religious Tract Society, 1872; New York, Dodd Mead, 1874.

The King's Servants.   London, Religious Tract Society, and New York, Dodd Mead, 1873.

Lost Gip.   London, King, and New York, Dodd Mead, 1873.

Cassy.   London, Religious Tract Society, and New York, Dodd Mead, 1874.

No Work No Bread.   London, Partridge, 1875.

Two Christmas Stories.   London, King, 1875.

Brought Home.   Glasgow, Scottish Temperance League, and New York, Dodd Mead, 1875.

Friends till Death and Other Stories.   London, King, 1875.

The Crew of the "Dolphin."   London, King, and New York, Dodd Mead, 1876.

A Night and a Day.   London, King, and New York, American Tract Society, 1876.

Michael Lorio's Cross and Other Stories.   London, King, 1876.

Old Transome.   London, King, 1876.

The Storm of Life.   London, King, and New York, American Tract Society, 1876.

The World of a Baby, and How Apple-Tree Court Was Won.   London, King, 1876.

A Man of His Word.   London, Kegan Paul, and New York, American Tract Society, 1878.

Mrs. Burton's Best Bedroom and Other Stories.   London, Religious Tract Society, 1878.

A Thorny Path.   London, Religious Tract Society, and New York, American Tract Society, 1879.

In Prison and Out, illustrated by R. Barnes.   London, Isbister, and New York, Dodd Mead, 1879.

Cobwebs and Cables, illustrated by Gordon Browne.   London, Religious Tract Society, and New York, Dodd Mead, 1881.

No Place Like Home.   London, Religious Tract Society, 1881.

Under the Old Roof.   London, Religious Tract Society, 1882.

The Lord's Purse-Bearers.   London, Nisbet, and Boston, Lothrop, 1882.

Carola.   London, Religious Tract Society, and New York, Dodd Mead, 1884.

Her Only Son.   Glasgow, Scottish Temperance League, and New York, Dodd Mead, 1887.

Left Alone.   London, Religious Tract Society, 1888.

Only a Dog.   London, Religious Tract Society, 1888.

A Miserable Christmas and a Happy New Year.   London, Religious Tract Society, 1888.

Sam Franklin's Savings Bank.   London, Religious Tract Society, 1888.

The Christmas Child.   London, Religious Tract Society, 1888.

An Acrobat's Girlhood.   London, S.P.C.K., 1889.

Half Brothers.   London, Religious Tract Society, and New York, Cassell, 1892.

Jessica's Mother.   London, Religious Tract Society, 1893; Philadelphia, Altemus, 1896.

The Highway of Sorrow at the Close of the Nineteenth Century, with Stepniak.   London, Cassell, and New York, Dodd Mead, 1894.

Two Secrets, and A Man of His Word.   London, Religious Tract Society, 1897.

In the Hollow of His Hand.   London, Religious Tract Society, 1897.

The Soul of Honour.   London, Isbister, 1898.

Other

The Sweet Story of Old ....   London, Religious Tract Society, 1860; New York, Whittaker, 1886.

The Wonderful Life.   London, Religious Tract Society, 1875; New York, American Tract Society, 1876; as *The Life of Christ,* Chicago, Monarch Book Company, 1895.

The Parables of Our Lord.   London, Religious Tract Society, 1903.

Editor, with H.L. Synnot, *Good Words from the Apocrypha.* London, Skeffington, 1903.

PUBLICATIONS FOR ADULTS

Novels

The Clives of Burcot. London, Tinsley, 3 vols., 1866; New York, Routledge, 1867.
Paul's Courtship. London, Wood, 3 vols., 1867.
David Lloyd's Last Will. London, Religious Tract Society, 2 vols., 1869; New York, Dodd Mead, 1873.
The Doctor's Dilemma. London, King, 3 vols., 1872; New York, Appleton, n.d.
Hester Morley's Promise. London, King, 3 vols., 1873; New York, Dodd Mead, 1873.
Through a Needle's Eye. London, Kegan Paul, 2 vols., 1878; New York, Dodd Mead, 1878.

Other

Editor, *Thoughts on Old Age: Good Words from Many Minds.* London, Religious Tract Society, 1906.

*   *   *

Jessica's First Prayer is one of those books known by its title to thousands who have never seen a copy. This simply told story of a destitute child, daughter of a gin-sodden actress, who hears the Christmas message and by her simple faith brings a new light into the lives of her elders was to initiate a new genre of evangelical writing, the street arab story, and to remain perhaps the best of them. It is not, however, the very first example. Mary Howitt, in *The Story of Little Cristal* (1863), probably inspired by Hans Andersen's *The Little Match Girl*, had described how a street waif's last hours had been comforted by the memory of a stained glass window depicting Christ blessing the children.

Jessica's First Prayer, originally published in *Sunday at Home* in 1866, was the first of Hesba Stretton's works to attract attention, and its success was phenomenal, not only in England but all over the world. Written no doubt as "family" reading rather than directly for children, it and its legion of imitations soon became adopted as standard Sunday reading for the young, replacing the Calvinistic tracts of Mrs. Sherwood and Mrs. Cameron that the early Victorians had been reared on, and the compilations of holy deaths of young people that had gone before these. The idea of the child evangelist unconsciously melting the cold and stubborn heart of an adult was to have a compelling effect on young readers, and for once children of their own age were the centre of the amazed attention of their elders. The result was a deluge of mawkish novelettes which did not subside until well on in the next century. But *Jessica's First Prayer* cannot be blamed for this. It is finely observed, economically told, and the child Jessica's awakening faith – very difficult to convey, as Miss Stretton's imitators were to find – is moving and convincing.

Miss Stretton followed it up with some 50 stories sometimes on the theme of the suffering poor, sometimes on the evil brought about by love of money. Unlike Charlotte Yonge and others in the squarson tradition, who wrote with rural church schools in mind, she could not agree that the existing social order was right. She had first-hand knowledge of slum conditions in London and Manchester; she knew all about grasping landlords, the heavy hand of officialdom, how unjust justice could be. In *In Prison and Out* she spoke with warm indignation of the deplorable difference in society's attitude towards a slum boy who had knocked down a man for insulting his mother, and a public schoolboy such as Tom Brown who did the same sort of thing. One would be sent to prison, the other commended. She was frequently to take the side of the employee against the employer, as in *Fern's Hollow*, and always to attack the folly of laying up treasures on earth.

Her accounts of the poor and destitute were always moving: the bare-footed crossing sweepers shivering in their rags, the feverish child grasping for fresh air in the mid-summer furnace of a stifling London courtyard, the street arab's search for a lost baby sister whom nobody cared about but himself, the shame and degradation of having at last to take refuge in the "House," the terror of being buried as a pauper. But they were to be repeated so often that they lost their first impact: "it is possible to have too many of them," as Charlotte Yonge wrote. It was in any case a time when journalists and philanthropists were working hard to open the public's eyes to the atrocious conditions in which the poor lived, and there was much literature on this theme.

Nevertheless, at her best, in books such as *Alone in London, Little Meg's Children, Lost Gip, Pilgrim Street* (all written in the earlier part of her career), she rose far above the level of the ordinary Sunday School reward book. Her successors could harrow the reader with their accounts of the mirk and misery and vice of the slums, but Hesba Stretton could also enter into the small pleasures of the poor: a feast of bloaters, a mug of hot coffee, the sight of a garden, a baby to love.

—Gillian Avery

TWAIN, Mark. Pseudonym for Samuel Langhorne Clemens. American. Born in Florida, Missouri, 30 November 1835. Grew up in Hannibal, Missouri. Married Olivia Langdon in 1870 (died, 1904); one son, three daughters. Printer's apprentice from age 12; helped brother with Hannibal newspapers, 1850–52; worked in St. Louis, New York, Philadelphia, Keokuk, Iowa, and Cincinnati, 1853–57. River pilot's apprentice, 1857, pilot license granted, 1859. Miner in Nevada, 1861; staff member, Virginia City *Territorial Enterprise*, Nevada, 1862–64. Lecturer from 1866. Editor, Buffalo *Express*, 1868–71. Associated with the Charles L. Webster Publishing Company from 1884, bankrupt, 1894 (last debts paid, 1898). M.A.: Yale University, New Haven, Connecticut, 1888; Litt.D.: Yale University, 1901; Oxford University, 1907; LL.D.: University of Missouri, Columbia, 1902. *Died 21 April 1910.*

PUBLICATIONS FOR CHILDREN

Fiction

> *The Adventures of Tom Sawyer*, illustrated by T.W. Williams. London, Chatto and Windus, and Hartford, Connecticut, American Publishing Company, 1876.
> *The Prince and the Pauper.* London, Chatto and Windus, and Boston, Osgood, 1881.
> *The Adventures of Huckleberry Finn (Tom Sawyer's Companion).* London, Chatto and Windus, 1884; New York, Webster, 1885.
> *Tom Sawyer Abroad, by Huck Finn, edited by Mark Twain.* New York, Webster, and London, Chatto and Windus, 1894.
> *Tom Sawyer Abroad, Tom Sawyer, Detective, and Other Stories.* New York, Harper, 1896; as *Tom Sawyer, Detective, as Told by Huck Finn, and Other Tales*, London, Chatto and Windus, 1897.
> *A Boy's Adventure.* Privately printed, 1928.
> *Mark Twain's Hannibal, Huck, and Tom*, edited by Walter Blair. Berkeley, University of California Press, 1969.

Other

Translator, *Slovenly Peter (Der Struwwelpeter)*. New York, Limited Editions Club, 1935.

PUBLICATIONS FOR ADULTS

Novels

The Innocents Abroad; or, The New Pilgrims' Progress .... Hartford, Connecticut, American Publishing Company, 1869; London, Routledge, 2 vols., 1872.
The Innocents at Home. London, Routledge, 1872.
The Gilded Age: A Tale of Today, with Charles Dudley Warner. Hartford, Connecticut, American Publishing Company, 1873; London, Routledge, 3 vols., 1874.
A Tramp Abroad. Hartford, Connecticut, American Publishing Company, and London, Chatto and Windus, 1880.
A Connecticut Yankee in King Arthur's Court. New York, Webster, and London, Chatto and Windus, 1889.
The American Claimant. New York, Webster, and London, Chatto and Windus, 1892.
Pudd'nhead Wilson: A Tale. London, Chatto and Windus, 1894; as *The Tragedy of Pudd'nhead Wilson*, Hartford, Connecticut, American Publishing Company, 1894.
Personal Recollections of Joan of Arc .... New York, Harper, and London, Chatto and Windus, 1896.
A Double Barrelled Detective Story. New York, Harper, and London, Chatto and Windus, 1902.
Extracts from Adam's Diary. New York and London, Harper, 1904.
Eve's Diary. New York and London, Harper, 1906.
A Horse's Tale. New York and London, Harper, 1907.
Simon Wheeler, Detective, edited by Franklin R. Rogers. New York, New York, Public Library, 1963.
The Complete Novels, edited by Charles Neider. New York, Doubleday, 2 vols., 1964.
The Adventures of Colonel Sellers, Being Mark Twain's Share of "The Gilded Age," edited by Charles Neider. New York, Doubleday, 1965.

Short Stories

The Celebrated Jumping Frog of Calaveras County and Other Sketches, edited by John Paul. New York, Webb, 1867.
A True Story and the Recent Carnival of Crime. Boston, Osgood, 1877.
Date 1601: Conversations as It Was by the Social Fireside in the Time of the Tudors. Privately printed, 1880; as *1601* ..., edited by Franklin J. Meine, Chicago, privately printed, 1939.
The Stolen White Elephant Etc. Boston, Osgood, 1882.
Merry Tales. New York, Webster, 1892.
The £1,000,000 Bank-Note and Other New Stories. New York, Webster, and London, Chatto and Windus, 1893.
The Man That Corrupted Hadleyburg and Other Stories and Essays. New York, Harper, and London, Chatto and Windus, 1900.
A Dog's Tale. London, National Anti-Vivisection Society, and New York, Harper, 1904.
The $30,000 Bequest and Other Stories. New York, Harper, 1906; London, Harper, 1907.

Extract from Captain Stormfield's Visit to Heaven. New York and London, Harper, 1909; revised edition, as *Report from Paradise*, edited by Dixon Wecter, New York, Harper, 1952.

The Mysterious Stranger: A Romance. New York, Harper, 1916; London, Harper, 1917.

The Curious Republic of Gondour and Other Whimsical Sketches. New York, Boni and Liveright, 1919.

The Mysterious Stranger and Other Stories. New York and London, Harper, 1922.

The Adventures of Thomas Jefferson Snodgrass, edited by Charles Honce. Chicago, Covici, 1928.

Jim Smiley and His Jumping Frog, edited by Albert B. Paine. Chicago, Pocahontas Press, 1940.

A Murder, A Mystery, and a Marriage. Privately printed, 1945.

The Complete Short Stories, edited by Charles Neider. New York, Hanover House, 1957.

The Complete Humorous Sketches and Tales, edited by Charles Neider. New York, Doubleday, 1961.

Mark Twain's Satires and Burlesques, edited by Franklin R. Rogers. Berkeley, University of California Press, 1967.

Mark Twain's Mysterious Stranger Manuscripts, edited by William M. Gibson. Berkeley, University of California Press, 1969.

Plays

Ah Sin, with Bret Harte, edited by Frederick Anderson (produced Washington, D.C., 1877). San Francisco, Book Club of California, 1961.

The Quaker City Holy Land Excursion: An Unfinished Play. Privately printed, 1927.

Verse

On the Poetry of Mark Twain, with Selections from His Verse, edited by Arthur L. Scott. Urbana, University of Illinois Press, 1966.

Other

Mark Twain's (Burlesque) Autobiography and First Romance. New York, Sheldon, 1871.

Memoranda: From the Galaxy. Toronto, Canadian News and Publishing Company, 1871.

Roughing It. London, Routledge, and Hartford, Connecticut, American Publishing Company, 1872.

A Curious Dream and Other Sketches. London, Routledge, 1872.

Screamers: A Gathering of Scraps of Humour, Delicious Bits, and Short Stories. London, Hotten, 1872.

Sketches. New York, American News Company, 1874.

Sketches, New and Old. Hartford, Connecticut, American Publishing Company, 1875.

Old Times on the Mississippi. Toronto, Belford, 1876.

Punch, Brothers, Punch! and Other Sketches. New York, Slote Woodman, 1878.

An Idle Excursion. Toronto, Belford, 1878.

A Curious Experience. Toronto, Gibson, 1881.

Life on the Mississippi. London, Chatto and Windus, and Boston, Osgood, 1883.

Facts for Mark Twain's Memory Builder. New York, Webster, 1891.

How to Tell a Story and Other Essays. New York, Harper, 1897; revised edition, 1900.

Following the Equator: A Journey Around the World. Hartford, Connecticut, American Publishing Company, 1897; as *More Tramps Abroad,* London, Chatto and Windus, 1897.

The Writings of Mark Twain. Hartford, Connecticut, American Publishing Company, and London, Chatto and Windus, 25 vols., 1899–1907.

The Pains of Lowly Life. London, London Anti-Vivisection Society, 1900.

English as She Is Taught. Boston, Mutual, 1900; revised edition, New York, Century, 1901.

To the Person Sitting in Darkness. New York, Anti-Imperialist League, 1901.

Edmund Burke on Croker, and Tammany (lecture). New York, Economist Press, 1901.

My Début as a Literary Person, with Other Essays and Stories. Hartford, Connecticut, American Publishing Company, 1903.

Mark Twain on Vivisection. New York, New York Anti-Vivisection Society, 1905(?).

King Leopold's Soliloquy: A Defense of His Congo Rule. Boston, Warren, 1905; revised edition, 1906; London, Unwin, 1907.

Editorial Wild Oats. New York, Harper, 1905.

What Is Man? (published anonymously). New York, DeVinne Press, 1906; as Mark Twain, London, Watts, 1910.

Mark Twain on Spelling (lecture). New York, Simplified Spelling Board, 1906.

The Writings of Mark Twain (Hillcrest Edition). New York and London, Harper, 25 vols., 1906–07.

Christian Science, with Notes Containing Corrections to Date. New York and London, Harper, 1907.

Is Shakespeare Dead? From My Autobiography. New York and London, Harper, 1909.

Mark Twain's Speeches, edited by F.A. Nast. New York and London, Harper, 1910; revised edition, 1923.

Queen Victoria's Jubilee. Privately printed, 1910.

Letter to the California Pioneers. Oakland, California, Dewitt and Snelling, 1911.

What Is Man? and Other Essays. New York, Harper, 1917; London, Chatto and Windus, 1919.

Mark Twain's Letters, Arranged with Comment, edited by Albert B. Paine. New York, Harper, 2 vols., 1917; shortened version, as *Letters,* London, Chatto and Windus, 1920.

Moments with Mark Twain, edited by Albert B. Paine. New York, Harper, 1920.

The Writings of Mark Twain (Definitive Edition), edited by Albert B. Paine. New York, Gabriel Wells, 37 vols., 1922–25.

Europe and Elsewhere. New York and London, Harper, 1923.

Mark Twain's Autobiography, edited by Albert B. Paine. New York and London, Harper, 2 vols., 1924.

Sketches of the Sixties by Bret Harte and Mark Twain ... from "The Californian," 1864–67. San Francisco, John Howell, 1926.

The Suppressed Chapter of "Following the Equator." Privately printed, 1928.

A Letter from Mark Twain to His Publisher, Chatto and Windus .... San Francisco, Penguin Press, 1929.

Mark Twain the Letter Writer, edited by Cyril Clemens. Boston, Meador, 1932.

Mark Twain's Works. New York, Harper, 23 vols., 1933.

The Family Mark Twain. New York, Harper, 1935.

The Mark Twain Omnibus, edited by Max J. Herzberg. New York, Harper, 1935.

Representative Selections, edited by Fred L. Pattee. New York, American Book Company, 1935.

Mark Twain's Notebook, edited by Albert B. Paine. New York, Harper, 1935.

Letters from the Sandwich Islands, Written for the "Sacramento Union," edited by G. Ezra Dane. San Francisco, Grabhorn Press, 1937; London, Oxford University Press, 1938.

The Washoe Giant in San Francisco, Being Heretofore Uncollected Sketches ..., edited by Franklin Walker. San Francisco, George Fields, 1938.

Mark Twain's Western Years, Together with Hitherto Unreprinted Clemens Western Items, by Ivan Benson. Stanford, Stanford University, 1938.

Letters from Honolulu Written for the "Sacramento Union," edited by Thomas Nickerson. Honolulu, Thomas Nickerson, 1939.

Mark Twain in Eruption: Hitherto Unpublished Pages about Men and Events, edited by Bernard De Voto. New York, Harper, 1940.

Travels with Mr. Brown, Being Heretofore Uncollected Sketches Written for the San Francisco "Alta California" in 1866 and 1867, edited by Franklin Walker and G. Ezra Dane. New York, Knopf, 1940.

Republican Letters, edited by Cyril Clemens. Webster Groves, Missouri, International Mark Twain Society, 1941.

Letters to Will Brown ..., edited by Theodore Hornberger. Austin, University of Texas, 1941.

Letters in the "Muscatine Journal," edited by Edgar M. Branch. Chicago, Mark Twain Association of America, 1942.

Washington in 1868, edited by Cyril Clemens. Webster Groves, Missouri, International Mark Twain Society, and London, Laurie, 1943.

Mark Twain, Business Man, edited by Samuel Charles Webster. Boston, Little Brown, 1946.

The Letters of Quintus Curtius Snodgrass, edited by Ernest E. Leisy. Dallas, Southern Methodist University Press, 1946.

The Portable Mark Twain, edited by Bernard De Voto. New York, Viking Press, 1946.

Mark Twain in Three Moods: Three New Items of Twainiana, edited by Dixon Wecter. San Marino, California, Friends of the Huntington Library, 1948.

The Love Letters of Mark Twain, edited by Dixon Wecter. New York, Harper, 1949.

Mark Twain to Mrs. Fairbanks, edited by Dixon Wecter. San Marino, California, Huntington Library, 1949.

Mark Twain to Uncle Remus, 1881–1885, edited by Thomas H. English. Atlanta, Emory University Library, 1953.

Twins of Genius (letters to George Washington Cable), edited by Guy A. Cardwell. East Lansing, Michigan State College Press, 1953.

Mark Twain of the "Enterprise" ..., edited by Henry Nash Smith and Frederick Anderson. Berkeley, University of California Press, 1957.

Traveling with Innocents Abroad: Mark Twain's Original Reports from Europe and the Holy Land, edited by Daniel Morley McKeithan. Norman, University of Oklahoma Press, 1958.

The Autobiography of Mark Twain, edited by Charles Neider. New York, Doubleday, 1959.

The Art, Humor, and Humanity of Mark Twain, edited by Minnie M. Brashear and Robert M. Rodney. Norman, University of Oklahoma Press, 1959.

Mark Twain and the Government, edited by Svend Petersen. Caldwell, Idaho, Caxton Printers, 1960.

The Correspondence of Samuel L. Clemens and William Dean Howells, 1872–1910, edited by Henry Nash Smith and William M. Gibson. Cambridge, Massachusetts, Harvard University Press, 2 vols., 1960; shortened version, as *Selected Mark Twain-Howells Letters*, 1967.

Your Personal Mark Twain .... New York, International Publishers, 1960.

Life as I Find It: Essays, Sketches, Tales, and Other Material, edited by Charles Neider. New York, Doubleday, 1961.

The Travels of Mark Twain, edited by Charles Neider. New York, Doubleday, 1961.

Contributions to "The Galaxy," 1868–1871, edited by Bruce R. McElderry. Gainesville, Florida, Scholars Facsimiles and Reprints, 1961.

Mark Twain on the Art of Writing, edited by Martin B. Fried. Buffalo, Salisbury Club, 1961.

Letters to Mary, edited by Lewis Leary. New York, Columbia University Press, 1961.

The Pattern for Mark Twain's "Roughing It": Letters from Nevada by Samuel and Orion Clemens, 1861–1862, edited by Franklin R. Rogers. Berkeley, University of California Press, 1961.

Letters from the Earth, edited by Bernard De Voto. New York, Harper, 1962.

Mark Twain on the Damned Human Race, edited by Janet Smith. New York, Hill and Wang, 1962.

Selected Shorter Writings, edited by Walter Blair. Boston, Houghton Mifflin, 1962.

The Complete Essays, edited by Charles Neider. New York, Doubleday, 1963.

Mark Twain's San Francisco, edited by Bernard Taper. New York, McGraw Hill, 1963.

The Forgotten Writings of Mark Twain, edited by Henry Duskus. New York, Citadel Press, 1963.

General Grant by Matthew Arnold, with a Rejoinder by Mark Twain (lecture), edited by John Y. Simon. Carbondale, Southern Illinois University Press, 1966.

Letters from Hawaii, edited by A. Grove Day. New York, Appleton Century Crofts, 1966; London, Chatto and Windus, 1967.

Which Was the Dream? and Other Symbolic Writings of the Later Years, edited by John S. Tuckey. Berkeley, University of California Press, 1967.

The Complete Travel Books, edited by Charles Neider. New York, Doubleday, 1967.

Letters to His Publishers, 1867–1894, edited by Hamlin Hill. Berkeley, University of California Press, 1967.

Clemens of the "Call": Mark Twain in California, edited by Edgar M. Branch. Berkeley, University of California Press, 1969.

Correspondence with Henry Huttleston Rogers, 1893–1909, edited by Lewis Leary. Berkeley, University of California Press, 1969.

Man Is the Only Animal That Blushes – or Needs to: The Wisdom of Mark Twain, edited by Michael Joseph. Los Angeles, Stanyan Books, 1970.

Mark Twain's Quarrel with Heaven: Captain Stormfield's Visit to Heaven and Other Sketches, edited by Roy B. Browne. New Haven, Connecticut, College and University Press, 1970.

Everybody's Mark Twain, edited by Caroline Thomas Harnsberger. South Brunswick, New Jersey, A.S. Barnes, 1972.

Fables of Man, edited by John S. Tuckey. Berkeley, University of California Press, 1972.

A Pen Warmed Up in Hell: Mark Twain in Protest, edited by Frederick Anderson. New York, Harper, 1972.

The Choice Humorous Works of Mark Twain. London, Chatto and Windus, 1973.

Mark Twain Speaking, edited by Paul Fatout. Iowa City, University of Iowa Press, 1976.

The Comic Mark Twain Reader ...., edited by Charles Neider. New York, Doubleday, 1977.

Editor, *Mark Twain's Library of Humour.* New York, Webster, and London, Chatto and Windus, 1888.

Bibliography: *A Bibliography of the Works of Mark Twain, Samuel Langhorne Clemens* ... by Merle Johnson, New York, Harper, revised edition, 1935; in *Bibliography of American Literature* by Jacob Blanck, New Haven, Connecticut, Yale University Press, vol. 2, 1957.

Manuscript Collections: University of California, Berkeley; Berg Collection, New York Public Library.

Critical Studies: *Mr. Clemens and Mark Twain* by Justin Kaplan, New York, Simon and Schuster, 1966; *Twentieth-Century Interpretations of "The Adventures of Huckleberry Finn,"* edited by Claude M. Simpson, Englewood Cliffs, New Jersey, Prentice Hall, 1968.

*   *   *

Ernest Hemingway wrote, in *Green Hills of Africa*, "All modern American literature comes from one book by Mark Twain called *Huckleberry Finn* ... it's the best book we've had. All American writing comes from that. There was nothing before. There has been nothing as good since."

As criticism Hemingway's statement is admittedly overstated. Samuel Clemens, or Mark Twain, has always been an enigma for critics, many of whom have had great difficulty in analyzing his works, and others in psychoanalyzing him. Hemingway, however, was not speaking as a critic, but rather as a reader, as a devotee, as a writer who recognized his debt to one who came before him. In that role he is an apt and accurate spokesman for all of us who rejoice in listening to the voice of Mark Twain. Just as Lincoln remains the folk symbol of the American spirit, for many Twain remains the folk symbol of the American writer.

It is significant that Hemingway specifically referred to *The Adventures of Huckleberry Finn*, for it is in that work, along with *The Adventures of Tom Sawyer* and *Life on the Mississippi* that Twain's narrative genius is self evident. Today *Tom Sawyer* is usually categorized as a book for children, while *Huck Finn* is considered adult fiction. Nevertheless, in any discussion of Twain's influence on American authors of children's books, both must be considered.

Oddly enough, when Twain wrote *Tom Sawyer* he did not have a child audience in mind. It wasn't until his friend William Dean Howells suggested that it was a story most appropriate for children that Twain "cleaned up" the manuscript and added a preface in which he said: "Although my book is intended mainly for the entertainment of boys and girls, I hope it will not be shunned by men and women on that account, for part of my plan has been to try to pleasantly remind adults of what they once were themselves, and of how they felt and thought and talked, and what queer enterprises they sometimes engaged in." That he did not consciously write it for children is perhaps the book's strongest attribute, though occasionally Twain as narrator speaks directly to the adult readers he originally had in mind. This is overwhelmingly outweighed by the absence of any condescension or moralizing. In fact at the time of its publication (1876) it came under attack as a children's book. The *New York Times* book review concluded: "In the books to be placed into children's hands for purposes of recreation, we have a preference for those of a milder type than *Tom Sawyer*."

Tom Sawyer is much more than a grown man's reminiscences about the idyllic joys and pains of childhood. Twain stands high on the list of eminent writers like Stevenson, Dickens, and Saroyan who successfully depicted how children "felt and thought and talked." Though they did not write specifically for children, they demonstrated for those who would how necessary it is to retain the heart of a child if your work is to have the ring of truth. Twain above all else sets out to entertain. One should not overlook the word "Adventures" in the titles of his "boy" books. He takes the blood and thunder stuff of the old-fashioned dime novels and the serial boy romances and makes it literature.

In *Huck Finn*, intended as a sequel to *Tom Sawyer*, Twain gets into the skin of Huck and tells the story through him, and by so doing he happens upon the narrative mode that is explicitly suited for his special talents. Huck, who could not possibly *write* a story, *tells* us the story. And that is how Twain himself would have it; as he says in his *Autobiography*: "With the pen in one's hand, narrative is a difficult art; narrative should flow as flows the brook down through the hills and leafy woodlands." This also was one of the reasons for Hemingway's acclaim, for he too, like many storytellers, was at heart a raconteur and a minstrel rather than a scribbler.

But there was even a more important reason. Hemingway recognized the straightforward honesty in *Huck Finn*. Twain possessed, as H.L. Mencken put it, "a truly amazing instinct for the truth." Today many writers of books for children and young adults have turned to first person narrative, with only a meager few of them handling it successfully. They would do well to look closely at *Huckleberry Finn*, for there they will find Mark Twain's greatest legacy to them – his integrity. He doesn't use the first person point of view as a literary device for simulating a peer relationship with young readers; but rather he turns over the complete narrative to Huck, allowing him to tell the story as only he can do it. And by so doing he must be content to let the work be found by those readers who are able and ready to receive it.

James E. Higgins

———————

YONGE, Charlotte (Mary).   British.   Born in Otterbourne, Hampshire, 13 August 1823. Editor, 1851–90, and Assistant Editor, 1891–95, *The Monthly Packet*; Editor, *The Monthly Paper of Sunday Teaching*, 1860–75, and *Mothers in Council*, 1890–1900. *Died 24 March 1901.*

PUBLICATIONS FOR CHILDREN

Fiction

> *Le Château de Melville; ou, Récreations du Cabinet d'Etude.*   London, Simkin, 1838.
> *Abbey Church; or, Self-Control and Self-Conceit* (published anonymously)   London, Mozley, 1844; with *Mystery of the Cavern*, 1872.
> *Scenes and Characters; or, Eighteen Months at Beechcroft.*   London, Mozley, 1847; as *Beechcroft*, New York, Appleton, 1871.
> *Henrietta's Wish; or, Domineering.*   London, Masters, 1850; New York, Munro, 1885.
> *Kenneth; or, The Rear Guard of the Grand Army.*   London, Parker, 1850; New York, Appleton, n.d.
> *Langley School.*   London, Mozley, 1850.
> *The Two Guardians; or, Home in This World.*   London, Masters, 1852; New York, Appleton, n.d.
> *The Heir of Redclyffe.*   London, Parker, 2 vols., 1853; New York, Appleton, 2 vols., 1853.
> *The Herb of the Field.*   London, Mozley, 1853; New York, Macmillan, 1887.
> *The Castle Builders; or, The Deferred Confirmation.*   London, Mozley, 1854; New York, Appleton, n.d.
> *Heartsease; or, The Brother's Wife.*   London, Parker, 1854; New York, Appleton, 2 vols, 1861.
> *The Little Duke; or, Richard the Fearless*, illustrated by Jane Blackburn.   London, Parker, 1854; as *Richard the Fearless*, New York, Appleton, 1856; as *The Little Duke*, New York, Macmillan, 1864.
> *The History of Sir Thomas Thumb*, illustrated by Jane Blackburn.   Edinburgh, Constable, 1855.
> *The Lances of Lynwood*, illustrated by Jane Blackburn.   London, Parker, 1855; New York, Appleton, 1856.
> *The Railroad Children.*   London, 1855.
> *Ben Sylvester's Word.*   London, Mozley, 1856; New York, Appleton, n.d.
> *The Daisy Chain; or, Aspirations: A Family Chronicle.*   London, 2 vols., 1856; New York, Appleton, n.d.
> *Harriet and Her Sister* (published anonymously).   London, Mozley, 1856.
> *Leonard the Lion-Heart.*   London, Mozley, 1856.

Dynevor Terrace; or, The Clue of Life. London, Parker, 2 vols., 1857; New York, Appleton, 2 vols., 1857.

The Christmas Mummers. London, Mozley, 1858; New York, Pott Young, 1876.

Friarswood Post Office. London, Mozley, 1860; New York, Appleton, n.d.

Hopes and Fears; or, Scenes from the Life of a Spinster. London, Parker, 2 vols., 1860; New York, Appleton, 1861.

The Mice at Play. London, 1860.

The Strayed Falcon. London, 1860.

The Pigeon Pie. London, Mozley, 1860; Boston, Roberts, 1864.

The Stokesley Secret. London, Mozley, 1861; New York, Appleton, 1862.

The Young Stepmother; or, A Chronicle of Mistakes. London, Macmillan, 1861; New York, Appleton, n.d.

Countess Kate. London, Mozley, 1862; Boston, Loring, n.d.

Sea Spleenwort and Other Stories. London, 1862.

Last Heartsease Leaves. Privately printed, 1862(?).

The Trial: More Links of the Daisy Chain. London, Macmillan, and New York, Appleton, 1864.

The Wars of Wapsburgh. London, Groombridge, 1864.

The Clever Woman of the Family. London, Macmillan, 2 vols., 1865; New York, Appleton, 1865.

The Dove in the Eagle's Nest. London, Macmillan, 2 vols., 1866; New York, Appleton, 1866.

The Prince and the Page: A Story of the Last Crusade, illustrated by R. Farren. London, Macmillan, 1866; New York, Macmillan, 1875.

The Danvers Papers: An Invention. London, Macmillan, 1867.

The Six Cushions. London, Mozley, 1867; Boston, Lee and Shepard, n.d.

The Chaplet of Pearls; or, The White and Black Ribaumont. London, Macmillan, 2 vols., 1868; New York, Appleton, 1869.

Kaffir Land; or, New Ground. London, Mozley, 1868.

The Caged Lion. London and New York, Macmillan, 1870.

Little Lucy's Wonderful Globe, illustrated by L. Frölich. London, Macmillan, 1871; Boston, Lothrop, 1872.

P's and Q's; or, The Question of Putting Upon. London and New York, Macmillan, 1872.

The Pillars of the House; or, Under Wode, Under Rode. London, Macmillan, 4 vols., 1873; New York, Macmillan, 2 vols., 1874.

Lady Hester; or, Ursula's Narrative. London and New York, Macmillan, 1874.

My Young Alcides: A Faded Photograph. London, Macmillan, 2 vols., 1875; New York, Macmillan, 1876.

The Three Brides. London, Macmillan, and New York, Appleton, 1876

The Disturbing Element; or, Chronicles of the Blue-Bell Society. London, Ward, 1878; New York, Appleton, 1879.

Burnt Out: A Story for Mothers' Meetings. London, Walter Smith, 1879.

Magnus Bonum; or, Mother Carey's Brood. London, Macmillan, 3 vols., 1879; New York, Macmillan, 1879.

Bye-Words: A Collection of Tales New and Old. London, Macmillan, 1880.

Love and Life: An Old Story in Eighteenth-Century Costume. London, Macmillan, 2 vols., 1880; New York, Macmillan, 1880.

Mary and Norah; or, Queen Katharine's School, with *Nelly and Margaret.* London and New York, Warne, 1880 (?).

Cheap Jack. London, Walter Smith, 1881.

Frank's Debt. London, Walter Smith, 1881.

Lads and Lasses of Langley. London, Walter Smith, 1881.

Wolf. London, Walter Smith, 1881.

Given to Hospitality. London, Walter Smith, 1882.

Langley Little Ones: Six Stories. London, Walter Smith, 1882.

Pickle and His Page Boy; or, Unlooked For. London, Walter Smith, 1882; New York, Dutton, 1883.

Sowing and Sewing: A Sexagesima Story. London, Walter Smith, 1882.

Unknown to History: A Story of the Captivity of Mary of Scotland. London, Macmillan, 2 vols., 1882; New York, Macmillan, 1882.

Stray Pearls: Memoirs of Margaret de Ribaumont, Viscountess of Bellaise. London and New York, Macmillan, 1883.

Langley Adventures. London, Walter Smith, and New York, Appleton, 1884.

The Armourer's 'Prentices, illustrated by J.W. Hennessy. London, Macmillan, 2 vols., 1884; New York, Macmillan, 1884.

Nuttie's Father. London, Macmillan, 2 vols., 1885; New York, Macmillan, 1885.

The Two Sides of the Shield. London, Macmillan, and New York, Munro, 1885.

Astray: A Tale of a Country Town, with others. London, Hatchards, 1886.

Chantry House. London, Macmillan, 2 vols., 1886; New York, Macmillan, 1886.

The Little Rick-Burners. London, Skeffington, 1886.

A Modern Telemachus. London, Macmillan, 2 vols., 1886; New York, Macmillan, 1886.

Under the Storm; or, Steadfast's Charge. London, National Society, and New York, Munro, 1887.

Beechcroft at Rockstone. London and New York, Macmillan, 1888.

Nurse's Memories, illustrated by F. Marriott and Florence Maplestone. London, Eyre and Spottiswoode, and New York, Young, 1888.

Our New Mistress; or, Changes at Brookfield Earl. London, National Society, and New York, Munro, 1888.

The Cunning Woman's Grandson: A Tale of Cheddar a Hundred Years Ago. London, National Society, and New York, Whittaker, 1889.

4 Reputed Changeling; or, Three Seventh Years Two Centuries Ago. London, Macmillan, 2 vols., 1889.

The Slaves of Sabinus: Jew and Gentile. London, National Society, and New York, Whittaker, 1890.

More Bywords (stories and poems). London and New York, Macmillan, 1890.

The Constable's Tower; or, The Times of Magna Carta. London, National Society, and New York, Whittaker, 1891.

Two Penniless Princesses. London, Macmillan, 2 vols., 1891; New York, Macmillan, 1891.

The Cross Roads; or, A Choice in Life. London, National Society, and New York, Whittaker, 1892.

That Stick. London and New York, Macmillan, 1892.

Grisly Grisell; or, The Laidly Lady of Whitburn: A Tale of the Wars of the Roses. London and New York, Macmillan, 2 vols., 1893.

Strolling Players: A Harmony of Contrasts, with Christabel Coleridge. London and New York, Macmillan, 1893.

The Treasures in the Marshes, illustrated by W.S. Stacey. London, National Society, and New York, Whittaker, 1893.

The Cook and the Captive; or, Attalus the Hostage, illustrated by W.S. Stacey. London, National Society, and New York, Whittaker, 1894.

The Rubies of St. Lô. London and New York, Macmillan, 1894.

The Carbonels. London, National Society, and New York, Whittaker, 1895.

The Long Vacation. London and New York, Macmillan, 1895.

The Release; or, Caroline's French Kindred. London and New York, Macmillan, 1896.

The Wardship of Steepcombe, illustrated by W.S. Stacey. London, National Society, and New York, Whittaker, 1896.

The Pilgrimage of the Ben Beriah. London and New York, Macmillan, 1897.

Founded on Paper; or, Uphill and Downhill Between the Two Jubilees, illustrated by W.S. Stacey. London, National Society, and New York, Whittaker, 1897.

The Patriots of Palestine: A Story of the Maccabees, illustrated by W.S. Stacey. London, National Society, and New York, Whittaker, 1898.

Scenes from "Kenneth" .... London, Arnold, 1899.

The Herd Boy and His Hermit, illustrated by W.S. Stacey. London, National Society, and New York, Whittaker, 1899.

The Making of a Missionary; or, Daydreams in Earnest. London, National Society, and New York, Whittaker, 1900.

Modern Broods; or, Developments Unlooked for. London, Macmillan, and New York, Whittaker, 1900.

Plays

The Apple of Discord. London, Groombridge, 1864.
Historical Dramas. London, 1864.

Verse

Verses on the Gospel for Sundays and Holidays. London, Walter Smith, 1880.

Other

Kings of England: A History for Young Children. London, Mozley, 1848.

Landmarks of History. London, Mozley, 3 vols., 1852–57; New York, Leypoldt and Holt, 3 vols., 1867–68.

The Instructive Picture Book; or, Lessons from the Vegetable World, illustrated by R.M. Stark. Edinburgh, Edmonston and Douglas, 1857.

The Chosen People: A Compendium of Sacred and Church History for School Children. London, Mozley, 1861; New York, Pott Young, 1874.

A History of Christian Names. London, Parker, 1863; revised edition, London, and New York, Macmillan, 1884.

A Book of Golden Deeds of All Times and All Lands. London, Macmillan, 1864; Cambridge, Massachusetts, Sever and Francis, 1966.

Cameos from English History. London and New York, Macmillan, 9 vols., 1868–99.

The Pupils of St. John the Divine. London and New York, Macmillan, 1868.

A Book of Worthies, Gathered from the Old Histories and Now Written Out Anew. London, and New York, Macmillan, 1869.

Keynotes of the First Lessons for Every Day in the Year. London, S.P.C.K., 1869.

Musings over the "Christian Year" and "Lyra Innocentium" .... Oxford, Parker, 1871.

A Parallel History of France and England .... London and New York, Macmillan, 1871.

Pioneers and Founders; or, Recent Works in the Mission Field. London and New York, Macmillan, 1871.

Scripture Readings for Schools, with Comments. London and New York, Macmillan, 5 vols., 1871–79.

Questions on the Prayer-Book [Collects, Epistles, Gospels, Psalms]. London, Mozley, 5 vols., 1872–81.

Aunt Charlotte's Stories of English [French, Bible, Greek, German, Roman] History for the Little One. London, Ward, 6 vols., 1873–77; as *Young Folks' History* ..., Boston, Lothrop, 2 vols., and Estes and Lauriet, 4 vols., 1878–80.

Womankind. London, Mozley, 1875; New York, Macmillan, 1887.

Eighteen Centuries of Beginnings of Church History. London, Mozley, and New York, Pott Young, 1876.

The Story of the Christians and Moors in Spain. London and New York, Macmillan, 1878.
Short English Grammar for Use in Schools. London, 1879.
Aunt Charlotte's Evenings at Home with the Poets .... London, Ward, 1880.
English History Reading Books .... London, National Society, 6 vols., 1881–83; as *Westminster Historical Reading Books,* 6 vols., 1891–92.
Talks about the Laws We Live Under; or, At Langley Night-School. London, Walter Smith, 1882.
A Pictorial History of the World's Great Nations .... New York, Hess, 1882.
Aunt Charlotte's Stories of American History, with J.H. Hastings Weld. London, Ward, and New York, Appleton, 1883.
English Church History .... London, National Society, 1883.
Landmarks of Recent History, 1770–1883. London, Walter Smith, 1883.
The Daisy Chain Birthday-Book, edited by Eadgyth. London, Walter Smith, 1884.
A Key to the Waverley Novels, vol. 1. Boston, Ginn Heath, 1885.
Teachings on the Catechism: For the Little Ones. London, Walter Smith, 1886.
The Victorian Half-Century: A Jubilee Book. London and New York, Macmillan, 1886.
What Books to Lend and What to Give. London, National Society, 1887.
Preparation of Prayer-Book Lessons. London, Walter Smith, 1888.
Conversations on the Prayer Book. London, 1888.
Deacon's Book of Dates: A Manual of the World's Chief Historical Landmarks and an Outline of Universal History. London, Deacon, 1888.
Life of H.R.H. the Prince Consort. London, W.H. Allen, 1890.
Seven Heroines of Christendom. London, Sonnenschein, 1891.
Simple Stories Relating to English History. London, 1891.
Twelve Stories from Early English History. London, National Society, 1891.
Twenty Stories and Biographies from 1066 to 1485. London, 1891.
The Hanoverian [Stuart, Tudor] Period, with Biographies of Leading Persons. London, National Society, 3 vols., 1892.
The Girl's Little Book. London, Skeffington, 1893.
The Story of Easter. London, Ward, 1894.

Editor, *Biographies of Good Women.* London, Mozley, 2 vols., 1862–65.
Editor, *Readings from Standard Authors.* London, 1864.
Editor, with E. Sewell, *Historical Selections: A Series of Readings in English and European History.* London, Macmillan, 2 vols., 1868–70; as *European History.* New York, Macmillan, 2 vols., 1872–73.
Editor, *A Storehouse of Stories.* London and New York, Macmillan, 2 vols., 1870–72.
Editor, *Beneath the Cross: Readings for Children in Our Lord's Seven Sayings.* London, Masters, 1881.
Editor, *Historical Ballads.* London, National Society, 3 vols., 1882–83.
Editor, *Shakespeare's Plays for Schools, Abridged and Annotated.* London and New York, Macmillan, 1883.
Editor, *Higher Reading Book for Schools, Colleges, and General Use.* London, National Society, 1885.
Editor, *Chips from the Royal Image, Being Fragments of the "Eikon Basilike" of Charles I,* by A.E.M. Anderson Morshead. London, Masters, 1887.

Translator, *Marie Thérèse de Lamourous, Foundress of the House of La Misericorde at Bordeaux,* by Abbé Pouget. Oxford, Parker, 1858.
Translator, *Two Years of School Life,* by Elise de Pressensé. London, Warne, and New York, Scribner, 1869.
Translator, *The Population of an Old Pear Tree; or, Stories of Insect Life,* by E. van Bruyssel, illustrated by Becker. London, Macmillan, 1870.

Translator, *Life and Adventures of Count Beugnot, Minister of State under Napoleon I*, by Count H. d'Ideville. London, Hurst and Blackett, 1871.

Translator, *Dames of High Estate*, by H. de Witt. London, Warne, 1872.

Translator, *Recollections of a Page at the Court of Louis XVI*, by Felix Count de France d'Hézecques. London, Hurst and Blackett, 1873.

Translator, *Recollections of Colonel de Gonville*. London, 1875.

Translator, *A Man of Other Days: Recollections of the Marquis Henry Joseph Costa de Beauregard*. London, Hurst and Blackett, 1877.

Translator, *The Youth of Queen Elizabeth, 1533–58*, by L. Wiesener. London, Hurst and Blackett, 2 vols., 1879.

Translator, *Catherine of Aragon, and the Sources of the English Reformation*, by Albert du Boys. London, Hurst and Blackett, 1881; New York, Franklin, 1968.

Translator, *Behind the Hedges; or, The War in the Vendee*, by H. de Witt. London, Warne, 1882.

Translator, *Sparks of Light for Every Day*, by H. de Witt. London, Masters, 1882.

PUBLICATIONS FOR ADULTS

Other

In Memoriam Bishop Patteson. London, 1872.

Life of John Coleridge Patteson, Missionary Bishop to the Melanesian Islands. London and New York, Macmillan, 2 vols., 1874.

Hints on the Religious Education of Children of the Wealthier Classes. London, n.d.

How to Teach the New Testament. London, National Society, 1881.

Practical Work in Sunday Schools. London, National Society, 1881; New York, Kellogg, 1888.

Hannah More (biography). London, W.H. Allen, and Boston, Roberts, 1888.

The Parent's Power (lecture). Winchester, Warren, 1891.

Old Times at Otterbourne. Winchester, Warren, 1891.

An Old Woman's Outlook in a Hampshire Village. London and New York, Macmillan, 1892.

Chimes for the Mothers: A Reading for Each Week in the Year. London, Wells Gardner, 1893.

John Keble's Parishes: A History of Hursley and Otterbourne. London and New York, Macmillan, 1898.

Reasons Why I Am a Catholic and Not a Roman Catholic. London, Wells Gardner, 1901.

Critical Studies: *Charlotte Mary Yonge: Her Life and Letters* by Christabel Coleridge, London, Macmillan, 1903; *Charlotte Mary Yonge: The Story of an Uneventful Life* by Georgina Battiscombe, London, Constable, 1943; *Victorian Best-Seller* by Margaret Mare and Alicia C. Percival, London, Harrap, 1947; *A Chaplet for Charlotte Yonge* edited by Georgina Battiscombe and Marghanita Laski, London, Cresset Press, 1965.

*   *   *

Charlotte Yonge's was the voice of the early Victorian daughter of the squirearchy, earnest in her fervour to do her duty in that state of life to which God had called her, eager to help others to do the same. Her first book was published in 1838, her last in 1901. Between those dates she wrote over 150 works – domestic stories for cottage and drawing room, historical tales, books of instruction both religious and secular, lengthy sagas of family life. But her outlook scarcely changed at all in over 60 years of authorship.

She never wrote for purely literary ends, but always directly or indirectly for the promotion of Christian truth, and the truth as it had been taught to her by John Keble when he prepared her for confirmation. Her duty as she had been taught it by her parents remained her touchstone of excellence; she desired no other guide. To the early and mid-Victorian girl she herself was a guide, providing them with chronicles of large and life-like upper class families whose characters are so real that a devoted coterie still discusses and analyses them today. Nor was it only the schoolroom who read her; in the 1850's *The Heir of Redclyffe* was received with enthusiasm by bishops and statesmen, undergraduates and Guards officers; it was one of the most popular Tractarian novels of its day.

The fascination of works such as *The Daisy Chain* and *The Pillars of the House* and their successors lies in the way they are interwoven, that one can walk in them as in Barsetshire, viewing characters from all aspects, in youth and middle life; as central figures in one book, as peripheral ones in another. The creation of personalities, in whom she believed as well as the reader, was her particular gift; plots were a secondary matter and she had no great skill in manipulating them. In her rather solitary childhood, cut off from all contemporaries except during rare and ecstatic visits to cousins, she had paced the gravel walks of her father's small Hampshire estate, inventing large families.

Within the framework of her family sagas is contained Miss Yonge's teaching on the girl and young woman's role in life. It was, in fact, her own role of ardent submission to those in authority, be it clergyman, teacher or parent. On the duty of those who achieved the status of authority she had nothing to say. "For her the newest, *youngest* thing was to do home and family duties more perfectly. What greater happiness can be given to youth?" wrote Christabel Coleridge in her memoir of 1903, and two generations of girls loved the chronicles of the Mays and the Underwoods, the Mohuns and the Merrifields. Their lofty ideals, their intellectual pursuits and conversation, their happy family relationship presented a way of life that they themselves yearned to imitate.

To a privileged few who named themselves her "goslings," she was Mother Goose and guided their strivings to educate and improve themselves. Some of these, like Christabel Coleridge, Florence Wilford, Frances Peard, subsequently themselves wrote for children. But, although she had thousands of admirers all over the world, as the century went on her message had increasingly little appeal to a generation of girls very different from her own, with whom she found it difficult to sympathise. Her implacable hostility to the idea of girls being educated outside the home circle – at the new High Schools and at universities, for instance – did at last modify a little, and a little uneasily in her last novels she allowed the daughters of some of her original characters to enter Oxford or Cambridge. But she made it clear that she felt rather wary of such girls.

Her outlook was narrow, parochial even, since during the whole of her long life she barely moved beyond the Hampshire village where she had been born. Her literary work came second in her mind to her parish duties there, her attendance at Otterbourne church and her devotion to its school whose girls she had known and lovingly taught from her own childhood. For them she wrote many tales of cottage life as it should be lived, with decency, order and deference towards the "great house," and above all stressing their duty to the church into which they had been baptized. Even in these didactic stories her gift for characterisation, for sketching a social background, shines out and makes them charming evocations of a vanished way of life.

—Gillian Avery

CHILDREN'S BOOKS
IN TRANSLATION

Throughout this century, and especially in recent years, children's books of high quality translated from other languages have been appearing in the English-speaking countries. They form a small but interesting and valuable part of the body of literature for young people which children may encounter.

The importance of making good foreign books available to children was stressed by Jella Lepman, the founder of the Munich International Youth Library. Her vision, springing from the desolate aftermath of the Second World War, is expressed in the title of her own *A Bridge of Children's Books*: she saw a world in which children of different countries, having grown up knowing each other through their children's literature, would be incapable of fighting one another. The same ideal was stated in the U.S.A. by Mildred L. Batchelder: "Interchange of children's books between countries, through translation, influences communication between the people of those countries." Communication of this nature is a far cry from those well-meaning but inevitably patronizing series which used to appear before the war, describing the lives of children of other lands with much ethnic detail; when it comes to portraying a country's way of life and of thought, both differences and similarities are much more tellingly presented from within. The Western reader may be startled by this piece of vintage Victorian advice given a teenage Russian boy in Vadim Frolov's *What It's All About* by his admired and sympathetic father: "My father had told me once that there was nothing wrong about some of the feelings involved in growing up ... but you should think as little as possible about them ... the best thing of all was to take up athletics seriously." But in fact the narrator's adolescent development is most sensitively described, as is his coming to terms with the fact of his parents' separation. Again, an English reader could be rather surprised by the almost casual alacrity with which a teenage girl who suspects she is pregnant is offered an abortion as a matter of course in Inge Krog's *Fourteen Days Overdue*, from Denmark, but the Swedish heroine of Gunnel Beckman's *Mia*, in the same predicament, evokes sympathetic recognition of a common female situation through the skill with which her complicated web of feelings about her whole family life as well as her possible pregnancy is described.

Only time can show which of the many foreign children's books published in English-language versions will become international classics like those nineteenth-century works (such as *Heidi*, *Pinocchio*, *The Swiss Family Robinson*) which have become assimilated into a common heritage of children's literature. But it is perhaps fitting that one of the major translated works of this century, Selma Lagerlöf's *The Wonderful Adventures of Nils*, stands with one foot, as it were, in the previous one. Its leisurely pace and strong moral tone reach back to the nineteenth century, as little Nils Holgersson, transformed to elf-size because of his own selfish naughtiness, learns to feel for the weak or threatened through his own experiences as he travels with the wild geese; its deep feeling for nature (it originated in a publisher's request for a geographical primer about Sweden) also looks forward to later works by other writers in this century.

Animal stories, in fact, comprise some of the best-remembered titles published in English in the years between the two World Wars. There is an understanding of animals and delicacy of touch in the books of Felix Salten (the pseudonym of Sigmund Salzmann) which inevitably became blurred in the famous Disney film of *Bambi*, though no doubt the film prolonged the story's popularity. No such fate overtook the fine *Père Castor* series of animal picture-books from France. Other books too appeared at this period which can now be seen to have attained the status of modern classics: notably Erich Kästner's *Emil and the Detectives*, prototype of the urban adventure story in which a gang of children outwit villainous adults (and still infinitely more lively and realistic than most of its followers), and Jean de Brunhoff's *The Story of Babar*. Babar, his family and his companions have been firm favourites ever since their first appearance; the series was sadly cut short by the author's early death, but continued by de Brunhoff's son Laurent. Strictly speaking, Babar is inimitable; all the same, Laurent de Brunhoff's sequels have given a lot of children a lot of pleasure. And it is pleasant to note that the English translation of *Babar the Elephant* has recently been re-issued in its original large format, with handwritten script instead of type.

However, it is in post-war publishing that one finds the real expansion of the market for translated foreign books. It must be admitted at once that we cannot quite be said to have achieved Jella Lepman's ideal of complete internationality in children's literature: publishers, after all, are in business, and it is inevitable that the vast majority of translated books come from European countries with publishing industries developed to the same level. This means, in effect, Scandinavia, Holland, Germany, France, with a most welcome and encouraging entry into the field of recent years from the U.S.S.R. and Eastern European countries.

There is one big exception, but again from a highly industrialized and much Westernized country: the phenomenon of the Japanese picture book. This is something which has emerged over the last decade. Not all the texts of these picture books are originally Japanese; for instance, one of the first books by Chiyoko Nakatani to attract Western notice was *The Animals' Lullaby* (1967), in which the artist's pictures were fitted to words taken from an Icelandic poem. But in other books by the same artist the texts are written by her or by other Japanese writers. Among other Japanese contributors to the picture book *genre* are Chihiro Iwasaki, with the *Momoko* books, and Kozo Kakimoto who illustrates the *Mr. Bear* stories by Chizuko Kuratomi. Westernized some of these books may be, but a Japanese delicacy of line and colour remains to make its own unique effect.

Obviously the picture book field is one of the simplest in which to achieve Frau Lepman's international ideal: the pictures matter as much as, and often more than, the words. And often a distinguished foreign artist, such as Katrin Brandt or Ruth Hürlimann, will take a traditional tale from Grimm or some other familiar source to illustrate. Countries which otherwise are not very well represented in English translated children's literature have made contributions here: Italy, for example, with Bruno Munari (*The Lorry Driver*, *Animals for Sale*, and other titles), with Emanuele Luzzati (*Ronald and the Wizard Calico*), and a story by the distinguished Italian writer Mario Soldati, illustrated by Alberto Longoni, *The Octopus and the Pirates*, which gives a most attractive picture of North Italian life by the sea. Mention must also be made of the books for rather older children by Andersen award winner Gianni Rodari. *The Befana's Toyshop*, *Mr. Cat in Business*, and *A Pie in the Sky* are international representatives of Italian children's literature. There have been arrivals from Eastern Europe too: Josef Lada's *Purrkin the Talking Cat*, originally Czech, comes to us from a German version made by Otfried Preussler, and there is a delightful rollicking translation by Richard N. Coe, illustrated by William Papas, of Kornei Chukovsky's *Dr. Concocter*, a kind of Dr. Dolittle in verse.

There are also very small, square format books, designed for very young children to hold comfortably themselves, and dealing usually with simple everyday events: a great many series of this kind come from the Continent. Probably the best-known practitioner of the art is Dick Bruna from Holland. His small, brightly and simply illustrated books range from brief educational texts, through stories about characters of his own, to simplified fairy tales: he has attracted a certain amount of criticism for *over*-simplification of effect, but is undoubtedly popular with his young readers – and surely easier on the adult eye than some of the pre-war artists who went in for over-prettification in picture-books. Other small-format books, such as those of Gunilla Wolde and Inger and Lasse Sandberg, come from Scandinavia, with texts on everyday matters which, again, are adapted rather than translated, though idea as well as illustrations are the authors' own.

With books for older children, one comes across a great many titles which are like their English and American counterparts in the areas of fantasy, the historical novel, the modern adventure story – and yet often, and in a very stimulating manner, not *quite* like them. Certainly there is no one else *quite* like Astrid Lindgren's *Pippi Longstocking*, first published a few years after the war. This is one of those books which does seem destined to become a modern classic; nine-year-old Pippi, immensely strong, kind-hearted, who lives on her own with a horse and a suitcase full of gold pieces, and breaks all the accepted rules of "good behaviour," is the personification of every child's dream of anarchism. Astrid Lindgren, a winner of the Hans Andersen international award, was not, however, a writer to keep repeating herself; there are two sequels to *Pippi Longstocking*, and she has also created another superbly naughty character in the hero of *Emil in the Soup Tureen* and other stories about the same little boy (both in picture book and in longer narrative form), but she has branched out into many other fields, and quite recently, with *The Brothers Lionheart*, has produced something new and original: a fantasy which raises moral questions and is set in a world-after-death with yet another world-after-death beyond it.

Another fine Swedish fantasy, *The Glassblower's Children*, is by Maria Gripe, who has written a number of stories of everyday life, yet stories with children at the centre of them who don't quite fit into an ordinary background, such as the attractive heroine of *Pappa Pellerin's Daughter*. Fantasy in Holland is well represented by Paul Biegel (*The King of the Copper Mountains*, and other works); while a writer of Biegel's stature really resembles no one but himself, yet a book like *The Seven-Times Search* has a touch of Hans Andersen about it. European fantasies, like those written in the U.S.A. and the U.K., are often based, distantly or not so distantly (as in Tolkien's *The Hobbit*), on European mythology and folklore. Otfried Preussler made his name in Germany with amusing fantasies about the exploits of such traditional figures as *The Little Witch* and *The Little Ghost*, and went on to write *The Satanic Mill*, a powerful tale for older readers about a pact with the Devil, based on South German legends and set at the time of the Thirty Years' War. James Krüss, of Germany, has written stories such as *My Great-Grandfather and I*, with strong elements of the poetic and the marvellous. The comic, the poetic and the magical are all intertwined in the popular *Moomintroll* series by Tove Jansson of Finland. Alf Prøysen of Norway has created a delightful comic-fantastic character for younger readers in his *Little Old Mrs. Pepperpot*. And one must mention Reiner Zimnik's *The Crane*, a book not really classifiable under any heading, but a fine fable which is bleak, haunting and humorous by turns.

The stock historical figure of the Viking is put to comic use in Runer Jonsson's *Viki Viking*, from Denmark. But serious historical novels of high quality have reached us from Germany in particular. One might note for special mention the work of Hans Baumann, including *Sons of the Steppe* and *The Barque of the Brothers*, and of Barbara Bartos-Höppner (*The Cossacks*, *Save the Khan*, and *Storm over the Caucasus*). Adventure stories pure and simple are not so much in fashion at the present time as they once were, but in post-war years excellent examples have come to us from Norway (Leif Hamre's adventure novels such as *Otter Three Two Calling!*), from Holland, notably in the work of An Rutgers van der Loeff with stories such as *Avalanche!* and *Children on the Oregon Trail*, and the more domestic type of adventure, in the *Emil and the Detectives* tradition, from France in the stories of Paul Berna (e.g. *A Hundred Million Francs*).

One should, perhaps, comment in parenthesis about France in general, because to some extent French children's literature stands apart from that of the rest of Europe. Eminent French men of letters have the habit – engaging or annoying, according to the way you look at it – of tossing off one or just possibly two works for children: these include *Fattypuffs and Thinifers* by André Maurois, *The Wonderful Farm* by Marcel Aymé, *Tistou of the Green Fingers* by Maurice Druon, and, perhaps the most important of them, Antoine de Saint-Exupéry's *The Little Prince*. These works can be – as in Maurois' and Saint-Exupéry's books – basically of a political or philosophical nature, though with an amusing and readable story to cover the message. One of the most recent additions to the *genre* must be Michel Tournier's *Friday and Robinson*, a junior version of his novel *Vendredi*, in which the Crusoe/ Man Friday situation is turned upside down and the savage becomes the educative influence. Then, on the other hand, we have a few good, very prolific authors in more conventional styles, such as Paul Berna and René Guillot, with adventure stories and animal stories. But only a few; the mass of less distinguished writing does not, naturally, get accepted by publishers and appear in translation. However, the Belgian Hergé's *Tintin* (from 1959), and Goscinny and Uderzo's *Asterix the Gaul* (from 1969), have imparted a degree of sophistication and literacy to the European strip cartoon for children which was not previously present.

A particularly important and interesting area of translated literature from Europe is that of the war story: not the hearty British adventures of Biggles and his like, but stories from countries which actually underwent German occupation. And here it is only right for English-speaking readers, who may have suffered greatly from the war but whose countries were never occupied, and for their children, the later generations of readers of young people's literature, to sit quiet and listen. The classic of them all, alas, is true: Anne Frank's *The Diary of a Young Girl* (1952). Close to Anne Frank, and also in Holland, are the experiences described by Johanna Reiss in *The Upstairs Room*, with its recent sequel *The Journey Back*. From Norway comes Aimée Sommerfelt's account of the friendship between a Jewish girl, *Miriam*, and her non-Jewish friend Hanne; from Greece, Alki Zei's *Petros' War*. From Germany itself we have a stark, semi-autobiographical trilogy by Hans Peter Richter: *Friedrich*, *I Was There*, and *The Time of the Young Soldiers*. And from Austria, Christine Nöstlinger gives us another autobiographical account of what it was like to be a small girl in Vienna when the Russians marched in at the end of the war (*Fly Away Home*).

The actual political setting of Anne Holm's *I Am David*, from Denmark, is purposely less clear; all we know is that the young hero, allowed to escape from an Eastern European concentration camp, is scared to death of being recaptured by *them*, whoever *they* are, as he makes his way gradually back to a long-lost mother. His character as it unfolds is perhaps rather over-saintly for some, but the concentration-camp mentality which has been induced in him is precisely and most movingly conveyed. The political background to Alki Zei's *Wildcat under Glass* (to which the translator, Edward Fenton, adds a useful foreword) is clear enough to the reader, the story being set in 1936 when the Fascists under Metaxas took power, but only dimly understood by the two little girls at the centre of the story. Moving again is the fact that in this book we catch echoes of the Spanish Civil War, in the songs sung and the tales half-told to the girls by their student cousin Niko, the freedom fighter. Perhaps we may now hope for more contributions to world children's literature from Spain itself: there has been very little translated work except for José María Sánchez-Silva's *Marcelino* and one or two other titles by the same author. Even from Portugal – an English translation exists of the famous Portuguese writer Miguel Torga's *Farrusco the Blackbird*, but although the book consists mainly of animal fables they are not specifically for children. More works of quality for older children from Italy would also be welcome, although Renée Reggiani's *The Adventures of Five Children and a Dog* states, through the medium of entertainment, the plight of the poorer regions of Southern Italy as compared with the richer industrial North.

There is now a very pleasing amount of Russian and Eastern European literature being translated into English: one has only to look down the list of awards and nominees for the Mildred L. Batchelder Award to find, since its institution in 1968 in the U.S.A. to mark the best translated work of the year, eight Russian titles mentioned and two Czech titles. Among them are *The Little Chalk Man* by Václav Ctvrtek; *Escape* by Ota Hofman; *There, Far Beyond the River* by Yuri Korinetz (from Hans Baumann's German version); and *The White Ship* by Chingiz Aitmatov. The last-named appears under an adult imprint in the U.K. and is of particular interest because of the stir it created in the U.S.S.R. on its appearance there, when Aitmatov, widely regarded by his countrymen as a formative influence on the young (especially with his earlier novel, *Farewell, Gul'sary*), was accused of transgressing against social realism with the use of a tragic ending and a tragic Kirghiz folk tale, and skilfully and effectively defended himself against such criticism. To the Western reader there would appear to be two parallel trends in the Eastern European literature we see in translation: the nostalgic (as exemplified in the book by Korinetz), evoking a near-timeless Russian atmosphere, and the socially aware (as in Frolov's *What It's All About*). Sometimes the two are successfully and sensitively combined. And it may well be that the tragically early death of Jan Prochazka has deprived Czechoslovakia of a major children's writer; his story of a twelve-year-old boy and his horse, *Long Live the Republic*, won the German Youth Prize in the late 1960's.

Not that social awareness is the particular property of Eastern Europe: the first half of the 1970's has seen the very strong emergence of what can loosely be called the Social Problem book in children's literature throughout the English-speaking countries and in those European nations that have contributed to our young people's literature. Such books can be directed to very young children; some critics have said *too* young, in particular of Monica Gydal's and Thomas Danielsson's series *Olly Sees It Through*, recently published in England and deriving from Sweden, which is for very young children: little Olly has to face events such as the death of a grandparent, a visit to hospital, the birth of a baby brother, the divorce of his friend Gemma's parents. One suspects that any critic must suffer from reading the entire well-intended series at one go, as a child would not, and that taken separately they can only be helpful. With a slightly older age group, we notice that the Social Problem is not, after all, an entirely modern phenomenon: Erich Kästner tackled the question of divorce, though in light-hearted vein, in *Lottie and Lisa*, over a quarter of a century ago. It is amusing, too, to see what a gap of less than ten years can do to feminist (or anti-feminist) attitudes: Edith Unnerstad's *Little O*, from Sweden, in itself a charming, lively collection of stories about the youngest girl in a large family, intended for children of six upwards, has the heroine playing a game of "families" with her brother, who acts the "big, clever daddy in charge of the work. Little O alternated between being a helper and a mummy bringing fruit drinks or coffee to her thirsty husband." This was first published in England in 1965, while the first English publication of Anne-Cath. Vestly's *Hallo Aurora!*, from Norway, was in 1973; the latter book is all about a family where successful role reversal between Aurora's parents has occurred, the precise opposite of Little O's game: mother works full time as a lawyer while father keeps house. However, both books are warm and lively stories; Anne-Cath. Vestly observes the necessity of putting character and action before the Social Problem.

Naturally enough, the Social Problems figure most importantly in books for the oldest reading-age group. For instance, Christine Nöstlinger's *The Cucumber King*, for children of around ten or eleven, contains a radical view of society intertwined with comedy and fantasy much as a latter-day E. Nesbit might have devised it. In the older age-group, politics as a subject definitely takes second place to human relationships. Sex, drugs, the generation gap, colour questions, the women's movement all appear. Naturally enough, while a good deal of mediocre stuff is written in this vein, upon the whole it is only the really good examples that come through to us in English translation: the books where the author has plainly thought first of a character or a predicament, only second of a generalized social problem. Notable among these good examples of the *genre* are the books of Gunnel Beckman, whose *Mia* was quoted earlier, and one may observe that while Mia's suspected pregnancy is a common enough situation for most girls to be able to identify imaginatively with it, that of Annika in the same author's earlier *Admission to the Feast* is not. Annika finds she has leukaemia and will probably live only for a few months – not, happily, a common predicament among nineteen-year-old girls, though tragic when it does strike. But Gunnel Beckman makes the plight of both her heroines, and their courage in facing it, equally poignant.

Far more could be said about the relationship between literature for the young originally written in English, and that translated from other languages, than the scope of this brief survey allows – and many more names could – and should – have been named. It is a tenable theory that translations have a unique part to play in children's as distinct from adult literature, unique in that except for the tiny, lucky minority of the bilingual, the child reader will be simply unable to read a good book in a foreign language while he or she is still a child. And a considerable responsibility rests upon the publishers and translators who make such books available. Let us hope, then, for continued intercommunication with Europe, for yet more books from Eastern Europe, and eventually for a warm welcome for children's books from the Third World.

—Anthea Bell

*   *   *

Selected books in translation (dates are of first English-language editions):

AITMATOV, Chingiz.   Russian.   *Farewell, Gul'sary*, 1970; *The White Ship* (*The White Steamship*), 1972.

AYME, Marcel.   French.   *The Wonderful Farm*, 1951.

BARTOS-HOPPNER, Barbara.   German.   *The Cossacks*, 1962; *Save the Khan*, 1963; *Avalanche Dog*, 1966; *Storm over the Caucasus*, 1968; *Hunters of Siberia*, 1969.

BAUMANN, Hans. German. *Sons of the Steppe*, 1958; *The Barque of the Brothers*, 1958; *Jackie the Pit Pony*, 1958; *Angelina and the Birds*, 1959; *The Lion and the Unicorn*, 1959; *The Dragon Next Door*, 1960; *The Bear and His Brothers*, 1962; *Caspar and His Friends*, 1967; *The Circus Is Here*, 1967; *Fenny*, 1970; *Dimitri and the False Tsars*, 1972; *The Hare's Race*, 1976.

BECKMAN, Gunnel. Swedish. *The Girl Without a Name*, 1970; *Admission to the Feast* (*19 Is Too Young to Die*), 1971; *A Room of His Own*, 1973; *Mia*, 1974; *The Loneliness of Mia* (*Mia Alone*), 1975; *That Early Spring*, 1977.

BERNA, Paul. French. *A Hundred Million Francs* (*The Horse Without a Head*), 1957; *Continent in the Sky*, 1959; *The Street Musician*, 1960; *Flood Warning*, 1962; *The Mystery of Saint-Salgue*, 1963; *The Clue of the Black Cat*, 1964; *The Secret of the Missing Boat*, 1966; *The Mule of the Motorway* (*The Mule of the Expressway*), 1967; *A Truckload of Rice*, 1968; *They Didn't Come Back*, 1969; *The Myna Bird Mystery*, 1970; *Gaby and the New Money Fraud*, 1971; *Vagabonds of the Pacific*, 1973.

BIEGEL, Paul. Dutch. *The King of the Copper Mountains*, 1969; *The Little Captain*, 1971; *The Seven-Times Search*, 1971; *Twelve Robbers*, 1974; *The Gardens of Dorr*, 1975.

BRUNA, Dick. Dutch. *The Happy Apple*, 1959; *Tilly and Tissa*, 1962; *The Circus*, 1963; *The Fish*, 1963; *Kitten Nell*, 1963; *Miffy*, 1964; *The Egg*, 1964; *The King*, 1964; *Hop-o'-My-Thumb*, 1966; *The School*, 1966; *Snuffy*, 1970; *Lisa and Lynn*, 1975.

BRUNHOFF, Jean de. French. *The Story of Babar, The Little Elephant*, 1933; *The Travels of Babar*, 1934; *Babar the King*, 1935; *Babar and Father Christmas*, 1940; *Babar and Zephir*, 1942; *Babar and His Children*, 1948.

BRUNHOFF, Laurent de. French. Continuation of Jean de Brunhoff's *Babar* series, from 1948; *Serafina* series, from 1961; *Anatole and the Donkey*, 1963; *Gregory and the Lady Turtle in the Valley of the Music Trees*, 1971.

CHUKOVSKY, Kornei. Russian. *Crocodile*, 1931; *The Telephone*, 1961; *Wash 'em Clean*, 1962; *Dr. Concocter*, 1967; *The Silver Crest*, 1977.

CTVRTEK, Václav. Czechoslovakian. *The Little Chalk Man*, 1970.

PERE CASTOR (pseudonym for Lida). French. *Wild Animal Books: Bourru, Frou, Mischief, Plouf, Scaf, Quipic, Martin, Cuckoo*, 1937–42.

DRUON, Maurice. French. *Tistou of the Green Fingers* (*Tistou of the Green Thumbs*), 1958.

FROLOV, Vadim. Russian. *What It's All About*, 1968.

GRIPE, Maria. Swedish. *Papa Pellerin's Daughter*, 1966; *Hugo and Josephine*, 1969; *The Night Daddy*, 1971; *The Glassblower's Children*, 1974; *The Land Beyond*, 1974; *Julia's House*, 1975; *Elvis and His Friends*, 1976.

GUILLOT, René. French. *Companions of Fortune*, 1952; *Sirga*, 1953; *The 397th White Elephant*, 1954; *The King's Corsair*, 1954; *Kpo the Leopard*, 1955; *The Wind of Chance*, 1955; *A Boy and Five Huskies*, 1957; *Prince of the Jungle*, 1958; *Elephant Road*, 1959; *Grishka and the Bear*, 1959; *Nicolette and the Mill*, 1960; *The Fantastic Brother*, 1961; *Sama*, 1961; *The Troubadour*, 1965; *The Champion of Olympia*, 1968; *Little Dog Lost*, 1969; *Castle in Spain*, 1970.

GYDAL, Monica. Swedish. *Olly Sees It Through* series (with Thomas Danielsson), from 1976.

HAMRE, Leif. Norwegian. *Otter Two Three Calling!* (*Leap into Danger*), 1959; *Edge of Disaster*, 1960; *Perilous Wings*, 1961; *Blue Two − Bale Out!*, 1961; *Ready for Take-Off*, 1962; *Contact Lost*, 1967; *Operation Arctic*, 1973.

HOFMAN, Ota. Czechoslovakian. *Escape*, 1970.

HOLM, Anne. Danish. *I Am David* (*North to Freedom*), 1965.

IWASAKI, Chihiro. Japanese. *Staying at Home on a Rainy Day*, 1969; *Momoko* series, from 1972; *The Birthday Wish*, 1974; *Will You Be My Friend?*, 1974.

JANSSON, Tove. Finnish. *Moomintroll* series, from 1958; *Who Will Comfort Toffle?*, 1960.

JONSSON, Runer. Danish. *Viki Viking* (*Vicke the Viking*), 1968.

KASTNER, Erich. German. *Emil and the Detectives*, 1930; *Annaluise and Anton*, 1932; *The 35th of May*, 1933; *The Flying Classroom*, 1934; *Emil and the Three Twins*, 1935; *The Animals' Conference*, 1949; *Lottie and Lisa* (*Lisa and Lottie*), 1950; *The Little Man*, 1966.

KORINETZ, Yuri. Russian. *There, Far Beyond the River*, 1973; *In the Middle of the World*, 1976.

KROG, Inge. Danish. *Fourteen Days Overdue*, 1975.

KRUSS, James. German. *My Great Grandfather and I*, 1964; *Eagle and Dove*, 1965; *3 × 3*, 1965; *The Happy Islands Behind the Winds*, 1966; *Florentine*, 1967; *The Animal Parade*, 1968; *The Lighthouse on the Lobster Cliffs*, 1969; *The Proud Wooden Drummer*, 1969; *Letters to Pauline*, 1971; *My Great-Grandfather, the Heroes, and I*, 1973.

KURATOMI, Chizuko. Japanese. *Mr. Bear* series, from 1967.

LADA, Josef. Czechoslovakian. *Purrkin the Talking Cat*, 1966.

LAGERLOF, Selma. Swedish. *The Wonderful Adventures of Nils*, 1907; *The Further Adventures of Nils*, 1911.

LINDGREN, Astrid. Swedish. *Pippi Longstocking*, 1950; *Bill Bergson, Master Detective*, 1952; *Mio, My Son*, 1956; *Kati in Paris*, 1961; *Rasmus and the Tramp* (*Rasmus and the Vagabond*), 1961; *Tomten*, 1961; *Noisy Village* (*Bullerby*) series, from 1962; *The Children on Troublemaker Street*, 1962; *Seacrow Island*, 1968; *Emil in the Soup Tureen*, 1970; *Christmas in the Stable*, 1970; *The Brothers Lionheart*, 1975; *Karlson on the Roof*, 1975.

LOEFF, An Rutgers van der. Dutch. *Avalanche!*, 1954; *They're Drowning Our Village*, 1959; *Children on the Oregon Trail* (*Oregon at Last!*), 1961; *Rossie*, 1964; *Great Day in Holland*, 1965; *Vassilis on the Run*, 1965; *Flight from the Polar Night*, 1968.

LUZZATI, Emanuele. Italian. *Ronald and the Wizard Calico*, 1969; *Punch and the Magic Fish*, 1972.

MAUROIS, André. French. *Fattypuffs and Thinifers*, 1941.

MUNARI, Bruno. Italian. *The Lorry Driver*, 1953; *Animals for Sale*, 1957; *In the Dark of the Night*, 1961; *Zoo*, 1963; *The Circus in the Mist*, 1969; *A Flower with Love*, 1974.

NAKATANI, Chiyoko. Japanese. *The Day Chiro Was Lost*, 1968; *Fumio and the Dolphins*, 1970; *The Zoo in My Garden*, 1973; *My Teddy Bear*, 1976.

NOSTLINGER, Christine. Austrian. *Fly Away Home*, 1975; *The Cucumber King*, 1975; *Fiery Frederica*, 1975; *Girl Missing*, 1976.

PREUSSLER, Otfried. German. *The Little Witch*, 1961; *Thomas Scarecrow*, 1963; *The Robber Hotzenplotz* series, from 1964; *The Little Ghost*, 1967; *The Adventures of Strong Vanya*, 1970; *The Satanic Mill*, 1972; *The Wise Men of Schilda*, 1974.

PROCHAZKA, Jan. Czechoslovakian. *Long Live the Republic*, 1973; *The Carp*, 1977.

PRØYSEN, Alf. Norwegian. *Little Old Mrs. Pepperpot* series, from 1959.

REGGIANI, Renée. Italian. *The Adventures of Five Children and a Dog*, 1963; *The Sun Train*, 1966; *Tomorrow and the Next Day*, 1967.

REISS, Johanna. Dutch. *The Upstairs Room*, 1972; *The Journey Back*, 1976.

RICHTER, Hans Peter. German. *Friedrich*, 1970; *I Was There*, 1972; *The Time of the Young Soldiers*, 1976.

RODARI, Gianni. Italian. *Telephone Tales*, 1965; *The Befana's Toyshop*, 1970; *A Pie in the Sky*, 1971; *Mr. Cat in Business*, 1975.

SAINT-EXUPERY, Antoine de. French. *The Little Prince*, 1943.

SALTEN, Felix. German. *Bambi: A Life in the Woods*, 1928; *Fifteen Rabbits*, 1930; *The Hound of Florence*, 1930; *Florian*, 1934; *Perri*, 1938; *Bambi's Children*, 1939; *Renni the Rescuer*, 1940.

SANCHEZ-SILVA, José María. Spanish. *Marcelino* (*The Miracle of Marcelino*), 1954; *The Boy and the Whale*, 1964; *Ladis and the Ant*, 1968; *Second Summer with Ladis*, 1969.

SANDBERG, Inger and **Lasse.** Swedish. *Little Anna* series, from 1964; *Nicholas' Red Day*, 1967; *Little Ghost Godfrey*, 1968; *The Boy with 100 Cars*, 1968; *The Boy with Many Houses*, 1970; *Come on Out, Daddy*, 1971; *Johan's Year*, 1971; *Daniel* series, from 1973; *Let's Play Desert* (*Desert Game*), 1974; *Kate* series, from 1974; *Let's Be Friends*, 1976.

SOLDATI, Mario. Italian. *The Octopus and the Pirates*, 1974.

SOMMERFELT, Aimée. Norwegian. *The Road to Agra*, 1961; *Miriam*, 1963; *The White Bungalow*, 1963; *My Name Is Pablo*, 1966; *No Easy Way*, 1967.

TORGA, Miguel. Portuguese. *Farrusco the Blackbird*, 1950.

TOURNIER, Michel. French. *Friday and Robinson*, 1972.

UNNERSTAD, Edith. Swedish. *The Saucepan Journey*, 1951; *Pysen*, 1955; *Little O*, 1957; *The Spettecake Holiday*, 1958; *The Journey with Grandmother* (*Grandmother's Journey*), 1960; *A Journey to England*, 1961; *The Cats from Summer Island*, 1963; *The*

Picnic, 1964; *The Urchin*, 1964; *The Pip-Larssons Go Sailing*, 1966; *Toppen and I at the Croft*, 1966; *Larry Makes Music*, 1967; *Two Little Gigglers*, 1967; *A House for Spinner's Grandmother*, 1970; *Mickie*, 1971.

VESTLY, Anne-Cath.   Norwegian.   *Aurora* series, from 1973; *Eight Children* series, from 1973.

WOLDE, Gunilla.   Swedish.   *Tommy* (*Thomas*) series, from 1971; *Betsy* (*Emma*) series, from 1975.

ZEI, Alki.   Greek.   *Wildcat under Glass*, 1968; *Petros' War*, 1972.

ZIMNIK, Reiner.   German.   *Jonah and the Fisherman*, 1956; *The Proud White Circus Horse*, 1957; *Little Owl*, 1962; *The Bear on the Motorcycle*, 1963; *The Crane*, 1969; *The Bear and the People*, 1971; *Billy's Balloon Ride*, 1973.

NOTES
ON
ADVISERS
AND
CONTRIBUTORS

ANDERSON, William D. Professor of English, California State University, Northridge. Author of *A New Look at Children's Literature* (with Patrick Groff), 1972. **Essays:** William H. Armstrong; Julia W. Cunningham; Norton Juster.

APPIAH, Peggy. See her own entry.

ASHDOWN, Fran. Children's Literature Specialist, Midwestern Regional Library System, Kitchener, Ontario; Chairman, Canadian Association of Children's Librarians, 1976; Reviewer for *In Review* and *Canadian Children's Literature*. **Essays:** Doris Andersen; Esther Averill; Sheila Burnford; Christie Harris; Markoosie; Richard Scarry.

AVERY, Gillian. See her own entry. **Essays:** Evelyn Everett-Green; Juliana Horatia Ewing (appendix); Amy Le Feuvre; Arthur Ransome; Hesba Stretton (appendix); Charlotte Yonge (appendix).

BAKER, Janet E. Assistant Professor of English, St. Mary's University, Halifax, Nova Scotia. **Essays:** Mabel Dunham; Hubert Evans; Lorrie McLaughlin; Delbert A. Young.

BARBER, Raymond W. Assistant Professor, Graduate School of Library Science, Drexel University, Philadelphia. **Essay:** John R. Tunis.

BARTHOLOMEW, Ann. Editor, Children's Book Centre's *Children's Newsletter*, London. **Essays:** Carol Ryrie Brink; Grace Hogarth; Kate Seredy.

BELL, Anthea. Free-lance Translator, specializing in French and German children's books. Has translated over 60 books, including *The Cat and the Mouse Who Shared a House* by Ruth Hürlimann, 1976. Author of *E. Nesbit*, 1960. **Essays:** Christianna Brand; Anthony Buckeridge; Charles Causley; Leon Garfield; Norman Hunter; Ruth Manning-Sanders; Children's Books in Translation.

BOEGEHOLD, Betty. Senior Associate Editor, Bank Street College of Education Publications Division, New York. Formerly, teacher, assistant principal, and librarian in public and private schools. Author of *Three to Get Ready*, 1965; *Pawpaw's Run*, 1968; *Pippa Mouse*, 1973; *What the Wind Told*, 1974; *Here's Pippa Again!*, 1975. **Essays:** Eleanor Clymer; Jean Merrill; Evaline Ness.

BRINKLEY-WILLSHER, Valerie. Children's Library Organiser, Surrey County; Library Association Lecturer in Library Work with Children; Regular Reviewer of children's books. Author of *Across Time*, 1973. **Essays:** Joan Clarke; Pauline Clarke; E.W. Hildick; Elisabeth Kyle; Ann Lawrence; Susan Price; Gwynedd Rae.

BULLA, Clyde Robert. See his own entry. **Essays:** Valenti Angelo; Irene Hunt.

BURNS, Mary Mehlman. Coordinator, Curriculum Library, and Children's Literature Specialist, Framingham State College, Massachusetts; Reviewer, *Horn Book* magazine. Essay "There Is Enough for All: Robert Lawson's America" published in *Horn Book*, 1972. **Essay:** Robert Lawson.

BUTLER, Dorothy. Bookseller in Auckland, and Lecturer. Contributor to *Horn Book* magazine, *Signal*, and other periodicals. **Essays:** Maurice Duggan; E.M. Ellin; Phyllis Krasilovsky; Diana Moorhead; Eve Sutton.

BUTLER, Francelia. Professor of English, University of Connecticut, Storrs; Editor of the journal *Children's Literature*. Founder, Seminar on Children's Literature, Modern Language Association; Member of the Founding Board, Children's Literature Association. Author of

Children's Literature: A Module, 1975; *Sharing Literature with Children*, 1977; *Masterworks of Children's Literature I: 1550–1739*, 1977; and of books on Shakespeare and 17th-century drama. **Essays:** Natalie Savage Carlson; Gail E. Haley; Phyllis McGinley; Kate Douglas Wiggin.

BUTTS, Dennis. Principal Lecturer in English, Bulmershe College of Higher Education, Reading, Berkshire. Author of *Living Words* (with John Merrick), 1966, and *R.L. Stevenson*, 1966. Editor of *Pergamon Poets 8*, 1970, and *Good Writers for Young Readers*, 1977. Contributor to *The Faber Book of Greek Legends*, 1973. **Essays:** Russell Hoban; Robert Louis Stevenson (appendix).

CADOGAN, Mary. Secretary of an educational trust; Governor of an international school. Author of *The Greyfriars' Characters* (with John Wernham), 1975; *You're a Brick, Angela: A New Look at Girls' Fiction from 1839 to 1975* (with Patricia Craig), 1976; *Women and Children First: Aspects of War and Literature* (with Patricia Craig), 1978. **Essays:** Gillian Avery; Elinor Brent-Dyer; Dorita Fairlie Bruce; Elsie Oxenham; Philippa Pearce; P.L. Travers.

CAMPBELL, Alasdair K.D. Tutor Librarian, Institute of Education, University of Keele, Staffordshire; Contributor to *The School Librarian*, *Books for Your Children*, and other journals. Author of *The School Novel*, 1970. **Essays:** Elizabeth Goudge; C. Fox Smith.

CAMPBELL, Margaret. Free-lance Writer. Author of *Lend a Hand: Social Work for the Young*, 1966. Editor of *The Countryman Animal Book*, *Bird Book*, and *Book of Humour*, 3 vols., 1973–75. **Essays:** Ruth Ainsworth; Val Biro; Donald Bisset; Lettice Cooper; Dorothy Edwards; Eleanor Farjeon; Barbara C. Freeman; Frank Knight; Naomi Mitchison; John Pudney; James Reeves; John Symonds.

CARTER, Anne. Free-lance Writer and Translator. **Essays:** John Burningham; Charles Keeping; Josephine Poole; Mary Treadgold.

CAUSLEY, Charles. See his own entry. **Essays:** Kevin Crossley-Holland; Ted Hughes; Brian Patten.

CHANG, Charity. Serials Librarian and Library Consultant for Children's Literature, University of Connecticut, Storrs. Author of Preface to Mary De Morgan volume of *Classics of Children's Literature*; prepared bibliography for *Masterworks of Children's Literature I: 1550–1739* by Francelia Butler, 1977. **Essays:** Carolyn Sherwin Bailey; Eric Kelly; Eloise Jarvis McGraw; Doris Orgel; Monica Shannon; Elizabeth Yates.

CHRISTIAN, Mary Blount. Creator and Moderator, *Children's Bookshelf* television program, Houston; Children's Books Reviewer for Houston *Chronicle* and Houston *Post*. Author of over 20 children's books, including the *Goosehill Gang* mystery series, and, most recently, *Hats Are for Watering Horses*, 1977. **Essays:** Robert Burch; Robert Kraus.

CLARK, Berna C. Schools Librarian and Senior Assistant to the County of Avon Education Department Children's Librarian, Bristol. Former National Chairman of the Library Association Youth Library Group. **Essays:** Martin Ballard; Anne Mainwaring Barrett; Antonia Ridge.

CLARK, Leonard. See his own entry. **Essay:** Walter de la Mare.

CLEAVER, Pamela. Free-lance Journalist and Author; Reviewer for *Children's Book Review*, *Books and Bookmen*, and *Foundation*; contributor of stories and articles to anthologies. **Essays:** William Mayne; Ronald Welch; Barbara Willard.

COSGRAVE, Mary Silva. Editor of "The Outlook Tower" column in *Horn Book* magazine. Children's Librarian for 15 years; Editor of Children's Books for Houghton Mifflin and Pantheon Books for 11 years. **Essays:** Thomas Bailey Aldrich (appendix); Maureen Daly.

CRAIG, Patricia. Free-lance Critic and Reviewer. Author of *You're a Brick, Angela: A New Look at Girls' Fiction from 1839 to 1975* (with Mary Cadogan), 1976, and *Women and Children First: Aspects of War and Literature* (with Mary Cadogan), 1978. **Essays:** Nina Beachcroft; Judy Blume; Lucy Boston; Patricia Lynch; Meta Mayne Reid; Geraldine Symons.

CROUCH, Marcus. Deputy County Librarian, Kent. Author of *Beatrix Potter*, 1960; *Treasure Seekers and Borrowers*, 1962; *The Nesbit Tradition*, 1971. **Essays:** Hilaire Belloc; Elisabeth Beresford; Margery Williams Bianco; Helen Cresswell; J.G. Fyson; Richard Hughes; Eric Linklater; Stephanie Plowman.

CROXSON, Mary. Senior Lecturer in English, and Co-Director of the summer school in children's literature, Worcester College of Higher Education; Reviewer for *The School Librarian*. Author of *Using the Library*, 1966, and "The Emancipated Child in the Novels of E. Nesbit" in *Signal*, 1974. **Essays:** Rex Benedict; Vera and Bill Cleaver; Walt Morey; C. Everard Palmer; George Selden; Eleanor Spence; Theodore Taylor.

CULPAN, Norman. Former Head of the English Department, St. Paul's College of Education, Cheltenham; former Review Editor, *The School Librarian*. Author of *Modern Adult Fiction: For School and College Libraries*, 1955; and *Contemporary Adult Fiction, 1945–65* (with W.J. Messer), 1966. Editor of *Dialogue and Drama* (with James Reeves), 1950. **Essays:** Andre Norton; Barbara Euphan Todd.

DAY, Alan Edwin. Principal Lecturer, Leeds Polytechnic School of Librarianship. Author of *History: A Reference Handbook*, 1976, and *Archaeology: A Reference Handbook*, 1977; essay on Biggles in *Children's Literature in Education*, 1974. **Essays:** Richard Church; Samuel Rutherford Crockett; Roy Fuller; Ronald Syme; John Verney.

DOYLE, Brian. Free-lance Writer; Contributor to the *Guardian, Books and Bookmen*, and *Collectors' Digest*. Author of *The Who's Who of Boys' Writers and Illustrators*, 1964, and *The Who's Who of Children's Literature*, 1968. **Essays:** Peter Dawlish; S.G. Hulme Beaman; Hilda Lewis; Talbot Baines Reed (appendix); Frank Richards; Malcolm Saville; David Severn; Donald Suddaby; Elleston Trevor.

du SAUTOY, Peter. Chairman of Faber and Faber Ltd., London. **Essay:** Alison Uttley.

ELLEMAN, Barbara. Free-lance Writer; Children's Book Reviewer, American Library Association *Booklist*, Chicago. **Essay:** Constance C. Greene.

ELLIS, Anne W. Assistant Librarian, Christ's College, Liverpool Institute of Higher Education. Author of *The Family Story in the 1960's*, 1970. **Essays:** Antonia Forest; Eleanor Graham; Laurence Meynell; Sheena Porter.

ENGLAND, A.W. Lecturer in Drama, Division of Education, University of Sheffield. Author of an article on Walter Macken in *Use of English*, of two television plays for children, and of a television adaptation of Sylvia Sherry's *A Pair of Jesus Boots*. Editor of *Man and Superman* by George Bernard Shaw, 1969, and of the anthologies *Looking at Scenes*, 1969, *Two Ages of Man*, 1971, *Caves*, 1973, and *Islands*, 1974. **Essays:** Walter Macken; Sylvia Sherry.

ERISMAN, Fred.   Associate Professor of English, Texas Christian University, Fort Worth. Author of *Frederic Remington*, 1975, and of articles on L. Frank Baum, Kate Douglas Wiggin, Laura Ingalls Wilder, Donald Hamilton, and Len Deighton. **Essays:** Mary O'Hara; Jack Schaefer.

FICK, Martha J.   Librarian, Elizabeth Haddon School, Haddonfield, New Jersey. **Essays:** Peggy Parish; Bernard Waber; Gene Zion.

FITZGIBBON, Tom.   Principal Lecturer and Head of the English Department, North Shore Teachers College, Auckland. Author of teaching syllabuses and reviews in periodicals. Editor of New Zealand *Children's Literature Association Yearbook*, 1974 and 1975. **Essays:** R.L. Bacon; Anne de Roo; Joyce West.

FORDYCE, Rachel.   Associate Professor of English, Virginia Polytechnic Institute and State University, Blacksburg; Contributing Editor, *Children's Literature*. Author of *Children's Theatre and Creative Dramatics*, 1975; *Caroline Drama*, 1977. **Essays:** Joan Walsh Anglund; Betsy Byars; Alice Dalgliesh; Edward Fenton; Rachel Field; Joanna Halpert Kraus; Bill Peet; Louis Slobodkin; Bertha Upton.

FOX, Geoff.   Lecturer in Education, Exeter University School of Education; Joint Editor of the journal *Children's Literature in Education*. Taught at the Harvard-Newton Summer School, Boston, and the University of British Columbia, Vancouver. Joint Editor of *Writers, Critics, and Children*, 1976. Regular Reviewer, *Times Educational Supplement*. **Essays:** C. Day Lewis; S.E. Hinton; Reginald Maddock; Paul Zindel.

FREEMAN, Gillian.   Novelist, Screenwriter, and Journalist. Author of several novels – the most recent being *The Alabaster Egg*, 1970, and *The Marriage Machine*, 1975 – and of *The Story of Albert Einstein* (for children), 1960; *The Undergrowth of Literature*, 1967; *The Schoolgirl Ethic: The Life and Work of Angela Brazil*, 1976. **Essays:** Angela Brazil; Susan Coolidge (appendix).

FRYATT, Norma R.   Free-lance Writer and Editor. Former Managing Editor of *Horn Book* magazine. Author of *Sarah Josepha Hale*, 1975. Editor of *A Horn Book Sampler*, 1976. **Essays:** E.M. Almedingen; Lucy Fitch Perkins; Brinton Turkle.

GIBBS, Matyelok.   Artistic Director of the Unicorn Theatre for Young People, London.

GIBLIN, James C.   Vice-President and Associate Publisher of Seabury Press, New York, and Editor-in-Chief of Seabury's Clarion Books for young people. Lecturer and Writer on children's book publishing. **Essays:** Beatrice Schenk de Regniers; Mildred Lee; Alvin Tresselt; Jan Wahl; Jane Yolen.

GILDERDALE, Betty.   Lecturer in English, North Shore Teachers College, Auckland. Reviewer for the New Zealand *Herald* and the New Zealand Broadcasting Company; Corresponding Editor for New Zealand, *Phaedrus*. Founding Member and Past President, Children's Literature Association of New Zealand. **Essays:** Ruth Dallas; Roberta Elliott; Lilith Norman; Patricia Wrightson.

GORDON, Cecilia.   Librarian in London schools for 10 years, and Inner London Education Authority Library Organiser, 1972–76; National Chairman of the School Library Association. Reviewer for the *Times Educational Supplement*, *Times Literary Supplement*, *Children's Book Review*, and *The School Librarian*. **Essays:** Joseph E. Chipperfield; Joan Lingard; Janet McNeill.

GREAVES, Margaret. See her own entry. **Essays:** Joyce Gard; Nicholas Stuart Gray; Rosemary Harris; Margery Sharp; Rosemary Weir.

GREEN, Roger Lancelyn. See his own entry. **Essays:** Lewis Carroll (appendix); Rudyard Kipling; Andrew Lang (appendix).

GROFF, Patrick. Professor of Education, San Diego State University; Contributing Editor, Chircorel Library Publishing Corporation. Author of *A New Look at Children's Literature* (with William D. Anderson), 1972, and of articles for *Elementary English, Horn Book, The School Librarian, Wilson Library Journal,* and other periodicals. **Essays:** Robert Bright; Carolyn Haywood; William Lipkind; Clare Turlay Newberry; Helen Sewell; Esphyr Slobodkina; William Jay Smith; Phil Stong.

HAAS, Irene. Free-lance Illustrator; has illustrated books by Sesyle Joslin, Elizabeth Enright, Myra Cohn Livingston, and others. Author of *The Maggie B.,* 1976. **Essays:** Jacqueline Ayer; Elizabeth Enright; Sesyle Joslin.

HALL, Dennis. Free-lance Journalist and Boundary Rider. Formerly, Children's Librarian, Public Library of South Australia, Adelaide, and Assistant Editor, *School Magazine.* **Essay:** Norman Lindsay.

HAMMOND, Graham. Lecturer in Education, Exeter University; Joint Editor of the journal *Children's Literature in Education.* Joint Editor of *Writers, Critics, and Children,* 1976. **Essays:** Mary Cockett; Eilís Dillon; Roger Lancelyn Green; Josephine Kamm; Clive King; Jean MacGibbon; Madeleine A. Polland.

HAVILAND, Virginia. Head of the Children's Book Section, Library of Congress, Washington, D.C. Author of the *Favorite Fairy Tales* series, from 1959, and *Ruth Sawyer,* 1965. Editor of *Children's Literature: A Guide to Reference Sources,* 1966; *The Fairy Tale Treasury,* 1972; *Children and Literature: Views and Reviews,* 1973; *Yankee Doodle's Literary Sampler,* 1974. Reviewer, *Horn Book* magazine.

HAY, Ann G. Teacher and Librarian. Reviewer for *British Book News.* **Essays:** Marchette Chute; Rose Fyleman; Jonathan Gathorne-Hardy; Cynthia Harnett; Margaret Storey; D.J. Watkins-Pitchford.

HAYNES, Renée. Free-lance Writer and Critic; Editor of the *Journal of the Society for Psychical Research.* Author of *Pan, Caesar, and God,* 1938; *The Hidden Springs,* 1961; *Philosopher King,* 1973; *The Seeing Eye, the Seeing I,* 1976. **Essay:** J.B.S. Haldane.

HEARNE, Betsy. Editor, Children's Books Section, American Library Association *Booklist,* Chicago. Has taught children's literature at the University of Illinois, Chicago Circle Campus, and been a children's librarian and storyteller. Author of the children's novel *South Star,* 1977. **Essays:** John Donovan; Virginia Hamilton.

HEEKS, Peggy. Assistant County Librarian, Berkshire. Lecturer and Writer on children's reading. **Essays:** Roy Brown; Gordon Cooper; Penelope Farmer; Geraldine Kaye; Rosemary Manning.

HEINS, Ethel L. Editor, *Horn Book* magazine, Boston. Author of many articles and reviews for *Horn Book* and other periodicals. **Essay:** Caroline Dale Snedeker.

HELSON, Ravenna. Research Psychologist, Institute of Personality Assessment and Research, University of California, Berkeley. Author of "Fantasy and Self Discovery" in *Horn Book,* 1970, "The Psychological Origins of Fantasy for Children in Mid-Victorian

England" in *Children's Literature 2*, 1974, and other articles on authors of fantasy for children in *Psychology Today*, *Arts in Society*, and other periodicals. **Essays:** Scott Corbett; Edward Eager.

HIGGINS, James E. Professor of Education, Queens College, City University of New York; Literature Consultant, Series R Reading Program, Macmillan Inc., New York. Author of *Beyond Words: Mystical Fancy in Children's Literature*, 1970. **Essays:** Ann Nolan Clark; Marie Hall Ets; Marguerite Henry; Robert McCloskey; Scott O'Dell; H.A. and Margret Rey; Mark Twain (appendix); Leonard Wibberley.

HOLE, John. Theatre Director of the Queens Theatre, Hornchurch, Essex. Theatre Director of the Swan Theatre, Worcester, 1967–74. **Essay:** David Wood.

HOLLINDALE, Peter. Senior Lecturer in English and Education, University of York; General Editor of the Macmillan Shakespeare series. Author of *Choosing Books for Children*, 1974. **Essays:** Margaret Jowett; Jenny Overton; Emma Smith; Ruth Tomalin; Philip Turner.

HOME, Anna. Executive Producer of Children's Programmes, BBC-TV, London. Has adapted several children's novels for television, including a 10-part series based on Peter Dickinson's *Changes* trilogy. **Essay:** Mary Norton.

HOYLE, Karen Nelson. Curator of the Kerlan Collection, Walter Library, University of Minnesota, Minneapolis. **Essays:** Helen Dore Boylston; Edgar and Ingri Parin d'Aulaire; Aileen Fisher; Wanda Gág; Jim Kjelgaard; Jean Lee Latham; Eleanor Lattimore; Patricia Miles Martin; Katherine Milhous; Else Minarik; Mary Rodgers; Glen Rounds; Zilpha Keatley Snyder; Sydney Taylor; Eve Titus; Yoshiko Uchida; Nora S. Unwin; Kurt Wiese.

INGLIS, Fred. Lecturer in Advanced Studies, University of Bristol; Editor, *New University Quarterly*. Author of *The Imagery of Power*, 1972; *Ideology and the Imagination*, 1975; *The Name of the Game*, 1977; *Literature and Children*, 1978. **Essay:** Catherine Storr.

ISRAEL, Callie. Coordinator of Adult and Children's Services, Windsor Public Library, Ontario. Reviewer for *In Review*, *Canadian Library Journal*, *Ontario Library Review*, and *Quill and Quire*. **Essays:** Jean Little; Louise Riley.

JACKSON, Clara O. Associate Professor of Library Science, Kent State University, Ohio. **Essays:** Syd Hoff; Holling C. Holling; Leo Lionni; Ann Petry; Ruth Sawyer.

JAGO, Wendy. Senior Lecturer in Education, Brighton Polytechnic. Formerly, Lecturer in English, University of Sussex. Author of the children's novel *Alias Podge*, 1965. **Essay:** Elsie Locke.

JENNINGS, Coleman A. Associate Professor of Drama, University of Texas, Austin; President of the Children's Theatre Association of America, 1975–77. Author of the children's play *The Honorable Urashima Taro* and of a doctoral thesis on Aurand Harris. Editor of *Children's Theatre Review* for two years, and of *Six Plays for Children* by Aurand Harris, 1977. **Essay:** Aurand Harris.

JONES, Ursula M. Resident Director, Unicorn Theatre for Young People, London; Actress. Author of 15 plays for children. **Essays:** Mary Melwood; Olwen Wymark.

KAMM, Antony. Development Manager of the International Division, and Regional Manager (Caribbean), Oxford University Press. Editor-in-Chief, Brockhampton Press, 1960–72; Senior Education Officer, Commonwealth Secretariat, 1972–74; former Chairman of the Publishers Association Children's Book Group and of the Children's Book Circle. Author of *Books and the Teacher* (with Boswell Taylor), 1966; *The Story of Islam* (for children), 1976; *Choosing Books for Younger Children*, 1977. **Essays:** Alexander Cordell; David Scott Daniell; Rosemary Sutcliff; H.E. Todd; Henry Treece.

KELLY, R. Gordon. Assistant Professor of English, Virginia Commonwealth University, Richmond. Author of *Mother Was a Lady: Self and Society in Selected American Children's Periodicals, 1865–1890.* Editor of the children's literature issue of *American Literary Realism.* **Essays:** Mary Mapes Dodge (appendix); Lucretia P. Hale (appendix); Frank R. Stockton (appendix).

KEMBALL-COOK, Jessica. Librarian of Thomas Tallis School, Greenwich, London; Secretary of the Tolkien Society, and Editor of the Society's bulletin. Reviewer for *The School Librarian* and *Children's Book Review*; Contributor to *New Society.* **Essays:** Richard Adams; Winifred Finlay; Diana Wynne Jones; Beverley Nichols; Mary Ray; J.R.R. Tolkien.

KEMP, Edward. Acquisitions Librarian, University of Oregon, Eugene. Editor of a series of bio-bibliographies of children's authors and illustrators, including one on James Daugherty in *Imprint: Oregon*, 1975. **Essay:** James Daugherty.

KINGMAN Lee. See her own entry. **Essays:** Virginia Lee Burton; Esther Forbes; Florence Crannell Means; Howard Pyle (appendix).

KINGSTON, Carolyn T. Free-lance Writer. Author of *The Tragic Mode in Children's Literature*, 1974, and of several articles for the *Christian Science Monitor.* **Essays:** Claire Huchet Bishop; Meindert De Jong; Emily Cheney Neville; Hilda Van Stockum.

LEFFALL, Dolores C. Librarian, and Book Review Editor of the *Journal of Negro Education*, Washington, D.C.; Consultant to the Minority Research Center. Has compiled numerous bibliographies dealing with Black literature and education. **Essays:** Olivia Coolidge; Lorenz Graham; Jesse Jackson; Stephen W. Meader; Rutherford Montgomery; Howard Pease; Donald J. Sobol.

LEWIS, Claudia. Teacher of Children's Literature and Publications Consultant, Bank Street College of Education, New York. Author of several children's books, including *Children of the Cumberland*, 1946, *When I Go to the Moon*, 1961, and *Poems of Earth and Space*, 1967, and of *Writing for Young Children*, 1954. **Essays:** Ludwig Bemelmans; Beverly Cleary; David McCord; John Steptoe.

LEWIS, Naomi. Writer, Critic, and Broadcaster. Recent books include *A Peculiar Music*, 1973, and *Fantasy Books*, revised edition, 1977. Author of introductory essays to works on or by Hans Christian Andersen, J.M. Barrie, Eleanor Farjeon, Eric Kelly, E. Nesbit, Christina Rossetti, Lore Segal, Arthur Waley, and others. Contributor to *The Observer, New Statesman, Times Literary Supplement, Listener, Encounter, New Review, British Book News, New York Times*, and other newspapers and periodicals. **Essays:** J.M. Barrie; Ewan Clarkson; Kenneth Grahame; G.D. Griffiths; Helen Griffiths; Jean Ingelow (appendix); C.S. Lewis; Laura Ingalls Wilder.

LICKTEIG, Mary J. Professor, Department of Elementary and Early Childhood Education, University of Nebraska, Omaha. Author of *An Introduction to Children's Literature*, 1975. **Essays:** Jean Craighead George; Berta and Elmer Hader.

LIVINGSTON, Myra Cohn. See her own entry. **Essays:** Harry Behn; John Ciardi; Randall Jarrell; Maud and Miska Petersham.

LUKENS, Rebecca J.   Assistant Professor of English, Miami University, Oxford, Ohio. Author of *A Critical Handbook of Children's Literature*, 1976. Reviewer for the Children's Book Review Service. **Essays:** Rebecca Caudill; Walter Farley; Louise Fatio; Will James; Myra Cohn Livingston; Gene Stratton Porter; Ester Wier.

LYNSKEY, Alan M.   Head Teacher, Greenbank School, Rochdale, Lancashire. Author of *Children and Themes*, 1974. **Essay:** Andrew Salkey.

MacCANN, Donnarae.   Free-lance Consultant and Writer about children's books. Formerly, Children's Librarian, Los Angeles Public Library, and Head Librarian, University of California Elementary School, Los Angeles. Author of *The Black American in Books for Children: Readings in Racism*, 1972; *The Child's First Books: A Critical Study of Pictures and Texts*, 1973; *Cultural Conformity in Books for Children: Further Readings in Racism*, 1977. **Essays:** Virginia Kahl; Carol Kendall; Maurice Sendak; Dr. Seuss.

MacLEOD, Anne S.   Assistant Professor, College of Library and Information Services, University of Maryland, College Park. **Essays:** Natalie Babbitt; Crockett Johnson; Lois Lenski; Laura E. Richards; William O. Steele; William Steig; Mary Stolz.

MANDER, Gertrud.   Free-lance Writer and Translator. Arts Correspondent for several German-language newspapers and magazines; has translated fiction and books on film and psychiatry. Author of books on Shaw, Shakespeare's contemporaries, Molière, and Giraudoux in a German series on dramatists. **Essays:** Graham Greene; Ezra Jack Keats; Judith Kerr.

MARSH, Gwen.   Children's Book Editor for Harrap Ltd. and J.W. Dent Ltd., London, 1958–76. Author of the novels *French Greeting*, 1944, and *Land of No Strangers*, 1950. Translator of more than 20 books by René Guillot, from 1952. **Essays:** Richard Armstrong; Arthur Catherall; Rosalie K. Fry; Joyce Stranger; Lorna Wood.

MARSHALL, Margaret R.   Senior Lecturer in Children's Literature and Librarianship, Leeds Polytechnic. Regular Reviewer for *British Book News*; former National Chairman of the Library Association Youth Libraries Group. Author of *Libraries and Literature for Teenagers*, 1975, and *Each According to His Ability: Books for the Mentally Handicapped Child*, 1976. **Essay:** Fiona French.

MASON, Bobbie Ann.   Assistant Professor of English and Journalism, Mansfield State College, Pennsylvania. Author of *Nabokov's Garden: A Guide to Ada*, 1974, and *The Girl Sleuth*, 1976. **Essays:** Betty Cavanna; Phyllis A. Whitney.

MAXWELL, Margaret.   Associate Professor, Graduate Library School, University of Arizona, Tucson. Reviewer for *Library Journal*. Author of *Shaping a Library: William L. Clements as Collector*, 1973. Editor of *Voices from the Southwest* (with Donald C. Dickinson and W. David Laird), 1976. **Essays:** Betty Baker; N.M. Bodecker; Mabel Leigh Hunt; Karla Kuskin; Richard Peck; Marjorie Weinman Sharmat.

McCASLIN, Nellie.   Associate Director of the University Without Walls and Professor in the Program in Educational Theatre, both at New York University. Author of several plays for children – including *Legends in Action*, 1945, *Pioneers in Petticoats*, 1961, and *The Little Snow Girl*, 1963 – and of *Creative Dramatics in the Classroom*, 1968; *Theatre for Children in the United States: A History*, 1971; *Give Them Roots and Wings*, 1972; *Act Now!* (for children), 1975. Editor of *Children and Drama: A Collection of Essays*, 1975. **Essays:** Flora B. Atkin; Charlotte Chorpenning; Constance D'Arcy Mackay; Madge Miller; Stuart Walker.

McCORD, David. See his own entry. **Essays:** L. Frank Baum; Walter D. Edmonds; Joel Chandler Harris (appendix); Charles G.D. Roberts; Elizabeth Madox Roberts; James Thurber; Eliza Orne White; E.B. White.

McDONOUGH, Irma. Coordinator of Children's Library Services, Ontario Provincial Library Service, Toronto; Founding Editor of *In Review: Canadian Books for Children.* Editor, *Ontario Library Review,* 1966–75. Reviewer for *Quill and Quire, Saturday Night, School Library Journal, Emergency Librarian,* and other periodicals. Editor of *Profiles,* revised edition, 1975, and of *Canadian Books for Children,* 1976. **Essays:** Ruth Nichols; James Reaney; Kerry Wood.

McDOWELL, Myles. Deputy Headmaster, J.H. Whiteley School, Halifax, Yorkshire. Essay "Fiction for Children and Adults: Some Essential Differences" published in *Writers, Critics, and Children,* 1976. **Essays:** Margaret Greaves; Aylmer Hall; Aaron Judah; Benjamin Lee; A.C. Stewart.

McGRATH, Joan. Teacher-Librarian, Toronto Board of Education. Reviewer for *In Review* and *Quill and Quire.* **Essays:** Herbert Best; Ralph Connor; John Craig; Marguerite de Angeli; Nat Hentoff; Lee Kingman; E.L. Konigsburg; Ellen MacGregor; Keith Robertson; Marilyn Sachs; Edith Sharp; Louisa R. Shotwell; Virginia Sorensen; Tomi Ungerer; Scott Young.

McKENZIE, Dorothy Clayton. Professor of English, California State University, Los Angeles; Editor of *Bibliophile,* a bi-monthly book review. **Essays:** Mary Buff; Leo Politi.

McVITTY, Walter. Children's Literature Specialist, Melbourne State College. Author of *Australian Children's Writers,* 1978. **Essays:** Alan Garner; Bette Greene; Ted Greenwood; David Martin; Christobel Mattingley; Joan Phipson; William Rayner; Ethel Turner.

MEEK, Margaret. Lecturer, University of London Institute of Education; Reviews Editor of *The School Librarian.* Contributor to the *Times Literary Supplement.* Author of *Geoffrey Trease,* 1960. Editor of *The Cool Web: The Pattern of Children's Reading* (with Griselda Barton and Aidan Warlow), 1977. **Essays:** Honor Arundel; Jane Gardam; Shirley Hughes; Geoffrey Trease.

MENDELSOHN, Leonard R. Director of the Graduate Program and Associate Professor of English, Concordia University, Montreal. Articles on Milton, Kafka, Renaissance drama, and children's literature and education published in *Comparative Drama, Studies in Short Fiction, Language Arts, Children's Literature,* and other periodicals. **Essays:** Ann Blades; Lyn Cook; William Pène du Bois; Ernest Thompson Seton.

MERCIER, Jean F. Children's Books Editor, *Publishers Weekly,* New York; Free-lance Editor. Stories and articles published in various American magazines. Author of the novel *Whatever You Do, Don't Panic,* 1961. **Essays:** Nathaniel Benchley; Frank Bonham; Roger Duvoisin; Jean Fritz; Hardie Gramatky; Felice Holman; Ruth Krauss; Tasha Tudor; Barbara Wersba; Charlotte Zolotow.

MEYERS, Susan. Instructor in the Extension Writer's Program, University of California, Los Angeles; Children's Books Editor, *BooksWest* magazine. Member of the Board of Directors, Society of Children's Book Writers. Author of the children's stories *Melissa Finds a Mystery,* 1966; *The Cabin on the Fjord,* 1968; *The Mysterious Bender Bones,* 1970. **Essay:** E.C. Spykman.

MILLS, Joan. Assistant Director of Theatre Powys, Brecon. Former Director of the Young People's Theatre, Royal Court Theatre, London. **Essay:** Ann Jellicoe.

MITCHISON, Naomi.   See her own entry. **Essays:** Peggy Appiah; Margaret MacPherson; John Masefield; Rhoda Power.

MOE, Christian H.   Professor of Theatre, Southern Illinois University, Carbondale; Member of the Advisory Board, Institute of Outdoor Drama; Bibliographer, American Theatre Association. Publicist for the Cornell University Theatre, 1956–58; Chairman of the Publications Committee, American Theatre Association, 1966–71; Associate Editor, *Bibliographic Annual of Speech Communication*, 1972–75. Fulbright Lecturer, Flinders University, Bedford Park, South Australia, 1975. Author of *Creating Historical Drama* (with George McCalmon), 1965, an essay on D.H. Lawrence as playwright, an article in *The William and Mary Theatre: A Chronicle, 1926–1956*, 1968, and of the children's plays *The Strolling Players* (with Darwin Payne), 1971, *Six New Plays* (with Payne), 1971, and *Santa Claus Comes to Simpson's Crossing* (with Cameron Garbutt), 1975. **Essays:** Betty Jean Lifton; Marjorie Kinnan Rawlings; Colin Thiele.

MOLSON, Francis J.   Associate Professor of English, Central Michigan University, Mount Pleasant. Author of a chapter on juvenile science fiction in *Anatomy of Wonder* edited by Neil Barron, 1976, and of periodical articles on Emily Dickinson, Louise Fitzhugh, Frances Hodgson Burnett, and Francis Finn. **Essays:** Eleanor Cameron; Jane Curry; Sylvia Engdahl; Robert Heinlein; Jane Langton; Ursula K. Le Guin; Madeleine L'Engle.

MOORE, Doris Langley.   Writer and Historian of Costume. Founder and Former Adviser, Museum of Costume, Assembly Rooms, Bath. Designer of period clothes for films and ballet. Author of many books: novels include *A Winter's Passion*, 1932; *They Knew Him When ...*, 1938; *All Done by Kindness*, 1951; *My Caravaggio Style*, 1959; other books include *E. Nesbit: A Biography*, 1933 (revised, 1966); *Pleasure, A Discursive Guide Book*, 1953; *The Late Lord Byron*, 1961, and *Lord Byron: Accounts Rendered*, 1974; and other biographies, books on the history of fashion and taste, and screenplays. O.B.E., 1971. **Essay:** E. Nesbit.

MOOREHEAD, Caroline.   Free-lance Writer and Journalist. Reviewer for *The Times*, London, and the *Times Literary Supplement* and *Times Educational Supplement*. **Essay:** Hugh Lofting.

MUIR, Marcie.   Author and Bibliographer. Author of *A Bibliography of Australian Children's Books*, 2 vols., 1970 and 1976; Editor of *Strike-a-Light, The Bushranger*, 1972. **Essays:** Mary Durack; May Gibbs; Noreen Shelley.

NEILL, Heather.   Assistant Literary Editor, *Times Educational Supplement*, London. **Essay:** James Roose-Evans.

NETTLEFOLD, Mary.   Principal Educational Resources Librarian, Ayr Division, Strathclyde, Scotland; Editor of Library Association Youth Library Group's *Storyline*. **Essays:** Monica Edwards; Mollie Hunter.

NEWMAN, Janet E.   Children's Librarian, Inner Ring Zone, Birmingham. **Essays:** Margaret Mahy; Alison Morgan.

NOAKES, Vivien.   Free-lance Writer. Author of *Edward Lear: The Life of a Wanderer*, 1968. **Essay:** Edward Lear (appendix).

OSLER, Ruth.   Assistant Coordinator of Boys and Girls Resources, Toronto Public Library. **Essays:** Catherine Anthony Clark; Laurence Hyde; William Stevenson.

PATON WALSH, Jill.   See her own entry. **Essays:** Nina Bawden; Violet Bibby; C. Walter Hodges; John Rowe Townsend; Robert Westall.

QUAYLE, Eric. Free-lance Writer. Author of *Ballantyne the Brave*, 1967, and a bibliography of Ballantyne; *The Ruin of Sir Walter Scott*, 1968; *The Collector's Book of Books, Children's Books, Detective Fiction*, and *Boys' Stories*, 4 vols., 1971–73; *Old Cook Books: An Illustrated History*, 1978. **Essay:** R.M. Ballantyne (appendix).

RAY, Sheila G. Lecturer, City of Birmingham Polytechnic. Contributor to *Children's Literature Abstracts*. Author of *Children's Fiction*, 1972, and *Library Service to Schools*, 1972. **Essays:** Prudence Andrew; Ruth Arthur; Enid Blyton; Virginia Pye.

RAYNER, Mary. Free-lance Writer and Illustrator. Author of the children's books *The Witch-Finder*, 1975, and *Mr. and Mrs. Pig's Evening Out*, 1976. **Essays:** Joyce Lankester Brisley; Eve Garnett; Dhan Gopal Mukerji; Ann Schlee; Ian Serraillier.

READY, William. Professor of Bibliography and University Librarian, McMaster University, Hamilton, Ontario. Author of *The Great Disciple* (short stories), 1950; *The Poor Hater* (novel), 1960; *The Tolkien Relation*, 1968; *Necessary Russell* (biography), 1971. **Essays:** Padriac Colum; Farley Mowat; David Walker; T.H. White.

REES, David. Lecturer at St. Luke's College, Exeter, Devon. Author of the children's novels *Storm Surge*, 1975; *Quintin's Man*, 1976; *The Missing German*, 1976; *Landslip*, 1977; *The Spectrum*, 1977. **Essays:** Alec Lea; Rodie Sudbery; Meriol Trevor.

REEVES, James. See his own entry. **Essay:** Edward Ardizzone.

ROGER, Mae Durham. Lecturer, School of Library and Information Studies, University of California, Berkeley. Contributor to professional journals. Author of *Tit for Tat and Other Latvian Folk Tales*, 1967, and *Tobei: A Japanese Folktale*, 1974. Editor of *Literature Sampler: Junior Edition*, 1964. **Essays:** Clyde Robert Bulla; Don Freeman; Ruth Stiles Gannett; Erik Haugaard; Sulamith Ish-Kishor; Elizabeth Gray Vining.

ROGINSKI, James W. Director of Library Promotion, Follett Publishing Company, Chicago. Formerly, librarian and bookseller. Author of essay "The Cabinet of Lilliput" in *Horn Book*, 1976. **Essays:** Walter R. Brooks; Fred Gipson; Munro Leaf; Sharon Bell Mathis; Judith Viorst.

ROOSE-EVANS, James. See his own entry. **Essays:** Margaret J. Baker; Susan Cooper; W. Towrie Cutt.

RUBIO, Mary. Associate Editor of *Canadian Children's Literature*, Guelph, Ontario; Part-time Lecturer in English, University of Guelph. Editor of *Kanata: An Anthology of Canadian Children's Literature* (with Glenys Stow), 1976. **Essays:** Clare Bice; Norman Duncan.

RUSSELL, Jean. Editor of *Books for Your Children*, Guildford, Surrey. Chairman, Federation of Children's Book Groups, 1975–76, and Editor of the Federation's Yearbook. **Essays:** Angela Bull; Roald Dahl; Rumer Godden; David McKee; Joan Tate; Ann Thwaite.

SADLER, Glenn Edward. Professor of English, Point Loma College, San Diego. Editor of *The Gifts of the Child Christ: Fairytales and Stories for the Childlike* by George MacDonald, 1973. **Essay:** George MacDonald (appendix).

SAUNDERS, Rubie. Editorial Director of Children's Magazines, Parents' Magazine Enterprises Inc., New York. **Essays:** Anita Lobel; Arnold Lobel; Robert Newton Peck; Lee Wyndham.

SAXBY, H.M. Head of the English Department, Kuring-gai College of Advanced Education, Lindfield, New South Wales. Author of *A History of Australian Children's Literature, 1841–1941* and *1941–1970,* 2 vols., 1969, 1971; *Teaching the New English in Primary Schools* (with Cliff Turney), 1974. **Essays:** Margaret Balderson; Mary Grant Bruce; Nan Chauncy; Elyne Mitchell; Reginald Ottley; Leslie Rees.

SCHEINMANN, Vivian J. Free-lance Writer and Researcher; Book Editor, *New Directions for Women* quarterly, Dover, New Jersey. Reviews published in the *New York Times,* Washington *Post,* and other periodicals. **Essays:** John and Patricia Beatty; Crosby Bonsall; Paula Fox; M.E. Kerr; Joan M. Lexau; Eve Merriam; Miriam Schlein; Elizabeth George Speare; Janice Udry; Maia Wojciechowska.

SCHMIDT, Nancy J. Head of the Tozzer Library, Peabody Museum of Archaelogy and Ethnology, Harvard University, Cambridge, Massachusetts; Contributing Editor, *Conch Review.* Children's and Young People's Editor, *Africana Library Journal,* 1971–74; former Visiting Professor, University of Illinois, Urbana. Author of "The Writer as Teacher: A Comparison of the African Adventure Stories of G.A. Henty, René Guillot, and Barbara Kimenye" in *African Studies Review 19,* 1976, and of articles on Nigerian fiction, African folklore and other topics in African literature for *Journal of the New African Literature and the Arts, Africa Report, Research in African Literatures,* and other journals. Editor of *Children's Books on Africa and Their Authors: An Annotated Bibliography,* 1975. **Essays:** Cyprian Ekwensi; Jenny Seed; Efua Sutherland.

SEGUN, Mabel D. Secretary, Nigerian Book Development Council, Lagos; Free-lance Journalist and Broadcaster. Has taught in primary and secondary schools and teacher training colleges. Author of *My Father's Daughter* (reader), 1966; *Friends, Nigerians, Countrymen* (radio broadcast talks), 1977; *Poetry for Primary Schools 1* (with Neville Grant), 1977. **Essays:** Barbara Kimenye; Kola Onadipe.

SHEPHERDSON, Nancy. Free-lance Writer. **Essays:** Nance Donkin; Mary Elwyn Patchett; Barbara Softly.

SILES, Dorothy D. Assistant Professor and Head of the Catalog Department, Ithaca College, New York. Rare Pamphlet Cataloger, American Antiquarian Society, Worcester, Massachusetts, 1974-76. Reviewer in American history and social sciences for *Library Journal.* **Essays:** Richard Armour; Dorothy Canfield Fisher; Grey Owl.

SMILEY, Barbara. Assistant Editor, *In Review* and *Ontario Library Review,* both Toronto. **Essays:** Mary Alice Downie; Adelaide Leitch.

SORFLEET, John Robert. Associate Professor of English and Canadian Studies, Concordia University, Montreal; Editor, *Canadian Children's Literature*; Editor and Managing Editor, *Journal of Canadian Fiction*; Corresponding Editor for Canada, *Phaedrus*; Member of the Advisory Editorial Board, *Owl: The Canadian Magazine for Children.* Author of *The Poems of Bliss Carman,* 1976, *L. M. Montgomery: An Assessment,* 1976, and other books. **Essays:** Cliff Faulknor; John F. Hayes; James A. Houston; Dennis Lee; L. M. Montgomery; Anne Wilkinson.

STERCK, Kenneth J. Senior Lecturer in English, College of St. Mark and St. John, Plymouth; Member of the Editorial Committee, *Children's Literature in Education.* Joint Editor of *Writers, Critics, and Children,* 1976. **Essays:** Jacynth Hope-Simpson; Percy Westerman.

STERN, Madeleine B. Partner in Leona Rostenberg-Rare Books, New York; Free-lance Writer. Author of *Louisa May Alcott,* 1950; *Imprints on History: Book Publishers and*

American Frontiers, 1956; *We the Women: Career Firsts of 19th-Century America*, 1963; *Heads and Headlines: The Phrenological Fowlers*, 1971; *Old and Rare: Thirty Years in the Book Business* (with Leona Rostenberg), 1975; and of adult biographies of Margaret Fuller, Mrs. Frank Leslie, and Stephen Pearl Andrews, and juvenile biographies of Mrs. Frank Leslie and Dr. Isabel Barrows. Editor of *Women on the Move*, 1972; *The Victoria Woodhull Reader*, 1974; and *Louisa's Wonder Book*, 1975, *Behind a Mask*, 1975, and *Plots and Counterplots*, 1976, all by Louisa May Alcott. **Essay:** Louisa May Alcott (appendix).

STONES, Rosemary. Children's Book Reviewer and Commentator; Member of the Children's Rights Workshop, London. Co-Editor, *Papers in Children's Literature* series: *Racist and Sexist Images in Children's Books*, 1975, *Sexism in Children's Books*, 1976, *Children's Books and Class Society*, 1977; Co-Editor, *Mother Goose Comes to Cable Street*, 1977. **Essays:** Bernard Ashley; Leila Berg; Peter Carter; Marjorie Darke; Louise Fitzhugh; Michael Foreman; Robert Leeson.

STOTT, Jon C. Associate Professor of English, University of Alberta, Edmonton; Editor and Publisher, *The World of Children's Books* (semi-annual review); Founding Director and President, Children's Literature Association. **Essays:** Doris Gates; Roderick Haig-Brown; Jean MacKenzie.

SUTHERLAND, Zena. Lecturer, University of Chicago Graduate Library School; Editor, *Bulletin of the Center for Children's Books*; Children's Books Editor of the Chicago *Tribune*. Contributing Editor of the *Saturday Review*, 1966-72. Author of *History in Children's Books*, 1967; *Children and Books* (with May Hill Arbuthnot), 1972; *The Best in Children's Books*, 1973; and of the children's literature article in *World Book Encyclopedia*. Editor of *An Arbuthnot Anthology*, 1976. **Essays:** Richard Atwater; Martha Bacon; Marie Halun Bloch; Patricia Clapp; James Flora; Florence Hightower; Harold Keith; Evelyn Lampman; Mildred Lawrence; Joseph Wharton Lippincott; Cornelia Meigs; Sterling North.

THOMAS, Gillian. Assistant Professor of English, St. Mary's University, Halifax, Nova Scotia. Author of numerous articles and reviews about 19th-century fiction and children's literature. **Essays:** Joseph Krumgold; Edward Ormondroyd; Mary Q. Steele.

THWAITE, Ann. See her own entry. **Essays:** M. E. Atkinson; Angela Banner; Frances Hodgson Burnett; V. H. Drummond; Mary K. Harris; Penelope Lively.

TOTTEN, Eileen. Free-lance Writer. Contributor to the *Guardian, The Observer, Financial Times,* and *Radio Times.* Author of three information books for children, the most recent being *Caring for Your Pets*, 1976. **Essay:** Jill Paton Walsh.

TOWNSEND, John Rowe. See his own entry. **Essays:** Joan Aiken; John Christopher; William Corlett; Peter Dickinson; John Gordon; A. A. Milne; Ivan Southall.

TREASE, Geoffrey. See his own entry. **Essays:** Kitty Barne; Frederick Grice; G. A. Henty (appendix); Charlotte Hough; W. E. Johns; Barbara Sleigh; L. A. G. Strong; Elfrida Vipont.

TRESSELT, Alvin. See his own entry. **Essays:** Margaret Wise Brown; Jay Williams.

TYE, Margaret M. Principal Tutor Librarian, Padgate College of Higher Education, Warrington, Cheshire. **Essays:** Bruce Carter; Dorothy Clewes; Carola Oman; Barbara Leonie Picard; Philip Rush; Barbara Ker Wilson.

VANSITTART, Peter. Novelist, Historian and Critic. Author of more than 25 books including *Enemies*, 1948; *The Overseer*, 1949; *The Game and the Ground*, 1955; *The Siege*, 1959; *The Storyteller*, 1968; *Pastimes of a Red Summer*, 1969; *Dictators*, 1973; *Worlds and*

Underworlds, 1974; *Quintet*, 1976; also author of three children's books, *The Dark Tower*, 1964, *The Shadow Land*, 1966; and *Green Knights, Black Angels*, 1967. **Essays:** Leonard Clark; Robert Nye; Joan G. Robinson.

WALKER, Margaret. Chairman of the Scottish Children's Book Association, Glasgow; Editor of *Book Window*. **Essays:** Michael Bond; Kathleen Fidler; Angus MacVicar; Iona McGregor; Allan Campbell McLean.

WARD, Joan. Editor of educational books. **Essay:** Elizabeth Stucley.

WARLOW, Aidan. Teacher; Deputy Warden of the Centre for Language in Primary Education, London. Editor of *The Cool Web: The Pattern of Children's Reading* (with Griselda Barton and Margaret Meek), 1977. **Essays:** Richmal Crompton; Robert C. O'Brien; Anna Sewell (appendix).

WEBER, Rosemary. Associate Professor, Graduate School of Library Science, Drexel University, Philadelphia. Author of *Building a Children's Literature Collection*, 1975, and of chapters in *Children and Books*, 1977. Editor of *Library Materials for Younger Children*, 1976. **Essays:** Lloyd Alexander; Eleanor Estes.

WEEKS, Brigitte. Managing Editor and Children's Books Review Editor of *Washington Post* "Book World." **Essays:** Isabelle Holland; Kristin Hunter; Norma Klein; Ellen Raskin.

WHALLEY, Joyce I. Assistant Keeper, Victoria and Albert Museum Library, London. Organised Beatrix Potter exhibition at the Victoria and Albert Museum, 1972. Author of *English Handwriting, 1540-1843*, 1969; *Writing Implements and Accessories*, 1975; *Cobwebs to Catch Flies: Illustrated Books for Nursery and Schoolroom, 1700-1900*, 1975. **Essays:** Mary Louisa Molesworth (appendix); Beatrix Potter.

WHITBY, Joy. Head of Children's Programmes for Yorkshire Television, Leeds. Creator of *Play School* and *Jackanory* series for BBC Television, and *Catweezle* series for London Weekend Television. Author of the children's novel *Grasshopper Island*, 1971. **Essays:** Nicholas Fisk; Anita Hewett; K. M. Peyton; Diana Ross.

WHITEHEAD, Frank. Reader in English and Education, University of Sheffield. Chairman, National Association for the Teaching of English, 1965-67; Editor, *The Use of English*, 1969-73. Author of *The Disappearing Dais*, 1966; *Creative Experiment*, 1970; *Children's Reading Interests* (with A.C. Capey and W. Maddron), 1974. **Essays:** Helen Bannerman; Hester Burton; Kathleen Hale; Annabell and Edgar Johnson; Armstrong Sperry.

WHITEHEAD, Winifred. Lecturer in English Literature and Curriculum Studies, Sheffield City Polytechnic. **Essays:** L. Leslie Brooke; Winifred Cawley; Elizabeth Borton de Treviño; Marjorie Flack; Ursula Moray Williams.

WIGAN, Angela. Member of the Books Section, *Time* magazine, New York. Reviewer for several magazines, including *Time, Bookletter*, and *SoHo News*. **Essays:** Elizabeth Coatsworth; Isaac Bashevis Singer.

WILLIAMS, Gladys A. Reviewer of Children's Books for *Good Housekeeping* magazine, London. Former Assistant Editor, *Books and Bookmen*. Author of *Children and Their Books*, 1970, and several books for children, including the *Semolina Silkpaws* series, 1963-72, *Garry the Goblin*, 1973, and *Percy the Pigeon*, 1973. **Essays:** Mabel Esther Allan; Richard Parker; Jenifer Wayne.

WILSON, Barbara Ker. See her own entry. **Essays:** H. F. Brinsmead; Mavis Thorpe Clark; Max Fatchen; George Finkel; Elisabeth MacIntyre; Ruth Park; Noel Streatfeild.

WOODY, Jacqueline Brown. Young Adult Age-Level Specialist, Prince George's County Library System, Greenbelt, Maryland; Volunteer, Reading Is Fundamental program. **Essays:** Lucille Clifton; Nikki Giovanni; Rosa Guy; June Jordan.

WYNDHAM, Lee. See her own entry.

YOLEN, Jane. See her own entry. **Essays:** Sid Fleischman; F. N. Monjo; Clyde Watson.